Christopher Floyd QC
11 South Square
Gray's Inn
London WC1R 5EU
Tel: 0171 405 1222

THE

INTELLECTUAL PROPERTY CITATOR

AUSTRALIA
LBC Information Services
Sydney

CANADA and USA
Carswell
Toronto

NEW ZEALAND
Brooker's
Auckland

SINGAPORE and MALAYSIA
Thomson Information (S.E. Asia)
Singapore

THE
INTELLECTUAL
PROPERTY
CITATOR

VOLUME 2

1982–1996

by

Michael FYSH, Q.C., S.C.
of the Inner Temple and King's Inns, Dublin
Barrister-at-Law.
Barrister, Supreme Court of N.S.W.
Advocate, High Court at Bombay
and Supreme Court of India

and

Robert WILSON THOMAS
of the Inner Temple
Barrister-at-Law.

London
Sweet & Maxwell
1997

Published in 1997 by
Sweet & Maxwell Limited
of 100 Avenue Road
Swiss Cottage, London NW3 3PF.
Photoset by MFK Information Services Ltd, Hitchin, Herts.
Printed and bound in Great Britain by Hartnolls Ltd, Bodmin.

A CIP catalogue record for this book
is available from The British Library

ISBN 0 421 52820 6

No natural forests were destroyed to make this product;
only farmed timber was used and replanted.

Contents

Acknowledgements

We should like to thank our many colleagues both in the United Kingdom and elsewhere who have enabled us to prepare what we hope and intend to be a reliable and comprehensive Citator. Particular mention should be made of Richard Lloyd who undertook the first independent review of the Main Index, of Jason Chan of Messrs Allen & Gledhill of Singapore and of Manoj Menda, advocate, Bombay, for their assistance in making available, respectively, Singapore and Malaysian and Indian references and of Genevieve Tan, advocate, Singapore.

Lastly, we would also like to thank Marion Thorley very much indeed.

MICHAEL FYSH, Q.C., S.C.
ROBERT WILSON THOMAS

Lincoln's Inn
October 1996

This volume covers cases reported up to:

F.S.R.	*July 1996*
R.P.C.	*July 1996*
C.M.L.R.	*July 1996*
Other series:	*most recently available*

Introduction

This is the second volume in the series and companion volume to the *Industrial Property Citator* which was published in 1982. This volume contains all relevant cases from 1982 until mid 1996 and includes all cases cited in both the 1985 and the 1988 supplements to the *Industrial Property Citator*.

It will not go without notice that this volume, at almost 1200 pages, is four times the size of the original work. This is due to a number of factors.

First, the material available has increased substantially. In the first volume, we cited about 3,000 intellectual property cases, reported over the 26 years covered by that volume. By comparison, only 15 years since its publication has yielded almost 5,000 reported cases. This shows as much a growing awareness of intellectual property rights as a willingness on the part of editors to report cases involving them.

Secondly, most of the overseas cases are now treated as comprehensively as cases from the United Kingdom and Europe. Whilst this has enlarged the text, we anticipate that this will be a welcome addition to the usefulness of the citator. On the other hand we have departed from the practice of providing a list of cases, with citations, before each subject matter section.

The original version of the *Industrial Property Citator* is being re-issued, with corrections.

Abbreviations

| W.A.R. | Western Australia Reports |
| W.L.R. | Weekly Law Reports |

COURTS

AAT	Administrative Appeals Tribunal (Australia)
A.D.	Appellate Division (South Africa)
AIPO	Australian Intellectual Property Office
BoT	Board of Trade
C.–G.	Comptroller-General
C.A.	Court of Appeal (England and Wales), Hof van Beroep (Belgium), Cour d'Appel (France), Oberlandesgericht (Germany), Corte de Appello (Italy)
C.A.(NSW)	Court of Appeal (New South Wales)
C.J.	Chief Justice (Benelux)
Comm. Crt	Commercial Court
CPD	Cape Province Division (South Africa)
Cprt Brd	Copyright Board
Cprt Trib.	Copyright Tribunal
D&CLD	Durban & Cape Local Division (South Africa)
D.C.	District Court
D.C.	(France) District Court (Tribunal de Grande Instance)
D.C.	(Denmark) Divisional Court
D.Reg.	Design Registry
E.C. Comm.	European Community Commission
CFI	European Court of the First Instance, Europe
ECHR	European Court of Human Rights
ECJ	European Court of Justice
EPO	European Patent Office
FCTD	Federal Court, Territorial Division
Fed. C.A.	Federal Court of Appeal
Fed. Ct	Federal Court (Australia)
Fed. Terr. Cr. App. Ct	Federal Territory Criminal Appeal Court
H.C.	High Court
H.L.	House of Lords
I.H.	Inner House (Scotland)
MMC	Monopolies and Mergers Commission (U.K.)
NPD	Natal Provincial Division (South Africa)
OCJ	Office of the Chief Justice (Malaysia)
O.H.	Outer House (Scotland)
Pat. C.C.	Patent County Court
Pat. Ct	Patents Court
Pat. Off.	Patents Office
P.C.	Privy Council
PRT	Performing Rights Tribunal
Q.B.D.	Queen's Bench Division
RDAT	Registered Design Appeal Tribunal
Reg.	Registry
RPCt	Restrictive Practices Court
S.C.	Supreme Court
S.C.	Federal Supreme Court (Bundesgerichtshof) (Germany)
S.C.	Supreme Court (Cour de Cassation) (France)
S.C.(ACT)	Supreme Court (Australian Capital Territory)
S.C.(NSW)	Supreme Court (New South Wales)

S.C.(Qd.)	Supreme Court (Queensland)
S.C.(S.A.)	Supreme Court (South Australia)
S.C.(Vic.)	Supreme Court (Victoria)
SECLD	South East Cape Local Division (South Africa)
T.M. Opp. Bd	Trade Mark Opposition Board (Canada)
T.M.Reg.	Trade Mark Registry
TPC	Trade Practices Commission (Australia)
TPD	Transvaal Provincial Division (South Africa)
WLD	Local Division (South Africa)

GENERAL ABBREVIATIONS

AB	Aktiebokaget
AG	Aktiengesellschaft
AIRC	Association of Independent Radio Companies
BV	Besloten Vennootschap (Public Limited Company) (Holland)
C.D.&P.A.88	Copyright, Designs and Patents Act 1988 (U.K.)
D&MPPA58	Dramatic & Music Performers Protection Act 1958 (U.K.)
EEA	European Economic Area (Treaty)
EPC	European Patent Convention
GmbH	Gesellschaft mit beschränkter Haftung (Public Limited Company) (Germany)
KK	Kabushiki Kaisha
NV	Naamloze Vennootschap (Public Limited Company) (Holland)
Ord.	Order
P.A.49	Patents Act 1949 (U.K.)
P.A.52	Patents Act 1952 (Cth) (Australia)
P.A.77	Patents Act 1977 (U.K.)
RSC	Rules of the Supreme Court (U.K.)
SACEM	Société des Auteurs, Compositeurs et Editeurs de Musique
TMA38	Trade Marks Act 1938 (U.K.)
TMA94	Trade Marks Act 1994 (U.K.)

Part I
ALPHABETICAL AND NUMERICAL INDICES

A. Alphabetical List of Cases

10th Cantanae Pty Ltd v. Shoshana Pty Ltd (TRADE PRACTICES: CONSUMER PROTECTION: PASSING OFF: CHARACTER MERCHANDISING: INNOCENT INFRINGEMENT: MISLEADING OR DECEPTIVE CONDUCT: FALSE REPRESENTATIONS AS TO APPROVAL: DAMAGES: ASSESSMENT: Australia: Fed. Ct) 79 A.L.R. 279; 10 I.P.R. 289
(Appeal: Fed. Ct) 79 A.L.R. 299; 1 I.P.R. 249

115778 Canada Inc. (t/a Microcom) v. Apple Computer Inc., *sub nom.* Mackintosh Computers Ltd v. Apple Computer Inc.

2000 TWO THOUSAND Trade Mark (TRADE MARK: APPLICATION: NUMERAL MARKS: PRACTICE: T.M.Reg.) [1992] R.P.C. 65

3D Geoshapes Australia Pty Ltd v. Registrar of Designs (DESIGN: REGISTRATION: APPLICATION FOR EXTENSION OF TIME REFUSED: APPEAL: Australia: Fed. Ct) 30 I.P.R. 474

682330 Ontario Inc. v. Cineplex Odean Corp. (COPYRIGHT: INFRINGEMENT: PLEADINGS: SCULPTURE: MORAL RIGHTS: PASSING OFF: Canada: FCTD) 33 C.P.R. (3d) 408

A. & K. Aluminium Pty Ltd v. Lidco Systems Sales Pty Ltd (PATENT: OPPOSITION: NOVELTY: PRIOR PUBLICATION: MATTERS ARISING UNDER SECTION 40: OBTAINING: Australia: Pat. Off.) 18 I.P.R. 597

A.C. Corp. Pty Ltd v. Jadon Investments Pty Ltd (REGISTERED DESIGN: WHETHER FRAUDULENT IMITATION: KNOWLEDGE OF DESIGN: DESIGNER NOT CALLED AS WITNESS: SMALL DIFFERENCES: REGISTERED DESIGN NOT DISSIMILAR TO PRIOR ART: EXPERT EVIDENCE: ADMISSIBILITY: Australia: H.C.)
(1992) 59 S.A.S.R. 265

A.C. Edwards Ltd v. Acme Signs & Displays Ltd, *sub nom.* Edwards (A.C.) Ltd v. Acme Signs & Displays Ltd

A Company's Application (CONFIDENTIAL INFORMATION: BREACH OF CONFIDENCE: PUBLIC INTEREST: FORMER EMPLOYEE OF COMPANY PROVIDING FINANCIAL SERVICES: THREAT TO DISCLOSE CONFIDENTIAL INFORMATION TO REGULATORY BODY AND INLAND REVENUE: NO THREAT OF DISCLOSURE TO PUBLIC: ENTITLEMENT TO INJUNCTION: Ch.D.)
[1989] 2 All E.R. 248; [1989] 1 Ch. 477; [1989] 3 W.L.R. 265

A Couple a Cowboys Pty Ltd v. Ward (PATENT: APPLICATION: OPPOSITION: Australia: AIPO) 31 I.P.R. 45

A.M. & S. Ltd v. E.C. Comm. (ADMINISTRATIVE PROCEDURE: LAWYERS: CONFIDENTIALITY: PRIVILEGE: Case 155/79: ECJ)
[1982] 2 C.M.L.R. 264; [1982] E.C.R. 1747; [1982] F.S.R. 474;
[1983] 3 W.L.R. 17

A v. B (X Intervening) (MAREVA INJUNCTION: APPLICATION BY INTERVENER: VARIATION: Q.B.D.) [1983] 2 Lloyd's Rep. 532

A.&M. Records v. Video Collection International Limited (COPYRIGHT: INFRINGEMENT: SOUND RECORDINGS: OWNERSHIP: EQUITABLE OWNERSHIP: ADDITIONAL DAMAGES: Ch.D.) [1995] E.M.L.R. 25

A.D.D.–70 Trade Mark (APPLICATION: SERVICE MARK: T.M.Reg.)
[1986] R.P.C. 89

AB Asea-Atom v. Boyle *sub nom.* Asea-Atom AB v. Boyle

AB v. CDE (BREACH OF CONFIDENCE: ANTON PILLER PRACTICE: Q.B.D.)
[1982] R.P.C. 509

Abbot/Oral proceedings (EUROPEAN PATENT: APPLICATION: ORAL PROCEEDINGS: PROCEDURE: INTERVIEW WITH EXAMINING DIVISION: MANDATORY IF REQUESTED: "SUGGESTION" AS A REQUEST: SPIRIT OF THE GUIDELINES: FEES: REIMBURSEMENT OF APPEAL FEE: T283/88: EPO)   [1989] E.P.O.R. 225

Abbott Laboratories' (Chu's) Patent (PATENT: PATENT OFFICE PRACTICE: APPLICATION FOR REVOCATION WITHDRAWN: COMPTROLLER'S PUBLIC DUTY TO CONSIDER VALIDITY THEREAFTER: C.-G.)   [1992] R.P.C. 487

Abella v. Anderson (PRACTICE: INJUNCTION: *Mareva* INJUNCTION: FORM OF ORDER: Australia: S.C.(Qd.))   [1987] 2 Qd.R. 1

Abkco Music & Records Inc. v. Music Collection International Ltd (COPYRIGHT: INFRINGEMENT: SOUND RECORDINGS: AUTHORISATION: WHETHER AUTHORISATION ABROAD IS AN INFRINGEMENT: C.A.)
[1995] E.M.L.R. 449; [1995] R.P.C. 657

Abundant Earth Pty Ltd v. R. & C. Products Pty Ltd (TRADE PRACTICES: MISLEADING AND DECEPTIVE CONDUCT: SIMILAR NAMED GOODS: Australia: Fed. Ct)   59 A.L.R. 211; [1985] 4 I.P.R. 387

A.C. Components Pty Ltd v. Jadon Investments Pty Ltd (DESIGNS: INFRINGEMENT: VALIDITY: NO OBVIOUS IMITATION: FRAUDULENT IMITATION FOUND: DESIGN REGISTRATION VALID: AIRCONDITIONING DIFFUSER: South Africa: S.C.)   [1992] A.L.M.D. 4195; 23 I.P.R. 594

Accounting Systems 2000 (Developments) Pty Ltd v. CCH Australia Ltd (COPYRIGHT: INFRINGEMENT: COMPUTER PROGRAMS: REPRODUCTION OR ADAPTATION: REPRODUCTION OF SUBSTANTIAL PART: EFFECT OF EXPENDITURE OF TIME AND EFFORT IN DEVELOPING COMPUTER PROGRAM: Australia: Fed. Ct)   114 A.L.R. 355; 20 I.P.R. 555

Accounting Systems 2000 (Developments) Pty Ltd v. CCH Australia Ltd (COPYRIGHT: COMPUTER PROGRAMS: REPRODUCTION OF SUBSTANTIAL PART: Australia: Fed. Ct)   27 I.P.R. 133

Accurist Watches Ltd v. King (TRADE MARK: INFRINGEMENT: MARK APPLIED BY MANUFACTURER UNDER CONTRACT WITH REGISTERED USER: RESERVATION OF TITLE: MANUFACTURER RETAKING POSSESSION ON REGISTERED USER'S INSOLVENCY: WHETHER INFRINGEMENT FOR MANUFACTURER TO SELL GOODS WITHOUT REMOVING MARK: SUMMARY JUDGMENT: STATUTORY DEFENCE: Ch.D.)   [1992] F.S.R. 80

ACI Australia Ltd v. Glamour Glaze Pty Ltd (TRADE PRACTICES: STATUTORY INFRACTION: REGISTRATION BY ANOTHER OF FORMER BUSINESS NAME OF ACQUIRED BUSINESS: Australia: Fed. Ct)   11 I.P.R. 269

A Clouet & Co. Pte. Ltd v. Maya Toba Sdn. Bhd. (TRADE MARK: INFRINGEMENT: PASSING OFF: SIMILARITY OF LABELS AND GET-UP: AYAM BRAND/BOTAN BRAND: LABEL COMMON TO THE TRADE: PRACTICE: LIMITATION PERIOD: Malaysia: H.C.)   [1996] 1 M.L.J. 251

Acme Merchandising v. Jamison *sub nom.* Tony Blain Pty Ltd (t/a Acme Merchandising) v. Jamison

ACNO/Calculation of aggregate time limits (EUROPEAN PATENT: PROCEDURE: INTERVIEW WITH EXAMINING DIVISION: TIME LIMITS, COMPUTATION OF: J09/82: E.P.O.)   [1978–85] E.P.O.R. A118

ACO/Drainage channel (EUROPEAN PATENT: OPPOSITION: PROCEDURE: FRESH GROUND ON APPEAL: PRIOR ART: PRIOR USE: PHOTOGRAPHIC EVIDENCE: T442/88: E.P.O.)   [1992] E.P.O.R. 515

Acorn Computer Ltd v. MCS Microcomputer System Pty Ltd (COPYRIGHT: ASSIGNMENT: REQUIREMENT OF WRITING: EQUITABLE OWNERSHIP: JOINT OWNERSHIP: Australia: Fed. Ct)   57 A.L.R. 389:4 I.P.R. 214

Actil Ltd v. Collector of Customs (South Australia) (ADMINISTRATIVE LAW: PAYMENT OF BOUNTY: MEANING OF PATTERN: Australia: A.A.T.)
8 I.P.R. 660

Action Bolt (Pty) Ltd v. Tool Wholesale Holdings (Pty) Ltd (TRADE MARK: REGISTRATION: VALIDITY: SERVICE MARK: PERSON AGGRIEVED: SELLING GOODS DOES NOT CONSTITUTE SERVICE: REGISTRATION FOR RETAIL AND WHOLESALE SERVICES CONTRARY TO STATUTE: South Africa: TPD)
1988 (4) S.A. 752; [1989] 1 F.S.R. 275
(AD) 1991 (2) S.A. 80; [1991] R.P.C. 251

Acushnet Co. v. Spalding Australia Pty Ltd (PATENTS: APPLICATION: OPPOSITION: PRIOR PUBLICATION: PRIOR USE: PRIOR SALES ON BALANCE OF PROBABILITIES: Australia: Pat. Off.)   11 I.P.R. 349

Acushnet Co. v. Spalding Australia Pty Ltd (PATENT: AMENDMENT: OPPOSITION: INTERPRETATION OF CLAIMS: INCLUSION OF PERCENTAGE RANGES IN CLAIMS: Australia: Pat. Off.)   16 I.P.R. 333

Acushnet Co. v. Spalding Australia Pty Ltd (PATENT: APPEAL FROM REFUSAL BY COMMISSIONER: CROSS-APPEAL: ORDER FOR FILING AFFIDAVITS: Australia: Fed. Ct)   17 I.P.R. 136

Acushnet Co. v. Spalding Australia Pty Ltd (PRACTICE AND PROCEDURE: PATENT APPEALS: EXISTENCE OF EARLIER INTERIM DECISION OF COMMISSIONER OF PATENTS: COMPETENCE OF APPEAL FROM FINAL DECISION BASED UPON AMENDED CLAIMS: Australia: Fed. Ct)   96 A.L.R. 493; 18 I.P.R. 364

Ada Productions Pty Ltd's Application (TRADE MARK: SURNAME: DISTINCTIVENESS: Australia: Pat. Off.)   (1985) 6 I.P.R. 611

Adams v. E.C. Commission (CONFIDENTIAL INFORMATION: DUTY OF E.C. COMM.: Cases 145/83 and 53/84: ECJ)
[1986] C.M.L.R. 506; [1986] F.S.R. 617; [1986] 2 W.L.R. 367

Adidas Sàrl (TRADE MARK: OPPOSITION: PRACTICE: EXTENSIONS OF TIME: CERTIORARI: Q.B.D.)   [1983] R.P.C. 262; (1984) 9 I.P.L.R. 170

Adidas Sportschuhfabriken Adi Dassler KG v. Chas O'Neill & Co. Ltd (PASSING OFF: GET-UP: SPORTSWEAR: REPUTATION IN IRELAND AND ABROAD: Ireland: S.C.)   [1983] F.S.R. 76

Advance Magazine Publishing Inc. v. Redwood Publishing Ltd (PASSING OFF: INTERLOCUTORY INJUNCTION: MAGAZINE TITLES: GOURMET: Ch.D.)   [1993] F.S.R. 449

Advanced Building Systems Pty Ltd v. Ramset (PATENT: VALIDITY: REVOCATION: ANTICIPATION: MOSAIC: OBVIOUSNESS: ENTITLEMENT AND INVENTOR NOT BEING A PERSON ENTITLED TO APPLY FOR PATENT: Australia: Fed. Ct)
26 I.P.R. 171

Advanced Hair Studio of America Pty Ltd's Application (TRADE MARK: APPLICATION: INVENTED WORD: COMPARISON WITH ORDINARY AND EXISTING WORDS: Australia: Pat. Off.)   7 I.P.R. 11

Advanced Hair Studio of America Pty Ltd v. Registrar of Trade Marks (TRADE MARKS: APPEAL AGAINST REGISTRARS DECISION: RELATIONSHIP BETWEEN MARK AND CHARACTER OR QUALITY OF SERVICES: INVENTED WORD: INHERENTLY DISTINCTIVE: EVIDENCE OF USE OF THE MARK: Australia: S.C.(Vic.))   10 I.P.R. 583

Advanced Hair Studio Pty Ltd v. TVW Enterprises Ltd (TRADE PRACTICES: MISLEADING AND DECEPTIVE CONDUCT: FALSE STATEMENT: CONSUMER'S STATEMENT OF COMPLAINT: INTERIM INJUNCTION: Australia: Fed. Ct)
10 I.P.R. 97

Advance Portfolio Technologies Inc. v. Ainsworth (PASSING OFF: MISUSE OF CONFIDENTIAL INFORMATION: PROCEEDINGS IN NEW YORK ON SAME FACTS: WHETHER *forum conveniens* WAS ENGLAND: APPLICATIONS FOR STAY: INJUNCTION AGAINST JOINDER OF DEFENDANT IN N.Y. PROCEEDINGS: Ch.D.)   [1996] F.S.R. 217

Advanced Semiconductor Products II/Limiting feature (EUROPEAN PATENT: OPPOSITION: REVOCATION: LIMITING FEATURE: NOT DISCLOSED IN APPLICATION AS FILED: REFERRAL ON APPEAL: CONFLICTING REQUIREMENTS OF EPC ARTICLE 123(2) AND 123(3): G01/93: T384/91: EPO)   [1995] E.P.O.R. 97

Adventure Film Productions SA v. Tully (WRONGFUL INTERFERENCE WITH GOODS: COPYRIGHT: FILM: INTERLOCUTORY ORDER FOR DELIVERY UP: STRENGTH OF CASE TO OWNERSHIP OF FILM AND COPYRIGHT: BALANCE OF CONVENIENCE: Ch.D.)   [1993] E.M.L.R. 376

Advertising by patent agents (EUROPEAN PATENT: PROFESSIONAL REPRESENTATIVES: ADVERTISING: EUROPEAN CONVENTION ON HUMAN RIGHTS: D12/88: EPO)   [1992] E.P.O.R. 248; [1991] O.J. EPO 591

AE plc/Exclusion of documents from file inspection (EUROPEAN PATENT: OPPOSITION: PROCEDURE: NOTICES OF THE EPO: ORAL PROCEEDINGS: DUTY OF EPO TO ADVISE OF WITHDRAWAL OF: FEES: REIMBURSEMENT OF APPEAL FEE: T811/90: EPO)   [1994] E.P.O.R. 271; [1993] O.J. EPO 1993, 728

AE plc/Re-establishment of rights (EUROPEAN PATENT: RE-ESTABLISHMENT OF RIGHTS: LARGE COMPANY: DUTY OF CARE DURING REORGANISATION: REPRESENTATIVE'S KNOWLEDGE OF EPC: T516/91: EPO)
                                                           [1993] E.P.O.R. 225

AECI/Thermoplastics sockets (EUROPEAN PATENT: INVENTIVE STEP: IRRELEVANT FEATURES: LEVEL OF INVENTION: CLAIMS: PREAMBLE: PRESUPPOSING POSSIBLY INVENTIVE FEATURE: PRODUCT V. PROCESS: PRIOR ART: PATENT PUBLICATIONS IN SAME CLASS: RELEVANCE OF: NATIONAL LAWS, RELATIONSHIP OF EPC TO: T1/81: EPO)
                          [1979–85] E.P.O.R. B273; [1981] O.J. EPO 439

AEG Telefunken's Agreement (RESTRICTIVE PRACTICES: SELECTIVE DISTRIBUTION: E.C. Comm.)   [1982] 2 C.M.L.R. 386

AEG Telefunken v. E.C. Comm. (RESTRICTIVE PRACTICES: PROCEDURE: INVESTIGATION: SEIZURE OF DOCUMENTS: Case 107/82 ECJ)
                          [1984] 3 C.M.L.R. 325; [1983] E.C.R. 3151

Aerospatiale and Alcatel's Agreement (RESTRICTIVE PRACTICES: TELECOMMUNICATIONS: CO-OPERATION IN CARRYING OUT SATELLITE REPAIRS: INFORMATION EXCHANGE: SPECIALISATION: INTENTION TO APPROVE: NOTICE: E.C. Comm.)   [1994] 4 C.M.L.R. 705

Aérospatiale Society Nationale Industrielle v. Aérospatiale Helicopters Pty Ltd (TRADE PRACTICES: PASSING OFF: NATURE OF CONDUCT: Australia: Fed. Ct)
                                                                7 I.P.R. 219

Aérospatiale/Interlocutory revision (EUROPEAN PATENT: APPEAL: PROCEDURE: INTERLOCUTORY REVISION, ABSENCE OF, IMPLYING OTHER GROUNDS FOR DECISION: STATEMENT OF GROUNDS, REQUIREMENTS OF: T313/90: EPO)   [1991] E.P.O.R. 354

Aetiology Today C.C. (t/a Somerset Schools) v. Van Aswegen (UNLAWFUL COMPETITION: PUBLIC POLICY: COMPETITION BETWEEN SCHOOLS: TEACHERS MOVING TO NEW SCHOOL: INJURIOUS FALSEHOOD: RESTRAINT OF TRADE: INTERDICT: South Africa: WLD)   1992 (1) S.A. 807

Agarwal (M.K.) v. Union of India (PASSING OFF: NEWSPAPERS WITH IDENTICAL NAMES: FOREIGN PROPRIETORS: India: H.C.)   (1994) 19 I.P.L.R. 139

AGL Sydney Ltd v. Shortland County Council (COPYRIGHT: INFRINGEMENT: REPLY TO COMPETITOR'S ADVERTISEMENT: TAKING ESSENTIAL FEATURES: PARODY: Australia: Fed. Ct) 17 I.P.R. 99

Agricultural Dairy Industry Authority of Epirus, Dodoni S.A. v. Dimtsis (TRADE MARKS: OPPOSITION: PROPRIETORSHIP: USE LIKELY TO DECEIVE OR CAUSE CONFUSION: REGISTRABILITY: Australia: Pat. Off.) 22 I.P.R. 643

Ahlstrom Oy v. E.C. Commission *sub nom.* Wood Pulp Cartel (Re) A. Ahlstrom Oy v. E.C. Commission

Ahmad/Additional period for renewal fee (EUROPEAN PATENT: CONVENTIONS: INTERPRETATION, TELEOLOGICA: RENEWAL FEES, PERMITTED EXTENSION OF TIME FOR PAYING: REIMBURSEMENT OF RE-ESTABLISHMENT FEE: *Effet utile*: *In claris non fit interpretatio*: *Sens clair*: J04/91: EPO)
[1994] E.P.O.R. 365; [1992] O.J. EPO 402

Ahmedabad Textile Industries Research Association v. The Bombay Textile Research Association (PATENT: OPPOSITION: PROCESS PATENT: India: Pat. Off.) (1978) 3 I.P.L.R. 91

Ainsworth Nominees Pty Ltd v. Andclar Pty Ltd (COPYRIGHT: INFRINGEMENT: DIFFERENT SECTIONS OF TABLE CONSTITUTING SEPARATE WORKS: REPRODUCTION OF A SUBSTANTIAL PART: USE OF DIFFERENT SYMBOLS AND FORMAT: Australia: Fed. Ct) 12 I.P.R. 551

Air Products/Cryogenic liquid dispenser (EUROPEAN PATENT: APPLICATION: PROCEDURE: REMITTAL TO EXAMINING DIVISION: CLAIMS: CONSTRUCTION: NOVELTY: "FOR" CLAUSE, EFFECT OF: T617/90: EPO)
[1994] E.P.O.R. 396

Air Products/Pressure swing adsorption (EUROPEAN PATENT: OPPOSITION: PROCEDURE: LATE FILING OF ADDITIONAL PRIOR ART: EXAMINATION: BY EPO OF ITS OWN MOTION: T156/84: EPO)
[1989] E.P.O.R. 47; [1988] O.J. EPO 372

Air Products/Priority (EUROPEAN PATENT: PRIORITY: NOVELTY: DISCLAIMER, NATURE OF THE INVENTION: T255/91: EPO)
[1993] E.P.O.R. 544; [1993] O.J. EPO 318

Air Products/Redox catalyst (EUROPEAN PATENT: DISCLOSURE: SUFFICIENCY: COMMON GENERAL KNOWLEDGE EXPECTED: DEFICIENCIES IN EXAMPLES: T171/84: EPO) [1986] E.P.O.R. 210; [1986] O.J. EPO 95

Air Products/Removal of hydrogen sulphide and carbonyl sulphide (EUROPEAN PATENT: AMENDMENT AND CORRECTION: REMOVAL OF INCONSISTENCY: OPPOSITION: PROCEDURE: FRESH DOCUMENTS ON APPEAL: INVENTIVE STEP: COMBINATION OF CHEMICAL ENGINEERING STEPS: COMBINATION OF CITATIONS: OPPONENT'S OWN FAILURE TO RECOGNISE ADVANTAGE: T271/84: EPO) [1987] E.P.O.R. 23; [1987] O.J. EPO 405

AIRC Ltd v. PPL, *sub nom.* Association of Independent Radio Companies Ltd (The) v. Phonographic Performance Ltd

AIRC Ltd v. PPL, BBC Intervening, *sub nom.* Association of Independent Radio Companies Ltd v. Phonographic Performance Ltd, BBC Intervening

Aisin Seiki KK's Application (PATENT: APPLICATION: PRACTICE: EXTENSION OF TIME LIMIT: DISCRETION: Pat. Ct) [1984] R.P.C. 191

Aisin/Late submission of amendment (EUROPEAN PATENT: APPEAL: PROCEDURE: LATE AMENDMENTS: PRIOR ART, FAILURE TO EXAMINE: DISCLOSURE: IMPLIED TEACHING: INVENTIVE STEP: TECHNICAL ADVANTAGE: T95/83: EPO) [1979–85] E.P.O.R. C815; [1985] O.J. EPO 75

Aitken v. Neville Jeffress Pidler Pty Ltd (COPYRIGHT: JOURNALISTS' BY-LINED ARTICLES: ALLEGED INFRINGEMENT BY MEDIA MONITORING SERVICE: RIGHT TO OBTAIN RELIEF: PRELIMINARY DISCOVERY OF SUBSCRIBER LISTS AND COPIED ARTICLES: SCOPE OF PRELIMINARY DISCOVERY: Australia: Fed. Ct)
22 I.P.R. 605

Ajay Industrial Corp. v. Kanao (PATENT: REVOCATION: JURISDICTION: India: H.C.)   (1983) 8 I.P.L.R. 95

Ajinomoto/Composite plasmid (EUROPEAN PATENT: OPPOSITION: PROCEDURE: ONUS OF PROOF: T109/91: EPO)   [1992] E.P.O.R. 163

Aktiebolaget Astra v. Schering Corp., *sub nom*. Astra (AB) v. Schering Corporation

Aktiebolaget Hassle v. Commissioner of Patents, *sub nom*. Hassle (AB) v. Commissioner of Patents

AKZO Chemie BV v. E.C. Commission (RESTRICTIVE PRACTICES: DOMINANT POSITION: ABUSE: BUSINESS SECRETS: NATURE OF: COMMUNICATION TO COMPLAINANT: ROLE OF E.C. COMM.: Case 53/85: ECJ)
[1987] 1 C.M.L.R. 231; [1986] E.C.R. 1965

AKZO Chemie BV v. E.C. Commission (RESTRICTIVE PRACTICES: EUROPEAN COURT PROCEDURE: ADMINISTRATIVE PROCEDURE: DISCOVERY OF DOCUMENTS: DOMINANT POSITION: RELEVANT PRODUCT MARKET: MARKET SHARE: PRICING: ABUSE: Case C–62/86R: ECJ)
[1993] 5 C.M.L.R. 215; [1994] F.S.R. 25

AKZO Chemie BV v. E.C. Commission (RESTRICTIVE PRACTICES: EUROPEAN COURT PROCEDURE: INTERIM MEASURES: DOMINANT POSITION: UNDERCUTTING: REQUEST FOR INTERIM SUSPENSION: REFUSAL: Case C–62/86: ECJ)
[1987] 1 C.M.L.R. 225; [1986] E.C.R. 1503; [1987] F.S.R. 203

AKZO Chemie BV v. E.C. Commission (RESTRICTIVE PRACTICES: SEARCH AND SEIZURE: SEARCH WARRANT: PRACTICE: Case 5/85; ECJ)
[1987] 3 C.M.L.R. 716; [1986] E.C.R. 2585; [1988] F.S.R. 55

AKZO/Automatic revocation (EUROPEAN PATENT: APPEAL: PROCEDURE: ADMISSIBILITY OF APPEAL: CONVENTIONS: INTERPRETATION: ECJ APPROACH: DIFFERENT LANGUAGE TEXTS: *Travaux préparatoires*: ENLARGED BOARD OF APPEAL: REFERENCE REFUSED: FEES: FAILURE TO PAY: REIMBURSEMENT OF APPEAL FEE: OPPOSITION: AMENDMENT: FAILURE OF SUBSEQUENT COMPLIANCE: REVOCATION: AUTOMATIC REVOCATION: T26/88: EPO)   [1990] E.P.O.R. 21; [1991] O.J. EPO 30

AKZO/Dry jet-wet spinning (EUROPEAN PATENT: INVENTIVE STEP: OBVIOUS TO TRY: PREJUDICE: V. TREND: NOVELTY: TESTING FOR NON–IDENTITY THROUGH PROPERTIES: OPPOSITION: PROCEDURE: FRESH ARGUMENT ON APPEAL: FRESH DOCUMENTS ON APPEAL: T253/85: EPO)
[1987] E.P.O.R. 198

AKZO/Fibre (EUROPEAN PATENT: CLAIMS: FEATURES NECESSARY FOR SOLUTION OF PROBLEM: FUNCTIONAL FEATURES: PARAMETERS, OPEN–ENDED: PRIOR ART: PRIOR USE: DISTINCTION BETWEEN WHAT WAS DONE AND WHAT WAS MADE: T129/88: EPO)   [1994] E.P.O.R. 176; [1993] O.J. EPO 598

AKZO/Rainwear (EUROPEAN PATENT: CLAIMS: RELIANCE UPON DICTIONARIES: INVENTIVE STEP: NEIGHBOURING FIELD: OPPOSITION: PROCEDURE: CLARITY OF AMENDED CLAIM: STATE OF THE ART: COMBINATION OF SEPARATE TEACHINGS IN SINGLE DOCUMENT: T215/90: EPO)   [1992] E.P.O.R. 1

AL BASSAM Trade Mark (TRADE MARK: APPLICATION: OPPOSITION: ARABIC DEVICE MARK: HEADSHAWLS: EXPORTED GOODS: ENTITLEMENT TO APPLY FOR REGISTRATION: WHETHER A TRADE MARK: SURNOMINAL SIGNIFICATION: PRACTICE: SCOPE OF APPLICATIONS: Ch.D.)
[1994] R.P.C. 315
(PROPRIETORSHIP: BONA FIDE CLAIM, WHETHER SUFFICIENT: OPPOSITION: MARK IN ARABIC SCRIPT INCLUDING ARABIC SURNAME: WHETHER CAPABLE OF DISTINGUISHING: C.A.) [1995] R.P.C. 511

Al Nahkel (etc.) Ltd v. Lowe (PRACTICE: WRIT: *Ne exeat regno*: APPLICATION: *Mareva* INJUNCTION: ALLEGED THIEF: FORM OF WRIT: Q.B.D.)
[1986] 1 All E.R. 729; [1986] 1 Q.B. 235; [1986] 2 W.L.R. 317

Alan H. Reid Engineering Ltd v. Ramset Fasteners (N.Z.) Ltd (TRADE LIBEL: MALICIOUS FALSEHOOD: RULE AGAINST RESTRAINT OF PUBLICATION WHERE JUSTIFICATION CLAIMED: COMPARATIVE ADVERTISING: INTERLOCUTORY INJUNCTION: New Zealand: H.C.) 20 I.P.R. 15

Albany International/Papermaking fabric (EUROPEAN PATENT: INVENTIVE STEP: SKILLED PERSON, CAPABILITIES OF: PREFERENCE FOR LEAST EXTENSIVE MODIFICATION: T406/89: EPO) [1992] E.P.O.R. 94

Albany/Shower fittings (EUROPEAN PATENT: INFRINGEMENT: RIGHT TO WORK: INVENTIVE STEP: STANDARD DESIGN, DEPARTURE: OPPOSITION: PROCEDURE: FRESH GROUND ON APPEAL: PRIOR ART: PRIOR USE: REQUIREMENTS: T194/86: EPO) [1994] E.P.O.R. 335

Albion Hat & Cap Co. Pty Ltd (Re) (DESIGNS: APPLICATION: DERIVATIVE DESIGN: OBJECTION: PARENT DESIGN DIFFERENT ONLY IN IMMATERIAL DETAILS OR FEATURES COMMONLY USED IN THE RELEVANT TRADE: Australia: Pat. Off.)
21 I.P.R. 558

Albright & Wilson Ltd v. Colgate Palmolive Co. (PATENT: APPLICATION: OPPOSITION: EXTENSION OF TIME LIMIT: Australia: Pat. Off.) 9 I.P.R. 669

Albright & Wilson/Extraction of uranium (EUROPEAN PATENT: INVENTIVE STEP: COULD/WOULD TEST: PREJUDICE: ABSENCE OF IMPROVEMENT: NOVELTY: INCIDENTAL DISCLOSURE: OPPOSITION: PROCEDURE: AMENDMENT OF CLAIM ON APPEAL: FRESH DOCUMENTS ON APPEAL: T223/84: EPO)
[1986] E.P.O.R. 66

Albright & Wilson/Fee reduction (EUROPEAN PATENT: EPO: GOOD FAITH TOWARDS PARTIES: PROCEDURE: EPO PRACTICES, PROMPT OFFICIAL ANNOUNCEMENT OF: FEES: PAYMENT BY DEBIT ORDER: REDUCTION FOR FILING IN NON-OFFICIAL LANGUAGE: SMALL AMOUNT EXCEPTION: *De minimus non curat lex*: T905/90: EPO) [1994] E.P.O.R. 585

Alcan/Aluminium alloys (EUROPEAN PATENT: INVENTIVE STEP: PROBLEM AND SOLUTION APPROACH: T465/92: EPO) [1995] E.P.O.R. 501

Alcan/Exhaust silencer (EUROPEAN PATENT: CLAIMS: QUALITATIVE EXPRESSION: SKILLED PERSON: KNOWLEDGE OF: T47/84: EPO)
[1979–85] E.P.O.R. C940

Alcatel Espace SA and Ant Nachrichtentechnik's Agreement (RESTRICTIVE PRACTICES: SATELLITE COMMUNICATIONS EQUIPMENT: JOINT RESEARCH AND DEVELOPMENT, PRODUCTION AND MARKETING: CAUGHT BY ARTICLE 85(1): JOINT TENDERING, SO INELIGIBLE FOR GROUP EXEMPTION: INDIVIDUAL EXEMPTION GRANTED: E.C. Comm.) [1991] 4 C.M.L.R. 208

Alcatel Espace SA and Ant Nachrichtentechnik GmbH's Agreement (RESTRICTIVE PRACTICES: JOINT RESEARCH AND DEVELOPMENT, MANUFACTURING AND MARKETING: SATELLITE COMMUNICATIONS EQUIPMENT: INTENTION TO APPROVE: E.C. Comm.) [1990] 4 C.M.L.R. 16

Alexander Bihi Zenou v. Michel Colucci (COPYRIGHT: COMPILATION OF STORIES: France: C.A.)   [1986] E.C.C. 528

Alexander Fergusson & Co. v. Matthews McClay & Manson (PASSING OFF: USE OF GET-UP: ABANDONMENT OF GET-UP: BALANCE OF CONVENIENCE: TRADE MARKS AND NAMES: Scotland: O.H.)   1989 S.L.T. 795

Alexander v. Tait-Jamison (TRADE MARK: APPLICATION: OPPOSITION: PROPRIETORSHIP: WHETHER MARKS NEARLY OR SUBSTANTIALLY IDENTICAL: WHETHER GOODS OF THE SAME DESCRIPTION: USE OF BUSINESS NAME: WHETHER USE AS MARK: Australia: AIPO)   28 I.P.R. 103

Alexander von Füner, *sub nom.* von Füner, Alexander

Alfa Laval Cheese Systems Ltd v. Wincanton Engineering Ltd (COPYRIGHT: INFRINGEMENT: INTERLOCUTORY INJUNCTION: SERIOUS ISSUE: BREACH OF CONFIDENCE: PUBLICATION OF CONFIDENTIAL INFORMATION BY SUPPLY OF MACHINES: INJUNCTION PRACTICE: UNQUANTIFIABLE HARM: BALANCE OF CONVENIENCE: Ch.D.)   [1990] F.S.R. 583

Alfa-Laval/Belated translation (EUROPEAN PATENT: OPPOSITION: PROCEDURE: NOTICE OF OPPOSITION: LATE FILING OF TRANSLATION: COSTS: APPORTIONMENT: FEES: REIMBURSEMENT OF OPPOSITION FEE GRANTED: T193/87: EPO)   [1992] E.P.O.R. 63; [1993] O.J. EPO 207

Algie v. Dorminy (TRADE MARK: APPLICATION: OPPOSITION: WHETHER PRIOR USE: WHETHER DECEPTIVE OR CONFUSING: Australia: AIPO)   30 I.P.R. 15

Allen & Hanbury's Ltd v. Generics (U.K.) Ltd (PATENT: INFRINGEMENT: INJUNCTION: LICENCES OF RIGHT: PARALLEL IMPORTS: EXHAUSTION OF RIGHTS: Pat. Ct)   [1985] 1 C.M.L.R. 619; [1985] F.S.R. 229

Allen & Hanbury's Ltd v. Generics (U.K.) Ltd (PATENTS: IMPORTS: PHARMACEUTICALS: FOLLOW-UP TO EARLIER EUROPEAN COURT RULING: H.L.)   [1989] 2 C.M.L.R. 325
(ECJ) 14 I.P.R. 131

Allen & Hanbury's Ltd's (Salbutamol) Patent (PATENT: PHARMACEUTICAL SUBSTANCE: LICENCE OF RIGHT: SETTLEMENT OF TERMS: ROYALTY: IMPORTATION: SUB-CONTRACTING PROVISION: PATENTEE'S POSITION AS MANUFACTURER: PRACTICE: NATURE OF APPEAL TO PATENT COURT: EFFECT OF COMPTROLLER'S DECISION ON OPERATION OF LICENCE: C.-G.: Pat. Ct: C.A.)   [1987] R.P.C. 327

Allen & Hanbury's Ltd v. Generics (U.K.) Ltd (R v. Comptroller-General of Patents, etc., ex p. Gist-Brocades NV) (PATENT: IMPORTS: LICENCES OF RIGHT: TERMS OF LICENCE: EFFECTIVE DATE OF LICENCE: CONSTRUCTION: EXHAUSTION OF RIGHTS: Ch.D.)   [1986] 2 F.T.L.R. 100
(C.A.) [1986] 1 C.M.L.R. 101; [1985] F.S.R. 610; [1986] R.P.C. 203
(INTERIM JUDGMENT: H.L.)
[1985] F.S.R. 610; [1986] 1 F.T.L.R. 283; [1986] R.P.C. 203; [1986] 1 W.L.R. 51
(Case 434/85: ECJ) [1988] 4 C.M.L.R. 701; [1988] E.C.R. 1275;
[1988] F.S.R. 312

Allen-Bradley/Electromagnetically operated switch (EUROPEAN PATENT: CLAIMS: CLARITY: IMPRECISE TERMS: INVENTIVE STEP: BONUS EFFECT: ONE-WAY STREET: PRIOR ART IN CLOSELY RELATED FIELD: T21/81: EPO)
[1979–85] E.P.O.R. B342; [1983] O.J. EPO 15

Allgas Energy Ltd v. East West International Gas Equipment Pty Ltd (PRACTICE: INTERLOCUTORY INJUNCTION: SERIOUS QUESTION TO BE TRIED: Australia: Fed. Ct)   30 I.P.R. 269

Allibert SA v. O'Connor (COPYRIGHT: INFRINGEMENT: ASSESSMENT OF DAMAGES: INTEREST: Ireland: H.C.)   [1982] I.L.R.M. 40

Allied Arab Bank Ltd v. Hajjar (PRACTICE: *Mareva* INJUNCTION: *Writ ne exeat regno*:
PURPOSE OF WRIT: PREJUDICE TO DEFENDANT: Q.B.D.)
[1987] 3 All E.R. 739; [1987] 1 F.T.L.R. 455

Allied Colloids Ltd v. S.C. Johnson & Son Inc. (TRADE MARK: APPLICATION:
OPPOSITION: EARLIER MARK REGISTERED FOR OVERLAPPING GOODS:
SUBSTANTIAL IDENTITY OR DECEPTIVE SIMILARITY: WHETHER USE LIKELY
TO DECEIVE OR CAUSE CONFUSION: USE OF MARK IN PRACTICE ONLY IN
INDUSTRIAL APPLICATION: Australia: Pat. Off.)   19 I.P.R. 447

Allied Colloids/Intervention (EUROPEAN PATENT: OPPOSITION: PROCEDURE:
FRESH GROUND ON APPEAL: INTERVENTION: ADMISSIBILITY: ENLARGED
BOARD OF APPEAL: INVITATION TO EPO PRESIDENT TO COMMENT:
REFERENCE MADE BY TECHNICAL BOARD OF APPEAL OF ITS OWN:
CONVENTIONS: INTERPRETATION: *Travaux préparatoires decisive*: T169/92:
EPO)   [1994] E.P.O.R. 491

Allied Industries (Jaipur West) v. Allied Industries (Jaipur South) (TRADE MARK:
ARBITRATION AWARD DECLARING EQUAL RIGHTS: RECTIFICATION:
APPLICATION: India: T.M.Reg.)   (1986) 11 I.P.L.R. 22

Allied Signal/Proportioning valve (EUROPEAN PATENT: OPPOSITION: PROCEDURE:
NOTICE OF OPPOSITION: GENERAL INTERRUPTION IN MAIL: RE-
ESTABLISHMENT OF RIGHTS: ADMISSIBILITY OF APPLICATION BY OPPONENT:
CONVENTIONS: NATIONAL LAWS, RELATIONSHIP OF EPC TO: T702/89:
EPO)   [1993] E.P.O.R. 580; [1994] O.J. EPO 472

Allied/Beryllium-substituted iron-boron alloy (EUROPEAN PATENT: INVENTIVE
STEP: GENERAL APPROACH: CLOSEST PRIOR ART: PROBLEM, DEFINITION OF:
OPPOSITION: PROCEDURE: DUTY TO RECTIFY FAILURE OF EXAMINING
DIVISION: REMITTAL TO FIRST INSTANCE: T113/83: EPO)
[1979–85] E.P.O.R. C829

Allied/Cobalt foils (EUROPEAN PATENT: NOVELTY: SELECTION: INVENTIVE STEP:
COULD/WOULD TEST: EVIDENCE: COMPARATIVE TESTS: EXTRAPOLATION
FROM: T265/84: EPO)   [1987] E.P.O.R. 193

Allied/Garnet laser (EUROPEAN PATENT: INVENTIVE STEP: AGED ART:
COMBINATION OF CITATIONS: T263/87: EPO)   [1988] E.P.O.R. 243

Allsop Inc. v. Bintang Ltd (PATENT: INFRINGEMENT: TWO PATENTS FOR DEVICES
FOR CLEANING CASSETTE PLAYERS: WHETHER INFRINGED BY RESPONDENTS
"FLEXIBAR": CONSTRUCTION OF CLAIMS: Australia: Fed. Ct)   15 I.P.R. 686

Allworth Constructions Pty Ltd v. Dixon Investments Pty Ltd (TRADE MARK:
APPLICATION: OPPOSITION: PROPRIETORSHIP: USE OF TRADE MARK: GOODS
OR SERVICES: Australia: AIPO)   27 I.P.R. 263

ALOHA SWANFU Trade Mark, *sub nom.* Beyer Electrical Enterprise Pte Ltd v.
Swanfu Trading Pte Ltd

Alpha Industries Pty Ltd v. Vita-Craft Ltd (TRADE MARK: PROPRIETORSHIP:
SCANDALOUS AND IMPROPER: Australia: Pat. Off.)   3 I.P.R. 239

Alphapharm Pty Ltd v. Secretary, Department of Community Services & Health, *sub
nom.* Smith Kline & French Laboratories (Aust.) Ltd v. Secretary, Department of
Community Services & Health

Alpine Audio Accoustic v. Alpine Electronic Inc. (TRADE MARK: APPLICATION:
OPPOSITION: OVERSEAS REPUTATION: Australia: Pat. Off.)   4 I.P.R. 358

Alt, Peter/Inspection of files (EUROPEAN PATENT: APPLICATION: PROCEDURE: INSPECTION OF FILE: CONFIDENTIALITY: ORAL HEARING: ABRIDGEMENT OF NOTICE: EVIDENCE: OBJECTIVE EFFECT V. SUBJECTIVE INTENTION: ENLARGED BOARD OF APPEAL: REFERENCE REFUSED: EPO: OBSERVATIONS BY PRESIDENT: CONVENTIONS: DIFFERENT LANGUAGE TEXTS: NATIONAL LAW: PROCEDURAL PRINCIPLES: RELEVANCE OF: PROCEDURAL V. SUBSTANTIVE LAW: EPC PROVISIONS AND EPC RULES: PRECEDENCE: J14/91: EPO)
[1994] E.P.O.R. 184; [1993] O.J. EPO 479

Altertext Inc. v. Advanced Data Communications Ltd (COPYRIGHT: INFRINGEMENT: PASSING OFF: ANTON PILLER PRACTICE: LEAVE TO SERVE ABROAD: Ch.D.)
[1985] 1 All E.R. 395; [1985] E.C.C. 375; [1986] F.S.R. 21

Altos Computer Systems v. The Purchasing Agent Ltd (PRACTICE: *ex parte* INJUNCTION: NON-DISCLOSURE: SETTING ASIDE: New Zealand: H.C.)
(1985) 5 I.P.R. 70

Aluminium Specialties Pty Ltd's Application (DESIGN: EXTENSION: NOVELTY: PRIOR PUBLICATION: MATERIAL OF FUNCTIONAL FEATURES: Australia: Pat. Off.)
23 I.P.R. 86

Aluminium Specialties Pty Ltd v. Ibis Building Products Pty Ltd (DESIGN: CANCELLATION: ORIGINALITY: Australia: S.C.)   (1982) 42 A.L.R. 127

Alupower-Chloride Ltd (Re) (RESTRICTIVE PRACTICES: JOINT VENTURE: JOINT DEVELOPMENT, PRODUCTION AND DISTRIBUTION OF ALUMINIUM/AIR BATTERY: INTENTION TO ISSUE COMFORT LETTER: E.C. Comm.)
[1990] 4 C.M.L.R. 739

ALWAYS Trade Mark (TRADE MARK: APPLICATION: DISTINCTIVENESS: Ch.D.)   [1986] R.P.C. 93

Alwinco Products Ltd v. Crystal Glass Industries Ltd, *sub nom.* Crystal Glass Industries Ltd v. Alwinco Products Ltd

Alza/Infusor (EUROPEAN PATENT: DIVISIONAL APPLICATION: CRITERIA FOR: AMENDMENT AND CORRECTION: HYPOTHETICAL CORRECTION, NON-OBVIOUS: T514/88: EPO)   [1990] E.P.O.R. 157; [1992] O.J. EPO 570

Amalgamated Mining Services Pty Ltd v. Warman International Ltd (COPYRIGHT: ENGINEERING DRAWINGS: WHETHER ARTISTIC WORKS: OVERLAP WITH DESIGN PROTECTION: ADDITIONAL DAMAGES: DESIGNS: OVERLAP WITH COPYRIGHT PROTECTION: REGISTRABILITY: C.-G.)   24 I.P.R. 461

Amalgamated TV Services Pty Ltd v. Australian Broadcasting Tribunal (BROADCASTING: TELEVISION: LICENSING FEES: PRACTICE: Australia: Fed. Ct)   [1984] 54 A.L.R. 57

Amalgamated TV Services Pty. Ltd v. Foxtel Digital Cable Television Pty. Ltd (COPYRIGHT: BROADCASTING: RE-TRANSMISSION OF TELEVISION PROGRAMMES: EXEMPTION FROM REGULATORY REGIME: Australia: Fed. Ct)
136 A.L.R. 3

Amar Nath Sehgal v. Union of India (COPYRIGHT: ARTISTIC WORK: MURAL: DESTRUCTION: DETERIORATION: *ex parte* INTERIM INJUNCTION TO PREVENT LOSS: India: H.C.)   (1994) 19 I.P.L.R. 160

Amateur Athletic Association's Applications (PATENT: APPLICATION: ENTITLEMENT: PRIORITY DATE: C.-G.)   [1989] R.P.C. 717

Amco Wrangler Ltd v. Jacques Konckier (TRADE MARKS: APPLICATION FOR REGISTRATION: PART B OF THE REGISTER: OPPOSITION: LIKELIHOOD OF DECEPTION OR CONFUSION: SURNAMES: Australia: Pat. Off.)   10 I.P.R. 376

Amcor Ltd v. Visy Board Pty Ltd (PATENT: OPPOSITION TO GRANT: OPPOSITION TO AMENDMENT: WHETHER CLAIMS PRIOR PUBLISHED: NO NOVELTY IN PURPOSE: PURPOSE COMMON KNOWLEDGE: CLAIMS 1, 2, 3 PRIOR PUBLISHED: CLAIM 5 NOT NOVEL: PROPOSED AMENDMENTS ALLOWABLE: AMENDED CLAIMS NOT NOVEL: Australia: Pat. Off.) 18 I.P.R. 621

American Chemical Society's Application (TRADE MARKS: NON-REGISTRABLE: DESCRIPTIVE: EVIDENCE OF LONG USE: DISTINCTIVE OF ORIGIN OF USE TO RELEVANT SECTION OF COMMUNITY: MARK INHERENTLY INCAPABLE OF DISTINGUISHING GOODS: Australia: Pat. Off.) 15 I.P.R. 105

American Colloid/Clay layer (EUROPEAN PATENT: CLAIMS: FUNCTIONAL FEATURES: SUPPORT FOR: T610/90: EPO) [1993] E.P.O.R. 1

American Cyanamid Co.'s (Fenbufen) Patent (PATENT: LICENCE OF RIGHT: SETTLEMENT OF TERMS: EFFECT OF PATENTEES' EXCEPTIONAL PROMOTIONAL EFFORTS: Pat. Ct) [1990] R.P.C. 309
(C.A.) [1991] R.P.C. 409

American Cyanamid Co. v. Alcoa of Australia Ltd (CONFIDENTIAL INFORMATION: MOTION TO STRIKE OUT PLEADINGS: PATENT SPECIFICATION: WHETHER INFORMATION SUFFICIENTLY IDENTIFIED: Australia: Fed. Ct) 27 I.P.R. 16

American Cyanamid Co. v. Nalco Chemical Co. (PATENT: OPPOSITION: EVIDENCE: CROSS-EXAMINATION: WITNESSES: REQUEST FOR THE COMMISSIONER OF PATENTS TO SUMMON WITNESSES: PATENT OFFICE PRACTICE: Australia: Pat. Off.) 24 I.P.R. 131

American Cyanamid/Acrylonitrile polymer fibre (EUROPEAN PATENT: INVENTIVE STEP: COULD/WOULD TEST: NOVELTY: SELECTION: EVIDENCE: COMPARATIVE TESTS: NOT CHALLENGED: T90/84: EPO)
[1979–85] E.P.O.R. C952

American Cyanamid/Melt spinning (EUROPEAN PATENT: T49/85: EPO)
[1989] E.P.O.R. 234

American Express Co. v. NV Amev (TRADE MARK: APPLICATION: OPPOSITION: AMEX/AMEV: SUBSTANTIALLY IDENTICAL MARKS: Australia: Pat. Off.)
5 I.P.R. 267

American Express International Inc. v. D. Thomas Associates Pty Ltd (CONFIDENTIAL INFORMATION: ESSENTIALS OF CAUSE OF ACTION: CHARGE CARD SCHEME: ASSOCIATED WINE SOCIETY: WHETHER LIST OF MEMBERS CONFIDENTIAL INFORMATION OF PROMOTER OF CARD SCHEME: Australia: S.C.(NSW)) 19 I.P.R. 574

American Geophysical Union v. Texaco Inc. (COPYRIGHT: INFRINGEMENT: PHOTOCOPYING: SCIENTIFIC JOURNALS: CORPORATE RESEARCH: COMMERCIAL PURPOSE: FAIR USE: U.S.A.: D.C.) 24 I.P.R. 417
(C.A.) 29 I.P.R. 381

American Greeting Corp.'s Application, sub nom. HOLLY HOBBIE Trade Mark

American Home Products Corp. v. Commissioner of Patents (PATENT: EXTENSION: MATTERS TO BE CONSIDERED: EXCEPTIONAL CASE: RELEVANCE OF LAWS REQUIRING APPROVAL ON DELAY IN MARKETING: Australia: Fed. Ct)
16 I.P.R. 252

American Home Products Corp. v. Mac Laboratories Pvt Ltd, sub nom. DRISTAN Trade Mark

American Home Products Corp. v. Mini Pharma (TRADE MARK: APPLICATION: OPPOSITION: PARIN/SPARINE: India: T.M.Reg.) (1992) 17 I.P.L.R. 271

American International Group Inc. v. London American International Corp. Ltd (PASSING OFF: LIBERTY TO DISCONTINUE ACTION: Ch.D.)
[1982] F.S.R. 441

American National Can Co. v. W.R. Grace & Co.–Conn. (PATENT: APPLICATION: OPPOSITION: COSTS: Australia: AIPO)   30 I.P.R. 292

American Optical Corp. v. Allergan Pharmaceuticals Pty Ltd (PATENT: TRADE PRACTICES: JOINT CLAIM: PRACTICE: Australia: Fed. Ct)   [1985] 4 I.P.R. 1

American Supplier Institute Inc.'s Application (TRADE MARKS: APPLICATION: GENERIC TERMS: UNADAPTED TO DISTINGUISH: INCAPABLE OF BECOMING DISTINCTIVE: FOREIGN TRADE MARK REGISTRATIONS: Australia: Pat. Off.)   24 I.P.R. 119

Americaya Singapore Pte Ltd v. Americaya Malaysia Shn Bhd (TRADE MARK: REGISTRATION: INFRINGEMENT: PASSING OFF: APPLICATION FOR STAY PENDING HEARING OF APPLICATION TO EXPUNGE: INTERLOCUTORY INJUNCTION: BALANCE OF CONVENIENCE: Malaysia: H.C.)   [1994] 1 M.L.J. 695

Amersham International's Joint Venture (RESTRICTIVE PRACTICES: E.C. Comm.)   [1983] 1 C.M.L.R. 619; [1983] F.S.R. 380; [1982] O.J. L314/34

Amersham International plc v. Corning Ltd (PATENT: INFRINGEMENT: PRACTICE: EUROPEAN PATENT: OPPOSITION AT EPO: MOTION FOR STAY IN HIGH COURT: *Forum conveniens*: STAY REFUSED: Pat. Ct)   [1987] R.P.C. 53

Ametex Fabrics Inc. v. C. & F. Fabrics Pty Ltd (COPYRIGHT: DESIGN APPLIED TO FABRIC: STATUTORY INTERPRETATION: Australia: Fed. Ct)   111 A.L.R. 565; 24 I.P.R. 449

Amoco Corporation/Alternative claims (EUROPEAN PATENT: APPLICATION: PROCEDURE: PRIOR ART, FAILURE TO EXAMINE: FRESH CLAIMS: NOVELTY: CROSS-REFERENCED DOCUMENTS: T153/85: EPO)   [1988] E.P.O.R. 116; [1988] O.J. EPO 01

Amoco/Polyarylates (EUROPEAN PATENT: NOVELTY: DOCUMENT: TOTAL INFORMATION CONTENT: T424/86: EPO)   [1992] E.P.O.R. 509

AMP/Coaxial connector (EUROPEAN PATENT: APPLICATION: PROCEDURE: CONTENTS OF APPLICATION: BROADENING CLAIM BY OMISSION: EVIDENCE: EXPERT'S AFFIDAVIT DISCOUNTED: CONVENTIONS: NATIONAL CASE LAW, NEED TO DEMONSTRATE RELEVANCE OF: T260/85: EPO)   [1989] E.P.O.R. 403; [1989] O.J. EPO 105

AMP/Connector (EUROPEAN PATENT: AMENDMENT AND CORRECTION: BROADENING CLAIM BY OMISSION: DRAWINGS: TEACHING OF: T66/85: EPO)   [1989] E.P.O.R. 283; [1989] O.J. EPO 167

AMP/Electrical connector (EUROPEAN PATENT: OPPOSITION: PROCEDURE: AMENDMENTS NOT PROPOSED: AMENDMENT AND CORRECTION: ADDITIONAL FEATURES IN CLAIM: INVENTIVE STEP: NOVELTY: NATURE OF EXAMINATION: FEES: REIMBURSEMENT OF APPEAL FEE: T133/83: EPO)   [1979–85] E.P.O.R. C850

AMP/Electrical contact (EUROPEAN PATENT: NOVELTY: ACCIDENTAL ANTICIPATION: IMPLICIT DISCLOSURE: PROCEDURE: OPPORTUNITY TO COMMENT ON REASONS: T161/82: EPO)   [1979–85] E.P.O.R. C660; [1984] O.J. EPO 551

Amper SA's Design application (REGISTERED DESIGN: APPLICATION: DIVISIONAL APPLICATION: PRACTICE: COSTS: RDAT)   [1993] R.P.C. 453

Ampex Corp. v. Amper SA (TRADE MARK: OPPOSITION: EXTENSION OF TIME TO SERVE EVIDENCE: SETTLEMENT NEGOTIATIONS: PUBLIC INTEREST: Australia: AIPO)   29 I.P.R. 501

Ampex Corporation/Clarity (EUROPEAN PATENT: CLAIMS: CLARITY AND SUFFICIENCY DISTINGUISHED: INTERPRETATION OF ARTICLE 84: PRECISE SCOPE OF PROTECTION: ALL ESSENTIAL FEATURES: FUNCTIONAL FEATURES: PRIOR ART DISTINGUISHED: T1055/92: EPO)
[1995] E.P.O.R. 469; [1995] O.J. EPO 214

Ampex/*Restitutio in integrum* (EUROPEAN PATENT: APPEAL: PROCEDURE: STATEMENT OF GROUNDS, REQUIREMENTS OF: RE-ESTABLISHMENT OF RIGHTS: COMPUTER FAILURE: T253/90: EPO)   [1992] E.P.O.R. 118

Amrad Corp. Ltd v. Genentech Inc. (PATENT: APPLICATION: OPPOSITION: NOTICE: EXTENSION OF TIME: ERROR OR OMISSION: Australia: AIPO)   29 I.P.R. 218

Amrutanjan Ltd v. Amrachand Sobachand (TRADE MARK: INFRINGEMENT: PASSING OFF: NO SALE UNDER INFRINGING MARK: PERMANENT INJUNCTION: India: H.C.)   (1992) 17 I.P.L.R. 1
(JURISDICTION: H.C.)   (1992) 17 I.P.L.R.

Amrutanjan Ltd v. Ashwin Fine Chemicals & Pharmaceuticals (TRADE MARK: INFRINGEMENT: AMRUTANJAN/ASHWIN: PASSING OFF: INTERIM INJUNCTION: India: H.C.)   (1995) 20 I.P.L.R. 48

Amstrad Consumer Electronics plc v. The British Phonograph Industry Ltd (COPYRIGHT: INFRINGEMENT: HOME TAPING: DOUBLE-HEADED CASSETTE RECORDERS: DECLARATION: EFFECT OF COPYRIGHT WARNING NOTICE: KNOWLEDGE AND INTENT: NEGLIGENCE: DUTY OF CARE: CRIMINAL LIABILITY: INCITEMENT: Ch.D.)
[1986] E.C.C. 531; [1986] F.S.R. 159; [1986] 1 F.T.L.R. 73
(C.A.) [1986] F.S.R. 159

An Bord Trachtala v. Waterford Foods plc (PASSING OFF: INTERLOCUTORY INJUNCTION: ATTEMPT TO RESTRICT ACTS COMMITTED ABROAD: JURISDICTION: WHETHER SERIOUS ISSUE TO BE TRIED: EVIDENCE: INJUNCTION REFUSED: Ireland: H.C.)   [1994] F.S.R. 316

An Post, National Treasury Management Agency v. Irish Permanent plc (PASSING OFF: PURPOSE OF REMEDY: USE OF DESCRIPTIVE NAME: TEST: PROOF OF ACTUAL DECEPTION: LIKELIHOOD OF DECEPTION: SAVINGS CERTIFICATES: TAX-FREE INVESTMENT GUARANTEED BY GOVERNMENT: LAUNCH OF PRODUCT UNDER SAME NAME: NEITHER TAX-FREE NOR GUARANTEED BY GOVERNMENT: LIKELIHOOD OF CONFUSION: INTERLOCUTORY INJUNCTION: SERIOUS QUESTION TO BE TRIED: DELAY: TRIAL DATE FIXED: WHETHER GROUNDS FOR REFUSAL: PUBLIC POLICY: Ireland: H.C.)   [1995] 1 I.R. 140

Anacon Corp. Ltd v. Environmental Research Technology Ltd (COPYRIGHT: INFRINGEMENT: CIRCUIT DIAGRAMS: WHETHER INFRINGED AS ARTISTIC WORKS BY "NET LISTS" AND CIRCUIT BOARDS: WHETHER INFRINGED AS LITERARY WORKS: Ch.D.)   [1994] F.S.R. 659

Anaesthetic Supplies Pty Ltd v. Rescare Ltd, *sub nom.* Rescare Ltd v. Anaesthetic Supplies Pty Ltd

Ancare Distributors Limited v. Merck Patent GmbH, *sub nom.* Merck Patent GmbH v. Virbac (Australia) Pty Ltd

Anchor Building Products Ltd v. Redland Roof Tiles Ltd (PATENT: INFRINGEMENT: STRIKING OUT: CONSTRUCTION: C.A.)   [1990] R.P.C. 283

Anderson & Lembke Ltd v. Anderson & Lembke Inc. (PASSING OFF: INTERLOCUTORY INJUNCTION: COMMON ORIGIN OF TRADING NAMES: Ch.D.)   [1989] R.P.C. 124

Andoy Pty Ltd v. S. & M Cannon Pty Ltd (PATENT: CONTRACT: EXCLUSIVE
LICENCE: WORLDWIDE EXPLOITATION OF PATENT: DETERMINATION UPON
BREACH: BREACH OF BEST ENDEAVOURS CLAUSE: INTERLOCUTORY
INJUNCTION: Australia: S.C.(Vic.))   17 I.P.R. 533

Andritz Sprout-Bauer Australia Pty Ltd v. Rowland Engineering Sales Pty Ltd
(COPYRIGHT: INFRINGEMENT: UNCONSCIOUS COPYING: ASSIGNMENT: SALE
OF OTHER ASSETS: Australia: Fed. Ct)   28 I.P.R. 29

Anglo French Drug Co. (Eastern) Ltd v. Belco Pharmaceuticals (TRADE MARK:
INFRINGEMENT: INJUNCTION: India: H.C.)   (1985) 9 I.P.L.R. 149

Anglo French Drug Co. (The) v. Brihans Laboratories (TRADE MARK: APPLICATION:
OPPOSITION: BRIPLEX/BEPLEX: India: H.C.)   (1995) 20 I.P.L.R. 7

Anglo-French Drug Co. (Eastern) Ltd v. Hony-N-Bois (APPLICATION: OPPOSITION:
HEPASYP/HEPAX: OPPOSITION DISMISSED BY REGISTRAR: APPEAL TO
HIGH COURT ALLOWED: India: H.C.)   (1989) 13 I.P.L.R. 193

Angoves Pty Ltd v. Johnson (TRADE MARK: INFRINGEMENT: EXCLUSIVE USE BY
PROPRIETOR: GOOD FAITH: Australia: Fed. Ct)   [1983] 43 A.L.R. 349

Angus & Coote Pty Ltd v. Render (CONFIDENTIAL INFORMATION: EX-EMPLOYEE:
WHETHER INFORMATION HAS QUALITY OF CONFIDENCE: NO PROOF
INFORMATION TAKEN IN WRITTEN FORM: EMPLOYEE'S FIDUCIARY DUTY
AND DUTY OF GOOD FAITH: CONTRACT OF EMPLOYMENT: IMPLIED TERM OF
GOOD FAITH: INJUNCTION: LENGTH OF RESTRAINT: DELIVERY UP: CLEAN
HANDS: Australia: S.C.(NSW))   16 I.P.R. 387

Anheuser Busch Inc. v. Controller of Patents, Designs & Trade marks (TRADE MARK:
DECISION OF REGISTRY: JUDICIAL REVIEW: NATURAL JUSTICE: Ireland:
H.C.)   [1988] F.S.R. 23

Anheuser-Busch Inc. v. Castlebrae Pty Ltd (COPYRIGHT: WHETHER DRAWINGS OF
DOG ARTISTIC OR LITERARY WORKS: WHETHER BREACH OF COPYRIGHT:
TRADE MARKS: APPLICATION: PRIOR REGISTRATION BY RESPONDENT:
CHARACTER MERCHANDISING: Australia: Fed. Ct)   23 I.P.R. 54

Anheuser-Busch v. Budejovicky Budvar NP (PASSING OFF: BUDWEISER BEER:
HONEST CONCURRENT USER: USE AT U.S. BASES IN U.K.: GOODWILL:
REPUTATION: ESTOPPEL: ACQUIESCENCE: Ch.D.: C.A.)   [1984] F.S.R. 413
see also, *sub nom.* BUD Trade Mark

ANI Corp. Ltd v. Celtite Aust. Pty Ltd (CONFIDENTIAL INFORMATION: DUTIES OF
EX-EMPLOYEE'S: WHETHER INFORMATION GAINED DURING EMPLOYMENT
HAS QUALITY OF CONFIDENCE: PUBLICATION BY PATENTS: INTERLOCUTORY
INJUNCTION: Australia: Fed. Ct)   19 I.P.R. 506

Anstoetz's (Jab Josef's) Application (TRADE MARKS: REMOVAL: NON-USE: PERSON
AGGRIEVED: USE BY DISTRIBUTOR: Australia: Pat. Off.)   22 I.P.R. 412

Antiphon AB's Application (PATENT: APPLICATION: PRACTICE: CLERICAL ERROR:
Pat. Ct)   [1984] R.P.C. 1

Antox India (Pvt.) Ltd v. State Drug Controller, Tamil Nadu (TRADE MARK: STATE
MANUFACTURING LICENCE: *Mandamus:* India: H.C.)   (1991) 16 I.P.L.R. 264

Anup Engr. Ltd v. Controller of Patents (PATENT: RIGHT TO LODGE: India:
H.C.)   (1983) 8 I.P.L.R. 22

Anvil Jewellery Ltd v. Riva Ridge Holdings Ltd (COPYRIGHT: SUBSISTENCE:
ASSIGNMENT: AGREEMENT FOR SALE OF ASSETS: CONSTRUCTION:
INTERLOCUTORY INJUNCTION: ANTON PILLER ORDERS: DISCHARGE: New
Zealand: H.C.)   8 I.P.R. 161; [1987] 1 N.Z.L.R. 35

Aoki's Application (PATENT: APPLICATION: PRACTICE: RULE 100; IRREGULARITY
IN PROCEDURE: DISCRETION: Pat. Ct)   [1987] R.P.C. 133

Apac Rowena Ltd v. Norpol Packaging Ltd (COPYRIGHT: ASSIGNED MATTERS: COUNSEL'S DUTY TO COURT: INTERLOCUTORY RELIEF: FAILURE TO SERVE STATEMENT OF CLAIM: Ch.D.) [1991] F.S.R. 273

Appellate jurisdiction (EUROPEAN PATENT: PCT APPLICATION: PROCEDURE: PRELIMINARY EXAMINATION AUTHORITY: PCT CASES: CONVENTIONS: PCT, APPLICABILITY OF EPC PROCEDURES UNDER: BOARD OF APPEAL: JURISDICTION: J20/89: EPO) [1991] E.P.O.R. 436; [1991] O.J. EPO 375

Apple Computer Inc. v. Apple Corps. SA (TRADE MARKS: EXPUNGEMENT OF NEW ZEALAND TRADE MARK: EXISTENCE OF DISPUTE BETWEEN SAME PARTIES IN U.K. CONCERNING THE SAME MARKS: SOLE JURISDICTION CLAUSE IN U.K. AGREEMENT: New Zealand: H.C.) 17 I.P.R. 123

Apple Computer Inc. v. Apple Leasing & Industries Ltd (TRADE MARK: PASSING OFF: INTERIM INJUNCTION: India: H.C.) (1993) 18 I.P.L.R. 63

Apple Computer Inc. v. Apple Leasing Industries Ltd (PASSING OFF: RESTRAINT OF USE OF UNREGISTERED MARKS FOR PROVISION OF SERVICES: INTERNATIONAL REPUTATION: COMMON FIELD OF ACTIVITY: LIKELIHOOD OF DECEPTION OR CONFUSION: NATURE OF GOODWILL: LACHES AND ACQUIESCENCE: India: H.C.) 22 I.P.R. 257

Apple Computer Inc. v. Computer Edge Pty Ltd (COPYRIGHT: INFRINGEMENT: COMPUTER PROGRAMS: WHETHER SOURCE CODE ADAPTATION OF SOURCE CODE: Australia: Fed. Ct)
(1984) 50 A.L.R. 581; [1983] A.T.P.R. 44, 884; 1 I.P.L. 353; [1984] F.S.R. 246
(Fed. Ct) (1984) 53 A.L.R. 225; [1984] A.T.P.R. 45, 235; 2 I.P.L. 1;
[1984] F.S.R. 481
(Full Ct) 53 A.L.R. 225
(H.C.) 65 A.L.R. 33; 161 C.L.R.J. 171; 6 I.P.R. 1; [1986] F.S.R. 537

Apple Computer Inc. v. Microsoft Corp. (COPYRIGHT: COMPUTER PROGRAMS: "LOOK AND FEEL" OF VISUAL DISPLAYS OF PROGRAM: SUBSISTENCE OF COPYRIGHT IN VISUAL DISPLAYS: MERGER OF IDEA AND EXPRESSION: INDISPENSABLE EXPRESSION: *Scenes a faire*: MERE FUNCTIONALITY: U.S.A.: D.C.) 24 I.P.R. 362

Apple Computer Inc. v. Microsoft Corp. (COPYRIGHT: COMPUTER PROGRAMS: "LOOK AND FEEL": SUBSISTENCE OF COPYRIGHT IN VISUAL DISPLAYS: LICENCE: SCOPE: INTERPRETATION: U.S.A.: D.C.) 21 I.P.R. 287

Apple Computer Inc. v. New-Con Technologies Ltd (COPYRIGHT: INFRINGEMENT: COMPUTER SOFTWARE: PRINTED CIRCUITS: Israel: D.C.) 8 I.P.R. 353

Apple Computer Inc. v. Popiolek (PRACTICE: PROCEDURE: Australia: S.C.) 2 I.P.L. 94

Apple Computer Inc. v. Rowney (COPYRIGHT: COMPUTER PROGRAMS: PRACTICE: ANTON PILLER PROCEEDINGS: FORM OF ORDER: Australia: S.C.(NSW)) 5 I.P.R. 350

Apple Computer Inc. v. Segimex Sàrl (COPYRIGHT: COMPUTER PROGRAMS: France) [1985] E.C.C. 383; [1985] F.S.R. 608

Apple Corps. Ltd v. Apple Computer Inc. ("No challenge interlocutory") (TRADE MARKS: DELIMITATION AGREEMENT SUBJECT TO ENGLISH LAW: NO CHALLENGE CLAUSE: CONFLICT OF LAWS: EXTENT OF RELEVANCE OF FOREIGN LAW: *American Cyanamid* PRINCIPLES: RESTRAINT OF FOREIGN PROCEEDINGS: COSTS: Ch.D.) [1992] F.S.R. 431; [1992] R.P.C. 70

Apple Corps. Ltd v. Apple Computer Inc. (RESTRICTIVE PRACTICES: TRADE MARKS: NATIONAL PROCEEDINGS IN PARALLEL WITH E.C. COMMISSION PROCEEDINGS: CONFIDENTIAL EVIDENCE BEFORE NATIONAL COURT TO BE HANDED TO E.C. COMMISSION: Ch.D.)
[1992] 1 C.M.L.R. 969; [1992] F.S.R. 389

Apple Corps Ltd v. Apple Computer Ltd (TRADE MARKS: DELIMITATION AGREEMENT: RESTRICTION TO OWN LINES: RESTRICTIVE PRACTICES: COMPATIBILITY WITH ARTICLE 85: WHETHER VALIDITY RELEVANT: USE: C.A.)   [1991] 3 C.M.L.R. 49

Apple Corps. Ltd v. Cooper (COPYRIGHT: PHOTOGRAPHS: OWNERSHIP OF COPYRIGHT: COMMISSIONED WORK: ESTOPPEL: Ch.D.)   [1993] F.S.R. 286

Apple Corps. Ltd v. EMI Records Ltd (CONTRACT: BREACH: CONSTRUCTION: RECTIFICATION: BEATLES RECORDINGS: RED AND BLUE ALBUMS: SETTLEMENT AGREEMENT PROHIBITING RELEASE OF CERTAIN RECORDS WITHOUT PRIOR WRITTEN CONSENT: ALBUMS IN NEW FORMAT: WHETHER AGREEMENT APPLIED TO BOXED SET: C.A.)   [1994] E.M.L.R. 73

Appleton Papers Inc. v. Tomasetti Paper Pty Ltd (PATENT: INFRINGEMENT: INTERLOCUTORY INJUNCTION: Australia: S.C.(NSW))
(1983) 50 A.L.R. 428; 1 I.P.L. 569; [1983] 3 N.S.W.L.R. 208

Appleton Papers/Pressure-sensitive recording material (EUROPEAN PATENT: INVENTIVE STEP: ADDITIONAL EFFECT: DISCOURAGING ART: *Ex post facto* APPROACH: OBVIOUS TO TRY: T286/84: EPO)   [1987] E.P.O.R. 212

Appleton v. Harnischfeger Corporation (COPYRIGHT: SUBSISTENCE: ENGINEERING DRAWINGS MADE OVERSEAS: APPLICABLE LEGISLATION GOVERNING RECOGNITION OF COPYRIGHT IN DRAWINGS: South Africa: A.D.)
1995 (2) S.A. 247

Appliances Emporium v. m/s Usha Industries (India) New Delhi (TRADE MARK: INFRINGEMENT: INTERIM INJUNCTION: India: H.C.)   (1986) 11 I.P.L.R. 95

Application des Gaz's Application (PATENT: APPLICATION: PRACTICE: FILING TRANSLATION: RULE 100: Pat. Ct)   [1987] R.P.C. 279

Applied Liquor Merchants Ltd v. Independent Liquor (N.Z.) Ltd (MISLEADING AND DECEPTIVE CONDUCT: LABELLING OF ALCOHOLIC SPIRITS: USE OF NAMES GIN, WHISKY, VODKA, RUM ON DILUTED SPIRITS: MISLEADING ADVERTISING BY THIRD PARTIES: New Zealand: H.C.)   17 I.P.R. 79

Approved Prescription Services Ltd's Application (TRADE MARKS: APPLICATION: REGISTRABILITY: LETTERS AND INITIALS: INVENTED WORK: ADAPTED TO DISTINGUISH: DISTINCTIVE: PRIOR REGISTRATIONS: OFFICE PRACTICE: Australia: Pat. Off.)   17 I.P.R. 179

Aquaculture Corp. v. New Zealand Green Mussel Co. Ltd (AVAILABILITY OF DAMAGES FOR BREACH OF DUTY OF CONFIDENCE: EXEMPLARY DAMAGES: New Zealand: C.A.)   19 I.P.R. 527; [1990] 3 N.Z.L.R. 299

Aquaculture Corp. v. New Zealand Green Mussel Co. Ltd (CONFIDENTIAL INFORMATION: MUSSEL PREPARATION FOR TREATMENT OF ILLNESS: RELEASE INTO PUBLIC DOMAIN: New Zealand: H.C.)   5 I.P.R. 353

Aquaculture Corp. v. New Zealand Green Mussel Co. Ltd (No. 2) (CONFIDENTIAL INFORMATION: INJUNCTION: ASSESSMENT OF DAMAGES: EVALUATION OF LOST OPPORTUNITY: EXEMPLARY DAMAGES: ACCOUNT PROFITS REFUSED: New Zealand: H.C.)   10 I.P.R. 319

Aqualon Company/Water-soluble cellulose ether (EUROPEAN PATENT: CLAIM: CLARITY: RELATIVE TERM: INTERPRETATION IN THE LIGHT OF DESCRIPTION: REIMBURSEMENT OF APPEAL FEE (NO): T860/93: EPO)
[1995] E.P.O.R. 391; [1995] O.J. EPO 47

Aravind Laboratories v. Padmini Products (TRADE MARK: PASSING OFF: INTERIM INJUNCTION: India: H.C.) (1991) 16 I.P.L.R. 1

Aravind Laboratories v. V.A. Samy Chemical Works (TRADE MARK: INFRINGEMENT: QUALIFICATION TO FILE SUIT: VALIDITY OF ASSIGNMENT AND RENEWAL OF TRADE MARK: INJUNCTION: India: H.C.) (1988) 13 I.P.L.R. 4

Arbed SA and Unimetal SA's Agreements (RESTRICTIVE PRACTICES: COAL AND STEEL: SPECIALISATION AGREEMENTS: PRODUCT EXCHANGE: EXEMPTION GRANTED: E.C. Comm.) [1989] 4 C.M.L.R. 74

Arenhold/Priority right (EUROPEAN PATENT: APPLICATION: PROCEDURE: PRIORITY CLAIM: PRIORITY: DESIGN APPLICATION: CONVENTIONS: PARIS CONVENTION, RELATIONSHIP WITH EPC: J15/80: EPO) [1979–85] E.P.O.R. A56; [1981] O.J. EPO 213

Argos Films SA v. Ivens (COPYRIGHT: *Droit moral*: EXPLANATORY NOTE IN CREDITS OF FILM: BREACH IF FORBIDDEN BY AUTHOR: France: S.C.) [1992] E.C.C. 336; [1992] F.S.R. 547

Aristograf Graphics Inc. v. Northover (EX-EMPLOYEE: CUSTOMERS: FIDUCIARY RELATIONSHIP: INTERLOCUTORY: INJUNCTION: Canada: H.C.(Ont.)) 33 C.P.R. (3d) 310

ARLITE Trade Mark (TRADE MARK: RECTIFICATION: NON-USE: WHETHER PRIMA FACIE CASE OF NON-USE ESTABLISHED: T.M.Reg.) [1995] R.P.C. 504

Armaturjonsson AB's Application (PATENT: APPLICATION: PRACTICE: TIME LIMITS: Pat. Ct) [1985] R.P.C. 213

Armstrong v. Larocca (PATENT: APPLICATION: OPPOSITION: PRIOR USE: DESIRABILITY OF CORROBORATION: Australia: Pat. Off.) 26 I.P.R. 362

ARNOLD PALMER Trade mark (TRADE MARK: REGISTRATION: RECTIFICATION: BONA FIDE INTENTION TO USE: TRAFFICKING: Singapore: H.C.) [1987] M.L.J. 681

Arnotts Ltd v. Trace Practices Commission (TRADE PRACTICES: DISCLOSURE: LEGAL PROFESSIONAL PRIVILEGE: CONDITIONS: Australia: Fed. Ct) 87 A.L.R. 73

Arriba Pty Limited v. Cuisine To Go Pty Ltd (PASSING OFF: INTERLOCUTORY INJUNCTION: COPYRIGHT: LOGO: LACK OF CANDOUR AS TO ORIGIN: POSSIBILITY OF ORIGIN: Australia: Fed. Ct) 29 I.P.R. 584

Arrowin Ltd v. Trimguard (U.K.) Ltd (COPYRIGHT: INFRINGEMENT: IMPORTATION: KNOWLEDGE: Ch.D.) [1984] R.P.C. 581

Arthur Martin (Sales) Ltd v. Electra Mechanics (1975) Ltd (TRADE MARKS: MARK INITIALLY BELONGING TO MANUFACTURER CAN BECOME DISTINCTIVE OF DEALER: New Zealand: H.C.) 13 I.P.R. 122

Artifakts Design Group Ltd v. N. P. Rigg Ltd (COPYRIGHT: COMPILATION OF COMMON FEATURES: PASSING OFF: GOODWILL IN GET-UP: New Zealand: H.C.) [1993] 1 N.Z.L.R. 196

Artware Sàrl v. Groupe D'Utilisation Francophone D'Informatique (SOFTWARE SALES: COPYRIGHT: RIGHT TO MAKE BACK-UP COPIES: COMPUTER SOFTWARE: ANTI-PROTECTION PROCESSES: France: S.C.) [1993] E.C.C. 279; [1993] F.S.R. 703

Arumugam v. State of Tamil Nadu (TRADE MARK: CRIMINAL OFFENCE: FORGERY AND COUNTERFEITING: India: H.C.) (1992) 17 I.P.L.R. 54

Asahi Kasei KKK/Resin composition (EUROPEAN PATENT: OPPOSITION: PROCEDURE: FRESH EVIDENCE ON APPEAL, ALLOWED: NOVELTY: NEW PARAMETER: TECHNICAL FEATURE: PRIOR USE: BURDEN OF PROOF: BOARD OF APPEAL: POWERS OF: T627/88: EPO) [1991] E.P.O.R. 81

Asahi Kasei Kogyo KK's Application (PATENT: APPLICATION: PRIORITY DATE: ANTICIPATION: CO-PENDING APPLICATIONS: WHETHER PRIORITY CONFERRED BY DISCLOSURE OF CLAIMS WITHOUT ENABLING DISCLOSURE: Pat. Ct) [1991] R.P.C. 485
(C.A.) [1990] F.S.R. 546; [1991] R.P.C. 485
(H.L.) [1991] R.P.C. 485
Asahi Kasei Kogyo KK v. W.R. Grace & Co. (PATENT: REVOCATION: NOVELTY: OBVIOUSNESS: DISTINCTION BETWEEN: TESTS OF: WHETHER MATERIAL PART OF COMMON GENERAL KNOWLEDGE: NEW PRODUCT USED IN MANUFACTURE: WANT OF INVENTIVENESS: Australia: Fed. Ct)
22 I.P.R. 491
Asahi/Polyamide fibre (EUROPEAN PATENT: AMENDMENT AND CORRECTION: NUMERICAL ERROR: CLAIMS: CLARITY: OPEN-ENDED DEFINITIONS: PRODUCT-BY-PROCESS: INVENTIVE STEP: COMBINATION OF CITATIONS: SUFFICIENCY: SURPRISING RESULT, FOLLOWING OTHER ERROR IN DESCRIPTION: T487/89: EPO) [1992] E.P.O.R. 32
Asahi/Polyethylene terephthalate fibres (EUROPEAN PATENT: CLAIMS: PRODUCT-BY-PROCESS: T189/88: EPO) [1990] E.P.O.R. 543
Asahi/Polyphenylene ether compositions (EUROPEAN PATENT: APPEAL: PROCEDURE: LATE AUXILIARY REQUESTS: LATE EVIDENCE: EVIDENCE: BURDEN OF PROOF: PRIOR ART: PRIOR USE: BURDEN OF PROOF: BOARD OF APPEAL: JUDICIAL BODY: T270/90: EPO)
[1992] E.P.O.R. 365; [1993] O.J. EPO 725
Asea-Atom AB v. Boyle (PATENT: AGREEMENT: ALLEGED BREACH: ARBITRATION CLAUSE: OPERATION: Australia: S.C.(NSW)) 7 I.P.R. 353
Ashmore v. Douglas-Home (COPYRIGHT: INFRINGEMENT: DRAMATIC WORK: ALTERATION TO ORIGINAL WORK: TRANSLATION: COMPILATION: ADAPTATION: CONFIDENTIAL INFORMATION: LIBEL: Ch.D.)
[1987] F.S.R. 553
Ashtiani v. Kashi (PRACTICE: MAREVA INJUNCTION: DISCOVERY: FOREIGN ASSETS: POWER OF COURT: C.A.) [1986] 2 All E.R. 970; [1986] 3 W.L.R. 647
Asia Television Ltd v. Mega Video Recording Supply Centre (COPYRIGHT: FOREIGN OWNERS: ENTITLEMENT: Malaysia: H.C.) [1985] M.L.J. 250
Asia Television Ltd v. Vina Video Sdn Bhd (COPYRIGHT: CINEMATOGRAPH FILM: VIDEO TAPES: CENSORSHIP: Malaysia: H.C.) [1983] 2 M.L.J. 409
(Appeal; Malaysia; Fed. Ct) [1984] 2 M.L.J. 304
Assidoman Multipack Limited v. The Mead Corp. (PATENTS: PETITION FOR REVOCATION AND DECLARATION OF NON-INFRINGEMENT: P.A. 49 AND P.A. 77: CLAIMS: PURPOSIVE CONSTRUCTION: *Catnic* PRINCIPLES: OBVIOUSNESS: FAIR BASIS: INSUFFICIENCY: EXTENSION OF DISCLOSURE: Pat. Ct)
[1995] R.P.C. 321
(C.A.) [1995] F.S.R. 254
Associated Board RSM v. Renner Piano Co., *sub nom.* Peters Edition Ltd v. Renner
Associated Electronics & Electricals Industries Pvt Ltd v. Sharp Tools (COPYRIGHT: ARTISTIC WORKS: REMOVAL FROM COPYRIGHT REGISTER: APPEAL: India: H.C.) (1992) 17 I.P.L.R. 96
Associated Engineering Italy/Decisions by Formalities Officers (EUROPEAN PATENT: AMENDMENT AND CORRECTION: DESIGNATION OF STATES: FORMALITIES OFFICERS, POWERS OF: RETROSPECTIVE EFFECT OF CORRECTION: FEES: REIMBURSEMENT OF APPEAL FEE: J03/83: EPO)
[1979–85] E.P.O.R. A164; [1995] O.J. EPO 102

Associated Newspapers Group plc v. Insert Media Ltd (PASSING OFF: INJUNCTION: JURISDICTION: PLEADINGS: AMENDMENT: UNFAIR TRADING: DAMAGE: Ch.D.) [1988] 2 All E.R. 420; [1988] 1 W.L.R. 509

Associated Newspapers Group plc v. News Group Newspapers Ltd (COPYRIGHT: INFRINGEMENT: THE WINDSOR CORRESPONDENCE: FAIR DEALING: DEFENCES: INTERLOCUTORY INJUNCTION: Ch.D.) [1986] R.P.C. 515

Associated Newspapers plc v. Insert Media Ltd (PASSING OFF: JOURNAL: ALTERATION OF COPIES WITHOUT AUTHORITY: NEWSPAPER: INSERTION OF ADVERTISING MATERIAL IN NEWSPAPERS WITHOUT CONSENT OF PROPRIETOR: WHETHER INSERTS AMOUNT TO MISREPRESENTATION: WHETHER INSERTS CAUSED DAMAGE TO GOODWILL AND REPUTATION ATTACHING TO NEWSPAPERS: Ch.D.)
[1991] F.S.R. 380; [1991] 3 All E.R. 535; [1991] 1 W.L.R. 571 (INTERLOCUTORY APPEAL: C.A.)
[1990] 2 All E.R. 803; [1990] 1 W.L.R. 900; 18 I.P.R. 345

Association of Independent Radio Companies Ltd (The) v. Phonographic Performance Ltd (COPYRIGHT: LICENCE TO BROADCAST SOUND RECORDINGS: PRACTICE: PRT: Ch.D.) [1983] F.S.R. 637

Association of Independent Radio Companies Ltd (The) v. Phonographic Performance Ltd, BBC Intervening (COPYRIGHT: COMMERCIAL RADIO: LICENCE TO BROADCAST SOUND RECORDINGS: SETTLEMENT OF TERMS: PRINCIPLES TO BE EXERCISED: RELEVANCE OF EARLIER PRT DECISION: ASSESSMENT OF ROYALTY: BASIS: Cprt Trib.)
[1994] R.P.C. 143; [1993] E.M.L.R. 181

Association of Plant Breeders of the EEC (Comasso's) Application (RESTRICTIVE PRACTICES: PLANT BREEDERS' VARIETIES: FRENCH MANAGEMENT GROUP: STANDARD LICENSING AGREEMENTS: EXPORT PROHIBITIONS: INTENTION TO APPROVE: E.C. Comm.) [1990] 4 C.M.L.R. 259
see also, *sub nom.* Société d'Intérêt Collectif Agricole des Sélectionneurs Obtenteurs de Variétés Végétales (SICASOV's) Agreement

Association of Retailer-Owner (AROW) v. Bureau National (BNIC) (RESTRICTIVE PRACTICES: TRADE ASSOCIATIONS: ARTICLE 85(1): E.C. Comm.)
[1983] 2 C.M.L.R. 238; [1983] F.S.R. 425

Association Pharmaceutique Belge (APB's) Application (RESTRICTIVE PRACTICES: PARAPHARMACEUTICALS: COLLECTIVE QUALITY CONTROL: STANDARD FORM DISTRIBUTION AGREEMENT OFFERED BY PHARMACIST'S TRADE ASSOCIATION: RIGHT TO AFFIX SEAL OF APPROVAL TO GOODS: SALE NEGATIVE CLEARANCE: E.C. Comm.) [1990] 4 C.M.L.R. 619

Association Pharmaceutique Belge (APB's) Application (RESTRICTIVE PRACTICES: SELECTIVE DISTRIBUTION: PARAPHARMACEUTICALS: QUALITY INSPECTION BY CHEMIST'S TRADE ASSOCIATION: INTENTION TO APPROVE: E.C. Comm.) [1990] 4 C.M.L.R. 176

ASTA/Cytostatic combination (EUROPEAN PATENT: PATENTABILITY: MEDICAL INDICATION: CLAIMS: NOVELTY: KIT OF KNOWN PARTS: CONVENTIONS: DIFFERENT LANGUAGE TEXTS: T9/81: EPO)
[1979–85] E.P.O.R. B303; [1983] O.J. EPO 372

Asten Group/Papermaking fabric (EUROPEAN PATENT: CLAIM: CLARITY: QUALITATIVE PARAMETER: NUMERICAL RANGE FOR SAME: OPPOSITION PROCEDURE: REMITTAL: T124/85: EPO) [1995] E.P.O.R. 464

ASTERIX Trade Mark (TRADE MARK: COPYRIGHT: COMIC STRIPS: UNAUTHORISED SALE: INJUNCTION: VICARIOUS LIABILITY: Germany: C.A.)
[1987] E.C.C. 308; [1987] F.S.R. 534

Astra (AB) v. Schering Corp. (TRADE MARK: APPLICATION: OPPOSITION: DECEPTIVELY SIMILAR: CONFUSION: HABITS OF MEDICAL PRACTITIONERS IN WRITING PRESCRIPTIONS AND PHARMACISTS IN READING THEM: VISUAL SIMILARITY: HEALTH CONSEQUENCES OF DECEPTION OR CONFUSION: Australia: Pat. Off.)   22 I.P.R. 485

Astra Laemedal AG v. Commissioner of Patents (PATENT: EXTENSION: PHARMACEUTICAL SUBSTANCE: WHETHER EXTENSION AVAILABLE: Australia: Fed. Ct)   31 I.P.R. 1

Astra Lakenedel AB (PATENT: EXTENSION: APPLICATION: OBJECTION: MARKETING APPROVAL CERTIFICATE: IN SUBSTANCE DISCLOSED: PHARMACEUTICAL SUBSTANCE: Australia: AIPO)   29 I.P.R. 183

Astra/IDL Ltd v. The Pharma Ltd (TRADE MARK: INFRINGEMENT: BETALONG/ BETALOC: PASSING OFF: PRESCRIPTIONS: WEIGHT TO BE ATTRIBUTED TO: PUBLIC INTEREST: India: H.C.)   (1991) 16 I.P.L.R. 207

Asulab II/Fee reduction (EUROPEAN PATENT: APPEAL: PROCEDURE: TRANSLATION OF NOTICE OF APPEAL, DATE OF FILING: CONVENTIONS: INTENT AND PURPOSE: ENLARGED BOARD OF APPEAL: INVITATION TO EPO PRESIDENT TO COMMENT: FEES: REDUCTION FOR FILING IN NON–OFFICIAL LANGUAGE: G06/91: EPO)   [1993] E.P.O.R. 231; [1992] O.J. EPO 491

ASX Operations Pty Ltd v. Pont Data Australia Pty Ltd (TRADE PRACTICES: MISLEADING AND DECEPTIVE CONDUCT: WHETHER OBLIGED BY CONTRACT TO ENGAGE IN: WHETHER AGREEMENT COMPELS MISLEADING STATEMENTS: WHETHER TERMS VALID: SUPPLY OF ELECTRONICALLY DISSEMINATED INFORMATION ON STOCK EXCHANGE DEALINGS: WHETHER GOODS: Australia: Fed. Ct)   19 I.P.R. 323

Atari Games Corp. v. Nintendo of America Inc. (COPYRIGHT: SUBSISTENCE: COMPUTER PROGRAMS: CIRCUIT IN SILICON CHIP: SCOPE OF PROTECTION: MERGER OF IDEA AND EXPRESSION: INFRINGEMENT IN "REVERSE ENGINEERING": U.S.A.: D.C.)   21 I.P.R. 45

Atari Inc. v. Fairstar Electronics Pty Ltd (TRADE MARK: INFRINGEMENT: VIDEO COMPUTER SYSTEMS: PARALLEL IMPORTATION: Australia: Fed. Ct)   (1984) 50 A.L.R. 274; 1 I.P.L. 291

Atari Inc. v. Philips Electronics, etc., Ltd (COPYRIGHT: INFRINGEMENT: COMPUTER PROGRAM: INSPECTION: PRACTICE: Ch.D.)   [1988] F.S.R. 416

Atari Ireland Ltd v. Valadon (TRADE MARK: INFRINGEMENT: COPYRIGHT: VIDEO GAMES: France: C.A.)   [1985] E.C.C. 393; [1986] F.S.R. 1
(S.C.) [1987] E.C.C. 212; [1987] F.S.R. 208

Athol Thomas Kelly's Application (TRADE MARK: APPLICATION: DISTINCTIVENESS: LIKELIHOOD OF DECEPTION OR CONFUSION: PRIOR REGISTRATION: HONEST CONCURRENT USE: IMPERFECT RECOLLECTION DOCTRINE: Australia: Pat. Off.)   8 I.P.R. 667

Atkinson Footwear Ltd v. Hodgskin International Services (COPYRIGHT: INFRINGEMENT: INTERLOCUTORY INJUNCTION SOUGHT TO RESTRAIN ACTS IN NEW ZEALAND AND AUSTRALIA: JURISDICTION *in personam, in rem*: New Zealand: H.C.)   31 I.P.R. 186

Atlas (RESTRICTIVE PRACTICES: JOINT VENTURES: GLOBAL TELECOMMUNICATIONS SERVICES: INTENTION TO APPROVE: E.C. Comm.)   [1996] 4 C.M.L.R. 265

Atlas Powder Co's Patent (PATENT: RESTORATION: Malaysia: Pat. Ct)   [1995] R.P.C. 357

Atlas Powder Co.'s Patent (PATENT: RESTORATION: PATENT REGISTERED AND EXCLUSIVELY LICENCED IN MALAYSIA: DELIBERATE BUT MISTAKEN DECISION NOT TO RENEW U.K. PATENT: CONSTRUCTION: SECTION 28(3): C.A.)
[1995] R.P.C. 666
Atlas Powder Co. v. ICI Australia Operations Pty Ltd (PATENT: OPPOSITION: AMENDMENT: AMBIGUITY: FAIR BASIS: Australia: Pat. Off.)   15 I.P.R. 34
Atomic Skifabrik Alois Rohmoser v. Registrar of Trade Marks (TRADE MARK: OPPOSITION: APPLICATION FOR EXTENSION OF PERIOD: Australia: Fed. Ct)
7 I.P.R. 551
Atomic Skifabrik Alois Rohmoser v. Sasdor Pty Ltd (TRADE MARKS: APPLICATION FOR REMOVAL: EXTENSION OF TIME TO LODGE NOTICE OF OPPOSITION: Australia: Pat. Off.)   11 I.P.R. 605
ATT/Inviting observations (EUROPEAN PATENT: OPPOSITION: PROCEDURE: OBSERVATIONS BY PARTIES, INVITATION NECESSARY: MISLEADING COMMUNICATION BY EPO: INVENTIVE STEP: TRIAL-AND-ERROR APPROACH: FEES: REIMBURSEMENT OF APPEAL FEE: APPEAL: ARTICLE 101(2): T669/90: EPO)   [1993] E.P.O.R. 397; [1992] O.J. EPO 739
Attorney General v. Blake (COPYRIGHT: FIDUCIARY DUTY: PART OF AUTOBIOGRAPHY BASED ON INFORMATION ACQUIRED WHILST EMPLOYED IN SECRET INTELLIGENCE SERVICE: DUTY TO CROWN: EQUITY: ACCOUNT OF PROFITS: Ch.D)   [1996] E.M.L.R. 382
Attorney-General (ex rel. Elisha) v. Holy Apostolic & Catholic Church of the East (Assyrian) Australia NSW Parish Association (TRADE PRACTICES: FALSE OR MISLEADING CONDUCT: WHETHER TRADE OR COMMERCE: USE OF CHURCH NAME BY BODY FORMED FOR RELIGIOUS PURPOSES: PASSING OFF: PROTECTION OF GOODWILL OF RELIGIOUS ORGANISATION: Australia: S.C.(NSW))   98 A.L.R. 327
sub nom. Holy Apostolic & Catholic Church of the East (Assyrian) Australia NSW Parish Association v. Attorney-General (ex rel.) Elisha (C.A.(NSW))
16 I.P.R. 619
Attorney-General v. Brandon Book Publishers Ltd (CONFIDENTIAL INFORMATION: FIDUCIARY DUTY: IRELAND: BRITISH SECURITY SERVICE EX-EMPLOYEE: BOOK: *One Girl's War.* CONSTITUTIONAL RIGHTS: Ireland: H.C.)
[1989] 1 F.S.R. 37
Attorney-General v. Guardian Newspaper Ltd, Observer Ltd, Times Newspapers Ltd (CONFIDENTIAL INFORMATION: *Spycatcher.* FULL ACTION: BREACH OF FIDUCIARY DUTY: INJUNCTION: PUBLICATION AND AVAILABILITY OF BOOK WITHOUT AND WITHIN U.K.: BALANCING PUBLIC INTEREST IN FREEDOM OF SPEECH AND PRESS AGAINST PUBLIC INTEREST IN MAINTAINING CONFIDENTIALITY: DEFENCE OF INIQUITY: INJUNCTIONS AGAINST FUTURE BREACHES: *Spycatcher 2*: "NO MAN SHALL PROFIT FROM HIS OWN WRONG": THIRD PARTY IN POSSESSION OF CONFIDENTIAL INFORMATION: KNOWLEDGE: *Turpis causa*: ACCOUNT OF PROFITS: Ch.D.: C.A.)
[1989] 2 F.S.R. 181; [1988] 3 All E.R. 545; [1988] 2 W.L.R. 805
(H.L.) [1989] 2 F.S.R. 181; [1988] 3 All E.R. 545; [1988] 3 W.L.R. 776;
13 I.P.R. 75
Attorney-General v. Guardian Newspapers Ltd (Derbyshire County Council Intervening) (CONTEMPT: *Spycatcher.* APPLICATION TO DETERMINE WHETHER BOOK COULD BE IMPORTED FOR DISPLAY IN PUBLIC LIBRARIES: IMPORTATION FROM EEC COUNTRY: STATUTORY DUTY OF PUBLIC LIBRARY: EXTENT: DUTY QUALIFIED SO AS NOT TO INTERFERE WITH DUE ADMINISTRATION OF JUSTICE: WHETHER LACK OF CENSORSHIP BY COUNCIL A CONTEMPT: Ch.D.)   [1989] 2 F.S.R. 163; [1988] 1 All E.R. 385

Attorney-General v. Guardian Newspapers Ltd and The Observer Ltd (*Spycatcher*: FORMER CROWN EMPLOYEE: INTERLOCUTORY INJUNCTION: APPLICATION TO DISCHARGE: MATERIAL CHANGE IN CIRCUMSTANCES SINCE INTERLOCUTORY INJUNCTION: PUBLICATION OF BOOK IN U.S.A. AND WIDE AVAILABILITY IN U.K.: EXERCISE OF DISCRETION: "EQUITY DOES NOT ACT IN VAIN": VALUE OF *Admiral Byng* INJUNCTION: Ch.D.)

[1989] 2 F.S.R. 81; [1987] 3 All E.R. 316
(C.A., H.L.) [1989] 2 F.S.R. 81; [1987] 3 All E.R. 316; [1987] 1 W.L.R. 1248

Attorney-General v. Guardian Newspapers Ltd and The Observer Ltd (INTERLOCUTORY INJUNCTION: *Spycatcher*: NEWSPAPER ARTICLE OUTLINING ALLEGATIONS TO BE PUBLISHED IN BOOK: NEWSPAPERS NOT HAVING ACCESS TO AUTHOR'S MANUSCRIPT: PRIOR RESTRAINT OF PUBLICATION: PUBLIC INTEREST: ALLEGATIONS OF MISCONDUCT BY SECURITY SERVICE: AUTHOR'S DUTY OF CONFIDENTIALITY TO CROWN: MATERIAL IN PUBLIC DOMAIN: FORM OF INJUNCTION: Ch.D.: C.A.)   [1989] 2 F.S.R. 3

Attorney-General v. Heinemann Publishers Australia Pty Ltd and Wright (BREACH OF CONFIDENCE: *Spycatcher*: BOOK IN MANUSCRIPT FORM: BREACH OF FIDUCIARY DUTY: INJUNCTIONS: NATURE OF DEFENDANT'S EMPLOYMENT BY CROWN: NATURE OF DUTY OF CONFIDENTIALITY: WHETHER INFORMATION IN PUBLIC DOMAIN: PRIOR PUBLICATION OF INFORMATION BY THIRD PARTY, WITH AGREEMENT OR ACQUIESCENCE OF BRITISH GOVERNMENT: PUBLIC POLICY: PUBLIC INTEREST: EVIDENCE: CREDIBILITY OF CROWN WITNESS: EQUITY: DEFENCE OF INIQUITY: CLEAN HANDS DEFENCE: Australia: S.C.(NSW): C.A.(NSW))

10 I.P.R. 153; [1989] 2 F.S.R. 349

Attorney-General v. Heinemann Publishers Australia Pty Ltd and Wright (*Spycatcher*: APPLICATION FOR STAY OF ORDER OF COURT OF APPEAL OF NSW PENDING HEARING OF APPLICATION FOR SPECIAL LEAVE TO APPEAL: PRACTICE AND PROCEDURE: JURISDICTION: *Admiral Byng* INJUNCTION: APPLICATION DISMISSED: Australia: H.C.)   10 I.P.R. 261; [1989] 2 F.S.R. 623

Attorney-General v. Newspaper Publishing plc (CONTEMPT OF COURT: *Spycatcher* MATERIAL: CRIMINAL CONTEMPT: NEWSPAPERS NOT DIRECTLY BOUND BY INJUNCTION: INTENTION: *Actus reus: Mens rea*: FINES: COSTS: Ch.D.)

[1989] 1 F.S.R. 457

Attorney-General v. Newspaper Publishing plc (CONTEMPT: *Spycatcher*: BREACH OF CONFIDENCE: CRIMINAL CONTEMPT: NEWSPAPERS NOT BOUND BY INJUNCTION NOT TO PUBLISH: INTENTION OF PUBLICATION: NATURAL JUSTICE: Ch.D.: C.A.)

[1989] 2 F.S.R. 27; [1987] 3 All E.R. 316; [1987] 1 W.L.R. 1248

Attorney-General v. Newspaper Publishing plc (PRACTICE: CONTEMPT OF COURT: THIRD PARTY: WHETHER BREACH OF INJUNCTION CONTEMPT: Ch.D.: C.A.)   [1987] 3 All E.R. 276; [1987] 3 W.L.R. 942

Attorney-General v. Observer Ltd (Re Derbyshire CC's Application) (CONFIDENTIAL INFORMATION: INJUNCTION: CONTEMPT: ADMINISTRATION OF JUSTICE: WHETHER LIBRARY BOUND BY TERMS: Q.B.D.)   [1988] 1 All E.R. 385; [1989] 2 F.S.R. 163

Attorney-General v. South China Morning Post Ltd (BREACH OF CONFIDENCE: BREACH OF FIDUCIARY DUTY: FORMER CROWN SERVANT: *Spycatcher*: SERIAL RIGHTS TO BOOK: SINGLE EXTRACT IN NEWSPAPER: *Ex parte* INTERLOCUTORY INJUNCTION: DISCHARGE: APPEAL: LEAVE TO APPEAL TO PRIVY COUNCIL: INFORMATION FREELY AVAILABLE OUTSIDE HONG KONG: BALANCING COMPETING INTERESTS OF PUBLIC SECURITY AND FREEDOM OF SPEECH: INJUNCTIVE RELIEF TO CONTINUE UNTIL TRIAL OF ACTION: BALANCING COMPETING INTERESTS OF PUBLIC SECURITY AND FREEDOM OF SPEECH: Hong Kong: C.A.)   [1988] 1 H.K.L.R. 143; [1989] 2 F.S.R. 653

Attorney-General v. Times Newspapers Ltd v. Attorney-General (BREACH OF CONFIDENCE: *Spycatcher*: CONTEMPT: PUBLICATION: APPELLANT NOT PARTY TO INJUNCTIONS RESTRAINING BREACH OF CONFIDENCE: APPEAL: H.L.)   [1991] 2 All E.R. 398; [1991] 2 W.L.R. 994; 20 I.P.R. 609

Attorney-General v. Turnaround Distribution Ltd (BREACH OF CONTRACT: BREACH OF CONFIDENCE: *One Girl's War*: EX-MI5 AUTHORESS: Q.B.D.)   [1989] 1 F.S.R. 169

Attorney-General v. Wellington Newspapers Ltd (CONFIDENTIAL INFORMATION: *Spycatcher*: GOVERNMENT SECRETS: FREEDOM OF THE PRESS: STATUS OF INTELLIGENCE AGENTS: EQUITABLE DUTY OF CONFIDENCE: FIDUCIARY OBLIGATION OF CONFIDENCE: PUBLIC INTEREST IN RESTRAINING PUBLICATION: PRIVATE INTERNATIONAL LAWS: MATERIAL IN PUBLIC DOMAIN: EFFECT OF PUBLICATION OUTSIDE NEW ZEALAND: EXEMPLARY DAMAGES: DECLARATION: ACCOUNT OF PROFITS: DEFENCE OF INIQUITY: New Zealand: H.C.: C.A.)   [1989] 2 F.S.R. 691

AU PRINTEMPS Trade Mark (TRADE MARK: APPLICATION: MARK IN FOREIGN LANGUAGE: EVIDENCE OF REPUTATION: T.M.Reg.)   [1990] R.P.C. 518

Auckland Harbour Cruise Co. Ltd v. Fullers Captain Cook Cruises Ltd (PASSING OFF: TOURIST YACHT CRUISES: SAIL COLOURS AND VESSELS' NAMES SIMILAR: TERRITORIAL NATURE OF GOODWILL: INTERIM INJUNCTION: New Zealand: H.C.)   8 I.P.R. 185

Auditel (RESTRICTIVE PRACTICES: BROADCASTING: JOINT VENTURE: EXCLUSIVE USE OF AUDIENCE RATING SYSTEM: CAUGHT BY ARTICLE 85(1): EXEMPTION REFUSED: E.C. Comm.)   [1995] 5 C.M.L.R. 719

Auer-Sog/Light reflecting slats (EUROPEAN PATENT: INVENTIVE STEP: KNOWN FEATURE SOLVING DIFFERENT PROBLEM: T39/82: EPO)
                          [1979–85] E.P.O.R. B441; [1982] O.J. EPO 419

Auld/Decorative emblems (EUROPEAN PATENT: APPEAL: PROCEDURE: DOCUMENTS FOUND BY BOARD OF APPEAL OF ITS OWN MOTION: CLAIMS: FUNCTIONAL FEATURES: EVIDENCE: POSTING, OF LETTER: INVENTIVE STEP: COMBINATION OF CITATIONS: SKILLED PERSON: KNOWLEDGE OF: SUFFICIENCY: T183/82: EPO)   [1979–85] E.P.O.R. C684

Aumac Ltd's Patent (PATENT: REVOCATION: DIVISIONAL APPLICATION TO EPO DESIGNATING U.K.: POSSIBILITY OF FURTHER INFRINGEMENT PROCEEDINGS IN U.K.: *See v. Scott-Paine* ORDER BY CONSENT: WHETHER CONSENSUAL ORDER IS A CONTRACT: INTENTION OF COURT: JURISDICTION TO VARY, DISCHARGE OR ADD TO ORDER: Pat. Ct)   [1995] F.S.R. 501

Ausonia/Withdrawal of application (EUROPEAN PATENT: PROCEDURE: ABANDONMENT V. WITHDRAWAL: WITHDRAWAL, WHAT CONSTITUTES: WHETHER RETRACTABLE AFTER PUBLICATION: CONVENTIONS: NATIONAL LAW, RELEVANCE OF, PROCEDURAL V. SUBSTANTIVE LAW: J15/86: EPO)   [1989] E.P.O.R. 152; [1988] O.J. EPO 417

Aussat Pty Ltd (Re) (TRADE MARK: APPLICATION: REGISTRABILITY: SUBSTANTIALLY IDENTICAL: DECEPTIVELY SIMILAR: CLOSELY RELATED: GOODS AND SERVICES: Australia: AIPO)   27 I.P.R. 309

Austgen Biojet Holdings Pty Ltd v. Goronszy (PATENT: OPPOSITION: OBTAINING: INVENTOR: TRANSITIONAL APPLICATION: Australia: Fed. Ct)   32 I.P.R. 193

Austin Knight (U.K.) Ltd v. Hinds (EMPLOYMENT CONTRACTS: RESTRICTIVE COVENANT: NON-SOLICITATION CLAUSE: WHETHER PLAINTIFF'S BUSINESS PROTECTABLE: WHETHER RESTRICTION REASONABLE: MISUSE OF CONFIDENTIAL INFORMATION: INTERLOCUTORY INJUNCTION: Ch.D.)   [1994] F.S.R. 52

Austin Rover Group Ltd & Unipart Group Ltd (RESTRICTIVE PRACTICES: FORMER FELLOW SUBSIDIARIES WITHIN SAME GROUP: ARTICLE 85(1): DISTRIBUTION AGREEMENT: BLOCK EXEMPTION: E.C. Comm.)   [1988] 4 C.M.L.R. 513

Austoft Industries Limited v. Cameco Industries Limited (PATENT: OPPOSITION: EXTENSION OF TIME TO FILE EVIDENCE: PUBLIC INTEREST: Australia: AIPO)   29 I.P.R. 425

Australasian Performing Right Association Ltd's Reference (COPYRIGHT: MUSICAL WORK: PERFORMING RIGHTS OWNED BY ASSOCIATION: REFERENCES TO TRIBUNAL: Australia: Cprt Trib.)   5 I.P.R. 449

Australasian Performing Right Association Ltd v. Ceridale Pty Ltd (COPYRIGHT: INFRINGEMENT: TRADE PRACTICES: PERFORMING RIGHTS: COPYRIGHT OWNER WITH MONOPOLY POWER: REFUSAL TO GRANT LICENCE TO PERFORM WORKS IN PUBLIC: USE OF POWER TO EXTRACT PAYMENT OF DISPUTED DEBT: WHETHER POWER EXERCISED FOR EXTRANEOUS PURPOSE: LICENCE FEES: CONDITIONS: Australia: S.C.(Qd.))
96 A.L.R. 432; 18 I.P.R. 245
(Fed. Ct) 97 A.L.R. 497; 19 I.P.R. 1

Australasian Performing Right Association Ltd v. Commonwealth Bank of Australia (COPYRIGHT: MUSICAL WORK: PERFORMED AT PLACE OF EMPLOYMENT: MEMBERS OF THE PUBLIC EXCLUDED: WHETHER PERFORMANCE "IN PUBLIC": Australia: Fed. Ct)   111 A.L.R. 671; 25 I.P.R. 157

Australasian Performing Right Association Ltd v. Jain (COPYRIGHT: INFRINGEMENT: AUTHORISING ACTS: EXECUTIVE DIRECTOR: POWER TO AUTHORISE PERFORMANCE OF WORKS IN PUBLIC: Australia: Fed. Ct)
96 A.L.R. 619; 18 I.P.R. 663

Australasian Performing Right Association Ltd v. Telstra Corp. Ltd (COPYRIGHT: DIFFUSION SERVICE: WHETHER MUSIC HEARD BY TELEPHONE USERS PLACED ON HOLD CONSTITUTES A PERFORMANCE IN PUBLIC OR A BROADCAST TO THE PUBLIC: Australia: Fed. Ct)
118 A.L.R. 684; 27 I.P.R. 357; [1994] R.P.C. 299
(APPEAL: Fed. Ct)   131 A.L.R. 141; 31 I.P.R. 289

Australasian Performing Right Association Ltd v. Tolbush Pty Ltd (COPYRIGHT: INFRINGEMENT: PUBLIC PERFORMANCE: AUTHORISATION: DIRECTORS OF CORPORATION: Australia: S.C.(Qd.))   62 A.L.R. 521

Australasian Performing Right Association Ltd v. Valamo Pty Ltd (COPYRIGHT: INFRINGEMENT: COMPANY INFRINGED COPYRIGHT: WHETHER DIRECTOR PERSONALLY LIABLE FOR INFRINGEMENT: AUTHORISATION: Australia: Fed. C.A.)   18 I.P.R. 216

Australian Airlines Ltd's Application (TRADE MARKS: APPLICATION: REFUSAL TO REGISTER UNLESS CONSENT TO DISCLAIMER: Australia: Pat. Off.)   20 I.P.R. 405

Australian Bacon Ltd v. Mulfric Foods Pty Ltd (TRADE MARKS: APPLICATION FOR REMOVAL: OPPOSITION: EVIDENCE: NON-USE: Australia: Pat. Off.)
                                                              12 I.P.R. 372
Australian Broadcasting Commission (ex parte Australasian Performing Right Association Ltd) (COPYRIGHT: "SERVICES OF THE COMMONWEALTH": AGENT OR INSTRUMENTALITY: Australia: Cprt Trib.)   (1982) 42 A.L.R. 58
                                                      (Fed. Ct) (1982) 45 A.L.R. 153
Australian Broadcasting Corporation's Application (TRADE MARKS: APPLICATION: APPLICATION FOR EXTENSION OF TIME TO FILE NOTICE OF OPPOSITION: INCORRECT REASONS: SECOND APPLICATION FILED: WHETHER AMENDMENT OR SUBSTITUTION NECESSARY: MATERIAL SUFFICIENT TO DISCHARGE ONUS: PUBLIC INTEREST: Australia: Pat. Off.)   10 I.P.R. 269
Australian Computer Evaluation Consultants Pty Ltd v. Datbury Pty Ltd (COPYRIGHT: INFRINGEMENT: COMPUTER PROGRAM: PASSING OFF: Fed. Ct)   30 I.P.R. 423
Australian Consolidated Industries Ltd v. Scholle Industries Pty Ltd (PATENT: INFRINGEMENT: PRACTICE: PROCEEDINGS IN TWO JURISDICTIONS: Australia: S.C.(S.A.))   [1982] 62 F.L.R. 289
Australian Consumers' Association for Review of Trade Practices Commission Authorisation of Certain Codes of the Media Council of Australia's Application (ADVERTISING CODES OF PRACTICE: Australia: TPT)   11 I.P.R. 162
Australian Design Council v. Peter Borello (t/a Buccaneer Pools) (TRADE MARK: INFRINGEMENT: CONTEMPT: FALSE REPRESENTATION: CONDUCT: INJUNCTION: CONTINUING USE OF MARK IN BREACH OF INJUNCTION: DELIBERATE BREACH: PUBLIC INTEREST: HONESTY IN ADVERTISING: FINE: Australia: Fed. Ct)   17 I.P.R. 389
Australian Iron & Steel Pty Ltd v. Buck (MAREVA INJUNCTION: VARIATION: Australia: S.C.(NSW))   [1982] 2 N.S.W.L.R. 659
Australian Mining & Smelting Europe Ltd, *sub nom.* A.M. & S. Ltd
Australian National Airlines Commission (TRADE MARKS: APPLICATIONS: CHARACTER OR QUALITY OF GOODS OR SERVICES: NON-DISTINCTIVE: SPECIAL CIRCUMSTANCES: DISCLAIMER: Australia: Pat. Off.)   16 I.P.R. 270
Australian National University/Metal complexes (EUROPEAN PATENT: INVENTIVE STEP: ANALOGOUS SUBSTITUTION: COMPLICATED CHEMICAL COMPOUNDS: SIGNPOST IN PRIOR ART: T154/82: EPO)   [1979–85] E.P.O.R. C648
Australian Ocean Line Pty Ltd v. West Australian Newspapers Ltd (TRADE PRACTICES: MISLEADING AND DECEPTIVE CONDUCT: PUBLICATION OF NEWS: Australia: Fed. Ct)   [1985] 4 I.P.R. 579
Australian Olympic Committee Inc. v. Brennan (TRADE MARK: APPLICATION: OPPOSITION: APPLICATION FOR EXTENSION OF TIME FOR SERVICE OF EVIDENCE: FACTORS TO BE CONSIDERED: Australia: AIPO)   30 I.P.R. 44
Australian Paper Manufacturers Ltd v. CIL Ltd (PATENTS: APPLICATION: OPPOSITION: NOVELTY: ANTICIPATION: PRIOR CLAIMING: PRIOR PUBLICATION: Australia: Pat. Off.)   [1985] 4 I.P.R. 612
Australian Soccer Federation Marketing Ltd v. Questor Corp. (TRADE MARK: OPPOSITION: LIKELIHOOD OF DECEPTION: Australia: Pat. Off.)   5 I.P.R. 446
Australian Society of Accountants v. Federation of Australian Accountants Inc. (PASSING OFF: TRADE PRACTICES: MISLEADING CONDUCT: USE OF LETTERS "CPA": Australia: Fed. Ct)   9 I.P.R. 282
Australian Tape Manufacturers Association Ltd v. Commonwealth of Australia (JOINTER OF PARTIES: COPYRIGHT: CHALLENGE TO VALIDITY OF PART OF COPYRIGHT ACT 1968; PROCEDURE: Australia: H.C.)
                                                      94 A.L.R. 641; 18 I.P.R. 175

Australian Tape Manufacturers Association Ltd v. Commonwealth of Australia (COPYRIGHT: SOUND RECORDINGS: UNAUTHORISED DOMESTIC COPYING: SCHEME FOR COMPENSATION: ROYALTY ON BLANK TAPES: COLLECTING SOCIETY: DISTRIBUTED TO COPYRIGHT OWNERS: CONSTITUTIONAL VALIDITY OF AMENDING LEGISLATION: Australia: H.C.)
112 A.L.R. 53; 177 C.L.R. 480; 25 I.P.R. 1

Australian Telecommunication Corp. v. Centec International Corp. Pty Ltd (TRADE MARKS: OPPOSITION: ADDRESS FOR SERVICE: EVIDENCE, SERVICE OF: DECEPTION AND CONFUSION: BLAMEWORTHY CONDUCT: Australia: Pat. Off.)
24 I.P.R. 170

Australian Telecommunications Corp. v. Hutchison Telecommunications (Australia) Ltd (TRADE PRACTICES: MISLEADING OR DECEPTIVE CONDUCT: PASSING OFF: SIMILARITY OF NEW TRADING NAME HUTCHISON TELECOMS TO WELL-ESTABLISHED NAME TELECOM: CORPORATIONS IN COMPETITION: WHETHER TELECOM A DESCRIPTIVE WORD: WHETHER POTENTIAL CLIENTS LIKELY TO BE MISLED OR DECEIVED: INTERLOCUTORY INJUNCTIONS: BALANCE OF CONVENIENCE: Australia: Fed. Ct)
17 I.P.R. 615

Austro-Mechana GmbH v. Gramola Winter & Co. (COPYRIGHT: EFTA: ENFORCEMENT: Austria: S.C.)   [1984] 2 C.M.L.R. 626; [1985] F.S.R. 8

Authors' Workshop v. Bileru Pty Ltd (INJUNCTION: INTERLOCUTORY: MOTION TO SET ASIDE *ex parte* ORDERS: WHETHER ORDERS AKIN TO ANTON PILLER ORDER AND SUBJECT TO SAME PRE-CONDITIONS: CLAIM OF PRIVILEGE AGAINST SELF-INCRIMINATION: COMMON LAW PRINCIPLES: Australia: Fed. Ct)
16 I.P.R. 661

Autobake Pty Ltd v. Budd & Grainger (TRADE PRACTICES: FRANCHISE: WHETHER CONTRACT UNFAIR, UNCONSCIONABLE OR HARSH: Australia: Ind Comm.)
8 I.P.R. 435

Autodesk Australia Pty Ltd v. Cheung (COPYRIGHT: COMPUTER PROGRAMS: INFRINGEMENT: SALE OF UNAUTHORISED REPRODUCTIONS: DAMAGES: MEASURE OF COMPENSATORY DAMAGES: ADDITIONAL DAMAGES: CLAIM BY COPYRIGHT OWNER AND AUSTRALIAN DISTRIBUTOR: Australia: Fed. Ct)
17 I.P.R. 69

Autodesk Australia Pty Ltd v. Dyason (PRACTICE: AFFIDAVITS: USE AGAINST THIRD PARTIES: UNDERTAKINGS: Australia: Fed. Ct)   30 I.P.R. 469

Autodesk Inc. v. Dyason (COPYRIGHT: COMPUTER PROGRAMS: WHETHER ELECTRICAL CIRCUIT IS A "COMPUTER PROGRAM": WHETHER "SET OF INSTRUCTIONS" AND "DATA PROCESSING DEVICE" NEED BE SEPARATE: INFRINGEMENT: REPRODUCTION: AUTHORISATION: DEVICE ENABLING BREACH OF "SHRINK-WRAP LICENCE": Australia: Fed. Ct)   15 I.P.R. 1

Autodesk Inc. v. Dyason (COPYRIGHT: COMPUTER PROGRAMS: WHETHER ELECTRICAL CIRCUIT CAN BE A "COMPUTER PROGRAM": INFRINGEMENT: REPRODUCTION: AUTHORISATION: WHETHER SUPPLY OF DEVICE ENABLING COMPUTER PROGRAM TO BE USED ON MORE THAN ONE COMPUTER AT A TIME MAY BE AUTHORISATION OF INFRINGEMENT: Australia: Fed. Ct)
96 A.L.R. 57; 173 C.L.R. 330; 18 I.P.R. 109

Autodesk Inc. v. Dyason (COPYRIGHT: INFRINGEMENT: AUSTRALIA: COMPUTER PROGRAM: ORIGINALITY: SUBSTANTIAL PART: APPELLANT'S DEVICE TO PREVENT ITS COMPUTER PROGRAMS BEING RUN ON A COMPUTER WITHOUT DEVICE: Australia: H.C.)   104 A.L.R. 563; 22 I.P.R. 163; [1992] R.P.C. 575

Autodesk Inc. v. Dyason (No. 2) (COPYRIGHT: INFRINGEMENT: AUSTRALIA: COMPUTER PROGRAM: ORIGINALITY: SUBSTANTIAL PART: APPELLANT'S DEVICE TO PREVENT ITS COMPUTER PROGRAMS BEING RUN ON A COMPUTER WITHOUT DEVICE: Australia: H.C.)
111 A.L.R. 385; 25 I.P.R. 33; [1993] R.P.C. 259
Autoliv Development AB's Patent (PATENT: AMENDMENT: DELAY: COVETOUSNESS: DISCRETION: LEAVE TO AMEND REFUSED: Pat. Ct) [1988] R.P.C. 425
Autopia Terakat Accessories Ltd v. Gwent Auto Fabrications Ltd (PATENT: INFRINGEMENT: VALIDITY: AMENDMENT: RELIEF FOR PART VALID PATENT: PUBLIC INTEREST: DECLARATION: Pat. Ct) [1991] F.S.R. 517
Autospin (Oil Seals) Ltd v. Beehive Spinning (COPYRIGHT: INFRINGEMENT: ANTECEDENT SKETCHES: BEST EVIDENCE: TABLES FOR CALCULATING CRITICAL DIMENSIONS: WHETHER THREE-DIMENSIONAL ARTICLE INFRINGES LITERARY WORK: Ch.D.) [1995] R.P.C. 683
Autronic AG v. Switzerland (HUMAN RIGHTS: FREEDOM OF EXPRESSION: BROADCASTING LICENCES: RECEIPT OF SATELLITE TRANSMISSIONS: NECESSITY IN A DEMOCRATIC SOCIETY: ECHR) [1991] F.S.R. 55; 12 E.H.R.R. 485
Auvi Pte Ltd v. Seah Siew Tee (COPYRIGHT: TRADE MARK: AUVI: COPYING MARK: SUBSTANTIAL SIMILARITY: PROTECTION: ORIGINALITY OF LOGO: WHETHER ARTISTIC WORK: APPLICATION TO EXPUNGE FROM REGISTER: PERSONS AGGRIEVED: *Locus standii*: AMENDMENT: DISCRETION: Singapore: H.C.)
[1992] 2 S.L.R. 639; [1995] F.S.R. 288; 24 I.P.R. 41
AUVI Trade mark, *sub nom.* Auvi Pte Ltd v. Seah Siew Tee
Availability to the public (EUROPEAN PATENT: PRIOR ART: PRIOR USE: ANALYSABILITY: STATE OF THE ART: PRIOR PRODUCT, ANALYSIS: G01/92: EPO) [1993] E.P.O.R. 241; [1993] O.J. EPO 277
Avedis Zildjian Company's Application (TRADE MARKS: APPLICATION: NAME OF PERSON: NOT REPRESENTED IN A SPECIAL OR PARTICULAR MANNER: C.-G.)
18 I.P.R. 474
Avel Pty Ltd v. Multicoin Amusements Pty Ltd (COPYRIGHT: INFRINGEMENT: MEANING OF "PUBLISH": UNITED STATES MANUFACTURER: PROPOSED IMPORT OF USED GOODS: THREATS: EXCLUSIVE LICENSEE: ONUS OF PROOF: PARALLEL IMPORTATION: ONUS OF PROOF: EXCLUSIVE LICENCE: Australia: H.C.) 97 A.L.R. 19; 18 I.P.R. 443
Avel Pty Ltd v. Wells (CIRCUIT LAYOUTS: INTEGRATED CIRCUIT: DEFENCE TO PARALLEL IMPORTATION OF COPYRIGHT MATERIAL: COPYRIGHT: COMPUTER PROGRAMS: INFRINGEMENT: PARALLEL IMPORTATION AND SALE: STATUTORY DEFENCE: Australia: Fed. Ct) 22 I.P.R. 305
Avel Pty Ltd v. Wells (CIRCUIT LAYOUTS: PARALLEL IMPORTATION OF ELIGIBLE LAYOUTS FOR VIDEO GAMES: COPYRIGHT: ELIGIBLE LAYOUTS CONTAINING SUBSTANTIAL PARTS OF COMPUTER PROGRAMS, THE COPYRIGHT IN WHICH WAS OWNED BY ONE OR OTHER OF THE APPELLANTS: WHETHER IMPORTATION OF SUCH ELIGIBLE LAYOUTS CONSTITUTED AN INFRINGEMENT OF APPELLANTS' COPYRIGHT IN COMPUTER PROGRAMS: Australia: Fed. Ct) 105 A.L.R. 635; 23 I.P.R. 353
Avion Engineering Pty Ltd v. Fisher & Paykel Healthcare Pty Ltd, *sub nom.* Fisher & Paykel Healthcare Pty Ltd v. Avion Engineering Pty Ltd
Avirone Pty Ltd v. ICI Australia Operations Pty Ltd (TRADE MARKS: APPLICATION FOR REGISTRATION: OPPOSITION: WANT OF PROSECUTION: REPUTATION OF OPPONENT'S MARKS FOR CAR PAINT: MANNER OF USE OF MARKS IN MOTOR INDUSTRY: MARK ALLUDED TO MOTOR INDUSTRY: USE IN RELATION TO CLOTHING LIKELY TO DECEIVE: Australia: Pat. Off.) 17 I.P.R. 262

AVON Trade Mark (TRADE MARK: APPLICATION: PRACTICE: SURVEY EVIDENCE: CAPABLE OF DISTINGUISHING: T.M.Reg.) [1985] R.P.C. 43
Avontuur/Piston compressor (EUROPEAN PATENT: AMENDMENT AND CORRECTION: DRAWINGS: TEACHING OF: INTERPRETATION OF TECHNICAL TERM: T182/86: EPO) [1988] E.P.O.R. 183
Avtex Airservices Pty Ltd v. Bartsch (COPYRIGHT: OWNERSHIP: COMPUTERISED TEACHING SYSTEM OF WORKBOOKS, SLIDES AND COMPUTER PROGRAMS: Australia: Fed. Ct) 23 I.P.R. 469; 107 A.L.R. 539
AWA Ltd v. Future Software Pty Ltd (TRADE MARK: APPLICATION: POTENTIAL OPPOSITION: EXTENSION TO TIME FOR OPPOSITION: APPLICATION WITHIN TIME PRESCRIBED OPPOSED: PUBLIC INTEREST: POSSIBILITY OF NEGOTIATED SETTLEMENT BETWEEN PARTIES: Australia: Pat. Off.) 19 I.P.R. 421
Aztech Systems Pte Ltd v. Creative Technology Ltd (COPYRIGHT: INFRINGEMENT: COMPUTER SOUND CARDS: DESIGNING COMPATIBLE SOUND CARDS: FAIR DEALING FOR THE PURPOSE OF PRIVATE STUDY: DEROGATION FROM GRANT: IMPLIED LICENCE: Singapore: H.C.) [1996] F.S.R. 54

B. & R. Relay Ltd's Application (PATENT: AMENDMENT: CLAIM BROADENING: Pat. Ct) [1985] R.P.C. 1
B&S Ltd v. Irish Auto Trader Ltd (PASSING OFF: ADVERTISING MAGAZINES: AUTOTRADER: INTERLOCUTORY INJUNCTION: PRINCIPLES: PRESERVATION OF *status quo*: BALANCE OF CONVENIENCE: Ireland: H.C.) [1995] 2 I.R. 142
B. & W. Cabs Ltd v. Brisbane Cabs Pty Ltd (MISLEADING STATEMENTS: INJUNCTION: STATEMENTS THOUGH STRICTLY TRUE LIKELY TO MISLEAD: Australia: Fed. Ct) 21 I.P.R. 563
B.F. Goodrich Co. v. ICI Australia Operations Pty Ltd (PATENT: APPLICATION: OPPOSITION: WHETHER CLAIMS FAIRLY BASED: PRIOR PUBLICATION: OBVIOUSNESS: COMBINATION INVENTION: MANNER OF NEW MANUFACTURE: PRIOR USE: PRIOR SECRET USE: STANDARD OF PROOF: Australia: AIPO) 31 I.P.R. 133
Babolat Maillot Witt SA v. Pachot (COPYRIGHT: France) [1984] E.C.C. 282; [1985] F.S.R. 1
BACH FLOWER REMEDIES Trade Mark (TRADE MARK: RECTIFICATION: PERSON AGGRIEVED: T.M.Reg.) [1992] R.P.C. 439
BACTA v. (&c), *sub nom.* British Amusement Catering Trades Association v. (&c)
Badische Karton- und Pappenfabrik/Dust-tight folding carton (EUROPEAN PATENT: APPEAL: PROCEDURE: REMITTAL NOT ORDERED: *De facto* CONSIDERATION BY OPPOSITION DIVISION: OPPOSITION: PROCEDURE: LATE-FILED ARGUMENTS BASED ON DOCUMENTS CITED IN PATENT: T536/88: EPO) [1993] E.P.O.R. 202; [1992] O.J. EPO 638
Bailey & Co. Ltd v. Boccaccio Pty Ltd (COPYRIGHT: INFRINGEMENT: ARTISTIC WORK ON BOTTLE LABEL: PARALLEL IMPORTATION: IMPLIED LICENCE: NON-DEROGATION FROM GRANT: DESIGNS: Australia: S.C.(NSW)) 6 I.P.R. 279; [1986] 4 N.S.W.L.R. 701; 77 A.L.R. 177
Bailey v. Namol Pty Ltd (COPYRIGHT: INFRINGEMENT: ARTISTIC WORKS: DESIGN DRAWING: DAMAGES: REFERENCE TO EXPECTED PROFITS: AGGRAVATED OR EXEMPLARY DAMAGES: Australia: Fed. Ct) 30 I.P.R. 147
Bailey v. Namol Pty Ltd (COPYRIGHT: INFRINGEMENT: ARTISTIC WORKS: DESIGN DRAWINGS: COMPENSATORY DAMAGES: ASSESSMENT: CALCULATION BY REFERENCE TO EXPECTED PROFITS: AGGRAVATED OR EXEMPLARY DAMAGES: Australia: Fed. Ct) 125 A.L.R. 228

Bajaj Electricals Ltd v. Metal & Applied Products (TRADE MARK: BAJAJ: INFRINGEMENT: PASSING OFF: USE OF FAMILY NAME: INTERIM INJUNCTION: APPEAL: India: H.C.)   (1988) 13 I.P.L.R. 77

Baker & Priem's Application (DESIGNS: APPLICATION FOR EXTENSION: WHETHER NEW OR ORIGINAL: WHETHER COPYRIGHT SUBSISTED IN ARTISTIC WORKS CORRESPONDING TO DESIGN: ESSENTIAL FEATURES NOT IN TEMPLATE: WHETHER BULL-BAR A SCULPTURE OR WORK OF ARTISTIC CRAFTSMANSHIP: NO PREVIOUS USE OF PHOTOGRAPHS: Australia: Pat. Off.)   15 I.P.R. 671

Baker & Priem's Application (No. 1) (DESIGN: APPLICATION FOR RESTORATION: NOTICE OF OPPOSITION LODGED: GROUNDS OF VALIDITY OF A REGISTERED DESIGN NOT APPROPRIATE FOR OPPOSITION PROCEEDINGS TO RESTORATION: Australia: Pat. Off.)   15 I.P.R. 655

Baker & Priems Application (No. 2) (DESIGN: APPLICATION FOR EXTENSION: DESIGN NEW OR ORIGINAL: EVIDENCE: CORRESPONDING DESIGN: PUBLICATION: INDUSTRIALLY APPLIED: ARTISTIC WORK: SCULPTURE: WORK OF ARTISTIC CRAFTSMANSHIP: Australia: Pat. Off.)   15 I.P.R. 660

Baker v. Peuren Agencies Ltd (PATENT: OPPOSITION: FAIR BASIS: DEFINITION NOT UNDERSTANDABLE: AMENDMENT OF SPECIFICATION: COSTS: Australia: Pat. Off.)   7 I.P.R. 340

Baldock v. Addison (COPYRIGHT: INFRINGEMENT: PRACTICE: DISCOVERY SPLIT TRIAL: WHETHER PLAINTIFF ENTITLED TO DISCOVERY OF QUANTUM DOCUMENTS BEFORE TRIAL ON LIABILITY: Ch.D.)   [1994] F.S.R. 665; [1995] 1 W.L.R. 158

Ballabil Holdings Pty Ltd v. Hospital Products Ltd (PRACTICE: DISCOVERY: MAREVA INJUNCTION: POWER OF COURT: Australia: S.C.)   [1985] 1 N.S.W.L.R. 155

Bally Gaming International Inc. v. Scandic International Pty Ltd (PATENT: OPPOSITION: NOVELTY: OBVIOUSNESS: MANNER OF NEW MANUFACTURE: FAIR BASIS: SECTION 40; SMART CARD FOR DATA TRANSFER BETWEEN AMUSEMENT MACHINES AND CENTRAL COMPUTER: TIME FOR AMENDMENTS ALLOWED: Australia: AIPO)   29 I.P.R. 87

Balston Ltd v. Headline Filters Ltd (BREACH OF CONFIDENCE: BREACH OF DUTY OF GOOD FAITH: EX-EMPLOYEE: Ch.D.)   [1987] F.S.R. 330

Balston Ltd v. Headline Filters Ltd (BREACH OF FIDUCIARY DUTY: COMPANY DIRECTOR: BREACH OF CONFIDENCE: BREACH OF DUTY OF FIDELITY: CONFIDENTIAL INFORMATION: DIRECTOR PLANNING WHILE UNDER NOTICE TO COMPLETE: Ch.D.)   [1990] F.S.R. 385

Banik Rubber Industries v. Sree K.B. Rubber Industries (TRADE MARK: REGISTRATION: OPPOSITION: ABANDONMENT: RECTIFICATION: India: H.C.)   (1989) 13 I.P.L.R. 80

Bank Mellat v. Nikpour (PRACTICE: *Ex parte* RELIEF: MAREVA INJUNCTION: C.A.)   [1985] F.S.R. 87

Bank of Credit & Commerce International SA (PRACTICE: MAREVA INJUNCTION: GEOGRAPHICAL SCOPE: LEAVE TO COMMENCE PROCEEDINGS ABROAD: C.A.)   [1994] 3 All E.R. 764; [1994] 1 W.L.R. 708

Bank of Queensland Ltd v. Grant (MAREVA INJUNCTION: GROUNDS: Australia: S.C.(NSW))   [1984] 1 N.S.W.L.R. 409

Banks v. CBS Songs Ltd (COPYRIGHT: INFRINGEMENT: LYRICS IN RECORDED POP SONG: FURTHER INFRINGEMENTS ALLEGED AFTER ISSUE OF WRIT: WHETHER CONTINUOUS CAUSE OF ACTION: PRACTICE: SUMMONS TO AMEND ISSUED BEFORE BUT HEARD AFTER COMING INTO FORCE OF ACT: WHETHER CLAIM FOR CONVERSION DAMAGES STATUTE BARRED: Ch.D.: C.A.)   [1992] F.S.R. 278; [1996] E.M.L.R. 440

Bansal Plastic Industries v. Neeraj Toys Industries (REGISTERED DESIGN: INFRINGEMENT: INTERIM INJUNCTION: India: H.C.)   (1989) 14 I.P.L.R. 75

Barastoc Pty Ltd's Application (TRADE MARKS: APPLICATION FOR REGISTRATION: EXAMINER'S OBJECTION: DEVICE MARKS: Australia: Pat. Off.)   18 I.P.R. 212

Bargal Pty Ltd v. Force (TRADE PRACTICES: DECEPTION: Australia: H.C.)
1 I.P.R. 193

Barlow Clowes Gilt Managers Ltd (PRACTICE: DISCOVERY: PUBLIC INTEREST IMMUNITY: CONFIDENTIALITY: INFORMATION OBTAINED IN COMPULSORY LIQUIDATION OF COMPANY: COMPANY'S OFFICERS CHARGED WITH CRIMINAL OFFENCES: WITNESS SUMMONS ISSUED IN CRIMINAL PROCEEDINGS REQUIRING COMPANY'S LIQUIDATORS TO DISCLOSE CONFIDENTIAL INFORMATION: WHETHER INFORMATION TO BE DISCLOSED: Ch.D.)
[1991] 4 All E.R. 385; [1992] Ch. 208; [1992] W.L.R. 36

Barr's Application (TRADE MARKS: OBJECTIONS TO REGISTRATION: DESCRIPTIVE WORDS: FOREIGN LANGUAGE WORDS: WORDS OF COLOUR IN RESPECT OF CLOTHING: REGISTRATION REFUSED: Australia: Pat. Off.)   18 I.P.R. 196

Barry v. Lake Jindabyne Reservation Centre Pty Ltd (TRADE PRACTICES: MISLEADING OR DECEPTIVE CONDUCT: SIMILAR BUSINESS NAMES: Australia: Fed. Ct)   5 I.P.R. 191

Bars Products International Ltd v. Holt Lloyd Ltd (MISLEADING AND DECEPTIVE CONDUCT: GET-UP: PASSING   OFF: WINDSCREEN   CLEANERS: INTERLOCUTORY INJUNCTION: RECALL OF PRODUCT DISTRIBUTED: New Zealand: H.C.)   20 I.P.R. 87

Barson Computers (N.Z.) Ltd v. John Gilbert & Co. Ltd (COPYRIGHT: INFRINGEMENT: COMPUTER PRODUCTS: IMPORTATION: IRRELEVANCE OF HYPOTHETICAL MAKER: New Zealand: H.C.)
4 I.P.R. 533; [1985] F.S.R. 489

Barson Computers Australasia Ltd v. Southern Technology Pty Ltd (COPYRIGHT: COMPUTER PROGRAMS: OPERATING SYSTEMS IN ROM: SUBSISTENCE: INFRINGEMENT: REVERSE ENGINEERING BY DISASSEMBLY: SUBSTANTIAL PART: CONTRIBUTORY INFRINGEMENT: USE OF GENUINE COPY FOR TESTING AND DEMONSTRATION: TRADE PRACTICES: MISLEADING OR DECEPTIVE CONDUCT: ADVERTISING OF FUTURE PRODUCT: Australia: Fed. Ct)   10 I.P.R. 597

Barton v. Croner Trading Pty Ltd (TRADE PRACTICES: CONSUMER PROTECTION: LABELS: Australia: Fed. Ct)   [1985] 5 I.P.R. 42

Bartos v. Scott (CONTRACT: TIME FOR PERFORMANCE: NOTICE TO COMPLETE: COPYRIGHT: CO-AUTHORS: PERSON SUPPLYING TABLES AND IDEAS FOR WORK: NOT AN AUTHOR: Australia: S.C.(NSW))   26 I.P.R. 27

BASF Bell/Withdrawal of appeal (EUROPEAN PATENT: OPPOSITION: PROCEDURE: WITHDRAWAL OF APPEAL BY OPPONENT: ENLARGED BOARD OF APPEAL: POINT OF LAW, ANSWERED: DISPOSITION MAXIM: G07/91: EPO)
[1993] E.P.O.R. 440; [1993] O.J. EPO 356

BASF Corp. v. ICI Australia Operations Pty Ltd (PATENT: OPPOSITION: APPLICATION FOR EXTENSION OF TIME WITHIN WHICH TO SERVE EVIDENCE-IN-SUPPORT: ONUS OF PROOF ON APPLICANT: Australia: Pat. Off.)
13 I.P.R. 458

BASF/Bis-epoxy ethers (EUROPEAN PATENT: INVENTIVE STEP: CHEMICAL INTERMEDIATES: MULTISTAGE CHEMICAL PROCESS: SURPRISING EFFECT: T22/82: EPO)   [1979–85] E.P.O.R. B414; [1982] O.J. EPO 341

BASF/Debit order I (EUROPEAN PATENT: PROCEDURE: INTERLOCUTORY DECISION: FEES: REIMBURSEMENT OF APPEAL FEE: T152/82: EPO)
[1979–85] E.P.O.R. C644; [1984] O.J. EPO 301

BASF/Grounds for opposition (EUROPEAN PATENT: OPPOSITION: PROCEDURE: ADMISSIBILITY: PURPOSE OF PROCEDURAL LAW: FEES: REIMBURSEMENT OF APPEAL FEE: T2/89: EPO)   [1991] E.P.O.R. 220; [1991] O.J. EPO 51

BASF/Hydroxy-pyrazoles (EUROPEAN PATENT: UNITY: CHEMICAL INTERMEDIATES: T35/87: EPO) [1988] E.P.O.R. 260; [1988] O.J. EPO 134

BASF/Incrustation inhibitors (EUROPEAN PATENT: AMENDMENT AND CORRECTION: PRE- AND POST-GRANT, DISTINCTION BETWEEN: OPPOSITION: PROCEDURE: OPPOSITION DIVISION: REQUESTS BY: *Venire contra factum proprium*: T123/85: EPO)   [1989] E.P.O.R. 476; [1989] O.J. EPO 336

BASF/Metal refining (EUROPEAN PATENT: INVENTIVE STEP: COMBINATION OF CITATIONS: OBJECTIVE ASSESSMENT: PROBLEM AND SOLUTION: SKILLED PERSON: TECHNICAL ADVANTAGE: T24/81: EPO)
[1979–85] E.P.O.R. B354; [1983] O.J. EPO 133

BASF/Paint line supply system (EUROPEAN PATENT: OPPOSITION: PROCEDURE: AMENDMENT, COMMUNICATION OF, DISPENSED WITH: CONVENTIONS: INTENT AND PURPOSE: T185/84: EPO)
[1987] E.P.O.R. 34; [1986] O.J. EPO 373

BASF/Paper dyeing (EUROPEAN PATENT: APPEAL: PROCEDURE: NEW SEARCH: REMITTAL ORDERED: FOR ADDITIONAL SEARCH AND FURTHER EXAMINATION: INVENTIVE STEP: PROBLEM AND SOLUTION: REMOTE TECHNICAL FIELD: SPECULATIVE TEACHING IN PRIOR ART: T8/83: EPO)   [1986] E.P.O.R. 186

BASF/R,R,R-alpha-tocopherol (EUROPEAN PATENT: INVENTIVE STEP: CHEMICAL INTERMEDIATES: T648/88: EPO)
[1991] E.P.O.R. 305; [1991] O.J. EPO 292

BASF/Revocation at proprietor's request (EUROPEAN PATENT: OPPOSITION: PROCEDURE: REVOCATION AT INSTIGATION OF PATENTEE: TEXT OF PATENT: WITHDRAWAL OF APPROVAL: T186/84: EPO)
[1986] E.P.O.R. 165; [1986] O.J. EPO 79

BASF/Triazole derivatives (EUROPEAN PATENT: NOVELTY: NEW PURPOSE/USE FOR KNOWN SUBSTANCE/EQUIPMENT: FEES: REIMBURSEMENT OF APPEAL FEE: T231/85: EPO)   [1989] E.P.O.R. 293; [1989] O.J. EPO 74

BASF/Zeolites (EUROPEAN PATENT: CLAIMS: CONSTRUCTION: NON-LITERAL: PRODUCT-BY-PROCESS: INVENTIVE STEP: PREJUDICE: RISK IN DEPARTURE FROM KNOWN METHOD: OPPOSITION: PROCEDURE: OBSERVATIONS BY PARTIES ON AMENDMENTS: EVIDENCE: ONUS OF PROOF: ENLARGED BOARD OF APPEAL: REFERENCE REFUSED: T219/83: EPO)
[1986] E.P.O.R. 247; [1986] O.J. EPO 211

Basic Books Inc. v. Kinko's Graphics Corp. (COPYRIGHT: INFRINGEMENT: CLASSROOM GUIDELINES: EXCESSIVE COPYING: DEFENSES: MISUSE: ESTOPPEL: REMEDIES: INJUNCTION: STATUTORY DAMAGES: WILFUL INFRINGEMENT: FAIR USE DOCTRINE: COMMERCIAL PURPOSES: MARKET EFFECT: FACTUAL MATTER: USA: D.C.)   23 I.P.R. 565

Basset v. Société des Auteurs, Compositeurs et Editeurs de Musique (SACEM) (COPYRIGHT: PHONOGRAMS: RESTRICTIVE PRACTICES: COPYRIGHT MANAGEMENT SOCIETIES: RESTRICTION OF CIRCULATION: ROYALTIES: ARTICLE 30: ARTICLE 86: Case 402/85: ECJ)
[1987] 3 C.M.L.R. 173; [1987] E.C.R. 1747; [1987] F.S.R. 572

Basset v. Société des Auteurs, Compositeurs et Editeurs de Musique (SACEM) (COPYRIGHT: RESTRICTIVE PRACTICES: COLLECTING SOCIETIES: France S.C.)   [1984] 3 C.M.L.R. 233; [1985] F.S.R. 39

Bassey v. Icon Entertainment plc (COPYRIGHT: PERFORMER'S RIGHTS: PROPRIETORSHIP: RECORDING OF PERFORMANCES: SUMMARY JUDGMENT: TRIABLE ISSUE: CONSENT: Ch.D.) [1995] E.M.L.R. 596
BAT Cigaretten-Fabriken GmbH v. E.C. Comm., *sub nom.* TOLTECS and DORCET Trade Marks
Bata India Ltd v. m/s Pyarelal & Co. (TRADE MARK: INFRINGEMENT: PASSING OFF: BATA/BATAFORM: India: H.C.) (1986) 10 I.P.L.R. 385
BATCHELORS SNACKPOT Trade Mark (TRADE MARK: REMOVAL: NON-USE: PERSON AGGRIEVED: USE OF ASSOCIATED MARK: T.M.Reg.)
[1995] R.P.C. 555
Bateman v. Slatyer (TRADE PRACTICES: MISLEADING AND DECEPTIVE CONDUCT: SALE OF STORE FRANCHISE: REPRESENTATIONS ABOUT PROFITABILITY: DIRECTORS' LIABILITY: MEASURE OF DAMAGES: Australia: Fed. Ct)
8 I.P.R. 33
Bates & Partners Pty Ltd v. The Law Book Company Ltd (CONFIDENTIAL INFORMATION: PRIZE LIST: EMBARGOED NEWS RELEASE: CORRECTIVE ADVERTISING: APPLICATION FOR INTERLOCUTORY MANDATORY INJUNCTION: WHETHER DAMAGES AN ADEQUATE REMEDY: Australia: S.C.(NSW)) 29 I.P.R. 11
Bates Saddlery Pty Ltd v. Becville Pty Ltd (PATENT: PETTY PATENT: EXTENSION OF TERM: NOVELTY: OBVIOUSNESS: Australia: Pat. Off.) 19 I.P.R. 161
Batjac Productions Inc. v. Simitar Entertainment (U.K.) Ltd (COPYRIGHT: EQUITABLE TITLE: REQUIREMENT TO JOIN LEGAL OWNER: ACQUISITION OF LEGAL TITLE BEFORE JUDGMENT: WHETHER SUFFICIENT: SUMMARY JUDGMENT: STANDARD OF PROOF: EVIDENCE: SECONDARY EVIDENCE OF CONTENTS OF DOCUMENTS: Ch.D.) [1996] F.S.R. 139
Battelle/Fluidised bed combustion sanitation (EUROPEAN PATENT: APPEAL: PROCEDURE: STATEMENT OF GROUNDS, REQUIREMENTS OF: OPPOSITION: REVOCATION ON GROUNDS NOT RAISED BY OPPONENT: PRECEDENT: RELEVANCE OF OTHER DECISIONS ON DIFFERENT SUBJECT-MATTER: T450/87: EPO) [1990] E.P.O.R. 448
Bausch & Lomb Inc. v. Allergan Inc. (PATENT: APPLICATION: ACCEPTANCE: OPPOSITION: FAIR BASIS: PRIOR PUBLICATION: OBVIOUSNESS: LACK OF NOVELTY: NON-COMPLIANCE WITH SECTION 40: Australia: Pat. Off.)
24 I.P.R. 310
Baux v. Société Co-operative de Calce (TRADING NAME: WINE: APPELATION: CHÂTEAU: CONFLICT BETWEEN OCCUPANTS OF CHÂTEAU AND VINEGROWERS OCCUPYING LAND PREVIOUSLY PART OF CHÂTEAU: REFERENCE TO ECJ: France, S.C.) [1992] 2 C.M.L.R. 873
Baverstock Ltd v. Haycock (PRACTICE: PROCEDURE: ANTON PILLER ORDER: PRE-TRIAL DISCHARGE OF ORDER: EFFECT: VARIATION: COSTS: DAMAGES: New Zealand: H.C.) [1986] 1 N.Z.L.R. 342
Baxter International Inc. and Nestlé SA's Joint Ventures (RESTRICTIVE PRACTICES: MERGERS: CO-OPERATIVE JOINT VENTURES: CONTINUED PRESENCE OF PARENT COMPANIES ON THE SAME MARKETS: NOT CONCENTRATIVE WHERE PARENTS DO NOT COMPLETELY AND PERMANENTLY WITHDRAW FROM THE MARKET AND STATUS QUO CAN BE RESTORED AT ANY TIME, AND WHERE PARENTS RETAIN JOINT OWNERSHIP OF RELEVANT INTELLECTUAL PROPERTY RIGHTS: MERGER REGULATION: E.C. Comm.)
[1992] 5 C.M.L.R. M33; [1993] F.S.R. 167

Baxter International/Liquid-gas-bubble separator (EUROPEAN PATENT: CLAIMS: MECHANICAL SUB-COMBINATIONS: AMENDMENT AND CORRECTION: BROADENING CLAIM BY OMISSION: APPEAL: PROCEDURE: REMITTAL ORDERED: TO CONSIDER AMENDED CLAIM AND TO CONSIDER MATTERS OTHER THAN CLARITY: FEES: REIMBURSEMENT OF APPEAL FEE: "*Ab ovo*": T888/90: EPO)   [1994] E.P.O.R. 98; [1994] O.J. EPO 162

Baxter Travenol Laboratories Inc. v. Cutter Laboratories Inc. (SC: OPPOSITION: EXTENSION OF TIME LIMIT FOR LODGING EVIDENCE: Australia: Pat. Off.)
9 I.P.R. 36

Baxter/One-year period (EUROPEAN PATENT: RE-ESTABLISHMENT OF RIGHTS: STATEMENT OF GROUNDS: WHEN DUE TIME LIMIT FOR: J06/90: EPO)
[1994] E.P.O.R. 304; [1993] O.J. EPO 794

Bayer AG's (Meyer)'s Application (PATENT: APPLICATION: DRUGS: METHOD OF THERAPY: NOVELTY: C.-G.)   [1984] R.P.C. 11

Bayer AG and Gist-Brocades NV's Agreement (RESTRICTIVE PRACTICES: PHARMACEUTICALS: SPECIALISATION AGREEMENTS: RECIPROCAL LONG-TERM SUPPLY CONTRACTS: INTENTION TO EXTEND EXEMPTION: E.C. Comm.)   [1990] 4 C.M.L.R. 516

Bayer AG v. Alphapharm Pty Ltd (PATENT: INFRINGEMENT: INVALIDITY: OBVIOUSNESS: LACK OF INVENTIVE STEP: FALSE SUGGESTION: BEST METHOD: Australia: S.C.(NSW))   8 I.P.R. 559

Bayer AG v. Controller of Patents (PATENT: RECTIFICATION: India: H.C.)
[1981] I.P.L.R. 6

Bayer AG v. Harris Pharmaceuticals Ltd (PATENT: PRACTICE: DISCOVERY: WHETHER REQUIRED TO TRANSLATE FOREIGN-LANGUAGE DOCUMENTS: Ch.D.)   [1991] F.S.R. 170

Bayer AG v. Minister for Health of the Commonwealth of Australia (PATENT: EXTENSION: PHARMACEUTICAL DRUG: ADEQUACY OF REMUNERATION: NOTIONAL ROYALTY: DATE OF ASSESSMENT: ALLOWANCE FOR RESEARCH AND DEVELOPMENT: FOREIGN EARNINGS: EARNINGS SINCE DATE OF EXPIRY: NATURE OF MERITS OF INVENTION: PUBLIC INTEREST: REQUIREMENT OF CANDOUR AND GOOD FAITH: PROPER TERM OF EXTENSION: Australia: S.C.(NSW))   13 I.P.R. 225

Bayer AG v. Pacific Pharmaceuticals Ltd (PASSING OFF: GET-UP: COLOURED CAPSULES: DISTINCTIVENESS: INTERLOCUTORY INJUNCTION: New Zealand: H.C.)   7 I.P.R. 227

Bayer AG v. Pan Laboratories Pty Ltd (Australia: AIPO)   29 I.P.R. 556

Bayer AG v. Süllhöfer (JUDICIAL PROCEDURE: PRELIMINARY RULINGS: MULTIPLE CLAIMS: PATENT LICENSING: RESTRICTIVE PRACTICES: ANTI-COMPETITIVE PRACTICES: COMMUNITY LAW AND NATIONAL LAW: NO-CHALLENGE CLAUSE: APPEAL ON POINT OF LAW: Germany: S.C.)
[1993] E.C.C. 1; [1993] F.S.R. 414

Bayer AG v. Süllhöfer (RESTRICTIVE PRACTICES: INDUSTRIAL PROPERTY: AGREEMENTS: PATENT LICENSING: NO-CHALLENGE CLAUSES: COMMUNITY LAW: COMPATIBILITY WITH ARTICLES 30 AND 85: Case 65/86: ECJ)
[1990] 4 C.M.L.R. 182; [1988] E.C.R. 5249; [1990] F.S.R. 300

Bayer AG v. Winter (No. 2) (PRACTICE: INTERLOCUTORY PROCEEDINGS: CROSS-EXAMINATION OF DEFENDANT: JURISDICTION: Ch.D.)
[1986] 2 All E.R. 43; [1986] 2 F.T.L.R. 111; [1986] 1 W.L.R. 540

Bayer AG v. Winter (PRACTICE: INTERLOCUTORY INJUNCTION: MAREVA AND ANTON PILLER ORDERS: DELIVERY UP OF PASSPORTS: C.A.)
[1986] 1 All E.R. 733; [1986] 1 W.L.R. 497

Bayer AG v. Winter (PRACTICE: JURISDICTION: FORUM SHOPPING: FOREIGN
  PROCEEDING SEEKING PROTECTIVE MEASURES: Ch.D.)   [1986] E.C.C. 465
Bayer AG, BP Chemicals International Ltd & Erdölchemie GmbH's Agreements
  (RESTRICTIVE PRACTICES: PETROCHEMICALS: DISTRIBUTION AND
  TECHNICAL CO-OPERATION: INTENTION TO GRANT EXEMPTION: E.C.
  Comm.)   [1988] 4 C.M.L.R. 92
Bayer AG, BP Chemicals International Ltd & Erdölchemie GmbH's Agreements
  (RESTRICTIVE PRACTICES: AGREEMENTS: RESTRICTION OF COMPETITION:
  TECHNICAL CO-OPERATION: RESEARCH AND DEVELOPMENT:
  RESTRUCTURING: INTER-STATE TRADE: NEGATIVE CLEARANCE REFUSED:
  EXEMPTION GRANTED: E.C. Comm.)   [1989] 4 C.M.L.R. 24
Bayer (Second medical indication: G01/83, G05/83, G06/83), *sub nom.* Eisai, Bayer,
  Pharmuka (Second medical indication)
Bayer/Acetophenone derivatives (EUROPEAN PATENT: INVENTIVE STEP: CHEMICAL
  INTERMEDIATES: MULTISTAGE CHEMICAL PROCESS: T163/84: EPO)
                               [1987] E.P.O.R. 284; [1987] O.J. EPO 301
Bayer/Admissibility of opposition (EUROPEAN PATENT: OPPOSITION: PROCEDURE:
  ADMISSIBILITY: INTERLOCUTORY DECISION: COSTS: UNNECESSARY
  HEARING: AWARDED: T10/82: EPO)
                               [1979–85] E.P.O.R. B381; [1983] O.J. EPO 407
Bayer/Amino-acid derivatives (EUROPEAN PATENT: APPEAL: PROCEDURE:
  REMITTAL ORDERED: TO CONSIDER POSSIBLE FRESH OBJECTION: NOVELTY:
  SELECTION: WHOLE CONTENTS: T12/90: EPO)   [1991] E.P.O.R. 312
Bayer/Benzyl esters (EUROPEAN PATENT: UNITY: CHEMICAL INTERMEDIATES:
  T110/82: EPO)   [1979–85] E.P.O.R. B546; [1984] O.J. EPO 274
Bayer/Carbonless copying paper (EUROPEAN PATENT: APPEAL: PROCEDURE: FRESH
  EVIDENCE: INVENTIVE STEP: OBJECTIVE ASSESSMENT: PROBLEM AND
  SOLUTION: SELECTION: T1/80: EPO)
                               [1979–85] E.P.O.R. B250; [1981] O.J. EPO 206
Bayer/Catalyst (EUROPEAN PATENT: NOVELTY: COMBINATION OF SEPARATE
  TEACHINGS IN SINGLE DOCUMENT: T291/85: EPO)
                               [1988] E.P.O.R. 371; [1988] O.J. EPO 302
Bayer/Clarity of claims (EUROPEAN PATENT: CLAIMS: FUNCTIONAL FEATURES:
  T26/82: EPO)   [1979–85] E.P.O.R. B423
Bayer/Copolycarbonates (EUROPEAN PATENT: UNITY: SOLUTION TO MULTIPLE
  PROBLEMS: T57/82: EPO)   [1979–85] E.P.O.R. B474; [1982] O.J. EPO 306
Bayer/Cyclopropane (EUROPEAN PATENT: INVENTIVE STEP: CHEMICAL
  INTERMEDIATES: T65/82: EPO)
                               [1979–85] E.P.O.R. B484; [1983] O.J. EPO 327
Bayer/Diastereomers (EUROPEAN PATENT: APPEAL: PROCEDURE: LATE
  PRESENTATION OF CLAIM: INVENTIVE STEP: SELECTION: NOVELTY:
  INEVITABLE RESULT: T12/81: EPO)
                               [1979–85] E.P.O.R. B308; [1982] O.J. EPO 296
Bayer/Fibre composites (EUROPEAN PATENT: AMENDMENT AND CORRECTION:
  DISCREPANCY BETWEEN CLAIM AND DESCRIPTION: NOVELTY: ORAL
  DESCRIPTION: PRODUCT OF ORALLY-DESCRIBED PROCESS: PRIOR ART:
  PRIOR ORAL DESCRIPTION: PRIOR USE: FEATURES INFERRABLE FROM
  INSPECTION: T177/83: EPO)   [1979–85] E.P.O.R. C884
Bayer/Immunostimulant (EUROPEAN PATENT: PATENTABILITY: THERAPY:
  T780/89: EPO)   [1993] E.P.O.R. 377; [1993] O.J. EPO 440
Bayer/Moulding compositions (EUROPEAN PATENT: INVENTIVE STEP: ANALOGOUS
  SUBSTITUTION: BONUS EFFECT: ONE-WAY STREET: T192/82: EPO)
                               [1979–85] E.P.O.R. C705; [1984] O.J. EPO 415

Bayer/Nimodipin (I) (EUROPEAN PATENT: PATENTABILITY: SECOND MEDICAL INDICATION: ENLARGED BOARD OF APPEAL: PRESIDENT OF THE EPO: T17/81: EPO) [1979–85] E.P.O.R. B320; [1985] O.J. EPO 130

Bayer/Plant growth regulating agent (EUROPEAN PATENT: NOVELTY: NEW PURPOSE/USE FOR KNOWN SUBSTANCE/EQUIPMENT: G06/88: EPO) [1990] E.P.O.R. 257

Bayer/Plant growth regulation (EUROPEAN PATENT: NOVELTY: NEW PURPOSE/USE FOR KNOWN SUBSTANCE/EQUIPMENT: PRECEDENT: EXAMINING DIVISION, NON-OBSERVANCE BY: FEES: REIMBURSEMENT OF APPEAL FEE: ENLARGED BOARD OF APPEAL: PRESIDENT OF THE EPO: T208/88: EPO) [1992] E.P.O.R. 74; [1992] O.J. EPO 22

Bayer/Polyamide moulding compositions (EUROPEAN PATENT: CLAIMS: CONTRADICTION IN: T2/80: EPO) [1979–85] E.P.O.R. B257; [1981] O.J. EPO 431

Bayer/Polyamide–6 (EUROPEAN PATENT: OPPOSITION: PROCEDURE: FRESH DOCUMENTS ON APPEAL: INVENTIVE STEP: REVERSAL OF TREND: SIMPLICITY OF SOLUTION: T9/86: EPO) [1988] E.P.O.R. 83; [1988] O.J. EPO 12

Bayer/Polyether polyols (EUROPEAN PATENT: CLAIMS: DISCLAIMER: T4/80: EPO) [1979–85] E.P.O.R. B260; [1982] O.J. EPO 149

Bayer/Polyurethane plastics (EUROPEAN PATENT: CLAIMS: NOVELTY: DISCLAIMER: PRIOR ART: SIMULTANEOUS APPLICATIONS: T123/82: EPO) [1979–85] E.P.O.R. B575

Bayer/Pulp production (EUROPEAN PATENT: OPPOSITION: PROCEDURE: CONSOLIDATION OF APPEALS: FEES: REIMBURSEMENT OF APPEAL FEE: FORMALITIES SECTION: POWERS OF: T114/82: EPO) [1979–85] E.P.O.R. B558; [1983] O.J. EPO 323

Bayer/Thermoplastic moulding compound (EUROPEAN PATENT: GUIDELINES FOR EXAMINATION: NOT BINDING: T344/88: EPO) [1994] E.P.O.R. 508

Bayer/Thermoplastic moulding compound (EUROPEAN PATENT: OPPOSITION: PROCEDURE: IDENTIFICATION OF CITATION: ADMISSIBILITY: EVIDENCE: COMPARATIVE TESTS: MUST BE BASED ON CLOSEST PRIOR ART: INVENTIVE STEP: CLOSEST PRIOR ART: COMBINATION OF CITATIONS: PROBLEM, DEFINITION OF: T69/83: EPO) [1979–85] E.P.O.R. C771; [1984] O.J. EPO 357

Bayer/Titanyl sulphate (EUROPEAN PATENT: INVENTIVE STEP: CLOSEST PRIOR ART: COMBINATION OF CITATIONS: ROUTINE POWERS OF A SKILLED MAN: NOVELTY: COMBINATION OF SEPARATE TEACHINGS IN SINGLE DOCUMENT: T183/84: EPO) [1986] E.P.O.R. 174

Bayer/Tolylfluanid (EUROPEAN PATENT: OPPOSITION: PROCEDURE: LATE EVIDENCE: INVENTIVE STEP: COMPARATIVE TESTS: OBVIOUS TO TRY: SKILLED PERSON: APPEAL: FRESH PRIOR ART: T57/84: EPO) [1987] E.P.O.R. 131; [1987] O.J. EPO 53

Bayer/Vaccine (EUROPEAN PATENT: "AND": T171/89: EPO) [1990] E.P.O.R. 126

Bayliner Marine Corp. v. Doral Boats Ltd (COPYRIGHT: INFRINGEMENT: PLANS FOR BOAT HULLS: WHETHER REGISTRABLE AS DESIGNS: STATUTORY EXCLUSION: NOVELTY: Canada: Fed. C.A.) [1987] F.S.R. 497

Bayo-N-Ox (Re). *See, sub nom.* Community v. Bayer AG (Re Bayo-N-Ox)

BBC Brown Boveri AG and NGK Insulators Ltd's Agreement (RESTRICTIVE PRACTICES: CO-OPERATION AGREEMENTS: JOINT VENTURES: JOINT DEVELOPMENT: INTENTION TO APPROVE: E.C. Comm.) [1988] 4 C.M.L.R. 427

BBC Brown Boveri and NGK Insulators Ltd's Agreements (RESTRICTIVE PRACTICES: JOINT VENTURE: GERMAN-JAPANESE JOINT RESEARCH AND DEVELOPMENT: EXCLUSIVE LICENSING: KNOW-HOW: GROUP EXEMPTION: INAPPLICABILITY OF REGULATION 418/85: INDIVIDUAL EXEMPTION GRANTED: E.C. Comm.)   [1989] 4 C.M.L.R. 610

BBC Enterprises Ltd v. Hi-Tech Xtravision Ltd (BROADCASTING RIGHTS: COPYRIGHT: UNAUTHORISED RECEPTION: ENCRYPTED SATELLITE BROADCASTS RECEIVABLE OUTSIDE U.K.: MONOPOLY AGREEMENT: LICENSING: SALE OF UNAUTHORISED DECODERS: CONSTRUCTION OF STATUTES: C.P.&D.A. 88: Ch.D.)

[1991] E.C.C. 71; [1990] F.S.R. 217; [1992] R.P.C. 167 (C.A.) [1990] 2 All E.R. 118; [1990] 1 Ch. 609; [1991] E.C.C. 71; [1990] F.S.R. 217; [1992] R.P.C. 167; [1990] 2 W.L.R. 1123; 20 I.P.R. 368 (H.L.) [1991] 2 A.C. 327; [1991] 3 All E.R. 257; [1992] R.P.C. 167; [1991] 3 W.L.R. 1; 18 I.P.R. 63

BBC v. British Satellite Broadcasting Ltd (COPYRIGHT: INFRINGEMENT: FAIR DEALING: USE OF EXTRACTS FROM BROADCASTS OF FOOTBALL MATCHES IN SPORTS NEWS PROGRAMME: EXTRACTS SHORT AND ACCOMPANIED BY VERBAL REPORTS: WHETHER FOR PURPOSE OF REPORTING CURRENT EVENTS: WHETHER FAIR DEALING: C.D.&P.A. 88: Ch.D.)

[1991] 3 All E.R. 833; [1992] Ch. 141; [1991] 3 W.L.R. 174 (*sub nom.* BBC v. British Sky Broadcasting Ltd) 1 I.P.R. 503

BBC v. Celebrity Centre Productions Ltd (COPYRIGHT: INFRINGEMENT: PASSING OFF: *EastEnders* TV SERIES: *A to Z of EastEnders* MAGAZINE: MISREPRESENTATION OF AUTHORISATION: Ch.D.)   15 I.P.R. 333

BBC v. E.C. Commission (RESTRICTIVE PRACTICES: BROADCASTING: WEEKLY LISTINGS OF TV PROGRAMMES: COPYRIGHT: REFUSAL TO PERMIT REPRODUCTION IN INDEPENDENT TV GUIDE: ARTICLE 86: COMMISSION ENTITLED TO REQUIRE LICENSING FOR REPRODUCTION OF THE LISTINGS: Case T-70/89: CFI)

[1991] 4 C.M.L.R. 669; [1991] E.C.R. 535; 22 I.P.R. 31

BBC/Colour television signal (EUROPEAN PATENT: INVENTIVE STEP: HINT IN PRIOR ART: PATENTABILITY: PRESENTATION OF INFORMATION: T163/85: EPO)   [1990] E.P.O.R. 599; [1990] O.J. EPO 379

BBC v. Marshall Cavendish (TRADE MARK: PASSING OFF: SEWING KIT: INTERLOCUTORY INJUNCTION: ADEQUACY OF DAMAGES: Ch.D.)

(1994) 81 L.S.Gaz. 436

Beatrice Companies Inc.'s Application (TRADE MARKS: APPLICATION: REGISTRABILITY: INHERENTLY DISTINCTIVE: CAPABLE OF BECOMING DISTINCTIVE: USE IN AUSTRALIA: Australia: Pat. Off.)   18 I.P.R. 265

Beattie/Marker (EUROPEAN PATENT: PATENTABILITY: MIX OF TECHNICAL AND NON-TECHNICAL ELEMENTS: MUSICAL AID: ENLARGED BOARD OF APPEAL: REFERENCE REFUSED: *Acte clair.* CONTRADICTION WITH GUIDELINES FOR EXAMINATION: T603/89: EPO) [1992] E.P.O.R. 221; [1992] O.J. EPO 230

Beckman Instruments Inc. v. Bockringer Mannheim GmbH (PATENT: VALIDITY: NOVELTY: OBVIOUSNESS: Australia: Pat. Off.)   3 I.P.R. 205

Becton/Radiation stabilisation (EUROPEAN PATENT: INVENTIVE STEP: SELECTION OF ONE OF SEVERAL POSSIBLE APPROACHES: NOVELTY: GENERAL V. SPECIFIC DISCLOSURE: WHOLE CONTENTS: PRIORITY: SPECIFIC EXAMPLE NOT INCLUDED IN PRIORITY DOCUMENT: PROCEDURE: WAIVER, PROPOSED NARROWER CLAIMS NOT AMOUNTING TO: APPEAL: BROADER CLAIMS AT ORAL PROCEEDINGS: T94/87: EPO)   [1989] E.P.O.R. 264

Bee Tek (Import & Export) Pte Ltd v. Kenner Parker Toys Inc. (TRADE MARK: APPLICATION FOR EXTENSION OF TIME TO FILE EVIDENCE IN REPLY: PUBLIC INTEREST: WHETHER INDULGENCES ALREADY GIVEN EXCESSIVE: Australia: Pat. Off.) 15 I.P.R. 640

Beecham Group Ltd's Application (PATENT: APPLICATION: OPPOSITION: MANNER OF NEW MANUFACTURE: NOVELTY: Australia: Pat. Off.) 3 I.P.R. 26

Beecham Group Ltd's Irish Patent Application (PATENT: APPLICATION: PROCEDURE: Ireland: S.C.) [1983] F.S.R. 355

Beecham Group plc v. Banafi (TRADE MARK: INFRINGEMENT: HAIR PREPARATIONS: BRYLCREEM/STELLACREAM: GET-UP: EXTENT OF TRADE MARK PROTECTION: WHETHER CONFUSION POSSIBLE BY CONSUMER OF AVERAGE PRODUCT: INJUNCTION: IMPORT AND SALE ENJOINED: SAUDI ARABIA: COURT OF GRIEVANCES) [1994] F.S.R. 685

Beecham Group plc v. Gist-Brocades NV, *sub nom.* R. v. Comptroller-General, *ex p.* Gist-Brocades

Beecham Group plc v. Southern Transvaal Pharmaceutical Pricing Bureau (Pty) Ltd (TRADE MARK: INFRINGEMENT: USE IN THE COURSE OF TRADE: GOODS FOR WHICH MARK REGISTERED: STATUTORY INTERPRETATION: South Africa: WLD) 1992 (2) S.A. 213

COMPUTER SOFTWARE SYSTEM PROVIDING INFORMATION ON GENERIC ALTERNATIVE MEDICINES AVAILABLE AFTER EXPIRY OF PATENT: South Africa: A.D.) 1993 (1) S.A. 546

Beecham-Wuelfing/PVD (EUROPEAN PATENT: EVIDENCE: EXPERT'S AFFIDAVIT DISCOUNTED: INVENTIVE STEP: CLOSEST PRIOR ART: OBVIOUS TO TRY: NOVELTY: SELECTION: THERAPEUTIC USE: T541/89: EPO) [1992] E.P.O.R. 193

Beecham/3–thienylmalonic acid (EUROPEAN PATENT: INVENTIVE STEP: CHEMICAL INTERMEDIATES: PROBLEM AND SOLUTION: T65/83: EPO) [1979–85] E.P.O.R. C766

Beecham/Antacid composition (EUROPEAN PATENT: INVENTIVE STEP: COULD/WOULD TEST: PREJUDICE: ROUTINE EXPERIMENTATION: T255/85: EPO) [1987] E.P.O.R. 351

Beecham/Corrected decision (EUROPEAN PATENT: AMENDMENT AND CORRECTION: RETROSPECTIVE EFFECT OF CORRECTION: FEES: REIMBURSEMENT OF APPEAL FEE: T116/90: EPO) [1991] E.P.O.R. 155

Beerens' Application (DESIGN: APPLICATION: STATEMENT OF MONOPOLY: DISCLAIMER: EFFECT: Australia: Pat. Off.) 7 I.P.R. 413

Beggars Banquet Records Ltd v. Carlton Television Ltd (COPYRIGHT: WRONGFUL INTERFERENCE WITH GOODS: FILM FOOTAGE: APPLICATION FOR INTERLOCUTORY ORDER FOR DELIVERY UP, INJUNCTIONS AND DISCOVERY: OWNERSHIP OF COPYRIGHT: Ch.D.) [1993] E.M.L.R. 349

Behr-Thomson Dehnstroffrengler Verwaltungs GmbH v. Western Thomson Controls Ltd (PATENT: INFRINGEMENT: PRACTICE: PLEADINGS: COUNTERCLAIM: See v. Scott-Paine ORDER: Pat. Ct) [1990] R.P.C. 569

Behr/Time limit for appeal (EUROPEAN PATENT: APPEAL: PROCEDURE: PREMATURE FILING: INVENTIVE STEP: DISCOURAGING ART: T389/86: EPO) [1988] E.P.O.R. 381; [1988] O.J. EPO 87

Behringwerke AG (PATENTS: AMENDMENT OF REGISTER: SUBSTITUTION OF NAME: CLERICAL ERROR: Australia: Pat. Off.) 7 I.P.R. 59

Beiersdorf AG's Application (TRADE MARK: APPLICATION: OPPOSITION: OVERSEAS REPUTATION: Australia: Pat. Off.) 2 I.P.R. 402

Bell & Howell/Vehicle guidance system (EUROPEAN PATENT: CLAIMS: GENERALISATION OF FEATURE: FEES: SMALL AMOUNT EXCEPTION: T130/82: EPO) [1979–85] E.P.O.R. B598; [1984] O.J. EPO 172

Bell Fruit Manufacturing Co. Ltd v. Twinfalcon Ltd (PATENT: INFRINGEMENT: PRACTICE: PATENT AGENTS: COSTS: BASIS FOR CALCULATION: DEFENCE STRUCK OUT: WHETHER AGENT ACTING WITHOUT INSTRUCTIONS: Pat. C.C.) [1995] F.S.R. 144

Bell Maschinenfabrik/Withdrawal of appeal (EUROPEAN PATENT: OPPOSITION: PROCEDURE: WITHDRAWAL OF APPEAL BY OPPONENT: ENLARGED BOARD OF APPEAL: POINT OF LAW, ANSWERED: G08/91: EPO) [1993] E.P.O.R. 445; [1993] O.J. EPO 346

Bella Cohen, *sub nom.* Cohen (Bella)

Belle Jardiniere's Application (TRADE MARKS: APPLICATION: SIGNATURE OF LIVING PERSON: SIGNATURE NOT THAT OF APPLICANT: NAME NOT DISTINCTIVE: WHETHER CONSENT TO USE SIGNATURE: Australia: Pat. Off.) 14 I.P.R. 159

Beloit Technologies Inc. v. Valmet Paper Machinery Inc. (PATENT: INFRINGEMENT: CONSTRUCTION: *Catnic*: PRIORITY: ENTITLEMENT: ANTICIPATION: OBVIOUSNESS: EXPERT EVIDENCE: COMMERCIAL SUCCESS: ADDED MATTER: Pat. Ct) [1995] R.P.C. 705

Bendix/Braking apparatus (EUROPEAN PATENT: INVENTIVE STEP: PRIOR ART: AGED ART: BONUS EFFECT: COMBINATION OF CITATIONS: T55/86: EPO) [1988] E.P.O.R. 285

Bendix/Braking system (EUROPEAN PATENT: OPPOSITION: PROCEDURE: AMENDMENT OF CLAIM ON APPEAL: COSTS: LATE FILING OF PROPOSED NEW CLAIMS: T99/87: EPO) [1989] E.P.O.R. 499

Bendix/Disc brake (EUROPEAN PATENT: OPPOSITION: PROCEDURE: AUXILIARY REQUEST, NEED FOR: T108/86: EPO) [1989] E.P.O.R. 494

Bendix/Governor valve (EUROPEAN PATENT: APPEAL: PROCEDURE: INTERLOCUTORY REVISION: T139/87: EPO) [1990] E.P.O.R. 234; [1990] O.J. EPO 69

Bendix/Telegraphic money order (EUROPEAN PATENT: CONVENTIONS: DIFFERENT LANGUAGE TEXTS: FEES: TELEGRAPHIC MONEY ORDER: T2/87: EPO) [1988] E.P.O.R. 415; [1988] O.J. EPO 264

Benetton Group SpA's Application (TRADE MARKS: APPLICATION: MARK DIRECTLY DESCRIPTIVE: NO EVIDENCE OF USE: Australia: Pat. Off.) 14 I.P.R. 198

BENJI Trade Mark (TRADE MARK: OPPOSITION: WITHDRAWAL OF OPPONENTS CONSENT: ESTOPPEL: T.M.Reg.) [1988] R.P.C. 251

BENSYL Trade Mark (TRADE MARK: APPLICATION: GOODS OF THE SAME DESCRIPTION: PRACTICE: BoT) [1992] R.P.C. 529

Bentley Fragrances Pty Ltd v. GDR Consultants Pty Ltd (TRADE PRACTICES: CONSUMER PROTECTION: MISLEADING OR DECEPTIVE CONDUCT: Australia: Fed. Ct) 5 I.P.R. 183

Bentley Lingerie Inc. v. Greta Lingerie (Aust.) Limited (TRADE MARK: APPLICATION: OPPOSITION: LATE APPLICATION FOR EXTENSION OF TIME TO FILE EVIDENCE: SPECIAL CIRCUMSTANCES: Australia: AIPO) 29 I.P.R. 375

Berkeley Administration Inc. v. McClelland (BREACH OF CONFIDENCE: EX-EMPLOYEE'S: FINANCIAL INFORMATION: WHETHER CONFIDENTIAL: WHETHER USED: Q.B.D.) [1990] F.S.R. 505
(SPECIFIC DISCOVERY: C.A.) [1990] F.S.R. 381
(PRACTICE: COSTS: ABANDONED PARTS OF ACTION: DISCRETION: COMPLAINT OF JUDICIAL BIAS: JUDGE'S DUTY: Q.B.D.) [1990] F.S.R. 565

Bernard Leser Publications Pty Ltd v. Spiritual Sky Group Co. Pty Ltd (TRADE MARK: APPLICATION: OPPOSITION: Australia: Pat. Off.) 5 I.P.R. 149

Besson (AP) Ltd v. Fulleon Ltd (COPYRIGHT: INNOCENT INFRINGEMENT: DIRECTORS' PERSONAL LIABILITY: Ch.D.) [1986] F.S.R. 319

Best Australia Ltd v. Aquagas Marketing Pty Ltd (PATENT: PRACTICE AND PROCEDURE: APPLICATION TO SET ASIDE SERVICE OUTSIDE AUSTRALIA: CASE AGAINST FOREIGN RESPONDENT OF CLAIMED INFRINGEMENT OF PATENT: Australia: Fed. Ct) 12 I.P.R. 143 (PATENT: INFRINGEMENT: FOREIGN RESPONDENT PARTICIPATED WITHIN AUSTRALIA WITH OTHER RESPONDENTS: CONFIDENTIAL INFORMATION: CLAIM FOR BREACH: PRACTICE AND PROCEDURE: APPLICATION TO SET ASIDE SERVICE OUTSIDE AUSTRALIA: DISCRETION OF COURT: Australia: Fed. Ct) 83 A.L.R. 217; 13 I.P.R. 600

Best v. Caltex Oil (Australia) Pty Ltd (TRADE AND COMMERCE: PETROLEUM RETAIL MARKETING FRANCHISE: FRANCHISE AGREEMENT: REVOCATION OF LICENCE: TRADE MARK AND RELATED SIGNS: INTERPRETATION OF STATUTE: Australia: Fed. Ct) 87 A.L.R. 1

Bestworth Ltd v. Wearwell Ltd (COPYRIGHT: INFRINGEMENT: PRACTICE: DISMISSAL FOR WANT OF PROSECUTION: Ch.D.) [1986] R.P.C. 527

Beta Computers (Europe) Ltd v. Adobe Systems (Europe) Ltd (CONTRACT: SHRINK-WRAPPED SOFTWARE LICENCE: SUPPLY OF COMPUTER SOFTWARE: NO CONCLUDED CONTRACT UNTIL ACCEPTANCE OF LICENCE CONDITIONS BY PURCHASER: NO NEED FOR IMPLIED TERM: LICENCE CONDITIONS IMPOSED BY COPYRIGHT OWNER: DOCTRINE OF *ius quaesitum tertio*: Scotland: O.H.) [1996] F.S.R. 367

Betsen v. CBS United Kingdom Ltd (COPYRIGHT: INFRINGEMENT: STRIKING OUT: MUSICAL WORK: WHETHER SUFFICIENT OBJECTIVE SIMILARITY: WHETHER PERCUSSION AND BASS LINE A SUBSTANTIAL PART: Ch.D.) [1994] E.M.L.R. 467

Bevanere Pty Ltd v. Lubidineuse (TRADE PRACTICES: CONSUMER PROTECTION: SALE OF BUSINESS: MISLEADING OF DECEPTIVE CONDUCT: Australia: Fed. Ct) 59 A.L.R. 334; 4 I.P.R. 467

Bevis v. Lyons (COPYRIGHT: DESIGNS: BOARD GAME: WRITTEN RULES: INFRINGEMENT: INTERLOCUTORY INJUNCTION: CROSS APPLICATION BY DEFENDANT FOR INFRINGEMENT OF COPYRIGHT AND REGISTERED DESIGN: BALANCE OF CONVENIENCE: Australia: S.C.(Qd.)) 7 I.P.R. 141

Bexford/Reflex copying (EUROPEAN PATENT: INVENTIVE STEP: AGED ART: ONE-WAY STREET: PRIOR ART: AGED PUBLICATIONS: T10/83: EPO) [1979–85] E.P.O.R. C726

Beyer Electrical Enterprise Pte Ltd v. Swanfu Trading Pte Ltd (TRADE MARK: ALOHA SWANFU: APPLICATION TO EXPUNGE FROM REGISTER: BONA FIDE USE: ONUS OF PROOF: Singapore: H.C.) [1993] 1 S.L.R. 293; 25 I.P.R. 215 (C.A.) [1994] 1 S.L.R. 625

Bharaj Manufacturing Co. v. Shiv Metal Works (TRADE MARK: REGISTRATION: OPPOSITION: India: T.M.Reg.) (1983) 8 I.P.L.R. 59

Bhimji v. Chatwani (PRACTICE: DISCOVERY: ANTON PILLER ORDER: LEGAL ADVICE: DELAY: SETTING ASIDE: BREACH: CONTEMPT: COMMITTAL ORDER: Ch.D.) [1991] 1 All E.R. 705; [1991] 1 W.L.R. 989

Bibby Bulk Carriers Ltd v. Cansulex Ltd (PRACTICE: DISCOVERY: USE OF DOCUMENTS: DOCUMENT READ IN OPEN COURT: DISCLOSURE TO CLAIMANT IN ARBITRATION PROCEEDINGS: IMPLIED UNDERTAKING NOT TO USE DOCUMENT IN OTHER PROCEEDINGS: WHETHER NEW RULES RETROSPECTIVE IN EFFECT: Q.B.D.) [1988] 2 All E.R. 820; [1989] 1 Q.B. 155

BICC plc v. Burndy Corp. (PATENT: JOINT OWNERSHIP: CONTRACT: SPECIFIC
PERFORMANCE: SET OFF: RELIEF AGAINST FORFEITURE: Pat. Ct)
[1985] R.P.C. 273
(C.A.) [1985] R.P.C. 273; [1985] 1 All E.R. 417; [1985] Ch. 232;
[1985] 2 W.L.R. 132
BICC/Radiation processing (EUROPEAN PATENT: APPEAL: PROCEDURE:
REJECTION OF CLAIMS PASSED BY EXAMINING DIVISION: PRIOR ART, FAILURE
TO EXAMINE: REMITTAL ORDERED: OBJECTIVE STATE OF THE ART NOT
CONSIDERED: CLAIMS: PRODUCT-BY-PROCESS: CONVENTIONS: NATIONAL
PRACTICES IRRELEVANT: T248/85: EPO)
[1986] E.P.O.R. 311; [1986] O.J. EPO 261
Big Country Developments Pty Ltd v. TGI Fridays Inc. (TRADE MARKS:
ACCEPTANCE FOR REGISTRATION IN PART A: OPPOSITION:
PROPRIETORSHIP: USE BY OPPONENT AS A MARK: Australia: Pat. Off.)
23 I.P.R. 523
Bijoli Grill Spencer's Products v. Spencers & Co. Ltd (TRADE MARK: INJUNCTION:
DECLARATION: India: H.C.) (1983) 8 I.P.L.R. 49
Bill Acceptance Corp. Ltd v. GWA Ltd (TRADE PRACTICES: DECEPTION: Australia:
Fed. Ct) 1 I.P.R. 496
Billhöfer Maschinenfabrik GmbH v. T.H. Dixon & Co. Ltd (COPYRIGHT
INFRINGEMENT: MECHANICAL DRAWING: WHETHER SUBSTANTIAL PART
COPIED: ENGINEER, NOT LAYMAN, TO ASSESS RELEVANT FEATURE:
Ch.D.) [1990] F.S.R. 105
Binon (S.A.) & Cie v. S.A. Agence et Messageries de la Presse (RESTRICTIVE
PRACTICES: SELECTIVE DISTRIBUTION: NEWSPAPERS: ARTICLE 85(1): Case
243/83: ECJ) [1985] 3 C.M.L.R. 800; [1985] E.C.R. 2015
Bio Energy Systems Inc. v. Lawrence John Walton (PATENT: APPLICATION:
OPPOSITION: LACK OF FAIR BASIS AND CLEAR DEFINITION: NOVELTY: PRIOR
PUBLICATION: Australia: Pat. Off.) 10 I.P.R. 566
Bioforce AG Roggwil TG's Application (TRADE MARKS: OBJECTION: DECEPTIVE
SIMILARITY TO CITED MARKS: COMMONALITY OF NON-DOMINANT
ELEMENT: DISCLAIMER: CONSENT OF PROPRIETOR OF CITED MARKS:
Australia: Pat. Off.) 14 I.P.R. 93
Biogen Inc. v. Medeva plc (PATENT: GENETIC ENGINEERING: HEPATITIS B. VIRUS:
SUFFICIENCY: PRIORITY DATE: OBVIOUSNESS: INTERPRETATION OF CLAIM:
FAIR BASIS: SUFFICIENCY: DATE OF ASSESSMENT: BURDEN OF PROOF: Pat.
Ct) [1995] R.P.C. 25
(C.A.) [1995] F.S.R. 4; [1995] R.P.C. 25
Biogen Inc. v. Medeva plc (PATENT: PRACTICE: INFRINGEMENT: DISCOVERY:
INVALIDITY: INJUNCTION: DECLARATION: DAMAGES: Pat. Ct)
[1993] R.P.C. 475
Biogen Inc./Hepatitis B (EUROPEAN PATENT: INTERVENTION: BELATED ENTRY:
ADMISSIBILITY: PRIOR ENTITLEMENT: ESSENTIAL ELEMENTS: REFERENCE TO
ENLARGED BOARD (NO): CITABILITY OF DOCUMENT: DESIGNATED
PUBLICATION DATE: INVENTIVE STEP: BIOTECHNOLOGICAL INVENTION:
REASONABLE EXPECTATION OF SUCCESS V. HOPE TO SUCCEED: ORAL
PROCEEDINGS: SUBSEQUENT FURTHER OBSERVATIONS: T296/93:
EPO) [1995] E.P.O.R. 1

Biogen Inc/Recombinant DNA (EUROPEAN PATENT: NOVELTY: AVAILABILITY: PRIORITY: MULTIPLE PRIORITY APPLICATIONS: PRIOR ART: OPPOSITION: PROCEDURE: AMENDMENT OF CLAIM, CLARITY AND SUPPORT: CLAIMS: OBJECTION TO CLARITY OF: SUFFICIENCY: CLAIMED SUBJECT-MATTER, REPRODUCIBILITY OF: FUNCTIONAL DEFINITIONS: ENLARGED BOARD OF APPEAL: REFERENCE REFUSED: T301/87: EPO)
[1990] E.P.O.R. 190; [1990] O.J. EPO 335

Bioglan Laboratories (Aust.) Pty Ltd v. Crooks (PATENT: APPLICATION: OPPOSITION: LACK OF NOVELTY: PRIOR DISCLOSURES: WHETHER PRIOR COMMERCIAL DEALING CONSTITUTES PRIOR USE: PRIOR PUBLICATION: NON COMPLIANCE WITH STATUTORY REQUIREMENTS: CLAIM NOT FAIRLY BASED: Australia: Pat. Off.)   17 I.P.R. 328

Biological Patents Directive (Draft) (PATENTS: BIOTECHNICAL INVENTIONS: PATENTABILITY OF LIVING MATTER: SCOPE OF PROTECTION: DEPENDENCY LICENCES FOR PLANT VARIETIES: DEPOSIT AND ACCESS TO DEPOSITED MATERIAL: BURDEN OF PROOF: DRAFT LEGISLATION: E.C. Council)
[1989] 1 C.M.L.R. 494; [1989] 1 F.S.R. 526

Biotrading and Financing OY v. Biohit Ltd (COPYRIGHT: INFRINGEMENT: ITERATIVE DRAWINGS: ORIGINALITY: RELEVANCE OF TITLE TO EARLIER DRAWINGS: Ch.D.)   [1996] F.S.R. 393

Bishwanath Prasad Radhay Sham v. Hindustan Metal Industries (PATENT: INFRINGEMENT: PERMANENT INJUNCTION: India: S.C.)   (1983) 8 I.P.L.R. 1

BK Engineering Co. v. UBHI Enterprises (PASSING OFF: USE OF HOUSE MARK: India: H.C.)   (1985) 10 I.P.L.R. 209

BK Products' Application (TRADE MARK: OPPOSITION: FORMIS/CHARMIS: India: T.M.Reg.)   (1986) 1 I.P.L.R. 40

Black & Decker Corp. v. Akarana Abrasive Industries Ltd (TRADE MARKS: APPLICATION FOR EXTENSION OF TIME TO FILE EVIDENCE IN SUPPORT: USUAL TIME REQUIRED FOR PREPARATION OF EVIDENCE: INCONVENIENCE OF APPLICANT: PUBLIC INTEREST: COSTS: Australia: Pat. Off.)   15 I.P.R. 399

Black & Decker Inc. v. Flymo Ltd (PATENT: INFRINGEMENT: PRACTICE: VALIDITY: OBVIOUSNESS: SPECIFIC DISCOVERY BASED ON WITNESS STATEMENT EXCHANGED BEFORE TRIAL: PRIVILEGE: DISCOVERY: WHETHER PRIVILEGE LOST BY EXCHANGE OF WITNESS STATEMENTS: Ch.D.)
[1991] F.S.R. 93; [1991] 3 All E.R. 158; [1991] 1 W.L.R. 753

Black & Decker/Brush assembly (EUROPEAN PATENT: AMENDMENT AND CORRECTION: INTERMEDIATE GENERALISATION: INVENTIVE STEP: COMBINATION OF CITATIONS: OPPOSITION: PROCEDURE: FRESH DOCUMENTS ON APPEAL: STATUTORY GROUNDS, RESTRICTION TO: *Cum grano salis*: T174/86: EPO)   [1989] E.P.O.R. 277

Black Clawson/Pulp delignification (EUROPEAN PATENT: APPLICATION: PROCEDURE: ORAL HEARING: FAILURE TO ATTEND: NOVELTY: NEW PURPOSE/USE FOR KNOWN SUBSTANCE/EQUIPMENT: T215/84: EPO)
[1986] E.P.O.R. 6

BLACK N' RED Trade Mark (TRADE MARK: APPLICATION: DISTINCTIVENESS: EVIDENCE: T.M.Reg.)   [1993] R.P.C. 25

Blackburn v. Boon Engineering & Construction Sdn Bhd (PATENT: LIFE: COMPULSORY LICENSING: WHETHER PA49 APPLICABLE: Brunei: H.C.)
[1988] 2 M.L.J. 572; [1991] F.S.R. 391

Blackwell v. Wadsworth (COPYRIGHT: INFRINGEMENT: AUTHORISING INFRINGING ACTS: LICENCE: Australia: S.C.(NSW))   (1982) 64 C.L.R. 145

Blazer plc v. Yardley & Co. Ltd (PASSING OFF: INTERLOCUTORY INJUNCTION: BLAZER: PLAINTIFF TRADING IN MEN'S CLOTHES AND DEFENDANT IN TOILETRIES: BALANCE OF CONVENIENCE: NO COMPETITION YET BETWEEN PARTIES: STATUS QUO: INJUNCTION REFUSED: Ch.D.)   [1992] F.S.R. 501

Bleiman v. News Media (Auckland) Ltd (COPYRIGHT: INFRINGEMENT: COMPETITION BASED ON RESULTS OF SPORTING EVENTS: COPYING: SUBSTANTIAL PART: TEST FOR ASSESSING BREACH: INTERIM INJUNCTION: New Zealand: C.A.)   [1994] 2 N.Z.L.R. 673

Blendax/Claims fees—Austria (EUROPEAN PATENT: CONVENTIONS: NON-LITERAL: FEES: EXTRA CLAIMS FEES, COMPUTATION: J08/84: EPO)
[1979–85] E.P.O.R. A204; [1985] O.J. EPO 261

Blockbuster Entertainment Corp. v. Registrar of Trade Marks (TRADE MARK: REGISTRATION: NON-DESCRIPTIVE AND PURELY DESCRIPTIVE MARK: BLOCKBUSTER/CHARTBUSTER: VIDEO RENTAL INDUSTRY: SERVICE MARK: South Africa: TPD)   1994 (3) S.A. 402

Blue Boats Ltd v. Gulf Tourist Services (1982) Ltd (PASSING OFF: SIMILARLY-COLOURED HARBOUR SHIPS: OTHER SHIPS SIMILARLY COLOURED: WHETHER DISTINCTIVE GET-UP: New Zealand: H.C.)   6 I.P.R. 256

Blue Cross & Blue Shield Association v. Blue Cross Health Clinic (TRADE MARK: INFRINGEMENT: PASSING OFF: INJUNCTION: India: H.C.)
(1990) 15 I.P.L.R. 92

Bluewater/Admissibility (EUROPEAN PATENT: AMENDMENT AND CORRECTION: AGREEMENT TO AMENDMENTS NOT PREVIOUSLY FORMULATED: ADMISSIBILITY: PARTY ADVERSELY AFFECTED: T156/90: EPO)
[1994] E.P.O.R. 515

BMW/Air-conditioning system (EUROPEAN PATENT: CONVENTIONS: *Travaux préparatoires*: FEES: REPAYMENT: J04/86: EPO)
[1988] E.P.O.R. 273; [1988] O.J. EPO 119

BMW/Non-appealing party (EUROPEAN PATENT: OPPOSITION PROCEDURE: MAINTENANCE OF PATENT IN AMENDED FORM: APPEAL BY ONE PARTY: EXTENT OF OTHER PARTY'S RIGHTS ON APPEAL: G09/92; T60/91; T96/92: EPO)   [1995] E.P.O.R. 169; [1994] O.J. EPO 875

Board of Control of Michigan Technological University v. Deputy Commissioner of Patents (PATENT: APPLICATION: RESTORATION: EXTENSION OF TIME LIMIT: UNDUE DELAY: Australia: H.C.)   (1981) 40 A.L.R. 577

Bodegas Rioja Santiago SA v. Barossa Co-operative Winery Ltd (TRADE MARK: OPPOSITION: PRIOR REGISTRATION: COMMON DESCRIPTIVE ELEMENTS: Australia: Pat. Off.)   (1985) 5 I.P.R. 1

Bodenrader/International application (EUROPEAN PATENT: AMENDMENT AND CORRECTION: DESIGNATION OF STATES: RE-ESTABLISHMENT OF RIGHTS: CONVENTIONS: EURO-PCT APPLICATIONS: SIMILAR PRINCIPLES APPLIED: FEES, FAILURE TO PAY: J03/81: EPO)
[1979–85] E.P.O.R. A74; [1982] O.J. EPO 100

Bodenseewerk Perkin-Elmer GmbH v. Varian Australia Pty Ltd (PATENT: APPLICATION: OPPOSITION: CLARITY: FAIR BASING: PRIOR PUBLICATION: OBVIOUSNESS: NOVELTY: EXPERT EVIDENCE: COMMON GENERAL KNOWLEDGE: OPPONENT'S RIGHT TO BE HEARD: Australia: Fed. Ct)
32 I.P.R. 110

Body Shop International plc v. Rawle (FRANCHISES: INTERLOCUTORY RELIEF: PASSING OFF: REPUDIATION: AFFIRMATION: DAMAGE: Ch.D.)   27 I.P.R. 255

Bodyline Cosmetics Ltd v. Brot Bodyline (TRADE MARK: OPPOSITION: PROPRIETORSHIP: FIRST USE: HONEST CONCURRENT USE: Australia: AIPO)   27 I.P.R. 315

Boehringer Mannheim GmbH v. Genzyme Ltd (PATENT: INFRINGEMENT: EUROPEAN PATENT (U.K.): VALIDITY: OBVIOUSNESS: PRACTICE: WHETHER CASE TO BE OPENED BY DEFENDANT WHEN ONLY VALIDITY IN ISSUE: Pat. Ct) [1993] F.S.R. 716

Boehringer Mannheim/Detection of redox preactions (EUROPEAN PATENT: INVENTIVE STEP: LONG-FELT WANT: REVERSAL OF TREND: T165/85: EPO) [1987] E.P.O.R. 125

Boehringer/Diagnostic agent (EUROPEAN PATENT: INVENTIVE STEP: PROBLEM, DEFINITION OF: NOVELTY: IMPLICIT DISCLOSURE: OPPOSITION: PROCEDURE: AMENDMENT OF CLAIM ON APPEAL: T99/85: EPO) [1987] E.P.O.R. 337; [1987] O.J. EPO 413

Boehringer/Reflection photometer (EUROPEAN PATENT: AMENDMENT AND CORRECTION: NOVELTY TEST: ADDED SUBJECT-MATTER: EQUIVALENTS, NOT INDICATED IN ORIGINAL DISCLOSURE: GENERALISATION: T416/86: EPO) [1989] E.P.O.R. 327; [1989] O.J. EPO 309

Boeing Co. v. DMH Imports (Aust.) Pty Ltd (TRADE MARK: DECEPTION OR CONFUSION: BOEING: OPPOSITION: ENTITLEMENT TO PROTECTION: Australia: AIPO) 31 I.P.R. 621

Boeing/Extendible airfoil track assembly (EUROPEAN PATENT: CLAIMS: PARENT AND SUBSIDIARY: INVENTIVE STEP: PROBLEM AND SOLUTION: PRIOR ART: PRIOR USE: SINGLE SALE MAKES ARTICLE AVAILABLE: GUIDELINES FOR EXAMINATION: NOT BINDING: T249/84: EPO) [1979–85] E.P.O.R. C997

Boeing/General technical knowledge (EUROPEAN PATENT: APPLICATION: PROCEDURE: ORAL HEARING: NEW GROUND FOR REJECTION AT: INVENTIVE STEP: COMMON GENERAL KNOWLEDGE: STATE OF THE ART: PRIOR ART: NEIGHBOURING FIELDS: T195/84: EPO) [1986] E.P.O.R. 190; [1986] O.J. EPO 121

Boeing/Obvious error in claims (EUROPEAN PATENT: AMENDMENT AND CORRECTION: MISTAKE, WHAT CONSTITUTES: TRANSCRIPTION ERROR: OBVIOUS CORRECTION WHEN TEXT READ IN ISOLATION: T200/89: EPO) [1990] E.P.O.R. 407; [1992] O.J. EPO 46

Boeing/Spoiler device (EUROPEAN PATENT: INVENTIVE STEP: PROBLEM, PERCEPTION OF: T225/84: EPO) [1986] E.P.O.R. 263

Bohemia Crystal Pty Ltd v. D. Swarovski (TRADE MARKS: PRACTICE AND PROCEDURE: POWER OF COURT TO VACATE CONSENT ORDERS: NEW ALLEGATION OF REGISTRATION HAVING BEEN PROCURED BY FRAUD: PRINCIPLES OF PLEADING: Australia: S.C.(NSW)) 14 I.P.R. 201

Bolesta's (Dymtro) Application (PATENT: LEAVE TO AMEND: SCOPE OF ACCEPTED CLAIMS: APPROPRIATENESS OF REASONS FOR AMENDMENTS: Australia: Pat. Off.) 20 I.P.R. 469

Bolestas Application (PATENT: OBJECTION: CONVERSION OF MOLECULAR ENERGY INTO POWER: FAIR BASIS: CLARITY: SUFFICIENCY OF DESCRIPTION: ADEQUACY OF DEFINITION: COMMISSIONER'S LACK OF POWER TO CONSIDER UTILITY: Australia: Pat. Off.) 13 I.P.R. 196; 13 I.P.R. 317

Bolland/Weight sensing apparatus (EUROPEAN PATENT: STATE OF THE ART: UNIVERSITY THESIS: DATE OF PUBLICATION: BURDEN OF PROOF: NECESSITY FOR EVIDENCE: OPPORTUNITY FOR OBTAINING EVIDENCE: NOVELTY: SCHEMATIC TEACHING: ENABLEMENT: FORM OF CLAIM: T405/94: EPO) [1995] E.P.O.R. 619

Bombay Oil Industries Pvt. Ltd v. Ballarpur Industries Ltd (TRADE MARK: INFRINGEMENT: SAFFOLA/SHAPOLA: INTERIM INJUNCTION: India: H.C.) (1989) 14 I.P.L.R. 16

BON MATIN Trade Mark (TRADE MARK: RECTIFICATION: NON-USE: CALCULATING PERIOD OF NON-USE: T.M.Reg.)   [1988] R.P.C. 553
(Ch.D.) [1989] R.P.C. 537; (1990) 15 I.P.L.R. 335

Bondax Carpets Ltd v. Advance Carpet Tiles (PATENT: INFRINGEMENT: PRACTICE: TITLE TO SUE: PLAINTIFF'S PROPRIETOR, SALES AND MARKETING COMPANY, AND MANUFACTURER: APPLICATION TO STRIKE OUT SECOND AND THIRD PLAINTIFFS: WHETHER TERMS OF LICENCE AGREEMENT CONSTRUABLE AS EXCLUSIVE LICENCE: MANUFACTURING LICENCE DISTINGUISHED: Ch.D.)   [1993] F.S.R. 162

Bondor Pty Ltd v. National Panels Pty Ltd (DESIGNS: INFRINGEMENT: REGISTERED DESIGN OF "PANELS" WITH NO SPECIFICATION OF PROPORTIONS: WHETHER MONOPOLY COVERS SHAPE AS IN REGISTERED REPRESENTATION: SIGNIFICANCE OF PROPORTIONS OF DESIGN: Australia: Fed. Ct)
98 A.L.R. 114; 102 A.L.R. 65; 19 I.P.R. 101

Bondor Pty Ltd v. National Panels Pty Ltd (DESIGNS: INFRINGEMENT: VALIDITY: WHETHER BUILDING PANEL OF INDEFINITE DIMENSIONS CAPABLE OF REGISTRATION: Australia: Fed. Ct)   23 I.P.R. 289

Bonz Group (Pty) Ltd v. Cooke (COPYRIGHT: INFRINGEMENT: ARTISTIC WORK: MODEL: HANDKNITTED GARMENTS: PROTOTYPE: OBJECTIVE SIMILARITY: INDEPENDENT SKILL, EFFORT AND LABOUR: ORIGINALITY: New Zealand: H.C.)   [1994] 3 N.Z.L.R. 216

Bonzel & Schneider (Europe) AG v. Intervention Ltd, *sub nom.* Bonzel v. Intervention Ltd

Bonzel v. Intervention Ltd (PATENT: INFRINGEMENT: PRACTICE: DISCOVERY: EPO: OPPOSITION: Pat. Ct)   [1991] R.P.C. 43

Bonzel v. Intervention Ltd (No. 2) (PATENT: INFRINGEMENT: PRACTICE: DISCLOSURE OF PRIVILEGED DOCUMENTS: *In camera* HEARING: Pat. Ct)
[1991] R.P.C. 231

Bonzel v. Intervention Ltd (No. 3) (PATENT: INFRINGEMENT: VALIDITY: EXTENSION OF DISCLOSURE THROUGH PRE-GRANT AMENDMENTS: OBVIOUSNESS: Pat. Ct)   [1991] R.P.C. 231

Booker McConnell plc v. Plascow (BREACH OF CONFIDENCE: ANTON PILLER PRACTICE: DISCHARGE OF ORDER: C.A.)   [1985] R.P.C. 425

Bookmakers' Afternoon Greyhound Services Ltd v. Wilf Gilbert (Staffordshire) Ltd (COPYRIGHT: SUBSISTENCE: OWNERSHIP: GREYHOUND CARDS AND RACE FORECAST DIVIDENDS: INFRINGEMENT: WHETHER DISPLAY ON TV MONITOR REPRODUCTION IN MATERIAL FORM: WHETHER WORKS PERFORMED IN PUBLIC: CONTRACTUAL LICENCE: AGENCY: BENEFIT OF PROMISE HELD ON TRUST: UNJUST ENRICHMENT: Ch.D.)   [1994] F.S.R. 723

Boot Tree Ltd v. Robinson (PASSING OFF: IMPORTED GOODS: ASSIGNMENT OF TRADE MARK WITHOUT GOODWILL: Ch.D.)   [1984] F.S.R. 545

Boots Co. Ltd v. Approved Prescription Services Ltd (PASSING OFF: COLOURED PILLS: INTERLOCUTORY INJUNCTION: C.A.)   [1988] F.S.R. 45

Borachem Industries Pvt. Ltd v. Fabril Gasosa (TRADE MARK: APPLICATION: OPPOSITION: BONITA/BONILA: India: T.M.Reg.)   (1992) 17 I.P.L.R. 266

Borden Inc. v. Elkem A/S (PATENT: OPPOSITION: ADEQUACY OF STATEMENT: GROUNDS FOR DISMISSAL: DISMISSAL OF OPPOSITION: Australia: Pat. Off.)
24 I.P.R. 146

Borg-Warner Corp.'s Patent (PATENT: PRACTICE: RESTORATION: C.-G.)
[1986] R.P.C. 137

Bosal Afrika Pty Ltd v. Grapnel Pty Ltd (COPYRIGHT: INFRINGEMENT: DRAWINGS: PROTOTYPE: ADAPTATIONS: South Africa: CPD)   1985 (4) S.A. 882

Bosch/Electronic computer components (EUROPEAN PATENT: PATENTABILITY: COMPUTER PROGRAM: SKILLED PERSON: KNOWLEDGE OF PROGRAM: T164/92: EPO) [1995] E.P.O.R. 585; [1995] O.J. EPO 305

Bosch/Hearing aid (EUROPEAN PATENT: INVENTIVE STEP: INACTIVE ART: LONG-FELT WANT: NEIGHBOURING FIELD, SOLUTION IN: PRIOR ART: PRIOR USE: T109/82: EPO) [1979–85] E.P.O.R. B539; [1984] O.J. EPO 473

Bosch/Power supply (EUROPEAN PATENT: PROCEDURE: INCORRECT FORM: ORIGINAL DECISION, WHAT CONSTITUTES: RE-ESTABLISHMENT OF RIGHTS: ADMISSIBILITY OF APPLICATION BY OPPONENT: T105/89: EPO) [1991] E.P.O.R. 360

Bosch/Test piece (EUROPEAN PATENT: AMENDMENT AND CORRECTION: ESSENTIAL FEATURE: EXTENSION OF SUBJECT-MATTER: ARTICLE 123(2) v. RULE 88; CONVENTIONS: PRECEDENCE OVER RULES: T401/88: EPO) [1990] E.P.O.R. 640; [1990] O.J. EPO 297

Bossert KG/Two-part claim (EUROPEAN PATENT: CLAIMS: ONE PART v. TWO PART: T170/84: EPO) [1987] E.P.O.R. 82; [1986] O.J. EPO 400

Bostick Ltd v. Sellotape GB Ltd (PASSING OFF: BLUE ADHESIVE TACK: WHETHER CONFUSION AT POINT OF SALE: INTERLOCUTORY INJUNCTION: Ch.D.) [1994] R.P.C. 556

Boswell-Wilkie Circus (Pty) Ltd v. Brian Boswell Circus (Pty) Ltd (TRADE MARK: PASSING OFF: USE OF OWN NAME: DECEPTION: South Africa: NPD) 1984 (1) S.A. 734; [1985] F.S.R. 434 (S.C.) [1986] F.S.R. 479

Botha v. Carapax Shadeports (Pty) Ltd (CESSION OF BUSINESS: SALE OF GOODWILL: TRANSFER OF RESTRAINT OF TRADE OBLIGATIONS: South Africa: A.D.) 1992 (1) S.A. 202

Boundy Insulations Pty Ltd's Application (TRADE MARK: OPPOSITION: PRIOR USE BY FOREIGN OPPONENT: OVERSEAS USE: MAGAZINES: INVITATION TO PURCHASE: Australia: Pat. Off.) 9 I.P.R. 345

Bourjois Ltd's Application (DESIGNS: APPLICATION: AMENDMENT OF STATEMENT OF MONOPOLY: ORNAMENTATION: PATTERN: COLOUR: Australia: Pat. Off.) 11 I.P.R. 625

Bousquet v. Barmish Inc. (TRADE MARKS: ADOPTION OF FOREIGN MARK ON DIFFERENT WARES: PREVIOUS USE IN CANADA REQUIRED: FIVE-YEAR DELAY CREATES HIGHER BURDEN: DISTINCTIVENESS: MESSAGE TO THE PUBLIC: EXPUNGEMENT: NAME OF DESIGNER: SIGNIFICANT REPUTATION REQUIRED: Canada: F.C.) 23 I.P.R. 273

Boussac Saint Frères/Interventions (EUROPEAN PATENT: APPEAL: PROCEDURE: INTERVENTIONS: T338/89: EPO) [1991] E.P.O.R. 268

Boussois SA and Interpane & Co. KG's Agreement (RESTRICTIVE PRACTICES: PATENT LICENCE: GROUP EXEMPTION: RELEVANCE: DECISION: E.C. Comm.) [1988] 4 C.M.L.R. 124; [1988] F.S.R. 215

Boussois SA and Interpane & Co. KG's Agreement (RESTRICTIVE PRACTICES: PATENT LICENCE: UNPATENTED KNOW-HOW: EXCLUSIVE LICENCE TO MANUFACTURE: IMPROVEMENT KNOW-HOW: INTENTION TO EXEMPT: E.C. Comm.) [1986] 3 C.M.L.R. 222

Bowden Controls Ltd v. Acco Cable Controls Ltd (PATENT: THREATS: Pat. Ct) [1990] R.P.C. 427

Bowles/Divisional application (EUROPEAN PATENT: APPLICATION: PROCEDURE: ORAL HEARING: NEW REQUEST AT: DIVISIONAL APPLICATION: FOREIGN LEGAL PROCEEDINGS, RESULTING FROM: CONVENTIONS: RECOGNITION OF FOREIGN LEGAL DECISIONS: ENTITLEMENT: EMPLOYER V. EMPLOYEE: ASSIGNMENT: CONSTRUCTION OF: UNSIGNED, WHETHER EFFECTIVE: J34/86: EPO)   [1988] E.P.O.R. 266

BP Chemicals Ltd and ECP-Enichem Polimeri Srl's Agreements (RESTRICTIVE PRACTICES: JOINT RESEARCH AND DEVELOPMENT: LICENSING: INTENTION TO APPROVE: NOTICE: E.C. Comm.)   [1994] 4 C.M.L.R. 116

BP International Ltd & M.W. Kellogg Company's Application (RESTRICTIVE PRACTICES: JOINT RESEARCH AND DEVELOPMENT: PRODUCTION OF AMMONIA: INTENTION TO EXEMPT: ARTICLE 85(3): E.C. Comm.)   [1985] 3 C.M.L.R. 198

BP Nutrition (U.K.) Ltd's Application (PATENT: APPLICATION: OBJECTION: NOVELTY: WHETHER CLAIMS DEFINE MORE THAN ONE INVENTION: OPTICAL COMPONENTS IN CLAIMS: Australia: Pat. Off.)   11 I.P.R. 506

BP/Theta-1 (EUROPEAN PATENT: COSTS: CRITERIA FOR AWARD: OPPOSITION: PROCEDURE: DECISION OF OPPOSITION DIVISION, CORRECTION OF: FRESH EVIDENCE ON APPEAL, ALLOWED: PRIORITY: NO CHANGE IN CHARACTER: SUFFICIENCY: AVAILABLE STARTING MATERIALS: T212/88: EPO)   [1990] E.P.O.R. 518; [1992] O.J. EPO 28

Braas & Co. GmbH v. Humes Ltd (PATENT: APPLICATION: SECTION 40: PRINCIPLES OF CONSTRUCTION: NOVELTY: ACCIDENTAL PRIOR USE: OBVIOUSNESS: VALUE OF EVIDENCE OF "OVER-QUALIFIED" EXPERTS: Australia: Pat. Off.)   26 I.P.R. 273

Bradley v. Wingnut Films Ltd (MALICIOUS FALSEHOOD: MALICE: WHETHER FILM SUGGESTED PLAINTIFF'S INVOLVEMENT: SCENE SHOT IN CEMETERY INCLUDING FAMILY TOMBSTONE IN BACKGROUND: BREACH OF PRIVACY: EMOTIONAL DISTRESS: New Zealand: H.C.)   [1993] 1 N.Z.L.R. 415; [1994] E.M.L.R. 217

Brady v. Chemical Process Equipment Pvt. Ltd (COPYRIGHT: MACHINE DRAWINGS: INFRINGEMENT: BREACH OF CONFIDENCE: THREE-DIMENSIONAL REPRODUCTION: APPLICABILITY OF ENGLISH AUTHORITIES: INTERIM INJUNCTION: India: H.C.)   (1987) 12 I.P.L.R. 125; [1988] F.S.R. 457

Braemar Appliances Pty Ltd v. Rank Electric Housewares Ltd (TRADE PRACTICES: DECEPTION: INTERLOCUTORY INJUNCTION: Australia: Fed. Ct)   2 I.P.R. 77

Brain v. Ingledew Brown Bennison (PATENT: THREATS: PENDING APPLICATION: CONDITIONAL THREATS: ADDRESSEE: AGGRIEVED PERSON: Ch.D.)   [1995] F.S.R. 552

(THREATS RELATING TO PENDING APPLICATION: WHETHER ACTIONABLE: WHETHER JUDGE AT LIBERTY TO MAKE DECLARATIONS UNDER ORDER 14A: C.A.)   [1966] F.S.R. 341

Brandella Pty Ltd's Application (TRADE MARK: APPLICATION: KANGAROO DEVICE: UNADAPTED TO DISTINGUISH: Australia: Pat. Off.)   9 I.P.R. 315

Branov v. Sleep Better Bedding Mfg Pty Ltd (TRADE MARK: OPPOSITION: APPLICATION FOR EXTENSION OF TIME TO LODGE OPPOSITION: Australia: AIPO)   32 I.P.R. 171

Brass Band Instruments Ltd v. Boosey & Hawkes plc (RESTRICTIVE PRACTICES: REFUSAL TO SUPPLY: PROCEDURE: INTERIM MEASURES: E.C. Comm.)   [1988] 4 C.M.L.R. 67; [1988] F.S.R. 213

Bravado Mechandising Services Ltd v. Mainstream Publishing (Edinburgh) Ltd (TRADE MARK: NAME OF POP GROUP REGISTERED *inter alia* FOR BOOKS: USE OF NAME OF GROUP ON BOOK ABOUT THE GROUP: INFRINGEMENT: WHETHER USE IN TRADE MARK SENSE: AVAILABILITY OF DEFENCE UNDER T.M.A. 94, s. 11(2): Scotland: O.H.) [1996] F.S.R. 205

Bredero/Inadmissible language of opposition (EUROPEAN PATENT: OPPOSITION: PROCEDURE: LANGUAGE OF NOTICE: T149/85: EPO)
[1986] E.P.O.R. 223; [1986] O.J. EPO 103

Bress Designs (Pty) Ltd v. G.Y. Lounge Suite Manufacturers (Pty) Ltd (COPYRIGHT: DIMENSIONAL WORK: LOUNGE SUITE: CREATION FROM PHOTOGRAPH: PASSING OFF: UNLAWFUL COMPETITION: South Africa: WLD)
1991 (2) S.A. 455

Breville Europe plc v. Thorn EMI Domestic Appliances Ltd (COPYRIGHT: REGISTERED DESIGN: INFRINGEMENT: TEST: SANDWICH TOASTERS: DRAWINGS: PLASTERCASTS OF TOASTED SANDWICHES: WHETHER SCULPTURES: PROPER PROPRIETOR: COMMISSIONED WORK: Pat. Ct)
[1995] F.S.R. 77

Brian Davis & Co. Pty Ltd's Application (TRADE MARK: APPLICATION: PROFESSIONAL: LAUDATORY WORD: INHERENT DISTINCTIVENESS: Australia: Pat. Off.) 7 I.P.R. 252

Brian Davis & Co. Pty Ltd's Application (TRADE MARK: APPLICATION: WATERWELL: CONJOINED USE: CAPACITY TO DISTINGUISH: Australia: Pat. Off.) 8 I.P.R. 192

Brickwood Holdings Pty Ltd v. ACI Operations Pty Ltd (PATENT: APPLICATION: OPPOSITION: APPEAL: Australia: S.C.(Vic.)) [1983] 2 V.R. 587

Bridge & Plate Constructions Pty Ltd v. Mannesmann Demag Pty Ltd (PATENT: OPPOSITION: NOVELTY: PRIOR PUBLICATION: DIFFERENTIATING FEATURES NOT COMMON GENERAL KNOWLEDGE: PART OF PATENTABLE COMBINATION: MERIT OF INVENTION: Australia: Pat. Off.) 13 I.P.R. 449

Bridges v. Bridge Stockbrokers Ltd (TRADE PRACTICES: CONSUMER PROTECTION: SIMILAR TRADE NAMES: Australia: Fed. Ct)
(1985) 57 A.L.R. 401; [1984] A.T.P.R. 45, 475; (1985) 5 I.P.R. 81

Bridgestone/Rubber composition (EUROPEAN PATENT: CLAIMS: CONSTRUCTION: MEANINGLESS LIMITATION: COMMON GENERAL KNOWLEDGE: INGREDIENTS OF: OPPOSITION: PROCEDURE: CLAIMS: OBJECTION TO CLARITY: FRESH DOCUMENTS ON APPEAL: T228/87: EPO) [1990] E.P.O.R. 483

Briggs v. Jaden Marketing Pty Ltd (TRADE MARK: APPLICATION TO REMOVE: NON-USE: UNAUTHORISED USE: DISCRETION: Australia: AIPO) 31 I.P.R. 128

Brij Mohan Dutta v. Jallo Subsidiary Industries Co. (India) Pvt. Ltd (TRADE MARK: INFRINGEMENT: LION BRAND/LION ELEPHANT: INTERIM INJUNCTION: APPEAL: DISSIMILAR PRODUCTS: India: H.C.)
(1990) 15 I.P.L.R. 332

Brink's Mat Ltd v. Elcombe (MAREVA INJUNCTION: MATERIAL NON-DISCLOSURE: DISCRETION: C.A.) [1989] 1 F.S.R. 211

Brintons Ltd v. Feltex Furnishings of New Zealand Ltd (No. 1) (COPYRIGHT: INFRINGEMENT: AUTHORISATION: INDEMNITY AND CONTRIBUTION: PRACTICE AND PROCEDURE: STRIKING OUT: New Zealand: H.C.)
[1991] 2 N.Z.L.R. 677

Brintons Ltd v. Feltex Furnishings of New Zealand Ltd (No. 2) (COPYRIGHT: INNOCENT INFRINGEMENT: KNOWLEDGE: MEASURE OF DAMAGES: LOSS OF PROFIT: CONVERSION DAMAGES: MEASURE OF CONTRIBUTION BY THIRD PARTY: New Zealand: H.C.) [1991] 2 N.Z.L.R. 683

Brisalebe Ltd v. Searle (PATENT: PROVISIONAL SPECIFICATION: REQUEST FOR INSPECTION: OBTAINING: ASSIGNMENT: Australia: AIPO)   30 I.P.R. 91

Brisbane Aluminium Fabricators & Supplies Pty Ltd v. Techni Interiors Pty Ltd (DESIGN: INFRINGEMENT: REGISTRATION: VALIDITY OF: SHAPE AND CONFIGURATION: INDEFINITE LENGTH: ORIGINALITY: TRADE VARIANT: Australia: Fed. Ct)   23 I.P.R. 107

Bristol Conservatories Ltd v. Conservatories Custom Built Ltd (PASSING OFF: "REVERSE" PASSING OFF: C.A.)   [1989] R.P.C. 455

Bristol-Myers Co.'s Application (TRADE MARKS: DISTINCTIVENESS: EVIDENCE: ACQUIRED DISTINCTIVENESS: ADAPTED TO DISTINGUISH: GEOGRAPHIC NAME: Australia: Pat. Off.)   16 I.P.R. 149

Bristol-Myers Co. v. David Bull Laboratories Pty Ltd (PATENT: PETITION FOR EXTENSION OF PATENT TERM: APPLICATION FOR EXTENSION OF TIME WITHIN WHICH TO PETITION FOR AN EXTENSION OF PATENT TERM: Australia: Fed. Ct)   12 I.P.R. 219

Bristol-Myers Co. v. L'Oréal (PATENT: OPPOSITION TO APPLICATION FOR A PATENT: PRIOR PUBLICATION: NOVELTY: ANTICIPATION: OBVIOUSNESS: INVENTION NOT FULLY DESCRIBED: Australia: Pat. Off.)   16 I.P.R. 652

Bristol-Myers Co. v. L'Oréal (PATENTS: OPPOSITION: OBVIOUSNESS: NO EVIDENCE OF COMMON GENERAL KNOWLEDGE: PRIOR PUBLICATION: SELECTION PATENT: MANNER OF NEW MANUFACTURE: PACKAGE CLAIMS: Australia: Pat. Off.)   12 I.P.R. 275

Bristol Myers Squibb v. Paranova (TRADE MARKS: PARALLEL IMPORTS: REPACKAGING OF GOODS: EXHAUSTION OF RIGHTS: RESTRICTIONS FOR PROTECTION OF INDUSTRIAL AND COMMERCIAL PROPERTY: DISGUISED RESTRICTION ON TRADE BETWEEN MEMBER STATES: ECJ Cases C-427, 429 and 436/93)   [1996] F.S.R. 225
[*conjoined cases:* Eurim-Pharm v. Beiersdorf, ECJ Cases C-71, 72 and 73/93; MPA Pharma v. Rhône Poulenc, ECJ Case C-232/94]

Britannia Industries Ltd v. Bharat Biscuits Co. Pvt. Ltd (TRADE MARK: INFRINGEMENT: BRITANNIA SNAX/BHARAT SNACKS: PASSING OFF: INTERIM INJUNCTION: REFUSED: India: H.C.)   (1988) 14 I.P.L.R. 122

Britax/Inventive step (EUROPEAN PATENT: APPEAL: PROCEDURE: FRESH PRIOR ART: FILLING MISSING LINK IN ARGUMENT, ADMITTED IN VIEW OF RELEVANCE: REMITTAL NOT ORDERED: NO NEW LINE OF ATTACK: INVENTIVE STEP: COMBINATION OF CITATIONS: OPPOSITION: FRESH DOCUMENTS ON APPEAL: T142/84: EPO)
[1987] E.P.O.R. 148; [1987] O.J. EPO 112

British Aerospace (Wiring loom: T262/89), *sub nom.* Lansing Bagnall, British Aerospace (Wiring loom: T262/89)

British Airways and British Caledonian (RESTRICTIVE PRACTICES: MERGERS: CIVIL AVIATION: AUTHORISATION: E.C. Comm.)   [1988] 4 C.M.L.R. 258

British American Tobacco Co. Ltd v. E.C. Commission (EUROPEAN COURT PROCEDURE: RESTRICTIVE PRACTICES: ORAL ARGUMENTS: BUSINESS SECRETS: EVIDENCE: DISCOVERY: Cases 142 and 156/84: ECJ)
[1987] 2 C.M.L.R. 551; [1987] E.C.R. 4566

British American Tobacco Co. Ltd v. E.C. Commission (RESTRICTIVE PRACTICES: COMPANY OWNERSHIP: ACQUISITION OF EQUITY INTEREST IN COMPETITOR: EFFECT: ARTICLE 85: POWER TO INFLUENCE CONDUCT: COMPLAINANTS: ECJ Case 35/83: ECJ)   [1988] 4 C.M.L.R. 24
Earlier proceedings, *sub nom.* TOLTECS and DORCET Trade Marks

British Amusement Catering Trades Association (BACTA) v. Phonographic Performance Ltd (COPYRIGHT: SOUND RECORDINGS: LICENCE SCHEME: BACKGROUND MUSIC FROM JUKEBOXES: FEES: COSTS: Cprt. Trib.)
[1992] R.P.C. 149

British Amusement Catering Trades Association (BACTA) v. Westminster City Council (LICENSING: CINEMATOGRAPH EXHIBITION: AMUSEMENT ARCADE: VIDEO GAMES: H.L.)   [1988] 1 All E.R. 740; [1988] 2 W.L.R. 48

British Association of Aesthetic Plastic Surgeons v. Cambright Ltd (PASSING OFF: INTERLOCUTORY INJUNCTION: Ch.D.)   [1987] R.P.C. 549

British Broadcasting Corp., *sub nom.* BBC

British Coal Corp. v. Dennis Rye Ltd (No. 2) (CONFIDENTIAL INFORMATION: EVIDENCE: PRIVILEGE: LEGAL ADVISERS: DOCUMENTS CREATED FOR CIVIL PROCEEDINGS SUBSEQUENTLY HANDED TO POLICE: EFFECT OF LEGAL PROFESSIONAL PRIVILEGE: ATTORNEY-GENERAL'S GUIDELINES: VOLUNTARY DISCLOSURE IN COURSE OF CRIMINAL TRIAL: WHETHER PRIVILEGE WAIVED: WHETHER ENTITLEMENT TO RETURN OF DOCUMENTS: C.A.)
[1988] 3 All E.R. 816; [1988] 1 W.L.R. 1113

British Dental Trade Association's Exhibition Rules (RESTRICTIVE PRACTICES: TRADE FAIRS: RULES FOR PARTICIPATION: INTENTION TO APPROVE: E.C. Comm.)   [1987] 2 C.M.L.R. 606

British Diabetic Association (The) v. Diabetic Society (The) (PASSING OFF: CHARITIES: ENTITLEMENT TO SUE: REPUTATION: WHETHER EXTENDED TO SOCIETY OR RELATED TRADING STYLES: ASSOCIATION/SOCIETY: WHETHER CONFUSABLY SIMILAR: INJUNCTION: Ch.D.)   [1996] F.S.R. 1

British Gas/Coal gasification (EUROPEAN PATENT: APPEAL: PROCEDURE: COMMUNICATIONS BY BOARD OF APPEAL, PURPOSE AND SIGNIFICANCE: T109/83: EPO)   [1979–85] E.P.O.R. C823

British Gas/Mains replacement method (EUROPEAN PATENT: EVIDENCE: FAILURE TO DISTINGUISH BETWEEN PERSONAL AND PUBLIC KNOWLEDGE: PRIOR ART: PRIOR USE: REQUIREMENTS FOR: T448/90: EPO)   [1994] E.P.O.R. 105

British Gas/Offshore platforms (EUROPEAN PATENT: AMENDMENT AND CORRECTION: NO RESTRICTION TO PARTIAL COMBINATION: REMITTAL TO EXAMINING DIVISION: T687/90: EPO)   [1993] E.P.O.R. 274

British Leyland Motor Corp. Ltd v. Armstrong Patents Co. Ltd (COPYRIGHT: INFRINGEMENT: CAR EXHAUST: OWNERS' RIGHT TO REPAIR: C.A.)
[1986] R.P.C. 279
(H.L.) [1986] A.C. 577; [1986] 1 All E.R. 850; [1986] E.C.C. 534; [1986] F.S.R. 221; [1986] F.T.L.R. 65; [1986] R.P.C. 279; [1986] 2 W.L.R. 400

British Leyland Motor Corp. Ltd v. E.C. Commission (RESTRICTIVE PRACTICES: DOMINANT POSITION: SUPPLY OF CERTIFICATES OF CONFORMITY FOR IMPORTED MOTOR VEHICLES: RELEVANT MARKET: DISCRIMINATORY FEES: ABUSE: Case 226/84: ECJ)   [1987] 1 C.M.L.R. 184; [1986] E.C.R. 3263

British Leyland Motor Corp. v. Armstrong Patents Co. Ltd (COPYRIGHT: INFRINGEMENT: REPLACEMENT EXHAUST PIPES: IMPLIED LICENCE TO REPAIR: ACQUIESCENCE: REFERENCE TO ECJ: Ch.D.)   [1982] F.S.R. 481

British Leyland Motor Corp. v. Armstrong Patents Co. Ltd (COPYRIGHT: INFRINGEMENT: U.K. DESIGN COPYRIGHT: ARTICLES 36, 85 & 86: Ch.D.)
[1983] E.C.C. 67; [1983] F.S.R. 50

British Leyland Motor Corp. v. Armstrong Patents Co. Ltd (COPYRIGHT: INFRINGEMENT: U.K. DESIGN COPYRIGHT: REFUSAL TO REFER TO ECJ UNDER ARTICLE 177: C.A.)   [1984] 3 C.M.L.R. 102; [1984] F.S.R. 591

British Petroleum/Diamond identification (EUROPEAN PATENT: APPEAL: PROCEDURE: OBJECTION BY BOARD, FAILURE TO RESPOND TO: CLAIMS: CLARITY: UNANSWERED OBJECTION BY BOARD: INVENTIVE STEP: SIMPLIFICATION OF PRIOR ART: SUFFICIENCY: SKILLED PERSON, KNOWLEDGE OF: T787/89: EPO)   [1991] E.P.O.R. 178

British Phonographic Industry Ltd v. Cohen (COPYRIGHT: INFRINGEMENT: ANTON PILLER: PRACTICE: Scotland: I.H.)   [1984] F.S.R. 159; 1983 S.L.T. 137

British Phonographic Industry Ltd v. Mechanical Copyright Protection Society Ltd (COPYRIGHT: ROYALTY RATE: TRIBUNAL CONSIDERING PROPOSED LICENSING SCHEME FOR MECHANICAL RECORDINGS: JURISDICTION: OMISSION OF EXPRESS JURISDICTION OVER DISTRIBUTION RIGHTS: PRINCIPLES OF LICENSING SCHEME: COMPARABLE SCHEMES: RELEVANCE OF "AVAILABLE PROFITS" OF RECORDING COMPANIES TO QUESTION OF RATE: Cprt. Trib.)   22 I.P.R. 325

British Phonographic Industry Ltd v. Mechanical Copyright Protection Society Ltd (No. 1) (COPYRIGHT: MECHANICAL COPYRIGHT: REFERENCE TO TRIBUNAL OF PROPOSED LICENSING SCHEME: APPLICATION FOR INTERIM ORDER: Cprt. Trib.)   [1993] E.M.L.R. 83

British Phonographic Industry Ltd v. Mechanical Copyright Protection Society Ltd (No. 2) (COPYRIGHT: MECHANICAL COPYRIGHT: SETTLEMENT OF SYSTEMS TERMS AND ROYALTY RATE: Cprt. Trib.)   [1993] E.M.L.R. 86

British Phonographic Industry Ltd v. Mechanical Copyright Protection Society Ltd (No. 3) (COPYRIGHT: MECHANICAL COPYRIGHT: REFERENCE TO TRIBUNAL OF PROPOSED LICENSING SCHEME: FINAL DECISION AND ORDER: Cprt. Trib.)
[1993] E.M.L.R. 139

British Sky Broadcasting Group Ltd v. Lyons (COPYRIGHT: SATELLITE BROADCASTING: DECODERS: INFRINGEMENT: EURO-DEFENCE: CD&PA 88, SECTION 298; QUANTITATIVE RESTRICTION: Ch.D.)   [1995] F.S.R. 357

British Steel plc's Patent (PATENT: EMPLOYEE'S INVENTION: APPLICATION FOR COMPENSATION: ACTUAL AND POTENTIAL BENEFIT TO EMPLOYER: WHETHER "OUTSTANDING BENEFIT": C.-G.)   [1992] R.P.C. 117

British Sugar plc v. James Robertson & Sons Ltd (TRADE MARK: INFRINGEMENT: USE IN THE COURSE OF TRADE: USE AS TRADE MARK: IDENTITY OF GOODS: SIMILARITY OF GOODS: VALIDITY: DEVOID OF DISTINCTIVE CHARACTER: PROOF: STATUTORY INTERPRETATION: Ch.D)   [1996] R.P.C. 281

British Technology Group/Contraceptive method (EUROPEAN PATENT: PATENTABILITY: CONTRACEPTIVE METHOD: T74/93: EPO)
[1995] E.P.O.R. 279

British Telecommunications (Re), *sub nom.* Italy v. E.C. Commission (Re British Telecommunications)

British Telecommunications plc and MCI's Agreement (RESTRICTIVE PRACTICES: PROVISION OF GLOBAL TELECOMMUNICATION SERVICES: STAKE IN U.S. FIRM ACQUIRED BY U.K. OPERATOR: JOINT VENTURE: PROVISION OF GLOBAL SERVICES: INTENTION TO APPROVE: E.C. Comm.)   [1994] 5 C.M.L.R. 167 (PARTIES POTENTIAL AND ACTUAL COMPETITORS: CO-OPERATIVE JOINT VENTURE: RESTRICTIONS OUTSIDE EEA: NON-COMPETE AND EXCLUSIVE PURCHASING PROVISIONS: EXEMPTION GRANTED: E.C. Comm.)
[1995] 4 C.M.L.R. 285

British Telecommunications/Oral proceedings (EUROPEAN PATENT: INVENTIVE STEP: FEATURE DISREGARDED UNLESS CONTRIBUTING TO SOLUTION OF PROBLEM: OPPOSITION: PROCEDURE: ORAL PROCEEDINGS, WITHDRAWAL OF REQUEST FOR: T3/90: EPO)
[1993] E.P.O.R. 366; [1992] O.J. EPO 737

British-American Tobacco Co. Ltd v. Philip Morris Ltd (PATENT: APPLICATION: OPPOSITION: EVIDENCE: EXTENSION OF TIME TO LODGE EVIDENCE: Australia: Pat. Off.) 18 I.P.R. 655

Brockhouse plc's Patent (PATENT: PRACTICE: PROPRIETORSHIP: PATENT OFFICE PROCEEDINGS: LEGAL AID: C.-G.) [1985] R.P.C. 332

Broderbund Software Inc. v. Computermate Products (Australia) Pty Ltd (COPYRIGHT: COMPUTER PROGRAMS: INFRINGEMENT: PARALLEL IMPORTATION AND SALE: IMPLIED LICENCE OF IMPORTER: WHETHER DISTRIBUTOR AN EXCLUSIVE LICENSEE: EVIDENCE: MARKET SURVEY: RESTRICTIVE PRACTICES: MARKET POWER: EXCLUSIONARY PROVISIONS: ANTI-COMPETITIVE AGREEMENTS: EXCLUSIVE DEALING: USE OF SURVEY EVIDENCE: Australia: Fed. Ct) 22 I.P.R. 215

Brooke Bond (India) Ltd v. Balaji Tea (India) Pvt. Ltd (TRADE MARK: COPYRIGHT: INFRINGEMENT: PASSING OFF: INJUNCTION: India: H.C.)
(1989) 16 I.P.L.R. 133

Brooke Bond India Ltd v. Balaji Tea (India) Pvt. Ltd (TRADE MARK: INFRINGEMENT: PASSING OFF: RED LABEL/RED APPLE TEA: PACKETS FILLED IN INDIA AND EXPORTED: India: H.C.) (1987) 12 I.P.L.R. 143

Brooke Bond India Ltd v. Balaji Tea (India) Pvt. Ltd (TRADE MARK: COPYRIGHT: INFRINGEMENT: PASSING OFF: PATENT: INFRINGEMENT: JOINDER OF ACTIONS: India: H.C.) (1989) 14 I.P.L.R. 127

Brooke Bond India Ltd v. Balaji Tea (India) Pvt. Ltd (TRADE MARK: COPYRIGHT: INFRINGEMENT: PASSING OFF: JOINDER OF ACTIONS: ABUSE OF PROCESS: STATUTORY INTERPRETATION: India: H.C.) (1990) 15 I.P.L.R. 266

Brooke Bond India Ltd v. Raj Kamal Enterprises (REGISTERED DESIGN: COPYRIGHT: PACKAGE LABEL: INFRINGEMENT: INTERIM INJUNCTION: India: H.C.) (1989) 14 I.P.L.R. 126

Brooke Bond Indian Ltd v. Balaji Tea (India) Pvt. Ltd (TRADE MARK: COPYRIGHT: INFRINGEMENT: SUPER DUST TEA: INTERIM INJUNCTION: India: H.C.)
(1993) 18 I.P.L.R. 14

Brooktree Corp. v. Advanced Micro Devices Inc. (CIRCUIT LAYOUTS: MASK WORKS: COPYRIGHT: WHETHER CIRCUIT LAYOUT DICTATED BY FUNCTION: INFRINGEMENT: STANDARD OF SIMILARITY REQUIRED: "SUBSTANTIALLY COPIED": REVERSE ENGINEERING: USA: D.C.) 14 I.P.R. 85

Brossmann's Application (PATENT: INTERNATIONAL APPLICATIONS: PRACTICE: PCT FILLING: PRIORITY DOCUMENTS FILED LATE: C.-G.)
[1983] R.P.C. 109

Brown, Boveri/Reasons for decision (EUROPEAN PATENT: OPPOSITION: PROCEDURE: REASONED DECISION, NECESSITY OF: FEES: REIMBURSEMENT OF APPEAL FEE: T271/90: EPO) [1990] E.P.O.R. 541

Brown, Boveri/Statement of Grounds of appeal (EUROPEAN PATENT: RE-ESTABLISHMENT OF RIGHTS: ASSISTANT'S FAULT: EVIDENCE REQUIRED: FEES: REIMBURSEMENT OF APPEAL FEE: T13/82: EPO)
[1979–85] E.P.O.R. B405; [1983] O.J. EPO 411

Browne & Williamson Tobacco Corp. v. Philip Morris Inc. (PATENTS: APPLICATION: OPPOSITION: FAIR BASIS: LACK OF CLARITY: ANTICIPATION: NOVELTY: AMENDMENT: Australia: Pat. Off.) 9 I.P.R. 243

Browne & Williamson Tobacco Corp. v. Philip Morris Inc. (No. 2) (PATENT: AMENDMENT: OPPOSITION: WHETHER AMENDED CLAIM OUTSIDE SCOPE OF ORIGINAL: NEW OMNIBUS CLAIM: Australia: Pat. Off.) 9 I.P.R. 662

Browne v. S. Smith & Son Pty Ltd (TRADE MARK: INFRINGEMENT: REMOVAL FOR NON-USE: JURISDICTION: Australia: Fed. Ct) 60 A.L.R. 431

Brugger v. Medicaid (COPYRIGHT: INFRINGEMENT: INQUIRY: ELECTION AS TO DAMAGES OR AN ACCOUNT: WHETHER PLAINTIFF CAN CLAIM ADDITIONAL DAMAGES IN INQUIRY ALTHOUGH NOT ORIGINALLY PLEADED: *Calderbank* LETTER: WHETHER COSTS SHOULD BE DETERMINED AFTER INQUIRY: Pat. Ct) [1996] F.S.R. 362

Bruker/Non-invasive measurement (EUROPEAN PATENT: CONVENTIONS: EXCEPTION TO GENERAL PRINCIPLE CONSTRUED STRICTLY: PATENTABILITY: DIAGNOSTIC METHOD: T385/86: EPO) [1988] E.P.O.R. 357; [1988] O.J. EPO 380

Brundaban Sahu v. Rajendra Subudhi Subudhi (TRADE MARK: COPYRIGHT: UNREGISTERED MARK AND LABEL: COGNIZANCE OF COMPLAINT: India: H.C.) (1986) 11 I.P.L.R. 129

Brunswick/Re-establishment of rights refused (EUROPEAN PATENT: RE-ESTABLISHMENT OF RIGHTS: AGENT'S HASTE: T287/84: EPO) [1986] E.P.O.R. 46; [1985] O.J. EPO 333

Brunswick/Restitutio (EUROPEAN PATENT: RE-ESTABLISHMENT OF RIGHTS: AGENT'S DUTIES: J27/90: EPO) [1994] E.P.O.R. 82

Brupat Ltd v. Sandford Marine Products Ltd (PATENT: INFRINGEMENT: INTERLOCUTORY RELIEF: PAYMENT OF "ROYALTY" INTO JOINT ACCOUNT: C.A.) [1983] R.P.C. 61

Brupat Ltd v. Smith (PATENT: INFRINGEMENT: CERTIFICATE OF VALIDITY: Scotland: O.H.) [1985] F.S.R. 156

BRUT DE MER Trade Mark (TRADE MARK: APPLICATION: PART B. MARK: WORDS IN FOREIGN LANGUAGE: T.M.Reg.) [1989] R.P.C. 555

Bruynzeel Plastics/Flat torsion spring (EUROPEAN PATENT: AMENDMENT AND CORRECTION: DELETION OF SUPERFLUOUS LIMITATION: RELATIONSHIP BETWEEN ARTICLE 123(2) AND (3): CLAIMS: CONSTRUCTION: MEANINGLESS FEATURE: CONVENTIONS: AVOIDING ABSURDITY: T231/89: EPO) [1993] E.P.O.R. 418; [1993] O.J. EPO 13

BSH Industries Ltd's Patents (PATENT: REVOCATION: CONSTRUCTION: INTERPRETATION OF DRAWING: OBVIOUSNESS: COMMERCIAL SUCCESS: Pat. Ct) [1995] R.P.C. 183

BT, *sub nom.* Italy v. E.C. Commission (Re British Telecommunications)

BUD Trade Mark (TRADE MARK: APPLICATION: OPPOSITION: USE BY BOTH PARTIES OF BUDWEISER FOR BEER: CONFUSION AND DECEPTION: HONEST CONCURRENT USER: TRIPLE IDENTITY RULE: Ch.D.) [1988] R.P.C. 535 see also, Anheuser-Busch v. Budejovicky Budvar NP

BUDGET Service Mark (SERVICE MARK: APPLICATION: CAR HIRE: DISTINCTIVENESS: BoT) [1991] R.P.C. 9

Bull SA v. Micro Controls Ltd (TRADE MARK: OPPOSITION: PRIOR REGISTERED MARK: LIKELIHOOD OF DECEPTION OR CONFUSION: SUBSTANTIAL IDENTITY WITH OR DECEPTIVE SIMILARITY TO PRIOR MARK: ONUS: WHETHER GOODS OF THE SAME DESCRIPTION: Australia: Pat. Off.) 19 I.P.R. 299

Bull/Identification system (EUROPEAN PATENT: AMENDMENT AND CORRECTION: ABSTRACT, MAY NOT BE BASED ON: DISCLOSURE: ABSTRACT DOES NOT FORM PART: T246/86: EPO) [1989] E.P.O.R. 344; [1989] O.J. EPO 199

Bulten-Kanthal/Electrical heating element (EUROPEAN PATENT: INVENTIVE STEP: STATE OF THE ART: T240/85: EPO) [1986] E.P.O.R. 240

Bundy American Corp. v. Rent-A-Wreck (Vic.) Pty Ltd (TRADE MARK: OPPOSITION: EXTENSION OF TIME LIMITS: INTER-PARTY NEGOTIATION: PUBLIC INTEREST: Australia: Pat. Off.) 5 I.P.R. 307

Bureau Européen des Média de l'Industrie Musicale v. Commission for the European Communities (RESTRICTIVE PRACTICES: COMPLAINT: BREACH OF ARTICLE 85 AND ARTICLE 86 BY SACEM: REFERENCE TO NATIONAL COURTS: APPLICATION FOR ANNULMENT: Case T–114/92: CFI)
[1996] 4 C.M.L.R. 306; [1996] E.M.L.R. 97

Bureau Européen des Unions Consommateurs v. E.C. Commission (RESTRICTIVE PRACTICES: DISCRETIONARY POWERS OF COMMISSION: REFUSAL TO TAKE UP COMPLAINT: Case T–37/92: CFI)
[1995] C.M.L.R. 167

Burgess/Claims fee (EUROPEAN PATENT: CONVENTIONS: NATIONAL PRACTICES IRRELEVANT: *Travaux préparatoires*: UNAMBIGUOUS TEXT: FEES: EXTRA CLAIMS FEES, COMPUTATION: J09/84: EPO)
[1979–85] E.P.O.R. A209; [1985] O.J. EPO 233

Burlington/Return of documents (EUROPEAN PATENT: OPPOSITION PROCEDURE: EVIDENCE FILED: BREACH OF ORDER OF FOREIGN COURT: T760/89: EPO)
[1995] E.P.O.R. 224

Burns (W.) Tractors Ltd v. Sperry New Holland (RESTRICTIVE PRACTICES: CONTRACTS: EXPORT BANS: REFUSAL TO SUPPLY: PARALLEL TRADE: EXEMPTION: FINES: NOTIFICATION: E.C. Comm.)
[1988] 4 C.M.L.R. 306; [1988] F.S.R. 381

Burr-Brown/Assignment (EUROPEAN PATENT: APPLICATION: PROCEDURE: EVIDENCE OF NATIONAL LAW: ENTITLEMENT: ASSIGNMENT, WHETHER EFFECTIVE: PRIORITY: SUCCESSOR IN TITLE IN EQUITY: CONVENTIONS: NATIONAL LAWS, RELATIONSHIP TO EPC: J19/87: EPO)
[1988] E.P.O.R. 350

Burroughs Wellcome (India) Ltd v. American Home Products Corp. (TRADE MARK: APPLICATION: OPPOSITION: ACTICEPH/ACTIFED: India: T.M.Reg.)
(1992) 17 I.P.L.R. 277

Burroughs Wellcome (India) Ltd v. G.K. Sharma & King Scientific Research Centre (TRADE MARK: SEPTRIN/CETRAN: COPYRIGHT: INFRINGEMENT: PASSING OFF: JURISDICTION OF COURT TO ENTERTAIN COMPOSITE SUIT: CLAUSE 14 OF LETTERS PATENT: INTERIM INJUNCTION GRANTED: India: H.C.)
(1989) 14 I.P.L.R. 60

Busby v. Thorne EMI Video Programmes Ltd (PRACTICE: ANTON PILLER ORDER: PRIVILEGE AGAINST SELF-INCRIMINATION: COPYRIGHT: INFRINGEMENT: SEARCH AND SEIZURE: JURISDICTION: CONDITIONS: New Zealand: C.A.)
[1984] 1 N.Z.L.R. 461

Business Marketing Australia Pty Ltd v. Australian Telecommunication Commission (TRADE MARK: REGISTRABILITY: GENERIC TERMS: DISTINCTIVENESS: DIRECT REFERENCE: Australia: AIPO)
28 I.P.R. 589

Business Name (Use of) (FIRM NAME: Germany)
[1985] E.C.C. 495; [1986] F.S.R. 40

Bussche/Filing notice of appeal by telegram (EUROPEAN PATENT: FEES: APPEAL FEE, FAILURE TO PAY: PROCEDURE: TELEGRAM NOT CONFIRMED: J01/79: EPO)
[1979–85] E.P.O.R. A5; [1980] O.J. EPO 34

Butt v. Butt (PRACTICE: MOTIONS: UNDERTAKINGS: C.A.)
[1987] F.S.R. 574

Butt v. Schultz (COPYRIGHT: INFRINGEMENT: UNFAIR COMPETITION: USE OF BOAT AS MOULD: South Africa: ECD)
1984 (3) S.A. 568

Butterworths & Co. (Publ.) Ltd v. Ng Sui Nam (COPYRIGHT: INFRINGEMENT: CONSTRUCTION OF 1911 COPYRIGHT ACT: Singapore: H.C.)
[1985] 1 M.L.J. 196; [1987] R.P.C. 485; [1987] 2 F.T.L.R. 198; 4 I.P.R. 395
(S.C.) [1987] 2 M.L.J. 5

Buying Systems (Australia) Pty Ltd v. Studio Srl (TRADE MARK: OPPOSITION: PROPRIETORSHIP: PRIOR USE BY OPPONENT: CONNECTION IN THE COURSE OF TRADE: Australia: AIPO)
30 I.P.R. 517

BWN Industries v. Delawood Pty Ltd, *sub nom.* Secton Pty Ltd (t/a BWN Industries)
v. Delawood Pty Ltd
BYSTANDER Trade Mark (TRADE MARK: OPPOSITION: AUTHORISATION OF
AGENT: ISSUE ESTOPPEL: DISCRETION: T.M.Reg.)   [1991] R.P.C. 279

C. & H. Engineering v. F. Klucznik & Sons Ltd (COPYRIGHT: INFRINGEMENT:
DESIGN RIGHTS: PRACTICE: COSTS: WHETHER "WITHOUT PREJUDICE"
CORRESPONDENCE AFTER *Calderbank* LETTER PRIVILEGED: WHETHER
PLAINTIFF SHOULD HAVE ACCEPTED TERMS OFFERED: Ch.D.)
[1992] F.S.R. 667
C. & H. Engineering v. F. Klucznik & Sons Ltd (COPYRIGHT: INFRINGEMENT: TEST:
DESIGN RIGHTS: FUNCTIONAL OBJECTS: SIMPLICITY: MODIFICATION AND
AMENDMENT: COUNTERCLAIM: LAMB CREEP FEEDER: PIG FENDER:
WHETHER DRAWING ORIGINAL: WHETHER DESIGN COMMONPLACE:
CREATOR: COPYING: TWO DIMENSIONAL AND THREE DIMENSIONAL WORKS:
OWNERSHIP: Ch.D.)   [1992] F.S.R. 421; 26 I.P.R. 133
Caboolture Motel v. Jedsminster Pty Ltd, *sub nom.* Street (t/a Caboolture Motel) v.
Jedsminster Pty Ltd
Cabot Corp. v. Minnesota Mining & Manufacturing Ltd (PATENT: INFRINGEMENT:
INTERLOCUTORY INJUNCTION: PRINCIPLES TO BE APPLIED: PRIMA FACIE
CASE: BALANCE OF CONVENIENCE: Australia: S.C.(NSW))
11 I.P.R. 487; (1988) 91 F.L.R. 142
Cabot Safety Corp. (PATENT: LICENCE OF RIGHT: SETTLEMENT OF TERMS:
KOMMANDITGESELLSCHAFT AS LICENCEE: ROYALTY RATE: RELEVANCE OF
VALIDITY: DELAY: C.-G.: Pat. Ct)   [1992] R.P.C. 39
Cadbury Ltd v. Ulmer GmbH (TRADE MARK: INFRINGEMENT: PASSING OFF:
STRIKING OUT: JOINT TORTFEASORS: GET-UP: SHAPE OF CHOCOLATE BAR:
"BADGE OF FRAUD": Ch.D.)   [1988] F.S.R. 385
Cadbury Schweppes Pty Ltd's Application (TRADE MARK: APPLICATION: DIRECT
REFERENCE: INHERENT DISTINCTIVENESS: CAPABLE OF BECOMING
DISTINCTIVE: Australia: AIPO)   30 I.P.R. 645
Cafe Do Brasil SpA v. Scrava Pty Ltd (TRADE MARKS: REMOVAL: NON-USE:
EVIDENCE: PRIMA FACIE CASE: SPECIAL CIRCUMSTANCES: Australia: Pat. Off.)
22 I.P.R. 359
Caisse Palette Diffusion/Correction of drawings (EUROPEAN PATENT: AMENDMENT
AND CORRECTION: DRAWINGS: COMPETENCE OF RECEIVING SECTION: EPO:
COMPETENCE OF RECEIVING SECTION: GUIDELINES FOR EXAMINATION:
CONVENTIONS, CANNOT AMEND: J33/89: EPO)
[1991] E.P.O.R. 521; [1991] O.J. EPO 288
Caj Amadio Constructions Pty Ltd v. Kitchen (COPYRIGHT: INFRINGEMENT OF
COPYRIGHT IN PLANS OF HOUSE: MEASURE OF DAMAGES: WHETHER
DAMAGES TO BE ASSESSED ON BASIS OF LOSS OF PROFITS OR ON BASIS OF LOSS
OF LICENCE FEE: Australia: SC(S.A.))   23 I.P.R. 284
Cala Homes (South) Ltd v. Alfred McAlpine Homes East Ltd (COPYRIGHT:
INFRINGEMENT: ARCHITECT'S DRAWINGS: COMMISSIONED DRAWINGS:
OWNERSHIP: JOINT OWNERSHIP: SUBSTANTIAL REPRODUCTION:
FLAGRANCY: ADDITIONAL DAMAGES, ASSESSMENT: CONTRACT: INDUCING
BREACH: IMPLIED TERM: PRACTICE: EXPERTS' REPORTS: FUNCTION OF
EXPERT WITNESS: Ch.D.)   [1995] F.S.R. 818
Cala Homes (South) Ltd v. Alfred McAlpine Homes East Ltd (No. 2) (COPYRIGHT:
INFRINGEMENT: ARCHITECT'S DRAWINGS: ELECTION FOR ACCOUNT OF
PROFITS: WHETHER ADDITIONAL STATUTORY DAMAGES AVAILABLE, FORM
OF ORDER: Ch.D.)   [1996] F.S.R. 36

Calmao Pty Ltd v. Stradbroke Waters Co-Owners Co-Operative Society Ltd (TRADE PRACTICES: LIMITATIONS OF ACTION MISLEADING AND DECEPTIVE CONDUCT: CAUSE OF ACTION: Australia: Fed. Ct)   16 I.P.R. 265

Calsil Ltd v. Riekie & Simpfendorfer (PATENT: APPLICATION: OPPOSITION: OBVIOUSNESS: LACK OF NOVELTY: COMMON GENERAL KNOWLEDGE: EVIDENCE: COSTS: Australia: Pat. Off.)   16 I.P.R. 399

Calsil Ltd v. Riekie & Simpfendorfer (PATENT: OPPOSITION: EXTENSION OF TIME FOR SERVICE OF OPPONENTS' EVIDENCE: Australia: Pat. Off.)   14 I.P.R. 219

Caltex Petroleum Corp. v. Veedol International Ltd (TRADE MARK: APPLICATION ACCEPTED: OPPOSITION: WHETHER MARKS DECEPTIVE OR CONFUSING: WHETHER SUBSTANTIALLY IDENTICAL WITH OTHER REGISTERED MARKS: Australia: AIPO)   29 I.P.R. 169

Calvin Klein Inc. v. International Apparel Syndicate (PASSING OFF: INTERNATIONAL FASHION GARMENTS: NO LOCAL BUSINESS: OVERSEAS REPUTATION: INJUNCTION: India: H.C.)   [1995] F.S.R. 515

Cambridge Plan AG v. Moore (TRADE MARK: INFRINGEMENT: PASSING OFF: DIETARY PREPARATION: SIMILAR PRODUCT APPELLATION: DISCLAIMER IN REGISTRATION: South Africa: D&CLD)   1987 (4) S.A. 821

Camera Care Ltd v. Victor Hasselblad AB (PROCEDURE: TORT: SERVICE ABROAD: ARTICLES 85 & 85: C.A.)   [1986] E.C.C. 373; [1986] 1 F.T.L.R. 348

Camera Care Ltd v. Victor Hasselblad AB (RESTRICTIVE PRACTICES: EXCLUSIVE DEALING: AFTER-SALES SERVICES: E.C. Comm.)
          [1982] 2 C.M.L.R. 233; [1982] F.S.R. 477; [1982] O.J. L161/18

Cameron Real Estate Pty Ltd v. D.J. Cameron (TRADE MARK: INTERLOCUTORY INJUNCTION: OPPOSITION TO CHANGE OF COMPANY NAME: Australia: S.C.(ACT))   6 I.P.R. 311

Camiceria Pancaldi and B. Srl v. Le Cravatte Di Pancaldi Srl (TRADE MARK: APPLICATIONS: OPPOSITION: PRIOR INCONSISTENT REGISTRATION: DECEPTION AND CONFUSION: INTENTION TO USE: Australia: AIPO)
          30 I.P.R. 547

Camlin Pvt. Ltd v. National Pencil Industries (TRADE MARK: COPYRIGHT: INFRINGEMENT: PASSING OFF: CAMLIN FLORA/TIGER FLORE: TRADE MARK AND CARTON DIFFERENT: GET-UP AND DESIGN OF PENCIL LIKELY TO CONFUSE SMALL CHILDREN: INTERIM INJUNCTION: India: H.C.)
          (1989) 13 I.P.L.R. 215

Camlin Pvt. Ltd v. National Pencil Industries (TRADE MARK: DESIGN ON CARTON: COPYRIGHT: INFRINGEMENT: PASSING OFF: India: H.C.)
          (1987) 11 I.P.L.R. 139

Camlin Pvt. Ltd v. National Pencil Industries (TRADE MARK: INFRINGEMENT PASSING OFF: APPEAL: INTERIM ORDER: India: H.C.) (1987) 12 I.P.L.R. 85.

Canadian Occidental Petroleum Ltd v. Oxychem Canada Inc. (TRADE MARKS: OPPOSITION: NON-USE: Canada: T.M. Opp. Bd)   33 C.P.R. (3d) 345

Canadian Olympic Assoc. v. Konica Canada Inc. (TRADE MARKS: OFFICIAL MARKS: OLYMPIC: PRE-EXISTING RIGHTS: NOT ACCEPTED BY PUBLIC NOTICE: USE WITH OTHER WARES NOT PERMITTED: Canada: Fed. Ct)   24 I.P.R. 216

Cannings' United States Application (PATENT: APPLICATION: INTERNATIONAL APPLICATION: ENTITLEMENT: PRACTICE: ASSIGNMENT: C.-G.)
          [1992] R.P.C. 459

Cannon KK's Application (PATENT: REVOCATION: PRACTICE: CERTIFICATE OF CONTESTED VALIDITY: TRANSITIONAL PROVISIONS OF P.A.77: Pat. Ct)
          [1982] R.P.C. 549

Canon KK v. Brook (t/a Canon Watch Company) (TRADE MARK: APPLICATION: OPPOSITION: SUBSTANTIALLY IDENTICAL: DECEPTIVELY SIMILAR: GOODS OF THE SAME DESCRIPTION: HONEST CONCURRENT USE: Australia: AIPO)
          30 I.P.R. 525

Canon KK v. Canon Electronics Pvt. Ltd (TRADE MARK: INFRINGEMENT: PASSING OFF: EX PARTE AD INTERIM INJUNCTION: APPEAL: India: H.C.)
(1990) 15 I.P.L.R. 213
Canon KK v. Green Cartridge Company (Hong Kong) Ltd (PATENT: INFRINGEMENT: STATUTORY INTERPRETATION: EFFECT OF P.A.77 IN: EXTENT OF RIGHT TO REPAIR: COPYRIGHT: INFRINGEMENT: REPLACEMENT PARTS: CONSUMABLES: NON-DEROGATION FROM GRANT: EXTENT OF RIGHT TO REPAIR: Hong Kong: S.C.)   [1995] F.S.R. 877
Canon/Denmark – expressly (EUROPEAN PATENT: APPLICATION: AMENDMENT AND CORRECTION: DESIGNATION OF STATES: LANGUAGE IN WHICH AMENDMENTS FORMULATED: RE-DATING APPLICATION: BOARD OF APPEAL: INVITATION TO PRESIDENT OF EPO: observations by president: J18/90: EPO)
[1992] E.P.O.R. 559; [1992] O.J. EPO 511
Cantarella Bros v. Kona Coffee Roastery & Equipment Supplies (TRADE MARK: INFRINGEMENT: WHETHER USE DESCRIPTIVE OF CHARACTER OR QUALITY: USE IN GOOD FAITH: Australia: Fed. Ct)   28 I.P.R. 176
Capelvenere v. Omega Development Corp. Pty Ltd (TRADE PRACTICES: DECEPTION: Australia: Fed. Ct)   1 I.P.R. 456
Cappe/Date of which payment is made (EUROPEAN PATENT: FEES: NOTIFICATION OF PAYMENT: J26/80: EPO)   [1979–85] E.P.O.R. A67; [1982] O.J. EPO 07
Car Parts (Re) (RESTRICTIVE PRACTICES: SPARE PARTS: EXCLUSIVE PACKAGING: DOMINANT POSITION: DESIGN COPYRIGHT: U.K. MONOPOLIES COMMISSION)   [1983] E.C.C. 100; [1983] F.S.R. 115
Carbon Gas Technologie GmbH (RESTRICTIVE PRACTICES: JOINT VENTURE: E.C. Comm.)   [1983] 3 C.M.L.R. 169; [1984] F.S.R. 589; [1983] O.J. C376/17
Cardin Laurant Ltd v. The Commerce Commission (FAIR TRADING: SUPPLY OF CHILDREN'S NIGHTCLOTHES: COMPLIANCE WITH SAFETY STANDARD: PROCURING OFFENCE: AIDING AND ABETTING OFFENCE: DEFENCES: REASONABLE MISTAKE: REASONABLE RELIANCE: New Zealand: H.C.)
17 I.P.R. 440
Carew Phipson Ltd v. Deejay Distilleries Pvt. Ltd (PASSING OFF: PRE-MIXED ALCOHOLIC DRINKS: RIVAL MARKS NOT DECEPTIVELY SIMILAR: INTERIM INJUNCTION: India: H.C.)   (1995) 20 I.P.L.R. 65
Carflow Products (U.K.) Ltd v. Linwood Securities (Birmingham) Ltd (REGISTERED DESIGN: UNREGISTERED DESIGN RIGHT: WHETHER DEFENDANT'S PROTOTYPE SHOWN TO BUYER IN CONFIDENCE: PRIOR USER: Pat. Ct)
[1996] F.S.R. 424
Cargill BV v. E.C. Commission (PROCEDURE: INTERIM MEASURES: SERIOUS AND IRREPARABLE DAMAGE: NOT IF PURELY FINANCIAL: Case 229/88R: ECJ)
[1989] 1 C.M.L.R. 304; [1990] I E.C.R. 1303
Carlsberg Beers (Re) (RESTRICTIVE PRACTICES: SUPPLY AGREEMENTS: TRADE MARK AND KNOW-HOW LICENCE: INTENTION TO APPROVE: E.C. Comm.)   [1984] 1 C.M.L.R. 305; [1984] O.J. C27/4
Carlsberg Beers v. De Forenede A/S & Grand Metropolitan Ltd (RESTRICTIVE PRACTICES: LONG-TERM CONTRACTS: 11 YEARS: EQUIVALENT TO EXCLUSIVITY: EXEMPTION UNDER ARTICLE 85(3): E.C. Comm.)
[1985] 1 C.M.L.R. 735
Carlton & United Breweries Ltd v. Castlemaine Tooheys Ltd (PRACTICE: JURISDICTION: TRADE PRACTICES: Australia: H.C.)   7 I.P.R. 17
Carlton & United Breweries Ltd v. Hahn Brewing Co. Ltd (PASSING OFF: DISCOVERY: FRAUDULENT INTENT NOT PLEADED: RELEVANCE IN PASSING OFF ACTION: VALUE IN EVIDENCE: Australia: Fed. Ct)   28 I.P.R. 545

Carlton & United Breweries Ltd v. Miller Brewing Co. (TRADE MARK: OPPOSITION: EXTENSION OF TIME LIMIT: REASONS: Australia: Pat. Off.)   9 I.P.R. 295

Carlton & United Breweries Ltd v. Tooth & Co. Ltd (CONTRACT: IMPLIED TERMS: GOODWILL OF BUSINESS: INJUNCTION RELIEF: Australia: S.C.(NSW))
    6 I.P.R. 319

Carlton & United Breweries Ltd v. Tooth & Co. Ltd (CONTRACT: IMPLIED TERMS: GOODWILL OF BUSINESS: INDUCEMENT TO BREAK CONTRACT: RESTRAINT OF TRADE: AGENCY: DISCRETION: Australia: S.C.(NSW))   7 I.P.R. 581

Carlton & United Breweries Ltd v. Tooth & Co. Ltd (TRADE PRACTICES: DEFENCES: JURISDICTION: Australia: Fed. Ct: S.C.(NSW))   6 I.P.R. 295

Carnation Australia Pty Ltd v. Commissioner of Stamp Duties (TRADE MARKS: WHETHER "PROPERTY OUTSIDE QUEENSLAND": WHETHER AGREEMENT FOR SALE OF BUSINESS LIABLE FOR STAMP DUTY BY REFERENCE TO THE VALUE OF TRADE MARKS OF THE BUSINESS: Australia: S.C.(Qd.))
    (1994) 2 Qd.R. 402; 26 I.P.R. 443

Carnaud/Toothed wheel welding process (EUROPEAN PATENT: INVENTIVE STEP: DEFINITION OF PROBLEM: OPPOSITION: PROCEDURE: EQUALITY OF TREATMENT: T190/90: EPO)   [1994] E.P.O.R. 527

Carnival Cruise Lines Inc. v. Sitmar Cruises Ltd (TRADE MARKS: SERVICE MARKS: OPPOSITION: APPEAL: USE IN COURSE OF TRADE: FUN SHIP: DECEPTIVE SIMILARITY: WHETHER SUFFICIENT IDENTITY BETWEEN MARKS AND SERVICES: PROPRIETORSHIP: Australia: Fed. Ct)
    120 A.L.R. 495; 31 I.P.R. 375

Caroma Industries Ltd (DESIGN: APPLICATION: REGISTRABILITY: Australia: AIPO)   29 I.P.R. 237

Carpenter v. Sue Agencies Pty Ltd (PATENT: OPPOSITION: NOVELTY: OBVIOUSNESS: Australia: Pat. Off.)   10 I.P.R. 48

sub nom. Sue v. Carpenter (PATENT: PATENT OFFICE PROCEDURE: SPECIAL LEAVE TO ADDUCE FURTHER EVIDENCE: Australia: Pat. Off.)   19 I.P.R. 187

Carpenter v. Sue (PATENT: OPPOSITION TO GRANT: DEFECTS IN CLAIMS: LACK OF NOVELTY: OBVIOUSNESS: Australia: Pat. Off.)   23 I.P.R. 63

Carroll & Harper's Applications (PATENTS: APPLICATIONS: Australia: Pat. Off.)
    1 I.P.R. 537

Carrozzeria Grazia v. Volvo Italia (RESTRICTIVE PRACTICES: DOMINANT POSITION: ABUSE: MOTOR CARS: TYPE APPROVAL: CERTIFICATES OF CONFORMITY: REFUSAL TO SUPPLY: CASE SETTLED: NOTICE: E.C. Comm.)
    [1988] 4 C.M.L.R. 423

Cartier International BV Co. Ltd v. Ramesh Kumar Sawhney (TRADE MARK: INFRINGEMENT: CARTIER: INTERNATIONAL REPUTATION: GOODS OF DIFFERENT DESCRIPTION: INTERIM INJUNCTION: India: H.C.)
    (1994) 19 I.P.L.R. 214

Cartier International BV v. Lee Hock Lee (TRADE MARK: INFRINGEMENT: PRESUMPTION: CONTEMPT: APPLICATION FOR COMMITTAL: EVIDENCE: SUFFICIENCY: HEARSAY: ADMISSIBILITY: Singapore: H.C.)
    [1993] 1 S.L.R. 616

Cassini v. Golden Era Shirt Co. Pty Ltd, *sub nom.* Golden Era Shirt Co. Pty Ltd v. Cassini

Castlebrae Pty Ltd v. Anheuser-Busch Inc. (TRADE MARK: OPPOSITION: Australia: AIPO)   27 I.P.R. 273

Castlemaine Tooheys Ltd v. State of South Australia (PRACTICE: INTERLOCUTORY INJUNCTION: PRINCIPLES: Australia: H.C.)   67 A.L.R. 553

Castleton/Re-establishment of rights (EUROPEAN PATENT: RE-ESTABLISHMENT OF RIGHTS: TIME-LIMIT FOR CORRECTION OF DEFICIENCIES: PROCEDURE: PRINCIPLE OF GOOD FAITH: PROTECTION OF LEGITIMATE EXPECTATIONS: J13/90: EPO)   [1994] E.P.O.R. 76

Caston Ltd v. Reeva Forman (Pty) Ltd (TRADE LIBEL: RIGHT TO SUE: DAMAGES: SPECIAL DAMAGES: QUANTITY: TRADE MARK: South Africa: A.D.)
1990 (3) S.A. 547

Castrol Ltd v. Automotive Oil Supplies Ltd (TRADE MARK: INFRINGEMENT: PARALLEL IMPORTS: NOTICES TO PURCHASERS: Ch.D.)   [1983] R.P.C. 315

Cataldo/Cause of non-compliance (EUROPEAN PATENT: RE-ESTABLISHMENT OF RIGHTS: TIME-LIMIT FOR: FEES: REIMBURSEMENT OF APPEAL FEE, UNNECESSARY APPLICATION FOR: REIMBURSEMENT GRANTED: J07/82: EPO)   [1979–85] E.P.O.R. A108; [1982] O.J. EPO 391

Cataldo/Re-establishment – insolvency (EUROPEAN PATENT: RE-ESTABLISHMENT OF RIGHTS: INSOLVENCY: J11/83: EPO)   [1979–85] E.P.O.R. A191

Caterpillar Tractor Co. v. Caterpillar Loader Hire (Holdings) Pty Ltd (TRADE MARK: INFRINGEMENT: SERVICE MARK: GOOD FAITH: Australia: S.C.(S.A.))
(1982) 44 A.L.R. 377; 31 S.A.S.R. 80
(Fed. Ct.) (1983) 48 A.L.R. 511; 1 I.P.R. 265

Caterpillar/Form of decision (EUROPEAN PATENT: FEES: PROCEDURE: DECISION, WHAT CONSTITUTES: REFUND FOR INTERNATIONAL SEARCH: J08/81: EPO)   [1979–85] E.P.O.R. A92; [1982] O.J. EPO 10

Caterpillar/Refund of examination fee (EUROPEAN PATENT: FEES: REPAYMENT: ENLARGED BOARD OF APPEAL: REFERENCE REFUSED: J06/83: EPO)
[1979–85] E.P.O.R. A169; [1985] O.J. EPO 97

Caterpillar/Self-purging heat exchanger (EUROPEAN PATENT: ENLARGED BOARD OF APPEAL: REFERENCE REFUSED: FEES: REIMBURSEMENT OF APPEAL FEE: ACTION IN ACCORDANCE WITH PREVAILING PRACTICE: J09/83: EPO)   [1979–85] E.P.O.R. A185

Catnic Components Ltd v. C. Evans & Co. Ltd (PATENT: INFRINGEMENT: VALIDITY: MODEL: RELIEF: DELIVERY UP OF FRANKED ARTICLES: Pat. Ct)
[1983] F.S.R. 401

Catnic Components Ltd v. Hill & Smith Ltd (PATENT: INFRINGEMENT: INQUIRY AS TO DAMAGES: INTEREST: LOSS OF PROFITS: PRESUMPTION OF LOST SALES: NOTIONAL ROYALTY: COMPOUND INTEREST AS HEAD OF DAMAGE: EXEMPLARY DAMAGES: SIMPLE INTEREST: Pat. Ct)   [1983] F.S.R. 512

Cave Holdings Pty Ltd v. Taperline Pty Ltd (PATENTS: INFRINGEMENT: MANUFACTURING AND SALE: PRACTICE: DISCOVERY: PREPARATORY DESIGN DRAWINGS: Australia: Fed. Ct)   4 I.P.R. 476

Cayne v. Global Natural Resources plc (PRACTICE: INTERLOCUTORY INJUNCTION: PRINCIPLES: TRIABLE ISSUE: EVIDENCE OF RIGID TIMETABLE: GUIDELINES: C.A.)   [1984] 1 All E.R. 225

CBA's Application (RESTRICTIVE PRACTICES: PLANT BREEDERS' RIGHTS: LICENSING AGREEMENTS: INTENTION TO ISSUE COMFORT LETTERS: NOTICE: E.C. Comm.)   [1995] 5 C.M.L.R. 730

CBS Inc. v. Ames Records & Tapes Ltd (COPYRIGHT: INFRINGEMENT: AUTHORISING BY HIRING OUT: Ch.D.)
[1981] 2 All E.R. 812; [1982] Ch. 91

CBS Inc. v. Blue Suede Music Ltd (TRADE MARK: INFRINGEMENT: SEIZURE OF GOODS BY CUSTOMS: PRACTICE: Ch.D.)   [1982] R.P.C. 523

CBS Records Australia Ltd v. Guy Gross (COPYRIGHT: MUSICAL WORK: SUBSISTENCE: AUTHORSHIP: OWNERSHIP: INFRINGEMENT: SUBSTANTIAL PART: QUALITY AND QUANTITY DISTINGUISHED: Australia: Fed. Ct)
15 I.P.R. 385

CBS Records Australia Ltd v. Telmak Teleproducts (Aust.) Pty Ltd (COPYRIGHT: SOUND RECORDINGS: SOUND-ALIKE RECORDS: WHETHER COPIES OF ORIGINAL ARTISTS: QUESTION TO BE TRIED ON AGREED STATEMENT OF FACTS: Australia: Fed. Ct)　　　　　　79 A.L.R. 604; 9 I.P.R. 440

CBS Records Australia Ltd v. Telmak Teleproducts (Aust.) Pty Ltd (TRADE PRACTICES: SOUND-ALIKE RECORDINGS: EVIDENCE OF CONFUSION: PASSING OFF: COPYRIGHT: INTERLOCUTORY INJUNCTION: COSTS: Fed. Ct)
8 I.P.R. 473

CBS Songs Ltd v. Amstrad Consumer Electronics plc (COPYRIGHT: INFRINGEMENT: HOME TAPING: AMENDMENT OF PLEADINGS: DISCOVERY: PRACTICE: USE IN PRESENT ACTION OF DOCUMENTS DISCLOSED BY DEFENDANT IN PREVIOUS ACTION: C.A.)　　　　　　[1987] R.P.C. 417; [1988] 1 W.L.R. 364

CBS Songs Ltd v. Amstrad Consumer Electronics plc and Dixons Ltd (COPYRIGHT: INFRINGEMENT: SOUND RECORDING: MUSICAL WORK: HOME TAPING AUTHORISATION: JOINT TORTFEASORS: INCITEMENT TO COMMIT A TORT: INCITEMENT TO COMMIT A CRIME: NEGLIGENCE: H.L.)
[1988] R.P.C. 567; [1988] A.C. 1013; [1988] 2 All E.R. 484; 11 I.P.R. 1

CBS Songs Ltd v. Amstrad Consumer Electronics plc (No. 2) (COPYRIGHT: INFRINGEMENT: HOME TAPING: REPRESENTATIVE ACTION BY COPYRIGHT OWNERS: PLEADINGS: INCITEMENT TO COMMIT OFFENCE UNDER COPYRIGHT ACT: LEAVE TO AMEND REFUSED: Ch.D.)　　　[1987] R.P.C. 429
(C.A.) [1987] R.P.C. 429; [1987] 3 All E.R. 151; [1988] Ch. 61; [1987] 1
F.T.L.R. 488; [1987] 3 W.L.R. 144
(H.L.) [1988] 2 W.L.R. 1191

CBS United Kingdom Ltd v. Lambert (COPYRIGHT: INFRINGEMENT: ANTON PILLER ORDER: MAREVA INJUNCTION: PRACTICE: REPRESENTATIVE ACTIONS: C.A.)
[1983] F.S.R. 127; [1982] 3 All E.R. 237; [1983] 1 Ch. 37; [1982] 3 W.L.R. 746

CBS United Kingdom Ltd v. Perry (COPYRIGHT: INFRINGEMENT: PRACTICE: ANTON PILLER: CROSS-EXAMINATION: Ch.D.)　　　　　　[1985] F.S.R. 421

CBS/Sony (Hong Kong) Ltd v. Television Broadcasts Ltd (COPYRIGHT: INFRINGEMENT: TAPE RECORDINGS: REPRESENTATIVE ACTIONS: STRIKING OUT: Hong Kong: H.C.)　　　　　　[1987] H.K.L.R. 306; 7 I.P.R. 267
(S.C) [1987] F.S.R. 262

CCH Australia Ltd v. Accounting Systems 2000 (Developments) Pty Ltd, *sub nom.* Accounting Systems 2000 (Developments) Pty Ltd v. CCH Australia Ltd

Ccom Pty Ltd v. Jiejung Pty Ltd (COPYRIGHT: COMPILATION OF CHINESE CHARACTERS IN DATABASE: INFRINGEMENT: CAUSAL LINK BETWEEN MATERIAL AND ALLEGED COPY: PATENT: COMPUTER PROCESS FOR ASSEMBLING CHINESE LANGUAGE CHARACTERS: VALIDITY: INFRINGEMENT: WHETHER SALE OF PROGRAM FOR USE IN STANDARD COMPUTER INFRINGES PATENTED APPARATUS CLAIM: CONTRIBUTORY INFRINGEMENT: Australia: Fed. Ct)　　　　　　27 I.P.R. 577

Ccom Pty Ltd v. Jiejung Pty Ltd (PATENT: COMPUTER PROCESS FOR ASSEMBLING CHINESE LANGUAGE CHARACTERS: INFRINGEMENT: CLAIMS: FAIRLY BASED: PRIORITY DATE: ANTICIPATION: NOVELTY: METHOD OF MANUFACTURE: Australia: Fed. Ct)　　　　　　122 A.L.R. 417; 28 I.P.R. 481

CEA-Framatome/Spacer grid (EUROPEAN PATENT: FEES: REIMBURSEMENT OF APPEAL FEE: INVENTIVE STEP: NOVELTY, RELATION TO: OPPOSITION: PROCEDURE: DUTY OF OPPOSITION DIVISION TO CONSIDER ALL GROUNDS: T493/88: EPO)　　　　　　[1991] E.P.O.R. 393; [1991] O.J. EPO 380

Ceat Tyres of India Ltd v. Jay Industrial Services (TRADE MARK: INFRINGEMENT: PASSING OFF: *Ad interim* INJUNCTION: India: H.C.)　　　(1989) 16 I.P.L.R. 77

Cebal/Plastic screw cap (EUROPEAN PATENT: OPPOSITION: PROCEDURE: LATE
FILING OF ADDITIONAL PRIOR ART: TERM OF OPPOSITION, COMMENCEMENT
OF: T438/87: EPO)   [1989] E.P.O.R. 489
Cedarapids Inc.'s Application (TRADE MARKS: APPLICATION: GEOGRAPHICAL
NAMES: INVENTED OR COINED WORDS: DISCLAIMERS: Australia: Pat. Off.)
                                                            13 I.P.R. 297
Cedars-Sinai/Treatment of plasma (EUROPEAN PATENT: AMENDMENT AND
CORRECTION: EXTENSION OF SUBJECT-MATTER: DISCLOSURE: CROSS-
REFERENCED DOCUMENT: SUFFICIENCY: FATAL EFFECT: FUNCTIONAL
DEFINITIONS: TEST PROCEDURE, AVAILABILITY OF: T449/90: EPO)
                                                            [1993] E.P.O.R. 54
Celanese/Polybutylene terephthalate (EUROPEAN PATENT: COSTS: PREMATURE
REQUEST FOR ORAL PROCEEDINGS: INVENTIVE STEP: COMBINATION OF
CITATIONS: LAPSE OF TIME, RELEVANCE OF: STATE OF THE ART:
INTERPRETATION OF DOCUMENT BY LATER DOCUMENT OUTSIDE ARTICLE
54(2): T507/89: EPO)   [1992] E.P.O.R. 229
Celine SA's Trade Mark Applications (TRADE MARK: APPLICATIONS: OPPOSITION:
DEVICE MARKS: PRACTICE: EVIDENCE: Ch.D.)   [1985] R.P.C. 381
Celltech Ltd, *sub nom.* R. v. The Comptroller-General of Patents. ex p Celltech Ltd
Celtrix/Cartilage-inducing factors (EUROPEAN PATENT: AMENDMENT AND
CORRECTION: TYPOGRAPHICAL ERROR: ENLARGED BOARD OF APPEAL:
REFERENCE MADE: SIMILAR ISSUES TO PENDING REFERENCE: T184/91:
EPO)   [1992] E.P.O.R. 419
Celtrix/Correction of errors (EUROPEAN PATENT: AMENDMENT AND
CORRECTION: DECLARATORY NATURE OF CORRECTION: CORRECTION
UNDER RULE 88 MUST COMPLY WITH ARTICLE 123(2): COMMON GENERAL
KNOWLEDGE: EVIDENCE ADMISSIBLE IN SUPPORT OF CORRECTION:
CONVENTIONS: EPC RULES TO COMPLY WITH CONVENTION: G11/91:
EPO)   [1993] E.P.O.R. 245; [1993] O.J. EPO 125
Cement & Concrete Association (PATENT: RESTORATION: REASONABLE CARE: Pat.
Ct)   [1984] R.P.C. 131
Central Wine Buyers Ltd v. Moet et Chandon Ltd (RESTRICTIVE PRACTICES:
EXPORT PROHIBITION: FINES: E.C. Comm.)
                 [1982] 2 C.M.L.R. 166; [1982] F.S.R. 479; [1982] O.J. L94/7
Centre Belge d'Etudes de Marché-Télé-Marketing SA v. Comp. Luxembourgeoise
de Télédiffusion SA (RESTRICTIVE PRACTICES: DOMINANT POSITION:
REMOVAL OF COMPETITION THROUGH LEGISLATION: ABUSE: Case 311/84:
ECJ)   [1986] 2 C.M.L.R. 558; [1985] E.C.R. 3261
Centocor Inc.'s SPC Application (PATENT: SUPPLEMENTARY PROTECTION
CERTIFICATE: WHETHER PRODUCT PROTECTED BY BASIC PATENT:
C.-G.)   [1996] R.P.C. 118
Centronics Systems Pty Ltd v. Nintendo Co. Ltd (CIRCUIT LAYOUT: INTEGRATED
CIRCUIT: OWNER OF E.L. RIGHTS IN AN ORIGINAL CIRCUIT LAYOUT:
INFRINGEMENT: WHETHER MADE IN ACCORDANCE WITH ORIGINAL
LAYOUT: PURPOSE OF EVALUATION OR ANALYSIS: SHRINKING/SCALING:
KNOWLEDGE: Australia: Fed. Ct)   23 I.P.R. 119
Centronics Systems Pty Ltd v. Nintendo Co. Ltd (CIRCUIT LAYOUT: INTEGRATED
CIRCUIT: COMMERCIAL EXPLOITATION: INTERPRETATION OF STATUTE:
IMPORTATION: INFRINGEMENT: Australia: Fed. Ct)
                                                     111 A.L.R. 13; 24 I.P.R. 481
(APPEAL: KNOWLEDGE OR CONSTRUCTIVE KNOWLEDGE OF LICENCE OR OF
PROPERTY RIGHT: H.C.)   121 A.L.R. 577; 28 I.P.R. 431

Century Communications Ltd v. Mayfair Entertainment U.K. Ltd (COPYRIGHT: SUBSISTENCE: INFRINGEMENT: FILM: DISTRIBUTION: WHETHER PREDECESSOR IN TITLE HAD UNDERTAKEN ARRANGEMENTS TO MAKE FILM: INFORMALLY LICENCE TO DISTRIBUTE: *Quantum meruit* CLAIM CONCEDED: Ch.D.) [1993] E.M.L.R. 335

Century Electronics Ltd v. CVS Enterprises Ltd (PASSING OFF: INTERLOCUTORY INJUNCTION: REPUTATION MONOPOLY IN GROUP OF LETTERS: HONEST CONCURRENT TRADING: USE *de minimis*: DELAY: Ch.D.) [1983] F.S.R. 1

Cerebos Food Corp. Ltd v. Diverse Foods SA (Pty) Ltd (ANTON PILLER APPLICATION: NATURE AND SCOPE: LIMITATION: South Africa: T.D.) 1984 (4) S.A. 149

Challenger Technologies Pte Ltd v. Public Prosecutor (TRADE MARK: FALSE APPLICATION OF REGISTERED MARK: OFFENCE: ACTUAL OR IMPLIED CONSENT OF PROPRIETOR: Singapore: H.C.) [1994] 2 S.L.R. 446

Chambre Syndicale Nationale de la Discothéque (SYNDIS) v. Société des Auteurs, Compositeurs et Editeurs de Musique (SACEM) (RESTRICTIVE PRACTICES: PERFORMING RIGHTS SOCIETIES: INTER-STATE TRADE: ROYALTY ENTITLEMENT: France: D.C.) [1986] E.C.C. 400

Champagne Louis Roederer v. Resource Management Services Pty Ltd (TRADE MARK: APPLICATION: OPPOSITION: SUBSTANTIALLY IDENTICAL: DECEPTIVELY SIMILAR: GOODS OF THE SAME DESCRIPTION: BLAMEWORTHY CONDUCT: DISENTITLEMENT TO PROTECTION: PRACTICE: Australia: AIPO) 30 I.P.R. 553

Chan Li Chai Medical Factory (H.K.) Ltd's Application (TRADE MARK: APPLICATION: THREE CHINESE CHARACTERS: GOODS OF SAME DESCRIPTION: DECEPTIVELY SIMILAR: NO OBJECTION UNDER SECTION 28: Australia: Pat. Off.) 19 I.P.R. 140

Chancellor, Master & Scholars of the University of Oxford, *sub nom.* Oxford University Press

Chandra Bhan Dembla Trading v. Bharat Sewing Machine Co. (TRADE MARK: INFRINGEMENT: PASSING OFF: India: H.C.) (1982) 6 I.P.L.R. 1

Chanel Ltd v. Chantal Chemical & Pharmaceutical Corp. (TRADE MARKS: APPLICATION: OPPOSITION: WHETHER APPLICANT PROPRIETOR OF MARK: NO EVIDENCE OF USE BY OTHERS: CHANTAL/CHANEL: SUBSTANTIALLY IDENTICAL OR DECEPTIVELY SIMILAR: NO RISK OF DECEPTION: BASE FOR OPPOSITION: Australia: Pat. Off.) 19 I.P.R. 108

Chanel Ltd v. Chronogem Ltd (TRADE MARKS: APPLICATION: OPPONENT'S EARLIER PART B MARK REGISTERED FOR SAME GOODS: SUBSTANTIAL IDENTITY OR DECEPTIVE SIMILARITY: MARKS DISTINGUISHABLE: WHETHER USE LIKELY TO DECEIVE OR CAUSE CONFUSION: WHETHER MARK OTHERWISE NOT ENTITLED TO PROTECTION: Australia: Pat. Off.) 19 I.P.R. 21

Chanel Ltd v. L'Arome (U.K.) Ltd (TRADE MARK: MULTI-LEVEL MARKETING: INFRINGEMENT: IMPORTING A REFERENCE: SMELL-ALIKE PERFUMES: COMPARISON CHART: WHETHER ADVERTISEMENT ISSUED TO THE PUBLIC: Ch.D.) [1991] R.P.C. 335; 22 I.P.R. 364
sub nom. Chanel Ltd (C.A.) v. Triton Packaging Ltd
(C.A.) [1993] R.P.C. 32; (1993) 18 I.P.L.R. 47

Chanel Ltd v. Produits Ella Bache Laboratoire Suzy (TRADE MARK: OPPOSITION: DECEPTIVE SIMILARITY: GOODS OF SAME DESCRIPTION: BLAMEWORTHY CONDUCT: Australia: AIPO) 27 I.P.R. 245

Chanel SA's Application (RESTRICTIVE PRACTICES: SELECTIVE DISTRIBUTION: MODIFICATION OF ADMISSION PROCEDURE: INTENTION TO ISSUE COMFORT LETTER: E.C. Comm.) [1995] 4 C.M.L.R. 108

Chappell v. United Kingdom (COPYRIGHT: INFRINGEMENT: ANTON PILLER ORDER: EXECUTION TOGETHER WITH SEARCH WARRANT: RIGHT TO RESPECT FOR PRIVATE LIFE: NECESSITY IN A DEMOCRATIC SOCIETY: PROPORTIONALITY: ECHR) [1989] 1 F.S.R. 617

Charak Pharmaceuticals v. M.J. Exports Pvt. Ltd, *sub nom.* M.J. Exports Pvt. Ltd v. Charak Pharmaceuticals

Charan Dass & Veer Industries (India) v. Bombay Crockery House (TRADE MARK: COPYRIGHT: DESIGN: INFRINGEMENT: PASSING OFF: PERFECT/SWASTIK PERFECT: INTERIM INJUNCTION: India: H.C.) (1984) 9 I.P.L.R. 51

Charbonnages/Venturi (EUROPEAN PATENT: DISCLOSURE: DIAGRAM, TEACHING OF: NOVELTY: DIAGRAMMATIC REPRESENTATION IN CITED ART: DRAWINGS, TEACHING OF: T204/83: EPO) [1986] E.P.O.R. 1; [1985] O.J. EPO 310

Charisma Waterbeds Ltd v. Registrar of Companies (COMPANY NAME: USE OF NAME: CHARISMA: CHANGE OF NAME: APPEAL: New Zealand: H.C.)
8 I.P.R. 1

Charles Church Developments plc v. Cronin (PASSING OFF: PRACTICE: PLEADINGS: APPEARANCE OF HOUSE: MAREVA INJUNCTION: ENJOINED AMOUNT REDUCED IN LINE WITH LIKELY FIGURE RECOVERABLE ON ACCOUNT OF PROFITS: Ch.D.) [1990] F.S.R. 1

Charles of the Ritz Group Ltd v. Jory (TRADE MARK: INFRINGEMENT: PRACTICE: DISCOVERY: NAMES OF SUPPLIERS: Ch.D.) [1986] F.S.R. 14

Charles Stark Draper Laboratory/Inertial sensor (EUROPEAN PATENT: INVENTIVE STEP: COMMERCIAL SUCCESS: LONG-FELT WANT: T140/82: EPO)
[1979–85] E.P.O.R. B614

Charleston v. News Group Newspapers Ltd (DEFAMATION: NEWSPAPER ARTICLE: PHOTOGRAPHS: ACTORS' FACES SUPERIMPOSED ON PORNOGRAPHIC PICTURES: EXPLANATORY TEXT: CONTEXT: C.A.) [1994] E.M.L.R. 186
(H.L.) [1995] E.M.L.R. 129

Chase Manhattan Overseas Corp. v. Chase Corp. Ltd (TRADE PRACTICES: PASSING OFF: COMPANY NAMES WITH COMMON WORD: EVIDENCE: INTERVIEWS WITH PUBLIC: PRACTICE: Australia: Fed. Ct) 63 A.L.R. 345; 6 I.P.R. 59
(Full Ct) 70 A.L.R. 303; 8 I.P.R. 69

Chater & Chater Productions Ltd v. Rose (COPYRIGHT: MUSIC: INFRINGEMENT: PERFORMANCE: PRIOR DISCLOSURE OF MUSIC TO DEFENDANTS: INTERLOCUTORY INJUNCTION APPLICATION: JURISDICTION: ARM-TWISTING INJUNCTION: EARLY DISCOVERY REFUSED: Ch.D.)
[1994] E.M.L.R. 217; [1994] F.S.R. 491

Chauvier v. Pelican Pools (Pty) Ltd (PATENT: INFRINGEMENT: *Locus standi*: PATENTEE DECEASED: EXECUTOR: DOMINIUM IN PATENT VESTING IN EXECUTOR WHO SHOULD SUE IN HIS OWN RIGHT IN RESPECT OF ANY INFRINGEMENT: South Africa: TPD) 1992 (2) S.A. 39

Chawrana Tobacco Co. v. Bhagwandas (TRADE MARK: COPYRIGHT: INFRINGEMENT: INTERIM INJUNCTION: India: H.C.) (1988) 13 I.P.L.R. 93

CHC Software Card Ltd v. Hopkins & Wood (MALICIOUS FALSEHOOD: LIBEL: COPYRIGHT INFRINGEMENT: PRACTICE: TRANSFER BETWEEN DIVISIONS: SOLICITOR'S DUTY: DISCOVERY: CONFIDENTIALITY: LEGAL PROFESSIONAL PRIVILEGE: INTERROGATORIES: Ch.D.) [1993] F.S.R. 241

CHEETAH Trade Mark (TRADE MARK: INFRINGEMENT: SUMMARY JUDGMENT: MARK USED ONLY ON INVOICES: WHETHER USED IN RELATION TO GOODS AND/OR IN COURSE OF TRADE: EEC: FREE MOVEMENT OF GOODS: EXHAUSTION OF RIGHTS: Ch.D.)   [1993] F.S.R. 263

Chelsea Man Menswear Ltd v. Chelsea Girl Ltd (PASSING OFF: CHELSEA MAN: REPUTATION: Ch.D.)   [1985] F.S.R. 567
(RELIEF: SCOPE OF INJUNCTION C.A.) [1987] R.P.C. 189

Chelsea Man plc v. Chelsea Girl Ltd (No. 2) (PASSING OFF: CONTEMPT: PRACTICE: Ch.D.)   [1988] F.S.R. 217

CHELSEA MAN Trade Mark (TRADE MARK: APPLICATION: INHERENT CAPACITY TO DISTINGUISH: HONEST CONCURRENT USER: OPPOSITION BASED ON CHELSEA GIRL: Ch.D.)   [1989] R.P.C. 111

Chemby Marketing Ltd v. Willoughby (INTERIM INJUNCTION: SERIOUS QUESTION TO BE TRIED: EFFECT OF UNDERTAKING BY DEFENDANT: New Zealand: H.C.)
13 I.P.R. 38

Chemie Linz/Reinforced channels (EUROPEAN PATENT: INVENTIVE STEP: ONLY REASONABLE CHOICE: OPPOSITION: PROCEDURE: FRESH EVIDENCE ON APPEAL, REFUSED: T242/85: EPO)   ·   [1988] E.P.O.R. 77

Chenel Pty Ltd v. Rayner (CONFIDENTIAL INFORMATION: WHAT CONSTITUTES: INTERLOCUTORY INJUNCTION: SERIOUS ISSUE TO BE TRIED: BALANCE OF CONVENIENCE: Australia: S.C.(Vic.))   28 I.P.R. 638

Cheng Kang Pte Ltd v. Sze Jishian (TRADE MARK: RECTIFICATION: AGGRIEVED PERSONS: *Locus standii*: DEVICE MARK REPRESENTING INGOT: WHETHER MARK HAS DIRECT REFERENCE TO GOODS: WHETHER ADAPTED TO DISTINGUISH: WHETHER COMMON TO TRADE: Singapore: H.C.)
[1992] 2 S.L.R. 214; [1992] F.S.R. 621

Chia v. Haw Par Brothers International Ltd (CONFIDENTIAL INFORMATION: MANUFACTURING PROCESS: WHETHER APPLICANT FOR INJUNCTION REQUIRED TO SPECIFY CONFIDENTIAL ASPECTS OF THE PROCESS: PASSING OFF: TIGER BALM: SIMILARITY OF GET-UP: FORM OF ORDER: ADEQUACY OF DAMAGES: Singapore: C.A.)   27 I.P.R. 55

Chiarapurk Jack v. Haw Paw Brothers International Ltd (CONFIDENTIAL INFORMATION: ESSENTIAL ELEMENTS OF CAUSE OF ACTION: INTERLOCUTORY INJUNCTION: PARTICULARS OF INFORMATION REQUIRED: Singapore: C.A.)   [1993] 3 S.L.R. 285

Chili's Inc.'s Application (TRADE MARK: APPLICATION: OBJECTION BY EXAMINER: DECEPTIVE SIMILARITY: INHERENT CAPABILITY TO BE DISTINCTIVE: FOREIGN MARKET: DISTINCTIVENESS: Australia: Pat. Off.)   10 I.P.R. 92

Chinoin's Application (PATENT: APPLICATION: MICRO-ORGANISMS: COMPLETENESS OF DESCRIPTION: AMENDMENT: Pat. Ct)   [1986] R.P.C. 39

Chiron Corp. v. Murex Diagnostics Australia Pty Ltd (PATENT: APPLICATION FOR REVOCATION: PATENTEE NOT INVENTOR: EFFECT OF TRANSITIONAL PROVISIONS: DISCOVERY: DISCRETION: PLEADINGS: APPLICATION TO STRIKE OUT: SECURITY FOR COSTS: Australia: Fed. Ct)
128 A.L.R. 525; 30 I.P.R. 277

Chiron Corp. v. Murex Diagnostics Ltd (No. 2) (RESTRICTIVE PRACTICES: NATIONAL COURTS: PROCEDURE: DOMINANT POSITION: ABUSE: INTER-STATE TRADE: MUST BE AFFECTED BY ABUSE, NOT MERELY BY DOMINANT POSITION ITSELF: PLEADING MUST ALLEGE SUCH EFFECT: PLEAS DEFECTIVE: PATENT: INFRINGEMENT: ALLEGED REFUSAL TO LICENSE: EURO-DEFENCES: C.A.)   [1994] 1 C.M.L.R. 410; [1994] F.S.R. 187

Chiron Corp. v. Murex Diagnostics Ltd (No. 3) (PATENT: INFRINGEMENT:
VALIDITY: OBVIOUSNESS: SIGNIFICANCE OF THIRD PARTY RESEARCH:
INSUFFICIENCY: WHETHER INVENTION DISCOVERY AS SUCH: WHETHER
CAPABLE OF INDUSTRIAL APPLICATION: P.A.77, SECTION 44: WHETHER
SECTION 44 DEFENCE AVAILABLE: Pat. Ct)   [1994] F.S.R. 202
Chiron Corp. v. Murex Diagnostics Ltd (No. 4) (PATENT: INFRINGEMENT: LICENCE
AGREEMENT HELD AT TRIAL TO OFFEND P.A.77, SECTION 44: AMENDMENT OF
AGREEMENT: APPLICATION TO AMEND PLEADINGS AFTER TRIAL:
JURISDICTION: DISCRETION: LEAVE REFUSED: Pat. Ct)   [1994] F.S.R. 252
Chiron Corp. v. Murex Diagnostics Ltd (No. 5) (PATENT: AMENDMENT: DELETION
OF CLAIMS HELD INVALID AT TRIAL: OPPOSITION ON BASIS OF UNAMENDED
VALID CLAIMS NOT SUPPORTED BY DESCRIPTION OR AMENDMENT
ALLOWABLE ONLY IF SUBJECT MATTER OF INVALID CLAIMS DISCLAIMED FROM
PRINCIPAL CLAIMS: PLAINTIFF'S APPLICATION TO STRIKE OUT: P.A.77, S.74:
RELEVANCE OF EUROPEAN PATENT OFFICE PROCEDURE: Pat. Ct)
[1994] F.S.R. 258
Chiron Corp. v. Murex Diagnostics Ltd (No. 8) (EUROPEAN LAW: TREATY OF
ROME: ARTICLE 177; INTERPRETATION: "PRELIMINARY": PRACTICE AND
PROCEDURE: APPEALS: PETITION FOR LEAVE TO APPEAL: WHETHER REFUSAL
BY HOUSE OF LORDS AN ADMINISTRATIVE OR JUDICIAL ACT: C.A.)
[1995] F.S.R. 309
Chiron Corp. v. Murex Diagnostics Ltd (No. 9) (PATENT: INFRINGEMENT: SECOND
ACTION AFTER AMENDMENT OF AGREEMENT HELD CONTRARY TO P.A.77,
S.44: PLEADINGS: AMENDMENT: WHETHER DEFENCE STRUCK OUT IN
EARLIER ACTION CAN BE RAISED IN LATER ACTION: *Res judicata:* ARTICLE 177:
Acte clair. Pat. Ct)   [1995] F.S.R. 318
Chiron Corp. v. Murex Diagnostics Ltd (No. 10) (PATENT: INFRINGEMENT: FINAL
INJUNCTION: DAMAGES IN LIEU OF INJUNCTION: DISCRETION: Pat. Ct)
[1994] F.S.R. 325
Chiron Corp. v. Murex Diagnostics Ltd (No. 12) (PATENT: HEPATITIS C VIRUS:
DIAGNOSTIC TEST: VALIDITY: CLAIMS: WHETHER DISCOVERY AS SUCH:
CAPABLE OF INDUSTRIAL APPLICATION: SUFFICIENCY: MORE THAN ONE
INVENTION: LICENCE AGREEMENT: VOID CONDITIONS: DATE OF
AGREEMENT: EXCLUSIVE LICENSEE: C.A.)   [1996] F.S.R. 153
Chiron Corp. v. Organon Teknika Ltd (RESTRICTIVE PRACTICES: PATENT:
DOMINANT POSITION: ABUSE: RELEVANT MARKET: REFUSAL TO LICENSE:
INTERLOCUTORY INJUNCTION: MEDICAL PRODUCT: COMPLAINT THAT
COMPETITION WOULD DRIVE DOWN PRICES WHICH WOULD BE TOO
DIFFICULT TO RAISE AGAIN: HEALTH AUTHORITY MIGHT EXERCISE
STATUTORY POWERS: INJUNCTION REFUSED: Pat. Ct)
[1992] 3 C.M.L.R. 813; [1992] F.S.R. 512
Chiron Corp. v. Organon Teknika Ltd (No. 2); Chiron Corp. v. Murex Diagnostics
Ltd (PATENT: INFRINGEMENT: DIAGNOSTIC TEST: PRIVATE INTERNATIONAL
LAW: "EURO-DEFENCE": STRIKING OUT: ARTICLE 86: WHETHER REFUSAL TO
LICENSE ABUSE: EFFECT ON TRADE BETWEEN MEMBER STATES: CONTRACT
SUBJECT TO FOREIGN LAW: SECTION 44 DEFENCE: Pat. Ct)
[1993] F.S.R. 324
(C.A.) [1993] F.S.R. 567
Chiron Corp. v. Organon Teknika Ltd (No. 3), *sub nom.* Chiron Corp. v. Murex
Diagnostics Ltd (No. 3)
Chiron Corp. v. Organon Teknika Ltd (No. 4), *sub nom.* Chiron Corp. v. Murex
Diagnostics Ltd (No. 4)

Chiron Corp. v. Organon Teknika Ltd (No. 5), *sub nom.* Chiron Corp. v. Murex Diagnostics Ltd (No. 5)

Chiron Corp. v. Organon Teknika Ltd (No. 6), *sub nom.* Chiron Corp. v. Murex Diagnostics Ltd (No. 6) (PATENT INFRINGEMENT: VALIDITY: NOVELTY: OBVIOUSNESS: *Res judicata*: CAUSE OF ACTION ESTOPPEL: ISSUE ESTOPPEL: PRACTICE: STRIKING OUT: Pat. Ct)   [1994] F.S.R. 448

Chiron Corp. v. Organon Teknika Ltd (No. 7), *sub nom.* Chiron Corp. v. Murex Diagnostics Ltd (No. 7) (PATENT INFRINGEMENT: PARTIALLY INVALID PATENT: AMENDMENT: DISCRETION: DAMAGES AND COSTS: WHETHER SPECIFICATION FRAMED IN GOOD FAITH WITH REASONABLE SKILL AND KNOWLEDGE: Pat. Ct)   [1994] F.S.R. 458

Chiron Corp. v. Organon Teknika Ltd (No. 11) (PATENT: PARTIAL INVALIDITY: AMENDMENT BY DELETION OF INVALID CLAIMS: DESCRIPTION: WHETHER VALID CLAIMS SUPPORTED: C.A.)   [1995] F.S.R. 589

Chiron Corp. v. Organon Teknika Ld (No. 12) *sub nom.* Chiron Corp. v. Murex Diagnostics Ltd (No. 12)

Chivato/Combustion chamber (EUROPEAN PATENT: APPEAL: PROCEDURE: NOTICE OF APPEAL, WHAT CONSTITUTES: T66/91: EPO)
[1992] E.P.O.R. 142

Chloe Production Sàrl v. Gaumont (COPYRIGHT: FILMS: DISTRIBUTION CONTRACT: France)   [1983] E.C.C. 279; [1983] F.S.R. 579

Chong Fok Shang v. Lily Handicraft (PASSING OFF: SERIOUS QUESTION TO BE TRIED: BALANCE OF CONVENIENCE: WHETHER DAMAGES ADEQUATE COMPENSATION: Malaysia: H.C.)   16 I.P.R. 247

Chong Loy Sen v. Public Prosecutor (COPYRIGHT: CROSS-EXAMINATION ON AFFIDAVIT: Malaysia: H.C.)   [1986] 2 M.L.J. 364

Chopra (S.M.) & Sons v. Rajendra Prosad Srivastava (TRADE MARK: RAJA: RECTIFICATION BY PROPRIETORS OF MAHRAJA: APPEAL: India: H.C.)   (1988) 13 I.P.L.R. 169

Chris Ford Enterprises Pty Ltd v. Badenhop Pty Ltd (DESIGNS: AUTHORSHIP: OWNERSHIP: AGREEMENT: INFRINGEMENT: AMENDMENT: PASSING OFF: Australia: Fed. Ct)   60 A.L.R. 400; 4 I.P.R. 485

Christian Franceries/Traffic regulation (EUROPEAN PATENT: PATENTABILITY: SCHEME FOR ECONOMIC ACTIVITY: T16/83: EPO)   [1988] E.P.O.R. 65

Christian Salvesen (Oil Services) Ltd v. Odfjell Drilling & Construction Co. (U.K.) Ltd (PATENT: INFRINGEMENT: RIGHTS OF EXCLUSIVE SUB-LICENSEE: KNOWLEDGE: Scotland: O.H.)   [1985] R.P.C. 569

Christine Hoden India (Pvt.) Ltd v. Johnson & Johnson, *sub nom.* Johnson & Johnson v. Christine Hoden India (Pvt.) Ltd

Chrysalis Records Ltd v. Vere (COPYRIGHT: INFRINGEMENT: SOUND RECORDINGS: IMPORTATION: Australia: S.C.(Qd.))   (1983) 43 A.L.R. 440

Chubb Australia Ltd's Application (TRADE MARKS: APPLICATION: REFUSAL TO REGISTER: Australia: Pat. Off.)   20 I.P.R. 175

Chubb/Failure to forward a European patent application (EUROPEAN PATENT: RE-ESTABLISHMENT OF RIGHTS: NATIONAL PATENT OFFICE, FAILURE BY: SECRECY ORDER: J03/80: EPO)
[1979–85] E.P.O.R. A23; [1980] O.J. EPO 92

Chugai Seiyaku/Inadmissible appeal (EUROPEAN PATENT: APPEAL: PROCEDURE: ADMISSIBILITY OF APPEAL: AMENDMENT AND CORRECTION: APPROVAL AFTER: CONVENTIONS: EPC RESERVATIONS: J12/83: EPO)
[1979–85] E.P.O.R. A196; [1985] O.J. EPO 06

Chuiaram Aggarwal v. Aggarwal Sweet Corner (PASSING OFF: CRIMINAL COMPLAINT AGAINST UNKNOWN PERSONS: MAGISTRATE'S ORDER FOR POLICE INQUIRY AND SEARCH WARRANTS: COMPLAINANT AWARE OF PETITIONER'S BUSINESS: ON REVISION PETITION, ORDER OF SEARCH WARRANT SET ASIDE: INHERENT POWER OF HIGH COURT WHEN EXERCISABLE ON INTERLOCUTORY ORDERS: India: H.C.)
(1990) 15 I.P.L.R. 237

Ciba Geigy AG's Application (PATENT: EXTENSION: Australia: S.C.(NSW))
1 I.P.R. 171

Ciba Geigy Australia Ltd v. Eli Lilly & Co. (TRADE MARK: APPLICATION: OPPOSITION: DISTINCTIVENESS: CHARACTER OF GOODS: Australia: Pat. Off.)
2 I.P.R. 353

CIBA Trade Mark (SURNAME: WHETHER DISTINCTIVE: Ch.D.) [1983] R.P.C. 75

Ciba-Geigy AG's Patent (PATENT: STATUTORY POLICY: LICENCE OF RIGHT: IMPORTATION: DISCRETION: Pat. Ct)   [1986] R.P.C. 403

Ciba-Geigy AG v. Douglas Pharmaceuticals Ltd (PATENT: EXTENSION OF TERM: APPEAL FROM REFUSAL: ADEQUATE REMUNERATION: NOTIONAL ROYALTY: ONUS OF PROOF: WORLDWIDE PROFITS: WHETHER EXCEPTIONAL CASE: New Zealand: H.C.)   10 I.P.R. 549

Ciba-Geigy Canada Ltd v. Apotex Inc. (PASSING OFF: GET-UP: SIZE, SHAPE AND COLOUR OF PHARMACEUTICAL TABLET: "PUBLIC" TO BE CONSIDERED FOR TEST OF CONFUSION INCLUDES CONSUMER: Canada: S.C.)   24 I.P.R. 652

Ciba-Geigy Ltd v. Sun Pharmaceuticals Industries (TRADE MARK: INFRINGEMENT: ANAFRANIL/CLOROFANIL: DISTINCTIVENESS: INTERIM INJUNCTION: APPEAL: India: H.C.)   (1994) 19 I.P.L.R. 43

Ciba-Geigy Ltd v. Torrent Laboratories Pvt. Ltd (TRADE MARK: APPLICATION: OPPOSITION: ULCIBAN/CIBA: India: H.C.)   (1993) 18 I.P.L.R. 137

Ciba-Geigy plc v. Parke Davis & Co. Ltd (PASSING OFF: INJURIOUS FALSEHOOD: INTERLOCUTORY INJUNCTION: REPRESENTATION THAT DEFENDANT'S PRODUCT A SUBSTITUTE FOR PLAINTIFF'S BY USE OF UNREGISTERED TRADE MARK: FREEDOM OF SPEECH: Ch.D.)   [1994] F.S.R. 8

Ciba-Geigy/Benzothiopyran derivatives (EUROPEAN PATENT: APPLICATION: PROCEDURE: EXAMINING DIVISION, DUTIES OF AND OWN KNOWLEDGE: INVENTIVE STEP: CHEMICAL COMPOUNDS, STRUCTURAL OBVIOUSNESS OF: T20/83: EPO)   [1979–85] E.P.O.R. C746; [1983] O.J. EPO 419

Ciba-Geigy/Diglycidyl ethers (EUROPEAN PATENT: CLAIMS: CLARITY: LIST OF COMPOUNDS: LIST OF CHEMICAL COMPOUNDS: T156/82: EPO)
[1979–85] E.P.O.R. C657

Ciba-Geigy/Dyeing of linear polyamides (EUROPEAN PATENT: APPEAL: PROCEDURE: NOTICE OF APPEAL: T7/81: EPO)
[1979–85] E.P.O.R. B301; [1983] O.J. EPO 98

Ciba-Geigy/Propagating material (EUROPEAN PATENT: PATENTABILITY: PLANTS: NOVELTY: PRODUCT OF PROCESS: T49/83: EPO)
[1979–85] E.P.O.R. C758; [1984] O.J. EPO 112

Ciba-Geigy/Spiro compounds (EUROPEAN PATENT: INVENTIVE STEP: CHEMICAL COMPOUNDS, STRUCTURAL OBVIOUSNESS OF: COMPARATIVE TESTS: PROBLEM, REFORMULATION OF: TECHNICAL ADVANTAGE: EVIDENCE: COMPARATIVE TESTS: MUST BE BASED ON CLOSEST PRIOR ART: DISCLOSURE: INEVITABLE RESULT: ENLARGED BOARD OF APPEAL: REFERENCE REFUSED: T181/82: EPO)   [1979–85] E.P.O.R. C672; [1984] O.J. EPO 401

Ciba-Geigy/Synergistic herbicides (EUROPEAN PATENT: CLAIMS: FUNCTIONAL FEATURES: INVENTIVE STEP: ANALOGOUS SUBSTITUTION: SUFFICIENCY: CLAIMS: T68/85: EPO)   [1987] E.P.O.R. 302; [1987] O.J. EPO 228

Cipla Ltd v. Unicure Pharmaceuticals (TRADE MARK: PIROX: RECTIFICATION: INTERLOCUTORY PETITION: JURISDICTION: India: T.M.Reg.)
(1988) 13 I.P.L.R. 183

Citizen Watch Co. Ltd's Patent (PATENT: REVOCATION BY COMPTROLLER: DOUBLE PATENTING WITH EUROPEAN PATENT (U.K.): PRACTICE: C.-G.) [1993] R.P.C. 1

Clafton Pty Ltd v. Forbes Engineering Holdings Pty Ltd (PATENT: OPPOSITION: FAIR BASIS: PRIOR CLAIMING: DIVISIONAL APPLICATION: PRIORITY DATE: PRIOR PUBLICATION: PUBLIC DOMAIN: ANTICIPATION: NOVELTY: WORKSHOP IMPROVEMENT: OBVIOUSNESS: EVIDENCE OF EXPERTS WHO ARE INVENTIVE OR OVERQUALIFIED OF LIMITED VALUE ON OBVIOUSNESS: Australia: Pat. Off.) 19 I.P.R. 29

Clark v. David Allan & Co. Ltd (COPYRIGHT: ARTISTIC WORK: DESIGN DRAWINGS: INFRINGEMENT: GARMENT: WHETHER FINISHED GARMENT CONSTITUTES REPRODUCTION: VISUAL IMPACT: Scotland: O.H.) 1987 S.L.T. 271

Clay v. ICI Australia Operations Pty Ltd (PATENTS: OPPOSITION: CLARITY OF CLAIMS: OBVIOUSNESS: COMMON GENERAL KNOWLEDGE: PRIOR PUBLICATION: Australia: Pat. Off.) 3 I.P.R. 439

Cleckheaton Australia Pty Ltd's Application (TRADE MARKS: OBJECTION: ADAPTATION TO DISTINGUISH: TEST: CONFUSION WITH CITED MARK: Australia: Pat. Off.) 17 I.P.R. 625

Clemco International Sales Co. v. Bolrette Pty Ltd (PETTY PATENT: UNFAIR TRADING: INTERLOCUTORY INJUNCTION: Australia: Fed. Ct) 6 I.P.R. 83

Cling Adhesive Products Pty Ltd's Application (TRADE MARK: APPLICATION: OBJECTION BY EXAMINER: WHETHER DESCRIPTIVE: WORDS JOINED BY HYPHEN: INHERENT DISTINCTIVENESS: EVIDENCE OF USE: Australia: AIPO) 29 I.P.R. 161

Clouth/Selection among designations (EUROPEAN PATENT: AMENDMENT AND CORRECTION: EPO DECISIONS, OF: DESIGNATION OF STATES: WHEN MUST BE SPECIFIED: EVIDENCE: ORIGINAL DOCUMENTS MUST BE CHECKED: FEES: DATE OF RECEIPT: PURPOSE OF, NEED NOT BE SPECIFIED WITHIN TIME LIMIT: REIMBURSEMENT OF APPEAL FEE: J23/82: EPO)
[1979–85] E.P.O.R. A154; [1983] O.J. EPO 127

Clouth/Selection among designations (EUROPEAN PATENT: PROCEDURE: CORRECTION OF DECISIONS: J23/82: EPO) [1979–85] E.P.O.R. A154

CLUB Trade Mark (TRADE MARK: SERVICE MARK: APPLICATION: AIRLINE SERVICES: WHETHER DISTINCTIVE: PRACTICE: T.M.Reg.)
[1994] R.P.C. 527

Clune v. Collins Angus & Robertson Publishers Pty Ltd (COPYRIGHT: PUBLICATION SHORTLY AFTER ARTIST'S DEATH OF BOOK CONTAINING COPYRIGHT WORKS: ISSUE WHETHER ARTIST LICENSED THE USE OF THE WORKS: ALLEGED ORAL LICENCE: EVIDENCE: CREDIT OF WITNESS: Australia: Fed. Ct) 25 I.P.R. 246

CNL-Sucal NV, SA v. HAG GF AG (TRADE MARKS: IMPORTS: EXHAUSTION OF RIGHTS: GERMAN AND BELGIAN MARKS OF COMMON ORIGIN: CONFUSION: IDENTICAL MARKS: CONFISCATION OF ENEMY PROPERTY OUTSIDE GERMANY: PREVIOUS EUROPEAN COURT JUDGMENT: Case C–10/89: ECJ) [1990] 3 C.M.L.R. 571; [1990] I E.C.R. 3711; [1991] F.S.R. 99

Coal Industry (Patents) Ltd's Application (PATENT: APPLICATION: PRACTICE: IRREGULARITY ATTRIBUTABLE TO PATENT OFFICE: CONDITIONS: DISCRETION: Pat. Ct) [1986] R.P.C. 57

COAPI, sub nom. Coleg de Agentes de la Propriedad Industrial (COAPI)

Coats/Synthetic yarn (EUROPEAN PATENT: AMENDMENT AND CORRECTION: ADDED DEFINITION OF RESULT OF DISCLOSED PROCESS STEP: SUFFICIENCY: CLAIMS: MANUFACTURER'S RECOMMENDATIONS: T596/88: EPO)
[1994] E.P.O.R. 37

Coca Cola Company v. Peter John Gilbey (TRADE MARK: INFRINGEMENT: PASSING OFF: COUNTERFEIT GOODS: PRACTICE: ANTON PILLER ORDER: DISCLOSURE OF INFORMATION: PRIVILEGE AGAINST SELF-INCRIMINATION: RISK OF PERSONAL JEOPARDY: WHETHER GROUNDS TO DISCHARGE ORDER: WHETHER PERMISSSIBLE FOR DEFENDANT TO GIVE EVIDENCE *in camera* IN THE ABSENCE OF PLAINTIFFS OR THEIR LEGAL REPRESENTATIVES: Ch.D.: C.A.)
[1996] F.S.R. 23

Coca Cola Trade Marks (TRADE MARK: APPLICATION: SHAPE OF BOTTLE: Ch.D.)   [1986] R.P.C. 421
(C.A.) [1985] F.S.R. 315; [1986] R.P.C. 421
(H.L) [1986] R.P.C. 421; [1986] F.S.R. 472; [1986] 2 All E.R. 274; [1986] 2 F.T.L.R. 236; [1986] 1 W.L.R. 695

Coca-Cola Co. v. Captain Icecream Pty Ltd (TRADE MARKS: OPPOSITION: USE LIKELY TO DECEIVE OR CAUSE CONFUSION: SUBSTANTIALLY IDENTICAL OR DECEPTIVELY SIMILAR MARKS: Australia: Pat. Off.)   24 I.P.R. 113

Cockerill Sambre/*Force majeure* (EUROPEAN PATENT: FEES: SMALL AMOUNT EXCEPTION: RE-ESTABLISHMENT OF RIGHTS: ARTICLE 122, EXHAUSTIVE: IMPOSSIBILITY OF: J18/82: EPO)
[1979–85] E.P.O.R. A140; [1983] O.J. EPO 441

Coco v. Newnham (EVIDENCE: TAPES AND TRANSCRIPTS: PRODUCED BY LISTENING DEVICES: PRIVATE CONVERSATION OBTAINED BY USE OF DEVICE: WHETHER COMPLETE PROHIBITION OR DISCRETIONARY GROUND OF EXCLUSION: ADMISSIBILITY: Australia: S.C.(Qd.))   97 A.L.R. 419

Codex Corp. v. Racal-Milgo Ltd (PATENT: INFRINGEMENT: DELIVERY UP: ACCOUNT OF PROFITS: WHETHER INFRINGING ARTICLES FRANKED BY TAKING ACCOUNT: Pat. Ct)   [1984] F.S.R. 87

Codex Corp. v. Racal-Milgo Ltd (PATENT: INFRINGEMENT: PURPOSIVE CONSTRUCTION OF CLAIMS: AMENDED SPECIFICATION: EFFECT OF AMENDMENTS ON ACCOUNT OF PROFITS: C.A.)   [1983] R.P.C. 369

Coditel SA v. Ciné Vog Films SA (COPYRIGHT: PERFORMING RIGHTS: RESTRICTIVE PRACTICES: EXCLUSIVE LICENCE: Case 262/81: ECJ)
[1983] 1 C.M.L.R. 49; [1982] E.C.R. 3381; [1983] F.S.R. 148

Codman/Second surgical use (EUROPEAN PATENT: LACK OF CLARITY: INDEFINITE PARAMETER: LACK OF NOVELTY: GENERIC CLAIM ANTICIPATED BY A SPECIFIC DISCLOSURE: RELATIONS BETWEEN USE AND DEVICE BY PROCESS CLAIMS: PATENTABILITY: SECOND SURGICAL USE DISTINGUISHED FROM SECOND THERAPEUTIC USE: T227/91: EPO)[1995] E.P.O.R. 82; [1994] O.J. EPO 291

Cohen (Bella) v. Chaine (Catherine) (COPYRIGHT: CO-AUTHORSHIP: POSTHUMOUS PUBLICATION: *droit moral*: LIABILITY OF PUBLISHER: France)   [1983] E.C.C. 318; [1983] F.S.R. 580

Cohen/Registering of licence (EUROPEAN PATENT: LICENCES: GRANTED PATENT, REGISTRABILITY OF: J17/91: EPO)
[1994] E.P.O.R. 317; [1994] O.J. EPO 225

Cointreau et Cie SA v. Pagan International (TRADE MARK: INFRINGEMENT: CONTAINER MARK: BOTTLE: SHAPE: THREE-DIMENSIONAL MARK: UTILITARIAN OR FUNCTIONAL FEATURE: LACK OF DISTINGUISHING FEATURES: South Africa: A.D.)   1991 (4) S.A. 705

Cole v. Australian Char Pty Ltd (TRADE MARK: APPLICATION: OPPOSITION: ABANDONMENT: INTENTION TO USE: LIKELIHOOD OF DECEPTION OR CONFUSION: BLAMEWORTHY CONDUCT: Australia: AIPO)   30 I.P.R. 51

Coleg de Agentes de la Propriedad Industrial (COAPI) (RESTRICTIVE PRACTICES: INDUSTRIAL PROPERTY AGENTS: SUBJECT TO COMPETITION RULES: FIXING OF MINIMUM FEES BY NATIONAL ASSOCIATION CAUGHT BY ARTICLE 85; IRRELEVANT THAT BREACH SANCTIONED BY NATIONAL LEGISLATION: EXEMPTION REFUSED: NO FINE IMPOSED: E.C. Comm.)
[1995] 5 C.M.L.R. 468

Coles & Co. Ltd's Application (TRADE MARK: APPLICATION: DISTINCTIVENESS: INVENTED WORD: DIRECT REFERENCE TO CHARACTER OR QUALITY OF GOODS: Australia: Pat. Off.)   7 I.P.R. 39

Colgate Palmolive Co. v. Erasmo De Sequeria (TRADE MARK: APPLICATION: OPPOSITION: FABRIL/FAB: India: T.M.Reg.)   (1992) 17 I.P.L.R. 231

Colgate-Palmolive Co. v. Cussons Pty Ltd (PATENT: INFRINGEMENT: VALIDITY: COMBINATION OF KNOWN INTEGERS: INVENTION IN CLAIMS LIMITED BY RESULT: WHETHER THE SPECIFICATION DESCRIBES THE BEST METHOD OF PERFORMING THE INVENTION: OBVIOUSNESS: NOVELTY: ALTERNATIVE CONSTRUCTIONS OF SPECIFICATION: Australia: Fed. Ct)   26 I.P.R. 311

Colgate-Palmolive Co. v. Cussons Pty Ltd (PATENT: VALIDITY: INDEMNITY COSTS: EXERCISE OF DISCRETION TO AWARD: Australia: Fed. Ct)   28 I.P.R. 561

Colgate-Palmolive Co. v. Unilever Ltd (PATENT: APPLICATION: PERSON "SKILLED IN THE ART": South Africa: TPD)   1983 (4) S.A. 249

Colgate-Palmolive Ltd v. Markwell Finance Ltd (PASSING OFF: TRADE MARK: INFRINGEMENT: TOOTHPASTE: PARALLEL IMPORTS: Ch.D.)
[1988] R.P.C. 283
(C.A.) [1989] R.P.C. 197; (1990) 15 I.P.L.R. 136
(PRACTICE: COSTS: PAYMENT INTO COURT: Ch.D.)   [1990] R.P.C. 497

Collaborative/Preprorennin (EUROPEAN PATENT: PRIORITY: CRITERIA FOR ACCORDING: SUFFICIENCY: FUTURE AND/OR INACCESSIBLE VARIANTS: T81/87: EPO)   [1990] E.P.O.R. 361; [1990] O.J. EPO 250

Collier Constructions Pty Ltd v. Foskett Pty Ltd (COPYRIGHT: INFRINGEMENT: DEFENCES: PLANS FOR PROJECT HOUSES: WHETHER SUBSTANTIAL PART TAKEN: WHETHER THE PUBLIC INTEREST IS A DEFENCE TO INFRINGEMENT: WHETHER LACK OF CLEAN HANDS: TRADE PRACTICES: COMPARATIVE ADVERTISING: Australia: Fed. Ct)   97 A.L.R. 460; 19 I.P.R. 44
(COPYRIGHT: INFRINGEMENT: WHETHER REPRODUCTION OF PERIMETER OF PLAN FOR PROJECT HOME: SUBSTANTIAL PART: Australia: Fed. Ct)
20 I.P.R. 666

Collins (Phil) v. Imtrat Handelsgesellschaft mbH, *sub nom.* Phil Collins v. Imtrat Handelsgesellschaft mbH

Colonial Arms Motor Inn Ltd v. Twentieth Century-Fox Films Corp. (COPYRIGHT: INFRINGEMENT: PRACTICE: ANTON PILLER: JURISDICTION: FORUM: New Zealand: C.A.)   [1985] 1 N.Z.L.R. 382

Colorado School of Mines/Photovoltaic cell (EUROPEAN PATENT: APPLICATION PROCEDURE: DEVICE CLAIM: INTRODUCTION OF METHOD CLAIM ALLOWED: PERMISSIBLE SCOPE OF METHOD CLAIM: SEVERAL OBJECTS OF INVENTION: NEED TO RESTRICT DEVICE CLAIM TO ATTAINMENT OF ALL OBJECTS: T802/92: EPO)   [1995] E.P.O.R. 568

COLORCOAT Trade Mark (TRADE MARK: PART A REGISTRATION: EVIDENCE: BoT)   [1990] R.P.C. 511

Columbia Picture Industries Inc. v. Robinson (COPYRIGHT: INFRINGEMENT: PRACTICE: ANTON PILLER ORDER: INTERLOCUTORY MOTION: *Ex parte* PROCEEDINGS: DUTY TO DISCLOSE: Ch.D.)
[1986] F.S.R. 367; [1986] 3 All E.R. 338; [1987] 1 Ch. 38; [1986] 3 W.L.R. 542
Columbia Pictures Industries Inc. v. Videorent Parkmore (COPYRIGHT: INFRINGEMENT: KNOWLEDGE: South Africa: H.C.)   1982 (1) S.A. 49
Comité des Industries Cinématographiques des E.C. v. E.C. Commission (RESTRICTIVE PRACTICES: ABUSE OF DOMINANT POSITION: BROADCASTING: FILMS: FEES: COMPLAINT: Case 298/83: ECJ)
[1986] 1 C.M.L.R. 486; [1985] E.C.R. 1105
Comite Interprofessionnel du Vin de Champagne v. Wineworths Groups Ltd (TORT: PASSING OFF: TRADE NAME: CHAMPAGNE: AUSTRALIAN SPARKLING WINE LABELLED "CHAMPAGNE": New Zealand: H.C.)
[1991] 2 N.Z.L.R. 432; 23 I.P.R. 435; [1992] 2 N.Z.L.R. 327
Comlink Information Systems Inc. v. Technology One Pty Ltd (TRADE MARK: OPPOSITION: FINANCE ONE: LOGO: PROPRIETORSHIP: Australia: AIPO)
31 I.P.R. 578
Commissariat á l'Energie Atomique/Reference voltage generator (EUROPEAN PATENT: DISCLOSURE: OMISSION FROM DIAGRAM: T32/84: EPO)
[1986] E.P.O.R. 94; [1986] O.J. EPO 09
Commissioner of Patents v. Wellcome Foundation Ltd, *sub nom.* Wellcome Foundation Ltd v. Commissioner of Patents
Commissioner of Taxation v. Just Jeans Pty Ltd (INCOME TAX: SALE OF UNREGISTERED TRADE MARK WITHOUT GOODWILL: EFFECT: Australia: Fed. Ct)   8 I.P.R. 622
Commissioners of Customs & Excise v. Hamlin Slowe (COPYRIGHT: INFRINGEMENT: ANTON PILLER PRACTICE: Ch.D.)   [1986] F.S.R. 346
Commonwealth Industrial Gases Ltd v. Liquid Air Australia Ltd (PATENT: OPPOSITION: NOVELTY: ANTICIPATION: PRIOR CLAIMING: MANNER OF NEW MANUFACTURE: Australia: Pat. Off.)   7 I.P.R. 309
Commonwealth Industrial Gases Ltd v. MWA Holdings Pty Ltd (PATENT: INFRINGEMENT: DEPARTURE FROM ESSENTIAL FEATURE: VALIDITY: INVENTIVENESS: PRIOR USE: PRIOR PUBLICATION: COMBINATION OF NON-ESSENTIAL FEATURES: WORKSHOP IMPROVEMENTS: Australia: H.C.)
180 C.L.R. 160
Commonwealth Scientific & Industrial Research Organisation v. HBH Technological Industries Pty Ltd (PATENT: OPPOSITION: EVIDENCE: REQUEST BY OPPONENT TO EXTEND TIME: UNCERTAINTY: Australia: Pat. Off.)
24 I.P.R. 90
Commonwealth Scientific & Industrial Research Organisation v. Western Mining Corp. Ltd (PATENT: OPPOSITION: OBJECTION TO APPLICATION FOR EXTENSION OF TIME WITHIN WHICH TO SERVE EVIDENCE-IN-SUPPORT: WHETHER OPPOSITION "SERIOUS": PUBLIC INTEREST: COSTS: Australia: Pat. Off.)   13 I.P.R. 424
Commonwealth Scientific & Industrial Research Organisation's and Gilbert's Applications (PATENT: JOINT APPLICATIONS: DISPUTE BETWEEN APPLICANTS: ENTITLEMENT TO INVENTIONS: Australia: AIPO)   31 I.P.R. 67
Commonwealth Scientific & Industrial Research Organisation v. Western Mining Corp. Ltd (PATENT: OPPOSITION: EXTENSION OF TIME TO SERVE EVIDENCE: OBJECTION: PRINCIPLES: PUBLIC INTEREST: Australia: Pat. Off.)
16 I.P.R. 538

Communication Credit Union Ltd v. National Westminster Finance Australia Ltd
(PASSING OFF: MISLEADING CONDUCT: Australia: Fed. Ct)
(1984) 51 A.L.R. 375; 1 I.P.R. 507
Communications de Mobile Cellulaire SA (CMC) (RESTRICTIVE PRACTICES: JOINT
VENTURE: TELECOMMUNICATIONS: INTENTION TO APPROVE: NOTICE: E.C.
Comm.)   [1994] 5 C.M.L.R. 486
Communications Satellite/Inadmissible appeal (EUROPEAN PATENT: APPEAL:
PROCEDURE: ADMISSIBILITY OF APPEAL: T831/90: EPO)
[1992] E.P.O.R. 56
Community Computer Programs (Directive 91/250 of May 14, 1991) (COMPUTER
PROGRAMS: LEGAL PROTECTION: E.C. Council)   [1991] O.J. L122/42
Community Computer Programs (Draft Directive) (COPYRIGHT: COMPUTER
PROGRAMS: E.C. Council)   [1989] 2 C.M.L.R. 180; [1989] 1 F.S.R. 550
Community for Creative Non-Violence v. James Earl Reid (COPYRIGHT: WORK
MADE FOR HIRE: EMPLOYEE: INDEPENDENT CONTRACTOR: AGENT: USA:
C.A.)   17 I.P.R. 367
Community Franchise Agreements Regulation (4087/88) (FRANCHISE
AGREEMENTS: APPLICATION OF ARTICLE 85(3): E.C. Comm.)
[1988] O.J. L359/46
Community Patent Appeal Court Privileges Protocol (PROTOCOL ON PRIVILEGES
AND IMMUNITIES OF THE COMMON APPEAL COURT)   [1990] C.M.L.R. 226
Community Patent Appeal Court Statute (PROTOCOL ON THE STATUTE OF THE
COMMON APPEAL COURT: STRUCTURE AND PROCEDURE OF COMMON
APPEAL COURT)   [1990] 2 C.M.L.R. 219
Community Patent Convention (PATENT: EUROPEAN PATENT: 1989
LUXEMBOURG AGREEMENT: E.C. Council)   [1989] O.J. L401/1
Community Patent Licensing Agreements Regulation (2349/84) (PATENTS:
LICENSING: APPLICATION OF ARTICLE 85(3): E.C. Comm.)
[1984] O.J. L219/15
Community Patent Licensing Regulation 1984–92 (2349/84) (RESTRICTIVE
PRACTICES: GROUP EXEMPTION: PATENT LICENSING: TEXT OF REGULATION
2349/84 AS AMENDED BY REGULATION 151/93: E.C. Comm.)
[1993] 4 C.M.L.R. 177
Community Patent Litigation Protocol (PROTOCOL ON SETTLEMENT OF
LITIGATION CONCERNING INFRINGEMENT AND VALIDITY OF COMMUNITY
PATENTS: COMMUNITY PATENT COURTS: COMMON APPEAL COURT:
INTERNATIONAL JURISDICTION AND ENFORCEMENT: FIRST INSTANCE:
SECOND INSTANCE: THIRD INSTANCE AND PRELIMINARY RULING
PROCEDURE: COMMON PROVISIONS FOR COMMUNITY PATENT COURTS OF
FIRST AND SECOND INSTANCE)   [1990] 2 C.M.L.R. 201
Community Plants Variety Rights Council Regulation 2100/94 (PLANTS VARIETY
RIGHTS: REGULATION: E.C. Council)   [1995] F.S.R. 396
Community Rental Right and Lending Right Directive (92/100) (COPYRIGHT:
RENTAL RIGHT: LENDING RIGHT: E.C. Council)   [1992] O.J. L346/61
Community Research and Development Agreements Regulation (418/85)
(RESEARCH AND DEVELOPMENT AGREEMENTS: APPLICATION OF ARTICLE
85(3): E.C. Comm.)   [1985] O.J. L53/5
Community Satellite Broadcasting and Cable Retransmission Directive (93/83)
(COPYRIGHT: SATELLITE BROADCASTING AND CABLE RETRANSMISSION: E.C.
Council)   [1993] O.J. L248/15
Community Semiconductor Products Directive (87/54) (SEMICONDUCTOR
PRODUCTS: TOPOGRAPHIES: LEGAL PROTECTION: E.C. Council)
[1987] O.J. 24/36

Community Trade Mark (First Council Directive) (89/104) (TRADE MARKS: APPROXIMATE OF THE LAWS OF EEC MEMBER STATES: E.C. Council)
[1989] O.J. L40/1
Community Trade Mark Regulation (40/94) (E.C. Council)   [1994] O.J. L11/1
Community Technology Transfer Agreements Regulation (Draft) (RESTRICTIVE PRACTICES: GROUP EXEMPTION: TECHNOLOGY TRANSFER: PATENT: KNOW-HOW: E.C. Comm.)   [1994] 5 C.M.L.R. 109; [1996] F.S.R. 397
Community v. Bayer AG (Re Bayo-N-Ox) (RESTRICTIVE PRACTICES: SELECTIVE DISTRIBUTION: RESALE BAN: MARKET POSITIONING: FEEDINGSTUFF ADDITIVES: EXPIRY OF PATENT IN ONE STATE: PARALLEL TRADE ARTICLE 85(1): FINE: E.C. Comm.)   [1990] 4 C.M.L.R. 930; [1991] F.S.R. 168
Community v. Bayer AG (RESTRICTIVE PRACTICES: AGREEMENTS: RESALE RESTRICTIONS: TRADE MARKS: EXPORT BANS: PACKAGING: E.C. Comm.)   [1992] 4 C.M.L.R. 61; [1992] F.S.R. 201
Community v. Fanuc Ltd and Siemens AG (RESTRICTIVE PRACTICES: EXCLUSIVE DEALING: MARKET PARTITIONING: JOINT RESEARCH AND DEVELOPMENT: GROUP EXEMPTION NOT APPLICABLE: EXCLUSIVE DEALING: NO NOTIFICATION, SO NO INDIVIDUAL EXEMPTION: BREACH OF ARTICLE 85(1): FINES IMPOSED: E.C. Comm.)   [1988] 4 C.M.L.R. 945
Community v. Fiat Auto (RESTRICTIVE PRACTICES: DISTRIBUTION AGREEMENTS: TYING CLAUSES: SETTLEMENT: E.C. Comm.)   [1988] 4 C.M.L.R. 425
Community v. International Business Machines (RESTRICTIVE PRACTICES: DOMINANT POSITION: ABUSE: NEW COMPUTERS: TECHNICAL INFORMATION: BUNDLING: E.C. Comm.)   [1984] 3 C.M.L.R. 147
Community v. National Panasonic (Belgium) NV (RESTRICTIVE PRACTICES: E.C. Comm.)   [1982] 2 C.M.L.R. 410; [1982] F.S.R. 528; [1982] O.J. L113/18
Community v. Syntex Corp. (RESTRICTIVE PRACTICES: SIMILAR TRADE MARKS: MARKET PETITIONING: NOT CLEAR WHETHER EARLIER TRADE MARK COULD BE ENFORCED IN MEMBER-STATES: DELIMITATION AGREEMENT TO AVOID CONFUSION: CAUGHT BY ARTICLE 85(1): CASE SETTLED: E.C. Comm.)
[1990] 4 C.M.L.R. 343; [1990] F.S.R. 529
Community v. Unilever NV (RESTRICTIVE PRACTICES: EXCHANGE OF SALES INFORMATION: RESTRICTIVE OF COMPETITION: INFRINGEMENT: FINE IMPOSED: E.C. Comm. Decision IV/31.128)   [1989] 4 C.M.L.R. 445
Community v. United States of America (Du Pont de Nemours/Akzo Dispute) (IMPORTS: GATT: NATIONAL TREATMENT: NOT IDENTICAL TREATMENT, BUT COVERS BREACH OF U.S. PATENTS: RULES RESTRICTING IMPORTS MORE ONEROUS THAN DOMESTIC PATENT INFRINGEMENT PROCEEDINGS: BREACH OF ARTICLE III.4 GATT: UNNECESSARY TO SECURE COMPLIANCE WITH U.S. PATENT LAWS: SO NOT SAVED BY EXCEPTION IN ARTICLE XX(D) GATT: GATT Panel)   [1989] 1 C.M.L.R. 715
Compagnie Générale d'Électricité/Calculation of fee for printing (EUROPEAN PATENT: FEES: CALCULATION OF PRINTING FEE: CONVENTIONS: NOTE BY EPO PRESIDENT INDICATING INTENTION OF RULE: J04/81: EPO)
[1979–85] E.P.O.R. A80; [1981] O.J. EPO 543
Compagnie Luxembourgeoise de Télédiffusion (BROADCASTING FRANCHISES: ADMINISTRATIVE PROCEDURE: JUDICIAL REVIEW: *Locus standi*: France: Conseil d'Etat)   [1988] 4 C.M.L.R. 193
Compagnie Royale Asturienne des Mines SA v. E.C. Comm. (RESTRICTIVE PRACTICES: EXPORT RESTRICTIONS: Cases 29–30/83: ECJ)
[1985] 1 C.M.L.R. 688; [1984] E.C.R. 1679
Company's Application, *sub nom*. A Company's Application

Compaq Computer Corp. v. Dell Computer Corp. Ltd (TRADE MARK: INFRINGEMENT: COMPARATIVE ADVERTISING: INVALIDITY: TRIABLE ISSUE: BALANCE OF CONVENIENCE: WHETHER PLAINTIFF'S CONDUCT BAR TO GRANT OF INJUNCTION: INJURIOUS FALSEHOOD: APPROACH TO INJUNCTION APPLICATION WHEN DEFENDANT DENIES STATEMENT: FREEDOM OF SPEECH AN ELEMENT OF BALANCE OF CONVENIENCE TEST: Ch.D.)
[1992] F.S.R. 93

Comparative Advertising Draft Directive (COMPARATIVE ADVERTISING: TO BE ALLOWED: CONDITIONS: NATIONAL CONTROLS: AMENDMENT OF MISLEADING ADVERTISING DIRECTIVE 84/450: E.C. Council)
[1991] 3 C.M.L.R. 470

Composite Gutters Ltd v. Pre-Formed Components Ltd (PATENT: INFRINGEMENT: TRANSFER TO PAT. C.C.: PLAINTIFFS' FINANCIAL POSITION: DISCRETION: Pat. Ct)   [1993] F.S.R. 305

Compulsory Patent Licences (Re), sub nom. E.C. Commission v. United Kingdom and Italy

Compusales Holdings N.Z. Ltd v. Sperry Ltd & Burroughs Ltd (PASSING OFF: COMPUTER DEVELOPMENT COMPANIES: TRADE NAME: UNISYS: INTERIM INJUNCTION: UNDERTAKING AS TO DAMAGES: New Zealand: H.C.)
8 I.P.R. 56

Computer Associates International, Inc. v. Altai, Inc. (COPYRIGHT: COMPUTER SOFTWARE: NON-LITERAL ELEMENTS PROTECTABLE: SUBSTANTIAL SIMILARITY TEST: TRADE SECRETS: FEDERAL PREEMPTION: USA: C.A.)
23 I.P.R. 385

Computer Programs (Draft Directive), sub nom. Community Computer Programs (Draft Directive)

Computer Programs Directive, sub nom. Community Computer Programs

Computer Generation of Chinese Characters (PATENT: APPLICATION: COMPUTER PROGRAM: CHINESE CHARACTERS: WHETHER PATENTABLE: WHETHER APPLICATION OF "TECHNICAL NATURE": APPLICATION REFUSED: Germany: S.C.)   [1993] F.S.R. 315

Computer Machinery Co. Ltd v. Drescher (CONFIDENTIAL INFORMATION: INTERLOCUTORY INJUNCTION: FORMER EMPLOYEE'S: EVIDENCE: Ch.D.)   [1983] 3 All E.R. 153

Computer People Pty Ltd (TRADE MARK: APPLICATION: AMENDMENT: DISCLAIMER: DESCRIPTION OF APPLICANT'S SERVICES: Australia: Pat. Off.)
4 I.P.R. 450

Computer Programs (Protection of) (COPYRIGHT: COMPUTER PROGRAMS: MARKETING RIGHTS: Germany: S.C.)   [1986] E.C.C. 498

Computer Workshops Ltd v. Banner Capital Market Brokers Ltd (BREACH OF CONFIDENCE: IMPLIED: EVIDENCE: Canada: C.A.)   33 C.P.R. (3d) 416

Computerland Europe SA's Franchise Agreements (FRANCHISING: RESTRICTIVE PRACTICES: AGREEMENTS: NOT CAUGHT BY ARTICLE 85(1) WHERE COMPETITIVE MARKET CONDITIONS PREVAIL: NON-COMPETITION CLAUSE: NOT CAUGHT PRIMA FACIE: CONTROL OF BUSINESS METHODS: EXCLUSIVE TERRITORIAL RIGHTS: SALE RESTRICTIONS: INTER-STATE TRADE: NON-APPLICABILITY OF BLOCK EXEMPTIONS UNDER REGULATION 67/67 AND REGULATION 1983/83: INDIVIDUAL EXEMPTION GRANTED: E.C. Comm.)   [1989] 4 C.M.L.R. 259; [1989] 1 F.S.R. 397

Computerland Europe SA (RESTRICTIVE PRACTICES: FRANCHISING AGREEMENTS: INTENTION TO APPROVE: E.C. Comm.)   [1987] 2 C.M.L.R. 389

Computermate Products (Aust.) Pty Ltd v. Ozi-Soft Pty Ltd (COPYRIGHT: LICENCE TO IMPORT COPYRIGHT MATERIAL: COMPUTER DISKETTES: NATURE AND DEFINITION OF LICENCE WITHIN STATUTORY DEFINITION: "LICENCE" INTERCHANGEABLE WITH "CONSENT" AND "PERMISSION": ONUS OF PROVING EXISTENCE OF LICENCE: Australia: Fed. Ct)
83 A.L.R. 492; 12 I.P.R. 487

Comshare Incorporated's Application (DESIGN: APPLICATION: "APPLICATION TO AN ARTICLE": "PATTERN OR ORNAMENT": Australia: Pat. Off.)   23 I.P.R. 145

Conagra Inc. v. McCain Foods (Aust.) Pty Ltd (PASSING OFF: ELEMENTS: REPUTATION: WHETHER NECESSARY TO HAVE A PLACE OF BUSINESS WITHIN THE JURISDICTION TO MAINTAIN ACTION: SIGNIFICANCE OF FRAUDULENT INTENTION: MISLEADING OR DECEPTIVE CONDUCT: PACKAGING: SIMILARITY OF NAME AND GET-UP: WHETHER MISREPRESENTATION OF SPONSORSHIP, APPROVAL OR AFFILIATION: Australia: Fed. Ct)
101 A.L.R. 461; 23 I.P.R. 193

Conagra Inc. v. McCain Foods (Aust.) Pty Ltd (PASSING OFF: MISLEADING OR DECEPTIVE CONDUCT: DESCRIPTION OF PRODUCTS: PACKAGING: GET-UP: SIMILARITY OF NAME AND GET-UP TO THAT USED BY APPLICANT FOR SIMILAR GOODS OUTSIDE THE JURISDICTION: Australia: Fed. Ct)
106 A.L.R. 465; 22 I.P.R. 175

Concept Factory v. Heyl (RESTRAINT OF TRADE: REASONABLENESS: DESIGN AND IDEAS IN PUBLIC DOMAIN: COPYING: UNLAWFUL COMPETITION: GENERAL PRINCIPLES: South Africa: TPD)   1994 (2) S.A. 105

Concept Television Products Pty Ltd v. Australian Broadcasting Corp. (TRADE PRACTICES: WHETHER REQUIREMENTS OF FALSITY OR RECKLESSNESS SUFFICIENTLY SHOWN TO WARRANT INJUNCTION: Australia: Fed. Ct)
12 I.P.R. 129

CONCORD Trade Mark (TRADE MARK: NON-USE: RECTIFICATION: USE ON LIMITED SCALE: Ch.D.)   [1987] F.S.R. 209

Concorde Trading Pty Ltd v. Croner Trading Pty Ltd (PATENT: OPPOSITION: APPLICATION FOR DISMISSAL: VEXATIOUS OR ABUSE OF PROCESS: COSTS: Australia: AIPO)   29 I.P.R. 507

Concrete Constructions (NSW) Pty Ltd v. Nelson (TRADE PRACTICES: MISLEADING AND DECEPTIVE CONDUCT: IN TRADE OR COMMERCE: FALSE REPRESENTATION BY FOREMAN TO FELLOW EMPLOYEE: WHETHER CONDUCT IN TRADE OR COMMERCE: CONSUMER PROTECTION: Australia: H.C.)   17 I.P.R. 39

Conde Nast Publications Pty Ltd v. Mango Pty Ltd (TRADE MARK: OPPOSITION: VOGUE: WHETHER DESCRIPTIVE: SIMILAR GOODS: CONFUSION: Australia: Fed. Ct)   28 I.P.R. 374

Condec/Extension apparatus (EUROPEAN PATENT: COMMON GENERAL KNOWLEDGE: NO NEED FOR DOCUMENTARY PROOF: EVIDENCE: WELL-KNOWN FACTS, NO NEED TO BE PROVED BY DOCUMENTS: INVENTIVE STEP: CONVENTIONAL USE: SIMPLICITY OF CONCEPT: SKILLED PERSON, CAPABILITIES OF: T66/82: EPO)   1979–85] E.P.O.R. B491

Conder International Ltd v. Hibbing Ltd (PATENT: INFRINGEMENT: INTERLOCUTORY INJUNCTION: SNOWBALL EFFECT: C.A.)
[1984] F.S.R. 312

Conegate Ltd v. Customs & Excise Commissioners (EEC: IMPORTS: PROHIBITION: QUALITATIVE RESTRICTIONS: PUBLIC MORALITY: OBSCENE GOODS: INFLATABLE DOLLS: Case 121/85: ECJ)
[1986] 2 All E.R. 688; [1986] C.M.L.R. 739; [1986] E.C.R. 1007

Connell v. L.D. Nathan & Co. Ltd, *sub nom.* Connell v. The Farmers' Trading Co. (Wellington) Ltd

Connell v. The Farmers Trading Co. (Wellington) Ltd (FAIR TRADING: CHILDREN'S NIGHT CLOTHES: FAILURE TO COMPLY WITH SAFETY STANDARDS: FALSE REPRESENTATIONS THAT CLOTHES WERE OF CERTAIN STANDARD: ADEQUACY OF PENALTY: GENERAL APPROACH TO LEVYING PENALTIES: New Zealand: H.C.)   17 I.P.R. 278

Conoco Specialty Products Inc. v. Merpro Montassa Ltd (No. 1) (PATENT: INFRINGEMENT: INTERIM INTERDICT: ALLEGED DIFFERENCES: WHETHER PRIMA FACIE CASE: BALANCE OF CONVENIENCE: Scotland: O.H.)
                                                                    1991 S.L.T. 222

Conoco Specialty Products Inc. v. Merpro Montassa Ltd (PATENT: INFRINGEMENT: CONSTRUCTION: GENERALLY CYLINDRICAL: VALIDITY: ANTICIPATION: OBVIOUSNESS: Scotland: O.H.)   [1994] F.S.R. 99; 1992 S.L.T. 444

Conry v. Atlas Air Aust. Pty Ltd (PATENT: OPPOSITION: EXTENSION OF TIME IN WHICH TO LODGE NOTICE OF OPPOSITION: Australia: Pat. Off.)
                                                                      18 I.P.R. 285

Consejo Regulador de las Denominaciones "Jerez-Xeres-Sherry" y "Manzanilla de Sanlucar de Barrameda" v. Mathew Clark & Sons Ltd (PASSING OFF: EUROPEAN REGULATIONS: BEVERAGE CONTAINING BRITISH WINE AND SHERRY: USE OF "SHERRY" ON LABELS: E.C. REGULATIONS 823/97 AND 2043/89: INTERLOCUTORY INJUNCTION: Ch.D.)   [1992] F.S.R. 525

Consolidation (EUROPEAN PATENT: APPLICATION: PROCEDURE: CONSOLIDATION: EVIDENCE: MEDICAL CERTIFICATE, INADEQUATE: FEES: DUTIES OF EPO: FAILURE TO PAY: J000/87: EPO)
                                          [1988] E.P.O.R. 333; [1988] O.J. EPO 177

Consorzio del Prosciutto di Parma v. Marks & Spencer plc (PASSING OFF: INTERLOCUTORY INJUNCTION: PRE-SLICED PARMA HAM: REPRESENTATIVE ACTION: *Locus standi*: BALANCE OF CONVENIENCE: ITALIAN LEGISLATION: Ch.D.)   [1990] F.S.R. 530; [1991] R.P.C. 351
                                    (C.A.) [1991] R.P.C. 351; 16 I.P.R. 117

Consorzio Italiano della Componentistica di Ricambio per Autoveicoli v. Regie Nationale des Usines Renault (COMMUNITY LAW AND NATIONAL LAW: INDUSTRIAL DESIGNS: RESTRICTIVE PRACTICES: DOMINANT POSITION: ABUSE: SPARE PARTS: Case 53/87: ECJ)   [1990] F.S.R. 544

Construction Engineering (Aust.) Pty Ltd v. Tambel (Aust.) Ltd (PRACTICE: MAREVA INJUNCTION: EVIDENCE: Australia: S.C.(NSW))   [1984] 1 N.S.W.L.R. 274

Construction Industry Long Service Leave Board v. Odco Pty Ltd (TRADE PRACTICES: MISLEADING OR DECEPTIVE CONDUCT: PUBLICATION OF STATEMENTS IN BROCHURE: Australia: Fed. Ct)   11 I.P.R. 577

Consumers Glass/Late correction (EUROPEAN PATENT: AMENDMENT AND CORRECTION: DESIGNATION OF STATES: CONVENTIONS: PRECEDENCE OVER RULES: J21/84: EPO)   [1986] E.P.O.R. 146; [1986] O.J. EPO 75

Consumers Glass/Late correction (EUROPEAN PATENT: RE-ESTABLISHMENT OF RIGHTS: INADMISSIBLE: AMENDMENT AND CORRECTION: BROADENING CLAIM BY OMISSION: T172/82: EPO)
                                       [1979–85] E.P.O.R. C668; [1983] O.J. EPO 493

Contal Co. Pty Ltd v. Szozda (TRADE NAMES: SIMILARITY: INTERLOCUTORY INJUNCTION: PRACTICE: Australia: S.C.(NSW))   7 I.P.R. 373

Continental Group Inc.'s Application (PATENT: APPLICATION: OBJECTION BY EXAMINER: AMENDED SPECIFICATION: NOVELTY: MANNER OF NEW MANUFACTURE: Australia: Pat. Off.)   7 I.P.R. 362

Continental Gummi-Werke AG and Compagnie Generale des Etablissements Michelin, Michelin et Cie's Agreement (RESTRICTIVE PRACTICES: JOINT VENTURES: JOINT RESEARCH AND DEVELOPMENT: INDEPENDENT DEVELOPMENT OF SIMILAR PRODUCTS ABANDONED: COMMON ENTITY TO EXPLOIT FUTURE PATENTS AND KNOW-HOW: LICENSING: MARKET IMPACT: INTER-STATE TRADE: E.C. Comm.)
[1989] 4 C.M.L.R. 920; [1990] F.S.R. 159

Continental Linen Co. (Pty) Ltd v. Kenpet Agency (Pty) Ltd (PATENT: INFRINGEMENT: THREATS: JUSTIFICATION: RELIEF: South Africa: TPD)
1986 (4) S.A. 703

Continental Manufacturing & Sales Inc.'s Patent (PATENT: RESTORATION: REASONABLE CARE: LICENSEE: Pat. Ct)   [1994] R.P.C. 535

Continental White Cap Inc. v. W.R. Grace & Co. (PATENT: APPLICATION: OPPOSITION: HEARING: WITHDRAWAL OF PARTY BEFORE HEARING: Australia: Pat. Off.)   24 I.P.R. 410

Continental Wholesalers v. Fashion Fantasy (Pty) Ltd (TRADE MARK: INFRINGEMENT: INTERIM INJUNCTION: HEARING *in camera:* South Africa: D&CLD)   1983 (1) S.A. 683

Control Systems/Ticket-issuing machines (EUROPEAN PATENT: INVENTIVE STEP: SUFFICIENCY: ELECTRONIC MEANS: RELATION TO SUFFICIENCY OF DISCLOSURE: T292/87: EPO)   [1989] E.P.O.R. 333

Cooper Chasney Ltd v. Commissioners of Customs & Excise (VAT: TRADE MARK INFRINGEMENT: SETTLEMENT OF LEGAL PROCEEDINGS: VAT Tribunal, London)   [1990] 3 C.M.L.R. 509; [1992] F.S.R. 298

Cooper Industries Inc. v. Metal Manufactures Ltd (PATENT: OPPOSITION: PROCEDURE: NON-COMPLIANCE WITH SECTION 40: EVIDENCE: OBVIOUSNESS: COMMON GENERAL KNOWLEDGE: Australia: AIPO)
29 I.P.R. 106

Coopers Animal Health Australia Ltd v. Western Stock Distributors Pty Ltd (PATENT: PROVISIONAL SPECIFICATION AND SUBSEQUENT PETTY PATENT: PRIORITY DATES: Australia: Fed. Ct)   11 I.P.R. 20

Coopers Animal Health Australia Ltd v. Western Stock Distributors Ltd (PATENT: PETTY PATENT: CLAIM BASED ON EARLIER SPECIFICATION: NOVELTY: OBVIOUSNESS: UTILITY: REVOCATION: Australia: Fed. Ct)
67 A.L.R. 390; 6 I.P.R. 545

Coopers Animal Health Australia Ltd v. Western Stock Distributors Ltd (PATENT: PETTY PATENT: EXTENSION: OBJECTION: OPPOSITION: INVALIDITY: ANTICIPATION: PRIOR USE: Australia: Pat. Off.)   7 I.P.R. 208
(Fed. Ct) 76 A.L.R. 429

Cope Allman (Marrickville) Ltd v. Farrow (COPYRIGHT: OWNERSHIP: ENGRAVINGS: COMMISSIONED WORK: CONFIDENTIAL INFORMATION: COMPUTER PROGRAMS: Australia: S.C.(NSW))   3 I.P.R. 567

Copperart Pty Ltd v. Floan (TRADE PRACTICES: FALSE AND MISLEADING CONDUCT: REPRESENTATION AS TO FUTURE EVENTS: Australia: Fed. Ct) 20 I.P.R. 519

Copyright Agency Ltd v. Department of Education of NSW (COPYRIGHT: COPYING BY EDUCATIONAL ESTABLISHMENTS: REMUNERATION: Australia: Cprt. Trib.)   4 I.P.R. 5; 59 A.L.R. 172

Copyright Agency Ltd v. Haines (COPYRIGHT: INFRINGEMENT: FAIR DEALING: AUTHORISING INFRINGEMENT: MULTIPLE COPYING: SCHOOLS: Australia: S.C.(NSW))   (1982) 40 A.L.R. 264
(Fed. Ct) (1982) 42 A.L.R. 549

Copyright Agency Ltd v. Victoria University of Technology (COPYRIGHT: MULTIPLE COPYING OF WORK BY EDUCATIONAL INSTITUTIONS: WHETHER AUTHORISED SALE OR USE OF COPIES SO MADE: OPERATION OF LICENSING SCHEME: Australia: Fed. Ct)   125 A.L.R. 278; 29 I.P.R. 263
                    (Appeal; Fed. Ct) 128 A.L.R. 482; 30 I.P.R. 140
Copyright (Ancillary Rights) Draft Directive (COPYRIGHT: RENTAL AND LENDING RIGHTS: PERFORMER'S RIGHTS: DURATION OF PROTECTION: E.C. Council)   [1992] 1 C.M.L.R. 205
Copyright (Broadcasting) Draft Direcive (SATELLITE BROADCASTING: CABLE RE-TRANSMISSION: COPYRIGHT AND NEIGHBOURING RIGHTS: SPECIAL BROADCASTING RIGHTS: PERFORMERS' RIGHTS: SPECIAL RULE FOR BROADCAST OF PHONOGRAMS: COMPETITION RULES: E.C. Council)
                                        [1992] 1 C.M.L.R. 166
Copyright Harmonising Directive (93/98) (COPYRIGHT TERM: HARMONISATION: E.C. Council)   [1993] O.J. L290/9
Copyright in Court Proceedings (COPYRIGHT: LAWYERS' PLEADINGS: TEST: PROTECTION: PUBLICATION: Germany: S.C.)
                                [1988] E.C.C. 4; [1988] F.S.R. 379
Copyright in Maps & Plans (COPYRIGHT: "MAP FOR MEN": IMMORALITY: SWITZERLAND)   [1985] E.C.C. 549; [1986] F.S.R. 38
Copyright in Tender Documents (COPYRIGHT: Germany)
                                [1985] E.C.C. 562; [1986] F.S.R. 36
Cormandel Fertilizers Ltd v. Cormandel Cements Ltd (TRADE MARK: INFRINGEMENT: PASSING OFF: AMENDMENT OF PLEADINGS: India: H.C.)   (1989) 16 I.P.L.R. 6
Corning Glass Works & Corning Ltd's Amendment Application (PATENT: AMENDMENT: DISCLAIMER: EXPLANATION: C.A.)   [1984] R.P.C. 459
Corning Glass/Moulding (EUROPEAN PATENT: INVENTIVE STEP: ADVANTAGES, NOT NECESSARILY REQUIRED TO SHOW NON-OBVIOUSNESS: AGED ART: COMBINATION OF CITATIONS: T366/89: EPO)   [1993] E.P.O.R. 266
Coromandel Fertilizers Ltd v. Coromandel Cements Ltd (TRADE MARK: INFRINGEMENT: Ad interim INJUNCTION VACATED: India: H.C.)
                                        (1989) 14 I.P.L.R. 105
Coronet Property Group Ltd v. Coronet Equities Ltd (PASSING OFF: INTERIM INJUNCTION: SERIOUS QUESTION TO BE TRIED: BALANCE OF CONVENIENCE: PARTIES' ACTIVITIES NOT IN COMPETITION: New Zealand: H.C.)11 I.P.R. 46
Corporate Group Holdings Ltd v. Corporate Resources Group Ltd (CONFIDENTIAL INFORMATION: DOCUMENT: RESTRAINT ON USE: New Zealand: H.C.)
                                        [1991] 1 N.Z.L.R. 115
Corrs Pavey Whiting & Byrne v. Collector of Customs for Victoria (ADMINISTRATIVE LAW: PATENT: ACCESS TO DOCUMENTS: STATUTORY RIGHT TO ACCESS: INTERPRETATION: Australia: Fed. Ct)   10 I.P.R. 53
Corvina Quality Foods Pty Ltd's Application (TRADE MARKS: OBJECTION: DISCLAIMER: DISTINCTIVENESS: MARKS NOT INHERENTLY DISTINCTIVE: MARKS NOT DISTINCTIVE IN FACT: REGISTRATION IN PART B REFUSED: Australia: Pat. Off.)   22 I.P.R. 66
COS Trade Mark (TRADE MARK: APPLICATION: GEOGRAPHICAL NAME: DISCLAIMER: T.M.Reg.)   [1993] R.P.C. 67
Costa v. G.R. & I.E. Daking Pty Ltd (PETTY PATENT: SECTION 28 NOTICE: OBTAINING: PRIOR USE: WHETHER FOR REASONABLE TRIAL: LACK OF NOVELTY: JOINT INVENTORSHIP: Australia: AIPO)   29 I.P.R. 241

Costelloe v. Johnston, Johnston and We Fit Doors Ltd (t/a Doorways) (COPYRIGHT: DESIGN: INFRINGEMENT: DOOR: WHETHER NEW OR ORIGINAL: WHETHER PRIOR PUBLICATION RENDERING EXISTING REGISTRATION INVALID: COUNTERCLAIM: FORM OF RELIEF: EXPUNCTION: Ireland: H.C.)
[1991] 1 I.R. 305

Cotterill v. Trenton Pty Ltd (PATENT: APPLICATION: OPPOSITION: DIRECTIONS ON PROVISION OF FURTHER AND BETTER PARTICULARS: Australia: AIPO)
28 I.P.R. 629

Cougar Marine Ltd v. Roberts (TRADE MARK: OPPOSITION: DIVISIONAL APPLICATION: PROPRIETORSHIP: ABANDONMENT BY PRIOR USERS: PRIOR REGISTRATION: GOODS OF THE SAME DESCRIPTION: HONEST CONCURRENT USER: Australia: AIPO)   27 I.P.R. 530

Counterfeit Goods Draft Regulation (CUSTOMS: TRADE IN COUNTERFEIT AND PIRATED GOODS: PROHIBITION: E.C. Council)
[1994] 1 C.M.L.R. 37; [1994] F.S.R. 325

COUNTRY CLASSICS Trade Marks (TRADE MARK: APPLICATION: PART B: EVIDENCE: PRACTICE: DoT)   [1993] R.P.C. 524

Country Road Clothing Pty Ltd v. Najee Nominees Pty Ltd (TRADE PRACTICES: MISLEADING OR DECEPTIVE CONDUCT: COMPARATIVE ADVERTISEMENT: INVITATION TO COMPARE DIFFERENT PRODUCTS: FACTUAL ACCURACY OF ADVERTISEMENT: Australia: Fed. Ct)   20 I.P.R. 419

County Sound plc v. Ocean Sound Ltd (PASSING OFF: INTERLOCUTORY INJUNCTION: ARGUABLE CASE: RADIO PROGRAMME TITLES: *The Gold AM*: DISTINCTIVENESS: REPUTATION, CONFUSION AND DAMAGE: C.A.)
[1991] F.S.R. 367; 16 I.P.R. 211

Courtaulds Textiles (Holdings) Ltd's Application (TRADE MARK: APPLICATION: ADJECTIVAL COMPOUND INDICATING QUALITY OR CHARACTER: SIGNIFICANT OVERSEAS USE: CAPABLE OF BECOMING DISTINCTIVE: Australia: A.I.P.O.)   30 I.P.R. 624

Cowan v. Avel Pty Ltd (COPYRIGHT: THREATS: DAMAGES: COMPUTATION: LOSS OF SALES: EFFECT OF TAXABILITY OF PROFITS: Australia: Fed. Ct)   32 I.P.R. 96

CPC (United Kingdom) Ltd v. Keenan (TRADE MARK: INFRINGEMENT: PASSING OFF: OXFORD MARMALADE: Ch.D.)   [1986] F.S.R. 527

CPC/Amylolytic enzymes (EUROPEAN PATENT: MICRO-ORGANISMS: DEPOSIT AND AVAILABILITY: T118/87: EPO)
[1990] E.P.O.R. 298; [1991] O.J. EPO 474

CPC/Cheese spreads (EUROPEAN PATENT: OPPOSITION: PROCEDURE: FRESH DOCUMENTS AT ORAL PROCEEDINGS: FRESH DOCUMENTS ON APPEAL: T559/88: EPO)   [1990] E.P.O.R. 430

CPC/Flavour concentrates (EUROPEAN PATENT: NOVELTY: INEVITABLE RESULT: UNEXPECTED EFFECT, ATTAINMENT OF BY ONLY PART OF CLAIMED SUBJECT-MATTER: T303/86: EPO)   [1989] E.P.O.R. 95

CPC/Micro-organisms (EUROPEAN PATENT: DISCLOSURE: NATURE OF REQUIREMENT: MICRO-ORGANISMS: DEPOSIT OF CULTURES: PROCEDURE: FAIRNESS TO APPLICANTS: T39/88: EPO)
[1990] E.P.O.R. 41; [1989] O.J. EPO 499

CQR Security Systems Ltd's Patent (PATENT PRACTICE: PETITION FOR REVOCATION: JOINDER OF CO-PETITIONER: WHETHER JUST AND CONVENIENT: WHETHER NECESSARY TO GIVE SECURITY FOR COSTS: AMENDMENT OF PLEADINGS: COSTS: APPLICATION TO AMEND PARTICULARS OF OBJECTIONS AFTER CLAIM AMENDED: APPROPRIATE ORDER AND DATE FOR TAXATION: Pat. Ct)   [1992] F.S.R. 303

Crespo (FREE MOVEMENT OF GOODS: TRANSIT: DESIGN RIGHTS: SPARE PARTS: INDUSTRIAL PROPERTY PROTECTION ONLY OFFERED IN TRANSIT STATE: WHETHER JURISDICTION TO HEAR INDUSTRIAL PROPERTY ACTION: France: S.C.)   [1992] 1 C.M.L.R. 1029; [1992] F.S.R. 430

Crest Homes plc v. Marks (COPYRIGHT: INFRINGEMENT: ANTON PILLER: PRACTICE: DISCOVERY: USE OF DOCUMENTS IN CONTEMPT PROCEEDINGS IN EARLIER ACTION: C.A.)   [1987] F.S.R. 305; [1987] 3 W.L.R. 48 (PRIVILEGE AGAINST SELF-INCRIMINATION: APPEAL DISMISSED: H.L.)
[1987] A.C. 829; [1987] 2 All E.R. 1074; [1988] R.P.C. 21; [1987] 3 W.L.R. 293

Criminal Justice Commission v. Nationwide News Pty Ltd (CONFIDENTIAL INFORMATION: INFORMATION MOSTLY IN PUBLIC DOMAIN: INJUNCTION: SERIOUS QUESTION TO BE TRIED: BALANCING HARM DONE BY PUBLICATION AGAINST PUBLIC INTEREST: STAY: CIRCUMSTANCES: Australia: Fed. Ct)
28 I.P.R. 360

Critikon/Infusion apparatus (EUROPEAN PATENT: AMENDMENT AND CORRECTION: GENERALISATION: T691/90: EPO)   [1994] E.P.O.R. 51

Crittall Windows Ltd v. Stormseal (UPVC) Window Systems Ltd (TRADE MARK: INFRINGEMENT: SUMMARY JUDGMENT: BREACH OF REGISTERED USER AGREEMENT: WHETHER BREACHES CAPABLE OF REMEDY: RELIEF FROM FORFEITURE: Ch.D.)   [1991] R.P.C. 265

Crocker v. Papunya Tula Artists Pty Ltd (TRADE PRACTICES: MISLEADING OR DECEPTIVE CONDUCT: COPYRIGHT: SECOND EDITION OF BOOK: AMENDMENTS: Australia: Fed. Ct)   61 A.L.R. 529; 5 I.P.R. 426

Crocodile Marketing Ltd v. Griffith Vintners Pty Ltd (TRADE PRACTICES: SALE OF LOW ALCOHOL WINE TO OVERSEAS PURCHASER: REPRESENTATIONS AS TO ALCOHOL, CALORIE AND OTHER CONTENT OF WINE: Australia: S.C.(NSW))   16 I.P.R. 222

Crooks Michell Peacock Pty Ltd v. Kaiser (TRADE MARK: OPPOSITION: PROPRIETORSHIP: DISTINCTIVENESS: DECEPTION AND CONFUSION: ESTOPPEL: HONEST ADOPTION OF MARK: GOOD FAITH: Australia: AIPO)
29 I.P.R. 225

Cruise (Tom) and Kidman (Nicole) v. Southdown Press Pty Ltd, *sub nom.* Tom Cruise and Nicole Kidman v. Southdown Press Pty Ltd

Crusader Oil N.L. v. Crusader Minerals N.Z. Ltd (PASSING OFF: FOREIGN PLAINTIFF: REPUTATION: New Zealand: H.C.)   3 I.P.R. 171

Crusta Fruit Juices Pty Ltd v. Cadbury Schweppes Pty Ltd (TRADE MARK: INFRINGEMENT: CRESTA/CRUSTA: INTERLOCUTORY INJUNCTION: BALANCE OF CONVENIENCE: IMPERFECT RECOLLECTION: Australia: Fed. Ct)   31 I.P.R. 471

Crystal Glass Industries Ltd v. Alwinco Products Ltd (COPYRIGHT: INFRINGEMENT: THREE-DIMENSIONAL REPRODUCTION: INDIRECT COPYING: JOINT TORTFEASORS: CONVERSION DAMAGES: New Zealand: C.A.)
(1986) 5 I.P.R. 192; [1985] 1 N.Z.L.R. 716; [1986] R.P.C. 259

Crystal Knitters v. Bombay Vestors (TRADE MARK: INFRINGEMENT: CRYSTAL/COASTAL: INTERIM INJUNCTION: THREATS: India: H.C.)
(1989) 16 I.P.L.R. 39

Cselt/Parabolic reflector antenna (EUROPEAN PATENT: PRIORITY: GENERIC CHEMICAL FORMULAE, VARIATION IN: INVENTIVE STEP: COMPUTER CALCULATIONS: CONFLICTING GOALS: T36/82: EPO)
[1979–85] E.P.O.R. B433; [1983] O.J. EPO 269

CSIRO v. Asterol International (PATENT: OPPOSITION: APPLICATION FOR
EXTENSION OF TIME TO LODGE NOTICE OF OPPOSITION: Australia: AIPO)
27 I.P.R. 48

CSIRO v. CEM Corp. (PATENT: APPLICATION: OPPOSITION: STATEMENT OF
GROUNDS AND PARTICULARS: DISMISSAL: REQUEST: DIRECTIONS: Australia:
AIPO) 29 I.P.R. 72

CSIRO/Arthropodicidal compounds (EUROPEAN PATENT: PRIORITY: GENUS/
SPECIES: T85/87: EPO) [1989] E.P.O.R. 24

Cue Design Pty Ltd v. Playboy Enterprises Pty Ltd (TRADE PRACTICES: PASSING OFF:
CONFUSION: RELEVANT AUDIENCE: Australia: Fed. Ct)
(1983) 45 A.L.R. 535

Cuisine Nature CLG Inc.'s Application (TRADE MARK: APPLICATION: DESCRIPTIVE
WORDS: DISCLAIMER: REFUSAL OF REGISTRATION: Australia: Pat. Off.)
17 I.P.R. 143

Cummins/Reimbursement (EUROPEAN PATENT: FEES: REIMBURSEMENT OF
APPEAL FEE: PROCEDURE: INHERENT JURISDICTION OF BOARDS OF APPEAL:
T99/82: EPO) [1979–85] E.P.O.R. B528

Cunard Lines Ltd's Application (TRADE MARK: APPLICATION: DISTINCTIVENESS:
LETTERS AND NUMERALS: IMPLIED ROYAL PATRONAGE OR AUTHORITY:
GOODS SOLD ON BOARD PASSENGER LINER: Australia: AIPO) 27 I.P.R. 527

Cutsforth v. Mansfield Inns Ltd (RESTRICTIVE PRACTICES: BREWERY: TIED
HOUSES: RESTRICTIONS ON GAMING MACHINES: ARTICLE 85(1): Q.B.D.)
[1986] 1 C.M.L.R. 1; [1986] 1 F.T.L.R. 65

Cyanamid/Melt spinning (EUROPEAN PATENT: APPEAL: PROCEDURE: FRESH
PRIOR ART: TO REBUT NEWLY EMPHASISED REASONS: INVENTIVE STEP:
PREJUDICE: MEANING OF: T49/85: EPO) [1989] E.P.O.R. 234

Cyberexact/Printer ribbon errors (EUROPEAN PATENT: CLAIMS: AMBIGUITY
RESULTING IN INSUFFICIENCY: RELATION TO CLARITY: SUFFICIENCY:
T684/89: EPO) [1993] E.P.O.R. 173

Cycle Corp. of India Ltd v. T.I. Raleigh Industries Ltd (TRADE MARK:
RECTIFICATION: NON-OBSERVANCE OF QUALITY CONTROL: India:
H.C.) (1992) 17 I.P.L.R. 155

D'Urban Inc. v. Canpio Pty Ltd (TRADE MARKS: APPLICATION FOR REMOVAL:
NEED TO PROVE NON-USE: EFFECTIVE SERVICE: EVIDENCE SERVED OUT OF
TIME: FAILURE TO SEEK EXTENSION OF TIME: "SPECIAL CIRCUMSTANCES":
Australia: Pat. Off.) 17 I.P.R. 486

D'Vaiz Chemical v. Kundu Coatar Co. (TRADE MARK: COPYRIGHT:
REGISTRATION: PRIOR RIGHTS: PRIOR USER: INTERLOCUTORY
INJUNCTION: India: H.C.) (1990) 15 I.P.L.R. 80

D2B Systems Co. Ltd (Re) (RESTRICTIVE PRACTICES: JOINT VENTURES: JOINT
DEVELOPMENT OF STANDARD COMMAND FRAMEWORK FOR HOME
ENTERTAINMENT BROADCASTING EQUIPMENT: INTENTION TO EXEMPT:
E.C. Comm.) [1991] 4 C.M.L.R. 905

Da Gama Textile Co. Ltd v. Vision Creations C.C. (COPYRIGHT: INFRINGEMENT:
SCOPE OF PROTECTION: THREE-DIMENSIONAL REPRODUCTION OF ARTISTIC
WORK: South Africa: D&CLD) 1995 (1) S.A. 398

Daca/Suppression device (EUROPEAN PATENT: FEES: SMALL AMOUNT EXCEPTION:
OPPOSITION: PROCEDURE: EXPEDITION: T290/90: EPO)
[1992] E.P.O.R. 278; [1992] O.J. EPO 368

Daido Kogyo KK's Patent (PATENT: RESTORATION: TIME LIMITS: PROTECTION OF
THIRD PARTIES: Pat. Ct: C.A.) [1984] R.P.C. 97

Daikin Kogyo/Interruption in delivery of mail (EUROPEAN PATENT: FEES: REFUNDED WHERE APPLICATION WITHOUT PURPOSE: PROCEDURE: GENERAL INTERRUPTION IN MAIL: T192/84: EPO)
[1979–85] E.P.O.R. C984; [1985] O.J. EPO 39
Daily v. Etablissements Fernand Berchet (PATENT: INFRINGEMENT: VALIDITY: CONSTRUCTION: "GILLETTE DEFENCE": Pat. C.C.) [1991] R.P.C. 587
(Appeal allowed: C.A.) [1992] F.S.R. 533; [1993] R.P.C. 357
Daimaru Pty Ltd v. Daimaru KK (TRADE MARKS: OPPOSITION TO REGISTRATION: PROPRIETORSHIP: INTENTION TO USE: USE LIKELY TO DECEIVE OR CAUSE CONFUSION: Australia: Pat. Off.) 19 I.P.R. 129
Daimer Industries Pty Ltd v. Daimaru KK (TRADE MARK: OPPOSITION: DAIMARU/DAIMER: PROPRIETORSHIP: FIRST USE BY OPPONENT ONLY BRIEFLY BEFORE APPLICATION BY APPLICANT: LIKELIHOOD OF CONFUSION: BONA FIDE INTENTION TO USE: USE ON PRICE TICKET: Australia: AIPO)
27 I.P.R. 124
Daimler Benz AG v. Hybo Hindustan (TRADE MARK: INFRINGEMENT: PASSING OFF: BENZ: GOODS OF DIFFERENT DESCRIPTION: INTERIM INJUNCTION: India: H.C.) (1994) 19 I.P.L.R. 224
Dalgety Australia Operations Ltd v. F.F. Seeley Nominees Pty Ltd (DESIGN: INFRINGEMENT: WHETHER FEATURE OF A DIMENSION CONSTITUTES A DESIGN: IMITATION: Australia: S.C.(S.A.)) 68 A.L.R. 458; 5 I.P.R. 97
(Fed. Ct) 64 A.L.R. 421; 6 I.P.R. 361
Dalgety Foods Holland BV v. Deb-Its Ltd (PRACTICE: SETTLEMENT: INTENTION TO OBTAIN CONSENT ORDER INCORPORATING UNDERTAKINGS: ACTUAL WORDING NOT AGREED: WHETHER AGREEMENT BINDING: Ch.D.)
[1994] F.S.R. 125
Dalgety Spillers Foods Ltd v. Food Brokers Ltd (PASSING OFF: GET-UP: POT NOODLES: INTERLOCUTORY INJUNCTION: EVIDENCE: Ch.D.)
[1994] F.S.R. 504
Dan-Pal/Light transmitting wall panels (EUROPEAN PATENT: FEES: REIMBURSEMENT OF APPEAL FEE: INVENTIVE STEP: SIMPLICITY: OPPOSITION: PROCEDURE: DEPENDENT CLAIMS NOT CHALLENGED: T293/88: EPO)
[1992] E.P.O.R. 240; [1992] O.J. EPO 220
Dana Corp. v. Unidrive (TRADE MARK: APPLICATION: OPPOSITION: PROPRIETORSHIP: DISTINCTIVENESS: SUBSTANTIALLY IDENTICAL OR DECEPTIVELY SIMILAR: Australia: AIPO) 32 I.P.R. 163
see also, *sub nom.* Unidrive v. Dana Corp.
Danby Pty Ltd v. Commissioner of Patents (PATENT: TIME FOR LODGING NOTICE OF OPPOSITION TO GRANT: EXTENSION OF TIME: STATUTORY INTERPRETATION: Australia: Fed. Ct) 82 A.L.R. 491; 12 I.P.R. 151
Danby Pty Ltd v. Rib Loc Group Ltd (PATENT: OPPOSITION: APPLICATION FOR EXTENSION OF TIME FOR LODGING NOTICE OF OPPOSITION: Australia: Pat. Off.) 10 I.P.R. 277
Danco Clothing (Pty) Ltd v. Nu-Care Marketing Sales & Promotions (Pty) Ltd (TRADE MARK: EXPUNGEMENT: LOCUS STANDI: AGGRIEVED PERSON: South Africa: TPD) 1990 (2) S.A. 619
(A.D.) 1991 (4) S.A. 850
Dandenong Rangers Bakery's Application (TRADE MARKS: WITHDRAWAL OF ACCEPTANCE FOR REGISTRATION: EXAMINER'S IGNORANCE OF A RELEVANT APPLICATION: WHETHER POWER TO DIRECT READVERTISEMENT OF ACCEPTANCE: POWER TO IMPOSE DIFFERENT CONDITIONS AND LIMITATIONS: DECEPTIVE SIMILARITY WITH CITED MARK: WITHDRAWAL OF ACCEPTANCE: Australia: Pat. Off.) 19 I.P.R. 65

Dart Industries Inc. v. Decor Corp. Pty Ltd (PRACTICE AND PROCEDURE: INTERLOCUTORY JUDGMENT: LEAVE TO APPEAL: DISCRETION: PATENT INFRINGEMENT: ACCOUNT OF PROFITS: Australia: Fed. Ct)
104 A.L.R. 621; 23 I.P.R. 1

Dart Industries Inc. v. Decor Corp. Pty Ltd (PATENT: INFRINGEMENT: CONSTRUCTION OF CLAIMS: INVALIDITY: WHETHER CLAIMS FAIRLY BASED ON INVENTION DESCRIBED IN SPECIFICATION: INUTILITY: CLARITY: Australia: Fed. Ct)
13 I.P.R. 385

Dart Industries Inc. v. Decor Corp. Pty Ltd (DESIGN: INFRINGEMENT: DEFINITION OF "ARTICLE": INVALIDITY OF REGISTERED DESIGN: VISUAL COMPARISON: COMPARISON WITH PRIOR ART: Australia: S.C.(Vic.))
11 I.P.R. 134

Dart Industries Inc. v. Decor Corp. Pty Ltd (DESIGN: SUBJECT-MATTER OF PROTECTION: INFRINGEMENT: CONSIDERATION OF PRIOR ART: Australia: Fed. Ct)
15 I.P.R. 403

Dart Industries Inc. v. Decor Corp. Pty Ltd (PATENTS: INFRINGEMENT: ACCOUNT OF PROFITS: DEDUCTION FOR INFRINGER'S GENERAL OVERHEAD COSTS: WHETHER ALLOWABLE: QUANTIFICATION OF: ONUS OF PROOF CONCERNING: MANUFACTURE AND SALE OF COMPOSITE GOODS INCLUDING PATENTED INVENTION: KITCHEN CONTAINERS FITTED WITH PATENTED SEAL: WHETHER ACCOUNT SHOULD ALSO INCLUDE PROFIT FROM CONTAINERS: Australia: H.C.)
116 A.L.R. 385; 179 C.L.R. 101; 26 I.P.R. 193; [1994] F.S.R. 567

Dart Industries Inc. v. Decor Corp. Pty Ltd (PRACTICE AND PROCEDURE: INTERLOCUTORY JUDGMENT: LEAVE TO APPEAL: DISCRETION: PATENT INFRINGEMENT: ACCOUNT OF PROFITS: Australia: Fed. Ct)
104 A.L.R. 621; 23 I.P.R. 1

Dart Industries Inc. v. Grace Bros Pty Ltd (PRACTICE AND PROCEDURE: PATENTS: PROVISION OF PARTICULARS OF INFRINGEMENTS: REQUIREMENT FOR PARTICULARS UNDER P.A.52, S.117: Australia: S.C.(Vic.))
18 I.P.R. 87

Dart Industries Inc. v. Prestige Group (Aust.) Pty Ltd (PATENT: CLAIMS: CONSTRUCTION: REPRESENTATIONS TO EXAMINER: MISREPRESENTATION: Australia: S.C.(Vic.))
16 I.P.R. 235

Dash Ltd v. Philip King Tailoring Ltd (TRADE MARKS: TRADE NAMES: PASSING OFF: SIMILAR NAMES DASH/DASCH: SIMILAR BUSINESSES: INTERIM INTERDICT: BALANCE OF CONVENIENCE: PROTECTION OF LONG ESTABLISHED BUSINESS AGAINST NEWLY-FORMED BUSINESS: Scotland: I.H.)
1989 S.L.T. 39

Data East USA Inc. v. Epyx Inc. (COPYRIGHT: INFRINGEMENT: SUBSTANTIAL SIMILARITY: RELATIONSHIP BETWEEN IDEAS AND EXPRESSION: SUFFICIENCY OF EVIDENCE OF CONTENTS OF AUDIO-VISUAL WORK: USA: C.A.)
13 I.P.R. 620

Davide Campari Milano SpA's Application (RESTRICTIVE PRACTICES: DISTRIBUTION SYSTEM: APPLICATION TO RENEW EXEMPTION: COMFORT LETTER INSTEAD: E.C. Comm.)
[1989] 4 C.M.L.R. 139

Davidoff Extension SA v. Davidoff Commercio E Industria Ltda (TRADE MARK: USE OF ANOTHER COMPANY'S MARK: APPLICATION FOR EXPUNGEMENT: REPUTATION: DECEPTION OF PUBLIC: DISCRETION: Singapore: H.C.)
[1988] 1 M.L.J. 234

Davis (J. & S.) (Holdings) Ltd v. Wright Health Group Ltd (COPYRIGHT: INFRINGEMENT: DENTAL IMPRESSION TRAYS: ORIGINALITY: DRAWINGS: SCULPTURES: NON-EXPERT DEFENCE: SUBSTANTIAL PART: Ch.D.)
[1988] R.P.C. 403

Davis v. Commonwealth of Australia (CONSTITUTIONAL LAW: POWERS OF COMMONWEALTH EXECUTIVE: AUSTRALIA BICENTENARY: TRADE MARKS: Australia: H.C.) 168 C.L.R. 79

Dawson v. Hinshaw Music Inc. (COPYRIGHT: INFRINGEMENT: PRIMA FACIE CASE: SUBSTANTIAL SIMILARITY: TWO PRONG TEST: "TOTAL CONCEPT AND FEEL": ORDINARY OR LAY OBSERVER VERSUS INTENDED AUDIENCE: EVIDENCE: SUBSTANTIAL SIMILARITY OF COPYRIGHTABLE WORKS: TESTIMONY FROM MEMBERS OF INTENDED AUDIENCE: EXPERT TESTIMONY ON INTENDED AUDIENCE: SHEET MUSIC VERSUS AUDIO RECORDINGS: USA: C.A.)
18 I.P.R. 256

DDD Ltd and Delta Chemie's Agreement (RESTRICTIVE PRACTICES: KNOW-HOW: EXCLUSIVE DEALING: TRADE MARKS: NOTICE: E.C. Comm.)
[1988] 4 C.M.L.R. 742; [1989] F.S.R. 52
(LICENCE CAUGHT BY ARTICLE 85(1): GROUP EXEMPTION: REGULATION 1983/83 NOT APPLICABLE: INDIVIDUAL EXEMPTION GRANTED: E.C. Comm.)
[1989] 4 C.M.L.R. 535; [1989] 1 F.S.R. 497

De Beers Industrial Diamond Division (Pty) Ltd v. General Electric Co. (PATENT: VALIDITY: CLAIMS: INCORPORATION BY REFERENCE: APPEAL: South Africa: TPD) 1987 (4) S.A. 362
(SPECIFICATION: FUNCTION: REASONABLE CERTAINTY: SKILLED ADDRESSEE: TEACHING OF: INSTRUCTIONS CONTAINED IN SPECIFICATION AS TO HOW INVENTION WORKS, OR HOW TO MAKE OR OPERATE IT: INCORPORATION BY REFERENCE OF THE TEACHING OF ANOTHER PATENT SPECIFICATION: AVAILABILITY OF OTHER PATENT SPECIFICATION: South Africa: A.D.)
1988 (4) S.A. 886

De Beers Industrial Diamond Division (Pty) Ltd v. General Electric Co. (PATENT: EXTENSION: INADEQUATE REMUNERATION: South Africa: A.D.)
1983 (1) S.A. 207

De Erven G. De Boer BV/Opponent-identifiability (EUROPEAN PATENT: OPPOSITION: PROCEDURE: IDENTIFICATION OF OPPONENT: T635/88: EPO) [1994] E.P.O.R. 358; [1993] O.J. EPO 698

De Garis v. Neville Jeffress Pidler Pty Ltd (COPYRIGHT: ARTICLE IN NEWSPAPERS: PRESS-CLIPPING AND MEDIA MONITORING SERVICE: ARTICLE WRITTEN ON COMMISSION: OTHER ARTICLES WRITTEN BY JOURNALIST EMPLOYED UNDER CONTRACT OF SERVICE: OWNERSHIP OF COPYRIGHT IN ARTICLES WRITTEN BY EMPLOYED JOURNALIST: WHETHER ANY OF "FAIR DEALING" DEFENCES APPLY: WHETHER IMPLIED LICENCE TO REPRODUCE: WHETHER RESPONDENT'S SERVICE CONSTITUTED NEWSPAPER, MAGAZINE OR SIMILAR PERIODICAL: INFRINGEMENT NOT EXCUSED BY FAIR DEALING DEFENCES: JOURNALIST OWNS RELEVANT COPYRIGHT: INJUNCTIONS GRANTED: Australia: Fed. Ct) 18 I.P.R. 292

De La Rue Systems/Apportionment of costs (EUROPEAN PATENT: APPEAL: PROCEDURE: STATEMENT OF GROUNDS: ADMISSIBILITY: COSTS: UNNECESSARY HEARING: APPORTIONED: EPO: INTERNAL PROMPTITUDE: T154/90: EPO) [1994] E.P.O.R. 284; [1993] O.J. EPO 505

De Laval-Stork (RESTRICTIVE PRACTICES: JOINT VENTURES: INTENTION TO RENEW EXEMPTION: E.C. Comm.) [1988] 4 C.M.L.R. 187

De Verenigde Bloemenveilingen Aalsmeer BA (RESTRICTIVE PRACTICES: AGRICULTURE: FLOWER AUCTIONS: AUCTION RULES AND STANDARD FORM CONTRACTS: INTENTION TO APPROVE: E.C. Comm.)
[1988] 4 C.M.L.R. 22

Deacons v. Bridge (RESTRAINT OF TRADE: SOLICITORS: PARTNERSHIP: WIDTH OF COVENANT: Hong Kong: P.C.) [1984] 2 All E.R. 19; [1984] A.C. 705

Deane v. Brian Hickey Invention Research Pty Ltd (TRADE PRACTICES: MISLEADING CONDUCT: SALE OF BUSINESS: FORM OF RELIEF: Australia: Fed. Ct)   11 I.P.R. 651

Dearborn Chemical Co. Ltd v. Rohm and Haas Co. (PATENT: APPLICATION: OPPOSITION: AMENDMENT: OPPOSITION TO AMENDMENT: IN SUBSTANCE DISCLOSED: INCONSISTENCY: ESSENTIAL FEATURES: ALLOWABILITY: REFUSAL: Australia: AIPO)   31 I.P.R. 121

Decina Bathroomware Pty Ltd's Application (TRADE MARKS: APPLICATION: DISTINCTIVENESS: EVIDENCE NECESSARY: INHERENTLY ADAPTED TO DISTINGUISH: Australia: Pat. Off.)   24 I.P.R. 95

Decor Corp. Pty Ltd v. Dart Industries Inc., *sub nom.* Dart Industries Inc. v. Decor Corp. Pty Ltd

Decor Corp. Pty Ltd v. Deeko Australia Pty Ltd (TRADE MARKS: OPPOSITION: WHETHER MARKS SUBSTANTIALLY IDENTICAL OR DECEPTIVELY SIMILAR: CIRCUMSTANCES OF TRADE: LESS WEIGHT ON PHONETIC COMPARISON: WHETHER INTENTION TO USE FOR ALL GOODS SPECIFIED: ABSENCE OF CLEAR EVIDENCE TO THE CONTRARY: REFERENCE TO CHARACTER OF GOODS: WORD NOT DISTINCTIVE IN FACT: WORD CAPABLE OF BECOMING DISTINCTIVE: Australia: Pat. Off.)   11 I.P.R. 531

Decorflex Ltd's Application (PATENT: APPLICATION: PRACTICE: EXTENDING TIME LIMITS: DISCRETION: Pat. Ct)   [1984] R.P.C. 55

Decro Paint & Hardware (Pty) Ltd v. Plascon-Evans Paints (Tvl) Ltd (TRADE MARK: INFRINGEMENT: CONFUSION: South Africa: TPD)   1982 (4) S.A. 213
(Appeal: A.D.) 1984 (3) S.A. 647

Dee Corp. plc's Applications (TRADE MARKS: APPLICATIONS: SERVICE MARKS: WHETHER RETAILING A SERVICE: Ch.D.)
[1989] 1 F.S.R. 267; [1990] R.P.C. 159
(C.A.) [1990] R.P.C. 159

Deekonda Pedda Chinniah v. Mangalore Ganesh Beedi Works (TRADE MARK: INFRINGEMENT: PASSING OFF: INTERIM INJUNCTION: APPEAL: India: H.C.)   (1989) 16 I.P.L.R. 53

Deere/Coupling rod (EUROPEAN PATENT: OPPOSITION: PROCEDURE: ADMISSIBILITY: NOTICE OF OPPOSITION: PRIOR ART: REQUIREMENTS OF IN PRIOR USE CASES: PRELIMINARY COMMUNICATION, WHEN REQUIRED: FEES: REIMBURSEMENT OF APPEAL FEE: NO PREJUDICE: T538/89: EPO)
[1991] E.P.O.R. 445

Deere/Mention of grant (EUROPEAN PATENT: APPLICATION: PROCEDURE: MENTION OF GRANT, INCOMPLETE, WHETHER VALID: COMPENSATION CLAIM AGAINST EPO: FEES: REIMBURSEMENT OF APPEAL FEE: J14/87: EPO)
[1988] E.P.O.R. 419; [1988] O.J. EPO 295

Def Lepp Music v. Stuart-Brown (COPYRIGHT: INFRINGEMENT: SERVICE OUTSIDE JURISDICTION: TERRITORIALITY: Ch.D.)   [1986] R.P.C. 273

Deforeit's Patent (PATENT: EUROPEAN PATENT (U.K.): PRACTICE: RESTORATION: C.-G.)   [1986] R.P.C. 142

Degussa/Furnace blacks (EUROPEAN PATENT: NOVELTY: DIFFERENT OBJECT: T53/82: EPO)   [1979–85] E.P.O.R. B463

Dellareed Ltd v. Delkim Developments (PATENT: INFRINGEMENT: IMPLIED LICENCE: EXHAUSTION OF RIGHTS: MODIFICATION OF PRODUCT: PRACTICE: ACQUIESCENCE: DECLARATION: ACCOUNT OF PROFITS: Ch.D.)
[1988] F.S.R. 329

Delphic Wholesalers Pty Ltd v. Elco Food Co. Pty Ltd (CONTRACT: INDUCEMENT TO BREACH: TRADE MARK: INFRINGEMENT: REGISTERED USER AS PLAINTIFF: PARALLEL IMPORTATION: Australia: S.C.(Vic.))   8 I.P.R. 545

Delta/Transfer of opposition (EUROPEAN PATENT: ENLARGED BOARD OF APPEAL: PRESIDENT OF THE EPO: OPPOSITION: PROCEDURE: TRANSFER OF OPPOSITION: T349/86: EPO)   [1989] E.P.O.R. 59; [1988] O.J. EPO 345

De Maudsley v. Palumbo (BREACH OF CONFIDENCE: IDEA FOR A NIGHT CLUB: WHETHER INFORMATION IMPARTED UNDER OBLIGATION OF CONFIDENCE: WHETHER INFORMATION TOO VAGUE AS TO QUALIFY AS CONFIDENTIAL: USE OF INFORMATION: Ch.D.)   [1996] F.S.R. 447; [1996] E.M.L.R. 460

Dempster's Application (TRADE MARKS: SERIES: WHAT CONSTITUTES SERIES: EFFECT OF HYPHEN: DIVISIONAL APPLICATION: Australia: Pat. Off.)
23 I.P.R. 669

Denev/Cancer cells and lymphocytes game (EUROPEAN PATENT: RE-ESTABLISHMENT OF RIGHTS: STATEMENT OF GROUNDS: INSUFFICIENT: J03/85: EPO)   [1986] E.P.O.R. 150

Dennison Manufacturing Co. v. Monarch Marking Systems Inc. (PATENTS: APPLICATION: OPPOSITION: OBVIOUSNESS: NOVELTY: EXPERT EVIDENCE: Australia: Fed. Ct)   66 A.L.R. 265; 1 I.P.R. 431

Dentsply International Inc. v. Bayer AG (PATENT: OPPOSITION: EXTENSION OF TIME LIMIT: Australia: Pat. Off.)   7 I.P.R. 408

Dentsply/Cartridge for filling dental cavities (EUROPEAN PATENT: APPLICATION: PROCEDURE: THIRD-PARTY OBSERVATIONS: LATE SUBMISSIONS: INVENTIVE STEP: PROBLEM NEED NOT BE SPECIFIED IN EXPRESS TERMS IN PRIOR ART: STIMULATED TO GENERATE TEST: T793/90: EPO)   [1993] E.P.O.R. 168

Dentsply/Inadmissible late filing (EUROPEAN PATENT: OPPOSITION: PROCEDURE: FRESH CITATION ON APPEAL: DELIBERATE ABUSE: PRINCIPLE OF GOOD FAITH: T534/89: EPO)   [1994] E.P.O.R. 540

Derby & Co. Ltd v. Weldon (No. 9) (COMPUTER DATABASE: PRACTICE: DISCOVERY: INSPECTION: WHETHER "DOCUMENT": EXTENT TO WHICH INSPECTION TO BE ORDERED: Ch.D.)   [1991] 1 W.L.R. 652

Dermatone Laboratories Inc. v. Omni-Pharm SA (TRADE MARKS: APPLICATION: OPPOSITION: SHARED ELEMENT COMMON TO TRADE: Australia: Pat. Off.)
21 I.P.R. 667

Derria AG's Application (TRADE MARK: APPLICATION: OPPOSITION: DECEPTION AND CONFUSION: Australia: Pat. Off.)   4 I.P.R. 433

Detras/Target apparatus (EUROPEAN PATENT: BOARD OF APPEAL: FAILURE TO REPLY TO PRELIMINARY COMMUNICATION, EFFECT OF: NOVELTY: INHERENT FUNCTION OF APPARATUS: PRIORITY: IDENTITY OF INVENTION: T229/88: EPO)   [1991] E.P.O.R. 407

Deutsche Gelatine-Fabriken, Stoess & Co./Opponent – identifiability (EUROPEAN PATENT: OPPOSITION: PROCEDURE: IDENTIFICATION OF OPPONENT: AMENDMENT AND CORRECTION: OPPONENT'S NAME: T25/85: EPO)
[1986] E.P.O.R. 158; [1986] O.J. EPO 81

Deutsche Renault AG v. Audi AG (QUATTRO Trade mark) (TRADE MARKS: IMPORTS: WHETHER PROTECTION OF ITALIAN NUMERAL IN WORDS AS A TRADE MARK FOR MOTOR CARS IN GERMANY AGAINST IMPORTS FROM OTHER MEMBER STATES CONSTITUTES AN UNLAWFUL RESTRICTION ON IMPORTS CONTRARY TO ARTICLE 30: Germany: S.C.)
[1993] 1 C.M.L.R. 421
(Reference to European Court: Case C–317/91: ECJ)   [1993] F.S.R. 759
(TRADE MARK: NATIONAL LAW: LIMITED PROTECTION: IMPORTATION: CONFUSION: QUATTRO/QUADRA: TEST: Case C–317/91: ECJ)
[1995] 1 C.M.L.R. 461; [1995] F.S.R. 738

Deutsche Schachtbau- und Tiefbohrgesellschaft GmbH v. Ras Al Khaimah National Oil Co. (PRACTICE: ARBITRATION: AWARD: ENFORCEMENT: PRE-TRIAL RELIEF: MAREVA INJUNCTION: C.A.)   [1987] 2 All E.R. 769

Devefi Pty Ltd v. Mateffy Pearl Nagy Pty Ltd (COPYRIGHT: LICENCES: ARTISTIC WORKS: ARCHITECT'S PLANS TO COMPLETE BUILDING: ASSIGNMENT: ARCHITECT AND BUILDER: WHETHER RIGHT TO PERFORMANCE ASSIGNABLE: Australia: Fed. Ct)   113 A.L.R. 225; [1993] R.P.C. 493

Deyhle's Design Applications (REGISTERED DESIGN: CONVENTION APPLICATION: PRIORITY DATE: NATURE OF DESIGN: RDAT)   [1982] R.P.C. 526

Dial-An-Angel Pty Ltd v. Sagitaur Services Systems Pty Ltd (TRADE MARKS: INFRINGEMENT: DIAL-AN-ANGEL/GUARDIAN ANGEL: COMMON ELEMENTS: Australia: Fed. Ct)   96 A.L.R. 181; 19 I.P.R. 171

Diamond Scientific Co. v. CSL Ltd (PATENT: APPLICATION: OPPOSITION: STATEMENT OF GROUNDS AND PARTICULARS: AMENDMENT: ALLOWABILITY: Australia: AIPO)   26 I.P.R. 15

Diamond Shamrock Technologies SA's Patent (PATENT: LICENCES OF RIGHT: PRACTICE: CONFIDENTIALITY OF INFORMATION: Pat. Ct) [1987] R.P.C. 91

Diazo Copying Materials' Agreements (RESTRICTIVE PRACTICES: AGREEMENT TO DESIGN, MANUFACTURE AND MARKET PHOTOCOPYING MACHINE: SALE RESTRICTION: R.P.C.)   [1984] I.C.R. 429

Digby International (Australia) Pty Ltd v. Beyond Imagination Pty Ltd (TRADE MARK: INFRINGEMENT: EXTREME/POWERADE EXTREMISTS: INTERLOCUTORY INJUNCTION: SERIOUS QUESTION TO BE TRIED: BALANCE OF CONVENIENCE: ADEQUACY OF DAMAGES: Australia: Fed. Ct)
                                        31 I.P.R. 410

Digital & Philips' Information Systems' Merger (MERGER: TAKEOVER OF COMPUTER BUSINESS: MARKET BREAKDOWN ACCORDING TO COMPUTER TYPE: NO DOMINANCE ON ANY MARKET: ANCILLARY RESTRAINTS: MERGER CLEARED: E.C. Comm.)   [1994] 4 C.M.L.R. M4

Digital Equipment Corp. and Ing C. Olivetti & Co. SpA's Agreement (RESTRICTIVE PRACTICES: CO-OPERATION AGREEMENT: COMPUTER SYSTEMS: TECHNOLOGY TRANSFER: INTENTION TO APPROVE: NOTICE: E.C. Comm.)   [1994] 4 C.M.L.R. 499

Digital Equipment Corp. v. Australian Telecommunication Commission (TRADE MARK: APPLICATION: OPPOSITION: DISTINCTIVENESS: Australia: AIPO)
                                        28 I.P.R. 663

Digital Equipment Corp. v. Darkcrest Ltd (PRACTICE: ANTON PILLER: COPYRIGHT: INFRINGEMENT: CROSS-UNDERTAKING IN DAMAGES: Ch.D.)
        [1984] 3 All E.R. 381; [1984] Ch. 512; [1984] 3 W.L.R. 617

Digmesa/Further search fee (EUROPEAN PATENT: ABANDONMENT: OMISSION: UNITY: AMENDMENT OF CLAIMS PRIOR TO EXAMINATION: CONTINUING REQUIREMENT: SEARCH DIVISION, DECISION BY: T87/88: EPO)
                                        [1994] E.P.O.R. 57

Dillon v. J.P. Products Pty Ltd (CONFIDENTIAL INFORMATION: PATENT: INFRINGEMENT: INTERLOCUTORY INJUNCTION: Australia: S.C.(NSW))
                                        4 I.P.R. 372

Dimtsis v. Agricultural Dairy Industry Authority of Epirus, Dodoni SA (PRACTICE AND PROCEDURE: TRADE MARKS OFFICE: APPLICATION FOR EXTENSION OF TIME TO FILE EVIDENCE: OBJECTION TO: SPECIAL CIRCUMSTANCES CONSTITUTED BY ERRORS OR OMISSIONS BY AGENTS OF PARTIES: Australia: Pat. Off.)   17 I.P.R. 273

Director General of Education v. Public Service Association of NSW (COPYRIGHT: CONFIDENTIAL INFORMATION: FAIR DEALING: PUBLIC INTEREST: Australia: S.C.(NSW)) 4 I.P.R. 552

Dirt Magnet Trade Mark (TRADE MARK: RECTIFICATION: PRACTICE: PARALLEL PROCEEDINGS IN SCOTLAND AND ENGLAND: IDENTICAL ISSUES: APPLICANTS NOT PARTIES TO SCOTTISH PROCEEDINGS: WHETHER DUPLICATION: COSTS: Ch.D.) [1991] F.S.R. 136

Discount Inter-Shopping Co. Ltd v. Micrometro Ltd (COPYRIGHT: SOUND RECORDING: LICENSING: ROYALTIES: Ch.D.) [1984] Ch. 369; [1984] R.P.C. 198; [1984] 2 W.L.R. 919

Discovision/Appealable decision (EUROPEAN PATENT: EPO: OBSERVATIONS BY PRESIDENT: PROCEDURE: BIAS: NATURAL JUSTICE: G05/91: EPO) [1993] E.P.O.R. 120; [1992] O.J. EPO 617

Discovision/Lens assembly (EUROPEAN PATENT: AMENDMENT AND CORRECTION: BROADENING CLAIM BY OMISSION: CLAIMS: IMPLICIT LIMITATION: ENLARGED BOARD OF APPEAL: REFERENCE REFUSED: T24/85: EPO) [1988] E.P.O.R. 247

Disney v. Plummer (PRACTICE: INDEMNITY COSTS: C.A.) [1991] F.S.R. 165

Dispensoroll & Therma-Wrap's Application, *sub nom.* Gatward's (t/a Dispensoroll & Therma-Wrap)'s Application

Distillers Co. plc's Application (RESTRICTIVE PRACTICES: EXCLUSIVE DEALING: RESTRICTIONS ON MANUFACTURER AND DISTRIBUTOR: REGULATION 67/67: INDIVIDUAL EXEMPTION: E.C. Comm.) [1986] 2 C.M.L.R. 664

Distillers Co. plc (NOTICE: E.C. COMM.) [1984] 3 C.M.L.R. 173; [1984] F.S.R. 28

Distillers Corp. (SA) Ltd's Application (TRADE MARKS: APPLICATION FOR REGISTRATION: CITATION OBJECTIONS: GOODS OF THE SAME DESCRIPTION: LETTER OF CONSENT: Australia: Pat. Off.) 21 I.P.R. 223

Distributori Automatici Italia SpA v. Holford General Trading Co. Ltd (PRACTICE: ANTON PILLER: POST-JUDGMENT ORDER IN AID OF EXECUTION: Q.B.D.) [1985] 3 All E.R. 750; [1985] 1 W.L.R. 1066

Divisional Application (EUROPEAN PATENT: DIVISIONAL APPLICATION: LATEST DATE FOR FILING: WHETHER EPC RULE 25 CONSISTENT WITH EPC ARTICLE 76(5): G10/92: EPO) [1995] E.P.O.R. 265; O.J. EPO 199

Divisional Application/Whether filing justified (EUROPEAN PATENT: DIVISIONAL APPLICATION: JURISDICTION TO DETERMINE WHETHER EXTENSION BEYOND FILED: LATE FILING: J13/85: EPO) [1988] E.P.O.R. 125; [1987] O.J. EPO 523

Divisional Trading Officer v. Kingley Clothing Ltd (TRADE MARK: FALSE TRADE DESCRIPTION: Q.B.D.) [1989] R.P.C. 695

Dixon Investments Pty Ltd v. Hall (COPYRIGHT: ALLEGED COPYING OF PROJECT HOUSE DESIGN DRAWINGS: RESPONDENTS' DESIGN DERIVED ORIGINALLY FROM APPLICANTS' PLAN: PRINCIPLES GOVERNING SIMPLE AND COMMONPLACE DRAWINGS: WHETHER RESPONDENTS' HOUSE A REPRODUCTION OF APPLICANT'S HOUSE PLAN OR A SUBSTANTIAL PART OF IT: WHAT CONSTITUTES "SUBSTANTIAL PART": DEFENCE: DAMAGES: Australia: Fed. Ct) 18 I.P.R. 481; 18 I.P.R. 490

Dodds Family Investments Pty Ltd (formerly Solar Tint Pty Ltd) v. Lane Industries Pty Ltd (PASSING OFF: APPEAL: DESCRIPTIVE TRADE NAMES: NECESSITY TO ACQUIRE A DISTINCTIVE OR SECONDARY MEANING: EVIDENCE REQUIRED TO ESTABLISH A SECONDARY MEANING: EVIDENCE OF MERE CONFUSION OR BELIEF BY INDIVIDUALS INSUFFICIENT: COSTS: Australia: Fed. Ct) 26 I.P.R. 261

Dodds Family Investments Pty Ltd v. Lane Industries Pty Ltd (TRADE MARK: WHETHER TRADE MARK DISTINCTIVE OF CERTAIN SERVICES: DETERMINATION OF WHEN A TRADE MARK SHOULD BE EXPUNGED FROM THE REGISTER: WHEN TRADE MARK WILL BE LIKELY TO DECEIVE AND CONFUSE: EXISTENCE OF BLAMEWORTHY CONDUCT: DISTINCTIVENESS OF DEVICE MARKS: Australia: Fed. Ct)   25 I.P.R. 197

Dohmeier v. Eisen-Und Drahtwerk Erlau AG (PATENT: OPPOSITION: NOVELTY: PRIOR PUBLICATION: Australia: Pat. Off.)   13 I.P.R. 131

Dolphin Showers Ltd v. Farmiloe (PATENT: INFRINGEMENT: PRACTICE: STRIKING OUT: ENTITLEMENT: ASSIGNMENT: PLEADINGS: Pat. Ct)   [1989] 1 F.S.R. 1

Domestic Appliances v. Globe Super Parts (REGISTERED DESIGN: INFRINGEMENT: CANCELLATION: India: H.C.)   (1983) 7 I.P.L.R. 16

DOMGARDEN Trade Mark (TRADE MARK: WINE LABELS: USE LIMITED TO WINES OF GERMAN ORIGIN: Ch.D.)   [1983] 1 C.M.L.R. 179; [1983] R.P.C. 155

Dominion Rent-A-Car Ltd v. Budget Rent-A-Car System (1970) Ltd (PASSING OFF: FOREIGN PLAINTIFF: INTERNATIONAL REPUTATION: SHARED REPUTATION: COPYRIGHT: INFRINGEMENT: LICENCE: ACQUIESCENCE: LACHES: DELAY: INTERFERENCE WITH TRADE: UNFAIR TRADING: New Zealand: C.A.)
9 I.P.R. 367

Domino's Pizza Inc. v. Eagle Boys Dial-a-Pizza Australia Pty Ltd (TRADE MARK: OPPOSITION: DECEPTION AND CONFUSION: PROPRIETORSHIP: SURVEY EVIDENCE: Australia: AIPO)   31 I.P.R. 592

Donaldson Co. Inc.'s Patent (PATENT: AMENDMENT: DISCLAIMER: DISCRETION: Pat. Ct)   [1986] R.P.C. 1

Doris/Abandonment (EUROPEAN PATENT: ABANDONMENT: WHAT CONSTITUTES: J11/87: EPO)   [1989] E.P.O.R. 54; [1989] O.J. EPO 367

Dormeuil Frères SA v. Feraglow Ltd (TRADE MARK: INFRINGEMENT: PASSING OFF: INQUIRY AS TO DAMAGES: INTERIM PAYMENT: BASIS OF DAMAGES: REMOTENESS: INTEREST: Ch.D.)   [1990] R.P.C. 449

Dormeuil Frères SA v. Nicolian International (Textiles) Ltd (TRADE MARK: INFRINGEMENT: ANTON PILLER PRACTICE: SETTING ASIDE OF ORDER: DUTY OF FULL DISCLOSURE: RETURN OF GOODS SEIZED: Ch.D.)
[1989] 1 F.S.R. 256

DORMEUIL Trade Mark (TRADE MARK: TRADE MARK AGENT'S PRIVILEGE: Ch.D.)   [1983] R.P.C. 131

Dory v. Richard Wolf GmbH (PATENT: INFRINGEMENT: PRACTICE: DISCOVERY: USE OF LISTS IN OTHER JURISDICTIONS: Pat. Ct)   [1990] F.S.R. 266

Dory v. Sheffield Health Authority (PATENT: INFRINGEMENT: CROWN USE: RETROSPECTIVE AUTHORISATION: STATUS OF ACTION BEGUN BEFORE AUTHORISATION: WHETHER HEALTH AUTHORITY TREATABLE AS CROWN: Pat. Ct)   [1991] F.S.R. 221

Douglas Pharmaceuticals Ltd v. Ciba-Geigy AG (PATENT: CELOTEX CONDITIONS: APPLICATION IN NEW ZEALAND: PROTECTION AGAINST CLAIMS OF INFRINGEMENT BETWEEN EXPIRY OF PATENT AND ORDER EXTENDING IT: INADEQUATE REMUNERATION: EXTENSION: RELEVANCE OF FOREIGN REMUNERATION: New Zealand: C.A.) [1990] 2 N.Z.L.R. 46; 18 I.P.R. 603

Dover Fisheries Pty Ltd v. Bottrill Research Pty Ltd (CONFIDENTIAL INFORMATION: WHAT CONSTITUTES: UNEXECUTED CONTRACT: WHETHER BREACH OF CONDITION OF CONFIDENTIALITY IS BREACH OF AN ESSENTIAL TERM: COMMON LAW RIGHTS: Australia: S.C.(S.A.))   30 I.P.R. 360

Dow Chemical AG v. Spence Bryson & Co. Ltd (PATENT: INFRINGEMENT: VALIDITY: ANTICIPATION: OBVIOUSNESS: INUTILITY: FALSE SUGGESTION: JOINT TORTFEASORS: Pat. Ct: C.A.)   [1984] R.P.C. 359

Dow Chemical Co. v. C.H. Boehringer Sohn KG (TRADE MARK: OPPOSITION: PRIOR REGISTRATION OF SIMILAR WORD: IMPERFECT RECOLLECTION: Australia: Pat. Off.)   9 I.P.R. 360

Dow Chemical Co. v. ICI plc (PATENT: EXTENSION: Australia: Pat. Off.)
1 I.P.R. 542

Dow Chemical Co. v. Ishihara Sangyo KK (PATENT: OPPOSITION: EXTENSION OF TIME LIMIT: Australia: Pat. Off.)   1 I.P.R. 298

Dow Chemical Co. v. Ishihara Sangyo KK (PATENT: REVOCATION: PLEADINGS: EUROPEAN PATENT: Pat. Ct)   [1985] F.S.R. 4

Dow Chemical Co. v. Ishihara Sangyo KK (PATENTS: REVOCATION: PARTICULARS OF OBJECTION: APPLICATION TO STRIKE OUT: FALSE SUGGESTION: INSUFFICIENCY: New Zealand: H.C.)   5 I.P.R. 415

Dow Chemical Nederland BV v. E.C. Commission (EUROPEAN COURT PROCEDURE: INTERIM MEASURES: SEARCH AND SEIZURE: Case 87/87R: ECJ)   [1988] 4 C.M.L.R. 439

Dow Chemical/Re-establishment (EUROPEAN PATENT: RE-ESTABLISHMENT OF RIGHTS: CLERK'S FAILURE: T72/83: EPO)   [1979–85] E.P.O.R. C780

Dow/Contaminant removal (EUROPEAN PATENT: INVENTIVE STEP: CONTEMPORARY EXPERT OPINION: PREJUDICE: T137/83: EPO)
[1987] E.P.O.R. 15

Dow/Divisional application (EUROPEAN PATENT: DIVISIONAL APPLICATION: LATEST DATE FOR FILING: RE-ESTABLISHMENT OF RIGHTS: TIME-LIMIT FOR: CONVENTIONS: GENERAL LEGAL PRINCIPLES: PROCEDURE OVER RULES: EPO: ADMINISTRATIVE COUNCIL, POWERS OF: OBSERVATIONS BY PRESIDENT: PRESIDENT: *Res judicata*: J11/91; J16/91: EPO)
[1994] E.P.O.R. 235; [1994] O.J. EPO 28

Dow/New citation (EUROPEAN PATENT: COSTS: LATE CITATIONS AND EVIDENCE: APPORTIONED: OPPOSITION: PROCEDURE: REQUEST TO FIRST INSTANCE: T622/89: EPO)   [1994] E.P.O.R. 488

Dow/Pyrimidines (EUROPEAN PATENT: INVENTIVE STEP: CHEMICAL INTERMEDIATES: T18/88: EPO) [1992] E.P.O.R. 184; [1992] O.J. EPO 107

Dow/Sequestering agent (EUROPEAN PATENT: NOVELTY: INHERENT FUNCTIONAL FEATURE: NEW PURPOSE/USE FOR KNOWN SUBSTANCE/EQUIPMENT: OPPOSITION: PROCEDURE: LATE SUBMISSION CONSIDERED: PATENTABILITY: TECHNICAL EFFECT: T958/90: EPO)   [1994] E.P.O.R. 1

Dowson & Mason Ltd v. Potter (CONFIDENTIAL INFORMATION: BREACH OF CONFIDENCE: INFORMATION READILY AVAILABLE ELSEWHERE: ASSESSMENT OF DAMAGES: C.A.)   [1986] 2 All E.R. 418; [1986] 1 W.L.R. 1419

Dr Rentschler Biotechnologie GmbH v. Boehringer Ingelheim International GmbH (PATENT: APPLICATION: PROCESS: TREATMENT: DISEASE: NOVELTY: Australia: AIPO)   31 I.P.R. 12

Draco/Xanthines (EUROPEAN PATENT: INVENTIVE STEP: COULD/WOULD TEST: *Ex post facto* APPROACH: OBJECTIVE ASSESSMENT: TRIAL–AND–ERROR APPROACH: NOVELTY: COMBINATION OF TWO SETS OF VARIANTS: GENERIC DISCLOSURE: SELECTION: T7/86: EPO)
[1989] E.P.O.R. 65; [1988] O.J. EPO 381

Draenert/Single general concept (EUROPEAN PATENT: UNITY: GENERAL CONCEPT NOT INVENTIVE: W06/90: EPO)
[1991] E.P.O.R. 516; [1991] O.J. EPO 438

Draft Counterfeit Goods Regulation, *sub nom.* Counterfeit Goods Draft Regulation

Draping of Curtains/Unsubstantiated protest (EUROPEAN PATENT: INTERNATIONAL APPLICATION: PROTEST MUST BE SUBSTANTIATED: W16/92: EPO)   [1994] E.P.O.R. 443

Drayton Controls (Engineering) Ltd v. Honeywell Control Systems Ltd (COPYRIGHT: INTERLOCUTORY INJUNCTION: EVIDENCE RELEVANT FOR INTERLOCUTORY STAGE: ORIGINALITY: VISUAL SIGNIFICANCE OF MINOR ALTERATIONS: DURATION OF COPYRIGHT PROTECTION FOR ARTICLE MADE BY INDUSTRIAL PROCESS WHERE PART NOT INTENDED TO BE SOLD SEPARATELY: PASSING OFF: GET-UP: PURCHASE BY NAME, NOT VISUAL APPEARANCE: DESIGN OF PARTS COMMON TO TRADE: REPUTATION: Ch.D.) [1992] F.S.R. 245

Drazil (PATENT: INTERNATIONAL APPLICATION: PRACTICE: PCT: RECTIFICATION OF ERROR: Q.B.D.) [1992] R.P.C. 479

DRG/Printing sleeve (EUROPEAN PATENT: CLAIMS: DISCLAIMER: INVENTIVE STEP: CLOSEST PRIOR ART: NOVELTY: CLOSE READING OF PRIOR ART: PROCEDURE: INTERPRETERS, LATE REQUEST FOR, REFUSED: MICROPHONE DISCONNECTED: T155/87: EPO) [1990] E.P.O.R. 455

Dricon Air Pty Ltd v. Waztech Pty Ltd (PATENT: APPLICATION: OPPOSITION: STANDING TO OPPOSE: NO *locus standi*: OPPOSITION CONTINUES AS BAR-TO-SEALING ACTION: PAPER ANTICIPATION: SPECIFICATION AS ITS OWN DICTIONARY: COSTS: Australia: Pat. Off.) 24 I.P.R. 398

DRISTAN Trade Mark (TRADE MARK: RECTIFICATION: OVERSEAS PROPRIETOR: INDIAN SUBSIDIARY: NON-USE: BONA FIDE INTENTION TO USE AT DATE OF REGISTRATION: REGISTERED USER: India: H.C.) [1984] F.S.R. 215 (S.C.) (1985) 10 I.P.L.R. 303; [1986] R.P.C. 161

Dronpool Pty Ltd v. Hunter (COPYRIGHT: INFRINGEMENT: ARCHITECTS' PLANS: SUBSTANTIAL REPRODUCTION: PRACTICE: INJUNCTIONS: Australia: S.C.(NSW)) 3 I.P.R. 310

Du Pont de Nemours (E.I.) & Co. (Blades') Patent (Licence of Right) (PATENT: PRACTICE: STAY: LICENCE OF RIGHT: SETTLEMENT OF TERMS: INFRINGEMENT: VALIDITY: APPEAL: ELECTION: APPROBATING AND REPROBATING: STAY REFUSED: Pat. Ct) [1988] R.P.C. 479

Du Pont de Nemours (E.I.) & Co. (Buege)'s Application (PATENT: APPLICATION: CLAIM DRAFTING: C.-G.) [1984] R.P.C. 17

Du Pont de Nemours (E.I.) & Co. and AKZO NV (INTERNATIONAL TRADE: U.S. LITIGATION: UNFAIR COMMERCIAL PRACTICES: IMPORTS: PATENTS: PARALLEL IMPORTS: DISCRIMINATION: GATT PROCEDURE: E.C. Comm.) [1987] 2 C.M.L.R. 545

Du Pont de Nemours (E.I.) & Co. v. Cadbury Schweppes Pty Ltd (PATENT: EXTENSION: OPPOSITION: CHALLENGE TO VALIDITY BY OPPONENT: Australia: Fed. Ct) 9 I.P.R. 643

Du Pont de Nemours (E.I.) & Co. v. Cadbury Schweppes Pty Ltd (PATENT: EXTENSION OF TERM: CHALLENGE TO VALIDITY: WHETHER OPPONENT TO EXTENSION CAN PLEAD INVALIDITY: CROSS-CLAIM FOR REVOCATION: DISTINCTION BETWEEN "PLAIN" OR "MANIFEST" AND "MERE" INVALIDITY: Australia: Fed. Ct) 10 I.P.R. 641

Du Pont de Nemours (E.I.) & Co. v. Commissioner of Patents (PATENTS: EXTENSION OF TERM: WHETHER OPPONENT MAY CHALLENGE VALIDITY: Australia: S.C.(NSW)) 72 A.L.R. 88; 8 I.P.R. 293

Du Pont de Nemours (E.I.) & Co. v. Commissioner of Patents (PATENT: EXTENSION OF TERM: DISCOVERY: WHETHER GENERAL DISCOVERY SHOULD BE ORDERED PRIOR TO FILING OF AFFIDAVITS: PRACTICE AND PROCEDURE: CONSENT ORDERS: INTERLOCUTORY: POWER OF COURT TO SET ASIDE CONSENT ORDER FOR DISCOVERY: PRACTICE AND PROCEDURE: DISCOVERY: PATENT CASE: WHETHER GENERAL DISCOVERY SHOULD BE ORDERED PRIOR TO FILING OF AFFIDAVITS: Australia: Fed. Ct)
83 A.L.R. 499; 12 I.P.R. 536

Du Pont de Nemours (E.I.) & Co. v. Commissioner of Patents (No. 1) (PATENT: EXTENTION OF TERM: APPLICATION BY COMPETITOR FOR EXTENSION OF TIME TO FILE CAVEAT AGAINST GRANTING OF EXTENSION: Australia: S.C.(NSW))
15 I.P.R. 280

Du Pont de Nemours (E.I.) & Co. v. Commissioner of Patents (No. 2) (PATENT: EXTENSION OF TERM: EXCLUSIVE LICENSEE: DISCLOSURE OF PROFITS: Australia: S.C.(NSW))
15 I.P.R. 289; (1989) 16 N.S.W.L.R. 641

Du Pont de Nemours (E.I.) & Co. v. Commissioner of Patents (No. 3) (PATENT: EXTENSION OF TERM: WHETHER INVENTION OF MORE THAN ORDINARY UTILITY: RELEVANCE OF MERIT OF INVENTIVE STEP: PROFITS OF PATENTEE: RESEARCH AND DEVELOPMENT COSTS: Australia: S.C.(NSW)) 15 I.P.R. 296

Du Pont de Nemours (E.I.) & Co. v. Commissioner of Patents (No. 4) (PATENT: EXTENSION OF TERM: APPLICATION BY PATENTEE: EXCLUSIVE LICENSEE: APPLICATION TO IMPOSE CONDITIONS ON GRANT OF EXTENSION: PRIMA FACIE EVIDENCE OF HIGH PRICES: NO EVIDENCE OF PROFITS OF EXCLUSIVE LICENSEE: WHETHER APPLICATION FOR COMPULSORY LICENCE A SUITABLE ALTERNATIVE REMEDY: PA52, ss.94, 108, 110: Australia: S.C.(NSW))
87 A.L.R. 89; 15 I.P.R. 315; (1989) 16 N.S.W.L.R. 641

Du Pont de Nemours (E.I.) & Co. v. Commissioner of Patents (No. 5) (PARTIES: JOINDER: WHETHER COURT HAS JURISDICTION OR POWER TO JOIN ADDITIONAL PARTIES TO APPLICATION: WHETHER APPLICANTS ARE PERSONS INTERESTED: WHETHER *amici curiae*: Australia: S.C.(NSW))
87 A.L.R. 491; (1989) 17 N.S.W.L.R. 389

Du Pont De Nemours (E.I.) & Co. v. Commissioner of Patents (No. 7) (PATENT: EXTENSION OF TERM: APPLICATION TO IMPOSE CONDITIONS ON EXTENSION: APPLICATION FOR SECURITY FOR COSTS AGAINST INTERVENOR: WHETHER INTERVENOR A "DEFENDANT": DISCRETIONARY CONSIDERATIONS: SECURITY FORECASTS: Australia: S.C.(NSW))
18 I.P.R. 643

Du Pont De Nemours (E.I.) & Co. v. Commissioner of Patents (No. 8) (PATENT: SETTLEMENT BY CONSENT ON TERMS THAT PATENT BE EXTENDED: WHETHER APPROPRIATE TO MAKE ORDERS IN THE PUBLIC INTEREST: Australia: S.C.(NSW))
18 I.P.R. 652

Du Pont de Nemours (E.I.) & Co. v. DowElanco (PATENT: APPLICATION: OPPOSITION: EXTENSION OF TIME TO FILE EVIDENCE: JUSTIFICATION: FULL AND FRANK DISCLOSURE OF FACTS: Australia: AIPO)
28 I.P.R. 59

(PATENT: OPPOSITION: STATEMENT OF GROUNDS AND PARTICULARS: REQUEST TO AMEND: REQUIREMENTS OF CONTENTS: AMENDMENT AFTER EVIDENCE FILED: Australia: AIPO)
29 I.P.R. 131

(PATENT: OPPOSITION: REQUEST FOR FURTHER AND BETTER PARTICULARS: Australia: AIPO)
30 I.P.R. 25

Du Pont de Nemours (E.I.) & Co. v. Enka AG (PATENT: AMENDMENT: PRACTICE: CROSS-EXAMINATION ON AFFIDAVITS IN AMENDMENT PROCEEDINGS: C.A.)
[1986] R.P.C. 417

Du Pont de Nemours (E.I.) & Co. v. Enka BV (PATENT: INFRINGEMENT: KEVLAR: VALIDITY: FAIR BASIS: INSUFFICIENCY: OPEN-ENDED PRODUCT CLAIMING: BEST METHOD: INUTILITY: Pat. Ct)   [1988] F.S.R. 69

Du Pont de Nemours (E.I.) & Co. v. Enka BV (No. 2) (PATENT INFRINGEMENT: PRACTICE: STAY OF INJUNCTION PENDING APPEAL: LICENCE OF RIGHT: JURISDICTION: DISCRETION: Pat. Ct)   [1988] R.P.C. 497

Du Pont de Nemours (E.I.) & Co./Admissibility of opposition (EUROPEAN PATENT: OPPOSITION: PROCEDURE: NOTICE OF OPPOSITION: MEANING OF 'SUFFICIENT INDICATION': PRECEDENT: *Ratio decidendi* OF BOARD OF APPEAL DECISION: GUIDELINES FOR EXAMINATION: MERE GUIDANCE: T204/91: EPO)   [1993] E.P.O.R. 348

Du Pont de Nemours (E.I.) & Co./Appetite suppressant (EUROPEAN PATENT: PATENTABILITY: COSMETIC INDICATION: INDUSTRIAL APPLICATION: T144/83: EPO)   [1987] E.P.O.R. 6; [1986] O.J. EPO 301

Du Pont de Nemours (E.I.) & Co./Copolymers (EUROPEAN PATENT: OPPOSITION: PROCEDURE: FRESH ARGUMENT ON APPEAL: T124/87: EPO)
[1989] E.P.O.R. 33; [1989] O.J. EPO 491

Du Pont de Nemours (E.I.) & Co./Correction of priority date (EUROPEAN PATENT: AMENDMENT AND CORRECTION: PRIORITY CLAIM: J06/91: EPO)
[1993] E.P.O.R. 318; [1994] O.J. EPO 349

Du Pont de Nemours (E.I.) & Co./Entitlement to request (EUROPEAN PATENT: APPEAL: PROCEDURE: RESPONDENT'S RIGHTS, ARGUMENT OF OTHER ISSUES: CONVENTIONS: EPC ACCESSIONS: T576/89: EPO)
[1994] E.P.O.R. 213; [1993] O.J. EPO 543

Du Pont de Nemours (E.I.) & Co./Flange formation process (2) (EUROPEAN PATENT: OPPOSITION: PROCEDURE: LATE OBJECTION OF INSUFFICIENCY: RECONSIDERATION OF CITED PRIOR ART: SUFFICIENCY: RELATION TO INVENTIVE STEP: CLAIMS: CONSTRUCTION: IMPLICIT INCLUSION OF OMITTED FEATURES: T7/88: EPO)   [1990] E.P.O.R. 149

Du Pont de Nemours (E.I.) & Co./Hollow filaments (EUROPEAN PATENT: CLAIMS: CONSTRUCTION: FUNCTIONAL FEATURES: CONSTRUCTION: IMPLICIT FEATURES: NOVELTY: CROSS-REFERENCED DOCUMENTS: PURPOSE, WHETHER NOVEL: OPPOSITION: PROCEDURE: AMENDMENT OF CLAIM, CLARITY AND SUPPORT: T361/88: EPO)   [1991] E.P.O.R. 1

Du Pont de Nemours (E.I.) & Co./Late submission (EUROPEAN PATENT: OPPOSITION PROCEDURE: LATE EXPERIMENTAL RESULTS: ADMISSIBILITY: NOVELTY: INVENTIVE STEP: SUFFICIENCY: BURDEN OF PROOF: REFERENCE TO ENLARGED BOARD (NO): REIMBURSEMENT OF APPEAL FEE (NO): COSTS AGAINST EPO (NO): T951/91: EPO)
[1995] E.P.O.R. 398; [1995] O.J. EPO 202

Du Pont de Nemours (E.I.) & Co./Nonwoven sheet (EUROPEAN PATENT: INVENTIVE STEP: OBVIOUS TO TRY: SUFFICIENCY: INUTILE STARTING MATERIALS, NEED FOR EXPERIMENTAL EVIDENCE OF: OPEN-ENDED DEFINITION: T297/90: EPO)   [1993] E.P.O.R. 389

Du Pont de Nemours (E.I.) & Co./Phenylenediamine (EUROPEAN PATENT: INVENTIVE STEP: ANALOGOUS SUBSTITUTION: NOVELTY: IMPLICIT DISCLOSURE: T103/86: EPO)   [1987] E.P.O.R. 265

Du Pont de Nemours (E.I.) & Co./Polyamide composition (EUROPEAN PATENT: OPPOSITION: PROCEDURE: FRESH DOCUMENTS ON APPEAL: IN THE EPO, GENERAL PRINCIPLES: COSTS: FRESH DOCUMENTS, MITIGATING CIRCUMSTANCES: T326/87: EPO)
[1991] E.P.O.R. 47; [1992] O.J. EPO 522

Du Pont de Nemours (E.I.) & Co./Yarn finish applicator (EUROPEAN PATENT: OPPOSITION: PROCEDURE: FRESH DOCUMENTS ON APPEAL: PRIOR ART: PAMPHLET, NECESSITY FOR STRICT PROOF AS TO PUBLICATION DATE: T308/87: EPO)   [1991] E.P.O.R. 464

Du Pont de Nemours (E.I.) & Co./Copolymers (EUROPEAN PATENT: NOVELTY: GENERAL DISCLOSURE: T124/87: EPO)   [1989] E.P.O.R. 33

Du Pont de Nemours/Akzo Dispute, *sub nom.* Community v. United States of America

Dubuffet v. Régie Nationale des Usines Renault (COPYRIGHT: ARCHITECTURAL WORKS: *Droit moral*: France)   [1982] E.C.C. 463; [1983] F.S.R. 31

Duco/Paint layers (EUROPEAN PATENT: INVENTIVE STEP: UNSUBSTANTIATED EFFECT: OPPOSITION: PROCEDURE: LATE FILING OF TRANSLATION OF ABSTRACTED CITATION: T94/84: EPO)
                                 [1987] E.P.O.R. 37; [1986] O.J. EPO 337

Duijnstee v. Goderbauer (PATENT: EMPLOYEE INVENTOR: FULL FAITH AND CREDIT: JURISDICTION: Case 288/82: ECJ)
                    [1985] 1 C.M.L.R. 220; [1983] E.C.R. 3663; [1985] F.S.R. 221

Duke & Sons Ltd v. Union of India (TRADE MARK: GOVERNMENT POLICY: USE OF FOREIGN BRAND NAMES: PROHIBITION: HYBRID NAME: PEPSI LAHER: India: H.C.)   (1990) 15 I.P.L.R. 293

Dukhovskoi's Applications (PATENT: APPLICATION: PRACTICE: ERROR OF TRANSLATION: Pat. Ct)   [1985] R.P.C. 8

Dun & Bradstreet (Singapore) Pte Ltd v. Dun & Bradstreet (Malaysia) Sdn Bhd (TRADE MARK: PASSING OFF: IDENTICAL BUSINESS NAMES: DIFFERENT SCOPE OF ACTIVITY: REPUTATION AND GOODWILL: Malaysia: H.C.)
                                                      [1994] 1 M.L.J. 32

Dun & Bradstreet Ltd v. Typesetting Facilities Ltd (COPYRIGHT INFRINGEMENT: BREACH OF CONFIDENCE: COMPUTERISED DATABASE: APPLICATION FOR INSPECTION: INFORMATION IN ELECTRONIC FORM, SO VISUAL INSPECTION OF DISKS USELESS: DISCLOSURE OF CONTENTS REQUIRED: PRACTICE: INSPECTION BEFORE SERVICE OF STATEMENT OF CLAIM: REQUIREMENTS: INSPECTION ORDERED: Ch.D.)   [1992] F.S.R. 320

Duncan Agro Industries Ltd v. Somabhai Tea Processors (Pvt.) Ltd (TRADE MARK: PASSING OFF: FIRST TO ENTER MARKET: INTERIM INJUNCTION: APPEAL: India: H.C.)   (1994) 19 I.P.L.R. 229

Dunlop Ltd and Pirelli General plc (Agreements between) (RESTRICTIVE PRACTICES: JOINT VENTURE: HYDRAULIC AND ELECTRO-HYDRAULIC UMBILICALS: INTENTION TO APPROVE: E.C. Comm.)
                                                  [1986] 2 C.M.L.R. 192

Dunlop Olympic Ltd v. Cricket Hosiery Inc. (TRADE MARKS: APPLICATION: OPPOSITION: DISTINCTIVENESS: LIKELIHOOD OF DECEPTION OR CONFUSION: USE OF MARK OVERSEAS: PROPRIETORSHIP: Australia: Pat. Off.)
                                                           20 I.P.R. 475

Dunn v. Ward (PATENTS: OPPOSITION: DATE OF LODGEMENT: Australia: Pat. Off.)
                                                            1 I.P.R. 595

Duphar/Pigs II (EUROPEAN PATENT: PATENTABILITY: SECOND MEDICAL INDICATION: THERAPY: T19/86: EPO)
                                     [1988] E.P.O.R. 10; [1989] O.J. EPO 25

Dupps Co. v. Stord Bartz A/S (PATENT: APPLICATION: OPPOSITION: EVIDENCE: APPLICATION FOR SPECIAL LEAVE TO ADDUCE FURTHER EVIDENCE: Australia: Pat. Off.)   18 I.P.R. 499; 19 I.P.R. 17

Dupps Co. v. Stord Bartz A/S (PATENT: APPLICATION: OPPOSITION: NUMEROUS EXTENSIONS OF TIME FOR SERVICE OF EVIDENCE: Australia: Pat. Off.)
17 I.P.R. 157

Dupps Co. v. Stord Bartz A/S (PATENT: OPPOSITION TO APPLICATION FOR A PATENT: NUMEROUS EXTENSIONS OF TIME WITHIN WHICH TO LODGE EVIDENCE IN SUPPORT: FAILURE TO LODGE APPLICATION FOR EXTENSION WITHIN TIME: Australia: Pat. Off.)
17 I.P.R. 397

Duracell Australia Pty Ltd v. Union Carbide Australia (TRADE PRACTICES: MISLEADING OR DECEPTIVE CONDUCT: COMPARATIVE ADVERTISING: MANNER IN WHICH COMPARATIVE ADVERTISING MAY MISLEAD: CLAIM THAT TESTS PROVED RESPONDENT'S BATTERY LASTED LONGER THAN APPLICANT'S: DISCRETIONARY FACTORS IN THE CASE OF COMPARATIVE ADVERTISING: Australia: Fed. Ct)
14 I.P.R. 293

Duracell International Inc. v. Ever Ready Ltd (TRADE MARK: INFRINGEMENT: INTERLOCUTORY INJUNCTION: "KNOCKING" ADVERTISING: GET-UP IN TRADE MARK: Ch.D.)
[1989] 1 F.S.R. 71

Duracell International Inc. v. Ever Ready Ltd (TRADE MARK: INFRINGEMENT: VALIDITY: EURO-DEFENCES: STRIKING OUT: Ch.D.)
[1989] R.P.C. 731

Durack v. Associated Pool Builders Pty Ltd (PATENT: PETTY PATENT: INFRINGEMENT: VALIDITY: INTERLOCUTORY INJUNCTION: Australia: Fed. Ct)
1 I.P.R. 545

Durai Swamy v. Subhaiyam (TRADE MARK: INFRINGEMENT: THREATS: RECTIFICATION: STAY: India: H.C.)
(1991) 16 I.P.L.R. 11

Durham Trading Standards v. Kingsley Clothing (TRADE MARK: INFRINGEMENT: CRIMINAL OFFENCE: SUBJECTIVE TEST: C.A.)
(1990) 154 J.P.N. 74

Durion Co. Inc. v. Jennings & Co. Ltd (COPYRIGHT: INFRINGEMENT: ORIGINALITY: C.A.)
[1984] F.S.R. 1

Duriron/Re-establishment of rights (EUROPEAN PATENT: RE-ESTABLISHMENT OF RIGHTS: EXAMINATION FEE OUT OF TIME: PROCEDURE: EQUALITY OF TREATMENT: CONVENTIONS: EQUALITY OF TREATMENT UNDER PCT AND EPC: G06/92: EPO)
[1994] E.P.O.R. 381

Dyason v. Autodesk Inc., *sub nom.* Autodesk Inc. v. Dyson

Dymo/Magazine file assembly (EUROPEAN PATENT: OPPOSITION: PROCEDURE: FRESH DOCUMENTS AT ORAL PROCEEDINGS: COSTS: LATE CITATIONS: REFUSED: EPO: AGREEMENTS BETWEEN PARTIES OUTSIDE COMPETENCE: PROFESSIONAL REPRESENTATIVES: ORAL PROCEEDINGS, EXPECTED TO REACT TO NEW SITUATION: T330/88: EPO)
[1990] E.P.O.R. 467

Dynamic Lifter Pty Ltd v. Incitec Ltd (TRADE PRACTICES: ADVERTISING BROCHURE: WHETHER REPRESENTATION ALLEGED REASONABLY DERIVED FROM BROCHURE: CLASS OF PEOPLE TO WHOM STATEMENT DIRECTED: Australia: Fed. Ct)
30 I.P.R. 198

Dynapac/Poker vibrator (EUROPEAN PATENT: RE-ESTABLISHMENT OF RIGHTS: TEMPORARY SYSTEM: APPEAL: PROCEDURE: FRESH CLAIMS: INVENTIVE STEP: COMMON GENERAL KNOWLEDGE, APPLICATION OF TO PARTICULAR DEVICE: COMPARATIVE TESTS: T27/86: EPO)
[1987] E.P.O.R. 179; [1989] E.P.O.R. 100

Dyson Refractories/Catalyst production (EUROPEAN PATENT: APPEAL: PROCEDURE: REMITTAL ORDERED: TO CONSIDER DEPENDENT CLAIMS: CLAIMS: SUPPORT FOR: INVENTIVE STEP: AGED ART: CLOSEST PRIOR ART: SUFFICIENCY: DEFICIENCIES IN EXAMPLES: T95/87: EPO)
[1988] E.P.O.R. 171

E's Applications (Energy Conversion Devices Inc.'s Applications) (PATENT: APPLICATION: PRACTICE: IRREGULARITY IN PROCEDURE: DISCRETION: INTERPRETATION OF INTERNATIONAL TREATY: Pat. Ct: C.A.)
[1983] R.P.C. 231
(H.L.) [1982] F.S.R. 544; [1983] R.P.C. 231; [1982] Com.L.R. 219
E.I. Du Pont De Nemours & Co. cases, *sub nom.* Du Pont de Nemours (E.I.) & Co
E.R. Squibb & Sons Inc. v. Pacific Pharmaceuticals Ltd (PATENTS: EXTENSION: FACTORS RELEVANT: ADEQUATE REMUNERATION OF: RELATIONSHIP OF NATURE AND MERITS OF INVENTION TO THE PUBLIC GOOD: New Zealand: H.C.)
[1993] 3 N.Z.L.R. 240
East India Pharmaceutical Works Ltd v. G. & G. Pharmaceuticals Ltd (TRADE MARK: INJUNCTION: GEOGRAPHICAL EXTENT: India: H.C.)   (1993) 18 I.P.L.R. 264
East India Pharmaceutical Works Ltd v. G.G. Pharmaceuticals (TRADE MARK: INFRINGEMENT: PASSING OFF: INJUNCTION: LIMITATION: STAY REFUSED: India: H.C.)   (1989) 16 I.P.L.R. 247
East West Design Inc.'s Application (DESIGN: EXTENSION: NOVELTY: ORIGINALITY: PRIOR PUBLICATION: Australia: Pat. Off.)   7 I.P.R. 459
Eastman Kodak/Anhydrous iodine compounds (EUROPEAN PATENT: OPPOSITION: PROCEDURE: FRESH CITATION ON APPEAL: FRESH GROUND OF OBJECTION AT ORAL PROCEEDINGS: ONUS OF PROOF: SUFFICIENCY: CLAIMS AND DESCRIPTION TO BE TAKEN INTO ACCOUNT: T291/89: EPO)
[1992] E.P.O.R. 399
Eastman Kodak/Photographic element/1 (EUROPEAN PATENT: OPPOSITION PROCEDURE: BOARD OF APPEAL: ALLEGED PARTIALITY: ORAL STATEMENT BY EXPERT: REMITTAL TO OPPOSITION DIVISION: ADAPTATION OF DESCRIPTION: T843/91: EPO)   [1995] E.P.O.R. 116
Eastman Kodak/Photographic element/2 (EUROPEAN PATENT: OPPOSITION PROCEDURE: REMITTAL TO OPPOSITION DIVISION: ADAPTATION OF DESCRIPTION: FINDINGS OF FACT: BINDING NATURE: GERMAN LAW: EVIDENCE OF LAW OF OTHER CONTRACTING STATES: REFERENCE TO ENLARGED BOARD OF APPEAL (NO): T843/91: EPO)   [1995] E.P.O.R. 126
Eastman Kodak/Preparation of acetic anhydride (EUROPEAN PATENT: INVENTIVE STEP: BONUS EFFECT: COULD/WOULD TEST: DISCOURAGING ART: T236/88: EPO)   [1990] E.P.O.R. 227
Eastman Kodak/Thermal recording (EUROPEAN PATENT: INVENTIVE STEP: COMBINATION OF CITATIONS: T40/83: EPO)   [1986] E.P.O.R. 20
Easycare Inc. v. Bryan Lawrence & Co. (PATENT: THREATS: MALICIOUS FALSEHOOD: FREEDOM OF SPEECH: INTERLOCUTORY INJUNCTION REFUSED: Pat. Ct)   [1995] F.S.R. 597
Easyfind (NSW) Pty Ltd v. Paterson (COPYRIGHT: CALENDAR WITH ADVERTISEMENTS IN PARTICULAR FORM: SUBSISTENCE: ORIGINALITY: INFRINGEMENT: REPRODUCTION OF A SUBSTANTIAL PART: MISTAKE: UNILATERAL MISTAKE: TERMS OF CONSENT ORDERS: DUTIES OF COUNSEL: Australia: S.C.(NSW))   10 I.P.R. 464
Easyfind International (S.A.) (Pty) Ltd v. Instaplan Holdings (TRADE MARK: INFRINGEMENT: PASSING OFF: ANTON PILLER APPLICATION: South Africa: WLD)   1983 (3) S.A. 917
Eaton/Blocked speed transmission (EUROPEAN PATENT: CLAIMS: NUMERICAL RANGE: INVENTIVE STEP: PERCEPTIVE ANALYSIS: PROBLEM, DEFINITION OF: PURPOSEFUL IMAGINATION: SKILLED PERSON, POWERS OF: PRIOR ART: NEIGHBOURING FIELDS: T46/82: EPO)   [1979–85] E.P.O.R. B454

Eau De Cologne and Parfumerie-Fabrik Glockengasse No. 4711 Gegenuber der Pferdepost von Ferd Mulhens's Application (TRADE MARKS: APPLICATION: REFUSAL OF APPLICATION: DECEPTIVELY SIMILAR: SPECIFICATION OF GOODS: PRIOR REGISTRANTS CONSENT: Australia: Pat. Off.)   17 I.P.R. 540

E.C. Commission v. Germany (Champagne-type bottles) (IMPORTS: WINE: GET-UP: RIGHT TO LEGISLATE: ARTICLE 30: CONFLICT: PROTECTION OF CONSUMER: Case 179/85: ECJ)
[1988] 1 C.M.L.R. 135; [1986] E.C.R. 3879; [1988] F.S.R. 113

E.C. Commission v. Italy (Subsidy for Italian Motor Vehicles) (IMPORTS: QUANTITIVE RESTRICTIONS: NO *de minimis* FOR ARTICLE 30: Case 103/84: ECJ)   [1987] 2 C.M.L.R. 825; [1986] E.C.R. 1759

E.C. Commission v. United Kingdom and Italy (Re Compulsory Patent Licences) (IMPORTS: PATENTS: COMPULSORY LICENCE IF NO EXPLOITATION WITHIN COUNTRY: IMPORTS FROM ELSEWHERE IN COMMUNITY NOT COUNTED AS INTERNAL EXPLOITATION: HINDRANCE TO IMPORTS: SO P.A.77, S.48 INFRINGES ARTICLE 30: SIMILAR ITALIAN PROVISIONS LIKEWISE: Cases C–235/89 and 30/90: ECJ)   [1992] 2 C.M.L.R. 709;
[1982] I E.C.R. 777; [1993] F.S.R. 1; [1993] R.P.C. 283

Ecolab Inc. v. Reddish Savilles Ltd (PATENT: INFRINGEMENT: PRACTICE: PLEADINGS: AMENDMENT OF PARTICULARS OF OBJECTION: *See v. Scott-Paine* ORDER: DATE OF OPERATION OF ORDER: Pat. Ct)   [1993] F.S.R. 193

Econlite Manufacturing Pte Ltd v. Technochem Holdings Pte Ltd (TRADE MARK: PASSING OFF: TRADE NAME: ECONLITE: WHETHER DESCRIPTIVE: LIKELIHOOD OF CONFUSION OR DECEPTION: OVERLAP IN FIELD OF ACTIVITY: DAMAGES: Singapore: H.C.)   [1994] 2 S.L.R. 454

Economic Data Processing (Pty) Ltd v. Pentreath (ANTON PILLER: NATURE AND SCOPE: South Africa: SLD)   1984 (2) S.A. 605

ECONOVENT Trade Mark (TRADE MARK: REMOVAL: NON-USE: ONUS OF PROOF: Australia: Pat. Off.)   6 I.P.R. 92

ECR 900 (Re) (RESTRICTIVE PRACTICE: JOINT VENTURE: JOINT DEVELOPMENT, PRODUCTION AND DISTRIBUTION OF HI-TECH TELECOMMUNICATIONS SYSTEM: NOT FEASIBLE FOR PARTIES TO PRODUCE IT INDIVIDUALLY: NEGATIVE CLEARANCE GRANTED: E.C. Comm.)   [1992] 4 C.M.L.R. 54

Eden Technology Pty Ltd v. Intel Corp. (TRADE MARKS: APPLICATION TO REGISTER: OPPOSITION: WITHDRAWAL OF TRADE MARK APPLICATION: COSTS: Australia: Pat. Off.)   18 I.P.R. 92

Edinburgh Laboratories (Australia) Pty Ltd v. Lantigen (England) Ltd (PROCEDURE: PROPER LAW OF CONTRACT: JURISDICTION: Australia: S.C.(NSW))
31 I.P.R. 499

Editions Gallimard v. Hamish Hamilton Ltd (COPYRIGHT: *Droit moral:* France)
[1986] F.S.R. 42; [1985] E.C.C. 574

Edwards (A.C.) Ltd v. Acme Signs & Displays Ltd (PATENT: INFRINGEMENT: CONSTRUCTION OF CLAIM: VALIDITY: NOVELTY: OBVIOUSNESS: COMMON GENERAL KNOWLEDGE: COMMERCIAL SUCCESS: Pat. Ct)   [1990] R.P.C. 621

Edwards (A.C.) Ltd v. Acme Signs & Displays Ltd (PATENT: AMENDMENT OF CLAIMS DURING PROSECUTION: ADDED MATTER: EPO DECISIONS APPLIED: C.A.)   [1992] R.P.C. 131

Edwards Hot Water Systems v. S.W. Hart & Co. Pty Ltd, *sub nom.* Hart (S.W.) & Co. v. Edwards Hot Water

Efamol/Pharmaceutical compositions (EUROPEAN PATENT: CLAIMS: FUNCTIONAL FEATURES: T139/85: EPO)   [1987] E.P.O.R. 229

Effem Foods Pty Ltd v. Design Concepts Pty Ltd (TRADE MARKS: OPPOSITION TO APPLICATION FOR REGISTRATION: APPLICATION TO EXTEND TIME TO FILE EVIDENCE IN SUPPORT OF OPPOSITION: EXTENSION OPPOSED: INTENTION TO OPPOSE A SECOND APPLICATION FOR REGISTRATION INSUFFICIENT GROUND TO JUSTIFY FURTHER EXTENSIONS: Australia: Pat. Off.)
19 I.P.R. 569

Effem Foods Pty Ltd v. Trade Consultants Ltd (CONFIDENTIAL INFORMATION: INTERNATIONAL TRADE ADVISOR: DUTIES OWED TO EX-CLIENT: *Quia timet* INJUNCTION: New Zealand: H.C.)   15 I.P.R. 45

Eirpage Ltd (Re) (RESTRICTIVE PRACTICES: TELECOMMUNICATIONS: JOINT VENTURE SETTING UP AND OPERATING NATIONWIDE PAGING SYSTEM: INTENTION TO EXEMPT: E.C. Comm.)   [1991] 4 C.M.L.R. 233
(INDIVIDUAL EXEMPTION GRANTED: E.C. Comm.)   [1993] 4 C.M.L.R. 64

Eisai, Bayer, Pharmuka/Second medical indication (EUROPEAN PATENT: G01/83: EPO)   [1979–85] E.P.O.R. B241; [1985] O.J. EPO 60

Eisai, Bayer, Pharmuka/Second medical indication (EUROPEAN PATENT: CLAIMS: SECOND PHARMACEUTICAL INDICATION: SWISS STYLE: PATENTABILITY: SECOND MEDICAL INDICATION: CONVENTIONS: HARMONISED APPROACH: VIENNA CONVENTION RULES: ENLARGED BOARD OF APPEAL: POINT OF LAW, ANSWERED: G05/83: EPO) [1979–85] E.P.O.R. B241; [1985] O.J. EPO 64

Eisai, Bayer, Pharmuka/Second medical indication (EUROPEAN PATENT: G06/83: EPO)   [1979–85] E.P.O.R. B241; [1985] O.J. EPO 67

Eisai/Antihistamines (EUROPEAN PATENT: APPEAL: PROCEDURE: REMITTAL ORDERED: TO CONSIDER FRESH EVIDENCE: INVENTIVE STEP: EVIDENCE: COMPARATIVE TESTS: MUST BE BASED ON CLOSEST PRIOR ART: NOVELTY: SELECTION: OVERLAPPING CLASS: T164/83: EPO)
[1987] E.P.O.R. 205; [1987] O.J. EPO 149

Eisai/Remittal (EUROPEAN PATENT: APPLICATION: REFUSAL ON ONE GROUND: OBSERVATION ON OTHER GROUND: APPEAL: AMENDMENT: REMITTAL: T311/94: EPO)   [1995] E.P.O.R. 597

Elan Digital Systems Ltd v. Elan Computers Ltd (PASSING OFF: INJUNCTION: WHETHER TRIABLE ISSUE: PRACTICE ON INJUNCTION APPEALS: C.A.)
[1984] F.S.R. 373

Elazac Pty Ltd v. Commissioner of Patents (PATENTS: AMENDMENT: OPPOSITION: *Locus standii* OF PERSON WHO FAILED TO OPPOSE: RIGHT OF APPEAL: Australia: AIPO)   125 A.L.R. 663; 29 I.P.R. 479

Elconnex Pty Ltd v. Gerard Industries Pty Ltd (DESIGNS: WHETHER OBVIOUS LIMITATION: APPEARANCE: DELIBERATE COPYING WITH CHANGES TO DISGUISE COPYING: FRAUDULENT IMITATION: PATENT: AMBIGUITY: CONSTRUCTION: OBVIOUSNESS: PRINCIPLES: PETTY PATENT: FAIRLY BASED ON PROVISIONAL OR COMPLETE SPECIFICATION FROM WHICH IT WAS DERIVED: TRADE PRACTICES: SILENCE: FAILURE TO DISCLOSE DEFECT RENDERING USE OF GOODS SOLD ILLEGAL: WHETHER MISLEADING AND DECEPTIVE CONDUCT: WORDS "PAT PEND" ENDORSED ON GOODS: GOODS NOT THE SUBJECT OF ANY PATENT APPLICATION: Australia: Fed. Ct)
105 A.L.R. 247; 22 I.P.R. 551

Elconnex Pty Ltd v. Gerard Industries Pty Ltd (PETTY PATENT: OBVIOUSNESS: ADMISSIBILITY OF EVIDENCE OF EXPERT WITNESSES: WHETHER PETTY PATENT FAIRLY BASED ON COMPLETE SPECIFICATION: WHETHER CLAIM OF THE PETTY PATENT AMBIGUOUS: INFRINGEMENT: PRACTICE: DISCRETION TO AWARD COSTS: Australia: Fed. Ct)   25 I.P.R. 173

Elconnex Pty Ltd v. Gerard Industries Pty Ltd (PATENT: OPPOSITION: OBVIOUSNESS: RELATED PETTY PATENT: Australia: AIPO)   28 I.P.R. 609

Elders IXL Ltd v. Australian Estates Pty Ltd (TRADE PRACTICES: MISLEADING AND DECEPTIVE CONDUCT: USE OF NAME OF OLD ESTABLISHED BUSINESS: USE OF ABANDONED NAME: PASSING OFF: RESIDUAL GOODWILL: Australia: Fed. Ct)
10 I.P.R. 575

Eleanor A. Consulting Ltd v. Eleanor's Fashions Ltd (TRADE MARK: INFRINGEMENT: INTERLOCUTORY INJUNCTION: DAMAGES: HONEST CONCURRENT USER: Canada: FCTD)   33 C.P.R. (3d) 320

Eleco Holdings plc and Mitek Holdings Inc.'s Agreement (RESTRICTIVE PRACTICES: DIVESTITURE OF U.K. SUBSIDIARY WITH LICENCE TO CONTINUE MANUFACTURE OF EXISTING PRODUCT: TRADE MARKS DELIMITATION AGREEMENT: INTENTION TO APPROVE: E.C. Comm.) [1992] 4 C.M.L.R. 70

Electric Furnace Co. v. Selas Corp. of America (PATENT: INFRINGEMENT: PRACTICE: LEAVE TO SERVE DEFENDANT OUT OF JURISDICTION: APPEAL: C.A.)   [1987] R.P.C. 23

Electricité de France (EDF's) Patents and Commissariat a L'Énergie Atomique's Patents (PATENT: RESTORATION: NON-PAYMENT OF RENEWAL FEES: Pat. Ct)   [1992] R.P.C. 205

Electricity Trust of South Australia v. Zellweger Uster Pty Ltd (PATENT: OPPOSITION: NOTIONAL ADDRESSEE: COMMON GENERAL KNOWLEDGE: PRIOR PUBLICATION: NOVELTY: ANTICIPATION: FAIR BASIS: Australia: Pat. Off.)   7 I.P.R. 491

Electro-Catheter/Protest (EUROPEAN PATENT: UNITY: LACK OF, RESULTING FROM ANTICIPATION OF CLAIM 1: W08/87: EPO)   [1989] E.P.O.R. 390

Electrolux AB and AEG AG (Re the Agreements Between) (RESTRICTIVE PRACTICES: SPECIALISATION AGREEMENTS: PRODUCTION OF DOMESTIC APPLIANCES: CROSS-SHAREHOLDINGS: INTENTION TO APPROVE: NOTICE: E.C. Comm.)   [1994] 4 C.M.L.R. 112

Electrolux/Automatic dispenser (EUROPEAN PATENT: AMENDMENT AND CORRECTION: DRAWINGS: TEACHING OF: CLAIMS: CONSTRUCTION: DICTIONARY, RELIANCE UPON: INVENTIVE STEP: SIMPLIFICATION OF PRIOR ART: T428/88: EPO)   [1990] E.P.O.R. 385

Eli Lilly and Co. v. Novopharm Ltd (PATENT: PROCESS: MANUFACTURE OF PHARMACEUTICAL: WHETHER INFRINGING PROCESS USED: DOCTRINE OF EQUIVALENTS: PURPOSIVE CONSTRUCTION: STATUTORY NOTICE UNDER PATENTED MEDICINES REGULATION: PROHIBITION ON ISSUE: Canada: Fed. Ct)   [1996] R.P.C. 1

Eli Lilly/Antibiotic (EUROPEAN PATENT: AMENDMENT AND CORRECTION: CHEMICAL FORMULA, CORRECTION OF: APPEAL: PROCEDURE: REMITTAL ORDERED: TO RECONSIDER UNFAVOURABLE INDICATION: T161/86: EPO)   [1987] E.P.O.R. 366

Elida Gibbs (Pty) Ltd v. Colgate Palmolive (Pty) Ltd (TRADE PRACTICES: UNLAWFUL COMPETITION: ADVERTISEMENT: TEST: *Boni mores* OF SOCIETY: South Africa: WLD)   1988 (2) S.A. 350

Elida Gibbs Ltd v. Colgate-Palmolive Ltd (PASSING OFF: TOOTHPASTE ADVERTISING: *Quia timet* RELIEF: REPUTATION: COMPETING TRADE: Ch.D.)   [1983] F.S.R. 95

Elley Ltd v. Wairoa-Harrison & McCarthy (CONFIDENTIAL INFORMATION: EX-EMPLOYEE: DELIVERY-UP OF DOCUMENTS: New Zealand: H.C.)
8 I.P.R. 423

Elopak v. Tetra Pak (RESTRICTIVE PRACTICES: DOMINANT POSITION: RELEVANT MARKET: PRODUCT MARKET: GEOGRAPHICAL MARKET: TAKE-OVERS: EXCLUSIVE LICENSING: INTER-STATE TRADE: E.C. Comm.)
[1990] 4 C.M.L.R. 47; [1990] F.S.R. 263

Elopak Italia Srl v. Tetra Pak (No. 2) (RESTRICTIVE PRACTICES: DOMINANT POSITION: ABUSE: RELEVANT PRODUCT MARKET: SALES CONTRACTS: TYING CLAUSES: EXCLUSIVE SUPPLY: ELIMINATORY PRICING: DISCRIMINATORY PRICING: E.C. Comm.) [1992] 4 C.M.L.R. 551; [1992] F.S.R. 542

Elram International Actuators Ltd v. Fluid Power Engineering Ltd (COPYRIGHT: INFRINGEMENT: REQUEST FOR PARTICULARS OF ORIGINALITY: PARTICULARS ORDERED: Ch.D.) [1984] F.S.R. 151

Elton John v. James, *sub nom.* John (Elton) v. James

Elton/Delay in post (EUROPEAN PATENT: APPLICATION: PROCEDURE: DATE OF FILING: DISCRETION TO EXTEND TIME LIMITS: CONVENTIONS: NATIONAL LAWS, RELATIONSHIP OF EPC TO: J04/87: EPO)
  [1988] E.P.O.R. 346; [1988] O.J. EPO 172

Eltra Corp.'s Trade Mark Applications (TRADE MARK: APPLICATIONS: NAMES OF TYPEFACES: DISTINCTIVENESS: T.M.Reg.) [1985] R.P.C. 50

Email Ltd v. Sharp KK (TRADE MARK: APPLICATION: OPPOSITION: REFERENCE TO QUALITY OR CHARACTER OF GOODS: Australia: Pat. Off.) 3 I.P.R. 331

Emdon Investments Pty Ltd v. Shell International Petroleum Co. Ltd (TRADE MARKS: OPPOSITION: PRIOR REGISTERED MARKS: SUBSTANTIAL IDENTITY OR DECEPTIVE SIMILARITY: Australia: Pat. Off.) 12 I.P.R. 525

EMI Electrola GmbH v. Patricia IM-und Export Verwaltungs GmbH (COPYRIGHT: IMPORTS: PHONOGRAMS: SOUND RECORDING RIGHTS: ARTICLE 36: EXERCISE OF COPYRIGHT: ARTIFICIAL PARTITIONING: EXHAUSTION OF RIGHTS: EXPIRY OF COPYRIGHT PERIOD IN DENMARK, NOT IN GERMANY: Case 341/87: ECJ)
  [1989] 2 C.M.L.R. 413; [1989] E.C.R. 79; [1989] 1 F.S.R. 544

EMI Music Publishing Ltd v. Papathanasiou (COPYRIGHT: INFRINGEMENT: MUSICAL WORK: *Chariots of Fire* THEME: SUBCONSCIOUS COPYING: INNOCENCE: Ch.D.) [1993] E.M.L.R. 306

EMI Records Ltd v. Kudhail (COPYRIGHT: INFRINGEMENT: ANTON PILLER PRACTICE: REPRESENTATIVE CLASS OF DEFENDANTS: COMMON INTEREST: C.A.) [1985] F.S.R. 36

EMI Records Ltd v. The CD Specialists Ltd (COPYRIGHT: INFRINGEMENT: SOUND RECORDING RIGHTS: BOOTLEG RECORDS: INTERLOCUTORY INJUNCTION: GERMAN IMPORTS: ARTICLE 30 DEFENCE: WHETHER COPYRIGHT OWNER CONSENTED: EXHAUSTION OF RIGHTS: Ch.D.) [1992] F.S.R. 70

Encompass Europe (Re) (RESTRICTIVE PRACTICES: JOINT VENTURES: JOINT OPERATION OF COMPUTERISED CARGO LOGISTICS INFORMATION SYSTEM: INTENTION TO APPROVE CONDITIONAL ON SYSTEM BEING OPERATED IN LINE WITH GROUP EXEMPTION ON COMPUTERISED RESERVATION SYSTEMS: E.C. Comm.) [1992] 5 C.M.L.R. 537

ENDLESS VACATION Trade Mark, *sub nom.* THE ENDLESS VACATION Trade Mark

Energy Conversion Devices Inc.'s Applications, *sub nom.* E's Applications

Energy Conversion/Silicon deposition (EUROPEAN PATENT: EVIDENCE: INVENTIVE STEP, ROLE IN DISPROVING: INVENTIVE STEP: EVIDENCE OF SKILLED PERSON: SIMPLICITY: T490/89: EPO) [1993] E.P.O.R. 46

Engineering & Chemical Supplies (Epsom & Glos.) Ltd v. AKZO Chemie BV (RESTRICTIVE PRACTICES: DOMINANT POSITION: RELEVANT MARKET: PRODUCT MARKET: RELEVANT CRITERIA: E.C. Comm.)
  [1986] 3 C.M.L.R. 273

Engineering & Pulp Producers Pvt. Ltd v. Raj Kumar Shah & Cons. (REGISTERED DESIGN: CANCELLATION: India: H.C.) (1987) 12 I.P.L.R. 88

Engineering Dynamics Ltd v. Reid & Harrison (1980) Ltd (COPYRIGHT: INFRINGEMENT: TEST: SUBSTANTIAL PART: INDIRECT COPYING: VERBAL AND VISUAL INSTRUCTIONS: CONVERSION DAMAGES: New Zealand: H.C.)
9 I.P.R. 17

English & American Insurance Co. Ltd v. Herbert Smith (CONFIDENTIAL INFORMATION: EVIDENCE: LEGAL PROFESSIONAL PRIVILEGE: INNOCENT RECEIPT OF INFORMATION: Ch.D.)   [1988] F.S.R. 232

English Clays/Gravure printing (EUROPEAN PATENT: INVENTIVE STEP: EMPIRICAL FIELD: PRIOR ART: ACADEMIC SEMINAR PAPER DISREGARDED: NEIGHBOURING FIELDS, DIFFERENT PROBLEM: T64/82: EPO)
[1979–85] E.P.O.R. B479

Enichem SpA and ICI's Agreements (RESTRICTIVE PRACTICES: JOINT VENTURES: EXEMPTION GRANTED: E.C. Comm.)   [1989] 4 C.M.L.R. 54

Ente Nazionale Idrocarburi (ENI) & Montedison (RESTRICTIVE PRACTICES: SPECIALISATION AGREEMENTS: RATIONALISATION: OVERLAPPING PRODUCTS: REDUCTION OF CAPACITY: EXEMPTION: E.C. Comm.)
[1988] 4 C.M.L.R. 444

Entec (Pollution Control) Ltd v. Abacus Mouldings (COPYRIGHT: INFRINGEMENT: SEPTIC TANKS: INTERLOCUTORY INJUNCTION: SIMPLE SKETCHES WITH DIMENSIONS: BALANCE OF RISK OF INJUSTICE: Ch.D.: C.A.)
[1992] F.S.R. 332

Enthone/Electroless plating (EUROPEAN PATENT: INVENTIVE STEP: PROBLEM AND SOLUTION: NOVELTY: CLEARLY, UNMISTAKABLY AND FULLY DERIVABLE TEST: T450/89: EPO)   [1994] E.P.O.R. 326

Enviro-Clear Co. Inc. v. Commissioner of Patents (PATENT: EXTENSION: DISCOVERY: PRINCIPLES: Australia: S.C.(NSW))   9 I.P.R. 129

Enviro-Spray Systems Inc.'s Patents (PATENT: COMPULSORY LICENCE: ABILITY TO WORK INVENTION: C.-G.)   [1986] R.P.C. 147

Enviro-Spray/Self-pressuring dispenser container (EUROPEAN PATENT: INVENTIVE STEP: ADVANTAGES OUTWEIGHING DISADVANTAGES: T207/84: EPO)   [1979–85] E.P.O.R. C993

Environmental Information Directive (Draft) (FREEDOM OF ACCESS TO INFORMATION ON THE ENVIRONMENT: E.C. Council)
[1989] 1 C.M.L.R. 666

Envirotech Australia Pty Ltd v. Enviroclear Co. Inc. (PATENT: PETITION FOR REVOCATION: PATENTEE UNDERTAKING NOT TO TAKE ANY PROCEEDINGS AGAINST THE PETITIONER RELYING OF LETTERS PATENT: APPLICATION TO DISMISS PETITION AS FRIVOLOUS, VEXATIOUS OR AN ABUSE OF PROCESS: Australia: Fed. Ct)   10 I.P.R. 657

Enzed Holdings Ltd v. Wynthea Pty Ltd (COPYRIGHT: INFRINGEMENT: FOREIGN AUTHOR: RIGHT OF ACTION: Australia: Fed. Ct)   (1985) 57 A.L.R. 167

Enzed Holdings Ltd v. Wynthea Pty Ltd (COPYRIGHT: OWNERSHIP: COMMISSIONED WORK: FOREIGN AUTHOR: *Locus standi:* Australia: Fed. Ct)
57 A.L.R. 167; 3 I.P.R. 619

EPC Rules/Amendment – (EUROPEAN PATENT: PROCEDURE: FILING BY FACSIMILE, ETC.: EPO)   [1987] E.P.O.R. 336

EPC Rules/Amendment – Late payment, etc. (EUROPEAN PATENT: APPLICATION: PROCEDURE: DATES FOR ORAL HEARINGS: COMMUNICATION UNDER RULE 51(4), EFFECT OF: EPO)   [1987] E.P.O.R. 335

Epikhiriseon Metalleftikon Viomikhanikon Kai Naftiliakon AE v. E.C. Comm. Council and E.C. Commission (EUROPEAN COURT PROCEDURE: DISCOVERY OF DOCUMENTS: PROCEDURAL DELAYS: Cases 121–122/86R: ECJ)
[1987] 2 C.M.L.R. 558; [1986] E.C.R. 2063

Era/Static inverter (EUROPEAN PATENT: AMENDMENT AND CORRECTION: CLARIFICATION OF SUCCINCT INITIAL DESCRIPTION: REFERENCE NUMERALS ADDED: INVENTIVE STEP: NON-OBVIOUS FEATURES OF COMBINATION: PROBLEM, FEATURES NECESSARY FOR SOLUTION OF: T167/82: EPO)
[1986] E.P.O.R. 137

Erauw-Jacquéry (Louis) Sprl v. La Hesbignonne Société Co-opérative (RESTRICTIVE PRACTICES: PLANT BREEDERS RIGHTS: LICENSING AGREEMENTS: SALES BAN: EXPORT BAN: ARTICLE 85(1): INTER-STATE TRADE: Case 27/87: ECJ)
[1988] 4 C.M.L.R. 576; [1988] E.C.R. 1919; [1988] F.S.R. 572

Erica Vale Australia Pty Limited v. Thompson & Morgan (Ipswich) Limited (COPYRIGHT: LITERARY WORK: ADAPTATION: OWNERSHIP: CONTRACT: IMPLIED TERM: DAMAGES: COSTS INCURRED IN MITIGATION OF LOSS: LOST PROFITS: Australia: Fed. Ct)
29 I.P.R. 589

Eriksson/Foam plastic filter (EUROPEAN PATENT: NOVELTY: MERE VERBAL DISTINCTION: T114/86: EPO)   [1988] E.P.O.R. 25; [1987] O.J. EPO 485

Erven Warnink BV v. J. Townend & Sons (Hull) Ltd (PASSING OFF: PRACTICE: COSTS: INTEREST ON COSTS: TIME OF ENTERING JUDGMENT: C.A.)
[1982] R.P.C. 511

E.S. & M.J. Heard Pty Ltd v. Phillips (PATENT: OPPOSITION: EVIDENCE: REQUEST TO SUMMON A WITNESS: WHETHER CONFLICT ON THE FACTS: REQUEST REFUSED: Australia: AIPO)
26 I.P.R. 461

Esanda Ltd v. Esanda Finance Ltd (PASSING OFF: COMPANY NAME: INTERIM INJUNCTION: OVERSEAS REPUTATION: SPILL-OVER OF REPUTATION FROM AUSTRALIA: New Zealand: H.C.)
[1984] N.Z.L.R. 748; 2 I.P.R. 182; [1984] F.S.R. 96

ESB/Follow-on appeal (EUROPEAN PATENT: APPEAL: PROCEDURE: FOLLOW-ON APPEAL, NO INQUEST: AMENDMENT AND CORRECTION: PRIOR ART, ACKNOWLEDGEMENT FOLLOWING OPPOSITION DECISION: DISCLOSURE: OPPOSITION: CONSEQUENTIAL AMENDMENT OF DESCRIPTION: T757/91: EPO)
[1993] E.P.O.R. 595

Escherich Developments (Pty) Ltd v. Andrew Mentis Steel Sales (Pty) Ltd (TRADE MARK: UNLAWFUL COMPETITION: South Africa: WLD)
1983 (3) S.A. 810

Esco Corp.'s Application (TRADE MARK: APPLICATION: AMENDMENT: DISTINCTIVENESS: Australia: Pat. Off.)
4 I.P.R. 457

Esdan/Electric fusion pipe fittings (EUROPEAN PATENT: INVENTIVE STEP: COMBINATION OF CITATIONS: T232/86: EPO)   [1988] E.P.O.R. 89

Esquire Electronics Ltd v. Executive Video (TRADE MARK: INFRINGEMENT: PRE-RECORDED VIDEO TAPES: South Africa: A.D.)
1986 (2) S.A. 576

Esquire Electronics Ltd v. Roopanand Bros (Pty) Ltd (TRADE MARK: INFRINGEMENT: MAGNETICALLY RECORDED IMAGES: WHETHER REPRODUCTION ESTABLISHED: South Africa: D&CLD)
1984 (4) S.A. 409; [1985] R.P.C. 83
(S.C) 1986 (2) S.A. 576; [1991] R.P.C. 425

ESSCO Sanitations v. Mascot Industries (TRADE MARK: INFRINGEMENT: INJUNCTION: India: H.C.)
(1982) 7 I.P.L.R. 25

Esselte Letraset Ltd's Application (TRADE MARKS: OPPOSITION: EXTENSION OF TIME: CIRCUMSTANCES BEYOND CONTROL: Australia: Pat. Off.)
21 I.P.R. 517

Essex Electric (Pte) Ltd v. IPC Computers (U.K.) Ltd (PASSING OFF: COPYRIGHT: INFRINGEMENT: TRADE MARK: OWNED BY SINGAPORE COMPANY USED WORLDWIDE: EXCLUSIVE DISTRIBUTION AGREEMENT IN U.K.: WHETHER OWNERSHIP OF U.K. GOODWILL VESTED IN PLAINTIFF OR EXCLUSIVE DISTRIBUTOR: Ch.D.)
[1991] F.S.R. 690; 19 I.P.R. 639

Esswein/Automatic programmer (EUROPEAN PATENT: INVENTIVE STEP: PRIOR ART IN DIFFERENT FIELD: PROBLEM, PERCEPTION OF: PATENTABILITY: NON-TECHNICAL PROBLEM: CONVENTIONS: PURPOSE OF PATENT SYSTEM: ENLARGED BOARD OF APPEAL: REFERENCE REFUSED: T579/88: EPO)
[1991] E.P.O.R. 120
Estate Agents Co-operative Ltd's Application (TRADE MARKS: APPLICATION: REALTOR: WHETHER DESCRIPTIVE: USED IN COURSE OF TRADE: NO DIRECT SALES OF GOODS: SALES TAX PAYABLE IN GOODS: Australia: Pat. Off.)
20 I.P.R. 547
Estate Agents Co-operative Ltd v. National Association of Realtors (TRADE MARKS: APPLICATION TO REMOVE MARK FOR NON-USE: USE IN RESPECT OF SERVICES: CLASSIFICATION OF SERVICES PROVIDED TO MEMBERS OF AN ASSOCIATION: Australia: Pat. Off.)
11 I.P.R. 467
Estée Lauder Cosmetics Ltd v. Registrar of Trade Marks (TRADE MARK: REGISTRATION: DISCLAIMER OF PART OF MARK: APPLICATION FOR ESTÉE LAUDER BEAUTIFUL: NON-DISTINCTIVE CHARACTER: South Africa: TPD)
1993 (3) S.A. 43
ETA Fabriques d'Ebauches SA v. DK Investment SA (RESTRICTIVE PRACTICES: EXCLUSIVE DEALING: DISTRIBUTION NETWORK: RESTRICTION ON SELLING OUTSIDE CONTRACT TERRITORY: Case 31/85: ECJ)
[1986] 2 C.M.L.R. 674; [1985] E.C.R. 3933
ETA/Watch (EUROPEAN PATENT: INVENTIVE STEP: AESTHETIC CONTRIBUTIONS IRRELEVANT: COMMERCIAL SUCCESS: RELEVANT ONLY IN CASE OF DOUBT: PATENTABILITY: AESTHETIC FEATURES: T456/90: EPO)
[1993] E.P.O.R. 252
État Français/Correction of drawings (EUROPEAN PATENT: APPEAL: PROCEDURE: REMITTAL ORDERED: TO INVESTIGATE WHETHER MISTAKE HAD BEEN MADE: AMENDMENT AND CORRECTION: DRAWINGS: REPLACEMENT OF: J04/85: EPO)
[1986] E.P.O.R. 331; [1986] O.J. EPO 205
État Français/Portable hyperbar box structure (EUROPEAN PATENT: APPEAL: PROCEDURE: FRESH PRIOR ART: ADMITTED IN VIEW OF RELEVANCE: REMITTAL NOT ORDERED: NO OBJECTION TO ADMISSION OF FRESH CITATIONS: OPPOSITION: PROCEDURE: FRESH DOCUMENTS ON APPEAL: T258/84: EPO)
[1987] E.P.O.R. 154; [1987] O.J. EPO 119
Etri Fans Ltd v. NMB (U.K.) Ltd (PRACTICE: COPYRIGHT: INFRINGEMENT: ARBITRATION CLAUSE: STAY OF ACTION: C.A.)
[1987] F.S.R. 389; [1987] 2 All E.R. 763; [1987] 1 W.L.R. 1110
Eurim-Pharm v. Beiersdorf *sub nom.* Bristol Myers Squibb v. Paranova
Euro-Celtique/6–Thioxanthine derivatives (EUROPEAN PATENT: APPLICATION: PROCEDURE: DISCRETION UNDER RULE 86(3): AMENDMENT AND CORRECTION: APPROVAL AFTER: COMMUNICATION UNDER RULE 51(6), EFFECT OF: EPO: FUNCTIONS OF: GENERAL PUBLIC INTEREST, REGARD TO: FEES: REIMBURSEMENT OF APPEAL FEE: INSUBSTANTIAL PROCEDURAL VIOLATION: T675/90: EPO)
[1994] E.P.O.R. 66; [1994] O.J. EPO 58
Eurofix Ltd and Bauco (U.K.) Ltd v. Hilti AG (RESTRICTIVE PRACTICES: RESPONSIBILITY OF PARENT COMPANY FOR ACTIONS OF SUBSIDIARIES: DOMINANT POSITION: SAFETY WORRIES DO NOT JUSTIFY ABUSIVE CONDUCT WHERE ADEQUATE STANDARDS EXIST THROUGHOUT E.C.: DOMINANT COMPANY RESTRICTING AVAILABILITY OF PATENTED PRODUCT: OBSTRUCTING INDEPENDENT MANUFACTURERS OF PRODUCTS ONLY CAPABLE OF USE WITH THE PATENTED PRODUCT FROM PENETRATING MARKET: ABUSE: FINE IMPOSED: E.C. Comm.)
[1989] 4 C.M.L.R. 677; [1988] F.S.R. 473; [1990] F.S.R. 45

Europcar International S.A. and Interrent Autovermietung GmbH's Merger (RESTRICTIVE PRACTICES: MERGERS: JOINT VENTURE: CAR RENTAL: INTENTION TO EXEMPT: E.C. Comm.)   [1989] 4 C.M.L.R. 119

European Broadcasting Unions Application (RESTRICTIVE PRACTICES: BROADCASTING: JOINT ACQUISITION OF TV RIGHTS TO SPORTS EVENTS: EXCHANGE SYSTEM FOR PROGRAMMES: INTENTION TO APPROVE: E.C. Comm.)   [1991] 4 C.M.L.R. 228

European Broadcasting Union (RESTRICTIVE PRACTICES: BROADCASTING: EXCHANGE OF NEWS ITEMS BETWEEN UNION MEMBERS: USE BY NON-MEMBERS: RATES AND CONDITIONS: E.C. Comm.)   [1987] 1 C.M.L.R. 390

European Committee for Co-operation of the Machine Tool Industries (CECIMO) Application (RESTRICTIVE PRACTICES: TRADE FAIRS: INTENTION TO RENEW EXEMPTION: E.C. Comm.)   [1989] 4 C.M.L.R. 17

European Community v. (xxxx), *sub nom.* Community v. (xxxx)

European Ltd v. The Economist Newspapers Ltd *sub nom.* The European Ltd v. The Economist Newspapers Ltd

European Music Satellite Venture (RESTRICTIVE PRACTICES: JOINT VENTURE: CABLE TV BY SATELLITE: INTENTION TO APPROVE: E.C. Comm.)
          [1984] 3 C.M.L.R. 162; [1984] O.J. C209/3

European Pacific Banking Corp. v. Fourth Estate Publications Ltd (CONFIDENTIAL INFORMATION: INJUNCTION: "INIQUITY RULE": PUBLIC INTEREST: EFFECT OF DOCUMENTS ALREADY IN PUBLIC DOMAIN: New Zealand: H.C.)
          [1993] 1 N.Z.L.R. 559

European Telecommunication Standards Institute (ESTI) Interim Intellectual Property Rights Policy (RESTRICTIVE PRACTICES: TELECOMMUNICATIONS: TECHNICAL STANDARDS: INTELLECTUAL PROPERTY: LICENSING: INTENTION TO EXEMPT: E.C. Comm.)   [1995] 4 C.M.L.R. 352

European Vinyls Corp. (RESTRICTIVE PRACTICES: JOINT VENTURE: INTENTION TO APPROVE: E.C. Comm.)   [1991] 4 C.M.L.R. 327

European Vinyls Corp. (RESTRICTIVE PRACTICES: JOINT VENTURE: RATIONALISATION PROGRAMME: INTENTION TO GRANT EXEMPTION: E.C. Comm.)   [1988] 4 C.M.L.R. 15

European Wastepaper Information Service (RESTRICTIVE PRACTICES: COMMERCIAL INFORMATION EXCHANGE: INTENTION TO APPROVE: E.C. Comm.)   [1988] 4 C.M.L.R. 173

Eurosport (Re) (RESTRICTIVE PRACTICES: BROADCASTING: OPERATION OF SINGLE PAN-EUROPEAN SPORTS CHANNEL BY CONSORTIUM OF NATIONAL BROADCASTERS: INTENTION TO APPROVE: E.C. Comm.)
          [1993] 4 C.M.L.R. 392

Eurotunnel (Re) (RESTRICTIVE PRACTICES: JOINT VENTURES: NOTICE: E.C. Comm.)   [1988] 4 C.M.L.R. 746

Evans & Sons Ltd v. Spritebrand Ltd (COPYRIGHT: INFRINGEMENT: COMPANY DIRECTOR: DIRECTORS' KNOWLEDGE: AUTHORISATION: C.A.)
          [1985] F.S.R. 267; [1985] 2 All E.R. 415; [1985] 1 W.L.R. 317

Evening Standard Co. Ltd v. Henderson (RESTRICTIVE COVENANT: EMPLOYEE: C.A.)   [1987] F.S.R. 165

Everest Pictures Circuit v. Karuppannan (COPYRIGHT: INFRINGEMENT: CINEMATOGRAPH FILM: India: H.C.)   (1982) 7 I.P.L.R. 1

Ewins v. Buderim Imports Pty Ltd (COURTS AND JUDGES: JURISDICTION: CONFERRAL OF JURISDICTION ON SUPREME COURT: CONVENIENCE OF TRANSFER OF PROCEEDING: Australia: Fed. Ct)   11 I.P.R. 327

Ex-Cell-O/Laminated paperboard container (EUROPEAN PATENT: APPEAL: PROCEDURE: AMENDMENT OF CLAIM ON APPEAL: FORMULATION OF PROBLEM: INVENTIVE STEP: COMMERCIAL SUCCESS: SKILLED PERSON, RELEVANT FIELD: STATE OF THE ART: TREND OF THE ART: T80/88: EPO) [1991] E.P.O.R. 596

Excelsior Pte Ltd v. Excelsior Sport (C) Pte Ltd (TRADE NAME: PASSING OFF: CONFUSION: Malaysia: H.C.) [1986] 1 M.L.J. 130

Exotic Products Ltd's Application (TRADE MARKS: APPLICATION: LAUDATORY WORD: NOT DISTINCTIVE: DISCLAIMER: RATIONALE BEHIND THE DISCLAIMER REQUIREMENT: Australia: Pat. Off.) 21 I.P.R. 580

Expanded Metal Manufacturing Pte Ltd v. Expanded Metal Co. Ltd (COPYRIGHT: INFRINGEMENT: *Ex parte* APPLICATION FOR INJUNCTION: ANTON PILLER ORDER: PRIVILEGE AGAINST SELF-INCRIMINATION: INFERENCE TO BE DRAWN: Singapore: C.A.) [1995] 1 S.L.R. 673

Express Bottlers Services Pvt. Ltd v. Pepsico Inc., *sub nom.* Pepsico Inc. v. Express Bottlers Services Pvt. Ltd

Express Newspapers plc v. Liverpool Daily Post & Echo plc (COPYRIGHT: INFRINGEMENT: ORIGINALITY: WORK PERFORMED BY COMPUTER: LOTTERIES: Ch.D.) [1985] F.S.R. 306; [1985] 3 All E.R. 680; [1986] E.C.C. 204; [1985] 1 W.L.R. 1089

Express Newspapers plc v. News (U.K.) Ltd (COPYRIGHT: INFRINGEMENT: COUNTERCLAIM: ORDER 14 APPLICATION: MUTUAL COPYING OF NEWS STORIES: FAIR DEALING: PUBLIC INTEREST: CUSTOM OF THE TRADE: IMPLIED LICENCE: Ch.D.) [1990] F.S.R. 359 (SUMMARY JUDGMENT: COUNTERCLAIM IN IDENTICAL TERMS: "TIT FOR TAT" COPYING OF NEWSPAPER STORIES: SUBSISTENCE OF COPYRIGHT: WHETHER REPORTER'S COPYRIGHT STILL EXISTED IN LAW: FAIR DEALING DEFENCE: MEANING OF "SUFFICIENT ACKNOWLEDGEMENT": PUBLIC INTEREST DEFENCE: IMPLIED LICENCE: APPROBATION AND REPROBATION: SUMMARY JUDGMENT GRANTED: Ch.D.) [1991] F.S.R. 37; 18 I.P.R. 201

Extrude Hone Corp. (PATENT: COMPULSORY LICENCE: DATE OF LICENCE: COSTS: C.-G.) [1984] F.S.R. 105

EXXATE Trade Mark (TRADE MARK: APPLICATION: PHONETIC EQUIVALENCE: Ch.D.) [1986] R.P.C. 567

Exxon Chemical International Inc. & Shell International Chemical Company Ltd (RESTRICTIVE PRACTICES: PRODUCTION JOINT VENTURE: AGREEMENT: AMENDMENT: INTENTION TO APPROVE: E.C. Comm.) [1993] 5 C.M.L.R. 76

Exxon Corp. v. Exxon Insurance Consultants International Ltd (COPYRIGHT: PASSING OFF: WHETHER SINGLE WORD ORIGINAL LITERARY WORK: Ch.D.) [1991] 2 All E.R. 495; [1982] Ch. 119; [1982] R.P.C. 69; [1981] 1 W.L.R. 624 (C.A.) [1981] 3 All E.R. 241; [1982] R.P.C. 69

Exxon Corporation, U.S.A v. Exxon Packing Systems Pvt. Ltd, Hyderabad (TRADE MARK: THREATS: PASSING OFF: INTERIM APPLICATION: APPEAL: India: H.C.) (1989) 14 I.P.L.R. 53

Exxon/Alumina spinel (EUROPEAN PATENT: APPLICATION: PROCEDURE: TELEPHONIC COMMUNICATION WITH EXAMINER, REQUEST FOR: APPEAL: REMITTAL ORDERED: NO FINAL CONCLUSION ON NOVELTY AND INVENTIVE STEP: GUIDELINES FOR EXAMINATION: NOT BINDING: T42/84: EPO) [1988] E.P.O.R. 387; [1988] O.J. EPO 251

Exxon/Arranging oral proceedings (EUROPEAN PATENT: OPPOSITION: PROCEDURE: ORAL PROCEEDINGS: FIXING DATE OF: T320/88: EPO)
[1989] E.P.O.R. 372; [1990] O.J. EPO 359
Exxon/Correction of errors (EUROPEAN PATENT: AMENDMENT AND CORRECTION: INCORRECT FIGURES: SUFFICIENCY: EXAMPLE, MISLEADING: T134/82: EPO) [1979–85] E.P.O.R. B605
Exxon/Fuel oils (EUROPEAN PATENT: CLAIMS: FEATURES NECESSARY FOR SOLUTION OF PROBLEM: FUNCTIONAL FEATURES: SUPPORT FOR: SUFFICIENCY: PURPOSE OF ARTICLE 83: WHOLE OF CLAIMED RANGE: T409/91: EPO) [1994] E.P.O.R. 149; [1994] O.J. EPO 953
Exxon/Gelation (EUROPEAN PATENT: INVENTIVE STEP: ANALOGY PROCESS: PREJUDICE: ONUS: NOVELTY: PRODUCT OF PROCESS: T119/82: EPO) [1979–85] E.P.O.R. B566; [1984] O.J. EPO 217
Exxon/Lubricating oil additive (EUROPEAN PATENT: AMENDMENT: EXTENSION OF SUBJECT MATTER: NEW RANGE: EXTRAPOLATION FROM SPECIFIC EXAMPLES: T562/92: EPO) [1995] E.P.O.R. 306
Exxon/Purification of sulphonic acids (EUROPEAN PATENT: INVENTIVE STEP: DIFFERENT PURPOSE: MULTISTAGE CHEMICAL PROCESS: T4/83: EPO)
[1979–85] E.P.O.R. C721; [1983] O.J. EPO 498

Fabcon Corp. Inc. U.S.A v. Industrial Engineering Corp. Ghaziabad (PATENT: INFRINGEMENT: TRANSFER OF SUIT: India: H.C.) (1988) 13 I.P.L.R. 1
Fablaine Ltd v. Leygill Ltd (No. 2) (COPYRIGHT: INFRINGEMENT: Ch.D.)
[1982] F.S.R. 427
Fabre/Toothbrush fibres (EUROPEAN PATENT: CLAIMS: CLARITY: REFERENCE TO DRAWINGS: ONE PART V. TWO PART: OPPOSITION: PROCEDURE: AMENDMENT OF CLAIM, CLARITY AND SUPPORT: T434/87: EPO)
[1990] E.P.O.R. 141
Fabrique Ebel SA v. Syarikat Permiagaan Tukang Jam City Port (CIVIL PROCEDURE: APPLICATION FOR FINAL JUDGMENT: CONDITIONS LAID DOWN: TRADE MARK: INFRINGEMENT: PROOF REQUIREMENTS: WHETHER DEFENDANTS HAVE SHOWN AN ARGUABLE CASE: Malaysia: H.C.)
[1988] 1 M.L.J. 188; 13 I.P.R. 47
Fabriques de Tabac Réunis SA's Application (TRADE MARK: APPLICATION: GEOGRAPHICAL NAME: ORDINARY DESCRIPTIVE TERM: DORADO: Australia: Pat. Off.) 10 I.P.R. 124
Fabritius II/Re-establishment of rights (EUROPEAN PATENT: PROCEDURE: FAIRNESS TO APPLICANTS: FEES: RE-ESTABLISHMENT FEE, FAILURE TO PAY: CONVENTIONS: PCT AND EPC, INTERPRETATION AND INTERRELATION OF: G03/91: EPO) [1993] E.P.O.R. 361; [1993] O.J. EPO 8
Fabritius/Re-establishment of rights (EUROPEAN PATENT: RE-ESTABLISHMENT OF RIGHTS: ADMISSIBILITY IN RELATION TO GRACE PERIODS: ENLARGED BOARD OF APPEAL: REFERENCE MUST BE NECESSARY TO DECISION: *Praeter legem*: J16/90: EPO) [1992] E.P.O.R. 271; [1992] O.J. EPO 260
Faccenda Chicken Ltd v. Fowler (BREACH OF CONFIDENCE: CONSPIRACY: SALES INFORMATION: MASTER AND SERVANT: DUTY OF FIDELITY: Ch.D.)
[1985] F.S.R. 105; [1985] 1 All E.R. 724;[1984] I.R.L.R. 61
(C.A.)[1986]1AllE.R.617;[1986]1Ch.117;[1986]F.S.R.291;[1986]I.R.L.R.69
Faessler v. Neale (PASSING OFF: ASSOCIATION WITH NAME: ONUS OF PROOF: Australia: Fed. Ct) 29 I.P.R. 1

Fai Insurances Ltd v. Advance Bank Australia Ltd (TRADE PRACTICES: MISLEADING
OR DECEPTIVE CONDUCT: AMBIGUOUS STATEMENTS COMPARING COMPANY
PROFITS: COPYRIGHT: PROXY FORM: IMPLIED LICENCE TO USE:
INTERLOCUTORY INJUNCTION: Australia: Fed. Ct)
68 A.L.R. 133; 7 I.P.R. 217
Fairdeal Corp. (Pvt.) Ltd v. Vijay Pharmaceuticals (TRADE MARK: INFRINGEMENT:
Ex parte INJUNCTION: APPEAL: India: H.C.)   (1985) 10 I.P.L.R. 227
Fairfax (Dental Equipment) Ltd v. Filhol (S.J.) Ltd (PATENT: VALIDITY:
INFRINGEMENT: CONSTRUCTION: C.A.)   [1986] R.P.C. 499
sub nom. Filhol (S.J.) Ltd v. Fairfax (Dental Equipment) Ltd (PATENT: DECLARA-
TION OF NON-INFRINGEMENT: DECLARATION UNDER INHERENT JURISDIC-
TION: Pat. Ct)   [1990] R.P.C. 293
Falcon Travel Ltd v. Owners Abroad Group plc (t/a Falcon Leisure Group) (TRADE
NAME: PROTECTION: PASSING OFF: REPUTATION: GOODWILL:
MISAPPROPRIATION: PROOF: DAMAGE: REMEDY: TRAVEL BUSINESS:
RELATIVE SIZE OF PARTIES: SCALE AND SCOPE OF TRADING ENVIRONMENT:
DISTINCT BUSINESS ACTIVITIES AS WHOLESALERS AND RETAILERS:
CONFUSION IN TRADE AND BY PUBLIC: WHETHER TRADE NAME
PROPRIETARY RIGHT: DISCRETION: WHETHER DAMAGES PREFERABLE TO
INJUNCTION: Ireland: H.C.)   [1991] 1 I.R. 175
Falconer v. Australian Broadcasting Corp. (CONFIDENTIAL INFORMATION:
INJUNCTION: INTERLOCUTORY: IDENTITY OF POLICE INFORMER: Australia:
S.C.(Vic.))   22 I.P.R. 205
Family Assurance Society's Service Mark (SERVICE MARK: APPLICATION: PRACTICE:
DISCLAIMER: T.M.Reg.)   [1992] R.P.C. 253
FANTASTIC SAM's Service Mark (SERVICE MARK: APPLICATION:
DISTINCTIVENESS: PRACTICE: T.M.Reg.)   [1990] R.P.C. 531
Farbenfabriken Bayer AG v. Christopher John (TRADE MARK: APPLICATION:
OPPOSITION: APPEAL: India: H.C.)   (1984) 9 I.P.L.R. 81
Farchione & Scrimizzis Application (TRADE MARK: APPLICATION: LAPSE DUE TO
NON-PAYMENT OF REGISTRATION FEE: APPLICATION FOR EXTENSION OF
TIME: UNDUE DELAY: Australia: AIPO)   28 I.P.R. 127
Farmitalia Carlo Erba Srl's Application (PATENT: SUPPLEMENTARY PROTECTION
CERTIFICATE: DURATION OF CERTIFICATE: WHETHER EARLIER VETERINARY
AUTHORISATION WAS FIRST AUTHORISATION: C.-G.)   [1996] R.P.C. 111
Farmitalia Carlo Erba SrL v. Delta West Pty Ltd (PATENT: INFRINGEMENT:
REVOCATION: PRACTICE: SECURITY FOR COSTS: APPLICANT ORDINARILY
RESIDENT OUTSIDE AUSTRALIA: DISCRETION: Australia: Fed. Ct)
28 I.P.R. 336
Fastrack Racing Pty Ltd's Application (TRADE MARK: APPLICATION: OBJECTIONS BY
EXAMINERS: POWER OF REGISTRAR TO SET DOWN FOR HEARING:
APPLICATION IN MULTIPLE CLASSES: AMENDMENT OF CLASS: DIVISIONAL
FILINGS: DESCRIPTIVE MARK: Australia: AIPO)   29 I.P.R. 193
Fateh Singh Mehta v. O. P. Singhal (COPYRIGHT: PH.D THESIS: INJUNCTION TO
PREVENT UNIVERSITY FROM AWARDING PH.D: India: H.C.)
(1990) 15 I.P.L.R. 69
Fatima Tile Works v. Sudarson Trading Co. Ltd (TRADE MARK: RECTIFICATION:
NON-USE: USE BY SUBSIDIARY COMPANY: India: H.C.)
(1992) 17 I.P.L.R. 174
Fatty Acids (Re), *sub nom.* Community v. Unilever NV.
Fawns & McAllan Pty Ltd v. Burns-Biotec Laboratories Inc. (TRADE MARK:
OPPOSITION: REMOVAL FOR NON-USE: PERSON AGGRIEVED: Australia:
T.M.Reg.)   7 I.P.R. 343

Fax Directories (Pty) Ltd v. SA Fax Listings C.C. (COPYRIGHT: SUBSISTENCE: LITERARY WORK: AUTHOR OWNERSHIP: COMPANY: INFRINGEMENT: TELEFAX DIRECTORY: South Africa: D&CLD) 1990 (2) S.A. 164

FBC Trade Mark (APPLICATION: DISTINCTIVENESS OF THREE-LETTER MASK ON "GRID" BACKGROUND: REGISTRATION: Ch.D.) [1985] R.P.C. 103

Fearis v. Davies (PRACTICE: PLEADINGS: REQUEST FOR FURTHER AND BETTER PARTICULARS: CONSENT ORDER: CONSTRUCTION OF ORDER: C.A.) [1989] 1 F.S.R. 555

Federaciónde Distribuidores Cinematográficos v. Spain (FILMS: DISTRIBUTION: LICENCES TO DUB FILMS FROM NON-MEMBER STATES INTO SPANISH: NATIONAL LEGISLATION RESTRICTING LICENCES TO DISTRIBUTORS OF SPANISH FILMS: ECJ) [1994] E.M.L.R. 153

Federal Computer Services Sdn Bhd v. Ang Jee Hai Eric (COPYRIGHT: SCOPE OF PROTECTION: COMPUTER SOFTWARE: INTERPRETATION OF STATUTE: Singapore: H.C.) [1993] 3 S.L.R. 388

Federation Internationale de Football v. Bartlett (PASSING OFF: CHARACTER MERCHANDISING: CONCEPT: REPUTATION: TRADE MARK: WORLD CUP USA 94; AMENDMENT: DISCLAIMER: MATTER COMMON TO THE TRADE: South Africa: TPD) 1994 (4) S.A. 722

Feist Publications, Inc. v. Rural Telephone Service Co. Inc. (COPYRIGHT: INFRINGEMENT: COPYING OF ORIGINAL ELEMENTS: COMPILATION: LACK OF CREATIVITY: FACT/EXPRESSION DICHOTOMY: USA: S.C.) 20 I.P.R. 129

Félicitas Sàrl v. Georges (TRADE MARK: LICENCE: OBLIGATIONS: France: C.A.) [1984] E.C.C. 28

Femis-Bank (Anguilla) Ltd v. Lazar (CONSPIRACY TO INJURE: DEFENDANTS PUBLISHING ALLEGATIONS THAT PLAINTIFF'S FINANCIALLY UNSOUND AND DISHONEST: INTENTION TO PROVE TRUTH OF ALLEGATIONS IN CONSPIRACY ACTION: WHETHER JURISDICTION TO GRANT INTERLOCUTORY INJUNCTION RESTRAINING PUBLICATION PENDING TRIAL: Ch.D.) [1991] 2 All E.R. 865; [1991] Ch. 391

Fender Australia Pty Ltd v. Beck (t/a Guitar Crazy) (TRADE MARKS: INFRINGEMENT: AUSTRALIAN TRADE MARK RIGHTS IN A U.S. TRADE MARK VESTED BY ASSIGNMENT IN DISTRIBUTOR IN AUSTRALIA: WHETHER OFFER FOR SALE IN AUSTRALIA OF SECOND-HAND GOODS BEARING OVERSEAS MANUFACTURERS TRADE MARK INFRINGES AUSTRALIAN TRADE MARK: Australia: Fed. Ct) 15 I.P.R. 257

Fender Australia Pty Ltd v. Sullivan (t/a St George Music Centre) (TRADE MARKS: INFRINGEMENT: AUSTRALIAN TRADE MARK RIGHTS IN A U.S. TRADE MARK VESTED BY ASSIGNMENT IN DISTRIBUTOR IN AUSTRALIA: SECOND-HAND GOODS: Australia: Fed. Ct) 15 I.P.R. 257

Fernholz/Vinyl acetate (EUROPEAN PATENT: AMENDMENT AND CORRECTION: DERIVED RANGE: DISCLAIMER: CLAIMS: INVENTIVE STEP: SELECTION: NOVELTY: INHERENT ADVANTAGE: PREVIOUSLY UNRECOGNISED ADVANTAGE: T188/83: EPO) [1979–85] E.P.O.R. C891; [1984] O.J. EPO 555

Ferocem Pty Ltd v. Commissioner of Patents (PATENT: OPPOSITION: EXTENSION OF TIME TO FILE EVIDENCE: PRINCIPLES: DISCRETION: Australia: Fed. Ct) 28 I.P.R. 243

Ferocem Pty Ltd v. High Tech Auto Tools Pty Ltd (PETTY PATENT: PRACTICE AND
PROCEDURE: NOTICE: INFORMATION: PENDING COURT PROCEEDINGS:
FEDERAL COURT: PATENT OFFICE PRACTICE: Australia: AIPO)
29 I.P.R. 144
(other proceedings, *sub nom.* High Tech Auto Tools Pty Ltd v. Ferocem Pty
Ltd) 29 I.P.R. 337
Ferrero/Unclear payment of fees (EUROPEAN PATENT: FEES: ALLOCATION: J16/84:
EPO) [1986] E.P.O.R. 141; [1985] O.J. EPO 357
Ferro Corp. v. Escol Products Ltd (PATENT: PRACTICE: STAY APPLICATION:
PROCEEDING IN PATENT OFFICE: Ch.D.) [1990] R.P.C. 651
Festival Records Pty Ltd v. Tenth Raymond Management Pty Ltd (INJUNCTION:
INTERLOCUTORY RELIEF: AGREEMENT TO SUPPLY RECORDS: WHETHER
IMPLIED TERM THAT SUPPLY COULD BE REFUSED ONLY IF COPYRIGHT
INFRINGEMENT ESTABLISHED: Australia: S.C.(Vic.)) 11 I.P.R. 61
Fiat and Hitachi's Joint Venture (RESTRICTIVE PRACTICES: JOINT VENTURE:
PARENT COMPANIES REMAINING POTENTIAL COMPETITORS: TERRITORIAL
PROTECTION: ARTICLE 85(1): EXEMPTION GRANTED: E.C. Comm.)
[1994] 4 C.M.L.R. 571
Fiat Geotech Technologie Per La Terra SpA and Deere & Company's Agreement
(RESTRICTIVE PRACTICES: JOINT VENTURES: JOINT RESEARCH AND
DEVELOPMENT: INTENTION TO EXEMPT: E.C. Comm.)
[1992] 4 C.M.L.R. 501
Fiat Geotech Technologie Per La Terra SpA and Hitachi Construction Machinery
Co. Ltd's Joint Venture (RESTRICTIVE PRACTICES: JOINT VENTURES: JOINT
MANUFACTURE, DISTRIBUTION AND SALE OF HYDRAULIC EXCAVATORS:
COMMUNITY MARKET EXCLUSIVE TO JOINT VENTURE AND REST OF WORLD
EXCLUSIVE TO ONE PARENT COMPANY: BUT PASSIVE SALES INTO EACH
OTHERS TERRITORY PERMITTED: INTENTION TO EXEMPT: E.C.
Comm.) [1991] 4 C.M.L.R. 857
Fibre-Chem/Baled waste paper product (EUROPEAN PATENT: INVENTIVE STEP:
COMMERCIAL SUCCESS: ANALOGOUS PURPOSE: T191/82: EPO)
[1986] E.P.O.R. 88; [1985] O.J. EPO 189
Fibre-Chem/Re-establishment of rights (EUROPEAN PATENT: RE-ESTABLISHMENT
OF RIGHTS: TIME LIMIT FOR: VICARIOUS RESPONSIBILITY, INAPPLICABLE:
T191/82: EPO) [1979–85] E.P.O.R. C701; [1985] O.J. EPO 189
Fichera v. Flogates Ltd (PATENT: INFRINGEMENT: VALIDITY: OBVIOUSNESS:
STATUTORY DEFENCE: Pat. Ct) [1983] F.S.R. 198; [1984] R.P.C. 257
(C.A.) [1984] R.P.C. 257
Fichera v. Flogates Ltd and British Steel plc (PATENT: PRACTICE: STRIKING OUT:
WHETHER NON-PROSECUTION ABUSE OF PROCESS OR INEXCUSABLE:
WHETHER MISREPRESENTATION VITIATED STAY AGREEMENT OF WAS ABUSE
OF PROCESS: ADDITION OF NEW CAUSE OF ACTION OUT OF TIME: Pat.
Ct) [1992] F.S.R. 48
Fido Dido Inc. v. Venture Stores (Retailers) Pty Ltd (PASSING OFF: "FIDO DIDO"
CHARACTER: APPLICATION FOR CONTINUATION OF INTERLOCUTORY
INJUNCTION: MISLEADING AND DECEPTIVE CONDUCT: Australia: Fed. Ct)
16 I.P.R. 365
Figgins Holdings Pty Ltd v. Parfums Christian Dior (TRADE MARKS: APPLICATION
TO REMOVE MARK FOR NON-USE: EXTENSION OF TIME FOR FILING
EVIDENCE: Australia: Pat. Off.) 11 I.P.R. 560

Figgins Holdings Pty Ltd v. Registrar of Trade Marks (TRADE MARK: OPPOSITION: PROCEEDINGS SETTLED: ASSIGNMENT OF APPLICATION: REGISTRATION OF PROPRIETORSHIP: JURISDICTION TO ORDER: Australia: Fed. Ct)
32 I.P.R. 29

Filhol (S.J.) Ltd v. Fairfax (Dental Equipment) Ltd (PATENT: DECLARATION OF NON-INFRINGEMENT: DECLARATION UNDER INHERENT JURISDICTION: Pat. Ct) [1990] R.P.C. 293
sub nom. Fairfax (Dental Equipment) Ltd v. Filhol (S.J.) Ltd (PATENT: VALIDITY: INFRINGEMENT: CONSTRUCTION: C.A.) [1986] R.P.C. 499

Film Corp. of New Zealand v. Golden Editions Pty Ltd (COPYRIGHT: INFRINGEMENT: OWNERSHIP: PASSING OFF: DESCRIPTIVE OR DISTINCTIVE: MISLEADING OR DECEPTIVE CONDUCT: Australia: Fed. Ct) 28 I.P.R. 1

Filmtec/Costs (EUROPEAN PATENT: COSTS: LATE CITATIONS AND EVIDENCE: APPORTIONED: OPPOSITION: PROCEDURE: FRESH DOCUMENTS ON APPEAL: FRESH EVIDENCE ON APPEAL, REFUSED: T117/86: EPO)
[1989] E.P.O.R. 504; [1989] O.J. EPO 401

Filtration/Fluid filter cleaning system (EUROPEAN PATENT: CLAIMS: CLARITY: MATHEMATICAL EXPRESSION: FAIR BASIS: SUFFICIENCY: EXAMPLE, ABSENCE OF: T126/89: EPO) [1990] E.P.O.R. 292

Fina/Appeal not filed (EUROPEAN PATENT: APPEAL: APPEAL FEE PAID: NOTICE OF APPEAL LACKING: RE-ESTABLISHMENT: DUE CARE: EXAMINATION PROCEDURE: REQUEST FOR GRANT: REQUEST FOR ORAL PROCEEDINGS: SUBSTANTIAL PROCEDURAL VIOLATION (NO): REFERENCE TO ENLARGED BOARD (NO): T371/92: EPO) [1995] E.P.O.R. 485

Finaf SpA and Procter & Gambles Joint Ventures (RESTRICTIVE PRACTICES: JOINT VENTURES: JOINT PRODUCTION AND DISTRIBUTION: CONDITIONAL APPROVAL INTENDED: E.C. Comm.) [1992] 4 C.M.L.R. 486

Financial Times Ltd v. Evening Standard Co. Ltd (PASSING OFF: INTERIM INJUNCTION: NEWSPAPERS: USE OF PINK PAPER FOR BUSINESS SECTION OF *Evening Standard*: WHETHER CONFUSION: DELAY: Ch.D.) [1991] F.S.R. 7

Financial Times Ltd v. Sàrl Ecopress (COPYRIGHT: NEWSPAPER ARTICLES: France) [1982] E.C.C. 459; [1983] F.S.R. 29

Findlay v. Rimfire Films Ltd (TRADE MARKS: APPLICATION: CROCODILE DUNDEE: OPPOSITION: REGISTRABILITY: USE LIKELY TO DECEIVE OR CAUSE CONFUSION: Australia: T.M.Reg.) 18 I.P.R. 59

Finers v. Miro (CONFIDENTIAL INFORMATION: SOLICITOR: CLIENT RELATIONSHIP: TRANSFER OF CLIENTS ASSETS TO OVERSEAS COMPANIES UNDER SOLICITOR'S CONTROL: C.A.) [1991] 1 All E.R. 182; [1991] 1 W.L.R. 35

FINGALS Trade Mark (TRADE MARK: APPLICATION: OFFICIAL OBJECTION: SERVICE MARK: WHETHER GOODS AND SERVICES ASSOCIATED: T.M.Reg.) [1993] R.P.C. 21

Finlay Mills Ltd v. National Textile Corp. (TRADE MARK: UNAUTHORISED USE BY MANAGED COMPANY: ENTITLEMENT TO ENFORCE: India: H.C.)
(1992) 17 I.P.L.R. 20

Fire Nymph Products Ltd v. Jalco Products (W.A.) Pty Ltd (COPYRIGHT: DESIGNS: INDUSTRIAL APPLICATION OF ARTISTIC WORK: Australia: Fed. Ct)
1 I.P.R. 79

Firmaframe Nominees Pty Ltd v. Automatic Roller Doors Aust. Pty Ltd (PATENT: OPPOSITION: EXTENTION OF TIME: OMISSION BY PATENT ATTORNEY: Australia: Pat. Off.) 4 I.P.R. 137

Firmagroup Australia Pty Ltd v. Byrne & Davidson Doors (Vic.) Pty Ltd (DESIGNS: INFRINGEMENT: ARTICLE COMPOSED WHOLLY OR CHIEFLY OF METAL: OBVIOUS IMITATION: FRAUDULENT IMITATION: NOVEL FEATURES: Australia: Fed. Ct)   67 A.L.R. 29; 4 I.P.R. 631;
(S.C.) 6 I.P.R. 377
(APPEAL: Australia: H.C.)   9 I.P.R. 353
First Green Park v. Lantech Inc., *sub nom.* Lantech Inc. v. First Green Park
First Tiffany Holdings Pty Ltd v. Tiffany & Co. (TRADE MARKS: OPPOSITION: PROPRIETORSHIP: AUTHORISED USE AND CONTROL: CONNECTION IN THE COURSE OF TRADE: USE LIKELY TO DECEIVE AND CAUSE CONFUSION: AMENDMENT TO SPECIFICATION OF GOODS: COSTS: Australia: Pat. Off.)
13 I.P.R. 589
Fiscal Technology Co. Ltd v. Johnson (CONFIDENTIAL INFORMATION: NON-DISCLOSURE AGREEMENT: BREACH OF CONTRACTUAL OBLIGATIONS: DAMAGES: COPYRIGHT: INFRINGEMENT: ADAPTATION INVOLVING SIGNIFICANT SKILL AND EXPERTISE: RELIEF: INJUNCTION: DELIVERY UP: DAMAGES: APPROPRIATENESS OF EXEMPLARY DAMAGES: New Zealand: H.C.)   23 I.P.R. 555
Fischer & Porter/Flowmeter (EUROPEAN PATENT: PRIORITY: APPLICANT'S STILL EARLIER APPLICATION: IDENTITY OF INVENTION: T400/90: EPO)
[1992] E.P.O.R. 14
Fischer Pharmaceuticals Ltd's Application (TRADE MARK: APPLICATION: REGISTRABILITY: INVENTED WORD: DESCRIPTIVENESS: Australia: AIPO)
30 I.P.R. 583
Fischer Scientific/Postal strike (EUROPEAN PATENT: J03/90: EPO)
[1992] E.P.O.R. 148; [1991] O.J. EPO 550
Fisher & Paykel Healthcare Pty Ltd v. Avion Engineering Pty Ltd (DESIGNS: INFRINGEMENT: WHETHER OBVIOUS OR FRAUDULENT IMITATION: SAME FUNDAMENTAL OR BASIC DESIGN: PATENTS: PETTY PATENT: VALIDITY: CONSTRUCTION OF CLAIM: PRINCIPLES: OBVIOUSNESS: COMBINATION OF COMMON INTEGERS: INFRINGEMENT: APPLICABLE PRINCIPLES: Australia: Fed. Ct)   103 A.L.R. 239; 22 I.P.R. 1
Fisher & Paykel Healthcare Pty Ltd v. Avion Engineering Pty Ltd (DESIGN: INFRINGEMENT: OBVIOUS IMITATION: FRAUDULENT IMITATION: RECTIFICATION: LACK OF NOVELTY AND VAGUE AND AMBIGUOUS REPRESENTATION: PATENT: COMBINATION PATENT: INFRINGEMENT: PITH AND MARROW DOCTRINE: SCOPE: PETTY PATENT: REVOCATION: OBVIOUSNESS: LACK OF FAIR BASING: Australia: Fed. Ct)   20 I.P.R. 23
Fisher & Paykel/Inwardly flanged curved members (EUROPEAN PATENT: PRIOR ART: DIFFERENT FIELD: SKILLED PERSON: IDENTITY OF: T168/82: EPO)   [1979–85] E.P.O.R. C664
Fisons Pharmaceuticals Ltd's Petition (PATENT: EXTENSION: INADEQUATE REMUNERATION: R&D COSTS: APPEAL: Ireland: S.C.)
[1984] I.L.R.M. 393; [1983] I.R. 129; [1984] F.S.R. 59
Fisons plc v. Norton Healthcare Ltd (TRADE MARK: INFRINGEMENT: INTERLOCUTORY INJUNCTION: EYE-CROM/VICROM: EXPORTED GOODS: RECTIFICATION: NON-USE IN U.K.: NO SERIOUS DEFENCE: NO SERIOUS RISK OF INJUSTICE: Ch.D.)   [1994] F.S.R. 745
Fives-Cail Babcock/Cleaning apparatus for conveyor belt (EUROPEAN PATENT: INVENTIVE STEP: SKILLED PERSON, RELEVANT FIELD: T32/81: EPO)
[1979–85] E.P.O.R. B377; [1982] O.J. EPO 225

Flachglas/Denmark – tacit (EUROPEAN PATENT: APPLICATION: PROCEDURE: RE-
DATING APPLICATION: AMENDMENT AND CORRECTION: DESIGNATION OF
STATES: BOARD OF APPEAL: INVITATION TO PRESIDENT OF EPO:
OBSERVATIONS BY PRESIDENT: J14/90: EPO)
[1992] E.P.O.R. 553; [1992] O.J. EPO 505

Flagstaff Investments Pty Ltd v. Guess? Inc. (TRADE MARKS: APPLICATION: GUESS:
OPPOSITION: PROPRIETORSHIP: USE: FOREIGN PUBLICATIONS ADVERTISING:
DECEPTION OR CONFUSION: ABSENCE OF EVIDENCE: Australia: Pat. Off.)
16 I.P.R. 311

Flamingo Park Pty Ltd v. Dolly Dolly Creation Pty Ltd (CONTRACT: DESIGN:
COMMISSIONED WORK: COPYRIGHT: PASSING OFF: CONFIDENTIAL
INFORMATION: Australia: Fed. Ct)
65 A.L.R. 500

FLASHPOINT Trade Mark (TRADE MARK: RECTIFICATION: NON-USE:
T.M.Reg.)
[1988] R.P.C. 561

Fleming (India) v. Ambalal Sarabhai Enterprises (TRADE MARK: PASSING OFF: USE OF
BRAND NAMES UNDER DRUG CONTROLLERS LICENCE: INJUNCTION: APPEAL:
India: H.C.)
(1989) 16 I.P.L.R. 198

Fleming Fabrications Ltd v. Albion Cylinders Ltd (PATENT: INFRINGEMENT:
INTERLOCUTORY INJUNCTION: CROSS-UNDERTAKING: BALANCE OF
CONVENIENCE: C.A.)
[1989] R.P.C. 47

Flexible Directional Indicators Ltd's Application (PATENT: APPLICATION:
AMENDMENT CLAIM BROADENING BEFORE GRANT: Pat. Ct)
[1994] R.P.C. 207

Floridienne/Late' request for examination (EUROPEAN PATENT: APPLICATION:
PROCEDURE: REQUEST FOR EXAMINATION, NOT IMPLIED BY PAYMENT OF
FEE: RE-ESTABLISHMENT OF RIGHTS: EXCLUDED: CONVENTIONS: HEADINGS
NOT AFFECTING SUBSTANTIVE PROVISIONS: J12/82: EPO)
[1979–85] E.P.O.R. A125; [1983] O.J. EPO 221

Flower Tobacco Co. v. Mottaahedah Bros (TRADE MARK: CRIMINAL ACTION:
COPYRIGHT: INFRINGEMENT: India: H.C.)
(1986) 11 I.P.L.R. 112

Flower Tobacco Co. v. Wajidsous Pvt. Ltd (TRADE MARK: APPLICATION:
OPPOSITION: India: T.M.Reg.)
(1985) 10 I.P.L.R. 258

Flude (H) & Co. (Hinkley) Ltd's Patent (PATENT: PATENT OFFICE PRACTICE:
PLEADINGS: REVOCATION: NON-INFRINGEMENT: WITHDRAWAL OF CERTAIN
GROUNDS OF INVALIDITY: C.-G.)
[1993] R.P.C. 197

FMC/Costs (EUROPEAN PATENT: COSTS: UNNECESSARY HEARING, BOTH PARTIES
AT FAULT, REFUSED: T336/86: EPO)
[1989] E.P.O.R. 291

Foo Loke Ying v. Television Broadcasts Ltd (COPYRIGHT: SUBSISTANCE:
PUBLICATION: ACQUISITION OF COPYRIGHT IN FOREIGN CINEMATOGRAPH
FILMS: STATUTORY CONSTRUCTION: Malaysia: S.C.)
[1985] M.L.J. 35; [1987] F.S.R. 57

Food Marketers Pty Ltd v. Maconochie Seafoods Ltd (TRADE MARKS: EXTENSION OF
TIME FOR LODGING NOTICE OF OPPOSITION: SPECIAL CIRCUMSTANCES:
PUBLIC INTEREST: Australia: Pat. Off.)
20 I.P.R. 219

Food Plus Ltd's Application (TRADE MARK: APPLICATION: DESCRIPTIVE: INABILITY
TO DISTINGUISH: USE: Australia: Pat. Off.)
9 I.P.R. 251

Foodland Associated Ltd v. John Weeks Pty Ltd (TRADE MARK: EVIDENCE: SERVICE:
EXTENSION OF TIME LIMITS: COSTS: HEARING FEES: REFUND: STATUTORY
PROVISIONS: Australia: Pat. Off.)
9 I.P.R. 289
(APPLICATION FOR GEOGRAPHICAL RESTRICTION OF REGISTRATION:
APPEAL FROM REGISTRAR FOLLOWING COMMENCEMENT OF NEW STATUTE:
TRANSITIONAL PROVISIONS: Australia: Pat. Off.)
11 I.P.R. 145
(APPEAL: Fed. Ct)
11 I.P.R. 158

For Eyes Optical Co.'s Application (TRADE MARK: DISTINCTIVENESS: Australia: Pat. Off.)   2 I.P.R. 381

Ford Motor Co. Ltd's Design Applications, *sub nom.* Ford Motor Co. Ltd and Iveco Fiat SpA's Design Applications

Ford Motor Co. Ltd's Replacement Parts Policy (RESTRICTIVE PRACTICES: U.K. MMC)   [1986] E.C.C. 106; [1986] F.S.R. 147

Ford Motor Co. Ltd and Iveco Fiat SpA's Design Applications (R v. Registered Designs Appeal Tribunal) (REGISTERED DESIGN: APPLICATIONS: PRACTICE: PARTS FOR MOTOR VEHICLES: "MUST MATCH" EXCEPTION: PATTERN AND ORNAMENT: REFERENCE TO *Hansard*: RDAT)   [1993] R.P.C. 399 (WHETHER FEATURES DICTATED BY FUNCTION: STATUTORY INTERPRET- ATION: REFERENCE TO PARLIAMENTARY MATERIAL: Q.B.D.)   [1994] R.P.C. 545 (APPEAL: H.L.) [1995] 1 W.L.R. 18; 30 I.P.R. 648 (*sub nom.* Ford Motor Co. Ltd and Iveco Fiat SpA's Design Applications) (H.L.) [1995] R.P.C. 167

Ford Motor Co. Ltd and Iveco Industrial Vehicles Corp. BV's Agreements (RESTRICTIVE PRACTICES: JOINT VENTURE: JOINT PRODUCTION AND MARKETING: INTENTION TO APPROVE: NOTICE: E.C. Comm.)   [1988] 4 C.M.L.R. 331 (EXEMPTION GRANTED: E.C. Comm.)   [1989] 4 C.M.L.R. 40

Ford New Holland Ltd (RESTRICTIVE PRACTICES: TERRITORIAL PROTECTION: BAN ON PARALLEL TRADE AGREED BETWEEN MANUFACTURER AND LOCAL DISTRIBUTORS: REBATES DEPENDENT UPON NON-EXPORT OF PRODUCTS BY CUSTOMERS: ARTICLE 85: INFRINGEMENT: E.C. Comm.)   [1995] 5 C.M.L.R. 89

Ford of Europe and Volkswagen's Joint Venture (RESTRICTIVE PRACTICES: JOINT VENTURES: JOINT DEVELOPMENT AND PRODUCTION OF MULTI-PURPOSE MOTOR VEHICLE FOR 10 YEARS: FINISHED VEHICLES TO BE DIFFERENTIATED AND DISTRIBUTED SEPARATELY: INTENTION TO APPROVE SUBJECT TO CONDITIONS ON DIFFERENTIATION AND DURATION: E.C. Comm.)   [1991] 4 C.M.L.R. 798 (CAUGHT BY ARTICLE 85(1): EXEMPTION GRANTED: E.C. Comm.)   [1993] 5 C.M.L.R. 617

Ford Werke's Agreement (EEC: RESTRICTIVE PRACTICES: SELECTIVE DISTRIBUTION: MARKET PARTITIONING: NOTIFICATION: E.C. Comm.)   [1982] 2 C.M.L.R. 267; [1983] F.S.R. 48; [1982] O.J. L256/20

Ford Werke's Agreement (No. 2) (EEC: RESTRICTIVE PRACTICES: EXCLUSIVE DEALERSHIP: E.C. Comm.)   [1984] 1 C.M.L.R. 596; [1984] F.S.R. 319; [1983] O.J. L327/31

Ford Werke v. E.C. Comm. (EEC: RESTRICTIVE PRACTICES: INTERLOCUTORY PROCEEDINGS: PROCEDURE: Cases 228 and 229/82R: ECJ)   [1982] 3 C.M.L.R. 673; [1982] I E.C.R. 2849

Ford/Debit order II (EUROPEAN PATENT: T17/83: EPO)   [1979–85] E.P.O.R. C743; [1984] O.J. EPO 307

Ford/Novelty (EUROPEAN PATENT: APPEAL: PROCEDURE: INTERLOCUTORY REVISION: DISCLOSURE: DIAGRAM, TEACHING OF: AMENDMENT CLAIMS: NOVELTY: CITATION TO BE READ IN ISOLATION: CLEARLY, UNMISTAKABLY AND FULLY DERIVABLE TEST: DRAWINGS, TEACHING OF: GENERAL KNOWLEDGE SHOULD NOT BE COMBINED WITH CITED DOCUMENT: IMMEDIATELY APPARENT TEST: T356/89: EPO)   [1990] E.P.O.R. 370

Foresheda/Divisional application (EUROPEAN PATENT: AMENDMENT AND CORRECTION: ADDED RESTRICTION, NO EXTENSION OF SUBJECT-MATTER: JAPANESE YEAR: DRAWINGS: DELETION OF CONFUSING LIMITATION OF FEATURES FROM: INTERMEDIATE GENERALISATION: DIVISIONAL APPLICATION: NO ABANDONMENT OF SUBJECT-MATTER FROM PARENT APPLICATION: ENLARGED BOARD OF APPEAL: REFERENCE REFUSED: INVENTIVE STEP: COULD/WOULD TEST: T118/91: EPO)
[1994] E.P.O.R. 557

Forgery of Copyright Videotapes, Re (VIDEOTAPES: FORGERY: DOCUMENTS: COPYRIGHT: Greece: S.C.)   [1993] E.C.C. 283; [1993] F.S.R. 704

Form Tubes Ltd v. Guinness Bros plc (COPYRIGHT: PRACTICE: STRIKING OUT: ABUSE OF PROCESS: Ch.D.)   [1989] F.S.R. 41

Format Communications Manufacturing Ltd v. ITT (U.K.) Ltd (BREACH OF CONFIDENCE: COPYRIGHT: INFRINGEMENT: COMPUTER PROGRAMS: PRACTICE: DISCOVERY AND INSPECTION: SAFEGUARDS: C.A.)
[1983] F.S.R. 473

Formstein (PATENT: INFRINGEMENT: CONSTRUCTION OF CLAIMS: EPC: PROTOCOL ON INTERPRETATION OF ARTICLE 69: EQUIVALENTS: PRIOR USER: Germany: S.C.)   [1991] R.P.C. 597

Fortnum & Mason plc v. Fortnam Ltd (PASSING OFF: COMMON FIELDS OF ACTIVITY: CONFUSION: MOTION DISMISSED: Ch.D.)   [1994] F.S.R. 438

Foujita v. Sàrl Art Conception Realisation (COPYRIGHT: DECEASED AUTHOR: *droit moral*: ABUSE: France: C.A.)   [1988] E.C.C. 309; [1988] F.S.R. 523

FOUNDATION Trade Mark (TRADE MARK: APPLICATION: GOODS OF SAME DESCRIPTION: COMPUTER SYSTEMS: PRACTICE: T.M.Reg.)
[1994] R.P.C. 41

Fractionated Cane Technology Ltd v. Ruiz-Avila (CONFIDENTIAL INFORMATION: IDEA: SIMULTANEOUS ACQUISITION OF INFORMATION: SPRING-BOARD DOCTRINE: CONTRACTUAL: FAILURE OF CONSIDERATION: Australia: S.C.(Qd))   8 I.P.R. 502; 1988 1 Qd.R. 51

Fractionated Cane Technology Ltd v. Ruiz-Avila (CONFIDENTIAL INFORMATION: EXPERIMENTAL TRIALS: NO OBLIGATION OF CONFIDENCE: PROFESSORS LETTER: RESULTS OF UNIVERSITY TESTS: LIMITED OBLIGATION OF CONFIDENCE: "SPRINGBOARD" DOCTRINE: Australia: S.C.(Qd.))
13 I.P.R. 609; 1988 2 Qd.R. 610

Franchise Agreements Regulation, *sub nom.* Community Franchise Agreements Regulation

Franchising Agreements Draft Regulation (RESTRICTIVE PRACTICES: GROUP EXEMPTION: FRANCHISING AGREEMENTS: E.C. Comm.)
[1988] 4 C.M.L.R. 542

Franchising Agreements Regulation 1988 (4087/88) (RESTRICTIVE PRACTICES: GROUP EXEMPTION: FRANCHISE AGREEMENTS: LEGISLATION: E.C. Comm.)   [1989] 4 C.M.L.R. 387; [1989] 1 F.S.R. 499

Francome v. Mirror Group Newspapers Ltd (CONFIDENTIAL INFORMATION: INTERLOCUTORY INJUNCTION: ILLEGAL TELEPHONE TAPPING: C.A.)
[1984] 2 All E.R. 408; [1984] 1 W.L.R. 892

Franconi Holdings Pty Ltd v. Gunning (PASSING OFF: BUSINESS NAME: REGISTRATION: INTERLOCUTORY INJUNCTION: Australia: S.C.(W.A.))
1982 1 S.R.(W.A.) 341

Frank & Hirsch (Pty) Ltd v. Roopanand Brothers (Pty) Ltd (TRADE MARK: INFRINGEMENT: EXCLUSIVE DISTRIBUTOR: IMPORTATION: PASSING OFF: South Africa: D.&C.L.D.)   1987 (3) S.A. 165

Frank & Hirsch (Pty) Ltd v. A. Roopanand Brothers (Pty) Ltd (COPYRIGHT: INFRINGEMENT: IMPORTATION: EXCLUSIVE DISTRIBUTOR: GET-UP: TRADE DRESS: LABELS: South Africa: D&CLD)   1991 (3) S.A. 240; 29 I.P.R. 465

Franklin International Export Ltd v. Wattie Exports Ltd (PASSING OFF: INJUNCTION AGAINST: WHAT QUALIFIES AS "STATUS QUO": WHETHER GET-UP SUFFICIENTLY RESEMBLES THAT OF PLAINTIFF: New Zealand: H.C.)
12 I.P.R. 358

Franklin Machinery Ltd v. Albany Farm Centre Ltd (COPYRIGHT: *Obiter dictum* ON EXTENT OF USE OF COPYRIGHT TO PROTECT INDUSTRIAL DESIGNS IN NEW ZEALAND: INTERLOCUTORY INJUNCTION: CONSENT ORDER: APPLICATION FOR DECLARATION THAT REVISED PRODUCTS OUTSIDE TERMS OF ORDER: VARIATION OF ORDER: PRINCIPLES: New Zealand: H.C.)   23 I.P.R. 649

Franklin/Missing drawings (EUROPEAN PATENT: APPLICATION: PROCEDURE: MISSING DRAWINGS: AMENDMENT AND CORRECTION: DRAWINGS: OMITTED: J19/80: EPO)   [1979–85] E.P.O.R. A62; [1981] O.J. EPO 65

Fraser & Neame Ltd v. Yeo Hiap Seng Ltd (TRADE MARK: INFRINGEMENT: PASSING OFF: ESSENTIAL FEATURES: Malaysia: H.C.)   [1982] 1 M.L.J. 122

Fraser v. Thames Television Ltd (CONFIDENTIAL INFORMATION: ORIGINAL IDEA FOR TV SERIES: ORAL COMMUNICATION: Q.B.D.)
[1983] 2 All E.R. 101; [1984] Q.B.D. 44; [1983] 2 W.L.R. 917

Freeman v. Pohlner Pty Ltd (PATENT: REVOCATION: PATENTABILITY: NOVELTY: DESCRIPTION OF INVENTION: Australia: Fed. Ct)   29 I.P.R. 663
(PATENT: REVOCATION: PATENTABILITY: NOVELTY: SKILLED ADDRESSEE: DESCRIPTION: BEST METHOD: Australia: Fed. Ct)   30 I.P.R. 377

Freestone v. Caterpillar Tractor Co. (TRADE MARK: APPLICATION: WHETHER DESCRIPTIVE AND CONFUSING: Australia: T.M.Reg.)   5 I.P.R. 296

Freighter Australia Manufacturing Pty Ltd's Application (DESIGNS: APPLICATION FOR EXTENSION OF THE PERIOD: INFORMANT: NOVELTY: ORIGINALITY: PRIOR PUBLICATION: Australia: Pat. Off.)   11 I.P.R. 512

Freistaat Bayern v. Eurim-Pharm GmbH (IMPORTS: PHARMACEUTICALS: NEED FOR AUTHORISATION: ARTICLE 30: HEALTH OF HUMANS: ARTICLE 36; GERMAN REQUIREMENT THAT IMPORTED MEDICINES BEAR MARKINGS IN GERMAN AT TIME OF IMPORTATION: IMPORTER'S INTENTION TO AFFIX MARKS AFTER IMPORTATION BUT BEFORE ONWARD SALE INSUFFICIENT: IMPORTS AUTHORISED IN EXPORTING MEMBER STATE: GERMAN RULE BREACHES ARTICLE 30: NOT SAVED BY ARTICLE 36: Case C–347/89: ECJ)
[1993] 1 C.M.L.R. 616; [1991] I E.C.R. 1747

Freixenet SA v. Bull (TRADE MARK: OPPOSITION: AMENDMENT OF STATEMENT OF GOODS: Australia: AIPO)   28 I.P.R. 587

Friedrich Grohe Armaturenfabrik GmbH & Co.'s Application (RESTRICTIVE PRACTICES: EXCLUSIVE DEALING: SELECTIVE DISTRIBUTION: E.C. Comm.)   [1988] 4 C.M.L.R. 612

Frisco-Findus/Frozen fish (EUROPEAN PATENT: INVENTIVE STEP: LONG-FELT WANT: T90/89: EPO)   [1991] E.P.O.R. 42

Fritz & Farni/Tree surround (EUROPEAN PATENT: AMENDMENT AND CORRECTION: BROADENING CLAIM BY OMISSION: INVENTIVE STEP: AGED ART: COMBINATION OF CITATIONS: T147/90: EPO)   [1992] E.P.O.R. 131

Fuji Photo Film Co. Ltd v. Carr's Paper Ltd (PATENT: INFRINGEMENT: VALIDITY: OBVIOUSNESS: PRACTICE: DISCOVERY: Pat. Ct)   [1989] R.P.C. 713

Fuji, Canon, Minolta and Nikon's Joint Venture (RESTRICTIVE PRACTICES: JOINT VENTURE: JOINT RESEARCH AND DEVELOPMENT: ADVANCED PHOTOGRAPHIC SYSTEM: LICENSING OF RESULTS: NOTICE: E.C. Comm.)   [1994] 4 C.M.L.R. 715

Fuji/Coloured disk jacket (EUROPEAN PATENT: PATENTABILITY: AESTHETIC
CREATION: PRESENTATION OF INFORMATION: T119/88: EPO)
[1990] E.P.O.R. 615; [1990] O.J. EPO 395

Fuji/Electron microscope image (EUROPEAN PATENT: APPLICATION: PROCEDURE:
REMITTAL TO EXAMINING DIVISION: BOARD OF APPEAL: INVESTIGATION OF
OWN MOTION: CLAIMS: ONE PART V. TWO PART: INVENTIVE STEP:
SURPRISING EFFECT: STATE OF THE ART: CROSS-REFERENCED DOCUMENT:
T747/90: EPO) [1994] E.P.O.R. 430

Fuji/Heat developable colour photographic materials (EUROPEAN PATENT:
AMENDMENT AND CORRECTION: CHANGE IN CLAIM CATEGORY: EXTENSION
OF PROTECTION: INVENTIVE STEP: OBVIOUS TO TRY: T402/89: EPO)
[1993] E.P.O.R. 81

Fuji/Multilayer photographic material (EUROPEAN PATENT: AMENDMENT AND
CORRECTION: APPEAL, ON: NOVELTY: PRECISE DISCLOSURE:
REPRODUCIBILITY OF PRIOR TEACHING: WHOLE CONTENTS: OPPOSITION:
PROCEDURE: AMENDMENT, UNNECESSARY: T763/89: EPO)
[1994] E.P.O.R. 384

Fuji/Photographic material (EUROPEAN PATENT: INVENTIVE STEP: CLOSEST PRIOR
ART: NOVELTY: CROSS-REFERENCED DOCUMENTS: MOST RELEVANT ART:
OPPOSITION: PROCEDURE: AMENDMENT OF CLAIMS AT ORAL PROCEEDINGS:
T267/88: EPO) [1991] E.P.O.R. 168

Fuji/Transmission apparatus (EUROPEAN PATENT: AMENDMENT AND
CORRECTION: GENERALISATION: CLAIMS: CONSTRUCTION: REFERENCE TO
DESCRIPTION, DRAWINGS AND FILE WRAPPER: T371/88: EPO)
[1992] E.P.O.R. 341; [1992] O.J. EPO 157

Fujitsu Ltd and Advanced Micro Devices Inc.'s Joint Venture (RESTRICTIVE
PRACTICES: JOINT VENTURES: LICENSING: JOINT RESEARCH AND
DEVELOPMENT: CROSS-SHAREHOLDING: INTENTION TO APPROVE: NOTICE:
E.C. Comm.) [1994] 5 C.M.L.R. 468

Fujitsu/Avalanche diode (EUROPEAN PATENT: DIVISIONAL APPLICATION:
PRIORITY CLAIM FOR, REFUSED: PRIORITY: WIDTH OF CLAIM IN PRIORITY
DOCUMENT: SKILLED PERSON: OPTIMISATION OF PRIOR ART PARAMETERS:
T409/90: EPO) [1991] E.P.O.R. 423; [1993] O.J. EPO 40

Fujitsu/Designation of inventors (EUROPEAN PATENT: CONVENTIONS: VIENNA
CONVENTION RULES: INVENTORS: RECTIFICATION OF DESIGNATION,
WHETHER CONSENT REQUIRED: J08/82: EPO)
[1979–85] E.P.O.R. A111; [1984] O.J. EPO 155

Fujitsu/Memory circuit (EUROPEAN PATENT: AMENDMENT AND CORRECTION:
ABSTRACT, MAY NOT BE BASED ON: DISCLOSURE, EXTENT OF: DRAWINGS:
NUMERAL IN: T407/86: EPO) [1988] E.P.O.R. 254

Fujitsu/Oral proceedings (EUROPEAN PATENT: PROCEDURE: ORAL PROCEEDINGS:
FEES: REIMBURSEMENT OF APPEAL FEE: T19/87: EPO)
[1988] E.P.O.R. 393; [1988] O.J. EPO 268

Fujitsu/Printer (EUROPEAN PATENT: APPLICATION: PROCEDURE: AMENDMENT
AFTER RULE 51(4) COMMUNICATION: AMENDMENT AND CORRECTION:
BROADENING CLAIM BY OMISSION: ESSENTIALITY TEST: NOVELTY TEST:
T685/90: EPO) [1993] E.P.O.R. 183

Fujitsu/Semiconductor (EUROPEAN PATENT: INVENTIVE STEP: SIMPLIFICATION OF
MANUFACTURING PROCESS: SKILLED PERSON, WILLINGNESS OF TO
EXPERIMENT: T128/83: EPO) [1979–85] E.P.O.R. C841

Fujitsu/Surface acoustic wave device (EUROPEAN PATENT: AMENDMENT AND CORRECTION: PRIOR ART, ERRONEOUS STATEMENT OF: APPEAL: PROCEDURE: INTERIM DECISION: OBJECTION BY BOARD, MET BY EXPLANATION: DISCLOSURE: COMMON GENERAL KNOWLEDGE: INVENTIVE STEP: COMBINATION OF CITATIONS: SUFFICIENCY: COMMON GENERAL KNOWLEDGE EXPECTED: T22/83: EPO) [1988] E.P.O.R. 234

Fulton (J.K.) (Pty) Ltd v. Logic Engineering Enterprises (Pty) Ltd (COPYRIGHT: EXCLUSIVE LICENCE: NOT NECESSARY FOR LICENCE TO COVER ALL ACTS MENTIONED IN RELEVANT ACT: South Africa: WLD) 1983 (1) S.A. 735; [1983] F.S.R. 435

Furnitureland Ltd v. Harris (TRADE MARK: INFRINGEMENT: FURNITURELAND/FURNITURE CITY: TRADE USAGE: Ch.D.) [1989] 1 F.S.R. 536

Furr v. C. D. Truline (Building Products) Ltd (PATENT: INFRINGEMENT: CONSTRUCTION OF CLAIMS: ESTOPPEL BY ACTION TAKEN TO SECURE GRANT: Pat. Ct) [1985] F.S.R. 553

FWS Joint Sports Claimants v. The Copyright Board (COPYRIGHT: INTERPRETATION OF CONTRACT: ASSIGNMENT OF PARTIAL RIGHTS: SUBJECT MATTER: NO COPYRIGHT IN *Broadcast day*: COMPILATION OF TV PROGRAMS: RETRANSMISSION OF TV SIGNALS: Canada: Fed. C.A.) 22 I.P.R. 429

Fyfe & Tana v. Amalgamated Food & Poultry Pty Ltd (TRADE MARK: OPPOSITION: SUBSTANTIAL SIMILARITY TO EXISTING REGISTERED MARK: Australia: T.M.Reg.) 5 I.P.R. 311

Fyffes plc v. Chiquita Brands International Inc. (REGISTERED AND UNREGISTERED TRADE MARKS: COVENANT NOT TO USE OUTSIDE U.K. AND IRELAND: STATUS OF E.C. COMMISSIONS PRELIMINARY FINDINGS: PROPRIETORSHIP: GOODWILL: RESTRAINT OF TRADE: COVENANTS: RESTRICTION OF ACTS OUTSIDE JURISDICTION: RESTRICTION OF USE OF MARKS: EFFECT ON PURCHASER: Ch.D.) [1993] F.S.R. 83

Gabon (The State of) v. Société Nationale de Télévision en Coulours "Antenne 2" (COPYRIGHT: *Droit moral*: FILM PRODUCTION: France: S.C.) [1988] E.C.C. 316; [1988] F.S.R. 524

Gacoli Pty Ltd v. Sterling Pharmaceuticals Pty Ltd (TRADE MARK: APPLICATION: OPPOSITION: LIKELIHOOD OF DECEPTION: SIMILARITY: Australia: T.M.Reg.) 7 I.P.R. 401

Gajjars Application (PATENT: APPLICATION: PRIOR PUBLICATION: India: H.C.) (1992) 17 I.P.L.R. 219

Gala of London Ltd v. Chandler Ltd (TRADE MARKS: INFRINGEMENT: SUMMARY JUDGEMENT: COUNTERCLAIM FOR NON-USE: INTERLOCUTORY INJUNCTION: BALANCE OF CONVENIENCE: PASSING OFF: INJUNCTION REFUSED: Ch.D.) [1991] F.S.R. 294

Galago Publishers (Pty) Ltd v. Erasmus (COPYRIGHT: INFRINGEMENT: TEST OF: OBJECTIVE SIMILARITY: ASSIGNED COPYRIGHT: STATUS OF AUTHOR: ABRIDGEMENT: South Africa: A.D.) 1989 (1) S.A. 276

Galaxay International Pty Ltd's Application (TRADE MARKS: APPLICATION: CAPABLE OF BECOMING DISTINCTIVE: INHERENTLY UNADAPTED TO DISTINGUISH: Australia: Pat. Off.) 13 I.P.R. 433

Galaxia Maritime SA v. Mineralimportexport, The Elftherios (MAREVA INJUNCTION: PROTECTION OF THIRD PARTY INTERESTS: C.A.) [1982] 1 All E.R. 796

Gales Application (PATENT APPLICATION: COMPUTER-RELATED INVENTIONS: DEDICATED ROM: WHETHER EXCLUDED FROM PATENTABILITY: APPLICATION REFUSED: C.-G.: Pat. Ct: C.A.)   [1991] R.P.C. 305

Galfa Laboratories Pvt. Ltd v. Rekvina Pharmaceuticals (TRADE MARK: APPLICATION: OPPOSITION: PRIOR REGISTRATION: PETITION TO CANCEL OPPONENTS REGISTRATION: STAY: India: H.C.)   (1993) 18 I.P.L.R. 128

Galileo and Covia Computer Reservation Systems' Combination (RESTRICTIVE PRACTICES: COMBINATION OF NORTH AMERICAN AND EUROPEAN COMPUTER RESERVATION SYSTEMS: INTENTION TO APPROVE: E.C. Comm.)   [1993] 4 C.M.L.R. 638

Gallaher (Dublin) Ltd v. The Health Education Bureau (TRADE MARK: USE "IN RELATION TO GOODS": Ireland: H.C.)
          [1982] I.L.R.M. 240; [1982] F.S.R. 464

Games Workshop Ltd v. Transworld Publishers Ltd (TRADE MARK: INFRINGEMENT: TITLE OF SERIES OF BOOKS: USE AS TRADE MARK: ADEQUACY OF DAMAGES: BALANCE OF CONVENIENCE: PRACTICE: PATENT AND TRADE MARK LICENCE AGREEMENTS CONTRASTED: C.A.)   [1993] F.S.R. 705

Gamlen Chemical Co. (U.K.) Ltd v. Rochem Ltd (CONSPIRACY TO INJURE: BREACH OF CONFIDENCE: DISCOVERY: LEGAL PRIVILEGE: Ch.D.)
          [1983] R.P.C. 1

Gang-Nail Australia Ltd v. Multinail Truss Systems Pty Ltd (PATENT: INFRINGEMENT ACTION: CONSTRUCTION OF LICENCE AGREEMENT: IMPLIED TERM: CONSTRUCTION OF CLAIM IN PATENT SPECIFICATION: IDENTIFYING ESSENTIAL INTEGERS OF CLAIM: Australia: Fed. Ct)   23 I.P.R. 73

Gansu Research Institution of Chemical Industry v. ICI Australia Operations Pty Ltd (PATENT: APPLICATION: OPPOSITION: EVIDENCE: EXTENSION OF TIME TO LODGE EVIDENCE: Australia: Pat. Off.)   19 I.P.R. 657

Gantenbrink v. BBC (COPYRIGHT: PRACTICE: FILM: UNDERTAKINGS: LIBERTY TO APPLY: Ch.D.)   [1995] F.S.R. 162

Garcia/Storage device (EUROPEAN PATENT: AMENDMENT AND CORRECTION: DRAWINGS: REPLACEMENT OF ROUGH BY FAIR: FEES: REIMBURSEMENT OF APPEAL FEE: REAL GROUNDS OF DECISION NOT: T546/90: EPO)
          [1993] E.P.O.R. 214

Gardam v. George Wills & Co. Ltd (TRADE PRACTICES: PROSECUTION: FALSELY REPRESENTING GOODS TO BE OF PARTICULAR STANDARD: WHETHER GENERALLY RECOGNISED STANDARD IS REQUIRED: Australia: Fed. Ct)
          12 I.P.R. 194

Garden Co. Ltd v. Gardenia Overseas Pty Ltd (TRADE MARK: OPPOSITION: DECEPTIVE SIMILARITY: MARKS APPLIED TO LOW VALUE GOODS ORDINARILY PURCHASED IN SUPERMARKETS: PARTIES SOUGHT TO INTRODUCE EXTENSIVE MATERIAL AT HEARING OF OPPOSITION: Australia: AIPO)
          27 I.P.R. 237
     See also, *sub nom.* Gardenia Overseas Pte Ltd v. The Garden Co. Ltd

Garden Cottage Foods Ltd v. Milk Marketing Board (NATIONAL COURTS: RESTRICTIVE PRACTICES: H.L.)   [1984] A.C. 130;
          [1983] 2 All E.R. 770; [1983] 3 C.M.L.R. 43; [1984] F.S.R. 23

Gardenia Overseas Pte Ltd v. The Garden Co. Ltd (TRADE MARK: OPPOSITION: COMMON ELEMENT: GARDEN/GARDENIA: LIKELIHOOD OF DECEPTION OR CONFUSION: AURAL AND VISUAL COMPARISONS: Australia: AIPO)
          29 I.P.R. 485
     See also, *sub nom.* Garden Co. Ltd v. Gardenia Overseas Pte Ltd

Gardex Ltd v. Sorata (REGISTERED DESIGN: COPYRIGHT: INFRINGEMENT: VALIDITY: EYE APPEAL: PATENT DRAWING: OWNERSHIP: Ch.D.)
[1986] R.P.C. 623

Garvin v. Domus Publishing Ltd (PRACTICE: DISCOVERY: USE OF DOCUMENTS: DOCUMENTS SEIZED IN EXECUTION OF ANTON PILLER ORDER: APPLICATION FOR LEAVE TO USE DOCUMENTS IN PROCEEDINGS FOR CONTEMPT OF COURT: WHETHER COMMITTAL PROCEEDINGS CIVIL PROCEEDINGS: WHETHER LEAVE TO BE REFUSED ON PRINCIPLE AGAINST SELF-INCRIMINATION: Ch.D.)   [1989] 2 All E.R. 344; [1989] 1 Ch. 335

Garware Plastics & Polyester Ltd v. Telelink (COPYRIGHT: INFRINGEMENT: EXHIBITION OF VIDEO FILMS OVER CABLE TV NETWORK: INJUNCTION: India: H.C.)   (1990) 15 I.P.L.R. 24

Gaskell & Chambers Ltd v. Measure Master Ltd (REGISTERED DESIGN: INFRINGEMENT: EFFECT OF PRIOR ART: Pat. Ct)   [1993] R.P.C. 76

Gates v. CML Assurance Society Ltd (TRADE PRACTICES: MISLEADING OR DECEPTIVE CONDUCT: FALSE REPRESENTATION: MEASURE OF DAMAGES: Australia: H.C.)   160 C.L.R. 1; 6 I.P.R. 462

Gatwards' (t/a Dispensoroll & Therma-Wrap)'s Application (TRADE MARKS: APPLICATION FOR EXTENSION OF TIME TO LODGE NOTICE OF OPPOSITION: APPLICATION NOT WITHIN SCOPE OF SECTION 49(1): APPLICATION NOT AUTHORISED BY SECTION 131; FAILURE DUE TO ERROR BY AGENT: FAILURE NOT BY REASON OF "CIRCUMSTANCES BEYOND THE CONTROL OF THE PERSON CONCERNED": Australia: Pat. Off.)   11 I.P.R. 447

Gay & Lunettas' (Gianfranco's) Application (TRADE MARKS: APPLICATION FOR REGISTRATION: COMPOSITE MARK: FAME: DIRECTLY DESCRIPTIVE: OTHER MATTER NON-DISTINCTIVE: MARK AS A WHOLE NOT DISTINCTIVE: MARK NOT CAPABLE OF BECOMING DISTINCTIVE: Australia: Pat. Off.)
18 I.P.R. 221

Gebhardts Patent (PATENT: COMPULSORY LICENCE: TREATY OF ROME: IMPORTATION FROM EEC MEMBER STATE: WHETHER GROUND FOR COMPULSORY LICENCE: PRACTICE: EVIDENCE: Pat. Ct)   [1992] R.P.C. 1

GEC Alsthom Ltd's Patent (PATENT: PETITION FOR REVOCATION: RELIANCE ON ADDITIONAL PRIOR ART: AMENDMENT OF PARTICULARS SOUGHT THREE WEEKS PRIOR TO TRIAL: COSTS: WHETHER See v. Scott-Paine FORM OF ORDER APPROPRIATE: Pat. Ct)   [1996] F.S.R. 415

GEC Alsthom/Homogenising immiscible fluids (EUROPEAN PATENT: AMENDMENT AND CORRECTION: BROADENING CLAIM BY OMISSION: CATEGORY OF CLAIM: EQUITABLE CONSIDERATIONS: T192/89: EPO)
[1990] E.P.O.R. 287

GEC Avionics Ltd's Patent (PATENT: EMPLOYEE'S INVENTION: APPLICATION FOR COMPENSATION: RELEVANCE OF FOREIGN EQUIVALENT PATENT: WHETHER OUTSTANDING BENEFIT: C.-G.)   [1992] R.P.C. 107

GEC-Marconi Ltd v. XYLLYX Viewdata Terminals Pte Ltd (PATENT: REVOCATION: PRACTICE: TRANSFER TO PATENTS COUNTY COURT: Pat. Ct)
[1991] F.S.R. 319

Gelman Sciences/Fresh ground (EUROPEAN PATENT: OPPOSITION PROCEDURE: DUTIES OF OPPOSITION DIVISION: NEED FOR CLEAR SUMMONS: LATE FILING OF EXPERIMENTAL REPORT: FRESH GROUND: PRODUCT BY PROCESS CLAIMS: REIMBURSEMENT OF APPEAL FEE: T817/93: EPO)
[1995] E.P.O.R. 557

GEMA's Reproduction Tariffs (COPYRIGHT: MUSICAL WORKS: VIDEOCASSETTES AND FILMS: LICENCE FEES: INFRINGEMENT: ASSESSMENT OF DAMAGES: Germany: S.C.)   [1988] E.C.C. 52; [1988] F.S.R. 253

GEMA (Re) (RESTRICTIVE PRACTICES: COPYRIGHT: COLLECTING SOCIETIES: INWARD PROCESSING: CUSTOM PRESSING: E.C. Comm.)
[1985] 2 C.M.L.R. 1
GEMA (Re) (RESTRICTIVE PRACTICES: COPYRIGHT: E.C. Comm.)
[1982] 2 C.M.L.R. 482; [1982] F.S.R. 561; [1982] O.J. L94/12
Gen Set SpA v. Mosarc Ltd (PATENT: PRACTICE: STAY OF PROCEEDINGS: Pat. Ct)
[1985] F.S.R. 302
Gencorp's Application (TRADE MARK: APPLICATION: PART B: TRADEMARK: NON-DISTINCTIVE: DECEPTION AND CONFUSION: AIPO)   28 I.P.R. 94
Genentech I/Polypeptide expression (EUROPEAN PATENT: APPEAL: PROCEDURE: ORAL EVIDENCE: THIRD PARTY OBSERVATIONS: CLAIMS: FUNCTIONAL FEATURES: SUPPORT FOR: INVENTIVE STEP: IMMEDIATE RECOGNITION: SPECULATIVE TEACHING IN PRIOR ART: SUFFICIENCY: COMMON GENERAL KNOWLEDGE EXPECTED: FUTURE AND/OR INACCESSIBLE VARIANTS: T292/85: EPO)   [1989] E.P.O.R. 1; [1989] O.J. EPO 275
Genentech Inc.'s (Human Growth Hormone) Patent (PATENT: REVOCATION: GENETIC ENGINEERING: RECOMBINANT DNA TECHNOLOGY: GENETIC ENGINEERING: HUMAN TISSUE PLASMINOGEN ACTIVATOR: DISCOVERY OF DNA AND AMINO-ACID SEQUENCE: NOVELTY: INVENTIVE STEP: COMMON GENERAL KNOWLEDGE: PRIORITY DATE: ADDRESSEE: Pat. Ct)
[1989] R.P.C. 147
(VALIDITY: INVENTION OR DISCOVERY: SUFFICIENCY OF DESCRIPTION: WHETHER DEPOSIT OF MICRO-ORGANISM NECESSARY: OBVIOUSNESS: PERSON SKILLED IN THE ART: AMENDMENT: CONVENTION COURT: STATUS OF RULINGS: APPLICATION OF DISCOVERY: C.A.)
[1989] R.P.C. 203; 15 I.P.R. 423
Genentech Inc.'s Patent (PATENT: GENETIC ENGINEERING: REVOCATION: NOVELTY: OBVIOUSNESS: SUFFICIENCY OF DESCRIPTION: AMBIGUITY: Pat. Ct)   [1987] R.P.C. 553
Genentech Inc.'s Patent (Pat. Ct)   [1989] R.P.C. 613
Genentech Inc. v. Wellcome Foundation Ltd (PATENT: OPPOSITION: APPLICATION FOR EXTENSION OF TIME IN WHICH TO SERVE EVIDENCE IN SUPPORT OF OPPOSITION: APPLICATION FOR EXTENSION OF TIME LODGED AFTER THE EXPIRATION OF THE TIME SOUGHT TO BE EXTENDED: ERRORS OR OMISSIONS OF PATENT ATTORNEY: "SPECIAL CIRCUMSTANCES": Australia: Pat. Off.)
11 I.P.R. 401
General Datacomm/Correction of description (EUROPEAN PATENT: AMENDMENT AND CORRECTION: APPENDIX MISSING: J13/82: EPO)
[1979-85] E.P.O.R. A129; [1983] O.J. EPO 12
General Electric Co.'s Amendment Application (PATENT: APPLICATION TO AMEND: DESCRIPTION: COVETOUSNESS: C.-G.)   [1984] R.P.C. 311
General Electric Company/Thermoplastic resin (EUROPEAN PATENT: AMENDMENT AND CORRECTION: CLARITY, IMPRECISE TERMS: CLAIMS: CLARITY: IMPRECISE TERMS: OPPOSITION: PROCEDURE: JURISDICTION TO CONSIDER LACK OF CLARITY: T472/88: EPO)   [1991] E.P.O.R. 486
General Electric/Disclosure of computer-related apparatus (EUROPEAN PATENT: PATENTABILITY: COMPUTER-RELATED INVENTIONS: AMENDMENT AND CORRECTION: BROADENING CLAIM BY "FOR" CLAUSE: CATEGORY OF CLAIM: CLAIMS: CONSTRUCTION: "FOR" CLAUSE: T784/89: EPO)
[1992] E.P.O.R. 446; [1992] O.J. EPO 438
General Electric/Retroactive change in language (EUROPEAN PATENT: APPLICATION: PROCEDURE: LANGUAGE OF PROCEEDINGS: T232/85: EPO)   [1986] E.P.O.R. 107; [1986] O.J. EPO 19

General Foods/Caffeine (EUROPEAN PATENT: CLAIMS: CONSTRUCTION: "CONSISTING ESSENTIALLY OF": T340/89: EPO)   [1992] E.P.O.R. 199

General Hospital/Contraceptive method (EUROPEAN PATENT: PATENTABILITY: CONTRACEPTIVE METHOD CONCURRENT THERAPEUTIC STEP: SWISS-STYLE CLAIM: CLARITY: FUNCTIONAL DEFINITIONS: T820/92: EPO)
[1995] E.P.O.R. 446; [1995] O.J. EPO 113

General Motors Holdens Ltd v. David Syme & Co. Ltd (CONFIDENTIAL INFORMATION: PRACTICE: EXCLUDING MEMBERS OF THE PUBLIC: ARGUABLE CASE: Australia: S.C.(NSW))   [1984] 2 N.S.W.L.R. 294; 2 I.P.R. 276

General Motors Holdens Ltd v. Premier Automobiles Ltd (TRADE MARK: REGISTRATION: INDIA)   (1983) 8 I.P.L.R. 66

General Motors/High voltage power supply (EUROPEAN PATENT: AMENDMENT AND CORRECTION: EXTENSION OF SUBJECT-MATTER: CIRCUMSTANCES OF EACH CASE MUST BE TAKEN INTO ACCOUNT: INTERMEDIATE GENERALISATION: INVENTIVE STEP: HINT IN PRIOR ART: PRECEDENT: BOARD OF APPEAL DECISION NOT BINDING: T415/91: EPO)
[1993] E.P.O.R. 279

General Motors/Zinc electrodes (EUROPEAN PATENT: AMENDMENT AND CORRECTION: NOVELTY TEST: GENERALISATION: "COMPREHENDS": T194/84: EPO)   [1989] E.P.O.R. 351; [1990] O.J. EPO 59

General Nutrition Ltd v. Pattni (COPYRIGHT: INFRINGEMENT: ANTON PILLER PRACTICE: Ch.D.)   [1984] F.S.R. 403

Generics (U.K.) Ltd's Application, *sub nom.* Allen & Hanbury's Ltd v. Generics (U.K.) Ltd

Generics (U.K.) Ltd v. Smith Kline & French Laboratories Ltd (PATENTS: IMPORTS: PHARMACEUTICALS: COMPULSORY LICENCES: INTRA-STATE CONDITIONS: DISCRIMINATING IMPORT RESTRICTIONS: LICENSEE STATUTORILY PERMITTED TO IMPORT FROM OUTSIDE EEC: PARALLEL IMPORTS: DISCRIMINATION: UNJUSTIFIABLE INTERFERENCE WITH INTRA-COMMUNITY TRADE: ARTICLES 30 AND 36: SPAIN AND PORTUGAL: Case C–191/90: ECJ)   [1993] 1 C.M.L.R. 89;
[1992] I E.C.R. 5335; [1993] F.S.R. 592; [1993] R.P.C. 333
(C.A.) [1990] 1 C.M.L.R. 416

Genetics Institute Inc. v. Johnson & Johnson (PATENT: APPLICATION: OPPOSITION: EVIDENCE: TIME LIMITS: APPLICATION FOR EXTENSION OF TIME: OBJECTION: DIRECTION: PRACTICE AND PROCEDURE: Australia: AIPO)   27 I.P.R. 277

Genetics International Inc. v. Serono Diagnostics Ltd (PATENT: OPPOSITION: APPLICATION FOR EXTENSION OF TIME IN WHICH TO LODGE NOTICE OF OPPOSITION: ERROR OR OMISSION OF AGENTS OR ATTORNEYS: Australia: Pat. Off.)   13 I.P.R. 31

Geo Meccanica Idrotecnica/Language of application (EUROPEAN PATENT: FEES: REDUCTION FOR FILING IN NON-OFFICIAL LANGUAGE: J04/88: EPO)
[1990] E.P.O.R. 69; [1989] O.J. EPO 483

Geoffrey Manners & Co. Ltd v. Mega Pharma Laboratories (TRADE MARK: OPPOSITION: MEGAVITE/MEGAVIT: India: H.C.)   (1986) 1 I.P.L.R. 9

Geographia Ltd v. Penguin Books Ltd (COPYRIGHT: INFRINGEMENT: MAPS: Ch.D.)
[1985] F.S.R. 208

Georg Fischer/Grounds of appeal (EUROPEAN PATENT: APPEAL: PROCEDURE: STATEMENT OF GROUNDS, REQUIREMENTS: T213/85: EPO)
[1988] E.P.O.R. 45; [1987] O.J. EPO 482

George L. Kregos (t/a American Sports Wire) v. The Associated Press (COPYRIGHT: INFRINGEMENT: PROTECTABILITY OF COMPILATION OF FACTS: ORIGINALITY: MINIMAL CREATIVITY: IDEA/EXPRESSION MERGER DOCTRINE: BLANK FORM DOCTRINE: SPORT STATISTICS FORM: USA: C.A.) 23 I.P.R. 13

George Michael v. Sony Music Entertainment (U.K.) Ltd, *sub nom.* Panayiotou v. Sony Music Entertainment (U.K.) Ltd

George Ward (Moxley) Ltd v. Richard Sankey Ltd (COPYRIGHT: INFRINGEMENT: ARTISTIC WORK: COPYING AN IDEA: Ch.D.) [1988] F.S.R. 66

Georgia Pacific Corp.'s Application (PATENT: APPLICATION: PRACTICE: PRIORITY DATES: C.-G.) [1984] R.P.C. 467

Gerber Garment Technology Inc. v. Lectra Systems Ltd (PATENT: INFRINGEMENT: PRACTICE: INQUIRY AS TO DAMAGES: PATENTEE MANUFACTURER: LOSSES OF ASSOCIATE SALES: ROYALTY BASIS: LOSSES SUSTAINED BY SUBSIDIARY: EFFECT OF ENDORSEMENT OF LICENCES OF RIGHT: ADVERTISING TO SUPPLY: WHETHER INFRINGEMENT: Pat. Ct) [1995] R.P.C. 383

Gerber Garment Technology Inc. v. Lectra Systems Ltd (PATENT: INFRINGEMENT: OBVIOUSNESS: RECITAL OF PRIOR ART IN PATENT: WHETHER PATENTEE CAN RESILE: BEST METHOD: PARTIAL INVALIDITY: DATE FROM WHICH DAMAGES SHOULD BE CALCULATED: C.A.) [1995] F.S.R. 492

Gerber Garment Technology Inc. v. Lectra Systems Ltd (PATENT: INFRINGEMENT: PARTIAL INVALIDITY: AMENDMENT: DAMAGES: PRACTICE: EXPERT WITNESS: Pat. Ct) [1994] F.S.R. 471

Gerber Scientific Products Inc. v. L. Vogel & Sons Pty Ltd (PATENT: OPPOSITION: PATENT OFFICE PROCEDURE: APPLICATION FOR EXTENSION OF TIME TO SERVE EVIDENCE IN REPLY: FACTORS RELEVANT: COSTS WHEN EXTENSION GRANTED: Australia: Pat. Off.) 19 I.P.R. 92

Gerber Scientific Products Inc. v. North Broken Hill Ltd (PETTY PATENT: APPLICATION UNDER SECTION 68B(3): LACK OF NOVELTY: OBVIOUSNESS: INVENTION NOT FULLY DESCRIBED: Australia: Pat. Off.) 18 I.P.R. 78

Germinal Holdings Ltd v. H. R. Fell & Sons Ltd (PLANT BREEDERS RIGHTS: INFRINGEMENT: "REPRODUCTIVE MATERIAL": WHETHER INFRINGEMENT TO MAKE SEED OVER TO ANOTHER FOR MULTIPLICATION: WHETHER INFRINGEMENT TO MULTIPLY AND SUPPLY SEED: SALE OF TURF GROWN FROM THE SEED: Ch.D.) [1993] F.S.R. 343

Gesellschaft zur Verwertung von Leistungsschutzrechten v. E.C. Comm. (RESTRICTIVE PRACTICES: ADMINISTRATIVE PROCEDURE: COPYRIGHT: MARKET PARTITIONING: INTER-STATE TRADE: DOMINANT POSITION: ABUSE: Case 7/82: ECJ) [1983] 3 C.M.L.R. 645; [1993] E.C.R. 483; [1984] F.S.R. 155

GFI Group Inc. v. Eaglestone (EMPLOYMENT CONTRACT: RESTRICTIVE COVENANT: HIGHLY-PAID SERVICES BROKER: WORKING RELATIONSHIP VERY PROFITABLE FOR EMPLOYER: GOODWILL: INTENTION TO FLOUT NOTICE PERIOD: INJUNCTION: ADEQUACY OF DAMAGES: BALANCE OF CONVENIENCE: DISCRETION: Ch.D.) [1994] F.S.R. 535

GI Marketing CC v. Fraser-Johnston (PATENT: VALIDITY: LACK OF NOVELTY: CLAIMING: DISTINCTION BETWEEN WORDS DESCRIBING PURPOSE OF INVENTION AND WORDS IMPORTING LIMITATION OF QUALITY OF ESSENTIAL INTEGER OF INVENTION: STATUTORY INTERPRETATION: South Africa: A.D.) 1996 (1) S.A. 939

GI Trade Mark (TRADE MARK: APPLICATION: LETTER MARK: DISTINCTIVENESS: BoT) [1986] R.P.C. 100

Gianfrancos Application *sub nom.* Gay & Lunettas (Gianfranco's) Application

Gianitsios v. Karagiannis (COPYRIGHT: INFRINGEMENT: CINEMATOGRAPHIC FILM: PRACTICE: ANTON PILLER: Australia: S.C.(NSW))   7 I.P.R. 36

GIDEONS INTERNATIONAL Service Mark (SERVICE MARK: APPLICATION: FREE DISTRIBUTION OF BIBLES: MONEYS WORTH: T.M.Reg.)
[1991] R.P.C. 141

Gilfoyle Shipping Services Ltd v. Binosi Pty Ltd (PRACTICE: MAREVA INJUNCTION: THIRD PARTY'S RIGHTS: JURISDICTION: New Zealand: H.C.)
[1984] N.Z.L.R. 742

Gill v. Chipman Ltd (PATENT: INFRINGEMENT: PRACTICE: PLEADINGS: EARTH CLOSET ORDERS: Pat. Ct)   [1987] R.P.C. 209

Gillette U.K. Ltd v. Edenwest Ltd (TRADE MARK: INFRINGEMENT: PASSING OFF: SUMMARY JUDGMENT: INQUIRY AS TO DAMAGES: INNOCENCE: Ch.D.)
[1994] R.P.C. 279

Gillette/Inconsistent documents for grant (EUROPEAN PATENT: AMENDMENT AND CORRECTION: APPROVAL AFTER: APPEAL: PROCEDURE: REMITTAL ORDERED: TO REMOVE INCONSISTENCY: APPROVED TEXT: T171/85: EPO)   [1986] E.P.O.R. 107; [1987] O.J. EPO 160

Gillman Engineering Ltd v. Simon Ho Shek On (CONFIDENTIAL INFORMATION: DUTY OF EX-EMPLOYEE: Hong Kong: S.C.)   8 I.P.R. 313

Gist-Brocades/Biomass preparation (EUROPEAN PATENT: AMENDMENT AND CORRECTION: ESSENTIAL FEATURE: INESSENTIAL LIMITATION: T32/85: EPO)   [1986] E.P.O.R. 267

Glamagard Pty Ltd v. Enderslea Productions Pty Ltd (DESIGNS: APPLICATION: UNREGISTERED: NO MONOPOLY RIGHT: NO RELIEF: Australia: S.C.(NSW))
29 A.L.R. 740; 4 I.P.R. 113; [1985] 1 N.S.W.L.R. 138

GLASSCAN Trade Mark (TRADE MARK: APPLICATION: DISTINCTIVENESS: T.M.Reg.)   [1994] R.P.C. 23

Glatt's Application (PATENT: APPLICATION: WHETHER CLAIM SUPPORTED BY DESCRIPTION: Pat. Ct)   [1983] R.P.C. 122

Glaverbel's Patent (PATENT: LICENCES OF RIGHT: APPLICATION TO CANCEL ENDORSEMENT: OPPOSITION: *Locus standii*: Pat. Ct)   [1987] R.P.C. 89
(C.A.) [1987] F.S.R. 153; [1987] R.P.C. 73

Glaverbel SA v. British Coal Corp. (PATENT: INFRINGEMENT: VALIDITY: DISCOVERY RELATING TO ANTICIPATION AND OBVIOUSNESS: PRACTICE: DISCOVERY REFUSED: Pat. Ct)   [1992] F.S.R. 642

Glaverbel SA v. British Coal Corp. (PATENT: INFRINGEMENT: VALIDITY: CONSTRUCTION OF CLAIMS: AMBIGUITY: FAIR BASIS: ANTICIPATION: OBVIOUSNESS: PRACTICE: WITNESSES: Pat. Ct)   [1994] R.P.C. 443
(C.A.) [1995] F.S.R. 254; [1995] R.P.C. 255

Glaverbel SA v. British Coal Corp. (No. 2) (PATENT: INFRINGEMENT: CONSTRUCTION: EVIDENCE: Pat. Ct)   [1993] R.P.C. 90

Glaverbel SA v. British Coal Corp. (No. 3) (PATENT: PRACTICE: PLEADINGS: WITNESS STATEMENT: OBJECT OF PARTICULARS: OBVIOUSNESS: CROSS-EXAMINATION: Pat. Ct)   [1993] F.S.R. 478

Glaxo Group Ltd v. Apotex NZ Ltd (PATENTS: PHARMACEUTICAL PATENT: DIFFERENT CRYSTALLINE FORMS: APPLICATION FOR PRE-TRIAL DISCOVERY TO OBTAIN DETAILS OF CRYSTALLINE FORM AND ROUTE OF SYNTHESIS: New Zealand: H.C.)   30 I.P.R. 665
(INFRINGEMENT: PRACTICE: APPLICATION TO STRIKE OUT: ALLEGED ABUSE OF PROCESS: EVIDENCE IN SUPPORT: AFFIDAVITS: NEW ZEALAND: H.C.)
[1996] 1 N.Z.L.R. 682

Glaxo Group Ltd v. Commissioner of Patents (PATENTS: APPLICATION: COMPULSORY LICENCE: PRIMA FACIE CASE: JUDICIAL REVIEW: EVIDENCE FOR FINDINGS: New Zealand: C.A.)   [1991] 3 N.Z.L.R. 179

Glaxo Group Ltd v. Pathstream Ltd (TRADE MARK: OPPOSITION: LIKELIHOOD OF DECEPTION AND CONFUSION: INTERNATIONAL AND NON-PROPRIETARY NAMES: Australia: Pat. Off.)   9 I.P.R. 95

Glaxo Operations U.K. Ltd v. Rama Bhaktha Hanuman Candle & Camphor Works (COPYRIGHT: TRADE MARK: INFORMATION: JOINDER OF CAUSE OF ACTION: JURISDICTION: INTERIM INJUNCTION: India: H.C.)   (1991) 16 I.P.L.R. 45

Glaxo plc v. Glaxo-Wellcome Ltd (PASSING OFF: REGISTRATION OF COMPANY NAME: DEMAND FOR PAYMENT TO CHANGE NAME: MANDATORY INJUNCTION GRANTED: Ch.D)   [1996] F.S.R. 388

Glenleith Holdings Ltd's Application (TRADE MARKS: APPLICATION: "NAME OF A PERSON NOT REPRESENTED IN A SPECIAL OR PARTICULAR MANNER": DISTINCTIVENESS: "SUBSTANTIALLY IDENTICAL WITH OR DECEPTIVELY SIMILAR TO": Australia: Pat. Off.)   15 I.P.R. 555

GLENLIVET Trade Marks, *sub nom.* THE GLENLIVET Trade Marks

Global European Network (RESTRICTIVE PRACTICES: TELECOMMUNICATIONS: TECHNICAL CO-OPERATION BETWEEN NATIONAL TELECOMMUNICATIONS ORGANISATIONS: PROVISION OF FIBRE OPTIC CAPACITY BETWEEN INTERNATIONAL LINES: NOTICE: E.C. Comm.)   [1994] 4 C.M.L.R. 712

Global Logistics System Europe Co. for Cargo Information Services GmbH (Re) (RESTRICTIVE PRACTICES: JOINT VENTURES: OPERATION OF COMPUTERISED AIR CARGO INFORMATION SYSTEM: INTENTION TO APPROVE: E.C. Comm.)   [1993] 4 C.M.L.R. 632

Globe Super Parts v. Blue Super Flame Industries (PASSING OFF: TRADE MARK: INFRINGEMENT: INJUNCTION: India: H.C.)   (1986) 11 I.P.L.R. 47

Goddard v. Nationwide Building Society (EVIDENCE: PROFESSIONALLY PRIVILEGED NOTE: USE OF COPIES RESTRAINED: C.A.)
          [1986] 3 All E.R. 264; [1987] Q.B. 670; [1986] 3 W.L.R. 734

Goddin and Rennie's Application (PATENT: APPLICATION: ENTITLEMENT: JOINT CONTRIBUTORS TO INVENTION: COMMISSIONED CONTRIBUTION: OWNERSHIPS: C.-G.; Court of Session)   [1996] R.P.C. 141

Godecke/Naphthyridinone derivatives (EUROPEAN PATENT: CLAIMS: DISCLAIMER: REQUIREMENT FOR PRECISION OF: NOVELTY: SELECTION: OVERLAPPING CLASS: T11/89: EPO)   [1991] E.P.O.R. 336

Godfrey v. Lees (COPYRIGHT: INFRINGEMENT: JOINT WORKS: ARRANGEMENTS: CONTRIBUTION: OWNERSHIP: BREACH OF CONTRACT: IMPLIED LICENCE: Ch.D.)   [1995] E.M.L.R. 307

Godrej Soaps Ltd v. Hindustan Lever Ltd (PATENT: INFRINGEMENT: INTERIM INJUNCTION: APPEAL: MANUFACTURE OF PRODUCT PRIOR TO GRANT OF PATENT: India: H.C.)   (1994) 19 I.P.L.R. 60

Gold Seal Engineering Products Pvt. Ltd v. Hindustan Manufacturers (TRADE MARK: INFRINGEMENT: COPYRIGHT: PASSING OFF: JURISDICTION: JOINDER OF CAUSES OF ACTION: India: H.C.)   (1993) 18 I.P.L.R. 205

Golden Editions Pty. Ltd v. Polygram Pty. Ltd (COPYRIGHT: INFRINGEMENT: DEFENCE: KNOWLEDGE OR SUSPICION THAT ACT WAS INFRINGEMENT: STATUTORY INTERPRETATION: RELEVANCE OF KNOWLEDGE OF IDENTITY OF OWNER: PRACTICE: APPEALS: FACTUAL FINDINGS AND ERRORS OF LAW: Australia: Fed. Ct)   135 A.L.R. 638

Golden Era Shirt Co. Pty Ltd v. Cassini (TRADE MARK: APPLICATION TO REMOVE: NON-USE: INTENTION TO USE: Australia: S.C.(NSW))   6 I.P.R. 247

Golden Era Shirt Co. Pty Ltd v. Cassini (TRADE MARK: APPLICATION TO REMOVE:
NON-USE: INTENTION TO USE: DISCRETION: AIPO)   28 I.P.R. 122
GOLDEN PAGES Trade Mark (APPLICATION: USE ON TELEPHONE DIRECTORIES:
Ireland: S.C.)   [1984] 2 I.L.T. 190; [1985] F.S.R. 27
Golf Lynx v. Golf Scene Pty Ltd (TRADE MARK: INFRINGEMENT: PASSING OFF:
ANTON PILLER ORDER: DAMAGE: *Ex parte* ORDER: Australia: S.C.(NSW))
3 I.P.R. 243; 59 A.L.R. 343
Gollel Holdings Pty Ltd v. Kenneth Maurer Funerals Pty Ltd (TRADE PRACTICES:
MISLEADING AND DECEPTIVE CONDUCT: INTERLOCUTORY INJUNCTION:
BALANCE OF CONVENIENCE: DELAY: PROOF OF LOSS: Australia: Fed. Ct)
9 I.P.R. 109
Goodman Fielder Industries Ltd's Application (TRADE MARKS: APPLICATIONS FOR
REGISTRATION: SUBSTANTIALLY IDENTICAL OR DECEPTIVELY SIMILAR
MARKS: DISTINCTIVENESS: Australia: Pat. Off.)   18 I.P.R. 637
Goodrich/Vinyl monomers (EUROPEAN PATENT: OPPOSITION: PROCEDURE: LATE
SUBMISSION CONSIDERED: SUFFICIENCY: PARAMETER: ILL-DEFINED:
T340/88: EPO)   [1990] E.P.O.R. 377
Goodyear Tire & Rubber Co. v. Silverstone Tire & Rubber Co. Sdn Bhd
(COPYRIGHT: INFRINGEMENT: SCOPE OF PROTECTION: TRADE MARK:
PASSING OFF: GET-UP OF TYRES: REPUTATION AND GOODWILL: Malaysia:
H.C.)   [1994] 1 M.L.J. 348
Goodyear/Thermoforming polyester articles (EUROPEAN PATENT: INVENTIVE STEP:
PREJUDICE: SINGLE SPECIFICATION: T519/89: EPO)   [1994] E.P.O.R. 9
Gordon & Rena Merchant Pty Ltd v. Barrymores Pty Ltd (TRADE MARK:
OPPOSITION: EXTENSION OF TIME: EVIDENCE IN ANSWER: SPECIAL
CIRCUMSTANCES: ONUS OF PROOF: Australia: AIPO)   28 I.P.R. 71
Gordon & Rena Merchant Pty Ltd v. Ocky Docket (Aust.) Pty Ltd (TRADE MARKS:
REMOVAL: OPPOSITION: NON-USE: PERSON AGGRIEVED: ONUS: TRADE
MARK CONSISTED OF A PERSON'S NICKNAME: TRADE MARK USED
DECORATIVELY: Australia: Pat. Off.)   24 I.P.R. 357
Gore W.L. & Associates Inc. v. Kimal Scientific Products Ltd (PATENT: VALIDITY:
PRIOR USE: PROCESS CLAIMS: PROCESS CARRIED OUT ABROAD:
IMPORTATION BEFORE PRIORITY DATE: Pat. Ct)   [1988] R.P.C. 137
Gosawami v. Hammons (COPYRIGHT: THESIS: REPUBLICATION: DAMAGES:
C.A.)   (1985) 129 S.J. 653
Gould Inc.'s Application (PATENT: APPLICATION: COMMISSIONERS POWER TO
REFUSE GRANT AFTER ACCEPTANCE BUT PRIOR TO SEALING, WHERE NO
OPPOSITION: Australia: Pat. Off.)   13 I.P.R. 644
Grace (W. R.) & Co. v. Betz International Inc. (PATENT: OPPOSITION: APPLICATION
FOR EXTENSION OF TIME WITHIN WHICH TO LODGE NOTICE OF OPPOSITION:
EXCEPTIONAL CIRCUMSTANCES: DUE DILIGENCE: UNREASONABLE DELAY:
SERIOUS OPPOSITION: Australia: Pat. Off.)   13 I.P.R. 55
Grace Bros Pty Ltd v. Magistrates, Local Courts of New South Wales (TRADE
PRACTICES: JURISDICTION OF FEDERAL COURT: SUMMONS UNDER STATE
CONSUMER PROTECTION STATUTE: Australia: Fed. Ct)   12 I.P.R. 600
Grace Bros Pty Ltd v. Magistrates, Local Court of New South Wales (TRADE
PRACTICES: REPRESENTATION AS TO ORIGIN OF GOODS: INCONSISTENCY
BETWEEN STATUTES: JURISDICTION OF FEDERAL COURT: Australia: Fed.
Ct)   16 I.P.R. 129
Grace/Nitro compounds (EUROPEAN PATENT: INVENTIVE STEP: PROBLEM,
DEFINITION OF: PRIOR ART: TEACHING OF SCIENTIFIC PAPER, TECHNICAL
PROBLEM DISTINGUISHED FROM: T121/91: EPO)   [1994] E.P.O.R. 114

Graf v. Milward-Bason (PATENT: OPPOSITION: NOVELTY: PRIOR USE: SECRET USE:
EXPERIMENTAL USE: BUILDING FOUNDATION METHOD CLAIM: BUILDING
ERECTED ON PRIVATE PROPERTY USING METHOD BEFORE PRIORITY DATE:
PATENT NOT NOVEL: Australia: Pat. Off.)   18 I.P.R. 566
Grafton Industries Pty Ltd v. Wyborn (PATENT: APPLICATION: OPPOSITION:
APPLICATION FOR AN EXTENSION OF TIME: ERROR OR OMISSION: Australia:
Pat. Off.)   20 I.P.R. 285
Graham v. Delderfield (CONFIDENTIAL INFORMATION: INTERLOCUTORY
INJUNCTION: *American Cyanamid* PRACTICE: STATUS QUO: C.A.)
                                                          [1992] F.S.R. 313
Grain Processing Corporation/Re-establishment of rights (EUROPEAN PATENT:
PROFESSIONAL REPRESENTATIVES: DUTY TO SEEK TIMELY INSTRUCTIONS:
RE-ESTABLISHMENT OF RIGHTS: LATE INSTRUCTIONS MISDIRECTED: T30/90:
EPO)   [1992] E.P.O.R. 424
Gramaphone Co. of India Ltd v. Birendra Bahadur Pande (COPYRIGHT: MUSICAL
RECORDS: IMPORT: India: S.C.)   (1985) 9 I.P.L.R. 359
Gramaphone Co. of India Ltd v. Electroband (India) Pvt. Ltd (COPYRIGHT:
INFRINGEMENT: RECORDS, CASSETTES: INTERIM ORDER: India: H.C.)
                                                          (1993) 18 I.P.L.R. 187
Gramaphone Co. of India Ltd v. The Oriental Gramophone Records Co.
(COPYRIGHT: INFRINGEMENT: RECORDS, CASSETTES: INTERIM INJUNCTION:
India: H.C.)   (1993) 18 I.P.L.R. 189
Grammophone Co. of India Ltd v. Pandey (COPYRIGHT: IMPORTATION:
INTERNATIONAL COPYRIGHT: India: S.C.)   [1985] F.S.R. 136
Granby Marketing Services Ltd v. Interlego AG (COPYRIGHT: INFRINGEMENT:
THREATS: UNLAWFUL INTERFERENCE WITH CONTRACTUAL RELATIONS:
STRIKING OUT: Ch.D.)   [1984] R.P.C. 209
GRAND MARNIER Liqueur (IMPORTS: GET-UP: PASSING OFF: GRAND
MARNIER: TWO QUALITIES, YELLOW (GOOD) AND RED (BETTER): IDENTICAL
PACKAGING EXCEPT FOR COLOUR OF STOPPER AND LABELS: USE OF
NATIONAL COMPETITION LAW INFRINGES ARTICLE 30: Germany: C.A.)
                                    [1994] 2 C.M.L.R. 123; [1994] F.S.R. 61
Grant's Application (TRADE MARK: APPLICATION: INHERENT ADAPTABILITY TO
DISTINGUISH: USE: Australia: Pat. Off.)   9 I.P.R. 57
Grant & Sons Ltd v. William Cadenhead Ltd (TRADE MARK: INFRINGEMENT:
PASSING OFF: WHISKY: GEOGRAPHICAL NAME: Scotland: O.H.)
                                                          1985 S.L.T. 291
Grant v. Procurator Fiscal (CONFIDENTIAL INFORMATION: COPIES OF COMPUTER
PRINT-OUTS: WHETHER DISHONEST EXPLOITATION OF THE CONFIDENTIAL
INFORMATION OF ANOTHER CRIME: Scotland: H.C.)   [1988] R.P.C. 41
Greater Glasgow Health Board's Application (PATENT: APPLICATION: OWNERSHIP:
EMPLOYEE INVENTOR: REGISTRAR AT HOSPITAL: WHETHER DUTIES EXTEND
TO RESEARCH: C.-G.; Pat. Ct)   [1996] R.P.C. 207
Greek City Co. Ltd v. Demetriou (COPYRIGHT: FAILURE TO SERVE STATEMENT OF
CLAIM: STRIKING OUT: DISCRETION: Ch.D.)
                                    [1983] F.S.R. 442; [1983] 2 All E.R. 921
Green v. Broadcasting Corp. of New Zealand (COPYRIGHT: INFRINGEMENT:
PASSING OFF: U.K. TV PROGRAMME: *Opportunity Knocks*: LITERARY OR
DRAMATIC WORK: FEATURES OF FOREIGN PROGRAMME COPIED: GOODWILL
IN NEW ZEALAND: SCRIPTS: SUBSISTENCE OF COPYRIGHT: WRITING OR
OTHER MATERIAL FORM: VIDEO TAPES: New Zealand: H.C.)   2 I.P.R. 191
                    16 I.P.R. 1; [1988] 2 N.Z.L.R. 490; [1989] R.P.C. 469
        (P.C.) [1989] 3 N.Z.L.R. 18; [1989] R.P.C. 700; [1989] 2 All E.R. 609

Greenberg v. Pearson (COPYRIGHT: INFRINGEMENT: PRACTICE: DISCOVERY: PRODUCTION OF DOCUMENTS: COMPUTER PRINTOUTS: SOURCE CODES: INVOICES AND OTHER SECONDARY DOCUMENTS: South Africa: WLD)
1994 (3) S.A. 264

Greenfield Products Pty Ltd v. Rover-Scott Bonnar Ltd (COPYRIGHT: OWNERSHIP: AGREEMENT FOR SALE OF BUSINESS: TAX AVOIDANCE SCHEME: NO EXPRESS ASSIGNMENT: COPYRIGHT ASSIGNMENT IMPLIED: ASSIGNMENT IN WRITING: AUTHORSHIP: EMPLOYEE'S: COPYRIGHT AND DESIGN OVERLAP: CROWN COPYRIGHT: THREE DIMENSIONAL OBJECTS: MOULDS AND ARTICLES MADE THEREFROM: MEANING OF "ENGRAVING": DRAWINGS: DEFENCE: Australia: Fed. Ct)
95 A.L.R. 275; 17 I.P.R. 417

Greg Cotton Motors Pty Ltd v. Neil & Ross Neilson Pty Ltd (TRADE PRACTICES: MISLEADING AND DECEPTIVE CONDUCT: RIGHT TO USE OWN NAME: Australia: Fed. Ct)
2 I.P.R. 214

Grehal/Shear (EUROPEAN PATENT: NOVELTY: COMBINATION OF SEPARATE TEACHINGS IN SINGLE DOCUMENT: PRIOR ART: CATALOGUE, NATURE OF DOCUMENT REPRESENTED BY: T305/87: EPO)
[1991] E.P.O.R. 389; [1991] O.J. EPO 429

Griffin & Sons Ltd v. R. (1988) Ltd (PASSING OFF: INTERLOCUTORY INJUNCTION: SIMILAR PACKAGING FOR CONFECTIONERY: DIVERSIONS OF TRADE: MODE OF SALE: New Zealand: H.C.)
19 I.P.R. 471

Griffon Laboratories (P.) Ltd v. Indian National Drug Co. P. Ltd (TRADE MARK: INFRINGEMENT: SORBILINE/SORBITON: INTERIM INJUNCTION: India: H.C.)
(1989) 14 I.P.L.R. 9

Grisebach/Divisional application (EUROPEAN PATENT: PROCEDURE: INTERPRETATION OF LETTERS: DIVISIONAL APPLICATION: TIME LIMIT: J24/82, J25/82, J26/82: EPO)
[1979–85] E.P.O.R. A159; [1984] O.J. EPO 467

Grofam Pty Ltd v. KPMG Peat Marwick (CONFIDENTIAL INFORMATION: SUPPLIED TO ACCOUNTANTS: SUSPICION THAT OFFENCE COMMITTED IN COURSE OF ACCOUNTANTS' DUTIES: WHETHER ACCOUNTANTS MAY DISCLOSE INFORMATION TO POLICE: Australia: Fed. Ct)
27 I.P.R. 215

Groko Maskin AB's Application (PATENT: OPPOSITION: EXTENSION OF TIME: PUBLIC INTEREST: ERROR OR OMISSION: DELAY: Australia: Pat. Off.)
3 I.P.R. 614

Grolsch NV's Application (TRADE MARKS: APPLICATION: REGISTRABILITY: BOTTLE SHAPE: DISTINCTIVE: INHERENT ADAPTABILITY: DISTINCTIVE THROUGH USE: Australia: Pat. Off.)
20 I.P.R. 302

Group Exemptions (Amendment) Regulation 1992 (RESTRICTIVE PRACTICES: GROUP EXEMPTIONS: SPECIALISATION AGREEMENTS: JOINT RESEARCH AND DEVELOPMENT: PATENT LICENSING: KNOW-HOW LICENSING: E.C. Comm.)
[1993] 4 C.M.L.R. 151

Grower v. BBC (DRAMATIC & MUSICAL PERFORMERS' PROTECTION ACT 1958: RECORDING MADE FOR BROADCAST LICENSED FOR DISTRIBUTION AS RECORD: CONSENT OF ONE AUTHOR NOT OBTAINED: JOINT TORTFEASORS: BREACH OF CONTRACT: Ch.D.)
[1990] F.S.R. 595

Grundig's Agreements (RESTRICTIVE PRACTICES: SELECTIVE DISTRIBUTION SYSTEM: ADMISSION CRITERIA: VALID IN SO FAR AS QUALITATIVE AND APPLIED IN NON–DISCRIMINATORY MANNER: EXEMPTION RENEWED: E.C. Comm.)
[1995] 4 C.M.L.R. 658

Grundy Television Pty Ltd v. Startrain Ltd (PASSING OFF: NEIGHBOURS TV SERIES: LOGO IN PARTICULAR SCRIPT: WHETHER *Neighbours Who's Who* MAGAZINE WITH IDENTICAL LOGO ACTIONABLE IN PASSING OFF: DISCLAIMER: MISREPRESENTATION OF AUTHORITY TO USE NAME: DAMAGE TO FUTURE MERCHANDISING AS HEAD OF DAMAGES: Ch.D.)
13 I.P.R. 585; [1988] F.S.R. 581

Gruzman Pty Ltd v. Percy Marks Pty Ltd (COPYRIGHT: ARTISTIC WORK: INFRINGEMENT: REPRODUCTION IN A MATERIAL FORM: THREE-DIMENSIONAL VERSION OF A TWO-DIMENSIONAL WORK: IMPLIED LICENCE: ARCHITECTURAL PLANS AND DRAWINGS: Australia: S.C.(NSW))
16 I.P.R. 87

GTC Industries Ltd v. ITC Ltd (TRADE MARK: APPLICATION: OPPOSITION: WINEX/WINNER: APPEAL: India: H.C.)   (1995) 20 I.P.L.R. 15

GTE/Silicon nitride cutting tools (EUROPEAN PATENT: APPEAL: PROCEDURE: PROBLEM, REFORMULATION OF: INVENTIVE STEP: BONUS EFFECT: T344/89: EPO)   [1993] E.P.O.R. 209

GTM/Sound-absorbent wall (EUROPEAN PATENT: CLAIMS: CLARITY: MINIMUM V. MAXIMUM REQUIREMENTS: UNITY: AMENDMENT OF CLAIMS IN OPPOSITION PROCEEDINGS: REQUIREMENTS OF *a priori v. a posteriori* EXAMINATIONS: T80/82: EPO)   [1979–85] E.P.O.R. B500

Guccio Gucci SpA v. Paolo Gucci (PASSING OFF: TRADE MARK INFRINGEMENT: EVIDENCE OF CONFUSION: TRADE EVIDENCE: Ch.D.)   [1991] F.S.R. 89

Guccio Gucci SpA v. Sukhdav Singh (TRADE MARK: POST-JUDGMENT DISCOVERY: PAST ACTS OF INFRINGEMENT: PRIVILEGE AGAINST SELF-INCRIMINATION: Singapore: H.C.)   [1992] 1 S.L.R. 553

Guertler's Application (PATENT: EXTENSION OF PETTY PATENT: OPPOSITION: OBVIOUSNESS: EVIDENCE: Australia: Pat. Off.)   4 I.P.R. 208

Guertler v. Antenna Engineering Australia Pty Ltd (PATENT: PETTY PATENT: OBVIOUSNESS: EXTENSION: Australia: Pat. Off.)   6 I.P.R. 170

Guess? Inc. v. Lee (PRACTICE: ANTON PILLER: NON-DISCLOSURE: Hong Kong: C.A.)   [1987] F.S.R. 125; 7 I.P.R. 321

Guest Keen Williams Ltd v. Controller of Patents & Designs (PATENT: PROCEEDINGS BEFORE CONTROLLER: EVIDENCE: India: H.C.)   (1986) 10 I.P.L.R. 414

Guilford Kapwood Ltd v. Embsay Fabrics Ltd (COPYRIGHT: INFRINGEMENT: SECTION 9(8) DEFENCE: Ch.D.)   [1983] F.S.R. 567

Guinness Peat Properties Ltd v. Fitzroy Robinson Partnership (DISCOVERY: LEGAL PROFESSIONAL PRIVILEGE: COMMUNICATION BETWEEN DEFENDANT AND INSURERS: INADVERTENT DISCLOSURE: C.A.)
[1987] 2 All E.R. 716; [1987] 1 W.L.R. 1027

Gulf Oil (G.B.) Ltd v. Page (CONSPIRACY TO INJURE: INTERLOCUTORY INJUNCTION: JURISDICTION: C.A.)
[1987] 3 All E.R. 14; [1987] Ch.D. 327; [1987] 3 W.L.R. 166

Gumley's Application (PATENT: PATENT APPLICATION: ADVERTISED AS ACCEPTED: NOTICE OF OPPOSITION: APPLICATION FOR EXTENSION OF TIME FOR FILING EVIDENCE IN SUPPORT OF OPPOSITION: APPLICATION OPPOSED: THREE-MONTH EXTENSION GRANTED: Australia: Pat. Off.)   17 I.P.R. 107

Gunn's Application (PATENT: APPLICATION: OBJECTIONS TO REGISTRATION: Australia: Pat. Off.)   17 I.P.R. 605

GUNTRUM Trade Mark (TRADE MARK: OPPOSITION: SURNAME: PARTNERSHIP: DECEPTION: EFFECT OF PROCEEDINGS IN ANOTHER JURISDICTION: T.M.Reg.)   [1990] R.P.C. 27

Gurshant Engineering Co. Pvt. Ltd v. DLF Universals Ltd (TRADE MARK: INFRINGEMENT: PASSING OFF: COPYRIGHT: APPEAL: India: H.C.)
(1987) 11 I.P.L.R. 156

Gussinyer/Calcium sulphate filler (EUROPEAN PATENT: INTERVENTION: ADMISSIBILITY: PRIOR ART: DOCUMENT TO BE READ AS OF ITS DATE: INVENTIVE STEP: AGED ART: CLOSEST PRIOR ART: NOVELTY: CROSS-REFERENCED DOCUMENTS: OPPOSITION: PROCEDURE: FRESH DOCUMENTS ON APPEAL: T390/90: EPO)   [1993] E.P.O.R. 424; [1994] O.J. EPO 03

Habeebur Rehman & Sons v. Ram Babu & Brothers (TRADE MARK: INFRINGEMENT: PASSING OFF: COPYRIGHT IN LABEL: INFRINGEMENT: DEFENDANT PRIOR REGISTRANT: INTERIM INJUNCTION: APPEAL: India: H.C.)   (1990) 15 I.P.L.R. 329

Hacharis Heat Treatment (Pty) Ltd v. Iscor (CONFIDENTIAL INFORMATION: UNLAWFUL INTERFERENCE WITH TRADE: South Africa: TPD)
1983 (1) S.A. 548

Haddonstone Pty Ltd v. Haddonstone Ltd (TRADE MARK: APPLICATION: ACCEPTANCE: OPPOSITION: PROPRIETORSHIP: MANUFACTURER OR DISTRIBUTOR: ESTOPPEL: ROLE OF REGISTRAR: DECEPTION OR CONFUSION: Australia: AIPO)   31 I.P.R. 79

HAG Coffee (TRADE MARKS: HAG: SPECIFIC SUBJECT-MATTER: CONSEQUENCES: EXHAUSTION OF RIGHTS: IMPORTS: BREAK OF CHAIN OF OWNERSHIP BY EXPROPRIATION: GERMAN HAG ABLE TO RESIST IMPORT INTO GERMANY OF BELGIAN HAG COFFEE: *acte claire* FROM EUROPEAN COURT JUDGMENT IN *Pharmon v. Hoechst*: NO ARTICLE 177 REFERENCE: Germany: C.A.)
[1989] 3 C.M.L.R. 154; [1990] F.S.R. 47

Haggar & Co. v. S.A. Tailorscraft (Pty) Ltd (TRADE MARK: PASSING OFF: REPUTATION: EVIDENCE: DAMAGES: QUANTUM: South Africa: TPD)
1985 (4) S.A. 569

Hai-O Enterprise BHD v. Nguang Chan (TRADE MARKS: MANUFACTURER OWNER OF TRADE MARK IN CHINA: MALAYSIAN IMPORTER OF CHINESE PRODUCT: IMPORTER REGISTERING TRADE MARK IN OWN NAME: TRADE DESCRIPTION ORDER: SEIZURE OF GOODS: EXPUNGEMENT OF MARK: WHETHER WRONGLY REGISTERED: ON REGISTER SEVEN YEARS: FRAUD: CLASS OF GOODS: WHETHER NON-REGISTRATION IN CORRECT CLASS RESULTED IN NON-USER OF MARK: PARALLEL IMPORT: Malaysia: H.C.)   23 I.P.R. 527

Hakoune/Inadequate description (EUROPEAN PATENT: SUFFICIENCY: PROCESS CONDITIONS, FAILURE TO SPECIFY: T219/85: EPO)
[1987] E.P.O.R. 30; [1986] O.J. EPO 376

Hal Computer Products's Application (TRADE MARKS: APPLICATION: CONFLICTING MARK CITED: WHETHER USE PRE-DATES FIRST USE AND REGISTRATION OF CITED MARK: ONUS OF PROOF: Australia: Pat. Off.)   15 I.P.R. 323

Halbach & Braun v. Polymaze Pty Ltd (TRADE MARK: OPPOSITION: APPLICATION FOR EXTENSION OF TIME TO SERVE EVIDENCE IN ANSWER TO OPPOSITION: Australia: AIPO)   32 I.P.R. 178

Halcon SD Group Inc.'s Patents (PATENT: COMPULSORY LICENCE: JURISDICTION: STRIKING OUT: ESTOPPEL: ELECTION: EVIDENCE: DISCOVERY: Pat. Ct)
[1989] R.P.C. 1

Hallen Co. v. Brabantia (U.K.) Ltd (PATENT: INFRINGEMENT: AMENDMENT: WHETHER PARTIALLY VALID: WHETHER SPECIFICATION FRAMED IN GOOD FAITH: WHETHER TO IMPOSE TERMS OR LIMIT DAMAGES: Pat. Ct)
[1990] F.S.R. 134; [1991] R.P.C. 195
(C.A.) [1991] R.P.C. 195

Hallen Co. v. Brabantia (U.K.) Ltd (PATENT: INFRINGEMENT: CORKSCREW: CONSTRUCTION: VALIDITY: OBVIOUSNESS: COMMERCIAL SUCCESS: SELECTION INVENTION: AMENDMENT: PRACTICE: Pat. Ct)
[1989] R.P.C. 307

Hamburger/Road vehicle (EUROPEAN PATENT: NOVELTY: DRAWINGS, TEACHING OF: PICTORIAL REPRESENTATION IN CITED ART, MAGNIFICATION OF: T127/83: EPO)   [1979–85] E.P.O.R. C838

Hami Brothers v. Hami & Co. (TRADE MARK: RECTIFICATION: DISTINCTIVENESS: India: H.C.)   (1985) 10 I.P.L.R. 233

Hamish Robertson & Co. Ltd's Application (TRADE MARKS: APPLICATION FOR REGISTRATION: DECEPTIVELY SIMILAR MARKS: LIKELIHOOD OF DECEPTION OR CONFUSION: CRESTS: GOODS SOLD THROUGH SELF-SERVICE OUTLETS: Australia: Pat. Off.)   13 I.P.R. 69

Hampo Systems (Pty) Ltd v. Audiolens (Cape) (Pty) Ltd (TRADE MARK: INFRINGEMENT: APPLICATION TO PREVENT AUTHORISED DEALER FROM PARALLEL SELLING: South Africa: CPD)   1985 (4) S.A. 257
sub nom. Protective Mining & Industrial Equipment Systems v. Audiolens (Cape) (Pty) Ltd   1987 (2) S.A. 961

Handmade Films (Productions) Ltd v. Express Newspapers plc (COPYRIGHT: INFRINGEMENT: UNLAWFUL INTERFERENCE WITH GOODS: PHOTOGRAPHS: PRACTICE: DISCOVERY: Ch.D.)   [1986] F.S.R. 463

Hans Continental Smallgoods Pty Ltd's Application (TRADE MARK: APPLICATION: REGISTRABILITY: DESCRIPTIVE: UNCOMMON COMBINATION OF WORDS: Australia: AIPO)   27 I.P.R.412

Hansly's Application (DESIGNS: REGISTRATION OF HOUSE DESIGN: WHETHER "PLANS": WHETHER DESIGN APPLICABLE TO AN ARTICLE: REGISTRATION REFUSED: Australia: Pat. Off.)   10 I.P.R. 365

Happy Landings Pty Ltd v. Magazine Promotions Pty Ltd (TRADE PRACTICES: SIMILAR BOOK TITLES: DECEPTION: Australia: Fed. Ct)   2 I.P.R. 347

Haralambides v. Pastrikos (TRADE MARK: APPLICATION: OPPOSITION: LIKELIHOOD OF CONFUSION OR DECEPTION: Australia: Pat. Off.)   7 I.P.R. 437

Harben Pumps (Scotland) Ltd v. Lafferty (CONFIDENTIAL INFORMATION: EX EMPLOYEE: TRADE SECRETS: IMPLIED TERMS OF CONTRACT: Scotland: O.H.)   1989 S.L.T. 752
(TRADE MARK: EXPUNGEMENT: NON-USE: APPEAL: SPECIAL CIRCUMSTANCES: IMPORT BAN: India: H.C.)   (1991) 16 I.P.L.R. 234

Hardie Trading Ltd v. Addison Paints & Chemicals Ltd (TRADE MARK: OVERSEAS PROPRIETOR: USE BY AGENT: REGISTERED USER: APPLICATION BY INDIAN COMPANY: OPPOSITION: APPLICATION FOR STAY: India: H.C.)
(1991) 16 I.P.L.R. 276

Hardings Patent (PATENT: VALIDITY: REVOCATION: ADDED SUBJECT-MATTER: AMENDMENT: Pat. Ct)   [1988] R.P.C. 515

Hardings Manufacturers Pty Ltd's Application (TRADE MARK: APPLICATION: OPPOSITION : WYANDRA GOLDEN CRUMPETS: DECEPTIVE SIMILARITY: DISCLAIMER: EVIDENCE OF USE: REPUTATION: Australia: Pat. Off.)   8 I.P.R. 147

Harnischfeger Corp. v. Appleton (COPYRIGHT: EVIDENCE: INFRINGEMENT: OWNERSHIP: FOREIGN LAW: South Africa: WLD)   1993 (4) S.A. 479

Harris' Patent (PATENT: EMPLOYEE'S INVENTION: OBLIGATIONS OF EMPLOYEE: Pat. Ct)   [1985] R.P.C. 19
see also, sub nom., Reiss Engineering Co. v. Harris [1987] R.P.C. 171

Harris v. CSIRO (PATENT: APPLICATION: INVENTION: JOINT INVENTORSHIP: DECLARATION SOUGHT CONCERNING ELIGIBLE PERSON IN RELATION TO INVENTIONS: COSTS: Australia: Pat. Off.)   26 I.P.R. 469

Harrison v. Project & Design Co. (Redcar) Ltd (PATENT: INFRINGEMENT: ENQUIRY AS TO DAMAGES: PRACTICE: MODIFICATION OF INFRINGING ARTICLE: *Res judicata*: CONSTRUCTION OF CLAIMS: C.A.) [1987] R.P.C. 151

Harrods Ltd v. Schwartz-Sackin & Co. Ltd (PASSING OFF: TRADE MARK: INFRINGEMENT: HARRODS: UNFAIR COMPETITION: BREACH OF CONTRACT: ADVERTISEMENT OF LAPSED CONCESSION: USE AS TRADE MARK: INTERLOCUTORY INJUNCTION: BALANCE OF CONVENIENCE: Ch.D.)
[1986] F.S.R. 490
(C.A.) [1991] F.S.R. 209

Hart (S.W.) & Co. Pty Ltd v. Edwards Hot Water Systems (COPYRIGHT: ARTISTIC WORK: DUAL PROTECTION: Australia: Fed. Ct)
[1983] 49 A.L.R. 605; 1 I.P.R. 228

Hart (S.W.) & Co. Pty Ltd v. Edwards Hot Water Systems (COPYRIGHT: INFRINGEMENT: REPRODUCTION IN THREE DIMENSIONAL FORM: NON-EXPERT TEST: Australia: H.C.)
61 A.L.R. 251; 159 C.L.R. 466; 5 I.P.R. 13; [1986] F.S.R. 575

Hart (S.W.) & Co. Pty Ltd v. Edwards Hot Water Systems (PRACTICE: PROCEDURE: JURISDICTION: COPYRIGHT: INFRINGEMENT: REOPENING LITIGATION: Australia: Fed. Ct) 5 I.P.R. 289

Harvard/Fusion proteins (EUROPEAN PATENT: APPEAL: PROCEDURE: POWERS OF BOARD OF APPEAL: NOVELTY: PRIOR ART: PRIOR ORAL DESCRIPTION: SKILLED PERSON: IDENTITY OF: SUFFICIENCY: COMMON GENERAL KNOWLEDGE EXPECTED, BUT NOT MORE: T60/89: EPO)
[1992] E.P.O.R. 320; [1990] O.J. EPO 268

Harvard/Onco-mouse (EUROPEAN PATENT: CLAIMS: GENERALISATION OF FEATURE: PATENTABILITY: ANIMALS: BIOLOGICAL PROCESS: MORALITY: THIRD PARTY OBSERVATIONS: SUFFICIENCY: FUTURE AND/OR INACCESSIBLE VARIANTS: CONVENTIONS: CHANGING CIRCUMSTANCES: DIFFERENT LANGUAGE TEXTS: T19/90: EPO)
[1990] E.P.O.R. 501; [1990] O.J. EPO 476

Harvard/Onco-mouse (EUROPEAN PATENT: PATENTABILITY: ANIMALS: MORALITY: PRECEDENT: *Ratio decidendi* OF BOARD OF APPEAL DECISION: SUFFICIENCY: EXTRAPOLATION: CONVENTIONS: DIFFERENT LANGUAGE TEXTS: INTENTION AT TIME OF DRAFTING: APPLICATION 85 304 490.7: EPO)
[1990] E.P.O.R. 4; [1991] E.P.O.R. 525

Hasmonay/Plug for affixing screws (EUROPEAN PATENT: CLAIMS: CLARITY: BY SKILLED PERSON ATTENTIVELY READING: INVENTIVE STEP: COMMERCIAL SUCCESS: T91/83: EPO) [1979–85] E.P.O.R. C807

Hasselblad (G.B.) Ltd v. E.C. Comm. (PARALLEL IMPORTS: PRACTICE: Case 86/82: ECJ) [1984] 1 C.M.L.R. 559; [1984] E.C.R. 883; [1984] F.S.R. 321

Hassle (A.B.) v. Commissioner of Patents (PATENT: EXTENSION: EXCEPTIONAL CASE: NATURE AND MERITS OF INVENTION: PATENTEE'S PROFITS: ADEQUACY OF REMUNERATION: LACK OF CANDOUR: WORLDWIDE PROFITS: PUBLIC INTEREST: BENEFIT TO PUBLIC: DELAY IN GETTING INVENTION ON TO MARKET: Australia: S.C.(NSW)) 98 A.L.R. 287

Hassle (A.B.) v. Pacific Pharmaceuticals Ltd (PRACTICE: DISCOVERY: CONFIDENTIALITY: PATENT EXTENSION: FINANCIAL INFORMATION: PROFESSIONAL PRIVILEGE: New Zealand: H.C.) [1991] 3 N.Z.L.R. 186

HAVE A BREAK Trade Mark (TRADE MARK: APPLICATION: OPPOSITIONS: SLOGAN: WHETHER A TRADE MARK: SURVEY EVIDENCE: WHETHER CAPABLE OF DISTINGUISHING: Ch.D.) [1993] R.P.C. 217

Hawke (Aust.) Ltd's Application (TRADE MARKS: APPLICATION FOR REGISTRATION: TIMELESS CREATION: MERE LAUDATORY EXPRESSION: INHERENT NON-DISTINCTIVENESS: NO USE OF MARK: Australia: Pat. Off.)
12 I.P.R. 494

Hawker Siddeley Dynamics Engineering Ltd v. Real Time Developments Ltd (PATENT: INFRINGEMENT: DECLARATION OF NON-INFRINGEMENT: STAY OF HIGH COURT PROCEEDINGS: PRACTICE: Pat. Ct)   [1983] R.P.C. 395

Hazel Grove (Superleague) Ltd v. Euro-League Leisure Products Ltd (PATENT: INFRINGEMENT: MODIFICATIONS OR REPAIRS: PROMISSORY ESTOPPEL: Pat. C.C.)   [1995] R.P.C. 529

Hazel Grove Music Co. Ltd v. Elster Enterprises (ANTON PILLER: PRACTICE: Ch.D.)   [1983] F.S.R. 379

Hearst Corp. v. Pacific Dunlop Ltd (TRADE MARKS: APPLICATION: OPPOSITION: PROPRIETORSHIP: LIKELIHOOD OF DECEPTION OR CONFUSION: Australia: Pat. Off.)   21 I.P.R. 587

Heatex Group Ltd's Application (PATENT: APPLICATION: SUBSTANTIVE EXAMINATION: EXTENSION OF TIME: DECISION NOT TO PROCEED: CHANGE OF MIND: C.-G.)   [1995] R.P.C. 546

Heidelberger Drückmaschinen/Microchip (EUROPEAN PATENT: APPEAL: PROCEDURE: FRESH CITATIONS ON APPEAL: AT ORAL PROCEEDINGS: COSTS: APPORTIONMENT: REFUSED: RESPONSIBLE DEFENCE OF RIGHTS: PRIOR ART: PRIOR USE: FEATURES INFERRABLE FROM INSPECTION: PRIOR USE: PROGRAM IN MACHINE CODE: T461/88: EPO)
[1993] E.P.O.R. 529; [1993] O.J. EPO 295

Heimann/Glue (EUROPEAN PATENT: NOVELTY: DOCUMENT: INTERPRETATION OF IN LIGHT OF COMMON GENERAL KNOWLEDGE: T364/90: EPO)
[1994] E.P.O.R. 445

Heinen v. Pancontinental Mining Ltd (PATENT: OPPOSITION: AMENDMENT OF UNSUCCESSFUL APPLICATION: SECTION 40 DEFECTS SUFFICIENTLY OVERCOME: Australia: Pat. Off.)   14 I.P.R. 119

Heisel/Late payment of appeal fee (EUROPEAN PATENT: FEES: LATE PAYMENT: REIMBURSEMENT OF APPEAL FEE: J21/80: EPO)
[1979–85] E.P.O.R. A65; [1981] O.J. EPO 101

Heithersays Application (DESIGN: EXTENSION: NOVELTY: ORIGINALITY: SET OF ARTICLES: Australia: Pat. Off.)   7 I.P.R. 425

Helitune Ltd v. Stewart Hughes Ltd (PATENT: INFRINGEMENT: COUNTERCLAIM FOR REVOCATION: CONSTRUCTION OF CLAIM: INDIRECT INFRINGEMENT: SUFFICIENCY OF DESCRIPTION: ADDRESSEE OF SPECIFICATION: WHETHER PROPER ADDRESSEE WOULD HAVE CORRECTED ERROR IN SPECIFICATION: PRIOR USE: Pat. Ct)   [1991] F.S.R. 171

Helitune Ltd v. Stewart Hughes Ltd (PATENT: INFRINGEMENT: PRACTICE: REVOCATION: PRIOR USE: AMENDMENT OF PLEADING: EARTH CLOSET ORDER: COSTS: Pat. Ct)   [1991] R.P.C. 78

Helitune Ltd v. Stewart Hughes Ltd (PRACTICE: INTERLOCUTORY INJUNCTION: CROSS-UNDERTAKING: INQUIRY AS TO DAMAGES: STRIKING OUT PLEADING: ABUSE OF PROCESS: PRACTICE: CONFIDENTIAL EXHIBIT: SPECIFIC DISCOVERY: REMOTENESS OF DAMAGE: Ch.D.)   [1994] F.S.R. 422

HELLEBREKERS Advocaat (IMPORTS: DRINKS: LIQUEURS: ADDITIVES: DUTCH
ADVOCAAT IMPORTED INTO GERMANY: TOO MUCH ADDITIVE: TOO LITTLE
EGG YOLK: DECEPTION OF GERMAN CONSUMER: LAWFUL MAKE-UP IN
NETHERLANDS: INJUNCTION AGAINST SALE IN GERMANY IN DECEPTIVE
GET-UP: NO OUTRIGHT BAN ON SALES: LEGITIMATE MANDATORY
REQUIREMENT UNDER *Cassis de Dijon*: NO BREACH OF ARTICLE 30: Germany:
C.A.)   [1993] 2 C.M.L.R. 61
Heller Financial Services Ltd v. John Brice (TRADE MARK: TRANSFER: SALE OF
    BUSINESS: GOODWILL: SUBSISTENCE: Australia: S.C.(Qd))   9 I.P.R. 469
Hellewell v. Chief Constable of Derbyshire (CONFIDENTIAL INFORMATION:
    BREACH OF CONFIDENCE: OFFENDER PHOTOGRAPHED BY POLICE:
    DISCLOSURE: PUBLIC INTEREST: Q.B.D.)   [1995] 1 W.L.R. 804
Heng Lee Handbags Co. Pte Ltd v. Public Prosecutor (TRADE MARK:
    INFRINGEMENT: CRIMINAL PROCEDURE: SEARCH WARRANT:
    JUSTIFICATION: APPLICATION TO QUASH: Singapore: H.C.)
                                                    [1994] 2 S.L.R. 760
Henjo Investments Pty Ltd v. Collins Marrickville Pty Ltd (TRADE PRACTICES:
    DAMAGES: CAUSATION: MEASURE OF DAMAGES IN RESPECT OF SALE OF
    RESTAURANT BUSINESS INDUCED BY MISREPRESENTATIONS: SILENCE
    CONSTITUTING MISLEADING CONDUCT: CONSTRUCTIVE NOTICE OF
    MATTERS WHICH SOLICITORS ACTING FOR APPLICANT WOULD HAVE
    DISCOVERED ON PROPER INQUIRY: OPERATION OF EXCLUSION CLAUSES AS
    DEFENCE: DISCRETION: ORDER FOR RESTITUTION: CIRCUMSTANCES:
    CONSEQUENTIAL LOSSES FLOWING FROM CONDUCT OF BUSINESS BY
    PURCHASER: ASSESSMENT OF DAMAGES FOR BURDEN OF UNECONOMIC
    LEASE: Australia: Fed. Ct)   79 A.L.R. 83; 16 I.P.R. 623
Henkel Kommanditgesellschaft Auf Aktien v. Fina Research SA (PATENT:
    APPLICATION: OPPOSITION: NOTICE: TIME LIMITS: APPLICATION FOR
    EXTENSION OF TIME: OBJECTION: Australia: AIPO)   27 I.P.R. 289
Henkel/Separate set of claims (EUROPEAN PATENT: AMENDMENT AND
    CORRECTION: APPROVAL AFTER: T166/86: EPO)
                              [1987] E.P.O.R. 371; [1987] O.J. EPO 372
Henkel/Surface active agents (EUROPEAN PATENT: APPEAL: PROCEDURE:
    INCORRECT REFERENCE TO CITED DOCUMENT: T185/88: EPO)
                              [1990] E.P.O.R. 649; [1990] O.J. EPO 451
Henkel/Zeolite suspensions (EUROPEAN PATENT: EPO AS IPEA: INVITATION TO PAY
    ADDITIONAL EXAMINATION FEES: UTILITY PROTEST: REVIEW: EXAMINATION
    OF UNITY: W04/93: EPO)   [1995] E.P.O.R. 251; [1994] O.J. EPO 939
Henri Jullien BV v. Verschuere Norbert (TRADE MARK: REGISTRATION:
    OPPOSITION: SIMILARITY: Benelux)   [1984] E.C.C. 14
Henri Vidals Application (PATENT: EXTENSION: INADEQUATE REMUNERATION:
    RELEVANCE OF FUTURE AND FOREIGN INCOME: Australia: S.C.)
                                                        [1983] V.R. 16
Heptulla v. Orient Longman Ltd (COPYRIGHT: JOINT AUTHORSHIP: GHOST-
    WRITTEN MEMOIRS: DEFINITION OF AUTHOR: HEIRS OF AUTHOR:
    AGREEMENT TO ASSIGN COPYRIGHT: PUBLICATION OF EXTRACT: INTERIM
    INJUNCTION: ESTOPPEL: BALANCE OF CONVENIENCE: India: H.C.)
                              (1989) 14 I.P.L.R. 36; [1989] 1 F.S.R. 598
Hérault v. Société des Auteurs, Compositeurs et Editeurs de Musique (SACEM)
    (COPYRIGHT: PERFORMING RIGHT: COLLECTING SOCIETY: DOMINANT
    POSITION: MUSIC: LICENCE: France: C.A.)
                              [1983] 1 C.M.L.R. 36; [1983] F.S.R. 212

Hercules NV, SA v. E.C. Commission (RESTRICTIVE PRACTICES: ADMINISTRATIVE PROCEDURE: SUPPLY OF DOCUMENTS: CONFIDENTIALITY: Case T–7/89: CFI)　　　　　　[1992] 4 C.M.L.R. 84; [1991] II E.C.R. 1711
Hermès SA v. Swift & Co. Pty Ltd (TRADE MARK: APPLICATION: FOREIGN REPUTATION: Australia: Pat. Off.)　　　　　　　　2 I.P.R. 432
Hermes Sweeteners Ltd v. Hermes (TRADE MARKS: APPLICATIONS: OPPOSITION: OPPONENT RELYING ON ITS OWN REGISTERED MARKS: SUBSTANTIALLY IDENTICAL OR DECEPTIVELY SIMILAR: SAME GOODS OR OF SIMILAR DESCRIPTION: USE LIKELY TO DECEIVE OR CAUSE CONFUSION: OPPOSITION FAILED: COSTS TO APPLICANT: Australia: Pat. Off.)　　　　17 I.P.R. 382
Herron Pharmaceuticals Pty Ltd v. Sterling Winthrop Pty Ltd (TRADE MARK: NON-USE: APPLICATION TO REMOVE: OPPOSITION: PERSON AGGRIEVED: *Locus standii* BASED ON PRIOR REGISTERED MARKS: ADMISSION OF FURTHER EVIDENCE: Australia: AIPO)　　　　　　　　30 I.P.R. 304
Herzberger Papierfabrik/Packaging magazine (EUROPEAN PATENT: INVENTIVE STEP: COMBINATION OF CITATIONS: UNITY: INDEPENDENT CLAIMS: T173/84: EPO)　　　　　　　　　　[1986] E.P.O.R. 181
Heublein Inc. v. Paterson Simons & Co. (S.) Pte Ltd (TRADE MARK: PASSING OFF: INJUNCTION: BALANCE OF CONVENIENCE: Malaysia: C.A.)[1985] 1 M.L.J. 177
Heublein Inc. v. Paterson Simons & Co. (Singapore) Pte Ltd (TRADE MARK: PASSING OFF: FRANCHISE: KENTUCKY FRIED CHICKEN: INJUNCTION: COUNTERCLAIM: BALANCE OF CONVENIENCE: Singapore: C.A.)
[1985] 1 M.L.J. 177
Heublin Inc. v. Golden Fried Chicken (Pty) Ltd (TRADE MARK: EXPUNGEMENT: IT'S FINGER LICKIN' GOOD: DISTINCTIVENESS: South Africa: TPD)
1982 (4) S.A. 84
(Appeal) 1983 (3) S.A. 911
Heylen v. Davies Collison Cave (PETTY PATENT: EXTENSION: NOTICE: COMPLETE SPECIFICATION: AMENDMENT: IN SUBSTANCE DISCLOSED: FAIR BASIS: NOVELTY: INVENTIVE STEP: OBVIOUSNESS: EVIDENTIARY BURDEN: PATENT ATTORNEYS: COSTS: Australia: AIPO)　　　　　　　30 I.P.R. 1
Hickman v. Andrews (PATENT: INFRINGEMENT: WORKMATE WORKBENCH: ANTICIPATION: OBVIOUSNESS: AMBIGUITY: *Gillette* DEFENCE: Ch.D.: C.A.)　　　　　　　　　　　[1983] R.P.C. 147
Hidesign v. Hi-Design Creations (TRADE MARK: PASSING OFF: HIDESIGN/ HI-DESIGN CREATIONS: *Ad interim* INJUNCTION: India: H.C.)
(1992) 17 I.P.L.R. 69
HIGH LIFE Trade Mark (TRADE MARK: PRACTICE: RECTIFICATION: NON-USE: STRIKING OUT: DELAY: Ch.D.)　　　　　　　[1991] R.P.C. 445
High Tech Auto Tools Pty Ltd v. Ferocem Pty Ltd (PETTY PATENT: EXTENSION: OBJECTION: NOTICE: CLAIMS: PRIORITY DATE: MANNER OF MANUFACTURE: OBVIOUS MISTAKE: NOVELTY: OBVIOUSNESS: EVIDENCE: PRACTICE AND PROCEDURE: CLARITY: UNCERTAINTY: Australia: AIPO)　　29 I.P.R. 337
Other proceedings, *sub nom.* Ferocem Pty Ltd v. High Tech Auto Tools Pty Ltd
29 I.P.R. 144
Highland Distilleries Co. plc v. Speymalt Whisky Distributors Ltd (TRADE MARK: TRADE NAMES: INFRINGEMENT: PASSING OFF: GEOGRAPHICAL NAME: Scotland: O.H.)　　　　　　　　　　　1985 S.L.T. 85
Hille International Ltd v. Tiong Hin Engineering Pty Ltd (TRADE MARK: INFRINGEMENT: PASSING OFF: DECEPTIVE SIMILARITY: Malaysia: H.C.)
[1983] 1 M.L.J. 145

Hillegom Municipality v. Hillenius (BANKING: CONFIDENTIALITY: NATIONAL COURTS: CIVIL PROCEEDINGS: PROFESSIONAL PRIVILEGE: Case 110/84: ECJ)
[1986] 3 C.M.L.R. 422; [1985] E.C.R. 3947
Hillier Parker May & Rowdens Applications (TRADE MARK: APPLICATION: DISTINCTIVENESS: WORD COMBINATIONS: TWO SURNAMES: Australia: Pat. Off.)   27 I.P.R. 470
Hilti AG's Patent (PATENT: LICENCES OF RIGHT: SUB-LICENSING: PERIOD OF NOTICE: "PASSING OFF" TERM: Pat. Ct)
[1987] F.S.R. 594; [1988] R.P.C. 51
Hilti AG (RESTRICTIVE PRACTICES: DOMINANT POSITION: ABUSE: TYING ARRANGEMENTS: INTERIM MEASURES: NOTICE: E.C. Comm.)
[1985] 3 C.M.L.R. 619; [1986] F.S.R. 105
Hilti AG v. E.C. Commission (RESTRICTIVE PRACTICES: RELEVANT PRODUCT MARKET: SPARE PARTS: BURDEN OF PROOF: EVIDENCE: COURT OF FIRST INSTANCE PROCEDURE: REASONING: APPELLATE JURISDICTION OF ECJ: Case C–53/92P: ECJ)   [1994] 4 C.M.L.R. 614; [1994] F.S.R. 760
Hilti AG v. E.C. Commission (CONFIDENTIALITY OF BUSINESS SECRETS: INTERVENERS: LEGAL PROFESSIONAL PRIVILEGE: APPLICABLE TO WRITTEN COMMUNICATIONS BETWEEN INDEPENDENT LAWYER AND CLIENT COMPANY: INTERESTS OF RIGHT OF DEFENCE: PROCEDURE: Case T–30/89A: CFI)   [1990] 4 C.M.L.R. 602; [1990] II E.C.R. 163
Hilti AG v. E.C. Commission (RESTRICTIVE PRACTICES: DOMINANT COMPANY: COMPULSORY PATENT LICENCES: EXTORTIONATE FEES: SELECTIVE AND DISCRIMINATORY SALES POLICY: ABUSE: NOT JUSTIFIED BY SAFETY WORRIES: Cases T–30/89, T–30/89A: CFI)
[1992] 4 C.M.L.R. 16; [1992] II E.C.R. 1439; [1992] F.S.R. 210
Himachal Pradesh Horticulture Produce Marketing v. Mohan Meakin Breweries Ltd (TRADE MARK: INFRINGEMENT: PASSING OFF: India: H.C.)
(1981) 6 I.P.L.R. 1
Hind Azad Factory v. Azad Factory (TRADE MARK: OPPOSITION: DELAY IN FILING EVIDENCE: COSTS: REVIEW: India: T.M.Reg.)   (1986) 11 I.P.L.R. 133
Hindustan Lever Ltd v. V. V. Dhanushkodi Nadar & Sons (REGISTERED DESIGN: INFRINGEMENT: PASSING OFF: INTERIM INJUNCTION: EXPIRED: TRANSFER OF SUIT: India: H.C.)   (1989) 3 I.P.L.R. 97
Hindustan Pencils Pvt. Ltd v. India Stationery Products Co. (TRADE MARK: INFRINGEMENT: INTERIM INJUNCTION: REGISTRATION UNDER COPYRIGHT ACT: *Ex parte* INJUNCTION: DELAY, LACHES AND ACQUIESCENCE: India: H.C.)   (1990) 15 I.P.L.R. 116
Hindustan Radiators Co. v. Hindustan Radiators Ltd (PASSING OFF: IDENTICAL TRADING STYLE AND MARK FOR IDENTICAL GOODS: INTERIM INJUNCTION: India: H.C.)   (1987) I.P.L.R. 21
Hiralal Parudas v. Ganesh Trading Co. (TRADE MARK: RECTIFICATION: APPEAL: India: H.C.)   (1984) 9 I.P.L.R. 41
Hiring of Video Games Cassettes (COPYRIGHT: VIDEO GAMES: Germany)
[1985] E.C.C. 397; [1985] F.S.R. 606
Hitachi Ltd's Application (PATENT APPLICATION: COMPUTER-RELATED INVENTION: WHETHER PATENTABLE: C.-G.)   [1991] R.P.C. 415
Hitachi Ltd v. Hoover (Aust.) Pty Ltd (PATENT: OPPOSITION: AMENDMENT TO STATEMENT OF CLAIM: ANTICIPATION: OBVIOUSNESS: COMMON KNOWLEDGE: Australia: Pat. Off.)   5 I.P.R. 569
Hitachi Maxell/Procedural violation (EUROPEAN PATENT: AMENDMENT: DECISION ON BASIS OF TEXT INCORPORATING PART OF AMENDMENT: T647/93: EPO)
[1995] E.P.O.R. 195; [1995] O.J. EPO 132

Hitachi/Engine control (EUROPEAN PATENT: AMENDMENT AND CORRECTION: REFERENCE SIGNS IN CLAIM: CLAIMS: REFERENCE NUMERALS/SIGNS, EFFECT OF: T145/89: EPO)   [1991] E.P.O.R. 137

Hitachi/Re-establishment of rights (RE-ESTABLISHMENT OF RIGHTS: ALTERNATIVE REMEDY: J12/87: EPO)   [1989] E.P.O.R. 443; [1989] O.J. EPO 366

HMT Ld v. Girnar Ltd (COPYRIGHT: ARTISTIC WORK: EARLIER REGISTRATION OF HMT AS TRADE MARK: India: Cprt Brd)   (1993) 18 I.P.L.R. 217

HMT Ltd v. Olympic Agencies (TRADE MARKS: INFRINGEMENT: PASSING OFF: HMT-SONA, HMT-ASHA/OLYMPIC SONA, OLYMPIC ASHA—FOR WATCHES: India: H.C.)   (1991) 16 I.P.L.R. 61

Hock Choo Hoe Sdn Bhd v. Public Prosecutor (TRADE MARK: FALSE TRADE DESCRIPTION: CORPORATION: WHETHER STATUTORY DEFENCE AVAILABLE: BURDEN OF PROOF: Malaysia: H.C.)   [1994] 1 M.L.J. 332

Hodge Clemco Ltd v. Airblast Ltd (PASSING OFF: SPARES TO "SUIT" PLAINTIFF'S PRODUCT: MISREPRESENTATION THAT PRODUCT FITTED WITH SPARES WOULD COMPLY WITH SAFETY REGULATIONS: ARGUABLE CAUSE OF ACTION: INTERLOCUTORY INJUNCTION REFUSED: Ch.D.)   [1995] F.S.R. 806

Hodgkinson & Corby Ltd v. Ward's Mobility Services Ltd (PASSING OFF: INGREDIENTS OF TORT: GET-UP: DECEPTION: EFFECT OF APPEARANCE ON ULTIMATE CONSUMER: WHEELCHAIR CUSHIONS: NO EVIDENCE OF LIKELIHOOD OF DECEPTION OF ORIGIN: Ch.D.)
[1995] F.S.R. 169; [1994] 1 W.L.R. 1564

Hoechst (Société Française) v. Allied Colloids Ltd (PATENT: INFRINGEMENT: PRACTICE: DISCOVERY: PRIVILEGE: CONTENTS OF NOTICE OF EXPERIMENTS: Pat. Ct)   [1991] R.P.C. 245

Hoechst (Société Française) v. Allied Colloids Ltd (PATENT: INFRINGEMENT: PRACTICE: DISCOVERY: REPORT PREPARED BY DEFENDANTS AFTER COMMENCEMENT OF PARALLEL PROCEEDINGS IN FRANCE: PRIVILEGE: Pat. Ct)   [1992] F.S.R. 66

Hoechst AG's Application (No. 2) (PATENT: EXAMINER'S OBJECTION: PLURALITY OF INVENTION: NOVELTY: FAIR BASIS: REQUEST BY APPLICANT FOR A DECISION: Australia: Pat. Off.)   11 I.P.R. 433

Hoechst AG's Application (PATENT: APPLICATION: OBJECTION BY EXAMINER: NEW OBJECTION RAISED AT HEARING: FAIR BASIS: Australia: Pat. Off.)
11 I.P.R. 283

Hoechst AG v. American Home Products Corp. (PATENT: APPLICATION: OPPOSITION: PRIOR CLAIMING: ANTICIPATION: PRIOR PUBLICATION: MATTERS ARISING UNDER SECTION 40: Australia: Pat. Off.)   21 I.P.R. 121

Hoechst AG v. E.C. Commission (EUROPEAN COURT PROCEDURE: INTERIM MEASURES: SEARCH AND SEIZURE: RESTRICTIVE PRACTICES: JUDICIAL REVIEW: Case 46/87R: ECJ)   [1988] 4 C.M.L.R. 430; [1987] E.C.R. 1549

Hoechst Pharmaceuticals (Pty) Ltd v. The Beauty Box (Pty) Ltd (TRADE MARK: PASSING OFF: EVIDENCE: MARKET SURVEYS: WEIGHT: South Africa: A.D.)
1987 (2) S.A. 600

Hoechst Pharmaceuticals Ltd v. Government of India (BRAND NAMES: AMENDMENT OF DRUG RULES: India: H.C.)   (1982) 7 I.P.L.R. 1

Hoechst U.K. Ltd v. Chemiculture Ltd (CONFIDENTIAL INFORMATION: INFORMATION OBTAINED IN EXERCISE OF STATUTORY POWERS: WHETHER DISCLOSURE TO THIRD PARTY BREACH OF CONFIDENCE: PRACTICE: ANTON PILLER ORDER: APPLICATION TO DISCHARGE: ALLEGED NON-DISCLOSURE ON *ex parte* APPLICATION: Ch.D.)   [1993] F.S.R. 270

Hoechst/Ace inhibitors (EUROPEAN PATENT: OPPOSITION PROCEDURE: ADMISSIBILITY: TRUE IDENTITY OF OPPONENT: BURDEN OF PROOF: STAGE OF OPPOSITION: T289/91: EPO)   [1995] E.P.O.R. 32

Hoechst/Admissibility of appeal by opponent (EUROPEAN PATENT: ENLARGED BOARD OF APPEAL: PRESIDENT OF THE EPO: OPPOSITION: PROCEDURE: RULE 58(4) COMMUNICATION: T271/85: EPO)
                    [1989] E.P.O.R. 62; [1988] O.J. EPO 341

Hoechst/Correction of mistakes (EUROPEAN PATENT: PUBLISHED APPLICATION) (EUROPEAN PATENT: CONVENTIONS: NATIONAL LAWS, RELATIONSHIP OF EPC TO: PUBLISHED APPLICATION AMENDMENT AND CORRECTION: DESIGNATION OF STATES: J12/80: EPO)
                    [1979–85] E.P.O.R. A52; [1981] O.J. EPO 143

Hoechst/Enantiomers (EUROPEAN PATENT: NOVELTY: RACEMATE/ENANTIOMER: CLAIMS: DISCLAIMER: INVENTIVE STEP: BONUS EFFECT: T296/87: EPO)
                    [1990] E.P.O.R. 337; [1990] O.J. EPO 195

Hoechst/Herbicides (EUROPEAN PATENT: UNITY: CHEMICAL COMBINATIONS: W15/91: EPO)   [1994] E.P.O.R. 226

Hoechst/Melting point (EUROPEAN PATENT: AMENDMENT AND CORRECTION: TRANSCRIPTION ERROR: T3/88: EPO)   [1988] E.P.O.R. 377

Hoechst/Metallic paint coating (EUROPEAN PATENT: ENLARGED BOARD OF APPEAL: REFERENCE REFUSED: INVENTIVE STEP: LOTTERY: OPPOSITION: PROCEDURE: FRESH DOCUMENTS ON APPEAL: FRESH GROUND ON APPEAL: T122/84: EPO)   [1987] E.P.O.R. 218; [1987] O.J. EPO 177

Hoechst/Opponent's silence (EUROPEAN PATENT: OPPOSITION: PROCEDURE: RULE 58(4) COMMUNICATION: CONVENTIONS: LOGIC OF CONVENTION: ROMAN LAW, RELIANCE ON: ENLARGED BOARD OF APPEAL: POINT OF LAW, ANSWERED: G01/88: EPO)   [1989] E.P.O.R. 421; [1989] O.J. EPO 189

Hoechst/Plasmid pSG2 (EUROPEAN PATENT: INVENTIVE STEP: PROBLEM, DEFINITION OF: SELECTION: T162/86: EPO)
                    [1989] E.P.O.R. 107; [1988] O.J. EPO 452

Hoechst/Polyvinylester dispersion (EUROPEAN PATENT: CLAIMS: CONSTRUCTION: NOVELTY: PRIOR USE, NEED FOR FULL CHARACTERISATION OF: STATE OF THE ART: PRIOR PRODUCT, ANALYSIS OF: T93/89: EPO)
                    [1992] E.P.O.R. 155; [1992] O.J. EPO 718

Hoechst/Thiochloroformates (EUROPEAN PATENT: INVENTIVE STEP: CONFLICTING GOALS: NOVELTY: SELECTION FROM KNOWN NUMERICAL RANGE: T198/84: EPO)   [1979–85] E.P.O.R. C987; [1985] O.J. EPO 209

Hoechst/Vinyl ester-crotonic acid copolymers (EUROPEAN PATENT: INVENTIVE STEP: MECHANISM OF PRIOR CHEMICAL PROCESS: NOVELTY: PRODUCT OF PROCESS: T205/83: EPO)   [1986] E.P.O.R. 57; [1985] O.J. EPO 363

Hoffman-La Roche Ltd v. Apotex Inc. (PATENT: IMPEACHMENT: ANTICIPATION: OBVIOUSNESS: CLAIMS AMBIGUOUS: CLAIMS FAIL TO EXPLICITLY STATE WHAT IS THE INVENTION: CLAIMS BROADER THAN THE INVENTION MADE: REISSUE: Canada: Fed. C.A.)   14 I.P.R. 97

Hoffman-La Roche/Pyrrolidine derivatives (EUROPEAN PATENT: PATENTABILITY: FIRST MEDICAL INDICATION: CLAIMS: NOVELTY: THERAPEUTIC USE: VIENNA CONVENTION RULES: INTERPRETATION: T128/82: EPO)
                    [1979–85] E.P.O.R. B591; [1984] O.J. EPO 164

Hoffmann-La Roche AG v. Centrafarm GmbH (TRADE MARK: IMPORTS: REPACKAGING: Germany: S.C.)   [1984] 2 C.M.L.R. 561; [1985] F.S.R. 6

Hoffmann-La Roche AG v. Dumex A/S (PATENT: INFRINGEMENT: CONSTRUCTION: Denmark: S.C.)   [1985] F.S.R. 40

Hogan v. Koala Dundee Pty Ltd (TRADE MARKS: TRADE NAME: PASSING OFF: PROTECTION OF WELL-KNOWN IMAGE UNCONNECTED WITH ANY BUSINESS: MERCHANDISING RIGHTS: ASSIGNMENT OF RIGHT TO USE SUCH IMAGE: SUCH ASSIGNMENT NEED NOT BE AS PART OF A BUSINESS: PASSING OFF: LOSS NECESSARY TO FOUND INJUNCTION: LOST CHANCE OF GETTING FEE FROM WRONG-DOER: FORM OF INJUNCTION: DAMAGES: WHETHER PROOF OF FRAUD NECESSARY: Australia: Fed. Ct)   83 A.L.R. 187; 12 I.P.R. 508

Hogan v. Pacific Dunlop Ltd (PASSING OFF: MISREPRESENTATION OF COMMERCIAL CONNECTION: IMPLIED BY USE OF IMAGE ASSOCIATED WITH CELEBRITY: WHAT AMOUNTS TO DECEPTION: RELEVANCE OF SURROUNDING CIRCUMSTANCES: CHARACTER MERCHANDISING, SPONSORSHIP AND TESTIMONIAL ADVERTISING: IMPLICATION OF COMMERCIAL ARRANGEMENT BETWEEN PARTIES WHICH IS NON-EXISTENT: COMMON FIELD OF ACTIVITY: WHETHER ERRONEOUS ASSUMPTION DOCTRINE APPLIES: PASSING: PECUNIARY REMEDIES: RIGHT TO ELECT BETWEEN DAMAGES AND ACCOUNT OF PROFITS: Australia: Fed. Ct)   83 A.L.R. 403

Hogan v. Pacific Dunlop Ltd (TRADE PRACTICES: MISLEADING OR DECEPTIVE CONDUCT: CHARACTER MERCHANDISING: ADVERTISEMENTS BASED ON SCENE FROM POPULAR FILM: WHETHER SIGNIFICANT SECTION OF PUBLIC WOULD BE MISLED INTO BELIEVING THAT PARTIES HAD ENTERED INTO COMMERCIAL ARRANGEMENT TO GRANT PERMISSION TO USE CHARACTER: PASSING OFF: CHARACTER MERCHANDISING: WHETHER ADVERTISEMENTS AMOUNTED TO MISREPRESENTATION AS TO COMMERCIAL ARRANGEMENT OF PERMISSION TO USE CHARACTER: Australia: Fed. Ct)
87 A.L.R. 14; 14 I.P.R. 398

Hollisters Inc.'s Application (PATENT: APPLICATION: PRACTICE: PRELIMINARY SEARCH: PLURALITY OF INVENTION: Pat. Ct)   [1983] R.P.C. 10

HOLLY HOBBIE Trade Mark (APPLICATION: REGISTERED USER: TRAFFICKING: CHARACTER MERCHANDISING: WHETHER QUALITY CONTROL BY PROPRIETORS CONSTITUTES TRADE CONNECTION: Ch.D.)
[1983] F.S.R. 138; [1984] R.P.C. 329
(C.A.) [1983] F.S.R. 581; [1984] R.P.C. 329
(H.L.) [1984] F.S.R. 199; [1984] R.P.C. 329; (1985) 8 I.P.L.R. 265
Cited as American Greeting Corp's Application (Ch.D.) [1983] 2 All E.R. 434
(C.A.) [1983] 2 All E.R. 609; [1983] 1 W.L.R. 912
(H.L.) [1984] 1 All E.R. 434; [1984] 1 W.L.R. 189

Hollywood Curl (Pty) Ltd v. Twins Products (Pty) Ltd (No. 1) (PASSING OFF: UNREGISTERED TRADE MARK: REPUTATION: SIMILAR GET-UP: ASSOCIATION IN MINDS OF PUBLIC: South Africa: A.D.)   1989 (1) S.A. 236

Holmes v. DPP (COPYRIGHT: INFRINGEMENT: CRIMINAL OFFENCE: RELEVANT TIME OF MAKING COPY: D.C.)   [1990] C.O.D. 150

Holmess Application (TRADE MARKS: APPLICATION: OPPOSITION: LIKELIHOOD OF DECEPTION OR CONFUSION: PERMACRAFT: NO EVIDENCE OF USE OF OPPONENTS MARK: OPPONENTS MARK COMMON TO TRADE MARKS NOT DECEPTIVELY SIMILAR: VENETIAN BLINDS AND FURNITURE NOT GOODS OF SAME DESCRIPTION: Australia: Pat. Off.)   10 I.P.R. 653

Holmsund Golv AB, Golvgripen AB & Amstrong World Industries' Agreements (RESTRICTIVE PRACTICES: DISTRIBUTION AGREEMENTS: AGENCY: JOINT PRODUCT DEVELOPMENT: INTENTION TO APPROVE: NOTICE: EFTA Surveillance Authority)   [1995] 4 C.M.L.R. 673

Homecraft Steel Industries (Pty) Ltd v. Hare & Sons (Pty) Ltd (COPYRIGHT: DESIGN: REGISTRABILITY: South Africa: A.D.)   1984 (3) S.A. 681

Honey v. Australian Airlines Ltd (TRADE PRACTICES: MISLEADING AND DECEPTIVE
CONDUCT: USE OF PHOTOGRAPH OF CHAMPION AMATEUR ATHLETE IN
CONDUCT OF BUSINESS ACTIVITIES: FALSE REPRESENTATION AS TO
SPONSORSHIP, APPROVAL OR AFFILIATION: SECTION OF THE PUBLIC:
OBJECTIVE ASSESSMENT OF OVERALL IMPRESSION ON VIEWERS OF THE USE OF
THE PHOTOGRAPH: WEIGHT TO BE GIVEN TO CONCLUSIONS OF PRIMARY
JUDGE: Australia: Fed. Ct)   14 I.P.R. 264; 18 I.P.R. 185
Honeywell Bull Inc.'s Application (PATENT: APPLICATION: COMPUTER PROGRAM:
MATHEMATICAL ALGORITHM: MANNER OF MANUFACTURE: Australia: Pat.
Off.)   22 I.P.R. 463
Honeywell Inc.'s Application (TRADE MARKS: APPLICATION: INHERENTLY
DISTINCTIVE: CAPABLE OF BECOMING DISTINCTIVE: USE IN AUSTRALIA:
DECEPTIVE SIMILARITY: Australia: Pat. Off.)   19 I.P.R. 70
Hong Kong & Shanghai Banking Corp. Ltd's Applications (TRADE MARKS:
APPLICATIONS FOR REGISTRATION: TRADE MARK CONSISTING OF CHINESE
CHARACTERS: REGISTRABILITY UNDER SECTION 24: Australia: Pat. Off.)
          19 I.P.R. 223
Hong Kong Toy Centre Ltd v. Tomy U.K. Ltd (PATENT: THREATS:
INTERLOCUTORY INJUNCTION: PRACTICE: *Ex parte* ORDER: SUBSEQUENT
AGREEMENT AS TO DATES FOR FILING EVIDENCE AND HEARING *inter partes*:
11-MONTH DELAY IN BRINGING MOTION FOR HEARING: INEXCUSABLE AND
INORDINATE: RELIEF REFUSED: OBSERVATIONS ON PUBLIC PURPOSE OF
PATENTS COURT: Pat. Ct)   [1994] F.S.R. 593
Hood Computers Pty Ltd v. On-Line Furniture Pty Ltd (PATENT: OPPOSITION: FAIR
BASIS: OBVIOUSNESS: NON-INVENTIVE SKILLED WORKER: COSTS: Australia:
AIPO)   28 I.P.R. 347
Hoogerdyk v. Condon (BUSINESS NAME: SALE OF BUSINESS: BREACH OF
CONTRACT: GOODWILL IN NAME: DAMAGES: ASSESSMENT: Australia: H.C.)
          (1990) 22 N.S.W.L.R. 171
Hooi v. Brophy (COPYRIGHT: INFRINGEMENT: CONSTRUCTIVE KNOWLEDGE:
Australia: SC(S.A.))   (1984) 52 A.L.R. 710; 3 I.P.R. 16
Hooper Trading/T–cell growth factor (EUROPEAN PATENT: INVENTIVE STEP:
Desideratum: SIMPLICITY: NOVELTY: CLEAR AND UNAMBIGUOUS DISCLOSURE,
TEST FOR: ORAL DESCRIPTION: PRIOR ART: PRIOR ORAL DESCRIPTION:
ENLARGED BOARD OF APPEAL: REFERENCE REFUSED: T877/90: EPO)
          [1993] E.P.O.R. 6
Hoover plc v. George Hulme (Stockport) Ltd (COPYRIGHT: REPLACEMENT PARTS:
KNOWLEDGE OF INFRINGEMENT: ACQUIESCENCE: ABUSE OF DOMINANT
POSITION: Ch.D.)   [1982] 3 C.M.L.R. 186; [1982] F.S.R. 565
Hoover SA (Pty) Ltd v. Fisher & Paykel Ltd (PATENT: EXTENSION: INADEQUATE
REMUNERATION: PROFITS MADE BY EXCLUSIVE LICENSEE: South Africa:
TPD)   1986 (4) S.A. 570
Hormann/Publication of a European patent application (EUROPEAN PATENT:
APPLICATION: PROCEDURE: PUBLICATION: CONVENTIONS: ENLARGED
BOARD OF APPEAL: REFERENCE REFUSED: FEES: REIMBURSEMENT OF APPEAL
FEE: *Argumentum a contrario*: J05/81: EPO)
          [1979–85] E.P.O.R. A83; [1982] O.J. EPO 155
Horwitz Grahame Books Ltd v. Performance Publications Pty Ltd (TRADE
PRACTICES: MISLEADING CONDUCT: STATEMENTS MADE IN MAGAZINE
SUGGESTING CONNECTION WITH ANOTHER MAGAZINE: INTERLOCUTORY
INJUNCTION: Australia: Fed. Ct)   8 I.P.R. 25

Hosokawa Micron International Inc. v. Fortune (COPYRIGHT: DESIGNS: COPYRIGHT AND DESIGNS OVERLAP: INFRINGEMENT: DEFENCES: COPYRIGHT IN DRAWING DATED 1972: WHETHER DRAWING CAPABLE OF REGISTRATION UNDER DESIGNS ACT 1906 BEFORE DESIGNS AMENDMENT ACT 1981: REGISTRABILITY OF FUNCTIONAL DESIGNS: Australia: Fed. Ct)
97 A.L.R. 615
(S.C.(Vic.)) 19 I.P.R. 531
Hospitals Contribution Fund of Australia Ltd v. Switzerland Australia Health Fund Pty Ltd (TRADE PRACTICES: HEALTH INSURERS: COMPARATIVE ADVERTISING: WHETHER MISLEADING OR DECEPTIVE: WHETHER TRIAL JUDGE HAS POWER TO ORDER CORRECTIVE ADVERTISEMENT: Australia: Fed. Ct)
11 I.P.R. 549
Houdaille/Removal of feature (EUROPEAN PATENT: AMENDMENT AND CORRECTION: BROADENING CLAIM BY OMISSION: T331/87: EPO)
[1991] E.P.O.R. 194; [1991] O.J. EPO 22
House of Spring Gardens Ltd v. Point Blank Ltd (BREACH OF CONFIDENCE: COPYRIGHT: INFRINGEMENT: BREACH OF CONTRACT: BULLETPROOF VESTS: APPLICABILITY IN IRELAND OF ENGLISH AUTHORITIES: SPRINGBOARD DOCTRINE: DIRECTORS LIABILITY FOR COMMISSION OF TORTS: Ireland: H.C.)
[1984] I.R. 690; [1983] F.S.R. 213
(S.C.) [1984] I.R. 611; [1985] F.S.R. 327
House of Spring Gardens Ltd v. Point Blank Ltd (BREACH OF CONFIDENCE: COPYRIGHT: INFRINGEMENT: BREACH OF CONTRACT: DAMAGES: ACCOUNT OF PROFITS: WHETHER ROYALTY FOR BREACH OF CONTRACT PRECLUDES FURTHER PECUNIARY AWARD FOR BREACH OF COPYRIGHT AND CONFIDENCE: OVERLAPPING HEADS OF DAMAGE: ABATEMENT: Ireland: H.C.)
[1983] F.S.R. 489
(S.C.) [1984] I.R. 611; [1985] F.S.R. 327
House of Spring Gardens Ltd v. Waite (CONFIDENTIAL INFORMATION: CONFLICT OF LAWS: FOREIGN JUDGMENT: JURISDICTION TO ENFORCE: JUDGMENT OF FOREIGN COURT FOR DAMAGES AGAINST DEFENDANTS: SUBSEQUENT JUDGMENT OF SAME COURT THAT PRIOR JUDGMENT NOT OBTAINED BY FRAUD: WHETHER DEFENDANTS ESTOPPED FROM ALLEGING IN ENGLISH PROCEEDINGS THAT JUDGMENT IN QUESTION OBTAINED BY FRAUD: WHETHER ABUSE OF PROCESS TO RE-LITIGATE ISSUE OF FRAUD: C.A.)
[1990] 2 All E.R. 990; [1991] 1 Q.B. 241
House of Spring Gardens Ltd v. Waite (PRACTICE: MAREVA INJUNCTION: PROCEEDINGS IN TWO JURISDICTIONS: LEGAL COSTS: Ch.D.)
[1984] F.S.R. 277
House of Spring Gardens Ltd v. Waite (PRACTICE: ORDER FOR DISCLOSURE OF ASSETS: C.A.)   [1985] F.S.R. 173
Howard Florey/Relaxin (EUROPEAN PATENT: BIOTECHNOLOGICAL INVENTION: H2–RELAXIN: PRESENCE IN HUMAN BODY: NOVELTY: INVENTIVE STEP: DISCOVERY: CONTRARY TO MORALITY: ADMISSIBILITY OF OPPOSITION: APPLICATION NO. 83 307 553: EPO)   [1995] E.P.O.R. 541
Howard/Snackfood (EUROPEAN PATENT: INVENTIVE STEP: COMMERCIAL SUCCESS: PRIORITY: CRITERIA FOR ACCORDING: OPPOSITION: PROCEDURE: ONUS OF PROOF: UPHOLDING ON OTHER GROUNDS: FEES: REIMBURSEMENT OF APPEAL FEE: T73/88: EPO)   [1990] E.P.O.R. 112; [1992] O.J. EPO 557
HPM Industries Pty Ltd's Registered Design (DESIGNS: APPLICATION FOR EXTENSION OF TERM: STATUTORY NOTICE: Australia: Pat. Off.)
12 I.P.R. 188

Hsiung's Patent (PATENT: REVOCATION: AMENDMENT: CORRECTION: DISCRETION: SUFFICIENCY: BEST METHOD: PRACTICE ON AMENDMENT: Pat. Ct: C.A.)   [1992] R.P.C. 497

HTX International Pty Ltd v. Semco Pty Ltd (TRADE PRACTICES: DECEPTION: Australia: Fed. Ct)   1 I.P.R. 403

Hüls/2,2,6,6–tetramethylpiperidone-(4) (EUROPEAN PATENT: INVENTIVE STEP: COMBINATION OF CITATIONS: OPPOSITION: PROCEDURE: AMENDMENT OF CLAIM ON APPEAL: FRESH DOCUMENTS ON APPEAL: T132/84: EPO)   [1986] E.P.O.R. 303

Hüls/Grounds for appeal (EUROPEAN PATENT: OPPOSITION: PROCEDURE: GROUNDS FOR APPEAL, REQUIREMENTS OF: INVENTIVE STEP: SELECTION: T220/83: EPO)   [1987] E.P.O.R. 49; [1986] O.J. EPO 249

Hung Ka Ho v. A-1 Office System Pte Ltd (COPYRIGHT: REGISTERED DESIGN: INFRINGEMENT: ANTON PILLER: APPLICATION TO DISCHARGE: INTERROGATORIES: PRIVILEGE AGAINST SELF–INCRIMINATION: Singapore: H.C.)   [1992] 2 S.L.R. 379

Hunter & Partners v. Wellings & Partners (PRACTICE: OPPOSED *ex parte* MOTION: COPYRIGHT: INFRINGEMENT: APPEAL: DISCRETION: C.A.)   [1987] F.S.R. 83

Hunters Products Pty Ltd v. R. & C. Products Pty Ltd (TRADE PRACTICES: MISLEADING OR DECEPTIVE CONDUCT: Fed. Ct)   8 I.P.R. 591

Hunt-Wesson Inc.'s Trade Mark Application (TRADE MARK: SWISS MISS: OPPOSITION: WHETHER DECEPTIVE: APPEAL FROM DECISION OF REGISTRAR: PRINCIPLES FOR ADMISSION OF FURTHER EVIDENCE ON APPEAL: REGISTRAR'S PRACTICE: Ch.D.)   [1996] R.P.C. 233

Hüppe/Assignment (EUROPEAN PATENT: ENTITLEMENT: REGISTER OF EUROPEAN PATENTS, EFFECT OF REGISTRATION IN: OPPOSITION: PROCEDURE: ADMISSIBILITY: T653/89: EPO)   [1991] E.P.O.R. 217

Husky Injection Molding Systems Ltd's Application (PATENT: EXTENSION OF TIME TO MAKE APPLICATION PURSUANT TO SECTION 51: COMMISSIONER'S POWERS TO EXTEND TIME: Australia: Pat. Off.)   98 A.L.R. 133
(Fed. Ct) 18 I.P.R. 505

Husky Injection Molding Systems Ltd v. Commissioner of Patents (PATENT: EXTENSION OF TIME: WHETHER COMMISSIONER HAS POWER TO EXTEND TIME IN RELATION TO A FURTHER APPLICATION WHEN ORIGINAL APPLICATION HAS PROCEEDED TO GRANT: Australia: Fed. Ct)   19 I.P.R. 193

Hutchison Personal Communications Ltd v. Hook Advertising Ltd (COPYRIGHT: INFRINGEMENT: AUTHORISING: COUNTERCLAIM STRUCK OUT: SECONDARY INFRINGEMENT: POSSESSION OF INFRINGING COPIES: PROPRIETORSHIP: Ch.D.)   [1995] F.S.R. 365

Hydroplan Engineering Ltd v. Naan Metal Works (PATENT: INFRINGEMENT: PRACTICE: DISCOVERY: VALIDITY: OBVIOUSNESS: NATURE AND SCOPE OF DISCOVERY: PATENT AGENTS: PRIVILEGE: Israel: D.C.)   [1985] F.S.R. 255

Hydrotherm Gerätebau GmbH v. Compact de Dott Ing Mario Andreoli & CSAS (RESTRICTIVE PRACTICES: EXCLUSIVE DEALING: BLOCK EXEMPTION: REGULATION 67/67; TRADE MARK LICENCE: Case 46/87R: ECJ)   [1985] 3 C.M.L.R. 224; [1987] E.C.R. 2999

Hytrac Conveyors Ltd v. Conveyors International Ltd (COPYRIGHT: BREACH OF CONFIDENCE: ANTON PILLER PRACTICE: INTERLOCUTORY INJUNCTION: Ch.D.)   [1983] F.S.R. 63
(C.A.) [1982] 3 All E.R. 415; [1983] F.S.R. 63; [1983] 1 W.L.R. 44

I CAN'T BELIEVE IT'S YOGURT Trade Mark (TRADE MARK: APPLICATION: WHETHER PHRASE A TRADE MARK: WHETHER MARK DISTINCTIVE OR LAUDATORY: PART B. REGISTRATION ALLOWED: BoT)
[1992] R.P.C. 533; (1992) 17 I.P.L.R. 283

I-Co Global Communications Ltd and Inmarsat's Agreements (RESTRICTIVE PRACTICES: TELECOMMUNICATIONS SERVICES: MOBILE SATELLITE SYSTEMS: INTENTION TO APPROVE: E.C. Comm.) [1996] 4 C.M.L.R. 244

I.Q. Trade Mark (TRADE MARK: APPLICATION: TWO LETTER MARK: PRACTICE: T.M.Reg.) [1993] R.P.C. 379

Ibcos Computers Ltd v. Barclays Mercantile Highland Finance Ltd (COPYRIGHT: COMPUTER SOFTWARE: SOURCE CODE: SUBSISTENCE AND EXTENT OF PROTECTION: INFRINGEMENT: SUBSTANTIAL PART: BREACH OF CONFIDENCE: FILE TRANSFER PROGRAM: BRITISH LEYLAND DEFENCE: RESTRICTIVE COVENANT: CONSTRUCTION: Ch.D.)
[1994] F.S.R. 275; 29 I.P.R. 25

IBM (Barclay & Bigar)'s Application (PATENT: APPLICATION: SECOND GRANT: PRACTICE: C.-G.) [1983] R.P.C. 283

IBM United Kingdom Ltd v. Prima Data International Ltd (PRACTICE: ANTON PILLER ORDER: PRIVILEGE: RULE AGAINST SELF-INCRIMINATION: Ch.D.) [1994] 1 W.L.R. 719

IBM v. Commissioner of Patents (PATENT: "ALGORITHM": TEST OF PATENTABILITY: DISTINCTION BETWEEN INVENTION AND DISCOVERY OR MATHEMATICAL PRINCIPLE: INTERPRETATION OF CLAIM IN CONTEXT OF SPECIFICATION: NATURE OF "APPEAL": PRINCIPLES IN GRANTING OR REFUSING PATENT APPLICATION: Australia: Fed. Ct)
105 A.L.R. 388; 22 I.P.R. 417

IBM v. Computer Imports Ltd (COPYRIGHT: INFRINGEMENT: COMPUTER TECHNOLOGY: THREE-DIMENSIONAL REPRODUCTION OF CABINET AND INTERNAL LAYOUT OF PERSONAL COMPUTER: COPYING OF COMPUTER PROGRAM: IMPORTATION AND SALE: SOURCE CODE: WHETHER OBJECT CODE (SILICON CHIP): TRANSFER OF LITERARY WORK: New Zealand: H.C.) [1989] 2 N.Z.L.R. 395; 14 I.P.R. 225

IBM v. Phoenix International Computers Ltd (PASSING OFF: TRADE MARK INFRINGEMENT: PRACTICE: STRIKING OUT: SUMMARY JUDGMENT: EURO-DEFENCES: ACQUIESCENCE: ESTOPPEL: Ch.D.) [1994] R.P.C. 251

IBM v. Phoenix International Computers Ltd (PRACTICE: DISCOVERY: LEGAL PROFESSIONAL PRIVILEGE: ADVICE FROM FOREIGN LAWYER ON U.K. LAW: INSPECTION OF DOCUMENTS: WHETHER PRIVILEGE WAIVED: PRODUCTION OF DOCUMENTS BY MISTAKE: WHETHER MISTAKE OBVIOUS: REMEDIES: Ch.D.) [1995] F.S.R. 184

IBM v. Smith, *sub nom.* IBM v. Commissioner of Patents

IBM/Brushless D.C. motor (EUROPEAN PATENT: AMENDMENT AND CORRECTION: CLAIM, LACK OF CLARITY: OPPOSITION: PROCEDURE: AMENDMENT OF CLAIM, CLARITY AND SUPPORT: LATE FILING OF ADDITIONAL PRIOR ART: T194/89: EPO) [1991] E.P.O.R. 411

IBM/Card reader (EUROPEAN PATENT: PATENTABILITY: METHOD FOR DOING BUSINESS: MIX OF TECHNICAL AND NON-TECHNICAL ELEMENTS: INVENTIVE STEP: PREJUDICE: SKILLED PERSON: KNOWLEDGE OF: T854/90: EPO)
[1994] E.P.O.R. 89

IBM/Commutation device (EUROPEAN PATENT: INVENTIVE STEP: KNOWN FUNCTION OF INDIVIDUAL INTEGERS: T48/83: EPO) [1986] E.P.O.R. 84

IBM/Computer-related invention (EUROPEAN PATENT: PATENTABILITY: COMPUTER-RELATED INVENTIONS: CLAIMS: FUNCTIONAL FEATURES: T115/85: EPO)   [1990] E.P.O.R. 107; [1990] O.J. EPO 30

IBM/Data processor network (EUROPEAN PATENT: PATENTABILITY: COMPUTER-RELATED INVENTIONS: TECHNICAL EFFECT: DISCLOSURE: CONVENTIONAL PROGRAMMING: REFERENCE TO APPLICANT'S MANUALS: T6/83: EPO)
[1990] E.P.O.R. 91; [1990] O.J. EPO 05

IBM/Document abstracting and retrieving (EUROPEAN PATENT: PATENTABILITY: COMPUTER-RELATED INVENTIONS: SUFFICIENCY: TECHNICAL FIELD AND PROBLEM MUST BE DEFINED: CLAIMS: DRAFTING CANNOT CIRCUMVENT CONVENTION: TECHNICAL FEATURES: NATIONAL PRACTICE: RULES, OF: T22/85: EPO)   [1990] E.P.O.R. 98; [1990] O.J. EPO 12

IBM/Editable document form (EUROPEAN PATENT: PATENTABILITY: METHOD OF CONVERTING DOCUMENTS BETWEEN WORD-PROCESSORS: T110/90: EPO)   [1995] E.P.O.R. 185

IBM/Insufficient disclosure (EUROPEAN PATENT: SUFFICIENCY: PRIOR ART: MUST BE DESCRIBED: T165/88: EPO)   [1989] E.P.O.R. 157

IBM/Ion etching (EUROPEAN PATENT: NOVELTY: ORAL DESCRIPTION: OPPOSITION: PROCEDURE: WITNESS, EVIDENCE OF: PRIOR ART: PRIOR ORAL DESCRIPTION: T534/88: EPO)   [1991] E.P.O.R. 18

IBM/Lack of unity (EUROPEAN PATENT: APPLICATION: PROCEDURE: UNITY, LACK OF, PROCEDURE TO BE FOLLOWED: REQUIREMENT THROUGHOUT EXAMINATION: T178/84: EPO)   [1989] E.P.O.R. 364; [1989] O.J. EPO 157

IBM/Magnetic transducer head support assemblies (EUROPEAN PATENT: AMENDMENT AND CORRECTION: DRAWINGS: NEW CLAIMS BASED ON: T75/82: EPO)   [1986] E.P.O.R. 103

IBM/Recording apparatus (EUROPEAN PATENT: INVENTIVE STEP: LOGICAL DERIVATION TEST: SERIES OF STEPS BETWEEN INVENTION AND PRIOR ART: SIMPLICITY: T113/82: EPO) [1979–85] E.P.O.R. B553; [1984] O.J. EPO 10

IBM/*Restitutio in integrum* (EUROPEAN PATENT: RE-ESTABLISHMENT OF RIGHTS: ASSISTANT'S FAULT: MONITORING SYSTEM: REPRESENTATIVE'S DUTIES: STRICT STANDARD: T715/91: EPO)   [1993] E.P.O.R. 76

IBM/Semantically-related expressions (EUROPEAN PATENT: PATENTABILITY: COMPUTER-RELATED INVENTIONS: T52/85: EPO)   [1989] E.P.O.R. 454

IBM/Text clarity processing (EUROPEAN PATENT: PATENTABILITY: MENTAL ACTS: INVENTIVE STEP: NO CONTRIBUTION IN PATENTABLE FIELD: T38/86: EPO)   [1990] E.P.O.R. 606; [1990] O.J. EPO 384

IBM/Text processing (EUROPEAN PATENT: PATENTABILITY: COMPUTER-RELATED INVENTIONS: T65/86: EPO)   [1990] E.P.O.R. 181

ICI's Petition (PATENT: EXTENSION: INADEQUATE REMUNERATION: INVALID PATENT: EFFECT: Australia: S.C.(Vic.))   [1983] 1 V.R. 1

ICI Americas/Polyisocyanurates (EUROPEAN PATENT: AMENDMENT AND CORRECTION: ARITHMETICAL ERROR: T13/83: EPO)
[1979–85] E.P.O.R. C732; [1984] O.J. EPO 428

ICI Australia Operations Pty Ltd v. Commercial Polymers Pty Ltd (PATENT: OPPOSITION: APPLICATION FOR EXTENSION OF TIME TO APPLY FOR FURTHER TIME TO FILE EVIDENCE: ATTORNEY'S ERROR AMOUNTS TO SPECIAL CIRCUMSTANCES: APPLICATION FOR EXTENSION OF TIME TO FILE EVIDENCE: SERIOUS OPPOSITION FORESHADOWED: PUBLIC INTEREST: RELEVANCE OF OTHER OPPOSITION: Australia: Pat. Off.)   24 I.P.R. 153

ICI plc/Optical sensing apparatus (EUROPEAN PATENT: INVENTIVE STEP: APPLICATION OF COMMON GENERAL KNOWLEDGE: PLURALITY OF OBVIOUS SOLUTIONS TO INDEPENDENT PROBLEMS: CLARITY: UNFEASIBLE COMBINATION OF FEATURES: NO FURTHER AMENDMENTS WITHOUT PATENTEE'S CONSENT: T454/89: EPO)   [1995] E.P.O.R. 600

ICI v. E.C. Commission (EUROPEAN COURT PROCEDURE: RESTRICTIVE PRACTICES: DISCOVERY OF DOCUMENTS: HEARING OFFICER'S REPORT: ˘ INCONSISTENCY BETWEEN REASONING IN JUDGMENTS AND MOTIVES REVEALED IN PRESS STATEMENTS: RELEVANCY: Case 212/86: ECJ)
[1987] 2 C.M.L.R. 500

ICI v. Irenco Inc. (PATENT: APPLICATION: OPPOSITION: STATEMENT OF GROUNDS AND PARTICULARS: ADEQUACY: DIRECTIONS: Australia: AIPO)
26 I.P.R. 154

ICI v. Mitsubishi Gas Chemical Co. (PATENT: APPLICATION: OPPOSITION: EVIDENCE: FURTHER EVIDENCE AFTER EVIDENCE IN REPLY: OBJECTION: PRACTICE AND PROCEDURE: Australia: AIPO)   29 I.P.R. 285

ICI v. Montedison (U.K.) Ltd (PATENT: INFRINGEMENT: CONSTRUCTION: CONFLICT BETWEEN RIVAL SCIENTIFIC THEORIES: WHETHER COURT OBLIGED TO CHOOSE BETWEEN THEORIES: FRESH EVIDENCE ON APPEAL: Pat. Ct)   [1995] R.P.C. 449

ICI v. Ram Bathrooms (PATENT: AMENDMENTS: PRACTICE: SETTLEMENT OF ACTION: WHETHER JURISDICTION TO ALLOW AMENDMENT: P.C.)
[1994] F.S.R. 181

ICI/Cartridge end closure (EUROPEAN PATENT: INVENTIVE STEP: COMBINATION OF CITATIONS: T74/82: EPO)   [1986] E.P.O.R. 74

ICI/Cleaning plaque (EUROPEAN PATENT: INVENTIVE STEP: AGED ART: COMPARATIVE TESTS: INVENTOR'S SUBSEQUENT REMARKS: NOVELTY: DISCLAIMED SPECIFIC EXAMPLES: PATENTABILITY: COSMETIC INDICATION: T290/86: EPO)   [1991] E.P.O.R. 157; [1992] O.J. EPO 414

ICI/Containers (EUROPEAN PATENT: CLAIMS: SUPPORT FOR: DISCLOSURE: PROBLEM, REQUIREMENT TO IDENTIFY: INVENTIVE STEP: PROBLEM AND SOLUTION: UNITY: SOLUTION TO MULTIPLE PROBLEMS: T26/81: EPO)
[1979–85] E.P.O.R. B362; [1982] O.J. EPO 211

ICI/Continuation of opposition proceedings (EUROPEAN PATENT: FEES: REIMBURSEMENT OF APPEAL FEE: OPPOSITION: PROCEDURE: WITHDRAWAL OF OPPONENT, CONTINUATION OF PROCEEDINGS UPON: T197/88: EPO)
[1990] E.P.O.R. 243; [1989] O.J. EPO 412

ICI/Control circuit (EUROPEAN PATENT: TEXT OF PATENT: APPROVAL BY APPLICANT REQUIRED: APPEAL: PROCEDURE: APPROVED TEXT: DECISION ONLY POSSIBLE ON: CLAIMS: FAIR BASIS: RESPONSIBILITY OF APPLICANT TO DRAFT: T32/82: EPO)   [1979–85] E.P.O.R. B426; [1984] O.J. EPO 354

ICI/Diphenyl ethers (EUROPEAN PATENT: INVENTIVE STEP: CHEMICAL INTERMEDIATES: T372/86: EPO)   [1988] E.P.O.R. 93

ICI/Emulsion explosive (EUROPEAN PATENT: PRIOR USE: HIDDEN BUT ENABLING: NOVELTY: DISCLAIMER: INVENTIVE STEP: SATISFACTORY EXISTING COMMERCIAL PRODUCT: INCENTIVE TO CHANGE: CLARITY OF CLAIM: T627/91: EPO)   [1995] E.P.O.R. 286

ICI/Fibre-reinforced compositions (EUROPEAN PATENT: AMENDMENT AND CORRECTION: LIMITATION BASED ON EXEMPLIFIED DISADVANTAGES: OPPOSITION: CLAIMS: PROCEDURE: ORAL PROCEEDINGS: PATENTEE'S STATEMENTS IN ORAL PROCEEDINGS: PRODUCT-BY-PROCESS: NOVELTY: PRODUCT OF PROCESS: T257/89: EPO)   [1992] E.P.O.R. 332

ICI/Fusecord (EUROPEAN PATENT: INVENTIVE STEP: COMMERCIAL SUCCESS: PREJUDICE: SECONDARY INDICATION: T270/84: EPO)
[1987] E.P.O.R. 357

ICI/Gamma-sorbitol (EUROPEAN PATENT: NOVELTY: INEVITABLE RESULT: OPPOSITION: PROCEDURE: COMMUNICATIONS FROM OPPOSITION DIVISION, FUNCTION OF: GENERAL PRINCIPLES UNDERLYING: SUFFICIENCY: TRIAL AND ERROR: T173/89: EPO)
[1991] E.P.O.R. 62

ICI/Gear crimped yarn (EUROPEAN PATENT: CLAIMS: PARAMETERS DEFINING PRODUCT: INVENTIVE STEP: PRODUCT CLAIM: ASSESSMENT INDEPENDENT OF PROCESS FOR MAKING PRODUCT: T94/82: EPO)
[1979–85] E.P.O.R. B513; [1984] O.J. EPO 75

ICI/Latex composition (EUROPEAN PATENT: INVENTIVE STEP: INCOMPATIBLE INCENTIVES: NOVELTY: ERRONEOUS ABSTRACT OF CITATION: OPPOSITION: PROCEDURE: FRESH DOCUMENTS ON APPEAL: FRESH EVIDENCE ON APPEAL, ALLOWED: PRIOR ART: ABSTRACT, ERRONEOUS: SKILLED PERSON: APPROACH TO TECHNICAL TEACHING: T77/87: EPO)
[1989] E.P.O.R. 246; [1990] O.J. EPO 280

ICI/Manufacture of fusecord (EUROPEAN PATENT: AMENDMENT AND CORRECTION: DISCLOSURE, EXTENT OF: INVENTIVE STEP: STATE OF THE ART: T17/84: EPO)
[1986] E.P.O.R. 274

ICI/Modified diisocyanates (EUROPEAN PATENT: AMENDMENT AND CORRECTION: ARBITRARY LIMITATION: OPPOSITION: PROCEDURE: FRESH DOCUMENTS ON APPEAL: FRESH EVIDENCE ON APPEAL, REFUSED: INVENTIVE STEP: ONLY REASONABLE CHOICE: SURPRISING EFFECT: NOVELTY: COMBINATION OF SEPARATE TEACHINGS IN SINGLE DOCUMENT: PRODUCT OF PROCESS: T433/86: EPO)
[1988] E.P.O.R. 97

ICI/Polyester crystallisation (EUROPEAN PATENT: ABANDONMENT: IMPOSSIBILITY OF REVIVING: PRIORITY: NOVEL SELECTION FROM PRIORITY DOCUMENT: T61/85: EPO)
[1988] E.P.O.R. 20

ICI/Polyester polyols (EUROPEAN PATENT: OPPOSITION: PROCEDURE: FRESH DOCUMENTS ON APPEAL: CLAIMS: FUNCTIONAL FEATURES: INVENTIVE STEP: COMBINATION OF CITATIONS: *Ex post facto* APPROACH: THEORETICAL PRINCIPLES, APPLICATION OF: SUFFICIENCY: FUNCTIONAL DEFINITIONS: T229/84: EPO)
[1988] E.P.O.R. 217

ICI/Polyetherketones (EUROPEAN PATENT: OPPOSITION: PROCEDURE: AMENDMENT OF CLAIM, CLARITY AND SUPPORT: OBSERVATIONS BY PARTIES, LIMITATIONS ON: OPPOSITION DIVISION: EXERCISE OF PROPER CONTROL BY: T295/87: EPO)   [1991] E.P.O.R. 56; [1990] O.J. EPO 470

ICI/Pyridine herbicides (EUROPEAN PATENT: COMMON GENERAL KNOWLEDGE: INGREDIENTS OF: DISCLOSURE: NON-ENABLING: NOVELTY: REPRODUCIBILITY OF PRIOR TEACHING: SUFFICIENCY: IDENTITY OF TEST UNDER ARTICLES 54(2) AND 83: T206/83: EPO)
[1986] E.P.O.R. 232; [1987] O.J. EPO 58
(Editor's Note: T206/83: EPO)   [1987] E.P.O.R. 112; [1987] O.J. EPO 05

ICI/Re-establishment of rights (EUROPEAN PATENT: FEES: PAYMENT BY DEBIT ORDER: RE-ESTABLISHMENT OF RIGHTS: TEMPORARY CLERK, FAILURE TO SUPERVISE: T105/85: EPO)   [1987] E.P.O.R. 186

ICI/Removal of hydrogen sulphide (EUROPEAN PATENT: RE-ESTABLISHMENT OF RIGHTS: PROCEDURE: INCAPACITY OF REPRESENTATIVE: CLERK'S FAILURE: T301/85: EPO)   [1986] E.P.O.R. 340

ICI/Triazoles (EUROPEAN PATENT: DIVISIONAL APPLICATION: CLASS OF CHEMICAL COMPOUND: INVENTIVE STEP: COMBINATION OF CITATIONS: T176/90: EPO)   [1994] E.P.O.R. 401

ICI/Unity (EUROPEAN PATENT: UNITY: CHEMICAL INTERMEDIATES: REIMBURSEMENT OF APPEAL FEES: MISINTERPRETATION OF BOARD: T470/91: EPO) [1994] E.P.O.R. 231

ICI/Zeolites (EUROPEAN PATENT: EPO: JURISDICTION: OPPOSITION: PROCEDURE: PARTIAL ATTACK: T9/87: EPO) [1990] E.P.O.R. 46; [1989] O.J. EPO 438

Idaho/Submitting culture deposit information (EUROPEAN PATENT: AMENDMENT AND CORRECTION: MICRO-ORGANISM DEPOSIT NUMBER: FEES: REIMBURSEMENT OF APPEAL FEE: REIMBURSEMENT OF RE-ESTABLISHMENT FEE: J08/87: EPO) [1989] E.P.O.R. 170; [1989] O.J. EPO 09

Idaho/Submitting culture deposit information (EUROPEAN PATENT: MICRO-ORGANISMS: DEPOSIT, ACCESSION NUMBER: J08/87: EPO) [1989] E.P.O.R. 170; [1989] O.J. EPO 09

Ideal-Standard GmbH's Application (RESTRICTIVE PRACTICES: EXCLUSIVE DEALING: SELECTIVE DISTRIBUTION SYSTEMS: WHOLESALERS: PLUMBING FITTINGS: E.C. Comm.) [1988] 4 C.M.L.R. 627; [1988] F.S.R. 574

IFF/Claim categories (EUROPEAN PATENT: CONVENTIONS: NATIONAL PRACTICES IRRELEVANT: T150/82: EPO) [1979–85] E.P.O.R. C629; [1984] O.J. EPO 309

IHT International Heiztechnik GmbH v. Ideal-Standard GmbH (TRADE MARK: IDEAL STANDARD: EXHAUSTION OF RIGHTS: COMMON ORIGIN: UNITARY CONTROL: SALE IN ONE MEMBER STATE: EXPORT TO ANOTHER: INJUNCTION: ECJ) [1994] 3 C.M.L.R. 857; [1995] F.S.R. 59

Ikaplast/Small amount lacking (EUROPEAN PATENT: FEES: SMALL AMOUNT EXCEPTION: J11/85: EPO) [1986] E.P.O.R. 110; [1986] O.J. EPO 01

Ikarian Reefer, The (PRACTICE: EXPERT WITNESSES: DUTIES AND RESPONSIBILITIES OF EXPERT WITNESS: Comm. Ct) [1993] F.S.R. 563

Ikida Koki Seisakusho KK v. Duro-Matic Pty Ltd (PATENT: OPPOSITION: EXTENSION OF TIME LIMIT: Australia: Pat. Off.) 1 I.P.R. 309

IMA AG v. Windsurfing International Inc. (RESTRICTIVE PRACTICES: E.C. Comm.) [1984] 1 C.M.L.R. 1; [1984] F.S.R. 146; [1983] O.J. L229/1

Image Enterprises CC v. Eastman Kodak Co. (TRADE MARKS REGISTERED IN SOUTH AFRICA: PROPRIETOR'S DECISION TO WITHDRAW: APPLICANT'S WISH TO REGISTER SAME MARKS: WHETHER MARKS ABANDONED: South Africa: S.C.) [1989] 1 F.S.R. 353

Imagic Inc. v. Futuretronics (Aust.) Pty Ltd (PATENT ATTORNEYS: COMMUNICATIONS WITH CLIENT: WHETHER PRIVILEGED: Australia: S.C.(NSW)) 1 I.P.R. 302

Imagic Inc. v. Futuretronics (Aust.) Pty Ltd (TRADE MARK: APPLICATION: EXCLUSIVE AGENCY CONTRACT: Australia: S.C.(NSW)) (1984) 51 A.L.R. 122

IMH Investments Ltd v. Trinidad Home Developers Ltd (PATENT: KNOW-HOW: LICENCE AGREEMENT: CONSTRUCTION: UNPAID ROYALTIES: SUMMARY JUDGMENT: LICENSED PATENTS NEVER REGISTERED BUT ROYALTIES PAID UNDER AGREEMENT FOR SEVEN YEARS: RECISSION BY LICENSEE: MISREPRESENTATION: ESTOPPEL: JUDGEMENT: APPEAL: STATUTORY AND CONTRACTUAL INTEREST: DISCRETION: Trinidad & Tobago: C.A.) [1994] F.S.R. 616

Imperial Chemical Industries, *sub nom.* ICI

Imperial Group plc v. Philip Morris Ltd (PASSING OFF: GET-UP: BLACK CIGARETTE PACKETS: FEATURES COMMON TO TRADE: STATUS OF SURVEY EVIDENCE: Ch.D.) [1984] R.P.C. 293

Import of Drugs from Italy (RESTRICTIVE PRACTICES: UNFAIR COMPETITION: PRICE: PARALLEL IMPORTS: RESTRAINT OF COMPETITION: Germany: S.C.)   [1988] 4 C.M.L.R. 246; [1988] F.S.R. 377
Imprimerie (SA) Thône v. Fernand Geubelle (COPYRIGHT: INTELLIGENCE TEST: PUBLISHER AS CO-AUTHOR: *Locus standi*: Belgium)
     [1983] E.C.C. 339; [1983] F.S.R. 511
Improver Corp. v. Raymond Industrial Ltd (PATENT: EUROPEAN PATENT: PROTOCOL ON INTERPRETATION: INFRINGEMENT: VALIDITY: PURPOSIVE CONSTRUCTION: RECONCILIATION OF PRINCIPLES IN *Catnic Components v. Hill & Smith*: OBVIOUSNESS: EPC: INCONSISTENT PRIOR EUROPEAN DECISIONS: Hong Kong: H.C.)   [1990] F.S.R. 422; 16 I.P.R. 92
Improver Corp. v. Raymond Industrial Ltd (PATENT: DEPILATORY DEVICE: CONSTRUCTION OF CLAIM: OBVIOUSNESS: CERTAINTY: NO INFRINGEMENT: Hong Kong: C.A.)   [1991] F.S.R. 233
Improver Corp. v. Remington Consumer Products Ltd (PATENT: INFRINGEMENT: DEPILATORY DEVICE: EUROPEAN PATENT: CONSTRUCTION: VALIDITY: OBVIOUSNESS: INSUFFICIENCY: Pat. Ct)   [1990] F.S.R. 181
Improver Corp. v. Remington Consumer Products Ltd (STRIKING OUT: INTERLOCUTORY INJUNCTION: BALANCE OF CONVENIENCE: C.A.)
     [1989] R.P.C. 69
Improver/Depilatory device (EUROPEAN PATENT: APPEAL: PROCEDURE: APPEAL BEFORE GROUNDS OF FIRST INSTANCE DECISION: INVENTIVE STEP: CLOSEST PRIOR ART: *Ex post facto* APPROACH: LANGUAGES: CONSENT OF PARTIES TO DIFFERENT LANGUAGE OF PROCEEDINGS: T754/89: EPO)
     [1993] E.P.O.R. 153
INADINE Trade Mark (TRADE MARK: APPLICATION: OPPOSITION: INADINE/ANADIN: GOODS OF SAME DESCRIPTION: APPLICATION REFUSED: Ch.D.)   [1992] R.P.C. 421
Incapacity (EUROPEAN PATENT: APPEAL: PROCEDURE: ADMISSIBILITY OF APPEAL: APPLICATION: PROCEDURE: ERRONEOUS INFORMATION FROM EPO: INTERRUPTION OF PROCEEDINGS: INCAPACITY OF REPRESENTATIVE: PROCEDURE: INCAPACITY OF REPRESENTATIVE: PROFESSIONAL REPRESENTATIVES: INCAPACITY: RE-ESTABLISHMENT OF RIGHTS: INCAPACITY OF REPRESENTATIVE: *Nemini licet venire contra factum proprium*: J000/87: EPO)   [1989] E.P.O.R. 73; [1988] O.J. EPO 323
Ind Coope Ltd v. Paine & Co. Ltd (TRADE MARK: INFRINGEMENT: PRACTICE: Ch.D.)   [1983] R.P.C. 326
Independent Locksmiths (NSW) Pty Ltd v. Aardvark (A.) Master Locksmiths Pty Ltd (TRADE PRACTICES: CONSUMER PROTECTION: SIMILAR NAMES: TELEPHONE DIRECTORY ENTRIES: Australia: Fed. Ct)   7 I.P.R. 432
Independent Management Resources Pty Ltd v. Brown (CONFIDENTIAL INFORMATION: EMPLOYER AND EMPLOYEE: INFORMATION GAINED IN EMPLOYMENT: NECESSARY QUALITY OF CONFIDENCE: EMPLOYEE SUBSEQUENTLY COMPETING: BREACH OF CONFIDENCE: DUTY OF FIDELITY: Australia: S.C.(Vic.))   [1987] V.R. 605; 9 I.P.R. 1
Independent Television Publications Ltd v. E.C. Commission (RESTRICTIVE PRACTICES: BROADCASTING: WEEKLY LISTINGS OF TV PROGRAMMES: COPYRIGHT: REFUSAL TO PERMIT REPRODUCTION IN INDEPENDENT TV GUIDE: ARTICLE 86: COMMISSION ENTITLED TO REQUIRE LICENSING FOR REPRODUCTION OF THE LISTINGS: Case T−76/89: CFI)
     [1991] 4 C.M.L.R. 745; [1991] II E.C.R. 575
SUBSEQUENT APPEAL CONJOINED WITH (AND REPORTED *sub nom.*) Radio Telefis Eireann v. E.C. Commission

Independent Television Publications Ltd v. Time Out Ltd (COPYRIGHT: INFRINGEMENT: TV PROGRAMME SCHEDULES: COMPILATION: Ch.D.)
[1984] F.S.R. 64

India Videogram Association Ltd v. Patel (PRACTICE: WRIT: SERVICE: SERVICE BY INSERTION THROUGH DEFENDANT'S LETTER-BOX: NO AFFIDAVIT OF DUE SERVICE: DEFENDANT OUTSIDE JURISDICTION: LEARNING OF WRIT ON HER RETURN PRIOR TO ITS EXPIRY: WHETHER SERVICE EFFECTED DURING CURRENCY OF WRIT: R.S.C. ORDER 10, r.1(3)(b)(i): Ch.D.)
[1991] 1 All E.R. 214; [1991] 1 W.L.R. 173

Indian Institute of Human Resources Development v. National Institute of Human Resources Development (PASSING OFF: INSTITUTES CARRYING ON UNAUTHORISED BUSINESS OF TRAINING AND AWARDING DIPLOMAS: INJUNCTION AGAINST BOTH FOR FRAUDULENT ACTIVITIES: India: H.C.)   (1994) 19 I.P.L.R. 183

Indoor Cricket Arenas (Australia) Pty Ltd v. Australian Indoor Cricket Federation (PATENT: APPLICATION: OPPOSITION: MANNER OF NEW MANUFACTURE: EVIDENCE: PERSON INTERESTED: NOVELTY: Australia: Pat. Off.)
9 I.P.R. 273
(FURTHER HEARING: Pat. Off.)   10 I.P.R. 115

Industrial Containers (Aust.) Pty Ltd's Application (TRADE MARKS: APPLICATION: REFUSAL TO REGISTER: Australia: Pat. Off.)   18 I.P.R. 469

Industrial Equity Ltd v. North Broken Hill Holdings Ltd (TRADE PRACTICES: ADVERTISEMENTS IN DEFENCE OF TAKEOVER BID: WHETHER SHAREHOLDERS CONSUMERS: Australia: Fed. Ct)   6 I.P.R. 317

Industrie Diensten Groep BV v. J.A. Beele Handelmaatschappij BV (IMPORTS: QUANTITATIVE RESTRICTIONS: UNFAIR COMPETITION: PROPORTIONALITY: Case 6/81: ECJ)
[1982] 3 C.M.L.R. 102; [1982] E.C.R. 707; [1983] F.S.R. 119

Infabrics Ltd v. Jaytex (COPYRIGHT: INFRINGEMENT: KNOWLEDGE: PUBLICATION: Ch.D.: C.A.)   [1980] All E.R. 669; [1984] R.P.C. 405
(H.L.) [1982] A.C. 1; [1981] All E.R. 1057; [1984] R.P.C. 405
(INQUIRY AS TO DAMAGES: OVERLAPPING HEADS OF DAMAGE: Ch.D.)
[1985] F.S.R. 75
(APPEAL: PRACTICE: COSTS: C.A.)   [1987] F.S.R. 529

Informed Sources Pty Ltd's Application (TRADE MARKS: APPLICATION: OBJECTION: "INFORMED SOURCES" DESCRIPTIVE OF INFORMATION SERVICES: LACK OF INHERENT DISTINCTIVENESS: EVIDENCE OF USE NOT APPROPRIATE WHERE MARK NOT ADAPTED TO DISTINGUISH: Australia: Pat. Off.) 23 I.P.R. 141

Ingersoll-Rand Co. and Dresser Industries Inc. (JOINT VENTURE: CONCENTRATIVE: NO MORE THAN 10 PER CENT SHARE OF COMPETITIVE MARKET: SOPHISTICATED BUYERS: MERGER CLEARED: NOTICES: E.C. Comm.)
[1993] 5 C.M.L.R. M67

Inglis v. Mayson (COPYRIGHT: INFRINGEMENT: SUBSTANTIAL REPRODUCTION: DRAWINGS IN PATENT SPECIFICATION: PATENT: INFRINGEMENT: ESSENTIAL INTEGERS: INVALIDITY: New Zealand: H.C.)   3 I.P.R. 588

Ink Group Pty Ltd v. Collector of Customs (CUSTOMS: WHETHER ROYALTY PAYMENT PART OF DUTIABLE PRICE OF IMPORTED GOODS: INTERPRETATION: STATUTE: Australia: AAT)   13 I.P.R. 480

Inland Steel/Bismuth-containing steel (EUROPEAN PATENT: APPEAL: PROCEDURE: STATEMENT OF GROUNDS, REQUIREMENTS OF: NOVELTY: DISCLAIMED SPECIFIC EXAMPLES: OPPOSITION: ADMISSIBILITY: T105/87: EPO)
[1991] E.P.O.R. 206

Inland Steel/Retraction of withdrawal (EUROPEAN PATENT: AMENDMENT AND CORRECTION: DESIGNATION OF STATES: J10/87: EPO)
[1989] E.P.O.R. 437; [1989] O.J. EPO 323
Inland Steel/Tellurium-containing steel (EUROPEAN PATENT: NOVELTY: COMBINATION OF SEPARATE TEACHINGS IN SINGLE DOCUMENT: FEATURE NOT CLEARLY DEFINED IN CLAIM: SELECTION FROM KNOWN NUMERICAL RANGE: T75/87: EPO)   [1994] E.P.O.R. 475
INR/Substitution of applicant (EUROPEAN PATENT: APPEAL: PROCEDURE: NEW FACTUAL SITUATION: ENTITLEMENT: APPLICATION FOR RECOGNITION BEFORE NATIONAL DECISION: J05/88: EPO)   [1989] E.P.O.R. 320
INRA/a-lactalbumin product (EUROPEAN PATENT: NOVELTY: PRODUCT OF PROCESS: OPPOSITION: PROCEDURE: FRESH DOCUMENTS ON APPEAL: GROUNDS OF OPPOSITION: T128/86: EPO)   [1989] E.P.O.R. 461
Insamcor (Pty) Ltd v. Maschinenfabriek Sidler Stadler AG (COPYRIGHT: INFRINGEMENT: ORIGINALITY: PROOF: EVIDENCE: SUFFICIENCY: South Africa: WLD)   1987 (4) S.A. 660
Insta-foam Products' Application (TRADE MARK: APPLICATION: INHERENTLY UNADAPTED TO DISTINGUISH: Australia: Pat. Off.)   6 I.P.R. 429
Instance v. Denny Bros Printing Ltd (PATENT: INFRINGEMENT: PLEADINGS: PRACTICE: *See v. Scott-Paine* ORDER: SECTION 64 DEFENCE: PROPOSED AMENDMENTS EMBARRASSING: AMENDMENT NOT ALLOWED: Pat. Ct)
[1994] F.S.R. 396
Instituform Technical Services Ltd v. Inliner U.K. plc (PATENT: INFRINGEMENT: CONSTRUCTION: VALIDITY: PRIORITY DATE: FAIR BASIS: EXCLUSIVE LICENCE: REGISTRATION: WHETHER EXCLUSIVE LICENSEE ENTITLED TO RELIEF FOR INFRINGEMENT: Pat. Ct)   [1992] R.P.C. 83
Institut Cerac/Pump impeller (EUROPEAN PATENT: COSTS: UNNECESSARY HEARING: APPORTIONED: T909/90: EPO)   [1993] E.P.O.R. 373
Intalite International NV v. Cellular Ceilings Ltd (No. 1) (PATENT: INFRINGEMENT: PRACTICE: DISCOVERY: Pat. Ct)   [1987] R.P.C. 532
Intalite International NV v. Cellular Ceilings Ltd (No. 2) (PATENT: INFRINGEMENT: VALIDITY: OBVIOUSNESS: FALSE SUGGESTION: Pat. Ct)   [1987] R.P.C. 537
Intel Corp. v. General Instrument Corp. (PATENT: INFRINGEMENT: PRACTICE: PLEADINGS: DISCOVERY AND PARTICULARS BEFORE DEFENCE SERVED: ORDERS REFUSED: Pat. Ct)   [1989] 1 F.S.R. 640
Intel Corp. v. General Instrument Corp. (No. 2) (PATENT: INFRINGEMENT: PRACTICE: JOINT TORTFEASORS: SERVICE OUTSIDE JURISDICTION: Pat. Ct)   [1991] R.P.C. 235
Intel Corp. v. ULSI System Technology, Inc. (PATENT: INFRINGEMENT: PRELIMINARY INJUNCTION: CROSS-LICENSING: USA: Fed. Ct)
27 I.P.R. 379
Intelligence Quotient International Ltd's Application (PATENT: APPLICATION: INTERNATIONAL APPLICATION: RECEIVING OFFICE: FAILURE TO FILE REQUEST FORM DESIGNATING CONTRACTING STATES: WHETHER RECTIFICATION OF ERROR ALLOWABLE: WHETHER U.K. PATENTS RULES APPLICABLE TO RECEIVING OFFICE: C.-G.)   [1996] R.P.C. 245
Intelligence Quotient International Ltd's Application (PATENT: APPLICATION: NATIONAL PHASE: DOCUMENTS FOR INTERNATIONAL APPLICATION FILED WITHOUT REQUEST FORM: INTERNATIONAL FILING DATE REFUSED UNTIL RECEIPT OF FORM: WHETHER FAILURE TO ACCORD DATE AN ERROR OR OMISSION OF RECEIVING OFFICE: CORRECTION OF IRREGULARITY: C.-G.)   [1996] R.P.C. 258

Inter-footwear Ltd's Applications (TRADE MARK: APPLICATION: HI-TEC: DESCRIPTION OF CHARACTER OF GOODS: EVIDENCE OF USE OVERSEAS: Australia: Pat. Off.) 8 I.P.R. 63

Intera Corp.'s Application (PATENT: APPLICATION: PREPARATIONS FOR PUBLICATION: WITHDRAWAL OF PUBLICATION: WHETHER PUBLICATION MANDATORY: Pat. Ct: C.A.) [1986] R.P.C. 459

Interact Machine Tools (NSW) Pty Ltd v. Yamazaki Mazak Corp. (PETTY PATENT: MACHINE TOOL COMPRISING COMBINATION OF INTEGERS: INFRINGEMENT: INVALIDITY: FAIR BASIS: WHETHER PETTY PATENTS FAIRLY BASED ON SPECIFICATIONS OF PETTY PATENTS, ON PARENT COMPLETE SPECIFICATION AND ON PRIORITY JAPANESE SPECIFICATIONS: Australia: Fed. Ct)
27 I.P.R. 83

Intercontex v. Schmidt (PASSING OFF: INJUNCTION: MISREPRESENTATION OUTSIDE U.K.: PLAINTIFF'S NON-COMPLIANCE WITH UNDERTAKINGS TO COURT: MISREPRESENTATION OF PROPRIETORSHIP OF REGISTERED MARKS: Ch.D.) [1988] F.S.R. 575

Intergraph Corp. v. Solid Systems CAD Services Ltd (COPYRIGHT: COMPUTER SOFTWARE: PRACTICE: APPLICATION TO DISCHARGE ANTON PILLER ORDER: MATERIAL NON-DISCLOSURE: MISREPRESENTATION: DELAY: Ch.D.)
[1993] F.S.R. 617

Interlego AG v. Alex Foley (Vic.) Pty Ltd (COPYRIGHT: INFRINGEMENT: EFFECT OF REGISTERED DESIGN: EXPIRED DESIGNS: TERM OF COPYRIGHT: WHETHER DESIGNS WERE CAPABLE OF REGISTRATION: WHETHER NOVELTY OF DESIGN WAS RELEVANT TO QUESTION OF REGISTRABILITY: Ch.D.)
10 I.P.R. 441; [1987] F.S.R. 283

Interlego AG v. Croner Trading Pty Ltd (COPYRIGHT: DRAWINGS: MODIFICATIONS TO REFLECT CHANGES IN MANUFACTURING PROCESS: PASSING OFF: COMPATIBILITY AND INTERCHANGEABILITY: TOY BRICKS: APPEARANCE: REPRESENTATION: SURVEY EVIDENCE: Australia: Fed. Ct)
102 A.L.R. 379; 25 I.P.R. 65

Interlego AG v. Tyco Industries Inc. (COPYRIGHT: INFRINGEMENT: ARTISTIC WORK: LEGO TOYS: ORIGINALITY: MOULDS AS ENGRAVINGS: NON-EXPERT DEFENCE: ADDITIONAL DAMAGES: DESIGN: REGISTRABILITY: Hong Kong: S.C.) 7 I.P.R. 513
(NOVELTY: ORIGINALITY: PUBLIC ESTOPPEL: EXPIRY OF REGISTRATION: ABANDONMENT OF COPYRIGHT: ADDITIONAL DAMAGES: C.A.)
[1987] H.K.L.R. 619; [1987] F.S.R. 409; 9 I.P.R. 133
(ALTERATIONS TO ENGINEERING DRAWINGS: NON-EXPERT DEFENCE: REGISTERED DESIGN: WHETHER DESIGN CAPABLE OF REGISTRATION: NOVELTY: EYE APPEAL: WHETHER FEATURES OF BRICK DICTATED SOLELY BY FUNCTION: P.C.)
[1989] A.C. 217; [1988] R.P.C. 343; [1988] 3 W.L.R. 678; 12 I.P.R. 97

Interlego AG v. Tyco Industries Inc. (PASSING OFF: GET-UP: INTERLOCUTORY INJUNCTION: MISREPRESENTATION: Hong Kong: H.C.)
[1986] H.K.L.R. 730; 7 I.P.R. 439
(APPEAL: C.A.) [1986] H.K.L.R. 50; 7 I.P.R. 417

Intermed Communications Inc.'s Application (TRADE MARK: APPLICATION: DIRECT DESCRIPTION OF GOODS: INHERENTLY ADAPTED: Australia: T.M.Reg.) 5 I.P.R. 341

International Business Machines Corp., *sub nom*. IBM

International Chemical Engineering AG's Application (DESIGNS: OBJECTIONS TO REGISTRATION: MEANING OF DESIGN: IRREGULAR FEATURES: SUBSTITUTION OF REPRESENTATION: Australia: Pat. Off.) 11 I.P.R. 601

International Computers (Australia) Pty Ltd v. Franhaem Pty Ltd (COPYRIGHT: INFRINGEMENT: PARTICULARS: STRIKING OUT: LEAVE TO APPEAL: Australia: S.C.(Vic.)) 8 I.P.R. 465

International Computers Ltd's Application (TRADE MARK: APPLICATION: DRS: DISTINCTIVENESS: EVIDENCE: Australia: Pat. Off.) 8 I.P.R. 222

International Computers Ltd and Fujitsu Ltd (RESTRICTIVE PRACTICES: JOINT DEVELOPMENT: COMPUTER COMPONENTS: INTENTION TO APPROVE: E.C. Comm.) [1986] 3 C.M.L.R. 154

International Control Automation Finance v. Controller of Patents & Designs (PATENT: ASSIGNMENT: REASSIGNMENT: RECORDAL OF PROPER ASSIGNEE: India: H.C.) (1994) 19 I.P.L.R. 176

International Dental Exhibition (Participation in) (RESTRICTIVE PRACTICES: TRADE FAIRS: RULES FOR PARTICIPATION: INTENTION TO EXEMPT UNDER ARTICLE 85(3): E.C. Comm.) [1987] 3 C.M.L.R. 606

International House of Heraldry v. Grant (TRADE MARK: PASSING OFF: SIMILAR NAMES: DESCRIPTIVE NAMES: INTERNATIONAL ART OF HERALDRY: WHETHER DESCRIPTIVE: WHETHER SLIGHT DIFFERENCE SUFFICIENT TO DISTINGUISH: INTERIM INTERDICT: BALANCE OF CONVENIENCE: PROTECTION OF ESTABLISHED BUSINESS AGAINST NEWLY-FORMED BUSINESS: Scotland: O.H.) 1992 S.L.T. 1021

International Private Satellite Partners (Re) (RESTRICTIVE PRACTICES: TELECOMMUNICATIONS: JOINT VENTURE: OPERATION OF INTERNATIONAL "ONE-STOP" DATA TRANSFER SERVICES FOR BUSINESSES: INTENTION TO APPROVE: NOTICE: E.C. Comm.) [1994] 4 C.M.L.R. 119

International Private Satellite Partners (Re) (No. 2) (RESTRICTIVE PRACTICES: TELECOMMUNICATIONS: EXTENSION OF NOTIFICATION TO COVER ARTICLE 53 EEA: INTENTION TO APPROVE: NOTICE: E.C. Comm.) [1994] 5 C.M.L.R. 478

International Standard Electric/Water-soluble glass (EUROPEAN PATENT: APPLICATION: PROCEDURE: ADMISSIBLE CLAIMS, NECESSITY OF EXAMINING ON BASIS OF: CLAIMS: NOVELTY: DISCLAIMED RANGE: SELECTION: T71/85: EPO) [1987] E.P.O.R. 113

INTERNATIONAL TELESIS GROUP Service Mark (SERVICE MARK: APPLICATION: OPPOSITION: WHETHER MARK CAPABLE OF DISTINGUISHING: WHETHER MARK LIKELY TO CAUSE CONFUSION: EARLIER CONFLICTING MARKS: PROCEEDINGS IN USA: WHETHER ESTOPPEL: HEARSAY EVIDENCE: HONEST CONCURRENT USER: T.M.Reg.) [1996] R.P.C. 45

International Writing Institute v. Rimila Pty Ltd (CONFIDENTIAL INFORMATION: BREACH OF CONTRACT: EXCLUSIVE LICENCE TO DISTRIBUTE: FIDUCIARY DUTY: COPYRIGHT: SUBSISTENCE: INFRINGEMENT: Australia: Fed. Ct) 27 I.P.R. 546

Interpress Associates Ltd v. Pacific Coilcoaters Ltd (PATENT: INFRINGEMENT: PLEADINGS: APPLICATION FOR FURTHER AND BETTER PARTICULARS AS TO ESSENTIAL INTEGERS: New Zealand: H.C.) 29 I.P.R. 635

INVICTA Trade Marks (TRADE MARKS: APPLICATION: GOODS OF THE SAME DESCRIPTION: BoT) [1992] R.P.C. 541

IPC Magazines Ltd v. Black & White Music Corp. (PASSING OFF: JUDGE DREDD: CHARACTER MERCHANDISING: Ch.D.) [1983] F.S.R. 348

Ireco/Blasting compositions (EUROPEAN PATENT: AMENDMENT AND CORRECTION: OPPOSITION PROCEEDINGS: DISCREPANCY BETWEEN EXAMPLE AND CLAIM: PROCEDURE: AMENDMENT, CORRELATION WITH GROUNDS OF OPPOSITION: T127/85: EPO) [1989] E.P.O.R. 358; [1989] O.J. EPO 271

Irish Distillers Ltd v. Smith & Son Pty Ltd (PASSING OFF: WINE COOLERS: ADVERTISEMENTS: REPUTATION: DISBELIEF OF EVIDENCE: MERE CONFUSION OR UNCERTAINTY: INTENTION TO DECEIVE: Australia: Fed. Ct) 7 I.P.R. 509

Ironside v. HM Attorney-General (COPYRIGHT INFRINGEMENT: COINAGE DESIGNS: OWNERSHIP OF COPYRIGHT: CROWN COPYRIGHT: Ch.D.)
[1988] R.P.C. 197

Irsid/Opposition Division (EUROPEAN PATENT: OPPOSITION: PROCEDURE: OPPOSITION DIVISION: IMPROPER CONSTITUTION OF: FEES: REIMBURSEMENT OF APPEAL FEE: T251/88: EPO)   [1990] E.P.O.R. 246

Irvine v. Carson (COPYRIGHT: CRIMINAL OFFENCE: POSSESSION OF INFRINGING COPIES OF COMPUTER PROGRAMS FOR THE PURPOSE OF DISTRIBUTING: CONVICTION: APPROPRIATE PENALTY: ORDER FOR FORFEITURE OF COMPUTERS USED FOR MAKING INFRINGING COPIES: Australia: Fed. Ct)
22 I.P.R. 107

Irvine v. Hanna-Rivero (COPYRIGHT: INFRINGING COPIES OF COMPUTER PROGRAMS MADE FOR "SWAP" TRADE: DEFENDANT PLEADED GUILTY: CONSIDERATION OF APPROPRIATE PENALTY: ORDER FOR FORFEITURE OF SOME HARDWARE EQUIPMENT USED IN MAKING INFRINGING COPIES: Australia: Fed. Ct)   23 I.P.R. 295

Ishihara Sangyo KK v. Dow Chemical Co. (PATENT: INFRINGEMENT: PRACTICE: PLEADINGS: FAIR BASIS: STRIKING OUT: C.A.)   [1987] F.S.R. 137
see also, *sub nom.* Dow Chemical Co. v. Ishihara Sangyo KK

Island Records Ltd v. Tring International plc (COPYRIGHT: INQUIRY AS TO DAMAGES: ACCOUNT OF PROFITS: ELECTION: TIME FOR ELECTION: INFORMED CHOICE: WHETHER ORDER RELEVANT TO DISCOVERY: Ch.D.)   [1995] F.S.R. 560

Island Trading Co. v. Anchor Brewing Co. (PASSING OFF: INTERLOCUTORY INJUNCTION: EVIDENCE: Ch.D.)   [1989] R.P.C. 287a

Isotube/Elevator (EUROPEAN PATENT: APPLICATION: PROCEDURE: ERROR BY APPLICANT MUST BE CORRECTED: FEES: REIMBURSEMENT OF APPEAL FEE: T76/82: EPO)   [1979–85] E.P.O.R. B495

ISS Management (Aust.) Pty Ltd v. Vulcan Australia Ltd (TRADE MARK: OPPOSITION: IDENTICAL MARKS: GOODS OF SAME DESCRIPTION: Australia: Pat. Off.)   4 I.P.R. 129

Isuzu/Correction of designation (EUROPEAN PATENT: AMENDMENT AND CORRECTION: DESIGNATION OF STATES: EVIDENCE: NATIONAL LAW, AS TO: J08/89: EPO)   [1990] E.P.O.R. 55

Italy v. Caldana (CONSUMER PROTECTION: PRODUCT SAFETY: LABELLING: DIFFERENCE BETWEEN DANGEROUS SUBSTANCES AND DANGEROUS PREPARATIONS: Case 187/84: ECJ)
[1989] 1 C.M.L.R. 137; [1985] E.C.R. 3013

Italy v. E.C. Commission (Re British Telecommunications) (RESTRICTIVE PRACTICES: MONOPOLIES: STATE ENTERPRISES: ECJ PROCEDURE: TREATIES: Case 41/83: ECJ)
[1985] 2 C.M.L.R. 368; [1985] E.C.R. 3013; [1985] F.S.R. 510

ITC Film Distributors Ltd v. Video Exchange Ltd (COPYRIGHT: INFRINGEMENT: ADMISSIBILITY OF EVIDENCE OBTAINED BY TRICKERY IN COURT PRECINCT: PUBLIC POLICY: Ch.D.)   [1982] 2 All E.R. 241; [1982] Ch. 431

Item/Inspection of files (EUROPEAN PATENT: APPLICATION: PROCEDURE: INSPECTION OF FILE: LOST PURPOSE: INSPECTION: INVOCATION OF RIGHTS: J27/87: EPO)   [1988] E.P.O.R. 282

ITP Pty Ltd v. United Capital Pty Ltd (COPYRIGHT: INFRINGEMENT: LITERARY
WORK: COMPILATION: INTERLOCUTORY INJUNCTION: Australia: S.C.(Qd))
5 I.P.R. 315
Ivoclar AG's Agreement (No. 2) (RESTRICTIVE PRACTICES: EXCLUSIVE
DISTRIBUTION AGREEMENT: INTENTION TO EXTEND EXEMPTION: NOTICE:
E.C. Comm.) [1994] 4 C.M.L.R. 578
Ixora Trading Incorporated v. Jones (BREACH OF CONFIDENCE: BREACH OF DUTY
OF FIDELITY: EX-EMPLOYEE'S: STATEMENT OF CLAIM FRIVOLOUS AND
VEXATIOUS: Ch.D.) [1990] F.S.R. 251

J. & W. Hardie Ltd v. Joseph E. Seargram & Sons Inc. (TRADE MARK: APPLICATION:
ANTIQUE/THE ANTIQUARY: HONEST CONCURRENT USER: India:
H.C.) (1991) 16 I.P.L.R. 255
J. N. Nicholas (Vimto) Ltd v. Rose & Thistle (TRADE MARK: APPLICATION:
WIMTO: CONFUSION WITH VIMTO AND VINTO: APPLICATION TO
EXPUNGE VINTO FOR NON-USE: SPECIAL CIRCUMSTANCES: APPEAL: India:
H.C.) (1995) 20 I.P.L.R. 32
See also, *sub nom.* Rose & Thistle v. J. N. Nicholas (Vimto) Ltd
Jackson v. Sterling Industries Ltd (TRADE PRACTICES: MAREVA INJUNCTION:
JURISDICTION: DAMAGES: UNDERTAKING: FAILURE OF COURT TO OBTAIN:
EFFECT: Australia: Fed. Ct) 8 I.P.R. 113
Jacuzzi Inc.'s Application (TRADE MARKS: WITHDRAWAL OF ACCEPTANCE FOR
REGISTRATION: CONFLICT WITH EARLIER APPLICATION: RELEVANCE OF
VALIDITY OF AMENDMENT OF CLASS OF GOODS IN RESPECT OF WHICH CITED
MARK WAS FILED: ACCEPTANCE IN ERROR: Australia: Pat. Off.)
17 I.P.R. 414
Jade Engineering (Coventry) Ltd v. Antiference Window Systems Ltd (DESIGN
RIGHT: INFRINGEMENT: IDENTITY OF SUPPLIER OF INFRINGING GOODS
SOUGHT: SUPPLIER NOT PARTY TO ACTION: *Norwich Pharmacal* ORDER:
WHETHER TORTFEASOR MUST BE IN U.K.: JURISDICTION: DISCOVERY:
PURPOSE: EXTENT: Ch.D.) [1996] F.S.R. 461
Jaguar Trade Mark (TRADE MARK: APPLICATION TO EXPUNGE: DISCRETION:
SIMILARITY BETWEEN MARKS: INTENTION TO DECEIVE: LIKELIHOOD OF
CONFUSION: Singapore: H.C.) [1993] 2 S.L.R. 466
Jain & Bros KK v. Paras Enterprises (TRADE MARK: INFRINGEMENT: PASSING OFF:
INTERIM INJUNCTION: India: H.C.) (1987) 11 I.P.L.R. 163
James Burrough Distillers plc v. Speymalt Whisky Distributors Ltd (TRADE MARK:
INFRINGEMENT ABROAD: PASSING OFF: INTERNATIONAL LAW: DOUBLE
ACTIONABILITY REQUIREMENT: NATURE OF TRADE MARKS: Scotland,
O.H.) 1989 S.L.T. 561; [1991] R.P.C. 130
James Hardie & Co. Pty Ltd v. Hardboards Australia Ltd (PATENT: OPPOSITION:
AMENDED SPECIFICATION: LACK OF NOVELTY: OBVIOUSNESS: Australia: Pat.
Off.) 3 I.P.R. 339
James Hardy Irrigation Pty Ltd v. Hydro Plan Engineering Ltd (PATENT:
APPLICATION: OPPOSITION: WITHDRAWAL: COSTS: Australia: AIPO)
28 I.P.R. 669
James Howden Australia Pty Ltd v. Flakt AB (PATENT: OPPOSITION: PRIOR
PUBLICATION: WORKING DRAWING AND BROCHURE SENT FROM OVERSEAS
MANUFACTURER: WHETHER CONFIDENTIAL: EVIDENCE: ANTICIPATION:
Australia: Pat. Off.) 8 I.P.R. 197

James Industries Ltd's Patent (PATENT: REVOCATION: PRIOR PUBLICATION: CONFIDENTIALITY OF DOCUMENT: ENTITLEMENT: WHETHER IMPLIED CONTRACTUAL TERM TO SHARE INVENTION: C.-G.)   [1987] R.P.C. 235

James North & Sons Ltd v. North Cape Textiles Ltd (PASSING OFF: TRADE MARK: INFRINGEMENT: PRACTICE: INJUNCTION: Scotland: England: C.A.)
[1985] E.C.C. 541; [1986] F.S.R. 28

James v. Australia & New Zealand Banking Group Ltd (PRACTICE: NO-CASE SUBMISSION: ELECTION NOT TO CALL EVIDENCE: Australia: Fed. Ct)
6 I.P.R. 540

James v. Australia & New Zealand Banking Group Ltd (TRADE PRACTICES: CONSUMER PROTECTION: MISLEADING CONDUCT: FINANCIAL ADVICE INDUCING AGREEMENT: PRACTICE: Australia: Fed. Ct)   4 I.P.R. 559

Jamesigns (Leeds) Ltd's Application (PATENT: OBVIOUSNESS: C.A.)
[1983] R.P.C. 68

Jamieson v. American Dairy Queen Corp. (TRADE MARKS: APPLICATION: OPPOSITION: PROPRIETORSHIP: Australia: Pat. Off.)   18 I.P.R. 101

Janak Mathuradas v. Union of India (TRADE MARK: LICENCE: PROHIBITION OF USE OF FOREIGN BRAND NAMES FOR INTERNAL SALES NOT A BAR TO GRANT: India: H.C.)   (1987) 12 I.P.L.R. 1

Janssen Pharmaceutica Pty Ltd v. Pfeizer Pty Ltd (TRADE PRACTICES: MISLEADING ADVERTISING: MANDATORY INJUNCTION TO PUBLISH CORRECTION: Australia: Fed. Ct)   6 I.P.R. 227

Japan Capsule Computers (U.K.) Ltd v. Sonic Games Sales (CONTEMPT: WANT OF PROSECUTION: APPLICATION TO DISMISS: DELAY: BLAME: C.A.)
[1988] F.S.R. 256

Japan Styrene Paper/Foam particles (EUROPEAN PATENT: ENLARGED BOARD OF APPEAL: REFERENCE REFUSED: PRIOR ART: UNINSPECTED PATENT APPLICATION: T444/88: EPO)   [1991] E.P.O.R. 94

Japan Styrene/Foamed articles (EUROPEAN PATENT: INVENTIVE STEP: BONUS EFFECT: OBVIOUS SELECTION OF KNOWN ALTERNATIVE: PREJUDICE: NOT TO BE EQUATED WITH ABSENCE OF DISCLOSURE IN PRIOR ART: T513/90: EPO)   [1994] E.P.O.R. 129

Jarvis v. Doman (PATENT: OPPOSITION: PRIOR PUBLICATION BY USE: KNOWLEDGE OR CONSENT OF APPLICANT: EVIDENCE: QUESTIONNAIRES: Australia: Pat. Off.)   3 I.P.R. 300

Jawahar Engineering Co. v. Jovahar Engineers Pvt. Ltd (TRADE MARK: INFRINGEMENT: PASSING OFF: India: H.C.)   (1983) 8 I.P.L.R. 116

Jean Patou Parfumeur v. Crisena Corp. Pty Ltd (TRADE MARKS: APPLICATION: OPPOSITION: IDENTICAL MARK REGISTERED FOR GOODS OF SAME DESCRIPTION: WHETHER HONEST CONCURRENT USER: Australia: Pat. Off.)   20 I.P.R. 660

Jeep Corp. v. Lion Industries (TRADE MARK: REGISTRATION: JEEP/CHHAP: India: T.M.Reg.)   (1978) 3 I.P.L.R. 119

Jeffrey Rogers Knitwear Productions Ltd v. Vinda (Knitwear) Manufacturing Co. (COPYRIGHT: INFRINGEMENT: PRACTICE: Ch.D.)   [1985] F.S.R. 184

Jellied Beef Trade Marks, Re (TRADE MARKS: NON-USE: JUSTIFICATION BY ILLEGALITY OF EXCLUSION FROM MARKET CONTRARY TO EEC LAWS: Germany: C.A.)   [1993] 1 C.M.L.R. 309; [1993] F.S.R. 484

Jelly's Music Hall Inc. v. Tripl-M Broadcasting Co. (PASSING OFF: INTERLOCUTORY INJUNCTION: ALLEGED PASSING OFF BY INTERRELATED RESPONDENT COMPANIES, EACH OPERATING A RADIO STATION, OF A NAME AND CONCEPT OPERATED BY THE APPLICANT AND KNOWN AS RADIO FREE: Australia: Fed. Ct)   26 I.P.R. 127

JENNY WREN Trade Mark (TRADE MARK: REGISTRATION: CLOTHING: SURNAME: PART A. REGISTRATION: SPECIAL CIRCUMSTANCES: BoT) [1991] R.P.C. 385

JGL Investments Proprietary's Application (TRADE MARK: REGISTRABILITY: ADAPTED TO DISTINGUISH: INHERENT ADAPTABILITY: DISTINCTIVE: DESCRIPTIVE: MISLEADING: CONFUSING AND DECEPTIVE: Australia: Pat. Off.) 13 I.P.R. 347

Jian Tools For Sales Inc. v. Roderick Manhattan Group Ltd (PASSING OFF: SOFTWARE FOR BUSINESS PLANS: BIZPLAN BUILDER: WHETHER DESCRIPTIVE: U.S. COMPANY WITHOUT PLACE OF BUSINESS IN U.K.: REPUTATION: ADEQUACY OF DAMAGES ON ROYALTY BASIS: EFFECT OF FORCED CHANGE OF NAME: BALANCE OF CONVENIENCE: DEFENDANTS AWARENESS OF PLAINTIFF'S OBJECTIONS: PRESERVATION OF STATUS QUO: Ch.D.) [1995] F.S.R. 947

JMK Magnusson/Locking device (EUROPEAN PATENT: APPLICATION: PROCEDURE: RE-DATING APPLICATION: EPO ACT WHERE APPLICANT MISLED: ABANDONMENT: ABANDONMENT OF PRIORITY DOES NOT REVIVE RIGHTS ALREADY LOST: J05/89: EPO) [1990] E.P.O.R. 248

JOB Trade Mark (TRADE MARK: RECTIFICATION: JOB FOR CIGARETTE PAPERS, ETC: REGISTERED USER AGREEMENT: WHETHER ESTOPPEL BY CONDUCT FROM APPLYING FOR RECTIFICATION: SUFFICIENCY OF CONTROL BY REGISTERED USER: DECEPTIVE USE OF MARK: T.M.Reg.) [1993] F.S.R. 118

JOCKEY Trade Mark (TRADE MARK: APPLICATION: NON-ALCOHOLIC DRINKS: OPPOSITION: WHETHER MARK DISTINCTIVE OR CAPABLE OF DISTINGUISHING: WHETHER DECEPTIVE IF NOT USED FOR DRINKS FOR JOCKEYS OR HAVING REGARD TO MARK JOKER/JOCKEY: LACK OF EVIDENCE: APPLICATION ALLOWED: T.M.Reg.) [1994] F.S.R. 269

Jogendra Nath Sen v. State (COPYRIGHT: INFRINGEMENT: CRIMINAL COMPLAINT: India: H.C.) (1993) 18 I.P.L.R. 201

Joginder Singh v. M/s Tobu Enterprises (P.) Ltd (REGISTERED DESIGN: TRICYCLES AND SEATS: CANCELLATION: PRIOR PUBLICATION: LACK OF NOVELTY: India: H.C.) (1989) 14 I.P.L.R. 24

Johann A. Wulfing v. Chemical Industrial & Pharmaceutical Laboratories Ltd (TRADE MARK: APPLICATION: OPPOSITION: CIPLAMINA/COMPLAMINA: India: H.C.) (1984) 9 I.P.L.R. 26

Johansson v. Institut National de la Propriete Industrielle (PATENTS: MEDICINES: SUPPLEMENTARY PROTECTION: France: C.A.) [1994] 1 C.M.L.R. 269

John (Elton) v. James (COPYRIGHT: ROYALTIES: PUBLISHING, RECORDING AND MANAGEMENT AGREEMENTS: LICENSING, SUB-PUBLISHING AGREEMENTS WITH PUBLISHERS' SUBSIDIARIES: UNDUE INFLUENCE: FIDUCIARY OBLIGATIONS: BREACH OF CONFIDENCE: FAIR DEALING: LIMITATION: LACHES: ACQUIESCENCE: ESTOPPEL: Ch.D.) [1991] F.S.R. 397

John (Elton) v. James, sub nom. Elton John v. James

John Baptiste Nella v. Kingia Pty Ltd (TRADE PRACTICES: MISLEADING AND DECEPTIVE CONDUCT: SALE OF BUSINESS: REPRESENTATION AS TO PROFITABILITY: Australia: Fed. Ct) 7 I.P.R. 55

John Deks Ltd v. Aztec Washer Co. (PATENT: INFRINGEMENT: PRACTICE: PLEADINGS: COMMERCIAL SUCCESS: Pat. Ct) [1989] R.P.C. 413

John Dumergue Charters's Application (PATENT: APPLICATION: EXAMINER'S OBJECTIONS: FAIRLY BASED: Australia: Pat. Off.) 16 I.P.R. 325

John Guest (Southern) Ltd's Patent (PATENT: REVOCATION: OFFICE PRACTICE: OBVIOUSNESS: DISCOVERY: Pat. Ct) [1987] R.P.C. 259

John Michael Design plc v. Cooke (RESTRAINT OF TRADE: EMPLOYMENT: AGREEMENT: TIME LIMITATION: INTERLOCUTORY INJUNCTION: C.A.)
[1987] F.S.R. 402; [1987] 2 All E.R. 332

John Richardson Computers Ltd v. Flanders (COPYRIGHT: PRACTICE: DISCHARGE OR VARIATION OF CONSENT ORDER ON CHANGE OF CIRCUMSTANCES: DUTY OF DUE DILIGENCE: WHETHER CONTEMPT OF COURT OR UNLAWFUL INTERFERENCE WITH TRADE: Ch.D.) [1992] F.S.R. 391

John Richardson Computers Ltd v. Flanders (COPYRIGHT: INFRINGEMENT: COMPUTER SOFTWARE: TITLE TO PORTIONS OF PROGRAM WRITTEN BY INDEPENDENT CONTRACTORS: WHETHER COPYING: WHETHER SUBSTANTIAL PART REPRODUCED: NO COPYING OF SOURCE CODE: APPROPRIATE TEST: ESTOPPEL: Ch.D.) [1993] F.S.R. 497; 26 I.P.R. 367

John Richardson Computers Ltd v. Flanders (COPYRIGHT: COMPUTER SOFTWARE: MINOR INFRINGEMENTS: FORM OF ORDER AND INJUNCTION: DAMAGES: PLAINTIFF'S RIGHT TO INQUIRY WHERE INFRINGEMENT SLIGHT: DEFENDANT'S RIGHT TO INQUIRY AS TO DAMAGES ON PLAINTIFF'S CROSS-UNDERTAKING: COSTS: APPROPRIATE ORDER WHERE WHOLESALE INFRINGEMENT ALLEGED BUT ONLY MINOR ESTABLISHED: Ch.D.)
[1994] F.S.R. 144

John Walker & Sons Ltd v. Douglas Laing & Co. Ltd (TRADE MARK: PASSING OFF: SCOTCH WHISKY: INTERDICT: BREACH: EXPORT OF SPIRIT CONTAINING MIXTURE OF SCOTCH WHISKY AND CANE SPIRIT: LABLES AND BOTTLES: ENABLING PASSING OFF: Scotland: O.H.) 1993 S.L.T. 156

John Weeks Pty Ltd v. Foodland Associated Ltd (TRADE MARK: REGISTRATION: RECTIFICATION: NON-USE: JURISDICTION: Australia: Fed. Ct) 74 A.L.R. 248

John Wyeth & Brother Ltd's Coloured Tablet Trade Mark (TRADE MARK: APPLICATION: OPPOSITION: COLOUR, SHAPE AND SIZE OF PHARMACEUTICAL TABLETS: DISTINCTIVENESS: T.M.Reg.) [1988] R.P.C. 233

John Wyeth & Brother Ltd's Application: Schering AG's Application (PATENT: APPLICATIONS: PHARMACEUTICAL USE: SECOND MEDICAL ACTIVITY OF KNOWN DRUG: NOVELTY: INDUSTRIAL APPLICATION: Pat. Ct)
[1985] R.P.C. 545

John Wyeth & Brother Ltd v. M. & A. Pharmachem Ltd (PASSING OFF: INTERLOCUTORY INJUNCTION: GET-UP: COLOURED PILL: SHAPE OF PILL: Ch.D.) [1988] F.S.R. 26

Johns v. Australian Securities Commission (CONFIDENTIAL INFORMATION: ROYAL COMMISSION INVESTIGATION: RELEASE OF TRANSCRIPTS: PUBLIC DOMAIN: REMEDIES: WHETHER ENTITLED TO ORDER RESTRAINING PUBLICATION OF TRANSCRIPTS: Australia: Fed. Ct) 108 A.L.R. 277
(H.C.) 116 A.L.R. 567

Johnson & Bloy (Holdings) Ltd v. Wolstenholme Rink plc (BREACH OF CONFIDENCE: EX-EMPLOYEE: NATURE OF INFORMATION: SCOPE OF INJUNCTION: C.A.) [1989] 1 F.S.R. 135

Johnson & Johnson's Application (TRADE MARK: APPLICATION: SERIES OF MARKS, WHAT CONSTITUTES: Australia: AIPO) 28 I.P.R. 167

Johnson & Johnson's Application (TRADE MARK: OPPOSITION: INADINE/ANADIN: Ch.D.) (1992) 17 I.P.L.R. 195

Johnson & Johnson's Application (TRADE MARK: PRACTICE: APPEAL: NOTICE OF ORIGINATING MOTION: Ch.D.) [1991] R.P.C. 1

Johnson & Johnson Australia Pty Ltd v. Sterling Pharmaceuticals Pty Ltd (TRADE MARKS: REGISTRATION: CAPLETS: MEDICATED TABLETS FOR HUMAN USE: NON-USE: INFRINGEMENT: USE AS A TRADE MARK: SURVEY EVIDENCE: Australia: Fed. Ct) 101 A.L.R. 700; 21 I.P.R. 1

Johnson & Johnson v. Boehringer Ingelheim KG (TRADE MARK: OPPOSITION: RESTRICTION OF STATEMENT OF GOODS: FURTHER DECISION: Australia: AIPO) 32 I.P.R. 220

Johnson & Johnson v. Christine Hoden India (Pvt.) Ltd (TRADE MARK: INFRINGEMENT: PASSING OFF: STAYFREE: INTERIM INJUNCTION: India: H.C.) (1986) 11 I.P.L.R. 37
(INTERIM INJUNCTION: APPEAL: H.C.) (1988) 13 I.P.L.R. 57

Johnson & Johnson v. Christine Hoden India (Pvt.) Ltd (TRADE MARK: APPLICATION: STAYFREE: OPPOSITION: DESCRIPTIVE: INCAPABLE OF DISTINGUISHING: DISCRETION: India: T.M.Reg.) (1990) 15 I.P.L.R. 96

Johnson & Johnson v. Kalnin (TRADE MARKS: APPLICATION FOR REGISTRATION: OPPOSITION: EXISTING REGISTRATION BY OPPONENT: WHETHER LIKELIHOOD FOR DECEPTION OR CONFUSION: Australia: Fed. Ct)
26 I.P.R. 435

Johnson & Johnson v. S.C. Johnson & Son Inc. (TRADE MARK: WHETHER CONFUSING: PROPRIETORSHIP: HONEST CONCURRENT USE: Australia: T.M.Reg.) 3 I.P.R. 429

Johnson & Johnson/Polylactide (EUROPEAN PATENT: AMENDMENT AND CORRECTION: OBVIOUS MISTAKE, STANDARD OF PROOF: INVENTIVE STEP: REVERSAL OF TREND: PRIOR ART: INTERPRETATION AS A DATE OF PUBLICATION: T581/91: EPO) [1994] E.P.O.R. 259

Johnson & Son Inc. v. Klensan (Pty) Ltd t/a Markrite (TRADE NAME: PASSING OFF: REPUTATION: South Africa: TPD) 1982 (4) S.A. 579

Johnson (H. & R.) Tiles Ltd v. Candy Tiles Ltd (PATENT: INFRINGEMENT: PRACTICE: LATE APPLICATION TO SUBMIT EVIDENCE: Ch.D.)
[1985] F.S.R. 253

Johnson (S.C.) & Son Inc.'s Application (TRADE MARKS: APPLICATION: DESCRIPTIVE: TECHNICAL MEANING NOT RELEVANT: DIRECT REFERENCE TO GOODS: EVIDENCE OF USE NOT PERSUASIVE: NOT REGISTRABLE IN PART A OR PART B OF THE REGISTER: Australia: Pat. Off.) 15 I.P.R. 349

Johnson Electric Industrial Manufactory Ltd v. Mabuchi-Motor KK (PATENT: AMENDMENT BY DELETION: DELAY: DISCRETION: INFRINGEMENT: IMMATERIAL VARIANT: VALIDITY: OBVIOUSNESS: COMBINATION OF KNOWN TECHNIQUES: Pat. Ct) [1996] F.S.R. 93
(PATENT: INFRINGEMENT: THREATS: JURISDICTION: Pat. Ct)
[1996] F.S.R. 280

Johnson Matthey/Priority declaration (EUROPEAN PATENT: AMENDMENT AND CORRECTION: PRIORITY CLAIM: FEES: REIMBURSEMENT OF APPEAL FEE: J14/82: EPO) [1979–85] E.P.O.R. A132; [1983] O.J. EPO 121

Johnstone Safety Ltd v. Peter Cook (International) plc (COPYRIGHT: INFRINGEMENT: ROAD CONES: CREDIBILITY OF WITNESS: TEST FOR SUBSTANTIAL PART: C.A.) [1990] F.S.R. 161

Joint Research & Development Regulation 1984–92 (418/85) (RESTRICTIVE PRACTICES: GROUP EXEMPTION: JOINT RESEARCH AND DEVELOPMENT: TEXT OF REGULATION 418/85 AS AMENDED BY REGULATION 151/93: E.C. Comm.) [1993] 4 C.M.L.R.163

Jonathan Sceats Design Pty Ltd's Application (TRADE MARKS: OBJECTION TO ALLOWANCE OF EXTENSION OF TIME FOR SERVICE OF EVIDENCE IN SUPPORT OF OPPOSITION: Australia: Pat. Off.) 15 I.P.R. 59

Jonsered Motor AB's Application (TRADE MARK: APPLICATION: CITATION: DECEPTIVE SIMILARITY: GOODS OF THE SAME DESCRIPTION: GEOGRAPHICAL NAME: TRADE MARK USED IN PLURAL FORM: Australia: AIPO) 27 I.P.R. 267

Joose Agencies Pty Ltd v. Maglificio Biellese Fratelli Fila SpA (TRADE MARK: OPPOSITION: LIKELIHOOD OF DECEPTION OR CONFUSION: MANNER OF USE: EVIDENCE OF USE: Australia: Pat. Off.) 5 I.P.R. 411

Jordache Enterprises Inc. v. Millenium Pte Ltd (TRADE MARK: INFRINGEMENT: JEANS: PRONUNCIATION OF TRADE NAME: DECEPTION AND CONFUSION: PASSING OFF: REPUTATION: PRACTICE: COSTS: Singapore: H.C.)
[1988] 2 M.L.J. 281; 7 I.P.R. 575

Jorge UA v. Registro de la Propiedad Industrial (TRADE MARKS: BIOLOGICAL VARIETIES: GENERIC TERMS: Spain: S.C.) [1988] 3 C.M.L.R. 133

Jos Schlitz Brewing Co. v. Containers Ltd (PATENT: APPLICATION: OPPOSITION: PRIOR PUBLICATION: NOVELTY: CONFIDENTIALITY: Australia: Pat. Off.)
8 I.P.R. 491

Joyce v. Sengupta (PRACTICE: PLEADINGS: STRIKING OUT: ABUSE OF PROCESS OF COURT: NEWSPAPER ARTICLE GIVING RISE TO CAUSES OF ACTION FOR DEFAMATION AND MALICIOUS FALSEHOOD: LEGAL AID GRANTED FOR ACTION FOR MALICIOUS FALSEHOOD: WHETHER ACTION ABUSE OF PROCESS OF COURT: MALICIOUS FALSEHOOD: LIBEL AND SLANDER: CHOICE OF ACTION: DEFENDANT MAKING FALSE STATEMENT ABOUT PLAINTIFF: DAMAGES: NATURE: C.A.) [1993] 1 All E.R. 897; [1993] 1 W.L.R. 337

JSR/Block copolymer (EUROPEAN PATENT: CLAIMS: CONSTRUCTION: IMPLICIT FEATURES: COSTS: APPORTIONMENT: OPPOSITION: PROCEDURE: FRESH DOCUMENTS ON APPEAL: T416/87: EPO)
[1991] E.P.O.R. 25; [1990] O.J. EPO 415

JSR/Impact resistant resin composition (EUROPEAN PATENT: OPPOSITION: PROCEDURE: FRESH GROUND ON APPEAL: ORAL PROCEEDINGS: ABSOLUTE ENTITLEMENT: SUFFICIENCY: EXCESSIVE EXPERIMENTATION: COSTS: LOCATION OF PARTY IRRELEVANT: REQUEST FOR ORAL PROCEEDINGS DOES NOT JUSTIFY SPECIAL ORDER: T79/88: EPO) [1992] E.P.O.R. 387

Jus-Rol Ltd and Rich Products Corp.'s Agreement (RESTRICTIVE PRACTICES: KNOW-HOW: MANUFACTURE OF FROZEN YEAST DOUGH: LICENCE AGREEMENT: INTENTION TO APPROVE: NOTIFICATION: E.C. Comm.)
[1988] 4 C.M.L.R. 12
(DECISION: E.C. COMM.) [1988] 4 C.M.L.R. 527; [1988] F.S.R. 528

Just Jeans Pty Ltd v. Westco Jeans (Aust.) Pty Ltd (TRADE MARKS: MISLEADING OR DECEPTIVE CONDUCT: SIMILAR ADVERTISING SIGNS: EFFECT OF DELIBERATE COPYING: Australia: Fed. Ct) 12 I.P.R. 403

Just Jeans Pty Ltd v. Westco Jeans (Aust.) Pty Ltd (TRADE PRACTICES: MISLEADING OR DECEPTIVE CONDUCT: SIMILAR ADVERTISING SIGNS: Australia: Fed. Ct)
13 I.P.R. 661

Juta & Co. Ltd v. De Koker (COPYRIGHT: INFRINGEMENT: SUBSTANTIAL PART: South Africa: TPD) 1994 (3) S.A. 499

K Mart Corp. v. A-Mart Allsports Pty Ltd (TRADE MARKS: APPLICATIONS: OPPOSITION: GOODS AND SERVICES: RETAILING: SUBSTANTIAL IDENTITY: DECEPTIVE SIMILARITY: USE: CONCURRENT USE: HONEST USE: CONDITION OF REGISTRATION: Australia: Pat. Off.) 23 I.P.R. 161

K Mart Corp. v. Artline Furnishers Supermarkets Pty Ltd (TRADE MARK: APPLICATION: OPPOSITION: SUBSTANTIAL IDENTITY: DECEPTIVE SIMILARITY: USE: CONCURRENT USE: HONEST USE: CONDITION OF REGISTRATION: Australia: Pat. Off.) 23 I.P.R. 149

K.R. Jadayappa Mudaliar v. K.S. Venkatachalam (TRADE MARK: UNLICENSED USE: INJUNCTION VACATED: India: H.C.) (1989) 14 I.P.L.R. 111

K. SABATIER Trade Mark (TRADE MARK: RECTIFICATION: IMPORTER'S OR MANUFACTURER'S MARK: T.M.Reg.) [1993] R.P.C. 97

K.T. Technology (S.) Pte Ltd v. Tomlin Holdings Pty Ltd (TRADE MARKS: APPLICATION: OPPOSITION: EXTENSION OF TIME: Australia: Pat. Off.) 20 I.P.R. 446

K-Corporation of Japan/*Restitutio in integrum* (EUROPEAN PATENT: RE-ESTABLISHMENT OF RIGHTS: NON-RECEIPT OF INFORMATION FROM EPO: J23/87: EPO) [1988] E.P.O.R. 52

Ka Wah International Merchant Finance Ltd v. Asean Resources Ltd (PRACTICE: PROCEDURE: MAREVA INJUNCTION: FOREIGN ASSETS: Hong Kong: H.C.) 8 I.P.R. 241

Ka-Te System/Intervention (EUROPEAN PATENT: INTERVENTION: ADMISSIBILITY: T27/92: EPO) [1994] E.P.O.R. 501; [1994] O.J. EPO 853

Kabelmetal/Combination claim (EUROPEAN PATENT: CLAIMS: EXTENT OF PROTECTION: T175/84: EPO) [1989] E.P.O.R. 181; [1989] O.J. EPO 71

Kabushiki Kaisha Sigma, *sub nom.* Sigma, KK

Kaken Pharmaceutical Co. Ltd's Patent (PATENT: LICENCE OF RIGHT: PRACTICE: INTERVENTION BY FORMER EXCLUSIVE LICENCEE: C.-G.) [1990] R.P.C. 72

Kakkar v. Szelke (EUROPEAN PATENT: ENTITLEMENT: JURISDICTION TO DETERMINE: C.A.) [1989] E.P.O.R. 284

Kalamazoo (Aust.) Pty Ltd v. Compact Business Systems Pty Ltd (COPYRIGHT: NATURE AND SUBJECT-MATTER: ORIGINAL LITERARY WORK: COMPILATION: INFRINGEMENT: REMEDIES: DAMAGES: MATTERS AFFECTING RIGHT TO DAMAGES: Australia: H.C.) (1990) 1 Qd.R. 231

Kali Aerated Water Works v. Rashid (TRADE MARK: PASSING OFF: KALI MARK/ SRI NEW KALI MARK: AERATED WATER: DECLARATION: INJUNCTION: India: H.C.) (1989) 13 I.P.L.R. 223

Kall-Kwik Printing (U.K.) Ltd v. Bell (FRANCHISE AGREEMENT: RESTRICTIVE COVENANT: ENFORCEABILITY: ARTICLE 85: REASONABLENESS: INTERLOCUTORY INJUNCTION: Ch.D.) [1994] F.S.R. 674

Kall-Kwik Printing (U.K.) Ltd v. Frank Clarence Rush (FRANCHISE AGREEMENT: RESTRICTIVE COVENANT: CONSTRUCTION ENFORCEABILITY: REASONABLENESS: INTERLOCUTORY INJUNCTION: Ch.D.) [1996] F.S.R. 114

Kalyani Breweries Ltd v. Khoday Brewing & Distilling Industries Ltd (TRADE MARK: INFRINGEMENT: KALYANI BLACK LABEL/KHODAY BLACK LABEL: INJUNCTION: India: H.C.) (1993) 18 I.P.L.R. 132

Kamal Trading Co. v. Gillette U.K. Ltd (PASSING OFF: TRADE MARK: INFRINGEMENT: 7 O'CLOCK: INTERLOCUTORY INJUNCTION: APPEAL: India: H.C.) (1988) 12 I.P.L.R. 135

Kambrook Distributing Pty Ltd v. Delaney (COPYRIGHT: REPRODUCTION OF ORIGINAL DRAWINGS: ORIGINAL LOST OR DESTROYED: MODELS MADE FROM ORIGINAL DRAWINGS: MODELS LOST OR DESTROYED: EPOXY MOULDS MADE FROM MODELS: EPOXY MOULDS MOSTLY LOST AND DESTROYED: DIES MADE FROM EPOXY MOULDS: DIES STILL IN EXISTENCE: WHETHER DRAWING, MODELS, DIES AND PRODUCT CONSTITUTE ARTISTIC WORKS: ARTISTIC WORKS: INFRINGEMENT: OWNERSHIP: SKETCHES PREPARED BY MANAGING DIRECTOR: INTENTION AS TO OWNERSHIP OF RIGHTS IN DRAWINGS: CONFIRMATORY ASSIGNMENT FOR PURPOSE OF PROCEEDINGS: ORIGINAL SKETCHES REPRODUCED FROM MEMORY FOR PURPOSE OF PROCEEDINGS: INTERLOCUTORY INJUNCTIONS: SERIOUS QUESTION TO BE TRIED: BALANCE OF CONVENIENCE: DELAY: Ch.D.) 4 I.P.R. 79

Kanegafuchi/Coating compositions (EUROPEAN PATENT: INVENTIVE STEP: COMPARATIVE TESTS: NOVELTY: CROSS-REFERENCED DOCUMENTS: OPPOSITION: PROCEDURE: FRESH EVIDENCE ON APPEAL, ALLOWED: ONUS OF PROOF: T67/88: EPO) [1991] E.P.O.R. 88

Kansai Paint/Disapproval of specification by proprietor (EUROPEAN PATENT: REVOCATION: OPPOSITION: PROPRIETOR: TEXT OF PATENT: WITHDRAWAL OF APPROVAL: T230/84: EPO) [1986] E.P.O.R. 44

Karrimor International Ltd v. Ho Choong Fun (TRADE MARKS: EXPUNGEMENT: OWNERSHIP OF MARK: WORLDWIDE REPUTATION OF APPLICANT: PHONETIC SIMILARITY: SIMILARITY OF APPEARANCE BETWEEN PRODUCT: CONFUSION: Singapore: H.C.) [1989] 3 M.L.J. 467; 16 I.P.R. 171

Karu Pty Ltd v. Jose (TRADE MARK: REGISTRATION: OPPOSITION: APPEAL: GOODS IN DIFFERENT CLASSES: SUBSTANTIALLY IDENTICAL MARKS: Australia: Fed. Ct) 30 I.P.R. 407

Kastner v. Rizla Ltd (PATENT: INFRINGEMENT: INTERLEAVED CIGARETTE PAPERS: CONSTRUCTION: WHETHER *Catnic* APPROACH CONSISTENT WITH PROTOCOL: OBVIOUSNESS: C.A.) [1995] R.P.C. 585

Kawasaki Steel Corp. v. Broken Hill Pty Co. Ltd (PATENT: APPLICATION: OPPOSITION TO GRANT OF REQUEST TO AMEND: Australia: Pat. Off.) 13 I.P.R. 168

Kawasaki/Grain-oriented silicon sheet (EUROPEAN PATENT: OPPOSITION PROCEDURE: ORAL PROCEEDINGS: SUBSEQUENT FURTHER OBSERVATIONS: INVENTIVE STEP: PRODUCT: KNOWN *desideratum*: CAPABILITY OF MANUFACTURE: T595/90: EPO) [1995] E.P.O.R. 36; [1994] O.J. EPO 695

Kaye v. Robertson (PASSING OFF: MALICIOUS FALSEHOOD: LIBEL: TRESPASS TO THE PERSON: BREACH OF PRIVACY: NEWSPAPER INTERVIEW IN HOSPITAL WITH ACTOR WITH SEVERE HEAD INJURIES: CONSENT: JOURNALISTS GAINING ACCESS AND "INTERVIEWING" ACTOR: RIGHT TO PROTECTION OF PRIVACY: INTERLOCUTORY INJUNCTION: APPEAL: C.A.) [1991] F.S.R. 62; 19 I.P.R. 147

Keays v. Dempster (COPYRIGHT: PHOTOGRAPH: INFRINGEMENT: AUTHORISING COPYING: C.C., City of London) [1994] F.S.R. 554; [1994] E.M.L.R. 443

KEDS Trade Mark (TRADE MARKS: REGISTRY PRACTICE: REGISTRATION OF ASSIGNMENT OF MARK THE SUBJECT OF RECTIFICATION PROCEEDINGS: NO GROUNDS FOR REFUSAL: ASSOCIATED MARKS: REGISTRATION OF MARK TO BE ASSOCIATED NOT COMPLETE UNTIL ASSOCIATION ALSO ENTERED IN REGISTER: Ch.D.) [1993] F.S.R. 72

Keith Harris & Co. Ltd's Application (TRADE MARKS: OPPOSITION: PROPRIETORSHIP: FIRST USE: USE LIKELY TO DECEIVE OR CAUSE CONFUSION: DESCRIPTIVE MARK: JOINT USE OF TRADE MARKS: Australia: Pat. Off.) 15 I.P.R. 273

Kelly Services Inc. v. Drake Personnel Ltd (TRADE PRACTICES: MISLEADING OR DECEPTIVE CONDUCT: PASSING OFF: WHETHER NECESSARY FOR BUSINESS TO BE CARRIED ON IN THIS COUNTRY: Australia: Fed. Ct) 12 I.P.R. 367

Kennard v. Lewis (COPYRIGHT: INFRINGEMENT: CND PAMPHLET: FAIR DEALING: Ch.D.) [1983] F.S.R. 346

Kenner Parker Toys Inc.'s Application (TRADE MARK: OBJECTION: SURNAME: EXTENSIVE "HOUSE" MARK USER: Australia: Pat. Off.) 13 I.P.R. 29

Kenning v. Eve Construction Ltd (CONFIDENTIAL INFORMATION: EXPERT EVIDENCE: DISCLOSURE: REPORT SENT TO WRONG PARTY: Q.B.D.) [1989] 1 W.L.R. 1189

KENT Trade Mark (APPLICATION: GEOGRAPHICAL NAME: SURVEY EVIDENCE: PRACTICE: T.M.Reg.) [1985] R.P.C. 117

Kent-Moore Corp. v. Environmental Products Amalgamated Pty Ltd (PATENT: APPLICATION: OPPOSITION: APPLICATION FOR EXTENSION OF TIME FOR FILING EVIDENCE IN OPPOSITION: WHETHER EXTENSION JUSTIFIED: STATEMENT OF GROUNDS AND PARTICULARS: EFFECT OF STATEMENT ON APPLICATION FOR EXTENSION: FULL AND FRANK DISCLOSURE OF FACTS: Australia: Pat. Off.)   25 I.P.R. 233

Kentucky Tobacco Corp. (Pty) Ltd v. Registrar of Trade Marks (TRADE MARK: APPLICATION: KENTUCKY: GEOGRAPHICAL SIGNIFICANCE: COMPOSITE MARK: South Africa: TPD)   1984 (2) S.A. 335

Keown/Spring element (EUROPEAN PATENT: CLAIMS: ONE PART V. TWO PART: T278/86: EPO)   [1987] E.P.O.R. 299

Kerber/Wire link bands (EUROPEAN PATENT: INVENTIVE STEP: PATENTEE'S ASSOCIATION DISREGARDED: REMOTE ART: OPPOSITION: PROCEDURE: OBJECTION BY ONE OPPONENT PURSUED BY SECOND OPPONENT: PRIOR ART: NEIGHBOURING FIELDS: T28/87: EPO)
          [1989] E.P.O.R. 377; [1989] O.J. EPO 383

KERLONE Trade Mark (TRADE MARK: PARALLEL IMPORTS OF PHARMACEUTICALS FROM FRANCE TO GERMANY: DIFFERENT PACKAGING REQUIREMENTS: REPACKAGING: VISIBILITY OF MARK THROUGH WINDOW IN NEW PACKAGING: INFRINGEMENT: ARTICLE 36(1): Germany: C.A.)
          [1993] C.M.L.R. 190

Kerr v. Morris (RESTRAINT OF TRADE: NHS DOCTOR: VALIDITY OF COVENANT: PUBLIC INTEREST: C.A.)
          [1986] 3 All E.R. 217; [1987] 1 Ch. 90; [1986] 3 W.L.R. 662

Kervan Trading Pty Ltd v. Aktas (COPYRIGHT: FILMS: STATUTORY PROVISIONS: LICENCE: EXCLUSIVITY: CONSTRUCTION OF DOCUMENT: Australia: S.C.(NSW))   8 I.P.R. 583

Kettle Chip Co. Pty Ltd v. Apand Pty Ltd (formerly CCA Snack Foods Pty Ltd) (PASSING OFF: USE OF NAME, SYMBOL AND GET-UP RESEMBLING THOSE OF APPLICANT: TEST FOR COMPARISON: SIMILARITY OF PACKAGING: COMMON ELEMENTS: USE OF WORD "KETTLE" TO DESCRIBE GOODS: ACCOUNT OF PROFITS: SURVEY EVIDENCE: ADMISSIBILITY: STATEMENTS ADMITTING DECEPTION: Australia: Fed. Ct)   119 A.L.R. 156; 27 I.P.R. 321
sub nom. Apand Pty Ltd v. Kettle Chip Co. Pty Ltd   30 I.P.R. 337

Kettle Chip Co. Pty Ltd v. Pepsico Australia Pty Ltd (TRADE MARK: KETTLE THINS/DOUBLE CRUNCH KETTLE COOKED POTATO CHIPS: DESCRIPTIVE WORDS: QUALITY OF GOODS: Australia: Fed. Ct)
          132 A.L.R. 286; 32 I.P.R. 302
(TRADE MARK: APPEAL: Australia: Fed. Ct)   135 A.L.R. 192

Keurkoop BV v. Nancy Kean Gifts BV (INDUSTRIAL DESIGN: APPLICATION OF ARTICLE 36: Case 144/81: ECJ)
          [1983] 2 C.M.L.R. 47; [1983] F.S.R. 381; [1982] E.C.R. 2853

Kevin McNamara Pty Ltd's Application (DESIGNS: APPLICATION: NOVELTY: ORIGINALITY: TENNIS COURT FENCE: WHETHER "ARTICLE" WITHIN MEANING OF ACT: Australia: D.Reg)   7 I.P.R. 335

Kevlacat Pty Ltd v. Trailcraft Marine Pty Ltd (COPYRIGHT: ARTISTIC WORKS: REPRODUCTION: INFRINGEMENT: DEFENCE: INDUSTRIAL APPLICATION: CORRESPONDING DESIGN: DUAL PROTECTION UNDER COPYRIGHT AND DESIGN LEGISLATION: Australia: Fed. Ct)   11 I.P.R. 77; 81 A.L.R. 534

Keybrand Foods Inc. v. Guinchard (EX-EMPLOYEE: PRODUCT RECIPE: PROOF: INTERLOCUTORY INJUNCTION: Canada: H.C.(Ont. Div.))33 C.P.R. (3d) 381

Khaitan (India) Ltd v. Metropolitan Appliances (REGISTERED DESIGN: SUBSEQUENT REGISTRATION OF IDENTICAL DESIGN: CANCELLATION: India: H.C.)
(1993) 18 I.P.L.R. 251

Khanshiram Surinder Kumar v. Thakurdas Deomal Rohira (TRADE MARK: RECTIFICATION: APPEAL: India: H.C.) (1983) 7 I.P.L.R. 4

K.I. George v. Cheriyan (COPYRIGHT: EXCLUSIVE LICENCE: JURISDICTION: India: H.C.) (1986) 11 I.P.L.R. 9

Kiama Constructions v. M.C. Casella Building Co. Pty Ltd (COPYRIGHT: HOUSE PLANS: "ARTISTIC WORK": ORIGINALITY: WHETHER DRAWINGS INFRINGED COPYRIGHT: WHETHER HOUSE INFRINGED COPYRIGHT: NON-EXPERT DEFENCE: Australia: S.C.(W.A.)) 10 I.P.R. 345

Kickers International S.A. v. Paul Kettle Agencies Ltd (PRACTICE: INTERLOCUTORY INJUNCTION: COSTS: BALANCING RISKS OF INJUSTICE: WHEN TO BE TAXED: Ch.D.) [1990] F.S.R. 436

Kikken Sohansha KK's (Nikken Sohansha Corp.'s) Application (TRADE MARK: APPLICATION: DISCOVERY OF MARK AS BOTANICAL TERM SUBSEQUENT TO ACCEPTANCE: ACCEPTANCE WITHDRAWN: Australia: AIPO) 28 I.P.R. 599

Kimberly-Clark Corp. v. Procter & Gamble Co. (PATENT: OPPOSITION: APPLICATION FOR EXTENSION OF TIME TO FILE EVIDENCE IN SUPPORT: APPLICABILITY OF OLD ACT LAW: WHETHER SERIOUS OPPOSITION IN TRAIN: PUBLIC INTEREST: EXTENSIONS GRANTED: Costs: Australia: Pat. Off.)
20 I.P.R. 425; 24 I.P.R. 345

Kimberly-Clark Ltd v. Commissioner of Patent (PATENT: EXTENSION OF TIME FOR LODGING NOTICE OF OPPOSITION TO THE GRANT OF A PATENT: ADMINISTRATIVE DECISIONS: JUDICIAL REVIEW: STAY OR DISMISSAL OF PROCEEDINGS: EXISTENCE OF OTHER RIGHTS OF REVIEW: Australia: Fed. Ct) 84 A.L.R. 685; 13 I.P.R. 62

Kimberly-Clark Ltd v. Commissioner of Patents (JUDICIAL REVIEW: DISCRETION TO REFUSE BECAUSE OF OTHER RIGHTS AVAILABLE: PATENT: APPLICATION: OPPOSITION: EXTENSION OF TIME WITHIN WHICH TO LODGE NOTICE OF OPPOSITION TO GRANT: ALTERNATIVE GROUNDS FOR EXTENSION: Australia: Fed. Ct) 83 A.L.R. 714

Kimberly-Clark Ltd v. Commissioner of Patents (No. 2) (ADMINISTRATIVE LAW: ADMINISTRATIVE APPEALS TRIBUNAL (COMMONWEALTH): REVIEW OF DECISIONS: AWARD OF COSTS: PATENT: OPPOSITION TO GRANT: EXTENSION OF TIME: RELEVANT MATTERS: Australia: AAT) 13 I.P.R. 551

Kimberly-Clark Ltd v. Commissioner of Patents (No. 3) (PATENT: OPPOSITION TO GRANT: EXTENSION OF TIME: CONSTRUCTION: "ERROR OR OMISSION": "BY REASON OF": Australia: Fed. Ct) 13 I.P.R. 569

Kingdom of Spain v. Council of the European Union, *sub nom.* Spain v. Council of the European Union.

Kirin-Amgen/Erythropoietin (EUROPEAN PATENT: SUFFICIENCY OF CLAIM: BURDEN OF PROOF: BEST MODE: NOVELTY: INVENTIVE STEP: SKILLED PERSON: TEAM: PROCESS-BY-PROCESS CLAIM: AMENDMENT: RELATIVE TERM: GREY AREA: OPPOSITION PROCEDURE: FUNCTION OF ORAL PROCEEDINGS: ASSOCIATED LITIGATION ELSEWHERE: LIMITATION OF EPO PROCEEDINGS: T412/93: EPO) [1995] E.P.O.R. 629

Kirra Collectables Pty Ltd v. Pewter Products Pty Ltd (TRADE MARK: OPPOSITION: KIRRA: EARLIER REGISTRATION: WHETHER GOODS OF THE SAME DESCRIPTION: Australia: AIPO) 31 I.P.R. 657

Kissan Industries v. Punjab Food Corp. (TRADE MARK: PASSING OFF: COPYRIGHT: INFRINGEMENT: India: H.C.) (1984) 8 I.P.L.R. 131

Kitechnology BV v. Unicor GmbH Plastmaschinen (CONFIDENTIAL INFORMATION: BREACH OF CONTRACT: PRACTICE: PLEADINGS: STRIKING OUT: JURISDICTION: EEC JUDGMENTS CONVENTION: C.A.)   [1995] F.S.R. 765
Kitechnology BV v. Unicorn GmbH Rahn Plastmaschinen (JURISDICTION: E.C. JUDGMENTS CONVENTION: PLACE OF COMMISSION OF TORT: CONFIDENTIAL INFORMATION: BREACH: Ch.D.)   [1994] I.L.Pr. 560; [1994] I.L.Pr. 568
Kiwi Coders Corp.'s Application (PATENT: APPLICATION: DIVISIONAL APPLICATION: PRACTICE: DISCRETION: Pat. Ct)   [1986] R.P.C. 106
Kleeneze Ltd v. DRG (U.K.) Ltd (COPYRIGHT: INFRINGEMENT: WHETHER CONCEPT OR SKILL AND LABOUR IN DRAWING COPIED: Ch.D.)
      [1984] F.S.R. 399
Klein Schanzlin & Becker AG's Application (PATENT: PRACTICE: DECLARATION OF PRIORITY: C.-G.)   [1985] R.P.C. 241
Klep Valves (Pty) Ltd v. Saunders Valve Co. Ltd (COPYRIGHT: SUBSISTENCE OF: INFRINGEMENT: TRADE MARK: INFRINGEMENT: South Africa: A.D.)
      1987 (2) S.A. 1
KLINT Trade Marks (TRADE MARK: IMPORTS: COMMON ORIGIN: SEPARATELY CREATED TRADE MARK FOR SAME PRODUCT: ARTICLE 30: INFRINGEMENT: Germany: S.C.)   [1988] 1 C.M.L.R. 340; [1988] F.S.R. 264
Klissers Farmhouse Bakeries Ltd v. Harvest Bakeries Ltd (No. 2) (INTERIM INJUNCTION: PRACTICE: H.C.: C.A.)   5 I.P.R. 399; [1985] 2 N.Z.L.R. 129
Klissers Farmhouse Bakeries Ltd v. Harvest Bakeries Ltd (No. 2) (PASSING OFF: COPYRIGHT: FEATURES COMMON TO THE TRADE: New Zealand: H.C.)
      [1985] 2 N.Z.L.R. 143; 5 I.P.R. 533
Klissers Farmhouse Bakeries Ltd v. Harvest Bakeries Ltd (PASSING OFF: MISREPRESENTATION: GET-UP: DISTINCTIVENESS: BREAD BAGS: DESIGN: ELEMENTS COMMON TO TRADE: PROTECTION WITHIN LIMITED GEOGRAPHICAL AREA: New Zealand: C.A.)
      10 I.P.R. 481; [1988] 1 N.Z.L.R. 16; [1989] R.P.C. 27
Klöckner Stahl GmbH, Krupp Stahl AG and Thyssen Stahl AG (joint venture between) (RESTRICTIVE PRACTICES: COAL AND STEEL: AUTHORISATION: E.C. Comm.)   [1988] 4 C.M.L.R. 753
Klostermann/Steel radiators (EUROPEAN PATENT: OPPOSITION: PROCEDURE: COMMUNICATION BY BOARD, WHEN REQUIRED: LATE SUBMISSION, TIME FOR RESPONSE: ORAL PROCEEDINGS: POSTPONEMENT: T275/89: EPO)   [1992] E.P.O.R. 260; [1992] O.J. EPO 126
Knoll International Gavina SpA v. Sàrl Aliotta Diffusion (IMPORTS: DESIGN COPYRIGHT: EXHAUSTION OF RIGHTS: NO DESIGN RIGHT UNDER ITALIAN LAW: ARTICLE 36(1) EEC: France: S.C.)   [1991] 2 C.M.L.R. 597
Know-How Licences (Draft Regulation) (RESTRICTIVE PRACTICES: GROUP EXEMPTIONS: KNOW-HOW AGREEMENTS: E.C. Comm.)
      [1987] 3 C.M.L.R. 144
Know-How Licensing Agreements (Post Term Use Bans), *sub nom.* Know-how Licensing Agreements (Post Term Use Bans)
Know-How Licensing Agreements Regulation (556/89) (KNOW-HOW LICENSING AGREEMENTS: APPLICATION OF ARTICLE 85(3): E.C. Comm.)
      [1989] O.J. L61 11
Know-How Licensing Regulation 1988 (RESTRICTIVE PRACTICES: GROUP EXEMPTION: KNOW-HOW LICENSING: E.C. Comm.) [1989] 4 C.M.L.R. 774
Know-How Licensing Regulation 1988–92 (RESTRICTIVE PRACTICES: GROUP EXEMPTION: KNOW-HOW LICENSING: TEXT OF REGULATION 556/89 AS AMENDED BY REGULATION 151/93: E.C. Comm.)   [1993] 4 C.M.L.R. 195

Knox D'Arcy Ltd v. Jamieson (TRADE MARK: UNLAWFUL COMPETITION: CONFIDENTIAL INFORMATION: EX-EMPLOYEE: DISTINCTION BETWEEN "TRADE SECRETS" AND OTHER CONFIDENTIAL INFORMATION: South Africa: WLD) 1992 (3) S.A. 520

Koch & Sterzel/X-ray apparatus (EUROPEAN PATENT: PATENTABILITY: COMPUTER-RELATED INVENTIONS: NATIONAL PRACTICES IRRELEVANT: ENLARGED BOARD OF APPEAL: REFERENCE REFUSED: T26/86: EPO)
[1988] E.P.O.R. 72; [1988] O.J. EPO 19

Kodak Ltd v. Reed International plc (PRACTICE: MOTION: ADJOURNED MOTION TO TRIAL: COSTS: Ch.D.) [1986] F.S.R. 477

Kodak/Crown ether (EUROPEAN PATENT: CLAIMS: FUNCTIONAL FEATURES: SUPPORT FOR: SUFFICIENCY: CLAIMED SUBJECT-MATTER, REPRODUCIBILITY OF: T238/88: EPO) [1993] E.P.O.R. 100; [1992] O.J. EPO 709

Kodak/Photographic couplers (EUROPEAN PATENT: INVENTIVE STEP: COMPARATIVE TESTS: T197/86: EPO)
[1989] E.P.O.R. 395; [1989] O.J. EPO 371

KODIAK Trade Mark (TRADE MARK: RECTIFICATION: NON-USE: PERSON AGGRIEVED: C.A.) [1987] R.P.C. 269

Kodiak Trade Mark (TRADE MARK: RECTIFICATION: NON-USE: USE ON GOODS ADVERTISING OTHER GOODS: WHETHER USE AS TRADE MARK: Ch.D.)
[1990] F.S.R. 49

Koelman v. E.C. Commission (RESTRICTIVE PRACTICES: BROADCASTING: RETRANSMISSION OF PROGRAMMES BY CABLE: STANDARD AGREEMENT: COPYRIGHT: OWNERSHIP: RADIO MATERIAL: COLLECTING SOCIETY: ALLEGED BREACH OF ARTICLES 85 AND 86: Case T-575/93: CFI)
[1996 4 C.M.L.R. 636

Kogyo Gijutsuin/Photosensitive resins (EUROPEAN PATENT: OPPOSITION: ADMISSIBILITY: IDENTIFICATION OF OPPONENT: TYPE OF EVIDENCE NECESSARY: SERIOUS PROCEDURAL VIOLATION (NO): T590/93: EPO)
[1995] E.P.O.R. 478; [1995] O.J. EPO 337

Koh Electronics Trading v. Libra Electronics Pty Ltd (TRADE MARK: OPPOSITION: PROPRIETORSHIP: FIRST USE: LIKELIHOOD OF DECEPTION OR CONFUSION: BLAMEWORTHY CONDUCT: IDENTICAL MARKS: COPYING OF OVERSEAS MARK: COPYRIGHT PROPRIETORSHIP ON TRADE MARK: GOODS OF SAME DESCRIPTION: Australia: AIPO) 29 I.P.R. 562

Kohler Company's Trade Mark Application (TRADE MARK: APPLICATION: PRACTICE: DEVICE MARK: Ch.D.) [1984] R.P.C. 125

Kolbenschmidt/Competence of Legal Board of Appeal (EUROPEAN PATENT: ENLARGED BOARD OF APPEAL: COMPETENCE: WHETHER DELEGABLE TO VICE-PRESIDENTS: T272/90: EPO)[1991] E.P.O.R. 493; [1991] O.J. EPO 205

Kolbenschmidt/Responsibility of the Legal Board of Appeal (EUROPEAN PATENT: EPO: OBSERVATIONS BY PRESIDENT: LEGAL BOARD OF APPEAL: POWERS OF: FORMALITIES SECTION: POWERS OF: G02/90: EPO)
[1992] E.P.O.R. 125; [1992] O.J. EPO 10

Kollmorgen/Consent for amendments (EUROPEAN PATENT: AMENDMENT AND CORRECTION: APPEAL, ON: APPEAL: PROCEDURE: REMITTAL ORDERED: FOR EXERCISE OF DISCRETION TO ALLOW AMENDMENT: T63/86: EPO)
[1988] E.P.O.R. 316; [1988] O.J. EPO 224

Kolotex Glo Australia Pty Ltd v. Sara Lee Personal Products (Australia) Pty Ltd (TRADE MARKS: REGISTRATION OF THE WORDS SHEER RELIEF AS MARK IN CONNECTION WITH WOMEN'S HOSIERY: WHETHER WORDS MERELY DESCRIPTIVE OF THE GOODS: USE AS A TRADE MARK: Australia: Fed. Ct)
26 I.P.R. 1

Komesaroff v. Mickle (TRADE PRACTICES: PASSING OFF: COPYRIGHT: INFRINGEMENT: ARTISTIC WORK: Australia: S.C.(Vic.))
77 A.L.R. 502; 7 I.P.R. 295; [1987] V.R. 703; [1988] R.P.C. 204

Komesaroff v. Mizzi (PATENT: PETTY PATENT: EXTENSION: OPPOSITION: OBJECTION: EVIDENCE: INVALIDITY: NOVELTY: OBVIOUSNESS: Australia: Pat. Off.)
9 I.P.R. 457

Kommerling/Profile member (EUROPEAN PATENT: INVENTIVE STEP: COLLOCATION: COMBINATION OF CITATIONS: PROBLEM, MULTIPLE: SKILLED PERSON: GENERAL TECHNICAL KNOWLEDGE, APPLICATION OF: T130/89: EPO)
[1992] E.P.O.R. 98; [1991] O.J. EPO 514

Kongskilde/Legal loophole (EUROPEAN PATENT: APPLICATION: PROCEDURE: DESIGNATION OF STATES, WHEN FEES DUE: CONVENTIONS: EPC RULES: FEES: DESIGNATION OF STATES: De minore ad majorem: J05/91: EPO)
[1994] E.P.O.R. 205; [1993] O.J. EPO 657

Konica/Colour photographic material (EUROPEAN PATENT: INVENTIVE STEP: SELECTION FROM SEVERAL OBVIOUS POSSIBILITIES: T162/89: EPO)
[1992] E.P.O.R. 24

Konica/Late citation (EUROPEAN PATENT: OPPOSITION PROCEDURE: AMENDMENT: APPEAL: FRESH PRIOR ART: REMITTAL: COSTS: T867/92: EPO)
[1995] E.P.O.R. 683

Konica/Photographic material (EUROPEAN PATENT: INVENTIVE STEP: EXPECTATION OF SUCCESS: PROBLEM, DEFINITION OF: EVIDENCE: COMPARATIVE TESTS: MUST BE BASED ON CLOSEST PRIOR ART: SUBMITTED EVIDENCE CANNOT BE DISREGARDED: T759/89: EPO) [1992] E.P.O.R. 483

Konica/Photographic material (EUROPEAN PATENT: BOARD OF APPEAL: JUDICIAL STATUS: COSTS: COMPETENCE OF BOARDS OF APPEAL: DECISION: FINALITY OF: FEES: REIMBURSEMENT OF APPEAL FEE: INADMISSIBLE APPEAL: PROCEDURE: DECISION, WHAT CONSTITUTES: Res judicata: Ratio decidendi: T934/91: EPO)
[1993] E.P.O.R. 219; [1993] O.J. EPO 685

Konica/Remittal (EUROPEAN PATENT: REMITTAL: OUTSTANDING REQUEST FOR HEARING: TERMINATION OF PROCEEDINGS WITHOUT PRIOR NOTIFICATION: SUBSTANTIAL PROCEDURAL VIOLATION: T892/92: EPO)
[1995] E.P.O.R. 238; [1994] O.J. EPO 664

Konica/Sensitising (EUROPEAN PATENT: AMENDMENT AND CORRECTION: CATEGORY OF CLAIM: INVENTIVE STEP: CLOSEST PRIOR ART: T423/89: EPO)
[1994] E.P.O.R. 142

Konishiroku/Photographic film (EUROPEAN PATENT: INVENTIVE STEP: COMPARATIVE TESTS: PRIOR ART: AVAILABILITY TO PUBLIC: PRIOR USE: SAMPLES: T390/88: EPO)
[1990] E.P.O.R. 417

Konishiroku/Photographic material (EUROPEAN PATENT: COSTS: LATE CITATIONS: APPORTIONED: T323/89: EPO) [1992] E.P.O.R. 210; [1992] O.J. EPO 169

Koo (Linda Chih Ling) v. Lam Tai Hing (CONFIDENTIAL INFORMATION: UNAUTHORISED DISCLOSURE: BREACH OF COPYRIGHT: QUESTIONNAIRES USED IN SCIENTIFIC SURVEY: Hong Kong: S.C.)   23 I.P.R. 607

Kopran Chemicals Co. Ltd v. Kent Pharmaceuticals (India) Pvt. Ltd (TRADE MARK: INFRINGEMENT: RIFINEX/RIFISON: INFRINGEMENT: PASSING OFF: INJUNCTION: India: H.C.)   (1990) 15 I.P.L.R. 319

Kornelis' Kunsthars Producten Industrie BV v. W.R. Grace & Co. (PATENT: AMENDMENT: CONSTRUCTION OF CLAIMS: NOT IN SUBSTANCE DISCLOSED: Australia: Fed. Ct)   28 I.P.R. 471

Kraft Foods Inc. v. Gaines Pet Foods Corporation (TRADE MARK: REMOVAL FOR NON-USE: PRACTICE: Locus standii: PERSON AGGRIEVED: ONUS OF PROOF: Australia: Fed. Ct)   135 A.L.R. 68

Kraft General Foods Inc. v. Gaines Pet Foods Corp. (TRADE MARK: REMOVAL FROM
REGISTER: NON-USE: ONUS OF PROOF: EFFECT OF CONTRACTUAL TERMS:
PERSON AGGRIEVED: DISCRETION OF REGISTRAR: DEROGATION FROM
GRANT: Australia: AIPO) 28 I.P.R. 617
(Fed. Ct) 31 I.P.R. 439
Kraftwerk Union/Eddy-current testing device (EUROPEAN PATENT: INVENTIVE
STEP: DISADVANTAGES OF COMPONENT IN CLOSEST PRIOR ART: T15/81:
EPO) [1979–85] E.P.O.R. B316; [1982] O.J. EPO 02
Kramer & Grebe/Lost cheque (EUROPEAN PATENT: EVIDENCE: BURDEN OF PROOF:
FEES, WHEN RECEIVED: ONUS OF PROOF: T128/87: EPO)
[1989] E.P.O.R. 485; [1989] O.J. EPO 406
Kreepy Krauly (Pty) Ltd v. Hofmann (PATENT: SPECIFICATION: ADDRESSEES:
IMPLEMENTATION: South Africa: A.D.) 1987 (2) S.A. 286
Krohne/Appeal fees (EUROPEAN PATENT: APPEAL: PROCEDURE: CROSS-APPEAL:
RESPONDENT, STATUS OF: WITHDRAWAL OF APPEAL: FEES: REIMBURSEMENT
OF APPEAL FEE: MULTIPLE PARTIES: G02/91: EPO)
[1992] E.P.O.R. 407; [1992] O.J. EPO 206
Kronborg Isager v. Boboli International Inc. (TRADE MARKS: OPPOSITION TO
ACCEPTANCE USE OF A MARK: Australia: Pat. Off.) 18 I.P.R. 526
(JOINT RESEARCH AND DEVELOPMENT: JOINT PRODUCTION: COMPONENTS
FOR PUMPS ASSEMBLED AND MARKETED BY THE PARTIES INDIVIDUALLY:
INTENTION TO APPROVE: E.C. Comm.) [1990] 4 C.M.L.R. 248
KSB AG, Lowara SpA, Goulds Pumps Inc, and ITT Fluid Handling Division's
Agreements (RESTRICTIVE PRACTICES: JOINT DEVELOPMENT AND
PRODUCTION OF HIGH TECHNOLOGY PRODUCTS: CAUGHT BY ARTICLE
85(1): RESEARCH AND DEVELOPMENT GROUP EXEMPTION INAPPLICABLE:
INDIVIDUAL EXEMPTION GRANTED: E.C. Comm.) [1992] 5 C.M.L.R. 55
Kubat/Cellulose composites (EUROPEAN PATENT: APPEAL: PROCEDURE: COMMON
GENERAL KNOWLEDGE: NEED FOR SUBSTANTIATION: T157/87: EPO)
[1989] E.P.O.R. 221
Kubat/Method of producing plastic composites (EUROPEAN PATENT: CLAIMS:
CLARITY: CONSTRUCTION: INVENTIVE STEP: CLOSEST PRIOR ART: PROBLEM
AND SOLUTION: SUFFICIENCY: FUNCTIONAL DEFINITIONS: T17/92:
EPO) [1993] E.P.O.R. 52
KUDOS Trade Mark (TRADE MARK: APPLICATION: DISTINCTIVENESS: BoT)
[1995] R.P.C. 242
Kureha Kagaku/Unreasoned decision (EUROPEAN PATENT: PROCEDURE:
UNREASONED DECISION: *Res judicata:* J27/86: EPO) [1988] E.P.O.R. 48
Kureha/Inadmissible appeal (EUROPEAN PATENT: AMENDMENT AND
CORRECTION: APPROVAL AFTER: J12/85: EPO)
[1986] E.P.O.R. 336; [1986] O.J. EPO 155
Kurosaki Refractories Co. Ltd v. Flogates Ltd (PATENT: APPLICATION: OPPOSITION:
WITHDRAWAL OF OPPOSITION: COSTS: PARTY AND PARTY: TAXATION: South
Africa: TPD) 1986 (1) S.A. 269
Kwality Icecreams Ltd v. India (TRADE MARK: PASSING OFF: USE OF LICENCED
MARK AFTER TERMINATION OF AGREEMENT: India: H.C.)
(1992) 17 I.P.L.R. 133
Kwan v. Queensland Corrective Services Commission (PETTY PATENT: EXTENSION:
SECTION 28 NOTICE: INVENTION MADE BY PRISONERS: WHETHER
INVENTORS EMPLOYEE'S OF CORRECTIONAL FACILITY: FAIR BASIS:
SUFFICIENCY: NOVELTY: OBVIOUSNESS: Australia: AIPO) 31 I.P.R. 25
Kwik-Lok Corp.'s Application (PATENT: APPLICATION: NOVELTY: FAIR BASIS:
HEARING: Australia: Pat. Off.) 5 I.P.R. 301

Kyowa Hakko Kogyo Co. Ltd v. Schering Corp. (TRADE MARKS: APPLICATION: OPPOSITION: NON-USE: STATEMENT OF USER: SUBSTANTIALLY IDENTICAL: DECEPTIVELY SIMILAR: LIKELY TO DECEIVE OR CAUSE CONFUSION: Australia: Pat. Off.)   17 I.P.R. 129

L'Air Liquide, SA pour L'Étude et L'Exploitation des Procedes Georges Claude v. The Commonwealth Industrial Gases Ltd (PATENT: OPPOSITION: INSUFFICIENT PARTICULARISATION OF GROUNDS: Australia: Pat. Off.)
      24 I.P.R. 77
L'AMY Trade Mark (APPLICATION: HONEST CONCURRENT USER: T.M.Reg.)   [1983] R.P.C. 137
L'Oréal's Application (PATENT: APPLICATION: NOVELTY: STATUS OF EUROPEAN APPLICATION: PRIORITY DATE: Pat. Ct)   [1986] R.P.C. 19
La Baigue Magiglo v. Multiglow Fires (PATENT: INFRINGEMENT: PLEADINGS: PRACTICE: See v. Scott-Paine practice: Pat. Ct)   [1994] R.P.C. 295
LA Gear Inc. v. Hi-Tec Sports plc (COPYRIGHT: INFRINGEMENT: SUMMARY JUDGMENT: ORIGINALITY: INDIRECT COPYING: IMPORTATION OF INFRINGING COPIES: POSSESSION IN COURSE OF BUSINESS: ORDER 14: Ch.D, C.A.)   [1992] F.S.R. 121
La Télémécanique Électrique/Power supply unit (EUROPEAN PATENT: EVIDENCE: DOCUMENTS, UNSIGNED: FREE EVALUATION: WITNESSES: EMPLOYEE OF PARTY NOT EXCLUDED: PRIOR ART: PRIOR USE: SINGLE SALE MAKES ARTICLE AVAILABLE: CONVENTIONS: NATIONAL LAW PRINCIPLES OF MAJORITY OF CONTRACTING: T482/89: EPO) [1993] E.P.O.R. 259; [1992] O.J. EPO 646
La Télémécanique Électrique/Power measuring device (EUROPEAN PATENT: APPEAL: PROCEDURE: CONDITION, FAILURE TO COMPLY WITH: REMITTAL ORDERED: TO CONSIDER AMENDED DESCRIPTION: T126/84: EPO)
      [1986] E.P.O.R. 342
LaBounty (Roy Edward) v. Hydraulic Machinery Co. of New Zealand Ltd (PATENT: APPLICATION: OPPOSITION: EVIDENCE: Australia: Pat. Off.)   22 I.P.R. 659
Labyrinth Media Ltd v. Brave World Limited (No. 2) (PRACTICE: INTERLOCUTORY INJUNCTION: APPLICATION FOR ADJOURNMENT AFTER DISCHARGE OF ex parte ORDER FOR PLAINTIFF'S TO GATHER EVIDENCE: WHETHER ABUSE OF PROCESS: Ch.D.)   [1995] E.M.L.R. 58
Labyrinth Media Ltd v. Brave World Limited (PASSING OFF: INTERLOCUTORY INJUNCTION: Ex parte ORDER: PROSPECTIVE RELEASES OF RIVAL VIDEOS UNDER SAME TITLE: WHETHER PRE-LAUNCH PUBLICITY SUFFICIENT TO ESTABLISH GOODWILL: REPUTATION: EVIDENCE: ARGUABLE CASE: Ch.D.)   [1995] E.M.L.R. 38
Lac Minerals Ltd v. International Corona Resources Ltd (CONFIDENTIAL INFORMATION: MISUSE: TEST FOR BREACH: REVERSE ONUS BY RECIPIENT TO SHOW NO MISUSE: ABSENCE OF CONFIDENTIALITY AGREEMENT NOT FATAL: EXPERT EVIDENCE: INDUSTRY PRACTICE: Canada: S.C.)   16 I.P.R. 27
Lac Minerals Ltd v. International Corona Resources Ltd (TRADE SECRETS AND CONFIDENTIAL INFORMATION: TRUST AND TRUSTEES: FIDUCIARY RELATIONSHIP: CONFIDENTIAL INFORMATION: BREACH OF DUTY: CONSTRUCTIVE TRUST: MINING EXPLORATION RESULTS: ACQUISITION OF PROPERTY: Canada: S.C.)   (1990) 26 C.P.R. (3d) 97; [1990] F.S.R. 441
LACTEL Trade Mark (TRADE MARK: APPLICATION: DEVICE MARK: WHETHER MARK DISTINCTIVE OR CAPABLE OF DISTINGUISHING: T.M.Reg.)
      [1994] R.P.C. 37

Lagenes Ltd v. It's At (U.K.) Ltd (COPYRIGHT: PRACTICE: *Ex parte* INJUNCTION: MISLEADING STATEMENTS: COPYRIGHT: DELIVERY UP: DISCOVERY OF IDENTITY OF TRADE CUSTOMERS: Ch.D.)   [1991] F.S.R. 492

Lake's Application (PATENT: PETTY PATENT: APPLICATION FOR EXTENSION OF TERM: INFORMATION LODGED AGAINST EXTENSION: ANTICIPATION: OBVIOUSNESS: PRIOR USE: SECRET USE: SUFFICIENCY: OBTAINING: LATE EVIDENCE: SPECIAL PLEA BASED ON EMPLOYMENT: Australia: Pat. Off.)
24 I.P.R. 281

Lakshmi PVC Products Pvt. Ltd v. Lakshmi Polymers (TRADE MARK: PASSING OFF: *Ad interim* INJUNCTION: India: H.C.)   (1991) 16 I.P.L.R. 32

Lallier v. Lux (TRADE MARK: REGISTRATION: OWNERSHIP: PRIOR USE: COPYRIGHT: IDEAS: GAMES: France: C.A.)   [1983] E.C.C. 465

Lamba Brothers Ltd v. Lamba Brothers (COPYRIGHT: INFRINGEMENT: BROCHURE NOT INDICATING CLAIM TO COPYRIGHT: India: H.C.)
(1993) 18 I.P.L.R. 246

Lance Court Furnishings Pte Ltd v. Public Prosecutor (COPYRIGHT: SCOPE OF PROTECTION: DESIGNS INDUSTRIALLY APPLIED: SEARCH WARRANTS: WHETHER PROPERLY OBTAINED: Singapore: H.C.)   [1993] 3 S.L.R. 969

LANCER Trade Mark (TRADE MARK: APPLICATION: OPPOSITION: PHONETIC CONFUSION WITH LANCIA: APPLICATION ALLOWED: Ch.D.: C.A.)
[1987] R.P.C. 303
sub nom. Mitsubishi v. Fiat   [1987] 1 F.T.L.R. 260

Land Power International Holdings Ltd v. Inter-Land Properties (H.K.) Ltd (PASSING OFF: TRADE MARK: COMMON DESCRIPTIVE WORDS USED AS MARK: LITTLE DIFFERENCES SUFFICE TO AVOID CONFUSION: Hong Kong: C.A.)
31 I.P.R. 163

Lane v. Diners Club International Ltd (TRADE MARKS: APPLICATION FOR REMOVAL FOR NON-USE: OPPOSITION: ONUS OF PROOF: NEED FOR APPLICANT TO ESTABLISH PRIMA FACIE CASE: Australia: Pat. Off.)   11 I.P.R. 371

Lang Bros Ltd v. Goldwell Ltd (PASSING OFF: UNFAIR TRADING: WEE McGLEN: Scotland: O.H.)   1977 S.L.R. 120; [1977] F.S.R. 353
(I.H.) 1982 S.L.R. 309; [1983] R.P.C. 289

Lansing Bagnall Ltd v. Buccaneer Lift Parts Ltd (COPYRIGHT: INFRINGEMENT: TREATY OF ROME: EURO-DEFENCE: C.A.)
[1984] 1 C.M.L.R. 224; [1984] F.S.R. 241

Lansing Bagnell, British Aerospace/Wiring loom (EUROPEAN PATENT: INVENTIVE STEP: AUTOMATION: SUFFICIENCY: DILIGENCE BUT NO IMAGINATION REQUIRED TO CARRY OUT INVENTION: T262/89: EPO)
[1991] E.P.O.R. 34

Lansing Bagnell/Control circuit (EUROPEAN PATENT: AMENDMENT AND CORRECTION: ADVANTAGES OVER PRIOR ART: PRIOR ART REFERENCE, ADMISSIBLE: APPEAL: PROCEDURE: COMMUNICATIONS BY BOARD OF APPEAL, PURPOSE AND SIGNIFICANCE: SUFFICIENCY: ADVANTAGES OVER PRIOR ART: DIFFERENT LANGUAGE TEXTS: T11/82: EPO)
[1979–85] E.P.O.R. B385; [1983] O.J. EPO 479

Lansing Linde Ltd v. Kerr (CONFIDENTIAL INFORMATION: EX-EMPLOYEE: INTERLOCUTORY INJUNCTION: RESTRAINT OF TRADE: RESTRICTIVE COVENANT IN CONTRACT OF EMPLOYMENT: ACTION FOR BREACH: WHETHER INFORMATION ACQUIRED BY EMPLOYEE PROTECTABLE AS TRADE SECRETS: WHETHER INTERIM INJUNCTION TO BE GRANTED: C.A.)
[1991] 1 All E.R. 418; [1991] 1 W.L.R. 251; 21 I.P.R. 529

Lantech Inc. v. First Green Park (PATENT: INFRINGEMENT: SPECIFICATION: CONSTRUCTION: REVOCATION: INVALIDITY: SECTION 40 GROUNDS: INUTILITY: Australia: Fed. Ct)   30 I.P.R. 99

Lasercare (Aust.) Pty Ltd v. Christiansen (PATENT: PETTY PATENT: EXTENSION: OBVIOUSNESS: LACK OF NOVELTY: PRIOR PUBLICATION: PRIOR USER: Australia: Pat. Off.)   5 I.P.R. 555

Lasercomb America Inc. v. Job Reynolds (COPYRIGHT: INFRINGEMENT: MISUSE: EQUITABLE DEFENCE: LIMITED MONOPOLY: SOFTWARE LICENSING RESTRICTIONS: NON-COMPETITION PROVISIONS: USA: C.A.) 19 I.P.R. 115

Latchways/Unlawful applicant (EUROPEAN PATENT: ENTITLEMENT: EUROPEAN APPLICATION WRONGFULLY MADE BUT ABANDONED: FRESH APPLICATION: MAJORITY DECISION OF ENLARGED BOARD: J01/91: G03/92: EPO)
[1995] E.P.O.R. 141; [1994] O.J. EPO 607

Late submission of protest (EUROPEAN PATENT: INTERNATIONAL SEARCHING AUTHORITY: PROTEST, ADMISSIBILITY OF: UNITY: INTERNATIONAL SEARCH: INADMISSIBLE PROTEST: W04/87: EPO)
[1989] E.P.O.R. 105; [1988] O.J. EPO 425

Latzke/Magnetic plaster (EUROPEAN PATENT: EVIDENCE: COMPARATIVE TESTS: NO REASON TO DOUBT: INVENTIVE STEP: PROBLEM, DEFINITION OF, *ex post facto*: PROBLEM, PERCEPTION OF: SELECTION OF SPECIFIC VALUE: T268/89: EPO)   [1994] E.P.O.R. 469

Laura Ashley Ltd v. Coloroll Ltd (TRADE MARK: INFRINGEMENT: LOGO: EVIDENCE: TACHISTOSCOPE: Ch.D.)   [1987] R.P.C. 1

LAURA ASHLEY Trade Mark (TRADE MARK: APPLICATION: PERSONAL NAME AND DEVICE: "OTHER CIRCUMSTANCES": BoT)   [1990] R.P.C. 539

Laverlochere/Bank cash payment (EUROPEAN PATENT: FEES: DATE OF PAYMENT: J07/81: EPO)   [1979–85] E.P.O.R. A88; [1983] O.J. EPO 89

Law Society of England and Wales v. Griffiths (PASSING OFF: LEGAL SERVICES: TELEPHONE NUMBERS: Ch.D.)   [1995] R.P.C. 16

Lawrence David Ltd v. Ashton (CONTRACT: RESTRAINT OF TRADE: CONFIDENTIAL INFORMATION: INTERLOCUTORY INJUNCTION: PRACTICE: TRADE SECRETS: INTERLOCUTORY INJUNCTION: EX-EMPLOYEE: PERIOD OF RESTRAINT: C.A.)   [1989] 1 F.S.R. 87; 20 I.P.R. 244

Le Bloc Fibre Quebec Inc. v. Les Entreprises Arsenault & Frs (PATENTS: INFRINGEMENT: JOINDER OF PARTIES: Canada: Fed. Ct)   3 I.P.R. 227

Le Monde (Sàrl) v. Société Microfor Inc. (COPYRIGHT: COLLECTIVE WORKS: OWNER'S RIGHTS: CONSENTS: REPRODUCTION: INDEXES: INTELLECTUAL CONTENT: DERIVED WORKS: PRESS REVIEW: BIBLIOGRAPHIES AND EXTRACTS: France: S.C.)   [1984] E.C.C. 271; [1985] F.S.R. 2
(C.A.) [1987] E.C.C. 205; [1987] F.S.R. 206
(S.A.) [1988] E.C.C. 297; [1988] F.S.R. 519

Leader Products Pty Ltd v. Allflex International Ltd (PATENT: APPLICATION: OPPOSITION: POWER OF COMMISSIONER: NOVELTY: PERSON SKILLED IN THE ART: TAX: Australia: Pat. Off.)   9 I.P.R. 649

Leara Trading Co. Ltd's Designs (REGISTERED DESIGN: CANCELLATION: JURISDICTION: DISCRETION: Designs Reg.)   [1991] R.P.C. 609

Lebelson's Application (PATENT: APPLICATION: PRACTICE: TIME LIMIT: Pat. Ct)
[1984] R.P.C. 136

Lech Pawlowski v. Seeley (FF) Nominees Pty Ltd (PATENT: PETTY PATENT: EXTENSION: APPLICATION: OBVIOUSNESS: LACK OF NOVELTY: COMMON GENERAL KNOWLEDGE: WHAT CONSTITUTES: Australia: Pat. Off.)
6 I.P.R. 635

Led Builders Pty Ltd v. Masterton Homes (NSW) Pty Ltd (COPYRIGHT: SUBSISTENCE: BUILDERS' PLANS: INFRINGEMENT: LACHES, ACQUIESCENCE AND DELAY: Australia: Fed. Ct) 30 I.P.R. 447

Lee Man Tat & Lee Man Lok (t/a Lee Kum Kee)'s Application (TRADE MARKS: APPLICATION FOR REGISTRATION: SURNAMES: DISTINCTIVENESS: Australia: Pat. Off.) 12 I.P.R. 212

Lee Thin Tuan v. Louis Vuitton, *sub nom.* Louis Vuitton v. Lee Thin Tuan

Legal & General Life of Australia Ltd v. Carlton-Jones & Associates Pty Ltd (TRADE MARK: OPPOSITION: PRIOR REGISTRATION REMOVED: DISCLAIMER: EFFECT: PROPRIETORSHIP: TRAFFICKING: Australia: Pat. Off.) 9 I.P.R. 447

Legal Practitioner (EUROPEAN PATENT: PROFESSIONAL REPRESENTATIVES: LEGAL PRACTITIONER, WHAT CONSTITUTES: J19/89: EPO)
[1991] E.P.O.R. 441; [1991] O.J. EPO 425

Legal Protection of Computer Programs Regulations 1993 (PROTECTION OF COMPUTER PROGRAMS AS LITERARY WORKS: ENACTMENT OF E.C. COUNCIL DIRECTIVE 91/250: ORIGINALITY: NON-PROTECTION OF UNDERLYING IDEAS AND PRINCIPLES: ENUMERATION OF RIGHTHOLDER'S EXCLUSIVE RIGHTS: RESTRICTIONS ON USE OF INFORMATION: ACTIONABLE INFRINGEMENTS: Ireland: Minister for Enterprise and Employment)
[1993] F.S.R. 636

Lego Australia Pty Ltd v. Paul's (Merchant) Pty Ltd (TRADE PRACTICES: DECEPTION: Australia: Fed. Ct) (1982) 42 A.L.R. 344

Lego System A/S v. Lego M. Lemelstrich Ltd (PASSING OFF: LEGO: *Quia timet* RELIEF: WHETHER COMMON FIELD OF ACTIVITY: MISREPRESENTATION: INJUNCTION: EVIDENCE: Pat. Ct) [1983] F.S.R. 155

Lehtovaara v. Acting Deputy Commissioner of Patents (PATENT: APPLICATION: EXTENSION OF TIME LIMITS: LAPSE: POWER: Australia: Fed. Ct)
(1982) 39 A.L.R. 103

Leisure Data v. Bell (COPYRIGHT: INFRINGEMENT: COMPUTER PROGRAM: PRACTICE: MANDATORY INJUNCTION: C.A.) [1988] F.S.R. 367

Lelah v. Associated Communication Corp. of Australia Pty Ltd (PRACTICE: INJUNCTION: MISLEADING ADVERTISEMENTS: Australia: Fed. Ct) 4 I.P.R. 461

Leland Stanford/Postal strike (EUROPEAN PATENT: PROCEDURE: GENERAL INTERRUPTION IN MAIL: J11/88: EPO)
[1990] E.P.O.R. 50; [1989] O.J. EPO 433

Leland/Light source (EUROPEAN PATENT: AMENDMENT: BEFORE GRANT: GENERALISATION: SERIOUS CONTEMPLATION TEST: T187/91: EPO)
[1995] E.P.O.R. 199

Lending Right Directive, *sub nom.* Community Rental Right and Lending Right Directive

Lenin's Monument (Re) (COPYRIGHT: STATUE: PUBLIC OWNERSHIP: SCULPTOR'S RIGHTS: PROSPECTIVE DAMAGE: STORAGE: Germany: C.A.)
[1992] E.C.C. 202; [1992] F.S.R. 265

Lennox v. Megray Pty Ltd (TRADE PRACTICES: PROSECUTIONS: FALSE REPRESENTATION OF APPROVAL: Australia: Fed. Ct) 6 I.P.R. 543

Leonard's Application (PATENT: APPLICATION: ARRANGEMENT OF INFORMATION: MECHANICAL FUNCTION: MANNER OF MANUFACTURE: NOVELTY: EXAMINERS OBJECTION: PATENT OFFICE PRACTICE: Australia: Pat. Off.)
18 I.P.R. 240

Leonardis v. St Alban (PATENTS: OPPOSITION: LATE NOTIFIED CITATIONS NOT PART OF OPPOSITION: LATE NOTIFIED CITATIONS PART OF BAR-TO-SEALING PROCEDURE: WHETHER OPPOSITION CONCLUDED AN OPPONENT HAS NO FURTHER ROLE: COSTS: Australia: Pat. Off.) 24 I.P.R. 351

Lesaffre's Patent (PATENT: REVOCATION: FAIR BASIS: OBVIOUSNESS: C.A.)
[1994] R.P.C. 523
Lesaffre/Composition of Opposition Division (EUROPEAN PATENT: PROCEDURE: CHANGE OF COMPOSITION OF DIVISION: FEES: REIMBURSEMENT OF APPEAL FEE: T243/87: EPO)   [1990] E.P.O.R. 136
Lesaffre/Yeast (EUROPEAN PATENT: CLAIMS: BREADTH: EFFECT ON SUFFICIENCY AND INVENTIVE STEP: EVIDENCE: REPETITION OF PATENTEE'S EXAMPLES: INVENTIVE STEP: CLAIMS TOO BROAD: SUFFICIENCY: CLAIMS: SINGLE EMBODIMENT: T740/90: EPO)   [1993] E.P.O.R. 459
LEUCO Great-Britain Trade Mark (TRADE MARK: APPLICATION: GREAT-BRITAIN IN MARK: DECEPTION AND CONFUSION: CONDITIONS: REGISTRATION: BoT)   [1985] R.P.C. 587
Levi Strauss & Co.'s Label Trade Mark (TRADE MARK: APPLICATION: LABEL SEWN INTO GARMENT: DISTINCTIVENESS: T.M.Reg.)   [1991] R.P.C. 441
Levi Strauss & Co. v. Barclays Trading Corp. Inc. (PRACTICE: DISCLOSURE OF NAMES: WHETHER PLAINTIFF ESTOPPED FROM USING INFORMATION DISCLOSED AGAINST THIRD PARTIES: IMPLIED UNDERTAKING ON DISCOVERY: PROPER TIME FOR APPLICATION: PRIVILEGE AGAINST SELF-INCRIMINATION: BALANCE OF CONVENIENCE: Ch.D.)   [1993] F.S.R. 179
Levi Strauss & Co. v. Dino Clothing Co. Ltd (TRADE MARK: INFRINGEMENT: TABS ON JEANS: ARCUATE STITCHING: INTERLOCUTORY INJUNCTION: BALANCE OF CONVENIENCE: New Zealand: H.C.)   8 I.P.R. 208
Levi Strauss & Co. v. Kimbyr Investments Ltd (TRADE MARKS: SCOPE OF REGISTRATION: PICTORIAL REPRESENTATION: WRITTEN DESCRIPTION: INFRINGEMENT: LIKELIHOOD OF DECEPTION OR CONFUSION: RECTIFICATION: EXPERT EVIDENCE: SURVEY EVIDENCE: ADMISSIBILITY: TRADE PRACTICES: MISLEADING AND DECEPTIVE CONDUCT: PASSING OFF: TABS ON JEANS POCKETS: STATUTORY INTERPRETATION: NON-USE: DAMAGE: New Zealand: H.C.)
[1994] 1 N.Z.L.R. 332; 28 I.P.R. 249; [1994] F.S.R. 335
Levi Strauss & Co. v. Robertsons Ltd (PASSING OFF: GET-UP AND LABELLING OF JEANS: TRADE MARK: INFRINGEMENT: DIFFERENCE BETWEEN WRITTEN DESCRIPTION AND PICTORIAL REPRESENTATION IN CERTIFICATE OF REGISTRATION: REMOVAL: New Zealand: H.C.)   20 I.P.R. 227
Levi Strauss & Co. v. Shah (TRADE MARK: INFRINGEMENT: TABS ON JEANS: RECTIFICATION: NON-USER: Ch.D.)   [1985] R.P.C. 371
Levi Strauss & Co. v. The French Connection Ltd (TRADE MARK: INFRINGEMENT: REGISTERED USER: Ch.D.)   [1982] F.S.R. 443
Levi Strauss & Co. v. Wingate Marketing Pty Ltd (TRADE MARKS: TRADE PRACTICES: PASSING OFF: SALE OF SECOND-HAND GOODS BEARING REGISTERED TRADE MARKS BY PERSON OTHER THAN REGISTERED PROPRIETOR: REVISE/LEVI'S: WHETHER MARK DECEPTIVELY SIMILAR: IMPORTANCE OF MANNER OF SALE OF PRODUCT: WHETHER SALE OF SECOND-HAND ALTERED AND UNALTERED GOODS INFRINGES REGISTERED MARKS: Australia: Fed. Ct)   116 A.L.R. 298; 26 I.P.R. 215
(PHONETIC SIMILARITY: REVISE/LEVI'S: SECOND-HAND JEANS: ALTER-ATIONS: CONFUSION AS TO ORIGIN: Fed. Ct) 121 A.L.R. 191; 28 I.P.R. 193
Lewis & Co. Ltd v. Trade Winds Furniture Ltd (DESIGNS: REGISTRABILITY: ORIGINALITY: New Zealand: H.C.)   4 I.P.R. 621

Lewis Galoob Toys Inc. v. Nintendo of America Inc. (COPYRIGHT: AUDIOVISUAL DISPLAYS OF COMPUTER PROGRAMS: INFRINGEMENT: AUTHORISATION: DERIVATIVE WORKS: WHETHER MODIFICATION OF VISUAL DISPLAYS BY A DEVICE NOT AFFECTING THE COMPUTER PROGRAM ITSELF IS AN INFRINGEMENT: FAIR USE: USA: D.C.)   22 I.P.R. 379
Lewis Trusts v. Bambers Stores Ltd (COPYRIGHT: INFRINGEMENT: GARMENTS: CONVERSION DAMAGES: WHETHER OVERLAPPING WITH DAMAGES FOR INFRINGEMENT OF COPYRIGHT: POINT OF CONVERSION: C.A.)
[1983] F.S.R. 453
Licht Druck/Copying process (EUROPEAN PATENT: AMENDMENT AND CORRECTION: SELECTION FROM ORIGINAL APPLICATION: T7/80: EPO)
[1979–85] E.P.O.R. B269; [1982] O.J. EPO 95
Liederman's Application (TRADE MARKS: APPLICATION FOR REGISTRATION: EXAMINER'S OBJECTIONS: SURNAME: CAPABLE OF BECOMING DISTINCTIVE: EVIDENCE OF OVERSEAS DISTINCTIVENESS: Australia: Pat. Off.)
16 I.P.R. 241
Liesenfeld/Courtesy service (EUROPEAN PATENT: PROCEDURE: MISLEADING COMMUNICATION BY EPO: GOOD FAITH TOWARDS PARTIES: FEES: LATE PAYMENT: J01/89: EPO)   [1992] E.P.O.R. 284; [1992] O.J. EPO 17
Life Underwriters Association of Canada v. Provincial Association of Quebec Life Underwriters (TRADE MARKS: INFRINGEMENT: CERTIFICATION MARK: CLU: Canada: Fed. C.A.)   33 C.P.R. (3d) 293
Lift Verkaufsgerate GmbH v. Fischer Plastics Pty Ltd (DESIGNS: INFRINGEMENT: FRAUDULENT OR OBVIOUS IMITATION: WHETHER THE ESSENTIAL FEATURES OF THE APPLICANTS DESIGNS REPEATED IN THE RESPONDENT'S PRODUCT: KNOWLEDGE: Australia: Fed. Ct)   27 I.P.R. 187
Light Signatures/Authenticator device (EUROPEAN PATENT: AMENDMENT AND CORRECTION: INTERPRETATION TO AVOID OBJECTION: CLAIMS: INVALIDITY, TO AVOID: INVENTIVE STEP: OBVIOUS SELECTION OF KNOWN ALTERNATIVE: T164/90: EPO)   [1991] E.P.O.R. 289
Lilypak Industries Ltd v. Poly Containers (N.Z.) Ltd (COPYRIGHT: DISPOSABLE PLASTIC CUPS: USE WITH PLASTIC HOLDERS: ARTISTIC WORKS: New Zealand: H.C.)   8 I.P.R. 363
Lind Engineering Pty Ltd v. Leeton Steel Works Pty Ltd (TRADE MARK: OPPOSITION: TIME LIMITS: EXTENSION: SUFFICIENCY OF REASON: Australia: Pat. Off.)   4 I.P.R. 445
Linde AG v. Air Products & Chemicals Inc. (PATENT: APPLICATION: OPPOSITION: NOVELTY: OBVIOUSNESS: NON-COMPLIANCE WITH SECTION 40: Australia: Fed. Ct)   28 I.P.R. 525
Lindholm/Breathing apparatus (EUROPEAN PATENT: CLAIMS: CLARITY: FUNCTIONAL FEATURES: CONSTRUCTION: FUNCTIONAL FEATURES: FUNCTIONAL FEATURES: T204/90: EPO)   [1992] E.P.O.R. 282
Linpac Mouldings Ltd v. Eagleton Direct Export Ltd (COPYRIGHT: SECONDARY INFRINGEMENT: IMPORTATION OF INFRINGING COPIES: KNOWLEDGE: THREAT TO INFRINGE: SUMMARY JUDGMENT: PRACTICE: Quia timet INJUNCTION ON ABANDONMENT OF DAMAGES CLAIM: DISCRETION: C.A.)   [1994] F.S.R. 545
Lintrend/Shrink treatment of linen (EUROPEAN PATENT: APPLICATION: PROCEDURE: EVIDENCE: ONUS ON APPLICANT: SUBSIDIARY CLAIMS NEED NOT BE CONSIDERED: ONUS OF PROOF: SUBJECTIVE ATTRIBUTE: FEES: REIMBURSEMENT OF APPEAL FEE: INVENTIVE STEP: EVIDENCE OF ADVANTAGES REQUIRED: NOVELTY: FORMAL TEST INSUFFICIENT: INEVITABLE RESULT: T76/83: EPO)   [1979–85] E.P.O.R. C782

Lion Laboratories Ltd v. Evans (CONFIDENTIAL INFORMATION: PUBLICATION: PUBLIC INTEREST: C.A.)
[1984] 2 All E.R. 417; [1984] 3 W.L.R. 539; [1985] Q.B. 526; 3 I.P.R. 276

Liposome Company, Inc.'s Application (PATENT: APPLICATION FOR GRANT OF A PATENT: CLAIMS TOO WIDE: NO CLEAR DISCLOSURE IN SPECIFICATION: CLAIMS LACKED CLARITY AND WERE NOT FAIRLY BASED: Australia: Pat. Off.)
22 I.P.R. 100

Liquid Air Aust. Ltd v. Commonwealth Industrial Gases Ltd (PATENT: OPPOSITION: EXTENSION OF TIME LIMIT: Australia: Pat. Off.)
1 I.P.R. 145

Liquid Retaining Structures (Aust.) Pty Ltd v. Delta Corp. Ltd (PATENT: OPPOSITION: TIME FOR LODGING EVIDENCE: Australia: Pat. Off.)
13 I.P.R. 363

LITE-LINE Trade Mark (TRADE MARK: REGISTRATION: REFERENCE TO CHARACTER AND QUALITY OF GOODS: SPECIAL CIRCUMSTANCES: T.M.Reg.)
[1991] R.P.C. 390

Little Tykes Co. v. Ciardullo (TRADE MARK: OPPOSITION: LITTLE TYKE/LITTLE TIKES: SUBSTANTIALLY IDENTICAL: DECEPTIVELY SIMILAR: GOODS OF THE SAME DESCRIPTION: CHARACTER MERCHANDISING: Australia: AIPO)
31 I.P.R. 571

Little v. Registrar of High Court of Australia (TRADE PRACTICES: TRADE PRACTICES ACT: WHETHER STATUTORY PRESCRIPTION OF PRACTISING FEE AND PROFESSIONAL INDEMNITY INSURANCE CONTRAVENES SECTION 46: Australia: Fed. Ct)
98 A.L.R. 145

Liversidge v. British Telecommunications plc (PATENT: INFRINGEMENT: REVOCATION: PARTICULARS OF OBJECTIONS: OBJECTION BASED ON PRE-GRANT AMENDMENT: Pat. Ct)
[1991] R.P.C. 229

LMG/Sterilising pouch (EUROPEAN PATENT: AMENDMENT AND CORRECTION: ENDPOINT OF RANGE, LIMITATION TO: INVENTIVE STEP: COMBINATION OF CITATIONS: T212/87: EPO)
[1991] E.P.O.R. 144

Lock International plc v. Beswick (PRACTICE: ANTON PILLER ORDER: PLAINTIFF TO PAY DAMAGES: CONFIDENTIAL INFORMATION: EX-EMPLOYEE: INJUNCTION: TRADE SECRETS: Ch.D.)
[1989] 3 All E.R. 373; [1989] 1 W.L.R. 1268; 16 I.P.R. 497

Lock/Windscreen removal device (EUROPEAN PATENT: APPEAL: PROCEDURE: FRESH PRIOR ART: FILLING MISSING LINK IN ARGUMENT: IN RESPONSE TO AMENDMENT: OPPOSITION: ABUSE: COSTS: LATE CITATIONS: APPORTIONED: T101/87: EPO)
[1990] E.P.O.R. 476

Logan v. Coulter (TRADE MARK: OPPOSITION: DECEPTIVE SIMILARITY: INTENTION TO USE: PRIOR USE: COPYRIGHT IN MARK: SUBSISTENCE: Australia: AIPO)
30 I.P.R. 304

Long John International Ltd v. Stellenbosch Wine Trust (Pty) Ltd (TRADE MARK: UNLAWFUL COMPETITION: MISREPRESENTATION: CHARACTER, COMPOSITION OF ORIGIN OF GOODS: REPUTATION: South Africa: D&CLD)
1990 (4) S.A. 136

Longman Group Ltd v. Carrington Technical Institite Board of Governors (COPYRIGHT: COMPILATION OF EXTRACTS FROM BOOKS BY TUTOR AT TECHNICAL INSTITUTE: INFRINGEMENT: DEFENCE OF FAIR DEALING: ADMISSIBLE EVIDENCE TO DETERMINE FAIR DEALING: "REASONABLE PROPORTION": New Zealand: H.C.) 20 I.P.R. 264; [1991] 2 N.Z.L.R. 574 *sub nom.* Carrington Technical Institite Board of Governors v. Longman Group Ltd
(C.A.) 17 I.P.R. 175

Longman Group Ltd v. Carrington Technical Institute Board of Governers (COPYRIGHT: INFRINGEMENT: SUBSTANTIALITY OF REPRODUCTION: FAIR DEALING: RESEARCH OR PRIVATE STUDY: USE BY AGENT OF CROWN: New Zealand: H.C.)   [1991] 2 N.Z.L.R. 574

Lonrho plc v. Fayed (UNLAWFUL INTERFERENCE WITH BUSINESS: TAKEOVER BID: MISREPRESENTATION TO SECRETARY OF STATE TO PREVENT BID BEING REFERRED TO MONOPOLIES & MERGERS COMMISSION: COMPETITOR PREVENTED FROM BIDDING FOR SHARE CAPITAL: CONSPIRACY: WHETHER CASE TO BE MET: WHETHER STATEMENT OF CLAIM TO BE STRUCK OUT: C.A.)   [1989] 2 All E.R. 65; [1989] 3 W.L.R. 631
(H.L.) [1991] 3 All E.R. 303; [1991] 3 W.L.R. 188

Lord Advocate v. Scotsman Publications Ltd (BREACH OF CONFIDENCE: MI5; BOOK, *Inside Intelligence*: DUTY ON THIRD PARTIES IN INNOCENT RECEIPT OF INFORMATION: INTERDICT: BALANCE OF CONVENIENCE: Scotland: O.H.)   [1989] 1 F.S.R. 281
(SCOTLAND: H.L.)   [1989] 3 W.L.R. 358
(BOOK, *Inside Intelligence*: NON-CONTENTS CASE: PUBLIC INTEREST: WHETHER SUFFICIENT PROOF FOR INTERDICT: RECLAIMING MOTION REFUSED: Scotland: I.H.)   [1989] 1 F.S.R. 310
(BOOK, *Inside Intelligence*: POSITION OF NEWSPAPERS: EFFECT OF *Spycatcher*: EFFECT OF OFFICIAL SECRETS ACT 1989: H.L.)
[1989] 1 F.S.R. 580: [1990] 1 A.C. 812

Lord Bloody Wog Rolo v. United Artists Corp. (TRADE MARKS: APPLICATION: OPPOSITION: APPLICATION FOR EXTENSION OF TIME: Australia: Pat. Off.)
11 I.P.R. 516

Lorenzo & Sons Pty Ltd v. Roland Corp., *sub nom.* Roland Corp. v. Lorenzo & Sons Pty Ltd

Lorraine's Application (TRADE MARK: APPLICATION: CATERER'S CHOICE: WHETHER ADAPTED TO DISTINGUISH: Australia: Pat. Off.)   8 I.P.R. 157

Losfeld/Public holiday (EUROPEAN PATENT: FEES: DATE OF PAYMENT: REIMBURSEMENT OF APPEAL FEE: J01/81: EPO)
[1979–85] E.P.O.R. A70; [1983] O.J. EPO 53

Lotus Development Corp. v. Mayne Nickless Ltd (TRADE PRACTICES: MISLEADING OR DECEPTIVE CONDUCT: "TRADE OR COMMERCE": REPRESENTATIONS BY ONE EMPLOYEE OF A CORPORATION TO ANOTHER: Australia: Fed. Ct)
20 I.P.R. 257

Lotus Development Corp. v. Paperback Software International (COPYRIGHT: COMPUTER PROGRAMS: USER INTERFACE: COPYRIGHTABILITY OF NONLITERAL ELEMENTS: IDEA/EXPRESSION: "LOOK AND FEEL": COPYRIGHT ACT 1976 (U.S.): USA: D.C.)   18 I.P.R. 1

Lotus Development Corp. v. Vacolan Pty Ltd (COPYRIGHT: INFRINGEMENT: PARALLEL IMPORTATION: ORDERS RECEIVED AND FILLED BY AUSTRALIAN AGENT OF FOREIGN VENDOR: COMMON DESIGN: Australia: Fed. Ct)
16 I.P.R. 143

Louis Erauw-Jacquéry Sprl v. La Hesbignonne Société Co-opérative, *sub nom.* Erauw-Jacquéry (Louis) Sprl v. La Hesbignonne Société Co-opérative

Louis Vuitton v. Lee Thin Tuan (TRADE MARK: INFRINGEMENT: INTERIM INJUNCTION: EVIDENCE: PRODUCTION OF DOCUMENTS: Singapore: H.C.)   [1989] 3 M.L.J. 465
(APPEAL: PRODUCTION OF DOCUMENTS: PRIVILEGE AGAINST SELF-INCRIMINATION: C.A.)   [1992] 2 S.L.R. 273

Lovatt v. Consolidated Magazines Pty Ltd (TRADE PRACTICES: MISLEADING AND
DECEPTIVE CONDUCT: ALLEGED FALSE STATEMENTS AS TO QUALITY AND
SPONSORSHIP: "PRESCRIBED INFORMATION PROVIDER": Australia: Fed. Ct)
12 I.P.R. 261
LSK Microwave Advance Technology Pty Ltd v. Rylead Pty Ltd (PASSING OFF:
WHETHER "MICROWAVE CUISINE" IS DISTINCTIVE OF BUSINESS OR USES
ORDINARY DESCRIPTIVE WORDS: PRINCIPLES OF PASSING OFF: Australia: Fed.
Ct)   16 I.P.R. 107
Lubrizol Corp. v. Esso Petroleum Co. Ltd (No. 1) (PATENT: INFRINGEMENT:
PRACTICE: JOINDER OF ADDITIONAL DEFENDANT: SERVICE OUT OF
JURISDICTION: JOINT TORTFEASANCE: PRIOR USE: Pat. Ct)
[1992] R.P.C. 281
(C.A.) [1992] R.P.C. 467
Lubrizol Corp. v. Esso Petroleum Co. Ltd (PRACTICE: DISCOVERY: WHETHER COPY
DOCUMENTS PRIVILEGED: Ch.D.)   [1992] 1 W.L.R. 957
Lubrizol Corp. v. Esso Petroleum Co. Ltd (No. 2) (PATENT: INFRINGEMENT:
PRACTICE: DISCOVERY: CONFIDENTIALITY: RESTRICTED INSPECTION OF
DISCOVERY DOCUMENTS: WHETHER ORDER DISAPPLYING ORDER 24, R.14A
TO BE GRANTED: INJUNCTION RESTRAINING USE OF AFFIDAVITS: *In camera*
HEARINGS: Pat. Ct)   [1993] F.S.R. 53
Lubrizol Corp. v. Esso Petroleum Co. Ltd (No. 3) (PATENT: INFRINGEMENT:
PRACTICE: PARTICULARS OF INFRINGEMENTS: WHETHER COMPLYING WITH
ORDER 104 R.5(2): Pat. Ct)   [1993] F.S.R. 59
Lubrizol Corp. v. Esso Petroleum Co. Ltd (No. 4) (PATENT: INFRINGEMENT:
PRACTICE: DISCOVERY: INSPECTION: EXPERTS AFFIDAVITS SWORN IN
FOREIGN PROCEEDINGS: WHETHER SUBJECT TO LEGAL PROFESSIONAL
PRIVILEGE: Pat. Ct)   [1993] F.S.R. 64
Lubrizol/Fuel products (EUROPEAN PATENT: UNITY: INTERNATIONAL SEARCH:
INADMISSIBLE PROTEST: W01/87: EPO)
[1988] E.P.O.R. 326; [1988] O.J. EPO 182
Lubrizol/Hybrid plants (EUROPEAN PATENT: PATENTABILITY: BIOLOGICAL
PROCESS: PLANTS: CLAIMS: PRODUCT-BY-PROCESS: EXCEPTION TO GENERAL
PRINCIPLE CONSTRUED STRICTLY: T320/87: EPO)
[1990] E.P.O.R. 173; [1990] O.J. EPO 71
Lubrizol/Lubricants (EUROPEAN PATENT: INVENTIVE STEP: PROBLEM,
REFORMULATION OF: NOVELTY: COMBINATION OF SEPARATE TEACHINGS IN
SINGLE DOCUMENT: DOCUMENT: TOTAL INFORMATION CONTENT:
OPPOSITION: PROCEDURE: REMITTAL, TO ENABLE FRESH EVIDENCE:
T618/90: EPO)   [1993] E.P.O.R. 19
Lucas/Combustion engine (EUROPEAN PATENT: INVENTIVE STEP: COMMON
GENERAL KNOWLEDGE: T426/88: EPO)
[1992] E.P.O.R. 458; [1992] O.J. EPO 427
Lucas/Ignition system (EUROPEAN PATENT: APPLICATION: PROCEDURE:
ADMISSION BY APPLICANT: ORAL HEARING: FAILURE TO ATTEND: INVENTIVE
STEP: HINT IN PRIOR ART: IMPLICIT TEACHING OF DIAGRAM IN PRIOR ART:
T22/81: EPO)   [1979–85] E.P.O.R. B348; [1983] O.J. EPO 226
Lucasfilm Ltd v. Krix (PATENT: APPLICATION: OPPOSITION: ANTICIPATION: PRIOR
PUBLICATION: NOVELTY: OBVIOUSNESS: Australia: Pat. Off.)   20 I.P.R. 357
Lucazeau v. Société des Auteurs, Compositeurs et Editeurs de Musique (SACEM), *sub
nom*. Ministère Public v. Lucazeau (SACEM, *partie civile*)

Luchtenberg/Rear-view mirror (EUROPEAN PATENT: APPEAL: PROCEDURE: ORAL EVIDENCE: EVIDENCE: ORAL EVIDENCE OF PRIOR USE: FEES: REIMBURSEMENT OF APPEAL FEE: PRIOR ART: PRIOR USE: FEATURES INFERRABLE FROM INSPECTION: PRIOR USE: PRIVATE CAR USED ON PUBLIC ROADS, IN: T84/83: EPO) [1979–85] E.P.O.R. C796

Luminous Pty Ltd v. Nitto Electric Industrial Co. Ltd (PATENT: OPPOSITION: NOVELTY: OBVIOUSNESS: SECTION 40; PRIOR PUBLICATION: COMBINATION PATENT: ESSENTIAL INTEGERS: INSUFFICIENCY: EVIDENCE: FAIR BASIS: Australia: AIPO) 29 I.P.R. 117

Lundia/Diffusion device (EUROPEAN PATENT: AMENDMENT AND CORRECTION: GENERALISATION: DIVISIONAL APPLICATION: BROADENING AS COMPARED TO PARENT APPLICATION: T265/88: EPO) [1990] E.P.O.R. 399

Lux Traffic Controls Ltd v. Pike Signals Ltd and Faronwise Ltd (PATENTS: INFRINGEMENT: VALIDITY: NOVELTY: PRIOR USE: ENABLING DISCLOSURE: OBVIOUSNESS: WHETHER AN INVENTION: ESTOPPEL: Pat. Ct)
[1993] R.P.C. 107

Lux Traffic Controls Ltd v. Staffordshire Public Works Co. Ltd (PATENT: INFRINGEMENT: PRACTICE: FURTHER AND BETTER PARTICULARS: PARTICULARS OF CONSTRUCTION OF CLAIMS: Pat. Ct) [1991] R.P.C. 73

Lyons v. Registrar of Trade Marks (TRADE MARKS: APPLICATION: EXTENSION OF TIME LIMITS: Australia: Fed. Ct) (1983) 50 A.L.R. 496; 1 I.P.R. 416

Lyons v. The J.M. Smucker Co. (PATENT: PETTY PATENT: APPLICATION FOR EXTENSION OF TIME TO FILE NOTICE OF OPPOSITION TO EXTENSION OF TERM: WHETHER ERROR BY ATTORNEY: WHETHER SERIOUS OPPOSITION: COSTS: Australia: Pat. Off.) 23 I.P.R. 664

Lyson Australia Pty Ltd's Application (TRADE MARK: APPLICATION: SERIES OF MARKS: WHAT CONSTITUTES: Australia: Pat. Off.) 9 I.P.R. 350

M's Application (PATENT: APPLICATION: PRACTICE: PROCEDURAL ERROR: TIME LIMITS: Pat. Ct: C.A.) [1985] R.P.C. 249

Maag Gear Wheel & Machine Co. Ltd's Patent (PATENT: U.K. AND EUROPEAN (U.K.) HAVING SAME PRIORITY DATE FILED BY SAME APPLICANT: WHETHER PATENTS GRANTED FOR THE SAME INVENTION: C.-G.) [1985] R.P.C. 572

Macallan-Glenlivet plc v. Speyside Whisky Distributors Ltd (TRADE MARK: INFRINGEMENT: PASSING OFF: WHISKY: Scotland: O.H.) 1983 S.L.T. 348

Macarthys/Chloral derivatives (EUROPEAN PATENT: APPLICATION: PROCEDURE: REFUSAL AFTER ONE COMMUNICATION: APPEAL: FRESH CITATIONS ON APPEAL: DIFFERENT SPECIES: T84/82: EPO)
[1979–85] E.P.O.R. B507; [1983] O.J. EPO 451

Macaulay v. Screenkarn Ltd (COPYRIGHT: INFRINGEMENT: EFFECT OF SETTLEMENT: WHETHER CLAIM EXTINGUISHED: Ch.D.) [1987] F.S.R. 257

Machinefabriek G.J. Nijhuis/Stunning apparatus (EUROPEAN PATENT: INVENTIVE STEP: PROBLEM, PERCEPTION OF: SKILLED PERSON, COMMON KNOWLEDGE OF: T90/83: EPO) [1979–85] E.P.O.R. C802

Machinery Market Ltd v. Sheen Publishing Ltd (COPYRIGHT: INFRINGEMENT: ORDER 14 RELIEF: WHETHER ADVERTISEMENT LITERARY WORK: PRINTER'S LIABILITY: CONVERSION: Ch.D.) [1983] F.S.R. 431

Mack Trucks Inc. v. Satberg Pty Ltd (INJUNCTION: INTERLOCUTORY: TRADE MARK INFRINGEMENT: WHETHER INFRINGEMENT REQUIRES USE OF IDENTICAL MARK: USE BY PREDECESSOR IN BUSINESS UNDER TRADE MARKS ACT, SECTION 64(1)(C): PERSONAL LIABILITY OF DIRECTORS: Australia: Fed. Ct) 22 I.P.R. 437

Mackintosh Computers Ltd v. Apple Computer Inc. (COPYRIGHT: SUBJECT-MATTER: COMPUTER PROGRAM: PROGRAM STORED IN ELECTRONIC FORM ON CHIP: REPRODUCTION: MERGER OF IDEA AND EXPRESSION: TRANSLATION: Canada: S.C.) 17 I.P.R. 611

Mackintosh Computers v. Apple Computer Inc. (COPYRIGHT: INFRINGEMENT: COMPUTER PROGRAMS: REPRODUCTION: ADAPTATION: CONTRIVANCE: MACHINE PARTS: Canada: Fed. Ct: C.A.) 9 I.P.R. 621

Macmillan Publishers Ltd v. Thomas Reed Publications Ltd (COPYRIGHT: INFRINGEMENT: CHARTS: SUMMARY JUDGMENT: ORIGINALITY: Ch.D.) [1993] F.S.R. 455

Macor Marine Systems/Secrecy agreement (EUROPEAN PATENT: AVAILABILITY TO THE PUBLIC: PRIOR USE: CONFIDENTIAL CIRCUMSTANCES: NO WRITTEN AGREEMENT: T830/90: EPO) [1995] E.P.O.R. 21; [1994] O.J. EPO 713

Macron Fire Protection Ltd v. Angus Fire Armour Ltd (RESTRICTIVE PRACTICES: DOMINANT POSITION: ABUSE: PRICES: E.C. Comm.) [1987] 3 C.M.L.R. 715; [1988] F.S.R. 54

MACY'S Trade Mark (TRADE MARK: OPPOSITION: OVERSEAS REPUTATION: T.M.Reg) [1989] R.P.C. 546

Macy & Co. Inc. v. Trade Accents (TRADE MARKS: OWNERSHIP: RECTIFICATION: AGGRIEVED PERSON: INTERNATIONAL AND LOCAL GOODWILL AND REPUTATION: FALSE CLAIM TO PROPRIETORSHIP OF TRADE MARK: CONFUSION OR DECEPTION: Singapore: H.C.) [1992] 1 S.L.R. 581; 22 I.P.R. 587

Mad Hat Music Ltd v. Pulse 8 Records Ltd (COPYRIGHT: INFRINGEMENT: INTERLOCUTORY INJUNCTION: SOUND RECORDINGS: OWNERSHIP: AUTHOR: PERFORMER'S RIGHTS: CONSENT TO MAKING STUDIO RECORDINGS: WHETHER FURTHER CONSENT NECESSARY FOR MAKING COMMERCIAL RECORDS: Ch.D.) [1993] E.M.L.R. 172

Madhavan v. S.K. Nayar (COPYRIGHT: ALLEGED COPYING OF NOVEL BY CINEMATOGRAPH FILM: INFRINGEMENT: APPEAL: India: H.C.) (1988) 13 I.P.L.R. 41

Magazines in Hairdressing Establishments (COPYRIGHT COLLECTING SOCIETY: *Locus standi*: ENTITLEMENT TO FEES ON LENDING OR HIRING WORKS FOR COMMERCIAL PURPOSES: Germany: S.C.) [1987] E.C.C. 467

Magee v. Farrell (PATENT: AMENDMENT: OPPOSITION: Australia: Pat. Off.) 7 I.P.R. 288

MAGIC SAFE Trade Mark (TRADE MARK: APPLICATION: DISTINCTIVENESS: BoT) [1993] R.P.C. 470

Magill TV Guide Ltd v. Independent Television Publications Ltd. See also, *sub nom.* Radio Telefis Eireann v. E.C. Commission

Magill TV Guide Ltd v. Independent Television Publications Ltd, BBC and Radio Telefis Eireann (RESTRICTIVE PRACTICES: PUBLIC BROADCASTING ORGANISATIONS: TV GUIDES: BROADCASTERS IN UNITED KINGDOM AND IRELAND: "UNDERTAKINGS" WITHIN ARTICLE 86: SUBSIDIARY AND PARENT: SINGLE ENTITY WITHIN ARTICLE 86: E.C. Comm. Decision IV/31.851) [1989] 4 C.M.L.R. 757; [1990] F.S.R. 71

Mail Newspapers plc v. Express Newspapers plc (COPYRIGHT: INFRINGEMENT: INTERLOCUTORY INJUNCTION: WEDDING PHOTOGRAPHS: WHETHER CO-OWNER LEGALLY DEAD: Ch.D.) [1987] F.S.R. 90

Mail Newspapers plc v. Insert Media Ltd (PASSING OFF: NEWSPAPERS: RIGHT OF PROPERTY: ADVERTISING INSERTS: DISCLAIMERS: Q.B.D.) [1987] R.P.C. 521

Mainbridge Industries Pty Ltd v. Whitewood & Ibbett Pty Ltd (COPYRIGHT: ARTISTIC WORK: REPRODUCTION: INFRINGEMENT: NON-EXPERT DEFENCE: CONFIDENTIAL INFORMATION: Australia: S.C.(NSW))   4 I.P.R. 97
Mainbridge Industries Pty Ltd v. Whitewood & Ibbett Pty Ltd (COPYRIGHT: REPRODUCTION IN THREE-DIMENSIONAL FORM: SIMILARITY: VISUAL COMPARISON: Australia: S.C.(NSW))   6 I.P.R. 239
Mainmet Holdings plc v. Austin (BREACH OF CONFIDENCE: EX-EMPLOYEE: NOT IN COMPETITION WITH EX-EMPLOYER: TRADE SECRETS: MALICIOUS FALSEHOOD: WHETHER INJUNCTION APPROPRIATE: Q.B.D.)
[1991] F.S.R. 538
Maison Lejay Lagoute SA v. l'Héritier Guyot SA (TRADE MARK: KIR: REGISTRATION: France: D.C.)   [1984] E.C.C. 22
Maize Seed, *sub nom.* Nungesser (L.C.) v. E.C. Comm.
Makita (Australia) Pty Ltd v. Black & Decker (Australasia) Pty Ltd (TRADE PRACTICES: COMPARATIVE ADVERTISING: ALLEGED REPRESENTATIONS AS TO PERFORMANCE OF DRILL IN TORTURE TEST: REQUIREMENTS OF SUITABLE CORRECTIVE ADVERTISING: Australia: Fed. Ct)   18 I.P.R. 270
Malaysian Milk Sdn Bhd's Registered Design (REGISTERED DESIGN: PRACTICE: STRIKING OUT: DELAY: CONTRACT: EFFECT OF AGREEMENT BETWEEN PARTIES ON STRIKING OUT: YOGHURT BOTTLE: RECTIFICATION OF REGISTER: DELAY: ESTOPPEL: Ch.D.)   [1993] F.S.R. 254
(APPEAL PROCEDURE: SETTING ASIDE LEAVE TO APPEAL: C.A.)
[1993] R.P.C. 151
Malcolm v. Oxford University Press (The Chancellor, Masters and Scholars of The University of Oxford) (CONTRACT: PUBLISHING: ORAL COMMITMENT TO PUBLISH BOOK AT ROYALTY RATE: WHETHER ENFORCEABLE CONTRACT IN ABSENCE OF AGREEMENT AS TO PRINT RUN, FORMAT, AND SALE PRICE: WHETHER INTENTION TO CREATE LEGAL RELATIONS: C.A.)
[1994] E.M.L.R. 17
MAN/Admissible (EUROPEAN PATENT: OPPOSITION: PROCEDURE: ADMISSIBILITY: REVOCATION AT INSTIGATION OF PATENTEE: T459/88: EPO)   [1991] E.P.O.R. 72; [1990] O.J. EPO 425
MAN/Intermediate layer for reflector (EUROPEAN PATENT: INVENTIVE STEP: COMBINATION OF CITATIONS: T6/80: EPO)
[1979–85] E.P.O.R. B265; [1981] O.J. EPO 434
MAN/Transfer of Opposition (EUROPEAN PATENT: OPPOSITION: PROCEDURE: TRANSFER OF PENDING PROCEEDINGS: G04/88: EPO)
[1990] E.P.O.R. 1; [1989] O.J. EPO 480
Management Publications Ltd v. Blenheim Exhibitions Group plc (PASSING OFF: INTERLOCUTORY INJUNCTION: MAGAZINE TITLES: BALANCE OF CONVENIENCE: Ch.D.)   [1991] F.S.R. 348
(C.A.) [1991] F.S.R. 550
Manhattan Confectioners v. United Tobacco Co., *sub nom.* Royal Beech-Nut (Pty) Ltd (t/a Manhattan Confectioners) v. United Tobacco Co.
Mannesmann Kienzle GmbH v. Microsystem Design Ltd (PATENT: INFRINGEMENT: PRACTICE: TRANSFER TO PATENTS COUNTY COURT: Pat. Ct)
[1992] R.P.C. 569
Mannesmann/Payment of fees (EUROPEAN PATENT: FEES: DATE OF RECEIPT: NATIONAL PRACTICES IRRELEVANT: T47/88: EPO)
[1990] E.P.O.R. 167; [1990] O.J. EPO 35
Manoj Plastic Industries v. Bhola Plastic Industries (TRADE MARK: PASSING OFF: SAME TRADE MARK FOR IDENTICAL GOODS: INTERIM INJUNCTION: India: H.C.)   (1985) 9 I.P.L.R. 143

Manor Electronics Ltd v. Dickson (BREACH OF CONFIDENCE: ANTON PILLER PRACTICE: Q.B.D.)   [1988] R.P.C. 618

Mantruck Services Ltd and Manton & Co. Ltd v. Ballinlough Electrical Refrigeration Co. Ltd (PASSING OFF: MISREPRESENTATION OF AGENCY: INTERFERENCE WITH CONTRACTUAL RELATIONS: INJURIOUS FALSEHOOD: SOLE DISTRIBUTORSHIP AGREEMENT: ARTICLE 85: Ireland: S.C.)
23 I.P.R. 500; [1992] 1 I.R. 351; [1992] 1 C.M.L.R. 325

Manufacture de Bonneterie C. Mawet v. Kaydale Apparel Ltd (TRADE MARK: OWNERSHIP: DECEPTION OR CONFUSION: GEOGRAPHIC NAME: Australia: Pat. Off.)   5 I.P.R. 178

Mar-Con Corp. Pty Ltd v. Campbell Capital Ltd (CONFIDENTIAL INFORMATION: WHETHER CONFIDENTIAL QUALITY: WHETHER IMPARTED IN CONFIDENCE: EXTENT OF DUTY OF CONFIDENCE: SPRINGBOARD DOCTRINE: JOINT VENTURE: WHETHER UNDER FIDUCIARY DUTY: UNJUST ENRICHMENT: BASIS OF LIABILITY: Australia: S.C.(NSW))   16 I.P.R. 153

Marcel v. Commissioner of Police of the Metropolis (CONFIDENTIAL INFORMATION: BREACH OF CONFIDENCE: PUBLIC INTEREST: SEIZURE BY POLICE UNDER STATUTORY POWERS DURING CRIMINAL INVESTIGATIONS: *Subpoena duces tecum* SEEKING PRODUCTION BY POLICE OF DOCUMENTS FOR USE IN CIVIL PROCEEDINGS: OBJECTION TO PRODUCTION: Ch.D.)
[1991] 1 All E.R. 845; [1991] 2 W.L.R. 1118; 20 I.P.R. 532
(C.A.) [1992] 1 All E.R. 72; [1992] Ch. 225; [1992] 2 W.L.R. 50

Marconi/Re-establishment of rights by opponent appellant (EUROPEAN PATENT: FEES: REIMBURSEMENT OF APPEAL FEE: RE-ESTABLISHMENT OF RIGHTS: ADMISSIBILITY OF APPLICATION BY OPPONENT: T210/89: EPO)
[1991] E.P.O.R. 403; [1991] O.J. EPO 433

Marcus Publishing plc v. Hutton-Wild Communications Ltd (PASSING OFF: NEWSPAPER TITLES: C.A.)   [1990] R.P.C. 575

Marello/Postal strike (EUROPEAN PATENT: FEES: REIMBURSEMENT OF APPEAL FEE: PROCEDURE: DUE PROCESS: INQUIRIES BY EPO MUST BE OBJECTIVE: POSTAL STRIKE: J04/90: EPO)   [1990] E.P.O.R. 576

Marengo v. Daily Sketch and Daily Graphic Ltd (PASSING OFF: PSEUDONYM: KEM/ KIM: CARTOONISTS' *noms de plume*: NO DOT ON "i" OF "KIM": MERE CONFUSION NOT ACTIONABLE: APPEAL ALLOWED: C.A.)   [1992] F.S.R. 1

Marie Claire Album SA v. Hartstone Hosiery Ltd (PRACTICE: PASSING OFF: TRAP ORDER: COSTS: Ch.D.)   [1993] F.S.R. 692

Markman v. Westview Instruments Inc. (PATENT: INFRINGEMENT: CONSTRUCTION: SUMMARY JUDGMENT: RIGHT TO JURY TRIAL: Australia: Fed. Ct)   32 I.P.R. 221

Marks and Spencer plc v. San Miguel Corp. (TRADE MARKS: OPPOSITION: LIKELIHOOD OF DECEPTION OR CONFUSION WITH PRIOR REGISTERED MARK: ST MICHAEL/SAN MIGUEL: Australia: Pat. Off.)   13 I.P.R. 499

Marlboro/Transfer (EUROPEAN PATENT: ENTITLEMENT: JURISDICTION TO DETERMINE: EPO: AGREEMENTS BETWEEN PARTIES OUTSIDE COMPETENCE: COMPETENCE OF BOARD OF APPEAL: OPPOSITION: PROCEDURE: TRANSFER OF PATENT PROPRIETORSHIP, EFFECT: T553/90: EPO) [1994] E.P.O.R. 440

Marley Roof Tile Co. Ltd's Patent (EUROPEAN AND U.K. PATENTS: PRACTICE: U.K. AND EUROPEAN PATENT APPLICATIONS IN NAME OF SAME PROPRIETOR WITH SAME SUBJECT-MATTER AND PRIORITY DATE: WHETHER PATENTS GRANTED FOR SAME INVENTION: CLAIMS TO PRODUCT IN U.K. PATENT AND TO PROCESS AND PRODUCT BY PROCESS IN EUROPEAN PATENT: WHETHER CLAIMS TO SAME INVENTION: CONSTRUCTION OF CLAIMS: ORDER FOR REVOCATION DISCHARGED: Pat. Ct) [1992] F.S.R. 614
(C.A.) [1994] R.P.C. 231

Marron Blanco/Re-establishment (EUROPEAN PATENT: RE-ESTABLISHMENT OF RIGHTS: E.P.O.'S DUTY TO WARN OF DEFICIENCIES IN APPLICATION: TIME LIMIT FOR: PROFESSIONAL REPRESENTATIVES: DUTY OF DUE CARE: SOLE PRACTITIONER: INCAPACITY: J41/92: EPO)
[1994] E.P.O.R. 375; [1995] O.J. EPO 93

Mars GB Ltd v. Cadbury Ltd (TRADE MARK: INFRINGEMENT: TREETS/TREAT SIZE: CONFECTIONERY: RECTIFICATION: Ch.D.) [1987] R.P.C. 387

Mars II/Glucomannan (EUROPEAN PATENT: INVENTIVE STEP: NEW USE OF KNOWN SUBSTANCE: T112/92: EPO) [1994] E.P.O.R. 249

Mars Incorporated v. Candy World (Pty) Ltd (TRADE MARK: EXPUNGEMENT: PERSON AGGRIEVED: APPLICATION: DEFENSIVE REGISTRATION: South Africa: A.D.) 1991 (1) S.A. 567

Marston Fastener Corp.'s Application (TRADE MARK: APPLICATION: OPPOSITION: RELEVANT PRIOR USE: DISTINCTIVENESS: Australia: Pat. Off.) 4 I.P.R. 40

Martin Cellars Pty Ltd v. Kies Pty Ltd (TRADE MARK: OPPOSITION: PROPRIETORSHIP: LIKELIHOOD OF DECEPTION OR CONFUSION: Australia: AIPO) 27 I.P.R. 567

Martin Engineering Co. v. Nicaro Holdings Pty Ltd (DAMAGES: PATENTS: COMPANIES: AUTHORISATION OF INFRINGEMENT: DIRECTOR'S PERSONAL LIABILITY: Australia: Fed. Ct) 100 A.L.R. 358; 20 I.P.R. 241

Martin Engineering Co. v. Trison Holdings Pty Ltd (PATENT: INFRINGEMENT OF STANDARD PATENT: APPLICATION FOR INTERLOCUTORY INJUNCTION TO RESTRAIN: VALIDITY PUT IN ISSUE: Australia: Fed. Ct)
81 A.L.R. 543; 11 I.P.R. 611
(CONSTRUCTION OF CLAIM: WHETHER CLAIM MAY BE CONSTRUED BY REFERENCE TO SPECIFICATION: Australia: Fed. Ct) 14 I.P.R. 330

Martinez (Re) (PATENT: DECLARATION OF NON-INFRINGEMENT: "EXISTING PATENT": PRACTICE: VALIDITY: C.-G.) [1983] R.P.C. 307

Masi AG v. Coloroll (PATENT: PRACTICE: TRIAL OF PRELIMINARY POINT: Pat. Ct)
[1986] R.P.C. 483

Mask Works (Protection of) (U.K. SEMICONDUCTOR CHIPS PROTECTION ACT: RECIPROCITY: INTERIM PROTECTION FOR EEC MEMBER STATES: U.S. Comm of Patents & Trade Marks) [1987] 1 C.M.L.R. 170

Massey v. Noack (PATENTS: PETTY PATENT: EXTENSION OF TERM: OBTAINING: MATTERS ARISING UNDER SECTION 40: Australia: Pat. Off.) 11 I.P.R. 632

Massey-Ferguson Ltd v. Bepco France SA (COPYRIGHT: SPARE PARTS: TRADE MARK: PACKAGING: UNFAIR COMPETITION: France)
[1983] E.C.C. 91; [1983] F.S.R. 117

Masterfoods Ltd v. HB Ice Cream Ltd (COMMUNITY LAW AND NATIONAL LAW: RESTRICTIVE PRACTICES: PRIORITY OF COMMUNITY LAW: NATIONAL COURTS: STANDARD OF PROOF: PENALTIES: INTER-STATE TRADE: RETAIL TRADE: VERTICAL AGREEMENTS: EXCLUSIVE DEALING: PROVISIONAL VALIDITY: DOMINANT POSITION: RELEVANT MARKET: ABUSE: REFERENCE TO E.C. COMMISSION: EXCLUSIVE DEALING AGREEMENTS: EVIDENCE: Ireland: H.C.) [1992] 3 C.M.L.R. 830; [1994] F.S.R. 1

Masterman's Design (REGISTERED DESIGN: APPLICATION: PRACTICE: WHETHER DESIGN CONTRARY TO MORALITY: DISCRETION: RDAT) [1991] R.P.C. 89

Masuda's Application (PATENT: PRACTICE: INTERNATIONAL APPLICATION: ERROR IN TRANSLATION: COMPTROLLERS POWER TO CORRECT MISTAKE: Pat. Ct) [1987] R.P.C. 37

Mateffy Perl Nagy Pty Ltd v. Devefi Pty Ltd (COPYRIGHT: ASSIGNMENT AND LICENCES: LICENCE TO USE ENGINEER'S PLANS FOR CONSTRUCTION OF BUILDING: SALE OF SITE BY LICENCE HOLDER TO THIRD PARTY: WHETHER IMPLIED LICENCE IN FAVOUR OF THIRD PARTY: WHETHER INFRINGEMENT BY THIRD PARTY: WHETHER COPYRIGHT OWNER ESTOPPED FROM CLAIMING INFRINGEMENT BY THIRD PARTY: MEASURE OF DAMAGES: Australia: Fed. Ct) 23 I.P.R. 505

Matshini (*ex parte*) (PRACTICE: ANTON PILLER ORDERS: SEARCH: South Africa: E.C.D.) 1986 (3) S.A. 605; [1986] F.S.R. 454

Matsushita Electric Industrial Co. Ltd's Application (TRADE MARKS: APPLICATION: LACK OF DISTINCTIVENESS: NOT INHERENTLY ADAPTED TO DISTINGUISH: DESCRIPTIVE WORDS: EVIDENCE OF SALES FIGURES: Australia: Pat. Off.) 15 I.P.R. 125

Matsushita Electric Works Ltd's Application (PATENT: INTERNATIONAL APPLICATION: PRACTICE: PCT FILING: PRIORITY DATE: C.-G.) [1983] R.P.C. 195

Matsushita/Dye transfer sheet (EUROPEAN PATENT: INVENTIVE STEP: INEVITABLE RESULT OF OBVIOUS ADAPTATION: MODERNISATION OF EXISTING ART: OPPOSITION: PROCEDURE: FRESH EVIDENCE ON APPEAL, REFUSED: STATE OF THE ART: SEPARATE STATES IN ONE DOCUMENT: T319/90: EPO) [1994] E.P.O.R. 460

Matsushita/Extension of time limit (EUROPEAN PATENT: FEES: REIMBURSEMENT OF FEE FOR FURTHER PROCESSING: J37/89: EPO) [1993] E.P.O.R. 356; [1993] O.J. EPO 201

Mattel Inc. v. Tonka Corp. (COPYRIGHT: INFRINGEMENT: BARBIE DOLL: GOOD ARGUABLE CASE: WHETHER DEFENDANT IMPORTED INTO HONG KONG: MEANING OF IMPORT: AGENT: PROCUREMENT OF BREACH: TRADE MARK: INFRINGEMENT: GOOD ARGUABLE CASE: WHETHER DEFENDANT PROCURED PRINTING OF PACKAGING: *ex parte* ORDER: SERVICE ABROAD: WHETHER ORDER GRANTED ON INNOCENT MISTAKE OF FACT SHOULD BE DISCHARGED: ORDER DISCHARGED: Hong Kong: H.C.) [1992] F.S.R. 28 (MEANING OF "IMPORT" IN SECTION 5(2) OF U.K. COPYRIGHT ACT 1956 AS EXTENDED TO HONG KONG: DISCHARGE OF ANTON PILLER ORDER FOR MIS-LEADING EVIDENCE: SERVICE OUT OF THE JURISDICTION: S.C.) 23 I.P.R. 91

Mauri Brothers & Thomson (Aust.) Pty Ltd v. Containers Ltd (PATENT: APPLICATION: OPPOSITION: NOVELTY: PRIOR PUBLICATION: MATTERS ARISING UNDER SECTION 40: Australia: Pat. Off.) 11 I.P.R. 477

Mauri/Plastics chain (EUROPEAN PATENT: COSTS: UNNECESSARY HEARING: APPORTIONED: T189/83: EPO) [1979–85] E.P.O.R. C897

Max Factor & Co. v. MGM/UA Entertainment Co. (PRACTICE: INTERLOCUTORY INJUNCTION: SAVING MOTION TO ANOTHER DAY: Ch.D.) [1983] F.S.R. 577

Maxam Food Products Pty Ltd's Application (TRADE MARKS: APPLICATION: REGISTRABILITY: INVENTED WORD: DESCRIPTIVE: CAPABLE OF BECOMING DISTINCTIVE: DISCLAIMER: Australia: Pat. Off.) 20 I.P.R. 381

Maxtor/Media storage system (EUROPEAN PATENT: FEES: INCORRECT INFORMATION BY TELEPHONE: DUTIES OF EPO TO INVESTIGATE PROMPTLY AND REPORT FINDINGS OBJECTIVELY: COURTESY SERVICES: RELIANCE MUST BE ESTABLISHED AND REASONABLE: ALTERNATIVE REMEDIES: DISCRETION TO OVERLOOK SMALL AMOUNT: DEFINITION OF SMALL AMOUNT (20 PER CENT): J27/92: EPO) [1995] E.P.O.R. 688; [1995] O.J. EPO 288

Maxwell v. Pressdram Ltd (EVIDENCE: PRIVILEGE: NEWSPAPER REPORTER: SOURCE OF INFORMATION: DISCLOSURE OF SOURCE: INTERESTS OF JUSTICE: C.A.) [1987] 1 All E.R. 656

Mayceys Confectionery Ltd v. Beckmann (COPYRIGHT: INFRINGEMENT: FLAGRANCY: CONVERSION DAMAGES: DAMAGES: ADDITIONAL DAMAGES: New Zealand: H.C.) 30 I.P.R. 331

Mayfair Hams & Bacon Co.'s Application (TRADE MARK: APPLICATION: REGISTERED USER: Australia: Pat. Off.) 2 I.P.R. 423

Mayfair International Pty Ltd's Application (TRADE MARK: APPLICATION: OPPOSITION WITHDRAWN: ADVERTISEMENT OF ACCEPTANCE BUT FAILURE TO REGISTER WITHIN PRESCRIBED TIME: EXTENSION OF TIME LIMIT: DISCRETION: Australia: AIPO) 28 I.P.R. 643

Mayne Nickless Ltd's Application (TRADE MARK: APPLICATION: COMPUTA-PAY: ADAPTED TO DISTINGUISH: Australia: Pat. Off.) 5 I.P.R. 345

McAlpine/Relief valve (EUROPEAN PATENT: OPPOSITION PROCEDURE: APPEAL FROM ORDER FOR REVOCATION: WITHDRAWAL BY OPPONENT: WHETHER EFFECTIVE: EXAMINATION BY BOARD OF OWN MOTION: T789/89: EPO) [1995] E.P.O.R. 213; [1994] O.J. EPO 482

McCain Foods (Aust.) Pty Ltd (TRADE MARK: APPLICATION: ENDORSEMENT: DISTINCTIVENESS: DESCRIPTIVENESS: COMBINATION OF COMMON WORDS: Australia: AIPO) 28 I.P.R. 557

McDonald's Corporation v. Coffee Hut Stores Ltd (TRADE MARK: APPEAL: OBJECTION TO INCORRECT CORPORATE NAME ON APPLICATION: JURISDICTION: SURNAME: FAMILY OF MARKS: Australia: Fed. Ct) 30 I.P.R. 318

McDonald's Hamburgers Ltd v. Burgerking (U.K.) Ltd (PASSING OFF: TRADE LIBEL: Ch.D.) [1986] F.S.R. 45
(PRACTICE: INQUIRY AS TO DAMAGES: INTEREST: C.A.) [1987] F.S.R. 112

McDonald v. Graham (COPYRIGHT: "Z CARDS": PATENTS COUNTY COURT PRACTICE: JURISDICTION: *Res judicata*: ANTON PILLER AND MAREVA PRACTICE: PATENT: INFRINGEMENT: EXPERIMENTAL USE: BANKRUPTCY OF DEFENDANT: Pat. C.C.: C.A.) [1994] R.P.C. 407

McGloin (J.) Pty Ltd's Application (TRADE MARKS: APPLICATION FOR REGISTRATION: DESCRIPTIVE MARK: EVIDENCE OF USE: REGISTRABILITY IN PART B: Australia: Pat. Off.) 22 I.P.R. 669

McGuinness v. Kellogg Co. of Great Britain Ltd (CONFIDENTIAL INFORMATION: PRACTICE: DISCOVERY: NON-DISCLOSURE OF EVIDENCE BEFORE TRIAL: DOCUMENTARY: REBUTTAL OF BONA FIDES: APPLICATION FOR LEAVE NOT TO DISCLOSE UNTIL TRIAL: PROCEDURE: C.A.) [1988] 1 W.L.R. 913

McIlwraith McEachern Operations Ltd v. Parcel Holdings Pty Ltd (PATENT: APPLICATION TO RESTORE LAPSED APPLICATION: ORDER TO PRODUCE DOCUMENTS: PRIVILEGE: WAIVER BY IMPLICATION: POWER OF COMMISSIONER TO ORDER DISCOVERY: DIFFERENCES BETWEEN PRODUCTION AND DISCOVERY: NATURE OF ORDER REQUIRED: Australia: Pat. Off.) 23 I.P.R. 177

McKenzie v. Uwatec Pty Ltd (PATENT: OPPOSITION: APPLICATION TO DISMISS: ADEQUACY OF STATEMENT OF GROUNDS AND PARTICULARS: Australia: AIPO)   30 I.P.R. 575

McManamey (David Fraser)'s Application (TRADE MARKS: APPLICATION: ROARING FORTIES: DISCLAIMER REQUIRED AS TO FORTIES: DISTINCTIVENESS OF NUMERALS: Australia: Pat. Off.)   16 I.P.R. 582

McManus's Application (PATENT: APPLICATION: EGGSHELLS AS ORAL MEDICAMENTS FOR TREATING OF ULCERS: SWISS-TYPE CLAIM: WHETHER SUPPORTED BY DESCRIPTION: ENFORCEMENT OF COSTS ORDER AGAINST APPELLANT IN PERSON: Pat. Ct)   [1994] F.S.R. 558

McNeil Inc. v. Sterling Pharmaceuticals Pty Ltd (PATENT: APPLICATION: OPPOSITION: USE OF REGISTERED TRADE MARK IN SPECIFICATION: MATTERS ARISING UNDER SECTION 40: PRIOR APPLICATION: Australia: Fed. Ct)   24 I.P.R. 297

MCT Labels SA v. Gemelli C.C. (TRADE MARK: INFRINGEMENT: USE AS TRADE MARK: "UNAUTHORISED" USE: South Africa: D&CLD)   1991 (1) S.A. 53

MCT Unilabels SA v. Peter Katholos (TRADE MARK: OPPOSITION: DECEPTIVELY SIMILAR: SUBSTANTIALLY IDENTICAL: PROPRIETORSHIP: Australia: AIPO)   27 I.P.R. 176

McWhirter/PCT form (EUROPEAN PATENT: PCT APPLICATION: PROCEDURE: DESIGNATION OF STATES ON OUT-OF-DATE FORM: AMENDMENT AND CORRECTION: MISTAKES BY NATIONAL PATENT OFFICE: CONVENTIONS: COMPETENCE OF EPO: J26/87: EPO)   [1989] E.P.O.R. 430; [1989] O.J. EPO 329

Mead/Printing plate (EUROPEAN PATENT: STATE OF THE ART: JAPANESE ABSTRACT: APPLICATION PROCEDURE: TELEPHONE DISCUSSIONS: CONFLICTING RECOLLECTIONS: FORMAL DENIAL OF RESPONSE: NOVELTY: INVENTIVE STEP: T160/92: EPO)   [1995] E.P.O.R. 424

Mecaniver SA and PPG Industries (Agreement between) (RESTRICTIVE PRACTICES: COMPANY TRANSFER: SALE OF SHARES: MARKET SHARE: DOMINANT POSITION: E.C. Comm.)   [1985] 3 C.M.L.R. 359

Mechanical Handling Engineering (S.) Pte Ltd v. Material Handling Engineering Pte Ltd (TRADE MARK: PASSING OFF: NAMES OF CORPORATIONS: DESCRIPTIVE NAME: SAME INDUSTRY: REPUTATION: DATE ESTABLISHED: SHARED REPUTATION DOCTRINE: WHETHER RELEVANT: INITIALS: MHE: EVIDENCE OF CONFUSION: DELAY: LACHES, ACQUIESENCE AND ESTOPPEL: Singapore: H.C.)   [1993] 2 S.L.R. 205

Medical Biological Sciences/Oral prosthesis (EUROPEAN PATENT: APPLICATION: PROCEDURE: COMMUNICATION UNDER RULE 51(4), EFFECT OF: APPEAL: STATEMENT OF GROUNDS, REQUIREMENTS OF: RE-ESTABLISHMENT OF RIGHTS: EPO PRACTICE, ERRONEOUS, RELIANCE ON: J22/86: EPO)   [1987] E.P.O.R. 87; [1987] O.J. EPO 280

Meditex Ltd v. New Horizonz Pty Ltd (TRADE MARKS: OPPOSITION TO REGISTRATION: PROPRIETORSHIP: EXTENSION OF TIME: COSTS: Australia: AIPO)   26 I.P.R. 497

Medtronic Inc.'s Application (TRADE MARK: APPLICATION: WHETHER DISTINCTIVE: Australia: Pat. Off.)   2 I.P.R. 276

Medtronic/Administrative Agreement (EUROPEAN PATENT: EPO: EUROPEAN COMMUNITY LAW, RELEVANCE TO: PRESIDENT'S FUNCTIONS AND POWERS: PROCEDURE: EPO ACT WHERE APPLICANT MISLED: LEGITIMATE EXPECTATIONS: G05/88: G07/88: G08/88: EPO)   [1991] E.P.O.R. 225; [1991] O.J. EPO 137

Medtronic/Cardiac defibrillator (EUROPEAN PATENT: INVENTIVE STEP: TRIAL-
AND-ERROR APPROACH: IMPRACTICABLE: T348/86: EPO)
[1988] E.P.O.R. 159
Medtronic/German Patent Office (EUROPEAN PATENT: ENLARGED BOARD OF
APPEAL: PRESIDENT OF THE EPO: T117/87: EPO)
[1989] E.P.O.R. 287; [1989] O.J. EPO 127
Medtronic/Synchronized intracardiac cardioverter (EUROPEAN PATENT: APPEAL:
PROCEDURE: FRESH CITATIONS BY BOARD OF APPEAL, REMITTAL NOT
ORDERED: CLAIMS: FUNCTIONAL FEATURES: EFFECT ON INVENTIVE STEP:
INVENTIVE STEP: COLLOCATION: OPPOSITION: FRESH CITATIONS BY BOARD
OF APPEAL FROM SEARCH REPORT: T387/89: EPO)
[1993] E.P.O.R. 113; [1992] O.J. EPO 583
Melbourne v. Terry Fluid Controls Pty Ltd (PATENTS: NOVELTY: PRIOR USE:
SECRET USE: ARTICLE DELIVERED TO POTENTIAL PURCHASER FOR TRIAL
AND EVALUATION: CIRCUMSTANCES IN WHICH THAT USE IS SECRET USE
CONSIDERED: OBVIOUSNESS: INUTILITY: Australia: Fed. Ct)   26 I.P.R. 292
(OPPOSITION: NOVELTY: OBVIOUSNESS: REFERENCE TO BODY OF
SPECIFICATION: IMPLIED LIMITATION BASED OF EXPECTATION OF THOSE
SKILLED IN THE ART: Australia: Fed. Ct)   28 I.P.R. 302
Meldrum v. Grego (TRADE MARKS: OPPOSITION: SUBSTANTIALLY IDENTICAL OR
DECEPTIVELY SIMILAR: ESSENTIAL FEATURES: Australia: Pat. Off.)
24 I.P.R. 201
Memco-Med Ltd (PATENT: EMPLOYEE'S INVENTION: APPLICATION FOR
COMPENSATION: WHETHER "OUTSTANDING BENEFIT": ONUS: PRACTICE:
DISCOVERY: Pat. Ct)   [1992] R.P.C. 403
Memminger-Iro GmbH v. Trip-Lite Ltd (PATENT: INFRINGEMENT: PRACTICE:
TRANSFER TO COUNTY COURT: FACTORS TO BE TAKEN INTO ACCOUNT:
COSTS: Pat. Ct)   [1991] F.S.R. 322; [1992] R.P.C. 210;
(TRANSFER OF ACTION TO COUNTY COURT: DISCRETION: C.A.)
[1992] R.P.C. 210
MEMPHIS Trade Mark (APPLICATION: DISTINCTIVENESS: T.M.Reg.)
[1985] R.P.C. 54
Memtec/Membranes (EUROPEAN PATENT: PROCEDURE: KNOWLEDGE OF RULES
EXPECTED: MISLEADING COMMUNICATION BY EPO: FEES: REIMBURSEMENT
OF APPEAL FEE: REIMBURSEMENT OF SURCHARGE: J03/87: EPO)
[1989] E.P.O.R. 175; [1989] O.J. EPO 03
Mentor Corp. v. Colorplast A/S (PATENT: INFRINGEMENT: PRACTICE: TRANSFER
FROM PATENTS COUNTY COURT TO HIGH COURT: COSTS: C.A.)
[1994] F.S.R. 175
Mentor Corp. v. Hollister Inc. (PATENT: INFRINGEMENT: OBVIOUSNESS:
INTERROGATORY: AWARENESS OF PRIOR ART: Pat. Ct)   [1990] F.S.R. 577
(VALIDITY: SUFFICIENCY: C.A.)   [1993] R.P.C. 7
Mercantile Group (Europe) AG v. Aiyela, The (PRACTICE: MAREVA INJUNCTION:
Norwich Pharmacal ORDER: JURISDICTION TO MAKE ORDERS: MAREVA
INJUNCTIONS AGAINST PERSONS INVOLVED IN TORTIOUS WRONGDOING OF
OTHERS: Q.B.D.)   [1993] F.S.R. 745
Merchandising Corp. of America Inc. v. Harpbond Ltd (COPYRIGHT:
INFRINGEMENT: ADAM ANT: FACIAL MAKE-UP AS "ARTISTIC WORK":
INDIRECT COPYING: REPRODUCTION OF SUBSTANTIAL PART: PASSING OFF:
Ch.D.: C.A.)   [1983] F.S.R. 32
Merck & Co.'s Application (TRADE MARK: OPPOSITION: LIKELIHOOD OF
DECEPTION OR CONFUSION: VISUAL AND AURAL TESTS: Australia: Pat. Off.)
5 I.P.R. 513

Merck & Co. Inc.'s Application (PATENT: EXTENSION: INADEQUATE REMUNERATION: EXCEPTIONAL CIRCUMSTANCES: Australia: S.C.(NSW))
1 I.P.R. 583; [1983] 2 N.S.W.L.R. 645

Merck & Co. Inc. and Pasteur-Merieux Serums et Vaccins (RESTRICTIVE PRACTICES: JOINT VENTURES: PHARMACEUTICALS: JOINT RESEARCH AND DEVELOPMENT OF VACCINES: INTENTION TO APPROVE: E.C. Comm.)
[1994] 5 C.M.L.R. 281

Merck & Co. Inc. v. Pacific Pharmaceuticals Ltd (PATENTS: EXTENSION: INADEQUATE REMUNERATION: OPPOSITION: NOTICE: ONUS OF PROOF: New Zealand: H.C.)   8 I.P.R. 393; [1987] 1 N.Z.L.R. 242
(APPEAL: C.A.)   [1990] 2 N.Z.L.R. 55

Merck & Co. Inc. v. Primecrown Ltd (PATENT: INFRINGEMENT: PARALLEL IMPORTS: WHETHER *Merck v. Stephar* STILL GOOD LAW: CONSTRUCTION: TRANSITIONAL PROVISIONS OF ACT OF ACCESSION OF SPAIN AND PORTUGAL: INTERLOCUTORY RELIEF: WHETHER REVISED VIEW OF *Merck v. Stephar* MAY BE TAKEN INTO ACCOUNT: REFERRAL TO ECJ: Pat. Ct)   [1995] F.S.R. 909

Merck & Co. Inc. v. Sankyo Co. Ltd (PATENT: AMENDED APPLICATION ACCEPTED: OPPOSITION: PRIORITY DATE: CLAIMING NEW MATTER: ANTICIPATION: CLAIM NOT FAIRLY BASED: Australia: Pat. Off.)   22 I.P.R. 529
(TESTS: *Locus standii*: COMMISSIONER OF PATENTS: Fed. Ct)   23 I.P.R. 415

Merck & Co. Inc. v. Syntex Corp. (TRADE MARKS: APPLICATION: OPPOSITION: SUBSTANTIALLY IDENTICAL OR DECEPTIVELY SIMILAR MARKS: GOODS OF SAME DESCRIPTION: Australia: Pat. Off.)   11 I.P.R. 318

Merck Patent GmbH v. Virbac (Australia) Pty Ltd (PATENT: APPLICATION FOR EXTENSION OF TERM: OPPOSITION: WHETHER CLAIMS ARE IN RESPECT OF A PHARMACEUTICAL SUBSTANCE: WHETHER CLAIMS MUST EXCLUDE USES OTHER THAN IN HUMANS: Australia: Pat. Off.)   26 I.P.R. 70
sub nom. Virbac (Australia) Pty Ltd v. Merck Patent GmbH (EXTENSION OF TERM: PHARMACEUTICAL SUBSTANCE: COSTS: Australia: Fed. Ct)
29 I.P.R. 548

Merck Patent/Chroman derivatives (EUROPEAN PATENT: CHEMICAL COMPOUNDS: GENERIC FORMULA: ERROR: CORRECTION (NO): PROCESS-BY-PROCESS PROTECTION: T552/91: EPO)   [1995] E.P.O.R. 455; [1995] O.J. EPO 100

Merck/Starting compounds (EUROPEAN PATENT: AMENDMENT AND CORRECTION: PRIOR ART REFERENCE, ADMISSIBLE: APPEAL: PROCEDURE: REMITTAL ORDERED: FOR INSERTION OF PRIOR ART ACKNOWLEDGEMENT: COMMON GENERAL KNOWLEDGE: PATENT APPLICATION, MAY INCLUDE: ENLARGED BOARD OF APPEAL: REFERENCE REFUSED: SUFFICIENCY: COMMON GENERAL KNOWLEDGE EXPECTED: T51/87: EPO)
[1991] E.P.O.R. 329; [1991] O.J. EPO 177

Mercury Communications Ltd v. Mercury Interactive (U.K.) Ltd (TRADE MARK: INFRINGEMENT: COMPUTER SOFTWARE: SUMMARY JUDGMENT: BONA FIDE USE OF OWN NAME: SCOPE OF REGISTRATION: Ch.D.)   [1995] F.S.R. 850

Meredith & Finlayson v. Canada (Registrar of Trade Marks) (TRADE MARKS: SUMMARY EXPUNGEMENT: APPEALS: SCOPE OF APPEAL FROM REGISTRAR'S DECISION: SUMMARY PROCEEDINGS: Canada: FCTD)   33 C.P.R. (3d) 396

MERIT Trade Marks (TRADE MARK: APPLICATION: COMPOSITE MARK: DISCLAIMER: Ch.D.)   [1989] R.P.C. 687

Merlet v. Mothercare plc (COPYRIGHT: INFRINGEMENT: BABY CAPE: WHETHER WORK OF ARTISTIC CRAFTSMANSHIP: SECTION 9(8) DEFENCE: Ch.D.)
[1984] F.S.R. 358; [1986] R.P.C. 115
(C.A.) [1986] R.P.C. 115

Merrell Dow Pharmaceuticals' Petition (PATENT: PHARMACEUTICAL COMPOUND: APPLICATION FOR PERMISSION TO IMPORT AND MARKET IN AUSTRALIA MADE 11 YEARS AFTER PRIORITY DATE FOR THE AUSTRALIAN PATENT: PETITION FOR EXTENSION: INADEQUATE REMUNERATION: Australia: Fed. Ct) 20 I.P.R. 347

Merrell Dow Pharmaceuticals Inc.'s (Terfenadine) Patent (PATENT: PRACTICE: DISCOVERY IN PATENT OFFICE: PRINCIPLES: Pat. Ct) [1991] R.P.C. 221

Merrell Dow Pharmaceuticals Inc. (PATENT: EXTENSION: LOST TIME IN EXPLOITATION: NO FAULT OF PATENTEE: EFFECT OF DELAYS IN REGULATORY APPROVAL: New Zealand: H.C.) [1994] 2 N.Z.L.R. 706

Merrell Dow Pharmaceuticals Inc. v. H.N. Norton & Co. Ltd (PATENT: INFRINGEMENT: VALIDITY: *Gillette* DEFENCE: ANTICIPATION: ENABLING DISCLOSURE: PRIOR USE: MEDICAL TREATMENT: PRACTICE: SUMMARY JUDGMENT: Pat. Ct) [1994] R.P.C. 1
(C.A.) [1995] R.P.C. 233
(PATENT: APPLICATION: PRIOR USE: PRIOR DISCLOSURE: USE OF KNOWN PHARMACEUTICAL: WHETHER INVENTION MADE AVAILABLE TO PUBLIC: TERFENADINE METABOLITE: METABOLITE INEVITABLY FORMED IN HUMAN BODY: H.L.) [1996] R.P.C. 76

Merrill Lynch Inc.'s Application (PATENT: APPLICATION: BUSINESS SYSTEM, WHETHER PATENTABLE: Pat. Ct) [1988] R.P.C. 1
(C.A.) [1989] R.P.C. 561

Merson v. British Leyland plc (RESTRICTIVE PRACTICES: DOMINANT POSITION: IMPORT RESTRICTIONS: FINES: E.C. Comm.)
[1984] 3 C.M.L.R. 92; [1984] O.J. L207/11

Merv Brown Pty Ltd v. David Jones (Aust.) Pty Ltd (TRADE PRACTICES: MISLEADING OR DECEPTIVE CONDUCT: PASSING OFF: Australia: Fed. Ct) 5 I.P.R. 517

Merv Brown Pty Ltd v. David Jones (Aust.) Pty Ltd (TRADE PRACTICES: MISLEADING OR DECEPTIVE CONDUCT: TRADE MARK: REGISTRATION: VALIDITY: REPUTATION AND GOODWILL: ASSIGNMENT WITHOUT GOODWILL: SUFFICIENCY: Australia: Fed. Ct) 8 I.P.R. 504

Merv Brown Pty Ltd v. David Jones (Aust.) Pty Ltd (TRADE PRACTICES: MISLEADING OR DECEPTIVE CONDUCT: PASSING OFF: TRADE MARK: INFRINGEMENT: VALIDITY: DECEPTION OR CONFUSION: VALIDITY OF ASSIGNMENT WITHOUT GOODWILL: Australia: Fed. Ct) 9 I.P.R. 321

Metal Box South Africa Ltd v. Midpak Blow-Moulders (Pty) Ltd (TRADE MARK: INFRINGEMENT: USE OF CONTAINER: RELEVANCE OF BELIEF OF PUBLIC AS TO ORIGIN OF GOODS: South Africa: TPD) 1988 (2) S.A. 446

Metal-Fren/Friction pad assembly (EUROPEAN PATENT: AMENDMENT: INCORPORATION INTO CLAIM 1 OF ONE (OUT OF SEVERAL) FEATURES OF DEPENDENT CLAIM: PRIORITY: NOVELTY: INVENTIVE STEP: DESCRIPTION: DISPARAGING REMARKS: T582/91: EPO) [1995] E.P.O.R. 574

Meter Systems Holdings Ltd v. Venter (CONFIDENTIAL INFORMATION: UNLAWFUL COMPETITION: FIDUCIARY RELATIONSHIPS: RESTRAINT OF TRADE: ENFORCEMENT: EX EMPLOYEE: South Africa: WLD) 1993 (1) S.A. 409

Methylomonas (XZB30/84: EPO) [1986] E.P.O.R. 325

Metrans Pty Ltd v. Courtney-Smith (CONFIDENTIAL INFORMATION: EMPLOYEE: PERSONAL SKILL: Australia: S.C.) 1 I.P.R. 185

Metro-SB-Großmärkte GmbH & Co. KG v. Cartier SA (RESTRICTIVE PRACTICES: SELECTIVE DISTRIBUTION: LUXURY WATCHES: REFUSAL BY MANUFACTURER TO HONOUR WATCHES ACQUIRED OUTSIDE EEC BY UNAUTHORISED DEALER AND SOLD IN GERMANY: WHETHER BREACH OF ARTICLE 85: Case C-376/92: ECJ) [1994] 5 C.M.L.R. 331

Metro-SB-Großmärkte GmbH & Co. KG v. E.C. Commission (No. 2)
(RESTRICTIVE PRACTICES: EXEMPTION: RENEWAL: NEED FOR COMMISSION
RE-EXAMINATION: SELECTIVE DISTRIBUTION: Case 75/84: ECJ)
[1987] 1 C.M.L.R. 118; [1986] E.C.R. 3121
Metropolitan Dairies Pty Ltd v. Pura Natural Spring Waters Pty Ltd (TRADE MARKS:
REGISTRATION: RENEWAL: LAPSED REGISTRATION: EXTENSION OF TIME:
ERROR OR OMISSION: NATURAL JUSTICE: *Locus standi*: PUBLIC POLICY:
Australia: Pat. Off.) 18 I.P.R. 436
Meyers v. Caterpillar Inc. (PATENT: APPLICATION: OPPOSITION: AMENDMENT:
COSTS: Australia: Pat. Off.) 19 I.P.R. 499
Michael (George) v. Sony Music Entertainment (U.K.) Ltd, *sub nom.* Panayiotou v.
Sony Music Entertainment (U.K.) Ltd
Michaelsen/Packing machine (EUROPEAN PATENT: INVENTIVE STEP: CHANGE OF
DIRECTION: COMMERCIAL SUCCESS: LONG-FELT WANT: SECONDARY
INDICATIONS: SIMPLICITY: T106/84: EPO)
[1979–85] E.P.O.R. C959; [1985] O.J. EPO 132
Michelin NV v. E.C. Commission, *sub nom.* Nederlandsche Banden-Industrie
Michelin NV v. E.C. Commission
Micro Pen Research Associates/Ink system for producing circuit patterns
(EUROPEAN PATENT: EXAMINATION PROCEDURE: FORMAL
CONSIDERATIONS FIRST: AMENDMENT AND CORRECTION: ADDED SUBJECT–
MATTER: T01/91: EPO) [1994] E.P.O.R. 71
Micro-Organisms (EUROPEAN PATENT: CONVENTIONS: EPO PRACTICE: REJECTED
BY NATIONAL COURT: MICRO–ORGANISMS: PATENTABILITY UNDER
AUSTRIAN LAW: B52/84: EPO) [1986] E.P.O.R. 204
Microcom v. Apple Computer Inc., *sub nom.* 115778 Canada Inc. (t/a Microcom) v.
Apple Computer Inc
Micronair (Aerial) Ltd v. Waikerie Co-operative Producers Ltd (PATENT:
OPPOSITION TO ACCEPTANCE: NOVELTY: OBVIOUSNESS: Australia: Pat.
Off.) 16 I.P.R. 460
Microsonics Corp.'s Applications (PATENT: APPLICATION: ANTICIPATION:
EVIDENCE: C.-G.) [1984] R.P.C. 29
Miele et Cie GmbH & Co. v. Evro Electrical (Pty) Ltd (TRADE MARK:
INFRINGEMENT: USE IN THE COURSE OF TRADE: South Africa: A.D.)
1988 (2) S.A. 583
Milcap Publishing Group AB v. Coranto Corporation Pty Ltd (PRACTICE: ANTON
PILLER: SETTING ASIDE: WHETHER FULL DISCLOSURE HAD BEEN MADE:
DOCTRINE OF *ex debito justitae*: Australia: Fed. Ct) 32 I.P.R. 34
Mildura Fruit Juices Pty Ltd v. Bannerman (TRADE PRACTICES: DECEPTION:
Australia: Fed. Ct) 1 I.P.R. 56
Miles/Test device (EUROPEAN PATENT: INVENTIVE STEP: CLOSEST PRIOR ART:
GENERAL APPROACH: OBJECTIVE ASSESSMENT: T31/84: EPO)
[1987] E.P.O.R. 10; [1986] O.J. EPO 369
Milk Marketing Board's Application (TRADE MARK: APPLICATION: DEVICE:
WHETHER MARK INHERENTLY ADAPTED TO DISTINGUISH: BoT)
[1988] R.P.C. 124
Millar v. Bassey (CONTRACT: INDUCING BREACH: APPLICATION TO STRIKE OUT
STATEMENT OF CLAIM: INTENTION OF DEFENDANT: KNOWLEDGE:
C.A.) [1994] E.M.L.R. 44

Milliken Denmark AS v. Walk Off Mats Ltd (PATENT: INFRINGEMENT: VALIDITY: RUBBER OR PLASTIC BACKED WASHABLE FLOOR MATS: CONSTRUCTION: AMBIGUITY: INSUFFICIENCY: ADDED MATTER: NOVELTY: PRIOR USE: ENABLING DISCLOSURE: OBVIOUSNESS: COMMERCIAL SUCCESS: Pat. Ct) [1996] F.S.R. 292

Mills' Application (PATENT: APPLICATION: PRACTICE: TIME LIMITS: ERROR IN PROCEDURE: Pat. Ct: C.A.) [1985] R.P.C. 339

Milltronics Ltd v. Hycontrol Ltd (COPYRIGHT: COMPUTER PROGRAMS: CANADIAN AUTHOR: QUALIFYING PERSON: C.A.) [1990] F.S.R. 273

Millwell Holdings Ltd v. Johnson (CONFIDENTIAL INFORMATION: DEVICES ASSEMBLED FROM COMMONPLACE COMPONENTS AND ON PUBLIC VIEW: EX-EMPLOYEE: DIRECTOR: ASSIGNMENT: New Zealand: H.C.) 12 I.P.R. 378

Milpurrurru v. Indofurn Pty Ltd (COPYRIGHT: ABORIGINAL ARTWORK: IMPORTATION: REPRODUCTION: SUBSTANTIAL PART: OWNERSHIP: KNOWLEDGE: DIRECTORS' LIABILITY: DELIVERY UP: CONVERSION DAMAGES: Australia: Fed. Ct) 130 A.L.R. 659; 30 I.P.R. 209

Milward-Bason and Burgess' Applications (PATENT: DIRECTIONS: JOINT OWNERS AND APPLICANTS: EFFECT OF AGREEMENT ON COMMISSIONER'S POWERS: EFFECT OF ONE OWNER'S DISINTEREST AND OBSTRUCTION: Australia: Pat. Off.) 11 I.P.R. 567

MINI-LIFT Trade Mark (TRADE MARK: OPPOSITION: NORMAL AND FAIR USE: EVIDENCE: T.M.Reg.) [1995] R.P.C. 128

Miniskips Ltd v. Sheltan Pty Ltd (TRADE PRACTICES: MISLEADING AND DECEPTIVE CONDUCT: FRANCHISE AGREEMENT: TERMINATION OF FRANCHISE AGREEMENT BY FRANCHISOR: RELIEF AGAINST FORFEITURE: FRANCHISEE CONTINUING TO TRADE USING FRANCHISOR'S TRADE MARK AND LOGO: INJUNCTION: INTERLOCUTORY: SERIOUS QUESTION TO BE TRIED: BALANCE OF CONVENIENCE: Australia: Fed. Ct) 11 I.P.R. 459

Minister of Agriculture's Patent (PATENT: AMENDMENT: OPPOSITION: VALIDITY: PRACTICE: PLEADINGS IN PATENT OFFICE: DISCRETION: Pat. Ct) [1990] R.P.C. 61

Ministère Public v. Deserbais (TRADE NAMES: CHEESE: EDAM GENERIC: NOT DESIGNATION OF ORIGIN: GERMAN EDAM WITH LOWER FAT CONTENT THAN ALLOWED IN FRANCE FOR FRENCH EDAM: REFUSED ENTRY INTO FRANCE: NO GOOD REASON: CONSUMERS PROTECTED ADEQUATELY BY LABELLING: MULTILATERAL TREATIES: NOT PLEADABLE AGAINST COMMUNITY LAW IF ONLY EEC MEMBER STATES INVOLVED: Case 286/86: ECJ) [1989] 1 C.M.L.R. 516; [1987] E.C.R. 4907

Ministère Public v. Lucazeau (Société des Auteurs, Compositeurs et Editeurs de Musique (SACEM) *partie civile*) (COPYRIGHT: INFRINGEMENT: COLLECTION AGENCIES: STATUS: CRIMINAL OFFENCE: PERFORMANCE: EEC: RESTRICTIVE PRACTICES: DOMINANT POSITION: ABUSE: France: C.A.) [1989] E.C.C. 66; [1989] 1 F.S.R. 209, *sub nom.* Ministère Public v. Tournier (Cases 395/87: ECJ) [1991] 4 C.M.L.R. 248; [1989] E.C.R. 2521; [1991] F.S.R. 465 *sub nom.* Lucazeau v. Société des Auteurs, Compositeurs et Editeurs de Musique (SACEM) (Cases 110/88 and 241–242/88: ECJ) [1991] 4 C.M.L.R. 248; [1989] E.C.R. 2521; [1991] F.S.R. 465

Minnesota Mining & Manufacturing Co. v. C. Jeffries Pty Ltd (PATENT: AUSTRALIA: PRACTICE: INFRINGEMENT: DISCOVERY: ELECTION FOR DAMAGES OR ACCOUNT OF PROFITS: WHETHER ELECTION TO BE MADE BEFORE DEFENDANT PROVIDES DISCOVERY: Australia: Fed. Ct (NSW)) 24 I.P.R. 413; [1993] F.S.R. 189

Minnesota Mining & Manufacturing Co. v. Rennicks (U.K.) Ltd (PATENT: INFRINGEMENT: DAMAGES: POSITION OF EXCLUSIVE LICENSEE WHO FAILED TO REGISTER: Pat. Ct)   [1992] F.S.R. 118
(CONSTRUCTION: VALIDITY: OBVIOUSNESS: INSUFFICIENCY: FALSE SUGGESTION: DAMAGES: EXCLUSIVE LICENCE: STAY OF INJUNCTION: Pat. Ct)
[1992] R.P.C. 331

Minnesota Mining & Manufacturing Co. v. Rennicks (U.K.) Ltd (PRACTICE: DISCOVERY: CONFIDENTIAL DOCUMENTS USED IN U.S. PROCEEDINGS: U.S. PROTECTIVE ORDER: PRIVILEGE: Ch.D.)   [1991] F.S.R. 97

Minnesota/Amendments (EUROPEAN PATENT: APPLICATION: PROCEDURE: INFORMAL COMMUNICATIONS: ORAL PROCEEDINGS MUST BE REQUESTED: TELEPHONIC COMMUNICATION WITH EXAMINER: REFUSAL: AMENDMENT AND CORRECTION: DISCLAIMER: NOVELTY: "REACTIVE WITH" INSUFFICIENT TO DISTINGUISH: T300/89: EPO)
[1991] E.P.O.R. 502; [1991] O.J. EPO 480

Minnesota/Insulating powder (EUROPEAN PATENT: UNITY: INTERNATIONAL SEARCH: MIXTURE AND COMPONENT: PCT AND EPC, COMMON JURISPRUDENCE: W07/85: EPO) [1988] E.P.O.R. 329; [1988] O.J. EPO 211

Minogue v. Grundy Television Pty Ltd (INJUNCTION: INTERLOCUTORY INJUNCTION: WHETHER SUBSTANTIAL QUESTION TO BE INVESTIGATED AT TRIAL AND WHETHER BALANCE OF CONVENIENCE FAVOURS INJUNCTION: APPLICATION OF BALANCE OF CONVENIENCE WHERE PROSPECTS OF SUCCESS AT TRIAL SLIGHT: Australia: S.C.(Vic.))   17 I.P.R. 596

MIPS Computer Systems Inc. v. MIPS Computer Resources Pty Ltd (TRADE PRACTICES: FALSE OR MISLEADING CONDUCT: COMPANY TRADING IN ITS OWN NAME WHERE NAME SUBSTANTIALLY SIMILAR TO ESTABLISHED COMPETITORS: LACHES: DELAY: INTERLOCUTORY INJUNCTION: BALANCE OF CONVENIENCE: Australia: Fed. Ct)   18 I.P.R. 577

Mirage Studios v. Counter-Feat Clothing Co. Ltd (PASSING OFF: COPYRIGHT INFRINGEMENT: CHARACTER MERCHANDISING: TEENAGE MUTANT NINJA TURTLES: INTERLOCUTORY INJUNCTION: FACTORS EVENLY BALANCED: PLAINTIFF'S NOT MANUFACTURING OR MARKETING: WHETHER PASSING OFF ARGUABLE: Ch.D.)   [1991] F.S.R. 145; 21 I.P.R. 302

Mirage Studios v. Thompson (TRADE MARK: OPPOSITION: FIRST USE IN AUSTRALIA: COWABUNGA: WHETHER USE AS A MARK OR AS EXCLAMATION: Australia: AIPO)   28 I.P.R. 517

Miro BV (IMPORTS: DRINKS: APPELATION: GENEVA: DECEPTION OF CONSUMER: STRENGTHS: Case 182/84: ECJ) [1986] 3 C.M.L.R. 545; [1983] E.C.R. 3461

Mirror Newspapers Ltd v. Queensland Newspapers Pty Ltd (COPYRIGHT: ORIGINAL LITERARY WORK: NEWSPAPER BINGO: Australia: S.C.(Qd.))
[1982] Qd.R. 305

Missing Link Software v. Magee (COPYRIGHT: INFRINGEMENT: WORK MADE IN COURSE OF EMPLOYMENT: TO WHOM DOES WORK OF MOONLIGHTING EMPLOYEE BELONG: Ch.D.)   [1989] 1 F.S.R. 361

MISTER DONUT Trade Mark (APPLICATION: PRACTICE: MISTER MARKS: T.M.Reg.)   [1983] R.P.C. 117; (1984) 8 I.P.L.R. 76

MITA/Representation (1) (EUROPEAN PATENT: PROFESSIONAL REPRESENTATIVES: ORAL PROCEEDINGS: AUTHORISED AND QUALIFIED: T80/84: EPO)   [1979–85] E.P.O.R. C946; [1985] O.J. EPO 269

MITA/Representation (2) (EUROPEAN PATENT: COSTS: ABORTIVE HEARING: AWARDED: T80/84: EPO)   [1986] E.P.O.R. 345; [1985] O.J. EPO 269

Mitchell Cotts Air Filtration Ltd (RESTRICTIVE PRACTICES: JOINT VENTURE: AIR
FILTERS FOR NUCLEAR, BIOLOGICAL, CHEMICAL AND COMPUTER MARKETS:
USE OF KNOW-HOW: INTENTION TO APPROVE: E.C. Comm.)
[1986] 3 C.M.L.R. 370

Mitchell Cotts Air Filtration Ltd (RESTRICTIVE PRACTICES: JOINT VENTURES:
POSITION OF PARENT: RELEVANT GEOGRAPHICAL MARKET: ARTICLE 85;
EXCLUSION FROM: KNOW-HOW LICENCE: PARTIAL NEGATIVE CLEARANCE:
E.C. Comm.)   [1988] 4 C.M.L.R. 111

Mitchelstown Co-operative Society Ltd v. Société des Produits Nestlé SA (TRADE
MARK LICENCE: JURISDICTION: ARBITRATION: BALANCE OF CONVENIENCE:
Ireland: S.C.)   [1989] 1 F.S.R. 345

Mitel Corp.'s Application (TRADE MARK: APPLICATION: SUPERSWITCH:
DISTINCTIVENESS: Australia: Pat. Off.)   5 I.P.R. 260

Mitsubishi Chemical Industries Ltd v. Asahi Kasei Kogyo KK (PATENT: OPPOSITION:
PRACTICE AND PROCEDURE: OPPORTUNITY GIVEN TO APPLICANT TO
RESPOND TO EVIDENCE-IN-REPLY: ERROR OR OMISSION BY EMPLOYEE OF
PATENT ATTORNEY: SPECIAL CIRCUMSTANCES: PUBLIC INTEREST: Australia:
Pat. Off.)   10 I.P.R. 591; 13 I.P.R. 160

Mitsubishi Denki KK/Semiconductor device (EUROPEAN PATENT: INVENTIVE
STEP: PREJUDICE: NOT TO BE EQUATED WITH ABSENCE OF DISCLOSURE IN
PRIOR SKILLED PERSON, RELEVANT FIELD: T607/90: EPO)
[1991] E.P.O.R. 569

Mitsubishi Jidosha Kogyo KK's Application (PATENT: APPLICATION:
INTERNATIONAL APPLICATION: PRACTICE: EXTENSION OF TIME: DEFAULT:
DISCRETION: Pat. Ct)   [1988] R.P.C. 449

Mitsubishi v. Fiat, *sub nom.* LANCER Trade Mark

Mitsuboshi Belting Ltd/Power transmission belt manufacture (EUROPEAN PATENT:
OPPOSITION: PROCEDURE: PROCEDURAL AND SUBSTANTIVE ISSUES SHOULD
BE HEARD TOGETHER: EXTENSIONS OF TIME: SHOULD NOT BE REPEATED
SAVE IN EXCEPTIONAL: ORAL PROCEEDINGS: APPEAL: REMITTAL ORDERED:
WITH RELUCTANCE IN PROTRACTED PROCEEDINGS: T352/89: EPO)
[1991] E.P.O.R. 249

Mitsuboshi/Endless power transmission belt (EUROPEAN PATENT: INVENTIVE STEP:
AGED ART: COMBINATION OF CITATIONS: FURTHER ADVANTAGES:
OPPOSITION: PROCEDURE: AUXILIARY REQUEST, NEED FOR: PRIOR ART:
AGED PUBLICATIONS: T169/84: EPO)
[1987] E.P.O.R. 120; [1995] O.J. EPO 193

Mitsui Engineering & Shipbuilding Co. Ltd's Application (PATENT:
INTERNATIONAL APPLICATION: FILING OF TRANSLATIONS: Pat. Ct)
[1984] R.P.C. 471

Mitsui/Ethylene copolymer (EUROPEAN PATENT: APPEAL: PROCEDURE:
STATEMENT OF GROUNDS, REQUIREMENTS OF: ADMISSIBILITY OF FRESH
CASE: REMITTAL, FRESH CATEGORY OF CLAIM ON APPEAL: OPPOSITION:
FRESH PRIOR USE ON APPEAL: EXPEDITED DETERMINATION: T611/90:
EPO)   [1991] E.P.O.R. 481; [1993] O.J. EPO 50

Mitsui/Titanium catalyst (EUROPEAN PATENT: OPPOSITION: PROCEDURE: ONUS
OF PROOF: PROCEEDINGS: EVIDENCE: COMPARATIVE TESTS: MUST BE
CARRIED OUT IN SOME WAY: INVENTIVE STEP: SIMPLICITY OF SOLUTION:
NOVELTY: IMPLICIT DISCLOSURE: T209/85: EPO)   [1987] E.P.O.R. 235

M.J. Exports Pvt. Ltd v. Charak Pharmaceuticals (TRADE MARK: REFUSAL OF
REGISTRATION: OPPOSITION: MJTONE/M2TONE: APPEAL: India:
H.C.)   (1991) 16 I.P.L.R. 255
(APPEAL: FURTHER APPEAL: India: H.C.)   (1993) 18 I.P.L.R. 39

MMD Design & Consultancy Ltd's Patent (PATENT: DECLARATION OF NON-
INFRINGEMENT: PRACTICE: C.-G.) [1989] R.P.C. 131
Mobay Corp. v. Dow Chemical Co. (PATENT: OPPOSITION: PRACTICE AND
PROCEDURE: APPLICATION TO DELETE CERTAIN PARTS OF OPPONENT'S
STATEMENT OF GROUNDS AND PARTICULARS: APPROPRIATE ANALOGY OF
PLEADING PRINCIPLES: POWER TO DISMISS OPPOSITION: NO POWER TO
AMEND GROUNDS OR PARTICULARS: POWER TO ORDER FURTHER AND
BETTER PARTICULARS: NO POWER TO STRIKE OUT PARTICULARS: Australia:
Pat. Off.) 24 I.P.R. 379
Mobay/Methylenebis (phenyl isocyanate) (EUROPEAN PATENT: AMENDMENT AND
CORRECTION: DERIVED RANGE: INVENTIVE STEP: COMBINATION OF
CITATIONS: SIMPLIFICATION OF PRIOR ART: T2/81: EPO)
[1979–85] E.P.O.R. B280; [1982] O.J. EPO 394
Mobil Oil Corp. v. Foodland Associated Ltd (TRADE MARK: APPLICATION:
OPPOSITION: PROPRIETORSHIP: AMENDMENT OF MARK: DISCLAIMER:
Australia: T.M.Reg.) 7 I.P.R. 382
Mobil Oil Corp. v. Registrar of Trade Marks (TRADE MARKS: REGISTRABILITY:
INVENTED WORD: Australia: S.C.(Vic.)) [1984] V.R. 25; 1 I.P.R. 366
Mobil Oil Corp. v. Registrar of Trade Marks (TRADE MARK: REGISTRABILITY:
INVENTED WORD: Australia: S.C.(NSW)) 5 I.P.R. 735
Mobil Oil/Admissibility (EUROPEAN PATENT: OPPOSITION: PROCEDURE:
ADMISSIBILITY: PRIOR NATIONAL RIGHTS: NATIONAL LAWS, DIVERGENCE IN:
WHETHER GROUND OF OPPOSITION: ENLARGED BOARD OF APPEAL:
REFERENCE REFUSED: *Acte clair.* T550/88: EPO)
[1990] E.P.O.R. 391; [1992] O.J. EPO 117
Mobil Oil/Amendment of claims (EUROPEAN PATENT: AMENDMENT AND
CORRECTION: DISCLOSURE: CROSS–REFERENCED DOCUMENT REFERRED
TO IN APPLICATION DOCUMENTS: INCLUSION OF FEATURES: NOVELTY:
SIMILAR PROCESS WITH DIFFERENT PURPOSE: T6/84: EPO)
[1979–85] E.P.O.R. C924; [1985] O.J. EPO 238
Mobil Oil/Catalyst (EUROPEAN PATENT: CLAIMS: FAIR BASIS: INVENTIVE STEP:
COULD/WOULD TEST: REVERSAL OF TREND: SURPRISING EFFECT: T392/86:
EPO) [1988] E.P.O.R. 178
Mobil Oil/Debit order III (EUROPEAN PATENT: OPPOSITION: PROCEDURE:
ADMISSIBILITY: COSTS: IMPROPER BEHAVIOUR REQUIRED: REFUSED:
ENLARGED BOARD OF APPEAL: REFERENCE REFUSED: FEES: PAYMENT BY
DEBIT ORDER: T170/83: EPO)
[1979–85] E.P.O.R. C877; [1984] O.J. EPO 605
Mobil Oil/Disclosure (EUROPEAN PATENT: AMENDMENT AND CORRECTION:
TEACHING OF DOCUMENT AS A WHOLE: DISCLOSURE: DERIVED RANGE:
T54/82: EPO) [1979–85] E.P.O.R. B469; [1983] O.J. EPO 446
Mobil Oil/Film (EUROPEAN PATENT: INVENTIVE STEP: CLOSEST PRIOR ART:
STATE OF THE ART: UNASCERTAINABLE FEATURES OF PRIOR PRODUCT:
T405/86: EPO) [1992] E.P.O.R. 178
Mobil Oil/Friction reducing additive (1) (EUROPEAN PATENT: NOVELTY: NEW
PURPOSE/USE FOR KNOWN SUBSTANCE/EQUIPMENT: INEVITABLE RESULT:
AMENDMENT AND CORRECTION: CATEGORY OF CLAIM: ENLARGED BOARD
OF APPEAL: PRESIDENT OF THE EPO: T59/87: EPO)
[1989] E.P.O.R. 80; [1991] O.J. EPO 561
Mobil Oil/Friction reducing additive (2) (EUROPEAN PATENT: AMENDMENT AND
CORRECTION: CATEGORY OF CLAIM: NOVELTY: NEW PURPOSE/USE FOR
KNOWN SUBSTANCE/EQUIPMENT: G02/88: EPO)
[1990] E.P.O.R. 73; [1990] O.J. EPO 93

Mobil Oil/Friction reducing additive (3) (EUROPEAN PATENT: T59/87: EPO)
[1990] E.P.O.R. 514; [1991] O.J. EPO 561
Mobil Oil/Metal-coated film (EUROPEAN PATENT: EVIDENCE: CONFLICT: INVENTIVE STEP: ONUS OF PROOF: OPPOSITION: PROCEDURE: EXPERIMENTAL PROTOCOL: ORAL PROCEEDINGS: NO CONTINUATION OF: T547/88: EPO) [1994] E.P.O.R. 349
Mobil Oil/Opposition against own patent (EUROPEAN PATENT: ENLARGED BOARD OF APPEAL: PRESIDENT OF THE EPO: T130/84: EPO)
[1979–85] E.P.O.R. C971; [1984] O.J. EPO 613
Mobil Oil/Opposition by proprietor (2) (EUROPEAN PATENT: REVOCATION: PROPRIETOR: OPPOSITION: PROCEDURE: LIMITATION AT INSTANCE OF PATENTEE: ENLARGED BOARD OF APPEAL: POINT OF LAW, ANSWERED: G01/84: EPO) [1986] E.P.O.R. 39; [1985] O.J. EPO 299
Mobil Oil/Poly P-methylstyrene articles (EUROPEAN PATENT: EVIDENCE: COMPARATIVE TESTS: UNRELIABLE METHOD: INVENTIVE STEP: PROBLEM, RE-STATEMENT OF: T184/82: EPO)
[1979–85] E.P.O.R. C690; [1984] O.J. EPO 261
Mobil Oil/Reformate upgrading (EUROPEAN PATENT: CLAIMS: CLARITY: T136/84: EPO) [1979–85] E.P.O.R. C973
Mobil Oil/Thermoplastic film laminate (EUROPEAN PATENT: COSTS: RESERVED FOR LATER CONSIDERATION: INVENTIVE STEP: MULTIPLE APPROACHES: OPPOSITION: PROCEDURE: FRESH DOCUMENTS ON APPEAL: T43/85: EPO) [1987] E.P.O.R. 272
Mobius/Pencil sharpener (EUROPEAN PATENT: INVENTIVE STEP: REMOTE TECHNICAL FIELD: STATE OF THE ART: PRIOR ART: NEIGHBOURING FIELDS: T176/84: EPO) [1986] E.P.O.R. 117; [1986] O.J. EPO 50
Mogul/Divisional application (EUROPEAN PATENT: DIVISIONAL APPLICATION: TIME LIMIT: APPEAL: PROCEDURE: POWERS OF BOARD OF APPEAL: FEES: REIMBURSEMENT OF APPEAL FEE: J38/89: EPO) [1992] E.P.O.R. 214
Mohamad Khalil v. The State of Maharashtra (TRADE MARK: REVISION: CRIMINAL APPLICATION: India: H.C.) (1982) 7 I.P.L.R. 25
Mohan Meakin Ltd v. The Pravara Sahakari Sakhar Karkhana Ltd (TRADE MARK: INFRINGEMENT: BLACK KNIGHT/ROYAL KNIGHT: PASSING OFF: STATUTORY NOTICE PERIOD: JURISDICTION: APPEAL: India: H.C.)
(1990) 15 I.P.L.R. 191
Mohan Meaking Ltd v. Kashmiri Dreamland Distilleries (TRADE MARK: COPYRIGHT: PASSING OFF: M.M.B./M.B.B.: JURISDICTION: India: H.C.)
(1990) 15 I.P.L.R. 321
Mohanlal Gupta v. The Board of School Education, Haryana (COPYRIGHT: INFRINGEMENT: India: H.C.) (1978) 3 I.P.L.R. 83
Mokhtar Haji Jamaludin v. Pustaka Sistem Pelajaran (COPYRIGHT: INFRINGEMENT: DAMAGES: Malaysia: H.C.) [1986] 2 M.L.J. 376
Mölnlycke AB v. Procter & Gamble Ltd (PATENT: DECLARATION OF NON-INFRINGEMENT: PATENT HELD INVALID IN OTHER PROCEEDINGS: MOTION FOR JUDGMENT: COSTS: Pat. Ct) [1990] R.P.C. 267
Mölnlycke AB v. Procter & Gamble Ltd (No. 2) (PATENT: INFRINGEMENT: INTERLOCUTORY INJUNCTION: AMENDMENT: Pat. Ct) [1990] R.P.C. 487
Mölnlycke AB v. Procter & Gamble Ltd (No. 3) (PATENT: INFRINGEMENT: PRACTICE: DISCOVERY: OBVIOUSNESS: COMMERCIAL SUCCESS: INSUFFICIENCY: Pat. Ct) [1990] R.P.C. 498

Mölnlycke AB v. Procter & Gamble Ltd (No. 4) (PATENT: INFRINGEMENT: JOINT TORTFEASOR: COMMON DESIGN: PRACTICE: DISCOVERY: JOINDER OF NEW DEFENDANT FOR PURPOSE OF DISCOVERY: WHETHER ABUSE OF PROCESS OR IMPROPER: C.A.)
[1992] 4 All E.R. 47; [1992] R.P.C. 21; [1992] 1 W.L.R. 1112
Mölnlycke AB v. Procter & Gamble Ltd (No. 5) (PATENT: CONSTRUCTION: PRACTICE: OBVIOUSNESS: RELEVANCE OF OTHER INVENTORS HAVING SAME IDEA: REACTIONS OF COMPETITORS: WHETHER AMBIGUITY NOT AMOUNTING TO INSUFFICIENCY GROUND FOR REVOCATION: ADDED MATTER: SECTION 2(3) CITATION: REASONABLE SKILL AND KNOWLEDGE: WHETHER FAILURE TO INCLUDE DETAILS OF METHOD RELEVANT: LACK OF CLARITY IN DRAFTING: WHETHER ENTRY OF NOTICE OF APPLICATION AMOUNTS TO REGISTRATION OF EXCLUSIVE LICENCE: WHETHER COMPLEXITY OF INQUIRY SPECIAL REASON JUSTIFYING STAY: COSTS: CERTIFICATE OF CONTESTED VALIDITY: Pat. Ct) [1992] F.S.R. 549
(VALIDITY: OBVIOUSNESS: ADDED MATTER: AMENDMENT: EXCLUSIVE LICENCE: PATENT OFFICE PRACTICE: COSTS: CERTIFICATE OF CONTESTED VALIDITY: Pat. Ct: C.A.) [1994] R.P.C. 49
Mölnlycke AB v. Procter & Gamble Ltd (No. 6) (PATENT: PRACTICE: COSTS: ENQUIRY FOR DAMAGES PENDING: WHETHER PLAINTIFF'S ENTITLED TO IMMEDIATE TAXATION: WHETHER AMENDMENT UNDER SLIP RULE PERMISSIBLE: Pat. Ct) [1993] F.S.R. 154
Mölnlycke/Dry salt compress (EUROPEAN PATENT: INVENTIVE STEP: AGED ART: ONE-WAY STREET: SMALL BUT NECESSARY MODIFICATION: SURPRISING EFFECT: PRIOR ART: AGED PUBLICATIONS: T102/82: EPO)
[1979–85] E.P.O.R. B530
Monde (Sàrl) etc, *sub nom.* Le Monde (Sàrl)
Monier Ltd v. Metalwork Tiling Co. of Australia Ltd (No. 2) (PRACTICE: COSTS: DISCRETION: EXERCISE AGAINST SUCCESSFUL PARTY: Australia: S.C.(NSW))
7 I.P.R. 562
Monks Ferry (Ship Breaking) Ltd and George Cohen Sons & Co. Ltd (RESTRICTIVE PRACTICES: COAL AND STEEL: SCRAP METAL: CONCENTRATION: AUTHORISATION OF TAKEOVER: E.C. Comm.) [1988] 4 C.M.L.R. 192
Mono Pumps (N.Z.) Ltd v. Amalgamated Pumps Ltd (COPYRIGHT: INFRINGEMENT: INJUNCTION: ORIGINAL ARTISTIC WORK: WHETHER DRAWINGS ILLUSTRATING AN IDEA CAPABLE OF COPYRIGHT PROTECTION: LICENSING AGREEMENT: IMPLIED TERMS: DESIGN: REGISTRABILITY: New Zealand: H.C.) [1992] 1 N.Z.L.R. 728
Mono Pumps (N.Z.) Ltd v. Karinya Industries Ltd (COPYRIGHT: INFRINGEMENT: LICENSEE OF OVERSEAS PATENT: IDEA AND EXPRESSION: INTERLOCUTORY INJUNCTION: New Zealand: H.C.) 4 I.P.R. 505
Mono Pumps (N.Z.) Ltd v. Karinya Industries Ltd (COURTS: JUDICIAL PRECEDENT: DECISIONS OF U.K. HOUSE OF LORDS: New Zealand: H.C.) 7 I.P.R. 25
Monsanto's CCP Patent (PATENT: COMPULSORY LICENCE: CARBONLESS COPYING PAPER: BURDEN OF PROOF: BEST EVIDENCE: C.-G.) [1990] F.S.R. 93
Monsanto Co.'s Application (PATENT: APPLICATION: CLAIMS: FAIRLY BASED: PRIOR PUBLICATION: Australia: Pat. Off.) 8 I.P.R. 108
Monsanto Co. v. Stauffer Chemical Co. (N.Z.) (PATENT: INFRINGEMENT: EXPERIMENTAL USE: INTERLOCUTORY RELIEF: New Zealand: H.C.)
[1984] F.S.R. 559
Monsanto Co. v. Stauffer Chemical Co. (PATENT: INFRINGEMENT: CONSTRUCTION OF CLAIM: CHEMICAL SUBSTANCE: INTERLOCUTORY INJUNCTION: C.A.) [1984] F.S.R. 574

Monsanto Co. v. Stauffer Chemical Co. (PATENT: INFRINGEMENT: EXPERIMENTAL
USE: MODIFICATION OF INTERLOCUTORY INJUNCTION: Pat. Ct)
3 I.P.R. 353; [1985] F.S.R. 55; [1985] R.P.C. 515
(C.A.) [1985] R.P.C. 675
Monsoon Ltd v. India Imports of Rhode Island Ltd (COPYRIGHT: PRINTED FABRICS:
SECONDARY INFRINGEMENT: PERIOD OF GRACE BEFORE FIXED WITH
KNOWLEDGE: Ch.D.) [1993] F.S.R. 486
Mont (J.A.) (U.K.) Ltd v. Mills (RESTRICTIVE PRACTICES: EX-EMPLOYEE'S
SEVERANCE AGREEMENT: VALIDITY OF COVENANT: BREACH OF
CONFIDENCE: FORM OF INJUNCTION: APPROACH TO CONSTRUCTION OF
RESTRICTIVE COVENANTS: GOOD FAITH: C.A.) [1993] F.S.R. 577
Montana Wines Ltd v. Villa Maria Wines Ltd, *sub nom.* Villa Maria Wines Ltd v.
Montana Wines Ltd
Montedison/Ethylene polymers (EUROPEAN PATENT: CLAIMS: PRODUCT-BY-
PROCESS: T93/83: EPO) [1987] E.P.O.R. 144
Montedison/Polymer (EUROPEAN PATENT: AMENDMENT AND CORRECTION:
DISCREPANCY BETWEEN CLAIM AND DESCRIPTION: OBVIOUS CORRECTION
WHEN TEXT READ IN ISOLATION: CLAIMS: CONSTRUCTION: ORIGINAL
LANGUAGE, SIGNIFICANCE OF: OPPOSITION: PROCEDURE: SUBSEQUENT
WRITTEN DECISION: CONFORMITY OF: REMITTAL TO FIRST INSTANCE:
ENLARGED BOARD OF APPEAL: FUNCTION OF: POWERS AND DUTIES OF:
T337/88: EPO) [1990] E.P.O.R. 533
Montres Rolex SA v. Kleynhams (TRADE MARK: INFRINGEMENT: ACCOUNT OF
PROFITS: South Africa: CPD) 1985 (1) S.A. 55
Moog/Change of category (EUROPEAN PATENT: AMENDMENT AND CORRECTION:
CATEGORY OF CLAIM: T378/86: EPO)
[1989] E.P.O.R. 85; [1988] O.J. EPO 386
Moons Products Pty Ltd v. Herbs of Gold Pty Ltd (CONSUMER PROTECTION:
PASSING OFF: MISLEADING OR DECEPTIVE CONDUCT: INTERLOCUTORY
INJUNCTION: SIMILARLY NAMED PRODUCTS: CELERY 2000+: WHETHER
CASE LIKELY TO SUCCEED AT TRIAL: Australia: Fed. Ct) 21 I.P.R. 577
Moore Paragon Aust. Ltd v. Multiform Printers (PATENTS: OPPOSITION: LACK OF
NOVELTY: PRIOR PUBLICATION: OBVIOUSNESS: MANNER OF NEW
MANUFACTURE: Australia: Pat. Off.) 3 I.P.R. 270
Moorgate Tobacco Co. Ltd v. Philip Morris Ltd (CONTRACT: LICENCE:
CONSTRUCTION: TRADE MARK: CONFIDENTIAL INFORMATION: Australia:
S.C.(NSW)) [1985] 56 A.L.R. 193; (1985) R.P.C. 219
(H.C.) (1982) 64 C.L.R. 387
Moorhead v. Paul Brennan (t/a Primavera Press) (COPYRIGHT: LITERARY WORK:
EXCLUSIVE LICENCE TO PUBLISH: IMPLIED OBLIGATIONS: Australia:
S.C.(NSW)) 20 I.P.R. 161
Moosehead Breweries Ltd and Whitbread and Co. plc's Agreement (RESTRICTIVE
PRACTICES: LICENCE FOR PRODUCTION AND SALE OF CANADIAN BEER IN
UNITED KINGDOM: NON-EXCLUSIVE WITH APPROPRIATE ANCILLARY
RESTRICTIONS FOR KNOW-HOW: PROHIBITION ON SALE OUTSIDE U.K. AND
SALE OF COMPETING BRANDS AND EXCLUSIVITY FOR TRADE MARK: ARTICLE
85(1): TRADE MARK NO CHALLENGE CLAUSE: OWNERSHIP: POSSIBLY
RESTRICTIVE AS REGARDS VALIDITY: COMPARATIVELY NEW TO U.K.:
EXEMPTION GRANTED: E.C. Comm.) [1991] 4 C.M.L.R. 391

Morgan & Banks Pty Ltd v. Select Personnel Pty Ltd (PASSING OFF: WHETHER REPUTATION ESTABLISHED: WHETHER DESCRIPTIVE WORDS ESTABLISHED A DISTINCTIVE NAME: WHETHER ADVERTISEMENTS RELEVANTLY MISREPRESENTED: SUFFICIENCY OF EVIDENCE OF CONFUSION: Australia: S.C.(NSW))   20 I.P.R. 289

Morgan-Grampian plc v. Training Personnel Ltd (PASSING OFF: MAGAZINE TITLES: CHANGE OF TITLE: INTERLOCUTORY INJUNCTION: BALANCE OF CONVENIENCE: STATUS QUO: Ch.D.)   [1992] F.S.R. 267

Moriarty's Application (PATENT: APPLICATION: DISPUTE BETWEEN APPLICANTS: REQUEST: INTERESTED PARTY: COSTS: Australia: Pat. Off.)   26 I.P.R. 21

Moroka Swallows Football Club Ltd v. The Birds Football Club (TRADE MARK: PASSING OFF: NAME OF SOCCER TEAM: GOODWILL: South Africa: WLD)   1987 (2) S.A. 511

Morrison Leahy Music Ltd v. Lightbond Ltd (COPYRIGHT: INFRINGEMENT: INTERLOCUTORY INJUNCTION: DEFENDANTS PRODUCING MEDLEY OF SECOND PLAINTIFF'S SONGS AND OBTAINING MCPS CLEARANCE: WHETHER CHARACTER OF MUSICAL WORKS ALTERED: WHETHER LYRICS MODIFIED MORAL RIGHTS: RIGHT OF INTEGRITY: INFRINGEMENT: WHETHER TREATMENT AMOUNTING TO MUTILATION OR DISTORTION: Ch.D.)   [1993] E.M.L.R. 144

Morton v. Black (TRADE PRACTICES: WHETHER SALE OF A FARM "IN TRADE OR COMMERCE": REPRESENTATIONS BY TELEPHONE: WHETHER WITHIN PRINCIPLE OF *Bevanere v. Lubidineuse*: Australia: Fed. Ct)   12 I.P.R. 408

Mothercare U.K. Ltd v. Penguin Books Ltd (PASSING OFF: TRADE MARK: INFRINGEMENT: INTERLOCUTORY INJUNCTION: MISREPRESENTATION: DESCRIPTIVE WORDS: BOOK TITLE: MOTHERCARE/MOTHER CARE/OTHER CARE: LIKELIHOOD OF DAMAGE: SURVEY EVIDENCE: PRACTICE: C.A.)   [1988] R.P.C. 113

Motorola/Admissibility (EUROPEAN PATENT: APPLICATION: PROCEDURE: COMMUNICATION UNDER RULE 51(4)—MISLEADING AND VOID: GOOD FAITH GOVERNING RELATIONS BETWEEN EPO AND APPLICANTS: PRACTICE CONTRARY TO RULES: VOIDNESS OF EPO ACT WHERE APPLICANT MISLED: CONVENTIONS: EPO PRACTICE: EFFECT OF: J02/87: EPO)   [1989] E.P.O.R. 42; [1988] O.J. EPO 330

Motorola/Isolated mistake-restitution (EUROPEAN PATENT: APPEAL: PROCEDURE: FRESH EVIDENCE: RE-ESTABLISHMENT OF RIGHTS: CHANGE IN APPLICANT'S PROCEDURES: J02/86; J03/86: EPO)   [1987] E.P.O.R. 394; [1987] O.J. EPO 362

Motorola/Restitution (EUROPEAN PATENT: RE-ESTABLISHMENT OF RIGHTS: COMMENCEMENT OF PERIOD FOR: FEES: REIMBURSEMENT OF APPEAL FEE: DIFFERENT MEANING OF GERMAN TEXT: J07/83: EPO)   [1979–85] E.P.O.R. A226; [1984] O.J. EPO 211

Mouchet/Interruption of proceedings (EUROPEAN PATENT: PROCEDURE: INTERRUPTION, EFFECT ON TIME LIMITS: J07/83: EPO)   [1979–85] E.P.O.R. A174

MOULIN Winter Wheat (PLANT BREEDERS RIGHTS: UNIFORMITY: PLANT VARIETIES AND SEEDS TRIBUNAL)   [1985] F.S.R. 283

MPA Pharma v. Rhône Poulenc *sub nom.* Bristol Myers Squibb v. Paranova

MPD Technology/Priority claim (EUROPEAN PATENT: APPLICATION: PROCEDURE: PRIORITY CLAIM: FEES: REIMBURSEMENT OF APPEAL FEE: J09/80: EPO)   [1979–85] E.P.O.R. A45

MRF Ltd v. Metro Tyres Ltd (TRADE MARK: INFRINGEMENT: NYLOGRIP/ RADIALGRIP: PASSING OFF: DECEPTIVE USE OF TYRE TREAD PATTERN: INTERIM INJUNCTION: India: H.C.) (1991) 16 I.P.L.R. 165

MS Associates Ltd v. Power (COPYRIGHT: INFRINGEMENT: COMPUTER PROGRAMS: INTERLOCUTORY INJUNCTION: TRANSLATOR PROGRAMS: SIMILARITIES: ARGUABLE CASE: BALANCE OF CONVENIENCE: Ch.D.) [1988] F.S.R. 242

MTV Europe v. BMG Records (U.K.) Ltd (RESTRICTIVE PRACTICES: ALLEGED BREACH OF ARTICLE 85; ACTION FOR DAMAGES: OVERLAPPING ACTION BEFORE COMMISSION: APPLICATION TO STAY: JURISDICTION: Ch.D.) [1995] 1 C.M.L.R. 437

Muckross Park Hotel Ltd v. Randles (PASSING OFF: HOTEL: MUCKROSS PARK HOTEL: NEW BUSINESS MUCKROSS COURT HOTEL: LIKELIHOOD OF DECEPTION: DETERMINATION: SECONDARY MEANING: THE MUCKROSS: GOODWILL: Ireland: H.C.) [1995] 1 I.R. 130

Mückter/Lithium salts (EUROPEAN PATENT: UNITY: INTERNATIONAL SEARCH: REQUIREMENT TO GIVE REASONS: W07/86: EPO) [1987] E.P.O.R. 176; [1987] O.J. EPO 67

Müllverbrennungsanlage Wuppertal/No-challenge obligation (EUROPEAN PATENT: OPPOSITION: PROCEDURE: NO-CHALLENGE OBLIGATION: PUBLIC INTEREST: PURPOSE: CONVENTIONS: EEC LAW, RELEVANCE OF: NATIONAL LAWS, RELATIONSHIP OF EPC TO: Patent No. 0 157 920: EPO) [1993] E.P.O.R. 479

Multi Tube Systems (Pty) Ltd v. Ponting (CONFIDENTIAL INFORMATION: MASTER AND SERVANT: INTERIM INJUNCTION: South Africa: D&CLD) 1984 (3) S.A. 182

Multicoin Amusements Pty Ltd v. British Amusements (North Coast) Corp. Pty Ltd (COPYRIGHT: THREATENED INFRINGEMENT: THREATS: IMPORTATION: PARALLEL IMPORTATION: EXCLUSIVE LICENCE: MISLEADING AND DECEPTIVE CONDUCT ARISING FROM UNJUSTIFIABLE THREATS: Australia: S.C.(Qd.)) 15 I.P.R. 63

Multotech Manufacturing (Pty) Ltd v. Screenex Wire Weaving Manufacturers (Pty) Ltd (PATENT: VALIDITY: ESSENTIAL FEATURES: South Africa: A.D.) 1983 (1) S.A. 709

Mun Loong Co. Sdn Bhd v. Chai Tuck Kin (PASSING OFF: BUSINESS NAME: MONOPOLY RIGHT: Malaysia: H.C.) [1982] 1 M.L.J. 356

Munro v. Tooheys Ltd (TRADE PRACTICES: MISLEADING AND DECEPTIVE CONDUCT: REPRESENTATION THAT A CUSTOMER CAN DRINK NOT INSIGNIFICANT AMOUNTS OF "LIGHT" BEER AND NOT EXCEED PRESCRIBED ALCOHOL LIMIT: Australia: Fed. Ct) 21 I.P.R. 268

Murdock Overseas Corp. v. Saramar Corp. (TRADE MARKS: PRACTICE AND PROCEDURE: APPLICATION OUT OF TIME FOR EXTENSION OF TIME FOR FILING EVIDENCE: OMISSION BY ATTORNEY: PUBLIC POLICY: Australia: Pat. Off.) 17 I.P.R. 451

Murex Diagnostics Australia Pty. Ltd v. Chiron Corp (PRACTICE: DISCOVERY: DOCUMENT OR CLASS OF DOCUMENT: Australia: Fed. Ct) 133 A.L.R. 737

Murex Diagnostics Pty Ltd v. Chiron Corp., *sub nom.* Chiron Corp. v. Murex Diagnostics Ltd

Murray Goulburn Co-operative Co. Ltd v. New South Wales Dairy Corp. (TRADE MARKS: APPLICATION FOR REMOVAL OF MARK FOR NON-USE: "GOODS OF THE SAME DESCRIPTION": NO "USE IN GOOD FAITH": Australia: Fed. Ct) 14 I.P.R. 26

MY MUMS COLA Trade Mark (TRADE MARK: APPLICATION: LAUDATORY ELEMENT: WHETHER MARK DESCRIPTIVE OF DISTINCTIVE: BoT)
[1988] R.P.C. 130

N. & P. Windows v. Cego Ltd (COPYRIGHT: INFRINGEMENT: PRACTICE: PARTICULARS OF SIMILARITIES: Ch.D.)   [1989] F.S.R. 56
Nabisco/Micro-organisms (EUROPEAN PATENT: APPLICATION: PROCEDURE: FAIRNESS, REQUIREMENT FOR: CONVENTIONS: BUDAPEST TREATY: MICRO-ORGANISMS: DEPOSIT AND AVAILABILITY: T239/87: EPO)
[1988] E.P.O.R. 311
Nachf's Application (PRACTICE: APPEAL TO PATENT COURT: EXTENSION OF TIME TO APPEAL: Pat. Ct)   [1983] R.P.C. 87
Naf Naf SA v. Dickens (London) Ltd (PASSING OFF: PRACTICE: APPLICATION TO DISCHARGE: ANTON PILLER ORDER: INSUFFICIENT EVIDENCE TO WARRANT GRANT: MATERIAL NON-DISCLOSURE: APPLICATION TO PREVENT PLAINTIFF'S FROM USING EVIDENCE GAINED ON EXECUTION: INDEMNITY COSTS: IMMEDIATE TAXATION: Ch.D.)   [1993] F.S.R. 424
Naimer/Computer-controlled switch (EUROPEAN PATENT: OPPOSITION: PROCEDURE: CLAIMS: OBJECTION TO CLARITY OF, INADMISSIBLE: T23/86: EPO)   [1987] E.P.O.R. 383; [1987] O.J. EPO 316
Namol Pty Ltd v. A. W. Baulderstone Pty Ltd (COPYRIGHT: INFRINGEMENT: WORKING DRAWINGS FOR DOORS AND WINDOWS: WHETHER DIRECTOR OF INFRINGING COMPANY A JOINT TORTFEASOR: WHETHER COMPANY DIRECTOR IN BREACH OF FIDUCIARY DUTY: ASSESSMENT OF DAMAGES FOR COPYRIGHT INFRINGEMENT: Australia: Fed. Ct)   27 I.P.R. 1
Napier Brown & Co. Ltd v. British Sugar plc (RESTRICTIVE PRACTICES: ABUSE OF DOMINANT POSITION: REFUSAL TO SUPPLY SUGAR: UNDERTAKINGS: SETTLEMENT: E.C. Comm.)   [1986] 3 C.M.L.R. 594
Napp Laboratories v. Pfizer Inc. (PATENT: REVOCATION: PRACTICE: SERVICE OF PETITION FOR REVOCATION: WHETHER LEAVE REQUIRED FOR SERVICE OUT OF JURISDICTION: WHETHER SERVICE IRREGULAR BECAUSE NO ENDORSEMENT: Ch.D.)   [1993] F.S.R. 150
Narhex Australia Pty Ltd v. Sunspot Products Pty Ltd (TRADE PRACTICES: MISLEADING OR DECEPTIVE CONDUCT: ADVERTISING AND LABELLING REPRESENTATIONS AS TO QUALITIES AND PROVENANCE OF PRODUCT: CROSS-LINKED ELASTIN CREAM FOR SKIN WRINKLES: CORRECTIVE ADVERTISING: FACTORS RELEVANT: Australia: Fed. Ct)   18 I.P.R. 535
NAT/Bagging plant (EUROPEAN PATENT: PATENTABILITY: METHOD FOR DOING BUSINESS: AMENDMENT AND CORRECTION: INTERNATIONAL STANDARD: CLAIMS: FUNCTIONAL FEATURES: SCOPE VARYING WITH TIME: INVENTIVE STEP: COMBINATION OF CITATIONS: ADAPTATION REQUIRED: SUFFICIENCY: STANDARD DIMENSIONS: T636/88: EPO)   [1993] E.P.O.R. 517
National Association of Realtors v. Estate Agents Co-operative Ltd (TRADE MARK: APPLICATION: OPPOSITION: "CALCULATED TO DECEIVE OR CONFUSE": DISTINCTIVENESS: USE IN COURSE OF TRADE: Australia: Pat. Off.)
5 I.P.R. 439
National Garments v. National Apparels (PASSING OFF: TRADE MARK: M.M.B./ M.B.B.: GET-UP: COVER OF BOXES: DECEPTION: INTERIM INJUNCTION: APPEAL: India: H.C.)   (1990) 15 I.P.L.R. 262
National Geographic Society's Application (TRADE MARK: APPLICATION: INCAPABLE OF BECOMING DISTINCTIVE: Australia: AIPO)   27 I.P.R. 229

National Information Utilities Corporation/Education utility (EUROPEAN PATENT: APPEAL: PROCEDURE: FUNCTION OF APPEAL: ORAL PROCEEDINGS FOR SAME SUBJECT: FRESH CITATIONS ON APPEAL: DAY BEFORE ORAL PROCEEDINGS: COMMUNICATION BY BOARD: RESPONSE NOT BONA FIDE: INVENTIVE STEP: ELECTRONIC IMPLEMENTATION OF CONVENTIONAL SYSTEM: T25/91: EPO)   [1993] E.P.O.R. 466

National Research Development Corporation's Application (PATENT: APPLICATION: OBJECTION BY EXAMINER: NOVELTY: SELECTION PATENT: WHETHER CLAIM NOVEL SPECIFYING LOWER DOSAGE OF KNOWN PHARMACEUTICAL: Australia: Pat. Off.)   24 I.P.R. 123

National Research Development Corporation's Application (PATENT: APPLICATION: OBJECTIONS BY EXAMINER: NOVELTY: INVENTIVENESS: COMBINATION OF KNOWN SUBSTANCES: Australia: Pat. Off.)   11 I.P.R. 666

National Research Development Corporation, *sub nom*. NRDC

National Treasury Management Agency v. Irish Permanent plc, *sub nom*. An Post, National Treasury Management Agency v. Irish Permanent plc

Nationwide Building Society v. Nationwide Estate Agents Ltd (PASSING OFF: ESTATE AGENCY: REPUTATION IN ALLIED FIELD: EVIDENCE: OPINION POLL: Ch.D.)   [1987] F.S.R. 579

Nationwide News Pty Ltd v. Copyright Agency Ltd (COPYRIGHT: COLLECTING SOCIETIES: COPYING BY EDUCATIONAL INSTITUTIONS: NEWSPAPERS, MAGAZINES AND PERIODICALS: JOURNALIST'S COPYRIGHT: COMPILATION: INFRINGEMENT: SUBSTANTIALITY: COPYING OF SINGLE ITEM: Australia: Fed. Ct)   128 A.L.R. 285; 30 I.P.R. 159
(APPEAL: CASES ON LITERARY WORTH DISTINGUISHED: Fed. Ct)   136 A.C.R. 273

Natural Gas Corp. Holdings Ltd v. Grant (INJUNCTION: PRACTICE AND PROCEDURE: MAREVA INJUNCTION: RULE AGAINST SELF-INCRIMINATION: New Zealand: H.C.)   [1994] 2 N.Z.L.R. 252

Natural Paper v. Spastic Centre of New South Wales (TRADE MARK: APPLICATION: OPPOSITION: LACK OF INTENTION TO USE: NON-USE: PROPRIETORSHIP: DECEPTION OR CONFUSION: Australia: AIPO)   30 I.P.R. 297

Natural Selection Clothing Ltd v. Commissioner of Trade Marks (TRADE MARKS: REGISTRATION: OPPOSITION: OVERSEAS OPPONENT: STRUCK OFF COMPANY: *Locus standii*: New Zealand: H.C.)   [1995] 3 N.Z.L.R. 599

Nautical Services Pty Ltd v. Hitech Distillation (Aust.) Pty Ltd (PATENT: OPPOSITION: EVIDENCE: EXTENSION OF TIME LIMITS TO SERVE: *Locus standii*: PUBLIC INTEREST: COSTS: Australia: Pat. Off.)   7 I.P.R. 567

Naylor v. Hutson (MOTOR VEHICLE: CORPORATE OWNER: SALE AND LEASEBACK: RECEIVERSHIP: TRANSFER OF LEASED ASSETS: BAILMENT: ENTITLEMENT TO TRANSFER OF REGISTRATION MARK: COSTS: Ch.D.)   [1994] F.S.R. 63

NEC Corp. v. Intel Corp. (COPYRIGHT: COMPUTER PROGRAMS: MICROCODE IN MICROPROCESSOR CHIPS: SUBSISTENCE: MINIMAL VERBAL STRUCTURES: WORKS DICTATED BY FUNCTION: FORFEITURE OF COPYRIGHT: NON-USE OF COPYRIGHT NOTICE: SCOPE OF LICENCE: INFRINGEMENT: WHETHER MODIFICATION OF EARLIER COPY AVOIDS INFRINGEMENT: USA: D.C.)   14 I.P.R. 1

Nederlandsche Banden-Industrie Michelin NV v. E.C. Comm. (RESTRICTIVE PRACTICES: DOMINANT POSITION: PRACTICE: Case 322/81: ECJ)   [1985] 1 C.M.L.R. 282; [1983] E.C.R. 3461; [1985] F.S.R. 250

Nederlandse Bankiersvereniging's Application (RESTRICTIVE PRACTICES: BANKING: ASSOCIATIONS OF UNDERTAKINGS: INTENTION TO APPROVE: E.C. Comm.)   [1989] 4 C.M.L.R. 10

Nederlandse Omroep-Programma Stichting's Application (RESTRICTIVE PRACTICES: BROADCASTING: CO-ORDINATION OF PURCHASE AND PRODUCTION OF TV PROGRAMMES BY BROADCASTERS: INTENTION TO APPROVE: E.C. Comm.) [1991] 4 C.M.L.R. 916

Neev Investment & Trading Pvt. Ltd v. Sasia Express Couriers Pvt. Ltd (PASSING OFF: SIMILAR SERVICES: INTERIM INJUNCTION: India: H.C.)
(1993) 18 I.P.L.R. 195

Neild v. Rockley (PATENT: INFRINGEMENT: THREATS: Pat. Ct) [1986] F.S.R. 3

Nellcor/Re-establishment (EUROPEAN PATENT: PROCEDURE: LEGITIMATE EXPECTATIONS: RE-ESTABLISHMENT OF RIGHTS: ARTICLE 122(5), SCOPE OF: G05/93: EPO) [1994] E.P.O.R. 169; [1994] O.J. EPO 447

Nelson v. Hillmark Industries Pty Ltd (PATENT: PROVISIONAL SPECIFICATION: PRIORITY DATE: PRIOR PUBLICATION: NOVELTY: OBVIOUSNESS: MATTERS ARISING UNDER SECTION 40: Australia: Pat. Off.) 19 I.P.R. 628

Nelson v. Rye (COPYRIGHT: INFRINGEMENT: MUSICAL WORKS: MANUFACTURE AND SALE AFTER EXPIRY OF LICENCE: POP MUSICIAN AND MANAGER: ACCOUNT: TERMS OF RETAINER: LIMITATION PERIOD: LACHES AND ACQUIESENCE: Ch.D.) [1996] E.M.L.R. 37; [1996] F.S.R. 313

Neorx/Claims fees (EUROPEAN PATENT: FEES: CLAIM, WHAT CONSTITUTES: J15/88: EPO) [1991] E.P.O.R. 76; [1990] O.J. EPO 445

Nestlé, *sub nom.* Société des Produits Nestlé SA

Nestlé/Cryogenic aroma recovery (EUROPEAN PATENT: APPEAL: PROCEDURE: FRESH GROUND TAKEN BY BOARD: T277/89: EPO) [1991] E.P.O.R. 323

Net Book Agreements (*sub nom.* Publishers Association's Agreement) (RESTRICTIVE PRACTICES: BOOKS: RESALE PRICE MAINTENANCE: COLLECTIVE SYSTEM OPERATED BY UNITED KINGDOM PUBLISHERS: E.C. Comm.)
[1989] 4 C.M.L.R. 825

(*sub nom.* Publishers Association v. E.C. Commission) (EUROPEAN COURT PROCEDURE: INTERIM MEASURES: RESTRICTIVE PRACTICES: BOOKS: U.K. COLLECTIVE RESALE PRICE MAINTENANCE SCHEME: Case 56/89R: ECJ)
[1989] 4 C.M.L.R. 816; [1989] E.C.R. 1693

(*sub nom.* Publishers Association v. E.C. Comm.) (RESTRICTIVE PRACTICES: BOOKS: RESALE PRICE MAINTENANCE: COLLECTIVE SYSTEM OPERATED BY U.K. PUBLISHERS: EFFECT ON INTER-STATE TRADE: ARTICLE 85(1) AND INELIGIBLE FOR EXEMPTION: ADMINISTRATIVE LAW: DECISIONS: Case T-66/89 CFI) [1992] 5 C.M.L.R. 120

(*sub nom.* Publishers Association v. E.C. Commission) (RESTRICTIVE PRACTICES: BOOKS: RESALE PRICE MAINTENANCE: COLLECTIVE SYSTEM OPERATED BY U.K. PUBLISHERS: REFUSAL TO EXEMPT, UPHELD BY CFI: EFFECT OF SINGLE LANGUAGE MARKET, U.K. AND IRELAND: Case 360/92P: ECJ)
[1995] 5 C.M.L.R. 33; [1995] E.M.L.R. 185; [1996] F.S.R. 33

NETWORK 90 Trade Mark (APPLICATION: PRACTICE: EVIDENCE: Ch.D.)
[1984] R.P.C. 549

NEUTROGENA Trade Mark (RECTIFICATION: NON-USE: INTERVENER: *locus*: APPEAL: PRACTICE: REGISTRATION: Ch.D.) [1984] R.P.C. 563

New Flex/Date of filing (EUROPEAN PATENT: APPLICATION: PROCEDURE: DATE OF FILING: CONVENTIONS: PURPOSE AND CONSEQUENCES: DESIGNATION OF STATES: AMENDMENT AND CORRECTION PRECAUTIONARY: J25/88: EPO) [1990] E.P.O.R. 59; [1989] O.J. EPO 486

New South Wales Dairy Corporation v. Murray Goulburn Co-operative Co. Ltd, *sub nom.* Murray Goulburn Co-operative Co. Ltd v. New South Wales Dairy Corporation

New York University v. Nissin Molecular Biology Institute Inc. (PATENT: APPLICATION: REQUEST FOR CERTIFICATION: USE OF DEPOSIT FOR EXPERIMENTAL PURPOSES: UNDERTAKING: Australia: AIPO)   29 I.P.R. 173
New York University v. Nissin Molecular Biology Institute Inc. (PATENT: APPLICATION: REQUEST FOR CERTIFICATION: UNDERTAKING: CONDITIONS FOR RELEASE OF SAMPLE OF MICRO–ORGANISM: Australia: AIPO)
30 I.P.R. 73
New York Yacht Club's Application (TRADE MARK: APPLICATION: AMERICA'S CUP: WHETHER USED AS A TRADE MARK: Australia: Pat. Off.)   9 I.P.R. 102
New Zealand Industrial Gases Ltd v. Oxyman (TRADE: INFRINGEMENT: INSERTING GAS INTO CONTAINERS BELONGING TO PLAINTIFF AND MARKED WITH ITS TRADE MARKS WAS NOT USE OF THE MARK: INTERFERING WITH CONTRACTUAL RELATION: New Zealand: H.C.)   24 I.P.R. 161
New Zealand Natural Pty Ltd's Application (TRADE MARK: APPLICATION: PART A: BALANCING DISTINCTIVE AND NON–DISTINCTIVE ELEMENTS IN MARK: DISTINCTIVE ELEMENTS ASSUMING SECONDARY ROLE: Australia: AIPO)
28 I.P.R. 22
New Zealand Natural Pty Ltd v. Granny's Natural New Zealand Ice Cream Pty Ltd (TRADE PRACTICES: RIVAL TRADERS: ALLEGED MISLEADING CONDUCT: RESPONDENTS TRADING UNDER NAME INCLUDING ALL ELEMENTS OF APPLICANT'S NAME: NO SECONDARY MEANING ALLEGED: RELEVANT MEMBERS OF THE PUBLIC: EFFECT OF SIMILARITY OR DISSIMILARITY OF GET–UP: SIMILARITY OF FUNCTION: Australia: Fed. Ct)   19 I.P.R. 214
Newitt & Co. Ltd v. Dunlop Slazenger International Ltd (RESTRICTIVE PRACTICES: DISTRIBUTION AGREEMENTS: PARALLEL IMPORTS: EXPORT BANS: REFUSAL TO SUPPLY: EXCLUSIVE DEALING: CONCERTED PRACTICES: PRICES: SUBSIDIES: BUY–BACK SCHEMES: DISCRIMINATION: E.C. Comm.)
[1993] 5 C.M.L.R. 352; [1994] F.S.R. 123
Newman/Perpetual motion (EUROPEAN PATENT: SUFFICIENCY: PERPETUAL MOTION: T5/86: EPO)   [1988] E.P.O.R. 301
News Datacom Ltd v. Satellite Decoding Systems (COPYRIGHT: COMPUTER PROGRAMS: BREACH: INTERLOCUTORY INJUNCTION: BALANCE OF CONVENIENCE: Ireland: H.C.)   [1995] F.S.R. 201
News Group Newspapers Ltd v. Independent Television Publications Ltd (COPYRIGHT: BROADCASTS: TV PROGRAMME LISTINGS: DUTY TO MAKE AVAILABLE: TERMS OF PAYMENT: Cprt. Trib.)
[1993] E.M.L.R. 1; [1993] R.P.C. 173
News Group Newspapers Ltd v. Independent Television Publications Ltd (No. 2) (TV LISTINGS: SETTLEMENT OF TERMS FOR PROVISION OF STATUTORY INFORMATION BY BROADCASTERS TO PUBLISHERS: APPEAL COMPROMISED BY PARTIES: CONSENT ORDER: Cprt. Trib.)   [1993] E.M.L.R. 133
News Group Newspapers Ltd v. The Mirror Group Newspapers (1988) Ltd (TRADE MARK: COPYRIGHT: INFRINGEMENT: THE SUN: MASTHEADS: "KNOCKING" ADVERTISING: Ch.D.)   [1989] 1 F.S.R. 126
News Group Newspapers Ltd v. The Mirror Group Newspapers (1988) Ltd (TRADE MARK: INFRINGEMENT: INTERLOCUTORY INJUNCTION: PRACTICE: DELAY IN PROCEEDINGS AFTER INJUNCTION GRANTED: Ch.D.)
[1991] F.S.R. 487; 21 I.P.R. 583
Nexoft Corporation's Application (TRADE MARK: APPLICATION: OBJECTION: INHERENT DISTINCTIVENESS: PORTABLE CARRY-ALL: Australia: AIPO)   28 I.P.R. 427
NEXT Trade Mark (TRADE MARK: APPLICATION: OBJECTION: DISTINCTIVENESS: USE IN ADVERTISING: APPLICATION REFUSED: BoT)   [1992] R.P.C. 455

Nexus/Unconfirmed telex (EUROPEAN PATENT: APPEAL: PROCEDURE: STRIKING OUT MANIFESTLY UNFOUNDED APPEAL: T298/89: EPO)
[1990] E.P.O.R. 252

Neylan v. Toisin Holdings Pty Ltd (PASSING OFF: NEWSPAPERS: PROPERTY IN NAME: Australia: S.C.(Qd)) [1983] 1 Qd.R. 600

Neynaber/Basic lead salts (EUROPEAN PATENT: OPPOSITION PROCEDURE: PATENT REVOKED BY OPPOSITION DIVISION: APPEAL: WIDER CLAIM 1; FAILURE BY PATENTEE TO ATTEND ORAL PROCEEDINGS: ARTICLE 123(3) OBJECTION AT ORAL PROCEEDINGS: T341/92: EPO) [1995] E.P.O.R. 563

Ng Chye Mong Pte Ltd v. Public Prosecutor (TRADE MARKS: FUNCTION: COUNTERFEIT LABELS: EXPLANATION OF: WHETHER NEED TO PROVE THAT CONTENTS OF BOTTLES ALSO NOT GENUINE: NATURE OF CRIMINAL OFFENCE: CONSTRUCTION: Singapore: H.C.)
[1988] F.S.R. 441; [1988] 1 F.T.L.R. 540; 13 I.P.R. 485

NGK Insulators/Ferrite crystal (EUROPEAN PATENT: PATENTABILITY: MERE DISCOVERY: PRIORITY: IDENTITY OF INVENTION: T184/84: EPO)
[1986] E.P.O.R. 169

NGK/Oral proceedings (EUROPEAN PATENT: PROCEDURE: ORAL PROCEEDINGS: "MAY" CONSTRUED AS REQUEST: T494/90: EPO) [1992] E.P.O.R. 60

NI Industries/Filler mass (EUROPEAN PATENT: AMENDMENT AND CORRECTION: ESSENTIAL FEATURE: INVENTIVE STEP: DIFFERENT TECHNICAL FIELD, RELIANCE UPON: T560/89: EPO) [1994] E.P.O.R. 120

Nicaro Holdings Pty Ltd v. Martin Engineering Co. (PATENT: INFRINGEMENT: VALIDITY: NOVELTY: ANTICIPATION: PRIOR PUBLICATION IN THREE UNITED STATES PATENTS: MOSAIC: PRIOR USE: Australia: Fed. Ct)
91 A.L.R. 513; 16 I.P.R. 545

Nichator AB's Application (PATENT: APPLICATION: EXAMINATION: PRIOR PUBLICATION: NOVELTY: Australia: Pat. Off.) 7 I.P.R. 504

Nicholas Saba Sportswear Pty Ltd v. Daryl K. Linane (TRADE MARKS: APPLICATION: OPPOSITION: FAILURE TO PROCEED WITH OPPOSITION: COSTS: PRACTICE AND PROCEDURE: Australia: Pat. Off.) 20 I.P.R. 545

Nicholas v. Borg (PASSING OFF: REPUTATION: MELBOURNE CUP: INTERLOCUTORY INJUNCTION: BALANCE OF CONVENIENCE: Australia: S.C.(S.A.)) 7 I.P.R. 1

Nichols Advanced Vehicle Systems Inc. v. Rees (No. 2) (COPYRIGHT: INFRINGEMENT: DAMAGES: PRACTICE: DELAY IN PURSUING INQUIRY: C.A.) [1985] R.P.C. 445

Nichols Advanced Vehicle Systems Inc. v. Rees (No. 3) (COPYRIGHT: INFRINGEMENT: RACING CARS: INQUIRY AS TO DAMAGES: CONVERSION DAMAGES: ASSESSMENT OF AGGRAVATED DAMAGES: INTEREST: Ch.D.: C.A.) [1988] R.P.C. 71

Nickelodeon U.K. (RESTRICTIVE PRACTICES: BROADCASTING: JOINT VENTURE: CHILDREN'S TV CHANNEL: E.C. Comm.) [1994] 5 C.M.L.R. 104

Nickmar Pty Ltd v. Preservatrice Skandia Insurance Ltd (PRACTICE: DISCOVERY: LEGAL PROFESSIONAL PRIVILEGE: USE OF DOCUMENTS: Australia: H.C.)
[1985] 3 N.S.W.L.R. 44

Nicolon/Statement of grounds (EUROPEAN PATENT: APPEAL: PROCEDURE: STATEMENT OF GROUNDS, REQUIREMENTS OF: T145/88: EPO)
[1991] E.P.O.R. 357; [1991] O.J. EPO 251

Nigel Louez Graphic Design Pty Ltd's Application (DESIGN: APPLICATION FOR
REGISTRATION: COLOURED PANELS ON BALL: PATTERN: ORNAMENTATION:
COLOUR: INHERENTLY REGISTRABLE: NOT NOVEL: JUDGED BY EYE OF
REGISTRAR: FUNCTION OF ARTICLE IRRELEVANT: Australia: Pat. Off.)
15 I.P.R. 570
Nijs v. Ciba-Geigy AG (TRADE MARK: USE: DOCTOR'S PRESCRIPTION: Benelux:
C.J.) [1985] E.C.C. 165
Nikken Sohansha Corp.'s Application, *sub nom.* Kikken Sohansha KK's Application
Niky Tasha India Pvt. Ltd v. Faridabad Gas Gadgets Pvt. Ltd (DESIGNS:
INFRINGEMENT: INTERLOCUTORY INJUNCTION: India: H.C.)
(1984) 9 I.P.L.R. 59
Niled/Electrical connecting apparatus (EUROPEAN PATENT: FEES: REIMBURSEMENT
OF APPEAL FEE: PRIOR ART: POST-PRIORITY DOCUMENTS AS EVIDENCE:
SKILLED PERSON: NATURE OF: T316/86: EPO) [1990] E.P.O.R. 217
Nimemia Maritime Corp. v. Trave Schiffahrt GmbH & Co. KG (MAREVA
INJUNCTION: PRINCIPLES: Ch.D.: C.A.)
[1984] 1 All E.R. 398; [1983] 1 W.L.R. 1412
Nintendo Co. Ltd v. Centronics Systems Pty Ltd, *sub nom.* Centronics Systems Pty
Ltd v. Nintendo Co. Ltd
Nintendo Co. Ltd v. Golden China TV-Game Centre Ltd (COPYRIGHT: PARALLEL
IMPORTATION: VIDEO GAMES: AUTHORSHIP: South Africa: S.C.)
28 I.P.R. 313
Nippon Gaishi KK's Application (PATENT: APPLICATION: PRACTICE: EXTENSION
OF PERIOD FOR REQUESTING SUBSTANTIVE EXAMINATION: DISCRETION: Pat.
Ct) [1983] R.P.C. 388
Nippon Piston Ring Co. Ltd's Applications (PATENT: INFRINGEMENT: PRACTICE:
RULE 100; INVENTOR'S NAME: ENTITLEMENT: Pat. Ct) [1987] R.P.C. 120
Nippon/Examination procedure (EUROPEAN PATENT: APPLICATION PROCEDURE:
GROUND OF OBJECTION: APPLICANT'S FAILURE TO REFUTE SERIOUSLY:
FINDING OF LACK OF GOOD FAITH: IMMEDIATE REFUSAL OF APPLICATION:
· T640/91: EPO) [1995] E.P.O.R. 243; [1994] O.J. EPO 918
Nippondenso/Vehicle display (EUROPEAN PATENT: PATENTABILITY: DISPLAY OF
INFORMATION: INVENTIVE STEP: SKILLED PERSON, FIELD OF EXPERIENCE OF:
PROCEDURE: TRANSLATION OF PRIOR ART: BOARD OF APPEAL: RELIANCE
ON MINUTES BELOW: SKILLED PERSON: FIELD OF EXPERIENCE OF: FEES:
REIMBURSEMENT OF APPEAL FEE: T683/89: EPO) [1992] E.P.O.R. 429
Nirex Industries (Pvt.) Ltd v. Manchand Footwears (TRADE MARK: COPYRIGHT:
INFRINGEMENT: JURISDICTION: INTERIM INJUNCTION: India: H.C.)
(1984) 9 I.P.L.R. 70
Nishika Corp. v. Goodchild (PASSING OFF: INTERLOCUTORY INJUNCTION:
PLAINTIFF'S TRADING ABROAD ONLY: DEFENDANTS' MISREPRESENTATION:
WHETHER PROTECTABLE U.K. GOODWILL: Ch.D.) [1990] F.S.R. 371
Nissan Motor Co. (Australia) Pty Ltd v. Vector Aeromotive Corp. (TRADE MARK:
APPLICATION: OPPOSITION: PROPRIETORSHIP: USE OF TRADE MARK: GOODS
OR SERVICES: Australia: AIPO) 27 I.P.R. 296
Nissan/Cylinder block (EUROPEAN PATENT: CLAIMS: INCONSISTENT WITH
DRAWINGS: INVENTIVE STEP: AGED ART: CLOSEST PRIOR ART: T726/89:
EPO) [1991] E.P.O.R. 107
Nissan/Fuel injector valve (EUROPEAN PATENT: COSTS: UNNECESSARY HEARING:
AWARDED: NOVELTY: WHOLE CONTENTS: T167/84: EPO)
[1987] E.P.O.R. 344; [1987] O.J. EPO 369
Nissei/Injection moulding machine (EUROPEAN PATENT: INVENTIVE STEP:
CLOSEST PRIOR ART: T335/88: EPO) [1990] E.P.O.R. 552

Nisshin/Steroid (EUROPEAN PATENT: INVENTIVE STEP: CLOSEST PRIOR ART: PROBLEM, REFORMULATION OF: PRIOR ART: TEXTBOOK, CREDIBILITY OF GENERAL CHEMICAL METHOD: T181/91: EPO)   [1994] E.P.O.R. 135
Nitto Boseki/Traversing motion (EUROPEAN PATENT: AMENDMENT AND CORRECTION: PROBLEM, REFORMULATION OF: T262/84: EPO)
[1979–85] E.P.O.R. C1001
NN/Re-establishment of rights (EUROPEAN PATENT: UNITY: OBJECTION BY EPO AS ISA: PROTEST BY APPLICANT: DELAY BETWEEN DATE OF OBJECTION AND DATE OF POSTING: BOARD NOT INFORMED: PROTEST HELD INADMISSIBLE ON GROUND OF DELAY: RE-ESTABLISHMENT SOUGHT AND GRANTED: REASONS FOR OBJECTION INSUFFICIENT: PROTEST UPHELD: W03/93: EPO)
[1995] E.P.O.R. 351; [1994] O.J. EPO 931
NN/Register of European Patents (EUROPEAN PATENT: APPLICATION: PROCEDURE: JOINT OWNERSHIP: J18/84: EPO)
[1987] E.P.O.R. 321; [1987] O.J. EPO 215
Noah v. Shuba (COPYRIGHT: INFRINGEMENT: LIBEL: FALSE ATTRIBUTION OF AUTHORSHIP: EMPLOYEE'S WORK: SCOPE OF IMPLIED LICENCE: MEANING OF "WORK": QUANTUM: Ch.D.)   [1991] F.S.R. 14
Noel Leeming Television Ltd v. Noel's Appliance Centre Ltd (PASSING OFF: MISREPRESENTATION: CONFUSION: REPUTATION: OWN NAME: SURVEY EVIDENCE: INJUNCTION: DAMAGES: New Zealand: H.C.)   5 I.P.R. 249
Nogier/Magnetic therapy (EUROPEAN PATENT: DISCLOSURE: PATENTABLE INVENTION NOT DISCLOSED: PATENTABILITY: THERAPY: T30/83: EPO)   [1979–85] E.P.O.R. C755
Nolek Systems AB v. Analytical Instruments Ltd (PATENT: INFRINGEMENT: PLEADINGS: PARTICULARS OF INFRINGEMENT: Pat. Ct)   [1984] R.P.C. 556
Nomad Films International Pty Ltd v. Export Development Grants Board (COPYRIGHT: APPLICATION FOR GRANT: WHETHER ELIGIBLE: FILM: EXCLUSIVE LICENCE: Australia: Fed. Ct)   66 A.L.R. 427; 6 I.P.R. 321
Nomad Structures International Ltd v. Heyring Pty Ltd (PATENT: APPLICATION: OPPOSITION: EVIDENCE: FAIR BASIS: PRIOR USE AND PUBLICATION: NOVELTY: OBVIOUSNESS: OBTAINING: Australia: Pat. Off.)   24 I.P.R. 185
Non-payment of further search fees (EUROPEAN PATENT: DIVISIONAL APPLICATION: UTILITY LACKING IN PATENT: ENLARGED BOARD OF APPEAL: INVITATION TO EPO PRESIDENT TO COMMENT: PRESIDENT OF EPO, REFERENCE BY: FEES: FAILURE TO PAY FURTHER SEARCH FEES: PROCEDURE: EXAMINATION: SEARCHED SUBJECT-MATTER ONLY: UNITY: SEARCH DIVISION, DECISION BY: G02/92: EPO)   [1994] E.P.O.R. 278; [1993] O.J. EPO 591
Noncyp Ltd v. Bow Street Magistrates' Court (IMPORTS: OBSCENE PUBLICATIONS: COVERED BY MORALITY CLAUSE IN ARTICLE 36: DIFFERENCE IN DEFINITION FOR IMPORTS AND DOMESTIC SALES: C.A.)   [1989] 1 C.M.L.R. 634
Normalec Ltd v. Britton (RESTRICTIVE COVENANT: AREA AGREEMENTS: Ch.D.)   [1983] F.S.R. 318
Norris's Patent (PATENT: APPLICATION: ENTITLEMENT: PRACTICE: EVIDENCE: CROSS-EXAMINATION IN PATENT OFFICE: CONFIDENTIALITY OF FILED EVIDENCE: DISCOVERY: C.-G.: Pat. Ct)   [1988] R.P.C. 159
North Cope Ltd v. Allman Properties (Aust.) Pty Ltd (PRACTICE: MAREVA INJUNCTION: NATURE OF EVIDENCE REQUIRED: Australia: S.C.(Qd))
(1994) 2 Qd.R. 409
Northern & Shell plc v. Condé Nast & National Magazines P.E. Ltd (PATENT: INFRINGEMENT: REGISTERED USER/LICENSEE: RIGHTS OF REGISTERED USER TO SUE: NATURE OF REGISTERED USER: Pat. Ct)   [1995] R.P.C. 117

Northern Telecom Ltd's Application (TRADE MARK: APPLICATION: WHETHER ADAPTED TO DISTINGUISH: INHERENT DISTINCTIVENESS: DISTINCTIVENESS ACQUIRED THROUGH USE: PART B: SUPERNODE: Australia: AIPO)
29 I.P.R. 659

Norwood Industries Pty Ltd v. Macbird Floraprint Pty Ltd (PATENT: OPPOSITION: GROUNDS AND PARTICULARS OF OPPOSITION: SUFFICIENCY OF: APPLICATION TO DISMISS: Australia: Pat. Off.) 24 I.P.R. 368

Nottingham Building Society v. Eurodynamics Systems plc (CONTRACT: COMPUTER SOFTWARE: REPUDIATION: DELIVERY UP OF SOFTWARE: DISPUTED DEBT: INTERLOCUTORY ORDER FOR DELIVERY UP: APPLICATION FOR LEAVE TO ADDUCE FURTHER EVIDENCE: INTERNAL COMPANY DOCUMENTS: RELEVANCY: C.A.) [1995] F.S.R. 605

Nottingham Building Society v. Eurodynamics Systems plc (DELIVERY UP: MANDATORY INJUNCTION: Ch.D.) [1993] F.S.R. 468

Novatome II/Final decision (EUROPEAN PATENT: PROCEDURE: DECISION: EFFECTIVE DATE OF: *In camera: In statu nascendi*: G12/91: EPO)
[1994] E.P.O.R. 309; [1994] O.J. EPO 285

Novell, Inc. v. Ong Seow Pheng (COPYRIGHT: SCOPE OF PROTECTION: COMPUTER SOFTWARE AND MANUALS: FIRST PUBLICATION IN USA: ADDITIONAL DAMAGES: TRADE MARK: INFRINGEMENT: INJUNCTION: Singapore: H.C.) [1993] 3 S.L.R. 700

Novopharm Ltd v. Syntex Inc. (INTERLOCUTORY INJUNCTION: CONSIDERATIONS BEFORE GRANTING: MERITS NOT TO BE DECIDED: INFRINGEMENT OF TRADE MARKS IS NOT *per se* IRREPARABLE HARM: PRODUCTS ARE INTERCHANGEABLE: NO IRREPARABLE HARM TO PLAINTIFF: PATENT: COMPULSORY LICENCE TO PHARMACEUTICAL OF NO EFFECT TO TRADE MARK RIGHTS: TRADE MARK: INFRINGEMENT: SHAPE AND COLOUR OF TABLET OF MEDICINE: Canada: Fed. C.A.) 21 I.P.R. 494

NRDC's Irish Application (PATENT: APPLICATION: MICRO-ORGANISM: WHETHER AN INVENTION: Ireland: Pat. Off.) [1986] F.S.R. 620

NRDC/*Eimeria necatrix* (EUROPEAN PATENT: SUFFICIENCY: CLAIMED SUBJECT-MATTER, REPRODUCIBILITY OF: CLAIMS: PRIOR METHOD RELEVANCE REPRODUCIBILITY OF: APPEAL: PROCEDURE: REMITTAL ORDERED: DESPITE APPLICANT'S PREFERENCE FOR DECISION WITHOUT DELAY: T48/85: EPO) [1987] E.P.O.R. 138

NRDC/Examination by a board of appeal of its own motion (EUROPEAN PATENT: AMENDMENT AND CORRECTION: APPEAL: PROCEDURE: POWERS OF BOARD OF APPEAL: J04/80: EPO) [1979–85] E.P.O.R. A27; [1980] O.J. EPO 351

NRDC/Polyurethane compositions (EUROPEAN PATENT: APPEAL: PROCEDURE: LATE AUXILIARY REQUESTS: TEXT OF PATENT: UNIT OF MEASUREMENT: T589/89: EPO) [1994] E.P.O.R. 17

NRDC/Thromboxane antagonists (EUROPEAN PATENT: UNITY: REASONS FOR LACK OF MUST BE GIVEN: W09/86: EPO)
[1988] E.P.O.R. 34; [1987] O.J. EPO 459

Nucron Pharmaceuticals Pvt. Ltd v. International Pharmaceuticals (TRADE MARK: INFRINGEMENT: SEPMAX/SELMAX: APPLIED TO MEDICINES FOR DIFFERENT MEDICAL CONDITIONS: DECEPTIVE SIMILARITY: LIKELIHOOD OF DISASTEROUS CONSEQUENCES: LEAVE TO APPLY FOR *ad interim* INJUNCTION: India: H.C.) (1994) 19 I.P.L.R. 56

Nungesser (L.C.) KG v. E.C. Commission (RESTRICTIVE PRACTICES: PLANT VARIETIES: MAIZE SEEDS: EXCLUSIVE LICENCE: Case 258/78: ECJ)
[1983] 1 C.M.L.R. 278; [1983] F.S.R. 309; [1982] E.C.R. 2015

Nusser/Payment order (EUROPEAN PATENT: FEES: 10-DAY RULE: J22/85: EPO)   [1988] E.P.O.R. 56; [1987] O.J. EPO 455
Nuts Chocoladefabriek BV v. Cadbury Ltd (TRADE MARK: APPLICATION: LIKELIHOOD OF CONFUSION: Australia: Pat. Off.)   5 I.P.R. 77
Nylex Corp. Ltd v. Sabco Ltd (TRADE PRACTICES: MISLEADING AND DECEPTIVE CONDUCT: SIMILAR PRODUCTS: DISCOVERY: IDENTITY OF SUPPLIER OR DISTRIBUTOR: Australia: Fed. Ct)   7 I.P.R. 275

O'Brien and Associates v. Orton & Burns Engineering Pty Ltd (TRADE MARKS: ACCEPTANCE FOR PART B REGISTRATION: OPPOSITION: EVIDENCE: DISTINCTIVENESS: PROPRIETORSHIP: Australia: Pat. Off.)   20 I.P.R. 511
O'Brien v. Komesaroff (COPYRIGHT: LEGAL PRECEDENTS: OWNERSHIP: BREACH OF CONFIDENCE: Australia: H.C.)   (1982) 41 A.L.R. 255; (1982) 150 C.L.R. 310
O'Connor v. Stevenson (TRADE PRACTICES: PROSECUTIONS: WHETHER CIVIL OR CRIMINAL: WHETHER SEVERAL PROSECUTIONS TO PROCEED IN JOINT OR SEPARATE TRIALS: SIMILAR FACT EVIDENCE: ADMISSIBILITY IN CIVIL TRIALS: Australia: Fed. Ct)   13 I.P.R. 145
O'Hara Manufacturing Ltd v. Eli Lilly & Co. and Thomas Engineering Ltd (PATENT: INFRINGEMENT: CLAIM CONSTRUCTION: PITH AND SUBSTANCE: Canada: Fed. C.A.)   14 I.P.R. 303
O'Neill & St George's Application (PATENT: APPLICATION: CO-APPLICANTS: DISPUTE: DETERMINATION: DIRECTIONS: Australia: AIPO)   30 I.P.R. 637
O'Sullivan v. Management Agency & Music Ltd (PRACTICE: UNDUE INFLUENCE: MANAGER AND ENTERTAINER: ACCOUNT OF PROFITS: INTEREST: C.A.)   [1985] 3 All E.R. 351; [1985] Q.B. 350; [1984] 3 W.L.R. 448
OBSA Pty Ltd v. T.F. Thomas and Sons Pty Ltd (DESIGN: WHETHER INTERLOCUTORY INJUNCTION AVAILABLE IN RESPECT OF ALLEGED INFRINGEMENT OF A REGISTERED DESIGN: Australia: Fed. Ct) 20 I.P.R. 155
Ocean Pacific Sunwear Ltd v. Ocean Pacific Enterprises Pty Ltd (PASSING OFF: APPLICANT ESTABLISHED REPUTATION AND GOODWILL IN TRADE MARKS IN RESPECT OF CLOTHING: USE OF MARKS IN RELATION TO CLOTHING CONSTITUTED PASSING OFF: NAME OF RESPONDENT INCORPORATED WORDS COMPRISING APPLICANT'S MARK: RESPONDENT HAD ESTABLISHED GOODWILL IN ITS NAME IN OTHER FIELDS OF ACTIVITY: WHETHER RESPONDENT SHOULD BE REQUIRED TO CHANGE ITS NAME: USE OF MARK OR NAME IN SCRIPT STYLE CONSTITUTED PASSING OFF: Australia: Fed. Ct)   17 I.P.R. 405
Odin Developments Ltd (RESTRICTIVE PRACTICES: JOINT RESEARCH AND DEVELOPMENT: CONTAINERS FOR UHT FOOD: INTENTION TO APPROVE: E.C. Comm.)   [1987] 3 C.M.L.R. 550
Odin Developments Ltd (RESTRICTIVE PRACTICES: JOINT VENTURES: JOINT DEVELOPMENT, PRODUCTION AND DISTRIBUTION OF NEW HIGH TECHNOLOGY PRODUCT: JOINT DISTRIBUTION EXCLUDES APPLICATION OF REGULATION 418/85: PARTIES NOT COMPETITORS AND UNABLE TO ENTER THE MARKET INDIVIDUALLY AND NO FORECLOSURE EFFECTS ON POTENTIAL THIRD PARTY COMPETITORS: CREATION OF JOINT VENTURE NOT CAUGHT BY ARTICLE 85(1): KNOW-HOW: LICENSED BY PARENTS TO JOINT VENTURE: ANCILLARY RESTRAINTS ONLY INCLUDED: NEGATIVE CLEARANCE GRANTED: E.C. Comm.)   [1991] 4 C.M.L.R. 832
Oehlschlager's Opposition (TRADE MARK: REMOVAL: OPPOSITION: USE ON INVOICES AND BUSINESS CORRESPONDENCE: FIELD OF USE: COPYRIGHT: JURISDICTION: Australia: Pat. Off.)   27 I.P.R. 663

Ofenbau/Slag discharge (EUROPEAN PATENT: FEES: INCREASE, WHEN APPLICABLE: J18/85: EPO)   [1987] E.P.O.R. 400; [1987] O.J. EPO 356

Office of Fair Trading/Review of restrictions on the patent agent's profession (EUROPEAN PATENT: PROFESSIONAL REPRESENTATIVES: PROFESSIONAL RESTRICTIONS: September 1986: EPO)   [1986] E.P.O.R. 348

Ogawa Chemical Industries Ltd's Applications (PATENT: APPLICATION: PRACTICE: GRANT: AMENDMENT: DIVISION: Pat. Ct)   [1986] R.P.C. 63

Ogden Industries Pty Ltd v. Kis (Australia) Ltd (COPYRIGHT: INFRINGEMENT: DRAWINGS FOR KEY BLANKS: NON-EXPERT DEFENCE: NON-REGISTRATION OF DESIGN: EXPIRES PATENT: Australia: S.C.(NSW))   (1983) 45 A.L.R. 129; [1982] 2 N.S.W.L.R. 283; [1983] F.S.R. 619

Oh Cheng Hai v. Ong Yong Yew (TRADE MARK: CRIMINAL PROCEDURE: PRIVATE PROSECUTION: *Locus standii*: COSTS: POSSESSION OF INLAY CARDS FOR AUDIO TAPES: WHETHER OFFENCE UNDER STATUTE: Singapore: H.C.)   [1993] 3 S.L.R. 930; [1988] 2 M.L.J. 150

OHI Seisakusho Co. Ltd's Application (PATENT: APPLICATION: PRACTICE: INTERNATIONAL APPLICATION: TRANSLATION NOT FILED: TIME LIMITS: Pat. Ct)   [1984] R.P.C. 219

OKI/Grounds for appeal (EUROPEAN PATENT: APPEAL: PROCEDURE: STATEMENT OF GROUNDS, REQUIREMENTS OF: T432/88: EPO)   [1990] E.P.O.R. 38

Olgeirsson v. Kitching (TRADE DESCRIPTION: DEALER'S SALE OF CAR: OWNER'S FALSE DESCRIPTION: D.C.)   [1986] 3 All E.R. 747; [1986] 1 W.L.R. 304

Olin Corp. v. Pacemaker Pool Supplies (TRADE MARK: CONFUSION: HONEST CONCURRENT USE: Australia: Pat. Off.)   4 I.P.R. 526

Olin Corp. v. Super Cartridge Co. Pty Ltd (PATENT: INFRINGEMENT: REVOCATION: VALIDITY: INVENTIVENESS: WHETHER CLAIMS CLEAR AND DISTINCTIVE: FAIRLY BASED: INVENTIVE STEP: Australia: H.C.)   180 C.L.R. 98

Oliver Homes (Manufacturing) v. Hamilton (COPYRIGHT: INFRINGEMENT: BUILDING PLANS AND DESIGNS: HOUSE KIT PLANS: USE OF PLANS NOT LICENSED SEPARATELY FROM SALE OF HOUSE KIT: DAMAGES: METHOD OF CALCULATION: ENTITLEMENT TO DAMAGES FOR LOSS OF PROFIT ON SALE OF HOUSE KIT: Scotland: O.H.)   1992 S.L.T. 892

Olivetti & Co. SpA and Canon Inc. (Joint Venture) (RESTRICTIVE PRACTICES: JOINT VENTURES: FURTHER COMPETITION BETWEEN PARTIES AT PRODUCTION STAGE PRECLUDED: PRODUCTS OF JOINT VENTURE COMPANY: BRANDING: E.C. Comm.)   [1989] 4 C.M.L.R. 940

Olivetti & Co. SpA and Canon Inc. (RESTRICTIVE PRACTICES: JOINT VENTURE: INTENTION TO EXEMPT: E.C. Comm.)   [1988] 4 C.M.L.R. 177

On Tat Bakelite Electric & Metal Works' Application (REGISTERED DESIGN: PRACTICE: ASSOCIATED DESIGN: EXTENSION OF TIME FOR RENEWAL: RDAT)   [1983] R.P.C. 297

One Girl's War
     sub nom. Attorney-General v. Turnaround Distribution Ltd (Q.B.D. proceedings)   [1989] 1 F.S.R. 169
     sub nom. Attorney-General for England and Wales v. Brandon Book Publishers Ltd (PROCEEDINGS IN IRELAND: Ireland: H.C.)   [1989] 1 F.S.R. 37

Opsvik v. Bad Back Centre Pty Ltd (PATENT: NOVELTY: OBVIOUSNESS: COMBINATION OF KNOWN IDEAS: FAIR BASIS: PRIORITY DATE: INTERNATIONAL APPLICATION: Australia: S.C.(NSW))   8 I.P.R. 217

Optech International Ltd v. Buxton Hicrarium Ltd (PATENT: APPLICATION: OPPOSITION: COSTS: EVIDENCE: ANTICIPATION: NOVELTY: OBVIOUSNESS: MANNER OF MANUFACTURE: OBTAINING: Australia: AIPO)   28 I.P.R. 649

Optical Coating Laboratory Inc. v. Pilkington PE Ltd (PATENT: INFRINGEMENT: SOLAR PANELS: EXCLUSIVE LICENCE: WHETHER PROPRIETOR AS WELL AS EXCLUSIVE LICENSEE ENTITLED TO DAMAGES FOR LOSS OF PROFIT: PRACTICE: STAY OF INJUNCTION: Pat. C.C.)   [1993] F.S.R. 310
(Pat. C.C. JURISDICTION: C.A.)   [1995] R.P.C. 145
Optical Laboratories Ltd v. Hayden Laboratories Ltd (No. 1) (PATENT: INFRINGEMENT: PRACTICE: EXPERT WITNESSES: COSTS OF WITNESSES: C.A.)   [1993] R.P.C. 204
Optrex India Ltd v. Optrex Ltd (TRADE MARK: INFRINGEMENT: USE AS MARK AND PART OF COMPANY NAME: PREVENTION OF USE AFTER TERMINATION OF REGISTERED USER AGREEMENT: INTERIM INJUNCTION: India: H.C.)
(1990) 15 I.P.L.R. 298
Organon Teknika Ltd v. F. Hoffmann-La Roche AG (PATENT: CLAIM FOR DECLARATION OF NON-INFRINGEMENT: APPLICATION TO STRIKE OUT CLAIMS REFERRING TO VALIDITY: APPLICATION TO AMEND TO INCLUDE CLAIM FOR REVOCATION: JURISDICTION TO ALLOW AMENDMENT: Pat. Ct)   [1996] F.S.R. 383
ORIENT EXPRESS Trade Mark (TRADE MARK: REMOVAL: NON-USE: USE OF COMPANY NAME: WHETHER USE AS A TRADE MARK: CONFLICT OF EVIDENCE: PRACTICE: CROSS-EXAMINATION BEFORE REGISTRAR: T.M.Reg.: Ch.D.)   [1996] R.P.C. 25
Origins Natural Resources Inc. v. Origin Clothing Limited (TRADE MARK: INFRINGEMENT: ASSOCIATED MARKS: OVERLAPPING SPECIFICATIONS: VALIDITY OF SECOND MARK: NON-USE: BONA-FIDE INTENTION TO USE: LIKELIHOOD OF CONFUSION: HONEST CONCURRENT USER: ORDER 14: SERVICE OF DEFENCE AND COUNTERCLAIM: Ch.D.)   [1995] F.S.R. 280
Orkney Seafoods Ltd's Petition (TRADE MARK: PASSING OFF: SIMILAR NAMES: DESCRIPTIVE NAME: ORKNEY SEAFOODS: WHETHER COMBINATION OF DESCRIPTIVE WORDS CALCULATED TO CAUSE CONFUSION: INTERIM INTERDICT: BALANCE OF CONVENIENCE: PROTECTION OF ESTABLISHED BUSINESS AGAINST NEWLY-FORMED BUSINESS: Scotland: O.H.)
1991 S.L.T. 891
Ornstein/Humidity control (EUROPEAN PATENT: RE-ESTABLISHMENT OF RIGHTS: EVIDENCE: OTHER FILES: FEES: REIMBURSEMENT OF APPEAL FEE: J01/84: EPO)   [1979–85] E.P.O.R. A200
Ortho/Monoclonal antibody (EUROPEAN PATENT: SUFFICIENCY: CLAIMED SUBJECT-MATTER, REPRODUCIBILITY OF: SUFFICIENCY: FUNCTIONAL DEFINITIONS: T495/89: EPO)   [1992] E.P.O.R. 48
Ortho/Monoclonal antibody (EUROPEAN PATENT: SUFFICIENCY: CULTURE DEPOSIT: NOT CORRESPONDING TO WRITTEN DESCRIPTION: T418/89: EPO)   [1993] E.P.O.R. 338; [1993] O.J. EPO 20
Orton & Burns Engineering Pty Ltd v. John L. O'Brien and Associates (TRADE MARKS: OPPOSITION TO REGISTRATION: APPLICATION FOR SPECIAL LEAVE TO ADDUCE FURTHER EVIDENCE: MEANING OF "FURTHER EVIDENCE": UNAVAILABLE TO APPLICANT WHO HAS FILED NO EVIDENCE: Australia: Pat. Off.)   17 I.P.R. 308
Orwell Steel (Erection & Fabrication) Ltd v. Asphalt & Tarmac (U.K.) Ltd (MAREVA INJUNCTION: APPLICATION AFTER FINAL JUDGMENT: JURISDICTION: Q.B.D.)   [1985] 3 All E.R. 747; [1984] 1 W.L.R. 1097
Osler, Hoskin & Harcourt v. Southwestern Bell Telecommunications, Inc. (SUMMARY EXPUNGEMENT: FREEDOM PHONE FOR TELEPHONE EQUIPMENT: USE OF COMPOSITE MARK: Canada: T.M. Hearing Officer)
33 C.P.R. (3d) 308

Östbo/Heat exchanger (EUROPEAN PATENT: CLAIMS: ESSENTIAL INTEGERS: INVENTIVE STEP: COMBINATION OF CITATIONS: IMPROVEMENT, GRADUAL OR SUBSTANTIAL: SURPRISING EFFECT, RELEVANCE OF: OPPOSITION: PROCEDURE: RE-DRAFTING TO ACKNOWLEDGE CLOSEST PRIOR ART: T100/90: EPO) [1991] E.P.O.R. 553

Osterman's Patent (PATENT: REVOCATION: PATENT OFFICE PROCEDURE: Pat. Ct) [1985] R.P.C. 579

Ostolski/Re-establishment of rights (EUROPEAN PATENT: EXAMINATION PROCEDURE: DUTY OF EPO TO WARN OF IMPENDING LOSS OF RIGHTS: J25/92: EPO) [1994] E.P.O.R. 298

Otep/Concrete hardening (EUROPEAN PATENT: APPEAL: PROCEDURE: FRESH PRIOR ART: CITED BY BOARD OF APPEAL: FEES: REIMBURSEMENT OF APPEAL FEE: T28/81: EPO) [1979–85] E.P.O.R. B367

Ottung v. Klee & Weilbach A/S (RESTRICTIVE PRACTICES: PATENTS: LICENSING AGREEMENT: OBLIGATION TO PAY ROYALTIES INDEFINITELY WHILE AGREEMENT SUBSISTING: EXPIRY OF PATENT: OUTSIDE ARTICLE 85(1) WHERE LICENSEE MAY TERMINATE FREELY ON REASONABLE NOTICE: Case 320/87: ECJ) [1990] 4 C.M.L.R. 915; [1989] E.C.R. 1177

Ovard/Splash bar (EUROPEAN PATENT: AMENDMENT AND CORRECTION: DISCLOSURE OF OBSCURE SUBSIDIARY CLAIM: CLAIMS: CONSTRUCTION: IN LIGHT OF TECHNICAL PROBLEM AND SOLUTION: T270/89: EPO) [1991] E.P.O.R. 540

Ownit Homes Pty Ltd v. D. & F. Mancuso Investments Pty Ltd (COPYRIGHT: ARCHITECT'S PLANS: SERIES OF DRAWINGS: WHETHER DRAWINGS OR HOUSE INFRINGED COPYRIGHT: REPRODUCTION OF SUBSTANTIAL PART: Australia: S.C.(Qd)) 9 I.P.R. 88; (1990) 6 Const. L.J. 161

Oxford University Press v. Registrar of Trade Marks (TRADE MARKS: APPLICATION: REFUSAL OF REGISTRATION: DISTRIBUTION: GEOGRAPHICAL NAME: OXFORD: WHETHER REGISTRABLE: DISTINCTIVENESS: INHERENT ADAPTABILITY TO DISTINGUISH: USE AS A TRADE MARK: BURDEN OF PROOF: Australia: S.C.(Vic.)) 15 I.P.R. 646
(Fed. Ct) 94 A.L.R. 269; 17 I.P.R. 509

OXY U.S.A Inc./Gel-forming composition (EUROPEAN PATENT: INVENTIVE STEP: CLOSEST PRIOR ART: ACKNOWLEDGED ART: MULTIPLICITY OF CLAIMING: T246/91: EPO) [1995] E.P.O.R. 526

Oy Airam AB v. Osram GmbH (RESTRICTIVE PRACTICES: TRADE MARK: DOMINANT POSITION: E.C. Comm.)
[1982] 3 C.M.L.R. 614; [1983] F.S.R. 108

Oy v. Canada (Registrar of Trade Marks) (TRADE MARK: APPEAL: REGISTRATION: WHETHER DECISION TO REGISTER APPEALABLE: Canada: FCTD)
33 C.P.R. (3d) 304

Ozi-Soft Pty Ltd v. Wong (COPYRIGHT: COMPUTER PROGRAMS: CONTRIBUTORY INFRINGEMENT: IMPORTATION OF DISKETTES PURCHASES FROM COPYRIGHT OWNERS: IMPLIED LICENCE: DOCTRINE OF NATIONAL TREATMENT: Australia: Fed. Ct) 10 I.P.R. 520

P's Applications (PATENT: APPLICATION: PRACTICE: EXTENSION OF TIME LIMIT: DIVISIONAL APPLICATION: C.-G.) [1983] R.P.C. 269

P.M. Diesels Ltd v. S.M. Diesels (TRADE MARK: COPYRIGHT IN MARK: INFRINGEMENT: FIELD MARSHAL/SONAMARSHAL: TRADING STYLE: INTERIM INJUNCTION: India: H.C.) (1995) 20 I.P.L.R. 73

P.M. Diesels Pvt. Ltd v. Thukral Mechanical Works (TRADE MARK: FIELD MARSHAL: RECTIFICATION: ENTITLEMENT TO USE MARK: INJUNCTION VACATED: India: H.C.)   (1988) 13 I.P.L.R. 151
Paccar/Excess claims fees (EUROPEAN PATENT: RE-ESTABLISHMENT OF RIGHTS: ADMISSIBILITY OF APPLICATION BY OPPONENT: FEES: EXCESS CLAIMS: FAILURE TO PAY: J29/86: EPO)   [1988] E.P.O.R. 194; [1988] O.J. EPO 84
Pacific Access Pty Ltd's Application (TRADE MARK: APPLICATION: SUBSEQUENT SEARCH: SIMILAR MARKS: Australia: AIPO)   27 I.P.R. 417
Pacific Basin Exploration Pty Ltd v. XLX (N.L.) (PRACTICE: DISCOVERY: DISCLOSURE OF DISCOVERED DOCUMENTS: BREACH OF UNDERTAKING: CONTEMPT OF COURT: Australia: S.C.(W.A.))   2 I.P.R. 489
Pacific Dunlop Ltd v. Australian Rubber Gloves Pty Ltd (COPYRIGHT: PRACTICE AND PROCEDURE: INSPECTION OF PROPERTY PRIOR TO ISSUING PROCEEDINGS: MACHINE FOR MANUFACTURE OF RUBBER GLOVES: PLANS: Australia: Fed. Ct)   23 I.P.R. 456
Pacific Dunlop Ltd v. Bonny Sports Corp. (TRADE MARK: APPLICATION: OPPOSITION: REGISTRATION: COMPOSITE MARK: BONNY PLUS DEVICE: ESSENTIAL FEATURES: USE: DECEPTION: CONFUSION: DISTINCTIVENESS: Australia: AIPO)   31 I.P.R. 511
Pacific Dunlop Ltd v. Fruit of the Loom Inc. (TRADE MARKS: OPPOSITION TO APPLICATION FOR REMOVAL: APPLICATION FOR EXTENSION OF TIME TO FILE EVIDENCE IN ANSWER: TIME NEEDED TO GATHER EVIDENCE ON USE: BALANCE OF CONVENIENCE: PUBLIC INTEREST: Australia: Pat. Off.)
                                                   17 I.P.R. 286
Pacific Dunlop Ltd v. Hogan, *sub nom.* Hogan v. Pacific Dunlop Ltd
Pacific Hotels Pty Ltd v. Asian Pacific International Ltd (PASSING OFF: HOTEL NAMES: DECEPTIVE CONDUCT: INTERLOCUTORY INJUNCTION: Australia: Fed. Ct)
                                                    7 I.P.R. 239
Pacific Pharmaceuticals Ltd v. Merck & Co. Inc. (PATENT: EXTENSION OF PATENT: INADEQUATE REMUNERATION: DISCRETION: New Zealand: H.C.)
                                                   18 I.P.R. 612
Pall Corp. v. Commercial Hydraulics (Bedford) Ltd (PATENT: INFRINGEMENT: ORATION: VALIDITY: PRACTICE: HIGH COURT AND EPO PROCEEDINGS: WHETHER STAY IN U.K. SHOULD BE ORDERED: STAY REFUSED: Pat. Ct)
                             [1988] F.S.R. 274; [1989] R.P.C. 703
                                          (C.A.) [1989] R.P.C. 703
      (COSTS: PRIOR USE: PRIOR PUBLICATION: Pat. Ct)   [1990] F.S.R. 329
PALM Trade Mark (TRADE MARK: RECTIFICATION: NON-USE: PERSON AGGRIEVED: SERVICE MARK: T.M.Reg.)   [1992] R.P.C. 258
Panayiotou v. Sony Music Entertainment (U.K.) Ltd (CONTRACT: RECORDING AGREEMENT: RESTRAINT OF TRADE: CHALLENGE TO ENFORCEABILITY OF AGREEMENT: ENTITLEMENT: EARLIER COMPROMISE OF PROCEEDINGS: REASONABLENESS OF TERMS: CONDUCT OF DEFENDANT: AFFECT ON TRADE BETWEEN MEMBER STATES: Ch.D.)   [1994] E.M.L.R. 229
Pancontinental Mining Ltd v. Commissioner of Stamp Duties (CONFIDENTIAL INFORMATION: WHETHER A TRANSFER OF VALUABLE CONFIDENTIAL INFORMATION IS A TRANSFER OF PROPERTY: Australia: S.C.(Qd))
                                                   15 I.P.R. 612

Pankaj Group v. The Good Year Tyre and Rubber Co. (TRADE MARK: NON-INTENTION TO USE: RECTIFICATION: India: T.M.Reg.)
(1987) 12 I.P.L.R. 53
(TRADE MARK: NON-APPEARANCE DURING RECTIFICATION PROCEEDINGS: LATE RECEIPT OF APPLICATION FOR RECTIFICATION: India: T.M.Reg.)
(1987) 12 I.P.L.R. 102
Papeteries de Golbey SA (RESTRICTIVE PRACTICES: JOINT VENTURE: PAPERMILL: JOINT MARKETING AND DISTRIBUTION: OPPOSITION BY COMMISSION: JOINT PRODUCTION ONLY: INTENTION TO APPROVE: E.C. Comm.)
[1994] 5 C.M.L.R. 96
Par Excellence Colour Printing (Pty) Ltd v. Ronnie Cox Graphic Supplies (Pty) Ltd (PATENT: INFRINGEMENT: VALIDITY: ONUS: South Africa: A.D.)
1983 (1) S.A. 295
(Order: A.D.) 1983 (1) S.A. 1142
Paragini Footwear Pty Ltd v. Paragon Shoes Pty Ltd (TRADE MARKS: APPLICATION: OPPOSITION: APPLICATION FOR LEAVE TO LODGE FURTHER EVIDENCE: Australia: Pat. Off.)
10 I.P.R. 477
Paragold Distributors Pty Ltd's Application (TRADE MARKS: OBJECTION TO REGISTRATION: SUPER SKIN FOR HANDBAGS: DIRECT REFERENCE TO CHARACTER OR QUALITY OF GOODS: NON-REGISTRABILITY IN PARTS A AND B: Australia: AIPO)
26 I.P.R. 307
Paragon Shoes Pty Ltd v. Paragini Distributors (NSW) Pty Ltd (TRADE PRACTICES: CONSUMER PROTECTION: MISLEADING AND DECEPTIVE CONDUCT: PASSING OFF: COPYING OF PRODUCT STYLE COMBINED WITH SIMILARITY OF NAME: DIFFERENCE IN PRODUCT PRICE: CATEGORY OF PERSONS LIKELY TO BE DECEIVED: Australia: Fed. Ct)
13 I.P.R. 323
Paramount Pictures Corp. v. Cablelink Ltd (COPYRIGHT: INFRINGEMENT: INTERLOCUTORY: INJUNCTION: TV CABLE DIFFUSION SERVICE: DAMAGES: LAW IN CINEMATOGRAPH FILM: ABUSE OF DOMINANT POSITION: ARTICLES 85 AND 86: Ireland: H.C.)
[1991] 1 I.R. 521
Paramount Pictures Corp. v. Video Parktown North (Pty) Ltd (COPYRIGHT: FILM: EXCLUSIVE LICENSEE: RIGHTS: South Africa: TPD)
1983 (2) S.A. 1
Parfums Givenchy SA's Application (RESTRICTIVE PRACTICES: SELECTIVE DISTRIBUTION SYSTEM: CAUGHT BY ARTICLE 85(1): EXEMPTION GRANTED: E.C. Comm.)
[1993] 5 C.M.L.R. 579
Parfums Givenchy SA v. Designer Alternatives Ltd (TRADE MARK: INFRINGEMENT: PRACTICE: EVIDENCE OF PRONUNCIATION: C.A.)
[1994] R.P.C. 243
Parkash Metal Works v. Square Automation (Pvt.) Ltd (TRADE MARK: INFRINGEMENT: PASSING OFF: HOT FLO/PMW HOT FLO: INJUNCTION: India: H.C.)
(1992) 17 I.P.L.R. 57
Parkash Roadlines Ltd v. Parkash Parcel Services (Pvt.) Ltd (TRADE MARK: COPYRIGHT: INFRINGEMENT: PASSING OFF: INTERIM INJUNCTION: India: H.C.)
(1992) 17 I.P.L.R. 251
Parke Davis & Co.'s Application (PATENT: EXTENSION: PROPERTIES OF PHARMACEUTICAL DRUG: RESEARCH AND DEVELOPMENT COSTS: REMUNERATION: Australia: S.C.(NSW))
14 I.P.R. 310
Parke Davis Pty Ltd v. Sanofi & Commissioner of Patents (PATENT: EXPIRATION: EXTENSION OF TIME LIMIT FOR PETITION: Australia: Fed. Ct)
(1983) 43 A.L.R. 487
(H.C.) (1983) 49 A.L.R. 1
Parker Knoll plc v. Knoll Overseas Ltd (PASSING OFF: TRADE MARK: USE OF OWN NAME: CONTEMPT OF COURT: Ch.D.)
[1985] F.S.R. 349

Parmenter v. Malt House Joinery (REGISTERED DESIGN: INFRINGEMENT: VALIDITY: PRACTICE: AMENDMENT OF PLEADINGS DURING TRIAL: EVIDENCE: *Res Judicata*: INTERLOCUTORY APPEAL ALLOWED: C.A.)   [1993] F.S.R. 680

Parsons Control/Scraper chain conveyor (EUROPEAN PATENT: OPPOSITION: PROCEDURE: FRESH DOCUMENTS ON APPEAL: ORAL PROCEEDINGS: UNNECESSARY: T61/89: EPO)   [1992] E.P.O.R. 205

Passoni/Stand structure (EUROPEAN PATENT: PARIS CONVENTION, RELATIONSHIP WITH EPC: *Travaux préparatoires*: STATE OF THE ART: EVIDENT ABUSE: Application no. 82 107 958.9: EPO)   [1992] E.P.O.R. 79

Patents Court Practice Explanation (PATENTS COURT PRACTICE EXPLANATION: TELEPHONE SUMMONSES: AGREED INTERLOCUTORY ORDERS: INFORMATION SHEETS AT SUMMONS FOR DIRECTIONS: PRE-TRIAL REVIEWS: RIGHTS OF AUDIENCE: SITTINGS OUTSIDE LONDON: Pat. Ct)
[1996] R.P.C. 73

Patent Licensing Agreements Regulation, *sub nom.* Community Patent Licensing Agreements Regulation

Patents Licensing Regulation, *sub nom.* Community Patents Licensing Regulations

Patented Bandaging Material (PATENTS: EXHAUSTION OF RIGHTS: IMPORTS: Germany)   [1988] 2 C.M.L.R. 359; [1988] F.S.R. 505

Paterson Zochonis Ltd v. Merfarken Packaging Ltd (COPYRIGHT: INFRINGEMENT: NEGLIGENCE: PRINTER'S INNOCENCE: PRINTER'S DUTY OF CARE: DAMAGES: VENUS DE MILO SKIN CREME: FORSEEABILITY: LOSS BY PASSING OFF: STRIKING OUT: C.A.)   [1983] F.S.R. 273; [1986] 3 All E.R. 522

PATON CALVERT CORDON BLEU Trade Mark (TRADE MARK: APPLICATION: OPPOSITION: WHETHER OPPONENTS TRUE PROPRIETOR OF CORDON BLEU: WHETHER MARK APPLIED FOR DECEPTIVE: EFFECT OF DISCLAIMERS: DISCRETION: T.M.Reg.)   [1996] R.P.C. 94

Patricia Im-und Export Verwaltungsgesellschaft mbH v. EMI Electrola GmbH, *sub nom.* Phil Collins v. Imtrat Handelsgesellschaft mbH

Patten v. Burke Publishing Co. Ltd (COPYRIGHT: AUTHOR'S RIGHTS: PRACTICE: JUDGMENT BY DEFAULT: DECLARATION: PUBLISHERS' CONTRACTUAL RIGHT TO PUBLISH AUTHOR'S WORKS: AUTHOR SEEKING DECLARATION THAT PARTIES NO LONGER BOUND BY CONTRACT: JUDGMENT IN DEFAULT OF PUBLISHERS GIVING NOTICE OF INTENTION TO DEFEND ACTION: WHETHER DECLARATION TO BE GRANTED: Ch.D.)
[1991] F.S.R. 483; [1991] 1 W.L.R. 541

Pavel v. Sony Corp. (COUNTY COURT: APPEAL TO COURT OF APPEAL: PERIOD OF SERVING NOTICE OF APPEAL: WHEN DOES TIME BEGIN TO RUN: Pat. C.C.)   [1993] F.S.R. 177

Payen Components S.A. Ltd v. Bovic Gaskets CC (COPYRIGHT: INFRINGEMENT: SUBSTANTIAL PART: REMEDIES: INJUNCTION: BREACH: INTERFACE BETWEEN UNLAWFUL COMPETITION AND COPYRIGHT, TRADE MARK, DESIGN AND PASSING OFF ACTIONS: South Africa, A.D.)   1995 (4) S.A. 441

Pavunny v. Mathew (PASSING OFF: TRADE NAMES: INJUNCTION: India: H.C.)
(1983) 8 I.P.L.R. 36

Paxus Services Ltd v. People Bank Pty Ltd (PRACTICE AND PROCEDURE: DISCOVERY BEFORE ACTION: CONFIDENTIAL INFORMATION IN COMPUTER DATABASES: WHETHER COMPUTER DATABASE A "DOCUMENT": CONSIDERATIONS FOR EXERCISE OF DISCRETION: Australia: Fed. Ct)
20 I.P.R. 79

Payen Components SA Ltd v. Bovic Gaskets C.C. (COPYRIGHT: SUBSISTENCE: LITERARY WORK: COMPUTERISED CATALOGUING SYSTEM: WORK PRODUCED BY PROGRAM: ASSIGNMENT OF COPYRIGHT TO OVERSEAS PARENT COMPANY: EXCLUSIVE LICENSEE: UNLAWFUL COMPETITION: South Africa: WLD)   1994 (2) S.A. 464

Payne's Application (PATENT: APPLICATION: PRIORITY DATE: CORRECTION OF CLERICAL ERROR: Pat. Ct)   [1985] R.P.C. 193

PCUK's Application (PATENT: APPLICATION: INVENTIVE STEP: PATENT OFFICE PROCEEDINGS: PRACTICE: Pat. Ct)   [1984] R.P.C. 482

PCW (Underwriting Agencies) Ltd v. Dixon (MAREVA INJUNCTION: PROTECTION OF THIRD PARTIES' INTERESTS: Q.B.D.)   [1983] 2 All E.R. 158
(C.A.) [1983] 2 All E.R. 697

PDL Packaging Ltd v. Labplas (N.Z.) Ltd (COPYRIGHT: INFRINGEMENT: MOULD OF BOTTLE: New Zealand: H.C.)   8 I.P.R. 331

Peabody International's Application (PATENT: APPLICATION: PRACTICE: PUBLICATION OF APPLICATION: WITHDRAWAL: C.-G.)   [1986] R.P.C. 521

Pearce v. Paul Kingston Pty Ltd (PATENT: INFRINGEMENT: VALIDITY: NOVELTY: LACK OF FAIR BASIS: LACK OF UTILITY: PAPER ANTICIPATION: WORKSHOP VARIATIONS: ALLEGED FAILURE TO DEFINE THE INVENTION: Australia: S.C.(Vic.))   23 I.P.R. 303

Pearce v. Waterhouse (PRACTICE: MAREVA INJUNCTION: JURISPRUDENCE: INHERENT POWER: PRINCIPLES: Australia: S.C.(Vic.))   [1986] V.R. 603

Pegulan/Surface finish (EUROPEAN PATENT: INVENTIVE STEP: PROBLEM AND SOLUTION: FORMULATION OF PROBLEM: PROBLEM AS DESCRIBED: WHEN ALTERNATIVE PROBLEM JUSTIFIED: T495/91: EPO)   [1995] E.P.O.R. 516

Pelikan International Handelsgesellschaft mbH & Co. KG v. Lifinia Pty Ltd (TRADE MARK: APPLICATION: ACCEPTANCE: OPPOSITION: DECEPTIVE OR CONFUSING: SUBSTANTIALLY IDENTICAL: EVIDENCE: Australia: AIPO)
30 I.P.R. 615

Pendax AB v. Anders & Kern (U.K.) Ltd (PATENT: INFRINGEMENT: PLEADINGS: AMENDMENT OF PATENT, STATEMENT OF CLAIM AND PARTICULARS OF OBJECTIONS: WHETHER A *See* v. *Scott-Paine* ORDER APPROPRIATE: COSTS: Pat. Ct)   [1993] F.S.R. 743

Penerbit Fajar Bakti Sdn Bhd v. Cahaya Surya Buku dan Alat Tulis (COPYRIGHT: COLLECTION OF SHORT STORIES AND POEMS: SUBSISTENCE OF COPYRIGHT: Malaysia: H.C.)   15 I.P.R. 122

Penfold v. Fairbrass (COPYRIGHT: INFRINGEMENT: STRIKING OUT: MUSICAL WORK: AFFIDAVIT EVIDENCE: WHETHER ADMISSIBLE: TAPE RECORDING OF SONGS: WHETHER ADMISSIBLE: Ch.D.)   [1994] E.M.L.R. 471

Penfolds Wines (N.Z.) v. Leo Buring Pty Ltd (TRADE MARK: APPLICATION: OPPOSITION: DECEPTIVE OR CONFUSING: New Zealand: Pat. Off.)
3 I.P.R. 233

Penguin Books Ltd v. India Book Distributors (COPYRIGHT: INFRINGEMENT: CONSENT DECREE IN USA: APPEAL: INTERLOCUTORY INJUNCTION: India: H.C.)   (1985) 9 I.P.L.R. 162; [1985] F.S.R. 120

Peninsular Real Estate Ltd v. Harris (CONFIDENTIAL INFORMATION: EX-EMPLOYEES: CLIENT LIST: NO RESTRAINT OF TRADE CLAUSE: New Zealand: H.C.)   [1992] 2 N.Z.L.R. 216

Pennys Pty Ltd's Application (TRADE MARK: APPLICATION: ACCEPTANCE IN ERROR: GEOGRAPHICAL NAME: STRATHSPEY: DISCRETION: Australia: AIPO)   31 I.P.R. 652

Pepsico Australia Pty. Ltd v. Kettle Chip Co Pty. Ltd *sub nom.* Kettle Chip Co Pty. Ltd v. Pepsico Australia Pty. Ltd

Pepsico Inc. v. Express Bottlers Services Pvt. Ltd (TRADE MARK: INFRINGEMENT: PEPSI/PEPSICOLA: NON-USE: RECTIFICATION PROCEEDINGS PENDING: INJUNCTION REFUSED: APPEAL: India: H.C.)   (1987) I.P.L.R. 71 (RECTIFICATION: WHETHER SALES TO EMBASSIES AMOUNT TO BONA FIDE USE OF MARK: India: H.C.)   (1988) 13 I.P.L.R. 99

Pepsico Inc. v. United Tobacco Co. Ltd (PASSING OFF: REPUTATION: ONUS OF PROOF: PRE-LAUNCH PUBLICITY: South Africa: WLD)   1988 (2) S.A. 334

Peptide Technology Ltd v. The Wellcome Foundation Ltd (PATENT: APPLICATION: OPPOSITION: MANNER OF NEW MANUFACTURE: SUFFICIENCY OF SPECIFICATION: FAIRLY BASED: AMBIGUITY: OBVIOUSNESS: COMMON GENERAL KNOWLEDGE: NOVELTY: Australia: Pat. Off.)   23 I.P.R. 319

Perceptual Development Corp. v. Versi Pty Ltd (CONTRACT: RESTRAINT OF TRADE: INFORMATION IN PUBLIC DOMAIN: TECHNIQUE FOR DIAGNOSIS AND TREATMENT OF DYSLEXIA: Australia: Fed. Ct)   11 I.P.R. 358

Performing Right Societies (RESTRICTIVE PRACTICES: COPYRIGHT: COLLECTING SOCIETIES: PARALLEL IMPORTS: ROYALTIES: NOTICE: E.C. Comm.)   [1984] 1 C.M.L.R. 308

Performing Right Society Ltd v. Marlin Communal Aerials Ltd (COPYRIGHT: BROADCASTING: CABLE TV: Ireland: S.C.)   [1982] I.L.R.M. 269; [1982] E.C.C. 30; [1983] F.S.R. 30

Performing Right Society Ltd v. The British Entertainment & Dancing Association Ltd (COPYRIGHT: PERFORMING RIGHT: DISCOTHÉQUES: APPEAL FROM DECISION OF COPYRIGHT TRIBUNAL: DETERMINATION OF ROYALTY RATE: COSTS: PRINCIPLES: Ch.D.)   [1993] E.M.L.R. 325

Performing Right Society Ltd v. Working Men's Club & Institute Union Ltd (COPYRIGHT: MUSICAL WORKS: LICENCE SCHEME: WHETHER NEW TARIFF WAS LICENCE SCHEME: REFERENCE TO TRIBUNAL: Ch.D.)   [1988] F.S.R. 586

Perkin-Elmer Corp. v. Varian Techtron Pty Ltd (PATENTS: OPPOSITION: AMENDMENT OF SPECIFICATION: INTERIM HEARING: FAIR BASIS: Australia: Pat. Off.)   5 I.P.R. 321

PERMO Trade Mark (TRADE MARK: RECTIFICATION: PRACTICE: CROSS-EXAMINATION: T.M.Reg.)   [1985] R.P.C. 597

Pernod Ricard SA v. Allswell Trading Pte Ltd (PASSING OFF: ELEMENTS OF TORT: GET-UP: MERE COPYING OF UTILITARIAN FEATURES INSUFFICIENT: Singapore: H.C.)   [1994] S.L.R. 603

Perrin v. Drennan (COPYRIGHT: REGISTERED DESIGN: INFRINGEMENT: COPYING: SIMILAR FACT EVIDENCE: Ch.D.)   [1991] F.S.R. 81

Personal Plating Meters Pty Ltd's Application (TRADE MARK: APPLICATION: PART A: EXAMINATION: OBJECTION: LACK OF INHERENT ABILITY TO DISTINGUISH: Australia: AIPO)   29 I.P.R. 496

Perth Building Society's Application (TRADE MARK: APPLICATION: DISTINCTIVENESS: Australia: Pat. Off.)   2 I.P.R. 385

Perth Mint v. Mickelberg (MAREVA INJUNCTION: PRINCIPLES, FOR GRANT: Australia: S.C.(W.A.))   [1984] W.A.R. 230

Perth Mint v. Mickelberg (No. 2) (PRACTICE: INTERLOCUTORY INJUNCTION: MAREVA INJUNCTION: RISK OF DISSIPATION OF ASSETS: Australia: S.C.(W.A.))   [1985] W.A.R. 117

Pestre v. Oril SA (PATENT: LICENSING AGREEMENT: KNOW-HOW: ROYALTIES: TERM: 50 YEARS: VALIDITY AFTER EXPIRY OF PATENT: France: C.A.)   [1994] 2 C.M.L.R. 515

Pet Plan Ltd v. Protect-A-Pet Ltd (CONFIDENTIAL INFORMATION: LISTS OF
CUSTOMERS: PRACTICE: CONSENT ORDER: APPLICATION TO DISCHARGE:
C.A.)   [1988] F.S.R. 34

Pete Waterman Ltd v. CBS United Kingdom Ltd (PASSING OFF: SERVICES:
PLAINTIFF'S ACQUIRING NICKNAME BUT NOT TRADING UNDER THAT NAME:
DISTINCTIVENESS: MISREPRESENTATION: SECONDARY   MEANING:
LIKELIHOOD OF DAMAGE: INTERNATIONAL REPUTATION: Ch.D.)
                                         [1993] E.M.L.R. 27; 20 I.P.R. 185

Peter Isaacson Publications Pty Ltd v. Nationwide News Pty Ltd (TRADE PRACTICES:
PASSING OFF: EXCLUSIVE REPUTATION: UNFAIR COMPETITION: CONSUMER
PROTECTION: MISLEADING CONDUCT: INJUNCTION: DAMAGES: Australia:
Fed. Ct)   56 A.L.R. 595; 3 I.P.R. 255

Peter Pan Electric Pty Ltd v. Newton Grace Pty Ltd (PETTY PATENT: VALIDITY:
INTERLOCUTORY INJUNCTION: PROCEDURE: Australia: Fed. Ct)
                                         70 A.L.R. 731; 4 I.P.R. 567

Peters Edition Ltd v. Renner Piano Co. (CIVIL PROCEDURE: ANTON PILLER ORDER:
GENUINE AND PIRATED GOODS MIXED: PLAINTIFF SEISING BOTH: WHETHER
PLAINTIFF UNDER A DUTY TO RETURN GENUINE GOODS: WHETHER
PLAINTIFF HAD GOOD REASON FOR NOT RETURNING GOODS: LIMITS OF
ANTON PILLER ORDER TO BE METICULOUSLY OBEYED: Singapore: H.C.)
                                                        18 I.P.R. 95

Petersville Sleigh Ltd v. Sugarman (PASSING OFF: PRINCIPLES TO BE APPLIED:
WHETHER TANGIBLE PROBABILITY OF DECEPTION OR OF DAMAGE:
INNOCENT PASSING OFF: DECEPTION AND INJURY COULD NOT BE INFERRED:
NO ACTUAL OR PROBABLE DAMAGE: PARTIES NOT ENGAGED IN COMMON
FIELD OF ACTIVITY: NO PRESUMPTION OF DAMAGE: Australia: S.C.(Vic.))
                                                        10 I.P.R. 501

Petre & Madco (Pty) Ltd v. Sanderson-Kasner (ANTON PILLER: APPLICATION:
CONDUCT OF SEARCH: PRACTICE: South Africa: WLD)   1984 (3) S.A. 850

Peugeot & Citroen II/Opposition by patent proprietor (EUROPEAN PATENT:
OPPOSITION BY PATENT PROPRIETOR: WHETHER ADMISSIBLE (NO):
REVERSAL OF PREVIOUS DECISION OF ENLARGED BOARD: PROSPECTIVE
EFFECT ONLY: G09/93: EPO)   [1995] E.P.O.R. 260; [1994] O.J. EPO 891

Peugeot SA and Fiat Auto SpA's Joint Venture (RESTRICTIVE PRACTICES: JOINT
VENTURE: JOINT PRODUCTION OF COMMERCIAL MOTOR VEHICLE:
INTENTION TO APPROVE: NOTICE: E.C. Comm.)   [1994] 4 C.M.L.R. 510

Peugeot/Electric motor (EUROPEAN PATENT: APPEAL: PROCEDURE: STATEMENT
OF GROUNDS, REQUIREMENTS OF: FRESH PRIOR ART: ADMITTED IN VIEW OF
RELEVANCE: EVIDENCE: ORAL EXAMINATION OF WITNESS: CREDIBILITY OF
WITNESS: PRIOR ART: PRIOR USE: CREDIBILITY OF EMPLOYEE OF ASSOCIATED
COMPANY: T124/88: EPO)   [1991] E.P.O.R. 255

Peugeot/Electric motor (EUROPEAN PATENT: T102/91: EPO)
                                                        [1993] E.P.O.R. 198

Pfizer Inc.'s Application (PATENT: EXTENSION: INADEQUATE REMUNERATION:
EXCEPTIONAL CASE: CHARACTER OF INVENTION: Australia: S.C.(NSW))
                       65 A.L.R. 289; 6 I.P.R. 527; [1986] 4 N.S.W.L.R. 566

Pfizer Inc. v. Chemo-Pharma Laboratories Ltd (TRADE MARK: OPPOSITION: LATE
FILED EVIDENCE: ABANDONMENT OF OPPOSITION: India: T.M.Reg.)
                                                  (1987) 12 I.P.L.R. 65

Pfizer Inc. v. Jiwa International (H.K.) Co. (PATENT: INFRINGEMENT:
REGISTRATION OF U.K. PATENT UNDER LOCAL ORDINANCE: EFFECT OF
REGISTRATION: POSITION OF LICENSEE: EFFECT OF PATENT UNDER
COMMON LAW: Hong Kong: H.C.)   [1988] R.P.C. 15

Pfizer Inc. v. South African Druggists Ltd (PATENT: EXTENSION: APPLICATION: APPEAL: PRACTICE: South Africa: TPD) 1987 (1) S.A. 259

Pfizer Pty Ltd v. Warner Lambert Pty Ltd (PATENT: PATENT ATTORNEY: PRIVILEGED COMMUNICATIONS WITH: WHETHER PRIVILEGE EXTENDS TO COMMUNICATIONS BETWEEN PATENT ATTORNEY AND CLIENT IN THE COURSE OF CONDUCT: Australia: Fed. Ct) 89 A.L.R. 625; 16 I.P.R. 667

Pfizer/Correction of chemical name (EUROPEAN PATENT: AMENDMENT AND CORRECTION: CHEMICAL NAME: ACKNOWLEDGED PRIOR ART, REFERENCE TO: FEES: REIMBURSEMENT OF APPEAL FEE: SUPEREROGATORY REASONING: T990/91: EPO) [1992] E.P.O.R. 351

Pfizer/Penem (EUROPEAN PATENT: NOVELTY: CHEMICAL COMPOUND: MIXTURE OF DIASTEREOMERS: T1048/92: EPO) [1995] E.P.O.R. 207

Pharma Plast A/S v. Bard Ltd (PATENTS COUNTY COURT PROCEDURE: TRANSFER TO HIGH COURT: Pat. C.C.) [1993] F.S.R. 686

Pharma Research & Analytical Labs v. Jal Pvt. Ltd (TRADE MARK: APPLICATION: OLIN: India: T.M.Reg.) (1986) 11 I.P.L.R. 16

Pharmon BV v. Hoechst AG (PATENTS: PARALLEL IMPORTS: COMPULSORY LICENCES: Case 19/84: ECJ)
[1985] 3 C.M.L.R. 775; [1985] E.C.R. 2281; [1986] F.S.R. 108

Pharmuka/Polysaccharides from heparin (EUROPEAN PATENT: APPEAL: PROCEDURE: STATEMENT OF GROUNDS, REQUIREMENTS OF: ADMISSIBILITY OF APPEAL: SUFFICIENCY: EXCESSIVE EXPERIMENTATION: T169/89: EPO) [1991] E.P.O.R. 262

Phil Collins v. Imtrat Handelsgesellschaft mbH (DISCRIMINATION: NATIONALITY: COPYRIGHT LAWS: PHONOGRAMS: BOOTLEG RECORDINGS: REMEDY UNDER GERMAN LAW AVAILABLE TO GERMAN NATIONALS: DISCRIMINATION: NATIONALITY: DIRECT EFFECT: NOT TO BRITONS: ARTICLE 7(1) EFFECTIVE DIRECTLY AND ON ITS OWN: BREACH OF ARTICLE 7(1): COPYRIGHT: SPECIFIC OBJECT: COVERED BY FREE MOVEMENT RULES: Case C–92/92: ECJ)
[1993] 3 C.M.L.R. 773; [1994] E.M.L.R. 108; [1994] F.S.R. 166

Philip Morris Belgium SA v. Golden Tobacco Co. Ltd (TRADE MARK: INFRINGEMENT: INTERIM INJUNCTION: India: H.C.) (1986) 11 I.P.L.R. 1

Philip Morris Inc. v. Brown and Williamson Tobacco Corp. (PATENT: APPLICATION: OPPOSITION: AMENDMENT: REQUEST TO AMEND: IN SUBSTANCE DISCLOSED: FAIR BASIS: COMPLETE SPECIFICATION: FURTHER REQUEST TO AMEND: PRACTICE AND PROCEDURE: Australia: AIPO) 29 I.P.R. 299

Philip Morris Inc. v. GTC Industries Ltd (TRADE MARK: INFRINGEMENT: BAN ON IMPORTS: EXPORT OF PRODUCTS USING PLAINTIFF'S NAME: INTERIM INJUNCTION: India: H.C.) (1992) 17 I.P.L.R. 237

Philip Morris Inc. v. Marlboro Shirt Co. SA Ltd (PASSING OFF: TRADE MARK: EXPUNGEMENT: USE: CONFUSION: South Africa: A.D.) 1991 (2) S.A. 720

Philips Electronic & Associated Industries Ltd's Patent (PATENT: EUROPEAN PATENT: AMENDMENT: C.-G.) [1987] R.P.C. 244

Philips Export BV and John Fluke Manufacturing Co. Inc.'s Agreements (RESTRICTIVE PRACTICES: RECIPROCAL EXCLUSIVE DISTRIBUTION AGREEMENTS: PARTIES DIRECT COMPETITORS IN SOME PRODUCTS, SO NOT COVERED BY GROUP EXEMPTION REGULATION 1983/83: INTENTION TO GRANT INDIVIDUAL EXEMPTION: E.C. Comm.) [1990] 4 C.M.L.R. 166

Philips Gloeilampenfabrieken (NV) v. Mirabella International Pty Ltd (PATENT: INFRINGEMENT: WHETHER INVENTION FULLY DESCRIBED: FAILURE TO DESCRIBE PARTICULAR MATERIALS: FAIR BASIS: WHETHER SPECIFICATION OF SUITABLE CHARACTERISTICS OF KNOWN MATERIAL FOR KNOWN USE CONSTITUTES A "PATENTABLE INVENTION" OR A "MANNER OF NEW MANUFACTURE": UTILITY: NOVELTY: Australia: Fed. Ct)
117 A.L.R. 79; 24 I.P.R. 1

Philips Gloeilampenfabrieken (NV) v. Ultralite International Pty Ltd (PATENT: INTERLOCUTORY INJUNCTION: BALANCE OF CONVENIENCE INJUNCTION REFUSED BUT UNDERTAKINGS ACCEPTED TO KEEP ACCOUNTS AND PAY $1.00 PER UNIT INTO COURT CONTROLLED FUND: COSTS: Australia: Fed. Ct)
22 I.P.R. 57

(PATENT: NEW USE FOR OLD SUBSTANCE: MANNER OF NEW MANUFACTURE: APPEAL: Fed. Ct)   132 A.L.R. 117

Philips International BV's Application (RESTRICTIVE PRACTICES: JOINT DEVELOPMENT OF DIGITAL COMPACT CASSETTES: PATENT LICENSING: COPYRIGHT PROTECTION: INTENTION TO APPROVE: E.C. Comm.)
[1993] 4 C.M.L.R. 286

Philips International BV and Osram GmbH (RESTRICTIVE PRACTICES: JOINT VENTURE: EXTENSION OF NOTIFICATION TO COVER ARTICLE 53 EEA: INTENTION TO APPROVE: NOTICE: E.C. Comm.)   [1994] 5 C.M.L.R. 491

Philips Petroleum Co. v. Joint Controller of Patents & Designs (PATENT: APPLICATION: PROCESS AND PASSIVE AGENT: OBJECTIONS RAISED AFTER ACCEPTANCE AND ADVERTISEMENT OF COMPLETE SPECIFICATION: India: H.C.)   (1994) 19 I.P.L.R. 10

Philips/Diagnostic method (EUROPEAN PATENT: PATENTABILITY: DIAGNOSTIC METHOD: T45/84: EPO)   [1979–85] E.P.O.R. C937

Philips/Display tube (EUROPEAN PATENT: INVENTIVE STEP: AGED ART: LATER DEVELOPMENTS BY PIONEER TEACHING AWAY: PRIOR ART: AGED PUBLICATIONS: T321/86: EPO)   [1989] E.P.O.R. 199

Philips/Image enhancement circuit (EUROPEAN PATENT: CLAIMS: CLARITY: NON-WORKING EXAMPLES: SPECULATIVE: AMENDMENT AND CORRECTION: INTERMEDIATE GENERALISATION: DISCLOSURE: IMPLIED TEACHING: NEED FOR EXCESSIVE INTENSITY OF BRAIN WORK: T770/90: EPO)
[1992] E.P.O.R. 438

Philips/Interchangeable disks (EUROPEAN PATENT: AMENDMENT AND CORRECTION: BROADENING CLAIM BY OMISSION: T147/85: EPO)
[1988] E.P.O.R. 111

Philips/Optical scanning apparatus (EUROPEAN PATENT: T165/82: EPO)
[1986] E.P.O.R. 133

Philips/Reference signs (EUROPEAN PATENT: AMENDMENT AND CORRECTION: EXPLANATION OF REFERENCE NUMERALS IN CLAIM: CLAIMS: REFERENCE NUMERALS/SIGNS, EFFECT OF: T237/84: EPO)
[1987] E.P.O.R. 310; [1987] O.J. EPO 309

Philips/Video disc apparatus (EUROPEAN PATENT: APPEAL: PROCEDURE: INTERLOCUTORY REVISION: CLAIMS: SPECULATIVE AND VAGUE: NOVELTY: SPECULATIVE AND VAGUE CLAIMS: PRECEDENT: *Ratio decidendi* OF BOARD OF APPEAL DECISION: T378/88: EPO)   [1990] E.P.O.R. 571

Phillips Petroleum/Passivation of catalyst (EUROPEAN PATENT: INVENTIVE STEP: PROBLEM, DEFINITION OF: STATE OF THE ART: T155/85: EPO)
[1988] E.P.O.R. 164; [1988] O.J. EPO 87

Phillips Petroleum/Re-establishment (EUROPEAN PATENT: CONVENTIONS: CPC
NEGOTIATIONS: FEES: REIMBURSEMENT OF APPEAL FEE: RE-ESTABLISHMENT
OF RIGHTS: EVIDENCE NEED NOT BE FILED WITHIN TIME-LIMIT FOR
APPLYING: LARGE COMPANY: MUST HAVE EFFECTIVE SYSTEM OF STAFF:
T324/90: EPO)   [1993] E.P.O.R. 507; [1993] O.J. EPO 33
Phillips v. Holmes (COPYRIGHT: PROSECUTION: MEANING OF "SALE":
Q.B.D.)   [1988] R.P.C. 613
Phillips/Cash payment to Post Office (EUROPEAN PATENT: FEES: DATE OF RECEIPT:
REIMBURSEMENT OF APPEAL FEE: J24/86: EPO)
                                                        [1988] E.P.O.R. 59; [1987] O.J. EPO 399
Phillips/Cracking catalyst (EUROPEAN PATENT: INVENTIVE STEP: OBVIOUS TO TRY:
T274/87: EPO)   [1989] E.P.O.R. 207
Phillips/Number of claims incurring fees (EUROPEAN PATENT: AMENDMENT AND
CORRECTION: CLAIM TO EMBODIMENT: TEXT OF PATENT: CLAIMS V.
DESCRIPTION: FEES: CLAIM, WHAT CONSTITUTES: J05/87: EPO)
                                                        [1987] E.P.O.R. 316; [1987] O.J. EPO 295
PHOENIX Trade Mark (APPLICATION: OPPOSITION: GEOGRAPHICAL NAME:
SURVEY EVIDENCE: T.M.Reg.)   [1985] R.P.C. 122
Phoenix (RESTRICTIVE PRACTICES: JOINT VENTURES: GLOBAL
TELECOMMUNICATIONS SERVICES: INTENTION TO APPROVE: E.C
Comm.)   [1996] 4 C.M.L.R. 285
Phonographic Performance (Ireland) Ltd v. J. Somers (Inspector of Taxes) (REVENUE:
VALUE ADDED TAX: TAX PAYABLE ON SUPPLY OF SERVICES: COPYRIGHT:
SOUND RECORDINGS: REMUNERATION FOR BROADCASTING OF SOUND
RECORDINGS: AGREEMENT: WHETHER APPELLANT SUPPLYING A SERVICE:
WHETHER ATTRACTING VALUE ADDED TAX: Ireland: H.C.)
                                                                          [1993] 1 I.R. 195
Phonographic Performance (South East Asia) Ltd v. California Entertainments Ltd
(COPYRIGHT: OWNERSHIP: BURDEN OF PROOF: INFRINGEMENT: Hong
Kong: C.A.)   14 I.P.R. 163
Phonographic Performance Ltd v. Grosvenor Leisure Ltd (COPYRIGHT:
INFRINGEMENT: SOUND RECORDINGS: COUNTERCLAIM: ARTICLE 86 EEC:
Ch.D.)   [1984] F.S.R. 24
Phonographic Performance Ltd v. Retail Broadcast Services Ltd (COPYRIGHT:
SOUND RECORDING RIGHTS: STATUTORY LICENCE TO BROADCAST: NOTICE
TO LICENSING BODY PRIOR TO EXERCISING RIGHT: WHETHER STRICT
COMPLIANCE WITH STATUTORY REQUIREMENTS MANDATORY:
Ch.D.)   [1995] F.S.R. 813
PHOTO-SCAN Trade Mark (TRADE MARK: APPLICATION: WHETHER
DESCRIPTIVE OR DECEPTIVE: BoT)   [1987] R.P.C. 213
Pickwick International Inc. (G.B.) Ltd v. Demon Records Ltd (TRADE MARK:
INFRINGEMENT: IMP: SPECIFICATION OF GOODS: C.A.)   [1988] F.S.R. 423
Pidilite Industries Pvt. Ltd v. Mittees Corp. (TRADE MARK: INFRINGEMENT:
FEVICOL/TREVICOL: COPYRIGHT: INTERIM INJUNCTION: THREATS:
India: H.C.)   (1989) 14 I.P.L.R. 67
Pierre Fabre SA v. Marion Laboratories Inc. (TRADE MARK: REMOVAL FOR NON-
USE: OPPOSITION: ONUS OF PROOF: Australia: T.M.Reg.)   7 I.P.R. 387
Pierre Fabre SA v. Ronco Teleproducts Inc. (PASSING OFF: PRACTICE: ORDER 14
PROCEDURE: Ch.D.)   [1984] F.S.R. 148
Pioneer Concrete Services Ltd v. Lorenzo Galli (CONFIDENTIAL INFORMATION:
IMPLIED OBLIGATION: RESTRAINT OF TRADE: INJUNCTION: DECLARATION:
DAMAGES: Australia: S.C.(Vic.))   4 I.P.R. 227

Pioneer Electronics Capital Inc. v. Warner Music Manufacturing Europe GmbH (PATENT: INFRINGEMENT: WHETHER PRODUCTS OBTAINED DIRECTLY BY PATENTED PROCESS: STRIKING OUT: Pat. Ct) [1995] R.P.C. 487

Pioneer Hi-bred International Inc. USA v. Pioneer Seed Co. Ltd (TRADE MARK: REGISTERED USER ARRANGEMENT: REFUSAL TO GIVE INSPECTION: SUIT FOR PERMANENT INJUNCTION AGAINST REGISTERED USER: INJUNCTION: India: H.C.) (1990) 15 I.P.L.R. 1

Pioneer Hi-Bred Ltd v. Commissioner of Patents (PATENT: APPLICATION: SUFFICIENCY OF DISCLOSURE: Canada: S.C.) 15 I.P.R. 109

Pioneer KK's Application (TRADE MARK: APPLICATION: DISTINCTIVENESS: LASER DISC: Australia: Pat. Off.) 5 I.P.R. 285

Piped Music in Prisons, Re (COPYRIGHT: ROYALTIES: EXEMPTIONS: MUSIC PLAYED IN PRISONS: Germany: C.A.) [1993] E.C.C. 267; [1993] F.S.R. 575

Pirtek Fluid Systems Pty Ltd v. Kaydon Holdings Pty Ltd (TRADE PRACTICES: MISLEADING OR DECEPTIVE CONDUCT: FRANCHISE AGREEMENT: FRANCHISEE IN FINANCIAL DIFFICULTIES: WHETHER MISLEADING FORECASTS BY FRANCHISOR: WHETHER BREACH OF FRANCHISE AGREEMENT: Australia: Fed. Ct) 22 I.P.R. 117

Pitney Bowes Inc. v. Francotyp-Postalia GmbH (PATENT: INFRINGEMENT: EURO-DEFENCES: DOMINANT POSITION: ABUSE: WHETHER ALLEGATIONS A DEFENCE TO THE ACTION: THREATS: Ch.D.)
[1991] E.C.C. 25; [1991] F.S.R. 72

Piver (L.T.) Sàrl v. S. & J. Perfume Co. Ltd (ANTON PILLER PRACTICE: Ch.D.)
[1987] F.S.R. 159

Planet Earth Productions Inc. v. Rowlands (COPYRIGHT: PHOTOGRAPHS AND NEGATIVES: SEIZURE: OWNERSHIP OF COPYRIGHT: PHOTOGRAPHS ORDERED BY ANOTHER: Canada: S.C.(Ont.)) 20 I.P.R. 431

Plant Genetic Systems/Glutamine synthetase inhibitors (EUROPEAN PATENT: PATENTABILITY: *Ordre public*: MORALITY: PLANT VARIETIES: BIOLOGICAL PROCESS FOR PRODUCTION OF PLANTS: MICROBIOLOGICAL PROCESS: T356/93: EPO) [1995] E.P.O.R. 357

Plant Variety Rights (Draft Regulation) (CREATION OF COMMUNITY PLANT VARIETY RIGHT: ADMINISTRATIVE AND LEGAL RULES APPLICABLE THERETO: E.C. Council) [1990] 3 C.M.L.R. 196

Plants Variety Rights Council Regulation, *sub nom.* Community Plants Variety Rights Council Regulation 2100/94

Plascon-Evans Paints Ltd v. Van Riebeeck Paints (Pty) Ltd (TRADE MARK: INFRINGEMENT: NOTIONAL USE: South Africa: A.D.) 1984 (3) S.A. 623

Plastella M/s v. Controller of Patents & Designs (DESIGN CANCELLATION: PRIOR PUBLICATION: APPEAL: India: H.C.) (1989) 13 I.P.L.R. 202

Plastus Kreativ AB v. Minnesota Mining and Manufacturing Company (PATENT: DECLARATION OF NON–INFRINGEMENT: FOREIGN PATENTS: JURISDICTION: STRIKING OUT: Pat. Ct) [1995] R.P.C. 438

Playboy Enterprises Inc. v. Fitwear Ltd (TRADE MARKS: OPPOSITION: LIKELY TO DECEIVE OR CAUSE CONFUSION: SUBSTANTIALLY IDENTICAL OR DECEPTIVELY SIMILAR: NON-USE: Australia: Pat. Off.) 12 I.P.R. 310

Playground Supplies Pty Ltd's Application (TRADE MARK: OPPOSITION: EXTENSION OF TIME LIMIT: PUBLIC INTEREST: Australia: Pat. Off.) 5 I.P.R. 433

PLG Research Ltd v. Ardon International Ltd (PATENT: INFRINGEMENT: PRACTICE: MOTIVE OF PLAINTIFF'S IN SEEKING TO JOIN DIRECTOR DEFENDANT: Pat. Ct) [1992] F.S.R. 59

PLG Research Ltd v. Ardon International Ltd (PATENT: PLASTICS NET: INFRINGEMENT: VALIDITY: CONSTRUCTION: ANTICIPATION: OBVIOUSNESS: PRIOR USE: WHETHER PRODUCT MADE INVENTION AVAILABLE TO MEMBER OF PUBLIC FREE IN LAW AND EQUITY TO USE IT: TORT: JOINT TORTFEASOR: DIRECTOR'S LIABILITY: Pat. Ct) [1993] F.S.R. 197
(C.A.) [1995] F.S.R. 116; [1995] R.P.C. 287
PLG Research Ltd v. Ardon International Ltd (No. 2) (PATENT: PRACTICE: INFRINGEMENT: AMENDMENT: CLAIM FOUND VALID AND INFRINGED AT TRIAL BUT SUBSEQUENTLY AMENDED: WHETHER PLAINTIFF ENTITLED TO COSTS OF THAT ACTION IN RESPECT OF THAT CLAIM: Pat. Ct)
[1993] F.S.R. 698
Plix Products Ltd v. Frank M. Winstone (Merchants) (COPYRIGHT: INFRINGEMENT: KIWI FRUIT "POCKET PACKS": PUBLIC LICENCE: INEVITABLE DESIGN: COMMISSIONED WORK: PASSING OFF: GET-UP: New Zealand: H.C.)
3 I.P.R. 373; [1986] F.S.R. 63
(C.A.) 5 I.P.R. 156; [1985] 1 N.Z.L.R. 376; [1986] F.S.R. 608
Plume Clothing Pty Ltd & Bossnac (Aust.) Pty Ltd's Application (TRADE MARKS: APPLICATION FOR REGISTRATION: PART B REGISTRATION: INHERENT ADAPTABILITY TO DISTINGUISH: DISTINCTIVENESS IN FACT: DESCRIPTIVE MARK: Australia: Pat. Off.) 21 I.P.R. 315
Plüss–Staufer/Filler (EUROPEAN PATENT: AMENDMENT AND CORRECTION: DERIVED RANGE: NOVELTY: SELECTION FROM KNOWN NUMERICAL RANGE: T17/85: EPO) [1987] E.P.O.R. 66; [1986] O.J. EPO 406
Poddar Tyres Ltd v. Bedrock Sales Corporation (TRADE MARK: INFRINGEMENT: PASSING OFF: USE IN CORPORATE NAME: INTERIM INJUNCTION: India: H.C.)
(1993) 18 I.P.L.R. 153
Polar Industries v. The Jay Engineering Works Ltd (PATENT: NOVELTY: REVOCATION: India: H.C.) (1991) 16 I.P.L.R. 150
Polar Vac Pty Ltd v. Spoutvac Manufacturing Pty Ltd (PATENT: OPPOSITION: PRIOR PUBLICATION: SECRET USE: OBVIOUSNESS: COMMON GENERAL KNOWLEDGE: Australia: AIPO) 29 I.P.R. 521
Police v. B. (GAINING ACCESS TO COMPUTER CENTRE WITHOUT AUTHORISATION: USE OF MECHANICAL MEANS THROUGH INNOCENT AGENT: OFFENCE: New Zealand: C.A.) [1991] 2 N.Z.L.R. 527
Polistil SpA & Arbois-Modelud (Re Agreement Between) (RESTRICTIVE PRACTICES: EXCLUSIVE DEALING: PARALLEL IMPORTS: E.C. Comm.)
[1984] 2 C.M.L.R. 594; [1985] F.S.R. 7; [1984] O.J. L136/9
Politechnika Ipari Szovetkezet v. Dallas Print Transfers Ltd (COPYRIGHT: INFRINGEMENT: PASSING OFF: "RUBIK" CUBES: KNOWLEDGE: Ch.D.)
[1982] F.S.R. 529
Polo Textile Industries Pty Ltd v. Domestic Textile Corp. Pty Ltd (TRADE MARKS: INFRINGEMENT: POLO/POLO CLUB: TRADE MARKS ACT (CTH) 1955, SECTION 62(1): DEFENCES: ACTUAL LIKELIHOOD OF DECEPTION: EXPUNGEMENT: DISTINCTIVENESS OF MARK: FOREIGN SURNAME: EXPUNGEMENT: NON-USE: SUFFICIENCY OF USE: EVIDENCE: GOODS OF THE SAME DESCRIPTION: Australia: Fed. Ct) 114 A.L.R. 157; 26 I.P.R. 246
Poltrock v. Ennor (PATENT: OPPOSITION: EXTENSION OF TIME LIMIT TO LODGE NOTICE: WANT OF EVIDENCE IN SUPPORT: Australia: Pat. Off.) 8 I.P.R. 217
Poly Lina Ltd v. Finch (BREACH OF CONFIDENCE: FORMER EMPLOYEE: WHETHER CONFIDENTIAL INFORMATION: EMBARGO ON ENGAGEMENTS WITH COMPETITOR: WIDTH OF COVENANT: ADEQUECY OF UNDERTAKING NOT TO DISCLOSE: Q.B.D.) [1995] F.S.R. 751

Polygram Pty Ltd v. Golden Editions Pty Ltd (COPYRIGHT: INFRINGEMENT: SOUND RECORDINGS: INNOCENT INFRINGEMENT: STATUTORY DEFENCES: Australia: Fed. Ct)   30 I.P.R. 183

Polygram Records Pty Ltd v. Manash Records (Aust.) Pty Ltd (COPYRIGHT: DESIGN: INDUSTRIAL APPLICATION: NON-REGISTRATION: PRACTICE: ANTON PILLER ORDERS: JURISDICTION: Australia: Fed. Ct)   6 I.P.R. 423

Polygram Records Sdn Bhd v. Phua Tai Eng (COPYRIGHT: INFRINGEMENT: INJUNCTION: CONTEMPT: Malaysia: H.C.)   [1986] 2 M.L.J. 87

Polygram, Sony Music Entertainment and Warner Music Group Inc. (RESTRICTIVE PRACTICES: JOINT VENTURES: CLUB SALES OF COMPACT DISCS AND VIDEOS THROUGH SERIES OF JOINT SUBSIDIARIES: INTENTION TO APPROVE: E.C. Comm.)   [1995] 4 C.M.L.R. 111

Polypropylene Cartel (Re The), *sub nom.* SA Hercules NV v. E.C. Commission.

Pomagalski/Cable car (EUROPEAN PATENT: FEES: REIMBURSEMENT OF APPEAL FEE: THOUGH NOT SOUGHT: OPPOSITION: PROCEDURE: FRESH DOCUMENTS AT ORAL PROCEEDINGS: NOTICE OF OPPOSITION: INTERPRETATION OF: RIGHT TO BE HEARD: T484/90: EPO)   [1993] E.P.O.R. 571; [1993] O.J. EPO 448

Pontello v. Ceselli (COPYRIGHT: INFRINGEMENT: CRIMINAL SANCTIONS: Australia: Fed. Ct)   16 I.P.R. 645

Pontello v. Giannotis (COPYRIGHT: OFFENCE: POSSESSION OF FILMS IN WHICH COPYRIGHT SUBSISTS FOR THE PURPOSE OF LETTING FOR HIRE OR, BY WAY OF TRADE OFFERING OR EXPOSING FOR HIRE: INFRINGING COPIES OF WORKS IN WHICH COPYRIGHT SUBSISTS: WHETHER THE DEFENDANT KNEW OR "OUGHT REASONABLY TO HAVE KNOWN" THAT FILMS WERE INFRINGING COPIES: POSSESSION BY PARTNERS: Australia: Fed. Ct)   16 I.P.R. 174

Ponty v. Chamberland (COPYRIGHT: COLLABORATIVE WORKS: *Droit moral*: WHO MAY SUE: France: S.C.)   [1992] E.C.C. 59; [1992] F.S.R. 141

Pop-A-Shot Inc. v. Filtration & Pumping (Commercial) Ltd (COPYRIGHT: ARTISTIC WORKS: REPRODUCTION: PASSING OFF: GOODWILL: MISLEADING AND DECEPTIVE CONDUCT: GOODWILL AND REPUTATION: INJUNCTION: BALANCE OF CONVENIENCE: IMPECUNIOUS DEFENDANT: New Zealand: H.C.)   14 I.P.R. 451

Populin v. H.B. Nominees Pty Ltd (PATENT: COMBINATION: ALLEGED INFRINGEMENT: ESSENTIAL INTEGERS: Australia: Fed. Ct)   (1982) 41 A.L.R. 471

Porcelain Products Pty Ltd's Application (DESIGNS: APPLICATION: SET OF ARTICLES: APPLICABILITY: Australia: Designs Reg.)   7 I.P.R. 367

Portakabin Ltd v. Powerblast Ltd (TRADE MARK: INFRINGEMENT: PREFIX MARK PORTA: SPECIFICATION OF GOODS: Ch.D.)   [1990] R.P.C. 471

Porter v. Arbortech Investments Pty Ltd (PATENT: APPLICATION: OPPOSITION: OBJECTION TO ALLOWANCE OF A REQUEST TO AMEND STATEMENT OF GROUNDS AND PARTICULARS: Australia: AIPO)   31 I.P.R. 169

Porter v. Victoria's Secret Inc. (PROCEDURE: CROSS-EXAMINATION OF WITNESS: COSTS: Australia: AIPO)   28 I.P.R. 143

Ports International Ltd v. Ipco Corp. (TRADE MARKS: OPPOSITION: CONFUSING TRADE MARK: SURROUNDING CIRCUMSTANCES: OUTLET FOR PRODUCT: Canada: T.M. Opp. Bd)   33 C.P.R. (3d) 339

Porzelack KG v. Porzelack (U.K.) Ltd (PRACTICE: COSTS: EEC PLAINTIFF: DISCRETION TO ORDER SECURITY FOR COSTS: Ch.D.)
[1987] 2 C.M.L.R. 333; [1987] E.C.C. 407; [1987] F.S.R. 353;
[1987] 1 W.L.R. 420

Posso/Minicassette box (EUROPEAN PATENT: FEES: REIMBURSEMENT OF APPEAL
FEE: THOUGH NOT SOUGHT: INVENTIVE STEP: ADAPTATION OF PRIOR ART,
NOT OBVIOUS: COMBINATION OF CITATIONS: PROCEDURE: RIGHT TO BE
HEARD: APPLICANT'S OBVIOUS MISTAKE MUST BE POINTED: T185/82:
EPO)   [1979–85] E.P.O.R. C696; [1984] O.J. EPO 174
Post Office v. Interlink Express Parcels Ltd (TRADE MARK: INFRINGEMENT:
INTERLOCUTORY INJUNCTION: BALANCE OF CONVENIENCE: Ch.D.)
                                                    [1989] 1 F.S.R. 369
Post Term Use Bans in Know-How Licensing Agreements (Re) (RESTRICTIVE
PRACTICES: KNOW-HOW LICENSING AGREEMENTS: POST TERM USE BANS:
NOT CAUGHT BY ARTICLE 85(1) OR 86 AS A RULE: COMPLAINT OF FORMER
LICENSEE REJECTED: E.C. Comm.) [1989] 4 C.M.L.R. 851; [1990] F.S.R. 21
Potton Ltd v. Yorkclose Ltd (COPYRIGHT: INFRINGEMENT: ARCHITECTURAL
DRAWINGS: APPORTIONMENT OF PROFITS: Ch.D.)   [1990] F.S.R. 11
POUND PUPPIES Trade Mark (TRADE MARK: APPLICATION: DESCRIPTIVENESS:
WHETHER MARK DECEPTIVE: BoT)   [1988] R.P.C. 530
Power Control Appliances Co. v. Sumit Machines Pvt. Ltd (PASSING OFF: FAMILY
BUSINESS: RIVAL BUSINESS ESTABLISHED BY FAMILY MEMBER: INTERIM
INJUNCTION: APPEAL: India: H.C.)   (1994) 19 I.P.L.R. 117
Powerscourt Estates v. Gallagher (MAREVA INJUNCTION: JURISDICTION: Ireland:
H.C.)   [1984] I.L.R.M. 123
PPG Industries Inc.'s Patent (PATENT: AMENDMENT: OBVIOUS MISTAKE:
DISCRETION: C.A.)   [1987] R.P.C. 469
PPG Industries Inc. v. Stauffer Chemical Co. (PATENTS: OPPOSITION: NOVELTY:
ANTICIPATION: PRIOR CLAIMING: FAIR BASIS: Australia: Pat. Off.)
                                                       5 I.P.R. 496
PPG/Pigment grinding vehicle (EUROPEAN PATENT: FEES: REIMBURSEMENT OF
APPEAL FEE: OPPOSITION: PROCEDURE: AMENDMENT OF SPECIFICATION
CONSEQUENTIAL TO AMENDMENT OF: T273/90: EPO) [1992] E.P.O.R. 104
PPG/Ungelled polyesters (EUROPEAN PATENT: OPPOSITION: PROCEDURE: NOTICE
OF OPPOSITION: MINIMUM REQUIREMENTS: T222/85: EPO)
                                    [1987] E.P.O.R. 99; [1988] O.J. EPO 128
PPI Industries Pty Ltd's Application (TRADE MARKS: APPLICATION FOR
REGISTRATION: PRIOR REGISTRATIONS: SUBSTANTIALLY IDENTICAL WITH:
DECEPTIVELY SIMILAR TO: GOODS OF THE SAME DESCRIPTION: GOODS THAT
ARE CLOSELY RELATED: Australia: Pat. Off.)   17 I.P.R. 667
Practice Direction (Chancery: Master's Powers) (PRACTICE: CHANCERY
CHAMBERS: AUTHORISATION FOR HEARING BEFORE MASTER: Ch.D.)
                                                    [1990] F.S.R. 215
Practice Direction (Chancery: Reading Guide in Patent Actions) (PRACTICE:
PATENTS COURT: JUDGE'S PRE-TRIAL READING: "READING GUIDE": Ch.D.)
                [1990] 1 All E.R. 192; [1990] F.S.R. 216; [1990] R.P.C. 60;
                                                    [1990] 1 W.L.R. 106
Practice Direction (CHANCERY: SUMMONS FOR DIRECTIONS: Ch.D.)
                                                    [1989] 1 F.S.R. 400
Practice Direction (Patent action summonses) (PATENT ACTION SUMMONSES:
PATENT COURT USERS' COMMITTEE: Ch.D.)   [1990] F.S.R. 328
Practice Direction (PATENTS: DESIGNS: RECTIFICATION OF REGISTER: AGREED
DIRECTIONS: PROCEDURE: R.S.C. Order 104, R. 17: Ch.D.)
                                                   [1985] 1 All E.R. 192
Practice Direction (PRACTICE: PATENT OFFICE: Pat. Off.)   [1995] R.P.C. 381
Practice Direction – Patents (RECTIFICATION OF REGISTER: AGREED DIRECTIONS:
Ch.D.)   [1985] 1 All E.R. 192

Practice Direction 1/94   [1994] R.P.C. 21
Practice Direction: (PRACTICE: PATENTS COURT: PROCEDURE: Ch.D.)
                                                        [1995] 1 W.L.R. 1578
Practice Explanation (PRACTICE: EXPLANATION: Pat. Ct)   [1995] R.P.C. 422
Practice Note (SIMPLIFIED TRIALS: TRIALS ON AFFIDAVIT EVIDENCE: DIRECTIONS:
    Pat. Ct)   [1994] F.S.R. 334; [1994] R.P.C. 229
Practice Note: patent Action Summonses (PATENT ACTION SUMMONSES: PATENT
    COURT USERS COMMITTEE: Ch.D.)   [1990] F.S.R. 328
Practice Statement (HEARING DATES: Ch.D.)   [1994] F.S.R. 470
Prangley's Application (PATENT: APPLICATION: PRACTICE: PCT: DEFECT IN
    PROCEDURE: C.A.)   [1988] R.P.C. 187
Presentaciones Musicales SA v. Secunda (COPYRIGHT: OWNERSHIP:
    INFRINGEMENT: SOUND RECORDINGS: COUNTERCLAIM: APPLICATION TO
    STRIKE OUT: PARTIAL SUMMARY JUDGMENT: Ch.D.)   [1995] E.M.L.R. 118
Press Form Pty Ltd v. Henderson's Ltd (DESIGNS: VALIDITY OF DESIGN: WHETHER
    DESIGN HAS BEEN APPLIED INDUSTRIALLY: WHETHER DEEMING CLAUSE IS
    INCLUSIVE OR EXHAUSTIVE: Australia: Fed. Ct)
                                             112 A.L.R. 671; 26 I.P.R. 113
Press Metal Corp. Ltd v. Noshir Sorabji (PATENT: OPPOSITION: PRIOR
    PUBLICATION: India: H.C.)   (1982) 7 I.P.L.R. 1
Pressings & Plastics (Pty) Ltd v. Sohnius (PATENT: RECTIFICATION: FRAUDULENT
    APPLICATION: South Africa: TPD)   1985 (4) S.A. 524
Prestige Group (Australia) Pty Ltd v. Dart Industries Inc. (PATENT: INVALIDITY:
    FALSE SUGGESTION OR REPRESENTATION: GROUNDS FOR REPEAL OF GRANT
    BY WRIT OF *scire facias*: WHETHER DOCTRINE OF FILE WRAPPER ESTOPPEL
    APPLIES UNDER AUSTRALIAN LAW: CONSTRUCTION OF CLAIM: Australia: Fed.
    Ct)   95 A.L.R. 533; 19 I.P.R. 275; [1992] F.S.R. 143
PRIMASPORT Trade Mark (TRADE MARK: APPLICATION: OPPOSITION
    PRIMASPORT/PRIMARK: GOODS OF THE SAME DESCRIPTION: WHETHER
    DISTINCTIVE: WHETHER DANGER OF CONFUSION AND DECEPTION:
    QUESTIONNAIRE TO OPPONENT'S SUPPLIERS: APPLICATION ALLOWED:
    T.M.Reg.)   [1992] F.S.R. 515
Prince Manufacturing Inc. v. Abac Corp. Aust. Pty Ltd (TRADE PRACTICES: PASSING
    OFF: TRADE MARKS: INFRINGEMENT: SIMILAR GOODS: TENNIS RACQUETS:
    Australia: Fed. Ct)   (1985) 57 A.L.R. 159; 4 I.P.R. 104
Print Investments Pty Ltd v. Art-Vue Printing Ltd (CONFIDENTIAL INFORMATION:
    EMPLOYEE: Australia: S.C.)   1 I.P.R. 149
Priority interval (EUROPEAN PATENT: PRIORITY: MULTIPLE PRIORITY
    APPLICATIONS: STATE OF THE ART: PUBLICATION FOLLOWING PRIORITY
    APPLICATION: ENLARGED BOARD OF APPEAL: FUNCTION OF: PRESIDENT OF
    EPO, REFERENCE BY: *Obiter dictum*: G03/93: EPO)
                                    [1994] E.P.O.R. 521; [1995] O.J. EPO 18
Priority Records (Pty) Ltd v. Ban-Nab Radio & TV (COPYRIGHT: INFRINGEMENT:
    DAMAGES: ADDITIONAL DAMAGES: South Africa: D&CLD)   1988 (2) S.A. 28
Private Research Ltd v. Brosnan (COPYRIGHT: INFRINGEMENT: BREACH OF
    CONFIDENCE: EMPLOYER AND EMPLOYEE: MISUSE OF CONFIDENTIAL
    INFORMATION: INTERLOCUTORY INJUNCTION: FAIR QUESTION TO BE
    TRIED: ADEQUACY OF DAMAGES: BALANCE OF CONVENIENCE: Ireland:
    H.C.)   [1995] I.R. 1 534

Procatalyse/Catalyst (EUROPEAN PATENT: CLAIMS: CLARITY: DISTINCTION
BETWEEN INTEGERS: CONSTRUCTION: IN OPPOSITION PROCEEDINGS:
OPPOSITION: PROCEDURE: ONUS OF PROOF: PRIORITY: FRESH
QUANTITATIVE RESTRICTION IN CLAIM 1: NO CHANGE IN CHARACTER:
SUFFICIENCY: CLAIMED SUBJECT-MATTER, REPRODUCIBILITY OF: T16/87:
EPO)   [1992] E.P.O.R. 305; [1992] O.J. EPO 212
Process Development Ltd v. Hogg (CONFIDENTIAL INFORMATION: ANTON PILLER
ORDER: UNDERTAKING TO RETAIN ITEMS IN SAFE CUSTODY: PROPERTY OF
PLAINTIFF: WHETHER PERMISSIBLE TO REPORT TO POLICE: C.A.)
                                                      [1996] F.S.R. 45
Procter & Gamble Co.'s Application (PATENT: APPLICATION: OPPOSITION:
SUFFICIENCY: EVIDENCE: C.A.)   [1982] R.P.C. 473; (1983) 8 I.P.L.R. 22
Procter & Gamble Co. v. Kimberly-Clark Corp. (PATENT: APPLICATION ACCEPTED:
OPPOSITION: VALIDITY: AMENDMENT OF OPPOSITION: OBTAINING:
APPLICATIONS FOR EXTENSION OF TIME TO LODGE EVIDENCE: Australia: Pat.
Off.)   23 I.P.R. 45
Procter & Gamble Co. v. Kimberly-Clark Corp. (PATENT: APPLICATION:
OPPOSITION: AMENDMENT OF OPPOSITION: OBTAINING: TRANSITIONAL
PROVISIONS: Australia: Pat. Off.)   23 I.P.R. 34
Procter & Gamble Co. v. Kimberly-Clark Corp. see also, *sub nom.* Kimberly-Clark
Corp. v. Procter & Gamble Co.
Procter & Gamble Co. v. Peaudouce (U.K.) (PATENT: INFRINGEMENT:
AMENDMENT OF CLAIMS INVALID FOR AMBIGUITY: CLAIMS INFRINGED IF
VALID: LATE APPLICATION FOR AMENDMENT: LEAVE TO APPLY TO AMEND
REFUSED: C.A.)   [1989] 1 F.S.R. 614
Procter & Gamble Co. v. Peaudouce (U.K.) Ltd (PATENT INFRINGEMENT:
VALIDITY: AMBIGUITY: OBVIOUSNESS: EXCLUSIVE LICENCE: PRACTICE: C.A.)
                                                    [1989] 1 F.S.R. 180
Procter & Gamble/Detergent composition (EUROPEAN PATENT: OPPOSITION:
PROCEDURE: PARTIES, VOLITIONAL AND AUTOMATIC, RIGHTS OF: RE-
ESTABLISHMENT OF RIGHTS: ISOLATED MISTAKE BY REPRESENTATIVE:
T369/91: EPO)   [1993] E.P.O.R. 497; [1993] O.J. EPO 561
Procter & Gamble/Pouring and measuring package (EUROPEAN PATENT:
INVENTIVE STEP: AWARD FOR TECHNICAL EXCELLENCE, SIGNIFICANCE OF:
COMBINATION OF CITATIONS: LAUDATORY ARTICLES, SIGNIFICANCE OF:
INVENTIVE STEP: TECHNICAL ADVANTAGE: OPPOSITION: PROCEDURE: FRESH
DOCUMENTS ON APPEAL: T521/90: EPO)   [1993] E.P.O.R. 558
Procter & Gamble/STW detergents (EUROPEAN PATENT: OPPOSITION:
PROCEDURE: FRESH DOCUMENTS ON APPEAL: NOTICE OF OPPOSITION: MUST
ADDRESS DEPENDENT CLAIMS: T100/88: EPO)   [1991] E.P.O.R. 529
Procter & Gamble/STW-laundry detergents (EUROPEAN PATENT: AMENDMENT
AND CORRECTION: EXTENSION OF PROTECTION: COMMON GENERAL
KNOWLEDGE: NEED FOR SUBSTANTIATION: EVIDENCE: LABORATORY TESTS
NOT ADEQUATE: T104/88: EPO)   [1991] E.P.O.R. 586
Procter & Gamble/Flavour (EUROPEAN PATENT: SUFFICIENCY: FUNCTIONAL
DEFINITIONS: CLAIMS: FUNCTIONAL LIMITATIONS: IMPLICIT LIMITATION:
SKILLED PERSON: TEAM: T295/88: EPO)   [1991] E.P.O.R. 458
Procter/Surfactant (EUROPEAN PATENT: OPPOSITION: PROCEDURE: FOREIGN
DECISIONS, IRRELEVANCE OF: INVENTIVE STEP: *Ex post facto* APPROACH:
MULTIPLE APPROACHES: BOARD OF APPEAL: FOREIGN DECISIONS, NEITHER
BINDING NOR RELEVANT: T216/90: EPO)   [1993] E.P.O.R. 66

Procurator Fiscal in the Lyon Court v. P. Baird Construction Ltd (HERALDRY: ILLEGAL USE OF ARMS: COMPLAINT: INTERDICT: PENALTY: Scotland: Lyon Ct) (1992) 32 S.L.T. 2; [1993] F.S.R. 362

Procureur de la République & SA Vêtements Goguet Sport v. Hechter (RESTRICTIVE PRACTICES: FRANCHISE AGREEMENTS: RESALE PRICE MAINTENANCE: REFUSAL TO SELL: France: D.C.) [1986] E.C.C. 583

Progro Pharmaceuticals (Pvt.) Ltd v. Deputy Registrar of Trade Marks (TRADE MARK: OPPOSITION: DELAY IN FILING COUNTERSTATEMENT: EXTENSION OF TIME LIMITS: India: H.C.) (1986) 11 I.P.L.R. 125

Project Development Co. Ltd SA v. KMK Securities Ltd (Syndicate Bank intervening) (MAREVA INJUNCTION: COSTS OF INNOCENT THIRD PARTY: VARIATION OF INJUNCTION: Comm. Ct) [1983] 1 All E.R. 465

Promedia SA v. Borght (COPYRIGHT: REGISTERED DESIGN: PROTECTED PRODUCT: ADVERTISING MATERIAL: Belgium: C.A.)
[1987] E.C.C. 318; [1987] F.S.R. 536

Prontaprint plc v. Landon Litho Ltd (RESTRICTIVE COVENANT: FRANCHISING: REASONABLENESS OF COVENANT: Ch.D.) [1987] F.S.R. 315

Pronuptia de Paris SA (Agreements) (RESTRICTIVE PRACTICES: FRANCHISES: E.C. Comm.) [1989] 4 C.M.L.R. 355; [1989] 1 F.S.R. 416

Prosimmon Golf (Aust.) Pty Ltd v. Dunlop Australia Ltd (TRADE MARK: REMOVAL: NON-USE: PERSON AGGRIEVED: EVIDENCE: ADEQUACY: Australia: Pat. Off.)
9 I.P.R. 425

Protective Mining & Industrial Equipment v. Audiolens etc, *sub nom.* Hampo Systems v. Audiolens

Protim Ltd v. Roberts Consolidated Industries Inc. (TRADE MARK: OPPOSITION: COMMON SUFFIX: LIKELIHOOD OF CONFUSION: Australia: T.M.Reg.)
2 I.P.R. 532

Protoned BV's Application (PATENT: APPLICATION: AMENDMENT: Pat. Ct)
[1983] F.S.R. 110

Prout v. British Gas plc (PATENT: INFRINGEMENT: VALIDITY: PUBLIC EXPERIMENTAL PRIOR USE UNDER P.A.77: "STATE OF THE ART": CONTRAST WITH POSITION UNDER P.A.77: ABSENCE OF U.K. AUTHORITY ON EXPERIMENTAL USER UNDER P.A.49: REVIVAL OF PRE-EXISTING COMMON LAW: REFERENCE TO COMMENTARY ON GERMAN LAW: PATENT NOT INFRINGED: BREACH OF CONFIDENCE: WHETHER DISCLOSURE BY EMPLOYEE UNDER EMPLOYEES' SUGGESTION SCHEME BINDING ON DEFENDANT: FIDUCIARY RELATIONSHIP: SPRINGBOARD DOCTRINE: Pat. C.C.)
[1992] F.S.R. 478
(APPEAL ON COSTS ALONE: PATENT COUNTY COURT: PRACTICE: C.A.)
[1994] F.S.R. 160

Provident Financial plc v. Halifax Building Society (TRADE MARKS: INFRINGEMENT: PASSING OFF: INTERLOCUTORY INJUNCTION: FINANCIAL SERVICES: WHETHER SERIOUS TRIABLE ISSUE: SECTIONS 5(2) AND 8 DEFENCES: Ch.D.) [1994] F.S.R. 81

Proweco/*Restitutio in integrum* (EUROPEAN PATENT: EPO: VOLUNTARY ACTS BY: PROFESSIONAL REPRESENTATIVES: DUTY OF DUE CARE: RE-ESTABLISHMENT OF RIGHTS: FEES: FAILURE TO PAY, VOLUNTARY NOTICE OF: J12/84: EPO) [1979–85] E.P.O.R. A217; [1985] O.J. EPO 108

PRS Ltd v. Working Men's Club & Institute Union, *sub nom.* Working Men's Club & Institute Union v. PRS Ltd

Prudential Building & Investment Society of Canterbury v. Prudential Assurance Co. of N.Z. Ltd (PASSING OFF: INSURANCE COMPANY WHICH OPERATED NATIONALLY AND A BUILDING SOCIETY WHICH OPERATED PROVINCIALLY BOTH USED THE NAME "PRUDENTIAL": GEOGRAPHICAL EXPANSION OF BUSINESS AND EMPHASIS ALTERED ON PART OF NAME: New Zealand: C.A.)
13 I.P.R. 353; [1988] 2 N.Z.L.R. 653

Prudhoe v. ICI Australian Operations Pty Ltd (PATENT: OPPOSITION: OPPOSITION WITHDRAWN: PATENT GRANTED: COSTS OF APPLICANT: WHETHER PROCEEDINGS STILL BEFORE COMMISSIONER: Australia: AIPO)
27 I.P.R. 100

PRURIDERM Trade Mark (APPLICATION: OPPOSITION: PRACTICE: T.M.Reg.)   [1985] R.P.C. 187

PSM International plc v. Specialised Fastener Products (Southern) Ltd (COPYRIGHT: JURISDICTION OF PATENT COUNTY COURT WHERE COPYRIGHT ALLEGED TO SUBSIST IN DESIGN DRAWINGS: PRACTICE: STRIKING OUT: AMENDMENT: Pat. C.C.)   [1993] F.S.R. 113

PSM International plc v. Whitehouse (BREACH OF CONFIDENCE: EX-EMPLOYEE: WHETHER INJUNCTION MAY BE GRANTED TO RESTRAIN EX-EMPLOYEE FROM FULFILLING CONTRACT ALREADY MADE WITH THIRD PARTY: PRACTICE: INJUNCTION GRANTED: C.A.)   [1992] F.S.R. 489

Public Prosecutor v. Basheer Ahmad (COPYRIGHT: INFRINGEMENT: PROCEDURE: Malaysia: Fed. Terr. Cr. App. Ct)   [1982] 2 M.L.J. 78

Public Prosecutor v. Oh Teck Soon (COPYRIGHT: TIME FOR PROSECUTION UNDER COPYRIGHT ACT 1969: Malaysia: S.C.)   [1986] 1 M.L.J. 488

Public Prosecutor v. Teo Al Nee (COPYRIGHT: PARALLEL IMPORTATION: INFRINGEMENT: SCOPE OF PROTECTION: SUBSISTENCE: ONUS OF PROOF: Singapore: H.C.)   [1994] 1 S.L.R. 452

Public Prosecutor v. Teo Al Nee (COPYRIGHT: INFRINGEMENT: SECONDARY INFRINGEMENT: KNOWLEDGE: TEST: REQUISITE STATE OF MIND: Singapore: H.C.)   [1995] 2 S.L.R. 69

Publishers Association's Agreement, *sub nom.* Net Book Agreements

Publishers Association v. E.C. Commission, *sub nom.* Net Book Agreements

Pumps 'N' Pipes Pty Ltd's Application (TRADE MARKS: OBJECTIONS TO REGISTRATION: DISTINCTIVENESS: INDICATION OF ORIGIN: RETAILER SEEKING REGISTRATION IN RESPECT OF GOODS SOLD: REGISTRATION IN PART B REFUSED: Australia: Pat. Off.)   18 I.P.R. 378

Purity Requirements for Beer (IMPORTS: MANUFACTURING STANDARDS: BEER: ANCIENT GERMAN PURITY RULES: *Reinheitsgebot*: BAN ON ADDITIVES: Case 178/84: ECJ)   [1988] 1 C.M.L.R. 780; [1987] E.C.R. 1227

Purolator Courier Ltd v. Mayne Nickless Transport Inc. (TRADE MARKS: COMPARATIVE ADVERTISING: FALSE AND MISLEADING STATEMENTS TENDING TO DISCREDIT A COMPETITOR: GOODWILL IN MARK: INTERLOCUTORY INJUNCTION: Canada: FCTD)   33 C.P.R. (3d) 391

Puschner v. Tom Palmer (Scotland) Ltd (PATENT: INFRINGEMENT: JOINT TORTFEASORS: PRACTICE: SERVICE OUT OF THE JURISDICTION: Pat. Ct)   [1989] R.P.C. 430

Q. H. Tours Ltd v. Ship Design & Management (Aust.) Pty Ltd (TRADE PRACTICES: CONTRACTUAL ARBITRATION CLAUSE: WHETHER A CLAIM UNDER TRADE PRACTICES ACT 1974 CAN BE RESOLVED AT ARBITRATION: WHETHER AN ARBITRATOR CAN RESOLVE A DISPUTE WHERE THE RELIEF SOUGHT INCLUDES A DECLARATION THAT THE CONTRACT IS VOID *ab initio*: WHETHER ARBITRATOR DETERMINING QUESTIONS AS TO BREACHES OF TRADE PRACTICES ACT 1974 EXERCISING JUDICIAL POWER: Australia: Fed. Ct)
22 I.P.R. 447

QDSV Holdings Pty Ltd (t/a Bush Friends Australia) v. Trade Practices Commission (TRADE PRACTICES: FALSE AND MISLEADING STATEMENTS: LABELS ATTACHED TO TOY KOALAS: ALL COMPONENTS MANUFACTURED ABROAD: ASSEMBLY IN AUSTRALIA: LABEL USING "MADE IN AUSTRALIA": WHETHER MISLEADING OR DECEPTIVE: TEST: Australia: Fed. Ct)   32 I.P.R. 1

QSF Marketing Pty Ltd v. Adidas Fabrique de Chaussures de Sport (TRADE MARKS: OPPOSITION: SUBSTANTIALLY IDENTICAL: DECEPTIVELY SIMILAR: USE LIKELY TO DECEIVE OR CAUSE CONFUSION: INTENTION TO USE THE TRADE MARK: Australia: Pat. Off.)   14 I.P.R. 173

Quaker Oats Company's Application (TRADE MARKS: APPLICATION: MARK DIRECTLY DESCRIPTIVE: LACK OF INHERENT DISTINCTIVENESS: EVIDENCE OF USE SCANT: Australia: Pat. Off.)   14 I.P.R. 481

Quantel Ltd v. Electronic Graphics Ltd (PATENT: INFRINGEMENT: EURO-DEFENCES: ARTICLE 86: Pat. Ct)   [1990] R.P.C. 272

Quantel Ltd v. Shima Seiki Europe Ltd (PATENT INFRINGEMENT: VALIDITY: INTERLOCUTORY INJUNCTION: EFFECT OF EARLIER ACTION: BALANCE OF CONVENIENCE: Pat. Ct)   [1990] R.P.C. 436

Quantel Ltd v. Spaceward Microsystems Ltd (No. 2) (PATENT: INFRINGEMENT: STAY OF INJUNCTION PENDING APPEAL: C.A.)   [1990] R.P.C. 147

Quantel Ltd v. Spaceward Microsystems Ltd (PATENT: INFRINGEMENT: VALIDITY: VIDEO GRAPHICS SYSTEMS: ANTICIPATION: PRIOR USE: ENABLING DISCLOSURE: SUFFICIENCY: DIVISIONAL SPECIFICATION: AMENDMENT: DISCRETION: PRACTICE: Pat. Ct)   [1990] R.P.C. 83

QUATTRO Trade Mark, *sub nom.* Deutsche Renault AG v. Audi AG

QUEEN DIANA Trade Mark (TRADE MARK: APPLICATION: SCOTCH WHISKY: ROYAL PATRONAGE: DISCRETION: T.M.Reg.)   [1989] R.P.C. 557
(BoT) [1991] R.P.C. 395

Queensland Plumbing Pty Ltd v. Trade Waste Diversion Pty Ltd (PATENT: APPLICATION: OPPOSITION: SUCCESS OF OPPONENT: LEAVE TO AMEND SPECIFICATION: APPLICATION TO AMEND: OPPONENT'S COMMENTS: PRACTICE AND PROCEDURE: Australia: AIPO)   27 I.P.R. 303

Queensland Rugby Football League (TRADE MARK: APPLICATION: REGISTRABILITY: DISTINCTIVENESS: GENERIC TERMS: Australia: AIPO)
28 I.P.R. 603

Queensland Wire Industries Pty Ltd v. The Broken Hill Pty Co. Ltd (RESTRICTIVE PRACTICES: DOMINANT POSITION: RELEVANT MARKET: PRODUCT SUBSTITUTABILITY: Australia: H.C.)
[1989] 3 C.M.L.R. 169; [1990] F.S.R. 23

Quintessence Incorporated v. Jovani Enterprises Pty Ltd (TRADE MARK: OPPOSITION: MARKS DECEPTIVELY SIMILAR: GOODS NOT OF THE SAME DESCRIPTION: ASSOCIATED MARKS: Australia: AIPO)   28 I.P.R. 365

Quotations from Published Works (COPYRIGHT: INFRINGEMENT: PERMISSIBLE EXTENT: Germany: S.C.)   [1988] E.C.C. 207; [1988] F.S.R. 439

R. & C. Products Pty Ltd (t/a Samuel Taylor) v. S.C. Johnson & Sons Pty Ltd (TRADE PRACTICES: TV ADVERTISEMENTS: WHETHER PUBLICATION CONSTITUTES PASSING OFF OR MISLEADING AND DECEPTIVE CONDUCT IN BREACH OF SECTION 52 OF TRADE PRACTICES ACT: WHETHER ELEMENTS OF ADVERTISING SO IDENTIFIED WITH ONE TRADER THAT USE BY A COMPETITOR WILL MISLEAD OR DECEIVE: WHETHER SUFFICIENT DISTINCTION BETWEEN COMPETING PRODUCTS AND MANUFACTURERS: Australia: Fed. Ct)   113 A.L.R. 487; 26 I.P.R. 98

R. & C. Products Pty Ltd (t/a Samuel Taylor) v. Sterling Winthrop Pty Ltd (TRADE MARK: INFRINGEMENT: PINE ACTION/PINE-O-CLEEN: PASSING OFF: GET-UP OF PRODUCT: Australia: Fed. Ct)   27 I.P.R. 223

R. & C. Products Pty Ltd v. Bathox Bathsalts Pty Ltd (TRADE MARKS: OPPOSITION: CONFLICTING MARKS: COMMON ELEMENT: BATH TIME: WHETHER SUBSTANTIAL SIMILARITY: DECEPTIVELY SIMILAR: PREVIOUS DECISION DOES NOT EXCLUDE SUCH FINDINGS: Australia: Pat. Off.)   21 I.P.R. 547
(SUCCESSFUL OPPOSITION: AWARD OF COSTS: Australia: Pat. Off.)
          24 I.P.R. 278

R.H. Macey & Co. Inc. v. Trade Accents, *sub nom.* Macey & Co. Inc. v. Trade Accents

R.J. Reynolds Tobacco Co. v. ITC Ltd (TRADE MARK: NOW: INFRINGEMENT: PASSING OFF: INTERIM INJUNCTION: India: H.C.)   (1987) 11 I.P.L.R. 180

R.P. Locks Co. v. Sehgal Locks Co. (TRADE MARK: INFRINGEMENT: HARRISON/ HARICON: INTERIM *ex parte* INJUNCTION: India: H.C.)
          (1988) 13 I.P.L.R. 165

R. v. Bridgeman and Butt (CRIMINAL LAW: CONSPIRACY TO DEFRAUD: SATELLITE BROADCASTING FROM U.K. TO SPAIN: AMBIT OF LICENCE: JURISDICTION: ENCRYPTED TRANSMISSIONS: DECODING DEVICES: NATURE OF RIGHTS AND REMEDIES: EVIDENCE: C.C.)   [1996] F.S.R. 528

R. v. Broadcasting Complaints Commission, *ex p.* BBC and, *ex p.* Lloyd (BROADCASTING COMPLAINTS COMMISSION: TV DOCUMENTARY: INFRINGEMENT OF PRIVACY AND UNFAIR TREATMENT: APPLICATIONS BY BROADCASTER AND BY COMPLAINANT FOR JUDICIAL REVIEW: JURISDICTION OF COMMISSION TO CONSIDER COMPLAINT WHERE MATERIAL IN QUESTION NOT BROADCAST: WHETHER COMMISSION HAD GIVEN APPLICANT PROPER OPPORTUNITY TO BE HEARD: Q.B.D.)   [1993] E.M.L.R. 419

R. v. Broadcasting Complaints Commission, *ex p.* Granada Television Ltd (INFRINGEMENT OF PRIVACY AND UNFAIR TREATMENT: TV DOCUMENTARIES: APPLICATIONS BY BROADCASTER FOR JUDICIAL REVIEW: WHETHER COMMISSION HAD JURISDICTION TO CONSIDER INVASION OF PRIVACY OF PERSON WHO DID NOT TAKE PART IN PROGRAMME: Q.B.D.)   [1993] E.M.L.R. 426
          (C.A.) [1995] E.M.L.R. 163

R. v. Carter (COPYRIGHT: INFRINGEMENT: DISTRIBUTION AND MAKING OF INFRINGING COPIES: CRIMINAL CONVICTION: APPEAL AGAINST SENTENCE: C.A., Crim. Div.)   [1993] F.S.R. 303

R. v. Chan Hing-Kin (COPYRIGHT: COMPUTER PROGRAMS: CASINGS FOR PERSONAL COMPUTERS: INFRINGEMENT: POSSESSION: FUNCTIONAL WORKS: ARTISTIC MERIT: IMPLIED LICENCE: LAY RECOGNITION TEST: Hong Kong: North Kowloon Magistrates Court)   9 I.P.R. 225

R. v. Comptroller-General of Patents, *ex p.* Celltech Ltd (PATENT: INTERNATIONAL APPLICATION: PCT: AGENT'S MISTAKE: Q.B.D.)   [1991] R.P.C. 475

R. v. Comptroller-General of Patents *ex p.* Gist-Brocades NV, *sub nom.* Allen & Hanbury's Ltd v. Generics (U.K.) Ltd

R. v. Cropp (COMPUTERS: HACKING: UNAUTHORISED ACCESS: UNAUTHORISED MODIFICATION: ALTERATION OF DATA ON COMPUTER: INTERPRETATION OF STATUTE: U.K. Crown Court, Snaresbrook)   22 I.P.R. 444

R. v. Licensing Authority established under Medicines Act 1968,, *ex p.* Smith Kline & French Laboratories Ltd (CONFIDENTIAL INFORMATION: ORIGINAL SCIENTIFIC RESEARCH: MEDICINAL PRODUCTS: SUPPLY OF DRUG MANUFACTURER'S CONFIDENTIAL DATA TO STATUTORY BODY FOR LICENCE TO MARKET DRUG: WHETHER LICENSING AUTHORITY ENTITLED TO USE DATA WHEN CONSIDERING OTHER APPLICANTS FOR PRODUCT LICENCES OF DRUG: MEDICINES ACT 1968, SS.6, 7(2): Q.B.D.)

[1988] 2 C.M.L.R. 883; [1989] 1 F.S.R. 9;
(C.A.) [1989] 1 All E.R. 175; [1988] 3 C.M.L.R. 301; [1989] 1 F.S.R. 11;
[1988] 3 W.L.R. 896
(H.L.) [1989] 2 All E.R. 113; [1989] 2 C.M.L.R. 137; [1989] 1 F.S.R. 440;
[1989] 2 W.L.R. 397; 14 I.P.R. 183

R. v. Licensing Authority established under Medicines Act 1968, *ex p.* Smith Kline & French Laboratories Ltd (No. 2) (HIGH COURT: PROCEDURE: INJUNCTIVE RELIEF: MANUFACTURER'S CONFIDENTIAL RESEARCH DATA SUPPLIED TO LICENSING AUTHORITY TO OBTAIN PRODUCT LICENCE: LICENSING AUTHORITY SEEKING TO USE RESEARCH DATA WHEN ASSESSING OTHER APPLICATIONS FOR PRODUCT LICENCES: C.A.)

[1989] 2 All E.R. 113; [1990] 1 Q.B. 574

R. v. Lloyd (COPYRIGHT: CRIME: TAKING FILMS TO COPY: NOT CONSPIRACY TO STEAL CONSPIRACY TO STEAL: C.A., Crim. Div.)
[1985] 2 All E.R. 758; [1986] E.C.C. 64; [1986] F.S.R. 138; [1985] Q.B. 829;
[1985] 3 W.L.R. 30

R. v. Monopolies & Mergers Commission, *ex p.* Elders IXL Ltd (CONFIDENTIAL INFORMATION: DISCLOSURE BY MMC: PUBLIC INTEREST: Q.B.D.)
[1986] 2 F.T.L.R. 201

R. v. Ng Wen Chein (TRADE MARK: INFRINGEMENT: FORGERY: CRIMINAL PENALTIES: IMPRISONMENT: Hong Kong: S.C.)   8 I.P.R. 499

R. v. Pharmaceutical Society of Great Britain, *ex p.* Association of Pharmaceutical Importers (IMPORTS: MEDICINES: MEASURES BY PHARMACEUTICAL SOCIETY COVERED BY ARTICLE 30 EEC: CHEMISTS NOT ALLOWED TO SUBSTITUTE IMPORTED EQUIVALENT (OR IDENTICAL) MEDICINES WITH DIFFERENT NAMES FOR BRANDED PREPARATIONS NAMED IN DOCTOR'S PRESCRIPTION: CAUGHT BY ARTICLE 30, BUT JUSTIFIED BY PUBLIC HEALTH UNDER ARTICLE 36: Q.B.D.)   [1987] B.T.L.C. 196
(C.A.) [1987] 33 C.M.L.R. 939
(Cases 266 and 267/86: ECJ) [1989] 2 All E.R. 758; [1989] 2 C.M.L.R. 751;
[1989] E.C.R. 1295; [1990] 2 W.L.R. 445

R. v. Registered Designs Appeal Tribunal *ex p.* Ford Motor Co. Ltd, *sub nom.* Ford Motor Co. Ltd and Iveco Fiat SpA's Design Applications

R. v. Secretary of State for Social Services, *ex p.* Wellcome Foundation Ltd (TRADE MARK: SEPTRIN: INFRINGEMENT: MEDICINAL PRODUCTS: PARALLEL IMPORTS INTO UNITED KINGDOM: SALE OF IMPORTED PRODUCTS ALLEGED TO BE INFRINGEMENT OF TRADE MARK: DUTY OF LICENSING AUTHORITY: WHETHER TRADE MARK CONSIDERATIONS RELEVANT TO GRANT OF LICENCES: MEDICINES ACT 1968, SECTION 19(A): Q.B.D.) [1987] R.P.C. 220
(C.A.) [1987] 2 All E.R. 1025; [1987] 3 C.M.L.R. 333; [1987] 1 W.L.R. 1166
(H.L.) [1988] 3 C.M.L.R. 95; [1988] 1 W.L.R. 635

R. v. Secretary of State for the National Heritage, *ex p.* Continental Television BVIO (BROADCASTING: APPLICATION FOR JUDICIAL REVIEW: PORNOGRAPHIC SATELLITE TV SERVICE TRANSMITTED FROM DENMARK: DECISION AND ORDER OF SECRETARY OF STATE TO PROSCRIBE: WHETHER COMPATIBLE WITH BROADCASTING DIRECTIVE: WHETHER "RETRANSMISSION" TO BE INTERPRETED LITERALLY OR PURPOSIVELY: REFERENCE TO ECJ: INJUNCTION REFUSED: APPEAL DISMISSED: Div. Ct; C.A.)
[1993] E.M.L.R. 389
R. v. Veys (FALSE TRADE DESCRIPTION: REGISTERED TRADE MARK: CRIMINAL OFFENCE: COAT OF ARMS: POSSIBLE TRADE MARK INFRINGEMENT: RELEVANCE TO OFFENCE UNDER TRADE DESCRIPTIONS ACT: C.A., Crim. Div.)
[1993] F.S.R. 366
R. v. Whiteley (COMPUTER HACKING: CRIMINAL DAMAGE: INTANGIBLE DAMAGE TO TANGIBLE PROPERTY: CONVICTION UPHELD: C.A., Crim. Div.)
[1993] F.S.R. 168
RAC Motoring Service Ltd v. RAC (Publishing) Ltd (PASSING OFF: CONTEMPT: COMMITTAL OF INDIVIDUAL DEFENDANTS: Ch.D.)   [1988] R.P.C. 321
Racal Group Services' Application (RESTRICTIVE PRACTICES: "UNDERTAKINGS": PARENT COMPANY AND SUBSIDIARIES: ARTICLES 85 AND 86; DOMINANT POSITION: RELEVANT MARKET: PROTECTION OF MONOPOLY POSITION THROUGH MARKET ALLOCATION AGREEMENT: COERCION OF UNWILLING PARTIES: ABUSIVE: USE OF COPYRIGHT AS BASIS OF AGREEMENTS ILLEGAL: JUSTIFICATION: E.C. Comm.)   [1990] 4 C.M.L.R. 627
Raccah/Hairdrying apparatus (EUROPEAN PATENT: COSTS: LATE CITATIONS: APPORTIONED: OPPOSITION: PROCEDURE: LATE FILING OF ADDITIONAL PRIOR ART: T632/88: EPO)   [1990] E.P.O.R. 130
Radakovic/Re-establishment of rights (EUROPEAN PATENT: RE-ESTABLISHMENT OF RIGHTS: FINANCIAL HARDSHIP: *Travaux préparatoires*: J22/88: EPO)
[1990] E.P.O.R. 495; [1990] O.J. EPO 244
Radford Chemical Co. Pty Ltd's Application (TRADE MARKS: APPLICATION: COMMAND/COMMAND PERFORMANCE: GOODS OF SAME DESCRIPTION: Australia: Pat. Off.)   16 I.P.R. 615
Radio Telefis Eireann v. E.C. Commission (Magill TV Guide) (EUROPEAN COURT PROCEDURE: INTERIM MEASURES: RESTRICTIVE PRACTICES: BROADCASTERS PROGRAMME LISTING: Cases 76 and 77/89R and 91/89R: ECJ)   [1989] 4 C.M.L.R. 749; [1989] E.C.R. 1141; [1990] F.S.R. 87
Radio Telefis Eireann v. E.C. Commission (RESTRICTIVE PRACTICES: BROADCASTING: WEEKLY LISTINGS OF TV PROGRAMMES: COPYRIGHT: REFUSAL TO PERMIT REPRODUCTION IN INDEPENDENT TV GUIDE: ARTICLE 86 EEC: COMMISSION ENTITLED TO REQUIRE LICENSING FOR REPRODUCTION OF THE LISTINGS: ADMINISTRATIVE PROCEDURE: ADVISORY COMMITTEE ON RESTRICTIVE PRACTICES AND DOMINANT POSITIONS: MINUTES OF ORAL HEARINGS: NOTICE OF SITTING: Case T–69/89: CFI)   [1991] 4 C.M.L.R. 586; [1991] II E.C.R. 485 (APPEAL, *conjoined with* Independent Television Publications Ltd v. E.C. Commission: CFI)   [1991] 4 C.M.L.R. 745; [1991] II E.C.R. 575; (ECJ) [1995] 4 C.M.L.R. 718; [1995] F.S.R. 530; [1995] E.M.L.R. 337
Radio Telefis Eireann v. Magill TV Guide Ltd (COPYRIGHT: RADIO AND TV SCHEDULES: "LITERARY WORK": RESTRICTIVE PRACTICES: COMMUNITY LAW AND NATIONAL LAW: JUDICIAL PROCEDURE: EVIDENCE: Ireland: H.C.)
[1989] 4 C.M.L.R. 749; [1986] E.C.C. 273; [1986] E.C.R. 574; [1990] F.S.R. 87

Rael Marcus v. Sabra International Pty Ltd (TRADE MARK: OPPOSITION: APPEAL: PRIOR USE: OVERSEAS VENDOR: EFFECT OF PREVIOUS, NOW–LAPSED REGISTRATION OF MARK AND LICENCE TO USE IT: DISTINCTION BETWEEN NON–USE AND ABANDONMENT: RESIDUAL GOODWILL: VALIDITY OF ASSIGNMENTS AT COMMON LAW: Australia: Fed. Ct) 30 I.P.R. 261

Rafidain Bank v. Agom Universal Sugar Trading Co. Ltd (PRACTICE: DISCOVERY: INSPECTION: REFERENCE IN AFFIDAVITS TO DOCUMENTS NOT IN PARTY'S POSSESSION: EFFECT: C.A.) [1987] 3 All E.R. 859; [1987] 1 W.L.R. 1606

Rahim (M.A.) v. Aravind Laboratories (TRADE MARK: INFRINGEMENT: EYETEX/ EYERIS: DECEPTIVE SIMILARITY: INTERIM INJUNCTION: RECTIFICATION: EXPUNGEMENT: APPEAL: DESIGN OF LABEL AMENDED TO AVOID CONFLICT: WITHDRAWAL OF INTERIM INJUNCTION: India: H.C.)
(1994) 19 I.P.L.R. 250

Raindrop Data Systems Ltd v. Systemics Ltd (PRACTICE: INTERLOCUTORY INJUNCTION: BALANCE OF CONVENIENCE: Ch.D.) [1988] F.S.R. 354

Raj Steel Rolling Mills v. Vij Iron & Steel Co. (TRADE MARK: APPLICATION: OPPOSITION: AGREEMENT: REQUEST FOR REVIEW REFUSED: India: H.C.) (1993) 18 I.P.L.R. 181

Rajan v. Ministry for Industry & Commerce (PATENTS: PATENT OFFICE DISPUTE: EXAMINATION: POWERS OF CONTROLLER: Ireland: H.C.) [1988] F.S.R. 9

Ram Pratap v. The Bhabha Atomic Research Centre (PATENT: APPLICATION: DIFFUSION PUMP: India: Pat. Off.) (1976) 1 I.P.L.R. 28

Ranbaxy Laboratories Ltd v. Dua Pharmaceuticals Pvt. Ltd (TRADE MARK: CALMPOSE/CALMPROSE: INFRINGEMENT: PASSING OFF: INTERIM INJUNCTION: India: H.C.) (1988) 13 I.P.L.R. 161

Rank Film Distributors Ltd v. Video Information Centre (COPYRIGHT: DISCOVERY: SELF–INCRIMINATION: C.A.) [1982] A.C. 380;
[1980] 2 All E.R. 273; [1980] F.S.R. 242; [1980] 3 W.L.R. 668
(H.L.) [1982] A.C. 380; [1981] 2 All E.R. 76; [1981] F.S.R. 363;
[1981] 2 W.L.R. 668

Rank Film Production Ltd v. Dodds (COPYRIGHT: INFRINGEMENT: CINEMATOGRAPH FILM: PUBLIC PERFORMANCE: Australia: S.C.(NSW))
2 I.P.R. 113; [1983] 2 N.S.W.L.R. 553

Ransburg-Gema AG v. Electrostatic Plant Systems Ltd (COPYRIGHT: PRACTICE: PLEADINGS: AMENDMENT: CAUSES OF ACTION: CLAIM TO CONVERSION DAMAGES NOT LOST IN RESPECT OF AMENDMENTS MADE AFTER COMMENCEMENT OF CD&PA88; C.A.) [1991] F.S.R. 508

Ransburg-Gema AG v. Electrostatic Plant Systems Ltd (INDUSTRIAL PROPERTY: EURO–DEFENCES: RESTRICTIVE PRACTICES: WHETHER ABUSE OF DOMINANT POSITION: ONLY IF EXERCISE OF INDUSTRIAL PROPERTY RIGHT ABUSIVE: MUST BE PROPERLY PLEASED: BAD PLEADING: STRUCK OUT: Ch.D.)
[1989] 2 C.M.L.R. 712; [1990] F.S.R. 287

Rapee (J.) & Co. Pty Ltd v. Kas Cushions Pty Ltd (DESIGNS: INFRINGEMENT: VALIDITY: PRIOR PUBLICATION OR PRIOR USER: WHETHER "SUBSTANTIAL" NOVELTY OF DESIGN: USES COMMON IN TRADE PRIOR TO REGISTRATION: PUBLIC POLICY: NON–CHALLENGE CLAUSE: Australia: Fed. Ct)
90 A.L.R. 288; 15 I.P.R. 577

Ratheon Co. v. Comptroller of Patents & Designs (PATENT: APPLICATION: IMAGE SYSTEM: India: H.C.) (1976) 1 I.P.L.R. 21

Raubenheimer v. Kreepy Krauly (Pty) Ltd (PATENT: INFRINGEMENT: CONSTRUCTION OF SPECIFICATION: PITH AND MARROW: South Africa: A.D.) 1987 (2) S.A. 650

Rawal Industries (Pvt.) Ltd v. Duke Enterprises (TRADE MARK: PASSING OFF: INFRINGEMENT: TRADING STYLE: INTERIM INJUNCTION: India: H.C.)(1983) 8 I.P.L.R. 121

Raychem Corp. v. Thermon (U.K.) Ltd (PATENT: INFRINGEMENT: PRACTICE: PLEADINGS: AMBIGUITY: Pat. Ct)　　　[1989] R.P.C. 578

(LEAVE TO SERVE WRIT OUT OF JURISDICTION: Pat. Ct)　[1989] R.P.C. 423

Raychem Ltd's Applications (PATENT: APPLICATIONS: AMENDMENT: DISCLOSURE: Pat. Ct)　　　[1986] R.P.C. 547

Raychem/Event detector (EUROPEAN PATENT: AMENDMENT AND CORRECTION: CROSS-REFERENCED DOCUMENT, INCLUSION OF FEATURES FROM: DISCLOSURE, EXTENT OF: ENLARGED BOARD OF APPEAL: REFERENCE REFUSED: T689/90: EPO)　[1994] E.P.O.R. 157; [1993] O.J. EPO 616

Raychem/Heat curable composition (EUROPEAN PATENT: TEXT OF PATENT: UNIT OF MEASUREMENT: T561/91: EPO)　　　[1994] E.P.O.R. 255

Raytheon Co.'s Application (PATENT: APPLICATION: "MENTAL ACT": "PROGRAM FOR COMPUTER": WHETHER INVENTION: Pat. Ct)　　　[1993] R.P.C. 427

RCA Corp. v. Pollard (TORT: STATUTORY OFFENCE: PERFORMERS PROTECTION ACTS 1958 TO 1972: APPLICATION TO STRIKE OUT: "BOOTLEGGING": Ch.D.)　　　[1982] 1 W.L.R. 979; [1982] 2 All E.R. 486
(C.A.) [1983] F.S.R.9; [1982] 3All E.R. 711; [1983] Ch. 135; [1982] 3 W.L.R. 1007

RCA/TV receiver (EUROPEAN PATENT: APPEAL: PROCEDURE: FRESH CITATIONS ON APPEAL: STATE OF THE ART: CONFIDENTIAL DOCUMENT: T300/86: EPO) [1994] E.P.O.R. 339

Really Useful Group Ltd (The) v. Gordon & Gotch Ltd (PASSING OFF: LIKELIHOOD TO DECEIVE OR MISLEAD THE PUBLIC: INTERLOCUTORY INJUNCTION: Australia: Fed. Ct)　　　29 I.P.R. 19

Rear v. Drilling Tools Australia Pty Ltd (PATENT: OPPOSITION: EXTENSION OF TIME: EVIDENCE-IN-SUPPORT: GROUNDS FOR GRANT OF EXTENSION OF TIME: ROLE OF COMMISSIONER OF PATENTS: INTERESTS OF PARTIES: INTEREST OF PUBLIC IN ENSURING AGAINST GRANT OF INVALID PATENTS: Australia: Pat. Off.)　　　13 I.P.R. 473

Rebsechini v. Miles Laboratories (Aust.) Ltd (COPYRIGHT: REPRODUCTION OF PLANS: COMMON-PRODUCTS: Australia: S.C.(Vic.))　　　1 I.P.R. 159

Reckitt & Colman of India Ltd v. Medicross Pharmaceuticals Pvt. Ltd (TRADE MARK: INFRINGEMENT: DISPRIN/MEDISPRIN: DISTINCTIVENESS: NOTICE OF MOTION: India: H.C.)　　　(1994) 19 I.P.L.R. 31

Reckitt & Colman Products Ltd v. Biorex Laboratories Ltd (PATENT: DECLARATION OF NON-INFRINGEMENT: STRIKING OUT: Pat. Ct)　　　[1985] F.S.R. 94

Reckitt & Colman Products Ltd v. Borden Inc. (PASSING OFF: GET-UP: PLASTIC LEMONS: INTERLOCUTORY INJUNCTION: C.A.)　　　[1987] F.S.R. 228

Reckitt & Colman Products Ltd v. Borden Inc. (PASSING OFF: GET-UP: PLASTIC LEMONS FOR LEMON JUICE: EFFECT OF EVIDENCE: SECONDARY MEANING: Ch.D.)　　　[1987] F.S.R. 505; [1990] R.P.C. 341
(REPUTATION: C.A.)　　　[1988] F.S.R. 601; [1990] R.P.C. 341
(H.L.) [1990] 1 All E.R. 873; [1990] R.P.C. 341; [1990] 1 W.L.R. 491; 17 I.P.R. 1

Reckitt & Colman Products Ltd v. Borden Inc. (No. 2) (PRACTICE: PASSING OFF: EVIDENCE: MARKET RESEARCH WITNESS: Ch.D.)　　　[1987] F.S.R. 407

Reckitt & Colman SA (Pty) Ltd v. S.C. Johnson & Son (S.A.) (Pty) Ltd (TRADE MARK: PASSING OFF: UNFAIR COMPETITION: DECEPTION AND CONFUSION AS TO ORIGIN OF GOODS: SIMILARITY OF MARKS: NEUTRA AIR/NEUTRA FRESH: APPLICATION FOR INTERIM INTERDICT: South Africa: TPD) 1995 (1) S.A. 725

Reckitt & Colman SA (Pty) Ltd v. S.C. Johnson & Son SA (Pty) Ltd (TRADE MARK: PASSING OFF: GET-UP: LIKELIHOOD OF CONFUSION OR DECEPTION: EVIDENCE OF PSYCHOLOGISTS AND LINGUISTIC EXPERTS: ROLE: MARKET OR PUBLIC OPINION SURVEY: EVIDENCE: South Africa: A.D.)   1993 (2) S.A. 307

Red Tulip Chocolates Pty Ltd (TRADE MARK: APPLICATION: DISTINCTIVENESS: GEOGRAPHICAL NAME: Australia: Pat. Off.)   2 I.P.R. 388

Red Tulip Imports Pty Ltd's Application (No. 2) (TRADE MARK: REGISTRATION: SURNAME: DISTINCTIVENESS: Australia: Pat. Off.)   2 I.P.R. 221

Red Tulip Imports Pty Ltd's Application (TRADE MARK: REGISTRATION: SURNAME: "ORIGINAL MEANING": Australia: Pat. Off.)   2 I.P.R. 109

Redic Industries Pty Ltd v. J.A.L. Chemicals Pty Ltd (CONFIDENTIAL INFORMATION: DISCOVERY: INSPECTION OF FINANCIAL AND SALES RECORDS OF COMPANY OF FORMER EMPLOYEE'S: Australia: S.C.(Vic.))   11 I.P.R. 310

Rediffusion Simulation Ltd v. Link Miles Ltd (PATENT: INFRINGEMENT: APPLICATION TO AMEND: DELAY: AFFIDAVIT EVIDENCE IN SUPPORT OF APPLICATION TO AMEND: WITHOUT PREJUDICE NEGOTIATIONS REFERRED TO IN AFFIDAVIT: APPLICATION TO STRIKE OUT REFUSED: Ch.D.)
[1992] F.S.R. 195

Rediffusion Simulation Ltd v. Link-Miles Ltd (PATENT: FLIGHT SIMULATORS: CONSTRUCTION OF CLAIMS: WHETHER TO TREAT DATA AS IF DRAWN TO SCALE: VALIDITY: AMBIGUITY: EFFECT OF CONSISTORY CLAUSES: SUFFICIENCY: AMENDMENT: DISCRETION: WHETHER PERMISSIBLE TO DELAY IN CONTEMPLATION OF PROCEEDINGS: WHETHER SPECIFICATION FRAMED WITH REASONABLE SKILL: PRACTICE: PLEADING: BEST METHOD: COSTS: DISCRETION: ALLEGATIONS ACCEPTED IN PART: Pat. Ct)   [1993] F.S.R. 369

Redland/Artificial slate (EUROPEAN PATENT: APPEAL: PROCEDURE: FRESH PRIOR ART: CITED BY APPLICANT: REMITTAL ORDERED: NEW STATE OF THE ART HAVING EMERGED: INVENTIVE STEP: COMBINATION OF CITATIONS: T130/83: EPO)   [1979–85] E.P.O.R. C846

Reebok International Ltd v. Royal Corp. (TRADE MARK: INFRINGEMENT: DISCOVERY: ANTON PILLER: *Riddick* PRINCIPLE: WHETHER ARTICLES SEIZED UNDER ANTON PILLER ORDER CAN BE USED IN FOREIGN CIVIL PROCEEDINGS AGAINST THIRD PARTIES: Singapore: H.C.)   [1992] 2 S.L.R. 136

Reed Exhibitions Pte. Ltd v. Khoo Yak Chuan Thomas (PASSING OFF: RESTRAINT OF TRADE: LICENSEES' COVENANT NOT TO ENTER TRADE SIMILAR TO LICENSOR FOR ONE YEAR FROM TERMINATION OF LICENCE: PRACTICE: INTERLOCUTORY INJUNCTION: SERIOUS QUESTION TO BE TRIED: WHETHER DAMAGES AN ADEQUATE REMEDY: BALANCE OF CONVENIENCE: Singapore; C.A.)   [1995] 3 S.L.R. 657

Regency Industries Ltd v. Kedar Builders (PASSING OFF: USE OF PLAINTIFF'S NAME FOR BUILDINGS: SUIT TO PREVENT PASSING OFF: INTERIM INJUNCTION: India: H.C.)   (1990) 15 I.P.L.R. 56

Regent Decorators Sdn Bhd v. Chee (PASSING OFF: FORMER EMPLOYEE'S: CONFUSION: MAREVA INJUNCTIONS: Malaysia: S.C.)   [1984] 2 M.L.J. 78

Regent Lock/Locking handle device (EUROPEAN PATENT: INVENTIVE STEP: COMBINATION OF CITATIONS: PROBLEM AND SOLUTION: OPPOSITION: PROCEDURE: LATE FILING OF ADDITIONAL PRIOR ART: T56/84: EPO)
[1986] E.P.O.R. 24

Regie Nationale des Usines Renault v. Roland Thevenoux (IMPORTS: INDUSTRIAL PROPERTY: SPARE PARTS: MOTOR CAR SPARE PARTS: SUBJECT TO STATUTORY PROTECTION: France: D.C.)
[1988] 3 C.M.L.R. 686; [1989] 1 F.S.R. 125

Registrar of Trade Marks v. Hawg Iron Inc. (SUMMARY EXPUNGEMENT: HAWG FOR MOTOR CYCLES: EVIDENCE FILED DEMONSTRATING MARK IN USE: Canada: T.M. Senior Hearing Officer)   33 C.P.R. (3d) 307

Rehm Pty Ltd v. Websters Security Systems (International) Pty Ltd (PATENT: INFRINGEMENT: USE OF SPECIFICATION TO CLARIFY CLAIM: USE OF ORIGINAL FORM OF CLAIM TO AID CONSTRUCTION: VALIDITY: Australia: Fed. Ct)
                                                        11 I.P.R. 289

Rehm Pty Ltd v. Websters Security Systems (International) Pty Ltd (PATENT: INFRINGEMENT: SECURITY APPARATUS: CLAIMS FASHIONED WITH PROGRESSIVE NARROWING OF INVENTION CLAIMED: WHETHER PERMISSIBLE TO QUALIFY CLAIM BY REFERENCE TO SPECIFICATION: LIMITATION OF CLAIM: PITH AND MARROW: VALIDITY: FAIR BASIS: UTILITY: QUALIFIED READER: Australia: Fed. Ct)   (1988) 81 A.L.R. 79

Reich v. Country Life Bakeries Pty Ltd (TRADE MARK: APPLICATION: OPPOSITION: PROPRIETORSHIP: LIKELY TO DECEIVE OR CONFUSE: DIVISIONAL APPLICATION: REGISTRAR'S DISCRETION: Australia: AIPO)   28 I.P.R. 54

Reichert/Anti-snoring means (EUROPEAN PATENT: PATENTABILITY: COSMETIC INDICATION: PAIN, DISCOMFORT, ETC.: THERAPY: CLAIMS: SECOND PHARMACEUTICAL INDICATION: SWISS STYLE: T584/88: EPO)
                                                        [1989] E.P.O.R. 449

Reiss Engineering Co. v. Harris (PATENT: EMPLOYEE'S INVENTION: OWNERSHIP: P.A. 77, SECTIONS 37, 39: Ch.D.)   [1985] I.R.L.R. 232

Reiss Engineering Co. Ltd v. Harris (PATENT: PRACTICE: COSTS: TAXATION OF PATENT AGENT'S COSTS ON APPEAL TO PATENTS COURT: RIGHT OF AUDIENCE: Pat. Ct)   [1987] R.P.C. 171

Reject Shop plc v. Robert Manners, *sub nom.* The Reject Shop plc v. Robert Manners

Remia BV v. E.C. Commission (EUROPEAN COURT PROCEDURE: RESTRICTIVE PRACTICES: Case 42/84: ECJ)   [1987] 1 C.M.L.R. 1; [1987] F.S.R. 190

Remington Products Inc.'s Application (TRADE MARKS: APPLICATION FOR REGISTRATION: MARK ACCEPTED IN PART B: WHETHER MARK ACCEPTED IN ERROR: OVERLOOKING OF EARLIER APPARENTLY CONFLICTING DECISION: WHETHER "ERROR" ENTITLING REGISTRAR TO WITHDRAW ACCEPTANCE: WHETHER WORDS "SMOOTH" AND "SILKY" RESPECTIVELY DIRECTLY DESCRIPTIVE: Australia: Pat. Off.)   18 I.P.R. 251

Remus Innovation Forschungs-Und Abgasanlagen-Produktiongesellschaft MbH v. Hong Boon Siong (COPYRIGHT: INFRINGEMENT: PARALLEL IMPORTATION: PRACTICE: INTERLOCUTORY INJUNCTION: STANDARD OF PROOF: DISCRETION: CHANCE OF INJUSTICE: Singapore: H.C.)   [1995] 2 S.L.R. 148

Renault v. Thevenoux, *sub nom.* Regie Nationale des Usines Renault v. Roland Thevenoux

Rent A Ute Pty Ltd v. Golden 44 Pty Ltd (PASSING OFF: PROTECTION OF BUSINESS NAME: SIMILAR NAME FOR SERVICES: DESCRIPTIVENESS: EVIDENCE: Australia: Fed. Ct)   9 I.P.R. 12

Rescare Ltd v. Anaesthetic Supplies Pty Ltd (PATENT: INFRINGEMENT: METHOD CLAIMS: VALIDITY: DISCLOSURE OF BEST METHOD OF PERFORMING THE INVENTION: PAPER ANTICIPATION: COMBINATION PATENT: UTILITY: PATENTABILITY OF METHODS OR PROCESSES FOR TREATING THE HUMAN BODY: FAIR BASIS: AMENDMENT OF CLAIMS: Australia: Fed. Ct)
                                            122 A.L.R. 141; 25 I.P.R. 119

Rescare Ltd v. Anaesthetic Supplies Pty Ltd (PATENT: VALIDITY: FAIR BASIS: METHOD OF TREATMENT OF DISEASE: PATENTABILITY: Australia: Fed. Ct)
                                                        28 I.P.R. 383

Rescare Ltd v. Anaesthetic Supplies Pty Ltd (PATENTS: VALIDITY: REVOCATION: INFRINGEMENT: APPARATUS AND METHOD CLAIMS: DEVICE FOR TREATMENT OF OBSTRUCTIVE SLEEP APNOEA (OSA): PATENT GRANTED UNDER 1952 ACT AND REVOCATION SOUGHT UNDER 1990 ACT: BEST METHOD OF PERFORMING INVENTION: FAIR BASING UPON PROVISIONAL SPECIFICATION: LACK OF NOVELTY: OBVIOUSNESS: UTILITY: WHETHER METHODS OR PROCESSES FOR TREATING THE HUMAN BODY ARE PATENTABLE: WHETHER CLAIM LIMITED BY RESULT OR DISGUISED PROCESS CLAIM: Australia: Fed. Ct) 111 A.L.R. 205

Research and Development Agreements Regulation, *sub nom.* Community Research and Development Agreements Regulation

Research Corp.'s Supplementary Protection Certificate (PATENT: EXPIRED PATENT FOR MEDICAL PRODUCT: CARBOPLATIN: SUPPLEMENTARY PROTECTION CERTIFICATE: LICENCES OF RIGHT: PATENT OFFICE PRACTICE: REFERENCE TO ECJ REFUSED: C.-G.) [1994] R.P.C. 387

Research Corporation's (Carboplatin) Patent (PATENT: LICENCES OF RIGHT: SETTLEMENT OF TERMS: REASONABLE REMUNERATION: Pat. Ct) [1990] R.P.C. 663

Research Corporation/Publication (EUROPEAN PATENT: APPEAL: PROCEDURE: LATE AUXILIARY REQUESTS: PRIOR ART: AVAILABILITY TO PUBLIC: DATE OF PUBLICATION: T381/87: EPO) [1989] E.P.O.R. 138; [1990] O.J. EPO 213

Research Specialties for Labs Pvba v. Chrompack NV (TRADE MARK: ADVERTISING: ORIGIN OF GOODS: Benelux C.J.) [1983] E.C.C. 471

Retain Nurserymen's Products Co-operative Ltd's Application (TRADE MARK: APPLICATION: INHERENT DISTINCTIVENESS: DESCRIPTIVE OF GOODS: USE: EVIDENCE: Australia: Pat. Off.) 9 I.P.R. 255

Retec Ltd's Application (TRADE MARKS: APPLICATION: "SUBSTANTIALLY IDENTICAL WITH OR DECEPTIVELY SIMILAR TO": PHONETIC SIMILARITY: RESTRICTED CLASS OF PURCHASERS: Australia: Pat. Off.) 12 I.P.R. 413

Revertex Ltd v. Slim Rivertex Shn Bhd (TRADE MARK: REGISTRAR OF COMPANIES REFUSAL NOT TO REGISTER SIMILAR NAME: PASSING OFF: LIKELIHOOD OF DECEPTION: Malaysia: H.C.) [1991] 1 M.L.J. 508

Revlon Inc. v. Kemco Chemicals (PASSING OFF: FOREIGN PLAINTIFF: NO LOCAL IMMOVABLE ASSETS STRIKING OUT: SECURITY FOR COSTS: India: H.C.) (1987) I.P.L.R. 32

Revocation of a patent (EUROPEAN PATENT: OPPOSITION: PROCEDURE: AMENDMENT, FAILURE OF SUBSEQUENT COMPLIANCE: REVOCATION: AUTOMATIC REVOCATION: APPEAL: ADMISSIBILITY: GENERAL LEGAL PRINCIPLES: *Travaux préparatoires*: ENLARGED BOARD OF APPEAL: POINT OF LAW, ANSWERED: PRESIDENT OF EPO, REFERENCE BY: G01/90: EPO) [1991] E.P.O.R. 343; [1991] O.J. EPO 275

REVUETRONIC Trade Mark (TRADE MARK: APPLICATION: DISCLAIMER OF PART OF MARK: T.M.Reg.) [1983] R.P.C. 401; (1984) 8 I.P.L.R. 33

Rexnold Inc. v. Ancon Ltd (COPYRIGHT: INFRINGEMENT: ORDER 14: UPDATED WORKING DRAWINGS: ORIGINALITY: Ch.D.) [1983] F.S.R. 662

Reynolds (R.J.) Tobacco Co. v. Philip Morris Inc. (TRADE MARKS: OPPOSITION: DISTINCTIVENESS: COMPOSITE MARK WITH NON-DISTINCTIVE ELEMENT: COLOUR LIMITATION: EFFECT OF DISCLAIMER: Australia: Pat. Off.) 12 I.P.R. 256

R.H. Macy & Co. Inc. v. Trade Accents, *sub nom.* Macy & Co. Inc. v. Trade Accents

RHM Foods Ltd v. Bovril Ltd (PASSING OFF: PRACTICE: DISCOVERY: C.A.) [1982] 1 All E.R. 673; [1983] R.P.C. 275; [1982] 1 W.L.R. 661

Rhône-Poulenc AG Co. v. Dikloride Herbicides Sdn Bhd (PATENT: AGRICULTURAL METHODS: INFRINGEMENT: VALIDITY: Malaysia: H.C.)
[1988] F.S.R. 282; 13 I.P.R. 653
Rhône-Poulenc Agrochemie SA v. UIM Chemical Services Pty Ltd (PATENT: INFRINGEMENT: PITH AND MARROW: Australia: Fed. Ct)
6 I.P.R. 607; 68 A.L.R. 77
Rhône-Poulenc Agrochemie SA v. UIM Chemical Services Pty Ltd (PATENT: INFRINGEMENT: PITH AND MARROW: EVIDENCE: INJUNCTION: DISCRETION: Australia: Fed. Ct) 6 I.P.R. 394
Rhône-Poulenc SA's (Ketoprofen) Patent (PATENT: LICENCE OF RIGHT: PATENT OFFICE PRACTICE: STRIKING OUT: Pat. Ct) [1989] R.P.C. 570
Rhône-Poulenc Santé's European Patent (U.K.) (PATENT: CLERICAL ERROR IN TRANSLATION: NARROWER PROTECTION CONFERRED BY TRANSLATION: WHETHER CORRECTION ALLOWABLE UNDER GENERAL STATUTORY PROVISION: WHETHER CORRECTION UNDER SPECIFIC PROVISION PERMISSIBLE BEFORE TRANSLATION PUBLISHED: C.-G.) [1996] R.P.C. 125
Rhône-Poulenc/Silico-aluminate (EUROPEAN PATENT: OPPOSITION: PROCEDURE: APPEAL: FRESH DOCUMENTS: REMITTAL ORDERED: T273/84: EPO) [1987] E.P.O.R. 44; [1986] O.J. EPO 346
Rhône-Poulenc/International applications (EUROPEAN PATENT: APPEAL: PROCEDURE: POWERS OF BOARD OF APPEAL: RE-ESTABLISHMENT OF RIGHTS: GENERAL PROCEDURAL PRINCIPLE OF THE EPC: EPO NOTICE, ERRONEOUS, RELIANCE ON: CONVENTIONS: EURO-PCT APPLICATIONS: DIFFERENT REGIME: FEES: REIMBURSEMENT OF APPEAL FEE: J06/79: EPO) [1979–85] E.P.O.R. A10; [1980] O.J. EPO 225
Rhône-Poulenc/Official language (EUROPEAN PATENT: APPEAL: PROCEDURE: TRANSLATION OF NOTICE OF APPEAL: T323/87: EPO)
[1989] E.P.O.R. 412; [1989] O.J. EPO 343
Rhône-Poulenc/Silane (EUROPEAN PATENT: INVENTIVE STEP: CITATION: STATE OF THE ART: AMBIGUOUS TEACHING: T70/90: EPO) [1994] E.P.O.R. 452
Rib Loc/Correction of mistakes (EUROPEAN PATENT: AMENDMENT AND CORRECTION: DESIGNATION OF STATES: *Travaux préparatoires*: J08/80: EPO) [1979–85] E.P.O.R. A40; [1980] O.J. EPO 293
Ricardo International plc v. Orital Engine Co. (Aust.) Pty Ltd (PATENT: OPPOSITION: PRIOR CLAIMING: NOVELTY: TRANSITIONAL APPLICATION: DIVISIONAL STATUS: FAIR BASIS: Australia: AIPO) 29 I.P.R. 353
Richardson Vicks Inc. v. Medico Laboratories (TRADE MARK: INFRINGEMENT: PASSING OFF: INJUNCTION: India: H.C.) (1986) 10 I.P.L.R. 420
Richardson Vicks Inc. v. Vikas Pharmaceuticals (TRADE MARK: COPYRIGHT: INFRINGEMENT: PASSING OFF: *Ad interim* INJUNCTION MADE ABSOLUTE: India: H.C.) (1990) 15 I.P.L.R. 44
Richardson-Vicks Inc.'s Patent (PATENT: REVOCATION: OBVIOUSNESS: SYNERGY SHOWN ONLY BY LATER EXPERIMENTS: AMENDMENT: NEW MATTER: SAME AMENDMENT SOUGHT IN EPO: DISCRETION: PRACTICE: RELIANCE ON EXPERIMENTS CARRIED OUT FOR OTHER PURPOSES: Pat. Ct)
[1995] R.P.C. 568
Richco Plastic Co.'s Patent (PATENT: PATENT OFFICE PRACTICE: COMPULSORY LICENCE: ABUSE OF PROCESS: EVIDENCE: DISCOVERY: C.-G.)
[1989] R.P.C. 722
Richsell Pty Ltd v. Khoury (DESIGNS: PRIOR PUBLICATION AND USE: ONUS OF PROOF: Australia: Fed. Ct) 30 I.P.R. 129

Rickless v. United Artists Corp. (DRAMATIC & MUSICAL PERFORMERS PROTECTION ACT 1958; OUT-TAKES FROM FILMS: PETER SELLERS' *Pink Panther*. USE AFTER DEATH OF STAR: KNOWLEDGE AND INTENT: INTERFERENCE WITH CONTRACTUAL RELATIONS: LIABILITY: CRIMINAL SANCTIONS: CIVIL REMEDIES: ASSESSMENT OF DAMAGES: Q.B.D.)
[1986] F.S.R. 502
(C.A.) [1987] 1 All E.R. 679; [1987] F.S.R. 362; [1988] Q.B. 40; [1987] 2 W.L.R. 945

Rider/Simethicone tablet (EUROPEAN PATENT: INVENTIVE STEP: COULD/WOULD TEST: T2/83: EPO)   [1979–85] E.P.O.R. C715; [1984] O.J. EPO 265

Ridgeway v. Consolidated Energy Corp. Pty Ltd (RESTRICTIVE PRACTICES: REPRESENTATIONS OF EXCLUSIVE LICENCE TO DISTRIBUTE PRODUCT: KNOWLEDGE OF FACTS AND MATTERS: Australia: Fed. Ct)   7 I.P.R. 452

Riedel-de-Haen AG v. Liew Keng Pang (CIVIL PROCEDURE: INTERLOCUTORY INJUNCTION: ANTON PILLER ORDER: DISCLOSURE OF NAMES OF SUPPLIERS AND CUSTOMERS OF COUNTERFEIT GOODS: WHETHER INFRINGEMENT OF PRIVILEGE AGAINST SELF-INCRIMINATION: Singapore: H.C.)   14 I.P.R. 285

Rieter/Winding apparatus (EUROPEAN PATENT: AMENDMENT AND CORRECTION: COMMON FEATURE OF PRIOR ART AND APPLICATION: PREAMBLE OF CLAIM: T52/82: EPO)   [1979–85] E.P.O.R. B459; [1983] O.J. EPO 416

Rifa/Capacitor roll (EUROPEAN PATENT: INVENTIVE STEP: ANALOGOUS USE: CLOSEST PRIOR ART: COMBINATION OF CITATIONS: OPPOSITION: PROCEDURE: FRESH DOCUMENTS ON APPEAL: STATE OF THE ART: PRIOR PROSPECTUS: T602/90: EPO)   [1992] E.P.O.R. 8

Rightway v. Rightways Footwear (TRADE MARK: TRADE NAME: PASSING OFF: PRIOR USE: INTERIM INJUNCTION: India: H.C.)   (1986) 11 I.P.L.R. 120

RIJN STAAL Trade Mark (TRADE MARK: REGISTRATION: DISTINCTIVENESS: BoT)   [1991] R.P.C. 400

Riker Laboratories Aust. Pty Ltd v. Westwood Pharmaceuticals Inc. (PATENT ATTORNEYS: COMMUNICATIONS WITH CLIENT: WHETHER PRIVILEGED: Australia: S.C.(NSW))   1 I.P.R. 122

Riker/Withdrawal (EUROPEAN PATENT: ABANDONMENT: WHAT CONSTITUTES: UNEQUIVOCAL STATEMENT BY REPRESENTATIVE: PRECEDENT: SIMILAR BUT NOT IDENTICAL FACTS: NATIONAL PRACTICES IRRELEVANT: J06/86: EPO)   [1988] E.P.O.R. 277; [1988] O.J. EPO 124

Riley Leisure Products Pty Ltd v. Dokyo Co. Ltd (PASSING OFF: TRADE NAME: INTERLOCUTORY INJUNCTION: Hong Kong: C.A.)   7 I.P.R. 464

Rippes/Computer fault (EUROPEAN PATENT: FEES: DATE OF RECEIPT: J05/84: EPO)   [1986] E.P.O.R. 53; [1985] O.J. EPO 306

Risis Pte Ltd v. Polar Gems Pte Ltd (REGISTERED DESIGN: WHETHER DESIGN NEW OR ORIGINAL: INFRINGEMENT: NOVELTY: PRINCIPLES IN JUDGING: Singapore: H.C.)   [1995] 1 S.L.R. 88

Rite-Hite Corp. v. Kelly Co. Inc. (PATENT: INFRINGEMENT: DAMAGES: LOST PROFITS: INJUNCTION: FAILURE TO PRACTICE INVENTION: U.S.A.: C.A., Fed. Ct)   [1996] F.S.R. 469

Ritz Hotel London Ltd's Application (TRADE MARK: APPLICATION: OPPOSITION: NOTICE: EXTENSION OF TIME LIMIT: Australia: Pat. Off.)   7 I.P.R. 546

Ritz Hotel Ltd v. Charles of The Ritz Ltd (TRADE MARKS: EXPUNGEMENT: PERSON AGGRIEVED: PRESCRIPTIVE VALIDITY: ENTRIES WRONGLY MADE IN REGISTER: ENTRIES WRONGLY REMAINING IN REGISTER: Australia: S.C.(NSW))
88 A.L.R. 217; 12 I.P.R. 417; (1988) 15 N.S.W.L.R. 158; [1989] R.P.C. 333

Ritz Hotel Ltd v. Charles of The Ritz Ltd (TRADE MARKS: RECTIFICATION: PERSON AGGRIEVED: QUALITY CONTROL: IMPORTED PACKAGING: LIKELY TO DECEIVE OR CONFUSE: South Africa: A.D.)
1988 (3) S.A. 290; [1988] F.S.R. 549
Ritz Hotel Ltd v. Parfums Yves Saint Laurent Ltd (TRADE MARKS: REMOVAL: ORDERS SERVED ON REGISTRAR: SUBSEQUENT APPEAL: Australia: Fed. Ct)
15 I.P.R. 328
Riv-Oland Marble Co. (Vic.) Pty Ltd v. Settef SpA (TRADE MARKS: VALIDITY: USE LIKELY TO CAUSE CONFUSION: LIABILITY TO EXPUNGEMENT: DISTINCTIVE: Australia: Fed. Ct)   83 A.L.R. 677; 12 I.P.R. 321
Riviera Leisurewear Pty Ltd v. J. Hepworth & Son plc (TRADE MARK: APPLICATION: OPPOSITION: PROPRIETORSHIP: REPUTATION: DECEPTION AND CONFUSION: Australia: Pat. Off.)   9 I.P.R. 305
Rizla International BV v. L. Suzman Distributors (Pty.) Ltd (PASSING OFF: NAME: GET-UP: PUBLIC DOMAIN: TEST: WHETHER USE CALCULATED TO DECEIVE: EXTENT OF LEGITIMATE IMITATION: DUTY TO DISTINGUISH GOODS FROM COMPETITOR: South Africa: C.P.D.)   1996 (2) S.A. 527
Rizla Ltd's Application (PATENT: PRACTICE: COSTS: REFERENCE TO COMPTROLLER UNDER SECTION 12 SUBSEQUENTLY DISMISSED ON WITHDRAWAL OF REFEROR: COMPTROLLER'S AUTHORITY TO AWARD COSTS: REASONABLE COSTS: PARTIES CONDUCT: C.-G.)   [1992] F.S.R. 659
(APPEAL: Pat. Ct)   [1993] R.P.C. 365
Rizla Ltd v. Bryant & May Ltd (PASSING OFF: GET-UP: CIGARETTE PAPERS: COLOUR OF PACKETS: Ch.D.)   [1986] R.P.C. 389
Robbins/Rotary cutterhead (EUROPEAN PATENT: NOVELTY: WHOLE CONTENTS: PRIORITY: IDENTITY OF INVENTION: T116/84: EPO)
[1979–85] E.P.O.R. C966
Robert Bosch GmbH v. Solo Industries Pty Ltd (PATENT: NOVELTY: OBVIOUSNESS: PRIORITY DATE OF COGNATED DISCLOSURES: FAIRLY BASED: Australia: Pat. Off.)   2 I.P.R. 482
Robert John Powers School Inc. v. Tessensohn (COPYRIGHT: INFRINGEMENT: SCOPE OF PROTECTION: COMPILATION: INVERSE PASSING OFF: MISLEADING ACCOUNT OF ACHIEVEMENT IN RÉSUMÉ: Singapore: H.C.)
[1993] 3 S.L.R. 724
(APPEAL: INVERSE PASSING OFF: Singapore: C.A.)
[1994] 3 S.L.R. 308; [1995] F.S.R. 947
Robert v. Société Crehallet-Folliot-Recherche et Publicité (COPYRIGHT: COLLECTIVE WORKS: INDIVIDUAL AUTHOR'S RIGHTS: EDITOR'S NAME: UNFAIR COMPETITION: France: S.C.)   [1987] E.C.C. 322; [1987] F.S.R. 537
Roberts v. Northwest Fixings (BREACH OF CONFIDENCE: CUSTOMER LIST: ANTON PILLER PRACTICE: LEGAL AID: PRACTICE: OBSERVATIONS ON COUNTY COURT JURISDICTION BY AGREEMENT: C.A.)   [1993] F.S.R. 281
Robertshaw Controls Co. v. GSA Industries Ltd (PATENT: AMENDMENT: OPPOSITION TO AMENDMENT: AMBIGUITY: SUFFICIENCY: Australia: Pat. Off.)   20 I.P.R. 307
Robinson v. Cooper Corp. of SA (Pty) Ltd (DESIGNS: INFRINGEMENT: FUNCTIONAL INTEGER: South Africa: TPD)   1983 (1) S.A. 88
Rocco Cartella's Application (PATENT: APPLICATION FOR EXTENSION OF TIME TO LODGE SUBSTITUTE COMPLETE SPECIFICATION: Australia: Pat. Off.)
11 I.P.R. 242
Rock Engineering Pty Ltd v. A. Noble & Son Ltd (PATENT: ACCEPTANCE: OPPOSITION: LAPSE: FAILURE TO PAY CONTINUATION FEE: APPLICATION TO RESTORE: Australia: Pat. Off.)   20 I.P.R. 525

Rockefeller/Deposit number (EUROPEAN PATENT: AMENDMENT AND CORRECTION: NUMBER OF MICRO-ORGANISM DEPOSIT, NOT PERMITTED: *Travaux préparatoires*: EPO: AGREEMENTS BETWEEN PARTIES OUTSIDE COMPETENCE: EPO)   [1990] E.P.O.R. 303

Rockwell International Corp. & Iveco's Agreements (RESTRICTIVE PRACTICES: E.C. Comm.)
[1983] 3 C.M.L.R. 709; [1984] F.S.R. 145; [1983] O.J. L224/19

Rockwell International Corp. v. Serck Industries Ltd (COPYRIGHT: INFRINGEMENT: PRACTICE: INTERROGATORIES: DEFENDANT'S DESIGN PROCESS: Ch.D.: C.A.)   [1988] F.S.R. 187

Rockwell International Corp. v. Serck Industries Ltd (PRACTICE: PATENT AGENT'S PRIVILEGE: Ch.D.)   [1987] R.P.C. 89

Roecar/Decisions by Formalities Officers (EUROPEAN PATENT: PROCEDURE: JURISDICTION OF FORMALITIES OFFICERS: FEES: REIMBURSEMENT OF APPEAL FEE: EPO: INTERNAL ORGANISATION: J10/82: EPO)
[1979–85] E.P.O.R. A122; [1983] O.J. EPO 94

Roelofs' Patent (PATENT: PETTY PATENT: EXTENSION OF TERM: STATUTORY NOTICE: FAIRLY BASED: PRIORITY DATE: PRIOR DATE: Australia: AIPO)
28 I.P.R. 131

Roger Bullivant Ltd v. Ellis (BREACH OF CONFIDENCE: EX-EMPLOYEE: SPRINGBOARD DOCTRINE: CUSTOMER CARD INDEX: C.A.)
[1987] F.S.R. 172; [1987] I.C.R. 468

Röhm & Haas/Power to examine (EUROPEAN PATENT: OPPOSITION: PROCEDURE: ADMINISTRATIVE CHARACTER: FRESH GROUNDS: ADMISSIBILITY: REVOCATION: STATEMENT OF GROUNDS: UNOPPOSED PARTS OF PATENT, COMPETENCE TO CONSIDER: APPEAL: PURPOSE OF EPO APPEAL PROCEDURE: PRECEDENT: JUDICIAL CHARACTER: *Volenti non fit injuria*: G09/91: G10/91: EPO)   [1993] E.P.O.R. 485; [1993] O.J. EPO 408; [1993] O.J. EPO 420

Röhm/Film coating (EUROPEAN PATENT: INVENTIVE STEP: PREJUDICE: DISCOUNTED: T19/81: EPO)
[1979–85] E.P.O.R. B330; [1982] O.J. EPO 51

Röhm/Ultra-violet emitters (EUROPEAN PATENT: CLAIMS: FAIR BASIS: T283/84: EPO)   [1988] E.P.O.R. 16

Röhm/Withdrawal of a European patent application (EUROPEAN PATENT: ABANDONMENT: WHAT CONSTITUTES: J11/80: EPO)
[1979–85] E.P.O.R. A48; [1981] O.J. EPO 141

Rohrmoser v. Registrar of Trade Marks (TRADE MARK: OPPOSITION: APPLICATION FOR EXTENSION OF TIME LIMIT: Australia: Fed. Ct)   70 A.L.R. 613

Roland Corp. v. Lorenzo & Sons Pty Ltd (COPYRIGHT: DRAWING OF SINGLE LETTER: COMPUTER PRINTOUT: ORIGINAL CREATED ON FLOPPY DISK: TRADE MARKS: DESIGNS: DEFENCE: PHOTOGRAPH IN BOOK: IMPORTATION: TRADE MARK: COPYRIGHT IN LOGO DEVICES REGULATED UNDER STATUTE: Australia: Fed. Ct)   105 A.L.R. 623; 22 I.P.R. 245

Roland Corp. v. Lorenzo & Sons Pty Ltd (COPYRIGHT: STYLISED REPRESENTATIONS OF THE LETTERS "R" AND "B": INSTRUCTION MANUALS FOR ELECTRONIC EQUIPMENT AND ASSOCIATED LITERATURE: INFRINGEMENT: UNAUTHORISED REPRODUCTION: PARALLEL IMPORTATION AND SALE: IMPLIED LICENCE TO IMPORT AND SELL: IMPLIED LICENCE TO REPRODUCE: Australia: Fed. Ct)   23 I.P.R. 376

Rolex Chemical Industries' Application (TRADE MARK: APPLICATION: OPPOSITION: ROLEX: India: T.M.Reg.)   (1976) 1 I.P.L.R. 37

Rollbits Pty Ltd v. Rowntree Mackintosh plc (TRADE MARK: SERVICE OF DOCUMENTS: EXTENSION OF TIME: PUBLIC INTEREST: PRESENTATION OF EVIDENCE AND ARGUMENTS: Australia: Pat. Off.)   6 I.P.R. 292

Rolled Zinc Products (RESTRICTIVE PRACTICES: PARALLEL IMPORTS: E.C. Comm.)   [1983] 2 C.M.L.R. 285; [1984] F.S.R. 31; [1982] O.J. L362/40

Roman Roller CC v. Speedmark Holdings (Pty.) Ltd (PATENT: VALIDITY OBVIOUSNESS: LACK OF CLARITY: STATUTORY INTERPRETATION: South Africa: A.D.)   1996 (1) S.A. 405

Rorer/Dysmenorrhea (EUROPEAN PATENT: PATENTABILITY: PAIN, DISCOMFORT, ETC.: THERAPY: T81/84: EPO)   [1988] E.P.O.R. 297; [1988] O.J. EPO 207

Rose & Thistle v. J.N. Nicholas (Vimto) Ltd (TRADE MARK: VIMTO: NON-USE: USE OF ASSOCIATED MARK: RECTIFICATION TO ALLOW REGISTRATION OF WIMTO: India: H.C.)   (1991) 16 I.P.L.R. 88
  see also, sub nom. J. N. Nicholas (Vimto) Ltd v. Rose & Thistle

ROSE GARDEN Trade Mark (TRADE MARK: APPLICATION: OPPOSITION: CONFUSING SIMILARITY: T.M.Reg.)   [1995] R.P.C. 246

Rose Plastics GmbH v. Wm. Beckett & Co. (Plastics) Ltd (COPYRIGHT INFRINGEMENT: SECTION 9(8) DEFENCE: "*Catnic*" DEFENCE: Ch.D)
                                                          [1989] 1 F.S.R. 113

Rose Records v. Motown Record Corp. (COPYRIGHT: INFRINGEMENT: EFFECT OF SETTLEMENT: SUCCESSION OF DEALINGS WITH INFRINGING GOODS: WHETHER GOODS "FRANKED": Ch.D.)   [1983] F.S.R. 361

Rose v. Information Services Ltd (COPYRIGHT: INFRINGEMENT: TITLE OF DIARY: SUBSISTENCE OF COPYRIGHT: Ch.D.)   [1987] F.S.R. 254

Rosebank Plastics Pty Ltd v. Duncan & Wigley Pty Ltd (t/a D. & W. Australia School Suppliers) (DESIGNS: REGISTERED DESIGN: OBVIOUS IMITATION: VISUAL COMPARISON: EXPERT EVIDENCE AS TO SIMILARITY: CONTENT OF STATEMENT OF NOVELTY: PASSING OFF: INFRINGEMENT OF COPYRIGHT IN DESIGN DRAWING: MISLEADING AND DECEPTIVE CONDUCT: FALSE REPRESENTATION AS TO SPONSORSHIP, APPROVAL AND AFFILIATION: Australia: Fed. Ct)   11 I.P.R. 413

Rosen's Application (PATENT: OBJECTION BY EXAMINER ON PROPOSED CLAIMS: MATTER NOT IN SUBSTANCE DISCLOSED IN SPECIFICATION AS LODGED: Australia: Pat. Off.)   17 I.P.R. 33

Rothmans of Pall Mall Ltd v. New Tobacco Co. Ltd (TRADE MARK: CAMBRIDGE FOR CIGARETTES: NON-USE: NON-AVAILABILITY OF MARK: India: H.C.)
                                                        (1988) 12 I.P.L.R. 103

ROTHSCHILD Trade Mark (TRADE MARK: APPLICATION: OPPOSITION: PRACTICE: DEVICE MARK INCORPORATING SURNAME: DISCLAIMER: T.M.Reg.)   [1985] R.P.C. 593; (1986) 11 I.P.L.R. 90

Roussel-Uclaf's (Clemence & Le Martret) Patent (PATENT: LICENCES OF RIGHT: PRACTICE: Pat. Ct)   [1987] R.P.C. 109
(STAY: COMPTROLLER'S JURISDICTION: VEXATIOUS PROCEEDINGS: Pat. Ct)
                                                          [1989] R.P.C. 405

Roussel-Uclaf v. Helopharm W. Petrik & Co. (TRADE MARK: OPPOSITION: SUBSTANTIALLY IDENTICAL: DECEPTIVELY SIMILAR: PHARMACEUTICAL PRODUCT: CONFUSION, SERIOUS IMPLICATIONS OF: Australia: AIPO)
                                                            27 I.P.R. 657

Roussel-Uclaf v. ICI (No. 2) (PATENT: INFRINGEMENT: PRACTICE: PROCESS CLAIMS: DISCLOSURE OF CONFIDENTIAL DESCRIPTION OF DEFENDANT'S PROCESS TO PLAINTIFF'S EMPLOYEE: TERMS OF DISCLOSURE: Pat. Ct)
                                  [1990] F.S.R. 25; [1990] R.P.C. 45
                                                (C.A.) [1990] R.P.C. 45

Roussel-Uclaf v. ICI (PATENT: INFRINGEMENT: PRACTICE: PROCESS CLAIMS: DISCLOSURE OF SECRET PROCESS: Ch.D.: C.A.)   [1989] R.P.C. 59

Roussel-Uclaf v. ICI (PATENT: INFRINGEMENT: VALIDITY: AMENDMENT: FUNCTIONAL CLAIMS: PROCESS CLAIMS: INSUFFICIENCY: INUTILITY: AMENDMENT BY EXPLANATION: DISCRETION: PRINCIPAL AMENDMENTS ALLOWED: Pat. C.C.)   [1991] R.P.C. 51

Roussel-Uclaf v. Pan Laboratories Pty Ltd (PATENT: GOODS INFRINGING PATENTS IN AUSTRALIA: EXPORT TO PAPUA NEW GUINEA: JURISDICTION TO ORDER DELIVERY UP: DISCRETION: Australia: AIPO)   29 I.P.R. 556

Roussel-Uclaf v. Shell Internationale Research Maatschappij BV (PATENT: OPPOSITION: EXTENSION OF TIME LIMITS: EVIDENCE IN SUPPORT: PUBLIC INTEREST: Australia: Pat. Off.)   9 I.P.R. 475

Roussel-Uclaf/Divisional application (EUROPEAN PATENT: DIVISIONAL APPLICATION: ABANDONED CLAIMS: INVITATION TO FILE: J13/84: EPO)   [1979–85] E.P.O.R. A221; [1985] O.J. EPO 34

Roussel-Uclaf/Tetrahydropyridinyl-indole derivatives (EUROPEAN PATENT: CLAIMS: DISCLAIMER: FIRST PHARMACEUTICAL USE: CONVENTIONS: INDEFINITE ARTICLE INTERPRETED AS GENERIC PLURAL: T43/82: EPO)   [1979–85] E.P.O.R. B448

Roussel-Uclaf/Thenoyl peroxide (EUROPEAN PATENT: PATENTABILITY: COSMETIC INDICATION: INDUSTRIAL APPLICATION: MEDICAL INDICATION: T36/83: EPO)   [1987] E.P.O.R. 1; [1986] O.J. EPO 295

Rovex Ltd v. Prima Toys (Pty) Ltd (TRADE MARK: DOLL: FIRST LOVE/BABY LOVE: PASSING OFF: CONFUSION: South Africa: CPD)   1982 (2) S.A. 403

Rowe v. Walt Disney Productions (COPYRIGHT: CONFLICT OF LAWS: *Droit moral*: France: C.A.)   [1987] F.S.R. 36

Rowntree plc v. Rollbits Pty Ltd (TRADE MARKS: DECEPTIVE SIMILARITY: MEANING OF "CONFECTIONERY": GOODS OF THE SAME DESCRIPTION: EVIDENCE OF THE PLAINTIFF'S EXTENSIVE REPUTATION: BURDEN OF PROOF: Australia: S.C.(NSW))   10 I.P.R. 539

Royal Beech-Nut (Pty) Ltd (t/a Manhattan Confectioners) v. United Tobacco Co. Ltd t/a Willards Foods (TRADE MARK: PASSING OFF: SIMILAR MARKS: IMPLIED REPRESENTATION OF CONNECTION IN TRADE: South Africa: A.D.)   1992 (4) S.A. 118

Royal Melbourne Hospital v. Mattews (CONFIDENTIAL INFORMATION: SEARCH WARRANT: PATIENT IN HOSPITAL: WHETHER HOSPITAL OBLIGED TO SUPPLY INFORMATION: Australia: H.C.)   [1993] 1 V.R. 665

Royale & Co. (Aust.) Pty Ltd v. Maxims Ltd (TRADE MARK: EXPUNGEMENT FOR NON-USE: EVIDENCE: EXTENSION OF TIME LIMITS: Australia: Pat. Off.)   9 I.P.R. 237

Royon v. Meilland (RESTRICTIVE PRACTICES: PLANT BREEDER'S RIGHTS: LICENCE AGREEMENT: GRANT BACK: NO-CHALLENGE CLAUSE: ARTICLE 85(1): INFRINGEMENT: REFUSAL OF EXEMPTION: E.C. Comm.)   [1988] 4 C.M.L.R. 193; [1988] F.S.R. 305

RS-Reklam/Edging (EUROPEAN PATENT: INVENTIVE STEP: SIMPLICITY OF SOLUTION: T83/83: EPO)   [1979–85] E.P.O.R. C793

Rubycliff Ltd v. Plastic Engineers Ltd (COPYRIGHT: INFRINGEMENT: DAMAGES: CROSS UNDERTAKING IN DAMAGES: SECTION 9(8): CONSEQUENTIAL DAMAGES: Ch.D.)   [1986] R.P.C. 573

Rühland/Exchange of invention (EUROPEAN PATENT: AMENDMENT AND CORRECTION: SUBSTITUTION OF DOCUMENTS: CONVENTIONS: DIFFERENT LANGUAGE TEXTS: J21/85: EPO)   [1986] E.P.O.R. 226; [1986] O.J. EPO 117

Rules of Court in Scotland 1994 (CAUSES RELATING TO INTELLECTUAL PROPERTY) [1995] R.P.C. 1

Rutman v. Société Des Gens de Lettres (COPYRIGHT: AUDIOVISUAL WORKS: WHETHER TECHNICAL WORK OR INTELLECTUAL CREATION: France: D.C.) [1988] E.C.C. 48; [1988] F.S.R. 273

Ryan v. Lum (FAIR TRADING: SIMILARITY OF TYPE OF PRODUCT, INSTRUCTIONS AND GET-UP: DAMAGES OR ACCOUNT OF PROFITS: COPYRIGHT: BREACHES ON PACKAGING OF PRODUCTS: PATENT: LACK OF NOVELTY AND OBVIOUSNESS: REVOCATION: ONUS OF PROOF: PROCUREMENT OF INFRINGEMENT: Australia: S.C.(NSW)) (1989) 86 A.L.R. 670: 16 N.S.W.L.R. 518

S. & M. Motor Repairs Pty Ltd v. Caltex Oil (Australia) Pty Ltd (PASSING OFF: WHAT CONSTITUTES: PETROL: PETROL STATIONS: GET-UP: SIGNS ON PUMPS: UNDERTAKING: Australia: S.C.(NSW)) 11 I.P.R. 97; (1988) 15 N.S.W.L.R. 358

S.M. Enterprises v. Hyderabad Lamps Ltd (TRADE MARK: SOLAR: CHOKES FOR FLUORESCENT TUBES: INFRINGEMENT: INTERIM INJUNCTION VACATED: India: H.C.) (1988) 13 I.P.L.R. 135

SPS Jayam & Co. v. Gajalakshmi (TRADE MARK: INFRINGEMENT: PASSING OFF: JOINDER OF PARTIES: INTERIM INJUNCTION: India: H.C.) (1992) 17 I.P.L.R. 46

SPS Selvaraj v. Muthuswamy Naicker (TRADE MARK: INFRINGEMENT: CIVIL AND CRIMINAL PROCEEDINGS: CONTEMPT: India: H.C.) (1991) 16 I.P.L.R. 98

S. v. Nxumalo (COPYRIGHT: OFFENCES: SALE OF INFRINGING COPIES: *Mens rea*: FORM: KNOWLEDGE: South Africa: TPD) 1993 (3) S.A. 456

S4C, *sub nom.* Sianel Pedwar Cymru

SAB/Vehicle brakes (EUROPEAN PATENT: AMENDMENT AND CORRECTION: PRE- AND POST-GRANT, DISTINCTION BETWEEN: APPEAL: PROCEDURE: NOTICE OF APPEAL, INTERPRETATION OF: T89/85: EPO) [1988] E.P.O.R. 105

SABATIER Trade Mark *sub nom.* K. SABATIER Trade Mark

Sabazo Pty Ltd v. Ruddiman (TRADE NAMES: PASSING OFF: LOWER QUALITY GOODS: DAMAGES: ASSESSMENT: Australia: S.C.(NSW)) 8 I.P.R. 599

Sabra International Pty Ltd's Application (TRADE MARKS: APPLICATION FOR REGISTRATION: MARK DIRECTLY DESCRIPTIVE: LACK OF INHERENT DISTINCTIVENESS: MARK NOT REGISTRABLE IN PART A OR PART B OF REGISTER: INSUFFICIENT EVIDENCE: Australia: Pat. Off.) 18 I.P.R. 181

Sabre v. Russ Kalvin's Hair Care Co. (TRADE SECRETS: PRACTICE AND PROCEDURE: PRODUCTION OF DOCUMENTS IN CONTROL OF THIRD PARTY: Australia: Fed. Ct) 27 I.P.R. 372

SAF Trade Mark (TRADE MARK: APPLICATION: COLLECTION OF LETTERS: DISTINCTIVENESS: Ireland: H.C.) [1982] I.L.R.M. 207; [1983] F.S.R. 6

SAF Trade Mark, *sub nom.* Soudure Autogéne Française SA

Safe Sport Australia Pty Ltd v. Puma Australia Pty Ltd (COPYRIGHT: DESIGN: INFRINGEMENT: VALIDITY: NOVELTY: PRIOR PUBLICATION: Australia: S.C.(Vic.)) 4 I.P.R. 120

Safetell Pty Ltd's Application (PATENT: APPLICATION: OBJECTIONS BY EXAMINER: AMENDMENT TO STATEMENT OF CLAIMS: MATTER NOT IN SUBSTANCE DISCLOSED IN THE SPECIFICATION AS LODGED: PRIOR PUBLICATION: Australia: Pat. Off.) 11 I.P.R. 40

Saga Foodstuffs Manufacturing (Pte) Ltd v. Best Food Pte Ltd (PASSING OFF: GET-UP: SIMILARITY: CONFUSION OF PUBLIC: RELEVANCE OF INTENTION TO DECEIVE: EVIDENCE: MARKET SURVEY: HEARSAY: Singapore: H.C.)
[1995] 1 S.L.R. 739

Saga Foodstuffs Manufacturing (Pte) Ltd v. Best Food Pte Ltd (TRADE MARK: REGISTRATION: INFRINGEMENT: ASSIGNMENT OF APPLICATION BEFORE DATE OF WRIT: PLEADINGS: AMENDMENT: Singapore: H.C.)
[1994] 2 S.L.R. 802

Sage Holdings Ltd v. Financial Mail (Pty) Ltd (CONFIDENTIAL INFORMATION: DIRECTOR: EMPLOYEE'S: PUBLIC POLICY: South Africa: WLD)
1991 (2) S.A. 117

Säger v. Dennemeyer & Co. Ltd (Services: patents: monitoring and renewal: patents Agents: statutory monopoly: Germany: foreign renewers to be licensed: Case C–76/90: ECJ)   [1993] 3 C.M.L.R. 639; [1991] I E.C.R.

Saidco/Water resistant cable (EUROPEAN PATENT: EVIDENCE: EXPERT'S AFFIDAVIT DISCOUNTED: INVENTIVE STEP: COMBINATION OF CITATIONS: PRIOR ART: AGED PUBLICATIONS: MISSED BY OTHERS: OBJECTIVE ASSESSMENT: T151/82: EPO)   [1979–85] E.P.O.R. C635

Sale and Buy-back of Records (COPYRIGHT: PERFORMING RIGHTS: SALE WITH OPTION TO RETURN: EXHAUSTION OF PRODUCER'S RIGHTS: PUBLIC INTEREST: FREE MOVEMENT OF GOODS: Germany: S.C.)   [1988] E.C.C. 70

Salminen/Pigs III (EUROPEAN PATENT: PATENTABILITY: THERAPY: ENLARGED BOARD OF APPEAL: REFERENCE REFUSED: T58/87: EPO)
[1989] E.P.O.R. 125; [1988] O.J. EPO 347

Salon Services (Hairdressing Supplies) Ltd v. Direct Salon Services Ltd (TRADE MARK: PASSING OFF: DESCRIPTIVE NAME: REPUTATION: Scotland: O.H.)
1988 S.L.T. 414

Salvage Association (The) v. CAP Financial Services Ltd (COMPUTER CONTRACT: BREACH: LIMITATION CLAUSE: APPLICABILITY OF UNFAIR CONTRACT TERMS ACT: Q.B.D.)   [1995] F.S.R. 654

Samir Senray's Design Application (DESIGN: PRELIMINARY OBJECTION ABOUT LACK OF JURISDICTION TO HEAR THE MATTER: India: Pat. Off.)
(1988) 13 I.P.L.R. 71

Samsung Electronics Co. Ltd v. ASDA Holdings Ltd (COPYRIGHT WORKS FROM NON-CONVENTION COUNTRY: PARALLEL IMPORTATION OF TV SETS: EXCLUSIVE DISTRIBUTORSHIP: UNAUTHORISED IMPORTATION: INTERIM INJUNCTION APPLICATION: New Zealand: H.C.)   19 I.P.R. 227

Samuel Taylor v. S.C. Johnson & Sons Pty Ltd, *sub nom.* R. & C. Products Pty Ltd (t/a Samuel Taylor) v. S.C. Johnson & Sons Pty Ltd

San Pellegrino SpA v. Coca-Cola Export Corp.—Filiale Italiana (RESTRICTIVE PRACTICES: DISTRIBUTION AGREEMENTS: REBATES: ABUSE OF DOMINANT POSITION: FIDELITY REBATES AND PRODUCTION TARGET REBATES: SETTLEMENT ON UNDERTAKING TO DISCONTINUE REBATES: E.C. Comm.)   [1989] 4 C.M.L.R. 137

Sandoz Ltd v. Fujisawa Pharmaceutical Co. Ltd (PATENT: APPLICATION: PRACTICE AND PROCEDURE: EXTENSION OF TIME FOR FILING EVIDENCE IN SUPPORT: NEED FOR FULL AND FRANK DISCLOSURE: Australia: Pat. Off.)
26 I.P.R. 426

Sandoz Ltd v. Fujisawa Pharmaceutical Co. Ltd (PATENT: APPLICATION: OPPOSITION: EVIDENCE: APPLICATION: FOR EXTENSION OF TIME TO SERVE FURTHER EVIDENCE IN SUPPORT: OBJECTION: PRACTICE AND PROCEDURE: Australia: Pat. Off.)   27 I.P.R. 421

Sandoz Ltd v. Pharmaceutical & Chemical Industries (TRADE MARK: OPPOSITION: HONEST CONCURRENT USE: *Res judicata*: India: T.M.Reg.)
(1987) 12 I.P.L.R. 40

Sandoz/Reimbursement of appeal fee (EUROPEAN PATENT: APPEAL: PROCEDURE: DISCRETION OF BOARD OF APPEAL: JURISDICTION OF BOARD OF APPEAL: FEES: REIMBURSEMENT OF APPEAL FEE: T41/82: EPO)
[1979–85] E.P.O.R. B446; [1982] O.J. EPO 256

Sandvik AB v. Boart International Ltd (PATENT: APPLICATION: OPPOSITION: PRIOR PUBLICATION: NOVELTY: CONVENTION APPLICATION: PRIORITY DATE: FAIR BASIS: FALSE SUGGESTION: Australia: Pat. Off.) 8 I.P.R. 571

Sandvik/Unpaid opposition fee (EUROPEAN PATENT: FEES: FAILURE TO PAY: T152/85: EPO) [1987] E.P.O.R. 258; [1987] O.J. EPO 191

Sanita Manufacturing (Malaysia) Sdn Bhd v. Chanchai Aroonratanawongse (TRADE MARK: REGISTRATION BY AGENT: ALTERATION WITHOUT AUTHORITY: APPLICATION TO EXPUNGE ALTERATION: Malaysia: S.C.)
[1987] 2 M.L.J. 219

Sankyo Co. Ltd v. Merck & Co. Inc. (PATENT: APPLICATION ACCEPTED: OPPOSITION: ANTICIPATION: PRIOR CLAIMING: PRIOR PUBLICATION: CLAIM NOT FAIRLY BASED: Australia: Pat. Off.) 22 I.P.R. 544

Sankyo/Diamond saw (EUROPEAN PATENT: APPLICATION: PROCEDURE: EXAMINING DIVISION, DUTY OF TO CONSIDER SUBMITTED TEXT: DISCRETION OF EXAMINING DIVISION: FRESH INDEPENDENT CLAIMS ON AMENDMENT: T55/89: EPO) [1991] E.P.O.R. 416

Sanofi (Re) (PATENT: EXTENSION: INADEQUATE REMUNERATION: ASSIGNMENT OF RIGHT TO APPLY: Australia: S.C.(Vic.)) [1983] 1 V.R. 25

Sanofi v. Parke Davis Pty Ltd (PATENT: EXTENSION: TIME LIMITS: Australia: H.C.) (1983) 152 C.L.R. 1; 1 I.P.R. 383

Santa Fe International Corp. v. Napier Shipping SA (PRACTICE: CONFIDENTIALITY: PATENT: INFRINGEMENT: PATENT AGENTS PRIVILEGE: Scotland: O.H.)
1985 S.L.T. 481; [1986] R.P.C. 72

Saphena Computing Ltd v. Allied Collection Agencies Ltd (COMPUTER CONTRACT: WHETHER STANDARD TERMS INCORPORATED: COPYRIGHT: WHETHER ASSIGNED IN EQUITY: RIGHT OR LICENCE TO REPAIR OR IMPROVE: INFRINGEMENT: WHETHER INNOCENT: FITNESS FOR PURPOSE: WHETHER OBLIGATION SURVIVED TERMINATION: Q.B.D., C.A.) [1995] F.S.R. 616

Sappi Fine Papers (Pty) Ltd v. ICI Canada Inc. (Formerly CIL Inc) (PATENT: SPECIFICATION: CONSTRUCTION: PERSONS SKILLED IN THE ART: REVOCATION: MISREPRESENTATION: South Africa: A.D.) 1992 (3) S.A. 306

Sartas No. 1 Pty Ltd v. Koukouou & Partners Pty Ltd (PATENT: METHOD CLAIMS: PRODUCT CLAIMS: INFRINGEMENT: AUTHORISATION: SUPPLY TO THIRD PARTY: VALIDITY: FAIR BASING: NOVELTY: ALLEGED PRIOR PUBLICATION: OBVIOUSNESS: DOUBLE CLAIMING: LACK OF TITLE: FALSE SUGGESTION: Australia: AIPO) 30 I.P.R. 479

Sartek Pty Ltd's Application (TRADE MARKS: APPLICATION: PROPOSED WITHDRAWAL OF ACCEPTANCE: PRIOR APPLICATION NOT CITED BEFORE ACCEPTANCE: EXERCISE OF DISCRETION: Australia: Pat. Off.) 22 I.P.R. 317

Sasdor Pty Ltd v. Atomic Skifabrik Alois Rohrmoser (TRADE MARKS: REMOVAL FOR NON-USE: OPPOSITION: PERSON AGGRIEVED: COSTS: PART SUCCESS: PRACTICE AND PROCEDURE: Australia: Pat. Off.) 20 I.P.R. 593

Satam Brandt/Refrigeration plant (EUROPEAN PATENT: AMENDMENT AND CORRECTION: ISOLATING FEATURE FROM COMBINATION AS DISCLOSED: T17/86: EPO) [1989] E.P.O.R. 347; [1989] O.J. EPO 297

Satellite Broadcasting and Cable Retransmission Directive, *sub nom.* Community
Satellite Broadcasting and Cable Retransmission Directive
Satellite Television Broadcasting (COPYRIGHT: CONTRACT: APPLICABLE LAW:
BROADCASTING RIGHTS: SATELLITE TV BROADCASTS: Austria: Regional
C.A.)   [1993] E.C.C. 439
(APPEAL: S.C.)   [1994] E.C.C. 526; [1995] F.S.R. 73
Saturno's Norwood Hotel Pty Ltd's Application (TRADE MARKS: APPLICATION:
OPPOSITION: PROPRIETORSHIP: FIRST USE BY APPLICANTS: LIKELIHOOD OF
DECEPTION OR CONFUSION: Australia: Pat. Off.)   12 I.P.R. 579
Saunders Valve Co. Ltd v. Klep Valves (COPYRIGHT: INFRINGEMENT: REMEDIES:
PRESUMPTION OF ORIGINALITY: South Africa: TPD)   1985 (1) S.A. 646
Savio Plastica/Fee reduction (EUROPEAN PATENT: FEES: SMALL AMOUNT
EXCEPTION: OPPOSITION: PROCEDURE: ACCELERATED PROCESSING:
ADMISSIBILITY: MULTIPLE OPPONENTS: T290/90: EPO)
                                  [1991] E.P.O.R. 200; [1992] O.J. EPO 368
Scanditronix/Radiation beam collimation (EUROPEAN PATENT: APPEAL:
PROCEDURE: OBJECTIONS BY BOARD OF ITS OWN MOTION: PRIOR ART:
DISCLOSURE: DIAGRAM: DOCUMENT TO BE READ AS A WHOLE: TEACHING OF:
NOVELTY: CLEARLY, UNMISTAKABLY AND FULLY DERIVABLE TEST: SKILLED
PERSON: T56/87: EPO)   [1990] E.P.O.R. 352; [1990] O.J. EPO 188
Sceats v. Jonathan Sceats Design Pty Ltd (TRADE MARKS: REMOVAL FOR NON-USE:
DISCRETIONARY REMEDY: EXERCISE OF DISCRETION: SUMMARY JUDGMENT:
Australia: Fed. Ct)   17 I.P.R. 28
Schering AG's Application (PATENT: APPLICATION: EXAMINER'S OBJECTIONS:
MERE COLLOCATION OF KNOWN INTEGERS: Australia: Pat. Off.)
                                                          22 I.P.R. 632
Schering AG's Patent (PATENT: PRACTICE: LICENCES OF RIGHT: PATENT AGENTS:
CONFIDENTIAL DOCUMENTS: AGENTS IN-HOUSE AND IN PRIVATE PRACTICE:
Pat. Ct)   [1986] R.P.C. 30
Schering Agrochemicals Ltd v. ABM Chemicals Ltd (PATENT: VALIDITY: PRACTICE:
DISCOVERY: Pat. Ct)   [1987] R.P.C. 185
Schering Biotech Corp.'s Application (PATENT: APPLICATION: BIOTECHNOLOGY:
WHETHER CLAIMS SUPPORTED BY DESCRIPTION: AMENDMENT: PRACTICE:
Pat. Ct)   [1993] R.P.C. 249
Schering Corp. v. Kilitch Co. (Pharma) Pvt. Ltd (TRADE MARK: INFRINGEMENT:
QUADRIDERM/CORIDERM: APPEAL: India: H.C.) (1994) 19 I.P.L.R. 1
Schering Corp. v. Perk Pharmaceutical Services (TRADE MARK: INFRINGEMENT:
GARAMYCIN/GAMAMYCIN: INTERIM   RELIEF: APPEAL: India:
H.C.)   (1993) 18 I.P.L.R. 33
Schering Corp. v. The Controller of Patents, Designs & Trademarks (PATENTS:
APPLICATION: DELAY: CONTROLLERS POWERS: CONVENTION APPLICATION:
REFUSAL TO DEEM APPLICATION: RECEIPT WITHIN STATUTORY PERIOD:
JUSTIFIED: Ireland: H.C.)   [1993] 2 I.R. 524
Schering/Confidential papers (EUROPEAN PATENT: INVENTIVE STEP: PROBLEM,
FORMULATION MUST NOT CONTAIN POINTERS TO SOLUTION: STATE OF THE
ART: MUST NOT BE ARTIFICIAL: EVIDENCE: COMPARATIVE TESTS: ARTIFICIAL
STATE OF THE ART, MUST NOT BE BASED ON: CONFIDENTIALITY: T516/89:
EPO)   [1992] E.P.O.R. 476; [1992] O.J. EPO 436
Schering/Dipeptides (EUROPEAN PATENT: OPPOSITION: ADMISSIBILITY: NO
ADVERSE EFFECT: MAN OF STRAW: INSUFFICIENCY: WIDE CLAIM:
PERFORMANCE ACROSS WHOLE WIDTH: INVENTIVE STEP: UNEXPECTED
RESULT: T548/91: EPO)   [1995] E.P.O.R. 327

Schick/Heat exchanger (EUROPEAN PATENT: PROCEDURE: REASONS, FUNDAMENTAL REQUIREMENT: UNITY: REASONS FOR LACK OF MUST BE GIVEN: W04/85: EPO) [1994] E.P.O.R. 437; [1987] O.J. EPO 63

Schindler Lifts Australia Pty Ltd v. Debelak (TRADE LIBEL: INJURIOUS FALSEHOOD: INDUCING BREACH OF CONTRACT: GENERAL SOLICITING OF BUSINESS: EMPLOYEE'S DUTY: INJUNCTION: DAMAGES: Australia: Fed. Ct)
89 A.L.R. 275

Schlegel Corp. & CPIO (NOTICE: INTENTION TO APPROVE: E.C. Comm.)
[1983] 3 C.M.L.R. 171; [1983] O.J. C208/7

Schlegel Corp. & CPIO (AGREEMENTS BETWEEN) (KNOW-HOW: NEGATIVE CLEARANCE: EXCLUSIVE SUPPLY: EXEMPTION: E.C. Comm.)
[1984] 2 C.M.L.R. 179; [1983] O.J. L351/20

Schmalbach-Lubeca AG v. Carnaud SA (RESTRICTIVE PRACTICES: MERGERS: CONCERTED PRACTICES: DOMINANT POSITION: E.C. Comm.)
[1988] 4 C.M.L.R. 262

Schmid/Etching process (EUROPEAN PATENT: INVENTIVE STEP: PROBLEM, DEFINITION OF: REVERSAL OF TREND: T229/85: EPO)
[1987] E.P.O.R. 279; [1987] O.J. EPO 237

Schmidt's Application (PATENT: EXTENSION: OPPOSITION: EVIDENCE: Australia: Pat. Off.) 1 I.P.R. 519

Schultz v. Butt (TRADE MARK: UNFAIR COMPETITION: COPYRIGHT: REGISTRATION: BOAT HULLS: South Africa: A.D.) 1986 (3) S.A. 1

Schupbach/Hot-sealing layer combination (EUROPEAN PATENT: INVENTIVE STEP: COMPARATIVE TESTS: T55/84: EPO) [1987] E.P.O.R. 53

Schwarz Italia/Abandonment (EUROPEAN PATENT: ABANDONMENT: ACTIVE AND PASSIVE: FEES: REIMBURSEMENT OF APPEAL FEE: J07/87: EPO)
[1989] E.P.O.R. 91; [1988] O.J. EPO 422

Schweizerische Interpreten-Gesellschaft v. X and Z (COPYRIGHT: WORKS OF ART AND LITERATURE: DISPUTES: PROTECTION: PERSONAL RIGHTS: BOOTLEGGING: UNFAIR COMPETITION: Switzerland: Fed. Ct)
[1986] E.C.C. 384; [1986] F.S.R. 500

Schweppes Ltd v. Wellingtons Ltd (COPYRIGHT: INFRINGEMENT: ORDER 14; SCHWEPPES/SCHLURPPES: WHETHER PARODY ARGUABLE DEFENCE: SUMMARY JUDGMENT: Ch.D.) [1984] F.S.R. 210

Schwiete/Concrete restoration (EUROPEAN PATENT: OPPOSITION: PROCEDURE: FRESH PRIOR ART, DOCUMENT ACKNOWLEDGED IN PATENT: INDEPENDENT OF APPLICATION: ENLARGED BOARD OF APPEAL: REFERENCE REFUSED: T198/88: EPO) [1991] E.P.O.R. 455; [1991] O.J. EPO 254

Sciaky/Surface hardening (EUROPEAN PATENT: INVENTIVE STEP: OVERLOOKED BY PIONEER: SECONDARY INDICATIONS: T12/82: EPO)
[1979–85] E.P.O.R. B395

Scott Bader/Ceramic tile adhesives (EUROPEAN PATENT: CLAIMS: CONSTRUCTION: "FOR" CLAUSE: EVIDENCE: COMPARATIVE TESTS: NOT CONTRADICTED BY COUNTER-EVIDENCE: INVENTIVE STEP: DIFFERENT PURPOSE: NOVELTY: COMBINATION OF SEPARATE TEACHINGS IN SINGLE DOCUMENT: T332/87: EPO) [1991] E.P.O.R. 575

Scott Ltd v. Nice-Pak Products Ltd (PASSING OFF: GET-UP: TUBS FOR BABY WIPES: Ch.D.) [1988] F.S.R. 125
(C.A.) [1989] 1 F.S.R. 100

Scott Paper Company/Release coating and release paper product (EUROPEAN PATENT: INVENTIVE STEP: *Ex post facto* APPROACH: PRIOR ART: DOCUMENT TO BE READ AS A WHOLE: PROCEDURE: ORAL PROCEEDINGS: RIGHT TO REPEAT ARGUMENTS: COSTS: T125/89: EPO) [1992] E.P.O.R. 41

Scott v. Watermaid (Pty) Ltd (TRADE MARK: PASSING OFF: *Mala fides*: South Africa: CPD) 1985 (1) S.A. 211

Scottish Milk Marketing Board v. Drybrough & Co. Ltd (TRADE MARK AND TRADE NAME: PASSING OFF: SCOTTISH PRIDE: INTERIM INTERDICT: Scotland: O.H.) 1985 S.L.T. 253

Screensport v. European Broadcasting Union (RESTRICTIVE PRACTICES: BROADCASTING: JOINT VENTURE SETTING UP TRANSNATIONAL TV SPORTS CHANNEL: PARTIES POTENTIAL COMPETITORS: ONE AND ONLY EXISTING COMPETITOR AT SERIOUS COMPETITIVE DISADVANTAGE: CAUGHT BY ARTICLE 85(1): EXEMPTION REFUSED: E.C. Comm.) [1992] 5 C.M.L.R. 273

Scruples Imports Pty Ltd v. Crabtree & Evelyn Pty Ltd (CONFIDENTIAL INFORMATION: CONFLICT OF LAWS: EXPERT EVIDENCE: Australia: S.C.(NSW)) 1 I.P.R. 315

SDRM's Practices (RESTRICTIVE PRACTICES: COLLECTING SOCIETIES: FOREIGN WORKS: IMPORTS: COPYRIGHT: DISCRIMINATORY PRACTICES: DOMINANT POSITION: France: Competition Commission) [1987] E.C.C. 490

SDS Biotech U.K. Ltd v. Power Agrichemicals Ltd (PASSING OFF: FUNGICIDES: USE OF MAFF NUMBERS DENOTING GOVERNMENT APPROVAL: WHETHER UNAUTHORISED USE GIVES RISE TO CAUSE OF ACTION BY AUTHORISED TRADERS: APPLICATIONS FOR SUMMARY JUDGMENT REFUSED: Ch.D.) [1995] F.S.R. 797

Sea Harvest Corp. (Pty) Ltd v. Irvin & Johnson Ltd (TRADE MARK: UNLAWFUL COMPETITION: ORDINARY OR LAUDATORY WORDS: South Africa: CPD) 1985 (2) S.A. 351

SEA ISLAND COTTON Certification Trade Marks (CERTIFICATION TRADE MARKS: RECTIFICATION: COMPETENCE TO CERTIFY: BoT) [1989] R.P.C. 87

Seabed Observatories Pty Ltd v. Tarca (COPYRIGHT: IDEAS AND CONCEPTS: FACTORS: Australia: S.C.(Qd)) 7 I.P.R. 559

Seaforth Maritine Ltd's Trade Mark (TRADE MARK: ALTERATION: T.M.Reg.) [1993] R.P.C. 72

Searle & Co. v. Commissioner of Patents (PATENT: EXTENSION OF TIME: ARTIFICIAL FOOD SWEETENER: Australia: S.C.(Vic.)) 8 I.P.R. 225

Searle & Co. v. Drug Houses of Aust. Pty Ltd (PATENT: EXTENSION: CAVEATS: PRACTICE: Australia: Fed. Ct) (1984) 53 A.L.R. 637; 3 I.P.R. 184

Searle Canada Inc. v. Novapharm Ltd (TRADE MARK: PASSING OFF: GET-UP: TABLETS: CONFUSION: INTERLOCUTORY INJUNCTION: BALANCE OF CONVENIENCE: Canada: C.A.) 30 I.P.R. 59

Searle Canada Inc. v. Novopharm Ltd (TRADE MARK: SUBSTITUTION: INDUCING SUBSTITUTION: EVIDENCE: Canada: FCTD) 33 C.P.R. (3d) 386

Searles Industrials (Pty) Ltd v. International Power Marketing Ltd (TRADE MARK: INFRINGEMENT: PASSING OFF: TEST: SALIENT FEATURES: South Africa: TPD) 1982 (4) S.A. 123
(APPEAL: TPD) 1983 (4) S.A. 163

Sears plc v. Sears, Roebuck & Co. (PASSING OFF: TRADE MARK RECTIFICATIONS AND APPLICATIONS IN REGISTRY: PRACTICE: CHOICE OF TRIBUNAL: INJUNCTION: *Res judicata*: Ch.D.) [1993] R.P.C. 385

Sears/Lockable closure (EUROPEAN PATENT: AMENDMENT AND CORRECTION: INACCURATE TECHNICAL FEATURE: INVENTIVE STEP: TECHNICAL ADVANTAGE: DERIVATION FROM CLAIMED FEATURES: T108/91: EPO) [1993] E.P.O.R. 407; [1994] O.J. EPO 228

Seasonmakers (Australia) Pty Ltd v. North Coast Woodwool Pty Ltd (PATENT: APPLICATION: OPPOSITION: ANTICIPATION: OBVIOUSNESS: Australia: Pat. Off.) 9 I.P.R. 433

Seawind Maritime Inc. v. Roumanian Bank (MAREVA INJUNCTION: THIRD PARTY INTERESTS: Q.B.D.) [1983] 1 W.L.R. 1295

Sebel & Co. Ltd v. National Article Metal Co. Pty Ltd (COPYRIGHT: DESIGN: REGISTRATION: INVALIDITY: ONUS OF PROOF: INFRINGEMENT: Australia: S.C.(NSW)) (1965) 10 FLT 224

Sebel Furniture Ltd's Application (DESIGNS: APPLICATION: WHETHER SUITE OF FURNITURE A SET OF ARTICLES: Australia: Pat. Off.) 10 I.P.R. 286

Secher/Oral proceedings (EUROPEAN PATENT: APPLICATION: PROCEDURE: ORAL HEARING: FAILURE TO REQUEST: T299/86: EPO) [1988] E.P.O.R. 204; [1988] O.J. EPO 88

Second Sight Ltd v. Novell U.K. Ltd (TRADE MARK: INFRINGEMENT: SUMMARY JUDGMENT: RECTIFICATION: NON-USE: ABANDONMENT: RESTORATION: HONEST CONCURRENT USER: USE OF ® SYMBOL: CRIMINAL OFFENCE: INQUIRY AS TO DAMAGES: Ch.D.) 32 I.P.R. 599; [1995] R.P.C. 423

Secretary of State for Defence (U.K.) v. Rheinmetall GmbH (PATENT: OPPOSITION: OBVIOUSNESS: MANNER OF NEW MANUFACTURE: AMENDMENT: WHETHER IN SUBSTANCE DISCLOSED: Australia: Pat. Off.) 11 I.P.R. 645

Secretary of State for Defence (U.K.) v. Rheinmetall GmbH, *sub nom.* United Kingdom Government (Secretary of State for Defence) v. Rheinmetall GmbH

Secretary of State For Defence (United Kingdom)/Grounds for appeal (EUROPEAN PATENT: PROCEDURE: APPEAL: ADMISSIBILITY: T22/88: EPO) [1993] E.P.O.R. 353; [1993] O.J. EPO 143

Secretary of State for Defence v. Guardian Newspapers Ltd (COPYRIGHT: OWNERSHIP OF SECRET CROWN DOCUMENT: PROTECTION OF NEWSPAPER SOURCE: C.A.) [1984] 1 All E.R. 453; [1984] Ch. 156; [1984] 2 W.L.R. 268 (H.L.) [1984] 3 W.L.R. 986

Secretary of State for the Home Department v. Central Broadcasting Ltd (COPYRIGHT: INFRINGEMENT: INTERVIEW WITH SERIAL KILLER: FILM: AUTHOR: ARRANGEMENTS FOR MAKING FILM: CONTRACT: BREACH: INTERLOCUTORY INJUNCTION SOUGHT BY HOME SECRETARY TO RESTRAIN INCLUSION OF EXTRACT IN DOCUMENTARY: BALANCE OF CONVENIENCE: WHETHER PUBLIC INTEREST REQUIRED BROADCAST TO BE RESTRAINED: RELEVANCE OF FREEDOM OF SPEECH: INJUNCTION REFUSED: APPEAL DISMISSED: Ch.D.: C.A.) [1993] E.M.L.R. 253

Secton Pty Ltd (t/a BWN Industries) v. Delawood Pty Ltd (CONFIDENTIAL INFORMATION: TRADE SECRETS: WHETHER SPECULATIVE CONCEPTS MAY QUALIFY AS TRADE SECRETS: NOVELTY: OBVIOUSNESS: VALUE: CLARITY OF DESCRIPTION OF ALLEGED TRADE SECRETS IN PARTICULARS: Australia: S.C.(Vic.)) 21 I.P.R. 136

Sedlbauer/Holding device (EUROPEAN PATENT: INVENTIVE STEP: COLLOCATION: COMBINATION OF CITATIONS: OPPOSITION: PROCEDURE: WITHDRAWAL OF OPPONENT, CONTINUATION OF PROCEEDINGS: T629/90: EPO) [1993] E.P.O.R. 147; [1992] O.J. EPO 654

See-Shell/Bloodflow (EUROPEAN PATENT: PATENTABILITY: METHOD OF SURGERY: FEES: REIMBURSEMENT OF APPEAL FEE: T182/90: EPO) [1994] E.P.O.R. 320; [1994] O.J. EPO 641

Seet Chuan Seng v. Tee Yih Jia Foods Manufacturing Pte Ltd (TRADE MARK: PASSING OFF: SIMILAR NAME AND MARK: DISTINCTIVENESS AND LIKELIHOOD OF DECEPTION: GOODS IN DIRECT COMPETITION: Malaysia: S.C.) [1994] 2 M.L.J. 770

Sefton's Application (TRADE MARK: RESTORATION: APPLICATION MORE THAN 12 MONTHS AFTER LAPSE: RIGHTS OF OTHER APPLICANTS: MARK RESTORED: Australia: Pat. Off.)   11 I.P.R. 424

Sega Enterprises Ltd v. Alca Electronics (COPYRIGHT: INFRINGEMENT: ANTON PILLER PRACTICE: DISCOVERY: C.A.)   [1982] F.S.R. 516

Sega Enterprises Ltd v. Richards (COPYRIGHT: COMPUTER PROGRAM: INTERLOCUTORY RELIEF: Ch.D.)   [1983] F.S.R. 73

Seiko & Toshiba/Contents of decision (EUROPEAN PATENT: APPEAL: PROCEDURE: INTERLOCUTORY REVISION: DECISION, WHAT CONSTITUTES: T99/88: EPO)   [1990] E.P.O.R. 568

Selas Corp. of America v. Electric Furnace Co. (PATENT: VALIDITY: INUTILITY: South Africa: A.D.)   1983 (1) S.A. 1043

Select Personnel Pty Ltd v. Morgan & Banks Pty Ltd (PASSING OFF: USE OF SAME ORDINARY ENGLISH WORD IN BUSINESS NAME: PRIMA FACIE DISTINCTIVE BY MANNER OF USE: Australia: S.C.(NSW))   12 I.P.R. 167

Selectrode Industries Inc. v. Selectrode Pty Ltd (PASSING OFF: MISLEADING CONDUCT: OVERSEAS SUPPLIER OF WELDING CONSUMABLES: PRIVATE LABEL ARRANGEMENT: AUSTRALIAN PRODUCT: DIFFERENT LEVELS OF SUPPLY: DECEPTION: INTERLOCUTORY INJUNCTION: DELAY: BALANCE OF CONVENIENCE: ADEQUACY OF DAMAGES: Australia: Fed. Ct)   30 I.P.R. 399

Selero (Pty) Ltd v. Chauvier (PATENT: INFRINGEMENT: SECURITY FOR COSTS: South Africa: TPD)   1982 (3) S.A. 519
(A.D.) 1984 (1) S.A. 128

Selero (Pty) Ltd v. Mostert (PATENT: APPLICATION: CONVERSION TO PATENT OF ADDITION: REGISTRAR'S POWER TO AUTHORISE: South Africa: TPD)   1989 (1) S.A. 41

Selskar Pty Ltd's Application (TRADE MARK: OPPOSITION: HONEST CONCURRENT USE: CONFLICTING EVIDENCE: Australia: AIPO)   27 I.P.R. 352

Selson (Europe) Pty Ltd v. Selson (Australasia) Pty Ltd (TRADE MARK: OPPOSITION: CONFUSION: SIMILAR GOODS: Australia: Pat. Off.)   4 I.P.R. 60

Semiconductor Products Directive, *sub nom.* Community Semiconductor Products Directive

Sent v. Jet Corp. of Australia Pty Ltd (TRADE PRACTICES: CAUSING A MISREPRESENTATION: DIRECTORS: Australia: Fed. Ct)   160 C.L.R. 540; 4 I.P.R. 145

Sent v. Jet Corp. of Australia Pty Ltd (TRADE PRACTICES: LEAVE TO AMEND STATEMENT OF CLAIM: COMPENSATORY RELIEF: DAMAGES: TIME LIMITATION: Australia: H.C.)   6 I.P.R. 417

Sepa Waste Water Treatment Pty Ltd v. JMT Welding Pty Ltd (PRACTICE: EVIDENCE: PATENT AGENTS' PRIVILEGE: ADVICE ON DESIGNS INFRINGEMENT: Australia: S.C.(NSW))   7 I.P.R. 52

SEPTRIN Trade Mark, *sub nom.* R. v. Secretary of State for Social Services, ex p. Wellcome Foundation

Series 5 Software Ltd v. Philip Clarke (CONFIDENTIAL INFORMATION: COMPUTER SOURCE CODES: SOLICITATION OF CUSTOMERS: INTERLOCUTORY RELIEF: DELAY: INTERLOCUTORY INJUNCTIONS: PRINCIPLES: HISTORICAL SURVEY OF *American Cyanamid* CASES: Ch.D)   [1996] F.S.R. 273

Service Station Association Ltd v. Berg Bennett & Associates Pty Ltd (TRADE PRACTICES: RIVAL TRADE PUBLICATIONS: WHETHER MISLEADING OR DECEPTIVE CONDUCT: Australia: Fed. Ct)   27 I.P.R. 23

Servicemaster Ltd (Franchise Agreements of) (RESTRICTIVE PRACTICES: FRANCHISING: INTENTION TO APPROVE: E.C. Comm.)   [1988] 4 C.M.L.R. 895

Servicemaster Ltd (Franchise Agreements of) (RESTRICTIVE PRACTICES: FRANCHISING: SERVICES: SERVICE FRANCHISES TREATED IN SAME WAY AS DISTRIBUTION AGREEMENTS: PROTECTION OF KNOW-HOW OUTSIDE ARTICLE 85(1): TERRITORIAL PROTECTION CAUGHT: INTERSTATE TRADE: INTRA-BRAND COMPETITION: INDIVIDUAL EXEMPTION GRANTED: E.C. Comm.) [1989] 4 C.M.L.R. 581

Serwane II/Withdrawal of opposition (EUROPEAN PATENT: APPEAL BY UNSUCCESSFUL OPPONENT: OPPOSITION WITHDRAWN: IMMEDIATE TERMINATION OF PROCEEDINGS: G08/93: T148/89: EPO)
[1995] E.P.O.R. 271; [1994] O.J. EPO 887

Settef SpA v. Riv-Oland Marble Co. (Vic.) Pty Ltd (TRADE MARKS: INFRINGEMENT: PROPRIETORSHIP OF MARK: WHETHER DISTINCTIVE, DECEPTIVE AND CONFUSING: RECTIFICATION OF REGISTER: NON-USE: USE IN GOOD FAITH: ABANDONMENT: Australia: S.C.(Vic.)) 10 I.P.R. 402

Sevcon Ltd v. Lucas CAV Ltd (PATENT: INFRINGEMENT: CAUSE OF ACTION: INFRINGEMENT COMMITTED AFTER PUBLICATION BUT BEFORE SEALING: TIME LIMITATION: C.A.) [1985] F.S.R. 545
(H.L.) [1986] F.S.R. 338; [1986] R.P.C. 609; [1986] 2 All E.R. 104; [1986] 1 W.L.R. 462

Seven Measures (EUROPEAN PATENT: NOTICE CONCERNING ACCELERATED PROSECUTION OF EUROPEAN PATENT APPLICATIONS: AMENDMENT AND CORRECTION: APPLICATION PROCEDURE—EXPEDITION: EPO)
[1992] E.P.O.R. 362

Seven-up Co. v. Bubble Up Co. Ltd (TRADE MARK: APPLICATION: APPEAL AGAINST DECISION OF REGISTRAR: DISTINCTIVENESS: DECEPTION OR CONFUSION: DECEPTIVELY SIMILAR MARKS: Australia: S.C.(Vic.)) 9 I.P.R. 259

Sew Hoy & Sons Ltd v. Skill Print Pty Ltd (TRADE MARKS: APPLICATION FOR REMOVAL FROM REGISTER: OPPOSITION: "PERSON AGGRIEVED": PRIMA FACIE CASE OF NON-USE: SUFFICIENCY OF EVIDENCE: Australia: Pat. Off.)
17 I.P.R. 361

SGS/Unacceptable generalisation (EUROPEAN PATENT: AMENDMENT AND CORRECTION: GENERALISATION: ENLARGED BOARD OF APPEAL: REFERENCE REFUSED: PRECEDENT: ISOLATED EARLIER DECISION: T248/88: EPO)
[1990] E.P.O.R. 274

Shacklady v. Atkins (COPYRIGHT: SUBSISTENCE: DESIGN: REPRODUCTION: CORRESPONDING DESIGNS: WHETHER INFRINGEMENT OF COPYRIGHT: DESIGN OF YACHT, WHETHER REGISTRABLE: Australia: Fed. Ct)
30 I.P.R. 387

SHAMROCK Trade Mark (TRADE MARK: INFRINGEMENT: NATIONAL SYMBOL: Germany: S.C.) [1985] A.C. 337; [1984] 3 All E.R. 601; [1986] F.S.R. 271

Shanton Apparel Ltd v. Thornton Hall Manufacturing Ltd, *sub nom.* Thornton Hall Manufacturing Ltd v. Shanton Apparel Ltd (COPYRIGHT: ARTISTIC WORKS: ORIGINALITY: CAUSAL CONNECTION: INFRINGEMENT: DAMAGES: TIME FOR MAKING ELECTION BETWEEN ACCOUNT OF PROFITS OR DAMAGES: TRIAL LIMITED TO LIABILITY: INCIDENTAL FINDINGS OF "FLAGRANCY": WHETHER PRE-DETERMINATION OR BIAS FOR SUBSEQUENT DAMAGES TRIAL: New Zealand: C.A.) 17 I.P.R. 311

Shea/Denmark—PCT (EUROPEAN PATENT: PCT APPLICATION: PROCEDURE: STATE BECOMING PARTY TO EPC SUBSEQUENT TO PCT: EPO ACT WHERE APPLICANT MISLED: BOARD OF APPEAL: INVITATION TO PRESIDENT OF EPO: OBSERVATIONS BY PRESIDENT: J30/90: EPO)
[1992] E.P.O.R. 564; [1992] O.J. EPO 516

Shell International Petroleum Co. Ltd's Application (TRADE MARK: APPLICATION: OPPOSITION: LIKELIHOOD OF DECEPTION AND CONFUSION: VISUAL AND AURAL DIFFERENCES: RELEVANCE OF IMPERFECT RECOLLECTION: Australia: Pat. Off.)   5 I.P.R. 393

Shell Internationale Research Maatschappij (PATENTS: APPLICATION: OPPOSITION: NOVELTY: AMENDED SPECIFICATION: METHOD CLAIM: Australia: Pat. Off.)
                                                                                 4 I.P.R. 439

Shell/Amino-triazine (EUROPEAN PATENT: NOVELTY: COMBINATION OF SEPARATE TEACHINGS IN SINGLE DOCUMENT: OPPOSITION: PROCEDURE: FRESH EVIDENCE ON APPEAL, REFUSED: OPPOSITION DIVISION: DUTY TO CONSIDER ALL OBJECTIONS: T137/90: EPO)   [1991] E.P.O.R. 381

Shell/Aryloxybenzaldehydes (EUROPEAN PATENT: INVENTIVE STEP: COMPARATIVE TESTS: T20/81: EPO)   [1979–85] E.P.O.R. B335; [1982] O.J. EPO 217

Shell/Changed composition of division (EUROPEAN PATENT: OPPOSITION: PROCEDURE: RULE 58(4) COMMUNICATION: WRITTEN CONFIRMATION SIGNED BY DIFFERENT MEMBERS: FEES: REIMBURSEMENT OF APPEAL FEE: T390/86: EPO)   [1989] E.P.O.R. 162; [1989] O.J. EPO 30

Shell/Gasification of solid fuel (EUROPEAN PATENT: APPEAL: PROCEDURE: APPEALABLE DECISION, REQUIREMENTS: RE-ESTABLISHMENT OF RIGHTS: APPEAL TREATED AS APPLICATION FOR: FEES: REIMBURSEMENT OF APPEAL FEE: EPO ACT WHERE APPLICANT MISLED: T522/88: EPO)
                                                                                 [1990] E.P.O.R. 237

Shell/Lead alloys (EUROPEAN PATENT: AMENDMENT AND CORRECTION: NOVELTY TEST: INTERMEDIATE GENERALISATION: T201/83: EPO)
                                   [1979–85] E.P.O.R. C905: [1984] O.J. EPO 481

Shell/Polysaccharide solutions (EUROPEAN PATENT: PRIORITY: FRESH QUANTITATIVE RESTRICTION IN CLAIM 1; T581/89: EPO)
                                                                                 [1992] E.P.O.R. 170

Shell/Removal of acid gases (EUROPEAN PATENT: INVENTIVE STEP: COMBINATION OF CHEMICAL ENGINEERING STEPS: COMBINATION OF CITATIONS: PRIOR ART: AMBIT: T119/86: EPO)   [1988] E.P.O.R. 290

Shell/Sinking tubular element (EUROPEAN PATENT: INVENTIVE STEP: RECOGNITION OF DISADVANTAGES OF KNOWN METHOD: SKILLED PERSON: POWERS OF GENERALISATION: T127/82: EPO)   [1979–85] E.P.O.R. B587

Shell/Water-thinnable binder (EUROPEAN PATENT: APPLICATION: PROCEDURE: ADJOURNMENT OF ORAL HEARING: INVENTIVE STEP: SURPRISING EFFECT: T44/85: EPO)   [1986] E.P.O.R. 258

Shelley Films Ltd v. Rex Features Ltd (COPYRIGHT: INFRINGEMENT: INTERLOCUTORY INJUNCTION: PHOTOGRAPH OF FILM COSTUMES, PROSTHESES AND SET: SUBSISTENCE OF COPYRIGHT: BREACH OF CONFIDENCE: INJUNCTION: Ch.D.)   [1994] E.M.L.R. 134

Shelley v. Cunane (PERFORMERS' PROTECTION ACTS: BOOTLEGGING: STRIKING OUT: Ch.D.)   [1983] F.S.R. 390

Shelltrie Distribution Sàrl v. SNTF (COPYRIGHT: FILMS: France)
                                         [1984] E.C.C. 479; [1985] F.S.R. 26

Shiley Inc.'s Patent (PATENT: LICENCE OF RIGHT: SURGICAL DEVICE: ROYALTY: TRADE LIBEL CLAUSE: Pat. Ct)   [1988] R.P.C. 97

Shimano Industrial Co. Ltd v. Silstar Australia Pty Ltd (DESIGNS: INFRINGEMENT: COMMON FEATURES: RECTIFICATION OF REGISTER: CONJUNCTION OF OLD FEATURES: Australia: Fed. Ct)   20 I.P.R. 451

Shippam (C.) Ltd v. Princes-Buitoni Ltd (COPYRIGHT: INFRINGEMENT: PLEADINGS: REQUIREMENTS OF STATEMENTS OF CLAIM: COSTS: Ch.D.)
                                                                                 [1983] F.S.R. 427

Shoketsu Kinzoku Kogyu KK's Patent (PATENT: VALIDITY: NOT LEGITIMATE TO TAKE FEATURES OF CLAIMED COMBINATION ONE AT A TIME IN LIGHT OF KNOWLEDGE OF THE INVENTION: EVIDENCE OF HAPPENINGS AT PRIORITY DATE: Pat. Ct) [1992] F.S.R. 184

Shop-Vac Corporations Application (TRADE MARKS: WITHDRAWAL OF ACCEPTANCE FOR REGISTRATION: "ACCEPTANCE IN ERROR": EXAMINER'S IGNORANCE OF RELEVANT DICTIONARY DEFINITION: DESCRIPTIVE OF SPECIFIED GOODS: ACCEPTANCE WITHDRAWN: Australia: Pat. Off.)
18 I.P.R. 523

Shoshana Pty Ltd v. 10th Cantanae Pty Ltd, *sub nom.* 10th Cantanae Pty Ltd v. Shoshana Pty Ltd

Shotover Gorge Jet Boats Ltd v. Marine Enterprises Ltd (PASSING OFF: TRADE MARK DESCRIPTIVE OF SERVICE: SECONDARY MEANING: New Zealand: H.C.)
[1984] 2 N.Z.L.R. 154; 4 I.P.R. 516

Shri Prem Singh v. Ceeam Auto Industries (COPYRIGHT: INFRINGEMENT: GET-UP: PIRACY: LACK OF EQUITY: India: H.C.) (1990) 15 I.P.L.R. 248

Sianel Pedwar Cymru, *ex p.* (PERFORMERS' RIGHTS: APPLICATION TO TRIBUNAL FOR CONSENT ON BEHALF OF PERFORMERS THE IDENTITY OR WHEREABOUTS OF WHOM CANNOT BE ASCERTAINED BY REASONABLE INQUIRY: Cprt Trib.) [1993] E.M.L.R. 251

Sibex Construction (S.A.) (Pty) Ltd v. Injectaseal C.C. (CONFIDENTIAL INFORMATION: UNLAWFUL COMPETITION: EX-EMPLOYEE'S: PRICE LIST: DUTY OF FIDELITY: DIRECTORS: South Africa: TPD) (1988) (2) S.A. 54

Siddons Pty Ltd v. Stanley Works Pty Ltd (TRADE PRACTICES: MISLEADING OR DECEPTIVE CONDUCT: REPRESENTATION AS TO ORIGIN: "MADE IN AUSTRALIA": USE OF "AUSTRALIA" ON GOODS: PASSING OFF: MEANING CONVEYED AS TO HISTORY AND ORIGIN OF GOODS: NATURE OF AN EFFECT ON TARGET AUDIENCE: Australia: Fed. Ct)
99 A.L.R. 497; 18 I.P.R. 630; 20 I.P.R. 1

SIDEWINDER Trade Mark (TRADE MARK: OPPOSITION: PROPRIETORSHIP: OVERSEAS PROPRIETORS' REPUTATION: BoT) [1988] R.P.C. 261

Sidharth Wheels Pvt. Ltd v. Bedrock Ltd (TRADE MARK: THREATS: DECLARATION: INTERLOCUTORY INJUNCTION: NATURE: India: H.C.)
(1988) 12 I.P.L.R. 146

Siemens AG's Application (TRADE MARK: TELETEX: REGISTRATION: Australia: Pat. Off.) 1 I.P.R. 1

Siemens/Character form (EUROPEAN PATENT: PATENTABILITY: COMPUTER-RELATED INVENTIONS: TECHNICAL EFFECT: T158/88: EPO)
[1992] E.P.O.R. 69; [1991] O.J. EPO 566

Siemens/Clarity of claim (EUROPEAN PATENT: CLAIMS: FAIR BASIS: T132/82: EPO) [1979–85] E.P.O.R. B602

Siemens/Data bank system (EUROPEAN PATENT: APPEAL: PROCEDURE: OBJECTION BY BOARD, FAILURE TO RESPOND TO: SUFFICIENCY: INVENTION, NATURE OF: T107/83: EPO) [1986] E.P.O.R. 323

Siemens/Diagnostic method (EUROPEAN PATENT: PATENTABILITY: DIAGNOSTIC METHOD: T83/87: EPO) [1988] E.P.O.R. 365

Siemens/Electrode slide (EUROPEAN PATENT: CLAIMS: PRIOR ART: PREAMBLE: OBJECTIVE PRIOR ART, SHOULD BE BASED ON: T6/81: EPO)
[1979–85] E.P.O.R. B294; [1982] O.J. EPO 183

Siemens/Electromedical device (EUROPEAN PATENT: CLAIMS: PREAMBLE: FICTITIOUS STATE OF THE ART: T21/81: EPO) [1979–85] E.P.O.R. B409

Siemens/Filing priority documents (EUROPEAN PATENT: APPLICATION: PROCEDURE: FILING OF PRIORITY DOCUMENTS, DEFICIENCY IN: PATENTABILITY: INDUSTRIAL APPLICATION: PRIORITY: TIME FOR FILING OF PRIORITY DOCUMENT: FEES: REIMBURSEMENT OF APPEAL FEE AND RE-ESTABLISHMENT FEE: J01/80: EPO)
[1979–85] E.P.O.R. A15; [1980] O.J. EPO 289

Siemens/Flow measurement (EUROPEAN PATENT: PATENTABILITY: THERAPY: T245/87: EPO)   [1989] E.P.O.R. 241; [1989] O.J. EPO 171

Siemens/Insulin infusion device (EUROPEAN PATENT: AMENDMENT AND CORRECTION: DISCREPANCY BETWEEN PREAMBLE AND CHARACTERISING PART OF CLAIM: INVENTIVE STEP: TECHNICAL ADVANTAGE: OPPOSITION: PROCEDURE: AMENDMENT OF CLAIM ON APPEAL: T191/84: EPO)
[1986] E.P.O.R. 318

Siemens/Low-tension switch (EUROPEAN PATENT: AMENDMENT AND CORRECTION: IMPLICIT SIGNIFICANCE: INVENTIVE STEP: FEATURE DISREGARDED UNLESS CONTRIBUTING TO SOLUTION OF PROBLEM: DISCLOSURE: SIGNIFICANCE OF CHARACTERISING FEATURE, OBLIGATION TO SPECIFY: T37/82: EPO)   [1979–85] E.P.O.R. B437; [1984] O.J. EPO 71

Siemens/Pacemaker (EUROPEAN PATENT: AMENDMENT AND CORRECTION: CATEGORY OF CLAIM: CLAIMS: CONSTRUCTION: CONCEALED APPARATUS CLAIM: PATENTABILITY: THERAPY: T426/89: EPO)
[1992] E.P.O.R. 149; [1992] O.J. EPO 172

Siemens/Party adversely affected by a decision (EUROPEAN PATENT: APPEAL: PROCEDURE: ADMISSIBILITY OF APPEAL: RE-ESTABLISHMENT OF RIGHTS: PRIORITY: THIRD PARTY RIGHTS: J05/79: EPO)
[1979–85] E.P.O.R. A7; [1980] O.J. EPO 71

Siemens/Priority claim (EUROPEAN PATENT: APPLICATION: PROCEDURE: PRIORITY CLAIM: FEES: REIMBURSEMENT OF APPEAL FEE AND RE-ESTABLISHMENT FEE: J02/80: EPO)   [1979–85] E.P.O.R. A19

Siemens/Sensor (EUROPEAN PATENT: PCT APPLICATION: EPO PHASE: AMENDED TEXT: OBJECTION UNDER ARTICLE 123(2) BY EXAMINING DIVISION: APPEAL TO BOARD: ADDITIONAL OBJECTION: REFERRAL TO ENLARGED BOARD: T933/92: EPO)   [1995] E.P.O.R. 66

Siemens/Stimulating electrode (EUROPEAN PATENT: OPPOSITION: PROCEDURE: NOTICE OF OPPOSITION: REQUIREMENTS OF: T448/89: EPO)
[1992] E.P.O.R. 540; [1992] O.J. EPO 361

Siemens/Unity (EUROPEAN PATENT: OPPOSITION: PROCEDURE: AMENDMENT OF CLAIMS ON APPEAL, REQUIREMENT FOR UNITY: UNITY: AMENDMENT OF CLAIMS IN OPPOSITION PROCEEDINGS: PURPOSE OF REQUIREMENT: CONVENTIONS: RULES UNDER, EFFECT OF: G01/91: EPO)
[1992] E.P.O.R. 356; [1992] O.J. EPO 253

Sigma KK v. Olympic Amusements Pty Ltd (TRADE MARK: APPLICATION: OPPOSITION: PROPRIETORSHIP: WHETHER SUFFICIENT ACTIVITY IN AUSTRALIA TO ESTABLISH PROPRIETORSHIP: Australia: AIPO)   31 I.P.R. 99

Sigma/Classifying areas (EUROPEAN PATENT: APPLICATION: PROCEDURE: FAIRNESS, REQUIREMENT FOR: OBSERVATIONS BY APPLICANT: CLAIMS: ONE PART V. TWO PART: GUIDELINES FOR EXAMINATION: NOT BINDING: INVENTIVE STEP: KNOWN PRINCIPLE, APPLICATION OF: T162/82: EPO)
[1987] E.P.O.R. 375; [1987] O.J. EPO 533

Silicon Graphics Inc. v. Indigo Graphic Systems (U.K.) Ltd (TRADE MARK: INFRINGEMENT: PASSING OFF: INTERLOCUTORY INJUNCTION: DIGITAL PRINTING PRESS: BALANCE OF CONVENIENCE: INJUNCTION REFUSED: COSTS: Ch.D.)   [1994] F.S.R. 403

Sillitoe v. McGraw-Hill Book Co. (U.K.) Ltd (COPYRIGHT: INFRINGEMENT: STUDY
NOTES FOR STUDENTS: WHETHER SUBSTANTIAL REPRODUCTION: FAIR
DEALING: KNOWLEDGE: SUFFICIENT ACKNOWLEDGEMENT: ADAPTATIONS:
INJUNCTIONS: DAMAGES: Ch.D.) [1983] F.S.R. 545
Silly Wizard Ltd v. Shaughnessy (COPYRIGHT: SOUND RECORDINGS: PERFORMERS'
PROTECTION: RIGHT OF ACTION: REMEDIES: INJUNCTION: Scotland:
O.H.) [1984] E.C.C. 1; [1984] F.S.R. 163
Silver Crystal Trading (Pty) Ltd v. Namibia Diamond Corp. (TRADE MARK:
UNLAWFUL COMPETITION: South Africa: D&CLD) 1983 (4) S.A. 884
Silver Seiko Co. Ltd v. Kaisha (TRADE MARK: APPLICATION: APPEAL: PRACTICE:
South Africa: TPD) 1982 (1) S.A. 632
Silver Systems/Further processing (EUROPEAN PATENT: TIME LIMITS: PERIOD OF
GRACE FOR FILING REQUEST FOR EXAMINATION: FURTHER PROCESSING
(NO): J47/92: EPO) [1995] E.P.O.R. 495; [1995] O.J. EPO 180
Silvercrest Sales Ltd v. Gainsborough Printing Co. Ltd (CONFIDENTIAL
INFORMATION: SIMPLE SECRET: NO CONTRACT NECESSARY:
CIRCUMSTANCES OF DISCLOSURE: NEGOTIATIONS: INTERLOCUTORY
INJUNCTION: New Zealand: H.C.) 7 I.P.R. 123
Silvertone Records Ltd v. Mountfield (CONTRACT: POP GROUP: RECORDING
AGREEMENT AND PUBLISHING AGREEMENT: RESTRAINT OF TRADE:
WHETHER UNREASONABLE: ESTOPPEL: WAIVER OF OBJECTION: WHETHER
AGREEMENTS SEVERABLE: Q.B.D.) [1993] E.M.L.R. 152
Silvertone Records Ltd v. Mountfield, *sub nom.* Zomba Music Publishers Ltd v.
Mountfield
Simac SpA Macchine Alimentari's Application (TRADE MARK: OPPOSITION:
DECEPTIVE SIMILARITY: SAME GOODS: USE: EVIDENCE: RELEVANT DATES:
Australia: Pat. Off.) 10 I.P.R. 81
Simla Chemicals Pvt. Ltd v. MJSP Products (India) (TRADE MARK: OPPOSITION:
VIMCO/SIMCO: India: T.M.Reg.) (1977) 1 I.P.L.R. 191
Simplicity Funerals Ltd v. Simplicity Funerals Pty Ltd (TRADE PRACTICES:
PRACTICE: PROCEDURE: PERPETUAL STAY: MOTION: PREVIOUS
UNSUCCESSFUL PROCEEDINGS IN SUPREME COURT: DUPLICATION OF
PROCEEDINGS: Australia: Fed. Ct) 76 A.L.R. 410; 10 I.P.R. 369
Simtech Advanced Training and Simulation Systems Ltd v. Jasmin Simtec Ltd
(CONFIDENTIAL INFORMATION: CONTRACT: COLLABORATION AGREEMENT:
PARTIALLY AGREED CONTRACT: INTERLOCUTORY RELIEF: SPECIFIC
PERFORMANCE: INTERLOCUTORY PROCEEDINGS: BALANCE OF JUSTICE:
Ch.D.) [1995] F.S.R. 475
Sinclair/Unity (EUROPEAN PATENT: UNITY: TIME OF DETERMINATION: T101/88:
EPO) [1990] E.P.O.R. 489
Singapore Broadcasting Corp. v. The Performing Right Society Ltd (COPYRIGHT:
LICENCE SCHEME IN RESPECT OF THE BROADCASTING OF MUSICAL WORKS:
REASONABLENESS: AMOUNT OF ROYALTIES TO BE PAID BY NATIONAL
BROADCASTER: COSTS: INTEREST: Singapore: Cprt. Trib.)
[1991] F.S.R. 573; 21 I.P.R. 595
Site Microsurgical Systems/Ophthalmic microsurgical system (EUROPEAN PATENT:
APPLICATION: PROCEDURE: DISCRETION TO ALLOW AMENDMENTS:
AMENDMENT AND CORRECTION: AFTER RULE 51(4) COMMUNICATION:
T375/90: EPO) [1993] E.P.O.R. 588
Sitma/Packaging machine (EUROPEAN PATENT: APPLICATION: PROCEDURE:
ABSTRACT OF SPECIFICATION: SKILLED PERSON: ORIENTED TOWARDS
PRACTICALITIES: T160/83: EPO) [1979–85] E.P.O.R. C860

Sizzler Restaurants International Inc. v. Sabra International Pty Ltd (TRADE MARKS: APPLICATION: OPPOSITION: Australia: Pat. Off.)   20 I.P.R. 331

Skedeleski v. Underwood (DESIGNS: VALIDITY: NEW OR ORIGINAL: WHETHER PREVIOUS USE OF ARTISTIC WORK FROM WHICH IT IS DERIVED MAY VALIDATE REGISTRATION DESPITE ABSENCE OF NEWNESS OR ORIGINALITY: Australia: Fed. Ct)   17 I.P.R. 161

SKF/Correction of mistakes (Languages) (EUROPEAN PATENT: APPLICATION: PROCEDURE: AMENDMENT AND CORRECTION: APPLICANT'S NAME: LANGUAGE OF PROCEEDINGS: PROFESSIONAL REPRESENTATIVES: AUTHORISATION: J07/80: EPO)
[1979–85] E.P.O.R. A36; [1981] O.J. EPO 137

SKF/Prevention of fretting corrosion (EUROPEAN PATENT: COMMON GENERAL KNOWLEDGE: RELEVANT FIELD: SUFFICIENCY: FUNCTIONAL DEFINITIONS: T111/89: EPO)   [1992] E.P.O.R. 376

SKM SA v. Wagner Spraytech (U.K.) Ltd (PATENT: INFRINGEMENT: PRACTICE: DISCOVERY: C.A.)   [1982] R.P.C. 497

Sky Channel (No. 2) (COPYRIGHT: CABLE TV: INTERPRETATION OF DECODING SATELLITE SIGNALS: ROYALTY: Austria: S.C.)   [1987] E.C.C. 449

Slaney's Application (TRADE MARK: APPLICATION: LIKELIHOOD OF DECEPTION: DESCRIPTIVE MARK: CONTRARY TO LAW: Australia: Pat. Off.)   6 I.P.R. 307

Slazengers Ltd v. Seaspeed Ferries International Ltd (PRACTICE: COSTS: SECURITY FOR COSTS: PLAINTIFF RESIDENT OUT OF JURISDICTION: Comm. Ct.)
[1987] 2 All E.R. 905
(C.A.) [1987] 3 All E.R. 967

SLOPHYLLIN Trade Mark (TRADE MARK: APPLICATION: OPPOSITION: SLOW RELEASE PHARMACEUTICAL: DISTINCTIVENESS: T.M.Reg.)
[1984] R.P.C. 39

Slow Indicator v. Monitoring Systems Ltd (PATENT: PRACTICE: TRANSFER FROM HIGH COURT TO PATENTS COUNTY COURT: APPLICATION REFUSED: Pat. Ct)   [1995] F.S.R. 867

Smale v. North Sales Ltd (PATENTS: REVOCATION: INFRINGEMENT: YACHT SALES: REVOCATION: PRIOR PUBLICATION AND OBVIOUSNESS: WHETHER INVENTION WAS NEW: LACK OF INVENTIVE STEP: New Zealand: H.C.)
[1991] 3 N.Z.L.R. 19

Smalls Application (TRADE MARKS: DESCRIPTIVE: DIRECT REFERENCE TO CHARACTER OF SERVICES: NO EVIDENCE TO SHOW ACQUIRED DISTINCTIVENESS NOT CAPABLE OF BECOMING DISTINCTIVE: Australia: Pat. Off.)   14 I.P.R. 82

Small & Associates Pty Ltd v. Robert Half Incorporated (TRADE MARK: REGISTRATION: REMOVAL: NON-USE: Australia: AIPO)   22 I.P.R. 600

Smith/Title of invention (EUROPEAN PATENT: OPPOSITION: PROCEDURE: IDENTIFICATION OF CONTESTED PATENT: T317/86: EPO)
[1989] E.P.O.R. 415; [1989] O.J. EPO 378

Smith & Nephew Plastics (Australia) Pty Ltd v. Sweetheart Holding Corp. (TRADE MARK: INFRINGEMENT: IMPORTATION: Australia: S.C.(Vic.))   8 I.P.R. 285

Smith (J.) & Nephew Ltd v. 3M United Kingdom plc (PATENT: INFRINGEMENT: INTERLOCUTORY RELIEF: WHETHER SERIOUS ISSUE TO BE TRIED: TRADE LIBEL: JUSTIFICATION: C.A.)   [1983] R.P.C. 92

Smith Kline & French Laboratories (Australia) Ltd v. Secretary, Department of Community Services and Health (PRACTICE: USUAL UNDERTAKING AS TO DAMAGES: WHETHER A NON-PARTY TO LITIGATION MAY BE A PARTY ADVERSELY AFFECTED BY AN INTERLOCUTORY INJUNCTION: SUBSEQUENT EXTENT OF UNDERTAKING TO INCLUDE SUCH PARTY: Australia: Fed. Ct)
16 I.P.R. 281

Smith Kline & French Laboratories (Australia) Ltd v. Secretary, Department of Community Services & Health (CONFIDENTIAL INFORMATION: DATA SUPPLIED FOR MARKETING APPROVAL: USE FOR ANOTHER APPLICATION: WHETHER REGULATORY AUTHORITY SUBJECT TO DUTY OF CONFIDENTIALITY: PUBLIC INTEREST DEFENCE: PATENT LICENSING: EXERCISE OF DUTIES BY LICENSING AUTHORITY: CONSTITUTIONAL LAW: Australia: Fed. Ct)   17 I.P.R. 545; 20 I.P.R. 643; [1990] F.S.R. 617

Smith Kline & French Laboratories Ltd's (Bavin's) Patent (PATENT: AMENDMENT: DISCRETION: INVALIDITY: PRACTICE: OPPOSITION: STRIKING OUT: C.-G.)   [1988] R.P.C. 224

Smith Kline & French Laboratories Ltd's (Cimetidine) Patents (PATENT: LICENCE OF RIGHT: LICENCE TO IMPORT: PRACTICE: Pat. Ct):   [1988] R.P.C. 148 (REASONABLE REMUNERATION: APPROACHES TO ASSESSMENT: TERMS OF LICENCE: WHETHER EXPORT AN INFRINGEMENT: IMPORTATION FROM OUTSIDE EEC: ARTICLES 30, 36 AND 177: ROYALTY SET AT 45 PER CENT: APPEAL: REFERENCES TO ECJ: Pat. Ct: C.A.)   [1990] R.P.C. 203

Smith Kline & French Laboratories Ltd's Cimetidine Trade Mark (TRADE MARK: APPLICATION: OPPOSITION: PHARMACEUTICAL: COLOURED TABLETS: WHETHER TRADE MARK: APPLICATION REFUSED: Ch.D.) [1991] R.P.C. 17

Smith Kline & French Laboratories Ltd v. Attorney-General (PATENT: LICENCE OF RIGHT: CIMETIDINE: BREACH OF CONFIDENCE: CONFIDENTIAL INFORMATION SUPPLIED TO HEALTH DEPARTMENT BY PHARMACEUTICAL MANUFACTURER: USE OF INFORMATION TO GRANT CONSENT TO RIVAL GENERIC DRUG: USE OF INFORMATION INTERNAL TO DEPARTMENT: USE NOT UNAUTHORISED NOR DETRIMENTAL TO PLAINTIFF'S: SUPPLY OF SAMPLE MEDICINE TO HEALTH DEPARTMENT IN SUPPORT OF APPLICATION FOR CONSENT TO DISTRIBUTE GENERIC DRUG PRIOR TO EXPIRY OF PATENT: NO INFRINGEMENT: New Zealand: H.C.)   16 I.P.R. 339; [1989] 1 F.S.R. 418

Smith Kline & French Laboratories Ltd v. Attorney-General (PATENT: INFRINGEMENT: EXPIRY: IMPORTATION: SUBMISSION TO GOVERNMENT BODY FOR APPROVAL AFTER EXPIRY: WHETHER SUBMISSION "USE": New Zealand: C.A.)   22 I.P.R. 143; [1991] 2 N.Z.L.R. 560

Smith Kline & French Laboratories Ltd v. Commissioner of Patents (PATENT: EXTENSION: MATTERS TO BE CONSIDERED: Australia: S.C.(NSW))
18 I.P.R. 513

Smith Kline & French Laboratories Ltd v. Doncaster Pharmaceuticals Ltd (PATENT: INFRINGEMENT: CIMETIDINE: PRACTICE: DELIVERY UP: DAMAGES: Pat. Ct)   [1989] 1 F.S.R. 401

Smith Kline & French Laboratories Ltd v. Douglas Pharmaceuticals Ltd (PATENT: INFRINGEMENT: CIMETIDINE: IMPORT OF SAMPLE FOR PURPOSES OF APPLICATION FOR PRODUCT LICENCE: USE FOR COMMERCIAL ADVANTAGE: INFRINGEMENT ESTABLISHED: New Zealand: C.A.)   [1991] F.S.R. 522

Smith Kline & French Laboratories Ltd v. Evans Medical Ltd (PATENT: CIMETIDINE: EXPERIMENTS IN CONNECTION WITH OPPOSITION: WHETHER PATENT OFFICE EXPERIMENTS PRIVILEGED AS EVIDENCE: Pat. Ct)
[1989] 1 F.S.R. 513

Smith Kline & French Laboratories Ltd v. Evans Medical Ltd (PATENT: CIMETIDINE: INFRINGEMENT: AMENDMENT: DELAY: WHETHER REASONABLE CAUSE FOR DELAY: Pat. Ct)   [1989] 1 F.S.R. 561
Smith Kline & French Laboratories Ltd v. Global Pharmaceutics Ltd (PATENT: INFRINGEMENT: PRACTICE: DISCOVERY OF IDENTITY OF OVERSEAS SUPPLIER: C.A.)   [1986] R.P.C. 394
Smith Kline & French Laboratories Ltd v. Harris Pharmaceuticals Ltd (PATENT: PHARMACEUTICALS: INFRINGEMENT: LICENCE OF RIGHT: BACK DOOR ASSIGNMENT: WHETHER TERMINATION PERMITTED: MANDATORY INJUNCTION FOR DESTRUCTION OF STOCKS: PRACTICE: SUMMARY JUDGMENT: JURISDICTION TO DETERMINE QUESTION OF CONSTRUCTION: Ch.D.)   [1992] F.S.R. 110
Smith Kline & French Laboratories Ltd v. Higson (TRADE MARK: INFRINGEMENT: PHARMACEUTICAL CAPSULES: COLOURS: Ch.D.)   [1988] F.S.R. 115
Smith Kline & French Laboratories Ltd v. Salim (Malaysia) Sdn Bhd (PATENT: CIMETIDINE: DRUG MANUFACTURED IN BRITAIN AND OTHER COUNTRIES: PATENTS IN RESPECT OF DRUG REGISTERED BY PLAINTIFF'S IN UNITED KINGDOM AND THEN IN MALAYSIA: DEFENDANTS IMPORTING AND RESELLING DRUG IN MALAYSIA WITHOUT NOTICE OF ANY RESTRICTION IN RESPECT OF IMPORT AND RESALE: WHETHER PLAINTIFFS' RIGHTS INFRINGED: Malaysia: H.C.)   15 I.P.R. 677; [1989] 1 F.S.R. 407
Smith Myers Communications Ltd v. Motorola Ltd (COPYRIGHT: INFRINGEMENT: PRACTICE: APPLICATION FOR INSPECTION OF DOCUMENTS BEFORE STATEMENT OF CLAIM SERVED: Ch.D.)   [1991] F.S.R. 262
Smith Pty Ltd v. E.A. Browne (TRADE MARK: APPLICATION FOR REMOVAL: INTENTION TO USE: NON-USE: Australia: Pat. Off.)   7 I.P.R. 45
Smith v. Greenfield (COPYRIGHT: INFRINGEMENT: TERM OF PROTECTION: CONVERSION DAMAGES: INNOCENCE: Northern Ireland: H.C.)
                    [1984] 6 N.I.J.B.; [1984] N.I.J.B. 125; [1985] F.S.R. 9
Smithkline Beecham Consolidated S.A. (Pty) Ltd v. Unilever plc (TRADE MARK: REGISTRATION: DISCLAIMER: EFFECT OF: WHETHER DISCLAIMED MATTER TO BE CONSIDERED IN COMPARISON WITH LATER APPLICATION FOR SIMILAR MARK: STRIPED TOOTHPASTE: South Africa: A.D.)   1995 (2) S.A. 903
SMS/Abandoned patent (EUROPEAN PATENT: OPPOSITION: PROCEDURE: REVOCATION AT INSTIGATION OF PATENTEE: T237/86: EPO)
                    [1988] E.P.O.R. 397; [1988] O.J. EPO 261
SMS/Revocation at the instigation of the patent proprietor (EUROPEAN PATENT: REVOCATION: PROPRIETOR, BY: TEXT OF PATENT: APPROVAL OF PROPRIETOR REQUIRED: T73/84: EPO)
                    [1979–85] E.P.O.R. C944; [1985] O.J. EPO 241
Smt Mannu Bhandari v. Kala Vikas Pictures Pvt. Ltd (COPYRIGHT: FILMING RIGHTS: ASSIGNMENT: AUTHOR'S RIGHTS: India: H.C.)   (1987) 12 I.P.L.R. 6
Smt Moneka Chawla v. National Trading Co. (REGISTERED DESIGN: INFRINGEMENT: INTERIM INJUNCTION: APPLICATION TO VACATE: India: H.C.)   (1993) 18 I.P.L.R. 177
Smucker (J.M.) Co.'s Petty Patent (PATENT: PETTY PATENT: EXTENSION: OPPOSITION: NOVELTY: OBVIOUSNESS: MANNER OF NEW MANUFACTURE: INCONVENIENT SPECIFICATION: NON–COMPLIENCE WITH SECTION 40: PROCEDURE: Australia: AIPO)   29 I.P.R. 311
SNIA/Deployable antenna reflector (EUROPEAN PATENT: APPEAL: PROCEDURE: REMITTAL NOT ORDERED: NO NEW LINE OF ATTACK: INVENTIVE STEP: COMBINING DIFFERENT PARTS OF SAME DOCUMENT: SKILLED PERSON: CAPABILITIES OF: T425/87: EPO)   [1990] E.P.O.R. 623

SNIA/Lack of due care (EUROPEAN PATENT: APPEAL: PROCEDURE: STATEMENT OF
GROUNDS, DOCUMENT POSSESSED BY THIRD PARTY: RE-ESTABLISHMENT OF
RIGHTS: DUE CARE: THIRD PARTY DOCUMENT NOT OBTAINED WITHIN TIME
LIMIT: T250/89: EPO)   [1992] E.P.O.R. 534; [1992] O.J. EPO 355
SNPE/Combustible sleeve (EUROPEAN PATENT: APPLICATION: PROCEDURE:
REFUSAL AFTER ONE COMMUNICATION: CLAIMS: FILE WRAPPER ESTOPPEL:
GUIDELINES FOR EXAMINATION: NOT BINDING: T149/82: EPO)
[1979–85] E.P.O.R. B621
Snyman v. Cooper (TRADE PRACTICES: MISLEADING OR DECEPTIVE CONDUCT:
REPRESENTATION IN TELECOM *Yellow Pages*: WHETHER CONDUCT INVOLVED
USE OF TELEPHONIC SERVICES: WHETHER PERSONS "KNOWINGLY ASSISTED"
IN CONTRAVENTION: PASSING OFF: WRONGFUL APPROPRIATION OF
GEOGRAPHICAL LOCATION OF A BUSINESS: WHETHER ACTIONABLE:
DAMAGES: EXEMPLARY DAMAGES: Australia: Fed. Ct)
91 A.L.R. 209; 16 I.P.R. 585
Snyman v. Cooper (PASSING OFF: FLORIST: ADVERTISEMENT IN *Yellow Pages*:
INJURY TO GOODWILL: MAJOR SHOPPING CENTRE USED AS INDICATION OF
LOCALITY: PREMISES 14KM FROM CENTRE: USE OF INDICIA OF APPELLANT'S
BUSINESS: DIRECTIONAL COMPONENT: PASSING OFF OF BUSINESS FOR
BUSINESS OF ONLY FLORIST IN SHOPPING CENTRE: DAMAGES: ASSESSMENT:
EXEMPLARY DAMAGES NOT AWARDED: Australia: Fed. Ct)
97 A.L.R. 653; 19 I.P.R. 471
Società Italiana Degli Autori ed Editori (SIAE) v. Domenico Pompa (COPYRIGHT:
INTELLECTUAL PRODUCT: BASIS OF PROTECTION: COMPUTER SOFTWARE:
Italy: S.C.)   [1989] E.C.C. 240; [1989] 1 F.S.R. 559
Société d'Intérêt Collectif Agricole des Sélectionneurs Obtenteurs de Variétés
Végétales (SICASOV) Agreement (RESTRICTIVE PRACTICES: PLANT
BREEDERS RIGHTS: SEED LICENSING AGREEMENTS: INTENTION TO APPROVE:
NOTICE: E.C. Comm.)   [1995] 5 C.M.L.R. 100
see also, *sub nom.* Association of Plant Breeders of the EEC (Comasso's)
Application
Société de Vente de Ciments et Betons de l'Est SA v. Kerpen & Kerpen GmbH & Co.
KG (RESTRICTIVE PRACTICES: EXHAUSTION OF RIGHTS: Case 319/82:
ECJ)   [1985] 1 C.M.L.R. 511; [1983] E.C.R. 4173; [1985] F.S.R. 281
Société des Produits Nestlé SA v. Midland Trading Co. (TRADE MARK: OPPOSITION:
DECEPTIVE SIMILARITY: AURAL SIMILARITY OF MARKS: Australia: AIPO)
27 I.P.R. 209
Société des Produits Nestlé SA v. Penaten Pharmazeutische Fabrik Dr Med Rieze &
Co. GmbH (TRADE MARK: APPLICATION: OPPOSITION: EXTENSION OF TIME
LIMIT TO LODGE EVIDENCE: COSTS: HEARING BEFORE REGISTRAR: Australia:
Pat. Off.)   9 I.P.R. 270
Société des Produits Nestlé SA v. Strasburger Enterprises Inc. (TRADE MARK:
OPPOSITION: QUIX:QUIK: DECEPTION OR CONFUSION: PROPRIETORSHIP:
Australia: AIPO)   31 I.P.R. 639
Société Française de Development de la Boîte-Boissons (SOFREB) (RESTRICTIVE
PRACTICES: JOINT SUBSIDIARY: INTENTION TO APPROVE: COMFORT LETTER:
E.C. Comm.)   [1986] 1 C.M.L.R. 226
Société Française de Transmissions Florales Interflora & Téléfleurs France
(RESTRICTIVE PRACTICES: DOMINANT POSITION: EXCLUSIVITY CLAUSE:
PROTECTION OF TRADE MARK: MINIMUM TARIFF ORDER: France: Copyright
Commission)   [1987] E.C.C. 515

Société Française des Viandes et Salaisons du Pacifique v. Société des Produits Nestlé SA (TRADE MARKS: OPPOSITION: SUBSTANTIALLY IDENTICAL OR DECEPTIVELY SIMILAR: IMPERFECT RECOLLECTION PRINCIPLE: GOODS OF SAME OR SIMILAR DESCRIPTION: Australia: Pat. Off.) 15 I.P.R. 89
Société Française Hoechst, *sub nom.* Hoechst (Société Française)
Société Microfor Inc. v. Le Monde Sàrl, *sub nom.* Le Monde Sàrl v. Société Microfor Inc
Société Nouvelle des Bennes Saphem v. Edbro Ltd (PATENT: INFRINGEMENT: CONSTRUCTION: Pat. Ct: C.A.) [1983] R.P.C. 345
Société Parisienne/*Restitutio in integrum* (EUROPEAN PATENT: RE-ESTABLISHMENT OF RIGHTS: PROFESSIONAL REPRESENTATIVES: DUTY OF DUE CARE: FEES: EXTENSION OF TIME TO PAY: J05/80: EPO)
[1979–85] E.P.O.R. A31; [1981] O.J. EPO 343
Société Princesse SA v. Société des Auteurs, Compositeurs et Editeurs de Musique (SACEM) (PERFORMING RIGHTS: ABUSE OF DOMINANT POSITION: France: D.C.) [1985] 2 C.M.L.R. 194; [1983] E.C.C. 322; [1983] F.S.R. 574
Société Rannou Graphie v. CNPRI (COPYRIGHT: PHOTOCOPIES: France: S.C.) [1985] E.C.C. 559; [1986] F.S.R. 44
Société Romanaise de la Chaussure SA v. British Shoe Corp. Ltd (COPYRIGHT: INFRINGEMENT: ITALIAN INFRINGER: DISCOVERY INTENDED TO SHOW IF ITALIAN ACTION WORTHWHILE: Ch.D.) [1991] F.S.R. 1
Société Technique de Pulverisation (STEP) v. Emson Europe Ltd (PATENT: INFRINGEMENT: CONSTRUCTION: OBVIOUSNESS: C.A.) [1993] R.P.C. 513
Socoil Corp. Berhad v. Ng Foo Cheng (TRADE MARK: GOLDEN DRAGON: Malaysia: Fed. Ct) [1981] 2 M.L.J. 7
(P.C.) [1984] 2 M.L.J. 85; 2 I.P.R. 300
Socoil Corp Bhd v. N.G. Brothers Import and Export Co. (TRADE MARK: INFRINGEMENT: CRIMINAL OFFENCE: FALSE TRADE DESCRIPTION: Malaysia: Pat. Ct) (1984) 134 New L.J. 991
Soda Ash (RESTRICTIVE PRACTICES: EXCLUSIVE PURCHASING AGREEMENTS: E.C. Comm.) [1982] 3 C.M.L.R. 495; [1983] F.S.R. 61
(TRADE MARK: INFRINGEMENT: GAS CYLINDERS: South Africa: TPD)
1984 (4) S.A. 425
Sodastream Ltd v. Berman Brothers (Pty) Ltd (TRADE MARK: INFRINGEMENT: SIMILAR GOODS: DIFFERENT CLASSES: South Africa: A.D.) 1986 (3) S.A. 209
Sodastream Ltd v. Thorn Cascade Co. Ltd (PASSING OFF: GET-UP: COLOURED GAS CYLINDERS: INTERLOCUTORY INJUNCTION: C.A.) [1982] R.P.C. 459
Soepenberg/Starch product (EUROPEAN PATENT: APPLICATION: PROCEDURE: EXAMINING DIVISION, OWN KNOWLEDGE: CLAIMS: CONSTRUCTION: "SUITABLE FOR" CLAUSE, NON-LIMITATIVE: NOVELTY: BURDEN OF PROOF: PRIOR ART: PERSONAL KNOWLEDGE OF EXAMINER: T21/83: EPO)
[1979–85] E.P.O.R. C751
SOFREB, *sub nom.* Société Française de Development de la Boîte-Boissons
Solco/Skin and mucous membrane preparation (EUROPEAN PATENT: UNITY: MEANS SPECIFICALLY DESIGNED FOR PROCESS: DISCLOSURE: CLAIM, TEACHING OF: T202/83: EPO) [1979–85] E.P.O.R. C912
Solicitors (Re a firm of) (CONFIDENTIAL INFORMATION: SOLICITOR RETAINED IN PATENT LITIGATION: FORMERLY PARTNER IN FIRM RETAINED BY OTHER PARTY: Ch.D.) [1995] F.S.R. 783

Solicitors (Re a firm of) (SOLICITOR: FIDUCIARY RELATIONSHIP WITH CLIENT: CONFIDENTIAL INFORMATION: ACQUISITION FROM COMPANIES CLOSELY ASSOCIATED WITH CLIENT: WHETHER DUTIES EXTEND TO ASSOCIATED COMPANIES: C.A.)
[1992] 1 All E.R. 353; [1992] 1 Q.B. 959; [1992] 2 W.L.R. 809

SOLID FUEL ADVISORY SERVICE Service Mark (SERVICE MARK: APPLICATION: DISTINCTIVENESS: T.M.Reg.)   [1990] R.P.C. 535

Solvay/Olefin polymers (EUROPEAN PATENT: APPLICATION: PROCEDURE: RELIANCE ON APPLICANT'S CITATION FOR DIFFERENT PURPOSE: FEES: REIMBURSEMENT OF APPEAL FEE: INVENTIVE STEP: PROBLEM DIFFERING FROM THAT OF PRIOR ART: SELECTION: T18/81: EPO)
[1979–85] E.P.O.R. B325; [1985] O.J. EPO 166

Solvay/Production of hollow thermoplastic objects (EUROPEAN PATENT: APPLICATION: PROCEDURE: REASONS REQUIRED: FEES: REIMBURSEMENT OF APPEAL FEE: INVENTIVE STEP: COMBINATION OF CITATIONS: SKILLED PERSON: ATTRIBUTES OF: T5/81: EPO)
[1979–85] E.P.O.R. B287; [1982] O.J. EPO 249

Somartec/Therapy with interference currents (EUROPEAN PATENT: OPPOSITION: PROCEDURE: ADMISSIBILITY: AUXILIARY REQUEST, GENERAL CONSIDERATIONS CONCERNING: FEES: REIMBURSEMENT OF APPEAL FEE: T234/86: EPO)   [1989] E.P.O.R. 303; [1989] O.J. EPO 79

Somerset Schools v. Van Aswegen, *sub nom.* Aetiology Today C.C. (t/a Somerset Schools) v. Van Aswegen

Somfy's Application (TRADE MARK: APPLICATION: DESCRIPTION OF METHOD OF OPERATION OF GOODS: DISTINCTIVENESS: Australia: Pat. Off.)   7 I.P.R. 305

Sommer Allibert (U.K.) Ltd v. Flair Plastics Ltd (REGISTRATION DESIGN: INFRINGEMENT: VALIDITY: PLASTIC GARDEN CHAIRS: STATEMENT OF NOVELTY: GROOVES MOULDED ON CHAIRS: WHETHER SHAPE OR CONFIGURATION: Pat. Ct: C.A.)   [1987] R.P.C. 599

Song Book for Schools (COPYRIGHT: STATUTORY EXCEPTIONS: SCHOOL BOOKS: EXTERNAL CHARACTERISTICS: INTERNAL CHARACTERISTICS: DEFINITIONS: Germany: S.C.)   [1993] E.C.C. 153; [1993] F.S.R. 431

Sonic Tape plc's Patent (PATENT: APPLICATION: PRACTICE: CONFIDENTIALITY OF DOCUMENTS: PRIVILEGE: C.-G.)   [1987] R.P.C. 251

Sonoco Products Co.'s Application (TRADE MARKS: APPLICATION: PART A REGISTRATION: INHERENT DISTINCTIVENESS: COMPOSITE MARK: DISCLAIMER AS TO ELEMENT OF MARK: SIGNIFICANCE OF HYPHEN IN MARK: Australia: Pat. Off.)   24 I.P.R. 269

Sony Corporation's Patent (PATENT: RESTORATION: MISTAKE BY PROPRIETOR'S EMPLOYEE: Pat. Ct)   [1990] R.P.C. 152

Sony Corporation v. Elite Optical Co. (TRADE MARK: OPPOSITION: GOODS TOTALLY DIFFERENT: India: T.M.Reg.)   (1987) 12 I.P.L.R. 92

Sony España SA (RESTRICTIVE PRACTICES: EXCLUSIVE AND SELECTIVE DISTRIBUTION AGREEMENT: INTENTION TO EXEMPT: NOTICE: E.C. Comm.)   [1994] 4 C.M.L.R. 581

Sony KK's Application (TRADE MARK: APPLICATION: GENERIC NAMES: INHERENTLY ADAPTED TO DISTINGUISH: Australia: Pat. Off.)   9 I.P.R. 466

Sony KK v. Saray Electronics (London) Ltd (PASSING OFF: AUTHORISED DEALERSHIP: C.A.)   [1983] F.S.R. 302

Sony KK v. Shamrao Maskar (TRADE MARK: OPPOSITION: SONY: India: H.C.)   (1986) 10 I.P.L.R. 405

Sony Music Australia Ltd v. Tansing (t/a Apple House Music) (PASSING OFF:
INTERLOCUTORY INJUNCTION: UNAUTHORISED RECORDINGS: EFFECT OF
DISCLAIMER ON PACKAGING: Australia: Fed. Ct)   27 I.P.R. 640
Sony Pan-European Dealer Agreement (RESTRICTIVE PRACTICES: SELECTIVE
DISTRIBUTION OF ELECTRICAL GOODS: E.C. Comm.)
                                              [1994] 5 C.M.L.R. 101
Sopharma SA's Application (PATENT: APPLICATION: NOVELTY: SUBSTANCE FOR
USE IN TREATMENT OF HUMAN BODY: C.-G.)   [1983] R.P.C. 195
Sorata Ltd v. Gardex Ltd (PATENT: INFRINGEMENT: PLEADINGS: Pat. Ct)
                          [1984] F.S.R. 81; [1984] R.P.C. 317
                                         (C.A.) [1984] R.P.C. 317
Soudure Autogène Française v. Controller of Patents, *sub nom.* SAF Trade Mark
South African Broadcasting Corporation v. Pollecutt (COPYRIGHT: PERFORMERS'
RIGHTS: RESTRICTION ON USE OF PERFORMANCE: SOUND RECORDING:
OWNERSHIP: STATUTORY INTERPRETATION: South Africa: A.D.)
                                              1996 (1) S.A. 547
South African Druggists Ltd v. Bayer AG (PATENT: EXTENSION: POST-EXPIRY
APPLICATION: South Africa: TPD)   1988 (1) S.A. 819
South African Historical Mint (Pty) Ltd v. Sutcliffe (TRADE MARK: UNFAIR
COMPETITION: FORMER EMPLOYEE: TRADE SECRETS: South Africa:
CPD)   1983 (2) S.A. 84
South African Music Rights Organisation Ltd v. Svenmill Fabrics (Pty) Ltd
(COPYRIGHT: INFRINGEMENT: MUSIC: BROADCAST: South Africa: CPD)
                                              1983 (1) S.A. 608
South African Railways & Harbours v. Standard Car Truck Co. (PATENT:
EXTENSION: INADEQUATE REMUNERATION: South Africa: A.D.)
                                              1982 (1) S.A. 806
South East Queensland Electricity Board v. Techmark-Miers Pty Ltd (PATENT:
APPLICATION: OPPOSITION: APPOINTMENT OF RECEIVER AND MANAGER TO
OPPONENT: NON-PURSUIT OF OPPOSITION: WITHDRAWAL OF OPPOSITION:
COSTS: PETTY PATENT: Australia: Pat. Off.)   24 I.P.R. 594
South Pacific Tyres NZ Ltd v. David Craw Cars Ltd (TRADE MARKS:
INFRINGEMENT: SECOND-HAND TYRES IMPORTED INTO AND SOLD IN NEW
ZEALAND BEARING IDENTICAL MARKS TO THE PLAINTIFFS' REGISTERED
MARKS: MARKS APPLIED TO TYRES IN JAPAN: NO CONNECTION OR
ARRANGEMENT WITH OWNER OR LEGITIMATE USER OF MARKS IN JAPAN:
New Zealand: H.C.)   24 I.P.R. 99
Southco Inc. v. Dzus Fastener Europe Ltd (PATENT: INFRINGEMENT:
CONSTRUCTION: VALIDITY: OBVIOUSNESS: EFFECT OF PRE-GRANT
AMENDMENT: Pat. Ct)   [1990] R.P.C. 587
                                         (C.A.) [1992] R.P.C. 299
Southco Inc. v. Dzus Fastener Europe Ltd (PATENT: INFRINGEMENT: STRIKING
OUT: CONSTRUCTION: PRACTICE: Pat. Ct)   [1989] R.P.C. 82
Spain v. Council of the European Union (PATENT: EEC: SUPPLEMENTARY
PROTECTION CERTIFICATES: VALIDITY OF REGULATION: COMMUNITY
COMPETENCE: LEGAL BASIS: Case C–350/92: ECJ)
                                 [1996] C.M.L.R. 415; [1996] F.S.R. 73
Spanset Inter/Appeal by intervener (EUROPEAN PATENT: ENLARGED BOARD OF
APPEAL: PRESIDENT OF THE EPO: intervention: admissibility: T202/89:
EPO)   [1992] E.P.O.R. 266; [1992] O.J. EPO 223
Spanset/Intervention (EUROPEAN PATENT: OPPOSITION: PROCEDURE:
INTERVENOR, RIGHT TO APPEAL: INTERVENTION: ADMISSIBILITY: G04/91:
EPO)   [1993] E.P.O.R. 565; [1993] O.J. EPO 707

Sparevirke/Notice of opposition (EUROPEAN PATENT: OPPOSITION: PROCEDURE: AUTHORISATION, NOT FILED: INTERVENOR: T355/86: EPO)
[1987] E.P.O.R. 331

Spectravest Inc. v. Aperknit Ltd (COPYRIGHT: INFRINGEMENT: CATS-IN-BOOTS DESIGN: CONTEMPT: WHETHER SUBSISTENCE AND OWNERSHIP TO BE PRESUMED: MITIGATION: Ch.D.)
[1988] F.S.R. 161

Speed Seal Products Ltd v. Paddington (BREACH OF CONFIDENCE: MASTER AND SERVANT: STRIKING OUT: ACTIONABLE ABUSE OF PROCESS: PLEADINGS: C.A.)
[1986] F.S.R. 309; [1986] 1 All E.R. 91; [1986] 1 W.L.R. 1327
(PLEADINGS: FURTHER AND BETTER PARTICULARS: Ch.D.)
[1984] F.S.R. 77

Speed Up Holdings Ltd v. Gough & Co. (Handly) Ltd (PRACTICE: CORPORATE PLAINTIFF: SECURITY FOR COSTS: Ch.D.)
[1986] F.S.R. 330

Sperry/Reformulation of the problem (EUROPEAN PATENT: AMENDMENT AND CORRECTION: PROBLEM, REFORMULATION OF: REFORMULATION OF CLAIMS IN LIGHT OF PRIOR ART: APPEAL: PROCEDURE: REMITTAL ORDERED: CLAIMS: ONE PART V. TWO PART: PREAMBLE: OBJECTIVE PRIOR ART, SHOULD BE BASED ON: INVENTIVE STEP: PROBLEM, REFORMULATION OF: T13/84: EPO)
[1986] E.P.O.R. 289; [1986] O.J. EPO 253

Spier Estate v. Die Bergkelder BPK (TRADE MARK: INFRINGEMENT: CANCELLATION PROCEEDINGS: JURISDICTION: South Africa: S.C.)
1988 (1) S.A. 94

Spiritual Sky Group Co. Pty Ltd v. Bernard Leser Publications Pty Ltd (TRADE MARK: APPLICATION: OPPOSITION: VOGUE: DECEPTIVE SIMILARITY: Australia: Pat. Off.)
7 I.P.R. 318

Spiro-flex Industries Ltd v. Progressive Sealing Inc. (COPYRIGHT: INDIRECT COPYING: REPRODUCTION OF THREE DIMENSIONAL REPRESENTATION OF ORIGINAL DRAWINGS: SALES BROCHURE: CO-OWNERSHIP: Canada: S.C.(B.C.))
8 I.P.R. 449

Sport Internationaal Bussum BV v. Inter-Footwear Ltd (TRADE MARK: LICENCE: FORFEITURE: RELIEF: DELAY: JURISDICTION: C.A.)
[1984] 1 All E.R. 376
(H.L.) [1986] 1 All E.R. 321; [1984] 1 W.L.R. 776

Split Roller Bearing Co. Ltd's Licence of Right (Copyright) Application (COPYRIGHT: LICENCE OF RIGHT APPLICATION: WHETHER APPLICATION MAY BE MADE IN RESPECT OF MORE THAN ONE DESIGN: WHETHER FAILURE TO INDICATE MANNER OF EXPLOITATION AN ABUSE OF PROCESS: C.-G.)
[1996] R.P.C. 225

Sport International Bussum BV v. Hi-Tech Sports Ltd (TRADE MARK: OPPOSITION: LICENSEE OPPOSING REGISTRATION: Q.B.D.)
[1990] F.S.R. 312
(SETTLEMENT BY LICENSING AGREEMENT: COMMUNITY LAW: INJUNCTION: C.A.)
[1988] R.P.C. 329

Sportscraft Consolidated Pty Ltd v. General Sportcraft Co. Ltd (TRADE MARK: OPPOSITION: PROPRIETORSHIP: DECEPTION: CONFUSION: SUBSTANTIALLY IDENTICAL: DECEPTIVELY SIMILAR: Australia: AIPO)
27 I.P.R. 74

Sportshoe (Pty) Ltd v. Pep Stores (S.A.) (Pty) Ltd (TRADE MARK: EXPUNGEMENT: ADAPTED TO DISTINGUISH: INFRINGEMENT: PASSING OFF: CONFUSION OR DECEPTION: PRODUCTS NOT COMPETING WITH ONE ANOTHER: DIFFERENCES IN PRICES, DESIGN, STRUCTURE AND OUTLETS OF PRODUCTS: South Africa: A.D.)
1990 (1) S.A. 722

Spotless Group Ltd v. Proplast Pty Ltd (PATENT: DESIGN: INFRINGEMENTS: STATE ACTION IN TWO JURISDICTIONS: APPLICATIONS TO SET ASIDE WRITS OR STAY OR TRANSFER: CONVENIENT FORUM: Australia: S.C.(Vic.))
10 I.P.R. 668

Spray Booths Aust. Pty Ltd's Application (TRADE MARKS: APPLICATION: MARKS
DIRECTLY DESCRIPTIVE: LACK OF INHERENT DISTINCTIVENESS: PART B:
Australia: Pat. Off.)   16 I.P.R. 360
Sprecher & Schuh/Toroidal transformer (EUROPEAN PATENT: OPPOSITION:
PROCEDURE: INTERLOCUTORY DECISION: T89/90: EPO)
                              [1992] E.P.O.R. 495; [1992] O.J. EPO 456
Springs Industries Inc.'s Application (TRADE MARKS: APPLICATIONS:
REGISTRABILITY: DISTINCTIVE: DESCRIPTIVE: ADAPTABILITY TO
DISTINGUISH: Australia: Pat. Off.)   23 I.P.R. 188
Spycatcher cases   ([1989] 2 F.S.R. *Spycatcher* volume)
sub nom. Attorney-General v. Guardian Newspaper Ltd, Observer Ltd, Times
Newspapers Ltd (THE GUARDIAN FULL ACTION: Ch.D: C.A.)
                              [1989] 2 F.S.R. 181; [1988] 2 W.L.R. 805
(H.L.) [1989] 2 F.S.R. 181; [1988] 1 A.C. 109; [1988] 3 All E.R. 545; [1988] 3
                                                                W.L.R. 776
sub nom. Attorney-General v. Guardian Newspapers Ltd (Derbyshire County
Council intervening) (PUBLIC LIBRARIES CASE: Ch.D.)
                              [1989] 2 F.S.R. 163; [1988] 1 All E.R. 385
sub nom. Attorney-General v. Guardian Newspapers Ltd and The Observer Ltd
(THE MILLETT INJUNCTION CASE: Ch.D: C.A.)   [1989] 2 F.S.R. 3
sub nom. Attorney-General v. Guardian Newspapers Ltd and The Observer Ltd
(THE GUARDIAN/OBSERVER DISCHARGE CASE: Ch.D.)   [1989] 2 F.S.R. 81
    (C.A.) [1989] 2 F.S.R. 81; [1987] 3 All E.R. 276; [1987] 1 W.L.R. 1248
    (H.L.) [1989] 2 F.S.R. 81; [1989] 3 All E.R. 316; [1987] 1 W.L.R. 1248
sub nom. Attorney-General v. Heinemann Publishers Australia Pty Ltd and
Wright (PROCEEDINGS IN THE NEW SOUTH WALES: Australia: S.C.(NSW):
C.A.(NSW))   10 I.P.R. 153; [1989] 2 F.S.R. 349
sub nom. Attorney-General v. Heinemann Publishers Australia Pty Ltd and
Wright (PROCEEDINGS IN AUSTRALIAN HIGH COURT: Australia H.C.)
                                     10 I.P.R. 261; [1989] 2 F.S.R. 623
sub nom. Attorney-General v. Heinemann Publishers Australia Pty Ltd and
Wright (CONFLICT OF LAWS: U.K. OFFICIAL SECRETS ACT: Australia: H.C.)
                                                                10 I.P.R. 261
sub nom. Attorney-General v. Heinemann Publishers Australia Pty Ltd and
Wright (DISCLOSURE OF INIQUITOUS CONDUCT: Australia: H.C.)
                                                                10 I.P.R. 129
sub nom. Attorney-General v. Newspaper Publishing plc (THE INDEPENDENT
CONTEMPT CASE: Ch.D.: C.A.)
            [1989] 2 F.S.R. 27; [1987] 3 All E.R. 316; [1987] 1 W.L.R. 1248
sub nom. Attorney-General v. Newspaper Publishing plc (CONTEMPT OF
COURT: *Spycatcher* MATERIAL: CRIMINAL CONTEMPT: NEWSPAPERS NOT
DIRECTLY BOUND BY INJUNCTION: INTENTION: *Actus reus: Mens rea*: FINES:
COSTS: Ch.D.)   [1989] 1 F.S.R. 457
sub nom. Attorney-General v. South China Morning Post (PROCEEDINGS IN
HONG KONG: Hong Kong: S.C.: C.A.)
                              [1988] 1 H.K.L.R. 143; [1989] 2 F.S.R. 653
sub nom. Attorney-General v. Times Newspapers Ltd (CONTEMPT: PUBLI-
CATION: APPELLANT NOT PARTY TO INJUNCTIONS RESTRAINING BREACH OF
CONFIDENCE: APPEAL: H.L.)
            [1991] 2 All E.R. 398; [1991] 2 W.L.R. 994; 20 I.P.R. 609
sub nom. Attorney-General v. Wellington Newspapers Ltd (PROCEEDINGS IN
NEW ZEALAND: H.C.: C.A.)   [1989] 2 F.S.R. 691

Squibb & Sons Pty Ltd v. Tully Corp. Pty Ltd (TRADE PRACTICES: MISLEADING OR DECEPTIVE CONDUCT: OBLIGATION ON RECIPIENT OF INFORMATION TO INVESTIGATE: REMEDIES: DECLARATION OF VOID CONTRACT: DAMAGES: INTEREST: Australia: Fed. Ct)   6 I.P.R. 489

St Albans City & District Council v. International Computers Ltd (COMPUTER CONTRACT: SOFTWARE: NEGLIGENT MISSTATEMENT: DEFICIENCY IN SOFTWARE RESULTING IN REDUCED REVENUE: WHETHER LOSS RECOVERABLE: LIMITATION CLAUSE: REASONABLENESS: WHETHER SOFTWARE GOODS: WHETHER PARTIES DEALING ON STANDARD TERMS: Q.B.D.)   [1995] F.S.R. 686

ST TRUDO Trade Mark (TRADE MARK: RECTIFICATION: EVIDENCE: REGISTRAR: HEARSAY RULES: APPLICABILITY AND SCOPE: Ch.D.)
[1995] F.S.R. 345; [1995] R.P.C. 370

Stacey v. 2020 Communications plc (PASSING OFF: TRADE NAME: SMALL-SCALE PLAINTIFF: DEFENDANT COMPANY: CONFUSION: TELECOMMUNICATIONS: NO INJUNCTION: Ch.D.)   [1991] F.S.R. 49

Stack v. Brisbane City Council (PATENT: INFRINGEMENT: USE BY STATE: AUTHORITY: SUPPLY OF WATER METERS: Australia: Fed. Ct)
131 A.L.R. 333; 32 I.P.R. 69

Stack v. Coast Securities (No. 9) Pty Ltd (TRADE PRACTICES: DECEPTION: Australia: Fed. Ct)   1 I.P.R. 193

Staeng Ltd's Patents (PATENT: OWNERSHIP: EMPLOYEE INVENTOR: WHETHER INVENTION MADE IN THE ORDINARY COURSE OF NORMAL DUTIES: JOINT INVENTORS: C.-G.)   [1996] R.P.C. 183

Stafford-Miller Ltd's Application (PATENT: APPLICATION: METHOD OF MEDICAL TREATMENT: Pat. Ct)   [1984] F.S.R. 258

Stafford-Miller Ltd v. Jean Patou Parfumeur (TRADE MARKS: APPLICATION: APPLICATION FOR EXTENSION OF TIME TO LODGE NOTICE OF OPPOSITION: Australia: Pat. Off.)   11 I.P.R. 409

Stamicarbon/Activated support (EUROPEAN PATENT: DISCLOSURE: CROSS-REFERENCED DOCUMENT: IMPLIED TEACHING: T288/84: EPO)
[1986] E.P.O.R. 217; [1986] O.J. EPO 128

Stamicarbon/Giro payment (EUROPEAN PATENT: FEES: NOTIFICATION OF PAYMENT: T214/83: EPO)   [1979–85] E.P.O.R. C920; [1985] O.J. EPO 10

Stamicarbon/Oxidation of toluene (EUROPEAN PATENT: CLAIMS: SUPPORT FOR: INVENTIVE STEP: SMALL IMPROVEMENT IN YIELD: T38/84: EPO)
[1979–85] E.P.O.R. C931; [1984] O.J. EPO 368

Stamicarbon/Polymer filaments (EUROPEAN PATENT: APPLICATION: PROCEDURE: FAILURE TO APPRECIATE EFFECT OF AMENDMENTS: FEES: REIMBURSEMENT OF APPEAL FEE: INTERLOCUTORY REVISION: T268/85: EPO)
[1989] E.P.O.R. 229

Standard Oil/Olefinic nitriles (EUROPEAN PATENT: INVENTIVE STEP: FAILED OBJECT: SIMPLIFICATION OF PRIOR ART: OPPOSITION: PROCEDURE: FRESH ARGUMENT AT ORAL PROCEEDINGS: FRESH GROUND ON APPEAL: T186/83: EPO)   [1986] E.P.O.R. 11

Standard Telephones and Cables Pty Ltd's Application (DESIGNS: OBJECTIONS TO REGISTRATION: MEANING OF DESIGN: DIVISION: WHETHER DEPICTIONS OF DIFFERENT CONFIGURATIONS OF SAME ARTICLE CONSTITUTE SEPARATE DESIGNS: Australia: Pat. Off.)   10 I.P.R. 609

Standen Engineering Ltd v. A. Spalding & Sons Ltd (COPYRIGHT: INFRINGEMENT: AUTHORISING INFRINGEMENT: Ch.D.)   [1984] F.S.R. 554

Stansfield v. Sovereign Music Ltd (PERFORMERS' RIGHTS: INFRINGEMENT: INTERLOCUTORY INJUNCTION: CONSENT TO RELEASE OF RECORDS: RECORDING AGREEMENT: ASSIGNMENT: Ch.D.)   [1994] E.M.L.R. 224

Star Micronics Pty Ltd v. Five Star Computers Pty Ltd (COPYRIGHT: COMPUTER PROGRAMS: WHETHER ROM IN PRINTER A COMPUTER PROGRAM: ORIGINALITY: SECONDARY INFRINGEMENT: SALE OF IMPORTED PRINTERS INCLUDING PROGRAM IN ROM: PASSING OFF: SUPPLY OF FOREIGN SUPPLIED PRINTERS ASSOCIATED WITH AUSTRALIAN SUPPLIER: SUPPLY OF 220v PRINTERS AS INTENDED BY MANUFACTURER FOR DISTRIBUTION IN AUSTRALIA: Australia: Fed. Ct)   18 I.P.R. 225
(DAMAGES: BREACH OF COPYRIGHT, PASSING OFF AND MISLEADING OR DECEPTIVE CONDUCT: MEANING OF FRAUD IN CONTEXT OF PASSING OFF: WHETHER ESTABLISHED: LACK OF CLEAR EVIDENCE OF ACTUAL DAMAGE: DAMAGES FOR LOSS OF REPUTATION: DAMAGES FOR DIMINUTION IN VALUE OF COPYRIGHT: Australia: Fed. Ct)   22 I.P.R. 473

STAR Trade Mark (TRADE MARK: APPLICATION: HONEST CONCURRENT USER: T.M.Reg.)   [1990] R.P.C. 522

State Government Insurance Corp. v. Government Insurance Office of NSW (TRADE PRACTICES: COMPETING STATE GOVERNMENT INSURANCE OFFICES: RESEMBLANCE OF LOGOS INDUCING ERROR: APPLICANT'S LOGO COPIED FROM RESPONDENTS: SURVEY EVIDENCE: Australia: Fed. Ct)   21 I.P.R. 65

State Government Insurance Corp. v. Government Insurance Office of NSW (TRADE PRACTICES: MISLEADING AND DECEPTIVE CONDUCT: CONDUCT LIKELY TO MISLEAD OR DECEIVE: LOGOS AND ACRONYMS OF STATE GOVERNMENT: WHETHER NECESSARY THAT CONDUCT SHOULD INDUCE OR BE LIKELY TO INDUCE SPECIFIC TRANSACTION: SUFFICIENCY OF DISCLAIMER: Australia: Fed. Ct)   19 I.P.R. 232

State of Oregon/Claims fees (EUROPEAN PATENT: FEES: CLAIM, WHAT CONSTITUTES: REIMBURSEMENT OF APPEAL FEE: J16/88: EPO)
[1990] E.P.O.R. 64

Stauffer Chemical Co. v. Safsan Marketing & Distributing Co. (Pty) Ltd (PATENT: INFRINGEMENT: PITH AND MARROW: PRACTICE: COSTS: South Africa: A.D.)   1987 (2) S.A. 331

Stauffer Chemicals v. Chesebrough-Ponds (Pty) Ltd (PATENT: INFRINGEMENT: REMEDIES: DELIVERY UP: EXPIRY OF PATENT: South Africa: TPD)
1988 (1) S.A. 805

Staver Co. Inc. v. Digitext Display Ltd (COPYRIGHT: INFRINGEMENT: INTERLOCUTORY JUDGMENT: WHETHER INJUNCTION WORKABLE: WHETHER VARIATION POSSIBLE: Ch.D.)   [1985] F.S.R. 512

STC plc's Application (TRADE MARKS: ACRONYMS, INITIALS: WHETHER DISTINCTIVE: WHETHER ADAPTED TO DISTINGUISH: Australia: Pat. Off.)
15 I.P.R. 419

Steel Bros (N.Z.) Ltd's Application (TRADE MARK: APPLICATION: SIDELIFTER: DIRECTLY DESCRIPTIVE OF SPECIFIED GOODS: MARK NOT INHERENTLY DISTINCTIVE: NOT AN INVENTED WORD: Australia: Pat. Off.) 19 I.P.R. 467

Steer, Clive, Allen/Wheelbarrow (EUROPEAN PATENT: INVENTIVE STEP: COMBINATION OF CITATIONS: APPEAL: PROCEDURE: REMITTAL NOT ORDERED: AMENDMENTS MINOR: DISCRETION UNDER RULE 86(3): FEES: REIMBURSEMENT OF APPEAL FEE: NO PREJUDICE: T183/89: EPO)
[1991] E.P.O.R. 298

STEMRA (EEC: RESTRICTIVE PRACTICES: COPYRIGHT: LICENSING: E.C. Comm.)   [1982] 3 C.M.L.R. 494; [1983] F.S.R. 107

Stenada Marketing Ltd v. Nazareno (TRADE SECRETS AND CONFIDENTIAL INFORMATION: RELATIONSHIP GIVING RISE TO PROTECTED INFORMATION: TRADE AND CONTRACTUAL RELATIONSHIPS: BUSINESS RELATIONSHIP: INTERLOCUTORY INJUNCTION: EQUITY: WINDOW BLIND CLEANING SERVICE: PURCHASE OF DRYING MACHINE FROM U.S. COMPANY: WHETHER UNIQUE SYSTEM: DISCLOSURE FOR PURPOSE OF SALE OF FRANCHISE: MATERIAL AVAILABLE TO PUBLIC: SPRINGBOARD PRINCIPLE: UNIQUE FEATURE CREATED BY PLAINTIFF NOT USED BY DEFENDANT: MATERIAL OBTAINED FROM INDEPENDENT U.S. COMPANY: NO BREACH OF CONFIDENCE: INTERLOCUTORY INJUNCTION REFUSED: Canada: S.C.(B.C.))   33 C.P.R. (3d) 367

Stephens v. Avery (CONFIDENTIAL INFORMATION: BREACH OF CONFIDENCE: RECIPIENT'S DUTY: LESBIAN RELATIONSHIP DISCLOSED TO RECIPIENT IN CONFIDENCE: RECIPIENT COMMUNICATING INFORMATION TO NEWSPAPER: WHETHER SUCH BREACH OF CONFIDENCE ACTIONABLE: CAUSE OF ACTION: WHETHER INFORMATION CAPABLE OF PROTECTION: DUTY OF CONFIDENCE: SEXUAL CONDUCT: Ch.D.)
    [1988] 2 All E.R. 477; [1988] Ch. 449; [1988] F.S.R. 510; [1988] 2 W.L.R. 1280; 11 I.P.R. 439

Stephenson & Donner's Application (PATENT: APPLICATION: JOINT APPLICANTS: PROCEED IN ONE NAME ONLY: Australia: Pat. Off.)   24 I.P.R. 108

Sterling Industries Ltd v. Nim Services Pty Ltd (PRACTICE: MAREVA INJUNCTION: APPLICATION: SUFFICIENCY OF REMEDY: DISCRETION: Australia: Fed. Ct)
                                                          66 A.L.R. 657

Sterling Pharmaceuticals Pty Ltd v. Johnson & Johnson Aust. Pty Ltd (PRACTICE AND PROCEDURE: EVIDENCE: ADMISSIBILITY AND RELEVANCE: HEARSAY: SURVEY EVIDENCE OF PUBLIC ON KNOWLEDGE AND USE OF MARK: ADMISSIBILITY OF EVIDENCE OF MEANINGS OF WORDS TO AID STATUTORY CONSTRUCTION AND FOR OTHER PURPOSES: INADMISSIBILITY OF EVIDENCE AS TO ULTIMATE ISSUE: Australia: Fed. Ct)   96 A.L.R. 277; 18 I.P.R. 309

Sterling Winthrop Pty Ltd v. Stephen Hunter Pty Ltd (TRADE MARK: OPPOSITION: APPLICATION: REGISTRATION: PHARMACEUTICAL: WORD COMMON TO THE TRADE: SIMILARITY: USE: DECEPTION: CONFUSION: Australia: AIPO)
                                                          32 I.P.R. 105

Sternheimer/Harmonic vibrations (EUROPEAN PATENT: PATENTABILITY: MUSIC: T366/87: EPO)   [1989] E.P.O.R. 131

Stevelift Pty Ltd v. Fomark Pty Ltd (PATENT: APPLICATION: OPPOSITION: STATEMENT OF GROUNDS AND PARTICULARS: AMENDMENT: REQUEST: DELAY: Australia: AIPO)   29 I.P.R. 154

Stewart v. Sheldon Abend, DBA Authors Research Co. (COPYRIGHT: ASSIGNMENT OF RENEWAL RIGHTS: DEATH OF AUTHOR BEFORE RENEWAL: DERIVATIVE WORKS: PRE-EXISTING WORKS: TERMINATION PROVISIONS: FAIR USE: SUBSTANTIAL PORTION: USA: S.C.)   17 I.P.R. 457

Stibbard v. The Commissioner of Patents (PATENT: COMPLETE SPECIFICATION: EXTENSION OF TIME LIMIT: Australia: AAT)   7 I.P.R. 337

Stichting Sigarettenindustries Agreements (RESTRICTIVE PRACTICES: PROCEDURE: EVIDENCE: DISCOUNTS: RETAILERS: E.C. Comm.)
              [1982] 3 C.M.L.R. 702; [1983] F.S.R. 102; [1982] O.J. L232/1

Stiga AB & Noma Outdoor Products Inc. v. SLM Canada Inc. (PASSING OFF: APPEARANCE OF WARES: TRI-SKI SNOW SLED: SECONDARY MEANING IN GET-UP A PREREQUISITE FOR ACTION: PATENT: INFRINGEMENT: OBVIOUSNESS: ANTICIPATION: REGISTRATION OF ASSIGNMENT: Canada: Fed. Ct)   21 I.P.R. 235

Still (W.M.) & Sons Ltd (RESTRICTIVE PRACTICES: SPARE PARTS: DISCOUNTS:
OFT) [1983] E.C.C. 128; [1983] F.S.R. 114
Stimtech/Transcutaneous electrical nerve stimulation (EUROPEAN PATENT: CLAIMS:
INDICATION OF HOW INVENTION WORKS NOT REQUIRED: PATENTABILITY:
THERAPY: SUFFICIENCY: CLAIMS: T94/83: EPO) [1979–85] E.P.O.R. C811
Stingray Surf Co. Pty Ltd v. Lister & Brown (TRADE MARK: APPLICATION:
OPPOSITION: PROPRIETORSHIP: HONEST CONCURRENT USER: Australia:
AIPO) 28 I.P.R. 581
Stockburger/Coded distinctive mark (EUROPEAN PATENT: APPLICATION:
PROCEDURE: AUXILIARY REQUEST, ABSENCE OF: PATENTABILITY: METHOD
FOR DOING BUSINESS: T51/84: EPO)
[1986] E.P.O.R. 229; [1986] O.J. EPO 226
Stord Bartz A/S v. Dupps Co., *sub nom.* Dupps Co. v. Stord Bartz A/S
Stork Pompen BV v. Weir Pumps Ltd (PATENT: OPPOSITION: EXTENSION OF TIME
TO LODGE NOTICE OF OPPOSITION: WHETHER ERROR OR OMISSION BY
PROPOSED OPPONENT: PRE-CONDITIONS TO EXERCISE OF COMMISSIONER'S
DISCRETION: APPLICATION REFUSED: Australia: Pat. Off.) 11 I.P.R. 542
Strabag, Krüger/Facsimile application (EUROPEAN PATENT: APPLICATION:
PROCEDURE: FACSIMILE TRANSMISSION, FILING BY: J23/85: EPO)
[1987] E.P.O.R. 165; [1987] O.J. EPO 95
Strack v. E.C. Commission (SECRECY: CIVIL SERVICE: EURATOM EMPLOYEE
EXPOSED TO RADIOACTIVE CONTAMINATION: PROCEEDINGS FOR
RECOGNITION OF INDUSTRIAL DISEASE: ACCESS TO MEDICAL INFORMATION:
NOT ON PERSONAL FILE: MADE AVAILABLE TO CLAIMANTS DOCTOR BUT NOT
TO CLAIMANT: ADEQUATE COMPLIANCE WITH RULE OF ACCESS:
COMMISSION'S GRUDGING AND UNINFORMATIVE REPLY TO REQUESTS FOR
ACCESS: MALADMINISTRATION: COMMISSION WINS CASE BUT ALL COSTS
AWARDED AGAINST IT: ECJ) [1990] 2 C.M.L.R. 347
Stratco Metal Pty Ltd's Application (TRADE MARK: OPPOSITION: ERROR IN
NOTICE: MISDESCRIPTION OF OPPONENT: AMENDMENT: LIKELIHOOD OF
DECEPTION OR CONFUSION: Australia: Pat. Off.) 4 I.P.R. 48
Street (t/a Caboolture Motel) v. Jedsminster Pty Ltd (TRADE PRACTICES:
CONSUMER PROTECTION: MISLEADING OR DECEPTIVE CONDUCT: PASSING
OFF: INTERLOCUTORY INJUNCTION: USE OF SIMILAR DESCRIPTIVE NAMES:
TWO MOTELS IN SMALL TOWN: CABOOLTURE MOTEL/CABOOLTURE
HOTEL MOTEL INN: GEOGRAPHICALLY DESCRIPTIVE NAME: BALANCE OF
CONVENIENCE: Australia: Fed. Ct) 11 I.P.R. 520
Stringfellow v. McCain Foods (G.B.) Ltd (PASSING OFF: STRINGFELLOWS:
NIGHTCLUB: CHIPPED POTATOES: NIGHTCLUB'S REPUTATION: RELEVANCE
OF MARKET SURVEY: WHETHER MISREPRESENTATION: WHETHER
DEFENDANTS' ACTIVITIES DAMAGE PLAINTIFF'S: MERCHANDISING RIGHTS
AND PRODUCT ENDORSEMENT: INJUNCTION: Ch.D.)
[1984] F.S.R. 175; [1984] R.P.C. 501
(C.A.) [1984] R.P.C. 501
Strix Ltd v. Otter Controls Ltd (PATENT: INFRINGEMENT: CONSTRUCTION:
ANTICIPATION: WHETHER PRIOR DISCLOSURE CONFIDENTIAL:
OBVIOUSNESS: AMENDMENT: NEW MATTER: WHETHER AMENDED CLAIM
CLEAR AND CONCISE: Pat. Ct) [1995] R.P.C. 607
Strix Ltd v. Otter Controls Ltd (PATENT INFRINGEMENT: PRACTICE: STRIKING
OUT: COSTS: Pat. Ct) [1991] F.S.R. 163
(C.A.) [1991] F.S.R. 354

Strix Ltd v. Otter Controls Ltd (No. 2) (PATENT: INFRINGEMENT: INQUIRY AS TO DAMAGES: PROCEDURE: DIRECTIONS AS TO CONDUCT OF INQUIRY: Pat. Ct) [1995] R.P.C. 655

Strix Ltd v. Otter Controls Ltd (No. 3) (PATENT: INFRINGEMENT: INQUIRY AS TO DAMAGES: STAY PENDING APPEAL: LATE APPLICATION: DISCRETION: Pat. Ct) [1995] R.P.C. 675

Stuart v. Barrett (COPYRIGHT: OWNERSHIP: POP GROUP: WHETHER PARTNERSHIP: EFFECT OF EXPULSION OF MEMBER: SONGS: COMPOSITION BEFORE MEMBER JOINED: WHETHER WORK OF JOINT OWNERSHIP: Ch.D.) [1994] E.M.L.R. 448

Studio Australia Pty Ltd v. Softsel Computer Products Inc. (TRADE MARKS: APPLICATION FOR REMOVAL OF REGISTRATION: ALLEGED NON-USE: EVIDENCE OF STATEMENT FROM TRADE MEMBERS: FAILURE TO SHOW PRIMA FACIE CASE: NO CASE TO ANSWER: APPLICATION FAILED: Australia: Pat. Off.) 19 I.P.R. 247

(TRADE MARKS: REMOVAL FROM REGISTER: NON-USE: *Locus standi*: ADEQUACY OF EVIDENCE TO ESTABLISH PRIMA FACIE CASE OF NON-USE: Australia: Pat. Off.) 19 I.P.R. 156

Studio SrL v. Buying Systems (Aust.) Pty Ltd (TRADE MARKS: APPLICATION: OPPOSITION: FURTHER EVIDENCE: SPECIAL LEAVE: Australia: Pat. Off.) 22 I.P.R. 580

(TRADE MARK: APPLICATION FOR REGISTRATION: OPPOSITION: PROPRIETORSHIP: PRIOR FOREIGN PROPRIETORSHIP BY OPPONENT: WHETHER CONFUSION: Australia: Pat. Off.) 26 I.P.R. 503

Stylesetter International Co. Pty Ltd v. Le Sportsac, Inc. (TRADE MARKS: APPLICATION FOR REGISTRATION: OPPOSITION: PROPRIETORSHIP: USE PRIOR TO APPLICATION: Australia: Pat. Off.) 17 I.P.R. 59

Sue v. Carpenter, *sub nom.* Carpenter v. Sue

SUISA (Swiss Society of Authors & Publishers) v. Rediffusion AG (COPYRIGHT: CABLE TV: FOREIGN BROADCASTS: Switzerland) [1982] E.C.C. 481; [1983] F.S.R. 27

Sulzer/Hot gas cooler (EUROPEAN PATENT: AMENDMENT AND CORRECTION: DRAWINGS: TEACHING OF: INVENTIVE STEP: PROBLEM AND SOLUTION: FURTHER SOLUTION: OPPOSITION: PROCEDURE: AMENDMENT AT ORAL PROCEEDINGS: T170/87: EPO) [1990] E.P.O.R. 14; [1989] O.J. EPO 441

Sumeet Machines Pvt. Ltd v. Sumeet Research & Holdings Ltd (TRADE MARK: COPYRIGHT: INFRINGEMENT: SIMULTANEOUS LAUNCHING OF CIVIL AND CRIMINAL PROCEEDINGS: India: H.C.) (1993) 18 I.P.L.R. 1

Sumitomo Chemical Co. Ltd v. Rhône-Poulenc Chimie (PATENT: APPLICATION: OPPOSITION: COMMON GENERAL KNOWLEDGE: ADMISSIONS IN SPECIFICATION: INVENTIVENESS: MANNER OF MANUFACTURE: SECTION 40: COSTS: Australia: Fed. Ct) 30 I.P.R. 591

Sumitomo Electrical Industries Ltd v. Metal Manufacturers Ltd (PATENT: SELECTION: APPLICATION: OPPOSITION: REHEARING: Australia: Fed. Ct) 32 I.P.R. 185

Sumitomo/Extent of opposition (EUROPEAN PATENT: ENLARGED BOARD OF APPEAL: REFERENCE REFUSED: UNDESIRABLE IN VIEW OF DELAY: EVIDENCE: REPETITION OF PATENTEE'S EXAMPLES: OPPOSITION: PROCEDURE: EXAMINATION OF OWN MOTION: UNSUPPORTED GROUNDS: SUFFICIENCY: EXAMPLES, REPRODUCIBILITY OF: T182/89: EPO) [1990] E.P.O.R. 438; [1991] O.J. EPO 391

Sumitomo/Polymer solution (EUROPEAN PATENT: OPPOSITION PROCEDURE: ADMISSIBILITY: EXTENT OF OPPOSITION: CLARITY (YES): T376/90: EPO)   [1995] E.P.O.R. 232
Sumitomo/Remittal (EUROPEAN PATENT: APPLICATION: PROCEDURE: AUXILIARY REQUESTS: INTERLOCUTORY REVISION: T47/90: EPO)
[1991] E.P.O.R. 513; [1991] O.J. EPO 486
Sumitomo/Vinyl chloride resins (EUROPEAN PATENT: SUFFICIENCY: CLAIMED SUBJECT-MATTER, REPRODUCIBILITY: T14/83: EPO)
[1979–85] E.P.O.R. C737; [1984] O.J. EPO 105
Sumitomo/Yellow dyes (EUROPEAN PATENT: INVENTIVE STEP: CLOSEST PRIOR ART: SURPRISING EFFECT: T254/86: EPO)
[1989] E.P.O.R. 257; [1989] O.J. EPO 115
Sun Earth Homes Pty Ltd v. Australian Broadcasting Corp. (TRADE PRACTICES: WHETHER TELECAST BY ABC PROTECTED BY STATUTE: WHETHER TELECAST AN ADVERTISEMENT OR OTHER PUBLICATION IN CONNECTION WITH SUPPLY OF GOODS OR SERVICES: WHETHER TV PROGRAM A SERVICE: Australia: Fed. Ct)   98 A.L.R. 101
Sun Newspapers Pty Ltd v. Brisbane TV Ltd (CONTEMPT OF COURT: INJUNCTION: NON-PARTY TO ORIGINAL ACTION: TERMS OF INJUNCTION READ OVER TELEPHONE: KNOWLEDGE OF ORDER: WHETHER PERSON CHARGED MUST BE AWARE OF FULL TERMS OF ORDER: STANDARD OF PROOF: Australia: Fed. Ct)   17 I.P.R. 113
Sunbeam Corp. v. Morphy-Richards (Aust.) Pty Ltd (PATENT: INFRINGEMENT: REVOCATION: VALIDITY: INVENTIVENESS: NOVELTY: SUBJECT-MATTER: OBVIOUSNESS: COMMON GENERAL KNOWLEDGE: MOSAIC: Australia: H.C.)   180 C.L.R. 98
Sundream Pty Ltd v. Hartland Investments Pty Ltd (TRADE MARKS: OPPOSITIONS TO REGISTRATION: PROPRIETORSHIP: LIKELIHOOD OF DECEPTION OR CONFUSION: ONUS OF PROOF: Australia: Pat. Off.)   13 I.P.R. 302
Sundstrand Corp. v. Safe Flight Instrument Corp. (PATENT: AIRCRAFT WIND SHEAR WARNING SYSTEM: DECLARATION OF NON-INFRINGEMENT: VALIDITY: DIFFERENT ALGORITHM: PURPOSIVE CONSTRUCTION: Pat. C.C.)
[1994] F.S.R. 599
Sunraysia Natural Beverage Co. Pty Ltd's Application (TRADE MARK: APPLICATION: OBJECTION BY EXAMINER: WHETHER CAPABLE OF BECOMING DISTINCTIVE: Australia: AIPO)   29 I.P.R. 165
Suntory/Repayment of examination fee (EUROPEAN PATENT: FEES: REPAYMENT: J14/85: EPO)   [1987] E.P.O.R. 171; [1987] O.J. EPO 47
Super Cassette Industries Ltd v. Bathla Cassettes India (Pvt.) Ltd (COPYRIGHT: SONGS OF PAKISTANI ARTISTS: THREATS: INJUNCTION: APPEAL TO VACATE: India: H.C.)   (1995) 20 I.P.L.R. 1
SUPERWOUND Trade Mark (TRADE MARK: REGISTRATION: DISTINCTIVENESS: LAUDATORY WORD: CONJOINED WORDS: BoT)   [1988] R.P.C. 272
Supply Of Ready Mixed Concrete (No. 2) (PRACTICE: CONTEMPT: BREACH OF INJUNCTION BY EMPLOYEE: LIABILITY OF EMPLOYER: H.L.)
[1994] 3 W.L.R. 1249
Surf Shirt Designs Pty Ltd (TRADE MARK: OPPOSITION TO REGISTRATION: PROPRIETORSHIP: USE LIKELY TO DECEIVE OR CAUSE CONFUSION: Australia: Pat. Off.)   23 I.P.R. 114
Surge Licensing Inc. v. Pearson (TRADE PRACTICES: MISLEADING OR DECEPTIVE CONDUCT: NO EVIDENCE OF CONSUMER BEING ACTUALLY MISLED OR DECEIVED: LOSS OF REPUTATION: DAMAGES: Australia: Fed. Ct)
21 I.P.R. 228

Surgikos/Disinfection (EUROPEAN PATENT: COMMON GENERAL KNOWLEDGE: SOURCES OF: INVENTIVE STEP: CLOSEST PRIOR ART: COMMERCIAL SUCCESS: COMMON GENERAL KNOWLEDGE: PROBLEM, REFORMULATION OF: T69/89: EPO) [1990] E.P.O.R. 632

Surjit Singh v. Alembic Glass Industries Ltd (TRADE MARK: PERFUMERY, COSMETICS ETC: APPLICATION: OPPOSITION: PROPRIETOR OF IDENTICAL MARK: DIFFERENT GOODS: India: H.C.) (1988) 13 I.P.L.R. 26

Sushil Vasudev (t/a Kwality Ice Cream Co) v. Kwality Frozen Foods Pvt. Ltd (TRADE MARK: KWALITY: TRADING STYLE: REGISTRATION: PRIOR USER: INTERIM INJUNCTION: India: H.C.) (1994) 19 I.P.L.R. 162

Swanfu Trading Pte Ltd v. Beyer Electrical Enterprise Pte Ltd, *sub nom.* Beyer Electrical Enterprise Pte Ltd v. Swanfu Trading Pte Ltd

Swedac Ltd v. Magnet & Southerns plc (COPYRIGHT INFRINGEMENT: STRIKING OUT: SOLICITORS' ERROR OF JUDGMENT: C.A.) [1990] F.S.R. 89

Swedac Ltd v. Magnet & Southerns plc (FRAUDULENT INTERFERENCE WITH TRADE: ANTON PILLER PRACTICE: DUTY OF DISCLOSURE: Ch.D.) [1989] 1 F.S.R. 243

Switzerland Australia Health Fund Pty Ltd v. Shaw (TRADE PRACTICES: TRADE AND COMMERCE: MISLEADING AND DECEPTIVE CONDUCT: REMEDIES: ABSENCE OF DAMAGE: Australia: Fed. Ct) 11 I.P.R. 331

Sybron Corp. v. Barclays Bank plc (CONFIDENTIAL INFORMATION: DISCOVERY AND INSPECTION: USE OF DOCUMENTS IN SUBSEQUENT LITIGATION: Ch.D.) [1985] Ch. 299; [1984] 3 W.L.R. 1055

Symbol Technologies Inc. v. Opticon Sensors Europe BV (No. 1) (PATENT: PRACTICE: SERVICE OF PETITION FOR REVOCATION: REGISTER OF PATENTS: Pat. Ct) [1993] R.P.C. 211

Symbol Technologies Inc. v. Opticon Sensors Europe BV (No. 2) (PATENT: INFRINGEMENT: PRACTICE: TRANSFER OF REVOCATION PETITION TO COUNTY COURT: Pat. Ct) [1993] R.P.C. 232

SYNDIS v. SACEM, *sub nom.* Chambre Syndicale Nationale de la Discothéque v. Société des Auteurs, Compositeurs et Editeurs de Musique

Syntex Corp.'s Patent (PATENT: LICENCES OF RIGHT: SETTLEMENT OF TERMS: ROYALTY: Pat. Ct) [1986] R.P.C. 585

Synthetic Moulders Ltd v. Semperit AG (TRADE MARK: INFRINGEMENT: INTERLOCUTORY INJUNCTION: India: H.C.) (1983) 7 I.P.L.R. 1

Systematica Ltd v. London Computer Centre Ltd (COPYRIGHT: INFRINGEMENT: ANTON PILLER PRACTICE: Ch.D.) [1983] F.S.R. 313

Taco Bell Pty Ltd v. Taco Co. of Australia Ltd (PASSING OFF: TRADE PRACTICES: DECEPTION: Australia: Fed. Ct) (1982) 40 A.L.R. 153
(APPEAL: S.C.) (1982) 42 A.L.R. 177

TAG/Suspension of proceedings (EUROPEAN PATENT: APPLICATION: PROCEDURE: STAY OF EPO EXAMINATION: PENDING NATIONAL ENTITLEMENT PROCEEDINGS: T146/82: EPO) [1979–85] E.P.O.R. B618; [1985] O.J. EPO 267

Tai Muk Kwai v. Luen Hup Medical Co. (TRADE MARKS: COPYRIGHT: RIVAL CLAIM OF OWNERSHIP OF MARKS: GOODS MANUFACTURED BY PLAINTIFF'S AND SOLD AND DISTRIBUTED EXCLUSIVELY BY DEFENDANT AS SOLE IMPORTER: WHETHER ASSIGNMENT OF MARKS CONFERS OWNERSHIP: PASSING OFF: BONA FIDE PURCHASER FOR VALUE WITHOUT NOTICE: Singapore: H.C.) [1988] 3 M.L.J. 69;14 I.P.R. 484

Taisho/Correction—priority (EUROPEAN PATENT: AMENDMENT AND CORRECTION: PRIORITY CLAIM: J03/82: EPO)
[1979–85] E.P.O.R. A99; [1983] O.J. EPO 171

Taito/Television game machine (EUROPEAN PATENT: APPLICATION: PROCEDURE: EURO-PCT APPLICATION, TIME LIMIT FOR FILING TRANSLATION: J10/89: EPO)
[1992] E.P.O.R. 218

Taittinger SA v. Allbev Ltd (PASSING OFF: MISREPRESENTATION: ELDERFLOWER CHAMPAGNE: CONFUSION: DAMAGE MINIMAL: ENGLISH LAW REMEDY FOR BREACH OF COMMUNITY REGULATIONS: REGULATION 823/87: WINE APPELLATION RULES: LACK OF COMMUNITY REMEDIAL RULE: ADOPTION OF RELEVANT ENGLISH RULE: *De minimis*: DISCRETION: INJUNCTION REFUSED: Ch.D.)
[1993] 1 C.M.L.R. 597; [1993] F.S.R. 641
(APPEAL: ENFORCEMENT OF COMMUNITY LAW: DIRECT EFFECT: INJUNCTION NOT DISPROPORTIONATE REMEDY AND GRANTED: C.A.)
[1993] 2 C.M.L.R. 741; [1993] F.S.R. 641; 27 I.P.R. 105

Taiwan Yamani Inc. v. Giorgio Armani SpA (TRADE MARKS: APPLICATION FOR REGISTRATION: OPPOSITION: SUBSTANTIALLY IDENTICAL OR DECEPTIVELY SIMILAR MARKS: USE NOT LIKELY TO CAUSE DECEPTION OR CONFUSION: VISUAL DIFFERENCES MORE IMPORTANT THAN AURAL SIMILARITY IN RELATION TO CLOTHING: USE OF OPPONENTS MARKS NOT GREAT: Australia: Pat. Off.)
17 I.P.R. 92

Takeda/Postponement of examination (EUROPEAN PATENT: APPLICATION: PROCEDURE: STAY: PENDING REFERENCE TO ENLARGED BOARD OF APPEAL: ENLARGED BOARD OF APPEAL: EFFECT OF REFERENCE ON OTHER CASES: FEES: REIMBURSEMENT OF APPEAL FEE: T166/84: EPO)
[1979–85] E.P.O.R. C981; [1984] O.J. EPO 489

Takemoto Yushi/Lubricating agents (EUROPEAN PATENT: APPEAL: FUNCTION OF APPEAL: INVENTIVE STEP: CLOSEST PRIOR ART: NOVELTY: SELECTION: DOCUMENT CITED WITH HINDSIGHT: OPPOSITION: FRESH GROUNDS: ON APPEAL: REMITTAL TO FIRST INSTANCE: PRIOR ART: DIFFERENT FIELD: T97/90: EPO)
[1993] E.P.O.R. 135; [1993] O.J. EPO 719

Talk of the Town Pty Ltd v. Hagstrom (COPYRIGHT: ENGRAVING: FUNCTIONAL OBJECTS: DRAWINGS AND DIES: RESTRAINT OF TRADE: VALIDITY OF COVENANT: Australia: Fed. Ct)
99 A.L.R. 130

Tamworth Herald Co. Ltd v. Thomson Free Newspapers Ltd (PASSING OFF: INTERLOCUTORY INJUNCTION: NEWSPAPER TITLES: BALANCE OF CONVENIENCE: Ch.D.)
[1991] F.S.R. 337

Tanabe Seiyaku Co. Ltd (Re) (PATENT: PETITION FOR EXTENSION OF TERM: CAVEAT: DILTIAZEM: EXCEPTIONAL CASE: MERIT: PUBLIC UTILITY: INADEQUATE REMUNERATION: REGRANT FOR 10 YEARS: Australia: S.C.(Vic.))
13 I.P.R. 177

Tandy Corp.'s Application (TRADE MARK: REGISTRABILITY: ORDINARY MEANING: Australia: Pat. Off.)
3 I.P.R. 221

Tandy Corporation's Application (TRADE MARK: APPLICATION: OPPOSITION: APPLICATION FOR EXTENSION OF TIME IN WHICH TO LODGE OPPOSITION: Australia: Pat. Off.)
22 I.P.R. 639

Tansing v. Musidor (TRADE MARK: INFRINGEMENT: DECLARATION: USE AS MARK: DISCLAIMER: USE IN GOOD FAITH: Australia: Fed. Ct)
28 I.P.R. 111

Targetts Pty Ltd v. Target Aust. Pty Ltd (TRADE PRACTICES: MISLEADING AND DECEPTIVE CONDUCT: LOCAL TRADER SEEKING TO PREVENT LARGE MAINLAND TRADER FROM ENTERING LAUNCESTON MARKET IN SAME TRADE UNDER SIMILAR NAME AND LOGO: WHETHER CONSUMERS MISLED DESPITE DIFFERENT STYLES OF BUSINESS: PASSING OFF: INTERLOCUTORY INJUNCTION: Australia: Fed. Ct)   26 I.P.R. 51

Tata Oil Mills Co. Ltd v. Reward Soap Works (TRADE MARK: COPYRIGHT: INFRINGEMENT: 501/507: INTERIM INJUNCTION: India: H.C.)
(1983) 8 I.P.L.R. 91

Tata Oil Mills Co. Ltd v. WIPRO Ltd (TRADE MARK: INFRINGEMENT: PASSING OFF: INTERIM INJUNCTION: India: H.C.)   (1986) 11 I.P.L.R. 99

Tatra Nominees Pty Ltd's Application (TRADE MARK: APPLICATION: OBJECTION BY EXAMINER: WHETHER DESCRIPTIVE: EXISTING REGISTRATIONS: Australia: AIPO)   29 I.P.R. 151

Tattilo Editrice SpA v. Playboy Enterprises Inc. (TRADE MARK: OPPOSITION: WITHDRAWAL: COSTS: BILL OF COSTS: HEARING FEE: Australia: T.M.Reg.)
7 I.P.R. 333

Tattinger v. Allbev Ltd, *sub nom.* Taittinger v. Allbev Ltd

Tavefar Pty Ltd v. Life Savers (Australasia) Ltd (TRADE MARKS: OPPOSITION: LIKELIHOOD OF DECEPTION OR CONFUSION: PROPRIETORSHIP: Australia: Pat. Off.)   12 I.P.R. 159

Taylor's Application (TRADE MARKS: APPLICATION: REGISTRABILITY: DISTINCTIVE: Australia: Pat. Off.)   22 I.P.R. 426

Taylor & Horne (Pty) Ltd v. Dentall (Pty) Ltd (TRADE MARK: UNFAIR COMPETITION: EXCLUSIVE DISTRIBUTION AGREEMENT: LEGITIMATE SALE OF GOODS BY THIRD PARTY: South Africa: A.D.)   1991 (1) S.A. 412

Taylor Bros Ltd v. Taylors Group Ltd (PASSING OFF: COMPANY NAME: TAYLORS: TRADE PRACTICES: MISLEADING OR DECEPTIVE CONDUCT: SIMILAR TRADES: DIFFERENT GEOGRAPHICAL AREAS OF OPERATION: DRYCLEANING LINEN HIRE: WHETHER COMMON FIELD OF ACTIVITY: New Zealand: H.C.)
[1988] 2 N.Z.L.R. 1; 19 I.P.R. 615
(C.A.) [1988] 2 N.Z.L.R. 1;19 I.P.R. 624
(INTERIM INJUNCTION PERMITTING LIMITED USE OF TAYLORS: SUB-SEQUENT PERMANENT INJUNCTION RESTRAINING TRADE UNDER AND BY REFERENCE TO TAYLORS: RESPONDENTS USE OF LAYTONS TO CREATE IMPRESSION OF CONTINUITY: CONTINUED USE OF TAYLORS FOR GOODS HIRED: WHETHER LAYTONS A BREACH OF PERMANENT INJUNCTION: NO CONTINUING CONFUSION: REMEDIES: New Zealand: C.A.)
[1990] 1 N.Z.L.R. 19; 14 I.P.R. 353

Taylor Made Golf Company Inc v. Rata & Rata (a firm) (PRACTICE: CONTEMPT: FAILURE TO COMPLY WITH ANTON PILLER ORDER: APPLICATION FOR COMMITTAL: WHETHER CUSTODIAL SENTENCE APPROPRIATE PENALTY: FINANCIAL PENALTY: QUANTUM: Ch.D.)   [1996] F.S.R. 528

Taylor v. Rotowax Trading Ltd (RESTRAINT OF TRADE: COVENANT: SALE OF COMPANY: NON-COMPETITION CLAUSE IN BREACH OF COVENANT: ACQUISITION OF GOODWILL OF VENDOR COMPANY: New Zealand: C.A.: P.C.)   [1988] 1 N.Z.L.R. 674

Taypar Pty Ltd v. Santic (COPYRIGHT: INFRINGEMENT: QUALITATIVE ASSESSMENT OF SIMILARITIES: WHETHER APPROPRIATION OF IDEA OR CONCEPT OR OF EXPRESSION OF THAT CONCEPT: Australia: Fed. Ct)   17 I.P.R. 146

Tayto (Northern Ireland) Ltd v. McKee (TRADE MARKS: RESTRICTIVE PRACTICES: PRE-EEC MARKET-PARTITIONING AGREEMENT FOR USE OF IDENTICAL TRADE MARK: ABANDONED AND NO CONTINUING EFFECTS: FAILURE TO USE TRADE MARK IN COMPETITOR'S TERRITORY NOT TAINTED BY ORIGINAL AGREEMENT: Northern Ireland: Ch.D.)   [1991] 3 C.M.L.R. 269

TDK Electronics Co. Ltd's Application (DESIGNS: REGISTRABILITY: Australia: Pat. Off.)   1 I.P.R. 529

TEC & Thomas (Aust.) Pty Ltd v. Matsumiya Computer Co. Pty Ltd (TRADE PRACTICES: DECEPTION: USE OF REGISTERED BUSINESS NAME: Australia: Fed. Ct)   2 I.P.R. 81

Technicolor Inc. v. R. & C. Products Pty Ltd (TRADE MARKS: OPPOSITION: PROPRIETORYSHIP: PRIOR USE: DECEPTION AND CONFUSION: REGISTRARS DIRECTION: Australia: Pat. Off.)   24 I.P.R. 177

Techniplast Gazzada/Re-establishment (EUROPEAN PATENT: RE-ESTABLISHMENT OF RIGHTS: FAILURE, DATE OF AWARENESS OF: T81/83: EPO)   [1979–85] E.P.O.R. C791

Technobiotic Ltd's Patent (PATENT: TERM: EXTENSION: INADEQUATE REMUNERATION: PHARMACEUTICAL COMPOUND: LENGTHY DEVELOPMENT PERIOD: SMALL DOMESTIC MARKET: WHETHER EXCEPTIONAL CASE: Ireland: H.C.)   [1990] 2 I.R. 499

Technology Transfer Agreement Regulations, *sub nom.*, Community Technology Transfer Agreement Regulations

Technology Transfer Regulations, *sub nom.*, Community Technology Transfer Regulations

Technology Transfer Regulation 1996 (RESTRICTIVE PRACTICES: GROUP EXEMPTION: PATENT LICENSING: KNOW-HOW LICENSING: APPLICATION OF ARTICLE 85(3) TO CERTAIN CATEGORIES OF TECHNOLOGY TRANSFER AGREEMENTS: E.C. Comm.)   [1996] 4 C.M.L.R. 405

Tefex Pty Ltd v. Bowler (COPYRIGHT: REGISTERED DESIGN: INFRINGEMENT: ARTICLE: Australia: S.C.(NSW))   (1982) 49 A.L.R. 362

Teijin/Cotton yarn-like composite yarn (EUROPEAN PATENT: INVENTIVE STEP: COMBINATION OF CITATIONS: PROCESS CLAIM: ASSESSMENT INDEPENDENT OF PRODUCT: OPPOSITION: PROCEDURE: TRANSLATION OF CITATION, CHALLENGE TO: T169/88: EPO)   [1991] E.P.O.R. 281

Teijin/Polyester composition (EUROPEAN PATENT: AMENDMENT AND CORRECTION: EXTENSION OF SUBJECT-MATTER: T938/90: EPO)   [1993] E.P.O.R. 287

Tekdata Ltd's Application (PATENT: RESTORATION: Pat. Ct)   [1985] R.P.C. 201

Tektronix/Schottky barrier diode (EUROPEAN PATENT: NOVELTY: IMPLICIT TEACHING: RELEVANT DATE: SUFFICIENCY: RELEVANT DATE: INVENTIVE STEP: T694/91: EPO)   [1995] E.P.O.R. 384

Télé-Métropole Inc. v. Bishop (COPYRIGHT: INFRINGEMENT BY BROADCAST PRERECORDING: EPHEMERAL RECORDINGS: STATUTORY INTERPRETATION: IMPLIED CONSENT NOT INCLUDED IN LICENCE TO PERFORM WORK: EFFECT OF U.K. COPYRIGHT LAW: Canada: S.C.)   20 I.P.R. 318

TELECHECK Trade Mark (TRADE MARK: APPLICATION: WORD DEVICE MARK: PRACTICE: BoT)   [1986] R.P.C. 77

Telecom Directories Ltd v. A.D. Viser (N.Z.) Ltd (COMPARATIVE ADVERTISING: PENALTIES: New Zealand: H.C.)   26 I.P.R. 37

Telecommunications Terminal Equipment (Antitrust) (Directive 1988–94 (Directive 475/88/301) (RESTRICTIVE PRACTICES: TELECOMMUNICATIONS: COMPETITION IN TERMINAL EQUIPMENT MARKETS: TEXT OF DIRECTIVE 88/ 301 AS AMENDED BY DIRECTIVE 94/96: E.C. Comm.)
[1996] 4 C.M.L.R. 87
Telecommunications Terminal Equipment and Services (Antitrust Amendment) Directive 1994 (Directive 94/96) (RESTRICTIVE PRACTICES: TELECOMMUNICATIONS: COMPETITION IN SERVICES AND TERMINAL EQUIPMENT MARKETS: E.C. Comm.) [1996] 4 C.M.L.R. 69
Telecommunications Terminal Services (Antitrust) Directive 1990–94 (Directive 90/388) (RESTRICTIVE PRACTICES: TELECOMMUNICATIONS: COMPETITION IN SERVICES MARKETS: TEXT OF DIRECTIVE 90/388 AS AMENDED BY DIRECTIVE 94/96: E.C. Comm.) [1996] 4 C.M.L.R. 69
Telecommunications/Antioxidant (EUROPEAN PATENT: FEES: DATE OF RECEIPT: INVENTIVE STEP: COMBINATION OF CITATIONS: CONSEQUENTIAL SIDE EFFECT: STATE OF THE ART: EVIDENT ABUSE: T173/83: EPO)
[1988] E.P.O.R. 133; [1987] O.J. EPO 465
Teleflora (Australia) Inc.'s Applications (TRADE MARK: APPLICATIONS: REGISTRABILITY: SUBSTANTIALLY IDENTICAL: DECEPTIVELY SIMILAR: GOODS AND SERVICES OF SAME DESCRIPTION: Australia: AIPO) 31 I.P.R. 92
Télémécanique Électrique, *sub nom.* La Télémécanique Électrique
Telesat Canada v. Ogden (TRADE MARKS: OPPOSITION: DESCRIPTIVE MARK: TELEPORT 1 & DESIGN: USE AS REGISTERED: Canada: T.M. Opp. Bd)
33 C.P.R. (3d) 361
Telespeed Services Ltd v. U.K. Post Office (RESTRICTIVE PRACTICES: DOMINANT POSITION: E.C. Comm.)
[1983] 1 C.M.L.R. 457; [1983] F.S.R. 359; [1982] O.J. L360/36
Television Broadcasts Ltd v. Golden Line Video & Marketing Pte Ltd (COPYRIGHT: PLAINTIFF'S: CINEMATOGRAPHIC FILMS: EXHIBITION OF THE FILMS OF VIDEOTAPES: RENTAL WITHOUT LICENCE OF PLAINTIFF'S: VIDEOTAPES NOT PIRATED COPIES: Singapore: H.C.) 13 I.P.R. 439
Television Broadcasts Ltd v. Mandarin Video Holdings Sdn Bhd (COPYRIGHT: INFRINGEMENT: ANTON PILLER PRACTICE: PRIVILEGE AGAINST SELF-INCRIMINATION: Malaysia: H.C.) [1983] 2 M.L.J. 346; [1984] F.S.R. 111
Television Broadcasts Ltd v. Seremban Video Centre Sdn Bhd (COPYRIGHT: INFRINGEMENT: APPEAL: ANTON PILLER ORDER: Malaysia: H.C.)
[1985] 1 M.L.J. 171
Television Broadcasts Ltd v. Thi Phuong Nguyen (PRACTICE AND PROCEDURE: ANTON PILLER ORDER: LIMITED RIGHT OF INSPECTION: PRIVILEGE AGAINST SELF INCRIMINATION: UNDERTAKING AS TO DAMAGES: Australia: Fed. Ct)
15 I.P.R. 97
Television Broadcasts Ltd v. Tu (COPYRIGHT: USE BY RESPONDENTS OF APPLICANTS' VIDEO CASSETTES AFTER EXPIRY OF LICENCE: FLAGRANT BREACH: DAMAGES: CALCULATION: TRADE MARKS: SUPERIMPOSED LABEL ON VIDEO CASSETTES NOT ADEQUATELY COVERING APPLICANTS' MARK: Australia: Fed. Ct) 19 I.P.R. 307
Television New Zealand Ltd v. Gloss Cosmetic Supplies Ltd (TV SOAP OPERA BROADCAST USING THE NAME GLOSS: LICENCE GRANTED TO SECOND PLAINTIFF TO PRODUCE COSMETICS UNDER SAME NAME: NOT YET ON MARKET: DEFENDANT PRODUCING COSMETICS UNDER NAME GLOSS: CONFUSION AND DECEPTION: New Zealand: H.C.) 19 I.P.R. 663

Television New Zealand Ltd v. Newsmonitor Services Ltd (COPYRIGHT:
INFRINGEMENT: TV BROADCASTS: SCRIPT OF NEWS: LITERARY COPYRIGHT:
DRAMATIC COPYRIGHT: COPYING FOR PRIVATE PURPOSES: FAIR DEALING:
PRIVATE RESEARCH OR STUDY: IMPLIED LICENCE: REPRODUCTION FOR
JUDICIAL PROCEEDINGS: New Zealand: C.A.)   [1991] 3 N.Z.L.R. 179
Television N.Z. v. Newsmonitor Services Ltd (COPYRIGHT: INFRINGEMENT: TV
PROGRAMMES: RECORDING BY NEWS MONITORING SERVICE: TRANSCRIPTS:
FAIR DEALING: IMPLIED LICENCE: New Zealand: H.C.)
                              27 I.P.R. 441; [1994] 2 N.Z.L.R. 91
Television Radio Centre (Pty) Ltd v. Sony KK (TRADE MARK: INFRINGEMENT:
REGISTERED USER: ALTERATION OF GOODS: South Africa: A.D.)
                                           1987 (2) S.A. 994
Telmak Teleproducts (Australia) Pty Ltd v. Coles Myer Ltd (PASSING OFF:
PACKAGING OF SIMILAR PRODUCTS: LABELLED WITH SAME DESCRIPTIVE
WORDS: NECESSITY TO PROVE DISTINCTIVENESS: NO SECONDARY MEANING
ACQUIRED: REQUIREMENT OF MISREPRESENTATION: WHETHER PROOF OF
FRAUDULENT INTENT SUFFICIENT TO GROUND ACTION: PROOF OF INTENT
ONLY EVIDENTIAL WEIGHT: Australia: Fed. Ct)
                                   84 A.L.R. 437; 12 I.P.R. 297
Telmak Teleproducts (Australia) Pty Ltd v. Coles Myer Ltd (TRADE PRACTICES:
MISLEADING AND DECEPTIVE CONDUCT: DESCRIPTION OF PRODUCTS:
PACKAGING GET-UP: SIMILARITY OF NAME AND GET-UP TO THAT USED BY
APPELLANT FOR SIMILAR GOODS: PASSING OFF: ELEMENTS: Australia: Fed.
Ct)   89 A.L.R. 48; 15 I.P.R. 362
Ten-Ichi Co. Ltd v. Jancar Ltd (TRADE MARK: PASSING OFF: WHETHER ACTION LIES
WHERE NO ACTIVE BUSINESS IN JURISDICTION: INTERNATIONAL
REPUTATION: WHETHER DAMAGES RECOVERABLE: INJUNCTION GRANTED:
Hong Kong: H.C.)   [1990] F.S.R. 351
TERBULINE Trade Mark (TRADE MARK: APPLICATION: WHETHER SPECIAL
CIRCUMSTANCES: BoT)   [1990] R.P.C. 21
Testro Bros v. Tennant (PASSING OFF: UNFAIR TRADING: MISREPRESENTATION:
INTERLOCUTORY INJUNCTION: Australia: S.C.)   2 I.P.R. 469
Tetra Pak International AB v. J. Gadsden Pty Ltd (PATENT: OPPOSITION: NOVELTY:
ANTICIPATION: OBVIOUSNESS: COMMON GENERAL KNOWLEDGE: FAIR BASIS:
AMENDMENT OF COMPLETE SPECIFICATION: Australia: Pat. Off.)
                                           10 I.P.R. 529
Tetra Pak Rausing SA v. E.C. Commission (CONSTITUTIONAL LAW: EEC TREATY:
RESTRICTIVE PRACTICES: DOMINANT POSITION: ABUSE: EXCLUSIVE
LICENCES: GROUP EXEMPTIONS: LEGAL CERTAINTY: POWER OF NATIONAL
COURTS: Case T–51/89: ECJ)   [1991] 4 C.M.L.R. 334; [1991] F.S.R. 654
Teva/Missing drawings (EUROPEAN PATENT: AMENDMENT AND CORRECTION:
DRAWINGS: OMITTED: CONVENTIONS: *Lex specialis*: J01/82: EPO)
                          [1979–85] E.P.O.R. A96; [1982] O.J. EPO 293
Texaco/Re-establishment (EUROPEAN PATENT: RE-ESTABLISHMENT OF RIGHTS:
MONITORING SYSTEM: PRINCIPAL OF PROPORTIONALITY: T869/90: EPO)
                                           [1994] E.P.O.R. 581
Texaco/Reaction injection moulded elastomer (EUROPEAN PATENT: CLAIMS:
CONSTRUCTION: NOVELTY: CROSS-REFERENCED DOCUMENTS: PRIOR
UNPUBLISHED APPLICATION: SELECTION FROM KNOWN NUMERICAL RANGE:
WHOLE CONTENTS: PRIOR ART: PRIOR UNPUBLISHED APPLICATIONS:
T279/89: EPO)   [1992] E.P.O.R. 294

Texas Alkyls/Dialkylmagnesium compositions (EUROPEAN PATENT: PRIOR ART: INACCURATE STATEMENTS: T116/82: EPO)   [1979–85] E.P.O.R. B562
Texas/Amendments (EUROPEAN PATENT: AMENDMENT AND CORRECTION: PRE-PUBLICATION: EPO: PRINCIPLES OF OPERATION: J10/84: EPO)
[1979–85] E.P.O.R. A213; [1985] O.J. EPO 71
Textron Inc.'s Patent (PATENT: RESTORATION: EVIDENCE: JUNIOR EMPLOYEE'S MISTAKE: FAILURE OF EMPLOYEE TO CARRY OUT INSTRUCTIONS: C.A.)   [1988] R.P.C. 177
(H.L.) [1989] R.P.C. 441; [1980] 1 F.T.L.R. 210; 13 I.P.R. 1
Thackray/Surgical instruments (EUROPEAN PATENT: UNITY: AMENDMENT OF CLAIMS IN OPPOSITION PROCEEDINGS: *A priori*: T249/89: EPO)
[1992] E.P.O.R. 137
Thai Gypsum Products Co. Ltd v. Waring and Gillow Pty Ltd (TRADE MARK: PROPRIETOR OF MARK: LEVEL OF USE: USE IN AUSTRALIA: USE IN CONNECTION WITH GOODS: USE ON BROCHURES: Australia: Fed. Ct)
29 I.P.R. 99
Thai World Import & Export Co. Ltd v. Shuey Shing Pty Ltd (PASSING OFF: MARKING AND GET-UP: WHETHER ANY REPUTATION HAD FALLEN INTO DESUETUDE BY THE TIME OF THE ALLEGED REPRESENTATION: PROOF OF GEOGRAPHICAL COVERAGE OF THE ALLEGED REPUTATION AND REPRESENTATION: Australia: Fed. Ct)   17 I.P.R. 289
Thakur Ayurvedic Pharmacy v. Pandit D.P. Sharma (TRADE MARKS: APPLICATION: OPPOSITION DISMISSED: REVIEW PETITIONS ALSO DISMISSED: APPEAL: India: H.C.)   (1990) 13 I.P.L.R. 233
Thames & Hudson Ltd v. Design and Artists Copyright Society Ltd (COPYRIGHT: INFRINGEMENT: CRIMINAL PROSECUTION BY COLLECTING SOCIETY AGAINST PUBLISHERS AND DIRECTORS: DECLARATION OF NON-INFRINGEMENT: FAIR DEALING: STAY: Ch.D.)   [1995] F.S.R. 153
Thapsons Pvt. Ltd v. Ashoka Food Industries (TRADE MARK: INFRINGEMENT: PASSING OFF: SIMILAR MARKS: COMMON TO THE TRADE: *Ad interim* INJUNCTION: India: H.C.)   (1992) 17 I.P.L.R. 85
The Body Shop International plc, *sub nom.* Body Shop International plc
The British Diabetic Association v. The Diabetic Society, *sub nom.* British Diabetic Association (The) v. Diabetic Society (The)
THE CLUB Trade Mark (TRADE MARK: APPLICATION: DEVICE MARK: WHETHER MARK DISTINCTIVE OR CAPABLE OF DISTINGUISHING: T.M.Reg.)
[1994] R.P.C. 33
The Concept Factory v. Heyl, *sub nom.* Concept Factory v. Heyl
THE ENDLESS VACATION Trade Mark (APPLICATION: WHETHER USE AS TRADE MARK: Ch.D.)   [1984] R.P.C. 148
The European Ltd v. The Economist Newspapers Ltd (TRADE MARK: DEVICE MARKS: THE EUROPEAN/EUROPEAN VOICE: WHETHER SIMILAR: WHETHER CONFUSING: EVIDENCE OF CONFUSION: T.M.A. 94: s.11(2)(b): SURVEY EVIDENCE: Ch.D.)   [1996] F.S.R. 431; [1996] E.M.L.R. 394
The Garden Co. Ltd v. Gardenia Overseas Pty Ltd, *sub nom.* Garden Co. Ltd v. Gardenia Overseas Pty Ltd
THE GLENLIVET Trade Marks (TRADE MARK: APPLICATIONS: GEOGRAPHICAL NAME: WHETHER DISTINCTIVE: BoT)   [1993] R.P.C. 461
The Really Useful Group Ltd v. Gordon & Gotch Ltd, *sub nom.* Really Useful Group Ltd (The) v. Gordon & Gotch Ltd

The Reject Shop plc v. Robert Manners (COPYRIGHT: SECONDARY INFRINGEMENT: SUBSISTANCE: ENLARGED PHOTOCOPIES: ORIGINALITY: WHETHER SKILL AND LABOUR INVOLVED: CRIMINAL PROCEEDINGS: APPEAL BY WAY OF CASE STATED: PRACTICE: COSTS: Q.B.D.)   [1995] F.S.R. 870

Theodor Kohl KG v. Ringelhan & Rennett SA (IMPORTS: PHARMACEUTICALS: TRADE MARK: GET-UP: USE BY SEVERAL SUCCESSORS TO SPLIT COMPANY: LIKELIHOOD OF CONFUSION: INFRINGEMENT: Germany: Case 177/83: ECJ)   [1985] 3 C.M.L.R. 340; [1986] F.S.R. 8

Therm-A-Stor Ltd v. Weatherseal Windows Ltd (No. 2) (PATENT: INFRINGEMENT: VALIDITY: AMENDMENT: FAIR BASIS: PRACTICE: C.A.)   [1984] F.S.R. 323

THERMAX Trade Mark (TRADE MARK: RECTIFICATION: NON-USER: INTENTION TO USE: OPPOSITION: T.M.Reg.)   [1985] R.P.C. 403

Thermo Produktor/Refrigeration apparatus (EUROPEAN PATENT: OPPOSITION: PRIOR USE: EVIDENCE: SUGGESTIONS BY OPPOSITION DIVISION: INVENTIVE STEP: T804/92: EPO)   [1995] E.P.O.R. 89; [1994] O.J. EPO 862

Thermo Technic Ltd's Application (PATENT: APPLICATION: PRACTICE: TIME LIMITS: Pat. Ct)   [1985] R.P.C. 109

Thermos Ltd v. Micropore International Ltd (TRADE MARKS: APPLICATION: OPPOSITION: ADAPTED TO DISTINGUISH: SUBSTANTIALLY IDENTICAL OR DECEPTIVELY SIMILAR MARKS: USE LIKELY TO DECEIVE OR CAUSE CONFUSION: Australia: Pat. Off.)   13 I.P.R. 504

THERMOS PRIMA Trade Mark (TRADE MARK: OPPOSITION: DATE AS OF WHICH LIKELIHOOD OF DECEPTION TO BE CONSIDERED: T.M.Reg.)
    [1991] R.P.C. 120

Thetford Corp. v. Fiamma SpA (PATENT: INFRINGEMENT: EURO-DEFENCE: ARTICLE 36: C.A.)   [1987] F.S.R. 244; [1987] 1 F.T.L.R. 162

Thetford Corp. v. Fiamma SpA (PATENT: INFRINGEMENT: NOVELTY: PA49 CASE: "50-YEAR RULE": REMEDITES: EEC LAW: COMMUNITY LAW CONFLICT WITH NATIONAL LAW: VALIDITY: RELATIVE NOVELTY: Case 35/87: ECJ)
    [1988] 3 C.M.L.R. 549; [1989] 1 F.S.R. 57; [1990] 2 W.L.R. 1394; 20 I.P.R. 117

Theurer/Assistant: substitute (EUROPEAN PATENT: FEES: REIMBURSEMENT OF APPEAL FEE: RE-ESTABLISHMENT OF RIGHTS: SUBSTITUTE, FAILURE TO SUPERVISE: J16/82: EPO)   [1979–85] E.P.O.R. A137; [1983] O.J. EPO 262

Thomas & Garnhams Application (PATENT: APPLICATION: OBJECTION BY EXAMINER: REQUEST TO COMMISSIONER TO EXERCISE DISCRETIONARY POWER: COMPUTER PROCESSING APPARATUS FOR ASSEMBLING TEXT, PARTICULARLY IN CHINESE CHARACTERS: PATENTABILITY: NOVELTY: PRIORITY DATE: Australia: AIPO)   29 I.P.R. 278

Thomas & Stohr's Application (PETTY PATENT: OPPOSITION TO EXTENSION OF TERM: COMPUTER INVENTION: OBVIOUSNESS: IDEA: ANTICIPATION: Australia: Pat. Off.)   21 I.P.R. 55

Thomas (Arthur Edward) Ltd v. Barcrest (PATENT: PATENTS COUNTY COURT: PRACTICE: SECURITY FOR COSTS: Pat. C.C.)   [1995] R.P.C. 138

Thomas (V.T.) v. Malayala Manorama Co. Ltd (COPYRIGHT: CARTOON CHARACTERS: BOBAN AND MOLLY: PETITION FOR STAY OF *ex parte* INJUNCTION: India: H.C.)   (1989) 14 I.P.L.R. 1

Thomas (V.T.) v. Malayala Manorama Co. Ltd (COPYRIGHT: CARTOONS: EX-EMPLOYEE: PREVENT PUBLICATION AFTER TERMINATION OF EMPLOYMENT: *ad interim ex parte* INJUNCTION VACATED: India: H.C.)
    (1988) 13 I.P.L.R. 172

Thomas Brandt v. Comptroller of Patents & Designs (APPLICATION FOR PROCESS PATENT: APPLICATION REJECTED BY COMPTROLLER: ON APPEAL APPLICATION REMANDED BACK TO COMPTROLLER: India: H.C.)
(1990) 15 I.P.L.R. 37

Thomas v. Jiejung Pty Ltd (PATENT: APPLICATION: EXTENSION OF TIME FOR ACCEPTANCE: ERROR OF COMMISSIONER: INCORRECT ADVICE FROM PATENT OFFICE: Australia: AIPO) 29 I.P.R. 441

Thomson Brandts Application (PATENT: APPLICATION: ARTICLE OR SUBSTANCE: STATUTORY INTERPRETATION: India: Pat. Off.) (1990) 15 I.P.L.R. 280

Thomson-Brandt/Admissibility (EUROPEAN PATENT: OPPOSITION: PROCEDURE: INADMISSIBLE OPPOSITION: NO JURISDICTION TO EXAMINE OF OWN: NOTICE OF OPPOSITION: REQUIREMENTS OF IN PRIOR USE CASES: TIME LIMIT FOR FULFILLING MINIMUM: T328/87: EPO)
[1993] E.P.O.R. 191; [1992] O.J. EPO 701

Thomson-CSF/Collector for high-frequency tube (EUROPEAN PATENT: AMENDMENT AND CORRECTION: BROADENING CLAIM BY OMISSION: T151/84: EPO) [1988] E.P.O.R. 29

Thomson-CSF/Spooling process for optical fibre gyroscope (EUROPEAN PATENT: AMENDMENT AND CORRECTION: BROADENING CLAIM BY OMISSION: T467/90: EPO) [1991] E.P.O.R. 115

Thomson-CSF/Tomodensitometry (1) (EUROPEAN PATENT: PATENTABILITY: DIAGNOSTIC METHOD: T61/83: EPO) [1979–85] E.P.O.R. C763

Thomson-CSF/Tomodensitometry (2) (EUROPEAN PATENT: PATENTABILITY: DIAGNOSTIC METHOD: T208/83: EPO) [1979–85] E.P.O.R. C917

Thomson-CSF/Transistor structure (EUROPEAN PATENT: CLAIMS: ONE PART V. TWO PART: INVENTIVE STEP: CONFLICTING GOALS: T15/86: EPO)
[1987] E.P.O.R. 291

Thorn EMI Video Programmes Ltd v. Kitching (COPYRIGHT: INFRINGEMENT: ANTON PILLER PRACTICE: PRIVILEGE AGAINST SELF-INCRIMINATION: New Zealand: H.C.) [1984] F.S.R. 342
sub nom. Busby v. Thorn EMI Video Programmes Ltd
(C.A.) 2 I.P.R. 304; [1984] N.Z.L.R. 461

Thorn EMI/Discharge lamps (EUROPEAN PATENT: CLAIMS: ONE PART V. TWO PART: INVENTIVE STEP: COMBINATION OF CITATIONS: STATE OF THE ART: T137/86: EPO) [1988] E.P.O.R. 187

Thorn EMI/Re-establishment of rights (EUROPEAN PATENT: RE-ESTABLISHMENT OF RIGHTS: DUE CARE: UNUSUALLY HIGH WORKLOAD: T137/86: EPO)
[1987] E.P.O.R. 183

Thorn/Thermal limiting device (EUROPEAN PATENT: NOVELTY: WHOLE CONTENTS: PRIORITY DATE: PRIOR USE: DEMONSTRATION AT EXHIBITION: BURDEN OF PROOF: T326/93: EPO) [1995] E.P.O.R. 297

Thornton Hall Manufacturing Ltd v. Shanton Apparel Ltd (COPYRIGHT: INFRINGEMENT: ARTISTIC WORK: DRESS: SAMPLE: WHETHER THREE-DIMENSIONAL REPRODUCTION OF AN ORIGINAL ARTISTIC WORK: SUBSISTENCE OF COPYRIGHT: New Zealand: H.C.) [1989] 1 N.Z.L.R. 239
(APPEAL: C.A.) [1989] 3 N.Z.L.R. 304

Thornton Hall Manufacturing Ltd v. Shanton Apparel Ltd (No. 2) (COPYRIGHT: SUBSISTENCE: SKETCHES, PATTERNS AND SAMPLE DRESS: ARTISTIC WORKS: ORIGINALITY: OWNERSHIP: INFRINGEMENT: New Zealand: H.C.)
13 I.P.R. 463

Thorp v. C. A. Imports Pty Ltd (TRADE PRACTICES: FALSE OR MISLEADING REPRESENTATION CONCERNING THE PLACE OF ORIGIN OF GOODS: REASONABLE RELIANCE ON INFORMATION SUPPLIED BY ANOTHER PERSON: Australia: Fed. Ct)   16 I.P.R. 511

Thrustcode Ltd v. WW Computing Ltd (COPYRIGHT: INFRINGEMENT: COMPUTER PROGRAMS: INTERLOCUTORY INJUNCTION: WHETHER COPYRIGHT CAN SUBSIST IN A COMPUTER PROGRAM: DIFFICULTY IN ESTABLISHING INFRINGEMENT: EVIDENCE OF COPYING: BALANCE OF CONVENIENCE: Ch.D.)   [1983] F.S.R. 502

Tiheti Pty Ltd v. Guard Dog Patrol & Security Services Pty Ltd (TRADE PRACTICES: MISLEADING CONDUCT: USE OF SIMILAR TRADING NAME: APPLICATION FOR ORDER FOR RESPONDENT TO INSTALL RECORDED MESSAGE ON TELEPHONE SERVICE GIVING APPLICANT'S TELEPHONE NUMBER: Australia: Fed. Ct)   19 I.P.R. 251

(APPEAL: APPEAL FROM SINGLE JUDGES ORDER FOR RECORDED MESSAGE REDIRECTING INQUIRIES: WHETHER JUDGE'S DISCRETION MISCARRIED: Australia: Fed. Ct)   19 I.P.R. 259

Timberland Co. v. Speedo Knitting Mills Pty Ltd (TRADE MARKS: NON-USE: APPLICATION TO REMOVE: OPPOSITION: DISCRETION OF REGISTRAR: EVIDENCE: PRACTICE AND PROCEDURE: Australia: Pat. Ct)   18 I.P.R. 555

Timbs v. Miller (COPYRIGHT: INFRINGEMENT: DRAWINGS OF BOATS: Australia: S.C.(NSW))   1 I.P.R. 128

Time Warner Entertainments Co. LP v. Channel Four Television Corp. plc (COPYRIGHT: INFRINGEMENT: FILM: *A Clockwork Orange*: EXCERPTS SHOWN ON TV: WHETHER FAIR DEALING FOR PURPOSE OF CRITICISM OR REVIEW: C.A.)   [1994] E.M.L.R. 1; 28 I.P.R. 459

Times Media Ltd v. South African Broadcasting Corp. (TRADE AND TRADE MARK: UNLAWFUL COMPETITION: PUBLIC BROADCASTING CORPORATION REFUSING TO TELEVISE ADVERTISEMENT: GOODWILL: UNLAWFUL BOYCOTT: South Africa: WLD)   1990 (4) S.A. 604

Times Newspapers Ltd v. Attorney-General, *sub nom.* Attorney-General v. Times Newspapers Ltd

Times Newspapers Ltd v. MGN Ltd (BREACH OF CONFIDENCE: INTERLOCUTORY INJUNCTION: THATCHER MEMOIRS: BOOK NOT YET PUBLISHED: EXCLUSIVE RIGHT TO NEWSPAPER SERIALISATION: DEFENDANT PUBLISHING ARTICLES BASED ON AND QUOTING FROM BOOK: WHETHER MATERIAL POSSESSING NECESSARY QUALITY OF CONFIDENCE: PUBLIC INTEREST IN PUBLICATION: CLARITY AND PRECISION OF INJUNCTION SOUGHT: C.A.)   [1993] E.M.L.R. 443

Tinna Enterprises Pvt. Ltd v. International Rubber Industries (TRADE MARK: INFRINGEMENT: PASSING OFF: TINNA/TANY: INTERIM INJUNCTION: India: H.C.)   (1986) 10 I.P.L.R. 427

Tioxide/Pigments (EUROPEAN PATENT: CLAIMS: CLARITY: CHALLENGE TO IN OPPOSITION: EVIDENCE: BURDEN OF PROOF; CLOSEST PRIOR ART: INVENTIVE STEP: COMBINATION OF CITATIONS: NOVELTY: INEVITABLE RESULT: OPPOSITION: PROCEDURE: CLAIMS: OBJECTION TO CLARITY OF, ADMISSIBLE: T525/90: EPO)   [1994] E.P.O.R. 408

Tippens/Reversing plate mill (EUROPEAN PATENT: PATENTABILITY: PRODUCTIVITY IMPROVEMENT METHOD: T209/91: EPO)   [1992] E.P.O.R. 289

Titan Group Pty Ltd v. Steriline Manufacturing Pty Ltd (CONFIDENTIAL INFORMATION: CONTENTS OF PATENT APPLICATIONS: DISCLOSURE IN CONFIDENCE: KNOWLEDGE OF RECIPIENT: SPRINGBOARD PERIOD: WHEN INFORMATION ENTERED PUBLIC DOMAIN: USE OF INFORMATION BEFORE EXPIRY OF SPRINGBOARD PERIOD BUT NO PROFITS DERIVED UNTIL AFTER EXPIRY: NO DAMAGE SUFFERED: CONTRACT: SETTLEMENT AGREEMENT: PROHIBITION ON USE OF PROPRIETARY INFORMATION AFTER EXPIRATION OF THREE-MONTH PERIOD: BREACH NOT ESTABLISHED: Australia: Fed. Ct)
19 I.P.R. 353
Titan Manufacturing Co. Pty Ltd v. John Terence Coyne (TRADE MARKS: APPLICATION: OPPOSITION: Australia: Pat. Off.)   22 I.P.R. 613
Titan Mining & Engineering Pty Ltd v. Arnall's Engineering Pty Ltd (PATENT: COMMISSIONERS DECISION: NATURE OF APPEAL: WITHDRAWAL OF OPPONENT AND INTERVENTION OF COMMISSIONER: JURISDICTION OF COURT: INVALIDITY: LACK OF NOVELTY: FAILURE OF SPECIFICATION TO FULLY DESCRIBE: Australia: S.C.(NSW))
86 A.L.R. 290; 10 I.P.R. 661; (1988) 12 N.S.W.L.R. 73
TJM Products Pty Ltd v. A. & P. Tyres Pty Ltd (TRADE PRACTICES: MISLEADING AND DECEPTIVE CONDUCT: SIMILAR BUSINESS NAMES: LOGOS: GET-UP: PASSING OFF: CONFIDENTIAL INFORMATION: Australia: Fed. Ct)
8 I.P.R. 527
Toa Nenryo/Elastomer (EUROPEAN PATENT: AMENDMENT AND CORRECTION: PUBLISHED TEXT: APPEAL: PROCEDURE: EXTENT LIMITED TO ORIGINAL REQUEST: CLAIMS: IMPLICIT LIMITATION: TEXT OF PATENT: BASIS FOR GRANT SOLE AUTHENTIC TEXT: CONVENTIONS: DIFFERENT LANGUAGE TEXTS: INVENTIVE STEP: COMBINATION OF CITATIONS: PROBLEM DIFFERING FROM THAT OF PRIOR ART: NOVELTY: DISTINCTION BY PARAMETER: T299/89: EPO)   [1992] E.P.O.R. 107
Tobacco Institute of Australia Ltd v. Australian Federation of Consumer Organisations Inc. (TRADE PRACTICES: CONSUMER PROTECTION: ADVERTISEMENTS CLAIMING THAT PASSIVE SMOKING NOT SHOWN TO BE HARMFUL TO HEALTH OF NON-SMOKERS: WHETHER MISLEADING OR DECEPTIVE: INJUNCTIVE RELIEF: Australia: Fed. Ct)   24 I.P.R. 529
Tobacco Institute of Australia Ltd v. Australian Federation of Consumer Organisations Inc. (TRADE PRACTICES: PRACTICE AND PROCEDURE: INJUNCTIVE RELIEF: WHETHER CLASSES OF APPLICANTS ARE ALTERNATIVE OR CUMULATIVE: Australia: Fed. Ct)   12 I.P.R. 499
Tobias/Photoelectric densitometer (EUROPEAN PATENT: EVIDENCE: DATING DOCUMENT FROM COPYRIGHT NOTICE: DEMONSTRATION AT ORAL PROCEEDINGS: INVENTIVE STEP: COMPUTERISATION: PRIOR ART: BROCHURE: T287/86: EPO)   [1989] E.P.O.R. 214
Tobu Interprises Pvt. Ltd v. Tokyo Cycle Industries (TRADE MARK: COPYRIGHT: INFRINGEMENT: PASSING OFF: TOBU/TOHO: India: H.C.)
(1984) 10 I.P.L.R. 150
Toby Construction Products Pty Ltd v. Computer Bar Sales Pty Ltd (COMPUTER SOFTWARE: SALE OF "GOODS": WHETHER GOODS: Australia: S.C.(NSW))
1 I.P.R. 334
Tohtonku Sdn Bhd v. Superace (M.) Sdn Bhd (TRADE MARKS: REGISTERED PROPRIETOR OF TRADE MARK: INFRINGEMENT: *Ex parte* APPLICATION FOR RELIEF: Malaysia: H.C.)   [1989] 2 M.L.J. 298; I.P.R. 356
(S.C.) [1992] 2 M.L.J. 63
Tokan Kogyo KK's Application (PATENT: APPLICATION: PRACTICE: PROCEDURAL ERROR: DISCRETION: C.-G.)   [1985] R.P.C. 244

Tokyo Shibaura/Ultrasonic diagnostic apparatus (EUROPEAN PATENT: ABANDONMENT: WHETHER UNAMBIGUOUS LIMITATION OF PROTECTION, NO: CLAIMS: CONSTRUCTION: IN LIGHT OF LIMITATION: OPPOSITION: PROCEDURE: REVIVAL OF ORIGINAL CLAIMS AT ORAL HEARING: T64/85: EPO)   [1988] E.P.O.R. 225

Toledo/Correction of designation (EUROPEAN PATENT: RE-ESTABLISHMENT OF RIGHTS: TIME LIMIT, WHAT CONSTITUTES: AMENDMENT AND CORRECTION: DESIGNATION OF STATES: ENLARGED BOARD OF APPEAL: REFERENCE REFUSED: J07/90: EPO)   [1993] E.P.O.R. 329; [1993] O.J. EPO 133

Tolima (Pty) Ltd v. Cugacius Motor Accessories (Pty) Ltd (COPYRIGHT: 3-D FORM OF 2-D DRAWING: INDIRECT COPYING: South Africa: WLD)
1983 (3) S.A. 504

TOLTECS and DORCET Trade Marks (RESTRICTIVE PRACTICES: TRADE MARKS: DORCET AND TOLTECS SPECIAL: DORMANT MARK: SIMILARITY: INFRINGEMENT OF ARTICLE 85 EEC: E.C. Comm.)
[1983] 1 C.M.L.R. 412; [1983] F.S.R. 327; [1982] O.J. L379/19
(E.C. COMM. UPHELD: FINES: Case 35/83: ECJ)
[1985] 2 C.M.L.R. 470; [1985] E.C.R. 363; [1985] F.S.R. 533
See further, *sub nom.* British American Tobacco Co. Ltd v. E.C. Commission

Tom Cruise and Nicole Kidman v. Southdown Press Pty Ltd (INJUNCTION: COPYRIGHT: IMPENDING PUBLICATION OF PHOTOGRAPHS OF CHILD: WHETHER RIGHT OF PRIVACY: MISUSE OF CONFIDENTIAL INFORMATION: BREACH OF COPYRIGHT: DEFAMATION: Australia: Fed. Ct)   26 I.P.R. 125

Tomy Kogyo Co. Inc.'s Applications (REGISTERED DESIGN: CONVENTION APPLICATION: PRACTICE: DISCRETION UNDER RULES TO EXTEND TIME: RDAT)   [1983] R.P.C. 207

Tong Guan Food Products Pte Ltd v. Hoe Huat Hng Foodstuffs Pte Ltd (PASSING OFF: GET-UP: SIMILARITY: DECEPTION OR CONFUSION: REPUTATION: Singapore: C.A.)   [1991] 2 M.L.J. 361

Tonka Corp. v. Chong (TRADE MARK: OPPOSITION: DECEPTIVE SIMILARITY: BLAMEWORTHY CONDUCT: Australia: AIPO)   29 I.P.R. 253

Tony Blain Pty Ltd (t/a Acme Merchandising) v. Jamison (PRACTICE AND PROCEDURE: REPRESENTATIVE ORDER: *Ex parte* ORDER: REPRESENTATION OF GROUP: ANTON PILLER: CIRCUMSTANCES: SAFEGUARDS: Australia: Fed. Ct)   26 I.P.R. 8

Tony Blain Pty Ltd v. Splain (PASSING OFF: TRADE MARKS: COPYRIGHT: INFRINGEMENT: INTERIM INJUNCTION: POP CONCERTS: COMMERCIAL EXPLOITATION OF NAMES AND ACTIVITIES OF ARTISTS AND OTHERS: PROTECTION OF LICENSEES: PRACTICE: ANTON PILLER ORDER AGAINST PERSONS UNKNOWN: New Zealand: H.C.)
[1993] 3 N.Z.L.R. 185; [1994] F.S.R. 497

Tooheys Ltd's Application (TRADE MARKS: APPLICATION: REGISTRABILITY: SURNAME: DISTINCTIVE: CAPABLE OF BECOMING DISTINCTIVE: Australia: Pat. Off.)   20 I.P.R. 507

Tool Wholesale Holdings (Pty) Ltd v. Action Bolt (Pty) Ltd, *sub nom.* Action Bolt (Pty) Ltd v. Tool Wholesale Holdings (Pty) Ltd

Toray Industries/Photosensitive resin (EUROPEAN PATENT: EVIDENCE: COMPARATIVE TESTS: CONFLICTING: NOVELTY: INEVITABLE RESULT: T310/88: EPO)   [1991] E.P.O.R. 10

Toray/Flame retarding polyester composition (EUROPEAN PATENT: INVENTIVE STEP: BONUS EFFECT: COULD/WOULD TEST: *Ex post facto* APPROACH: T227/89: EPO)   [1993] E.P.O.R. 107

Toray/Partial withdrawal of appeal (EUROPEAN PATENT: AMENDMENT AND CORRECTION: JURISDICTION OF FORMALITIES SECTION: APPEAL: PROCEDURE: POINTS TAKEN BY BOARD OF ITS OWN MOTION: WITHDRAWAL OF PART OF APPEAL: EPO: INTERNAL ORGANISATION: FEES: REIMBURSEMENT OF APPEAL FEE: APPELLANT'S COMMENDABLE CONDUCT OF: J19/82: EPO)　　　　[1979–85] E.P.O.R. A145; [1984] O.J. EPO 06

Toray/Ultrasonic transducer (EUROPEAN PATENT: INVENTIVE STEP: SKILLED PERSON, FIELD OF EXPERIENCE OF: TRIAL-AND-ERROR APPROACH: APPLIED: T48/86: EPO)　　　　[1988] E.P.O.R. 143

Torgersen/Door structure (EUROPEAN PATENT: INVENTIVE STEP: PROBLEM, RECOGNITION OF, NO CONTRIBUTION TO: SIMPLIFICATION OF PRIOR ART: T144/84: EPO)　　　　[1979–85] E.P.O.R. C976

Toro Companys Applications (TRADE MARK: APPLICATION: OBJECTION: DESCRIPTIVE MARK: CONSISTANCY BY REGISTRAR: PRACTICE: SURVEY EVIDENCE: Australia: AIPO)　　　　30 I.P.R. 569

Torras/Tractor (EUROPEAN PATENT: APPLICATION: PROCEDURE: REMITTAL TO EXAMINING DIVISION: CLAIMS: CLARITY: OPEN-ENDED DEFINITIONS: T577/88: EPO)　　　　[1991] E.P.O.R. 149

TORRE NOVA Trade Mark (TRADE MARK: OPPOSITION: LABEL MARK: HONEST CONCURRENT USE: T.M.Reg.)　　　　[1991] R.P.C. 109

Torrington/Reimbursement of appeal fees (EUROPEAN PATENT: APPEAL: PROCEDURE: CROSS-APPEAL: EXAMINATION BY BOARD OF APPEAL OF ITS OWN MOTION: FEES: REIMBURSEMENT OF APPEAL FEE: OPPOSITION: CROSS-APPEAL: T89/84: EPO)　　　　[1979–85] E.P.O.R. C949; [1984] O.J. EPO 562

Tosca (COPYRIGHT: OPERA: PERIOD OF PROTECTION: FOREIGN AUTHORS: EVIDENCE: INTERNATIONAL CONVENTION AND NATIONAL LAWS: Germany: S.C.)　　　　[1987] E.C.C. 455

Toshiba Appliances Co. v. Toshiba KK (TRADE MARK: RECTIFICATION: NON-USE FOR FIVE YEARS: NON-INTENTION TO USE: IMPORT BAN: India: H.C.)
　　　　(1992) 17 I.P.L.R. 107
(APPEAL: EXPUNGEMENT CONFIRMED: H.C.)　　　　(1994) 19 I.P.L.R. 79

Toshiba/Display device for a machine (EUROPEAN PATENT: APPEAL: PROCEDURE: REIMBURSEMENT OF APPEAL FEES: OPPOSITION: AMENDMENTS PROPOSED BY OPPOSITION DIVISION AT START OF ORAL: T783/89: EPO)
　　　　[1991] E.P.O.R. 472

Toshiba/Semiconductor device (EUROPEAN PATENT: CLAIMS: FUNCTIONAL INTERPRETATION: SUFFICIENCY: EXAMPLE, ABSENCE OF: T407/87: EPO)
　　　　[1989] E.P.O.R. 470

Toshiba/Thickness of magnetic layers (EUROPEAN PATENT: APPEAL: PROCEDURE: OBJECTION BY BOARD, NEW: INVENTIVE STEP: SURPRISING EFFECT: NOVELTY: AVAILABILITY: NUMERICAL RANGES, OVERLAP: T26/85: EPO)　　　　[1990] E.P.O.R. 267; [1990] O.J. EPO 22

Tot Toys Ltd v. Mitchell (PASSING OFF: ELEMENTS: KIWI BEE/BUZZY BEE: TRADE MARK: ASSIGNABILITY OF MARK: New Zealand: H.C.)
　　　　[1993] 1 N.Z.L.R. 325

Total Information Processing Systems Ltd v. Daman Ltd (COPYRIGHT: COMPUTER SOFTWARE: COPYRIGHT IN SOFTWARE INTERFACE: MERGER OF IDEA WITH EXPRESSION: WHETHER PRINCIPLE OF DEROGATION FROM GRANT CONFINED TO COMPANIES WITH DOMINANT POSITION: EVIDENCE FOR INTERLOCUTORY APPLICATION: Ch.D.)　　　　[1992] F.S.R. 171; 22 I.P.R. 71

Totara Vineyards Sye Ltd v. Villa Maria Estate Ltd (PASSING OFF: INTERIM INJUNCTION: GEOGRAPHICAL OF DESCRIPTIVE NAME: New Zealand: H.C.)
　　　　8 I.P.R. 51

Townsend Controls Pty Ltd v. Gilead (PATENT: PRACTICE AND PROCEDURE: EQUITABLE ASSIGNEE: INFRINGEMENT: REVOCATION: Australia: Fed. Ct)
14 I.P.R. 443; 16 I.P.R. 469
Townsend Controls Pty Ltd v. Gilead (PATENT: THREATS: DAMAGES: Australia: Fed. Ct) 21 I.P.R. 520
Toyama Chemical Co. Ltd's Application (PATENT APPLICATION: NOVELTY: PRIORITY DATE: ENABLING DISCLOSURE: PRACTICE: EVIDENCE ON APPEAL: COSTS: Pat. Ct) [1990] R.P.C. 555
Toyo Seikan Kaisha Ltd v. Nordson Corp. (PATENT: OPPOSITION: NOTICE: EXTENSION OF TIME LIMIT: ERROR OR OMISSION: TIMELINESS: Australia: Pat. Off.) 5 I.P.R. 388
Toyota/Apparatus for measuring tyre uniformity (EUROPEAN PATENT: APPEAL: PROCEDURE: FRESH PRIOR ART: ADMITTED IN VIEW OF RELEVANCE: COSTS: APPORTIONMENT: REFUSED: FRESH CITATIONS ON APPEAL: T638/89: EPO) [1991] E.P.O.R. 101
Tracey Lee Wickham, *sub nom.* Wickham v. Associated Pool Builders Pty
Tracto-Technik/Telecopy filings (EUROPEAN PATENT: OPPOSITION: ADMISSIBILITY: NOTICE OF OPPOSITION: FILING AT GERMAN PATENT OFFICE: PROCEDURE: LEGITIMATE EXPECTATIONS: T485/89: EPO)
[1993] E.P.O.R. 475; [1993] O.J. EPO 214
Tradam Trading Co. (Bahamas) Ltd's Trade Mark (TRADE MARKS: RECTIFICATION: REGISTERED PROPRIETOR IN DEFAULT: APPLICATION BY ALLEGED ASSIGNEE TO INTERVENE: Ch.D.) [1990] F.S.R. 200
Trade Facilities Pte Ltd v. Public Prosecutor (TRADE MARK: COUNTERFEIT GOODS: IMPORTATION: SALE ABROAD: GOODS RETURNED BY FOREIGN BUYER: JURISDICTION: Singapore: H.C.) [1995] 2 S.L.R. 475
Trade Fairs & Promotions (Pty) Ltd v. Thomson (ANTON PILLER: NATURE AND SCOPE: EXCLUSION OF RIGHT OF SEARCH: South Africa: WLD)
1984 (4) S.A. 177
Trade Mark (Council Regulation), *sub nom.* Community Trade Mark Regulation
Trade Practices Commission v. Glo Juice Co. Pty Ltd (TRADE PRACTICES: MISLEADING AND DECEPTIVE CONDUCT: MISREPRESENTATION AS TO STRENGTH OF RECONSTITUTED DRINK MADE FROM CONCENTRATE: INJUNCTION: FORM: CONTEMPT: DISCRETION: Australia: Fed. Ct)
9 I.P.R. 63
Trade Practices Commission v. International Technology Holdings Pty Ltd (TRADE MARK: PRACTICE AND PROCEDURE: DISCOVERY AND INSPECTION: LEGAL PROFESSIONAL PRIVILEGE: PATENT ATTORNEYS: Australia: Fed. Ct)
31 I.P.R. 466
Transocean Marine Paint Association (No. 5) (RESTRICTIVE PRACTICES: JOINT PRODUCTION AND DISTRIBUTION: TERRITORIAL PROTECTION: FURTHER RENEWAL OF EXEMPTION GRANTED: E.C. Comm.) [1989] 4 C.M.L.R. 621
Tremblay v. E.C. Comm. *sub nom.* Bureau Européen des Medias de l'Industrie Musicale v. E.C. Comm.
Trepper v. Miss Selfridge Ltd (TRADE MARKS: APPLICATIONS FOR REGISTRATION: OPPOSITION: HONEST CONCURRENT USE: "PERSON AGGRIEVED": ONUS: EVIDENCE: SPECIAL CIRCUMSTANCES: DISCRETION: Australia: Pat. Off.)
23 I.P.R. 335
Tri-ang Pedigree (S.A.) (Pty) Ltd v. Prime Toys (Pty) Ltd (TRADE MARK: INFRINGEMENT: ONUS: South Africa: A.D.) 1985 (1) S.A. 448
Triangle Corp. Pty Ltd v. Carnsew (CONFIDENTIAL INFORMATION: CONFIDENTIALITY CLAUSE: DUTY OF EX-EMPLOYEE: CUSTOMER LISTS: CATEGORIES OF INFORMATION: Australia: Fed. Ct) 29 I.P.R. 69

Tribe & Rankins Application (PATENT: JOINT APPLICATION: PRACTICE AND
PROCEDURE: Australia: Pat. Off.) 1 I.P.R. 561
Triple Five Corp. v. Walt Disney Productions (TRADE MARK: PASSING OFF:
ELEMENTS: GOODWILL OR REPUTATION: MISREPRESENTATION:
CONFUSION: GENERAL RECOLLECTION: EVIDENCE: SURVEY EVIDENCE: ROLE
OF APPELLATE COURT: DAMAGE: USE OF MARK: FROM DIFFERENT
JURISDICTION: Australia: S.C.) 29 I.P.R. 639
Triple Three Leisure Ltd v. Turkovic (TRADE MARK: APPLICATION: OPPOSITION:
PROPRIETORSHIP: INHERENT DISTINCTIVENESS: USE OUTSIDE AUSTRALIA:
COPYRIGHT: Australia: AIPO) 27 I.P.R. 430
Trippit (C.) & Son's Application (TRADE MARKS: APPLICATION: EXAMINER'S
OBJECTION: GEOGRAPHICAL NAME: DESCRIPTIVE WORDS: Australia: Pat. Off.)
11 I.P.R. 596
TROOPER Trade Mark (TRADE MARK: RECTIFICATION: NON-USE: USE BY
UNREGISTERED USER: T.M.Reg.) [1994] R.P.C. 26
Trotman Australia Pty Ltd v. Hobsons Press (Australia) Pty Ltd (TRADE PRACTICES:
INJUNCTIONS: INTERLOCUTORY RELIEF: FALSE AND MISLEADING
COMPARISON OF GRADUATE CAREER DIRECTORIES: EVIDENCE OF PERSONS
ACTUALLY MISLED: PRINCIPLES GOVERNING ORDER FOR CORRECTIVE
PUBLICATIONS AT INTERLOCUTORY STAGE: Australia: Fed. Ct)
22 I.P.R. 397
Trucco/Re-establishment of rights (EUROPEAN PATENT: RE-ESTABLISHMENT OF
RIGHTS: MISLEADING INFORMATION GIVEN BY EPO: J32/86: EPO)
[1987] E.P.O.R. 249
Tube Couplings (Re Distribution of) (EXCLUSIVE DISTRIBUTION AGREEMENT:
INDUSTRIAL PROPERTY RIGHTS: MINIMUM PURCHASE OBLIGATION: EEC
COMPETITION LAW: Germany: C.A.) [1991] E.C.C. 11
Turbo Tek Enterprises Inc. v. Sperling Enterprises Pty Ltd (DESIGN: OBVIOUS OR
FRAUDULENT IMITATION: ELEMENTS: WHETHER ARTICLE MANUFACTURED
PRIOR TO REGISTRATION CAN BE A FRAUDULENT IMITATION OF
SUBSEQUENT REGISTRATION: Australia: Fed. Ct)
88 A.L.R. 524; 13 I.P.R. 368
(Fed. Ct) 15 I.P.R. 617
Turelin Nominees Pty Ltd v. Dainford Ltd (COURTS: JURISDICTION: TRADE
PRACTICES: Australia: Fed. Ct) 1 I.P.R. 69
Turner & Newall Ltd's Patent (PATENT: APPLICATION: PRACTICE: EUROPEAN
PATENT FOR SAME INVENTION: SURRENDER OF EUROPEAN PATENT:
AMENDMENT OF U.K. PATENT: C.-G.) [1984] R.P.C. 49
Twentieth Century Fox Film Corp. v. Anthony Black Films (Pty) Ltd (COPYRIGHT:
INFRINGEMENT: PARALLEL IMPORTS: South Africa: WLD) 1982 (3) S.A. 582
Twentieth Century Fox Film Corp. v. Tryrare Ltd (COPYRIGHT: INFRINGEMENT:
ANTON PILLER PRACTICE: THIRD PARTY RIGHTS: DISCLOSURE OF
INFORMATION OBTAINED: Ch.D.) [1991] F.S.R. 58
Two Pesos Inc. v. Taco Cabana Inc. (TRADE MARKS: TRADE DRESS: INHERENT
DISTINCTIVENESS: SECONDARY MEANING NOT REQUIRED: USA: S.C.)
24 I.P.R. 61
Tyburn Productions Ltd v. Conan Doyle (COPYRIGHT: LITERARY CHARACTERS:
SHERLOCK HOLMES: APPLICATION FOR DECLARATION OF NO SUBSISTING
COPYRIGHT IN U.S. AND INJUNCTION TO PREVENT THE MAKING OF SUCH
ASSERTIONS: WHETHER JUSTICIABLE IN ENGLAND: TRANSITORY AND LOCAL
ACTIONS: Ch.D.) [1990] 1 All E.R. 909;
[1990] R.P.C. 185; [1991] Ch. 75; [1990] 3 W.L.R. 167; 19 I.P.R. 455

Tyco Industries Inc. v. Interlego, *sub nom.* Interlego v. Tyco

Tye-Sil Corp. Ltd v. Diversified Products Corp. (PATENT: VALIDITY: PRESUMPTION: EVIDENTIARY BURDEN: Canada: Fed. Ct)   20 I.P.R. 574

TYLER Trade Mark (EEC: RESTRICTIVE PRACTICES: TRADE MARK: EXCLUSIVE LICENSING: E.C. Comm.)   [1982] 3 C.M.L.R. 613; [1983] F.S.R. 109

Typing Centre of NSW Pty Ltd v. Northern Business College Ltd (TRADE PRACTICES: MISLEADING CONDUCT: COMPARATIVE ADVERTISING: ALLEGED SUPERIORITY OF COURSES OFFERED BY RESPONDENTS: DAMAGES: Australia: Fed. Ct)   13 I.P.R. 627

Tytel Pty Ltd v. Australian Telecommunications Commission (TRADE PRACTICES: MISLEADING CONDUCT: FALSE REPRESENTATIONS: MONOPOLISATION: "AIDED, ABETTED, COUNSELLED OR PROCURED": Australia: Fed. Ct)   11 I.P.R. 223

Ueno Seiyaku/2-hydroxy-naphthalene-3-carboxylic acid (BON-3-acid) (EUROPEAN PATENT: INVENTIVE STEP: PROBLEM AND SOLUTION: FORMULATION OF PROBLEM: AGED ART: AVOIDANCE OF ARTIFICIALITY: CHEMICAL PROCESS: PROMISED RESULT: ALL EMBODIMENTS: EXPERIMENTS BY OPPONENT: NEED FOR EXERCISE OF APPROPRIATE SKILL: T741/91: EPO)   [1995] E.P.O.R. 533; [1993] O.J. EPO 630

Uhde/Re-establishment (EUROPEAN PATENT: APPEAL: PROCEDURE: APPEAL CONSTRUED AS RE-ESTABLISHMENT APPLICATION: EPO: GOOD FAITH TOWARDS PARTIES: RE-ESTABLISHMENT OF RIGHTS: REORGANISATION OF COMPANY: T14/89: EPO)   [1990] E.P.O.R. 656; [1990] O.J. EPO 432

Uhde/Reduction in NOx content (EUROPEAN PATENT: APPEAL: PROCEDURE: AMENDMENT OF RULES, EFFECT ON: UNITY: ASSESSED ON BASIS OF CLAIMS ALONE: CONVENTIONS: AMENDMENT OF RULES, EFFECT ON: T544/88: EPO)   [1990] E.P.O.R. 652; [1990] O.J. EPO 429

UKAEA/Fluidic flow control (EUROPEAN PATENT: CLAIMS: ONE PART V. TWO PART: INVENTIVE STEP: REMOTE ART: T135/82: EPO)   [1979–85] E.P.O.R. B608

Ulrich Labels Pty Ltd v. Printing & Allied Trades Employers Federation of Australia (PATENT: OPPOSITION: EXTENSION OF TIME TO FILE NOTICE OF OPPOSITION: *locus standi:* Australia: Pat. Off.)   20 I.P.R. 410

Unauthorised Reproduction of Sound Recordings in Indonesia (ILLICIT COMMERCIAL PRACTICES: NO PROTECTION AGAINST COPYING IN INDONESIA: INJURY TO EEC INDUSTRY: PROCEDURE: E.C. Comm.)   [1987] 3 C.M.L.R. 547

Unauthorised Reproduction of Sound Recordings in Indonesia (ILLICIT COMMERCIAL PRACTICES: SUSPENSION OF PROCEEDINGS: E.C. Comm.)   [1988] 1 C.M.L.R. 387

Underwood v. Toby Construction Products Pty Ltd (PATENT: OPPOSITION: APPLICATION FOR EXTENSION OF TIME WITHIN WHICH TO SERVE EVIDENCE-IN-SUPPORT OF OPPOSITION: Australia: Pat. Off.)   13 I.P.R. 140

Uni-Charm/Priority declaration (correction) (EUROPEAN PATENT: AMENDMENT AND CORRECTION: AFTER PUBLICATION: FEES: REIMBURSEMENT OF APPEAL FEE: J03/91: EPO)   [1994] E.P.O.R. 566; [1994] O.J. EPO 365

Unicomp Srl v. Italcomputers Srl (COPYRIGHT: CREATIVE WORK: COMPUTER PROGRAMS: Italy; Pisa; Magistrates Ct)   [1986] E.C.C. 216

Unidoor Ltd v. Marks & Spencer plc (TRADE MARK: INFRINGEMENT: PASSING OFF: INTERLOCUTORY INJUNCTION: COAST TO COAST: WHETHER USE AS TRADE MARK: Ch.D.)   [1988] R.P.C. 275

Unidrive v. Dana Corp. (TRADE MARK: APPLICATION: OPPOSITION: PROPRIETORSHIP: DECEPTION OR CONFUSION: Australia: AIPO)
32 I.P.R. 163

Unie Van Kunstmestfabrieken/Urea synthesis (EUROPEAN PATENT: INVENTIVE STEP: LEVEL OF INVENTION: UNSUBSTANTIATED EFFECT: T124/84: EPO)   [1986] E.P.O.R. 297

Uniglobe Holdings Pty Ltd v. Uniglobe Travel (International) Inc. (TRADE MARKS: CLERICAL ERROR: APPLICATION TO AMEND FORM: OBVIOUS MISTAKE: Australia: Pat. Off.)   11 I.P.R. 658

Unik Time Co. Ltd v. Unik Time Ltd (PASSING OFF: CONSPIRACY: DAMAGES: DELAY: Ch.D.)   [1983] F.S.R. 121

Unilever Australia Ltd v. ABC Tissue Products Pty Ltd (TRADE MARK: OPPOSITION: IDENTICAL MARKING OTHER CLASS: LIKELIHOOD OF DECEPTION OR CONFUSION: Australia: AIPO)   29 I.P.R. 578

Unilever Ltd's (Striped Toothpaste No. 2) Trade Marks (TRADE MARK: APPLICATION: DEVICE MARK: WHETHER MARKS: Ch.D.)
[1987] R.P.C. 13; (1987) 12 I.P.L.R. 109

Unilever Ltd (Davis)'s Application (PATENT: APPLICATION: METHOD OF TREATMENT OF ANIMAL BODY BY THERAPY: Pat. Ct)   [1983] R.P.C. 219

Unilever NV/Hexagonal liquid crystal gel (EUROPEAN PATENT: SUFFICIENCY: INGREDIENT OF CHEMICAL COMPOUND: FUNCTIONAL DEFINITION: T435/91: EPO)   [1995] E.P.O.R. 314; [1995] O.J. EPO 188

Unilever plc's Trade Mark Application (TRADE MARK: APPLICATION: OPPOSITION: DEVICE MARK: TOOTHPASTE ON BRUSH: EVIDENCE: Ch.D.)
[1984] R.P.C. 155

Unilever plc v. Chefaro Proprietaries Ltd (PATENT: INFRINGEMENT: OBVIOUSNESS: WHETHER CLAIMS SUPPORTED BY DESCRIPTION: DAMAGES: FORM OF ORDER: Pat. Ct)   [1994] R.P.C. 567

Unilever plc v. Chefaro Proprietaries Ltd (PATENT: PRACTICE: INFRINGEMENT: OBVIOUSNESS: DISCOVERY: JOINT TORTFEASORS: MULTI-NATIONAL GROUP: WHETHER SHAREHOLDER CONTROL BY ULTIMATE HOLDING COMPANY SUFFICIENT TO INFER ASSISTANCE TO PRIMARY INFRINGER OR COMMON DESIGN: C.A.)   [1994] F.S.R. 135

Unilever plc v. Gillette (U.K.) Ltd (PATENT: INFRINGEMENT: PRACTICE: DISCOVERY: Pat. Ct)   [1988] R.P.C. 416

Unilever plc v. Gillette (U.K.) Ltd (PATENT: INFRINGEMENT: JOINT TORTFEASORS: SERVICE OUT OF JURISDICTION: Pat. Ct: C.A.)   [1989] R.P.C. 583

Unilever plc v. Gillette (U.K.) Ltd (PATENT: INFRINGEMENT: PRACTICE: PLEADING: COMMERCIAL SUCCESS: Pat. Ct)   [1989] R.P.C. 417

Unilever plc v. Johnson Wax Ltd (TRADE MARKS: INFRINGEMENT: TOILET DUCK: SPECIFICATION OF GOODS: RECTIFICATION: NON-USE: ASSOCIATED MARKS: SURVEY EVIDENCE: Ch.D.)   [1989] 1 F.S.R. 145

Unilever plc v. Pearce (PATENT: INFRINGEMENT: PROCESS CLAIMS: INSPECTION OF PROCESS: JURISDICTION: Pat. Ct)   [1985] F.S.R. 475

Unilever plc v. Schöller Lebensmittel GmbH & Co. KG (PATENT: INFRINGEMENT: STRIKING OUT: CONSTRUCTION OF CLAIM: Ch.D.)   [1988] F.S.R. 596

Unilever/Coloured composition (EUROPEAN PATENT: INVENTIVE STEP: PREJUDICE: PATENTABILITY: AESTHETIC CREATION: PRIOR ART: ABSTRACT AND DOCUMENT, RELATION THEREOF: T228/90: EPO)
[1993] E.P.O.R. 309

Unilever/Deodorant products (EUROPEAN PATENT: APPLICATION: PROCEDURE:
ORAL HEARING: NEW EVIDENCE AT: CLAIMS: BIOLOGICAL TEST: INVENTIVE
STEP: COLLOCATION: NOVELTY: COLLOCATION: OPPOSITION: FRESH
DOCUMENTS AT ORAL PROCEEDINGS: ORAL PROCEEDINGS: CONDUCT OF:
SUFFICIENCY: BIOLOGICAL TEST: FUNCTIONAL DEFINITIONS: T98/84:
EPO)   [1986] E.P.O.R. 30
Unilever/Detergent composition (EUROPEAN PATENT: INVENTIVE STEP:
COMBINATION OF CITATIONS: PROBLEM, DEFINITION OF: SURPRISING
EFFECT: T146/83: EPO)   [1986] E.P.O.R. 128
Unilever/Detergent compositions (EUROPEAN PATENT: OPPOSITION:
PROCEDURE: PARTIAL ATTACK: SUPERVISORY JURISDICTION: T227/88:
EPO)   [1990] E.P.O.R. 424; [1990] O.J. EPO 292
Unilever/Detergent speckles (EUROPEAN PATENT: INVENTIVE STEP: SURPRISING
EFFECT: T226/84: EPO)   [1986] E.P.O.R. 123
Unilever/Grounds of appeal (EUROPEAN PATENT: APPEAL: PROCEDURE:
ADMISSIBILITY OF APPEAL: REMITTAL ORDERED: T195/90: EPO)
                                                        [1990] E.P.O.R. 646
Unilever/Interesterification process (EUROPEAN PATENT: NOVELTY: SELECTION
FROM KNOWN NUMERICAL RANGE: OPPOSITION: PROCEDURE: REMITTAL
TO FIRST INSTANCE: T366/90: EPO)   [1993] E.P.O.R. 383
Unilever/Multicoloured detergent bars (EUROPEAN PATENT: EVIDENCE: POSTING,
OF LETTER: INVENTIVE STEP: PROBLEM, RELATION TO PRIOR ART: T98/82:
EPO)   [1979–85] E.P.O.R. B522
Unilever/Perborate (EUROPEAN PATENT: NOVELTY: PRIOR USE, BURDEN OF
PROOF: PRIOR ART: PRIOR USE: ANALYSIS OF LATER SAMPLE, RELIANCE ON:
SUFFICIENCY: TEST RESULTS, REPRODUCIBILITY OF: T600/90: EPO)
                                                        [1993] E.P.O.R. 28
Unilever/Perfumed cartons (EUROPEAN PATENT: INVENTIVE STEP: COMBINATION
OF CITATIONS: PRIOR ART: ABSOLUTE TEST: SKILLED PERSON: CHOICE
BETWEEN KNOWN METHODS: ELEMENTARY EXPERIMENTATION: READS AND
COMPREHENDS ALL RELEVANT CITATIONS: T107/82: EPO)
                                                        [1979–85] E.P.O.R. B534
Unilever/Preprothaumatin (EUROPEAN PATENT: APPLICATION: PROCEDURE:
TENTATIVE OBJECTIONS BY EXAMINING DIVISION: APPEAL: REMITTAL
ORDERED: WITH NON–BINDING OBSERVATIONS: SUFFICIENCY: EXAMPLES,
REPRODUCIBILITY OF: T281/86: EPO)
                                  [1989] E.P.O.R. 313; [1989] O.J. EPO 202
Unilever/Right to be heard (EUROPEAN PATENT: FEES: REIMBURSEMENT OF
APPEAL FEE: RIGHT TO BE HEARD VIOLATED: OPPOSITION: PROCEDURE:
PROPRIETOR MUST BE INFORMED OF OWN OPPOSITION: T716/89: EPO)
                                  [1992] E.P.O.R. 256; [1992] O.J. EPO 132
Unilever/Stable bleaches (EUROPEAN PATENT: APPEAL: PROCEDURE: FRESH
EVIDENCE: SUFFICIENCY: CLAIMED SUBJECT–MATTER, REPRODUCIBILITY OF:
T226/85: EPO)   [1989] E.P.O.R. 18; [1988] O.J. EPO 336
Unilever/Viscosity reduction (EUROPEAN PATENT: APPEAL: PROCEDURE:
FUNCTION OF APPEAL: LANGUAGE AT ORAL PROCEEDINGS: EVIDENCE:
COMPARATIVE TESTS: MINOR DIFFERENCE NOT PREVENTING COMPARISON:
INVENTIVE STEP: COULD/WOULD TEST: POINTERS, ABSENCE OF: STATE OF
THE ART: MUST NOT BE ARTIFICIAL: PRIOR ART: ACKNOWLEDGEMENT IN
PATENT, SHOULD BE CLEAR AND UNAMBIGUOUS: T34/90: EPO)
                                  [1992] E.P.O.R. 466; [1992] O.J. EPO 454

Unilever/Washing composition (EUROPEAN PATENT: NOVELTY: AVAILABILITY TO THE PUBLIC: DOCUMENT: TOTAL INFORMATION CONTENT: SELECTION FROM KNOWN NUMERICAL RANGE: T666/89: EPO)
[1992] E.P.O.R. 501; [1993] O.J. EPO 495

Union Carbide Agricultural Products Co. Inc.'s Petition (PATENT: EXTENSION: INSUFFICIENT REMUNERATION: JUSTIFICATION: Australia: S.C.(Vic.))
[1986] A.I.P.C. 90; 8 I.P.R. 16

Union Carbide Australia Ltd v. Duracell Australia Pty Ltd (TRADE PRACTICES: COMPARATIVE ADVERTISING: POINT OF SALE MATERIAL: TV COMMERCIALS: COMPARISON OF PRODUCTS VALUES: Australia: Fed. Ct)   7 I.P.R. 481

Union Carbide Corp. v. B.P. Chemicals Ltd (PATENT: INFRINGEMENT: PRACTICE: DISCOVERY: APPLICATION IN SCOTLAND TO AID INFRINGEMENT PROCEEDINGS IN ENGLAND: APPLICATION BEFORE SERVICE OF STATEMENT OF CLAIM AND PARTICULARS OF INFRINGEMENT: WHETHER NECESSARY TO ENABLE PATENTEE ADEQUATELY TO PLEAD PARTICULARS IN ENGLAND: DISCRETION: CONFIDENTIAL DOCUMENTS: DISCLOSURE: TERMS: Scotland: O.H.: I.H.)   [1995] F.S.R. 449

Union Carbide Corp. v. Naturin Ltd (BREACH OF CONFIDENCE: SAUSAGE SKINS: STOLEN INFORMATION: CONVICTIONS PLEADED: CIVIL EVIDENCE ACT: STRIKING OUT: C.A.)   [1987] F.S.R. 538

Union Carbide/Atmospheric vaporizer (EUROPEAN PATENT: OPPOSITION: PROCEDURE: FRESH DOCUMENTS ON APPEAL: PRIOR ART: PRIOR USE: NEED TO ESTABLISH NON-CONFIDENTIALITY OF: PRIVATE GROUND, ON: T245/88: EPO)   [1991] E.P.O.R. 373

Union Carbide/Coatings (EUROPEAN PATENT: SUFFICIENCY: PARAMETER: FAILURE TO TEACH METHOD OF MEASUREMENT: T654/90: EPO)
[1994] E.P.O.R. 483

Union Carbide/Ethylene copolymers (EUROPEAN PATENT: AMENDMENT AND CORRECTION: ARBITRARY RANGES: APPEAL: PROCEDURE: FRESH CITATIONS ON APPEAL: AT ORAL PROCEEDINGS: NOVELTY: PRIOR USE, NEED FOR CLEAR AND UNAMBIGUOUS RECOGNITION THEREFROM: T245/88: EPO)   [1991] E.P.O.R. 129

Union Carbide/High tear strength polymers (EUROPEAN PATENT: APPEAL: RESPONDENT'S NOTICE TO REARGUE ISSUES UNNECESSARY: NOVELTY: BURDEN OF PROOF: EQUIVALENCE OF PARAMETERS: INEVITABLE RESULT: EXACT REPETITION REQUIRED: OPPOSITION: CONCESSIONS AT ORAL PROCEEDINGS: PROCEDURE: FORMAL SEPARATION OF FACTS, EVIDENCE AND ARGUMENT, NOT: T396/89: EPO)   [1992] E.P.O.R. 312

Union Carbide/Hydroformylation (EUROPEAN PATENT: CLAIMS: CONSTRUCTION: IN LIGHT OF SPECIFICATION: CONSTRUCTION: UNSPECIFIED INGREDIENTS, WHETHER EXCLUDED: INVENTIVE STEP: ONE-WAY STREET: T619/89: EPO)   [1991] E.P.O.R. 561

Union Carbide/Polyacrylate molding composition (EUROPEAN PATENT: INVENTIVE STEP: COMMON GENERAL KNOWLEDGE: NOVELTY: NEW PURPOSE/USE FOR KNOWN SUBSTANCE/EQUIPMENT: OVERLAPPING NOVEL RANGES IN PRIOR ART: T25/87: EPO)   [1989] E.P.O.R. 381

Union Carbide/Polyalkyline polyamines (EUROPEAN PATENT: EVIDENCE: ONUS IN OPPOSITION PROCEEDINGS: INVENTIVE STEP: GENERAL PRIOR ART TEACHING DISCOUNTED BY CLOSEST PRIOR ART: NOVELTY: "NOT CRITICAL" DOES NOT CONSTITUTE DISCLOSURE OF ALTERNATIVES: T23/90: EPO)   [1994] E.P.O.R. 30

Union Carbide/Polymer-polyol compositions (EUROPEAN PATENT: NOVELTY: IMPLICIT DISCLOSURE: NEW TECHNICAL EFFECT: T20/88: EPO)
[1990] E.P.O.R. 212

Union Carbide/Restitution (EUROPEAN PATENT: APPEAL: PROCEDURE: ADMISSIBILITY OF APPEAL: RE-ESTABLISHMENT OF RIGHTS: OBJECTIVE INABILITY: T413/91: EPO)   [1993] E.P.O.R. 504

Union Carbide/Separation of air (EUROPEAN PATENT: COMMON GENERAL KNOWLEDGE: FRESH EVIDENCE OF, ADMISSIBLE ON APPEAL: INVENTIVE STEP: ADVANTAGES UNSUBSTANTIATED SO OBVIOUS EQUIVALENT: OPPOSITION: PROCEDURE: FRESH EVIDENCE ON APPEAL, ALLOWED: T379/88: EPO)
[1991] E.P.O.R. 274

Union Carbide/Threaded connections (EUROPEAN PATENT: INVENTIVE STEP: KNOWN MEANS TO SOLVE NEW PROBLEM: PROBLEM, DEFINITION OF: SKILLED PERSON: ABILITY TO DISCRIMINATE BETWEEN PARAMETERS: POWERS OF GENERALISATION: T124/82: EPO)   [1979–85] E.P.O.R. B580

Union Laitière Normande's Trade Mark Application (TRADE MARK: APPLICATION: DEVICE MARK: T.M.Reg.)   [1993] R.P.C. 87

Union Wine Ltd v. E. Snell & Co. Ltd (PASSING OFF: GET-UP: COMPARISON: South Africa: D&CLD)   1990 (2) S.A. 180
(CPD) 1990 (2) S.A. 189

Unique Transmission Co. India Ltd v. ESBI Transmission Pvt. Ltd (PATENT: FLEXIBLE COUPLINGS: APPLICATION FOR REVOCATION: INVENTION NEITHER NEW, NOR NOVEL, BEING FREELY USED BY MANUFACTURERS: PATENT OBTAINED ON A FALSE CLAIM OF IMPROVEMENT ON EXISTING INVENTION: India: H.C.)   (1990) 15 I.P.L.R. 216

Uniroyal Inc. v. Maxpharma (TRADE MARK: APPLICATION: OPPOSITION: VITAMAX/VITAVAX: India: T.M.Reg.)   (1984) 8 I.P.L.R. 161

Uniroyal/Lubricating composition (EUROPEAN PATENT: EVIDENCE: CONFLICT: INVENTIVE STEP: CLOSEST PRIOR ART: OPPONENT'S OWN CONDUCT: OPPOSITION: PROCEDURE: FRESH EVIDENCE ON APPEAL, ALLOWED: FRESH GROUND ON APPEAL: PRIOR ART: PRIOR USE: ANALYSABILITY: T852/90: EPO)   [1992] E.P.O.R. 522

United Bank Ltd v. Standard Bank of South Africa Ltd (TRADE MARK: EXPUNGEMENT: NO BONA FIDE USE FOR A PERIOD OF FIVE YEARS: South Africa: TPD)   1991 (4) S.A. 810

United Biomedical Inc. v. Genetics Systems Corp. (PATENT: OPPOSITION: PRIOR CLAIMING: PRIOR PUBLICATION: OBVIOUSNESS: Australia: AIPO)
27 I.P.R. 393

United Biscuits (U.K.) Ltd v. Burtons Biscuits Ltd (PASSING OFF: GET-UP: JAFFA CAKES: PACKAGING: INTERLOCUTORY INJUNCTION: RELIABILITY OF SURVEY EVIDENCE: THREE KINDS: RELIEF REFUSED: Ch.D.)
[1992] F.S.R. 14

United International Pictures BV's Application (RESTRICTIVE PRACTICES: JOINT VENTURE: FRANCHISING: THEATRICAL DISTRIBUTION OF FILMS: INTENTION TO EXEMPT: E.C. Comm.)   [1989] 4 C.M.L.R. 109

United Kingdom Government (Secretary of State for Defence) v. Rheinmetall GmbH (PATENTS: OPPOSITION: EVIDENCE: TIME LIMITS: EXTENSION: ONUS OF PROOF: PUBLIC INTEREST: DELAY: Australia: Pat. Off.)   5 I.P.R. 529

United Kingdom Government (Secretary of State for Defence) v. Rheinmetall GmbH (PATENTS: OPPOSITION: NOVELTY: ANTICIPATION: OBVIOUSNESS: Australia: Pat. Off.)   8 I.P.R. 173

United States of America II/Hepatitis A virus (EUROPEAN PATENT: MICRO-
ORGANISM: FAILURE TO INDICATE DEPOSIT NUMBER WITHIN TIME LIMIT:
WHETHER IRREMEDIAL DEFICIENCY: ALTERNATIVE REFERENCE IN
DESCRIPTION: REFERENCE TO ENLARGED BOARD OF APPEAL: LEGAL
CHARACTER OF TIME LIMIT: PRINCIPLE OF GOOD FAITH AND PROTECTION
OF LEGITIMATE EXPECTATIONS: G02/93: EPO)
[1995] E.P.O.R. 437; [1995] O.J. EPO 275
United States of America/Hepatitis A virus (EUROPEAN PATENT: SUFFICIENCY:
CULTURE DEPOSIT: BELATED UNDUE BURDEN: T815/90: EPO)
[1994] E.P.O.R. 421
United States of America/Priority declaration (EUROPEAN PATENT: AMENDMENT
AND CORRECTION: PRIORITY CLAIM: REPLACEMENT OF WRONG PRIORITY
DOCUMENT: CORRECTION AFTER PUBLICATION: TYPOGRAPHICAL ERROR:
PUBLIC INTEREST: FEES: REIMBURSEMENT OF APPEAL FEE: J02/92:
EPO) [1994] E.P.O.R. 547; [1994] O.J. EPO 375
United States Shoe Corp. v. Premiere Vision Inc. (TRADE MARKS: OPPOSITION:
PERSON NOT ENTITLED: PREVIOUS USE: NON-USE: Canada: T.M.Opp. Bd)
33 C.P.R. (3d) 353
UNIVER Trade Mark (TRADE MARK: APPLICATION: GOODS OF SAME
DESCRIPTION: CHANNELS OF TRADE: PHARMACEUTICAL AND VETERINARY
PRODUCTS: Ch.D.) [1993] R.P.C. 239; (1990) 19 I.P.L.R. 102
Universal City Studios Inc. v. Frankenstein Pty Ltd (TRADE MARK: ACCEPTANCE:
OPPOSITION: EVIDENCE IN SUPPORT: EXTENSION OF TIME: BURDEN OF
PROOF: NEGOTIATIONS, MEANING OF: Australia: AIPO) 28 I.P.R. 137
Universal City Studios Inc. v. Hubbard (COPYRIGHT: INFRINGEMENT: ANTON
PILLER PRACTICE: PRIVILEGE AGAINST SELF-INCRIMINATION: Ch.D.)
[1993] 2 All E.R. 596; [1983] Ch. 241; [1983] 2 W.L.R. 882
(C.A.) [1994] 1 All E.R. 661; [1994] Ch. 225; [1984] R.P.C. 43; [1984] 2
W.L.R. 492
Universal Pharmacy v. Classic Pharmaceuticals (TRADE MARK: OPPOSITION:
REQUEST FOR FURTHER EXTENSION OF TIME TO FILE EVIDENCE: OPPOSITION
DEEMED ABANDONED: PETITION FOR REVIEW: REGISTRAR'S POWER: India:
T.M.Reg.) (1989) 13 I.P.L.R. 231
Universal Press Pty Ltd v. Provest Ltd (COPYRIGHT: INFRINGEMENT: MAPS: STREET
DIRECTORIES: APPLICATION TO STRIKE OUT STATEMENT OF CLAIM: Australia:
Fed. Ct) 87 A.L.R. 497
Universal Smo-King Ovens Pty Ltd v. Guinn (COPYRIGHT: SUBSTANTIAL
REPRODUCTION: DESIGNS: INFRINGEMENT: FAILURE TO REGISTER: Australia:
S.C.(NSW)) 1 I.P.R. 602
Universal Telecasters (Queensland) Ltd v. Ainsworth Consolidated Ind Ltd (TRADE
PRACTICES: DECEPTION: STATEMENTS IN NEWSCAST: Australia: Fed. Ct)
1 I.P.R. 260
Universal Thermosensors Ltd v. Hibben (BREACH OF CONFIDENCE: STOLEN
CUSTOMER INFORMATION: EX-EMPLOYEE'S COMPETING BUSINESS:
DAMAGES: ASSESSMENT: INTERLOCUTORY ORDER BY CONSENT: SCOPE OF
INJUNCTIONS IN BREACH OF CONFIDENCE: SPRINGBOARD DOCTRINE:
DISCRETION: ANTON PILLER PRACTICE: Ch.D.)
[1992] 3 All E.R. 257; [1992] F.S.R. 361; [1992] 1 W.L.R. 840
University of California/Dimeric oligopeptides (EUROPEAN PATENT: AMENDMENT
AND CORRECTION: APPROVAL AFTER: APPEAL: PROCEDURE:
DISCRETIONARY DECISIONS—BOARD OF APPEAL'S ROLE: DISCRETION OF
EXAMINING DIVISION, EXERCISE OF: T182/88: EPO)
[1989] E.P.O.R. 147; [1990] O.J. EPO 287

University of Sydney v. Werner & Mertz GmbH (PATENT: OPPOSITION: COLLOCATION: FAIR BASING: AMENDMENT OF SPECIFICATION: COSTS: Australia: AIPO)   30 I.P.R. 606

Untell Pty Ltd v. Manenti Holdings Pty Ltd (TRADE MARKS: OPPOSITION: PROPRIETORSHIP, DISTINCTIVENESS: INHERENT ADAPTABILITY TO DISTINGUISH: ACCEPTANCE BASED ON EVIDENCE OF USE: Australia: Pat. Off.)   23 I.P.R. 641

Upjohn Co.'s Application (PATENT: APPLICATION: OBJECTION: CLAIMS: REDUNDANCY: METHOD: PRODUCT: NEW USE OF OLD SUBSTANCE: Australia: AIPO)   29 I.P.R. 548

Upjohn Co. v. Merck (TRADE MARK: INFRINGEMENT: LIKELIHOOD OF CONFUSION: South Africa: TPD)   1987 (3) S.A. 221

Upjohn Co. v. Schering Aktiengesellschaft (TRADE MARK: OPPOSITION: DECEPTIVE SIMILARITY: COMMON PREFIX: Australia: AIPO)   29 I.P.R. 548

Upjohn Co. v. T. Kerfoot & Co. Ltd (PATENT: INFRINGEMENT: PHARMACEUTICAL: TESTING TO OBTAIN PRODUCT LICENCE: STRIKING OUT: Pat. Ct)
[1988] F.S.R. 1

Upjohn/Refund of search fee (EUROPEAN PATENT: FEES: REIMBURSEMENT SEARCH FEE: J20/87: EPO)   [1989] E.P.O.R. 298; [1989] O.J. EPO 67

UPL Group Ltd v. Dux Engineers Ltd (DESIGNS: INFRINGEMENT: TESTS: DEGREE OF NOVELTY ORIGINALITY RELEVANT TO SCOPE OF DESIGNS: WHETHER INFRINGEMENT: New Zealand: C.A.)   [1989] 3 N.Z.L.R. 135; 13 I.P.R. 15

Uruguay Round Treaties (REPORTING, *inter alia* GATT: INTELLECTUAL PROPERTY: COUNTERFEIT GOODS: TRIPS RULES PROHIBITING RELEASE INTO FREE CIRCULATION: ECJ)   [1995] C.M.L.R. 205

USN & EF/Cold roll manufacturing (EUROPEAN PATENT: INVENTIVE STEP: CLOSEST PRIOR ART: NEIGHBOURING FIELD, SIMILARITY OF PROBLEM: PREJUDICE V. RATIONAL ARGUMENT: NOVELTY: IDENTITY TEST: IMPLICIT STRUCTURAL DIFFERENCES: PROPERTIES OF PRODUCT: USE OF PRODUCTS: PRIOR ART: TYPOGRAPHICAL ERROR IN PRIOR ART DOCUMENTS: SKILLED PERSON: CONSTRAINED BY CURRENT TECHNICAL ENVIRONMENT: SUFFICIENCY: DISCREPANCY IN RANGES: DOCUMENT MUST BE READ AS A WHOLE: UNATTAINABLE RESULT: T179/87: EPO)   [1990] E.P.O.R. 585

USS Engineers/Coke oven patching (EUROPEAN PATENT: AMENDMENT AND CORRECTION: INTERMEDIATE GENERALISATION: T139/83: EPO)
[1979–85] E.P.O.R. C855

Utting v. Clyde Industries Ltd (PATENTS: OPPOSITION: CESSATION OF PATENT: APPLICATION FOR RESTORATION: FAILURE TO PAY FEE: INTENTION: DELAY: Australia: Pat. Off.)   8 I.P.R. 16

V.T. Thomas v. Malayala Manorama Co. Ltd, *sub nom.* Thomas (V.T.) v. Malayala Manorama Co. Ltd

VAG France v. Etablissements Magne SA (RESTRICTIVE PRACTICES: MOTOR VEHICLES: GROUP EXEMPTION: REGULATION 123/85: EFFECT ON DISTRIBUTION CONTRACTS: Case 10/86: ECJ)
[1988] 4 C.M.L.R. 98; [1986] E.C.R. 4071

Val Lessina/Crepe fabric (EUROPEAN PATENT: PRIOR ART: LANGUAGE: NEIGHBOURING FIELDS: T106/86: EPO)   [1988] E.P.O.R. 401

Valeo Vision SA v. Flexible Lamps Ltd (REGISTERED DESIGN: COPYRIGHT: CONFIDENTIAL INFORMATION: INFRINGEMENT: VALIDITY OF DESIGN: NOVELTY: FUNCTIONALITY OF DESIGN: LICENCE OF RIGHT: WHETHER INNOCENT THIRD PARTY CONSCIENCE BOUND: FORM OF RELIEF: Pat. Ct)   [1995] R.P.C. 205

Vallourec & Nyby Uddeholm AB's Agreement (RESTRICTIVE PRACTICES: FRANCO-SWEDISH JOINT VENTURE: JOINT SUBSIDIARY: INTENTION TO APPROVE: COMFORT LETTER: E.C. Comm.) [1986] 2 C.M.L.R. 194

Vamuta Pty Ltd (t/a Sogo Jewellers) v. Sogo Co. Ltd (TRADE MARK: SOGO: PROPRIETORSHIP: IDENTICAL MARKS: USE AS A TRADE MARK: ADVERTISEMENTS: Australia: AIPO) 31 I.P.R. 557

Van Camp Chocolates Ltd v. Aulsebrooks Ltd (CONFIDENTIAL INFORMATION: MISUSE: TORT: New Zealand: C.A.) 2 I.P.R. 337; [1984] 1 N.Z.L.R. 354

Van Castricum v. Theunissen (TRADE MARK: UNLAWFUL COMPETITION: CONFIDENTIAL INFORMATION: EX-EMPLOYEE: CUSTOMER LISTS: South Africa: TPD) 1993 (2) S.A. 726

Van der Lely (C.) NV's Application (PATENT: APPLICATION: DIVISIONAL APPLICATION: DISCLOSURE: Pat. Ct) [1987] R.P.C. 61

Van der Lely (C.) NV v. Maulden Engineering Co. (Beds) Ltd (PATENT: INFRINGEMENT: PRACTICE: ORDER 14: BREACH OF UNDERTAKING SETTLING ACTION: WHETHER VALIDITY A DEFENCE: WHETHER INFRINGEMENT WITHIN CLAIMS OF PATENT IN SUIT: LEAVE TO DEFEND: Pat. Ct) [1984] F.S.R. 157

Van der Lely (C.) NV v. Ruston's Engineering Co. Ltd (PATENT: POWER HARROW: VALIDITY: BEST METHOD: AMBIGUITY: FAIR BASIS: CONSTRUCTION: COSTS: C.A.) [1993] R.P.C. 45

Van der Lely (C.) NV v. Ruston's Engineering Co. Ltd (PATENT: REVOCATION: CONSTRUCTION: NOVELTY: OBVIOUSNESS: AMBIGUITY: FAIR BASIS: C.A.) [1985] R.P.C. 461

Van der Watt v. Humansdorp Marketing C.C. (PASSING OFF: USE OF OWN NAME OR MERE DESCRIPTIVE WORDS: SECONDARY MEANING: South Africa: SECLD) 1993 (4) S.A. 779

Vanitone Pty Ltd v. Formica Technology, Inc. (PATENT: OPPOSITION: EXTENSION OF TIME TO LODGE EVIDENCE IN SUPPORT OF OPPOSITION: ONUS ON PARTY SEEKING EXTENSION: PUBLIC INTEREST IN COMMISSIONER HAVING PERTINENT MATERIAL: COSTS WHERE PARTIES DECLINE HEARING: Australia: Pat. Off.) 22 I.P.R. 158

Vapocure Technologies Ltd's Application (PATENT: APPLICATION: PCT: OBVIOUS ERROR: DELAY: CORRECTION: Pat. Ct: C.A.) [1990] R.P.C. 1

Varma v. South Pacific Recordings Pty Ltd (TRADE MARKS: APPLICATION: OPPOSITION: ADJOURNMENT: CONCURRENT PROCEEDINGS IN FEDERAL COURT: Australia: Pat. Off.) 26 I.P.R. 167

VAW/Aluminium trihydroxide (EUROPEAN PATENT: OPPOSITION: PROCEDURE: AMENDED TEXT, FAILURE TO OBJECT TO: CONVENTIONS: ROMAN LAW, RELIANCE ON: T244/85: EPO) [1988] E.P.O.R. 319; [1988] O.J. EPO 216

Vax Appliances Ltd v. Hoover plc (PATENT: INFRINGEMENT: PLEADINGS: AMENDMENT OF COUNTERCLAIM TO BRING IN SECTION 71 DECLARATION: Ch.D.) [1990] R.P.C. 656

Vax Appliances Ltd v. Hoover plc (PATENT: INFRINGEMENT: VALIDITY: EVIDENCE: PRIOR USE: DEMONSTRATION OF DEVICE AFTER FILING OF FIRST PROVISIONAL: PRIORITY DATE: WHETHER "USE": Pat. Ct) [1991] F.S.R. 307

VBBB & VBVB v. E.C. Commission (RESTRICTIVE PRACTICES: CONDUCT OF HEARINGS: DISCOVERY: RESALE PRICE MAINTENANCE: INFRINGEMENT OF ARTICLE 85(1): EXEMPTION: PRECEDENTS: Cases 43 and 63/82: ECJ) [1985] 1 C.M.L.R. 27; [1984] E.C.R. 19

VBBB & VBVBs' Agreement (RESTRICTIVE PRACTICES: TRADE ASSOCIATIONS: COLLECTIVE RESALE PRICE MAINTENANCE: E.C. Comm.) [1982] 2 C.M.L.R. 344; [1982] F.S.R. 564; [1982] O.J. L54/36

VDU Installations Ltd v. Integrated Computer Systems & Cybernetics Ltd (COPYRIGHT: INFRINGEMENT: ANTON PILLER ORDER: IMPROPER EXECUTION: NEGLIGENT IMPROPRIETY: CONTEMPT: Ch.D.)
[1989] 1 F.S.R. 378
VEB Kombinat Walzlager und Normteile's Application (PATENT: APPLICATION: PRACTICE: DRAWINGS: Pat. Ct)   [1987] R.P.C. 405
Veech/Haemodialysis processes and solutions (EUROPEAN PATENT: APPLICATION: PROCEDURE: REFUSAL AFTER ONE COMMUNICATION: CLAIMS: CLARITY: CONCISENESS: FUNCTIONAL FEATURES: INDEPENDENT CLAIMS: DECISION: ANCILLARY POINTS RAISED FOR THE FIRST TIME: FEES: REIMBURSEMENT OF APPEAL FEE: GUIDELINES FOR EXAMINATION: NOT BINDING: INTERLOCUTORY REVISION: REIMBURSEMENT OF APPEAL FEE: T79/91: EPO)   [1993] E.P.O.R. 91
Veidekke/Dam core machine (EUROPEAN PATENT: PRIOR ART: PRIOR USE: FEATURES INFERRABLE FROM INSPECTION: NOVELTY: PRIOR USE, BURDEN OF PROOF: NOTICE OF OPPOSITION, REQUIREMENTS OF: PROOF OF: T232/89: EPO)   [1993] E.P.O.R. 37
Velcro SA v. Aplix SA (RESTRICTIVE PRACTICES: PATENT AND TRADE MARK LICENCES: EXCLUSIVITY: EXPORT BAN: EXTENSION BEYOND EXPIRY OF RIGHTS: NON-COMPETITION OBLIGATION: IMPROVEMENT PATENTS: ESSENTIAL FUNCTION OF TRADE MARK: EXEMPTION REFUSED: CEASE AND DESIST ORDER ISSUED: E.C. Comm.)   [1989] 4 C.M.L.R. 157
Venice Simplon Orient Express Inc.'s Applications (SERVICE MARKS: CERTIORARI: CONFLICTING APPLICATIONS: REGISTRARS REFUSAL TO REGISTER UNTIL PARTIES RIGHTS DETERMINED BY HIGH COURT, OR BY AGREEMENT: ONE APPLICATION DEEMED ABANDONED FOR FAILURE TO RESPOND: EXTENSION OF TIME REFUSED: NATURAL JUSTICE: RESTORAL OF APPLICATION: RELIEF: Singapore: H.C.)   [1994] 3 S.L.R. 346; [1995] F.S.R. 103
(APPEAL: C.A.)   [1995] 2 S.L.R. 20
Verband der Sachversicherer eV v. E.C. Commission (RESTRICTIVE PRACTICES: EXCLUSIONS: INSURANCE: NATIONAL LAW: TRADE ASSOCIATIONS: COMPETITION: Case 45/85: ECJ)
[1988] 4 C.M.L.R. 264; [1987] E.C.R. 405; [1988] F.S.R. 383
Vereinigte Metallwerke/Wall element (EUROPEAN PATENT: AMENDMENT AND CORRECTION: DRAWINGS: NEW CLAIMS BASED ON: CONVENTIONS: NATIONAL CASE LAW, NEED TO DEMONSTRATE RELEVANCE OF: INVENTIVE STEP: *Ex post facto* APPROACH: SUFFICIENCY: PURPOSE OF ARTICLE 83: T169/83: EPO)   [1979–85] E.P.O.R. C865; [1985] O.J. EPO 193
Verenigde Bedrijven Nutricia NV's Agreements (RESTRICTIVE PRACTICES: TRANSFER OF GOODWILL: NON-COMPETITION AGREEMENT: E.C. Comm.)   [1984] 2 C.M.L.R. 165; [1984] F.S.R. 388; [1983] O.J. L376/22
Vestar Inc. v. Liposome Technology Inc. (PATENT: INFRINGEMENT: PRACTICE: *See v. Scott-Paine* ORDER: FORM AND CONSTRUCTION: WRITTEN SUBMISSIONS: Patent C.C.)   [1995] F.S.R. 391
VEW Trade Mark (TRADE MARK: APPLICATION: SERVICE MARK: T.M.Reg.)
[1986] R.P.C. 82
Vickers plc v. Horsell Graphic Industries Ltd (PATENT INFRINGEMENT: VALIDITY: PRACTICE: DISCOVERY: Pat. Ct)   [1988] R.P.C. 421
Vicom/Computer-related invention (EUROPEAN PATENT: NOVELTY: NEW PURPOSE/USE FOR KNOWN SUBSTANCE/EQUIPMENT: PATENTABILITY: COMPUTER-RELATED INVENTIONS: T208/84: EPO)
[1987] E.P.O.R. 74; [1987] O.J. EPO 14

Victorian Dairy Industry Authority's Application (TRADE MARKS: APPLICATION: MILK CARTONS: DESCRIPTIVE WORDS: NON–DISTINCTIVE DEVICE: Australia: Pat. Off.)   12 I.P.R. 295

Video Arts Ltd v. Paget Industries Ltd (COPYRIGHT: INFRINGEMENT: INTERLOCUTORY INJUNCTION: FORM: Ch.D.)
[1986] F.S.R. 623; [1988] F.S.R. 501

Video Parktown North (Pty) Ltd v. Paramount Pictures Corp. (COPYRIGHT: INFRINGEMENT: CINEMATOGRAPHIC FILM: EXCLUSIVE LICENCEE: REMEDIES: PRACTICE: ACCOUNT OF PROFITS: South Africa: TPD)   1986 (2) S.A. 623

Viho Europe BV v. Parker Pen Ltd (RESTRICTIVE PRACTICES: DISTRIBUTION AGREEMENTS: EXPORT BANS: LIABILITY: E.C. Comm.)
[1993] 5 C.M.L.R. 382; [1994] F.S.R. 122

Villa Maria Wines Ltd v. Montana Wines Ltd (TRADE MARK: INFRINGEMENT: COMPARATIVE ADVERTISING: SUGGESTION OF PARITY OF QUALITY: CONNECTION IN THE COURSE OF TRADE: New Zealand: C.A.)
4 I.P.R. 65; [1984] 2 N.Z.L.R. 422; [1985] R.P.C. 412

Villa Maria Wines Ltd v. Montana Wines Ltd (TRADE MARK: INFRINGEMENT: COMPARATIVE ADVERTISING: New Zealand: H.C.)   2 I.P.R. 203

Villeroy & Boch KG and Villeroy & Boch Sàrl's Agreements (RESTRICTIVE PRACTICES: SELECTIVE DISTRIBUTION: RETAILERS: QUALITATIVE CRITERIA: LOCATION CLAUSE: SALES PROMOTIONS OBLIGATIONS: RESALE RESTRICTIONS: NEGATIVE CLEARANCE: E.C. Comm.)
[1988] 4 C.M.L.R. 461

Vinide Ltd v. National Home Products (Pty) Ltd (TRADE MARK: STATUTORY PROVISIONS: RESTRICTIVE PRACTICES: IMPORTS: South Africa: H.C.)
1988 (1) S.A. 60

Virbac (Australia) Pty Ltd v. Merck Patent GmbH, *sub nom.* Merck Patent GmbH v. Virbac (Australia) Pty Ltd

Virendra Dresses v. Varindera Garments (PASSING OFF: INTERIM INJUNCTION: India: H.C.)   (1983) 8 I.P.L.R. 30

Virtual Reality & Reality v. W. Industries Ltd (TRADE MARK: APPLICATION: OPPOSITION: EVIDENCE: EXTENSION OF TIME: PRACTICE: Australia: AIPO)
28 I.P.R. 455

Visa International Services Association v. Beiser Corp. Pty Ltd (No. 1) (TRADE PRACTICES: CONSUMER PROTECTION: DECEPTION: Australia: Fed. Ct)
1 I.P.R. 471

Visa International Services Association v. Beiser Corp. Pty Ltd (No. 2) (TRADE PRACTICES: INTERLOCUTORY INJUNCTION: APPEAL: Australia: Fed. Ct)
1 I.P.R. 482

VISA Trade Mark (TRADE MARK: APPLICATION: BANK CARDS AND TRAVELLERS CHEQUES: CONNECTION IN THE COURSE OF TRADE: Ch.D.)
[1985] R.P.C. 323

Visco Sport Ltd's Application (TRADE MARKS: OPPOSITION: SORBOLITE: WHETHER CONFUSINGLY SIMILAR: IMPORTANCE OF FIRST SYLLABLE: EFFECT OF COMMON PARTS: Australia: Pat. Off.)   14 I.P.R. 22

Vishnudas Kishindas Zarda Factory v. Vazir Sultan Tobacco Co. Ltd (TRADE MARK: RECTIFICATION: NON–USE: REGISTRABILITY: India: H.C.)
(1991) 16 I.P.L.R. 111

Vishwa Mitter of Vijay Bharat Cigarette Stores v. O.P. Poddar (TRADE MARK: STATUTORY OFFENCE: COMPLAINANT'S QUALIFICATIONS: India: S.C.)
(1984) I.P.L.R. 19

Viskase Corp. v. W.R. Grace & Co.-Conn. (PATENT: OPPOSITION: APPLICATION FOR EXTENSION OF TIME FOR SERVICE OF EVIDENCE: AMENDMENTS TO CLAIMS: Australia: AIPO)   30 I.P.R. 84

Visnjic/*Restitutio in integrum* (EUROPEAN PATENT: APPEAL: PROCEDURE: ADMISSIBILITY OF APPEAL: FEES: REIMBURSEMENT OF APPEAL FEE: RE-ESTABLISHMENT OF RIGHTS: ERROR OF LAW: T248/91: EPO)
[1992] E.P.O.R. 145

Vitamins Australia Ltd v. Beta-Carotene Industries Pty Ltd (PATENTS: EXCLUSIVE LICENCE: CANCELLATION: EFFECT: Australia: S.C.(W.A.))   9 I.P.R. 41

Viziball Ltd's Application (PATENT: APPLICATION: ENTITLEMENT: WHEN INVENTION MADE: Pat. Ct)   [1988] R.P.C. 213

VMI EPE/Tyre (EUROPEAN PATENT: UNQUALIFIED REPRESENTATIVE: WHETHER COMPETENT TO PLEAD AT ORAL PROCEEDINGS: PERMISSION AND SUPERVISION: T598/91: EPO)   [1995] E.P.O.R. 342; [1993] O.J. EPO 12

VMX/Electronic audio communication system (EUROPEAN PATENT: AMENDMENT AND CORRECTION: NOVELTY TEST (EUROPEAN PATENT: ADDED SUBJECT-MATTER): EXTENSION OF SUBJECT-MATTER: T339/89: EPO)
[1991] E.P.O.R. 545

VNU Publications Ltd v. Ziff Davis (U.K.) Ltd (COPYRIGHT: INFRINGEMENT: "SEED ENTRIES" IN DIRECTORY: PRACTICE: INTERLOCUTORY INJUNCTION: CONFIDENTIAL EXHIBIT: EVIDENCE: Ch.D.)   [1992] R.P.C. 269

Voest Alpine/Re-establishment of opponent (EUROPEAN PATENT: CONVENTIONS: GENERAL LEGAL PRINCIPLES: ROMAN LAW, RELIANCE ON: ENLARGED BOARD OF APPEAL: POINT OF LAW, ANSWERED: RE-ESTABLISHMENT OF RIGHTS: ADMISSIBILITY OF APPLICATION BY OPPONENT: *Cessante ratione cessat ipsa lex*: G01/86: EPO)   [1987] E.P.O.R. 388; [1987] O.J. EPO 447

Voest Alpine/Re-establishment of rights (EUROPEAN PATENT: RE-ESTABLISHMENT OF RIGHTS: ADMISSIBILITY OF APPLICATION BY OPPONENT: T110/85: EPO)   [1987] E.P.O.R. 256; [1987] O.J. EPO 157

Volkswagenwerke AG & MAN's Agreement (RESTRICTIVE PRACTICES: SPECIALISATION AGREEMENT: JOINT R&D: EXEMPTION: E.C. Comm.)
[1984] 1 C.M.L.R. 621; [1983] O.J. L376/11

Voll/Container (EUROPEAN PATENT: J28/86: EPO)   [1988] O.J. EPO 85

Voll/Refund of Examination Fee (EUROPEAN PATENT: J33/86: EPO)
[1988] O.J. EPO 84

Volvo AB's Application (PATENT: EXAMINATION AND SPECIFICATION: AMENDMENT: Australia: Pat. Off.)   1 I.P.R. 554

Volvo AB v. Erik Veng (U.K.) Ltd (RESTRICTIVE PRACTICES: INDUSTRIAL DESIGN RIGHTS: SPARE PARTS: ABUSE OF DOMINANT POSITION: REFUSAL TO LICENSE: NOT *per se* ABUSIVE: Case 238/87: ECJ)
[1989] 4 C.M.L.R. 122; [1988] E.C.R. 6211

Volvo Flygmotor AB & Sauer Getriebe AG (Agreement Between) (RESTRICTIVE PRACTICES: JOINT PRODUCTION AND JOINT SALE: INTENTION TO EXEMPT: E.C. Comm.)   [1985] 1 C.M.L.R. 663

von Blücher/Air-cleaning apparatus (EUROPEAN PATENT: APPEAL: PROCEDURE: REMITTAL NOT ORDERED: UNREASONED DECISION: OPPOSITION: PROCEDURE: AUXILIARY REQUESTS: T5/89: EPO)
[1992] E.P.O.R. 546; [1992] O.J. EPO 348

von Blücher/Interlocutory decision (EUROPEAN PATENT: APPEAL: PROCEDURE: NO SEPARATE APPEAL: PROCEDURE: INTERLOCUTORY DECISION: T762/90: EPO)   [1991] E.P.O.R. 213

von Blücher/Surface filter (EUROPEAN PATENT: AMENDMENT AND CORRECTION: GENERALISATION: BOARD OF APPEAL: ADDITION OF TECHNICALLY SPECIALISED MEMBER AT PARTY'S REQUEST: ENLARGED BOARD OF APPEAL: REFERENCE REFUSED: OPPOSITION: PROCEDURE: ADDITION OF TECHNICALLY SPECIALISED MEMBER TO BOARD: AMENDMENT OF CLAIM, CLARITY AND SUPPORT: T762/90: EPO)   [1993] E.P.O.R. 296
von Füner, Alexander/Family name (EUROPEAN PATENT: PROFESSIONAL REPRESENTATIVES: LIST, ENTRY ON: J01/78: EPO)
                     [1979–85] E.P.O.R. A1; [1979] O.J. EPO 285
Vondrovsky/Display signs (EUROPEAN PATENT: APPEAL: PROCEDURE: FRESH CITATIONS ON APPEAL: WHEN THEY SHOULD BE FILED: COSTS: LATE AMENDMENTS: T51/90: EPO)   [1992] E.P.O.R. 412
Voyager Distributing Co. Pty Ltd v. Cherry Lane Fashion Group Ltd (TRADE PRACTICES: MISLEADING AND DECEPTIVE CONDUCT: INTERLOCUTORY INJUNCTION: Australia: Fed. Ct)   4 I.P.R. 247
Vrajlal Manilal & Co. v. N.S. Bidi Co. (TRADE MARK: BIDIS: INFRINGEMENT: INTERIM INJUNCTION: India: H.C.)   (1988) 13 I.P.L.R. 33
Vulcan Aust. Ltd v. Braemar Appliances Pty Ltd (PATENT: INFRINGEMENT: VALIDITY: COUNTERCLAIM FOR REVOCATION: OBVIOUSNESS: NOVELTY: INVALIDITY: Australia: Pat. Off.)   (S.C.(Vic.)) 6 I.P.R. 516
                     6 I.P.R. 142
Vulcan Australia Ltd v. M.L. D'Astoli & Co. Pty Ltd (TRADE MARK: INFRINGEMENT: STAY: CO-PENDING APPLICATION FOR SIMILAR MARK: Australia: Fed. Ct)
                     32 I.P.R. 25
Vulcan-Hart Corporation v. Vulcan Australia Ltd (TRADE MARK: REMOVAL: PRACTICE: CORRECTION OF REGISTER: MISNOMER IN ORIGINAL APPLICATION: Australia: AIPO)   30 I.P.R. 441

W. v. Egdell (CONFIDENTIAL INFORMATION: BREACH OF CONFIDENCE: PUBLIC INTEREST: PLAINTIFF DETAINED AS MENTAL PATIENT IN SECURE HOSPITAL: PSYCHIATRIST INSTRUCTED BY PLAINTIFF TO PREPARE INDEPENDENT REPORT FOR USE AT MENTAL HEALTH REVIEW TRIBUNAL: APPLICATION TO TRIBUNAL WITHDRAWN IN VIEW OF UNFAVOURABLE NATURE OF REPORT: PSYCHIATRISTS DISCLOSURE OF REPORT TO HOSPITAL: COPIES SENT TO HOME OFFICE AND TRIBUNAL: WHETHER BREACH OF DUTY OF CONFIDENCE: Ch.D.)
[1989] 1 All E.R. 1089; [1990] 1 Ch. 359; [1989] 2 W.L.R. 689; 17 I.P.R. 646
     (C.A.) [1990] 1 All E.R. 835; [1990] 1 Ch. 359; [1990] 2 W.L.R. 471;
                     17 I.P.R. 646
Wabco/Grounds of Appeal (EUROPEAN PATENT: APPEAL: PROCEDURE: ADMISSIBILITY OF APPEAL: T287/90: EPO)   [1992] E.P.O.R. 531
Wacker-Chemie/Crosslinkable organopolysiloxanes (EUROPEAN PATENT: CLAIMS: FAIR BASIS: T115/83: EPO)   [1979–85] E.P.O.R. C834
Wacker/Trichloroethylene (EUROPEAN PATENT: OPPOSITION: PROCEDURE: AMENDMENT OF CLAIM ON APPEAL, BELATED: BOARD OF APPEAL'S POWERS: CLAIMS: OBJECTION TO CLARITY OF, INADMISSIBLE: T406/86: EPO)
                     [1989] E.P.O.R. 338; [1989] O.J. EPO 302
Waddingtons Ltd's Patent (PATENT: AMENDMENT: PRACTICE: REASONS: DISCRETION: C.-G.)   [1986] R.P.C. 158

Wagamama Ltd v. City Centre Restaurants plc (TRADE MARK: INFRINGEMENT:
PASSING OFF: WAGAMAMA/RAJAMAMA: ORIENTAL THEME
RESTAURANTS: STATUTORY CONSTRUCTION: INTENTION OF E.C.
DIRECTIVE: HISTORICAL FUNCTION OF TRADE MARKS: ASSOCIATION
WITHOUT CONFUSION AS TO ORIGIN: DILUTION OF GOODWILL: EVIDENCE:
SURVEY EVIDENCE: EXPERT EVIDENCE: ADMISSIBILITY: Ch.D.)
[1995] F.S.R. 713; 32 I.P.R. 535
Wagner/Fixing device (EUROPEAN PATENT: AMENDMENT AND CORRECTION:
DRAWINGS: TEACHING OF: T255/88: EPO)   [1992] E.P.O.R. 87
Walch/Non-payment of the fee for appeal (EUROPEAN PATENT: FEES: LACK OF
MEANS: J02/78: EPO)   [1979–85] E.P.O.R. A3; [1979] O.J. EPO 283
Wall (T.) & Sons Ltd v. Rasa Sayang Ice Cream (TRADE MARK: INFRINGEMENT:
APPLICATION: OPPOSITION: STAY: BALANCE OF CONVENIENCE: Malaysia:
H.C.)   1981 2 M.L.J. 271
Walt Disney Productions Ltd v. Gurvitz (COPYRIGHT: CONTEMPT: TRAP ORDER:
Agent provocateur. Ch.D.)   [1982] F.S.R. 446
Walt Disney Productions v. Fantasyland Hotel Inc. (PASSING OFF: TRADE NAME:
COMPONENTS OF CAUSE OF ACTION: REPUTATION: MISREPRESENTATION:
DAMAGES: ISSUE ESTOPPEL: EVIDENCE: USE OF WORD ASSOCIATION:
RELEVANCE TO CONFUSION: Canada: Q.B.)   31 I.P.R. 233
Wander Ltd v. Antox India Pvt. Ltd (TRADE MARK: CONFLICT BETWEEN
LICENCEES: PASSING OFF: INTERIM INJUNCTION: APPEAL AND FURTHER
APPEAL: India: H.C.)   (1991) 16 I.P.L.R. 225
Wanem Pty Ltd v. John Tekiela (DESIGNS: INFRINGEMENT: REPRODUCTION OR
OBVIOUS IMITATION OF DESIGN: NO CLAIM OF FRAUDULENT IMITATION:
PRINCIPLES IN DETERMINING INFRINGEMENT: Australia: Fed. Ct)
19 I.P.R. 435
Wang Laboratories Inc.'s Application (PATENT: APPLICATION: PATENTABILITY:
COMPUTER-RELATED INVENTION: TECHNICAL CONTRIBUTION: Pat. Ct)
[1991] R.P.C. 463
Ward's Applications (PATENT: APPLICATIONS: NOVELTY: LACK OF INVENTIVE STEP:
AMENDMENT: C.-G.)   [1986] R.P.C. 50
Wardle Fabrics Ltd v. G. Myristis Ltd (COPYRIGHT: INFRINGEMENT: ANTON PILLER
PRACTICE: CONTEMPT: DISCHARGE OF ORDER: Ch.D.)   [1984] F.S.R. 263
Warheit/Identity of applicant (EUROPEAN PATENT: APPLICATION: PROCEDURE:
IDENTIFICATION OF APPLICANT: J25/86: EPO)
[1988] E.P.O.R. 40; [1987] O.J. EPO 475
Warman International Ltd v. Envirotech Australia Pty Ltd (DESIGN: COPYRIGHT:
INFRINGEMENT: INDUSTRIAL APPLICATION: BREACH OF CONFIDENCE:
PRACTICE: ANTON PILLER: EVIDENCE: PRIVILEGE AGAINST SELF-
INCRIMINATION: Australia: Fed. Ct)   67 A.L.R. 253; 6 I.P.R. 578
Warmestelle Steine und Erden/Annular shaft kiln (EUROPEAN PATENT:
AMENDMENT AND CORRECTION: BROADENING CLAIM BY OMISSION:
INVENTIVE STEP: SIMPLIFICATION OF PRIOR ART: T20/84: EPO)
[1986] E.P.O.R. 197
Warner Bros Records Inc. v. Parr (COPYRIGHT: INFRINGEMENT: BOOTLEGGING:
WHETHER ACTIONABLE BY RECORD COMPANIES: DMPPA 58: PERFORMERS
PROTECTION ACT 1963: Ch.D.)
[1982] 2 All E.R. 455; [1982] 1 W.L.R. 993

Warner Brothers Inc. v. Christiansen (COPYRIGHT: LENDING RIGHT: VIDEO BOUGHT IN SHOP IN ENGLAND WHERE NO LENDING RIGHT: RENTED FROM SHOP IN DENMARK WHERE LENDING RIGHT APPLIES: WHETHER SALE IN ENGLAND EXHAUSTS COPYRIGHT IN THE BOUGHT VIDEO: EXTENT OF EXHAUSTION: NOT APPLICABLE TO RENTAL: NO RIGHT TO RENT OUT ENGLISH VIDEO IN DENMARK WITHOUT AUTHORISATION: Case 158/86: ECJ) [1990] 3 C.M.L.R. 684; [1988] E.C.R. 2605; [1991] F.S.R. 161

Warner Brothers Inc. v. The Roadrunner Ltd (COPYRIGHT: ARTISTIC WORK: SUBSISTENCE: REGISTERED DESIGN: PRACTICE: SUMMARY JUDGMENT: Ch.D.) [1988] F.S.R. 292

Warner-Lambert Co. and BIC SA v. The Gillette Co. and Eemland Holdings NV (RESTRICTIVE PRACTICES: COMPANY OWNERSHIP: ACQUISITION BY DOMINANT COMPANY OF SUBSTANTIAL HOLDING IN MAJOR COMPETITOR: ABUSE CAUGHT BY ARTICLE 86 EEC: AGREEMENT TO ASSIGN NON-COMMUNITY BUSINESS AND TRADE MARKS TO DOMINANT FIRM: VIOLATION OF ARTICLE 85(1): ORDER TO DIVEST INTEREST IN COMPETITOR AND REASSIGN BUSINESS AND TRADE MARKS IN COUNTRIES BORDERING COMMUNITY: E.C. Comm.) [1993] 5 C.M.L.R. 559

Warner-Lambert Co. v. Harel (TRADE MARK: APPLICATION: OPPOSITION: PROPRIETORSHIP: DECEPTION OR CONFUSION: BLAMEWORTHY CONDUCT: Australia: AIPO) 32 I.P.R. 189

Warner-Lambert/Different sets of claims (EUROPEAN PATENT: APPLICATION: PROCEDURE: DOCUMENTS RECEIVED MUST BE PLACED ON FILE: PRIOR NATIONAL RIGHTS: WHEN SEPARATE CLAIMS PERMISSIBLE: J21/82: EPO) [1979–85] E.P.O.R. A149; [1984] O.J. EPO 65

Warnink BV v. J. Townend & Sons (Hull) Ltd, *sub nom.* Erven Warnink BV v. J. Townend & Sons (Hull) Ltd

Warren v. Mendy (RESTRAINT OF TRADE: INJUNCTION: INTERLOCUTORY: BOXER'S MANAGER SEEKING TO RESTRAIN DEFENDANT FROM ACTING FOR BOXER: RELATIONSHIP DEPENDENT ON MUTUAL TRUST AND CONFIDENCE: WHETHER EFFECT OF GRANTING RELIEF TO COMPEL BOXER TO PERFORM CONTRACT WITH MANAGER: WHETHER RELIEF APPROPRIATE: C.A.) [1989] 3 All E.R. 103; [1989] 1 W.L.R. 853

Warwickshire County Council v. Verco (TRADE DESCRIPTIONS: COUNTERFEIT GOODS SOLD AS BRANDED GOODS: USE OF REASONABLE DILIGENCE: Q.B.D.) 31 I.P.R. 423

Waste-Tech (Pty) Ltd v. Wade Refuse (Pty) Ltd (CONFIDENTIAL INFORMATION: DISCOVERY AND INSPECTION: ANTON PILLER ORDERS: NATURE AND SCOPE: South Africa: WLD) 1993 (1) S.A. 833

Water Renovation (Pty) Ltd v. Gold Fields of SA Ltd (PATENT: REVOCATION: AMENDMENT: DISCRETION: PRIOR ART: RESEARCH PAPER: South Africa: A.D.) 1994 (2) S.A. 588

Waterbed Association of Retailers & Manufacturers' Application (TRADE MARKS: APPLICATION FOR REGISTRATION IN PART B: COMPOSITE MARK: ACRONYM: DESCRIPTIVE: INHERENT ADAPTABILITY TO DISTINGUISH: DISCLAIMER: Australia: Pat. Off.) 20 I.P.R. 605

Waterford Glass Group Ltd's Application (TRADE MARK: APPLICATION: WATERFORD: GEOGRAPHICAL NAMES: INHERENTLY ADAPTED TO DISTINGUISH: Australia: Pat. Off.) 9 I.P.R. 339

WATERFORD Trade Mark (PART B: WHETHER CAPABLE OF DISTINGUISHING: SUBSTANTIAL USER: Ireland: H.C.) [1982] I.L.R.M. 91 (S.C.) [1984] I.L.R.M. 565; [1984] 2 I.L.T. 104; [1984] F.S.R. 390

Waterlow Directories Ltd v. Reed Information Services Ltd (COPYRIGHT: INFRINGEMENT: INTERLOCUTORY INJUNCTION: LEGAL DIRECTORIES: COPYING NAMES AND ADDRESSES FROM COMPUTER MAIL-SHOT TO COMPILE OWN DIRECTORY: WHETHER REPRODUCTION: WHETHER SUBSTANTIAL: EURO-DEFENCES: NON-DEROGATION FROM GRANT: QUANTIFIABILITY OF DAMAGE: ADEQUACY OF UNDERTAKINGS: BALANCE OF CONVENIENCE: Ch.D.) [1992] F.S.R. 409; 20 I.P.R. 69

Waterlow Publishers Ltd v. Rose (COPYRIGHT: INFRINGEMENT: COPYRIGHT IN PUBLISHED COMPILATION: SOLICITORS' DIRECTORY AND DIARY: AUTHORSHIP OF A COMPILATION: CO-AUTHORSHIP: NO AUTHORSHIP CREDIT IN PUBLISHED WORK: WHETHER COPYRIGHT COULD SUBSIST WHERE THERE WAS NO IDENTIFIABLE AUTHOR: PRESUMPTION AS TO AUTHORSHIP: PRESUMPTION UPHELD: INFRINGEMENT FOUND: APPEAL DISMISSED: Ch.D.) 17 I.P.R. 493
(C.A.) [1995] F.S.R. 207

Watson v. Bristol-Myers Co. (PATENTS: OPPOSITION: EXTENSION OF TIME: CIRCUMSTANCES BEYOND CONTROL OF PERSON CONCERNED: Australia: Pat. Off.) 5 I.P.R. 333

Watson v. Dolmark Industries Ltd (COPYRIGHT: INFRINGEMENT: COPYING OF PART OF BOOK: DEGREE OF ORIGINALITY: INTERIM INJUNCTION: New Zealand: H.C.) 7 I.P.R. 279

Watson v. Dolmark Industries Ltd (DECEIT: WHETHER CAUSE OF ACTION ESTABLISHED: FIDUCIARY DUTY: LICENSORS MOULDS AND DIES BAILED TO LICENSEE: USE OF DIES FOR LICENSEES OWN PURPOSES: BREACH OF DUTY: UNFAIR SPRINGBOARD ADVANTAGE: PASSING OFF: DUTY TO ACCOUNT: LIABILITY OF SUBSTANTIAL PROPRIETOR OF LICENSEE: New Zealand: C.A.) 23 I.P.R. 363

Watson v. Prager (CONTRACT: PROFESSIONAL BOXER AND MANAGER: AGREEMENT: RESTRAINT OF TRADE: REASONABLENESS: Ch.D.) [1993] E.M.L.R. 275

Wavin/Belated division and amendment (EUROPEAN PATENT: AMENDMENT AND CORRECTION: APPROVAL AFTER: CONVENTIONS: NATIONAL PRACTICES IRRELEVANT: DIVISIONAL APPLICATION: LATE FILING: T92/85: EPO) [1986] E.P.O.R. 281; [1986] O.J. EPO 352

Wavin/Interconnected bags (EUROPEAN PATENT: DIVISIONAL APPLICATION: CRITERIA FOR: T527/88: EPO) [1991] E.P.O.R. 184

Waylite Diaries C.C. v. First National Bank Ltd (COPYRIGHT: SUBSISTENCE: "ARTISTIC WORK": DRAWINGS: LITERARY WORK: WRITTEN TABLES AND COMPILATIONS: DIARY: South Africa: WLD) 1993 (2) S.A. 128;
(A.D.) 1995 (1) S.A. 645

W.D. & H.O. Wills (Australia) Ltd and Benson & Hedges Co. Pty Ltd's Application (TRADE MARKS: OBJECTION: PRIOR REGISTRATION: SUBSTANTIAL IDENTITY, DECEPTIVE SIMILARITY: COMPOSITE AS AGAINST PRIOR WORD ONLY MARK: Australia: Pat. Off.) 13 I.P.R. 9

WEA International Inc. v. Hanimex Corp. Ltd (TRADE PRACTICES: RADIO ADVERTISEMENTS: COPYRIGHT: SOUND RECORDINGS: CONTRIBUTORY INFRINGEMENT: AUTHORISATION: ADVERTISEMENT FOR BLANK TAPE: Australia: Fed. Ct) 77 A.L.R. 456; 10 I.P.R. 349

WEA Records Ltd v. Visions Channel 4 Ltd (COPYRIGHT: INFRINGEMENT: ANTON PILLER PRACTICE: JURISDICTION TO ENTERTAIN APPEAL: C.A.) [1983] 2 All E.R. 589; [1984] F.S.R. 404; [1983] 1 W.L.R. 721

WEA Records Pty Ltd (COPYRIGHT: BROADCASTS: ROYALTY: RELEVANT MATTERS: Australia: Cprt. Trib.) (1982) 40 A.L.R. 111

WEA Records Pty Ltd v. Stereo FM Pty Ltd (COPYRIGHT: SOUND RECORDINGS: BROADCASTS: ROYALTY: OWNERS' AGENT: OWNERS' EXCLUSIVE LICENSEE: Australia: Cprt. Trib.) (1983) 43 A.L.R. 91; 1 I.P.R. 6

WEATHERSHIELDS Trade Mark (TRADE MARK: APPLICATION: OPPOSITION: WHETHER NAME OF WELL-KNOWN ARTICLE: T.M.Reg.) [1991] R.P.C. 451

Webb/Interruption of proceedings (EUROPEAN PATENT: APPLICATION: PROCEDURE: INTERRUPTION OF PROCEEDINGS: PROFESSIONAL REPRESENTATIVES: INCAPACITY: CONVENTIONS: PCT AND EPC, INTERRELATION OF: J23/88: EPO) [1989] E.P.O.R. 272

Weber-Stephen Products Co. v. Alrite Engineering (Pty) Ltd (TRADE MARK: PASSING OFF: DISTINCTION BETWEEN ARTICLE AND ITS GET-UP: REPUTATION OF PRODUCT ATTACHING TO ITS SHAPE: South Africa: TPD) 1990 (2) S.A. 718

(FORM OF INTERDICT: EFFECT OF NOTICE ON DEFENDANTS PRODUCT: INTERDICT INFRINGED: S.C.) 1992 (2) S.A. 489; [1992] R.P.C. 549

Weber-Stephen Products Co. v. Registrar of Trade Marks (TRADE MARK: REGISTRATION: SHAPE AND CONFIGURATION: South Africa: TPD) 1994 (3) S.A. 611

Wegener/Jurisdiction (EUROPEAN PATENT: BOARD OF APPEAL: JURISDICTION: RE-ESTABLISHMENT OF RIGHTS: DEFICIENT REQUEST, APPLICANT NOT NOTIFIED: JURISDICTION OF FIRST INSTANCE: T473/91: EPO) [1994] E.P.O.R. 292; [1993] O.J. EPO 630

Weigand v. Schutzverband Deutscher Wein eV (WINE LABELS: TRADE MARKS: FALSE IMPRESSION OF ORIGIN: Germany: S.C.) [1983] 1 C.M.L.R. 168 (ECJ Case 56/80) [1983] 1 C.M.L.R. 146; [1981] E.C.R. 583

Weir Pumps Ltd and Commissioner of Patents & Stork Pompen BV (PATENT: EXTENSION OF TIME TO LODGE NOTICE OF OPPOSITION: APPLICATION AFTER PATENT APPLICATION ADVERTISED AS ACCEPTED AND EXPIRY OF THREE-MONTH OPPOSITION PERIOD: Australia: AAT) 13 I.P.R. 163

Weir Pumps Ltd v. CML Pumps Ltd (COPYRIGHT: INFRINGEMENT: BREACH OF CONFIDENCE: LICENCE TO REPAIR: TERM OF COPYRIGHT: REVERSE ENGINEERING: Ch.D.) [1984] F.S.R. 33

Weitman/Heat recovery (EUROPEAN PATENT: AMENDMENT AND CORRECTION: CATEGORY OF CLAIM: APPEAL: PROCEDURE: REMITTAL, FRESH CATEGORY OF CLAIM ON APPEAL: T531/88: EPO) [1991] E.P.O.R. 433

Welgro/Bulk carrier (EUROPEAN PATENT: INVENTIVE STEP: COMBINATION OF CITATIONS: LEVEL OF INVENTION: PRIOR ART: SIGNIFICANCE OF SUBSIDIARY FEATURES: T187/85: EPO) [1986] E.P.O.R. 79

Wella AG's Application (TRADE MARKS: OBJECTIONS: DESCRIPTIVE MARK: INHERENT DISTINCTIVENESS: RELEVANCE OF EVIDENCE OF USE AFTER APPLICATION: Australia: Pat. Off.) 11 I.P.R. 452

Wellcome Foundation (Hitching)'s Application (PATENT: APPLICATION: NEW THERAPEUTIC USE FOR KNOWN DRUG: New Zealand: C.A.) [1983] F.S.R. 593

Wellcome Foundation Ltd's Two Patent Applications (PATENT: APPLICATIONS: DOUBLE PATENTING: Pat. Ct) [1983] R.P.C. 200

Wellcome Foundation Ltd v. Commissioner of Patents (PATENTS: APPLICATION: METHOD OF TREATMENT: MANNER OF NEW MANUFACTURE: New Zealand: C.A.) 2 I.P.R. 156; [1983] N.Z.L.R. 385

Wellcome Foundation Ltd v. Discpharm Ltd (No. 2) (PATENT: PRACTICE: COSTS: Pat. C.C.) [1993] F.S.R. 444

Wellcome Foundation Ltd v. Discpharm Ltd (PATENT: INFRINGEMENT: PARALLEL IMPORTS: WHETHER IMPLIED LICENCE TO IMPORT FROM SPAIN TO PORTUGAL: DEROGATION FROM GRANT: EXHAUSTION OF RIGHTS: ARTICLE 30: TREATY OF IBERIAN ACCESSION: WHETHER PATENT A PRODUCT PATENT: Pat. C.C.)   [1993] F.S.R. 433

Wellcome/3-Amino-pyrazoline derivatives (EUROPEAN PATENT: CLAIMS: LIST OF CHEMICAL COMPOUNDS: NOVELTY: ADAPTATION COMPARED TO SUITABILITY: PHARMACEUTICAL COMPOSITION: T289/84: EPO)
[1987] E.P.O.R. 58

Wellcome/Pigs I (EUROPEAN PATENT: PATENTABILITY: INDUSTRIAL APPLICATION: THERAPY: T116/85: EPO)
[1988] E.P.O.R. 1; [1989] O.J. EPO 13

Weller v. TGI Friday's Application (TRADE MARK: OPPOSITION: OPPONENT SEEKING SPECIAL LEAVE TO ADDUCE FURTHER EVIDENCE: Australia: AIPO)
29 I.P.R. 61

Wellington Newspapers Ltd v. Dealers Guide Ltd (COPYRIGHT: INFRINGEMENT: FLAGRANT COPYING: PUNITIVE OR EXEMPLARY DAMAGES: New Zealand: C.A.)   4 I.P.R. 417; [1984] 2 N.Z.L.R. 66

Werner (R.D.) & Co. Inc. v. Bailey Aluminium Products Pty Ltd (PATENT: APPLICATION: OPPOSITION: GROUNDS: LACK OF NOVELTY: RELATIONSHIP BETWEEN LACK OF NOVELTY AND OBVIOUSNESS: SPECIFICITY OF CLAIM: Australia: Fed. Ct)   85 A.L.R. 679; 13 I.P.R. 513

Werner Co. Inc. v. Bailey Aluminium Products Pty Ltd (PATENT: OPPOSITION: Australia: S.C.(Vic.))   8 I.P.R. 339

Westaflex (Aust.) Pty Ltd v. Wood, *sub nom.* Wood v. Westaflex (Aust.) Pty Ltd

Westco Jeans (Aust.) Pty Ltd's Application (TRADE MARKS: APPLICATION: REGISTRABILITY: KNOCKOUT: ADAPTED TO DISTINGUISH: INHERENT ADAPTABILITY: DESCRIPTIVE: Australia: Pat. Off.)   16 I.P.R. 493

Western Electric/Refund of examination fee (EUROPEAN PATENT: ENLARGED BOARD OF APPEAL: REFERENCE REFUSED: FEES: REIMBURSEMENT OF APPEAL FEE: ACTION IN ACCORDANCE WITH PREVAILING: J08/83: EPO)
[1979–85] E.P.O.R. A179; [1985] O.J. EPO 102

Western Front Ltd v. Vestron Inc. (COPYRIGHT: FILM: LICENCE AGREEMENT: STRIKING OUT: UNLAWFUL INTERFERENCE WITH CONTRACTUAL RELATIONS: NEGLIGENCE: DEFAMATION: Ch.D.)   [1987] F.S.R. 66

Westinghouse/Payment by cheque (EUROPEAN PATENT: APPEAL: PROCEDURE: OWN INQUIRIES BY BOARD OF APPEAL: FEES: DATE OF RECEIPT: J01/85: EPO)
[1979–85] E.P.O.R. A230; [1995] O.J. EPO 126

Westminster City Council v. Pierglow Ltd (PASSING OFF: FALSE TRADE DESCRIPTION: COUNTERFEITING: LEVI'S JEANS: DUE DILIGENCE DEFENCE: Q.B.D.)   29 I.P.R. 572

Westpac Banking Corp. v. Goodmaker Leasing Corp. Berhad (PASSING OFF: FOREIGN PLAINTIFF: GOODWILL: FANCY NAME: Malaysia: H.C.)   8 I.P.R. 9

Westpac Banking Corp. v. John Fairfax Group Pty Ltd (BREACH OF CONFIDENCE: PUBLIC POLICY: WHAT CONSTITUTES: Australia: S.C.(NSW))   19 I.P.R. 513

Westpac Banking Corp. v. Northern Metals Pty Ltd (TRADE PRACTICES: RELATIONSHIP BETWEEN MISLEADING AND DECEPTIVE CONDUCT AND CONDUCT LIABLE TO MISLEAD THE PUBLIC: Australia: Fed. Ct)
14 I.P.R. 499

Wham-O Manufacturing Co. v. Lincoln Industries Ltd (COPYRIGHT: INFRINGEMENT: "PATENT" DRAWINGS: ACQUIESCENCE: DAMAGES: TRADE MARK: INFRINGEMENT: New Zealand: H.C.)
[1981] 2 N.Z.L.R. 628; [1982] R.P.C. 281
(C.A.) 3 I.P.R. 115; [1984] 1 N.Z.L.R. 641; [1985] R.P.C. 127
Wheatley's Application (PATENT: APPLICATION: PRIOR DEALING: WHETHER PRIOR USE: C.A.) (1984) 81 L.S.Gaz. 741
Wheatley v. Bell (BREACH OF CONFIDENCE: INNOCENT RECEIPT OF CONFIDENTIAL INFORMATION: WHETHER INJUNCTIVE RELIEF AVAILABLE: Australia: S.C.(NSW)) [1984] F.S.R. 16
Wheelan Associates Inc. v. Jaslow Dental Laboratories Inc. (COPYRIGHT: INFRINGEMENT: COMPUTER PROGRAMS: COPYING OF STRUCTURE: SUBSTANTIAL PART: USA: C.A.) [1987] F.S.R. 1
Wheeler Grace & Pierucci Pty Ltd v. Wright (TRADE PRACTICES: MISLEADING AND DECEPTIVE CONDUCT: PREDICTION MADE IN UNQUALIFIED TERMS: IMPLIED REPRESENTATION THAT MAKER OF PREDICTION KNEW OF FACTS WHICH IN AN OBJECTIVE SENSE WOULD JUSTIFY HIS BELIEF: WHETHER MISLEADING OR DECEPTIVE: Australia: Fed. Ct) 16 I.P.R. 189
Whisky and Gin (Sole Distribution Agreements) (RESTRICTIVE PRACTICES: EXCLUSIVE DISTRIBUTION: GROUP EXEMPTION: INTENTION TO EXEMPT: E.C. Comm.) [1985] 3 C.M.L.R. 337
Whitby II/Late amendments (EUROPEAN PATENT: ADMISSIBILITY OF AMENDMENTS AFTER APPROVAL OF TEXT: EXAMINING DIVISIONS DISCRETION: EFFECT OF COMMUNICATION UNDER EPC ARTICLE 167(2): REFERRAL ON INTERPRETATION OF EPC: G07/93; T830/91: EPO)
[1995] E.P.O.R. 49; [1994] O.J. EPO 775
Whitco Pty Ltd v. Austral Lock Industries Pty Ltd (PATENT: OPPOSITION: INVENTION: NOT DISCLOSURE: LACK OF FAIR BASIS: PRIOR PUBLICATION: LACK OF NOVELTY: OBVIOUSNESS: Australia: Pat. Off.) 13 I.P.R. 115
White Horse Distillers Ltd v. Gregson Associates Ltd (PASSING OFF: SCOTCH WHISKY: ADMIXTURE TRADE IN URUGUAY: LABELS: TORT COMMITTED IN ENGLAND: LIABILITY OF DIRECTORS: Ch.D.) [1984] R.P.C. 61
White Horse Distillers Ltd v. The Upper Doab Sugar Mills Ltd (TRADE MARK: INFRINGEMENT: PASSING OFF: Ex parte INJUNCTION: APPEAL: WHITE HORSE/FLYING HORSE: India: H.C.) (1985) 9 I.P.L.R. 156
Wickham v. Associated Pool Builders Pty Ltd (TRADE PRACTICES: AGREEMENT: USE OF BUSINESS NAME: PRACTICE: INTERLOCUTORY INJUNCTION: GRANT: ADEQUACY OF DAMAGES: DELAY: Australia: Fed. Ct) 7 I.P.R. 392
Wickham v. Associated Pool Builders Pty Ltd (TRADE PRACTICES: CONSUMER PROTECTION: MISLEADING OR DECEPTIVE CONDUCT: PASSING OFF: PROMOTIONS AGREEMENT BETWEEN SWIMMING CHAMPION AND POOL DISTRIBUTING COMPANY: Australia: Fed. Ct) 12 I.P.R. 567
Wickstrand v. Förening Svenska Tonsättares Internationella Musikbyrå (COPYRIGHT: DAMAGES: EXPLOITATION RIGHTS: PUBLIC PERFORMANCE: PRIVATE USE: Sweden: S.C.) [1988] E.C.C. 301; [1988] F.S.R. 521
Widen/Three-stroke engine (EUROPEAN PATENT: CLAIMS: QUALITATIVE EXPRESSION: NOVELTY: MERE VERBAL DISTINCTION: T67/87: EPO)
[1991] E.P.O.R. 498
Widmaier v. SPADEM (COPYRIGHT: Droit moral: COPYRIGHT MANAGEMENT SOCIETY: France: S.C.) [1993] F.S.R. 341
Wiederhold/Two-component polyurethane lacquer (EUROPEAN PATENT: INVENTIVE STEP: SELECTION: TRIAL-AND-ERROR APPROACH: PRIOR ART: INOPERATIVE EMBODIMENT: T259/85: EPO) [1988] E.P.O.R. 209

Wigginton v. Brisbane TV Ltd (COPYRIGHT: CINEMATOGRAPH FILM: FAIR
DEALING: CONFIDENTIAL INFORMATION: WHETHER INFORMATION FREELY
AVAILABLE: Australia: S.C.(Qd))   25 I.P.R. 58
Wilden Pump & Engineering Co. v. Fusfield (PRACTICE: DISCOVERY: SCOPE OF
IMPLIED UNDERTAKING: CONTEMPT: Ch.D.)   [1985] F.S.R. 581
Wilden Pump Engineering Co. v. Fusfield (PRACTICE: COPYRIGHT: PATENT
AGENTS' PRIVILEGE: C.A.)   [1985] F.S.R. 159
Wilder Days Pty Ltd v. Karhugh Properties Ltd (TRADE MARK: OPPOSITION:
INTENTION TO USE: DECEPTIVE SIMILARITY: Australia: AIPO) 27 I.P.R. 473
Wilkinson Sword Ltd's Application (TRADE MARKS: APPLICATION: PIVOT:
DESCRIPTIVENESS: DISTINCTIVENESS: Australia: Pat. Off.)   12 I.P.R. 138
Willemijn Houdstermaatschappij BV v. Madge Networks Ltd (PATENT:
INFRINGEMENT: COMPUTERS: CONSTRUCTION: ESSENTIAL INTEGER:
INESSENTIAL VARIANT: C.A.)   [1992] R.P.C. 386
Willems (Re) (PATENT: APPLICATION: APPLICANTS: INVENTORS: PERSON
ENTITLED TO HAVE PATENT ASSIGNED TO IT: REFUSAL BY ONE APPLICANT TO
PROCEED WITH APPLICATION: Australia: Pat. Off.)   21 I.P.R. 569
William E. Selkin Ltd v. Proven Products Ltd (PATENT: INFRINGEMENT: CLAIMS:
CONSTRUCTION: OBVIOUSNESS: NOVELTY: SIMILAR APPARATUS: INTERIM
INTERDICT: WEIGHT TO BE GIVEN TO EXISTANCE OF PATENT: BALANCE OF
CONVENIENCE: PROTECTION OF LONG ESTABLISHED BUSINESS AGAINST
NEWLY FORMED BUSINESS: ADEQUACY OF DAMAGES: Scotland: V.C.)
                                1992 S.L.T. 983
William Grant & Sons Ltd v. Cape Wine & Distillers Ltd (TRADE MARK: UNLAWFUL
COMPETITION: CONDUCT: REPRESENTATION: CONFUSION OR DECEPTION:
PUBLIC POLICY: South Africa: CPD)   1990 (3) S.A. 897
William Grant & Sons Ltd v. McDowell & Co. Ltd (PASSING OFF: COPYRIGHT:
INTERLOCUTORY INJUNCTION: SINGLE MALT SCOTCH WHISKEY: DESIGN
AND DEFINITION OF LABEL: GET-UP: TRANS-BORDER REPUTATION OF
PRODUCT AVAILABLE IN INDIA: EROSION OF REPUTATION: GENERIC
NATURE OF PRODUCT: India: H.C.)   [1994] F.S.R. 690
Williams & Humbert Ltd v. International Distillers & Vintners Ltd (TRADE MARK:
INFRINGEMENT: SUMMARY JUDGMENT: COUNTERCLAIM: Ch.D.)
                                [1986] F.S.R. 150
Williams & Humbert Ltd v. W. & H. Trade Marks (Jersey) Ltd (CONFLICT OF LAWS:
FOREIGN LAW: ENFORCEMENT: CONFISCATION OF ASSETS: TRADE MARK:
Ch.D.)   [1985] 2 All E.R. 208; [1985] 3 W.L.R. 501
                 (C.A.) [1985] 2 All E.R. 619; [1985] 3 W.L.R. 501
      (H.L.) [1986] A.C. 368; [1986] 1 All E.R. 129; [1986] 1 F.T.L.R. 298;
                                [1986] W.L.R. 24
Williamson Music Ltd v. The Pearson Partnership Ltd (COPYRIGHT:
INFRINGEMENT: PARODY: Ch.D.)   [1987] F.S.R. 97
Williamson v. Moldline Ltd (PATENT: INFRINGEMENT: PRACTICE: PLEADINGS:
COSTS: EARTH CLOSET ORDER: DISCRETION: C.A.)   [1986] R.P.C. 556
Willow Lea Pastoral Co. Pty Ltd's Application (TRADE MARKS: APPLICATION:
REFUSAL TO REGISTER: Australia: Pat. Off.)   20 I.P.R. 180
Wilson v. Broadcasting Corp. of New Zealand (COPYRIGHT: INFRINGEMENT:
FORMAT OR CONCEPT FOR A TV PROGRAMME: BREACH OF
CONFIDENTIALITY: FEASIBILITY STUDY: EXEMPLARY DAMAGES: New Zealand:
H.C.)   12 I.P.R. 173; [1990] 2 N.Z.L.R. 565
Wimmera Industrial Minerals Pty Ltd v. RGC Mineral Dand Ltd (PATENT:
REVOCATION: WHETHER SECTION 64(2) A BASIS FOR VOIDING A PATENT:
PREROGATIVE RELIEF: Australia: Fed. Ct)   32 I.P.R. 89

Windsurfing International Inc. v. E.C. Commission (RESTRICTIVE PRACTICES: PATENT LICENSING: RELEVANT MARKET: COMPONENTS: PATENT PROTECTION: COMMISSION'S POWERS TO INTERPRET NATIONAL LAW: JUDICIAL REVIEW: TYING CLAUSE: NO-CHALLENGE CLAUSES: TRADE MARK: Case 193/83: ECJ)   [1986] 3 C.M.L.R. 489; [1986] E.C.R. 611

Windsurfing International Inc. v. Petit (PATENT: INFRINGEMENT: SALE OF KIT OF PARTS: CONSTRUCTION: NOVELTY: Australia: S.C.(NSW))
[1984] 2 N.S.W.L.R. 196

Windsurfing International Inc. v. Sailboards Australia Pty Ltd (TRADE MARK: CONTEMPT OF COURT: BREACH OF UNDERTAKING: ONUS OF PROOF: LIABILITY: ASSESSMENT OF FINE: Australia: Fed. Ct)   69 A.L.R. 534

Windsurfing International Inc. v. Tabur Marine (G.B.) Ltd (PATENT: VALIDITY: OBVIOUSNESS: ANTICIPATION: AMENDMENT: PRACTICE: DISCRETION: C.A.)
[1985] R.P.C. 59

Wineworths Group Ltd v. Comite Interprofessional du Vin de Champagne *sub nom.* Comite Interprofessional du Vin de Champagne v. Wineworths Group Ltd

Wingate Marketing Pty Ltd v. Levi Strauss & Co., *sub nom.* Levi Strauss & Co. v. Wingate Marketing Pty Ltd

Winner v. Ammar Holdings Pty Ltd (PATENT: INFRINGEMENT: REVOCATION: INVENTIVE STEP: OBVIOUSNESS: NOVELTY: DISTINCTION BETWEEN: COMMON GENERAL KNOWLEDGE: DISCOVERY OF PROBLEM: DESCRIPTION OF INVENTION: COMBINATION: MOSAIC: FRAUD: FALSE SUGGESTION OR MISREPRESENTATION: MISREPRESENTATION OF PRIOR ART IN UNITED STATES, NON-DISCLOSURE OF FATE OF OVERSEAS APPLICATION: Australia: Fed. Ct)   113 A.L.R. 63; 24 I.P.R. 137

Winner v. Morey Haigh & Associates (Australasia) Pty Ltd (PATENT: INFRINGEMENT: REVOCATION OF PATENT IN SUIT AT OTHER PROCEEDINGS: DISMISSAL OF INFRINGEMENT PROCEEDINGS: COSTS: INDEMNITY BASIS: Australia: Fed. Ct)   30 I.P.R. 419

Winning Appliances Pty Ltd v. Dean Appliances Pty Ltd (TRADE PRACTICES: TRADE NAME: USE OF NAME IN COMPANY NAME: WHETHER MISLEADING AND DECEPTIVE CONDUCT: ASSIGNMENT OF TRADING NAME: WHETHER GOODWILL ASSIGNED: Australia: Fed. Ct)   32 I.P.R. 43

Winning Appliances Pty Ltd v. Dean Appliances Pty Ltd (TRADE PRACTICES: MISLEADING AND DECEPTIVE CONDUCT: ASSESSMENT OF DAMAGES: GENERAL DAMAGES: EVIDENCE: Australia: Fed. Ct)   32 I.P.R. 65

Winthrop Products Inc. v. Sun Ocean (M.) Sdn Bhd (TRADE MARKS: PARALLEL IMPORTS: PRODUCT MANUFACTURED IN U.K. SOLD IN MALAYSIA: INFRINGEMENT: PASSING OFF: Malaysia: H.C.)
[1988] 2 M.L.J. 317; [1988] F.S.R. 430; 13 I.P.R. 307

Wiseman v. George Weidenfeld & Nicholson Ltd (COPYRIGHT: INFRINGEMENT: DRAMATIC WORK: JOINT AUTHORSHIP: Ch.D.)   [1985] F.S.R. 525

Wissen Pty Ltd v. Kenneth Mervyn Lown (PATENT: COMPULSORY LICENCE: APPLICATION: REASONABLE REQUIREMENTS OF PUBLIC: Australia: Pat. Off.)
9 I.P.R. 124

Wistar Institute's Application (PATENT: APPLICATION: OBVIOUSNESS: EVIDENCE: PRACTICE: Pat. Ct)   [1983] R.P.C. 255

Wistyn Enterprises (Pty) Ltd v. Levi Strauss & Co. (TRADE MARK: EXPUNGEMENT: REGISTERED USER: JOINDER: USE: South Africa: TPD)   1984 (4) S.A. 796

Wollard's Patent (PATENT: DECLARATION OF NON-INFRINGEMENT: PRACTICE: C.-G.)   [1989] R.P.C. 141

Wood Pulp Cartel (Re): A. Ahlstrom Oy v. E.C. Commission (RESTRICTIVE PRACTICES: EXTRATERRITORIAL JURISDICTION: CONCERTED PRACTICES: EFFECT ON COMPETITION WITHIN COMMUNITY: STREAM OF COMMERCE DOCTRINE: TERRITORIALITY: INTERNATIONAL LAW: INTERNATIONAL COMITY: EXPORT CARTELS: Cases 89/85, 104/85, 114/85, 116 and 117/85, 125 and 129/85: ECJ) [1988] 4 C.M.L.R. 901; [1988] E.C.R. 5193

Wood v. Kempe (COPYRIGHT: INFRINGEMENT: ARCHITECTS PLANS: INTERLOCUTORY INJUNCTION: BALANCE OF CONVENIENCE: Australia: Fed. Ct) 32 I.P.R. 37

Wood v. Uniflex (Aust.) Pty Ltd, *sub nom.* Wood v. Westaflex (Aust.) Pty Ltd

Wood v. Westaflex (Aust.) Pty Ltd (PATENT: VALIDITY: NOVELTY: PRIOR PUBLICATION: FOREIGN DISCLOSURE TO EMPLOYEE OF AUSTRALIAN COMPANY: australia: S.C.(Vic.)) 20 I.P.R. 387
(INFRINGEMENT: INJUNCTION: STAY PENDING APPEAL: PRINCIPLES ON WHICH GRANTED: WHETHER SPECIAL RULE FOR INJUNCTIONS IN PATENT CASES: PRACTICE AND PROCEDURE: APPEAL: APPROPRIATE UNDERTAKINGS AND CONDITIONS: Australia: Fed. Ct) 18 I.P.R. 168

Woodcap/Appeal of proprietor (EUROPEAN PATENT: APPEAL: PROCEDURE: ADMISSIBILITY OF APPEAL: OPPOSITION: PROCEDURE: ESTOPPEL OF PATENTEE: OPPOSITION DIVISION: AGREEMENT BY PATENTEE TO LIMITED RE-ESTABLISHMENT OF RIGHTS: DELAY BY EPO: T506/91: EPO)
[1994] E.P.O.R. 197

Working Mens Club & Institute Union Ltd v. Performing Right Society Ltd (COPYRIGHT: REFERENCE TO TRIBUNAL: NON-PROFIT-MAKING MEMBERS CLUBS TARIFF: PRACTICE: Cprt Trib.) [1992] R.P.C. 227

Work Model Enterprises Ltd v. Ecosystem Ltd (COPYRIGHT: INFRINGEMENT: COPYING WORDS OF BROCHURE: CLAIM FOR DAMAGES RESULTING FROM COMPETITION GENERATED BY INFRINGING BROCHURE: Ch.D.)
[1996] F.S.R. 356

Worrallo v. Hales (PATENT: NON-PAYMENT OF RENEWAL FEE: PATENT LAPSED: APPLICATION FOR RESTORATION OF PATENT: OPPOSITION TO APPLICATION FOR RESTORATION: APPLICATION FOR SPECIAL LEAVE TO LODGE FURTHER EVIDENCE: Australia: Pat. Off.) 24 I.P.R. 273

Wright v. Gasweld Pty Ltd (CONFIDENTIAL INFORMATION: EX-EMPLOYEE: Australia: S.C.(NSW)) 20 I.P.R. 481

Wulro BV v. Tuchtgerecht van de Stichting Scharreleieren-Controle (TRADE MARK: FOOD: LABELLING: INDICATION OF FREE-RANGE OR BATTERY EGGS: ILLEGALITY OF DUTCH RULES: Case 130/85: ECJ)
[1988] 1 C.M.L.R. 496; [1986] E.C.R. 2035

Wundowie Foundry Pty Ltd v. Milson Foundry Pty Ltd (PATENT: INFRINGEMENT: DISCOVERY: DOCUMENTS RELATING TO DESIGN AND DEVELOPMENT OF INVENTION: PATENT ATTORNEY AND CLIENT PRIVILEGE: Australia: Fed. Ct) 27 I.P.R. 202

Wyko Group plc v. Cooper Roller Bearings Co. Ltd (COPYRIGHT: ENGINEERING DRAWINGS: DECLARATION OF NON-INFRINGEMENT: SPARE PARTS DEFENCE: PRACTICE: DECLARATORY RELIEF: SCOPE OF COURTS'S POWER: STRIKING OUT WRIT AND STATEMENT OF CLAIM: Ch.D.) [1996] F.S.R. 126

X Health Authority v. Y. (BREACH OF CONFIDENCE: INJUNCTION: INFORMATION OBTAINED FROM CONFIDENTIAL HOSPITAL RECORDS: DOCTORS WITH AIDS: IDENTITY: INTERLOCUTORY INJUNCTION AGAINST NEWSPAPER PROHIBITING PUBLICATION: PUBLIC INTEREST: WHETHER PUBLICATION IN BREACH OF INJUNCTION A CONTEMPT: Q.B.D.)
[1988] 2 All E.R. 648; [1988] R.P.C. 379; 13 I.P.R. 202

X Pte Ltd v. CDE (CONFIDENTIAL INFORMATION: GROUNDS: BREACH: ELEMENTS TO BE SATISFIED: EQUITABLE OBLIGATION OF CONFIDENCE: INTERLOCUTORY INJUNCTION: SERIOUS QUESTION TO BE TRIED: APPROPRIATENESS OF DAMAGES: Singapore: H.C.) [1992] 2 S.L.R. 996

X-Cyte Inc. v. Tablek Electronics Pty Ltd (PATENT: PRACTICE AND PROCEDURE: OPPOSITION: WITHDRAWAL: EFFECT: Australia: AIPO) 27 I.P.R. 372

X/Basis for decisions (EUROPEAN PATENT: OPPOSITION: PROCEDURE: ORAL PROCEEDINGS: BASIS FOR DECISION: ENLARGED BOARD OF APPEAL: PRESIDENT OF EPO, REFERENCE BY: G04/92: EPO)
[1994] E.P.O.R. 392; [1994] O.J. EPO 149

X/Beta-blockers (EUROPEAN PATENT: UNITY: INTERNATIONAL SEARCH: W31/88: EPO) [1990] E.P.O.R. 317; [1990] O.J. EPO 134

X/Correction under Rule 88, second sentence (EUROPEAN PATENT: G03/89: EPO) [1993] E.P.O.R. 376; [1993] O.J. EPO 117

X/Fibre fleece (EUROPEAN PATENT: UNITY: PROBLEM SOLVED BY INVENTION MUST BE ANALYSED: REASONS FOR LACK OF MUST BE GIVEN: W11/89: EPO) [1993] E.P.O.R. 514; [1992] O.J. EPO 225

X/Immunoassay process and apparatus (EUROPEAN PATENT: UNITY: PROCESS AND APPARATUS CLAIM: W32/88: EPO)
[1990] E.P.O.R. 321; [1990] O.J. EPO 138

X/Interruption of proceedings (EUROPEAN PATENT: PROCEDURE: INCAPACITY OF REPRESENTATIVE: *Travaux préparatoires*, REQUEST FOR COPIES OF: CONVENTIONS: AUTONOMOUS STANDARD UNDER EPC: EVIDENCE: MEDICAL EVIDENCE OF INCAPACITY: JXX/XX: EPO)
[1979–85] E.P.O.R. A234; [1985] O.J. EPO 159

X/Jurisdiction of board of appeal (EUROPEAN PATENT: BOARD OF APPEAL: JURISDICTION, LACK OF: J15/91: EPO) [1994] E.P.O.R. 574

X/Lubricants (EUROPEAN PATENT: INTERNATIONAL APPLICATION: UNITY— SUBSTANTIVE EXAMINATION: INTERNATIONAL SEARCH: INADMISSIBLE PROTEST: W03/88: EPO) [1990] E.P.O.R. 309; [1990] O.J. EPO 126

X/Lubricants—Polysuccinate esters (EUROPEAN PATENT: INTERNATIONAL APPLICATION: UNITY—SUBSTANTIVE EXAMINATION: SUBSTANTIVE EXAMINATION OF INTERNATIONAL APPLICATION: W12/89: EPO)
[1990] E.P.O.R. 333; [1990] O.J. EPO 152

X/Open Group (RESTRICTIVE PRACTICES: COMPUTER OPERATING SYSTEM: UNIX: AGREEMENT TO STANDARDISE: OPEN INDUSTRY STANDARD: INTENTION TO APPROVE: NOTICE: E.C. Comm.) [1986] 3 C.M.L.R. 373
(DECISION: E.C. Comm.) [1988] 4 C.M.L.R. 542; [1988] F.S.R. 530

X/Polysuccinate esters (EUROPEAN PATENT: ENLARGED BOARD OF APPEAL: JURISDICTION: EPO: PRESIDENT'S FUNCTIONS AND POWERS: G01/89: G02/89: EPO)
[1991] E.P.O.R. 239; [1991] O.J. EPO 155; [1991] O.J. EPO 166

X/Professional representative—legal incapacity (EUROPEAN PATENT: PROFESSIONAL REPRESENTATIVES: INCAPACITY: FEES: REIMBURSEMENT OF APPEAL FEE: J00/86: EPO) [1988] E.P.O.R. 129; [1987] O.J. EPO 528

X/Synergic combination of additives (EUROPEAN PATENT: INTERNATIONAL APPLICATION: UNITY—SUBSTANTIVE EXAMINATION: W44/88: EPO)
[1990] E.P.O.R. 323; O.J. EPO 1990,140

Xerox Corp. v. Apple Computer Inc. (COMPUTER PROGRAMS: "LOOK AND FEEL" OF USER INTERFACE: REMEDIES FOR INFRINGEMENT: WHETHER ORDER STRIKING OUT COPYRIGHT REGISTRATION AVAILABLE: WHETHER REMEDY OF CONSTRUCTIVE TRUST AVAILABLE: USA: S.C.)   17 I.P.R. 629

Xerox/Amendments (EUROPEAN PATENT: AMENDMENT AND CORRECTION: NOVELTY TEST (EUROPEAN PATENT: ADDED SUBJECT-MATTER): GENERALISATION: CLAIMS: SUPPORT FOR: T133/85: EPO)
[1989] E.P.O.R. 116; [1988] O.J. EPO 441

Xerox/Finality of decision (EUROPEAN PATENT: APPLICATION: PROCEDURE: COMMUNICATION UNDER RULE 51(4), EFFECT OF: APPEAL: DISCRETION TO DETERMINE NEW REQUESTS AS SINGLE INSTANCE: SINGLE INSTANCE, DISCRETION TO ACT AS, ON NEW REQUEST: ENLARGED BOARD OF APPEAL: NOT A THIRD INSTANCE: REFERENCE REFUSED: PROCEDURE: DECISION: FINALITY OF: T79/89: EPO)   [1990] E.P.O.R. 558; [1992] O.J. EPO 283

Yale Security Products Ltd v. Newman (COPYRIGHT INFRINGEMENT: ESTOPPEL: EURO-DEFENCES: FREE MOVEMENT OF GOODS: DOMINANT POSITION: ABUSE: Ch.D.)   [1990] F.S.R. 320

Yamaha Corp.'s Application (TRADE MARKS: APPLICATION: REGISTRABILITY: OBJECTION: DESCRIPTIVE: NON-DISTINCTIVE: Australia: Pat. Off.)
18 I.P.R. 359

Yamazaki Mazak Corp.'s Application (PATENT: PETTY PATENTS: APPLICATIONS FOR EXTENSION OF TERMS: INFORMATION AGAINST EXTENSION: APPLICATION FOR ADJOURNMENT OF HEARING: Australia: Pat. Off.)
24 I.P.R. 321

Yamazaki Mazak Corp. v. Interact Machine Tools (NSW) Pty Ltd (PATENT: PETTY PATENTS: INFRINGEMENT: VALIDITY: OBVIOUSNESS: FAIR BASING OF CLAIM UPON MATTER DESCRIBED IN SPECIFICATION: NOVELTY: WHETHER CONVENTION PRIORITY DATE PRECEDED DATE OF ALLEGED ANTICIPATION: WHETHER FOR THAT PURPOSE CLAIMS FAIRLY BASED ON DISCLOSURE IN FOREIGN BASIC APPLICATIONS: WHETHER PETTY PATENTS OBTAINED ON FALSE SUGGESTION OR REPRESENTATION: Australia: Fed. Ct)   22 I.P.R. 79

Yandill Holdings Pty Ltd v. Insurance Co. of North America (PRACTICE: MAREVA INJUNCTION: Australia: H.C.)   [1987] 7 N.S.W.L.R. 571

Yardley & Co. Ltd v. Higson (PASSING OFF: INJUNCTION: FAILURE TO DISCLOSE MATERIAL FACT: PARALLEL IMPORTS: C.A.)   [1984] F.S.R. 304

Yardley of London (Australia) Pty Ltd v. Chapman & Lester, The Sales Promotion Agency Pty Ltd (TRADE PRACTICES: MISLEADING OR DECEPTIVE CONDUCT: WHETHER "AUSTRALIAN FOOTBALLER OF THE YEAR" CREATED BY APPLICANT OR RESPONDENT: Australia: Fed. Ct)   17 I.P.R. 345

Yarmirr v. Australian Telecommunications Corp. (TRADE PRACTICES: IMPLIED REPRESENTATION: WHETHER RELIANCE OR DAMAGE: Australia: Fed. Ct)
19 I.P.R. 75

Yomeishu Seizo Co. Ltd v. Sinma Medical Products (Singapore) Pte Ltd (TRADE MARK: INFRINGEMENT: CHINESE CHARACTERS READABLE IN CHINESE AND JAPANESE: NO MEANING IN JAPANESE BUT CHINESE NAME DESCRIPTIVE OF PRODUCT: FRAUD ON REGISTRY: PART A MARK REGISTERED IN U.K. AND SUBSEQUENT REGISTRATIONS ELSEWHERE: INTERLOCUTORY RELIEF REFUSED: Singapore: H.C.)   [1991] F.S.R. 278; [1991] 3 M.L.J. 251

YORK Trade Mark (TRADE MARK: APPLICATION: YORK: GEOGRAPHICAL SIGNIFICANCE: DISTINCTIVENESS: Ch.D.)
[1981] F.S.R. 33; [1984] R.P.C. 231; 8 I.P.R. 250
(H.L.) [1982] 1 All E.R. 257; [1982] F.S.R. 111; [1984] R.P.C. 231;
8 I.P.R. 250
York Trailer Holdings Ltd v. Registrar of Trade Marks, *sub nom.* YORK Trade Mark
Yorkwain Automatic Doors Ltd v. Newman Tonks Pty Ltd (PATENT: INFRINGEMENT: APPLICATION FOR MAREVA INJUNCTION: MEASURE OF DAMAGE: NECESSITY OF DELIBERATELY SEEKING TO AVOID JUDGMENT: Australia: S.C.(Vic.))   12 I.P.R. 290
Yoshida Kogyo/Priority declaration (EUROPEAN PATENT: AMENDMENT AND CORRECTION: EVIDENCE REQUIRED: PRIORITY CLAIM: MISTAKE, WHAT CONSTITUTES: PUBLIC INTEREST: PROCEDURE: EVIDENCE, REASONABLE TIME MUST BE GIVEN FOR FILING: PARIS CONVENTION, APPLICABILITY OF: EVIDENCE: MISTAKE, PROOF OF: FEES: REIMBURSEMENT OF APPEAL FEE: J04/82: EPO)   [1979–85] E.P.O.R. A102; [1982] O.J. EPO 385
YOURT Trade Mark (TRADE MARK: APPLICATION: WHETHER INVENTED WORD: PRACTICE: T.M.Reg.)   [1985] R.P.C. 363
Yumbulul v. Reserve Bank of Australia (COPYRIGHT: ARTISTIC WORKS BY ABORIGINAL ARTIST: PERMANENT PUBLIC DISPLAY IN MUSEUM: COPYRIGHT COLLECTING AGENCY: EXCLUSIVE LICENCE TO COLLECTING AGENCY: SUB-LICENCE TO RESERVE BANK: WHETHER ARTIST MISLED AS TO NATURE OF LICENCE AND INTENDED USE OF WORK: WHETHER ESTOPPEL OR MISTAKE: Australia: Fed. Ct)   21 I.P.R. 481
Yves Rocher's Franchise Agreements (RESTRICTIVE PRACTICES: FRANCHISE AGREEMENTS BETWEEN UNDERTAKINGS: COMPETITION: RESTRICTION ON COMMERCIAL FREEDOM: INDUSTRIAL PROPERTY: EXCLUSIVE TERRITORIAL RIGHTS: DISTRIBUTION: BLOCK EXEMPTION: PRICES: INTER-STATE TRADE: KNOW-HOW: ARTICLE 85(1) APPLICATION FOR NEGATIVE CLEARANCE: E.C. Comm.)   [1988] 4 C.M.L.R. 592; [1988] F.S.R. 569

Z. Ltd v. A. (MAREVA INJUNCTION: PROTECTION OF THIRD PARTIES' INTERESTS: GUIDELINES: C.A.)
[1982] 1 All E.R. 556; [1982] Q.B. 558; [1982] 2 W.L.R. 288
Z.S. Projects Pty Ltd v. G. & R. Investments Pty Ltd (COPYRIGHT: BUILDING PLANS: INFRINGEMENT: DAMAGES: ACCOUNT OF PROFITS: DEFENCE: SUMMARY JUDGMENT: PRACTICE: Australia: S.C.(NSW))   8 I.P.R. 460
Zang Tumb Tuum Records Ltd v. Johnson (CONTRACT: POP GROUP: RECORDING AGREEMENT AND PUBLISHING AGREEMENT: UNREASONABLE RESTRAINT OF TRADE: ENFORCEABILITY: WAIVE OF OBJECTION: SCOPE OF INQUIRY AS TO DAMAGES: C.A.)   [1993] E.M.L.R. 61
Zeccola v. Universal City Studios Inc. (COPYRIGHT: INFRINGEMENT: JAWS: INTERLOCUTORY INJUNCTION: DISCRETION: Australia: Fed. Ct)
(1983) 46 A.L.R. 189
Zeiss/Spectacle lens (EUROPEAN PATENT: INVENTIVE STEP: COMBINATION OF CITATIONS: PROBLEM AND SOLUTION: FRESH DOCUMENTS AT ORAL PROCEEDINGS: T263/86: EPO)   [1988] E.P.O.R. 150
Zenith/Missing claims (EUROPEAN PATENT: APPLICATION: PROCEDURE: FAIRNESS, REQUIREMENT FOR: MISSING CLAIMS: APPEAL: PROCEDURE: REMITTAL NOT ORDERED: UNFAIR AFTER LAPSE OF TIME: J20/85: EPO)   [1987] E.P.O.R. 157; [1987] O.J. EPO 102
Zinc Producer Group (RESTRICTIVE PRACTICES: E.C. Comm.)
[1985] 2 C.M.L.R. 108; [1985] F.S.R. 431

Zink/Vaporisation (EUROPEAN PATENT: FEES: REIMBURSEMENT OF APPEAL FEE: PROCEDURE: RIGHT TO BE HEARD: T30/81: EPO)
[1979–85] E.P.O.R. B373

Zokor/Naming of opponent (EUROPEAN PATENT: AMENDMENT AND CORRECTION: NAMING OF OPPONENT: OPPOSITION: PROCEDURE: IDENTIFICATION OF OPPONENT: PRECEDENT: *Obiter dicta* NOT APPLIED: T219/86: EPO)   [1988] E.P.O.R. 407; [1988] O.J. EPO 254

Zomba Music Publishers Ltd v. Mountfield (CONTRACT: POP GROUP: RECORDING AGREEMENT AND PUBLISHING AGREEMENT: RESTRAINT OF TRADE: ENFORCEABILITY: ESTOPPEL: WAIVER: SEVERABILITY OF AGREEMENTS: Q.B.D.)   [1993] E.M.L.R. 152

Zoueki/Filing date (EUROPEAN PATENT: APPLICATION: PROCEDURE: DATE OF FILING: CONVENTIONS: NATIONAL LAWS, RELATIONSHIP OF EPC TO: J18/86: EPO)   [1988] E.P.O.R. 338; [1988] O.J. EPO 165

Zunis Holding SA v. E C. Commission (RESTRICTIVE PRACTICES: MERGER: CLEARED BY COMMISSION: REQUEST BY SHAREHOLDERS TO REOPEN CASE: REFUSAL: JUDICIAL REVIEW: WHETHER APPEAL POSSIBLE: *Locus standii*: CFI)   [1994] 5 C.M.L.R. 154

ZYX Music GmbH v. King (COPYRIGHT: INFRINGEMENT: DISCO ARRANGEMENT OF POPULAR SONG: INNOCENT INFRINGEMENT BY PLAINTIFF: WHETHER COPYRIGHT ENFORCEABLE: ENTITLEMENT TO RELIEF: SECONDARY INFRINGEMENT: ADDITIONAL DAMAGES: FLAGRANCY OF INFRINGEMENT: INJUNCTION: Ch.D.)
[1995] E.M.L.R. 281; [1995] F.S.R. 566; 31 I.P.R. 207

B. Numerical List of European Community Cases

The European Court of Justice and The European Court of First Instance

258/78, Nungesser KG v. E.C. Commission (RESTRICTIVE PRACTICES: PLANT VARIETIES: MAIZE SEEDS: EXCLUSIVE LICENCE: ECJ)
[1983] 1 C.M.L.R. 278; [1983] F.S.R. 309; [1982] E.C.R. 2015

155/79, A.M. & S. Ltd v. E.C. Commission (ADMINISTRATIVE PROCEDURE: LAWYERS: CONFIDENTIALITY: PRIVILEGE: ECJ)   [1982] 2 C.M.L.R. 264; [1982] E.C.R. 1747; [1982] F.S.R. 474; [1983] 3 W.L.R. 17

56/80, Weigand v. Schutzerverband Deutscher Wein eV (WINE LABELS: TRADE MARKS: FALSE IMPRESSION OF ORIGIN: Germany: S.C.)
[1983] 1 C.M.L.R. 168
(ECJ) [1983] 1 C.M.L.R. 146; [1981] E.C.R. 583

6/81, Industrie Diensten Groep v. J.A. Beele Handelmaatschappij BV (IMPORTS: QUANTITATIVE RESTRICTIONS: UNFAIR COMPETITION: PROPORTIONALITY: ECJ)   [1982] 3 C.M.L.R. 102; [1982] E.C.R. 707; [1983] F.S.R. 119

144/81, Keurkoop BV v. Nancy Kean Gifts BV (INDUSTRIAL DESIGN: APPLICATION OF ARTICLE 36 EEC: ECJ)
[1983] 2 C.M.L.R. 47; [1983] F.S.R. 381; [1982] E.C.R. 2853

262/81, Coditel SA v. Cin Vog Films SA (COPYRIGHT: PERFORMING RIGHTS: RESTRICTIVE PRACTICES: EXCLUSIVE LICENCE: ECJ)
[1983] 1 C.M.L.R. 49; [1982] E.C.R. 3381; [1983] F.S.R. 148

322/81, Nederlandsche Banden-Industrie Michelin NV v. E.C. Commission (RESTRICTIVE PRACTICES: DOMINANT POSITION: PRACTICE: ECJ)
[1985] 1 C.M.L.R. 282; [1983] E.C.R. 3461; [1985] F.S.R. 250

7/82, Gesellschaft zur Verwertung von Leistungsschutzrechten v. E.C. Commission (RESTRICTIVE PRACTICES: ADMINISTRATIVE PROCEDURE: COPYRIGHT: MARKET PARTITIONING: INTER-STATE TRADE: DOMINANT POSITION: ABUSE: ECJ)   [1983] 3 C.M.L.R. 645; [1993] E.C.R. 483; [1984] F.S.R. 155

43 & 63/82, VBBB and VBVB v. E.C. Commission (RESTRICTIVE PRACTICES: CONDUCT OF HEARINGS: DISCOVERY: RESALE PRICE MAINTENANCE: INFRINGEMENT OF ARTICLE 85(1): EXEMPTION: PRECEDENTS: ECJ)
[1985] 1 C.M.L.R. 27; [1984] E.C.R. 19

86/82, Hasselblad (G.B.) Ltd v. E.C. Commission (PARALLEL IMPORTS: PRACTICE: ECJ)   [1984] 1 C.M.L.R. 559; [1984] E.C.R. 883; [1984] F.S.R. 321

107/82, AEG Telefunken v. E.C. Commission (RESTRICTIVE PRACTICES: PROCEDURE: INVESTIGATION: SEIZURE OF DOCUMENTS: ECJ)
[1984] 3 C.M.L.R. 325; [1983] E.C.R. 3151

228 & 229/82R, Ford Werke v. E.C. Commission (RESTRICTIVE PRACTICES: INTERLOCUTORY PROCEEDINGS: PROCEDURE: ECJ)
[1982] 3 C.M.L.R. 673; [1982] I E.C.R. 2849

288/82, Duijnstee v. Goderbauer (PATENT: EMPLOYEE INVENTOR: FULL FAITH AND
CREDIT: JURISDICTION: ECJ)
[1985] 1 C.M.L.R. 220; [1983] E.C.R. 3663; [1985] F.S.R. 221

319/82, Société de Vente de Ciments v. Kerpen & Kerpen GmbH (RESTRICTIVE
PRACTICES: EXHAUSTION OF RIGHTS: ECJ)
[1985] 1 C.M.L.R. 511; [1983] E.C.R. 4173; [1985] F.S.R. 281

29 & 29/83, Compagnie Royale Asturienne des Mines S.A. v. E.C. Commission
(RESTRICTIVE PRACTICES: EXPORT RESTRICTIONS: ECJ)
[1985] 1 C.M.L.R. 688; [1984] E.C.R. 1679

35/83, TOLTECS and DORCET Trade marks, British American Tobacco
Company Ltd v. E.C. Commission (RESTRICTIVE PRACTICES: TRADE MARKS:
DORCET AND TOLTECS SPECIAL: DORMANT MARK: SIMILARITY:
INFRINGEMENT OF ARTICLE 85: E.C. Comm.)
[1983] 1 C.M.L.R. 412; [1983] F.S.R. 327; [1982] O.J. L379/19
(E.C. COMMISSION UPHELD: FINES: ECJ)
[1985] 2 C.M.L.R. 470; [1985] E.C.R. 363; [1985] F.S.R. 533
(RESTRICTIVE PRACTICES: COMPANY OWNERSHIP: ACQUISITION OF EQUITY
INTEREST IN COMPETITOR: EFFECT: ARTICLE 85: POWER TO INFLUENCE
CONDUCT: COMPLAINANTS: ECJ) [1988] 4 C.M.L.R. 24; [1985] E.C.R. 363

41/83, Italy v. E.C. Commission (Re BT) (RESTRICTIVE PRACTICES: MONOPOLIES:
STATE ENTERPRISES: ECJ PROCEDURE: TREATIES: ECJ)
[1985] 2 C.M.L.R. 368; [1985] E.C.R. 3013; [1985] F.S.R. 510

145/83, & 53/84, Adams v. E.C. Commission (CONFIDENTIAL INFORMATION:
DUTY OF E.C. Comm.: ECJ)   [1986] F.S.R. 617; [1986] 2 W.L.R. 367

170/83, Hydrotherm Gerätebau GmbH v. Compact de Dott Ing Mario Andreoli &
CSAS (RESTRICTIVE PRACTICES: EXCLUSIVE DEALING: BLOCK EXEMPTION:
REGULATION 67/67: TRADE MARK LICENCE: ECJ)
[1985] 3 C.M.L.R. 224; [1987] E.C.R. 2999

177/83, Theodor Kohl KG v. Ringelhan & Rennett S.A. (IMPORTS:
PHARMACEUTICALS: TRADE MARK: GET-UP: USE BY SEVERAL SUCCESSORS TO
SPLIT COMPANY: LIKELIHOOD OF CONFUSION: INFRINGEMENT: Germany:
ECJ)   [1985] 3 C.M.L.R. 340; [1986] F.S.R. 8

193/83, Windsurfing International Inc. v. E.C. Commission (RESTRICTIVE
PRACTICES: PATENT LICENSING: RELEVANT MARKET: COMPONENTS: PATENT
PROTECTION: COMMISSION'S POWERS TO INTERPRET NATIONAL LAW:
JUDICIAL REVIEW: TYING CLAUSE: NO-CHALLENGE CLAUSES: TRADE MARK:
ECJ)   [1986] 3 C.M.L.R. 489; [1986] E.C.R. 611

243/83, Binon (SA) & Cie v. SA Agence et Messageries de la Presse (RESTRICTIVE
PRACTICES: SELECTIVE DISTRIBUTION: NEWSPAPERS: ARTICLE 85(1):
ECJ)   [1985] 3 C.M.L.R. 800; [1985] E.C.R. 2015

298/83, Comité des Industries Cinématographiques des E.C. v. E.C. Commission
(RESTRICTIVE PRACTICES: ABUSE OF DOMINANT POSITION: BROADCASTING:
FILMS: FEES: COMPLAINT: ECJ) [1986] 1 C.M.L.R. 486; [1985] E.C.R. 1105

19/84, Pharmon BV v. Hoechst (PATENTS: PARALLEL IMPORTS: COMPULSORY
LICENCES: ECJ)
[1985] 3 C.M.L.R. 775; [1985] E.C.R. 2281; [1986] F.S.R. 108

42/84, Remia BV v. Verenigde Bedrijven Nutricia BV (EUROPEAN COURT
PROCEDURE: RESTRICTIVE PRACTICES: ECJ)   [1987] F.S.R. 190

53/84 & 145/83, Adams v. E.C. Commission (CONFIDENTIAL INFORMATION:
DUTY OF E.C. Comm.: ECJ)   [1986] F.S.R. 617; [1986] 2 W.L.R. 367

75/84, Metro-SB-Großmärkte (RESTRICTIVE PRACTICES: EXEMPTION: RENEWAL:
NEED FOR COMMISSION RE-EXAMINATION: SELECTIVE DISTRIBUTION:
ECJ)   [1987] 1 C.M.L.R. 118; [1986] E.C.R. 3121

103/84, E.C. Commission v. Italy (SUBSIDY FOR ITALIAN MOTOR VEHICLES)
(IMPORTS: QUANTITIVE RESTRICTIONS: No *de minimis* FOR ARTICLE 30:
ECJ)   [1987] 2 C.M.L.R. 825; [1986] E.C.R. 1759

110/84, Hillegom Municipality v. Hillenius (BANKING: CONFIDENTIALITY:
NATIONAL COURTS: CIVIL PROCEEDINGS: PROFESSIONAL PRIVILEGE:
ECJ)   [1986] 3 C.M.L.R. 422; [1985] E.C.R. 3947

142 & 156/84, British American Tobacco Co. Ltd v. E.C. Commission (EUROPEAN
COURT PROCEDURE: RESTRICTIVE PRACTICES: ORAL ARGUMENTS:
BUSINESS SECRETS: EVIDENCE: DISCOVERY: ECJ)
[1987] 2 C.M.L.R. 551; [1987] E.C.R. 4566

178/84, Purity Requirements for Beer (IMPORTS: MANUFACTURING STANDARDS:
BEER: ANCIENT GERMAN PURITY RULES: *Reinheitsgebot*: BAN ON ADDITIVES:
ECJ)   [1988] 1 C.M.L.R. 780; [1987] E.C.R. 1227

182/84, Miro BV (IMPORTS: DRINKS: APPELATION: "GENEVA": DECEPTION OF
CONSUMER: STRENGTHS: ECJ) [1986] 3 C.M.L.R. 545; [1983] E.C.R. 3461

187/84, Italy v. Caldana (CONSUMER PROTECTION: PRODUCT SAFETY: LABELLING:
DIFFERENCE BETWEEN DANGEROUS SUBSTANCES AND DANGEROUS
PREPARATIONS: ECJ)   [1989] 1 C.M.L.R. 137; [1985] E.C.R. 3013

226/84, British Leyland Motor Corp. Ltd v. E.C. Commission (RESTRICTIVE
PRACTICES: DOMINANT POSITION: SUPPLY OF CERTIFICATES OF
CONFORMITY FOR IMPORTED MOTOR VEHICLES: RELEVANT MARKET:
DISCRIMINATORY FEES: ABUSE: ECJ)
[1987] 1 C.M.L.R. 184; [1986] E.C.R. 3263

311/84, Centre Belge d'Etudes de Marché-Télé-Marketing SA v. Comp
Luxembourgeoise de Télédiffusion SA (RESTRICTIVE PRACTICES: DOMINANT
POSITION: REMOVAL OF COMPETITION THROUGH LEGISLATION: ABUSE:
ECJ)   [1986] 2 C.M.L.R. 558; [1985] E.C.R. 3261

5/85, AKZO Chemie BV v. E.C. Commission (RESTRICTIVE PRACTICES: SEARCH AND SEIZURE: SEARCH WARRANT: PRACTICE: ECJ)
[1987] 3 C.M.L.R. 716; [1986] E.C.R. 2585; [1988] F.S.R. 55

31/85, ETA Fabriques d'Ebauches SA v. DK Investment SA (RESTRICTIVE PRACTICES: EXCLUSIVE DEALING: DISTRIBUTION NETWORK: RESTRICTION ON SELLING OUTSIDE CONTRACT TERRITORY: ECJ)
[1986] 2 C.M.L.R. 674; [1985] E.C.R. 3933

45/85, Verband der Sachversicherer eV v. E.C. Commission (RESTRICTIVE PRACTICES: EXCLUSIONS: INSURANCE: NATIONAL LAW: TRADE ASSOCIATIONS: COMPETITION: ECJ).
[1988] 4 C.M.L.R. 264; [1987] E.C.R. 405; [1988] F.S.R. 383

53/85, AKZO Chemie BV v. E.C. Commission (RESTRICTIVE PRACTICES: DOMINANT POSITION: ABUSE: BUSINESS SECRETS: NATURE OF: COMMUNICATION TO COMPLAINANT: ROLE OF E.C. Comm.: ECJ)
[1987] 1 C.M.L.R. 231; [1986] E.C.R. 1965

89, 104, 114, 116, 117, 125 & 129/85, Wood Pulp Cartel (Re) A. Ahlstrom Oy v. E.C. Commission (RESTRICTIVE PRACTICES: EXTRATERRITORIAL JURISDICTION: CONCERTED PRACTICES: EFFECT ON COMPETITION WITHIN COMMUNITY: STREAM OF COMMERCE DOCTRINE: TERRITORIALITY: INTERNATIONAL LAW: INTERNATIONAL COMITY: EXPORT CARTELS: ECJ)
[1988] 4 C.M.L.R. 901; [1988] E.C.R. 5193

121/85, Conegate Ltd v. Customs & Excise Commissioners (IMPORTS: PROHIBITION: QUALITATIVE RESTRICTIONS: PUBLIC MORALITY: OBSCENE GOODS: INFLATABLE DOLLS: ECJ)
[1986] 2 All E.R. 688; [1986] C.M.L.R. 739; [1986] E.C.R. 1007

125 & 129, 89 & 104, 114, 116 & 117/85, Wood Pulp Cartel (Re) A. Ahlstrom Oy v. E.C. Commission (RESTRICTIVE PRACTICES: EXTRATERRITORIAL JURISDICTION: CONCERTED PRACTICES: EFFECT ON COMPETITION WITHIN COMMUNITY: STREAM OF COMMERCE DOCTRINE: TERRITORIALITY: INTERNATIONAL LAW: INTERNATIONAL COMITY: EXPORT CARTELS: ECJ)
[1988] 4 C.M.L.R. 901; [1988] E.C.R. 5193

130/85, Wulro BV v. Tuchtgerecht van de Stichting Scharreleieren-Controle (TRADE MARK: FOOD: LABELLING: INDICATION OF FREE-RANGE OR BATTERY EGGS: ILLEGALITY OF DUTCH RULES: ECJ)
[1988] 1 C.M.L.R. 496; [1986] E.C.R. 2035

179/85, E.C. Commission v. Germany (Champagne-type bottles) (IMPORTS: WINE: GET-UP: RIGHT TO LEGISLATE: ARTICLE 30: CONFLICT: PROTECTION OF CONSUMER: ECJ)
[1988] 1 C.M.L.R. 135; [1986] E.C.R. 3879

402/85, Basset v. Société des Auteurs, Compositeurs et Editeurs de Musique (SACEM) (COPYRIGHT: PHONOGRAMS: RESTRICTIVE PRACTICES: COPYRIGHT MANAGEMENT SOCIETIES: RESTRICTION OF CIRCULATION: ROYALTIES: ARTICLE 30: ARTICLE 86: ECJ)
[1987] 3 C.M.L.R. 173; [1987] E.C.R. 1747; [1987] F.S.R. 572

434/85, Allen & Hanburys Ltd v. Generics (U.K.) Ltd (PATENT: IMPORTS: LICENCES OF RIGHT: TERMS OF LICENCE: EFFECTIVE DATE OF LICENCE: CONSTRUCTION: EXHAUSTION OF RIGHTS: Ch.D.)   [1986] 2 F.T.L.R. 100 (C.A.) [1986] 1 C.M.L.R. 101; [1985] F.S.R. 610; [1986] R.P.C. 203 (INTERIM JUDGMENT: H.L.)   [1985] F.S.R. 610; [1986] R.P.C. 203 (Case 434/85: ECJ)
[1988] 4 C.M.L.R. 701; [1988] E.C.R. 1275; [1988] F.S.R. 312

10/86, VAG France v. Etablissements Magne SA (RESTRICTIVE PRACTICES: MOTOR VEHICLES: GROUP EXEMPTION: REGULATION 123/85: EFFECT ON DISTRIBUTION CONTRACTS: ECJ)
[1988] 4 C.M.L.R. 98; [1986] E.C.R. 4071

62/86, AKZO Chemie BV v. E.C. Commission (RESTRICTIVE PRACTICES: EUROPEAN COURT PROCEDURE: INTERIM MEASURES: DOMINANT POSITION: UNDERCUTTING: REQUEST FOR INTERIM SUSPENSION: REFUSAL: ECJ)
[1987] 1 C.M.L.R. 225; [1986] E.C.R. 1503; [1987] F.S.R. 203

62/86R, AKZO Chemie BV v. E.C. Commission (RESTRICTIVE PRACTICES: EUROPEAN COURT PROCEDURE: ADMINISTRATIVE PROCEDURE: DISCOVERY OF DOCUMENTS: DOMINANT POSITION: RELEVANT PRODUCT MARKET: MARKET SHARE: PRICING: ABUSE: ECJ)
[1993] 5 C.M.L.R. 215; [1994] F.S.R. 25

65/86, Bayer AG and Maschinenfabrik Hennecke GmbH v. Sullhofer (RESTRICTIVE PRACTICES: INDUSTRIAL PROPERTY: AGREEMENTS: PATENT LICENSING: NO-CHALLENGE CLAUSES: COMMUNITY LAW: COMPATIBILITY WITH ARTICLES 30 AND 85: ECJ)   [1990] 4 C.M.L.R. 182; [1988] E.C.R. 5249; [1990] F.S.R. 300

121 & 122/86R, Epikhiriseon Metalleftikon Viomikhanikon Kai Naftiliakon AE v. E.C. Commission Council and E.C. Commission (EUROPEAN COURT PROCEDURE: DISCOVERY OF DOCUMENTS: PROCEDURAL DELAYS: ECJ)   [1987] 2 C.M.L.R. 558; [1986] E.C.R. 2063

158/86, Warner Brothers Inc. v. Christiansen (COPYRIGHT: LENDING RIGHT: VIDEO BOUGHT IN SHOP IN ENGLAND WHERE NO LENDING RIGHT: RENTED OUT FROM SHOP IN DENMARK WHERE LENDING RIGHT APPLIES: WHETHER SALE IN ENGLAND EXHAUSTS COPYRIGHT IN THE BOUGHT VIDEO: EXTENT OF EXHAUSTION: NOT APPLICABLE TO RENTAL: NO RIGHT TO RENT OUT ENGLISH VIDEO IN DENMARK WITHOUT APPROPRIATE AUTHORISATION: ECJ)   [1990] 3 C.M.L.R. 684; [1988] E.C.R. 2605; [1991] F.S.R. 161

212/86, Imperial Chemical Industries plc v. E.C. Commission (EUROPEAN COURT PROCEDURE: RESTRICTIVE PRACTICES: DISCOVERY OF DOCUMENTS: HEARING OFFICER'S REPORT: INCONSISTENCY BETWEEN REASONING IN JUDGMENTS AND MOTIVES REVEALED IN PRESS STATEMENTS: RELEVANCY: ECJ)   [1987] 2 C.M.L.R. 500

266 & 267/86, R. v. Pharmaceutical Society of Great Britain, *ex p.* Association of Pharmaceutical Importers (IMPORTS: MEDICINES: MEASURES BY PHARMACEUTICAL SOCIETY COVERED BY ARTICLE 30: CHEMISTS NOT ALLOWED TO SUBSTITUTE IMPORTED EQUIVALENT (OR IDENTICAL) MEDICINES WITH DIFFERENT NAMES FOR BRANDED PREPARATIONS NAMED IN DOCTORS PRESCRIPTION: CAUGHT BY ARTICLE 30: BUT JUSTIFIED BY PUBLIC HEALTH UNDER ARTICLE 36: ECJ)
[1989] 2 C.M.L.R. 751; [1989] E.C.R. 1295; [1990] 2 W.L.R. 445

286/86, Ministere Public v. Deserbais (TRADE NAMES: CHEESE: EDAM GENERIC: NOT DESIGNATION OF ORIGIN: GERMAN EDAM WITH LOWER FAT CONTENT THAN ALLOWED IN FRANCE FOR FRENCH EDAM: REFUSED ENTRY INTO FRANCE: NO GOOD REASON: CONSUMERS PROTECTED ADEQUATELY BY LABELLING: MULTILATERAL TREATIES: NOT PLEADABLE AGAINST COMMUNITY LAW IF ONLY EEC MEMBER-STATES INVOLVED: ECJ)
[1989] 1 C.M.L.R. 516; [1987] E.C.R. 4907

27/87, Erauw-Jacquéry Sprl v. La Hesbignonne Société Co-opérative (RESTRICTIVE PRACTICES: PLANT BREEDERS' RIGHTS: LICENSING AGREEMENTS: SALES BAN: EXPORT BAN: ARTICLE 85(1): INTER-STATE TRADE: ECJ)
[1988] 4 C.M.L.R. 576; [1988] E.C.R. 1919; [1988] F.S.R. 572

35/87, Thetford Corporation v. Fiamma SpA (PATENT: INFRINGEMENT: NOVELTY: PA49 CASE: "50-YEAR RULE": REMEDITES: EEC LAW: COMMUNITY LAW CONFLICT WITH NATIONAL LAW: VALIDITY: RELATIVE NOVELTY: ECJ)
[1988] 3 C.M.L.R. 549; [1989] F.S.R. 57; [1990] 2 W.L.R. 1394; 20 I.P.R. 117

46/87R, Hoechst AG v. E.C. Commission (EUROPEAN COURT PROCEDURE: INTERIM MEASURES: SEARCH AND SEIZURE: RESTRICTIVE PRACTICES: JUDICIAL REVIEW: ECJ)
[1988] 4 C.M.L.R. 430; [1987] E.C.R. 1549; [1992] F.S.R. 210

53/87, Consorzio Italiano della Componentistica di Ricambio per Autoveicoli and Maxicar v. Regie Nationale des Usines Renault (COMMUNITY LAW AND NATIONAL LAW: INDUSTRIAL DESIGNS: RESTRICTIVE PRACTICES: DOMINANT POSITION: ABUSE: SPARE PARTS: ECJ)   [1990] F.S.R. 544

87/87R, Dow Chemical Nederland BV v. E.C. Commission (EUROPEAN COURT PROCEDURE: INTERIM MEASURES: SEARCH AND SEIZURE: ECJ)
[1988] 4 C.M.L.R. 439

238/87, Volvo AB v. Erik Veng (U.K.) Ltd (RESTRICTIVE PRACTICES: INDUSTRIAL DESIGN RIGHTS: SPARE PARTS: ABUSE OF DOMINANT POSITION: REFUSAL TO LICENSE: NOT *per se* ABUSIVE: ECJ)
[1989] 4 C.M.L.R. 122; [1988] E.C.R. 6211

320/87, Ottung v. Klee & Weilbach A/S (RESTRICTIVE PRACTICES: PATENTS: LICENSING AGREEMENT: OBLIGATION TO PAY ROYALTIES INDEFINITELY WHILE AGREEMENT SUBSISTING: EXPIRY OF PATENT: OUTSIDE ARTICLE 85(1) WHERE LICENSEE MAY TERMINATE FREELY ON REASONABLE NOTICE: ECJ)   [1990] 4 C.M.L.R. 915; [1989] E.C.R. 1177

341/87, EMI Electrola GmbH v. Patricia IM- und Export Verwaltungs GmbH (COPYRIGHT: IMPORTS: PHONOGRAMS: SOUND RECORDING RIGHTS: ARTICLE 36: EXERCISE OF COPYRIGHT: ARTIFICIAL PARTITIONING: EXHAUSTION OF RIGHTS: EXPIRY OF COPYRIGHT PERIOD IN DENMARK, NOT IN GERMANY: ECJ)
[1989] 2 C.M.L.R. 413; [1989] E.C.R. 79; [1989] F.S.R. 544

395/87, Ministere Public v. Lucazeau (Société des Auteurs, Compositeurs et Editeurs de Musique (SACEM), *partie civile*) (COPYRIGHT: INFRINGEMENT: COLLECTION AGENCIES: STATUS: CRIMINAL OFFENCE: PERFORMANCE: RESTRICTIVE PRACTICES: DOMINANT POSITION: ABUSE: France: C.A.)
[1989] E.C.C. 66; [1989] F.S.R. 209, *sub nom.* Lucazeau v. Société des Auteurs, Compositeurs et Editeurs de Musique (SACEM) (ECJ)
[1991] 4 C.M.L.R. 248; [1989] E.C.R. 2521; [1991] F.S.R. 465

229/88R, Cargill BV v. E.C. Commission (PROCEDURE: INTERIM MEASURES: SERIOUS AND IRREPARABLE DAMAGE: NOT IF PURELY FINANCIAL: ECJ)
[1989] 1 C.M.L.R. 304; [1990] I E.C.R. 1303

T–7/89, Hercules NV, SA v. E.C. Commission (RESTRICTIVE PRACTICES: ADMINISTRATIVE PROCEDURE: SUPPLY OF DOCUMENTS: CONFIDENTIALITY: CFI)
[1992] 4 C.M.L.R. 84; [1991] II E.C.R. 1711

C–10/89, CNL-Sucal NV, SA v. HAG GF AG (TRADE MARKS: IMPORTS: EXHAUSTION OF RIGHTS: GERMAN AND BELGIAN MARKS OF COMMON ORIGIN: CONFUSION: IDENTICAL MARKS CONFISCATION OF ENEMY PROPERTY OUTSIDE GERMANY: PREVIOUS EUROPEAN COURT JUDGMENT: ECJ)
[1990] 3 C.M.L.R. 571; [1990] I E.C.R. 3711; [1991] F.S.R. 99

T–30/89, Hilti AG v. E.C. Commission (RESTRICTIVE PRACTICES: DOMINANT COMPANY: COMPULSORY PATENT LICENCES: EXTORTIONATE FEES: SELECTIVE AND DISCRIMINATORY SALES POLICY: ABUSE: NOT JUSTIFIED BY SAFETY WORRIES: CFI)
[1992] 4 C.M.L.R. 16

T–30/89A, Hilti AG v. E.C. Commission (CONFIDENTIALITY OF BUSINESS SECRETS: INTERVENERS: LEGAL PROFESSIONAL PRIVILEGE: APPLICABLE TO WRITTEN COMMUNICATIONS BETWEEN INDEPENDENT LAWYER AND CLIENT COMPANY: INTERESTS OF RIGHT OF DEFENCE: PROCEDURE: CFI)
[1990] 4 C.M.L.R. 602; [1990] II E.C.R. 163

T–51/89, Tetra Pak Rausing SA v. E.C. Commission (CONSTITUTIONAL LAW: EEC TREATY: RESTRICTIVE PRACTICES: DOMINANT POSITION: ABUSE: EXCLUSIVE LICENCES: GROUP EXEMPTIONS: LEGAL CERTAINTY: POWER OF NATIONAL COURTS: ECJ)
[1991] 4 C.M.L.R. 334; [1991] F.S.R. 654

56/89R, Net Book Agreements (Publishers Association v. E.C. Commission) (EUROPEAN COURT PROCEDURE: INTERIM MEASURES: RESTRICTIVE PRACTICES: BOOKS: U.K. COLLECTIVE RESALE PRICE MAINTENANCE SCHEME: ECJ)
[1989] 4 C.M.L.R. 816; [1989] E.C.R. 1693

T–66/89, Net Book Agreements (*sub nom.* Publishers Association v. E.C. Commission) (RESTRICTIVE PRACTICES: BOOKS: RESALE PRICE MAINTENANCE: COLLECTIVE SYSTEM OPERATED BY U.K. PUBLISHERS: EFFECT ON INTER-STATE TRADE: ARTICLE 85(1): INELIGIBLE FOR EXEMPTION: ADMINISTRATIVE LAW: DECISIONS: CFI)   [1992] 5 C.M.L.R. 120

T–69/89, Radio Telefis Eireann v. E.C. Commission (RESTRICTIVE PRACTICES: BROADCASTING: WEEKLY LISTINGS OF TV PROGRAMMES: COPYRIGHT: REFUSAL TO PERMIT REPRODUCTION IN INDEPENDENT TV GUIDE: ARTICLE 86: COMMISSION ENTITLED TO REQUIRE LICENSING FOR REPRODUCTION OF THE LISTINGS: ADMINISTRATIVE PROCEDURE: ADVISORY COMMITTEE ON RESTRICTIVE PRACTICES AND DOMINANT POSITIONS: MINUTES OF ORAL HEARINGS: NOTICE OF SITTING: CFI)
[1991] 4 C.M.L.R. 586; [1991] II E.C.R. 485

T–70/89, British Broadcasting Corporation v. E.C. Commission (RESTRICTIVE PRACTICES: BROADCASTING: WEEKLY LISTINGS OF TV PROGRAMMES: COPYRIGHT: REFUSAL TO PERMIT REPRODUCTION IN INDEPENDENT TV GUIDE: ARTICLE 86: COMMISSION ENTITLED TO REQUIRE LICENSING FOR REPRODUCTION OF THE LISTINGS: CFI)
[1991] 4 C.M.L.R. 669; [1991] E.C.R. 535; 22 I.P.R. 31

T–76 & T–77/89R, Independent Television Publications Ltd v. E.C. Commission (RESTRICTIVE PRACTICES: BROADCASTING: WEEKLY LISTINGS OF TV PROGRAMMES: COPYRIGHT: REFUSAL TO PERMIT REPRODUCTION IN INDEPENDENT TV GUIDE: ARTICLE 86: COMMISSION ENTITLED TO REQUIRE LICENSING FOR REPRODUCTION OF THE LISTINGS: CFI)
[1991] 4 C.M.L.R. 745; [1991] II E.C.R. 575

77, 76 & 91/89R, Radio Telefis Eireann v. E.C. Commission (Magill TV Guide) (EUROPEAN COURT PROCEDURE: INTERIM MEASURES: RESTRICTIVE PRACTICES: BROADCASTERS PROGRAMME LISTING: ECJ)
[1989] 4 C.M.L.R. 749; [1989] E.C.R. 1141; [1990] F.S.R. 87

C–235/89 & C–30/90, E.C. Commission v. United Kingdom and Italy (Re Compulsory Patent Licences) (IMPORTS: PATENTS: COMPULSORY LICENCE IF NO EXPLOITATION WITHIN COUNTRY: IMPORTS FROM ELSEWHERE IN COMMUNITY NOT COUNTED AS INTERNAL EXPLOITATION: HINDRANCE TO IMPORTS: U.K. P.A.77, S.48 INFRINGES ARTICLE 30: SIMILAR ITALIAN PROVISIONS LIKEWISE: ECJ)
[1992] 2 C.M.L.R. 709; [1982] I E.C.R. 777; [1993] F.S.R. 1

C–347/89, Freistaat Bayern v. Eurim-Pharm GmbH (IMPORTS: PHARMACEUTICALS: NEED FOR AUTHORISATION: CAUGHT BY ARTICLE 30: HEALTH OF HUMANS: IMPORTANT ITEM IN ARTICLE 36: GERMAN REQUIREMENT THAT IMPORTED MEDICINES BEAR MARKINGS IN GERMAN AT TIME OF IMPORTATION: IMPORTERS INTENTION TO AFFIX TRADE MARKS AFTER IMPORTATION BUT BEFORE ONWARD SALE INSUFFICIENT: IMPORTS AUTHORISED IN EXPORTING MEMBER-STATE: GERMAN RULE BREACHES ARTICLE 30: NOT SAVED BY ARTICLE 36: ECJ)
[1993] 1 C.M.L.R. 616; [1991] I E.C.R. 1747

C–30/90 & C–235/89, Commission v. United Kingdom and Italy (Re Compulsory Patent Licences) (IMPORTS: PATENTS: COMPULSORY LICENCE IF NO EXPLOITATION WITHIN COUNTRY: IMPORTS FROM ELSEWHERE IN COMMUNITY NOT COUNTED AS INTERNAL EXPLOITATION: HINDRANCE TO IMPORTS: P.A.77, S.48 INFRINGES ARTICLE 30: SIMILAR ITALIAN PROVISIONS LIKEWISE: ECJ)
[1992] 2 C.M.L.R. 709; [1982] I E.C.R. 777; [1993] F.S.R. 1

C–76/90, Sager v. Dennemeyer & Co. Ltd (SERVICES: PATENTS: MONITORING AND RENEWAL: PATENTS AGENTS: STATUTORY MONOPOLY: GERMANY: FOREIGN RENEWERS TO BE LICENSED: ECJ)   [1993] 3 C.M.L.R. 639; [1991] I E.C.R.

C–191/90, Generics (U.K.) Ltd v. Smith Kline & French Laboratories Ltd (PATENTS: IMPORTS: PHARMACEUTICALS: COMPULSORY LICENCES: INTRA-STATE CONDITIONS: LICENSEE STATUTORILY PERMITTED TO IMPORT FROM OUTSIDE EEC: PARALLEL IMPORTS: DISCRIMINATION: SPAIN AND PORTUGAL: ECJ)   [1993] 1 C.M.L.R. 89; [1992] I E.C.R. 5335; [1993] F.S.R. 592

C–92/92, Phil Collins v. Imtrat Handelsgesellschaft mbH (DISCRIMINATION: NATIONALITY: COPYRIGHT LAWS: PHONOGRAMS: BOOTLEG RECORDINGS: REMEDY UNDER GERMAN LAW AVAILABLE TO GERMAN NATIONALS: DISCRIMINATION: NATIONALITY: DIRECT EFFECT: NOT TO BRITONS: ARTICLE 7(1) EFFECTIVE DIRECTLY AND ON ITS OWN: BREACH OF ARTICLE 7(1): COPYRIGHT: SPECIFIC OBJECT: COVERED BY FREE MOVEMENT RULES: ECJ)   [1993] 3 C.M.L.R. 773; [1994] E.M.L.R. 108; [1994] F.S.R. 166

T–114/92, Bureau Européen des Média de l'Industrie Musicale v. Commission for the European Communities (RESTRICTIVE PRACTICES: COMPLAINT: BREACH OF ARTICLE 85 AND ARTICLE 86 BY SACEM: REFERENCE TO NATIONAL COURTS: APPLICATION FOR ANNULMENT: CFI)
[1996] 4 C.M.L.R. 305; [1996] E.M.L.R. 97

C–350/92, Spain v. Council of the European Union (SUPPLEMENTARY PROTECTION CERTIFICATES: VALIDITY OF REGULATION: COMMUNITY COMPETENCE: LEGAL BASIS: ECJ)   [1996] 4 C.M.L.R. 415; [1996] F.S.R. 73

360/92P, Net Book Agreements (Publishers Association v. E.C. Commission) (RESTRICTIVE PRACTICES: BOOKS: RESALE PRICE MAINTENANCE: COLLECTIVE SYSTEM OPERATED BY U.K. PUBLISHERS: REFUSAL TO EXEMPT, UPHELD BY CFI: EFFECT OF SINGLE LANGUAGE MARKET, U.K. AND IRELAND: ECJ)   [1995] 5 C.M.L.R. 33; [1995] E.M.L.R. 185

C–376/92, Metro-SB-Großmärkte GmbH & Co. KG v. Cartier SA (RESTRICTIVE PRACTICES: SELECTIVE DISTRIBUTION: LUXURY WATCHES: REFUSAL BY MANUFACTURER TO HONOUR WATCHES ACQUIRED OUTSIDE EEC BY UNAUTHORISED DEALER AND SOLD IN GERMANY: WHETHER BREACH OF ARTICLE 85: ECJ)   [1994] 5 C.M.L.R. 331

C–71/93, Eurim-Pharm v. Beiersdorf *sub nom.* Bristol Myers Squibb v. Paranova (TRADE MARKS: EUROPEAN COMMUNITY: PARALLEL IMPORTS: REPACKAGING OF GOODS: EXHAUSTION OF RIGHTS: RESTRICTIONS FOR PROTECTION OF INDUSTRIAL AND COMMERCIAL PROPERTY: DISGUISED RESTRICTION ON TRADE BETWEEN MEMBER STATES: ECJ)
[1996] F.S.R. 225

C–72/93, Eurim-Pharm v. Beiersdorf *sub nom.* Bristol Myers Squibb v. Paranova
(TRADE MARKS: EUROPEAN COMMUNITY: PARALLEL IMPORTS: REPACKAGING OF GOODS: EXHAUSTION OF RIGHTS: RESTRICTIONS FOR PROTECTION OF INDUSTRIAL AND COMMERCIAL PROPERTY: DISGUISED RESTRICTION ON TRADE BETWEEN MEMBER STATES: ECJ)
[1996] F.S.R. 225

C–73/93, Eurim-Pharm v. Beiersdorf *sub nom.* Bristol Myers Squibb v. Paranova
(TRADE MARKS: EUROPEAN COMMUNITY: PARALLEL IMPORTS: REPACKAGING OF GOODS: EXHAUSTION OF RIGHTS: RESTRICTIONS FOR PROTECTION OF INDUSTRIAL AND COMMERCIAL PROPERTY: DISGUISED RESTRICTION ON TRADE BETWEEN MEMBER STATES: ECJ)
[1996] F.S.R. 225

C–427/93, Bristol Myers Squibb v. Paranova (TRADE MARKS: EUROPEAN COMMUNITY: PARALLEL IMPORTS: REPACKAGING OF GOODS: EXHAUSTION OF RIGHTS: RESTRICTIONS FOR PROTECTION OF INDUSTRIAL AND COMMERCIAL PROPERTY: DISGUISED RESTRICTION ON TRADE BETWEEN MEMBER STATES: ECJ)
[1996] F.S.R. 225

C–429/93, Bristol Myers Squibb v. Paranova (TRADE MARKS: EUROPEAN COMMUNITY: PARALLEL IMPORTS: REPACKAGING OF GOODS: EXHAUSTION OF RIGHTS: RESTRICTIONS FOR PROTECTION OF INDUSTRIAL AND COMMERCIAL PROPERTY: DISGUISED RESTRICTION ON TRADE BETWEEN MEMBER STATES: ECJ)
[1996] F.S.R. 225

C–436/93, Bristol Myers Squibb v. Paranova (TRADE MARKS: EUROPEAN COMMUNITY: PARALLEL IMPORTS: REPACKAGING OF GOODS: EXHAUSTION OF RIGHTS: RESTRICTIONS FOR PROTECTION OF INDUSTRIAL AND COMMERCIAL PROPERTY: DISGUISED RESTRICTION ON TRADE BETWEEN MEMBER STATES: ECJ)
[1996] F.S.R. 225

T–575/93, Koelman v. E.C. Commission (RESTRICTIVE PRACTICES: BROADCASTING: RETRANSMISSION OF PROGRAMMES BY CABLE: STANDARD AGREEMENT: COPYRIGHT: OWNERSHIP: RADIO MATERIAL: COLLECTING SOCIETY: ALLEGED BREACH OF ARTICLES 85 AND 86: CFI)
[1996] 4 C.M.L.R. 636

C–232/94, MPA Pharma v. Rhône Poulenc *sub nom.* Bristol Myers Squibb v. Paranova (TRADE MARKS: EUROPEAN COMMUNITY: PARALLEL IMPORTS: REPACKAGING OF GOODS: EXHAUSTION OF RIGHTS: RESTRICTIONS FOR PROTECTION OF INDUSTRIAL AND COMMERCIAL PROPERTY: DISGUISED RESTRICTION ON TRADE BETWEEN MEMBER STATES: ECJ)
[1996] F.S.R. 225

T–5/95, Tremblay v. E.C. Commission. (RESTRICTIVE PRACTICES: MUSIC: COPYRIGHT: MANAGEMENT SOCIETIES: ALLEGED INFRINGEMENTS OF ARTICLES 85 AND 86: MARKET SHARING: PRICE FIXING: NATIONAL COURTS, POWER OF INVESTIGATION: CFI)
[1996] 4 C.M.L.R. 305

C. Numerical List of European Patent Office Cases

Application no. 82 107 958.9 Passoni/Stand structure   [1992] E.P.O.R. 79

Application no. 83 307 553 Howard Florey/Relaxin   [1995] E.P.O.R. 541

Application no. 85 304 490.7 Harvard/Onco-mouse
     [1990] E.P.O.R. 4; [1991] E.P.O.R. 525

Patent no. 0 157 920 Müllverbrennungsanlage Wuppertal/No-challenge obligation   [1993] E.P.O.R. 479

B52/84 Micro-organisms   [1986] E.P.O.R. 204

XZB30/84 Methylomonas   [1986] E.P.O.R. 325

D12/88 Advertising by patent agents   [1992] E.P.O.R. 248; [1991] O.J. EPO 591

G01/83 Eisai, Bayer, Pharmuka/Second medical indication
     [1979–85] E.P.O.R. B241; [1985] O.J. EPO 60

G05/83 Eisai, Bayer, Pharmuka/Second medical indication
     [1979–85] E.P.O.R. B241; [1985] O.J. EPO 64

G06/83 Eisai, Bayer, Pharmuka/Second medical indication
     [1979–85] E.P.O.R. B241; [1985] O.J. EPO 67

G01/84 Mobil Oil/Opposition by proprietor (2)
     [1986] E.P.O.R. 39; [1985] O.J. EPO 299

G01/86 Voest-Alpine/Re-establishment of opponent
     [1987] E.P.O.R. 388; [1987] O.J. EPO 447

G01/88 Hoechst/Opponent's silence   [1989] E.P.O.R. 421; [1989] O.J. EPO 189

G02/88 Mobil Oil/Friction reducing additive
     [1990] E.P.O.R. 73; [1990] O.J. EPO 93

G04/88 MAN/Transfer of opposition   [1990] E.P.O.R. 1; [1989] O.J. EPO 480

G05/88 Medtronic/Administrative agreement
     [1991] E.P.O.R. 225; [1991] O.J. EPO 137

G06/88 Bayer/Plant growth regulating agent
     [1990] E.P.O.R. 257; [1990] O.J. EPO 114

G07/88 Medtronic/Administrative agreement
     [1991] E.P.O.R. 225; [1991] O.J. EPO 137

G08/88 Medtronic/Administrative agreement
     [1991] E.P.O.R. 225; [1991] O.J. EPO 137

G01/89 X/Polysuccinate esters   [1991] E.P.O.R. 239; [1991] O.J. EPO 155

G02/89 X/Non-unity *a posteriori*   [1991] E.P.O.R. 239; [1991] O.J. EPO 166

G03/89 Correction under Rule 88, second sentence
     [1993] E.P.O.R. 376; [1993] O.J. EPO 117

G01/90 Revocation of a patent   [1991] E.P.O.R. 343; [1991] O.J. EPO 275

G02/90 Kolbenschmidt/Responsibility of the Legal Board of Appeal
     [1992] E.P.O.R. 125; [1992] O.J. EPO 10

G01/91 Siemens/Unity   [1992] E.P.O.R. 356; [1992] O.J. EPO 253

G02/91 Krohne/Appeal fees   [1992] E.P.O.R. 407; [1992] O.J. EPO 206

G03/91 Fabritius II/Re-establishment of rights
                                   [1993] E.P.O.R. 361; [1993] O.J. EPO 8

G04/91 Spanset/Intervention   [1993] E.P.O.R. 565; [1993] O.J. EPO 707

G05/91 Discovision/Appealable decision
                                   [1993] E.P.O.R. 120; [1992] O.J. EPO 617

G06/91 Asulab II/Fee reduction   [1993] E.P.O.R. 231; [1992] O.J. EPO 491

G07/91 BASF Bell/Withdrawal of appeal
                                   [1993] E.P.O.R. 440; [1993] O.J. EPO 356

G08/91 Bell Maschinenfabrik/Withdrawal of appeal
                                   [1993] E.P.O.R. 445; [1993] O.J. EPO 346

G09/91 Röhm & Haas/Power to examine
                                   [1993] E.P.O.R. 485; [1993] O.J. EPO 408

G10/91 Röhm & Haas/Power to examine
                                   [1993] E.P.O.R. 485; [1993] O.J. EPO 420

G11/91 Celtrix/Correction of errors   [1993] E.P.O.R. 245; [1993] O.J. EPO 125

G12/91 Novatome II/Final decision   [1994] E.P.O.R. 309; [1994] O.J. EPO 285

G01/92 Availability to the public   [1993] E.P.O.R. 241; [1993] O.J. EPO 277

G02/92 Non-payment of further search fees
                                   [1994] E.P.O.R. 278; [1993] O.J. EPO 591

G03/92 ; J01/91 Latchways/Unlawful applicant
                                   [1995] E.P.O.R. 141; [1994] O.J. EPO 607

G04/92 XXX/Basis for decisions   [1994] E.P.O.R. 392; [1994] O.J. EPO 149

G06/92 Duriron/Re-establishment of rights   [1994] E.P.O.R. 381

G09/92 ; T60/91; T96/92 BMW/Non-appealing party
                                   [1995] E.P.O.R. 169; [1994] O.J. EPO 875

G10/92 Divisional application   [1995] E.P.O.R. 265; O.J. EPO 199

G01/93 ; T384/91 Advanced Semiconductor Products II/Limiting feature
                                   [1995] E.P.O.R. 97

G02/93 United States of America II/Hepatitis A virus
                                   [1995] E.P.O.R. 437; [1995] O.J. EPO 275

G03/93 Priority interval   [1994] E.P.O.R. 521; [1995] O.J. EPO 18

G05/93 Nellcor/Re-establishment   [1994] E.P.O.R. 169; [1994] O.J. EPO 447

G07/93 ; T830/91 Whitby II/Late amendments
                                   [1995] E.P.O.R. 49; [1994] O.J. EPO 775

G08/93 ; T148/89 Serwane II/Withdrawal of opposition
                                   [1995] E.P.O.R. 271; [1994] O.J. EPO 887

G09/93 Peugeot & Citroën II/Opposition by patent proprietor
                                   [1995] E.P.O.R. 260; [1994] O.J. EPO 891

G01/94 ; T169/92 Allied Colloids/Intervention   [1995] E.P.O.R. 491

J01/78 Alexander von Füner/Family name
                                   [1979–85] E.P.O.R. A1; [1979] O.J. EPO 285

J02/78 Walch/Non-payment of the fee for appeal
[1979–85] E.P.O.R. A3; [1979] O.J. EPO 283

J01/79 Bussche/Filing notice of appeal by telegram
[1979–85] E.P.O.R. A5; [1980] O.J. EPO 34

J05/79 Siemens/Party adversely affected by a decision
[1979–85] E.P.O.R. A7; [1980] O.J. EPO 71

J06/79 Rhône-Poulenc/International applications
[1979–85] E.P.O.R. A10; [1980] O.J. EPO 225

J01/80 Siemens/Filing priority documents
[1979–85] E.P.O.R. A15; [1980] O.J. EPO 289

J02/80 Siemens/Priority claim   [1979–85] E.P.O.R. A19

J03/80 Chubb/Failure to forward a European patent application
[1979–85] E.P.O.R. A23; [1980] O.J. EPO 92

J04/80 NRDC/Examination by a Board of Appeal of its own motion
[1979–85] E.P.O.R. A27; [1980] O.J. EPO 351

J05/80 Société Parisienne/*Restitutio in integrum*
[1979–85] E.P.O.R. A31; [1981] O.J. EPO 343

J07/80 SKF/Correction of mistakes-languages
[1979–85] E.P.O.R. A36; [1981] O.J. EPO 137

J08/80 Rib Loc/Correction of mistakes
[1979–85] E.P.O.R. A40; [1980] O.J. EPO 293

J09/80 MPD Technology/Priority claim   [1979–85] E.P.O.R. A45

J11/80 Röhm/Withdrawal of a European patent application
[1979–85] E.P.O.R. A48; [1981] O.J. EPO 141

J12/80 Hoechst/Correction of mistakes (published application)
[1979–85] E.P.O.R. A52; [1981] O.J. EPO 143

J15/80 Arenhold/Priority right   [1979–85] E.P.O.R. A56; [1981] O.J. EPO 213

J19/80 Franklin/Missing drawings   [1979–85] E.P.O.R. A62; [1981] O.J. EPO 65

J21/80 Heisel/Late payment of appeal fee
[1979–85] E.P.O.R. A65; [1981] O.J. EPO 101

J26/80 Cappe/Date of which payment is made
[1979–85] E.P.O.R. A67; [1982] O.J. EPO 07

J01/81 Losfeld/Public holiday   [1979–85] E.P.O.R. A70; [1983] O.J. EPO 53

J03/81 Bodenrader/International application
[1979–85] E.P.O.R. A74; [1982] O.J. EPO 100

J04/81 Compagnie Générale D'Électricité/Calculation of the fee for printing
[1979–85] E.P.O.R. A80; [1981] O.J. EPO 543

J05/81 Hormann/Publication of a European patent application
[1979–85] E.P.O.R. A83; [1982] O.J. EPO 155

J07/81 Laverlochere/Bank cash payment
[1979–85] E.P.O.R. A88; [1983] O.J. EPO 89

J08/81 Caterpillar/Form of decision
[1979–85] E.P.O.R. A92; [1982] O.J. EPO 10

J01/82 Teva/Missing drawings   [1979–85] E.P.O.R. A96; [1982] O.J. EPO 293

J03/82 Taisho/Correction—priority
[1979–85] E.P.O.R. A99; [1983] O.J. EPO 171

J04/82 Yoshida Kogyo/Priority declaration
[1979–85] E.P.O.R. A102; [1982] O.J. EPO 385

J07/82 Cataldo/Cause of non-compliance
[1979–85] E.P.O.R. A108; [1982] O.J. EPO 391

J08/82 Fujitsu/Designation of inventors
[1979–85] E.P.O.R. A111; [1984] O.J. EPO 155

J09/82 Acno/Calculation of aggregate time limits
[1979–85] E.P.O.R. A118; [1983] O.J. EPO 57

J10/82 Roecar/Decisions by Formalities Officers
[1979–85] E.P.O.R. A122; [1983] O.J. EPO 94

J12/82 Floridienne/Late request for examination
[1979–85] E.P.O.R. A125; [1983] O.J. EPO 221

J13/82 General Datacomm/Correction of description
[1979–85] E.P.O.R. A129; [1983] O.J. EPO 12

J14/82 Johnson Matthey/Priority declaration
[1979–85] E.P.O.R. A132; [1983] O.J. EPO 121

J16/82 Theurer/Assistant: substitute
[1979–85] E.P.O.R. A137; [1983] O.J. EPO 262

J18/82 Cockerill Sambre/*Force majeure*
[1979–85] E.P.O.R. A140; [1983] O.J. EPO 441

J19/82 Toray/Partial withdrawal of appeal
[1979–85] E.P.O.R. A145; [1984] O.J. EPO 06

J21/82 Warner-Lambert/Different sets of claims
[1979–85] E.P.O.R. A149; [1984] O.J. EPO 65

J23/82 Clouth/Selection among designations
[1979–85] E.P.O.R. A154; [1983] O.J. EPO 127

J24/82 Grisebach/Divisional application
[1979–85] E.P.O.R. A159; [1984] O.J. EPO 467

J25/82 Grisebach/Divisional application
[1979–85] E.P.O.R. A159; [1984] O.J. EPO 467

J26/82 Grisebach/Divisional application
[1979–85] E.P.O.R. A159; [1984] O.J. EPO 467

J03/83 Associated Engineering Italy/Decisions by formalities officers
[1979–85] E.P.O.R. A164; [1995] O.J. EPO 102

J06/83 Caterpillar/Refund of examination fee
[1979–85] E.P.O.R. A169; [1985] O.J. EPO 97

J07/83 Mouchet/Interruption of proceedings
[1979–85] E.P.O.R. A174; [1984] O.J. EPO 211

J08/83 Western Electric/Refund of examination fee
[1979–85] E.P.O.R. A179; [1985] O.J. EPO 102

J09/83 Caterpillar/Self-purging heat exchanger   [1979–85] E.P.O.R. A185

J11/83 Cataldo/Re-establishment—insolvency   [1979–85] E.P.O.R. A191

J12/83 Chugai Seiyaku/Inadmissible appeal
　　　　　　[1979–85] E.P.O.R. A196; [1985] O.J. EPO 06

J01/84 Ornstein/Humidity control   [1979–85] E.P.O.R. A200

J05/84 Rippes/Computer fault   [1986] E.P.O.R. 53; [1985] O.J. EPO 306

J08/84 Blendax/Claims fees—Austria
　　　　　　[1979–85] E.P.O.R. A204; [1985] O.J. EPO 261

J09/84 Burgess/Claims fee   [1979–85] E.P.O.R. A209; [1985] O.J. EPO 233

J10/84 Texas/Amendments   [1979–85] E.P.O.R. A213; [1985] O.J. EPO 71

J12/84 Proweco/*Restitutio in integrum*
　　　　　　[1979–85] E.P.O.R. A217; [1985] O.J. EPO 108

J13/84 Roussel-Uclaf/Divisional application
　　　　　　[1979–85] E.P.O.R. A221; [1985] O.J. EPO 34

J15/84 Motorola/Restitution   [1979–85] E.P.O.R. A226

J16/84 Ferrero/Unclear payment of fees
　　　　　　[1986] E.P.O.R. 141; [1985] O.J. EPO 357

J18/84 NN/Register of European Patents
　　　　　　[1987] E.P.O.R. 321; [1987] O.J. EPO 215

J20/84 ; J23/85 Strabag, Krüger/Facsimile application
　　　　　　[1987] E.P.O.R. 165; [1987] O.J. EPO 95

J21/84 Consumers Glass/Late correction
　　　　　　[1986] E.P.O.R. 146; [1986] O.J. EPO 75

Jxx/xx X/Interruption of proceedings
　　　　　　[1979–85] E.P.O.R. A234; [1985] O.J. EPO 159

J01/85 Westinghouse/Payment by cheque
　　　　　　[1979–85] E.P.O.R. A230; [1995] O.J. EPO 126

J03/85 Denev/Cancer cells and lymphocytes game   [1986] E.P.O.R. 150

J04/85 État Français/Correction of drawings
　　　　　　[1986] E.P.O.R. 331; [1986] O.J. EPO 205

J11/85 Ikaplast/Small amount lacking   [1986] E.P.O.R. 110; [1986] O.J. EPO 01

J12/85 Kureha/Inadmissible appeal   [1986] E.P.O.R. 336; [1986] O.J. EPO 155

J13/85 Divisional Application/Whether filing justified
　　　　　　[1988] E.P.O.R. 125; [1987] O.J. EPO 523

J14/85 Suntory/Repayment of examination fee
　　　　　　[1987] E.P.O.R. 171; [1987] O.J. EPO 47

J15/85 X/Abandonment of claim   [1987] E.P.O.R. 108; [1985] O.J. EPO 395

J18/85 Ofenbau/Slag discharge   [1987] E.P.O.R. 400; [1987] O.J. EPO 356

J20/85 Zenith/Missing claims   [1987] E.P.O.R. 157; [1987] O.J. EPO 102

J21/85 Ruhland/Exchange of invention
　　　　　　[1986] E.P.O.R. 226; [1986] O.J. EPO 117

J22/85 Nusser/Payment order   [1988] E.P.O.R. 56; [1987] O.J. EPO 455

J23/85; J20/84 Strabag, Krüger/Facsimile application
        [1987] E.P.O.R. 165; [1987] O.J. EPO 95

J00/86 X/Professional representative—legal incapacity
        [1988] E.P.O.R. 129; [1987] O.J. EPO 528

J02/86 Motorola/Isolated mistake/restitution
        [1987] E.P.O.R. 394; [1987] O.J. EPO 362

J03/86 Motorola/Isolated mistake/restitution
        [1987] E.P.O.R. 394; [1987] O.J. EPO 362

J04/86 BMW/Air-conditioning system
        [1988] E.P.O.R. 273; [1988] O.J. EPO 119

J06/86 Riker/Withdrawal   [1988] E.P.O.R. 277; [1988] O.J. EPO 124

J15/86 Ausonia/Withdrawal of application
        [1989] E.P.O.R. 152; [1988] O.J. EPO 417

J18/86 Zoueki/Filing date   [1988] E.P.O.R. 338; [1988] O.J. EPO 165

J22/86 Medical Biological Sciences/Oral prosthesis
        [1987] E.P.O.R. 87; [1987] O.J. EPO 280

J24/86 Phillips/Cash payment to Post Office
        [1988] E.P.O.R. 59; [1987] O.J. EPO 399

J25/86 Warheit/Identity of applicant   [1988] E.P.O.R. 40; [1987] O.J. EPO 475

J27/86 Kureha Kagaku/Unreasoned decision   [1988] E.P.O.R. 48

J28/86 Voll/Container   [1988] O.J. EPO 85

J29/86 Paccar/Excess claims fees   [1988] E.P.O.R. 194; [1988] O.J. EPO 84

J32/86 Trucco/Re-establishment of rights   [1987] E.P.O.R. 249

J33/86 Voll/Refund of examination fee   [1988] O.J. EPO 84

J34/86 Bowles/Divisional application   [1988] E.P.O.R. 266

Jxx/87 Consolidation   [1988] E.P.O.R. 333; [1988] O.J. EPO 177

Jxxx/87 Incapacity   [1989] E.P.O.R. 73; [1988] O.J. EPO 323

J02/87 Motorola/Admissibility   [1989] E.P.O.R. 42; [1988] O.J. EPO 330

J03/87 Memtec/Membranes   [1989] E.P.O.R. 175; [1989] O.J. EPO 03

J04/87 Elton/Delay in post   [1988] E.P.O.R. 346; [1988] O.J. EPO 172

J05/87 Phillips/Number of claims incurring fees
        [1987] E.P.O.R. 316; [1987] O.J. EPO 295

J07/87 Schwarz Italia/Abandonment   [1989] E.P.O.R. 91; [1988] O.J. EPO 422

J08/87 Idaho/Submitting culture deposit information
        [1989] E.P.O.R. 170; [1989] O.J. EPO 09

J09/87 Idaho/Submitting culture deposit information
        [1989] E.P.O.R. 170; [1989] O.J. EPO 09

J10/87 Inland Steel/Retraction of withdrawal
        [1989] E.P.O.R. 437; [1989] O.J. EPO 323

J11/87 Doris/Abandonment   [1989] E.P.O.R. 54; [1989] O.J. EPO 367

J12/87 Hitachi/Re-establishment of rights
        [1989] E.P.O.R. 443; [1989] O.J. EPO 366

J14/87 Deere/Mention of grant   [1988] E.P.O.R. 419; [1988] O.J. EPO 295

J19/87 Burr-Brown/Assignment   [1988] E.P.O.R. 350

J20/87 Upjohn/Refund of search fee   [1989] E.P.O.R. 298; [1989] O.J. EPO 67

J23/87 K-Corporation of Japan/*Restitutio in integrum*   [1988] E.P.O.R. 52

J26/87 McWhirter/PCT form   [1989] E.P.O.R. 430; [1989] O.J. EPO 329

J27/87 Item/Inspection of files   [1988] E.P.O.R. 282

J04/88 Geo Meccanica Idrotecnica/Language of application
        [1990] E.P.O.R. 69; [1989] O.J. EPO 483

J05/88 INR/Substitution of applicant   [1989] E.P.O.R. 320

J11/88 Leland Stanford/Postal strike   [1990] E.P.O.R. 50; [1989] O.J. EPO 433

J15/88 Neorx/Claims fees   [1991] E.P.O.R. 76; [1990] O.J. EPO 445

J16/88 State of Oregon/Claims fees   [1990] E.P.O.R. 64

J22/88 Radakovic/Re-establishment of rights
        [1990] E.P.O.R. 495; [1990] O.J. EPO 244

J23/88 Webb/Interruption of proceedings   [1989] E.P.O.R. 272

J25/88 New Flex/Date of filing   [1990] E.P.O.R. 59; [1989] O.J. EPO 486

J01/89 Liesenfeld/Courtesy service   [1992] E.P.O.R. 284; [1992] O.J. EPO 17

J05/89 JMK Magnusson/Locking device   [1990] E.P.O.R. 248

J08/89 Isuzu/Correction of designation   [1990] E.P.O.R. 55

J10/89 Taito/Television game machine   [1992] E.P.O.R. 218

J19/89 Legal practitioner   [1991] E.P.O.R. 441; [1991] O.J. EPO 425

J20/89 Appellate jurisdiction (PCT cases)
        [1991] E.P.O.R. 436; [1991] O.J. EPO 375

J33/89 Caisse Palette Diffusion/Correction of drawings
        [1991] E.P.O.R. 521; [1991] O.J. EPO 288

J37/89 Matsushita/Extension of time limit
        [1993] E.P.O.R. 356; [1993] O.J. EPO 201

J38/89 Mogul/Divisional application   [1992] E.P.O.R. 214

J03/90 Fischer Scientific/Postal strike   [1992] E.P.O.R. 148; [1991] O.J. EPO 550

J04/90 Marello/Postal strike   [1990] E.P.O.R. 576

J06/90 Baxter/One-year period   [1994] E.P.O.R. 304; [1993] O.J. EPO 794

J07/90 Toledo/Correction of designation
        [1993] E.P.O.R. 329; [1993] O.J. EPO 133

J13/90 Castleton/Re-establishment of rights   [1994] E.P.O.R. 76

J14/90 Flachglas/Denmark—tacit   [1992] E.P.O.R. 553; [1992] O.J. EPO 505

J16/90 Fabritius/Re-establishment of rights
        [1992] E.P.O.R. 271; [1992] O.J. EPO 260

J18/90 Canon/Denmark—Expressly   [1992] E.P.O.R. 559; [1992] O.J. EPO 511

J27/90 Brunswick/*Restitutio*   [1994] E.P.O.R. 82

J30/90 Shea/Denmark—PCT   [1992] E.P.O.R. 564; [1992] O.J. EPO 516

J01/91; G03/92 Latchways/Unlawful applicant
   [1995] E.P.O.R. 141; [1993] O.J. EPO 281

J03/91 Uni-Charm/Priority declaration (correction)
   [1994] E.P.O.R. 566; [1994] O.J. EPO 365

J04/91 Ahmad/Additional period for renewal fee
   [1994] E.P.O.R. 365; [1992] O.J. EPO 402

J05/91 Kongskilde/Legal loophole   [1994] E.P.O.R. 205; [1993] O.J. EPO 657

J06/91 Du Pont de Nemours (E.I.) & Co./Correction of priority date
   [1993] E.P.O.R. 318; [1994] O.J. EPO 349

J11/91; J16/91 Dow/Divisional application
   [1994] E.P.O.R. 235; [1994] O.J. EPO 28

J14/91 Alt, Peter/Inspection of files   [1994] E.P.O.R. 184; [1993] O.J. EPO 479

J15/91 X/Jurisdiction of Board of Appeal   [1994] E.P.O.R. 574

J16/91; J11/91 Dow/Divisional application
   [1994] E.P.O.R. 235; [1994] O.J. EPO 28

J17/91 Cohen/Registering of licence   [1994] E.P.O.R. 317; [1994] O.J. EPO 225

J02/92 United States of America/Priority declaration
   [1994] E.P.O.R. 547; [1994] O.J. EPO 375

J25/92 Ostolski/Re-establishment of rights   [1994] E.P.O.R. 298

J27/92 Maxtor/Media storage system   [1995] E.P.O.R. 688; [1995] O.J. EPO 288

J41/92 Marron Blanco/Re-establishment
   [1994] E.P.O.R. 375; [1995] O.J. EPO 93

J47/92 Silver Systems/Further processing
   [1995] E.P.O.R. 495; [1995] O.J. EPO 180

T1/80 Bayer/Carbonless copying paper
   [1979–85] E.P.O.R. B250; [1981] O.J. EPO 206

T2/80 Bayer/Polyamide moulding compositions
   [1979–85] E.P.O.R. B257; [1981] O.J. EPO 431

T4/80 Bayer/Polyether polyols   [1979–85] E.P.O.R. B260; [1982] O.J. EPO 149

T6/80 MAN/Intermediate layer for reflector
   [1979–85] E.P.O.R. B265; [1981] O.J. EPO 434

T7/80 Licht Druck/Copying process
   [1979–85] E.P.O.R. B269; [1982] O.J. EPO 95

T1/81 AECI/Thermoplastics sockets
   [1979–85] E.P.O.R. B273; [1981] O.J. EPO 439

T2/81 Mobay/Methylenebis (phenyl isocyanate)
   [1979–85] E.P.O.R. B280; [1982] O.J. EPO 394

T5/81 Solvay/Production of hollow thermoplastic objects
   [1979–85] E.P.O.R. B287; [1982] O.J. EPO 249

T6/81 Siemens/Electrode slide   [1979–85] E.P.O.R. B294; [1982] O.J. EPO 183

T7/81 Ciba-Geigy/Dyeing of linear polyamides
                    [1979–85] E.P.O.R. B301; [1983] O.J. EPO 98

T9/81 ASTA/Cytostatic combination
                    [1979–85] E.P.O.R. B303; [1983] O.J. EPO 372

T12/81 Bayer/Diastereomers   [1979–85] E.P.O.R. B308; [1982] O.J. EPO 296

T15/81 Kraftwerk Union/Eddy-current testing device
                    [1979–85] E.P.O.R. B316; [1982] O.J. EPO 02

T17/81 Bayer/Nimodipin (I)   [1979–85] E.P.O.R. B320; [1985] O.J. EPO 130

T17/81 Bayer/Nimodipin (II)   [1979–85] E.P.O.R. B323; [1985] O.J. EPO 130

T18/81 Solvay/Olefin polymers [1979–85] E.P.O.R. B325; [1985] O.J. EPO 166

T19/81 Röhm/Film coating   [1979–85] E.P.O.R. B330; [1982] O.J. EPO 51

T20/81 Shell/Aryloxybenzaldehydes
                    [1979–85] E.P.O.R. B335; [1982] O.J. EPO 217

T21/81 Allen-Bradley/Electromagnetically operated switch
                    [1979–85] E.P.O.R. B342; [1983] O.J. EPO 15

T22/81 Lucas/Ignition system   [1979–85] E.P.O.R. B348; [1983] O.J. EPO 226

T24/81 BASF/Metal refining   [1979–85] E.P.O.R. B354; [1983] O.J. EPO 133

T26/81 ICI plc/Containers   [1979–85] E.P.O.R. B362; [1982] O.J. EPO 211

T28/81 Otep/Concrete hardening   [1979–85] E.P.O.R. B367

T30/81 Zink/Vaporisation   [1979–85] E.P.O.R. B373

T32/81 Fives-Cail Babcock/Cleaning apparatus for conveyor belt
                    [1979–85] E.P.O.R. B377; [1982] O.J. EPO 225

T10/82 Bayer/Admissibility of opposition
                    [1979–85] E.P.O.R. B381; [1983] O.J. EPO 407

T11/82 Lansing Bagnall/Control circuit
                    [1979–85] E.P.O.R. B385; [1983] O.J. EPO 479

T12/82 Sciaky/Surface hardening   [1979–85] E.P.O.R. B395

T13/82 Brown, Boveri/Statement of grounds of appeal
                    [1979–85] E.P.O.R. B405; [1983] O.J. EPO 411

T21/82 Siemens/Electromedical device   [1979–85] E.P.O.R. B409

T22/82 BASF/Bis-epoxy ethers [1979–85] E.P.O.R. B414; [1902] O.J. EPO 341

T26/82 Bayer/Clarity of claims   [1979–85] E.P.O.R. B423

T32/82 ICI plc/Control circuit [1979–85] E.P.O.R. B426; [1984] O.J. EPO 354

T36/82 Cselt/Parabolic reflector antenna
                    [1979–85] E.P.O.R. B433; [1983] O.J. EPO 269

T37/82 Siemens/Low-tension switch
                    [1979–85] E.P.O.R. B437; [1984] O.J. EPO 71

T39/82 Auer-Sog/Light reflecting slats
                    [1979–85] E.P.O.R. B441; [1982] O.J. EPO 419

T41/82 Sandoz/Reimbursement of appeal fee
                    [1979–85] E.P.O.R. B446; [1982] O.J. EPO 256

T43/82 Roussel-Uclaf/Tetrahydropyridinyl-indole derivatives
                              [1979–85] E.P.O.R. B448

T46/82 Eaton/Blocked speed transmission   [1979–85] E.P.O.R. B454

T52/82 Rieter/Winding apparatus
                    [1979–85] E.P.O.R. B459; [1983] O.J. EPO 416

T53/82 Degussa/Furnace blacks   [1979–85] E.P.O.R. B463

T54/82 Mobil/Disclosure   [1979–85] E.P.O.R. B469; [1983] O.J. EPO 446

T57/82 Bayer/Copolycarbonates
                    [1979–85] E.P.O.R. B474; [1982] O.J. EPO 306

T64/82 English Clays/Gravure printing   [1979–85] E.P.O.R. B479

T65/82 Bayer/Cyclopropane   [1979–85] E.P.O.R. B484; [1983] O.J. EPO 327

T66/82 Condec/Extrusion apparatus   [1979–85] E.P.O.R. B491

T74/82 ICI plc/Cartridge end closure   [1986] E.P.O.R. 74

T75/82 IBM/Magnetic transducer head support assemblies   [1986] E.P.O.R. 103

T76/82 Isotube/Elevator   [1979–85] E.P.O.R. B495

T80/82 GTM/Sound-absorbent wall   [1979–85] E.P.O.R. B500

T84/82 Macarthys/Chloral derivatives
                    [1979–85] E.P.O.R. B507; [1983] O.J. EPO 451

T94/82 ICI plc/Gear crimped yarn
                    [1979–85] E.P.O.R. B513; [1984] O.J. EPO 75

T98/82 Unilever/Multicoloured detergent bars   [1979–85] E.P.O.R. B522

T99/82 Cummins/Reimbursement   [1979–85] E.P.O.R. B528

T102/82 Mölnlycke/Dry salt compress   [1979–85] E.P.O.R. B530

T107/82 Unilever/Perfumed cartons   [1979–85] E.P.O.R. B534

T109/82 Bosch/Hearing aid   [1979–85] E.P.O.R. B539; [1984] O.J. EPO 473

T110/82 Bayer/Benzyl esters   [1979–85] E.P.O.R. B546; [1984] O.J. EPO 274

T113/82 IBM/Recording apparatus
                    [1979–85] E.P.O.R. B553; [1984] O.J. EPO 10

T114/82 Bayer/Pulp production
                    [1979–85] E.P.O.R. B558; [1983] O.J. EPO 323

T115/82 Bayer/Pulp production
                    [1979–85] E.P.O.R. B558; [1983] O.J. EPO 323

T116/82 Texas Alkyls/Dialkylmagnesium compositions
                              [1979–85] E.P.O.R. B562

T119/82 Exxon/Gelation   [1979–85] E.P.O.R. B566; [1984] O.J. EPO 217

T123/82 Bayer/Polyurethane plastics   [1979–85] E.P.O.R. B575

T124/82 Union Carbide/Threaded connections   [1979–85] E.P.O.R. B580

T127/82 Shell/Sinking tubular element [1979–85] E.P.O.R. B587

T128/82 Hoffman-La Roche/Pyrrolidine derivatives
[1979–85] E.P.O.R. B591; [1984] O.J. EPO 164

T130/82 Bell & Howell/Vehicle Guidance system
[1979–85] E.P.O.R. B598; [1984] O.J. EPO 172

T132/82 Siemens/Clarity of claim [1979–85] E.P.O.R. B602

T134/82 Exxon/Correction of errors [1979–85] E.P.O.R. B605

T135/82 UKAEA/Fluidic flow control [1979–85] E.P.O.R. B608

T140/82 Charles Stark Draper Laboratory/Inertial sensor
[1979–85] E.P.O.R. B614

T146/82 TAG/Suspension of proceedings
[1979–85] E.P.O.R. B618; [1985] O.J. EPO 267

T149/82 SNPE/Combustible sleeve [1979–85] E.P.O.R. B621

T150/82 IFF/Claim categories [1979–85] E.P.O.R. C629; [1984] O.J. EPO 309

T151/82 Saidco/Water resistant cable [1979–85] E.P.O.R. C635

T152/82 BASF/Debit order I [1979–85] E.P.O.R. C644; [1984] O.J. EPO 301

T154/82 Australian National University/Metal complexes
[1979–85] E.P.O.R. C648

T156/82 Ciba-Geigy/Diglycidyl ethers [1979–85] E.P.O.R. C657

T161/82 AMP/Electrical contact
[1979–85] E.P.O.R. C660; [1984] O.J. EPO 551

T162/82 Sigma/Classifying areas [1987] E.P.O.R. 375; [1987] O.J. EPO 533

T165/82 Philips/Optical scanning apparatus [1986] E.P.O.R. 133

T167/82 ERA/Static inverter [1986] E.P.O.R. 137

T168/82 Fisher & Paykel/Inwardly flanged curved members
[1979–85] E.P.O.R. C664

T172/82 Contraves/Particle analyser
[1979–85] E.P.O.R. C668; [1983] O.J. EPO 493

T181/82 Ciba-Geigy/Spiro compounds
[1979–85] E.P.O.R. C672; [1984] O.J. EPO 401

T183/82 Auld/Decorative emblems [1979–85] E.P.O.R. C684

T184/82 Mobil/Poly (p-methylstyrene) articles
[1979–85] E.P.O.R. C690; [1984] O.J. EPO 261

T185/82 Posso/Minicassette box
[1979–85] E.P.O.R. C696; [1984] O.J. EPO 174

T191/82 Fibre-Chem/Baled waste paper product
[1986] E.P.O.R. 88; [1985] O.J. EPO 189

T191/82 Fibre-Chem/Re-establishment of rights
[1979–85] E.P.O.R. C701; [1985] O.J. EPO 189

T192/82 Bayer/Moulding compositions
[1979–85] E.P.O.R. C705; [1984] O.J. EPO 415

T2/83 Rider/Simethicone tablet
[1979–85] E.P.O.R. C715; [1984] O.J. EPO 265

T4/83 Exxon/Purification of sulphonic acids
[1979–85] E.P.O.R. C721; [1983] O.J. EPO 498

T6/83 IBM/Data processor network   [1990] E.P.O.R. 91; [1990] O.J. EPO 05

T8/83 BASF/Paper dyeing   [1986] E.P.O.R. 186

T10/83 Bexford/Reflex copying   [1979–85] E.P.O.R. C726

T13/83 ICI Americas/Polyisocyanurates
[1979–85] E.P.O.R. C732; [1984] O.J. EPO 428

T14/83 Sumitomo/Vinyl chloride resins
[1979–85] E.P.O.R. C737; [1984] O.J. EPO 105

T16/83 Christian Franceries/Traffic regulation   [1988] E.P.O.R. 65

T17/83 Ford/Debit order II   [1979–85] E.P.O.R. C743; [1984] O.J. EPO 307

T20/83 Ciba-Geigy/Benzothiopyran derivatives
[1979–85] E.P.O.R. C746; [1983] O.J. EPO 419

T21/83 Soepenberg/Starch product   [1979–85] E.P.O.R. C751

T22/83 Fujitsu/Surface acoustic wave device   [1988] E.P.O.R. 234

T30/83 Nogier/Magnetic therapy   [1979–85] E.P.O.R. C755

T36/83 Roussel-Uclaf/Thenoyl peroxide[1987] E.P.O.R. 1; [1986] O.J. EPO 295

T40/83 Eastman Kodak/Thermal recording   [1986] E.P.O.R. 20

T48/83 IBM/Commutation device   [1986] E.P.O.R. 84

T49/83 Ciba-Geigy/Propagating material
[1979–85] E.P.O.R. C758; [1984] O.J. EPO 112

T61/83 Thomson-CSF/Tomodensitometry (1)   [1979–85] E.P.O.R. C763

T65/83 Beecham/3–thienylmalonic acid   [1979–85] E.P.O.R. C766

T69/83 Bayer/Thermoplastic moulding compositions
[1979–85] E.P.O.R. C771; [1984] O.J. EPO 357

T72/83 Dow Chemical/Re-establishment   [1979–85] E.P.O.R. C780

T76/83 Lintrend/Shrink treatment of linen   [1979–85] E.P.O.R. C782

T81/83 Techniplast Gazzada/Re-establishment   [1979–85] E.P.O.R. C791

T83/83 RS-Reklam/Edging   [1979–85] E.P.O.R. C793

T84/83 Luchtenberg/Rear-view mirror   [1979–85] E.P.O.R. C796

T90/83 Machinefabriek G.J. Nijhuis/Stunning apparatus
[1979–85] E.P.O.R. C802

T91/83 Hasmonay/Plug for affixing screws   [1979–85] E.P.O.R. C807

T93/83 Montedison/Ethylene polymers   [1987] E.P.O.R. 144

T94/83 Stimtech/Transcutaneous electrical nerve stimulation
[1979–85] E.P.O.R. C811

T95/83 Aisin/Late submission of amendment
[1979–85] E.P.O.R. C815; [1985] O.J. EPO 75

T107/83 Siemens/Data bank system [1986] E.P.O.R. 323

T109/83 British Gas/Coal gasification [1979–85] E.P.O.R. C823

T113/83 Allied/Beryllium-substituted iron-boron alloy
[1979–85] E.P.O.R. C829

T115/83 Wacker-Chemie/Crosslinkable organopolysiloxanes
[1979–85] E.P.O.R. C834

T127/83 Hamburger/Road vehicle [1979–85] E.P.O.R. C838

T128/83 Fujitsu/Semiconductor [1979–85] E.P.O.R. C841

T130/83 Redland/Artificial slate [1979–85] E.P.O.R. C846

T133/83 AMP/Electrical connector [1979–85] E.P.O.R. C850

T137/83 Dow/Contaminant removal [1987] E.P.O.R. 15

T139/83 USS Engineers/Coke oven patching [1979–85] E.P.O.R. C855

T144/83 Du Pont de Nemours (E.I.) & Co./Appetite suppressant
[1987] E.P.O.R. 6; [1986] O.J. EPO 301

T146/83 Unilever/Detergent composition [1986] E.P.O.R. 128

T160/83 Sitma/Packaging machine [1979–85] E.P.O.R. C860

T164/83 Eisai/Antihistamines [1987] E.P.O.R. 205; [1987] O.J. EPO 149

T169/83 Vereinigte Metallwerke/Wall element
[1979–85] E.P.O.R. C865; [1985] O.J. EPO 193

T170/83 Mobil Oil/Debit order III
[1979–85] E.P.O.R. C877; [1984] O.J. EPO 605

T173/83 Telecommunications/Antioxidant
[1988] E.P.O.R. 133; [1987] O.J. EPO 465

T177/83 Bayer/Fibre composites [1979–85] E.P.O.R. C884

T186/83 Standard Oil/Olefinic nitriles [1986] E.P.O.R. 11

T188/83 Fernholz/Vinyl acetate
[1979–85] E.P.O.R. C891; [1984] O.J. EPO 555

T189/83 Mauri/Plastics chain [1979–85] E.P.O.R. C897

T201/83 Shell/Lead alloys [1979–85] E.P.O.R. C905; [1904] O.J. EPO 481

T202/83 Solco/Skin and mucous membrane preparation
[1979–85] E.P.O.R. C912

T204/83 Charbonnages/Venturi [1986] E.P.O.R. 1; [1985] O.J. EPO 310

T205/83 Hoechst/Vinyl ester-crotonic acid copolymers
[1986] E.P.O.R. 57; [1985] O.J. EPO 363

T206/83 ICI plc/Pyridine herbicides [1986] E.P.O.R. 232; [1987] O.J. EPO 58

T206/83 ICI plc/Pyridine herbicides (Editor's Note)
[1987] E.P.O.R. 112; [1987] O.J. EPO 05

T208/83 Thomson-CSF/Tomodensitometry (2) [1979–85] E.P.O.R. C917

T214/83 Stamicarbon/Giro payment
[1979–85] E.P.O.R. C920; [1985] O.J. EPO 10

T219/83 BASF/Zeolites   [1986] E.P.O.R. 247; [1986] O.J. EPO 211

T220/83 Hüls/Grounds for appeal   [1987] E.P.O.R. 49; [1986] O.J. EPO 249

T6/84 Mobil/Amendment of claims
                                       [1979–85] E.P.O.R. C924; [1985] O.J. EPO 238

T13/84 Sperry/Reformulation of the problem
                                       [1986] E.P.O.R. 289; [1986] O.J. EPO 253

T17/84 ICI plc/Manufacture of fusecord   [1986] E.P.O.R. 274

T20/84 Warmestelle Steine Und Erden/Annular shaft kiln   [1986] E.P.O.R. 197

T31/84 Miles/Test device   [1987] E.P.O.R. 10; [1986] O.J. EPO 369

T32/84 Commissariat À L'Énergie Atomique/Reference voltage generator
                                       [1986] E.P.O.R. 94; [1986] O.J. EPO 09

T38/84 Stamicarbon/Oxidation of toluene
                                       [1979–85] E.P.O.R. C931; [1984] O.J. EPO 368

T42/84 Exxon/Alumina spinel   [1988] E.P.O.R. 387; [1988] O.J. EPO 251

T45/84 Philips/Diagnostic method   [1979–85] E.P.O.R. C937

T47/84 Alcan/Exhaust silencer   [1979–85] E.P.O.R. C940

T51/84 Stockburger/Coded distinctive mark
                                       [1986] E.P.O.R. 229; [1986] O.J. EPO 226

T55/84 Schupbach/Hot-sealing layer combination   [1987] E.P.O.R. 53

T56/84 Regent Lock/Locking handle device   [1986] E.P.O.R. 24

T57/84 Bayer/Tolylfluanid   [1987] E.P.O.R. 131; [1987] O.J. EPO 53

T73/84 SMS/Revocation at the instigation of the patent proprietor
                                       [1979–85] E.P.O.R. C944; [1985] O.J. EPO 241

T80/84 MITA/Representation (1)
                                       [1979–85] E.P.O.R. C946; [1985] O.J. EPO 269

T80/84 MITA/Representation (2)   [1986] E.P.O.R. 345; [1985] O.J. EPO 269

T81/84 Rorer/Dysmenorrhea   [1988] E.P.O.R. 297; [1988] O.J. EPO 207

T89/84 Torrington/Reimbursement of appeal fees
                                       [1979–85] E.P.O.R. C949; [1984] O.J. EPO 562

T90/84 American Cyanamid/Acrylonitrile polymer fibre
                                       [1979–85] E.P.O.R. C952

T94/84 Duco/Paint layers   [1987] E.P.O.R. 37; [1986] O.J. EPO 337

T98/84 Unilever/Deodorant products   [1986] E.P.O.R. 30

T106/84 Michaelsen/Packing machine
                                       [1979–85] E.P.O.R. C959; [1985] O.J. EPO 132

T116/84 Robbins/Rotary cutterhead   [1979–85] E.P.O.R. C966

T122/84 Hoechst/Metallic paint coating
                                       [1987] E.P.O.R. 218; [1987] O.J. EPO 177

T124/84 Unie Van Kunstmestfabrieken/Urea synthesis   [1986] E.P.O.R. 297

T126/84 La Télémécanique Électrique/Power measuring device
                                       [1986] E.P.O.R. 342

T130/84 Mobil Oil/Opposition against own patent
[1979–85] E.P.O.R. C971; [1984] O.J. EPO 613

T132/84 Hüls/2,2,6,6-tetramethylpiperidone-4   [1986] E.P.O.R. 303

T136/84 Mobil/Reformate upgrading   [1979–85] E.P.O.R. C973

T142/84 Britax/Inventive step   [1987] E.P.O.R. 148; [1987] O.J. EPO 112

T144/84 Torgersen/Door structure   [1979–85] E.P.O.R. C976

T151/84 Thomson-CSF/Collector for high-frequency tube   [1988] E.P.O.R. 29

T156/84 Air Products/Pressure swing adsorption
[1989] E.P.O.R. 47; [1988] O.J. EPO 372

T163/84 Bayer/Acetophenone derivatives
[1987] E.P.O.R. 284; [1987] O.J. EPO 301

T166/84 Takeda/Postponement of examination
[1979–85] E.P.O.R. C981; [1984] O.J. EPO 489

T167/84 Nissan/Fuel injector valve   [1987] E.P.O.R. 344; [1987] O.J. EPO 369

T169/84 Mitsuboshi/Endless power transmission belt
[1987] E.P.O.R. 120; [1995] O.J. EPO 193

T170/84 Bossert KG/Two-part claim   [1987] E.P.O.R. 82; [1986] O.J. EPO 400

T171/84 Air Products/Redox catalyst   [1986] E.P.O.R. 210; [1986] O.J. EPO 95

T173/84 Herzberger Papierfabrik/Packaging magazine   [1986] E.P.O.R. 181

T175/84 Kabelmetal/Combination claim
[1989] E.P.O.R. 181; [1989] O.J. EPO 71

T176/84 Möbius/Pencil sharpener   [1986] E.P.O.R. 117; [1986] O.J. EPO 50

T178/84 IBM/Lack of unity   [1989] E.P.O.R. 364; [1989] O.J. EPO 157

T183/84 Bayer/Titanyl sulphate   [1986] E.P.O.R. 174

T184/84 NGK Insulators/Ferrite crystal   [1986] E.P.O.R. 169

T185/84 BASF/Paint line supply system
[1987] E.P.O.R. 34; [1906] O.J. EPO 373

T186/84 BASF/Revocation at proprietor's request
[1986] E.P.O.R. 165; [1986] O.J. EPO 79

T191/84 Siemens/Insulin infusion device   [1986] E.P.O.R. 318

T192/84 Daikin Kogyo/Interruption in delivery of mail
[1979–85] E.P.O.R. C984; [1985] O.J. EPO 39

T194/84 General Motors/Zinc electrodes (cellulose fibres)
[1989] E.P.O.R. 351; [1990] O.J. EPO 59

T195/84 Boeing/General technical knowledge
[1986] E.P.O.R. 190; [1986] O.J. EPO 121

T198/84 Hoechst/Thiochloroformates
[1979–85] E.P.O.R. C987; [1985] O.J. EPO 209

T207/84 Enviro-Spray/Self-pressuring dispenser container
[1979–85] E.P.O.R. C993

T208/84 Vicom/Computer-related invention
[1987] E.P.O.R. 74; [1987] O.J. EPO 14

T215/84 Black Clawson/Pulp delignification   [1986] E.P.O.R. 6

T223/84 Albright & Wilson/Extraction of uranium   [1986] E.P.O.R. 66

T225/84 Boeing/Spoiler device   [1986] E.P.O.R. 263

T226/84 Unilever/Detergent speckles   [1986] E.P.O.R. 123

T229/84 ICI plc/Polyester polyols   [1988] E.P.O.R. 217

T230/84 Kansai Paint/Disapproval of specification by proprietor
[1986] E.P.O.R. 44

T237/84 Philips/Reference signs   [1987] E.P.O.R. 310; [1987] O.J. EPO 309

T249/84 Boeing/Extendible airfoil track assembly   [1979–85] E.P.O.R. C997

T258/84 État Français/Portable hyperbar box structure
[1987] E.P.O.R. 154; [1987] O.J. EPO 119

T262/84 Nitto Boseki/Traversing motion   [1979–85] E.P.O.R. C1001

T265/84 Allied/Cobalt foils   [1987] E.P.O.R. 193

T270/84 ICI plc/Fusecord   [1987] E.P.O.R. 357

T271/84 Air Products/Removal of hydrogen sulphide and carbonyl sulphide
[1987] E.P.O.R. 23; [1987] O.J. EPO 405

T273/84 Rhône-Poulenc/Silico-aluminate
[1987] E.P.O.R. 44; [1986] O.J. EPO 346

T283/84 Röhm/Ultra-violet emitters   [1988] E.P.O.R. 16

T286/84 Appleton Papers/Pressure-sensitive recording material
[1987] E.P.O.R. 212

T287/84 Brunswick/Re-establishment of rights refused
[1986] E.P.O.R. 46; [1985] O.J. EPO 333

T288/84 Stamicarbon/Activated support
[1986] E.P.O.R. 217; [1986] O.J. EPO 128

T289/84 Wellcome/3-Amino-pyrazoline derivatives   [1987] E.P.O.R. 58

T17/85 Plüss-Staufer/Filler   [1987] E.P.O.R. 66; [1986] O.J. EPO 406

T22/85 IBM/Document abstracting and retrieving
[1990] E.P.O.R. 98; [1990] O.J. EPO 12

T24/85 Discovision/Lens assembly   [1988] E.P.O.R. 247

T25/85 Deutsche Gelatine-Fabriken, Stoess & Co./Opponent—
identifiability   [1986] E.P.O.R. 158; [1986] O.J. EPO 81

T26/85 Toshiba/Thickness of magnetic layers
[1990] E.P.O.R. 267; [1990] O.J. EPO 22

T32/85 Gist-Brocades/Biomass preparation   [1986] E.P.O.R. 267

T43/85 Mobil Oil/Thermoplastic film laminate   [1987] E.P.O.R. 272

T44/85 Shell/Water-thinnable binder   [1986] E.P.O.R. 258

T48/85 NRDC/Eimeria necatrix   [1987] E.P.O.R. 138

T49/85 American Cyanamid/Melt spinning   [1989] E.P.O.R. 234

T52/85 IBM/Semantically-related expressions   [1989] E.P.O.R. 454

T61/85 ICI plc/Polyester crystallisation   [1988] E.P.O.R. 20

T64/85 Tokyo Shibaura/Ultrasonic diagnostic apparatus   [1988] E.P.O.R. 225

T66/85 AMP/Connector   [1989] E.P.O.R. 283; [1989] O.J. EPO 167

T68/85 Ciba-Geigy/Synergistic herbicides
                                  [1987] E.P.O.R. 302; [1987] O.J. EPO 228

T71/85 International Standard Electric/Water-soluble glass   [1987] E.P.O.R. 113

T89/85 SAB/Vehicle brakes   [1988] E.P.O.R. 105

T92/85 Wavin/Belated division and amendment
                                  [1986] E.P.O.R. 281; [1986] O.J. EPO 352

T99/85 Boehringer/Diagnostic agent   [1987] E.P.O.R. 337; [1987] O.J. EPO 413

T105/85 ICI plc/Re-establishment of rights   [1987] E.P.O.R. 186

T110/85 Voest-Alpine/Re-establishment of rights
                                  [1987] E.P.O.R. 256; [1987] O.J. EPO 157

T115/85 IBM/Computer-related invention
                                  [1990] E.P.O.R. 107; [1990] O.J. EPO 30

T116/85 Wellcome/Pigs I   [1988] E.P.O.R. 1; [1989] O.J. EPO 13

T123/85 BASF/Incrustation inhibitors
                                  [1989] E.P.O.R. 476; [1989] O.J. EPO 336

T124/85 Lasten Group/Papermaking fabric   [1995] E.P.O.R. 464

T127/85 Ireco/Blasting compositions
                                  [1989] E.P.O.R. 358; [1989] O.J. EPO 271

T133/85 Xerox/Amendments   [1989] E.P.O.R. 116; [1988] O.J. EPO 441

T139/85 Efamol/Pharmaceutical compositions   [1987] E.P.O.R. 229

T147/85 Philips/Interchangeable disks   [1988] E.P.O.R. 111

T149/85 Bredero/Inadmissible language of opposition
                                  [1986] E.P.O.R. 223; [1986] O.J. EPO 103

T152/85 Sandvik/Unpaid opposition fee
                                  [1987] E.P.O.R. 258; [1987] O.J. EPO 191

T153/85 Amoco Corporation/Alternative claims
                                  [1988] E.P.O.R. 116; [1988] O.J. EPO 01

T155/85 Phillips Petroleum/Passivation of catalyst
                                  [1988] E.P.O.R. 164; [1988] O.J. EPO 87

T163/85 BBC/Colour television signal
                                  [1990] E.P.O.R. 599; [1990] O.J. EPO 379

T165/85 Boehringer Mannheim/Detection of redox reactions
                                                              [1987] E.P.O.R. 125

T171/85 Gillette/Inconsistent documents for grant
                                  [1986] E.P.O.R. 107; [1987] O.J. EPO 160

T187/85 Welgro/Bulk carrier [1986] E.P.O.R. 79

T209/85 Mitsui/Titanium catalyst [1987] E.P.O.R. 235

T213/85 Georg Fischer/Grounds of appeal
[1988] E.P.O.R. 45; [1987] O.J. EPO 482

T219/85 Hakoune/Inadequate description
[1987] E.P.O.R. 30; [1986] O.J. EPO 376

T222/85 PPG/Ungelled polyesters [1987] E.P.O.R. 99; [1988] O.J. EPO 128

T226/85 Unilever/Stable bleaches [1989] E.P.O.R. 18; [1988] O.J. EPO 336

T229/85 Schmid/Etching process [1987] E.P.O.R. 279; [1987] O.J. EPO 237

T231/85 BASF/Triazole derivatives [1989] E.P.O.R. 293; [1989] O.J. EPO 74

T232/85 General Electric/Retroactive change in language of proceedings
[1986] E.P.O.R. 107; [1986] O.J. EPO 19

T242/85 Chemie Linz/Reinforced channels [1988] E.P.O.R. 77

T244/85 VAW/Aluminium trihydroxide
[1988] E.P.O.R. 319; [1988] O.J. EPO 216

T248/85 BICC/Radiation processing
[1986] E.P.O.R. 311; [1986] O.J. EPO 261

T253/85 AKZO/Dry jet-wet spinning [1987] E.P.O.R. 198

T255/85 Beecham/Antacid composition [1987] E.P.O.R. 351

T256/85 Bulten-Kanthal/Electrical heating element [1986] E.P.O.R. 240

T259/85 Wiederhold/Two-component polyurethane lacquer
[1988] E.P.O.R. 209

T260/85 AMP/Coaxial connector [1989] E.P.O.R. 403; [1989] O.J. EPO 105

T268/85 Stamicarbon/Polymer filaments [1989] E.P.O.R. 229

T271/85 Hoechst/Admissibility of appeal by opponent
[1989] E.P.O.R. 62; [1988] O.J. EPO 341

T291/85 Bayer/Catalyst [1988] E.P.O.R. 371; [1988] O.J. EPO 302

T292/85 Genentech I/Polypeptide expression
[1989] E.P.O.R. 1; [1989] O.J. EPO 275

T301/85 ICI plc/Removal of hydrogen sulphide [1986] E.P.O.R. 340

T5/86 Newman/Perpetual motion [1988] E.P.O.R. 301

T7/86 Draco/Xanthines [1989] E.P.O.R. 65; [1988] O.J. EPO 381

T9/86 Bayer/Polyamide-6 [1988] E.P.O.R. 83; [1988] O.J. EPO 12

T15/86 Thomson-CSF/Transistor structure [1987] E.P.O.R. 291

T17/86 Satam Brandt/Refrigeration plant
[1989] E.P.O.R. 347; [1989] O.J. EPO 297

T19/86 Duphar/Pigs II [1988] E.P.O.R. 10; [1989] O.J. EPO 25

T23/86 Naimer/Computer-controlled switch
[1987] E.P.O.R. 383; [1987] O.J. EPO 316

T26/86 Koch & Sterzel/X-ray apparatus
[1988] E.P.O.R. 72; [1988] O.J. EPO 19

T27/86 Dynapac/Poker vibrator (1)   [1987] E.P.O.R. 179

T27/86 Dynapac/Poker vibrator (2)   [1989] E.P.O.R. 100

T38/86 IBM/Text clarity processing   [1990] E.P.O.R. 606; [1990] O.J. EPO 384

T48/86 Toray/Ultrasonic transducer   [1988] E.P.O.R. 143

T55/86 Bendix/Braking apparatus   [1988] E.P.O.R. 285

T63/86 Kollmorgen/Consent for amendments
[1988] E.P.O.R. 316; [1988] O.J. EPO 224

T65/86 IBM/Text processing   [1990] E.P.O.R. 181

T103/86 Du Pont de Nemours (E.I.) & Co./Phenylenediamine
[1987] E.P.O.R. 265

T106/86 Val Lessina/Crepe fabric   [1988] E.P.O.R. 401

T108/86 Bendix/Disc brake   [1989] E.P.O.R. 494

T114/86 Eriksson/Foam plastic filter   [1988] E.P.O.R. 25; [1987] O.J. EPO 485

T117/86 Filmtec/Costs   [1989] E.P.O.R. 504; [1989] O.J. EPO 401

T119/86 Shell/Removal of acid gases   [1988] E.P.O.R. 290

T128/86 INRA/A-Lactalbumin Product   [1989] E.P.O.R. 461

T137/86 Thorn EMI/Discharge lamps   [1988] E.P.O.R. 187

T137/86 Thorn EMI/Re-establishment of rights   [1987] E.P.O.R. 183

T161/86 Eli Lilly/Antibiotic   [1987] E.P.O.R. 366

T162/86 Hoechst/Plasmid pSG2   [1989] E.P.O.R. 107; [1988] O.J. EPO 452

T166/86 Henkel/Separate set of claims
[1987] E.P.O.R. 371; [1987] O.J. EPO 372

T174/86 Black & Decker/Brush assembly   [1989] E.P.O.R. 277

T182/86 Avontuur/Piston compressor   [1988] E.P.O.R. 183

T194/86 Albany/Shower fittings   [1994] E.P.O.R. 335

T197/86 Kodak/Photographic couplers
[1989] E.P.O.R. 395; [1989] O.J. EPO 371

T219/86 Zokor/Naming of opponent
[1988] E.P.O.R. 407; [1998] O.J. EPO 254

T232/86 Esdan/Electric fusion pipe fittings   [1988] E.P.O.R. 89

T234/86 Somartec/Therapy with interference currents
[1989] E.P.O.R. 303; [1989] O.J. EPO 79

T237/86 SMS/Abandoned patent   [1988] E.P.O.R. 397; [1988] O.J. EPO 261

T246/86 Bull/Identification system   [1989] E.P.O.R. 344; [1989] O.J. EPO 199

T254/86 Sumitomo/Yellow dye   [1989] E.P.O.R. 257; [1989] O.J. EPO 115

T263/86 Zeiss/Spectacle lens   [1988] E.P.O.R. 150

T278/86 Keown/Spring element   [1987] E.P.O.R. 299

T281/86 Unilever/Preprothaumatin   [1989] E.P.O.R. 313; [1989] O.J. EPO 202

T287/86 Tobias/Photoelectric densitometer   [1989] E.P.O.R. 214

T290/86 ICI plc/Cleaning plaque   [1991] E.P.O.R. 157; [1992] O.J. EPO 414

T299/86 Secher/Oral proceedings   [1988] E.P.O.R. 204; [1988] O.J. EPO 88

T300/86 RCA/TV receiver   [1994] E.P.O.R. 339

T303/86 CPC/Flavour concentrates   [1989] E.P.O.R. 95

T316/86 Niled/Electrical connecting apparatus   [1990] E.P.O.R. 217

T317/86 Smidth/Title of invention   [1989] E.P.O.R. 415; [1989] O.J. EPO 378

T321/86 Philips/Display tube   [1989] E.P.O.R. 199

T336/86 FMC/Costs   [1989] E.P.O.R. 291

T348/86 Medtronic/Cardiac defibrillator   [1988] E.P.O.R. 159

T349/86 Delta/Transfer of opposition   [1989] E.P.O.R. 59; [1988] O.J. EPO 345

T355/86 Sparevirke/Notice of opposition   [1987] E.P.O.R. 331

T372/86 ICI plc/Diphenyl ethers   [1988] E.P.O.R. 93

T378/86 Moog/Change of category   [1989] E.P.O.R. 85; [1988] O.J. EPO 386

T385/86 Bruker/Non-invasive measurement
                                    [1988] E.P.O.R. 357; [1988] O.J. EPO 380

T389/86 Behr/Time limit for appeal   [1988] E.P.O.R. 381; [1988] O.J. EPO 87

T390/86 Shell/Changed composition of division
                                    [1989] E.P.O.R. 162; [1989] O.J. EPO 30

T392/86 Mobil/Catalyst   [1988] E.P.O.R. 178

T405/86 Mobil Oil/Film   [1992] E.P.O.R. 178

T406/86 Wacker/Trichloroethylene   [1989] E.P.O.R. 338; [1989] O.J. EPO 302

T407/86 Fujitsu/Memory circuit   [1988] E.P.O.R. 254

T416/86 Boehringer/Reflection photometer
                                    [1989] E.P.O.R. 327; [1989] O.J. EPO 309

T424/86 Amoco/Polyarylates   [1992] E.P.O.R. 509

T433/86 ICI plc/Modified diisocyanates   [1988] E.P.O.R. 97

T2/87 Bendix/Telegraphic money order
                                    [1988] E.P.O.R. 415; [1988] O.J. EPO 264

T9/87 ICI plc/Zeolites   [1990] E.P.O.R. 46; [1989] O.J. EPO 438

T16/87 Procatalyse/Catalyst   [1992] E.P.O.R. 305; [1992] O.J. EPO 212

T19/87 Fujitsu/Oral proceedings   [1988] E.P.O.R. 393; [1988] O.J. EPO 268

T25/87 Union Carbide/Polyacrylate molding composition   [1989] E.P.O.R. 381

T28/87 Kerber/Wire link bands   [1989] E.P.O.R. 377; [1989] O.J. EPO 383

T35/87 BASF/Hydroxy-pyrazoles   [1988] E.P.O.R. 260; [1988] O.J. EPO 134

T51/87 Merck/Starting compounds   [1991] E.P.O.R. 329; [1991] O.J. EPO 177

T56/87 Scanditronix/Radiation beam collimation
[1990] E.P.O.R. 352; [1990] O.J. EPO 188

T58/87 Salminen/Pigs III   [1989] E.P.O.R. 125; [1988] O.J. EPO 347

T59/87 Mobil/Friction reducing additive (1)
[1989] E.P.O.R. 80; [1991] O.J. EPO 561

T59/87 Mobil/Friction reducing additive (3)
[1990] E.P.O.R. 514; [1991] O.J. EPO 561

T67/87 Widen/Three-stroke engine   [1991] E.P.O.R. 498

T75/87 Inland Steel/Tellurium-containing steel   [1994] E.P.O.R. 475

T77/87 ICI plc/Latex composition   [1989] E.P.O.R. 246; [1990] O.J. EPO 280

T81/87 Collaborative/Preprorennin   [1990] E.P.O.R. 361; [1990] O.J. EPO 250

T83/87 Siemens/Diagnostic method   [1988] E.P.O.R. 365

T85/87 Csiro/Arthropodicidal compounds   [1989] E.P.O.R. 24

T94/87 Becton/Radiation stabilisation   [1989] E.P.O.R. 264

T95/87 Dyson Refractories/Catalyst production   [1988] E.P.O.R. 171

T99/87 Bendix/Braking system   [1989] E.P.O.R. 499

T101/87 Lock/Windscreen removal device   [1990] E.P.O.R. 476

T105/87 Inland Steel/Bismuth-containing steel   [1991] E.P.O.R. 206

T117/87 Medtronic/German patent office
[1989] E.P.O.R. 287; [1989] O.J. EPO 127

T118/87 CPC/Amylolytic enzymes   [1990] E.P.O.R. 298; [1991] O.J. EPO 474

T124/87 Du Pont de Nemours (E.I.) & Co./Copolymers
[1989] E.P.O.R. 33; [1989] O.J. EPO 491

T128/87 Kramer & Grebe/Lost cheque
[1989] E.P.O.R. 485; [1989] O.J. EPO 406

T139/87 Bendix/Governor valve   [1990] E.P.O.R. 234; [1990] O.J. EPO 69

T155/87 DRG/Printing sleeve   [1990] E.P.O.R. 455

T157/87 Kubat/Cellulose composites   [1989] E.P.O.R. 221

T170/87 Sulzer/Hot gas cooler   [1990] E.P.O.R. 14; [1989] O.J. EPO 441

T179/87 USN & EF/Cold roll manufacturing   [1990] E.P.O.R. 585

T193/87 Alfa-Laval/Belated translation
[1992] E.P.O.R. 63; [1993] O.J. EPO 207

T212/87 LMG/Sterilising pouch   [1991] E.P.O.R. 144

T228/87 Bridgestone/Rubber composition   [1990] E.P.O.R. 483

T239/87 Nabisco/Micro-organisms   [1988] E.P.O.R. 311

T243/87 Lesaffre/Composition of opposition division   [1990] E.P.O.R. 136

T245/87 Siemens/Flow measurement
[1989] E.P.O.R. 241; [1989] O.J. EPO 171

T263/87 Allied/Garnet laser [1988] E.P.O.R. 243

T274/87 Phillips/Cracking catalyst [1989] E.P.O.R. 207

T292/87 Control Systems/Ticket-issuing machines [1989] E.P.O.R. 333

T295/87 ICI plc/Polyetherketones [1991] E.P.O.R. 56; [1990] O.J. EPO 470

T296/87 Hoechst/Enantiomers [1990] E.P.O.R. 337; [1990] O.J. EPO 195

T301/87 Biogen/Recombinant DNA
[1990] E.P.O.R. 190; [1990] O.J. EPO 335

T305/87 Grehal/Shear [1991] E.P.O.R. 389; [1991] O.J. EPO 429

T308/87 Du Pont de Nemours (E.I.) & Co./Yarn finish applicator
[1991] E.P.O.R. 464

T320/87 Lubrizol/Hybrid plants [1990] E.P.O.R. 173; [1990] O.J. EPO 71

T323/87 Rhône-Poulenc/Official language
[1989] E.P.O.R. 412; [1989] O.J. EPO 343

T326/87 Du Pont de Nemours (E.I.) & Co./Polyamide composition
[1991] E.P.O.R. 47; [1992] O.J. EPO 522

T328/87 Thomson-Brandt/Admissibility
[1993] E.P.O.R. 191; [1992] O.J. EPO 701

T331/87 Houdaille/Removal of feature
[1991] E.P.O.R. 194; [1991] O.J. EPO 22

T332/87 Scott Bader/Ceramic tile adhesives [1991] E.P.O.R. 575

T366/87 Sternheimer/Harmonic vibrations [1989] E.P.O.R. 131

T381/87 Research Corporation/Publication
[1989] E.P.O.R. 138; [1990] O.J. EPO 213

T407/87 Toshiba/Semiconductor device [1989] E.P.O.R. 470

T416/87 JSR/Block copolymer [1991] E.P.O.R. 25; [1990] O.J. EPO 415

T425/87 SNIA/Deployable antenna reflector [1990] E.P.O.R. 623

T434/87 Fabre/Toothbrush fibres [1990] E.P.O.R. 141

T438/87 Cebal/Plastic screw cap [1989] E.P.O.R. 489

T450/87 Battelle/Fluidised bed combustion sanitation [1990] E.P.O.R. 448

T3/88 Hoechst/Melting point [1988] E.P.O.R. 377

T7/88 Du Pont de Nemours (E.I.) & Co./Flange formation process
[1990] E.P.O.R. 149

T18/88 Dow/Pyrimidines [1992] E.P.O.R. 184; [1992] O.J. EPO 107

T20/88 Union Carbide/Polymer-polyol compositions [1990] E.P.O.R. 212

T22/88 Secretary of State for Defence (United Kingdom)/Grounds for appeal
[1993] E.P.O.R. 353; [1993] O.J. EPO 143

T26/88 AKZO/Automatic revocation [1990] E.P.O.R. 21; [1991] O.J. EPO 30

T39/88 CPC/Micro-organisms [1990] E.P.O.R. 41; [1989] O.J. EPO 499

T47/88 Mannesmann/Payment of fees [1990] E.P.O.R. 167; [1990] O.J. EPO 35

T67/88 Kanegafuchi/Coating compositions [1991] E.P.O.R. 88

T73/88 Howard/Snackfood [1990] E.P.O.R. 112; [1992] O.J. EPO 557

T79/88 JSR/Impact resistant resin composition [1992] E.P.O.R. 387

T80/88 Ex-Cell-O/Laminated paperboard container [1991] E.P.O.R. 596

T87/88 Digmesa/Further search fee [1994] E.P.O.R. 57

T99/88 Seiko & Toshiba/Contents of decision [1990] E.P.O.R. 568

T100/88 Procter & Gamble/STW detergents [1991] E.P.O.R. 529

T101/88 Sinclair/Unity [1990] E.P.O.R. 489

T104/88 Procter & Gamble/STW-laundry detergents [1991] E.P.O.R. 586

T119/88 Fuji/Coloured disk jacket [1990] E.P.O.R. 615; [1990] O.J. EPO 395

T124/88 Peugeot/Electric motor [1991] E.P.O.R. 255

T129/88 AKZO/Fibre [1994] E.P.O.R. 176; [1993] O.J. EPO 598

T145/88 Nicolon/Statement of grounds
[1991] E.P.O.R. 357; [1991] O.J. EPO 251

T158/88 Siemens/Character form [1992] E.P.O.R. 69; [1991] O.J. EPO 566

T165/88 IBM/Insufficient disclosure [1989] E.P.O.R. 157

T169/88 Teijin/Cotton yarn-like composite yarn [1991] E.P.O.R. 281

T182/88 University of California/Dimeric oligopeptides
[1989] E.P.O.R. 147; [1990] O.J. EPO 287

T185/88 Henkel/Surface active agents
[1990] E.P.O.R. 649; [1990] O.J. EPO 451

T189/88 Asahi/Polyethylene terephthalate fibres [1990] E.P.O.R. 543

T197/88 ICI plc/Continuation of opposition proceedings
[1990] E.P.O.R. 243; [1989] O.J. EPO 412

T198/88 Schwiete/Concrete restoration
[1991] E.P.O.R. 455; [1991] O.J. EPO 254

T208/88 Bayer/Plant growth regulation
[1989] E.P.O.R. 323; [1992] O.J. EPO 22

T208/88 Bayer/Growth regulation [1992] E.P.O.R. 74; [1992] O.J. EPO 22

T212/88 British Petroleum/Theta-1 [1990] E.P.O.R. 518; [1992] O.J. EPO 28

T227/88 Unilever/Detergent compositions
[1990] E.P.O.R. 424; [1990] O.J. EPO 292

T229/88 Detras/Target apparatus [1991] E.P.O.R. 407

T236/88 Eastman Kodak/Preparation of acetic anhydride [1990] E.P.O.R. 227

T238/88 Kodak/Crown ether [1993] E.P.O.R. 100; [1992] O.J. EPO 709

T245/88 Union Carbide/Atmospheric vaporizer [1991] E.P.O.R. 373

T248/88 SGS/Unacceptable generalisation [1990] E.P.O.R. 274

T251/88 Irsid/Opposition division [1990] E.P.O.R. 246

T255/88 Wagner/Fixing device   [1992] E.P.O.R. 87

T265/88 Lundia/Diffusion device   [1990] E.P.O.R. 399

T267/88 Fuji/Photographic material   [1991] E.P.O.R. 168

T283/88 Abbot/Oral proceedings   [1989] E.P.O.R. 225

T293/88 Dan-Pal/Light transmitting wall panels
                        [1992] E.P.O.R. 240; [1992] O.J. EPO 220

T295/88 Procter/Flavour   [1991] E.P.O.R. 458

T310/88 Toray Industries/Photosensitive resin   [1991] E.P.O.R. 10

T320/88 Exxon/Arranging oral proceedings
                        [1989] E.P.O.R. 372; [1990] O.J. EPO 359

T330/88 Dymo/Magazine file assembly   [1990] E.P.O.R. 467

T335/88 Nissei/Injection moulding machine   [1990] E.P.O.R. 552

T337/88 Montedison/Polymer   [1990] E.P.O.R. 533

T340/88 Goodrich/Vinyl monomers   [1990] E.P.O.R. 377

T344/88 Bayer/Thermoplastic moulding compound   [1994] E.P.O.R. 508

T361/88 Du Pont de Nemours (E.I.) & Co./Hollow filaments
                                                                [1991] E.P.O.R. 1

T371/88 Fuji/Transmission apparatus [1992] E.P.O.R. 341; [1992] O.J. EPO 157

T378/88 Philips/Video disc apparatus   [1990] E.P.O.R. 571

T379/88 Union Carbide/Separation of air   [1991] E.P.O.R. 274

T390/88 Konishiroku/Photographic film   [1990] E.P.O.R. 417

T401/88 Bosch/Test piece   [1990] E.P.O.R. 640; [1990] O.J. EPO 297

T426/88 Lucas/Combustion engine   [1992] E.P.O.R. 458; [1992] O.J. EPO 427

T428/88 Electrolux/Automatic dispenser   [1990] E.P.O.R. 385

T432/88 OKI/Grounds for appeal   [1990] E.P.O.R. 38

T442/88 ACO/Drainage channel   [1992] E.P.O.R. 515

T444/88 Japan Styrene Paper/Foam particles   [1991] E.P.O.R. 94

T459/88 MAN/Admissible   [1991] E.P.O.R. 72; [1990] O.J. EPO 425

T461/88 Heidelberger Drückmaschinen/Microchip
                        [1993] E.P.O.R. 529; [1993] O.J. EPO 295

T472/88 General Electric Company/Thermoplastic resin   [1991] E.P.O.R. 486

T493/88 CEA-Framatome/Spacer grid
                        [1991] E.P.O.R. 393; [1991] O.J. EPO 380

T514/88 ALZA/Infusor   [1990] E.P.O.R. 157; [1992] O.J. EPO 570

T522/88 Shell/Gasification of solid fuel   [1990] E.P.O.R. 237

T527/88 Wavin/Interconnected bags   [1991] E.P.O.R. 184

T531/88 Weitman/Heat recovery   [1991] E.P.O.R. 433

T534/88 IBM/Ion etching [1991] E.P.O.R. 18

T536/88 Badische Karton-und Pappenfabrik/Dust-tight folding carton
[1993] E.P.O.R. 202; [1992] O.J. EPO 638

T544/88 UHDE/Reduction in NOx content
[1990] E.P.O.R. 652; [1990] O.J. EPO 429

T547/88 Mobil/Metal-coated film [1994] E.P.O.R. 349

T550/88 Mobil/Admissibility [1990] E.P.O.R. 391; [1992] O.J. EPO 117

T559/88 CPC/Cheese spreads [1990] E.P.O.R. 430

T577/88 Torras/Tractor [1991] E.P.O.R. 149

T579/88 Esswein/Automatic programmer [1991] E.P.O.R. 120

T584/88 Reichert/Anti-snoring means [1989] E.P.O.R. 449

T596/88 Coats/Synthetic yarn [1994] E.P.O.R. 37

T627/88 Asahi Kasei KKK/Resin composition [1991] E.P.O.R. 81

T632/88 Raccah/Hairdrying apparatus [1990] E.P.O.R. 130

T635/88 De Erven G. De Boer BV/Opponent—identifiability
[1994] E.P.O.R. 358; [1993] O.J. EPO 698

T648/88 BASF/R,R,R-alpha-tocopherol
[1991] E.P.O.R. 305; [1991] O.J. EPO 292

T2/89 BASF/Grounds for opposition [1991] E.P.O.R. 220; [1991] O.J. EPO 51

T5/89 von Blücher/Air-cleaning apparatus
[1992] E.P.O.R. 546; [1992] O.J. EPO 348

T11/89 Godecke/Naphthyridinone derivatives [1991] E.P.O.R. 336

T14/89 Uhde/Re-establishment [1990] E.P.O.R. 656; [1990] O.J. EPO 432

T38/89 Union Carbide/Ethylene copolymers [1991] E.P.O.R. 129

T55/89 Sankyo/Diamond saw [1991] E.P.O.R. 416

T60/89 Harvard/Fusion proteins [1992] E.P.O.R. 320; [1990] O.J. EPO 268

T61/89 Parsons Control/Scraper chain conveyor [1992] E.P.O.R. 205

T69/89 Surgikos/Disinfection [1990] E.P.O.R. 632

T79/89 Xerox/Finality of decision [1990] E.P.O.R. 558; [1992] O.J. EPO 283

T90/89 Frisco-Findus/Frozen fish [1991] E.P.O.R. 42

T93/89 Hoechst/Polyvinylester dispersion
[1992] E.P.O.R. 155; [1992] O.J. EPO 718

T105/89 Bosch/Power supply [1991] E.P.O.R. 360

T111/89 SKF/Prevention of fretting corrosion [1992] E.P.O.R. 376

T125/89 Scott Paper Company/Release coating and release paper product
[1992] E.P.O.R. 41

T126/89 Filtration/Fluid filter cleaning system [1990] E.P.O.R. 292

T130/89 Kommerling/Profile member
[1992] E.P.O.R. 98; [1991] O.J. EPO 514

T145/89 Hitachi/Engine control [1991] E.P.O.R. 137

T162/89 Konica/Colour photographic material [1992] E.P.O.R. 24

T169/89 Pharmuka/Polysaccharides from heparin [1991] E.P.O.R. 262

T171/89 Bayer/Vaccine [1990] E.P.O.R. 126

T173/89 ICI plc/Gamma-sorbitol [1991] E.P.O.R. 62

T182/89 Sumitomo/Extent of opposition
[1990] E.P.O.R. 438; [1991] O.J. EPO 391

T183/89 Steer, Clive, Allen/Wheelbarrow [1991] E.P.O.R. 298

T192/89 GEC Alsthom/Homogenising immiscible fluids [1990] E.P.O.R. 287

T194/89 IBM/Brushless DC motor [1991] E.P.O.R. 411

T200/89 Boeing/Obvious error in claims
[1990] E.P.O.R. 407; [1992] O.J. EPO 46

T202/89 Spanset Inter/Appeal by intervener
[1992] E.P.O.R. 266; [1992] O.J. EPO 223

T210/89 Marconi/Re-establishment of rights by opponent appellant
[1991] E.P.O.R. 403; [1991] O.J. EPO 433

T227/89 Toray/Flame retarding polyester composition [1993] E.P.O.R. 107

T231/89 Bruynzeel Plastics/Flat torsion spring
[1993] E.P.O.R. 418; [1993] O.J. EPO 13

T232/89 Veidekke/Dam core machine [1993] E.P.O.R. 37

T249/89 Thackray/Surgical instruments [1992] E.P.O.R. 137

T250/89 SNIA/Lack of due care [1992] E.P.O.R. 534; [1992] O.J. EPO 355

T257/89 ICI plc/Fibre-reinforced compositions [1992] E.P.O.R. 332

T262/89 Lansing Bagnall, British Aerospace/Wiring loom [1991] E.P.O.R. 34

T268/89 Latzke/Magnetic plaster [1994] E.P.O.R. 469

T270/89 Ovard/Splash bar [1991] E.P.O.R. 540

T275/89 Klostermann/Steel radiators
[1992] E.P.O.R. 260; [1992] O.J. EPO 126

T277/89 Nestlé/Cryogenic aroma recovery [1991] E.P.O.R. 323

T279/89 Texaco/Reaction injection moulded elastomer [1992] E.P.O.R. 294

T291/89 Eastman Kodak/Anhydrous iodine compounds [1992] E.P.O.R. 399

T298/89 Nexus/Unconfirmed telex [1990] E.P.O.R. 252

T299/89 Toa Nenryo/Elastomer [1992] E.P.O.R. 107

T300/89 Minnesota/Amendments [1991] E.P.O.R. 502; [1991] O.J. EPO 480

T323/89 Konishiroku/Photographic material
[1992] E.P.O.R. 210; [1992] O.J. EPO 169

T338/89 Boussac Saint Frères/Interventions [1991] E.P.O.R. 268

T339/89 VMX/Electronic audio communication system [1991] E.P.O.R. 545

T340/89 General Foods/Caffeine [1992] E.P.O.R. 199

T344/89 GTE/Silicon nitride cutting tools [1993] E.P.O.R. 209

T352/89 Mitsuboshi Belting/Power transmission belt manufacture
[1991] E.P.O.R. 249

T356/89 Ford/Novelty [1990] E.P.O.R. 370

T366/89 Corning Glass/Moulding [1993] E.P.O.R. 266

T387/89 Medtronic/Synchronised intracardiac cardioverter
[1993] E.P.O.R. 113; [1992] O.J. EPO 583

T396/89 Union Carbide/High tear strength polymers [1992] E.P.O.R. 312

T402/89 Fuji/Heat developable colour photographic materials
[1993] E.P.O.R. 81

T406/89 Albany International/Papermaking fabric [1992] E.P.O.R. 94

T418/89 Ortho/Monoclonal antibody [1993] E.P.O.R. 338; [1993] O.J. EPO 20

T423/89 Konica/Sensitising [1994] E.P.O.R. 142

T426/89 Siemens/Pacemaker [1992] E.P.O.R. 149; [1992] O.J. EPO 172

T448/89 Siemens/Stimulating electrode
[1992] E.P.O.R. 540; [1992] O.J. EPO 361

T450/89 Enthone/Electroless plating [1994] E.P.O.R. 326

T454/89 ICI plc/Optical sensing apparatus [1995] E.P.O.R. 600

T482/89 Télémecanique/Power supply unit
[1993] E.P.O.R. 259; [1992] O.J. EPO 646

T485/89 Tracto-Technik/Telecopy filings
[1993] E.P.O.R. 475; [1993] O.J. EPO 214

T487/89 Asahi/Polyamide fibre [1992] E.P.O.R. 32

T490/89 Energy Conversion/Silicon deposition [1993] E.P.O.R. 46

T495/89 Ortho/Monoclonal antibody [1992] E.P.O.R. 48

T507/89 Celanese/Polybutylene terephthalate [1992] E.P.O.R. 229

T516/89 Schering/Confidential papers
[1992] E.P.O.R. 476; [1992] O.J. EPO 436

T519/89 Goodyear/Thermoforming polyester articles [1994] E.P.O.R. 9

T534/89 Dentsply/Inadmissible late filing [1994] E.P.O.R. 540

T538/89 Deere/Coupling rod [1991] E.P.O.R. 445

T541/89 Beecham-Wuelfing/PVD [1992] E.P.O.R. 193

T560/89 N.I. Industries/Filler mass [1994] E.P.O.R. 120

T576/89 Du Pont de Nemours (E.I.) & Co./Entitlement to request
[1994] E.P.O.R. 213; [1993] O.J. EPO 543

T581/89 Shell/Polysaccharide solutions [1992] E.P.O.R. 170

T589/89 NRDC/Polyurethane compositions [1994] E.P.O.R. 17

T603/89 Beattie/Marker   [1992] E.P.O.R. 221; [1992] O.J. EPO 230

T619/89 Union Carbide/Hydroformylation   [1991] E.P.O.R. 561

T622/89 Dow/New citation   [1994] E.P.O.R. 488

T636/89 NAT/Bagging plant   [1993] E.P.O.R. 517

T638/89 Toyota/Apparatus for measuring tyre uniformity   [1991] E.P.O.R. 101

T653/89 Hüppe/Assignment   [1991] E.P.O.R. 217

T666/89 Unilever/Washing composition
                 [1992] E.P.O.R. 501; [1993] O.J. EPO 495

T683/89 Nippondenso/Vehicle display   [1992] E.P.O.R. 429

T684/89 Cyberexact/Printer ribbon errors   [1993] E.P.O.R. 173

T695/89 Bell Maschinenfabrik/Withdrawal of approval
                 [1993] E.P.O.R. 445; [1993] O.J. EPO 152

T702/89 Allied Signal/Proportioning valve
                 [1993] E.P.O.R. 580; [1994] O.J. EPO 472

T716/89 Unilever/Right to be heard
                 [1992] E.P.O.R. 256; [1992] O.J. EPO 132

T726/89 Nissan/Cylinder block   [1991] E.P.O.R. 107

T739/89 Konica/Photographic material   [1992] E.P.O.R. 483

T754/89 Improver/Depilatory device   [1993] E.P.O.R. 153

T760/89 Burlington/Return of documents   [1995] E.P.O.R. 224

T763/89 Fuji/Multilayer photographic material   [1994] E.P.O.R. 384

T780/89 Bayer/Immunostimulant   [1993] E.P.O.R. 377; [1993] O.J. EPO 440

T783/89 Toshiba/Display device for a machine   [1991] E.P.O.R. 472

T784/89 General Electric/Disclosure of computer-related apparatus
                 [1992] E.P.O.R. 446; [1992] O.J. EPO 438

T787/89 British Petroleum/Diamond identification   [1991] E.P.O.R. 178

T789/89 McAlpine/Relief valve   [1995] E.P.O.R. 213; [1994] O.J. EPO 482

T3/90 British Telecommunications/Oral proceedings
                 [1993] E.P.O.R. 366; [1992] O.J. EPO 737

T12/90 Bayer/Amino acid derivatives   [1991] E.P.O.R. 312

T19/90 Harvard/Onco-mouse   [1990] E.P.O.R. 501; [1990] O.J. EPO 476

T23/90 Union Carbide/Polyalkyline polyamines   [1994] E.P.O.R. 30

T30/90 Grain Processing Corporation/Re-establishment of rights
                 [1992] E.P.O.R. 424

T34/90 Unilever/Viscosity reduction [1992] E.P.O.R. 466; [1992] O.J. EPO 454

T47/90 Sumitomo/Remittal   [1991] E.P.O.R. 513; [1991] O.J. EPO 486

T51/90 Vondrovsky/Display signs   [1992] E.P.O.R. 412

T70/90 Rhône-Poulenc/Silane   [1994] E.P.O.R. 452

T89/90 Sprecher & Schuh/Toroidal transformer
[1992] E.P.O.R. 495; [1992] O.J. EPO 456

T97/90 Takemoto Yushi/Lubricating agents
[1993] E.P.O.R. 135; [1993] O.J. EPO 719

T100/90 Östbo/Heat exchanger   [1991] E.P.O.R. 553

T110/90 IBM/Editable document form   [1995] E.P.O.R. 185

T116/90 Beecham/Corrected decision   [1991] E.P.O.R. 155

T137/90 Shell/Amino-triazine   [1991] E.P.O.R. 381

T147/90 Fritz & Farni/Tree surround   [1992] E.P.O.R. 131

T154/90 De La Rue Systems/Apportionment of costs
[1994] E.P.O.R. 284; [1993] O.J. EPO 505

T156/90 Bluewater/Admissibility   [1994] E.P.O.R. 515

T164/90 Light Signatures/Authenticator device   [1991] E.P.O.R. 289

T176/90 ICI plc/Triazoles   [1994] E.P.O.R. 401

T182/90 See-Shell/Bloodflow   [1994] E.P.O.R. 320; [1994] O.J. EPO 641

T190/90 Carnaud/Toothed wheel welding process   [1994] E.P.O.R. 527

T195/90 Unilever/Grounds of appeal   [1990] E.P.O.R. 646

T204/90 Lindholm/Breathing apparatus   [1992] E.P.O.R. 282

T215/90 AKZO/Rainwear   [1992] E.P.O.R. 1

T216/90 Procter & Gamble/Surfactant   [1993] E.P.O.R. 66

T228/90 Unilever/Coloured composition   [1993] E.P.O.R. 309

T253/90 Ampex/*Restitutio in integrum*   [1992] E.P.O.R. 118

T270/90 Asahi/Polyphenylene ether compositions
[1992] E.P.O.R. 365; [1993] O.J. EPO 725

T271/90 Brown, Boveri/Reasons for decision   [1990] E.P.O.R. 541

T272/90 Kolbenschmidt/Competence of Legal Board of Appeal
[1991] E.P.O.R. 493; [1991] O.J. EPO 205

T273/90 PPG/Pigment grinding vehicle   [1992] E.P.O.R. 104

T287/90 Wabco/Grounds of appeal   [1992] E.P.O.R. 531

T290/90 Savio Plastica/Fee reduction
[1991] E.P.O.R. 200; [1992] O.J. EPO 368

T290/90 Daca/Suppression device   [1992] E.P.O.R. 278; [1992] O.J. EPO 368

T297/90 Du Pont de Nemours (E.I.) & Co./Non-woven sheet
[1993] E.P.O.R. 389

T313/90 Aerospatiale/Interlocutory revision   [1991] E.P.O.R. 354

T319/90 Matsushita/Dye transfer sheet   [1994] E.P.O.R. 460

T324/90 Phillips Petroleum/Re-establishment
[1993] E.P.O.R. 507; [1993] O.J. EPO 33

T364/90 Heimann/Glue   [1994] E.P.O.R. 445

T366/90 Unilever/Interesterification process   [1993] E.P.O.R. 383

T375/90 Site Microsurgical Systems/Ophthalmic microsurgical system
                                                        [1993] E.P.O.R. 588

T376/90 Sumitomo/Polymer solution   [1995] E.P.O.R. 232

T390/90 Gussinyer/Calcium sulphate filler
                        [1993] E.P.O.R. 424; [1994] O.J. EPO 03

T400/90 Fischer & Porter/Flowmeter   [1992] E.P.O.R. 14

T409/90 Fujitsu/Avalanche photo diodes
                        [1991] E.P.O.R. 423; [1993] O.J. EPO 40

T448/90 British Gas/Mains replacement method   [1994] E.P.O.R. 105

T449/90 Cedars-Sinai/Treatment of plasma   [1993] E.P.O.R. 54

T456/90 ETA/Watch   [1993] E.P.O.R. 252

T467/90 Thomson-CSF/Spooling process for optical fibre gyroscope
                                                        [1991] E.P.O.R. 115

T484/90 Pomagalski/Cable car   [1993] E.P.O.R. 571; [1993] O.J. EPO 448

T490/90. *See* T409/90; [1993] O.J. EPO 40 (incorrectly reported as T490/90)
                                                        [1991] E.P.O.R. 423

T494/90 NGK/Oral proceedings   [1992] E.P.O.R. 60

T513/90 Japan Styrene/Foamed articles   [1994] E.P.O.R. 129

T521/90 Procter & Gamble/Pouring and measuring package
                                                        [1993] E.P.O.R. 558

T525/90 Tioxide/Pigments   [1994] E.P.O.R. 408

T546/90 Garcia/Storage device   [1993] E.P.O.R. 214

T553/90 Marlboro/Transfer   [1994] E.P.O.R. 440

T595/90 Kawasaki/Grain-oriented silicon sheet
                        [1995] E.P.O.R. 36; [1994] O.J. EPO 695

T600/90 Unilever/Perborate   [1993] E.P.O.R. 28

T602/90 RIFA/Capacitor roll   [1992] E.P.O.R. 8

T607/90 Mitsubishi/Semiconductor device   [1991] E.P.O.R. 569

T610/90 American Colloid/Clay layer   [1993] E.P.O.R. 1

T611/90 Mitsui/Ethylene copolymer   [1991] E.P.O.R. 481; [1993] O.J. EPO 50

T617/90 Air Products/Cryogenic liquid dispenser   [1994] E.P.O.R. 396

T618/90 Lubrizol/Lubricants   [1993] E.P.O.R. 19

T629/90 Sedblauer/Holding device   [1993] E.P.O.R. 147; [1992] O.J. EPO 654

T654/90 Union Carbide/Coatings   [1994] E.P.O.R. 483

T669/90 ATT/Inviting observations   [1993] E.P.O.R. 397; [1992] O.J. EPO 739

T675/90 Euro-Celtique/6-Thioxanthine derivatives
                        [1994] E.P.O.R. 66; [1994] O.J. EPO 58

T685/90 Fujitsu/Printer [1993] E.P.O.R. 183

T687/90 British Gas/Offshore platforms [1993] E.P.O.R. 274

T689/90 Raychem/Event detector [1994] E.P.O.R. 157; [1993] O.J. EPO 616

T691/90 Critikon/Infusion apparatus [1994] E.P.O.R. 51

T740/90 Lesaffre/Yeast [1993] E.P.O.R. 459

T747/90 Fuji/Electron microscope image [1994] E.P.O.R. 430

T762/90 von Blücher/Interlocutory decision [1991] E.P.O.R. 213

T762/90 von Blücher /Surface filter [1993] E.P.O.R. 296

T770/90 Philips/Image enhancement circuit [1992] E.P.O.R. 438

T793/90 Dentsply/Cartridge for filling dental cavities [1993] E.P.O.R. 168

T811/90 AE plc/Exclusion of documents from file inspection
[1994] E.P.O.R. 271; [1993] O.J. EPO 728

T815/90 United States of America/Hepatitis A virus [1994] E.P.O.R. 421

T830/90 Macor Marine Systems/Secrecy agreement
[1995] E.P.O.R. 21; [1994] O.J. EPO 713

T831/90 Communications Satellite/Inadmissible appeal [1992] E.P.O.R. 56

T852/90 Uniroyal/Lubricating composition [1992] E.P.O.R. 522

T854/90 IBM/Card reader [1994] E.P.O.R. 89

T869/90 Texaco/Re-establishment [1994] E.P.O.R. 581

T877/90 Hooper Trading/T-cell growth factor [1993] E.P.O.R. 6

T888/90 Baxter International/Liquid-gas-bubble separator
[1994] E.P.O.R. 98; [1994] O.J. EPO 162

T905/90 Albright & Wilson/Fee reduction [1994] E.P.O.R. 585

T909/90 Institut Cerac/Pump impeller [1993] E.P.O.R. 373

T938/90 Teijin/Polyester composition [1993] E.P.O.R. 287

T958/90 Dow/Sequestering agent [1994] E.P.O.R. 1

T01/91 Micro Pen Research Associates/Ink system for producing circuit
patterns [1994] E.P.O.R. 71

T25/91 National Information Utilities Corporation/Education utility
[1993] E.P.O.R. 466

T66/91 Chivato/Combustion chamber [1992] E.P.O.R. 142

T79/91 Veech/Haemodialysis processes and solutions [1993] E.P.O.R. 91

T102/91 Peugeot/Electric motor [1993] E.P.O.R. 198

T108/91 Sears/Lockable closure [1993] E.P.O.R. 407; [1994] O.J. EPO 228

T109/91 Ajinomoto/Composite plasmid [1992] E.P.O.R. 163

T118/91 Forsheda/Divisional application [1994] E.P.O.R. 557

T121/91 Grace/Nitro compounds [1994] E.P.O.R. 114

T181/91 Nisshin/Steroid   [1994] E.P.O.R. 135

T184/91 Celtrix/Cartilage-inducing factors   [1992] E.P.O.R. 419

T187/91 Leland/Light source   [1995] E.P.O.R. 199

T204/91 Du Pont de Nemours (E.I.) & Co./Admissibility of opposition
   [1993] E.P.O.R. 348

T209/91 Tippens/Reversing plate mill   [1992] E.P.O.R. 289

T227/91 Codman/Second surgical use
   [1995] E.P.O.R. 82; [1994] O.J. EPO 291

T246/91 OXY U.S.A. Inc./Gel-forming composition   [1995] E.P.O.R. 526

T248/91 Visnjic/*Restitutio in integrum*   [1992] E.P.O.R. 145

T255/91 Air Products/Priority   [1993] E.P.O.R. 544; [1993] O.J. EPO 318

T289/91 Hoechst/Ace inhibitors   [1995] E.P.O.R. 32

T369/91 Procter & Gamble/Detergent composition
   [1993] E.P.O.R. 497; [1993] O.J. EPO 561

T409/91 Exxon/Fuel oils   [1994] E.P.O.R. 149; [1994] O.J. EPO 953

T413/91 Union Carbide/Restitution   [1993] E.P.O.R. 504

T415/91 General Motors/High voltage power supply   [1993] E.P.O.R. 279

T435/91 Unilever NV/Hexagonal liquid crystal gel
   [1995] E.P.O.R. 314; [1995] O.J. EPO 188

T470/91 ICI plc/Unity   [1994] E.P.O.R. 231

T473/91 Wegener/Jurisdiction   [1994] E.P.O.R. 292; [1993] O.J. EPO 630

T495/91 Tarkett Pegulan/Surface finish   [1995] E.P.O.R. 516

T500/91 Biogen/Alpha-interferon II   [1995] E.P.O.R. 69

T506/91 Woodcap/Appeal of proprietor   [1994] E.P.O.R. 197

T516/91 AE plc/Re-establishment of rights   [1993] E.P.O.R. 225

T548/91 Schering/Dipeptides   [1995] E.P.O.R. 327

T552/91 Merck Patent/Chroman derivatives
   [1995] E.P.O.R. 455; [1995] O.J. EPO 100

T561/91 Raychem/Heat curable composition   [1994] E.P.O.R. 255

T581/91 Johnson & Johnson/Polylactide   [1994] E.P.O.R. 259

T582/91 Metal-Fren/Friction pad assembly   [1995] E.P.O.R. 574

T598/91 VMI EPE/Tyre   [1995] E.P.O.R. 342; [1993] O.J. EPO 12

T627/91 ICI plc/Emulsion explosive   [1995] E.P.O.R. 286

T640/91 Nippon/Examination procedure
   [1995] E.P.O.R. 243; [1994] O.J. EPO 918

T694/91 Tektronix/Schottky barrier diode   [1995] E.P.O.R. 384

T715/91 IBM/*Restitutio in integrum*   [1993] E.P.O.R. 76

T741/91 Ueno Seiyaku/2-hydroxy-naphthalene-3-carboxylic acid
   [1995] E.P.O.R. 533; [1993] O.J. EPO 630

T757/91 ESB/Follow-on appeal   [1993] E.P.O.R. 595

T843/91 Eastman Kodak/Photographic element (1)   [1995] E.P.O.R. 116

T843/91 Eastman Kodak/Photographic element (2)   [1995] E.P.O.R. 126

T934/91 Konica/Photographic material
         [1993] E.P.O.R. 219; [1993] O.J. EPO 685

T951/91 Du Pont de Nemours (E.I.) & Co./Late submission
         [1995] E.P.O.R. 398; [1995] O.J. EPO 202

T990/91 Pfizer/Correction of chemical name   [1992] E.P.O.R. 351

T17/92 Kubat/Method of producing plastic composites   [1993] E.P.O.R. 552

T27/92 Ka-Te System/Intervention   [1994] E.P.O.R. 501; [1994] O.J. EPO 853

T112/92 Mars II/Glucomannan   [1994] E.P.O.R. 249

T160/92 Mead/Printing plate   [1995] E.P.O.R. 424

T164/92 Bosch/Electronic computer components
         [1995] E.P.O.R. 585; [1995] O.J. EPO 305

T341/92 Neynaber/Basic lead salts   [1995] E.P.O.R. 563

T371/92 Fina/Appeal not filed   [1995] E.P.O.R. 485

T465/92 Alcan/Aluminium alloys   [1995] E.P.O.R. 501

T562/92 Exxon/Lubricating oil additive   [1995] E.P.O.R. 306

T802/92 Colorado School of Mines/Photovoltaic cell   [1995] E.P.O.R. 568

T804/92 Thermo Produktor/Refrigeration apparatus
         [1995] E.P.O.R. 89; [1994] O.J. EPO 862

T820/92 General Hospital/Contraceptive method
         [1995] E.P.O.R. 446; [1995] O.J. EPO 113

T867/92 Konica/Late citation   [1995] E.P.O.R. 683

T892/92 Konica/Remittal   [1995] E.P.O.R. 238; [1994] O.J. EPO 664

T1048/92 Pfizer/Penem   [1995] E.P.O.R. 207

T1055/92 Ampex Corporation/Clarity
         [1995] E.P.O.R. 469; [1995] O.J. EPO 214

T74/93 British Technology Group/Contraceptive method   [1995] E.P.O.R. 279

T296/93 Biogen Inc./Hepatitis B   [1995] E.P.O.R. 1

T326/93 Thorn/Thermal limiting device   [1995] E.P.O.R. 297

T356/93 Plant Genetic Systems/Glutamine synthetase inhibitors
         [1995] E.P.O.R. 357

T412/93 Kirin-Amgen/Erythropoietin   [1995] E.P.O.R. 629

T590/93 Kogyo Gijutsuin/Photosensitive resins
         [1995] E.P.O.R. 478; [1995] O.J. EPO 337

T647/93 Hitachi Maxwell/Procedural violation
         [1995] E.P.O.R. 195; [1995] O.J. EPO 132

T817/93 Gelman Sciences/Fresh ground   [1995] E.P.O.R. 557

T860/93 Aqualon Company/Water-soluble cellulose ether
[1995] E.P.O.R. 391; [1995] O.J. EPO 47

T311/94 Eisai/Remittal   [1995] E.P.O.R. 597 *·

T405/94 Bolland/Weight-sensing apparatus   [1995] E.P.O.R. 619

W04/85 Schick/Heat exchanger   [1994] E.P.O.R. 437; [1987] O.J. EPO 63

W07/85 Minnesota/Insulating powder
[1988] E.P.O.R. 329; [1988] O.J. EPO 211

W07/86Mückter/Lithium salts   [1987] E.P.O.R. 176; [1987] O.J. EPO 67

W09/86 NRDC/Thromboxane antagonists
[1988] E.P.O.R. 34; [1987] O.J. EPO 459

W01/87 Lubrizol/Fuel products   [1988] E.P.O.R. 326; [1988] O.J. EPO 182

W04/87 Late submission of protest   [1989] E.P.O.R. 105; [1988] O.J. EPO 425

W08/87 Electro-Catheter/Protest   [1989] E.P.O.R. 390; [1989] O.J. EPO 123

W03/88 X/Lubricants   [1990] E.P.O.R. 309; [1990] O.J. EPO 126

W31/88 X/Beta-blockers   [1990] E.P.O.R. 317; [1990] O.J. EPO 134

W32/88 X/Immunoassay process and apparatus
[1990] E.P.O.R. 321; [1990] O.J. EPO 138

W44/88 X/Synergic combination of additives
[1990] E.P.O.R. 323; [1990] O.J. EPO 140

W11/89 X/Fibre fleece   [1993] E.P.O.R. 514; [1992] O.J. EPO 225

W12/89 X/Lubricants—Polysuccinate esters
[1990] E.P.O.R. 333; [1990] O.J. EPO 152

W06/90 Draenert/Single general concept
[1991] E.P.O.R. 516; [1991] O.J. EPO 438

W15/91 Hoechst/Herbicides   [1994] E.P.O.R. 226

W16/92 Draping of Curtains/Unsubstantiated protest   [1994] E.P.O.R. 443

W03/93 NN/Re-establishment of rights
[1995] E.P.O.R. 351; [1994] O.J. EPO 931

W04/93 Henkel/Zeolite suspensions   [1995] E.P.O.R. 251; [1994] O.J. EPO 939

A. UNITED KINGDOM AND EUROPEAN CASES

Confidential Information and Breach of Confidence

Account of Profits. *See* **Practice** (*Account of profits*)

Abuse of Process

Helitune Ltd v. Stewart Hughes Ltd (Ch.D.)
House of Spring Gardens Ltd v. Waite (WHETHER ABUSE TO RELITIGATE ISSUE OF FRAUD: C.A.)
Speed Seal Products Ltd v. Paddington (ACTIONABLE ABUSE: PLEADINGS: Ch.D.: C.A.)

Anton Piller. *See* **Practice** (*Anton Piller*)

Breach

Kitechnology BV v. Unicorn GmbH Rahn Plastmaschinen (JURISDICTION: E.C. JUDGMENTS CONVENTION: PLACE OR COMMISSION OF TORT: Ch.D.)

Breach of Confidence

De Maudsley v. Palumbo (IDEA FOR A NIGHT CLUB: WHETHER INFORMATION IMPARTED UNDER OBLIGATION OF CONFIDENCE: WHETHER INFORMATION TOO VAGUE AS TO QUALIFY AS CONFIDENTIAL: USE OF INFORMATION: Ch.D.)
Private Research Ltd v. Brosnan (COPYRIGHT: INFRINGEMENT: EMPLOYER AND EMPLOYEE: MISUSE OF CONFIDENTIAL INFORMATION: INTERLOCUTORY INJUNCTION: FAIR QUESTION TO BE TRIED: ADEQUACY OF DAMAGES: BALANCE OF CONVENIENCE: Ireland: H.C.)

British Leyland Defence

Ibcos Computers Ltd v. Barclays Mercantile Highland Finance Ltd (Ch.D.)

Company Director

Balston Ltd v. Headline Filters Ltd (BREACH OF FIDUCIARY DUTY: DUTY OF FIDELITY: Ch.D.)

Computer Programs

Dun & Bradstreet Ltd v. Typesetting Facilities Ltd (COMPUTERISED DATABASE: Ch.D.)
Format Communications Manufacturing Ltd v. ITT (U.K.) Ltd (C.A.)
Grant v. Procurator Fiscal (COPIES OF COMPUTER PRINT-OUTS: Scotland: H.C.)
Ibcos Computers Ltd v. Barclays Mercantile Highland Finance Ltd (SOURCE CODE: SUBSISTENCE AND EXTENT OF PROTECTION: Ch.D.)
Series 5 Software Ltd v. Philip Clarke (SOLICITATION OF CUSTOMERS: INTERLOCUTORY RELIEF: DELAY: INTERLOCUTORY INJUNCTIONS: PRINCIPLES: HISTORICAL SURVEY OF *American Cyanamid* CASES: Ch.D.)

Conflict of Laws

House of Spring Gardens Ltd v. Waite (FOREIGN JUDGMENT: JURISDICTION TO ENFORCE: JUDGMENT OF FOREIGN COURT: C.A.)

Contempt. *See also under* Spycatcher

Attorney-General v. Newspaper Publishing plc (*Spycatcher*: CRIMINAL CONTEMPT: Ch.D.: C.A.)

Attorney-General v. Observer Ltd (Re Derbyshire CC's Application) (ADMINISTRATION OF JUSTICE: WHETHER LIBRARY BOUND BY TERMS: Q.B.D.)

Times Newspapers Ltd v. Her Majesty's Attorney-General (*Spycatcher*: PUBLICATION: APPELLANT NOT PARTY TO INJUNCTIONS RESTRAINING BREACH OF CONFIDENCE: APPEAL: H.L.)

X Health Authority v. Y (DOCTORS WITH AIDS: IDENTITY: INTERLOCUTORY INJUNCTION AGAINST NEWSPAPER PROHIBITING PUBLICATION: PUBLIC INTEREST: WHETHER PUBLICATION IN BREACH OF INJUNCTION A CONTEMPT: Q.B.D.)

Contract

Kitechnology BV v. Unicor GmbH Plastmaschinen (BREACH: PRACTICE: PLEADINGS: STRIKING OUT: JURISDICTION: EEC JUDGMENTS CONVENTION: C.A.)

Simtech Advanced Training and Simulation Systems Ltd v. Jasmin Simtec Ltd (COLLABORATION AGREEMENT: PARTIALLY AGREED CONTRACT: INTERLOCUTORY RELIEF: SPECIFIC PERFORMANCE: INTERLOCUTORY PROCEEDINGS: BALANCE OF JUSTICE: Ch.D.)

Crown Employee. *See also* Employment Contracts

Attorney-General v. Guardian Newspapers Ltd and The Observer Ltd (*Spycatcher*: AUTHOR'S DUTY OF CONFIDENTIALITY TO CROWN: Ch.D.: C.A.)

Attorney-General v. The Times Newspapers Ltd (SPECIAL POSITION OF CROWN AS CONFIDER OF INFORMATION: PUBLIC INTEREST CONSIDERATIONS: H.L.)

Attorney-General v. Guardian Newspapers Ltd (*Spycatcher*: FORMER CROWN EMPLOYEE: Ch.D.: C.A.: H.L.)

Lord Advocate v. Scotsman Publications Ltd (BOOK, *Inside Intelligence*: DUTY ON THIRD PARTIES IN INNOCENT RECEIPT OF INFORMATION: INTERDICT: BALANCE OF CONVENIENCE: Scotland: O.H.: H.L.)

Lord Advocate v. Scotsman Publications Ltd (BOOK, *Inside Intelligence*: NON-CONTENTS CASE: PUBLIC INTEREST: WHETHER SUFFICIENT PROOF FOR INTERDICT: RECLAIMING MOTION REFUSED: Scotland: I.H.)

Lord Advocate v. Scotsman Publications Ltd (BOOK, *Inside Intelligence*: POSITION OF NEWSPAPERS: EFFECT OF *Spycatcher*: EFFECT OF OFFICIAL SECRETS ACT 1989: H.L.)

Customer Information or Lists

Pet Plan Ltd v. Protect-A-Pet Ltd (C.A.)

Roberts v. Northwest Fixings (ANTON PILLER PRACTICE: LEGAL AID: C.A.)

Roger Bullivant Ltd v. Ellis (EX-EMPLOYEE: SPRINGBOARD DOCTRINE: C.A.)

Universal Thermosensors Ltd v. Hibben (STOLEN INFORMATION: EX-EMPLOYEES' COMPETING BUSINESS: ASSESSMENT OF DAMAGES: SPRINGBOARD DOCTRINE: ANTON PILLER PRACTICE: Ch.D.)

Defence

Attorney-General v. Guardian Newspaper Ltd, Observer Ltd, Times Newspapers Ltd (*Spycatcher*: FULL ACTION: DEFENCE OF INIQUITY: Ch.D.: C.A.: H.L.)

Hilti AG v. E.C. Commission (INTERESTS OF RIGHT OF DEFENCE: PROCEDURE: CFI)

Ibcos Computers Ltd v. Barclays Mercantile Highland Finance Ltd (BRITISH LEYLAND DEFENCE: Ch.D.)

Disclosure by MMC

R. v. Monopolies and Mergers Commission, *ex p.* Elders IXL Ltd (PUBLIC INTEREST: Q.B.D.)

Ex-employees. *See also* Crown Employee, Fiduciary Duty/Fiduciary Relationship and Restrictive Covenant/Restraint of Trade

Attorney-General v. Brandon Book Publishers Ltd (FIDUCIARY DUTY: BRITISH SECURITY SERVICE EX-EMPLOYEE: BOOK: *One Girl's War*: CONSTITUTIONAL RIGHTS: Ireland: H.C.)

Attorney-General v. Guardian Newspapers Ltd (*Spycatcher*: FORMER CROWN EMPLOYEE: INTERLOCUTORY INJUNCTION: SUBSEQUENT PUBLICATION OUTSIDE JURISDICTION: Ch.D.: C.A.: H.L.)

Austin Knight (U.K.) Ltd v. Hinds (EMPLOYMENT CONTRACTS: NON-SOLICITATION CLAUSE: WHETHER PLAINTIFF'S BUSINESS PROTECTABLE: WHETHER RESTRICTION REASONABLE: Ch.D.)

Balston Ltd v. Headline Filters Ltd (DUTY OF GOOD FAITH: Ch.D.)

Berkeley Administration Inc. v. McClelland (FINANCIAL INFORMATION: WHETHER CONFIDENTIAL: WHETHER USED: Q.B.D.)

Company's Application (PUBLIC INTEREST: FORMER EMPLOYEE PROVIDING FINANCIAL SERVICES: THREAT TO DISCLOSE CONFIDENTIAL INFORMATION TO REGULATORY BODY AND REVENUE: NO THREAT OF DISCLOSURE TO PUBLIC: Ch.D.)

Computer Machinery Co. Ltd v. Drescher (EVIDENCE: Ch.D.)

Faccenda Chicken Ltd v. Fowler (CONSPIRACY: SALES INFORMATION: MASTER AND SERVANT: DUTY OF FIDELITY: Ch.D.: C.A.)

Harben Pumps (Scotland) Ltd v. Lafferty (TRADE SECRETS: IMPLIED TERMS OF CONTRACT: Scotland: O.H.)

Ixora Trading Incorporated v. Jones (BREACH OF DUTY OF FIDELITY: Ch.D.)

Johnson & Bloy (Holdings) Ltd v. Wolstenholme Rink plc (NATURE OF INFORMATION: SCOPE OF INJUNCTION: C.A.)

Lansing Linde Ltd v. Kerr (RESTRAINT OF TRADE: RESTRICTIVE COVENANT IN CONTRACT OF EMPLOYMENT: BREACH: WHETHER INFORMATION PROTECTABLE AS TRADE SECRETS: C.A.)

Lawrence David Ltd v. Ashton (CONTRACT: RESTRAINT OF TRADE: PERIOD OF RESTRAINT: C.A.)

Lock International plc v. Beswick (INJUNCTION: TRADE SECRETS: Ch.D.)

Lord Advocate v. Scotsman Publications Ltd (BREACH OF CONFIDENCE: MI5: BOOK, *Inside Intelligence*: DUTY ON THIRD PARTIES IN INNOCENT RECEIPT OF INFORMATION: INTERDICT: BALANCE OF CONVENIENCE: Scotland: O.H.: H.L.)

Lord Advocate v. Scotsman Publications Ltd (BOOK, *Inside Intelligence*: NON-CONTENTS CASE: PUBLIC INTEREST: WHETHER SUFFICIENT PROOF FOR INTERDICT: RECLAIMING MOTION REFUSED: Scotland: I.H.)

Lord Advocate v. Scotsman Publications Ltd (BOOK, *Inside Intelligence*: POSITION OF
  NEWSPAPERS: EFFECT OF *Spycatcher*: EFFECT OF OFFICIAL SECRETS ACT 1989:
  H.L.)
Mainmet Holdings plc v. Austin (NOT IN COMPETITION WITH EX-EMPLOYER:
  TRADE SECRETS: MALICIOUS FALSEHOOD: WHETHER INJUNCTION
  APPROPRIATE: Q.B.D.)
Mont (J.A.) (U.K.) Ltd v. Mills (RESTRICTIVE PRACTICES: SEVERANCE
  AGREEMENT: VALIDITY OF COVENANT: FORM OF INJUNCTION: APPROACH
  TO CONSTRUCTION OF RESTRICTIVE COVENANTS: GOOD FAITH: C.A.)
Private Research Ltd v. Brosnan (COPYRIGHT: INFRINGEMENT: INTERLOCUTORY
  INJUNCTION: FAIR QUESTION TO BE TRIED: ADEQUACY OF DAMAGES:
  BALANCE OF CONVENIENCE: Ireland H.C.)
PSM International plc v. Whitehouse (WHETHER INJUNCTION MAY BE GRANTED
  TO RESTRAIN EX-EMPLOYEE FROM FULFILLING CONTRACT ALREADY MADE
  WITH THIRD PARTY: PRACTICE: C.A.)
Roger Bullivant Ltd v. Ellis (SPRINGBOARD DOCTRINE: CUSTOMER CARD INDEX:
  C.A.)
Solicitors (Re a firm of) (SOLICITOR RETAINED IN PATENT LITIGATION: FORMERLY
  PARTNER IN FIRM RETAINED BY OTHER PARTY: Ch.D.)
Speed Seal Products Ltd v. Paddington (MASTER AND SERVANT: STRIKING OUT:
  ACTIONABLE ABUSE OF PROCESS: PLEADINGS: Ch.D.: C.A.)
Universal Thermosensors Ltd v. Hibben (STOLEN CUSTOMER INFORMATION: EX-
  EMPLOYEES' COMPETING BUSINESS: ASSESSMENT OF DAMAGES:
  INTERLOCUTORY ORDER BY CONSENT: SCOPE OF INJUNCTIONS:
  SPRINGBOARD DOCTRINE: Ch.D.)

Fiduciary Duty/Fiduciary Relationship

Attorney-General v. Brandon Book Publishers Ltd (BRITISH SECURITY SERVICE EX-
  EMPLOYEE: BOOK: *One Girl's War*: CONSTITUTIONAL RIGHTS: Ireland: H.C.)
Attorney-General v. Guardian Newspaper Ltd, Observer Ltd, Times Newspapers Ltd
  (*Spycatcher*: FULL ACTION: Ch.D.: C.A.: H.L.)
Balston Ltd v. Headline Filters Ltd (COMPANY DIRECTOR: BREACH OF DUTY OF
  FIDELITY: CONFIDENTIAL INFORMATION: DIRECTOR PLANNING WHILE
  UNDER NOTICE TO COMPLETE: Ch.D.)
Lord Advocate v. Scotsman Publications Ltd (MI5: BOOK, *Inside Intelligence*: DUTY ON
  THIRD PARTIES IN INNOCENT RECEIPT OF INFORMATION: Scotland: O.H.:
  H.L.)
Solicitors (Re a firm of) (SOLICITOR: FIDUCIARY RELATIONSHIP WITH CLIENT:
  CONFIDENTIAL INFORMATION: ACQUISITION FROM COMPANIES CLOSELY
  ASSOCIATED WITH CLIENT: WHETHER DUTIES EXTEND TO ASSOCIATED
  COMPANIES: C.A.)

Freedom of Speech and Press

Attorney-General v. Guardian Newspaper Ltd, Observer Ltd, Times Newspapers Ltd
  (*Spycatcher*: FULL ACTION: PUBLICATION AND AVAILABILITY OF BOOK
  WITHOUT AND WITHIN U.K.: BALANCING PUBLIC INTEREST IN FREEDOM OF
  SPEECH AND PRESS AGAINST PUBLIC INTEREST IN MAINTAINING
  CONFIDENTIALITY: Ch.D.: C.A.: H.L.)

Idea

De Maudsley v. Palumbo (IDEA FOR A NIGHT CLUB: WHETHER INFORMATION
  IMPARTED UNDER OBLIGATION OF CONFIDENCE: WHETHER INFORMATION
  TOO VAGUE AS TO QUALIFY AS CONFIDENTIAL: USE OF INFORMATION: Ch.D.)

Identity of Doctors with AIDS

X Health Authority v. Y (INJUNCTION: INFORMATION OBTAINED FROM CONFIDENTIAL HOSPITAL RECORDS: INTERLOCUTORY INJUNCTION AGAINST NEWSPAPER PROHIBITING PUBLICATION: PUBLIC INTEREST: WHETHER PUBLICATION IN BREACH OF INJUNCTION A CONTEMPT: Q.B.D.)

Illegal Telephone Tapping

Francome v. Mirror Group Newspapers Ltd (INTERLOCUTORY INJUNCTION: C.A.)

Implied Terms of Contract

Harben Pumps (Scotland) Ltd v. Lafferty (EX-EMPLOYEE: TRADE SECRETS: Scotland: O.H.)

Iniquity

Attorney-General v. Guardian Newspaper Ltd, Observer Ltd, Times Newspapers Ltd (*Spycatcher*: FULL ACTION: Ch.D.: C.A.: H.L.)

Innocent Receipt of Information

English & American Insurance Co. Ltd v. Herbert Smith (LEGAL PROFESSIONAL PRIVILEGE: INNOCENT RECEIPT OF INFORMATION: Ch.D.)
Lord Advocate v. Scotsman Publications Ltd (DUTY ON THIRD PARTIES: INTERDICT: BALANCE OF CONVENIENCE: Scotland: O.H.: H.L.)

Inspection. *See* **Practice** (*Inspection*)

Interlocutory Injunction. *See* **Practice** (*Interlocutory injunction*)

Ireland

Attorney-General v. Brandon Book Publishers Ltd (H.C.)
House of Spring Gardens Ltd v. Point Blank Ltd (H.C.: S.C.)
Private Research Ltd v. Brosnan (H.C.)

Legal Aid

Roberts v. Northwest Fixings (PRACTICE: C.A.)

Lesbian Relationship

Stephens v. Avery (RELATIONSHIP DISCLOSED TO RECIPIENT IN CONFIDENCE: INFORMATION COMMUNICATED TO NEWSPAPER: WHETHER BREACH OF CONFIDENCE ACTIONABLE: CAUSE OF ACTION: WHETHER INFORMATION CAPABLE OF PROTECTION: DUTY OF CONFIDENCE: SEXUAL CONDUCT: Ch.D.)

Malicious Falsehood

CHC Software Card Ltd v. Hopkins & Wood (LIBEL: TRANSFER BETWEEN DIVISIONS: SOLICITOR'S DUTY: DISCOVERY: CONFIDENTIALITY: LEGAL PROFESSIONAL PRIVILEGE: INTERROGATORIES: Ch.D.)
Mainmet Holdings plc v. Austin (WHETHER INJUNCTION APPROPRIATE: Q.B.D.)

Material in Public Domain

Attorney-General v. Guardian Newspapers Ltd and The Observer Ltd (*Spycatcher*: INTERLOCUTORY INJUNCTION: FORM OF INJUNCTION: Ch.D.: C.A.)

Master and Servant. *See also under* **Ex-employees**

Faccenda Chicken Ltd v. Fowler (CONSPIRACY: SALES INFORMATION: DUTY OF FIDELITY: Ch.D.: C.A.)

Speed Seal Products Ltd v. Paddington (STRIKING OUT: ACTIONABLE ABUSE OF PROCESS: PLEADINGS: Ch.D.: C.A.)

Natural Justice

Attorney-General v. Newspaper Publishing plc (*Spycatcher*: CONTEMPT: CRIMINAL CONTEMPT: NEWSPAPERS NOT BOUND BY INJUNCTION NOT TO PUBLISH: INTENTION OF PUBLICATION: Ch.D.: C.A.)

Official Secrets Act 1989

Lord v. Scotsman Publications Ltd (EFFECT: BREACH OF CONFIDENCE: MI5: DUTY ON THIRD PARTIES IN INNOCENT RECEIPT OF INFORMATION: POSITION OF NEWSPAPERS: EFFECT OF *Spycatcher*: BOOK, *Inside Intelligence*: H.L.)

One Girl's War

Attorney-General v. Brandon Book Publishers Ltd (Ireland: H.C.)

Attorney-General v. Turnaround Distribution Ltd (Q.B.D.)

Pleadings. *See* **Practice** (*Pleadings*)

Practice

Account of profits

Attorney-General v. Guardian Newspaper Ltd, Observer Ltd, Times Newspapers Ltd (*Spycatcher*: FULL ACTION: Ch.D.: C.A.: H.L.)

Attorney-General v. The Times Newspapers Ltd (UNJUST ENRICHMENT: H.L.)

House of Spring Gardens Ltd v. Point Blank Ltd (WHETHER ROYALTY FOR BREACH OF CONTRACT PRECLUDES FURTHER PECUNIARY AWARD FOR BREACH OF CONFIDENCE: OVERLAPPING HEADS: Ireland: H.C.)

My Kinda Town Ltd v. Soll (Ch.D., C.A.)

Administrative procedure

Hercules NV, SA v. E.C. Commission (CFI)

American Cyanamid practice

Graham v. Delderfield (STATUS QUO: C.A.)

Anton Piller practice

AB v. CDE (Q.B.D.)

Booker McConnell plc v. Plascow (DISCHARGE OF ORDER: C.A.)

Hoechst U.K. Ltd v. Chemiculture Ltd (APPLICATION TO DISCHARGE: ALLEGED NON-DISCLOSURE ON *ex p.* APPLICATION: Ch.D.)

Hytrac Conveyors Ltd v. Conveyors International Ltd (INTERLOCUTORY INJUNCTION: C.A.)

Lock International plc v. Beswick (PLAINTIFF TO PAY DAMAGES: Ch.D.)

Discretion

Berkeley Administration Inc. v. McClelland (COSTS: ABANDONED PARTS OF ACTION: DISCRETION: Q.B.D.)
Dun & Bradstreet Ltd v. Typesetting Facilities Ltd (COMPUTERISED DATABASE: APPLICATION FOR INSPECTION: INFORMATION IN ELECTRONIC FORM, SO VISUAL INSPECTION OF DISKS USELESS: DISCLOSURE OF CONTENTS REQUIRED: INSPECTION BEFORE SERVICE OF STATEMENT OF CLAIM: REQUIREMENTS: INSPECTION ORDERED: Ch.D.)

Civil Evidence Act

Union Carbide Corp. v. Naturin Ltd (STOLEN INFORMATION: CONVICTIONS PLEADED: STRIKING OUT: C.A.)

Discovery

Barlow Clowes Gilt Managers Ltd (PUBLIC INTEREST IMMUNITY: INFORMATION OBTAINED IN COMPULSORY LIQUIDATION OF COMPANY: COMPANY'S OFFICERS CHARGED WITH CRIMINAL OFFENCES: WITNESS SUMMONS ISSUED IN CRIMINAL PROCEEDINGS REQUIRING COMPANY'S LIQUIDATORS TO DISCLOSE CONFIDENTIAL INFORMATION: WHETHER INFORMATION TO BE DISCLOSED: Ch.D.)
Berkeley Administration Inc. v. McClelland (SPECIFIC DISCOVERY: C.A.)
CHC Software Card Ltd v. Hopkins & Wood (SOLICITOR'S DUTY: CONFIDENTIALITY: LEGAL PROFESSIONAL PRIVILEGE: INTERROGATORIES: Ch.D.)
Format Communications Manufacturing Ltd v. ITT (U.K.) Ltd (COMPUTER PROGRAMS: SAFEGUARDS: C.A.)
Gamlen Chemical Co. (U.K.) Ltd v. Rochem Ltd (CONSPIRACY TO INJURE: LEGAL PRIVILEGE: Ch.D.)
Helitune Ltd v. Stewart Hughes Ltd (CONFIDENTIAL EXHIBIT: SPECIFIC DISCOVERY: Ch.D.)
McGuinness v. Kellogg Co. of Great Britain Ltd (NON-DISCLOSURE OF EVIDENCE BEFORE TRIAL: DOCUMENTARY: REBUTTAL OF BONA FIDES: C.A.)
Minnesota Mining & Manufacturing Co. v. Rennicks (U.K.) Ltd (CONFIDENTIAL DOCUMENTS USED IN U.S. PROCEEDINGS: U.S. PROTECTIVE ORDER: PRIVILEGE: Ch.D.)
Sybron Corp. v. Barclays Bank plc (DISCOVERY AND INSPECTION: USE OF DOCUMENTS IN SUBSEQUENT LITIGATION: Ch.D.)

Discretion

Berkeley Administration Inc. v. McClelland (COSTS: ABANDONED PARTS OF ACTION: COMPLAINT OF JUDICIAL BIAS: JUDGE'S DUTY: Q.B.D.)
Universal Thermosensors Ltd v. Hibben (SCOPE OF INJUNCTIONS: SPRINGBOARD DOCTRINE: Ch.D.)

EEC Judgments Convention

Kitechnology BV v. Unicor GmbH Plastmaschinen (BREACH OF CONTRACT: PLEADINGS: STRIKING OUT: JURISDICTION: EEC JUDGMENTS CONVENTION: C.A.)

Evidence

British Coal Corporation v. Dennis Rye Ltd (No. 2) (PRIVILEGE: LEGAL ADVISERS: DOCUMENTS CREATED FOR CIVIL PROCEEDINGS SUBSEQUENTLY HANDED TO POLICE: EFFECT OF LEGAL PROFESSIONAL PRIVILEGE: ATTORNEY-GENERAL'S GUIDELINES: VOLUNTARY DISCLOSURE IN COURSE OF CRIMINAL TRIAL: WHETHER PRIVILEGE WAIVED: WHETHER ENTITLEMENT TO RETURN OF DOCUMENTS: C.A.)

Computer Machinery Co. Ltd v. Drescher (INTERLOCUTORY INJUNCTION: Ch.D.)

English & American Insurance Co. Ltd v. Herbert Smith (LEGAL PROFESSIONAL PRIVILEGE: INNOCENT RECEIPT OF INFORMATION: Ch.D.)

Kenning v. Eve Construction Ltd (EXPERT EVIDENCE: DISCLOSURE: REPORT SENT TO WRONG PARTY: Q.B.D.)

McGuinness v. Kellogg Co. of Great Britain Ltd (NON-DISCLOSURE OF EVIDENCE BEFORE TRIAL: C.A.)

Union Carbide Corp. v. Naturin Ltd (STOLEN INFORMATION: CONVICTIONS PLEADED: CIVIL EVIDENCE ACT: C.A.)

VNU Publications Ltd v. Ziff Davis (U.K.) Ltd (INTERLOCUTORY INJUNCTION: CONFIDENTIAL EXHIBIT: Ch.D.)

Ex Parte application

Hoechst U.K. Ltd v. Chemiculture Ltd (ALLEGED NON-DISCLOSURE ON *ex p.* APPLICATION: Ch.D.)

Expert evidence

Kenning v. Eve Construction Ltd (DISCLOSURE: REPORT SENT TO WRONG PARTY: Q.B.D.)

McGuinness v. Kellogg Co. of Great Britain Ltd (NON-DISCLOSURE OF EVIDENCE BEFORE TRIAL: DOCUMENTARY: REBUTTAL OF BONA FIDES: C.A.)

VNU Publications Ltd v. Ziff Davis (U.K.) Ltd (CONFIDENTIAL EXHIBIT: Ch.D.)

Inspection. See also under *Discovery*

Dun & Bradstreet Ltd v. Typesetting Facilities Ltd (INSPECTION BEFORE SERVICE OF STATEMENT OF CLAIM: REQUIREMENTS: INSPECTION ORDERED: Ch.D.)

Format Communications Manufacturing Ltd v. ITT (U.K.) Ltd (COMPUTER PROGRAMS: DISCOVERY AND INSPECTION: SAFEGUARDS: C.A.)

Sybron Corp. v. Barclays Bank plc (DISCOVERY AND INSPECTION: USE OF DOCUMENTS IN SUBSEQUENT LITIGATION: Ch.D.)

Injunction

Alfa Laval Cheese Systems Ltd v. Wincanton Engineering Ltd (Ch.D.)

Lock International plc v. Beswick (EX-EMPLOYEE: INJUNCTION: TRADE SECRETS: Ch.D.)

Mont (J.A.) (U.K.) Ltd v. Mills (FORM OF INJUNCTION: APPROACH TO CONSTRUCTION OF RESTRICTIVE COVENANTS: C.A.)

PSM International plc v. Whitehouse (EX-EMPLOYEE: WHETHER INJUNCTION LIES TO RESTRAIN EX-EMPLOYEE FROM FULFILLING CONTRACT ALREADY MADE WITH THIRD PARTY: C.A.)

Inspection

Dun & Bradstreet Ltd v. Typesetting Facilities Ltd (APPLICATION: INFORMATION IN ELECTRONIC FORM, SO VISUAL INSPECTION OF DISKS USELESS: DISCLOSURE OF CONTENTS REQUIRED: INSPECTION BEFORE SERVICE OF STATEMENT OF CLAIM: REQUIREMENTS: Ch.D.)

Format Communications Manufacturing Ltd v. ITT (U.K.) Ltd (COMPUTER PROGRAMS: DISCOVERY AND INSPECTION: SAFEGUARDS: C.A.)

Sybron Corp. v. Barclays Bank plc (USE OF DOCUMENTS IN SUBSEQUENT LITIGATION: Ch.D.)

Interlocutory injunction

Attorney-General v. Guardian Newspapers Ltd and The Observer Ltd (*Spycatcher:* PRIOR RESTRAINT OF PUBLICATION: FORM OF INJUNCTION: Ch.D.: C.A.)

Attorney-General v. Guardian Newspapers Ltd (*Spycatcher:* Ch.D.: C.A.: H.L.)

Austin Knight (U.K.) Ltd v. Hinds (Ch.D.)

Computer Machinery Co. Ltd v. Drescher (FORMER EMPLOYEES: EVIDENCE: Ch.D.)

Francome v. Mirror Group Newspapers Ltd (ILLEGAL TELEPHONE TAPPING: C.A.)

Graham v. Delderfield (*American Cyanamid* PRACTICE: STATUS QUO: C.A.)

Helitune Ltd v. Stewart Hughes Ltd (CROSS-UNDERTAKING: Ch.D.)

Hytrac Conveyors Ltd v. Conveyors International Ltd (ANTON PILLER PRACTICE: C.A.)

Lansing Linde Ltd v. Kerr (EX-EMPLOYEE: WHETHER INFORMATION ACQUIRED PROTECTABLE AS TRADE SECRETS: WHETHER INTERIM INJUNCTION TO BE GRANTED: C.A.)

Lawrence David Ltd v. Ashton (EX-EMPLOYEE: PERIOD OF RESTRAINT: C.A.)

Shelley Films Ltd v. Rex Features Ltd (Ch.D.)

Simtech Advanced Training and Simulation Systems Ltd v. Jasmin Simtec Ltd (PARTIALLY AGREED CONTRACT: SPECIFIC PERFORMANCE: Ch.D.)

Times Newspapers Ltd v. MGN Ltd (THATCHER MEMOIRS: CLARITY AND PRECISION OF INJUNCTION SOUGHT: C.A.)

Universal Thermosensors Ltd v. Hibben (SCOPE OF INJUNCTIONS IN BREACH OF CONFIDENCE: SPRINGBOARD DOCTRINE: ANTON PILLER PRACTICE: Ch.D.)

VNU Publications Ltd v. Ziff Davis (U.K.) Ltd (CONFIDENTIAL EXHIBIT: EVIDENCE: Ch.D.)

X Health Authority v. Y (IDENTITY OF DOCTORS WITH AIDS: PROHIBITION AGAINST PUBLICATION BY NEWSPAPER: PUBLIC INTEREST: WHETHER PUBLICATION IN BREACH OF INJUNCTION A CONTEMPT: Q.B.D.)

Interlocutory injunction—adequacy of damages

Private Research Ltd v. Brosnan (EMPLOYER AND EMPLOYEE: MISUSE OF CONFIDENTIAL INFORMATION: FAIR QUESTION TO BE TRIED: BALANCE OF CONVENIENCE: Ireland: H.C.)

Interlocutory injunction—balance of convenience

Alfa Laval Cheese Systems Ltd v. Wincanton Engineering Ltd (UNQUANTIFIABLE HARM: Ch.D.)

Lord Advocate v. Scotsman Publications Ltd (Scotland: O.H.: H.L.)

Simtech Advanced Training and Simulation Systems Ltd v. Jasmin Simtec Ltd (COLLABORATION AGREEMENT: PARTIALLY AGREED CONTRACT: SPECIFIC PERFORMANCE: INTERLOCUTORY PROCEEDINGS: Ch.D.)

Private Research Ltd v. Brosnan (EMPLOYER AND EMPLOYEE: MISUSE OF CONFIDENTIAL INFORMATION: FAIR QUESTION TO BE TRIED: ADEQUACY OF DAMAGES: Ireland: H.C.)

Interlocutory Injunction—fair question to be tried

Private Research Ltd v. Brosnan (BREACH OF CONFIDENCE: EMPLOYER AND EMPLOYEE: MISUSE OF CONFIDENTIAL INFORMATION: ADEQUACY OF DAMAGES: BALANCE OF CONVENIENCE: Ireland: H.C.)

Interlocutory injunctions—principles

Series 5 Software Ltd v. Philip Clarke (COMPUTER SOURCE CODES: SOLICITATION OF CUSTOMERS: HISTORICAL SURVEY OF *American Cyanamid* CASES: Ch.D)

Interrogatories

CHC Software Card Ltd v. Hopkins & Wood (CONFIDENTIALITY: LEGAL PROFESSIONAL PRIVILEGE: Ch.D.)

Judge's duty

Berkeley Administration Inc. v. McClelland (COMPLAINT OF JUDICIAL BIAS: Q.B.D.)

Jurisdiction

Kitechnology BV v. Unicorn GmbH Rahn Plastmaschinen (E.C. JUDGMENTS CONVENTION: PLACE OF COMMISSION OF TORT: Ch.D.: C.A.)

Legal aid

Roberts v. Northwest Fixings (C.A.)

Pleadings

Helitune Ltd v. Stewart Hughes Ltd (INQUIRY AS TO DAMAGES: STRIKING OUT: ABUSE OF PROCESS: Ch.D.)

Kitechnology BV v. Unicor GmbH Plastmaschinen (BREACH OF CONTRACT: STRIKING OUT: JURISDICTION: EEC JUDGMENTS CONVENTION: C.A.)

Speed Seal Products Ltd v. Paddington (STRIKING OUT: ACTIONABLE ABUSE OF PROCESS: Ch.D.: C.A.)

Union Carbide Corp. v. Naturin Ltd (CRIMINAL CONVICTIONS: CIVIL EVIDENCE ACT: STRIKING OUT: C.A.)

Public interest immunity

Barlow Clowes Gilt Managers Ltd (Ch.D.)

Solicitor's duty

CHC Software Card Ltd v. Hopkins & Wood (Ch.D.)

Specific performance

Simtech Advanced Training and Simulation Systems Ltd v. Jasmin Simtec Ltd (COLLABORATION AGREEMENT: PARTIALLY AGREED: INTERLOCUTORY RELIEF: INTERLOCUTORY PROCEEDINGS: BALANCE OF JUSTICE: Ch.D.)

Striking out

Helitune Ltd v. Stewart Hughes Ltd (INQUIRY AS TO DAMAGES: ABUSE OF PROCESS: Ch.D.)

Kitechnology BV v. Unicor GmbH Plastmaschinen (BREACH OF CONTRACT: JURISDICTION: EEC JUDGMENTS CONVENTION: C.A.)

Speed Seal Products Ltd v. Paddington (ACTIONABLE ABUSE OF PROCESS: Ch.D.: C.A.)

Union Carbide Corp. v. Naturin Ltd (CRIMINAL CONVICTIONS: CIVIL EVIDENCE ACT: C.A.)

Subpoena Duces Tecum

Marcel v. Commissioner of Police of the Metropolis (SEIZURE BY POLICE UNDER STATUTORY POWERS DURING INVESTIGATIONS: *Subpoena duces tecum* SEEKING PRODUCTION OF DOCUMENTS FOR USE IN CIVIL PROCEEDINGS: Ch.D.: C.A.)

Transfer between divisions

CHC Software Card Ltd v. Hopkins & Wood (SOLICITOR'S DUTY: Ch.D.)

Undertaking

Poly Lina Ltd v. Finch (FORMER EMPLOYEE: WHETHER INFORMATION CONFIDENTIAL: EMBARGO ON ENGAGEMENTS WITH COMPETITOR: WIDTH OF COVENANT: ADEQUACY OF UNDERTAKING NOT TO DISCLOSE: Q.B.D.)

Process Development Ltd v. Hogg (ANTON PILLER ORDER: UNDERTAKING TO RETAIN ITEMS IN SAFE CUSTODY: PROPERTY OF PLAINTIFF: WHETHER PERMISSIBLE TO REPORT TO POLICE: C.A.)

Witness summons

Barlow Clowes Gilt Managers Ltd (Ch.D.)

Privilege and Legal Professional Privilege

A.M. & S. Ltd v. E.C. Commission (ADMINISTRATIVE PROCEDURE: LAWYERS: CONFIDENTIALITY: ECJ)

British Coal Corporation v. Dennis Rye Ltd (No. 2) (EVIDENCE: LEGAL ADVISERS: DOCUMENTS CREATED FOR CIVIL PROCEEDINGS SUBSEQUENTLY HANDED TO POLICE: EFFECT OF PRIVILEGE: ATTORNEY-GENERAL'S GUIDELINES: VOLUNTARY DISCLOSURE IN COURSE OF CRIMINAL TRIAL: WHETHER PRIVILEGE WAIVED: ENTITLEMENT TO RETURN OF DOCUMENTS: C.A.)

CHC Software Card Ltd v. Hopkins & Wood (SOLICITOR'S DUTY: DISCOVERY: CONFIDENTIALITY: LEGAL PROFESSIONAL PRIVILEGE: INTERROGATORIES: Ch.D.)

English & American Insurance Co. Ltd v. Herbert Smith (EVIDENCE: LEGAL PROFESSIONAL PRIVILEGE: INNOCENT RECEIPT OF INFORMATION: Ch.D.)

Finers v. Miro (CONFIDENTIAL INFORMATION: SOLICITOR: CLIENT RELATIONSHIP: TRANSFER OF CLIENT'S ASSETS TO OVERSEAS COMPANIES UNDER SOLICITOR'S CONTROL: C.A.)

Gamlen Chemical Co. (U.K.) Ltd v. Rochem Ltd (CONSPIRACY TO INJURE: DISCOVERY: Ch.D.)

Hillegom Municipality v. Hillenius (BANKING: CONFIDENTIALITY: NATIONAL COURTS: CIVIL PROCEEDINGS: PROFESSIONAL PRIVILEGE: ECJ)

Hilti AG v. E.C. Commission (CONFIDENTIALITY OF BUSINESS SECRETS: INTERVENERS: APPLICABLE TO WRITTEN COMMUNICATIONS BETWEEN INDEPENDENT LAWYER AND CLIENT COMPANY: INTERESTS OF RIGHT OF DEFENCE: PROCEDURE: CFI)

Minnesota Mining & Manufacturing Co. v. Rennicks (U.K.) Ltd (CONFIDENTIAL DOCUMENTS USED IN U.S. PROCEEDINGS: U.S. PROTECTIVE ORDER: Ch.D.)

Santa Fe International Corp. v. Napier Shipping SA (PRACTICE: CONFIDENTIALITY: PATENT: INFRINGEMENT: PATENT AGENT'S PRIVILEGE: Scotland: O.H.)

Schering AG's Patent (PATENT: PRACTICE: LICENCES OF RIGHT: PATENT AGENTS: CONFIDENTIAL DOCUMENTS: AGENTS IN-HOUSE AND IN PRIVATE PRACTICE: Pat. Ct)

Solicitors (Re a firm of) (SOLICITOR: FIDUCIARY RELATIONSHIP WITH CLIENT: CONFIDENTIAL INFORMATION: ACQUISITION FROM COMPANIES CLOSELY ASSOCIATED WITH CLIENT: WHETHER DUTIES EXTEND TO ASSOCIATED COMPANIES: C.A.)

Public Interest

Attorney-General v. Guardian Newspaper Ltd, Observer Ltd, Times Newspapers Ltd (*Spycatcher*: FULL ACTION: BALANCING PUBLIC INTEREST IN FREEDOM OF SPEECH AND PRESS AGAINST PUBLIC INTEREST IN MAINTAINING CONFIDENTIALITY: Ch.D.: C.A.: H.L.)

Attorney-General v. Guardian Newspapers Ltd and The Observer Ltd (*Spycatcher*: INTERLOCUTORY INJUNCTION: NEWSPAPER ARTICLE OUTLINING ALLEGATIONS TO BE PUBLISHED IN BOOK: NEWSPAPERS NOT HAVING ACCESS TO AUTHOR'S MANUSCRIPT: PRIOR RESTRAINT OF PUBLICATION: Ch.D.: C.A.)

Attorney-General v. The Times Newspapers Ltd (SPECIAL POSITION OF CROWN AS CONFIDER OF INFORMATION: PUBLIC INTEREST CONSIDERATIONS: H.L.)

Barlow Clowes Gilt Managers Ltd (PRACTICE: DISCOVERY: PUBLIC INTEREST IMMUNITY: INFORMATION OBTAINED IN COMPULSORY LIQUIDATION OF COMPANY: COMPANY'S OFFICERS CHARGED WITH CRIMINAL OFFENCES: WITNESS SUMMONS ISSUED IN CRIMINAL PROCEEDINGS REQUIRING LIQUIDATORS TO DISCLOSE CONFIDENTIAL INFORMATION: WHETHER INFORMATION TO BE DISCLOSED: Ch.D.)

Company's Application (FORMER EMPLOYEE OF COMPANY PROVIDING FINANCIAL SERVICES: THREAT TO DISCLOSE CONFIDENTIAL INFORMATION TO REGULATORY BODY AND REVENUE: Ch.D.)

Hellewell v. Chief Constable of Derbyshire (OFFENDER PHOTOGRAPHED BY POLICE: DISCLOSURE: Q.B.D.)

Lion Laboratories Ltd v. Evans (PUBLICATION: C.A.)

Lord Advocate v. Scotsman Publications Ltd (BOOK, *Inside Intelligence*: NON-CONTENTS CASE: WHETHER SUFFICIENT PROOF FOR INTERDICT: Scotland: I.H.)

Marcel v. Commissioner of Police of the Metropolis (SEIZURE BY POLICE UNDER STATUTORY POWERS DURING CRIMINAL INVESTIGATIONS: *Subpoena duces tecum* SEEKING PRODUCTION BY POLICE OF DOCUMENTS FOR USE IN CIVIL PROCEEDINGS: OBJECTION TO PRODUCTION: Ch.D.: C.A.)

R. v. Monopolies and Mergers Commission, *ex p.* Elders IXL Ltd (DISCLOSURE BY MMC: Q.B.D.)

Times Newspapers Ltd v. MGN Ltd (INTERLOCUTORY INJUNCTION: THATCHER MEMOIRS: PUBLIC INTEREST IN PUBLICATION: C.A.)

W v. Egdell (PLAINTIFF DETAINED AS MENTAL PATIENT IN SECURE HOSPITAL: PSYCHIATRIST INSTRUCTED BY PLAINTIFF TO PREPARE INDEPENDENT REPORT FOR USE AT MENTAL HEALTH REVIEW TRIBUNAL: APPLICATION TO TRIBUNAL WITHDRAWN IN VIEW OF UNFAVOURABLE NATURE OF REPORT: PSYCHIATRIST'S DISCLOSURE OF REPORT TO HOSPITAL: COPIES SENT TO HOME OFFICE AND TRIBUNAL: WHETHER PSYCHIATRIST IN BREACH OF DUTY OF CONFIDENCE OWED TO PLAINTIFF: Ch.D.: C.A.)

X Health Authority v. Y (IDENTITY OF DOCTORS WITH AIDS: INFORMATION OBTAINED FROM CONFIDENTIAL HOSPITAL RECORDS: WHETHER PUBLICATION IN BREACH OF INJUNCTION A CONTEMPT: Q.B.D.)

Public Interest Immunity

Barlow Clowes Gilt Managers Ltd (PRACTICE: DISCOVERY: INFORMATION OBTAINED IN COMPULSORY LIQUIDATION OF COMPANY: COMPANY'S OFFICERS CHARGED WITH CRIMINAL OFFENCES: WITNESS SUMMONS ISSUED IN CRIMINAL PROCEEDINGS REQUIRING LIQUIDATORS TO DISCLOSE CONFIDENTIAL INFORMATION: WHETHER INFORMATION TO BE DISCLOSED: Ch.D.)

Restrictive Covenant (also known as **Restraint of Trade**). *See also under* **Crown Employee, Ex-employees** and **Fiduciary Duty/Fiduciary Relationship**

Austin Knight (U.K.) Ltd v. Hinds (NON-SOLICITATION CLAUSE IN EMPLOYMENT CONTRACT: WHETHER RESTRICTION REASONABLE: Ch.D.)

Ibcos Computers Ltd v. Barclays Mercantile Highland Finance Ltd (CONSTRUCTION: Ch.D.)

Lansing Linde Ltd v. Kerr (EX-EMPLOYEE: INTERLOCUTORY INJUNCTION: RESTRICTIVE COVENANT IN CONTRACT OF EMPLOYMENT: ACTION FOR BREACH: WHETHER INFORMATION ACQUIRED BY EMPLOYEE PROTECTABLE AS TRADE SECRETS: WHETHER INTERIM INJUNCTION TO BE GRANTED: C.A.)

Lawrence David Ltd v. Ashton (EX-EMPLOYEE: PERIOD OF RESTRAINT: C.A.)

Mont (J.A.) (U.K.) Ltd v. Mills (EX-EMPLOYEE'S SEVERANCE AGREEMENT: VALIDITY OF COVENANT: FORM OF INJUNCTION: APPROACH TO CONSTRUCTION OF RESTRICTIVE COVENANTS: GOOD FAITH: C.A.)

Poly Lina Ltd v. Finch (FORMER EMPLOYEE: WHETHER CONFIDENTIAL INFORMATION: EMBARGO ON ENGAGEMENTS WITH COMPETITOR: WIDTH OF COVENANT: ADEQUACY OF UNDERTAKING NOT TO DISCLOSE: Q.B.D.)

Scotland

Grant v. Procurator Fiscal (H.C.)
Harben Pumps (Scotland) Ltd v. Lafferty (O.H.)
Lord Advocate v. Scotsman Publications Ltd (I.H.)
Lord Advocate v. Scotsman Publications Ltd (O.H.: H.L.)
Santa Fe International Corp. v. Napier Shipping SA (O.H.)

Security Service

Attorney-General v. Brandon Book Publishers Ltd (*One Girl's War*. Ireland: H.C.)
Attorney-General v. Guardian Newspapers Ltd and The Observer Ltd (*Spycatcher*. Ch.D.: C.A.)

Seizure by Police

Marcel v. Commissioner of Police of the Metropolis (PUBLIC INTEREST: SEIZURE BY POLICE UNDER STATUTORY POWERS DURING CRIMINAL INVESTIGATIONS: *Subpoena duces tecum* SEEKING PRODUCTION BY POLICE OF DOCUMENTS FOR USE IN CIVIL PROCEEDINGS: OBJECTION TO PRODUCTION: Ch.D.: C.A.)

Sexual Conduct

Stephens v. Avery (LESBIAN RELATIONSHIP DISCLOSED TO RECIPIENT IN CONFIDENCE: RECIPIENT'S DUTY: COMMUNICATION OF INFORMATION TO NEWSPAPER: WHETHER BREACH OF CONFIDENCE ACTIONABLE: CAUSE OF ACTION: WHETHER INFORMATION CAPABLE OF PROTECTION: DUTY OF CONFIDENCE: Ch.D.)

Solicitation of customers

Series 5 Software Ltd v. Philip Clarke (COMPUTER SOURCE CODES: INTERLOCUTORY RELIEF: DELAY: INTERLOCUTORY INJUNCTIONS: PRINCIPLES: Ch.D.)

Springboard Doctrine

House of Spring Gardens Ltd v. Point Blank Ltd (DIRECTORS' LIABILITY FOR
COMMISSION OF TORTS: Ireland: H.C.: S.C.)
Roger Bullivant Ltd v. Ellis (EX-EMPLOYEE: CUSTOMER CARD INDEX: C.A.)
Universal Thermosensors Ltd v. Hibben (SCOPE OF INJUNCTIONS IN BREACH OF
CONFIDENCE: DISCRETION: ANTON PILLER PRACTICE: Ch.D.)

Spycatcher. See also under **Australia, Hong Kong, New Zealand,** etc.

Attorney-General v. Guardian Newspaper Ltd, Observer Ltd, Times Newspapers Ltd
(FULL ACTION: BREACH OF FIDUCIARY DUTY: INJUNCTION: PUBLICATION
AND AVAILABILITY OF BOOK WITHOUT AND WITHIN U.K.: BALANCING PUBLIC
INTEREST IN FREEDOM OF SPEECH AND PRESS AGAINST PUBLIC INTEREST IN
MAINTAINING CONFIDENTIALITY: DEFENCE OF INIQUITY: INJUNCTIONS
AGAINST FUTURE BREACHES: *Spycatcher 2*: "NO MAN SHALL PROFIT FROM HIS
OWN WRONG": THIRD PARTY IN POSSESSION OF CONFIDENTIAL
INFORMATION: KNOWLEDGE: *Turpis causa*: ACCOUNT OF PROFITS: Ch.D.:
C.A.: H.L.)
Attorney-General v. Guardian Newspapers Ltd and The Observer Ltd
(INTERLOCUTORY INJUNCTION: NEWSPAPER ARTICLE OUTLINING
ALLEGATIONS TO BE PUBLISHED IN BOOK: NEWSPAPERS NOT HAVING ACCESS
TO AUTHOR'S MANUSCRIPT: PRIOR RESTRAINT OF PUBLICATION: PUBLIC
INTEREST: ALLEGATIONS OF MISCONDUCT BY SECURITY SERVICE: AUTHOR'S
DUTY OF CONFIDENTIALITY TO CROWN: MATERIAL IN PUBLIC DOMAIN:
FORM OF INJUNCTION: Ch.D.: C.A.)
Attorney-General v. Newspaper Publishing plc (CONTEMPT: BREACH OF
CONFIDENCE: CRIMINAL CONTEMPT: NEWSPAPERS NOT BOUND BY
INJUNCTION NOT TO PUBLISH: INTENTION OF PUBLICATION: NATURAL
JUSTICE: Ch.D.: C.A.)
Attorney-General v. Guardian Newspapers Ltd (FORMER CROWN EMPLOYEE:
INTERLOCUTORY INJUNCTION: SUBSEQUENT PUBLICATION OUTSIDE
JURISDICTION: Ch.D.: C.A.: H.L.)
Times Newspapers Ltd v. Her Majesty's Attorney-General (CONTEMPT:
PUBLICATION: APPELLANT NOT PARTY TO INJUNCTIONS RESTRAINING
BREACH OF CONFIDENCE: APPEAL: H.L.)

Stolen Information

Union Carbide Corp. v. Naturin Ltd (CONVICTIONS PLEADED: CIVIL EVIDENCE
ACT: STRIKING OUT: C.A.)
Universal Thermosensors Ltd v. Hibben (STOLEN CUSTOMER INFORMATION: EX-
EMPLOYEES' COMPETING BUSINESS: ASSESSMENT OF DAMAGES: SCOPE OF
INJUNCTIONS IN BREACH OF CONFIDENCE: SPRINGBOARD DOCTRINE:
Ch.D.)

Thatcher Memoirs

Times Newspapers Ltd v. MGN Ltd (C.A.)

Trade Secrets

Harben Pumps (Scotland) Ltd v. Lafferty (EX-EMPLOYEE: IMPLIED TERMS OF
CONTRACT: Scotland: O.H.)

Copyright

Abuse of Dominant Position

Acquiescence

Adaptation

Agent Provocateur

Alteration to Original Work

Antecedent Works

Anton Piller Practice. *See* **Practice** (*Anton Piller Practice*)

Architectural Drawings

Cala Homes (South) Ltd v. Alfred McAlpine Homes East Ltd (No. 2) (INFRINGEMENT: ELECTION FOR ACCOUNT OF PROFITS: WHETHER ADDITIONAL STATUTORY DAMAGES AVAILABLE, FORM OF ORDER: Ch.D.)
Dubuffet (Jean) v. Régie Nationale des Usines Renault (*Droit moral*: France)
Potton Ltd v. Yorkclose Ltd (INFRINGEMENT: APPORTIONMENT OF PROFITS: Ch.D.)

Artistic Works

Amalgamated Mining Services Pty Ltd v. Warman International Ltd (ENGINEERING DRAWINGS: OVERLAP WITH DESIGN PROTECTION: ADDITIONAL DAMAGES: DESIGNS: C.-G.)
Clark v. David Allan & Co. Ltd (DESIGN DRAWINGS: INFRINGEMENT: GARMENT: WHETHER FINISHED GARMENT CONSTITUTES REPRODUCTION: VISUAL IMPACT: Scotland: O.H.)
Kambrook Distributing Pty Ltd v. Delaney (REPRODUCTION OF ORIGINAL DRAWINGS: ORIGINAL LOST OR DESTROYED: INFRINGEMENT: OWNERSHIP: SKETCHES PREPARED BY MANAGING DIRECTOR: INTENTION AS TO OWNERSHIP: Ch.D.)
Merchandising Corp. of America Inc. v. Harpbond Ltd (ADAM ANT: FACIAL MAKE-UP AS ARTISTIC WORK: C.A.)
Merlet v. Mothercare plc (INFRINGEMENT: BABY CAPE: WHETHER WORK OF ARTISTIC CRAFTSMANSHIP: SECTION 9(8) DEFENCE: Ch.D.: C.A.)
Ward (Geo.) (Moxley) Ltd v. Richard Sankey Ltd (INFRINGEMENT: COPYING AN IDEA: Ch.D.)
Warner Brothers Inc. v. The Roadrunner Ltd (SUBSISTENCE: Ch.D.)

Assignment

Stansfield v. Sovereign Music Ltd (PERFORMERS' RIGHTS: INFRINGEMENT: INTERLOCUTORY INJUNCTION: CONSENT TO RELEASE OF RECORDS: RECORDING AGREEMENT: Ch.D.)

Austria

Austro-Mechana GmbH v. Gramola Winter & Co. (EFTA: ENFORCEMENT: S.C.)
Sky Channel (No. 2) (CABLE TELEVISION: INTERPRETATION OF DECODING SATELLITE SIGNALS: ROYALTY: S.C.)
Satellite Television Broadcasting (CONTRACT: APPLICABLE LAW: BROADCASTING RIGHTS: SATELLITE TELEVISION BROADCASTS: Regional C.A.)

Authorising Copying

Abkco Music & Records Inc. v. Music Collection International Ltd (INFRINGEMENT: SOUND RECORDINGS: LICENCE GRANTED TO MANUFACTURE AND SELL OUTSIDE U.K.: C.A.)
Hutchison Personal Communications Ltd v. Hook Advertising Ltd (COUNTERCLAIM STRUCK OUT: SECONDARY INFRINGEMENT: Ch.D.)
Keays v. Dempster (PHOTOGRAPH: INFRINGEMENT: C.C., City of London)

Belgium

Imprimerie (SA) Thône v. Fernand Geubelle (INTELLIGENCE TEST: PUBLISHER AS CO-AUTHOR: *Locus standi*)

Promedia SA v. Borght (REGISTERED DESIGN: PROTECTED PRODUCT: ADVERTISING MATERIAL: C.A.)

Bootleg Records. *See under* **Sound Recordings**

Breach of Confidence

Alfa Laval Cheese Systems Ltd v. Wincanton Engineering Ltd (Ch.D.)
Ashmore v. Douglas-Home (Ch.D.)
CHC Software Card Ltd v. Hopkins & Wood (Ch.D.)
Dun & Bradstreet Ltd v. Typesetting Facilities Ltd (Ch.D.)
Format Communications Manufacturing Ltd v. ITT (U.K.) Ltd (C.A.)
House of Spring Gardens Ltd v. Point Blank Ltd (Ireland: H.C.: S.C.)
Hytrac Conveyors Ltd v. Conveyors International Ltd (C.A.)
Ibcos Computers Ltd v. Barclays Mercantile Highland Finance Ltd (Ch.D.)
John (Elton) v. James (Ch.D.)
Shelley Films Ltd v. Rex Features Ltd (Ch.D.)
VNU Publications Ltd v. Ziff Davis (U.K.) Ltd (Ch.D.)
Weir Pumps Ltd v. CML Pumps Ltd (Ch.D.)

Breach of Contract

House of Spring Gardens Ltd v. Point Blank Ltd (Ireland: H.C.: S.C.)
House of Spring Gardens Ltd v. Point Blank Ltd (DAMAGES: Ireland: H.C.)

Broadcasts and Broadcasting Rights

AIRC Ltd v. PPL (LICENCE TO BROADCAST SOUND RECORDINGS: PERFORMING RIGHT TRIBUNAL: Ch.D.)
AIRC Ltd v. Phonographic Performance Ltd (COMMERCIAL RADIO: LICENCE TO BROADCAST SOUND RECORDINGS: PRINCIPLES TO BE EXERCISED: RELEVANCE OF EARLIER PERFORMING RIGHT TRIBUNAL DECISION: ASSESSMENT OF ROYALTY: BASIS: Cprt Trib.)
BBC Enterprises Ltd v. Hi-Tech Xtravision Ltd (UNAUTHORISED RECEPTION: ENCRYPTED SATELLITE BROADCASTS RECEIVABLE OUTSIDE U.K.: Ch.D.: C.A.: H.L.)
BBC v. British Satellite Broadcasting Ltd (FAIR DEALING: USE OF EXTRACTS FROM BROADCASTS OF FOOTBALL MATCHES IN SPORTS NEWS PROGRAMME: EXTRACTS SHORT AND ACCOMPANIED BY VERBAL REPORTS: Ch.D.)
BBC v. E.C. Commission (WEEKLY LISTINGS OF TV PROGRAMMES: REFUSAL TO PERMIT REPRODUCTION IN INDEPENDENT TV GUIDE: ARTICLE 86: CFI)
Copyright (Broadcasting) Draft Directive (SATELLITE BROADCASTING: CABLE RE-TRANSMISSION: COPYRIGHT AND NEIGHBOURING RIGHTS: PERFORMERS' RIGHTS: SPECIAL RULE FOR BROADCAST OF PHONOGRAMS: COMPETITION RULES: E.C. Council)
Independent Television Publications Ltd v. E.C. Commission (WEEKLY LISTINGS OF TV PROGRAMMES: REFUSAL TO PERMIT REPRODUCTION IN INDEPENDENT TV GUIDE: ARTICLE 86: CFI)
Koelman v. E.C. Commission (RE-TRANSMISSION OF PROGRAMMES BY CABLE: STANDARD AGREEMENT: OWNERSHIP: RADIO MATERIAL: COLLECTING SOCIETY: ALLEGED BREACH OF ARTICLES 85 AND 86: Case T–575/93: CFI)
News Group Newspapers Ltd v. Independent Television Publications Ltd (TELEVISION LISTINGS: SETTLEMENT OF TERMS FOR PROVISION OF STATUTORY INFORMATION BY BROADCASTERS TO PUBLISHERS: Cprt Trib.)

Performing Right Society Ltd v. Marlin Communal Aerials Ltd (CABLE TELEVISION: Ireland: S.C.)

Phonographic Performance (Ireland) Ltd v. J. Somers (Inspector of Taxes) (VAT PAYABLE ON SUPPLY OF SERVICES: REMUNERATION FOR BROADCASTING OF SOUND RECORDINGS: Ireland: H.C.)

Phonographic Performance Ltd v. Retail Broadcast Services Ltd (STATUTORY LICENCE TO BROADCAST: NOTICE TO LICENSING BODY PRIOR TO EXERCISING RIGHT: WHETHER STRICT COMPLIANCE WITH STATUTORY REQUIREMENTS MANDATORY: Ch.D.)

Radio Telefis Eireann v. E.C. Commission (WEEKLY LISTINGS OF TV PROGRAMMES: REFUSAL TO PERMIT REPRODUCTION IN INDEPENDENT TV GUIDE: ARTICLE 86: CFI)

Satellite Television Broadcasting (CONTRACT: APPLICABLE LAW: BROADCASTING RIGHTS: Austria: Regional C.A.)

Secretary of State for the Home Department v. Central Broadcasting Ltd (INTERVIEW WITH SERIAL KILLER: WHETHER PUBLIC INTEREST REQUIRED BROADCAST TO BE RESTRAINED: RELEVANCE OF FREEDOM OF SPEECH: Ch.D.: C.A.)

SUISA (Swiss Society of Authors & Publishers) v. Rediffusion AG (CABLE TELEVISION: FOREIGN BROADCASTS: Switzerland)

Brochure

Work Model Enterprises Ltd v. Ecosystem Ltd (INFRINGEMENT: COPYING WORDS OF BROCHURE: CLAIM FOR DAMAGES RESULTING FROM COMPETITION GENERATED BY INFRINGING BROCHURE: Ch.D.)

Building Plans

Oliver Homes (Manufacturing) v. Hamilton (INFRINGEMENT: BUILDING PLANS AND DESIGNS: HOUSE KIT PLANS: USE OF PLANS NOT LICENCES SEPARATELY FROM SALE OF KIT: Scotland: O.H.)

Cable Television. *See under* **Television**

Collaborative Works

Ponty v. Chamberland (COLLABORATIVE WORKS: *Droit moral*: WHO MAY SUE: France: S.C.)

Collecting Societies

Basset v. SACEM (RESTRICTIVE PRACTICES: S.C.: France)

GEMA (Re) (RESTRICTIVE PRACTICES: INWARD PROCESSING: CUSTOM PRESSING: E.C. Comm.)

Hérault v. SACEM (PERFORMING RIGHT: DOMINANT POSITION: MUSIC: LICENCE: France: C.A.)

Koelman v. E.C. Commission (STANDARD AGREEMENT: OWNERSHIP: RADIO MATERIAL: ALLEGED BREACH OF ARTICLES 85 AND 86: Case T–575/93: CFI)

Magazines in Hairdressing Establishments (*Locus standi*: ENTITLEMENT TO FEES ON LENDING OR HIRING WORKS FOR COMMERCIAL PURPOSES: Germany: S.C.)

Ministère Public v. Lucazeau (SACEM, *partie civile*) (INFRINGEMENT: STATUS: CRIMINAL OFFENCE: PERFORMANCE: RESTRICTIVE PRACTICES: DOMINANT POSITION: ABUSE: France: C.A.)

Performing Right Societies (RESTRICTIVE PRACTICES: PARALLEL IMPORTS: ROYALTIES: NOTICE: E.C. Comm.)

SDRM's Practices (RESTRICTIVE PRACTICES: FOREIGN WORKS: IMPORTS: DISCRIMINATORY PRACTICES: DOMINANT POSITION: France: Competition Commission)

Thames & Hudson Ltd v. Design and Artists Copyright Society Ltd (INFRINGEMENT: CRIMINAL PROSECUTION BY COLLECTING SOCIETY AGAINST PUBLISHERS AND DIRECTORS: DECLARATION OF NON-INFRINGEMENT: FAIR DEALING: STAY: Ch.D.)

Collective Works

Robert (Daniel) v. Soc. Crehallet-Folliot-Recherche et Publicité (INDIVIDUAL AUTHOR'S RIGHTS: EDITOR'S NAME: UNFAIR COMPETITION: France: S.C.)

Le Monde (Sàrl) v. Société Microfor Inc. (OWNER'S RIGHTS: CONSENTS: REPRODUCTION: INDEXES: INTELLECTUAL CONTENT: DERIVED WORKS: PRESS REVIEW: BIBLIOGRAPHIES AND EXTRACTS: France: S.C.)

Commissioned Work

Apple Corps. Ltd v. Cooper (OWNERSHIP: ESTOPPEL: Ch.D.)

Breville Europe plc v. Thorn EMI Domestic Appliances Ltd (REGISTERED DESIGN: INFRINGEMENT: TEST: SANDWICH TOASTERS: DRAWINGS: PLASTERCASTS OF TOASTED SANDWICHES: WHETHER SCULPTURES: PROPER PROPRIETOR: Pat. Ct)

Compilation of Stories

Alexander Bihi Zenou v. Michel Colucci (France: C.A.)

Ashmore v. Douglas-Home (INFRINGEMENT: DRAMATIC WORK: ALTERATION TO ORIGINAL WORK: TRANSLATION: Ch.D.)

Independent Television Publications Ltd v. Time Out Ltd (INFRINGEMENT: TV PROGRAMME SCHEDULES: Ch.D.)

Waterlow Directories Ltd v. Reed Information Services Ltd (INFRINGEMENT: LEGAL DIRECTORIES: COPYING OF NAMES AND ADDRESSES TO COMPILE OWN DIRECTORY: Ch.D.)

Computer Programs and Software

Alexander Bihi Zenou v. Michel Colucci (COMPILATION OF STORIES: France: C.A.)

Anacon Corporation Ltd v. Environmental Research Technology Ltd (CIRCUIT DIAGRAMS: WHETHER ARTISTIC WORKS BY NET LISTS AND CIRCUIT BOARDS OR LITERARY WORKS: Ch.D.)

Apple Computer Inc. v. Segimex Sàrl (France)

Artware (Sárl) v. Groupe D'Utilisation Francophone D'Informatique (RIGHT TO MAKE BACK-UP COPIES: ANTI-PROTECTION PROCESSES: France: S.C.)

Atari Inc. v. Philips Electronics Ltd (INFRINGEMENT: INSPECTION: PRACTICE: Ch.D.)

Computer Programs (draft directive) (E.C. Council)

Computer Programs (protection of) (MARKETING RIGHTS: Germany: S.C.)

Dun & Bradstreet Ltd v. Typesetting Facilities Ltd (COMPUTERISED DATABASE: INSPECTION BEFORE SERVICE OF STATEMENT OF CLAIM: INFORMATION IN ELECTRONIC FORM, SO VISUAL INSPECTION OF DISKS USELESS: DISCLOSURE OF CONTENTS REQUIRED: PRACTICE: Ch.D.)

Express Newspapers plc v. Liverpool Daily Post & Echo plc (INFRINGEMENT: ORIGINALITY: WORK PERFORMED BY COMPUTER: LOTTERIES: Ch.D.)

Format Communications Manufacturing Ltd v. ITT (U.K.) Ltd (INFRINGEMENT: DISCOVERY AND INSPECTION: SAFEGUARDS: C.A.)

Contract

Contract, Inducing Breach

Contract, Publishing

Copyright Management Society

Costs. *See* **Practice** (*Costs*)

Counsel's Duty to Court

Apac Rowena Ltd v. Norpol Packaging Ltd (ASSIGNED MATTERS: INTERLOCUTORY RELIEF: FAILURE TO SERVE STATEMENT OF CLAIM: Ch.D.)

Counterfeit Goods

Uruguay Round Treaties (reporting, *inter alia*: GATT: INTELLECTUAL PROPERTY: TRIPS RULES PROHIBITING RELEASE INTO FREE CIRCULATION: ECJ)

Criminal Liability Offence

Amstrad Consumer Electronics plc v. The British Phonograph Industry Ltd (INFRINGEMENT: HOME TAPING: DOUBLE-HEADED CASSETTE RECORDERS: DECLARATION: EFFECT OF COPYRIGHT WARNING NOTICE: KNOWLEDGE AND INTENT: INCITEMENT: Ch.D.: C.A.)
Holmes v. DPP (RELEVANT TIME OF MAKING COPY: D.C.)
Thames & Hudson Ltd v. Design and Artists Copyright Society Ltd (INFRINGEMENT: PROSECUTION BY COLLECTING SOCIETY AGAINST PUBLISHERS AND DIRECTORS: DECLARATION OF NON-INFRINGEMENT: FAIR DEALING: STAY: Ch.D.)
The Reject Shop plc v. Robert Manners (SECONDARY INFRINGEMENT: SUBSISTENCE: ENLARGED PHOTOCOPIES: ORIGINALITY: WHETHER SKILL AND LABOUR INVOLVED: APPEAL BY WAY OF CASE STATED: PRACTICE: COSTS: Q.B.D.)

Crown Copyright

Ironside v. H.M. Attorney-General (INFRINGEMENT: COINAGE DESIGNS: Ch.D.)

Damages

A.&M. Records v. Video Collection International Limited (INFRINGEMENT: SOUND RECORDINGS: OWNERSHIP: EQUITABLE OWNERSHIP: ADDITIONAL DAMAGES: Ch.D.)
Allibert SA v. O'Connor (ASSESSMENT OF DAMAGES: INTEREST: Ireland: H.C.)
Amalgamated Mining Services Pty Ltd v. Warman International Ltd (ADDITIONAL DAMAGES: C.-G.)
Banks v. CBS Songs Ltd (WHETHER CLAIM FOR CONVERSION DAMAGES STATUTE BARRED: Ch.D.: C.A.)
Digital Equipment Corp. v. Darkcrest Ltd (CROSS-UNDERTAKING IN DAMAGES: Ch.D.)
GEMA's Reproduction Tariffs (MUSICAL WORKS: VIDEOCASSETTES AND FILMS: INFRINGEMENT: ASSESSMENT OF DAMAGES: Germany: S.C.)
House of Spring Gardens Ltd v. Point Blank Ltd (OVERLAPPING HEADS OF DAMAGE: Ireland: H.C.)
Infabrics Ltd v. Jaytex (INQUIRY AS TO DAMAGES: OVERLAPPING HEADS OF DAMAGE: Ch.D.)
John Richardson Computers Ltd v. Flanders (DEFENDANT'S RIGHT TO INQUIRY AS TO DAMAGES ON PLAINTIFF'S CROSS-UNDERTAKING: Ch.D.)

Lewis Trusts v. Bambers Stores Ltd (GARMENTS: CONVERSION DAMAGES: WHETHER OVERLAPPING WITH DAMAGES FOR INFRINGEMENT: POINT OF CONVERSION: C.A.)

Nichols Advanced Vehicle Systems Inc. v. Rees (No. 3) (RACING CARS: INQUIRY AS TO DAMAGES: CONVERSION DAMAGES: ASSESSMENT OF AGGRAVATED DAMAGES: Ch.D.)

Nichols Advanced Vehicle Systems Inc. v. Rees (No. 2) (PRACTICE: DELAY IN PURSUING ENQUIRY: C.A.)

Paramount Pictures Corporation v. Cablelink Ltd (TELEVISION CABLE DIFFUSION SERVICE: LAW IN CINEMATOGRAPH FILM: H.C.)

Paterson Zochonis Ltd v. Merfarken Packaging Ltd (PRINTER'S DUTY OF CARE: STRIKING OUT: C.A.)

Ransburg-Gema AG v. Electrostatic Plant Systems Ltd (CLAIM TO CONVERSION DAMAGES NOT LOST IN RESPECT OF AMENDMENTS MADE AFTER COMMENCEMENT OF CD&P.A.88: C.A.)

Rubycliff Ltd v. Plastic Engineers Ltd (CROSS UNDERTAKING IN DAMAGES: SECTION 9(8): CONSEQUENTIAL DAMAGES: Ch.D.)

Sillitoe v. McGraw-Hill Book Co. (U.K.) Ltd (Ch.D.)

Smith v. Greenfield (CONVERSION DAMAGES: INNOCENCE: Northern Ireland: H.C.)

Wickstrand v. Förening Svenska Tonsättares Internationella Musikbyrå (EXPLOITATION RIGHTS: PUBLIC PERFORMANCE: PRIVATE USE: Sweden: S.C.)

Deceased Author

Foujita v. Sàrl Art Conception Realisation (*Droit moral*: ABUSE: France: S.C.)

Declaration. *See* Practice (*Declaration*)

Defamation

Charleston v. News Group Newspapers Ltd (NEWSPAPER ARTICLE: PHOTOGRAPHS: ACTORS' FACES SUPERIMPOSED ON PORNOGRAPHIC PICTURES: EXPLANATORY TEXT: CONTEXT: C.A.)

Defences

Associated Newspapers Group plc v. News Group Newspapers Ltd (THE WINDSOR CORRESPONDENCE: FAIR DEALING: INTERLOCUTORY INJUNCTION: Ch.D.)

Davis (J.&S.) (Holdings) Ltd v. Wright Health Group Ltd (INFRINGEMENT: DENTAL IMPRESSION TRAYS: ORIGINALITY: DRAWINGS: SCULPTURES: NON-EXPERT DEFENCE: SUBSTANTIAL PART: Ch.D.)

EMI Records Ltd v. The CD Specialists Ltd (SOUND RECORDING RIGHTS: BOOTLEG RECORDS: ARTICLE 30 DEFENCE: WHETHER COPYRIGHT OWNER CONSENTED: EXHAUSTION OF RIGHTS: Ch.D.)

Express Newspapers plc v. News (U.K.) Ltd (FAIR DEALING DEFENCE: MEANING OF SUFFICIENT ACKNOWLEDGEMENT: PUBLIC INTEREST DEFENCE: IMPLIED LICENCE: APPROBATION AND REPROBATION: Ch.D.)

Guilford Kapwood Ltd v. Embsay Fabrics Ltd (SECTION 9(8) DEFENCE: Ch.D.)

Ibcos Computers Ltd v. Barclays Mercantile Highland Finance Ltd (COMPUTER SOFTWARE: SOURCE CODE: *British Leyland* DEFENCE: Ch.D.)

Lansing Bagnall Ltd v. Buccaneer Lift Parts Ltd (INFRINGEMENT: EURO-DEFENCE: C.A.)

Merlet v. Mothercare plc (INFRINGEMENT: BABY CAPE: WHETHER WORK OF ARTISTIC CRAFTSMANSHIP: SECTION 9(8) DEFENCE: Ch.D.: C.A.)

Rose Plastics GmbH v. Wm Beckett & Co. (Plastics) Ltd (SECTION 9(8) DEFENCE: *Catnic* DEFENCE: Ch.D.)

Schweppes Ltd v. Wellingtons Ltd (INFRINGEMENT: ORDER 14: SCHWEPPES: SCHLURPPES: WHETHER PARODY ARGUABLE DEFENCE: SUMMARY JUDGMENT: Ch.D.)

Waterlow Directories Ltd v. Reed Information Services Ltd (EURO-DEFENCES: Ch.D.)

Wyko Group plc v. Cooper Roller Bearings Co. Ltd (ENGINEERING DRAWINGS: DECLARATION OF NON-INFRINGEMENT: SPARE PARTS DEFENCE: Ch.D.)

Yale Security Products Ltd v. Newman (EURO-DEFENCES: Ch.D.)

Delivery Up. *See* **Practice** (*Delivery Up*)

Derived Works

Le Monde (Sàrl) v. Société Microfor Inc. (INDEXES: INTELLECTUAL CONTENT: PRESS REVIEW: BIBLIOGRAPHIES AND EXTRACTS: France: S.C.: C.A.)

Design Copyright. *See under* **Registered Design & Design Copyright Cases**

Directors' Liability/Directors' Personal Liability

Besson (A.P.) Ltd v. Fulleon Ltd (INNOCENT INFRINGEMENT: DIRECTORS' PERSONAL LIABILITY: Ch.D.)

Evans & Sons Ltd v. Spritebrand Ltd (INFRINGEMENT: COMPANY DIRECTOR: AUTHORISATION: C.A.)

House of Spring Gardens Ltd v. Point Blank Ltd (SPRINGBOARD DOCTRINE: DIRECTORS' LIABILITY FOR COMMISSION OF TORTS: Ireland: H.C.: S.C.)

Kambrook Distributing Pty Ltd v. Delaney (OWNERSHIP: SKETCHES PREPARED BY MANAGING DIRECTOR: INTENTION AS TO OWNERSHIP: CONFIRMATORY ASSIGNMENT FOR PURPOSE OF PROCEEDINGS: Ch.D.)

Dramatic and Musical Performers' Protection Act 1958

Warner Bros Records Inc. v. Parr (BOOTLEGGING: WHETHER ACTIONABLE BY RECORD COMPANIES: D&MPPACT: PERFORMERS' PROTECTION ACT 1963: Ch.D.: C.A.)

Dramatic Work

Ashmore v. Douglas-Home (INFRINGEMENT: ALTERATION TO ORIGINAL WORK: TRANSLATION: COMPILATION: ADAPTATION: Ch.D.)

Wiseman v. George Weidenfeld & Nicholson Ltd (INFRINGEMENT: JOINT AUTHORSHIP: Ch.D.)

Drawings

Biotrading and Financing OY v. Biohit Ltd (INFRINGEMENT: ORIGINALITY: RELEVANCE OF TITLE TO EARLIER DRAWINGS: Ch.D.)

Breville Europe plc v. Thorn EMI Domestic Appliances Ltd (INFRINGEMENT: TEST: SANDWICH TOASTERS: PLASTERCASTS OF TOASTED SANDWICHES: WHETHER SCULPTURES: PROPER PROPRIETOR: COMMISSIONED WORK: Pat. Ct)

Droit Moral

Argos Films, SA v. Ivens (EXPLANATORY NOTE IN CREDITS OF FILM: BREACH IF FORBIDDEN BY AUTHOR: France: S.C.)

Cohen (Bella) v. Chaine (Catherine) (CO-AUTHORSHIP: POSTHUMOUS PUBLICATION: LIABILITY OF PUBLISHER: France)

Dubuffet (Jean) v. Régie Nationale des Usines Renault (ARCHITECTURAL WORKS: France)

Editions Gallimard v. Hamish Hamilton Ltd (France)

Foujita v. Sàrl Art Conception Realisation (DECEASED AUTHOR: ABUSE: France: S.C.)

Gabon (The State of) v. Société Nationale de Télévision en Couleurs "Antenne 2" (FILM PRODUCTION: France: S.C.)

Morrison Leahy Music Ltd v. Lightbond Ltd (MEDLEY OF SONGS: WHETHER CHARACTER OF MUSICAL WORKS ALTERED: WHETHER LYRICS MODIFIED RIGHTS: RIGHT OF INTEGRITY: Ch.D.)

Ponty v. Chamberland (COLLABORATIVE WORKS: WHO MAY SUE: France: S.C.)

Rowe v. Walt Disney Productions (CONFLICT OF LAWS: France: S.C.)

Widmaier v. SPADEM (COPYRIGHT MANAGEMENT SOCIETY: France: S.C.)

Duration of Protection

Copyright (Ancillary Rights) Draft Directive (RENTAL AND LENDING RIGHTS: PERFORMERS' RIGHTS: E.C. Council)

Duty of Care

Amstrad Consumer Electronics plc v. The British Phonograph Industry Ltd (INFRINGEMENT: HOME TAPING: KNOWLEDGE AND INTENT: NEGLIGENCE: Ch.D.: C.A.)

Paterson Zochonis Ltd v. Merfarken Packaging Ltd (INFRINGEMENT: NEGLIGENCE: PRINTER'S INNOCENCE: PRINTER'S DUTY OF CARE: C.A.)

Employer and Employee

Private Research Ltd v. Brosnan (INFRINGEMENT: INTERLOCUTORY INJUNCTION: BREACH OF CONFIDENCE: MISUSE OF CONFIDENTIAL INFORMATION: Ireland: H.C.)

Enforceability

ZYX Music GmbH v. King (INFRINGEMENT: DISCO ARRANGEMENT OF POPULAR SONG: INNOCENT INFRINGEMENT BY PLAINTIFF: ENTITLEMENT TO RELIEF: SECONDARY INFRINGEMENT: ADDITIONAL DAMAGES: FLAGRANCY OF INFRINGEMENT: INJUNCTION: Ch.D.)

Engineering Drawings. *See under* Mechanical or Engineering Drawings

Exclusive Licence

Coditel SA v. Ciné Vog Films SA (PERFORMING RIGHTS: RESTRICTIVE PRACTICES: ECJ)

Exhaustion of Rights

EMI Electrola GmbH v. Patricia IM- und Export Verwaltungs GmbH (IMPORTS: ARTICLE 36 EEC: EXERCISE OF COPYRIGHT: ARTIFICIAL PARTITIONING: EXPIRY OF COPYRIGHT PERIOD IN DENMARK, NOT IN GERMANY: ECJ)

EMI Records Ltd v. The CD Specialists Ltd (INFRINGEMENT: GERMAN IMPORTS: ARTICLE 30 DEFENCE: WHETHER COPYRIGHT OWNER CONSENTED: Ch.D.)

Knoll International Gavina SpA v. Sàrl Aliotta Diffusion (IMPORTS: DESIGN COPYRIGHT: NO DESIGN RIGHT UNDER ITALIAN LAW: ARTICLE 36(1): France: S.C.)

Musik-Vertrieb Membran GmbH v. GEMA (IMPORTS: Germany)

Warner Brothers Inc. v. Christiansen (LENDING RIGHTS: SPECIFIC SUBJECT-MATTER: IMPORTS: VIDEOS: ECJ)

Exploitation Rights

Wickstrand v. Förening Svenska Tonsättares Internationella Musikbyrå (DAMAGES: "PUBLIC PERFORMANCE": PRIVATE USE: Sweden: S.C.)

Fair Dealing

Associated Newspapers Group plc v. News Group Newspapers Ltd (INFRINGEMENT: THE WINDSOR CORRESPONDENCE: Ch.D.)

BBC v. British Satellite Broadcasting Ltd (INFRINGEMENT: USE OF EXTRACTS FROM BROADCASTS OF FOOTBALL MATCHES IN SPORTS NEWS PROGRAMME: EXTRACTS SHORT AND ACCOMPANIED BY VERBAL REPORTS: WHETHER FOR PURPOSE OF REPORTING CURRENT EVENTS: C.D.&P.A.88: Ch.D.)

Express Newspapers plc v. News (U.K.) Ltd ("TIT FOR TAT" COPYING OF NEWSPAPER STORIES: SUBSISTENCE OF: WHETHER REPORTER'S COPYRIGHT STILL EXISTED IN LAW: MEANING OF "SUFFICIENT ACKNOWLEDGEMENT": Ch.D.)

Express Newspapers plc v. News (U.K.) Ltd (ORDER 14 APPLICATION: MUTUAL COPYING OF NEWS STORIES: Ch.D.)

John (Elton) v. James (LIMITATION: LACHES: ACQUIESCENCE: ESTOPPEL: Ch.D.)

Kennard v. Lewis (INFRINGEMENT: CND PAMPHLET: Ch.D.)

Sillitoe v. McGraw-Hill Book Co. (U.K.) Ltd (INFRINGEMENT: STUDY NOTES FOR STUDENTS: WHETHER SUBSTANTIAL REPRODUCTION: KNOWLEDGE: SUFFICIENT ACKNOWLEDGEMENT: Ch.D.)

Thames & Hudson Ltd v. Design and Artists Copyright Society Ltd (INFRINGEMENT: CRIMINAL PROSECUTION BY COLLECTING SOCIETY AGAINST PUBLISHERS AND DIRECTORS: DECLARATION OF NON-INFRINGEMENT: STAY: Ch.D.)

Time Warner Entertainments Company LP v. Channel Four Television Corporation plc (INFRINGEMENT: FILM: *A Clockwork Orange*: WHETHER EXCERPTS SHOWN ON TELEVISION FAIR DEALING FOR PURPOSE OF CRITICISM OR REVIEW: C.A.)

Fees

BACTA v. Phonographic Performance Ltd (SOUND RECORDINGS: LICENCE SCHEME: BACKGROUND MUSIC FROM JUKEBOXES: Cprt Trib.)

GEMA's Reproduction Tariffs (MUSICAL WORKS: VIDEOCASSETTES AND FILMS: LICENCE FEES: Germany: S.C.)

Magazines in Hairdressing Establishments (COPYRIGHT COLLECTING SOCIETY: *Locus standi*: ENTITLEMENT TO FEES ON LENDING OR HIRING WORKS FOR COMMERCIAL PURPOSES: Germany: S.C.)

Film

Adventure Film Productions SA v. Tully (WRONGFUL INTERFERENCE WITH GOODS: INTERLOCUTORY ORDER FOR DELIVERY UP: STRENGTH OF CASE TO OWNERSHIP OF FILM: Ch.D.)

Argos Films, SA v. Ivens (*Droit moral*: EXPLANATORY NOTE IN CREDITS: France: S.C.)

Beggars Banquet Records Ltd v. Carlton Television Ltd (WRONGFUL INTERFERENCE WITH GOODS: FILM FOOTAGE: OWNERSHIP: Ch.D.)

Century Communications Ltd v. Mayfair Entertainment U.K. Ltd (SUBSISTENCE: INFRINGEMENT: THEATRICAL DISTRIBUTION: Ch.D.)

Chloe Production Sàrl v. Gaumont (DISTRIBUTION CONTRACT: France: S.C.)

Gabon (The State of) v. Société Nationale de Télévision en Coulours "Antenne 2" (*Droit moral*: France: S.C.)

Gantenbrink v. BBC (UNDERTAKINGS: LIBERTY TO APPLY: Ch.D.)

GEMA's Reproduction Tariffs (MUSICAL WORKS: VIDEOCASSETTES AND FILMS: LICENCE FEES: INFRINGEMENT: ASSESSMENT OF DAMAGES: Germany: S.C.)

Federaciónde Distribuidores Cinematográficos v. Spain (DISTRIBUTION: LICENCES TO DUB FILMS FROM NON-MEMBER STATES INTO SPANISH: NATIONAL LEGISLATION RESTRICTING LICENCES TO DISTRIBUTORS OF SPANISH FILMS: ECJ)

Musa v. Le Maitre (PROSECUTION: WHETHER FILM PUBLISHED: CRIMINAL PRACTICE: Q.B.D.)

Paramount Pictures Corporation v. Cablelink Ltd (INFRINGEMENT: TELEVISION CABLE DIFFUSION SERVICE: DAMAGES: LAW IN CINEMATOGRAPH FILM: ABUSE OF DOMINANT POSITION: ARTICLES 85 AND 86: Ireland: H.C.)

R. v. Lloyd (CRIME: TAKING FILMS TO COPY: CONSPIRACY TO STEAL: C.A.)

Secretary of State for the Home Department v. Central Broadcasting Ltd (INFRINGEMENT: INTERVIEW WITH SERIAL KILLER: AUTHOR: ARRANGEMENTS FOR MAKING FILM: Ch.D.: C.A.)

Shelley Films Ltd v. Rex Features Ltd (INFRINGEMENT: PHOTOGRAPH OF FILM COSTUMES, PROSTHESES AND SET: Ch.D.)

Shelltrie Distribution Sàrl v. SNTF (France)

Time Warner Entertainments Company LP v. Channel Four Television Corporation plc (INFRINGEMENT: *A Clockwork Orange*: WHETHER EXCERPTS SHOWN ON TELEVISION FAIR DEALING FOR PURPOSE OF CRITICISM OR REVIEW: C.A.)

Western Front Ltd v. Vestron Inc. (LICENCE AGREEMENT: STRIKING OUT: UNLAWFUL INTERFERENCE WITH CONTRACTUAL RELATIONS: NEGLIGENCE: DEFAMATION: Ch.D.)

Foreign Broadcasts

SUISA (Swiss Society of Authors & Publishers) v. Rediffusion AG (CABLE TELEVISION: Switzerland)

France

Alexander Bihi Zenou v. Michel Colucci (COMPILATION OF STORIES: C.A.)

Apple Computer Inc. v. Segimex Sàrl (COMPUTER PROGRAMS)

Argos Films, SA v. Ivens (*Droit moral*: EXPLANATORY NOTE IN CREDITS OF FILM: BREACH IF FORBIDDEN BY AUTHOR: S.C.)

Artware (Sàrl) v. Groupe D'Utilisation Francophone D'Informatique (SOFTWARE SALES: RIGHT TO MAKE BACK-UP COPIES: COMPUTER SOFTWARE: ANTI-PROTECTION PROCESSES: S.C.)

Atari Ireland Ltd v. Valadon (VIDEO GAMES)

Babolat Maillot Witt SA v. Pachot

Basset v. SACEM (RESTRICTIVE PRACTICES: COLLECTING SOCIETIES: S.C.)

Chloe Production Sàrl v. Gaumont (FILMS: DISTRIBUTION CONTRACT: S.C.)

Cohen (Bella) v. Chaine (Catherine) (CO-AUTHORSHIP: POSTHUMOUS PUBLICATION: *Droit moral*: LIABILITY OF PUBLISHER)

Dubuffet (Jean) v. Régie Nationale des Usines Renault (ARCHITECTURAL WORKS: *Droit moral*)

Editions Gallimard v. Hamish Hamilton Ltd (*Droit moral*)

Financial Times Ltd v. Sàrl Ecopress (NEWSPAPER ARTICLES)

Foujita v. Sàrl Art Conception Realisation (COPYRIGHT: DECEASED AUTHOR: *Droit moral*: ABUSE: S.C.)

Gabon (The State of) v. Société Nationale de Télévision en Coulours "Antenne 2" (*Droit moral*: FILM PRODUCTION: S.C.)

Hérault v. SACEM (PERFORMING RIGHT: COLLECTING SOCIETY: DOMINANT POSITION: MUSIC: LICENCE: C.A.)

Knoll International Gavina SpA v. Sàrl Aliotta Diffusion (IMPORTS: DESIGN EXHAUSTION OF RIGHTS: NO DESIGN RIGHT UNDER ITALIAN LAW: ARTICLE 36(1): S.C.)

Lallier v. Lux (TRADE MARK: REGISTRATION: OWNERSHIP: PRIOR USE: IDEAS: GAMES: C.A.)

Le Monde (Sàrl) v. Société Microfor Inc. (COPYRIGHT: COLLECTIVE WORKS: OWNER'S RIGHTS: CONSENTS: REPRODUCTION: INDEXES: INTELLECTUAL CONTENT: DERIVED WORKS: PRESS REVIEW: BIBLIOGRAPHIES AND EXTRACTS: S.C.: C.A.)

Massey-Ferguson Ltd v. Bepco France SA (SPARE PARTS: TRADE MARK: PACKAGING: UNFAIR COMPETITION)

Ministère Public v. Lucazeau (SACEM, *partie civile*) (INFRINGEMENT: COLLECTION AGENCIES: STATUS: CRIMINAL OFFENCE: PERFORMANCE: RESTRICTIVE PRACTICES: DOMINANT POSITION: ABUSE: C.A.)

Ponty v. Chamberland (COLLABORATIVE WORKS: *Droit moral*: WHO MAY SUE: S.C.)

Robert (Daniel) v. Soc. Crehallet-Folliot-Recherche et Publicite (COLLECTIVE WORKS: INDIVIDUAL AUTHOR'S RIGHTS: EDITOR'S NAME: UNFAIR COMPETITION: S.C.)

Rowe v. Walt Disney Productions (CONFLICT OF LAWS: *Droit moral*: S.C.)

Rutman v. Société Des Gens de Lettres (AUDIOVISUAL WORKS: WHETHER TECHNICAL WORK OR INTELLECTUAL CREATION: D.C.)

SDRM's Practices (RESTRICTIVE PRACTICES: COLLECTING SOCIETIES: FOREIGN WORKS: IMPORTS: DISCRIMINATORY PRACTICES: DOMINANT POSITION: COMPETITION COMMISSION)

Shelltrie Distribution Sàrl v. SNTF (FILMS)

Société Française de Transmissions Florales Interflora & Téléfleurs France (RESTRICTIVE PRACTICES: DOMINANT POSITION: EXCLUSIVITY CLAUSE: PROTECTION OF TRADE MARK: MINIMUM TARIFF ORDER: Copyright Commission)

Société Rannou Graphie v. CNPRI (PHOTOCOPIES: S.C.)

Widmaier v. SPADEM (*Droit moral*: COPYRIGHT MANAGEMENT SOCIETY: S.C.)

Knoll International Gavina SpA v. Sàrl Aliotta Diffusion (IMPORTS: DESIGN EXHAUSTION OF RIGHTS: NO DESIGN RIGHT UNDER ITALIAN LAW: ARTICLE 36(1): S.C.)

Germany

ASTERIX Trade Mark (TRADE MARK: COMIC STRIPS: UNAUTHORISED SALE: INJUNCTION: VICARIOUS LIABILITY: C.A.)

Computer Programs (Protection of) (COMPUTER PROGRAMS: MARKETING RIGHTS: S.C.)

Copyright in Court Proceedings (LAWYERS' PLEADINGS: TEST: PROTECTION: PUBLICATION: S.C.)

Copyright in Tender Documents

GEMA's Reproduction Tariffs (MUSICAL WORKS: VIDEOCASSETTES AND FILMS: LICENCE FEES: INFRINGEMENT: ASSESSMENT OF DAMAGES: S.C.)

Hiring of Video Games Cassettes (VIDEO GAMES)

Lenin's Monument (Re) (STATUE: PUBLIC OWNERSHIP: SCULPTOR'S RIGHTS: PROSPECTIVE DAMAGE: STORAGE: C.A.)

Magazines in Hairdressing Establishments (COPYRIGHT COLLECTING SOCIETY: *Locus standi*: ENTITLEMENT TO FEES ON LENDING OR HIRING WORKS FOR COMMERCIAL PURPOSES: S.C.)

Musik-Vertrieb Membran GmbH v. GEMA (IMPORTS: EXHAUSTION OF RIGHTS)

Piped Music in Prisons, Re (ROYALTIES: EXEMPTIONS: MUSIC PLAYED IN PRISONS: C.A.)

Quotations from Published Works (INFRINGEMENT: PERMISSIBLE EXTENT: S.C.)

Sale and Buy-back of Records (PERFORMING RIGHTS: SALE WITH OPTION TO RETURN: EXHAUSTION OF PRODUCER'S RIGHTS: PUBLIC INTEREST: FREE MOVEMENT OF GOODS: S.C.)

Song Book for Schools (STATUTORY EXCEPTIONS: SCHOOL BOOKS: EXTERNAL CHARACTERISTICS: INTERNAL CHARACTERISTICS: DEFINITIONS: S.C.)

Tosca (OPERA: PERIOD OF PROTECTION: FOREIGN AUTHORS: EVIDENCE: INTERNATIONAL CONVENTION AND NATIONAL LAWS: S.C.)

Greece

Forgery of Copyright Videotapes, Re (VIDEOTAPES: FORGERY: "DOCUMENTS": S.C.)

Home Taping

Amstrad Consumer Electronics plc v. The British Phonograph Industry Ltd (INFRINGEMENT: DOUBLE-HEADED CASSETTE RECORDERS: DECLARATION: EFFECT OF COPYRIGHT WARNING NOTICE: KNOWLEDGE AND INTENT: NEGLIGENCE: DUTY OF CARE: CRIMINAL LIABILITY: INCITEMENT: Ch.D.: C.A.)

CBS Songs Ltd v. Amstrad Consumer Electronics plc (INFRINGEMENT: C.A.: H.L.)

CBS Songs Ltd v. Amstrad Consumer Electronics plc (No. 2) (INFRINGEMENT: REPRESENTATIVE ACTION BY COPYRIGHT OWNERS: Ch.D.: C.A.: H.L.)

Implied Licence

British Leyland Motor Corp. v. Armstrong Patents Co. Ltd (INFRINGEMENT: REPLACEMENT EXHAUST PIPES: ACQUIESCENCE: REFERENCE TO ECJ: Ch.D.)

Express Newspapers plc v. News (U.K.) Ltd ("TIT FOR TAT" COPYING OF NEWSPAPER STORIES: APPROBATION AND REPROBATION: Ch.D.)

Express Newspapers plc v. News (U.K.) Ltd (MUTUAL COPYING OF NEWS STORIES: CUSTOM OF THE TRADE: Ch.D.)

Godfrey v. Lees (INFRINGEMENT: JOINT WORKS: ARRANGEMENTS: CONTRIBUTION: OWNERSHIP: BREACH OF CONTRACT: Ch.D.)

BBC v. British Satellite Broadcasting Ltd (Ch.D.)
BBC v. Celebrity Centre Productions Ltd (Ch.D.)
Besson (A.P.) Ltd v. Fulleon Ltd (Ch.D.)
Bestworth Ltd v. Wearwell Ltd (Ch.D.)
Betsen v. CBS United Kingdom Ltd (Ch.D.)
Billhöfer Maschinenfabrik BmgH v. T.H. Dixon & Co. Ltd (Ch.D.)
Biotrading and Financing OY v. Biohit Ltd (Ch.D.)
Bookmakers' Afternoon Greyhound Services Ltd v. Wilf Gilbert (Staffordshire) Ltd
    (Ch.D.)
British Leyland Motor Corp. Ltd v. Armstrong Patents Co. Ltd (Ch.D.)
British Leyland Motor Corp. Ltd v. Armstrong Patents Co. Ltd (C.A.: H.L.)
British Phonographic Industry Ltd v. Cohen (Scotland: I.H.)
British Sky Broadcasting Group Ltd v. Lyons (Ch.D.)
Brugger v. Medicaid (Pat. Ct)
C. & H. Engineering v. F. Klucznik & Sons Ltd (Ch.D.)
Cala Homes (South) Ltd v. Alfred McAlpine Homes East Ltd (Ch.D.)
Cala Homes (South) Ltd v. Alfred McAlpine Homes East Ltd (No. 2) (Ch.D.)
CBS Inc. v. Ames Records & Tapes Ltd (Ch.D.)
CBS Songs Ltd v. Amstrad Consumer Electronics plc (C.A.: H.L.)
CBS Songs Ltd v. Amstrad Consumer Electronics plc (No. 2) (Ch.D.: C.A.: H.L.)
CBS United Kingdom Ltd v. Lambert (C.A.)
CBS United Kingdom Ltd v. Perry (Ch.D.)
Century Communications Ltd v. Mayfair Entertainment U.K. Ltd (Ch.D.)
Chappell v. United Kingdom (ECHR)
Chater & Chater Productions Ltd v. Rose (Ch.D.)
Chater and Chater Productions Ltd v. Rose (Ch.D.)
CHC Software Card Ltd v. Hopkins & Wood (Ch.D.)
Clark v. David Allan & Co. Ltd (Scotland: O.H.)
Columbia Picture Industries Inc. v. Robinson (Ch.D.)
Commissioners of Customs & Excise v. Hamlin Slowe (Ch.D.)
Costelloe v. Johnston, Johnston and We Fit Doors Ltd (t/a Doorways) (Ireland: H.C.)
Crest Homes plc v. Marks (C.A.: H.L.)
Davis (J.&S.) (Holdings) Ltd v. Wright Health Group Ltd (Ch.D.)
Def Lepp Music v. Stuart-Brown (Ch.D.)
Digital Equipment Corp. v. Darkcrest Ltd (Ch.D.)
Dun & Bradstreet Ltd v. Typesetting Facilities Ltd (Ch.D.)
Durion Co. Inc. v. Jennings & Co. Ltd (Ch.D.)
EMI Music Publishing Ltd v. Papathanasiou (Ch.D.)
EMI Records Ltd v. Kudhail (C.A.)
EMI Records Ltd v. The CD Specialists Ltd (Ch.D.)
Entec (Pollution Control) Ltd v. Abacus Mouldings (Ch.D., C.A.)
Etri Fans Ltd v. NMB (U.K.) Ltd (C.A.)
Evans & Sons Ltd v. Spritebrand Ltd (C.A.)
Express Newspapers plc v. Liverpool Daily Post & Echo plc (Ch.D.)
Express Newspapers plc v. News (U.K.) Ltd (Ch.D.)
Fablaine Ltd v. Leygill Ltd (No. 2) (Ch.D.)
Form Tubes Ltd v. Guinness Bros plc (Ch.D.)
Format Communications Manufacturing Ltd v. ITT (U.K.) Ltd (C.A.)
Gardex Ltd v. Sorata (Ch.D.)
GEMA's Reproduction Tariffs (Germany: S.C.)
General Nutrition Ltd v. Pattni (Ch.D.)
Geographia Ltd v. Penguin Books Ltd (Ch.D.)
Godfrey v. Lees (JOINT WORKS: ARRANGEMENTS: Ch.D.)
Granby Marketing Services Ltd v. Interlego AG (Ch.D.)

Politechnika Ipari Szovetkezet v. Dallas Print Transfers Ltd (Ch.D.)
Potton Ltd v. Yorkclose Ltd (Ch.D.)
PPL v. Grosvenor Leisure Ltd (Ch.D.)
Presentaciones Musicales SA v. Secunda (SOUND RECORDINGS: Ch.D.)
Private Research Ltd v. Brosnan (Ireland: H.C.)
Quotations from Published Works (Germany: S.C.)
R. v. Carter (C.A.)
Rexnold Inc. v. Ancon Ltd (Ch.D.)
Rockwell International Corp. v. Serck Industries Ltd (Ch.D.: C.A.)
Rose Plastics GmbH v. Wm Beckett & Co. (Plastics) Ltd (Ch.D.)
Rose Records v. Motown Record Corp. (Ch.D.)
Rose v. Information Services Ltd (Ch.D.)
Rubycliff Ltd v. Plastic Engineers Ltd (Ch.D.)
Saphena Computing Ltd v. Allied Collection Agencies Ltd (COMPUTER CONTRACT:
    Q.B.D.: C.A.)
Schweppes Ltd v. Wellingtons Ltd (Ch.D.)
Secretary of State for the Home Department v. Central Broadcasting Ltd (Ch.D.:
    C.A.)
Sega Enterprises Ltd v. Alca Electronics (C.A.)
Shelley Films Ltd v. Rex Features Ltd (Ch.D.)
Shippam (C.) Ltd v. Princes-Buitoni Ltd (Ch.D.)
Sillitoe v. McGraw-Hill Book Co. (U.K.) Ltd (Ch.D.)
Smith Myers Communications Ltd v. Motorola Ltd (Ch.D.)
Smith v. Greenfield (Northern Ireland: H.C.)
Société Romanaise de la Chaussure SA v. British Shoe Corp. Ltd (Ch.D.)
Spectravest Inc. v. Aperknit Ltd (Ch.D.)
Standen Engineering Ltd v. A. Spalding & Sons Ltd (Ch.D.)
Stansfield v. Sovereign Music Ltd (Ch.D.)
Staver Co. Inc. v. Digitext Display Ltd (Ch.D.)
Swedac Ltd v. Magnet & Southerns plc (C.A.)
Systematica Ltd v. London Computer Centre Ltd (Ch.D.)
Thames & Hudson Ltd v. Design and Artists Copyright Society Ltd (Ch.D.)
The Reject Shop plc v. Robert Manners (Q.B.D.)
Thrustcode Ltd v. WW Computing Ltd (Ch.D.)
Time Warner Entertainments Company LP v. Channel Four Television Corporation
    plc (C.A.)
Twentieth Century Fox Film Corp. v. Tryrare Ltd (Ch.D.)
Universal City Studios Inc. v. Hubbard (Ch.D.: C.A.)
Valeo Vision SA v. Flexible Lamps Ltd (Pat. Ct)
VDU Installations Ltd v. Integrated Computer Systems & Cybernetics Ltd (Ch.D.)
Video Arts Ltd v. Paget Industries Ltd (Ch.D.)
VNU Publications Ltd v. Ziff Davis (U.K.) Ltd (Ch.D.)
Ward (Geo.) (Moxley) Ltd v. Richard Sankey Ltd (Ch.D.)
Wardle Fabrics Ltd v. G. Myristis Ltd (Ch.D.)
Warner Bros Records Inc. v. Parr (Ch.D.: C.A.)
Waterlow Directories Ltd v. Reed Information Services Ltd (Ch.D.)
WEA Records Ltd v. Visions Channel 4 Ltd (C.A.)
Weir Pumps Ltd v. CML Pumps Ltd (Ch.D.)
Williamson Music Ltd v. The Pearson Partnership Ltd (Ch.D.)
Wiseman v. George Weidenfeld & Nicholson Ltd (Ch.D.)
Work Model Enterprises Ltd v. Ecosystem Ltd (Ch.D.)
Wyko Group v. Cooper Roller Bearings Co. Ltd (Ch.D.)
Yale Security Products Ltd v. Newman (Ch.D.)
ZYX Music GmbH v. King (Ch.D.)

Innocent Infringement

ZYX Music GmbH v. King (DISCO ARRANGEMENT OF SONG: WHETHER COPYRIGHT ENFORCEABLE: ENTITLEMENT TO RELIEF: SECONDARY INFRINGEMENT: ADDITIONAL DAMAGES: Ch.D.)

Intellectual Content

Le Monde (Sàrl) v. Société Microfor Inc. (INDEXES: DERIVED WORKS: PRESS REVIEW: BIBLIOGRAPHIES AND EXTRACTS: France: S.C.: C.A.)

Intent

Amstrad Consumer Electronics plc v. The British Phonograph Industry Ltd (INFRINGEMENT: EFFECT OF COPYRIGHT WARNING NOTICE: Ch.D.: C.A.)

Interest

Allibert SA v. O'Connor (INFRINGEMENT: ASSESSMENT OF DAMAGES: Ireland: H.C.)

Nichols Advanced Vehicle Systems Inc. v. Rees (No. 3) (INFRINGEMENT: RACING CARS: INQUIRY AS TO DAMAGES: CONVERSION DAMAGES: ASSESSMENT OF AGGRAVATED DAMAGES: Ch.D.: C.A.)

Interlocutory Injunction. *See* **Practice** (*Interlocutory injunction*)

Injunction. See **Practice** (*Injunction*)

Ireland/Northern Ireland

Allibert SA v. O'Connor (INFRINGEMENT: ASSESSMENT OF DAMAGES: INTEREST: H.C.)

Costelloe v. Johnston, Johnston and We Fit Doors Ltd (t/a Doorways) (DESIGN: INFRINGEMENT: DOOR: WHETHER DESIGN NEW OR ORIGINAL: WHETHER PRIOR PUBLICATION EXISTING RENDERING REGISTRATION INVALID: COUNTERCLAIM: FORM OF RELIEF: EXPUNCTION FROM REGISTER: H.C.)

House of Spring Gardens Ltd v. Point Blank Ltd (BREACH OF CONFIDENCE: INFRINGEMENT: BREACH OF CONTRACT: BULLETPROOF VESTS: APPLICABILITY IN IRELAND OF ENGLISH AUTHORITIES: SPRINGBOARD DOCTRINE: DIRECTORS' LIABILITY FOR COMMISSION OF TORTS: H.C.: S.C.)

House of Spring Gardens Ltd v. Point Blank Ltd (BREACH OF CONFIDENCE: INFRINGEMENT: BREACH OF CONTRACT: DAMAGES: ACCOUNT OF PROFITS: WHETHER ROYALTY FOR BREACH OF CONTRACT PRECLUDES FURTHER PECUNIARY AWARD FOR BREACH OF COPYRIGHT AND CONFIDENCE: OVERLAPPING HEADS OF DAMAGE: ABATEMENT: H.C.)

News Datacom Ltd v. Satellite Decoding Systems (COMPUTER PROGRAMS: BREACH: INTERLOCUTORY INJUNCTION: BALANCE OF CONVENIENCE: H.C.)

Paramount Pictures Corporation v. Cablelink Ltd (INFRINGEMENT: INTERLOCUTORY: INJUNCTION: TELEVISION CABLE DIFFUSION SERVICE: DAMAGES: LAW IN CINEMATOGRAPH FILM: ABUSE OF DOMINANT POSITION: ARTICLES 85 AND 86: H.C.)

Performing Right Society Ltd v. Marlin Communal Aerials Ltd (BROADCASTING: CABLE TELEVISION: S.C.)

Phonographic Performance (Ireland) Ltd v. J. Somers (Inspector of Taxes) (REVENUE: VALUE ADDED TAX: TAX PAYABLE ON SUPPLY OF SERVICES: SOUND RECORDINGS: REMUNERATION FOR BROADCASTING OF SOUND RECORDINGS: AGREEMENT: WHETHER APPELLANT SUPPLYING A SERVICE: WHETHER ATTRACTING VALUE ADDED TAX: H.C.)

Private Research Ltd v. Brosnan (INFRINGEMENT: BREACH OF CONFIDENCE: EMPLOYER AND EMPLOYEE: MISUSE OF CONFIDENTIAL INFORMATION: INTERLOCUTORY INJUNCTION: FAIR QUESTION TO BE TRIED: ADEQUACY OF DAMAGES: BALANCE OF CONVENIENCE: H.C.)

Radio Telefis Eireann v. Magill TV Guide Ltd (RADIO AND TELEVISION SCHEDULES: "LITERARY WORK": RESTRICTIVE PRACTICES: COMMUNITY LAW AND NATIONAL LAW: JUDICIAL PROCEDURE: EVIDENCE: H.C.)

Radio Telefis Eireann v. Magill TV Guide Ltd (TELEVISION PROGRAMMES: PUBLIC INTEREST: RESTRICTIVE PRACTICES: H.C.)

Smith v. Greenfield (INFRINGEMENT: TERM OF PROTECTION: CONVERSION DAMAGES: INNOCENCE: H.C.)

Issuing to the Public

Nelson v. Mark Rye and Cocteau Records Ltd (AUTHORISING: ISSUING TO THE PUBLIC: LICENCE: Ch.D.)

Italy

Società Italiana Degli Autori ed Editori (SIAE) v. Domenico Pompa (INTELLECTUAL PRODUCT: BASIS OF PROTECTION: COMPUTER SOFTWARE: S.C.)

Unicomp Srl v. Italcomputers Srl (CREATIVE WORK: COMPUTER PROGRAMS: Magistrates Ct: Pisa)

Iterative Drawings

Biotrading and Financing OY v. Biohit Ltd (INFRINGEMENT: ORIGINALITY: RELEVANCE OF TITLE TO EARLIER DRAWINGS: Ch.D.)

Joint Ownership/Joint Works

Godfrey v. Lees (INFRINGEMENT: ARRANGEMENTS: CONTRIBUTION: OWNERSHIP: BREACH OF CONTRACT: IMPLIED LICENCE: Ch.D.)

Stuart v. Barrett (POP GROUP: WHETHER PARTNERSHIP: EFFECT OF EXPULSION OF MEMBER: SONGS: COMPOSITION BEFORE MEMBER JOINED: Ch.D.)

Kits

Oliver Homes (Manufacturing) v. Hamilton (INFRINGEMENT: BUILDING PLANS AND DESIGNS: HOUSE KIT PLANS: USE OF PLANS NOT LICENCES SEPARATELY FROM SALE OF HOUSE KIT: DAMAGES: METHOD OF CALCULATION: ENTITLEMENT TO DAMAGES FOR LOSS OF PROFITS ON SALE OF HOUSE KIT: Scotland: O.H.)

"Knocking" Advertising

News Group Newspapers Ltd v. The Mirror Group Newspapers (1988) Ltd (INFRINGEMENT: THE SUN: MASTHEADS: Ch.D.)

Knowledge

Amstrad Consumer Electronics plc v. The British Phonograph Industry Ltd (INFRINGEMENT: EFFECT OF COPYRIGHT WARNING NOTICE: Ch.D.: C.A.)

Arrowin Ltd v. Trimguard (U.K.) Ltd (INFRINGEMENT: IMPORTATION: Ch.D.)

Hoover plc v. George Hulme (Stockport) Ltd (REPLACEMENT PARTS: ACQUIESCENCE: ABUSE OF DOMINANT POSITION: Ch.D.)

Infabrics Ltd v. Jaytex (INFRINGEMENT: PUBLICATION: Ch.D.: C.A.: H.L.)

Linpac Mouldings Ltd v. Eagleton Direct Export Ltd (SECONDARY INFRINGEMENT: IMPORTATION OF INFRINGING COPIES: THREATS: SUMMARY JUDGMENT: C.A.)

Millar v. Bassey (CONTRACT: INDUCING BREACH: APPLICATION TO STRIKE OUT STATEMENT OF CLAIM: INTENTION OF DEFENDANT: C.A.)

Politechnika Ipari Szovetkezet v. Dallas Print Transfers Ltd (INFRINGEMENT: PASSING OFF: "RUBIK" CUBES: Ch.D.)

Sillitoe v. McGraw-Hill Book Co. (U.K.) Ltd (INFRINGEMENT: STUDY NOTES FOR STUDENTS: Ch.D.)

Lending Right

Warner Brothers Inc. v. Christiansen (VIDEO BOUGHT IN ENGLAND WHERE NO LENDING RIGHT: RENTED IN DENMARK WHERE LENDING RIGHT APPLIES: EXTENT OF EXHAUSTION: ECJ)

Licence of Right

Split Roller Bearing Co. Ltd's Licence of Right (Copyright) Application (WHETHER APPLICATION MAY BE MADE IN RESPECT OF MORE THAN ONE DESIGN: WHETHER FAILURE TO INDICATE MANNER OF EXPLOITATION AN ABUSE OF PROCESS: C.-G.)

Licences

Nelson v. Rye (INFRINGEMENT: MUSICAL WORKS: MANUFACTURE AND SALE AFTER EXPIRY OF LICENCE: POP MUSICIAN AND MANAGER: ACCOUNT: TERMS OF RETAINER: LIMITATION PERIOD: LACHES AND ACQUIESCENCE: Ch.D.)

Oliver Homes (Manufacturing) v. Hamilton (INFRINGEMENT: BUILDING PLANS AND DESIGNS: HOUSE KIT PLANS: USE OF PLANS NOT LICENCES SEPARATELY FROM SALE OF HOUSE KIT: Scotland: O.H.)

Performing Right Society Ltd v. Working Men's Club & Institute Union Ltd (MUSICAL WORKS: WHETHER NEW TARIFF WAS LICENCE SCHEME: REFERENCE TO TRIBUNAL: Ch.D.)

Saphena Computing Ltd v. Allied Collection Agencies Ltd (COMPUTER CONTRACT: RIGHT OR LICENCE TO REPAIR OR IMPROVE: Q.B.D.: C.A.)

Literary Work

Autospin (Oil Seals) Ltd v. Beehive Spinning (INFRINGEMENT: TABLES FOR CALCULATING CRITICAL DIMENSIONS: WHETHER THREE-DIMENSIONAL ARTICLE INFRINGES LITERARY WORK: Ch.D.)

Locus Standi. *See* **Practice** (*Locus Standi*)

Management Contract

Nelson v. Mark Rye and Cocteau Records Ltd (ACCOUNT OF MONEYS RECEIVED: WHETHER CLAIM STATUTE-BARRED: LACHES: COUNTERCLAIM FOR COMMISSION AND EXPENSES: CONVERSION: MASTER RECORDINGS: Ch.D.)

Maps

Copyright in Maps and Plans ("MAP FOR MEN": IMMORALITY: Switzerland)

Geographia Ltd v. Penguin Books Ltd (INFRINGEMENT: Ch.D.)

Mechanical or Engineering Drawings

Amalgamated Mining Services Pty Ltd v. Warman International Ltd (ENGINEERING DRAWING: WHETHER "ARTISTIC WORKS": OVERLAP WITH DESIGN PROTECTION: C.-G.)

Billhöfer Maschinenfabrik BmgH v. T.H. Dixon & Co. Ltd (INFRINGEMENT: MECHANICAL DRAWING: WHETHER SUBSTANTIAL PART COPIED: ENGINEER, NOT LAYMAN, TO ASSESS RELEVANT FEATURE: Ch.D.)

Wyko Group plc v. Cooper Roller Bearings Co. Ltd (DECLARATION OF NON-INFRINGEMENT: SPARE PARTS DEFENCE: PRACTICE: DECLARATORY RELIEF: SCOPE OF COURT'S POWERS: STRIKING OUT WRIT AND STATEMENT OF CLAIM: Ch.D.)

Morality

Copyright in Maps and Plans ("MAP FOR MEN": IMMORALITY: Switzerland)

Masterman's Design (REGISTERED DESIGN: APPLICATION: PRACTICE: WHETHER DESIGN CONTRARY TO MORALITY: DISCRETION: RDAT)

Musical Work

BACTA v. Phonographic Performance Ltd (SOUND RECORDINGS: LICENCE SCHEME: BACKGROUND MUSIC FROM JUKEBOXES: FEES: COSTS: Cprt Trib.)

Bassey v. Icon Entertainment plc (PROPRIETORSHIP: RECORDING OF PERFORMANCES: SUMMARY JUDGMENT: TRIABLE ISSUE: CONSENT: Ch.D.)

Betsen v. CBS United Kingdom Ltd (INFRINGEMENT: STRIKING OUT: WHETHER SUFFICIENT OBJECTIVE SIMILARITY: WHETHER PERCUSSION AND BASS LINE A SUBSTANTIAL PART: Ch.D.)

CBS Songs Ltd v. Amstrad Consumer Electronics plc (INFRINGEMENT: HOME TAPING AUTHORISATION: JOINT TORTFEASORS: INCITEMENT TO COMMIT A TORT: INCITEMENT TO COMMIT A CRIME: NEGLIGENCE: H.L.)

Chater & Chater Productions Ltd v. Rose (INFRINGEMENT: PERFORMANCE: PRIOR DISCLOSURE OF MUSIC TO DEFENDANTS: Ch.D.)

EMI Music Publishing Ltd v. Papathanasiou (*Chariots of Fire* THEME: SUBCONSCIOUS COPYING: INNOCENCE: Ch.D.)

GEMA's Reproduction Tariffs (LICENCE FEES: INFRINGEMENT: ASSESSMENT OF DAMAGES: Germany: S.C.)

Hérault v. SACEM (PERFORMING RIGHT: COLLECTING SOCIETY: DOMINANT POSITION: LICENCE: France: C.A.)

Mad Hat Music Ltd v. Pulse 8 Records Ltd (INFRINGEMENT: INTERLOCUTORY INJUNCTION: OWNERSHIP: AUTHOR: PERFORMER'S RIGHTS: CONSENT TO MAKING STUDIO RECORDINGS: WHETHER FURTHER CONSENT NECESSARY FOR MAKING COMMERCIAL RECORDS: Ch.D.)

Morrison Leahy Music Ltd v. Lightbond Ltd (INFRINGEMENT: MEDLEY OF SONGS WITH MCPS CLEARANCE: WHETHER CHARACTER OF WORKS ALTERED: WHETHER LYRICS MODIFIED *droit moral* RIGHTS: RIGHT OF INTEGRITY: INFRINGEMENT: WHETHER TREATMENT AMOUNTING TO MUTILATION OR DISTORTION: Ch.D.)

Nelson v. Rye (INFRINGEMENT: MANUFACTURE AND SALE AFTER EXPIRY OF LICENCE: POP MUSICIAN AND MANAGER: ACCOUNT: TERMS OF RETAINER: LIMITATION PERIOD: LACHES AND ACQUIESCENCE: Ch.D.)

Penfold v. Fairbrass (INFRINGEMENT: STRIKING OUT: AFFIDAVIT EVIDENCE: WHETHER ADMISSIBLE: TAPE RECORDING OF SONGS: WHETHER ADMISSIBLE: Ch.D.)

Performing Right Society Ltd v. Working Men's Club & Institute Union Ltd (LICENCE SCHEME: WHETHER NEW TARIFF WAS LICENCE SCHEME: REFERENCE TO TRIBUNAL: Ch.D.)

Piped Music in Prisons, Re (ROYALTIES: EXEMPTIONS: MUSIC PLAYED IN PRISONS: Germany: C.A.)

Warner Bros Records Inc. v. Parr (INFRINGEMENT: BOOTLEGGING: WHETHER ACTIONABLE BY RECORD COMPANIES: DMPPA58: PERFORMERS' PROTECTION ACT 1963: Ch.D.: C.A.)

Williamson Music Ltd v. The Pearson Partnership Ltd (INFRINGEMENT: PARODY: Ch.D.)

Negligence

Amstrad Consumer Electronics plc v. The British Phonograph Industry Ltd (HOME TAPING: DOUBLE-HEADED CASSETTE RECORDERS: EFFECT OF COPYRIGHT WARNING NOTICE: KNOWLEDGE AND INTENT: DUTY OF CARE: Ch.D.: C.A.)

CBS Songs Ltd v. Amstrad Consumer Electronics plc and Dixons Ltd (HOME TAPING: AUTHORISATION: JOINT TORTFEASORS: INCITEMENT TO COMMIT A TORT: INCITEMENT TO COMMIT A CRIME: H.L.)

Paterson Zochonis Ltd v. Merfarken Packaging Ltd (INFRINGEMENT: PRINTER'S INNOCENCE: PRINTERS' DUTY OF CARE: C.A.)

Western Front Ltd v. Vestron Inc. (FILM: LICENCE AGREEMENT: STRIKING OUT: UNLAWFUL INTERFERENCE WITH CONTRACTUAL RELATIONS: Ch.D.)

Neighbouring Rights

Copyright (Broadcasting) Draft Directive (SATELLITE BROADCASTING: CABLE RE-TRANSMISSION: SPECIAL BROADCASTING RIGHTS: PERFORMERS' RIGHTS: SPECIAL RULE FOR BROADCAST OF PHONOGRAMS: COMPETITION RULES: E.C. Council)

Newspaper

Charleston v. News Group Newspapers Ltd (DEFAMATION: NEWSPAPER ARTICLE: PHOTOGRAPHS: ACTORS' FACES SUPERIMPOSED ON PORNOGRAPHIC PICTURES: EXPLANATORY TEXT: CONTEXT: C.A.)

Originality

Biotrading and Financing OY v. Biohit Ltd (INFRINGEMENT: ITERATIVE DRAWINGS: RELEVANCE OF TITLE TO EARLIER DRAWINGS: Ch.D.)

C. & H. Engineering v. F. Klucznik & Sons Ltd (INFRINGEMENT: TEST: DESIGN RIGHTS: FUNCTIONAL OBJECTS: SIMPLICITY: MODIFICATION AND AMENDMENT: LAMB CREEP FEEDER: PIG FENDER: WHETHER DRAWING ORIGINAL: WHETHER DESIGN COMMONPLACE: TWO-DIMENSIONAL AND THREE-DIMENSIONAL WORKS: Ch.D.)

Costelloe v. Johnston, Johnston and We Fit Doors Ltd (t/a Doorways) (INFRINGEMENT: DOOR: WHETHER DESIGN NEW OR ORIGINAL: Ireland: H.C.)

Davis (J.&S.) (Holdings) Ltd v. Wright Health Group Ltd (INFRINGEMENT: DENTAL IMPRESSION TRAYS: DRAWINGS: SCULPTURES: NON-EXPERT DEFENCE: Ch.D.)

Drayton Controls (Engineering) Ltd v. Honeywell Control Systems Ltd (VISUAL SIGNIFICANCE OF MINOR ALTERATIONS: Ch.D.)

Durion Co. Inc. v. Jennings & Co. Ltd (INFRINGEMENT: C.A.)

Elram International Actuators Ltd v. Fluid Power Engineering Ltd (INFRINGEMENT: REQUEST FOR PARTICULARS OF ORIGINALITY: Ch.D.)

Express Newspapers plc v. Liverpool Daily Post & Echo plc (INFRINGEMENT: WORK PERFORMED BY COMPUTER: LOTTERIES: Ch.D.)

Exxon Corp. v. Exxon Insurance Consultants International Ltd (PASSING OFF: WHETHER SINGLE WORD ORIGINAL LITERARY WORK: Ch.D.: C.A.)

LA Gear Inc. v. Hi-Tec Sports plc (INFRINGEMENT: SUMMARY JUDGMENT: INDIRECT COPYING: Ch.D.: C.A.)

Macmillan Publishers Ltd v. Thomas Reed Publications Ltd (INFRINGEMENT: CHARTS: SUMMARY JUDGMENT: Ch.D.)

Rexnold Inc. v. Ancon Ltd (INFRINGEMENT: UPDATED WORKING DRAWINGS: Ch.D.)

The Reject Shop plc v. Robert Manners (ENLARGED PHOTOCOPIES: WHETHER SKILL AND LABOUR INVOLVED: Q.B.D.)

Ownership

Adventure Film Productions SA v. Tully (STRENGTH OF CASE TO OWNERSHIP: Ch.D.)

A.&M. Records v. Video Collection International Limited (INFRINGEMENT: SOUND RECORDINGS: OWNERSHIP: EQUITABLE OWNERSHIP: ADDITIONAL DAMAGES: Ch.D.)

Apple Corps. Ltd v. Cooper (PHOTOGRAPHS: COMMISSIONED WORK: ESTOPPEL: Ch.D.)

Bassey v. Icon Entertainment plc (PERFORMER'S RIGHTS: RECORDING OF PERFORMANCES: SUMMARY JUDGMENT: TRIABLE ISSUE: CONSENT: Ch.D.)

Beggars Banquet Records Ltd v. Carlton Television Ltd (WRONGFUL INTERFERENCE WITH GOODS: FILM FOOTAGE: Ch.D.)

Bookmakers' Afternoon Greyhound Services Ltd v. Wilf Gilbert (Staffordshire) Ltd (GREYHOUND CARDS AND RACE FORECAST DIVIDENDS: SUBSISTENCE: INFRINGEMENT: Ch.D.)

Breville Europe plc v. Thorn EMI Domestic Appliances Ltd (REGISTERED DESIGN: INFRINGEMENT: TEST: SANDWICH TOASTERS: DRAWINGS: PLASTERCASTS OF TOASTED SANDWICHES: WHETHER SCULPTURES: PROPER PROPRIETOR: COMMISSIONED WORK: Pat. Ct)

C. & H. Engineering v. F. Klucznik & Sons Ltd (WHETHER DRAWING ORIGINAL: WHETHER DESIGN COMMONPLACE: CREATOR: COPYING: TWO-DIMENSIONAL AND THREE-DIMENSIONAL WORKS: Ch.D.)

Cala Homes (South) Ltd v. Alfred McAlpine Homes East Ltd (INFRINGEMENT: ARCHITECT'S DRAWINGS: COMMISSIONED DRAWINGS: JOINT OWNERSHIP: Ch.D.)

Gardex Ltd v. Sorata (PATENT DRAWING: Ch.D.)

Godfrey v. Lees (INFRINGEMENT: JOINT WORKS: ARRANGEMENTS: CONTRIBUTION: Ch.D.)

Hutchison Personal Communications Ltd v. Hook Advertising Ltd (POSSESSION OF INFRINGING COPIES: Ch.D.)

Ironside v. H.M. Attorney-General (COINAGE DESIGNS: CROWN COPYRIGHT: Ch.D.)

Kambrook Distributing Pty Ltd v. Delaney (SKETCHES PREPARED BY MANAGING DIRECTOR: INTENTION AS TO OWNERSHIP OF RIGHTS IN DRAWINGS: CONFIRMATORY ASSIGNMENT FOR PURPOSE OF PROCEEDINGS: Ch.D.)

Koelman v. E.C. Commission (RADIO MATERIAL: COLLECTING SOCIETY: ALLEGED BREACH OF ARTICLES 85 AND 86: Case T–575/93: CFI)

Le Monde (Sàrl) v. Société Microfor Inc. (COLLECTIVE WORKS: OWNER'S RIGHTS: CONSENTS: REPRODUCTION: France: S.C.: C.A.)

Lenin's Monument (Re) (STATUE: PUBLIC OWNERSHIP: SCULPTOR'S RIGHTS: Germany: C.A.)

Mad Hat Music Ltd v. Pulse 8 Records Ltd (SOUND RECORDINGS: AUTHOR: PERFORMER'S RIGHTS: CONSENT TO MAKING STUDIO RECORDINGS: Ch.D.)

Mail Newspapers plc v. Express Newspapers plc (WEDDING PHOTOGRAPHS: WHETHER CO-OWNER LEGALLY DEAD: Ch.D.)

Missing Link Software v. Magee (WORK MADE IN COURSE OF EMPLOYMENT: TO WHOM DOES WORK OF MOONLIGHTING EMPLOYEE BELONG: Ch.D.)

Presentaciones Musicales SA v. Secunda (INFRINGEMENT: SOUND RECORDINGS: COUNTERCLAIM: APPLICATION TO STRIKE OUT: PARTIAL SUMMARY JUDGMENT: Ch.D.)

Secretary of State for Defence v. Guardian Newspapers Ltd (SECRET CROWN DOCUMENT: PROTECTION OF NEWSPAPER SOURCE: C.A.: H.L.)

Spectravest Inc. v. Aperknit Ltd (CATS-IN-BOOTS DESIGN: WHETHER SUBSISTENCE AND OWNERSHIP TO BE PRESUMED: Ch.D.)

Stuart v. Barrett (POP GROUP: WHETHER PARTNERSHIP: EFFECT OF EXPULSION OF MEMBER: SONGS: COMPOSITION BEFORE MEMBER JOINED: WHETHER WORK OF JOINT OWNERSHIP: Ch.D.)

Owner's Rights

Le Monde (Sàrl) v. Société Microfor Inc. (COLLECTIVE WORKS: CONSENTS: REPRODUCTION: INDEXES: INTELLECTUAL CONTENT: DERIVED WORKS: PRESS REVIEW: BIBLIOGRAPHIES AND EXTRACTS: France: S.C.: C.A.)

Parody

Schweppes Ltd v. Wellingtons Ltd (WHETHER PARODY ARGUABLE DEFENCE: SUMMARY JUDGMENT: Ch.D.)

Williamson Music Ltd v. The Pearson Partnership Ltd (INFRINGEMENT: Ch.D.)

Passing Off

Altertext Inc. v. Advanced Data Communications Ltd (INFRINGEMENT: ANTON PILLER PRACTICE: Ch.D.)

BBC v. Celebrity Centre Productions Ltd (INFRINGEMENT: *EastEnders* TELEVISION SERIES: *A to Z of EastEnders* MAGAZINE: MISREPRESENTATION OF AUTHORISATION: Ch.D.)

Drayton Controls (Engineering) Ltd v. Honeywell Control Systems Ltd (GET-UP: PURCHASE BY NAME, NOT VISUAL APPEARANCE: DESIGN OF PARTS COMMON TO TRADE: REPUTATION: Ch.D.)

Exxon Corp. v. Exxon Insurance Consultants International Ltd (WHETHER SINGLE WORD ORIGINAL LITERARY WORK: Ch.D.: C.A.)

Merchandising Corp. of America Inc. v. Harpbond Ltd (INFRINGEMENT: ADAM ANT: FACIAL MAKE-UP AS "ARTISTIC WORK": INDIRECT COPYING: REPRODUCTION OF SUBSTANTIAL PART: C.A.)

Mirage Studios v. Counter-Feat Clothing Co. Ltd (INFRINGEMENT: CHARACTER MERCHANDISING: TEENAGE MUTANT NINJA TURTLES: ARGUABLE CASE: Ch.D.)

Politechnika Ipari Szovetkezet v. Dallas Print Transfers Ltd (INFRINGEMENT: RUBIK CUBES: KNOWLEDGE: Ch.D.)

Performers' Protection Act 1963

Warner Bros Records Inc. v. Parr (BOOTLEGGING: WHETHER ACTIONABLE BY RECORD COMPANIES: DMPPA58: Ch.D.: C.A.)

Performers' Rights

Bassey v. Icon Entertainment plc (PROPRIETORSHIP: RECORDING OF PERFORMANCES: SUMMARY JUDGMENT: TRIABLE ISSUE: CONSENT: Ch.D.)

Copyright (Ancillary Rights) Draft Directive (RENTAL AND LENDING RIGHTS: DURATION OF PROTECTION: E.C. Council)

Stansfield v. Sovereign Music Ltd (PERFORMERS' RIGHTS: INFRINGEMENT: INTERLOCUTORY INJUNCTION: CONSENT TO RELEASE OF RECORDS: RECORDING AGREEMENT: ASSIGNMENT: Ch.D.)

Performing Right Tribunal

AIRC Ltd v. PPL (LICENCE TO BROADCAST SOUND RECORDINGS: PRACTICE: Ch.D.)

AIRC Ltd v. PPL (BBC intervening) (COMMERCIAL RADIO: SETTLEMENT OF TERMS FOR LICENCE TO BROADCAST SOUND RECORDINGS: PRINCIPLES TO BE EXERCISED: RELEVANCE OF EARLIER TRIBUNAL DECISION: Cprt Trib.)

Photographs

Apple Corps. Ltd v. Cooper (OWNERSHIP: COMMISSIONED WORK: ESTOPPEL: Ch.D.)

Charleston v. News Group Newspapers Ltd (DEFAMATION: NEWSPAPER ARTICLE: PHOTOGRAPHS: ACTORS FACES SUPERIMPOSED ON PORNOGRAPHIC PICTURES: EXPLANATORY TEXT: CONTEXT: C.A.)

Handmade Films (Productions) Ltd v. Express Newspapers plc (INFRINGEMENT: UNLAWFUL INTERFERENCE WITH GOODS: Ch.D.)

Mail Newspapers plc v. Express Newspapers plc (WEDDING PHOTOGRAPHS: WHETHER CO-OWNER LEGALLY DEAD: Ch.D.)

Shelley Films Ltd v. Rex Features Ltd (PHOTOGRAPH OF FILM COSTUMES, PROSTHESES AND SET: SUBSISTENCE OF COPYRIGHT: Ch.D.)

Plastercasts

Breville Europe plc v. Thorn EMI Domestic Appliances Ltd (REGISTERED DESIGN: INFRINGEMENT: TEST: SANDWICH TOASTERS: DRAWINGS: PLASTERCASTS OF TOASTED SANDWICHES: WHETHER SCULPTURES: PROPER PROPRIETOR: COMMISSIONED WORK: Pat. Ct)

Practice

Abuse of process

Form Tubes Ltd v. Guinness Bros plc (STRIKING OUT: Ch.D.)

Split Roller Bearing Co. Ltd's Licence of Right (Copyright) Application (WHETHER FAILURE TO INDICATE MANNER OF EXPLOITATION AN ABUSE OF PROCESS: C.-G.)

Account

Nelson v. Rye (INFRINGEMENT: MUSICAL WORKS: MANUFACTURE AND SALE AFTER EXPIRY OF LICENCE: POP MUSICIAN AND MANAGER: TERMS OF RETAINER: LIMITATION PERIOD: LACHES AND ACQUIESCENCE: Ch.D.)

Account of moneys received

Nelson v. Mark Rye and Cocteau Records Ltd (MANAGEMENT CONTRACT: WHETHER CLAIM STATUTE-BARRED: LACHES: COUNTERCLAIM FOR COMMISSION AND EXPENSES: CONVERSION: MASTER RECORDINGS: DELIVERY UP: COPYRIGHT: AUTHORISING: ISSUING TO THE PUBLIC: LICENCE: Ch.D.)

Account of profits

Cala Homes (South) Ltd v. Alfred McAlpine Homes East Ltd (No. 2) (INFRINGEMENT: WHETHER ADDITIONAL STATUTORY DAMAGES AVAILABLE, FORM OF ORDER: Ch.D.)

Island Records Ltd v. Tring International plc (INQUIRY AS TO DAMAGES: ELECTION: TIME FOR ELECTION: INFORMED CHOICE: WHETHER ORDER RELEVANT TO DISCOVERY: Ch.D.)

Additional damages

A.&M. Records v. Video Collection International Limited (INFRINGEMENT: SOUND RECORDINGS: OWNERSHIP: EQUITABLE OWNERSHIP: ADDITIONAL DAMAGES: Ch.D.)

Cala Homes (South) Ltd v. Alfred McAlpine Homes East Ltd (No. 2) (ARCHITECT'S DRAWINGS: ELECTION FOR ACCOUNT OF PROFITS: WHETHER ADDITIONAL STATUTORY DAMAGES AVAILABLE, FORM OF ORDER: Ch.D.)

Affidavit evidence

Penfold v. Fairbrass (INFRINGEMENT: STRIKING OUT: MUSICAL WORK: WHETHER ADMISSIBLE: TAPE RECORDING OF SONGS: WHETHER ADMISSIBLE: Ch.D.)

Anton Piller practice

Altertext Inc. v. Advanced Data Communications Ltd (INFRINGEMENT: PASSING OFF: Ch.D.)

British Phonographic Industry Ltd v. Cohen (Scotland: I.H.)

CBS United Kingdom Ltd v. Lambert (CROSS-EXAMINATION: Ch.D.: C.A.)

CBS United Kingdom Ltd v. Perry (INFRINGEMENT: PRACTICE: ANTON PILLER: CROSS-EXAMINATION: Ch.D.)

Chappell v. United Kingdom (INFRINGEMENT: EXECUTION TOGETHER WITH SEARCH WARRANT: RIGHT TO RESPECT FOR PRIVATE LIFE: NECESSITY IN A DEMOCRATIC SOCIETY: PROPORTIONALITY: ECHR)

Columbia Picture Industries Inc. v. Robinson (INTERLOCUTORY MOTION: *ex parte* PROCEEDINGS: DUTY TO DISCLOSE: Ch.D.)

Commissioners of Customs & Excise v. Hamlin Slowe (Ch.D.)

Crest Homes plc v. Marks (USE OF DOCUMENTS FOR CONTEMPT PROCEEDINGS IN EARLIER ACTION: PRIVILEGE AGAINST SELF-INCRIMINATION: C.A.: H.L.)

Digital Equipment Corp. v. Darkcrest Ltd (CROSS-UNDERTAKING IN DAMAGES: Ch.D.)

EMI Records Ltd v. Kudhail (INFRINGEMENT: REPRESENTATIVE CLASS OF DEFENDANTS: C.A.)

General Nutrition Ltd v. Pattni (Ch.D.)

Hytrac Conveyors Ltd v. Conveyors International Ltd (INTERLOCUTORY INJUNCTION: C.A.)

Intergraph Corp. v. Solid Systems CAD Services Ltd (COMPUTER SOFTWARE: APPLICATION TO DISCHARGE ORDER: MATERIAL NON-DISCLOSURE: MISREPRESENTATION: DELAY: Ch.D.)

McDonald v. Graham ("Z CARDS": MAREVA PRACTICE: Pat C.C.: C.A.)

Sega Enterprises Ltd v. Alca Electronics (DISCOVERY: C.A.)

Systematica Ltd v. London Computer Centre Ltd (Ch.D.)

Twentieth Century Fox Film Corp. v. Tryrare Ltd (DISCLOSURE OF INFORMATION OBTAINED: Ch.D.)

Universal City Studios Inc. v. Hubbard (PRIVILEGE AGAINST SELF-INCRIMINATION: Ch.D.: C.A.)

VDU Installations Ltd v. Integrated Computer Systems & Cybernetics Ltd (IMPROPER EXECUTION: NEGLIGENT IMPROPRIETY: CONTEMPT: Ch.D.)

Wardle Fabrics Ltd v. G. Myristis Ltd (CONTEMPT: DISCHARGE OF ORDER: Ch.D.)

WEA Records Ltd v. Visions Channel 4 Ltd (JURISDICTION TO ENTERTAIN APPEAL: C.A.)

Best evidence

Autospin (Oil Seals) Ltd v. Beehive Spinning (INFRINGEMENT: ANTECEDENT SKETCHES: Ch.D.)

Calderbank letter

Brugger v. Medicaid (Pat. Ct)

C. & H. Engineering v. F. Klucznik & Sons Ltd (Ch.D.)

Case stated

The Reject Shop plc v. Robert Manners (CRIMINAL PROCEEDINGS: APPEAL BY WAY OF CASE STATED: Q.B.D.)

Cause of action

Banks v. CBS Songs Ltd (SUMMONS TO AMEND CAUSE ISSSUED BEFORE BUT HEARD AFTER COMING INTO FORCE OF ACT: WHETHER CLAIM FOR CONVERSION DAMAGES STATUTE BARRED: Ch.D.: C.A.)

Coming into force of C.D.&P.A. 1988

Banks v. CBS Songs Ltd (WHETHER CLAIM FOR CONVERSION DAMAGES STATUTE BARRED: Ch.D.: C.A.)

Ransburg-Gema AG v. Electrostatic Plant Systems Ltd (CLAIM TO CONVERSION DAMAGES NOT LOST IN RESPECT OF AMENDMENTS MADE AFTER COMMENCEMENT OF ACT: C.A.)

Consent

Bassey v. Icon Entertainment plc (PERFORMER'S RIGHTS: PROPRIETORSHIP: RECORDING OF PERFORMANCES: SUMMARY JUDGMENT: TRIABLE ISSUE: Ch.D.)

Consent order

John Richardson Computers Ltd v. Flanders (DISCHARGE OR VARIATION OF CONSENT ORDER ON CHANGE OF CIRCUMSTANCES: DUTY OF DUE DILIGENCE: Ch.D.)

Contempt

VDU Installations Ltd v. Integrated Computer Systems & Cybernetics Ltd (ANTON PILLER ORDER: IMPROPER EXECUTION: NEGLIGENT IMPROPRIETY: Ch.D.)

Wardle Fabrics Ltd v. G. Myristis Ltd (ANTON PILLER PRACTICE: DISCHARGE OF ORDER: Ch.D.)

Conversion

Nelson v. Mark Rye and Cocteau Records Ltd (MANAGEMENT CONTRACT: ACCOUNT OF MONEYS RECEIVED: MASTER RECORDINGS: DELIVERY UP: AUTHORISING: ISSUING TO THE PUBLIC: LICENCE: Ch.D.)

Costs

BACTA v. Phonographic Performance Ltd (SOUND RECORDINGS: LICENCE SCHEME: BACKGROUND MUSIC FROM JUKEBOXES: FEES: Cprt Trib.)

Brugger v. Medicaid (INFRINGEMENT: INQUIRY: *Calderbank* LETTER: WHETHER COSTS SHOULD BE DETERMINED AFTER INQUIRY: Pat. Ct)

C. & H. Engineering v. F. Klucznik & Sons Ltd (WHETHER WITHOUT PREJUDICE CORRESPONDENCE AFTER *Calderbank* LETTER PRIVILEGED: Ch.D.)

John Richardson Computers Ltd v. Flanders (SOFTWARE: MINOR INFRINGEMENTS: APPROPRIATE ORDER WHERE WHOLESALE INFRINGEMENT ALLEGED BUT ONLY MINOR ESTABLISHED: Ch.D.)

Performing Right Society Ltd v. The British Entertainment and Dancing Association Ltd (APPEAL FROM DECISION OF COPYRIGHT TRIBUNAL: DETERMINATION OF ROYALTY RATE: PRINCIPLES: Ch.D.)

Shippam (C.) Ltd v. Princes-Buitoni Ltd (INFRINGEMENT: PLEADINGS: REQUIREMENTS OF STATEMENTS OF CLAIM: Ch.D.)

The Reject Shop plc v. Robert Manners (SECONDARY INFRINGEMENT: CRIMINAL PROCEEDINGS: APPEAL BY WAY OF CASE STATED: Q.B.D.)

Counterclaim

Nelson v. Mark Rye and Cocteau Records Ltd (MANAGEMENT CONTRACT: ACCOUNT OF MONEYS RECEIVED: WHETHER CLAIM STATUTE-BARRED: LACHES: CONVERSION: MASTER RECORDINGS: DELIVERY UP: AUTHORISING: Ch.D)

Presentaciones Musicales SA v. Secunda (OWNERSHIP: INFRINGEMENT: SOUND RECORDINGS: COUNTERCLAIM: APPLICATION TO STRIKE OUT: PARTIAL SUMMARY JUDGMENT: Ch.D.)

Criminal practice

Musa v. Le Maitre (Q.B.D.)

Cross-examination

CBS United Kingdom Ltd v. Lambert (Ch.D.)

Cross-undertaking in damages

Digital Equipment Corp. v. Darkcrest Ltd (ANTON PILLER: INFRINGEMENT: Ch.D.)

Damages

Cala Homes (South) Ltd v. Alfred McAlpine Homes East Ltd (ARCHITECT'S DRAWINGS: SUBSTANTIAL REPRODUCTION: FLAGRANCY: ADDITIONAL DAMAGES, ASSESSMENT: Ch.D.)

Gosawami v. Hammons (THESIS: RE-PUBLICATION: C.A.)

Oliver Homes (Manufacturing) v. Hamilton (BUILDING PLANS AND DESIGNS: HOUSE KIT PLANS: USE OF PLANS NOT LICENCES SEPARATELY FROM SALE OF HOUSE KIT: METHOD OF CALCULATION: ENTITLEMENT TO DAMAGES FOR LOSS OF PROFITS ON SALE OF HOUSE KIT: Scotland: O.H.)

Work Model Enterprises Ltd v. Ecosystem Ltd (INFRINGEMENT: COPYING WORDS OF BROCHURE: CLAIM FOR DAMAGES RESULTING FROM COMPETITION GENERATED BY INFRINGING BROCHURE: Ch.D.)

ZYX Music GmbH v. King (DISCO ARRANGEMENT OF SONG: INNOCENT INFRINGEMENT: ENTITLEMENT TO RELIEF: SECONDARY INFRINGEMENT: ADDITIONAL DAMAGES: FLAGRANCY OF INFRINGEMENT: Ch.D.)

Declaration

Amstrad Consumer Electronics plc v. The British Phonograph Industry Ltd (Ch.D.: C.A.)

Patten v. Burke Publishing Co. Ltd (JUDGMENT BY DEFAULT OF PUBLISHERS GIVING NOTICE OF INTENTION TO DEFEND ACTION: Ch.D.)

Thames & Hudson Ltd v. Design and Artists Copyright Society Ltd (INFRINGEMENT: CRIMINAL PROSECUTION BY COLLECTING SOCIETY AGAINST PUBLISHERS AND DIRECTORS: FAIR DEALING: STAY: Ch.D.)

Tyburn Productions Ltd v. Conan Doyle (APPLICATION FOR DECLARATION OF NO SUBSISTING COPYRIGHT IN U.S. AND INJUNCTION TO PREVENT DEFENDANT FROM MAKING SUCH ASSERTIONS: Ch.D.)

Wyco Group plc v. Cooper Roller Bearings Co. Ltd (SCOPE OF COURT'S POWER: Ch.D.)

Delay in pursuing inquiry

Nichols Advanced Vehicle Systems Inc. v. Rees (No. 2) (C.A.)

Delivery up

Adventure Film Productions SA v. Tully (WRONGFUL INTERFERENCE WITH GOODS: FILM: INTERLOCUTORY ORDER: STRENGTH OF CASE TO OWNERSHIP OF FILM AND BALANCE OF CONVENIENCE: Ch.D.)

Beggars Banquet Records Ltd v. Carlton Television Ltd (WRONGFUL INTERFERENCE WITH GOODS: FILM FOOTAGE: APPLICATION FOR INTERLOCUTORY ORDER FOR DELIVERY UP, INJUNCTIONS AND DISCOVERY: Ch.D.)

Lagenes Ltd v. It's At (U.K.) Ltd (PRACTICE: *ex parte* INJUNCTION: MISLEADING STATEMENTS: DISCOVERY OF IDENTITY OF TRADE CUSTOMERS: Ch.D.)

Nelson v. Mark Rye and Cocteau Records Ltd (MANAGEMENT CONTRACT: MASTER RECORDINGS: AUTHORISING: ISSUING TO THE PUBLIC: LICENCE: Ch.D.)

Disclosure

Dun & Bradstreet Ltd v. Typesetting Facilities Ltd (Ch.D.)

Discovery

Baldock v. Addison (SPLIT TRIAL: WHETHER PLAINTIFF ENTITLED TO DISCOVERY OF QUANTUM DOCUMENTS BEFORE TRIAL ON LIABILITY: Ch.D.)

CBS Songs Ltd v. Amstrad Consumer Electronics plc (USE IN PRESENT ACTION OF DOCUMENTS DISCLOSED BY DEFENDANT IN PREVIOUS ACTION: C.A.)

Chater & Chater Productions Ltd v. Rose (Ch.D.)

CHC Software Card Ltd v. Hopkins & Wood (CONFIDENTIALITY: Ch.D.)

Crest Homes plc v. Marks (ANTON PILLER PRACTICE: USE OF DOCUMENTS FOR
    CONTEMPT PROCEEDINGS IN EARLIER ACTION: PRIVILEGE AGAINST SELF-
    INCRIMINATION: C.A.: H.L.)
Format Communications Manufacturing Ltd v. ITT (U.K.) Ltd (DISCOVERY AND
    INSPECTION: SAFEGUARDS: C.A.)
Handmade Films (Productions) Ltd v. Express Newspapers plc (Ch.D.)
Hunter & Partners v. Wellings & Partners (OPPOSED *ex parte* MOTION: C.A.)
Island Records Ltd v. Tring International plc (INQUIRY AS TO DAMAGES: ACCOUNT
    OF PROFITS: ELECTION: TIME: INFORMED CHOICE: WHETHER ORDER
    RELEVANT TO DISCOVERY: Ch.D.)
Sega Enterprises Ltd v. Alca Electronics (ANTON PILLER PRACTICE: C.A.)

Discretion

Linpac Mouldings Ltd v. Eagleton Direct Export Ltd (SECONDARY INFRINGEMENT:
    IMPORTATION OF INFRINGING COPIES: KNOWLEDGE: THREATS: *Quia timet*
    INJUNCTION ON ABANDONMENT OF DAMAGES CLAIM: C.A.)

Dismissal for want of prosecution

Bestworth Ltd v. Wearwell Ltd (Ch.D.)

Documents disclosed by defendant in previous action

CBS Songs Ltd v. Amstrad Consumer Electronics plc (C.A.)

Duty of due diligence

John Richardson Computers Ltd v. Flanders (DISCHARGE OR VARIATION OF
    CONSENT ORDER ON CHANGE OF CIRCUMSTANCES: Ch.D.)

Duty to disclose

Columbia Picture Industries Inc. v. Robinson (ANTON PILLER ORDER:
    INTERLOCUTORY MOTION: *Ex parte* PROCEEDINGS: Ch.D.)

Evidence

Batjac Productions Inc. v. Simitar Entertainment (U.K.) Ltd (EQUITABLE TITLE:
    REQUIREMENT TO JOIN LEGAL OWNER: ACQUISITION OF LEGAL TITLE
    BEFORE JUDGMENT: WHETHER SUFFICIENT: SUMMARY JUDGMENT:
    STANDARD OF PROOF: SECONDARY EVIDENCE OF CONTENTS OF
    DOCUMENTS: Ch.D.)
Penfold v. Fairbrass (AFFIDAVIT EVIDENCE: WHETHER ADMISSIBLE: TAPE
    RECORDING OF SONGS: WHETHER ADMISSIBLE: Ch.D.)
VNU Publications Ltd v. Ziff Davis (U.K.) Ltd (CONFIDENTIAL EXHIBIT: Ch.D.)

Ex parte actions

Lagenes Ltd v. It's At (U.K.) Ltd (Ch.D.)
Hunter & Partners v. Wellings & Partners (PRACTICE: OPPOSED *ex parte* MOTION:
    DISCRETION: C.A.)
Columbia Picture Industries Inc. v. Robinson (DUTY TO DISCLOSE: Ch.D.)

Experts' reports

Cala Homes (South) Ltd v. Alfred McAlpine Homes East Ltd (INFRINGEMENT:
    FUNCTION OF EXPERT WITNESS: Ch.D.)

Injunction

ASTERIX Trade Mark (COMIC STRIPS: UNAUTHORISED SALE: INJUNCTION: VICARIOUS LIABILITY: Germany: C.A.)

Sillitoe v. McGraw-Hill Book Co. (U.K.) Ltd (INFRINGEMENT: FAIR DEALING: KNOWLEDGE: SUFFICIENT ACKNOWLEDGEMENT: ADAPTATIONS: INJUNCTIONS: DAMAGES: Ch.D.)

Silly Wizard Ltd v. Shaughnessy (SOUND RECORDINGS: PERFORMERS' PROTECTION: RIGHT OF ACTION: REMEDIES: INJUNCTION: Scotland: O.H.)

Tyburn Productions Ltd v. Conan Doyle (LITERARY CHARACTERS: APPLICATION FOR DECLARATION OF NO SUBSISTING COPYRIGHT IN U.S. AND INJUNCTION TO PREVENT SUCH ASSERTIONS: WHETHER JUSTICIABLE IN ENGLAND: TRANSITORY AND LOCAL ACTIONS: Ch.D.)

Inquiry as to damages

Brugger v. Medicaid (INFRINGEMENT: ELECTION AS TO DAMAGES OR AN ACCOUNT: WHETHER PLAINTIFF CAN CLAIM ADDITIONAL DAMAGES IN INQUIRY ALTHOUGH NOT ORIGINALLY PLEADED: *Calderbank* LETTER: WHETHER COSTS SHOULD BE DETERMINED AFTER INQUIRY: Pat. Ct)

Island Records Ltd v. Tring International plc (ACCOUNT OF PROFITS: ELECTION: TIME FOR ELECTION: INFORMED CHOICE: WHETHER ORDER RELEVANT TO DISCOVERY: Ch.D.)

Inspection

Atari Inc. v. Philips Electronics Ltd (INFRINGEMENT: COMPUTER PROGRAM: PRACTICE: Ch.D.)

Dun & Bradstreet Ltd v. Typesetting Facilities Ltd (Ch.D.)

Format Communications Manufacturing Ltd v. ITT (U.K.) Ltd (DISCOVERY AND INSPECTION: SAFEGUARDS: C.A.)

Smith Myers Communications Ltd v. Motorola Ltd (APPLICATION FOR INSPECTION OF DOCUMENTS BEFORE STATEMENT OF CLAIM SERVED: Ch.D.)

Interlocutory injunction

Alfa Laval Cheese Systems Ltd v. Wincanton Engineering Ltd (SERIOUS ISSUE: UNQUANTIFIABLE HARM: BALANCE OF CONVENIENCE: Ch.D.)

Associated Newspapers Group plc v. News Group Newspapers Ltd (THE WINDSOR CORRESPONDENCE: FAIR DEALING: DEFENCES: Ch.D.)

Chater and Chater Productions Ltd v. Rose (ARM-TWISTING INJUNCTION: EARLY DISCOVERY REFUSED: Ch.D.)

Columbia Picture Industries Inc. v. Robinson (ANTON PILLER ORDER: *ex parte* PROCEEDINGS: DUTY TO DISCLOSE: Ch.D.)

Drayton Controls (Engineering) Ltd v. Honeywell Control Systems Ltd (EVIDENCE RELEVANT FOR INTERLOCUTORY STAGE: Ch.D.)

EMI Records Ltd v. The CD Specialists Ltd (GERMAN IMPORTS: ARTICLE 30 DEFENCE: WHETHER COPYRIGHT OWNER CONSENTED: EXHAUSTION OF RIGHTS: Ch.D.)

Entec (Pollution Control) Ltd v. Abacus Mouldings (BALANCE OF RISK OF INJUSTICE: Ch.D.: C.A.)

Hytrac Conveyors Ltd v. Conveyors International Ltd (ANTON PILLER PRACTICE: C.A.)

Kambrook Distributing Pty Ltd v. Delaney (SERIOUS QUESTION TO BE TRIED: BALANCE OF CONVENIENCE: DELAY: Ch.D.)

Mad Hat Music Ltd v. Pulse 8 Records Ltd (Ch.D.)

Mail Newspapers plc v. Express Newspapers plc (Ch.D.)
Mirage Studios v. Counter-Feat Clothing Co. Ltd (FACTORS EVENLY BALANCED: Ch.D.)
Morrison Leahy Music Ltd v. Lightbond Ltd (Ch.D.)
MS Associates Ltd v. Power (ARGUABLE CASE: BALANCE OF CONVENIENCE: Ch.D.)
News Datacom Ltd v. Satellite Decoding Systems (COMPUTER PROGRAMS: BREACH: BALANCE OF CONVENIENCE: Ireland: H.C.)
Secretary of State for the Home Department v. Central Broadcasting Ltd (BALANCE OF CONVENIENCE: PUBLIC INTEREST: RELEVANCE OF FREEDOM OF SPEECH: Ch.D.: C.A.)
Shelley Films Ltd v. Rex Features Ltd (Ch.D.)
Stansfield v. Sovereign Music Ltd (PERFORMERS' RIGHTS: INFRINGEMENT: CONSENT TO RELEASE OF RECORDS: RECORDING AGREEMENT: ASSIGNMENT: Ch.D.)
Thrustcode Ltd v. WW Computing Ltd (BALANCE OF CONVENIENCE: Ch.D.)
Video Arts Ltd v. Paget Industries Ltd (FORM OF ORDER: Ch.D.)
VNU Publications Ltd v. Ziff Davis (U.K.) Ltd (CONFIDENTIAL EXHIBIT: EVIDENCE: Ch.D.)
Waterlow Directories Ltd v. Reed Information Services Ltd (QUANTIFIABILITY OF DAMAGE: ADEQUACY OF UNDERTAKINGS: BALANCE OF CONVENIENCE: Ch.D.)

Interlocutory injunction—adequacy of undertakings

Private Research Ltd v. Brosnan (WHETHER FAIR QUESTION TO BE TRIED: BALANCE OF CONVENIENCE: Ireland: H.C.)
Waterlow Directories Ltd v. Reed Information Services Ltd (QUANTIFIABILITY OF DAMAGE: BALANCE OF CONVENIENCE: Ch.D.)

Interlocutory injunction—arguable case

Mirage Studios v. Counter-Feat Clothing Co. Ltd (PASSING OFF: TEENAGE MUTANT NINJA TURTLES: Ch.D.)
MS Associates Ltd v. Power (TRANSLATOR PROGRAMS: SIMILARITIES: BALANCE OF CONVENIENCE: Ch.D.)

Interlocutory injunction—balance of convenience

Adventure Film Productions SA v. Tully (WRONGFUL INTERFERENCE WITH GOODS: INTERLOCUTORY ORDER FOR DELIVERY UP: STRENGTH OF CASE TO OWNERSHIP OF FILM: Ch.D.)
Alfa Laval Cheese Systems Ltd v. Wincanton Engineering Ltd (SERIOUS ISSUE: UNQUANTIFIABLE HARM: Ch.D.)
Entec (Pollution Control) Ltd v. Abacus Mouldings (BALANCE OF RISK OF INJUSTICE: Ch.D.: C.A.)
Kambrook Distributing Pty Ltd v. Delaney (SERIOUS QUESTION TO BE TRIED: DELAY: Ch.D.)
MS Associates Ltd v. Power (TRANSLATOR PROGRAMS: SIMILARITIES: ARGUABLE CASE: Ch.D.)
News Datacom Ltd v. Satellite Decoding Systems (COMPUTER PROGRAMS: BREACH: Ireland: H.C.)
Private Research Ltd v. Brosnan (WHETHER FAIR QUESTION TO BE TRIED: ADEQUACY OF DAMAGES: Ireland: H.C.)
Secretary of State for the Home Department v. Central Broadcasting Ltd (INTERVIEW WITH SERIAL KILLER: WHETHER PUBLIC INTEREST REQUIRED BROADCAST TO BE RESTRAINED: RELEVANCE OF FREEDOM OF SPEECH: Ch.D.: C.A.)

Thrustcode Ltd v. WW Computing Ltd (DIFFICULTY IN ESTABLISHING INFRINGEMENT: EVIDENCE OF COPYING: Ch.D.)

Waterlow Directories Ltd v. Reed Information Services Ltd (QUANTIFIABILITY OF DAMAGE: ADEQUACY OF UNDERTAKINGS: Ch.D.)

Interlocutory injunction—quantifiable harm

Alfa Laval Cheese Systems Ltd v. Wincanton Engineering Ltd (SERIOUS ISSUE: BALANCE OF CONVENIENCE: Ch.D.)

Interlocutory injunction—serious issue to be tried

Alfa Laval Cheese Systems Ltd v. Wincanton Engineering Ltd (UNQUANTIFIABLE HARM: BALANCE OF CONVENIENCE: Ch.D.)

Bassey v. Icon Entertainment plc (PERFORMER'S RIGHTS: PROPRIETORSHIP: RECORDING OF PERFORMANCES: SUMMARY JUDGMENT: CONSENT: Ch.D.)

Kambrook Distributing Pty Ltd v. Delaney (BALANCE OF CONVENIENCE: DELAY: Ch.D.)

Interlocutory injunction—whether fair question to be tried

Private Research Ltd v. Brosnan (ADEQUACY OF DAMAGES: BALANCE OF CONVENIENCE: Ireland: H.C.)

Interrogatories

CHC Software Card Ltd v. Hopkins & Wood (Ch.D.)

Rockwell International Corp. v. Serck Industries Ltd (Ch.D.: C.A.)

Judgment by default

Patten v. Burke Publishing Co. Ltd (DECLARATION: JUDGMENT IN DEFAULT OF PUBLISHERS GIVING NOTICE OF INTENTION TO DEFEND ACTION: Ch.D.)

Jurisdiction

Abkco Music & Records Inc. v. Music Collection International Ltd (APPLICATION TO SET ASIDE SERVICE OUTSIDE JURISDICTION: C.A.)

Chater & Chater Productions Ltd v. Rose (MUSIC: INFRINGEMENT: PERFORMANCE: PRIOR DISCLOSURE OF MUSIC TO DEFENDANTS: INTERLOCUTORY INJUNCTION APPLICATION: EARLY DISCOVERY: Ch.D.)

Jurisdiction of Patent County Court

McDonald v. Graham ("Z CARDS": *Res judicata*: ANTON PILLER AND MAREVA PRACTICE: PATENT: INFRINGEMENT: EXPERIMENTAL USE: BANKRUPTCY OF DEFENDANT: Pat. C.C.: C.A.)

PSM International plc v. Specialised Fastener Products (Southern) Ltd (JURISDICTION OF PATENT COUNTY COURT WHERE COPYRIGHT ALLEGED TO SUBSIST IN DESIGN DRAWINGS: Pat. C.C.)

Laches and acquiescence

Nelson v. Rye (INFRINGEMENT: MUSICAL WORKS: MANUFACTURE AND SALE AFTER EXPIRY OF LICENCE: POP MUSICIAN AND MANAGER: ACCOUNT: TERMS OF RETAINER: LIMITATION PERIOD: Ch.D.)

Legal professional privilege

CHC Software Card Ltd v. Hopkins & Wood (Ch.D.)
Wilden Pump Engineering Co. v. Fusfield (PRACTICE: PATENT AGENTS' PRIVILEGE: C.A.)

Liberty to apply

Gantenbrink v. BBC (PRACTICE: FILM: UNDERTAKINGS: LIBERTY TO APPLY: Ch.D.)

Limitation period

Nelson v. Rye (INFRINGEMENT: MUSICAL WORKS: MANUFACTURE AND SALE AFTER EXPIRY OF LICENCE: POP MUSICIAN AND MANAGER: ACCOUNT: TERMS OF RETAINER: LACHES AND ACQUIESCENCE: Ch.D.)

Locus standi

Imprimerie (SA) Thône v. Fernand Geubelle (INTELLIGENCE TEST: PUBLISHER AS CO-AUTHOR: Belgium)
Magazines in Hairdressing Establishments (COPYRIGHT COLLECTING SOCIETY: ENTITLEMENT TO FEES ON LENDING OR HIRING WORKS FOR COMMERCIAL PURPOSES: Germany: S.C.)

Mandatory injunction

Leisure Data v. Bell (C.A.)

Mareva injunction

CBS United Kingdom Ltd v. Lambert (C.A.)
McDonald v. Graham ("Z CARDS": ANTON PILLER PRACTICE: PATENT INFRINGEMENT: Pat. C.C.: C.A.)

Order 14 (summary judgment)

Bassey v. Icon Entertainment plc (PERFORMER'S RIGHTS: PROPRIETORSHIP: RECORDING OF PERFORMANCES: TRIABLE ISSUE: CONSENT: Ch.D.)
Batjac Productions Inc. v. Simitar Entertainment (U.K.) Ltd (EQUITABLE TITLE: REQUIREMENT TO JOIN LEGAL OWNER: ACQUISITION OF LEGAL TITLE BEFORE JUDGMENT: WHETHER SUFFICIENT: STANDARD OF PROOF: EVIDENCE: SECONDARY EVIDENCE OF CONTENTS OF DOCUMENTS: Ch.D.)
Express Newspapers plc v. News (U.K.) Ltd (INFRINGEMENT: COUNTERCLAIM: MUTUAL COPYING OF NEWS STORIES: FAIR DEALING: PUBLIC INTEREST: CUSTOM OF THE TRADE: Ch.D.)
LA Gear Inc. v. Hi-Tec Sports plc (INFRINGEMENT: ORIGINALITY: INDIRECT COPYING: IMPORTATION OF INFRINGING COPIES: POSSESSION IN COURSE OF BUSINESS: Ch.D.: C.A.)
Linpac Mouldings Ltd v. Eagleton Direct Export Ltd (SECONDARY INFRINGEMENT: IMPORTATION OF INFRINGING COPIES: KNOWLEDGE: THREATS: C.A.)
Machinery Market Ltd v. Sheen Publishing Ltd (INFRINGEMENT: WHETHER ADVERTISEMENT LITERARY WORK: PRINTER'S LIABILITY: CONVERSION: Ch.D.)
Macmillan Publishers Ltd v. Thomas Reed Publications Ltd (CHARTS: Ch.D.)

Presentaciones Musicales SA v. Secunda (OWNERSHIP: INFRINGEMENT: SOUND
    RECORDINGS: COUNTERCLAIM: APPLICATION TO STRIKE OUT: PARTIAL
    SUMMARY JUDGMENT: Ch.D.)
Rexnold Inc. v. Ancon Ltd (INFRINGEMENT: UPDATED WORKING DRAWINGS:
    ORIGINALITY: Ch.D.)
Schweppes Ltd v. Wellingtons Ltd (INFRINGEMENT: SCHWEPPES/
    SCHLURPPES: WHETHER PARODY ARGUABLE DEFENCE: Ch.D.)
Warner Brothers Inc. v. The Roadrunner Ltd (Ch.D.)

Patent agents' privilege

Wilden Pump Engineering Co. v. Fusfield (C.A.)

Performing right tribunal

AIRC Ltd v. PPL (LICENCE TO BROADCAST SOUND RECORDINGS: PRACTICE:
    Ch.D.)

Pleadings

Brugger v. Medicaid (WHETHER PLAINTIFF CAN CLAIM ADDITIONAL DAMAGES IN
    INQUIRY ALTHOUGH NOT ORIGINALLY PLEADED: *Calderbank* LETTER: Pat. Ct)
N. & P. Windows v. Cego Ltd (PARTICULARS OF SIMILARITIES: Ch.D.)
Ransburg-Gema AG v. Electrostatic Plant Systems Ltd (C.A.)

Privilege against self-incrimination

Crest Homes plc v. Marks (C.A.: H.L.)
Universal City Studios Inc. v. Hubbard (ANTON PILLER PRACTICE: Ch.D.: C.A.)

Privilege

C. & H. Engineering v. F. Klucznik & Sons Ltd (*Calderbank* LETTER: Ch.D.)
Wilden Pump Engineering Co. v. Fusfield (PATENT AGENTS' PRIVILEGE: C.A.)

Quia timet injunction

Linpac Mouldings Ltd v. Eagleton Direct Export Ltd (SECONDARY INFRINGEMENT:
    IMPORTATION OF INFRINGING COPIES: KNOWLEDGE: THREAT TO INFRINGE:
    Quia timet INJUNCTION ON ABANDONMENT OF DAMAGES CLAIM:
    DISCRETION: C.A.)

Reference to copyright tribunal

Working Men's Club & Institute Union Ltd v. PRS Ltd (Cprt Trib.)

Solicitor's duty

CHC Software Card Ltd v. Hopkins & Wood (LEGAL PROFESSIONAL PRIVILEGE:
    INTERROGATORIES: Ch.D.)

Standard of proof

Batjac Productions Inc. v. Simitar Entertainment (U.K.) Ltd (EQUITABLE TITLE:
    REQUIREMENT TO JOIN LEGAL OWNER: ACQUISITION OF LEGAL TITLE
    BEFORE JUDGMENT: WHETHER SUFFICIENT: SUMMARY JUDGMENT:
    EVIDENCE: SECONDARY EVIDENCE OF CONTENTS OF DOCUMENTS: Ch.D.)

Statement of claim

Millar v. Bassey (CONTRACT: INDUCING BREACH: APPLICATION TO STRIKE OUT
    STATEMENT OF CLAIM: INTENTION OF DEFENDANT: KNOWLEDGE: C.A.)

Wyko Group plc v. Cooper Roller Bearings Co. Ltd (ENGINEERING DRAWINGS: DECLARATION OF NON-INFRINGEMENT: SPARE PARTS DEFENCE: DECLARATORY RELIEF: SCOPE OF COURT'S POWER: STRIKING OUT: Ch.D.)

Statute barred

Banks v. CBS Songs Ltd (WHETHER CLAIM FOR CONVERSION DAMAGES STATUTE BARRED: Ch.D.: C.A.)

Stay of action

Etri Fans Ltd v. NMB (U.K.) Ltd (C.A.)
Thames & Hudson Ltd v. Design and Artists Copyright Society Ltd (INFRINGEMENT: CRIMINAL PROSECUTION BY COLLECTING SOCIETY AGAINST PUBLISHERS AND DIRECTORS: DECLARATION OF NON-INFRINGEMENT: FAIR DEALING: Ch.D.)

Striking out

Betsen v. CBS United Kingdom Ltd (MUSICAL WORK: WHETHER SUFFICIENT OBJECTIVE SIMILARITY: WHETHER PERCUSSION AND BASS LINE A SUBSTANTIAL PART: Ch.D.)
Form Tubes Ltd v. Guinness Bros plc (ABUSE OF PROCESS: Ch.D.)
Hutchison Personal Communications Ltd v. Hook Advertising Ltd (COUNTERCLAIM STRUCK OUT: SECONDARY INFRINGEMENT: Ch.D.)
Penfold v. Fairbrass (INFRINGEMENT: MUSICAL WORK: AFFIDAVIT EVIDENCE: WHETHER ADMISSIBLE: TAPE RECORDING OF SONGS: WHETHER ADMISSIBLE: Ch.D.)
Presentaciones Musicales SA v. Secunda (OWNERSHIP: INFRINGEMENT: SOUND RECORDINGS: COUNTERCLAIM: APPLICATION TO STRIKE OUT: PARTIAL SUMMARY JUDGMENT: Ch.D.)
PSM International plc v. Specialised Fastener Products (Southern) Ltd (AMENDMENT: Pat. C.C.)
Thames & Hudson Ltd v. Design and Artists Copyright Society Ltd (INFRINGEMENT: CRIMINAL PROSECUTION BY COLLECTING SOCIETY AGAINST PUBLISHERS AND DIRECTORS: DECLARATION OF NON-INFRINGEMENT: FAIR DEALING: STAY: Ch.D.)
Wyko Group plc v. Cooper Roller Bearings Co. Ltd (ENGINEERING DRAWINGS: DECLARATION OF NON-INFRINGEMENT: SPARE PARTS DEFENCE: DECLARATORY RELIEF: SCOPE OF COURT'S POWER: STRIKING OUT WRIT AND STATEMENT OF CLAIM: Ch.D.)

Summary judgment. See under *Order 14*

Tape recording of songs

Penfold v. Fairbrass (WHETHER ADMISSIBLE: Ch.D.)

Transfer between divisions

CHC Software Card Ltd v. Hopkins & Wood (SOLICITOR'S DUTY: Ch.D.)

Undertakings

Gantenbrink v. BBC (PRACTICE: FILM: LIBERTY TO APPLY: Ch.D.)

Use of documents for contempt proceedings in earlier action

Crest Homes plc v. Marks (C.A.: H.L.)

Without prejudice correspondence

C. & H. Engineering v. F. Klucznik & Sons Ltd (Ch.D.)

Printer's Duty of Care

Paterson Zochonis Ltd v. Merfarken Packaging Ltd (INNOCENCE: DAMAGES: STRIKING OUT: C.A.)

Private Use

Wickstrand v. Förening Svenska Tonsättares Internationella Musikbyrå (DAMAGES: EXPLOITATION RIGHTS: "PUBLIC PERFORMANCE": Sweden: S.C.)

Privilege

C. & H. Engineering v. F. Klucznik & Sons Ltd (INFRINGEMENT: COSTS: WHETHER WITHOUT PREJUDICE CORRESPONDENCE AFTER *Calderbank* LETTER PRIVILEGED: WHETHER PLAINTIFF SHOULD HAVE ACCEPTED TERMS OFFERED: Ch.D.)

CHC Software Card Ltd v. Hopkins & Wood (MALICIOUS FALSEHOOD: SOLICITOR'S DUTY: DISCOVERY: CONFIDENTIALITY: LEGAL PROFESSIONAL PRIVILEGE: INTERROGATORIES: Ch.D.)

Crest Homes plc v. Marks (DISCOVERY: ANTON PILLER PRACTICE: USE OF DOCUMENTS FOR CONTEMPT PROCEEDINGS IN EARLIER ACTION: PRIVILEGE AGAINST SELF-INCRIMINATION: APPEAL DISMISSED: H.L.)

Universal City Studios Inc. v. Hubbard (INFRINGEMENT: ANTON PILLER PRACTICE: PRIVILEGE AGAINST SELF-INCRIMINATION: Ch.D.: C.A.)

Wilden Pump Engineering Co. v. Fusfield (PATENT AGENTS' PRIVILEGE: C.A.)

Proprietor. *See under* Ownership

Public Interest

Express Newspapers plc v. News (U.K.) Ltd ("TIT FOR TAT" COPYING OF NEWSPAPER STORIES: DEFENCE: Ch.D.)

Express Newspapers plc v. News (U.K.) Ltd (MUTUAL COPYING OF NEWS STORIES: FAIR DEALING: CUSTOM OF THE TRADE: IMPLIED LICENCE: Ch.D.)

Secretary of State for the Home Department v. Central Broadcasting Ltd (INTERVIEW WITH SERIAL KILLER: WHETHER PUBLIC INTEREST REQUIRED BROADCAST TO BE RESTRAINED: RELEVANCE OF FREEDOM OF SPEECH: Ch.D.: C.A.)

Public Performance

AIRC Ltd v. PPL (LICENCE TO BROADCAST SOUND RECORDINGS: PERFORMING RIGHT TRIBUNAL: Ch.D.)

AIRC Ltd v. PPL, BBC Intervening (COMMERCIAL RADIO: SETTLEMENT OF TERMS FOR LICENCE TO BROADCAST SOUND RECORDINGS: PRINCIPLES TO BE EXERCISED: RELEVANCE OF EARLIER PERFORMING RIGHT TRIBUNAL DECISION: ASSESSMENT OF ROYALTY: BASIS: Cprt Trib.)

BACTA v. PPL (SOUND RECORDINGS: LICENCE SCHEME: BACKGROUND MUSIC FROM JUKEBOXES: FEES: COSTS: Cprt Trib.)

Ministère Public v. Lucazeau (SACEM, *partie civile*) (COLLECTION AGENCIES: STATUS: CRIMINAL OFFENCE: France: C.A.)

Phonographic Performance (Ireland) Ltd v. J. Somers (Inspector of Taxes) (TAX PAYABLE ON SUPPLY OF SERVICES: SOUND RECORDINGS: REMUNERATION FOR BROADCASTING OF SOUND RECORDINGS: Ireland: H.C.)

Piped Music in Prisons, Re (ROYALTIES: EXEMPTIONS: MUSIC PLAYED IN PRISONS: Germany: C.A.)

PPL v. Grosvenor Leisure Ltd (INFRINGEMENT: SOUND RECORDINGS: COUNTERCLAIM: ARTICLE 86 EEC: Ch.D.)

Wickstrand v. Förening Svenska Tonsättares Internationella Musikbyrå (DAMAGES: EXPLOITATION RIGHTS: PRIVATE USE: Sweden: S.C.)

Recording Agreement

Panayiotou v. Sony Music Entertainment (U.K.) Ltd (RESTRAINT OF TRADE: CHALLENGE TO ENFORCEABILITY OF AGREEMENT: ENTITLEMENT: EARLIER COMPROMISE OF PROCEEDINGS: REASONABLENESS OF TERMS: CONDUCT OF DEFENDANT: AFFECT ON TRADE BETWEEN MEMBER STATES: Ch.D.)

Stansfield v. Sovereign Music Ltd (PERFORMERS' RIGHTS: INFRINGEMENT: INTERLOCUTORY INJUNCTION: CONSENT TO RELEASE OF RECORDS: ASSIGNMENT: Ch.D.)

Recording of Performances

Bassey v. Icon Entertainment plc (PERFORMER'S RIGHTS: PROPRIETORSHIP: SUMMARY JUDGMENT: TRIABLE ISSUE: CONSENT: Ch.D.)

Registrability. *See under* Registered Design & Design Copyright Cases

Rental and Lending Rights

Copyright (Ancillary Rights) Draft Directive (PERFORMERS' RIGHTS: DURATION OF PROTECTION: E.C. Council)

Replacement Parts/Spare Parts

Car Parts (Re) (RESTRICTIVE PRACTICES: EXCLUSIVE PACKAGING: DOMINANT POSITION: DESIGN: U.K. Monopolies Commission)

Hoover plc v. George Hulme (Stockport) Ltd (KNOWLEDGE OF INFRINGEMENT: ACQUIESCENCE: ABUSE OF DOMINANT POSITION: Ch.D.)

Massey-Ferguson Ltd v. Bepco France SA (TRADE MARK: PACKAGING: UNFAIR COMPETITION: France)

Restraint of Trade

Panayiotou v. Sony Music Entertainment (U.K.) Ltd (CONTRACT: RECORDING AGREEMENT: CHALLENGE TO ENFORCEABILITY OF AGREEMENT: ENTITLEMENT: EARLIER COMPROMISE OF PROCEEDINGS: REASONABLENESS OF TERMS: CONDUCT OF DEFENDANT: AFFECT ON TRADE BETWEEN MEMBER STATES: Ch.D.)

Restrictive Practices

Koelman v. E.C. Commission (BROADCASTING: RETRANSMISSION OF PROGRAMMES BY CABLE: STANDARD AGREEMENT: OWNERSHIP: RADIO MATERIAL: COLLECTING SOCIETY: ALLEGED BREACH OF ARTICLES 85 AND 86: Case T–575/93: CFI)

Reverse Engineering

Weir Pumps Ltd v. CML Pumps Ltd (INFRINGEMENT: LICENCE TO REPAIR: Ch.D.)

Royalties

AIRC v. PPL and BBC (RADIO BROADCASTING OF SOUND RECORDINGS: TREATY OF ROME: PRACTICE: Cprt Trib.)

Basset v. SACEM (PHONOGRAMS: RESTRICTIVE PRACTICES: COPYRIGHT MANAGEMENT SOCIETIES: RESTRICTION OF CIRCULATION: ECJ)

British Phonographic Industry Ltd v. Mechanical Copyright Protection Society Ltd (No. 2) (SETTLEMENT OF SYSTEMS TERMS AND ROYALTY RATE: Cprt Trib.)

British Phonographic Industry Ltd v. Mechanical Copyright Protection Society Ltd (TRIBUNAL CONSIDERING PROPOSED LICENSING SCHEME: JURISDICTION: Cprt Trib.)

Discount Inter-Shopping Co. Ltd v. Micrometro Ltd (SOUND RECORDING: LICENSING: Ch.D.)

House of Spring Gardens Ltd v. Point Blank Ltd (DAMAGES: ACCOUNT OF PROFITS: WHETHER ROYALTY FOR BREACH OF CONTRACT PRECLUDES FURTHER PECUNIARY AWARD FOR BREACH OF COPYRIGHT AND CONFIDENCE: Ireland: H.C.)

John (Elton) v. James (PUBLISHING, RECORDING AND MANAGEMENT AGREEMENTS: LICENSING, SUB-PUBLISHING AGREEMENTS WITH PUBLISHERS' SUBSIDIARIES: UNDUE INFLUENCE: Ch.D.)

Malcolm v. Oxford University Press (The Chancellor, Masters and Scholars of The University of Oxford) (ORAL COMMITMENT TO PUBLISH BOOK AT ROYALTY RATE: WHETHER ENFORCEABLE CONTRACT IN ABSENCE OF AGREEMENT AS TO PRINT RUN, FORMAT, AND SALE PRICE: WHETHER INTENTION TO CREATE LEGAL RELATIONS: C.A.)

Performing Right Societies (RESTRICTIVE PRACTICES: COLLECTING SOCIETIES: PARALLEL IMPORTS: NOTICE: E.C. Comm.)

Performing Right Society Ltd v. The British Entertainment and Dancing Association Ltd (PERFORMING RIGHT: DISCOTHÈQUES: APPEAL FROM DECISION OF COPYRIGHT TRIBUNAL: Ch.D.)

Piped Music in Prisons, Re (EXEMPTIONS: MUSIC PLAYED IN PRISONS: Germany: C.A.)

Sky Channel (No. 2) (CABLE TELEVISION: INTERPRETATION OF DECODING SATELLITE SIGNALS: Austria: S.C.)

Satellite Broadcasting. *See under* Broadcasting

Scotland

Beta Computers (Europe) Ltd v. Adobe Systems (Europe) Ltd (SHRINK-WRAPPED SOFTWARE LICENCE: SUPPLY OF SOFTWARE: NO CONCLUDED CONTRACT UNTIL ACCEPTANCE OF LICENCE CONDITIONS BY PURCHASER: NO NEED FOR IMPLIED TERM: LICENCE CONDITIONS IMPOSED BY COPYRIGHT OWNER: DOCTRINE OF *ius quaesitum tertio*: O.H.)

British Phonographic Industry Ltd v. Cohen (INFRINGEMENT: ANTON PILLER: PRACTICE: I.H.)

Clark v. David Allan & Co. Ltd (ARTISTIC WORK: DESIGN DRAWINGS: INFRINGEMENT: GARMENT: WHETHER FINISHED GARMENT CONSTITUTES REPRODUCTION: VISUAL IMPACT: O.H.)

Oliver Homes (Manufacturing) v. Hamilton (INFRINGEMENT: BUILDING PLANS AND DESIGNS: HOUSE KIT PLANS: USE OF PLANS NOT LICENCES SEPARATELY FROM SALE OF HOUSE KIT: DAMAGES: METHOD OF CALCULATION: ENTITLEMENT TO DAMAGES FOR LOSS OF PROFITS ON SALE OF HOUSE KIT: O.H.)

Silly Wizard Ltd v. Shaughnessy (SOUND RECORDINGS: PERFORMERS' PROTECTION: RIGHT OF ACTION: REMEDIES: INJUNCTION: O.H.)

Sculptures

Breville Europe plc v. Thorn EMI Domestic Appliances Ltd (REGISTERED DESIGN: INFRINGEMENT: TEST: SANDWICH TOASTERS: DRAWINGS: PLASTERCASTS OF TOASTED SANDWICHES: WHETHER SCULPTURES: PROPER PROPRIETOR: COMMISSIONED WORK: Pat. Ct)

Davis (J.&S.) (Holdings) Ltd v. Wright Health Group Ltd (DENTAL IMPRESSION TRAYS: ORIGINALITY: DRAWINGS: NON-EXPERT DEFENCE: Ch.D.)

Lenin's Monument (Re) (STATUE: PUBLIC OWNERSHIP: SCULPTOR'S RIGHTS: PROSPECTIVE DAMAGE: Germany: C.A.)

Secondary Infringement

Hutchison Personal Communications Ltd v. Hook Advertising Ltd (COUNTERCLAIM STRUCK OUT: SECONDARY INFRINGEMENT: POSSESSION OF INFRINGING COPIES: Ch.D.)

Linpac Mouldings Ltd v. Eagleton Direct Export Ltd (IMPORTATION OF INFRINGING COPIES: KNOWLEDGE: THREAT TO INFRINGE: C.A.)

The Reject Shop plc v. Robert Manners (SUBSISTENCE: ENLARGED PHOTOCOPIES: ORIGINALITY: Q.B.D.)

Section 9(8) Defence. See Defence

Serious Issue to be Tried. See Practice (Interlocutory injunction—serious issue to be tried)

Shrink-wrapped Licence

Beta Computers (Europe) Ltd v. Adobe Systems (Europe) Ltd (SUPPLY OF SOFTWARE: NO CONCLUDED CONTRACT UNTIL ACCEPTANCE OF LICENCE CONDITIONS BY PURCHASER: NO NEED FOR IMPLIED TERM: LICENCE CONDITIONS IMPOSED BY COPYRIGHT OWNER: SCOTTISH: DOCTRINE OF ius quaesitum tertio: Scotland: O.H.)

Software. See under Computer Programs and Software

Skill and Labour

The Reject Shop plc v. Robert Manners (SECONDARY INFRINGEMENT: SUBSISTENCE: ENLARGED PHOTOCOPIES: ORIGINALITY: CRIMINAL PROCEEDINGS: APPEAL BY WAY OF CASE STATED: PRACTICE: COSTS: Q.B.D.)

Sound Recordings. *See also* **Musical Works**

A.&M. Records v. Video Collection International Limited (INFRINGEMENT: OWNERSHIP: EQUITABLE OWNERSHIP: ADDITIONAL DAMAGES: Ch.D.)

Abkco Music & Records Inc. v. Music Collection International Ltd (INFRINGEMENT: AUTHORISATION: LICENCE GRANTED TO MANUFACTURE AND SELL OUTSIDE U.K.: APPLICATION TO SET ASIDE SERVICE OUTSIDE JURISDICTION: C.A.)

AIRC Ltd v. PPL (LICENCE TO BROADCAST: PRACTICE: Performing Right Tribunal: Ch.D.)

AIRC Ltd v. PPL (COMMERCIAL RADIO: SETTLEMENT OF TERMS FOR LICENCE: PRINCIPLES: RELEVANCE OF EARLIER PRT DECISION: Cprt Trib.)

Amstrad Consumer Electronics plc v. The British Phonograph Industry Ltd (HOME TAPING: EFFECT OF COPYRIGHT WARNING NOTICE: Ch.D.: C.A.)

Apple Corps. Ltd v. EMI Records Ltd (CONTRACT: BREACH: CONSTRUCTION: RECTIFICATION: BEATLES RECORDINGS: RED AND BLUE ALBUMS: SETTLEMENT AGREEMENT PROHIBITING RELEASE OF CERTAIN RECORDS WITHOUT PRIOR WRITTEN CONSENT: ALBUMS IN NEW FORMAT: WHETHER AGREEMENT APPLIED TO BOXED SET: C.A.)

BACTA v. PPL (LICENCE SCHEME: BACKGROUND MUSIC FROM JUKEBOXES: FEES: COSTS: Cprt Trib.)

Banks v. CBS Songs Ltd (LYRICS IN RECORDED POP SONG: Ch.D.: C.A.)

CBS Songs Ltd v. Amstrad Consumer Electronics plc and Dixons Ltd (INFRINGEMENT: MUSICAL WORK: HOME TAPING AUTHORISATION: JOINT TORTFEASORS: INCITEMENT TO COMMIT A TORT: INCITEMENT TO COMMIT A CRIME: NEGLIGENCE: H.L.)

Discount Inter-Shopping Co. Ltd v. Micrometro Ltd (LICENSING: ROYALTIES: Ch.D.)

John (Elton) v. James (ROYALTIES: PUBLISHING, RECORDING AND MANAGEMENT AGREEMENTS: Ch.D.)

EMI Electrola GmbH v. Patricia IM-und Export Verwaltungs GmbH (PHONOGRAMS: ARTICLE 36 EEC: EXHAUSTION OF RIGHTS: EXPIRY OF COPYRIGHT PERIOD IN DENMARK, NOT IN GERMANY: ECJ)

EMI Records Ltd v. The CD Specialists Ltd (INFRINGEMENT: BOOTLEG RECORDS: IMPORTS: EXHAUSTION OF RIGHTS: Ch.D.)

Mad Hat Music Ltd v. Pulse 8 Records Ltd (INFRINGEMENT: OWNERSHIP: AUTHOR: PERFORMER'S RIGHTS: CONSENT TO MAKING STUDIO RECORDINGS: WHETHER FURTHER CONSENT NECESSARY FOR MAKING COMMERCIAL RECORDS: Ch.D.)

Phil Collins v. Imtrat Handelsgesellschaft mbH (DISCRIMINATION: NATIONALITY: PHONOGRAMS: BOOTLEG RECORDINGS: REMEDY UNDER GERMAN LAW AVAILABLE TO GERMAN NATIONALS: DISCRIMINATION: ECJ)

Phonographic Performance (Ireland) Ltd v. J. Somers (Inspector of Taxes) (REMUNERATION FOR BROADCASTING OF SOUND RECORDINGS: Ireland: H.C.)

Phonographic Performance Ltd v. Retail Broadcast Services Ltd (STATUTORY LICENCE TO BROADCAST: NOTICE TO LICENSING BODY PRIOR TO EXERCISING RIGHT: WHETHER STRICT COMPLIANCE WITH STATUTORY REQUIREMENTS MANDATORY: Ch.D.)

PPL v. Grosvenor Leisure Ltd (INFRINGEMENT: COUNTERCLAIM: ARTICLE 86: Ch.D.)

Presentaciones Musicales SA v. Secunda (OWNERSHIP: INFRINGEMENT: COUNTERCLAIM: APPLICATION TO STRIKE OUT: PARTIAL SUMMARY JUDGMENT: Ch.D.)

Silly Wizard Ltd v. Shaughnessy (PERFORMERS' PROTECTION: RIGHT OF ACTION: REMEDIES: INJUNCTION: Scotland: O.H.)

Warner Bros Records Inc. v. Parr (BOOTLEGGING: WHETHER ACTIONABLE BY RECORD COMPANIES: Ch.D.: C.A.)

Subconscious Copying

EMI Music Publishing Ltd v. Papathanasiou (*Chariots of Fire* THEME: INNOCENCE: Ch.D.)

Subject–Matter

Architectural drawings

Cala Homes (South) Ltd v. Alfred McAlpine Homes East Ltd (Ch.D.)

Potton Ltd v. Yorkclose Ltd (Ch.D.)

Oliver Homes (Manufacturing) v. Hamilton (BUILDING PLANS AND DESIGNS: HOUSE KIT PLANS: Scotland: O.H.)

Audiovisual works

Rutman v. Société Des Gens de Lettres (France: D.C.)

Baby cape

Merlet v. Mothercare plc (Ch.D.: C.A.)

Bibliographies and extracts

Le Monde (Sàrl) v. Société Microfor Inc. (France: S.C.)

Bulletproof vests

House of Spring Gardens Ltd v. Point Blank Ltd (H.C.: S.C.)

Cable television

Sky Channel (No. 2) (INTERPRETATION OF DECODING SATELLITE SIGNALS: Austria: S.C.)

Performing Right Society Ltd v. Marlin Communal Aerials Ltd (Ireland: S.C.)

SUISA (Swiss Society of Authors & Publishers) v. Rediffusion AG (Switzerland)

CND pamphlet

Kennard v. Lewis (Ch.D.)

Circuit diagrams

Anacon Corporation Ltd v. Environmental Research Technology Ltd (WHETHER INFRINGED AS ARTISTIC WORKS BY "NET LISTS" AND CIRCUIT BOARDS: WHETHER INFRINGED AS LITERARY WORKS: Ch.D.)

Comic strips

ASTERIX Trade Mark (Germany: C.A.)

Computer mail-shot

Waterlow Directories Ltd v. Reed Information Services Ltd (LEGAL DIRECTORIES: Ch.D.)

Computer program

Elan Digital Systems Ltd v. Elan Computers Ltd (C.A.)
John Richardson Computers Ltd v. Flanders (Ch.D.)
Leisure Data v. Bell (C.A.)
MS Associates Ltd v. Power (TRANSLATOR PROGRAMS: Ch.D.)
Sega Enterprises Ltd v. Richards (Ch.D.)
Thrustcode Ltd v. WW Computing Ltd (Ch.D.)
Total Information Processing Systems Ltd v. Daman Ltd (Ch.D.)
Unicomp Srl v. Italcomputers Srl (Italy: Magistrates' Ct: Pisa)

Dental impression trays

Davis (J.&S.) (Holdings) Ltd v. Wright Health Group Ltd (Ch.D.)

Digital compact cassettes

Philips International BV's Application (E.C. Comm.)

Doors

Costelloe v. Johnston, Johnston and We Fit Doors Ltd (t/a Doorways) (Ireland: H.C.)

Dramatic work

Wiseman v. George Weidenfeld & Nicholson Ltd (Ch.D.)

Facial make-up

Merchandising Corp. of America Inc. v. Harpbond Ltd (C.A.)

Film costumes

Shelley Films Ltd v. Rex Features Ltd (PHOTOGRAPH OF FILM COSTUMES: Ch.D.)

Film

Musa v. Le Maitre (Q.B.D.)
Shelltrie Distribution Sàrl v. SNTF (France)
Time Warner Entertainments Company LP v. Channel Four Television Corporation
    plc (*A Clockwork Orange*: C.A.)
Western Front Ltd v. Vestron Inc. (Ch.D.)

Games

Lallier v. Lux (France: C.A.)

Garment

Clark v. David Allan & Co. Ltd (Scotland: O.H.)
Lewis Trusts v. Bambers Stores Ltd (C.A.)

Greyhound cards and race forecast dividends

Bookmakers' Afternoon Greyhound Services Ltd v. Wilf Gilbert (Staffs) Ltd (Ch.D.)

Indexes

Le Monde (Sàrl) v. Société Microfor Inc. (OWNERS' RIGHTS: REPRODUCTION:
    INDEXES: INTELLECTUAL CONTENT: DERIVED WORKS: France: S.C.: C.A.)

413

Lamb creep feeder

C. & H. Engineering v. F. Klucznik & Sons Ltd (Ch.D.)

Lawyers' pleadings

Copyright in Court Proceedings (Germany: S.C.)

Legal directories

Waterlow Directories Ltd v. Reed Information Services Ltd (COMPUTER MAIL-SHOT: Ch.D.)

Lotteries

Express Newspapers plc v. Liverpool Daily Post & Echo plc (Ch.D.)

Maps and charts

Copyright in Maps and Plans ("MAP FOR MEN": Switzerland)
Geographia Ltd v. Penguin Books Ltd (Ch.D.)
Macmillan Publishers Ltd v. Thomas Reed Publications Ltd (CHARTS: Ch.D.)

Mastheads

News Group Newspapers Ltd v. The Mirror Group Newspapers (1988) Ltd (Ch.D.)

Medley of songs

Morrison Leahy Music Ltd v. Lightbond Ltd (Ch.D.)

Music

Hérault v. SACEM (France: C.A.)
Penfold v. Fairbrass (Ch.D.)

Music played in prisons

Piped Music in Prisons, Re (Germany: C.A.)

Newspaper

Express Newspapers plc v. News (U.K.) Ltd (STORIES: Ch.D.)
Financial Times Ltd v. Sàrl Ecopress (ARTICLES: France)
Société Microfor v. Sàrl "Le Monde" (TITLES AND ARTICLES: INDEXES: PRESS REVIEW: BIBLIOGRAPHIES AND EXTRACTS: France: S.C.: C.A.)

Phonograms

Phil Collins v. Imtrat Handelsgesellschaft mbH (ECJ)

Photocopies

Société Rannou Graphie v. CNPRI (France: S.C.)

Photograph

Handmade Films (Productions) Ltd v. Express Newspapers plc (Ch.D.)

Keays v. Dempster (C.C., City of London)
Mail Newspapers plc v. Express Newspapers plc (WEDDING PHOTOGRAPHS: Ch.D.)
Shelley Films Ltd v. Rex Features Ltd (FILM COSTUMES: Ch.D.)

Pig fender

C. & H. Engineering v. F. Klucznik & Sons Ltd (Ch.D.)

Press review

Le Monde (Sàrl) v. Société Microfor Inc. (France: S.C.)

Racing cars

Nichols Advanced Vehicle Systems Inc. v. Rees (No. 3) (Ch.D.: C.A.)

Radio and television schedules

Radio Telefis Eireann v. Magill TV Guide Ltd (Ireland: H.C.)

Rubik cubes

Politechnika Ipari Szovetkezet v. Dallas Print Transfers Ltd (Ch.D.)

School books

Song Book for Schools (Germany: S.C.)

Sculptures

Davis (J.&S.) (Holdings) Ltd v. Wright Health Group Ltd (DENTAL IMPRESSION TRAYS: Ch.D.)

Septic tanks

Entec (Pollution Control) Ltd v. Abacus Mouldings (Ch.D.: C.A.)

Sherlock Holmes

Tyburn Productions Ltd v. Conan Doyle (Ch.D.)

Sound recordings

Phonographic Performance (Ireland) Ltd v. J. Somers (Inspector of Taxes) (Ireland: H.C.)
Silly Wizard Ltd v. Shaughnessy (Scotland: O.H.)

Source code

Ibcos Computers Ltd v. Barclays Mercantile Highland Finance Ltd (Ch.D.)

Statue

Lenin's Monument (Re) (Germany: C.A.)

Study notes for students

Sillitoe v. McGraw-Hill Book Co. (U.K.) Ltd (Ch.D.)

Teenage Mutant Ninja Turtles

Mirage Studios v. Counter-Feat Clothing Co. Ltd (Ch.D.)

Television cable diffusion service

Paramount Pictures Corporation v. Cablelink Ltd (Ireland: H.C.)

Television listings

Independent Television Publications Ltd v. E.C. Commission (CFI)
Independent Television Publications Ltd v. Time Out Ltd (Ch.D.)
News Group Newspapers Ltd v. Independent Television Publications Ltd (Cprt Trib.)
Radio Telefis Eireann v. E.C. Commission (CFI)
Radio Telefis Eireann v. Magill TV Guide Ltd (Ireland: H.C.)

Tender documents

Copyright in Tender Documents (Germany)

Thesis

Gosawami v. Hammons (RE-PUBLICATION: DAMAGES: C.A.)

The Windsor correspondence

Associated Newspapers Group plc v. News Group Newspapers Ltd (Ch.D.)

Video games

Hiring of Video Games Cassettes (Germany)

Videos

Warner Brothers Inc. v. Christiansen (ECJ)

Wedding photographs

Mail Newspapers plc v. Express Newspapers plc (Ch.D.)

Works of art and literature

Schweizerische Interpreten-Gesellschaft v. X and Z (Switzerland: Fed. Ct)

Subsistence

Bookmakers' Afternoon Greyhound Services Ltd v. Wilf Gilbert (Staffordshire) Ltd (GREYHOUND CARDS AND RACE FORECAST DIVIDENDS: OWNERSHIP: Ch.D.)
The Reject Shop plc v. Robert Manners (SECONDARY INFRINGEMENT: ENLARGED PHOTOCOPIES: ORIGINALITY: WHETHER SKILL AND LABOUR INVOLVED: Q.B.D.)

Substantial Part

Betsen v. CBS United Kingdom Ltd (MUSICAL WORK: WHETHER SUFFICIENT OBJECTIVE SIMILARITY: WHETHER PERCUSSION AND BASS LINE A SUBSTANTIAL PART: Ch.D.)
Billhöfer Maschinenfabrik BmgH v. T.H. Dixon & Co. Ltd (INFRINGEMENT: MECHANICAL DRAWING: ENGINEER, NOT LAYMAN, TO ASSESS RELEVANT FEATURE: Ch.D.)
Davis (J.&S.) (Holdings) Ltd v. Wright Health Group Ltd (INFRINGEMENT: DENTAL IMPRESSION TRAYS: DEFENCE: Ch.D.)
Ibcos Computers Ltd v. Barclays Mercantile Highland Finance Ltd (COMPUTER SOFTWARE: SOURCE CODE: SUBSISTENCE AND EXTENT OF PROTECTION: INFRINGEMENT: Ch.D.)
John Richardson Computers Ltd v. Flanders (INFRINGEMENT: SOFTWARE: TITLE TO PORTIONS OF PROGRAM WRITTEN BY INDEPENDENT CONTRACTORS: WHETHER COPYING: Ch.D.)
Johnstone Safety Ltd v. Peter Cook (International) plc (INFRINGEMENT: ROAD CONES: TEST: C.A.)

Merchandising Corp. of America Inc. v. Harpbond Ltd (INFRINGEMENT: ADAM ANT: FACIAL MAKE-UP AS "ARTISTIC WORK": INDIRECT COPYING: C.A.)

Sweden

Wickstrand v. Förening Svenska Tonsättares Internationella Musikbyrå (DAMAGES: EXPLOITATION RIGHTS: "PUBLIC PERFORMANCE": PRIVATE USE: S.C.)

Switzerland

Copyright in Maps and Plans ("MAP FOR MEN": IMMORALITY)
Schweizerische Interpreten-Gesellschaft v. X and Z (WORKS OF ART AND LITERATURE: DISPUTES: PROTECTION: PERSONAL RIGHTS: BOOTLEGGING: UNFAIR COMPETITION: Fed. Ct) `
SUISA (Swiss Society of Authors & Publishers) v. Rediffusion AG (CABLE TELEVISION: FOREIGN BROADCASTS)

Television Guides

BBC v. E.C. Commission (CFI)
Independent Television Publications Ltd v. E.C. Commission (CFI)
Independent Television Publications Ltd v. Time Out Ltd (Ch.D.)
News Group Newspapers Ltd v. Independent Television Publications Ltd (Cprt Trib.)
Paramount Pictures Corporation v. Cablelink Ltd (Ireland: H.C.)
Radio Telefis Eireann v. E.C. Commission (CFI)
Radio Telefis Eireann v. Magill TV Guide Ltd (Ireland: H.C.)

Term of Protection

Drayton Controls (Engineering) Ltd v. Honeywell Control Systems Ltd (DURATION OF PROTECTION FOR ARTICLE MADE BY INDUSTRIAL PROCESS WHERE PART NOT INTENDED TO BE SOLD SEPARATELY: Ch.D.)
Interlego AG v. A. Foley (Vic.) Pty Ltd (EFFECT OF REGISTERED DESIGN: Ch.D.)
Smith v. Greenfield (INFRINGEMENT: Northern Ireland: H.C.)
Weir Pumps Ltd v. CML Pumps Ltd (INFRINGEMENT: REVERSE ENGINEERING: Ch.D.)

Threats

Granby Marketing Services Ltd v. Interlego AG (UNLAWFUL INTERFERENCE WITH CONTRACTUAL RELATIONS: STRIKING OUT: Ch.D.)

Title

Batjac Productions Inc. v. Simitar Entertainment (U.K.) Ltd (EQUITABLE TITLE: REQUIREMENT TO JOIN LEGAL OWNER: ACQUISITION OF LEGAL TITLE BEFORE JUDGMENT: WHETHER SUFFICIENT: Ch.D.)

Translation

Ashmore v. Douglas-Home (DRAMATIC WORK: ALTERATION TO ORIGINAL WORK: COMPILATION: ADAPTATION: Ch.D.)
MS Associates Ltd v. Power (COMPUTER PROGRAMS: TRANSLATOR PROGRAMS: SIMILARITIES: Ch.D.)

Trap Order

Walt Disney Productions Ltd v. Gurvitz (CONTEMPT: *Agent provocateur*: Ch.D.)

Two-Dimensional and Three-Dimensional Works

Autospin (Oil Seals) Ltd v. Beehive Spinning (TABLES FOR CALCULATING CRITICAL
    DIMENSIONS: WHETHER THREE-DIMENSIONAL ARTICLE INFRINGES
    LITERARY WORK: Ch.D.)
C. & H. Engineering v. F. Klucznik & Sons Ltd (Ch.D.)
Entec (Pollution Control) Ltd v. Abacus Mouldings (Ch.D.: C.A.)

Unlawful Interference with Contractual Relations

Granby Marketing Services Ltd v. Interlego AG (THREATS: STRIKING OUT: Ch.D.)
Western Front Ltd v. Vestron Inc. (STRIKING OUT: UNLAWFUL INTERFERENCE
    WITH CONTRACTUAL RELATIONS: Ch.D.)

Video Games, Video Tapes and Video Cassettes

Atari Ireland Ltd v. Valadon (France)
Forgery of Copyright Videotapes, Re (FORGERY: "DOCUMENTS": Greece: S.C.)
GEMA's Reproduction Tariffs (MUSICAL WORKS: LICENCE FEES: INFRINGEMENT:
    ASSESSMENT OF DAMAGES: Germany: S.C.)
Hiring of Video Games Cassettes (Germany)
Warner Brothers Inc. v. Christiansen (LENDING RIGHTS: IMPORTS: EXHAUSTION OF
    RIGHTS: ECJ)

Wrongful Interference with Goods

Adventure Film Productions SA v. Tully (FILM: INTERLOCUTORY ORDER FOR
    DELIVERY UP: STRENGTH OF CASE TO OWNERSHIP OF FILM: Ch.D.)
Beggars Banquet Records Ltd v. Carlton Television Ltd (FILM FOOTAGE:
    APPLICATION FOR INTERLOCUTORY ORDER FOR DELIVERY UP,
    INJUNCTIONS AND DISCOVERY: Ch.D.)

Design Copyright and Registered Design

Advertising Material

Promedia SA v. Borght (PROTECTED PRODUCT: Belgium: C.A.)

Application

Amper SA's Design Application (DIVISIONAL APPLICATION: PRACTICE: COSTS:
    RDAT)
Ford Motor Co. Ltd's Design Applications (PARTS FOR MOTOR VEHICLE: "MUST
    MATCH" EXCEPTION: WHETHER FEATURES DICTATED BY FUNCTION:
    STATUTORY INTERPRETATION: REFERENCE TO PARLIAMENTARY
    MATERIAL: Q.B.D.)
Ford Motor Co. Ltd and Iveco Fiat SpA's Design Applications (PARTS FOR MOTOR
    VEHICLES: "MUST MATCH" EXCEPTION: "PATTERN AND ORNAMENT":
    REFERENCE TO *Hansard*: RDAT) (Appeal: H.L.)

Artistic Work

Clark v. David Allan & Co. Ltd (DESIGN DRAWINGS: INFRINGEMENT: GARMENT: WHETHER FINISHED GARMENT CONSTITUTES REPRODUCTION: VISUAL IMPACT: Scotland: O.H.)

Warner Brothers Inc. v. The Roadrunner Ltd (SUBSISTENCE: PRACTICE: SUMMARY JUDGMENT: Ch.D.)

Belgium

Promedia SA v. Borght (PROTECTED PRODUCT: ADVERTISING MATERIAL: Belgium: C.A.)

Coinage Designs

Ironside v. H.M. Attorney-General (INFRINGEMENT: COINAGE DESIGNS: OWNERSHIP: CROWN COPYRIGHT: Ch.D.)

Commissioned Work

Breville Europe plc v. Thorn EMI Domestic Appliances Ltd (INFRINGEMENT: TEST: SANDWICH TOASTERS: DRAWINGS: PLASTERCASTS OF TOASTED SANDWICHES: WHETHER SCULPTURES: PROPER PROPRIETOR: Pat. Ct)

Copying

C. & H. Engineering v. F. Klucznik & Sons Ltd (INFRINGEMENT: TEST: DESIGN RIGHTS: FUNCTIONAL OBJECTS: CREATOR: TWO-DIMENSIONAL AND THREE-DIMENSIONAL WORKS: Ch.D.)

Perrin v. Drennan (REGISTERED DESIGN: INFRINGEMENT: SIMILAR FACT EVIDENCE: Ch.D.)

Copyright Infringement

Ironside v. H.M. Attorney-General (COINAGE DESIGNS: OWNERSHIP OF COPYRIGHT: CROWN COPYRIGHT: Ch.D.)

Interlego AG v. A. Foley (Vic.) Pty Ltd (EFFECT OF REGISTERED DESIGN: TERM OF PROTECTION: Ch.D.)

Valeo Vision SA v. Flexible Lamps Ltd (INFRINGEMENT: VALIDITY: NOVELTY: FUNCTIONALITY: LICENCE OF RIGHT: WHETHER INNOCENT THIRD PARTY CONSCIENCE BOUND: FORM OF RELIEF: Pat. Ct)

Creator

C. & H. Engineering v. F. Klucznik & Sons Ltd (COPYING: TWO-DIMENSIONAL AND THREE-DIMENSIONAL WORKS: OWNERSHIP: Ch.D.)

Crown Ownership of Copyright

Ironside v. H.M. Attorney General (INFRINGEMENT: COINAGE DESIGNS: Ch.D.)

Damages

Amalgamated Mining Services Pty Ltd v. Warman International Ltd (OVERLAP WITH DESIGN PROTECTION: ADDITIONAL DAMAGES: C.-G.)

Design Copyright

British Leyland Motor Corp. v. Armstrong Patents Co. Ltd (INFRINGEMENT: U.K. DESIGN COPYRIGHT: ARTICLES 36, 85 & 86: Ch.D.) (REFUSAL TO REFER TO ECJ UNDER ARTICLE 177: C.A.)

Car Parts (Re) (RESTRICTIVE PRACTICES: SPARE PARTS: EXCLUSIVE PACKAGING: DOMINANT POSITION: DESIGN COPYRIGHT: U.K. Monopolies Commission)

Knoll International Gavina SpA v. Sàrl Aliotta Diffusion (IMPORTS: EXHAUSTION OF RIGHTS: NO DESIGN RIGHT UNDER ITALIAN LAW: ARTICLE 36(1): France: S.C.)

Design Drawings

Breville Europe plc v. Thorn EMI Domestic Appliances Ltd (INFRINGEMENT: TEST: SANDWICH TOASTERS: PLASTERCASTS OF TOASTED SANDWICHES: WHETHER SCULPTURES: PROPER PROPRIETOR: COMMISSIONED WORK: Pat. Ct)

Clark v. David Allan & Co. Ltd (ARTISTIC WORK: INFRINGEMENT: GARMENT: WHETHER FINISHED GARMENT CONSTITUTES REPRODUCTION: VISUAL IMPACT: Scotland: O.H.)

Design of Parts Common to Trade

Drayton Controls (Engineering) Ltd v. Honeywell Control Systems Ltd (ORIGINALITY: VISUAL SIGNIFICANCE OF MINOR ALTERATIONS: DURATION OF COPYRIGHT PROTECTION FOR ARTICLE MADE BY INDUSTRIAL PROCESS WHERE PART NOT INTENDED TO BE SOLD SEPARATELY: PURCHASE BY NAME, NOT VISUAL APPEARANCE: Ch.D.)

Divisional Application

Amper SA's Design Application (PRACTICE: COSTS: RDAT)

Dominant Position

Car Parts (Re) (RESTRICTIVE PRACTICES: SPARE PARTS: EXCLUSIVE PACKAGING: U.K. Monopolies Commission)

Duration of Protection. *See under* Term of Copyright

Engineering Drawings

Amalgamated Mining Services Pty Ltd v. Warman International Ltd (WHETHER "ARTISTIC WORKS": OVERLAP WITH COPYRIGHT PROTECTION: REGISTRABILITY: C.-G.)

European Court, Reference to

British Leyland Motor Corp. v. Armstrong Patents Co. Ltd (INFRINGEMENT: U.K. DESIGN COPYRIGHT: ARTICLES 36, 85 & 86: Ch.D.) (REFUSAL TO REFER TO ECJ UNDER ARTICLE 177: C.A.)

Evidence. *See* Practice *(Evidence)*

Exclusive Packaging

Car Parts (Re) (RESTRICTIVE PRACTICES: SPARE PARTS: DOMINANT POSITION: DESIGN COPYRIGHT: U.K. Monopolies Commission)

Exhaustion of Rights

Knoll International Gavina SpA v. Sàrl Aliotta Diffusion (IMPORTS: NO DESIGN RIGHT UNDER ITALIAN LAW: ARTICLE 36(1): France: S.C.)

Expired Registered Designs

Interlego AG v. Alex Folley (Vic.) Pty Ltd (COPYRIGHT: INFRINGEMENT: WHETHER DESIGNS WERE CAPABLE OF REGISTRATION: WHETHER NOVELTY OF DESIGN WAS RELEVANT TO QUESTION OF REGISTRABILITY: Ch.D.)

Expunction from Register

Costelloe v. Johnston, Johnston and We Fit Doors Ltd (t/a Doorways) (INFRINGEMENT: DOOR: WHETHER PRIOR PUBLICATION EXISTING RENDERING REGISTRATION INVALID: COUNTERCLAIM: FORM OF RELIEF: Ireland: H.C.)

Eye Appeal

Gardex Ltd v. Sorata (INFRINGEMENT: VALIDITY: PATENT DRAWING: OWNERSHIP: Ch.D.)

Form of Relief

Costelloe v. Johnston, Johnston and We Fit Doors Ltd (t/a Doorways) (WHETHER PRIOR PUBLICATION EXISTING RENDERING REGISTRATION INVALID: COUNTERCLAIM: EXPUNCTION FROM REGISTER: Ireland: H.C.)

France

Knoll International Gavina SpA v. Sàrl Aliotta Diffusion (IMPORTS: DESIGN EXHAUSTION OF RIGHTS: NO DESIGN RIGHT UNDER ITALIAN LAW: ARTICLE 36(1): S.C.)

Functional Objects

C. & H. Engineering v. F. Klucznik & Sons Ltd (INFRINGEMENT: TEST: DESIGN RIGHTS: SIMPLICITY: MODIFICATION AND AMENDMENT: TWO-DIMENSIONAL AND THREE-DIMENSIONAL WORKS: Ch.D.)

Functionality

Valeo Vision SA v. Flexible Lamps Ltd (COPYRIGHT: CONFIDENTIAL INFORMATION: INFRINGEMENT: VALIDITY: NOVELTY: LICENCE OF RIGHT: WHETHER INNOCENT THIRD PARTY CONSCIENCE BOUND: FORM OF RELIEF: Pat. Ct)

Garment

Clark v. David Allan & Co. Ltd (ARTISTIC WORK: DESIGN DRAWINGS: INFRINGEMENT: WHETHER FINISHED GARMENT CONSTITUTES REPRODUCTION: VISUAL IMPACT: Scotland: O.H.)

Implied Licence

British Leyland Motor Corp. v. Armstrong Patents Co. Ltd (COPYRIGHT: INFRINGEMENT: REPLACEMENT EXHAUST PIPES: ACQUIESCENCE: REFERENCE TO ECJ: Ch.D.)

Imports

Knoll International Gavina SpA v. Sàrl Aliotta Diffusion (EXHAUSTION OF RIGHTS: NO DESIGN RIGHT UNDER ITALIAN LAW: ARTICLE 36(1): France: S.C.)

Infringement

Breville Europe plc v. Thorn EMI Domestic Appliances Ltd (TEST: SANDWICH TOASTERS: DRAWINGS: PLASTERCASTS OF TOASTED SANDWICHES: WHETHER SCULPTURES: PROPER PROPRIETOR: COMMISSIONED WORK: Pat. Ct)

British Leyland Motor Corp. v. Armstrong Patents Co. Ltd (U.K. DESIGN COPYRIGHT: ARTICLES 36, 85 & 86: Ch.D.) (REFUSAL TO REFER TO ECJ UNDER ARTICLE 177: C.A.)

C. & H. Engineering v. F. Klucznik & Sons Ltd (COPYRIGHT AND DESIGN RIGHT INFRINGEMENT: PRACTICE: COSTS: WHETHER "WITHOUT PREJUDICE" CORRESPONDENCE AFTER *Calderbank* LETTER PRIVILEGED: WHETHER PLAINTIFF SHOULD HAVE ACCEPTED TERMS OFFERED: Ch.D.)

C. & H. Engineering v. F. Klucznik & Sons Ltd (TEST: DESIGN RIGHTS: FUNCTIONAL OBJECTS: Ch.D.)

Clark v. David Allan & Co. Ltd (ARTISTIC WORK: DESIGN DRAWINGS: GARMENT: WHETHER FINISHED GARMENT CONSTITUTES REPRODUCTION: VISUAL IMPACT: Scotland: O.H.)

Costelloe v. Johnston, Johnston and We Fit Doors Ltd (t/a Doorways) (DOOR: WHETHER DESIGN NEW OR ORIGINAL: WHETHER PRIOR PUBLICATION EXISTING RENDERING REGISTRATION INVALID: COUNTERCLAIM: FORM OF RELIEF: EXPUNCTION FROM REGISTER: Ireland: H.C.)

Gardex Ltd v. Sorata (VALIDITY: EYE APPEAL: PATENT DRAWING: OWNERSHIP: Ch.D.)

Gaskell & Chambers Ltd v. Measure Master Ltd (EFFECT OF PRIOR ART: Pat. Ct)

Interlego AG v. Alex Folley (Vic.) Pty Ltd (EXPIRED REGISTERED DESIGNS: WHETHER CAPABLE OF REGISTRATION: WHETHER NOVELTY RELEVANT TO REGISTRABILITY: Ch.D.)

Jade Engineering (Coventry) Ltd v. Antiference Window Systems Ltd (IDENTITY OF SUPPLIER OF INFRINGING GOODS SOUGHT: SUPPLIER NOT PARTY TO ACTION: *Norwich Pharmacal* ORDER: WHETHER TORTFEASOR MUST BE IN U.K.: JURISDICTION: DISCOVERY: PURPOSE: EXTENT: Ch.D)

Perrin v. Drennan (COPYING: SIMILAR FACT EVIDENCE: Ch.D.)

Valeo Vision SA v. Flexible Lamps Ltd (COPYRIGHT: CONFIDENTIAL INFORMATION: VALIDITY: NOVELTY: FUNCTIONALITY: LICENCE OF RIGHT: WHETHER INNOCENT THIRD PARTY CONSCIENCE BOUND: FORM OF RELIEF: Pat. Ct)

Interlocutory Injunction. *See* Practice (*Interlocutory injunction*)

Invalidity

Costelloe v. Johnston, Johnston and We Fit Doors Ltd (t/a Doorways) (DESIGN: INFRINGEMENT: DOOR: WHETHER DESIGN NEW OR ORIGINAL: PRIOR PUBLICATION: COUNTERCLAIM: FORM OF RELIEF: EXPUNCTION FROM REGISTER: Ireland: H.C.)

Ireland

Costelloe v. Johnston, Johnston and We Fit Doors Ltd (t/a Doorways) (DESIGN: INFRINGEMENT: DOOR: WHETHER DESIGN NEW OR ORIGINAL: WHETHER PRIOR PUBLICATION EXISTING RENDERING REGISTRATION INVALID: COUNTERCLAIM: FORM OF RELIEF: EXPUNCTION FROM REGISTER: H.C.)

Jurisdiction of Patent County Court. *See* Practice (*Jurisdiction*)

Licence of Right

Valeo Vision SA v. Flexible Lamps Ltd (COPYRIGHT: CONFIDENTIAL INFORMATION: INFRINGEMENT: VALIDITY: NOVELTY: FUNCTIONALITY: WHETHER INNOCENT THIRD PARTY CONSCIENCE BOUND: FORM OF RELIEF: Pat. Ct)

Modification and Amendment

C. & H. Engineering v. F. Klucznik & Sons Ltd (INFRINGEMENT: TEST: FUNCTIONAL OBJECTS: SIMPLICITY: Ch.D.)

Novelty of Design

Costelloe v. Johnston, Johnston and We Fit Doors Ltd (t/a Doorways) (INFRINGEMENT: DOOR: WHETHER DESIGN NEW OR ORIGINAL: WHETHER PRIOR PUBLICATION EXISTING RENDERING REGISTRATION INVALID: COUNTERCLAIM: EXPUNCTION FROM REGISTER: Ireland: H.C.)

Interlego AG v. Alex Folley (Vic.) Pty Ltd (INFRINGEMENT: EXPIRED REGISTERED DESIGNS: WHETHER DESIGNS WERE CAPABLE OF REGISTRATION: WHETHER NOVELTY RELEVANT TO QUESTION OF REGISTRABILITY: Ch.D.)

Valeo Vision SA v. Flexible Lamps Ltd (COPYRIGHT: CONFIDENTIAL INFORMATION: INFRINGEMENT: VALIDITY: FUNCTIONALITY: LICENCE OF RIGHT: WHETHER INNOCENT THIRD PARTY CONSCIENCE BOUND: FORM OF RELIEF: Pat. Ct)

Originality of Drawing

C. & H. Engineering v. F. Klucznik & Sons Ltd (FUNCTIONAL OBJECTS: SIMPLICITY: MODIFICATION AND AMENDMENT: COUNTERCLAIM: WHETHER DESIGN COMMONPLACE: CREATOR: COPYING: Ch.D.)

Overlap with Copyright Protection

Amalgamated Mining Services Pty Ltd v. Warman International Ltd (ENGINEERING DRAWINGS: WHETHER "ARTISTIC WORKS": REGISTRABILITY: C.-G.)

Breville Europe plc v. Thorn EMI Domestic Appliances Ltd (SANDWICH TOASTERS: DRAWINGS: PLASTERCASTS OF TOASTED SANDWICHES: WHETHER SCULPTURES: Pat. Ct)

Ownership

Breville Europe plc v. Thorn EMI Domestic Appliances Ltd (COMMISSIONED WORK: Pat. Ct)

C. & H. Engineering v. F. Klucznik & Sons Ltd (Ch.D.)

Gardex Ltd v. Sorata (INFRINGEMENT: VALIDITY: EYE APPEAL: PATENT DRAWING: Ch.D.)

Patent Drawing

Gardex Ltd v. Sorata (COPYRIGHT: INFRINGEMENT: VALIDITY: EYE APPEAL: OWNERSHIP: Ch.D.)

Pattern and Ornament

Ford Motor Co. Ltd and Iveco Fiat SpA's Design Applications (PARTS FOR MOTOR VEHICLES: "MUST MATCH" EXCEPTION: RDAT) (APPEAL: H.L.)

Plastercasts

Breville Europe plc v. Thorn EMI Domestic Appliances Ltd (INFRINGEMENT: TEST: SANDWICH TOASTERS: DRAWINGS: PLASTERCASTS OF TOASTED SANDWICHES: WHETHER SCULPTURES: PROPER PROPRIETOR: COMMISSIONED WORK: Pat. Ct)

Practice

Amendment

PSM International plc v. Specialised Fastener Products (Southern) Ltd (JURISDICTION OF PATENT COUNTY COURT WHERE COPYRIGHT ALLEGED TO SUBSIST IN DESIGN DRAWINGS: PRACTICE: STRIKING OUT: Pat. C.C.)

Appeal

Malaysian Milk Sdn Bhd's Registered Design (STRIKING OUT: DELAY: CONTRACT: EFFECT OF AGREEMENT BETWEEN PARTIES ON STRIKING OUT: SETTING ASIDE LEAVE TO APPEAL: Pat. Ct: C.A.)

Calderbank letter

C. & H. Engineering v. F. Klucznik & Sons Ltd (WITHOUT PREJUDICE CORRESPONDENCE AFTER *Calderbank* LETTER: WHETHER PRIVILEGED: WHETHER PLAINTIFF SHOULD HAVE ACCEPTED TERMS OFFERED: Ch.D.)

Costs

Amper SA's Design Application (DIVISIONAL APPLICATION: RDAT)
C. & H. Engineering v. F. Klucznik & Sons Ltd (WHETHER "WITHOUT PREJUDICE" CORRESPONDENCE AFTER *Calderbank* LETTER PRIVILEGED: WHETHER PLAINTIFF SHOULD HAVE ACCEPTED TERMS OFFERED: Ch.D.)

Counterclaim

C. & H. Engineering v. F. Klucznik & Sons Ltd (FUNCTIONAL OBJECTS: MODIFICATION AND AMENDMENT: Ch.D.)
Costelloe v. Johnston, Johnston and We Fit Doors Ltd (t/a Doorways) (INFRINGEMENT: FORM OF RELIEF: EXPUNCTION FROM REGISTER: Ireland: H.C.)

Delay

Malaysian Milk Sdn Bhd's Registered Design (STRIKING OUT: EFFECT OF AGREEMENT BETWEEN PARTIES ON STRIKING OUT: APPEAL PROCEDURE: SETTING ASIDE LEAVE TO APPEAL: Pat. Ct: C.A.)

Discovery

Jade Engineering (Coventry) Ltd v. Antiference Window Systems Ltd (IDENTITY OF SUPPLIER OF INFRINGING GOODS SOUGHT: SUPPLIER NOT PARTY TO ACTION: *Norwich Pharmacal* ORDER: WHETHER TORTFEASOR MUST BE IN U.K.: JURISDICTION: PURPOSE: EXTENT: Ch.D)

Evidence

Drayton Controls (Engineering) Ltd v. Honeywell Control Systems Ltd (EVIDENCE RELEVANT FOR INTERLOCUTORY STAGE: Ch.D.)
Perrin v. Drennan (INFRINGEMENT: SIMILAR FACT EVIDENCE: Ch.D.)

Form of relief

Valeo Vision SA v. Flexible Lamps Ltd (COPYRIGHT: CONFIDENTIAL
INFORMATION: INFRINGEMENT: VALIDITY: NOVELTY: FUNCTIONALITY:
LICENCE OF RIGHT: WHETHER INNOCENT THIRD PARTY CONSCIENCE
BOUND: Pat. Ct)

Hansard, reference to

Ford Motor Co. Ltd's Design Applications (PARTS FOR MOTOR VEHICLE: "MUST
MATCH" EXCEPTION: WHETHER FEATURES DICTATED BY FUNCTION:
STATUTORY INTERPRETATION: Q.B.D.)
Ford Motor Co. Ltd and Iveco Fiat SpA's Design Applications (PARTS FOR MOTOR
VEHICLES: "MUST MATCH" EXCEPTION: "PATTERN AND ORNAMENT":
RDAT) (APPEAL: H.L.)

Interlocutory injunction

Drayton Controls (Engineering) Ltd v. Honeywell Control Systems Ltd (EVIDENCE
RELEVANT FOR INTERLOCUTORY STAGE: Ch.D.)

Jurisdiction

Jade Engineering (Coventry) Ltd v. Antiference Window Systems Ltd
(INFRINGEMENT: IDENTITY OF SUPPLIER OF INFRINGING GOODS SOUGHT:
SUPPLIER NOT PARTY TO ACTION: *Norwich Pharmacal* ORDER: WHETHER
TORTFEASOR MUST BE IN U.K.: DISCOVERY: PURPOSE: EXTENT: Ch.D)
PSM International plc v. Specialised Fastener Products (Southern) Ltd (ALLEGATION
OF COPYRIGHT SUBSISTING IN DESIGN DRAWINGS: JURISDICTION OF PATENT
COUNTY COURT: Pat. C.C.)

Norwich Pharmacal order

Jade Engineering (Coventry) Ltd v. Antiference Window Systems Ltd (DESIGN
RIGHT: INFRINGEMENT: IDENTITY OF SUPPLIER OF INFRINGING GOODS
SOUGHT: SUPPLIER NOT PARTY TO ACTION: WHETHER TORTFEASOR MUST
BE IN U.K.: JURISDICTION: DISCOVERY: PURPOSE: EXTENT: Ch.D)

Patent County Court—jurisdiction

PSM International plc v. Specialised Fastener Products (Southern) Ltd (ALLEGATION
OF SUBSISTENCE OF COPYRIGHT IN DESIGN DRAWINGS: STRIKING OUT:
AMENDMENT: Pat. C.C.)

Privilege

C. & H. Engineering v. F. Klucznik & Sons Ltd (WHETHER "WITHOUT PREJUDICE"
CORRESPONDENCE AFTER *Calderbank* LETTER PRIVILEGED: Ch.D.)

Striking out

PSM International plc v. Specialised Fastener Products (Southern) Ltd (AMENDMENT:
Pat. C.C.)
Malaysian Milk Sdn Bhd's Registered Design (DELAY: EFFECT OF AGREEMENT
BETWEEN PARTIES ON STRIKING OUT: APPEAL PROCEDURE: SETTING ASIDE
LEAVE TO APPEAL: Pat. Ct: C.A.)

Similar fact evidence

Perrin v. Drennan (INFRINGEMENT: COPYING: Ch.D.)

Summary judgment

Warner Brothers Inc. v. The Roadrunner Ltd (Ch.D.)

Third party, whether conscience bound

Valeo Vision SA v. Flexible Lamps Ltd (COPYRIGHT: CONFIDENTIAL INFORMATION: INFRINGEMENT: VALIDITY: NOVELTY: FUNCTIONALITY: LICENCE OF RIGHT: WHETHER INNOCENT THIRD PARTY CONSCIENCE BOUND: FORM OF RELIEF: Pat. Ct)

Without prejudice correspondence

C. & H. Engineering v. F. Klucznik & Sons Ltd (CORRESPONDENCE AFTER *Calderbank* LETTER: WHETHER PRIVILEGED: WHETHER PLAINTIFF SHOULD HAVE ACCEPTED TERMS OFFERED: Ch.D.)

Prior Art

Gaskell & Chambers Ltd v. Measure Master Ltd (EFFECT OF: INFRINGEMENT: Pat. Ct)

Prior Publication

Costelloe v. Johnston, Johnston and We Fit Doors Ltd (t/a Doorways) (INFRINGEMENT: DOOR: WHETHER DESIGN NEW OR ORIGINAL: COUNTERCLAIM: Ireland: H.C.)

Prior User

Carflow Products (U.K.) Ltd v. Linwood Securities (Birmingham) Ltd (REGISTERED DESIGN: UNREGISTERED DESIGN RIGHT: WHETHER DEFENDANT'S PROTOTYPE SHOWN TO BUYER IN CONFIDENCE: Pat. Ct)

Proprietor

Breville Europe plc v. Thorn EMI Domestic Appliances Ltd (SANDWICH TOASTERS: DRAWINGS: PLASTERCASTS OF TOASTED SANDWICHES: WHETHER SCULPTURES: COMMISSIONED WORK: Pat. Ct)

Promedia SA v. Borght (REGISTERED DESIGN: ADVERTISING MATERIAL: Belgium: C.A.)

Registrability

Amalgamated Mining Services Pty Ltd v. Warman International Ltd (ENGINEERING DRAWINGS: WHETHER ARTISTIC WORKS: OVERLAP WITH COPYRIGHT PROTECTION: C.-G.)

Interlego AG v. Alex Folley (Vic.) Pty Ltd (EXPIRED REGISTERED DESIGNS: WHETHER CAPABLE OF REGISTRATION: WHETHER NOVELTY RELEVANT TO QUESTION OF REGISTRABILITY: Ch.D.)

Scotland

Clark v. David Allan & Co. Ltd (ARTISTIC WORK: DESIGN DRAWINGS: INFRINGEMENT: GARMENT: WHETHER FINISHED GARMENT CONSTITUTES REPRODUCTION: VISUAL IMPACT: O.H.)

Sculptures

Breville Europe plc v. Thorn EMI Domestic Appliances Ltd (SANDWICH TOASTERS: DRAWINGS: PLASTERCASTS OF TOASTED SANDWICHES: WHETHER SCULPTURES: Pat. Ct)

Simplicity

C. & H. Engineering v. F. Klucznik & Sons Ltd (INFRINGEMENT: TEST: DESIGN RIGHTS: FUNCTIONAL OBJECTS: Ch.D.)

Spare Parts. *See also under* Implied Licence *and* Design of Parts Common to Trade

Car Parts (Re) (RESTRICTIVE PRACTICES: EXCLUSIVE PACKAGING: DOMINANT POSITION: DESIGN COPYRIGHT: U.K. Monopolies Commission)

Subsistence of Copyright

Warner Brothers Inc. v. The Roadrunner Ltd (ARTISTIC WORK: REGISTERED DESIGN: PRACTICE: SUMMARY JUDGMENT: Ch.D.)

Term of Copyright

Drayton Controls (Engineering) Ltd v. Honeywell Control Systems Ltd (DURATION OF PROTECTION FOR ARTICLE MADE BY INDUSTRIAL PROCESS WHERE PART NOT INTENDED TO BE SOLD SEPARATELY: Ch.D.)
Interlego AG v. A. Foley (Vic.) Pty Ltd (COPYRIGHT: INFRINGEMENT: EFFECT OF REGISTERED DESIGN: Ch.D.)

Two-Dimensional and Three-Dimensional Works

C. & H. Engineering v. F. Klucznik & Sons Ltd (LAMB CREEP FEEDER: PIG FENDER: OWNERSHIP: Ch.D.)

Unregistered Design Right

Carflow Products (U.K.) Ltd v. Linwood Securities (Birmingham) Ltd (WHETHER DEFENDANT'S PROTOTYPE SHOWN TO BUYER IN CONFIDENCE: PRIOR USER: Pat. Ct)

Validity

Gardex Ltd v. Sorata (INFRINGEMENT: EYE APPEAL: PATENT DRAWING: OWNERSHIP: Ch.D.)
Valeo Vision SA v. Flexible Lamps Ltd (COPYRIGHT: CONFIDENTIAL INFORMATION: INFRINGEMENT: NOVELTY: FUNCTIONALITY: LICENCE OF RIGHT: WHETHER INNOCENT THIRD PARTY CONSCIENCE BOUND: FORM OF RELIEF: Pat. Ct)

Visual Impact

Clark v. David Allan & Co. Ltd (ARTISTIC WORK: DESIGN DRAWINGS: INFRINGEMENT: GARMENT: WHETHER FINISHED GARMENT CONSTITUTES REPRODUCTION: Scotland: O.H.)

Visual Significance of Minor Alterations

Drayton Controls (Engineering) Ltd v. Honeywell Control Systems Ltd (ORIGINALITY: Ch.D.)

Whether Design Commonplace

C. & H. Engineering v. F. Klucznik & Sons Ltd (FUNCTIONAL OBJECTS: WHETHER DRAWING ORIGINAL: Ch.D.)

Whether Design New or Original

Costelloe v. Johnston, Johnston and We Fit Doors Ltd (t/a Doorways) (INFRINGEMENT: DOOR: Ireland: H.C.)

Passing Off

Account of Profits. *See* **Practice** (*Account of profits*)

Acquiescence

Anheuser-Busch v. Budejovicky Budvar NP (HONEST CONCURRENT USER: USE AT U.S. BASES IN U.K.: GOODWILL: REPUTATION: ESTOPPEL: Ch.D.: C.A.)

Affirmation

Body Shop International plc v. Rawle (FRANCHISES: INTERLOCUTORY RELIEF: REPUDIATION: DAMAGE: Ch.D.)

Appearance

Hodgkinson & Corby Ltd v. Wards Mobility Services Ltd (GET-UP: EFFECT OF APPEARANCE ON ULTIMATE CONSUMER: Ch.D.)

Badge of Fraud

Cadbury Ltd v. Ulmer GmbH (SHAPE OF CHOCOLATE BAR: Ch.D.)

Cause of Action

SDS Biotech U.K. Ltd v. Power Agrichemicals Ltd (FUNGICIDES: USE OF MAFF NUMBERS DENOTING GOVERNMENT APPROVAL: WHETHER UNAUTHORISED USE GIVES RISE TO CAUSE OF ACTION BY AUTHORISED TRADERS: APPLICATIONS FOR SUMMARY JUDGMENT REFUSED: Ch.D.)

Character Merchandising

IPC Magazines Ltd v. Black & White Music Corp. (JUDGE DREDD: Ch.D.)
Mirage Studios v. Counter-Feat Clothing Co. Ltd (TEENAGE MUTANT NINJA TURTLES: Ch.D.)

Colour of Object

Boots Co. Ltd v. Approved Prescription Services Ltd (PILLS: INTERLOCUTORY INJUNCTION: C.A.)

GRAND MARNIER Liqueur (TWO QUALITIES, YELLOW (GOOD) AND RED (BETTER): IDENTICAL PACKAGING EXCEPT FOR COLOUR OF STOPPER AND LABELS: Germany: C.A.)
John Wyeth & Brother Ltd v. M. & A. Pharmachem Ltd (PILL: SHAPE: Ch.D.)
Rizla Ltd v. Bryant & May Ltd (CIGARETTE PAPERS: COLOUR OF PACKETS: Ch.D.)
Sodastream Ltd v. Thorn Cascade Co. Ltd (COLOURED GAS CYLINDERS: C.A.)

Common Field of Activity

Lego System A/S v. Lego M. Lemelstrich Ltd (MISREPRESENTATION: INJUNCTION: EVIDENCE: Pat. Ct)

Common Origin of Trading Names

Anderson & Lembke Ltd v. Anderson & Lembke Inc. (INTERLOCUTORY INJUNCTION: Ch.D.)

Combination of Descriptive Words

Orkney Seafoods Ltd's Petition (TRADE MARK: SIMILAR NAMES: DESCRIPTIVE NAME: ORKNEY SEAFOODS: WHETHER COMBINATION OF DESCRIPTIVE WORDS CALCULATED TO CAUSE CONFUSION: Scotland: O.H.)

Company Name

Glaxo plc v. Glaxo-Wellcome Ltd (REGISTRATION OF COMPANY NAME: DEMAND FOR PAYMENT TO CHANGE NAME: MANDATORY INJUNCTION GRANTED: Ch.D.)

Confusion

An Post, National Treasury Management Agency v. Irish Permanent plc (DESCRIPTIVE NAME: LIKELIHOOD OF DECEPTION: SAVINGS CERTIFICATES: Ireland: H.C.)
Bostick Ltd v. Sellotape G.B. Ltd (BLUE ADHESIVE TACK: WHETHER CONFUSION AT POINT OF SALE: INTERLOCUTORY INJUNCTION: Ch.D.)
British Diabetic Association (The) v. Diabetic Society (The) (CHARITIES: ENTITLEMENT TO SUE: REPUTATION: WHETHER EXTENDED TO SOCIETY OR RELATED TRADING STYLES: ASSOCIATION/SOCIETY: INJUNCTION: Ch.D.)
County Sound plc v. Ocean Sound Ltd (RADIO PROGRAMME TITLES: *The Gold AM*: DISTINCTIVENESS: REPUTATION AND DAMAGE: C.A.)
Falcon Travel Ltd v. Owners Abroad Group plc (t/a Falcon Leisure Group) (DISTINCT BUSINESS ACTIVITIES AS WHOLESALERS AND RETAILERS: CONFUSION IN TRADE AND BY PUBLIC: Ireland: H.C.)
Financial Times Ltd v. Evening Standard Co. Ltd (NEWSPAPERS: USE OF PINK PAPER FOR BUSINESS SECTION OF *Evening Standard*: Ch.D.)
Fortnum & Mason plc v. Fortnam Ltd (COMMON FIELDS OF ACTIVITY: Ch.D.)
Guccio Gucci SpA v. Paolo Gucci (TRADE MARK INFRINGEMENT: EVIDENCE: TRADE EVIDENCE: Ch.D.)
Marengo v. Daily Sketch and Daily Graphic Ltd (MERE CONFUSION NOT ACTIONABLE: C.A.)
My Kinda Town Ltd v. Soll (RESTAURANTS: CHICAGO PIZZA: Ch.D.: C.A.)
Stacey v. 2020 Communications plc (TRADE NAME: SMALL-SCALE PLAINTIFF: DEFENDANT COMPANY: Ch.D.)

Taittinger SA v. Allbev Ltd (ELDERFLOWER CHAMPAGNE: MISREPRESENTATION: DAMAGE: Ch.D.: C.A.)

Counterfeiting

Warwickshire County Council v. Verco (TRADE DESCRIPTIONS: COUNTERFEIT GOODS SOLD AS BRANDED GOODS: USE OF REASONABLE DILIGENCE: Q.B.D.)
Westminster City Council v. Pierglow Ltd (FALSE TRADE DESCRIPTION: LEVI'S JEANS: DUE DILIGENCE DEFENCE: Q.B.D.)

Damage

Associated Newspapers Group plc v. Insert Media Ltd (Ch.D.)
Associated Newspapers plc v. Insert Media Ltd (DAMAGE TO GOODWILL AND REPUTATION ATTACHING TO NEWSPAPERS: Ch.D.) (INTERLOCUTORY APPEAL: C.A.)
Body Shop International plc v. Rawle (REPUDIATION: AFFIRMATION: Ch.D.)
County Sound plc v. Ocean Sound Ltd (REPUTATION, CONFUSION AND DAMAGE: C.A.)
Grundy Television Pty Ltd v. Startrain Ltd (DAMAGE TO FUTURE MERCHANDISING AS HEAD OF DAMAGES: Ch.D.)
Mothercare U.K. Ltd v. Penguin Books Ltd (LIKELIHOOD OF DAMAGE: SURVEY EVIDENCE: C.A.)
Pete Waterman Ltd v. CBS United Kingdom Ltd (LIKELIHOOD OF DAMAGE: INTERNATIONAL REPUTATION: Ch.D.)
Stringfellow v. McCain Foods (GB) Ltd (WHETHER DEFENDANTS' ACTIVITIES DAMAGE PLAINTIFFS: MERCHANDISING RIGHTS AND PRODUCT ENDORSEMENT: Ch.D.: C.A.)
Taittinger SA v. Allbev Ltd (ELDERFLOWER CHAMPAGNE: MISREPRESENTATION: CONFUSION: Ch.D.: C.A.)

Damages

Dormeuil Frères SA v. Feraglow Ltd (INQUIRY AS TO DAMAGES: INTERIM PAYMENT: BASIS OF DAMAGES: REMOTENESS: Ch.D.)
Falcon Travel Ltd v. Owners Abroad Group plc (t/a Falcon Leisure Group) (WHETHER DAMAGES PREFERABLE TO INJUNCTION: Ireland: H.C.)
Grundy Television Pty Ltd v. Startrain Ltd (DAMAGE TO FUTURE MERCHANDISING AS HEAD OF DAMAGES: Ch.D.)
McDonald's Hamburgers Ltd v. Burgerking (U.K.) Ltd (INQUIRY AS TO DAMAGES: C.A.)
Unik Time Co. Ltd v. Unik Time Ltd (CONSPIRACY: DELAY: Ch.D.)

Deception

An Post, National Treasury Management Agency v. Irish Permanent plc (DESCRIPTIVE NAME: PROOF OF ACTUAL DECEPTION: SAVINGS CERTIFICATES: Ireland: H.C.)
Hodgkinson & Corby Ltd v. Ward's Mobility Services Ltd (INGREDIENTS OF TORT: WHEELCHAIR CUSHIONS: NO EVIDENCE OF LIKELIHOOD OF DECEPTION OF ORIGIN: Ch.D.)
Muckross Park Hotel Ltd v. Randles (HOTEL: MUCKROSS PARK HOTEL/ MUCKROSS COURT HOTEL: DETERMINATION: SECONDARY MEANING: THE MUCKROSS: GOODWILL: Ireland: H.C.)

Descriptive Name

An Post, National Treasury Management Agency v. Irish Permanent plc (PURPOSE OF REMEDY: TEST: PROOF OF ACTUAL DECEPTION: LIKELIHOOD OF DECEPTION: LIKELIHOOD OF CONFUSION: Ireland: H.C.)

Jian Tools For Sales Inc. v. Roderick Manhattan Group Ltd (SOFTWARE FOR BUSINESS PLANS: BIZPLAN BUILDER: WHETHER DESCRIPTIVE: Ch.D.)

Orkney Seafoods Ltd's Petition (SIMILAR NAMES: ORKNEY SEAFOODS: WHETHER COMBINATION OF DESCRIPTIVE WORDS CALCULATED TO CAUSE CONFUSION: Scotland: O.H.)

International House of Heraldry v. Grant (SIMILAR NAMES: INTERNATIONAL ART OF HERALDRY: WHETHER DESCRIPTIVE: WHETHER SLIGHT DIFFERENCE SUFFICIENT TO DISTINGUISH: Scotland: O.H.)

Enabling Passing off

John Walker & Sons Ltd v. Douglas Laing & Co. Ltd (SCOTCH WHISKY: INTERDICT: BREACH: EXPORT OF SPIRIT CONTAINING MIXTURE OF SCOTCH WHISKY AND CANE SPIRIT: LABELS AND BOTTLES: Scotland: O.H.)

Entitlement to Sue

British Diabetic Association (The) v. Diabetic Society (The) (CHARITIES: REPUTATION: WHETHER EXTENDED TO SOCIETY OR RELATED TRADING STYLES: ASSOCIATION/SOCIETY: WHETHER CONFUSABLY SIMILAR: INJUNCTION: Ch.D.)

Estoppel

Anheuser-Busch v. Budejovicky Budvar NP (HONEST CONCURRENT USER: USE AT U.S. BASES IN U.K.: GOODWILL: REPUTATION: Ch.D.: C.A.)

European Regulations

Consejo Regulador de las Denominaciones "Jerez-Xeres-Sherry" y "Manzanilla de Sanlucar de Barrameda" v. Mathew Clark & Sons Ltd (BEVERAGE CONTAINING BRITISH WINE AND SHERRY: USE OF "SHERRY" ON LABELS: E.C. REGULATIONS 823/97 AND 2043/89: Ch.D.)

Forced Change of Name, Effect

Jian Tools For Sales Inc. v. Roderick Manhattan Group Ltd (BALANCE OF CONVENIENCE: DEFENDANT'S AWARENESS OF PLAINTIFF'S OBJECTIONS: PRESERVATION OF STATUS QUO: Ch.D.)

Franchises

Body Shop International plc v. Rawle (INTERLOCUTORY RELIEF: REPUDIATION: AFFIRMATION: DAMAGE: Ch.D.)

Geographical Name

Grant & Sons Ltd v. William Cadenhead Ltd (TRADE MARK: INFRINGEMENT: WHISKY: Scotland: O.H.)

Highland Distilleries Co. plc v. Speymalt Whisky Distributors Ltd (TRADE MARK: INFRINGEMENT: Scotland: O.H.)

Get-up

Adidas Sportschuhfabriken v. Chas O'Neill & Co. Ltd (SPORTSWEAR: REPUTATION IN IRELAND AND ABROAD: Ireland: S.C.)

Alexander Fergusson & Co. v. Matthews McClay & Manson (USE OF GET-UP: ABANDONMENT OF GET-UP: BALANCE OF CONVENIENCE: TRADE MARKS AND NAMES: Scotland: O.H.)

Cadbury Ltd v. Ulmer GmbH (SHAPE OF CHOCOLATE BAR: BADGE OF FRAUD: Ch.D.)

Dalgety Spillers Foods Ltd v. Food Brokers Ltd (POT NOODLES: INTERLOCUTORY INJUNCTION: EVIDENCE: Ch.D.)

Drayton Controls (Engineering) Ltd v. Honeywell Control Systems Ltd (PURCHASE BY NAME, NOT VISUAL APPEARANCE: DESIGN OF PARTS COMMON TO TRADE: REPUTATION: Ch.D.)

GRAND MARNIER Liqueur (IMPORTS: GRAND MARNIER: IDENTICAL PACKAGING EXCEPT FOR COLOUR OF STOPPER AND LABELS: USE OF NATIONAL COMPETITION LAW INFRINGES ARTICLE 30: Germany: C.A.)

Hodgkinson & Corby Ltd v. Wards Mobility Services Ltd (EFFECT OF APPEARANCE ON ULTIMATE CONSUMER: Ch.D.)

Imperial Group plc v. Philip Morris Ltd (BLACK CIGARETTE PACKETS: FEATURES COMMON TO TRADE: Ch.D.)

John Wyeth & Brother Ltd v. M. & A. Pharmachem Ltd (INTERLOCUTORY INJUNCTION: COLOURED PILL: SHAPE OF PILL: Ch.D.)

Reckitt & Coleman Products Ltd v. Borden Inc. (PLASTIC LEMONS: INTERLOCUTORY INJUNCTION: C.A.)

Reckitt & Coleman Products Ltd v. Borden Inc. (PLASTIC LEMONS FOR LEMON JUICE: EFFECT OF EVIDENCE: SECONDARY MEANING: Ch.D.: H.L.)

Reckitt and Coleman Products Ltd v. Borden Inc. (APPEAL: PLASTIC LEMONS FOR LEMON JUICE: H.L.)

Reckitt & Coleman Products Ltd v. Borden Inc. (No. 3) (PLASTIC LEMONS: Ch.D.) (REPUTATION: C.A.)

Rizla Ltd v. Bryant & May Ltd (CIGARETTE PAPERS: COLOUR OF PACKETS: Ch.D.)

Scott Ltd v. Nice-Pak Products Ltd (TUBS FOR BABY WIPES: Ch.D.: C.A.)

Sodastream Ltd v. Thorn Cascade Co. Ltd (COLOURED GAS CYLINDERS: INTERLOCUTORY INJUNCTION: C.A.)

United Biscuits (U.K.) Ltd v. Burtons Biscuits Ltd (JAFFA CAKES: PACKAGING: INTERLOCUTORY INJUNCTION: Ch.D.)

Goodwill

Anheuser-Busch v. Budejovicky Budvar NP (USE AT U.S. BASES IN U.K.: REPUTATION: Ch.D.: C.A.)

Associated Newspapers plc v. Insert Media Ltd (WHETHER ADVERTISING INSERTS CAUSING DAMAGE TO GOODWILL AND REPUTATION ATTACHING TO NEWSPAPERS: Ch.D.) (INTERLOCUTORY APPEAL: C.A.)

Boot Tree Ltd v. Robinson (ASSIGNMENT OF TRADE MARK WITHOUT GOODWILL: Ch.D.)

Falcon Travel Ltd v. Owners Abroad Group plc (t/a Falcon Leisure Group) (TRADE NAME: PROTECTION: REPUTATION: MISAPPROPRIATION: PROOF: Ireland: H.C.)

Labyrinth Media Ltd v. Brave World Limited (INTERLOCUTORY INJUNCTION: *Ex parte* ORDER: PROSPECTIVE RELEASES OF RIVAL VIDEOS UNDER SAME TITLE: WHETHER PRE-LAUNCH PUBLICITY SUFFICIENT TO ESTABLISH GOODWILL: REPUTATION: EVIDENCE: ARGUABLE CASE: Ch.D.)

Muckross Park Hotel Ltd v. Randles (HOTEL: MUCKROSS PARK HOTEL/ MUCKROSS COURT HOTEL: LIKELIHOOD OF DECEPTION: DETERMINATION: SECONDARY MEANING: THE MUCKROSS: Ireland: H.C.)

Nishika Corporation v. Goodchild (INTERLOCUTORY INJUNCTION: PLAINTIFFS TRADING ABROAD ONLY: DEFENDANTS' MISREPRESENTATION: WHETHER PROTECTABLE: Ch.D.)

Honest Concurrent User

Anheuser-Busch v. Budejovicky Budvar NP (BUDWEISER BEER: USE AT U.S. BASES IN U.K.: GOODWILL: REPUTATION: Ch.D.: C.A.)

Inquiry as to Damages. *See* **Practice** (*Inquiry as to damages*)

Ireland

Adidas Sportschuhfabriken v. Chas O'Neill & Co. Ltd (GET UP: SPORTSWEAR: REPUTATION IN IRELAND AND ABROAD: S.C.)

An Bord Trachtala v. Waterford Foods plc (INTERLOCUTORY INJUNCTION: ATTEMPT TO RESTRICT ACTS COMMITTED ABROAD: JURISDICTION: WHETHER SERIOUS ISSUE TO BE TRIED: EVIDENCE: INJUNCTION REFUSED: H.C.)

An Post, National Treasury Management Agency v. Irish Permanent plc (PURPOSE OF REMEDY: USE OF DESCRIPTIVE NAME: TEST: PROOF OF ACTUAL DECEPTION: LIKELIHOOD OF DECEPTION: SAVINGS CERTIFICATES: TAX-FREE INVESTMENT GUARANTEED BY GOVERNMENT: LAUNCH OF PRODUCT UNDER SAME NAME: NEITHER TAX-FREE NOR GUARANTEED BY GOVERNMENT: LIKELIHOOD OF CONFUSION: INTERLOCUTORY INJUNCTION: SERIOUS QUESTION TO BE TRIED: DELAY: TRIAL DATE FIXED: WHETHER GROUNDS FOR REFUSAL: PUBLIC POLICY: H.C.)

B&S Ltd v. Irish Auto Trader Ltd (ADVERTISING MAGAZINES: AUTOTRADER: INTERLOCUTORY INJUNCTION: PRINCIPLES: PRESERVATION OF *status quo*: BALANCE OF CONVENIENCE: H.C.)

Falcon Travel Ltd v. Owners Abroad Group plc (t/a Falcon Leisure Group) (TRADE NAME: PROTECTION: REPUTATION: GOODWILL: MISAPPROPRIATION: PROOF: DAMAGE: REMEDY: TRAVEL BUSINESS: RELATIVE SIZE OF PARTIES: SCALE AND SCOPE OF TRADING ENVIRONMENT: DISTINCT BUSINESS ACTIVITIES AS WHOLESALERS AND RETAILERS: CONFUSION IN TRADE AND BY PUBLIC: WHETHER TRADE NAME PROPRIETARY RIGHT: DISCRETION: WHETHER DAMAGES PREFERABLE TO INJUNCTION: H.C.)

Mantruck Services Ltd and Manton & Company Ltd v. Ballinlough Electrical Refrigeration Company Ltd (MISREPRESENTATION OF AGENCY: INTERFERENCE WITH CONTRACTUAL RELATIONS: INJURIOUS FALSEHOOD: SOLE DISTRIBUTORSHIP AGREEMENT: ARTICLE 85: S.C.)

Muckross Park Hotel Ltd v. Randles (HOTEL: MUCKROSS PARK HOTEL: NEW BUSINESS MUCKROSS COURT HOTEL: LIKELIHOOD OF DECEPTION: DETERMINATION: SECONDARY MEANING: THE MUCKROSS: GOODWILL: H.C.)

Labels

Consejo Regulador de las Denominaciones "Jerez-Xeres-Sherry" y "Manzanilla de Sanlucar de Barrameda" v. Mathew Clark & Sons Ltd (BEVERAGE CONTAINING BRITISH WINE AND SHERRY: USE OF "SHERRY" ON LABELS: Ch.D.)

GRAND MARNIER Liqueur (IDENTICAL PACKAGING EXCEPT FOR COLOUR OF STOPPER AND LABELS: Germany: C.A.)

White Horse Distillers Ltd v. Gregson Associates Ltd (SCOTCH WHISKY: ADMIXTURE TRADE IN URUGUAY: TORT COMMITTED IN ENGLAND: LIABILITY OF DIRECTORS: Ch.D.)

Liability of Directors

White Horse Distillers Ltd v. Gregson Associates Ltd (SCOTCH WHISKY: ADMIXTURE TRADE IN URUGUAY: LABELS: TORT COMMITTED IN ENGLAND: LIABILITY OF DIRECTORS: Ch.D.)

Magazine or Newspaper Titles

Advance Magazine Publishing Inc. v. Redwood Publishing Ltd (INTERLOCUTORY INJUNCTION: GOURMET: Ch.D.)

Management Publications Ltd v. Blenheim Exhibitions Group plc (INTERLOCUTORY INJUNCTION: BALANCE OF CONVENIENCE: Ch.D.)

Marcus Publishing plc v. Hutton-Wild Communications Ltd (C.A.)

Morgan-Grampian plc v. Training Personnel Ltd (CHANGE OF TITLE: INTERLOCUTORY INJUNCTION: BALANCE OF CONVENIENCE: STATUS QUO: Ch.D.)

Mothercare U.K. Ltd v. Penguin Books Ltd (TRADE MARK: INFRINGEMENT: INTERLOCUTORY INJUNCTION: MISREPRESENTATION: DESCRIPTIVE WORDS: LIKELIHOOD OF DAMAGE: C.A.)

Tamworth Herald Company Ltd v. Thomson Free Newspapers Ltd (INTERLOCUTORY INJUNCTION: BALANCE OF CONVENIENCE: Ch.D.)

Malicious Falsehood

Kaye v. Robertson (LIBEL: TRESPASS TO THE PERSON: BREACH OF PRIVACY: NEWSPAPER INTERVIEW IN HOSPITAL WITH ACTOR WITH SEVERE HEAD INJURIES: C.A.)

Misrepresentation

Associated Newspapers plc v. Insert Media Ltd (JOURNAL: ALTERATION OF COPIES WITHOUT AUTHORITY: NEWSPAPER: INSERTION OF ADVERTISING MATERIAL IN NEWSPAPERS WITHOUT CONSENT OF NEWSPAPER PROPRIETOR: Ch.D.) (INTERLOCUTORY APPEAL: C.A.)

BBC v. Celebrity Centre Productions Ltd (*EastEnders* TELEVISION SERIES: *A to Z of EastEnders* MAGAZINE: AUTHORISATION: Ch.D.)

Grundy Television Pty Ltd v. Startrain Ltd (*Neighbours* TELEVISION SERIES: MISREPRESENTATION OF AUTHORITY TO USE NAME: Ch.D.)

Hodge Clemco Ltd v. Airblast Ltd (SPARES TO SUIT PLAINTIFF'S PRODUCT: MISREPRESENTATION THAT PRODUCT FITTED WITH SPARES WOULD COMPLY WITH SAFETY REGULATIONS: Ch.D.)

Intercontex v. Schmidt (INJUNCTION: MISREPRESENTATION OUTSIDE U.K.: PLAINTIFF'S NON-COMPLIANCE WITH UNDERTAKINGS TO COURT: MISREPRESENTATION OF PROPRIETORSHIP OF REGISTERED MARKS: Ch.D.)

Lego System A/S v. Lego M. Lemelstrich Ltd (LEGO: INJUNCTION: EVIDENCE: Pat. Ct)

Mantruck Services Ltd and Manton & Company Ltd v. Ballinlough Electrical Refrigeration Company Ltd (AGENCY: Ireland: S.C.)

Mothercare U.K. Ltd v. Penguin Books Ltd (TRADE MARK: INFRINGEMENT: INTERLOCUTORY INJUNCTION: DESCRIPTIVE WORDS: BOOK TITLE: C.A.)

Nishika Corporation v. Goodchild (INTERLOCUTORY INJUNCTION: PLAINTIFFS TRADING ABROAD ONLY: WHETHER GOODWILL PROTECTABLE IN U.K.: Ch.D.)

Pete Waterman Ltd v. CBS United Kingdom Ltd (PLAINTIFFS ACQUIRING NICKNAME BUT NOT TRADING UNDER THAT NAME: DISTINCTIVENESS: SECONDARY MEANING: LIKELIHOOD OF DAMAGE: INTERNATIONAL REPUTATION: Ch.D.)

Stringfellow v. McCain Foods (G.B.) Ltd (NIGHTCLUB'S REPUTATION: RELEVANCE OF MARKET SURVEY: Ch.D.: C.A.)

Taittinger SA v. Allbev Ltd (ELDERFLOWER CHAMPAGNE: CONFUSION: DAMAGE: Ch.D.) (APPEAL ALLOWED: C.A.)

Newspapers

Associated Newspapers plc v. Insert Media Ltd (JOURNAL: ALTERATION OF COPIES WITHOUT AUTHORITY: INSERTION OF ADVERTISING MATERIAL IN NEWSPAPERS WITHOUT CONSENT OF NEWSPAPER PROPRIETOR: WHETHER ADVERTISING INSERTS AMOUNTING TO MISREPRESENTATION: WHETHER ADVERTISING INSERTS CAUSING DAMAGE TO GOODWILL AND REPUTATION ATTACHING TO NEWSPAPERS: Ch.D.) (INTERLOCUTORY APPEAL: C.A.)

Financial Times Ltd v. Evening Standard Co. Ltd (INTERIM INJUNCTION: USE OF PINK PAPER FOR BUSINESS SECTION OF Evening Standard: WHETHER CONFUSION: DELAY: Ch.D.)

Kaye v. Robertson (MALICIOUS FALSEHOOD: LIBEL: TRESPASS TO THE PERSON: BREACH OF PRIVACY: NEWSPAPER INTERVIEW IN HOSPITAL WITH ACTOR WITH SEVERE HEAD INJURIES: CONSENT: JOURNALISTS GAINING ACCESS AND "INTERVIEWING" ACTOR: RIGHT TO PROTECTION OF PRIVACY: INTERLOCUTORY INJUNCTION: APPEAL: C.A.)

Mail Newspapers plc v. Insert Media Ltd (RIGHT OF PROPERTY: ADVERTISING INSERTS: DISCLAIMERS: Q.B.D.)

Marcus Publishing plc v. Hutton-Wild Communications Ltd (NEWSPAPER TITLES: C.A.)

Tamworth Herald Company Ltd v. Thomson Free Newspapers Ltd (INTERLOCUTORY INJUNCTION: NEWSPAPER TITLES: BALANCE OF CONVENIENCE: Ch.D.)

Origin of Goods

Hodgkinson & Corby Ltd v. Wards Mobility Services Ltd (INGREDIENTS OF TORT: DECEPTION: WHEELCHAIR CUSHIONS: NO EVIDENCE OF LIKELIHOOD OF DECEPTION OF ORIGIN: Ch.D.)

Packaging

GRAND MARNIER Liqueur (IMPORTS: GET-UP: GRAND MARNIER: TWO QUALITIES: IDENTICAL PACKAGING EXCEPT FOR COLOUR OF STOPPER AND LABELS: Germany: C.A.)

United Biscuits (U.K.) Ltd v. Burtons Biscuits Ltd (GET-UP: JAFFA CAKES: INTERLOCUTORY INJUNCTION: Ch.D.)

Parallel Imports

Colgate-Palmolive Ltd v. Markwell Finance Ltd (TRADE MARK: INFRINGEMENT: TOOTHPASTE: Ch.D.: C.A.)

435

Yardley & Co. Ltd v. Higson (INJUNCTION: FAILURE TO DISCLOSE MATERIAL FACT: C.A.)

Practice

Account of profits

Charles Church Developments plc v. Cronin (ENJOINED AMOUNT REDUCED IN LINE WITH LIKELY FIGURE RECOVERABLE ON ACCOUNT OF PROFITS: Ch.D.)
My Kinda Town Ltd v. Soll (PLEADINGS: Ch.D.: C.A.)

Acquiescence

International Business Machines Corporation v. Phoenix International (Computers) Ltd (TRADE MARK INFRINGEMENT: STRIKING OUT: SUMMARY JUDGMENT: EURO-DEFENCES: ESTOPPEL: Ch.D.)

Anton Piller

Altertext Inc. v. Advanced Data Communications Ltd (Ch.D.)
Coca Cola Company v. Peter John Gilbey (COUNTERFEIT GOODS: DISCLOSURE OF INFORMATION: PRIVILEGE AGAINST SELF-INCRIMINATION: RISK OF PERSONAL JEOPARDY: WHETHER GROUNDS TO DISCHARGE ORDER: WHETHER PERMISSIBLE FOR DEFENDANT TO GIVE EVIDENCE *in camera* IN THE ABSENCE OF PLAINTIFFS OR THEIR LEGAL REPRESENTATIVES: Ch.D.: C.A.)
Naf Naf SA v. Dickens (London) Ltd (APPLICATION TO DISCHARGE: INSUFFICIENT EVIDENCE TO WARRANT GRANT: MATERIAL NON-DISCLOSURE: Ch.D.)

Appeals

Elan Digital Systems Ltd v. Elan Computers Ltd (INJUNCTION APPEALS: Ch.D.: C.A.)

Arguable case

County Sound plc v. Ocean Sound Ltd (RADIO PROGRAMME TITLES: *The Gold AM*: DISTINCTIVENESS: C.A.)
Hodge Clemco Ltd v. Airblast Ltd (SPARES TO SUIT PLAINTIFF'S PRODUCT: MISREPRESENTATION THAT PRODUCT FITTED WITH SPARES WOULD COMPLY WITH SAFETY REGULATIONS: INTERLOCUTORY INJUNCTION REFUSED: Ch.D.)
Labyrinth Media Ltd v. Brave World Limited (INTERLOCUTORY INJUNCTION: *Ex parte* ORDER: PROSPECTIVE RELEASES OF RIVAL VIDEOS UNDER SAME TITLE: WHETHER PRE-LAUNCH PUBLICITY SUFFICIENT TO ESTABLISH GOODWILL: Ch.D.)

Choice of tribunal

Sears plc v. Sears, Roebuck & Co. (TRADE MARK RECTIFICATIONS AND APPLICATIONS IN REGISTRY: INJUNCTION: *Res judicata:* Ch.D.)

Contempt

Chelsea Man plc v. Chelsea Girl Ltd (No. 2) (Ch.D.)

Costs

Colgate Palmolive Ltd v. Markwell Finance Ltd (PAYMENT INTO COURT: Ch.D.)
Erven Warnink BV v. J. Townend & Sons (Hull) Ltd (INTEREST ON COSTS: TIME OF ENTERING JUDGMENT: C.A.)

Marie Claire Album SA v. Hartstone Hosiery Ltd (TRAP ORDER: Ch.D.)

Delay

An Post, National Treasury Management Agency v. Irish Permanent plc (TRIAL DATE FIXED: WHETHER GROUNDS FOR REFUSAL: PUBLIC POLICY: Ireland: H.C.)

Discovery

RHM Foods Ltd v. Bovril Ltd (C.A.)

Estoppel

International Business Machines Corporation v. Phoenix International (Computers) Ltd (TRADE MARK INFRINGEMENT: STRIKING OUT: SUMMARY JUDGMENT: EURO-DEFENCES: ACQUIESCENCE: Ch.D.)

Euro-defences

International Business Machines Corporation v. Phoenix International (Computers) Ltd (TRADE MARK INFRINGEMENT: STRIKING OUT: SUMMARY JUDGMENT: ACQUIESCENCE: ESTOPPEL: Ch.D.)

Evidence. See also under Survey evidence and Expert evidence

Coca Cola Company v. Peter John Gilbey (RISK OF PERSONAL JEOPARDY: WHETHER PERMISSIBLE FOR DEFENDANT TO GIVE EVIDENCE *in camera* IN THE ABSENCE OF PLAINTIFFS OR THEIR LEGAL REPRESENTATIVES: Ch.D.: C.A.)

Labyrinth Media Ltd v. Brave World Limited (PROSPECTIVE RELEASES OF RIVAL VIDEOS UNDER SAME TITLE: WHETHER PRE-LAUNCH PUBLICITY SUFFICIENT TO ESTABLISH GOODWILL: Ch.D.)

Mothercare U.K. Ltd v. Penguin Books Ltd (LIKELIHOOD OF DAMAGE: SURVEY EVIDENCE: PRACTICE: C.A.)

Naf Naf SA v. Dickens (London) Ltd (INSUFFICIENT EVIDENCE TO WARRANT GRANT OF ANTON PILLER ORDER: INDEMNITY COSTS: Ch.D.)

Reckitt & Coleman Products Ltd v. Borden Inc. (No. 2) (MARKET RESEARCH WITNESS: Ch.D.)

Wagamama Ltd v. City Centre Restaurants plc (SURVEY EVIDENCE: EXPERT EVIDENCE: ADMISSIBILITY: Ch.D.)

Evidence of confusion

Guccio Gucci SpA v. Paolo Gucci (TRADE EVIDENCE: Ch.D.)

Ex parte injunction

Labyrinth Media Ltd v. Brave World Limited (PROSPECTIVE RELEASES OF RIVAL VIDEOS UNDER SAME TITLE: WHETHER PRE-LAUNCH PUBLICITY SUFFICIENT TO ESTABLISH GOODWILL: REPUTATION: EVIDENCE: ARGUABLE CASE: Ch.D.)

Expert evidence

Wagamama Ltd v. City Centre Restaurants plc (SURVEY EVIDENCE: ADMISSIBILITY: Ch.D.)

Forum conveniens

Advanced Portfolio Technologies Inc v. Ainsworth (PROCEEDINGS IN NEW YORK ON SAME FACTS: WHETHER *forum conveniens* WAS ENGLAND: APPLICATION TO STAY: INJUNCTION AGAINST JOINDER OF DEFENDANT IN N.Y. PROCEEDINGS: Ch.D.)

Injunction

Intercontex v. Schmidt (MISREPRESENTATION OUTSIDE U.K.: PLAINTIFF'S NON-COMPLIANCE WITH UNDERTAKINGS TO COURT: MISREPRESENTATION OF PROPRIETORSHIP OF REGISTERED MARKS: Ch.D.)

James North & Sons Ltd v. North Cape Textiles Ltd (Scotland: England: C.A.)

Inquiry as to damages

Dormeuil Frères SA v. Feraglow Ltd (TRADE MARK: INFRINGEMENT: INTERIM PAYMENT: BASIS OF DAMAGES: Ch.D.)

McDonald's Hamburgers Ltd v. Burgerking (U.K.) Ltd (PRACTICE: INTEREST: C.A.)

Interlocutory injunction

Advance Magazine Publishing Inc. v. Redwood Publishing Ltd (MAGAZINE TITLES: GOURMET: Ch.D.)

An Bord Trachtala v. Waterford Foods plc (ATTEMPT TO RESTRICT ACTS COMMITTED ABROAD: JURISDICTION: WHETHER SERIOUS ISSUE TO BE TRIED: EVIDENCE: INJUNCTION REFUSED: Ireland: H.C.)

Anderson & Lembke Ltd v. Anderson & Lembke Inc. (COMMON ORIGIN OF TRADING NAMES: Ch.D.)

Blazer plc v. Yardley and Co. Ltd (BLAZER: PLAINTIFF TRADING IN MEN'S CLOTHES AND DEFENDANT IN TOILETRIES: BALANCE OF CONVENIENCE: NO COMPETITION YET BETWEEN PARTIES: STATUS QUO: INJUNCTION REFUSED: Ch.D.)

Boots Co. Ltd v. Approved Prescription Services Ltd (COLOURED PILLS: C.A.)

Bostick Ltd v. Sellotape G.B. Ltd (BLUE ADHESIVE TACK: WHETHER CONFUSION AT POINT OF SALE: Ch.D.)

British Association of Aesthetic Plastic Surgeons v. Cambright Ltd (Ch.D.)

Century Electronics Ltd v. CVS Enterprises Ltd (REPUTATION MONOPOLY IN GROUP OF LETTERS: HONEST CONCURRENT TRADING: USE OF *de minimis*: DELAY: Ch.D.)

Ciba-Geigy plc v. Parke Davis & Co. Ltd (INJURIOUS FALSEHOOD: REPRESENTATION THAT DEFENDANT'S PRODUCT A SUBSTITUTE FOR PLAINTIFF'S BY USE OF UNREGISTERED TRADE MARK: FREEDOM OF SPEECH: Ch.D.)

Consejo Regulador de las Denominaciones "Jerez-Xeres-Sherry" y "Manzanilla de Sanlucar de Barrameda" v. Mathew Clark & Sons Ltd (EUROPEAN REGULATIONS: BEVERAGE CONTAINING BRITISH WINE AND SHERRY: USE OF "SHERRY" ON LABELS: E.C. REGULATIONS 823/97 AND 2043/89: Ch.D.)

Consorzio del Prosciutto di Parma v. Marks and Spencer plc (PRE-SLICED PARMA HAM: REPRESENTATIVE ACTION: *Locus standi*: BALANCE OF CONVENIENCE: ITALIAN LEGISLATION: Ch.D.: C.A.)

County Sound plc v. Ocean Sound Ltd (ARGUABLE CASE: RADIO PROGRAMME TITLES: *The Gold AM*: DISTINCTIVENESS: REPUTATION, CONFUSION AND DAMAGE: C.A.)

Dalgety Spillers Foods Ltd v. Food Brokers Ltd (GET-UP: POT NOODLES: EVIDENCE: Ch.D.)

Harrods Ltd v. Schwartz-Sackin & Co. Ltd (ADVERTISEMENT OF LAPSED CONCESSION: USE AS TRADE MARK: BALANCE OF CONVENIENCE: Ch.D.)

Island Trading Co. v. Anchor Brewing Co. (EVIDENCE: Ch.D.)

Jian Tools For Sales Inc. v. Roderick Manhattan Group Ltd (COMPANY WITH NO PLACE OF BUSINESS IN U.K.: REPUTATION: ADEQUACY OF DAMAGES ON ROYALTY BASIS: EFFECT OF FORCED CHANGE OF NAME: DEFENDANT'S AWARENESS OF PLAINTIFF'S OBJECTIONS: PRESERVATION OF STATUS QUO: Ch.D.)

John Wyeth & Brother Ltd v. M. & A. Pharmachem Ltd (GET-UP: COLOURED PILL: SHAPE OF PILL: Ch.D.)

Kaye v. Robertson (MALICIOUS FALSEHOOD: LIBEL: TRESPASS TO THE PERSON: BREACH OF PRIVACY: NEWSPAPER INTERVIEW IN HOSPITAL WITH ACTOR WITH SEVERE HEAD INJURIES: CONSENT: JOURNALISTS GAINING ACCESS AND "INTERVIEWING" ACTOR: RIGHT TO PROTECTION OF PRIVACY: APPEAL: C.A.)

Management Publications Ltd v. Blenheim Exhibitions Group plc (MAGAZINE TITLES: BALANCE OF CONVENIENCE: Ch.D.)

Mirage Studios v. Counter-Feat Clothing Co. Ltd (COPYRIGHT INFRINGEMENT: CHARACTER MERCHANDISING: TEENAGE MUTANT NINJA TURTLES: FACTORS EVENLY BALANCED: PLAINTIFFS NOT MANUFACTURING OR MARKETING: WHETHER PASSING OFF ARGUABLE: Ch.D.)

Morgan-Grampian plc v. Training Personnel Ltd (MAGAZINE TITLES: CHANGE OF TITLE: BALANCE OF CONVENIENCE: STATUS QUO: Ch.D.)

Mothercare U.K. Ltd v. Penguin Books Ltd (TRADE MARK: INFRINGEMENT: LIKELIHOOD OF DAMAGE: SURVEY EVIDENCE: PRACTICE: C.A.)

Nishika Corporation v. Goodchild (PLAINTIFFS TRADING ABROAD ONLY: DEFENDANTS' MISREPRESENTATION: WHETHER PROTECTABLE IN U.K. GOODWILL: Ch.D.)

Provident Financial plc v. Halifax Building Society (TRADE MARKS: INFRINGEMENT: FINANCIAL SERVICES: WHETHER SERIOUS TRIABLE ISSUE: SECTIONS 5(2) AND 8 DEFENCES: Ch.D.)

Reckitt & Coleman Products Ltd v. Borden Inc. (GET-UP: PLASTIC LEMONS: C.A.)

Silicon Graphics Inc. v. Indigo Graphic Systems (U.K.) Ltd (TRADE MARK: INFRINGEMENT: DIGITAL PRINTING PRESS: BALANCE OF CONVENIENCE: INJUNCTION REFUSED: COSTS: Ch.D.)

Sodastream Ltd v. Thorn Cascade Co. Ltd (GET-UP: COLOURED GAS CYLINDERS: C.A.)

Tamworth Herald Company Ltd v. Thomson Free Newspapers Ltd (NEWSPAPER TITLES: BALANCE OF CONVENIENCE: Ch.D.)

Unidoor Ltd v. Marks & Spencer plc (TRADE MARK INFRINGEMENT: *Coast to Coast*: WHETHER USE AS TRADE MARK: Ch.D.)

United Biscuits (U.K.) Ltd v. Burtons Biscuits Ltd (GET-UP: JAFFA CAKES: PACKAGING: RELIABILITY OF SURVEY EVIDENCE: THREE KINDS: RELIEF REFUSED: Ch.D.)

Interlocutory injunction—adequacy of damages

BBC v. Marshall Cavendish (TRADE MARK: SEWING KIT: Ch.D.)

Interlocutory injunction—balance of convenience

Alexander Fergusson & Co. v. Matthews McClay & Manson (Scotland: O.H.)

B&S Ltd v. Irish Auto Trader Ltd (ADVERTISING MAGAZINES: AUTOTRADER: PRESERVATION OF *status quo*: Ireland: H.C.)

Blazer plc v. Yardley and Co. Ltd (NO COMPETITION YET BETWEEN PARTIES: STATUS QUO: Ch.D.)

Consorzio del Prosciutto di Parma v. Marks and Spencer plc (REPRESENTATIVE ACTION: *Locus standi*: ITALIAN LEGISLATION: Ch.D.: C.A.)

Dash Ltd v. Philip King Tailoring Ltd (PROTECTION OF LONG-ESTABLISHED BUSINESS AGAINST NEWLY-FORMED BUSINESS: Scotland: I.H.)

Gala of London Ltd v. Chandler Ltd (COUNTERCLAIM FOR NON-USE OF TRADE MARK: Ch.D.)

Harrods Ltd v. Schwartz-Sackin & Co. Ltd (ADVERTISEMENT OF LAPSED CONCESSION: Ch.D.)

International House of Heraldry v. Grant (INTERIM INTERDICT: PROTECTION OF ESTABLISHED BUSINESS AGAINST NEWLY FORMED BUSINESS: Scotland: O.H.)

Jian Tools For Sales Inc. v. Roderick Manhattan Group Ltd (COMPANY WITH NO PLACE OF BUSINESS IN U.K.: REPUTATION: ADEQUACY OF DAMAGES ON ROYALTY BASIS: EFFECT OF FORCED CHANGE OF NAME: DEFENDANT'S AWARENESS OF PLAINTIFF'S OBJECTIONS: PRESERVATION OF STATUS QUO: Ch.D.)

Management Publications Ltd v. Blenheim Exhibitions Group plc (MAGAZINE TITLES: Ch.D.)

Morgan-Grampian plc v. Training Personnel Ltd (CHANGE OF TITLE OF MAGAZINE: STATUS QUO: Ch.D.)

Orkney Seafoods Ltd's Petition (INTERIM INTERDICT: PROTECTION OF ESTABLISHED BUSINESS AGAINST NEWLY FORMED BUSINESS: Scotland: O.H.)

Silicon Graphics Inc. v. Indigo Graphic Systems (U.K.) Ltd (DIGITAL PRINTING PRESS: Ch.D.)

Tamworth Herald Company Ltd v. Thomson Free Newspapers Ltd (NEWSPAPER TITLES: Ch.D.)

Interlocutory injunction—delay

An Post, National Treasury Management Agency v. Irish Permanent plc (TRIAL DATE FIXED: WHETHER GROUNDS FOR REFUSAL: PUBLIC POLICY: Ireland: H.C.)

Interlocutory injunction—likelihood of damage

Mothercare U.K. Ltd v. Penguin Books Ltd (SURVEY EVIDENCE: PRACTICE: C.A.)

Interlocutory injunction—preservation of status quo

B&S Ltd v. Irish Auto Trader Ltd (ADVERTISING MAGAZINES: AUTOTRADER: BALANCE OF CONVENIENCE: Ireland: H.C.)

Interlocutory injunction—principles

B&S Ltd v. Irish Auto Trader Ltd (ADVERTISING MAGAZINES: AUTOTRADER: PRESERVATION OF *status quo*: BALANCE OF CONVENIENCE: Ireland: H.C.)

Interlocutory injunction—serious issue to be tried

An Bord Trachtala v. Waterford Foods plc (ATTEMPT TO RESTRICT ACTS COMMITTED ABROAD: JURISDICTION: EVIDENCE: Ireland: H.C.)

An Post, National Treasury Management Agency v. Irish Permanent plc (LIKELIHOOD OF DECEPTION: SAVINGS CERTIFICATES: LIKELIHOOD OF CONFUSION: DELAY: TRIAL DATE FIXED: WHETHER GROUNDS FOR REFUSAL: PUBLIC POLICY: Ireland: H.C.)

Interlocutory injunction—triable issue

Elan Digital Systems Ltd v. Elan Computers Ltd (PRACTICE ON INJUNCTION APPEALS: Ch.D.: C.A.)

Interest

Erven Warnink BV v. J. Townend & Sons (Hull) Ltd (INTEREST ON COSTS: TIME OF ENTERING JUDGMENT: C.A.)

McDonald's Hamburgers Ltd v. Burgerking (U.K.) Ltd (INQUIRY AS TO DAMAGES: C.A.)

Judgment

Erven Warnink BV v. J. Townend & Sons (Hull) Ltd (INTEREST ON COSTS: TIME OF
ENTERING JUDGMENT: C.A.)

Jurisdiction

An Bord Trachtala v. Waterford Foods plc (ATTEMPT TO RESTRICT ACTS
COMMITTED ABROAD: Ireland: H.C.)
Associated Newspapers Group plc v. Insert Media Ltd (PLEADINGS: AMENDMENT:
UNFAIR TRADING: DAMAGE: Ch.D.)

Laches

My Kinda Town Ltd v. Soll (CONFUSION: RESTAURANTS: CHICAGO PIZZA:
ACCOUNT OF PROFITS: PLEADINGS: Ch.D.: C.A.)

Mareva injunction

Charles Church Developments plc v. Cronin (APPEARANCE OF HOUSE: ENJOINED
AMOUNT REDUCED IN LINE WITH LIKELY FIGURE RECOVERABLE ON
ACCOUNT OF PROFITS: Ch.D.)

Opinion poll. See under *Survey evidence*

Order 14

Gillette U.K. Ltd v. Edenwest Ltd (TRADE MARK: INFRINGEMENT: INQUIRY AS TO
DAMAGES: INNOCENCE: Ch.D.)
International Business Machines Corporation v. Phoenix International (Computers)
Ltd (TRADE MARK INFRINGEMENT: STRIKING OUT: EURO-DEFENCES:
ACQUIESCENCE: ESTOPPEL: Ch.D.)
Pierre Fabre SA v. Ronco Teleproducts Inc. (Ch.D.)

Payment into court

Colgate Palmolive Ltd v. Markwell Finance Ltd (COSTS: Ch.D.)

Pleadings

Charles Church Developments plc v. Cronin (MAREVA INJUNCTION: ENJOINED
AMOUNT REDUCED IN LINE WITH LIKELY FIGURE RECOVERABLE ON
ACCOUNT OF PROFITS: Ch.D.)

Public policy

An Post, National Treasury Management Agency v. Irish Permanent plc (DELAY:
TRIAL DATE FIXED: WHETHER GROUNDS FOR REFUSAL: Ireland: H.C.)

Quia timet relief

Elida Gibbs Ltd v. Colgate-Palmolive Ltd (TOOTHPASTE ADVERTISING:
REPUTATION: COMPETING TRADE: Ch.D.)
Lego System A/S v. Lego M. Lemelstrich Ltd (WHETHER COMMON FIELD OF
ACTIVITY: MISREPRESENTATION: INJUNCTION: EVIDENCE: Pat. Ct)

Representative action

Consorzio del Prosciutto di Parma v. Marks and Spencer plc (PRE-SLICED PARMA HAM: Ch.D.: C.A.)

Res judicata

Sears plc v. Sears, Roebuck & Co. (TRADE MARK RECTIFICATIONS AND APPLICATIONS IN REGISTRY: CHOICE OF TRIBUNAL: INJUNCTION: Ch.D.)

Status quo, preservation

Jian Tools For Sales Inc. v. Roderick Manhattan Group Ltd (SOFTWARE FOR BUSINESS PLANS: BIZPLAN BUILDER: WHETHER DESCRIPTIVE: DEFENDANT'S AWARENESS OF PLAINTIFF'S OBJECTIONS: Ch.D.)

Stay, application for

Advanced Portfolio Technologies Inc v. Ainsworth (PROCEEDINGS IN NEW YORK ON SAME FACTS: WHETHER *forum conveniens* WAS ENGLAND: INJUNCTION AGAINST JOINDER OF DEFENDANT IN N.Y. PROCEEDINGS: Ch.D.)

Striking out

International Business Machines Corporation v. Phoenix International (Computers) Ltd (TRADE MARK INFRINGEMENT: SUMMARY JUDGMENT: EURO-DEFENCES: ACQUIESCENCE: ESTOPPEL: Ch.D.)

Survey evidence

Mothercare U.K. Ltd v. Penguin Books Ltd (C.A.)
Reckitt & Coleman Products Ltd v. Borden Inc. (No. 2) (MARKET RESEARCH WITNESS: Ch.D.)

Trap order

Marie Claire Album SA v. Hartstone Hosiery Ltd (COSTS: Ch.D.)

Undertaking

Process Development Ltd v. Hogg (ANTON PILLER ORDER: UNDERTAKING TO RETAIN ITEMS IN SAFE CUSTODY: PROPERTY OF PLAINTIFF: WHETHER PERMISSIBLE TO REPORT TO POLICE: C.A.)

Pseudonym

Marengo v. Daily Sketch and Daily Graphic Ltd (KEM/KIM: CARTOONISTS' *noms de plume*: NO DOT ON "*i*" OF *Kim*: MERE CONFUSION NOT ACTIONABLE: APPEAL ALLOWED: C.A.)

Purpose of Remedy

An Post, National Treasury Management Agency v. Irish Permanent plc (DESCRIPTIVE NAME: TEST: PROOF OF ACTUAL DECEPTION: LIKELIHOOD OF DECEPTION: SAVINGS CERTIFICATES: LIKELIHOOD OF CONFUSION: INTERLOCUTORY INJUNCTION: SERIOUS QUESTION TO BE TRIED: DELAY: TRIAL DATE FIXED: WHETHER GROUNDS FOR REFUSAL: PUBLIC POLICY: Ireland: H.C.)

Radio Programme Titles

County Sound plc v. Ocean Sound Ltd (*The Gold AM*: DISTINCTIVENESS: REPUTATION, CONFUSION AND DAMAGE: C.A.)

Reputation. *See also under* **Goodwill**

Adidas Sportschuhfabriken v. Chas O'Neill & Co. Ltd (REPUTATION IN IRELAND AND ABROAD: Ireland: S.C.)

Anheuser-Busch v. Budejovicky Budvar NP (USE AT U.S. BASES IN U.K.: GOODWILL: Ch.D.: C.A.)

Associated Newspapers plc v. Insert Media Ltd (WHETHER ADVERTISING INSERTS CAUSING DAMAGE TO GOODWILL AND REPUTATION ATTACHING TO NEWSPAPERS: Ch.D.) (INTERLOCUTORY APPEAL: C.A.)

British Diabetic Association (The) v. Diabetic Society (The) (WHETHER EXTENDED TO SOCIETY OR RELATED TRADING STYLES: ASSOCIATION: SOCIETY: Ch.D.)

Century Electronics Ltd v. CVS Enterprises Ltd (REPUTATION MONOPOLY IN GROUP OF LETTERS: HONEST CONCURRENT USE: USE *de minimis*: Ch.D.)

Chelsea Man Menswear Ltd v. Chelsea Girl Ltd (CHELSEA MAN: REPUTATION: Ch.D.)

County Sound plc v. Ocean Sound Ltd (RADIO PROGRAMME TITLES: *The Gold AM*: C.A.)

Drayton Controls (Engineering) Ltd v. Honeywell Control Systems Ltd (Ch.D.)

Elida Gibbs Ltd v. Colgate-Palmolive Ltd (TOOTHPASTE ADVERTISING: *Quia timet* RELIEF: Ch.D.)

Falcon Travel Ltd v. Owners Abroad Group plc (t/a Falcon Leisure Group) (TRADE NAME: PROTECTION: GOODWILL: TRAVEL BUSINESS: RELATIVE SIZE OF PARTIES: Ireland: H.C.)

Jian Tools For Sales Inc. v. Roderick Manhattan Group Ltd (COMPANY WITH NO PLACE OF BUSINESS IN U.K.: ADEQUACY OF DAMAGES ON ROYALTY BASIS: DEFENDANT'S AWARENESS OF PLAINTIFF'S OBJECTIONS: PRESERVATION OF STATUS QUO: Ch.D.)

Labyrinth Media Ltd v. Brave World Limited (PROSPECTIVE RELEASES OF RIVAL VIDEOS UNDER SAME TITLE: WHETHER PRE-LAUNCH PUBLICITY SUFFICIENT TO ESTABLISH GOODWILL: Ch.D.)

Nationwide Building Society v. Nationwide Estate Agents Ltd (ESTATE AGENCY: ALLIED FIELD: Ch.D.)

Pete Waterman Ltd v. CBS United Kingdom Ltd (INTERNATIONAL REPUTATION: Ch.D.)

Reckitt & Coleman Products Ltd v. Borden Inc. (No. 3) (GET-UP: PLASTIC LEMONS: C.A.)

Salon Services (Hairdressing Supplies) Ltd v. Direct Salon Services Ltd (TRADE MARK: DESCRIPTIVE NAME: Scotland: O.H.)

Stringfellow v. McCain Foods (G.B.) Ltd (NIGHTCLUB'S REPUTATION: RELEVANCE OF MARKET SURVEY: Ch.D.: C.A.)

Shape of Object

Cadbury Ltd v. Ulmer GmbH (CHOCOLATE BAR: Ch.D.)

John Wyeth & Brother Ltd v. M. & A. Pharmachem Ltd (PILL: Ch.D.)

Scotland

Alexander Fergusson & Co. v. Matthews McClay & Manson (USE OF GET-UP: ABANDONMENT OF GET-UP: BALANCE OF CONVENIENCE: TRADE MARKS AND NAMES: O.H.)

Dash Ltd v. Philip King Tailoring Ltd (TRADE MARKS: TRADE NAMES: SIMILAR NAMES DASH:DASCH: SIMILAR BUSINESSES: INTERIM INTERDICT: BALANCE OF CONVENIENCE: PROTECTION OF LONG-ESTABLISHED BUSINESS AGAINST NEWLY-FORMED BUSINESS: I.H.)

Grant & Sons Ltd v. William Cadenhead Ltd (TRADE MARK: INFRINGEMENT: WHISKY: GEOGRAPHICAL NAME: O.H.)

Highland Distilleries Co. plc v. Speymalt Whisky Distributors Ltd (TRADE MARK: TRADE NAMES: INFRINGEMENT: GEOGRAPHICAL NAME: O.H.)

International House of Heraldry v. Grant (TRADE MARK: SIMILAR NAMES: DESCRIPTIVE NAMES: INTERNATIONAL ART OF HERALDRY: WHETHER DESCRIPTIVE: WHETHER SLIGHT DIFFERENCE SUFFICIENT TO DISTINGUISH: INTERIM INTERDICT: BALANCE OF CONVENIENCE: PROTECTION OF ESTABLISHED BUSINESS AGAINST NEWLY-FORMED BUSINESS: O.H.)

James Burrough Distillers plc v. Speymalt Whisky Distributors Ltd (TRADE MARK: INFRINGEMENT ABROAD: INTERNATIONAL LAW: DOUBLE ACTIONABILITY REQUIREMENT: NATURE OF TRADE MARKS: O.H.)

James North & Sons Ltd v. North Cape Textiles Ltd (TRADE MARK: INFRINGEMENT: PRACTICE: INJUNCTION: England: C.A.)

John Walker & Sons Ltd v. Douglas Laing & Co. Ltd (TRADE MARK: SCOTCH WHISKY: INTERDICT: BREACH: EXPORT OF SPIRIT CONTAINING MIXTURE OF SCOTCH WHISKY AND CANE SPIRIT: LABELS AND BOTTLES: ENABLING: O.H.)

Lang Bros Ltd v. Goldwell Ltd (UNFAIR TRADING: WEE McGLEN: I.H.)

Macallan-Glenlivet plc v. Speyside Whisky Distributors Ltd (TRADE MARK: INFRINGEMENT: WHISKY: O.H.)

Salon Services (Hairdressing Supplies) Ltd v. Direct Salon Services Ltd (TRADE MARK: DESCRIPTIVE NAME: REPUTATION: O.H.)

Scottish Milk Marketing Board v. Drybrough & Co. Ltd (TRADE MARK AND TRADE NAME: "SCOTTISH PRIDE": INTERIM INTERDICT: O.H.)

Secondary Meaning

Muckross Park Hotel Ltd v. Randles (MUCKROSS PARK HOTEL: MUCKROSS COURT HOTEL: LIKELIHOOD OF DECEPTION: GOODWILL: Ireland: H.C.)

Similar Names

An Post, National Treasury Management Agency v. Irish Permanent plc (DESCRIPTIVE NAME: PROOF OF ACTUAL DECEPTION: LIKELIHOOD OF DECEPTION: SAVINGS CERTIFICATES: LIKELIHOOD OF CONFUSION: Ireland: H.C.)

International House of Heraldry v. Grant (DESCRIPTIVE NAMES: INTERNATIONAL ART OF HERALDRY: WHETHER DESCRIPTIVE: WHETHER SLIGHT DIFFERENCE SUFFICIENT TO DISTINGUISH: Scotland: O.H.)

Orkney Seafoods Ltd's Petition (DESCRIPTIVE NAME: ORKNEY SEAFOODS: WHETHER COMBINATION OF DESCRIPTIVE WORDS CALCULATED TO CAUSE CONFUSION: Scotland: O.H.)

Software

Jian Tools For Sales Inc. v. Roderick Manhattan Group Ltd (SOFTWARE FOR BUSINESS PLANS: BIZPLAN BUILDER: WHETHER DESCRIPTIVE: Ch.D.)

Subjects

Advertising magazines

B&S Ltd v. Irish Auto Trader Ltd (AUTOTRADER: Ireland: H.C.)

Book title

Mothercare U.K. Ltd v. Penguin Books Ltd (MOTHERCARE: MOTHER CARE: OTHER CARE: C.A.)

Cartoonists' noms de plume

Marengo v. Daily Sketch and Daily Graphic Ltd (C.A.)

Charities

British Diabetic Association (The) v. Diabetic Society (The) (Ch.D.)

Chicago Pizza

My Kinda Town Ltd v. Soll (Ch.D.: C.A.)

Cigarette packets

Imperial Group plc v. Philip Morris Ltd (BLACK CIGARETTE PACKETS: Ch.D.)

Cigarette papers

Rizla Ltd v. Bryant & May Ltd (COLOUR OF PACKETS: Ch.D.)

Elderflower Champagne

Taittinger SA v. Allbev Ltd (Ch.D.: C.A.)

Estate agency

Nationwide Building Society v. Nationwide Estate Agents Ltd (Ch.D.)

Grand Marnier

GRAND MARNIER Liqueur (Germany: C.A.)

Hotel

Muckross Park Hotel Ltd v. Randles (MUCKROSS PARK HOTEL: MUCKROSS COURT HOTEL: Ireland: H.C.)

Jaffa Cakes

United Biscuits (U.K.) Ltd v. Burtons Biscuits Ltd (Ch.D.)

Jeans

Westminster City Council v. Pierglow Ltd (LEVI'S JEANS: Q.B.D.)

Legal services

Law Society of England and Wales v. Griffiths (TELEPHONE NUMBERS: Ch.D.)

LEGO

Lego System A/S v. Lego M. Lemelstrich Ltd (Pat. Ct)

Nightclub

Stringfellow v. McCain Foods (G.B.) Ltd (STRINGFELLOWS: Ch.D.: C.A.)

OXFORD marmalade

CPC (United Kingdom) Ltd v. Keenan (Ch.D.)

Parma ham

Consorzio del Prosciutto di Parma v. Marks and Spencer plc (Ch.D.: C.A.)

Plastic lemons

Reckitt & Coleman Products Ltd v. Borden Inc. (Ch.D.: H.L.)
Reckitt & Coleman Products Ltd v. Borden Inc. (C.A.)
Reckitt & Coleman Products Ltd v. Borden Inc. (No. 3) (Ch.D.: C.A.)

Pot Noodles

Dalgety Spillers Foods Ltd v. Food Brokers Ltd (Ch.D.)

Restaurants

My Kinda Town Ltd v. Soll (*Chicago Pizza*: Ch.D.: C.A.)

Sewing kit

BBC v. Marshall Cavendish (Ch.D.)

Sherry

Consejo Regulador de las Denominaciones "Jerez-Xeres-Sherry" v. Mathew Clark
& Sons Ltd (Ch.D.)

Telephone numbers

Law Society of England and Wales v. Griffiths (LEGAL SERVICES: Ch.D.)

Television series

BBC v. Celebrity Centre Productions Ltd (*EastEnders*: Ch.D.)
Grundy Television Pty Ltd v. Startrain Ltd (*Neighbours*: Ch.D.)

Tubs for baby wipes

Scott Ltd v. Nice-Pak Products Ltd (Ch.D.: C.A.)

Videos

Labyrinth Media Ltd v. Brave World Limited (Ch.D.)

Whisky

Grant & Sons Ltd v. William Cadenhead Ltd (Scotland: O.H.)
Highland Distilleries Co. plc v. Speymalt Whisky Distributors Ltd (Scotland: O.H.)
James Burrough Distillers plc v. Speymalt Whisky Distributors Ltd (Scotland: O.H.)
John Walker & Sons Ltd v. Douglas Laing & Co. Ltd (Scotland: O.H.)
Macallan-Glenlivet plc v. Speyside Whisky Distributors Ltd (Scotland: O.H.)
White Horse Distillers Ltd v. Gregson Associates Ltd (Ch.D.)

Test of

An Post, National Treasury Management Agency v. Irish Permanent plc (PURPOSE
OF REMEDY: DESCRIPTIVE NAME: PROOF OF ACTUAL DECEPTION:
LIKELIHOOD OF DECEPTION: SAVINGS CERTIFICATES: Ireland: H.C.)

Trade Descriptions

Warwickshire County Council v. Verco (TRADE DESCRIPTIONS: COUNTERFEIT
GOODS SOLD AS BRANDED GOODS: USE OF REASONABLE DILIGENCE: Q.B.D.)

Trade Mark

Alexander Fergusson & Co. v. Matthews McClay & Manson (Scotland: O.H.)
BBC v. Marshall Cavendish (Ch.D.)

Boot Tree Ltd v. Robinson (Ch.D.)
Coca Cola Company v. Peter John Gilbey (Ch.D.: C.A.)
Cadbury Ltd v. Ulmer GmbH (Ch.D.)
Ciba-Geigy plc v. Parke Davis & Co. Ltd (Ch.D.)
Colgate Palmolive Ltd v. Markwell Finance Ltd (Ch.D.: C.A.)
CPC (United Kingdom) Ltd v. Keenan (Ch.D.)
Dash Ltd v. Philip King Tailoring Ltd (Scotland: I.H.)
Dormeuil Frères SA v. Feraglow Ltd (Ch.D.)
Gillette U.K. Ltd v. Edenwest Ltd (Ch.D.)
Grant & Sons Ltd v. William Cadenhead Ltd (Scotland: O.H.)
Guccio Gucci SpA v. Paolo Gucci (Ch.D.)
Harrods Ltd v. Schwartz-Sackin & Co. Ltd (Ch.D.)
Highland Distilleries Co. plc v. Speymalt Whisky Distributors Ltd (Scotland: O.H.)
Intercontex v. Schmidt (Ch.D.)
International Business Machines Corporation v. Phoenix International (Computers) Ltd (Ch.D.)
International House of Heraldry v. Grant (Scotland: O.H.)
James Burrough Distillers plc v. Speymalt Whisky Distributors Ltd (Scotland: O.H.)
James North & Sons Ltd v. North Cape Textiles Ltd (Scotland: England: C.A.)
Macallan-Glenlivet plc v. Speyside Whisky Distributors Ltd (Scotland: O.H.)
Mothercare U.K. Ltd v. Penguin Books Ltd (C.A.)
Orkney Seafoods Ltd's Petition (Scotland: O.H.)
Parker Knoll plc v. Knoll Overseas Ltd (Ch.D.)
Provident Financial plc v. Halifax Building Society (Ch.D.)
Salon Services (Hairdressing Supplies) Ltd v. Direct Salon Services Ltd (Scotland: O.H.)
Scottish Milk Marketing Board v. Drybrough & Co. Ltd (Scotland: O.H.)
Silicon Graphics Inc. v. Indigo Graphic Systems (U.K.) Ltd (Ch.D.)
Unidoor Ltd v. Marks & Spencer plc (Ch.D.)
Wagamama Ltd v. City Centre Restaurants plc (Ch.D.)

Unfair Trading

Associated Newspapers Group plc v. Insert Media Ltd (Damage: Ch.D.)
Lang Bros Ltd v. Goldwell Ltd (WEE McGLEN: Scotland: I.H.)
Westminster City Council v. Pierglow Ltd (FALSE TRADE DESCRIPTION: COUNTERFEITING: LEVI'S JEANS: DUE DILIGENCE DEFENCE: Q.B.D.)

Patents

Added Matter

Milliken Denmark AS v. Walk Off Mats Ltd (INFRINGEMENT: VALIDITY: RUBBER OR PLASTIC BACKED WASHABLE FLOOR MATS: CONSTRUCTION: AMBIGUITY: INSUFFICIENCY: NOVELTY: PRIOR USE: ENABLING DISCLOSURE: OBVIOUSNESS: COMMERCIAL SUCCESS: Pat. Ct)

Aggrieved Person

Brain v. Ingledew Brown Bennison (THREATS: PENDING APPLICATION: CONDITIONAL THREATS: ADDRESSEE: Ch.D.)

Ambiguity

Genentech Inc.'s Patent (Pat. Ct)

Hickman v. Andrews (Ch.D.: C.A.)

Milliken Denmark AS v. Walk Off Mats Ltd (INFRINGEMENT: VALIDITY: RUBBER
OR PLASTIC BACKED WASHABLE FLOOR MATS: CONSTRUCTION:
INSUFFICIENCY: ADDED MATTER: NOVELTY: PRIOR USE: ENABLING
DISCLOSURE: OBVIOUSNESS: COMMERCIAL SUCCESS: Pat. Ct)

Mölnlycke AB v. Procter & Gamble Ltd (WHETHER AMBIGUITY NOT AMOUNTING
TO INSUFFICIENCY GROUND FOR REVOCATION: Pat. Ct)

Procter & Gamble Co. v. Peaudouce (U.K.) (AMENDMENT OF CLAIMS INVALID FOR
AMBIGUITY: C.A.)

Raychem Corp. v. Thermon (U.K.) Ltd (Pat. Ct)

Rediffusion Simulation Ltd v. Link-Miles Ltd (Pat. Ct)

Van der Lely (C.) NV v. Ruston's Engineering Co. Ltd (C.A.)

Amendment to Claims

Autoliv Development AB's Patent (Pat. Ct)

Autopia Terakat Accessories Ltd v. Gwent Auto Fabrications Ltd (Pat. Ct)

B. & R. Relay Ltd's Application (CLAIM BROADENING: Pat. Ct)

Bonzel v. Intervention Ltd (No. 3) (EXTENSION OF DISCLOSURE THROUGH PRE-
GRANT AMENDMENTS: Pat. Ct)

Chinoin's Application (COMPLETENESS OF DESCRIPTION: Pat. Ct)

Chiron Corporation v. Murex Diagnostics Ltd (No. 5) (DELETING OF CLAIMS HELD
INVALID AT TRIAL: Pat. Ct)

Chiron Corporation v. Murex Diagnostics Ltd (No. 7) (DISCRETION: Pat. Ct)

Chiron Corp. v. Organon Teknika Ltd (No. 11) (PARTIAL INVALIDITY:
AMENDMENT BY DELETION OF INVALID CLAIMS: DESCRIPTION: WHETHER
VALID CLAIMS SUPPORTED: C.A.)

Codex Corp. v. Racal-Milgo Ltd (EFFECT ON ACCOUNT OF PROFITS: C.A.)

Corning Glass Works & Corning Ltd's Amendment Application (DISCLAIMER:
EXPLANATION: C.A.)

Donaldson Co. Inc's Patent (DISCLAIMER: DISCRETION: Pat. Ct)

Du Pont de Nemours & Co. v. Enka AG (CROSS-EXAMINATION ON AFFIDAVITS:
C.A.)

Edwards (A.C.) Ltd v. Acme Signs & Displays Ltd (AMENDMENT OF CLAIMS DURING
PROSECUTION: ADDED MATTER: EPO DECISIONS APPLIED: C.A.)

Flexible Directional Indicators Ltd's Application (CLAIM BROADENING BEFORE
GRANT: Pat. Ct)

GEC Alsthom Ltd's Patent (PETITION FOR REVOCATION: RELIANCE ON
ADDITIONAL PRIOR ART: AMENDMENT SOUGHT THREE WEEKS PRIOR TO
TRIAL: COSTS: WHETHER See v. Scott-Paine form of order appropriate: Pat. Ct)

Genentech Inc.'s (Human Growth Hormone) Patent (CONVENTION COURT:
STATUS OF RULINGS: C.A.)

Gerber Garment Technology Inc. v. Lectra Systems Ltd (Pat. Ct)

Hallen Company v. Brabantia (U.K.) Ltd (PRACTICE: Pat. Ct)

Harding's Patent (ADDED SUBJECT-MATTER: Pat. Ct)

Hsiung's Patent (CORRECTION: DISCRETION: SUFFICIENCY: BEST METHOD:
PRACTICE ON AMENDMENT: C.-G.: Pat. Ct: C.A.)

ICI v. Ram Bathrooms (PRACTICE: SETTLEMENT OF ACTION: WHETHER
JURISDICTION TO ALLOW: P.C.)

Instance v. Denny Bros Printing Ltd (See v. Scott-Paine ORDER: PROPOSED
AMENDMENTS EMBARRASSING: Pat. Ct)

Johnson Electric Industrial Manufactory v. Mabuchi Motor KK (AMENDMENT BY
DELETION; DELAY; DISCRETION: Pat. Ct)
Liversidge v. British Telecommunications plc (PRE-GRANT AMENDMENT: Pat. Ct)
Minister of Agriculture's Patent (OPPOSITION: VALIDITY: PRACTICE: PLEADINGS IN
PATENT OFFICE: DISCRETION: Pat. Ct)
Mölnlycke AB v. Procter & Gamble Ltd (No. 2) (Pat. Ct)
Mölnlycke AB v. Procter & Gamble Ltd (No. 5) (ADDED MATTER: EXCLUSIVE
LICENCE: Pat. Ct: C.A.)
Mölnlycke AB v. Procter & Gamble Ltd (No. 6) (WHETHER AMENDMENT UNDER
SLIP RULE PERMISSIBLE: Pat. Ct)
Ogawa Chemical Industries Ltd's Applications (Divisional Pat. Ct)
Organon Teknika Ltd v. F. Hoffmann-La Roche AG (PATENT: CLAIM FOR
DECLARATION OF NON-INFRINGEMENT: APPLICATION TO STRIKE OUT
CLAIMS REFERRING TO VALIDITY: APPLICATION TO AMEND TO INCLUDE
CLAIM FOR REVOCATION: JURISDICTION TO ALLOW AMENDMENT: Pat. Ct)
Philips Electronic & Associated Industries Ltd's Patent (European C.-G.)
PLG Research Ltd v. Ardon International Ltd (No. 2) (CLAIM VALID AND INFRINGED
BUT SUBSEQUENTLY AMENDED: ENTITLEMENT TO COSTS: Pat. Ct)
PPG Industries Inc's Patent (OBVIOUS MISTAKE: DISCRETION: C.A.)
Procter & Gamble Co. v. Peaudouce (U.K.) (AMENDMENT OF CLAIMS INVALID FOR
AMBIGUITY BUT INFRINGED IF VALID: LATE APPLICATION FOR AMENDMENT:
C.A.)
Protoned BV's Application (Pat. Ct)
Quantel Ltd v. Spaceward Microsystems Ltd (DISCRETION: PRACTICE: Pat. Ct)
Raychem Ltd's Applications (DISCLOSURE: Pat. Ct)
Rediffusion Simulation Ltd v. Link-Miles Ltd (DISCRETION: PRACTICE: PLEADING:
BEST METHOD: Pat. Ct)
Richardson-Vicks Inc.'s Patent (REVOCATION: OBVIOUSNESS: SYNERGY SHOWN
ONLY BY LATER EXPERIMENTS: NEW MATTER: SAME AMENDMENT SOUGHT
IN EPO: DISCRETION: Pat. Ct)
Roussel Uclaf v. ICI (FUNCTIONAL CLAIMS: PROCESS CLAIMS: INSUFFICIENCY:
INUTILITY: AMENDMENT BY EXPLANATION: DISCRETION: Pat. Ct)
Schering Biotech Corp's Application (BIOTECHNOLOGY: WHETHER CLAIMS
SUPPORTED BY DESCRIPTION: Pat. Ct)
Smith Kline & French Laboratories Ltd (Bavin's) Patent (DISCRETION: C.-G.)
Smith Kline & French Laboratories Ltd v. Evans Medical Ltd (Cimetidine) (DELAY:
Pat. Ct)
Southco Inc. v. Dzus Fastener Europe Ltd (EFFECT OF PRE-GRANT AMENDMENT:
Pat. Ct: C.A.)
Strix Ltd v. Otter Controls Ltd (CONSTRUCTION: ANTICIPATION: OBVIOUSNESS:
NEW MATTER: WHETHER AMENDED CLAIM CLEAR AND CONCISE: Pat. Ct)
Therm-A-Stor Ltd v. Weatherseal Windows Ltd (No. 2) (FAIR BASIS: PRACTICE:
C.A.)
Turner & Newall Ltd's Patent (SURRENDER OF EUROPEAN AMENDMENT OF U.K.
PATENT: C.-G.)
Waddingtons Ltd's Patent (PRACTICE: REASONS: DISCRETION: C.-G.)
Ward's Applications (C.-G.)
Windsurfing International Inc. v. Tabur Marine (G.B.) Ltd (PRACTICE: DISCRETION:
C.A.)

Anticipation

Asahi Kasei Kogyo KK's Application (CO-PENDING APPLICATIONS: ENABLING
DISCLOSURE: Pat. Ct: C.A.: H.L.)

Applications

Marley Roof Tile Co. Ltd's Patent (EUROPEAN AND U.K. PATENTS: U.K. AND EUROPEAN APPLICATIONS BY SAME PROPRIETOR WITH SAME SUBJECT-MATTER AND PRIORITY DATE: PRODUCT CLAIMS IN U.K. PATENT AND PROCESS AND PRODUCT BY PROCESS IN EUROPEAN: WHETHER CLAIMS TO SAME INVENTION: ORDER FOR REVOCATION DISCHARGED: Pat. Ct)

Masuda's Application (PRACTICE: INTERNATIONAL ERROR IN TRANSLATION: COMPTROLLER'S POWER TO CORRECT MISTAKE: Pat. Ct)

Matsushita Electric Works Ltd's Application (INTERNATIONAL APPLICATION: PRACTICE: PCT FILING: PRIORITY DATE: C.-G.)

McManus's Application (EGGSHELLS AS ORAL MEDICAMENTS FOR TREATING OF ULCERS: SWISS-TYPE CLAIM: WHETHER SUPPORTED BY DESCRIPTION: ENFORCEMENT OF COSTS ORDER AGAINST APPELLANT IN PERSON: Pat. Ct)

Merrell Dow Pharmaceuticals Inc v. H.N. Norton & Co. Ltd (PRIOR USE: PRIOR DISCLOSURE: USE OF KNOWN PHARMACEUTICAL: WHETHER INVENTION MADE AVAILABLE TO PUBLIC: TERFENADINE METABOLITE: METABOLITE INEVITABLY FORMED IN HUMAN BODY: H.L.)

Merrill Lynch Inc.'s Application (BUSINESS SYSTEM, WHETHER PATENTABLE: Pat. Ct: C.A.)

Microsonics Corp.'s Application (ANTICIPATION: EVIDENCE: C.-G.)

Mills' Application (PRACTICE: TIME LIMITS: ERROR IN PROCEDURE: Pat. Ct: C.A.)

Mitsubishi Jidosha Kogyo KK's Application (INTERNATIONAL APPLICATION: PRACTICE: EXTENSION OF TIME: DEFAULT: DISCRETION: Pat. Ct)

Mitsui Engineering & Shipbuilding Co. Ltd's Application (INTERNATIONAL APPLICATION: FILING OF TRANSLATIONS: Pat. Ct)

Mölnlycke AB v. Procter & Gamble Ltd (CONSTRUCTION: PRACTICE: OBVIOUSNESS: Pat. Ct)

Mutoh Industry Ltd's Application (OBVIOUSNESS: Pat. Ct)

Nachf's Application (PRACTICE: APPEAL TO PATENT COURT: EXTENSION OF TIME TO APPEAL: Pat. Ct)

Nippon Gaishi KK's Application (PRACTICE: EXTENSION OF PERIOD FOR REQUESTING SUBSTANTIVE EXAMINATION: DISCRETION: Pat. Ct)

Nippon Piston Ring Co. Ltd's Applications (INFRINGEMENT: PRACTICE: RULE 100: INVENTOR'S NAME: ENTITLEMENT: Pat. Ct)

Norris's Patent (ENTITLEMENT: PRACTICE: EVIDENCE: CROSS-EXAMINATION IN PATENT OFFICE: CONFIDENTIALITY OF FILED EVIDENCE: DISCOVERY: C.-G.: Pat. Ct)

NRDC's Irish Application (MICRO-ORGANISM: WHETHER AN INVENTION: Ireland: C.-G.)

Ogawa Chemical Industries Ltd's Applications (PRACTICE: GRANT: AMENDMENT: DIVISION: Pat. Ct)

OHI Seisakusho Co. Ltd's Application (PRACTICE: INTERNATIONAL APPLICATION: TRANSLATION NOT FILED: TIME LIMITS: Pat. Ct)

P's Applications (PRACTICE: EXTENSION OF TIME LIMIT: Divisional C.-G.)

Payne's Application (PRIORITY DATE: CORRECTION OF CLERICAL ERROR: Pat. Ct)

PCUK's Application (INVENTIVE STEP: PATENT OFFICE PROCEEDINGS: PRACTICE: Pat. Ct)

Peabody International's Application (PRACTICE: PUBLICATION OF WITHDRAWAL: C.-G.)

Prangley's Application (PRACTICE: PCT: DEFECT IN PROCEDURE: C.A.)

Procter & Gamble Co.'s Application (OPPOSITION: SUFFICIENCY: EVIDENCE: C.A.)

Protoned BV's Application (AMENDMENT: Pat. Ct)

R. v. The Comptroller-General of Patents, *ex parte* Celltech Ltd (INTERNATIONAL PATENT: PCT: AGENTS MISTAKE: Q.B.D.)

Raychem Ltd's Applications (AMENDMENT: DISCLOSURE: Pat. Ct)
Raytheon Co.'s Application ("MENTAL ACT": "PROGRAM FOR COMPUTER": WHETHER INVENTION: Pat. Ct)
Rizla Ltd's Application (PATENT OFFICE PRACTICE: COSTS: C.-G.: Pat. Ct)
Schering Biotech Corp.'s Application (BIOTECHNOLOGY: WHETHER CLAIMS SUPPORTED BY DESCRIPTION: AMENDMENT: PRACTICE: Pat. Ct)
Schering Corporation v. The Controller of Patents, Designs and Trademarks (CONVENTION APPLICATION: Ireland: H.C.)
Sonic Tape plc's Patent (CONFIDENTIALITY OF DOCUMENTS: PRIVILEGE: C.-G.)
Sopharma SA's Application (SUBSTANCE FOR USE IN TREATMENT OF HUMAN BODY: C.-G.)
Stafford-Miller Ltd's Application (METHOD OF MEDICAL TREATMENT: Pat. Ct)
Strix Ltd v. Otter Controls Ltd (INFRINGEMENT: CONSTRUCTION: WHETHER PRIOR DISCLOSURE CONFIDENTIAL: OBVIOUSNESS: Pat. Ct)
Thermo Technic Ltd's Application (TIME LIMITS: Pat. Ct)
Tokan Kogyo KK's Application (PROCEDURAL ERROR: DISCRETION: C.-G.)
Toyama Chemical Co. Ltd's Application (NOVELTY: PRIORITY DATE: ENABLING DISCLOSURE: EVIDENCE ON APPEAL: COSTS: Pat. Ct)
Turner & Newall Ltd's Patent (EUROPEAN PATENT FOR SAME INVENTION: SURRENDER OF EUROPEAN AMENDMENT OF U.K.: C.-G.)
Unilever Ltd (Davis)'s Application (METHOD OF TREATMENT OF ANIMAL BODY BY THERAPY: Pat. Ct)
Van der Lely's Application (DIVISIONAL APPLICATION: DISCLOSURE: Pat. Ct)
Vapocure Technologies Ltd's Application (PCT: OBVIOUS ERROR: DELAY: CORRECTION: Pat. Ct: C.A.)
VEB Kombinat Walzlager und Normteile's Application (DRAWINGS: Pat. Ct)
Viziball Ltd's Application (ENTITLEMENT: WHEN INVENTION MADE: Pat. Ct)
Wang Laboratories Inc.'s Application (PATENTABILITY: COMPUTER-RELATED INVENTION: TECHNICAL CONTRIBUTION: Pat. Ct)
Ward's Applications (NOVELTY: LACK OF INVENTIVE STEP: AMENDMENT: C.-G.)
Wellcome Foundation Ltd's Two Patent Applications (DOUBLE PATENTING: Pat. Ct)
Wistar Institute's Application (OBVIOUSNESS: EVIDENCE: PRACTICE: Pat. Ct)

Available to the Public

Merrell Dow Pharmaceuticals Inc v. H.N. Norton & Co. Ltd (APPLICATION: PRIOR USE: PRIOR DISCLOSURE: USE OF KNOWN PHARMACEUTICAL: TERFENADINE METABOLITE: METABOLITE INEVITABLY FORMED IN HUMAN BODY: H.L.)

Best Method

Du Pont de Nemours & Co. v. Enka BV (KEVLAR: Pat. Ct)
Gerber Garment Technology Inc. v. Lectra Systems Ltd (PARTIAL INVALIDITY: C.A.)
Hsiung's Patent (PRACTICE ON AMENDMENT: C.-G.: Pat. Ct: C.A.)
Rediffusion Simulation Ltd v. Link-Miles Ltd (FLIGHT SIMULATORS: PLEADING: Pat. Ct)
Van der Lely (C.) NV v. Ruston's Engineering Co. Ltd (POWER HARROW: VALIDITY: AMBIGUITY: FAIR BASIS: CONSTRUCTION: COSTS: C.A.)

Biotechnical and Medical Inventions

Biological Patents Directive (Draft) (BIOTECHNICAL INVENTION: PATENTABILITY OF LIVING MATTER: SCOPE OF PROTECTION: DEPENDENCY LICENCES FOR PLANT VARIETIES: DEPOSIT AND ACCESS TO DEPOSITED MATERIAL: BURDEN OF PROOF: DRAFT LEGISLATION: E.C. Council)

John Wyeth & Brother Ltd's Application: Schering AG's Application (PHARMACEUTICAL USE: SECOND MEDICAL ACTIVITY OF KNOWN DRUG: NOVELTY: INDUSTRIAL APPLICATION: Pat. Ct)

Smith Kline & French Laboratories Ltd v. Evans Medical Ltd (CIMETIDINE: EXPERIMENTS IN CONNECTION WITH OPPOSITION: WHETHER PATENT OFFICE EXPERIMENTS PRIVILEGED AS EVIDENCE: Pat. Ct)

Smith Kline & French Laboratories Ltd v. Evans Medical Ltd (CIMETIDINE: INFRINGEMENT: AMENDMENT: DELAY: WHETHER REASONABLE CAUSE FOR DELAY: Pat. Ct)

Stafford-Miller Ltd's Application (METHOD OF MEDICAL TREATMENT: Pat. Ct)

Sopharma SA's Application (NOVELTY: SUBSTANCE FOR USE IN TREATMENT OF HUMAN BODY: C.-G.)

Unilever Ltd (Davis)'s Application (METHOD OF TREATMENT OF ANIMAL BODY BY THERAPY: Pat. Ct)

Capable of Industrial Application

Chiron Corp v. Murex Diagnostics Ltd (No. 12) (HEPATITIS C VIRUS: DIAGNOSTIC TEST: VALIDITY: CLAIMS, WHETHER DISCOVERY AS SUCH: SUFFICIENCY: MORE THAN ONE INVENTION: LICENCE AGREEMENT: VOID CONDITIONS: DATE OF AGREEMENT: EXCLUSIVE LICENSEE: C.A.)

Catnic

Beloit Technologies Inc. v. Valmet Paper Machinery Inc. (INFRINGEMENT: CONSTRUCTION: Pat. Ct)

Kastner v. Rizla Ltd (CONSTRUCTION: WHETHER *Catnic* APPROACH CONSISTENT WITH PROTOCOL: OBVIOUSNESS: C.A.)

Certificate of Contested Validity

Cannon KK's Application (TRANSITIONAL PROVISIONS OF P.A.77: Pat. Ct)

Mölnlycke AB v. Procter & Gamble Ltd (Pat. Ct)

Certificate of Validity

Brupat Ltd v. Smith (INFRINGEMENT: Scotland: O.H.)

Claims

Assidoman Multipack Limited v. The Mead Corp. (PURPOSIVE CONSTRUCTION: *Catnic* PRINCIPLES: OBVIOUSNESS: FAIR BASIS: INSUFFICIENCY: EXTENSION OF DISCLOSURE: C.A.)

Biogen Inc. v. Medeva plc (GENETIC ENGINEERING: HEPATITIS B VIRUS: SUFFICIENCY: PRIORITY DATE: OBVIOUSNESS: INTERPRETATION OF CLAIM: FAIR BASIS: SUFFICIENCY: DATE OF ASSESSMENT: BURDEN OF PROOF: C.A.)

Chiron Corporation v. Murex Diagnostics Ltd (No. 5) (AMENDMENT DURING ACTION: P.A.77, S.74: EUROPEAN PATENT OFFICE PROCEDURE: Pat. Ct)

Chiron Corp. v. Organon Teknika Ltd (No. 11) (PARTIAL INVALIDITY: AMENDMENT BY DELETION OF INVALID CLAIMS: DESCRIPTION: WHETHER VALID CLAIMS SUPPORTED: C.A.)

Chiron Corp v. Murex Diagnostics Ltd (No. 12) (HEPATITIS C VIRUS: DIAGNOSTIC TEST: VALIDITY: CAPABLE OF INDUSTRIAL APPLICATION: SUFFICIENCY: MORE THAN ONE INVENTION: C.A.)

Codex Corp. v. Racal-Milgo Ltd ("PURPOSIVE CONSTRUCTION": C.A.)

CQR Security Systems Ltd's Patent (PRACTICE: APPLICATION TO AMEND PARTICULARS OF OBJECTIONS AFTER CLAIM AMENDED: Pat. Ct)

Claim Broadening

Combination of known techniques

Commercial Success

Beloit Technologies Inc. v. Valmet Paper Machinery Inc. (INFRINGEMENT: CONSTRUCTION: *Catnic*: PRIORITY: ENTITLEMENT: ANTICIPATION: OBVIOUSNESS: EXPERT EVIDENCE: Pat. Ct)

BSH Industries Ltd's Patents (REVOCATION: CONSTRUCTION: INTERPRETATION OF DRAWING: OBVIOUSNESS: Pat. Ct)

Common General Knowledge

Edwards (A.C.) Ltd v. Acme Signs & Displays Ltd (CONSTRUCTION OF CLAIM: VALIDITY: NOVELTY: OBVIOUSNESS: COMMERCIAL SUCCESS: Pat. Ct)

Genentech Inc.'s (Human Growth Hormone) Patent (REVOCATION: GENETIC ENGINEERING: RECOMBINANT DNA TECHNOLOGY: GENETIC ENGINEERING: HUMAN TISSUE PLASMINOGEN ACTIVATOR: DISCOVERY OF DNA AND AMINO-ACID SEQUENCE: NOVELTY: INVENTIVE STEP: PRIORITY DATE: ADDRESSEE: Pat. Ct)

Community Patent Procedure

Community Patent Appeal Court Statute (PROTOCOL ON THE STATUTE OF THE COMMON APPEAL COURT: STRUCTURE AND PROCEDURE OF COMMON APPEAL COURT)

Community Patent Litigation Protocol (PROTOCOL ON THE SETTLEMENT OF LITIGATION CONCERNING THE INFRINGEMENT AND VALIDITY OF COMMUNITY PATENTS: COMMUNITY PATENT COURTS: COMMON APPEAL COURT: INTERNATIONAL JURISDICTION AND ENFORCEMENT: FIRST INSTANCE: SECOND INSTANCE: THIRD INSTANCE AND PRELIMINARY RULING PROCEDURE: COMMON PROVISIONS FOR THE COMMUNITY PATENT COURTS OF FIRST AND SECOND INSTANCE)

Milliken Denmark AS v. Walk Off Mats Ltd (INFRINGEMENT: VALIDITY: ENABLING DISCLOSURE: OBVIOUSNESS: Pat. Ct)

Compulsory Licence

E.C. Commission v. United Kingdom and Italy (IMPORTS: FREE MOVEMENT OF GOODS: SPECIFIC SUBJECT-MATTER: SATISFACTION OF DEMAND BY IMPORT: ECJ)

E.C. Commission v. United Kingdom and Italy (IMPORTS: PATENTS: HINDRANCE TO IMPORTS: P.A.77, S.48 AND ARTICLE 30: SIMILAR ITALIAN PROVISIONS: ECJ)

Enviro-Spray Systems Inc.'s Patents (ABILITY TO WORK INVENTION: C.-G.)

Extrude Hone Corp. (DATE OF LICENCE: COSTS: C.-G.)

Gebhardt's Patent (TREATY OF ROME: IMPORTATION FROM EEC MEMBER STATE: WHETHER GROUNDS: PRACTICE: EVIDENCE: Pat. Ct)

Generics (U.K.) Ltd v. Smith Kline & French Laboratories Ltd (IMPORTS: MANUFACTURE IN BRITAIN AND IN OTHER MEMBER STATE: EXHAUSTION OF RIGHTS: TRANSITIONAL PERIOD FOR IBERIAN GOODS: PARALLEL IMPORT: C.A.)

Generics (U.K.) Ltd v. Smith Kline & French Laboratories Ltd (IMPORTS: PHARMACEUTICALS: COMPULSORY LICENCES: INTRA-STATE CONDITIONS: PARALLEL IMPORTS: DISCRIMINATION: SPAIN AND PORTUGAL: ECJ)

Halcon SD Group Inc.'s Patents (JURISDICTION: STRIKING OUT: ESTOPPEL: ELECTION: EVIDENCE: DISCOVERY: Pat. Ct)

Monsanto's CCP Patent (CARBONLESS COPYING PAPER: BURDEN OF PROOF: BEST EVIDENCE: C.-G.)

Pharmon BV v. Hoechst AG (PARALLEL IMPORTS: ECJ)

Richco Plastic Co.'s Patent (PATENT OFFICE PRACTICE: ABUSE OF PROCESS: EVIDENCE: DISCOVERY: C.-G.)

Computer-Related Invention

Computer Generation of Chinese Characters (APPLICATION: COMPUTER PROGRAM: CHINESE CHARACTERS: WHETHER PATENTABLE: WHETHER APPLICATION OF TECHNICAL NATURE: APPLICATION REFUSED: Germany: S.C.)

Gale's Application (APPLICATION: DEDICATED ROM: WHETHER EXCLUDED FROM PATENTABILITY: APPLICATION REFUSED: C.-G.: Pat. Ct: C.A.)

Hitachi Ltd's Application Patent application (WHETHER PATENTABLE: C.-G.)

Wang Laboratories Inc.'s Application (PATENTABILITY: TECHNICAL CONTRIBUTION: Pat. Ct)

Willemijn Houdstermaatschappij BV v. Madge Networks Ltd (INFRINGEMENT: COMPUTERS: CONSTRUCTION: ESSENTIAL INTEGER: INESSENTIAL VARIANT: C.A.)

Construction

Anchor Building Products Ltd v. Redland Roof Tiles Ltd (INFRINGEMENT: STRIKING OUT: C.A.)

Beloit Technologies Inc. v. Valmet Paper Machinery Inc. (*Catnic*: PRIORITY: ENTITLEMENT: ANTICIPATION: OBVIOUSNESS: EXPERT EVIDENCE: COMMERCIAL SUCCESS: ADDED MATTER: Pat. Ct)

BSH Industries Ltd's Patents (INTERPRETATION OF DRAWING: OBVIOUSNESS: COMMERCIAL SUCCESS: Pat. Ct)

Codex Corp. v. Racal-Milgo Ltd (INFRINGEMENT: "PURPOSIVE CONSTRUCTION": C.A.)

Conoco Specialty Products Inc. v. Merpro Montassa Ltd (INFRINGEMENT: GENERALLY CYLINDRICAL: Scotland: O.H.)

Daily v. Ets Fernand Berchet ("GILLETTE" DEFENCE: Pat. C.C.) (APPEAL ALLOWED: C.A.)

Edwards (A.C.) Ltd v. Acme Signs & Displays Ltd (Pat. Ct)

Fairfax (Dental Equipment) Ltd v. S.J. Filhol Ltd (VALIDITY: INFRINGEMENT: C.A.)

Formstein (INFRINGEMENT: EPC: PROTOCOL ON INTERPRETATION OF ARTICLE 69: Germany: S.C.)

Furr v. C.D. Truline (Building Products) Ltd (INFRINGEMENT: ESTOPPEL BY ACTION TAKEN TO SECURE GRANT: Pat. Ct)

Hallen Company v. Brabantia (U.K.) Ltd (INFRINGEMENT: CORKSCREW: Pat. Ct)

Harrison v. Project & Design Co. (Redcar) Ltd (C.A.)

Helitune Ltd v. Stewart Hughes Ltd (INDIRECT INFRINGEMENT: SUFFICIENCY OF DESCRIPTION: ADDRESSEE OF SPECIFICATION: ERROR IN SPECIFICATION: PRIOR USE: Pat. Ct)

Hoffmann-La Roche AG v. Dumex A/S (Denmark: S.C.)

ICI v. Montedison (U.K.) Ltd (CONFLICT BETWEEN RIVAL SCIENTIFIC THEORIES: WHETHER COURT OBLIGED TO CHOOSE BETWEEN THEORIES: FRESH EVIDENCE ON APPEAL: Pat. Ct)

Improver Corporation v. Remington Consumer Products Ltd (DEPILATORY DEVICE: EUROPEAN CONSTRUCTION: Pat. Ct)

Instituform Technical Services Ltd v. Inliner U.K. plc (INFRINGEMENT: Pat. Ct)

Kastner v. Rizla Ltd (WHETHER *Catnic* APPROACH CONSISTENT WITH PROTOCOL: OBVIOUSNESS: C.A.)

457

Damages. *See* **Practice** (*Damages*)

Damages—Interest

Declaration. *See* **Practice** (*Declaration*)

Declaration of Non-Infringement. *See* **Practice** (*Declaration of non-infringement*)

Declaration of Priority. *See* **Practice** (*Declaration of priority*)

Delay. *See* **Practice** (*Delay*)

Description

Chiron Corp. v. Organon Teknika Ltd (No. 11) (PARTIAL INVALIDITY: AMENDMENT BY DELETION OF INVALID CLAIMS: WHETHER VALID CLAIMS SUPPORTED: C.A.)

Schering Biotech Corp.'s Application (BIOTECHNOLOGY: WHETHER CLAIMS SUPPORTED BY DESCRIPTION: Pat. Ct)

Disclosure

Assidoman Multipack Limited v. The Mead Corp. (CLAIMS: PURPOSIVE CONSTRUCTION: *Catnic* PRINCIPLES: OBVIOUSNESS: FAIR BASIS: INSUFFICIENCY: EXTENSION OF DISCLOSURE: C.A.)

Bonzel v. Intervention Ltd (No. 3) (EXTENSION OF DISCLOSURE THROUGH PRE-GRANT AMENDMENTS: Pat. Ct)

Prout v. British Gas plc (DISCLOSURE BY EMPLOYEE UNDER EMPLOYEES' SUGGESTION SCHEME BINDING: Pat. C.C.)

Roussel Uclaf v. ICI (INFRINGEMENT: PROCESS CLAIMS: SECRET PROCESS: Ch.D.: C.A.)

Roussel Uclaf v. ICI (No. 2) (DISCLOSURE TO PLAINTIFF'S EMPLOYEE: TERMS OF DISCLOSURE: Pat. Ct: C.A.)

Disclosure of Privileged Documents

Bonzel v. Intervention Ltd (No. 2) (INFRINGEMENT: *In camera* HEARING: Pat. Ct)

Divisional Application

Aumac Ltd's Patent (REVOCATION: DIVISIONAL APPLICATION TO EPO DESIGNATING U.K.: POSSIBILITY OF FURTHER INFRINGEMENT PROCEEDINGS IN U.K.: Pat. Ct)

Kiwi Coders Corp.'s Application (APPLICATION: DIVISIONAL APPLICATION: PRACTICE: DISCRETION: Pat. Ct)

P's Applications (APPLICATION: PRACTICE: EXTENSION OF TIME LIMIT: DIVISIONAL APPLICATION: C.-G.)

Van der Lely's Application (APPLICATION: DIVISIONAL APPLICATION: DISCLOSURE: Pat. Ct)

Earth Closet Orders. *See* **Practice** (*Earth closet orders*)

Employee's Invention. *See also* **Ownership**

British Steel plc (APPLICATION FOR COMPENSATION: ACTUAL AND POTENTIAL BENEFIT TO EMPLOYER: OUTSTANDING BENEFIT: C.-G.)

European Patent Office/European Patent Court

Amersham International plc v. Corning Ltd (EUROPEAN OPPOSITION AT EPO: MOTION FOR STAY IN HIGH COURT: *Forum conveniens*: Pat. Ct)

Chiron Corporation v. Murex Diagnostics Ltd (No. 5) (RELEVANCE OF EPO PROCEDURE: Pat. Ct)

Dow Chemical Co. v. Ishihara Sangyo Kaisha Ltd (REVOCATION: PLEADINGS: European Pat. Ct)

Edwards (A.C.) Ltd v. Acme Signs & Displays Ltd (EPO DECISIONS APPLIED: C.A.)

Kakkar and Others v. Szelke (EUROPEAN ENTITLEMENT: EQUITABLE INTERESTS: JURISDICTION: Pat. Ct: C.A.)

Pall Corporation v. Commercial Hydraulics (Bedford) Ltd (INFRINGEMENT: VALIDITY: PRACTICE: OPPOSITION IN EUROPEAN PATENT OFFICE: WHETHER STAY OF PROCEEDINGS IN U.K. SHOULD BE ORDERED: Pat. Ct: C.A.)

Pall Corporation v. Commercial Hydraulics (Bedford) Ltd (STAY OF PROCEEDINGS: HIGH COURT AND EPO PROCEEDINGS: Pat. Ct)

Exclusive Licence

Bondax Carpets Ltd v. Advance Carpet Tiles (TERMS OF LICENCE AGREEMENT: Ch.D.)

Boussois SA and Interpane & Co. KG's Agreement (RESTRICTIVE PRACTICES: UNPATENTED KNOW-HOW: EXCLUSIVE LICENCE TO MANUFACTURE: IMPROVEMENT KNOW-HOW: E.C. Comm.)

Chiron Corp v. Murex Diagnostics Ltd (No. 12) (HEPATITIS C VIRUS: DIAGNOSTIC TEST: LICENCE AGREEMENT: VOID CONDITIONS: DATE OF AGREEMENT: C.A.)

Christian Salvesen (Oil Services) Ltd v. Odfjell Drilling & Construction Co. (U.K.) Ltd (INFRINGEMENT: RIGHTS OF EXCLUSIVE SUB-LICENSEE: Scotland: O.H.)

Instituform Technical Services Ltd v. Inliner U.K. plc (REGISTRATION: WHETHER EXCLUSIVE LICENSEE ENTITLED TO RELIEF FOR INFRINGEMENT: Pat. Ct)

Minnesota Mining & Manufacturing Co. v. Rennicks (U.K.) Ltd (DAMAGES: POSITION OF EXCLUSIVE LICENSEE WHO FAILED TO REGISTER: Pat. Ct)

Mölnlycke AB v. Procter & Gamble Ltd (WHETHER ENTRY OF NOTICE OF APPLICATION AMOUNTS TO REGISTRATION OF EXCLUSIVE LICENCE: Pat. Ct)

Mölnlycke AB v. Procter & Gamble Ltd (No. 5) (PATENT OFFICE PRACTICE: COSTS: CERTIFICATE OF CONTESTED VALIDITY: Pat. Ct: C.A.)

Optical Coating Laboratory Inc. v. Pilkington PE Ltd (INFRINGEMENT: SOLAR PANELS: ENTITLEMENT TO DAMAGES FOR LOSS OF PROFIT: Pat. C.C.)

Procter & Gamble Co. v. Peaudouce (U.K.) Ltd (PRACTICE: C.A.)

Exemplary Damages

Catnic Components Ltd v. Hill & Smith Ltd (Pat. Ct)

Exhaustion of Rights

Allen & Hanbury's Ltd v. Generics (U.K.) Ltd (Pat. Ct)

Allen & Hanbury's Ltd v. Generics (U.K.) Ltd (Ch.D.: C.A.) (INTERIM JUDGMENT: H.L.: ECJ)

Dellareed Ltd v. Delkim Developments (Ch.D.)

Generics (U.K.) Ltd v. Smith Kline & French Laboratories Ltd (C.A.)

Patented Bandaging Material (Germany)

Wellcome Foundation Ltd v. Discpharm Ltd (Pat. C.C.)

Experiments

Richardson-Vicks Inc.'s Patent (REVOCATION: OBVIOUSNESS: SYNERGY SHOWN ONLY BY LATER EXPERIMENTS: AMENDMENT: NEW MATTER: SAME AMENDMENT SOUGHT IN EPO: DISCRETION: RELIANCE ON EXPERIMENTS CARRIED OUT FOR OTHER PURPOSES: Pat. Ct)

Fair Basis

Assidoman Multipack Limited v. The Mead Corp. (CLAIMS: PURPOSIVE CONSTRUCTION: *Catnic* PRINCIPLES: OBVIOUSNESS: INSUFFICIENCY: EXTENSION OF DISCLOSURE: C.A.)

Biogen Inc. v. Medeva plc (GENETIC ENGINEERING: HEPATITIS B VIRUS: SUFFICIENCY: PRIORITY DATE: OBVIOUSNESS: INTERPRETATION OF CLAIM: SUFFICIENCY: DATE OF ASSESSMENT: BURDEN OF PROOF: C.A.)

Du Pont de Nemours & Co. v. Enka BV (Pat. Ct)

Instituform Technical Services Ltd v. Inliner U.K. plc (Pat. Ct)

Ishihara Sangyo Kaisha Ltd v. The Dow Chemical Co. (STRIKING OUT: C.A.)

Lesaffre's Patent (REVOCATION: OBVIOUSNESS: C.A.)

Therm-A-Stor Ltd v. Weatherseal Windows Ltd (No. 2) (PRACTICE: C.A.)

Van der Lely (C.) NV v. Ruston's Engineering Co. Ltd (C.A.)

False Suggestion

Dow Chemical AG v. Spence Bryson & Co. Ltd (Pat. Ct: C.A.)

Intalite International NV v. Cellular Ceilings Ltd (No. 2) (Pat. Ct)

Minnesota Mining & Manufacturing Co. v. Rennicks (U.K.) Ltd (Pat. Ct)

Fiduciary Relationship

Prout v. British Gas plc (DISCLOSURE BY EMPLOYEE UNDER EMPLOYEES' SUGGESTION: SPRINGBOARD DOCTRINE: Pat. C.C.)

Final Injunction. *See* **Practice** (*Final injunction*)

Genetic Engineering

Hepatitis B virus: Biogen Inc. v. Medeva plc (HEPATITIS B VIRUS: SUFFICIENCY: PRIORITY DATE: OBVIOUSNESS: INTERPRETATION OF CLAIM: FAIR BASIS: SUFFICIENCY: DATE OF ASSESSMENT: BURDEN OF PROOF: C.A.)

Gillette **Defence**

Merrell Dow Pharmaceuticals Inc. v. H.N. Norton & Co. Ltd (INFRINGEMENT: VALIDITY: ANTICIPATION: ENABLING DISCLOSURE: PRIOR USE: MEDICAL TREATMENT: Pat. Ct)

Implied Licences

Bondax Carpets Ltd v. Advance Carpet Tiles (TITLE TO SUE: WHETHER TERMS OF LICENCE AGREEMENT CONSTRUABLE AS EXCLUSIVE LICENCE: Ch.D.)

Dellareed Ltd v. Delkim Developments (INFRINGEMENT: EXHAUSTION OF RIGHTS: MODIFICATION OF PRODUCT: Ch.D.)

Importation

Allen & Hanbury's Ltd's (Salbutamol) Patent (C.-G.: Pat. Ct: C.A.)

Ciba-Geigy AG's Patent (STATUTORY POLICY: DISCRETION: Pat. Ct)

Infringement

Insufficiency. *See under* **Sufficiency**

Inquiry as to Damages. *See* **Practice** (*Inquiry as to damages*)

International Application

Interpretation of Drawing

Inutility

Invalidity. See under **Validity**

Invention, Definition

Ireland

Fisons Pharmaceuticals Ltd's Petition (EXTENSION: INADEQUATE REMUNERATION: Ireland: S.C.)

NRDC's Irish Application (MICRO-ORGANISM: WHETHER AN INVENTION: Ireland: C.-G.)

Rajan v. Ministry for Industry and Commerce (PATENT OFFICE DISPUTE: POWERS OF CONTROLLER: Ireland: H.C.)

Schering Corporation v. The Controller of Patents, Designs and Trademarks (APPLICATION: DELAY: POWERS OF CONTROLLER: CONVENTION APPLICATION: Ireland: H.C.)

Technobiotic Ltd's Patent (EXTENSION: INADEQUATE REMUNERATION: Ireland: H.C.)

Joint Contributors

Goddin and Rennie's Application (ENTITLEMENT: COMMISSIONED CONTRIBUTION: OWNERSHIP: C.-G.: Scotland: Court of Session)

Joint Ownership

BICC plc v. Burndy Corp. (CONTRACT: SPECIFIC PERFORMANCE: SET OFF: RELIEF AGAINST FORFEITURE: Pat. Ct: C.A.)

Lack of Inventive Step

Ward's Applications (NOVELTY: AMENDMENT: C.-G.)

Legal Aid. *See* Practice (*Legal aid*)

Licences of Right

Allen & Hanbury's Ltd v. Generics (U.K.) Ltd (PARALLEL IMPORTS: EXHAUSTION OF RIGHTS: Pat. Ct)

Allen & Hanbury's Ltd's (Salbutamol) Patent (PHARMACEUTICAL SUBSTANCE: SETTLEMENT OF TERMS: ROYALTY: IMPORTATION: SUB-CONTRACTING PROVISION: C.-G.: Pat. Ct: C.A.)

Allen & Hanbury's Ltd v. Generics (U.K.) Ltd (IMPORTS: TERMS OF LICENCE: EFFECTIVE DATE OF LICENCE: CONSTRUCTION: EXHAUSTION OF RIGHTS: Ch.D.: C.A.)
(INTERIM JUDGMENT: H.L.: ECJ)

American Cyanamid Co.'s (Fenbrufen) Patent (SETTLEMENT OF TERMS: EFFECT OF PATENTEES' EXCEPTIONAL PROMOTIONAL EFFORTS: Pat. Ct: C.A.)

Cabot Safety Corp. (SETTLEMENT OF TERMS: KOMMANDITGESELLSCHAFT AS LICENCEE: ROYALTY RATE: RELEVANCE OF VALIDITY: C.-G.: Pat. Ct)

Ciba-Geigy AG's Patent (STATUTORY POLICY: IMPORTATION: DISCRETION: Pat. Ct)

Diamond Shamrock Technologies SA's Patent (CONFIDENTIALITY OF INFORMATION: Pat. Ct)

Du Pont de Nemours (E.I.) & Co. (Blades') Patent (PRACTICE: STAY: SETTLEMENT OF TERMS: Pat. Ct)

Du Pont de Nemours (E.I.) & Co. v. Enka BV (No. 2) (JURISDICTION: DISCRETION: Pat. Ct)

Generics (U.K.) Ltd v. Smith Kline and French Laboratories Ltd (IMPORTS: DISCRIMINATING IMPORT RESTRICTIONS: PARALLEL IMPORTS FROM NON-EEC COUNTRIES AND SPAIN AND PORTUGAL: UNJUSTIFIABLE INTERFERENCE WITH INTRA-COMMUNITY TRADE: ARTICLES 30 AND 36: ECJ)

Gerber Garment Technology Inc. v. Lectra Systems Ltd (INFRINGEMENT: INQUIRY AS TO DAMAGES: EFFECT OF ENDORSEMENT OF LICENCES OF RIGHT: Pat. Ct)

Glaverbel's Patent (OPPOSITION: *Locus standi*: C.A.)

Hilti AG's Patent (SUB-LICENSING: PERIOD OF NOTICE: "PASSING OFF TERM": Pat. Ct)

Kaken Pharmaceutical Co. Ltd's Patent (PRACTICE: INTERVENTION BY FORMER EXCLUSIVE LICENCEE: C.-G.)

R. v. Comptroller-General of Patents *ex p.* Gist-Brocades NV (EXTENSION OF PATENT TO 20 YEARS: TERMS OF LICENCE: H.L.)

Research Corporation's (Carboplatin) Patent (SETTLEMENT OF TERMS: REASONABLE REMUNERATION: Pat. Ct)

Research Corp.'s Supplementary Protection Certificate (EXPIRED PATENT: MEDICAL PRODUCT: CARBOPLATIN: SUPPLEMENTARY PROTECTION CERTIFICATE: C.-G.)

Rhone Poulenc SA's (Ketoprofen) Patent (PATENT OFFICE PRACTICE: STRIKING OUT: Pat. Ct)

Roussel Uclaf's (Clemence & Le Martret) Patent (PRACTICE: STAY: COMPTROLLER'S JURISDICTION: VEXATIOUS PROCEEDINGS: Pat. Ct)

Schering AG's Patent (PRACTICE: PATENT AGENTS: CONFIDENTIAL DOCUMENTS: AGENTS IN-HOUSE AND IN PRIVATE PRACTICE: Pat. Ct)

Shiley Inc.'s Patent (SURGICAL DEVICE: ROYALTY: TRADE LIBEL CLAUSE: Pat. Ct)

Smith Kline & French Laboratories Ltd's (Cimetidine) Patents (REASONABLE REMUNERATION: APPROACHES TO ASSESSMENT: TERMS OF LICENCE: APPEAL: REFERENCES TO ECJ: Pat. Ct: C.A.) (LICENCE TO IMPORT: PRACTICE: Pat. Ct)

Smith Kline & French Laboratories Ltd v. Harris Pharmaceuticals Ltd (PHARMACEUTICALS: INFRINGEMENT: BACK DOOR ASSIGNMENT: WHETHER TERMINATION PERMITTED: MANDATORY INJUNCTION FOR DESTRUCTION OF STOCKS: Ch.D.)

Syntex Corp.'s Patent (SETTLEMENT OF TERMS: ROYALTY: Pat. Ct)

Malicious Falsehood

Easycare Inc. v. Bryan Lawrence & Co. (THREATS: FREEDOM OF SPEECH: INTERLOCUTORY INJUNCTION REFUSED: Pat. Ct)

Merck v. Stephar

Merck & Co. Inc. v. Primecrown Ltd (INFRINGEMENT: PARALLEL IMPORTS: WHETHER *Merck v. Stephar* STILL GOOD LAW: CONSTRUCTION: TRANSITIONAL PROVISIONS OF ACT OF ACCESSION OF SPAIN AND PORTUGAL: INTERLOCUTORY RELIEF: WHETHER REVISED VIEW OF *Merck v. Stephar* MAY BE TAKEN INTO ACCOUNT: REFERRAL TO ECJ: Pat. Ct)

Modifications or Repairs

Hazel Grove (Superleague) Ltd v. Euro-League Leisure Products Ltd (INFRINGEMENT: PROMISSORY ESTOPPEL: Pat. C.C.)

Multiple Claims

Bayer AG v. Süllhöfer (JUDICIAL PROCEDURE: PRELIMINARY RULINGS: Germany: S.C.)

Novelty

Bayer AG's (Meyer)'s Application (METHOD OF THERAPY: C.-G.)

Obvious Mistake

Obviousness

Wistar Institute's Application (EVIDENCE: PRACTICE: Pat. Ct)

Opposition

Amersham International plc v. Corning Ltd (EUROPEAN OPPOSITION AT EPO: MOTION FOR STAY IN HIGH COURT: *Forum conveniens:* Pat. Ct)
Bonzel v. Intervention Ltd (EPO OPPOSITION: Pat. Ct)
Leader Products Pty Ltd v. Allflex International Ltd (POWER OF COMMISSIONER: NOVELTY: PERSON SKILLED IN THE ART: TAX: C.-G.)
Minister of Agriculture's Patent (PRACTICE: PLEADINGS IN PATENT OFFICE: DISCRETION: Pat. Ct)
Pall Corporation v. Commercial Hydraulics (Bedford) Ltd (OPPOSITION IN EUROPEAN PATENT OFFICE: WHETHER STAY OF PROCEEDINGS IN U.K. SHOULD BE ORDERED: Pat. Ct: C.A.)
Procter & Gamble Co.'s Application (SUFFICIENCY: EVIDENCE: C.A.)
Smith Kline & French Laboratories Ltd (Bavin's) Patent (STRIKING OUT: C.-G.)
Smith Kline & French Laboratories Ltd v. Evans Medical Ltd (CIMETIDINE: EXPERIMENTS IN CONNECTION WITH OPPOSITION: WHETHER PATENT OFFICE EXPERIMENTS PRIVILEGED AS EVIDENCE: Pat. Ct)

Ownership

Goddin and Rennie's Application (JOINT CONTRIBUTORS TO INVENTION: COMMISSIONED CONTRIBUTION: C.-G.: Court of Session)
Greater Glasgow Health Board's Application (EMPLOYEE INVENTOR: REGISTRAR AT HOSPITAL: WHETHER DUTIES EXTEND TO RESEARCH: C.-G.: Pat. Ct)

Parallel Imports

Merck & Co. Inc. v. Primecrown Ltd (INFRINGEMENT: WHETHER *Merck v. Stephar* STILL GOOD LAW: CONSTRUCTION: TRANSITIONAL PROVISIONS OF ACT OF ACCESSION OF SPAIN AND PORTUGAL: INTERLOCUTORY RELIEF: WHETHER REVISED VIEW OF *Merck v. Stephar* MAY BE TAKEN INTO ACCOUNT: REFERRAL TO ECJ: Pat. Ct)

Patentability

Biological Patents Directive (Draft) (PATENTS: BIOTECHNICAL INVENTIONS: PATENTABILITY OF LIVING MATTER: SCOPE OF PROTECTION: DEPENDENCY LICENCES FOR PLANT VARIETIES: DEPOSIT AND ACCESS TO DEPOSITED MATERIAL: BURDEN OF PROOF: DRAFT LEGISLATION: E.C. Council)
Gale's Application (PATENT APPLICATION: COMPUTER RELATED INVENTIONS: DEDICATED ROM: WHETHER EXCLUDED FROM PATENTABILITY: APPLICATION REFUSED: C.-G.: Pat. Ct: C.A.)
Wang Laboratories Inc.'s Application (APPLICATION: PATENTABILITY: COMPUTER-RELATED INVENTION: TECHNICAL CONTRIBUTION: Pat. Ct)

Patent Agents

Rockwell International Corp. v. Serck Industries Ltd (PRIVILEGE: Ch.D.)
Santa Fe International Corp. v. Napier Shipping SA (PRIVILEGE: Scotland: O.H.)
Schering AG's Patent (CONFIDENTIAL DOCUMENTS: AGENTS IN-HOUSE AND IN PRIVATE PRACTICE: Pat. Ct)
Wilden Pump Engineering Co. v. Fusfield (COPYRIGHT: PRIVILEGE: C.A.)

Patent Co-operation Treaty

Brossmann's Application (INTERNATIONAL APPLICATIONS: PRACTICE: PCT FILING: PRIORITY DOCUMENTS FILED LATE: C.-G.)

Drazil (INTERNATIONAL APPLICATION: PRACTICE: PCT: RECTIFICATION OF ERROR: Q.B.D.)

Matsushita Electric Works Ltd's Application (INTERNATIONAL APPLICATION: PRACTICE: PCT FILING: PRIORITY DATE: C.-G.)

Prangley's Application (APPLICATION: PRACTICE: PCT: DEFECT IN PROCEDURE: C.A.)

R. v. The Comptroller-General of Patents, *ex p.* Celltech Ltd (INTERNATIONAL APPLICATION: PCT: AGENT'S MISTAKE: Q.B.D.)

Vapocure Technologies Ltd's Application (APPLICATION: PCT: OBVIOUS ERROR: DELAY: CORRECTION: Pat. Ct: C.A.)

Person Skilled in the Art

Genentech Inc.'s (Human Growth Hormone) Patent (OBVIOUSNESS: C.A.)

Leader Products Pty Ltd v. Allflex International Ltd (APPLICATION: OPPOSITION: POWER OF COMMISSIONER: NOVELTY: TAX: C.-G.)

Practice

I. High Court proceedings (U.K.)

Abuse of process

Fichera v. Flogates Ltd and British Steel plc (WHETHER NON-PROSECUTION ABUSE OF PROCESS OR INEXCUSABLE: Pat. Ct)

Mölnlycke AB v. Procter & Gamble Ltd (No. 4) (JOINDER OF NEW DEFENDANT FOR PURPOSE OF DISCOVERY: C.A.)

Account of profits

Dellareed Ltd v. Delkim Developments (Ch.D.)

Acquiescence

Dellareed Ltd v. Delkim Developments (Ch.D.)

Affidavits

Lubrizol Corporation v. Esso Petroleum Co. Ltd (No. 2) (INJUNCTION RESTRAINING USE: Pat. Ct)

Lubrizol Corporation v. Esso Petroleum Co. Ltd (No. 4) (EXPERTS' AFFIDAVITS IN FOREIGN PROCEEDINGS: LEGAL PROFESSIONAL PRIVILEGE: Pat. Ct)

Amendment

CQR Security Systems Ltd's Patent (AMENDMENT OF PLEADINGS: Pat. Ct)

Hallen Company v. Brabantia (U.K.) Ltd (Pat. Ct)

Appeal

Nachf's Application (APPEAL TO PATENT COURT: EXTENSION OF TIME TO APPEAL: Pat. Ct)

Reiss Engineering Co. Ltd v. Harris (APPEAL TO PATENT COURT: COSTS: TAXATION OF PATENT AGENT'S COSTS ON APPEAL: Pat. Ct)

Toyama Chemical Co. Ltd's Application (EVIDENCE: Pat. Ct)

Breach of undertaking

Van der Lely (C.) NV v. Maulden Engineering Co. (Beds) Ltd (BREACH OF UNDERTAKING SETTLING ACTION: ORDER 14: Pat. Ct)

Burden of proof

Biogen Inc. v. Medeva plc (INTERPRETATION OF CLAIM: FAIR BASIS: SUFFICIENCY: DATE OF ASSESSMENT: C.A.)

Cause of action estoppel. See under estoppel

Certificate of contested validity

Cannon KK's Application (Pat. Ct)
Mölnlycke AB v. Procter & Gamble Ltd (COSTS: Pat. Ct)
Mölnlycke AB v. Procter & Gamble Ltd (No. 5) (COSTS: Pat. Ct: C.A.)

Clerical error

Antiphon AB's Application (Pat. Ct)
Payne's Application (PRIORITY DATE: CORRECTION OF CLERICAL ERROR: Pat. Ct)

Comptroller's jurisdiction

Roussel Uclaf's (Clemence & Le Martret) Patent (STAY: VEXATIOUS PROCEEDINGS: Pat. Ct)

Comptroller's power

Masuda's Application (ERROR IN TRANSLATION: POWER TO CORRECT MISTAKE: Pat. Ct)

Confidential documents

Union Carbide Corp. v. BP Chemicals Ltd (DISCOVERY: APPLICATION IN SCOTLAND TO AID PROCEEDINGS IN ENGLAND: APPLICATION BEFORE SERVICE OF STATEMENT OF CLAIM AND PARTICULARS OF INFRINGEMENT: WHETHER NECESSARY TO ENABLE PATENTEE ADEQUATELY TO PLEAD PARTICULARS IN ENGLAND: DISCLOSURE: TERMS: Scotland: O.H.: I.H.)

Costs

Bell Fruit Manufacturing Co. Ltd v. Twinfalcon Ltd (PATENT AGENTS: BASIS FOR CALCULATION: Pat. C.C.)
Chiron Corporation v. Organon Teknika Ltd (No. 7) (INFRINGEMENT: PARTIAL INVALIDITY: AMENDMENT: DISCRETION: Pat. Ct)
CQR Security Systems Ltd's Patent (SECURITY FOR COSTS: AMENDMENT OF PLEADINGS: Pat. Ct)
GEC Alsthom Ltd's Patent (REVOCATION: RELIANCE ON ADDITIONAL PRIOR ART: AMENDMENT OF PARTICULARS SOUGHT THREE WEEKS PRIOR TO TRIAL: WHETHER *See v. Scott-Paine* FORM OF ORDER APPROPRIATE: Pat. Ct)
Helitune Ltd v. Stewart Hughes Ltd (AMENDMENT OF PLEADING: EARTH CLOSET ORDER: Pat. Ct)
McManus's Application (ENFORCEMENT OF COSTS ORDER AGAINST APPELLANT IN PERSON: Pat. Ct)
Memminger-Iro GmbH v. Trip-Lite Ltd (INFRINGEMENT: TRANSFER TO COUNTY COURT: FACTORS: Pat. Ct)
Mentor Corporation v. Colorplast A/S (TRANSFER FROM PATENT COUNTY COURT TO HIGH COURT: C.A.)
Mölnlycke AB v. Procter & Gamble Ltd (CONSTRUCTION: WHETHER COMPLEXITY OF INQUIRY SPECIAL REASON JUSTIFYING STAY: Pat. Ct)

Mölnlycke AB v. Procter & Gamble Ltd (No. 5) (CERTIFICATE OF CONTESTED
  VALIDITY: Pat. Ct: C.A.)
Mölnlycke AB v. Procter & Gamble Ltd (No. 6) (INQUIRY FOR DAMAGES PENDING:
  ENTITLEMENT TO IMMEDIATE TAXATION: Pat. Ct)
Optical Laboratories Ltd v. Hayden Laboratories Ltd (No. 1) (EXPERT WITNESSES:
  COSTS OF WITNESSES: C.A.)
Pall Corp. v. Commercial Hydraulics (Bedford) Ltd (INFRINGEMENT: VALIDITY: Pat.
  Ct)
Pendax AB v. Anders & Kern (U.K.) Ltd (INFRINGEMENT: PLEADINGS:
  AMENDMENT OF PATENT, STATEMENT OF CLAIM AND PARTICULARS OF
  OBJECTIONS: COSTS: Pat. Ct)
PLG Research Ltd v. Ardon International Ltd (No. 2) (INFRINGEMENT:
  AMENDMENT: CLAIM VALID AND INFRINGED BUT SUBSEQUENTLY AMENDED:
  ENTITLED TO COSTS: Pat. Ct)
Rediffusion Simulation Ltd v. Link–Miles Ltd (DISCRETION: Pat. Ct)
Reiss Engineering Co. Ltd v. Harris (TAXATION OF PATENT AGENT'S COSTS ON
  APPEAL TO PATENTS COURT: Pat. Ct)
Strix Ltd v. Otter Controls Ltd (INFRINGEMENT: STRIKING OUT: COSTS: Pat. Ct:
  C.A.)
Toyama Chemical Co. Ltd's Application (EVIDENCE ON APPEAL: COSTS: Pat. Ct)
Van der Lely (C.) NV v. Ruston's Engineering Co. Ltd (C.A.)
Williamson v. Moldline Ltd (INFRINGEMENT: PLEADINGS: EARTH CLOSET ORDER:
  DISCRETION: C.A.)

Counterclaim

Behr–Thomson Dehnstroffrengler Verwaltungs GmbH v. Western Thomson
  Controls Ltd (Pat. Ct)

Cross-examination

Du Pont de Nemours & Co. v. Enka AG (AFFIDAVITS IN AMENDMENT
  PROCEEDINGS: C.A.)
Glaverbel SA v. British Coal Corp. (No. 3) (WITNESS STATEMENT: Pat. Ct)

Damages

Biogen Inc. v. Medeva plc (INFRINGEMENT: DISCOVERY: INVALIDITY:
  INJUNCTION: DECLARATION: Pat. Ct)
Chiron Corporation v. Organon Teknika Ltd (No. 7) (INFRINGEMENT: PARTIAL
  INVALIDITY: Pat. Ct)
Gerber Garment Technology Inc. v. Lectra Systems Ltd (PARTIAL INVALIDITY: DATE
  FROM WHICH DAMAGES SHOULD BE CALCULATED: Pat. Ct: C.A.)
Hallen Co. v. Brabantia (U.K.) Ltd (WHETHER TO IMPOSE TERMS OR LIMIT
  DAMAGES: Pat. Ct)
Minnesota Mining & Manufacturing Co. v. Rennicks (U.K.) Ltd (INFRINGEMENT:
  POSITION OF EXCLUSIVE LICENSEE WHO FAILED TO REGISTER: Pat. Ct)
Optical Coating Laboratory Inc. v. Pilkington PE Ltd (WHETHER PROPRIETOR AS
  WELL AS EXCLUSIVE LICENSEE ENTITLED TO DAMAGES FOR LOSS OF PROFIT:
  Pat. C.C.)
Smith Kline & French Laboratories Ltd v. Doncaster Pharmaceuticals Ltd (DELIVERY
  UP: Pat. Ct)
Unilever plc v. Chefaro Proprietaries Ltd (FORM OF ORDER: Pat. Ct)

Drawings

478

Hong Kong Toy Centre Ltd v. Tomy U.K. Ltd (THREATS: INTERLOCUTORY INJUNCTION: *Ex parte* ORDER: SUBSEQUENT AGREEMENT AS TO DATES FOR FILING EVIDENCE AND HEARING *inter partes*: 11–MONTH DELAY IN BRINGING MOTION FOR HEARING: Pat. Ct)

ICI v. Montedison (U.K.) Ltd (CONSTRUCTION: CONFLICT BETWEEN RIVAL SCIENTIFIC THEORIES: WHETHER COURT OBLIGED TO CHOOSE BETWEEN THEORIES: FRESH EVIDENCE ON APPEAL: Pat. Ct)

Johnson (H. & R.) Tiles Ltd v. Candy Tiles Ltd (LATE APPLICATION TO SUBMIT EVIDENCE: Ch.D.)

Procter & Gamble Co.'s Application (C.A.)

Rediffusion Simulation Ltd v. Link Miles Ltd (AFFIDAVIT EVIDENCE: REFERENCE TO "WITHOUT PREJUDICE" NEGOTIATIONS: Ch.D.)

Richco Plastic Co.'s Patent (ABUSE OF PROCESS: DISCOVERY: C.-G.)

Shoketsu Kinzoku Kogyu KK's Patent (EVIDENCE OF HAPPENINGS AT PRIORITY DATE: Pat. Ct)

Smith Kline & French Laboratories Ltd v. Evans Medical Ltd (WHETHER PATENT OFFICE EXPERIMENTS PRIVILEGED AS EVIDENCE: Pat. Ct)

Textron Inc.'s Patent (RESTORATION: EVIDENCE: JUNIOR EMPLOYEE'S MISTAKE: FAILURE OF EMPLOYEE TO CARRY OUT INSTRUCTIONS: C.A.: H.L.)

Toyama Chemical Co. Ltd's Application (EVIDENCE ON APPEAL: Pat. Ct)

Vax Appliances Ltd v. Hoover plc (Ch.D.)

Wistar Institute's Application (Pat. Ct)

Exclusive licence

Procter & Gamble Co. v. Peaudouce (U.K.) Ltd (C.A.)

Ex parte orders

Hong Kong Toy Centre Ltd v. Tomy U.K. Ltd (THREATS: INTERLOCUTORY INJUNCTION: SUBSEQUENT AGREEMENT AS TO DATES FOR FILING EVIDENCE AND HEARING *inter partes*: 11–MONTH DELAY IN BRINGING MOTION FOR HEARING: Pat. Ct)

Experiments, notice of

Société Française Hoechst v. Allied Colloids Ltd (DISCOVERY: PRIVILEGE: Pat. Ct)

Expert witness

Black & Decker Inc. v. Flymo Ltd (Ch.D.)

Gerber Garment Technology Inc. v. Lectra Systems Ltd (Pat. Ct)

Extension of time limit

Aisin Seiki KK's Application (Pat. Ct)

Heatex Group Ltd's Application (SUBSTANTIVE EXAMINATION: DECISION NOT TO PROCEED: CHANGE OF MIND: C.-G.)

Mitsubishi Jidosha Kogyo KK's Application (DISCRETION: Pat. Ct)

Nachf's Application (APPEAL TO PATENT COURT: TIME TO APPEAL: Pat. Ct)

Nippon Gaishi KK's Application (PERIOD FOR REQUESTING SUBSTANTIVE EXAMINATION: DISCRETION: Pat. Ct)

Optical Laboratories Ltd v. Hayden Laboratories Ltd (No. 1) (COSTS OF WITNESSES: C.A.)

Fair basis

Ishihara Sangyo Kaisha Ltd v. The Dow Chemical Co. (STRIKING OUT: C.A.)
Therm-A-Stor Ltd v. Weatherseal Windows Ltd (No. 2) (C.A.)

Filing

Application des Gaz's Application (TRANSLATION: RULE 100: Pat. Ct)
Mitsui Engineering & Shipbuilding Co. Ltd's Application (INTERNATIONAL
   APPLICATION: TRANSLATIONS: Pat. Ct)

Forum conveniens

Amersham International plc v. Corning Ltd (Pat. Ct)

Further and better particulars

Lux Traffic Controls Ltd v. Staffordshire Public Works Company Ltd (PARTICULARS
   OF CONSTRUCTION OF CLAIMS: Pat. Ct)

In camera hearings

Bonzel v. Intervention Ltd (No. 2) (DISCLOSURE OF PRIVILEGED DOCUMENTS: Pat.
   Ct)
Lubrizol Corporation v. Esso Petroleum Co. Ltd (No. 2) (CONFIDENTIALITY:
   RESTRICTED INSPECTION OF DISCOVERY DOCUMENTS: Pat. Ct)

Injunction

Allen & Hanbury's Ltd v. Generics (U.K.) Ltd (Pat. Ct)
Chiron Corporation v. Murex Diagnostics Ltd (No. 10) (INFRINGEMENT: DAMAGES
   IN LIEU OF INJUNCTION: DISCRETION: Pat. Ct)
Du Pont de Nemours (E.I.) & Co. v. Enka BV (No. 2) (STAY PENDING APPEAL: Pat.
   Ct)
Lubrizol Corporation v. Esso Petroleum Co. Ltd (No. 2) (RESTRICTED INSPECTION
   OF DISCOVERY DOCUMENTS: INJUNCTION RESTRAINING USE OF AFFIDAVITS:
   Pat. Ct)
Minnesota Mining & Manufacturing Co. v. Rennicks (U.K.) Ltd (STAY OF
   INJUNCTION: Pat. Ct)
Optical Coating Laboratory Inc. v. Pilkington PE Ltd (STAY OF INJUNCTION: Pat.
   C.C.)
Quantel Ltd v. Spaceward Microsystems Ltd (No. 2) (STAY PENDING APPEAL: C.A.)
Smith Kline & French Laboratories Ltd v. Harris Pharmaceuticals Ltd (MANDATORY
   INJUNCTION FOR DESTRUCTION OF STOCKS: SUMMARY JUDGMENT: Ch.D.)

Inquiry as to damages

Catnic Components Ltd v. Hill & Smith Ltd (Pat. Ct)
Gerber Garment Technology Inc. v. Lectra Systems Ltd (INFRINGEMENT: PATENTEE
   MANUFACTURER: LOSS OF ASSOCIATE SALES: ROYALTY BASIS: LOSS
   SUSTAINED BY SUBSIDIARY: EFFECT OF ENDORSEMENT OF LICENCES OF
   RIGHT: Pat. Ct)
Harrison v. Project & Design Co. (Redcar) Ltd (C.A.)
Mölnlycke AB v. Procter & Gamble Ltd (No. 6) (ENTITLEMENT TO IMMEDIATE
   TAXATION WHEN INQUIRY PENDING: Pat. Ct)
Strix Ltd v. Otter Controls Ltd (No. 2) (INFRINGEMENT: PROCEDURE: DIRECTIONS
   AS TO CONDUCT OF INQUIRY: Pat. Ct)
Strix Ltd v. Otter Controls Ltd (No. 3) (INFRINGEMENT: STAY PENDING APPEAL:
   LATE APPLICATION: DISCRETION: Pat. Ct)

Inspection

Lubrizol Corporation v. Esso Petroleum Co. Ltd (No. 2) (CONFIDENTIALITY: RESTRICTED INSPECTION OF DISCOVERY DOCUMENTS: Pat. Ct)
Lubrizol Corporation v. Esso Petroleum Co. Ltd (No. 4) (EXPERTS' AFFIDAVITS SWORN IN FOREIGN PROCEEDINGS: Pat. Ct)

Intention of court

Aumac Ltd's Patent (*See v. Scott-Paine* ORDER BY CONSENT: WHETHER CONSENSUAL ORDER IS A CONTRACT: JURISDICTION TO VARY, DISCHARGE OR ADD TO ORDER: Pat. Ct)

Interlocutory injunction

Chiron Corporation v. Organon Teknika Ltd (REFUSED: Pat. Ct)
Conder International Ltd v. Hibbing Ltd ("SNOWBALL EFFECT": C.A.)
Conoco Specialty Products Inc. v. Merpro Montassa Ltd (No. 1) (WHETHER PRIMA FACIE CASE: BALANCE OF CONVENIENCE: Scotland: O.H.)
Easycare Inc. v. Bryan Lawrence & Co. (THREATS: MALICIOUS FALSEHOOD: FREEDOM OF SPEECH: Pat. Ct)
Fleming Fabrications Ltd v. Albion Cylinders Ltd (CROSS-UNDERTAKING: BALANCE OF CONVENIENCE: C.A.)
Improver Corporation v. Remington Consumer Products Ltd (STRIKING OUT: BALANCE OF CONVENIENCE: C.A.)
Merck & Co. Inc. v. Primecrown Ltd (TRANSITIONAL PROVISIONS OF ACT OF ACCESSION OF SPAIN AND PORTUGAL: WHETHER REVISED VIEW OF *Merck v. Stephar* MAY BE TAKEN INTO ACCOUNT: REFERRAL TO ECJ: Pat. Ct)
Mölnlycke AB v. Procter & Gamble Ltd (No. 2) (AMENDMENT: Pat. Ct)
Monsanto Co. v. Stauffer Chemical Co. (C.A.)
Monsanto Co. v. Stauffer Chemical Co. (MODIFICATION OF INTERLOCUTORY INJUNCTION: Pat. Ct: C.A.)
Monsanto Co. v. Stauffer Chemical Co. (VARIATION TO PERMIT EXPERIMENTATION: Ch.D.)
Quantel Ltd v. Shima Seiki Europe Ltd (EFFECT OF EARLIER ACTION: BALANCE OF CONVENIENCE: Pat. Ct)
William E. Selkin Ltd v. Proven Products Ltd (INFRINGEMENT: BALANCE OF CONVENIENCE: PROTECTION OF LONG ESTABLISHED BUSINESS AGAINST NEWLY FORMED BUSINESS: ADEQUACY OF DAMAGES: Scotland: V.C.)

Interlocutory orders

Patents Court Practice Explanation (TELEPHONE SUMMONSES: AGREED INTERLOCUTORY ORDERS: INFORMATION SHEETS AT SUMMONS FOR DIRECTIONS: PRE-TRIAL REVIEWS: RIGHTS OF AUDIENCE: SITTINGS OUTSIDE LONDON: Pat. Ct)

Issue estoppel. See under *Estoppel*

Joinder of party

CQR Security Systems Ltd's Patent (CO-PETITIONER: WHETHER JUST AND CONVENIENT: Pat. Ct)
Lubrizol Corporation v. Esso Petroleum Co. Ltd (No. 1) (ADDITIONAL DEFENDANT: SERVICE OUT OF JURISDICTION: Pat. Ct: C.A.)
Mölnlycke AB v. Procter & Gamble Ltd (No. 4) (NEW DEFENDANT FOR PURPOSE OF DISCOVERY: WHETHER ABUSE OF PROCESS OR IMPROPER: C.A.)

PLG Research Ltd v. Ardon International Ltd (DEFENDANT: MOTIVE OF PLAINTIFFS IN SEEKING TO JOIN DIRECTOR DEFENDANT: Pat. Ct)

Joint tortfeasance/Joint tortfeasor

Intel Corporation v. General Instrument Corporation (No. 2) (SERVICE OUTSIDE JURISDICTION: Pat. Ct)
Lubrizol Corporation v. Esso Petroleum Co. Ltd (No. 1) (Pat. Ct: C.A.)
Mölnlycke AB v. Procter & Gamble Ltd (No. 4) (COMMON DESIGN: C.A.)
Puschner v. Tom Palmer (Scotland) Ltd (SERVICE OUT OF THE JURISDICTION: Pat. Ct)
Unilever plc v. Chefaro Proprietaries Ltd (MULTI-NATIONAL GROUP: C.A.)

Jurisdiction

Du Pont de Nemours (E.I.) & Co. v. Enka BV (No. 2) (STAY OF INJUNCTION PENDING APPEAL: DISCRETION: Pat. Ct)
ICI v. Ram Bathrooms (JURISDICTION TO ALLOW AMENDMENT: Pat. Ct)
Organon Teknika Ltd v. F. Hoffmann-La Roche AG (PATENT: CLAIM FOR DECLARATION OF NON-INFRINGEMENT: APPLICATION TO STRIKE OUT CLAIMS REFERRING TO VALIDITY: APPLICATION TO AMEND TO INCLUDE CLAIM FOR REVOCATION: JURISDICTION TO ALLOW AMENDMENT: Pat. Ct)
Plastus Kreativ AB v. Minnesota Mining and Manufacturing Company (DECLARATION OF NON-INFRINGEMENT: FOREIGN PATENTS: STRIKING OUT: Pat. Ct)
Smith Kline & French Laboratories Ltd v. Harris Pharmaceuticals Ltd (DETERMINATION OF QUESTION OF CONSTRUCTION: Ch.D.)

Leave

Electric Furnace Co. v. Selas Corporation of America (LEAVE TO SERVE OUT OF JURISDICTION: APPEAL: C.A.)
Raychem Corporation v. Thermon (U.K.) Ltd (INFRINGEMENT: LEAVE TO SERVE WRIT OUT OF JURISDICTION: Pat. Ct)
Van der Lely (C.) NV v. Maulden Engineering Co. (Beds) Ltd (LEAVE TO DEFEND: Pat. Ct)

Legal professional privilege. See also *Privilege*

Lubrizol Corporation v. Esso Petroleum Co. Ltd (No. 4) (EXPERTS' AFFIDAVITS SWORN IN FOREIGN PROCEEDINGS: Pat. Ct)
Rockwell International Corporation v. Serck Industries Ltd (PATENT AGENT: Ch.D.)
Schering AG's Patent (PRACTICE: LICENCES OF RIGHT: PATENT AGENTS: CONFIDENTIAL DOCUMENTS: AGENTS IN-HOUSE AND IN PRIVATE PRACTICE: Pat. Ct)
Wilden Pump Engineering Co. v. Fusfield (COPYRIGHT: PATENT AGENTS' PRIVILEGE: C.A.)

Licence of right

Smith Kline & French Laboratories Ltd's Cimetidine Patents (Pat. Ct)

Licence to import

Smith Kline & French Laboratories Ltd's Cimetidine Patents (Pat. Ct)

Mandatory injunction. See under *Injunction*

Notice of experiments

Société Française Hoechst v. Allied Colloids Ltd (DISCOVERY: PRIVILEGE: Pat. Ct)

Onus of proof

Memco-Med Ltd (EMPLOYEE'S INVENTION: "OUTSTANDING BENEFIT": Pat. Ct)

Order 14

Brain v. Ingledew Brown Bennison & Garrett (PATENTS: THREATS RELATING TO PENDING APPLICATION: WHETHER ACTIONABLE: WHETHER JUDGE AT LIBERTY TO MAKE DECLARATIONS UNDER ORDER 14A: C.A.)

Van der Lely (C.) NV v. Maulden Engineering Co. (Beds) Ltd (BREACH OF UNDERTAKING SETTLING ACTION: Pat. Ct)

Order 24, r.14A

Lubrizol Corporation v. Esso Petroleum Co. Ltd (No. 2) (Pat. Ct)

Order 104

Lubrizol Corporation v. Esso Petroleum Co. Ltd (No. 3) (PARTICULARS OF INFRINGEMENTS: WHETHER COMPLYING: Pat. Ct)

Patent agents

Bell Fruit Manufacturing Co. Ltd v. Twinfalcon Ltd (COSTS: BASIS FOR CALCULATION: DEFENCE STRUCK OUT: WHETHER AGENT ACTING WITHOUT INSTRUCTIONS: Pat. C.C.)

Reiss Engineering Co. Ltd v. Harris (TAXATION OF PATENT AGENT'S COSTS ON APPEAL TO PATENTS COURT: Pat. Ct)

Rockwell International Corporation v. Serck Industries Ltd (PRIVILEGE: Ch.D.)

Schering AG's Patent (CONFIDENTIAL DOCUMENTS: AGENTS IN-HOUSE AND IN PRIVATE PRACTICE: Pat. Ct)

Wilden Pump Engineering Co. v. Fusfield (PATENT AGENTS' PRIVILEGE: C.A.)

Patent Office practice

John Guest (Southern) Ltd's Patent (Pat. Ct)
Rhône Poulenc SA's (Ketoprofen) Patent (STRIKING OUT: Pat. Ct)

Patent Office proceedings

PCUK's Application (Pat. Ct)

Pleadings

Behr-Thomson Dehnstroffrengler Verwaltungs GmbH v. Western Thomson Controls Ltd (Pat. Ct)

Chiron Corporation v. Murex Diagnostics Ltd (No. 9) (INFRINGEMENT: SECOND ACTION AFTER AMENDMENT OF AGREEMENT HELD CONTRARY TO P.A.77, s.44: AMENDMENT TO PLEADINGS: WHETHER DEFENCE STRUCK OUT IN EARLIER ACTION CAN BE RAISED IN LATER ACTION: *Res judicata*: ARTICLE 177: *Acte clair*: Pat. Ct)

Dolphin Showers Ltd v. Farmiloe (Pat. Ct)

Ecolab Inc. v. Reddish Savilles Ltd (AMENDMENT OF PARTICULARS OF OBJECTION: Pat. Ct)

Gill v. Chipman Ltd (EARTH CLOSET ORDERS: Pat. Ct)

Glaverbel SA v. British Coal Corp. (No. 3) (WITNESS STATEMENT: CROSS-EXAMINATION: Pat. Ct)

Helitune Ltd v. Stewart Hughes Ltd (AMENDMENT: Pat. Ct)

Instance v. Denny Bros Printing Ltd (*See v. Scott-Paine* ORDER: Pat. Ct)

Intel Corporation v. General Instrument Corporation (DISCOVERY AND PARTICULARS BEFORE DEFENCE SERVED: Pat. Ct)
Ishihara Sangyo Kaisha Ltd v. The Dow Chemical Co. (FAIR BASIS: STRIKING OUT: C.A.)
John Deks Ltd v. Aztec Washer Co. (Pat. Ct)
La Baigue Magiglo v. Multiglow Fires (INFRINGEMENT: *See v. Scott-Paine* PRACTICE: Pat. Ct)
Minister of Agriculture's Patent (Pat. Ct)
Pleadings Ishihara Sangyo Kaisha Ltd v. The Dow Chemical Co. (STRIKING OUT: C.A.)
Raychem Corporation v. Thermon (U.K.) Ltd (AMBIGUITY: Pat. Ct)
Rediffusion Simulation Ltd v. Link-Miles Ltd (Pat. Ct)
Unilever plc v. Gillette (U.K.) Ltd (Pat. Ct)
Williamson v. Moldline Ltd (C.A.)

Practice Directions

Practice Direction—Patents (CHANCERY: READING GUIDE IN PATENT ACTIONS: (Ch.D.)
Practice Direction—Patents (DESIGNS: RECTIFICATION OF REGISTER: AGREED DIRECTIONS: PROCEDURE: RSC ORDER 104, R.17: Ch.D.)
Practice Direction—Patents (RECTIFICATION OF REGISTER: AGREED DIRECTIONS: Ch.D.)
Practice Direction—Patent action summonses (PATENT ACTION SUMMONSES: PATENT COURT USERS' COMMITTEE: Ch.D.)
Practice Direction—Patents Court (PROCEDURE: Ch.D.)
Practice Direction—(PATENT OFFICE: Pat. Off.)

Practice Notes

Practice Note (PATENT ACTION SUMMONSES: PATENT COURT USERS' COMMITTEE: Ch.D.)

Preliminary point

Masi AG v. Coloroll (Pat. Ct)

Preliminary search

Hollister's Inc.'s Application (Pat. Ct)

Pre-trial Reviews

Patents Court Practice Explanation (TELEPHONE SUMMONSES: AGREED INTERLOCUTORY ORDERS: INFORMATION SHEETS AT SUMMONS FOR DIRECTIONS: Pat. Ct)

Privilege

Black & Decker Inc. v. Flymo Ltd (DISCOVERY: WHETHER PRIVILEGE LOST BY EXCHANGE OF WITNESS STATEMENTS: Ch.D.)
Bonzel v. Intervention Ltd (No. 2) (DISCLOSURE OF PRIVILEGED DOCUMENTS: *In camera* HEARING: Pat. Ct)
Lubrizol Corporation v. Esso Petroleum Co. Ltd (No. 4) (EXPERTS' AFFIDAVITS SWORN IN FOREIGN PROCEEDINGS: WHETHER SUBJECT TO LEGAL PROFESSIONAL PRIVILEGE: Pat. Ct)
Rockwell International Corporation v. Serck Industries Ltd (PATENT AGENTS' PRIVILEGE: Ch.D.)
Schering AG's Patent (CONFIDENTIAL DOCUMENTS: PATENT AGENTS IN-HOUSE AND IN PRIVATE PRACTICE: Pat. Ct)

Société Française Hoechst v. Allied Colloids Ltd (CONTENTS OF NOTICE OF
EXPERIMENTS: Pat. Ct)
Wilden Pump Engineering Co. v. Fusfield (COPYRIGHT: PATENT AGENTS'
PRIVILEGE: C.A.)

Procedural defect, error or irregularity

Aoki's Application (Pat. Ct)
Coal Industry (Patents) Ltd's Application (IRREGULARITY ATTRIBUTABLE TO
PATENT OFFICE: Pat. Ct)
Drazil (PCT: RECTIFICATION OF ERROR: Q.B.D.)
E's Applications (DISCRETION: Pat. Ct: C.A.: H.L.)
M's Application (Pat. Ct: C.A.)
Mills' Application (TIME LIMITS: Pat. Ct: C.A.)
Practice Direction (RECTIFICATION OF REGISTER: AGREED DIRECTIONS:
PROCEDURE: RSC ORDER 104, R.17: Ch.D.)
Prangley's Application (PCT: C.A.)

Procedure

Aoki's Application (IRREGULARITY: DISCRETION: Pat. Ct)
Chiron Corporation v. Murex Diagnostics Ltd (No. 2) (RESTRICTIVE PRACTICES:
NATIONAL COURTS: DOMINANT POSITION: C.A.)
Chiron Corporation v. Murex Diagnostics Ltd (No. 5) (EPO PROCEDURE,
RELEVANCE: Pat. Ct)
E's Applications (IRREGULARITY: DISCRETION: INTERPRETATION OF
INTERNATIONAL TREATY: Pat. Ct: C.A.: H.L.)
Mills' Application (TIME LIMITS: ERROR: Pat. Ct: C.A.)
Osterman's Patent (REVOCATION: PATENT OFFICE PROCEDURE: Pat. Ct)
Practice Direction—Patents Court (PROCEDURE: Ch.D.)
Prangley's Application (PCT: DEFECT IN PROCEDURE: C.A.)
Strix Ltd v. Otter Controls Ltd (No. 2) (DIRECTIONS AS TO CONDUCT OF INQUIRY:
Pat. Ct)

Res judicata

Chiron Corporation v. Organon Teknika Ltd (No. 6); Chiron Corporation v. Murex
Diagnostics Ltd (No. 6) (CAUSE OF ACTION ESTOPPEL: ISSUE ESTOPPEL:
PRACTICE: STRIKING OUT: Pat. Ct)
Chiron Corporation v. Murex Diagnostics Ltd (No. 9) (SECOND ACTION AFTER
AMENDMENT OF AGREEMENT HELD CONTRARY TO P.A.77, S.44: PLEADINGS:
AMENDMENT: WHETHER DEFENCE STRUCK OUT IN EARLIER ACTION CAN BE
RAISED IN LATER ACTION: ARTICLE 177: *Acte clair*: Pat. Ct)
Harrison v. Project & Design Co. (Redcar) Ltd (C.A.)

Right of audience

Patents Court Practice Explanation (TELEPHONE SUMMONSES: AGREED
INTERLOCUTORY ORDERS: INFORMATION SHEETS AT SUMMONS FOR
DIRECTIONS: PRE-TRIAL REVIEWS: SITTINGS OUTSIDE LONDON: Pat. Ct)
Reiss Engineering Co. Ltd v. Harris (PATENT AGENT: Pat. Ct)

Right to open

Boehringer Mannheim GmbH v. Genzyme Ltd (WHETHER DEFENDANT OPENS WHEN ONLY VALIDITY IN ISSUE: Pat. Ct)

Rule 100

Aoki's Application (Pat. Ct)
Application des Gaz's Application (Pat. Ct)
Nippon Piston Ring Co. Ltd's Applications (INVENTOR'S NAME: ENTITLEMENT: Pat. Ct)

Section 64 defence

Instance v. Denny Bros Printing Ltd (Pat. Ct)

Security for costs

CQR Security Systems Ltd's Patent (Pat. Ct)

See v. Scott-Paine order

Alsthom Ltd's Patent (PETITION FOR REVOCATION: RELIANCE ON ADDITIONAL PRIOR ART: AMENDMENT OF PARTICULARS SOUGHT THREE WEEKS PRIOR TO TRIAL: COSTS: Pat. Ct)
Behr-Thomson Dehnstroffrengler Verwaltungs GmbH v. Western Thomson Controls Ltd (Pat. Ct)
Ecolab Inc. v. Reddish Savilles Ltd (Pat. Ct)
Instance v. Denny Bros Printing Ltd (Pat. Ct)
La Baigue Magiglo v. Multiglow Fires (Pat. Ct)

Service of petition for revocation

Symbol Technologies Inc. v. Opticon Sensors Europe BV (No. 1) (REGISTER OF PATENTS: Pat. Ct)

Service out of jurisdiction

Intel Corporation v. General Instrument Corporation (No. 2) (Pat. Ct)
Lubrizol Corporation v. Esso Petroleum Co. Ltd (No. 1) (JOINDER OF ADDITIONAL DEFENDANT: Pat. Ct: C.A.)
Napp Laboratories v. Pfizer Inc. (WHETHER SERVICE IRREGULAR BECAUSE NO ENDORSEMENT: Ch.D.)
Napp Laboratories v. Pfizer Inc. (WHETHER LEAVE REQUIRED: Ch.D.)
Puschner v. Tom Palmer (Scotland) Ltd (JOINT TORTFEASORS: Pat. Ct)

Settlement of action

ICI v. Ram Bathrooms (Pat. Ct)

Slip rule

Mölnlycke AB v. Procter & Gamble Ltd (No. 6) (Pat. Ct)

Stay

Amersham International plc v. Corning Ltd (Pat. Ct)
Du Pont de Nemours (E.I.) & Co. (Blades') Patent (Licence of Right) (SETTLEMENT OF TERMS: Pat. Ct)
Du Pont de Nemours (E.I.) & Co. v. Enka BV (No. 2) (STAY OF INJUNCTION PENDING APPEAL: Pat. Ct)
Ferro Corporation v. Escol Products Ltd (PROCEEDING IN PATENT OFFICE: Ch.D.)
Gen Set SpA v. Mosarc Ltd (Pat. Ct)
Hawker Siddeley Dynamics Engineering Ltd v. Real Time Developments Ltd (Pat. Ct)

Mölnlycke AB v. Procter & Gamble Ltd (WHETHER COMPLEXITY OF INQUIRY SPECIAL REASON JUSTIFYING STAY: Pat. Ct)

Pall Corporation v. Commercial Hydraulics (Bedford) Ltd (OPPOSITION IN EPO: STAY IN U.K. REFUSED: Pat. Ct: C.A.)

Roussel Uclaf's (Clemence & Le Martret) Patent (COMPTROLLER'S JURISDICTION: VEXATIOUS PROCEEDINGS: Pat. Ct)

Strix Ltd v. Otter Controls Ltd (No. 3) (INFRINGEMENT: INQUIRY AS TO DAMAGES: LATE APPLICATION: DISCRETION: Pat. Ct)

Striking out

Anchor Building Products Ltd v. Redland Roof Tiles Ltd (INFRINGEMENT: CONSTRUCTION: C.A.)

Bell Fruit Manufacturing Co. Ltd v. Twinfalcon Ltd (Pat. C.C.)

Chiron Corporation v. Organon Teknika Ltd (No. 2) (EURO-DEFENCE: Pat. Ct: C.A.)

Chiron Corporation v. Organon Teknika Ltd (No. 6) (Pat. Ct)

Dolphin Showers Ltd v. Farmiloe (Pat. Ct)

Fichera v. Flogates Ltd and British Steel plc (WHETHER NON-PROSECUTION ABUSE OF PROCESS OR INEXCUSABLE: Pat. Ct)

Halcon SD Group Inc.'s Patents (ESTOPPEL: Pat. Ct)

Improver Corporation v. Remington Consumer Products Ltd (INTERLOCUTORY INJUNCTION: BALANCE OF CONVENIENCE: C.A.)

Ishihara Sangyo Kaisha Ltd v. The Dow Chemical Co. (INFRINGEMENT: FAIR BASIS: C.A.)

Organon Teknika Ltd v. F. Hoffmann-La Roch AG (PATENT: CLAIM FOR DECLARATION OF NON-INFRINGEMENT: APPLICATION TO STRIKE OUT CLAIMS REFERRING TO VALIDITY: APPLICATION TO AMEND TO INCLUDE CLAIM FOR REVOCATION: JURISDICTION TO ALLOW AMENDMENT: Pat. Ct)

Pioneer Electronics Capital Inc. v. Warner Music Manufacturing Europe GmbH (INFRINGEMENT: WHETHER PRODUCTS OBTAINED DIRECTLY BY PATENTED PROCESS: Pat. Ct)

Plastus Kreativ AB v. Minnesota Mining and Manufacturing Company (DECLARATION OF NON-INFRINGEMENT: FOREIGN PATENTS: JURISDICTION: Pat. Ct)

Reckitt & Coleman Products Ltd v. Biorex Laboratories Ltd (DECLARATION OF NON-INFRINGEMENT: Pat. Ct)

Rhône Poulenc SA's (Ketoprofen) Patent (LICENCE OF RIGHT: PATENT OFFICE PRACTICE: Pat. Ct)

Smith Kline & French Laboratories Ltd (Bavin's) Patent (OPPOSITION: C.-G.)

Southco Inc. v. Dzus Fastener Europe Ltd (INFRINGEMENT: CONSTRUCTION: Pat. Ct)

Strix Ltd v. Otter Controls Ltd (COSTS: Pat. Ct: C.A.)

Unilever plc v. Schöller Lebensmittel GmbH & Co. KG (CONSTRUCTION OF CLAIM: Ch.D.)

Upjohn Co. v. T. Kerfoot & Co. Ltd (INFRINGEMENT: PHARMACEUTICAL: TESTING TO OBTAIN PRODUCT LICENCE: Pat. Ct)

Summary judgment

Smith Kline & French Laboratories Ltd v. Harris Pharmaceuticals Ltd (MANDATORY INJUNCTION FOR DESTRUCTION OF STOCKS: Ch.D.)

Summons for directions

Patents Court Practice Explanation (TELEPHONE SUMMONSES: AGREED INTERLOCUTORY ORDERS: INFORMATION SHEETS AT SUMMONS FOR DIRECTIONS: PRE-TRIAL REVIEWS: RIGHTS OF AUDIENCE: SITTINGS OUTSIDE LONDON: INJUNCTION: Pat. Ct)

Taxation

CQR Security Systems Ltd's Patent (ORDER AND DATE: Pat. Ct)
Mölnlycke AB v. Procter & Gamble Ltd (No. 6) (ENTITLEMENT TO IMMEDIATE TAXATION WHEN INQUIRY FOR DAMAGES PENDING: Pat. Ct)

Telephone summonses

Patents Court Practice Explanation (AGREED INTERLOCUTORY ORDERS: INFORMATION SHEETS AT SUMMONS FOR DIRECTIONS: PRE-TRIAL REVIEWS: RIGHTS OF AUDIENCE: SITTINGS OUTSIDE LONDON: Pat. Ct)

Time limits

Armaturjonsson AB's Application (Pat. Ct)
Decorflex Ltd's Application (EXTENSION: DISCRETION: Pat. Ct)
Fichera v. Flogates Ltd and British Steel plc (ADDITION OF NEW CAUSE OF ACTION OUT OF TIME: Pat. Ct)
Lebelson's Application (Pat. Ct)
M's Application (Pat. Ct: C.A.)
Mills' Application (ERROR IN PROCEDURE: Pat. Ct: C.A.)
OHI Seisakusho Co. Ltd's Application (TRANSLATION NOT FILED: Pat. Ct)
Thermo Technic Ltd's Application (Pat. Ct)

Title to sue

Bondax Carpets Ltd v. Advance Carpet Tiles (Ch.D.)

Transfer from Patents County Court to High Court

Mentor Corporation v. Colorplast A/S (COSTS: C.A.)

Transfer to Patents County Court

Memminger-Iro GmbH v. Trip-Lite Ltd (FACTORS TO BE TAKEN INTO ACCOUNT: Pat. Ct)
GEC-Marconi Ltd v. XYLLYX Viewdata Terminals Pte Ltd (Pat. Ct)
Slow Indicator v. Monitoring Systems Ltd (APPLICATION REFUSED: Pat. Ct)
Symbol Technologies Inc. v. Opticon Sensors Europe BV (No. 2) (Pat. Ct)

Transitional provisions of 1977 Patents Act

Cannon KK's Application (Pat. Ct)

Translation

Application des Gaz's Application (Pat. Ct)
Bayer AG v. Harris Pharmaceuticals Ltd (WHETHER REQUIRED TO TRANSLATE FOREIGN-LANGUAGE DOCUMENTS: Ch.D.)
OHI Seisakusho Co. Ltd's (TRANSLATION NOT FILED: TIME LIMITS: Pat. Ct)

Vexatious proceedings

Roussel Uclaf's (Clemence & Le Martret) Patent (STAY: COMPTROLLER'S JURISDICTION: Pat. Ct)

Witness statement

Glaverbel SA v. British Coal Corp. (No. 3) (PLEADINGS: OBJECT OF PARTICULARS: CROSS-EXAMINATION: Pat. Ct)

II. Patents County Court and Appeals therefrom

Appeal on costs

Prout v. British Gas plc (C.A.)

Costs

Memminger-Iro GmbH v. Trip-Lite Ltd (Pat. Ct)
Mentor Corporation v. Colorplast A/S (INFRINGEMENT: TRANSFER FROM PATENTS COUNTY COURT TO HIGH COURT: C.A.)
Prout v. British Gas plc (APPEAL: C.A.)
Rizla Ltd's Application (Pat. Ct)
Wellcome Foundation Ltd v. Discpharm Ltd (No. 2) (Pat. C.C.)

Damages

Optical Coating Laboratory Inc. v. Pilkington PE Ltd (WHETHER PROPRIETOR AS WELL AS EXCLUSIVE LICENSEE ENTITLED TO DAMAGES FOR LOSS OF PROFIT: Pat. C.C.)

Declaration of non-infringement

Sundstrand Corporation v. Safe Flight Instrument Corporation (VALIDITY: DIFFERENT ALGORITHM: PURPOSIVE CONSTRUCTION: Pat. C.C.)

Discretion

Memminger-Iro GmbH v. Trip-Lite Ltd (TRANSFER OF ACTION TO COUNTY COURT: C.A.)

Estoppel

Hazel Grove (Superleague) Ltd v. Euro-League Leisure Products Ltd (INFRINGEMENT: PROMISSORY ESTOPPEL: MODIFICATIONS OR REPAIRS: Pat. C.C.)

European Court, referral to

Research Corp.'s Supplementary Protection Certificate (EXPIRED PATENT FOR MEDICAL PRODUCT: CARBOPLATIN: SUPPLEMENTARY PROTECTION CERTIFICATE: LICENCES OF RIGHT: REFERENCE TO ECJ REFUSED: C.-G.)

Injunction

Optical Coating Laboratory Inc. v. Pilkington PE Ltd (STAY OF INJUNCTION: Pat. C.C.)

Jurisdiction

Optical Coating Laboratory Inc. v. Pilkington PE Ltd (C.A.)

Pleadings

Flude (H.) & Co. (Hinkley) Ltd's Patent (REVOCATION: NON-INFRINGEMENT: WITHDRAWAL OF CERTAIN GROUNDS OF INVALIDITY: C.-G.)

Privilege

Sonic Tape plc's Patent (CONFIDENTIALITY OF DOCUMENTS: C.-G.)

Referral to ECJ. See European Court, referral to

Security for costs

Thomas (Arthur Edward) Ltd v. Barcrest (Pat. C.C.)

See v. Scott-Paine order

Vestar Inc. v. Liposome Technology Inc. (INFRINGEMENT: FORM AND CONSTRUCTION: WRITTEN SUBMISSIONS: Pat. C.C.)

Stay of injunction

Optical Coating Laboratory Inc. v. Pilkington PE Ltd (Pat. C.C.)

Transfer to County Court

GEC-Marconi Ltd v. XYLLYX Viewdata Terminals Pte Ltd (Pat. Ct)
Memminger-Iro GmbH v. Trip-Lite Ltd (FACTORS TO BE TAKEN INTO ACCOUNT: COSTS: Pat. Ct)
Memminger-Iro GmbH v. Trip-Lite Ltd (DISCRETION: C.A.)

Transfer to High Court

Mentor Corporation v. Colorplast A/S (COSTS: C.A.)

Withdrawal of grounds of invalidity

Flude (H.) & Co. (Hinkley) Ltd's Patent (PLEADINGS: REVOCATION: NON-INFRINGEMENT: C.-G.)

Written submissions

Vestar Inc. v. Liposome Technology Inc. (INFRINGEMENT: *See v. Scott-Paine* ORDER: FORM AND CONSTRUCTION: Pat. C.C.)

III. United Kingdom Patent Office and Appeals therefrom

Abuse of process

Richco Plastic Co.'s Patent (COMPULSORY LICENCE: EVIDENCE: DISCOVERY: C.-G.)

Amendment

Hsiung's Patent (REVOCATION: DISCRETION: C.-G.: Pat. Ct: C.A.)
Smith Kline & French Laboratories Ltd (Bavin's) Patent (DISCRETION: C.-G.)

Appeal to Patent Court

Allen & Hanbury's Ltd's (Salbutamol) Patent (C.-G.: Pat. Ct: C.A.)

Clerical error in translation

Rhône-Poulenc Santé's European Patent (U.K.) (NARROWER PROTECTION CONFERRED BY TRANSLATION: WHETHER CORRECTION ALLOWABLE UNDER GENERAL STATUTORY PROVISION: WHETHER CORRECTION UNDER SPECIFIC PROVISION PERMISSIBLE BEFORE TRANSLATION PUBLISHED: C.-G.)

Entitlement

Cannings' United States Application (C.-G.)
Norris's Patent (C.-G.: Pat. Ct)
Tokan Kogyo KK's Application (PROCEDURAL ERROR: DISCRETION: C.-G.)

Error or omission

Intelligence Quotient International Ltd's Application (NATIONAL PHASE: DOCUMENTS FOR INTERNATIONAL APPLICATION FILED WITHOUT REQUEST FORM: INTERNATIONAL FILING DATE REFUSED UNTIL RECEIPT OF FORM: WHETHER FAILURE TO ACCORD DATE AN ERROR OR OMISSION OF RECEIVING OFFICE: CORRECTION OF IRREGULARITY: C.-G.)

European patent for same invention

Turner & Newall Ltd's Patent (SURRENDER OF EUROPEAN PATENT: AMENDMENT OF U.K. PATENT: PATENT: C.-G.)

Evidence

Microsonics Corp.'s Application (C.-G.)
Monsanto's CCP Patent (BEST EVIDENCE: C.-G.)
Norris's Patent (CROSS-EXAMINATION IN PATENT OFFICE: CONFIDENTIALITY OF FILED EVIDENCE: DISCOVERY: C.-G.: Pat. Ct)
Richco Plastic Co.'s Patent (COMPULSORY LICENCE: ABUSE OF PROCESS: DISCOVERY: C.-G.)

Filing

Matsushita Electric Works Ltd's Application (PCT FILING: PRIORITY DATE: C.-G.)

Time limit

P's Applications (EXTENSION OF TIME LIMIT: DIVISIONAL APPLICATION: C.-G.)
Brossmann's Application (PCT FILING: PRIORITY DOCUMENTS FILED LATE: C.-G.)

Legal aid

Brockhouse plc's Patent (PROPRIETORSHIP: PATENT OFFICE PROCEEDINGS: C.-G.)

Licence of right

Kaken Pharmaceutical Co. Ltd's Patent (INTERVENTION BY FORMER EXCLUSIVE LICENSEE: C.-G.)

PCT filing

Matsushita Electric Works Ltd's Application (PRIORITY DATE: C.-G.)

Priority date

Matsushita Electric Works Ltd's Application (PCT FILING: C.-G.)
Georgia Pacific Corp.'s Application (C.-G.)

Privilege

Sonic Tape plc's Patent (CONFIDENTIALITY OF DOCUMENTS: C.-G.)

Procedural defect, error or irregularity

Tokan Kogyo KK's Application (DISCRETION: C.-G.)

Publication of application

Peabody International's Application (WITHDRAWAL OF APPLICATION: C.-G.)

Rectification of error

Intelligence Quotient International Ltd's Application (INTERNATIONAL APPLICATION: RECEIVING OFFICE: FAILURE TO FILE REQUEST FORM DESIGNATING CONTRACTING STATES: WHETHER RECTIFICATION OF ERROR ALLOWABLE: WHETHER U.K. PATENTS RULES APPLICABLE TO RECEIVING OFFICE: C.-G.)

Reference to comptroller under section 12

Rizla Ltd's Application (SUBSEQUENT DISMISSAL ON WITHDRAWAL OF REFERROR: COMPTROLLER'S AUTHORITY TO AWARD COSTS: C.-G.)

Restoration

Borg-Warner Corp.'s Patent (C.-G.)
Deforeit's Patent (European Patent (U.K.): C.-G.)

Second grant

IBM (Barclay & Bigar)'s Application (C.-G.)

Striking out

Smith Kline & French Laboratories Ltd (Bavin's) Patent (AMENDMENT: DISCRETION: C.-G.)

Substantive examination

Heatex Group Ltd's Application (EXTENSION OF TIME: DECISION NOT TO PROCEED: CHANGE OF MIND: C.-G.)

Surrender of European amendment of United Kingdom patent

Turner & Newall Ltd's Patent (EUROPEAN PATENT FOR SAME INVENTION: C.-G.)

Withdrawal of application

Peabody International's Application (PUBLICATION OF APPLICATION: C.-G.)

IV. European Patent Office

Discovery

Bonzel v. Intervention Ltd (EPO: OPPOSITION: Pat. Ct)

Forum Conveniens

Amersham International plc v. Corning Ltd (Pat. Ct)

Motion for stay in High Court

Amersham International plc v. Corning Ltd (Pat. Ct)

Privilege

Community Patent Appeal Court Privileges Protocol (PROTOCOL ON PRIVILEGES AND IMMUNITIES OF THE COMMON APPEAL COURT)

Stay of proceedings

Pall Corporation v. Commercial Hydraulics (Bedford) Ltd (OPPOSITION IN EPO: WHETHER STAY IN U.K. SHOULD BE ORDERED: Pat. Ct: C.A.)

Prior Art

GEC Alsthom Ltd's Patent (PETITION FOR REVOCATION: RELIANCE ON ADDITIONAL PRIOR ART: AMENDMENT OF PARTICULARS SOUGHT THREE WEEKS PRIOR TO TRIAL: COSTS: WHETHER *See v. Scott-Paine* FORM OF ORDER APPROPRIATE: Pat. Ct)

Gerber Garment Technology Inc. v. Lectra Systems Ltd (INFRINGEMENT: OBVIOUSNESS: RECITAL OF PRIOR ART IN: WHETHER PATENTEE CAN RESILE: C.A.)

Mentor Corporation v. Hollister Inc. (INTERROGATORY: AWARENESS OF PRIOR ART: Pat. Ct)

Priority

Beloit Technologies Inc. v. Valmet Paper Machinery Inc. (INFRINGEMENT: CONSTRUCTION: *Catnic*: ENTITLEMENT: ANTICIPATION: OBVIOUSNESS: EXPERT EVIDENCE: Pat. Ct)

Priority Date

Amateur Athletic Association's Application (ENTITLEMENT: C.-G.)

Asahi Kasei Kogyo KK's Application (ANTICIPATION: CO-PENDING APPLICATIONS: ENABLING DISCLOSURE: Pat. Ct: C.A.: H.L.)

Biogen Inc. v. Medeva plc (GENETIC ENGINEERING: HEPATITIS B VIRUS: FAIR BASIS: SUFFICIENCY: DATE OF ASSESSMENT: BURDEN OF PROOF: C.A.)

Brossmann's Application (DOCUMENTS FILED LATE: C.-G.)

Genentech Inc.'s (Human Growth Hormone) Patent (COMMON GENERAL KNOWLEDGE: ADDRESSEE: Pat. Ct)

Georgia Pacific Corp.'s Application (C.-G.)

Gore W.L. & Associates Inc. v. Kimal Scientific Products Ltd (IMPORTATION BEFORE PRIORITY DATE: Pat. Ct)

Instituform Technical Services Ltd v. Inliner U.K. plc (Pat. Ct)

L'Oréal's Application (STATUS OF EUROPEAN APPLICATION: Pat. Ct)

Maag Gear Wheel & Machine Co. Ltd's Patent (U.K. AND EUROPEAN (U.K.) PATENTS: C.-G.)

Marley Roof Tile Co. Ltd's Patent (EUROPEAN AND U.K. PATENTS: Pat. Ct)

Matsushita Electric Works Ltd's Application (PCT FILING: C.-G.)

Payne's Application (CORRECTION OF CLERICAL ERROR: Pat. Ct)

Shoketsu Kinzoku Kogyu KK's Patent (EVIDENCE OF HAPPENINGS AT PRIORITY DATE: Pat. Ct)

Toyama Chemical Co. Ltd's Application (NOVELTY: ENABLING DISCLOSURE: Pat. Ct)

Vax Appliances Ltd v. Hoover plc (DEMONSTRATION AFTER FILING OF FIRST PROVISIONAL: Ch.D.)

Prior Dealing

Wheatley's Application (WHETHER PRIOR USE: C.A.)

Prior disclosure

Merrell Dow Pharmaceuticals Inc v. H.N. Norton & Co. Ltd (APPLICATION: PRIOR USE: USE OF KNOWN PHARMACEUTICAL: WHETHER INVENTION MADE AVAILABLE TO PUBLIC: H.L.)

Strix Ltd v. Otter Controls Ltd (INFRINGEMENT: CONSTRUCTION: ANTICIPATION: WHETHER PRIOR DISCLOSURE CONFIDENTIAL: OBVIOUSNESS: Pat. Ct)

Prior Use

Lux Traffic Controls Ltd v. Pike Signals Ltd and Faronwise Ltd (NOVELTY: ENABLING DISCLOSURE: OBVIOUSNESS: WHETHER AN INVENTION: ESTOPPEL: Pat. Ct)
Merrell Dow Pharmaceuticals Inc. v. H.N. Norton & Co. Ltd (INFRINGEMENT: VALIDITY: GILLETTE DEFENCE: ANTICIPATION: ENABLING DISCLOSURE: MEDICAL TREATMENT: Pat. Ct: H.L.)
Milliken Denmark AS v. Walk Off Mats Ltd (INFRINGEMENT: VALIDITY: RUBBER OR PLASTIC BACKED WASHABLE FLOOR MATS: CONSTRUCTION: AMBIGUITY: INSUFFICIENCY: ADDED MATTER: NOVELTY: ENABLING DISCLOSURE: OBVIOUSNESS: COMMERCIAL SUCCESS: Pat. Ct)
Wheatley's Application (PRIOR DEALING: C.A.)

Public Interest

Autopia Terakat Accessories Ltd v. Gwent Auto Fabrications Ltd (RELIEF FOR PART VALID PATENT: DECLARATION: Pat. Ct)

Rectification of Error. *See* **Practice** (*Procedural defect, error or irregularity*)

Rectification of Register. *See* **Practice** (*Procedural defect, error or irregularity*)

Registered User

Northern & Shell plc v. Condé Nast & National Magazines PE Ltd (INFRINGEMENT: RIGHTS OF REGISTERED USER TO SUE: NATURE OF REGISTERED USER: Pat. Ct)

Res Judicata. *See* **Practice** (*Res judicata*)

Restoration

Atlas Powder Co.'s Patent (PATENT REGISTERED AND EXCLUSIVELY LICENCED IN MALAYSIA: DELIBERATE BUT MISTAKEN DECISION NOT TO RENEW U.K. PATENTS: CONSTRUCTION: SECTION 28(3): Pat. Ct: C.A.)
Borg-Warner Corp.'s Patent (C.-G.)
Cement & Concrete Association (REASONABLE CARE: Pat. Ct)
Continental Manufacturing and Sales Inc.'s Patent (REASONABLE CARE: LICENSEE: Pat. Ct)
Daido Kogyo KK's Patent (TIME LIMITS: PROTECTION OF THIRD PARTIES: Pat. Ct: C.A.)
Deforeit's Patent (EUROPEAN PATENT (U.K.): C.-G.)
Electricité de France (EDF's) Patents and Commissariat a L'Énergie Atomique's Patents (NON-PAYMENT OF RENEWAL FEES: Pat. Ct)
Sony Corporation's Patent (MISTAKE BY PROPRIETOR'S EMPLOYEE: Pat. Ct)
Tekdata Ltd's Application (Pat. Ct)
Textron Inc.'s Patent (EVIDENCE: JUNIOR EMPLOYEES MISTAKE: FAILURE OF EMPLOYEE TO CARRY OUT INSTRUCTIONS: C.A.: H.L.)

Revocation

Abbott Laboratories' (Chu's) Patent (APPLICATION FOR REVOCATION WITHDRAWN: COMPTROLLER'S PUBLIC DUTY TO CONSIDER VALIDITY THEREAFTER: C.-G.)
Assidoman Multipack Limited v. The Mead Corp. (PETITION FOR REVOCATION AND DECLARATION OF NON-INFRINGEMENT: P.A.49 AND P.A.77: CLAIMS: PURPOSIVE CONSTRUCTION: C.A.)

Right of Audience. See **Practice** (*Right of audience*)

Rights of Registered User to Sue. *See* **Registered User**

Royalty

Catnic Components Ltd v. Hill & Smith Ltd (INQUIRY AS TO DAMAGES: INTEREST: LOSS OF PROFITS: PRESUMPTION OF LOST SALES: NOTIONAL ROYALTY: Pat. Ct)

Shiley Inc.'s Patent (LICENCE OF RIGHT: Pat. Ct)

Smith Kline & French Laboratories Ltd's (Cimetidine) Patents (LICENCE OF RIGHT: REASONABLE REMUNERATION: APPROACHES TO ASSESSMENT: REFERENCES TO ECJ: Pat. Ct: C.A.)

Syntex Corp.'s Patent (LICENCES OF RIGHT: SETTLEMENT OF TERMS: Pat. Ct)

Section 28(3)

Atlas Powder Co.'s Patent (RESTORATION: PATENT REGISTERED AND EXCLUSIVELY LICENCED IN MALAYSIA: DELIBERATE BUT MISTAKEN DECISION NOT TO RENEW U.K. PATENT: CONSTRUCTION: Pat. Ct: C.A.)

Scotland

Brupat Ltd v. Smith (INFRINGEMENT: CERTIFICATE OF VALIDITY: O.H.)

Christian Salvesen (Oil Services) Ltd v. Odfjell Drilling & Construction Co. (U.K.) Ltd (INFRINGEMENT: RIGHTS OF EXCLUSIVE SUB-LICENSEE: KNOWLEDGE: O.H.)

Conoco Specialty Products Inc. v. Merpro Montassa Ltd (INFRINGEMENT: CONSTRUCTION: GENERALLY CYLINDRICAL: VALIDITY: ANTICIPATION: OBVIOUSNESS: O.H.)

Santa Fe International Corp. v. Napier Shipping SA (PRACTICE: CONFIDENTIALITY: INFRINGEMENT: PATENT AGENT'S PRIVILEGE: O.H.)

Union Carbide Corp. v. BP Chemicals Ltd (INFRINGEMENT: PRACTICE: DISCOVERY: APPLICATION IN SCOTLAND TO AID INFRINGEMENT PROCEEDINGS IN ENGLAND: APPLICATION BEFORE SERVICE OF STATEMENT OF CLAIM AND PARTICULARS OF INFRINGEMENT: WHETHER NECESSARY TO ENABLE PATENTEE ADEQUATELY TO PLEAD PARTICULARS IN ENGLAND: DISCRETION: CONFIDENTIAL DOCUMENTS: DISCLOSURE: TERMS: O.H.: I.H.)

William E. Selkin Ltd v. Proven Products Ltd (INFRINGEMENT: CLAIMS: CONSTRUCTION: OBVIOUSNESS: NOVELTY: SIMILAR APPARATUS: INTERIM INTERDICT: WEIGHT TO BE GIVEN TO EXISTANCE OF BALANCE OF CONVENIENCE: PROTECTION OF LONG ESTABLISHED BUSINESS AGAINST NEWLY FORMED BUSINESS: ADEQUACY OF DAMAGES: V.C.)

See v. Scott-Paine Order. *See* **Practice** (*See v. Scott-Paine order*)

Set Off

BICC plc v. Burndy Corp. (JOINT OWNERSHIP: CONTRACT: SPECIFIC PERFORMANCE: RELIEF AGAINST FORFEITURE: Pat. Ct: C.A.)

Specific Performance

BICC plc v. Burndy Corp. (JOINT OWNERSHIP: CONTRACT: SET OFF: RELIEF AGAINST FORFEITURE: Pat. Ct: C.A.)

Specification

Chiron Corporation v. Organon Teknika Ltd (No. 7); Chiron Corporation v. Murex Diagnostics Ltd (No. 7) (WHETHER FRAMED IN GOOD FAITH WITH REASONABLE SKILL AND KNOWLEDGE: Pat. Ct)

Codex Corp. v. Racal-Milgo Ltd ("PURPOSIVE CONSTRUCTION" OF CLAIMS:
EFFECT OF AMENDMENTS ON ACCOUNT OF PROFITS: C.A.)
Hallen Co. v. Brabantia (U.K.) Ltd (WHETHER FRAMED IN GOOD FAITH: Pat. Ct)
Helitune Ltd v. Stewart Hughes Ltd (WHETHER PROPER ADDRESSEE WOULD HAVE
CORRECTED ERROR: Pat. Ct)
Quantel Ltd v. Spaceward Microsystems Ltd (DIVISIONAL SPECIFICATION:
AMENDMENT: Pat. Ct)
Rediffusion Simulation Ltd v. Link-Miles Ltd (WHETHER FRAMED WITH
REASONABLE SKILL: BEST METHOD: Pat. Ct)

Springboard Doctrine

Prout v. British Gas plc (Pat. C.C.)

Sufficiency

Assidoman Multipack Limited v. The Mead Corp. (PETITION FOR REVOCATION
AND DECLARATION OF NON-INFRINGEMENT: P.A.49 AND P.A.77: CLAIMS:
PURPOSIVE CONSTRUCTION: *Catnic* PRINCIPLES: OBVIOUSNESS: FAIR BASIS:
INSUFFICIENCY: EXTENSION OF DISCLOSURE: C.A.)
Biogen Inc. v. Medeva plc (GENETIC ENGINEERING: HEPATITIS B VIRUS: PRIORITY
DATE: OBVIOUSNESS: INTERPRETATION OF CLAIM: FAIR BASIS: DATE OF
ASSESSMENT: BURDEN OF PROOF: C.A.)
Mentor Corporation v. Hollister Inc. (VALIDITY: C.A.)
Milliken Denmark AS v. Walk Off Mats Ltd (INFRINGEMENT: VALIDITY: RUBBER
OR PLASTIC BACKED WASHABLE FLOOR MATS: CONSTRUCTION: AMBIGUITY:
ADDED MATTER: NOVELTY: PRIOR USE: ENABLING DISCLOSURE:
OBVIOUSNESS: COMMERCIAL SUCCESS: Pat. Ct)

Supplementary Protection Certificate

Centocor Inc.'s SPC Application (WHETHER PRODUCT PROTECTED BY BASIC
PATENT: C.-G.)
Chiron Corp. v. Murex Diagnostics Ltd (No. 12) (HEPATITIS C VIRUS: DIAGNOSTIC
TEST: VALIDITY: CLAIMS, WHETHER DISCOVERY AS SUCH: CAPABLE OF
INDUSTRIAL APPLICATION: MORE THAN ONE INVENTION: LICENCE
AGREEMENT: VOID CONDITIONS: DATE OF AGREEMENT: EXCLUSIVE
LICENSEE: C.A.)
Farmitalia Carlo Erba Srl's Application (DURATION OF CERTIFICATE: WHETHER
EARLIER VETERINARY AUTHORISATION WAS FIRST AUTHORISATION: C.-G.)
Research Corp.'s Supplementary Protection Certificate (EXPIRED PATENT FOR
MEDICAL PRODUCT: CARBOPLATIN: LICENCES OF RIGHT: C.-G.)
Spain v. Council of the European Union (VALIDITY OF REGULATION: COMMUNITY
COMPETENCE: LEGAL BASIS: ECJ)

Terms of Licence

Bayer AG and Maschinenfabrik Hennecke GmbH v. Süllhöfer (NO-CHALLENGE
CLAUSES: ARTICLES 30 AND 85: ECJ)
Bayer AG v. Süllhöfer (ANTI-COMPETITIVE PRACTICES: COMMUNITY LAW AND
NATIONAL LAW: NO-CHALLENGE CLAUSE: Germany: S.C.)
Boussois SA and Interpane & Co. KG's Agreement (RESTRICTIVE PRACTICES:
GROUP EXEMPTION: RELEVANCE: E.C. Comm)
Games Workshop Ltd v. Transworld Publishers Ltd (PATENT AND TRADEMARK
LICENCE AGREEMENTS CONTRASTED: C.A.)

Group Exemptions (Amendment) Regulation 1992 (RESTRICTIVE PRACTICES: GROUP EXEMPTIONS: SPECIALISATION AGREEMENTS: JOINT RESEARCH AND DEVELOPMENT: PATENT LICENSING: KNOW-HOW LICENSING: E.C. Comm)

Ottung v. Klee & Weilbach A/S (OBLIGATION TO PAY ROYALTIES INDEFINITELY WHILE AGREEMENT SUBSISTING: ARTICLE 85(1): TERMINATION ON REASONABLE NOTICE: ECJ)

Patent Licensing Regulation 1984-92 (2349/84) (RESTRICTIVE PRACTICES: GROUP EXEMPTION: PATENT LICENSING: TEXT OF REGULATION 2349/84 AS AMENDED BY REGULATION 151/93: E.C. Comm)

Pestre v. Oril SA (LICENSING AGREEMENT: KNOW-HOW: ROYALTIES: TERM: 50 YEARS: VALIDITY AFTER EXPIRY OF PATENT: FRANCE: C.A.)

Velcro SA v. Aplix SA (EXPORT BAN: EXTENSION BEYOND EXPIRY OF RIGHTS: NON-COMPETITION OBLIGATION: IMPROVEMENT PATENTS: E.C. Comm)

Windsurfing International Inc. v. E.C. Commission (TYING CLAUSE: NO-CHALLENGE CLAUSES: ECJ)

Threats

Bowden Controls Ltd v. Acco Cable Controls Ltd (Pat. Ct)

Brain v. Ingledew Brown Bennison (PENDING APPLICATION: CONDITIONAL THREATS: ADDRESSEE: AGGRIEVED PERSON: Ch.D.: C.A.)

Easycare Inc. v. Bryan Lawrence & Co. (MALICIOUS FALSEHOOD: FREEDOM OF SPEECH: INTERLOCUTORY INJUNCTION REFUSED: Pat. Ct)

Hong Kong Toy Centre Ltd v. Tomy U.K. Ltd (INTERLOCUTORY INJUNCTION: *Ex parte order*: SUBSEQUENT AGREEMENT AS TO DATES FOR FILING EVIDENCE AND HEARING *inter partes*: 11-MONTH DELAY IN BRINGING MOTION FOR HEARING: INEXCUSABLE AND INORDINATE: Pat. Ct)

Johnson Electric Industrial Manufactory Ltd v. Mabuchi-Motor KK (INFRINGEMENT: JURISDICTION: Pat. Ct)

Neild v. Rockley (INFRINGEMENT: Pat. Ct)

Pitney Bowes Inc. v. Francotyp-Postalia GmbH (INFRINGEMENT: EURO-DEFENCES: DOMINANT POSITION: ABUSE: WHETHER ALLEGATIONS A DEFENCE TO THE ACTION: Ch.D.)

Time limits. *See* Practice (*Time limits*)

Transfer to Patents County Court. *See* Practice

Unpatented Know-How

Boussois SA and Interpane & Co. KG's Agreement (E.C. Comm)

Continental Gummi-Werke AG and Compagnie Generale des Etablissements Michelin, Michelin et Cies Agreement (E.C. Comm)

Group Exemptions (Amendment) Regulation 1992 (RESTRICTIVE PRACTICES: GROUP EXEMPTIONS: SPECIALISATION AGREEMENTS: JOINT RESEARCH AND DEVELOPMENT: PATENT LICENSING: KNOW-HOW LICENSING: E.C. Comm)

Pestre v. Oril SA (LICENSING AGREEMENT: ROYALTIES: TERM: 50 YEARS: VALIDITY AFTER EXPIRY OF: France: C.A.)

Transitional Provisions of Act of Accession of Spain and Portugal

Merck & Co. Inc. v. Primecrown Ltd (PARALLEL IMPORTS: WHETHER *Merck v. Stephar* STILL GOOD LAW: INTERLOCUTORY RELIEF: WHETHER REVISED VIEW OF *Merck v. Stephar* MAY BE TAKEN INTO ACCOUNT: REFERRAL TO ECJ: Pat. Ct)

Translation. *See* **Practice** (*Translation*)

Validity

Abbott Laboratories' (Chu's) Patent (COMPTROLLER'S PUBLIC DUTY TO CONSIDER VALIDITY AFTER APPLICATION FOR REVOCATION WITHDRAWN: C.-G.)

Autopia Terakat Accessories Ltd v. Gwent Auto Fabrications Ltd (AMENDMENT: RELIEF FOR PART VALID PATENT: PUBLIC INTEREST: Pat. Ct)

Biogen Inc. v. Medeva plc (PRACTICE: INFRINGEMENT: DISCOVERY: INVALIDITY: INJUNCTION: DECLARATION: DAMAGES: Pat. Ct)

• Black & Decker Inc. v. Flymo Ltd (OBVIOUSNESS: Ch.D.)

• Boehringer Mannheim GmbH v. Genzyme Ltd (EUROPEAN PATENT (U.K.): OBVIOUSNESS: Pat. Ct)

Bonzel v. Intervention Ltd (No. 3) (EXTENSION OF DISCLOSURE THROUGH PRE-GRANT AMENDMENTS: OBVIOUSNESS: Pat. Ct)

Cabot Safety Corp. (LICENCE OF RIGHT: SETTLEMENT OF TERMS: RELEVANCE OF VALIDITY: C.-G.: Pat. Ct)

Cannon KK's Application (CERTIFICATE OF CONTESTED VALIDITY: TRANSITIONAL PROVISIONS OF P.A.77: Pat. Ct)

Catnic Components Ltd v. C. Evans & Co. Ltd (Pat. Ct)

Chiron Corporation v. Murex Diagnostics Ltd (No. 3) (OBVIOUSNESS: SIGNIFICANCE OF THIRD PARTY RESEARCH: INSUFFICIENCY: WHETHER INVENTION DISCOVERY AS SUCH: WHETHER CAPABLE OF INDUSTRIAL APPLICATION: Pat. Ct)

Chiron Corporation v. Organon Teknika Ltd (No. 6) (NOVELTY: OBVIOUSNESS: Pat. Ct)

Chiron Corp. v. Organon Teknika Ltd (No. 11) (PARTIAL INVALIDITY: AMENDMENT BY DELETION OF INVALID CLAIMS: DESCRIPTION: WHETHER VALID CLAIMS SUPPORTED: C.A.)

Chiron Corp. v. Murex Diagnostics Ltd (No. 12) (HEPATITIS C VIRUS: DIAGNOSTIC TEST: CLAIMS, WHETHER DISCOVERY AS SUCH: CAPABLE OF INDUSTRIAL APPLICATION: SUFFICIENCY: MORE THAN ONE INVENTION: LICENCE AGREEMENT: VOID CONDITIONS: DATE OF AGREEMENT: EXCLUSIVE LICENSEE: C.A.)

Conoco Specialty Products Inc. v. Merpro Montassa Ltd (ANTICIPATION: OBVIOUSNESS: SCOTLAND: O.H.)

Daily v. Ets Fernand Berchet (CONSTRUCTION: *Gillette* DEFENCE: Pat. C.C.) (APPEAL ALLOWED: C.A.)

Dow Chemical AG v. Spence Bryson & Co. Ltd (ANTICIPATION: OBVIOUSNESS: INUTILITY: Pat. Ct: C.A.)

Du Pont de Nemours & Co. v. Enka BV (FAIR BASIS: INSUFFICIENCY: OPEN-ENDED PRODUCT CLAIMING: BEST METHOD: INUTILITY: Pat. Ct)

Du Pont de Nemours (E.I.) & Co. (Blades) Patent (APPEAL: Pat. Ct)

Edwards (A.C.) Ltd v. Acme Signs & Displays Ltd (CONSTRUCTION OF CLAIM: NOVELTY: OBVIOUSNESS: COMMON GENERAL KNOWLEDGE: COMMERCIAL SUCCESS: Pat. Ct)

Fairfax (Dental Equipment) Ltd v. S.J. Filhol Ltd (CONSTRUCTION: Ch.D.)

Fichera v. Flogates Ltd (OBVIOUSNESS: STATUTORY DEFENCE: Pat. Ct: C.A.)

Flude (H.) & Co. (Hinkley) Ltd's Patent (PATENT OFFICE PRACTICE: PLEADINGS: REVOCATION: NON-INFRINGEMENT: WITHDRAWAL OF CERTAIN GROUNDS OF INVALIDITY: C.-G.)

• Fuji Photo Film Co. Ltd v. Carr's Paper Ltd (OBVIOUSNESS: PRACTICE: DISCOVERY: Pat. Ct)

Quantel Ltd v. Shima Seiki Europe Ltd (Pat. Ct)
Quantel Ltd v. Spaceward Microsystems Ltd (VIDEO GRAPHICS SYSTEMS: ANTICIPATION: PRIOR USE: ENABLING DISCLOSURE: SUFFICIENCY: Pat. Ct)
Rediffusion Simulation Ltd v. Link-Miles Ltd (AMBIGUITY: EFFECT OF CONSISTORY CLAUSES: SUFFICIENCY: AMENDMENT: Pat. Ct)
Roussel Uclaf v. ICI (AMENDMENT: FUNCTIONAL CLAIMS: PROCESS CLAIMS: INSUFFICIENCY INUTILITY: Pat. Ct)
Schering Agrochemicals Ltd v. ABM Chemicals Ltd (PRACTICE: DISCOVERY: Pat. Ct)
Shoketsu Kinzoku Kogyu KK's Patent (NOT LEGITIMATE TO TAKE FEATURES OF CLAIMED COMBINATION ONE AT A TIME IN LIGHT OF KNOWLEDGE OF THE INVENTION: EVIDENCE OF HAPPENINGS AT PRIORITY DATE: Pat. Ct)
Smith Kline & French Laboratories Ltd (Bavin's) Patent (C.-G.)
Southco Inc. v. Dzus Fastener Europe Ltd (OBVIOUSNESS: EFFECT OF PRE-GRANT AMENDMENT: Pat. Ct: C.A.)
Sundstrand Corporation v. Safe Flight Instrument Corporation (AIRCRAFT WIND SHEAR WARNING SYSTEM: DECLARATION OF NON-INFRINGEMENT: DIFFERENT ALGORITHM: PURPOSIVE CONSTRUCTION: Pat. C.C.)
Therm-A-Stor Ltd v. Weatherseal Windows (No. 2) (AMENDMENT: FAIR BASIS: C.A.)
Thetford Corporation v. Fiamma SpA (RELATIVE NOVELTY: ECJ)
Van der Lely (C.) NV v. Maulden Engineering Co. (Beds) Ltd (WHETHER VALIDITY A DEFENCE TO ORDER 14 APPLICATION: Pat. Ct)
Van der Lely (C.) NV v. Ruston's Engineering Co. Ltd (POWER HARROW: BEST METHOD: AMBIGUITY: FAIR BASIS: CONSTRUCTION: COSTS: C.A.)
Vax Appliances Ltd v. Hoover plc (PRIOR USE: DEMONSTRATION OF DEVICE AFTER FILING OF FIRST PROVISIONAL: PRIORITY DATE: Ch.D.)
Vickers plc v. Horsell Graphic Industries Ltd (Pat. Ct)
Windsurfing International Inc. v. Tabur Marine (G.B.) Ltd (OBVIOUSNESS: ANTICIPATION: AMENDMENT: C.A.)

Use of Known Substance

Merrell Dow Pharmaceuticals Inc v. H.N. Norton & Co. Ltd (APPLICATION: PRIOR USE: PRIOR DISCLOSURE: USE OF KNOWN PHARMACEUTICAL: H.L.)

Plant Breeders Rights

Biological Patents

Biological Patents Directive (Draft) (E.C. Council)

Burden of Proof. *See* **Practice** (*Burden of Proof*)

Comfort Letter, Intention to Issue

CBA's Application (RESTRICTIVE PRACTICES: LICENSING AGREEMENTS: NOTICE: E.C. Comm.)

Dependency Licences for Plant Varieties

Biological Patents Directive (Draft) (PATENTS: BIOTECHNICAL INVENTIONS: E.C. Council)

Deposited Material

Biological Patents Directive (Draft) (PATENTABILITY OF LIVING MATTER: SCOPE OF PROTECTION: DEPENDENCY LICENCES FOR PLANT VARIETIES: DEPOSIT AND ACCESS TO DEPOSITED MATERIAL: BURDEN OF PROOF: E.C. Council)

Licensing Agreements

CBA's Application (RESTRICTIVE PRACTICES: INTENTION TO ISSUE COMFORT LETTERS: NOTICE: E.C. Comm)

Patentability of Living Matter

Biological Patents Directive (Draft) (BIOTECHNICAL INVENTIONS: SCOPE OF PROTECTION: DEPENDENCY LICENCES FOR PLANT VARIETIES: E.C. Council)

Plant Breeders Rights

MOULIN Winter Wheat (UNIFORMITY: Plant Varieties and Seeds Tribunal)

Plants Variety Rights

Plants Variety Rights Council Regulation 2100/94 (PLANTS VARIETY RIGHTS: REGULATION: E.C. Council)

Practice

Burden of proof

Biological Patents Directive (Draft) (DEPOSIT AND ACCESS TO DEPOSITED MATERIAL: E.C. Council)

Restrictive Practices

CBA's Application (LICENSING AGREEMENTS: INTENTION TO ISSUE COMFORT LETTERS: NOTICE: E.C. Comm)
Société d'Intérêt Collectif Agricole des Sélectionneurs Obtenteurs de Variétés Végétales (SICASOV) Agreement (SEED LICENSING AGREEMENTS: INTENTION TO APPROVE: NOTICE: E.C. Comm)

Seed Licensing Agreements

Société d'Intérêt Collectif Agricole des Sélectionneurs Obtenteurs de Variétés Végétales (SICASOV) Agreement (RESTRICTIVE PRACTICES: INTENTION TO APPROVE: NOTICE: E.C. Comm)

Uniformity

MOULIN Winter Wheat (PLANT BREEDERS RIGHTS: Plant Varieties and Seeds Tribunal)

Practice

- Excludes *Restrictive Practices* cases
- See also under *Practice* sections in the individual subject digests
- See also under **Practice Directions** and **Practice Notes** in the main section

Abandoned Parts of Action

Berkeley Administration Inc. v. McClelland (COSTS: DISCRETION: COMPLAINT OF JUDICIAL BIAS: JUDGES DUTY: Q.B.D.)

Abuse of Process

Fichera v. Flogates Ltd and British Steel plc (WHETHER NON-PROSECUTION OF PATENT ABUSE OF PROCESS OR INEXCUSABLE: Pat. Ct)
Form Tubes Ltd v. Guinness Bros plc (COPYRIGHT: STRIKING OUT: Ch.D.)
Helitune Ltd v. Stewart Hughes Ltd (Ch.D)
House of Spring Gardens Ltd v. Waite (WHETHER ABUSE OF PROCESS TO RELITIGATE ISSUE THAT PRIOR JUDGMENT NOT OBTAINED BY FRAUD: C.A.)
Joyce v. Sengupta (NEWSPAPER ARTICLE: DEFAMATION AND MALICIOUS FALSEHOOD: LEGAL AID GRANTED FOR MALICIOUS FALSEHOOD ACTION: WHETHER ABUSE: C.A.)
Labyrinth Media Ltd v. Brave World Limited (No. 2) (INTERLOCUTORY INJUNCTION: APPLICATION FOR ADJOURNMENT AFTER DISCHARGE OF *ex parte* ORDER FOR PLAINTIFFS TO GATHER EVIDENCE: Ch.D.)
Mölnlycke AB v. Procter & Gamble Ltd (No. 4) (JOINDER OF NEW DEFENDANT FOR PURPOSE OF DISCOVERY: WHETHER ABUSE OF PROCESS OR IMPROPER: C.A.)
Richco Plastic Co.'s Patent (COMPULSORY LICENCE: EVIDENCE: DISCOVERY: C.-G.)
Speed Seal Products Ltd v. Paddington (STRIKING OUT: ACTIONABLE ABUSE: Ch.D.: C.A.)

Account of Profits

Attorney-General v. The Times Newspapers Ltd (UNJUST ENRICHMENT: PERMANENT INJUNCTION: H.L.)
Cala Homes (South) Ltd v. Alfred McAlpine Homes East Ltd (No. 2) (ELECTION FOR ACCOUNT OF PROFITS: WHETHER ADDITIONAL STATUTORY DAMAGES AVAILABLE, FORM OF ORDER: Ch.D.)
Charles Church Developments plc v. Cronin (MAREVA INJUNCTION: ENJOINED AMOUNT REDUCED IN LINE WITH LIKELY FIGURE RECOVERABLE ON ACCOUNT OF PROFITS: Ch.D.)
Codex Corp. v. Racal-Milgo Ltd (DELIVERY UP: WHETHER INFRINGING ARTICLES "FRANKED" BY TAKING ACCOUNT: Pat. Ct)
Dellareed Ltd v. Delkim Developments (ACQUIESCENCE: DECLARATION: Ch.D.)
Island Records Ltd v. Tring International plc (INQUIRY AS TO DAMAGES: ELECTION: TIME FOR ELECTION: INFORMED CHOICE: WHETHER ORDER RELEVANT TO DISCOVERY: Ch.D.)
My Kinda Town Ltd v. Soll (LACHES: PLEADINGS: Ch.D.: C.A.)
O'Sullivan v. Management Agency & Music Ltd (UNDUE INFLUENCE: MANAGER AND ENTERTAINER: INTEREST: C.A.)

504

Acquiescence

Dellareed Ltd v. Delkim Developments (DECLARATION: ACCOUNT OF PROFITS: Ch.D.)

International Business Machines Corporation v. Phoenix International (Computers) Ltd (STRIKING OUT: SUMMARY JUDGMENT: EURO-DEFENCES: ESTOPPEL: Ch.D.)

Nelson v. Rye (INFRINGEMENT: MUSICAL WORKS: MANUFACTURE AND SALE AFTER EXPIRY OF LICENCE: POP MUSICIAN AND MANAGER: ACCOUNT: TERMS OF RETAINER: LIMITATION PERIOD: Ch.D.)

Admiral Byng

Attorney-General v. Guardian Newspapers Ltd and The Observer Ltd (Ch.D)

Affidavits

Du Pont de Nemours & Co. v. Enka AG (CROSS-EXAMINATION ON AFFIDAVITS IN PATENT AMENDMENT PROCEEDINGS: C.A.)

Lubrizol Corporation v. Esso Petroleum Co. Ltd (No. 2) (INJUNCTION RESTRAINING USE OF AFFIDAVITS: *In camera* HEARINGS: Pat. Ct)

Lubrizol Corporation v. Esso Petroleum Co. Ltd (No. 4) (EXPERTS' AFFIDAVITS SWORN IN FOREIGN PROCEEDINGS: WHETHER SUBJECT TO LEGAL PROFESSIONAL PRIVILEGE: Pat. Ct)

Penfold v. Fairbrass (AFFIDAVIT EVIDENCE: WHETHER ADMISSIBLE: Ch.D.)

Practice Note (SIMPLIFIED TRIALS: TRIALS ON AFFIDAVIT EVIDENCE: DIRECTIONS: Pat. Ct)

Rafidain Bank v. Agom Universal Sugar Trading Co. Ltd (REFERENCE IN AFFIDAVITS TO DOCUMENTS NOT IN PARTY'S POSSESSION: EFFECT: C.A.)

Anton Piller

AB v. CDE (BREACH OF CONFIDENCE: Q.B.D.)

Altertext Inc. v. Advanced Data Communications Ltd (LEAVE TO SERVE ABROAD: Ch.D.)

(COPYRIGHT: INFRINGEMENT: PASSING OFF: Ch.D.)

Bayer AG v. Winter (INTERLOCUTORY INJUNCTION: MAREVA INJUNCTION: DELIVERY UP OF PASSPORTS: C.A.)

Bhimji v. Chatwani (DISCOVERY: LEGAL ADVICE: DELAY: SETTING ASIDE: BREACH: CONTEMPT: COMMITTAL ORDER: Ch.D.)

Booker McConnell plc v. Plascow (BREACH OF CONFIDENCE: DISCHARGE OF ORDER: C.A.)

British Phonographic Industry Ltd v. Cohen (COPYRIGHT: INFRINGEMENT: Scotland: I.H.)

CBS United Kingdom Ltd v. Lambert (COPYRIGHT: INFRINGEMENT: MAREVA INJUNCTION: C.A.)

CBS United Kingdom Ltd v. Perry (COPYRIGHT: INFRINGEMENT: CROSS-EXAMINATION: Ch.D.)

Chappell v. United Kingdom (EXECUTION WITH SEARCH WARRANT: RIGHT TO RESPECT FOR PRIVATE LIFE: NECESSITY IN A DEMOCRATIC SOCIETY: PROPORTIONALITY: ECHR)

Coca Cola Company v. Peter John Gilbey (DISCLOSURE OF INFORMATION: PRIVILEGE AGAINST SELF INCRIMINATION: RISK OF PERSONAL JEOPARDY: WHETHER GROUNDS TO DISCHARGE ORDER: WHETHER PERMISSIBLE FOR DEFENDANT TO GIVE EVIDENCE IN CAMERA IN THE ABSENCE OF PLAINTIFFS OR THEIR LEGAL REPRESENTATIVES: Ch.D.: C.A.)

506

Taylor Made Golf Company Inc v. Rata & Rata (CONTEMPT: FAILURE TO COMPLY
WITH ORDER: APPLICATION FOR COMMITTAL: WHETHER CUSTODIAL
SENTENCE APPROPRIATE PENALTY: FINANCIAL PENALTY: QUANTUM: Ch.D.)

Twentieth Century Fox Film Corp. v. Tryrare Ltd (COPYRIGHT: INFRINGEMENT:
THIRD PARTY RIGHTS: DISCLOSURE OF INFORMATION OBTAINED: Ch.D.)

Universal City Studios Inc. v. Hubbard (COPYRIGHT: INFRINGEMENT: ANTON
PILLER: PRIVILEGE AGAINST SELF-INCRIMINATION: Ch.D.: C.A.)

Universal Thermosensors Ltd v. Hibben (BREACH OF CONFIDENCE: STOLEN
CUSTOMER INFORMATION: EX-EMPLOYEES' COMPETING BUSINESS:
ASSESSMENT OF DAMAGES: INTERLOCUTORY ORDER BY CONSENT: SCOPE OF
INJUNCTIONS IN BREACH OF CONFIDENCE: SPRINGBOARD DOCTRINE:
DISCRETION: Ch.D.)

VDU Installations Ltd v. Integrated Computer Systems & Cybernetics Ltd
(COPYRIGHT: INFRINGEMENT: IMPROPER EXECUTION: NEGLIGENT
IMPROPRIETY: CONTEMPT: Ch.D.)

Wardle Fabrics Ltd v. G Myristis Ltd (COPYRIGHT: INFRINGEMENT: ANTON PILLER:
CONTEMPT: DISCHARGE OF ORDER: Ch.D.)

WEA Records Ltd v. Visions Channel 4 Ltd (COPYRIGHT: INFRINGEMENT:
JURISDICTION TO ENTERTAIN APPEAL: C.A.)

Appeal Subjects

Allen & Hanburys Ltd's (Salbutamol) Patent (NATURE OF APPEAL TO PATENT
COURT)

Chiron Corporation v. Murex Diagnostics Ltd (No. 8) (EUROPEAN LAW: TREATY OF
ROME: ARTICLE 177: INTERPRETATION: "PRELIMINARY": PETITION FOR
LEAVE TO APPEAL: WHETHER REFUSAL BY HOUSE OF LORDS AN
ADMINISTRATIVE OR JUDICIAL ACT: C.A.)

Du Pont de Nemours (E.I.) & Co. v. Enka BV (No. 2) (PATENT INFRINGEMENT:
STAY OF INJUNCTION PENDING APPEAL: Pat. Ct)

Elan Digital Systems Ltd v. Elan Computers Ltd (PASSING OFF: INJUNCTION:
WHETHER TRIABLE ISSUE: PRACTICE ON INJUNCTION APPEALS: Ch.D.: C.A.)

Electric Furnace Co. v. Selas Corp. of America (LEAVE TO SERVE DEFENDANT OUT
OF JURISDICTION: C.A.)

Hunter & Partners v. Wellings & Partners (OPPOSED *ex parte* MOTION: DISCRETION:
C.A.)

Hunt-Wesson Inc.'s Trade Mark Application (APPEAL FROM DECISION OF TRADE
MARK REGISTER: PRINCIPLES FOR ADMISSION OF FURTHER EVIDENCE ON
APPEAL: REGISTRAR'S PRACTICE: Ch.D.)

Infabrics Ltd v. Jaytex Ltd (COSTS: APPEAL: C.A.)

Johnson & Johnson's Application (TRADE MARK: NOTICE OF ORIGINATING
MOTION: Ch.D.)

Malaysian Milk Sdn Bhd's Registered Design (STRIKING OUT: DELAY: CONTRACT:
EFFECT OF AGREEMENT BETWEEN PARTIES ON STRIKING OUT: SETTING ASIDE
LEAVE TO APPEAL: Pat. Ct: C.A.)

Nachf's Application (APPEAL TO PATENT COURT: EXTENSION OF TIME: Pat. Ct)

NEUTROGENA Trade Mark (RECTIFICATION: NON-USE: INTERVENER: *Locus*:
Ch.D.)

Parmenter v. Malt House Joinery (AMENDMENT OF PLEADINGS DURING TRIAL:
EVIDENCE: *Res judicata*: INTERLOCUTORY APPEAL: C.A.)

Prout v. British Gas plc (APPEAL ON COSTS ALONE: Pat. C.C.: C.A.)

Reiss Engineering Co. Ltd v. Harris (TAXATION OF PATENT AGENT'S COSTS ON
APPEAL TO PATENTS COURT: RIGHT OF AUDIENCE: Pat. Ct)

The Reject Shop plc v. Robert Manners (COPYRIGHT INFRINGEMENT: CRIMINAL
PROCEEDINGS: APPEAL BY WAY OF CASE STATED: Q.B.D.)

Toyama Chemical Co. Ltd's Application (EVIDENCE ON APPEAL: COSTS: Pat. Ct)
WEA Records Ltd v. Visions Channel 4 Ltd (COPYRIGHT: INFRINGEMENT: ANTON
    PILLER: JURISDICTION TO ENTERTAIN APPEAL: C.A.)
Zunis Holding SA v. E.C. Commission (RESTRICTIVE PRACTICES: MERGER:
    CLEARED BY COMMISSION: REQUEST BY SHAREHOLDERS TO REOPEN CASE:
    REFUSAL: JUDICIAL REVIEW: WHETHER APPEAL POSSIBLE: *Locus standii*: CFI)

Arbitration

Bibby Bulk Carriers Ltd v. Cansulex Ltd (DISCOVERY: USE OF DOCUMENTS:
    DOCUMENT READ IN OPEN COURT: DISCLOSURE TO CLAIMANT IN
    ARBITRATION PROCEEDINGS: IMPLIED UNDERTAKING NOT TO USE IN
    OTHER PROCEEDINGS: WHETHER NEW RULES RETROSPECTIVE IN EFFECT:
    Q.B.D.)
Deutsche Schachtbau- und Tiefbohrgesellschaft mbH v. Ras Al Khaimah National
    Oil Co. (AWARD: ENFORCEMENT: PRE-TRIAL RELIEF: MAREVA INJUNCTION:
    C.A.)
Etri Fans Ltd v. NMB (U.K.) Ltd (COPYRIGHT: INFRINGEMENT: ARBITRATION
    CLAUSE: STAY OF ACTION: C.A.)

Balance of Convenience. *See under* **Interlocutory Injunction** (*Balance of convenience*)

Bona Fides

McGuinness v. Kellogg Co. of Great Britain Ltd (CONFIDENTIAL INFORMATION:
    DISCOVERY: NON-DISCLOSURE OF EVIDENCE BEFORE TRIAL:
    DOCUMENTARY: REBUTTAL OF BONA FIDES: APPLICATION FOR LEAVE NOT
    TO DISCLOSE UNTIL TRIAL: PROCEDURE: C.A.)

Burden of Proof

Biogen Inc. v. Medeva plc (PATENT: GENETIC ENGINEERING: HEPATITIS B VIRUS:
    SUFFICIENCY: PRIORITY DATE: OBVIOUSNESS: INTERPRETATION OF CLAIM:
    FAIR BASIS: SUFFICIENCY: DATE OF ASSESSMENT: C.A.)

***Calderbank* Letter**

Brugger v. Medicaid (ELECTION AS TO DAMAGES OR AN ACCOUNT: WHETHER
    PLAINTIFF CAN CLAIM ADDITIONAL DAMAGES IN INQUIRY ALTHOUGH NOT
    ORIGINALLY PLEADED: WHETHER COSTS SHOULD BE DETERMINED AFTER
    INQUIRY: Pat. Ct)
C. & H. Engineering v. F. Klucznik & Sons Ltd (COSTS: WHETHER "WITHOUT
    PREJUDICE" CORRESPONDENCE AFTER *Calderbank* LETTER PRIVILEGED:
    WHETHER PLAINTIFF SHOULD HAVE ACCEPTED TERMS OFFERED: Ch.D.)

Case Stated

The Reject Shop plc v. Robert Manners (COPYRIGHT INFRINGEMENT: CRIMINAL
    PROCEEDINGS: APPEAL BY WAY OF CASE STATED: COSTS: Q.B.D.)

Cause of Action

Banks v. CBS Songs Ltd (FURTHER INFRINGEMENTS ALLEGED AFTER ISSUE OF
    WRIT: WHETHER CONTINUOUS CAUSE OF ACTION: Ch.D., C.A.)
Chiron Corporation v. Organon Teknika Ltd (No. 6) (*Res judicata*: CAUSE OF
    ACTION ESTOPPEL: ISSUE ESTOPPEL: STRIKING OUT: Pat. Ct)

Fichera v. Flogates Ltd and British Steel plc (ADDITION OF NEW CAUSE OF ACTION OUT OF TIME: Pat. Ct)

Cause of Action Estoppel. *See under* Cause of Action

Certiorari

Adidas Sàrl (TRADE MARK: OPPOSITION: EXTENSIONS OF TIME: Q.B.D.)

Choice of Tribunal. *See under* Tribunal, Choice of

Civil Evidence Act

Union Carbide Corp. v. Naturin Ltd (STOLEN INFORMATION: CONVICTIONS PLEADED: STRIKING OUT: C.A.)

Committal

Bhimji v. Chatwani (DISCOVERY: ANTON PILLER ORDER: LEGAL ADVICE: DELAY: SETTING ASIDE: BREACH: CONTEMPT: COMMITTAL ORDER: Ch.D.)

Garvin v. Domus Publishing Ltd (USE OF DOCUMENTS SEIZED IN EXECUTION OF ANTON PILLER ORDER: APPLICATION FOR LEAVE TO USE IN CONTEMPT PROCEEDINGS: WHETHER COMMITTAL PROCEEDINGS CIVIL PROCEEDINGS: PRINCIPLE AGAINST SELF-INCRIMINATION: Ch.D.)

Confidential Documents

Union Carbide Corp. v. BP Chemicals Ltd (COPYRIGHT INFRINGEMENT: DISCOVERY: DISCRETION: DISCLOSURE: TERMS: SCOTLAND: O.H.: I.H.)

Consent

Bassey v. Icon Entertainment plc (COPYRIGHT: PERFORMERS RIGHTS: PROPRIETORSHIP: RECORDING OF PERFORMANCES: SUMMARY JUDGMENT: TRIABLE ISSUE: Ch.D.)

Consent Orders

Dalgety Foods Holland BV v. Deb-Its Ltd (SETTLEMENT: INTENTION TO OBTAIN CONSENT ORDER INCORPORATING UNDERTAKINGS: ACTUAL WORDING NOT AGREED: WHETHER BINDING: Ch.D.)

Fearis v. Davies (REQUEST FOR FURTHER AND BETTER PARTICULARS: CONSTRUCTION OF ORDER: C.A.)

John Richardson Computers Ltd v. Flanders (DISCHARGE OR VARIATION OF CONSENT ORDER ON CHANGE OF CIRCUMSTANCES: DUTY OF DUE DILIGENCE: Ch.D.)

Pet Plan Ltd v. Protect-A-Pet Ltd (APPLICATION TO DISCHARGE: C.A.)

Universal Thermosensors Ltd v. Hibben (ASSESSMENT OF DAMAGES: INTERLOCUTORY ORDER BY CONSENT: SCOPE OF INJUNCTIONS IN BREACH OF CONFIDENCE: SPRINGBOARD DOCTRINE: Ch.D.)

Conspiracy to Defraud

R. v. Bridgeman and Butt (SATELLITE BROADCASTING FROM U.K. TO SPAIN: AMBIT OF LICENCE: JURISDICTION: ENCRYPTED TRANSMISSIONS: DECODING DEVICES: NATURE OF RIGHTS AND REMEDIES: EVIDENCE: C.C.)

Contempt

Attorney-General v. Guardian Newspapers Ltd (DERBYSHIRE COUNTY COUNCIL INTERVENING) (*Spycatcher*: WHETHER LACK OF CENSORSHIP BY COUNCIL A CONTEMPT: Ch.D.)

Attorney-General v. Newspaper Publishing plc (THIRD PARTY: WHETHER BREACH OF INJUNCTION CONTEMPT: Ch.D.: C.A.)

Bhimji v. Chatwani (DISCOVERY: ANTON PILLER ORDER: BREACH: COMMITTAL ORDER: Ch.D.)

Chelsea Man plc v. Chelsea Girl Ltd (No. 2) (PASSING OFF: Ch.D.)

Crest Homes plc v. Marks (ANTON PILLER: USE OF DOCUMENTS FOR CONTEMPT PROCEEDINGS IN EARLIER ACTION: PRIVILEGE AGAINST SELF-INCRIMINATION: C.A.: H.L.)

Garvin v. Domus Publishing Ltd (USE OF DOCUMENTS SEIZED IN EXECUTION OF ANTON PILLER ORDER: APPLICATION FOR LEAVE TO USE IN CONTEMPT PROCEEDINGS: Ch.D.)

Japan Capsule Computers (U.K.) Ltd v. Sonic Games Sales (WANT OF PROSECUTION: APPLICATION TO DISMISS: DELAY: BLAME: C.A.)

John Richardson Computers Ltd v. Flanders (DISCHARGE OR VARIATION OF CONSENT ORDER ON CHANGE OF CIRCUMSTANCES: DUTY OF DUE DILIGENCE: WHETHER CONTEMPT OR UNLAWFUL INTERFERENCE WITH TRADE: Ch.D.)

Supply of Ready Mixed Concrete (No. 2) (BREACH OF INJUNCTION BY EMPLOYEE: LIABILITY OF EMPLOYER: H.L.)

Taylor Made Golf Company Inc v. Rata & Rata (FAILURE TO COMPLY WITH ANTON PILLER ORDER: APPLICATION FOR COMMITTAL: WHETHER CUSTODIAL SENTENCE APPROPRIATE PENALTY: FINANCIAL PENALTY: QUANTUM: Ch.D.)

VDU Installations Ltd v. Integrated Computer Systems & Cybernetics Ltd (COPYRIGHT: INFRINGEMENT: ANTON PILLER ORDER: IMPROPER EXECUTION: NEGLIGENT IMPROPRIETY: Ch.D.)

Walt Disney Productions Ltd v. Gurvitz (TRAP ORDER: *Agent provocateur*: Ch.D.)

Wardle Fabrics Ltd v. G. Myristis Ltd (ANTON PILLER: DISCHARGE OF ORDER: Ch.D.)

Wilden Pump & Engineering Co. v. Fusfield (DISCOVERY: SCOPE OF IMPLIED UNDERTAKING: Ch.D.)

Costs. *See also under* Security for Costs

Amper SA's Design Application (RDAT)

Apple Corp.'s Ltd v. Apple Computer Inc. ("No challenge interlocutory") (*American Cyanamid* PRINCIPLES: RESTRAINT OF FOREIGN PROCEEDINGS: COSTS: Ch.D.)

Attorney-General v. Newspaper Publishing plc (CONTEMPT: FINES: Ch.D.: C.A.)

Bell Fruit Manufacturing Co. Ltd v. Twinfalcon Ltd (PATENT AGENTS: BASIS FOR CALCULATION: DEFENCE STRUCK OUT: WHETHER AGENT ACTING WITHOUT INSTRUCTIONS: Pat. C.C.)

Berkeley Administration Inc v. McClelland (ABANDONED PARTS OF ACTION: DISCRETION: COMPLAINT OF JUDICIAL BIAS: JUDGES DUTY: Q.B.D.)

Brugger v. Medicaid (*Calderbank* LETTER: WHETHER COSTS SHOULD BE DETERMINED AFTER INQUIRY: Pat. Ct)

C. & H. Engineering v. F. Klucznik & Sons Ltd (COSTS: WHETHER WITHOUT PREJUDICE CORRESPONDENCE AFTER *Calderbank* LETTER PRIVILEGED: WHETHER PLAINTIFF SHOULD HAVE ACCEPTED TERMS OFFERED: Ch.D.)

Colgate Palmolive Ltd v. Markwell Finance Ltd (PAYMENT INTO COURT: Ch.D.)

CQR Security Systems Ltd's Patent (PETITION FOR REVOCATION OF PATENT: JOINDER OF CO-PETITIONER: WHETHER JUST AND CONVENIENT: NECESSITY OF SECURITY FOR COSTS: AMENDMENT OF PLEADINGS: APPROPRIATE ORDER AND DATE FOR TAXATION: Pat. Ct)

Dirt Magnet Trade Mark (PARALLEL PROCEEDINGS IN SCOTLAND AND ENGLAND: IDENTICAL ISSUES: APPLICANTS NOT PARTIES TO SCOTTISH PROCEEDINGS: WHETHER DUPLICATION: Ch.D.)

Disney v. Plummer (INDEMNITY COSTS: C.A.)

Erven Warnink BV v. J. Townend & Sons (Hull) Ltd (INTEREST ON COSTS: TIME OF ENTERING JUDGMENT: C.A.)

GEC Alsthom Ltd's Patent (PETITION FOR REVOCATION: RELIANCE ON ADDITIONAL PRIOR ART: AMENDMENT OF PARTICULARS SOUGHT THREE WEEKS PRIOR TO TRIAL: COSTS: WHETHER See v. Scott-Paine FORM OF ORDER APPROPRIATE: Pat. Ct)

Helitune Ltd v. Stewart Hughes Ltd (EARTH CLOSET ORDER: Pat. Ct)

House of Spring Gardens Ltd v. Waite (MAREVA INJUNCTION: PROCEEDINGS IN TWO JURISDICTIONS: Ch.D.)

Infabrics Ltd v. Jaytex Ltd (Costs Appeal) (APPEAL: C.A.)

John Richardson Computers Ltd v. Flanders (APPROPRIATE ORDER FOR COSTS WHERE WHOLESALE INFRINGEMENT ALLEGED BUT ONLY MINOR ESTABLISHED: CH.D.

Kickers International SA v. Paul Kettle Agencies Ltd (INTERLOCUTORY INJUNCTION: BALANCING RISKS OF INJUSTICE: WHEN TO BE TAXED: Ch.D.)

Kodak Ltd v. Reed International plc (MOTION: ADJOURNED MOTION TO TRIAL: Ch.D.)

Marie Claire Album SA v. Hartstone Hosiery Ltd (TRAP ORDER: Ch.D.)

McManus's Application (PATENT: ENFORCEMENT OF COSTS ORDER AGAINST APPELLANT IN PERSON: Pat. Ct)

Memminger-Iro GmbH v. Trip-Lite Ltd (TRANSFER TO COUNTY COURT: FACTORS TO BE TAKEN INTO ACCOUNT: C.A.)

Mentor Corporation v. Colorplast A/S (TRANSFER FROM PATENTS COUNTY COURT TO HIGH COURT: C.A.)

Mölnlycke AB v. Procter & Gamble Ltd (No. 5) (PATENT OFFICE: CERTIFICATE OF CONTESTED VALIDITY: Pat. Ct: C.A.)

Mölnlycke AB v. Procter & Gamble Ltd (No. 6) (INQUIRY FOR DAMAGES PENDING: WHETHER PLAINTIFFS ENTITLED TO IMMEDIATE TAXATION: WHETHER AMENDMENT UNDER SLIP RULE PERMISSIBLE: Pat. Ct)

Naf Naf SA v. Dickens (London) Ltd (APPLICATION TO DISCHARGE ANTON PILLER ORDER: INDEMNITY COSTS: IMMEDIATE TAXATION: Ch.D.)

Optical Laboratories Ltd v. Hayden Laboratories Ltd (No. 1) (EXPERT WITNESSES: COSTS OF WITNESSES: C.A.)

Porzelack KG v. Porzelack (U.K.) Ltd (EEC PLAINTIFF: DISCRETION TO ORDER SECURITY FOR COSTS: Ch.D.)

Project Development Co. Ltd SA v. KMK Securities Ltd (Syndicate Bank intervening) (MAREVA INJUNCTION: COSTS OF INNOCENT THIRD PARTY: Q.B.D.)

Prout v. British Gas plc (PATENT: APPEAL ON COSTS ALONE: Pat. C.C.: C.A.)

Reiss Engineering Co. Ltd v. Harris (COSTS: TAXATION OF PATENT AGENTS' COSTS ON APPEAL TO PATENTS COURT: Pat. Ct)

Rizla Ltd's Application (Pat. Ct)

Shippam (C.) Ltd v. Princes-Buitoni Ltd (REQUIREMENTS OF STATEMENTS OF CLAIM: Ch.D.)

Silicon Graphics Inc v. Indigo Graphic Systems (U.K.) Ltd (DIGITAL PRINTING PRESS: BALANCE OF CONVENIENCE: Ch.D.)

Slazengers Ltd v. Seaspeed Ferries International Ltd (SECURITY FOR COSTS: PLAINTIFF RESIDENT OUT OF JURISDICTION: Comm. Ct.: C.A.)

Speed Up Holdings Ltd v. Gough & Co. (Handly) Ltd (CORPORATE PLAINTIFF: SECURITY FOR COSTS: Ch.D.)

Strix Ltd v. Otter Controls Ltd (STRIKING OUT: Pat. Ct.: C.A.)

The Reject Shop plc v. Robert Manners (COPYRIGHT INFRINGEMENT: CRIMINAL PROCEEDINGS: APPEAL BY WAY OF CASE STATED: Q.B.D.)

Van der Lely (C.) NV v. Ruston's Engineering Co. Ltd (C.A.)

Williamson v. Moldline Ltd (EARTH CLOSET ORDER: DISCRETION: C.A.)

Counterclaim

Behr-Thomson Dehnstroffrengler Verwaltungs GmbH v. Western Thomson Controls Ltd (*See v. Scott-Paine* ORDER: Pat. Ct)

Express Newspapers plc v. News (U.K.) Ltd (SUMMARY JUDGMENT: COUNTERCLAIM IN IDENTICAL TERMS: "TIT FOR TAT" COPYING OF NEWSPAPER STORIES: Ch.D.)

Express Newspapers plc v. News (U.K.) Ltd (ORDER 14 APPLICATION: MUTUAL COPYING OF NEWS STORIES: Ch.D.)

Nelson v. Mark Rye and Cocteau Records Ltd (MANAGEMENT CONTRACT: ACCOUNT OF MONEYS RECEIVED: WHETHER CLAIM STATUTE-BARRED: LACHES: COUNTERCLAIM FOR COMMISSION AND EXPENSES: Ch.D.)

Origins Natural Resources Inc. v. Origin Clothing Limited (ORDER 14: SERVICE OF DEFENCE AND COUNTERCLAIM: Ch.D.)

PPL v. Grosvenor Leisure Ltd (ARTICLE 86: Ch.D.)

Williams & Humbert Ltd v. International Distillers & Vintners Ltd (SUMMARY JUDGMENT: Ch.D.)

Court's Power, Scope

Wyko Group plc v. Cooper Roller Bearings Co. Ltd (DECLARATORY RELIEF: STRIKING OUT WRIT AND STATEMENT OF CLAIM: Ch.D.)

Criminal Practice

Barlow Clowes Gilt Managers Ltd (DISCOVERY: PUBLIC INTEREST IMMUNITY: CONFIDENTIALITY: INFORMATION OBTAINED IN COMPULSORY LIQUIDATION OF COMPANY: COMPANY'S OFFICERS CHARGED WITH CRIMINAL OFFENCES: WITNESS SUMMONS ISSUED IN CRIMINAL PROCEEDINGS REQUIRING COMPANY'S LIQUIDATORS TO DISCLOSE CONFIDENTIAL INFORMATION: WHETHER INFORMATION TO BE DISCLOSED: Ch.D.)

Musa v. Le Maitre (COPYRIGHT: FILM: PROSECUTION: WHETHER FILM PUBLISHED: Q.B.D.)

Cross-examination

Bayer AG v. Winter (No. 2) (INTERLOCUTORY PROCEEDINGS: CROSS-EXAMINATION OF DEFENDANT: JURISDICTION: Ch.D.)

CBS United Kingdom Ltd v. Perry (ANTON PILLER: Ch.D.)

Du Pont de Nemours & Co. v. Enka AG (CROSS-EXAMINATION ON AFFIDAVITS IN PATENT AMENDMENT PROCEEDINGS: C.A.)

Norris's Patent (CROSS-EXAMINATION IN PATENT OFFICE: CONFIDENTIALITY OF FILED EVIDENCE: DISCOVERY: C.-G.: Pat. Ct)

ORIENT EXPRESS Trade Mark (TRADE MARK: REMOVAL: CONFLICT OF
EVIDENCE: CROSS-EXAMINATION BEFORE REGISTRAR: T.M.Reg.: Ch.D.)
PERMO Trade Mark (T.M.Reg.)

Cross-undertaking in Damages. *See* **Interlocutory Injunction** (*Cross-undertaking in damages*)

Damages. *See also* **Inquiry as to Damages**

A.&M. Records v. Video Collection International Limited (COPYRIGHT:
INFRINGEMENT: SOUND RECORDINGS: OWNERSHIP: EQUITABLE
OWNERSHIP: ADDITIONAL DAMAGES: Ch.D.)
Biogen Inc. v. Medeva plc (PATENT: INFRINGEMENT: DECLARATION: Pat. Ct)
Brugger v. Medicaid (COPYRIGHT: INFRINGEMENT: INQUIRY: ELECTION AS TO
DAMAGES OR AN ACCOUNT: WHETHER PLAINTIFF CAN CLAIM ADDITIONAL
DAMAGES IN INQUIRY ALTHOUGH NOT ORIGINALLY PLEADED: Pat. Ct)
Cala Homes (South) Ltd v. Alfred McAlpine Homes East Ltd (COPYRIGHT
INFRINGEMENT: ARCHITECT'S DRAWINGS: FLAGRANCY: ADDITIONAL
DAMAGES, ASSESSMENT: Ch.D.)
Cala Homes (South) Ltd v. Alfred McAlpine Homes East Ltd (No. 2) (ELECTION FOR
ACCOUNT OF PROFITS: WHETHER ADDITIONAL STATUTORY DAMAGES
AVAILABLE, FORM OF ORDER: Ch.D.)
Digital Equipment Corp. v. Darkcrest Ltd (CROSS-UNDERTAKING IN DAMAGES:
Ch.D.)
Games Workshop Ltd v. Transworld Publishers Ltd (ADEQUACY OF DAMAGES:
BALANCE OF CONVENIENCE: C.A.)
Gerber Garment Technology Inc. v. Lectra Systems Ltd (PATENT INFRINGEMENT:
PARTIAL INVALIDITY: DATE FROM WHICH DAMAGES SHOULD BE
CALCULATED: C.A.)
Helitune Ltd v. Stewart Hughes Ltd (INQUIRY AS TO DAMAGES: CROSS-
UNDERTAKING AS TO DAMAGES: REMOTENESS OF DAMAGE: Ch.D.)
Joyce v. Sengupta (DEFENDANT MAKING FALSE STATEMENT ABOUT PLAINTIFF:
NATURE OF DAMAGES: C.A.)
Lock International plc v. Beswick (ANTON PILLER ORDER: PLAINTIFF TO PAY
DAMAGES: Ch.D.)
McDonald's Hamburgers Ltd v. Burgerking (U.K.) Ltd (INQUIRY AS TO DAMAGES:
INTEREST: C.A.)
Mölnlycke AB v. Procter & Gamble Ltd (No. 6) (INQUIRY FOR DAMAGES PENDING:
WHETHER PLAINTIFFS ENTITLED TO IMMEDIATE TAXATION: WHETHER
AMENDMENT UNDER SLIP RULE PERMISSIBLE: Pat. Ct)
Nichols Advanced Vehicle Systems Inc. v. Rees (No. 2) (DAMAGES: DELAY IN
PURSUING ENQUIRY: C.A.)
Oliver Homes (Manufacturing) v. Hamilton (COPYRIGHT INFRINGEMENT:
BUILDING PLANS AND DESIGNS: HOUSE KIT PLANS: USE OF PLANS NOT
LICENCES SEPARATELY FROM SALE OF HOUSE KIT: METHOD OF
CALCULATION: ENTITLEMENT TO DAMAGES FOR LOSS OF PROFITS ON SALE OF
HOUSE KIT: Scotland: O.H.)
Optical Coating Laboratory Inc. v. Pilkington PE Ltd (WHETHER PROPRIETOR AS
WELL AS EXCLUSIVE LICENSEE ENTITLED TO DAMAGES FOR LOSS OF PROFIT:
Pat. C.C.)
Smith Kline & French Laboratories Ltd v. Doncaster Pharmaceuticals Ltd (DELIVERY
UP: Pat. Ct)
Unilever plc v. Chefaro Proprietaries Ltd (FORM OF ORDER: Pat. Ct)

Universal Thermosensors Ltd v. Hibben (STOLEN CUSTOMER INFORMATION: EX-EMPLOYEES' COMPETING BUSINESS: ASSESSMENT OF DAMAGES: Ch.D.)

Work Model Enterprises Ltd v. Ecosystem Ltd (COPYRIGHT: INFRINGEMENT: COPYING WORDS OF BROCHURE: CLAIM FOR DAMAGES RESULTING FROM COMPETITION GENERATED BY INFRINGING BROCHURE: Ch.D.)

ZYX Music GmbH v. King (COPYRIGHT INFRINGEMENT: DISCO ARRANGEMENT OF SONG: INNOCENT INFRINGEMENT: ADDITIONAL DAMAGES: FLAGRANCY: Ch.D.)

Declaration

Biogen Inc. v. Medeva plc (PATENT: INFRINGEMENT: DISCOVERY: INVALIDITY: INJUNCTION: DAMAGES: Pat. Ct)

Dellareed Ltd v. Delkim Developments (PATENT: INFRINGEMENT: ACCOUNT OF PROFITS: Ch.D.)

Hawker Siddeley Dynamics Engineering Ltd v. Real Time Developments Ltd (PATENT: DECLARATION OF NON-INFRINGEMENT: STAY OF HIGH COURT PROCEEDINGS: Pat. Ct)

Martinez (PATENT: DECLARATION OF NON-INFRINGEMENT: "EXISTING PATENT": C.-G.)

Patten v. Burke Publishing Co. Ltd (PUBLISHERS' CONTRACTUAL RIGHT TO PUBLISH AUTHOR'S WORKS: AUTHOR SEEKING DECLARATION THAT PARTIES NO LONGER BOUND BY CONTRACT: JUDGMENT IN DEFAULT OF PUBLISHERS GIVING NOTICE OF INTENTION TO DEFEND ACTION: Ch.D.)

Wyko Group plc v. Cooper Roller Bearings Co. Ltd (SCOPE OF COURT'S POWER: STRIKING OUT WRIT AND STATEMENT OF CLAIM: Ch.D.)

Delay

Bhimji v. Chatwani (ANTON PILLER ORDER: LEGAL ADVICE: Ch.D.)

Century Electronics Ltd v. CVS Enterprises Ltd (Ch.D)

Epikhiriseon Metalleftikon Viomikhanikon Kai Naftiliakon AE v. E.C. Commission Council and E.C. Commission (EUROPEAN COURT PROCEDURE: DISCOVERY OF DOCUMENTS: PROCEDURAL DELAYS: ECJ)

HIGH LIFE Trade Mark (STRIKING OUT: Ch.D.)

Hong Kong Toy Centre Ltd v. Tomy U.K. Ltd (THREATS: INTERLOCUTORY INJUNCTION: *Ex parte* ORDER: SUBSEQUENT AGREEMENT AS TO DATES FOR FILING EVIDENCE AND HEARING *inter partes*: 11 MONTH DELAY IN BRINGING MOTION FOR HEARING: INEXCUSABLE AND INORDINATE: RELIEF REFUSED: Pat. Ct)

Intergraph Corp. v. Solid Systems CAD Services Ltd (APPLICATION TO DISCHARGE ANTON PILLER ORDER: MATERIAL NON-DISCLOSURE: MISREPRESENTATION: Ch.D.)

Japan Capsule Computers (U.K.) Ltd v. Sonic Games Sales (WANT OF PROSECUTION: APPLICATION TO DISMISS: BLAME: C.A.)

Johnson Electric Industrial Manufactory Ld v. Mabuchi Motor KK (DISCRETION: Pat. Ct)

Kambrook Distributing Pty Ltd v. Delaney (BALANCE OF CONVENIENCE: Ch.D.)

Malaysian Milk Sdn Bhd's Registered Design (STRIKING OUT: EFFECT OF AGREEMENT BETWEEN PARTIES ON STRIKING OUT: Pat. Ct: C.A.)

Newsgroup Newspapers Ltd v. The Mirror Group Newspapers (1986) Ltd (DELAY IN PROCEEDINGS AFTER INJUNCTION GRANTED: Ch.D.)

Nichols Advanced Vehicle Systems Inc. v. Rees (No. 2) (DELAY IN PURSUING INQUIRY: C.A.)

Sport Internationaal Bussum BV v. Inter-Footwear Ltd (FORFEITURE: RELIEF: JURISDICTION: H.L.)

Unik Time Co. Ltd v. Unik Time Ltd (CONSPIRACY: DAMAGES: Ch.D.)

Delivery Up

Bayer AG v. Winter (INTERLOCUTORY INJUNCTION: MAREVA AND ANTON PILLER ORDERS: DELIVERY UP OF PASSPORTS: C.A.)

Lagenes Ltd v. It's At (U.K.) Ltd (*Ex parte* INJUNCTION: MISLEADING STATEMENTS: DISCOVERY OF IDENTITY OF TRADE CUSTOMERS: Ch.D.)

Nelson v. Mark Rye and Cocteau Records Ltd (COPYRIGHT: MANAGEMENT CONTRACT: MASTER RECORDINGS: AUTHORISING: ISSUING TO THE PUBLIC: Ch.D.)

Nottingham Building Society v. Eurodynamics Systems plc (CONTRACT: REPUDIATION: DELIVERY UP OF SOFTWARE: DISPUTED DEBT: INTERLOCUTORY ORDER FOR DELIVERY UP: C.A.)

Discovery. *See also under* Discovery and Inspection *and under* Inspection

Ashtiani v. Kashi (MAREVA INJUNCTION: FOREIGN ASSETS: POWER OF COURT: C.A.)

Baldock v. Addison (SPLIT TRIAL: WHETHER PLAINTIFF ENTITLED TO DISCOVERY OF QUANTUM DOCUMENTS BEFORE TRIAL ON LIABILITY: Ch.D.)

Barlow Clowes Gilt Managers Ltd (PUBLIC INTEREST IMMUNITY: INFORMATION OBTAINED IN COMPULSORY LIQUIDATION OF COMPANY: COMPANY'S OFFICERS CHARGED WITH CRIMINAL OFFENCES: WITNESS SUMMONS ISSUED REQUIRING LIQUIDATORS TO DISCLOSE CONFIDENTIAL INFORMATION: WHETHER INFORMATION TO BE DISCLOSED: Ch.D.)

Bayer AG v. Harris Pharmaceuticals Ltd (PATENT: WHETHER REQUIRED TO TRANSLATE FOREIGN-LANGUAGE DOCUMENTS: Ch.D.)

Berkeley Administration Inc. v. McClelland (BREACH OF CONFIDENCE: SPECIFIC DISCOVERY: C.A.)

Bhimji v. Chatwani (ANTON PILLER ORDER: LEGAL ADVICE: DELAY: SETTING ASIDE: BREACH: CONTEMPT: COMMITTAL ORDER: Ch.D.)

Bibby Bulk Carriers Ltd v. Cansulex Ltd (USE OF DOCUMENTS READ IN OPEN COURT: DISCLOSURE TO CLAIMANT IN ARBITRATION PROCEEDINGS: IMPLIED UNDERTAKING NOT TO USE IN OTHER PROCEEDINGS: WHETHER NEW RULES RETROSPECTIVE IN EFFECT: Q.B.D.)

Biogen Inc. v. Medeva plc (PATENT INFRINGEMENT: INVALIDITY: Pat. Ct)

Black & Decker Inc. v. Flymo Ltd (SPECIFIC DISCOVERY BASED ON WITNESS STATEMENT EXCHANGED BEFORE TRIAL: WHETHER PRIVILEGE LOST BY EXCHANGE OF WITNESS STATEMENTS: Ch.D.)

CBS Songs Ltd v. Amstrad Consumer Electronics plc (USE IN PRESENT ACTION OF DOCUMENTS DISCLOSED BY DEFENDANT IN PREVIOUS ACTION: C.A.)

Charles of the Ritz Group Ltd v. Jory (NAMES OF SUPPLIERS: Ch.D.)

Chater & Chater Productions Ltd v. Rose (ARM-TWISTING INJUNCTION: EARLY DISCOVERY REFUSED: Ch.D.)

CHC Software Card Ltd v. Hopkins & Wood (TRANSFER BETWEEN DIVISIONS: SOLICITOR'S DUTY: CONFIDENTIALITY: LEGAL PROFESSIONAL PRIVILEGE: INTERROGATORIES: Ch.D.)

Crest Homes plc v. Marks (ANTON PILLER: USE OF DOCUMENTS FOR CONTEMPT PROCEEDINGS IN EARLIER ACTION: PRIVILEGE AGAINST SELF-INCRIMINATION: C.A.: H.L.)

Rafidain Bank v. Agom Universal Sugar Trading Co. Ltd (INSPECTION: REFERENCE IN AFFIDAVITS TO DOCUMENTS NOT IN PARTYS POSSESSION: EFFECT: C.A.)

RHM Foods Ltd v. Bovril Ltd (PASSING OFF: DISCOVERY BEFORE PLEADINGS: C.A.)

Richco Plastic Co.'s Patent (PATENT: COMPULSORY LICENCE: ABUSE OF PROCESS: EVIDENCE: C.-G.)

Sega Enterprises Ltd v. Alca Electronics (ANTON PILLER: CUSTOMERS' NAMES AND ADDRESSES: C.A.)

Smith Kline & French Laboratories Ltd v. Global Pharmaceutics Ltd (DISCOVERY OF IDENTITY OF OVERSEAS SUPPLIER: C.A.)

Unilever plc v. Chefaro Proprietaries Ltd (JOINT TORTFEASORS: MULTI-NATIONAL GROUP: WHETHER SHAREHOLDER CONTROL BY ULTIMATE HOLDING COMPANY SUFFICIENT TO INFER ASSISTANCE TO PRIMARY INFRINGER OR COMMON DESIGN: C.A.)

Union Carbide Corp. v. BP Chemicals Ltd (WHETHER NECESSARY TO ENABLE PATENTEE ADEQUATELY TO PLEAD PARTICULARS IN ENGLAND: DISCRETION: CONFIDENTIAL DOCUMENTS: DISCLOSURE: TERMS: Scotland: O.H.: I.H.)

Wilden Pump & Engineering Co. v. Fusfield (SCOPE OF IMPLIED UNDERTAKING: CONTEMPT: Ch.D.)

Discovery and Inspection. *See also under* **Discovery** and under **Inspection**

Format Communications Manufacturing Ltd v. ITT (U.K.) Ltd (COMPUTER PROGRAMS: SAFEGUARDS: C.A.)

Rafidain Bank v. Agom Universal Sugar Trading Co. Ltd (REFERENCE IN AFFIDAVITS TO DOCUMENTS NOT IN PARTY'S POSSESSION: EFFECT: C.A.)

Discretion

Aisin Seiki KK's Application (EXTENSION OF TIME LIMIT: Pat. Ct)

Aokis Application (RULE 100: IRREGULARITY IN PROCEDURE: Pat. Ct)

Berkeley Administration Inc. v. McClelland (BREACH OF CONFIDENCE: COSTS: ABANDONED PARTS OF ACTION: COMPLAINT OF JUDICIAL BIAS: JUDGE'S DUTY: Q.B.D.)

Chiron Corporation v. Murex Diagnostics Ltd (No. 10) (FINAL INJUNCTION: DAMAGES IN LIEU OF INJUNCTION: Pat. Ct)

Decorflex Ltd's Application (EXTENDING TIME LIMITS: Pat. Ct)

Du Pont de Nemours (E.I.) & Co. v. Enka BV (No. 2) (STAY OF INJUNCTION PENDING APPEAL: LICENCE OF RIGHT: JURISDICTION: Pat. Ct)

E's Applications (PATENT: IRREGULARITY IN PROCEDURE: INTERPRETATION OF INTERNATIONAL TREATY: Pat. Ct: C.A.: H.L.)

Hunter & Partners v. Wellings & Partners (OPPOSED *ex parte* MOTION: COPYRIGHT: INFRINGEMENT: APPEAL: C.A.)

Linpac Mouldings Ltd v. Eagleton Direct Export Ltd (*Quia timet* INJUNCTION ON ABANDONMENT OF DAMAGES CLAIM: C.A.)

Masterman's Design (WHETHER REGISTERED DESIGN CONTRARY TO MORALITY: RDAT)

Memminger-Iro GmbH v. Trip-Lite Ltd (TRANSFER OF ACTION TO COUNTY COURT: C.A.)

Mitsubishi Jidosha Kogyo KK's Application (EXTENSION OF TIME: DEFAULT: Pat. Ct)

Porzelack KG v. Porzelack (U.K.) Ltd (COSTS: EEC PLAINTIFF: DISCRETION TO ORDER SECURITY FOR COSTS: Ch.D.)

Strix Ltd v. Otter Controls Ltd (No. 3) (INQUIRY AS TO DAMAGES: STAY PENDING APPEAL: LATE APPLICATION: Pat. Ct)

Tokan Kogyo KK's Application (PATENT: APPLICATION: PROCEDURAL ERROR: C.-G.)

Tomy Kogyo Co. Inc.'s Applications (REGISTERED DESIGN: CONVENTION APPLICATION: DISCRETION UNDER RULES TO EXTEND TIME: RDAT)

Dalgety Spillers Foods Ltd v. Food Brokers Ltd (Ch.D.)

English & American Insurance Co. Ltd v. Herbert Smith (LEGAL PROFESSIONAL PRIVILEGE: INNOCENT RECEIPT OF INFORMATION: Ch.D.)

Gebhardt's Patent (Pat. Ct)

Glaverbel SA v. British Coal Corporation (No. 2) (PATENT: INFRINGEMENT: CONSTRUCTION: Pat. Ct)

Goddard v. Nationwide Building Society (PROFESSIONALLY PRIVILEGED NOTE: USE OF COPIES RESTRAINED: C.A.)

Guccio Gucci SpA v. Paolo Gucci (EVIDENCE OF CONFUSION: TRADE EVIDENCE: Ch.D.)

Hunt-Wesson Inc.'s Trade Mark Application (APPEAL FROM DECISION OF TRADE MARK REGISTRAR: PRINCIPLES FOR ADMISSION OF FURTHER EVIDENCE ON APPEAL: REGISTRAR'S PRACTICE: Ch.D.)

Imperial Group plc v. Philip Morris Ltd (STATUS OF SURVEY EVIDENCE: Ch.D.)

Island Trading Co. v. Anchor Brewing Co. (Ch.D.)

ITC Film Distributors Ltd v. Video Exchange Ltd (ADMISSIBILITY OF EVIDENCE OBTAINED BY TRICKERY IN COURT PRECINCT: PUBLIC POLICY: Ch.D.)

Johnson (H. & R.) Tiles Ltd v. Candy Tiles Ltd (LATE APPLICATION TO SUBMIT EVIDENCE: Ch.D.)

Kenning v. Eve Construction Ltd (EXPERT EVIDENCE: DISCLOSURE: REPORT SENT TO WRONG PARTY: Q.B.D.)

KENT Trade Mark (SURVEY EVIDENCE: T.M.Reg.)

Labyrinth Media Ltd v. Brave World Limited (PASSING OFF: REPUTATION: ARGUABLE CASE: Ch.D.)

Lego System A/S v. Lego M. Lemelstrich Ltd (Pat. Ct)

McGuinness v. Kellogg Co. of Great Britain Ltd (NON-DISCLOSURE OF EVIDENCE BEFORE TRIAL: DOCUMENTARY: REBUTTAL OF BONA FIDES: C.A.)

MINI-LIFT Trade Mark (OPPOSITION: NORMAL AND FAIR USE: T.M.Reg.)

Monsanto's CCP Patent (BURDEN OF PROOF: BEST EVIDENCE: C.-G.)

Mothercare U.K. Ltd v. Penguin Books Ltd (SURVEY EVIDENCE: C.A.)

Naf Naf SA v. Dickens (London) Ltd (ANTON PILLER ORDER: INSUFFICIENT EVIDENCE TO WARRANT GRANT: MATERIAL NON-DISCLOSURE: APPLICATION TO PREVENT PLAINTIFFS FROM USING EVIDENCE GAINED ON EXECUTION: Ch.D.)

Nationwide Building Society v. Nationwide Estate Agents Ltd (REPUTATION IN ALLIED FIELD: OPINION POLL: Ch.D.)

NETWORK 90 Trade Mark (Ch.D.)

Norris's Patent (CROSS-EXAMINATION IN PATENT OFFICE: CONFIDENTIALITY OF FILED EVIDENCE: C.-G.: Pat. Ct)

Nottingham Building Society v. Eurodynamics Systems plc (APPLICATION FOR LEAVE TO ADDUCE FURTHER EVIDENCE: INTERNAL COMPANY DOCUMENTS: RELEVANCY: C.A.)

ORIENT EXPRESS Trade Mark (CONFLICT OF EVIDENCE: CROSS-EXAMINATION BEFORE REGISTRAR: T.M.Reg.: Ch.D.)

Parfums Givenchy SA v. Designer Alternatives Ltd (TRADE MARK: INFRINGEMENT: EVIDENCE OF PRONUNCIATION: C.A.)

Parmenter v. Malt House Joinery (*Res judicata*: C.A.)

Penfold v. Fairbrass (AFFIDAVIT EVIDENCE: WHETHER ADMISSIBLE: TAPE RECORDING OF SONGS: WHETHER ADMISSIBLE: Ch.D.)

Perrin v. Drennan (SIMILAR FACT EVIDENCE: Ch.D.)

Practice Note (TRIALS ON AFFIDAVIT EVIDENCE: DIRECTIONS: Pat. Ct)

R. v. Bridgeman and Butt (CONSPIRACY TO DEFRAUD: SATELLITE BROADCASTING FROM U.K. TO SPAIN: AMBIT OF LICENCE: JURISDICTION: ENCRYPTED TRANSMISSIONS: DECODING DEVICES: NATURE OF RIGHTS AND REMEDIES: C.C.)

Reckitt & Coleman Products Ltd v. Borden Inc. (No. 2) (MARKET RESEARCH WITNESS: Ch.D.)
Reckitt & Coleman Products Ltd v. Borden Inc. (No. 3) (SURVEY EVIDENCE: Ch.D.)
Richco Plastic Co's Patent (ABUSE OF PROCESS: DISCOVERY: C.-G.)
Strix Ltd v. Otter Controls Ltd (No. 2) (DIRECTIONS AS TO CONDUCT OF INQUIRY: Pat. Ct)
Strix Ltd v. Otter Controls Ltd (No. 3) (STAY PENDING APPEAL: LATE APPLICATION: DISCRETION: Pat. Ct)
ST TRUDO Trade Mark (RECTIFICATION: REGISTRAR: HEARSAY RULES: APPLICABILITY AND SCOPE: Ch.D.)
Thrustcode Ltd v. WW Computing Ltd (EVIDENCE OF COPYING: BALANCE OF CONVENIENCE: Ch.D.)
Tosca (PERIOD OF PROTECTION: FOREIGN AUTHORS: INTERNATIONAL CONVENTION AND NATIONAL LAWS: Germany: S.C.)
Toyama Chemical Co. Ltd's Application (EVIDENCE ON APPEAL: Pat. Ct)
Unilever plc v. Johnson Wax Ltd (SURVEY EVIDENCE: Ch.D.)
United Biscuits (U.K.) Ltd v. Burtons Biscuits Ltd (RELIABILITY OF SURVEY EVIDENCE: THREE KINDS: RELIEF REFUSED: Ch.D.)
VNU Publications Ltd v. Ziff Davis (U.K.) Ltd (Ch.D.)
Wagamama Ltd v. City Centre Restaurants plc (DILUTION OF GOODWILL: SURVEY EVIDENCE: EXPERT EVIDENCE: ADMISSIBILITY: Ch.D.)
Wistar Institute's Application (Pat. Ct)

European Court, Referral to

Merck & Co. Inc. v. Primecrown Ltd (PARALLEL IMPORTS: WHETHER *Merck v. Stephar* STILL GOOD LAW: TRANSITIONAL PROVISIONS OF ACT OF ACCESSION OF SPAIN AND PORTUGAL: INTERLOCUTORY RELIEF: WHETHER REVISED VIEW OF *Merck v. Stephar* MAY BE TAKEN INTO ACCOUNT: Pat. Ct)
Research Corp.'s Supplementary Protection Certificate (EXPIRED PATENT FOR MEDICAL PRODUCT: CARBOPLATIN: SUPPLEMENTARY PROTECTION CERTIFICATE: LICENCES OF RIGHT: REFERENCE TO ECJ REFUSED: C.-G.)

Ex Parte **Relief**

Bank Mellat v. Nikpour (MAREVA INJUNCTION: C.A.)
Columbia Picture Industries Inc. v. Robinson (ANTON PILLER ORDER: INTERLOCUTORY MOTION: Ch.D.)
Hoechst U.K. Ltd v. Chemiculture Ltd (ANTON PILLER ORDER: APPLICATION TO DISCHARGE: ALLEGED NON-DISCLOSURE ON *ex parte* APPLICATION: Ch.D.)
Hong Kong Toy Centre Ltd v. Tomy U.K. Ltd (PATENT: THREATS: INTERLOCUTORY INJUNCTION: *Ex parte* ORDER: SUBSEQUENT AGREEMENT AS TO DATES FOR FILING EVIDENCE AND HEARING *inter partes*: 11-MONTH DELAY IN BRINGING MOTION FOR HEARING: INEXCUSABLE AND INORDINATE: RELIEF REFUSED: Pat. Ct)
Hunter & Partners v. Wellings & Partners (OPPOSED *ex parte* MOTION: C.A.)
Labyrinth Media Ltd v. Brave World Limited (PASSING OFF: INTERLOCUTORY INJUNCTION: PROSPECTIVE RELEASES OF RIVAL VIDEOS UNDER SAME TITLE: WHETHER PRE-LAUNCH PUBLICITY SUFFICIENT TO ESTABLISH GOODWILL: REPUTATION: EVIDENCE: ARGUABLE CASE: Ch.D.)
Lagenes Ltd v. Its At (U.K.) Ltd (*Ex parte* INJUNCTION: Ch.D.)

Expert Witness

Gerber Garment Technology Inc. v. Lectra Systems Ltd (PATENT: INFRINGEMENT: Pat. Ct)

Ikarian Reefer, The (DUTIES AND RESPONSIBILITIES: Comm. Ct)

Lubrizol Corporation v. Esso Petroleum Co. Ltd (No. 4) (EXPERTS' AFFIDAVITS SWORN IN FOREIGN PROCEEDINGS: WHETHER SUBJECT TO LEGAL PROFESSIONAL PRIVILEGE: Pat. Ct)

Optical Laboratories Ltd v. Hayden Laboratories Ltd (No. 1) (COSTS OF WITNESSES: C.A.)

Extension of Time Limit. *See under* Time Limits

Final Injunction

Chiron Corporation v. Murex Diagnostics Ltd (No. 10) (DAMAGES IN LIEU OF INJUNCTION: DISCRETION: Pat. Ct)

Foreign Assets

Ashtiani v. Kashi (MAREVA INJUNCTION: DISCOVERY: POWER OF COURT: C.A.)

Foreign Language Documents

Bayer AG v. Harris Pharmaceuticals Ltd (PATENT: DISCOVERY: WHETHER REQUIRED TO TRANSLATE FOREIGN-LANGUAGE DOCUMENTS: Ch.D.)

Foreign Lawyer

IBM v. Phoenix International Computers Ltd (DISCOVERY: LEGAL PROFESSIONAL PRIVILEGE: FOREIGN LAWYER'S ADVICE ON U.K. LAW: INSPECTION: WHETHER PRIVILEGE WAIVED: PRODUCTION OF DOCUMENTS BY MISTAKE: WHETHER MISTAKE OBVIOUS: REMEDIES: Ch.D.)

Foreign Proceedings

Bayer AG v. Winter (FORUM SHOPPING: FOREIGN PROCEEDING SEEKING PROTECTIVE MEASURES: Ch.D.)

Lubrizol Corporation v. Esso Petroleum Co. Ltd (No. 4) (EXPERTS' AFFIDAVITS SWORN IN FOREIGN PROCEEDINGS: WHETHER SUBJECT TO LEGAL PROFESSIONAL PRIVILEGE: Pat. Ct)

Forum

Amersham International plc v. Corning Ltd (EUROPEAN PATENT: OPPOSITION AT EPO: MOTION FOR STAY IN HIGH COURT: *Forum conveniens*: Pat. Ct)

Bayer AG v. Winter (FORUM SHOPPING: FOREIGN PROCEEDING SEEKING PROTECTIVE MEASURES: Ch.D.)

Forum Conveniens

Advanced Portfolio Technologies Inc v. Ainsworth (PROCEEDINGS IN NEW YORK ON SAME FACTS: WHETHER *forum conveniens* WAS ENGLAND: APPLICATION FOR STAY: INJUNCTION AGAINST JOINDER OF DEFENDANT IN N.Y. PROCEEDINGS: Ch.D.)

Fraudulent Interference With Trade

Swedac Ltd v. Magnet & Southerns plc (ANTON PILLER PRACTICE: DUTY OF DISCLOSURE: Ch.D.)

Further and Better Particulars

Fearis v. Davies (CONSENT ORDER: CONSTRUCTION OF ORDER: C.A.)

Lux Traffic Controls Ltd v. Staffordshire Public Works Company Ltd (PATENT: INFRINGEMENT: PARTICULARS OF CONSTRUCTION OF CLAIMS: Pat. Ct)

Speed Seal Products Ltd v. Paddington (BREACH OF CONFIDENCE: Ch.D.)

Hansard, **Reference to**

Ford Motor Co. Ltd's Design Applications (REGISTERED DESIGN APPLICATIONS: PARTS FOR MOTOR VEHICLE: "MUST MATCH" EXCEPTION: WHETHER FEATURES DICTATED BY FUNCTION: STATUTORY INTERPRETATION: Q.B.D.)

Ford Motor Co. Ltd and Iveco Fiat SpA's v. Design Applications (REGISTERED DESIGN: APPLICATIONS: PARTS FOR MOTOR VEHICLES: "MUST MATCH" EXCEPTION: "PATTERN AND ORNAMENT": RDAT) (APPEAL: H.L.)

Hearing. *See also under* **In Camera Hearings**

Practice Direction (CHANCERY: MASTER'S POWERS: CHANCERY CHAMBERS: AUTHORISATION FOR HEARING BEFORE MASTER: Ch.D.)

Practice Statement (HEARING DATES: Ch.D.)

Hearsay Rules

ST TRUDO Trade Mark (EVIDENCE: REGISTRAR: APPLICABILITY AND SCOPE: Ch.D.)

In Camera **hearings**

Bonzel v. Intervention Ltd (No. 2) (DISCLOSURE OF PRIVILEGED DOCUMENTS: Pat. Ct)

Coca Cola Company v. Peter John Gilbey (TRADE MARK: INFRINGEMENT: PASSING OFF: COUNTERFEIT GOODS: ANTON PILLER ORDER: DISCLOSURE OF INFORMATION: PRIVILEGE AGAINST SELF-INCRIMINATION: RISK OF PERSONAL JEOPARDY: WHETHER GROUNDS TO DISCHARGE ORDER: WHETHER PERMISSSABLE FOR DEFENDANT TO GIVE EVIDENCE *in camera* IN THE ABSENCE OF PLAINTIFFS OR THEIR LEGAL REPRESENTATIVES: Ch.D.: C.A.)

Lubrizol Corporation v. Esso Petroleum Co. Ltd (No. 2) (DISCOVERY: CONFIDENTIALITY: RESTRICTED INSPECTION OF DISCOVERY DOCUMENTS: WHETHER ORDER DISAPPLYING ORDER 24, R.14A TO BE GRANTED: INJUNCTION RESTRAINING USE OF AFFIDAVITS: Pat. Ct)

Injunction. *See also* **Interlocutory Injunction**

Attorney-General v. Newspaper Publishing plc (WHETHER BREACH OF INJUNCTION BY THIRD PARTY CONTEMPT: Ch.D.: C.A.)

Du Pont de Nemours (E.I.) & Co. v. Enka BV (No. 2) (STAY PENDING APPEAL: Pat. Ct)

GFI Group Inc. v. Eaglestone (ADEQUACY OF DAMAGES: BALANCE OF CONVENIENCE: DISCRETION: Ch.D.)

James North & Sons Ltd v. North Cape Textiles Ltd (Scotland: England: C.A.)
Lagenes Ltd v. It's At (U.K.) Ltd (*Ex parte* INJUNCTION: MISLEADING STATEMENTS: Ch.D.)
Leisure Data v. Bell (COMPUTER PROGRAM: MANDATORY INJUNCTION: C.A.)
Lock International plc v. Beswick (ANTON PILLER ORDER: PLAINTIFF TO PAY DAMAGES: CONFIDENTIAL INFORMATION: EX-EMPLOYEE: Ch.D.)
Optical Coating Laboratory Inc. v. Pilkington PE Ltd (STAY OF INJUNCTION: Pat. C.C.)
PSM International plc v. Whitehouse (WHETHER INJUNCTION MAY BE GRANTED TO RESTRAIN EX-EMPLOYEE FROM FULFILLING CONTRACT ALREADY MADE WITH THIRD PARTY: C.A.)
Smith Kline & French Laboratories Ltd v. Harris Pharmaceuticals Ltd (MANDATORY INJUNCTION FOR DESTRUCTION OF STOCKS: Ch.D.)
Supply of Ready Mixed Concrete (No. 2) (CONTEMPT: BREACH OF INJUNCTION BY EMPLOYEE: LIABILITY OF EMPLOYER: H.L.)

Inquiry

Brugger v. Medicaid (ELECTION AS TO DAMAGES OR AN ACCOUNT: WHETHER PLAINTIFF CAN CLAIM ADDITIONAL DAMAGES IN INQUIRY ALTHOUGH NOT ORIGINALLY PLEADED: *Calderbank* LETTER: WHETHER COSTS SHOULD BE DETERMINED AFTER INQUIRY: Pat. Ct)

Inquiry as to Damages

Gillette U.K. Ltd v. Edenwest Ltd (TRADE MARK: INFRINGEMENT: PASSING OFF: SUMMARY JUDGMENT: INNOCENCE: Ch.D.)
Harrison v. Project & Design Co. (Redcar) Ltd (PATENT: INFRINGEMENT: MODIFICATION OF INFRINGING ARTICLE: *Res judicata*: CONSTRUCTION OF CLAIMS: C.A.)
Helitune Ltd v. Stewart Hughes Ltd (INTERLOCUTORY INJUNCTION: CROSS-UNDERTAKING: STRIKING OUT PLEADING: ABUSE OF PROCESS: CONFIDENTIAL EXHIBIT: SPECIFIC DISCOVERY: REMOTENESS OF DAMAGE: Ch.D.)
Island Records Ltd v. Tring International plc (ACCOUNT OF PROFITS: ELECTION: TIME FOR ELECTION: INFORMED CHOICE: WHETHER ORDER RELEVANT TO DISCOVERY: Ch.D.)
McDonald's Hamburgers Ltd v. Burgerking (U.K.) Ltd (INTEREST: C.A.)

Inspection. *See also under* Discovery and Inspection

Atari Inc. v. Philips Electronics Ltd (COMPUTER PROGRAM: Ch.D.)
Derby & Co. Ltd v. Weldon (No. 9) (COMPUTER DATABASE: "WHETHER DOCUMENT": EXTENT TO WHICH INSPECTION TO BE ORDERED: Ch.D.)
Dun & Bradstreet Ltd v. Typesetting Facilities Ltd (COMPUTERISED DATABASE: INFORMATION IN ELECTRONIC FORM, SO VISUAL INSPECTION OF DISKS USELESS: DISCLOSURE OF CONTENTS REQUIRED: INSPECTION BEFORE SERVICE OF STATEMENT OF CLAIM: REQUIREMENTS: Ch.D.)
Format Communications Manufacturing Ltd v. ITT (U.K.) Ltd (COMPUTER PROGRAMS: DISCOVERY AND INSPECTION: SAFEGUARDS: C.A.)
IBM v. Phoenix International Computers Ltd (BURDEN OF PROOF: LEGAL PROFESSIONAL PRIVILEGE: ADVICE FROM FOREIGN LAWYER ON U.K. LAW: WHETHER PRIVILEGE WAIVED: PRODUCTION OF DOCUMENTS BY MISTAKE: WHETHER MISTAKE OBVIOUS: REMEDIES: Ch.D.)

Interest

Interlocutory Injunction

Acts committed abroad

Adequacy of damages

American Cyanamid practice

Anton Piller orders

Arm-twisting injunction

Chater & Chater Productions Ltd v. Rose (EARLY DISCOVERY REFUSED: Ch.D.)

Arguable case

County Sound plc v. Ocean Sound Ltd (C.A.)
Hodge Clemco Ltd v. Airblast Ltd (INTERLOCUTORY INJUNCTION REFUSED: Ch.D.)
Mirage Studios v. Counter-Feat Clothing Co. Ltd (FACTORS EVENLY BALANCED: Ch.D.)
MS Associates Ltd v. Power (BALANCE OF CONVENIENCE: Ch.D.)

Balance of convenience

Adventure Film Productions SA v. Tully (INTERLOCUTORY ORDER FOR DELIVERY UP: STRENGTH OF CASE TO OWNERSHIP OF FILM AND COPYRIGHT: Ch.D.)
Alexander Fergusson & Co. v. Matthews McClay & Manson (Scotland: O.H.)
Alfa Laval Cheese Systems Ltd v. Wincanton Engineering Ltd (SERIOUS ISSUE: PUBLICATION OF CONFIDENTIAL INFORMATION BY SUPPLY OF MACHINES: UNQUANTIFIABLE HARM: Ch.D.)
B&S Ltd v. Irish Auto Trader Ltd (PASSING OFF: ADVERTISING MAGAZINES: AUTOTRADER: PRINCIPLES: PRESERVATION OF *status quo*: Ireland: H.C.)
Blazer plc v. Yardley and Co. Ltd (STATUS QUO: Ch.D.)
Compaq Computer Corp. v. Dell Computer Corp. Ltd (COMPARATIVE ADVERTISING: INVALIDITY: TRIABLE ISSUE: FREEDOM OF SPEECH: Ch.D.)
Conoco Specialty Products Inc. v. Merpro Montassa Ltd (No. 1) (TRADE MARK: INFRINGEMENT: ALLEGED DIFFERENCES: PRIMA FACIE CASE: Scotland: O.H.)
Consorzio del Prosciutto di Parma v. Marks and Spencer plc (REPRESENTATIVE ACTION: *Locus standi*: ITALIAN LEGISLATION: Ch.D.: C.A.)
Fleming Fabrications Ltd v. Albion Cylinders Ltd (CROSS-UNDERTAKING: C.A.)
Gala of London Ltd v. Chandler Ltd (Ch.D.)
Games Workshop Ltd v. Transworld Publishers Ltd (ADEQUACY OF DAMAGES: C.A.)
Harrods Ltd v. Schwartz-Sackin & Co. Ltd (Ch.D.)
Improver Corporation v. Remington Consumer Products Ltd (STRIKING OUT: C.A.)
International House of Heraldry v. Grant (PROTECTION OF ESTABLISHED BUSINESS AGAINST NEWLY FORMED BUSINESS: Scotland: O.H.)
Jian Tools For Sales Inc. v. Roderick Manhattan Group Ltd (PASSING OFF: DEFENDANT'S AWARENESS OF PLAINTIFF'S OBJECTIONS: PRESERVATION OF STATUS QUO: Ch.D.)
Kambrook Distributing Pty Ltd v. Delaney (SERIOUS QUESTION TO BE TRIED: DELAY: Ch.D.)
Levi Strauss & Co. v. Barclays Trading Corp. Inc. (DISCLOSURE OF NAMES: WHETHER PLAINTIFF ESTOPPED FROM USING INFORMATION DISCLOSED AGAINST THIRD PARTIES: IMPLIED UNDERTAKING ON DISCOVERY: PROPER TIME FOR APPLICATION: PRIVILEGE AGAINST SELF-INCRIMINATION: Ch.D.)
Lord Advocate v. Scotsman Publications Ltd (INTERDICT: Scotland: O.H.: H.L.)
Management Publications Ltd v. Blenheim Exhibitions Group plc (MAGAZINE TITLES: Ch.D.)
Mitchelstown Co-operative Society Ltd v. Société des Produits Nestlé SA (JURISDICTION: ARBITRATION: Ireland: S.C.)
Morgan-Grampian plc v. Training Personnel Ltd (STATUS QUO: Ch.D.)
MS Associates Ltd v. Power (ARGUABLE CASE: Ch.D.)
News Datacom Ltd v. Satellite Decoding Systems (COPYRIGHT: COMPUTER PROGRAMS: BREACH: Ireland: H.C.)

Orkney Seafoods Ltd's Petition (PROTECTION OF ESTABLISHED BUSINESS AGAINST
  NEWLY-FORMED BUSINESS: Scotland: O.H.)
Post Office v. Interlink Express Parcels Ltd (Ch.D.)
Private Research Ltd v. Brosnan (WHETHER FAIR QUESTION TO BE TRIED:
  ADEQUACY OF DAMAGES: Ireland: H.C.)
Quantel Ltd v. Shima Seiki Europe Ltd (EFFECT OF EARLIER ACTION: Pat. Ct)
Raindrop Data Systems Ltd v. Systemics Ltd (Ch.D.)
Secretary of State for the Home Department v. Central Broadcasting Ltd (INTERVIEW
  WITH SERIAL KILLER: Ch.D.: C.A.)
Shelley Films Ltd v. Rex Features Ltd (Ch.D.)
Silicon Graphics Inc. v. Indigo Graphic Systems (U.K.) Ltd (COSTS: Ch.D.)
Tamworth Herald Company Ltd v. Thomson Free Newspapers Ltd (Ch.D.)
Thrustcode Ltd v. WW Computing Ltd (Ch.D.)
Waterlow Directories Ltd v. Reed Information Services Ltd (ADEQUACY OF
  UNDERTAKINGS: Ch.D.)

Consent

Universal Thermosensors Ltd v. Hibben (ASSESSMENT OF DAMAGES:
  INTERLOCUTORY ORDER BY CONSENT: Ch.D.)

Confusion at point of sale

Bostick Ltd v. Sellotape G.B. Ltd (PASSING OFF: BLUE ADHESIVE TACK: Ch.D.)

Costs

Kickers International SA v. Paul Kettle Agencies Ltd (BALANCING RISKS OF
  INJUSTICE: WHEN TO BE TAXED: Ch.D.)

Cross-undertaking

Digital Equipment Corp. v. Darkcrest Ltd (ANTON PILLER: COPYRIGHT:
  INFRINGEMENT: Ch.D.)
Fleming Fabrications Ltd v. Albion Cylinders Ltd (BALANCE OF CONVENIENCE:
  C.A.)
Helitune Ltd v. Stewart Hughes Ltd (INQUIRY AS TO DAMAGES: STRIKING OUT
  PLEADING: ABUSE OF PROCESS: Ch.D.)
John Richardson Computers Ltd v. Flanders (DEFENDANTS RIGHT TO INQUIRY AS
  TO DAMAGES ON PLAINTIFFS CROSS-UNDERTAKING: APPROPRIATE ORDER:
  Ch.D.)
Rubycliff Ltd v. Plastic Engineers Ltd (CROSS UNDERTAKING IN DAMAGES: Ch.D.)
Waterlow Directories Ltd v. Reed Information Services Ltd (ADEQUACY OF
  UNDERTAKINGS: BALANCE OF CONVENIENCE: Ch.D.)

Delay

An Post, National Treasury Management Agency v. Irish Permanent plc (TRIAL DATE
  FIXED: WHETHER GROUNDS FOR REFUSAL: PUBLIC POLICY: Ireland: H.C.)
Century Electronics Ltd v. CVS Enterprises Ltd (REPUTATION MONOPOLY IN
  GROUP OF LETTERS: HONEST CONCURRENT TRADING: USE *de minimis*:
  Ch.D.)
Newsgroup Newspapers Ltd v. The Mirror Group Newspapers (1986) Ltd (DELAY IN
  PROCEEDINGS AFTER GRANT: Ch.D.)
Series 5 Software Ltd v. Philip Clarke (INJUNCTIONS: PRINCIPLES: HISTORICAL
  SURVEY OF *American Cyanamid* CASES: Ch.D.)

Discharge

Attorney-General v. Guardian Newspapers Ltd and The Observer Ltd (APPLICATION TO DISCHARGE: MATERIAL CHANGE IN CIRCUMSTANCES SINCE GRANT: DISCRETION: Ch.D.)

Discretion

Attorney-General v. Guardian Newspapers Ltd and The Observer Ltd (Ch.D.)
Universal Thermosensors Ltd v. Hibben (SCOPE OF INJUNCTIONS IN BREACH OF CONFIDENCE: SPRINGBOARD DOCTRINE: Ch.D.)

Early discovery

Chater & Chater Productions Ltd v. Rose (COPYRIGHT: MUSIC: INFRINGEMENT: PERFORMANCE: PRIOR DISCLOSURE OF MUSIC TO DEFENDANTS: JURISDICTION: Ch.D.)

Equity does not act in vain

Attorney-General v. Guardian Newspapers Ltd and The Observer Ltd (Ch.D.)

Evidence

Dalgety Spillers Foods Ltd v. Food Brokers Ltd (Ch.D.)
Drayton Controls (Engineering) Ltd v. Honeywell Control Systems Ltd (EVIDENCE RELEVANT FOR INTERLOCUTORY STAGE: Ch.D.)
Island Trading Co. v. Anchor Brewing Co. (Ch.D.)
United Biscuits (U.K.) Ltd v. Burtons Biscuits Ltd (RELIABILITY OF SURVEY EVIDENCE: Ch.D.)

Ex-employee

Lawrence David Ltd v. Ashton (PERIOD OF RESTRAINT: C.A.)

Ex parte order

Hong Kong Toy Centre Ltd v. Tomy U.K. Ltd (THREATS: SUBSEQUENT AGREEMENT AS TO DATES FOR FILING EVIDENCE AND HEARING *inter partes*: 11-MONTH DELAY IN BRINGING MOTION FOR HEARING: Pat. Ct)
Labyrinth Media Ltd v. Brave World Limited (PASSING OFF: INTERLOCUTORY INJUNCTION: PROSPECTIVE RELEASES OF RIVAL VIDEOS UNDER SAME TITLE: WHETHER PRE-LAUNCH PUBLICITY SUFFICIENT TO ESTABLISH GOODWILL: REPUTATION: EVIDENCE: ARGUABLE CASE: Ch.D.)

Fair dealing defence

Associated Newspapers Group plc v. News Group Newspapers Ltd (THE WINDSOR CORRESPONDENCE: Ch.D.)

Form of order

Video Arts Ltd v. Paget Industries Ltd (Ch.D.)

Freedom of speech

Ciba-Geigy plc v. Parke Davis & Co. Ltd (INJURIOUS FALSEHOOD: REPRESENTATION THAT DEFENDANT'S PRODUCT A SUBSTITUTE FOR PLAINTIFFS BY USE OF UNREGISTERED TRADE MARK: Ch.D.)
Easycare Inc. v. Bryan Lawrence & Co. (THREATS: MALICIOUS FALSEHOOD: INTERLOCUTORY INJUNCTION REFUSED: Pat. Ct)

Jurisdiction

Chater & Chater Productions Ltd v. Rose (Ch.D.)
Femis-Bank (Anguilla) Ltd v. Lazar (Ch.D.)
Gulf Oil (G.B.) Ltd v. Page (C.A.)
Jurisdiction MTV Europe v. BMG Records (U.K.) Ltd (OVERLAPPING ACTION
    BEFORE COMMISSION: APPLICATION TO STAY: Ch.D.)

Likelihood of damage

Mothercare U.K. Ltd v. Penguin Books Ltd (SURVEY EVIDENCE: C.A.)

Mareva injunction

Bayer AG v. Winter (ANTON PILLER ORDERS: DELIVERY UP OF PASSPORTS: C.A.)

No serious defence

Fisons plc v. Norton Healthcare Ltd (TRADE MARK: INFRINGEMENT: EXPORTED
    GOODS: RECTIFICATION: NON-USE U.K.: NO SERIOUS RISK OF INJUSTICE:
    Ch.D.)

No serious risk of injustice

Fisons plc v. Norton Healthcare Ltd (TRADE MARK: INFRINGEMENT: EXPORTED
    GOODS: RECTIFICATION: NON-USE U.K.: NO. SERIOUS DEFENCE: Ch.D.)

Period of restraint

Lawrence David Ltd v. Ashton (EX-EMPLOYEE: C.A.)

Preservation of status quo

B&S Ltd v. Irish Auto Trader Ltd (PASSING OFF: ADVERTISING MAGAZINES:
    AUTOTRADER: BALANCE OF CONVENIENCE: Ireland: H.C.)

Principles

B&S Ltd v. Irish Auto Trader Ltd (PASSING OFF: ADVERTISING MAGAZINES:
    AUTOTRADER: PRESERVATION OF *status quo*: BALANCE OF CONVENIENCE:
    Ireland: H.C.)

Public interest

Attorney-General v. Guardian Newspapers Ltd and The Observer Ltd (*Spycatcher*:
    FORM OF INJUNCTION: Ch.D.: C.A.)
Secretary of State for the Home Department v. Central Broadcasting Ltd (INTERVIEW
    WITH SERIAL KILLER: Ch.D.: C.A.)
Times Newspapers Ltd v. MGN Ltd (THATCHER MEMOIRS: C.A.)
X Health Authority v. Y (IDENTITY OF DOCTORS WITH AIDS: Q.B.D.)

Reasonableness

Austin Knight (U.K.) Ltd v. Hinds (EMPLOYMENT CONTRACTS: RESTRICTIVE
    COVENANT: NON-SOLICITATION CLAUSE: Ch.D.)

Restrictive covenant, reasonableness

Kall-Kwik Printing (U.K.) Ltd v. Frank Clarence Rush (FRANCHISE AGREEMENT:
    CONSTRUCTION: ENFORCEABILITY: Ch.D.)

Risk of injustice

Entec (Pollution Control) Ltd v. Abacus Mouldings (Ch.D.: C.A.)
Kickers International SA v. Paul Kettle Agencies Ltd (Ch.D.)

Saving motion to another day

Max Factor & Co. v. MGM/UA Entertainment Co. (Ch.D.)

Scope of injunction

Universal Thermosensors Ltd v. Hibben (SPRINGBOARD DOCTRINE: DISCRETION: Ch.D.)

Serious issue/triable issue

An Bord Trachtala v. Waterford Foods plc (ATTEMPT TO RESTRICT ACTS COMMITTED ABROAD: Ireland: H.C.)

An Post, National Treasury Management Agency v. Irish Permanent plc (DELAY: TRIAL DATE FIXED: WHETHER GROUNDS FOR REFUSAL: PUBLIC POLICY: Ireland: H.C.)

Bassey v. Icon Entertainment plc (COPYRIGHT: PERFORMERS RIGHTS: PROPRIETORSHIP: RECORDING OF PERFORMANCES: SUMMARY JUDGMENT: CONSENT: Ch.D.)

Cayne v. Global Natural Resources plc (GUIDELINES: C.A.)

Elan Digital Systems Ltd v. Elan Computers Ltd (PRACTICE ON INJUNCTION APPEALS: Ch.D.: C.A.)

Kambrook Distributing Pty Ltd v. Delaney (BALANCE OF CONVENIENCE: DELAY: Ch.D.)

Provident Financial plc v. Halifax Building Society (Ch.D.)

Smith (J.) & Nephew Ltd v. 3M United Kingdom plc (C.A.)

Status quo

Blazer plc v. Yardley and Co. Ltd (Ch.D.)

Garden Cottage Foods v. Milk Marketing Board (H.L.)

Graham v. Delderfield (C.A.)

Morgan-Grampian plc v. Training Personnel Ltd (Ch.D.)

Unquantifiable harm

Alfa Laval Cheese Systems Ltd v. Wincanton Engineering Ltd (BALANCE OF CONVENIENCE: Ch.D.)

Interlocutory Proceedings (other than injunctions)

Delivery up

Nottingham Building Society v. Eurodynamics Systems plc (CONTRACT: REPUDIATION: DISPUTED DEBT: APPLICATION FOR LEAVE TO ADDUCE FURTHER EVIDENCE: INTERNAL COMPANY DOCUMENTS: RELEVANCY: C.A.)

Specific performance

Simtech Advanced Training and Simulation Systems Ltd v. Jasmin Simtec Ltd (CONFIDENTIAL INFORMATION: CONTRACT: COLLABORATION AGREEMENT: PARTIALLY AGREED CONTRACT: BALANCE OF JUSTICE: Ch.D.)

Interpretation of International Treaty

E's Applications (Pat. Ct: C.A.: H.L.)

Interrogatories

CHC Software Card Ltd v. Hopkins & Wood (DISCOVERY: CONFIDENTIALITY: LEGAL PROFESSIONAL PRIVILEGE: INTERROGATORIES: Ch.D.)

Rockwell International Corp. v. Serck Industries Ltd (DEFENDANT'S DESIGN PROCESS: Ch.D.: C.A.)

Irregularity Procedure

Aoki's Application (RULE 100: DISCRETION: Pat. Ct)

Coal Industry (Patents) Ltd's Application (IRREGULARITY ATTRIBUTABLE TO PATENT OFFICE: CONDITIONS: DISCRETION: Pat. Ct)

E's Applications (DISCRETION: INTERPRETATION OF INTERNATIONAL TREATY: Pat. Ct: C.A.: H.L.)

Napp Laboratories v. Pfizer Inc. (WHETHER LEAVE REQUIRED FOR SERVICE OUT OF JURISDICTION: WHETHER SERVICE IRREGULAR BECAUSE NO ENDORSEMENT: Ch.D.)

Issue Estoppel

BYSTANDER Trade Mark (AUTHORISATION OF AGENT: DISCRETION: T.M.Reg.)

Chiron Corporation v. Organon Teknika Ltd (No. 6) (*Res judicata*: CAUSE OF ACTION ESTOPPEL: STRIKING OUT: Pat. Ct)

International Business Machines Corporation v. Phoenix International (Computers) Ltd (STRIKING OUT: SUMMARY JUDGMENT: Ch.D.)

Joinder of Party

Advanced Portfolio Technologies Inc v. Ainsworth (PROCEEDINGS IN NEW YORK ON SAME FACTS: WHETHER *forum conveniens* WAS ENGLAND: APPLICATION FOR STAY: INJUNCTION AGAINST JOINDER OF DEFENDANT IN N.Y. PROCEEDINGS: Ch.D.)

CQR Security Systems Ltd's Patent (JOINDER OF CO-PETITIONER: WHETHER JUST AND CONVENIENT: WHETHER NECESSARY TO GIVE SECURITY FOR COSTS: Pat. Ct)

Lubrizol Corporation v. Esso Petroleum Co. Ltd (No. 1) (JOINDER OF ADDITIONAL DEFENDANT: SERVICE OUT OF JURISDICTION: JOINT TORTFEASANCE: Pat. Ct: C.A.)

Mölnlycke AB v. Procter & Gamble Ltd (No. 4) (JOINDER OF NEW DEFENDANT FOR PURPOSE OF DISCOVERY: WHETHER ABUSE OF PROCESS OR IMPROPER: C.A.)

Joint Tortfeasance/Joint Tortfeasors

Dow Chemical AG v. Spence Bryson & Co. Ltd (FALSE SUGGESTION: JOINT TORTFEASORS: Pat. Ct: C.A.)

Intel Corporation v. General Instrument Corporation (No. 2) (JOINT TORTFEASORS: SERVICE OUTSIDE JURISDICTION: Pat. Ct)

Lubrizol Corporation v. Esso Petroleum Co. Ltd (No. 1) (JOINDER OF ADDITIONAL DEFENDANT: SERVICE OUT OF JURISDICTION: JOINT TORTFEASANCE: Pat. Ct: C.A.)

Mölnlycke AB v. Procter & Gamble Ltd (No. 4) (JOINT TORTFEASOR: JOINDER OF NEW DEFENDANT FOR PURPOSE OF DISCOVERY: WHETHER ABUSE OF PROCESS OR IMPROPER: C.A.)

PLG Research Ltd v. Ardon International Ltd (JOINT TORTFEASOR: DIRECTORS LIABILITY: Pat. Ct)

Puschner v. Tom Palmer (Scotland) Ltd (JOINT TORTFEASORS: SERVICE OUT OF THE JURISDICTION: Pat. Ct)

Unilever plc v. Chefaro Proprietaries Ltd (JOINT TORTFEASORS: MULTI-NATIONAL GROUP: WHETHER SHAREHOLDER CONTROL BY ULTIMATE HOLDING COMPANY SUFFICIENT TO INFER ASSISTANCE TO PRIMARY INFRINGER OR COMMON DESIGN: C.A.)

Unilever plc v. Gillette (U.K.) Ltd (JOINT TORTFEASORS: SERVICE OUT OF JURISDICTION: Pat. Ct: C.A.)

Judgment

Patten v. Burke Publishing Co. Ltd (JUDGMENT BY DEFAULT: DECLARATION: PUBLISHERS' CONTRACTUAL RIGHT TO PUBLISH AUTHOR'S WORKS: AUTHOR SEEKING DECLARATION THAT PARTIES NO LONGER BOUND BY CONTRACT: JUDGMENT IN DEFAULT OF PUBLISHERS GIVING NOTICE OF INTENTION TO DEFEND ACTION: Ch.D.)

Smith Kline & French Laboratories Ltd v. Harris Pharmaceuticals Ltd (SUMMARY JUDGMENT: JURISDICTION TO DETERMINE QUESTION OF CONSTRUCTION: Ch.D.)

Judicial Bias

Berkeley Administration Inc. v. McClelland (DISCRETION: COMPLAINT OF JUDICIAL BIAS: JUDGE'S DUTY: Q.B.D.)

Jurisdiction

An Bord Trachtala v. Waterford Foods plc (INTERLOCUTORY INJUNCTION: ATTEMPT TO RESTRICT ACTS COMMITTED ABROAD: WHETHER SERIOUS ISSUE TO BE TRIED: Ireland: H.C.)

Associated Newspapers Group plc v. Insert Media Ltd (PLEADINGS: AMENDMENT: Ch.D.)

Aumac Ltd's Patent (*See v. Scott-Paine* ORDER BY CONSENT: WHETHER CONSENSUAL ORDER IS A CONTRACT: INTENTION OF COURT: JURISDICTION TO VARY, DISCHARGE OR ADD TO ORDER: Pat. Ct)

Bayer AG v. Winter (FORUM SHOPPING: FOREIGN PROCEEDING SEEKING PROTECTIVE MEASURES: Ch.D.)

Bayer AG v. Winter (No. 2) (CROSS-EXAMINATION OF DEFENDANT: Ch.D.)

Dory v. Richard Wolf GmbH (USE OF DISCOVERY LISTS IN OTHER JURISDICTIONS: Pat. Ct)

Du Pont de Nemours (E.I.) & Co. v. Enka BV (No. 2) (STAY OF INJUNCTION PENDING APPEAL: DISCRETION: Pat. Ct)

Electric Furnace Co. v. Selas Corp. of America (LEAVE TO SERVE DEFENDANT OUT OF JURISDICTION: APPEAL: C.A.)

Femis-Bank (Anguilla) Ltd v. Lazar (WHETHER JURISDICTION TO GRANT INTERLOCUTORY INJUNCTION RESTRAINING PUBLICATION PENDING TRIAL: Ch.D.)

Gulf Oil (G.B.) Ltd v. Page (INTERLOCUTORY INJUNCTION: C.A.)

GUNTRUM Trade Mark (EFFECT OF PROCEEDINGS IN ANOTHER JURISDICTION: T.M.Reg.)

Halcon SD Group Inc.'s Patents (STRIKING OUT: ESTOPPEL: ELECTION: EVIDENCE: DISCOVERY: Pat. Ct)

House of Spring Gardens Ltd v. Waite (CONFLICT OF LAWS: FOREIGN JUDGMENT: JURISDICTION TO ENFORCE: C.A.)

House of Spring Gardens Ltd v. Waite (MAREVA INJUNCTION: PROCEEDINGS IN TWO JURISDICTIONS: LEGAL COSTS: Ch.D.)

ICI v. Ram Bathrooms (SETTLEMENT OF ACTION: WHETHER JURISDICTION TO ALLOW AMENDMENT: P.C.)

Intel Corporation v. General Instrument Corporation (No. 2) (JOINT TORTFEASORS: SERVICE OUTSIDE JURISDICTION: Pat. Ct)

Jade Engineering (Coventry) Ltd v. Antiference Window Systems Ltd (DESIGN RIGHT: INFRINGEMENT: IDENTITY OF SUPPLIER OF INFRINGING GOODS SOUGHT: SUPPLIER NOT PARTY TO ACTION: *Norwich Pharmacal* ORDER: WHETHER TORTFEASOR MUST BE IN U.K.: JURISDICTION: DISCOVERY: PURPOSE: EXTENT: Ch.D.)

Johnson Electric Industrial Manufactory Ltd v. Mabuchi-Motor KK (THREATS: Pat. Ct)

Kakkar v. Szelke (Pat. Ct: C.A.)

Kitechnology BV v. Unicor GmbH Plastmaschinen (PLEADINGS: STRIKING OUT: EEC JUDGMENTS CONVENTION: C.A.)

Lubrizol Corporation v. Esso Petroleum Co. Ltd (No. 1) (JOINDER OF ADDITIONAL DEFENDANT: SERVICE OUT OF JURISDICTION: Pat. Ct: C.A.)

McDonald v. Graham (PATENTS COUNTY COURT: *Res judicata*: Pat. C.C.: C.A.)

Mercantile Group (Europe) AG v. Aiyela (MAREVA INJUNCTION: *Norwich Pharmacal* ORDER: JURISDICTION TO MAKE ORDERS: Q.B.D.)

Mitchelstown Co-operative Society Ltd v. Société des Produits Nestlé SA (JURISDICTION: ARBITRATION: BALANCE OF CONVENIENCE: Ireland: S.C.)

Napp Laboratories v. Pfizer Inc. (SERVICE OF PETITION FOR REVOCATION: WHETHER LEAVE REQUIRED FOR SERVICE OUT OF JURISDICTION: WHETHER SERVICE IRREGULAR BECAUSE NO ENDORSEMENT: Ch.D.)

Optical Coating Laboratory Inc. v. Pilkington PE Ltd (PATENTS COUNTY COURT JURISDICTION: C.A.)

Orwell Steel (Erection & Fabrication) Ltd v. Asphalt & Tarmac (U.K.) Ltd (MAREVA INJUNCTION: APPLICATION AFTER FINAL JUDGMENT: Q.B.D.)

Powerscourt Estates v. Gallagher (MAREVA INJUNCTION: Ireland: H.C.)

PSM International plc v. Specialised Fastener Products (Southern) Ltd (JURISDICTION OF PATENT COUNTY COURT WHERE COPYRIGHT ALLEGED TO SUBSIST IN DESIGN DRAWINGS: Pat. C.C.)

Puschner v. Tom Palmer (Scotland) Ltd (JOINT TORTFEASORS: SERVICE OUT OF THE JURISDICTION: Pat. Ct)

R. v. Bridgeman and Butt (CONSPIRACY TO DEFRAUD: SATELLITE BROADCASTING FROM U.K. TO SPAIN: AMBIT OF LICENCE: ENCRYPTED TRANSMISSIONS: DECODING DEVICES: NATURE OF RIGHTS AND REMEDIES: EVIDENCE: C.C.)

Roberts v. Northwest Fixings (OBSERVATIONS ON COUNTY COURT JURISDICTION BY AGREEMENT: C.A.)

Slazengers Ltd v. Seaspeed Ferries International Ltd (SECURITY FOR COSTS: PLAINTIFF RESIDENT OUT OF JURISDICTION: Comm. Ct: C.A.)

Smith Kline & French Laboratories Ltd v. Harris Pharmaceuticals Ltd (SUMMARY JUDGMENT: JURISDICTION TO DETERMINE QUESTION OF CONSTRUCTION: Ch.D.)

Sport Internationaal Bussum BV v. Inter-Footwear Ltd (RELIEF: DELAY: H.L.)

Unilever plc v. Gillette (U.K.) Ltd (JOINT TORTFEASORS: SERVICE OUT OF JURISDICTION: Pat. Ct: C.A.)

Unilever plc v. Pearce (INSPECTION OF PROCESS: Pat. Ct)

WEA Records Ltd v. Visions Channel 4 Ltd (ANTON PILLER: JURISDICTION TO ENTERTAIN APPEAL: C.A.)

Knowledge

Millar v. Bassey (CONTRACT: INDUCING BREACH: APPLICATION TO STRIKE OUT
STATEMENT OF CLAIM: INTENTION OF DEFENDANT: C.A.)

Laches

John (Elton) v. James (Ch.D.)
My Kinda Town Ltd v. Soll (Ch.D.: C.A.)
Nelson v. Rye (LIMITATION PERIOD: Ch.D.)

Leave

Altertext Inc. v. Advanced Data Communications Ltd (ANTON PILLER: LEAVE TO
SERVE ABROAD: Ch.D.)
Bank of Credit and Commerce International SA (MAREVA INJUNCTION:
GEOGRAPHICAL SCOPE: LEAVE TO COMMENCE PROCEEDINGS ABROAD: C.A.)
Electric Furnace Co. v. Selas Corp. of America (LEAVE TO SERVE DEFENDANT OUT
OF JURISDICTION: APPEAL: C.A.)
Garvin v. Domus Publishing Ltd (DISCOVERY: USE OF DOCUMENTS SEIZED UNDER
ANTON PILLER ORDER: APPLICATION FOR LEAVE TO USE DOCUMENTS IN
PROCEEDINGS FOR CONTEMPT OF COURT: WHETHER TO BE REFUSED ON
PRINCIPLE AGAINST SELF-INCRIMINATION: Ch.D.)
McGuinness v. Kellogg Co. of Great Britain Ltd (APPLICATION FOR LEAVE NOT TO
DISCLOSE EVIDENCE UNTIL TRIAL: C.A.
Napp Laboratories v. Pfizer Inc. (WHETHER LEAVE REQUIRED FOR SERVICE OUT OF
JURISDICTION: WHETHER SERVICE IRREGULAR BECAUSE NO
ENDORSEMENT: Ch.D.)
Raychem Corp. v. Thermon (U.K.) Ltd (LEAVE TO SERVE WRIT OUT OF
JURISDICTION: Pat. Ct)

Legal Professional Privilege. *See also* Privilege

CHC Software Card Ltd v. Hopkins & Wood (DISCOVERY: CONFIDENTIALITY:
INTERROGATORIES: Ch.D.)
Gamlen Chemical Co. (U.K.) Ltd v. Rochem Chem. Ltd (FRAUD: Ch.D.)
IBM v. Phoenix International Computers Ltd (ADVICE FROM FOREIGN LAWYER ON
U.K. LAW: INSPECTION: WHETHER WAIVE: Ch.D.)
Lubrizol Corporation v. Esso Petroleum Co. Ltd (No. 4) (EXPERTS' AFFIDAVITS
SWORN IN FOREIGN PROCEEDINGS: WHETHER SUBJECT TO LEGAL
PROFESSIONAL PRIVILEGE: Pat. Ct)
Rockwell International Corp. v. Serck Industries Ltd (PATENT AGENT'S PRIVILEGE:
Ch.D.)
Santa Fe International Corp. v. Napier Shipping SA (PATENT AGENT'S PRIVILEGE:
Scotland: O.H.)
Wilden Pump Engineering Co. v. Fusfield (PATENT AGENT'S PRIVILEGE: C.A.)

Liberty to Apply

Gantenbrink v. BBC (COPYRIGHT: FILM: UNDERTAKINGS: Ch.D.)

Liberty To Discontinue Action

American International Group Inc. v. London American International Corp. Ltd
(Ch.D.)

Limitation Period

Nelson v. Rye (INFRINGEMENT: MUSICAL WORKS: MANUFACTURE AND SALE
AFTER EXPIRY OF LICENCE: POP MUSICIAN AND MANAGER: ACCOUNT:
TERMS OF RETAINER: LACHES AND ACQUIESCENCE: Ch.D.)

Locus Standi

Compagnie Luxembourgeoise de Télédiffusion (BROADCASTING FRANCHISES:
ADMINISTRATIVE PROCEDURE: JUDICIAL REVIEW: France: Conseil d'Etat)
Consorzio del Prosciutto di Parma v. Marks and Spencer plc (REPRESENTATIVE
ACTION: BALANCE OF CONVENIENCE: ITALIAN LEGISLATION: Ch.D.: C.A.)
Imprimerie (SA) Thône v. Fernand Geubelle (PUBLISHER AS CO-AUTHOR: Belgium)
Zunis Holding SA v. E.C. Commission (MERGER: CLEARED BY COMMISSION:
REQUEST BY SHAREHOLDERS TO REOPEN CASE: REFUSAL: JUDICIAL REVIEW:
WHETHER APPEAL POSSIBLE: CFI)

Mandatory Injunction

Leisure Data v. Bell (C.A.)
Smith Kline & French Laboratories Ltd v. Harris Pharmaceuticals Ltd (MANDATORY
INJUNCTION FOR DESTRUCTION OF STOCKS: Ch.D.)

Mareva Injunction

A v. B (X Intervening) (APPLICATION BY INTERVENER: VARIATION: Q.B.D.)
Al Nahkel Ltd v. Lowe (WRIT: *Ne exeat regno*: APPLICATION: MAREVA INJUNCTION:
ALLEGED THIEF: FORM OF WRIT: Q.B.D.)
Allied Arab Bank Ltd v. Hajjar (WRIT *ne exeat regno*: PURPOSE OF WRIT: PREJUDICE
TO DEFENDANT: Q.B.D.)
Ashtiani v. Kashi (DISCOVERY: FOREIGN ASSETS: POWER OF COURT: C.A.)
Bank Mellat v. Nikpour (*Ex parte* RELIEF: C.A.)
Bank of Credit and Commerce International SA (GEOGRAPHICAL SCOPE: LEAVE TO
COMMENCE PROCEEDINGS ABROAD: C.A.)
Bayer AG v. Winter (INTERLOCUTORY INJUNCTION: ANTON PILLER ORDERS:
DELIVERY UP OF PASSPORTS: C.A.)
Brink's Mat Ltd v. Elcombe (MATERIAL NON-DISCLOSURE: DISCRETION: C.A.)
CBS United Kingdom Ltd v. Lambert (ANTON PILLER ORDER: C.A.)
Charles Church Developments plc v. Cronin (ENJOINED AMOUNT REDUCED IN
LINE WITH LIKELY FIGURE RECOVERABLE ON ACCOUNT OF PROFITS: Ch.D.)
Deutsche Schachtbau- und Tiefbohrgesellschaft mbH v. Ras Al Khaimah National
Oil Co. (ARBITRATION: AWARD: ENFORCEMENT: PRE-TRIAL RELIEF: C.A.)
Galaxia Maritime SA v. Mineralimportexport, The Elftherios (PROTECTION OF
THIRD PARTY INTERESTS: C.A.)
House of Spring Gardens Ltd v. Waite (PROCEEDINGS IN TWO JURISDICTIONS:
LEGAL COSTS: Ch.D.)
McDonald v. Graham (PATENTS COUNTY COURT: JURISDICTION: *Res judicata*:
ANTON PILLER AND MAREVA: Pat. C.C.: C.A.)
Mercantile Group (Europe) AG v. Aiyela (*Norwich Pharmacal* ORDER: JURISDICTION:
MAREVA INJUNCTIONS AGAINST PERSONS INVOLVED IN TORTIOUS
WRONGDOING OF OTHERS: Q.B.D.)
Nimemia Maritime Corp. v. Trave Schiffahrt GmbH & Co. KG (PRINCIPLES: C.A.)
Orwell Steel (Erection & Fabrication) Ltd v. Asphalt & Tarmac (U.K.) Ltd
(APPLICATION AFTER FINAL JUDGMENT: JURISDICTION: Q.B.D.)
PCW (Underwriting Agencies) Ltd v. Dixon (PROTECTION OF THIRD PARTIES'
INTERESTS: Q.B.D.: C.A.)
Powerscourt Estates v. Gallagher (JURISDICTION: Ireland: H.C.)

Project Development Co. Ltd SA v. KMK Securities Ltd (SYNDICATE BANK INTERVENING) (COSTS OF INNOCENT THIRD PARTY: VARIATION OF INJUNCTION: Q.B.D.)

Seawind Maritime Inc. v. Roumanian Bank (THIRD PARTY INTERESTS: Q.B.D.)

Z Ltd v. A (PROTECTION OF THIRD PARTIES' INTERESTS: GUIDELINES: C.A.)

Market Research Evidence. *See also under* **Survey Evidence**

Reckitt & Coleman Products Ltd v. Borden Inc. (No. 2) (Ch.D.)

Motions. *See also under* **Anton Piller,** *Ex parte* **Motions, Mareva Injunctions,** etc.

Amersham International plv v. Corning Ltd (EUROPEAN PATENT: OPPOSITION AT EPO: MOTION FOR STAY IN HIGH COURT: *Forum conveniens*: Pat. Ct)

Butt v. Butt (UNDERTAKINGS: C.A.)

Johnson & Johnson's Application (NOTICE OF ORIGINATING MOTION: Ch.D.)

Kodak Ltd v. Reed International plc (ADJOURNED MOTION TO TRIAL: COSTS: Ch.D.)

Max Factor & Co. v. MGM/UA Entertainment Co. (SAVING MOTION TO ANOTHER DAY: Ch.D.)

Ne Exeat Regno

Al Nahkel Ltd v. Lowe (APPLICATION: MAREVA INJUNCTION: ALLEGED THIEF: FORM OF WRIT: Q.B.D.)

Allied Arab Bank Ltd v. Hajjar (MAREVA INJUNCTION: PURPOSE OF WRIT: PREJUDICE TO DEFENDANT: Q.B.D.)

Norwich Pharmacal **Order**

Jade Engineering (Coventry) Ltd v. Antiference Window Systems Ltd (DESIGN RIGHT: INFRINGEMENT: IDENTITY OF SUPPLIER OF INFRINGING GOODS SOUGHT: SUPPLIER NOT PARTY TO ACTION: *Norwich Pharmacal* ORDER: WHETHER TORTFEASOR MUST BE IN U.K.: JURISDICTION: DISCOVERY: PURPOSE: EXTENT: Ch.D.)

Mercantile Group (Europe) AG v. Aiyela, The (JURISDICTION TO MAKE ORDERS: MAREVA INJUNCTIONS AGAINST PERSONS INVOLVED IN TORTIOUS WRONG-DOING OF OTHERS: Q.B.D.)

Order 14. *See under* **Summary judgment**

Payment Into Court

Colgate Palmolive Ltd v. Markwell Finance Ltd (COSTS: Ch.D.)

Pleadings

Associated Newspapers Group plc v. Insert Media Ltd (AMENDMENT: UNFAIR TRADING: DAMAGE: Ch.D.)

Behr-Thomson Dehnstoffrengler Verwaltungs GmbH v. Western Thomson Controls Ltd (COUNTERCLAIM: *See v. Scott-Paine* ORDER: Pat. Ct)

Charles Church Developments plc v. Cronin (MAREVA INJUNCTION: ENJOINED AMOUNT REDUCED IN LINE WITH LIKELY FIGURE RECOVERABLE ON ACCOUNT OF PROFITS: Ch.D.)

Copyright in Court Proceedings (LAWYERS PLEADINGS: TEST: PROTECTION: PUBLICATION: Germany: S.C.)

CQR Security Systems Ltd's Patent (AMENDMENT OF PLEADINGS: COSTS: APPLICATION TO AMEND PARTICULARS OF OBJECTIONS AFTER CLAIM AMENDED: APPROPRIATE ORDER AND DATE FOR TAXATION: Pat. Ct)

Dolphin Showers Ltd v. Farmiloe (STRIKING OUT: ENTITLEMENT: ASSIGNMENT: Pat. Ct.)

Ecolab Inc. v. Reddish Savilles Ltd (AMENDMENT OF PARTICULARS OF OBJECTION: *See v. Scott-Paine* ORDER: DATE OF OPERATION OF ORDER: Pat. Ct)

Fearis v. Davies (REQUEST FOR FURTHER AND BETTER PARTICULARS: CONSENT ORDER: CONSTRUCTION OF ORDER: C.A.)

Flude (H.) & Co. (Hinkley) Ltd's Patent (PATENT OFFICE: C.-G.)

Gill v. Chipman Ltd (EARTH CLOSET ORDERS: Pat. Ct)

Glaverbel SA v. British Coal Corp. (No. 3) (WITNESS STATEMENT: OBJECT OF PARTICULARS: OBVIOUSNESS: CROSS-EXAMINATION: Pat. Ct)

Helitune Ltd v. Stewart Hughes Ltd (AMENDMENT OF PLEADING: EARTH CLOSET ORDER: COSTS: Pat. Ct)

Helitune Ltd v. Stewart Hughes Ltd (STRIKING OUT: ABUSE OF PROCESS: Ch.D.)

Instance v. Denny Bros Printing Ltd (*See v. Scott-Paine* ORDER: Pat. Ct)

Intel Corp. v. General Instrument Corporation (DISCOVERY AND PARTICULARS BEFORE DEFENCE SERVED: Pat. Ct)

Ishihara Sangyo Kaisha Ltd v. The Dow Chemical Co. (FAIR BASIS: STRIKING OUT: C.A.)

Joyce v. Sengupta (STRIKING OUT: ABUSE OF PROCESS OF COURT: C.A.)

Kitechnology BV v. Unicor GmbH Plastmaschinen (STRIKING OUT: JURISDICTION: EEC JUDGMENTS CONVENTION: C.A.)

La Baigue Magiglo v. Multiglow Fires (*See v. Scott-Paine*: Pat. Ct)

Minister of Agriculture's Patent (PLEADINGS IN PATENT OFFICE: Pat. Ct)

Millar v. Bassey (INDUCING BREACH OF CONTRACT: APPLICATION TO STRIKE OUT STATEMENT OF CLAIM: INTENTION OF DEFENDANT: KNOWLEDGE: C.A.)

My Kinda Town Ltd v. Soll (LACHES: ACCOUNT OF PROFITS: Ch.D.: C.A.)

N. & P. Windows v. Cego Ltd (COPYRIGHT INFRINGEMENT: PARTICULARS OF SIMILARITIES: Ch.D.)

Parmenter v. Malt House Joinery (AMENDMENT OF PLEADINGS DURING TRIAL: EVIDENCE: C.A.)

Ransburg-Gema AG v. Electrostatic Plant Systems Ltd (AMENDMENT: CAUSES OF ACTION: CLAIM TO CONVERSION DAMAGES NOT LOST IN RESPECT OF AMENDMENTS MADE AFTER COMMENCEMENT OF CD&PA88: C.A.)

Raychem Corp. v. Thermon (U.K.) Ltd (AMBIGUITY: Pat. Ct)

Shippam (C.) Ltd v. Princes-Buitoni Ltd (REQUIREMENTS OF STATEMENTS OF CLAIM: COSTS: Ch.D.)

Speed Seal Products Ltd v. Paddington (STRIKING OUT: ACTIONABLE ABUSE OF PROCESS: Ch.D.: C.A.)

Speed Seal Products Ltd v. Paddington (FURTHER AND BETTER PARTICULARS: Ch.D.)

Unilever plc v. Gillette (U.K.) Ltd (COMMERCIAL SUCCESS: Pat. Ct)

Williamson v. Moldline Ltd (COSTS: EARTH CLOSET ORDER: DISCRETION: C.A.)

Wyko Group plc v. Cooper Roller Bearings Co. Ltd (STRIKING OUT: Ch.D.)

Post-judgment Order

Distributori Automatici Italia SpA v. Holford General Trading Co. Ltd (ANTON PILLER: POST-JUDGMENT ORDER IN AID OF EXECUTION: Q.B.D.)

Practice Directions

Practice Direction (Chancery: Masters Powers) (CHANCERY CHAMBERS: AUTHORISATION FOR HEARING BEFORE MASTER: Ch.D.)

Practice Direction (Chancery: Reading Guide in Patent Actions) (PATENTS COURT: JUDGE'S PRE-TRIAL READING: "READING GUIDE": Ch.D.)

Practice Direction (Patent action summonses) (PATENT ACTION SUMMONSES: PATENT COURT USERS' COMMITTEE: Ch.D.)

Practice Direction (PATENTS: DESIGNS: RECTIFICATION OF REGISTER: AGREED DIRECTIONS: PROCEDURE: RSC ORDER 104, R.17: Ch.D.)

Practice Direction—Patents (RECTIFICATION OF REGISTER: AGREED DIRECTIONS: Ch.D.)

Practice Direction 1/94

Practice Direction—(CHANCERY: SUMMONS FOR DIRECTIONS: Ch.D.)

Practice Direction—Simplified Trial

Practice Direction—(PATENTS COURT: PROCEDURE: Ch.D.)

Pre-trial Relief

Deutsche Schachtbau- und Tiefbohrgesellschaft mbH v. Ras Al Khaimah National Oil Co. (ARBITRATION: AWARD: ENFORCEMENT: PRE-TRIAL RELIEF: MAREVA INJUNCTION: C.A.)

Pre-trial Reviews

Patents Court Practice Explanation (INFORMATION SHEETS AT SUMMONS FOR DIRECTIONS: RIGHTS OF AUDIENCE: SITTINGS OUTSIDE LONDON: Pat. Ct)

Prejudice

Allied Arab Bank Ltd v. Hajjar (PURPOSE OF WRIT: PREJUDICE TO DEFENDANT: Q.B.D.)

Privilege. *See also under* Privilege against Self-incrimination and Legal Professional Privilege

A.M. & S. Ltd v. E.C. Commission (ADMINISTRATIVE PROCEDURE: LAWYERS: CONFIDENTIALITY: ECJ)

Black & Decker Inc. v. Flymo Ltd (SPECIFIC DISCOVERY BASED ON WITNESS STATEMENT EXCHANGED BEFORE TRIAL: WHETHER PRIVILEGE LOST BY EXCHANGE OF WITNESS STATEMENTS: Ch.D.)

Bonzel v. Intervention Ltd (No. 2) (DISCLOSURE OF PRIVILEGED DOCUMENTS: Pat. Ct)

British Coal Corporation v. Dennis Rye Ltd (No. 2) (EVIDENCE: LEGAL ADVISERS: DOCUMENTS CREATED FOR CIVIL PROCEEDINGS SUBSEQUENTLY HANDED TO POLICE: EFFECT OF LEGAL PROFESSIONAL PRIVILEGE: ATTORNEY-GENERAL'S GUIDELINES: VOLUNTARY DISCLOSURE IN COURSE OF CRIMINAL TRIAL: WHETHER PRIVILEGE WAIVED: WHETHER ENTITLEMENT TO RETURN OF DOCUMENTS: C.A.)

C. & H. Engineering v. F. Klucznik & Sons Ltd (WHETHER "WITHOUT PREJUDICE" CORRESPONDENCE AFTER *Calderbank* LETTER PRIVILEGED: Ch.D.)

DORMEUIL Trade Mark (TRADE MARK AGENT'S PRIVILEGE: Ch.D.)

English & American Insurance Co. Ltd v. Herbert Smith (CONFIDENTIAL INFORMATION: EVIDENCE: LEGAL PROFESSIONAL PRIVILEGE: INNOCENT RECEIPT OF INFORMATION: Ch.D.)

Gamlen Chemical Co. (U.K.) Ltd v. Rochem Ltd (CONSPIRACY TO INJURE: BREACH OF CONFIDENCE: DISCOVERY: LEGAL PRIVILEGE: Ch.D.)

Goddard v. Nationwide Building Society (EVIDENCE: PROFESSIONALLY PRIVILEGED NOTE: USE OF COPIES RESTRAINED: C.A.)

Hillegom Municipality v. Hillenius (BANKING: CONFIDENTIALITY: NATIONAL COURTS: CIVIL PROCEEDINGS: PROFESSIONAL PRIVILEGE: ECJ)

Hilti AG v. E.C. Commission (CONFIDENTIALITY OF BUSINESS SECRETS: INTERVENERS: LEGAL PROFESSIONAL PRIVILEGE: APPLICABLE TO WRITTEN COMMUNICATIONS BETWEEN INDEPENDENT LAWYER AND CLIENT COMPANY: INTERESTS OF RIGHT OF DEFENCE: PROCEDURE: CFI)

Lubrizol Corporation v. Esso Petroleum Co. Ltd (WHETHER COPY DOCUMENTS PRIVILEGED: Ch.D.)

Minnesota Mining & Manufacturing Co. v. Rennicks (U.K.) Ltd (CONFIDENTIAL DOCUMENTS USED IN U.S. PROCEEDINGS: U.S. PROTECTIVE ORDER: Ch.D.)

Société Française Hoechst v. Allied Colloids Ltd (CONTENTS OF NOTICE OF EXPERIMENTS: Pat. Ct)

Sonic Tape plc's Patent (CONFIDENTIALITY OF DOCUMENTS: C.-G.)

Privilege Against Self-incrimination

Coca Cola Company v. Peter John Gilbey (ANTON PILLER ORDER: DISCLOSURE OF INFORMATION: RISK OF PERSONAL JEOPARDY: WHETHER GROUNDS TO DISCHARGE ORDER: Ch.D.: C.A.)

Crest Homes plc v. Marks (USE OF DOCUMENTS FOR CONTEMPT PROCEEDINGS IN EARLIER ACTION: APPEAL DISMISSED: H.L.)

Levi Strauss & Co. v. Barclays Trading Corp. Inc. (DISCLOSURE OF NAMES: WHETHER PLAINTIFF ESTOPPED FROM USING INFORMATION DISCLOSED AGAINST THIRD PARTIES: IMPLIED UNDERTAKING ON DISCOVERY: PROPER TIME FOR APPLICATION: Ch.D.)

Universal City Studios Inc. v. Hubbard (ANTON PILLER: Ch.D.: C.A.)

Procedure

Strix Ltd v. Otter Controls Ltd (No. 2) (INQUIRY AS TO DAMAGES: DIRECTIONS AS TO CONDUCT OF INQUIRY: Pat. Ct)

Procedural Error

M's Application (PATENT: APPLICATION: TIME LIMITS: Pat. Ct: C.A.)

Tokan Kogyo KK's Application (PATENT: APPLICATION: DISCRETION: C.-G.)

Public Interest Immunity

Barlow Clowes Gilt Managers Ltd (Ch.D.)

Quia Timet Relief

Elida Gibbs Ltd v. Colgate-Palmolive Ltd (Ch.D.)

Lego System A/S v. Lego M. Lemelstrich Ltd (Pat. Ct)

Linpac Mouldings Ltd v. Eagleton Direct Export Ltd (*Quia timet* INJUNCTION ON ABANDONMENT OF DAMAGES CLAIM: DISCRETION: C.A.)

Referral to European Court of Justice. *See* European Court, Referral to

Res Judicata

Chiron Corporation v. Organon Teknika Ltd (No. 6) (CAUSE OF ACTION ESTOPPEL: ISSUE ESTOPPEL: STRIKING: OUT: Pat. Ct)

Chiron Corporation v. Murex Diagnostics Ltd (No. 9) (WHETHER DEFENCE STRUCK
OUT IN EARLIER ACTION CAN BE RAISED IN LATER ACTION: ARTICLE 177: *Acte
clair*: Pat. Ct)

Harrison v. Project & Design Co. (Redcar) Ltd (CONSTRUCTION OF CLAIMS: C.A.)

McDonald v. Graham (JURISDICTION: ANTON PILLER AND MAREVA: PATENT:
INFRINGEMENT: Pat. C.C.: C.A.)

Parmenter v. Malt House Joinery (EVIDENCE: INTERLOCUTORY APPEAL ALLOWED:
C.A.)

Sears plc v. Sears, Roebuck & Co. (CHOICE OF TRIBUNAL: INJUNCTION: Ch.D.)

Right of Audience

Patents Court Practice Explanation (TELEPHONE SUMMONSES: PRE-TRIAL REVIEWS:
SITTINGS OUTSIDE LONDON: Pat. Ct)

Reiss Engineering Co. Ltd v. Harris (TAXATION OF PATENT AGENT'S COSTS ON
APPEAL TO PATENTS COURT: Pat. Ct)

Risk of Injustice

Entec (Pollution Control) Ltd v. Abacus Mouldings (Ch.D.: C.A.)

Scotland

British Phonographic Industry Ltd v. Cohen (COPYRIGHT: INFRINGEMENT: ANTON
PILLER: I.H.)

Dirt Magnet Trade Mark (TRADE MARK: RECTIFICATION: PARALLEL PROCEEDINGS
IN SCOTLAND AND ENGLAND: IDENTICAL ISSUES: APPLICANTS NOT PARTIES
TO SCOTTISH PROCEEDINGS: WHETHER DUPLICATION: COSTS: Ch.D.)

James North & Sons Ltd v. North Cape Textiles Ltd (PASSING OFF: TRADE MARK:
INFRINGEMENT: INJUNCTION: England: C.A.)

Santa Fe International Corp. v. Napier Shipping SA (CONFIDENTIALITY: PATENT:
INFRINGEMENT: PATENT AGENT'S PRIVILEGE: O.H.)

Security for Costs

CQR Security Systems Ltd's Patent (JOINDER OF CO-PETITIONER: WHETHER JUST
AND CONVENIENT: WHETHER NECESSARY TO GIVE SECURITY FOR COSTS:
Pat. Ct)

Porzelack KG v. Porzelack (U.K.) Ltd (EEC PLAINTIFF: DISCRETION TO ORDER
SECURITY Ch.D.)

Slazengers Ltd v. Seaspeed Ferries International Ltd (PLAINTIFF RESIDENT OUT OF
JURISDICTION: Comm. Ct: C.A.)

Speed Up Holdings Ltd v. Gough & Co. (Handly) Ltd (CORPORATE PLAINTIFF:
Ch.D.)

Thomas (Arthur Edward) Ltd v. Barcrest (PATENT: Pat. C.C.)

See v. Scott-Paine Order

Behr-Thomson Dehnstroffrengler Verwaltungs GmbH v. Western Thomson
Controls Ltd (COUNTERCLAIM: Pat. Ct)

Ecolab Inc. v. Reddish Savilles Ltd (AMENDMENT OF PARTICULARS OF OBJECTION:
See v. Scott-Paine ORDER: DATE OF OPERATION OF ORDER: Pat. Ct)

GEC Alsthom Ltd's Patent (PETITION FOR REVOCATION: RELIANCE ON
ADDITIONAL PRIOR ART: AMENDMENT OF PARTICULARS SOUGHT THREE
WEEKS PRIOR TO TRIAL: COSTS: WHETHER *See v. Scott-Paine* FORM OF ORDER
APPROPRIATE: Pat. Ct)

Instance v. Denny Bros Printing Ltd (Pat. Ct)
La Baigue Magiglo v. Multiglow Fires (PLEADINGS: Pat. Ct)
Pendax AB v. Anders & Kern (U.K.) Ltd (APPROPRIATENESS: COSTS: Pat. Ct)
Vestar Inc. v. Liposome Technology Inc. (FORM AND CONSTRUCTION: WRITTEN
SUBMISSIONS: Pat. C.C.)

Seizure of Goods

CBS Inc. v. Blue Suede Music Ltd (SEIZURE BY CUSTOMS: Ch.D.)

Serious Issue. *See under* Interlocutory Injunction

Service, General

Symbol Technologies Inc. v. Opticon Sensors Europe BV (No. 1) (SERVICE OF
PETITION FOR REVOCATION OF PATENT: Pat. Ct)

Service out of the Jurisdiction

Abkco Music & Records Inc. v. Music Collection International Ltd (LICENCE
GRANTED TO MANUFACTURE AND SELL OUTSIDE U.K.: APPLICATION TO SET
ASIDE SERVICE OUTSIDE JURISDICTION: C.A.)
Puschner v. Tom Palmer (Scotland) Ltd (JOINT TORTFEASORS: Pat. Ct)
Unilever plc v. Gillette (U.K.) Ltd (JOINT TORTFEASORS: Pat. Ct: C.A.)

Setting Aside

Dormeuil Frères SA v. Nicolian International (Textiles) Ltd (ANTON PILLER BURDEN
OF PROOF: DUTY OF FULL DISCLOSURE: RETURN OF GOODS SEIZED: Ch.D.)

Solicitors' Error

Swedac Ltd v. Magnet & Southerns plc (STRIKING OUT: SOLICITORS' ERROR OF
JUDGMENT: C.A.)

Specific Performance

Simtech Advanced Training and Simulation Systems Ltd v. Jasmin Simtec Ltd
(CONFIDENTIAL INFORMATION: COLLABORATION AGREEMENT: PARTIALLY
AGREED CONTRACT: INTERLOCUTORY RELIEF: BALANCE OF JUSTICE: Ch.D.)

Springboard Doctrine

Universal Thermosensors Ltd v. Hibben (EX-EMPLOYEES' COMPETING BUSINESS:
SCOPE OF INJUNCTIONS IN BREACH OF CONFIDENCE: DISCRETION: ANTON
PILLER: Ch.D.)

Standard of Proof

Batjac Productions Inc. v. Simitar Entertainment (U.K.) Ltd (SUMMARY JUDGMENT:
EVIDENCE: SECONDARY EVIDENCE OF CONTENTS OF DOCUMENTS: Ch.D.)

Status Quo, Preservation of

Jian Tools For Sales Inc. v. Roderick Manhattan Group Ltd (PASSING OFF: SOFTWARE FOR BUSINESS PLANS: BIZPLAN BUILDER: WHETHER DESCRIPTIVE: COMPANY WITH NO U.K. PLACE OF BUSINESS: REPUTATION: EFFECT OF FORCED CHANGE OF NAME: BALANCE OF CONVENIENCE: DEFENDANT'S AWARENESS OF PLAINTIFF'S OBJECTIONS: Ch.D.)

Statute Barred

Banks v. CBS Songs Ltd (WHETHER CLAIM FOR CONVERSION DAMAGES STATUTE BARRED: Ch.D., C.A.)

Stay

Advanced Portfolio Technologies Inc v. Ainsworth (PROCEEDINGS IN NEW YORK ON SAME FACTS: WHETHER *forum conveniens* WAS ENGLAND: INJUNCTION AGAINST JOINDER OF DEFENDANT IN N.Y. PROCEEDINGS: Ch.D.)

Amersham International plc v. Corning Ltd (EUROPEAN PATENT: OPPOSITION AT EPO: MOTION FOR STAY IN HIGH COURT: *Forum conveniens*: Pat. Ct)

Du Pont de Nemours (E.I.) & Co. (Blades') Patent (Licence of Right) (LICENCE OF RIGHT: SETTLEMENT OF TERMS: Pat. Ct)

Du Pont de Nemours (E.I.) & Co. v. Enka BV (No. 2) (STAY OF INJUNCTION PENDING APPEAL: LICENCE OF RIGHT: JURISDICTION: DISCRETION: Pat. Ct)

Etri Fans Ltd v. NMB (U.K.) Ltd (ARBITRATION CLAUSE: C.A.)

Ferro Corporation v. Escol Products Ltd (PROCEEDING IN PATENT OFFICE: Ch.D.)

Fichera v. Flogates Ltd and British Steel plc (WHETHER MISREPRESENTATION VITIATED STAY AGREEMENT OF WAS ABUSE OF PROCESS: Pat. Ct)

Gen Set SpA v. Mosarc Ltd (Pat. Ct)

Hawker Siddeley Dynamics Engineering Ltd v. Real Time Developments Ltd (Pat. Ct)

Minnesota Mining & Manufacturing Co. v. Rennicks (U.K.) Ltd (STAY OF INJUNCTION: Pat. Ct)

Mölnlycke AB v. Procter & Gamble Ltd (WHETHER COMPLEXITY OF INQUIRY SPECIAL REASON JUSTIFYING STAY: Pat. Ct)

MTV Europe v. BMG Records (U.K.) Ltd (OVERLAPPING ACTION BEFORE COMMISSION: JURISDICTION: Ch.D.)

Optical Coating Laboratory Inc. v. Pilkington PE Ltd (STAY OF INJUNCTION: Pat. C.C.)

Pall Corporation v. Commercial Hydraulics (Bedford) Ltd (OPPOSITION IN EPO: WHETHER STAY IN U.K. SHOULD BE ORDERED: Pat. Ct: C.A.)

Quantel Ltd v. Spaceward Microsystems Ltd (No. 2) (STAY OF INJUNCTION PENDING APPEAL: C.A.)

Roussel Uclaf's (Clemence & Le Martret) Patent (COMPTROLLER'S JURISDICTION: VEXATIOUS PROCEEDINGS: Pat. Ct)

Strix Ltd v. Otter Controls Ltd (No. 3) (PATENT: INFRINGEMENT: INQUIRY AS TO DAMAGES: LATE APPLICATION: DISCRETION: Pat. Ct)

Striking Out

Dolphin Showers Ltd v. Farmiloe (ENTITLEMENT: ASSIGNMENT: PLEADINGS: Pat. Ct)

Subpoena Duces Tecum

Summary Judgment

Linpac Mouldings Ltd v. Eagleton Direct Export Ltd (THREAT TO INFRINGE: *Quia timet* INJUNCTION ON ABANDONMENT OF DAMAGES CLAIM: DISCRETION: C.A.)

Mercury Communications Ltd v. Mercury Interactive (U.K.) Ltd (TRADE MARK: INFRINGEMENT: SOFTWARE: BONA FIDE USE OF OWN NAME: SCOPE OF REGISTRATION: Ch.D.)

Merrell Dow Pharmaceuticals Inc. v. H.N. Norton & Co. Ltd (PATENT: INFRINGEMENT: VALIDITY: *Gillette* DEFENCE: ANTICIPATION: ENABLING DISCLOSURE: PRIOR USE: MEDICAL TREATMENT: Pat. Ct)

Origins Natural Resources Inc. v. Origin Clothing Limited (SERVICE OF DEFENCE AND COUNTERCLAIM: Ch.D.)

SDS Biotech U.K. Ltd v. Power Agrichemicals Ltd (PASSING OFF: USE OF MAFF NUMBERS DENOTING GOVERNMENT APPROVAL: WHETHER UNAUTHORISED USE GIVES RISE TO CAUSE OF ACTION BY AUTHORISED TRADERS: APPLICATIONS FOR SUMMARY JUDGMENT REFUSED: Ch.D.)

Williams & Humbert Ltd v. International Distillers & Vintners Ltd (COUNTERCLAIM: Ch.D.)

Summons

Banks v. CBS Songs Ltd (SUMMONS TO AMEND ISSUED BEFORE BUT HEARD AFTER COMING INTO FORCE OF ACT: WHETHER CLAIM FOR CONVERSION DAMAGES STATUTE BARRED: Ch.D.: C.A.)

Barlow Clowes Gilt Managers Ltd (WITNESS SUMMONS ISSUED IN CRIMINAL PROCEEDINGS REQUIRING COMPANY'S LIQUIDATORS TO DISCLOSE CONFIDENTIAL INFORMATION: WHETHER INFORMATION TO BE DISCLOSED: Ch.D.)

Practice Note: Patent Action Summonses (PATENT ACTION SUMMONSES: PATENT COURT USERS' COMMITTEE: Ch.D.)

Patents Court Practice Explanation (INFORMATION SHEETS AT SUMMONS FOR DIRECTIONS: PRE-TRIAL REVIEWS: Pat. Ct)

Survey Evidence. *See also under* Market Research Evidence

AVON Trade Mark (T.M.Reg.)

HAVE A BREAK Trade Mark (Ch.D.)

KENT Trade Mark (T.M.Reg.)

Mothercare U.K. Ltd v. Penguin Books Ltd (LIKELIHOOD OF DAMAGE: C.A.)

The European Ltd v. The Economist Newspapers Ltd (TRADE MARK: DEVICE MARKS: THE EUROPEAN/EUROPEAN VOICE: WHETHER SIMILAR: WHETHER CONFUSING: EVIDENCE OF CONFUSION: SURVEY EVIDENCE: Ch.D.)

Wagamama Ltd v. City Centre Restaurants plc (ADMISSIBILITY: Ch.D.)

Taxation

CQR Security Systems Ltd's Patent (APPLICATION TO AMEND PARTICULARS OF OBJECTIONS AFTER CLAIM AMENDED: APPROPRIATE ORDER AND DATE FOR TAXATION: Pat. Ct)

Mölnlycke AB v. Procter & Gamble Ltd (No. 6) (INQUIRY FOR DAMAGES PENDING: WHETHER PLAINTIFFS ENTITLED TO IMMEDIATE TAXATION: Pat. Ct)

Naf Naf SA v. Dickens (London) Ltd (INDEMNITY COSTS: IMMEDIATE TAXATION: Ch.D.)

Reiss Engineering Co. Ltd v. Harris (PATENT AGENT'S COSTS ON APPEAL TO PATENTS COURT: Pat. Ct)

Telephone Summonses

Patents Court Practice Explanation (AGREED INTERLOCUTORY ORDERS: INFORMATION SHEETS AT SUMMONS FOR DIRECTIONS: PRE-TRIAL REVIEWS: RIGHTS OF AUDIENCE: SITTINGS OUTSIDE LONDON: Pat. Ct)

Time Limits

Adidas Sàrl (EXTENSIONS OF TIME: CERTIORARI: Q.B.D.)
Aisin Seiki KK's Application (EXTENSION OF TIME LIMIT: DISCRETION: Pat. Ct)
Armaturjonsson AB's Application (Pat. Ct)
Decorflex Ltd's Application (EXTENDING TIME LIMITS: DISCRETION: Pat. Ct)
Erven Warnink BV v. J. Townend & Sons (Hull) Ltd (INTEREST ON COSTS: TIME OF ENTERING JUDGMENT: C.A.)
Fichera v. Flogates Ltd and British Steel plc (ADDITION OF NEW CAUSE OF ACTION OUT OF TIME: Pat. Ct)
Lebelson's Application (Pat. Ct)
Levi Strauss & Co. v. Barclays Trading Corp. Inc. (IMPLIED UNDERTAKING ON DISCOVERY: PROPER TIME FOR APPLICATION: Ch.D.)
M's Application (PROCEDURAL ERROR: TIME LIMITS: Pat. Ct: C.A.)
Mills' Application (TIME LIMITS: ERROR IN PROCEDURE: Pat. Ct: C.A.)
Mitsubishi Jidosha Kogyo KK's Application (INTERNATIONAL PATENT APPLICATION: EXTENSION OF TIME: DEFAULT: DISCRETION: Pat. Ct)
Nachf's Application (APPEAL TO PATENT COURT: EXTENSION OF TIME TO APPEAL: Pat. Ct)
Nippon Gaishi KK's Application (EXTENSION OF PERIOD FOR REQUESTING SUBSTANTIVE EXAMINATION: DISCRETION: Pat. Ct)
OHI Seisakusho Co. Ltd's Application (INTERNATIONAL APPLICATION: TRANSLATION NOT FILED: Pat. Ct)
On Tat Bakelite Electric & Metal Works' Application (DESIGN: EXTENSION OF TIME FOR RENEWAL: RDAT)
P's Applications (EXTENSION OF TIME LIMIT: DIVISIONAL PATENT APPLICATION: C.-G.)
Thermo Technic Ltd's Application (Pat. Ct)
Tomy Kogyo Co. Inc.'s Applications (CONVENTION DESIGN APPLICATION: DISCRETION UNDER RULES TO EXTEND TIME: RDAT)

Title to Sue

Bondax Carpets Ltd v. Advance Carpet Tiles (PLAINTIFFS PROPRIETOR, SALES AND MARKETING COMPANY, AND MANUFACTURER: Ch.D.)

Transfers

CHC Software Card Ltd v. Hopkins & Wood (TRANSFER BETWEEN DIVISIONS: Ch.D.)
GEC-Marconi Ltd v. XYLLYX Viewdata Terminals Pte Ltd (TRANSFER TO PATENTS COUNTY COURT: Pat. Ct)
Mannesmann Kienzle GmbH v. Microsystem Design Ltd (TRANSFER TO PATENTS COUNTY COURT: Pat. Ct)
Memminger-Iro GmbH v. Trip-Lite Ltd (TRANSFER TO COUNTY COURT: FACTORS: DISCRETION: C.A.)

Mentor Corporation v. Colorplast A/S (TRANSFER FROM PATENTS COUNTY COURT TO HIGH COURT: COSTS: C.A.)

Slow Indicator v. Monitoring Systems Ltd (PRACTICE: TRANSFER FROM HIGH COURT TO PATENTS COUNTY COURT: APPLICATION REFUSED: Pat. Ct)

Symbol Technologies Inc. v. Opticon Sensors Europe BV (No. 2) (TRANSFER OF PETITION FOR REVOCATION OF PATENT TO COUNTY COURT: Pat. Ct)

Trap Order

Walt Disney Productions Ltd v. Gurvitz (CONTEMPT: *Agent provocateur*: Ch.D.)

Triable Issue. *See under* **Interlocutory Injunction**

Tribunal, Choice of

Sears plc v. Sears, Roebuck & Co. (INJUNCTION: *Res judicata*: Ch.D.)

Undertakings. *See also under* **Interlocutory Injunction** (*Cross-undertaking in damages*)

Bibby Bulk Carriers Ltd v. Cansulex Ltd (USE OF DOCUMENTS READ IN OPEN COURT: DISCLOSURE TO CLAIMANT IN ARBITRATION PROCEEDINGS: IMPLIED UNDERTAKING NOT TO USE DOCUMENT IN OTHER PROCEEDINGS: WHETHER NEW RULES RETROSPECTIVE IN EFFECT: Q.B.D.)

Butt v. Butt (MOTIONS: C.A.)

Dalgety Foods Holland BV v. Deb-Its Ltd (SETTLEMENT: INTENTION TO OBTAIN CONSENT ORDER INCORPORATING UNDERTAKINGS: ACTUAL WORDING NOT AGREED: WHETHER AGREEMENT BINDING: Ch.D.)

Gantenbrink v. BBC (COPYRIGHT: FILM: LIBERTY TO APPLY: Ch.D.)

Levi Strauss & Co. v. Barclays Trading Corp. Inc. (DISCLOSURE OF NAMES: WHETHER PLAINTIFF ESTOPPED FROM USING INFORMATION DISCLOSED AGAINST THIRD PARTIES: IMPLIED UNDERTAKING ON DISCOVERY: PROPER TIME FOR APPLICATION: Ch.D.)

Van der Lely (C.) NV v. Maulden Engineering Co. (Beds) Ltd (BREACH OF UNDERTAKING SETTLING ACTION: WHETHER VALIDITY A DEFENCE: WHETHER INFRINGEMENT WITHIN CLAIMS OF PATENT IN SUIT: Pat. Ct)

Wilden Pump & Engineering Co. v. Fusfield (DISCOVERY: SCOPE OF IMPLIED UNDERTAKING: CONTEMPT: Ch.D.)

Undue Influence

O'Sullivan v. Management Agency & Music Ltd (MANAGER AND ENTERTAINER: ACCOUNT OF PROFITS: INTEREST: C.A.)

Unquantifiable Harm. *See under* **Interlocutory Injunction** (*Unquantifiable harm*)

Vexatious Proceedings

Ixora Trading Incorporated v. Jones (STATEMENT OF CLAIM FRIVOLOUS AND VEXATIOUS: Ch.D.)

Roussel Uclaf's (Clemence & Le Martret) Patent (Pat. Ct)

Want of Prosecution, Dismissal For

Bestworth Ltd v. Wearwell Ltd (Ch.D)

Without Prejudice Correspondence

C. & H. Engineering v. F. Klucznik & Sons Ltd (WHETHER "WITHOUT PREJUDICE" CORRESPONDENCE AFTER *Calderbank* LETTER PRIVILEGED: Ch.D.)

Witness

Barlow Clowes Gilt Managers Ltd (WITNESS SUMMONS ISSUED IN CRIMINAL PROCEEDINGS REQUIRING COMPANY'S LIQUIDATORS TO DISCLOSE CONFIDENTIAL INFORMATION: WHETHER INFORMATION TO BE DISCLOSED: Ch.D.)

Black & Decker Inc. v. Flymo Ltd (SPECIFIC DISCOVERY BASED ON WITNESS STATEMENT EXCHANGED BEFORE TRIAL: PRIVILEGE: DISCOVERY: WHETHER PRIVILEGE LOST BY EXCHANGE OF WITNESS STATEMENTS: Ch.D.)

Gerber Garment Technology Inc. v. Lectra Systems Ltd (EXPERT WITNESS: Pat. Ct)

Glaverbel SA v. British Coal Corp. (Pat. Ct)

Glaverbel SA v. British Coal Corp. (No. 3) (WITNESS STATEMENT: OBJECT OF PARTICULARS: CROSS-EXAMINATION: Pat. Ct)

Ikarian Reefer, The (EXPERT WITNESSES: DUTIES AND RESPONSIBILITIES OF: Comm. Ct)

Optical Laboratories Ltd v. Hayden Laboratories Ltd (No. 1) (EXPERT WITNESSES: COSTS OF WITNESSES: C.A.)

Reckitt & Coleman Products Ltd v. Borden Inc. (No. 2) (EVIDENCE: MARKET RESEARCH WITNESS: Ch.D.)

Writ

Al Nahkel Ltd v. Lowe (*Ne exeat regno*: APPLICATION: MAREVA INJUNCTION: ALLEGED THIEF: FORM OF WRIT: Q.B.D.)

Allied Arab Bank Ltd v. Hajjar (MAREVA INJUNCTION: *Ne exeat regno*: PURPOSE: PREJUDICE TO DEFENDANT: Q.B.D.)

Banks v. CBS Songs Ltd (FURTHER INFRINGEMENTS ALLEGED AFTER ISSUE OF WRIT: WHETHER CONTINUOUS CAUSE OF ACTION: Ch.D.: C.A.)

Wyko Group plc v. Cooper Roller Bearings Co. Ltd (STRIKING OUT: Ch.D.)

Restrictive Practices

(For specific references to Articles in the Community Treaty and in Regulations, Statutes and References thereto, see under **Regulations and other Legislation**)

Abuse of Dominant Position. *See also* **Dominant Position**

AKZO Chemie BV v. E.C. Commission (BUSINESS SECRETS: NATURE OF: COMMUNICATION TO COMPLAINANT: ROLE OF E.C. COMMISSION: ECJ)

AKZO Chemie BV v. E.C. Commission (EUROPEAN COURT PROCEDURE: ADMINISTRATIVE PROCEDURE: DISCOVERY OF DOCUMENTS: RELEVANT PRODUCT MARKET: MARKET SHARE: PRICING: ECJ)

British Leyland Motor Corp. Ltd v. E.C. Commission (SUPPLY OF CERTIFICATES OF CONFORMITY FOR IMPORTED MOTOR VEHICLES: RELEVANT MARKET: DISCRIMINATORY FEES: ECJ)

Carrozzeria Grazia v. Volvo Italia (MOTOR CARS: TYPE APPROVAL: CERTIFICATES OF CONFORMITY: REFUSAL TO SUPPLY: CASE SETTLED: NOTICE: E.C. Comm.)

Centre Belge d'Etudes de Marché-Télé-Marketing SA v. Comp Luxembourgeoise de Télédiffusion SA (REMOVAL OF COMPETITION THROUGH LEGISLATION: ECJ)

San Pellegrino SpA v. Coca-Cola Export Corporation—Filiale Italiana (DISTRIBUTION AGREEMENTS: REBATES: OF FIDELITY REBATES AND PRODUCTION TARGET REBATES: SETTLEMENT ON UNDERTAKING TO DISCONTINUE REBATES: E.C. Comm.)

Tetra Pak Rausing SA v. E.C. Commission (CONSTITUTIONAL LAW: EEC TREATY: EXCLUSIVE LICENCES: GROUP EXEMPTIONS: LEGAL CERTAINTY: POWER OF NATIONAL COURTS: ECJ)

Volvo AB v. Erik Veng (U.K.) Ltd (INDUSTRIAL DESIGN RIGHTS: SPARE PARTS: OF REFUSAL TO LICENSE: NOT *per se* ABUSIVE: ECJ)

Warner-Lambert Company and BIC SA v. The Gillette Company and Eemland Holdings NV (COMPANY OWNERSHIP: ACQUISITION BY DOMINANT COMPANY OF SUBSTANTIAL HOLDING IN MAJOR COMPETITOR: CAUGHT BY ARTICLE 86: AGREEMENT TO ASSIGN NON-COMMUNITY BUSINESS AND TRADE MARKS TO DOMINANT FIRM: VIOLATION OF ARTICLE 85(1): ORDER TO DIVEST INTEREST IN COMPETITOR AND REASSIGN BUSINESS AND TRADE MARKS IN COUNTRIES BORDERING COMMUNITY: E.C. Comm.)

Acte Clair

Chiron Corporation v. Murex Diagnostics Ltd (No. 9) (PATENT: INFRINGEMENT: SECOND ACTION AFTER AMENDMENT OF AGREEMENT HELD CONTRARY TO P.A.77, S.44: PLEADINGS: AMENDMENT: WHETHER DEFENCE STRUCK OUT IN EARLIER ACTION CAN BE RAISED IN LATER ACTION: *Res judicata*: ARTICLE 177: Pat. Ct)

Agency

Holmsund Golv AB, Golvgripen AB & Armstrong World Industrie's Agreements (DISTRIBUTION AGREEMENTS: JOINT PRODUCT DEVELOPMENT: INTENTION TO APPROVE: NOTICE: EFTA Surveillance Authority)

Agents

Coleg de Agentes de la Propriedad Industrial (COAPI) (INDUSTRIAL PROPERTY AGENTS: SUBJECT TO COMPETITION RULES: FIXING OF MINIMUM FEES BY NATIONAL ASSOCIATION: CAUGHT BY ARTICLE: IRRELEVANT THAT BREACH SANCTIONED BY NATIONAL LEGISLATION: EXEMPTION REFUSED: NO FINE IMPOSED: E.C. Comm.)

Agreement to Standardise. *See under* Specialisation and Standardisation Agreements

Anti-competitive Practices

Bayer AG v. Süllhöfer (JUDICIAL PROCEDURE: PRELIMINARY RULINGS: MULTIPLE CLAIMS: PATENT LICENSING: COMMUNITY LAW AND NATIONAL LAW: NO-CHALLENGE CLAUSE: APPEAL ON POINT OF LAW: Germany: S.C.)

Approval. *See also under* Intention to Approve

Ford of Europe and Volkswagen's Joint Venture (E.C. Comm.)
X/Open Group (DECISION: E.C. Comm.)

Block Exemption

Austin Rover Group Ltd & Unipart Group Ltd (FORMER FELLOW SUBSIDIARIES WITHIN SAME GROUP: ARTICLE 85(1): DISTRIBUTION AGREEMENT: E.C. Comm.)

Computerland Europe SA's Franchise Agreements (FRANCHISING: AGREEMENTS: NOT CAUGHT BY ARTICLE 85(1) WHERE COMPETITIVE MARKET CONDITIONS PREVAIL: NON-COMPETITION CLAUSE: NOT CAUGHT PRIMA FACIE: CONTROL OF BUSINESS METHODS: EXCLUSIVE TERRITORIAL RIGHTS: SALE RESTRICTIONS: INTER-STATE TRADE: NON-APPLICABILITY OF BLOCK EXEMPTIONS UNDER REGULATIONS 67/67 AND 1983/83: INDIVIDUAL EXEMPTION GRANTED: E.C. Comm.)

Hydrotherm Gerätebau GmbH v. Compact de Dott Ing Mario Andreoli & CSAS (EXCLUSIVE DEALING: REGULATION 67/67: TRADE MARK LICENCE: ECJ)

Yves Rocher's Franchise Agreements (FRANCHISE AGREEMENTS: COMPETITION: INDUSTRIAL PROPERTY: EXCLUSIVE TERRITORIAL RIGHTS: DISTRIBUTION: PRICES: INTER-STATE TRADE: APPLICATION FOR NEGATIVE CLEARANCE: E.C. Comm.)

Broadcasting

Auditel (JOINT VENTURE: EXCLUSIVE USE OF AUDIENCE RATING SYSTEM: CAUGHT BY ARTICLE 85(1): EXEMPTION REFUSED: E.C. Comm.)

Koelman v. E.C. Commission (BROADCASTING: RETRANSMISSION OF PROGRAMMES BY CABLE: STANDARD AGREEMENT: COPYRIGHT: OWNERSHIP: RADIO MATERIAL: COLLECTING SOCIETY: ALLEGED BREACH OF ARTICLES 85 AND 86: Case T–575/93: CFI)

Bundling

Community v. International Business Machines (DOMINANT POSITION: ABUSE: NEW COMPUTERS: TECHNICAL INFORMATION: ECC)

Business Secrets

AKZO Chemie BV v. E.C. Commission (NATURE OF: DOMINANT POSITION: ABUSE: COMMUNICATION TO COMPLAINANT: ROLE OF E.C. COMMISSION: ECJ)

British American Tobacco Co. Ltd v. E.C. Commission (ECJ PROCEDURE: ORAL ARGUMENTS: EVIDENCE: DISCOVERY: ECJ)

Hilti AG v. E.C. Commission (CONFIDENTIALITY OF BUSINESS SECRETS: INTERVENERS: LEGAL PROFESSIONAL PRIVILEGE: APPLICABLE TO WRITTEN COMMUNICATIONS BETWEEN INDEPENDENT LAWYER AND CLIENT COMPANY: INTERESTS OF RIGHT OF DEFENCE: PROCEDURE: CFI)

Cease and Desist Order

Velcro SA v. Aplix SA (PATENT AND TRADE MARK LICENCES: EXCLUSIVITY: EXPORT BAN: EXTENSION BEYOND EXPIRY OF RIGHTS: NON-COMPETITION OBLIGATION: IMPROVEMENT PATENTS: ESSENTIAL FUNCTION OF TRADE MARK: EXEMPTION REFUSED: E.C. Comm)

Collecting Societies

Basset v. SACEM (COPYRIGHT: France: S.C.)

GEMA (COPYRIGHT: INWARD PROCESSING: CUSTOM PRESSING: E.C. Comm.)

Koelman v. E.C. Commission (BROADCASTING: RETRANSMISSION OF PROGRAMMES BY CABLE: STANDARD AGREEMENT: COPYRIGHT: OWNERSHIP: RADIO MATERIAL: COLLECTING SOCIETY: ALLEGED BREACH OF ARTICLES 85 AND 86: Case T–575/93: CFI)

Performing Right Societies (COPYRIGHT: PARALLEL IMPORTS: ROYALTIES: NOTICE: E.C. Comm.)

SDRM's Practices (FOREIGN WORKS: IMPORTS: COPYRIGHT: DISCRIMINATORY PRACTICES: DOMINANT POSITION: France: Competition Commission)

Comfort Letter

Alupower-Chloride Ltd (JOINT VENTURE: JOINT DEVELOPMENT, PRODUCTION AND DISTRIBUTION OF ALUMINIUM/AIR BATTERY: INTENTION TO ISSUE COMFORT LETTER: E.C. Comm.)

CBA's Application (PLANT BREEDERS' RIGHTS: LICENSING AGREEMENTS: NOTICE: E.C. Comm.)

Chanel SA's Application (SELECTIVE DISTRIBUTION: MODIFICATION OF ADMISSION PROCEDURE: INTENTION TO ISSUE COMFORT LETTER: E.C.C)

Davide Campari Milano SpA's Application (DISTRIBUTION SYSTEM: APPLICATION TO RENEW EXEMPTION: COMFORT LETTER INSTEAD: E.C. Comm.)

Société Française de Dev't de la Boîte-Boissons (SOFREB) (JOINT SUBSIDIARY: INTENTION TO APPROVE: E.C. Comm.)

Vallourec and Nyby Uddeholm AB's Agreement (FRANCO-SWEDISH JOINT VENTURE: JOINT SUBSIDIARY: INTENTION TO APPROVE: E.C. Comm.)

Commission's Power

Bureau Européen des Unions Consommateurs v. E.C. Commission (DISCRETIONARY POWERS OF COMMISSION: REFUSAL TO TAKE UP COMPLAINT: Case T-37/92: CFI)

Complaint

Bureau Européen des Média de l'Industrie Musicale v. Commission for the European Communities (BREACH OF ARTICLE 85 AND ARTICLE 86 BY SACEM: REFERENCE TO NATIONAL COURTS: APPLICATION FOR ANNULMENT: CFI)

Compulsory Patent Licences. *See under* Patent Licensing

Confidentiality

A.M. & S. Ltd v. E.C. Commission (ADMINISTRATIVE PROCEDURE: LAWYERS: PRIVILEGE: ECJ)

Apple Corp.'s Ltd v. Apple Computer Inc. (RESTRICTIVE PRACTICES: TRADE MARKS: NATIONAL PROCEEDINGS IN PARALLEL WITH E.C. COMMISSION PROCEEDINGS: CONFIDENTIAL EVIDENCE BEFORE NATIONAL COURT TO BE HANDED TO E.C. COMMISSION: Ch.D.)

Hercules NV, SA v. E.C. Commission (ADMINISTRATIVE PROCEDURE: SUPPLY OF DOCUMENTS: CFI)

Hillegom Municipality v. Hillenius (BANKING: NATIONAL COURTS: CIVIL PROCEEDINGS: PROFESSIONAL PRIVILEGE: ECJ)

Hilti AG v. E.C. Commission (BUSINESS SECRETS: INTERVENERS: LEGAL PROFESSIONAL PRIVILEGE: APPLICABLE TO WRITTEN COMMUNICATIONS BETWEEN INDEPENDENT LAWYER AND CLIENT COMPANY: INTERESTS OF RIGHT OF DEFENCE: CFI)

Co-operation Agreements

BBC Brown Boveri AG and NGK Insulators Ltd's Agreement (JOINT VENTURES: JOINT DEVELOPMENT: INTENTION TO APPROVE: E.C. Comm.)

Digital Equipment Corporation and Ing C. Olivetti & Co. SpA's Agreement (COMPUTER SYSTEMS: TECHNOLOGY TRANSFER: INTENTION TO APPROVE: NOTICE: E.C. Comm.)

Copyright and Design Copyright

Basset v. SACEM (PHONOGRAMS: COPYRIGHT MANAGEMENT SOCIETIES: RESTRICTION OF CIRCULATION: ROYALTIES: ARTICLE 30: ARTICLE 86: ECJ)

Basset v. SACEM (COLLECTING SOCIETIES: France: S.C.)

British Broadcasting Corp. and Independent Television Publications Ltd (U.K. MMC Comm.)

BBC v. E.C. Commission (BROADCASTING: WEEKLY LISTINGS OF TV PROGRAMMES: REFUSAL TO PERMIT REPRODUCTION IN INDEPENDENT TV GUIDE: ARTICLE 86: COMMISSION ENTITLED TO REQUIRE LICENSING FOR REPRODUCTION OF THE LISTINGS: CFI)

Car Parts (SPARE PARTS: EXCLUSIVE PACKAGING: DOMINANT POSITION: DESIGN COPYRIGHT: U.K. Monopolies Commission)

Coditel SA v. CinéVog Films SA (PERFORMING RIGHTS: EXCLUSIVE LICENCE: ECJ)

Copyright in Court Proceedings (LAWYERS PLEADINGS: TEST: PROTECTION: PUBLICATION: Germany: S.C.)

GEMA (COLLECTING SOCIETIES: INWARD PROCESSING: CUSTOM PRESSING: E.C. Comm.)

GEMA (E.C. Comm.)

Gesellschaft zur Verwertung von Leistungsschutzrechten v. E.C. Commission (ADMINISTRATIVE PROCEDURE: MARKET PARTITIONING: INTER-STATE TRADE: DOMINANT POSITION: ABUSE: ECJ)

Imprimerie (SA) Thône v. Fernand Geubelle (INTELLIGENCE TEST: PUBLISHER AS CO-AUTHOR: *Locus standi*: Belgium)

Independent Television Publications Ltd v. E.C. Commission (BROADCASTING: WEEKLY LISTINGS OF TV PROGRAMMES: REFUSAL TO PERMIT REPRODUCTION IN INDEPENDENT TV GUIDE: ARTICLE 86: COMMISSION ENTITLED TO REQUIRE LICENSING FOR REPRODUCTION OF THE LISTINGS: CFI)

Koelman v. E.C. Commission (BROADCASTING: RETRANSMISSION OF PROGRAMMES BY CABLE: STANDARD AGREEMENT: COPYRIGHT: OWNERSHIP: RADIO MATERIAL: COLLECTING SOCIETY: ALLEGED BREACH OF ARTICLES 85 AND 86: Case T–575/93: CFI)

Ministère Public v. Lucazeau (SACEM, *partie civile*) (INFRINGEMENT: COLLECTION AGENCIES: STATUS: CRIMINAL OFFENCE: PERFORMANCE: DOMINANT POSITION: ABUSE: France: C.A.)

Performing Right Societies (COLLECTING SOCIETIES: PARALLEL IMPORTS: ROYALTIES: NOTICE: E.C. Comm.)

Philips International BV's Application (JOINT DEVELOPMENT OF DIGITAL COMPACT CASSETTES: PATENT LICENSING: INTENTION TO APPROVE: E.C. Comm.)

Racal Group Services' Application (ARTICLES 85 AND 86: DOMINANT POSITION: RELEVANT MARKET: PROTECTION OF MONOPOLY POSITION THROUGH MARKET ALLOCATION AGREEMENT: COERCION OF UNWILLING PARTIES: ABUSIVE: USE OF COPYRIGHT AS BASIS OF AGREEMENTS ILLEGAL: JUSTIFICATION: E.C. Comm.)

Radio Telefis Eireann v. E.C. Commission (BROADCASTING: WEEKLY LISTINGS OF TV PROGRAMMES: REFUSAL TO PERMIT REPRODUCTION IN INDEPENDENT TV GUIDE: ARTICLE 86: COMMISSION ENTITLED TO REQUIRE LICENSING FOR REPRODUCTION OF THE LISTINGS: ADMINISTRATIVE PROCEDURE: ADVISORY COMMITTEE ON RESTRICTIVE PRACTICES AND DOMINANT POSITIONS: MINUTES OF ORAL HEARINGS: NOTICE OF SITTING: CFI)

Radio Telefis Eireann v. Magill TV Guide Ltd (RADIO AND TELEVISION SCHEDULES: LITERARY WORK: COMMUNITY LAW AND NATIONAL LAW: JUDICIAL PROCEDURE: EVIDENCE: Ireland: H.C.)

SDRM's Practices (COLLECTING SOCIETIES: FOREIGN WORKS: IMPORTS: DISCRIMINATORY PRACTICES: DOMINANT POSITION: France: Competition Commission)

STEMRA (EEC: LICENSING: E.C. Comm.)

Tosca (OPERA: PERIOD OF PROTECTION: FOREIGN AUTHORS: EVIDENCE: INTERNATIONAL CONVENTION AND NATIONAL LAWS: Germany: S.C.)

Copyright Management Societies

Basset v. SACEM (COPYRIGHT: PHONOGRAMS: RESTRICTION OF CIRCULATION: ROYALTIES: ARTICLE 30: ARTICLE 86: ECJ)

Counterfeit Goods

Uruguay Round Treaties (REPORTING, *inter alia:* GATT: INTELLECTUAL PROPERTY: COUNTERFEIT GOODS: TRIPS RULES PROHIBITING RELEASE INTO FREE CIRCULATION: ECJ)

Court of First Instance Procedure. *See under* Procedure *(Court of First Instance procedure)*

Design Copyright. *See under* Copyright

Discovery. *See* Practice *(Discovery)*

Discrimination

Du Pont de Nemours & Co. and AKZO NV (INTERNATIONAL TRADE: U.S. LITIGATION: UNFAIR COMMERCIAL PRACTICES: IMPORTS: PATENTS: PARALLEL IMPORTS: GATT PROCEDURE: E.C. Comm.)

Newitt & Co. Ltd v. Dunlop Slazenger International Ltd (DISTRIBUTION AGREEMENTS: PARALLEL IMPORTS: EXPORT BANS: REFUSAL TO SUPPLY: EXCLUSIVE DEALING: CONCERTED PRACTICES: PRICES: SUBSIDIES: BUY-BACK SCHEMES: E.C. Comm.)

Discriminatory Fees or Pricing

British Leyland Motor Corp. Ltd v. E.C. Commission (DOMINANT POSITION: SUPPLY OF CERTIFICATES OF CONFORMITY FOR IMPORTED MOTOR VEHICLES: RELEVANT MARKET: ABUSE: ECJ)

Elopak Italia Srl v. Tetra Pak (No. 2) (DOMINANT POSITION: ABUSE: RELEVANT PRODUCT MARKET: SALES CONTRACTS: TYING CLAUSES: EXCLUSIVE SUPPLY: ELIMINATORY PRICING: E.C. Comm.)

Hilti AG v. E.C. Commission (DOMINANT COMPANY: COMPULSORY PATENT LICENCES: EXTORTIONATE FEES: SELECTIVE AND DISCRIMINATORY SALES POLICY: ABUSE: NOT JUSTIFIED BY SAFETY WORRIES: CFI)

Newitt & Co. Ltd v. Dunlop Slazenger International Ltd (DISTRIBUTION AGREEMENTS: PARALLEL IMPORTS: EXPORT BANS: REFUSAL TO SUPPLY: EXCLUSIVE DEALING: CONCERTED PRACTICES: PRICES: SUBSIDIES: BUY-BACK SCHEMES: E.C. Comm.)

Discriminatory Practices

SDRM's Practices (COLLECTING SOCIETIES: FOREIGN WORKS: IMPORTS: COPYRIGHT: DISCRIMINATORY PRACTICES: DOMINANT POSITION: France: Competition Commission)

Discriminatory Pricing. *See under* Discriminatory Fees or Pricing

Distribution Agreements

Association Pharmaceutique Belge (APB's) Application (PARAPHARMACEUTICALS: COLLECTIVE QUALITY CONTROL: STANDARD FORM AGREEMENT OFFERED BY PHARMACIST'S TRADE ASSOCIATION: RIGHT TO AFFIX SEAL OF APPROVAL TO GOODS: SALE NEGATIVE CLEARANCE: E.C. Comm.)

Austin Rover Group Ltd & Unipart Group Ltd (FORMER FELLOW SUBSIDIARIES WITHIN SAME GROUP: ARTICLE 85(1): BLOCK EXEMPTION: E.C. Comm.)

Community v. Fiat Auto (TYING CLAUSES: SETTLEMENT: E.C. Comm.)

Holmsund Golv AB, Golvgripen AB & Armstrong World Industries' Agreements (AGENCY: JOINT PRODUCT DEVELOPMENT: INTENTION TO APPROVE: NOTICE: EFTA Surveillance Authority)

Ivoclar AG's Agreement (No. 2) (EXCLUSIVE DISTRIBUTION AGREEMENT: INTENTION TO EXTEND EXEMPTION: NOTICE: E.C. Comm.)

Newitt & Co. Ltd v. Dunlop Slazenger International Ltd (PARALLEL IMPORTS: EXPORT BANS: REFUSAL TO SUPPLY: EXCLUSIVE DEALING: CONCERTED PRACTICES: PRICES: SUBSIDIES: BUY-BACK SCHEMES: DISCRIMINATION: E.C. Comm.)

Philips Export BV and John Fluke Manufacturing Co. Inc.'s Agreements (RECIPROCAL EXCLUSIVE DISTRIBUTION AGREEMENTS: PARTIES DIRECT COMPETITORS IN SOME PRODUCTS, SO NOT COVERED BY GROUP EXEMPTION REGULATION 1983/83: INTENTION TO GRANT INDIVIDUAL EXEMPTION: E.C. Comm.)

San Pellegrino SpA v. Coca-Cola Export Corp.—Filiale Italiana (REBATES: ABUSE OF DOMINANT POSITION: FIDELITY REBATES AND PRODUCTION TARGET REBATES: SETTLEMENT ON UNDERTAKING TO DISCONTINUE REBATES: E.C. Comm.)

Sony España SA (EXCLUSIVE AND SELECTIVE DISTRIBUTION AGREEMENT: INTENTION TO EXEMPT: NOTICE: E.C. Comm.)

Dominant Position. See also under **Abuse of Dominant Position**

AKZO Chemie BV v. E.C. Commission (EUROPEAN COURT PROCEDURE: INTERIM MEASURES: UNDERCUTTING: REQUEST FOR INTERIM SUSPENSION: REFUSAL: ECJ)

Car Parts (SPARE PARTS: EXCLUSIVE PACKAGING: DESIGN COPYRIGHT: U.K. Monopolies Commission)

Elopak v. Tetra Pak (RELEVANT MARKET: PRODUCT MARKET: GEOGRAPHICAL MARKET: TAKE-OVERS: EXCLUSIVE LICENSING: INTER-STATE TRADE: E.C. Comm.)

Engineering and Chemical Supplies (Epsom & Glos) Ltd v. AKZO Chemie BV (RELEVANT MARKET: PRODUCT MARKET: RELEVANT CRITERIA: E.C. Comm.)

Mecaniver SA and PPG Industries' Agreement (COMPANY TRANSFER: SALE OF SHARES: MARKET SHARE: E.C. Comm.)

Merson v. British Leyland plc (IMPORT RESTRICTIONS: FINES: E.C. Comm.)

Nederlandsche Banden-Industrie Michelin NV v. E.C. Commission (PRACTICE: ECJ)

Oy Airam AB v. Osram GmbH (EEC: TRADE MARK: E.C. Comm.)

Racal Group Services' Application ("UNDERTAKINGS": PARENT COMPANY AND SUBSIDIARIES: ARTICLES 85 AND 86: RELEVANT MARKET: PROTECTION OF MONOPOLY POSITION THROUGH MARKET ALLOCATION AGREEMENT: COERCION OF UNWILLING PARTIES: ABUSIVE: USE OF COPYRIGHT AS BASIS OF AGREEMENTS ILLEGAL: JUSTIFICATION: E.C. Comm.)

Radio Telefis Eireann v. E.C. Commission (BROADCASTING: WEEKLY LISTINGS OF TV PROGRAMMES: COPYRIGHT: REFUSAL TO PERMIT REPRODUCTION IN INDEPENDENT TV GUIDE: ARTICLE 86: COMMISSION ENTITLED TO REQUIRE LICENSING FOR REPRODUCTION OF THE LISTINGS: ADMINISTRATIVE PROCEDURE: ADVISORY COMMITTEE ON RESTRICTIVE PRACTICES AND DOMINANT POSITIONS: MINUTES OF ORAL HEARINGS: NOTICE OF SITTING: CFI)

Schmalbach-Lubeca AG v. Carnaud SA (MERGERS: CONCERTED PRACTICES: E.C. Comm.)

SDRM's Practices (COLLECTING SOCIETIES: FOREIGN WORKS: IMPORTS: COPYRIGHT: DISCRIMINATORY PRACTICES: France: Competition Commission)

Société Française de Transmissions Florales Interflora & Téléfleurs France (EXCLUSIVITY CLAUSE: PROTECTION OF TRADE MARK: MINIMUM TARIFF ORDER: France: Copyright Commission)

Telespeed Services Ltd v. U.K. Post Office (E.C. Comm.)

Eliminatory Pricing

Elopak Italia Srl v. Tetra Pak (No. 2) (DOMINANT POSITION: ABUSE: RELEVANT PRODUCT MARKET: SALES CONTRACTS: TYING CLAUSES: EXCLUSIVE SUPPLY: DISCRIMINATORY PRICING: E.C. Comm.)

European Court Procedure. See under **Procedure** (European Court procedure)

Exclusive Dealing

Camera Care Ltd v. Victor Hasselblad AB (AFTER-SALES SERVICES: E.C. Comm.)

Community v. Fanuc Ltd and Siemens AG (MARKET PARTITIONING: JOINT RESEARCH AND DEVELOPMENT: GROUP EXEMPTION NOT APPLICABLE: NO NOTIFICATION, SO NO INDIVIDUAL EXEMPTION: BREACH OF ARTICLE 85(1): FINES IMPOSED: E.C. Comm.)

DDD Ltd and Delta Chemie's Agreement (KNOW-HOW: TRADE MARKS: LICENCE CAUGHT BY ARTICLE 85(1): GROUP EXEMPTION: REGULATION 1983/83 NOT APPLICABLE: INDIVIDUAL EXEMPTION GRANTED: E.C. Comm.)

Distillers Company plc's Application (RESTRICTIONS ON MANUFACTURER AND DISTRIBUTOR: REGULATION 67/67: INDIVIDUAL EXEMPTION: E.C. Comm.)

ETA Fabriques d'Ebauches SA v. DK Investment SA (DISTRIBUTION NETWORK: RESTRICTION ON SELLING OUTSIDE CONTRACT TERRITORY: ECJ)

Ford Werke's Agreement (No. 2) (EXCLUSIVE DEALERSHIP: E.C. Comm.)

Friedrich Grohe Armaturenfabrik GmbH & Co.'s Application (SELECTIVE DISTRIBUTION: E.C. Comm.)

Hydrotherm Gertebau GmbH v. Compact de Dott Ing Mario Andreoli & CSAS (BLOCK EXEMPTION: REGULATION 67/67: TRADE MARK LICENCE: ECJ)

Ideal-Standard GmbH's Application (SELECTIVE DISTRIBUTION SYSTEMS: WHOLESALERS: PLUMBING FITTINGS: E.C. Comm.)

Masterfoods Ltd v. HB Ice Cream Ltd (COMMUNITY LAW AND NATIONAL LAW: PRIORITY OF COMMUNITY LAW: NATIONAL COURTS: STANDARD OF PROOF: PENALTIES: INTER-STATE TRADE: RETAIL TRADE: VERTICAL AGREEMENTS: PROVISIONAL VALIDITY: DOMINANT POSITION: RELEVANT MARKET: ABUSE: REFERENCE TO E.C. COMMISSION: EXCLUSIVE DEALING AGREEMENTS: EVIDENCE: Ireland: H.C.)

Newitt & Co. Ltd v. Dunlop Slazenger International Ltd (DISTRIBUTION AGREEMENTS: PARALLEL IMPORTS: EXPORT BANS: REFUSAL TO SUPPLY: CONCERTED PRACTICES: PRICES: SUBSIDIES: BUY-BACK SCHEMES: DISCRIMINATION: E.C. Comm.)

Polistil SpA & Arbois-Modelud's Agreement (PARALLEL IMPORTS: E.C. Comm.)

Exclusive Distribution Agreements

Whisky and Gin (Sole distribution agreements) (GROUP EXEMPTION: INTENTION TO EXEMPT: E.C. Comm.)

Yves Rocher's Franchise Agreements (FRANCHISE AGREEMENTS: COMPETITION: INDUSTRIAL PROPERTY: EXCLUSIVE TERRITORIAL RIGHTS: BLOCK EXEMPTION: PRICES: INTER-STATE TRADE: APPLICATION FOR NEGATIVE CLEARANCE: E.C. Comm.)

Exclusive Licensing

Auditel (BROADCASTING: JOINT VENTURE: EXCLUSIVE USE OF AUDIENCE RATING SYSTEM: CAUGHT BY ARTICLE 85(1): EXEMPTION REFUSED: E.C. Comm.)

BBC Brown Boveri and NGK Insulators Ltd's Agreements (JOINT VENTURE: GERMAN-JAPANESE JOINT RESEARCH AND DEVELOPMENT: KNOW-HOW: GROUP EXEMPTION: INAPPLICABILITY OF REGULATION 418/85: INDIVIDUAL EXEMPTION GRANTED: E.C. Comm.)

Boussois SA and Interpane & Co. KG's Agreement (PATENT LICENCE: UNPATENTED KNOW-HOW: EXCLUSIVE LICENCE TO MANUFACTURE: IMPROVEMENT KNOW-HOW: INTENTION TO EXEMPT: E.C. Comm.)

Elopak v. Tetra Pak (DOMINANT POSITION: RELEVANT MARKET: PRODUCT MARKET: GEOGRAPHICAL MARKET: TAKE-OVERS: INTER-STATE TRADE: E.C. Comm.)

Nungesser KG v. E.C. Commission (PLANT VARIETIES: MAIZE SEEDS: ECJ)

Tetra Pak Rausing SA v. E.C. Commission (CONSTITUTIONAL LAW: EEC TREATY: DOMINANT POSITION: ABUSE: GROUP EXEMPTIONS: LEGAL CERTAINTY: POWER OF NATIONAL COURTS: ECJ)

TYLER Trade Mark (EEC: TRADE MARK: E.C. Comm.)

Exclusive Packaging

Car Parts (SPARE PARTS: DOMINANT POSITION: DESIGN COPYRIGHT: U.K. Monopolies Commission)

Exclusive Territory

Computerland Europe SA's Franchise Agreements (FRANCHISING: AGREEMENTS: NOT CAUGHT BY ARTICLE 85(1) WHERE COMPETITIVE MARKET CONDITIONS PREVAIL: NON-COMPETITION CLAUSE: NOT CAUGHT PRIMA FACIE: CONTROL OF BUSINESS METHODS: SALE RESTRICTIONS: INTER-STATE TRADE: NON-APPLICABILITY OF BLOCK EXEMPTIONS UNDER REGULATIONS 67/67 AND 1983/83: INDIVIDUAL EXEMPTION GRANTED: E.C. Comm)

Fiat Geotech Technologie Per La Terra SpA and Hitachi Construction Machinery Co. Ltd's Joint Venture (JOINT VENTURES: JOINT MANUFACTURE, DISTRIBUTION AND SALE OF HYDRAULIC EXCAVATORS: COMMUNITY MARKET EXCLUSIVE TO JOINT VENTURE AND REST OF WORLD EXCLUSIVE TO ONE PARENT COMPANY: PASSIVE SALES INTO EACH OTHER'S TERRITORY PERMITTED: INTENTION TO EXEMPT: E.C. Comm.)

Moosehead Breweries Ltd and Whitbread and Company plc's Agreement (LICENCE FOR PRODUCTION AND SALE OF CANADIAN BEER IN U.K.: NON-EXCLUSIVE WITH ANCILLARY RESTRICTIONS FOR KNOW-HOW: PROHIBITION ON SALE OUTSIDE U.K. AND SALE OF COMPETING BRANDS AND EXCLUSIVITY FOR TRADE MARK: ARTICLE 85(1): NO CHALLENGE CLAUSE: OWNERSHIP: POSSIBLY RESTRICTIVE AS REGARDS VALIDITY: COMPARATIVELY NEW TO U.K.: EXEMPTION GRANTED: E.C. Comm.)

Newitt & Co. Ltd v. Dunlop Slazenger International Ltd (DISTRIBUTION AGREEMENTS: PARALLEL IMPORTS: EXPORT BANS: REFUSAL TO SUPPLY: EXCLUSIVE DEALING: CONCERTED PRACTICES: PRICES: SUBSIDIES: BUY-BACK SCHEMES: DISCRIMINATION: E.C. Comm.)

Yves Rocher's Franchise Agreements (FRANCHISE AGREEMENTS: COMPETITION: INDUSTRIAL PROPERTY: EXCLUSIVE TERRITORIAL RIGHTS: DISTRIBUTION: BLOCK EXEMPTION: PRICES: INTER-STATE TRADE: APPLICATION FOR NEGATIVE CLEARANCE: E.C. Comm.)

Exhaustion of Rights

Bristol Myers Squibb v. Paranova (PARALLEL IMPORTS: REPACKAGING OF GOODS: RESTRICTIONS FOR PROTECTION OF INDUSTRIAL AND COMMERCIAL PROPERTY: DISGUISED RESTRICTION ON TRADE BETWEEN MEMBER STATES: ECJ)

Hag Coffee (TRADE MARKS: HAG: SPECIFIC SUBJECT-MATTER: CONSEQUENCES: IMPORTS: BREAK OF CHAIN OF OWNERSHIP BY EXPROPRIATION: GERMAN HAG ABLE TO RESIST IMPORT INTO GERMANY OF BELGIAN HAG COFFEE: *Acte claire* FROM EUROPEAN COURT JUDGMENT IN *Pharmon v. Hoechst*: NO ARTICLE 177 REFERENCE: Germany: C.A.)

Société de Vente de Ciments et Betons de l'Est SA v. Kerpen & Kerpen GmbH & Co. KG (ECJ)

Export Bans

Burns (W.) Tractors Ltd v. Sperry New Holland (REFUSAL TO SUPPLY: PARALLEL TRADE: EXEMPTION: FINES: NOTIFICATION: E.C. Comm.)

Community v. Bayer AG (AGREEMENTS: RESALE RESTRICTIONS: TRADE MARKS: PACKAGING: E.C. Comm.)
Newitt & Co. Ltd v. Dunlop Slazenger International Ltd (DISTRIBUTION AGREEMENTS: PARALLEL IMPORTS: REFUSAL TO SUPPLY: EXCLUSIVE DEALING: CONCERTED PRACTICES: PRICES: SUBSIDIES: BUY-BACK SCHEMES: DISCRIMINATION: E.C. Comm.)
Viho Europe BV v. Parker Pen Ltd (DISTRIBUTION AGREEMENTS: LIABILITY: E.C. Comm.)

Extraterritorial Jurisdiction

Wood Pump Cartel A. Ahlstrom Oy v. E.C. Commission (CONCERTED PRACTICES: EFFECT ON COMPETITION WITHIN COMMUNITY: STREAM OF COMMERCE DOCTRINE: TERRITORIALITY: INTERNATIONAL LAW: INTERNATIONAL COMITY: EXPORT CARTELS: ECJ)

Fines

BAT Cigaretten-Fabriken GmbH v. E.C. Comm (TRADE MARKS: DORCET AND TOLTECS SPECIAL: DORMANT MARK: SIMILARITY: INFRINGEMENT OF ARTICLE 85: E.C. COMM. UPHELD: ECJ)
Burns (W.) Tractors Ltd v. Sperry New Holland (CONTRACTS: EXPORT BANS: REFUSAL TO SUPPLY: PARALLEL TRADE: EXEMPTION: NOTIFICATION: E.C. Comm.)
Central Wine Buyers Ltd v. Moet et Chandon Ltd (EXPORT PROHIBITION: E.C. Comm.)
Community v. Bayer AG (RESALE BAN: MARKET POSITIONING: FEEDINGSTUFF ADDITIVES: EXPIRY OF PATENT IN ONE STATE: PARALLEL TRADE ARTICLE 85(1): E.C. Comm.)
Community v. Fanuc Ltd and Siemens AG (EXCLUSIVE DEALING: MARKET PARTITIONING: JOINT RESEARCH AND DEVELOPMENT: GROUP EXEMPTION NOT APPLICABLE: EXCLUSIVE DEALING: NO NOTIFICATION, SO NO INDIVIDUAL EXEMPTION: BREACH OF ARTICLE 85(1): E.C. Comm.)
Community v. Unilever NV (EXCHANGE OF SALES INFORMATION: RESTRICTIVE OF COMPETITION: INFRINGEMENT: ECJ)
Eurofix Ltd and Bauco (U.K.) Ltd v. Hilti AG (RESPONSIBILITY OF PARENT COMPANY FOR ACTIONS OF SUBSIDIARIES: DOMINANT POSITION: SAFETY WORRIES DO NOT JUSTIFY ABUSIVE CONDUCT WHERE ADEQUATE STANDARDS EXIST THROUGHOUT EEC: DOMINANT COMPANY RESTRICTING AVAILABILITY OF PATENTED PRODUCT: OBSTRUCTING INDEPENDENT MANUFACTURERS OF PRODUCTS ONLY CAPABLE OF USE WITH THE PATENTED PRODUCT FROM PENETRATING MARKET: ABUSE: E.C. Comm.)
Merson v. British Leyland plc (DOMINANT POSITION: IMPORT RESTRICTIONS: E.C. Comm.)

Franchising and Franchising Agreements

Compagnie Luxembourgeoise de Télédiffusion (BROADCASTING FRANCHISES: ADMINISTRATIVE PROCEDURE: JUDICIAL REVIEW: *Locus standi*: France: Conseil d'Etat)
Computerland Europe SA's Franchise Agreements (AGREEMENTS: NOT CAUGHT BY ARTICLE 85(1) WHERE COMPETITIVE MARKET CONDITIONS PREVAIL: NON-COMPETITION CLAUSE: NOT CAUGHT PRIMA FACIE: CONTROL OF BUSINESS METHODS: EXCLUSIVE TERRITORIAL RIGHTS: SALE RESTRICTIONS: INTER-STATE TRADE: NON-APPLICABILITY OF BLOCK EXEMPTIONS UNDER REGULATIONS 67/67 AND 1983/83: INDIVIDUAL EXEMPTION GRANTED: E.C. Comm.)

Computerland Europe SA (INTENTION TO APPROVE: E.C. Comm.)
Franchising Agreements Draft Regulation (GROUP EXEMPTION: E.C. Comm.)
Franchising Agreements Regulation 1988 (4087/88) (GROUP EXEMPTION: LEGISLATION: E.C. Comm.)
Kall-Kwik Printing (U.K.) Ltd v. Bell (FRANCHISE AGREEMENT: RESTRICTIVE COVENANT: ENFORCEABILITY: ARTICLE 85: REASONABLENESS: INTERLOCUTORY INJUNCTION: Ch.D.)
Procureur de la République & SA Vêtements Goguet Sport v. Hechter (RESALE PRICE MAINTENANCE: REFUSAL TO SELL: France: D.C.)
Pronuptia de Paris SA (Agreements) (E.C. Comm.)
Servicemaster Ltd (Franchise Agreements) (SERVICE FRANCHISES TREATED IN SAME WAY AS DISTRIBUTION AGREEMENTS: PROTECTION OF KNOW-HOW OUTSIDE ARTICLE 85(1): TERRITORIAL PROTECTION CAUGHT: INTERSTATE TRADE: INTRA-BRAND COMPETITION: INDIVIDUAL EXEMPTION GRANTED: E.C. Comm.)
Servicemaster Ltd's Franchise Agreements (INTENTION TO APPROVE: ECC)
United International Pictures BV's Application (JOINT VENTURE: THEATRICAL DISTRIBUTION OF FILMS: INTENTION TO EXEMPT: E.C. Comm.)
Yves Rocher's Franchise Agreements (AGREEMENTS: RESTRICTION ON COMMERCIAL FREEDOM: KNOW-HOW: ARTICLE 85(1): E.C. Comm.)
Yves Rocher's Franchise Agreements (COMPETITION: INDUSTRIAL PROPERTY: EXCLUSIVE TERRITORIAL RIGHTS: DISTRIBUTION: BLOCK EXEMPTION: PRICES: INTER-STATE TRADE: APPLICATION FOR NEGATIVE CLEARANCE: E.C. Comm.)

Group Exemption

Alcatel Espace SA and Ant Nachrichtentechniks Agreement (SATELLITE COMMUNICATIONS EQUIPMENT: JOINT RESEARCH AND DEVELOPMENT, PRODUCTION AND MARKETING: CAUGHT BY ARTICLE 85(1): JOINT TENDERING, SO INELIGIBLE FOR GROUP EXEMPTION: INDIVIDUAL EXEMPTION GRANTED: E.C. Comm.)
BBC Brown Boveri and NGK Insulators Ltd's Agreements (JOINT VENTURE: GERMAN-JAPANESE JOINT RESEARCH AND DEVELOPMENT: EXCLUSIVE LICENSING: KNOW-HOW: INAPPLICABILITY OF REGULATION 418/85: INDIVIDUAL EXEMPTION GRANTED: E.C. Comm.)
Boussois SA and Interpane & Co. KG's Agreement (PATENT LICENCE: RELEVANCE: DECISION: E.C. Comm.)
Community v. Fanuc Ltd and Siemens AG (EXCLUSIVE DEALING: MARKET PARTITIONING: JOINT RESEARCH AND DEVELOPMENT: EXCLUSIVE DEALING: NO NOTIFICATION, SO NO INDIVIDUAL EXEMPTION: BREACH OF ARTICLE 85(1): FINES IMPOSED: E.C. Comm.)
DDD Ltd and Delta Chemie's Agreement (KNOW-HOW: EXCLUSIVE DEALING: TRADE MARKS: LICENCE CAUGHT BY ARTICLE 85(1): REGULATION 1983/83 NOT APPLICABLE: INDIVIDUAL EXEMPTION GRANTED: E.C. Comm.)
Encompass Europe (JOINT VENTURES: JOINT OPERATION OF COMPUTERISED CARGO LOGISTICS INFORMATION SYSTEM: INTENTION TO APPROVE CONDITIONAL ON SYSTEM BEING OPERATED IN LINE WITH GROUP EXEMPTION ON COMPUTERISED RESERVATION SYSTEMS: E.C. Comm.)
KSB AG, Lowara SpA, Goulds Pumps Inc, and ITT Fluid Handling Divisions Agreements (JOINT DEVELOPMENT AND PRODUCTION OF HIGH TECHNOLOGY PRODUCTS: CAUGHT BY ARTICLE 85(1): R&D GROUP EXEMPTION INAPPLICABLE: INDIVIDUAL EXEMPTION GRANTED: E.C. Comm.)

European Broadcasting Union's Application (BROADCASTING: JOINT ACQUISITION OF TELEVISION RIGHTS TO SPORTS EVENTS: EXCHANGE SYSTEM FOR PROGRAMMES: E.C. Comm.)

European Music Satellite Venture (JOINT VENTURE: CABLE TV BY SATELLITE: E.C. Comm.)

European Vinyls Corporation (JOINT VENTURE: E.C. Comm.)

European Wastepaper Information Service (COMMERCIAL INFORMATION EXCHANGE: E.C. Comm.)

Eurosport (BROADCASTING: OPERATION OF SINGLE PAN-EUROPEAN SPORTS CHANNEL BY CONSORTIUM OF NATIONAL BROADCASTERS: E.C. Comm.)

Exxon Chemical International Inc. & Shell International Chemical Company Ltd (PRODUCTION JOINT VENTURE: AGREEMENT: AMENDMENT: E.C. Comm.)

Ford Motor Company Ltd and Iveco Industrial Vehicles Corp. BV's Agreements (JOINT VENTURE: JOINT PRODUCTION AND MARKETING: NOTICE: E.C. Comm.)

Ford of Europe and Volkswagen's Joint Venture (JOINT VENTURES: JOINT DEVELOPMENT AND PRODUCTION OF MULTI-PURPOSE MOTOR VEHICLE FOR 10 YEARS: FINISHED VEHICLES TO BE DIFFERENTIATED AND DISTRIBUTED SEPARATELY: INTENTION TO APPROVE SUBJECT TO CONDITIONS ON DIFFERENTIATION AND DURATION: E.C. Comm.)

(CAUGHT BY ARTICLE 85(1): EXEMPTION GRANTED: E.C. Comm.)

Fujitsu Ltd and Advanced Micro Devices Inc.'s Joint Venture (JOINT VENTURES: LICENSING: JOINT RESEARCH AND DEVELOPMENT: CROSS-SHAREHOLDING: NOTICE: E.C. Comm.)

Galileo and Covia Computer Reservation Systems' Combination (COMBINATION OF NORTH AMERICAN AND EUROPEAN COMPUTER RESERVATION SYSTEMS: E.C. Comm.)

Global Logistics System Europe Company for Cargo Information Services GmbH (JOINT VENTURES: OPERATION OF COMPUTERISED AIR CARGO INFORMATION SYSTEM: E.C. Comm.)

Holmsund Golv AB, Golvgripen AB & Arnstrong World Industries' Agreements (DISTRIBUTION AGREEMENTS: AGENCY: JOINT PRODUCT DEVELOPMENT: EFTA Surveillance Authority)

I-Co Global Communications Ltd and Inmarsat's Agreements (TELECOMMUNICATIONS SERVICES: MOBILE SATELLITE SYSTEMS: E.C. Comm.)

International Computers Ltd and Fujitsu Ltd (JOINT DEVELOPMENT: COMPUTER COMPONENTS: E.C. Comm.)

International Private Satellite Partners (Re) (No. 2) (TELECOMMUNICATIONS: EXTENSION OF NOTIFICATION TO COVER ARTICLE 53 EEA: NOTICE: E.C. Comm.)

International Private Satellite Partners (TELECOMMUNICATIONS: JOINT VENTURE: OPERATION OF INTERNATIONAL "ONE-STOP" DATA TRANSFER SERVICES FOR BUSINESSES: NOTICE: E.C. Comm.)

Jus-Rol Ltd and Rich Products Corp.'s Agreement (KNOW-HOW: MANUFACTURE OF FROZEN YEAST DOUGH: LICENCE AGREEMENT: NOTIFICATION: E.C. Comm.)

(DECISION: E.C. Comm.)

KSB AG, Lowara SpA, Goulds Pumps Inc. and ITT Fluid Handling Division's Agreements (JOINT RESEARCH AND DEVELOPMENT: JOINT PRODUCTION: COMPONENTS FOR PUMPS ASSEMBLED AND MARKETED BY THE PARTIES INDIVIDUALLY: E.C. Comm.)

Merck & Co. Inc. and Pasteur-Merieux Serums et Vaccins (JOINT VENTURES: PHARMACEUTICALS: JOINT RESEARCH AND DEVELOPMENT OF VACCINES: APPROVE: E.C. Comm.)

Mitchell Cotts Air Filtration Ltd (JOINT VENTURE: AIR FILTERS FOR NUCLEAR, BIOLOGICAL, CHEMICAL AND COMPUTER MARKETS: USE OF KNOW-HOW: E.C. Comm.)
Nederlandse Bankiersvereniging's Application (BANKING: ASSOCIATIONS OF UNDERTAKINGS: E.C. Comm.)
Nederlandse Omroep-Programma Stichting's Application (BROADCASTING: CO-ORDINATION OF PURCHASE AND PRODUCTION OF TELEVISION PROGRAMMES BY BROADCASTERS: E.C. Comm.)
Odin Developments Ltd (JOINT RESEARCH AND DEVELOPMENT: CONTAINERS FOR UHT FOOD: E.C. Comm.)
Papeteries de Golbey SA (JOINT VENTURE: PAPERMILL: JOINT MARKETING AND DISTRIBUTION: OPPOSITION BY COMMISSION: JOINT PRODUCTION ONLY: E.C. Comm.)
Peugeot SA and Fiat Auto SpA's Joint Venture (JOINT VENTURE: JOINT PRODUCTION OF COMMERCIAL MOTOR VEHICLE: NOTICE: E.C. Comm.)
Philips International BV's Application (JOINT DEVELOPMENT OF DIGITAL COMPACT CASSETTES: PATENT LICENSING: COPYRIGHT PROTECTION: E.C. Comm.)
Philips International BV and Osram GmbH (JOINT VENTURE: EXTENSION OF NOTIFICATION TO COVER ARTICLE 53 EEA: NOTICE: E.C. Comm.)
Phoenix (JOINT VENTURES: GLOBAL TELECOMMUNICATIONS SERVICES: E.C. Comm.)
Polygram, Sony Music Entertainment and Warner Music Group Inc. (JOINT VENTURES: CLUB SALES OF COMPACT DISCS AND VIDEOS THROUGH SERIES OF JOINT SUBSIDIARIES: E.C. Comm.)
Servicemaster Ltd's Franchise Agreements (FRANCHISING: E.C. Comm.)
Société d'Intérêt Collectif Agricole des Sélectionneurs Obtenteurs de Variétés Végétales (SICASOV) Agreement (PLANT BREEDERS RIGHTS: SEED LICENSING AGREEMENTS: NOTICE: E.C. Comm.)
Société Française de Dev't de la Boîte-Boissons (SOFREB) (JOINT SUBSIDIARY: COMFORT LETTER: E.C. Comm.)
Vallourec and Nyby Uddeholm AB's Agreement (FRANCO-SWEDISH JOINT VENTURE: JOINT SUBSIDIARY: COMFORT LETTER: E.C. Comm.)
X/Open Group (COMPUTER OPERATING SYSTEM: UNIX: AGREEMENT TO STANDARDISE: OPEN INDUSTRY STANDARD: NOTICE: E.C. Comm.) (DECISION: E.C. Comm.)

Intention to Exempt

Boussois SA and Interpane & Co. KG's Agreement (PATENT LICENCE: UNPATENTED KNOW-HOW: EXCLUSIVE LICENCE TO MANUFACTURE: IMPROVEMENT KNOW-HOW: E.C. Comm.)
BP International Ltd & M.W. Kellogg Company's Application (JOINT RESEARCH AND DEVELOPMENT: PRODUCTION OF AMMONIA: ARTICLE 85(3): E.C. Comm.)
D2B Systems Co. Ltd (Re) (JOINT VENTURES: JOINT DEVELOPMENT OF STANDARD COMMAND FRAMEWORK FOR HOME ENTERTAINMENT BROADCASTING EQUIPMENT: E.C. Comm.)
Eirpage Ltd (Re) (TELECOMMUNICATIONS: JOINT VENTURE SETTING UP AND OPERATING NATIONWIDE PAGING SYSTEM: E.C. Comm.)
Europcar International SA and Interrent Autovermietung GmbH's Merger (MERGERS: JOINT VENTURE: CAR RENTAL: E.C. Comm.)
European Telecommunication Standards Institute (ESTI) Interim Intellectual Property Rights Policy (TELECOMMUNICATIONS: TECHNICAL STANDARDS: INTELLECTUAL PROPERTY: LICENSING: E.C. Comm.)

Fiat Geotech Technologie Per La Terra SpA and Deere & Company's Agreement (JOINT VENTURES: JOINT RESEARCH AND DEVELOPMENT: E.C. Comm.)

Fiat Geotech Technologie Per La Terra SpA and Hitachi Construction Machinery Co. Ltd's Joint Venture (JOINT VENTURES: JOINT MANUFACTURE, DISTRIBUTION AND SALE OF HYDRAULIC EXCAVATORS: COMMUNITY MARKET EXCLUSIVE TO JOINT VENTURE AND REST OF WORLD EXCLUSIVE TO ONE PARENT COMPANY: PASSIVE SALES INTO EACH OTHER'S TERRITORY PERMITTED: E.C. Comm.)

International Dental Exhibition (Participation in) TRADE FAIRS: RULES FOR PARTICIPATION: INTENTION TO EXEMPT UNDER ARTICLE 85(3): E.C. Comm.)

Olivetti & Co. SpA and Canon Inc. (JOINT VENTURE: E.C. Comm.)

Sony España SA (EXCLUSIVE AND SELECTIVE DISTRIBUTION AGREEMENT: NOTICE: E.C. Comm.)

United International Pictures BV's Application (JOINT VENTURE: FRANCHISING: THEATRICAL DISTRIBUTION OF FILMS: E.C. Comm.)

Volvo Flygmotor AB & Sauer Getriebe AG (Agreement Between) (JOINT PRODUCTION AND JOINT SALE: E.C. Comm.)

Whisky and Gin (Sole distribution agreements) (EXCLUSIVE DISTRIBUTION: GROUP EXEMPTION: E.C. Comm.)

Inter-State Trade

Bayer AG, BP Chemicals International Ltd and Erdölchemie GmbH's Agreements (RESTRICTION OF COMPETITION: TECHNICAL CO-OPERATION: RESEARCH AND DEVELOPMENT: RESTRUCTURING: NEGATIVE CLEARANCE REFUSED: EXEMPTION GRANTED: E.C. Comm.)

Chambre Syndicale Nationale de la Discothéque (SYNDIS) v. SACEM (PERFORMING RIGHTS SOCIETIES: ROYALTY ENTITLEMENT: France: D.C.)

Chiron Corporation v. Murex Diagnostics Ltd (No. 2) (NATIONAL COURTS: PROCEDURE: DOMINANT POSITION: ABUSE: MUST BE AFFECTED BY ABUSE, NOT MERELY BY DOMINANT POSITION ITSELF: PLEADING MUST ALLEGE SUCH EFFECT: PLEAS DEFECTIVE: PATENT: INFRINGEMENT: ALLEGED REFUSAL TO LICENSE: EURO-DEFENCES: C.A.)

Computerland Europe SA's Franchise Agreements (FRANCHISING: AGREEMENTS: NOT CAUGHT BY ARTICLE 85(1) WHERE COMPETITIVE MARKET CONDITIONS PREVAIL: NON-COMPETITION CLAUSE: NOT CAUGHT PRIMA FACIE: CONTROL OF BUSINESS METHODS: EXCLUSIVE TERRITORIAL RIGHTS: SALE RESTRICTIONS: NON-APPLICABILITY OF BLOCK EXEMPTIONS UNDER REGULATIONS 67/67 AND 1983/83: INDIVIDUAL EXEMPTION GRANTED: E.C. Comm.)

Computerland Europe SA (FRANCHISING AGREEMENTS: INTENTION TO APPROVE: E.C. Comm.)

Continental Gummi-Werke AG and Compagnie Generale des Etablissements Michelin, Michelin et Cie's Agreement (JOINT VENTURES: JOINT RESEARCH AND DEVELOPMENT: INDEPENDENT DEVELOPMENT OF SIMILAR PRODUCTS ABANDONED: COMMON ENTITY TO EXPLOIT FUTURE PATENTS AND KNOW-HOW: LICENSING: MARKET IMPACT: E.C. Comm.)

Elopak v. Tetra Pak (DOMINANT POSITION: RELEVANT MARKET: PRODUCT MARKET: GEOGRAPHICAL MARKET: TAKE-OVERS: EXCLUSIVE LICENSING: E.C. Comm.)

Erauw-Jacquéry (Louis) Sprl v. La Hesbignonne Société Co-operative (PLANT BREEDERS' RIGHTS: LICENCE AGREEMENT: SALES AND EXPORT BAN: ECJ)

Gesellschaft zur Verwertung von Leistungsschutzrechten v. E.C. Commission (ADMINISTRATIVE PROCEDURE: COPYRIGHT: MARKET PARTITIONING: DOMINANT POSITION: ABUSE: ECJ)

Masterfoods Ltd v. HB Ice Cream Ltd (COMMUNITY LAW AND NATIONAL LAW: PRIORITY OF COMMUNITY LAW: NATIONAL COURTS: STANDARD OF PROOF: PENALTIES: RETAIL TRADE: VERTICAL AGREEMENTS: EXCLUSIVE DEALING: PROVISIONAL VALIDITY: DOMINANT POSITION: RELEVANT MARKET: ABUSE: REFERENCE TO E.C. COMMISSION: EXCLUSIVE DEALING AGREEMENTS: EVIDENCE: Ireland: H.C.)

Mecaniver SA and PPG Industries Agreement (COMPANY TRANSFER: SALE OF SHARES: MARKET SHARE: DOMINANT POSITION: E.C. Comm.)

Servicemaster Ltd (Franchise Agreements) (SERVICE FRANCHISES TREATED IN SAME WAY AS DISTRIBUTION AGREEMENTS: PROTECTION OF KNOW-HOW OUTSIDE ARTICLE 85(1): TERRITORIAL PROTECTION CAUGHT: INTRA-BRAND COMPETITION: INDIVIDUAL EXEMPTION GRANTED: E.C. Comm.)

Yves Rocher's Franchise Agreements (FRANCHISE AGREEMENTS: COMPETITION: INDUSTRIAL PROPERTY: EXCLUSIVE TERRITORIAL RIGHTS: DISTRIBUTION: BLOCK EXEMPTION: PRICES: APPLICATION FOR NEGATIVE CLEARANCE: E.C. Comm.)

Interim Measures and Interlocutory Proceedings. *See* Procedure

International Law, Conventions and Practice

Du Pont de Nemours & Co. and AKZO NV (INTERNATIONAL TRADE: U.S. LITIGATION: UNFAIR COMMERCIAL PRACTICES: IMPORTS: PATENTS: PARALLEL IMPORTS: DISCRIMINATION: GATT PROCEDURE: E.C. Comm.)

Tosca (COPYRIGHT: OPERA: PERIOD OF PROTECTION: FOREIGN AUTHORS: EVIDENCE: INTERNATIONAL CONVENTION AND NATIONAL LAWS: Germany: S.C.)

Wood Pump Cartel A. Ahlstrom Oy v. E.C. Commission (EXTRATERRITORIAL JURISDICTION: CONCERTED PRACTICES: EFFECT ON COMPETITION WITHIN COMMUNITY: STREAM OF COMMERCE DOCTRINE: TERRITORIALITY: INTERNATIONAL LAW: INTERNATIONAL COMITY: EXPORT CARTELS: ECJ)

Intra-brand Competition

Servicemaster Ltd (Franchise Agreements) (SERVICE FRANCHISES TREATED IN SAME WAY AS DISTRIBUTION AGREEMENTS: PROTECTION OF KNOW-HOW OUTSIDE ARTICLE 85(1): TERRITORIAL PROTECTION CAUGHT: INTERSTATE TRADE: INDIVIDUAL EXEMPTION GRANTED: E.C. Comm.)

Investigation. *See* Practice (*Investigation*)

Joint Research and Development including Joint Development

Alcatel Espace SA and Ant Nachrichtentechnik's Agreement (SATELLITE COMMUNICATIONS EQUIPMENT: PRODUCTION AND MARKETING: CAUGHT BY ARTICLE 85(1): JOINT TENDERING, SO INELIGIBLE FOR GROUP EXEMPTION: INDIVIDUAL EXEMPTION GRANTED: E.C. Comm.)

Alcatel Espace SA and Ant Nachrichtentechnik GmbH's Agreement (JOINT RESEARCH AND DEVELOPMENT, MANUFACTURING AND MARKETING: SATELLITE COMMUNICATIONS EQUIPMENT: INTENTION TO APPROVE: E.C. Comm.)

Alupower-Chloride Ltd (JOINT VENTURE: JOINT DEVELOPMENT, PRODUCTION AND DISTRIBUTION OF ALUMINIUM/AIR BATTERY: INTENTION TO ISSUE COMFORT LETTER: E.C. Comm.)

BBC Brown Boveri AG and NGK Insulators Ltd's Agreement (CO-OPERATION AGREEMENTS: JOINT VENTURES: JOINT DEVELOPMENT: INTENTION TO APPROVE: E.C. Comm.)

BBC Brown Boveri and NGK Insulators Ltd's Agreements (JOINT VENTURE: GERMAN-JAPANESE JOINT RESEARCH AND DEVELOPMENT: EXCLUSIVE LICENSING: KNOW-HOW: GROUP EXEMPTION: INAPPLICABILITY OF REGULATION 418/85: INDIVIDUAL EXEMPTION GRANTED: E.C. Comm.)

BP Chemicals Ltd and ECP-Enichem Polimeri Srl's Agreements (JOINT RESEARCH AND DEVELOPMENT: LICENSING: INTENTION TO APPROVE: NOTICE: E.C. Comm.)

BP International Ltd & M.W. Kellogg Company's Application (JOINT RESEARCH AND DEVELOPMENT: PRODUCTION OF AMMONIA: INTENTION TO EXEMPT: ARTICLE 85: E.C. Comm.)

Community v. Fanuc Ltd and Siemens AG (EXCLUSIVE DEALING: MARKET PARTITIONING: JOINT RESEARCH AND DEVELOPMENT: GROUP EXEMPTION NOT APPLICABLE: EXCLUSIVE DEALING: NO NOTIFICATION, SO NO INDIVIDUAL EXEMPTION: BREACH OF ARTICLE 85(1): FINES IMPOSED: E.C. Comm.)

Continental Gummi-Werke AG and Compagnie Generale des Etablissements Michelin, Michelin et Cie's Agreement (JOINT VENTURES: JOINT RESEARCH AND DEVELOPMENT: INDEPENDENT DEVELOPMENT OF SIMILAR PRODUCTS ABANDONED: COMMON ENTITY TO EXPLOIT FUTURE PATENTS AND KNOW-HOW: LICENSING: MARKET IMPACT: INTER-STATE TRADE: E.C. Comm.)

D2B Systems Co. Ltd (JOINT VENTURES: JOINT DEVELOPMENT OF STANDARD COMMAND FRAMEWORK FOR HOME ENTERTAINMENT BROADCASTING EQUIPMENT: INTENTION TO EXEMPT: E.C. Comm.)

ECR 900 (RESTRICTIVE PRACTICE: JOINT VENTURE: JOINT DEVELOPMENT, PRODUCTION AND DISTRIBUTION OF HI-TECH TELECOMMUNICATIONS SYSTEM: NOT FEASIBLE FOR PARTIES TO PRODUCE IT INDIVIDUALLY: NEGATIVE CLEARANCE GRANTED: E.C. Comm.)

Fiat Geotech Technologie Per La Terra SpA and Deere & Company's Agreement (JOINT VENTURES: JOINT RESEARCH AND DEVELOPMENT: INTENTION TO EXEMPT: E.C. Comm.)

Ford of Europe and Volkswagen's Joint Venture (JOINT VENTURES: JOINT DEVELOPMENT AND PRODUCTION OF MULTI-PURPOSE MOTOR VEHICLE FOR 10 YEARS: FINISHED VEHICLES TO BE DIFFERENTIATED AND DISTRIBUTED SEPARATELY: INTENTION TO APPROVE SUBJECT TO CONDITIONS ON DIFFERENTIATION AND DURATION: E.C. Comm.)
(CAUGHT BY ARTICLE 85(1): EXEMPTION GRANTED: E.C. Comm.)

Fuji, Canon, Minolta and Nikon's Joint Venture (JOINT VENTURE: JOINT RESEARCH AND DEVELOPMENT: ADVANCED PHOTOGRAPHIC SYSTEM: LICENSING OF RESULTS: NOTICE: E.C. Comm.)

Fujitsu Ltd and Advanced Micro Devices Inc.'s Joint Venture (LICENSING: CROSS-SHAREHOLDING: INTENTION TO APPROVE: NOTICE: E.C. Comm.)

Group Exemptions (Amendment) Regulation 1992 (GROUP EXEMPTIONS: SPECIALISATION AGREEMENTS: JOINT RESEARCH AND DEVELOPMENT: PATENT LICENSING: KNOW-HOW LICENSING: E.C. Comm.)

Holmsund Golv AB, Golvgripen AB & Armstrong World Industries' Agreements (DISTRIBUTION AGREEMENTS: AGENCY: JOINT PRODUCT DEVELOPMENT: INTENTION TO APPROVE: NOTICE: EFTA Surveillance Authority)

International Computers Ltd and Fujitsu Ltd (JOINT DEVELOPMENT: COMPUTER COMPONENTS: INTENTION TO APPROVE: E.C. Comm.)

KSB AG, Lowara SpA, Goulds Pumps Inc. and ITT Fluid Handling Division's Agreements (JOINT RESEARCH AND DEVELOPMENT: JOINT PRODUCTION: COMPONENTS FOR PUMPS ASSEMBLED AND MARKETED BY THE PARTIES INDIVIDUALLY: INTENTION TO APPROVE: E.C. Comm.)

KSB AG, Lowara SpA, Goulds Pumps Inc, and ITT Fluid Handling Division's Agreements (JOINT DEVELOPMENT AND PRODUCTION OF HIGH TECHNOLOGY PRODUCTS: CAUGHT BY ARTICLE 85(1): RESEARCH AND DEVELOPMENT GROUP EXEMPTION INAPPLICABLE: INDIVIDUAL EXEMPTION GRANTED: E.C. Comm.)

Merck & Co. Inc. and Pasteur-Merieux Serums et Vaccins (JOINT VENTURES: PHARMACEUTICALS: JOINT RESEARCH AND DEVELOPMENT OF VACCINES: INTENTION TO APPROVE: E.C. Comm.)

Odin Developments Ltd (JOINT VENTURES: JOINT DEVELOPMENT, PRODUCTION AND DISTRIBUTION OF NEW HIGH TECHNOLOGY PRODUCT: JOINT DISTRIBUTION EXCLUDES APPLICATION OF REGULATION 418/85: PARTIES NOT COMPETITORS AND UNABLE TO ENTER THE MARKET INDIVIDUALLY AND NO FORECLOSURE EFFECTS ON POTENTIAL THIRD PARTY COMPETITORS: SO CREATION OF JOINT VENTURE NOT CAUGHT BY ARTICLE 85(1): KNOW-HOW: LICENSED BY PARENTS TO JOINT VENTURE: ANCILLARY RESTRAINTS ONLY INCLUDED: NEGATIVE CLEARANCE GRANTED: E.C. Comm.)

Odin Developments Ltd (JOINT RESEARCH AND DEVELOPMENT: CONTAINERS FOR UHT FOOD: INTENTION TO APPROVE: E.C. Comm.)

Papeteries de Golbey SA (JOINT VENTURE: PAPERMILL: JOINT MARKETING AND DISTRIBUTION: OPPOSITION BY COMMISSION: JOINT PRODUCTION ONLY: INTENTION TO APPROVE: E.C. Comm.)

Philips International BV's Application (JOINT DEVELOPMENT OF DIGITAL COMPACT CASSETTES: PATENT LICENSING: COPYRIGHT PROTECTION: INTENTION TO APPROVE: E.C. Comm.)

Joint Subsidiaries

Polygram, Sony Music Entertainment and Warner Music Group Inc. (CLUB SALES OF COMPACT DISCS AND VIDEOS THROUGH SERIES OF JOINT SUBSIDIARIES: INTENTION TO APPROVE: E.C. Comm.)

Joint Tendering

Alcatel Espace SA and Ant Nachrichtentechnik's Agreement (SATELLITE COMMUNICATIONS EQUIPMENT: JOINT RESEARCH AND DEVELOPMENT, PRODUCTION AND MARKETING: CAUGHT BY ARTICLE 85(1): JOINT TENDERING, SO INELIGIBLE FOR GROUP EXEMPTION: INDIVIDUAL EXEMPTION GRANTED: E.C. Comm.)

Joint Ventures

Alcatel Espace SA and Ant Nachrichtentechnik GmbH's Agreement (JOINT RESEARCH AND DEVELOPMENT, MANUFACTURING AND MARKETING: SATELLITE COMMUNICATIONS EQUIPMENT: INTENTION TO APPROVE: E.C. Comm.)

Alupower-Chloride Ltd (JOINT DEVELOPMENT, PRODUCTION AND DISTRIBUTION OF ALUMINIUM/AIR BATTERY: INTENTION TO ISSUE COMFORT LETTER: E.C. Comm.)

Amersham International's Joint Venture (E.C. Comm)

Atlas (GLOBAL TELECOMMUNICATIONS SERVICES: INTENTION TO APPROVE: E.C. Comm.)

Auditel (BROADCASTING: EXCLUSIVE USE OF AUDIENCE RATING SYSTEM: CAUGHT BY ARTICLE 85(1): EXEMPTION REFUSED: E.C. Comm.)

Baxter International Inc. and Nestlé SA's Joint Ventures (MERGERS: CO-OPERATIVE CONTINUED PRESENCE OF PARENT COMPANIES ON THE SAME MARKETS: NOT CONCENTRATIVE WHERE PARENTS DO NOT COMPLETELY AND PERMANENTLY WITHDRAW FROM THE MARKET AND STATUS QUO CAN BE RESTORED AT ANY TIME, AND WHERE PARENTS RETAIN JOINT OWNERSHIP OF RELEVANT INTELLECTUAL PROPERTY RIGHTS: MERGER REGULATION: E.C. Comm.)

BBC Brown Boveri and NGK Insulators Ltd's Agreements (GERMAN-JAPANESE JOINT RESEARCH AND DEVELOPMENT: EXCLUSIVE LICENSING: KNOW-HOW: GROUP EXEMPTION: INAPPLICABILITY OF REGULATION 418/85: INDIVIDUAL EXEMPTION GRANTED: E.C. Comm.)

British Telecommunications plc and MCI's Agreement (TELECOMMUNICATIONS: STAKE IN U.S. FIRM ACQUIRED BY U.K. OPERATOR: PROVISION OF GLOBAL SERVICES: INTENTION TO APPROVE: E.C. Comm.)
(EXEMPTION GRANTED: E.C. Comm.)

Carbon Gas Technologie GmbH (ECC)

Communications de Mobile Cellulaire SA (CMC) (Re) (TELECOMMUNICATIONS: INTENTION TO APPROVE: NOTICE: E.C. Comm.)

Continental Gummi-Werke AG and Compagnie Generale des Etablissements Michelin, Michelin et Cie's Agreement (JOINT RESEARCH AND DEVELOPMENT: INDEPENDENT DEVELOPMENT OF SIMILAR PRODUCTS ABANDONED: COMMON ENTITY TO EXPLOIT FUTURE PATENTS AND KNOW-HOW: LICENSING: MARKET IMPACT: INTER-STATE TRADE: E.C. Comm.)

D2B Systems Co. Ltd (JOINT DEVELOPMENT OF STANDARD COMMAND FRAMEWORK FOR HOME ENTERTAINMENT BROADCASTING EQUIPMENT: INTENTION TO EXEMPT: E.C. Comm.)

De Laval-Stork (INTENTION TO RENEW EXEMPTION: E.C. Comm.)

Dunlop Ltd and Pirelli General plc's Agreements (HYDRAULIC AND ELECTRO-HYDRAULIC UMBILICALS: INTENTION TO APPROVE: E.C. Comm.)

E.C.R 900 (RESTRICTIVE PRACTICE: JOINT DEVELOPMENT, PRODUCTION AND DISTRIBUTION OF HI-TECH TELECOMMUNICATIONS SYSTEM: NOT FEASIBLE FOR PARTIES TO PRODUCE IT INDIVIDUALLY: NEGATIVE CLEARANCE GRANTED: E.C. Comm.)

Eirpage Ltd (TELECOMMUNICATIONS: SETTING UP AND OPERATING NATIONWIDE PAGING SYSTEM: INTENTION TO EXEMPT: E.C. Comm.)
(INDIVIDUAL EXEMPTION GRANTED: E.C. Comm.)

Encompass Europe (JOINT OPERATION OF COMPUTERISED CARGO LOGISTICS INFORMATION SYSTEM: INTENTION TO APPROVE CONDITIONAL ON SYSTEM BEING OPERATED IN LINE WITH GROUP EXEMPTION ON COMPUTERISED RESERVATION SYSTEMS: E.C. Comm.)

Enichem SpA and ICI's Agreements (EXEMPTION GRANTED: E.C. Comm.)

Europcar International SA and Interrent Autovermietung GmbH's Merger (MERGERS: CAR RENTAL: INTENTION TO EXEMPT: E.C. Comm.)

European Broadcasting Union's Application (BROADCASTING: JOINT ACQUISITION OF TELEVISION RIGHTS TO SPORTS EVENTS: EXCHANGE SYSTEM FOR PROGRAMMES: INTENTION TO APPROVE: E.C. Comm.)

Klöckner Stahl GmbH, Krupp Stahl AG and Thyssen Stahl AG's Joint Venture (COAL AND STEEL: AUTHORISATION: E.C. Comm.)

Merck & Co. Inc. and Pasteur-Merieux Serums et Vaccins (PHARMACEUTICALS: JOINT RESEARCH AND DEVELOPMENT OF VACCINES: INTENTION TO APPROVE: E.C. Comm.)

Mitchell Cotts Air Filtration Ltd (AIR FILTERS FOR NUCLEAR, BIOLOGICAL, CHEMICAL AND COMPUTER MARKETS: USE OF KNOW-HOW: INTENTION TO APPROVE: E.C. Comm.)

Mitchell Cotts Air Filtration Ltd (POSITION OF PARENT: RELEVANT GEOGRAPHICAL MARKET: ARTICLE 85: EXCLUSION FROM: KNOW-HOW LICENCE: PARTIAL NEGATIVE CLEARANCE: E.C. Comm.)

Nickelodeon U.K. (BROADCASTING: CHILDREN'S TELEVISION CHANNEL: E.C. Comm.)

Odin Developments Ltd (JOINT DEVELOPMENT, PRODUCTION AND DISTRIBUTION OF NEW HIGH TECHNOLOGY PRODUCT: JOINT DISTRIBUTION EXCLUDES APPLICATION OF REGULATION 418/85: PARTIES NOT COMPETITORS AND UNABLE TO ENTER THE MARKET INDIVIDUALLY AND NO FORECLOSURE EFFECTS ON POTENTIAL THIRD PARTY COMPETITORS: SO CREATION OF JOINT VENTURE NOT CAUGHT BY ARTICLE 85(1): KNOW-HOW: LICENSED BY PARENTS TO ANCILLARY RESTRAINTS ONLY INCLUDED: NEGATIVE CLEARANCE GRANTED: E.C. Comm.)

Olivetti & C. SpA and Canon Inc. (JOINT VENTURE OF ING C.) (FURTHER COMPETITION BETWEEN PARTIES AT PRODUCTION STAGE PRECLUDED: PRODUCTS OF JOINT VENTURE COMPANY: BRANDING: E.C. Comm.)

Olivetti & Co. SpA and Canon Inc. (INTENTION TO EXEMPT: E.C. Comm.)

Papeteries de Golbey SA (PAPERMILL: JOINT MARKETING AND DISTRIBUTION: OPPOSITION BY COMMISSION: JOINT PRODUCTION ONLY: INTENTION TO APPROVE: E.C. Comm.)

Peugeot SA and Fiat Auto SpA's Joint Venture (JOINT PRODUCTION OF COMMERCIAL MOTOR VEHICLE: INTENTION TO APPROVE: NOTICE: E.C. Comm.)

Philips International BV and Osram GmbH (EXTENSION OF NOTIFICATION TO COVER ARTICLE 53 EEA: INTENTION TO APPROVE: NOTICE: E.C. Comm.)

Polygram, Sony Music Entertainment and Warner Music Group Inc. (CLUB SALES OF COMPACT DISCS AND VIDEOS THROUGH SERIES OF JOINT SUBSIDIARIES: INTENTION TO APPROVE: E.C. Comm.)

Screensport v. European Broadcasting Union (BROADCASTING: JOINT VENTURE SETTING UP TRANSNATIONAL TELEVISION SPORTS CHANNEL: PARTIES POTENTIAL COMPETITORS: ONE AND ONLY EXISTING COMPETITOR AT SERIOUS COMPETITIVE DISADVANTAGE: CAUGHT BY ARTICLE 85(1): EXEMPTION REFUSED: E.C. Comm.)

United International Pictures BV's Application (FRANCHISING: THEATRICAL DISTRIBUTION OF FILMS: INTENTION TO EXEMPT: E.C. Comm.)

Vallourec and Nyby Uddeholm AB's Agreement (FRANCO-SWEDISH JOINT SUBSIDIARY: INTENTION TO APPROVE: COMFORT LETTER: E.C. Comm.)

Know-How

BBC Brown Boveri and NGK Insulators Ltd's Agreements (JOINT VENTURE: GERMAN-JAPANESE JOINT RESEARCH AND DEVELOPMENT: EXCLUSIVE LICENSING: GROUP EXEMPTION: INAPPLICABILITY OF REGULATION 418/85: INDIVIDUAL EXEMPTION GRANTED: E.C. Comm.)

Boussois SA and Interpane & Co. KG's Agreement (PATENT LICENCE: UNPATENTED KNOW-HOW: EXCLUSIVE LICENCE TO MANUFACTURE: IMPROVEMENT KNOW-HOW: INTENTION TO EXEMPT: E.C. Comm.)

Listings of TV Programmes. *See* **TV Programmes**

Locus Standi. *See* **Practice** (*Locus Standii*)

Management Societies

Bureau Europeen des Medias de l'Industrie Musicale v. E.C. Commission (MUSIC COPYRIGHT: ALLEGED INFRINGEMENTS OF ARTICLES 85 AND 86: MARKET SHARING: PRICE FIXING: NATIONAL COURTS' POWER OF INVESTIGATION: CFI)

Market Petitioning

Community v. Syntex Corporation & Synthelabo (TRADE MARKS: E.C. Comm.)

Market Share

AKZO Chemie BV v. E.C. Commission (EUROPEAN COURT PROCEDURE: ADMINISTRATIVE PROCEDURE: DISCOVERY OF DOCUMENTS: DOMINANT POSITION: RELEVANT PRODUCT MARKET: PRICING: ABUSE: ECJ)

Bureau Europeen des Medias de l'Industrie Musicale v. E.C. Commission (MUSIC COPYRIGHT: MANAGEMENT SOCIETIES: ALLEGED INFRINGEMENTS OF ARTICLES 85 AND 86: PRICE FIXING: NATIONAL COURTS' POWER OF INVESTIGATION: CFI)

Mecaniver SA and PPG Industries' Agreement (COMPANY TRANSFER: SALE OF SHARES: DOMINANT POSITION: E.C. Comm.)

Mergers. *See also under* Takeovers

Baxter International Inc. and Nestlé SA's Joint Ventures (CO-OPERATIVE JOINT VENTURES: CONTINUED PRESENCE OF PARENT COMPANIES ON THE SAME MARKETS: NOT CONCENTRATIVE WHERE PARENTS DO NOT COMPLETELY AND PERMANENTLY WITHDRAW FROM THE MARKET AND STATUS QUO CAN BE RESTORED AT ANY TIME, AND WHERE PARENTS RETAIN JOINT OWNERSHIP OF RELEVANT INTELLECTUAL PROPERTY RIGHTS: MERGER REGULATION: E.C. Comm.)

British Airways and British Caledonian (CIVIL AVIATION: AUTHORISATION: E.C. Comm.)

Europcar International SA and Interrent Autovermietung GmbH's Merger (JOINT VENTURE: CAR RENTAL: INTENTION TO EXEMPT: E.C. Comm.)

Schmalbach-Lubeca AG v. Carnaud SA (CONCERTED PRACTICES: DOMINANT POSITION: E.C. Comm.)

Zunis Holding SA v. E.C. Commission (MERGER: CLEARED BY COMMISSION: REQUEST BY SHAREHOLDERS TO REOPEN CASE: REFUSAL: JUDICIAL REVIEW: WHETHER APPEAL POSSIBLE: *Locus standii*: CFI)

Minimum Fees

Coleg de Agentes de la Propriedad Industrial (COAPI) (INDUSTRIAL PROPERTY AGENTS: SUBJECT TO COMPETITION RULES: FIXING OF MINIMUM FEES BY NATIONAL ASSOCIATION: CAUGHT BY ARTICLE 85: IRRELEVANT THAT BREACH SANCTIONED BY NATIONAL LEGISLATION: EXEMPTION REFUSED: NO FINE IMPOSED: E.C. Comm.)

National Courts

Bureau Européen des Média de l'Industrie Musicale v. Commission for the European Communities (COMPLAINT: BREACH OF ARTICLE 85 AND ARTICLE 86 BY SACEM: REFERENCE TO NATIONAL COURTS: APPLICATION FOR ANNULMENT: CFI)

Chiron Corporation v. Murex Diagnostics Ltd (No. 2) (PROCEDURE: DOMINANT POSITION: ABUSE: INTER-STATE TRADE: MUST BE AFFECTED BY ABUSE, NOT MERELY BY DOMINANT POSITION ITSELF: PLEADING MUST ALLEGE SUCH EFFECT: PLEAS DEFECTIVE: PATENT: INFRINGEMENT: ALLEGED REFUSAL TO LICENSE: EURO-DEFENCES: C.A.)

Garden Cottage Foods Ltd v. Milk Marketing Board (H.L.)

Hillegom Municipality v. Hillenius (BANKING: CONFIDENTIALITY: CIVIL PROCEEDINGS: PROFESSIONAL PRIVILEGE: ECJ)

Kall-Kwik Printing (U.K.) Ltd v. Bell (FRANCHISE AGREEMENT: RESTRICTIVE COVENANT: ENFORCEABILITY: ARTICLE 85: REASONABLENESS: INTERLOCUTORY INJUNCTION: Ch.D.)

Masterfoods Ltd v. HB Ice Cream Ltd (COMMUNITY LAW AND NATIONAL LAW: PRIORITY OF COMMUNITY LAW: STANDARD OF PROOF: PENALTIES: INTER-STATE TRADE: RETAIL TRADE: VERTICAL AGREEMENTS: EXCLUSIVE DEALING: PROVISIONAL VALIDITY: DOMINANT POSITION: RELEVANT MARKET: ABUSE: REFERENCE TO E.C. COMMISSION: EXCLUSIVE DEALING AGREEMENTS: EVIDENCE: Ireland: H.C.)

Tetra Pak Rausing SA v. E.C. Commission (CONSTITUTIONAL LAW: EEC TREATY: DOMINANT POSITION: ABUSE: EXCLUSIVE LICENCES: GROUP EXEMPTIONS: LEGAL CERTAINTY: ECJ)

Negative Clearance (Negative clearance granted, unless otherwise indicated)

Association Pharmaceutique Belge (APB's) Application (PHARMACEUTICALS: COLLECTIVE QUALITY CONTROL: STANDARD FORM DISTRIBUTION AGREEMENT OFFERED BY PHARMACIST'S TRADE ASSOCIATION: RIGHT TO AFFIX SEAL OF APPROVAL TO GOODS: E.C. Comm.)

Bayer AG, BP Chemicals International Ltd and Erdölchemie GmbH's Agreements (AGREEMENTS: RESTRICTION OF COMPETITION: TECHNICAL CO-OPERATION: RESEARCH AND DEVELOPMENT: RESTRUCTURING: INTER-STATE TRADE: NEGATIVE CLEARANCE REFUSED: EXEMPTION GRANTED: E.C. Comm.)

ECR 900 (RESTRICTIVE PRACTICE: JOINT VENTURE: JOINT DEVELOPMENT, PRODUCTION AND DISTRIBUTION OF HI-TECH TELECOMMUNICATIONS SYSTEM: NOT FEASIBLE FOR PARTIES TO PRODUCE IT INDIVIDUALLY: E.C. Comm.)

Mitchell Cotts Air Filtration Ltd (JOINT VENTURES: POSITION OF PARENT: RELEVANT GEOGRAPHICAL MARKET: ARTICLE 85: EXCLUSION FROM: KNOW-HOW LICENCE: PARTIAL NEGATIVE CLEARANCE: E.C. Comm.)

Odin Developments Ltd (JOINT VENTURES: JOINT DEVELOPMENT, PRODUCTION AND DISTRIBUTION OF NEW HIGH TECHNOLOGY PRODUCT: JOINT DISTRIBUTION EXCLUDES APPLICATION OF REGULATION 418/85: PARTIES NOT COMPETITORS AND UNABLE TO ENTER THE MARKET INDIVIDUALLY AND NO FORECLOSURE EFFECTS ON POTENTIAL THIRD PARTY COMPETITORS: SO CREATION OF JOINT VENTURE NOT CAUGHT BY ARTICLE 85(1): KNOW-HOW: LICENSED BY PARENTS TO JOINT VENTURE: ANCILLARY RESTRAINTS ONLY INCLUDED: E.C. Comm.)

Odin Developments Ltd (JOINT RESEARCH AND DEVELOPMENT: CONTAINERS FOR UHT FOOD: INTENTION TO APPROVE: E.C. Comm.)

Villeroy & Boch KG and Villeroy & Boch Sàrl's Agreements (SELECTIVE DISTRIBUTION: RETAILERS: QUALITATIVE CRITERIA: LOCATION CLAUSE: SALES PROMOTIONS OBLIGATIONS: RESALE RESTRICTIONS: E.C. Comm.)
Yves Rocher's Franchise Agreements (FRANCHISE AGREEMENTS: COMPETITION: INDUSTRIAL PROPERTY: EXCLUSIVE TERRITORIAL RIGHTS: DISTRIBUTION: BLOCK EXEMPTION: PRICES: INTER-STATE TRADE: E.C. Comm.)

No-Challenge Clauses

Bayer AG and Maschinenfabrik Hennecke GmbH v. Süllhöfer (PATENT LICENSING: COMMUNITY LAW: COMPATIBILITY WITH ARTICLES 30 AND 85: ECJ)
Bayer AG v. Süllhöfer (JUDICIAL PROCEDURE: PRELIMINARY RULINGS: MULTIPLE CLAIMS: PATENT LICENSING: ANTI-COMPETITIVE PRACTICES: COMMUNITY LAW AND NATIONAL LAW: APPEAL ON POINT OF LAW: Germany: S.C.)
Royon v. Meilland (PLANT BREEDERS RIGHTS: LICENCE AGREEMENT: GRANT BACK: ARTICLE 85(1): INFRINGEMENT: REFUSAL OF EXEMPTION: E.C. Comm.)
Windsurfing International Inc. v. E.C. Commission (PATENT LICENSING: RELEVANT MARKET: COMPONENTS: PATENT PROTECTION: COMMISSION'S POWERS TO INTERPRET NATIONAL LAW: JUDICIAL REVIEW: TYING CLAUSE: TRADE MARK: ECJ)

Non-Competition Agreement

Verenigde Bedrijven Nutricia NV's Agreements (TRANSFER OF GOODWILL: E.C. Comm.)

Notice

Aerospatiale and Alcatel's Agreement (TELECOMMUNICATIONS: CO-OPERATION IN CARRYING OUT SATELLITE REPAIRS: INFORMATION EXCHANGE: SPECIALISATION: INTENTION TO APPROVE: E.C. Comm.)
BP Chemicals Ltd and ECP-Enichem Polimeri Srl's Agreements (JOINT RESEARCH AND DEVELOPMENT: LICENSING: INTENTION TO APPROVE: E.C. Comm.)
Carrozzeria Grazia v. Volvo Italia (DOMINANT POSITION: ABUSE: MOTOR CARS: TYPE APPROVAL: CERTIFICATES OF CONFORMITY: REFUSAL TO SUPPLY: CASE SETTLED: E.C. Comm.)
CBA's Application (PLANT BREEDERS' RIGHTS: LICENSING AGREEMENTS: INTENTION TO ISSUE COMFORT LETTERS: E.C. Comm.)
Communications de Mobile Cellulaire SA (CMC) (Re) (JOINT VENTURE: TELECOMMUNICATIONS: INTENTION TO APPROVE: E.C. Comm.)
Digital Equipment Corporation and Ing C. Olivetti & Co. SpA's Agreement (CO-OPERATION AGREEMENT: COMPUTER SYSTEMS: TECHNOLOGY TRANSFER: INTENTION TO APPROVE: E.C. Comm.)
Electrolux AB and AEG AG's Agreements (SPECIALISATION AGREEMENTS: PRODUCTION OF DOMESTIC APPLIANCES: CROSS-SHAREHOLDINGS: INTENTION TO APPROVE: E.C. Comm.)
Eurotunnel (JOINT VENTURES: E.C. Comm.)
Ford Motor Company Ltd and Iveco Industrial Vehicles Corp. BV's Agreements (JOINT VENTURE: JOINT PRODUCTION AND MARKETING: INTENTION TO APPROVE: E.C. Comm.)
Fuji, Canon, Minolta and Nikons Joint Venture (JOINT VENTURE: JOINT RESEARCH AND DEVELOPMENT: ADVANCED PHOTOGRAPHIC SYSTEM: LICENSING OF RESULTS: E.C. Comm.)
Fujitsu Ltd and Advanced Micro Devices Inc.'s Joint Venture (JOINT VENTURES: LICENSING: JOINT RESEARCH AND DEVELOPMENT: CROSS-SHAREHOLDING: INTENTION TO APPROVE: E.C. Comm.)

Global European Network (TELECOMMUNICATIONS: TECHNICAL CO-OPERATION BETWEEN NATIONAL TELECOMMUNICATIONS ORGANISATIONS: PROVISION OF FIBRE OPTIC CAPACITY BETWEEN INTERNATIONAL LINES: E.C. Comm.)

Hilti AG (DOMINANT POSITION: ABUSE: TYING ARRANGEMENTS: INTERIM MEASURES: E.C. Comm.)

International Private Satellite Partners (Re) (No. 2) (TELECOMMUNICATIONS: EXTENSION OF NOTIFICATION TO COVER ARTICLE 53 EEA: INTENTION TO APPROVE: E.C. Comm.)

International Private Satellite Partners (TELECOMMUNICATIONS: JOINT VENTURE: OPERATION OF INTERNATIONAL "ONE-STOP" DATA TRANSFER SERVICES FOR BUSINESSES: INTENTION TO APPROVE: E.C. Comm.)

Ivoclar AG's Agreement (No. 2) (EXCLUSIVE DISTRIBUTION AGREEMENT: INTENTION TO EXTEND EXEMPTION: E.C. Comm.)

Ottung v. Klee & Weilbach A/S (PATENTS: LICENSING AGREEMENT: OBLIGATION TO PAY ROYALTIES INDEFINITELY WHILE AGREEMENT SUBSISTING: EXPIRY OF PATENT: OUTSIDE ARTICLE 85(1) WHERE LICENSEE MAY TERMINATE FREELY ON REASONABLE NOTICE: ECJ)

Performing Right Societies (COPYRIGHT: COLLECTING SOCIETIES: PARALLEL IMPORTS: ROYALTIES: E.C. Comm.)

Peugeot SA and Fiat Auto SpA's Joint Venture (JOINT VENTURE: JOINT PRODUCTION OF COMMERCIAL MOTOR VEHICLE: INTENTION TO APPROVE: E.C. Comm.)

Philips International BV and Osram GmbH (JOINT VENTURE: EXTENSION OF NOTIFICATION TO COVER ARTICLE 53 EEA: INTENTION TO APPROVE: E.C. Comm.)

Radio Telefis Eireann v. E.C. Commission (BROADCASTING: WEEKLY LISTINGS OF TV PROGRAMMES: COPYRIGHT: REFUSAL TO PERMIT REPRODUCTION IN INDEPENDENT TV GUIDE: ARTICLE 86: COMMISSION ENTITLED TO REQUIRE LICENSING FOR REPRODUCTION OF THE LISTINGS: ADMINISTRATIVE PROCEDURE: ADVISORY COMMITTEE ON RESTRICTIVE PRACTICES AND DOMINANT POSITIONS: MINUTES OF ORAL HEARINGS: NOTICE OF SITTING: CFI)

Sony España SA (EXCLUSIVE AND SELECTIVE DISTRIBUTION AGREEMENT: INTENTION TO EXEMPT: E.C. Comm.)

X/Open Group (COMPUTER OPERATING SYSTEM: UNIX: AGREEMENT TO STANDARDISE: OPEN INDUSTRY STANDARD: INTENTION TO APPROVE: E.C. Comm.)
(DECISION: E.C. Comm.)

Ownership of Intellectual Property Rights

Baxter International Inc. and Nestlé SA's Joint Ventures (MERGERS: CO-OPERATIVE JOINT VENTURES: CONTINUED PRESENCE OF PARENT COMPANIES ON THE SAME MARKETS: MERGER REGULATION: E.C. Comm.)

Hag Coffee (TRADE MARKS: HAG: SPECIFIC SUBJECT-MATTER: CONSEQUENCES: EXHAUSTION OF RIGHTS: IMPORTS: BREAK OF CHAIN OF OWNERSHIP BY EXPROPRIATION: Germany: C.A.)

Moosehead Breweries Ltd and Whitbread and Company plc's Agreement (LICENCE FOR PRODUCTION AND SALE OF CANADIAN BEER IN U.K.: TRADE MARK NO CHALLENGE CLAUSE: POSSIBLY RESTRICTIVE AS REGARDS VALIDITY: E.C. Comm.)

Warner-Lambert Company and BIC SA v. The Gillette Company and Eemland Holdings NV (COMPANY OWNERSHIP: ACQUISITION BY DOMINANT COMPANY OF SUBSTANTIAL HOLDING IN MAJOR COMPETITOR: ABUSE CAUGHT BY ARTICLE 86: AGREEMENT TO ASSIGN NON-COMMUNITY BUSINESS AND TRADE MARKS TO DOMINANT FIRM: VIOLATION OF ARTICLE 85(1): ORDER TO DIVEST INTEREST IN COMPETITOR AND RE-ASSIGN BUSINESS AND TRADE MARKS IN COUNTRIES BORDERING COMMUNITY: E.C. Comm.)

Parallel Imports

Du Pont de Nemours & Co. and AKZO NV (INTERNATIONAL TRADE: U.S. LITIGATION: UNFAIR COMMERCIAL PRACTICES: IMPORTS: PATENTS: DISCRIMINATION: GATT PROCEDURE: E.C. Comm.)
Hasselblad (G.B.) Ltd v. E.C. Commission (PRACTICE: ECJ)
Import of Drugs from Italy (UNFAIR COMPETITION: PRICE: RESTRAINT OF COMPETITION: Germany: S.C.)
Merck & Co. Inc. v. Primecrown Ltd (PATENT: INFRINGEMENT: WHETHER *Merck v. Stephar* STILL GOOD LAW: CONSTRUCTION: TRANSITIONAL PROVISIONS OF ACT OF ACCESSION OF SPAIN AND PORTUGAL: INTERLOCUTORY RELIEF: WHETHER REVISED VIEW OF *Merck v. Stephar* MAY BE TAKEN INTO ACCOUNT: REFERRAL TO ECJ: Pat. Ct)
Newitt & Co. Ltd v. Dunlop Slazenger International Ltd (DISTRIBUTION AGREEMENTS: EXPORT BANS: REFUSAL TO SUPPLY: EXCLUSIVE DEALING: CONCERTED PRACTICES: PRICES: SUBSIDIES: BUY-BACK SCHEMES: DISCRIMINATION: E.C. Comm.)
Performing Right Societies (COPYRIGHT: COLLECTING SOCIETIES: ROYALTIES: NOTICE: E.C. Comm.)
Polistil SpA & Arbois-Modelud's Agreement (EXCLUSIVE DEALING: E.C. Comm.)
Rolled Zinc Products (E.C. Comm.)

Parallel Trade

Burns (W.) Tractors Ltd v. Sperry New Holland (CONTRACTS: EXPORT BANS: REFUSAL TO SUPPLY: EXEMPTION: FINES: NOTIFICATION: E.C. Comm.)
Community v. Bayer AG (RESALE BAN: MARKET POSITIONING: FEEDINGSTUFF ADDITIVES: EXPIRY OF PATENT IN ONE STATE: ARTICLE 85(1): FINE: E.C. Comm.)
Ford New Holland Ltd (TERRITORIAL PROTECTION: BAN ON PARALLEL TRADE AGREED BETWEEN MANUFACTURER AND LOCAL DISTRIBUTORS: REBATES DEPENDENT UPON NON-EXPORT OF PRODUCTS BY CUSTOMERS: ARTICLE 85: INFRINGEMENT: E.C. Comm.)

Patent Licensing including Compulsory Patent Licences

Bayer AG and Maschinenfabrik Hennecke GmbH v. Süllhöfer (INDUSTRIAL PROPERTY: AGREEMENTS: NO-CHALLENGE CLAUSES: COMMUNITY LAW: COMPATIBILITY WITH ARTICLES 30 AND 85: ECJ)
Bayer AG v. Süllhöfer (JUDICIAL PROCEDURE: PRELIMINARY RULINGS: MULTIPLE CLAIMS: ANTI-COMPETITIVE PRACTICES: COMMUNITY LAW AND NATIONAL LAW: NO-CHALLENGE CLAUSE: APPEAL ON POINT OF LAW: Germany: S.C.)
Boussois SA and Interpane & Co. KG's Agreement (GROUP EXEMPTION: RELEVANCE: DECISION: E.C. Comm.)

Boussois SA and Interpane & Co. KG's Agreement (UNPATENTED KNOW-HOW: EXCLUSIVE LICENCE TO MANUFACTURE: IMPROVEMENT KNOW-HOW: INTENTION TO EXEMPT: E.C. Comm.)

Continental Gummi–Werke AG and Compagnie Generale des Etablissements Michelin, Michelin et Cie's Agreement (JOINT VENTURES: JOINT RESEARCH AND DEVELOPMENT: INDEPENDENT DEVELOPMENT OF SIMILAR PRODUCTS ABANDONED: COMMON ENTITY TO EXPLOIT FUTURE PATENTS AND KNOW-HOW: LICENSING: MARKET IMPACT: INTER-STATE TRADE: E.C. Comm.)

Hilti AG v. E.C. Commission (DOMINANT COMPANY: COMPULSORY PATENT LICENCES: EXTORTIONATE FEES: SELECTIVE AND DISCRIMINATORY SALES POLICY: ABUSE: NOT JUSTIFIED BY SAFETY WORRIES: CFI)

Ottung v. Klee & Weilbach A/S (OBLIGATION TO PAY ROYALTIES INDEFINITELY WHILE AGREEMENT SUBSISTING: EXPIRY OF PATENT: OUTSIDE ARTICLE 85(1) WHERE LICENSEE MAY TERMINATE FREELY ON REASONABLE NOTICE: ECJ)

Philips International BV's Application (JOINT DEVELOPMENT OF DIGITAL COMPACT CASSETTES: COPYRIGHT PROTECTION: INTENTION TO APPROVE: E.C. Comm.)

Technology Transfer Agreements Regulation (Draft) (GROUP EXEMPTION: TECHNOLOGY TRANSFER: PATENT: KNOW-HOW: E.C. Comm.)

Technology Transfer Regulation 1996 (GROUP EXEMPTION: KNOW-HOW LICENSING: APPLICATION OF ARTICLE 85(3) TO CERTAIN CATEGORIES OF TECHNOLOGY TRANSFER AGREEMENTS: E.C. Comm.)

Velcro SA v. Aplix SA (PATENT AND TRADE MARK LICENCES: EXCLUSIVITY: EXPORT BAN: EXTENSION BEYOND EXPIRY OF RIGHTS: NON-COMPETITION OBLIGATION: IMPROVEMENT PATENTS: ESSENTIAL FUNCTION OF TRADE MARK: EXEMPTION REFUSED: CEASE AND DESIST ORDER ISSUED: E.C. Comm.)

Windsurfing International Inc. v. E.C. Commission (RELEVANT MARKET: COMPONENTS: PATENT PROTECTION: COMMISSION'S POWERS TO INTERPRET NATIONAL LAW: JUDICIAL REVIEW: TYING CLAUSE: NO-CHALLENGE CLAUSES: TRADE MARK: ECJ)

Performing Rights Societies

Chambre Syndicale Nationale de la Discothéque (SYNDIS) v. SACEM (INTER-STATE TRADE: ROYALTY ENTITLEMENT: France: D.C.)

Plant Breeders' Rights

Association of Plant Breeders of the EEC (Comasso's) Application (FRENCH MANAGEMENT GROUP: STANDARD LICENSING AGREEMENTS: EXPORT PROHIBITIONS: INTENTION TO APPROVE: E.C. Comm.)

CBA's Application (LICENSING AGREEMENTS: INTENTION TO ISSUE COMFORT LETTERS: NOTICE: E.C. Comm.)

Erauw-Jacquéry (Louis) Sprl v. La Hesbignonne Société Co-opérative (LICENSING AGREEMENTS: SALES BAN: EXPORT BAN: ARTICLE 85(1): ECJ)

Royon v. Meilland (LICENCE AGREEMENT: GRANT BACK: NO-CHALLENGE CLAUSE: ARTICLE 85(1): INFRINGEMENT: REFUSAL OF EXEMPTION: E.C. Comm.)

Plant Varieties

Nungesser KG v. E.C. Commission (MAIZE SEEDS: EXCLUSIVE LICENCE: ECJ)

Practice

Discovery

AKZO Chemie BV v. E.C. Commission (ECJ PROCEDURE: ADMINISTRATIVE PROCEDURE: DOMINANT POSITION: RELEVANT PRODUCT MARKET: MARKET SHARE: PRICING: ABUSE: ECJ)

British American Tobacco Co. Ltd v. E.C. Commission (ECJ PROCEDURE: ORAL ARGUMENTS: BUSINESS SECRETS: EVIDENCE: ECJ)

Epikhiriseon Metalleftikon Viomikhanikon Kai Naftiliakon AE v. E.C. Commission Council and E.C. Commission (ECJ PROCEDURE: PROCEDURAL DELAYS: ECJ)

ICI v. E.C. Commission (ECJ PROCEDURE: HEARING OFFICER'S REPORT: INCONSISTENCY BETWEEN REASONING IN JUDGMENTS AND MOTIVES REVEALED IN PRESS STATEMENTS: RELEVANCY: ECJ)

VBBB and VBVB v. E.C. Commission (CONDUCT OF HEARINGS: RESALE PRICE MAINTENANCE: INFRINGEMENT OF ARTICLE 85(1): EXTEMPTION: PRECEDENTS: ECJ)

Investigation

AEG Telefunken v. E.C. Commission (PROCEDURE: SEIZURE OF DOCUMENTS: ECJ)

Locus standii

Compagnie Luxembourgeoise de Télédiffusion (BROADCASTING FRANCHISES: ADMINISTRATIVE PROCEDURE: JUDICIAL REVIEW: France: Conseil d'Etat)

Imprimerie (SA) Thône v. Fernand Geubelle (COPYRIGHT: INTELLIGENCE TEST: PUBLISHER AS CO-AUTHOR: Belgium)

Privilege

A.M. & S. Ltd v. E.C. Commission (ADMINISTRATIVE PROCEDURE: LAWYERS: CONFIDENTIALITY: PRIVILEGE: ECJ)

Hillegom Municipality v. Hillenius (BANKING: CONFIDENTIALITY: NATIONAL COURTS: CIVIL PROCEEDINGS: PROFESSIONAL PRIVILEGE: ECJ)

Hilti AG v. E.C. Commission (CONFIDENTIALITY OF BUSINESS SECRETS: INTERVENERS: LEGAL PROFESSIONAL PRIVILEGE: APPLICABLE TO WRITTEN COMMUNICATIONS BETWEEN INDEPENDENT LAWYER AND CLIENT COMPANY: INTERESTS OF RIGHT OF DEFENCE: PROCEDURE: CFI)

Search and seizure

AKZO Chemie BV v. E.C. Commission (SEARCH AND SEIZURE: SEARCH WARRANT: PRACTICE: ECJ)

Dow Chemical Nederland BV v. E.C. Commission (ECJ PROCEDURE: INTERIM MEASURES: SEARCH AND SEIZURE: ECJ)

Hoechst AG v. E.C. Commission (ECJ PROCEDURE: INTERIM MEASURES: SEARCH AND SEIZURE: JUDICIAL REVIEW: ECJ)

AEG Telefunken v. E.C. Commission (PROCEDURE: INVESTIGATION: SEIZURE OF DOCUMENTS: ECJ)

Pricing. *See also* Resale Price Maintenance

AKZO Chemie BV v. E.C. Commission (ECJ PROCEDURE: ADMINISTRATIVE PROCEDURE: DISCOVERY OF DOCUMENTS: DOMINANT POSITION: RELEVANT PRODUCT MARKET: MARKET SHARE: ABUSE: ECJ)

Bureau Europeen des Medias de l'Industrie Musicale v. E.C. Commission (MUSIC COPYRIGHT: MANAGEMENT SOCIETIES: ALLEGED INFRINGEMENTS OF ARTICLES 85 AND 86: MARKET SHARING: NATIONAL COURTS' POWER OF INVESTIGATION: CFI)

Chiron Corporation v. Organon Teknika Ltd (REFUSAL TO LICENSE: MEDICAL
PRODUCT: COMPLAINT THAT COMPETITION WOULD DRIVE DOWN PRICES
WHICH WOULD BE TOO DIFFICULT TO RAISE AGAIN: HEALTH AUTHORITY
MIGHT EXERCISE STATUTORY POWERS: Pat. Ct)

Elopak Italia Srl v. Tetra Pak (No. 2) (DOMINANT POSITION: ABUSE: RELEVANT
PRODUCT MARKET: SALES CONTRACTS: TYING CLAUSES: EXCLUSIVE SUPPLY:
ELIMINATORY PRICING: DISCRIMINATORY PRICING: E.C. Comm.)

Erauw-Jacquéry (Louis) Sprl v. La Hesbignonne Société Co-opérative (PLANT
BREEDERS' RIGHTS: LICENCE AGREEMENTS: SALES BAN: EXPORT BAN:
ARTICLE 85: LICENCE AGREEMENTS: MINIMUM SALES PRICE: ECJ)

Import of Drugs from Italy (UNFAIR COMPETITION: PARALLEL IMPORTS:
RESTRAINT OF COMPETITION: Germany: S.C.)

Macron Fire Protection Ltd v. Angus Fire Armour Ltd (DOMINANT POSITION:
ABUSE: E.C. Comm.)

Newitt & Co. Ltd v. Dunlop Slazenger International Ltd (DISTRIBUTION
AGREEMENTS: PARALLEL IMPORTS: EXPORT BANS: REFUSAL TO SUPPLY:
EXCLUSIVE DEALING: CONCERTED PRACTICES: SUBSIDIES: BUY-BACK
SCHEMES: DISCRIMINATION: E.C. Comm.)

Procureur de la République & SA Vêtements Goguet Sport v. Hechter (FRANCHISE
AGREEMENTS: RESALE PRICE MAINTENANCE: REFUSAL TO SELL: France: D.C.)

Publishers Association's Agreement (BOOKS: RESALE PRICE MAINTENANCE: U.K.
COLLECTIVE RESALE PRICE MAINTENANCE SCHEME: E.C. Comm.)
(ECJ PROCEDURE: INTERIM MEASURES: ECJ)

Société d'Intérêt Collectif Agricole des Sélectionneurs Obtenteurs de Variétés
Végétales Agreement (SEED LICENSING AGREEMENTS: INTENTION TO
APPROVE: E.C. Comm.)

VBBB and VBVB's Agreement (TRADE ASSOCIATIONS: COLLECTIVE RESALE PRICE
MAINTENANCE: E.C. Comm.)

VBBB and VBVB v. E.C. Commission (CONDUCT OF HEARINGS: DISCOVERY:
RESALE PRICE MAINTENANCE: INFRINGEMENT OF ARTICLE 85(1):
EXTEMPTION: PRECEDENTS: ECJ)

Yves Rocher's Franchise Agreements (FRANCHISE AGREEMENTS: COMPETITION:
INDUSTRIAL PROPERTY: EXCLUSIVE TERRITORIAL RIGHTS: DISTRIBUTION:
BLOCK EXEMPTION: INTER-STATE TRADE: APPLICATION FOR NEGATIVE
CLEARANCE: E.C. Comm.)

Privilege. *See* **Practice** *(Privilege)*

Procedure

Administrative procedure

A.M. & S. Ltd v. E.C. Commission (LAWYERS: CONFIDENTIALITY: PRIVILEGE: ECJ)

Compagnie Luxembourgeoise de Télédiffusion (BROADCASTING FRANCHISES:
JUDICIAL REVIEW: *Locus standi*: France: Conseil d'Etat)

Gesellschaft zur Verwertung von Leistungsschutzrechten v. E.C. Commission
(COPYRIGHT: MARKET PARTITIONING: INTER-STATE TRADE: DOMINANT
POSITION: ABUSE: ECJ)

Hercules NV, SA v. E.C. Commission (SUPPLY OF DOCUMENTS:
CONFIDENTIALITY: CFI)

Radio Telefis Eireann v. E.C. Commission (ADVISORY COMMITTEE ON
RESTRICTIVE PRACTICES AND DOMINANT POSITIONS: MINUTES OF ORAL
HEARINGS: NOTICE OF SITTING: CFI)

European Commission procedure

Brass Band Instruments Ltd v. Boosey & Hawkes plc (REFUSAL TO SUPPLY: INTERIM MEASURES: E.C. Comm.)

Stichting Sigarettenindustries Agreements (PROCEDURE: EVIDENCE: DISCOUNTS: RETAILERS: E.C. Comm.)

Unauthorised Reproduction of Sound Recordings in Indonesia (ILLICIT COMMERCIAL PRACTICES: NO PROTECTION AGAINST COPYING IN INDONESIA: INJURY TO EEC INDUSTRY: PROCEDURE: E.C. Comm.)

European Court of First Instance procedure

Hilti AG v. E.C. Commission (RELEVANT PRODUCT MARKET: SPARE PARTS: BURDEN OF PROOF: EVIDENCE: COURT OF FIRST INSTANCE PROCEDURE: REASONING: APPELLATE JURISDICTION OF ECJ: ECJ)

Hilti AG v. E.C. Commission (CONFIDENTIALITY OF BUSINESS SECRETS: INTERVENERS: LEGAL PROFESSIONAL PRIVILEGE: APPLICABLE TO WRITTEN COMMUNICATIONS BETWEEN INDEPENDENT LAWYER AND CLIENT COMPANY: INTERESTS OF RIGHT OF DEFENCE: CFI)

Zunis Holding SA v. E.C. Commission (MERGER: CLEARED BY COMMISSION: REQUEST BY SHAREHOLDERS TO REOPEN CASE: REFUSAL: JUDICIAL REVIEW: WHETHER APPEAL POSSIBLE: *Locus standii*: CFI)

European Court procedure

AEG Telefunken v. E.C. Commission (INVESTIGATION: SEIZURE OF DOCUMENTS: ECJ)

AKZO Chemie BV v. E.C. Commission (DISCOVERY OF DOCUMENTS: DOMINANT POSITION: RELEVANT PRODUCT MARKET: MARKET SHARE: PRICING: ABUSE: ECJ)

AKZO Chemie BV v. E.C. Commission (INTERIM MEASURES: DOMINANT POSITION: UNDERCUTTING: REQUEST FOR INTERIM SUSPENSION: REFUSAL: ECJ)

British American Tobacco Co. Ltd v. E.C. Commission (ORAL ARGUMENTS: BUSINESS SECRETS: EVIDENCE: DISCOVERY: ECJ)

Cargill BV v. E.C. Commission (INTERIM MEASURES: SERIOUS AND IRREPARABLE DAMAGE: NOT IF PURELY FINANCIAL: ECJ)

Dow Chemical Nederland BV v. E.C. Commission (INTERIM MEASURES: SEARCH AND SEIZURE: ECJ)

Epikhiriseon Metalleftikon Viomikhanikon Kai Naftiliakon AE v. E.C. Commission Council and E.C. Commission (DISCOVERY OF DOCUMENTS: PROCEDURAL DELAYS: ECJ)

Ford Werke v. E.C. Commission (EEC: INTERLOCUTORY PROCEEDINGS: ECJ)

Hag Coffee (TRADE MARKS: HAG: SPECIFIC SUBJECT-MATTER: CONSEQUENCES: EXHAUSTION OF RIGHTS: IMPORTS: BREAK OF CHAIN OF OWNERSHIP BY EXPROPRIATION: GERMAN HAG ABLE TO RESIST IMPORT INTO GERMANY OF BELGIAN HAG COFFEE: *Acte claire* FROM EUROPEAN COURT JUDGMENT IN *Pharmon v. Hoechst*: NO ARTICLE 177 REFERENCE: Germany: C.A.)

Hoechst AG v. E.C. Commission (INTERIM MEASURES: SEARCH AND SEIZURE: JUDICIAL REVIEW: ECJ)

ICI v. E.C. Commission (DISCOVERY OF DOCUMENTS: HEARING OFFICER'S REPORT: INCONSISTENCY BETWEEN REASONING IN JUDGMENTS AND MOTIVES REVEALED IN PRESS STATEMENTS: RELEVANCY: ECJ)

Italy v. E.C. Commission (Re BT) (MONOPOLIES: STATE ENTERPRISES: TREATIES: ECJ)

Publishers Association v. E.C. Commission (INTERIM MEASURES: U.K. COLLECTIVE RESALE PRICE MAINTENANCE SCHEME: ECJ)

Radio Telefis Eireann and Others v. E.C. Commission (Magill TV Guide) (INTERIM MEASURES: BROADCASTERS' PROGRAMME LISTING: ECJ)

Remia BV v. E.C. Commission (ECJ)

GATT procedure

Du Pont de Nemours & Co. and AKZO NV (INTERNATIONAL TRADE: U.S. LITIGATION: UNFAIR COMMERCIAL PRACTICES: IMPORTS: PATENTS: PARALLEL IMPORTS: DISCRIMINATION: GATT PROCEDURE: E.C. Comm.)

Interim measures and interlocutory proceedings

AKZO Chemie BV v. E.C. Commission (ECJ PROCEDURE: DOMINANT POSITION: UNDERCUTTING: REQUEST FOR INTERIM SUSPENSION: REFUSAL: ECJ, President)

Brass Band Instruments Ltd v. Boosey & Hawkes plc (REFUSAL TO SUPPLY: PROCEDURE: E.C. Comm.)

Cargill BV v. E.C. Commission (PROCEDURE: SERIOUS AND IRREPARABLE DAMAGE: NOT IF PURELY FINANCIAL: ECJ)

Dow Chemical Nederland BV v. E.C. Commission (ECJ PROCEDURE: SEARCH AND SEIZURE: ECJ)

Ford Werke v. E.C. Commission (EEC: PROCEDURE: ECJ)

Hilti AG (DOMINANT POSITION: ABUSE: TYING ARRANGEMENTS: NOTICE: E.C. Comm.)

Hoechst AG v. E.C. Commission (ECJ PROCEDURE: SEARCH AND SEIZURE: JUDICIAL REVIEW: ECJ)

Net Book Agreements: Publishers Association v. E.C. Commission (ECJ PROCEDURE: U.K. COLLECTIVE RESALE PRICE MAINTENANCE SCHEME: ECJ)

Radio Telefis Eireann v. E.C. Commission (Magill TV Guide) (ECJ PROCEDURE: BROADCASTERS PROGRAMME LISTING: ECJ)

National courts' procedure

Bayer AG v. Süllhöfer (PRELIMINARY RULINGS: MULTIPLE CLAIMS: PATENT LICENSING: ANTI-COMPETITIVE PRACTICES: COMMUNITY LAW AND NATIONAL LAW: NO-CHALLENGE CLAUSE: APPEAL ON POINT OF LAW: Germany: S.C.)

Chiron Corporation v. Murex Diagnostics Ltd (No. 2) (NATIONAL COURTS: DOMINANT POSITION: ABUSE: INTER-STATE TRADE: MUST BE AFFECTED BY ABUSE, NOT MERELY BY DOMINANT POSITION ITSELF: PLEADING MUST ALLEGE SUCH EFFECT: PLEAS DEFECTIVE: PATENT: INFRINGEMENT: ALLEGED REFUSAL TO LICENSE: EURO-DEFENCES: C.A.)

Radio Telefis Eireann v. Magill TV Guide Ltd (COPYRIGHT: RADIO AND TELEVISION SCHEDULES: LITERARY WORK: COMMUNITY LAW AND NATIONAL LAW: JUDICIAL PROCEDURE: EVIDENCE: Ireland: H.C.)

Quantitative Restrictions

Industrie Diensten Groep BV v. J.A. Beele Handelmaatschappij BV (IMPORTS: UNFAIR COMPETITION: PROPORTIONALITY: ECJ)

Refusal to License

Chiron Corporation v. Murex Diagnostics Ltd (No. 2) (NATIONAL COURTS: PROCEDURE: DOMINANT POSITION: ABUSE: INTER-STATE TRADE: MUST BE AFFECTED BY ABUSE, NOT MERELY BY DOMINANT POSITION ITSELF: PLEADING MUST ALLEGE SUCH EFFECT: PLEAS DEFECTIVE: PATENT: INFRINGEMENT: EURO-DEFENCES: C.A.)

Chiron Corporation v. Organon Teknika Ltd (PATENT: DOMINANT POSITION: ABUSE: RELEVANT MARKET: MEDICAL PRODUCT: COMPLAINT THAT COMPETITION WOULD DRIVE DOWN PRICES WHICH WOULD BE TOO DIFFICULT TO RAISE AGAIN: HEALTH AUTHORITY MIGHT EXERCISE STATUTORY POWERS: Pat. Ct)

Independent Television Publications Ltd v. E.C. Commission (BROADCASTING: WEEKLY LISTINGS OF TV PROGRAMMES: COPYRIGHT: REFUSAL TO PERMIT REPRODUCTION IN INDEPENDENT TV GUIDE: ARTICLE 86: CFI)

Radio Telefis Eireann v. E.C. Commission (BROADCASTING: WEEKLY LISTINGS OF TV PROGRAMMES: COPYRIGHT: REFUSAL TO PERMIT REPRODUCTION IN INDEPENDENT TV GUIDE: ARTICLE 86: CFI)

Volvo AB v. Erik Veng (U.K.) Ltd (NOT *per se* ABUSIVE: INDUSTRIAL DESIGN RIGHTS: SPARE PARTS: ABUSE OF DOMINANT POSITION: ECJ)

Refusal to Sell or Refusal to Supply

Brass Band Instruments Ltd v. Boosey & Hawkes plc (PROCEDURE: INTERIM MEASURES: E.C. Comm.)

Burns (W.) Tractors Ltd v. Sperry New Holland (CONTRACTS: EXPORT BANS: PARALLEL TRADE: EXEMPTION: FINES: NOTIFICATION: E.C. Comm.)

Carrozzeria Grazia v. Volvo Italia (DOMINANT POSITION: ABUSE: MOTOR CARS: TYPE APPROVAL: CERTIFICATES OF CONFORMITY: CASE SETTLED: NOTICE: E.C. Comm.)

Napier Brown & Co. Ltd v. British Sugar plc (ABUSE OF DOMINANT POSITION: UNDERTAKINGS: SETTLEMENT: E.C. Comm.)

Newitt & Co. Ltd v. Dunlop Slazenger International Ltd (DISTRIBUTION AGREEMENTS: PARALLEL IMPORTS: EXPORT BANS: EXCLUSIVE DEALING: CONCERTED PRACTICES: PRICES: SUBSIDIES: BUY-BACK SCHEMES: DISCRIMINATION: E.C. Comm.)

Procureur de la République & SA Vêtements Goguet Sport v. Hechter (FRANCHISE AGREEMENTS: RESALE PRICE MAINTENANCE: France: D.C.)

Regulations and Other Legislation

Article 30

Basset v. SACEM (COPYRIGHT: PHONOGRAMS: COPYRIGHT MANAGEMENT SOCIETIES: RESTRICTION OF CIRCULATION: ROYALTIES: ARTICLE 86: ECJ)

Article 53 EEA

International Private Satellite Partners (Re) (No. 2) (TELECOMMUNICATIONS: EXTENSION OF NOTIFICATION TO COVER ARTICLE 53: INTENTION TO APPROVE: NOTICE: E.C. Comm.)

Philips International BV and Osram GmbH (JOINT VENTURE: EXTENSION OF NOTIFICATION TO COVER ARTICLE 53: INTENTION TO APPROVE: NOTICE: E.C. Comm.)

Article 85(1)

Alcatel Espace SA and Ant Nachrichtentechnik's Agreement (SATELLITE COMMUNICATIONS EQUIPMENT: JOINT RESEARCH AND DEVELOPMENT, PRODUCTION AND MARKETING: CAUGHT BY ARTICLE 85(1): JOINT TENDERING, SO INELIGIBLE FOR GROUP EXEMPTION: INDIVIDUAL EXEMPTION GRANTED: E.C. Comm.)

Apple Corps Ltd v. Apple Computer Ltd (TRADE MARKS: DELIMITATION AGREEMENT: RESTRICTION TO OWN LINES: WHETHER VALIDITY RELEVANT: USE: C.A.)

Auditel (BROADCASTING: JOINT VENTURE: EXCLUSIVE USE OF AUDIENCE RATING SYSTEM: EXEMPTION REFUSED: E.C. Comm.)

Austin Rover Group Ltd & Unipart Group Ltd (FORMER FELLOW SUBSIDIARIES WITHIN SAME GROUP: DISTRIBUTION AGREEMENT: BLOCK EXEMPTION: E.C. Comm.)

Bureau Européen des Média de l'Industrie Musicale v. Commission for the European Communities (COMPLAINT: BREACH OF ARTICLE 85 AND ARTICLE 86 BY SACEM: REFERENCE TO NATIONAL COURTS: APPLICATION FOR ANNULMENT: CFI)

Community v. Fanuc Ltd and Siemens AG (EXCLUSIVE DEALING: MARKET PARTITIONING: JOINT RESEARCH AND DEVELOPMENT: GROUP EXEMPTION NOT APPLICABLE: EXCLUSIVE DEALING: NO NOTIFICATION, SO NO INDIVIDUAL EXEMPTION: BREACH OF ARTICLE 85(1): FINES IMPOSED: E.C. Comm.)

Computerland Europe SA's Franchise Agreements (FRANCHISING: AGREEMENTS: NOT CAUGHT BY ARTICLE 85(1) WHERE COMPETITIVE MARKET CONDITIONS PREVAIL: NON-COMPETITION CLAUSE: NOT CAUGHT PRIMA FACIE: CONTROL OF BUSINESS METHODS: EXCLUSIVE TERRITORIAL RIGHTS: SALE RESTRICTIONS: INTER-STATE TRADE: NON-APPLICABILITY OF BLOCK EXEMPTIONS UNDER REGULATIONS 67/67 AND 1983/83: INDIVIDUAL EXEMPTION GRANTED: E.C. Comm.)

Community v. Bayer AG (RESALE BAN: MARKET POSITIONING: FEEDINGSTUFF ADDITIVES: EXPIRY OF PATENT IN ONE STATE: PARALLEL TRADE ARTICLE 85(1): FINE: E.C. Comm.)

Community v. Syntex Corporation (SIMILAR TRADE MARKS: MARKET PETITIONING: NOT CLEAR WHETHER EARLIER MARK COULD BE ENFORCED IN MEMBER STATES: DELIMITATION AGREEMENT TO AVOID CONFUSION: CAUGHT BY ARTICLE 85(1): E.C. Comm.)

Cutsforth v. Mansfield Inns Ltd (BREWERY: TIED HOUSES: RESTRICTIONS ON GAMING MACHINES: ARTICLE 85(1): Q.B.D.)

DDD Ltd and Delta Chemie's Agreement (KNOW-HOW: EXCLUSIVE DEALING: TRADE MARKS: LICENCE CAUGHT BY ARTICLE 85(1): GROUP EXEMPTION: REGULATION 1983/83 NOT APPLICABLE: INDIVIDUAL EXEMPTION GRANTED: E.C. Comm.)

Erauw-Jacquéry (Louis) Sprl v. La Hesbignonne Société Co-opérative (PLANT BREEDERS' RIGHTS: LICENSING AGREEMENTS: SALES BAN: EXPORT BAN: ARTICLE 85(1): ECJ)

Fiat and Hitachi's Joint Venture (JOINT VENTURES: PARENT COMPANIES REMAINING POTENTIAL COMPETITORS: BAN ON FOREIGN PARENT COMPANY ACTIVELY IMPORTING INTO COMMUNITY: ARTICLE 85(1): EXEMPTION GRANTED: E.C. Comm.)

Ford New Holland Ltd (TERRITORIAL PROTECTION: BAN ON PARALLEL TRADE AGREED BETWEEN MANUFACTURER AND LOCAL DISTRIBUTORS: REBATES DEPENDENT UPON NON-EXPORT OF PRODUCTS BY CUSTOMERS: INFRINGEMENT: E.C. Comm.)

Ford of Europe and Volkswagen's Joint Venture (JOINT VENTURES: JOINT DEVELOPMENT AND PRODUCTION OF MULTI-PURPOSE MOTOR VEHICLE FOR 10 YEARS: FINISHED VEHICLES TO BE DIFFERENTIATED AND DISTRIBUTED SEPARATELY: INTENTION TO APPROVE SUBJECT TO CONDITIONS ON DIFFERENTIATION AND DURATION: E.C. Comm.)
(ARTICLE 85(1): EXEMPTION GRANTED: E.C. Comm.)

Koelman v. E.C. Commission (BROADCASTING: RETRANSMISSION OF PROGRAMMES BY CABLE: STANDARD AGREEMENT: COPYRIGHT: OWNERSHIP: RADIO MATERIAL: COLLECTING SOCIETY: ALLEGED BREACH OF ARTICLES 85 AND 86: Case T–575/93: CFI)

KSB AG, Lowara SpA, Goulds Pumps Inc., and ITT Fluid Handling Division's Agreements (JOINT DEVELOPMENT AND PRODUCTION OF HIGH TECHNOLOGY PRODUCTS: CAUGHT BY ARTICLE 85(1): RESEARCH AND DEVELOPMENT GROUP EXEMPTION INAPPLICABLE: INDIVIDUAL EXEMPTION GRANTED: E.C. Comm.)

Kall-Kwik Printing (U.K.) Ltd v. Bell (FRANCHISE AGREEMENT: RESTRICTIVE COVENANT: ENFORCEABILITY: ARTICLE 85: REASONABLENESS: INTERLOCUTORY INJUNCTION: Ch.D.)

MTV Europe v. BMG Records (U.K.) Ltd (ALLEGED BREACH OF ARTICLE 85: ACTION FOR DAMAGES: OVERLAPPING ACTION BEFORE COMMISSION: APPLICATION TO STAY: JURISDICTION: Ch.D.)

Odin Developments Ltd (JOINT VENTURES: JOINT DEVELOPMENT, PRODUCTION AND DISTRIBUTION OF NEW HIGH TECHNOLOGY PRODUCT: JOINT DISTRIBUTION EXCLUDES APPLICATION OF REGULATION 418/85: PARTIES NOT COMPETITORS AND UNABLE TO ENTER THE MARKET INDIVIDUALLY AND NO FORECLOSURE EFFECTS ON POTENTIAL THIRD PARTY COMPETITORS: SO CREATION OF JOINT VENTURE NOT CAUGHT BY ARTICLE 85(1): KNOW-HOW: LICENSED BY PARENTS TO JOINT VENTURE: ANCILLARY RESTRAINTS ONLY INCLUDED: NEGATIVE CLEARANCE GRANTED: E.C. Comm.)

Ottung v. Klee & Weilbach A/S (PATENTS: LICENSING AGREEMENT: OBLIGATION TO PAY ROYALTIES INDEFINITELY WHILE AGREEMENT SUBSISTING: EXPIRY OF PATENT: OUTSIDE ARTICLE 85(1) WHERE LICENSEE MAY TERMINATE FREELY ON REASONABLE NOTICE: ECJ)

Parfums Givenchy SA's Application (SELECTIVE DISTRIBUTION SYSTEM: CAUGHT BY ARTICLE 85(1): EXEMPTION GRANTED: E.C. Comm.)

Post-Term Use Bans in Know-How Licensing Agreements (KNOW-HOW LICENSING AGREEMENTS: POST-TERM USE BANS: NOT CAUGHT BY ARTICLE 85(1) OR 86 AS A RULE: COMPLAINT OF FORMER LICENSEE REJECTED: E.C. Comm.)

Screensport v. European Broadcasting Union (BROADCASTING: JOINT VENTURE SETTING UP TRANSNATIONAL TELEVISION SPORTS CHANNEL: PARTIES POTENTIAL COMPETITORS: ONE AND ONLY EXISTING COMPETITOR AT SERIOUS COMPETITIVE DISADVANTAGE: ARTICLE 85(1): EXEMPTION REFUSED: E.C. Comm.)

Servicemaster Ltd (Franchise Agreements) (SERVICE FRANCHISES TREATED IN SAME WAY AS DISTRIBUTION AGREEMENTS: PROTECTION OF KNOW-HOW OUTSIDE ARTICLE 85(1): TERRITORIAL PROTECTION CAUGHT: INTERSTATE TRADE: INTRA-BRAND COMPETITION: INDIVIDUAL EXEMPTION GRANTED: E.C. Comm.)

VBBB and VBVB v. E.C. Commission (CONDUCT OF HEARINGS: DISCOVERY: RESALE PRICE MAINTENANCE: INFRINGEMENT OF ARTICLE 85(1): EXTEMPTION: PRECEDENTS: ECJ)

Warner-Lambert Company and BIC SA v. The Gillette Company and Eemland Holdings NV (COMPANY OWNERSHIP: ACQUISITION BY DOMINANT COMPANY OF SUBSTANTIAL HOLDING IN MAJOR COMPETITOR: ABUSE CAUGHT BY ARTICLE 86: AGREEMENT TO ASSIGN NON-COMMUNITY BUSINESS AND TRADE MARKS TO DOMINANT FIRM: VIOLATION OF ARTICLE 85(1): ORDER TO DIVEST INTEREST IN COMPETITOR AND REASSIGN BUSINESS AND TRADE MARKS IN COUNTRIES BORDERING COMMUNITY: E.C. Comm.)

Yves Rocher's Franchise Agreements (FRANCHISING: AGREEMENTS: RESTRICTION ON COMMERCIAL FREEDOM: KNOW-HOW: ARTICLE 85(1): E.C. Comm.)

Article 85(3)

BP International Ltd & M.W. Kellogg Company's Application (JOINT RESEARCH AND DEVELOPMENT: PRODUCTION OF AMMONIA: INTENTION TO EXEMPT: ARTICLE 85(3): E.C. Comm.)

Carlsberg Beers v. De Forenede A/S & Grand Metropolitan Ltd (LONG-TERM CONTRACTS: 11 YEARS: EQUIVALENT TO EXCLUSIVITY: EXEMPTION UNDER ARTICLE 85(3): E.C. Comm.)

International Dental Exhibition (Participation in) (TRADE FAIRS: RULES FOR PARTICIPATION: INTENTION TO EXEMPT UNDER ARTICLE 85(3): E.C. Comm.)

Technology Transfer Regulation 1996 (GROUP EXEMPTION: PATENT LICENSING: KNOW-HOW LICENSING: APPLICATION OF ARTICLE 85(3) TO CERTAIN CATEGORIES OF TECHNOLOGY TRANSFER AGREEMENTS: E.C. Comm.)

Article 86

Basset v. SACEM (COPYRIGHT: PHONOGRAMS: COPYRIGHT MANAGEMENT SOCIETIES: RESTRICTION OF CIRCULATION: ROYALTIES: ARTICLE 30: ARTICLE 86: ECJ)

BBC v. E.C. Commission (BROADCASTING: WEEKLY LISTINGS OF TV PROGRAMMES: COPYRIGHT: REFUSAL TO PERMIT REPRODUCTION IN INDEPENDENT TV GUIDE: ARTICLE 86: COMMISSION ENTITLED TO REQUIRE LICENSING FOR REPRODUCTION OF THE LISTINGS: CFI)

Bureau Européen des Média de l'Industrie Musicale v. Commission for the European Communities (COMPLAINT: BREACH OF ARTICLE 85 AND ARTICLE 86 BY SACEM: REFERENCE TO NATIONAL COURTS: APPLICATION FOR ANNULMENT: CFI)

Independent Television Publications Ltd v. E.C. Commission (BROADCASTING: WEEKLY LISTINGS OF TV PROGRAMMES: COPYRIGHT: REFUSAL TO PERMIT REPRODUCTION IN INDEPENDENT TV GUIDE: ARTICLE 86: COMMISSION ENTITLED TO REQUIRE LICENSING FOR REPRODUCTION OF THE LISTINGS: CFI)

Koelman v. E.C. Commission (BROADCASTING: RETRANSMISSION OF PROGRAMMES BY CABLE: STANDARD AGREEMENT: COPYRIGHT: OWNERSHIP: RADIO MATERIAL: COLLECTING SOCIETY: ALLEGED BREACH OF ARTICLES 85 AND 86: Case T–575/93: CFI)

Magill TV Guide Ltd v. Independent Television Publications Ltd, BBC and Radio Telefis Eireann (PUBLIC BROADCASTING ORGANISATIONS: TV GUIDES: BROADCASTERS IN UNITED KINGDOM AND IRELAND: "UNDERTAKINGS" WITHIN ARTICLE 86: SUBSIDIARY AND PARENT: SINGLE ENTITY WITHIN ARTICLE 86: E.C. Comm.)

Radio Telefis Eireann v. E.C. Commission (BROADCASTING: WEEKLY LISTINGS OF TV PROGRAMMES: COPYRIGHT: REFUSAL TO PERMIT REPRODUCTION IN INDEPENDENT TV GUIDE: ARTICLE 86: COMMISSION ENTITLED TO REQUIRE LICENSING FOR REPRODUCTION OF THE LISTINGS: ADMINISTRATIVE PROCEDURE: ADVISORY COMMITTEE ON RESTRICTIVE PRACTICES AND DOMINANT POSITIONS: MINUTES OF ORAL HEARINGS: NOTICE OF SITTING: CFI)

Warner-Lambert Company and BIC SA v. The Gillette Company and Eemland Holdings NV (COMPANY OWNERSHIP: ACQUISITION BY DOMINANT COMPANY OF SUBSTANTIAL HOLDING IN MAJOR COMPETITOR: ABUSE CAUGHT BY ARTICLE 86: AGREEMENT TO ASSIGN NON-COMMUNITY BUSINESS AND TRADE MARKS TO DOMINANT FIRM: VIOLATION OF ARTICLE 85(1): ORDER TO DIVEST INTEREST IN COMPETITOR AND RE-ASSIGN BUSINESS AND TRADE MARKS IN COUNTRIES BORDERING COMMUNITY: E.C. Comm.)

Article 177

Chiron Corporation v. Murex Diagnostics Ltd (No. 9) (PATENT: INFRINGEMENT: SECOND ACTION AFTER AMENDMENT OF AGREEMENT HELD CONTRARY TO P.A.77, S.44: PLEADINGS: AMENDMENT: WHETHER DEFENCE STRUCK OUT IN EARLIER ACTION CAN BE RAISED IN LATER ACTION: *Res judicata*: *Acte clair*. Pat. Ct)

Group Exemptions (Amendment) Regulation 1992

Group Exemptions (Amendment) Regulation 1992 (GROUP EXEMPTIONS: SPECIALISATION AGREEMENTS: JOINT RESEARCH AND DEVELOPMENT: PATENT LICENSING: KNOW-HOW LICENSING: E.C. Comm.)

Know-How Licences (Draft Regulation)

Know-How Licences (Draft Regulation) (GROUP EXEMPTIONS: KNOW-HOW AGREEMENTS: E.C. Comm.)

Know-How Licensing Regulation 1988

Know-How Licensing Regulation 1988 (GROUP EXEMPTION: KNOW-HOW LICENSING: E.C. Comm.)

Know-How Licensing Regulation 1988-92

Know-How Licensing Regulation 1988-92 (GROUP EXEMPTION: KNOW-HOW LICENSING: TEXT OF REGULATION 556/89 AS AMENDED BY REGULATION 151/93: E.C. Comm.)

Patent Licensing Regulation 1984-92 (2349/84)

Patent Licensing Regulation 1984-92 (2349/84) (GROUP EXEMPTION: PATENT LICENSING: TEXT OF REGULATION 2349/84 AS AMENDED BY REGULATION 151/93: E.C. Comm.)

Regulation 123/85

VAG France v. Etablissements Magne SA (MOTOR VEHICLES: GROUP EXEMPTION: EFFECT ON DISTRIBUTION CONTRACTS: ECJ)
Vallourec and Nyby Uddeholm AB's Agreement (FRANCO-SWEDISH JOINT VENTURE: JOINT SUBSIDIARY: INTENTION TO APPROVE: COMFORT LETTER: E.C. Comm.)

Regulation 151/93

Joint Research and Development Regulation 1984-92 (418/85) (GROUP EXEMPTION: JOINT RESEARCH AND DEVELOPMENT: TEXT OF REGULATION 418/85 AS AMENDED BY REGULATION 151/93: E.C. Comm.)
Know-How Licensing Regulation 1988-92 (GROUP EXEMPTION: KNOW-HOW LICENSING: TEXT OF REGULATION 556/89 AS AMENDED BY REGULATION 151/93: E.C. Comm.)

Patent Licensing Regulation 1984-92 (2349/84) (GROUP EXEMPTION: PATENT LICENSING: TEXT OF REGULATION 2349/84 AS AMENDED BY REGULATION 151/93: E.C. Comm.)

Regulation 1983/83

DDD Ltd and Delta Chemie's Agreement (KNOW-HOW: EXCLUSIVE DEALING: TRADE MARKS: LICENCE CAUGHT BY ARTICLE 85(1): GROUP EXEMPTION: REGULATION 1983/83 NOT APPLICABLE: INDIVIDUAL EXEMPTION GRANTED: E.C. Comm.)

Philips Export BV and John Fluke Manufacturing Company Inc.'s Agreements (RECIPROCAL EXCLUSIVE DISTRIBUTION AGREEMENTS: PARTIES DIRECT COMPETITORS IN SOME PRODUCTS, SO NOT COVERED BY GROUP EXEMPTION REGULATION 1983/83: INTENTION TO GRANT INDIVIDUAL EXEMPTION: E.C. Comm.)

Regulation 2349/84

Patent Licensing Regulation 1984-92 (2349/84) (GROUP EXEMPTION: PATENT LICENSING: TEXT OF REGULATION 2349/84 AS AMENDED BY REGULATION 151/93: E.C. Comm.)

Regulation 418/85

BBC Brown Boveri and NGK Insulators Ltd's Agreements (JOINT VENTURE: GERMAN-JAPANESE JOINT RESEARCH AND DEVELOPMENT: EXCLUSIVE LICENSING: KNOW-HOW: GROUP EXEMPTION: INAPPLICABILITY OF REGULATION 418/85: INDIVIDUAL EXEMPTION GRANTED: E.C. Comm.)

Joint Research and development Regulation 1984-92 (418/85) (GROUP EXEMPTION: JOINT RESEARCH AND DEVELOPMENT: TEXT OF REGULATION 418/85 AS AMENDED BY REGULATION 151/93: E.C. Comm.)

Odin Developments Ltd (JOINT VENTURES: JOINT DEVELOPMENT, PRODUCTION AND DISTRIBUTION OF NEW HIGH TECHNOLOGY PRODUCT: JOINT DISTRIBUTION EXCLUDES APPLICATION OF REGULATION 418/85: PARTIES NOT COMPETITORS AND UNABLE TO ENTER THE MARKET INDIVIDUALLY AND NO FORECLOSURE EFFECTS ON POTENTIAL THIRD PARTY COMPETITORS: SO CREATION OF JOINT VENTURE NOT CAUGHT BY ARTICLE 85(1): KNOW-HOW: LICENSED BY PARENTS TO JOINT VENTURE: ANCILLARY RESTRAINTS ONLY INCLUDED: NEGATIVE CLEARANCE GRANTED: E.C. Comm.)

Regulation 67/67

Hydrotherm Geratebau GmbH v. Compact de Dott Ing Mario Andreoli & CSAS (EXCLUSIVE DEALING: BLOCK EXEMPTION: TRADE MARK LICENCE: ECJ)

Technology Transfer Agreements Regulation

Technology Transfer Agreements Regulation (Draft) (GROUP EXEMPTION: TECHNOLOGY TRANSFER: PATENT: KNOW-HOW: E.C. Comm.)

Telecommunications directives

Telecommunications Terminal Equipment and Services (Antitrust Amendment) Directive 1994 (Directive 94/96) (COMPETITION IN SERVICES AND TERMINAL EQUIPMENT MARKETS: E.C. Comm.)

Telecommunications Terminal Equipment (Antitrust) Directive 1988-94 Directive 475/88/301) (COMPETITION IN TERMINAL EQUIPMENT MARKETS: TEXT OF DIRECTIVE 88/301 AS AMENDED BY DIRECTIVE 94/96: E.C. Comm.)

Telecommunications Terminal Services (Antitrust) Directive 1990-94 (Directive 90/388) (COMPETITION IN SERVICES MARKETS: TEXT OF DIRECTIVE 90/388 AS AMENDED BY DIRECTIVE 94/96: E.C. Comm.)

Relevant Market

British Leyland Motor Corp. Ltd v. E.C. Commission (DOMINANT POSITION: SUPPLY OF CERTIFICATES OF CONFORMITY FOR IMPORTED MOTOR VEHICLES: DISCRIMINATORY FEES: ABUSE: ECJ)

Chiron Corporation v. Organon Teknika Ltd (PATENT: DOMINANT POSITION: ABUSE: REFUSAL TO LICENSE: INTERLOCUTORY INJUNCTION: MEDICAL PRODUCT: COMPLAINT THAT COMPETITION WOULD DRIVE DOWN PRICES WHICH WOULD BE TOO DIFFICULT TO RAISE AGAIN: HEALTH AUTHORITY MIGHT EXERCISE STATUTORY POWERS: INJUNCTION REFUSED: Pat. Ct)

Elopak v. Tetra Pak (DOMINANT POSITION: PRODUCT MARKET: GEOGRAPHICAL MARKET: TAKEOVERS: EXCLUSIVE LICENSING: INTER-STATE TRADE: E.C. Comm.)

Engineering and Chemical Supplies (Epsom & Glos) Ltd v. AKZO Chemie BV (DOMINANT POSITION: PRODUCT MARKET: RELEVANT CRITERIA: E.C. Comm.)

Masterfoods Ltd v. HB Ice Cream Ltd (COMMUNITY LAW AND NATIONAL LAW: PRIORITY OF COMMUNITY LAW: NATIONAL COURTS: STANDARD OF PROOF: PENALTIES: INTER-STATE TRADE: RETAIL TRADE: VERTICAL AGREEMENTS: EXCLUSIVE DEALING: PROVISIONAL VALIDITY: DOMINANT POSITION: ABUSE: REFERENCE TO E.C. COMMISSION: EXCLUSIVE DEALING AGREEMENTS: EVIDENCE: Ireland: H.C.)

Racal Group Services' Application (PARENT COMPANY AND SUBSIDIARIES: ARTICLES 85 AND 86: DOMINANT POSITION: PROTECTION OF MONOPOLY POSITION THROUGH MARKET ALLOCATION AGREEMENT: COERCION OF UNWILLING PARTIES: ABUSIVE: USE OF COPYRIGHT AS BASIS OF AGREEMENTS ILLEGAL: JUSTIFICATION: E.C. Comm.)

Windsurfing International Inc. v. E.C. Commission (PATENT LICENSING: COMPONENTS: PATENT PROTECTION: COMMISSION'S POWERS TO INTERPRET NATIONAL LAW: JUDICIAL REVIEW: TYING CLAUSE: NO-CHALLENGE CLAUSES: TRADE MARK: ECJ)

Repackaging of Goods

Bristol Myers Squibb v. Paranova (PARALLEL IMPORTS: EXHAUSTION OF RIGHTS: RESTRICTIONS FOR PROTECTION OF INDUSTRIAL AND COMMERCIAL PROPERTY: DISGUISED RESTRICTION ON TRADE BETWEEN MEMBER STATES: ECJ)

Resale Price Maintenance

Publishers Association's Agreement (BOOKS: RESALE PRICE MAINTENANCE: COLLECTIVE SYSTEM OPERATED BY UNITED KINGDOM PUBLISHERS: E.C. Comm.)
sub nom. Net Book Agreements: Publishers Association v. E.C. Commission (ECJ PROCEDURE: INTERIM MEASURES: U.K. COLLECTIVE RESALE PRICE MAINTENANCE SCHEME: ECJ)

Procureur de la République & SA Vêtements Goguet Sport v. Hechter (FRANCHISE AGREEMENTS: RESALE PRICE MAINTENANCE: REFUSAL TO SELL: France: D.C.)

VBBB and VBVB's Agreement (TRADE ASSOCIATIONS: COLLECTIVE RESALE PRICE MAINTENANCE: E.C. Comm.)

VBBB and VBVB v. E.C. Commission (CONDUCT OF HEARINGS: DISCOVERY: RESALE PRICE MAINTENANCE: INFRINGEMENT OF ARTICLE 85(1): EXTEMPTION: PRECEDENTS: ECJ)

Royalties

Basset v. SACEM (COPYRIGHT: PHONOGRAMS: COPYRIGHT MANAGEMENT SOCIETIES: RESTRICTION OF CIRCULATION: ARTICLE 30: ARTICLE 86: ECJ)

Chambre Syndicale Nationale de la Discothéque (SYNDIS) v. SACEM (PERFORMING RIGHTS SOCIETIES: INTER-STATE TRADE: ROYALTY ENTITLEMENT: France: D.C.)

Ottung v. Klee & Weilbach A/S (PATENTS: LICENSING AGREEMENT: OBLIGATION TO PAY ROYALTIES INDEFINITELY WHILE AGREEMENT SUBSISTING: EXPIRY OF PATENT: OUTSIDE ARTICLE 85(1) WHERE LICENSEE MAY TERMINATE FREELY ON REASONABLE NOTICE: ECJ)

Performing Right Societies (COPYRIGHT: COLLECTING SOCIETIES: PARALLEL IMPORTS: NOTICE: E.C. Comm.)

Search and Seizure. See Practice (Search and seizure)

Selective Distribution

AEG Telefunken's Agreement (E.C. Comm)

Association Pharmaceutique Belge (APB's) Application (PHARMACEUTICALS: QUALITY INSPECTION BY CHEMIST'S TRADE ASSOCIATION: INTENTION TO APPROVE: E.C. Comm.)

Binon (SA) & Cie v. SA Agence et Messageries de la Presse (NEWSPAPERS: ARTICLE 85(1): ECJ)

Chanel SA's Application (MODIFICATION OF ADMISSION PROCEDURE: INTENTION TO ISSUE COMFORT LETTER: ECC)

Community v. Bayer AG (Re Bayo-N-Ox) (E.C. Comm)

Ford Werke's Agreement (MARKET PARTITIONING: NOTIFICATION: E.C. Comm.)

Friedrich Grohe Armaturenfabrik GmbH & Co's Application (EXCLUSIVE DEALING: E.C. Comm.)

Grundig's Agreements (ADMISSION CRITERIA: VALID IN SO FAR AS QUALITATIVE AND APPLIED IN NON-DISCRIMINATORY MANNER: EXEMPTION RENEWED: E.C. Comm.)

Ideal-Standard GmbH's Application (EXCLUSIVE DEALING: SYSTEMS: WHOLESALERS: PLUMBING FITTINGS: E.C. Comm.)

Metro-SB-Großmärkte GmbH & Co. KG v. E.C. Commission (No. 2) (EXEMPTION: RENEWAL: NEED FOR COMMISSION RE-EXAMINATION: ECJ)

Metro-SB-Großmärkte GmbH & Co. KG v. Cartier SA (LUXURY WATCHES: REFUSAL BY MANUFACTURER TO HONOUR WATCHES ACQUIRED OUTSIDE EEC BY UNAUTHORISED DEALER AND SOLD IN GERMANY: WHETHER BREACH OF ARTICLE 85: ECJ)

Parfums Givenchy SA's Application (ARTICLE 85(1): EXEMPTION GRANTED: E.C. Comm.)

Sony España SA (EXCLUSIVE AND SELECTIVE DISTRIBUTION AGREEMENT: INTENTION TO EXEMPT: NOTICE: E.C. Comm.)

Sony Pan-European Dealer Agreement (SELECTIVE DISTRIBUTION OF ELECTRICAL GOODS: E.C. Comm.)

Villeroy & Boch KG and Villeroy & Boch Sàrl's Agreements (RETAILERS: QUALITATIVE CRITERIA: LOCATION CLAUSE: SALES PROMOTIONS OBLIGATIONS: RESALE RESTRICTIONS: NEGATIVE CLEARANCE: E.C. Comm.)

Sole Distribution Agreements

Whisky and Gin (Sole distribution agreements) (EXCLUSIVE DISTRIBUTION: GROUP EXEMPTION: INTENTION TO EXEMPT: E.C. Comm.)

Spare Parts and Replacement Parts

Car Parts (SPARE PARTS: EXCLUSIVE PACKAGING: DOMINANT POSITION: DESIGN COPYRIGHT: U.K. Monopolies Commission)

Consorzio Italiano della Componentistica di Ricambio per Autoveicoli v. Regie Nationale des Usines Renault (COMMUNITY LAW AND NATIONAL LAW: INDUSTRIAL DESIGNS: DOMINANT POSITION: ABUSE: SPARE PARTS: ECJ)

Ford Motor Co. Ltd's Replacement Parts Policy (U.K. MMC)

Hilti AG v. E.C. Commission (RELEVANT PRODUCT MARKET: SPARE PARTS: BURDEN OF PROOF: EVIDENCE: COURT OF FIRST INSTANCE PROCEDURE: REASONING: APPELLATE JURISDICTION OF ECJ: ECJ)

Still (W.M.) & Sons Ltd (SPARE PARTS: DISCOUNTS: OFT)

Volvo A.B. v. Erik Veng (U.K.) Ltd (INDUSTRIAL DESIGN RIGHTS: SPARE PARTS: ABUSE OF DOMINANT POSITION: REFUSAL TO LICENSE: NOT *per se* ABUSIVE: ECJ)

Specialisation and Standardisation Agreements

Aerospatiale and Alcatel's Agreement (TELECOMMUNICATIONS: CO-OPERATION IN CARRYING OUT SATELLITE REPAIRS: INFORMATION EXCHANGE: INTENTION TO APPROVE: NOTICE: E.C. Comm.)

Arbed SA and Unimetal SA's Agreements (COAL AND STEEL: PRODUCT EXCHANGE: EXEMPTION GRANTED: E.C. Comm.)

Bayer AG and Gist-Brocades NV's Agreement (PHARMACEUTICALS: RECIPROCAL LONG-TERM SUPPLY CONTRACTS: INTENTION TO EXTEND EXEMPTION: E.C. Comm.)

Electrolux AB and AEG AG's Agreements (PRODUCTION OF DOMESTIC APPLIANCES: CROSS-SHAREHOLDINGS: INTENTION TO APPROVE: NOTICE: E.C. Comm.)

Ente Nazionale Idrocarburi (ENI) & Montedison (RATIONALISATION: OVERLAPPING PRODUCTS: REDUCTION OF CAPACITY: EXEMPTION: E.C. Comm.)

Volkswagenwerke AG & MAN's Agreement (JOINT R.&D.: EXTEMPTION: E.C. Comm.)

X/Open Group (COMPUTER OPERATING SYSTEM: UNIX: OPEN INDUSTRY STANDARD: INTENTION TO APPROVE: NOTICE: E.C. Comm.) (DECISION: E.C. Comm.)

Standard Agreements

Koelman v. E.C. Commission (BROADCASTING: RETRANSMISSION OF PROGRAMMES BY CABLE: STANDARD AGREEMENT: COPYRIGHT: OWNERSHIP: RADIO MATERIAL: COLLECTING SOCIETY: ALLEGED BREACH OF ARTICLES 85 AND 86: Case T–575/93: CFI)

Takeovers

Elopak v. Tetra Pak (DOMINANT POSITION: RELEVANT MARKET: PRODUCT MARKET: GEOGRAPHICAL MARKET: EXCLUSIVE LICENSING: INTER–STATE TRADE: E.C. Comm.)

Territorial Protection

Burns (W.) Tractors Ltd v. Sperry New Holland (CONTRACTS: EXPORT BANS: REFUSAL TO SUPPLY: EXEMPTION: FINES: NOTIFICATION: E.C. Comm.)

Community v. Bayer AG (RESALE BAN: MARKET POSITIONING: FEEDINGSTUFF ADDITIVES: EXPIRY OF PATENT IN ONE STATE: ARTICLE 85(1): FINE: E.C. Comm.)

Ford New Holland Ltd (BAN ON PARALLEL TRADE AGREED BETWEEN MANUFACTURER AND LOCAL DISTRIBUTORS: REBATES DEPENDENT UPON NON-EXPORT OF PRODUCTS BY CUSTOMERS: ARTICLE 85: INFRINGEMENT: E.C. Comm.)

Servicemaster Ltd (Franchise Agreements) (SERVICE FRANCHISES TREATED IN SAME WAY AS DISTRIBUTION AGREEMENTS: PROTECTION OF KNOW-HOW OUTSIDE ARTICLE 85(1): INTERSTATE TRADE: INTRA-BRAND COMPETITION: INDIVIDUAL EXEMPTION GRANTED: E.C. Comm.)

Trade Associations

Association of Retailer-Owner (AROW) v. Bureau National (BNIC) (ARTICLE 85(1): E.C. Comm.)

Association Pharmaceutique Belge (APB's) Application (PHARMACEUTICALS: COLLECTIVE QUALITY CONTROL: STANDARD FORM DISTRIBUTION AGREEMENT OFFERED BY PHARMACIST'S TRADE ASSOCIATION: RIGHT TO AFFIX SEAL OF APPROVAL TO GOODS: SALE NEGATIVE CLEARANCE: E.C. Comm.)

Association Pharmaceutique Belge (APB's) Application (SELECTIVE DISTRIBUTION: PHARMACEUTICALS: QUALITY INSPECTION BY CHEMIST'S TRADE ASSOCIATION: INTENTION TO APPROVE: E.C. Comm.)

British Dental Trade Association's Exhibition Rules (TRADE FAIRS: RULES FOR PARTICIPATION: INTENTION TO APPROVE: E.C. Comm.)

VBBB and VBVB's Agreement (TRADE ASSOCIATIONS: COLLECTIVE RESALE PRICE MAINTENANCE: E.C. Comm.)

Verband der Sachversicherer eV v. E.C. Commission (EXCLUSIONS: INSURANCE: NATIONAL LAW: COMPETITION: ECJ)

Trade Fairs

British Dental Trade Association's Exhibition Rules (RULES FOR PARTICIPATION: INTENTION TO APPROVE: E.C. Comm.)

European Committee for Co-operation of the Machine Tool Industries' (CECIMO) Application (INTENTION TO RENEW EXEMPTION: E.C. Comm.)

International Dental Exhibition (Participation in) (RULES FOR PARTICIPATION: INTENTION TO EXEMPT UNDER ARTICLE 85(3): E.C. Comm.)

Trade Marks

Apple Corp.'s Ltd v. Apple Computer Inc. (RESTRICTICE PRACTICES: NATIONAL PROCEEDINGS IN PARALLEL WITH E.C. COMMISSION PROCEEDINGS: CONFIDENTIAL EVIDENCE BEFORE NATIONAL COURT TO BE HANDED TO E.C. COMMISSION: Ch.D.)

BAT Cigaretten-Fabriken GmbH v. E.C. Commission (DORCET AND TOLTECS SPECIAL: DORMANT MARK: SIMILARITY: INFRINGEMENT OF ARTICLE 85: E.C. COMMISSION UPHELD: FINES: ECJ)

Carlsberg Beers (SUPPLY AGREEMENTS: TRADE MARK AND KNOW-HOW LICENCE: INTENTION TO APPROVE: ECJ)

Community v. Bayer AG (AGREEMENTS: RESALE RESTRICTIONS: EXPORT BANS: PACKAGING: E.C. Comm.)

Community v. Syntex Corporation (SIMILAR TRADE MARKS: MARKET PETITIONING: NOT CLEAR WHETHER EARLIER TRADE MARK COULD BE ENFORCED IN MEMBER STATES: DELIMITATION AGREEMENT TO AVOID CONFUSION: CAUGHT BY ARTICLE 85(1): CASE SETTLED: E.C. Comm.)

DDD Ltd and Delta Chemie's Agreement (KNOW-HOW: EXCLUSIVE DEALING: LICENCE CAUGHT BY ARTICLE 85(1): GROUP EXEMPTION: REGULATION 1983/83 NOT APPLICABLE: INDIVIDUAL EXEMPTION GRANTED: E.C. Comm.)

Eleco Holdings plc and Mitek Holdings Inc.'s Agreement (DIVESTITURE OF U.K. SUBSIDIARY WITH LICENCE TO CONTINUE MANUFACTURE OF EXISTING PRODUCT: TRADE MARKS DELIMITATION AGREEMENT: INTENTION TO APPROVE: E.C. Comm.)

Hag Coffee (HAG: SPECIFIC SUBJECT-MATTER: CONSEQUENCES: EXHAUSTION OF RIGHTS: IMPORTS: BREAK OF CHAIN OF OWNERSHIP BY EXPROPRIATION: GERMAN HAG ABLE TO RESIST IMPORT INTO GERMANY OF BELGIAN HAG COFFEE: *Acte claire* FROM EUROPEAN COURT JUDGMENT IN *Pharmon v. Hoechst*: NO ARTICLE 177 REFERENCE: Germany: C.A.

Hydrotherm Gerätebau GmbH v. Compact de Dott Ing Mario Andreoli & CSAS (EXCLUSIVE DEALING: BLOCK EXEMPTION: REGULATION 67/67: LICENCE: ECJ)

IHT International Heiztechnik GmbH v. Ideal-Standard GmbH (IDEAL STANDARD: EXHAUSTION OF RIGHTS: COMMON ORIGIN: UNITARY CONTROL: SALE IN ONE MEMBER STATE: EXPORT TO ANOTHER: INJUNCTION: ECJ)

Moosehead Breweries Ltd and Whitbread and Company plc' Agreement (LICENCE FOR PRODUCTION AND SALE OF CANADIAN BEER IN U.K.: NON-EXCLUSIVE WITH APPROPRIATE ANCILLARY RESTRICTIONS FOR KNOW-HOW: PROHIBITION ON SALE OUTSIDE U.K. AND SALE OF COMPETING BRANDS AND EXCLUSIVITY FOR MARK: ARTICLE 85(1): TRADE MARK NO CHALLENGE CLAUSE: OWNERSHIP: POSSIBLY RESTRICTIVE AS REGARDS VALIDITY: COMPARATIVELY NEW TO U.K.: EXEMPTION GRANTED: E.C. Comm.)

Oy Airam AB v. Osram GmbH (DOMINANT POSITION: E.C. Comm.)

Société Française de Transmissions Florales Interflora & Téléfleurs France (DOMINANT POSITION: EXCLUSIVITY CLAUSE: PROTECTION OF MARK: MINIMUM TARIFF ORDER: France: Copyright Commission)

Tayto (Northern Ireland) Ltd v. McKee (PRE-EEC MARKET-PARTITIONING AGREEMENT FOR USE OF IDENTICAL TRADE MARK: ABANDONED AND NO CONTINUING EFFECTS: FAILURE TO USE MARK IN COMPETITOR'S TERRITORY NOT TAINTED BY ORIGINAL AGREEMENT: Northern Ireland: Ch.D.)

TYLER Trade Mark (EXCLUSIVE LICENSING: E.C. Comm.)

Velcro SA v. Aplix SA (PATENT AND TRADE MARK LICENCES: EXCLUSIVITY: EXPORT BAN: EXTENSION BEYOND EXPIRY OF RIGHTS: NON-COMPETITION OBLIGATION: IMPROVEMENT PATENTS: ESSENTIAL FUNCTION OF TRADE MARK: EXEMPTION REFUSED: CEASE AND DESIST ORDER ISSUED: E.C. Comm.)

Warner-Lambert Company and BIC SA v. The Gillette Company and Eemland Holdings NV (COMPANY OWNERSHIP: ACQUISITION BY DOMINANT COMPANY OF SUBSTANTIAL HOLDING IN MAJOR COMPETITOR: ABUSE CAUGHT BY ARTICLE 86 EEC: AGREEMENT TO ASSIGN NON-COMMUNITY BUSINESS AND MARKS TO DOMINANT FIRM: VIOLATION OF ARTICLE 85(1): ORDER TO DIVEST INTEREST IN COMPETITOR AND RE-ASSIGN BUSINESS AND MARKS IN COUNTRIES BORDERING COMMUNITY: E.C. Comm.)

Windsurfing International Inc. v. E.C. Commission (PATENT LICENSING: RELEVANT MARKET: COMPONENTS: PATENT PROTECTION: COMMISSION'S POWERS TO INTERPRET NATIONAL LAW: JUDICIAL REVIEW: TYING CLAUSE: NO-CHALLENGE CLAUSES: ECJ)

TV Programmes

Radio Telefis Eireann v. Magill TV Guide Ltd (COPYRIGHT: TELEVISION PROGRAMMES: PUBLIC INTEREST: Ireland: H.C.)

Tying Clauses

Community v. Fiat Auto (DISTRIBUTION AGREEMENTS: SETTLEMENT: E.C. Comm.)
Elopak Italia Srl v. Tetra Pak (No. 2) (DOMINANT POSITION: ABUSE: RELEVANT PRODUCT MARKET: SALES CONTRACTS: EXCLUSIVE SUPPLY: ELIMINATORY PRICING: DISCRIMINATORY PRICING: E.C. Comm.)
Hilti AG (DOMINANT POSITION: ABUSE: INTERIM MEASURES: NOTICE: E.C. Comm.)
Windsurfing International Inc. v. E.C. Commission (PATENT LICENSING: RELEVANT MARKET: COMPONENTS: PATENT PROTECTION: COMMISSION'S POWERS TO INTERPRET NATIONAL LAW: JUDICIAL REVIEW: NO-CHALLENGE CLAUSES: TRADE MARK: ECJ)

Unfair Competition

Import of Drugs from Italy (PRICE: PARALLEL IMPORTS: RESTRAINT OF COMPETITION: Germany: S.C.)
Industrie Diensten Groep BV v. J.A. Beele Handelmaatschappij BV (IMPORTS: QUANTITATIVE RESTRICTIONS: PROPORTIONALITY: ECJ)

Trade Marks

Abandonment

Alexander Fergusson & Co. v. Matthews McClay & Manson (Scotland: O.H.)
Second Sight v. Novell U.K. Ltd (INFRINGEMENT: SUMMARY JUDGMENT: RECTIFICATION: NON-USE: RESTORATION: HONEST CONCURRENT USER: Ch.D.)

Advertising

Compaq Computer Corp. v. Dell Computer Corp. Ltd (COMPARATIVE ADVERTISING: Ch.D.)
Duracell International Inc. v. Ever Ready Ltd (KNOCKING ADVERTISING: Ch.D.)
Kodiak Trade Mark (USE ON GOODS ADVERTISING OTHER GOODS: Ch.D.)
News Group Newspapers Ltd v. The Mirror Group Newspapers (1988) Ltd (KNOCKING ADVERTISING: Ch.D.)
NEXT Trade Mark (USE IN ADVERTISING: BoT)
Research Specialties for Labs Pvba v. Chrompack NV (ORIGIN OF GOODS: Benelux: C.J.)

Alteration

Seaforth Maritine Ltd's Trade Mark (T.M.Reg.)

Anton Piller. *See* **Practice (***Anton Piller***)**

Application

2000 TWO THOUSAND Trade Mark (T.M.Reg.)
A.D.D.-70 Trade Mark (SERVICE MARK: T.M.Reg.)
AL BASSAM Trade Mark (ARABIC DEVICE MARK: Ch.D.: C.A.)
ALWAYS Trade Mark (Ch.D)
AU PRINTEMPS Trade Mark (MARK IN FOREIGN LANGUAGE: T.M.Reg.)
Avedis Zildjian Company's Application (NAME OF PERSON: C.-G.)
AVON Trade Mark (T.M.Reg.)
BENSYL Trade Mark (BoT)
BLACK N' RED Trade Mark (T.M.Reg.)
BRUT DE MER Trade Mark (PART B MARK: WORDS IN FOREIGN LANGUAGE: T.M.Reg.)
BUD Trade Mark (Ch.D)
BUDGET Service Mark (SERVICE MARK: BoT)
Celine SA's Trade Mark Applications (DEVICE MARKS: Ch.D.)
CHELSEA MAN Trade Mark (Ch.D)
CLUB Trade Mark (SERVICE MARK: T.M.Reg.)
Coca Cola Trade Marks (SHAPE OF BOTTLE: Ch.D.: C.A.: H.L.)
Compaq Computer Corp. v. Dell Computer Corp. Ltd (Ch.D)
COS Trade Mark (T.M.Reg.)
COUNTRY CLASSICS Trade Marks (PART B: BoT)
Dee Corporation plc's Applications (Ch.D.: C.A.)
Eltra Corp.'s Trade Mark Applications (T.M.Reg.)
EXXATE Trade Mark (Ch.D)
Family Assurance Society's Service Mark (SERVICE MARK: T.M.Reg.)
FANTASTIC SAM's Service Mark (SERVICE MARK: T.M.Reg.)
FBC Trade Mark (Ch.D)
FINGALS Trade Mark (SERVICE MARK: T.M.Reg.)
FOUNDATION Trade Mark (T.M.Reg.)
GI Trade Mark (T.M.Reg.)
GLASSCAN Trade Mark (T.M.Reg.)
GOLDEN PAGES Trade Mark (Ireland: S.C.)
HAVE A BREAK Trade Mark (SLOGAN: Ch.D.)
HOLLY HOBBIE Trade Mark (Ch.D.: C.A.: H.L.)
I CAN'T BELIEVE IT'S YOGURT Trade Mark (PART B REGISTRATION: BoT)
INADINE Trade Mark (Ch.D)
Industrial Containers (Aust.) Pty Ltd's Application (C.-G.)
INTERNATIONAL TELESIS GROUP Service Mark (T.M.Reg.)
INVICTA Trade Marks (BoT)
I.Q. Trade Mark (T.M.Reg.)
JOCKEY Trade Mark (T.M.Reg.)
John Wyeth & Bro Ltd's COLOURED TABLET Trade Mark (T.M.Reg.)
Johnson & Johnson's Application (Ch.D)
Johnson & Johnson's Application (OPPOSITION: INADINE/ANADIN: Ch.D.)
Jorge UA v. Registro de la Propiedad Industrial (Spain: S.C.)
K SABATIER Trade Mark (T.M.Reg.)
Keds Trade Mark (Ch.D)
KENT Trade Mark (T.M.Reg.: Ch.D.)
KLINT Trade Mark (Germany: S.C.)

Assignment

Keds Trade Mark (REGISTRATION OF ASSIGNMENT OF MARK THE SUBJECT OF RECTIFICATION PROCEEDINGS: NO GROUNDS FOR REFUSAL: ASSOCIATED MARKS: REGISTRATION OF MARK TO BE ASSOCIATED NOT COMPLETE UNTIL ASSOCIATION ALSO ENTERED IN REGISTER: Ch.D.)
Tradam Trading Company (Bahamas) Ltd's Trade Mark (RECTIFICATION: REGISTERED PROPRIETOR IN DEFAULT: APPLICATION BY ALLEGED ASSIGNEE TO INTERVENE: Ch.D.)
Warner-Lambert Company and BIC SA v. The Gillette Company and Eemland Holdings NV (RESTRICTIVE PRACTICES: AGREEMENT TO ASSIGN NON-COMMUNITY BUSINESS AND TRADE MARKS TO DOMINANT FIRM: VIOLATION OF ARTICLE 85(1): E.C. Comm.)

Associated Marks

BATCHELORS SNACKPOT Trade Mark (REMOVAL: NON-USE: USE OF ASSOCIATED MARK: T.M.Reg.)
Keds Trade Mark (REGISTRATION OF MARK TO BE ASSOCIATED NOT COMPLETE UNTIL ASSOCIATION ALSO ENTERED IN REGISTER: Ch.D.)
Origins Natural Resources Inc. v. Origin Clothing Limited (INFRINGEMENT: OVERLAPPING SPECIFICATIONS: VALIDITY OF SECOND MARK: NON-USE: BONA-FIDE INTENTION TO USE: LIKELIHOOD OF CONFUSION: HONEST CONCURRENT USER: ORDER 14: SERVICE OF DEFENCE AND COUNTERCLAIM: Ch.D.)
Unilever plc v. Johnson Wax Ltd (INFRINGEMENT: TOILET DUCK: SPECIFICATION OF GOODS: RECTIFICATION: NON-USE: SURVEY EVIDENCE: Ch.D.)

Authorisation of Agent

BYSTANDER Trade Mark (OPPOSITION: ISSUE ESTOPPEL: DISCRETION: T.M.Reg.)

Badge of Fraud

Cadbury Ltd v. Ulmer GmbH (SHAPE OF CHOCOLATE BAR: Ch.D.)

Balance of Convenience. *See* **Practice** *(Interlocutory injunction)*

Benelux

Henri Jullien BV v. Verschuere Norbert (REGISTRATION: OPPOSITION: SIMILARITY)
Nijs v. Ciba-Geigy AG (USE: DOCTOR'S PRESCRIPTION: C.J.)
Research Specialties for Labs Pvba v. Chrompack NV (ADVERTISING: ORIGIN OF GOODS: C.J.)

Biological Varieties

Jorge UA v. Registro de la Propiedad Industrial (GENERIC TERMS: Spain: S.C.)

Capable of Distinguishing

AL BASSAM Trade Mark (ARABIC SURNAME: Ch.D.: C.A.)

AVON Trade Mark (T.M.Reg.)
CHELSEA MAN Trade Mark (Ch.D)
INTERNATIONAL TELESIS GROUP Service Mark (OPPOSITION: WHETHER
    MARK LIKELY TO CAUSE CONFUSION: EARLIER CONFLICTING MARKS:
    T.M.Reg.)
JOCKEY Trade Mark (T.M.Reg.)
Milk Marketing Board's Application (BoT)
WATERFORD Trade Mark (PART B: Ireland: H.C.: S.C.)

Certiorari. *See* **Practice** (*Certiorari*)

Character Merchandising

HOLLY HOBBIE Trade Mark (TRAFFICKING: WHETHER QUALITY CONTROL
    CONSTITUTES TRADE CONNECTION: Ch.D.: C.A.: H.L.)

Colour of Object

John Wyeth & Bro. Ltd's COLOURED TABLET Trade Mark (COLOUR, SHAPE
    AND SIZE OF PHARMACEUTICAL TABLETS: DISTINCTIVENESS: T.M.Reg.)
Smith Kline & French Laboratories Ltd's Cimetidine Trade Mark
    (PHARMACEUTICAL: COLOURED TABLETS: Ch.D.)
Smith Kline & French Laboratories Ltd v. Higson (PHARMACEUTICAL CAPSULES:
    Ch.D.)

Combination of Descriptive Words

Orkney Seafoods Ltd's Petition (TRADE MARK: PASSING OFF: SIMILAR NAMES:
    DESCRIPTIVE NAME: ORKNEY SEAFOODS: WHETHER COMBINATION OF
    DESCRIPTIVE WORDS CALCULATED TO CAUSE CONFUSION: Scotland: O.H.)

Common Origin

CNL-Sucal NV, SA v. HAG GF AG (GERMAN AND BELGIAN MARKS OF COMMON
    ORIGIN: ECJ)
KLINT Trade Mark (SEPARATELY CREATED TRADE MARK FOR SAME PRODUCT:
    Germany: S.C.)
IHT International Heiztechnik GmbH v. Ideal-Standard GmbH (IDEAL
    STANDARD: EXHAUSTION OF RIGHTS: UNITARY CONTROL: SALE IN ONE
    MEMBER STATE: EXPORT TO ANOTHER: INJUNCTION: ECJ)

Conflicting Marks

INTERNATIONAL TELESIS GROUP Service Mark (OPPOSITION: EARLIER
    CONFLICTING MARKS: PROCEEDINGS IN USA: WHETHER ESTOPPEL: HEARSAY
    EVIDENCE: HONEST CONCURRENT USER: T.M.Reg.)

Confusing Similarity

ROSE GARDEN Trade Mark (APPLICATION: OPPOSITION: T.M.Reg.)

Confusion. *See also under* **Deception**

BUD Trade Mark (USE BY BOTH PARTIES OF BUDWEISER FOR BEER:
    CONFUSION AND DECEPTION: HONEST CONCURRENT USER: TRIPLE
    IDENTITY RULE: Ch.D.)

CNL-Sucal NV, SA v. HAG GF AG (GERMAN AND BELGIAN MARKS OF COMMON
ORIGIN: IDENTICAL MARKS: CONFISCATION OF ENEMY PROPERTY OUTSIDE
GERMANY: ECJ)

Community v. Syntex Corporation (RESTRICTIVE PRACTICES: SIMILAR TRADE
MARKS: MARKET PETITIONING: NOT CLEAR WHETHER EARLIER TRADE
MARK COULD BE ENFORCED IN MEMBER STATES: DELIMITATION
AGREEMENT TO AVOID CONFUSION: CAUGHT BY ARTICLE 85(1): E.C.
Comm.)

Deutsche Renault AG v. Audi AG (NATIONAL LAW: LIMITED PROTECTION:
IMPORTATION: QUATTRO/QUADRA: TEST: ECJ)

Guccio Gucci SpA v. Paolo Gucci (INFRINGEMENT: EVIDENCE: TRADE EVIDENCE:
Ch.D.)

INTERNATIONAL TELESIS GROUP Service Mark (OPPOSITION: WHETHER
MARK LIKELY TO CAUSE CONFUSION: EARLIER CONFLICTING MARKS:
T.M.Reg.)

LANCER Trade Mark (PHONETIC CONFUSION WITH LANCIA: Ch.D.)

LEUCO Great Britain Trade Mark (GREAT BRITAIN IN MARK: DECEPTION AND
CONFUSION: CONDITIONS: BoT)

Origins Natural Resources Inc. v. Origin Clothing Limited (ASSOCIATED MARKS:
OVERLAPPING SPECIFICATIONS: VALIDITY OF SECOND MARK: NON-USE:
BONA-FIDE INTENTION TO USE: LIKELIHOOD OF CONFUSION: HONEST
CONCURRENT USER: Ch.D.)

PRIMASPORT Trade Mark (OPPOSITION: DISTINCTIVENESS: QUESTIONNAIRE
TO OPPONENT'S SUPPLIERS: T.M.Reg.)

The European Ltd v. The Economist Newspapers Ltd (DEVICE MARKS: THE
EUROPEAN/EUROPEAN VOICE: WHETHER SIMILAR: WHETHER
CONFUSING: EVIDENCE OF CONFUSION: SURVEY EVIDENCE: Ch.D.)

Theodor Kohl KG v. Ringelhan & Rennett SA (USE BY SEVERAL SUCCESSORS TO
SPLIT COMPANY: LIKELIHOOD OF CONFUSION: Germany: ECJ)

Criminal Offence

Durham Trading Standards v. Kingsley Clothing (INFRINGEMENT: CRIMINAL
OFFENCE: SUBJECTIVE TEST: C.A.)

Damages. See Practice (Damages)

Deception

BUD Trade Mark (USE BY BOTH PARTIES OF BUDWEISER FOR BEER:
CONFUSION AND DECEPTION: HONEST CONCURRENT USER: TRIPLE
IDENTITY RULE: Ch.D.)

GUNTRUM Trade Mark (OPPOSITION: SURNAME: T.M.Reg.)

Hunt-Wesson Inc.'s Trade Mark Application (SWISS MISS: OPPOSITION: APPEAL
FROM DECISION OF REGISTRAR: PRINCIPLES FOR ADMISSION OF FURTHER
EVIDENCE ON APPEAL: REGISTRAR'S PRACTICE: Ch.D.)

LEUCO Great Britain Trade Mark (APPLICATION: GREAT BRITAIN IN MARK:
CONDITIONS: REGISTRATION: BoT)

PATON CALVERT CORDON BLEU Trade Mark (OPPOSITION: EFFECT OF
DISCLAIMERS: DISCRETION: T.M.Reg.)

PRIMASPORT Trade Mark (DANGER OF CONFUSION AND DECEPTION:
QUESTIONNAIRE TO OPPONENT'S SUPPLIERS: T.M.Reg.)

THERMOS PRIMA Trade Mark (DATE AS OF WHICH LIKELIHOOD OF DECEPTION TO BE CONSIDERED: T.M.Reg.)

Defences

Accurist Watches Ltd v. King (DEFENCE UNDER T.M.A. 1938: Ch.D.)

Bravado Merchandising Services Ltd v. Mainstream Publishing (Edinburgh) Ltd (NAME OF POP GROUP REGISTERED *inter alia* FOR BOOKS: USE OF NAME OF GROUP ON BOOK ABOUT THE GROUP: INFRINGEMENT: WHETHER USE IN TRADEMARK SENSE: T.M.A. 94, s.11(2): AVAILABILITY OF DEFENCE: Scotland: O.H.)

Duracell International Inc. v. Ever Ready Ltd (EURO-DEFENCES: Ch.D.)

Provident Financial plc v. Halifax Building Society (SECTIONS 5(2) AND 8 DEFENCES: Ch.D.)

The European Ltd v. The Economist Newspapers Ltd (T.M.A. 94, s.11(2)(b): Ch.D.)

Delimitation Agreement

Apple Corps Ltd v. Apple Computer Ltd (DELIMITATION AGREEMENT: RESTRICTION TO OWN LINES: RESTRICTIVE PRACTICES: COMPATIBILITY WITH ARTICLE 85: WHETHER VALIDITY RELEVANT: USE: C.A.)

Descriptive Names

International House of Heraldry v. Grant (INTERNATIONAL ART OF HERALDRY: WHETHER DESCRIPTIVE: WHETHER SLIGHT DIFFERENCE SUFFICIENT TO DISTINGUISH: Scotland: O.H.)

Orkney Seafoods Ltd's Petition (ORKNEY SEAFOODS: WHETHER COMBINATION OF DESCRIPTIVE WORDS CALCULATED TO CAUSE CONFUSION: Scotland: O.H.)

Descriptiveness

Mothercare U.K. Ltd v. Penguin Books Ltd (MOTHERCARE/MOTHER CARE/OTHER CARE: DESCRIPTIVE WORDS: C.A.)

MY MUMS COLA Trade Mark (LAUDATORY ELEMENT: BoT)

PHOTO-SCAN Trade Mark (BoT)

POUND PUPPIES Trade Mark (BoT)

Salon Services (Hairdressing Supplies) Ltd v. Direct Salon Services Ltd (Scotland: O.H.)

Device Mark

AL BASSAM Trade Mark (OPPOSITION: ARABIC DEVICE MARK: HEADSHAWLS: Ch.D.: C.A.)

Celine SA's Trade Mark Applications (Ch.D)

Kohler Company's Trade Mark Application (Ch.D)

ROTHSCHILD Trade Mark (DISCLAIMER: T.M.Reg.)

TELECHECK Trade Mark (BoT)

The European Ltd v. The Economist Newspapers Ltd (THE EUROPEAN/ EUROPEAN VOICE: WHETHER SIMILAR: WHETHER CONFUSING: EVIDENCE OF CONFUSION: SURVEY EVIDENCE: Ch.D.)

Unilever Ltd's (Striped Toothpaste No. 2) Trade Marks (Ch.D)

Unilever plc's Trade Mark Application (TOOTHPASTE ON BRUSH: Ch.D.)

Disclaimer

Family Assurance Society's Service Mark (T.M.Reg.)
MERIT Trade Marks (COMPOSITE MARK: Ch.D.)
PATON CALVERT CORDON BLEU Trade Mark (OPPOSITION: EFFECT OF
   DISCLAIMERS: DISCRETION: T.M.Reg.)
REVUETRONIC Trade Mark (DISCLAIMER OF PART OF MARK: T.M.Reg.)
ROTHSCHILD Trade Mark (DEVICE MARK INCORPORATING SURNAME:
   T.M.Reg.)

Distinctiveness

ALWAYS Trade Mark (Ch.D)
British Sugar plc v. James Robertson & Sons Ltd (INFRINGEMENT: DEVOID OF
   DISTINCTIVE CHARACTER: PROOF: STATUTORY INTERPRETATION: Ch.D.)
BUDGET Service Mark (CAR HIRE: BoT)
Ciba Trade Mark (SURNAME: Ch.D.)
Eltra Corp.'s Trade Mark Applications (NAMES OF TYPEFACES: T.M.Reg.)
FANTASTIC SAM's Service Mark (APPLICATION: PRACTICE: T.M.Reg.)
FBC Trade Mark (APPLICATION: DISTINCTIVENESS OF THREE-LETTER MASK ON
   GRID BACKGROUND: Ch.D.)
GI Trade Mark (APPLICATION: LETTER MARK: T.M.Reg.)
I CAN'T BELIEVE IT'S YOGURT Trade Mark (APPLICATION: WHETHER
   DISTINCTIVE OR LAUDATORY: PART B REGISTRATION: BoT)
JOCKEY Trade Mark (NON-ALCOHOLIC DRINKS: WHETHER DISTINCTIVE OR
   CAPABLE OF DISTINGUISHING: T.M.Reg.)
John Wyeth & Bro Ltd's Coloured Tablet Trade Mark (APPLICATION: T.M.Reg.)
KUDOS Trade Mark (APPLICATION: BoT)
Levi Strauss & Company's Label Trade Mark (LABEL SEWN INTO GARMENT:
   T.M.Reg.)
MEMPHIS Trade Mark (T.M.Reg.)
MY MUMS COLA Trade Mark (LAUDATORY ELEMENT: WHETHER MARK
   DESCRIPTIVE OF DISTINCTIVE: BoT)
NEXT Trade Mark (APPLICATION: OBJECTION: USE IN ADVERTISING: BoT)
PRIMASPORT Trade Mark (T.M.Reg.)
RIJN STAAL Trade Mark (BoT)
SLOPHYLLIN Trade Mark (SLOW RELEASE PHARMACEUTICAL: T.M.Reg.)
SOLID FUEL ADVISORY SERVICE Service Mark (SERVICE MARK: T.M.Reg.)
SAF Trade Mark (COLLECTION OF LETTERS: Ireland: H.C.)
SUPERWOUND Trade Mark (LAUDATORY WORD: CONJOINED WORDS: BoT)
YORK Trade Mark (YORK: GEOGRAPHICAL SIGNIFICANCE: Ch.D.: H.L.)

Entitlement to Apply

AL BASSAM Trade Mark (OPPOSITION: ARABIC DEVICE MARK: HEADSHAWLS:
   EXPORTED GOODS: WHETHER SURNOMINAL SIGNIFICATION: SCOPE OF
   APPLICATION: Ch.D.: C.A.)

European Court Procedure. *See* **Practice** (*European Court procedure*)

Evidence. *See* **Practice** (*Evidence*)

Exhaustion of Rights

Bristol Myers Squibb v. Paranova (PARALLEL IMPORTS: REPACKAGING OF GOODS: EXHAUSTION OF RIGHTS: RESTRICTIONS FOR PROTECTION OF INDUSTRIAL AND COMMERCIAL PROPERTY: DISGUISED RESTRICTION ON TRADE BETWEEN MEMBER STATES: ECJ)

Exported Goods

AL BASSAM Trade Mark (OPPOSITION: ARABIC DEVICE MARK: HEADSHAWLS: ENTITLEMENT TO APPLY FOR REGISTRATION: WHETHER SURNOMINAL SIGNIFICATION: SCOPE OF APPLICATIONS: Ch.D.: C.A.)

Fisons plc v. Norton Healthcare Ltd (INFRINGEMENT: INTERLOCUTORY INJUNCTION: RECTIFICATION: NON-USE IN U.K.: NO SERIOUS DEFENCE: NO SERIOUS RISK OF INJUSTICE: Ch.D.)

IHT International Heiztechnik GmbH v. Ideal-Standard GmbH (IDEAL STANDARD: EXHAUSTION OF RIGHTS: COMMON ORIGIN: UNITARY CONTROL: SALE IN ONE MEMBER STATE: EXPORT TO ANOTHER: INJUNCTION: ECJ)

France

Baux v. Société Co-operative de Calce (TRADING NAME: WINE: APPELATION: CHÂTEAU: CONFLICT BETWEEN OCCUPANTS OF CHÂTEAU AND VINEGROWERS OCCUPYING LAND PREVIOUSLY PART OF CHÂTEAU: REFERENCE TO ECJ: S.C.)

Function

Wagamama Ltd v. City Centre Restaurants plc (INTENTION OF E.C. DIRECTIVE: HISTORICAL FUNCTION OF TRADE MARKS: ASSOCIATION WITHOUT CONFUSION AS TO ORIGIN: Ch.D.)

Generic Terms

Jorge UA v. Registro de la Propiedad Industrial (BIOLOGICAL VARIETIES: Spain: S.C.)

Geographical Name

Grant & Sons Ltd v. William Cadenhead Ltd (Scotland: O.H.)
Highland Distilleries Co. plc v. Speymalt Whisky Distributors Ltd (Scotland: O.H.)
KENT Trade Mark (T.M.Reg.: C.-G.)
PHOENIX Trade Mark (T.M.Reg.)
YORK Trade Mark (Ch.D.: H.L.)

Germany

ASTERIX Trade Mark (COPYRIGHT: COMIC STRIPS: UNAUTHORISED SALE: INJUNCTION: VICARIOUS LIABILITY: C.A.)

HAG COFFEE (HAG: SPECIFIC SUBJECT-MATTER: CONSEQUENCES: EXHAUSTION OF RIGHTS: IMPORTS: BREAK OF CHAIN OF OWNERSHIP BY EXPROPRIATION: GERMAN HAG ABLE TO RESIST IMPORT INTO GERMANY OF BELGIAN HAG COFFEE: *Acte claire* FROM EUROPEAN COURT JUDGMENT IN *Pharmon v. Hoechst*: NO ARTICLE 177 REFERENCE: Germany: C.A.)

Hoffmann–La Roche AG v. Centrafarm GmbH (IMPORTS: REPACKAGING: S.C.)

JELLIED BEEF Trade Marks, Re (NON-USE: JUSTIFICATION BY ILLEGALITY OF EXCLUSION FROM MARKET CONTRARY TO EEC LAWS: C.A.)

KERLONE Trade Mark (PARALLEL IMPORTS OF PHARMACEUTICALS FROM FRANCE TO GERMANY: DIFFERENT PACKAGING REQUIREMENTS: REPACKAGING: VISIBILITY OF MARK THROUGH WINDOW IN NEW PACKAGING: INFRINGEMENT: ARTICLE 36(1): C.A.)

KLINT Trade Mark (IMPORTS: COMMON ORIGIN: SEPARATELY CREATED TRADE MARK FOR SAME PRODUCT: ARTICLE 30: INFRINGEMENT: S.C.)

QUATTRO Trade Mark (IMPORTS: WHETHER PROTECTION OF ITALIAN NUMERAL IN WORDS AS A TRADE MARK FOR MOTOR CARS IN GERMANY AGAINST IMPORTS FROM OTHER MEMBER STATES CONSTITUTES AN UNLAWFUL RESTRICTION ON IMPORTS CONTRARY TO ARTICLE 30: S.C.) (REFERENCE TO EUROPEAN COURT: ECJ)

SHAMROCK Trade Mark (INFRINGEMENT: NATIONAL SYMBOL: S.C.)

Theodor Kohl KG v. Ringelhan & Rennett SA (IMPORTS: PHARMACEUTICALS: GET-UP: USE BY SEVERAL SUCCESSORS TO SPLIT COMPANY: LIKELIHOOD OF CONFUSION: INFRINGEMENT: ECJ)

Weigand v. Schutzverband Deutscher Wein eV (WINE LABELS: FALSE IMPRESSION OF ORIGIN: S.C.: ECJ)

Get-up

Alexander Fergusson & Co. v. Matthews McClay & Manson (USE OF GET-UP: ABANDONMENT OF GET-UP: BALANCE OF CONVENIENCE: Scotland: O.H.)

Cadbury Ltd v. Ulmer GmbH (SHAPE OF CHOCOLATE BAR: Ch.D.)

Duracell International Inc. v. Ever Ready Ltd (KNOCKING ADVERTISING: GET-UP: Ch.D.)

Theodor Kohl KG v. Ringelhan & Rennett SA (USE BY SEVERAL SUCCESSORS TO SPLIT COMPANY: LIKELIHOOD OF CONFUSION: Germany: ECJ)

Goods of the Same Description

BENSYL Trade Mark (APPLICATION: PRACTICE: BoT)

INVICTA Trade Marks (APPLICATION: BoT)

PPI Industries Pty Ltd's Application (APPLICATION: PRIOR REGISTRATIONS: SUBSTANTIALLY IDENTICAL WITH: DECEPTIVELY SIMILAR: GOODS THAT ARE CLOSELY RELATED: C.-G.)

Goodwill

Boot Tree Ltd v. Robinson (ASSIGNMENT WITHOUT GOODWILL: Ch.D.)

Fyffes plc v. Chiquita Brands International Inc. (REGISTERED AND UNREGISTERED MARKS: COVENANT NOT TO USE OUTSIDE U.K. AND IRELAND: RESTRAINT OF TRADE: EFFECT ON PURCHASER: Ch.D.)

Wagamama Ltd v. City Centre Restaurants plc (INFRINGEMENT: ASSOCIATION WITHOUT CONFUSION AS TO ORIGIN: DILUTION OF GOODWILL: EVIDENCE: Ch.D.)

Honest Concurrent User

BUD Trade Mark (TRIPLE IDENTITY RULE: Ch.D.)

CHELSEA MAN Trade Mark (OPPOSITION BASED ON CHELSEA GIRL: Ch.D.)
INTERNATIONAL TELESIS GROUP Service Mark (OPPOSITION: WHETHER
MARK CAPABLE OF DISTINGUISHING: WHETHER MARK LIKELY TO CAUSE
CONFUSION: EARLIER CONFLICTING MARKS: HONEST CONCURRENT USER:
T.M.Reg.)
L'AMY Trade Mark (APPLICATION: T.M.Reg.)
Origins Natural Resources Inc. v. Origin Clothing Limited (ASSOCIATED MARKS:
OVERLAPPING SPECIFICATIONS: VALIDITY OF SECOND MARK: NON-USE:
BONA-FIDE INTENTION TO USE: LIKELIHOOD OF CONFUSION: ORDER 14:
SERVICE OF DEFENCE AND COUNTERCLAIM: Ch.D.)
Second Sight v. Novell U.K. Ltd (INFRINGEMENT: SUMMARY JUDGMENT:
RECTIFICATION: NON-USE: ABANDONMENT: RESTORATION: Ch.D.)
STAR Trade Mark (APPLICATION: T.M.Reg.)

Identity of Goods

British Sugar plc v. James Robertson & Sons Ltd (INFRINGEMENT: USE IN THE
COURSE OF TRADE: IDENTITY OF GOODS: SIMILARITY OF GOODS: VALIDITY:
DEVOID OF DISTINCTIVE CHARACTER: PROOF: STATUTORY
INTERPRETATION: Ch.D.)

Imports

Boot Tree Ltd v. Robinson (PASSING OFF: IMPORTED GOODS: ASSIGNMENT OF
MARK WITHOUT GOODWILL: Ch.D.)
Castrol Ltd v. Automotive Oil Supplies Ltd (INFRINGEMENT: PARALLEL IMPORTS:
NOTICES TO PURCHASERS: Ch.D.)
CNL-Sucal NV, SA v. HAG GF AG (EXHAUSTION OF RIGHTS: GERMAN AND
BELGIAN MARKS OF COMMON ORIGIN: ECJ)
Colgate-Palmolive Ltd v. Markwell Finance Ltd (PASSING OFF: INFRINGEMENT:
TOOTHPASTE: Ch.D.: C.A.)
Freistaat Bayern v. Eurim-Pharm GmbH (PHARMACEUTICALS: NEED FOR
AUTHORISATION: CAUGHT BY ARTICLE 30: ECJ)
HAG COFFEE (EXHAUSTION OF RIGHTS: Germany: C.A.)
Hoffmann-la Roche AG v. Centrafarm GmbH (REPACKAGING: Germany: S.C.)
KLINT Trade Mark (COMMON ORIGIN: SEPARATELY CREATED MARK FOR SAME
PRODUCT: Germany: S.C.)
QUATTRO Trade Mark (WHETHER PROTECTION OF ITALIAN NUMERAL IN
WORDS AS A TRADE MARK FOR MOTOR CARS IN GERMANY AGAINST
IMPORTS FROM OTHER MEMBER STATES CONSTITUTES AN UNLAWFUL
RESTRICTION ON IMPORTS CONTRARY TO ARTICLE 30: Germany: S.C.)
(REFERENCE TO EUROPEAN COURT: ECJ)
R. v. Secretary of State for Social Services ex parte Wellcome Foundation Ltd
(SEPTRIN Trade Mark) (PRODUCT LICENCE: IMPORTATION FROM EEC
MEMBER STATE: WHETHER INFRINGEMENT RELEVANT TO APPLICATION FOR
PRODUCT LICENCE: Q.B.D.: C.A.: H.L.)
Theodor Kohl KG v. Ringelhan & Rennett SA (PHARMACEUTICALS: Germany:
ECJ)

Importing a Reference

Chanel Ltd v. L'Arome (U.K.) Ltd (MULTI-LEVEL MARKETING: SMELL-ALIKE
PERFUMES: COMPARISON CHART: WHETHER ADVERTISEMENT ISSUED TO
THE PUBLIC: Ch.D.)

Infringement

Accurist Watches Ltd v. King (MARK APPLIED BY MANUFACTURER UNDER CONTRACT WITH REGISTERED USER: RESERVATION OF TITLE CLAUSE: Ch.D.)

Atari Ireland Ltd v. Valadon (France)

Bravado Merchandising Services Ltd v. Mainstream Publishing (Edinburgh) Ltd (NAME OF POP GROUP REGISTERED *inter alia* FOR BOOKS: USE OF NAME OF GROUP ON BOOK ABOUT THE GROUP: INFRINGEMENT: WHETHER USE IN TRADEMARK SENSE: AVAILABILITY OF DEFENCE UNDER T.M.A.94 s.11(2): Scotland: O.H.)

British Sugar plc v. James Robertson & Sons Ltd (USE IN THE COURSE OF TRADE: IDENTITY OF GOODS: SIMILARITY OF GOODS: VALIDITY: DEVOID OF DISTINCTIVE CHARACTER: PROOF: STATUTORY INTERPRETATION: Ch.D.)

Cadbury Ltd v. Ulmer GmbH (PASSING OFF: STRIKING OUT: JOINT TORTFEASORS: GET-UP: SHAPE OF CHOCOLATE BAR: "BADGE OF FRAUD": Ch.D.)

Castrol Ltd v. Automotive Oil Supplies Ltd (PARALLEL IMPORTS: NOTICES TO PURCHASERS: Ch.D.)

CBS Inc. v. Blue Suede Music Ltd (SEIZURE OF GOODS BY CUSTOMS: PRACTICE: Ch.D.)

Chanel Ltd v. L'Arome (U.K.) Ltd (MULTI-LEVEL MARKETING: IMPORTING A REFERENCE: SMELL-ALIKE PERFUMES: COMPARISON CHART: WHETHER ADVERTISEMENT ISSUED TO THE PUBLIC: Ch.D.)

Charles of the Ritz Group Ltd v. Jory (PRACTICE: DISCOVERY: NAMES OF SUPPLIERS: Ch.D.)

CHEETAH Trade Mark (SUMMARY JUDGMENT: MARK USED ONLY ON INVOICES: WHETHER USED IN RELATION TO GOODS AND/OR IN COURSE OF TRADE: EEC: FREE MOVEMENT OF GOODS: EXHAUSTION OF RIGHTS: Ch.D.)

Coca Cola Company v. Peter John Gilbey (PASSING OFF: COUNTERFEIT GOODS: PRACTICE: ANTON PILLER ORDER: DISCLOSURE OF INFORMATION: PRIVILEGE AGAINST SELF INCRIMINATION: RISK OF PERSONAL JEOPARDY: WHETHER GROUNDS TO DISCHARGE ORDER: WHETHER PERMISSSABLE FOR DEFENDANT TO GIVE EVIDENCE IN CAMERA IN THE ABSENCE OF PLAINTIFFS OR THEIR LEGAL REPRESENTATIVES: Ch.D.: C.A.)

Colgate Palmolive Ltd v. Markwell Finance Ltd (PASSING OFF: PRACTICE: COSTS: PAYMENT INTO COURT: Ch.D.)

Colgate-Palmolive Ltd v. Markwell Finance Ltd (PASSING OFF: TOOTHPASTE: PARALLEL IMPORTS: Ch.D.: C.A.)

Compaq Computer Corp. v. Dell Computer Corp. Ltd (COMPARATIVE ADVERTISING: Ch.D.)

Cooper Chasney Ltd v. Commissioners of Customs and Excise (VAT: SETTLEMENT OF LEGAL PROCEEDINGS: VAT Trib., London)

CPC (United Kingdom) Ltd v. Keenan (PASSING OFF: OXFORD MARMALADE: Ch.D.)

Crittall Windows Ltd v. Stormseal (UPVC) Window Systems Ltd (SUMMARY JUDGMENT: BREACH OF REGISTERED USER AGREEMENT: Ch.D.)

Dormeuil Frères SA v. Feraglow Ltd (PASSING OFF: INQUIRY AS TO DAMAGES: INTERIM PAYMENT: BASIS OF DAMAGES: Ch.D.)

Dormeuil Frères SA v. Nicolian International (Textiles) Ltd (ANTON PILLER PRACTICE: SETTING ASIDE OF ORDER: DUTY OF FULL DISCLOSURE: RETURN OF GOODS SEIZED: Ch.D.)

Duracell International Inc. v. Ever Ready Ltd (INTERLOCUTORY INJUNCTION: KNOCKING ADVERTISING: GET-UP: Ch.D.)

Duracell International Inc. v. Ever Ready Ltd (VALIDITY: EURO-DEFENCES: STRIKING OUT: Ch.D.)

Durham Trading Standards v. Kingsley Clothing (INFRINGEMENT: CRIMINAL OFFENCE: SUBJECTIVE TEST: C.A.)

Fisons plc v. Norton Healthcare Ltd (INTERLOCUTORY INJUNCTION: EYE-CROM/VICROM: EXPORTED GOODS: RECTIFICATION: NON-USE IN U.K.: NO SERIOUS DEFENCE: NO SERIOUS RISK OF INJUSTICE: Ch.D.)

Furnitureland Ltd v. Harris (FURNITURELAND/FURNITURE CITY: trade usage: Ch.D.)

Games Workshop Ltd v. Transworld Publishers Ltd (TITLE OF SERIES OF BOOKS: C.A.)

Grant & Sons Ltd v. William Cadenhead Ltd (PASSING OFF: WHISKY: GEOGRAPHICAL NAME: Scotland: O.H.)

Guccio Gucci SpA v. Paolo Gucci (PASSING OFF: EVIDENCE OF CONFUSION: TRADE EVIDENCE: Ch.D.)

Harrods Ltd v. Schwartz-Sackin & Co. Ltd (PASSING OFF: UNFAIR COMPETITION: Ch.D.)

Highland Distilleries Co. plc v. Speymalt Whisky Distributors Ltd (PASSING OFF: GEOGRAPHICAL NAME: Scotland: O.H.)

IHT International Heiztechnik GmbH v. Ideal-Standard GmbH (IDEAL STANDARD: EXHAUSTION OF RIGHTS: COMMON ORIGIN: UNITARY CONTROL: SALE IN ONE MEMBER STATE: EXPORT TO ANOTHER: INJUNCTION: ECJ)

Ind Coope Ltd v. Paine & Co. Ltd (PRACTICE: Ch.D.)

International Business Machines Corporation v. Phoenix International (Computers) Ltd (PASSING OFF: PRACTICE: STRIKING OUT: SUMMARY JUDGMENT: EURO-DEFENCES: ACQUIESCENCE: ESTOPPEL: Ch.D.)

James Burrough Distillers plc v. Speymalt Whisky Distributors Ltd (INFRINGEMENT ABROAD: PASSING OFF: INTERNATIONAL LAW: DOUBLE ACTIONABILITY REQUIREMENT: O.H.)

James North & Sons Ltd v. North Cape Textiles Ltd (PASSING OFF: PRACTICE: INJUNCTION: Scotland: England: C.A.)

KERLONE Trade Mark (PARALLEL IMPORTS OF PHARMACEUTICALS FROM FRANCE TO GERMANY: DIFFERENT PACKAGING REQUIREMENTS: REPACKAGING: VISIBILITY OF MARK THROUGH WINDOW IN NEW PACKAGING: INFRINGEMENT: ARTICLE 36(1): GERMANY: C.A.)

KLINT Trade Mark (IMPORTS: COMMON ORIGIN: SEPARATELY CREATED MARK FOR SAME PRODUCT: ARTICLE 30: Germany: S.C.)

Laura Ashley Ltd v. Coloroll Ltd (LOGO: EVIDENCE: TACHISTOSCOPE: Ch.D.)

LAURA ASHLEY Trade Mark (APPLICATION: PERSONAL NAME AND DEVICE: "OTHER CIRCUMSTANCES": BoT)

Levi Strauss & Co. v. Shah (TABS ON JEANS: RECTIFICATION: NON-USER: Ch.D.)

Levi Strauss & Co. v. The French Connection Ltd (REGISTERED USER: Ch.D.)

Macallan-Glenlivet plc v. Speyside Whisky Distributors Ltd (PASSING OFF: WHISKY: Scotland: O.H.)

Machinery Market Ltd v. Sheen Publishing Ltd (Ch.D)

Mars GB Ltd v. Cadbury Ltd (TREETS/TREAT SIZE: CONFECTIONERY: RECTIFICATION: Ch.D.)

Mercury Communications Ltd v. Mercury Interactive (U.K.) Ltd (COMPUTER SOFTWARE: SUMMARY JUDGMENT: BONA FIDE USE OF OWN NAME: SCOPE OF REGISTRATION: Ch.D.)

Mothercare U.K. Ltd v. Penguin Books Ltd (PASSING OFF: INTERLOCUTORY INJUNCTION: BOOK TITLE: LIKELIHOOD OF DAMAGE: SURVEY EVIDENCE: PRACTICE: C.A.)

Mothercare U.K. Ltd v. Penguin Books Ltd (PASSING OFF: MOTHERCARE/ MOTHER CARE/OTHER CARE: MISREPRESENTATION: DESCRIPTIVE WORDS: C.A.)

News Group Newspapers Ltd v. The Mirror Group Newspapers (1988) Ltd (COPYRIGHT: THE SUN: MASTHEADS: KNOCKING ADVERTISING: Ch.D.)

Newsgroup Newspapers Ltd v. The Mirror Group Newspapers (1986) Ltd (INTERLOCUTORY INJUNCTION: PRACTICE: DELAY IN PROCEEDINGS AFTER INJUNCTION GRANTED: Ch.D.)

Origins Natural Resources Inc. v. Origin Clothing Limited (ASSOCIATED MARKS: OVERLAPPING SPECIFICATIONS: VALIDITY OF SECOND MARK: NON-USE: BONA FIDE INTENTION TO USE: LIKELIHOOD OF CONFUSION: HONEST CONCURRENT USER: ORDER 14: SERVICE OF DEFENCE AND COUNTERCLAIM: Ch.D.)

Parfums Givenchy SA v. Designer Alternatives Ltd (PRACTICE: EVIDENCE OF PRONUNCIATION: C.A.)

Pickwick International Inc. (G.B.) Ltd v. Demon Records Ltd (IMP: SPECIFICATION OF GOODS: C.A.)

Portakabin Ltd v. Powerblast Ltd (PREFIX MARK PORTA: SPECIFICATION OF GOODS: Ch.D.)

Post Office v. Interlink Express Parcels Ltd (INTERLOCUTORY INJUNCTION: BALANCE OF CONVENIENCE: Ch.D.)

Provident Financial plc v. Halifax Building Society (PASSING OFF: INTERLOCUTORY INJUNCTION: FINANCIAL SERVICES: WHETHER SERIOUS TRIABLE ISSUE: SECTIONS 5(2) AND 8 DEFENCES: Ch.D.)

R. v. Secretary of State for Social Services *ex parte* Wellcome Foundation Ltd (SEPTRIN Trade Mark) (WHETHER INFRINGEMENT RELEVANT TO APPLICATION FOR PRODUCT LICENCE: Q.B.D.: C.A.: H.L.)

R. v. Veys (FALSE TRADE DESCRIPTION: CRIMINAL OFFENCE: COAT OF ARMS: RELEVANCE TO OFFENCE UNDER TRADE DESCRIPTIONS ACT: C.A., Crim. Div.)

Second Sight v. Novell U.K. Ltd (SUMMARY JUDGMENT: RECTIFICATION: NON-USE: ABANDONMENT: RESTORATION: Ch.D.)

SHAMROCK Trade Mark (NATIONAL SYMBOL: Germany: S.C.)

Silicon Graphics Inc. v. Indigo Graphic Systems (U.K.) Ltd (PASSING OFF: INTERLOCUTORY INJUNCTION: DIGITAL PRINTING PRESS: BALANCE OF CONVENIENCE: Ch.D.)

Smith Kline & French Laboratories Ltd v. Higson (PHARMACEUTICAL CAPSULES: COLOURS: Ch.D.)

Theodor Kohl KG v. Ringelhan & Rennett SA (IMPORTS: PHARMACEUTICALS: GET-UP: USE BY SEVERAL SUCCESSORS TO SPLIT COMPANY: LIKELIHOOD OF CONFUSION: Germany: ECJ)

Unidoor Ltd v. Marks & Spencer plc (PASSING OFF: INTERLOCUTORY INJUNCTION: *Coast to Coast*: WHETHER USE AS MARK: Ch.D.)

Unilever plc v. Johnson Wax Ltd (TOILET DUCK: Ch.D.)

Wagamama Ltd v. City Centre Restaurants plc (PASSING OFF: WAGAMAMA/ RAJAMAMA: ORIENTAL THEME RESTAURANTS: STATUTORY CONSTRUCTION: Ch.D.)

Williams & Humbert Ltd v. International Distillers & Vintners Ltd (SUMMARY JUDGMENT: Ch.D.)

Infringement—Marks in Issue

AUTOTRADER
    B&S Ltd v. Irish Auto Trader Ltd (Ireland: H.C.)

Injunction. *See* **Practice** (*Injunction*)

Interlocutory Injunction. *See* **Practice** (*Interlocutory Injunction*)

Ireland

Anheuser Busch Inc. v. Controller of Patents, Designs and Trade Marks (DECISION OF
T.M.REG.: JUDICIAL REVIEW: NATURAL JUSTICE: H.C.)

B&S Ltd v. Irish Auto Trader Ltd (PASSING OFF: ADVERTISING MAGAZINES:
AUTOTRADER: INTERLOCUTORY INJUNCTION: PRINCIPLES:
PRESERVATION OF *status quo*: BALANCE OF CONVENIENCE: H.C.)

Gallaher (Dublin) Ltd v. The Health Education Bureau (USE IN RELATION TO
GOODS: H.C.)

GOLDEN PAGES Trade Mark (APPLICATION: USE ON TELEPHONE DIRECTORIES:
S.C.)

Mitchelstown Co-operative Society Ltd v. Société des Produits Nestlé SA (LICENCE:
JURISDICTION: ARBITRATION: BALANCE OF CONVENIENCE: S.C.)

Schering Corporation v. The Controller of Patents, Designs and Trademarks
(PATENTS: APPLICATION: DELAY: CONTROLLER OF PATENTS, DESIGNS AND
TRADEMARKS: POWERS: CONVENTION APPLICATION: REFUSAL TO DEEM
APPLICATION: RECEIPT WITHIN STATUTORY PERIOD: JUSTIFIED: H.C.)

SAF Trade Mark (APPLICATION: COLLECTION OF LETTERS: DISTINCTIVENESS:
H.C.)

Tayto (Northern Ireland) Ltd v. McKee (RESTRICTIVE PRACTICES: PRE-EEC
MARKET-PARTITIONING AGREEMENT FOR USE OF IDENTICAL MARK:
ABANDONED AND NO CONTINUING EFFECTS: FAILURE TO USE TRADE MARK
IN COMPETITOR'S TERRITORY NOT TAINTED BY ORIGINAL AGREEMENT:
Ch.D.)

WATERFORD Trade Mark (PART B: WHETHER CAPABLE OF DISTINGUISHING:
SUBSTANTIAL USER: H.C.: S.C.)

Knocking Advertising. *See under* Advertising

Laudatory Epithet

I CAN'T BELIEVE IT'S YOGURT Trade Mark (PART B REGISTRATION
ALLOWED: BoT)

MY MUM'S COLA Trade Mark (WHETHER MARK DESCRIPTIVE OF DISTINCTIVE:
BoT)

SUPERWOUND Trade Mark (CONJOINED WORDS: BoT)

Likelihood of Damage

Mothercare U.K. Ltd v. Penguin Books Ltd (BOOK TITLE: SURVEY EVIDENCE:
PRACTICE: C.A.)

Pete Waterman Ltd v. CBS United Kingdom Ltd (PASSING OFF: DISTINCTIVENESS:
MISREPRESENTATION: SECONDARY MEANING: CONCURRENT USE:
INTERNATIONAL REPUTATION: Ch.D.)

Logo

Laura Ashley Ltd v. Coloroll Ltd (Ch.D)

Mark in Foreign Language

AU PRINTEMPS Trade Mark (EVIDENCE OF REPUTATION: T.M.Reg.)

BRUT DE MER Trade Mark (PART B MARK: WORDS IN FOREIGN LANGUAGE:
T.M.Reg.)

Market Research Witness. *See under* **Survey Evidence**

Misrepresentation

Intercontex v. Schmidt (PASSING OFF: INJUNCTION: MISREPRESENTATION OUTSIDE
U.K.: MISREPRESENTATION OF PROPRIETORSHIP OF REGISTERED MARKS:
Ch.D.)
Mothercare U.K. Ltd v. Penguin Books Ltd (DESCRIPTIVE WORDS: C.A.)
Pete Waterman Ltd v. CBS United Kingdom Ltd (SECONDARY MEANING:
CONCURRENT USE: Ch.D.)

National Symbol

SHAMROCK Trade Mark (INFRINGEMENT: Germany: S.C.)

Nature of Trade Marks

James Burrough Distillers plc v. Speymalt Whisky Distributors Ltd (Scotland: O.H.)

Non-User

ARLITE Trade Mark (RECTIFICATION: WHETHER PRIMA FACIE CASE OF NON-USE
ESTABLISHED: T.M.Reg.)
BATCHELORS SNACKPOT Trade Mark (REMOVAL: PERSON AGGRIEVED: USE
OF ASSOCIATED MARK: T.M.Reg.)
Fisons plc v. Norton Healthcare Ltd (INFRINGEMENT: EXPORTED GOODS:
RECTIFICATION: NON-USE IN U.K.: NO SERIOUS DEFENCE: NO SERIOUS RISK
OF INJUSTICE: Ch.D.)
Levi Strauss & Co. v. Shah (INFRINGEMENT: TABS ON JEANS: RECTIFICATION:
Ch.D.)
ORIENT EXPRESS Trade Mark (REMOVAL: USE OF COMPANY NAME: WHETHER
USE AS A CONFLICT OF EVIDENCE: PRACTICE: CROSS-EXAMINATION BEFORE
REGISTRAR: T.M.REG: Ch.D.)
Origins Natural Resources Inc. v. Origin Clothing Limited (ASSOCIATED MARKS:
OVERLAPPING SPECIFICATIONS: VALIDITY OF SECOND MARK: NON-USE:
BONA FIDE INTENTION TO USE: LIKELIHOOD OF CONFUSION: HONEST
CONCURRENT USER: Ch.D.)
Second Sight v. Novell U.K. Ltd (INFRINGEMENT: SUMMARY JUDGMENT:
RECTIFICATION: ABANDONMENT: RESTORATION: HONEST CONCURRENT
USER: Ch.D.)
THERMAX Trade Mark (RECTIFICATION: INTENTION TO USE: OPPOSITION:
T.M.Reg.)

Numeral Marks

2000 TWO THOUSAND Trade Mark (T.M.Reg.)
QUATTRO Trade Mark (WHETHER PROTECTION OF ITALIAN NUMERAL IN
WORDS AS A TRADE MARK FOR MOTOR CARS IN GERMANY AGAINST
IMPORTS FROM OTHER MEMBER STATES CONSTITUTES AN UNLAWFUL
RESTRICTION ON IMPORTS CONTRARY TO ARTICLE 30: Germany: S.C.)

Opposition

Adidas Sàrl (PRACTICE: EXTENSIONS OF TIME: CERTIORARI: Q.B.D.)
AL BASSAM Trade Mark (ARABIC DEVICE MARK: HEADSHAWLS: EXPORTED
GOODS: ENTITLEMENT TO APPLY FOR REGISTRATION: WHETHER
SURNOMINAL SIGNIFICATION: SCOPE OF APPLICATIONS: Ch.D.: C.A.)

Part B Mark

BRUT DE MER Trade Mark (APPLICATION: WORDS IN FOREIGN LANGUAGE: T.M.Reg.)

I CAN'T BELIEVE IT'S YOGURT Trade Mark (WHETHER PHRASE A TRADE MARK: WHETHER MARK DISTINCTIVE OR LAUDATORY: BoT)

WATERFORD Trade Mark (WHETHER CAPABLE OF DISTINGUISHING: SUBSTANTIAL USER: Ireland: H.C.: S.C.)

Partnership

GUNTRUM Trade Mark (T.M.Reg.)

Passing Off

Alexander Fergusson & Co. v. Matthews McClay & Manson (USE OF GET-UP: ABANDONMENT OF GET-UP: Scotland: O.H.)

B&S Ltd v. Irish Auto Trader Ltd (ADVERTISING MAGAZINES: AUTOTRADER: INTERLOCUTORY INJUNCTION: PRINCIPLES: PRESERVATION OF *status quo*: BALANCE OF CONVENIENCE: Ireland: H.C.)

BBC v. Marshall Cavendish (SEWING KIT: INTERLOCUTORY INJUNCTION: ADEQUACY OF DAMAGES: Ch.D.)

Boot Tree Ltd v. Robinson (IMPORTED GOODS: ASSIGNMENT OF TRADE MARK WITHOUT GOODWILL: Ch.D.)

Cadbury Ltd v. Ulmer GmbH (INFRINGEMENT: STRIKING OUT: Ch.D.)

Ciba-Geigy plc v. Parke Davis & Co. Ltd (INJURIOUS FALSEHOOD: REPRESENTATION THAT DEFENDANT'S PRODUCT A SUBSTITUTE FOR PLAINTIFF'S BY USE OF UNREGISTERED TRADE MARK: FREEDOM OF SPEECH: Ch.D.)

Coca Cola Company v. Peter John Gilbey (INFRINGEMENT: COUNTERFEIT GOODS: ANTON PILLER ORDER: Ch.D.: C.A.)

Colgate Palmolive Ltd v. Markwell Finance Ltd (INFRINGEMENT: PRACTICE: COSTS: PAYMENT INTO COURT: Ch.D.)

Colgate-Palmolive Ltd v. Markwell Finance Ltd (INFRINGEMENT: TOOTHPASTE: PARALLEL IMPORTS: Ch.D.: C.A.)

CPC (United Kingdom) Ltd v. Keenan (INFRINGEMENT: OXFORD MARMALADE: Ch.D.)

Dash Ltd v. Philip King Tailoring Ltd (SIMILAR NAMES DASH/DASCH: SIMILAR BUSINESSES: INTERIM INTERDICT: BALANCE OF CONVENIENCE: PROTECTION OF LONG-ESTABLISHED BUSINESS AGAINST NEWLY FORMED BUSINESS: Scotland: I.H.)

Dormeuil Frères SA v. Feraglow Ltd (INFRINGEMENT: INQUIRY AS TO DAMAGES: INTERIM PAYMENT: BASIS OF DAMAGES: Ch.D.)

Gillette U.K. Ltd v. Edenwest Ltd (INFRINGEMENT: SUMMARY JUDGMENT: INQUIRY AS TO DAMAGES: INNOCENCE: Ch.D.)

Grant & Sons Ltd v. William Cadenhead Ltd (INFRINGEMENT: WHISKY: Scotland: O.H.)

Guccio Gucci SpA v. Paolo Gucci (INFRINGEMENT: EVIDENCE OF CONFUSION: TRADE EVIDENCE: Ch.D.)

Harrods Ltd v. Schwartz-Sackin & Co. Ltd (INFRINGEMENT: UNFAIR COMPETITION: ADVERTISEMENT OF LAPSED CONCESSION: USE AS TRADE MARK: Ch.D.)

Highland Distilleries Co. plc v. Speymalt Whisky Distributors Ltd (INFRINGEMENT: GEOGRAPHICAL NAME: Scotland: O.H.)

Person Aggrieved

BACH FLOWER REMEDIES Trade Mark (T.M.Reg.)
BATCHELORS SNACKPOT Trade Mark (T.M.Reg.)
KODIAK Trade Mark (C.A.)
PALM Trade Mark (T.M.Reg.)

Personal Name as Trade Mark

Avedis Zildjian Company's Application (NAME OF PERSON: NOT REPRESENTED IN A
  SPECIAL OR PARTICULAR MANNER: C.-G.)
Ciba Trade Mark (SURNAME: WHETHER DISTINCTIVE: Ch.D.)
GUNTRUM Trade Mark (OPPOSITION: PARTNERSHIP: T.M.Reg.)
JENNY WREN Trade Mark (REGISTRATION: CLOTHING: PART A REGISTRATION:
  SPECIAL CIRCUMSTANCES: BoT)
LAURA ASHLEY Trade Mark (PERSONAL NAME AND DEVICE: OTHER
  CIRCUMSTANCES: BoT)
Parker Knoll plc v. Knoll Overseas Ltd (USE OF OWN NAME: CONTEMPT OF COURT:
  Ch.D.)
ROTHSCHILD Trade Mark (DEVICE MARK INCORPORATING SURNAME:
  DISCLAIMER: T.M.Reg.)

Phonetic Equivalence or Confusion

EXXATE Trade Mark (PHONETIC EQUIVALENCE: Ch.D.)
LANCER Trade Mark (PHONETIC CONFUSION WITH LANCIA: Ch.D.)

Practice

Acquiescence

International Business Machines Corporation v. Phoenix International (Computers)
  Ltd (INFRINGEMENT: STRIKING OUT: SUMMARY JUDGMENT: EURO-
  DEFENCES: ESTOPPEL: Ch.D.)

Anton Piller

Coca Cola Company v. Peter John Gilbey (DISCLOSURE OF INFORMATION:
  PRIVILEGE AGAINST SELF-INCRIMINATION: RISK OF PERSONAL JEOPARDY:
  WHETHER GROUNDS TO DISCHARGE ORDER: WHETHER PERMISSIBLE FOR
  DEFENDANT TO GIVE EVIDENCE *in camera* IN THE ABSENCE OF PLAINTIFFS OR
  THEIR LEGAL REPRESENTATIVES: Ch.D.: C.A.)
Dormeuil Frères SA v. Nicolian International (Textiles) Ltd (SETTING ASIDE OF
  ORDER: DUTY OF FULL DISCLOSURE: RETURN OF GOODS SEIZED: Ch.D.)

Appeal

Hunt-Wesson Inc.'s Trade Mark Application (APPEAL FROM DECISION OF
  REGISTRAR: PRINCIPLES FOR ADMISSION OF FURTHER EVIDENCE:
  REGISTRAR'S PRACTICE: Ch.D.)
Johnson & Johnson's Application (NOTICE OF ORIGINATING MOTION: Ch.D.)
NEUTROGENA Trade Mark (RECTIFICATION: NON-USE: INTERVENER: *Locus
  standii*: APPEAL: REGISTRATION: Ch.D.)

Assignment (registration of)

Keds Trade Mark (MARK SUBJECT OF RECTIFICATION PROCEEDINGS: NO
  GROUNDS FOR REFUSAL: Ch.D.)

Associated trade marks

Keds Trade Mark (REGISTRATION OF MARK TO BE ASSOCIATED NOT COMPLETE UNTIL ENTERED IN REGISTER: Ch.D.)

Certiorari

Adidas Sàrl (OPPOSITION: EXTENSIONS OF TIME: Q.B.D.)

Choice of tribunal

Sears plc v. Sears, Roebuck & Co. (RECTIFICATIONS AND APPLICATIONS IN REGISTRY: *Res judicata*: Ch.D.)

Costs

Colgate Palmolive Ltd v. Markwell Finance Ltd (PAYMENT INTO COURT: Ch.D.)
Dirt Magnet Trade Mark (PARALLEL PROCEEDINGS IN SCOTLAND AND ENGLAND: WHETHER DUPLICATION: Ch.D.)

Counterclaim

Williams & Humbert Ltd v. International Distillers & Vintners Ltd (INFRINGEMENT: SUMMARY JUDGMENT: Ch.D.)

Cross-examination

ORIENT EXPRESS Trade Mark (CROSS-EXAMINATION BEFORE REGISTRAR: T.M.Reg.: Ch.D.)
PERMO Trade Mark (T.M.Reg.)

Damages

Dormeuil Frères SA v. Feraglow Ltd (INQUIRY AS TO DAMAGES: INTERIM PAYMENT: BASIS OF DAMAGES: Ch.D.)
Games Workshop Ltd v. Transworld Publishers Ltd (ADEQUACY OF DAMAGES: C.A.)

Delay

HIGH LIFE Trade Mark (STRIKING OUT: Ch.D.)
Newsgroup Newspapers Ltd v. The Mirror Group Newspapers (1986) Ltd (DELAY IN PROCEEDINGS AFTER INJUNCTION GRANTED: Ch.D.)

Disclaimer

Family Assurance Society's Service Mark (T.M.Reg.)
ROTHSCHILD Trade Mark (T.M.Reg.)

Discovery

Charles of the Ritz Group Ltd v. Jory (NAMES OF SUPPLIERS: Ch.D.)

Discretion

PATON CALVERT CORDON BLEU Trade Mark (OPPOSITION: EFFECT OF DISCLAIMERS: DISCRETION: T.M.Reg.)

Distinctiveness

FANTASTIC SAM's Service Mark (T.M.Reg.)

Estoppel

International Business Machines Corporation v. Phoenix International (Computers) Ltd (STRIKING OUT: SUMMARY JUDGMENT: EURO-DEFENCES: ACQUIESCENCE: Ch.D.)

European Court procedure

CNL-Sucal NV, SA v. HAG GF AG (PREVIOUS EUROPEAN COURT JUDGMENT:
ECJ)
HAG COFFEE (*Acte claire* FROM EUROPEAN COURT JUDGMENT IN *Pharmon v.*
Hoechst: Germany: C.A.)
INTERNATIONAL TELESIS GROUP Service Mark (OPPOSITION: EARLIER
CONFLICTING MARKS: PROCEEDINGS IN USA: HEARSAY EVIDENCE: HONEST
CONCURRENT USER: T.M.Reg.)
QUATTRO Trade Mark (REFERENCE TO EUROPEAN COURT: ECJ)

Evidence

Apple Corp.'s Ltd v. Apple Computer Inc. (RESTRICTIVE PRACTICES:
CONFIDENTIAL EVIDENCE BEFORE NATIONAL COURT TO BE HANDED TO E.C.
COMMISSION: Ch.D.)
AU PRINTEMPS Trade Mark (MARK IN FOREIGN LANGUAGE: EVIDENCE OF
REPUTATION: T.M.Reg.)
AVON Trade Mark (SURVEY EVIDENCE: CAPABLE OF DISTINGUISHING: T.M.Reg.)
Celine SA's Trade Mark Applications (Ch.D)
Coca Cola Company v. Peter John Gilbey (ANTON PILLER ORDER: WHETHER
PERMISSIBLE FOR DEFENDANT TO GIVE EVIDENCE *in camera* IN THE ABSENCE
OF PLAINTIFFS OR THEIR LEGAL REPRESENTATIVES: Ch.D.: C.A.)
COLORCOAT Trade Mark (PART A REGISTRATION: BoT)
Guccio Gucci SpA v. Paolo Gucci (EVIDENCE OF CONFUSION: TRADE EVIDENCE:
Ch.D.)
Hunt-Wesson Inc.'s Trade Mark Application (APPEAL FROM DECISION OF
REGISTRAR: PRINCIPLES FOR ADMISSION OF FURTHER EVIDENCE ON APPEAL:
REGISTRAR'S PRACTICE: Ch.D.)
INTERNATIONAL TELESIS GROUP Service Mark (OPPOSITION: EARLIER
CONFLICTING MARKS: PROCEEDINGS IN USA: HEARSAY EVIDENCE: HONEST
CONCURRENT USER: T.M.Reg.)
JOCKEY Trade Mark (LACK OF EVIDENCE: T.M.Reg.)
KENT Trade Mark (SURVEY EVIDENCE: T.M.Reg.: C.-G.)
Laura Ashley Ltd v. Coloroll Ltd (LOGO: TACHISTOSCOPE: Ch.D.)
MINI-LIFT Trade Mark (OPPOSITION: NORMAL AND FAIR USE: T.M.Reg.)
Mothercare U.K. Ltd v. Penguin Books Ltd (SURVEY EVIDENCE: C.A.)
NETWORK 90 Trade Mark (Ch.D)
ORIENT EXPRESS Trade Mark (REMOVAL: NON-USE: USE OF CONFLICT OF
EVIDENCE: T.M.Reg.: Ch.D.)
PHOENIX Trade Mark (SURVEY EVIDENCE: T.M.Reg.)
ST TRUDO Trade mark (RECTIFICATION: REGISTRAR: HEARSAY RULES:
APPLICABILITY AND SCOPE: Ch.D.)
The European Ltd v. The Economist Newspapers Ltd (TRADE MARK: DEVICE
MARKS: THE EUROPEAN/EUROPEAN VOICE: WHETHER SIMILAR:
WHETHER CONFUSING: EVIDENCE OF CONFUSION: SURVEY EVIDENCE:
Ch.D.)
Unilever plc's Trade mark Application (Ch.D)
Unilever plc v. Johnson Wax Ltd (SURVEY EVIDENCE: Ch.D.)
Wagamama Ltd v. City Centre Restaurants plc (INFRINGEMENT: WAGAMAMA/
RAJAMAMA: DILUTION OF GOODWILL: SURVEY EVIDENCE: EXPERT
EVIDENCE: ADMISSIBILITY: Ch.D.)

Expert evidence

Wagamama Ltd v. City Centre Restaurants plc (HISTORICAL FUNCTION OF TRADE MARKS: ASSOCIATION WITHOUT CONFUSION AS TO ORIGIN: DILUTION OF GOODWILL: ADMISSIBILITY: Ch.D.)

Extensions of time

Adidas Sàrl (OPPOSITION: CERTIORARI: Q.B.D.)

Goods of the same description

BENSYL Trade Mark (BoT)

Inquiry as to damages

Dormeuil Frères SA v. Feraglow Ltd (INTERIM PAYMENT: BASIS OF DAMAGES: REMOTENESS: INTEREST: Ch.D.)

Gillette U.K. Ltd v. Edenwest Ltd (INFRINGEMENT: PASSING OFF: SUMMARY JUDGMENT: INNOCENCE: Ch.D.)

Injunction

ASTERIX Trade Mark (Germany: C.A.)

IHT International Heiztechnik GmbH v. Ideal-Standard GmbH (ECJ)

James North & Sons Ltd v. North Cape Textiles Ltd (PASSING OFF: INFRINGEMENT: PRACTICE: Scotland: England C.A.)

Sport International Bussum BV v. Hi-Tech Sports Ltd (Q.B.D.: C.A.)

Interest

Dormeuil Frères SA v. Feraglow Ltd (Ch.D)

Interlocutory injunction

Ciba-Geigy plc v. Parke Davis & Co. Ltd (REPRESENTATION THAT DEFENDANT'S PRODUCT A SUBSTITUTE FOR PLAINTIFF'S BY USE OF UNREGISTERED MARK: FREEDOM OF SPEECH: Ch.D.)

Compaq Computer Corp. v. Dell Computer Corp. Ltd (TRIABLE ISSUE: BALANCE OF CONVENIENCE: WHETHER PLAINTIFF'S CONDUCT BAR TO GRANT OF INJUNCTION: INJURIOUS FALSEHOOD: APPROACH TO INJUNCTION APPLICATION WHEN DEFENDANT DENIES STATEMENT: FREEDOM OF SPEECH AN ELEMENT OF BALANCE OF CONVENIENCE TEST: Ch.D.)

Duracell International Inc. v. Ever Ready Ltd (KNOCKING ADVERTISING: GET-UP: Ch.D.)

Fisons plc v. Norton Healthcare Ltd (EXPORTED GOODS: RECTIFICATION: NON-USE IN U.K.: NO SERIOUS DEFENCE: NO SERIOUS RISK OF INJUSTICE: Ch.D.)

Harrods Ltd v. Schwartz-Sackin & Co. Ltd (USE AS TRADE MARK: BALANCE OF CONVENIENCE: Ch.D.)

Mothercare U.K. Ltd v. Penguin Books Ltd (BOOK TITLE: LIKELIHOOD OF DAMAGE: SURVEY EVIDENCE: C.A.)

Newsgroup Newspapers Ltd v. The Mirror Group Newspapers (1986) Ltd (DELAY IN PROCEEDINGS AFTER INJUNCTION GRANTED: Ch.D.)

Post Office v. Interlink Express Parcels Ltd (BALANCE OF CONVENIENCE: Ch.D.)

Provident Financial plc v. Halifax Building Society (TRIABLE ISSUE: SECTIONS 5(2) AND 8 DEFENCES: Ch.D.)

Silicon Graphics Inc. v. Indigo Graphic Systems (U.K.) Ltd (BALANCE OF CONVENIENCE: COSTS: Ch.D.)

Unidoor Ltd v. Marks & Spencer plc (*Coast to Coast*: WHETHER USE AS MARK: Ch.D.)

Mothercare U.K. Ltd v. Penguin Books Ltd (LIKELIHOOD OF DAMAGE: SURVEY EVIDENCE: C.A.)

Intervener

NEUTROGENA Trade Mark (*Locus standii*: Ch.D.)

Likelihood of damage

Mothercare U.K. Ltd v. Penguin Books Ltd (INTERLOCUTORY INJUNCTION: SURVEY EVIDENCE: C.A.)

Locus standii

NEUTROGENA Trade Mark (INTERVENER: Ch.D.)

Notice of originating motion

Johnson & Johnson's Application (APPEAL: Ch.D.)

Numeral marks

2000 TWO THOUSAND Trade Mark (T.M.Reg.)

Order 14

Origins Natural Resources Inc. v. Origin Clothing Limited (SERVICE OF DEFENCE AND COUNTERCLAIM: Ch.D.)

Payment into court

Colgate Palmolive Ltd v. Markwell Finance Ltd (COSTS: Ch.D.)

Protection of established business against newly-formed business

Dash Ltd v. Philip King Tailoring Ltd (INTERIM INTERDICT: BALANCE OF CONVENIENCE: I.H.)
International House of Heraldry v. Grant (INTERIM INTERDICT: BALANCE OF CONVENIENCE: Scotland: O.H.)
Orkney Seafoods Ltd's Petition (INTERIM INTERDICT: BALANCE OF CONVENIENCE: Scotland: O.H.)

Privilege

DORMEUIL Trade Mark (TRADE MARK AGENT'S PRIVILEGE: Ch.D.)

Registration of assignment

Keds Trade Mark (MARK SUBJECT OF RECTIFICATION PROCEEDINGS: NO GROUNDS FOR REFUSAL: Ch.D.)

Res judicata

Sears plc v. Sears, Roebuck & Co. (PASSING OFF: RECTIFICATIONS AND APPLICATIONS IN T.M.REG.: CHOICE OF TRIBUNAL: INJUNCTION: Ch.D.)

Scope of applications

AL BASSAM Trade Mark (ENTITLEMENT TO APPLY FOR REGISTRATION: WHETHER A SURNOMINAL SIGNIFICATION: Ch.D.: C.A.)

Seizure of goods

CBS Inc. v. Blue Suede Music Ltd (INFRINGEMENT: SEIZURE OF GOODS BY CUSTOMS: Ch.D.)

Service

Origins Natural Resources Inc. v. Origin Clothing Limited (ORDER 14: SERVICE OF DEFENCE AND COUNTERCLAIM: Ch.D.)

Striking out

HIGH LIFE Trade Mark (DELAY: Ch.D.)

International Business Machines Corporation v. Phoenix International (Computers) Ltd (SUMMARY JUDGMENT: EURO-DEFENCES: ACQUIESCENCE: ESTOPPEL: Ch.D.)

Summary judgment

Accurist Watches Ltd v. King (Ch.D)

CHEETAH Trade Mark (MARK USED ONLY ON INVOICES: WHETHER USED IN RELATION TO GOODS AND/OR IN COURSE OF TRADE: Ch.D.)

Crittall Windows Ltd v. Stormseal (UPVC) Window Systems Ltd (INFRINGEMENT: BREACH OF REGISTERED USER AGREEMENT: WHETHER BREACHES CAPABLE OF REMEDY: Ch.D.)

Gillette U.K. Ltd v. Edenwest Ltd (INFRINGEMENT: PASSING OFF: INQUIRY AS TO DAMAGES: INNOCENCE: Ch.D.)

Mercury Communications Ltd v. Mercury Interactive (U.K.) Ltd (SOFTWARE: BONA FIDE USE OF OWN NAME: SCOPE OF REGISTRATION: Ch.D.)

Second Sight v. Novell U.K. Ltd (INFRINGEMENT: RECTIFICATION: NON-USE: ABANDONMENT: RESTORATION: HONEST CONCURRENT USER: Ch.D.)

Survey evidence

AVON Trade Mark (APPLICATION: PRACTICE: CAPABLE OF DISTINGUISHING: T.M.Reg.)

KENT Trade Mark (APPLICATION: GEOGRAPHICAL NAME: T.M.Reg.: C.-G.)

Mothercare U.K. Ltd v. Penguin Books Ltd (INTERLOCUTORY INJUNCTION: LIKELIHOOD OF DAMAGE: C.A.)

PHOENIX Trade Mark (APPLICATION: OPPOSITION: GEOGRAPHICAL NAME: T.M.Reg.)

The European Ltd v. The Economist Newspapers Ltd (TRADE MARK: DEVICE MARKS: THE EUROPEAN/EUROPEAN VOICE: WHETHER SIMILAR: WHETHER CONFUSING: EVIDENCE OF CONFUSION: SURVEY EVIDENCE: Ch.D.)

Unilever plc v. Johnson Wax Ltd (RECTIFICATION: NON-USE: ASSOCIATED MARKS: Ch.D.)

Wagamama Ltd v. City Centre Restaurants plc (ASSOCIATION WITHOUT CONFUSION AS TO ORIGIN: DILUTION OF GOODWILL: EXPERT EVIDENCE: ADMISSIBILITY: Ch.D.)

Prior Use

Lallier v. Lux (REGISTRATION: OWNERSHIP: PRIOR USE: COPYRIGHT: IDEAS: GAMES: France: C.A.)

PPI Industries Pty Ltd's Application (APPLICATION FOR REGISTRATION: PRIOR REGISTRATIONS: SUBSTANTIALLY IDENTICAL WITH: DECEPTIVELY SIMILAR TO: GOODS OF THE SAME DESCRIPTION: GOODS THAT ARE CLOSELY RELATED: C.-G.)

Privilege. *See* Practice *(Privilege)*

Proprietorship

AL BASSAM Trade Mark (BONA FIDE CLAIM, WHETHER SUFFICIENT: OPPOSITION: C.A.)

Fyffes plc v. Chiquita Brands International Inc. (GOODWILL: RESTRAINT OF TRADE: COVENANTS: EFFECT ON PURCHASER: Ch.D.)

HAG Coffee (BREAK OF CHAIN OF OWNERSHIP BY EXPROPRIATION: Germany: C.A.)

HOLLY HOBBIE Trade Mark (WHETHER QUALITY CONTROL BY PROPRIETORS CONSTITUTES TRADE CONNECTION: Ch.D.: C.A.: H.L.)

Intercontex v. Schmidt (PASSING OFF: MISREPRESENTATION OF PROPRIETORSHIP OF REGISTERED MARKS: Ch.D.)

Lallier v. Lux (France: C.A.)

Moosehead Breweries Ltd and Whitbread and Company plc's Agreement (NO CHALLENGE CLAUSE: E.C. Comm.)

SIDEWINDER Trade Mark (OPPOSITION: OVERSEAS PROPRIETORS' REPUTATION: BoT)

Tradam Trading Company (Bahamas) Ltd's Trade Mark (RECTIFICATION: REGISTERED PROPRIETOR IN DEFAULT: APPLICATION BY ALLEGED ASSIGNEE TO INTERVENE: Ch.D.)

Purchaser

Castrol Ltd v. Automotive Oil Supplies Ltd (INFRINGEMENT: PARALLEL IMPORTS: NOTICES TO PURCHASERS: Ch.D.)

Fyffes plc v. Chiquita Brands International Inc. (COVENANT NOT TO USE OUTSIDE U.K. AND IRELAND: RESTRAINT OF TRADE: RESTRICTION OF USE OF MARKS: EFFECT ON PURCHASER: Ch.D.)

Rectification

ARLITE Trade Mark (NON-USE: WHETHER PRIMA FACIE CASE OF NON-USE ESTABLISHED: T.M.Reg.)

BACH FLOWER REMEDIES Trade Mark (PERSON AGGRIEVED: T.M.Reg.)

BON MATIN Trade Mark (NON-USE: CALCULATING PERIOD OF NON-USE: T.M.Reg.: Ch.D.)

CONCORD Trade Mark (NON-USE: USE ON LIMITED SCALE: Ch.D.)

Dirt Magnet Trade Mark (PRACTICE: PARALLEL PROCEEDINGS IN SCOTLAND AND ENGLAND: IDENTICAL ISSUES: APPLICANTS NOT PARTIES TO SCOTTISH PROCEEDINGS: WHETHER DUPLICATION: COSTS: Ch.D.)

Fisons plc v. Norton Healthcare Ltd (EXPORTED GOODS: NON-USE IN U.K.: NO SERIOUS DEFENCE: NO SERIOUS RISK OF INJUSTICE: Ch.D.)

FLASHPOINT Trade Mark (NON-USE: T.M.Reg.)

HIGH LIFE Trade Mark (NON-USE: STRIKING OUT: DELAY: Ch.D.)

JOB Trade Mark (JOB FOR CIGARETTE PAPERS, ETC.: REGISTERED USER AGREEMENT: WHETHER ESTOPPEL BY CONDUCT FROM APPLYING FOR RECTIFICATION: T.M.Reg.)

Keds Trade Mark (PRACTICE: REGISTRATION OF ASSIGNMENT OF MARK THE SUBJECT OF RECTIFICATION PROCEEDINGS: NO GROUNDS FOR REFUSAL: ASSOCIATED MARKS: Ch.D.)

KODIAK Trade Mark (NON-USE: PERSON AGGRIEVED: C.A.)

Kodiak Trade Mark (NON-USE: USE ON GOODS ADVERTISING OTHER GOODS: WHETHER USE AS TRADE MARK: Ch.D.)

Levi Strauss & Co. v. Shah (INFRINGEMENT: TABS ON JEANS: NON-USER: Ch.D.)

Mars G.B. Ltd v. Cadbury Ltd (INFRINGEMENT: TREETS/TREAT SIZE: CONFECTIONERY: Ch.D.)

NEUTROGENA Trade Mark (NON-USE: INTERVENER: *Locus standii*: Ch.D.)

PALM Trade Mark (NON-USE: PERSON AGGRIEVED: SERVICE MARK: T.M.Reg.)

PERMO Trade Mark (PRACTICE: CROSS-EXAMINATION: T.M.Reg.)

SEA ISLAND COTTON Certification Trade Marks (CERTIFICATION TRADE MARKS: COMPETENCE TO CERTIFY: BoT)

Sears plc v. Sears, Roebuck & Co. (PASSING OFF: PRACTICE: CHOICE OF TRIBUNAL: INJUNCTION: *Res judicata*: Ch.D.)

Second Sight v. Novell U.K. Ltd (INFRINGEMENT: SUMMARY JUDGMENT: NON-USE: ABANDONMENT: RESTORATION: HONEST CONCURRENT USER: Ch.D.)

ST TRUDO Trade Mark (EVIDENCE: REGISTRAR: HEARSAY RULES: APPLICABILITY AND SCOPE: Ch.D.)

THERMAX Trade Mark (NON-USER: INTENTION TO USE: OPPOSITION: T.M.Reg.)

Tradam Trading Company (Bahamas) Ltd's Trade Mark (REGISTERED PROPRIETOR IN DEFAULT: APPLICATION BY ALLEGED ASSIGNEE TO INTERVENE: Ch.D.)

TROOPER Trade Mark (NON-USE: USE BY UNREGISTERED USER: T.M.Reg.)

Unilever plc v. Johnson Wax Ltd (INFRINGEMENT: TOILET DUCK: SPECIFICATION OF GOODS: NON-USE: ASSOCIATED MARKS: SURVEY EVIDENCE: Ch.D.)

Registered User

Accurist Watches Ltd v. King (MARK APPLIED BY MANUFACTURER UNDER REGISTERED USER CONTRACT: RESERVATION OF TITLE CLAUSE: RETAKING POSSESSION ON USER'S INSOLVENCY: WHETHER SALE WITHOUT REMOVING MARK IS INFRINGEMENT: Ch.D.)

Crittall Windows Ltd v. Stormseal (UPVC) Window Systems Ltd (INFRINGEMENT: BREACH OF AGREEMENT: WHETHER CAPABLE OF REMEDY: Ch.D.)

HOLLY HOBBIE Trade Mark (APPLICATION: TRAFFICKING: CHARACTER MERCHANDISING: WHETHER QUALITY CONTROL BY PROPRIETORS CONSTITUTES TRADE CONNECTION: WHETHER NECESSARY AND PROPER CO-PLAINTIFF: Ch.D.: C.A.: H.L.)

JOB Trade Mark (RECTIFICATION: JOB FOR CIGARETTE PAPERS, ETC.: REGISTERED USER AGREEMENT: WHETHER ESTOPPEL BY CONDUCT FROM APPLYING FOR RECTIFICATION: SUFFICIENCY OF CONTROL BY REGISTERED USER: T.M.Reg.)

Levi Strauss & Co. v. The French Connection Ltd (INFRINGEMENT: WHETHER NECESSARY AND PROPER CO-PLAINTIFF: Ch.D.)

Removal

BATCHELORS SNACKPOT Trade Mark (NON-USE: PERSON AGGRIEVED: USE OF ASSOCIATED MARK: T.M.Reg.)

ORIENT EXPRESS Trade Mark (NON-USE: USE OF COMPANY NAME: WHETHER USE AS A CONFLICT OF EVIDENCE: PRACTICE: CROSS-EXAMINATION BEFORE REGISTRAR: T.M.Reg.: Ch.D.)

Repackaging

Bristol Myers Squibb v. Paranova (PARALLEL IMPORTS: REPACKAGING OF GOODS: EXHAUSTION OF RIGHTS: RESTRICTIONS FOR PROTECTION OF INDUSTRIAL AND COMMERCIAL PROPERTY: DISGUISED RESTRICTION ON TRADE BETWEEN MEMBER STATES: ECJ)

Hoffmann-La Roche AG v. Centrafarm GmbH (IMPORTS: Germany: S.C.)

KERLONE Trade Mark (PARALLEL IMPORTS OF PHARMACEUTICALS FROM FRANCE TO GERMANY: DIFFERENT PACKAGING REQUIREMENTS: REPACKAGING: VISIBILITY OF MARK THROUGH WINDOW IN NEW PACKAGING: INFRINGEMENT: ARTICLE 36(1): Germany: C.A.)

Reputation

AU PRINTEMPS Trade Mark (APPLICATION: MARK IN FOREIGN LANGUAGE: EVIDENCE OF REPUTATION: T.M.Reg.)

MACY'S Trade Mark (OPPOSITION: OVERSEAS REPUTATION: T.M.Reg.)

Salon Services (Hairdressing Supplies) Ltd v. Direct Salon Services Ltd (PASSING OFF: DESCRIPTIVE NAME: REPUTATION: Scotland: O.H.)

SIDEWINDER Trade Mark (OPPOSITION: PROPRIETORSHIP: OVERSEAS PROPRIETORS' REPUTATION: BoT)

Restoration

Second Sight v. Novell U.K. Ltd (INFRINGEMENT: SUMMARY JUDGMENT: RECTIFICATION: NON-USE: ABANDONMENT: HONEST CONCURRENT USER: Ch.D.)

Restrictive Practices

Apple Corps Ltd v. Apple Computer Ltd (DELIMITATION AGREEMENT: RESTRICTION TO OWN LINES: RESTRICTIVE PRACTICES: COMPATIBILITY WITH ARTICLE 85: WHETHER VALIDITY RELEVANT: USE: C.A.)

Scope of Registration

Mercury Communications Ltd v. Mercury Interactive (U.K.) Ltd (INFRINGEMENT: SOFTWARE: SUMMARY JUDGMENT: BONA FIDE USE OF OWN NAME: Ch.D.)

Scotland

Alexander Fergusson & Co. v. Matthews McClay & Manson (PASSING OFF: USE OF GET UP: ABANDONMENT OF GET UP: BALANCE OF CONVENIENCE: TRADE MARKS AND NAMES: O.H.)

Bravado Merchandising Services Ltd v. Mainstream Publishing (Edinburgh) Ltd (NAME OF POP GROUP REGISTERED *inter alia* FOR BOOKS: USE OF NAME OF GROUP ON BOOK ABOUT THE GROUP: INFRINGEMENT: WHETHER USE IN TRADEMARK SENSE: AVAILABILITY OF DEFENCE UNDER T.M.A.94, s.11(2): O.H.)

Dash Ltd v. Philip King Tailoring Ltd (TRADE NAMES: PASSING OFF: SIMILAR NAMES DASH/DASCH: SIMILAR BUSINESSES: INTERIM INTERDICT: BALANCE OF CONVENIENCE: PROTECTION OF LONG ESTABLISHED BUSINESS AGAINST NEWLY FORMED BUSINESS: I.H.)

Dirt Magnet Trade Mark (RECTIFICATION: PRACTICE: PARALLEL PROCEEDINGS IN SCOTLAND AND ENGLAND: IDENTICAL ISSUES: APPLICANTS NOT PARTIES TO SCOTTISH PROCEEDINGS: WHETHER DUPLICATION: COSTS: Ch.D.)

Grant & Sons Ltd v. William Cadenhead Ltd (INFRINGEMENT: PASSING OFF: WHISKY: GEOGRAPHICAL NAME: O.H.)

Highland Distilleries Co. plc v. Speymalt Whisky Distributors Ltd (TRADE NAMES: INFRINGEMENT: PASSING OFF: GEOGRAPHICAL NAME: O.H.)

James Burrough Distillers plc v. Speymalt Whisky Distributors Ltd (INFRINGEMENT ABROAD: INTERNATIONAL LAW: DOUBLE ACTIONABILITY REQUIREMENT: NATURE OF TRADE MARKS: O.H.)

James North & Sons Ltd v. North Cape Textiles Ltd (PASSING OFF: TRADE MARK: INFRINGEMENT: PRACTICE: INJUNCTION: England: C.A.)

Macallan-Glenlivet plc v. Speyside Whisky Distributors Ltd (INFRINGEMENT: PASSING OFF: WHISKY: O.H.)

Salon Services (Hairdressing Supplies) Ltd v. Direct Salon Services Ltd (PASSING OFF: DESCRIPTIVE NAME: REPUTATION: O.H.)

Scottish Milk Marketing Board v. Drybrough & Co. Ltd (TRADE MARK AND TRADE
NAME: PASSING OFF: *Scottish Pride*: INTERIM INTERDICT: O.H.)

Seizure of Goods. *See* **Practice** (*Seizure of Goods*)

Service Marks

ADD-70 Trade Mark (T.M.Reg.)
BUDGET Service Mark (BoT)
Dee Corporation plc's Applications (WHETHER RETAILING A "SERVICE": Ch.D.:
C.A.)
Family Assurance Society's Service Mark (DISCLAIMER: T.M.Reg.)
FANTASTIC SAM's Service Mark (APPLICATION: DISTINCTIVENESS: PRACTICE:
T.M.Reg.)
PALM Trade Mark (RECTIFICATION: NON-USE: PERSON AGGRIEVED: T.M.Reg.)
SOLID FUEL ADVISORY SERVICE Service Mark (APPLICATION:
DISTINCTIVENESS: T.M.Reg.)
VEW Trade Mark (APPLICATION: T.M.Reg.)

Shape of Object

Cadbury Ltd v. Ulmer GmbH (SHAPE OF CHOCOLATE BAR: "BADGE OF FRAUD":
Ch.D.)
Coca Cola Trade Marks (APPLICATION: SHAPE OF BOTTLE: Ch.D.: C.A.: H.L.)
John Wyeth & Bro Ltd's Coloured Tablet Trade Mark (COLOUR, SHAPE AND SIZE OF
PHARMACEUTICAL TABLETS: DISTINCTIVENESS: T.M.Reg.)

Similarity of goods

British Sugar plc v. James Robertson & Sons Ltd (INFRINGEMENT: IDENTITY OF
GOODS: VALIDITY: DEVOID OF DISTINCTIVE CHARACTER: PROOF: Ch.D.)

Similar Marks or Names

BAT Cigaretten-Fabriken GmbH v. E.C. Commission (DORCET AND TOLTECS
SPECIAL: DORMANT MARK: SIMILARITY: INFRINGEMENT OF ARTICLE 85:
E.C. COMMISSION UPHELD: FINES: ECJ)
Community v. Syntex Corporation (RESTRICTIVE PRACTICES: NOT CLEAR
WHETHER EARLIER TRADE MARK COULD BE ENFORCED IN MEMBER STATES:
DELIMITATION AGREEMENT TO AVOID CONFUSION: E.C. Comm.)
Dash Ltd v. Philip King Tailoring Ltd (DASH/DASCH: SIMILAR BUSINESSES:
INTERIM INTERDICT: BALANCE OF CONVENIENCE: PROTECTION OF LONG-
ESTABLISHED BUSINESS AGAINST NEWLY FORMED BUSINESS: Scotland: I.H.)
Henri Jullien BV v. Verschuere Norbert (REGISTRATION: OPPOSITION: SIMILARITY:
Benelux)
International House of Heraldry v. Grant (DESCRIPTIVE NAMES:
INTERNATIONAL ART OF HERALDRY: WHETHER DESCRIPTIVE:
WHETHER SLIGHT DIFFERENCE SUFFICIENT TO DISTINGUISH: Scotland: O.H.)
Orkney Seafoods Ltd's Petition (DESCRIPTIVE NAME: ORKNEY SEAFOODS:
WHETHER COMBINATION OF DESCRIPTIVE WORDS CALCULATED TO CAUSE
CONFUSION: Scotland: O.H.)

Reservation of Title

Accurist Watches Ltd v. King (Ch.D)

Trade Marks Act 1938

Accurist Watches Ltd v. King (STATUTORY DEFENCE: Ch.D.)

Trade Mark Agent

BYSTANDER Trade Mark (AUTHORISATION: T.M.Reg.)
DORMEUIL Trade Mark (PRIVILEGE: Ch.D.)

Trade Usage

Furnitureland Ltd v. Harris (INFRINGEMENT: FURNITURELAND/
FURNITURE CITY: Ch.D.)

Trafficking

HOLLY HOBBIE Trade Mark (CHARACTER MERCHANDISING: WHETHER
QUALITY CONTROL BY PROPRIETORS CONSTITUTES TRADE CONNECTION:
Ch.D.: C.A.: H.L.)

Triple Identity Rule

BUD Trade Mark (Ch.D)

Unregistered Trade Marks

Ciba-Geigy plc v. Parke Davis & Co. Ltd (REPRESENTATION THAT DEFENDANT'S
PRODUCT A SUBSTITUTE FOR PLAINTIFF'S BY USE OF UNREGISTERED MARK:
Ch.D.)
Fyffes plc v. Chiquita Brands International Inc. (REGISTERED AND UNREGISTERED
MARKS: RESTRICTION OF USE OF TRADE MARKS: EFFECT ON PURCHASER:
Ch.D.)

Use. *See also under* **Non-use, Use of Own Name** and **Honest Concurrent Use**

Alexander Fergusson & Co. v. Matthews McClay & Manson (USE OF GET-UP:
Scotland: O.H.)
Bravado Merchandising Services Ltd v. Mainstream Publishing (Edinburgh) Ltd
(NAME OF POP GROUP REGISTERED *inter alia* FOR BOOKS: USE OF NAME OF
GROUP ON BOOK ABOUT THE GROUP: INFRINGEMENT: WHETHER USE IN
TRADEMARK SENSE: AVAILABILITY OF DEFENCE UNDER T.M.A.94, s.11(2):
Scotland: O.H.)
British Sugar plc v. James Robertson & Sons Ltd (INFRINGEMENT: SIMILARITY OF
GOODS: VALIDITY: DEVOID OF DISTINCTIVE CHARACTER: PROOF:
STATUTORY INTERPRETATION: Ch.D.)
CHEETAH Trade Mark (USE ONLY ON INVOICES: WHETHER USE IN RELATION TO
GOODS AND/OR IN COURSE OF TRADE: EEC: FREE MOVEMENT OF GOODS:
EXHAUSTION OF RIGHTS: Ch.D.)
Ciba-Geigy plc v. Parke Davis & Co. Ltd (REPRESENTATION BY USE OF
UNREGISTERED TRADE MARK: Ch.D.)
CONCORD Trade Mark (USE ON LIMITED SCALE: Ch.D.)
DOMGARDEN Trade Mark (USE LIMITED TO WINES OF GERMAN ORIGIN: Ch.D.)
Fyffes plc v. Chiquita Brands International Inc. (COVENANT NOT TO USE OUTSIDE
U.K. AND IRELAND: RESTRICTION OF USE OF TRADE MARKS: EFFECT ON
PURCHASER: Ch.D.)

Gallaher (Dublin) Ltd v. The Health Education Bureau (USE IN RELATION TO GOODS: Ireland: H.C.)

Games Workshop Ltd v. Transworld Publishers Ltd (SERIES OF BOOKS: USE AS TRADE MARK: C.A.)

GOLDEN PAGES Trade Mark (USE ON TELEPHONE DIRECTORIES: Ireland: S.C.)

Harrods Ltd v. Schwartz-Sackin & Co. Ltd (USE AS TRADE MARK: Ch.D.)

JOB Trade Mark (DECEPTIVE USE OF MARK: T.M.Reg.)

Kodiak Trade Mark (USE ON GOODS ADVERTISING OTHER GOODS: WHETHER USE AS TRADE MARK: Ch.D.)

MINI-LIFT Trade Mark (OPPOSITION: NORMAL AND FAIR USE: T.M.Reg.)

NEXT Trade Mark (USE IN ADVERTISING: BoT)

Nijs v. Ciba-Geigy AG (USE: DOCTOR'S PRESCRIPTION: Benelux: C.J.)

Parker Knoll plc v. Knoll Overseas Ltd (USE OF OWN NAME: Ch.D.)

Pete Waterman Ltd v. CBS United Kingdom Ltd (SECONDARY MEANING: CONCURRENT USE: Ch.D.)

Tayto (Northern Ireland) Ltd v. McKee (RESTRICTIVE PRACTICES: PRE-EEC MARKET-PARTITIONING AGREEMENT FOR USE OF IDENTICAL MARK: ABANDONED AND NO CONTINUING EFFECT: FAILURE TO USE IN COMPETITOR'S TERRITORY NOT TAINTED BY ORIGINAL AGREEMENT: Northern Ireland: Ch.D.)

THE ENDLESS VACATION Trade Mark (WHETHER USE AS TRADE MARK: Ch.D.)

Theodor Kohl KG v. Ringelhan & Rennett SA (USE BY SEVERAL SUCCESSORS TO SPLIT COMPANY: Germany: ECJ)

THERMAX Trade Mark (INTENTION TO USE: T.M.Reg.)

Unidoor Ltd v. Marks & Spencer plc (*Coast to Coast*: WHETHER USE AS TRADE MARK: Ch.D.)

WATERFORD Trade Mark (CAPABLE OF DISTINGUISHING: SUBSTANTIAL USER: Ireland: H.C.: S.C.)

Use of Company Name

ORIENT EXPRESS Trade Mark (REMOVAL: NON-USE: WHETHER USE AS A TRADE MARK: CONFLICT OF EVIDENCE: CROSS-EXAMINATION BEFORE REGISTRAR: T.M.REG.: Ch.D.)

Use of Own Name

Mercury Communications Ltd v. Mercury Interactive (U.K.) Ltd (BONA FIDE USE OF OWN NAME: SCOPE OF REGISTRATION: Ch.D.)

Parker Knoll plc v. Knoll Overseas Ltd (Ch.D.)

Validity

British Sugar plc v. James Robertson & Sons Ltd (INFRINGEMENT: USE IN THE COURSE OF TRADE: IDENTITY OF GOODS: SIMILARITY OF GOODS: Ch.D.)

Compaq Computer Corp. v. Dell Computer Corp. Ltd (INFRINGEMENT: COMPARATIVE ADVERTISING: INVALIDITY: Ch.D.)

Duracell International Inc. v. Ever Ready Ltd (INFRINGEMENT: EURO-DEFENCES: Ch.D.)

Moosehead Breweries Ltd and Whitbread and Company plc's Agreement (RESTRICTIVE PRACTICES: LICENCE FOR PRODUCTION AND SALE OF CANADIAN BEER IN U.K.: TRADE MARK NO CHALLENGE CLAUSE: POSSIBLY RESTRICTIVE AS REGARDS VALIDITY: E.C. Comm.)

Origins Natural Resources Inc. v. Origin Clothing Limited (ASSOCIATED MARKS: OVERLAPPING SPECIFICATIONS: VALIDITY OF SECOND MARK: Ch.D.)

Whisky

Grant & Sons Ltd v. William Cadenhead Ltd (Scotland: O.H.)
Highland Distilleries Co. plc v. Speymalt Whisky Distributors Ltd (Scotland: O.H.)
James Burrough Distillers plc v. Speymalt Whisky Distributors Ltd (Scotland: O.H.)
Macallan-Glenlivet plc v. Speyside Whisky Distributors Ltd (Scotland: O.H.)
QUEEN DIANA Trade Mark (T.M.Reg.: BoT)

B. EUROPEAN CASES BY COUNTRY

Austria

Austro-Mechana GmbH v. Gramola Winter & Co. (COPYRIGHT: EFTA: ENFORCEMENT: S.C.)

Satellite Television Broadcasting (COPYRIGHT: CONTRACT: APPLICABLE LAW: BROADCASTING RIGHTS: SATELLITE TELEVISION BROADCASTS: Regional C.A.)

Sky Channel (No. 2) (COPYRIGHT: CABLE TELEVISION: INTERPRETATION OF DECODING SATELLITE SIGNALS: ROYALTY: S.C.)

Belgium

CNL-Sucal NV, SA v. HAG GF AG (TRADE MARKS: IMPORTS: EXHAUSTION OF RIGHTS: GERMAN AND BELGIAN MARKS OF COMMON ORIGIN: CONFUSION: IDENTICAL MARKS: CONFISCATION OF ENEMY PROPERTY OUTSIDE GERMANY: PREVIOUS EUROPEAN COURT JUDGMENT: ECJ)

Hag Coffee (TRADE MARKS: HAG: SPECIFIC SUBJECT-MATTER: CONSEQUENCES: EXHAUSTION OF RIGHTS: IMPORTS: BREAK OF CHAIN OF OWNERSHIP BY EXPROPRIATION: GERMAN HAG ABLE TO RESIST IMPORT INTO GERMANY OF BELGIAN HAG COFFEE: *Acte claire* FROM EUROPEAN COURT JUDGMENT IN *Pharmon v. Hoechst*: NO ARTICLE 177 REFERENCE: Germany: C.A.)

Imprimerie (SA) Thône v. Fernand Geubelle (COPYRIGHT: INTELLIGENCE TEST: PUBLISHER AS CO-AUTHOR: *Locus standi*)

Promedia SA v. Borght (COPYRIGHT: REGISTERED DESIGN: PROTECTED PRODUCT: ADVERTISING MATERIAL: C.A.)

Denmark

EMI Electrola GmbH v. Patricia IM- und Export Verwaltungs GmbH (COPYRIGHT: IMPORTS: PHONOGRAMS: SOUND RECORDING RIGHTS: ARTICLE 36: EXERCISE OF COPYRIGHT: ARTIFICIAL PARTITIONING: EXHAUSTION OF RIGHTS: EXPIRY OF COPYRIGHT PERIOD IN DENMARK, NOT IN GERMANY: ECJ)

Hoffmann-La Roche AG v. Dumex A/S (PATENT: INFRINGEMENT: CONSTRUCTION: S.C.)

R. v. Secretary of State for the National Heritage, *ex parte* Continental Television BVIO (BROADCASTING: APPLICATION FOR JUDICIAL REVIEW: PORNOGRAPHIC SATELLITE TELEVISION SERVICE TRANSMITTED FROM DENMARK: DECISION AND ORDER OF SECRETARY OF STATE TO PROSCRIBE: WHETHER COMPATIBLE WITH BROADCASTING DIRECTIVE: WHETHER "RETRANSMISSION" TO BE INTERPRETED LITERALLY OR PURPOSIVELY: REFERENCE TO ECJ: INJUNCTION REFUSED: APPEAL DISMISSED: C.A.: D.C.)

Warner Brothers Inc. v. Christiansen (COPYRIGHT: LENDING RIGHT: VIDEO BOUGHT IN SHOP IN ENGLAND WHERE NO LENDING RIGHT: RENTED OUT FROM SHOP IN DENMARK WHERE LENDING RIGHT APPLIES: WHETHER SALE IN ENGLAND EXHAUSTS COPYRIGHT IN BOUGHT VIDEO: EXTENT OF EXHAUSTION: NOT APPLICABLE TO RENTAL: NO RIGHT TO RENT OUT ENGLISH VIDEO IN DENMARK WITHOUT APPROPRIATE AUTHORISATION: ECJ)

France

Alexander Bihi Zenou v. Michel Colucci (COPYRIGHT: COMPILATION OF STORIES: C.A.)

Apple Computer Inc. v. Segimex Sàrl (COPYRIGHT: COMPUTER PROGRAMS)

Argos Films, SA v. Ivens (COPYRIGHT: *Droit moral*: EXPLANATORY NOTE IN CREDITS OF FILM: BREACH IF FORBIDDEN BY AUTHOR: S.C.)

Artware (Sárl) v. Groupe d'Utilisation Francophone d'Informatique (SOFTWARE SALES: COPYRIGHT: RIGHT TO MAKE BACK-UP COPIES: COMPUTER SOFTWARE: ANTI-PROTECTION PROCESSES: S.C.)

Atari Ireland Ltd v. Valadon (COPYRIGHT: VIDEO GAMES)

Atari Ireland Ltd v. Valadon (TRADE MARK: INFRINGEMENT)

Babolat Maillot Witt SA v. Pachot (COPYRIGHT)

Basset v. SACEM (COPYRIGHT: RESTRICTIVE PRACTICES: COLLECTING SOCIETIES: S.C.)

Baux v. Société Co-operative de Calce (TRADING NAME: WINE: APPELATION: CHÂTEAU: CONFLICT BETWEEN OCCUPANTS OF CHÂTEAU AND VINEGROWERS OCCUPYING LAND PREVIOUSLY PART OF CHÂTEAU: REFERENCE TO ECJ: S.C.)

Chambre Syndicale Nationale de la Discothéque (SYNDIS) v. SACEM (RESTRICTIVE PRACTICES: PERFORMING RIGHTS SOCIETIES: INTER-STATE TRADE: ROYALTY ENTITLEMENT: D.C.)

Chloe Production Sàrl v. Gaumont (COPYRIGHT: FILMS: DISTRIBUTION CONTRACT: S.C.)

Cohen v. Chaine (COPYRIGHT: CO-AUTHORSHIP: POSTHUMOUS PUBLICATION: *Droit moral*: LIABILITY OF PUBLISHER)

Compagnie Luxembourgeoise de Télédiffusion (BROADCASTING FRANCHISES: ADMINISTRATIVE PROCEDURE: JUDICIAL REVIEW: *Locus standi*: Conseil d'Etat)

Dubuffet v. Régie Nationale des Usines Renault (COPYRIGHT: ARCHITECTURAL WORKS: *Droit moral*)

Editions Gallimard v. Hamish Hamilton Ltd (COPYRIGHT: *Droit moral*)

Félicitas Sàrl v. Georges (TRADE MARK: LICENCE: OBLIGATIONS: C.A.)

Financial Times Ltd v. Sàrl Ecopress (COPYRIGHT: NEWSPAPER ARTICLES)

Foujita v. Sàrl Art Conception Realisation (COPYRIGHT: DECEASED AUTHOR: *Droit moral*: Abuse: S.C.)

Gabon (The State of) v. Société Nationale de Télévision en Couleurs "Antenne 2" (COPYRIGHT: *Droit moral*: FILM PRODUCTION: S.C.)

Hérault v. SACEM (COPYRIGHT: PERFORMING RIGHT: COLLECTING SOCIETY: DOMINANT POSITION: MUSIC: LICENCE: C.A.)

Johansson v. Institut National de la Propriete Industrielle (PATENTS: MEDICINES: SUPPLEMENTARY PROTECTION: C.A.)

Lallier v. Lux (TRADE MARK: REGISTRATION: OWNERSHIP: PRIOR USE: COPYRIGHT: IDEAS: GAMES: C.A.)

Le Monde (Sàrl) v. Société Microfor Inc. (COPYRIGHT: COLLECTIVE WORKS: OWNER'S RIGHTS: CONSENTS: REPRODUCTION: INDEXES: INTELLECTUAL CONTENT: DERIVED WORKS: PRESS REVIEW: BIBLIOGRAPHIES AND EXTRACTS: S.C.: C.A.)

Maison Lejay Lagoute SA v. l'Héritier Guyot SA (TRADE MARK: KIR: REGISTRATION: D.C.)

Massey-Ferguson Ltd v. Bepco France SA (COPYRIGHT: SPARE PARTS: TRADE MARK: PACKAGING: UNFAIR COMPETITION)

Ministère Public v. Deserbais (TRADE NAMES: "EDAM" GENERIC: NOT
DESIGNATION OF ORIGIN: GERMAN EDAM WITH LOWER FAT CONTENT THAN
ALLOWED IN FRANCE FOR FRENCH EDAM: IMPORT REFUSED WITHOUT GOOD
REASON: CONSUMERS PROTECTED ADEQUATELY BY LABELLING:
MULTILATERAL TREATIES: NOT PLEADABLE AGAINST COMMUNITY LAW IF
ONLY EEC MEMBER STATES INVOLVED: ECJ)
Ministère Public v. Lucazeau (SACEM, *partie civile*) (COPYRIGHT: INFRINGEMENT:
COLLECTION AGENCIES: STATUS: CRIMINAL OFFENCE: PERFORMANCE: EEC:
RESTRICTIVE PRACTICES: DOMINANT POSITION: ABUSE: C.A.)
Pestre v. Oril SA (PATENT: LICENSING AGREEMENT: KNOW-HOW: ROYALTIES:
TERM: 50 YEARS: VALIDITY AFTER EXPIRY OF PATENT: C.A.)
Ponty v. Chamberland (COPYRIGHT: COLLABORATIVE WORKS: *Droit moral*: WHO
MAY SUE: S.C.)
Procureur de la République & SA Vêtements Goguet Sport v. Hechter (RESTRICTIVE
PRACTICES: FRANCHISE AGREEMENTS: RESALE PRICE MAINTENANCE:
REFUSAL TO SELL: D.C.)
Regie Nationale des Usines Renault v. Roland Thevenoux (IMPORTS: INDUSTRIAL
PROPERTY: SPARE PARTS: MOTOR CAR SPARE PARTS: SUBJECT TO
STATUTORY PROTECTION: D.C.)
Renault v. Thevenoux (Regie Nationale) (DESIGNS: SPARE PARTS FOR CARS)
Robert v. Société Crehallet-Folliot-Recherche et Publicité (COPYRIGHT:
COLLECTIVE WORKS: INDIVIDUAL AUTHOR'S RIGHTS: EDITOR'S NAME:
UNFAIR COMPETITION: S.C.)
Rowe v. Walt Disney Productions (COPYRIGHT: CONFLICT OF LAWS: *Droit moral*:
S.C.)
Rutman v. Société Des Gens de Lettres (COPYRIGHT: AUDIOVISUAL WORKS:
WHETHER TECHNICAL WORK OR INTELLECTUAL CREATION: D.C.)
SDRM's Practices (RESTRICTIVE PRACTICES: COLLECTING SOCIETIES: FOREIGN
WORKS: IMPORTS: COPYRIGHT: DISCRIMINATORY PRACTICES: DOMINANT
POSITION: Competition Commission)
Shelltrie Distribution Sàrl v. SNTF (COPYRIGHT: FILMS)
Société Française de Transmissions Florales Interflora & Téléfleurs France
(RESTRICTIVE PRACTICES: DOMINANT POSITION: EXCLUSIVITY CLAUSE:
PROTECTION OF TRADE MARK: MINIMUM TARIFF ORDER: Copyright
Commission)
Société Française Hoechst v. Allied Colloids Ltd (PATENT: INFRINGEMENT:
PRACTICE: DISCOVERY: REPORT PREPARED BY DEFENDANTS AFTER
COMMENCEMENT OF PARALLEL PROCEEDINGS IN FRANCE: PRIVILEGE: Pat.
Ct.)
Société Princesse SA v. SACEM (PERFORMING RIGHTS: ABUSE OF DOMINANT
POSITION: D.C.)
Société Rannou Graphie v. CNPRI (COPYRIGHT: PHOTOCOPIES: S.C.)
VAG France v. Etablissements Magne SA (RESTRICTIVE PRACTICES: MOTOR
VEHICLES: GROUP EXEMPTION: REGULATION 123/85: EFFECT ON
DISTRIBUTION CONTRACTS: ECJ)
Widmaier v. SPADEM (COPYRIGHT: *Droit moral*: COPYRIGHT MANAGEMENT
SOCIETY: S.C.)

Germany

ASTERIX Trade Mark (TRADE MARK: COPYRIGHT: COMIC STRIPS:
UNAUTHORISED SALE: INJUNCTION: VICARIOUS LIABILITY: C.A.)
Bayer AG v. Süllhöfer (JUDICIAL PROCEDURE: PRELIMINARY RULINGS: MULTIPLE
CLAIMS: PATENT LICENSING: RESTRICTIVE PRACTICES: ANTI-COMPETITIVE
PRACTICES: COMMUNITY LAW AND NATIONAL LAW: NO-CHALLENGE
CLAUSE: APPEAL ON POINT OF LAW: S.C.)

Holland

Ireland

Muckross Park Hotel Ltd v. Randles (PASSING OFF: HOTEL: MUCKROSS PARK HOTEL: NEW BUSINESS MUCKROSS COURT HOTEL: LIKELIHOOD OF DECEPTION: DETERMINATION: SECONDARY MEANING: THE MUCKROSS: GOODWILL: H.C.)

NRDC's Irish Application (PATENT: APPLICATION: MICRO-ORGANISM: WHETHER AN INVENTION: C.-G.)

Paramount Pictures Corporation v. Cablelink Ltd (COPYRIGHT: INTERLOCUTORY INFRINGEMENT: INJUNCTION: TELEVISION CABLE DIFFUSION SERVICE: DAMAGES: LAW IN CINEMATOGRAPH FILM: ABUSE OF DOMINANT POSITION: ARTICLES 85 AND 86: H.C.)

Performing Right Society Ltd v. Marlin Communal Aerials Ltd (COPYRIGHT: BROADCASTING: CABLE TELEVISION: S.C.)

Phonographic Performance (Ireland) Ltd v. J. Somers (Inspector of Taxes) (REVENUE: VALUE ADDED TAX: TAX PAYABLE ON SUPPLY OF SERVICES: COPYRIGHT: SOUND RECORDINGS: REMUNERATION FOR BROADCASTING OF SOUND RECORDINGS: AGREEMENT: WHETHER APPELLANT SUPPLYING A SERVICE: WHETHER ATTRACTING VALUE ADDED TAX: H.C.)

Powerscourt Estates v. Gallagher (MAREVA INJUNCTION: JURISDICTION: H.C.)

Private Research Ltd v. Brosnan (COPYRIGHT: INFRINGEMENT: INTERLOCUTORY INJUNCTION: BREACH OF CONFIDENCE: EMPLOYER AND EMPLOYEE: MISUSE OF CONFIDENTIAL INFORMATION: WHETHER FAIR QUESTION TO BE TRIED: ADEQUACY OF DAMAGES: BALANCE OF CONVENIENCE: Ireland: H.C.)

Radio Telefis Eireann v. Magill TV Guide Ltd (COPYRIGHT: RADIO AND TELEVISION SCHEDULES: LITERARY WORK: RESTRICTIVE PRACTICES: COMMUNITY LAW AND NATIONAL LAW: JUDICIAL PROCEDURE: EVIDENCE: H.C.)

Radio Telefis Eireann v. Magill TV Guide Ltd (COPYRIGHT: TELEVISION PROGRAMMES: PUBLIC INTEREST: RESTRICTIVE PRACTICES: H.C.)

Rajan v. Ministry for Industry and Commerce (PATENTS: PATENT OFFICE DISPUTE: EXAMINATION: POWERS OF CONTROLLER: H.C.)

Schering Corporation v. The Controller of Patents, Designs and Trademarks (PATENTS: APPLICATION: DELAY: CONTROLLER OF PATENTS, DESIGNS AND TRADEMARKS: POWERS: CONVENTION APPLICATION: REFUSAL TO DEEM APPLICATION: RECEIPT WITHIN STATUTORY PERIOD: JUSTIFIED: H.C.)

Soudure Autogne Française v. Controller of Patents (TRADE MARK: APPLICATION: COLLECTION OF LETTERS: DISTINCTIVENESS: H.C.)

Technobiotic Ltd's Patent (PATENT: TERM: EXTENSION: INADEQUATE REMUNERATION: PHARMACEUTICAL COMPOUND: LENGTHY DEVELOPMENT PERIOD: SMALL DOMESTIC MARKET: WHETHER EXCEPTIONAL CASE: H.C.)

WATERFORD Trade Mark (PART B: WHETHER CAPABLE OF DISTINGUISHING: SUBSTANTIAL USER: H.C.: S.C.)

Italy

Carrozzeria Grazia v. Volvo Italia (RESTRICTIVE PRACTICES: DOMINANT POSITION: ABUSE: MOTOR CARS: TYPE APPROVAL: CERTIFICATES OF CONFORMITY: REFUSAL TO SUPPLY: CASE SETTLED: NOTICE: E.C. Comm.)

Consorzio del Prosciutto di Parma v. Marks and Spencer plc (PASSING OFF: INTERLOCUTORY INJUNCTION: PRE-SLICED PARMA HAM: REPRESENTATIVE ACTION: Locus standi: BALANCE OF CONVENIENCE: ITALIAN LEGISLATION: Ch.D.: C.A.)

Consorzio Italiano della Componentistica di Ricambio per Autoveicoli v. Regie Nationale des Usines Renault (COMMUNITY LAW AND NATIONAL LAW: INDUSTRIAL DESIGNS: RESTRICTIVE PRACTICES: DOMINANT POSITION: ABUSE: SPARE PARTS: ECJ)

Distributori Automatici Italia SpA v. Holford General Trading Co. Ltd (PRACTICE: ANTON PILLER: POST-JUDGMENT ORDER IN AID OF EXECUTION: Q.B.D.)

E.C. Commission v. Italy (Subsidy for Italian Motor Vehicles) (IMPORTS: QUANTITIVE RESTRICTIONS: NO *de minimis* FOR ARTICLE 30: ECJ)

E.C. Commission v. United Kingdom and Italy (IMPORTS: PATENTS: FREE MOVEMENT OF GOODS: SPECIFIC SUBJECT-MATTER: COMPULSORY LICENCE: WHERE PATENTED PRODUCT BEING IMPORTED RATHER THAN MANUFACTURED DOMESTICALLY, CAPABLE OF HINDERING INTRA-COMMUNITY TRADE: WHETHER SATISFACTION OF DEMAND FOR PATENTED PRODUCT BY IMPORT CONSTITUTES INSUFFICIENT EXPLOITATION OF THE PATENT: ECJ)

E.C. Commission v. United Kingdom and Italy (Re Compulsory Patent Licences) (IMPORTS: PATENTS: COMPULSORY LICENCE IF NO EXPLOITATION WITHIN COUNTRY: IMPORTS FROM ELSEWHERE IN COMMUNITY NOT COUNTED AS INTERNAL EXPLOITATION: HINDRANCE TO IMPORTS: P.A.77: SIMILAR ITALIAN PROVISIONS LIKEWISE: ECJ)

Elopak Italia Srl v. Tetra Pak (No. 2) (RESTRICTIVE PRACTICES: DOMINANT POSITION: ABUSE: RELEVANT PRODUCT MARKET: SALES CONTRACTS: TYING CLAUSES: EXCLUSIVE SUPPLY: ELIMINATORY PRICING: DISCRIMINATORY PRICING: E.C. Comm.)

Italy v. Caldana (CONSUMER PROTECTION: PRODUCT SAFETY: LABELLING: DIFFERENCE BETWEEN DANGEROUS SUBSTANCES AND DANGEROUS PREPARATIONS: ECJ)

Italy v. E.C. Commission (Re BT) (RESTRICTIVE PRACTICES: MONOPOLIES: STATE ENTERPRISES: ECJ PROCEDURE: TREATIES: ECJ)

San Pellegrino SpA v. Coca-Cola Export Corporation—Filiale Italiana (RESTRICTIVE PRACTICES: DISTRIBUTION AGREEMENTS: REBATES: ABUSE OF DOMINANT POSITION: FIDELITY REBATES AND PRODUCTION TARGET REBATES: SETTLEMENT ON UNDERTAKING TO DISCONTINUE REBATES: E.C. Comm.)

Società Italiana Degli Autori ed Editori (SIAE) v. Domenico Pompa (COPYRIGHT: INTELLECTUAL PRODUCT: BASIS OF PROTECTION: COMPUTER SOFTWARE: S.C.)

Société Romanaise de la Chaussure SA v. British Shoe Corp. Ltd (COPYRIGHT: INFRINGEMENT: ITALIAN INFRINGER: DISCOVERY INTENDED TO SHOW IF ITALIAN ACTION WORTHWHILE: Ch.D.)

Unicomp Srl v. Italcomputers Srl (COPYRIGHT: CREATIVE WORK: COMPUTER PROGRAMS: Italy: Magistrates Ct)

Northern Ireland

Smith v. Greenfield (COPYRIGHT: INFRINGEMENT: TERM OF PROTECTION: CONVERSION DAMAGES: INNOCENCE: H.C.)

Tayto (Northern Ireland) Ltd v. McKee (TRADE MARKS: RESTRICTIVE PRACTICES: PRE-EEC MARKET-PARTITIONING AGREEMENT FOR USE OF IDENTICAL TRADE MARK: ABANDONED AND NO CONTINUING EFFECTS: FAILURE TO USE TRADE MARK IN COMPETITOR'S TERRITORY NOT TAINTED BY ORIGINAL AGREEMENT: Ch.D.)

Scotland

Alexander Fergusson & Co. v. Matthews McClay & Manson (PASSING OFF: USE OF GET UP: ABANDONMENT OF GET UP: BALANCE OF CONVENIENCE: TRADE MARKS AND NAMES: O.H.)

Beta Computers (Europe) Ltd v. Adobe Systems (Europe) Ltd (CONTRACT: SHRINK-WRAPPED SOFTWARE LICENCE: SUPPLY OF COMPUTER SOFTWARE: NO CONCLUDED CONTRACT UNTIL ACCEPTANCE OF LICENCE CONDITIONS BY PURCHASER: NO NEED FOR IMPLIED TERM: LICENCE CONDITIONS IMPOSED BY COPYRIGHT OWNER: *Jus quaesitum tertio*: O.H.)

Bravado Merchandising Services Ltd v. Mainstream Publishing (Edinburgh) Ltd (TRADE MARK: NAME OF POP GROUP REGISTERED *inter alia* FOR BOOKS: USE OF NAME OF GROUP ON BOOK ABOUT THE GROUP: INFRINGEMENT: WHETHER USE IN TRADEMARK SENSE: AVAILABILITY OF DEFENCE UNDER: T.M.A.94, S.11(2): O.H.)

British Phonographic Industry Ltd v. Cohen (COPYRIGHT: INFRINGEMENT: ANTON PILLER: PRACTICE: I.H.)

Brupat Ltd v. Smith (PATENT: INFRINGEMENT: CERTIFICATE OF VALIDITY: O.H.)

Christian Salvesen (Oil Services) Ltd v. Odfjell Drilling & Construction Co. (U.K.) Ltd (PATENT: INFRINGEMENT: RIGHTS OF EXCLUSIVE SUB-LICENSEE: KNOWLEDGE: O.H.)

Clark v. David Allan & Co. Ltd (COPYRIGHT: ARTISTIC WORK: DESIGN DRAWINGS: INFRINGEMENT: GARMENT: WHETHER FINISHED GARMENT CONSTITUTES REPRODUCTION: VISUAL IMPACT: O.H.)

Conoco Specialty Products Inc. v. Merpro Montassa Ltd (No. 1) (INFRINGEMENT: INTERIM INTERDICT: ALLEGED DIFFERENCES: WHETHER PRIMA FACIE CASE: BALANCE OF CONVENIENCE: O.H.)

Conoco Specialty Products Inc. v. Merpro Montassa Ltd (PATENT: INFRINGEMENT: CONSTRUCTION: GENERALLY CYLINDRICAL: VALIDITY: ANTICIPATION: OBVIOUSNESS: O.H.)

Dash Ltd v. Philip King Tailoring Ltd (TRADE MARKS: TRADE NAMES: PASSING OFF: SIMILAR NAMES: DASH/DASCH: SIMILAR BUSINESSES: INTERIM INTERDICT: BALANCE OF CONVENIENCE: PROTECTION OF LONG-ESTABLISHED BUSINESS AGAINST NEWLY FORMED BUSINESS: I.H.)

Dirt Magnet Trade Mark (TRADE MARK: RECTIFICATION: PRACTICE: PARALLEL PROCEEDINGS IN SCOTLAND AND ENGLAND: IDENTICAL ISSUES: APPLICANTS NOT PARTIES TO SCOTTISH PROCEEDINGS: WHETHER DUPLICATION: COSTS: Ch.D.)

Grant & Sons Ltd v. William Cadenhead Ltd (TRADE MARK: INFRINGEMENT: PASSING OFF: WHISKY: GEOGRAPHICAL NAME: O.H.)

Grant v. Procurator Fiscal (CONFIDENTIAL INFORMATION: COPIES OF COMPUTER PRINT-OUTS: WHETHER DISHONEST EXPLOITATION OF THE CONFIDENTIAL INFORMATION OF ANOTHER A CRIME: H.C.)

Harben Pumps (Scotland) Ltd v. Lafferty (CONFIDENTIAL INFORMATION: EX-EMPLOYEE: TRADE SECRETS: IMPLIED TERMS OF CONTRACT: O.H.)

Highland Distilleries Co. plc v. Speymalt Whisky Distributors Ltd (TRADE MARK: TRADE NAMES: INFRINGEMENT: PASSING OFF: GEOGRAPHICAL NAME: O.H.)

International House of Heraldry v. Grant (TRADE MARK: PASSING OFF: SIMILAR NAMES: DESCRIPTIVE NAMES: INTERNATIONAL ART OF HERALDRY: WHETHER DESCRIPTIVE: WHETHER SLIGHT DIFFERENCE SUFFICIENT TO DISTINGUISH: INTERIM INTERDICT: BALANCE OF CONVENIENCE: PROTECTION OF ESTABLISHED BUSINESS AGAINST NEWLY FORMED BUSINESS: O.H.)

James Burrough Distillers plc v. Speymalt Whisky Distributors Ltd (TRADE MARK: INFRINGEMENT ABROAD: PASSING OFF: INTERNATIONAL LAW: DOUBLE ACTIONABILITY REQUIREMENT: NATURE OF TRADE MARKS: O.H.)

James North & Sons Ltd v. North Cape Textiles Ltd (PASSING OFF: TRADE MARK: INFRINGEMENT: PRACTICE: INJUNCTION: England: C.A.)

John Walker & Sons Ltd v. Douglas Laing & Co. Ltd (TRADE MARK: PASSING OFF: SCOTCH WHISKY: INTERDICT: BREACH: EXPORT OF SPIRIT CONTAINING MIXTURE OF SCOTCH WHISKY AND CANE SPIRIT: LABELS AND BOTTLES: ENABLING PASSING OFF: O.H.)

Lang Bros Ltd v. Goldwell Ltd (PASSING OFF: UNFAIR TRADING: WEE McGLEN: I.H.)

Lord Advocate v. Scotsman Publications Ltd (BREACH OF CONFIDENCE: MI5: DUTY ON THIRD PARTIES IN INNOCENT RECEIPT OF INFORMATION: INTERDICT: BALANCE OF CONVENIENCE: O.H.: H.L.)
(NON-CONTENTS CASE: PUBLIC INTEREST: WHETHER SUFFICIENT PROOF FOR INTERDICT: RECLAIMING MOTION REFUSED: I.H.)
(POSITION OF NEWSPAPERS: EFFECT OF "*Spycatcher*": EFFECT OF OFFICIAL SECRETS ACT 1989: H.L.)

Macallan-Glenlivet plc v. Speyside Whisky Distributors Ltd (TRADE MARK: INFRINGEMENT: PASSING OFF: WHISKY: O.H.)

Oliver Homes (Manufacturing) v. Hamilton (INFRINGEMENT: BUILDING PLANS AND DESIGNS: HOUSE KIT PLANS: USE OF PLANS NOT LICENCES SEPARATELY FROM SALE OF HOUSE KIT: DAMAGES: METHOD OF CALCULATION: ENTITLEMENT TO DAMAGES FOR LOSS OF PROFITS ON SALE OF HOUSE KIT: O.H.)

Salon Services (Hairdressing Supplies) Ltd v. Direct Salon Services Ltd (TRADE MARK: PASSING OFF: DESCRIPTIVE NAME: REPUTATION: O.H.)

Santa Fe International Corp. v. Napier Shipping SA (PRACTICE: CONFIDENTIALITY: PATENT: INFRINGEMENT: PATENT AGENT'S PRIVILEGE: O.H.)

Scottish Milk Marketing Board v. Drybrough & Co. Ltd (TRADE MARK AND TRADE NAME: PASSING OFF: SCOTTISH PRIDE: INTERIM INTERDICT: O.H.)

Silly Wizard Ltd v. Shaughnessy (COPYRIGHT: SOUND RECORDINGS: PERFORMERS' PROTECTION: RIGHT OF ACTION: REMEDIES: INJUNCTION: O.H.)

Union Carbide Corp. v. BP Chemicals Ltd (PATENT: INFRINGEMENT: PRACTICE: DISCOVERY: APPLICATION IN SCOTLAND TO AID PROCEEDINGS IN ENGLAND: APPLICATION BEFORE SERVICE OF STATEMENT OF CLAIM AND PARTICULARS OF INFRINGEMENT: WHETHER NECESSARY TO ENABLE PATENTEE ADEQUATELY TO PLEAD PARTICULARS IN ENGLAND: DISCRETION: CONFIDENTIAL DOCUMENTS: DISCLOSURE: TERMS: O.H.: I.H.)

William E. Selkin Ltd v. Proven Products Ltd (PATENT: INFRINGEMENT: CLAIMS: CONSTRUCTION: OBVIOUSNESS: NOVELTY: SIMILAR APPARATUS: INTERIM INTERDICT: WEIGHT TO BE GIVEN TO EXISTENCE OF BALANCE OF CONVENIENCE: PROTECTION OF LONG-ESTABLISHED BUSINESS AGAINST NEWLY-FORMED BUSINESS: ADEQUACY OF DAMAGES: V.C.)

Spain

Generics (U.K.) Ltd v. Smith Kline and French Laboratories Ltd (IMPORTS: PATENTS: COMPULSORY LICENCES: INTER-STATE TRADE: PARALLEL IMPORTS: DISCRIMINATION: Spain and Portugal: ECJ)

Jorge UA v. Registro de la Propiedad Industrial (TRADE MARKS: BIOLOGICAL VARIETIES: GENERIC TERMS: S.C.)

Wellcome Foundation Ltd v. Discpharm Ltd (PATENT: INFRINGEMENT: PARALLEL IMPORTS: WHETHER IMPLIED LICENCE TO IMPORT FROM SPAIN TO PORTUGAL: DEROGATION FROM GRANT: EXHAUSTION OF RIGHTS: ARTICLE 30: TREATY OF IBERIAN ACCESSION: WHETHER PATENT A PRODUCT PATENT: Pat. C.C.)

Portugal

Generics (U.K.) Ltd v. Smith Kline and French Laboratories Ltd (IMPORTS: PATENTS: COMPULSORY LICENCES: INTER-STATE TRADE: PARALLEL IMPORTS: DISCRIMINATION: Spain and Portugal: ECJ)

Wellcome Foundation Ltd v. Discpharm Ltd (PATENT: INFRINGEMENT: PARALLEL IMPORTS: WHETHER IMPLIED LICENCE TO IMPORT FROM SPAIN TO PORTUGAL: DEROGATION FROM GRANT: EXHAUSTION OF RIGHTS: ARTICLE 30: TREATY OF IBERIAN ACCESSION: WHETHER PATENT A PRODUCT PATENT: Pat. C.C.)

Sweden

Wickstrand v. Förening Svenska Tonsättares Internationella Musikbyrå (COPYRIGHT: DAMAGES: EXPLOITATION RIGHTS: "PUBLIC PERFORMANCE": PRIVATE USE: S.C.)

Switzerland

Autronic AG v. Switzerland (HUMAN RIGHTS: FREEDOM OF EXPRESSION: BROADCASTING LICENCES: RECEIPT OF SATELLITE TRANSMISSIONS: NECESSITY IN A DEMOCRATIC SOCIETY: ECHR)

Copyright in Maps and Plans (COPYRIGHT: "MAP FOR MEN": IMMORALITY)

Schweizerische Interpreten-Gesellschaft v. X and Z (COPYRIGHT: WORKS OF ART AND LITERATURE: DISPUTES: PROTECTION: PERSONAL RIGHTS: BOOTLEGGING: UNFAIR COMPETITION: Fed. Ct.)

SUISA (Swiss Society of Authors & Publishers) v. Rediffusion AG (COPYRIGHT: CABLE TELEVISION: FOREIGN BROADCASTS)

C. EUROPEAN PATENT OFFICE CASES

Abandonment

Abandonment of priority does not revive rights already lost
JMK Magnusson/Locking device (J05/89)
Active and passive, distinction between
Schwarz Italia/Abandonment (J07/87)
European application wrongfully made but abandoned
Latchways/Unlawful applicant (J01/91; G03/92)
Impossibility of reviving
ICI/Polyester crystallisation (T61/85)
Omission, whether constitutes
Digmesa/Further search fee (T87/88)
Unequivocal statement by representative
Riker/Withdrawal (J06/86)
What constitutes
Doris/Abandonment (J11/87)
Riker/Withdrawal (J06/86)
Röhm/Withdrawal of a European patent application (J11/80)
Whether unambiguous limitation of protection (no)
Tokyo Shibaura/Ultrasonic diagnostic apparatus (T64/85)

Abuse, evident (*See* **Prior Art—Evident Abuse**)

Amendment and Correction

Abstract, may not be based on
Bull/Identification system (T246/86)
Fujitsu/Memory circuit (T407/86)
Acknowledged prior art, reference to
Pfizer/Correction of chemical name (T990/91)
Added definition of result of disclosed process step
Coats/Synthetic yarn (T596/88)
Additional features in claim
AMP/Electrical connector (T133/83)
Added restriction, no extension of subject-matter
Foresheda/Divisional application (T118/91)
Added subject-matter
Micro Pen Research Associates/Ink system for producing circular patterns (T01/91)
Admissibility after approval of text
Whitby II/Late amendments (G07/93; T830/91)
Advantages over prior art
Lansing Bagnall/Control circuit (T11/82)
After publication
Uni-Charm/Priority declaration (correction) (J03/91)
Agreement to amendments not previously formulated
Bluewater/Admissibility (T156/90)
Appeal, on
Fuji/Multilayer photographic material (T763/89)
Kollmorgen/Consent for amendments (T63/86)
Konica/Late citation (T867/92)

647

Revocation of a patent (G01/90)
Secretary of State For Defence (United Kingdom)/Grounds for appeal (T22/88)
Siemens/Party adversely affected by a decision (J05/79)
Unilever/Grounds of appeal (T195/90)
Union Carbide/Restitution (T413/91)
Visnjic/*Restitutio in integrum* (T248/91)
Wabco/Grounds of Appeal (T287/90)
Woodcap/Appeal of proprietor (T506/91)
Admissibility, costs alone
De La Rue Systems/Apportionment of costs (T154/90)
Admissibility of fresh case
Mitsui/Ethylene copolymer (T611/90)
Admissibility: party adversely affected
Bluewater/Admissibility (T156/90)
Amendment of claim on appeal
Ex-Cell-O/Laminated paperboard container (T80/88)
Amendment of rules, effect on
Uhde/Reduction in NOx content (T544/88)
Appealable decision, requirements of
Shell/Gasification of solid fuel (T522/88)
Appeal before grounds of first instance decision
Improver/Depilatory device (T754/89)
Appeal by one party
BMW/Non-appealing party (G09/92: T60/91: T96/92)
Appeal construed as re-establishment application
Uhde/Re-establishment (T14/89)
Approved text: decision only possible on
ICI/Control circuit (T32/82)
Broader claims at oral proceedings
Becton/Radiation stabilisation (T94/87)
Common general knowledge, reliance upon by Board
Kubat/Cellulose composites (T157/87)
Communication by Board: response not bona fide
National Information Utilities Corporation/ Education utility (T25/91)
Communications by Board of Appeal, purpose and significance (See also Objection by board)
British Gas/Coal gasification (T109/83)
Lansing Bagnell/Control circuit (T11/82)
Condition, failure to comply with
La Télémécanique Électrique/Power measuring device (T126/84)
Cross-appeal
Krohne/Appeal fees (G02/91)
Torrington/Reimbursement of appeal fees (T89/84)
Discretionary decisions—Board of Appeal's role
University of California/Dimeric oligopeptides (T182/88)
Discretion of Board of Appeal
Sandoz/Reimbursement of appeal fee (T41/82)
Discretion to determine new requests as single instance
Xerox/Finality of decision (T79/89)
Documents found by Board of Appeal of its own motion
Auld/Decorative emblems (T183/82)
Examination by Board of Appeal of its own motion
Torrington/Reimbursement of appeal fees (T89/84)
Expert evidence. See Oral evidence
Extent limited to original request
Toa Nenryo/Elastomer (T299/89)

Own inquiries by Board of Appeal
  Westinghouse/Payment by cheque (J01/8)
Points taken by Board of its own motion
  Toray/Partial withdrawal of appeal (J19/82)
Powers of Board of Appeal
  Harvard/Fusion proteins (T60/89)
  Mogul/Divisional application (J38/89)
  NRDC/Examination by a Board of Appeal of its own motion (J04/80)
  Rhône-Poulenc/International applications (J06/79)
Premature filing
  Behr/Time limit for appeal (T389/86)
Problem, reformulation of
  GTE/Silicon nitride cutting tools (T344/89)
Purpose of EPO appeal procedure—precedent
  Rohm & Haas/Power to examine (G09/91; G10/91)
Reimbursement of appeal fees
  Toshiba/Display device for a machine (T783/89)
Rejection of claims passed by Examining Division
  BICC/Radiation processing (T248/85)
Remittal, fresh category of claim on appeal
  Mitsui/Ethylene copolymer (T611/90)
  Weitman/Heat recovery (T531/88)
Remittal not ordered
  Amendments minor
    Steer, Clive, Allen/Wheelbarrow (T183/89)
  De facto consideration by opposition division
    Badische Karton-und Pappenfabrik/Dust-tight folding carton (T536/88)
  No new line of attack
    Britax/Inventive step (T142/84)
    SNIA/Deployable antenna reflector (T425/87)
  No objection to admission of fresh citations
    État Français/Portable hyperbar box structure (T258/84)
  Unfair after lapse of time
    Zenith/Missing claims (J20/85)
  Unreasoned decision
    von Blücher/Air-cleaning apparatus (T5/89)
Remittal ordered
  Despite applicant's preference for decision without delay
    NRDC/Eimeria necatrix (T48/85)
  For additional search and further examination
    BASF/Paper dyeing (T8/83)
  For exercise of discretion to allow amendment
    Kollmorgen/Consent for amendments (T63/86)
  For insertion prior of art acknowledgement
    Merck/Starting compounds (T51/87)
  New state of the art having emerged
    Redland/Artificial slate (T130/83)
  No final conclusion on novelty and inventive step
    Exxon/Alumina spinel (T42/84)
    Vicom/Computer-related invention (T208/84)
  Objective state of the art not considered
    BICC/Radiation processing (T248/85)
  To allow compliance with Board's decision on previously undecided point of law
    Sperry/Reformulation of the problem (T13/84)
  To consider amended claim
    Baxter International/Liquid-gas-bubble separator (T888/90)

Translation of notice of appeal
    Rhône-Poulenc/Official language (T323/87)
Translation of notice of appeal, date of filing
    Asulab/Fee reduction (G06/91)
Withdrawal of appeal
    Krohne/Appeal fees (G02/91)
Withdrawal by opponent
  Whether effective
      McAlpine/Relief valve (T789/89)
Withdrawal of part of appeal
    Toray/Partial withdrawal of appeal (J19/82)

Application Procedure (*See also* **Appeal Procedure, Amendment and Correction, Fees and Procedure (generally)**)
Abandonment. See main heading **Abandonment**
Abstract of specification
    Sitma/Packaging machine (T160/83)
Adjournment of oral hearing
    Shell/Water-thinnable binder (T44/85)
Admissible claims, necessity of examining on basis of
    International Standard Electric/Water-soluble glass (T71/85)
Admission by applicant
    Lucas/Ignition system (T22/81)
Amendment after rule 51(4) communication
    Fujitsu/Printer (T685/90)
Amendment/correction. See main heading **Amendment and Correction**
Auxiliary requests
    Sumitomo/Remittal (T47/90)
Auxiliary request, absence of (See also Subsidiary claims need not be considered)
    Stockburger/Coded distinctive mark (T51/84)
Common general knowledge. See main heading **Common General Knowledge**
Communication under rule 51(4), effect of
    EPC Rules/Amendment—Late payment, etc.)
    Medical Biological Sciences/Oral prosthesis (J22/86)
    Xerox/Finality of decision (T79/89)
Communication under rule 51(4)—misleading and void
    Motorola/Admissibility (J02/87)
Communication under rule 51(6), effect of
    Euro-Celtique/6-Thioxanthine derivatives (T675/90)
Confidentiality
    Alt, Peter/Inspection of files (J14/91)
Consolidation
    Consolidation (J000/87)
Contents of application
    AMP/Coaxial connector (T260/85)
Date of filing
    Elton/Delay in post (J04/87)
    New Flex/Date of filing (J25/88)
    Zoueki/Filing date (J18/86)
Designation of states, correction of. See under main heading **Amendment and Correction**
Designation of states, when fees due
    Kongskilde/Legal loophole (J05/91)
Discretion of Examining Division, exercise of
    Sankyo/Diamond saw (T55/89)
    University of California/Dimeric oligopeptides (T182/88)

Product-by-process
  Asahi/Polyamide fibre (T487/89)
  Asahi/Polyethylene terephthalate fibres (T189/88)
  BICC/Radiation processing (T248/85)
  BASF/Zeolites (T219/83)
  ICI/Fibre-reinforced compositions (T257/89)
  Lubrizol/Hybrid plants (T320/87)
  Montedison/Ethylene polymers (T93/83)
Product v. process
  AECI/Thermoplastics sockets (T1/81)
  Gelman Sciences/Fresh ground (T817/93)
Qualitative expression
  Alcan/Exhaust silencer (T47/84)
  Widen/Three-stroke engine (T67/87)
Reference numerals/signs, effect of
  Hitachi/Engine control (T145/89)
  Philips/Reference signs (T237/84)
Reliance upon dictionaries
  AKZO/Rainwear (T215/90)
Requirements of prev. post-substantive examination
  GTM/Sound-absorbent wall (T80/82)
Responsibility of applicant to draft
  ICI/Control circuit (T32/82)
Second pharmaceutical indication
  Eisai/Second medical indication (G05/83)
  Reichert/Anti-snoring means (T584/88)
Speculative
  Philips/Image enhancement circuit (T770/90)
Speculative and vague
  Philips/Video disc apparatus (T378/88)
Support for. See also Generalisation of feature and Functional features
  Dyson Refractories/Catalyst production (T95/87)
  Exxon/Fuel oils (T409/91)
  Genentech I/Polypeptide expression (T292/85)
  ICI/Containers (T26/81)
  Stamicarbon/Oxidation of toluene (T38/84)
  Xerox/Amendments (T133/85)
Swiss-style
  Eisai/Second medical indication (G05/83)
  Reichert/Anti-snoring means (T584/88)
Technical features
  IBM/Document abstracting and retrieving (T22/85)
Therapeutic use
  Hoffmann-La Roche/Pyrrolidine derivatives (T128/82)
"When programmed for" clause
  General Electric/Disclosure of computer-related apparatus (T784/89)

Common general knowledge

Evidence admissible in support of correction
  Celtrix/Correction of errors (G11/91)
Fresh evidence of, admissible on appeal
  Union Carbide/Separation of air (T379/88)
Ingredients of
  Bridgestone/Rubber composition (T228/87)
  ICI/Pyridine herbicides (T206/83)

Correction *See* **Amendment** and **Correction**

Costs

Refused
    Alfa-Laval/Belated translation (T193/87)
    Du Pont de Nemours (E.I.) & Co./Late submission (T951/91)
    Toyota/Apparatus for measuring tyre uniformity (T638/89)
Refused: responsible defence of rights
    Heidelberger Drückmaschinen/Microchip (T461/88)
Competence of Boards of Appeal
    Konica/Photographic material (T934/91)
Criteria for award
    BP/Theta-1 (T212/88)
Fresh citations on appeal
    Toyota/Apparatus for measuring tyre uniformity (T638/89)
Fresh documents, mitigating circumstances
    Du Pont de Nemours (E.I.) & Co./Polyamide composition (T326/87)
Improper behaviour required: refused
    Mobil Oil/Debit order III (T170/83)
Late amendments
    Vondrovsky/Display signs (T51/90)
Late citations and evidence: apportioned
    Dow/New citation (T622/89)
    Filmtec/Costs (T117/86)
Late citations: apportioned
    Konishiroku/Photographic material (T323/89)
    Lock/Windscreen removal device (T101/87)
    Raccah/Hairdrying apparatus (T632/88)
Late citations: refused
    Dymo/Magazine file assembly (T330/88)
Late filing of proposed new claims: refused
    Bendix/Braking system (T99/87)
Location of party irrelevant
    JSR/Impact resistant resin composition (T79/88)
Oral proceedings, apportioned (no)
    Scott Paper Company/Release coating and release paper product (T125/89)
Premature request for oral proceedings
    Celanese/Polybutylene terephthalate (T507/89)
Request for oral proceedings does not justify special order
    JSR/Impact resistant resin composition (T79/88)
Reserved for later consideration
    Mobil Oil/Thermoplastic film laminate (T43/85)
Unnecessary hearing: apportioned
    De La Rue Systems/Apportionment of costs (T154/90)
    Institut Cerac/Pump impeller (T909/90)
    Mauri/Plastics chain (T189/83)
Unnecessary hearing: awarded
    Bayer/Admissibility of opposition (T10/82)
    Nissan/Fuel injector valve (T167/84)
Unnecessary hearing, both parties at fault, refused
    FMC/Costs (T336/86)

Decision

Ancillary points raised for the first time
    Veech/Haemodialysis processes and solutions (T79/91)
Finality of
    Konica/Photographic material (T934/91)

Description. *See* **Sufficiency**

Designation of States

Correction. See Amendment and *correction precautionary designation*
New Flex/Date of filing (J25/88)
When must be specified
Clouth/Selection among designations (J23/82)

Diagram. *See under* **Disclosure**

Disclosure. *See also* **Sufficiency**

Abstract does not form part
Bull/Identification system (T246/86)
Acknowledgement of prior art, subjective element
ESB/Follow-on appeal (T757/91)
Claim, teaching of
Solco/Skin and mucous membrane preparation (T202/83)
Common general knowledge
Air Products/Redox catalyst (T171/84)
Fujitsu/Surface acoustic wave device (T22/83)
Conventional programming
IBM/Data processor network (T6/83)
Cross-referenced document
Cedars-Sinai/Treatment of plasma (T449/90)
Mobil/Amendment of claims (T6/84)
Stamicarbon/Activated support (T288/84)
Derived range
Mobay/Methylenebis(phenyl isocyanate) (T2/81)
Mobil/Disclosure (T54/82)
Diagram, teaching of
Charbonnages/Venturi (T204/83)
Ford/Novelty (T356/89)
Scanditronix/Radiation beam collimation (T56/87)
Implied teaching
Aisin/Late submission of amendment (T95/83)
Stamicarbon/Activated support (T288/84)
Implied teaching: need for excessive intensity of brain work
Philips/Image enhancement circuit (T770/90)
Inevitable result
Ciba-Geigy/Spiro compounds (T181/82)
Nature of requirement
Rockefeller/Deposit number
Micro-organisms
CPC/Micro-organisms (T39/88)
Non-enabling
ICI/Pyridine herbicides (T206/83)
Omission from diagram
Commissariat á l'Energie Atomique/Reference voltage generator (T32/84)
Patentable invention not disclosed
Nogier/Magnetic therapy (T30/83)
Problem, requirement to identify
ICI/Containers (T26/81)

Entitlement

European Patent Office

Evidence

Examination procedure

Failure to pay further search fees
Non-payment of further search fees (G02/92)
Failure to pay, voluntary notice of
Proweco/*Restitutio in integrum* (J12/84)
Increase, when applicable
Ofenbau/Slag discharge (J18/85)
Lack of means
Walch/Non-payment of the fee for appeal (J02/78)
Late payment
Heisel/Late payment of appeal fee (J21/80)
Liesenfeld/Courtesy service (J01/89)
Notification of payment
Cappe/Date of which payment is made (J26/80)
Stamicarbon/Giro payment (T214/83)
Payment by debit order
Albright & Wilson/Fee reduction (T905/90)
Ford/Debit order II
ICI/Re-establishment of rights (T105/85)
Mobil Oil/Debit order III (T170/83)
Purpose of, need not be specified within time limit
Clouth/Selection among designations (J23/82)
Reduction for filing in non-official language
Albright & Wilson/Fee reduction (T905/90)
Asulab/Fee reduction (G06/91)
Geo Meccanica Idrotecnica/Language of application (J04/88)
Re-establishment fee, failure to pay
Bodenrader/International application (J03/81)
Fabritius/Re-establishment of rights (G03/91)
Refund for international search
Caterpillar/Form of decision (J08/81)
Refunded where application without purpose
Daikin Kogyo/Interruption in delivery of mail (T192/84)
Reimbursement of appeal fee, application for, unnecessary
Cataldo/Cause of non-compliance (J07/82)
Reimbursement of appeal fee (granted)
Abbot/Oral proceedings (T283/88)
AE plc/Exclusion of documents from file inspection (T811/90)
AKZO/Automatic revocation (T26/88)
BASF/Debit order I (T152/82)
BASF/Grounds for opposition (T2/89)
BASF/Triazole derivates (T231/85)
Bayer/Pulp production (T114/82)
Beecham/Corrected decision (T116/90)
Cataldo/Cause of non-compliance (J07/82)
CEA-Framatome/Spacer grid (T493/88)
Clouth/Selection among designations (J23/82)
Dan-Pal/Light transmitting wall panels (T293/88)
Deere/Mention of grant (J14/87)
Gelman Sciences/Fresh ground (T817/93)
Heisel/Late payment of appeal fee (J21/80)
Hormann/Publication of a European patent application (J05/81)
Howard/Snackfood (T73/88)
ICI/Continuation of opposition proceedings (T197/88)
Idaho/Submitting culture deposit information (J08/87)

Du Pont de Nemours (E.I.) & Co./Late submission (T951/91)
Fujitsu/Oral proceedings (T19/87)
Lintrend/Shrink treatment of linen (T76/83)
Niled/Electrical connecting apparatus (T316/86)
Nippondenso/Vehicle display (T683/89)
Otep/Concrete hardening (T28/81)
Phillips/Cash payment to Post Office (J24/86)
Phillips Petroleum/Re-establishment (T324/90)
PPG/Pigment grinding vehicle (T273/90)
Sandoz/Reimbursement of appeal fee (T41/82)
See-Shell/Bloodflow (T182/90)
Solvay/Production of hollow thermoplastic objects (T5/81)
Torrington/Reimbursement of appeal fees (T89/84)
Uni-Charm/Priority declaration/correction) (J03/91)
Veech/Haemodialysis processes and solutions (T79/91)
Action in accordance with prevailing interpretation
Caterpillar/Self-purging heat exchanger (J09/83)
Western Electric/Refund of examination fee (J08/83)
Appeal unsuccessful
ATT/Inviting observations (T669/90)
Inadmissible appeal
Konica/Photographic material (T934/91)
Multiple parties
Krohne/Appeal fees (G02/91)
No prejudice
Deere/Coupling rod (T538/89)
Steer, Clive, Allen/Wheelbarrow (T183/89)
Supererogatory reasoning
Pfizer/Correction of chemical name (T990/91)
Reimbursement of fee for further processing
Matsushita/Extension of time limit (J37/89)
Reimbursement of opposition fee (granted)
Alfa-Laval/Belated translation (T193/87)
Reimbursement of re-establishment fee (granted)
Ahmad/Additional period for renewal fee (J04/91)
Idaho/Submitting culture deposit information (J08/87)
MPD Technology/Priority claim (J09/80)
Siemens/Filing priority documents (J01/80; J02/80)
Siemens/Priority claim (J02/80)
Reimbursement search fee
Upjohn/Refund of search fee (J20/87)
Reimbursement of surcharge
Memtec/Membranes (J03/87)
Renewal fees, permitted extension of time for paying
Ahmad/Additional period for renewal fee (J04/91)
Repayment
BMW/Air-conditioning system (J04/86)
Caterpillar/Refund of examination fee (J06/83)
Caterpillar/Self-purging heat exchanger (J09/83)
Maxtor/Media storage system (J27/92)
Suntory/Repayment of examination fee (J14/85)
Western Electric/Refund of examination fee (J08/83)

Small amount exception (inside)
    Bell & Howell/Vehicle guidance system (T130/82)
    Daca/Suppression device (T290/90)
    Ikaplast/Small amount lacking (J11/85)
    Savio Plastica/Fee reduction (T290/90)
Small amount exception (outside)
    Albright & Wilson/Fee reduction (T905/90)
    Cockerill Sambre/Force majeure (J18/82)
Telegraphic money order
    Bendix/Telegraphic money order (T2/87)
10-day rule
    Nusser/Payment order (J22/85)
When received (See Date of receipt)

Formalities Section

Powers of
    Bayer/Pulp production (T114/82)
    Kolbenschmidt/Responsibility of the Legal Board of Appeal (G02/90)

Guidelines for Examination

Conventions, cannot amend
    Caisse Palette Diffusion/Correction of drawings (J33/89)
Mere guidance
    Du Pont de Nemours (E.I.) & Co./Admissibility of opposition (T204/91)
Not binding
    Bayer/Thermoplastic moulding compound (T344/88)
    Beattie/Marker (T603/89)
    Boeing/Extendible airfoil track assembly (T249/84)
    Exxon/Alumina spinel (T42/84)
    Sigma/Classifying areas (T162/82)
    Snpe/Combustible sleeve (T149/82)
    Veech/Haemodialysis processes and solutions (T79/91)

Infringement

Right to work
    Albany/Shower fittings (T194/86)

Inspection

Invocation of rights
    Item/Inspection of files (J27/87)

Interlocutory Revision

Amendment claims
    Ford/Novelty (T356/89)
Reimbursement of appeal fee
    Veech/Haemodialysis processes and solutions (T79/91)

International Application

Protest must be substantiated
    Draping of curtains/Unsubstantiated protest (W16/92)

Unity—substantive examination
    X/Lubricants (W03/88)
    X/Lubricants—Polysuccinate esters (W12/89)
    X/Synergic combination of additives (W44/88)

International Searching Authority

Protest, admissibility of
    Late submission of protest (W04/87)

Interruption of Proceedings

Incapacity of representative
    Incapacity (J000/87)

Intervention

Admissibility
    Allied Colloids/Intervention (G01/94; T169/92)
    Biogen Inc./Hepatitis B (T296/93)
    Gussinyer/Calcium sulphate filler (T390/90)
    Ka-Te System/Intervention (T27/92)
    Spanset Inter/Appeal by intervener (T202/89)
    Appeal by intervenor
        Spanset/Intervention (G04/91)
Belated entry
    Biogen Inc./Hepatitis B (T296/93)

Inventive Step

Acknowledged art
    OXY USA Inc./Gel-forming composition (T246/91)
Adaptation of prior art, not obvious
    Posso/Minicassette box (T185/82)
Additional effect. See also Bonus effect
    Appleton Papers/Pressure-sensitive recording material (T286/84)
Advantages, not necessarily required to show non-obviousness
    Corning Glass/Moulding (T366/89)
Advantages outweighing disadvantages
    Enviro-Spray/Self-pressurising dispensing container (T207/84)
Advantages unsubstantiated so obvious equivalent
    Union Carbide/Separation of air (T379/88)
Aesthetic contributions irrelevant
    ETA/Watch (T456/90)
Aged art
    Allied/Garnet laser (T263/87)
    Bendix/Braking apparatus (T55/86)
    Bexford/Reflex copying (T10/83)
    Corning Glass/Moulding (T366/89)
    Dyson Refractories/Catalyst production (T95/87)
    Fritz & Farni/Tree surround (T147/90)
    Gussinyer/Calcium sulphate filler (T390/90)
    ICI/Cleaning plaque (T290/86)
    Mitsuboshi/Endless power transmission belt (T169/84)
    Mölnlycke/Dry salt compress (T102/82)
    Nissan/Cylinder block (T726/89)
    Philips/Display tube (T321/86)
    Saidco/Water resistant cable (T151/82)

Analogous purpose
  Fibre-Chem/Baled waste paper product (T191/82)
Analogous substitution
  Australian National University/Metal complexes (T154/82)
  Bayer/Moulding compositions (T192/82)
  Ciba-Geigy/Synergistic herbicides (T68/85)
  Du Pont de Nemours (E.I.) & Co./Phenylenediamine (T103/86)
Analogous use
  Rifa/Capacitor roll (T602/90)
Analogy process
  Exxon/Gelation (T119/82)
Automation
  Lansing Bagnell, British Aerospace/Wiring loom (T262/89)
Award for technical excellence, significance of
  Procter & Gamble/Pouring and measuring package (T521/90)
Biotechnological invention
  Howard Florey/Relaxin (Application No. 83 307 553)
Bonus effect
  Allen-Bradley/Electromagnetically-operated switch (T21/81)
  Bayer/Moulding compositions (T192/82)
  Bendix/Braking apparatus (T55/86)
  Eastman Kodak/Preparation of acetic anhydride (T236/88)
  GTE/Silicon nitride cutting tools (T344/89)
  Hoechst/Enantiomers (T296/87)
  Japan Styrene/Foamed articles (T513/90)
  Toray/Flame-retarding polyester composition (T227/89)
Change of direction
  Michaelsen/Packing machine (T106/84)
Chemical compounds, structural obviousness of
  Ciba-Geigy/Benzothiopyran derivatives (T20/83)
  Ciba-Geigy/Spiro compounds (T181/82)
Chemical intermediates
  BASF/Bis-epoxy ethers (T22/82)
  BASF/R,R,R–alpha-tocopherol (T648/88)
  Bayer/Acetophenone derivatives (T163/84)
  Bayer/Cyclopropane (T65/82)
  Beecham/3-thienylmalonic acid (T65/83)
  Dow/Pyrimidines (T18/88)
  ICI/Diphenyl ethers (T372/86)
Citation
  Rhône-Poulenc/Silane (T70/90)
Claims too broad
  Lesaffre/Yeast (T740/90)
Closest prior art
  Allied/Beryllium-substituted iron-boron alloy (T113/83)
  Bayer/Thermoplastic moulding compositions (T69/83)
  Bayer/Titanyl sulphate (T183/84)
  Beecham-Wuelfing/PVD (T541/89)
  DRG/Printing sleeve (T155/87)
  Dyson Refractories/Catalyst production (T95/87)
  Fuji/Photographic material (T267/88)
  Gussinyer/Calcium sulphate filler (T390/90)
  Improver/Depilatory device (T754/89)

Konica/Sensitizing (T423/89)
Kubat/Method of producing plastic composites (T17/92)
Miles/Test device (T31/84)
Mobil Oil/Film (T405/86)
Nissan/Cylinder block (T726/89)
Nisshin/Steroid (T181/91)
Nissei/Injection moulding machine (T335/88)
OXY USA Inc./Gel-forming composition (T246/91)
Rifa/Capacitor roll (T602/90)
Surgikos/Disinfection (T69/89)
Sumitomo/Yellow dyes (T254/86)
Takemoto Yushi/Lubricating agents (T97/90)
Tioxide/Pigments (T525/90)
Uniroyal/Lubricating composition (T852/90)
USN & EF/Cold roll manufacturing (T179/87)

Collocation
Kommerling/Profile member (T130/89)
Medtronic/Synchronized intracardiac cardioverter (T387/89)
Sedlbauer/Holding device (T629/90)
Unilever/Deodorant products (T98/84)

Combination of chemical engineering steps
Air Products/Removal of hydrogen sulphide and carbonyl sulphide (T271/84)
Shell/Removal of acid gases (T119/86)

Combination of citations
Air Products/Removal of hydrogen sulphide and carbonyl sulphide (T271/84)
Allied/Garnet laser (T263/87)
Asahi/Polyamide fibre (T487/89)
Auld/Decorative emblems (T183/82)
BASF/Metal refining (T24/81)
Bayer/Thermoplastic moulding compositions (T69/83)
Bayer/Titanyl sulphate (T183/84)
Bendix/Braking apparatus (T55/86)
Black & Decker/Brush assembly (T174/86)
Britax/Inventive step (T142/84)
Celanese/Polybutylene terephthalate (T507/89)
Corning Glass/Moulding (T366/89)
Eastman Kodak/Thermal recording (T40/83)
Esdan/Electric fusion pipe fittings (T232/86)
Fritz & Farni/Tree surround (T147/90)
Fujitsu/Surface acoustic wave device (T22/83)
Herzberger Papierfabrik/Packaging magazine (T173/84)
Hüls/2,2,6,6-tetramethylpiperidone-(4) (T132/84)
ICI/Cartridge end-closure (T74/82)
ICI/Polyester polyols (T229/84)
ICI plc/Triazoles (T176/90)
Kommerling/Profile member (T130/89)
LMG/Sterilising pouch (T212/87)
MAN/Intermediate layer for reflector (T6/80)
Mitsuboshi/Endless power transmission belt (T169/84)
Mobay/Methylenebis (PHENYL ISOCYANATE) (T2/81)
Östbo/Heat exchanger (T100/90)
Posso/Minicassette box (T185/82)
Procter & Gamble/Pouring and measuring package (T521/90)
Redland/Artificial slate (T130/83)

Regent Lock/Locking handle device (T56/84)
Rifa/Capacitor roll (T602/90)
Saidco/Water resistant cable (T151/82)
Sedlbauer/Holding device (T629/90)
Shell/Removal of acid gases (T119/86)
Solvay/Production of hollow thermoplastic objects (T5/81)
Steer, Clive, Allen/Wheelbarrow (T183/89)
Teijin/Cotton yarn-like composite yarn (T169/88)
Telecommunications/Antioxidant (T173/83)
Thorn EMI/Discharge lamps (T137/86)
Tioxide/Pigments (T525/90)
Toa Nenryo/Elastomer (T299/89)
Unilever/Detergent composition (T146/83)
Unilever/Perfumed cartons (T107/82)
Welgro/Bulk carrier (T187/85)
Zeiss/Spectacle lens (T263/86)
Adaptation required
  NAT/Bagging plant (T636/88)
Combining different parts of same document
  SNIA/Deployable antenna reflector (T425/87)
Commercial success
  Charles Stark Draper Laboratory/Inertial sensor (T140/82)
  Ex-Cell-O/Laminated paperboard container (T80/88)
  Fibre-Chem/Baled waste-paper product (T191/82)
  Hasmonay/Plug for affixing screws (T91/83)
  Howard/Snackfood (T73/88)
  ICI/Fusecord (T270/84)
  Michaelsen/Packing machine (T106/84)
  Surgikos/Disinfection (T69/89)
Commercial success: relevant only in case of doubt
  ETA/Watch (T456/90)
Common general knowledge
  Boeing/General technical knowledge (T195/84)
  ICI plc/Optical sensing apparatus (T454/89)
  Lucas/Combustion engine (T426/88)
  Surgikos/Disinfection (T69/89)
  Union Carbide/Polyacrylate molding composition (T25/87)
Common general knowledge, application of to particular device
  Dynapac/Poker vibrator (2) (T27/86)
Comparative tests
  Bayer/Tolylfluanid (T57/84)
  Ciba-Geigy/Spiro compounds (T181/82)
  Dynapac/Poker vibrator (T27/86)
  Eisai/Antihistamines (T164/83)
  ICI/Cleaning plaque (T290/86)
  Kanegafuchi/Coating compositions (T67/88)
  Kodak/Photographic couplers (T197/86)
  Konishiroku/Photographic film (T390/88)
  Schupbach/Hot-sealing layer combination (T55/84)
  Shell/Aryloxybenzaldehydes (T20/81)
Complicated chemical compounds
  Australian National University/Metal complexes (T154/82)
Computer calculations
  Cselt/Parabolic reflector antenna (T36/82)

Computerisation
Tobias/Photoelectric densitometer (T287/86)
Conflicting goals
Cselt/Parabolic reflector antenna (T36/82)
Hoechst/Thiochloroformates (T198/84)
Thomson-CSF/Transistor structure (T15/86)
Consequential side effect
Telecommunications/Antioxidant (T173/83)
Contemporary expert opinion
Dow/Contaminant removal (T137/83)
Conventional use
Condec/Extrusion apparatus (T66/82)
Could/would test
Albright & Wilson/Extraction of uranium (T223/84)
Allied/Cobalt foils (T265/84)
American Cyanamid/Acrylonitrile polymer fibre (T90/84)
Beecham/Antacid composition (T255/85)
Draco/Xanthines (T7/86)
Eastman Kodak/Preparation of acetic anhydride (T236/88)
Forsheda/Divisional application (T118/91)
Japan Styrene/Foamed articles (T513/90)
Mobil/Catalyst (T392/86)
Nissan/Cylinder block (T726/89)
Rider/Simethicone tablet (T2/83)
Toray/Flame retarding polyester composition (T227/89)
Unilever/Viscosity reduction (T34/90)
Desideratum
Hooper Trading/T-cell growth factor (T877/90)
Different purpose
Exxon/Purification of sulphonic acids (T4/83)
Scott Bader/Ceramic tile adhesives (T332/87)
Different technical field, reliance upon (yes)
NI Industries/Filler mass (T560/89)
Disadvantages of component in closest prior art
Kraftwerk Union/Eddy-current testing device (T15/81)
Discouraging art, see Prejudice (Dual problem)
Appleton Papers/Pressure-sensitive recording material (T286/84)
Behr/Time limit for appeal (T389/86)
Eastman Kodak/Preparation of acetic anhydride (T236/88)
Electronic implementation of conventional system
National Information Utilities Corporation/Education utility (T25/91)
Electronic means
Control Systems/Ticket-issuing machines (T292/87)
Empirical field
English Clays/Gravure printing (T64/82)
Evidence of advantages required
Lintrend/Shrink treatment of linen (T76/83)
Evidence of skilled person
Energy Conversion/Silicon deposition (T490/89)
Expectation of success
Konica/Photographic material (T759/89)

Secondary indication
    ICI/Fusecord (T270/84)
Single specification (no)
    Goodyear/Thermoforming polyester articles (T519/89)
v. rational argument
    USN & EF/Cold roll manufacturing (T179/87)
v. trend (See also Reversal of trend)
    AKZO/Dry jet-wet spinning (T253/85)
Would/could
    Beecham/Antacid composition (T255/85)
    Dow/Contaminant removal (T137/83)
Prior art in closely related field
    Allen-Bradley/Electromagnetically-operated switch (T21/81)
Prior art in different field
    Esswein/Automatic programmer (T579/88)
Problem, definition of
    Allied/Beryllium-substituted iron-boron alloy (T113/83)
    Bayer/Thermoplastic moulding compositions (T69/83)
    Boehringer/Diagnostic agent (T99/85)
    Carnaud/Toothed wheel welding process (T190/90)
    Eaton/Blocked speed transmission (T46/82)
    Grace/Nitro compounds (T121/91)
    Hoechst/Plasmid pSG2 (T162/86)
    Konica/Photographic material (T759/89)
    Phillips Petroleum/Passivation of catalyst (T155/85)
    Schmid/Etching process (T229/85)
    Unilever/Detergent composition (T146/83)
    Union Carbide/Threaded connections (T124/82)
Problem, definition of, ex post facto
    Latzke/Magnetic plaster (T268/89)
Problem differing from that of prior art
    Solvay/Olefin polymers (T18/81)
    Toa Nenryo/Elastomer (T299/89)
Problem, features necessary for solution of
    ERA/Static inverter (T167/82)
Problem, formulation must not contain pointers to solution
    Schering/Confidential papers (T516/89)
Problem, multiple
    Kommerling/Profile member (T130/89)
Problem need not be specified in express terms in prior art
    Dentsply/Cartridge for filling dental cavities (T793/90)
Problem, perception of
    Boeing/Spoiler device (T225/84)
    Esswein/Automatic programmer (T579/88)
    Latzke/Magnetic plaster (T268/89)
    Machinefabriek G.J. Nijhuis/Stunning apparatus (T90/83)
Problem, recognition of, no contribution to
    Torgersen/Door structure (T144/84)
Problem, reformulation of
    Ciba-Geigy/Spiro compounds (T181/82)
    Lubrizol/Lubricants (T618/90)
    Nisshin/Steroid (T181/91)
    Sperry/Reformulation of the problem (T13/84)
    Surgikos/Disinfection (T69/89)

Skilled person, relevant field
    Ex-Cell-O/Laminated paperboard container (T80/88)
    Fives-Cail Babcock/Cleaning apparatus for conveyor belt (T32/81)
    Kirin-Amgen/Erythropoietin (T412/93)
    Mitsubishi Denki KK/Semiconductor device (T607/90)
Skilled person, willingness of to experiment
    Fujitsu/Semiconductor (T128/83)
Small but necessary modification
    Mölnlycke/Dry salt compress (T102/82)
Small improvement in yield
    Stamicarbon/Oxidation of toluene (T38/84)
Speculative teaching in prior art
    BASF/Paper dyeing (T8/83)
    Genentech I/Polypeptide expression (T292/85)
Standard design, departure from
    Albany/Shower fittings (T194/86)
State of the art
    Boeing/General technical knowledge (T195/84)
    Bulten-Kanthal/Electrical heating element (T240/85)
    Ex-Cell-O/Laminated paperboard container (T80/88)
    ICI/Explosive fusecord (T17/84)
    Möbius/Pencil sharpener (T176/84)
    Phillips Petroleum/Passivation of catalyst (T155/85)
    Thorn EMI/Discharge lamps (T137/86)
  Must not be artificial
      Schering/Confidential papers (T516/89)
      Unilever/Viscosity reduction (T34/90)
Stimulated to generate test
    Dentsply/Cartridge for filling dental cavities (T793/90)
Surprising effect
    BASF/Bis-epoxy ethers (T22/82)
    Fuji/Electron microscope image (T747/90)
    ICI/Modified diisocyanates (T433/86)
    Mobil/Catalyst (T392/86)
    Mölnlycke/Dry salt compress (T102/82)
    Shell/Water-thinnable binder (T44/85)
    Sumitomo/Yellow dyes (T254/86)
    Toshiba/Thickness of magnetic layers (T26/85)
    Unilever/Detergent composition (T146/83)
    Unilever/Detergent speckles (T226/84)
Surprising effect, relevance of
    Östbo/Heat exchanger (T100/90)
Technical advantage
    Aisin/Late submission of amendment (T95/83)
    BASF/Metal refining (T24/81)
    Ciba-Geigy/Spiro compounds (T181/82)
    Procter & Gamble/Pouring and measuring package (T521/90)
    Siemens/Insulin infusion device (T191/84)
  Derivation from claimed features
      Sears/Lockable closure (T108/91)
Theoretical principles, application of
    ICI/Polyester polyols (T229/84)
Trend of the art
    Ex-Cell-O/Laminated paperboard container (T80/88)
    Mobay/Methylenebis(phenyl isocyanate) (T2/81)

Trial-and-error approach
   ATT/Inviting observations (T669/90)
   Draco/Xanthines (T7/86)
   Wiederhold/Two-component polyurethane lacquer (T259/85)
   Applied
      Toray/Ultrasonic transducer (T48/86)
   Impracticable
      Medtronic/Cardiac defibrillator (T348/86)
Unsubstantiated effect
   Duco/Paint layers (T94/84)
   Unie Van Kunstmestfabrieken/Urea synthesis (T124/84)
Unexpected result
   Schering/Dipeptides (T548/91)

Inventors

Rectification of designation, whether consent required
   Fujitsu/Designation of inventors (J08/82)

Languages

Consent of parties to different language of proceedings
   Improver/Depilatory device (T754/89)
Filing in non-official language
   Asulab/Fee reduction (G06/91)
Notice of Appeal, translation not filed
   Rhône-Poulenc/Official language (T323/87)
Notice of opposition
   Late filing of translation
      Alfa-Laval/Belated translation (T193/87)

Legal Board of Appeal

Powers of
   Kolbenschmidt/Responsibility of the Legal Board of Appeal (G02/90)

Legal Maxims

A jure nemo recedere praesumitur
   Hoechst/Opponent's silence (G01/88)
Argumentum a contrario
   Hormann/Publication of a European patent application (J05/81)
Cessante ratione cessat ipsa lex
   Voest Alpine/Reestablishment of opponent (G01/86)
Cum grano salis
   Black & Decker/Brush assembly (T174/86)
Delegatus non potest delegare
   Shell/Changed composition of division (T390/86)
De minimus non curat lex
   Albright & Wilson/Fee reduction (T905/90)
De minore ad majorem
   Kongskilde/Legal loophole (J05/91)
Disposition maxim
   BASF/Withdrawal of appeal (G07/91)
Effet utile
   Ahmad/Additional period for renewal fee (J04/91)

In camera
  Novatome II/Final decision (G12/91)
In claris non fit interpretatio
  Ahmad/Additional period for renewal fee (J04/91)
In statu nascendi
  Novatome II/Final decision (G12/91)
Nemini licet venire contra factum proprium
  Incapacity (J000/87)
Obiter dictum
  Priority interval (G03/93)
Praeter legem
  Fabritius/Re-establishment of rights (J16/90)
Principal of proportionality
  Texaco/Re-establishment (T869/90)
Qui tacet consentere indetur ubi loqui debuit
  Hoechst/Opponent's silence (G01/88)
Ratio decidendi
  Konica/Photographic material (T934/91)
Ratio legis
  Harvard/Onco-mouse (T19/90)
Res judicata
  Dow/Divisional application (J11/91; J16/91)
  Konica/Photographic material (T934/91)
Sens clair
  Ahmad/Additional period for renewal fee (J04/91)
Tu patere legem quam fecisti
  Motorola/Admissibility (J02/87)
Venire contra factum proprium
  BASF/Incrustation inhibitors (T123/85)
Volenti non fit injuria
  Rohm & Haas/Power to examine (G09/91; G10/91)

Licences

Granted patent, registrability of
  Cohen/Registering of licence (J17/91)

Micro-organisms

Deposit, accession number
  Idaho/Submitting culture deposit information (J08/87)
Deposit and availability
  CPC/Amylolytic enzymes (T118/87)
  Nabisco/Micro-organisms (T239/87)
Deposit of cultures
  CPC/Micro-organisms (T39/88)
Patentability under Austrian law
  Micro-organisms

National Laws (See Conventions)

Notices of the EPO

Opposition procedure ([1989] O.J. L 417/10)
  AE plc/Exclusion of documents from file inspection (T811/90)

Novelty

Accidental anticipation
    AMP/Electrical contact (T161/82)
Adaptation compared to suitability
    Wellcome/3-Amino-pyrazoline derivatives (T289/84)
Availability
    Biogen/Recombinant DNA (T301/87)
    Toshiba/Thickness of magnetic layers (T26/85)
    To the public
        Unilever/Washing composition (T666/89)
Burden of proof
    Soepenberg/Starch product (T21/83)
    Union Carbide/High tear strength polymers (T396/89)
Citation to be read in isolation
    Ford/Novelty (T356/89)
Clear and unambiguous disclosure, test for
    Hooper Trading/T-cell growth factor (T877/90)
Clearly, unmistakably and fully derivable test
    Enthone/Electroless plating (T450/89)
    Ford/Novelty (T356/89)
    Scanditronix/Radiation beam collimation (T56/87)
Close reading of prior art
    DRG/Printing sleeve (T155/87)
Collocation
    Unilever/Deodorant products (T98/84)
Combination of separate teachings in single document
    Bayer/Catalyst (T291/85)
    Bayer/Titanyl sulphate (T183/84)
    Grehal/Shear (T305/87)
    ICI/Modified diisocyanates (T433/86)
    Inland Steel/Tellurium-containing steel (T75/87)
    Lubrizol/Lubricants (T618/90)
    Scott Bader/Ceramic tile adhesives (T332/87)
    Shell/Amino-triazine (T137/90)
Combination of two sets of variants
    Draco/Xanthines (T7/86)
Cross-referenced documents
    Amoco Corporation/Alternative claims (T153/85)
    Du Pont de Nemours (E.I.) & Co./Hollow filaments (T361/88)
    Fuji/Photographic material (T267/88)
    Gussinyer/Calcium sulphate filler (T390/90)
    Kanegafuchi/Coating compositions (T67/88)
    Texaco/Reaction injection moulded elastomer (T279/89)
Diagrammatic representation in cited art
    Charbonnages/Venturi (T204/83)
Different object
    Degussa/Furnace blacks (T53/82)
Disclaimed range
    International Standard Electric/Water-soluble glass (T71/85)
Disclaimed specific examples
    ICI/Cleaning plaque (T290/86)
    ICI/Emulsion explosive (T627/91)
    Inland Steel/Bismuth-containing steel (T105/87)

Inevitable result
    Bayer/Diastereomers (T12/81)
    CPC/Flavour concentrates (T303/86)
    ICI/Gamma-sorbitol (T173/89)
    Lintrend/Shrink treatment of linen (T76/83)
    Mobil/Friction reducing additive (T59/87)
    Tioxide/Pigments (T525/90)
    Toray Industries/Photosensitive resin (T310/88)
       Exact repetition required
          Union Carbide/High tear strength polymers (T396/89)
Inherent advantage
    Fernholz/Vinyl acetate (T188/83)
Inherent function of apparatus
    Detras/Target apparatus (T229/88)
Inherent functional feature
    Dow/Sequestering agent (T958/90)
Inventive step, relation to
    CEA-Framatome/Spacer grid (T493/88)
    Du Pont de Nemours (E.I.) & Co./Late submission (T951/91)
    Mead/Printing plate (T160/92)
Kit of known parts
    Asta/Cytostatic combination (T9/81)
Mere verbal distinction
    Eriksson/Foam plastic filter (T114/86)
    Widen/Three-stroke engine (T67/87)
Most relevant art
    Fuji/Photographic material (T267/88)
Nature of examination
    AMP/Electrical connector (T133/83)
New parameter
    Asahi Kasei KKK/Resin composition (T627/88)
New purpose/use for known substance/equipment
    BASF/Triazole derivatives (T231/85)
    Bayer/Plant growth regulating agent (G06/88)
    Bayer/Plant growth regulation (T208/88)
    Black Clawson/Pulp delignification (T215/84)
    Dow/Sequestering agent (T958/90)
    Mobil/Friction reducing additive (1) (T59/87)
    Mobil/Friction reducing additive (2) (G02/88)
    Mobil/Friction reducing additive (3) (T59/87)
    Union Carbide/Polyacrylate molding composition (T25/87)
    Vicom/Computer-related invention (T208/84)
New technical effect
    Union Carbide/Polymer-polyol compositions (T20/88)
New use of old compound
    Bayer/Growth regulation (T208/88)
"Not critical" does not constitute disclosure of alternatives
    Union Carbide/Polyalkyline polyamines (T23/90)
Numerical ranges, overlap
    Toshiba/Thickness of magnetic layers (T26/85)
Oral description
    Bayer/Fibre composites (T177/83)
    Harvard/Fusion proteins (T60/89)
    Hooper Trading/T-cell growth factor (T877/90)
    IBM/Ion etching (T534/88)

Selection from known numerical range
    Hoechst/Thiochloroformates (T198/84)
    Inland Steel/Tellurium-containing steel (T75/87)
    Plüss-Staufer/Filler (T17/85)
    Texaco/Reaction injection moulded elastomer (T279/89)
    Unilever/Interesterification process (T366/90)
    Unilever/Washing composition (T666/89)
Selection: overlapping class
    Eisai/Antihistamines (T164/83)
    Godecke/Naphthyridinone derivatives (T11/89)
Similar process with different purpose
    Mobil/Amendment of claims (T6/84)
Speculative and vague claims
    Philips/Video disc apparatus (T378/88)
Technical feature
    Asahi Kasei/Resin composition (T627/88)
Testing for non-identity through properties
    AKZO/Dry jet-wet spinning (T253/85)
Therapeutic use
    Beecham-Wuelfing/PVD (T541/89)
    Hoffman-La Roche/Pyrrolidine derivatives (T128/82)
Unexpected effect, attainment of by only part of claimed subject-matter
    CPC/Flavour concentrates (T303/86)
Use of products
    USN & EF/Cold roll manufacturing (T179/87)
Whole contents
    Bayer/Amino acid derivatives (T12/90)
    Becton/Radiation stabilisation (T94/87)
    Fuji/Multilayer photographic material (T763/89)
    Nissan/Fuel injector valve (T167/84)
    Robbins/Rotary cutterhead (T116/84)
    Texaco/Reaction injection moulded elastomer (T279/89)
    Thorn/Thermal limiting device (T326/93)

Opposition Procedure *(See also* Appeal Procedure, Costs, Procedure (generally)*)*

Abuse
    Lock/Windscreen removal device (T101/87)
Accelerated processing
    Savio Plastica/Fee reduction (T290/90)
Addition of technically specialised member to Board
    von Blücher/Surface filter (T762/90)
Administrative character
    Rohm & Haas/Power to examine (G09/91; G10/91)
Admissibility. See also Notice of opposition and Grounds of opposition
    Hoechst/Ace inhibitors (T289/91)
    Kogyo Gijutsuin/Photosensitive resins (T590/93)
    Howard Florey/Relaxin (Application No. 83 307 553)
    Schering/Dipeptides (T548/91)
    Sumitomo/Polymer solution (T376/90)
    Bayer/Admissibility of Opposition (No. 2)
    Bayer/Thermoplastic moulding compound (T344/88)
    Deere/Coupling rod (T538/89)

Extensions of time: should not be repeated save in exceptional circumstances
    Mitsuboshi Belting/Power transmission belt manufacture (T352/89)
Foreign decisions, irrelevance of
    Procter/Surfactant (T216/90)
Fresh argument at oral proceedings
    Standard Oil/Olefinic nitriles (T186/83)
Fresh argument on appeal
    AKZO/Dry jet-wet spinning (T253/85)
    Du Pont de Nemours (E.I.) & Co./Copolymers (T124/87)
Fresh citation on appeal
    Eastman Kodak/Anhydrous iodine compounds (T291/89)
  Not admitted: deliberate abuse
        Dentsply/Inadmissible late filing (T534/89)
Fresh citations by Board of Appeal from Search Report
    Medtronic/Synchronised intracardiac cardioverter (T387/89)
Fresh documents at oral proceedings
    CPC/Cheese spreads (T559/88)
    Dymo/Magazine file assembly (T330/88)
    Pomagalski/Cable car (T484/90)
    Unilever/Deodorant products (T98/84)
    Zeiss/Spectacle lens (T263/86)
Fresh documents on appeal
    Air Products/Removal of hydrogen sulphide and carbonyl sulphide (T271/84)
    AKZO/Dry jet-wet spinning (T253/85)
    Albright & Wilson/Extraction of uranium (T223/84)
    Bayer/Polyamide-6 (T9/86)
    Black & Decker/Brush assembly (T174/86)
    Bridgestone/Rubber composition (T228/87)
    Britax/Inventive step (T142/84)
    CPC/Cheese spreads (T559/88)
    Du Pont de Nemours (E.I.) & Co./Polyamide composition (T326/87)
    Du Pont de Nemours (E.I.) & Co./Yarn finish applicator (T308/87)
    État Français/Portable hyperbar box structure (T258/84)
    Filmtec/Costs (T117/86)
    Gussinyer/Calcium sulphate filler (T390/90)
    Hoechst/Metallic paint coating (T122/84)
    Hüls/2,2,6,6-tetramethylpiperidone-(4) (T132/84)
    ICI/Latex composition (T77/87)
    ICI/Modified diisocyanates (T433/86)
    ICI/Polyester polyols (T229/84)
    INRA/a-lactalbumin product (T128/86)
    JSR/Block copolymer (T416/87)
    Mobil Oil/Thermoplastic film laminate (T43/85)
    Parsons Control/Scraper chain conveyor (T61/89)
    Procter & Gamble/Pouring and measuring package (T521/90)
    Procter & Gamble/STW detergents (T100/88)
    Rhône-Poulenc/Silico-aluminate (T273/84)
    Rifa/Capacitor roll (T602/90)
    Union Carbide/Atmospheric vaporiser (T245/88)
Fresh evidence on appeal, allowed
    Asahi Kasei/Resin composition (T627/88)
    BP/Theta-1 (T212/88)
    ICI/Latex composition (T77/87)

Kanegafuchi/Coating compositions (T67/88)
Union Carbide/Separation of air (T379/88)
Uniroyal/Lubricating composition (T852/90)
Fresh evidence on appeal, refused
Chemie Linz/Reinforced channels (T242/85)
Filmtec/Costs (T117/86)
ICI/Modified diisocyanates (T433/86)
Matsushita/Dye transfer sheet (T319/90)
Shell/Amino-triazine (T137/90)
Fresh ground on appeal
ACO/Drainage channel (T442/88)
Allied Colloids/Intervention (G01/94; T169/92)
Bridgestone/Rubber composition (T228/87)
Hoechst/Metallic paint coating (T122/84)
Standard Oil/Olefinic nitriles (T186/83)
Uniroyal/Lubricating composition (T852/90)
Fresh ground on appeal (no)
Albany/Shower fittings (T194/86)
JSR/Impact-resistant resin composition (T79/88)
Fresh ground of objection at oral proceedings
Eastman Kodak/Anhydrous iodine compounds (T291/89)
Fresh grounds
Admissibility
Rohm & Haas/Power to examine (G09/91; G10/91)
On appeal
Takemoto Yushi/Lubricating agents (T97/90)
Fresh prior art, document acknowledged in patent
Schwiete/Concrete restoration (T198/88)
Fresh prior use on appeal
Mitsui/Ethylene copolymer (T611/90)
General principles underlying
ICI/Gamma-sorbitol (T173/89)
Grounds for appeal, requirements of
Hüls/Grounds for appeal (T220/83)
Grounds of opposition
INRA/a-lactalbumin product (T128/86)
Identification of citation
Bayer/Thermoplastic moulding compound (T344/88)
Identification of contested patent
Smidth/Title of invention (T317/86)
Identification of opponent
Deutsche Gelatine-Fabriken, Stoess & Co./Opponent—identifiability (T25/85)
De Erven G. De Boer BV/Opponent-identifiability (T635/88)
Kogyo Gijutsuin/Photosensitive resins (T590/93)
Zokor/Naming of opponent (T219/86)
Inadmissible opposition: no jurisdiction to examine of own motion
Thomson-Brandt/Admissibility (T328/87)
Independent of application procedure
Schwiete/Concrete restoration (T198/88)
Interlocutory decision
Bayer/Admissibility of opposition (T10/82)
Sprecher & Schuh/Toroidal transformer (T89/90)

Revocation on grounds not raised by opponent
    Battelle/Fluidised bed combustion sanitation (T450/87)
Right to be heard
    Pomagalski/Cable car (T484/90)
Rule 58(4) communication
    Hoechst/Admissibility of appeal by opponent (T271/85)
    Hoechst/Opponent's silence (G01/88)
    Shell/Changed composition of division (T390/86)
Statement of Grounds, significance of
    Rohm & Haas/Power to examine (G09/91; G10/91)
Statutory grounds, restriction to
    Black & Decker/Brush assembly (T174/86)
Supervisory jurisdiction
    Unilever/Detergent compositions (T227/88)
Term of opposition, commencement of
    Cebal/Plastic screw cap (T438/87)
Transfer of opposition
    Delta/Transfer of opposition (T349/86)
Transfer of patent proprietorship, effect
    Marlboro/Transfer (T553/90)
Transfer of pending proceedings
    MAN/Transfer of opposition (G04/88)
Translation of citation, challenge to (unsuccessful)
    Teijin/Cotton yarn-like composite yarn (T169/88)
Unopposed parts of patent, competence to consider
    Rohm & Haas/Power to examine (G09/91; G10/91)
Unsupported grounds
    Sumitomo/Extent of opposition (T182/89)
Upholding on other grounds
    Howard/Snackfood (T73/88)
Withdrawal of appeal by opponent
    BASF/Withdrawal of appeal (G07/91)
    Bell Maschinenfabrik/Withdrawal of appeal (G08/91)
Withdrawal of opponent, continuation of proceedings upon
    ICI/Continuation of opposition proceedings (T197/88)
    Sedlbauer/Holding device (T629/90)
Witness, evidence of
    IBM/Ion etching (T534/88)

Patentability

Aesthetic features
    ETA/Watch (T456/90)
Mix of technical and non-technical elements
    Beattie/Marker (T603/89)
Musical aid
    Beattie/Marker (T603/89)
Productivity improvement method
    Tippens/Reversing plate mill (T209/91)

Patentable Subject–Matter

Aesthetic creation
    Fuji/Coloured disk jacket (T119/88)
    Unilever/Coloured composition (T228/90)

Animals
Harvard/Onco-mouse (Application No. 85 304 490.7)
Harvard/Onco-mouse (T19/90)
Biological process
Biogen Inc./Hepatitis B (T296/93)
Harvard/Onco-mouse (T19/90)
Lubrizol/Hybrid plants (T320/87)
Plant Genetic Systems/Glutamine synthetase inhibitors (T356/93)
Computer-related inventions
Bosch/Electronic computer components (T164/92)
General Electric/Disclosure of computer-related apparatus (T784/89)
IBM/Computer-related invention (T115/85)
IBM/Data processor network (T6/83)
IBM/Document abstracting and retrieving (T22/85)
IBM/Semantically-related expressions (T52/85)
IBM/Text processing (T65/86)
Koch & Sterzel/X-ray apparatus (T26/86)
Siemens/Character form (T158/88)
Vicom/Computer-related invention (T208/84)
Contraceptive method
British Technology Group/Contraceptive method (T74/93)
General Hospital/Contraceptive method (T820/92)
Cosmetic indication
Du Pont de Nemours (E.I.) & Co./Appetite suppressant (T144/83)
ICI/Cleaning plaque (T290/86)
Reichert/Anti-snoring means (T584/88)
Roussel-Uclaf/Thenoyl peroxide (T36/83)
Diagnostic method
Bruker/Non-invasive measurement (T385/86)
Philips/Diagnostic method (T45/84)
Siemens/Diagnostic method (T83/87)
Thomson-CSF/Tomodensitometry (1) (T61/83)
Thomson-CSF/Tomodensitometry (2) (T208/83)
Display of information
Nippondenso/Vehicle display (T683/89)
First medical indication
Hoffman-La-Roche/Pyrrolidine derivatives (T128/82)
Industrial application
Du Pont de Nemours (E.I.) & Co./Appetite suppressant (T144/83)
Roussel-Uclaf/Thenoyl peroxide (T36/83)
Siemens/Flow measurement (T245/87)
Wellcome/Pigs I (T116/85)
Medical indication. (See also First medical indication, Second medical indication)
Asta/Cytostatic combination (T9/81)
Roussel-Uclaf/Thenoyl peroxide (T36/83)
Mental acts
IBM/Text clarity processing (T38/86)
Mere discovery
NGK Insulators/Ferrite crystal (T184/84)
Method for doing business
IBM/Card reader (T854/90)
NAT/Bagging plant (T636/88)
Stockburger/Coded distinctive mark (T51/84)
Method of surgery
See-Shell/Bloodflow (T182/90)

Microbiological process
    Plant Genetic Systems/Glutamine synthetase inhibitors (T356/93)
Micro-organisms
    Micro-Organisms (B52/84)
Mix of technical and non-technical elements
    IBM/Card reader (T854/90)
Morality
    Harvard/Onco-mouse (T19/90)
    Harvard/Onco-mouse (Application No. 85 304 490.7)
Music
    Sternheimer/Harmonic vibrations (T366/87)
Non-technical problem
    Esswein/Automatic programmer (T579/88)
"Ordre public" (See Morality)
Pain, discomfort, etc.
    Reichert/Anti-snoring means (T584/88)
    Rorer/Dysmenorrhea (T81/84)
Plants
    Ciba-Geigy/Propagating material (T49/83)
    Lubrizol/Hybrid plants (T320/87)
Presentation of information
    BBC/Colour television signal (T163/85)
    Fuji/Coloured disk jacket (T119/88)
Scheme for economic activity
    Christian Franceries/Traffic regulation (T16/83)
Second medical indication
    Bayer/Nimodipin (I) (T17/81)
    Duphar/Pigs II (T19/86)
    Eisai/Second medical indication (G05/83)
  Distinguished from second therapeutic use
        Codman/Second surgical use (T227/91)
Technical effect
    Dow/Sequestering agent (T958/90)
    IBM/Data processor network (T6/83)
    Siemens/Character form (T158/88)
Therapy (generally) (see also Medical indication)
    Bayer/Immunostimulant (T780/89)
    Duphar/Pigs II (T19/86)
    Nogier/Magnetic therapy (T30/83)
    Reichert/Anti-snoring means (T584/88)
    Rorer/Dysmenorrhea (T81/84)
    Salminen/Pigs III (T58/87)
    Siemens/Flow measurement (T245/87)
    Siemens/Pacemaker (T426/89)
    Stimtech/Transcutaneous electrical nerve stimulation (T94/83)
    Wellcome/Pigs I (T116/85)
Word-processors
    IBM/Editable document form (T110/90)

PCT Application Procedure *(See also* **Procedure** (generally) and **Unity**)

Designation of states on out-of-date form
    McWhirter/PCT form (J26/87)
Preliminary examination authority
    Appellate jurisdiction (PCT cases) (J20/89)

707

Uninspected patent application
    Japan Styrene Paper/Foam particles (T444/88)

Priority

Abandonment. See main heading **Abandonment**
Applicant's still earlier application
    Fischer & Porter/Flowmeter (T400/90)
Change in nature of the invention (no)
    Air Products/Priority (T255/91)
Correction under rule 88. See under **Amendment and Correction**
Criteria for according
    Collaborative/Preprorennin (T81/87)
    Howard/Snackfood (T73/88)
Demonstration at exhibition
    Thorn/Thermal limiting device (T326/93)
Design application
    Arenhold/Priority right (J15/80)
Fresh quantitative restriction in claim 1
    Procatalyse/Catalyst (T16/87)
    Shell/Polysaccharide solutions (T581/89)
Generic chemical formulae, variation in
    CSIRO/Arthropodicidal compounds (T85/87)
Genus/species
    CSIRO/Arthropodicidal compounds (T85/87)
Identity of invention
    Detras/Target apparatus (T229/88)
    Fischer & Porter/Flowmeter (T400/90)
    NGK Insulators/Ferrite crystal (T184/84)
    Robbins/Rotary cutterhead (T116/84)
Multiple priority applications
    Biogen/Recombinant DNA (T301/87)
    Priority interval (G03/93)
No change in character
    BP/Theta-1 (T212/88)
    Procatalyse/Catalyst (T16/87)
Novel selection from priority document
    ICI/Polyester crystallisation (T61/85)
Re-establishment
    Siemens/Party adversely affected by a decision (J05/79)
Specific example not included in priority document
    Becton/Radiation stabilisation (T94/87)
Successor in title in equity
    Burr-Brown/Assignment (J19/87)
Time for filing of priority document
    Siemens/Filing priority documents (J01/80; J02/80)
Width of claim in priority document
    Fujitsu/Avalanche diode (T409/90)

Prior National Rights

When separate claims permissible
    Warner-Lambert/Different sets of claims (J21/82)
Whether ground of opposition (no)
    Mobil/Admissibility (T550/88)

Prior Use (*See main heading* **Prior Art**)

Procedure (generally) (*See also* **Appeal Procedure, PCT Application Procedure, Application Procedure, Opposition Procedure**)
Abandonment v. withdrawal
    Ausonia/Withdrawal of application (J15/86)
Abuse
    Dentsply/Inadmissible late filing (T534/89)
Bias
    Discovision/Appealable decision (G05/91)
Change of composition of division (See also Written confirmation signed by different members, void)
    Lesaffre/Composition of opposition division (T243/87)
Compensation claim against EPO: inadmissible
    Deere/Mention of grant (J14/87)
Correction of decisions
    Clouth/Selection among designations (J23/82)
Dates for oral hearings
    EPO Notice/Dates for oral hearings
Decision
  Effective date of
      Novatome II/Final decision (G12/91)
  Finality of
      Xerox/Finality of decision (T79/89)
Decision, what constitutes
    Caterpillar/Form of decision (J08/81)
    Konica/Photographic material (T934/91)
    Seiko & Toshiba/Contents of decision (T99/88)
Discretion
  Reasons must be given
      Steer, Clive, Allen/Wheelbarrow (T183/89)
  To overlook small amount
      Maxtor/Media storage system (J27/92)
Due process
    Marello/Postal strike (J04/90)
Duties of EPO
    Consolidation (J000/87)
EPO practices, prompt official announcement of
    Albright & Wilson/Fee reduction (T905/90)
Equality of treatment
    Duriron/Re-establishment of rights (G06/92)
Evidence, reasonable time must be given for filing
    Yoshida Kogyo/Priority declaration (J04/82)
Examination
  By EPO of its own motion
      Air Products/Pressure swing adsorption (T156/84)
  Searched subject-matter only
      Non-payment of further search fees (G02/92)
Expedited determination
    Mitsui/Ethylene copolymer (T611/90)
Fairness to applicants
    CPC/Micro-organisms (T39/88)
    Fabritius/Re-establishment of rights (G03/91)

Filing by facsimile, etc.
EPC Rules/Amendment—filing by facsimile
Formal separation of facts, evidence and argument not required
Union Carbide/High tear strength polymers (T396/89)
General interruption in mail
Allied Signal/Proportioning valve (T702/89)
Daikin Kogyo/Interruption in delivery of mail (T192/84)
Leland Stanford/Postal strike (J11/88)
*Good faith between EPO and parties (See also Legitimate expectations, Voidness of EPO act
where applicant misled)*
JMK Magnusson/Locking device (J05/89)
Medtronic/Administrative agreement (G05/88; G08/88)
Shea/Denmark—PCT (J30/90)
Shell/Gasification of solid fuel (T522/88)
Incapacity of representative
ICI/Removal of hydrogen sulphide (T301/85)
Incapacity (J000/87)
X/Interruption of proceedings (Jxx/xx)
Inherent jurisdiction of Boards of Appeal
Cummins/Reimbursement (T99/82)
Inquiries by EPO must be objective
Marello/Postal strike (J04/90)
Inquisitorial nature
Isotube/Elevator (T76/82)
Interlocutory decision
BASF/Debit order I (T152/82)
von Blücher/Interlocutory decision (T762/90)
Interlocutory revision
Stamicarbon/Polymer filaments (T268/85)
Sumitomo/Remittal (T47/90)
Interpretation of letters
Grisebach/Divisional application (J24/82; J25/82; J26/82)
Interpreters, late request for, refused
DRG/Printing sleeve (T155/87)
Interruption, effect on time limits
Mouchet/Interruption of proceedings (J07/83)
Incorrect form
Bosch/Power supply (T105/89)
Jurisdiction of formalities officers
Roecar/Decisions by Formalities Officers (J10/82)
Knowledge of rules expected
Memtec/Membranes (J03/87)
Legitimate expectations
Medtronic/Administrative agreement (G05/88; G08/88)
Nellcor/Re-establishment (G05/93)
Tracto-Technik/Telecopy filings (T485/89)
Microphone disconnected
DRG/Printing sleeve (T155/87)
Misleading communication by EPO
ATT/Inviting observations (T669/90)
Liesenfeld/Courtesy service (J01/89)
Memtec/Membranes (J03/87)
Natural justice
Discovision/Appealable decision (G05/91)

713

Professional Representatives

Re-establishment of Rights

Alternative remedy
    Hitachi/Re-establishment of rights (J12/87)
Appeal treated as application for
    Shell/Gasification of solid fuel (T522/88)
Article 122, exhaustive
    Cockerill Sambre/*Force majeure* (J18/82)
Article 122(5), scope of
    Nellcor/Re-establishment (G05/93)
Assistant's fault (See also Clerk's failure)
    Brown, Boveri/Statement of grounds of appeal (T13/82)
    IBM/*Restitutio in integrum* (T715/91)
Change in applicant's procedures
    Motorola/Isolated mistake-restitution (J02/86; J03/86)
Clerk's failure (See also Assistant's fault and Temporary clerk, failure to supervise)
    Dow Chemical/Re-establishment (T72/83)
    ICI/Removal of hydrogen sulphide (T301/85)
Commencement of period for
    Motorola/Restitution (J15/84)
Computer failure
    Ampex/*Restitutio in integrum* (T253/90)
Deficient request, applicant not notified
    Wegener/Jurisdiction (T473/91)
Delay by EPO
    Woodcap/Appeal of proprietor (T506/91)
Due care
    Proweco/*Restitutio in integrum* (J12/84)
    SNIA/Lack of due care (T250/89)
    Société Parisienne/*Restitutio in integrum* (J05/80)
    Thorn EMI/Re-establishment of rights (T137/86)
EPO's duty to warn of deficiencies in application
    Marron Blanco/Re-establishment (J41/92)
EPO notice, erroneous, reliance on
    Rhône-Poulenc/International applications (J06/79)
EPO practice, erroneous, reliance on
    Medical Biological Sciences/Oral prosthesis (J22/86)
Error of law
    Visnjic/*Restitutio in integrum* (T248/91)
Evidence in other files
    Ornstein/Humidity control (J01/84)
Evidence need not be filed within time limit for applying
    Phillips Petroleum/Re-establishment (T324/90)
Evidence required
    Brown, Boveri/Statement of grounds of appeal (T13/82)
Examination fee out of time
    Duriron/Re-establishment of rights (G06/92)
Excluded
    Floridienne/Late request for examination (J12/82)
Failure, date of awareness of
    Techniplast Gazzada/Re-establishment (T81/83)
Fees, failure to pay
    Bodenrader/International application (J03/81)
    Fabritius/Re-establishment of rights (G03/91)
Financial hardship (allowed)
    Radakovic/Re-establishment of rights (J22/88)

General procedural principle of the EPC
    Rhône-Poulenc/International applications (J06/79)
Impossibility of
    Cockerill Sambre/*Force majeure* (J18/82)
Inadmissible
    Consumers Glass/Late correction (J21/84)
  On ground of delay
      NN/Re-establishment of rights (W03/93)
Incapacity of representative
    ICI/Removal of hydrogen sulphide (T301/85)
    Incapacity (J000/87)
    Marron Blanco/Re-establishment (J41/92)
Jurisdiction of first instance
    Wegener/Jurisdiction (T473/91)
Insolvency
    Cataldo/Re-establishment—insolvency (J11/83)
Isolated mistake by representative
    Procter & Gamble/Detergent composition (T369/91)
Large company
  Duty of care during reorganisation
      AE plc/Re-establishment of rights (T516/91)
  Must have effective system of staff substitution
      Phillips Petroleum/Re-establishment (T324/90)
Late instructions misdirected
    Grain Processing Corporation/Re-establishment of rights (T30/90)
Misleading information given by EPO
    Trucco/Re-establishment of rights (J32/86)
Monitoring system
    IBM/*Restitutio in integrum* (T715/91)
    Texaco/Re-establishment (T869/90)
National patent office, failure by
    Chubb/Failure to forward a European patent application (J03/80)
Non-receipt of information from EPO
    K-Corporation of Japan/*Restitutio in integrum* (J23/87)
Objective inability
    Union Carbide/Restitution (T413/91)
Priority
    Siemens/Party adversely affected by a decision (J05/79)
Reorganisation of company
    Uhde/Re-establishment (T14/89)
Representative's duties
    IBM/Restitutio in integrum (T715/91)
Representative's knowledge of the EPC
    AE plc/Re-establishment of rights (T516/91)
Statement of grounds
  Insufficient
      Denev/Cancer cells and lymphocytes game (J03/85)
  When due
      Baxter/One-year period (J06/90)
Strict standard
    IBM/*Restitutio in integrum* (T715/91)
Substitute, failure to supervise
    Theurer/Assistant: substitute (J16/82)
Temporary clerk, failure to supervise
    ICI/Re-establishment of rights (T105/85)

Temporary system
  Dynapac Martin/Poker vibrator (T27/86)
Third party document not obtained within time limit
  SNIA/Lack of due care (T250/89)
  Time-limit for
      Baxter/One-year period (J06/90)
      Cataldo/Cause of non-compliance (J07/82)
      Dow/Divisional application (J11/91; J16/91)
      Fibre-Chem/Re-establishment of rights (T191/82)
      Marron Blanco/Re-establishment (J41/92)
    Time limit for correction of deficiencies
      Castleton/Re-establishment of rights (J13/90)
    Time limit, what constitutes
      Toledo/Correction of designation (J07/90)
Unusually high workload
    Thorn EMI/Re-establishment of rights (T137/86)
Vicarious responsibility, inapplicable
    Fibre-Chem/Re-establishment of rights (T191/82)

Reimbursement of Appeal Fees (Refused)

Costs against EPO
    Du Pont de Nemours (E.I.) & Co./Late submission (T951/91)
Interpretation in the light of description
    Aqualon Company/Water-soluble cellulose ether (T860/93)
Late experimental results
    Du Pont de Nemours (E.I.) & Co./Late submission (T951/91)
Misinterpretation of Board's jurisdiprudence not enough
    ICI plc/Unity (T470/91)

Reimbursement of Appeal Fee (Allowed)

  Gelman Sciences/Fresh ground (T817/93)

Restitution (*See* Re-establishment of Rights)

Revocation

Automatic revocation
    AKZO/Automatic revocation (T26/88)
    Revocation of a patent (G01/90)
Proprietor, by
    BASF/Revocation at proprietor's request
    Kansai Paint/Disapproval of specification by proprietor
    Mobil Oil/Opposition by proprietor
    SMS/Revocation at the instigation of the patent proprietor (T73/84)

Secrecy Order

  Chubb/Failure to forward a European patent application (J03/80)

Skilled Person

Ability to discriminate between parameters
    Union Carbide/Threaded connections (T124/82)

Approach to technical teaching
    ICI/Latex composition (T77/87)
Attributes of
    Solvay/Production of hollow thermoplastic objects (T5/81)
Capabilities of
    SNIA/Deployable antenna reflector (T425/87)
Choice between known methods
    Unilever/Perfumed cartons (T107/82)
Constrained by current technical environment
    USN & EF/Cold roll manufacturing (T179/87)
Elementary experimentation
    Unilever/Perfumed cartons (T107/82)
Field of experience of
    Nippondenso/Vehicle display (T683/89)
General technical knowledge, application of
    Kommerling/Profile member (T130/89)
Identity of
    Fisher & Paykel/Inwardly flanged curved members (T168/82)
    Harvard/Fusion proteins (T60/89)
Knowledge of
    Alcan/Exhaust silencer (T47/84)
    Auld/Decorative emblems (T183/82)
    Bosch/Electronic computer components (T164/92)
    IBM/Card reader (T854/90)
Nature of
    Biogen/Alpha-interferon II (T500/91)
    Niled/Electrical connecting apparatus (T316/86)
Optimisation of prior art parameters
    Fujitsu/Avalanche diode (T409/90)
Oriented towards practicalities
    Sitma/Packaging machine (T160/83)
Powers of generalisation
    Shell/Sinking tubular element (T127/82)
    Union Carbide/Threaded connections (T124/82)
Preference for least extensive modification
    Albany International/Papermaking fabric (T406/89)
Reads and comprehends all relevant citations
    Unilever/Perfumed cartons (T107/82)
Reads documents as a whole and does not isolate parts
    Scanditronix/Radiation beam collimation (T56/87)
Recognition of disadvantages of known method
    Shell/Sinking tubular element (T127/82)
Team
    Kirin-Amgen/Erythropoietin (T412/93)
    Procter/Flavour (T295/88)

State of the art

Ambiguous teaching
    Rhône-Poulenc/Silane (T70/90)
Combination of separate teachings in single document
    AKZO/Rainwear (T215/90)
Confidential document
    RCA/TV receiver (T300/86)

719

Technical Subject-matter

1-acylimidazolinones
Hoechst/Melting point (T3/88)
1,3-di-n-butyl-7-(2-oxopropyl)xanthine
Beecham-Wuelfing/PVD (T541/89)
1,6-naphthyridinone derivatives
Godecke/Naphthyridinone derivatives (T11/89)
2-hydroxy-naphthalene-3-carboxylic acid
Ueno Seiyaku/2-hydroxy-naphthalene-3-carboxylic acid (BON-3-acid)
(T741/91)
2-oxypyridyl derivatives
ICI plc/Unity (T470/91)
2,2,6,6-tetramethylpiperidone-(4)
Hüls/2,2,6,6-tetramethylpiperidone-(4) (T132/84)
3-thienylmalonic acid salts
Beecham/3-thienylmalonic acid (T65/83)
6-amino-6-deoxy-L-sorbose
Bayer/Clarity of claims (T26/82)
a-lactalbumin
INRA/a-lactalbumin product (T128/86)
q-azolyl-acetophenone oxime ethers
Bayer/Acetophenone derivatives (T169/83)
Ace inhibitors
Hoechst/Ace inhibitors (T289/91)
Acetic anhydride preparation
Eastman Kodak/Preparation of acetic anhydride (T236/88)
Acetylene storage vessels
NI Industries/Filler mass (T560/89)
Acrylonitrile polymer fibre
American Cyanamid/Acrylonitrile polymer fibre (T90/94)
Additives
X/Synergic combination of additives (W44/88)
Air-cleaning apparatus
von Blücher/Air-cleaning apparatus (T5/89)
Aircraft spoiler device
Boeing/Spoiler device (T225/84)
Airfoil track assembly
Boeing/Extendible airfoil track assembly (T249/84)
Air separation
Union Carbide/Separation of air (T379/88)
Alkyl esters
Hüls/Grounds for appeal (T220/83)
Alkyl styrene/nitrile copolymerisation
Sumitomo/Extent of opposition (T182/89)
Allergy treatment
Takeda/Postponement of examination (T166/84)
Alumina spinel sorbent
Exxon/Alumina spinel (T42/84)
Aluminium-based alloy
Boeing/Obvious error in claims (T200/89)
Aluminium trihydroxide
VAW/Aluminium trihydroxide (T244/85)

Biomass preparation
Gist-Brocades/Biomass preparation (T32/85)
Bis-epoxy ethers
BASF/Bis-epoxy ethers (T22/82)
Bismuth-containing steel
Inland Steel/Bismuth-containing steel (T105/87)
Blasting compositions
Ireco/Blasting compositions (T127/85)
Block copolymers
JSR/Block copolymer (T416/87)
Bloodflow measurement
See-Shell/Bloodflow (T182/90)
Blowing agents
Schering/Confidential papers (T516/89)
Blow moulding
Solvay/Production of hollow thermoplastic objects (T5/81)
BON-3-acid
Ueno Seiyaku/2-hydroxy-naphthalene-3-carboxylic acid
(BON-3-acid) (T741/91)
Braking system
Bendix/Braking system (T99/87)
Breathing apparatus
Lindholm/Breathing apparatus (T204/90)
Brushless DC motor
IBM/Brushless DC motor (T194/89)
Bulk carrier discharging means
Welgro/Bulk carrier (T187/85)
Buoys
Bluewater/Admissibility (T156/90)
Butoxybenzylhyoscyamine bromide
Eisai/Second medical indication (G05/83)
Butter flavour composition
Procter/Flavour (T295/88)
Butyraldehyde preparation
Union Carbide/Hydroformylation (T619/89)
Cable car
Pomagalski/Cable car (T484/90)
Caffeine recovery
General Foods/Caffeine (T430/89)
Calcium sulphate filler
Gussinyer/Calcium sulphate filler (T390/90)
Carbonless copying papers
Bayer/Carbonless copying paper (T1/80)
Cardiac assist device
Electro-Catheter/Protest (W08/87)
Cardiac defibrillation
Medtronic/Cardiac defibrillator (T348/86)
Cartilage-inducing factors
Celtrix/Cartilage-inducing factors (T184/91)
Cartridge end-closure
ICI/Cartridge end-closure (T74/82)
Cartridge for filling dental cavities
Dentsply/Cartridge for filling dental cavities (T793/90)
Catalytic dewaxing: synthetic offretite
Mobil/Amendment of claims (T6/84)

Cathode for gas discharge indicator
  Siemens/Clarity of claim (T132/82)
Cellulose fibres (See zinc electrodes)
Cheese spreads
  CPC/Cheese spreads (T559/88)
Chloral derivatives
  Macarthys/Chloral derivatives (T84/82)
Chroman derivatives
  Merck Patent/Chroman derivatives (T552/91)
Clostridium acetobutylicum
  CPC/Micro-organisms (T39/88)
Coal gasification
  British Gas/Coal gasification (T109/83)
  Exxon/Arranging oral proceedings (T320/88)
Coated TiO₂ compositions
  Tioxide/Pigments (T525/90)
Coating compositions
  Kanegafuchi/Coating compositions (T67/88)
  Containing alkylolated melemines
    Union Carbide/Coatings (T654/90)
Coaxial connector
  AMP/Coaxial connector (T260/85)
Cobalt foils
  Allied/Cobalt foils (T265/84)
Coke oven patching composition
  USS Engineers/Coke oven patching (T139/83)
Cold rolling equipment
  USN & EF/Cold roll manufacturing (T179/87)
Collector for high-frequency tube
  Thomson-CSF (T151/84)
Coloured aqueous hypochlorite compositions
  Unilever/Coloured compositions (T228/90)
Coloured disk jacket
  Fuji/Coloured disk jacket (T119/88)
Colour photographic material
  Konica/Colour photographic material (T162/89)
Combustible sleeve
  SNPE/Combustible sleeve (T149/82)
Combustion chamber
  Chivato/Combustion chamber (T66/91)
Compact measuring device
  Digmesa/Further search fee (T87/88)
Composite plasmid
  Ajinomoto/Composite plasmid (T109/91)
Composite plastics
  Kubat/Method of producing plastic composites (T17/92)
Compresses
  Mölnlycke/Dry salt compress (T102/82)
Computer generation of semantically-related expressions
  IBM/Semantically-related expressions (T52/85)
Computerised message display
  IBM/Computer-related invention (T115/85)
Computer program, character form
  Siemens/Character form (T158/88)

726

Magnetic transducer head support assemblies
   IBM/Magnetic transducer head support assemblies (T75/82)
Magnetotherapy
   Latzke/Magnetic plaster (T268/89)
Mains replacement
   British Gas/Mains replacement method (T448/90)
Media storage system
   Maxtor/Media storage system (J27/92)
Melt spinning
   Cyanamid/Melt spinning (T49/85)
Memory circuit
   Fujitsu/Memory circuit (T407/86)
Menstrual pain relief
   Rorer/Dysmenorrhea (T81/84)
Metal-coated polypropylene film
   Fuji/Multilayer photographic material (T763/89)
Metal co-ordination complexes
   Australian National University/Metal complexes (T154/82)
Metallic paint coating
   Hoechst/Metallic paint coating (T122/84)
Methylenebis(phenyl isocyanate)
   Mobay/Methylenebis(phenyl isocyanate) (T2/81)
Micro-organisms
   Micro–organisms (B52/84)
Mineral fillers
   Plüss–Staufer/Filler (T17/85)
Minicassette box
   Posso/Minicassette box (T185/82)
Modified diisocyanates
   ICI/Modified diisocyanates (T433/86)
Modified elastomers
   Toa Nenryo/Elastomer (T299/89)
Modified milbemycin compounds
   Merck/Starting compounds (T51/87)
Moisture-protected capacitor roll
   Rifa/Capacitor roll (T602/90)
Monoclonal antibody
   Ortho/Monoclonal antibody (T418/89)
   Ortho/Monoclonal antibody (T495/89)
Moulding of precision optical elements
   Corning Glass/Moulding (T366/89)
Multi-coloured detergent
   Unilever/Multicoloured detergent bars (T98/82)
Multilayer photographic film
   Fuji/Multi-layer photographic material (T763/89)
Multi-solid fluidised bed combustion product cleansing method
   Battelle/Fluidised bed combustion sanitation (T450/87)
Naltrexone appetite suppressant
   Du Pont de Nemours (E.I.) & Co./Appetite suppressant (T144/83)
Nappies
   Boussac Saint Frères/Interventions (T338/89)
Nimodipin
   Bayer/Nimodipin (I) (T17/81)
   Bayer/Nimodipin (II) (T17/81)

Portable hyperbar box structure
    État Français/Portable hyperbar box structure (T258/84)
Power supply apparatus
    Bosch/Power supply (T105/89)
Power supply unit
    La Télémécanique Électrique/Power supply unit (T482/89)
Power transmission belt
    Mitsuboshi/Endless power transmission belt (T169/84)
Power transmission belt manufacture
    Mitsuboshi Belting Ltd/Power transmission belt manufacture (T352/89)
p-Phenylenediamine production
    Du Pont de Nemours (E.I.) & Co./Phenylenediamine (T103/86)
Preprorennin
    Collaborative/Preprorennin (T81/87)
Preprothaumatin
    Unilever/Preprothaumatin (T281/86)
Pressure swing adsorption
    Air Products/Pressure swing adsorption (T156/84)
Printer ribbon errors
    Cyberexact/Printer ribbon errors (T684/89)
Printers
    Fujitsu/Printer (T685/90)
Printing plate
    Mead/Printing plate (T160/92)
Printing press
    Heidelberger Drückmaschinen/Microchip (T461/88)
Printing sleeves
    DRG/Printing sleeve (T155/87)
Production of cholesta-1,5,7-trien-3-ol
    Nisshin/Steroid (T181/91)
Production of nitroalkanes
    Grace/Nitro compounds (T121/91)
Programmable cardiac pacemaker
    Medtronic/Administrative agreement (G05/88; G08/88)
Prostaglandin derivatives
    Kureha/Inadmissible appeal (J12/85)
Protein excretion
    Harvard/Fusion proteins (T60/89)
Psoriasis treatment
    Visnjic/*Restitutio in integrum* (T248/91)
Pulp delignification
    Black Clawson/Pulp delignification (T215/84)
Pulp production
    Bayer/Pulp production (T114/82)
Purification of sulphonic acids
    Exxon/Purification of sulphonic acids (T4/83)
Pyridine herbicides
    ICI/Pyridine herbicides (T206/83)
Pyrimidine intermediates
    Dow/Pyrimidines (T18/88)
Pyrimidine-butanol derivatives
    Bayer/Plant growth regulating agent (G06/88)
    Bayer/Plant growth regulation (T208/88)
    Bayer/Growth regulation (T208/88)

Removal of organic pollutants
      Dow/Contaminant removal (T137/83)
Resin composition
      JSR/Impact resistant resin composition (T79/88)
Resin composition for injection moulding
      Asahi Kasei KKK/Resin composition (T627/88)
Reticulated polyolefines
      Telecommunications/Antioxidant (T173/83)
Reversing plate mill
      Tippens/Reversing plate mill (T209/91)
Revetment grids and mats
      Nicolon/Statement of grounds (T145/88)
Rotary cutterheads
      Robbins/Rotary cutterhead (T116/84)
Rubber composition
      Bridgestone/Rubber composition (T228/87)
Safety belt harness fastener
      Britax/Inventive step (T142/84)
Schottky barrier diode
      Tektronix/Schottky barrier diode (T694/91)
Scouring cleanser
      Unilever/Stable bleaches (T226/85)
Scraper chain conveyor
      Parsons Control/Scraper chain conveyor (T61/89)
Sealing cup
      Aisin/Late submission of amendment (T95/83)
Self-pressurising dispensing container
      Enviro-Spray/Self-pressurising dispensing container (T207/84)
Self-service machine
      IBM/Card reader (T854/90)
Semiconductor device
      Toshiba/Semiconductor device (T407/87)
Semiconductor device with pressure loading
      Mitsubishi/Semiconductor device (T607/90)
Semiconductor integrated circuits
      ATT/Inviting observations (T669/90)
Semiconductor manufacture
      Fujitsu/Semiconductor (T128/83)
Sequestering agent
      Dow/Sequestering agent (T958/90)
Serial storage interface
      IBM/Lack of unity (T178/84)
Shears
      Grehal/Shear (T305/87)
Shower fittings
      Albany/Shower fittings (T194/86)
Shrink treatment of linen
      Lintrend/Shrink treatment of linen (T76/83)
Silane production
      Rhône-Poulenc/Silane (T70/90)
Silicon layer deposition
      Energy Conversion/Silicon deposition (T490/89)
Silicon nitride-based cutting tools
      GTE/Silicon nitride cutting tools (T344/89)

Simethicone tablet
Rider/Simethicone tablet (T2/83)
Sinking tubular element
Shell/Sinking tubular element (T127/82)
Skirting boards
RS-Reklam/Edging (T83/83)
Softening detergent composition
Procter & Gamble/STW detergents (T100/88)
Procter & Gamble/STW-laundry detergents (T104/88)
Sound-absorbent wall
GTM/Sound-absorbent wall (T80/82)
Sound recording carriers
Stockburger/Coded distinctive mark (T51/84)
Spacer grids for nuclear reactors
CEA-Framatome/Spacer grid (T493/88)
Spheroidal polymer beads
Dow/New citation (T622/89)
Spiro-compounds
Ciba-Geigy/Spiro compounds (T181/82)
Splash bar
Ovard/Splash bar (T270/89)
Spot welding
Siemens/Electrode slide (T6/81)
Spring element construction
Keown/Spring element (T278/86)
SSTV encryption
Communications Satellite/Inadmissible appeal (T831/90)
Stabilisation of trichloroethylene
Wacker/Trichloroethylene (T406/86)
Stand structure
Passoni/Stand structure (Application No. 82 107 958.9)
Starch product
Soepenberg/Starch product (T21/83)
Static inverters
ERA/Static inverter (T167/82)
Sterilising pouch
LMG/Sterilising pouch (T212/87)
Stimulating electrodes
Siemens/Stimulating electrode (T448/89)
Storage device
Garcia/Storage device (T546/90)
Stretch-wrap film
Mobil Oil/Film (T405/86)
Stunning apparatus
Machinefabriek G.J. Nijhuis/Stunning apparatus (T90/83)
Surface acoustic wave devices
Fujitsu/Surface acoustic wave device (T22/83)
Surface filter
von Blücher/Surface filter (T762/90)
Surface finish
Pegulan/Surface finish (T495/91)
Surface hardening of metals
Sciaky/Surface hardening (T12/82)
Suspension polymerisation of vinyl monomers
Goodrich/Vinyl monomers (T340/88)

Switching devices
    Naimer/Computer-controlled switch (T23/86)
Synchronised intracardiac cardioverter
    Medtronic/Synchronised intracardiac cardioverter (T387/89)
T-cell growth factor
    Hooper Trading/T-cell growth factor (T877/90)
Tank flap device
    Bossert KG/Two-part claim (T170/84)
Target apparatus
    Detras/Target apparatus (T229/88)
Tear-resistant polymer
    Union Carbide/High tear strength polymers (T396/89)
Television receivers
    RCA/TV receiver (T300/86)
Television signal (colour)
    BBC/Colour television signal (T163/85)
Tellurium-containing steel
    Inland Steel/Tellurium-containing steel (T75/87)
Tetrahydropyridinyl-indole derivatives
    Roussel-Uclaf/Tetrahydropyridinyl-indole derivatives (T43/82)
Text clarity processor
    IBM/Text clarity processing (T38/86)
Thenoyl peroxide
    Roussel-Uclaf/Thenoyl peroxide (T36/83)
Theophylline derivatives
    Eisai/Antihistamines (T164/83)
Therapy with interference currents
    Somartec/Therapy with interference currents (T234/86)
Thermal limiting device
    Thorn/Thermal limiting device (T326/93)
Thermal recording methods
    Eastman Kodak/Thermal recording (T40/83)
Thermoforming polyester articles
    Goodyear/Thermoforming polyester articles (T519/89)
Thermoplastic film laminate
    Mobil Oil/Thermoplastic film laminate (T43/85)
Thermoplastic moulding compositions or compounds
    Bayer/Moulding compositions (T192/82)
    Bayer/Thermoplastic moulding compositions (T69/83)
    Bayer/Thermoplastic moulding compound (T344/88)
Thermoplastic resin
    General Electric Company/Thermoplastic resin (T472/88)
Thermoplastic sockets
    AECI/Thermoplastics sockets (T1/81)
Thermosetting coating composition
    Du Pont de Nemours (E.I.) & Co./Admissibility of opposition (T204/91)
Thiochloroformates
    Hoechst/Thiochloroformates (T198/84)
Threaded connections
    Union Carbide/Threaded connections (T124/82)
Three-stroke engine
    Widen/Three-stroke engine (T67/87)
Thromboxane antagonists
    NRDC/Thromboxane antagonists (W09/86)

Ultrasonic diagnostic apparatus
    Tokyo Shibaura/Ultrasonic diagnostic apparatus (T64/85)
Ultrasonic transducer
    Toray/Ultrasonic transducer (T48/86)
Ultra-violet emitters
    Rohm/Ultra-violet emitters (T283/84)
Urea synthesis
    Unie Van Kunstmestfabrieken/Urea synthesis (T124/84)
Vaccines
    Bayer/Vaccine (T171/89)
Vaporisation apparatus
    Zink/Vaporisation (T30/81)
Vehicle brakes
    SAB/Vehicle brakes (T89/85)
Vehicle display
    Nippondenso/Vehicle display (T683/89)
Vehicle guidance system
    Bell & Howell/Vehicle guidance system (T130/82)
Vehicle windscreen removing apparatus
    Lock/Windscreen removal device (T101/87)
Venturi devices
    Charbonnages/Venturi (T204/83)
Video disk system components
    Philips/Video disk apparatus (T378/88)
Vinyl acetate
    Fernholz/Vinyl acetate (T188/83)
Vinyl chloride resins
    Sumitomo/Vinyl chloride resins (T14/83)
Wall element
    Vereinigte Metallwerke/Wall element (T169/83)
Wall panels
    Dan-Pal/Light transmitting wall panels (T293/88)
Washing composition
    Unilever/Washing composition (T666/89)
Washing machine
    Thomson-Brandt/Admissibility (T328/87)
Watch
    ETA/Watch (T456/90)
Waterproof materials
    AKZO/Rainwear (T215/90)
Water-sealing clay layer
    American Colloid/Clay layer (T610/90)
Water-soluble cellulose ether
    Aqualon Company/Water-soluble cellulose ether (T860/93)
Water-soluble glass
    International Standard Electric/Water-soluble glass (T71/85)
Water-thinnable binder
    Shell/Water-thinnable binder (T44/85)
Weight-sensing apparatus
    Bolland/Weight-sensing apparatus (T405/94)
Welding
    Carnaud/Toothed wheel welding process (T190/90)
Wheelbarrow
    Steer, Clive, Allen/Wheelbarrow (T183/89)

Text of Patent

Therapy (*See* Patentable Subject-matter, Therapy)

Third Party Observations

Third Party Rights

Unity

Words and Phrases

"Subject-matter"
  Lansing Bagnell/Control circuit (T11/82)
"Sufficient indication for purposes of EPC Rule 55(C)"
  Du Pont de Nemours (E.I.) & Co./Admissibility of opposition (T204/91)

D. NON-EUROPEAN CASES

AUSTRALIA

Confidential Information and Breach of Confidence

Accountants' Duties. *See* **Fiduciary Duty**

Arguable Case. *See* **Practice** (*Arguable Case*)

Basis of Liability

Mar-Con Corp. Pty Ltd v. Campbell Capital Ltd (WHETHER CONFIDENTIAL QUALITY: WHETHER IMPARTED IN CONFIDENCE: EXTENT OF DUTY: SPRINGBOARD DOCTRINE: JOINT VENTURE: WHETHER UNDER FIDUCIARY DUTY: UNJUST ENRICHMENT: S.C.(NSW))

Common Law Rights

Dover Fisheries Pty Ltd v. Bottrill Research Pty Ltd (UNEXECUTED CONTRACT: WHETHER BREACH OF CONDITION OF CONFIDENTIALITY IS BREACH OF AN ESSENTIAL TERM: S.C.(S.A.))

Computer Programs

Cope Allman (Marrickville) Ltd v. Farrow (COPYRIGHT: OWNERSHIP: COMMISSIONED WORK: ENGRAVINGS: S.C.(NSW))
Paxus Services Ltd v. People Bank Pty Ltd (COMPUTER DATABASES: WHETHER A "DOCUMENT": CONSIDERATIONS FOR EXERCISE OF DISCRETION: Fed. Ct)

Conflict of Laws

Scruples Imports Pty Ltd v. Crabtree & Evelyn Pty Ltd (EXPERT EVIDENCE: S.C.(NSW))

Contract

Dover Fisheries Pty Ltd v. Bottrill Research Pty Ltd (UNEXECUTED CONTRACT: WHETHER BREACH OF CONDITION OF CONFIDENTIALITY IS BREACH OF AN ESSENTIAL TERM: COMMON LAW RIGHTS: S.C.(S.A.))

Contract of Employment. *See* **Employees and Ex-employees**

Corrective Advertising

Bates & Partners Pty Ltd v. The Law Book Company Ltd (PRIZE LIST: EMBARGOED NEWS RELEASE: APPLICATION FOR INTERLOCUTORY MANDATORY INJUNCTION: WHETHER DAMAGES AN ADEQUATE REMEDY: S.C.(NSW))

Customer or Member Lists

American Express International Inc. v. D. Thomas Associates Pty Ltd (CHARGE CARD SCHEME: ASSOCIATED WINE SOCIETY: WHETHER LIST OF MEMBERS CONFIDENTIAL INFORMATION OF PROMOTER OF CARD SCHEME: S.C.(NSW))

Triangle Corp. Pty Ltd v. Carnsew (CONFIDENTIALITY CLAUSE: DUTY OF EX-EMPLOYEE: CUSTOMER LISTS: CATEGORIES OF INFORMATION: Fed. Ct)

Discretion. *See* **Practice** (*Discretion*)

Duty of Fidelity

Independent Management Resources Pty Ltd v. Brown (EX-EMPLOYEE: BREACH: S.C.(Vic.))

Embargoed News Release

Bates & Partners Pty Ltd v. The Law Book Company Ltd (PRIZE LIST: CORRECTIVE ADVERTISING: APPLICATION FOR INTERLOCUTORY MANDATORY INJUNCTION: WHETHER DAMAGES AN ADEQUATE REMEDY: S.C.(NSW))

Employees and Ex-employees

Angus & Coote Pty Ltd v. Render (WHETHER INFORMATION HAS QUALITY OF CONFIDENCE: NO PROOF INFORMATION TAKEN IN WRITTEN FORM: FIDUCIARY DUTY: DUTY OF GOOD FAITH: CONTRACT OF EMPLOYMENT: IMPLIED TERM OF GOOD FAITH: INJUNCTION: LENGTH OF RESTRAINT: DELIVERY UP: CLEAN HANDS: S.C.(NSW))

ANI Corp. Ltd v. Celtite Aust. Pty Ltd (DUTIES OF EMPLOYEES AFTER EMPLOYMENT: WHETHER INFORMATION GAINED DURING EMPLOYMENT HAS QUALITY OF CONFIDENCE: PUBLICATION BY PATENTS: INTERLOCUTORY INJUNCTION: EX-EMPLOYEES: Fed. Ct)

Independent Management Resources Pty Ltd v. Brown (EX-EMPLOYEE: DUTY OF FIDELITY: BREACH: S.C.(Vic.))

Metrans Pty Ltd v. Courtney-Smith (EMPLOYEE: PERSONAL SKILL: S.C.)

Print Investments Pty Ltd v. Art-Vue Printing Ltd (EMPLOYEE: Australia: S.C.)

Redic Industries Pty Ltd v. JAL Chemicals Pty Ltd (DISCOVERY: INSPECTION OF FINANCIAL AND SALES RECORDS OF COMPANY OF FORMER EMPLOYEES: S.C.(Vic.))

Triangle Corp. Pty Ltd v. Carnsew (CONFIDENTIALITY CLAUSE: CUSTOMER LISTS: CATEGORIES OF INFORMATION: Fed. Ct)

Wright v. Gasweld Pty Ltd (EX-EMPLOYEE: C.A.(NSW))

Essentials of Cause of Action

American Express International Inc. v. D. Thomas Associates Pty Ltd (CHARGE CARD SCHEME: ASSOCIATED WINE SOCIETY: WHETHER LIST OF MEMBERS OF SOCIETY CONFIDENTIAL INFORMATION OF PROMOTER OF CARD SCHEME: S.C.(NSW))

Dover Fisheries Pty Ltd v. Bottrill Research Pty Ltd (WHAT CONSTITUTES: UNEXECUTED CONTRACT: WHETHER BREACH OF CONDITION OF CONFIDENTIALITY IS BREACH OF AN ESSENTIAL TERM: COMMON LAW RIGHTS: S.C.(S.A.))

Evidence. *See* **Practice** (*Evidence*)

Ex-employee. *See* **Employees and Ex-employees**

Fair Dealing

Director General of Education v. Public Service Association of NSW (COPYRIGHT: PUBLIC INTEREST: S.C.(NSW))

Wigginton v. Brisbane TV Ltd (COPYRIGHT: CINEMATOGRAPH FILM: WHETHER INFORMATION FREELY AVAILABLE: S.C.(Qd))

Fiduciary Duty

Grofam Pty Ltd v. KPMG Peat Marwick (INFORMATION SUPPLIED TO ACCOUNTANTS: SUSPICION THAT OFFENCE COMMITTED IN COURSE OF ACCOUNTANTS' DUTIES: WHETHER ACCOUNTANTS MAY DISCLOSE INFORMATION TO POLICE: Fed. Ct)

Mar-Con Corporation Pty Ltd v. Campbell Capital Ltd (WHETHER CONFIDENTIAL QUALITY: WHETHER IMPARTED IN CONFIDENCE: EXTENT OF DUTY OF CONFIDENCE: S.C.(NSW))

International Writing Institute v. Rimila Pty Ltd (BREACH OF CONTRACT: EXCLUSIVE LICENCE TO DISTRIBUTE: Fed. Ct)

Identity of Police Informer

Falconer v. Australian Broadcasting Corporation (INTERLOCUTORY INJUNCTION: S.C.(Vic.))

Implied Term

Angus & Coote Pty Ltd v. Render (CONTRACT OF EMPLOYMENT: IMPLIED TERM OF GOOD FAITH: S.C.(NSW))

Pioneer Concrete Services Ltd v. Lorenzo Galli (IMPLIED OBLIGATION: RESTRAINT OF TRADE: INJUNCTION: DECLARATION: DAMAGES: S.C.(Vic.))

Injunction. *See* Practice *(Injunction)*

Innocent Receipt of Information

Wheatley v. Bell (WHETHER INJUNCTIVE RELIEF AVAILABLE: S.C.(NSW))

Legal Precedents

O'Brien v. Komesaroff (COPYRIGHT: OWNERSHIP: BREACH OF CONFIDENCE: H.C.)

Length of Restraint. *See* Injunction *(Length of restraint)*

List of Members of Society. *See* Customer or Member Lists

Patent-Related Subjects

ANI Corp. Ltd v. Celtite Aust. Pty Ltd (DUTIES OF EMPLOYEES AFTER EMPLOYMENT: PUBLICATION BY PATENT: Fed. Ct)

Dillon v. J. P. Products Pty Ltd (INTERLOCUTORY INJUNCTION: S.C.(NSW))

James Howden Australia Pty Ltd v. Flakt AB (OPPOSITION: PRIOR PUBLICATION: WORKING DRAWING AND BROCHURE SENT FROM OVERSEAS MANUFACTURER: WHETHER CONFIDENTIAL: Pat. Off.)

Jos Schlitz Brewing Company v. Containers Ltd (OPPOSITION: PRIOR PUBLICATION: NOVELTY: CONFIDENTIALITY: Pat. Off.)

Smith Kline & French Laboratories (Australia) Ltd v. Secretary to the Department of Community Services and Health (WHETHER REGULATORY AUTHORITY SUBJECT TO DUTY OF CONFIDENTIALITY: PATENT LICENSING: EXERCISE OF DUTIES BY LICENSING AUTHORITY: Fed. Ct)

Practice

Anton Piller

Warman International Ltd v. Envirotech Australia Pty Ltd (EVIDENCE: PRIVILEGE
AGAINST SELF-INCRIMINATION: Fed. Ct)

Clean hands

Angus & Coote Pty Ltd v. Render (EX-EMPLOYEE: FIDUCIARY DUTY AND DUTY OF
GOOD FAITH: IMPLIED TERM OF GOOD FAITH: DELIVERY UP: S.C.(NSW))

Damages

Bates & Partners Pty Ltd v. The Law Book Company Ltd (WHETHER DAMAGES AN
ADEQUATE REMEDY: S.C.(NSW))
Pioneer Concrete Services Ltd v. Lorenzo Galli (S.C.(Vic.))

Declaration

Pioneer Concrete Services Ltd v. Lorenzo Galli (S.C.(Vic.))

Delivery up

Angus & Coote Pty Ltd v. Render (EX-EMPLOYEE: CLEAN HANDS: S.C.(NSW))

Discovery and inspection

Paxus Services Ltd v. People Bank Pty Ltd (CONFIDENTIAL INFORMATION IN
COMPUTER DATABASES: WHETHER A "DOCUMENT": CONSIDERATIONS FOR
EXERCISE OF DISCRETION: Fed. Ct)
Redic Industries Pty Ltd v. JAL Chemicals Pty Ltd (INSPECTION OF FINANCIAL AND
SALES RECORDS OF COMPANY OF FORMER EMPLOYEES: S.C.(Vic.))

Discretion

BEST Australia Ltd v. Aquagas Marketing Pty Ltd (PATENT: INFRINGEMENT: Fed.
Ct)
Paxus Services Ltd v. People Bank Pty Ltd (DISCOVERY: COMPUTER DATABASE:
CONSIDERATIONS FOR EXERCISE OF DISCRETION: Fed. Ct)

Evidence

Warman International Ltd v. Envirotech Australia Pty Ltd (ANTON PILLER:
PRIVILEGE AGAINST SELF-INCRIMINATION: Fed. Ct)

Injunction—adequacy of damages

Bates & Partners Pty Ltd v. The Law Book Company Ltd (PRIZE LIST: EMBARGOED
NEWS RELEASE: S.C.(NSW))

Injunction—balancing harm by publication against public interest

Criminal Justice Commission v. Nationwide News Pty Ltd (INFORMATION MOSTLY
IN PUBLIC DOMAIN: SERIOUS QUESTION TO BE TRIED: STAY:
CIRCUMSTANCES: Fed. Ct)

Injunction—innocent receipt of information

Wheatley v. Bell (WHETHER INJUNCTIVE RELIEF AVAILABLE: S.C.(NSW))

Injunction—length of restraint

Angus & Coote Pty Ltd v. Render (EX-EMPLOYEE: FIDUCIARY DUTY AND DUTY OF
GOOD FAITH: CONTRACT OF EMPLOYMENT: IMPLIED TERM OF GOOD FAITH:
DELIVERY UP: CLEAN HANDS: S.C.(NSW))

Interlocutory injunction—arguable case

General Motors Holden's Ltd v. David Syme & Co. Ltd (PRACTICE: EXCLUDING MEMBERS OF THE PUBLIC: S.C.(NSW))

Interlocutory injunction—balance of convenience

Chenel Pty Ltd v. Rayner (WHAT CONSTITUTES: SERIOUS ISSUE TO BE TRIED: S.C.(Vic.))

Interlocutory injunction—serious question to be tried

Chenel Pty Ltd v. Rayner (WHAT CONSTITUTES: BALANCE OF CONVENIENCE: S.C.(Vic.))

Criminal Justice Commission v. Nationwide News Pty Ltd (INFORMATION MOSTLY IN PUBLIC DOMAIN: BALANCING HARM DONE BY PUBLICATION AGAINST PUBLIC INTEREST: STAY: CIRCUMSTANCES: Fed. Ct)

Interlocutory mandatory injunction

Bates & Partners Pty Ltd v. The Law Book Company Ltd (WHETHER DAMAGES AN ADEQUATE REMEDY: S.C.(NSW))

Privilege against self incrimination

Warman International Ltd v. Envirotech Australia Pty Ltd (ANTON PILLER: EVIDENCE: Fed. Ct)

Search warrant

Royal Melbourne Hospital v. Matthews (SEARCH WARRANT: PATIENT IN HOSPITAL: WHETHER HOSPITAL OBLIGED TO SUPPLY INFORMATION: H.C.)

Public Domain

Criminal Justice Commission v. Nationwide News Pty Ltd (INFORMATION MOSTLY IN PUBLIC DOMAIN: INJUNCTION: SERIOUS QUESTION TO BE TRIED: BALANCING HARM DONE BY PUBLICATION AGAINST PUBLIC INTEREST: Fed. Ct)

Johns v. Australian Securities Commission (COMMISSION INVESTIGATION: RELEASE OF TRANSCRIPTS: REMEDIES: ENTITLEMENT TO ORDER RESTRAINING PUBLICATION: Fed. Ct)

Public Interest

Criminal Justice Commission v. Nationwide News Pty Ltd (INFORMATION MOSTLY IN PUBLIC DOMAIN: BALANCING HARM DONE BY PUBLICATION AGAINST PUBLIC INTEREST: Fed. Ct)

Director-General of Education v. Public Service Association of NSW (COPYRIGHT: FAIR DEALING: S.C.(NSW))

Smith Kline & French Laboratories (Aust.) Ltd v. Secretary, Department of Community Services and Health (DATA CONCERNING THERAPEUTIC SUBSTANCE FURNISHED FOR APPROVAL: USE FOR EVALUATION OF APPLICATION BY ANOTHER APPLICANT: EXTENT OF OBLIGATION OF CONFIDENCE: Fed. Ct)

Public Policy

Royal Melbourne Hospital v. Matthews (SEARCH WARRANT: PATIENT IN HOSPITAL: WHETHER HOSPITAL OBLIGED TO SUPPLY INFORMATION: H.C.)

Westpac Banking Corporation v. John Fairfax Group Pty Ltd (WHAT CONSTITUTES: S.C.(NSW))

Quality or Nature of Confidential Information

Mar-Con Corporation Pty Ltd v. Campbell Capital Ltd (WHETHER IMPARTED IN CONFIDENCE: EXTENT OF DUTY OF CONFIDENCE: SPRINGBOARD DOCTRINE: JOINT VENTURE: WHETHER UNDER FIDUCIARY DUTY: UNJUST ENRICHMENT: BASIS OF LIABILITY: S.C.(NSW))
Pancontinental Mining Ltd v. Commissioner of Stamp Duties (WHETHER A TRANSFER OF VALUABLE CONFIDENTIAL INFORMATION IS A TRANSFER OF PROPERTY: S.C.(Qd))
Secton Pty Ltd v. Delawood Pty Ltd (WHETHER SPECULATIVE CONCEPTS MAY QUALIFY AS TRADE SECRETS: NOVELTY: OBVIOUSNESS: VALUE: CLARITY OF DESCRIPTION OF ALLEGED TRADE SECRETS IN PARTICULARS: S.C.(Vic.))

Remedies

Johns v. Australian Securities Commission (ROYAL COMMISSION INVESTIGATION: RELEASE OF TRANSCRIPTS: PUBLIC DOMAIN: WHETHER ENTITLED TO ORDER RESTRAINING PUBLICATION OF TRANSCRIPTS: Fed. Ct)

Restraint of Trade

Pioneer Concrete Services Ltd v. Lorenzo Galli (IMPLIED OBLIGATION: INJUNCTION: DECLARATION: DAMAGES: S.C.(Vic.))

Right of Privacy

Tom Cruise and Nicole Kidman v. Southdown Press Pty Ltd (INJUNCTION: COPYRIGHT: IMPENDING PUBLICATION OF PHOTOGRAPHS OF CHILD: Fed. Ct)

Royal Commission Investigation, Release of Transcripts

Johns v. Australian Securities Commission (PUBLIC DOMAIN: REMEDIES: WHETHER ENTITLED TO ORDER RESTRAINING PUBLICATION OF TRANSCRIPTS: Fed. Ct)

Search Warrant. See Practice (Search warrant)

Serious Question to be Tried. See Practice (Interlocutory injunction)

Springboard Doctrine

Fractionated Cane Technology Ltd v. Joseph Ruiz-Avila (IDEA: SIMULTANEOUS ACQUISITION OF INFORMATION: FAILURE OF CONSIDERATION: S.C.(Qd))
Mar-Con Corporation Pty Ltd v. Campbell Capital Ltd (WHETHER CONFIDENTIAL QUALITY: WHETHER IMPARTED IN CONFIDENCE: EXTENT OF DUTY OF CONFIDENCE: S.C.(NSW))

Unjust Enrichment

Mar-Con Corporation Pty Ltd v. Campbell Capital Ltd (WHETHER INFORMATION IMPARTED IN CONFIDENCE: EXTENT OF DUTY OF CONFIDENCE: SPRINGBOARD DOCTRINE: JOINT VENTURE: WHETHER FIDUCIARY DUTY: BASIS OF LIABILITY: S.C.(NSW))

What Constitutes

Chenel Pty Ltd v. Rayner (INTERLOCUTORY INJUNCTION SERIOUS ISSUE TO BE TRIED: BALANCE OF CONVENIENCE: S.C.(Vic.))

Copyright

Account of Profits. *See* **Practice** (*Account of Profits*)

Adaptation

Accounting Systems 2000 (Developments) Pty Ltd v. CCH Australia Ltd (REPRODUCTION OF SUBSTANTIAL PART: EFFECT OF EXPENDITURE OF TIME AND EFFORT IN DEVELOPING COMPUTER PROGRAM: Fed. Ct)
Apple Computer Inc. v. Computer Edge Pty Ltd (Fed. Ct: H.C.)
Apple Computer Inc. v. Computer Edge Pty Ltd (WHETHER SOURCE CODE ADAPTATION OF SOURCE CODE: Fed. Ct)
Erica Vale Australia Pty Limited v. Thompson & Morgan (Ipswich) Limited (LITERARY WORK: OWNERSHIP: CONTRACT: IMPLIED TERM: DAMAGES: COSTS INCURRED IN MITIGATION OF LOSS: LOST PROFITS: Fed. Ct)

Agreed Statement of Facts. *See* **Practice** (*Agreed statement of facts*)

Anton Piller. *See* **Practice** (*Anton Piller*)

Appeal. *See* **Practice** (*Appeal*)

Architect, Architect's Plans

Devefi Pty Ltd v. Mateffy Pearl Nagy Pty Ltd (ARTISTIC WORKS: PLANS TO COMPLETE BUILDING: WHETHER RIGHT TO PERFORMANCE ASSIGNABLE: Fed. Ct)
Dronpool Pty Ltd v. Hunter (SUBSTANTIAL REPRODUCTION: S.C.(NSW))
Gruzman Pty Ltd v. Percy Marks Pty Ltd (ARTISTIC WORK: INFRINGEMENT: REPRODUCTION IN A MATERIAL FORM: THREE-DIMENSIONAL VERSION OF A TWO DIMENSIONAL WORK: S.C.(NSW))
Ownit Homes Pty Ltd v. D. & F. Mancuso Investments Pty Ltd (SERIES OF DRAWINGS: WHETHER DRAWINGS OR HOUSE INFRINGED: SUBSTANTIAL PART: S.C.(Qd))
Wood v. Kempe (INFRINGEMENT: INTERLOCUTORY INJUNCTION: BALANCE OF CONVENIENCE: Fed. Ct)

Artistic Works

Anheuser-Busch Inc. v. Castlebrae Pty Ltd (Fed. Ct)
Bailey & Co. Ltd v. Boccaccio Pty Ltd (INFRINGEMENT: ARTISTIC WORK ON BOTTLE LABEL: S.C.(NSW))
Bailey v. Namol Pty Ltd (INFRINGEMENT: DESIGN DRAWINGS: COMPENSATORY DAMAGES: ASSESSMENT: CALCULATION BY REFERENCE TO EXPECTED PROFITS: AGGRAVATED OR EXEMPLARY DAMAGES: Fed. Ct)
Baker and Priem's Application (WHETHER BULL-BAR A SCULPTURE OR WORK OF ARTISTIC CRAFTSMANSHIP: Pat. Off.)
Devefi Pty Ltd v. Mateffy Pearl Nagy Pty Ltd (ARCHITECT'S PLANS TO COMPLETE BUILDING: Fed. Ct)

Edwards Hot Water Systems v. S.W. Hart & Co. Pty Ltd (DUAL PROTECTION: Fed. Ct)

Fire Nymph Products Ltd v. Jalco Products (W.A.) Pty Ltd (INDUSTRIAL APPLICATION OF ARTISTIC WORK: Fed. Ct)

Gruzman Pty Ltd v. Percy Marks Pty Ltd (INFRINGEMENT: REPRODUCTION IN A MATERIAL FORM: THREE-DIMENSIONAL VERSION OF A TWO-DIMENSIONAL WORK: IMPLIED LICENCE: ARCHITECTURAL PLANS AND DRAWINGS: S.C.(NSW))

Kevlacat Pty Ltd v. Trailcraft Marine Pty Ltd (REPRODUCTION: INFRINGEMENT: DEFENCE: INDUSTRIAL APPLICATION: Fed. Ct)

Kiama Constructions v. M.C. Casella Building Co. Pty Ltd (HOUSE PLANS: ORIGINALITY: INFRINGEMENT: NON-EXPERT DEFENCE: S.C.(W.A.))

Koh Electronics Trading v. Libra Electronics Pty Ltd (COPYRIGHT PROPRIETORSHIP ON TRADE MARK: AIPO)

Komesaroff v. Mickle (INFRINGEMENT: S.C.(Vic.))

Mainbridge Industries Pty Ltd v. Whitewood & Ibbett Pty Ltd (REPRODUCTION: INFRINGEMENT: NON-EXPERT DEFENCE: S.C.(NSW))

Yumbulul v. Reserve Bank of Australia (ABORIGINAL ARTIST: PERMANENT PUBLIC DISPLAY IN MUSEUM: Fed. Ct)

Assignment

Acorn Computer Ltd v. MCS Microcomputer System Pty Ltd (REQUIREMENT OF WRITING: EQUITABLE OWNERSHIP: JOINT OWNERSHIP: Fed. Ct)

Andritz Sprout-Bauer Australia Pty Ltd v. Rowland Engineering Sales Pty Ltd (SALE OF OTHER ASSETS: Fed. Ct)

Devefi Pty Ltd v. Mateffy Pearl Nagy Pty Ltd (ARCHITECT AND BUILDER: WHETHER RIGHT TO PERFORMANCE ASSIGNABLE: Fed. Ct)

Greenfield Products Pty Ltd v. Rover-Scott Bonnar Ltd (SALE OF BUSINESS: NO EXPRESS ASSIGNMENT: COPYRIGHT ASSIGNMENT IMPLIED: ASSIGNMENT IN WRITING: Fed. Ct)

Mateffy Perl Nagy Pty Ltd v. Devefi Pty Ltd (LICENCE TO USE PLANS FOR CONSTRUCTION OF BUILDING: SALE OF SITE: WHETHER IMPLIED LICENCE IN FAVOUR OF PURCHASER: Fed. Ct)

Authorisation of Infringement

Australasian Performing Right Association Ltd v. Jain (EXECUTIVE DIRECTOR: POWER TO AUTHORISE PERFORMANCE OF WORKS IN PUBLIC: Fed. Ct)

Australasian Performing Right Association Ltd v. Tolbush Pty Ltd (PUBLIC PERFORMANCE: DIRECTORS: S.C.(Qd))

Australasian Performing Right Association Ltd v. Valamo Pty Ltd (PERSONAL LIABILITY OF DIRECTOR: Fed. C.A.)

Autodesk Inc. v. Dyason (COMPUTER PROGRAMS: DEVICE ENABLING BREACH OF SHRINK-WRAP LICENCE: Fed. Ct)

Autodesk Inc. v. Dyason (No. 2) (COMPUTER PROGRAM: PRACTICE: JURISDICTION TO REHEAR: H.C.)

Blackwell v. Wadsworth (LICENCE: S.C.(NSW))

Copyright Agency Ltd v. Haines (FAIR DEALING: MULTIPLE COPYING: SCHOOLS: S.C.(NSW))

WEA International Inc. v. Hanimex Corporation Ltd (SOUND RECORDINGS: CONTRIBUTORY INFRINGEMENT: ADVERTISEMENT FOR BLANK TAPE: Fed. Ct)

Balance of Convenience. *See* **Practice** (*Balance of Convenience*)

Builders Plans

Led Builders Pty Ltd v. Masterton Homes (NSW) Pty Ltd (SUBSISTENCE: INFRINGEMENT: LACHES, ACQUIESCENCE AND DELAY: Fed. Ct)

Broadcasts

Amalgamated TV Services Pty. Ltd v. Foxtel Digital Cable Television Pty. Ltd (RE-TRANSMISSION OF TELEVISION PROGRAMMES: EXEMPTION FROM REGULATORY REGIME: Fed. Ct)

Australasian Performing Right Association Ltd v. Telstra Corporation Ltd (DIFFUSION SERVICE: WHETHER MUSIC HEARD BY TELEPHONE USERS ON HOLD CONSTITUTES PERFORMANCE IN PUBLIC OR BROADCAST TO THE PUBLIC: Fed. Ct)

WEA Records Pty Ltd v. Stereo FM Pty Ltd (SOUND RECORDINGS: ROYALTY: OWNERS AGENT: OWNERS' EXCLUSIVE LICENSEE: Cprt Trib.)

Cinematographic Film

Gianitsios v. Karagiannis (INFRINGEMENT: PRACTICE: ANTON PILLER: S.C.(NSW))

Kervan Trading Pty Ltd v. Aktas (STATUTORY PROVISIONS: LICENCE: EXCLUSIVITY: CONSTRUCTION OF DOCUMENT: S.C.(NSW))

Nomad Films International Pty Ltd v. Export Development Grants Board (APPLICATION FOR GRANT: WHETHER ELIGIBLE: EXCLUSIVE LICENCE: Fed. Ct)

Pontello v. Giannotis (OFFENCE: POSSESSION OF FILMS FOR LETTING FOR HIRE OR, BY WAY OF TRADE OFFERING OR EXPOSING FOR HIRE: Fed. Ct)

Rank Film Production Ltd v. Dodds (INFRINGEMENT: PUBLIC PERFORMANCE: S.C.(NSW))

Wigginton v. Brisbane TV Ltd (FAIR DEALING: CONFIDENTIAL INFORMATION: WHETHER INFORMATION FREELY AVAILABLE: S.C.(Qd))

Circuit Layouts. *See* Computer Topics

Collecting Society

Australian Tape Manufacturers Association Ltd v. Commonwealth of Australia (SOUND RECORDINGS: UNAUTHORISED DOMESTIC COPYING: SCHEME FOR COMPENSATION: ROYALTY ON BLANK TAPES: DISTRIBUTED TO COPYRIGHT OWNERS: CONSTITUTIONAL VALIDITY OF AMENDING LEGISLATION: H.C.)

Nationwide News Pty Ltd v. Copyright Agency Ltd (COPYING BY EDUCATIONAL INSTITUTIONS: NEWSPAPERS, MAGAZINES AND PERIODICALS: JOURNALISTS COPYRIGHT: COMPILATION: INFRINGEMENT: SUBSTANTIALITY: COPYING OF SINGLE ITEM: Fed. Ct)

Commissioned Work

Cope Allman (Marrickville) Ltd v. Farrow (OWNERSHIP: ENGRAVINGS: CONFIDENTIAL INFORMATION: COMPUTER PROGRAMS: S.C.(NSW))

Enzed Holdings Ltd v. Wynthea Pty Ltd (OWNERSHIP: FOREIGN AUTHOR: *Locus standi*: Fed. Ct)

Flamingo Park Pty Ltd v. Dolly Dolly Creation Pty Ltd (CONTRACT: DESIGN: Fed. Ct)

759

Company Director

Australasian Performing Right Association Ltd v. Jain (POWER TO AUTHORISE
PERFORMANCE OF WORKS IN PUBLIC: Fed. Ct)
Australasian Performing Right Association Ltd v. Tolbush Pty Ltd (INFRINGEMENT:
PUBLIC PERFORMANCE: AUTHORISATION: DIRECTORS OF CORPORATION:
S.C.(Qd))
Australasian Performing Right Assn Ltd v. Valamo Pty Ltd (PERSONAL LIABILITY FOR
INFRINGEMENT: Fed. Ct: Fed. C.A.)
Milpurrurru v. Indofurn Pty Ltd (ABORIGINAL ARTWORK: IMPORTATION:
REPRODUCTION: SUBSTANTIAL PART: OWNERSHIP: KNOWLEDGE:
DIRECTORS' LIABILITY: Fed. Ct)
Namol Pty Ltd v. A.W. Baulderstone Pty Ltd (INFRINGEMENT: WHETHER
DIRECTOR OF INFRINGING COMPANY A JOINT TORTFEASOR: WHETHER IN
BREACH OF FIDUCIARY DUTY: ASSESSMENT OF DAMAGES: Fed. Ct)

Compilation

CCOM Pty Ltd v. Jiejung Pty Ptd (CHINESE CHARACTERS IN DATABASE:
INFRINGEMENT: CAUSAL LINK BETWEEN MATERIAL AND ALLEGED COPY: Fed.
Ct)
ITP Pty Ltd v. United Capital Pty Ltd (INFRINGEMENT: LITERARY WORK:
INTERLOCUTORY INJUNCTION: S.C.(Qd))
Nationwide News Pty Ltd v. Copyright Agency Ltd (COPYING BY EDUCATIONAL
INSTITUTIONS: NEWSPAPERS, MAGAZINES AND PERIODICALS: JOURNALISTS
COPYRIGHT: COMPILATION: INFRINGEMENT: SUBSTANTIALITY: COPYING OF
SINGLE ITEM: Fed. Ct)

Computer Topics

Accounting· Systems 2000 (Developments) Pty Ltd v. CCH Australia Ltd
(PROGRAMS: REPRODUCTION OR ADAPTATION: REPRODUCTION OF
SUBSTANTIAL PART: EFFECT OF EXPENDITURE OF TIME AND EFFORT IN
DEVELOPING PROGRAM: Fed. Ct)
Apple Computer Inc. v. Computer Edge Pty Ltd (INFRINGEMENT: MICRO
COMPUTER PROGRAMS: WHETHER SOURCE CODE ADAPTATION OF SOURCE
CODE: Fed. Ct)
Apple Computer Inc. v. Rowney (COMPUTER PROGRAMS: ANTON PILLER
PROCEEDINGS: FORM OF ORDER: S.C.(NSW))
Australian Computer Evaluation Consultants Pty Ltd v. Datbury Pty Ltd
(INFRINGEMENT: COMPUTER PROGRAM: PASSING OFF: Fed. Ct)
Autodesk Australia Pty Ltd v. Cheung (PROGRAMS: INFRINGEMENT: SALE OF
UNAUTHORISED REPRODUCTIONS: DAMAGES: MEASURE: ADDITIONAL
DAMAGES: CLAIM BY COPYRIGHT OWNER AND AUSTRALIAN DISTRIBUTOR:
Fed. Ct)
Autodesk Inc. v. Dyason (INFRINGEMENT: PROGRAM: ORIGINALITY: SUBSTANTIAL
PART: APPELLANT'S DEVICE TO PREVENT ITS COMPUTER PROGRAMS BEING
RUN ON A COMPUTER WITHOUT DEVICE: Fed. Ct: H.C.)
Autodesk Inc. v. Dyason (No. 2) (INFRINGEMENT: PROGRAM: ORIGINALITY:
SUBSTANTIAL PART: APPELLANTS DEVICE TO PREVENT ITS PROGRAMS BEING
RUN ON A COMPUTER WITHOUT DEVICE: H.C.)
Autodesk Inc. v. Dyason (No. 2) (INFRINGEMENT: PROGRAM: PRACTICE:
JURISDICTION TO REHEAR: H.C.)

Avel Pty Ltd v. Wells (CIRCUIT LAYOUTS: INTEGRATED CIRCUIT: DEFENCE TO PARALLEL IMPORTATION OF COPYRIGHT MATERIAL: PROGRAMS: INFRINGEMENT: PARALLEL IMPORTATION AND SALE: STATUTORY DEFENCE: Fed. Ct)

Avel Pty Ltd v. Wells (CIRCUIT LAYOUTS: PARALLEL IMPORTATION OF ELIGIBLE LAYOUTS FOR VIDEO GAMES: LAYOUTS CONTAINING SUBSTANTIAL PARTS OF COMPUTER PROGRAMS, THE COPYRIGHT OWNED BY ONE OF THE APPELLANTS: WHETHER IMPORTATION CONSTITUTED INFRINGEMENT OF COPYRIGHT IN PROGRAMS: Fed. Ct)

Avtex Airservices Pty Ltd v. Bartsch (OWNERSHIP: COMPUTERISED TEACHING SYSTEM OF WORKBOOKS, SLIDES AND COMPUTER PROGRAMS: Fed. Ct)

Barson Computers Australasia Ltd v. Southern Technology Pty Ltd (PROGRAMS: OPERATING SYSTEMS IN ROM: SUBSISTENCE: INFRINGEMENT: REVERSE ENGINEERING BY DISASSEMBLY: CONTRIBUTORY INFRINGEMENT: SUBSTANTIAL PART: USE OF GENUINE COPY FOR TESTING AND DEMONSTRATION: Fed. Ct)

Broderbund Software Inc. v. Computermate Products (Australia) Pty Ltd (PROGRAMS: INFRINGEMENT: PARALLEL IMPORTATION AND SALE: IMPLIED LICENCE OF IMPORTER: WHETHER DISTRIBUTOR AN EXCLUSIVE LICENSEE: MARKET SURVEY: SURVEY EVIDENCE: Fed. Ct)

CCOM Pty Ltd v. Jiejung Pty Ptd (COMPILATION OF CHINESE CHARACTERS IN DATABASE: INFRINGEMENT: CAUSAL LINK BETWEEN MATERIAL AND ALLEGED COPY: Fed. Ct)

Computermate Products (Aust.) Pty Ltd v. Ozi-Soft Pty Ltd (LICENCE TO IMPORT COPYRIGHT MATERIAL: COMPUTER DISKETTES: NATURE AND DEFINITION OF LICENCE WITHIN STATUTORY DEFINITION: Fed. Ct)

Cope Allman (Marrickville) Ltd v. Farrow (OWNERSHIP: COMMISSIONED WORK: ENGRAVINGS: CONFIDENTIAL INFORMATION: PROGRAMS: S.C.(NSW))

Irvine v. Carson (CRIMINAL OFFENCE: POSSESSION OF INFRINGING COPIES OF PROGRAMS FOR THE PURPOSE OF DISTRIBUTION: CONVICTION: APPROPRIATE PENALTY: ORDER FOR FORFEITURE OF COMPUTERS USED FOR MAKING INFRINGING COPIES: Fed. Ct)

Irvine v. Hanna-Rivero (INFRINGING COPIES OF PROGRAMS MADE FOR SWAP TRADE: CRIME: APPROPRIATE PENALTY: ORDER FOR FORFEITURE OF HARDWARE USED IN MAKING INFRINGING COPIES: Fed. Ct)

Ozi-Soft Pty Ltd v. Wong (PROGRAMS: CONTRIBUTORY INFRINGEMENT: IMPORTATION OF DISKETTES PURCHASES FROM COPYRIGHT OWNERS: IMPLIED LICENCE: DOCTRINE OF NATIONAL TREATMENT: Fed. Ct)

Roland Corporation v. Lorenzo & Sons Pty Ltd (DRAWING OF SINGLE LETTER: PRINTOUT: ORIGINAL CREATED ON FLOPPY DISK: COPYRIGHT IN LOGO DEVICES REGULATED UNDER STATUTE: Fed. Ct)

Star Micronics Pty Ltd v. Five Star Computers Pty Ltd (PROGRAMS: WHETHER ROM IN PRINTER A PROGRAM: ORIGINALITY: SECONDARY INFRINGEMENT: SALE OF IMPORTED PRINTERS INCLUDING PROGRAM IN ROM: Fed. Ct)

Consent Orders. *See* **Practice** (*Consent orders*)

Constructive Knowledge

Hooi v. Brophy (INFRINGEMENT: S.C.(S.A.))

Contributory Infringement

Barson Computers Australasia Ltd v. Southern Technology Pty Ltd (USE OF GENUINE COPY FOR TESTING AND DEMONSTRATION: Fed. Ct)

761

Ozi-Soft Pty Ltd v. Wong (COMPUTER PROGRAMS: IMPORTATION OF DISKETTES
    PURCHASES FROM COPYRIGHT OWNERS: IMPLIED LICENCE: DOCTRINE OF
    NATIONAL TREATMENT: Fed. Ct)
WEA International Inc. v. Hanimex Corporation Ltd (SOUND RECORDINGS:
    AUTHORISATION: ADVERTISEMENT FOR BLANK TAPE: Fed. Ct)

Copyright Collecting Agency

Yumbulul v. Reserve Bank of Australia (EXCLUSIVE LICENCE TO COLLECTING
    AGENCY: SUB-LICENCE TO RESERVE BANK: WHETHER ARTIST MISLED AS TO
    NATURE OF LICENCE AND INTENDED USE OF WORK: WHETHER ESTOPPEL OR
    MISTAKE: Fed. Ct)

Criminal Sanctions

Irvine v. Carson (POSSESSION OF INFRINGING COPIES OF COMPUTER PROGRAMS
    FOR PURPOSE OF DISTRIBUTING: CONVICTION: APPROPRIATE PENALTY:
    FORFEITURE OF COMPUTERS USED FOR MAKING INFRINGING COPIES: Fed.
    Ct)
Irvine v. Hanna-Rivero (INFRINGING COPIES OF PROGRAMS MADE FOR SWAP
    TRADE: CRIME: APPROPRIATE PENALTY: ORDER FOR FORFEITURE OF
    HARDWARE USED IN MAKING INFRINGING COPIES: Fed. Ct)
Pontello v. Ceselli (INFRINGEMENT: Fed. Ct)

Crown Copyright

Greenfield Products Pty Ltd v. Rover-Scott Bonnar Ltd (Fed. Ct)

Damages. *See* **Practice** (*Damages*)

Defence

Golden Editions Pty. Ltd v. Polygram Pty. Ld (INFRINGEMENT: KNOWLEDGE OR
    SUSPICION THAT ACT WAS INFRINGEMENT: STATUTORY INTERPRETATION:
    RELEVANCE OF KNOWLEDGE OF IDENTITY OF OWNER: PRACTICE: APPEALS:
    FACTUAL FINDINGS AND ERRORS OF LAW: Fed. Ct)

Design, Application

3D Geoshapes Australia Pty Ltd v. Registrar of Designs (REGISTRATION:
    APPLICATION FOR EXTENSION OF TIME REFUSED: APPEAL: Fed. Ct)
Caroma Industries Ltd (REGISTRABILITY: AIPO)

Design, Overlap between Copyright and Design

Greenfield Products Pty Ltd v. Rover-Scott Bonnar Ltd (Fed. Ct)
Hosokawa Micron International Inc. v. Fortune (DRAWING DATED 1972: WHETHER
    CAPABLE OF REGISTRATION UNDER DESIGNS ACT 1906 OR DESIGNS
    AMENDMENT ACT 1981: REGISTRABILITY OF FUNCTIONAL DESIGNS: Fed. Ct)

Designs Act 1906

Hosokawa Micron International Inc. v. Fortune (Fed. Ct)

Designs Amendment Act 1981

Hosokawa Micron International Inc. v. Fortune (Fed. Ct)

Design, Registrability

Caroma Industries Ltd (APPLICATION: AIPO)

Shacklady v. Atkins (REPRODUCTION: CORRESPONDING DESIGNS: WHETHER INFRINGEMENT OF COPYRIGHT: DESIGN OF YACHT, WHETHER REGISTRABLE: Fed. Ct)

Diffusion Service

Australasian Performing Right Association Ltd v. Telstra Corporation Ltd (WHETHER MUSIC HEARD BY TELEPHONE USERS PLACED ON HOLD CONSTITUTES A PERFORMANCE IN PUBLIC OR A BROADCAST TO THE PUBLIC: Fed. Ct)

Discretion. *See* **Practice** (*Discretion*)

Drawings

Anheuser-Busch Inc. v. Castlebrae Pty Ltd (Fed. Ct)

Dixon Investments Pty Ltd v. Hall (PROJECT HOUSE DESIGN DRAWINGS: DESIGN DERIVED ORIGINALLY FROM APPLICANTS PLAN: PRINCIPLES GOVERNING SIMPLE AND COMMONPLACE DRAWINGS: SUBSTANTIAL PART: Fed. Ct)

Greenfield Products Pty Ltd v. Rover-Scott Bonnar Ltd (Fed. Ct)

Gruzman Pty Ltd v. Percy Marks Pty Ltd (THREE-DIMENSIONAL VERSION OF TWO-DIMENSIONAL WORK: IMPLIED LICENCE: ARCHITECTURAL PLANS AND DRAWINGS: S.C.(NSW))

Hosokawa Micron International Inc. v. Fortune (Fed. Ct)

Interlego AG v. Croner Trading Pty Ltd (MODIFICATIONS TO REFLECT CHANGES IN MANUFACTURING PROCESS: Fed. Ct)

Kiama Constructions v. M.C. Casella Building Co. Pty Ltd (HOUSE PLANS: INFRINGEMENT: NON-EXPERT DEFENCE: S.C.(W.A.))

Namol Pty Ltd v. A.W. Baulderstone Pty Ltd (INFRINGEMENT: WORKING DRAWINGS FOR DOORS AND WINDOWS: Fed. Ct)

Ogden Industries Pty Ltd v. Kis (Australia) Ltd (INFRINGEMENT: DRAWINGS FOR KEY BLANKS: NON-EXPERT DEFENCE: S.C.(NSW))

Ownit Homes Pty Ltd v. D. & F. Mancuso Investments Pty Ltd (ARCHITECT'S PLANS: SERIES OF DRAWINGS: WHETHER DRAWINGS OR HOUSE INFRINGED COPYRIGHT: SUBSTANTIAL PART: S.C.(Qd))

Roland Corporation v. Lorenzo & Sons Pty Ltd (SINGLE LETTER: COMPUTER PRINTOUT: ORIGINAL CREATED ON FLOPPY DISK: Fed. Ct)

Talk of the Town Pty Ltd v. Hagstrom (ENGRAVING: FUNCTIONAL OBJECTS: Fed. Ct)

Timbs v. Miller (INFRINGEMENT: DRAWINGS OF BOATS: S.C.(NSW))

Educational Establishments

Copyright Agency Ltd v. Department of Education of NSW (COPYING BY EDUCATIONAL ESTABLISHMENTS: REMUNERATION: Cprt Trib.)

Copyright Agency Ltd v. Victoria University of Technology (MULTIPLE COPYING BY EDUCATIONAL ESTABLISHMENTS: LICENSING SCHEME: Fed. Ct)

Nationwide News Pty Ltd v. Copyright Agency Ltd (COLLECTING SOCIETIES: COPYING BY EDUCATIONAL INSTITUTIONS: NEWSPAPERS, MAGAZINES AND PERIODICALS: Fed. Ct)

Employees

Greenfield Products Pty Ltd v. Rover-Scott Bonnar Ltd (AUTHORSHIP: Fed. Ct)

Engravings

Cope Allman (Marrickville) Ltd v. Farrow (OWNERSHIP: COMMISSIONED WORK: S.C.(NSW))

Greenfield Products Pty Ltd v. Rover-Scott Bonnar Ltd (THREE-DIMENSIONAL OBJECTS: MOULDS AND ARTICLES MADE THEREFROM: Fed. Ct)

Talk of the Town Pty Ltd v. Hagstrom (FUNCTIONAL OBJECTS: DRAWINGS AND DIES: Fed. Ct)

Equitable Ownership. *See* **Ownership**

Essential Features

AGL Sydney Ltd v. Shortland County Council (INFRINGEMENT: REPLY TO COMPETITOR'S ADVERTISEMENT: Fed. Ct)

Baker and Priem's Application (SUBSISTANCE OF COPYRIGHT IN ARTISTIC WORKS CORRESPONDING TO DESIGN: Pat. Off.)

Estoppel

Yumbulul v. Reserve Bank of Australia (WHETHER ARTIST MISLED AS TO NATURE OF LICENCE AND INTENDED USE OF WORK: WHETHER ESTOPPEL OR MISTAKE: Fed. Ct)

Evidence. *See* **Practice** (*Evidence*)

Exclusive Licence. *See* **Licence**

Fair Dealing

Copyright Agency Ltd v. Haines (INFRINGEMENT: AUTHORISING INFRINGEMENT: MULTIPLE COPYING: SCHOOLS: S.C.(NSW))

De Garis v. Neville Jeffress Pidler Pty Ltd (PRESS-CLIPPING AND MEDIA MONITORING SERVICE: WHETHER IMPLIED LICENCE TO REPRODUCE: Fed. Ct)

Director-General of Education v. Public Service Association of NSW (PUBLIC INTEREST: S.C.(NSW))

Wigginton v. Brisbane TV Ltd (CINEMATOGRAPH FILM: S.C.(Qd))

Films. *See* **Cinematographic Films**

Flagrant Breach

Television Broadcasts Ltd v. Tu (ASSESSMENT OF DAMAGES: USE BY RESPONDENTS OF APPLICANTS' VIDEO CASSETTES AFTER EXPIRY OF LICENCE: HOW DAMAGES CALCULATED: Fed. Ct)

Forfeiture. *See* **Practice** (*Forfeiture*)

Fraudulent Imitation

A C. Corp. Pty Ltd v. Jadon Investments Pty Ltd (REGISTERED DESIGN: KNOWLEDGE OF DESIGN: DESIGNER NOT CALLED AS WITNESS: SMALL DIFFERENCES: REGISTERED DESIGN NOT DISSIMILAR TO PRIOR ART: H.C.)

Functional Objects

Hosokawa Micron International Inc. v. Fortune (REGISTRABILITY: Fed. Ct)

Talk of the Town Pty Ltd v. Hagstrom (ENGRAVING: DRAWINGS AND DIES: Fed. Ct)

House or Building Plans. *See also under* Architect, Architect's Plans

Caj Amadio Constructions Pty Ltd v. Kitchen (INFRINGEMENT: MEASURE OF DAMAGES: WHETHER DAMAGES TO BE ASSESSED ON BASIS OF LOSS OF PROFITS OR ON BASIS OF LOSS OF LICENCE FEE: S.C.(S.A.))

Collier Constructions Pty Ltd v. Foskett Pty Ltd (INFRINGEMENT: DEFENCES: SUBSTANTIAL PART: PUBLIC INTEREST: LACK OF CLEAN HANDS: Fed. Ct)

Devefi Pty Ltd v. Mateffy Pearl Nagy Pty Ltd (ARCHITECT'S PLANS TO COMPLETE BUILDING: WHETHER RIGHT TO PERFORMANCE ASSIGNABLE: Fed. Ct)

Dixon Investments Pty Ltd v. Hall (ALLEGED COPYING OF DESIGN DERIVED FROM APPLICANT'S PLAN: SIMPLE AND COMMONPLACE DRAWINGS: SUBSTANTIAL PART: Fed. Ct)

Dronpool Pty Ltd v. Hunter (INFRINGEMENT: SUBSTANTIAL REPRODUCTION: S.C.(NSW))

Gruzman Pty Ltd v. Percy Marks Pty Ltd (INFRINGEMENT: REPRODUCTION IN A MATERIAL FORM: THREE-DIMENSIONAL VERSION OF A TWO-DIMENSIONAL WORK: IMPLIED LICENCE: S.C.(NSW))

Kiama Constructions v. M.C. Casella Building Co. Pty Ltd (ORIGINALITY: WHETHER HOUSE INFRINGED COPYRIGHT: NON-EXPERT DEFENCE: S.C.(W.A.))

Mateffy Perl Nagy Pty Ltd v. Devefi Pty Ltd (LICENCE TO USE PLANS OF BUILDING: SALE OF SITE TO THIRD PARTY: WHETHER IMPLIED LICENCE: INFRINGEMENT: ESTOPPEL: MEASURE OF DAMAGES: Fed. Ct)

Ownit Homes Pty Ltd v. D. & F. Mancuso Investments Pty Ltd (SERIES OF DRAWINGS: WHETHER DRAWINGS OR HOUSE INFRINGED COPYRIGHT: SUBSTANTIAL PART: S.C.(Qd))

Z.S. Projects Pty Ltd v. G. & R. Investments Pty Ltd (INFRINGEMENT: DAMAGES: ACCOUNT OF PROFITS: S.C.(NSW))

Idea and Expression, Idea and Concept

Bartos v. Scott (CO-AUTHORS: PERSON SUPPLYING TABLES AND IDEAS FOR WORK: NOT AN AUTHOR: S.C.(NSW))

Seabed Observatories Pty Ltd v. Tarca (IDEAS AND CONCEPTS: FACTORS: S.C.(Qd))

Taypar Pty Ltd v. Santic (INFRINGEMENT: WHETHER APPROPRIATION OF IDEA OR CONCEPT OR OF EXPRESSION OF CONCEPT: Fed. Ct)

Implied Licence. *See* Licence

Implied Obligations

Erica Vale Australia Pty Limited v. Thompson & Morgan (Ipswich) Limited (LITERARY WORK: ADAPTATION: OWNERSHIP: CONTRACT: DAMAGES: COSTS INCURRED IN MITIGATION OF LOSS: LOST PROFITS: Fed. Ct)

Moorhead v. Paul Brennan (LITERARY WORK: EXCLUSIVE LICENCE TO PUBLISH: S.C.(NSW))

Importation

Avel Pty Ltd v. Multicoin Amusements Pty Ltd (INFRINGEMENT: U.S. MANUFACTURER: PROPOSED IMPORT OF USED GOODS: THREATS: EXCLUSIVE LICENSEE: ONUS OF PROOF: H.C.)

Avel Pty Ltd v. Wells (CIRCUIT LAYOUTS: INTEGRATED CIRCUIT: PARALLEL IMPORTATION: COMPUTER PROGRAMS: INFRINGEMENT: STATUTORY DEFENCE: Fed. Ct)

Bailey & Co. Ltd v. Boccaccio Pty Ltd (INFRINGEMENT: ARTISTIC WORK: IMPLIED LICENCE: NON-DEROGATION FROM GRANT: S.C.(NSW))

Broderbund Software Inc. v. Computermate Products (Australia) Pty Ltd (COMPUTER PROGRAMS: INFRINGEMENT: PARALLEL IMPORTATION AND SALE: IMPLIED LICENCE OF IMPORTER: Fed. Ct)

Chrysalis Records Ltd v. Vere (INFRINGEMENT: SOUND RECORDINGS: S.C.(Qd))

Lotus Development Corporation v. Vacolan Pty Ltd (INFRINGEMENT: PARALLEL IMPORTATION: ORDERS RECEIVED AND FILLED BY AUSTRALIAN AGENT OF FOREIGN VENDOR: Fed. Ct)

Multicoin Amusements Pty Ltd v. British Amusements (North Coast) Corporation Pty Ltd (THREATENED INFRINGEMENT: THREATS: IMPORTATION: PARALLEL IMPORTATION: EXCLUSIVE LICENCE: S.C.(Qd))

Ozi-Soft Pty Ltd v. Wong (COMPUTER PROGRAMS: CONTRIBUTORY INFRINGEMENT: IMPORTATION OF DISKETTES PURCHASES FROM COPYRIGHT OWNERS: IMPLIED LICENCE: DOCTRINE OF NATIONAL TREATMENT: Fed. Ct)

Roland Corporation v. Lorenzo & Sons Pty Ltd (INFRINGEMENT: UNAUTHORISED REPRODUCTION: PARALLEL IMPORTATION AND SALE: IMPLIED LICENCE TO IMPORT AND SELL: IMPLIED LICENCE: Fed. Ct)

In Public

Australasian Performing Right Association Ltd v. Ceridale Pty Ltd (INFRINGEMENT: PERFORMING RIGHTS: COPYRIGHT OWNER WITH MONOPOLY POWER: REFUSAL TO GRANT LICENCE TO PERFORM WORKS IN PUBLIC: S.C.(Qd))

Australasian Performing Right Association Ltd v. Commonwealth Bank of Australia (MUSICAL WORK: PERFORMED AT PLACE OF EMPLOYMENT: MEMBERS OF THE PUBLIC EXCLUDED: WHETHER PERFORMANCE IN PUBLIC: Fed. Ct)

Australasian Performing Right Association Ltd v. Jain (INFRINGEMENT: EXECUTIVE DIRECTOR: POWER TO AUTHORISE PERFORMANCE IN PUBLIC: Fed. Ct)

Australasian Performing Right Association Ltd v. Telstra Corporation Ltd (WHETHER MUSIC HEARD BY TELEPHONE USERS PLACED ON HOLD CONSTITUTES A PERFORMANCE IN PUBLIC OR A BROADCAST TO THE PUBLIC: Fed. Ct)

Infringement

Accounting Systems 2000 (Developments) Pty Ltd v. CCH Australia Ltd (COMPUTER PROGRAMS: Fed. Ct)

AGL Sydney Ltd v. Shortland County Council (TAKING ESSENTIAL FEATURES: PARODY: Fed. Ct)

Ainsworth Nominees Pty Ltd v. Andclar Pty Ltd (SUBSTANTIAL PART: Fed. Ct)

Aitken v. Neville Jeffress Pidler Pty Ltd (MEDIA MONITORING SERVICE: Fed. Ct)

Andritz Sprout-Bauer Australia Pty Ltd v. Rowland Engineering Sales Pty Ltd (UNCONSCIOUS COPYING: Fed. Ct)

Apple Computer Inc. v. Computer Edge Pty Ltd (ADAPTATIONS: Fed. Ct: H.C.)

Australasian Performing Right Assn Ltd v. Valamo Pty Ltd (DIRECTOR'S PERSONAL LIABILITY: Fed. Ct)

Australasian Performing Right Association Ltd v. Ceridale Pty Ltd (S.C.(Qd))

Australasian Performing Right Association Ltd v. Jain (EXECUTIVE DIRECTOR'S POWER TO AUTHORISE PERFORMANCE OF WORKS IN PUBLIC: Fed. Ct)

Australasian Performing Right Association Ltd v. Tolbush Pty Ltd (PUBLIC PERFORMANCE: AUTHORISATION: DIRECTOR: S.C.(Qd))

Australasian Performing Right Association Ltd v. Valamo Pty Ltd (DIRECTOR
   PERSONAL LIABILITY: AUTHORISATION: Fed. C.A.)
Australian Computer Evaluation Consultants Pty Ltd v. Datbury Pty Ltd (COMPUTER
   PROGRAM: PASSING OFF: Fed. Ct)
Autodesk Australia Pty Ltd v. Cheung (COMPUTER PROGRAMS: SALE OF
   UNAUTHORISED REPRODUCTIONS: Fed. Ct)
Autodesk Inc. v. Dyason (COMPUTER PROGRAMS: WHETHER ELECTRICAL CIRCUIT
   IS A COMPUTER PROGRAM: REPRODUCTION: AUTHORISATION: DEVICE
   ENABLING BREACH OF SHRINK-WRAP LICENCE: Fed. Ct: H.C.)
Autodesk Inc. v. Dyason (No. 2) (INFRINGEMENT: COMPUTER PROGRAM:
   ORIGINALITY: SUBSTANTIAL PART: APPELLANT'S DEVICE TO PREVENT ITS
   COMPUTER PROGRAMS BEING RUN ON A COMPUTER WITHOUT DEVICE:
   H.C.)
Avel Pty Ltd v. Multicoin Amusements Pty Ltd (PROPOSED IMPORT OF USED
   GOODS: THREATS: H.C.)
Avel Pty Ltd v. Wells (CIRCUIT LAYOUTS: INTEGRATED CIRCUIT: PARALLEL
   IMPORTATION: COMPUTER PROGRAMS: STATUTORY DEFENCE: Fed. Ct)
Bailey & Co. Ltd v. Boccaccio Pty Ltd (ARTISTIC WORK: PARALLEL IMPORTATION:
   IMPLIED LICENCE: NON-DEROGATION FROM GRANT: S.C.(NSW))
Barson Computers Australasia Ltd v. Southern Technology Pty Ltd (REVERSE
   ENGINEERING BY DISASSEMBLY: SUBSTANTIAL PART: CONTRIBUTORY
   INFRINGEMENT: USE OF GENUINE COPY FOR TESTING AND
   DEMONSTRATION: Fed. Ct)
Bevis v. Lyons (WRITTEN RULES OF BOARD GAME: S.C.(Qd))
Blackwell v. Wadsworth (AUTHORISING: LICENCE: S.C.(NSW))
Broderbund Software Inc. v. Computermate Products (Australia) Pty Ltd (PARALLEL
   IMPORTATION AND SALE: IMPLIED LICENCE OF IMPORTER: WHETHER
   DISTRIBUTOR AN EXCLUSIVE LICENSEE: Fed. Ct)
Caj Amadio Constructions Pty Ltd v. Kitchen (MEASURE OF DAMAGES: BASIS OF
   ASSESSMENT: S.C.(S.A.))
CBS Records Australia Ltd v. Guy Gross (SUBSTANTIAL PART: QUALITY AND
   QUANTITY DISTINGUISHED: Fed. Ct)
CCOM Pty Ltd v. Jiejung Pty Ptd (COMPILATION OF CHINESE CHARACTERS IN
   DATABASE: CAUSAL LINK BETWEEN MATERIAL AND ALLEGED COPY: Fed. Ct)
Chrysalis Records Ltd v. Vere (SOUND RECORDINGS: IMPORTATION: S.C.(Qd))
Collier Constructions Pty Ltd v. Foskett Pty Ltd (DEFENCES: PLANS FOR PROJECT
   HOUSES: SUBSTANTIAL PART: PUBLIC INTEREST: LACK OF CLEAN HANDS: Fed.
   Ct)
Collier Constructions Pty Ltd v. Foskett Pty Ltd (PERIMETER OF PLAN FOR PROJECT
   HOME: SUBSTANTIAL PART: Fed. Ct)
Copyright Agency Ltd v. Haines (FAIR DEALING: AUTHORISING INFRINGEMENT:
   MULTIPLE COPYING: SCHOOLS: S.C.(NSW))
Copyright Agency Ltd v. Victoria University of Technology (MULTIPLE COPYING:
   EDUCATIONAL INSTITUTIONS: WHETHER AUTHORISED SALE OR USE OF
   COPIES SO MADE: OPERATION OF LICENSING SCHEME: Fed. Ct)
De Garis v. Neville Jeffress Pidler Pty Ltd (PRESS-CLIPPING AND MEDIA
   MONITORING SERVICE: FAIR DEALING: Fed. Ct)
Dronpool Pty Ltd v. Hunter (ARCHITECTS' PLANS: SUBSTANTIAL REPRODUCTION:
   S.C.(NSW))
Easyfind (NSW) Pty Ltd v. Paterson (CALENDAR WITH ADVERTISEMENTS IN
   PARTICULAR FORM: REPRODUCTION OF A SUBSTANTIAL PART: S.C.(NSW))
Enzed Holdings Ltd v. Wynthea Pty Ltd (FOREIGN AUTHOR: RIGHT OF ACTION:
   Fed. Ct)

Polygram Pty Ltd v. Golden Editions Pty Ltd (SOUND RECORDINGS: INNOCENT INFRINGEMENT: STATUTORY DEFENCES: Fed. Ct)

Pontello v. Ceselli (CRIMINAL SANCTIONS: Fed. Ct)

Rank Film Production Ltd v. Dodds (CINEMATOGRAPH FILM: PUBLIC PERFORMANCE: S.C.(NSW))

Roland Corporation v. Lorenzo & Sons Pty Ltd (UNAUTHORISED REPRODUCTION: PARALLEL IMPORTATION AND SALE: IMPLIED LICENCE: Fed. Ct)

Rosebank Plastics Pty Ltd v. Duncan & Wigley Pty Ltd (DESIGN DRAWING: Fed. Ct)

Shacklady v. Atkins (SUBSISTENCE: DESIGN: REPRODUCTION: CORRESPONDING DESIGNS: WHETHER INFRINGEMENT OF COPYRIGHT: DESIGN OF YACHT, WHETHER REGISTRABLE: Fed. Ct)

Star Micronics Pty Ltd v. Five Star Computers Pty Ltd (ORIGINALITY: SECONDARY INFRINGEMENT: SALE OF IMPORTED PRINTERS INCLUDING PROGRAM IN ROM: Fed. Ct)

Taypar Pty Ltd v. Santic (QUALITATIVE ASSESSMENT OF SIMILARITIES: Fed. Ct)

Timbs v. Miller (DRAWINGS OF BOATS: S.C.(NSW))

Universal Press Pty Ltd v. Provest Ltd (MAPS: STREET DIRECTORIES: Fed. Ct)

Universal Smo-King Ovens Pty Ltd v. Guinn (SUBSTANTIAL REPRODUCTION: S.C.(NSW))

WEA International Inc. v. Hanimex Corporation Ltd (CONTRIBUTORY INFRINGEMENT: AUTHORISATION: ADVERTISEMENT FOR BLANK TAPE: Fed. Ct)

Wood v. Kempe (ARCHITECT'S PLANS: INTERLOCUTORY INJUNCTION: BALANCE OF CONVENIENCE: Fed. Ct)

Z.S. Projects Pty Ltd v. G. & R. Investments Pty Ltd (DAMAGES: ACCOUNT OF PROFITS: DEFENCE: S.C.(NSW))

Zeccola v. Universal City Studios Inc. (INTERLOCUTORY INJUNCTION: DISCRETION: Fed. Ct)

Injunctions. *See* **Practice** (*Injunctions*)

Integrated Circuit

Avel Pty Ltd v. Wells (CIRCUIT LAYOUTS: INTEGRATED CIRCUIT: DEFENCE TO PARALLEL IMPORTATION OF COPYRIGHT MATERIAL: COMPUTER PROGRAMS: INFRINGEMENT: PARALLEL IMPORTATION AND SALE: STATUTORY DEFENCE: Fed. Ct)

Innocent Infringement

Polygram Pty Ltd v. Golden Editions Pty Ltd (INFRINGEMENT: SOUND RECORDINGS: STATUTORY DEFENCES: Fed. Ct)

Interlocutory Injunction. *See* **Practice** (*Interlocutory injunction*)

Joint Authorship or Ownership

Acorn Computer Ltd v. MCS Microcomputer System Pty Ltd (Fed. Ct)

Murray v. King (S.C.(Qd))

Jurisdiction. *See* **Practice** *(Jurisdiction)*

Licence

Australasian Performing Right Association Ltd v. Ceridale Pty Ltd (REFUSAL TO
GRANT LICENCE TO PERFORM WORKS IN PUBLIC: USE OF POWER TO
EXTRACT PAYMENT OF DISPUTED DEBT: WHETHER POWER EXERCISED FOR
EXTRANEOUS PURPOSE: LICENCE FEES: CONDITIONS: S.C.(Qd))

Autodesk Inc. v. Dyason (DEVICE ENABLING BREACH OF SHRINK-WRAP LICENCE:
Fed. Ct)

Avel Pty Ltd v. Multicoin Amusements Pty Ltd (PARALLEL IMPORTATION: ONUS OF
PROOF: EXCLUSIVE LICENCE: H.C.)

Bailey & Co. Ltd v. Boccaccio Pty Ltd (IMPLIED LICENCE: NON-DEROGATION
FROM GRANT: S.C.(NSW))

Blackwell v. Wadsworth (INFRINGEMENT: AUTHORISING INFRINGING ACTS:
S.C.(NSW))

Broderbund Software Inc. v. Computermate Products (Australia) Pty Ltd (PARALLEL
IMPORTATION AND SALE: IMPLIED LICENCE: Fed. Ct)

Clune v. Collins Angus & Robertson Publishers Pty Ltd (ORAL LICENCE: Fed. Ct)

Computermate Products (Aust.) Pty Ltd v. Ozi-Soft Pty Ltd (LICENCE TO IMPORT:
Fed. Ct)

Copyright Agency Ltd v. Victoria University of Technology (MULTIPLE COPYING:
EDUCATIONAL INSTITUTIONS: WHETHER AUTHORISED SALE OR USE OF
COPIES SO MADE: OPERATION OF LICENSING SCHEME: Fed. Ct)

De Garis v. Neville Jeffress Pidler Pty Ltd (PRESS-CLIPPING AND MEDIA
MONITORING SERVICE: IMPLIED LICENCE: FAIR DEALING: Fed. Ct)

Devefi Pty Ltd v. Mateffy Pearl Nagy Pty Ltd (ARCHITECT'S PLANS TO COMPLETE
BUILDING: Fed. Ct)

Fai Insurances Ltd v. Advance Bank Australia Ltd (AMBIGUOUS STATEMENTS
COMPARING COMPANY PROFITS: PROXY FORM: IMPLIED LICENCE TO USE:
Fed. Ct)

Gruzman Pty Ltd v. Percy Marks Pty Ltd (REPRODUCTION IN A MATERIAL FORM:
THREE-DIMENSIONAL VERSION OF A TWO-DIMENSIONAL WORK: IMPLIED
LICENCE: S.C.(NSW))

International Writing Institute v. Rimila Pty Ltd (EXCLUSIVE LICENCE TO
DISTRIBUTE: FIDUCIARY DUTY: Fed. Ct)

Kervan Trading Pty Ltd v. Aktas (FILMS: STATUTORY PROVISIONS: EXCLUSIVITY:
CONSTRUCTION OF DOCUMENT: S.C.(NSW))

Roland Corporation v. Lorenzo & Sons Pty Ltd (PARALLEL IMPORTATION AND
SALE: IMPLIED LICENCE: Fed. Ct)

Mateffy Perl Nagy Pty Ltd v. Devefi Pty Ltd (LICENCE TO USE ENGINEER'S PLANS
FOR CONSTRUCTION OF BUILDING: SALE OF SITE BY LICENCE HOLDER: Fed.
Ct)

Moorhead v. Paul Brennan (EXCLUSIVE LICENCE TO PUBLISH: IMPLIED
OBLIGATIONS: S.C.(NSW))

Multicoin Amusements Pty Ltd v. British Amusements (North Coast) Corporation
Pty Ltd (PARALLEL IMPORTATION: EXCLUSIVE LICENCE: MISLEADING AND
DECEPTIVE CONDUCT ARISING FROM UNJUSTIFIABLE THREATS: S.C.(Qd))

Nomad Films International Pty Ltd v. Export Development Grants Board (FILM:
EXCLUSIVE LICENCE: Fed. Ct)

Ozi-Soft Pty Ltd v. Wong (IMPORTATION: IMPLIED LICENCE: DOCTRINE OF
NATIONAL TREATMENT: Fed. Ct)

Television Broadcasts Ltd v. Tu (USE AFTER EXPIRY OF LICENCE: FLAGRANT
BREACH: Fed. Ct)

Yumbulul v. Reserve Bank of Australia (ABORIGINAL ARTIST: PERMANENT PUBLIC
DISPLAY IN MUSEUM: EXCLUSIVE LICENCE: SUB-LICENCE: WHETHER ARTIST
MISLED AS TO NATURE OF LICENCE: Fed. Ct)

Literary Work

Anheuser-Busch Inc. v. Castlebrae Pty Ltd (WHETHER DRAWINGS ARTISTIC OR
LITERARY WORKS: Fed. Ct)
Erica Vale Australia Pty Limited v. Thompson & Morgan (Ipswich) Limited
(ADAPTATION: OWNERSHIP: CONTRACT: IMPLIED TERM: DAMAGES: COSTS
INCURRED IN MITIGATION OF LOSS: LOST PROFITS: Fed. Ct)
ITP Pty Ltd v. United Capital Pty Ltd (INFRINGEMENT: COMPILATION: S.C.(Qd))
Mirror Newspapers Ltd v. Queensland Newspapers Pty Ltd (NEWSPAPER BINGO:
S.C.(Qd))
Moorhead v. Paul Brennan (EXCLUSIVE LICENCE TO PUBLISH: IMPLIED
OBLIGATIONS: S.C.(NSW))

Literary Worth

Nationwide News Pty. Ltd v. Copyright Agency Ltd (CASES ON LITERARY WORTH
DISTINGUISHED: Fed. Ct)

Locus Standii. See **Practice** *(Locus standii)*

Market Survey. *See* **Practice** *(Market survey)*

Mistake

Easyfind (NSW) Pty Ltd v. Paterson (UNILATERAL MISTAKE: TERMS OF CONSENT
ORDERS: DUTIES OF COUNSEL: S.C.(NSW))
Yumbulul v. Reserve Bank of Australia (WHETHER ARTIST MISLED AS TO NATURE
OF LICENCE: WHETHER ESTOPPEL OR MISTAKE: Fed. Ct)

Non-Expert Test

Hart (S.W.) & Co. Pty Ltd v. Edwards Hot Water Systems (REPRODUCTION IN
THREE-DIMENSIONAL FORM: H.C.)
Kiama Constructions v. M.C. Casella Building Co. Pty Ltd (HOUSE PLANS:
S.C.(W.A.))
Mainbridge Industries Pty Ltd v. Whitewood & Ibbett Pty Ltd (ARTISTIC WORK:
REPRODUCTION: INFRINGEMENT: S.C.(NSW))
Ogden Industries Pty Ltd v. Kis (Australia) Ltd (INFRINGEMENT: DRAWINGS FOR
KEY BLANKS: S.C.(NSW))

Onus of Proof. *See* **Practice** *(Onus of proof)*

Operating Systems in ROM. *See* **Computer Topics**

Originality

Autodesk Inc. v. Dyason (COMPUTER PROGRAM: SUBSTANTIAL PART: H.C.)
Autodesk Inc. v. Dyason (No. 2) (COMPUTER PROGRAM: SUBSTANTIAL PART:
H.C.)
Easyfind (NSW) Pty Ltd v. Paterson (CALENDAR WITH ADVERTISEMENTS IN
PARTICULAR FORM: S.C.(NSW))

Kiama Constructions v. M.C. Casella Building Co. Pty Ltd (HOUSE PLANS: S.C.(W.A.))

Star Micronics Pty Ltd v. Five Star Computers Pty Ltd (SECONDARY INFRINGEMENT: Fed. Ct)

Ownership

Acorn Computer Ltd v. MCS Microcomputer System Pty Ltd (ASSIGNMENT: REQUIREMENT OF WRITING: EQUITABLE OWNERSHIP: JOINT OWNERSHIP: Fed. Ct)

Avtex Airservices Pty Ltd v. Bartsch (COMPUTERISED TEACHING SYSTEM OF WORKBOOKS, SLIDES AND COMPUTER PROGRAMS: Fed. Ct)

CBS Records Australia Ltd v. Guy Gross (MUSICAL WORK: SUBSISTENCE: AUTHORSHIP: Fed. Ct)

Cope Allman (Marrickville) Ltd v. Farrow (COMMISSIONED WORK: ENGRAVINGS: CONFIDENTIAL INFORMATION: COMPUTER PROGRAMS: S.C.(NSW))

De Garis v. Neville Jeffress Pidler Pty Ltd (PRESS-CLIPPING AND MEDIA MONITORING SERVICE: JOURNALISTS: CONTRACT OF SERVICE: Fed. Ct)

Enzed Holdings Ltd v. Wynthea Pty Ltd (COMMISSIONED WORK: FOREIGN AUTHOR: *Locus standi*: Fed. Ct)

Erica Vale Australia Pty Limited v. Thompson & Morgan (Ipswich) Limited (LITERARY WORK: ADAPTATION: CONTRACT: IMPLIED TERM: DAMAGES: COSTS INCURRED IN MITIGATION OF LOSS: LOST PROFITS: Fed. Ct)

Film Corporation of New Zealand v. Golden Editions Pty Ltd (INFRINGEMENT: PASSING OFF: DESCRIPTIVE OR DISTINCTIVE: MISLEADING OR DECEPTIVE CONDUCT: Fed. Ct)

Greenfield Products Pty Ltd v. Rover-Scott Bonnar Ltd (AGREEMENT FOR SALE OF BUSINESS: NO EXPRESS ASSIGNMENT: COPYRIGHT ASSIGNMENT IMPLIED: Fed. Ct)

O'Brien v. Komesaroff (LEGAL PRECEDENTS: Australia: H.C.)

Parallel Importation. *See* Importation

Parody

AGL Sydney Ltd v. Shortland County Council (INFRINGEMENT: REPLY TO COMPETITOR'S ADVERTISEMENT: TAKING ESSENTIAL FEATURES: Fed. Ct)

Performance in Public

Australasian Performing Right Association Ltd v. Commonwealth Bank of Australia (MUSICAL WORK: PERFORMED AT PLACE OF EMPLOYMENT: MEMBERS OF THE PUBLIC EXCLUDED: WHETHER PERFORMANCE IN PUBLIC: Fed. Ct)

Australasian Performing Right Association Ltd v. Jain (INFRINGEMENT: AUTHORISING ACTS: EXECUTIVE DIRECTOR: POWER TO AUTHORISE PERFORMANCE OF WORKS IN PUBLIC: Fed. Ct)

Australasian Performing Right Association Ltd v. Telstra Corporation Ltd (DIFFUSION SERVICE: WHETHER MUSIC HEARD BY TELEPHONE USERS PLACED ON HOLD CONSTITUTES A PERFORMANCE IN PUBLIC OR A BROADCAST TO THE PUBLIC: Fed. Ct)

Australasian Performing Right Association Ltd v. Tolbush Pty Ltd (AUTHORISATION: DIRECTORS: S.C.(Qd))

Rank Film Production Ltd v. Dodds (CINEMATOGRAPH FILM: S.C.(NSW))

Plans. *See also under* **House or Building Plans**

Pacific Dunlop Ltd v. Australian Rubber Gloves Pty Ltd (PRACTICE AND PROCEDURE: INSPECTION OF PROPERTY PRIOR TO ISSUING PROCEEDINGS: MACHINE FOR MANUFACTURE OF RUBBER GLOVES: PLANS: Fed. Ct)

Rebsechini v. Miles Laboratories (Aust.) Ltd (REPRODUCTION: COMMON PRODUCTS: Australia: S.C.(Vic.))

Practice

Account of profits

Ryan v. Lum (S.C.(NSW))

Z.S. Projects Pty Ltd v. G. & R. Investments Pty Ltd (S.C.(NSW))

Acquiescence

Led Builders Pty Ltd v. Masterton Homes (NSW) Pty Ltd (LACHES, ACQUIESCENCE AND DELAY: Fed. Ct)

Agreed statement of facts

CBS Records Australia Ltd v. Telmak Teleproducts (Aust.) Pty Ltd (SOUND RECORDINGS: SOUND-ALIKE RECORDS: WHETHER COPIES OF ORIGINAL ARTISTS: QUESTION TO BE TRIED ON AGREED STATEMENT OF FACTS: Fed. Ct)

Anton Piller

Apple Computer Inc. v. Rowney (FORM OF ORDER: S.C.(NSW))

Gianitsios v. Karagiannis (S.C.(NSW))

Polygram Records Pty Ltd v. Manash Records (Aust.) Pty Ltd (JURISDICTION: Fed. Ct)

Warman International Ltd v. Envirotech Australia Pty Ltd (EVIDENCE: PRIVILEGE AGAINST SELF-INCRIMINATION: Fed. Ct)

Appeal

Golden Editions Pty. Ltd v. Polygram Pty. Ltd (FACTUAL FINDINGS AND ERRORS OF LAW: Fed. Ct)

Interlego AG v. Tyco Industries Inc. (P.C.)

International Computers (Australia) Pty Ltd v. Franhaem Pty Ltd (STRIKING OUT: LEAVE TO APPEAL: S.C.(Vic.))

3D Geoshapes Australia Pty Ltd v. Registrar of Designs (APPLICATION FOR EXTENSION OF TIME REFUSED: Fed. Ct)

Consent orders

Easyfind (NSW) Pty Ltd v. Paterson (TERMS OF ORDER: DUTIES OF COUNSEL: S.C.(NSW))

Costs

Erica Vale Australia Pty Limited v. Thompson & Morgan (Ipswich) Limited (COSTS INCURRED IN MITIGATION OF LOSS: LOST PROFITS: Fed. Ct)

Damages

Autodesk Australia Pty Ltd v. Cheung (MEASURE OF COMPENSATORY DAMAGES: ADDITIONAL DAMAGES: Fed. Ct)

Bailey v. Namol Pty Ltd (COMPENSATORY DAMAGES: ASSESSMENT: CALCULATION BY REFERENCE TO EXPECTED PROFITS: AGGRAVATED OR EXEMPLARY DAMAGES: Fed. Ct)

Caj Amadio Constructions Pty Ltd v. Kitchen (MEASURE OF DAMAGES: WHETHER ASSESSED ON BASIS OF LOSS OF PROFITS OR ON LOSS OF LICENCE FEE: S.C.(S.A.))

Cowan v. Avel Pty Ltd (THREATS: COMPUTATION: LOSS OF SALES: EFFECT OF TAXABILITY OF PROFITS: Fed. Ct)

Dixon Investments Pty Ltd v. Hall (ALLEGED COPYING OF PROJECT HOUSE DESIGN DRAWINGS: Fed. Ct)

Erica Vale Australia Pty Limited v. Thompson & Morgan (Ipswich) Limited (CONTRACT: IMPLIED TERM: COSTS INCURRED IN MITIGATION OF LOSS: LOST PROFITS: Fed. Ct)

Kalamazoo (Aust.) Pty Ltd v. Compact Business Systems Pty Ltd (MATTERS AFFECTING RIGHT TO DAMAGES: H.C.)

Mateffy Perl Nagy Pty Ltd v. Devefi Pty Ltd (MEASURE OF DAMAGES: Fed. Ct)

Milpurrurru v. Indofurn Pty Ltd (ABORIGINAL ARTWORK: IMPORTATION: REPRODUCTION: SUBSTANTIAL PART: CONVERSION DAMAGES: Fed. Ct)

Namol Pty Ltd v. A.W. Baulderstone Pty Ltd (ASSESSMENT OF DAMAGES: Fed. Ct)

Ryan v. Lum (DAMAGES OR ACCOUNT OF PROFITS: BREACHES ON PACKAGING OF PRODUCTS: S.C.(NSW))

Star Micronics Pty Ltd v. Five Star Computers Pty Ltd (LACK OF CLEAR EVIDENCE OF ACTUAL DAMAGE: DAMAGES FOR LOSS OF REPUTATION: DAMAGES FOR DIMINUTION IN VALUE OF COPYRIGHT: Fed. Ct)

Television Broadcasts Ltd v. Tu (ASSESSMENT OF DAMAGES: USE BY RESPONDENTS OF APPLICANTS' VIDEO CASSETTES AFTER EXPIRY OF LICENCE: FLAGRANT BREACH: CALCULATION OF DAMAGES: Fed. Ct)

Z.S. Projects Pty Ltd v. G. & R. Investments Pty Ltd (ACCOUNT OF PROFITS: S.C.(NSW))

Delay

Led Builders Pty Ltd v. Masterton Homes (NSW) Pty Ltd (LACHES, ACQUIESCENCE AND DELAY: Fed. Ct)

Delivery up

Milpurrurru v. Indofurn Pty Ltd (Fed. Ct)

Discretion

Zeccola v. Universal City Studios Inc. (INTERLOCUTORY INJUNCTION: Fed. Ct)

Evidence

A.C. Corp. Pty Ltd v. Jadon Investments Pty Ltd (EXPERT EVIDENCE: ADMISSIBILITY: H.C.)

Broderbund Software Inc. v. Computermate Products (Australia) Pty Ltd (USE OF SURVEY EVIDENCE: Fed. Ct)

Clune v. Collins Angus & Robertson Publishers Pty Ltd (ALLEGED ORAL LICENCE: EVIDENCE: Fed. Ct)

Interlego AG v. Croner Trading Pty Ltd (SURVEY EVIDENCE: Fed. Ct)

Rosebank Plastics Pty Ltd v. Duncan & Wigley Pty Ltd (VISUAL COMPARISON: EXPERT EVIDENCE: Fed. Ct)

Warman International Ltd v. Envirotech Australia Pty Ltd (PRIVILEGE AGAINST SELF-INCRIMINATION: Fed. Ct)

Forfeiture

Irvine v. Hanna-Rivero (ORDER FOR FORFEITURE OF HARDWARE USED IN MAKING INFRINGING COPIES: Fed. Ct)

Irvine v. Carson (CRIMINAL OFFENCE: ORDER FOR FORFEITURE OF COMPUTERS USED FOR MAKING INFRINGING COPIES: Fed. Ct)

Inspection

Pacific Dunlop Ltd v. Australian Rubber Gloves Pty Ltd (INSPECTION OF PROPERTY PRIOR TO ISSUING PROCEEDINGS: Fed. Ct)

Injunctions

De Garis v. Neville Jeffress Pidler Pty Ltd (Fed. Ct)

Dronpool Pty Ltd v. Hunter (S.C.(NSW))

Tom Cruise and Nicole Kidman v. Southdown Press Pty Ltd (Fed. Ct)

Interlocutory injunctions

Bevis v. Lyons (BALANCE OF CONVENIENCE: S.C.(Qd))

CBS Records Australia Ltd v. Telmak Teleproducts (Aust.) Pty Ltd (EVIDENCE OF CONFUSION: COSTS: Fed. Ct)

Fai Insurances Ltd v. Advance Bank Australia Ltd (Fed. Ct)

Festival Records Pty Ltd v. Tenth Raymond Management Pty Ltd (S.C.(Vic.))

ITP Pty Ltd v. United Capital Pty Ltd (S.C.(Qd))

Zeccola v. Universal City Studios Inc. (DISCRETION: Fed. Ct)

Interlocutory injunction—balance of convenience

Bevis v. Lyons (CROSS APPLICATION BY DEFENDANT: S.C.(Qd))

Wood v. Kempe (INFRINGEMENT: ARCHITECT'S PLANS: Fed. Ct)

Jurisdiction

Autodesk Inc. v. Dyason (No. 2) (JURISDICTION TO REHEAR: H.C.)

Hart (S.W.) & Co. Pty Ltd v. Edwards Hot Water Systems (Fed. Ct)

Oehlschlager's Opposition (Pat. Off.)

Polygram Records Pty Ltd v. Manash Records (Aust.) Pty Ltd (ANTON PILLER ORDERS: Fed. Ct)

Knowledge

A.C. Corp. Pty Ltd v. Jadon Investments Pty Ltd (WHETHER FRAUDULENT IMITATION: KNOWLEDGE OF DESIGN: H.C.)

Golden Editions Pty. Ltd v. Polygram Pty. Ltd (STATUTORY INTERPRETATION: RELEVANCE OF KNOWLEDGE OF IDENTITY OF OWNER: Fed. Ct)

Laches

Led Builders Pty Ltd v. Masterton Homes (NSW) Pty Ltd (LACHES, ACQUIESCENCE AND DELAY: Fed. Ct)

Locus standii

Enzed Holdings Ltd v. Wynthea Pty Ltd (FOREIGN AUTHOR: Fed. Ct)

Lost profits

Erica Vale Australia Pty Limited v. Thompson & Morgan (Ipswich) Limited (DAMAGES: COSTS INCURRED IN MITIGATION OF LOSS: Fed. Ct)

Onus of proof

Avel Pty Ltd v. Multicoin Amusements Pty Ltd (H.C.)

Richsell Pty Ltd v. Khoury (PRIOR PUBLICATION AND USE: Fed. Ct)
Ryan v. Lum (S.C.(NSW))
Sebel & Co. Ltd v. National Art Metal Co. Pty Ltd (S.C.(NSW))

Procedure

Australian Tape Manufacturers Association Ltd v. Commonwealth of Australia
(CHALLENGE TO VALIDITY OF PART OF COPYRIGHT ACT 1968: H.C.)
Hart (S.W.) & Co. Pty Ltd v. Edwards Hot Water Systems (REOPENING LITIGATION: Fed. Ct)
Pacific Dunlop Ltd v. Australian Rubber Gloves Pty Ltd (INSPECTION OF PROPERTY PRIOR TO ISSUING PROCEEDINGS: Fed. Ct)

Striking out

International Computers (Australia) Pty Ltd v. Franhaem Pty Ltd (LEAVE TO APPEAL: S.C.(Vic.))
Universal Press Pty Ltd v. Provest Ltd (APPLICATION TO STRIKE OUT STATEMENT OF CLAIM: Fed. Ct)

Summary judgment

Z.S. Projects Pty Ltd v. G. & R. Investments Pty Ltd (S.C.(NSW))

Survey evidence

Broderbund Software Inc. v. Computermate Products (Australia) Pty Ltd (Fed. Ct)
Interlego AG v. Croner Trading Pty Ltd (Fed. Ct)

Time limits

3D Geoshapes Australia Pty Ltd v. Registrar of Designs (APPLICATION FOR EXTENSION OF TIME REFUSED: Fed. Ct)

Prior Publication and Use

Richsell Pty Ltd v. Khoury (ONUS OF PROOF: Fed. Ct)

Procedure. *See* **Practice** (*Procedure*)

Registrability

Shacklady v. Atkins (DESIGN OF YACHT, WHETHER REGISTRABLE: Fed. Ct)

Reproduction

Accounting Systems 2000 (Developments) Pty Ltd v. CCH Australia Ltd
(SUBSTANTIAL PART: EFFECT OF EXPENDITURE OF TIME AND EFFORT IN DEVELOPING COMPUTER PROGRAM: Fed. Ct)
Accounting Systems 2000 (Developments) Pty Ltd v. CCH Australia Ltd
(SUBSTANTIAL PART: Fed. Ct)
Ainsworth Nominees Pty Ltd v. Andclar Pty Ltd (SUBSTANTIAL PART: USE OF DIFFERENT SYMBOLS AND FORMAT: Fed. Ct)
Autodesk Inc. v. Dyason (AUTHORISATION: WHETHER SUPPLY OF DEVICE ENABLING COMPUTER PROGRAM TO BE USED ON MORE THAN ONE COMPUTER AT A TIME MAY BE AUTHORISATION OF INFRINGEMENT: Fed. Ct)
Collier Constructions Pty Ltd v. Foskett Pty Ltd (SUBSTANTIAL PART: Fed. Ct)
Dixon Investments Pty Ltd v. Hall (PRINCIPLES GOVERNING SIMPLE AND COMMONPLACE DRAWINGS: SUBSTANTIAL PART: Fed. Ct)

Dronpool Pty Ltd v. Hunter (SUBSTANTIAL REPRODUCTION: S.C.(NSW))

Easyfind (NSW) Pty Ltd v. Paterson (SUBSTANTIAL PART: MISTAKE: UNILATERAL MISTAKE: TERMS OF CONSENT ORDERS: DUTIES OF COUNSEL: S.C.(NSW))

Gruzman Pty Ltd v. Percy Marks Pty Ltd (MATERIAL FORM: THREE-DIMENSIONAL VERSION OF A TWO-DIMENSIONAL WORK: S.C.(NSW))

Hart (S.W.) & Co. Pty Ltd v. Edwards Hot Water Systems (THREE-DIMENSIONAL FORM: NON-EXPERT TEST: H.C.)

Kevlacat Pty Ltd v. Trailcraft Marine Pty Ltd (DEFENCE: DUAL PROTECTION UNDER COPYRIGHT AND DESIGN LEGISLATION: Fed. Ct)

Mainbridge Industries Pty Ltd v. Whitewood & Ibbett Pty Ltd (NON-EXPERT DEFENCE: S.C.(NSW))

Mainbridge Industries Pty Ltd v. Whitewood & Ibbett Pty Ltd (THREE-DIMENSIONAL FORM: SIMILARITY: VISUAL COMPARISON: S.C.(NSW))

Ownit Homes Pty Ltd v. D. & F. Mancuso Investments Pty Ltd (ARCHITECT'S PLANS: SERIES OF DRAWINGS: SUBSTANTIAL PART: S.C.(Qd))

Rebsechini v. Miles Laboratories (Aust.) Ltd (PLANS: COMMON PRODUCTS: Australia: S.C.(Vic.))

Roland Corporation v. Lorenzo & Sons Pty Ltd (PARALLEL IMPORTATION AND SALE: IMPLIED LICENCE: Fed. Ct)

Universal Smo-King Ovens Pty Ltd v. Guinn (SUBSTANTIAL REPRODUCTION: S.C.(NSW))

Royalty

Australian Tape Manufacturers Association Ltd v. Commonwealth of Australia (BLANK TAPES: COLLECTING SOCIETY: CONSTITUTIONAL VALIDITY OF AMENDING LEGISLATION: H.C.)

WEA Records Pty Ltd v. Stereo FM Pty Ltd (OWNERS' AGENT: OWNERS' EXCLUSIVE LICENSEE: Cprt Trib.)

Shrink-Wrap Licence. *See* Licence

Sound Recordings

Australian Tape Manufacturers Association Ltd v. Commonwealth of Australia (UNAUTHORISED DOMESTIC COPYING: SCHEME FOR COMPENSATION: ROYALTY ON BLANK TAPES: COLLECTING SOCIETY: DISTRIBUTED TO COPYRIGHT OWNERS: CONSTITUTIONAL VALIDITY OF AMENDING LEGISLATION: H.C.)

CBS Records Australia Ltd v. Telmak Teleproducts (Aust.) Pty Ltd (SOUND-ALIKE RECORDS: WHETHER COPIES OF ORIGINAL ARTISTS: QUESTION TO BE TRIED ON AGREED STATEMENT OF FACTS: Fed. Ct)

CBS Records Australia Ltd v. Telmak Teleproducts (Aust.) Pty Ltd (RECORDS AND CASSETTES: SOUND-ALIKE RECORDINGS: WHETHER COPIES: Fed. Ct)

CBS Records Australia Ltd v. Telmak Teleproducts (Aust.) Pty Ltd (TRADE PRACTICES: SOUND-ALIKE RECORDINGS: EVIDENCE OF CONFUSION: PASSING OFF: INTERLOCUTORY INJUNCTION: COSTS: Fed. Ct)

Chrysalis Records Ltd v. Vere (INFRINGEMENT: IMPORTATION: S.C.(Qd))

Polygram Pty Ltd v. Golden Editions Pty Ltd (INFRINGEMENT: INNOCENT INFRINGEMENT: STATUTORY DEFENCES: Fed. Ct)

WEA International Inc. v. Hanimex Corporation Ltd (CONTRIBUTORY INFRINGEMENT: AUTHORISATION: ADVERTISEMENT FOR BLANK TAPE: Fed. Ct)

WEA Records Pty Ltd v. Stereo FM Pty Ltd (BROADCASTS: ROYALTY: OWNERS' AGENT: OWNERS' EXCLUSIVE LICENSEE: Cprt Trib.)

Sound-Alike Records. *See* **Sound Recordings**

Striking Out. *See* **Practice** (*Striking out*)

Subsistence

Barson Computers Australasia Ltd v. Southern Technology Pty Ltd (COMPUTER PROGRAMS: OPERATING SYSTEMS IN ROM: Fed. Ct)
CBS Records Australia Ltd v. Guy Gross (MUSICAL WORK: AUTHORSHIP: OWNERSHIP: Fed. Ct)
Easyfind (NSW) Pty Ltd v. Paterson (CALENDAR WITH ADVERTISEMENTS IN PARTICULAR FORM: ORIGINALITY: S.C.(NSW))
International Writing Institute v. Rimila Pty Ltd (Fed. Ct)
Led Builders Pty Ltd v. Masterton Homes (NSW) Pty Ltd (BUILDERS' PLANS: INFRINGEMENT: LACHES, ACQUIESCENCE AND DELAY: Fed. Ct)
Shacklady v. Atkins (DESIGN: REPRODUCTION: CORRESPONDING DESIGNS: WHETHER INFRINGEMENT OF COPYRIGHT: DESIGN OF YACHT, WHETHER REGISTRABLE: Fed. Ct)

Substantial Part

Accounting Systems 2000 (Developments) Pty Ltd v. CCH Australia Ltd (EFFECT OF EXPENDITURE OF TIME AND EFFORT IN DEVELOPING COMPUTER PROGRAM: Fed. Ct)
Ainsworth Nominees Pty Ltd v. Andclar Pty Ltd (INFRINGEMENT: DIFFERENT SECTIONS OF TABLE CONSTITUTING SEPARATE WORKS: USE OF DIFFERENT SYMBOLS AND FORMAT: Fed. Ct)
Autodesk Inc. v. Dyason (H.C.)
Autodesk Inc. v. Dyason (No. 2) (H.C.)
Avel Pty Ltd v. Wells (CIRCUIT LAYOUTS: Fed. Ct)
Barson Computers Australasia Ltd v. Southern Technology Pty Ltd (REVERSE ENGINEERING BY DISASSEMBLY: CONTRIBUTORY INFRINGEMENT: Fed. Ct)
CBS Records Australia Ltd v. Guy Gross (QUALITY AND QUANTITY DISTINGUISHED: Fed. Ct)
Collier Constructions Pty Ltd v. Foskett Pty Ltd (Fed. Ct)
Dixon Investments Pty Ltd v. Hall (WHAT CONSTITUTES: Fed. Ct)
Easyfind (NSW) Pty Ltd v. Paterson (CALENDAR WITH ADVERTISEMENTS IN PARTICULAR FORM: S.C.(NSW))
Ownit Homes Pty Ltd v. D. & F. Mancuso Investments Pty Ltd (ARCHITECT'S PLANS: S.C.(Qd))

Substantiality

Nationwide News Pty Ltd v. Copyright Agency Ltd (NEWSPAPERS, MAGAZINES AND PERIODICALS: JOURNALISTS COPYRIGHT: COMPILATION: INFRINGEMENT: COPYING OF SINGLE ITEM: Fed. Ct)

Summary Judgment. *See* **Practice** (*Summary judgment*)

Survey Evidence. *See* **Practice** (*Survey evidence*)

Threats

Avel Pty Ltd v. Multicoin Amusements Pty Ltd (H.C.)
Cowan v. Avel Pty Ltd (DAMAGES: COMPUTATION: LOSS OF SALES: EFFECT OF TAXABILITY OF PROFITS: Fed. Ct)

Multicoin Amusements Pty Ltd v. British Amusements (North Coast) Corporation
Pty Ltd: (S.C.(Qd))

Television Programmes

Amalgamated TV Services Pty. Ltd v. Foxtel Digital Cable Television Pty. Ltd
(BROADCASTING: RE-TRANSMISSION OF TELEVISION PROGRAMMES:
EXEMPTION FROM REGULATORY REGIME: Fed. Ct)

Three-Dimensional Objects

Greenfield Products Pty Ltd v. Rover-Scott Bonnar Ltd (MOULDS AND ARTICLES:
Fed. Ct)
Gruzman Pty Ltd v. Percy Marks Pty Ltd (REPRODUCTION IN A MATERIAL FORM:
IMPLIED LICENCE: ARCHITECTURAL PLANS AND DRAWINGS: S.C.(NSW))
Hart (S.W.) & Co. Pty Ltd v. Edwards Hot Water Systems (NON-EXPERT TEST:
H.C.)
Mainbridge Industries Pty Ltd v. Whitewood & Ibbett Pty Ltd (SIMILARITY: VISUAL
COMPARISON: S.C.(NSW))

Trade Mark, Copyright Proprietorship in

Arriba Pty Limited v. Cuisine To Go Pty Ltd (LOGO: LACK OF CANDOUR AS TO
ORIGIN: POSSIBILITY OF ORIGIN: Fed. Ct)
Koh Electronics Trading v. Libra Electronics Pty Ltd (COPYING OF OVERSEAS MARK:
AIPO)

Visual Comparison

Mainbridge Industries Pty Ltd v. Whitewood & Ibbett Pty Ltd (REPRODUCTION IN
THREE-DIMENSIONAL FORM: SIMILARITY: S.C.(NSW))
Rosebank Plastics Pty Ltd v. Duncan & Wigley Pty Ltd (EXPERT EVIDENCE AS TO
SIMILARITY: CONTENT OF STATEMENT OF NOVELTY: Fed. Ct)

Passing-off and Trade Practices

Account of Profits. *See* **Practice** (*Account of profits*)

Advertisements and Advertising

10th Cantanae Pty Ltd v. Shoshana Pty Ltd (USE OF NAME CORRESPONDING TO
THAT IN ADVERTISEMENT FOR VIDEO RECORDER OF WELL-KNOWN MEDIA
PERSONALITY: Fed. Ct)
Australian Consumers Association for Review of Trade Practices Commission
Authorisation of Certain Codes of the Media Council of Australia's Application
(TPT)
Barson Computers Australasia Ltd v. Southern Technology Pty Ltd (ADVERTISING
OF FUTURE PRODUCT: Fed. Ct)
Country Road Clothing Pty Ltd v. Najee Nominees Pty Ltd (COMPARATIVE
ADVERTISEMENT: FACTUAL ACCURACY: Fed. Ct)

Duracell Australia Pty Ltd v. Union Carbide Australia (COMPARATIVE ADVERTISING: MANNER IN WHICH ADVERTISING MAY MISLEAD: Fed. Ct)

Dynamic Lifter Pty Ltd v. Incitec Ltd (ADVERTISING BROCHURE: WHETHER REPRESENTATION ALLEGED REASONABLY DERIVED FROM BROCHURE: CLASS OF PEOPLE TO WHOM STATEMENT DIRECTED: Fed. Ct)

Hogan v. Pacific Dunlop Ltd (MISREPRESENTATION OF COMMERCIAL CONNECTION: IMPLIED BY USE OF IMAGE ASSOCIATED WITH CELEBRITY: CHARACTER MERCHANDISING, SPONSORSHIP AND TESTIMONIAL ADVERTISING: Fed. Ct)

Hogan v. Pacific Dunlop Ltd (ADVERTISEMENTS BASED ON SCENE FROM FILM: WHETHER ADVERTISEMENTS AMOUNTED TO MISREPRESENTATION AS TO COMMERCIAL ARRANGEMENT OF PERMISSION TO USE CHARACTER: Fed. Ct)

Hospitals Contribution Fund of Australia Ltd v. Switzerland Australia Health Fund Pty Ltd (COMPARATIVE ADVERTISING: WHETHER TRIAL JUDGE HAS POWER TO ORDER CORRECTIVE ADVERTISEMENT: Fed. Ct)

Industrial Equity Ltd v. North Broken Hill Holdings Ltd (ADVERTISEMENTS IN DEFENCE OF TAKEOVER BID: Fed. Ct)

Irish Distillers Ltd v. Smith & Son Pty Ltd (REPUTATION: Fed. Ct)

Janssen Pharmaceutica Pty Ltd v. Pfeizer Pty Ltd (MISLEADING ADVERTISING: MANDATORY INJUNCTION TO PUBLISH CORRECTION: Fed. Ct)

Just Jeans Pty Ltd v. Westco Jeans (Aust.) Pty Ltd (SIMILAR ADVERTISING SIGNS: Fed. Ct)

Makita (Australia) Pty Ltd v. Black & Decker (Australasia) Pty Ltd (COMPARATIVE ADVERTISING: REQUIREMENTS OF SUITABLE CORRECTIVE ADVERTISING: Fed. Ct)

Morgan & Banks Pty Ltd v. Select Personnel Pty Ltd (WHETHER ADVERTISEMENTS RELEVANTLY MISREPRESENTED: C.A.(NSW))

Narhex Australia Pty Ltd v. Sunspot Products Pty Ltd (ADVERTISING AND LABELLING REPRESENTATIONS AS TO QUALITIES AND PROVENANCE OF PRODUCT: CORRECTIVE ADVERTISING: Fed. Ct)

R. & C. Products Pty Ltd v. S. C. Johnson & Sons Pty Ltd (TELEVISION ADVERTISEMENTS: WHETHER ELEMENTS OF ADVERTISING ARE SO IDENTIFIED WITH ONE TRADER THAT THEIR USE BY A COMPETITOR WILL MISLEAD OR DECEIVE: Fed. Ct)

Snyman v. Cooper (ADVERTISEMENT IN BRISBANE Yellow Pages: Fed. Ct)

Sun Earth Homes Pty Ltd v. Australian Broadcasting Corp. (WHETHER TELECAST AN ADVERTISEMENT OR OTHER PUBLICATION IN CONNECTION WITH SUPPLY OF GOODS OR SERVICES: Fed. Ct)

Tobacco Institute of Australia Ltd v. Australian Federation of Consumer Organisations Inc. (ADVERTISEMENTS CLAIMING THAT PASSIVE SMOKING NOT SHOWN TO BE HARMFUL TO HEALTH OF NON-SMOKERS: Fed. Ct)

Typing Centre of NSW Pty Ltd v. Northern Business College Ltd (COMPARATIVE ADVERTISING: Fed. Ct)

Union Carbide Australia Ltd v. Duracell Australia Pty Ltd (COMPARATIVE ADVERTISING: POINT OF SALE MATERIAL: Fed. Ct)

WEA International Inc. v. Hanimex Corp. Ltd (RADIO ADVERTISEMENTS: Fed. Ct)

Aiding, Abetting, Counselling or Procuring

Tytel Pty Ltd v. Australian Telecommunications Commission (FALSE REPRESEN-TATIONS: MONOPOLISATION: Fed. Ct)

Anton Piller Order. *See* **Practice** (*Anton Piller order*)

Appeal. *See* **Practice** (*Appeal*)

Balance of Convenience. *See* **Practice** (*Interlocutory injunction*)

Cause of Action

Calmao Pty Ltd v. Stradbroke Waters Co-Owners Co-Operative Society Ltd (Fed. Ct)

Character Merchandising. *See* **Merchandising Rights**

Common Field of Activity

Hogan v. Pacific Dunlop Ltd (WHETHER ERRONEOUS ASSUMPTION DOCTRINE APPLIES: Fed. Ct)

Hutchence v. South Seas Bubble Co. Pty Ltd (TRADING NAME: REPUTATION: USE OF DISCLAIMING LABELS: EFFECT ON PURCHASERS: Fed. Ct)

Petersville Sleigh Ltd v. Sugarman (INNOCENT PASSING OFF: DECEPTION AND INJURY NOT INFERRED: S.C.(Vic.))

Comparative Advertising. *See* **Advertising**

Confusion

CBS Records Australia Ltd v. Telmak Teleproducts (Aust.) Pty Ltd (SOUND-ALIKE RECORDINGS: EVIDENCE OF CONFUSION: Fed. Ct)

Cue Design Pty Ltd v. Playboy Enterprises Pty Ltd (RELEVANT AUDIENCE: Fed. Ct)

Dodds Family Investments Pty Ltd (formerly Solar Tint Pty Ltd) v. Lane Industries Pty Ltd (DESCRIPTIVE TRADE NAMES: NECESSITY TO ACQUIRE A DISTINCTIVE OR SECONDARY MEANING: EVIDENCE OF MERE CONFUSION OR BELIEF BY INDIVIDUALS INSUFFICIENT: COSTS: Fed. Ct)

Irish Distillers Ltd v. Smith & Son Pty Ltd (MERE CONFUSION OR UNCERTAINTY: INTENTION TO DECEIVE: Fed. Ct)

Morgan & Banks Pty Ltd v. Select Personnel Pty Ltd (SUFFICIENCY OF EVIDENCE: C.A.(NSW))

Really Useful Group Ltd (The) v. Gordon & Gotch Ltd (LIKELIHOOD TO DECEIVE OR MISLEAD THE PUBLIC: INTERLOCUTORY INJUNCTION: Fed. Ct)

Wingate Marketing Pty Ltd v. Levi Strauss & Co. (SECOND-HAND JEANS: ALTERATIONS: CONFUSION AS TO ORIGIN: Fed. Ct)

Consequential Loss

Henjo Investments Pty Ltd v. Collins Marrickville Pty Ltd (CONSEQUENTIAL LOSSES FLOWING FROM CONDUCT OF BUSINESS BY PURCHASER: ASSESSMENT OF DAMAGES FOR BURDEN OF UNECONOMIC LEASE: Fed. Ct)

Consumer Protection

10th Cantanae Pty Ltd v. Shoshana Pty Ltd (Fed. Ct) (APPEAL: Fed. Ct)

Barton v. Croner Trading Pty Ltd (LABELS: Fed. Ct)

Bentley Fragrances Pty Ltd v. GDR Consultants Pty Ltd (MISLEADING OR DECEPTIVE CONDUCT: Fed. Ct)

Bevanere Pty Ltd v. Lubidineuse (SALE OF BUSINESS: MISLEADING OF DECEPTIVE CONDUCT: Fed. Ct)

Sabazo Pty Ltd v. Ruddiman (LOWER QUALITY GOODS: ASSESSMENT: S.C.(NSW))
Sent v. Jet Corp. of Australia Pty Ltd (COMPENSATORY RELIEF: TIME LIMITATION: H.C.)
Snyman v. Cooper (INJURY TO GOODWILL: ASSESSMENT OF DAMAGES: EXEMPLARY DAMAGES NOT AWARDED: Fed. Ct)
Snyman v. Cooper (WRONGFUL APPROPRIATION OF GEOGRAPHICAL LOCATION OF A BUSINESS: WHETHER ACTIONABLE: EXEMPLARY DAMAGES: Fed. Ct)
Squibb & Sons Pty Ltd v. Tully Corp. Pty Ltd (DECLARATION OF VOID CONTRACT: INTEREST: Fed. Ct)
Star Micronics Pty Ltd v. Five Star Computers Pty Ltd (BREACH OF COPYRIGHT, PASSING OFF AND MISLEADING OR DECEPTIVE CONDUCT: DAMAGES FOR LOSS OF REPUTATION: DAMAGES FOR DIMINUTION IN VALUE OF COPYRIGHT: Fed. Ct)
Surge Licensing Inc. v. Pearson (LOSS OF REPUTATION: Fed. Ct)
Typing Centre of NSW Pty Ltd v. Northern Business College Ltd (COMPARATIVE ADVERTISING: ALLEGED SUPERIORITY OF COURSES OFFERED BY RESPONDENTS: Fed. Ct)
Wickham v. Associated Pool Builders Pty Ltd (AGREEMENT: USE OF BUSINESS NAME: ADEQUACY OF DAMAGES: Fed. Ct)

Deception

Bargal Pty Ltd v. Force (Australia: H.C.)
Bill Acceptance Corp. Ltd v. GWA Ltd (Fed. Ct)
Braemar Appliances Pty Ltd v. Rank Electric Housewares Ltd (INTERLOCUTORY INJUNCTION: Fed. Ct)
Capelvenere v. Omega Development Corp. Pty Ltd (Fed. Ct)
Happy Landings Pty Ltd v. Magazine Promotions Pty Ltd (SIMILAR BOOK TITLES: Fed. Ct)
Hogan v. Pacific Dunlop Ltd (IMPLIED BY USE OF IMAGE ASSOCIATED WITH CELEBRITY: RELEVANCE OF SURROUNDING CIRCUMSTANCES: CHARACTER MERCHANDISING, SPONSORSHIP AND TESTIMONIAL ADVERTISING: Fed. Ct)
HTX International Pty Ltd v. Semco Pty Ltd (Fed. Ct)
Kettle Chip Company Pty Ltd v. Apand Pty Ltd (USE OF NAME, SYMBOL AND GET-UP RESEMBLING THOSE OF APPLICANT: Fed. Ct)
Lego Australia Pty Ltd v. Pauls (Merchant) Pty Ltd (Fed. Ct)
Mildura Fruit Juices Pty Ltd v. Bannerman (Fed. Ct)
Petersville Sleigh Ltd v. Sugarman (PASSING OFF: PRINCIPLES TO BE APPLIED: WHETHER TANGIBLE PROBABILITY OF DECEPTION OR OF DAMAGE: S.C.(Vic.))
Really Useful Group Ltd (The) v. Gordon & Gotch Ltd (LIKELIHOOD TO DECEIVE OR MISLEAD THE PUBLIC: INTERLOCUTORY INJUNCTION: Fed. Ct)
Stack v. Coast Securities (No. 9) Pty Ltd (Fed. Ct)
Taco Bell Pty Ltd v. Taco Company of Australia Ltd (PASSING OFF: Fed. Ct)
TEC & Thomas (Aust.) Pty Ltd v. Matsumiya Computer Co. Pty Ltd (USE OF REGISTERED BUSINESS NAME: Fed. Ct)
Universal Telecasters (Queensland) Ltd v. Ainsworth Consolidated Ind Ltd (STATEMENTS IN NEWSCAST: Fed. Ct)
Visa International Services Association v. Beiser Corp. Pty Ltd (No. 1) (CONSUMER PROTECTION: Fed. Ct)

Delay. See Practice (Delay)

Directors' Liability

Bateman v. Slatyer (Fed. Ct)

Sent v. Jet Corp. of Australia Pty Ltd (CAUSING A MISREPRESENTATION: Fed. Ct)

Disclaimer

Hutchence v. South Seas Bubble Co. Pty Ltd (COMMON FIELD OF ACTIVITY: USE OF
DISCLAIMING LABELS: EFFECT ON PURCHASERS: Fed. Ct)
Sony Music Australia Ltd v. Tansing (UNAUTHORISED RECORDINGS: EFFECT OF
DISCLAIMER ON PACKAGING: Fed. Ct)
State Government Insurance Corp. v. Government Insurance office of NSW
(SUFFICIENCY OF DISCLAIMER: Fed. Ct)

Discovery. *See* Practice (*Discovery*)

Discretion. *See* Practice (*Discretion*)

Evidence. *See* Practice (*Evidence*)

Ex Parte Order. *See* Practice (*Ex parte order*)

False Representation or Statement

Advanced Hair Studio Pty Ltd v. TVW Enterprises Ltd (CONSUMER'S STATEMENT
OF COMPLAINT: Fed. Ct)
Lovatt v. Consolidated Magazines Pty Ltd (ALLEGED FALSE STATEMENTS AS TO
QUALITY AND SPONSORSHIP: Fed. Ct)
QDSV Holdings Pty Ltd v. Trade Practices Commission (LABELS ATTACHED TO TOY
KOALAS: ALL COMPONENTS MANUFACTURED ABROAD: ASSEMBLY IN
AUSTRALIA: LABEL USING MADE IN AUSTRALIA: WHETHER MISLEADING OR
DECEPTIVE: TEST: Fed. Ct)

Fraudulent Intent

Carlton and United Breweries Ltd v. Hahn Brewing Co. Ltd (RELEVANCE IN
PASSING OFF ACTION: VALUE IN EVIDENCE: Fed. Ct)

Get-up

Conagra Inc. v. McCain Foods (Aust.) Pty Ltd (PACKAGING: SIMILARITY OF NAME
AND GET-UP: WHETHER MISREPRESENTATION OF SPONSORSHIP, APPROVAL
OR AFFILIATION: Fed. Ct)
Conagra Inc. v. McCain Foods (Aust.) Pty Ltd (PACKAGING: SIMILARITY OF NAME
AND GET-UP TO THAT USED BY APPLICANT FOR SIMILAR GOODS OUTSIDE THE
JURISDICTION: Fed. Ct)
Kettle Chip Company Pty Ltd v. Apand Pty Ltd (USE OF NAME, SYMBOL AND GET-UP
RESEMBLING THOSE OF APPLICANT: TEST FOR COMPARISON: SIMILARITY OF
PACKAGING: COMMON ELEMENTS: USE OF WORD "KETTLE" TO DESCRIBE
GOODS: Fed. Ct)
New Zealand Natural Pty Ltd v. Granny's Natural New Zealand Ice Cream Pty Ltd
(RELEVANT MEMBERS OF THE PUBLIC: EFFECT OF SIMILARITY OR
DISSIMILARITY OF GET-UP: SIMILARITY OF FUNCTION: Fed. Ct)

R. & C. Products Pty Ltd v. Sterling Winthrop Pty Ltd (TRADE MARK: INFRINGEMENT: PINE ACTION/PINE-O-CLEEN: Fed. Ct)

S. & M. Motor Repairs Pty Ltd v. Caltex Oil (Australia) Pty Ltd (PETROL STATIONS: SIGNS ON PUMPS: S.C.(NSW))

Telmak Teleproducts (Australia) Pty Ltd v. Coles Myer Ltd (PACKAGING: SIMILARITY OF NAME AND GET-UP TO THAT USED BY APPELLANT FOR SIMILAR GOODS: PASSING OFF: ELEMENTS: Fed. Ct)

Thai World Import & Export Co. Ltd v. Shuey Shing Pty Ltd (PROOF OF GEOGRAPHICAL COVERAGE OF THE ALLEGED REPUTATION AND REPRESENTATION: Fed. Ct)

TJM Products Pty Ltd v. A. & P. Tyres Pty Ltd (SIMILAR BUSINESS NAMES: LOGOS: Fed. Ct)

Goodwill

Attorney-General (ex rel. Elisha) v. Holy Apostolic and Catholic Church of the East (Assyrian) Australia NSW Parish Association (FALSE OR MISLEADING CONDUCT: WHETHER IN TRADE OR COMMERCE: USE OF CHURCH NAME BY BODY FORMED FOR RELIGIOUS PURPOSES: S.C.(NSW))

Ocean Pacific Sunwear Ltd v. Ocean Pacific Enterprises Pty Ltd (APPLICANT ESTABLISHED REPUTATION AND GOODWILL IN TRADE MARKS IN RESPECT OF CLOTHING: Fed. Ct)

Triple Five Corp. v. Walt Disney Productions (ELEMENTS: S.C.)

Interim Injunction. *See* **Practice** (*Interim injunction*)

Interlocutory Injunctions. *See* **Practice** (*Interlocutory injunctions*)

Joint Claim. *See* **Practice** (*Joint claim*)

Jurisdiction. *See* **Practice** (*Jurisdiction*)

Labels

QDSV Holdings Pty Ltd v. Trade Practices Commission (FALSE AND MISLEADING STATEMENTS: ALL COMPONENTS MANUFACTURED ABROAD: ASSEMBLY IN AUSTRALIA: LABEL USING "MADE IN AUSTRALIA": WHETHER MISLEADING OR DECEPTIVE: TEST: Fed. Ct)

Laches. *See* **Practice** (*Laches*)

Leave. *See* **Practice** (*Leave*)

Legal Professional Privilege

Arnotts Ltd v. Trade Practices Commission (CONDITIONS: Fed. Ct)

Logo: Lack of Candour as to Origin
Arriba Pty Limited v. Cuisine To Go Pty Ltd (POSSIBILITY OF ORIGIN: Fed. Ct)

Made in Australia

QDSV Holdings Pty Ltd v. Trade Practices Commission (FALSE AND MISLEADING STATEMENTS: LABELS ATTACHED TO TOY KOALAS: ALL COMPONENTS MANUFACTURED ABROAD: ASSEMBLY IN LABEL USING "MADE IN AUSTRALIA": WHETHER MISLEADING OR DECEPTIVE: TEST: Fed. Ct)

Mandatory Injunction. *See* **Practice** (*Mandatory injunction*)

Mareva Injunction. *See* **Practice** (*Mareva injunction*)

Merchandising Rights

10th Cantanae Pty Ltd v. Shoshana Pty Ltd (CHARACTER MERCHANDISING: INNOCENT INFRINGEMENT: Fed. Ct)

Hogan v. Koala Dundee Pty Ltd (ASSIGNMENT OF RIGHT TO USE SUCH IMAGE: Fed. Ct)

Hogan v. Pacific Dunlop Ltd (IMPLIED BY USE OF IMAGE ASSOCIATED WITH CELEBRITY: RELEVANCE OF SURROUNDING CIRCUMSTANCES: CHARACTER MERCHANDISING: Fed. Ct)

Hogan v. Pacific Dunlop Ltd (CHARACTER MERCHANDISING: ADVERTISEMENTS BASED ON SCENE FROM POPULAR FILM: Fed. Ct)

Misleading or Deceptive Conduct or Statements

10th Cantanae Pty Ltd v. Shoshana Pty Ltd (Fed. Ct)

Abundant Earth Pty Ltd v. R. & C. Products Pty Ltd (SIMILAR NAMED GOODS: Fed. Ct)

Advanced Hair Studio Pty Ltd v. TVW Enterprises Ltd (FALSE STATEMENT: CONSUMER'S STATEMENT OF COMPLAINT: INTERIM INJUNCTION: Fed. Ct)

ASX Operations Pty Ltd v. Pont Data Australia Pty Ltd (WHETHER OBLIGED BY CONTRACT TO ENGAGE IN: Fed. Ct)

Attorney-General (ex rel. Elisha) v. Holy Apostolic and Catholic Church of the East (Assyrian) Australia NSW Parish Association (WHETHER IN TRADE OR COMMERCE: USE OF CHURCH NAME BY BODY FORMED FOR RELIGIOUS PURPOSES: S.C.(NSW))

Australian Ocean Line Pty Ltd v. West Australian Newspapers Ltd (PUBLICATION OF NEWS: Fed. Ct)

Australian Society of Accountants v. Federation of Australian Accountants Inc. (USE OF LETTERS "CPA": Fed. Ct)

Australian Telecommunications Corporation v. Hutchison Telecommunications (Australia) Ltd (SIMILARITY OF NEW TRADING NAME HUTCHISON TELECOMS TO WELL ESTABLISHED NAME TELECOM: Fed. Ct)

Barry v. Lake Jindabyne Reservation Centre Pty Ltd (SIMILAR BUSINESS NAMES: Fed. Ct)

Barson Computers Australasia Ltd v. Southern Technology Pty Ltd (ADVERTISING OF FUTURE PRODUCT: Fed. Ct)

Bateman v. Slatyer (SALE OF STORE FRANCHISE: REPRESENTATIONS ABOUT PROFITABILITY: DIRECTORS' LIABILITY: Fed. Ct)

Bentley Fragrances Pty Ltd v. GDR Consultants Pty Ltd (Fed. Ct)

Bevanere Pty Ltd v. Lubidineuse (SALE OF BUSINESS: Fed. Ct)

Calmao Pty Ltd v. Stradbroke Waters Co-Owners Co-Operative Society Ltd (CAUSE OF ACTION: Fed. Ct)

Communication Credit Union Ltd v. National Westminster Finance Australia Ltd (Fed. Ct)

Conagra Inc. v. McCain Foods (Aust.) Pty Ltd (PACKAGING: GET-UP: SIMILARITY OF NAME AND GET-UP TO THAT USED BY APPLICANT FOR SIMILAR GOODS OUTSIDE THE JURISDICTION: Fed. Ct)

Concrete Constructions (NSW) Pty Ltd v. Nelson (IN TRADE OR COMMERCE: FALSE REPRESENTATION BY FOREMAN TO FELLOW EMPLOYEE: H.C.)

Construction Industry Long Service Leave Board v. Odco Pty Ltd (PUBLICATION OF STATEMENTS IN BROCHURE: Fed. Ct)

Copperart Pty Ltd v. Floan (REPRESENTATION AS TO FUTURE EVENTS: Fed. Ct)

Country Road Clothing Pty Ltd v. Najee Nominees Pty Ltd (COMPARATIVE ADVERTISEMENT: INVITATION TO COMPARE DIFFERENT PRODUCTS: Fed. Ct)

Crocker v. Papunya Tula Artists Pty Ltd (SECOND EDITION OF BOOK: Fed. Ct)

Deane v. Brian Hickey Invention Research Pty Ltd (SALE OF BUSINESS: FORM OF RELIEF: Fed. Ct)

Duracell Australia Pty Ltd v. Union Carbide Australia (COMPARATIVE ADVERTISING: MANNER IN WHICH COMPARATIVE ADVERTISING MAY MISLEAD: Fed. Ct)

Elconnex Pty Ltd v. Gerard Industries Pty Ltd (FAILURE TO DISCLOSE DEFECT RENDERING USE OF GOODS SOLD ILLEGAL: WHETHER MISLEADING AND DECEPTIVE CONDUCT: Fed. Ct)

Elders IXL Ltd v. Australian Estates Pty Ltd (USE OF NAME OF OLD ESTABLISHED BUSINESS: USE OF ABANDONED NAME: RESIDUAL GOODWILL: Fed. Ct)

Fai Insurances Ltd v. Advance Bank Australia Ltd (AMBIGUOUS STATEMENTS COMPARING COMPANY PROFITS: Fed. Ct)

Fido Dido Inc. v. Venture Stores (Retailers) Pty Ltd (Fed. Ct)

Film Corporation of New Zealand v. Golden Editions Pty Ltd (COPYRIGHT: INFRINGEMENT: DESCRIPTIVE OR DISTINCTIVE: Fed. Ct)

Gates v. CML Assurance Society Ltd (FALSE REPRESENTATION: MEASURE OF DAMAGES: H.C.)

Gollel Holdings Pty Ltd v. Kenneth Maurer Funerals Pty Ltd (INTERLOCUTORY INJUNCTION: BALANCE OF CONVENIENCE: DELAY: PROOF OF LOSS: Fed. Ct)

Greg Cotton Motors Pty Ltd v. Neil & Ross Neilson Pty Ltd (RIGHT TO USE OWN NAME: Fed. Ct)

Henjo Investments Pty Ltd v. Collins Marrickville Pty Ltd (SILENCE CONSTITUTING MISLEADING CONDUCT: CONSTRUCTIVE NOTICE OF MATTERS DISCOVERABLE ON PROPER INQUIRY: Fed. Ct)

Honey v. Australian Airlines Ltd (USE OF PHOTOGRAPH OF CHAMPION AMATEUR ATHLETE IN CONDUCT OF BUSINESS ACTIVITIES: Fed. Ct)

Horwitz Grahame Books Ltd v. Performance Publications Pty Ltd (STATEMENTS MADE IN MAGAZINE SUGGESTING CONNECTION WITH ANOTHER MAGAZINE: INTERLOCUTORY INJUNCTION: Fed. Ct)

Hospitals Contribution Fund of Australia Ltd v. Switzerland Australia Health Fund Pty Ltd (COMPARATIVE ADVERTISING: WHETHER TRIAL JUDGE HAS POWER TO ORDER CORRECTIVE ADVERTISEMENT: Fed. Ct)

James v. Australia & New Zealand Banking Group Ltd (FINANCIAL ADVICE INDUCING AGREEMENT: Fed. Ct)

Janssen Pharmaceutica Pty Ltd v. Pfeizer Pty Ltd (MANDATORY INJUNCTION TO PUBLISH CORRECTION: Fed. Ct)

John Baptiste Nella v. Kingia Pty Ltd (SALE OF BUSINESS: REPRESENTATION AS TO PROFITABILITY: Fed. Ct)

Just Jeans Pty Ltd v. Westco Jeans (Aust.) Pty Ltd (SIMILAR ADVERTISING SIGNS: Fed. Ct)

Kelly Services Inc. v. Drake Personnel Ltd (WHETHER NECESSARY FOR BUSINESS TO BE CARRIED ON IN AUSTRALIA: Fed. Ct)

Lotus Development Corporation v. Mayne Nickless Ltd (REPRESENTATIONS BY ONE EMPLOYEE OF A CORPORATION TO ANOTHER: Fed. Ct)

Lovatt v. Consolidated Magazines Pty Ltd (ALLEGED FALSE STATEMENTS AS TO QUALITY AND SPONSORSHIP: PRESCRIBED INFORMATION PROVIDER: Fed. Ct)

Merv Brown Pty Ltd v. David Jones (Aust.) Pty Ltd (Fed. Ct)

Miniskips Ltd v. Sheltan Pty Ltd (FRANCHISE AGREEMENT: TERMINATION: RELIEF AGAINST FORFEITURE: Fed. Ct)

MIPS Computer Systems Inc. v. MIPS Computer Resources Pty Ltd (COMPANY TRADING IN NAME SUBSTANTIALLY SIMILAR TO ESTABLISHED COMPETITORS: Fed. Ct)

Moon's Products Pty Ltd v. Herbs of Gold Pty Ltd (SIMILARLY NAMED PRODUCTS: CELERY 2000+: Fed. Ct)

Munro v. Tooheys Ltd (REPRESENTATION THAT A CUSTOMER CAN DRINK NOT INSIGNIFICANT AMOUNTS OF LIGHT BEER AND NOT EXCEED PRESCRIBED ALCOHOL LIMIT: Fed. Ct)

Narhex Australia Pty Ltd v. Sunspot Products Pty Ltd (ADVERTISING AND LABELLING REPRESENTATIONS AS TO QUALITIES AND PROVENANCE OF PRODUCT: CORRECTIVE ADVERTISING: FACTORS RELEVANT: Fed. Ct)

New Zealand Natural Pty Ltd v. Granny's Natural New Zealand Ice Cream Pty Ltd (TRADING UNDER NAME INCLUDING ALL ELEMENTS OF APPLICANT'S NAME: NO SECONDARY MEANING ALLEGED: Fed. Ct)

Nylex Corp. Ltd v. Sabco Ltd (SIMILAR PRODUCTS: DISCOVERY: IDENTITY OF SUPPLIER OR DISTRIBUTOR: Fed. Ct)

Paragon Shoes Pty Ltd v. Paragini Distributors (NSW) Pty Ltd (COPYING OF PRODUCT STYLE COMBINED WITH SIMILARITY OF NAME: DIFFERENCE IN PRODUCT PRICE: Fed. Ct)

Peter Isaacson Publications Pty Ltd v. Nationwide News Pty Ltd (DAMAGES: Fed. Ct)

Pirtek Fluid Systems Pty Ltd v. Kaydon Holdings Pty Ltd (FRANCHISE AGREEMENT: FRANCHISEE IN FINANCIAL DIFFICULTIES: WHETHER MISLEADING FORECASTS BY FRANCHISOR: Fed. Ct)

R. & C. Products Pty Ltd v. S.C. Johnson & Sons Pty Ltd (TELEVISION ADVERTISEMENTS: DISTINCTION DRAWN BETWEEN COMPETING PRODUCTS: Fed. Ct)

Rosebank Plastics Pty Ltd v. Duncan & Wigley Pty Ltd (FALSE REPRESENTATION AS TO SPONSORSHIP, APPROVAL AND AFFILIATION: Fed. Ct)

Service Station Association Ltd v. Berg Bennett & Associates Pty Ltd (RIVAL TRADE PUBLICATIONS: Fed. Ct)

Siddons Pty Ltd v. Stanley Works Pty Ltd (REPRESENTATION AS TO ORIGIN: MADE IN AUSTRALIA: USE OF AUSTRALIA ON GOODS: Fed. Ct)

Snyman v. Cooper (REPRESENTATION IN TELECOM *Yellow Pages*: WHETHER CONDUCT INVOLVED USE OF TELEPHONIC SERVICES: KNOWINGLY ASSISTING IN CONTRAVENTION: Fed. Ct)

Squibb & Sons Pty Ltd v. Tully Corp. Pty Ltd (OBLIGATION ON RECIPIENT OF INFORMATION TO INVESTIGATE: Fed. Ct)

Star Micronics Pty Ltd v. Five Star Computers Pty Ltd (MEANING OF FRAUD IN CONTEXT OF PASSING OFF: Fed. Ct)

State Government Insurance Corp. v. Government Insurance office of NSW (LOGOS AND ACRONYMS OF STATE GOVERNMENT INSTRUMENTALITIES: WHETHER NECESSARY THAT CONDUCT SHOULD INDUCE OR BE LIKELY TO INDUCE SPECIFIC TRANSACTION: Fed. Ct)

Street v. Jedsminster Pty Ltd (USE OF SIMILAR DESCRIPTIVE NAMES: TWO MOTELS IN SMALL TOWN: CABOOLTURE MOTEL/CABOOLTURE HOTEL MOTEL INN: GEOGRAPHICALLY DESCRIPTIVE NAME: Fed. Ct)

Surge Licensing Inc. v. Pearson (NO EVIDENCE OF CONSUMER BEING ACTUALLY MISLED OR DECEIVED: LOSS OF REPUTATION: Fed. Ct)

Switzerland Australia Health Fund Pty Ltd v. Shaw (REMEDIES: ABSENCE OF DAMAGE: Fed. Ct)

Targetts Pty Ltd v. Target Aust. Pty Ltd (LOCAL TRADER SEEKING TO PREVENT LARGE TRADER FROM ENTERING MARKET IN SAME TRADE UNDER SIMILAR NAME AND LOGO: WHETHER CONSUMERS MISLED DESPITE DIFFERENT STYLES OF BUSINESS: Fed. Ct)

Telmak Teleproducts (Australia) Pty Ltd v. Coles Myer Ltd (DESCRIPTION OF PRODUCTS: PACKAGING GET-UP: Fed. Ct)

Thorp v. C.A. Imports Pty Ltd (ORIGIN OF GOODS: REASONABLE RELIANCE ON INFORMATION SUPPLIED BY ANOTHER PERSON: Fed. Ct)

Tiheti Pty Ltd v. Guard Dog Patrol & Security Services Pty Ltd (USE OF SIMILAR TRADING NAME: Fed. Ct)

TJM Products Pty Ltd v. A. & P. Tyres Pty Ltd (SIMILAR BUSINESS NAMES: LOGOS: GET-UP: Fed. Ct)

Tobacco Institute of Australia Ltd v. Australian Federation of Consumer Organisations Inc. (ADVERTISEMENTS CLAIMING THAT PASSIVE SMOKING NOT SHOWN TO BE HARMFUL TO HEALTH OF NON-SMOKERS: Fed. Ct)

Trade Practices Commission v. Glo Juice Co. Pty Ltd (MISREPRESENTATION AS TO STRENGTH OF RECONSTITUTED DRINK MADE FROM CONCENTRATE: Fed. Ct)

Trotman Australia Pty Ltd v. Hobsons Press (Australia) Pty Ltd (COMPARISON OF GRADUATE CAREER DIRECTORIES: EVIDENCE OF PERSONS ACTUALLY MISLED: Fed. Ct)

Typing Centre of NSW Pty Ltd v. Northern Business College Ltd (COMPARATIVE ADVERTISING: ALLEGED SUPERIORITY OF COURSES OFFERED BY RESPONDENTS: DAMAGES: Fed. Ct)

Tytel Pty Ltd v. Australian Telecommunications Commission (MONOPOLISATION: AIDED, ABETTED, COUNSELLED OR PROCURED: Fed. Ct)

Voyager Distributing Co. Pty Ltd v. Cherry Lane Fashion Group Ltd (Fed. Ct)

Westpac Banking Corporation v. Northern Metals Pty Ltd (RELATIONSHIP BETWEEN MISLEADING AND DECEPTIVE CONDUCT AND CONDUCT LIABLE TO MISLEAD THE PUBLIC: Fed. Ct)

Wheeler Grace & Pierucci Pty Ltd v. Wright (PREDICTION MADE IN UNQUALIFIED TERMS: IMPLIED REPRESENTATION THAT MAKER OF PREDICTION KNEW OF FACTS WHICH IN AN OBJECTIVE SENSE WOULD JUSTIFY HIS BELIEF: WHETHER MISLEADING OR DECEPTIVE: Fed. Ct)

Wickham v. Associated Pool Builders Pty Ltd (PROMOTIONS AGREEMENT BETWEEN SWIMMING CHAMPION AND POOL DISTRIBUTING COMPANY: Fed. Ct)

Winning Appliances Pty Ltd v. Dean Appliances Pty Ltd (ASSESSMENT OF DAMAGES: GENERAL DAMAGES: EVIDENCE: Fed. Ct)

Yardley of London (Australia) Pty Ltd v. Chapman & Lester The Sales Promotion Agency Pty Ltd (WHETHER CONDUCT OF AUSTRALIAN FOOTBALLER OF THE YEAR CREATED BY APPLICANT OR RESPONDENT: Fed. Ct)

Misrepresentation

Conagra Inc. v. McCain Foods (Aust.) Pty Ltd (MISREPRESENTATION OF SPONSORSHIP, APPROVAL OR AFFILIATION: Fed. Ct)

Henjo Investments Pty Ltd v. Collins Marrickville Pty Ltd (MEASURE OF DAMAGES IN RESPECT OF SALE OF RESTAURANT BUSINESS INDUCED BY MISREPRESENTATIONS: SILENCE CONSTITUTING MISLEADING CONDUCT: Fed. Ct)

Hogan v. Pacific Dunlop Ltd (COMMERCIAL CONNECTION: IMPLIED BY USE OF IMAGE ASSOCIATED WITH CELEBRITY: Fed. Ct)

Hogan v. Pacific Dunlop Ltd (WHETHER ADVERTISEMENTS AMOUNTED TO MISREPRESENTATION AS TO COMMERCIAL ARRANGEMENT OF PERMISSION TO USE CHARACTER: Fed. Ct)

Morgan & Banks Pty Ltd v. Select Personnel Pty Ltd (WHETHER ADVERTISEMENTS RELEVANTLY MISREPRESENTED: SUFFICIENCY OF EVIDENCE OF CONFUSION: C.A.(NSW))

Sent v. Jet Corp. of Australia Pty Ltd (CAUSING A MISREPRESENTATION: DIRECTORS: Fed. Ct)

Telmak Teleproducts (Australia) Pty Ltd v. Coles Myer Ltd (REQUIREMENT: WHETHER PROOF OF FRAUDULENT INTENT SUFFICIENT TO GROUND ACTION: Fed. Ct)

Testro Bros v. Tennant (INTERLOCUTORY INJUNCTION: S.C.)

Trade Practices Commission v. Glo Juice Co. Pty Ltd (STRENGTH OF RECONSTITUTED DRINK MADE FROM CONCENTRATE: Fed. Ct)

Triple Five Corp. v. Walt Disney Productions (CONFUSION: GENERAL RECOLLECTION: EVIDENCE: SURVEY EVIDENCE: ROLE OF APPELLATE COURT: DAMAGE: USE OF TRADE MARK: FROM DIFFERENT JURISDICTION: S.C.)

Motions. *See* **Practice** (*Motions*)

Practice

Account of profits

Hogan v. Pacific Dunlop Ltd (Fed. Ct)
Kettle Chip Company Pty Ltd v. Apand Pty Ltd (Fed. Ct)

Anton Piller order

Golf Lynx v. Golf Scene Pty Ltd (S.C.(NSW))

Appeal

10th Cantanae Pty Ltd v. Shoshana Pty Ltd (Fed. Ct)
Dodds Family Investments Pty Ltd v. Lane Industries Pty Ltd (Fed. Ct)
Tiheti Pty Ltd v. Guard Dog Patrol & Security Services Pty Ltd (Fed. Ct)
Visa International Services Association v. Beiser Corp. Pty Ltd (No. 2) (Fed. Ct)

Contempt

Trade Practices Commission v. Glo Juice Co. Pty Ltd (Fed. Ct)

Costs

CBS Records Australia Ltd v. Telmak Teleproducts (Aust.) Pty Ltd (Fed. Ct)
Dodds Family Investments Pty Ltd v. Lane Industries Pty Ltd (Fed. Ct)

Damages

Winning Appliances Pty Ltd v. Dean Appliances Pty Ltd (ASSESSMENT: GENERAL DAMAGES: EVIDENCE: Fed. Ct)

Delay

Gollel Holdings Pty Ltd v. Kenneth Maurer Funerals Pty Ltd (Fed. Ct)
MIPS Computer Systems Inc. v. MIPS Computer Resources Pty Ltd (Fed. Ct)
Selectrode Industries Inc. v. Selectrode Pty Ltd (INTERLOCUTORY INJUNCTION: BALANCE OF CONVENIENCE: ADEQUACY OF DAMAGES: Fed. Ct)
Wickham v. Associated Pool Builders Pty Ltd (Fed. Ct)

Discovery

Carlton and United Breweries Ltd v. Hahn Brewing Co. Ltd (FRAUDULENT INTENT NOT PLEADED: RELEVANCE IN PASSING OFF ACTION: VALUE IN EVIDENCE: Fed. Ct)
Nylex Corp. Ltd v. Sabco Ltd (Fed. Ct)

Discretion

Duracell Australia Pty Ltd v. Union Carbide Australia (Fed. Ct)
Henjo Investments Pty Ltd v. Collins Marrickville Pty Ltd (Fed. Ct)
Tiheti Pty Ltd v. Guard Dog Patrol & Security Services Pty Ltd (Fed. Ct)
Trade Practices Commission v. Glo Juice Co. Pty Ltd (Fed. Ct)

Evidence

Carlton and United Breweries Ltd v. Hahn Brewing Co. Ltd (FRAUDULENT INTENT
   NOT PLEADED: VALUE IN EVIDENCE: Fed. Ct)
CBS Records Australia Ltd v. Telmak Teleproducts (Aust.) Pty Ltd (Fed. Ct)
Chase Manhattan Overseas Corp. v. Chase Corp. Ltd (Fed. Ct)
Dodds Family Investments Pty Ltd v. Lane Industries Pty Ltd (Fed. Ct)
Interlego AG v. Croner Trading Pty Ltd (Fed. Ct)
Irish Distillers Ltd v. Smith & Son Pty Ltd (Fed. Ct)
Kettle Chip Company Pty Ltd v. Apand Pty Ltd (Fed. Ct)
Morgan & Banks Pty Ltd v. Select Personnel Pty Ltd (C.A.(NSW))
O'Connor v. Stevenson (Fed. Ct)
Rent A Ute Pty Ltd v. Golden 44 Pty Ltd (Fed. Ct)
Rosebank Plastics Pty Ltd v. Duncan & Wigley Pty Ltd (Fed. Ct)
Star Micronics Pty Ltd v. Five Star Computers Pty Ltd (Fed. Ct)
State Government Insurance Corp. v. Government Insurance Office of NSW (Fed.
   Ct)
Surge Licensing Inc. v. Pearson (Fed. Ct)
Trotman Australia Pty Ltd v. Hobsons Press (Australia) Pty Ltd (Fed. Ct)
Triple Five Corp. v. Walt Disney Productions (SURVEY EVIDENCE: ROLE OF
   APPELLATE COURT: S.C.)
Winning Appliances Pty Ltd v. Dean Appliances Pty Ltd (MISLEADING AND
   DECEPTIVE CONDUCT: ASSESSMENT OF DAMAGES: GENERAL DAMAGES: Fed.
   Ct)

Ex parte order

Golf Lynx v. Golf Scene Pty Ltd (ANTON PILLER ORDER: S.C.(NSW))

Interim or interlocutory injunctions

Arriba Pty Limited v. Cuisine To Go Pty Ltd (COPYRIGHT: LOGO: LACK OF
   CANDOUR AS TO ORIGIN: POSSIBILITY OF ORIGIN: Fed. Ct)
Australian Telecommunications Corporation v. Hutchison Telecommunications
   (Aust.) Ltd (BALANCE OF CONVENIENCE: Fed. Ct)
Braemar Appliances Pty Ltd v. Rank Electric Housewares Ltd (Fed. Ct)
CBS Records Australia Ltd v. Telmak Teleproducts (Aust.) Pty Ltd (COSTS: Fed. Ct)
Fai Insurances Ltd v. Advance Bank Australia Ltd (Fed. Ct)
Fido Dido Inc. v. Venture Stores (Retailers) Pty Ltd (Fed. Ct)
Franconi Holdings Pty Ltd v. Gunning (S.C.(W.A.))
Gollel Holdings Pty Ltd v. Kenneth Maurer Funerals Pty Ltd (BALANCE OF
   CONVENIENCE: DELAY: PROOF OF LOSS: Fed. Ct)
Horwitz Grahame Books Ltd v. Performance Publications Pty Ltd (Fed. Ct)
Jelly's Music Hall Inc. v. Tripl-M Broadcasting Co. (Fed. Ct)
MIPS Computer Systems Inc. v. MIPS Computer Resources Pty Ltd (BALANCE OF
   CONVENIENCE: Fed. Ct)
Moon's Products Pty Ltd v. Herbs of Gold Pty Ltd (WHETHER CASE LIKELY TO
   SUCCEED AT TRIAL: Fed. Ct)
Nicholas v. Borg (BALANCE OF CONVENIENCE: S.C.(S.A.))
Pacific Hotels Pty Ltd v. Asian Pacific International Ltd (Fed. Ct)

Selectrode Industries Inc. v. Selectrode Pty Ltd (DELAY: BALANCE OF CONVENIENCE: ADEQUACY OF DAMAGES: Fed. Ct)
Sony Music Australia Ltd v. Tansing (Fed. Ct)
Street v. Jedsminster Pty Ltd (BALANCE OF CONVENIENCE: Fed. Ct)
Targetts Pty Ltd v. Target Aust. Pty Ltd (Fed. Ct)
Testro Bros v. Tennant (S.C.)
Visa International Services Association v. Beiser Corp. Pty Ltd (No. 2) (APPEAL: Fed. Ct)
Voyager Distributing Co. Pty Ltd v. Cherry Lane Fashion Group Ltd (Fed. Ct)
Wickham v. Associated Pool Builders Pty Ltd (GRANT: ADEQUACY OF DAMAGES: Fed. Ct)

Interlocutory injunction—adequacy of damages

Selectrode Industries Inc. v. Selectrode Pty Ltd (DELAY: BALANCE OF CONVENIENCE: Fed. Ct)
Wickham v. Associated Pool Builders Pty Ltd (GRANT: Fed. Ct)

Interlocutory injunction—balance of convenience

Australian Telecommunications Corporation v. Hutchison Telecommunications (Australia) Ltd (Fed. Ct)
Gollel Holdings Pty Ltd v. Kenneth Maurer Funerals Pty Ltd (DELAY: PROOF OF LOSS: Fed. Ct)
Miniskips Ltd v. Sheltan Pty Ltd (Fed. Ct)
MIPS Computer Systems Inc. v. MIPS Computer Resources Pty Ltd (Fed. Ct)
Nicholas v. Borg (S.C.(S.A.))
Selectrode Industries Inc. v. Selectrode Pty Ltd (INTERLOCUTORY INJUNCTION: DELAY: ADEQUACY OF DAMAGES: Fed. Ct)
Street v. Jedsminster Pty Ltd (Fed. Ct)
Sun Earth Homes Pty Ltd v. Australian Broadcasting Corp. (Fed. Ct)

Interlocutory injunction—likelihood of success at trial

Moon's Products Pty Ltd v. Herbs of Gold Pty Ltd (Fed. Ct)

Interviews with public

Chase Manhattan Overseas Corp. v. Chase Corp. Ltd (EVIDENCE: PRACTICE: Fed. Ct)

Jurisdiction

Carlton & United Breweries Ltd v. Castlemaine Tooheys Ltd (H.C.)
Carlton & United Breweries Ltd v. Tooth & Co. Ltd (Fed. Ct: S.C.(NSW))
Conagra Inc. v. McCain Foods (Aust.) Pty Ltd (SIMILARITY OF NAME AND GET-UP TO THAT USED BY APPLICANT FOR SIMILAR GOODS OUTSIDE THE JURISDICTION: Fed. Ct)
Grace Bros Pty Ltd v. Magistrates, Local Court of New South Wales (JURISDICTION OF FEDERAL COURT: Fed. Ct)
Jackson v. Sterling Industries Ltd (MAREVA INJUNCTION: Fed. Ct)
Turelin Nominees Pty Ltd v. Dainford Ltd (Fed. Ct)

Laches

MIPS Computer Systems Inc. v. MIPS Computer Resources Pty Ltd (Fed. Ct)

Leave

Sent v. Jet Corp. of Australia Pty Ltd (LEAVE TO AMEND STATEMENT OF CLAIM: H.C.)

Mandatory injunction

Janssen Pharmaceutica Pty Ltd v. Pfeizer Pty Ltd (MANDATORY INJUNCTION TO PUBLISH CORRECTION: Fed. Ct)

Mareva injunction

Jackson v. Sterling Industries Ltd (JURISDICTION: DAMAGES: Fed. Ct)

Motion for stay

Simplicity Funerals Ltd v. Simplicity Funerals Pty Ltd (PERPETUAL STAY: PREVIOUS UNSUCCESSFUL PROCEEDINGS IN SUPREME COURT: Fed. Ct)

Onus of proof

Faessler v. Neale (Fed. Ct)

Order for restitution

Henjo Investments Pty Ltd v. Collins Marrickville Pty Ltd (CIRCUMSTANCES: Fed. Ct)

Power of judge

Honey v. Australian Airlines Ltd (WEIGHT TO BE GIVEN TO CONCLUSIONS OF PRIMARY JUDGE: Fed. Ct)
Hospitals Contribution Fund of Australia Ltd v. Switzerland Australia Health Fund Pty Ltd (WHETHER TRIAL JUDGE HAS POWER TO ORDER CORRECTIVE ADVERTISEMENT: Fed. Ct)
Tiheti Pty Ltd v. Guard Dog Patrol & Security Services Pty Ltd (APPEAL FROM SINGLE JUDGE'S ORDER FOR RECORDED MESSAGE REDIRECTING INQUIRIES: WHETHER JUDGE'S DISCRETION MISCARRIED: Fed. Ct)

Proof

Gollel Holdings Pty Ltd v. Kenneth Maurer Funerals Pty Ltd (PROOF OF LOSS: Fed. Ct)
Hogan v. Koala Dundee Pty Ltd (WHETHER PROOF OF FRAUD NECESSARY: Fed. Ct)
Telmak Teleproducts (Australia) Pty Ltd v. Coles Myer Ltd (WHETHER PROOF OF FRAUDULENT INTENT SUFFICIENT TO GROUND ACTION: Fed. Ct)
Thai World Import & Export Co. Ltd v. Shuey Shing Pty Ltd (PROOF OF GEOGRAPHICAL COVERAGE OF THE ALLEGED REPUTATION AND REPRESENTATION: Fed. Ct)

Serious question to be tried

Miniskips Ltd v. Sheltan Pty Ltd (Fed. Ct)

Statement of claim

Sent v. Jet Corp. of Australia Pty Ltd (LEAVE TO AMEND: H.C.)

Survey evidence

Interlego AG v. Croner Trading Pty Ltd (Fed. Ct)
Kettle Chip Company Pty Ltd v. Apand Pty Ltd (ADMISSIBILITY: Fed. Ct)
State Government Insurance Corp. v. Government Insurance Office of NSW (Fed. Ct)
Triple Five Corp. v. Walt Disney Productions (ROLE OF APPELLATE COURT: S.C.)

Time limitation

Sent v. Jet Corp. of Australia Pty Ltd (H.C.)

Undertaking

Jackson v. Sterling Industries Ltd (FAILURE OF COURT TO OBTAIN: EFFECT: Fed. Ct)
S. & M. Motor Repairs Pty Ltd v. Caltex Oil (Australia) Pty Ltd (S.C.(NSW))

Quality of Goods or Services

Lovatt v. Consolidated Magazines Pty Ltd (ALLEGED FALSE STATEMENTS AS TO
   QUALITY AND SPONSORSHIP: Fed. Ct)
Sabazo Pty Ltd v. Ruddiman (LOWER QUALITY GOODS: S.C.(NSW))

Prosecution

Gardam v. George Wills & Co. Ltd (Fed. Ct)
Lennox v. Megray Pty Ltd (FALSE REPRESENTATION OF APPROVAL: Fed. Ct)
O'Connor v. Stevenson (WHETHER CIVIL OR CRIMINAL: WHETHER SEVERAL
   PROSECUTIONS TO PROCEED IN JOINT OR SEPARATE TRIALS: Fed. Ct)

Protection of Goodwill. *See* Goodwill

Publication of Correction

Janssen Pharmaceutica Pty Ltd v. Pfeizer Pty Ltd (MANDATORY INJUNCTION TO
   PUBLISH CORRECTION: Fed. Ct)
Hospitals Contribution Fund of Australia Ltd v. Switzerland Australia Health Fund
   Pty Ltd (WHETHER TRIAL JUDGE HAS POWER TO ORDER CORRECTIVE
   ADVERTISEMENT: Fed. Ct)
Janssen Pharmaceutica Pty Ltd v. Pfeizer Pty Ltd (MANDATORY INJUNCTION TO
   PUBLISH CORRECTION: Fed. Ct)
Makita (Australia) Pty Ltd v. Black & Decker (Australasia) Pty Ltd (REQUIREMENTS
   OF SUITABLE CORRECTIVE ADVERTISING: Fed. Ct)
Narhex Australia Pty Ltd v. Sunspot Products Pty Ltd (CORRECTIVE ADVERTISING:
   FACTORS RELEVANT: Fed. Ct)
Trotman Australia Pty Ltd v. Hobsons Press (Australia) Pty Ltd (PRINCIPLES
   GOVERNING ORDER FOR CORRECTIVE PUBLICATIONS AT INTERLOCUTORY
   STAGE: Fed. Ct)

Representations

10th Cantanae Pty Ltd v. Shoshana Pty Ltd (APPROVAL OF GOODS: Fed. Ct)
Bateman v. Slatyer (PROFITABILITY: Fed. Ct)
Conagra Inc. v. McCain Foods (Aust.) Pty Ltd (MISREPRESENTATION OF
   SPONSORSHIP, APPROVAL OR AFFILIATION: Fed. Ct)
Concrete Constructions (NSW) Pty Ltd v. Nelson (REPRESENTATION BY FOREMAN
   TO FELLOW EMPLOYEE: H.C.)
Copperart Pty Ltd v. Floan (FUTURE EVENTS: Fed. Ct)
Crocodile Marketing Ltd v. Griffith Vintners Pty Ltd (ALCOHOL, CALORIE AND
   OTHER CONTENT OF WINE: S.C.(NSW))
Dynamic Lifter Pty Ltd v. Incitec Ltd (ADVERTISING BROCHURE: WHETHER
   REPRESENTATION ALLEGED REASONABLY DERIVED FROM BROCHURE: Fed.
   Ct)
Gardam v. George Wills & Co. Ltd (FALSELY REPRESENTING GOODS TO BE OF
   PARTICULAR STANDARD: Fed. Ct)
Gates v. CML Assurance Society Ltd (MEASURE OF DAMAGES: H.C.)
Grace Bros Pty Ltd v. Magistrates, Local Court of New South Wales (ORIGIN OF
   GOODS: Fed. Ct)

Henjo Investments Pty Ltd v. Collins Marrickville Pty Ltd (SALE OF BUSINESS INDUCED BY MISREPRESENTATIONS: SILENCE: Fed. Ct)

Hogan v. Pacific Dunlop Ltd (COMMERCIAL CONNECTION: Fed. Ct)

Honey v. Australian Airlines Ltd (FALSE REPRESENTATION AS TO SPONSORSHIP, APPROVAL OR AFFILIATION: Fed. Ct)

Interlego AG v. Croner Trading Pty Ltd (SURVEY EVIDENCE: Fed. Ct)

John Baptiste Nella v. Kingia Pty Ltd (PROFITABILITY: Fed. Ct)

Lennox v. Megray Pty Ltd (FALSE REPRESENTATION OF APPROVAL: Fed. Ct)

Lotus Development Corporation v. Mayne Nickless Ltd (REPRESENTATIONS BY ONE EMPLOYEE OF A CORPORATION TO ANOTHER: Fed. Ct)

Makita (Australia) Pty Ltd v. Black & Decker (Australasia) Pty Ltd (ALLEGED REPRESENTATIONS AS TO PERFORMANCE OF PRODUCT: Fed. Ct)

Morgan & Banks Pty Ltd v. Select Personnel Pty Ltd (WHETHER ADVERTISEMENTS RELEVANTLY MISREPRESENTED: C.A.(NSW))

Morton v. Black (REPRESENTATIONS BY TELEPHONE: WHETHER WITHIN PRINCIPLE OF *Bevanere v. Lubidineuse*: Fed. Ct)

Munro v. Tooheys Ltd (REPRESENTATION THAT A CUSTOMER CAN DRINK NOT INSIGNIFICANT AMOUNTS OF LIGHT BEER AND NOT EXCEED PRESCRIBED ALCOHOL LIMIT: Fed. Ct)

Narhex Australia Pty Ltd v. Sunspot Products Pty Ltd (QUALITIES AND PROVENANCE OF PRODUCT: Fed. Ct)

Rosebank Plastics Pty Ltd v. Duncan & Wigley Pty Ltd (FALSE REPRESENTATION AS TO SPONSORSHIP, APPROVAL AND AFFILIATION: Fed. Ct)

Sent v. Jet Corp. of Australia Pty Ltd (CAUSING A MISREPRESENTATION: DIRECTORS: Fed. Ct)

Siddons Pty Ltd v. Stanley Works Pty Ltd (ORIGIN: MADE IN AUSTRALIA: USE OF AUSTRALIA ON GOODS: Fed. Ct)

Snyman v. Cooper (REPRESENTATION IN TELECOM *Yellow Pages*: WHETHER CONDUCT INVOLVED USE OF TELEPHONIC SERVICES: Fed. Ct)

Telmak Teleproducts (Australia) Pty Ltd v. Coles Myer Ltd (REQUIREMENT OF MISREPRESENTATION: WHETHER PROOF OF FRAUDULENT INTENT SUFFICIENT: Fed. Ct)

Testro Bros v. Tennant (S.C.)

Thai World Import & Export Co. Ltd v. Shuey Shing Pty Ltd (WHETHER REPUTATION HAD FALLEN INTO DESUETUDE BY TIME OF ALLEGED REPRESENTATION: PROOF OF GEOGRAPHICAL COVERAGE OF ALLEGED REPUTATION AND REPRESENTATION: Fed. Ct)

Thorp v. C.A. Imports Pty Ltd (ORIGIN OF GOODS: REASONABLE RELIANCE ON INFORMATION SUPPLIED BY ANOTHER PERSON: Fed. Ct)

Trade Practices Commission v. Glo Juice Co. Pty Ltd (STRENGTH OF RECONSTITUTED DRINK MADE FROM CONCENTRATE: Fed. Ct)

Tytel Pty Ltd v. Australian Telecommunications Commission (MONOPOLISATION: AIDED, ABETTED, COUNSELLED OR PROCURED: Fed. Ct)

Wheeler Grace & Pierucci Pty Ltd v. Wright (IMPLIED REPRESENTATION THAT MAKER OF PREDICTION KNEW OF FACTS WHICH IN AN OBJECTIVE SENSE WOULD JUSTIFY HIS BELIEF: Fed. Ct)

Yarmirr v. Australian Telecommunications Corp. (IMPLIED REPRESENTATION: WHETHER RELIANCE OR DAMAGE: Fed. Ct)

Reputation

Conagra Inc. v. McCain Foods (Aust.) Pty Ltd (WHETHER NECESSARY TO HAVE A PLACE OF BUSINESS WITHIN THE JURISDICTION TO MAINTAIN ACTION: Fed. Ct)

Hutchence v. South Seas Bubble Co. Pty Ltd (COMMON FIELD OF ACTIVITY: Fed. Ct)
Irish Distillers Ltd v. Smith & Son Pty Ltd (DISBELIEF OF EVIDENCE: MERE
    CONFUSION OR UNCERTAINTY: Fed. Ct)
Morgan & Banks Pty Ltd v. Select Personnel Pty Ltd (WHETHER REPUTATION
    ESTABLISHED: C.A.(NSW))
Nicholas v. Borg (MELBOURNE CUP: S.C.(S.A.))
Ocean Pacific Sunwear Ltd v. Ocean Pacific Enterprises Pty Ltd (REPUTATION AND
    GOODWILL IN TRADE MARKS IN RESPECT OF CLOTHING: Fed. Ct)
Peter Isaacson Publications v. Nationwide News Pty Ltd (EXCLUSIVE REPUTATION:
    UNFAIR COMPETITION: Fed. Ct)
Star Micronics Pty Ltd v. Five Star Computers Pty Ltd (DAMAGES FOR LOSS OF
    REPUTATION: Fed. Ct)
Surge Licensing Inc. v. Pearson (LOSS OF REPUTATION: DAMAGES: Fed. Ct)
Thai World Import & Export Co. Ltd v. Shuey Shing Pty Ltd (WHETHER ANY
    REPUTATION HAD FALLEN INTO DESUETUDE BY THE TIME OF THE ALLEGED
    REPRESENTATION: PROOF OF GEOGRAPHICAL COVERAGE OF THE ALLEGED
    REPUTATION AND REPRESENTATION: Fed. Ct)
Triple Five Corp. v. Walt Disney Productions (ELEMENTS: GOODWILL OR
    REPUTATION: MISREPRESENTATION: S.C.)

Residual Goodwill. *See* **Goodwill**

Restitution

Henjo Investments Pty Ltd v. Collins Marrickville Pty Ltd (ORDER FOR
    RESTITUTION: CIRCUMSTANCES: Fed. Ct)

Sale of Business

Bevanere Pty Ltd v. Lubidineuse (MISLEADING OF DECEPTIVE CONDUCT: Fed. Ct)
Deane v. Brian Hickey Invention Research Pty Ltd (FORM OF RELIEF: Fed. Ct)
John Baptiste Nella v. Kingia Pty Ltd (REPRESENTATION AS TO PROFITABILITY: Fed.
    Ct)
Winning Appliances Pty Ltd v. Dean Appliances Pty Ltd (ASSIGNMENT OF TRADING
    NAME: WHETHER GOODWILL ASSIGNED: Fed. Ct)

Secondary Meaning

Dodds Family Investments Pty Ltd v. Lane Industries Pty Ltd (ACQUISITION OF
    DISTINCTIVE OR SECONDARY MEANING: EVIDENCE REQUIRED: MERE
    CONFUSION OR BELIEF INSUFFICIENT: Fed. Ct)
New Zealand Natural Pty Ltd v. Granny's Natural New Zealand Ice Cream Pty Ltd
    (NO SECONDARY MEANING ALLEGED: Fed. Ct)
Telmak Teleproducts (Australia) Pty Ltd v. Coles Myer Ltd (PACKAGING OF SIMILAR
    PRODUCTS: LABELLED WITH SAME DESCRIPTIVE WORDS: NO SECONDARY
    MEANING ACQUIRED: Fed. Ct)

Serious Question to be Tried. *See* **Practice** (*Serious question to be tried*)

Similar Fact Evidence. *See* **Practice** (*Evidence*)

Similar Names, Trade Names or Business Names

Abundant Earth Pty Ltd v. R. & C. Products Pty Ltd (SIMILAR NAMED GOODS: Fed. Ct)

Australian Telecommunications Corporation v. Hutchison Telecommunications (Australia) Ltd (SIMILARITY OF NEW TRADING NAME TO WELL-ESTABLISHED NAME: CORPORATIONS IN COMPETITION: Fed. Ct)

Barry v. Lake Jindabyne Reservation Centre Pty Ltd (SIMILAR BUSINESS NAMES: Fed. Ct)

Bridges v. Bridge Stockbrokers Ltd (SIMILAR TRADE NAMES: Fed. Ct)

Conagra Inc. v. McCain Foods (Aust.) Pty Ltd (SIMILARITY OF NAME AND GET-UP: WHETHER MISREPRESENTATION OF SPONSORSHIP, APPROVAL OR AFFILIATION: Fed. Ct)

Happy Landings Pty Ltd v. Magazine Promotions Pty Ltd (SIMILAR BOOK TITLES: Fed. Ct)

Independent Locksmiths (NSW) Pty Ltd v. Aardvark (A.) Master Locksmiths Pty Ltd (SIMILAR NAMES: TELEPHONE DIRECTORY ENTRIES: Fed. Ct)

Just Jeans Pty Ltd v. Westco Jeans (Aust.) Pty Ltd (SIMILAR ADVERTISING SIGNS: Fed. Ct)

Kettle Chip Company Pty Ltd v. Apand Pty Ltd (USE OF NAME, SYMBOL AND GET-UP RESEMBLING THOSE OF APPLICANT: SIMILARITY OF PACKAGING: COMMON ELEMENTS: Fed. Ct)

MIPS Computer Systems Inc. v. MIPS Computer Resources Pty Ltd (COMPANY TRADING IN ITS OWN NAME WHERE NAME SUBSTANTIALLY SIMILAR TO ESTABLISHED COMPETITORS: Fed. Ct)

Moon's Products Pty Ltd v. Herbs of Gold Pty Ltd (SIMILARLY NAMED PRODUCTS: CELERY 2000+: Fed. Ct)

New Zealand Natural Pty Ltd v. Granny's Natural New Zealand Ice Cream Pty Ltd (EFFECT OF SIMILARITY OR DISSIMILARITY OF GET-UP: SIMILARITY OF FUNCTION: Fed. Ct)

Nylex Corp. Ltd v. Sabco Ltd (SIMILAR PRODUCTS: Fed. Ct)

Paragon Shoes Pty Ltd v. Paragini Distributors (NSW) Pty Ltd (COPYING OF PRODUCT STYLE COMBINED WITH SIMILARITY OF NAME: Fed. Ct)

Prince Manufacturing Inc. v. ABAC Corp. Aust. Pty Ltd (SIMILAR GOODS: TENNIS RACQUETS: Fed. Ct)

Rent A Ute Pty Ltd v. Golden 44 Pty Ltd (SIMILAR NAME FOR SERVICES: Fed. Ct)

Street v. Jedsminster Pty Ltd (USE OF SIMILAR DESCRIPTIVE NAMES: TWO MOTELS IN SMALL TOWN: CABOOLTURE MOTEL/CABOOLTURE HOTEL MOTEL INN: Fed. Ct)

Targetts Pty Ltd v. Target Aust. Pty Ltd (TRADER SEEKING TO PREVENT LARGE TRADER ENTERING MARKET IN SAME TRADE UNDER SIMILAR NAME AND LOGO: Fed. Ct)

Telmak Teleproducts (Australia) Pty Ltd v. Coles Myer Ltd (SIMILARITY OF NAME AND GET-UP FOR SIMILAR GOODS: Fed. Ct)

Tiheti Pty Ltd v. Guard Dog Patrol & Security Services Pty Ltd (USE OF SIMILAR TRADING NAME: Fed. Ct)

TJM Products Pty Ltd v. A. & P. Tyres Pty Ltd (SIMILAR BUSINESS NAMES: Fed. Ct)

Triple Five Corp. v. Walt Disney Productions (USE OF TRADE MARK: FROM DIFFERENT JURISDICTION: S.C.)

Wingate Marketing Pty Ltd v. Levi Strauss & Co. (PHONETIC SIMILARITY: LEVI'S/ REVISE: Fed. Ct)

Statement of Claim. *See* **Practice** (*Statement of claim*)

Survey Evidence. *See* **Practice** (*Survey evidence*)

Time Limitation. *See* **Practice** (*Time limitation*)

Trade or Commerce

Attorney-General (ex rel. Elisha) v. Holy Apostolic and Catholic Church of the East
    (Assyrian) Australia NSW Parish Association (USE OF CHURCH NAME BY BODY
    FORMED FOR RELIGIOUS PURPOSES: S.C.(NSW))
Concrete Constructions (NSW) Pty Ltd v. Nelson (FALSE REPRESENTATION BY
    FOREMAN TO FELLOW EMPLOYEE: WHETHER CONDUCT IN TRADE OR
    COMMERCE: H.C.)
Faessler v. Neale (ASSOCIATION WITH NAME: ONUS OF PROOF: Fed. Ct)
Lotus Development Corporation v. Mayne Nickless Ltd (REPRESENTATIONS BY
    ONE EMPLOYEE OF A CORPORATION TO ANOTHER: Fed. Ct)

Trade Practices Act

Section 46

Little v. Registrar of High Court of Australia (Fed. Ct)

Section52

R. & C. Products Pty Ltd v. S.C. Johnson & Sons Pty Ltd (Fed. Ct)

Undertaking. *See* **Practice** (*Undertaking*)

Unfair Competition

Peter Isaacson Publications v. Nationwide News Pty Ltd (Fed. Ct)

Patents

Account of profits. *See* **Practice** (*Account of profits*)

Ambiguity

Atlas Powder Co. v. ICI Australia Operations Pty Ltd (FAIR BASIS: Pat. Off.)
Elconnex Pty Ltd v. Gerard Industries Pty Ltd (CONSTRUCTION: OBVIOUSNESS:
    PRINCIPLES: PETTY PATENT: Fed. Ct)
Peptide Technology Ltd v. The Wellcome Foundation Ltd (Pat. Off.)
Robertshaw Controls Co. v. GSA Industries Ltd (SUFFICIENCY: Pat. Off.)

Amendment of Register

Behringwerke AG (SUBSTITUTION OF NAME: CLERICAL ERROR: Pat. Off.)

Amendment of Specification

Acushnet Company v. Spalding Australia Pty Ltd (OPPOSITION: INTERPRETATION OF CLAIMS: INCLUSION OF PERCENTAGE RANGES IN CLAIMS: Pat. Off.)

Amcor Ltd v. Visy Board Pty Ltd (OPPOSITION TO GRANT: OPPOSITION TO AMENDMENT: Pat. Off.)

Atlas Powder Co. v. ICI Australia Operations Pty Ltd (OPPOSITION: AMBIGUITY: FAIR BASIS: Pat. Off.)

Baker v. Peuren Agencies Ltd (OPPOSITION: FAIR BASIS: DEFINITION NOT UNDERSTANDABLE: Pat. Off.)

Bally Gaming International Inc. v. Scandic International Pty Ltd (OPPOSITION: NOVELTY: OBVIOUSNESS: MANNER OF NEW MANUFACTURE: FAIR BASIS: SECTION 40: SMART CARD FOR DATA TRANSFER BETWEEN AMUSEMENT MACHINES AND CENTRAL COMPUTER: TIME FOR AMENDMENTS ALLOWED: AIPO)

Bolesta's (Dymtro) Application (LEAVE TO AMEND: SCOPE OF ACCEPTED CLAIMS: APPROPRIATENESS OF REASONS FOR AMENDMENTS: Pat. Off.)

Browne & Williamson Tobacco Corp. v. Philip Morris Inc. (No. 2) (OPPOSITION: WHETHER AMENDED CLAIM OUTSIDE SCOPE OF ORIGINAL: NEW OMNIBUS CLAIM: Pat. Off.)

Browne & Williamson Tobacco Corp. v. Philip Morris Inc. (Pat. Off.)

Dearborn Chemical Co. Ltd v. Rohm and Haas Co. (APPLICATION: OPPOSITION: OPPOSITION TO AMENDMENT: IN SUBSTANCE DISCLOSED: INCONSISTENCY: ESSENTIAL FEATURES: ALLOWABILITY: REFUSAL: AIPO)

Diamond Scientific Co. v. CSL Ltd (APPLICATION: OPPOSITION: STATEMENT OF GROUNDS AND PARTICULARS: ALLOWABILITY: AIPO)

Du Pont de Nemours (E.I.) & Co. v. DowElanco (OPPOSITION: STATEMENT OF GROUNDS AND PARTICULARS: REQUEST TO AMEND: REQUIREMENTS OF CONTENTS: AMENDMENT AFTER EVIDENCE FILED: AIPO)

Elazac Pty Ltd v. Commissioner of Patents (AMENDMENT: FAILURE TO OPPOSE: RIGHT OF APPEAL: AIPO)

Heinen v. Pancontinental Mining Ltd (OPPOSITION: UNSUCCESSFUL APPLICATION: SECTION 40 DEFECTS SUFFICIENTLY OVERCOME: Pat. Off.)

Heylen v. Davies Collison Cave (PETTY PATENT: EXTENSION: NOTICE: COMPLETE SPECIFICATION: IN SUBSTANCE DISCLOSED: FAIR BASIS: NOVELTY: INVENTIVE STEP: OBVIOUSNESS: EVIDENTIARY BURDEN: PATENT ATTORNEYS: COSTS: AIPO)

Kornelis' Kunsthars Producten Industrie BV v. W.R. Grace & Co. (CONSTRUCTION OF CLAIMS: NOT IN SUBSTANCE DISCLOSED: Fed. Ct)

Magee v. Farrell (OPPOSITION: Pat. Off.)

Merck & Co., Inc. v. Sankyo Co. Ltd (PROPOSED AMENDMENTS: TESTS: *Locus standii*: COMMISSIONER OF PATENTS: Fed. Ct)

Meyers v. Caterpillar Inc. (APPLICATION: OPPOSITION: COSTS: Pat. Off.)

Perkin-Elmer Corp. v. Varian Techtron Pty Ltd (OPPOSITION: Pat. Off.)

Philip Morris Inc. v. Brown and Williamson Tobacco Corp. (OPPOSITION: AMENDMENT: REQUEST TO AMEND: IN SUBSTANCE DISCLOSED: FAIR BASIS: COMPLETE SPECIFICATION: FURTHER REQUEST TO AMEND: PRACTICE AND PROCEDURE: AIPO)

Rescare Ltd v. Anaesthetic Supplies Pty Ltd (AMENDMENT OF CLAIMS: Fed. Ct)

Robertshaw Controls Co. v. GSA Industries Ltd (OPPOSITION: AMBIGUITY: SUFFICIENCY: Pat. Off.)

Secretary of State for Defence (U.K.) v. Rheinmetall GmbH (OPPOSITION: OBVIOUSNESS: MANNER OF NEW MANUFACTURE: WHETHER SUBSTANCE DISCLOSED: Pat. Off.)

Anticipation

Sankyo Company Ltd v. Merck & Co. Inc. (OPPOSITION: PRIOR CLAIMING: PRIOR
PUBLICATION: FAIR BASIS: Pat. Off.)
Seasonmakers (Australia) Pty Ltd v. North Coast Woodwool Pty Ltd (OPPOSITION:
OBVIOUSNESS: Pat. Off.)
Tetra Pak International AB v. J. Gadsden Pty Ltd (OPPOSITION: NOVELTY:
OBVIOUSNESS: COMMON GENERAL KNOWLEDGE: FAIR BASIS: Pat. Off.)
Thomas and Stohr's Application (PETTY PATENT: OPPOSITION TO EXTENSION:
COMPUTER INVENTION: OBVIOUSNESS: Pat. Off.)
United Kingdom Government (Secretary of State for Defence) v. Rheinmetall
GmbH (OPPOSITION: NOVELTY: OBVIOUSNESS: Pat. Off.)
Yamazaki Mazak Corporation v. Interact Machine Tools (NSW) Pty Ltd (PETTY
PATENT: INFRINGEMENT: OBVIOUSNESS: NOVELTY: CONVENTION PRIORITY
DATE: Fed. Ct)

Appeal. *See* **Practice** *(Appeal)*

Application

A Couple 'a Cowboys Pty Ltd v. Ward (OPPOSITION: AIPO)
American National Can Co. v. W.R. Grace & Co.-Conn. (OPPOSITION: COSTS:
AIPO)
B.F. Goodrich Co. v. ICI Australia Operations Pty Ltd (OPPOSITION: WHETHER
CLAIMS FAIRLY BASED: PRIOR PUBLICATION: OBVIOUSNESS: COMBINATION
INVENTION: MANNER OF NEW MANUFACTURE: PRIOR USE: PRIOR SECRET
USE: STANDARD OF PROOF: AIPO)
Bodenseewerk Perkin-Elmer GmbH v. Varian Australia Pty Ltd (OPPOSITION:
CLARITY: FAIR BASING: PRIOR PUBLICATION: OBVIOUSNESS: NOVELTY:
EXPERT EVIDENCE: COMMON GENERAL KNOWLEDGE: OPPONENT'S RIGHT
TO BE HEARD: Fed. Ct)
Commonwealth Scientific and Industrial Research Organisation's and Gilbert's
Applications (JOINT APPLICATIONS: DISPUTE BETWEEN APPLICANTS:
ENTITLEMENT TO INVENTIONS: AIPO)
Dearborn Chemical Co. Ltd v. Rohm and Haas Co. (OPPOSITION: AMENDMENT:
OPPOSITION TO AMENDMENT: IN SUBSTANCE DISCLOSED: INCONSISTENCY:
ESSENTIAL FEATURES: ALLOWABILITY: REFUSAL: AIPO)
Dr Rentschler Biotechnologie GmbH v. Boehringer Ingelheim International GmbH
(PROCESS: TREATMENT: DISEASE: NOVELTY: AIPO)
O'Neill & St George's Application (CO-APPLICANTS: DISPUTE: DETERMINATION:
DIRECTIONS: AIPO)
Porter v. Arbortech Investments Pty Ltd (OPPOSITION: OBJECTION TO ALLOWANCE
OF A REQUEST TO AMEND STATEMENT OF GROUNDS AND PARTICULARS:
AIPO)
Sumitomo Chemical Co. Ltd v. Rhône-Poulenc Chimie (OPPOSITION: COMMON
GENERAL KNOWLEDGE: ADMISSIONS IN SPECIFICATION: INVENTIVENESS:
MANNER OF MANUFACTURE: SECTION 40: COSTS: Fed. Ct)
Sumitomo Electrical Industries Ltd v. Metal Manufacturers Ltd (SELECTION PATENT:
OPPOSITION: REHEARING: Fed. Ct)

Arbitration

Asea-Atom AB v. Boyle (AGREEMENT: ALLEGED BREACH: OPERATION:
S.C.(NSW))

Assignment

Brisalebe Ltd v. Searle (PROVISIONAL SPECIFICATION: REQUEST FOR INSPECTION:
OBTAINING: AIPO)

Authorisation of Infringement

Martin Engineering Co. v. Nicaro Holdings Pty Ltd (DIRECTORS' PERSONAL LIABILITY: Fed. Ct)
Sartas No. 1 Pty Ltd v. Koukouou & Partners Pty Ltd (METHOD CLAIMS: PRODUCT CLAIMS: INFRINGEMENT: SUPPLY TO THIRD PARTY: VALIDITY: FAIR BASING: NOVELTY: ALLEGED PRIOR PUBLICATION: OBVIOUSNESS: DOUBLE CLAIMING: LACK OF TITLE: FALSE SUGGESTION: AIPO)

Best Endeavours

Andoy Pty Ltd v. S. & M. Cannon Pty Ltd (EXCLUSIVE LICENCE: WORLDWIDE EXPLOITATION OF PATENT: S.C.(Vic.))

Best Method

Bayer AG v. Alphapharm Pty Ltd (FALSE SUGGESTION: S.C.(NSW))
Colgate-Palmolive Co. v. Cussons Pty Ltd (INFRINGEMENT: VALIDITY: COMBINATION OF KNOWN INTEGERS: INVENTION IN CLAIMS LIMITED BY RESULT: WHETHER THE SPECIFICATION DESCRIBES THE BEST METHOD OF PERFORMING THE INVENTION: OBVIOUSNESS: NOVELTY: ALTERNATIVE CONSTRUCTIONS OF SPECIFICATION: Fed. Ct)
Freeman v. Pohlner Pty Ltd (REVOCATION: PATENTABILITY: NOVELTY: SKILLED ADDRESSEE: DESCRIPTION: Fed. Ct)
Rescare Ltd v. Anaesthetic Supplies Pty Ltd (INFRINGEMENT: METHOD CLAIMS: Fed. Ct)
Rescare Ltd v. Anaesthetic Supplies Pty Ltd (FAIR BASING UPON PROVISIONAL SPECIFICATION: Fed. Ct)

Certification

New York University v. Nissin Molecular Biology Institute Inc. (REQUEST FOR CERTIFICATION: UNDERTAKING: CONDITIONS FOR RELEASE OF SAMPLE OF MICRO-ORGANISM: AIPO)

Cessation

Utting v. Clyde Industries Ltd (OPPOSITION: APPLICATION FOR RESTORATION: Pat. Off.)

Claims

B.F. Goodrich Co. v. ICI Australia Operations Pty Ltd (APPLICATION: OPPOSITION: WHETHER CLAIMS FAIRLY BASED: AIPO)
High Tech Auto Tools Pty Ltd v. Ferocem Pty Ltd (PETTY PATENT: EXTENSION: OBJECTION: NOTICE: PRIORITY DATE: MANNER OF MANUFACTURE: OBVIOUS MISTAKE: NOVELTY: OBVIOUSNESS: EVIDENCE: PRACTICE AND PROCEDURE: CLARITY: UNCERTAINTY: AIPO)
Olin Corp. v. Super Cartridge Co. Pty Ltd (INVENTIVENESS: WHETHER CLAIMS CLEAR AND DISTINCTIVE: FAIRLY BASED: INVENTIVE STEP: H.C.)
Sartas No. 1 Pty Ltd v. Koukouou & Partners Pty Ltd (METHOD CLAIMS: PRODUCT CLAIMS: INFRINGEMENT: AUTHORISATION: SUPPLY TO THIRD PARTY: AIPO)
Upjohn Co.'s Application (OBJECTION: REDUNDANCY: METHOD: PRODUCT: NEW USE OF OLD SUBSTANCE: AIPO)
Viskase Corp. v. W.R. Grace & Co.-Conn. (OPPOSITION: APPLICATION FOR EXTENSION OF TIME FOR SERVICE OF EVIDENCE: AMENDMENTS TO CLAIMS: AIPO)

Clarity

Bodenseewerk Perkin-Elmer GmbH v. Varian Australia Pty Ltd (APPLICATION: OPPOSITION: FAIR BASING: PRIOR PUBLICATION: OBVIOUSNESS: NOVELTY: EXPERT EVIDENCE: Fed. Ct)

Clerical Error. *See* Practice (*Clerical error*)

Co-Applicants

O'Neill & St Georges Application (DISPUTE: DETERMINATION: DIRECTIONS: AIPO)

Collocation

University of Sydney v. Werner & Mertz GmbH (OPPOSITION: FAIR BASING: AMENDMENT OF SPECIFICATION: COSTS: AIPO)

Combination of Known Ideas or Substances

Avion Engineering Pty Ltd v. Fisher and Paykel Healthcare Pty Ltd (INFRINGEMENT: PITH AND MARROW DOCTRINE: Fed. Ct)
Avion Engineering Pty Ltd v. Fisher and Paykel Healthcare Pty Ltd (COMBINATION OF COMMON INTEGERS: Fed. Ct)
Colgate-Palmolive Co. v. Cussons Pty Ltd (COMBINATION OF KNOWN INTEGERS: Fed. Ct)
Commonwealth Industrial Gases Ltd v. MWA Holdings Pty Ltd (COMBINATION OF NON-ESSENTIAL FEATURES: WORKSHOP IMPROVEMENTS: H.C.)
Gang-Nail Australia Ltd v. Multinail Truss Systems Pty Ltd (INFRINGEMENT: CONSTRUCTION OF LICENCE: IMPLIED TERM: ESSENTIAL INTEGERS OF CLAIM: Fed. Ct)
Interact Machine Tools (NSW) Pty Ltd v. Yamazaki Mazak Corporation (PETTY PATENT: MACHINE TOOL COMPRISING COMBINATION OF INTEGERS: Fed. Ct)
Luminous Pty Ltd v. Nitto Electric Industrial Co. Ltd (OPPOSITION: NOVELTY: OBVIOUSNESS: SECTION 40: PRIOR PUBLICATION: ESSENTIAL INTEGERS: INSUFFICIENCY: EVIDENCE: FAIR BASIS: AIPO)
National Research Development Corporation's Application (Pat. Off.)
Opsvik v. Bad Back Centre Pty Ltd (FAIR BASIS: S.C.(NSW))
Populin v. HB Nominees Pty Ltd (ALLEGED INFRINGEMENT: ESSENTIAL INTEGERS: Fed. Ct)
Rescare Ltd v. Anaesthetic Supplies Pty Ltd (Fed. Ct)
Winner v. Ammar Holdings Pty Ltd (NOVELTY: MOSAIC: Fed. Ct)

Common General Knowledge

Asahi Kasei Kogyo KK v. W.R. Grace & Co. (DISTINCTION BETWEEN REVOCATION, NOVELTY AND OBVIOUSNESS: TESTS OF REVOCATION, NOVELTY AND OBVIOUSNESS: Fed. Ct)
Bodenseewerk Perkin-Elmer GmbH v. Varian Australia Pty Ltd (APPLICATION: OPPOSITION: CLARITY: FAIR BASING: PRIOR PUBLICATION: OBVIOUSNESS: NOVELTY: EXPERT EVIDENCE: OPPONENT'S RIGHT TO BE HEARD: Fed. Ct)
Bridge & Plate Constructions Pty Ltd v. Mannesmann Demag Pty Ltd (PART OF PATENTABLE COMBINATION: MERIT OF INVENTION: Pat. Off.)
Bristol-Myers Company v. L'Oreal (NO EVIDENCE OF COMMON GENERAL KNOWLEDGE: Pat. Off.)

Calsil Ltd v. Riekie & Simpfendorfer (EVIDENCE: Pat. Off.)

Clay v. ICI Australia Operations Pty Ltd (PRIOR PUBLICATION: Pat. Off.)

Cooper Industries Inc. v. Metal Manufactures Ltd (OPPOSITION: PROCEDURE: NON-COMPLIANCE WITH SECTION 40: EVIDENCE: OBVIOUSNESS: AIPO)

Electricity Trust of South Australia v. Zellweger Uster Pty Ltd (NOTIONAL ADDRESSEE: PRIOR PUBLICATION: NOVELTY: ANTICIPATION: FAIR BASIS: Pat. Off.)

Lech Pawlowski v. Seeley (F.F.) Nominees Pty Ltd (WHAT CONSTITUTES: Pat. Off.)

Murray Joseph Wright v. Ajax Davey Pty Ltd (OBVIOUSNESS: NOVELTY: Pat. Off.)

Peptide Technology Ltd v. The Wellcome Foundation Ltd (MANNER OF NEW MANUFACTURE: SUFFICIENCY: FAIR BASIS: AMBIGUITY: OBVIOUSNESS: NOVELTY: Pat. Off.)

Polar Vac Pty Ltd v. Spoutvac Manufacturing Pty Ltd (OPPOSITION: PRIOR PUBLICATION: SECRET USE: OBVIOUSNESS: AIPO)

Sumitomo Chemical Co. Ltd v. Rhône-Poulenc Chimie (APPLICATION: OPPOSITION: ADMISSIONS IN SPECIFICATION: INVENTIVENESS: MANNER OF MANUFACTURE: SECTION 40: COSTS: Fed. Ct)

Sunbeam Corp. v. Morphy-Richards (Aust.) Pty Ltd (INFRINGEMENT: REVOCATION: VALIDITY: INVENTIVENESS: NOVELTY: SUBJECT-MATTER: OBVIOUSNESS: MOSAIC: H.C.)

Tetra Pak International AB v. J. Gadsden Pty Ltd (ANTICIPATION: OBVIOUSNESS: FAIR BASIS: Pat. Off.)

Winner v. Ammar Holdings Pty Ltd (DISTINCTION BETWEEN OBVIOUSNESS AND NOVELTY: MOSAIC OF PRIOR PATENTS: Fed. Ct)

Complete Specification

Heylen v. Davies Collison Cave (PETTY PATENT: EXTENSION: NOTICE: AMENDMENT: IN SUBSTANCE DISCLOSED: FAIR BASIS: NOVELTY: INVENTIVE STEP: OBVIOUSNESS: EVIDENTIARY BURDEN: PATENT ATTORNEYS: COSTS: AIPO)

Philip Morris Inc. v. Brown and Williamson Tobacco Corp. (APPLICATION: OPPOSITION: AMENDMENT: REQUEST TO AMEND: IN SUBSTANCE DISCLOSED: FAIR BASIS: FURTHER REQUEST TO AMEND: AIPO)

Compulsory Licence

Du Pont de Nemours (E.I.) & Co. v. Commissioner of Patents (No. 4) (P.A.52, SECTIONS 94, 108, 110; S.C.(NSW))

Wissen Pty Ltd v. Kenneth Mervyn Lown (APPLICATION: REASONABLE REQUIREMENTS OF PUBLIC: Pat. Off.)

Computer

CCOM Pty Ltd v. Jiejung Pty Ptd (COMPUTER PROCESS FOR ASSEMBLING CHINESE LANGUAGE CHARACTERS: VALIDITY: INFRINGEMENT: WHETHER SALE OF PROGRAM FOR USE IN STANDARD COMPUTER INFRINGES PATENTED APPARATUS CLAIM: Fed. Ct)

Honeywell Bull Inc.'s Application (PROGRAM: MATHEMATICAL ALGORITHM: MANNER OF MANUFACTURE: Pat. Off.)

Thomas & Garnham's Application (OBJECTION BY EXAMINER: REQUEST TO COMMISSIONER TO EXERCISE DISCRETIONARY POWER: COMPUTER PROCESSING APPARATUS FOR ASSEMBLING TEXT, PARTICULARLY IN CHINESE CHARACTERS: PATENTABILITY: NOVELTY: PRIORITY DATE: AIPO)

Thomas and Stohrs Application (PETTY PATENT: OPPOSITION TO EXTENSION OF
TERM: COMPUTER INVENTION: OBVIOUSNESS: IDEA: ANTICIPATION: Pat.
Off.)

Construction

Allsop Inc. v. Bintang Ltd (Fed. Ct)
Braas & Co. GmbH v. Humes Ltd (APPLICATION: SECTION 40: Pat. Off.)
Colgate-Palmolive Co. v. Cussons Pty Ltd (COMBINATION OF KNOWN INTEGERS:
INVENTION IN CLAIMS LIMITED BY RESULT: Fed. Ct)
Dart Industries Inc. v. Prestige Group (Aust.) Pty Ltd (CLAIMS: REPRESENTATIONS
TO EXAMINER: MISREPRESENTATION: S.C.(Vic.))
Decor Corporation Pty Ltd v. Dart Industries Inc. (INFRINGEMENT: INVALIDITY:
WHETHER CLAIMS FAIRLY BASED ON INVENTION DESCRIBED IN
SPECIFICATION: Fed. Ct)
Elconnex Pty Ltd v. Gerard Industries Pty Ltd (PETTY PATENT: FAIR BASIS ON
PROVISIONAL OR COMPLETE SPECIFICATION: Fed. Ct)
Fisher & Paykel Healthcare Pty Ltd v. Avion Engineering Pty Ltd (PETTY PATENT:
PRINCIPLES: Fed. Ct)
Gang-Nail Australia Ltd v. Multinail Truss Systems Pty Ltd (INFRINGEMENT:
ESSENTIAL INTEGERS OF CLAIM: Fed. Ct)
Kimberly-Clark Ltd v. Commissioner of Patents (No. 3) (ERROR OR OMISSION: Fed.
Ct)
Kornelis' Kunsthars Producten Industrie BV v. W.R. Grace & Co. (AMENDMENT:
NOT IN SUBSTANCE DISCLOSED: Fed. Ct)
Lantech Inc. v. First Green Park (INFRINGEMENT: SPECIFICATION: REVOCATION:
INVALIDITY: SECTION 40 GROUNDS: INUTILITY: Fed. Ct)
Markman v. Westview Instruments Inc. (INFRINGEMENT: SUMMARY JUDGMENT:
RIGHT TO JURY TRIAL: Fed. Ct)
Martin Engineering Co. v. Trison Holdings Pty Ltd (CONSTRUCTION OF CLAIM BY
REFERENCE TO SPECIFICATION: Fed. Ct)
Prestige Group (Australia) Pty Ltd v. Dart Industries Inc. (Fed. Ct)
Rehm Pty Ltd v. Websters Security Systems (International) Pty Ltd (INFRINGEMENT:
USE OF SPECIFICATION TO CLARIFY CLAIM: USE OF ORIGINAL FORM OF CLAIM
TO AID CONSTRUCTION: Fed. Ct)
Windsurfing International Inc. v. Petit (INFRINGEMENT: SALE OF KIT OF PARTS:
NOVELTY: S.C.(NSW))

Contributory Infringement

CCOM Pty Ltd v. Jiejung Pty Ptd (Fed. Ct)

Convenient Forum. See **Practice** (*Convenient forum*)

Costs. See **Practice** (*Costs*)

Cross-examination. See **Practice** (*Cross-examination*)

Damages. See **Practice** (*Damages*)

Director's Liability

Martin Engineering Co. v. Nicaro Holdings Pty Ltd (Fed. Ct)

Discovery. *See* **Practice** (*Discovery*)

Discretion. *See* **Practice** (*Discretion*)

Divisional Application

Clafton Pty Ltd v. Forbes Engineering Holdings Pty Ltd (PRIORITY DATE: Pat. Off.)
Ricardo International plc v. Orital Engine Co. (Aust.) Pty Ltd (OPPOSITION: PRIOR
   CLAIMING: NOVELTY: TRANSITIONAL APPLICATION: FAIR BASIS: AIPO)

Double Claiming

Sartas No. 1 Pty Ltd v. Koukouou & Partners Pty Ltd (METHOD CLAIMS: PRODUCT
   CLAIMS: INFRINGEMENT: AUTHORISATION: SUPPLY TO THIRD PARTY:
   VALIDITY: FAIR BASING: NOVELTY: ALLEGED PRIOR PUBLICATION:
   OBVIOUSNESS: LACK OF TITLE: FALSE SUGGESTION: AIPO)

Employee

Mitsubishi Chemical Industries Ltd v. Asahi Kasei Kogyo KK (ERROR OR OMISSION
   BY EMPLOYEE OF PATENT ATTORNEY: SPECIAL CIRCUMSTANCES: Pat. Off.)
Wood v. Uniflex (Aust.) Pty Ltd (FOREIGN DISCLOSURE TO EMPLOYEE OF
   AUSTRALIAN COMPANY: S.C.(Vic.))

Entitlement

Advanced Building Systems Pty Ltd v. Ramset (Fed. Ct)
Commonwealth Scientific and Industrial Research Organisation's and Gilbert's
   Applications (JOINT APPLICATIONS: DISPUTE BETWEEN APPLICANTS: AIPO)

Errors. *See* **Practice** (*Errors*)

Essential Features Integers

Dearborn Chemical Co. Ltd v. Rohm and Haas Co. (OPPOSITION: AMENDMENT:
   OPPOSITION TO AMENDMENT: IN SUBSTANCE DISCLOSED: INCONSISTENCY:
   ALLOWABILITY: REFUSAL: AIPO)
Luminous Pty Ltd v. Nitto Electric Industrial Co. Ltd (OPPOSITION: NOVELTY:
   OBVIOUSNESS: SECTION 40: PRIOR PUBLICATION: COMBINATION PATENT:
   INSUFFICIENCY: EVIDENCE: FAIR BASIS: AIPO)
Validity Commonwealth Industrial Gases Ltd v. MWA Holdings Pty Ltd
   (INFRINGEMENT: DEPARTURE FROM ESSENTIAL FEATURE: COMBINATION OF
   NON-ESSENTIAL FEATURES: WORKSHOP IMPROVEMENTS: H.C.)

Evidence. *See* **Practice** (*Evidence*)

Exclusive Licence

Andoy Pty Ltd v. S. & M. Cannon Pty Ltd (DETERMINATION UPON BREACH:
   BREACH OF BEST ENDEAVOURS CLAUSE: S.C.(Vic.))
Vitamins Australia Ltd v. Beta-Carotene Industries Pty Ltd (CANCELLATION: EFFECT:
   S.C.(W.A.))

Experimental Use

Graf v. Milward-Bason (OPPOSITION: NOVELTY: PRIOR USE: SECRET USE: Pat. Off.)

Expired Patent

Ogden Industries Pty Ltd v. Kis (Australia) Ltd (NON-REGISTRATION OF DESIGN: S.C.(NSW))

Parke Davis Pty Ltd v. Sanofi & Commissioner of Patents (EXPIRATION: EXTENSION OF TIME LIMIT FOR PETITION: Fed. Ct)

Export

Roussel-Uclaf v. Pan Laboratories Pty Ltd (GOODS INFRINGING PATENTS IN AUSTRALIA: EXPORT TO PAPUA NEW GUINEA: JURISDICTION TO ORDER DELIVERY UP: DISCRETION: Fed. Ct)

Extension

American Home Products Corporation v. Commissioner of Patents (EXCEPTIONAL CASE: RELEVANCE OF LAWS REQUIRING APPROVAL ON DELAY IN MARKETING: Fed. Ct)

Anaesthetic Supplies Pty Ltd v. Rescare Ltd (Fed. Ct)

Astra Lakenedel AB (OBJECTION: MARKETING APPROVAL CERTIFICATE: IN SUBSTANCE DISCLOSED: PHARMACEUTICAL SUBSTANCE: AIPO)

Astra Laemedal AG v. Commissioner of Patents (PHARMACEUTICAL SUBSTANCE: WHETHER EXTENSION AVAILABLE: Fed. Ct)

Atlas Powder Co. v. ICI Australia Operations Pty Ltd (Pat. Off.)

Baker v. Peuren Agencies Ltd (DEFINITION NOT UNDERSTANDABLE: AMENDMENT OF SPECIFICATION: Pat. Off.)

Bates Saddlery Pty Ltd v. Becville Pty Ltd (PETTY PATENT: NOVELTY: OBVIOUSNESS: Pat. Off.)

Bausch & Lomb Inc. v. Allergan Inc. (Pat. Off.)

Bayer AG v. Minister for Health of the Commonwealth of Australia (DRUG: ADEQUACY OF REMUNERATION: NOTIONAL ROYALTY: DATE OF ASSESSMENT: ALLOWANCE FOR RESEARCH AND DEVELOPMENT: FOREIGN EARNINGS: EARNINGS SINCE DATE OF EXPIRY: NATURE OF MERITS OF INVENTION: S.C.(NSW))

Bio Energy Systems Inc. v. Lawrence John Walton (LACK OF CLEAR DEFINITION: Pat. Off.)

Bolesta's Application (CLARITY: SUFFICIENCY OF DESCRIPTION: ADEQUACY OF DEFINITION: Pat. Off.)

Bristol-Myers Co. v. David Bull Laboratories Pty Ltd (EXTENSION OF TIME LIMIT: Fed. Ct)

Browne & Williamson Tobacco Corp. v. Philip Morris Inc. (LACK OF CLARITY: Pat. Off.)

CCOM Pty Ltd v. Jiejung Pty Ptd (COMPUTER PROCESS FOR ASSEMBLING CHINESE LANGUAGE CHARACTERS: INFRINGEMENT: CLAIMS: PRIORITY DATE: ANTICIPATION: NOVELTY: METHOD OF MANUFACTURE: Fed. Ct)

Ciba Geigy AG's Application (EXTENSION: S.C.(NSW))

Clafton Pty Ltd v. Forbes Engineering Holdings Pty Ltd (Pat. Off.)

Coopers Animal Health Australia Ltd v. Western Stock Distributors Ltd (PETTY PATENT: Pat. Off.)

Dow Chemical Co. v. ICI PLC (Pat. Off.)

Du Pont de Nemours (E.I.) & Co. v. Cadbury Schweppes Pty Ltd (WHETHER OPPONENT TO EXTENSION CAN PLEAD INVALIDITY: Fed. Ct)

Du Pont de Nemours (E.I.) & Co. v. Commissioner of Patents (DISCOVERY: WHETHER GENERAL DISCOVERY SHOULD BE ORDERED PRIOR TO FILING OF AFFIDAVITS: Fed. Ct)

Du Pont de Nemours (E.I.) & Co. v. Commissioner of Patents (No. 2) (EXCLUSIVE LICENSEE: DISCLOSURE OF PROFITS: S.C.(NSW))

Du Pont de Nemours (E.I.) & Co. v. Commissioner of Patents (No. 3) (WHETHER INVENTION OF MORE THAN ORDINARY UTILITY: RELEVANCE OF MERIT OF INVENTIVE STEP: PROFITS OF PATENTEE: RESEARCH AND DEVELOPMENT COSTS: S.C.(NSW))

Du Pont de Nemours (E.I.) & Co. v. Commissioner of Patents (No. 4) (EXCLUSIVE LICENSEE: CONDITIONS ON GRANT OF EXTENSION: EVIDENCE OF HIGH PRICES: NO EVIDENCE OF PROFITS OF EXCLUSIVE LICENSEE: WHETHER APPLICATION FOR COMPULSORY LICENCE A SUITABLE ALTERNATIVE REMEDY: P.A.52, SECTIONS 94, 108, 110: S.C.(NSW))

Du Pont de Nemours (E.I.) & Co. v. Commissioner of Patents (No. 7) (APPLICATION TO IMPOSE CONDITIONS ON EXTENSION: S.C.(NSW))

Du Pont de Nemours (E.I.) & Co. v. Commissioner of Patents (WHETHER OPPONENT MAY CHALLENGE VALIDITY: S.C.(NSW))

Electricity Trust of South Australia v. Zellweger Uster Pty Ltd (ANTICIPATION: Pat. Off.)

Enviro-Clear Co. Inc. v. Commissioner of Patents (DISCOVERY: PRINCIPLES: S.C.(NSW))

High Tech Auto Tools Pty Ltd v. Ferocem Pty Ltd (PETTY PATENT: OBJECTION: NOTICE: CLAIMS: PRIORITY DATE: MANNER OF MANUFACTURE: OBVIOUS MISTAKE: NOVELTY: OBVIOUSNESS: EVIDENCE: CLARITY: UNCERTAINTY: AIPO)

Heylen v. Davies Collison Cave (PETTY PATENT: NOTICE: COMPLETE SPECIFICATION: AMENDMENT: IN SUBSTANCE DISCLOSED: FAIR BASIS: NOVELTY: INVENTIVE STEP: OBVIOUSNESS: EVIDENTIARY BURDEN: PATENT ATTORNEYS: COSTS: AIPO)

Kwan v. Queensland Corrective Services Commission (PETTY PATENT: SECTION 28 NOTICE: INVENTION MADE BY PRISONERS: WHETHER INVENTORS EMPLOYEES OF CORRECTIONAL FACILITY: FAIR BASIS: SUFFICIENCY: NOVELTY: OBVIOUSNESS: AIPO)

Smucker (J.M.) Co.'s Petty Patent (OPPOSITION TO EXTENSION: NOVELTY: OBVIOUSNESS: MANNER OF NEW MANUFACTURE: INCONVENIENT SPECIFICATION: NON-COMPLIENCE WITH SECTION 40: PROCEDURE: AIPO)

Virbac (Australia) Pty Ltd v. Merck Patent GmbH (PHARMACEUTICAL SUBSTANCE: COSTS: Fed. Ct)

Extension of Time Limit. *See* **Practice** (*Extension of time limit*)

Fair Basis

B.F. Goodrich Co. v. ICI Australia Operations Pty Ltd (APPLICATION: OPPOSITION: PRIOR PUBLICATION: OBVIOUSNESS: COMBINATION INVENTION: MANNER OF NEW MANUFACTURE: PRIOR USE: PRIOR SECRET USE: STANDARD OF PROOF: AIPO)

Bally Gaming International Inc. v. Scandic International Pty Ltd (OPPOSITION: NOVELTY: OBVIOUSNESS: MANNER OF NEW MANUFACTURE: SECTION 40: SMART CARD FOR DATA TRANSFER BETWEEN AMUSEMENT MACHINES AND CENTRAL COMPUTER: TIME FOR AMENDMENTS ALLOWED: AIPO)

Bodenseewerk Perkin-Elmer GmbH v. Varian Australia Pty Ltd (APPLICATION: OPPOSITION: CLARITY: PRIOR PUBLICATION: OBVIOUSNESS: NOVELTY: EXPERT EVIDENCE: COMMON GENERAL KNOWLEDGE: OPPONENTS RIGHT TO BE HEARD: Fed. Ct)

Guertler's Application (PETTY PATENT: Pat. Off.)

Rehm Pty Ltd v. Websters Security Systems (International) Pty Ltd (Fed. Ct)
Rescare Ltd v. Anaesthetic Supplies Pty Ltd (AMENDMENT OF CLAIMS: Fed. Ct)
Ricardo International plc v. Orital Engine Co. (Aust.) Pty Ltd (OPPOSITION: PRIOR
    CLAIMING: NOVELTY: TRANSITIONAL APPLICATION: DIVISIONAL STATUS:
    FAIR BASIS: AIPO)
Roelofs' Patent (PETTY PATENT: EXTENSION OF TERM: STATUTORY NOTICE:
    FAIRLY BASED: PRIORITY DATE: PRIOR DATE: AIPO)
Sandvik AB v. Boart International Ltd (FALSE SUGGESTION: Pat. Off.)
Sanofi (Re) (INADEQUATE REMUNERATION: ASSIGNMENT OF RIGHT TO APPLY:
    S.C.(Vic.))
Sanofi v. Parke Davis Pty Ltd (TIME LIMITS: H.C.)
Schmidt's Application (OPPOSITION: EVIDENCE: Pat. Off.)
Searle & Co. v. Drug Houses of Australia Pty Ltd (CAVEATS: Fed. Ct)
Smith Kline & French Laboratories Ltd v. Commissioner of Patents (MATTERS TO BE
    CONSIDERED: S.C.(NSW))
Tetra Pak International AB v. J. Gadsden Pty Ltd (AMENDMENT OF COMPLETE
    SPECIFICATION: Pat. Off.)
Union Carbide Agricultural Products Company Inc.'s Petition (INSUFFICIENT
    REMUNERATION: JUSTIFICATION: S.C.(Vic.))
University of Sydney v. Werner & Mertz GmbH (OPPOSITION: COLLOCATION:
    AMENDMENT: COSTS: AIPO)
Virbac (Australia) Pty Ltd v. Merck Patent GmbH (EXTENSION OF TERM:
    PHARMACEUTICAL SUBSTANCE: COSTS: Fed. Ct)
Whitco Pty Ltd v. Austral Lock Industries Pty Ltd (Pat. Off.)
Yamazaki Mazak Corp.'s Application (PETTY PATENT: INFORMATION AGAINST
    EXTENSION: APPLICATION FOR ADJOURNMENT OF HEARING: Pat. Off.)

False Suggestion

Bayer AG v. Alphapharm Pty Ltd (S.C.(NSW))
Prestige Group (Australia) Pty Ltd v. Dart Industries Inc. (Fed. Ct)
Sandvik AB v. Boart International Ltd (Pat. Off.)
Sartas No. 1 Pty Ltd v. Koukouou & Partners Pty Ltd (DOUBLE CLAIMING: LACK OF
    TITLE: FALSE SUGGESTION: AIPO)
Winner v. Ammar Holdings Pty Ltd (NON-DISCLOSURE OF THE FATE OF OVERSEAS
    APPLICATION: Fed. Ct)
Yamazaki Mazak Corporation v. Interact Machine Tools (NSW) Pty Ltd (Fed. Ct)

Filing Affidavits or Evidence. *See* **Practice** (*Filing affidavits or evidence*)

Full and Frank Disclosure

De Pont de Nemours (E.I.) & Co. v. Dowelanco (OPPOSITION: EXTENSION OF TIME
    TO FILE EVIDENCE: JUSTIFICATION: AIPO)
Kent-Moore Corp. v. Environmental Products Amalgamated Pty Ltd (Pat. Off.)
Sandoz Ltd v. Fujisawa Pharmaceutical Co. Ltd (Pat. Off.)

Imports and Importation

Merrell Dow Pharmaceuticals' Petition (APPLICATION FOR PERMISSION TO IMPORT
    AND MARKET IN AUSTRALIA MADE 11 YEARS AFTER PRIORITY DATE: Fed. Ct)

Inconsistency

Dearborn Chemical Co. Ltd v. Rohm and Haas Co. (OPPOSITION: AMENDMENT: OPPOSITION TO AMENDMENT: IN SUBSTANCE DISCLOSED: ESSENTIAL FEATURES: ALLOWABILITY: REFUSAL: AIPO)

Infringement

Allsop Inc. v. Bintang Ltd (Fed. Ct)
Appleton Papers Inc. v. Tomasetti Paper Pty Ltd (S.C.(NSW))
Australian Consolidated Industries Ltd v. Scholle Industries Pty Ltd (S.C.(S.A.))
Avion Engineering Pty Ltd v. Fisher and Paykel Healthcare Pty Ltd (Fed. Ct)
Bayer AG v. Alphapharm Pty Ltd (S.C.(NSW))
BEST Australia Ltd v. Aquagas Marketing Pty Ltd (Fed. Ct)
Cabot Corporation v. Minnesota Mining & Manufacturing Ltd (S.C.(NSW))
Cave Holdings Pty Ltd v. Taperline Pty Ltd (Fed. Ct)
CCOM Pty Ltd v. Jiejung Pty Ptd (CONTRIBUTORY INFRINGEMENT: Fed. Ct)
Colgate-Palmolive Co. v. Cussons Pty Ltd (Fed. Ct)
Commonwealth Industrial Gases Ltd v. MWA Holdings Pty Ltd (H.C.)
Dart Industries Inc. v. Decor Corporation Pty Ltd (H.C.)
Dart Industries Inc. v. Grace Bros Pty Ltd (S.C.(Vic.))
Decor Corporation Pty Ltd v. Dart Industries Inc. (Fed. Ct)
Dillon v. J.P. Products Pty Ltd (S.C.(NSW))
Durack v. Associated Pool Builders Pty Ltd (Fed. Ct)
Elconnex Pty Ltd v. Gerard Industries Pty Ltd (Fed. Ct)
Farmitalia Carlo Erba SrL v. Delta West Pty Ltd (Fed. Ct)
Fisher & Paykel Healthcare Pty Ltd v. Avion Engineering Pty Ltd (Fed. Ct)
Gang-Nail Australia Ltd v. Multinail Truss Systems Pty Ltd (Fed. Ct)
Interact Machine Tools (NSW) Pty Ltd v. Yamazaki Mazak Corporation (Fed. Ct)
Lantech Inc. v. First Green Park (AIPO: Fed. Ct)
Markman v. Westview Instruments Inc. (RIGHT TO JURY TRIAL: Fed. Ct)
Martin Engineering Co. v. Nicaro Holdings Pty Ltd (Fed. Ct)
Minnesota Mining & Manufacturing Co. v. C. Jeffries Pty Ltd (Fed. Ct (NSW))
Nicaro Holdings Pty Ltd v. Martin Engineering Co. (Fed. Ct)
Olin Corp. v. Super Cartridge Co. Pty Ltd (H.C.)
Pearce v. Paul Kingston Pty Ltd (S.C.(Vic.))
Philips Gloeilampenfabrieken (NV) v. Mirabella International Pty Ltd (Fed. Ct)
Populin v. HB Nominees Pty Ltd (Fed. Ct)
Rehm Pty Ltd v. Websters Security Systems (International) Pty Ltd (Fed. Ct)
Rescare Ltd v. Anaesthetic Supplies Pty Ltd (Fed. Ct)
Rhône Poulenc Agrochemie SA v. UIM Chemical Services Pty Ltd (Fed. Ct)
Roussel-Uclaf v. Pan Laboratories Pty Ltd (Fed. Ct)
Sartas No. 1 Pty Ltd v. Koukouou & Partners Pty Ltd (AIPO)
Stack v. Brisbane City Council (Fed. Ct)
Sunbeam Corp. v. Morphy-Richards (Aust.) Pty Ltd (MOSAIC: H.C.)
Townsend Controls Pty Ltd v. Gilead (Fed. Ct)
Vulcan Aust. Ltd v. Braemar Appliances Pty Ltd (Pat. Off.)
Westaflex (Aust.) Pty Ltd v. Wood (Fed. Ct)
Windsurfing International Inc. v. Petit (S.C.(NSW))
Winner v. Ammar Holdings Pty Ltd (Fed. Ct)
Winner v. Morey Haigh & Associates (Australasia) Pty Ltd (REVOCATION OF PATENT IN SUIT AT OTHER PROCEEDINGS: DISMISSAL OF PROCEEDINGS: Fed. Ct)
Wundowie Foundry Pty Ltd v. Milson Foundry Pty Ltd (Fed. Ct)
Yamazaki Mazak Corporation v. Interact Machine Tools (NSW) Pty Ltd (Fed. Ct)
Yorkwain Automatic Doors Ltd v. Newman Tonks Pty Ltd (S.C.(Vic.))

Injunction. *See* **Practice** (*Injunction*)

Insufficiency

Luminous Pty Ltd v. Nitto Electric Industrial Co. Ltd (OPPOSITION: NOVELTY: OBVIOUSNESS: SECTION 40: PRIOR PUBLICATION: COMBINATION PATENT: ESSENTIAL INTEGERS: EVIDENCE: FAIR BASIS: AIPO)

Interest. *See* **Practice** (*Interest*)

Interlocutory Injunction. *See* **Practice** (*Interlocutory injunction*)

International Applications

Opsvik v. Bad Back Centre Pty Ltd (S.C.(NSW))

Inutility. *See* **Utility**

Invention Made by Prisoners

Kwan v. Queensland Corrective Services Commission (PETTY PATENT: EXTENSION: SECTION 28 NOTICE: WHETHER INVENTORS EMPLOYEES OF CORRECTIONAL FACILITY: AIPO)

Inventive Step

Bayer AG v. Alphapharm Pty Ltd (S.C.(NSW))
Du Pont de Nemours (E.I.) & Co. v. Commissioner of Patents (No. 3) (EXTENSION OF TERM: RELEVANCE OF MERIT OF INVENTIVE STEP: S.C.(NSW))
Heylen v. Davies Collison Cave (PETTY PATENT: EXTENSION: NOTICE: COMPLETE SPECIFICATION: AMENDMENT: IN SUBSTANCE DISCLOSED: FAIR BASIS: NOVELTY: OBVIOUSNESS: AIPO)
Olin Corp. v. Super Cartridge Co. Pty Ltd (INFRINGEMENT: REVOCATION: VALIDITY: INVENTIVENESS: WHETHER CLAIMS CLEAR AND DISTINCTIVE: FAIRLY BASED: H.C.)
Winner v. Ammar Holdings Pty Ltd (REVOCATION: Fed. Ct)

Inventiveness

Commonwealth Industrial Gases Ltd v. MWA Holdings Pty Ltd (INFRINGEMENT: DEPARTURE FROM ESSENTIAL FEATURE: VALIDITY: COMBINATION OF NON-ESSENTIAL FEATURES: WORKSHOP IMPROVEMENTS: H.C.)
Olin Corp. v. Super Cartridge Co. Pty Ltd (INFRINGEMENT: REVOCATION: VALIDITY: WHETHER CLAIMS CLEAR AND DISTINCTIVE: INVENTIVE STEP: H.C.)
Sumitomo Chemical Co. Ltd v. Rhône-Poulenc Chimie (OPPOSITION: COMMON GENERAL KNOWLEDGE: ADMISSIONS IN SPECIFICATION: MANNER OF MANUFACTURE: SECTION 40: COSTS: Fed. Ct)
Sunbeam Corp. v. Morphy-Richards (Aust.) Pty Ltd (INFRINGEMENT: REVOCATION: VALIDITY: NOVELTY: SUBJECT-MATTER: OBVIOUSNESS: COMMON GENERAL KNOWLEDGE: MOSAIC: H.C.)

Inventor

Austgen Biojet Holdings Pty Ltd v. Goronszy (OPPOSITION: OBTAINING: TRANSITIONAL APPLICATION: Fed. Ct)

Joint Applicants, Owners or Inventors

Commonwealth Scientific and Industrial Research Organisation's and Gilbert's Applications (DISPUTE BETWEEN APPLICANTS: ENTITLEMENT TO INVENTIONS: AIPO)

Costa v. G.R. & I.E. Daking Pty Ltd (PETTY PATENT: SECTION 28 NOTICE: OBTAINING: PRIOR USE: WHETHER FOR REASONABLE TRIAL: LACK OF NOVELTY: AIPO)

Harris v. CSIRO (JOINT INVENTORSHIP: DECLARATION SOUGHT CONCERNING ELIGIBLE PERSON IN RELATION TO INVENTIONS: COSTS: AIPO)

Milward-Bason and Burgess, Applications (EFFECT OF AGREEMENT ON COMMISSIONER'S POWERS: EFFECT OF ONE OWNER'S DISINTEREST AND OBSTRUCTION: Pat. Off.)

O'Neill & St George's Application (CO-APPLICANTS: DISPUTE: DETERMINATION: DIRECTIONS: AIPO)

Stephenson and Donner's Application (PROCEED IN ONE NAME ONLY: Pat. Off.)

Tribe & Rankin's Application (PRACTICE AND PROCEDURE: Pat. Off.)

Joint Claim

American Optical Corp. v. Allergan Pharmaceuticals Pty Ltd (PRACTICE: Fed. Ct)

Jurisdiction

Australian Consolidated Industries Ltd v. Scholle Industries Pty Ltd (INFRINGEMENT: PRACTICE: PROCEEDINGS IN TWO JURISDICTIONS: Australia: S.C. (SA))

Du Pont de Nemours (E.I.) & Co. v. Commissioner of Patents (No. 5) (PARTIES: JOINDER: WHETHER COURT HAS JURISDICTION OR POWER TO JOIN ADDITIONAL PARTIES TO APPLICATION: S.C.(NSW))

Spotless Group Ltd v. Proplast Pty Ltd (STATE ACTION IN TWO JURISDICTIONS: APPLICATIONS TO SET ASIDE WRITS OR STAY OR TRANSFER: CONVENIENT FORUM: S.C.(Vic.))

Titan Mining & Engineering Pty Ltd v. Arnall's Engineering Pty Ltd (COMMISSIONER'S DECISION: S.C.(NSW))

Kit of Parts

Windsurfing International Inc. v. Petit (INFRINGEMENT: CONSTRUCTION: NOVELTY: S.C.(NSW))

Locus Standii. *See* Practice (*Locus standii*)

Manner of Manufacture

Sumitomo Chemical Co. Ltd v. Rhône-Poulenc Chimie (OPPOSITION: COMMON GENERAL KNOWLEDGE: ADMISSIONS IN SPECIFICATION: INVENTIVENESS: SECTION 40: COSTS: Fed. Ct)

Manner of New Manufacture

Bally Gaming International Inc. v. Scandic International Pty Ltd (OPPOSITION: NOVELTY: OBVIOUSNESS: FAIR BASIS: SECTION 40: SMART CARD FOR DATA TRANSFER BETWEEN AMUSEMENT MACHINES AND CENTRAL COMPUTER: AIPO)

Beecham Group Ltd's Application (Pat. Off.)
B. F. Goodrich Co. v. ICI Australia Operations Pty Ltd (OPPOSITION: WHETHER
    CLAIMS FAIRLY BASED: PRIOR PUBLICATION: OBVIOUSNESS: COMBINATION
    INVENTION: AIPO)
Bristol-Myers Company v. L'Oréal (SELECTION PATENT: PACKAGE CLAIMS: Pat.
    Off.)
Commonwealth Industrial Gases Ltd v. Liquid Air Australia Ltd (Pat. Off.)
Continental Group Inc.'s Application (Pat. Off.)
High Tech Auto Tools Pty Ltd v. Ferocem Pty Ltd (PETTY PATENT: EXTENSION:
    OBJECTION: NOTICE: CLAIMS: PRIORITY DATE: OBVIOUS MISTAKE: NOVELTY:
    OBVIOUSNESS: EVIDENCE: PRACTICE AND PROCEDURE: CLARITY:
    UNCERTAINTY: AIPO)
Indoor Cricket Arenas (Australia) Pty Ltd v. Australian Indoor Cricket Federation
    (Pat. Off.)
Moore Paragon Australia Ltd v. Multiform Printers (Pat. Off.)
Murray Joseph Wright v. Ajax Davey Pty Ltd (PETTY PATENT: Pat. Off.)
Optech International Ltd v. Buxton Hicrarium Ltd (OPPOSITION: ANTICIPATION:
    NOVELTY: OBVIOUSNESS: OBTAINING: AIPO)
Philips Gloeilampenfabrieken (NV) v. Mirabella International Pty Ltd (WHETHER
    SPECIFICATION OF SUITABLE CHARACTERISTICS OF KNOWN MATERIAL FOR
    KNOWN USE CONSTITUTES INVENTION OR MANNER OF NEW
    MANUFACTURE: Fed. Ct)
Philips Gloeilampenfabrieken (NV) v. Ultralite International Pty Ltd (NEW USE FOR
    OLD SUBSTANCE: APPEAL: Fed. Ct)
Secretary of State for Defence (U.K.) v. Rheinmetall GmbH (Pat. Off.)
Smucker (J.M.) Co.'s Petty Patent (EXTENSION OF TERM: OPPOSITION TO
    EXTENSION: NOVELTY: OBVIOUSNESS: INCONVENIENT SPECIFICATION: NON-
    COMPLIENCE WITH SECTION 40: AIPO)

Mosaic

Sunbeam Corp. v. Morphy-Richards (Aust.) Pty Ltd (INFRINGEMENT:
    REVOCATION: VALIDITY: INVENTIVENESS: NOVELTY: SUBJECT-MATTER:
    OBVIOUSNESS: COMMON GENERAL KNOWLEDGE: H.C.)

Nature and Merits of Invention. *See* Extension

New use of Old Substance

Philips Gloeilampenfabrieken (NV) v. Ultralite International Pty Ltd (MANNER OF
    NEW MANUFACTURE: APPEAL: Fed. Ct)
Upjohn Co.'s Application (APPLICATION: OBJECTION: CLAIMS: REDUNDANCY:
    METHOD: PRODUCT: AIPO)

Novelty

Petty patents

Bates Saddlery Pty Ltd v. Becville Pty Ltd (Pat. Off.)
Coopers Animal Health Australia Ltd v. Western Stock Distributors Ltd (Fed. Ct)
Costa v. G.R. & I.E. Daking Pty Ltd (SECTION 28 NOTICE: OBTAINING: PRIOR USE:
    WHETHER FOR REASONABLE TRIAL: AIPO)
Gerber Scientific Products Inc. v. North Broken Hill Ltd (Pat. Off.)
Heylen v. Davies Collison Cave (EXTENSION: OBVIOUSNESS: AIPO)
High Tech Auto Tools Pty Ltd v. Ferocem Pty Ltd (AIPO)

Kwan v. Queensland Corrective Services Commission (EXTENSION: SECTION 28
    NOTICE: FAIR BASIS: SUFFICIENCY: OBVIOUSNESS: AIPO)
Lech Pawlowski v. Seeley (F.F.) Nominees Pty Ltd (Pat. Off.)
Murray Joseph Wright v. Ajax Davey Pty Ltd (Pat. Off.)
Smucker (J.M.) Co.'s Petty Patent (AIPO)
Yamazaki Mazak Corporation v. Interact Machine Tools (NSW) Pty Ltd (Fed. Ct)

Full patent

A. & K. Aluminium Pty Ltd v. Lidco Systems Sales Pty Ltd (Pat. Off.)
Amcor Ltd v. Visy Board Pty Ltd (Pat. Off.)
Asahi Kasei Kogyo KK v. W.R. Grace & Co. (Fed. Ct)
Australian Paper Manufacturers Ltd v. CIL Ltd (Pat. Off.)
Bally Gaming International Inc. v. Scandic International Pty Ltd (AIPO)
Bausch & Lomb Inc. v. Allergan Inc. (Pat. Off.)
Beckman Instruments Inc. v. Bockringer Mannheim GmbH (Pat. Off.)
Beecham Group Ltd's Application (Pat. Off.)
Bio Energy Systems Inc. v. Lawrence John Walton (Pat. Off.)
Bioglan Laboratories (Aust.) Pty Ltd v. Crooks (Pat. Off.)
Bodenseewerk Perkin-Elmer GmbH v. Varian Australia Pty Ltd (Fed. Ct)
BP Nutrition (U.K.) Ltd's Application (Pat. Off.)
Braas & Co. GmbH v. Humes Ltd (Pat. Off.)
Bridge & Plate Constructions Pty Ltd v. Mannesmann Demag Pty Ltd (Pat. Off.)
Bristol-Myers Company v. L'Oréal (Pat. Off.)
Browne & Williamson Tobacco Corp. v. Philip Morris Inc. (Pat. Off.)
Calsil Ltd v. Riekie & Simpfendorfer (Pat. Off.)
Carpenter v. Sue Agencies Pty Ltd (Pat. Off.)
Clafton Pty Ltd v. Forbes Engineering Holdings Pty Ltd (Pat. Off.)
Colgate-Palmolive Co. v. Cussons Pty Ltd (Fed. Ct)
Commonwealth Industrial Gases Ltd v. Liquid Air Australia Ltd (Pat. Off.)
Continental Group Inc.'s Application (Pat. Off.)
Dennison Manufacturing Co. v. Monarch Marketing Systems Inc. (Fed. Ct)
Dohmeier v. Eisen-Und Drahtwerk Erlau AG (Pat. Off.)
Dr Rentschler Biotechnologie GmbH v. Boehringer Ingelheim International GmbH
    (TREATMENT: DISEASE: AIPO)
Electricity Trust of South Australia v. Zellweger Uster Pty Ltd (Pat. Off.)
Freeman v. Pohlner Pty Ltd (Fed. Ct)
Freeman v. Pohlner Pty Ltd (Fed. Ct)
Graf v. Milward-Bason (Pat. Off.)
Hoechst AG's Application (No. 2) (Pat. Off.)
Indoor Cricket Arenas (Australia) Pty Ltd v. Australian Indoor Cricket Federation
    (Pat. Off.)
James Hardie & Coy Pty Ltd v. Hardboards Australia Ltd (Pat. Off.)
Jos Schlitz Brewing Company v. Containers Ltd (Pat. Off.)
Komesaroff v. Mizzi (PETTY PATENT: Pat. Off.)
Kwik-Lok Corp.'s Application (Pat. Off.)
Lasercare (Aust.) Pty Ltd v. Christiansen (PETTY PATENT: Pat. Off.)
Leonard's Application (Pat. Off.)
Linde AG v. Air Products and Chemicals Inc. (Fed. Ct)
Lucasfilm Ltd v. Krix (Pat. Off.)
Luminous Pty Ltd v. Nitto Electric Industrial Co. Ltd (AIPO)
Mauri Brothers & Thomson (Aust.) Pty Ltd v. Containers Ltd (Pat. Off.)
Melbourne v. Terry Fluid Controls Pty Ltd (Fed. Ct)
Micronair (Aerial) Ltd v. Waikerie Co-operative Producers Ltd (Pat. Off.)
Moore Paragon Australia Ltd v. Multiform Printers (Pat. Off.)

National Research Development Corporation's Application (Pat. Off.)
Nelson v. Hillmark Industries Pty Ltd (Pat. Off.)
Nicaro Holdings Pty Ltd v. Martin Engineering Co. (Fed. Ct)
Nichator AB's Application (Pat. Off.)
Nomad Structures International Ltd v. Heyring Pty Ltd (Pat. Off.)
Opsvik v. Bad Back Centre Pty Ltd (S.C.(NSW))
Optech International Ltd v. Buxton Hicrarium Ltd (AIPO)
Pearce v. Paul Kingston Pty Ltd (S.C.(Vic.))
Peptide Technology Ltd v. The Wellcome Foundation Ltd (Pat. Off.)
Philips Gloeilampenfabrieken (NV) v. Mirabella International Pty Ltd (Fed. Ct)
PPG Industries Inc. v. Stauffer Chemical Co. (Pat. Off.)
Rescare Ltd v. Anaesthetic Supplies Pty Ltd (Fed. Ct)
Ricardo International plc v. Orital Engine Co. (Aust.) Pty Ltd (AIPO)
Robert Bosch GmbH v. Solo Industries Pty Ltd (Pat. Off.)
Ryan v. Lum (S.C.(NSW))
Sandvik AB v. Boart International Ltd (Pat. Off.)
Shell Internationale Research Maatschappij (Pat. Off.)
Sunbeam Corp. v. Morphy-Richards (Aust.) Pty Ltd (MOSAIC: H.C.)
Tetra Pak International AB v. J. Gadsden Pty Ltd (Pat. Off.)
Thomas & Garnham's Application (AIPO)
Titan Mining & Engineering Pty Ltd v. Arnall's Engineering Pty Ltd (S.C.(NSW))
United Kingdom Government (Secretary of State for Defence) v. Rheinmetall GmbH (Pat. Off.)
Vulcan Australia Ltd v. Braemar Appliances Pty Ltd (Pat. Off.)
Werner (R.D.) & Co. Inc. v. Bailey Aluminium Products Pty Ltd (Fed. Ct)
Whitco Pty Ltd v. Austral Lock Industries Pty Ltd (Pat. Off.)
Windsurfing International Inc. v. Petit (S.C.(NSW))
Winner v. Ammar Holdings Pty Ltd (Fed. Ct)
Wood v. Uniflex (Aust.) Pty Ltd (S.C.(Vic.))

Objection

Astra Lakenedel AB (EXTENSION: APPLICATION: OBJECTION: MARKETING APPROVAL CERTIFICATE: IN SUBSTANCE DISCLOSED: PHARMACEUTICAL SUBSTANCE: AIPO)

High Tech Auto Tools Pty Ltd v. Ferocem Pty Ltd (PETTY PATENT: EXTENSION: NOTICE: CLAIMS: PRIORITY DATE: MANNER OF MANUFACTURE: OBVIOUS MISTAKE: NOVELTY: OBVIOUSNESS: EVIDENCE: PRACTICE AND PROCEDURE: CLARITY: UNCERTAINTY: AIPO)

Thomas & Garnham's Application (APPLICATION: OBJECTION BY EXAMINER: REQUEST TO COMMISSIONER TO EXERCISE DISCRETIONARY POWER: COMPUTER PROCESSING APPARATUS FOR ASSEMBLING TEXT, PARTICULARLY IN CHINESE CHARACTERS: PATENTABILITY: NOVELTY: PRIORITY DATE: AIPO)

Upjohn Co.'s Application (APPLICATION: CLAIMS: REDUNDANCY: METHOD: PRODUCT: NEW USE OF OLD SUBSTANCE: AIPO)

Obtaining

A. & K. Aluminium Pty Ltd v. Lidco Systems Sales Pty Ltd (MATTERS ARISING UNDER SECTION 40: Pat. Off.)

Austgen Biojet Holdings Pty Ltd v. Goronszy (OPPOSITION: INVENTOR: TRANSITIONAL APPLICATION: Fed. Ct)

Lakes Application (PETTY PATENT: Pat. Off.)

Massey v. Noack (MATTERS ARISING UNDER SECTION 40: Pat. Off.)

Nomad Structures International Ltd v. Heyring Pty Ltd (Pat. Off.)
Optech International Ltd v. Buxton Hicrarium Ltd (AIPO)
Procter & Gamble Company v. Kimberly-Clark Corporation (Pat. Off.)
Procter & Gamble Company v. Kimberly-Clark Corporation (TRANSITIONAL PROVISIONS: Pat. Off.)

Obviousness

Petty patent

Avion Engineering Pty Ltd v. Fisher and Paykel Healthcare Pty Ltd (REVOCATION: LACK OF FAIR BASING: Fed. Ct)
Bates Saddlery Pty Ltd v. Becville Pty Ltd (EXTENSION: NOVELTY: Pat. Off.)
Coopers Animal Health Australia Ltd v. Western Stock Distributors Ltd (CLAIM BASED ON EARLIER SPECIFICATION: NOVELTY: REVOCATION: Fed. Ct)
Elconnex Pty Ltd v. Gerard Industries Pty Ltd (ADMISSIBILITY OF EVIDENCE OF EXPERT WITNESSES: Fed. Ct)
Fisher & Paykel Healthcare Pty Ltd v. Avion Engineering Pty Ltd (COMBINATION OF COMMON INTEGERS: Fed. Ct)
Gerber Scientific Products Inc. v. North Broken Hill Ltd (INVENTION NOT FULLY DESCRIBED: Pat. Off.)
Guertler's Application (EXTENSION: EVIDENCE: Pat. Off.)
Guertler v. Antenna Engineering Australia Pty Ltd (EXTENSION: Pat. Off.)
Heylen v. Davies Collison Cave (EXTENSION: NOTICE: COMPLETE SPECIFICATION: AMENDMENT: IN SUBSTANCE DISCLOSED: FAIR BASIS: NOVELTY: INVENTIVE STEP: EVIDENTIARY BURDEN: AIPO)
High Tech Auto Tools Pty Ltd v. Ferocem Pty Ltd (EXTENSION: OBJECTION: NOTICE: CLAIMS: PRIORITY DATE: MANNER OF MANUFACTURE: OBVIOUS MISTAKE: NOVELTY: EVIDENCE: AIPO)
Komesaroff v. Mizzi (EXTENSION: EVIDENCE: INVALIDITY: NOVELTY: Pat. Off.)
Kwan v. Queensland Corrective Services Commission (EXTENSION: SECTION 28 NOTICE: FAIR BASIS: SUFFICIENCY: NOVELTY: AIPO)
Lake's Application (EXTENSION: ANTICIPATION: Pat. Off.)
Lasercare (Aust.) Pty Ltd v. Christiansen (EXTENSION: LACK OF NOVELTY: Pat. Off.)
Lech Pawlowski v. Seeley (F.F.) Nominees Pty Ltd (EXTENSION: LACK OF NOVELTY: COMMON GENERAL KNOWLEDGE: WHAT CONSTITUTES: Pat. Off.)
Murray Joseph Wright v. Ajax Davey Pty Ltd (EXTENSION: MANNER OF NEW MANUFACTURE: COMMON GENERAL KNOWLEDGE: Pat. Off.)
Smucker (J.M.) Co.'s Petty Patent (EXTENSION OF TERM: OPPOSITION TO EXTENSION: NOVELTY: MANNER OF NEW MANUFACTURE: INCONVENIENT SPECIFICATION: NON-COMPLIANCE WITH SECTION 40: PROCEDURE: AIPO)
Thomas and Stohr's Application (EXTENSION: COMPUTER INVENTION: IDEA: ANTICIPATION: Pat. Off.)
Yamazaki Mazak Corporation v. Interact Machine Tools (NSW) Pty Ltd (INFRINGEMENT: FAIR BASING OF CLAIM UPON MATTER DESCRIBED IN SPECIFICATION: NOVELTY: Fed. Ct)

Full patent

Advanced Building Systems Pty Ltd v. Ramset (VALIDITY: REVOCATION: ANTICIPATION: MOSAIC OF DIFFERENT PUBLICATIONS: Fed. Ct)
Asahi Kasei Kogyo KK v. W.R. Grace & Co. (REVOCATION: DISTINCTION BETWEEN NOVELTY AND OBVIOUSNESS: TESTS OF: COMMON GENERAL KNOWLEDGE: Fed. Ct)

Bally Gaming International Inc. v. Scandic International Pty Ltd (OPPOSITION: NOVELTY: MANNER OF NEW MANUFACTURE: FAIR BASIS: SECTION 40: SMART CARD FOR DATA TRANSFER BETWEEN AMUSEMENT MACHINES AND CENTRAL COMPUTER: TIME FOR AMENDMENTS ALLOWED: AIPO)

Bausch & Lomb Inc. v. Allergan Inc. (LACK OF NOVELTY: NON-COMPLIANCE WITH SECTION 40: Pat. Off.)

Bayer AG v. Alphapharm Pty Ltd (INFRINGEMENT: INVALIDITY: LACK OF INVENTIVE STEP: S.C.(NSW))

Beckman Instruments Inc. v. Bockringer Mannheim GmbH (VALIDITY: NOVELTY: Pat. Off.)

Bodenseewerk Perkin-Elmer GmbH v. Varian Australia Pty Ltd (OPPOSITION: CLARITY: FAIR BASING: PRIOR PUBLICATION: NOVELTY: EXPERT EVIDENCE: COMMON GENERAL KNOWLEDGE: Fed. Ct)

Braas & Co. GmbH v. Humes Ltd (SECTION 40: PRINCIPLES OF CONSTRUCTION: NOVELTY: ACCIDENTAL PRIOR USE: Pat. Off.)

Bristol-Myers Company v. L'Oréal (OPPOSITION: COMMON GENERAL KNOWLEDGE: Pat. Off.)

Bristol-Myers Company v. L'Oréal (OPPOSITION: PRIOR PUBLICATION: NOVELTY: ANTICIPATION: NOT FULLY DESCRIBED: Pat. Off.)

Calsil Ltd v. Riekie & Simpfendorfer (OPPOSITION: LACK OF NOVELTY: COMMON GENERAL KNOWLEDGE: Pat. Off.)

Carpenter v. Sue (OPPOSITION: DEFECTS IN CLAIMS: LACK OF NOVELTY: Pat. Off.)

Carpenter v. Sue Agencies Pty Ltd (OPPOSITION: NOVELTY: Pat. Off.)

Clafton Pty Ltd v. Forbes Engineering Holdings Pty Ltd (OPPOSITION: ANTICIPATION: NOVELTY: WORKSHOP IMPROVEMENT: EVIDENCE OF EXPERTS WHO ARE INVENTIVE OR OVERQUALIFIED OF LIMITED VALUE ON OBVIOUSNESS: Pat. Off.)

Clay v. ICI Australia Operations Pty Ltd (OPPOSITION: CLARITY OF CLAIMS: COMMON GENERAL KNOWLEDGE: Pat. Off.)

Colgate-Palmolive Co. v. Cussons Pty Ltd (INFRINGEMENT: NOVELTY: Fed. Ct)

Cooper Industries Inc. v. Metal Manufactures Ltd (OPPOSITION: PROCEDURE: NON-COMPLIANCE WITH SECTION 40: EVIDENCE: COMMON GENERAL KNOWLEDGE: AIPO)

Coopers Animal Health Australia Ltd v. Western Stock Distributors Ltd (CLAIM BASED ON EARLIER SPECIFICATION: NOVELTY: REVOCATION: Fed. Ct)

Dennison Manufacturing Co. v. Monarch Marking Systems Inc. (OPPOSITION: NOVELTY: EXPERT EVIDENCE: Fed. Ct)

Hitachi Ltd v. Hoover (Aust.) Pty Ltd (OPPOSITION: AMENDMENT TO STATEMENT OF CLAIM: ANTICIPATION: COMMON KNOWLEDGE: Pat. Off.)

Hood Computers Pty Ltd v. On-Line Furniture Pty Ltd (OPPOSITION: OBVIOUSNESS: NON-INVENTIVE SKILLED WORKER: COSTS: AIPO)

James Hardie & Coy Pty Ltd v. Hardboards Australia Ltd (OPPOSITION: AMENDED SPECIFICATION: LACK OF NOVELTY: Pat. Off.)

Linde AG v. Air Products and Chemicals Inc. (OPPOSITION: NOVELTY: NON-COMPLIANCE WITH SECTION 40: Fed. Ct)

Lucasfilm Ltd v. Krix (OPPOSITION: ANTICIPATION: NOVELTY: Pat. Off.)

Luminous Pty Ltd v. Nitto Electric Industrial Co. Ltd (OPPOSITION: NOVELTY: OBVIOUSNESS: SECTION 40: PRIOR PUBLICATION: COMBINATION PATENT: ESSENTIAL INTEGERS: INSUFFICIENCY: EVIDENCE: FAIR BASIS: AIPO)

Melbourne v. Terry Fluid Controls Pty Ltd (PATENTS: OPPOSITION: NOVELTY: OBVIOUSNESS: REFERENCE TO BODY OF SPECIFICATION: IMPLIED LIMITATION BASED OF EXPECTATION OF THOSE SKILLED IN THE ART: Fed. Ct)

Micronair (Aerial) Ltd v. Waikerie Co-operative Producers Ltd (OPPOSITION TO ACCEPTANCE: NOVELTY: OBVIOUSNESS: Pat. Off.)

Moore Paragon Australia Ltd v. Multiform Printers (OPPOSITION: LACK OF NOVELTY: Pat. Off.)

Nelson v. Hillmark Industries Pty Ltd (PROVISIONAL SPECIFICATION: PRIORITY DATE: PRIOR PUBLICATION: NOVELTY: MATTERS ARISING UNDER SECTION 40: Pat. Off.)

Nomad Structures International Ltd v. Heyring Pty Ltd (OPPOSITION: NOVELTY: OBTAINING: Pat. Off.)

Opsvik v. Bad Back Centre Pty Ltd (NOVELTY: COMBINATION OF KNOWN IDEAS: S.C.(NSW))

Optech International Ltd v. Buxton Hicrarium Ltd (OPPOSITION: ANTICIPATION: NOVELTY: OBVIOUSNESS: MANNER OF MANUFACTURE: AIPO)

Peptide Technology Ltd v. The Wellcome Foundation Ltd (OPPOSITION: COMMON GENERAL KNOWLEDGE: NOVELTY: Pat. Off.)

Polar Vac Pty Ltd v. Spoutvac Manufacturing Pty Ltd (OPPOSITION: PRIOR PUBLICATION: SECRET USE: OBVIOUSNESS: COMMON GENERAL KNOWLEDGE: AIPO)

Rescare Ltd v. Anaesthetic Supplies Pty Ltd (VALIDITY: REVOCATION: INFRINGEMENT: FAIR BASIS: LACK OF NOVELTY: Fed. Ct)

Robert Bosch GmbH v. Solo Industries Pty Ltd (NOVELTY: FAIRLY BASED: Pat. Off.)

Ryan v. Lum (LACK OF NOVELTY: REVOCATION: ONUS OF PROOF: S.C.(NSW))

Sartas No. 1 Pty Ltd v. Koukouou & Partners Pty Ltd (METHOD CLAIMS: PRODUCT CLAIMS: VALIDITY: FAIR BASING: NOVELTY: DOUBLE CLAIMING: LACK OF TITLE: FALSE SUGGESTION: AIPO)

Seasonmakers (Australia) Pty Ltd v. North Coast Woodwool Pty Ltd (OPPOSITION: ANTICIPATION: Pat. Off.)

Secretary of State for Defence (U.K.) v. Rheinmetall GmbH (OPPOSITION: MANNER OF NEW MANUFACTURE: AMENDMENT: WHETHER IN SUBSTANCE DISCLOSED: Pat. Off.)

Sunbeam Corp. v. Morphy-Richards (Aust.) Pty Ltd (INFRINGEMENT: REVOCATION: VALIDITY: INVENTIVENESS: NOVELTY: SUBJECT–MATTER: COMMON GENERAL KNOWLEDGE: MOSAIC: H.C.)

Tetra Pak International AB v. J. Gadsden Pty Ltd (OPPOSITION: NOVELTY: ANTICIPATION: COMMON GENERAL KNOWLEDGE: Pat. Off.)

United Biomedical Inc. v. Genetics Systems Corp. (OPPOSITION: PRIOR CLAIMING: PRIOR PUBLICATION: AIPO)

United Kingdom Government (Secretary of State for Defence) v. Rheinmetall GmbH (OPPOSITION: NOVELTY: ANTICIPATION: Pat. Off.)

Vulcan Australia Ltd v. Braemar Appliances Pty Ltd (INFRINGEMENT: VALIDITY: COUNTERCLAIM FOR REVOCATION: NOVELTY: INVALIDITY: Pat. Off.)

Werner (R.D.) & Co. Inc. v. Bailey Aluminium Products Pty Ltd (OPPOSITION: RELATIONSHIP BETWEEN LACK OF NOVELTY AND OBVIOUSNESS: Fed. Ct)

Whitco Pty Ltd v. Austral Lock Industries Pty Ltd (OPPOSITION: INVENTION: FAIR BASIS: PRIOR PUBLICATION: LACK OF NOVELTY: Pat. Off.)

Winner v. Ammar Holdings Pty Ltd (INFRINGEMENT: REVOCATION: LOCKING DEVICE: Fed. Ct)

Winner v. Ammar Holdings Pty Ltd (REVOCATION: DISTINCTION BETWEEN OBVIOUSNESS AND NOVELTY: COMMON GENERAL KNOWLEDGE: Fed. Ct)

Omnibus Claim

Browne & Williamson Tobacco Corp. v. Philip Morris Inc. (No. 2) (AMENDMENT: OPPOSITION: WHETHER AMENDED CLAIM OUTSIDE SCOPE OF ORIGINAL: Pat. Off.)

Onus. *See* **Practice** (*Onus*)

Opposition to Grant

For cases on opposition to amendment, extension or restoration, see the relevant subject-matter

A. & K. Aluminium Pty Ltd v. Lidco Systems Sales Pty Ltd (NOVELTY: PRIOR PUBLICATION: MATTERS ARISING UNDER SECTION 40: OBTAINING: Pat. Off.)

A Couple 'a Cowboys Pty Ltd v. Ward (APPLICATION: AIPO)

Acushnet Co. v. Spalding Australia Pty Ltd (PRIOR PUBLICATION: PRIOR USE: PRIOR SALES: Pat. Off.)

Acushnet Company v. Spalding Australia Pty Ltd (AMENDMENT: INTERPRETATION OF CLAIMS: Pat. Off.)

Albright & Wilson Ltd v. Colgate Palmolive Co. (EXTENSION OF TIME LIMIT: Pat. Off.)

American Cyanamid Company v. Nalco Chemical Company (EVIDENCE: CROSS-EXAMINATION: Pat. Off.)

American National Can Co. v. W.R. Grace & Co-Conn. (APPLICATION: COSTS: AIPO)

Amrad Corp. Ltd v. Genentech Inc. (NOTICE: EXTENSION OF TIME: ERROR OR OMISSION: AIPO)

Armstrong v. Larocca (PRIOR USE: DESIRABILITY OF CORROBORATION: Pat. Off.)

Austgen Biojet Holdings Pty Ltd v. Goronszy (OBTAINING: INVENTOR: TRANSITIONAL APPLICATION: Fed. Ct)

Austoft Industries Limited v. Cameco Industries Limited (EXTENSION OF TIME TO FILE EVIDENCE: PUBLIC INTEREST: AIPO)

Australian Paper Manufacturers Ltd v. CIL Ltd (NOVELTY: ANTICIPATION: PRIOR CLAIMING: PRIOR PUBLICATION: Pat. Off.)

B.F. Goodrich Co. v. ICI Australia Operations Pty Ltd (APPLICATION: WHETHER CLAIMS FAIRLY BASED: PRIOR PUBLICATION: OBVIOUSNESS: COMBINATION INVENTION: MANNER OF NEW MANUFACTURE: PRIOR USE: PRIOR SECRET USE: STANDARD OF PROOF: AIPO)

Baker v. Peuren Agencies Ltd (FAIR BASIS: DEFINITION NOT UNDERSTANDABLE: AMENDMENT OF SPECIFICATION: COSTS: Pat. Off.)

Bally Gaming International Inc. v. Scandic International Pty Ltd (NOVELTY: OBVIOUSNESS: MANNER OF NEW MANUFACTURE: FAIR BASIS: SECTION 40: SMART CARD FOR DATA TRANSFER BETWEEN AMUSEMENT MACHINES AND CENTRAL COMPUTER: TIME FOR AMENDMENTS ALLOWED: AIPO)

BASF Corporation v. ICI Australia Operations Pty Ltd (APPLICATION FOR EXTENSION OF TIME WITHIN WHICH TO SERVE EVIDENCE-IN-SUPPORT: ONUS OF PROOF ON APPLICANT: Pat. Off.)

Bausch & Lomb Inc. v. Allergan Inc. (ACCEPTANCE: FAIR BASIS: PRIOR PUBLICATION: OBVIOUSNESS: LACK OF NOVELTY: NON-COMPLIANCE WITH SECTION 40: Pat. Off.)

Baxter Travenol Laboratories Inc. v. Cutter Laboratories Inc. (EXTENSION OF TIME FOR LODGING EVIDENCE: Pat. Off.)

Beecham Group Ltd's Application (MANNER OF NEW MANUFACTURE: NOVELTY: Pat. Off.)

Bio Energy Systems Inc. v. Lawrence John Walton (LACK OF FAIR BASIS AND CLEAR DEFINITION: NOVELTY: PRIOR PUBLICATION: Pat. Off.)

Bioglan Laboratories (Aust.) Pty Ltd v. Crooks (LACK OF NOVELTY: PRIOR DISCLOSURES: Pat. Off.)

Bodenseewerk Perkin-Elmer GmbH v. Varian Australia Pty Ltd (CLARITY: FAIR BASING: PRIOR PUBLICATION: OBVIOUSNESS: NOVELTY: EXPERT EVIDENCE: COMMON GENERAL KNOWLEDGE: OPPONENT'S RIGHT TO BE HEARD: Fed. Ct)

Borden Inc. v. Elkem A/S (ADEQUACY OF STATEMENT: GROUNDS FOR DISMISSAL: Pat. Off.)

Brickwood Holdings Pty Ltd v. ACI Operations Pty Ltd (APPEAL: S.C.(Vic.))

Bridge & Plate Constructions Pty Ltd v. Mannesmann Demag Pty Ltd (NOVELTY: PRIOR PUBLICATION: Pat. Off.)

Bristol-Myers Company v. L'Oréal (OBVIOUSNESS: COMMON GENERAL KNOWLEDGE: PRIOR PUBLICATION: MANNER OF NEW MANUFACTURE: Pat. Off.)

Bristol-Myers Company v. L'Oréal (PRIOR PUBLICATION: NOVELTY: ANTICIPATION: OBVIOUSNESS: INVENTION NOT FULLY DESCRIBED: Pat. Off.)

British-American Tobacco Co. Ltd v. Philip Morris Ltd (EVIDENCE: EXTENSION OF TIME TO LODGE EVIDENCE: Pat. Off.)

Browne & Williamson Tobacco Corp. v. Philip Morris Inc. (FAIR BASIS: LACK OF CLARITY: ANTICIPATION: NOVELTY: AMENDMENT: Pat. Off.)

Calsil Ltd v. Riekie & Simpfendorfer (OBVIOUSNESS: LACK OF NOVELTY: COMMON GENERAL KNOWLEDGE: EVIDENCE: COSTS: Pat. Off.)

Calsil Ltd v. Riekie and Simpfendorfer (EXTENSION OF TIME FOR SERVICE OF OPPONENTS' EVIDENCE: Pat. Off.)

Carpenter v. Sue (DEFECTS IN CLAIMS: LACK OF NOVELTY: OBVIOUSNESS: Pat. Off.)

Carpenter v. Sue Agencies Pty Ltd (NOVELTY: OBVIOUSNESS: Pat. Off.)

Clafton Pty Ltd v. Forbes Engineering Holdings Pty Ltd (FAIR BASIS: PRIOR CLAIMING: PRIORITY DATE OF DIVISIONAL PATENT: PRIOR PUBLICATION: PUBLIC DOMAIN: ANTICIPATION: NOVELTY: WORKSHOP IMPROVEMENT: OBVIOUSNESS: Pat. Off.)

Clay v. ICI Australia Operations Pty Ltd (CLARITY OF CLAIMS: COMMON GENERAL KNOWLEDGE: Pat. Off.)

Clay v. ICI Australia Operations Pty Ltd (CLARITY OF CLAIMS: OBVIOUSNESS: COMMON GENERAL KNOWLEDGE: PRIOR PUBLICATION: Pat. Off.)

Commonwealth Industrial Gases Ltd v. Liquid Air Australia Ltd (NOVELTY: ANTICIPATION: PRIOR CLAIMING: MANNER OF NEW MANUFACTURE: Pat. Off.)

Commonwealth Scientific and Industrial Research Organisation v. HBH Technological Industries Pty Ltd (EVIDENCE: REQUEST BY OPPONENT TO EXTEND TIME: UNCERTAINTY: Pat. Off.)

Commonwealth Scientific and Industrial Research Organisation v. Western Mining Corporation Ltd (EXTENSION OF TIME TO SERVE EVIDENCE: OBJECTION: PRINCIPLES: PUBLIC INTEREST: Pat. Off.)

Commonwealth Scientific and Industrial Research Organisation v. Western Mining Corp. Ltd (OBJECTION TO APPLICATION FOR EXTENSION OF TIME WITHIN WHICH TO SERVE EVIDENCE-IN-SUPPORT: WHETHER OPPOSITION SERIOUS: PUBLIC INTEREST: COSTS: Pat. Off.)

Concorde Trading Pty Ltd v. Croner Trading Pty Ltd (APPLICATION FOR DISMISSAL: VEXATIOUS OR ABUSE OF PROCESS: COSTS: AIPO)

Conry v. Atlas Air Australia Pty Ltd (EXTENSION OF TIME IN WHICH TO LODGE NOTICE OF OPPOSITION: Pat. Off.)

Continental White Cap Inc. v. W.R. Grace & Co. (HEARING: WITHDRAWAL OF PARTY BEFORE HEARING: Pat. Off.)

Cooper Industries Inc. v. Metal Manufactures Ltd (PROCEDURE: NON-COMPLIANCE WITH SECTION 40: EVIDENCE: OBVIOUSNESS: COMMON GENERAL KNOWLEDGE: AIPO)

Cotterill v. Trenton Pty Ltd (DIRECTIONS ON PROVISION OF FURTHER AND BETTER PARTICULARS: AIPO)

CSIRO v. Asterol International (APPLICATION FOR EXTENSION OF TIME TO LODGE NOTICE OF OPPOSITION: AIPO)

Mitsubishi Chemical Industries Ltd v. Asahi Kasei Kogyo KK (RESPONSE TO
EVIDENCE-IN-REPLY: ERROR OR OMISSION BY EMPLOYEE OF PATENT
ATTORNEY: SPECIAL CIRCUMSTANCES: PUBLIC INTEREST: Pat. Off.)

Mobay Corp. v. Dow Chemical Co. (DELETE OF PART OF STATEMENT OF GROUNDS
AND PARTICULARS: Pat. Off.)

Moore Paragon Australia Ltd v. Multiform Printers (LACK OF NOVELTY: PRIOR
PUBLICATION: OBVIOUSNESS: MANNER OF NEW MANUFACTURE: Pat. Off.)

MXM v. Franke (PERSON INTERESTED: *Locus standii*: STANDING: PATENT
ATTORNEY: AGENCY: DISMISSAL OF PROCEEDINGS: Pat. Off.)

Nautical Services Pty Ltd v. Hitech Distillation (Aust.) Pty Ltd (EVIDENCE:
EXTENSION OF TIME LIMITS TO SERVE: *Locus standii*: PUBLIC INTEREST: COSTS:
Pat. Off.)

Nomad Structures International Ltd v. Heyring Pty Ltd (EVIDENCE: FAIR BASIS:
PRIOR USE AND PUBLICATION: NOVELTY: OBVIOUSNESS: OBTAINING: Pat.
Off.)

Norwood Industries Pty Ltd v. Macbird Floraprint Pty Ltd (GROUNDS AND
PARTICULARS OF SUFFICIENCY OF: APPLICATION TO DISMISS: Pat. Off.)

Optech International Ltd v. Buxton Hicrarium Ltd (COSTS: EVIDENCE:
ANTICIPATION: NOVELTY: OBVIOUSNESS: MANNER OF MANUFACTURE:
OBTAINING: AIPO)

Peptide Technology Ltd v. The Wellcome Foundation Ltd (MANNER OF NEW
MANUFACTURE: SUFFICIENCY OF SPECIFICATION: FAIRLY BASED:
AMBIGUITY: OBVIOUSNESS: COMMON GENERAL KNOWLEDGE: NOVELTY: Pat.
Off.)

Perkin-Elmer Corp. v. Varian Techtron Pty Ltd (AMENDMENT OF SPECIFICATION:
INTERIM HEARING: FAIR BASIS: Pat. Off.)

Philip Morris Inc. v. Brown and Williamson Tobacco Corp. (AMENDMENT:
REQUEST TO AMEND: IN SUBSTANCE DISCLOSED: FAIR BASIS: COMPLETE
SPECIFICATION: FURTHER REQUEST TO AMEND: PRACTICE AND
PROCEDURE: AIPO)

Polar Vac Pty Ltd v. Spoutvac Manufacturing Pty Ltd (PRIOR PUBLICATION: SECRET
USE: OBVIOUSNESS: COMMON GENERAL KNOWLEDGE: AIPO)

Poltrock v. Ennor (EXTENSION OF TIME LIMIT TO LODGE NOTICE: EVIDENCE IN
SUPPORT: Pat. Off.)

Porter v. Arbortech Investments Pty Ltd (APPLICATION: OBJECTION TO
ALLOWANCE OF A REQUEST TO AMEND STATEMENT OF GROUNDS AND
PARTICULARS: AIPO)

PPG Industries Inc. v. Stauffer Chemical Co. (NOVELTY: ANTICIPATION: PRIOR
CLAIMING: FAIR BASIS: Pat. Off.)

Procter & Gamble Company v. Kimberly-Clark Corporation (VALIDITY:
OBTAINING: APPLICATIONS FOR EXTENSION OF TIME TO LODGE EVIDENCE:
Pat. Off.)

Prudhoe v. ICI Australian Operations Pty Ltd (OPPOSITION WITHDRAWN: PATENT
GRANTED: COSTS OF APPLICANT: WHETHER PROCEEDINGS STILL BEFORE
COMMISSIONER: AIPO)

Queensland Plumbing Pty Ltd v. Trade Waste Diversion Pty Ltd (SUCCESS OF
OPPONENT: LEAVE TO AMEND: OPPONENTS COMMENTS: AIPO)

Rear v. Drilling Tools Australia Pty Ltd (EXTENSION OF TIME: EVIDENCE-IN-
SUPPORT: GROUNDS FOR GRANT OF EXTENSION OF TIME: ROLE OF
COMMISSIONER: Pat. Off.)

Ricardo International plc v. Orital Engine Co. (Aust.) Pty Ltd (PRIOR CLAIMING:
NOVELTY: TRANSITIONAL APPLICATION: DIVISIONAL STATUS: FAIR BASIS:
AIPO)

Rock Engineering Pty Ltd v. A. Noble & Son Ltd (ACCEPTANCE: LAPSE: FAILURE TO
PAY CONTINUATION FEE: APPLICATION TO RESTORE: Pat. Off.)

Watson v. Bristol-Myers Co. (EXTENSION OF TIME: CIRCUMSTANCES BEYOND
CONTROL OF PERSON CONCERNED: Pat. Off.)

Weir Pumps Ltd and Commissioner of Patent and Stork Pompen BV (Re)
(EXTENSION OF TIME TO LODGE NOTICE: LATE APPLICATION: ERROR OR
OMISSION: AAT)

Werner (R.D.) & Co. Inc. v. Bailey Aluminium Products Pty Ltd (LACK OF
NOVELTY: RELATIONSHIP BETWEEN LACK OF NOVELTY AND OBVIOUSNESS:
SPECIFICITY OF CLAIM: Fed. Ct)

Werner Co. Inc. v. Bailey Aluminium Products Pty Ltd (S.C.(Vic.))

Whitco Pty Ltd v. Austral Lock Industries Pty Ltd (NON-DISCLOSURE: LACK OF FAIR
BASIS: PRIOR PUBLICATION: LACK OF NOVELTY: OBVIOUSNESS: Pat. Off.)

X-Cyte Inc. v. Tablek Electronics Pty Ltd (WITHDRAWAL: EFFECT: AIPO)

Package Claims

Bristol-Myers Company v. L'Oréal (Pat. Off.)

Patent Agent or Attorney

Firmaframe Nominees Pty Ltd v. Automatic Roller Doors Australia Pty Ltd
(OMISSION BY PATENT ATTORNEY: Pat. Off.)

Genentech Inc. v. Wellcome Foundation Ltd (ERRORS OR OMISSIONS OF PATENT
ATTORNEY: SPECIAL CIRCUMSTANCES: Pat. Off.)

Petty Patent Heylen v. Davies Collison Cave (PETTY PATENT: EXTENSION: NOTICE:
COMPLETE SPECIFICATION: AMENDMENT: IN SUBSTANCE DISCLOSED: FAIR
BASIS: NOVELTY: INVENTIVE STEP: OBVIOUSNESS: EVIDENTIARY BURDEN:
PATENT ATTORNEYS: COSTS: AIPO)

Imagic Inc. v. Futuretronics (Aust.) Pty Ltd (COMMUNICATIONS WITH CLIENT:
WHETHER PRIVILEGED: S.C.(NSW))

Mitsubishi Chemical Industries Ltd v. Asahi Kasei Kogyo KK (ERROR OR OMISSION
BY EMPLOYEE OF PATENT ATTORNEY: SPECIAL CIRCUMSTANCES: PUBLIC
INTEREST: Pat. Off.)

MXM v. Franke (PERSON INTERESTED: Locus standii: STANDING: Pat. Off.)

Pfizer Pty Ltd v. Warner Lambert Pty Ltd (PRIVILEGED COMMUNICATIONS WITH:
WHETHER PRIVILEGE EXTENDS TO COMMUNICATIONS BETWEEN PATENT
ATTORNEY AND CLIENT IN THE COURSE OF CONDUCT: Fed. Ct)

Riker Laboratories Australia Pty Ltd v. Westwood Pharmaceuticals Inc.
(COMMUNICATIONS WITH CLIENT: WHETHER PRIVILEGED: S.C.(NSW))

Sepa Waste Water Treatment Pty Ltd v. JMT Welding Pty Ltd (PATENT AGENTS'
PRIVILEGE: ADVICE ON DESIGNS INFRINGEMENT: S.C.(NSW))

Wundowie Foundry Pty Ltd v. Milson Foundry Pty Ltd (DOCUMENTS RELATING TO
DESIGN AND DEVELOPMENT OF INVENTION: PATENT ATTORNEY AND CLIENT
PRIVILEGE: Fed. Ct)

Patent Office Practice. See Practice (Patent Office practice)

Patentability

Anaesthetic Supplies Pty Ltd v. Rescare Ltd (VALIDITY: FAIR BASIS: METHOD OF
TREATMENT OF DISEASE: Fed. Ct)

Freeman v. Pohlner Pty Ltd (REVOCATION: NOVELTY: DESCRIPTION OF
INVENTION: Fed. Ct)

International Business Machines Corporation v. Commissioner of Patents
(ALGORITHM: TEST OF PATENTABILITY: DISTINCTION BETWEEN INVENTION
AND DISCOVERY OR MATHEMATICAL PRINCIPLE: Fed. Ct)

Rescare Ltd v. Anaesthetic Supplies Pty Ltd (METHODS OR PROCESSES FOR TREATING THE HUMAN BODY: FAIR BASIS: Fed. Ct)

Thomas & Garnham's Application (OBJECTION BY EXAMINER: REQUEST TO COMMISSIONER TO EXERCISE DISCRETIONARY POWER: COMPUTER PROCESSING APPARATUS FOR ASSEMBLING TEXT, PARTICULARLY IN CHINESE CHARACTERS: NOVELTY: PRIORITY DATE: AIPO)

Patentee

Murex Diagnostics Australia Pty Ltd v. Chiron Corp. (APPLICATION FOR REVOCATION: PATENTEE NOT INVENTOR: EFFECT OF TRANSITIONAL PROVISIONS: Fed. Ct)

Petty Patent

Avion Engineering Pty Ltd v. Fisher and Paykel Healthcare Pty Ltd (DESIGN: INFRINGEMENT: OBVIOUS IMITATION: FRAUDULENT IMITATION: RECTIFICATION: LACK OF NOVELTY AND VAGUE AND AMBIGUOUS REPRESENTATION: COMBINATION INFRINGEMENT: PITH AND MARROW DOCTRINE: SCOPE: REVOCATION: OBVIOUSNESS: LACK OF FAIR BASING: Fed. Ct)

Baker v. Peuren Agencies Ltd (OPPOSITION: FAIR BASIS: DEFINITION NOT UNDERSTANDABLE: AMENDMENT OF SPECIFICATION: COSTS: Pat. Off.)

Bates Saddlery Pty Ltd v. Becville Pty Ltd (EXTENSION OF TERM: NOVELTY: OBVIOUSNESS: Pat. Off.)

Clemco International Sales Co. v. Bolrette Pty Ltd (UNFAIR TRADING: INTERLOCUTORY INJUNCTION: Fed. Ct)

Coopers Animal Health Australia Ltd v. Western Stock Distributors Pty Ltd (PROVISIONAL SPECIFICATION AND SUBSEQUENT PRIORITY DATES: Fed. Ct)

Coopers Animal Health Australia Ltd v. Western Stock Distributors Ltd (CLAIM BASED ON EARLIER SPECIFICATION: NOVELTY: OBVIOUSNESS: UTILITY: REVOCATION: Fed. Ct)

Coopers Animal Health Australia Ltd v. Western Stock Distributors Ltd (EXTENSION: OBJECTION: OPPOSITION: INVALIDITY: ANTICIPATION: PRIOR USE: Pat. Off.)

Costa v. G.R. & I.E. Daking Pty Ltd (PETTY PATENT: SECTION 28 NOTICE: OBTAINING: PRIOR USE: WHETHER FOR REASONABLE TRIAL: LACK OF NOVELTY: JOINT INVENTORSHIP: AIPO)

Durack v. Associated Pool Builders Pty Ltd (INFRINGEMENT: VALIDITY: INTERLOCUTORY INJUNCTION: Fed. Ct)

Elconnex Pty Ltd v. Gerard Industries Pty Ltd (CONSTRUCTION: OBVIOUSNESS: PRINCIPLES: FAIRLY BASED ON PROVISIONAL OR COMPLETE SPECIFICATION FROM WHICH IT WAS DERIVED: Fed. Ct)

Elconnex Pty Ltd v. Gerard Industries Pty Ltd (OBVIOUSNESS: ADMISSIBILITY OF EVIDENCE OF EXPERT WITNESSES: WHETHER FAIRLY BASED ON COMPLETE SPECIFICATION: WHETHER CLAIM OF THE AMBIGUOUS: INFRINGEMENT: Fed. Ct)

Elconnex Pty Ltd v. Gerard Industries Pty Ltd (OPPOSITION: OBVIOUSNESS: RELATED PETTY PATENT: AIPO)

Ferocem Pty Ltd v. High Tech Auto Tools Pty Ltd (PETTY PATENT: PRACTICE AND PROCEDURE: NOTICE: INFORMATION: PENDING COURT PROCEEDINGS: FEDERAL COURT: PATENT OFFICE PRACTICE: AIPO)

Fisher & Paykel Healthcare Pty Ltd v. Avion Engineering Pty Ltd (DESIGNS: INFRINGEMENT: WHETHER OBVIOUS OR FRAUDULENT IMITATION: SAME FUNDAMENTAL OR BASIC DESIGN: VALIDITY: CONSTRUCTION OF CLAIM: PRINCIPLES: OBVIOUSNESS: COMBINATION OF COMMON INTEGERS: INFRINGEMENT: APPLICABLE PRINCIPLES: Fed. Ct)

Gerber Scientific Products Inc. v. North Broken Hill Ltd (APPLICATION UNDER SECTION 68B(3): LACK OF NOVELTY: OBVIOUSNESS: INVENTION NOT FULLY DESCRIBED: Pat. Off.)

Guertler's Application (EXTENSION OF OPPOSITION: OBVIOUSNESS: EVIDENCE: Pat. Off.)

Gumley's Application (PATENT APPLICATION: ADVERTISED AS ACCEPTED: NOTICE OF OPPOSITION: APPLICATION FOR EXTENSION OF TIME FOR FILING EVIDENCE IN SUPPORT OF OPPOSITION: APPLICATION OPPOSED: THREE-MONTH EXTENSION GRANTED: Pat. Off.)

Heylen v. Davies Collison Cave (PETTY PATENT: EXTENSION: NOTICE: COMPLETE SPECIFICATION: AMENDMENT: IN SUBSTANCE DISCLOSED: FAIR BASIS: NOVELTY: INVENTIVE STEP: OBVIOUSNESS: EVIDENTIARY BURDEN: PATENT ATTORNEYS: COSTS: AIPO)

Heylen v. Davies Collison Cave (PETTY PATENT: EXTENSION: NOTICE: COMPLETE SPECIFICATION: AMENDMENT: IN SUBSTANCE DISCLOSED: FAIR BASIS: NOVELTY: INVENTIVE STEP: OBVIOUSNESS: EVIDENTIARY BURDEN: PATENT ATTORNEYS: COSTS: AIPO)

High Tech Auto Tools Pty Ltd v. Ferocem Pty Ltd (PETTY PATENT: EXTENSION: OBJECTION: NOTICE: CLAIMS: PRIORITY DATE: MANNER OF MANUFACTURE: OBVIOUS MISTAKE: NOVELTY: OBVIOUSNESS: EVIDENCE: PRACTICE AND PROCEDURE: CLARITY: UNCERTAINTY: AIPO)

High Tech Auto Tools Pty Ltd v. Ferocem Pty Ltd (PETTY PATENT: EXTENSION: OBJECTION: NOTICE: CLAIMS: PRIORITY DATE: MANNER OF MANUFACTURE: OBVIOUS MISTAKE: NOVELTY: OBVIOUSNESS: EVIDENCE: PRACTICE AND PROCEDURE: CLARITY: UNCERTAINTY: AIPO)

Interact Machine Tools (NSW) Pty Ltd v. Yamazaki Mazak Corporation (MACHINE TOOL COMPRISING COMBINATION OF INTEGERS: INFRINGEMENT: INVALIDITY: FAIR BASIS: WHETHER PETTY PATENTS FAIRLY BASED ON SPECIFICATIONS OF PARENT COMPLETE SPECIFICATION AND ON PRIORITY JAPANESE SPECIFICATIONS: Fed. Ct)

Komesaroff v. Mizzi (EXTENSION: OPPOSITION: OBJECTION: EVIDENCE: INVALIDITY: NOVELTY: OBVIOUSNESS: Pat. Off.)

Kwan v. Queensland Corrective Services Commission (EXTENSION: SECTION 28 NOTICE: INVENTION MADE BY PRISONERS: WHETHER INVENTORS EMPLOYEES OF CORRECTIONAL FACILITY: FAIR BASIS: SUFFICIENCY: NOVELTY: OBVIOUSNESS: AIPO)

Lake's Application (APPLICATION FOR EXTENSION OF TERM: INFORMATION LODGED AGAINST EXTENSION: ANTICIPATION: OBVIOUSNESS: PRIOR USE: SECRET USE: SUFFICIENCY: OBTAINING: LATE EVIDENCE: SPECIAL PLEA BASED ON EMPLOYMENT: Pat. Off.)

Lasercare (Aust.) Pty Ltd v. Christiansen (EXTENSION: OBVIOUSNESS: LACK OF NOVELTY: PRIOR PUBLICATION: PRIOR USER: Pat. Off.)

Lech Pawlowski v. Seeley (F.F.) Nominees Pty Ltd (EXTENSION: APPLICATION: OBVIOUSNESS: LACK OF NOVELTY: COMMON GENERAL KNOWLEDGE: WHAT CONSTITUTES: Pat. Off.)

Lyons v. The J.M. Smucker Co. (APPLICATION FOR EXTENSION OF TIME TO FILE NOTICE OF OPPOSITION TO EXTENSION OF TERM: WHETHER ERROR BY ATTORNEY: WHETHER SERIOUS OPPOSITION: COSTS: Pat. Off.)

Massey v. Noack (EXTENSION OF TERM: OBTAINING: MATTERS ARISING UNDER SECTION 40: Pat. Off.)

Murray Joseph Wright v. Ajax Davey Pty Ltd (EXTENSION: MANNER OF NEW MANUFACTURE: COMMON GENERAL KNOWLEDGE: OBVIOUSNESS: NOVELTY: Pat. Off.)

Peter Pan Electric Pty Ltd v. Newton Grace Pty Ltd (VALIDITY: INTERLOCUTORY INJUNCTION: PROCEDURE: Fed. Ct)

Roelofs' Patent (EXTENSION OF TERM: STATUTORY NOTICE: FAIRLY BASED: PRIORITY DATE: PRIOR DATE: AIPO)

Smucker (J.M.) Co.'s Petty Patent (PETTY PATENT: EXTENSION OF TERM: OPPOSITION TO EXTENSION: NOVELTY: OBVIOUSNESS: MANNER OF NEW MANUFACTURE: INCONVENIENT SPECIFICATION: NON-COMPLIANCE WITH SECTION 40: PROCEDURE: AIPO)

South East Queensland Electricity Board v. Techmark-Miers Pty Ltd (APPLICATION: OPPOSITION: APPOINTMENT OF RECEIVER AND MANAGER TO OPPONENT: NON-PURSUIT OF OPPOSITION: WITHDRAWAL OF OPPOSITION: COSTS: Pat. Off.)

Thomas and Stohrs Application (OPPOSITION TO EXTENSION OF TERM: COMPUTER INVENTION: OBVIOUSNESS: IDEA: ANTICIPATION: Pat. Off.)

Yamazaki Mazak Corp.'s Application (APPLICATIONS FOR EXTENSION OF TERMS: INFORMATION AGAINST EXTENSION: APPLICATION FOR ADJOURNMENT OF HEARING: Pat. Off.)

Yamazaki Mazak Corporation v. Interact Machine Tools (NSW) Pty Ltd (INFRINGEMENT: VALIDITY: OBVIOUSNESS: FAIR BASING OF CLAIM UPON MATTER DESCRIBED IN SPECIFICATION: NOVELTY: WHETHER CONVENTION PRIORITY DATE PRECEDED DATE OF ALLEGED ANTICIPATION: WHETHER FOR THAT PURPOSE CLAIMS FAIRLY BASED ON DISCLOSURE IN FOREIGN BASIC APPLICATIONS: WHETHER PATENTS OBTAINED ON FALSE SUGGESTION OR REPRESENTATION: Fed. Ct)

Pith and Marrow Doctrine

Avion Engineering Pty Ltd v. Fisher and Paykel Healthcare Pty Ltd (INFRINGEMENT: SCOPE: Fed. Ct)

Rehm Pty Ltd v. Websters Security Systems (International) Pty Ltd (INFRINGEMENT: LIMITATION OF CLAIM: Fed. Ct)

Rhône Poulenc Agrochemie SA v. UIM Chemical Services Pty Ltd (INFRINGEMENT: EVIDENCE: INJUNCTION: DISCRETION: Fed. Ct)

Plurality of Invention

Hoechst AG's Application (No. 2) (EXAMINERS OBJECTION: Pat. Off.)

Practice Subjects

Account of profits

Dart Industries Inc. v. Decor Corporation Pty Ltd (DEDUCTION FOR INFRINGER'S GENERAL OVERHEAD COSTS: WHETHER ALLOWABLE: QUANTIFICATION OF: ONUS OF PROOF CONCERNING: H.C.)

Decor Corporation Pty Ltd v. Dart Industries Inc. (Fed. Ct)

Minnesota Mining & Manufacturing Co. v. C. Jeffries Pty Ltd (ELECTION FOR DAMAGES OR ACCOUNT: WHETHER ELECTION TO BE MADE BEFORE DEFENDANT PROVIDES DISCOVERY: Fed. Ct (NSW))

Ryan v. Lum (DAMAGES OR ACCOUNT: S.C.(NSW))

Appeal subjects

Acushnet Co. v. Spalding Australia Pty Ltd (EXISTENCE OF EARLIER INTERIM DECISION: Fed. Ct)

Acushnet Co. v. Spalding Australia Pty Ltd (CROSS-APPEAL: ORDER FOR FILING AFFIDAVITS: Fed. Ct)

Brickwood Holdings Pty Ltd v. ACI Operations Pty Ltd (APPLICATION: OPPOSITION: S.C.(Vic.))

Decor Corporation Pty Ltd v. Dart Industries Inc. (INTERLOCUTORY JUDGMENT: LEAVE TO APPEAL: DISCRETION: Fed. Ct)

Elazac Pty Ltd v. Commissioner of Patents (AMENDMENT: FAILURE TO OPPOSE: RIGHT OF APPEAL: AIPO)

International Business Machines Corporation v. Commissioner of Patents (NATURE OF APPEAL: Fed. Ct)

Titan Mining & Engineering Pty Ltd v. Arnall's Engineering Pty Ltd (NATURE OF APPEAL: S.C.(NSW))

Westaflex (Aust.) Pty Ltd v. Wood (INFRINGEMENT: INJUNCTIONS: STAY PENDING APPEAL: PRINCIPLES: APPROPRIATE UNDERTAKINGS AND CONDITIONS: Fed. Ct)

Clerical error

Behringwerke AG (AMENDMENT OF REGISTER: SUBSTITUTION OF NAME: Pat. Off.)

Convenient forum

Spotless Group Ltd v. Proplast Pty Ltd (INFRINGEMENTS: STATE ACTION IN TWO JURISDICTIONS: S.C.(Vic.))

Costs

American National Can Co. v. W.R. Grace & Co.-Conn. (OPPOSITION: AIPO)

Colgate-Palmolive Co. v. Cussons Pty Ltd (INDEMNITY COSTS: EXERCISE OF DISCRETION TO AWARD: Fed. Ct)

Concorde Trading Pty Ltd v. Croner Trading Pty Ltd (OPPOSITION: APPLICATION FOR DISMISSAL: VEXATIOUS OR ABUSE OF PROCESS: COSTS: AIPO)

Farmitalia Carlo Erba SrL v. Delta West Pty Ltd (SECURITY FOR COSTS: APPLICANT ORDINARILY RESIDENT OUTSIDE JURISDICTION: DISCRETION: Fed. Ct)

Heylen v. Davies Collison Cave (PATENT ATTORNEYS: AIPO)

James Hardy Irrigation Pty Ltd v. Hydro Plan Engineering Ltd (OPPOSITION: WITHDRAWAL: AIPO)

Optech International Ltd v. Buxton Hicrarium Ltd (OPPOSITION: AIPO)

Sumitomo Chemical Co. Ltd v. Rhône-Poulenc Chimie (OPPOSITION: SECTION 40: Fed. Ct)

University of Sydney v. Werner & Mertz GmbH (AMENDMENT OF SPECIFICATION: AIPO)

Virbac (Australia) Pty Ltd v. Merck Patent GmbH (EXTENSION OF TERM: PHARMACEUTICAL SUBSTANCE: COSTS: Fed. Ct)

Winner v. Morey Haigh & Associates (Australasia) Pty Ltd (REVOCATION OF PATENT IN SUIT AT OTHER PROCEEDINGS: DISMISSAL OF INFRINGEMENT PROCEEDINGS: INDEMNITY BASIS: Fed. Ct)

Cross-examination

American Cyanamid Company v. Nalco Chemical Company (REQUEST FOR THE COMMISSIONER OF PATENTS TO SUMMON WITNESSES: PATENT OFFICE PRACTICE: Pat. Off.)

Damages

Martin Engineering Co. v. Nicaro Holdings Pty Ltd (AUTHORISATION OF INFRINGEMENT: DIRECTOR'S PERSONAL LIABILITY: Fed. Ct)

Minnesota Mining & Manufacturing Co. v. C. Jeffries Pty Ltd (ELECTION FOR DAMAGES OR ACCOUNT OF PROFITS: WHETHER ELECTION TO BE MADE BEFORE DEFENDANT PROVIDES DISCOVERY: Fed. Ct (NSW))

Delay

Stevelift Pty Ltd v. Fomark Pty Ltd (APPLICATION: OPPOSITION: STATEMENT OF
GROUNDS AND PARTICULARS: AMENDMENT: REQUEST: AIPO)

Directions

CSIRO v. CEM Corp. (OPPOSITION: STATEMENT OF GROUNDS AND
PARTICULARS: DISMISSAL: REQUEST FOR DIRECTIONS: AIPO)
O'Neill & St George's Application (CO-APPLICANTS: DISPUTE: DETERMINATION:
AIPO)

Discovery

Murex Diagnostics Australia Pty. Ltd v. Chiron Corp (DOCUMENT OR CLASS OF
DOCUMENT: Fed. Ct)
Murex Diagnostics Australia Pty Ltd v. Chiron Corp. (REVOCATION: PATENTEE
NOT INVENTOR: EFFECT OF TRANSITIONAL PROVISIONS: DISCRETION:
PLEADINGS: APPLICATION TO STRIKE OUT: SECURITY FOR COSTS: Fed. Ct)

Discretion

BEST Australia Ltd v. Aquagas Marketing Pty Ltd (APPLICATION TO SET ASIDE
SERVICE OUTSIDE AUSTRALIA: Fed. Ct)
Cave Holdings Pty Ltd v. Taperline Pty Ltd (PREPARATORY DESIGN DRAWINGS:
Fed. Ct)
Colgate-Palmolive Co. v. Cussons Pty Ltd (INDEMNITY COSTS: EXERCISE OF
DISCRETION TO AWARD: Fed. Ct)
Decor Corporation Pty Ltd v. Dart Industries Inc. (LEAVE TO APPEAL:
INFRINGEMENT: ACCOUNT OF PROFITS: Fed. Ct)
Du Pont de Nemours (E.I.) & Co. v. Commissioner of Patents (No. 7) (EXTENSION:
APPLICATION TO IMPOSE CONDITIONS: SECURITY FOR COSTS AGAINST
INTERVENOR: S.C.(NSW))
Du Pont de Nemours (E.I.) & Co. v. Commissioner of Patents (WHETHER GENERAL
DISCOVERY SHOULD BE ORDERED PRIOR TO FILING OF AFFIDAVITS: Fed. Ct)
Enviro-Clear Co. Inc. v. Commissioner of Patents (PRINCIPLES: S.C.(NSW))
Ferocem Pty Ltd v. Commissioner of Patents (EXTENSION OF TIME TO FILE
EVIDENCE: PRINCIPLES: Fed. Ct)
Kimberly-Clark Ltd v. Commissioner of Patents (JUDICIAL REVIEW: OTHER RIGHTS
AVAILABLE: Fed. Ct)
McIlwraith McEachern Operations Ltd v. Parcel Holdings Pty Ltd (POWER OF
COMMISSIONER TO ORDER DISCOVERY: DIFFERENCES BETWEEN
PRODUCTION AND DISCOVERY: NATURE OF ORDER REQUIRED: Pat. Off.)
Minnesota Mining & Manufacturing Co. v. C. Jeffries Pty Ltd (INFRINGEMENT:
ELECTION FOR DAMAGES OR ACCOUNT OF PROFITS: WHETHER ELECTION TO
BE MADE BEFORE DEFENDANT PROVIDES DISCOVERY: Fed. Ct (NSW))
Murex Diagnostics Australia Pty Ltd v. Chiron Corp. (APPLICATION FOR
REVOCATION: PATENTEE NOT INVENTOR: EFFECT OF TRANSITIONAL
PROVISIONS: DISCRETION: PLEADINGS: APPLICATION TO STRIKE OUT:
SECURITY FOR COSTS: Fed. Ct)
Rhône Poulenc Agrochemie SA v. UIM Chemical Services Pty Ltd (INJUNCTION:
Fed. Ct)
Roussel-Uclaf v. Pan Laboratories Pty Ltd (GOODS INFRINGING PATENTS IN
AUSTRALIA: EXPORT TO PAPUA NEW GUINEA: JURISDICTION TO ORDER
DELIVERY UP: Fed. Ct)

Stork Pompen BV v. Weir Pumps Ltd (EXTENSION OF TIME TO LODGE NOTICE OF OPPOSITION: PRE-CONDITIONS TO EXERCISE OF COMMISSIONERS DISCRETION: Pat. Off.)
Wundowie Foundry Pty Ltd v. Milson Foundry Pty Ltd (INFRINGEMENT: DOCUMENTS RELATING TO DESIGN AND DEVELOPMENT OF INVENTION: PATENT ATTORNEY AND CLIENT PRIVILEGE: Fed. Ct)

Errors

Behringwerke AG (CLERICAL ERROR: Pat. Off.)
Genentech Inc. v. Wellcome Foundation Ltd (ERRORS OR OMISSIONS OF PATENT ATTORNEY: Pat. Off.)
Genetics International Inc. v. Serono Diagnostics Ltd (APPLICATION FOR EXTENSION OF TIME IN WHICH TO LODGE NOTICE OF OPPOSITION: ERROR OR OMISSION OF AGENTS OR ATTORNEYS: Pat. Off.)
Grafton Industries Pty Ltd v. Wyborn (APPLICATION FOR AN EXTENSION OF TIME: ERROR OR OMISSION: Pat. Off.)
Groko Maskin AB's Application (EXTENSION OF TIME: PUBLIC INTEREST: ERROR OR OMISSION: Pat. Off.)
ICI Australia Operations Pty Ltd v. Commercial Polymers Pty Ltd (APPLICATION FOR EXTENSION OF TIME TO APPLY FOR FURTHER TIME TO FILE EVIDENCE: ATTORNEYS ERROR AMOUNTS TO SPECIAL CIRCUMSTANCES: Pat. Off.)
Kimberly-Clark Ltd v. Commissioner of Patents (No. 3) (EXTENSION OF TIME: ERROR OR OMISSION: Fed. Ct)
Lyons v. The J.M. Smucker Co. (APPLICATION FOR EXTENSION OF TIME TO FILE NOTICE OF OPPOSITION TO EXTENSION OF TERM: WHETHER ERROR BY ATTORNEY: Pat. Off.)
Mitsubishi Chemical Industries Ltd v. Asahi Kasei Kogyo KK (ERROR OR OMISSION BY EMPLOYEE OF PATENT ATTORNEY: SPECIAL CIRCUMSTANCES: PUBLIC INTEREST: Pat. Off.)
Stork Pompen BV v. Weir Pumps Ltd (EXTENSION OF TIME TO LODGE NOTICE OF OPPOSITION: WHETHER ERROR OR OMISSION BY PROPOSED OPPONENT: Pat. Off.)
Toyo Seikan Kaisha Ltd v. Nordson Corp. (EXTENSION OF TIME LIMIT: ERROR OR OMISSION: TIMELINESS: Pat. Off.)
Weir Pumps Ltd and Commissioner of Patent and Stork Pompen BV (EXTENSION OF TIME TO LODGE NOTICE OF OPPOSITION: ERROR OR OMISSION: CIRCUMSTANCES BEYOND THE CONTROL: AAT)

Evidence

American Cyanamid Company v. Nalco Chemical Company (CROSS-EXAMINATION: WITNESSES: REQUEST FOR THE COMMISSIONER TO SUMMON WITNESSES: PATENT OFFICE PRACTICE: Pat. Off.)
BASF Corporation v. ICI Australia Operations Pty Ltd (APPLICATION FOR EXTENSION OF TIME WITHIN WHICH TO SERVE EVIDENCE-IN-SUPPORT: ONUS OF PROOF ON APPLICANT: Pat. Off.)
Baxter Travenol Laboratories Inc. v. Cutter Laboratories Inc. (EXTENSION OF TIME FOR LODGING: Pat. Off.)
Bodenseewerk Perkin-Elmer GmbH v. Varian Australia Pty Ltd (OBVIOUSNESS: NOVELTY: EXPERT EVIDENCE: COMMON GENERAL KNOWLEDGE: Fed. Ct)
Braas & Co. GmbH v. Humes Ltd (VALUE OF EVIDENCE OF OVER QUALIFIED EXPERTS: Pat. Off.)
Bristol-Myers Company v. L'Oréal (OBVIOUSNESS: NO EVIDENCE OF COMMON GENERAL KNOWLEDGE: Pat. Off.)

British-American Tobacco Co. Ltd v. Philip Morris Ltd (EXTENSION OF TIME TO LODGE EVIDENCE: Pat. Off.)

Calsil Ltd v. Riekie and Simpfendorfer (EXTENSION OF TIME FOR SERVICE OF OPPONENTS' EVIDENCE: Pat. Off.)

Clafton Pty Ltd v. Forbes Engineering Holdings Pty Ltd (EVIDENCE OF EXPERTS WHO ARE INVENTIVE OR OVER-QUALIFIED OF LIMITED VALUE ON OBVIOUSNESS: Pat. Off.)

Commonwealth Scientific and Industrial Research Organisation v. HBH Technological Industries Pty Ltd (REQUEST BY OPPONENT TO EXTEND TIME: Pat. Off.)

Commonwealth Scientific and Industrial Research Organisation v. Western Mining Corporation Ltd (EXTENSION OF TIME TO SERVE EVIDENCE: OBJECTION: PRINCIPLES: PUBLIC INTEREST: Pat. Off.)

Cooper Industries Inc. v. Metal Manufactures Ltd (OPPOSITION: PROCEDURE: NON-COMPLIANCE WITH SECTION 40: OBVIOUSNESS: COMMON GENERAL KNOWLEDGE: AIPO)

Dennison Manufacturing Co. v. Monarch Marking Systems Inc. (EXPERT EVIDENCE: Fed. Ct)

Dupps Co. v. Stord Bartz A/S (APPLICATION FOR SPECIAL LEAVE TO ADDUCE FURTHER EVIDENCE: Pat. Off.)

Dupps Co. v. Stord Bartz A/S (NUMEROUS EXTENSIONS OF TIME WITHIN WHICH TO LODGE EVIDENCE-IN-SUPPORT: FAILURE TO LODGE APPLICATION FOR EXTENSION WITHIN TIME: Pat. Off.)

E.S. & M.J. Heard Pty Ltd v. Phillips (REQUEST TO SUMMON A WITNESS: WHETHER CONFLICT ON THE FACTS: AIPO)

Elconnex Pty Ltd v. Gerard Industries Pty Ltd (ADMISSIBILITY OF EVIDENCE OF EXPERT WITNESSES: Fed. Ct)

Ferocem Pty Ltd v. Commissioner of Patents (EXTENSION OF TIME TO FILE EVIDENCE: PRINCIPLES: Fed. Ct)

Gansu Research Institution of Chemical Industry v. ICI Australia Operations Pty Ltd (EXTENSION OF TIME TO LODGE EVIDENCE: Pat. Off.)

Genentech Inc. v. Wellcome Foundation Ltd (APPLICATION FOR EXTENSION OF TIME IN WHICH TO SERVE EVIDENCE IN SUPPORT OF OPPOSITION: Pat. Off.)

Genetics Institute Inc. v. Johnson & Johnson (TIME LIMITS: APPLICATION FOR EXTENSION OF TIME: AIPO)

Gerber Scientific Products Inc. v. L. Vogel and Sons Pty Ltd (APPLICATION FOR EXTENSION OF TIME TO SERVE EVIDENCE-IN-REPLY: FACTORS RELEVANT: Pat. Off.)

Guertler's Application (EXTENSION OF PETTY PATENT: EVIDENCE: Pat. Off.)

Gumley's Application (APPLICATION FOR EXTENSION OF TIME FOR FILING EVIDENCE IN SUPPORT OF OPPOSITION: Pat. Off.)

Heylen v. Davies Collison Cave (OBVIOUSNESS: EVIDENTIARY BURDEN: AIPO)

High Tech Auto Tools Pty Ltd v. Ferocem Pty Ltd (CLARITY: UNCERTAINTY: AIPO)

ICI Australia Operations Pty Ltd v. Commercial Polymers Pty Ltd (APPLICATION FOR EXTENSION OF TIME TO APPLY FOR FURTHER TIME TO FILE EVIDENCE: ATTORNEY'S ERROR AMOUNTS TO SPECIAL CIRCUMSTANCES: Pat. Off.)

ICI v. Mitsubishi Gas Chemical Co. (OPPOSITION: FURTHER EVIDENCE AFTER EVIDENCE-IN-REPLY: OBJECTION: AIPO)

Indoor Cricket Arenas (Australia) Pty Ltd v. Australian Indoor Cricket Federation (MANNER OF NEW MANUFACTURE: PERSON INTERESTED: Pat. Off.)

James Howden Australia Pty Ltd v. Flakt AB (WORKING DRAWING AND BROCHURE SENT FROM OVERSEAS MANUFACTURER: WHETHER CONFIDENTIAL: Pat. Off.)

Jarvis v. Doman (QUESTIONNAIRES: Pat. Off.)

Kent-Moore Corp. v. Environmental Products Amalgamated Pty Ltd (APPLICATION FOR EXTENSION OF TIME FOR FILING EVIDENCE-IN-OPPOSITION: Pat. Off.)

Kimberly-Clark Corp. v. Procter & Gamble Co. (APPLICATION FOR EXTENSION OF TIME TO FILE EVIDENCE-IN-SUPPORT: Pat. Off.)

Komesaroff v. Mizzi (PETTY PATENT: EXTENSION: Pat. Off.)

Lake's Application (PETTY PATENT: EXTENSION: LATE EVIDENCE: SPECIAL PLEA BASED ON EMPLOYMENT: Pat. Off.)

Liquid Retaining Structures (Aust.) Pty Ltd v. Delta Corporation Ltd (TIME FOR LODGING EVIDENCE: Pat. Off.)

Luminous Pty Ltd v. Nitto Electric Industrial Co. Ltd (OPPOSITION: NOVELTY: OBVIOUSNESS: SECTION 40: PRIOR PUBLICATION: COMBINATION PATENT: ESSENTIAL INTEGERS: INSUFFICIENCY: FAIR BASIS: AIPO)

Mitsubishi Chemical Industries Ltd v. Asahi Kasei Kogyo KK (RESPONSE TO EVIDENCE-IN-REPLY: Pat. Off.)

Nautical Services Pty Ltd v. Hitech Distillation (Aust.) Pty Ltd (EXTENSION OF TIME LIMITS TO SERVE: Pat. Off.)

Nomad Structures International Ltd v. Heyring Pty Ltd (Pat. Off.)

Optech International Ltd v. Buxton Hicrarium Ltd (OPPOSITION: AIPO)

Poltrock v. Ennor (EXTENSION OF TIME LIMIT TO LODGE NOTICE: WANT OF EVIDENCE-IN-SUPPORT: Pat. Off.)

Procter & Gamble Company v. Kimberly-Clark Corporation (APPLICATIONS FOR EXTENSION OF TIME TO LODGE EVIDENCE: Pat. Off.)

Rear v. Drilling Tools Australia Pty Ltd (EXTENSION OF TIME: EVIDENCE-IN-SUPPORT: GROUNDS FOR GRANT OF EXTENSION OF TIME: Pat. Off.)

Rhône Poulenc Agrochemie SA v. UIM Chemical Services Pty Ltd (PITH AND MARROW: Fed. Ct)

Roussel-Uclaf v. Shell Internationale Research Maatschappij BV (EXTENSION OF TIME LIMITS: EVIDENCE-IN-SUPPORT: Pat. Off.)

Sandoz Ltd v. Fujisawa Pharmaceutical Co. Ltd (EXTENSION OF TIME FOR FILING EVIDENCE-IN-SUPPORT: Pat. Off.)

Schmidt's Application (EXTENSION: Pat. Off.)

Sepa Waste Water Treatment Pty Ltd v. JMT Welding Pty Ltd (PATENT AGENTS' PRIVILEGE: ADVICE ON DESIGNS INFRINGEMENT: S.C.(NSW))

Sue v. Carpenter (SPECIAL LEAVE TO ADDUCE FURTHER EVIDENCE: Pat. Off.)

Underwood v. Toby Construction Products Pty Ltd (APPLICATION FOR EXTENSION OF TIME WITHIN WHICH TO SERVE EVIDENCE-IN-SUPPORT OF OPPOSITION: Pat. Off.)

United Kingdom Government (Secretary of State for Defence) v. Rheinmetall GmbH (TIME LIMITS: EXTENSION: ONUS OF PROOF: Pat. Off.)

Vanitone Pty Ltd v. Formica Technology, Inc. (EXTENSION OF TIME TO LODGE EVIDENCE-IN-SUPPORT OF OPPOSITION: ONUS ON PARTY SEEKING EXTENSION: Pat. Off.)

Worrallo v. Hales (APPLICATION FOR SPECIAL LEAVE TO LODGE FURTHER EVIDENCE: Pat. Off.)

Extension of time

Albright & Wilson Ltd v. Colgate Palmolive Co. (Pat. Off.)

Amrad Corp. Ltd v. Genentech Inc. (OPPOSITION: NOTICE: AIPO)

Austoft Industries Limited v. Cameco Industries Limited (EXTENSION OF TIME TO FILE EVIDENCE: PUBLIC INTEREST: AIPO)

BASF Corporation v. ICI Australia Operations Pty Ltd (SERVICE OF EVIDENCE-IN-SUPPORT: ONUS OF PROOF: Pat. Off.)

Baxter Travenol Laboratories Inc. v. Cutter Laboratories Inc. (LODGING EVIDENCE: Pat. Off.)

Board of Control of Michigan Technological University v. Deputy Commissioner of Patents (UNDUE DELAY: H.C.)

Bristol-Myers Co. v. David Bull Laboratories Pty Ltd (PETITIONING FOR EXTENSION OF TERM: Fed. Ct)

British-American Tobacco Co. Ltd v. Philip Morris Ltd (LODGING EVIDENCE: Pat. Off.)

Calsil Ltd v. Riekie and Simpfendorfer (SERVICE OF OPPONENTS' EVIDENCE: Pat. Off.)

Commonwealth Scientific and Industrial Research Organisation v. Western Mining Corporation Ltd (SERVICE OF EVIDENCE: Pat. Off.)

Commonwealth Scientific and Industrial Research Organisation v. Western Mining Corp. Ltd (SERVICE OF EVIDENCE-IN-SUPPORT OF OPPOSITION: Pat. Off.)

Conry v. Atlas Air Australia Pty Ltd (LODGING NOTICE OF OPPOSITION: Pat. Off.)

CSIRO v. Asterol International (LODGING NOTICE OF OPPOSITION: AIPO)

Danby Pty Ltd v. Commissioner of Patents (LODGING NOTICE OF OPPOSITION: Fed. Ct)

Danby Pty Ltd v. Rib Loc Group Ltd (LODGING NOTICE OF OPPOSITION: Pat. Off.)

Dentsply International Inc. v. Bayer AG (Pat. Off.)

Dow Chemical Co. v. Ishihara Sangyo Kaisha Ltd (Pat. Off.)

Du Pont de Nemours (E.I.) & Co. v. Commissioner of Patents (No. 1) (FILING CAVEAT AGAINST GRANTING OF EXTENSION: S.C.(NSW))

Gansu Research Institution of Chemical Industry v. ICI Australia Operations Pty Ltd (LODGING EVIDENCE: Pat. Off.)

Genentech Inc. v. Wellcome Foundation Ltd (SERVICE OF EVIDENCE-IN-SUPPORT OF OPPOSITION: APPLICATION LODGED AFTER THE EXPIRATION OF THE TIME SOUGHT TO BE EXTENDED: Pat. Off.)

Genetics Institute Inc. v. Johnson & Johnson (OBJECTION: DIRECTION: AIPO)

Genetics International Inc. v. Serono Diagnostics Ltd (LODGING NOTICE OF OPPOSITION: Pat. Off.)

Gerber Scientific Products Inc. v. L. Vogel and Sons Pty Ltd (SERVICE OF EVIDENCE-IN-REPLY: Pat. Off.)

Grace (W.R.) & Co. v. Betz International Inc. (LODGING NOTICE OF OPPOSITION: Pat. Off.)

Grafton Industries Pty Ltd v. Wyborn (ERROR OR OMISSION: Pat. Off.)

Groko Maskin AB's Application (PUBLIC INTEREST: ERROR OR OMISSION: DELAY: Pat. Off.)

Gumley's Application (FILING EVIDENCE-IN-SUPPORT OF OPPOSITION: APPLICATION OPPOSED: THREE-MONTH EXTENSION GRANTED: Pat. Off.)

Henkel Kommanditgesellschaft Auf Aktien v. Fina Research SA (OBJECTION: AIPO)

Husky Injection Molding Systems Ltd's Application (APPLICATION PURSUANT TO SECTION 51: COMMISSIONER'S POWERS TO EXTEND TIME: Pat Off:)

Husky Injection Molding Systems Ltd v. Commissioner of Patents (WHETHER COMMISSIONER HAS POWER TO EXTEND TIME IN RELATION TO A FURTHER APPLICATION WHEN ORIGINAL APPLICATION HAS PROCEEDED TO GRANT: Fed. Ct)

ICI Australia Operations Pty Ltd v. Commercial Polymers Pty Ltd (APPLICATION FOR EXTENSION OF TIME TO APPLY FOR FURTHER TIME TO FILE EVIDENCE: Pat. Off.)

Ikida Koki Seisakusho KK v. Duro-Matic Pty Ltd (OPPOSITION: Pat. Off.)

Kent-Moore Corp. v. Environmental Products Amalgamated Pty Ltd (FILING EVIDENCE IN OPPOSITION: Pat. Off.)

Kimberly-Clark Corp. v. Procter & Gamble Co. (FILING EVIDENCE-IN-SUPPORT: Pat. Off.)

Kimberly-Clark Ltd v. Commissioner of Patent (LODGING NOTICE OF OPPOSITION: Fed. Ct)

Filing affidavits or evidence

Sandoz Ltd v. Fujisawa Pharmaceutical Co. Ltd (EXTENSION OF TIME FOR FILING EVIDENCE-IN-SUPPORT: Pat. Off.)

Further and better particulars

Cotterill v. Trenton Pty Ltd (DIRECTIONS ON PROVISION OF: AIPO)
Dupont de Nemours (E.I.) & Co. v. DowElanco (OPPOSITION: AIPO)

Injunction

Rhône Poulenc Agrochemie SA v. UIM Chemical Services Pty Ltd (Fed. Ct)
Westaflex (Aust.) Pty Ltd v. Wood (Fed. Ct)
Yorkwain Automatic Doors Ltd v. Newman Tonks Pty Ltd (MAREVA INJUNCTION: S.C.(Vic.))

Inspection

Brisalebe Ltd v. Searle (PROVISIONAL SPECIFICATION: REQUEST FOR INSPECTION: OBTAINING: ASSIGNMENT: AIPO)

Interlocutory injunction—balance of convenience

Cabot Corporation v. Minnesota Mining & Manufacturing Ltd (S.C.(NSW))
Clemco International Sales Co. v. Bolrette Pty Ltd (PETTY PATENT: Fed. Ct)
Philips Gloeilampenfabrieken (NV) v. Ultralite International Pty Ltd (BALANCE OF CONVENIENCE INJUNCTION REFUSED BUT UNDERTAKINGS ACCEPTED TO KEEP ACCOUNTS AND PAY $1.00 PER UNIT INTO COURT CONTROLLED FUND: Fed. Ct)

Interlocutory injunction—cases

Andoy Pty Ltd v. S. & M. Cannon Pty Ltd (S.C.(Vic.))
ANI Corp. Ltd v. Celtite Australia Pty Ltd (Fed. Ct)
Appleton Papers Inc. v. Tomasetti Paper Pty Ltd (S.C.(NSW))
Cabot Corporation v. Minnesota Mining & Manufacturing Ltd (S.C.(NSW))
Clemco International Sales Co. v. Bolrette Pty Ltd (Fed. Ct)
Decor Corporation Pty Ltd v. Dart Industries Inc. (Fed. Ct)
Dillon v. J.P. Products Pty Ltd (S.C.(NSW))
Durack v. Associated Pool Builders Pty Ltd (PETTY PATENT: Fed. Ct)
Martin Engineering Co. v. Trison Holdings Pty Ltd (Fed. Ct)
Peter Pan Electric Pty Ltd v. Newton Grace Pty Ltd (PETTY PATENT: Fed. Ct)
Philips Gloeilampenfabrieken (NV) v. Ultralite International Pty Ltd (Fed. Ct)

Interlocutory injunction—prima facie case

Cabot Corporation v. Minnesota Mining & Manufacturing Ltd (S.C.(NSW))

Interlocutory injunction—principles and procedure

Cabot Corporation v. Minnesota Mining & Manufacturing Ltd (S.C.(NSW))
Decor Corporation Pty Ltd v. Dart Industries Inc. (LEAVE TO APPEAL: DISCRETION: Fed. Ct)
Martin Engineering Co. v. Trison Holdings Pty Ltd (VALIDITY PUT IN ISSUE: Fed. Ct)
Peter Pan Electric Pty Ltd v. Newton Grace Pty Ltd (PETTY PATENT: Fed. Ct)

Jurisdiction

Roussel-Uclaf v. Pan Laboratories Pty Ltd (GOODS INFRINGING PATENTS IN AUSTRALIA: EXPORT TO PAPUA NEW GUINEA: JURISDICTION TO ORDER DELIVERY UP: DISCRETION: Fed. Ct)

Locus standi

Dricon Air Pty Ltd v. Waztech Pty Ltd (STANDING TO OPPOSE: NO *locus standi*: Pat. Off.)

Elazac Pty Ltd v. Commissioner of Patents (AMENDMENT: OPPOSITION: RIGHT OF APPEAL: *Locus standii* OF PERSON WHO FAILED TO OPPOSE: Fed. Ct)

Merck & Co, Inc. v. Sankyo Co. Ltd (Commissioner of Fed. Ct)

MXM v. Franke (PERSON INTERESTED: STANDING: PATENT ATTORNEY: AGENCY: Pat. Off.)

Nautical Services Pty Ltd v. Hitech Distillation (Aust.) Pty Ltd (PUBLIC INTEREST: Pat. Off.)

Ulrich Labels Pty Ltd v. Printing and Allied Trades Employers' Federation of Australia (EXTENSION OF TIME TO FILE NOTICE OF OPPOSITION: Pat. Off.)

Onus

BASF Corporation v. ICI Australia Operations Pty Ltd (EXTENSION OF TIME TO SERVE EVIDENCE-IN-SUPPORT: Pat. Off.)

Dart Industries Inc. v. Decor Corporation Pty Ltd (ACCOUNT OF PROFITS: DEDUCTION FOR INFRINGER'S GENERAL OVERHEAD COSTS: QUANTIFICATION: H.C.)

Ryan v. Lum (PROCUREMENT OF INFRINGEMENT: S.C.(NSW))

United Kingdom Government (Secretary of State for Defence) v. Rheinmetall GmbH (PUBLIC INTEREST: Pat. Off.)

Vanitone Pty Ltd v. Formica Technology, Inc. (EXTENSION OF TIME TO LODGE EVIDENCE-IN-SUPPORT OF OPPOSITION: Pat. Off.)

Mareva injunction

Yorkwain Automatic Doors Ltd v. Newman Tonks Pty Ltd (S.C.(Vic.))

Obvious mistake

High Tech Auto Tools Pty Ltd v. Ferocem Pty Ltd (PETTY PATENT: EXTENSION: OBJECTION: NOTICE: CLAIMS: PRIORITY DATE: MANNER OF MANUFACTURE: AIPO)

Patent attorneys

Heylen v. Davies Collison Cave (COSTS: AIPO)

Patent Office matters

American Cyanamid Company v. Nalco Chemical Company (REQUEST FOR THE COMMISSIONER TO SUMMON WITNESSES: Pat. Off.)

Ferocem Pty Ltd v. High Tech Auto Tools Pty Ltd (NOTICE: INFORMATION: PENDING COURT PROCEEDINGS: FEDERAL COURT: PATENT OFFICE PRACTICE: AIPO)

Lantech Inc. v. First Green Park (INFRINGEMENT: NOTICE: INFORMATION: PENDING COURT PROCEEDINGS: FEDERAL COURT: AIPO)

Leonard's Application (EXAMINER'S OBJECTION: Pat. Off.)

Thomas v. Jiejung Pty Ltd (APPLICATION: EXTENSION OF TIME FOR ACCEPTANCE: ERROR OF COMMISSIONER: INCORRECT ADVICE FROM PATENT OFFICE: AIPO)

Pleadings

Murex Diagnostics Australia Pty Ltd v. Chiron Corp. (REVOCATION: APPLICATION: PATENTEE NOT INVENTOR: EFFECT OF TRANSITIONAL PROVISIONS: DISCOVERY: DISCRETION: APPLICATION TO STRIKE OUT: SECURITY FOR COSTS: Fed. Ct)

Stevelift Pty Ltd v. Fomark Pty Ltd (APPLICATION: OPPOSITION: STATEMENT OF GROUNDS AND PARTICULARS: AMENDMENT: REQUEST: DELAY: AIPO)

Privilege

Imagic Inc. v. Futuretronics (Aust.) Pty Ltd (PATENT ATTORNEYS: COMMUNICATIONS WITH CLIENT: WHETHER PRIVILEGED: S.C.(NSW))

Pfizer Pty Ltd v. Warner Lambert Pty Ltd (PATENT ATTORNEY: PRIVILEGED COMMUNICATIONS WITH: WHETHER PRIVILEGE EXTENDS TO COMMUNICATIONS BETWEEN PATENT ATTORNEY AND CLIENT IN THE COURSE OF CONDUCT: Fed. Ct)

Riker Laboratories Australia Pty Ltd v. Westwood Pharmaceuticals Inc. (PATENT ATTORNEYS: COMMUNICATIONS WITH CLIENT: WHETHER PRIVILEGED: S.C.(NSW))

Sepa Waste Water Treatment Pty Ltd v. JMT Welding Pty Ltd (PRACTICE: EVIDENCE: PATENT AGENTS' PRIVILEGE: ADVICE ON DESIGNS INFRINGEMENT: S.C.(NSW))

Wundowie Foundry Pty Ltd v. Milson Foundry Pty Ltd (INFRINGEMENT: DISCOVERY: DOCUMENTS RELATING TO DESIGN AND DEVELOPMENT OF INVENTION: PATENT ATTORNEY AND CLIENT PRIVILEGE: Fed. Ct)

Procedure

Gerber Scientific Products Inc. v. L. Vogel and Sons Pty Ltd (OPPOSITION: Pat. Off.)

Leonardis v. St Alban (LATE NOTIFIED CITATIONS PART OF BAR-TO-SEALING PROCEDURE: Pat. Off.)

Peter Pan Electric Pty Ltd v. Newton Grace Pty Ltd (PETTY PATENT: INTERLOCUTORY INJUNCTION: Fed. Ct)

Cooper Industries Inc. v. Metal Manufactures Ltd (OPPOSITION: NON-COMPLIANCE WITH SECTION 40: EVIDENCE: OBVIOUSNESS: COMMON GENERAL KNOWLEDGE: AIPO)

Smucker (J.M.) Co.'s Petty Patent (OPPOSITION TO EXTENSION OF TERM: NOVELTY: OBVIOUSNESS: MANNER OF NEW MANUFACTURE: INCONVENIENT SPECIFICATION: NON-COMPLIANCE WITH SECTION 40: AIPO)

Sue v. Carpenter (SPECIAL LEAVE TO ADDUCE FURTHER EVIDENCE: Pat. Off.)

Registrar's power

Thomas & Garnham's Application (OBJECTION BY EXAMINER: REQUEST TO COMMISSIONER TO EXERCISE DISCRETIONARY POWER: COMPUTER PROCESSING APPARATUS FOR ASSEMBLING TEXT, PARTICULARLY IN CHINESE CHARACTERS: AIPO)

Rehearing

Sumitomo Electrical Industries Ltd v. Metal Manufacturers Ltd (SELECTION PATENT: APPLICATION: OPPOSITION: Fed. Ct)

Right to jury trial

Markman v. Westview Instruments Inc. (INFRINGEMENT: CONSTRUCTION: SUMMARY JUDGMENT: Fed. Ct)

Right of appeal

Elazac Pty Ltd v. Commissioner of Patents (AMENDMENT: FAILURE TO OPPOSE: AIPO)

Murex Diagnostics Australia Pty Ltd v. Chiron Corp. (REVOCATION: PATENTEE NOT INVENTOR: EFFECT OF TRANSITIONAL PROVISIONS: DISCOVERY: DISCRETION: Fed. Ct)

Scire facias, writ of

Prestige Group (Aust.) Pty Ltd v. Dart Industries Inc. (FALSE SUGGESTION OR REPRESENTATION: GROUNDS FOR REPEAL BY WRIT OF *scire facias:* Fed. Ct)

Security for costs

Austoft Industries Limited v. Cameco Industries Limited (OPPOSITION: EXTENSION OF TIME TO FILE EVIDENCE: PUBLIC INTEREST: AIPO)

Farmitalia Carlo Erba SrL v. Delta West Pty Ltd (APPLICANT ORDINARILY RESIDENT OUTSIDE DISCRETION: Fed. Ct)

Murex Diagnostics Australia Pty Ltd v. Chiron Corp. (APPLICATION TO STRIKE OUT: Fed. Ct)

Special circumstances

Genentech Inc. v. Wellcome Foundation Ltd (ERRORS OR OMISSIONS OF PATENT ATTORNEY: Pat. Off.)

ICI Australia Operations Pty Ltd v. Commercial Polymers Pty Ltd (WHETHER ATTORNEY'S ERROR AMOUNTS TO SPECIAL CIRCUMSTANCES: Pat. Off.)

Mitsubishi Chemical Industries Ltd v. Asahi Kasei Kogyo KK (ERROR OR OMISSION BY EMPLOYEE OF PATENT ATTORNEY: Pat. Off.)

Striking out

Murex Diagnostics Australia Pty Ltd v. Chiron Corp. (REVOCATION: PATENTEE NOT INVENTOR: EFFECT OF TRANSITIONAL PROVISIONS: DISCOVERY: DISCRETION: PLEADINGS: SECURITY FOR COSTS: Fed. Ct)

Standard of proof

B.F. Goodrich Co. v. ICI Australia Operations Pty Ltd (PRIOR USE: PRIOR SECRET USE: AIPO)

Statement of claim

Porter v. Arbortech Investments Pty Ltd (OPPOSITION: OBJECTION TO ALLOWANCE OF A REQUEST TO AMEND STATEMENT OF GROUNDS AND PARTICULARS: AIPO)

Statement of grounds and particulars

McKenzie v. Uwatec Pty Ltd (OPPOSITION: APPLICATION TO DISMISS: ADEQUACY OF STATEMENT OF GROUNDS AND PARTICULARS: AIPO)

Summary judgment

Markman v. Westview Instruments Inc. (INFRINGEMENT: CONSTRUCTION: RIGHT TO JURY TRIAL: Fed. Ct)

Undertaking

New York University v. Nissin Molecular Biology Institute Inc. (REQUEST FOR CERTIFICATION: USE OF DEPOSIT FOR EXPERIMENTAL PURPOSES: AIPO)

Vexatious or abuse of process

Concorde Trading Pty Ltd v. Croner Trading Pty Ltd (OPPOSITION: APPLICATION FOR DISMISSAL: COSTS: AIPO)

Witnesses

American Cyanamid Company v. Nalco Chemical Company (REQUEST FOR THE COMMISSIONER OF PATENTS TO SUMMON WITNESSES: PATENT OFFICE PRACTICE: Pat. Off.)

Prior Art

Winner v. Ammar Holdings Pty Ltd (MOSAIC: ALLEGED MISREPRESENTATION OF STATE OF PRIOR ART IN THE UNITED STATES: Fed. Ct)

Prior Claiming

Australian Paper Manufacturers Ltd v. CIL Ltd (Pat. Off.)
Clafton Pty Ltd v. Forbes Engineering Holdings Pty Ltd (Pat. Off.)
Commonwealth Industrial Gases Ltd v. Liquid Air Australia Ltd (Pat. Off.)
Hoechst AG v. American Home Products Corp. (Pat. Off.)
Luminous Pty Ltd v. Nitto Electric Industrial Co. Ltd (AIPO)
Polar Vac Pty Ltd v. Spoutvac Manufacturing Pty Ltd (AIPO)
PPG Industries Inc. v. Stauffer Chemical Co. (Pat. Off.)
Ricardo International plc v. Orital Engine Co. (Aust.) Pty Ltd (AIPO)
Sankyo Company Ltd v. Merck & Co. Inc. (Pat. Off.)
United Biomedical Inc. v. Genetics Systems Corp. (AIPO)

Prior Publication

A. & K. Aluminium Pty Ltd v. Lidco Systems Sales Pty Ltd (Pat. Off.)
Australian Paper Manufacturers Ltd v. CIL Ltd (Pat. Off.)
Bausch & Lomb Inc. v. Allergan Inc. (Pat. Off.)
Bio Energy Systems Inc. v. Lawrence John Walton (Pat. Off.)
Bioglan Laboratories (Aust.) Pty Ltd v. Crooks (Pat. Off.)
Bodenseewerk Perkin-Elmer GmbH v. Varian Australia Pty Ltd (OPPOSITION: CLARITY: FAIR BASING: OBVIOUSNESS: NOVELTY: EXPERT EVIDENCE: COMMON GENERAL KNOWLEDGE: OPPONENTS RIGHT TO BE HEARD: Fed. Ct)
Bridge & Plate Constructions Pty Ltd v. Mannesmann Demag Pty Ltd (Pat. Off.)
Bristol-Myers Company v. L'Oréal (Pat. Off.)
Clafton Pty Ltd v. Forbes Engineering Holdings Pty Ltd (PUBLIC DOMAIN: Pat. Off.)
Clay v. ICI Australia Operations Pty Ltd (Pat. Off.)
Commonwealth Industrial Gases Ltd v. MWA Holdings Pty Ltd (COMBINATION OF NON-ESSENTIAL FEATURES: WORKSHOP IMPROVEMENTS: H.C.)
Dohmeier v. Eisen-Und Drahtwerk Erlau AG (Pat. Off.)
Electricity Trust of South Australia v. Zellweger Uster Pty Ltd (Pat. Off.)
Hoechst AG v. American Home Products Corp. (Pat. Off.)
James Howden Australia Pty Ltd v. Flakt AB (WORKING DRAWING AND BROCHURE SENT FROM OVERSEAS MANUFACTURER: WHETHER CONFIDENTIAL: Pat. Off.)
Jarvis v. Doman (PRIOR PUBLICATION BY USE: KNOWLEDGE OR CONSENT OF APPLICANT: Pat. Off.)
Jos Schlitz Brewing Company v. Containers Ltd (CONFIDENTIALITY: Pat. Off.)
Lasercare (Aust.) Pty Ltd v. Christiansen (PETTY PATENT: Pat. Off.)
Lucasfilm Ltd v. Krix (Pat. Off.)
Luminous Pty Ltd v. Nitto Electric Industrial Co. Ltd (COMBINATION PATENT: ESSENTIAL INTEGERS: INSUFFICIENCY: EVIDENCE: FAIR BASIS: AIPO)
Mauri Brothers & Thomson (Aust.) Pty Ltd v. Containers Ltd (Pat. Off.)
Monsanto Co.'s Application (Pat. Off.)
Moore Paragon Australia Ltd v. Multiform Printers (Pat. Off.)
Nelson v. Hillmark Industries Pty Ltd (Pat. Off.)
Nicaro Holdings Pty Ltd v. Martin Engineering Co. (UNITED STATES PATENTS: MOSAIC: Fed. Ct)
Nichator AB's Application (Pat. Off.)
Nomad Structures International Ltd v. Heyring Pty Ltd (Pat. Off.)

Polar Vac Pty Ltd v. Spoutvac Manufacturing Pty Ltd (OPPOSITION: SECRET USE: AIPO)
Safetell Pty Ltd's Application (Pat. Off.)
Sankyo Company Ltd v. Merck & Co. Inc. (Pat. Off.)
Sartas No. 1 Pty Ltd v. Koukouou & Partners Pty Ltd (ALLEGED PRIOR PUBLICATION: AIPO)
United Biomedical Inc. v. Genetics Systems Corp. (AIPO)
Whitco Pty Ltd v. Austral Lock Industries Pty Ltd (Pat. Off.)
Wood v. Uniflex (Aust.) Pty Ltd (FOREIGN DISCLOSURE TO EMPLOYEE OF AUSTRALIAN COMPANY: S.C.(Vic.))

Prior Sales

Acushnet Co. v. Spalding Australia Pty Ltd (APPLICATION: OPPOSITION: PRIOR PUBLICATION: PRIOR USE: PRIOR SALES ON BALANCE OF PROBABILITIES: Pat. Off.)

Prior Secret Use

B.F. Goodrich Co. v. ICI Australia Operations Pty Ltd (OPPOSITION: PRIOR PUBLICATION: OBVIOUSNESS: COMBINATION INVENTION: MANNER OF NEW MANUFACTURE: PRIOR USE: STANDARD OF PROOF: AIPO)

Prior Use

Acushnet Co. v. Spalding Australia Pty Ltd (PRIOR SALES ON BALANCE OF PROBABILITIES: Pat. Off.)
Armstrong v. Larocca (DESIRABILITY OF CORROBORATION: Pat. Off.)
Bioglan Laboratories (Aust.) Pty Ltd v. Crooks (WHETHER PRIOR COMMERCIAL DEALING CONSTITUTES PRIOR USE: Pat. Off.)
Braas & Co. GmbH v. Humes Ltd (ACCIDENTAL PRIOR USE: Pat. Off.)
Commonwealth Industrial Gases Ltd v. MWA Holdings Pty Ltd (INFRINGEMENT: PRIOR PUBLICATION: COMBINATION OF NON-ESSENTIAL FEATURES: WORKSHOP IMPROVEMENTS: H.C.)
Coopers Animal Health Australia Ltd v. Western Stock Distributors Ltd (PETTY PATENT: Pat. Off.)
Costa v. G.R. & I.E. Daking Pty Ltd (PETTY PATENT: WHETHER FOR REASONABLE TRIAL: AIPO)
Graf v. Milward-Bason (SECRET USE: EXPERIMENTAL USE: Pat. Off.)
Jarvis v. Doman (PRIOR PUBLICATION BY USE: Pat. Off.)
Lake's Application (PETTY PATENT: SECRET USE: Pat. Off.)
Lasercare (Aust.) Pty Ltd v. Christiansen (PETTY PATENT: Pat. Off.)
Melbourne v. Terry Fluid Controls Pty Ltd (SECRET USE: ARTICLE DELIVERED TO POTENTIAL PURCHASER FOR TRIAL AND EVALUATION: CIRCUMSTANCES IN WHICH THAT USE IS SECRET USE CONSIDERED: Fed. Ct)
Nicaro Holdings Pty Ltd v. Martin Engineering Co. (MOSAIC: Fed. Ct)
Nomad Structures International Ltd v. Heyring Pty Ltd (Pat. Off.)

Priority Date

Clafton Pty Ltd v. Forbes Engineering Holdings Pty Ltd (DIVISIONAL APPLICATION: Pat. Off.)

Coopers Animal Health Australia Ltd v. Western Stock Distributors Pty Ltd (PROVISIONAL SPECIFICATION AND SUBSEQUENT PETTY PATENT: Fed. Ct)

Graf v. Milward-Bason (SECRET USE: EXPERIMENTAL USE: BUILDING FOUNDATION METHOD CLAIM: BUILDING ERECTED ON PRIVATE PROPERTY USING METHOD BEFORE PRIORITY DATE: Pat. Off.)

High Tech Auto Tools Pty Ltd v. Ferocem Pty Ltd (PETTY PATENT: EXTENSION: OBJECTION: NOTICE: CLAIMS: MANNER OF MANUFACTURE: OBVIOUS MISTAKE: NOVELTY: OBVIOUSNESS: EVIDENCE: AIPO)

Merck & Co. Inc. v. Sankyo Company Ltd (Pat. Off.)

Merrell Dow Pharmaceuticals Petition (APPLICATION FOR PERMISSION TO IMPORT AND MARKET IN AUSTRALIA MADE 11 YEARS AFTER PRIORITY DATE: PETITION FOR EXTENSION: Fed. Ct)

Nelson v. Hillmark Industries Pty Ltd (PROVISIONAL SPECIFICATION: Pat. Off.)

Opsvik v. Bad Back Centre Pty Ltd (INTERNATIONAL APPLICATION: S.C.(NSW))

Robert Bosch GmbH v. Solo Industries Pty Ltd (COGNATED DISCLOSURES: Pat. Off.)

Roelofs' Patent (PETTY PATENT: EXTENSION OF TERM: STATUTORY NOTICE: FAIRLY BASED: AIPO)

Sandvik AB v. Boart International Ltd (CONVENTION APPLICATION: Pat. Off.)

Thomas & Garnham's Application (OBJECTION BY EXAMINER: REQUEST TO COMMISSIONER TO EXERCISE DISCRETIONARY POWER: COMPUTER PROCESSING APPARATUS FOR ASSEMBLING TEXT, PARTICULARLY IN CHINESE CHARACTERS: PATENTABILITY: NOVELTY: AIPO)

Yamazaki Mazak Corporation v. Interact Machine Tools (NSW) Pty Ltd (PETTY PATENT: WHETHER CONVENTION PRIORITY DATE PRECEDED DATE OF ALLEGED ANTICIPATION: Fed. Ct)

Privilege. *See* **Practice** (*Privilege*)

Procedure. *See* **Practice** (*Procedure*)

Provisional Specification

Brisalebe Ltd v. Searle (REQUEST FOR INSPECTION: OBTAINING: ASSIGNMENT: AIPO)

Public Interest

Austoft Industries Limited v. Cameco Industries Limited (OPPOSITION: EXTENSION OF TIME TO FILE EVIDENCE: PUBLIC INTEREST: AIPO)

Bayer AG v. Minister for Health of the Commonwealth of Australia (EXTENSION: PROPER TERM OF EXTENSION: S.C.(NSW))

Commonwealth Scientific and Industrial Research Organisation v. Western Mining Corporation Ltd (OPPOSITION: EXTENSION OF TIME TO SERVE EVIDENCE: OBJECTION: PRINCIPLES: Pat. Off.)

Du Pont De Nemours (E.I.) & Co. v. Commissioner of Patents (No. 8) (SETTLEMENT BY CONSENT ON TERMS THAT PATENT BE EXTENDED: S.C.(NSW))

Groko Maskin AB's Application (OPPOSITION: EXTENSION OF TIME: Pat. Off.)

Hassle (A.B.) v. Commissioner of Patents (EXTENSION: BENEFIT TO PUBLIC: DELAY IN GETTING INVENTION ON TO MARKET: S.C.(NSW))

ICI Australia Operations Pty Ltd v. Commercial Polymers Pty Ltd (OPPOSITION: APPLICATION FOR EXTENSION OF TIME TO FILE EVIDENCE: Pat. Off.)

Mitsubishi Chemical Industries Ltd v. Asahi Kasei Kogyo KK (OPPORTUNITY GIVEN TO APPLICANT TO RESPOND TO EVIDENCE-IN-REPLY: ERROR OR OMISSION BY EMPLOYEE OF PATENT ATTORNEY: Pat. Off.)

Nautical Services Pty Ltd v. Hitech Distillation (Aust.) Pty Ltd (EXTENSION OF TIME
  LIMITS TO SERVE EVIDENCE: Pat. Off.)
Roussel-Uclaf v. Shell Internationale Research Maatschappij BV (EXTENSION OF
  TIME LIMITS: Pat. Off.)
United Kingdom Government (Secretary of State for Defence) v. Rheinmetall
  GmbH (EXTENSION OF TIME LIMITS: Pat. Off.)
Vanitone Pty Ltd v. Formica Technology, Inc. (EXTENSION OF TIME TO LODGE
  EVIDENCE-IN-SUPPORT OF OPPOSITION: Pat. Off.)
Kimberly-Clark Corp. v. Procter & Gamble Co. (EXTENSION OF TIME TO FILE
  EVIDENCE-IN-SUPPORT: Pat. Off.)

Questionnaires. *See* **Practice** (*Questionnaires*)

Rectification

Avion Engineering Pty Ltd v. Fisher and Paykel Healthcare Pty Ltd (LACK OF
  NOVELTY AND VAGUE AND AMBIGUOUS REPRESENTATION: PETTY PATENT:
  OBVIOUSNESS: LACK OF FAIR BASING: Fed. Ct)

Redundancy

Upjohn Co.'s Application (OBJECTION: CLAIMS: METHOD: PRODUCT: NEW USE OF
  OLD SUBSTANCE: AIPO)

Restoration

Board of Control of Michigan Technological University v. Deputy Commissioner of
  Patents (APPLICATION: EXTENSION OF TIME LIMIT: UNDUE DELAY: H.C.)
Utting v. Clyde Industries Ltd (OPPOSITION: CESSATION OF PATENT: APPLICATION
  FOR RESTORATION: FAILURE TO PAY FEE: INTENTION: DELAY: Pat. Off.)
Worrallo v. Hales (APPLICATION FOR RESTORATION: NON-PAYMENT OF RENEWAL
  FEE: PATENT LAPSED: OPPOSITION: APPLICATION FOR SPECIAL LEAVE TO
  LODGE FURTHER EVIDENCE: Pat. Off.)

Revocation

Advanced Building Systems Pty Ltd v. Ramset (Fed. Ct)
Asahi Kasei Kogyo KK v. W.R. Grace & Co. (DISTINCTION BETWEEN NOVELTY
  AND OBVIOUSNESS: Fed. Ct)
Avion Engineering Pty Ltd v. Fisher and Paykel Healthcare Pty Ltd (PETTY PATENT:
  Fed. Ct)
Coopers Animal Health Australia Ltd v. Western Stock Distributors Ltd (PETTY
  PATENT: Fed. Ct)
Du Pont de Nemours (E.I.) & Co. v. Cadbury Schweppes Pty Ltd (EXTENSION:
  CROSS-CLAIM FOR REVOCATION: Fed. Ct)
Envirotech Australia Pty Ltd v. Enviroclear Co. Inc. (PETITION FOR REVOCATION:
  Fed. Ct)
Freeman v. Pohlner Pty Ltd (PATENTABILITY: NOVELTY: DESCRIPTION OF
  INVENTION: Fed. Ct)
Freeman v. Pohlner Pty Ltd (PATENTABILITY: NOVELTY: SKILLED ADDRESSEE:
  DESCRIPTION: BEST METHOD: Fed. Ct)

Lantech Inc. v. First Green Park (INFRINGEMENT: SPECIFICATION: CONSTRUCTION: INVALIDITY: SECTION 40 GROUNDS: INUTILITY: Fed. Ct)

Murex Diagnostics Australia Pty Ltd v. Chiron Corp. (APPLICATION FOR REVOCATION: PATENTEE NOT INVENTOR: EFFECT OF TRANSITIONAL PROVISIONS: DISCOVERY: DISCRETION: PLEADINGS: APPLICATION TO STRIKE OUT: SECURITY FOR COSTS: Fed. Ct)

Olin Corp. v. Super Cartridge Co. Pty Ltd (INFRINGEMENT: VALIDITY: INVENTIVENESS: WHETHER CLAIMS CLEAR AND DISTINCTIVE: FAIRLY BASED: INVENTIVE STEP: H.C.)

Rescare Ltd v. Anaesthetic Supplies Pty Ltd (INFRINGEMENT: PATENT GRANTED UNDER P.A.52 AND REVOCATION SOUGHT UNDER P.A.90: Fed. Ct)

Ryan v. Lum (LACK OF NOVELTY AND OBVIOUSNESS: ONUS OF PROOF: S.C.(NSW))

Sunbeam Corp. v. Morphy-Richards (Aust.) Pty Ltd (INFRINGEMENT: VALIDITY: INVENTIVENESS: NOVELTY: SUBJECT-MATTER: OBVIOUSNESS: COMMON GENERAL KNOWLEDGE: MOSAIC: H.C.)

Townsend Controls Pty Ltd v. Gilead (INFRINGEMENT: Fed. Ct)

Vulcan Australia Ltd v. Braemar Appliances Pty Ltd (INFRINGEMENT: COUNTERCLAIM FOR REVOCATION: Pat. Off.)

Wimmera Industrial Minerals Pty Ltd v. RGC Mineral Dand Ltd (WHETHER SECTION 64(2) A BASIS FOR VOIDING A PATENT: PREROGATIVE RELIEF: Fed. Ct)

Winner v. Ammar Holdings Pty Ltd (INFRINGEMENT: Fed. Ct)

Winner v. Morey Haigh & Associates (Australasia) Pty Ltd (INFRINGEMENT: REVOCATION OF PATENT IN SUIT AT OTHER PROCEEDINGS: DISMISSAL OF INFRINGEMENT PROCEEDINGS: COSTS: INDEMNITY BASIS: Fed. Ct)

Royalty

Bayer AG v. Minister for Health of the Commonwealth of Australia (EXTENSION: PHARMACEUTICAL DRUG: ADEQUACY OF REMUNERATION: NOTIONAL ROYALTY: DATE OF ASSESSMENT: S.C.(NSW))

Scire facias. See **Practice** (*Scire facias*)

Secret Use

Graf v. Milward-Bason (EXPERIMENTAL USE: Pat. Off.)

Lake's Application (PETTY PATENT: Pat. Off.)

Melbourne v. Terry Fluid Controls Pty Ltd (ARTICLE DELIVERED TO POTENTIAL PURCHASER FOR TRIAL AND EVALUATION: CIRCUMSTANCES IN WHICH THAT USE IS SECRET USE CONSIDERED: Fed. Ct)

Polar Vac Pty Ltd v. Spoutvac Manufacturing Pty Ltd (OPPOSITION: PRIOR PUBLICATION: SECRET USE: OBVIOUSNESS: COMMON GENERAL KNOWLEDGE: AIPO)

Section 28, Patents Act 1952(Cth) Cases

Costa v. G.R. & I.E. Daking Pty Ltd (AIPO)

Kwan v. Queensland Corrective Services Commission (AIPO)

Section 40, Patents Act 1952(Cth) Cases

A. & K. Aluminium Pty Ltd v. Lidco Systems Sales Pty Ltd (Pat. Off.)

Bally Gaming International Inc. v. Scandic International Pty Ltd (AIPO)

Bausch & Lomb Inc. v. Allergan Inc. (Pat. Off.)
Braas & Co. GmbH v. Humes Ltd (Pat. Off.)
Cooper Industries Inc. v. Metal Manufactures Ltd (AIPO)
Heinen v. Pancontinental Mining Ltd (Pat. Off.)
Hoechst AG v. American Home Products Corp. (Pat. Off.)
Linde AG v. Air Products and Chemicals Inc. (Fed. Ct)
Luminous Pty Ltd v. Nitto Electric Industrial Co. Ltd (AIPO)
Massey v. Noack (Pat. Off.)
Mauri Brothers & Thomson (Aust.) Pty Ltd v. Containers Ltd (Pat. Off.)
McNeil Inc. v. Sterling Pharmaceuticals Pty Ltd (Fed. Ct)
Nelson v. Hillmark Industries Pty Ltd (Pat. Off.)
Smucker (J.M.) Co.'s Petty Patent (AIPO)
Sumitomo Chemical Co. Ltd v. Rhône-Poulenc Chimie (COSTS: Fed. Ct)

Section 51, Patents Act 1952(Cth) Cases

Husky Injection Molding Systems Ltd's Application (Pat. Off.)

Section 64(2), Patents Act 1952(Cth) Cases

Wimmera Industrial Minerals Pty Ltd v. RGC Mineral Dand Ltd (WHETHER SECTION 64(2) A BASIS FOR VOIDING A PATENT: PREROGATIVE RELIEF: Fed. Ct)

Section 117, Patents Act 1952(Cth) Cases

Dart Industries Inc. v. Grace Bros Pty Ltd (S.C.(Vic.))

Selection Patent

Bristol-Myers Company v. L'Oréal (Pat. Off.)
National Research Development Corporations Application (Pat. Off.)
Sumitomo Electrical Industries Ltd v. Metal Manufacturers Ltd (OPPOSITION: REHEARING: Fed. Ct)

Skilled Addressee

Freeman v. Pohlner Pty Ltd (REVOCATION: PATENTABILITY: NOVELTY: DESCRIPTION: BEST METHOD: Fed. Ct)

Special Circumstances. *See* Practice (*Special circumstances*)

Springboard Doctrine

Titan Group Pty Ltd v. Steriline Manufacturing Pty Ltd (CONFIDENTIAL INFORMATION: CONTENTS OF PATENT APPLICATIONS: DISCLOSURE IN CONFIDENCE: KNOWLEDGE OF RECIPIENT: Fed. Ct)

State Use

Stack v. Brisbane City Council (INFRINGEMENT: USE BY STATE: AUTHORITY: SUPPLY OF WATER METERS: Fed. Ct)

Sufficiency

Kwan v. Queensland Corrective Services Commission (PETTY PATENT: EXTENSION: SECTION 28 NOTICE: NOVELTY: OBVIOUSNESS: AIPO)

Threats

Townsend Controls Pty Ltd v. Gilead (DAMAGES: Fed. Ct)

Time Limits. *See* **Practice** (*Time limits*)

Title

Sartas No. 1 Pty Ltd v. Koukouou & Partners Pty Ltd (LACK OF TITLE: FALSE SUGGESTION: AIPO)

Transitional Application

Austgen Biojet Holdings Pty Ltd v. Goronszy (OPPOSITION: OBTAINING: INVENTOR: Fed. Ct)

Ricardo International plc v. Orital Engine Co. (Aust.) Pty Ltd (OPPOSITION: PRIOR CLAIMING: NOVELTY: DIVISIONAL STATUS: FAIR BASIS: AIPO)

Murex Diagnostics Australia Pty Ltd v. Chiron Corp. (APPLICATION FOR REVOCATION: PATENTEE NOT INVENTOR: EFFECT OF TRANSITIONAL PROVISIONS: Fed. Ct)

Treatment

Dr Rentschler Biotechnologie GmbH v. Boehringer Ingelheim International GmbH (APPLICATION: PROCESS: DISEASE: NOVELTY: AIPO)

Utility, including Inutility

Bolesta's (Dymtro) Application (COMMISSIONER'S LACK OF POWER TO CONSIDER UTILITY: Pat. Off.)

Bolesta's Application (COMMISSIONER'S LACK OF POWER TO CONSIDER UTILITY: Pat. Off.)

Coopers Animal Health Australia Ltd v. Western Stock Distributors Ltd (PETTY PATENT: Fed. Ct)

Decor Corporation Pty Ltd v. Dart Industries Inc. (INFRINGEMENT: CONSTRUCTION OF CLAIMS: Fed. Ct)

Du Pont de Nemours (E.I.) & Co. v. Commissioner of Patents (No. 3) (EXTENSION: WHETHER INVENTION OF MORE THAN ORDINARY UTILITY: S.C.(NSW))

Lantech Inc. v. First Green Park (INFRINGEMENT: SPECIFICATION: CONSTRUCTION: REVOCATION: INVALIDITY: SECTION 40 GROUNDS: Fed. Ct)

Pearce v. Paul Kingston Pty Ltd (LACK OF UTILITY: PAPER ANTICIPATION: S.C.(Vic.))

Philips Gloeilampenfabrieken (NV) v. Mirabella International Pty Ltd (Fed. Ct)

Rehm Pty Ltd v. Websters Security Systems (International) Pty Ltd (QUALIFIED READER: Fed. Ct)

Rescare Ltd v. Anaesthetic Supplies Pty Ltd (PAPER ANTICIPATION: COMBINATION: PATENT: Fed. Ct)

Melbourne v. Terry Fluid Controls Pty Ltd (Fed. Ct)

Validity

Advanced Building Systems Pty Ltd v. Ramset (Fed. Ct)

Anaesthetic Supplies Pty Ltd v. Rescare Ltd (FAIR BASIS: METHOD OF TREATMENT OF DISEASE: PATENTABILITY: Fed. Ct)

Bayer AG v. Alphapharm Pty Ltd (S.C.(NSW))

Beckman Instruments Inc. v. Bockringer Mannheim GmbH (Pat. Off.)

CCOM Pty Ltd v. Jiejung Pty Ptd (Fed. Ct)

Commonwealth Industrial Gases Ltd v. MWA Holdings Pty Ltd (COMBINATION OF NON-ESSENTIAL FEATURES: WORKSHOP IMPROVEMENTS: H.C.)

Coopers Animal Health Australia Ltd v. Western Stock Distributors Ltd (PETTY PATENT: Pat. Off.)

Decor Corporation Pty Ltd v. Dart Industries Inc. (Fed. Ct)

Du Pont de Nemours (E.I.) & Co. v. Cadbury Schweppes Pty Ltd (Fed. Ct)

Du Pont de Nemours (E.I.) & Co. v. Commissioner of Patents (EXTENSION: WHETHER OPPONENT MAY CHALLENGE VALIDITY: S.C.(NSW))

Du Pont de Nemours (E.I.) & Co. v. Cadbury Schweppes Pty Ltd (EXTENSION: CHALLENGE TO VALIDITY: WHETHER OPPONENT TO EXTENSION CAN PLEAD INVALIDITY: Fed. Ct)

Durack v. Associated Pool Builders Pty Ltd (PETTY PATENT: Fed. Ct)

Fisher & Paykel Healthcare Pty Ltd v. Avion Engineering Pty Ltd (PETTY PATENT: CONSTRUCTION OF CLAIM: Fed. Ct)

Interact Machine Tools (NSW) Pty Ltd v. Yamazaki Mazak Corporation (PETTY PATENT: FAIR BASIS: Fed. Ct)

Komesaroff v. Mizzi (PETTY PATENT: EXTENSION: INVALIDITY: Pat. Off.)

Martin Engineering Co. v. Trison Holdings Pty Ltd (INFRINGEMENT: VALIDITY IN ISSUE: Fed. Ct)

Nicaro Holdings Pty Ltd v. Martin Engineering Co. (INFRINGEMENT: Fed. Ct)

Olin Corp. v. Super Cartridge Co. Pty Ltd (WHETHER CLAIMS CLEAR AND DISTINCTIVE: FAIRLY BASED: INVENTIVE STEP: H.C.)

Pearce v. Paul Kingston Pty Ltd (INFRINGEMENT: S.C.(Vic.))

Peter Pan Electric Pty Ltd v. Newton Grace Pty Ltd (PETTY PATENT: Fed. Ct)

Prestige Group (Australia) Pty Ltd v. Dart Industries Inc. (INVALIDITY: FALSE SUGGESTION OR REPRESENTATION: GROUNDS FOR REPEAL OF GRANT BY WRIT OF *scire facias*: DOCTRINE OF FILE WRAPPER ESTOPPEL: Fed. Ct)

Procter & Gamble Company v. Kimberly-Clark Corporation (APPLICATION: OPPOSITION: Pat. Off.)

Rehm Pty Ltd v. Websters Security Systems (International) Pty Ltd (INFRINGEMENT: Fed. Ct)

Rehm Pty Ltd v. Websters Security Systems (International) Pty Ltd (INFRINGEMENT: PITH AND MARROW: Fed. Ct)

Rescare Ltd v. Anaesthetic Supplies Pty Ltd (INFRINGEMENT: Fed. Ct)

Rescare Ltd v. Anaesthetic Supplies Pty Ltd (REVOCATION: INFRINGEMENT: GRANT UNDER P.A.52 AND REVOCATION UNDER P.A.90: Fed. Ct)

Sartas No. 1 Pty Ltd v. Koukouou & Partners Pty Ltd (ALLEGED PRIOR PUBLICATION: OBVIOUSNESS: DOUBLE CLAIMING: LACK OF TITLE: FALSE SUGGESTION: AIPO)

Sunbeam Corp. v. Morphy-Richards (Aust.) Pty Ltd (NOVELTY: SUBJECT-MATTER: OBVIOUSNESS: COMMON GENERAL KNOWLEDGE: MOSAIC: H.C.)

Titan Mining & Engineering Pty Ltd v. Arnall's Engineering Pty Ltd (OPPOSITION: JURISDICTION OF COURT: LACK OF NOVELTY: FAILURE OF SPECIFICATION TO FULLY DESCRIBE: S.C.(NSW))

Vulcan Australia Ltd v. Braemar Appliances Pty Ltd (INFRINGEMENT: COUNTERCLAIM FOR REVOCATION: Pat. Off.)

Wood v. Uniflex (Aust.) Pty Ltd (NOVELTY: PRIOR PUBLICATION: FOREIGN DISCLOSURE TO EMPLOYEE OF AUSTRALIAN COMPANY: S.C.(Vic.))

Yamazaki Mazak Corporation v. Interact Machine Tools (NSW) Pty Ltd (PETTY PATENT: INFRINGEMENT: OBVIOUSNESS: FAIR BASIS: PETTY PATENT: Fed. Ct)

Witnesses. *See* **Practice** (*Witnesses*)

Workshop Improvement

Clafton Pty Ltd v. Forbes Engineering Holdings Pty Ltd (NOVELTY: OBVIOUSNESS: EVIDENCE OF EXPERTS WHO ARE INVENTIVE OR OVER-QUALIFIED OF LIMITED VALUE ON OBVIOUSNESS: Pat. Off.)

Practice and Miscellaneous Subjects

Account of Profits

Dart Industries Inc. v. Decor Corporation Pty Ltd (PATENT: INFRINGEMENT: DEDUCTION FOR INFRINGER'S GENERAL OVERHEAD COSTS: WHETHER ALLOWABLE: QUANTIFICATION OF: ONUS OF PROOF: H.C.: Fed. Ct)
Hogan v. Pacific Dunlop Ltd (PECUNIARY REMEDIES: RIGHT TO ELECT BETWEEN DAMAGES AND ACCOUNT OF PROFITS: Fed. Ct)
Kettle Chip Company Pty Ltd v. Apand Pty Ltd (PASSING OFF: SURVEY EVIDENCE: ADMISSIBILITY: Fed. Ct)
Minnesota Mining & Manufacturing Co. v. C. Jeffries Pty Ltd (PATENT: INFRINGEMENT: WHETHER ELECTION FOR DAMAGES OR ACCOUNT OF PROFITS TO BE MADE BEFORE DEFENDANT PROVIDES DISCOVERY: Fed. Ct (NSW))
Ryan v. Lum (DAMAGES OR ACCOUNT OF PROFITS: S.C.(NSW))
Z.S. Projects Pty Ltd v. G. & R. Investments Pty Ltd (COPYRIGHT; INFRINGEMENT: DAMAGES: S.C.(NSW))

Acquiescence

Led Builders Pty Ltd v. Masterton Homes (NSW) Pty Ltd (LACHES AND DELAY: Fed. Ct)

Affidavits

Acushnet Company v. Spalding Australia Pty Ltd (APPEAL FROM REFUSAL BY COMMISSIONER OF PATENTS: CROSS-APPEAL: ORDER FOR FILING AFFIDAVITS: Fed. Ct)
Autodesk Australia Pty Ltd v. Dyason (USE AGAINST THIRD PARTIES: UNDERTAKINGS: Fed. Ct)
Du Pont de Nemours (E.I.) & Co. v. Commissioner of Patents (PATENT: EXTENSION: WHETHER GENERAL DISCOVERY SHOULD BE ORDERED PRIOR TO FILING OF AFFIDAVITS: Fed. Ct)

Anton Piller Proceedings

Apple Computer Inc. v. Rowney (FORM OF ORDER: S.C.(NSW))
Authors Workshop v. Bileru Pty Ltd (MOTION TO SET ASIDE *ex parte* ORDERS: WHETHER ORDERS AKIN TO ANTON PILLER ORDER SUBJECT TO SAME PRECONDITIONS: PRIVILEGE AGAINST SELF-INCRIMINATION: COMMON LAW PRINCIPLES: Fed. Ct)
Gianitsios v. Karagiannis (S.C.(NSW))
Milcap Publishing Group AB v. Coranto Corporation Pty Ltd (SETTING ASIDE: WHETHER FULL DISCLOSURE HAD BEEN MADE: DOCTRINE OF *ex debito justitae*: Fed. Ct)

Polygram Records Pty Ltd v. Manash Records (Aust.) Pty Ltd (JURISDICTION: Fed. Ct)

Television Broadcasts Ltd v. Thi Phuong Nguyen (LIMITED RIGHT OF INSPECTION: PRIVILEGE AGAINST SELF INCRIMINATION: UNDERTAKING AS TO DAMAGES: Fed. Ct)

Tony Blain Pty Ltd v. Jamison (REPRESENTATIVE ORDER: *Ex parte* ORDER: REPRESENTATION OF GROUP: CIRCUMSTANCES: SAFEGUARDS: Fed. Ct)

Warman International Ltd v. Envirotech Australia Pty Ltd (EVIDENCE: PRIVILEGE AGAINST SELF-INCRIMINATION: Fed. Ct)

Appeal

Acushnet Company v. Spalding Australia Pty Ltd (REFUSAL BY COMMISSIONER OF PATENTS: CROSS-APPEAL: ORDER FOR FILING AFFIDAVITS: Fed. Ct)

Attorney-General v. Heinemann Publishers Australia Pty Ltd and Wright (APPLICATION FOR STAY OF ORDER PENDING APPLICATION FOR LEAVE TO APPEAL: JURISDICTION: H.C.)

Decor Corporation Pty Ltd v. Dart Industries Inc. (INTERLOCUTORY JUDGMENT: LEAVE TO APPEAL: DISCRETION: Fed. Ct)

Golden Editions Pty. Ltd v. Polygram Pty. Ltd (FACTUAL FINDINGS AND ERRORS OF LAW: Fed. Ct)

Visa International Services Association v. Beiser Corp. Pty Ltd (No. 2) (INTERLOCUTORY INJUNCTION: Fed. Ct)

Westaflex (Aust.) Pty Ltd v. Wood (INJUNCTIONS TO RESTRAIN PATENT INFRINGEMENT: STAY PENDING APPEAL: PRINCIPLES: Fed. Ct)

Balance of Convenience. *See* **Interlocutory Injunction** (*Balance of convenience*)

Best Endeavours Clause

Andoy Pty Ltd v. S. & M. Cannon Pty Ltd (EXCLUSIVE LICENCE: WORLDWIDE EXPLOITATION OF PATENT: DETERMINATION UPON BREACH: BREACH: S.C.(Vic.))

Burden of Proof

Oxford University Press v. Registrar of Trade Marks (TRADE MARKS: INHERENT ADAPTABILITY TO DISTINGUISH: USE AS A TRADE MARK: S.C.(Vic.))

Rowntree PLC v. Rollbits Pty Ltd (EVIDENCE OF REPUTATION: S.C.(NSW))

Universal City Studios Inc. v. Frankenstein Pty Ltd (NEGOTIATIONS, MEANING OF: AIPO)

Caveat

Searle & Co. v. Drug Houses of Australia Pty Ltd (PATENT: EXTENSION: Fed. Ct)

Clean Hands

Angus & Coote Pty Ltd v. Render (EMPLOYEE'S FIDUCIARY DUTY AND DUTY OF GOOD FAITH: S.C.(NSW))

Attorney-General v. Heinemann Publishers Australia Pty Ltd and Wright (BREACH OF CONFIDENCE: *Spycatcher*. S.C.(NSW): C.A.(NSW))

Consent Orders

Bohemia Crystal Pty Ltd v. D. Swarovski (POWER OF COURT TO VACATE: S.C.(NSW))

Du Pont de Nemours (E.I.) & Co. v. Commissioner of Patents (POWER OF COURT TO SET ASIDE CONSENT ORDER FOR DISCOVERY: Fed. Ct)

Contempt

Australian Design Council v. Peter Borello (TRADE MARK: INFRINGEMENT: FALSE REPRESENTATION: CONDUCT: FINE: Fed. Ct)

Pacific Basin Exploration Pty Ltd v. XLX (N.L.) (DISCLOSURE OF DISCOVERED DOCUMENTS: BREACH OF UNDERTAKING: S.C.(W.A.))

Sun Newspapers Pty Ltd v. Brisbane TV Ltd (NON PARTY TO ORIGINAL ACTION: TERMS OF INJUNCTION READ OVER TELEPHONE: KNOWLEDGE: Fed. Ct)

Trade Practices Commission v. Glo Juice Co. Pty Ltd (DISCRETION: Fed. Ct)

Windsurfing International Inc. v. Sailboards Australia Pty Ltd (BREACH OF UNDERTAKING: ONUS OF PROOF: LIABILITY: ASSESSMENT OF FINE: Fed. Ct)

Convenient Forum

Spotless Group Ltd v. Proplast Pty Ltd (STATE ACTION IN TWO JURISDICTIONS: APPLICATIONS TO SET ASIDE WRITS OR STAY OR TRANSFER: S.C.(Vic.))

Costs. *See also* Security for Costs

American National Can Co. v. W.R. Grace & Co.-Conn. (PATENT: OPPOSITION: AIPO)

Baker v. Peuren Agencies Ltd (PATENT: OPPOSITION: AMENDMENT OF SPECIFICATION: Pat. Off.)

Black & Decker Corporation v. Akarana Abrasive Industries Ltd (APPLICATION FOR EXTENSION OF TIME TO FILE EVIDENCE-IN-SUPPORT: INCONVENIENCE OF APPLICANT: PUBLIC INTEREST: Pat. Off.)

Calsil Ltd v. Riekie & Simpfendorfer (PATENT: APPLICATION: Pat. Off.)

CBS Records Australia Ltd v. Telmak Teleproducts (Aust.) Pty Ltd (INTERLOCUTORY INJUNCTION: Fed. Ct)

Colgate-Palmolive Co. v. Cussons Pty Ltd (INDEMNITY COSTS: EXERCISE OF DISCRETION TO AWARD: Fed. Ct)

Commonwealth Scientific and Industrial Research Organisation v. Western Mining Corp. Ltd (OBJECTION TO APPLICATION FOR EXTENSION OF TIME TO SERVE EVIDENCE-IN-SUPPORT: PUBLIC INTEREST: Pat. Off.)

Concorde Trading Pty Ltd v. Croner Trading Pty Ltd (PATENT: OPPOSITION: APPLICATION FOR DISMISSAL: VEXATIOUS OR ABUSE OF PROCESS: AIPO)

Dodds Family Investments Pty Ltd v. Lane Industries Pty Ltd (PASSING OFF: Fed. Ct)

Dricon Air Pty Ltd v. Waztech Pty Ltd (PATENT: OPPOSITION: *Locus standii*: Pat. Off.)

Du Pont De Nemours (E.I.) & Co. v. Commissioner of Patents (No. 7) (PATENT: EXTENSION: APPLICATION FOR SECURITY FOR COSTS AGAINST INTERVENOR: S.C.(NSW))

Eden Technology Pty Ltd v. Intel Corp. (WITHDRAWAL OF TRADE MARK APPLICATION: Pat. Off.)

Elconnex Pty Ltd v. Gerard Industries Pty Ltd (DISCRETION TO AWARD: Fed. Ct)

Farmitalia Carlo Erba SrL v. Delta West Pty Ltd (PATENT: INFRINGEMENT: REVOCATION: SECURITY FOR COSTS: APPLICANT ORDINARILY RESIDENT OUTSIDE DISCRETION: Fed. Ct)

First Tiffany Holdings Pty Ltd v. Tiffany and Company (TRADE MARKS: Pat. Off.)

Foodland Associated Ltd v. John Weeks Pty Ltd (EXTENSION OF TIME LIMITS: HEARING FEES: REFUND: Pat. Off.)

Gerber Scientific Products Inc. v. L. Vogel and Sons Pty Ltd (APPLICATION FOR EXTENSION OF TIME TO SERVE EVIDENCE IN REPLY: FACTORS RELEVANT: Pat. Off.)

Heylen v. Davies Collison Cave (EVIDENTIARY BURDEN: PATENT ATTORNEYS: AIPO)

Harris v. CSIRO (PATENT: APPLICATION: AIPO)

Hermes Sweeteners Ltd v. Hermes (TRADE MARKS: OPPOSITION FAILED: Pat. Off.)

Hood Computers Pty Ltd v. On-Line Furniture Pty Ltd (AIPO)

Kimberly-Clark Corp. v. Procter & Gamble Co. (APPLICATION FOR EXTENSION OF TIME TO FILE EVIDENCE-IN-SUPPORT: PUBLIC INTEREST: Pat. Off.)

Kimberly-Clark Ltd v. Commissioner of Patents (No. 2) (ADMINISTRATIVE APPEALS TRIBUNAL (COMMONWEALTH): REVIEW OF DECISIONS: EXTENSION OF TIME: RELEVANT MATTERS: AAT)

Leonardis v. St Alban (PATENTS: LATE NOTIFIED CITATIONS NOT PART OF OPPOSITION: Pat. Off.)

Lyons v. The J.M. Smucker Co. (APPLICATION FOR EXTENSION OF TIME TO FILE NOTICE OF OPPOSITION TO EXTENSION OF PATENT TERM: WHETHER ERROR BY ATTORNEY: WHETHER SERIOUS OPPOSITION: Pat. Off.)

Meditex Ltd v. New Horizonz Pty Ltd (EXTENSION OF TIME: AIPO)

Meyers v. Caterpillar Inc. (PATENT: OPPOSITION: AMENDMENT: Pat. Off.)

Monier Ltd v. Metalwork Tiling Co. of Australia Ltd (No. 2) (DISCRETION: EXERCISE AGAINST SUCCESSFUL PARTY: S.C.(NSW))

Moriarty's Application (PATENT: DISPUTE BETWEEN APPLICANTS: INTERESTED PARTY: Pat. Off.)

Nautical Services Pty Ltd v. Hitech Distillation (Aust.) Pty Ltd (EXTENSION OF TIME LIMITS TO SERVE EVIDENCE: *Locus standii*: PUBLIC INTEREST: Pat. Off.)

Nicholas Saba Sportswear Pty Ltd v. Daryl K. Linane (TRADE MARKS: FAILURE TO PROCEED WITH OPPOSITION: Pat. Off.)

Philips Gloeilampenfabrieken (NV) v. Ultralite International Pty Ltd (INJUNCTION REFUSED BUT UNDERTAKINGS ACCEPTED TO KEEP ACCOUNTS AND PAY INTO COURT-CONTROLLED FUND: Fed. Ct)

Porter v. Victoria's Secret Inc. (CROSS-EXAMINATION OF WITNESS: AIPO)

Prudhoe v. ICI Australian Operations Pty Ltd (PATENT: OPPOSITION WITHDRAWN: PATENT GRANTED: COSTS OF APPLICANT: WHETHER PROCEEDINGS STILL BEFORE COMMISSIONER: AIPO)

R. & C. Products Pty Ltd v. Bathox Bathsalts Pty Ltd (TRADE MARKS: SUCCESSFUL OPPOSITION: Pat. Off.)

Sasdor Pty Ltd v. Atomic Skifabrik Alois Rohrmoser (TRADE MARKS: REMOVAL FOR NON-USE: OPPOSITION: PERSON AGGRIEVED: PART SUCCESS: Pat. Off.)

Société des Produits Nestlé SA v. Penaten Pharmazeutische Fabrik Dr Med Rieze & Co. GmbH (EXTENSION OF TIME LIMIT TO LODGE EVIDENCE: HEARING BEFORE REGISTRAR: Pat. Off.)

South East Queensland Electricity Board v. Techmark-Miers Pty Ltd (PATENT: OPPOSITION: APPOINTMENT OF RECEIVER AND MANAGER TO OPPONENT: NON-PURSUIT OF OPPOSITION: WITHDRAWAL OF OPPOSITION: Pat. Off.)

Tattilo Editrice SpA v. Playboy Enterprises Inc. (TRADE MARK: WITHDRAWAL OF OPPOSITION: BILL OF COSTS: HEARING FEE: T.M.Reg.)

Vanitone Pty Ltd v. Formica Technology, Inc. (EXTENSION OF TIME TO LODGE EVIDENCE-IN-SUPPORT OF OPPOSITION: PUBLIC INTEREST IN COMMISSIONER HAVING PERTINENT MATERIAL: COSTS WHERE PARTIES DECLINE HEARING: Pat. Off.)

Virbac (Australia) Pty Ltd v. Merck Patent GmbH (PATENT: EXTENSION OF TERM: PHARMACEUTICAL SUBSTANCE: Fed. Ct)

Cross-appeal

Acushnet Company v. Spalding Australia Pty Ltd (ORDER FOR FILING AFFIDAVITS: Fed. Ct)

Cross-examination

American Cyanamid Company v. Nalco Chemical Company (REQUEST FOR THE COMMISSIONER OF PATENTS TO SUMMON WITNESSES: Pat. Off.)

Damages

10th Cantanae Pty Ltd v. Shoshana Pty Ltd (PASSING OFF: ASSESSMENT OF DAMAGES: Fed. Ct) (CHARACTER MERCHANDISING: INNOCENT INFRINGEMENT: SUBSTANTIAL DAMAGES: MEASURE OF DAMAGES: Fed. Ct)

Autodesk Australia Pty Ltd v. Cheung (MEASURE OF COMPENSATORY DAMAGES: ADDITIONAL DAMAGES: Fed. Ct)

Bailey v. Namol Pty Ltd (COMPENSATORY DAMAGES: ASSESSMENT: CALCULATION BY REFERENCE TO EXPECTED PROFITS: AGGRAVATED OR EXEMPLARY DAMAGES: Fed. Ct)

Bateman v. Slatyer (SALE OF STORE FRANCHISE: REPRESENTATIONS ABOUT PROFITABILITY: MEASURE OF DAMAGES: Fed. Ct)

Caj Amadio Constructions Pty Ltd v. Kitchen (WHETHER DAMAGES FOR INFRINGEMENT OF COPYRIGHT TO BE ASSESSED ON BASIS OF LOSS OF PROFITS OR ON BASIS OF LOSS OF LICENCE FEE: S.C.(S.A.))

Dixon Investments Pty Ltd v. Hall (ALLEGED COPYING OF PROJECT HOUSE DESIGN DRAWINGS: Fed. Ct)

Erica Vale Australia Pty Limited v. Thompson & Morgan (Ipswich) Limited (COPYRIGHT: LITERARY WORK: ADAPTATION: OWNERSHIP: CONTRACT: IMPLIED TERM: COSTS INCURRED IN MITIGATION OF LOSS: LOST PROFITS: Fed. Ct)

Gates v. CML Assurance Society Ltd (MEASURE OF DAMAGES: H.C.)

Henjo Investments Pty Ltd v. Collins Marrickville Pty Ltd (MEASURE OF DAMAGES IN RESPECT OF SALE OF RESTAURANT BUSINESS INDUCED BY MISREPRESENTATIONS: ASSESSMENT OF DAMAGES FOR BURDEN OF UNECONOMIC LEASE: Fed. Ct)

Hogan v. Koala Dundee Pty Ltd (PASSING OFF: LOST CHANCE OF GETTING FEE FROM WRONG-DOER: WHETHER PROOF OF FRAUD NECESSARY: Fed. Ct)

Hogan v. Pacific Dunlop Ltd (CHARACTER MERCHANDISING, SPONSORSHIP AND TESTIMONIAL ADVERTISING: RIGHT TO ELECT BETWEEN DAMAGES AND ACCOUNT OF PROFITS: Fed. Ct)

Hoogerdyk v. Condon (BUSINESS NAME: SALE OF BUSINESS: BREACH OF CONTRACT: GOODWILL IN NAME: ASSESSMENT: H.C.)

Jackson v. Sterling Industries Ltd (TRADE PRACTICES: Fed. Ct)

Kalamazoo (Aust.) Pty Ltd v. Compact Business Systems Pty Ltd (COPYRIGHT: INFRINGEMENT: REMEDIES: MATTERS AFFECTING RIGHT TO DAMAGES: H.C.)

Martin Engineering Co. v. Nicaro Holdings Pty Ltd (AUTHORISATION OF INFRINGEMENT: DIRECTOR'S PERSONAL LIABILITY: Fed. Ct)

Mateffy Perl Nagy Pty Ltd v. Devefi Pty Ltd (MEASURE OF DAMAGES: Fed. Ct)

Minnesota Mining & Manufacturing Co. v. C. Jeffries Pty Ltd (WHETHER ELECTION FOR DAMAGES OR ACCOUNT OF PROFITS TO BE MADE BEFORE DISCOVERY: Fed. Ct (NSW))

Namol Pty Ltd v. A.W. Baulderstone Pty Ltd (ASSESSMENT OF DAMAGES FOR COPYRIGHT INFRINGEMENT: Fed. Ct)

Peter Isaacson Publications Pty Ltd v. Nationwide News Pty Ltd (Fed. Ct)

Pioneer Concrete Services Ltd v. Lorenzo Galli (CONFIDENTIAL INFORMATION: IMPLIED OBLIGATION: RESTRAINT OF TRADE: S.C.(Vic.))

Ryan v. Lum (SIMILARITY OF TYPE OF PRODUCT, INSTRUCTIONS AND GET-UP: DAMAGES OR ACCOUNT OF PROFITS: S.C.(NSW))

Sabazo Pty Ltd v. Ruddiman (PASSING OFF: LOWER QUALITY GOODS: ASSESSMENT OF DAMAGES: S.C.(NSW))

Schindler Lifts Australia Pty Ltd v. Debelak (TRADE LIBEL: INJURIOUS FALSEHOOD: INDUCING BREACH OF CONTRACT: Fed. Ct)

Sent v. Jet Corp. of Australia Pty Ltd (COMPENSATORY RELIEF: TIME LIMITATION: H.C.)

Smith Kline & French Laboratories (Australia) Ltd v. Secretary, Department of Community Services and Health (UNDERTAKING AS TO DAMAGES: Fed. Ct)

Snyman v. Cooper (PASSING OFF: INJURY TO GOODWILL: ASSESSMENT OF DAMAGES: EXEMPLARY DAMAGES: Fed. Ct)

Squibb & Sons Pty Ltd v. Tully Corp. Pty Ltd (OBLIGATION ON RECIPIENT OF INFORMATION TO INVESTIGATE: Fed. Ct)

Star Micronics Pty Ltd v. Five Star Computers Pty Ltd (BREACH OF COPYRIGHT, PASSING OFF AND MISLEADING OR DECEPTIVE CONDUCT: DAMAGES FOR LOSS OF REPUTATION: DAMAGES FOR DIMINUTION IN VALUE OF COPYRIGHT: Fed. Ct)

Surge Licensing Inc. v. Pearson (LOSS OF REPUTATION: Fed. Ct)

Television Broadcasts Ltd v. Thi Phuong Nguyen (ANTON PILLER ORDER: UNDERTAKING AS TO DAMAGES: Fed. Ct)

Television Broadcasts Ltd v. Tu (ASSESSMENT OF DAMAGES: FLAGRANT BREACH OF COPYRIGHT: HOW DAMAGES CALCULATED: Fed. Ct)

Townsend Controls Pty Ltd v. Gilead (PATENT: THREATS: Fed. Ct)

Typing Centre of NSW Pty Ltd v. Northern Business College Ltd (COMPARATIVE ADVERTISING: Fed. Ct)

Wickham v. Associated Pool Builders Pty Ltd (USE OF BUSINESS NAME: ADEQUACY OF DAMAGES: Fed. Ct)

Winning Appliances Pty Ltd v. Dean Appliances Pty Ltd (ASSESSMENT OF DAMAGES: GENERAL DAMAGES: EVIDENCE: Fed. Ct)

Z.S. Projects Pty Ltd v. G. & R. Investments Pty Ltd (COPYRIGHT: BUILDING PLANS: INFRINGEMENT: S.C.(NSW))

Declaration

Harris v. CSIRO (JOINT INVENTORSHIP: DECLARATION SOUGHT CONCERNING ELIGIBLE PERSON IN RELATION TO INVENTIONS: AIPO)

Pioneer Concrete Services Ltd v. Lorenzo Galli (CONFIDENTIAL INFORMATION: IMPLIED OBLIGATION: RESTRAINT OF TRADE: S.C.(Vic.))

Squibb & Sons Pty Ltd v. Tully Corp. Pty Ltd (DECLARATION OF VOID CONTRACT: Fed. Ct)

Defence

Attorney-General v. Heinemann Publishers Australia Pty Ltd and Wright (INIQUITY: CLEAN HANDS: S.C.(NSW): C.A.(NSW))

De Garis v. Neville Jeffress Pidler Pty Ltd (FAIR DEALING: IMPLIED LICENCE: Fed. Ct)

Henjo Investments Pty Ltd v. Collins Marrickville Pty Ltd (OPERATION OF EXCLUSION CLAUSES AS DEFENCE: Fed. Ct)

Delay

Led Builders Pty Ltd v. Masterton Homes (NSW) Pty Ltd (COPYRIGHT: INFRINGEMENT: LACHES AND ACQUIESCENCE: Fed. Ct)

Selectrode Industries Inc. v. Selectrode Pty Ltd (PASSING OFF: INTERLOCUTORY INJUNCTION: Fed. Ct)

Delivery Up

Angus & Coote Pty Ltd v. Render (S.C.(NSW))
Milpurrurru v. Indofurn Pty Ltd (COPYRIGHT: ABORIGINAL ARTWORK: IMPORTATION: REPRODUCTION: SUBSTANTIAL PART: OWNERSHIP: KNOWLEDGE: DIRECTOR'S LIABILITY: CONVERSION DAMAGES: Fed. Ct)

Director's Liability

Australasian Performing Right Association Ltd v. Jain (EXECUTIVE DIRECTOR: POWER TO AUTHORISE PERFORMANCE OF WORKS IN PUBLIC: Fed. Ct)
Australasian Performing Right Association Ltd v. Tolbush Pty Ltd (PUBLIC PERFORMANCE: AUTHORISATION: S.C.(Qd))
Australasian Performing Right Association Ltd v. Valamo Pty Ltd (Fed. Ct)
Bateman v. Slatyer (REPRESENTATIONS ABOUT PROFITABILITY: MEASURE OF DAMAGES: Fed. Ct)
Mack Trucks Inc. v. Satberg Pty Ltd (Fed. Ct)
Martin Engineering Co. v. Nicaro Holdings Pty Ltd (AUTHORISATION OF INFRINGEMENT: Fed. Ct)
Milpurrurru v. Indofurn Pty Ltd (COPYRIGHT: ABORIGINAL ARTWORK: KNOWLEDGE: CONVERSION DAMAGES: Fed. Ct)
Namol Pty Ltd v. A.W. Baulderstone Pty Ltd (WHETHER DIRECTOR OF INFRINGING COMPANY A JOINT TORTFEASOR: WHETHER IN BREACH OF FIDUCIARY DUTY: Fed. Ct)
Sent v. Jet Corp. of Australia Pty Ltd (CAUSING A MISREPRESENTATION: Fed. Ct)

Discovery and Inspection

Aitken v. Neville Jeffress Pidler Pty Ltd (SCOPE OF PRELIMINARY DISCOVERY: Fed. Ct)
Ballabil Holdings Pty Ltd v. Hospital Products Ltd (MAREVA INJUNCTION: POWER OF COURT: C.A.)
Cave Holdings Pty Ltd v. Taperline Pty Ltd (PREPARATORY DESIGN DRAWINGS: Fed. Ct)
Du Pont de Nemours (E.I.) & Co. v. Commissioner of Patents (WHETHER GENERAL DISCOVERY SHOULD BE ORDERED PRIOR TO FILING OF AFFIDAVITS: POWER OF COURT TO SET ASIDE CONSENT ORDER FOR DISCOVERY: Fed. Ct)
Enviro-Clear Co. Inc. v. Commissioner of Patents (PRINCIPLES: S.C.(NSW))
McIlwraith McEachern Operations Ltd v. Parcel Holdings Pty Ltd (POWER OF COMMISSIONER TO ORDER: DIFFERENCES BETWEEN PRODUCTION AND DISCOVERY: Pat. Off.)
Minnesota Mining & Manufacturing Co. v. C. Jeffries Pty Ltd (WHETHER ELECTION FOR DAMAGES OR ACCOUNT OF PROFITS TO BE MADE BEFORE DEFENDANT PROVIDES DISCOVERY: Fed. Ct (NSW))
Nickmar Pty Ltd v. Preservatrice Skandia Insurance Ltd (LEGAL PROFESSIONAL PRIVILEGE: USE OF DOCUMENTS: H.C.)
Nylex Corp. Ltd v. Sabco Ltd (IDENTITY OF SUPPLIER OR DISTRIBUTOR: Fed. Ct)
Pacific Basin Exploration Pty Ltd v. XLX (N.L.) (DISCLOSURE OF DISCOVERED DOCUMENTS: BREACH OF UNDERTAKING: CONTEMPT: S.C.(W.A.))
Paxus Services Ltd v. People Bank Pty Ltd (DISCOVERY BEFORE ACTION: CONFIDENTIAL INFORMATION IN COMPUTER DATABASES: CONSIDERATIONS FOR EXERCISE OF DISCRETION: Fed. Ct)
Redic Industries Pty Ltd v. J.A.L. Chemicals Pty Ltd (INSPECTION OF FINANCIAL AND SALES RECORDS OF COMPANY OF FORMER EMPLOYEES: S.C.(Vic.))

Trade Practices Commission v. International Technology Holdings Pty Ltd (TRADE
MARK: LEGAL PROFESSIONAL PRIVILEGE: PATENT ATTORNEYS: Fed. Ct)
Wundowie Foundry Pty Ltd v. Milson Foundry Pty Ltd (DOCUMENTS RELATING TO
DESIGN AND DEVELOPMENT OF INVENTION: PATENT ATTORNEY AND CLIENT
PRIVILEGE: Fed. Ct)

Discretion

BEST Australia Ltd v. Aquagas Marketing Pty Ltd (APPLICATION TO SET ASIDE
SERVICE OUTSIDE JURISDICTION: Fed. Ct)
Brisalebe Ltd v. Searle (PATENT: PROVISIONAL SPECIFICATION: REQUEST FOR
INSPECTION: OBTAINING: ASSIGNMENT: AIPO)
Coco v. Newnham (TAPES AND TRANSCRIPTS PRODUCED BY LISTENING DEVICES:
PRIVATE CONVERSATION OBTAINED BY USE OF DEVICE: WHETHER
COMPLETE PROHIBITION OR DISCRETIONARY GROUND OF EXCLUSION:
S.C.(Qd))
Decor Corporation Pty Ltd v. Dart Industries Inc. (INTERLOCUTORY JUDGMENT:
LEAVE TO APPEAL: Fed. Ct)
Du Pont De Nemours (E.I.) & Co. v. Commissioner of Patents (No. 7) (APPLICATION
FOR SECURITY FOR COSTS AGAINST INTERVENOR IN PATENT EXTENSION:
WHETHER INTERVENOR A "DEFENDANT": CONSIDERATIONS: S.C.(NSW))
Elconnex Pty Ltd v. Gerard Industries Pty Ltd (DISCRETION TO AWARD COSTS: Fed.
Ct)
Ferocem Pty Ltd v. Commissioner of Patents (EXTENSION OF TIME TO FILE
EVIDENCE: PRINCIPLES: Fed. Ct)
Henjo Investments Pty Ltd v. Collins Marrickville Pty Ltd (OPERATION OF
EXCLUSION CLAUSES AS DEFENCE: Fed. Ct)
Monier Ltd v. Metalwork Tiling Co. of Australia Ltd (No. 2) (COSTS: EXERCISE
AGAINST SUCCESSFUL PARTY: S.C.(NSW))
Paxus Services Ltd v. People Bank Pty Ltd (DISCOVERY BEFORE ACTION:
CONSIDERATIONS FOR EXERCISE OF DISCRETION: Fed. Ct)
Rhône Poulenc Agrochemie SA v. UIM Chemical Services Pty Ltd (INJUNCTION:
Fed. Ct)
Roussel-Uclaf v. Pan Laboratories Pty Ltd (PATENT: GOODS INFRINGING PATENTS
IN AUSTRALIA: EXPORT TO PAPUA NEW GUINEA: JURISDICTION TO ORDER
DELIVERY UP: DISCRETION: Fed. Ct)
Sterling Industries Ltd v. Nim Services Pty Ltd (MAREVA INJUNCTION: SUFFICIENCY
OF REMEDY: Fed. Ct)
Stork Pompen BV v. Weir Pumps Ltd (EXTENSION OF TIME TO LODGE NOTICE OF
OPPOSITION: PRE-CONDITIONS TO EXERCISE OF COMMISSIONER'S
DISCRETION: Pat. Off.)
Timberland Co. v. Speedo Knitting Mills Pty Ltd (TRADE MARKS: DISCRETION OF
REGISTRAR: Pat. Ct)
Trade Practices Commission v. Glo Juice Co. Pty Ltd (INJUNCTION: FORM:
CONTEMPT: Fed. Ct)
Trepper v. Miss Selfridge Ltd (TRADE MARKS: OPPOSITION: WHETHER SPECIAL
CIRCUMSTANCES EXIST: Pat. Off.)
Zeccola v. Universal City Studios Inc. (INTERLOCUTORY INJUNCTION: Fed. Ct)

Dismissal of Proceedings

Kimberly-Clark Ltd v. Commissioner of Patent (EXISTENCE OF OTHER RIGHTS OF
REVIEW: Fed. Ct)
MXM v. Franke (PERSON INTERESTED: *Locus standii*: STANDING: PATENT
ATTORNEY: Pat. Off.)

Error

Behringwerke AG (SUBSTITUTION OF NAME: CLERICAL ERROR: Pat. Off.)

Dimtsis v. Agricultural Dairy Industry Authority of Epirus, Dodoni SA (EXTENSION OF TIME TO FILE EVIDENCE: ERRORS OR OMISSIONS BY AGENTS OF PARTIES: Pat. Off.)

Gatward's Application (EXTENSION OF TIME TO LODGE NOTICE OF OPPOSITION: FAILURE DUE TO ERROR BY AGENT: Pat. Off.)

Genentech Inc. v. Wellcome Foundation Ltd (EXTENSION OF TIME IN WHICH TO SERVE EVIDENCE-IN-SUPPORT OF OPPOSITION: ERRORS OR OMISSIONS OF PATENT ATTORNEY: Pat. Off.)

Genetics International Inc. v. Serono Diagnostics Ltd (EXTENSION OF TIME TO LODGE NOTICE OF OPPOSITION: ERROR OR OMISSION OF AGENTS OR ATTORNEYS: Pat. Off.)

Grafton Industries Pty Ltd v. Wyborn (EXTENSION OF TIME: ERROR OR OMISSION: Pat. Off.)

Groko Maskin AB's Application (EXTENSION OF TIME: PUBLIC INTEREST: ERROR OR OMISSION: Pat. Off.)

ICI Australia Operations Pty Ltd v. Commercial Polymers Pty Ltd (EXTENSION OF TIME TO APPLY FOR TIME TO FILE EVIDENCE: ATTORNEY'S ERROR: Pat. Off.)

Jacuzzi Inc.'s Application (TRADE MARKS: ACCEPTANCE IN ERROR: Pat. Off.)

Kimberly-Clark Ltd v. Commissioner of Patents (No. 3) (EXTENSION OF TIME: Fed. Ct)

Lyons v. The J.M. Smucker Co. (EXTENSION OF TIME TO FILE NOTICE OF OPPOSITION TO PATENT EXTENSION: ERROR BY ATTORNEY: Pat. Off.)

Mitsubishi Chemical Industries Ltd v. Asahi Kasei Kogyo KK (ERROR OR OMISSION BY EMPLOYEE OF PATENT ATTORNEY: PUBLIC INTEREST: Pat. Off.)

Stork Pompen BV v. Weir Pumps Ltd (EXTENSION OF TIME TO LODGE NOTICE OF OPPOSITION: ERROR OR OMISSION BY PROPOSED OPPONENT: PRE-CONDITIONS TO EXERCISE OF COMMISSIONER'S DISCRETION: Pat. Off.)

Stratco Metal Pty Ltd's Application (ERROR IN NOTICE OF OPPOSITION TO TRADE MARK: Pat. Off.)

Toyo Seikan Kaisha Ltd v. Nordson Corp. (EXTENSION OF TIME LIMIT: ERROR OR OMISSION: TIMELINESS: Pat. Off.)

Uniglobe Holdings Pty Ltd v. Uniglobe Travel (International) Inc. (CLERICAL ERROR: APPLICATION TO AMEND: OBVIOUS MISTAKE: Pat. Off.)

Weir Pumps Ltd and Commissioner of Patent and Stork Pompen BV (EXTENSION OF TIME TO LODGE NOTICE OF OPPOSITION TO PATENT: AAT)

Evidence. *See also* **Extension of Time Limits, Survey Evidence and Questionnaires**

American Cyanamid Company v. Nalco Chemical Company (CROSS-EXAMINATION: WITNESSES: REQUEST FOR THE COMMISSIONER OF PATENTS TO SUMMON WITNESSES: Pat. Off.)

Attorney-General v. Heinemann Publishers Australia Pty Ltd and Wright (CREDIBILITY OF CROWN WITNESS: S.C.(NSW): C.A.(NSW))

Australian Telecommunication Corporation v. Centec International Corp. Pty Ltd (SERVICE: ADDRESS FOR SERVICE: Pat. Off.)

Bodenseewerk Perkin-Elmer GmbH v. Varian Australia Pty Ltd (PATENT: OPPOSITION: CLARITY: FAIR BASING: PRIOR PUBLICATION: OBVIOUSNESS: NOVELTY: EXPERT EVIDENCE: COMMON GENERAL KNOWLEDGE: Fed. Ct)

Braas & Co. GmbH v. Humes Ltd (VALUE OF EVIDENCE OF OVER-QUALIFIED EXPERTS: Pat. Off.)

Broderbund Software Inc. v. Computermate Products (Australia) Pty Ltd (USE OF SURVEY EVIDENCE: Fed. Ct)

Chase Manhattan Overseas Corp. v. Chase Corp. Ltd (INTERVIEWS WITH PUBLIC: Fed. Ct)

Clafton Pty Ltd v. Forbes Engineering Holdings Pty Ltd (PATENT: OPPOSITION: EVIDENCE OF EXPERTS WHO ARE INVENTIVE OR OVER-QUALIFIED OF LIMITED VALUE ON OBVIOUSNESS: Pat. Off.)

High Tech Auto Tools Pty Ltd v. Ferocem Pty Ltd (CLARITY: UNCERTAINTY: AIPO)

Clune v. Collins Angus & Robertson Publishers Pty Ltd (CREDIT OF WITNESS: Fed. Ct)

Coco v. Newnham (TAPES AND TRANSCRIPTS: PRODUCED BY LISTENING DEVICES: PRIVATE CONVERSATION OBTAINED BY USE OF DEVICE: WHETHER COMPLETE PROHIBITION OR DISCRETIONARY GROUND OF EXCLUSION: ADMISSIBILITY: S.C.(Qd))

Cooper Industries Inc. v. Metal Manufactures Ltd (PATENT: OPPOSITION: PROCEDURE: NON-COMPLIANCE WITH SECTION 40: OBVIOUSNESS: COMMON GENERAL KNOWLEDGE: AIPO)

D'Urban Inc. v. Canpio Pty Ltd (EVIDENCE SERVED OUT OF TIME: FAILURE TO SEEK EXTENSION: SPECIAL CIRCUMSTANCES: Pat. Off.)

Dennison Manufacturing Co. v. Monarch Marking Systems Inc. (NOVELTY: EXPERT EVIDENCE: Fed. Ct)

Dupps Co. v. Stord Bartz A/S (APPLICATION FOR SPECIAL LEAVE TO ADDUCE FURTHER EVIDENCE: Pat. Off.)

Dupps Co. v. Stord Bartz A/S (NUMEROUS EXTENSIONS OF TIME WITHIN WHICH TO LODGE EVIDENCE-IN-SUPPORT: FAILURE TO LODGE APPLICATION FOR EXTENSION WITHIN TIME: Pat. Off.)

Elconnex Pty Ltd v. Gerard Industries Pty Ltd (ADMISSIBILITY OF EVIDENCE OF EXPERT WITNESSES: Fed. Ct)

E.S. & M.J. Heard Pty Ltd v. Phillips (REQUEST TO SUMMON A WITNESS: WHETHER CONFLICT ON THE FACTS: AIPO)

Gordon & Rena Merchant Pty Ltd v. Barrymores Pty Ltd (EXTENSION OF TIME: EVIDENCE IN ANSWER: AIPO)

Herron Pharmaceuticals Pty Ltd v. Sterling Winthrop Pty Ltd (TRADE MARK: APPLICATION TO REMOVE: OPPOSITION: ADMISSION OF FURTHER EVIDENCE: AIPO)

Heylen v. Davies Collison Cave (OBVIOUSNESS: EVIDENTIARY BURDEN: PATENT ATTORNEYS: COSTS: AIPO)

ICI v. Mitsubishi Gas Chemical Co. (PATENT: APPLICATION: OPPOSITION: FURTHER EVIDENCE AFTER EVIDENCE IN REPLY: OBJECTION: AIPO)

Interlego AG v. Croner Trading Pty Ltd (SURVEY EVIDENCE: Fed. Ct)

James v. Australia & New Zealand Banking Group Ltd (NO-CASE SUBMISSION: ELECTION NOT TO CALL EVIDENCE: Fed. Ct)

Jarvis v. Doman (QUESTIONNAIRES: Pat. Off.)

Johnson & Johnson Australia Pty Ltd v. Sterling Pharmaceuticals Pty Ltd (SURVEY EVIDENCE: Fed. Ct)

Kettle Chip Company Pty Ltd v. Apand Pty Ltd (SURVEY EVIDENCE: ADMISSIBILITY: Fed. Ct)

Liederman's Application (TRADE MARKS: SURNAME: CAPABLE OF BECOMING DISTINCTIVE: EVIDENCE OF OVERSEAS DISTINCTIVENESS: Pat. Off.)

Luminous Pty Ltd v. Nitto Electric Industrial Co. Ltd (PATENT: OPPOSITION: NOVELTY: OBVIOUSNESS: SECTION 40: PRIOR PUBLICATION: COMBINATION PATENT: ESSENTIAL INTEGERS: INSUFFICIENCY: FAIR BASIS: AIPO)

North Cope Ltd v. Allman Properties (Aust.) Pty Ltd (MAREVA INJUNCTION: NATURE OF EVIDENCE REQUIRED: S.C.(Qd))

O'Connor v. Stevenson (SIMILAR FACT EVIDENCE: ADMISSIBILITY IN CIVIL TRIALS: Fed. Ct)

Orton & Burns Engineering Pty Ltd v. John L. O'Brien and Associates (APPLICATION FOR SPECIAL LEAVE TO ADDUCE FURTHER EVIDENCE: UNAVAILABLE TO APPLICANT WHO HAS FILED NO EVIDENCE: Pat. Off.)

Pacific Dunlop Ltd v. Fruit of the Loom Inc. (APPLICATION FOR EXTENSION OF TIME TO FILE EVIDENCE-IN-ANSWER: TIME NEEDED TO GATHER EVIDENCE ON USE: Pat. Off.)

Rollbits Pty Ltd v. Rowntree Mackintosh PLC (PRESENTATION OF EVIDENCE AND ARGUMENTS: Pat. Off.)

Rosebank Plastics Pty Ltd v. Duncan & Wigley Pty Ltd (VISUAL COMPARISON: EXPERT EVIDENCE AS TO SIMILARITY: Fed. Ct)

Scruples Imports Pty Ltd v. Crabtree & Evelyn Pty Ltd (CONFLICT OF LAWS: EXPERT EVIDENCE: S.C.(NSW))

Selskar Pty Ltd's Application (HONEST CONCURRENT USE: CONFLICTING EVIDENCE: AIPO)

Sepa Waste Water Treatment Pty Ltd v. JMT Welding Pty Ltd (PATENT AGENTS' PRIVILEGE: ADVICE ON DESIGNS INFRINGEMENT: S.C.(NSW))

Sew Hoy & Sons Ltd v. Skill Print Pty Ltd (SUFFICIENCY OF EVIDENCE: Pat. Off.)

State Government Insurance Corp. v. Government Insurance Office of NSW (SURVEY EVIDENCE: Fed. Ct)

Sterling Pharmaceuticals Pty Ltd v. Johnson & Johnson Australia Pty Ltd (ADMISSIBILITY AND RELEVANCE OF EVIDENCE: HEARSAY: SURVEY EVIDENCE OF PUBLIC AS TO KNOWLEDGE AND USE OF TRADE MARK: ADMISSIBILITY OF EVIDENCE OF MEANINGS OF WORDS TO AID STATUTORY CONSTRUCTION AND FOR OTHER PURPOSES: INADMISSIBILITY OF EVIDENCE AS TO ULTIMATE ISSUE: Fed. Ct)

Studio Australia Pty Ltd v. Softsel Computer Products Inc. (TRADE MARKS: NON-USE: ADEQUACY OF EVIDENCE TO ESTABLISH PRIMA FACIE CASE OF NON-USE: Pat. Off.)

Toro Company's Applications (TRADE MARK: OBJECTION: DESCRIPTIVE MARK: CONSISTENCY BY REGISTRAR: SURVEY EVIDENCE: AIPO)

Virtual Reality and Reality v. W. Industries Ltd (EXTENSION OF TIME: AIPO)

Winning Appliances Pty Ltd v. Dean Appliances Pty Ltd (ASSESSMENT OF DAMAGES: GENERAL DAMAGES: Fed. Ct)

Ex Parte Order

Authors Workshop v. Bileru Pty Ltd (INTERLOCUTORY INJUNCTION: MOTION TO SET ASIDE ex parte ORDERS: WHETHER ORDERS AKIN TO ANTON PILLER ORDER AND SUBJECT TO SAME PRE-CONDITIONS: Fed. Ct)

Tony Blain Pty Ltd v. Jamison (REPRESENTATIVE ORDER: Ex parte ORDER: REPRESENTATION OF GROUP: ANTON PILLER: CIRCUMSTANCES: SAFEGUARDS: Fed. Ct)

Expert Witnesses

Elconnex Pty Ltd v. Gerard Industries Pty Ltd (ADMISSIBILITY OF EVIDENCE OF: Fed. Ct)

Extension of Time Limit

Albright & Wilson Ltd v. Colgate Palmolive Co. (Pat. Off.)

Amrad Corp. Ltd v. Genentech Inc. (PATENT: OPPOSITION: NOTICE: ERROR OR OMISSION: AIPO)

Austoft Industries Limited v. Cameco Industries Limited (PATENT: OPPOSITION: PUBLIC INTEREST: AIPO)

Australian Olympic Committee Inc. v. Brennan (APPLICATION FOR EXTENSION OF TIME FOR SERVICE OF EVIDENCE: FACTORS TO BE CONSIDERED: AIPO)

Ampex Corp. v. Amper SA (TRADE MARK: OPPOSITION: SETTLEMENT NEGOTIATIONS: PUBLIC INTEREST: AIPO)

BASF Corporation v. ICI Australia Operations Pty Ltd (SERVICE OF EVIDENCE-IN-SUPPORT: ONUS OF PROOF: Pat. Off.)

Baxter Travenol Laboratories Inc. v. Cutter Laboratories Inc. (LODGING EVIDENCE: Pat. Off.)

Bee Tek (Import & Export) Pte Ltd v. Kenner Parker Toys Inc. (FILING EVIDENCE-IN-REPLY: PUBLIC INTEREST: Pat. Off.)

Black & Decker Corporation v. Akarana Abrasive Industries Ltd (FILING EVIDENCE-IN-SUPPORT: USUAL TIME REQUIRED FOR PREPARATION OF EVIDENCE: INCONVENIENCE OF APPLICANT: PUBLIC INTEREST: Pat. Off.)

Board of Control of Michigan Technological University v. Deputy Commissioner of Patents (UNDUE DELAY: H.C.)

British-American Tobacco Co. Ltd v. Philip Morris Ltd (LODGING EVIDENCE: Pat. Off.)

Bundy American Corp. v. Rent-A-Wreck (Vic.) Pty Ltd (INTER-PARTY NEGOTIATION: PUBLIC INTEREST: Pat. Off.)

Calsil Ltd v. Riekie and Simpfendorfer (SERVICE OF OPPONENTS' EVIDENCE: Pat. Off.)

Carlton & United Breweries Ltd v. Miller Brewing Co. (REASONS: Pat. Off.)

Commonwealth Scientific and Industrial Research Organisation v. Western Mining Corporation Ltd (SERVICE OF EVIDENCE: OBJECTION: PRINCIPLES: PUBLIC INTEREST: Pat. Off.)

D'Urban Inc. v. Canpio Pty Ltd (FAILURE TO SEEK EXTENSION OF TIME: SPECIAL CIRCUMSTANCES: Pat. Off.)

Dentsply International Inc. v. Bayer AG (Pat. Off.)

Du Pont de Nemours (E.I.) & Co. v. DowElanco (EXTENSION OF TIME TO FILE EVIDENCE: JUSTIFICATION: FULL AND FRANK DISCLOSURE OF FACTS: AIPO)

Dimtsis v. Agricultural Dairy Industry Authority of Epirus, Dodoni SA (FILING EVIDENCE: OBJECTION TO: SPECIAL CIRCUMSTANCES: Pat. Off.)

Dow Chemical Co. v. Ishihara Sangyo Kaisha Ltd (Pat. Off.)

Ferocem Pty Ltd v. Commissioner of Patents (EXTENSION OF TIME TO FILE EVIDENCE: PRINCIPLES: DISCRETION: Fed. Ct)

Figgins Holdings Pty Ltd v. Parfums Christian Dior (FILING EVIDENCE: Pat. Off.)

Foodland Associated Ltd v. John Weeks Pty Ltd (SERVICE OF EVIDENCE: COSTS: Pat. Off.)

Gansu Research Institution of Chemical Industry v. ICI Australia Operations Pty Ltd (LODGING EVIDENCE: Pat. Off.)

Gatward's Application (LODGE NOTICE OF OPPOSITION: ERROR BY AGENT: Pat. Off.)

Genentech Inc. v. Wellcome Foundation Ltd (SERVICE OF EVIDENCE-IN-SUPPORT OF OPPOSITION: ERRORS OR OMISSIONS OF PATENT ATTORNEY: SPECIAL CIRCUMSTANCES: Pat. Off.)

Genetics Institute Inc. v. Johnson & Johnson (OBJECTION: DIRECTION: AIPO)

Genetics International Inc. v. Serono Diagnostics Ltd (LODGING NOTICE OF OPPOSITION: ERROR OR OMISSION OF AGENTS OR ATTORNEYS: Pat. Off.)

Gerber Scientific Products Inc. v. L. Vogel and Sons Pty Ltd (SERVICE OF EVIDENCE-IN-REPLY: FACTORS RELEVANT: COSTS WHEN EXTENSION GRANTED: Pat. Off.)

Gordon & Rena Merchant Pty Ltd v. Barrymores Pty Ltd (EVIDENCE-IN-ANSWER: SPECIAL CIRCUMSTANCES: ONUS OF PROOF: AIPO)

Grafton Industries Pty Ltd v. Wyborn (ERROR OR OMISSION: Pat. Off.)

Groko Maskin AB's Application (PUBLIC INTEREST: ERROR OR OMISSION: Pat. Off.)

Gumley's Application (FILING EVIDENCE-IN-SUPPORT OF OPPOSITION: APPLICATION OPPOSED: Pat. Off.)

Henkel Kommanditgesellschaft Auf Aktien v. Fina Research SA (OBJECTION: AIPO)

ICI Australia Operations Pty Ltd v. Commercial Polymers Pty Ltd (FILING EVIDENCE: ATTORNEYS ERROR AMOUNTS TO SPECIAL CIRCUMSTANCES: PUBLIC INTEREST: Pat. Off.)

Ikida Koki Seisakusho KK v. Duro-Matic Pty Ltd (Pat. Off.)

Jonathan Sceats Design Pty Ltd's Application (SERVICE OF EVIDENCE-IN-SUPPORT OF OPPOSITION: Pat. Off.)

Kent-Moore Corp. v. Environmental Products Amalgamated Pty Ltd (FILING EVIDENCE IN OPPOSITION: Pat. Off.)

Kimberly-Clark Corp. v. Procter & Gamble Co. (FILING EVIDENCE-IN-SUPPORT: PUBLIC INTEREST: COSTS: Pat. Off.)

Kimberly-Clark Ltd v. Commissioner of Patent (LODGING NOTICE OF OPPOSITION TO THE GRANT OF A PATENT: ADMINISTRATIVE DECISIONS: Fed. Ct)

Kimberly-Clark Ltd v. Commissioner of Patents (No. 2) (RELEVANT MATTERS: AAT)

Kimberly-Clark Ltd v. Commissioner of Patents (No. 3) (CONSTRUCTION: ERROR OR OMISSION: Fed. Ct)

Lehtovaara v. Acting Deputy Commissioner of Patents (Fed. Ct)

Liquid Air Australia Ltd v. Commonwealth Industrial Gases Ltd (Pat. Off.)

Lyons v. Registrar of Trade Marks (Fed. Ct)

Lyons v. The J.M. Smucker Co. (FILING NOTICE OF OPPOSITION TO EXTENSION OF TERM: WHETHER ERROR BY ATTORNEY: WHETHER SERIOUS OPPOSITION: COSTS: Pat. Off.)

Meditex Ltd v. New Horizonz Pty Ltd (COSTS: AIPO)

Murdock Overseas Corporation v. Saramar Corporation (FILING EVIDENCE: OMISSION BY ATTORNEY: PUBLIC POLICY: Pat. Off.)

Nautical Services Pty Ltd v. Hitech Distillation (Aust.) Pty Ltd (FILING EVIDENCE: *Locus standi*: PUBLIC INTEREST: COSTS: Pat. Off.)

Pacific Dunlop Ltd v. Fruit of the Loom Inc. (FILING EVIDENCE: TIME NEEDED TO GATHER EVIDENCE ON USE: BALANCE OF CONVENIENCE: PUBLIC INTEREST: Pat. Off.)

Parke Davis Pty Ltd v. Sanofi & Commissioner of Patents (Fed. Ct)

Playground Supplies Pty Ltd's Application (PUBLIC INTEREST: Pat. Off.)

Poltrock v. Ennor (LODGING NOTICE: WANT OF EVIDENCE-IN-SUPPORT: Pat. Off.)

Procter & Gamble Company v. Kimberly-Clark Corporation (LODGING EVIDENCE: Pat. Off.)

Rear v. Drilling Tools Australia Pty Ltd (EVIDENCE-IN-SUPPORT: GROUNDS FOR GRANT OF EXTENSION OF TIME: ROLE OF COMMISSIONER OF PATENTS: INTERESTS OF PARTIES: Pat. Off.)

Ritz Hotel London Ltd's Application (Pat. Off.)

Rohrmoser v. Registrar of Trade Marks (Fed. Ct)

Rollbits Pty Ltd v. Rowntree Mackintosh PLC (SERVICE OF DOCUMENTS: PUBLIC INTEREST: Pat. Off.)

Roussel-Uclaf v. Shell Internationale Research Maatschappij BV (EVIDENCE-IN-SUPPORT: PUBLIC INTEREST: Pat. Off.)

Royale & Co. (Aust.) Pty Ltd v. Maxims Ltd (EVIDENCE: Pat. Off.)

Sandoz Ltd v. Fujisawa Pharmaceutical Co. Ltd (FILING EVIDENCE-IN-SUPPORT: NEED FOR FULL AND FRANK DISCLOSURE: Pat. Off.)

Sandoz Ltd v. Fujisawa Pharmaceutical Co. Ltd (SERVICE OF FURTHER EVIDENCE-IN-SUPPORT: OBJECTION: Pat. Off.)

Société des Produits Nestlé SA v. Penaten Pharmazeutische Fabrik Dr Med Rieze & Co. GmbH (LODGING OF EVIDENCE: COSTS: Pat. Off.)

Stafford-Miller Ltd v. Jean Patou Parfumeur (LODGING NOTICE OF OPPOSITION: Pat. Off.)

Stibbard v. The Commissioner of Patents (AAT)

Stork Pompen BV v. Weir Pumps Ltd (LODGING NOTICE OF OPPOSITION: ERROR OR OMISSION: PRE-CONDITIONS TO EXERCISE OF COMMISSIONER'S DISCRETION: Pat. Off.)

Tandy Corporation's Application (LODGING NOTICE OF OPPOSITION: Pat. Off.)

Toyo Seikan Kaisha Ltd v. Nordson Corp. (LODGING NOTICE OF OPPOSITION: ERROR OR OMISSION: TIMELINESS: Pat. Off.)

Ulrich Labels Pty Ltd v. Printing and Allied Trades Employers' Federation of Australia (FILING NOTICE OF OPPOSITION: *Locus standii*: Pat. Off.)

Underwood v. Toby Construction Products Pty Ltd (SERVICE OF EVIDENCE-IN-SUPPORT OF OPPOSITION: Pat. Off.)

Universal City Studios Inc. v. Frankenstein Pty Ltd (EVIDENCE-IN-SUPPORT: BURDEN OF PROOF: AIPO)

Vanitone Pty Ltd v. Formica Technology, Inc. (LODGING EVIDENCE-IN-SUPPORT OF OPPOSITION: ONUS ON PARTY SEEKING EXTENSION: PUBLIC INTEREST: COSTS: Pat. Off.)

Virtual Reality and Reality v. W. Industries Ltd (EVIDENCE: AIPO)

Viskase Corp. v. W.R. Grace & Co.-Conn. (APPLICATION FOR EXTENSION OF TIME FOR SERVICE OF EVIDENCE: AIPO)

Weir Pumps Ltd and Commissioner of Patent and Stork Pompen BV (LODGING NOTICE OF OPPOSITION: ERROR OR OMISSION: CIRCUMSTANCES BEYOND THE CONTROL: AAT)

Weller v. TGI Friday's Application (TRADE MARK: OPPOSITION: OPPONENT SEEKING SPECIAL LEAVE TO ADDUCE FURTHER EVIDENCE: AIPO)

Forfeiture

Irvine v. Carson (ORDER FOR FORFEITURE OF COMPUTERS USED FOR MAKING INFRINGING COPIES: Fed. Ct)

Further and Better Particulars

Du Pont de Nemours (E.I.) & Co. v. DowElanco (PATENT: OPPOSITION: AIPO)

Mobay Corp. v. Dow Chemical Co. (POWER TO ORDER: NO POWER TO STRIKE OUT PARTICULARS: Pat. Off.)

Inspection

Pacific Dunlop Ltd v. Australian Rubber Gloves Pty Ltd (INSPECTION PRIOR TO ISSUING PROCEEDINGS: Fed. Ct)

Redic Industries Pty Ltd v. J.A.L. Chemicals Pty Ltd (FINANCIAL AND SALES RECORDS OF COMPANY OF FORMER EMPLOYEES: S.C.(Vic.))

Injunction. *See also* Interlocutory Injunctions and Mareva Injunctions

Angus & Coote Pty Ltd v. Render (CONFIDENTIAL INFORMATION: EMPLOYEE'S FIDUCIARY DUTY AND DUTY OF GOOD FAITH: LENGTH OF RESTRAINT: S.C.(NSW))

Attorney-General v. Heinemann Publishers Australia Pty Ltd and Wright (*Admiral Byng* INJUNCTION: H.C.)

Australian Design Council v. Peter Borello (CONTINUING USE OF TRADE MARK IN BREACH OF INJUNCTION: DELIBERATE BREACH: PUBLIC INTEREST FACTORS: FINE: Fed. Ct)

B. & W. Cabs Ltd v. Brisbane Cabs Pty Ltd (STATEMENTS THOUGH STRICTLY TRUE LIKELY TO MISLEAD: Fed. Ct)

Carlton & United Breweries Ltd v. Tooth & Co. Ltd (IMPLIED TERMS: GOODWILL OF BUSINESS: S.C.(NSW))

Concept Television Products Pty Ltd v. Australian Broadcasting Corporation (TRADE PRACTICES: WHETHER REQUIREMENTS OF FALSITY OR RECKLESSNESS SUFFICIENTLY SHOWN TO WARRANT INJUNCTION: Fed. Ct)

De Garis v. Neville Jeffress Pidler Pty Ltd (Fed. Ct)

Dronpool Pty Ltd v. Hunter (S.C.(NSW))

Hogan v. Koala Dundee Pty Ltd (MERCHANDISING RIGHTS: PASSING OFF: LOSS NECESSARY TO FOUND INJUNCTION: FORM OF INJUNCTION: Fed. Ct)

Janssen Pharmaceutica Pty Ltd v. Pfeizer Pty Ltd (MANDATORY INJUNCTION TO PUBLISH CORRECTION: Fed. Ct)

Lelah v. Associated Communication Corp. of Australia Pty Ltd (MISLEADING ADVERTISEMENTS: Fed. Ct)

Peter Isaacson Publications Pty Ltd v. Nationwide News Pty Ltd (TRADE PRACTICES: CONSUMER PROTECTION: MISLEADING CONDUCT: Fed. Ct)

Pioneer Concrete Services Ltd v. Lorenzo Galli (CONFIDENTIAL INFORMATION: IMPLIED OBLIGATION: RESTRAINT OF TRADE: S.C.(Vic.))

Rhône Poulenc Agrochemie SA v. UIM Chemical Services Pty Ltd (PATENT: INFRINGEMENT: DISCRETION: Fed. Ct)

Schindler Lifts Australia Pty Ltd v. Debelak (TRADE LIBEL: INJURIOUS FALSEHOOD: INDUCING BREACH OF CONTRACT: EMPLOYEE'S DUTY: Fed. Ct)

Sun Newspapers Pty Ltd v. Brisbane TV Ltd (CONTEMPT OF COURT: NON-PARTY TO ORIGINAL ACTION: Fed. Ct)

Trade Practices Commission v. Glo Juice Co. Pty Ltd (MISLEADING AND DECEPTIVE CONDUCT: FORM: Fed. Ct)

Westaflex (Aust.) Pty Ltd v. Wood (PATENT: INJUNCTIONS TO RESTRAIN INFRINGEMENT: STAY PENDING APPEAL: PRINCIPLES: Fed. Ct)

Interlocutory and Interim Injunctions

Adequacy of damages

Bates & Partners Pty Ltd v. The Law Book Company Ltd (CONFIDENTIAL INFORMATION: PRIZE LIST: EMBARGOED NEWS RELEASE: CORRECTIVE ADVERTISING: APPLICATION FOR INTERLOCUTORY MANDATORY INJUNCTION: S.C.(NSW))

Digby International (Australia) Pty Ltd v. Beyond Imagination Pty Ltd (TRADE MARK: INFRINGEMENT: EXTREME/POWERADE EXTREMISTS: SERIOUS QUESTION TO BE TRIED: BALANCE OF CONVENIENCE: Fed. Ct)

Wickham v. Associated Pool Builders Pty Ltd (DELAY: Fed. Ct)

Appeal

Visa International Services Association v. Beiser Corp. Pty Ltd (No. 2) (Fed. Ct)

Balance of convenience

Australian Telecommunications Corporation v. Hutchison Telecommunications (Australia) Ltd (Fed. Ct)

Bevis v. Lyons (S.C.(Qd))

Cabot Corporation v. Minnesota Mining & Manufacturing Ltd (PRINCIPLES TO BE APPLIED: PRIMA FACIE CASE: S.C.(NSW))

Chenel Pty Ltd v. Rayner (SERIOUS ISSUE TO BE TRIED: S.C.(Vic.))

Criminal Justice Commission v. Nationwide News Pty Ltd (BALANCING HARM DONE BY PUBLICATION AGAINST PUBLIC INTEREST: Fed. Ct)

Crusta Fruit Juices Pty Ltd v. Cadbury Schweppes Pty Ltd (TRADE MARK: INFRINGEMENT: CRESTA/CRUSTA: IMPERFECT RECOLLECTION: Fed. Ct)

Digby International (Australia) Pty Ltd v. Beyond Imagination Pty Ltd (TRADE MARK: INFRINGEMENT: EXTREME/POWERADE EXTREMISTS: SERIOUS QUESTION TO BE TRIED: ADEQUACY OF DAMAGES: Fed. Ct)

Gollel Holdings Pty Ltd v. Kenneth Maurer Funerals Pty Ltd (TRADE PRACTICES: MISLEADING AND DECEPTIVE CONDUCT: DELAY: PROOF OF LOSS: Fed. Ct)

Miniskips Ltd v. Sheltan Pty Ltd (TRADE PRACTICES: MISLEADING AND DECEPTIVE CONDUCT: FRANCHISE AGREEMENT: TERMINATION OF FRANCHISE AGREEMENT BY FRANCHISOR: RELIEF AGAINST FORFEITURE: FRANCHISEE CONTINUING TO TRADE USING FRANCHISOR'S TRADE MARK AND LOGO: SERIOUS QUESTION TO BE TRIED: Fed. Ct)

Minogue v. Grundy Television Pty Ltd (INJUNCTION: INTERLOCUTORY INJUNCTION: WHETHER SUBSTANTIAL QUESTION TO BE INVESTIGATED AT TRIAL AND WHETHER BALANCE OF CONVENIENCE FAVOURS INJUNCTION: APPLICATION OF BALANCE OF CONVENIENCE WHERE PROSPECTS OF SUCCESS AT TRIAL SLIGHT: S.C.(Vic.))

MIPS Computer Systems Inc. v. MIPS Computer Resources Pty Ltd (TRADE PRACTICES: FALSE OR MISLEADING CONDUCT: COMPANY TRADING IN ITS OWN NAME WHERE NAME SUBSTANTIALLY SIMILAR TO ESTABLISHED COMPETITORS: LACHES: DELAY: Fed. Ct)

Nicholas v. Borg (PASSING OFF: REPUTATION: MELBOURNE CUP: S.C.(S.A.))

Pacific Dunlop Ltd v. Fruit of the Loom Inc. (TRADE MARKS: OPPOSITION TO APPLICATION FOR REMOVAL: APPLICATION FOR EXTENSION OF TIME TO FILE EVIDENCE-IN-ANSWER: TIME NEEDED TO GATHER EVIDENCE ON USE: PUBLIC INTEREST: Pat. Off.)

Philips Gloeilampenfabrieken (NV) v. Ultralite International Pty Ltd (PATENT: INJUNCTION REFUSED BUT UNDERTAKINGS ACCEPTED TO KEEP ACCOUNTS AND PAY $1.00 PER UNIT INTO COURT-CONTROLLED FUND: COSTS: Fed. Ct)

Selectrode Industries Inc. v. Selectrode Pty Ltd (PASSING OFF: DELAY: ADEQUACY OF DAMAGES: Fed. Ct)

Street v. Jedsminster Pty Ltd (TRADE PRACTICES: CONSUMER PROTECTION: MISLEADING OR DECEPTIVE CONDUCT: PASSING OFF: USE OF SIMILAR DESCRIPTIVE NAMES: TWO MOTELS IN SMALL TOWN: CABOOLTURE MOTEL/CABOOLTURE HOTEL MOTEL INN: GEOGRAPHICALLY DESCRIPTIVE NAME: Fed. Ct)

Wood v. Kempe (COPYRIGHT: INFRINGEMENT: ARCHITECTS PLANS: Fed. Ct)

Continuation of injunction

Fido Dido Inc. v. Venture Stores (Retailers) Pty Ltd (APPLICATION FOR CONTINUATION OF INTERLOCUTORY INJUNCTION: Fed. Ct)

Costs

CBS Records Australia Ltd v. Telmak Teleproducts (Aust.) Pty Ltd (Fed. Ct)

Philips Gloeilampenfabrieken (NV) v. Ultralite International Pty Ltd (BALANCE OF CONVENIENCE INJUNCTION REFUSED BUT UNDERTAKINGS ACCEPTED TO KEEP ACCOUNTS AND PAY INTO COURT-CONTROLLED FUND: Fed. Ct)

Delay

Gollel Holdings Pty Ltd v. Kenneth Maurer Funerals Pty Ltd (BALANCE OF CONVENIENCE: Fed. Ct)

Wickham v. Associated Pool Builders Pty Ltd (ADEQUACY OF DAMAGES: Fed. Ct)

Discretion

Zeccola v. Universal City Studios Inc. (Fed. Ct)

Likelihood of success at trial

Moon's Products Pty Ltd v. Herbs of Gold Pty Ltd (Fed. Ct)

Jurisdiction

Edinburgh Laboratories (Australia) Pty Ltd v. Lantigen (England) Ltd (PROCEDURE: PROPER LAW OF CONTRACT: S.C.(NSW))

Order for corrective publications

Trotman Australia Pty Ltd v. Hobsons Press (Australia) Pty Ltd (PRINCIPLES GOVERNING ORDER FOR CORRECTIVE PUBLICATIONS AT INTERLOCUTORY STAGE: Fed. Ct)

Payment into court-controlled fund

Philips Gloeilampenfabrieken (NV) v. Ultralite International Pty Ltd (BALANCE OF CONVENIENCE INJUNCTION REFUSED BUT UNDERTAKINGS ACCEPTED TO KEEP ACCOUNTS AND PAY $1.00 PER UNIT INTO COURT CONTROLLED FUND: Fed. Ct)

Prima facie case

Cabot Corporation v. Minnesota Mining & Manufacturing Ltd (BALANCE OF CONVENIENCE: S.C.(NSW))

Principles

Castlemaine Tooheys Ltd v. State of South Australia (H.C.)

Proof of loss

Gollel Holdings Pty Ltd v. Kenneth Maurer Funerals Pty Ltd (BALANCE OF CONVENIENCE: DELAY: Fed. Ct)

Serious question to be tried

Allgas Energy Its v. East West International Gas Equipment Pty Ltd (Fed. Ct)
Chenel Pty Ltd v. Rayner (CONFIDENTIAL INFORMATION: BALANCE OF CONVENIENCE: S.C.(Vic.))
Criminal Justice Commission v. Nationwide News Pty Ltd (CONFIDENTIAL INFORMATION: INFORMATION MOSTLY IN PUBLIC DOMAIN: BALANCING HARM DONE BY PUBLICATION AGAINST PUBLIC INTEREST: Fed. Ct)
Digby International (Australia) Pty Ltd v. Beyond Imagination Pty Ltd (TRADE MARK: INFRINGEMENT: EXTREME/POWERADE EXTREMISTS: BALANCE OF CONVENIENCE: ADEQUACY OF DAMAGES: Fed. Ct)
Miniskips Ltd v. Sheltan Pty Ltd (BALANCE OF CONVENIENCE: Fed. Ct)

Undertaking as to damages

Smith Kline & French Laboratories (Australia) Ltd v. Secretary, Department of Community Services and Health (USUAL UNDERTAKING: NON-PARTY TO LITIGATION: EXTENSION OF UNDERTAKING: Fed. Ct)

Whether injunction available

OBSA Pty Ltd v. T.F. Thomas and Sons Pty Ltd (Fed. Ct)

Jurisdiction to Act

Attorney-General v. Heinemann Publishers Australia Pty Ltd (*Admiral Byng* injunction: H.C.)

Autodesk Inc. v. Dyason (No. 2) (JURISDICTION TO REHEAR: H.C.)

Carlton & United Breweries Ltd v. Castlemaine Tooheys Ltd (H.C.)

Du Pont de Nemours (E.I.) & Co. v. Commissioner of Patents (No. 5) (JURISDICTION OR POWER TO JOIN ADDITIONAL PARTIES TO APPLICATION: WHETHER *amici curiae*: S.C.(NSW))

Edinburgh Laboratories (Australia) Pty Ltd v. Lantigen (England) Ltd (PROCEDURE: PROPER LAW OF CONTRACT: S.C.(NSW))

Hart (S.W.) & Co. Pty Ltd v. Edwards Hot Water Systems (REOPENING LITIGATION: Fed. Ct)

Jackson v. Sterling Industries Ltd (DAMAGES: UNDERTAKING: FAILURE OF COURT TO OBTAIN: EFFECT: Fed. Ct)

Polygram Records Pty Ltd v. Manash Records (Aust.) Pty Ltd (ANTON PILLER ORDERS: Fed. Ct)

Roussel-Uclaf v. Pan Laboratories Pty Ltd (PATENT: GOODS INFRINGING PATENTS IN AUSTRALIA: EXPORT TO PAPUA NEW GUINEA: JURISDICTION TO ORDER DELIVERY UP: DISCRETION: Fed. Ct)

Knowledge

Milpurrurru v. Indofurn Pty Ltd (COPYRIGHT: IMPORTATION: DIRECTOR'S LIABILITY: Fed. Ct)

Laches

Led Builders Pty Ltd v. Masterton Homes (NSW) Pty Ltd (COPYRIGHT: INFRINGEMENT: ACQUIESCENCE AND DELAY: Fed. Ct)

Leave

Attorney-General v. Heinemann Publishers Australia Pty Ltd (APPLICATION FOR STAY PENDING HEARING OF APPLICATION FOR SPECIAL LEAVE TO APPEAL: *Admiral Byng* INJUNCTION: H.C.)

Decor Corporation Pty Ltd v. Dart Industries Inc. (INTERLOCUTORY JUDGMENT: LEAVE TO APPEAL: DISCRETION: Fed. Ct)

Dupps Co. v. Stord Bartz A/S (SPECIAL LEAVE TO ADDUCE FURTHER EVIDENCE: Pat. Off.)

Orton & Burns Engineering Pty Ltd v. John L. O'Brien and Associates (SPECIAL LEAVE TO ADDUCE FURTHER EVIDENCE: POSITION OF APPLICANT WHO HAS FILED NO EVIDENCE: Pat. Off.)

Paragini Footwear Pty Ltd v. Paragon Shoes Pty Ltd (LEAVE TO LODGE FURTHER EVIDENCE: Pat. Off.)

Queensland Plumbing Pty Ltd v. Trade Waste Diversion Pty Ltd (LEAVE TO AMEND PATENT SPECIFICATION: AIPO)

Sent v. Jet Corp. of Australia Pty Ltd (LEAVE TO AMEND STATEMENT OF CLAIM: COMPENSATORY RELIEF: H.C.)

Studio SrL v. Buying Systems (Aust.) Pty Ltd (FURTHER EVIDENCE: Pat. Off.)

Sue v. Carpenter (SPECIAL LEAVE TO ADDUCE FURTHER EVIDENCE: Pat. Off.)

Worrallo v. Hales (SPECIAL LEAVE TO LODGE FURTHER EVIDENCE: Pat. Off.)

Locus standii

Dricon Air Pty Ltd v. Waztech Pty Ltd (STANDING TO OPPOSE PATENT: Pat. Off.)

Enzed Holdings Ltd v. Wynthea Pty Ltd (COPYRIGHT: OWNERSHIP: COMMISSIONED WORK: FOREIGN AUTHOR: Fed. Ct)

Herron Pharmaceuticals Pty Ltd v. Sterling Winthrop Pty Ltd (TRADE MARK: APPLICATION TO REMOVE: OPPOSITION: PERSON AGGRIEVED: *Locus standii* BASED ON PRIOR REGISTERED MARKS: ADMISSION OF FURTHER EVIDENCE: AIPO)

Kraft Foods Inc. v. Gaines Pet Foods Corporation (TRADE MARK: REMOVAL FOR NON-USE: PERSON AGGRIEVED: ONUS OF PROOF: Fed. Ct)

Merck & Co, Inc. v. Sankyo Co. Ltd (PATENT APPLICATION: Fed. Ct)

Metropolitan Dairies Pty Ltd v. Pura Natural Spring Waters Pty Ltd (TRADE MARKS: REGISTRATION: RENEWAL: LAPSED REGISTRATION: EXTENSION OF TIME: ERROR OR OMISSION: NATURAL JUSTICE: PUBLIC POLICY: Pat. Off.)

MXM v. Franke (PATENT: OPPOSITION: PERSON INTERESTED: PATENT ATTORNEY: Pat. Off.)

Nautical Services Pty Ltd v. Hitech Distillation (Aust.) Pty Ltd (EXTENSION OF TIME LIMITS TO SERVE EVIDENCE: PUBLIC INTEREST: COSTS: Pat. Off.)

Ulrich Labels Pty Ltd v. Printing and Allied Trades Employers Federation of Australia (EXTENSION OF TIME TO FILE NOTICE OF OPPOSITION: Pat. Off.)

Mareva Injunction

Damage

Yorkwain Automatic Doors Ltd v. Newman Tonks Pty Ltd (MEASURE OF DAMAGE: NECESSITY OF DELIBERATELY SEEKING TO AVOID JUDGMENT: S.C.(Vic.))

Damages

Jackson v. Sterling Industries Ltd (Fed. Ct)

Discretion

Sterling Industries Ltd v. Nim Services Pty Ltd (Fed. Ct)

Evidence

Construction Engineering (Aust.) Pty Ltd v. Tambel (Aust.) Ltd (S.C.(NSW))

North Cope Ltd v. Allman Properties (Aust.) Pty Ltd (NATURE OF EVIDENCE REQUIRED: S.C.(Qd))

Form of order

Abella v. Anderson (S.C.(Qd))

Grounds for grant

Bank of Queensland Ltd v. Grant (S.C.(NSW))

Jurisdiction

Jackson v. Sterling Industries Ltd (Fed. Ct)

Power of court

Ballabil Holdings Pty Ltd v. Hospital Products Ltd (DISCOVERY: C.A.)

Pearce v. Waterhouse (S.C.(Vic.))

Principles for grant

Pearce v. Waterhouse (S.C.(Vic.))

868

Perth Mint v. Mickelberg (S.C.(W.A.))
Yandill Holdings Pty Ltd v. Insurance Co. of North America (H.C.)

Risk of dissipation of assets

Perth Mint v. Mickelberg (No. 2) (S.C.(W.A.))

Sufficiency of remedy

Sterling Industries Ltd v. Nim Services Pty Ltd (DISCRETION: Fed. Ct)

Undertaking

Jackson v. Sterling Industries Ltd (Fed. Ct)

Variation

Australian Iron & Steel Pty Ltd v. Buck (S.C.(NSW))

Motion

American Cyanamid Company v. Alcoa of Australia Ltd (MOTION TO STRIKE OUT PLEADINGS: Fed. Ct)
Authors Workshop v. Bileru Pty Ltd (INTERLOCUTORY INJUNCTION: MOTION TO SET ASIDE *ex parte* ORDERS: WHETHER ORDERS AKIN TO ANTON PILLER ORDER AND SUBJECT TO SAME PRECONDITIONS: CLAIM OF PRIVILEGE AGAINST SELF-INCRIMINATION: COMMON LAW PRINCIPLES: Fed. Ct)
Simplicity Funerals Ltd v. Simplicity Funerals Pty Ltd (PERPETUAL STAY: DUPLICATION OF PROCEEDINGS: PREVIOUS UNSUCCESSFUL PROCEEDINGS IN SUPREME COURT; Fed. Ct)

Natural Justice

Metropolitan Dairies Pty Ltd v. Pura Natural Spring Waters Pty Ltd (TRADE MARKS: REGISTRATION: RENEWAL: LAPSED REGISTRATION: EXTENSION OF TIME: ERROR OR OMISSION: *Locus standii*: PUBLIC POLICY: Pat. Off.)

Onus of Proof

BASF Corporation v. ICI Australia Operations Pty Ltd (EXTENSION OF TIME TO SERVE EVIDENCE-IN-SUPPORT: ONUS OF PROOF ON APPLICANT: Pat. Off.)
Dart Industries Inc. v. Decor Corporation Pty Ltd (ACCOUNT OF PROFITS: DEDUCTION FOR GENERAL OVERHEAD COSTS: ONUS OF PROOF CONCERNING: H.C.)
Faessler v. Neale (PASSING OFF: ASSOCIATION WITH NAME: Fed. Ct)
Gordon & Rena Merchant Pty Ltd v. Barrymores Pty Ltd (EXTENSION OF TIME: EVIDENCE IN ANSWER: SPECIAL CIRCUMSTANCES: AIPO)
Kraft Foods Inc. v. Gaines Pet Foods Corporation (TRADE MARK: REMOVAL FOR NON-USE: *Locus standii*: PERSON AGGRIEVED: Fed. Ct)
Ryan v. Lum (PATENT: LACK OF NOVELTY AND OBVIOUSNESS: REVOCATION: PROCUREMENT OF INFRINGEMENT: S.C.(NSW))
Trepper v. Miss Selfridge Ltd (TRADE MARK: OPPOSITION: PERSON AGGRIEVED: Pat. Off.)
United Kingdom Government (Secretary of State for Defence) v. Rheinmetall GmbH (EXTENSION OF TIME LIMIT: PUBLIC INTEREST: Pat. Off.)
Vanitone Pty Ltd v. Formica Technology, Inc. (EXTENSION OF TIME TO LODGE EVIDENCE-IN-SUPPORT: PUBLIC INTEREST: Pat. Off.)
Windsurfing International Inc. v. Sailboards Australia Pty Ltd (CONTEMPT: BREACH OF UNDERTAKING: LIABILITY: Fed. Ct)

Patent Attorneys. *See also under* Privilege

Genentech Inc. v. Wellcome Foundation Ltd (EXTENSION OF TIME: ERRORS OR OMISSIONS OF PATENT ATTORNEY: Pat. Off.)

Heylen v. Davies Collison Cave (EVIDENTIARY BURDEN: PATENT ATTORNEYS: COSTS: AIPO)

Imagic Inc. v. Futuretronics (Aust.) Pty Ltd (COMMUNICATIONS WITH CLIENT: WHETHER PRIVILEGED: S.C.(NSW))

Mitsubishi Chemical Industries Ltd v. Asahi Kasei Kogyo KK (OPPORTUNITY GIVEN TO APPLICANT TO RESPOND TO EVIDENCE-IN-REPLY: ERROR OR OMISSION BY EMPLOYEE OF PATENT ATTORNEY: Pat. Off.)

MXM v. Franke (*Locus standii*: Pat. Off.)

Pfizer Pty Ltd v. Warner Lambert Pty Ltd (WHETHER PRIVILEGE EXTENDS TO COMMUNICATIONS BETWEEN PATENT ATTORNEY AND CLIENT IN THE COURSE OF CONDUCT: Fed. Ct)

Riker Laboratories Australia Pty Ltd v. Westwood Pharmaceuticals Inc. (COMMUNICATIONS WITH CLIENT: WHETHER PRIVILEGED: S.C.(NSW))

Trade Practices Commission v. International Technology Holdings Pty Ltd (TRADE MARK: DISCOVERY AND INSPECTION: LEGAL PROFESSIONAL PRIVILEGE: Fed. Ct)

Wundowie Foundry Pty Ltd v. Milson Foundry Pty Ltd (DISCOVERY: DOCUMENTS RELATING TO DESIGN AND DEVELOPMENT OF INVENTION: ATTORNEY AND CLIENT PRIVILEGE: Fed. Ct)

Pleadings

American Cyanamid Company v. Alcoa of Australia Ltd (MOTION TO STRIKE OUT: Fed. Ct)

Bohemia Crystal Pty Ltd v. D. Swarovski (POWER OF COURT TO VACATE CONSENT ORDERS: PRINCIPLES OF PLEADING: S.C.(NSW))

Mobay Corp. v. Dow Chemical Co. (APPLICATION TO DELETE PARTS OF STATEMENT OF GROUNDS AND PARTICULARS: APPROPRIATE ANALOGY OF PLEADING PRINCIPLES: Pat. Off.)

Power of Court

Ballabil Holdings Pty Ltd v. Hospital Products Ltd (DISCOVERY: MAREVA INJUNCTION: C.A.)

Bohemia Crystal Pty Ltd v. D. Swarovski (VACATION OF CONSENT ORDERS: PRINCIPLES OF PLEADING: S.C.(NSW))

Du Pont de Nemours (E.I.) & Co. v. Commissioner of Patents (POWER OF COURT TO SET ASIDE CONSENT ORDER FOR DISCOVERY: WHETHER GENERAL DISCOVERY SHOULD BE ORDERED PRIOR TO FILING OF AFFIDAVITS: Fed. Ct)

Prima Facie Case. *See* Interlocutory Injunction (*Prima facie case*)

Privilege. *See also* Privilege against Self-incrimination

Arnotts Ltd v. Trace Practices Commission (LEGAL PROFESSIONAL PRIVILEGE: CONDITIONS: Fed. Ct)

Imagic Inc. v. Futuretronics (Aust.) Pty Ltd (PATENT ATTORNEYS: COMMUNICATIONS WITH CLIENT: WHETHER PRIVILEGED: S.C.(NSW))

Nickmar Pty Ltd v. Preservatrice Skandia Insurance Ltd (DISCOVERY: LEGAL PROFESSIONAL PRIVILEGE: USE OF DOCUMENTS: H.C.)

Pfizer Pty Ltd v. Warner Lambert Pty Ltd (PATENT ATTORNEY: PRIVILEGED COMMUNICATIONS WITH: WHETHER PRIVILEGE EXTENDS TO COMMUNICATIONS BETWEEN PATENT ATTORNEY AND CLIENT IN THE COURSE OF CONDUCT: Fed. Ct)

Riker Laboratories Australia Pty Ltd v. Westwood Pharmaceuticals Inc. (PATENT ATTORNEYS: COMMUNICATIONS WITH CLIENT: WHETHER PRIVILEGED: S.C.(NSW))

Sepa Waste Water Treatment Pty Ltd v. JMT Welding Pty Ltd (EVIDENCE: PATENT AGENTS' PRIVILEGE: ADVICE ON DESIGNS INFRINGEMENT: S.C.(NSW))

Trade Practices Commission v. International Technology Holdings Pty Ltd (TRADE MARK: DISCOVERY AND INSPECTION: PATENT ATTORNEYS: Fed. Ct)

Wundowie Foundry Pty Ltd v. Milson Foundry Pty Ltd (DOCUMENTS RELATING TO DESIGN AND DEVELOPMENT OF INVENTION: PATENT ATTORNEY AND CLIENT PRIVILEGE: Fed. Ct)

Privilege against Self-incrimination

Authors Workshop v. Bileru Pty Ltd (*Ex parte* ORDERS: WHETHER ORDERS AKIN TO ANTON PILLER ORDER AND SUBJECT TO SAME PRE-CONDITIONS: COMMON LAW PRINCIPLES: Fed. Ct)

Television Broadcasts Ltd v. Thi Phuong Nguyen (ANTON PILLER ORDER: LIMITED RIGHT OF INSPECTION: UNDERTAKING AS TO DAMAGES: Fed. Ct)

Warman International Ltd v. Envirotech Australia Pty Ltd (ANTON PILLER: EVIDENCE: Fed. Ct)

Proceedings in Two Jurisdictions

Australian Consolidated Industries Ltd v. Scholle Industries Pty Ltd (PATENT: INFRINGEMENT: PRACTICE: S.C.(S.A.): Australia)

Spotless Group Ltd v. Proplast Pty Ltd (APPLICATIONS TO SET ASIDE WRITS OR STAY OR TRANSFER: CONVENIENT FORUM: S.C.(Vic.))

Public Interest

Attorney-General v. Heinemann Publishers Australia Pty Ltd and Wright (BREACH OF CONFIDENCE: DEFENDANTS EMPLOYMENT BY CROWN: PUBLIC POLICY: S.C.(NSW): C.A.(NSW))

Australian Design Council v. Peter Borello (CONTINUING USE OF TRADE MARK IN BREACH OF INJUNCTION: DELIBERATE BREACH: Fed. Ct)

Bee Tek (Import & Export) Pte Ltd v. Kenner Parker Toys Inc. (EXTENSION OF TIME TO FILE EVIDENCE-IN-REPLY: WHETHER INDULGENCES ALREADY GIVEN EXCESSIVE: Pat. Off.)

Black & Decker Corporation v. Akarana Abrasive Industries Ltd (APPLICATION FOR EXTENSION OF TIME TO FILE EVIDENCE-IN-SUPPORT: INCONVENIENCE OF APPLICANT: Pat. Off.)

Bundy American Corp. v. Rent-A-Wreck (Vic.) Pty Ltd (EXTENSION OF TIME LIMITS: INTER-PARTY NEGOTIATION: Pat. Off.)

Commonwealth Scientific and Industrial Research Organisation v. Western Mining Corporation Ltd (EXTENSION OF TIME TO SERVE EVIDENCE: OBJECTION: Pat. Off.)

Commonwealth Scientific and Industrial Research Organisation v. Western Mining Corp. Ltd (APPLICATION FOR EXTENSION OF TIME WITHIN WHICH TO SERVE EVIDENCE-IN-SUPPORT: Pat. Off.)

Groko Maskin AB's Application (EXTENSION OF TIME: Pat. Off.)
ICI Australia Operations Pty Ltd v. Commercial Polymers Pty Ltd (APPLICATION
FOR EXTENSION OF TIME TO APPLY FOR FURTHER TIME TO FILE EVIDENCE:
Pat. Off.)
Kimberly-Clark Corp. v. Procter & Gamble Co. (APPLICATION FOR EXTENSION OF
TIME TO FILE EVIDENCE: Pat. Off.)
Mitsubishi Chemical Industries Ltd v. Asahi Kasei Kogyo KK (OPPORTUNITY GIVEN
TO APPLICANT TO RESPOND TO EVIDENCE-IN-REPLY: ERROR OR OMISSION
BY EMPLOYEE OF PATENT ATTORNEY: Pat. Off.)
Nautical Services Pty Ltd v. Hitech Distillation (Aust.) Pty Ltd (EXTENSION OF TIME
LIMITS TO SERVE EVIDENCE: Pat. Off.)
Pacific Dunlop Ltd v. Fruit of the Loom Inc. (APPLICATION FOR EXTENSION OF
TIME TO FILE EVIDENCE-IN-ANSWER: Pat. Off.)
Playground Supplies Pty Ltd's Application (EXTENSION OF TIME LIMIT: Pat. Off.)
Rollbits Pty Ltd v. Rowntree Mackintosh PLC (SERVICE OF DOCUMENTS:
EXTENSION OF TIME: Pat. Off.)
Roussel-Uclaf v. Shell Internationale Research Maatschappij BV (EXTENSION OF
TIME LIMITS: EVIDENCE-IN-SUPPORT: Pat. Off.)
United Kingdom Government (Secretary of State for Defence) v. Rheinmetall
GmbH (EVIDENCE: TIME LIMITS: EXTENSION: Pat. Off.)
Vanitone Pty Ltd v. Formica Technology, Inc. (EXTENSION OF TIME TO LODGE
EVIDENCE-IN-SUPPORT OF OPPOSITION: PUBLIC INTEREST IN
COMMISSIONER HAVING PERTINENT MATERIAL: Pat. Off.)

Public Policy

Attorney-General v. Heinemann Publishers Australia Pty Ltd and Wright (BREACH
OF FIDUCIARY DUTY: CROWN EMPLOYEE: PRIOR PUBLICATION OF
INFORMATION BY THIRD PARTY, WITH AGREEMENT OR ACQUIESCENCE OF
BRITISH GOVERNMENT: S.C.(NSW): C.A.(NSW))
Murdock Overseas Corporation v. Saramar Corporation (OMISSION BY ATTORNEY:
PUBLIC POLICY: Pat. Off.)

Right to Jury Trial

Markman v. Westview Instruments Inc. (PATENT: INFRINGEMENT:
CONSTRUCTION: SUMMARY JUDGMENT: Fed. Ct)

Security for Costs

Du Pont De Nemours (E.I.) & Co. v. Commissioner of Patents (No. 7) (PATENT:
EXTENSION: APPLICATION FOR SECURITY FOR COSTS AGAINST
INTERVENOR: S.C.(NSW))
Farmitalia Carlo Erba SrL v. Delta West Pty Ltd (PATENT: INFRINGEMENT:
REVOCATION: SECURITY FOR COSTS: APPLICANT ORDINARILY RESIDENT
OUTSIDE DISCRETION: Fed. Ct)
Murex Diagnostics Australia Pty Ltd v. Chiron Corp. (PLEADINGS: APPLICATION TO
STRIKE OUT: Fed. Ct)

Serious Question to be Tried. See Interlocutory Injunctions (*Serious question to be tried*)

Setting Aside

Milcap Publishing Group AB v. Coranto Corporation Pty Ltd (ANTON PILLER:
WHETHER FULL DISCLOSURE HAD BEEN MADE: DOCTRINE OF *ex debito justitae*:
Fed. Ct)

Similar Fact Evidence. *See* **Evidence**

Special Circumstances

Cafe Do Brasil SpA v. Scrava Pty Ltd (TRADE MARKS: REMOVAL: NON-USE: Pat. Off.)

D'Urban Inc. v. Canpio Pty Ltd (EVIDENCE SERVED OUT OF TIME: FAILURE TO SEEK EXTENSION OF TIME: Pat. Off.)

Dimtsis v. Agricultural Dairy Industry Authority of Epirus, Dodoni SA (APPLICATION FOR EXTENSION OF TIME TO FILE EVIDENCE: OBJECTION TO: ERRORS OR OMISSIONS BY AGENTS OF PARTIES: Pat. Off.)

Genentech Inc. v. Wellcome Foundation Ltd (APPLICATION FOR EXTENSION OF TIME IN WHICH TO SERVE EVIDENCE LODGED AFTER THE EXPIRATION OF THE TIME SOUGHT TO BE EXTENDED: ERRORS OR OMISSIONS OF PATENT ATTORNEY: Pat. Off.)

ICI Australia Operations Pty Ltd v. Commercial Polymers Pty Ltd (APPLICATION FOR EXTENSION OF TIME TO APPLY FOR FURTHER TIME TO FILE EVIDENCE: ATTORNEY'S ERROR AMOUNTS TO SPECIAL CIRCUMSTANCES: Pat. Off.)

Mitsubishi Chemical Industries Ltd v. Asahi Kasei Kogyo KK (OPPORTUNITY GIVEN TO APPLICANT TO RESPOND TO EVIDENCE-IN-REPLY: ERROR OR OMISSION BY EMPLOYEE OF PATENT ATTORNEY: PUBLIC INTEREST: Pat. Off.)

Trepper v. Miss Selfridge Ltd (DISCRETION: Pat. Off.)

Statement of Claim

Sent v. Jet Corp. of Australia Pty Ltd (LEAVE TO AMEND: H.C.)

Striking Out

American Cyanamid Company v. Alcoa of Australia Ltd (MOTION TO STRIKE OUT PLEADINGS: Fed. Ct)

Mobay Corp. v. Dow Chemical Co. (APPLICATION TO DELETE CERTAIN PARTS OF OPPONENT'S STATEMENT OF GROUNDS AND PARTICULARS: POWER TO ORDER FURTHER AND BETTER PARTICULARS: Pat. Off.)

Murex Diagnostics Australia Pty Ltd v. Chiron Corp. (PLEADINGS: SECURITY FOR COSTS: Fed. Ct)

Sufficiency of Evidence. *See* **Evidence**

Sufficiency of Remedy

Sterling Industries Ltd v. Nim Services Pty Ltd (MAREVA INJUNCTION: APPLICATION: DISCRETION: Fed. Ct)

Summary Judgment

Markman v. Westview Instruments Inc. (PATENT: INFRINGEMENT: CONSTRUCTION: RIGHT TO JURY TRIAL: Fed. Ct)

Z.S. Projects Pty Ltd v. G. & R. Investments Pty Ltd (COPYRIGHT: BUILDING PLANS: INFRINGEMENT: DAMAGES: ACCOUNT OF PROFITS: DEFENCE: S.C.(NSW))

Survey Evidence and Questionnaires

Broderbund Software Inc. v. Computermate Products (Australia) Pty Ltd (USE OF SURVEY EVIDENCE: Fed. Ct)

Dominos Pizza Inc. v. Eagle Boys Dial-a-Pizza Australia Pty Ltd (TRADE MARK:
OPPOSITION: DECEPTION AND CONFUSION: PROPRIETORSHIP: AIPO)
Interlego AG v. Croner Trading Pty Ltd (SURVEY EVIDENCE: Fed, Ct)
Jarvis v. Doman (QUESTIONNAIRES: Pat. Off.)
Johnson & Johnson Australia Pty Ltd v. Sterling Pharmaceuticals Pty Ltd (SURVEY
EVIDENCE: Fed. Ct)
Kettle Chip Company Pty Ltd v. Apand Pty Ltd (SURVEY EVIDENCE: ADMISSIBILITY:
Fed. Ct)
State Government Insurance Corp. v. Government Insurance Office of NSW
(SURVEY EVIDENCE: Fed. Ct)
Sterling Pharmaceuticals Pty Ltd v. Johnson & Johnson Australia Pty Ltd (SURVEY
EVIDENCE AS TO KNOWLEDGE AND USE OF TRADE MARK: ADMISSIBILITY: Fed.
Ct)
Toro Company's Applications (TRADE MARK: APPLICATION: OBJECTION:
DESCRIPTIVE MARK: CONSISTANCY BY REGISTRAR: AIPO)

Undertaking

Autodesk Australia Pty Ltd v. Dyason (AFFIDAVITS: USE AGAINST THIRD PARTIES:
Fed. Ct)
Jackson v. Sterling Industries Ltd (MAREVA INJUNCTION: FAILURE OF COURT TO
OBTAIN UNDERTAKING: EFFECT: Fed. Ct)
New York University v. Nissin Molecular Biology Institute Inc. (PATENT:
APPLICATION: REQUEST FOR CERTIFICATION: CONDITIONS FOR RELEASE OF
SAMPLE OF MICRO-ORGANISM: AIPO)
Pacific Basin Exploration Pty Ltd v. XLX (N.L.) (DISCLOSURE OF DISCOVERED
DOCUMENTS: BREACH OF UNDERTAKING: CONTEMPT: S.C.(W.A.))
Philips Gloeilampenfabrieken (NV) v. Ultralite International Pty Ltd (BALANCE OF
CONVENIENCE INJUNCTION REFUSED BUT UNDERTAKINGS ACCEPTED TO
KEEP ACCOUNTS AND PAY INTO COURT CONTROLLED FUND: Fed. Ct)
S. & M. Motor Repairs Pty Ltd v. Caltex Oil (Australia) Pty Ltd (S.C.(NSW))
Smith Kline & French Laboratories (Australia) Ltd v. Secretary, Department of
Community Services and Health (USUAL UNDERTAKING AS TO DAMAGES:
WHETHER NON-PARTY TO LITIGATION MAY BE ADVERSELY AFFECTED BY
INTERLOCUTORY INJUNCTION: Fed. Ct)
Television Broadcasts Ltd v. Thi Phuong Nguyen (ANTON PILLER ORDER: LIMITED
RIGHT OF INSPECTION: UNDERTAKING AS TO DAMAGES: Fed. Ct)
Westaflex (Aust.) Pty Ltd v. Wood (PATENT INFRINGEMENT: STAY PENDING
APPEAL: APPEAL: APPROPRIATE UNDERTAKINGS AND CONDITIONS: Fed. Ct)
Windsurfing International Inc. v. Sailboards Australia Pty Ltd (CONTEMPT: BREACH
OF UNDERTAKING: ONUS OF PROOF: Fed. Ct)

Vexatious or Abuse of Process

Concorde Trading Pty Ltd v. Croner Trading Pty Ltd (PATENT: OPPOSITION:
APPLICATION FOR DISMISSAL: COSTS: AIPO)

Witnesses

American Cyanamid Company v. Nalco Chemical Company (EVIDENCE: CROSS-
EXAMINATION: REQUEST FOR THE COMMISSIONER OF PATENTS TO SUMMON
WITNESSES: Pat. Off.)
Attorney-General v. Heinemann Publishers Australia Pty Ltd and Wright
(CREDIBILITY OF CROWN WITNESS: S.C.(NSW): C.A.(NSW))

Clune v. Collins Angus & Robertson Publishers Pty Ltd (ALLEGED ORAL LICENCE: EVIDENCE: CREDIT OF WITNESS: Fed. Ct)

E.S. & M.J. Heard Pty Ltd v. Phillips (EVIDENCE: REQUEST TO SUMMON A WITNESS: WHETHER CONFLICT ON THE FACTS: AIPO)

Elconnex Pty Ltd v. Gerard Industries Pty Ltd (ADMISSIBILITY OF EVIDENCE OF EXPERT WITNESSES: Fed. Ct)

Porter v. Victoria's Secret Inc. (CROSS-EXAMINATION OF WITNESS: COSTS: AIPO)

Trade Marks

Abandonment

Cole v. Australian Char Pty Ltd (OPPOSITION: INTENTION TO USE: LIKELIHOOD OF DECEPTION OR CONFUSION: BLAMEWORTHY CONDUCT: AIPO)

Cougar Marine Ltd v. Roberts (ABANDONMENT BY PRIOR USERS: PRIOR REGISTRATION: HONEST CONCURRENT USER: AIPO)

Rael Marcus v. Sabra International Pty Ltd (OPPOSITION: EFFECT OF PREVIOUS, NOW-LAPSED REGISTRATION OF MARK AND LICENCE TO USE IT: DISTINCTION BETWEEN NON-USE AND ABANDONMENT: Fed. Ct)

Settef SpA v. Riv-Oland Marble Co. (Vic.) Pty Ltd (RECTIFICATION: USE IN GOOD FAITH: ABANDONMENT: S.C.(Vic.))

Acceptance

Haddonstone Pty Ltd v. Haddonstone Ltd (OPPOSITION: PROPRIETORSHIP: MANUFACTURER OR DISTRIBUTOR: ESTOPPEL: ROLE OF REGISTRAR: DECEPTION OR CONFUSION: AIPO)

Pelikan International Handelsgesellschaft mbH & Co. KG v. Lifinia Pty Ltd (OPPOSITION: DECEPTIVE OR CONFUSING: SUBSTANTIALLY IDENTICAL: EVIDENCE: AIPO)

Acquired Distinctiveness. *See* Distinctiveness

Acronyms

STC PLC's Application (INITIALS: WHETHER DISTINCTIVE: WHETHER ADAPTED TO DISTINGUISH: Pat. Off.)

Waterbed Association of Retailers & Manufacturers's Application (PART B APPLICATION: COMPOSITE MARK: DESCRIPTIVE: INHERENT ADAPTABILITY TO DISTINGUISH: DISCLAIMER: Pat. Off.)

Adapted to Distinguish

American Supplier Institute Inc.'s Application (GENERIC TERMS: UNADAPTED TO DISTINGUISH: INCAPABLE OF BECOMING DISTINCTIVE: Pat. Off.)

Approved Prescription Services Ltd's Application (REGISTRABILITY: LETTERS AND INITIALS: INVENTED WORK: Pat. Off.)

Brandella Pty Ltd's Application (KANGAROO DEVICE: UNADAPTED TO DISTINGUISH: Pat. Off.)

Bristol-Myers Co.'s Application (EVIDENCE: ACQUIRED DISTINCTIVENESS: GEOGRAPHIC NAME: Pat. Off.)

Decina Bathroomware Pty Ltd's Application (EVIDENCE: INHERENTLY ADAPTED TO DISTINGUISH: Pat. Off.)

Galaxay International Pty Ltd's Application (CAPABLE OF BECOMING DISTINCTIVE: INHERENTLY UNADAPTED TO DISTINGUISH: Pat. Off.)

Informed Sources Pty Ltd's Application (INFORMED SOURCES DESCRIPTIVE OF INFORMATION SERVICES: LACK OF INHERENT DISTINCTIVENESS: EVIDENCE OF USE: Pat. Off.)

Insta-foam Products' Application (INHERENTLY UNADAPTED TO DISTINGUISH: Pat. Off.)

JGL Investments Proprietary's Application (REGISTRABILITY: INHERENT ADAPTABILITY: DISTINCTIVE: DESCRIPTIVE: MISLEADING: CONFUSING AND DECEPTIVE: Pat. Off.)

Lorraine's Application (CATERER'S CHOICE: WHETHER ADAPTED TO DISTINGUISH: Pat. Off.)

Matsushita Electric Industrial Co. Ltd's Application (LACK OF DISTINCTIVENESS: NOT INHERENTLY ADAPTED TO DISTINGUISH: DESCRIPTIVE WORDS: EVIDENCE OF SALES FIGURES: Pat. Off.)

Mayne Nickless Ltd's Application (COMPUTA-PAY: ADAPTED TO DISTINGUISH: Pat. Off.)

Northern Telecom Ltd's Application (APPLICATION: WHETHER ADAPTED TO DISTINGUISH: INHERENT DISTINCTIVENESS: DISTINCTIVENESS ACQUIRED THROUGH USE: PART B: SUPERNODE: AIPO)

Oxford University Press v. Registrar of Trade Marks (GEOGRAPHICAL NAME: OXFORD: WHETHER REGISTRABLE: WHETHER A MARK WHICH IS 100 PER CENT DISTINCTIVE IN FACT MUST ALSO BE INHERENTLY ADAPTED TO DISTINGUISH IN ORDER TO BE REGISTRABLE: Fed. Ct)

Sony KK's Application (GENERIC NAMES: INHERENTLY ADAPTED TO DISTINGUISH: Pat. Off.)

STC PLC's Application (ACRONYMS, INITIALS: WHETHER DISTINCTIVE: WHETHER ADAPTED TO DISTINGUISH: Pat. Off.)

Thermos Ltd v. Micropore International Ltd (OPPOSITION: SUBSTANTIALLY IDENTICAL OR DECEPTIVELY SIMILAR MARKS: USE LIKELY TO DECEIVE OR CAUSE CONFUSION: Pat. Off.)

Waterford Glass Group Ltd's Application (WATERFORD: GEOGRAPHICAL NAMES: INHERENTLY ADAPTED TO DISTINGUISH: Pat. Off.)

Westco Jeans (Aust.) Pty Ltd's Application (REGISTRABILITY: KNOCKOUT: INHERENT ADAPTABILITY: DESCRIPTIVE: Pat. Off.)

Address for Service. *See* **Practice** *(Address for service)*

Advertisements

Vamuta Pty Ltd (t/a Sogo Jewellers) v. Sogo Co. Ltd (SOGO: PROPRIETORSHIP: IDENTICAL MARKS: USE AS ADVERTISEMENTS: AIPO)

Amendment

Computer People Pty Ltd (APPLICATION: DISCLAIMER: DESCRIPTION OF APPLICANT'S SERVICES: Pat. Off.)

Esco Corp.'s Application (DISTINCTIVENESS: Pat. Off.)

Fastrack Racing Pty Ltd's Application (APPLICATION IN MULTIPLE CLASSES: AMENDMENT OF CLASS: DIVISIONAL FILINGS: DESCRIPTIVE MARK: AIPO)

First Tiffany Holdings Pty Ltd v. Tiffany and Company (CONNECTION IN THE COURSE OF TRADE: USE LIKELY TO DECEIVE AND CAUSE CONFUSION: AMENDMENT TO SPECIFICATION OF GOODS: COSTS: Pat. Off.)

Freixenet SA v. Bull (OPPOSITION: AMENDMENT OF STATEMENT OF GOODS: AIPO)

Jacuzzi Inc.'s Application (WITHDRAWAL OF ACCEPTANCE FOR REGISTRATION: CONFLICT WITH EARLIER APPLICATION: RELEVANCE OF VALIDITY OF AMENDMENT OF CLASS OF GOODS IN RESPECT OF WHICH CITED MARK WAS FILED: ACCEPTANCE IN ERROR: Pat. Off.)

Mobil Oil Corp. v. Foodland Associated Ltd (APPLICATION: OPPOSITION: DISCLAIMER: T.M.Reg.)

Stratco Metal Pty Ltd's Application (OPPOSITION: ERROR IN NOTICE: MISDESCRIPTION OF OPPONENT: LIKELIHOOD OF DECEPTION OR CONFUSION: Pat. Off.)

Uniglobe Holdings Pty Ltd v. Uniglobe Travel (International) Inc. (CLERICAL ERROR: APPLICATION TO AMEND FORM: OBVIOUS MISTAKE: Pat. Off.)

Anton Piller Order. *See* **Practice** (*Anton Piller order*)

Appeal. *See* **Practice** (*Appeal*)

Applications

Ada Productions Pty Ltd's Application (SURNAME: DISTINCTIVENESS: Pat. Off.)

Advanced Hair Studio of America Pty Ltd's Application (INVENTED WORD: COMPARISON WITH ORDINARY AND EXISTING WORDS: Pat. Off.)

Alexander v. Tait-Jamison (OPPOSITION: PROPRIETORSHIP: WHETHER MARKS NEARLY OR SUBSTANTIALLY IDENTICAL: WHETHER GOODS OF THE SAME DESCRIPTION: USE OF BUSINESS NAME: WHETHER USE AS MARK: AIPO)

Algie v. Dorminy (OPPOSITION: WHETHER PRIOR USE: WHETHER DECEPTIVE OR CONFUSING: AIPO)

Allied Colloids Ltd v. S.C. Johnson & Son Inc. (OPPOSITION: EARLIER MARK REGISTERED FOR OVERLAPPING GOODS: SUBSTANTIAL IDENTITY OR DECEPTIVE SIMILARITY: Pat. Off.)

Allworth Constructions Pty Ltd v. Dixon Investments Pty Ltd (OPPOSITION: PROPRIETORSHIP: GOODS OR SERVICES: AIPO)

Alpine Audio Accoustic v. Alpine Electronic Inc. (OPPOSITION: OVERSEAS REPUTATION: Pat. Off.)

Amco Wrangler Ltd v. Jacques Konckier (PART B: OPPOSITION: LIKELIHOOD OF DECEPTION OR CONFUSION: SURNAMES: Pat. Off.)

American Chemical Society's Application (NON-REGISTRABLE: DESCRIPTIVE: EVIDENCE OF LONG USE: DISTINCTIVE OF ORIGIN OF USE TO RELEVANT SECTION OF COMMUNITY: MARK INHERENTLY INCAPABLE OF DISTINGUISHING GOODS: Pat. Off.)

American Express Co. v. NV Amev (OPPOSITION: AMEX/AMEV: SUBSTANTIALLY IDENTICAL MARKS: Pat. Off.)

American Supplier Institute Inc.'s Application (GENERIC TERMS: UNADAPTED TO DISTINGUISH: INCAPABLE OF BECOMING DISTINCTIVE: FOREIGN TRADE MARK REGISTRATIONS: Pat. Off.)

Anheuser-Busch Inc. v. Castlebrae Pty Ltd (PRIOR REGISTRATION BY RESPONDENT: CHARACTER MERCHANDISING: Fed. Ct)

Approved Prescription Services Ltd's Application (REGISTRABILITY: LETTERS AND INITIALS: INVENTED WORK: ADAPTED TO DISTINGUISH: DISTINCTIVE: PRIOR REGISTRATIONS: Pat. Off.)

Astra (AB) v. Schering Corporation (VISUAL SIMILARITY: Pat. Off.)

Athol Thomas Kelly's Application (DISTINCTIVENESS: LIKELIHOOD OF DECEPTION OR CONFUSION: PRIOR REGISTRATION: HONEST CONCURRENT USE: IMPERFECT RECOLLECTION DOCTRINE: Pat. Off.)

Aussat Pty Ltd (REGISTRABILITY: SUBSTANTIALLY IDENTICAL: DECEPTIVELY SIMILAR: CLOSELY RELATED: GOODS AND SERVICES: AIPO)

Camiceria Pancaldi and B. Srl v. Le Cravatte Di Pancaldi Srl (OPPOSITION: PRIOR
INCONSISTENT REGISTRATION: DECEPTION AND CONFUSION: INTENTION
TO USE: AIPO)

Canon KK v. Brook (OPPOSITION: SUBSTANTIALLY IDENTICAL: DECEPTIVELY
SIMILAR: GOODS OF THE SAME DESCRIPTION: HONEST CONCURRENT USE:
AIPO)

Cassini v. Golden Era Shirt Co. Pty Ltd (CASSINI FOR CLOTHING: WHETHER
DISTINCTIVE: S.C.(NSW))

Cedarapids Inc.'s Application (GEOGRAPHICAL NAMES: INVENTED OR COINED
WORDS: DISCLAIMERS: Pat. Off.)

Champagne Louis Roederer v. Resourse Management Services Pty Ltd
(OPPOSITION: SUBSTANTIALLY IDENTICAL: DECEPTIVELY SIMILAR: GOODS OF
THE SAME DESCRIPTION: BLAMEWORTHY CONDUCT: DISENTITLEMENT TO
PROTECTION: PRACTICE: AIPO)

Chan Li Chai Medical Factory (H.K.) Ltd's Application (THREE CHINESE
CHARACTERS: GOODS OF SAME DESCRIPTION: MARKS DECEPTIVELY SIMILAR:
Pat. Off.)

Chanel Ltd v. Chantal Chemical & Pharmaceutical Corp. (OPPOSITION: WHETHER
APPLICANT PROPRIETOR OF MARK: NO EVIDENCE OF USE BY OTHERS:
SUBSTANTIALLY IDENTICAL OR DECEPTIVELY SIMILAR: CHANTAL/
CHANEL: Pat. Off.)

Chanel Ltd v. Chronogem Ltd (EARLIER PART B MARK REGISTERED FOR SAME
GOODS: SUBSTANTIAL IDENTITY OR DECEPTIVE SIMILARITY: MARKS
DISTINGUISHABLE: Pat. Off.)

Chilis Inc.'s Application (OBJECTION BY EXAMINER: DECEPTIVE SIMILARITY:
INHERENT CAPABILITY TO BE DISTINCTIVE: FOREIGN MARKET:
DISTINCTIVENESS: Pat. Off.)

Chubb Australia Ltd's Application (REFUSAL TO REGISTER: Pat. Off.)

Ciba Geigy Australia Ltd v. Eli Lilly & Co. (OPPOSITION: DISTINCTIVENESS:
CHARACTER OF GOODS: Pat. Off.)

Cleckheaton Australia Pty Ltd's Application (OBJECTION: ADAPTATION TO
DISTINGUISH: TEST: CONFUSION WITH CITED MARK: Pat. Off.)

Cling Adhesive Products Pty Ltd's Application (OBJECTION BY EXAMINER:
WHETHER DESCRIPTIVE: WORDS JOINED BY HYPHEN: INHERENT
DISTINCTIVENESS: EVIDENCE OF USE: AIPO)

Cole v. Australian Char Pty Ltd (OPPOSITION: ABANDONMENT: INTENTION TO USE:
LIKELIHOOD OF DECEPTION OF CONFUSION: BLAMEWORTHY CONDUCT:
AIPO)

Coles & Co. Ltd's Application (DISTINCTIVENESS: INVENTED WORD: DIRECT
REFERENCE TO CHARACTER OR QUALITY OF GOODS: Pat. Off.)

Computer People Pty Ltd (AMENDMENT: DISCLAIMER: DESCRIPTION OF
APPLICANT'S SERVICES: Pat. Off.)

Conde Nast Publications Pty Ltd v. Mango Pty Ltd (OPPOSITION: VOGUE:
WHETHER DESCRIPTIVE: SIMILAR GOODS: CONFUSION: Fed. Ct)

Corvina Quality Foods Pty Ltd's Application (OBJECTION TO REGISTRATION:
DISCLAIMER: DISTINCTIVENESS: MARKS NOT INHERENTLY DISTINCTIVE:
MARKS NOT DISTINCTIVE IN FACT: REGISTRATION IN PART B REFUSED: Pat.
Off.)

Cougar Marine Ltd v. Roberts (OPPOSITION: DIVISIONAL PROPRIETORSHIP:
ABANDONMENT BY PRIOR USERS: PRIOR REGISTRATION: GOODS OF THE
SAME DESCRIPTION: HONEST CONCURRENT USER: AIPO)

Courtaulds Textiles (Holdings) Ltd's Application (ADJECTIVAL COMPOUND
INDICATING QUALITY OR CHARACTER: SIGNIFICANT OVERSEAS USE:
CAPABLE OF BECOMING DISTINCTIVE: AIPO)

Hawke (Aust.) Ltd's Application (TIMELESS CREATION: MERE LAUDATORY EXPRESSION: INHERENT NON-DISTINCTIVENESS: NO USE OF MARK: Pat. Off.)

Hearst Corp. v. Pacific Dunlop Ltd (OPPOSITION: PROPRIETORSHIP: LIKELIHOOD OF DECEPTION OR CONFUSION: Pat. Off.)

Hermès SA v. Swift & Co. Pty Ltd (FOREIGN REPUTATION: Pat. Off.)

Hermes Sweeteners Ltd v. Hermes (OPPOSITION: OPPONENT RELYING ON ITS OWN REGISTERED MARKS: SUBSTANTIALLY IDENTICAL OR DECEPTIVELY SIMILAR: SAME GOODS OR OF SIMILAR DESCRIPTION: USE LIKELY TO DECEIVE OR CAUSE CONFUSION: Pat. Off.)

Hillier Parker May & Rowden's Applications (DISTINCTIVENESS: WORD COMBINATIONS: TWO SURNAMES: Pat. Off.)

Holmes's Application (OPPOSITION: LIKELIHOOD OF DECEPTION OR CONFUSION: PERMACRAFT: NO EVIDENCE OF USE OF OPPONENT'S MARK: OPPONENT'S MARK COMMON TO TRADE MARKS NOT DECEPTIVELY SIMILAR: VENETIAN BLINDS AND FURNITURE NOT GOODS OF SAME DESCRIPTION: Pat. Off.)

Honeywell Inc.'s Application (INHERENTLY DISTINCTIVE: CAPABLE OF BECOMING DISTINCTIVE: USE: DECEPTIVE SIMILARITY: Pat. Off.)

Hongkong and Shanghai Banking Corp. Ltd's Applications (CHINESE CHARACTERS: REGISTRABILITY UNDER SECTION 24: Pat. Off.)

Informed Sources Pty Ltd's Application (OBJECTION: INFORMED SOURCES: DESCRIPTIVE OF INFORMATION SERVICES: LACK OF INHERENT DISTINCTIVENESS: EVIDENCE OF USE NOT APPROPRIATE WHERE MARK NOT ADAPTED TO DISTINGUISH: Pat. Off.)

Insta-foam Products' Application (INHERENTLY UNADAPTED TO DISTINGUISH: Pat. Off.)

Inter-footwear Ltd's Applications (HI-TEC: DESCRIPTION OF CHARACTER OF GOODS: EVIDENCE OF USE OVERSEAS: Pat. Off.)

Intermed Communications Inc.'s Application (DIRECT DESCRIPTION OF GOODS: INHERENTLY ADAPTED: T.M.Reg.)

International Computers Ltd's Application (DRS: DISTINCTIVENESS: EVIDENCE: Pat. Off.)

Jacuzzi Inc.'s Application (WITHDRAWAL OF ACCEPTANCE FOR REGISTRATION: CONFLICT WITH EARLIER RELEVANCE OF VALIDITY OF AMENDMENT OF CLASS OF GOODS IN RESPECT OF WHICH CITED MARK WAS FILED: ACCEPTANCE IN ERROR: Pat. Off.)

Jamieson v. American Dairy Queen Corporation (OPPOSITION: PROPRIETORSHIP: Pat. Off.)

Jean Patou Parfumeur v. Crisena Corporation Pty Ltd (OPPOSITION: IDENTICAL MARK REGISTERED FOR GOODS OF SAME DESCRIPTION: WHETHER HONEST CONCURRENT USER: Pat. Off.)

JGL Investments Proprietary's Application (REGISTRABILITY: ADAPTED TO DISTINGUISH: INHERENT ADAPTABILITY: DISTINCTIVE: DESCRIPTIVE: MISLEADING: CONFUSING AND DECEPTIVE: Pat. Off.)

Johnson & Johnson's Application (SERIES OF MARKS, WHAT CONSTITUTES: AIPO)

Johnson & Johnson v. Kalnin (OPPOSITION: EXISTING REGISTRATION BY OPPONENT: WHETHER LIKELIHOOD FOR DECEPTION OR CONFUSION: Fed. Ct)

Johnson (S.C.) & Son Inc.'s Application (DESCRIPTIVE: TECHNICAL MEANING NOT RELEVANT: DIRECT REFERENCE TO GOODS: EVIDENCE OF USE NOT PERSUASIVE: NOT REGISTRABLE IN PART A OR PART B OF THE REGISTER: Pat. Off.)

Jonathan Sceats Design Pty Ltd's Application (OBJECTION TO ALLOWANCE OF EXTENSION OF TIME FOR SERVICE OF EVIDENCE-IN-SUPPORT OF OPPOSITION: Pat. Off.)

Jonsered Motor AB's Application (CITATION: DECEPTIVE SIMILARITY: GOODS OF THE SAME DESCRIPTION: GEOGRAPHICAL NAME: TRADE MARK USED IN PLURAL FORM: AIPO)

K Mart Corporation v. A-Mart Allsports Pty Ltd (OPPOSITION: GOODS AND SERVICES: RETAILING: SUBSTANTIAL IDENTITY: DECEPTIVE SIMILARITY: USE: CONCURRENT USE: HONEST USE: CONDITION OF REGISTRATION: Pat. Off.)

K Mart Corporation v. Artline Furnishers Supermarkets Pty Ltd (OPPOSITION: SUBSTANTIAL IDENTITY: DECEPTIVE SIMILARITY: USE: CONCURRENT USE: HONEST USE: CONDITION OF REGISTRATION: Pat. Off.)

K.T. Technology (S.) Pte Ltd v. Tomlin Holdings Pty Ltd (OPPOSITION: EXTENSION OF TIME: Pat. Off.)

Keith Harris & Co. Ltd's Application (OPPOSITION: PROPRIETORSHIP: FIRST USE: USE LIKELY TO DECEIVE OR CAUSE CONFUSION: DESCRIPTIVE MARK: JOINT USE: Pat. Off.)

Kenner Parker Toys Inc.'s Application (OBJECTION: SURNAME: EXTENSIVE HOUSE MARK USER: Pat. Off.)

Kikken Sohansha KK's Application (DISCOVERY OF MARK AS BOTANICAL TERM SUBSEQUENT TO ACCEPTANCE: ACCEPTANCE WITHDRAWN: AIPO)

Kyowa Hakko Kogyo Co. Ltd v. Schering Corporation (OPPOSITION: NON-USE: STATEMENT OF USER: SUBSTANTIALLY IDENTICAL: DECEPTIVELY SIMILAR: LIKELY TO DECEIVE OR CAUSE CONFUSION: Pat. Off.)

Lee Man Tat and Lee Man Lok's Application (SURNAMES: DISTINCTIVENESS: Pat. Off.)

Liederman's Application (EXAMINER'S OBJECTIONS: SURNAME: CAPABLE OF BECOMING DISTINCTIVE: EVIDENCE OF OVERSEAS DISTINCTIVENESS: Pat. Off.)

Lord Bloody Wog Rolo v. United Artists Corporation (OPPOSITION: APPLICATION FOR EXTENSION OF TIME: Pat. Off.)

Lorraine's Application (CATERER'S CHOICE: WHETHER ADAPTED TO DISTINGUISH: Pat. Off.)

Lyons v. Registrar of Trade Marks (EXTENSION OF TIME LIMITS: Fed. Ct)

Lyson Australia Pty Ltd's Application (SERIES OF MARKS: WHAT CONSTITUTES: Pat. Off.)

Marston Fastener Corp.'s Application (OPPOSITION: RELEVANT PRIOR USE: DISTINCTIVENESS: Pat. Off.)

Matsushita Electric Industrial Co. Ltd's Application (LACK OF DISTINCTIVENESS: NOT INHERENTLY ADAPTED TO DISTINGUISH: DESCRIPTIVE WORDS: EVIDENCE OF SALES FIGURES: Pat. Off.)

Maxam Food Products Pty Ltd's Application (REGISTRABILITY: INVENTED WORD: DESCRIPTIVE: CAPABLE OF BECOMING DISTINCTIVE: DISCLAIMER: Pat. Off.)

Mayfair Hams & Bacon Co.'s Application (REGISTERED USER: Pat. Off.)

Mayfair International Pty Ltd's Application (OPPOSITION WITHDRAWN: ADVERTISEMENT OF ACCEPTANCE BUT FAILURE TO REGISTER WITHIN PRESCRIBED TIME: EXTENSION OF TIME LIMIT: DISCRETION: AIPO)

Mayne Nickless Ltd's Application (COMPUTA-PAY: ADAPTED TO DISTINGUISH: Pat. Off.)

McCain Foods (Aust.) Pty Ltd (ENDORSEMENT: DISTINCTIVENESS: DESCRIPTIVENESS: COMBINATION OF COMMON WORDS: AIPO)

McDonald's Corporation v. Coffee Hut Stores Ltd (APPEAL: OBJECTION TO INCORRECT CORPORATE NAME ON APPLICATION: JURISDICTION: SURNAME: FAMILY OF MARKS: Fed. Ct)

McGloin (J.) Pty Ltd's Application (DESCRIPTIVE MARK: EVIDENCE OF USE: REGISTRABILITY IN PART B: Pat. Off.)

McManamey (David Fraser)'s Application (ROARING FORTIES: DISCLAIMER REQUIRED AS TO FORTIES: DISTINCTIVENESS OF NUMERALS: Pat. Off.)

884

Visco Sport Ltd's Application (OPPOSITION: SORBOLITE: WHETHER CONFUSINGLY SIMILAR: IMPORTANCE OF FIRST SYLLABLE: EFFECT OF COMMON PARTS: Pat. Off.)

Warner-Lambert Co. v. Harel (OPPOSITION: PROPRIETORSHIP: DECEPTION OR CONFUSION: BLAMEWORTHY CONDUCT: AIPO)

Waterbed Association of Retailers & Manufacturers's Application (PART B COMPOSITE MARK: ACRONYM: DESCRIPTIVE: INHERENT ADAPTABILITY TO DISTINGUISH: DISCLAIMER: Pat. Off.)

Waterford Glass Group Ltd's Application (WATERFORD: GEOGRAPHICAL NAMES: INHERENTLY ADAPTED TO DISTINGUISH: Pat. Off.)

W.D. & H.O. Wills (Australia) Ltd and Benson & Hedges Co. Pty Ltd's Application (OBJECTION: PRIOR REGISTRATION: SUBSTANTIAL IDENTITY, DECEPTIVE SIMILARITY: COMPOSITE AS AGAINST PRIOR WORD ONLY MARK: Pat. Off.)

Wella AG's Application (OBJECTIONS: DESCRIPTIVE MARK: INHERENT DISTINCTIVENESS: RELEVANCE OF EVIDENCE OF USE AFTER: Pat. Off.)

Westco Jeans (Aust.) Pty Ltd's Application (REGISTRABILITY: KNOCKOUT: ADAPTED TO DISTINGUISH: INHERENT ADAPTABILITY: DESCRIPTIVE: Pat. Off.)

Wilkinson Sword Ltd's Application (PIVOT: DESCRIPTIVENESS: DISTINCTIVENESS: Pat. Off.)

Willow Lea Pastoral Co. Pty Ltd's Application (REFUSAL TO REGISTER: Pat. Off.)

Yamaha Corp.'s Application (REGISTRABILITY: OBJECTION: DESCRIPTIVE: NON-DISTINCTIVE: Pat. Off.)

Assignment or Sale without Goodwill

Commissioner of Taxation v. Just Jeans Pty Ltd (SALE OF UNREGISTERED TRADE MARK WITHOUT GOODWILL: EFFECT: Fed. Ct)

Figgins Holdings Pty Ltd v. Registrar of Trade Marks (OPPOSITION: PROCEEDINGS SETTLED: ASSIGNMENT OF APPLICATION: REGISTRATION OF PROPRIETORSHIP: JURISDICTION TO ORDER: Fed. Ct)

Merv Brown Pty Ltd v. David Jones (Aust.) Pty Ltd (VALIDITY: REPUTATION AND GOODWILL: SUFFICIENCY: Fed. Ct)

Murray Goulburn Co-operative Co. Ltd v. New South Wales Dairy Corporation (Fed. Ct)

Rael Marcus v. Sabra International Pty Ltd (VALIDITY OF ASSIGNMENTS AT COMMON LAW: Fed. Ct)

Winning Appliances Pty Ltd v. Dean Appliances Pty Ltd (USE OF NAME IN COMPANY NAME: ASSIGNMENT OF TRADING NAME: WHETHER GOODWILL ASSIGNED: Fed. Ct)

Associated Marks

Quintessence Incorporated v. Jovani Enterprises Pty Ltd (OPPOSITION: MARKS DECEPTIVELY SIMILAR: GOODS NOT OF THE SAME DESCRIPTION: AIPO)

Attorney. See Practice (Attorney)

Aural and Visual Comparisons

Gardenia Overseas Pte Ltd v. The Garden Co. Ltd (COMMON ELEMENT: GARDEN/ GARDENIA: LIKELIHOOD OF DECEPTION OR CONFUSION: Fed. Ct)

Balance of Convenience. *See* **Practice** (*Interlocutory injunction*)

Blameworthy Conduct

Champagne Louis Roederer v. Resourse Management Services Pty Ltd (DISENTITLEMENT TO PROTECTION: PRACTICE: AIPO)

Cole v. Australian Char Pty Ltd (OPPOSITION: ABANDONMENT: INTENTION TO USE: LIKELIHOOD OF DECEPTION OF CONFUSION: AIPO)

Tonka Corp. v. Chong (OPPOSITION: DECEPTIVE SIMILARITY: AIPO)

Business Name

Hoogerdyk v. Condon (SALE OF BUSINESS: BREACH OF CONTRACT: GOODWILL IN NAME: DAMAGES: ASSESSMENT: H.C.)

Capacity to Distinguish. *See also* **Adapted to Distinguish**

American Chemical Society's Application (DISTINCTIVE OF ORIGIN OF USE TO RELEVANT SECTION OF COMMUNITY: MARK INHERENTLY INCAPABLE OF DISTINGUISHING GOODS: Pat. Off.)

Brian Davis & Co. Pty Ltd's Application (WATERWELL) (CONJOINED USE: CAPACITY TO DISTINGUISH: Pat. Off.)

Food Plus Ltd's Application (DESCRIPTIVE: INABILITY TO DISTINGUISH: USE: Pat. Off.)

Character Merchandising. *See also under* **Merchandising Rights**

Anheuser-Busch Inc. v. Castlebrae Pty Ltd (Fed. Ct)

Little Tykes Co. v. Ciardullo (OPPOSITION: LITTLE TYKE/LITTLE TIKES: SUBSTANTIALLY IDENTICAL: DECEPTIVELY SIMILAR: GOODS OF THE SAME DESCRIPTION: AIPO)

Character or Quality of Goods or Services

Advanced Hair Studio of America Pty Ltd v. Registrar of Trade Marks (RELATIONSHIP BETWEEN MARK AND CHARACTER OR QUALITY OF THE SERVICES: S.C.(Vic.))

Australian National Airlines Commission (APPLICATIONS: NON-DISTINCTIVE: SPECIAL CIRCUMSTANCES: DISCLAIMER: Pat. Off.)

Cantarella Bros v. Kona Coffee Roastery & Equipment Supplies (INFRINGEMENT: USE IN GOOD FAITH: Fed. Ct)

Ciba Geigy Australia Ltd v. Eli Lilly & Co. (APPLICATION: OPPOSITION: DISTINCTIVENESS: Pat. Off.)

Coles & Co. Ltd's Application (DISTINCTIVENESS: INVENTED WORD: DIRECT REFERENCE TO CHARACTER OR QUALITY OF GOODS: Pat. Off.)

Decor Corporation Pty Ltd v. Deeko Australia Pty Ltd (OPPOSITION: WHETHER MARKS SUBSTANTIALLY IDENTICAL OR DECEPTIVELY SIMILAR: CIRCUMSTANCES OF TRADE: LESS WEIGHT ON PHONETIC COMPARISON: REFERENCE TO CHARACTER OF GOODS: Pat. Off.)

Email Ltd v. Sharp KK (OPPOSITION: Pat. Off.)

Inter-footwear Ltd's Applications (HI-TEC: EVIDENCE OF USE OVERSEAS: Pat. Off.)

Paragold Distributors Pty Ltd's Application (OBJECTION TO REGISTRATION: SUPER SKIN FOR HANDBAGS: NON-REGISTRABILITY IN PART A AND PART B: AIPO)

Small's Application (DESCRIPTIVE: NO EVIDENCE OF ACQUIRED DISTINCTIVENESS: Pat. Off.)

Athol Thomas Kelly's Application (TRADE MARK: APPLICATION: DISTINCTIVENESS: PRIOR REGISTRATION: HONEST CONCURRENT USE: IMPERFECT RECOLLECTION DOCTRINE: Pat. Off.)

Aussat Pty Ltd (APPLICATION: REGISTRABILITY: SUBSTANTIALLY IDENTICAL: DECEPTIVELY SIMILAR: CLOSELY RELATED GOODS AND SERVICES: AIPO)

Australian Telecommunication Corporation v. Centec International Corp. Pty Ltd (OPPOSITION: DECEPTION AND CONFUSION: BLAMEWORTHY CONDUCT: Pat. Off.)

Bioforce AG Roggwil TG's Application (OBJECTION: DECEPTIVE SIMILARITY TO CITED MARKS: COMMONALITY OF NON-DOMINANT ELEMENT: Pat. Off.)

Boeing Co. v. DMH Imports (Aust.) Pty Ltd (BOEING: OPPOSITION: ENTITLEMENT TO PROTECTION: AIPO)

Bull SA v. Micro Controls Ltd (OPPOSITION: PRIOR REGISTERED MARK: SUBSTANTIAL IDENTITY WITH OR DECEPTIVE SIMILARITY TO PRIOR REGISTERED MARK: Pat. Off.)

Caltex Petroleum Corp. v. Veedol International Ltd (APPLICATION ACCEPTED: OPPOSITION: WHETHER MARKS DECEPTIVE OR CONFUSING: WHETHER SUBSTANTIALLY IDENTICAL WITH OTHER REGISTERED MARKS: AIPO)

Camiceria Pancaldi and B. Srl v. Le Cravatte Di Pancaldi Srl (OPPOSITION: PRIOR INCONSISTENT REGISTRATION: INTENTION TO USE: AIPO)

Canon KK v. Brook (OPPOSITION: SUBSTANTIALLY IDENTICAL: GOODS OF THE SAME DESCRIPTION: HONEST CONCURRENT USE: AIPO)

Carnival Cruise Lines Inc. v. Sitmar Cruises Ltd (OPPOSITION: DECEPTIVE SIMILARITY: PROPRIETORSHIP: Fed. Ct)

Champagne Louis Roederer v. Resourse Management Services Pty Ltd (OPPOSITION: SUBSTANTIALLY IDENTICAL: GOODS OF THE SAME DESCRIPTION: BLAMEWORTHY CONDUCT: DISENTITLEMENT TO PROTECTION: PRACTICE: AIPO)

Chan Li Chai Medical Factory (H.K.) Ltd's Application (CHINESE CHARACTERS: GOODS OF SAME DESCRIPTION: MARKS DECEPTIVELY SIMILAR: Pat. Off.)

Chanel Ltd v. Chantal Chemical & Pharmaceutical Corp. (APPLICATION: OPPOSITION: CHANTAL/CHANEL SUBSTANTIALLY IDENTICAL OR DECEPTIVELY SIMILAR: NO RISK OF DECEPTION: Pat. Off.)

Chanel Ltd v. Chronogem Ltd (APPLICATION: EARLIER PART B MARK REGISTERED FOR SAME GOODS: SUBSTANTIAL IDENTITY OR DECEPTIVE SIMILARITY: Pat. Off.)

Chanel Ltd v. Produits Ella Bache Laboratoire Suzy (OPPOSITION: DECEPTIVE SIMILARITY: GOODS OF SAME DESCRIPTION: AIPO)

Chili's Inc.'s Application (OBJECTION BY EXAMINER: DECEPTIVE SIMILARITY: INHERENT CAPABILITY TO BE DISTINCTIVE: Pat. Off.)

Cleckheaton Australia Pty Ltd's Application (OBJECTION: ADAPTATION TO DISTINGUISH: TEST: CONFUSION WITH CITED MARK: Pat. Off.)

Coca-Cola Company v. Captain Icecream Pty Ltd (OPPOSITION: SUBSTANTIALLY IDENTICAL OR DECEPTIVELY SIMILAR MARKS: Pat. Off.)

Cole v. Australian Char Pty Ltd (OPPOSITION: ABANDONMENT: INTENTION TO USE: LIKELIHOOD OF DECEPTION OR CONFUSION: BLAMEWORTHY CONDUCT: AIPO)

Crooks Michell Peacock Pty Ltd v. Kaiser (OPPOSITION: PROPRIETORSHIP: DISTINCTIVENESS: DECEPTION AND CONFUSION: ESTOPPEL: HONEST ADOPTION OF MARK: GOOD FAITH: AIPO)

Daimaru Pty Ltd v. Daimaru KK (OPPOSITION: PROPRIETORSHIP: INTENTION TO USE: Pat. Off.)

Daimer Industries Pty Ltd v. Daimaru KK (OPPOSITION: DAIMARU/DAIMER: FIRST USE BY OPPONENT ONLY BRIEFLY BEFORE APPLICATION: LIKELIHOOD OF CONFUSION: AIPO)

Dandenong Rangers Bakery's Application (WITHDRAWAL OF ACCEPTANCE: EXAMINER'S IGNORANCE OF A RELEVANT APPLICATION: DECEPTIVE SIMILARITY WITH CITED MARK: WITHDRAWAL OF ACCEPTANCE: Pat. Off.)

Decor Corporation Pty Ltd v. Deeko Australia Pty Ltd (OPPOSITION: WHETHER MARKS SUBSTANTIALLY IDENTICAL OR DECEPTIVELY SIMILAR: CIRCUMSTANCES OF TRADE: Pat. Off.)

Derria AG's Application (OPPOSITION: DECEPTION AND CONFUSION: Pat. Off.)

Domino's Pizza Inc. v. Eagle Boys Dial-a-Pizza Australia Pty Ltd (OPPOSITION: PROPRIETORSHIP: SURVEY EVIDENCE: AIPO)

Dow Chemical Co. v. C.H. Boehringer Sohn KG (OPPOSITION: PRIOR REGISTRATION OF SIMILAR WORD: IMPERFECT RECOLLECTION: Pat. Off.)

Dunlop Olympic Ltd v. Cricket Hosiery Inc. (APPLICATION: OPPOSITION: DISTINCTIVENESS: Pat. Off.)

Eau De Cologne and Parfumerie-Fabrik Glockengasse No. 4711 Gegenuber der Pferdepost von Ferd Mulhens's Application (REFUSAL: DECEPTIVELY SIMILAR: Pat. Off.)

Emdon Investments Pty Ltd v. Shell International Petroleum Co. Ltd (OPPOSITION: PRIOR REGISTERED MARKS: SUBSTANTIAL IDENTITY OR DECEPTIVE SIMILARITY: Pat. Off.)

Findlay v. Rimfire Films Ltd (APPLICATION: CROCODILE DUNDEE: OPPOSITION: REGISTRABILITY: T.M.Reg.)

First Tiffany Holdings Pty Ltd v. Tiffany and Company (OPPOSITION: AUTHORISED USE AND CONTROL: CONNECTION IN THE COURSE OF TRADE: Pat. Off.)

Flagstaff Investments Pty Ltd v. Guess? Inc. (APPLICATION: GUESS?: OPPOSITION: ABSENCE OF EVIDENCE: Pat. Off.)

Fyfe & Tana v. Amalgamated Food & Poultry Pty Ltd (OPPOSITION: SUBSTANTIAL SIMILARITY TO EXISTING REGISTERED MARK: T.M.Reg.)

Gacoli Pty Ltd v. Sterling Pharmaceuticals Pty Ltd (APPLICATION: OPPOSITION: LIKELIHOOD OF DECEPTION: SIMILARITY: T.M.Reg.)

Garden Co. Ltd v. Gardenia Overseas Pty Ltd (OPPOSITION: DECEPTIVE SIMILARITY: MARKS APPLIED TO LOW VALUE GOODS ORDINARILY PURCHASED IN SUPERMARKETS: PARTIES SOUGHT TO INTRODUCE EXTENSIVE MATERIAL AT HEARING OF OPPOSITION: AIPO)

Gardenia Overseas Pte Ltd v. The Garden Co. Ltd (OPPOSITION: COMMON ELEMENT: GARDEN/GARDENIA: LIKELIHOOD OF DECEPTION OR CONFUSION: AURAL AND VISUAL COMPARISONS: AIPO)

Gencorp's Application (PART B: TRADEMARK: NON-DISTINCTIVE: AIPO)

Glaxo Group Ltd v. Pathstream Ltd (OPPOSITION: LIKELIHOOD OF DECEPTION AND CONFUSION: INTERNATIONAL AND NON-PROPRIETARY NAMES: Pat. Off.)

Glenleith Holdings Ltd's Application (SURNAME: DISTINCTIVENESS: SUBSTANTIALLY IDENTICAL WITH OR DECEPTIVELY SIMILAR TO: Pat. Off.)

Goodman Fielder Industries Ltd's Application (SUBSTANTIALLY IDENTICAL OR DECEPTIVELY SIMILAR MARKS: DISTINCTIVENESS: Pat. Off.)

Haddonstone Pty Ltd v. Haddonstone Ltd (ACCEPTANCE: OPPOSITION: PROPRIETORSHIP: MANUFACTURER OR DISTRIBUTOR: ESTOPPEL: ROLE OF REGISTRAR: AIPO)

Hamish Robertson & Co. Ltd's Application (DECEPTIVELY SIMILAR MARKS: LIKELIHOOD OF DECEPTION OR CONFUSION: CRESTS: GOODS SOLD THROUGH SELF-SERVICE OUTLETS: Pat. Off.)

Haralambides v. Pastrikos (APPLICATION: OPPOSITION: LIKELIHOOD OF CONFUSION OR DECEPTION: Pat. Off.)

Hardings Manufacturers Pty Ltd's Application (OPPOSITION: WYANDRA GOLDEN CRUMPETS: DECEPTIVE SIMILARITY: DISCLAIMER: EVIDENCE OF USE: Pat. Off.)

Hearst Corp. v. Pacific Dunlop Ltd (APPLICATION: OPPOSITION: LIKELIHOOD OF DECEPTION OR CONFUSION: Pat. Off.)

Hermes Sweeteners Ltd v. Hermes (APPLICATIONS: OPPOSITION: OPPONENT RELYING ON ITS OWN REGISTERED MARKS: SUBSTANTIALLY IDENTICAL OR DECEPTIVELY SIMILAR: Pat. Off.)

Holmes's Application (OPPOSITION: LIKELIHOOD OF DECEPTION OR CONFUSION: PERMACRAFT: NO EVIDENCE OF USE OF OPPONENT'S MARK: Pat. Off.)

Honeywell Inc.'s Application (INHERENTLY DISTINCTIVE: CAPABLE OF BECOMING DISTINCTIVE: DECEPTIVE SIMILARITY: Pat. Off.)

Johnson & Johnson v. Kalnin (APPLICATION: OPPOSITION: EXISTING REGISTRATION BY OPPONENT: WHETHER LIKELIHOOD FOR DECEPTION OR CONFUSION: Fed. Ct)

Jonsered Motor AB's Application (CITATION: DECEPTIVE SIMILARITY: GOODS OF THE SAME DESCRIPTION: AIPO)

Joose Agencies Pty Ltd v. Maglificio Biellese Fratelli Fila SpA (OPPOSITION: LIKELIHOOD OF DECEPTION OR CONFUSION: MANNER OF USE: EVIDENCE: Pat. Off.)

K Mart Corporation v. A-Mart Allsports Pty Ltd (APPLICATIONS: OPPOSITION: GOODS AND SERVICES: SUBSTANTIAL IDENTITY: DECEPTIVE SIMILARITY: USE: CONCURRENT USE: HONEST USE: Pat. Off.)

Keith Harris & Co. Ltd's Application (OPPOSITION: USE LIKELY TO DECEIVE OR CAUSE CONFUSION: DESCRIPTIVE MARK: Pat. Off.)

Koh Electronics Trading v. Libra Electronics Pty Ltd (OPPOSITION: PROPRIETORSHIP: FIRST USE: LIKELIHOOD OF DECEPTION OR CONFUSION: BLAMEWORTHY CONDUCT: IDENTICAL MARKS: COPYING OF OVERSEAS MARK: COPYRIGHT PROPRIETORSHIP ON GOODS OF SAME DESCRIPTION: AIPO)

Kyowa Hakko Kogyo Co. Ltd v. Schering Corporation (APPLICATION: OPPOSITION: NON-USE: STATEMENT OF USER: SUBSTANTIALLY IDENTICAL: DECEPTIVELY SIMILAR: LIKELY TO DECEIVE OR CAUSE CONFUSION: Pat. Off.)

Little Tykes Co. v. Ciardullo (OPPOSITION: LITTLE TYKE/LITTLE TIKES: SUBSTANTIALLY IDENTICAL: GOODS OF THE SAME DESCRIPTION: CHARACTER MERCHANDISING: AIPO)

Logan v. Coulter (OPPOSITION: INTENTION TO USE: PRIOR USE: COPYRIGHT IN MARK: SUBSISTENCE: AIPO)

Manufacture de Bonneterie C. Mawet v. Kaydale Apparel Ltd (OWNERSHIP: DECEPTION OR CONFUSION: GEOGRAPHIC NAME: Pat. Off.)

Marks and Spencer PLC v. San Miguel Corporation (OPPOSITION: LIKELIHOOD OF DECEPTION OR CONFUSION WITH PRIOR REGISTERED MARK: ST MICHAEL/SAN MIGUEL: Pat. Off.)

Martin Cellars Pty Ltd v. Kies Pty Ltd (OPPOSITION: PROPRIETORSHIP: LIKELIHOOD OF DECEPTION OR CONFUSION: AIPO)

MCT Unilabels SA v. Peter Katholos (OPPOSITION: DECEPTIVELY SIMILAR: SUBSTANTIALLY IDENTICAL: PROPRIETORSHIP: AIPO)

Meldrum v. Grego (OPPOSITION: SUBSTANTIALLY IDENTICAL OR DECEPTIVELY SIMILAR: ESSENTIAL FEATURES: Pat. Off.)

Merck & Co.'s Application (OPPOSITION: LIKELIHOOD OF DECEPTION OR CONFUSION: VISUAL AND AURAL TESTS: Pat. Off.)

Merck & Co. Inc. v. Syntex Corporation (APPLICATION: OPPOSITION: SUBSTANTIALLY IDENTICAL OR DECEPTIVELY SIMILAR MARKS: GOODS OF SAME DESCRIPTION: Pat. Off.)

Merv Brown Pty Ltd v. David Jones (Aust.) Pty Ltd (INFRINGEMENT: VALIDITY: DECEPTION OR CONFUSION: VALIDITY OF ASSIGNMENT WITHOUT GOODWILL: Fed. Ct)

Société des Produits Nestlé SA v. Strasburger Enterprises Inc. (OPPOSITION: QUIX/ QUIK: PROPRIETORSHIP: AIPO)

Société Française des Viandes et Salaisons du Pacifique v. Société des Produits Nestlé SA (OPPOSITION: SUBSTANTIALLY IDENTICAL OR DECEPTIVELY SIMILAR: IMPERFECT RECOLLECTION PRINCIPLE: GOODS OF SAME OR SIMILAR DESCRIPTION: Pat. Off.)

Spiritual Sky Group Co. Pty Ltd v. Bernard Leser Publications Pty Ltd (APPLICATION: OPPOSITION: VOGUE: DECEPTIVE SIMILARITY: Pat. Off.)

Sportscraft Consolidated Pty Ltd v. General Sportcraft Co. Ltd (OPPOSITION: PROPRIETORSHIP: DECEPTION: CONFUSION: SUBSTANTIALLY IDENTICAL: DECEPTIVELY SIMILAR: AIPO)

Sterling Winthrop Pty Ltd v. Stephen Hunter Pty Ltd (OPPOSITION: REGISTRATION: PHARMACEUTICAL: WORD COMMON TO THE TRADE: SIMILARITY: USE: DECEPTION: AIPO)

Stratco Metal Pty Ltd's Application (OPPOSITION: ERROR IN NOTICE: MISDESCRIPTION OF OPPONENT: AMENDMENT: LIKELIHOOD OF DECEPTION OR CONFUSION: Pat. Off.)

Studio Srl v. Buying Systems (Australia) Pty Ltd (APPLICATION: OPPOSITION: PROPRIETORSHIP: PRIOR FOREIGN PROPRIETORSHIP BY OPPONENT: WHETHER CONFUSION: Pat. Off.)

Sundream Pty Ltd v. Hartland Investments Pty Ltd (OPPOSITION: PROPRIETORSHIP: LIKELIHOOD OF DECEPTION OR CONFUSION: ONUS OF PROOF: Pat. Off.)

Surf Shirt Designs Pty Ltd (OPPOSITION: PROPRIETORSHIP: USE LIKELY TO DECEIVE OR CAUSE CONFUSION: Pat. Off.)

Taiwan Yamani Inc. v. Giorgio Armani SpA (APPLICATION: OPPOSITION: SUBSTANTIALLY IDENTICAL OR DECEPTIVELY SIMILAR MARKS: USE NOT LIKELY TO CAUSE DECEPTION OR CONFUSION: VISUAL DIFFERENCES MORE IMPORTANT THAN AURAL SIMILARITY IN RELATION TO CLOTHING: Pat. Off.)

Tavefar Pty Ltd v. Life Savers (Australasia) Ltd (OPPOSITION: LIKELIHOOD OF DECEPTION OR CONFUSION: PROPRIETORSHIP: Pat. Off.)

Technicolor Inc. v. R. & C. Products Pty Ltd (OPPOSITION: PRIOR USE: DECEPTION AND CONFUSION: REGISTRAR'S DIRECTION: Pat. Off.)

Teleflora (Australia) Inc.'s Applications (APPLICATIONS: REGISTRABILITY: SUBSTANTIALLY IDENTICAL: GOODS AND SERVICES OF SAME DESCRIPTION: AIPO)

Thermos Ltd v. Micropore International Ltd (APPLICATION: OPPOSITION: ADAPTED TO DISTINGUISH: SUBSTANTIALLY IDENTICAL OR DECEPTIVELY SIMILAR MARKS: USE LIKELY TO DECEIVE OR CAUSE CONFUSION: Pat. Off.)

Tonka Corp. v. Chong (OPPOSITION: BLAMEWORTHY CONDUCT: AIPO)

Unidrive v. Dana Corp. (OPPOSITION: PROPRIETORSHIP: AIPO)

Unilever Australia Ltd v. ABC Tissue Products Pty Ltd (OPPOSITION: IDENTICAL MARKING OTHER CLASS: LIKELIHOOD OF DECEPTION OR CONFUSION: AIPO)

Upjohn Co. v. Schering Aktiengesellschaft (OPPOSITION: COMMON PREFIX: Fed. Ct)

Visco Sport Ltd's Application (OPPOSITION: SORBOLITE: WHETHER CONFUSINGLY SIMILAR: IMPORTANCE OF FIRST SYLLABLE: EFFECT OF COMMON PARTS: Pat. Off.)

Warner-Lambert Co. v. Harel (OPPOSITION: PROPRIETORSHIP: BLAMEWORTHY CONDUCT: AIPO)

W.D. & H.O. Wills (Australia) Ltd and Benson & Hedges Co. Pty Ltd's Application (OBJECTION: PRIOR REGISTRATION: SUBSTANTIAL IDENTITY, DECEPTIVE SIMILARITY: COMPOSITE AS AGAINST PRIOR WORD ONLY MARK: Pat. Off.)

Wilder Days Pty Ltd v. Karhugh Properties Ltd (OPPOSITION: INTENTION TO USE: DECEPTIVE SIMILARITY: AIPO)

Wingate Marketing Pty Ltd v. Levi Strauss & Co. (INFRINGEMENT: PHONETIC SIMILARITY: LEVI'S/REVISE: SECOND-HAND JEANS: ALTERATIONS: CONFUSION AS TO ORIGIN: Fed. Ct)

Contempt. *See* **Practice** (*Contempt*)

Copyright Proprietorship of Trade Mark

Koh Electronics Trading v. Libra Electronics Pty Ltd (OPPOSITION: PROPRIETORSHIP: FIRST USE: LIKELIHOOD OF DECEPTION OR CONFUSION: BLAMEWORTHY CONDUCT: IDENTICAL MARKS: COPYING OF OVERSEAS MARK: GOODS OF SAME DESCRIPTION: AIPO)

Costs. *See* **Practice** (*Costs*)

Deceptively Similar Marks. *See* **Confusion and Deception**

Derogation from Grant

Kraft General Foods Inc. v. Gaines Pet Foods Corp. (REMOVAL FROM REGISTER: NON-USE: ONUS OF PROOF: EFFECT OF CONTRACTUAL TERMS: PERSON AGGRIEVED: DISCRETION OF REGISTRAR: AIPO)

Descriptiveness

Cling Adhesive Products Pty Ltd's Application (OBJECTION BY EXAMINER: WHETHER DESCRIPTIVE: WORDS JOINED BY HYPHEN: INHERENT DISTINCTIVENESS: EVIDENCE OF USE: AIPO)

Fastrack Racing Pty Ltd's Application (OBJECTIONS BY EXAMINERS: POWER OF REGISTRAR TO SET DOWN FOR HEARING: APPLICATION IN MULTIPLE CLASSES: AMENDMENT OF CLASS: DIVISIONAL FILINGS: DESCRIPTIVE MARK: AIPO)

Fischer Pharmaceuticals Ltd's Application (REGISTRABILITY: INVENTED WORD: AIPO)

Kettle Chip Co. Pty Ltd v. Pepsico Australia Pty Ltd (KETTLE THINS/DOUBLE CRUNCH KETTLE COOKED POTATO CHIPS: QUALITY OF GOODS: Fed. Ct)

Tatra Nominees Pty Ltd's Application (OBJECTION BY EXAMINER: WHETHER DESCRIPTIVE: EXISTING REGISTRATIONS: AIPO)

Toro Company's Applications (OBJECTION: DESCRIPTIVE MARK: CONSISTENCY BY REGISTRAR: PRACTICE: SURVEY EVIDENCE: AIPO)

Device Marks

Barastoc Pty Ltd's Application (EXAMINER'S OBJECTION: Pat. Off.)

Brandella Pty Ltd's Application (KANGAROO DEVICE: UNADAPTED TO DISTINGUISH: Pat. Off.)

Dodds Family Investments Pty Ltd v. Lane Industries Pty Ltd (DISTINCTIVENESS OF DEVICE MARKS: Fed. Ct)

Roland Corporation v. Lorenzo & Sons Pty Ltd (COPYRIGHT IN LOGO DEVICES REGULATED UNDER STATUTE: Fed. Ct)

Victorian Dairy Industry Authority's Application (MILK CARTONS: DESCRIPTIVE WORDS: NON-DISTINCTIVE DEVICE: Pat. Off.)

Direct Reference

Cadbury Schweppes Pty Ltd's Application (INHERENT DISTINCTIVENESS: CAPABLE OF BECOMING DISTINCTIVE: AIPO)

Disclaimers

Australian Airlines Ltd's Application (REFUSAL TO REGISTER UNLESS CONSENT TO DISCLAIMER: Pat. Off.)

Australian National Airlines Commission (CHARACTER OR QUALITY OF GOODS OR SERVICES: NON-DISTINCTIVE: SPECIAL CIRCUMSTANCES: Pat. Off.)

Bioforce AG Roggwil TG's Application (OBJECTION: COMMONALITY OF NON-DOMINANT ELEMENT: CONSENT OF PROPRIETOR OF CITED MARKS: Pat. Off.)

Cedarapids Inc.'s Application (GEOGRAPHICAL NAMES: INVENTED OR COINED WORDS: Pat. Off.)

Computer People Pty Ltd (AMENDMENT: DESCRIPTION OF APPLICANT'S SERVICES: Pat. Off.)

Cuisine Nature CLG Inc.'s Application (DESCRIPTIVE WORDS: REFUSAL OF REGISTRATION: Pat. Off.)

Exotic Products Ltd's Application (LAUDATORY WORD: RATIONALE BEHIND THE DISCLAIMER REQUIREMENT: Pat. Off.)

Hardings Manufacturers Pty Ltd's Application (OPPOSITION: WYANDRA GOLDEN CRUMPETS: DECEPTIVE SIMILARITY: EVIDENCE OF USE: REPUTATION: Pat. Off.)

Legal & General Life of Australia Ltd v. Carlton-Jones & Associates Pty Ltd (OPPOSITION: PRIOR REGISTRATION REMOVED: EFFECT: PROPRIETORSHIP: TRAFFICKING: Pat. Off.)

Maxam Food Products Pty Ltd's Application (REGISTRABILITY: INVENTED WORD: DESCRIPTIVE: Pat. Off.)

McManamey (David Fraser)'s Application (ROARING FORTIES: DISCLAIMER TO FORTIES: DISTINCTIVENESS OF NUMERALS: Pat. Off.)

Mobil Oil Corp. v. Foodland Associated Ltd (APPLICATION: OPPOSITION: AMENDMENT: T.M.Reg.)

Reynolds (R.J.) Tobacco Co. v. Philip Morris Inc. (COMPOSITE MARK WITH NON-DISTINCTIVE ELEMENT: COLOUR LIMITATION: EFFECT OF DISCLAIMER: Pat. Off.)

Sonoco Products Co.'s Application (COMPOSITE MARK: DISCLAIMER AS TO ELEMENT OF MARK: SIGNIFICANCE OF HYPHEN: Pat. Off.)

Waterbed Association of Retailers & Manufacturers's Application (PART B: COMPOSITE MARK: ACRONYM: Pat. Off.)

Discretion. *See* Practice (*Discretion*)

Disentitlement to Protection

Champagne Louis Roederer v. Resourse Management Services Pty Ltd (OPPOSITION: BLAMEWORTHY CONDUCT: AIPO)

Distinctiveness

Ada Productions Pty Ltd's Application (SURNAME: Pat. Off.)

897

899

Somfy's Application (DESCRIPTION OF METHOD OF OPERATION OF GOODS: Pat. Off.)

Sonoco Products Co.'s Application (PART A: INHERENT DISTINCTIVENESS: COMPOSITE MARK: DISCLAIMER AS TO ELEMENT OF MARK: SIGNIFICANCE OF HYPHEN: Pat. Off.)

Spray Booths Australia Pty Ltd's Application (MARKS DIRECTLY DESCRIPTIVE: LACK OF INHERENT DISTINCTIVENESS: PART B: Pat. Off.)

Springs Industries Inc.'s Application (REGISTRABILITY: DESCRIPTIVE: ADAPTABILITY TO DISTINGUISH: Pat. Off.)

STC PLC's Application (ACRONYMS, INITIALS: WHETHER ADAPTED TO DISTINGUISH: Pat. Off.)

Steel Bros (N.Z.) Ltd's Application (SIDELIFTER: DIRECTLY DESCRIPTIVE OF SPECIFIED GOODS: MARK NOT INHERENTLY DISTINCTIVE: NOT AN INVENTED WORD: Pat. Off.)

Sunraysia Natural Beverage Co. Pty Ltd's Application (OBJECTION BY EXAMINER: WHETHER CAPABLE OF BECOMING DISTINCTIVE: AIPO)

Taylor's Application (REGISTRABILITY: DISTINCTIVE: Pat. Off.)

Tooheys Ltd's Application (REGISTRABILITY: SURNAME: DISTINCTIVE: CAPABLE OF BECOMING DISTINCTIVE: Pat. Off.)

Triple Three Leisure Ltd v. Turkovic (APPLICATION: OPPOSITION: PROPRIETORSHIP: INHERENT DISTINCTIVENESS: AIPO)

Untell Pty Ltd v. Manenti Holdings Pty Ltd (OPPOSITION: INHERENT ADAPTABILITY TO DISTINGUISH: ACCEPTANCE BASED ON EVIDENCE OF USE: Pat. Off.)

Victorian Dairy Industry Authority's Application (MILK CARTONS: DESCRIPTIVE WORDS: NON-DISTINCTIVE DEVICE: Pat. Off.)

Wella AG's Application (OBJECTIONS: DESCRIPTIVE MARK: RELEVANCE OF EVIDENCE OF USE AFTER APPLICATION: Pat. Off.)

Wilkinson Sword Ltd's Application (PIVOT: DESCRIPTIVENESS: Pat. Off.)

Yamaha Corp.'s Application (REGISTRABILITY: OBJECTION: DESCRIPTIVE: Pat. Off.)

Divisional Filings

Fastrack Racing Pty Ltd's Application (OBJECTIONS BY EXAMINERS: POWER OF REGISTRAR TO SET DOWN FOR HEARING: APPLICATION IN MULTIPLE CLASSES: AMENDMENT OF CLASS: DESCRIPTIVE MARK: AIPO)

Entitlement to Protection

Boeing Co. v. DMH Imports (Aust.) Pty Ltd (DECEPTION OR CONFUSION: BOEING: OPPOSITION: AIPO)

Errors or Omissions. See Practice (Errors or omissions)

Essential Features

Pacific Dunlop Ltd v. Bonny Sports Corp. (APPLICATION: OPPOSITION: REGISTRATION: COMPOSITE MARK: BONNY PLUS DEVICE: USE: DECEPTION: CONFUSION: DISTINCTIVENESS: AIPO)

Evidence. See Practice (Evidence)

Evidence of Use. See Practice (Evidence of use)

***Ex Parte* Order.** *See* **Practice** (*Ex parte order*)

Expungement

Murray Goulburn Co-operative Company Ltd v. New South Wales Dairy
  Corporation (REMOVAL: NON-USE: PREVIOUS EXPUNGEMENT OF PART OF
  GOODS ORDER: WHETHER COURT SHOULD EXERCISE ITS DISCRETION TO
  EXPUNGE BALANCE OF REGISTRATION: Fed. Ct)
Polo Textile Industries Pty Ltd v. Domestic Textile Corporation Pty Ltd
  (INFRINGEMENT: POLO/POLO CLUB: DISTINCTIVENESS OF MARK: Fed.
  Ct)
Ritz Hotel Ltd v. Charles of The Ritz Ltd (PERSON AGGRIEVED: PRESCRIPTIVE
  VALIDITY: ENTRIES WRONGLY MADE IN REGISTER: ENTRIES WRONGLY
  REMAINING IN REGISTER: S.C.(NSW))
Riv-Oland Marble Co. (Vic.) Pty Ltd v. Settef SpA (VALIDITY: USE LIKELY TO CAUSE
  CONFUSION: LIABILITY TO EXPUNGEMENT: Fed. Ct)
Royale & Co. (Aust.) Pty Ltd v. Maxims Ltd (EXPUNGEMENT FOR NON-USE:
  EVIDENCE: Pat. Off.)

Extension of Time. *See* **Practice** (*Extension of time*)

Foreign Language Words or Surnames

Barrs Application (OBJECTIONS TO REGISTRATION: DESCRIPTIVE WORDS: Pat. Off.)
Polo Textile Industries Pty Ltd v. Domestic Textile Corporation Pty Ltd
  (EXPUNGEMENT: DISTINCTIVENESS: FOREIGN SURNAME: Fed. Ct)

Foreign Trade Mark Registrations

American Supplier Institute Inc.'s Application (GENERIC TERMS: UNADAPTED TO
  DISTINGUISH: INCAPABLE OF BECOMING DISTINCTIVE: FOREIGN TRADE
  MARK REGISTRATIONS: Pat. Off.)
Studio Srl v. Buying Systems (Australia) Pty Ltd (TRADE MARK: APPLICATION FOR
  REGISTRATION: OPPOSITION: PROPRIETORSHIP: PRIOR FOREIGN
  PROPRIETORSHIP BY OPPONENT: Pat. Off.)

Foreign Use or Reputation

Boundy Insulations Pty Ltd's Application (OPPOSITION: PRIOR USE BY FOREIGN
  OPPONENT: OVERSEAS USE: Pat. Off.)
Chili's Inc.'s Application (DECEPTIVE SIMILARITY: INHERENT CAPABILITY TO BE
  DISTINCTIVE: FOREIGN MARKET: DISTINCTIVENESS: Pat. Off.)
Flagstaff Investments Pty Ltd v. Guess? Inc. (GUESS?: USE: FOREIGN PUBLICATIONS
  ADVERTISING: Pat. Off.)
Hermès SA v. Swift & Co. Pty Ltd (APPLICATION: FOREIGN REPUTATION: Pat. Off.)

Generic Name

Business Marketing Australia Pty Ltd v. Australian Telecommunication Commission
  (REGISTRABILITY: DISTINCTIVENESS: DIRECT REFERENCE: AIPO)
Queensland Rugby Football League (REGISTRABILITY: DISTINCTIVENESS: AIPO)

Sony KK's Application (INHERENTLY ADAPTED TO DISTINGUISH: Pat. Off.)

Geographic Name

Bristol-Myers Co.'s Application (DISTINCTIVENESS: EVIDENCE: ACQUIRED DISTINCTIVENESS: ADAPTED TO DISTINGUISH: Pat. Off.)

Cedarapids Inc.'s Application (INVENTED OR COINED WORDS: DISCLAIMERS: Pat. Off.)

Fabriques de Tabac Réunis SA's Application (ORDINARY DESCRIPTIVE TERM: DORADO: Pat. Off.)

Foodland Associated Ltd v. John Weeks Pty Ltd (REGISTRATION FOR SERVICES: APPLICATION FOR GEOGRAPHICAL RESTRICTION OF REGISTRATION: Pat. Off.)

Jonsered Motor AB's Application (CITATION: DECEPTIVE SIMILARITY: GOODS OF THE SAME DESCRIPTION: USE IN PLURAL FORM: AIPO)

Manufacture de Bonneterie C. Mawet v. Kaydale Apparel Ltd (OWNERSHIP: DECEPTION OR CONFUSION: Pat. Off.)

Oxford University Press v. Registrar of Trade Marks (OXFORD: WHETHER A MARK WHICH IS 100 PER CENT DISTINCTIVE IN FACT MUST ALSO BE INHERENTLY ADAPTED TO DISTINGUISH IN ORDER TO BE REGISTRABLE: Fed. Ct)

Pennys Pty Ltd's Application (APPLICATION: ACCEPTANCE IN ERROR: STRATHSPEY: DISCRETION: AIPO)

Red Tulip Chocolates Pty Ltd (APPLICATION: DISTINCTIVENESS: Pat. Off.)

Trippit & Sons's Application (EXAMINER'S OBJECTION: DESCRIPTIVE WORDS: Pat. Off.)

Waterford Glass Group Ltd's Application (WATERFORD: INHERENTLY ADAPTED TO DISTINGUISH: Pat. Off.)

Goods of Same Description

Alexander v. Tait-Jamison (OPPOSITION: WHETHER MARKS NEARLY OR SUBSTANTIALLY IDENTICAL: AIPO)

Canon KK v. Brook (OPPOSITION: SUBSTANTIALLY IDENTICAL: DECEPTIVELY SIMILAR: HONEST CONCURRENT USE: AIPO)

Champagne Louis Roederer v. Resourse Management Services Pty Ltd (OPPOSITION: SUBSTANTIALLY IDENTICAL: DECEPTIVELY SIMILAR: BLAMEWORTHY CONDUCT: DISENTITLEMENT TO PROTECTION: AIPO)

Chan Li Chai Medical Factory (H.K.) Ltd's Application (CHINESE CHARACTERS: MARKS DECEPTIVELY SIMILAR: Pat. Off.)

Chanel Ltd v. Produits Ella Bache Laboratoire Suzy (OPPOSITION: DECEPTIVE SIMILARITY: AIPO)

Holmes's Application (OPPOSITION: LIKELIHOOD OF DECEPTION OR CONFUSION: PERMACRAFT: NO EVIDENCE OF USE OF OPPONENT'S MARK: VENETIAN BLINDS AND FURNITURE NOT GOODS OF SAME DESCRIPTION: Pat. Off.)

ISS Management (Aust.) Pty Ltd v. Vulcan Australia Ltd (OPPOSITION: IDENTICAL MARKS: Pat. Off.)

Jean Patou Parfumeur v. Crisena Corporation Pty Ltd (APPLICATION: OPPOSITION: IDENTICAL MARKS: WHETHER HONEST CONCURRENT USER: Pat. Off.)

Kirra Collectables Pty Ltd v. Pewter Products Pty Ltd (OPPOSITION: KIRRA: EARLIER REGISTRATION: AIPO)

Little Tykes Co. v. Ciardullo (OPPOSITION: LITTLE TYKE/LITTLE TIKES: SUBSTANTIALLY IDENTICAL: DECEPTIVELY SIMILAR: CHARACTER MERCHANDISING: AIPO)

Merck & Co. Inc. v. Syntex Corporation (APPLICATION: OPPOSITION: SUBSTANTIALLY IDENTICAL OR DECEPTIVELY SIMILAR MARKS: Pat. Off.)

Radford Chemical Company Pty Ltd's Application (COMMAND/COMMAND PERFORMANCE: Pat. Off.)

Teleflora (Australia) Inc.'s Applications (REGISTRABILITY: SUBSTANTIALLY IDENTICAL: DECEPTIVELY SIMILAR: GOODS AND SERVICES OF SAME DESCRIPTION: AIPO)

Goodwill

Commissioner of Taxation v. Just Jeans Pty Ltd (SALE OF UNREGISTERED TRADE MARK WITHOUT GOODWILL: EFFECT: Fed. Ct)

Heller Financial Services Ltd v. John Brice (SALE OF BUSINESS: SUBSISTENCE: S.C.(Qd))

Hoogerdyk v. Condon (BUSINESS NAME: SALE OF BUSINESS: BREACH OF CONTRACT: GOODWILL IN NAME: DAMAGES: ASSESSMENT: H.C.)

Merv Brown Pty Ltd v. David Jones (Aust.) Pty Ltd (ASSIGNMENT WITHOUT GOODWILL: SUFFICIENCY: Fed. Ct)

Murray Goulburn Co-operative Co. Ltd v. New South Wales Dairy Corporation (GROUND FOR REMOVAL FROM REGISTER: Fed. Ct)

Murray Goulburn Co-operative Company Ltd v. New South Wales Dairy Corporation (RECTIFICATION: Fed. Ct)

Ocean Pacific Sunwear Ltd v. Ocean Pacific Enterprises Pty Ltd (RESPONDENT'S GOODWILL IN OTHER FIELDS OF ACTIVITY: Fed. Ct)

Winning Appliances Pty Ltd v. Dean Appliances Pty Ltd (ASSIGNMENT OF TRADING NAME: WHETHER GOODWILL ASSIGNED: Fed. Ct)

Hearing Fees. See Practice (Hearing fees)

Honest Concurrent Use

Athol Thomas Kelly's Application (IMPERFECT RECOLLECTION DOCTRINE: Pat. Off.)

Bodyline Cosmetics Ltd v. Brot Bodyline (OPPOSITION: PROPRIETORSHIP: FIRST USE: AIPO)

Canon KK v. Brook (OPPOSITION: SUBSTANTIALLY IDENTICAL: DECEPTIVELY SIMILAR: GOODS OF THE SAME DESCRIPTION: AIPO)

Cougar Marine Ltd v. Roberts (OPPOSITION: DIVISIONAL APPLICATION: PROPRIETORSHIP: ABANDONMENT BY PRIOR USERS: PRIOR REGISTRATION: GOODS OF THE SAME DESCRIPTION: AIPO)

Jean Patou Parfumeur v. Crisena Corporation Pty Ltd (OPPOSITION: IDENTICAL MARK REGISTERED FOR GOODS OF SAME DESCRIPTION: Pat. Off.)

Johnson & Johnson v. S.C. Johnson & Son Inc. (WHETHER CONFUSING: PROPRIETORSHIP: T.M.Reg.)

Olin Corp. v. Pacemaker Pool Supplies (CONFUSION: Pat. Off.)

Selskar Pty Ltd's Application (OPPOSITION: CONFLICTING EVIDENCE: AIPO)

Stingray Surf Co. Pty Ltd v. Lister and Brown (OPPOSITION: PROPRIETORSHIP: AIPO)

Trepper v. Miss Selfridge Ltd (OPPOSITION: PERSON AGGRIEVED: Pat. Off.)

Hyphenated Words

Cling Adhesive Products Pty Ltd's Application (OBJECTION BY EXAMINER: WHETHER DESCRIPTIVE: INHERENT DISTINCTIVENESS: EVIDENCE OF USE: AIPO)

Identical Marks

Vamuta Pty Ltd (t/a Sogo Jewellers) v. Sogo Co. Ltd (SOGO: PROPRIETORSHIP: USE AS ADVERTISEMENTS: AIPO)

Identity Between Marks and Services

Carnival Cruise Lines Inc. v. Sitmar Cruises Ltd (SERVICE MARKS: OPPOSITION: APPEAL: USE IN COURSE OF TRADE: FUN SHIP: Fed. Ct)

Imperfect Recollection Doctrine

Athol Thomas Kelly's Application (DISTINCTIVENESS: LIKELIHOOD OF DECEPTION OR CONFUSION: PRIOR REGISTRATION: HONEST CONCURRENT USE: Pat. Off.)
Crusta Fruit Juices Pty Ltd v. Cadbury Schweppes Pty Ltd (INFRINGEMENT: CRESTA/CRUSTA: INTERLOCUTORY INJUNCTION: BALANCE OF CONVENIENCE: Fed. Ct)
Dow Chemical Co. v. C.H. Boehringer Sohn KG (OPPOSITION: PRIOR REGISTRATION OF SIMILAR WORD: Pat. Off.)
Shell International Petroleum Co. Ltd's Application (VISUAL AND AURAL DIFFERENCES: RELEVANCE OF IMPERFECT RECOLLECTION: Pat. Off.)
Société Française des Viandes et Salaisons du Pacifique v. Société des Produits Nestlé SA (OPPOSITION: SUBSTANTIALLY IDENTICAL OR DECEPTIVELY SIMILAR: GOODS OF SAME OR SIMILAR DESCRIPTION: Pat. Off.)

Indication of Origin. *See* Origin

Infringement

Angoves Pty Ltd v. Johnson (EXCLUSIVE USE BY PROPRIETOR: GOOD FAITH: Fed. Ct)
Atari Inc. v. Fairstar Electronics Pty Ltd (VIDEO COMPUTER SYSTEMS: PARALLEL IMPORTATION: Fed. Ct)
Australian Design Council v. Peter Borello (CONTEMPT: FALSE REPRESENTATION: CONDUCT: INJUNCTION: CONTINUING USE OF TRADE MARK IN BREACH OF INJUNCTION: DELIBERATE BREACH: PUBLIC INTEREST FACTORS: HONESTY IN ADVERTISING: FINE: Fed. Ct)
Browne v. S. Smith & Son Pty Ltd (REMOVAL FOR NON-USE: JURISDICTION OF FED. CT: Fed. Ct)
Cantarella Bros v. Kona Coffee Roastery & Equipment Supplies (WHETHER USE DESCRIPTIVE OF CHARACTER OR QUALITY: USE IN GOOD FAITH: Fed. Ct)
Caterpillar Tractor Co. v. Caterpillar Loader Hire (Holdings) Pty Ltd (SERVICE MARK: GOOD FAITH: S.C.(S.A.))
Crusta Fruit Juices Pty Ltd v. Cadbury Schweppes Pty Ltd (CRESTA/CRUSTA: INTERLOCUTORY INJUNCTION: BALANCE OF CONVENIENCE: IMPERFECT RECOLLECTION: Fed. Ct)
Delphic Wholesalers Pty Ltd v. Elco Food Co. Pty Ltd (CONTRACT: INDUCEMENT TO BREACH: PARALLEL IMPORTATION: S.C.(Vic.))
Dial-An-Angel Pty Ltd v. Sagitaur Services Systems Pty Ltd (DIAL-AN-ANGEL/ GUARDIAN ANGEL: COMMON ELEMENTS: Fed. Ct)
Digby International (Australia) Pty Ltd v. Beyond Imagination Pty Ltd (EXTREME/ POWERADE EXTREMISTS: INTERLOCUTORY INJUNCTION: SERIOUS QUESTION TO BE TRIED: BALANCE OF CONVENIENCE: ADEQUACY OF DAMAGES: Fed. Ct)

Fender Australia Pty Ltd v. Beck (AUSTRALIAN RIGHTS IN A U.S. MARK ASSIGNED TO
    AUSTRALIAN DISTRIBUTOR: SALE OF SECOND-HAND GOODS BEARING
    OVERSEAS MANUFACTURER'S TRADE MARK: Fed. Ct)
Golf Lynx v. Golf Scene Pty Ltd (PASSING OFF: ANTON PILLER ORDER: DAMAGE: *Ex
    parte* ORDER: S.C.(NSW))
Johnson & Johnson Australia Pty Ltd v. Sterling Pharmaceuticals Pty Ltd
    (REGISTRATION: CAPLETS: MEDICATED TABLETS FOR HUMAN USE: NON-
    USE: SURVEY EVIDENCE: Fed. Ct)
Mack Trucks Inc. v. Satberg Pty Ltd (INTERLOCUTORY INJUNCTION: WHETHER
    INFRINGEMENT REQUIRES USE OF IDENTICAL MARK: USE BY PREDECESSOR
    IN BUSINESS UNDER T.M.A.55, S.64(1): Fed. Ct)
Merv Brown Pty Ltd v. David Jones (Aust.) Pty Ltd (VALIDITY: DECEPTION OR
    CONFUSION: VALIDITY OF ASSIGNMENT WITHOUT GOODWILL: Fed. Ct)
Musidor BV v. Tansing (ROLLING STONES ON COVER OF COMPACT DISK:
    "UNAUTHORISED" COMPACT DISK: WHETHER BREACH OF MARK: Fed. Ct)
New South Wales Dairy Corporation v. Murray-Goulburn Co-operative Co. Ltd
    (NON-USE: RECTIFICATION: ASSIGNMENT WITHOUT GOODWILL: PASSING
    OFF: Fed. Ct)
Polo Textile Industries Pty Ltd v. Domestic Textile Corporation Pty Ltd (POLO/
    POLO CLUB: T.M.A.55, S.62(1): DEFENCES: Fed. Ct)
Prince Manufacturing Inc. v. ABAC Corp. Aust. Pty Ltd (SIMILAR GOODS: TENNIS
    RACQUETS: Fed. Ct)
R. & C. Products Pty Ltd v. Sterling Winthrop Pty Ltd (PINE ACTION/PINE-O-
    CLEEN: PASSING OFF: GET-UP OF PRODUCT: Fed. Ct)
Settef SpA v. Riv-Oland Marble Co. (Vic.) Pty Ltd (PROPRIETORSHIP: WHETHER
    DISTINCTIVE, DECEPTIVE AND CONFUSING: RECTIFICATION: NON-USE: USE
    IN GOOD FAITH: ABANDONMENT: S.C.(Vic.))
Smith and Nephew Plastics (Australia) Pty Ltd v. Sweetheart Holding Corp.
    (IMPORTATION: S.C.(Vic.))
Tansing v. Musidor (DECLARATION: USE AS MARK: DISCLAIMER: USE IN GOOD
    FAITH: Fed. Ct)
Vulcan Australia Ltd v. M.L. D'Astoli & Co. Pty Ltd (STAY: CO-PENDING
    APPLICATION FOR SIMILAR MARK: Fed. Ct)
Wingate Marketing Pty Ltd v. Levi Strauss & Co. (PHONETIC SIMILARITY: LEVI'S/
    REVISE: SECOND-HAND JEANS: ALTERATIONS: CONFUSION AS TO ORIGIN:
    Fed. Ct)

Inherently Distinctive. *See* **Distinctiveness**

Initials

Approved Prescription Services Ltd's Application (REGISTRABILITY: LETTERS AND
    INITIALS: INVENTED WORK: ADAPTED TO DISTINGUISH: Pat. Off.)
STC PLC's Application (ACRONYMS, WHETHER DISTINCTIVE: WHETHER ADAPTED
    TO DISTINGUISH: Pat. Off.)

Injunction. *See* **Practice** (*Injunction*)

Intention to Use

Camiceria Pancaldi and B. Srl v. Le Cravatte Di Pancaldi Srl (OPPOSITION: PRIOR
    INCONSISTENT REGISTRATION: DECEPTION AND CONFUSION: AIPO)
Cole v. Australian Char Pty Ltd (OPPOSITION: ABANDONMENT: LIKELIHOOD OF
    DECEPTION OF CONFUSION: BLAMEWORTHY CONDUCT: AIPO)

Logan v. Coulter (OPPOSITION: DECEPTIVE SIMILARITY: PRIOR USE: COPYRIGHT IN MARK: SUBSISTENCE: AIPO)

Natural Paper v. Spastic Centre of New South Wales (OPPOSITION: LACK OF INTENTION TO USE: NON-USE: PROPRIETORSHIP: DECEPTION OR CONFUSION: AIPO)

Interlocutory Injunction. *See* **Practice** (*Interlocutory injunction*)

International Goodwill. *See* **Goodwill**

Invented Word

Advanced Hair Studio of America Pty Ltd's Application (COMPARISON WITH ORDINARY AND EXISTING WORDS: Pat. Off.)

Advanced Hair Studio of America Pty Ltd v. Registrar of Trade Marks (RELATIONSHIP BETWEEN MARK AND CHARACTER OR QUALITY OF SERVICES: INHERENTLY DISTINCTIVE: EVIDENCE OF USE: S.C.(Vic.))

Coles & Co. Ltd's Application (DISTINCTIVENESS: DIRECT REFERENCE TO CHARACTER OR QUALITY OF GOODS: Pat. Off.)

Fischer Pharmaceuticals Ltd's Application (REGISTRABILITY: DESCRIPTIVENESS: AIPO)

Maxam Food Products Pty Ltd's Application (REGISTRABILITY: DESCRIPTIVE: CAPABLE OF BECOMING DISTINCTIVE: DISCLAIMER: Pat. Off.)

Mobil Oil Corp. v. Registrar of Trade Marks (REGISTRABILITY: S.C.(NSW))

Mobil Oil Corp. v. Registrar of Trade Marks (REGISTRABILITY: S.C.(Vic.))

Steel Bros (N.Z.) Ltd's Application (SIDELIFTER: DIRECTLY DESCRIPTIVE OF SPECIFIED GOODS: MARK NOT INHERENTLY DISTINCTIVE: NOT AN INVENTED WORD: Pat. Off.)

Injunction. *See* **Practice** (*Injunction*)

Jurisdiction. *See* **Practice** (*Jurisdiction*)

Label

Television Broadcasts Ltd v. Tu (SUPERIMPOSED LABEL ON VIDEO CASSETTES NOT ADEQUATELY COVERING APPLICANTS' MARK: Fed. Ct)

Lapsed Registration

Metropolitan Dairies Pty Ltd v. Pura Natural Spring Waters Pty Ltd (REGISTRATION: RENEWAL: EXTENSION OF TIME: ERROR OR OMISSION: NATURAL JUSTICE: *Locus standi*: PUBLIC POLICY: Pat. Off.)

Rael Marcus v. Sabra International Pty Ltd (OPPOSITION: APPEAL: PRIOR USE: OVERSEAS VENDOR: EFFECT OF PREVIOUS, NOW-LAPSED REGISTRATION OF MARK AND LICENCE TO USE IT: DISTINCTION BETWEEN NON-USE AND ABANDONMENT: RESIDUAL GOODWILL: Fed. Ct)

Laudatory Expression or Word

Brian Davis & Co. Pty Ltd's Application (PROFESSIONAL) (INHERENT DISTINCTIVENESS: Pat. Off.)

Exotic Products Ltd's Application (NOT DISTINCTIVE: DISCLAIMER: RATIONALE BEHIND THE DISCLAIMER REQUIREMENT: Pat. Off.)

Hawke (Aust.) Ltd's Application (TIMELESS CREATION: INHERENT NON-DISTINCTIVENESS: NO USE OF MARK: Pat. Off.)

Licence to Use

Rael Marcus v. Sabra International Pty Ltd (OPPOSITION: PRIOR USE: OVERSEAS VENDOR: EFFECT OF PREVIOUS, NOW–LAPSED REGISTRATION OF MARK AND LICENCE TO USE IT: DISTINCTION BETWEEN NON–USE AND ABANDONMENT: Fed. Ct)

Likelihood of Deception or Confusion. *See* **Confusion or Deception**

Limitation. *See* **Disclaimer**

Marks in Issue. *See* **Trade Marks Considered**

Merchandising rights/Character Merchandising

Anheuser-Busch Inc. v. Castlebrae Pty Ltd (Fed. Ct)
Hogan v. Koala Dundee Pty Ltd (Fed. Ct)

Nickname. *See* **Surname or Nickname**

Non-use

Anstoetz's (Jab Josef's) Application (APPLICATION FOR REMOVAL: PERSON AGGRIEVED: USE BY DISTRIBUTOR: Pat. Off.)
Australian Bacon Ltd v. Mulfric Foods Pty Ltd (APPLICATION FOR REMOVAL: OPPOSITION: EVIDENCE: Pat. Off.)
Briggs v. Jaden Marketing Pty Ltd (APPLICATION TO REMOVE: UNAUTHORISED USE: DISCRETION: AIPO)
Browne v. S. Smith & Son Pty Ltd (INFRINGEMENT: REMOVAL FOR NON–USE: JURISDICTION: Fed. Ct)
Cafe Do Brasil SpA v. Scrava Pty Ltd (APPLICATION FOR REMOVAL: EVIDENCE: PRIMA FACIE CASE: SPECIAL CIRCUMSTANCES: Pat. Off.)
Cassini v. Golden Era Shirt Co. Pty Ltd (APPLICATION: CASSINI FOR CLOTHING: WHETHER DISTINCTIVE: S.C.(NSW))
D'Urban Inc. v. Canpio Pty Ltd (APPLICATION FOR REMOVAL: NEED TO PROVE NON–USE: Pat. Off.)
ECONOVENT Trade Mark (APPLICATION FOR REMOVAL: ONUS OF PROOF: Pat. Off.)
Estate Agents Co-operative Ltd v. National Association of Realtors (APPLICATION TO REMOVAL: Pat. Off.)
Fawns & McAllan Pty Ltd v. Burns-Biotec Laboratories Inc. (REMOVAL: PERSON AGGRIEVED: T.M.Reg.)
Figgins Holdings Pty Ltd v. Parfums Christian Dior (APPLICATION FOR REMOVAL: Pat. Off.)
Golden Era Shirt Co. Pty Ltd v. Cassini (APPLICATION: CASSINI FOR CLOTHING: WHETHER DISTINCTIVE: AIPO)
Gordon & Rena Merchant Pty Ltd v. Ocky Docket (Aust.) Pty Ltd (REMOVAL: OPPOSITION: PERSON AGGRIEVED: ONUS: Pat. Off.)
Herron Pharmaceuticals Pty Ltd v. Sterling Winthrop Pty Ltd (APPLICATION TO REMOVE: OPPOSITION: PERSON AGGRIEVED: *Locus standii* BASED ON PRIOR REGISTERED MARKS: ADMISSION OF FURTHER EVIDENCE: AIPO)

John Weeks Pty Ltd v. Foodland Associated Ltd (REGISTRATION: RECTIFICATION: JURISDICTION: Fed. Ct)

Johnson & Johnson Australia Pty Ltd v. Sterling Pharmaceuticals Pty Ltd (REGISTRATION: CAPLETS: MEDICATED TABLETS FOR HUMAN USE: Fed. Ct)

Kraft General Foods Inc. v. Gaines Pet Foods Corp. (REMOVAL FROM REGISTER: ONUS OF PROOF: EFFECT OF CONTRACTUAL TERMS: PERSON AGGRIEVED: DISCRETION OF REGISTRAR: DEROGATION FROM GRANT: AIPO: Fed. Ct)

Kyowa Hakko Kogyo Co. Ltd v. Schering Corporation (APPLICATION: OPPOSITION: STATEMENT OF USER: Pat. Off.)

Lane v. Diners Club International Ltd (APPLICATION FOR REMOVAL: OPPOSITION: ONUS OF PROOF: NEED TO ESTABLISH PRIMA FACIE CASE: Pat. Off.)

Murray Goulburn Co-operative Company Ltd v. New South Wales Dairy Corporation (APPLICATION FOR REMOVAL: EXERCISE OF DISCRETION TO EXPUNGE: Fed. Ct)

Murray Goulburn Co-operative Company Ltd v. New South Wales Dairy Corporation (APPLICATION FOR REMOVAL: GOODS OF THE SAME DESCRIPTION: NO USE IN GOOD FAITH: Fed. Ct)

Murray Goulburn Co-operative Company Ltd v. New South Wales Dairy Corporation (REMOVAL: PREVIOUS EXPUNGEMENT OF PART OF GOODS: WHETHER COURT SHOULD EXERCISE ITS DISCRETION TO EXPUNGE BALANCE OF REGISTRATION: Fed. Ct)

Murray Goulburn Co-operative Company Ltd v. New South Wales Dairy Corporation (RECTIFICATION: ASSIGNMENT WITHOUT GOODWILL: Fed. Ct)

Natural Paper v. Spastic Centre of New South Wales (OPPOSITION: LACK OF INTENTION TO USE: PROPRIETORSHIP: DECEPTION OR CONFUSION: AIPO)

Pierre Fabre SA v. Marion Laboratories Inc. (REMOVAL: OPPOSITION: ONUS OF PROOF: T.M.Reg.)

Playboy Enterprises Inc. v. Fitwear Ltd (OPPOSITION: LIKELY TO DECEIVE OR CAUSE CONFUSION: SUBSTANTIALLY IDENTICAL OR DECEPTIVELY SIMILAR: Pat. Off.)

Polo Textile Industries Pty Ltd v. Domestic Textile Corporation Pty Ltd (INFRINGEMENT: EXPUNGEMENT: SUFFICIENCY OF USE: EVIDENCE: Fed. Ct)

Prosimmon Golf (Aust.) Pty Ltd v. Dunlop Australia Ltd (REMOVAL: PERSON AGGRIEVED: EVIDENCE: ADEQUACY: Pat. Off.)

Rael Marcus v. Sabra International Pty Ltd (OPPOSITION: DISTINCTION BETWEEN NON-USE AND ABANDONMENT: RESIDUAL GOODWILL: Fed. Ct)

Royale & Co. (Aust.) Pty Ltd v. Maxims Ltd (EXPUNGEMENT: EVIDENCE: Pat. Off.)

Sasdor Pty Ltd v. Atomic Skifabrik Alois Rohrmoser (REMOVAL: OPPOSITION: PERSON AGGRIEVED: Pat. Off.)

Sceats v. Jonathan Sceats Design Pty Ltd (REMOVAL: DISCRETIONARY REMEDY: EXERCISE OF DISCRETION: Fed. Ct)

Settef SpA v. Riv-Oland Marble Co. (Vic.) Pty Ltd (INFRINGEMENT: RECTIFICATION: USE IN GOOD FAITH: ABANDONMENT: S.C.(Vic.))

Sew Hoy & Sons Ltd v. Skill Print Pty Ltd (APPLICATION FOR REMOVAL: OPPOSITION: PERSON AGGRIEVED: PRIMA FACIE CASE: SUFFICIENCY OF EVIDENCE: Pat. Off.)

Small & Associates Pty Ltd v. Robert Half Incorporated (REGISTRATION: REMOVAL: AIPO)

Smith Pty Ltd v. E.A. Browne (APPLICATION FOR REMOVAL: INTENTION TO USE: Pat. Off.)

Studio Australia Pty Ltd v. Softsel Computer Products Inc. (APPLICATION FOR REMOVAL: ALLEGED NON-USE: EVIDENCE OF STATEMENT FROM TRADE MEMBERS: Pat. Off.)

Timberland Co. v. Speedo Knitting Mills Pty Ltd (APPLICATION FOR REMOVAL: OPPOSITION: DISCRETION OF REGISTRAR: EVIDENCE: Pat. Ct)

909

Numerals

Cunard Lines Ltd's Application (DISTINCTIVENESS: LETTERS AND NUMERALS: IMPLIED ROYAL PATRONAGE OR AUTHORITY: GOODS SOLD ON BOARD PASSENGER LINER: AIPO)

McManamey (David Fraser)'s Application (ROARING FORTIES: DISCLAIMER REQUIRED AS TO FORTIES: DISTINCTIVENESS OF NUMERALS: Pat. Off.)

Objection by Examiner. *See* **Practice** (*Objection by examiner*)

Onus of Proof. *See* **Practice** (*Onus of proof*)

Opposition

Agricultural Dairy Industry Authority of Epirus Dodoni SA v. Dimtsis (PROPRIETORSHIP: USE LIKELY TO DECEIVE OR CAUSE CONFUSION: REGISTRABILITY: Pat. Off.)

Alexander v. Tait-Jamison (PROPRIETORSHIP: WHETHER MARKS NEARLY OR SUBSTANTIALLY IDENTICAL: WHETHER GOODS OF THE SAME DESCRIPTION: USE OF BUSINESS NAME: WHETHER USE AS MARK: AIPO)

Algie v. Dorminy (OPPOSITION: WHETHER PRIOR USE: WHETHER DECEPTIVE OR CONFUSING: AIPO)

Allied Colloids Ltd v. S.C. Johnson & Son Inc. (EARLIER MARK REGISTERED FOR OVERLAPPING GOODS: SUBSTANTIAL IDENTITY OR DECEPTIVE SIMILARITY: MARKS DECEPTIVELY SIMILAR: WHETHER USE LIKELY TO DECEIVE OR CAUSE CONFUSION: USE OF MARK IN PRACTICE ONLY IN INDUSTRIAL APPLICATION: Pat. Off.)

Allworth Constructions Pty Ltd v. Dixon Investments Pty Ltd (PROPRIETORSHIP: USE OF TRADE MARK: GOODS OR SERVICES: AIPO)

Alpine Audio Accoustic v. Alpine Electronic Inc. (OVERSEAS REPUTATION: Pat. Off.)

Amco Wrangler Ltd v. Jacques Konckier (PART B: LIKELIHOOD OF DECEPTION OR CONFUSION: SURNAMES: Pat. Off.)

American Express Co. v. NV Amev (AMEX/AMEV: SUBSTANTIALLY IDENTICAL MARKS: Pat. Off.)

Ampex Corp. v. Amper SA (EXTENSION OF TIME TO SERVE EVIDENCE: SETTLEMENT NEGOTIATIONS: PUBLIC INTEREST: AIPO)

Astra (AB) v. Schering Corporation (DECEPTIVELY SIMILAR: CONFUSION: HABITS OF MEDICAL PRACTITIONERS IN WRITING PRESCRIPTIONS AND PHARMACISTS IN READING THEM: VISUAL SIMILARITY: HEALTH CONSEQUENCES OF DECEPTION OR CONFUSION: Pat. Off.)

Atomic Skifbrik Alois Rohmoser v. Registrar of Trade Marks (APPLICATION FOR EXTENSION OF PERIOD: Fed. Ct)

Australian Broadcasting Corporation's Application (APPLICATION FOR EXTENSION OF TIME TO FILE NOTICE OF OPPOSITION: Pat. Off.)

Australian Olympic Committee Inc. v. Brennan (APPLICATION FOR EXTENSION OF TIME FOR SERVICE OF EVIDENCE: FACTORS TO BE CONSIDERED: AIPO)

Australian Soccer Federation Marketing Ltd v. Questor Corp. (LIKELIHOOD OF DECEPTION: Pat. Off.)

Australian Telecommunication Corporation v. Centec International Corp. Pty Ltd (ADDRESS FOR SERVICE: EVIDENCE: Pat. Off.)

Avirone Pty Ltd v. ICI Australia Operations Pty Ltd (WANT OF PROSECUTION: MANNER OF USE: FIELDS OF USE: Pat. Off.)

AWA Ltd v. Future Software Pty Ltd (POTENTIAL OPPOSITION: EXTENSION TO TIME FOR OPPOSITION: Pat. Off.)

Beiersdorf AG's Application (OVERSEAS REPUTATION: Pat. Off.)

Bentley Lingerie Inc. v. Greta Lingerie (Aust.) Limited (LATE APPLICATION FOR EXTENSION OF TIME TO FILE EVIDENCE: SPECIAL CIRCUMSTANCES: AIPO)

Bernard Leser Publications Pty Ltd v. Spiritual Sky Group Co. Pty Ltd (Pat. Off.)

Big Country Developments Pty Ltd v. TGI Friday's Inc. (PART A: USE BY OPPONENT AS A MARK: Pat. Off.)

Bodegas Rioja Santiago SA v. Barossa Co-operative Winery Ltd (PRIOR REGISTRATION: COMMON DESCRIPTIVE ELEMENTS: Pat. Off.)

Bodyline Cosmetics Ltd v. Brot Bodyline (PROPRIETORSHIP: FIRST USE: HONEST CONCURRENT USE: AIPO)

Boeing Co. v. DMH Imports (Aust.) Pty Ltd (BOEING: ENTITLEMENT TO PROTECTION: AIPO)

Boundy Insulations Pty Ltd's Application (PRIOR USE BY FOREIGN OPPONENT: OVERSEAS USE: MAGAZINES: Pat. Off.)

Branov v. Sleep Better Bedding Mfg Pty Ltd (APPLICATION FOR EXTENSION OF TIME TO LODGE OPPOSITION: AIPO)

Bull SA v. Micro Controls Ltd (LIKELIHOOD OF DECEPTION OR CONFUSION: SUBSTANTIAL IDENTITY WITH OR DECEPTIVE SIMILARITY TO PRIOR REGISTERED MARK: WHETHER GOODS OF THE SAME DESCRIPTION: Pat. Off.)

Bundy American Corp. v. Rent-A-Wreck (Vic.) Pty Ltd (EXTENSION OF TIME LIMITS: INTER-PARTY NEGOTIATION: PUBLIC INTEREST: Pat. Off.)

Buying Systems (Australia) Pty Ltd v. Studio Srl (PROPRIETORSHIP: PRIOR USE BY OPPONENT: CONNECTION IN THE COURSE OF TRADE: AIPO)

Caltex Petroleum Corp. v. Veedol International Ltd (APPLICATION ACCEPTED: WHETHER MARKS DECEPTIVE OR CONFUSING: WHETHER SUBSTANTIALLY IDENTICAL WITH OTHER REGISTERED MARKS: AIPO)

Camiceria Pancaldi and B. Srl v. Le Cravatte Di Pancaldi Srl (PRIOR INCONSISTENT REGISTRATION: DECEPTION AND CONFUSION: INTENTION TO USE: AIPO)

Canon KK v. Brook (SUBSTANTIALLY IDENTICAL: DECEPTIVELY SIMILAR: GOODS OF THE SAME DESCRIPTION: HONEST CONCURRENT USE: AIPO)

Carlton & United Breweries Ltd v. Miller Brewing Co. (EXTENSION OF TIME LIMIT: REASONS: Pat. Off.)

Carnival Cruise Lines Inc. v. Sitmar Cruises Ltd (SERVICE MARKS: APPEAL: USE IN COURSE OF TRADE: FUN SHIP: WHETHER SUFFICIENT IDENTITY BETWEEN MARKS AND SERVICES: Fed. Ct)

Carnival Cruise Lines Inc. v. Sitmar Cruises Ltd (SERVICE MARKS: DECEPTIVE SIMILARITY: PROPRIETORSHIP: Fed. Ct)

Castlebrae Pty Ltd v. Anheuser-Busch Inc. (AIPO)

Champagne Louis Roederer v. Resourse Management Services Pty Ltd (SUBSTANTIALLY IDENTICAL: DECEPTIVELY SIMILAR: GOODS OF THE SAME DESCRIPTION: BLAMEWORTHY CONDUCT: DISENTITLEMENT TO PROTECTION: AIPO)

Chanel Ltd v. Chantal Chemical & Pharmaceutical Corp. (PROPRIETORSHIP: NO EVIDENCE OF USE OF MARK BY OTHERS: CHANTAL/CHANEL SUBSTANTIALLY IDENTICAL OR DECEPTIVELY SIMILAR: NO RISK OF DECEPTION: Pat. Off.)

Chanel Ltd v. Chronogem Ltd (OPPONENT'S EARLIER PART B MARK FOR SAME GOODS: SUBSTANTIAL IDENTITY OR DECEPTIVE SIMILARITY: MARKS DISTINGUISHABLE: WHETHER USE LIKELY TO DECEIVE OR CAUSE CONFUSION: Pat. Off.)

Chanel Ltd v. Produits Ella Bache Laboratoire Suzy (DECEPTIVE SIMILARITY: GOODS OF SAME DESCRIPTION: BLAMEWORTHY CONDUCT: AIPO)

Ciba Geigy Australia Ltd v. Eli Lilly & Co. (DISTINCTIVENESS: CHARACTER OF GOODS: Pat. Off.)

Coca-Cola Company v. Captain Ice cream Pty Ltd (USE LIKELY TO DECEIVE OR CAUSE CONFUSION: SUBSTANTIALLY IDENTICAL OR DECEPTIVELY SIMILAR MARKS: Pat. Off.)

Cole v. Australian Char Pty Ltd (ABANDONMENT: INTENTION TO USE: LIKELIHOOD OF DECEPTION OR CONFUSION: BLAMEWORTHY CONDUCT: AIPO)

Comlink Information Systems Inc. v. Technology One Pty Ltd (FINANCE ONE: LOGO: PROPRIETORSHIP: AIPO)

Conde Nast Publications Pty Ltd v. Mango Pty Ltd (VOGUE: WHETHER DESCRIPTIVE: SIMILAR GOODS: CONFUSION: Fed. Ct)

Cougar Marine Ltd v. Roberts (DIVISIONAL APPLICATION: PROPRIETORSHIP: ABANDONMENT BY PRIOR USERS: PRIOR REGISTRATION: GOODS OF THE SAME DESCRIPTION: HONEST CONCURRENT USER: AIPO)

Crooks Michell Peacock Pty Ltd v. Kaiser (PROPRIETORSHIP: DISTINCTIVENESS: DECEPTION AND CONFUSION: ESTOPPEL: HONEST ADOPTION OF MARK: GOOD FAITH: AIPO)

Daimaru Pty Ltd v. Daimaru KK (PROPRIETORSHIP: INTENTION TO USE: USE LIKELY TO DECEIVE OR CAUSE CONFUSION: Pat. Off.)

Daimer Industries Pty Ltd v. Daimaru KK (DAIMARU/DAIMER: PROPRIETORSHIP: FIRST USE BY OPPONENT ONLY BRIEFLY BEFORE APPLICATION BY APPLICANT: LIKELIHOOD OF CONFUSION: AIPO)

Dana Corp. v. Unidrive (PROPRIETORSHIP: DISTINCTIVENESS: SUBSTANTIALLY IDENTICAL OR DECEPTIVELY SIMILAR: AIPO)

Decor Corporation Pty Ltd v. Deeko Australia Pty Ltd (WHETHER MARKS SUBSTANTIALLY IDENTICAL OR DECEPTIVELY SIMILAR: CIRCUMSTANCES OF TRADE: Pat. Off.)

Dermatone Laboratories Inc. v. Omni-Pharm SA (SHARED ELEMENT COMMON TO TRADE: Pat. Off.)

Derria AG's Application (DECEPTION AND CONFUSION: Pat. Off.)

Digital Equipment Corporation v. Australian Telecommunication Commission (DISTINCTIVENESS: AIPO)

Domino's Pizza Inc. v. Eagle Boys Dial-a-Pizza Australia Pty Ltd (DECEPTION AND CONFUSION: PROPRIETORSHIP: SURVEY EVIDENCE: AIPO)

Dow Chemical Co. v. C.H. Boehringer Sohn KG (PRIOR REGISTRATION OF SIMILAR WORD: IMPERFECT RECOLLECTION: Pat. Off.)

Dunlop Olympic Ltd v. Cricket Hosiery Inc. (DISTINCTIVENESS: LIKELIHOOD OF DECEPTION OR CONFUSION: USE OF MARK OVERSEAS: PROPRIETORSHIP: Pat. Off.)

Eden Technology Pty Ltd v. Intel Corp. (WITHDRAWAL OF APPLICATION: Pat. Off.)

Effem Foods Pty Ltd v. Design Concepts Pty Ltd (APPLICATION TO EXTEND TIME TO FILE EVIDENCE IN SUPPORT OF OPPOSITION: Pat. Off.)

Email Ltd v. Sharp KK (REFERENCE TO QUALITY OR CHARACTER OF GOODS: Pat. Off.)

Emdon Investments Pty Ltd v. Shell International Petroleum Co. Ltd (PRIOR REGISTERED MARKS: SUBSTANTIAL IDENTITY OR DECEPTIVE SIMILARITY: Pat. Off.)

Esselte Letraset Ltd's Application (EXTENSION OF TIME: CIRCUMSTANCES BEYOND CONTROL: Pat. Off.)

Fawns & McAllan Pty Ltd v. Burns-Biotec Laboratories Inc. (REMOVAL FOR NON-USE: PERSON AGGRIEVED: T.M.Reg.)

Figgins Holdings Pty Ltd v. Registrar of Trade Marks (PROCEEDINGS SETTLED: ASSIGNMENT OF APPLICATION: REGISTRATION OF PROPRIETORSHIP: JURISDICTION TO ORDER: Fed. Ct)

Findlay v. Rimfire Films Ltd (CROCODILE DUNDEE: REGISTRABILITY: USE LIKELY TO DECEIVE OR CAUSE CONFUSION: T.M.Reg.)

First Tiffany Holdings Pty Ltd v. Tiffany and Company (PROPRIETORSHIP: AUTHORISED USE AND CONTROL: CONNECTION IN THE COURSE OF TRADE: USE LIKELY TO DECEIVE AND CAUSE CONFUSION: Pat. Off.)

Flagstaff Investments Pty Ltd v. Guess? Inc. (GUESS?: PROPRIETORSHIP: USE: FOREIGN PUBLICATIONS ADVERTISING: DECEPTION OR CONFUSION: ABSENCE OF EVIDENCE: Pat. Off.)

Food Marketers Pty Ltd v. Maconochie Seafoods Ltd (EXTENSION OF TIME FOR LODGING NOTICE OF OPPOSITION: SPECIAL CIRCUMSTANCES: Pat. Off.)

Fyfe & Tana v. Amalgamated Food & Poultry Pty Ltd (SUBSTANTIAL SIMILARITY TO EXISTING REGISTERED MARK: T.M.Reg.)

Gacoli Pty Ltd v. Sterling Pharmaceuticals Pty Ltd (LIKELIHOOD OF DECEPTION: SIMILARITY: T.M.Reg.)

Garden Co. Ltd v. Gardenia Overseas Pty Ltd (DECEPTIVE SIMILARITY: MARKS APPLIED TO LOW VALUE GOODS ORDINARILY PURCHASED IN SUPERMARKETS: AIPO)

Gardenia Overseas Pte Ltd v. The Garden Co. Ltd (COMMON ELEMENT: GARDEN/ GARDENIA: LIKELIHOOD OF DECEPTION OR CONFUSION: AURAL AND VISUAL COMPARISONS: Fed. Ct)

Gatward's Application (APPLICATION FOR EXTENSION OF TIME TO LODGE NOTICE OF OPPOSITION: ERROR BY AGENT: Pat. Off.)

Glaxo Group Ltd v. Pathstream Ltd (LIKELIHOOD OF DECEPTION AND CONFUSION: INTERNATIONAL AND NON-PROPRIETARY NAMES: Pat. Off.)

Gordon & Rena Merchant Pty Ltd v. Barrymores Pty Ltd (EXTENSION OF TIME: EVIDENCE IN ANSWER: SPECIAL CIRCUMSTANCES: ONUS OF PROOF: AIPO)

Haddonstone Pty Ltd v. Haddonstone Ltd (ACCEPTANCE: PROPRIETORSHIP: MANUFACTURER OR DISTRIBUTOR: ESTOPPEL: ROLE OF REGISTRAR: DECEPTION OR CONFUSION: AIPO)

Halbach & Braun v. Polymaze Pty Ltd (APPLICATION FOR EXTENSION OF TIME TO SERVE EVIDENCE IN ANSWER TO OPPOSITION: AIPO)

Haralambides v. Pastrikos (LIKELIHOOD OF CONFUSION OR DECEPTION: Pat. Off.)

Hardings Manufacturers Pty Ltd's Application (WYANDRA GOLDEN CRUMPETS: DECEPTIVE SIMILARITY: Pat. Off.)

Hearst Corp. v. Pacific Dunlop Ltd (PROPRIETORSHIP: LIKELIHOOD OF DECEPTION OR CONFUSION: Pat. Off.)

Hermes Sweeteners Ltd v. Hermes (OPPONENT RELYING ON ITS OWN REGISTERED MARKS: SUBSTANTIALLY IDENTICAL OR DECEPTIVELY SIMILAR: SAME GOODS OR OF SIMILAR DESCRIPTION: USE LIKELY TO DECEIVE OR CAUSE CONFUSION: Pat. Off.)

Herron Pharmaceuticals Pty Ltd v. Sterling Winthrop Pty Ltd (APPLICATION TO REMOVE: PERSON AGGRIEVED: *Locus standii* BASED ON PRIOR REGISTERED MARKS: AIPO)

Holmes's Application (LIKELIHOOD OF DECEPTION OR CONFUSION: PERMACRAFT: NO EVIDENCE OF USE OF OPPONENT'S MARK: OPPONENT'S MARK COMMON TO TRADE: Pat. Off.)

ISS Management (Aust.) Pty Ltd v. Vulcan Australia Ltd (IDENTICAL MARKS: GOODS OF SAME DESCRIPTION: Pat. Off.)

Jamieson v. American Dairy Queen Corporation (PROPRIETORSHIP: Pat. Off.)

Jean Patou Parfumeur v. Crisena Corporation Pty Ltd (IDENTICAL MARK REGISTERED FOR GOODS OF SAME DESCRIPTION: WHETHER HONEST CONCURRENT USER: Pat. Off.)

Johnson & Johnson v. Boehringer Ingelheim KG (RESTRICTION OF STATEMENT OF GOODS: FURTHER DECISION: AIPO)

Johnson & Johnson v. Kalnin (EXISTING REGISTRATION BY OPPONENT: WHETHER LIKELIHOOD FOR DECEPTION OR CONFUSION: Fed. Ct)

Jonathan Sceats Design Pty Ltd's Application (OBJECTION TO ALLOWANCE OF EXTENSION OF TIME FOR SERVICE OF EVIDENCE IN SUPPORT OF OPPOSITION: Pat. Off.)

Joose Agencies Pty Ltd v. Maglificio Biellese Fratelli Fila SpA (LIKELIHOOD OF DECEPTION OR CONFUSION: MANNER OF USE: EVIDENCE OF USE: Pat. Off.)

K Mart Corporation v. A-Mart Allsports Pty Ltd (GOODS AND SERVICES: RETAILING: SUBSTANTIAL IDENTITY: DECEPTIVE SIMILARITY: USE: CONCURRENT USE: HONEST USE: Pat. Off.)

K Mart Corporation v. Artline Furnishers Supermarkets Pty Ltd (SUBSTANTIAL IDENTITY: DECEPTIVE SIMILARITY: USE: CONCURRENT USE: HONEST USE: CONDITION OF REGISTRATION: Pat. Off.)

K.T. Technology (S.) Pte Ltd v. Tomlin Holdings Pty Ltd (EXTENSION OF TIME: Pat. Off.)

Karu Pty Ltd v. Jose (APPEAL: GOODS IN DIFFERENT CLASSES: SUBSTANTIALLY IDENTICAL MARKS: Fed. Ct)

Keith Harris & Co. Ltd's Application (PROPRIETORSHIP: FIRST USE: USE LIKELY TO DECEIVE OR CAUSE CONFUSION: DESCRIPTIVE MARK: Pat. Off.)

Kirra Collectables Pty Ltd v. Pewter Products Pty Ltd (KIRRA: EARLIER REGISTRATION: WHETHER GOODS OF THE SAME DESCRIPTION: AIPO)

Koh Electronics Trading v. Libra Electronics Pty Ltd (PROPRIETORSHIP: FIRST USE: LIKELIHOOD OF DECEPTION OR CONFUSION: BLAMEWORTHY CONDUCT: IDENTICAL MARKS: COPYING OF OVERSEAS MARK: COPYRIGHT PROPRIETORSHIP ON GOODS OF SAME DESCRIPTION: AIPO)

Kronborg Isager v. Boboli International Inc. (USE OF A MARK: Pat. Off.)

Kyowa Hakko Kogyo Co. Ltd v. Schering Corporation (NON-USE: STATEMENT OF USER: SUBSTANTIALLY IDENTICAL: DECEPTIVELY SIMILAR: LIKELY TO DECEIVE OR CAUSE CONFUSION: Pat. Off.)

Legal & General Life of Australia Ltd v. Carlton-Jones & Associates Pty Ltd (PRIOR REGISTRATION REMOVED: DISCLAIMER: EFFECT: PROPRIETORSHIP: Pat. Off.)

Lind Engineering Pty Ltd v. Leeton Steel Works Pty Ltd (TIME LIMITS: EXTENSION: SUFFICIENCY OF REASON: Pat. Off.)

Little Tykes Co. v. Ciardullo (LITTLE TYKE/LITTLE TIKES: SUBSTANTIALLY IDENTICAL: DECEPTIVELY SIMILAR: GOODS OF THE SAME DESCRIPTION: CHARACTER MERCHANDISING: AIPO)

Logan v. Coulter (DECEPTIVE SIMILARITY: INTENTION TO USE: PRIOR USE: COPYRIGHT IN MARK: SUBSISTENCE: AIPO)

Lord Bloody Wog Rolo v. United Artists Corporation (APPLICATION FOR EXTENSION OF TIME: Pat. Off.)

Marks and Spencer PLC v. San Miguel Corporation (LIKELIHOOD OF DECEPTION OR CONFUSION WITH PRIOR REGISTERED MARK: ST MICHAEL/SAN MIGUEL: Pat. Off.)

Marston Fastener Corp.'s Application (RELEVANT PRIOR USE: DISTINCTIVENESS: Pat. Off.)

Martin Cellars Pty Ltd v. Kies Pty Ltd (PROPRIETORSHIP: LIKELIHOOD OF DECEPTION OR CONFUSION: AIPO)

Mayfair International Pty Ltd's Application (OPPOSITION WITHDRAWN: ADVERTISEMENT OF ACCEPTANCE BUT FAILURE TO REGISTER WITHIN PRESCRIBED TIME: EXTENSION OF TIME LIMIT: DISCRETION: AIPO)

MCT Unilabels SA v. Peter Katholos (DECEPTIVELY SIMILAR: SUBSTANTIALLY IDENTICAL: PROPRIETORSHIP: AIPO)

Meditex Ltd v. New Horizonz Pty Ltd (PROPRIETORSHIP: EXTENSION OF TIME: COSTS: AIPO)

Meldrum v. Grego (SUBSTANTIALLY IDENTICAL OR DECEPTIVELY SIMILAR: ESSENTIAL FEATURES: Pat. Off.)

Surf Shirt Designs Pty Ltd (PROPRIETORSHIP: USE LIKELY TO DECEIVE OR CAUSE CONFUSION: Pat. Off.)

Taiwan Yamani Inc. v. Giorgio Armani SpA (SUBSTANTIALLY IDENTICAL OR DECEPTIVELY SIMILAR MARKS: USE UNLIKELY TO CAUSE DECEPTION OR CONFUSION: VISUAL DIFFERENCES MORE IMPORTANT THAN AURAL SIMILARITY: Pat. Off.)

Tandy Corporation's Application (APPLICATION FOR EXTENSION OF TIME IN WHICH TO LODGE OPPOSITION: Pat. Off.)

Tattilo Editrice SpA v. Playboy Enterprises Inc. (WITHDRAWAL: COSTS: T.M.Reg.)

Tavefar Pty Ltd v. Life Savers (Australasia) Ltd (LIKELIHOOD OF DECEPTION OR CONFUSION: PROPRIETORSHIP: Pat. Off.)

Technicolor Inc. v. R. & C. Products Pty Ltd (PROPRIETORSHIP: PRIOR USE: DECEPTION AND CONFUSION: Pat. Off.)

Thermos Ltd v. Micropore International Ltd (ADAPTED TO DISTINGUISH: SUBSTANTIALLY IDENTICAL OR DECEPTIVELY SIMILAR MARKS: USE LIKELY TO DECEIVE OR CAUSE CONFUSION: Pat. Off.)

Titan Manufacturing Company Pty Ltd v. John Terence Coyne (Pat. Off.)

Tonka Corp. v. Chong (DECEPTIVE SIMILARITY: BLAMEWORTHY CONDUCT: AIPO)

Trepper v. Miss Selfridge Ltd (HONEST CONCURRENT USE: PERSON AGGRIEVED: ONUS: Pat. Off.)

Triple Three Leisure Ltd v. Turkovic (PROPRIETORSHIP: INHERENT DISTINCTIVENESS: USE OUTSIDE AUSTRALIA: AIPO)

Unidrive v. Dana Corp. (PROPRIETORSHIP: DECEPTION OR CONFUSION: AIPO)

Unilever Australia Ltd v. ABC Tissue Products Pty Ltd (IDENTICAL MARKING OTHER CLASS: LIKELIHOOD OF DECEPTION OR CONFUSION: AIPO)

Universal City Studios Inc. v. Frankenstein Pty Ltd (EVIDENCE-IN-SUPPORT: EXTENSION OF TIME: BURDEN OF PROOF: NEGOTIATIONS, MEANING OF: AIPO)

Untell Pty Ltd v. Manenti Holdings Pty Ltd (PROPRIETORSHIP, DISTINCTIVENESS: INHERENT ADAPTABILITY TO DISTINGUISH: ACCEPTANCE BASED ON EVIDENCE OF USE: Pat. Off.)

Upjohn Co. v. Schering Aktiengesellschaft (DECEPTIVE SIMILARITY: COMMON PREFIX: Fed. Ct)

Varma v. South Pacific Recordings Pty Ltd (ADJOURNMENT: CONCURRENT PROCEEDINGS IN FEDERAL COURT: Pat. Off.)

Virtual Reality and Reality v. W. Industries Ltd (EVIDENCE: EXTENSION OF TIME: PRACTICE: AIPO)

Visco Sport Ltd's Application (SORBOLITE: WHETHER CONFUSINGLY SIMILAR: IMPORTANCE OF FIRST SYLLABLE: EFFECT OF COMMON PARTS: Pat. Off.)

Warner-Lambert Co. v. Harel (PROPRIETORSHIP: DECEPTION OR CONFUSION: BLAMEWORTHY CONDUCT: AIPO)

Weller v. TGI Friday's Application (OPPOSITION: OPPONENT SEEKING SPECIAL LEAVE TO ADDUCE FURTHER EVIDENCE: AIPO)

Wilder Days Pty Ltd v. Karhugh Properties Ltd (INTENTION TO USE: DECEPTIVE SIMILARITY: AIPO)

Origin

American Chemical Society's Application (DISTINCTIVE OF ORIGIN OF USE TO RELEVANT SECTION OF COMMUNITY: Pat. Off.)

Pumps 'N' Pipes Pty Ltd's Application (OBJECTIONS TO REGISTRATION: INDICATION OF ORIGIN: Pat. Off.)

Gencorp's Application (TRADEMARK: NON-DISTINCTIVE: DECEPTION AND CONFUSION: AIPO)

Johnson (S.C.) & Son Inc.'s Application (DESCRIPTIVE: TECHNICAL MEANING NOT RELEVANT: DIRECT REFERENCE TO GOODS: EVIDENCE OF USE NOT PERSUASIVE: NOT REGISTRABLE IN PART A OR PART B OF THE REGISTER: Pat. Off.)

McGloin (J.) Pty Ltd's Application (DESCRIPTIVE MARK: EVIDENCE OF USE: REGISTRABILITY IN PART B: Pat. Off.)

O'Brien and Associates v. Orton & Burns Engineering Pty Ltd (ACCEPTANCE FOR PART B REGISTRATION: OPPOSITION: EVIDENCE: DISTINCTIVENESS: PROPRIETORSHIP: Pat. Off.)

Plume Clothing Pty Ltd & Bossnac (Aust.) Pty Ltd's Application (APPLICATION: INHERENT ADAPTABILITY TO DISTINGUISH: DISTINCTIVENESS IN FACT: DESCRIPTIVE MARK: Pat. Off.)

Pumps 'N' Pipes Pty Ltd's Application (OBJECTIONS TO REGISTRATION: DISTINCTIVENESS: INDICATION OF ORIGIN: RETAILER SEEKING REGISTRATION IN RESPECT OF GOODS SOLD: REGISTRATION IN PART B REFUSED: Pat. Off.)

Remington Products Inc.'s Application (ACCEPTANCE IN PART B: WHETHER MARK ACCEPTED IN ERROR: OVERLOOKING OF EARLIER APPARENTLY CONFLICTING DECISION: Pat. Off.)

Sabra International Pty Ltd's Application (MARK DIRECTLY DESCRIPTIVE: LACK OF INHERENT DISTINCTIVENESS: MARK NOT REGISTRABLE IN PART A OR PART B OF REGISTER: INSUFFICIENT EVIDENCE: Pat. Off.)

Spray Booths Australia Pty Ltd's Application (MARKS DIRECTLY DESCRIPTIVE: LACK OF INHERENT DISTINCTIVENESS: Pat. Off.)

Waterbed Association of Retailers & Manufacturers's Application (COMPOSITE MARK: ACRONYM: DESCRIPTIVE: INHERENT ADAPTABILITY TO DISTINGUISH: DISCLAIMER: Pat. Off.)

Person Aggrieved

Anstoetz's (Jab Josef's) Application (REMOVAL: NON-USE: USE BY DISTRIBUTOR: Pat. Off.)

Fawns & McAllan Pty Ltd v. Burns-Biotec Laboratories Inc. (OPPOSITION: REMOVAL FOR NON-USE: T.M.Reg.)

Gordon & Rena Merchant Pty Ltd v. Ocky Docket (Aust.) Pty Ltd (REMOVAL: OPPOSITION: NON-USE: ONUS: Pat. Off.)

Herron Pharmaceuticals Pty Ltd v. Sterling Winthrop Pty Ltd (APPLICATION TO REMOVE: OPPOSITION: *Locus standii* BASED ON PRIOR REGISTERED MARKS: AIPO)

Kraft General Foods Inc. v. Gaines Pet Foods Corp. (REMOVAL FROM REGISTER: NON-USE: ONUS OF PROOF: EFFECT OF CONTRACTUAL TERMS: DISCRETION OF REGISTRAR: DEROGATION FROM GRANT: AIPO: Fed. Ct)

Prosimmon Golf (Aust.) Pty Ltd v. Dunlop Australia Ltd (REMOVAL: NON-USE: EVIDENCE: ADEQUACY: Pat. Off.)

Ritz Hotel Ltd v. Charles of The Ritz Ltd (EXPUNGEMENT PROCEEDINGS: PRESCRIPTIVE VALIDITY: ENTRIES WRONGLY MADE IN REGISTER: ENTRIES WRONGLY REMAINING IN REGISTER: S.C.(NSW))

Sasdor Pty Ltd v. Atomic Skifabrik Alois Rohrmoser (REMOVAL FOR NON-USE: OPPOSITION: COSTS: PART SUCCESS: Pat. Off.)

Sew Hoy & Sons Ltd v. Skill Print Pty Ltd (TRADE MARKS: APPLICATION FOR REMOVAL: OPPOSITION: PRIMA FACIE CASE OF NON-USE: SUFFICIENCY OF EVIDENCE: Pat. Off.)

Trepper v. Miss Selfridge Ltd (APPLICATIONS: OPPOSITION: HONEST CONCURRENT USE: ONUS: EVIDENCE: Pat. Off.)

Phonetic Comparison or Similarity

Decor Corporation Pty Ltd v. Deeko Australia Pty Ltd (OPPOSITION: WHETHER MARKS SUBSTANTIALLY IDENTICAL OR DECEPTIVELY SIMILAR: CIRCUMSTANCES OF TRADE: LESS WEIGHT ON PHONETIC COMPARISON: Pat. Off.)

Retec Ltd's Application (SUBSTANTIALLY IDENTICAL WITH OR DECEPTIVELY SIMILAR TO: RESTRICTED CLASS OF PURCHASERS: Pat. Off.)

Practice

Acceptance in error

Jacuzzi Inc.'s Application (WITHDRAWAL OF ACCEPTANCE FOR REGISTRATION: CONFLICT WITH EARLIER APPLICATION: RELEVANCE OF VALIDITY OF AMENDMENT OF CLASS OF GOODS IN RESPECT OF WHICH CITED MARK WAS FILED: Pat. Off.)

Kikken Sohansha KK's Application (DISCOVERY OF MARK AS BOTANICAL TERM SUBSEQUENT TO ACCEPTANCE: ACCEPTANCE WITHDRAWN: AIPO)

Remington Products Inc.'s Application (ACCEPTANCE IN PART B: Pat. Off.)

Shop-Vac Corporation's Application (WITHDRAWAL OF ACCEPTANCE FOR REGISTRATION: EXAMINER'S IGNORANCE OF RELEVANT DICTIONARY DEFINITION: Pat. Off.)

Address for service

Australian Telecommunication Corporation v. Centec International Corp. Pty Ltd (OPPOSITION: SERVICE OF EVIDENCE: Pat. Off.)

Anton Piller order

Golf Lynx v. Golf Scene Pty Ltd (INFRINGEMENT: PASSING OFF: DAMAGE: *Ex parte* order: S.C.(NSW))

Appeal

Advanced Hair Studio of America Pty Ltd v. Registrar of Trade Marks (DECISION OF REGISTRAR: S.C.(Vic.))

Carnival Cruise Lines Inc. v. Sitmar Cruises Ltd (SERVICE MARKS: OPPOSITION: USE IN COURSE OF TRADE: FUN SHIP: WHETHER SUFFICIENT IDENTITY BETWEEN MARKS AND SERVICES: Fed. Ct)

Foodland Associated Ltd v. John Weeks Pty Ltd (APPEAL FROM REGISTRAR FOLLOWING COMMENCEMENT OF NEW STATUTE: TRANSITIONAL PROVISIONS: Pat. Off.)

McDonald's Corporation v. Coffee Hut Stores Ltd (OBJECTION TO INCORRECT CORPORATE NAME ON APPLICATION: Fed. Ct)

Ritz Hotel Ltd v. Parfums Yves Saint Laurent Ltd (ORDERS SERVED ON REGISTRAR: SUBSEQUENT APPEAL: Fed. Ct)

Seven-Up Co. v. Bubble Up Co. Ltd (DECISION OF REGISTRAR: S.C.(Vic.))

Attorney or agent

Dimtsis v. Agricultural Dairy Industry Authority of Epirus, Dodoni SA (EXTENSION OF TIME TO FILE EVIDENCE: OBJECTION: SPECIAL CIRCUMSTANCES: ERRORS OR OMISSIONS BY AGENTS OF PARTIES: Pat. Off.)

Gatward's Application (EXTENSION OF TIME TO LODGE NOTICE OF OPPOSITION: OUTSIDE SCOPE OF SECTION 49(1) AND NOT AUTHORISED BY SECTION 131: FAILURE DUE TO ERROR BY AGENT: Pat. Off.)

Murdock Overseas Corporation v. Saramar Corporation (APPLICATION OUT OF-TIME FOR EXTENSION OF TIME FOR FILING EVIDENCE: OMISSION BY ATTORNEY: PUBLIC POLICY: Pat. Off.)

Consistency by registrar

Toro Company's Applications (OBJECTION: DESCRIPTIVE MARK: SURVEY EVIDENCE: AIPO)

Contempt

Australian Design Council v. Peter Borello (CONTINUING USE OF TRADE MARK IN BREACH OF INJUNCTION: DELIBERATE BREACH: PUBLIC INTEREST FACTORS: FINE: Fed. Ct)

Windsurfing International Inc. v. Sailboards Australia Pty Ltd (BREACH OF UNDERTAKING: ONUS OF PROOF: ASSESSMENT OF FINE: Fed. Ct)

Correction of register

Vulcan-Hart Corporation v. Vulcan Australia Ltd (MISNOMER IN ORIGINAL APPLICATION: AIPO)

Costs

Black & Decker Corporation v. Akarana Abrasive Industries Ltd (EXTENSION OF TIME TO FILE EVIDENCE IN SUPPORT: INCONVENIENCE OF APPLICANT: Pat. Off.)

Eden Technology Pty Ltd v. Intel Corp. (WITHDRAWAL OF TRADE MARK APPLICATION: Pat. Off.)

First Tiffany Holdings Pty Ltd v. Tiffany and Company (OPPOSITION: AMENDMENT TO SPECIFICATION OF GOODS: Pat. Off.)

Foodland Associated Ltd v. John Weeks Pty Ltd (EXTENSION OF TIME LIMITS FOR SERVICE OF EVIDENCE: HEARING FEES: REFUND: Pat. Off.)

Hermes Sweeteners Ltd v. Hermes (APPLICATION: FAILED OPPOSITION: Pat. Off.)

Meditex Ltd v. New Horizonz Pty Ltd (OPPOSITION: PROPRIETORSHIP: EXTENSION OF TIME: AIPO)

Nicholas Saba Sportswear Pty Ltd v. Daryl K. Linane (FAILURE TO PROCEED WITH OPPOSITION: Pat. Off.)

R. & C. Products Pty Ltd v. Bathox Bathsalts Pty Ltd (SUCCESSFUL OPPOSITION: AWARD OF COSTS: Pat. Off.)

Sasdor Pty Ltd v. Atomic Skifabrik Alois Rohrmoser (REMOVAL FOR NON-USE: OPPOSITION: PERSON AGGRIEVED: PART SUCCESS: Pat. Off.)

Société des Produits Nestlé SA v. Penaten Pharmazeutische Fabrik Dr Med Rieze & Co. GmbH (EXTENSION OF TIME LIMIT TO LODGE EVIDENCE: Pat. Off.)

Tattilo Editrice SpA v. Playboy Enterprises Inc. (OPPOSITION: WITHDRAWAL: BILL OF COSTS: HEARING FEE: T.M.Reg.)

Damages

Hoogerdyk v. Condon (ASSESSMENT: H.C.)

Discretion

Briggs v. Jaden Marketing Pty Ltd (APPLICATION TO REMOVE: NON-USE: UNAUTHORISED USE: AIPO)

Cassini v. Golden Era Shirt Co. Pty Ltd (APPLICATION TO REMOVE: NON-USE: INTENTION TO USE: S.C.(NSW))

Kraft General Foods Inc. v. Gaines Pet Foods Corp. (REMOVAL FROM REGISTER: NON-USE: ONUS OF PROOF: EFFECT OF CONTRACTUAL TERMS: PERSON AGGRIEVED: AIPO)

Mayfair International Pty Ltd's Application (APPLICATION: OPPOSITION WITHDRAWN: ADVERTISEMENT OF ACCEPTANCE BUT FAILURE TO REGISTER WITHIN PRESCRIBED TIME: EXTENSION OF TIME LIMIT: AIPO)

Murray Goulburn Co-operative Company Ltd v. New South Wales Dairy Corporation (APPLICATION FOR REMOVAL FOR NON-USE: EXERCISE OF DISCRETION TO EXPUNGE BALANCE OF A MARK WHERE MARK USED ONLY IN RELATION TO TWO TYPES OF GOODS: Fed. Ct)

Murray Goulburn Co-operative Company Ltd v. New South Wales Dairy Corporation (REMOVAL: NON-USE: PREVIOUS EXPUNGEMENT OF PART OF GOODS ORDER: WHETHER COURT SHOULD EXERCISE ITS DISCRETION TO EXPUNGE BALANCE OF REGISTRATION: Fed. Ct)

Pennys Pty Ltd's Application (ACCEPTANCE IN ERROR: GEOGRAPHICAL NAME: STRATHSPEY: AIPO)

Reich v. Country Life Bakeries Pty Ltd (DIVISIONAL APPLICATION: REGISTRAR'S DISCRETION: AIPO)

Sartek Pty Ltd's Application (PROPOSED WITHDRAWAL OF ACCEPTANCE: PRIOR APPLICATION NOT CITED BEFORE ACCEPTANCE: EXERCISE OF DISCRETION: Pat. Off.)

Sceats v. Jonathan Sceats Design Pty Ltd (REMOVAL FOR NON-USE: EXERCISE OF DISCRETION: Fed. Ct)

Timberland Co. v. Speedo Knitting Mills Pty Ltd (NON-USE: APPLICATION TO REMOVE: OPPOSITION: DISCRETION OF REGISTRAR: Pat. Ct)

Trepper v. Miss Selfridge Ltd (APPLICATION: OPPOSITION: PERSON AGGRIEVED: ONUS: EVIDENCE: WHETHER SPECIAL CIRCUMSTANCES: Pat. Off.)

Errors or omissions. See also under Acceptance in error

Dimtsis v. Agricultural Dairy Industry Authority of Epirus, Dodoni SA (EXTENSION OF TIME TO FILE EVIDENCE: OBJECTION: SPECIAL CIRCUMSTANCES: ERRORS OR OMISSIONS BY AGENTS OF PARTIES: Pat. Off.)

Gatward's Application (EXTENSION OF TIME TO LODGE NOTICE OF OPPOSITION: FAILURE DUE TO ERROR BY AGENT: Pat. Off.)

Metropolitan Dairies Pty Ltd v. Pura Natural Spring Waters Pty Ltd (REGISTRATION: RENEWAL: LAPSED REGISTRATION: EXTENSION OF TIME: ERROR OR OMISSION: NATURAL JUSTICE: *Locus standi*: PUBLIC POLICY: Pat. Off.)

Stratco Metal Pty Ltd's Application (OPPOSITION: ERROR IN NOTICE: MISDESCRIPTION OF OPPONENT: Pat. Off.)

Uniglobe Holdings Pty Ltd v. Uniglobe Travel (International) Inc. (CLERICAL ERROR: APPLICATION TO AMEND FORM: OBVIOUS MISTAKE: Pat. Off.)

Estoppel

Cole v. Australian Char Pty Ltd (OPPOSITION: ABANDONMENT: INTENTION TO USE: LIKELIHOOD OF DECEPTION OR CONFUSION: BLAMEWORTHY CONDUCT: AIPO)

Crooks Michell Peacock Pty Ltd v. Kaiser (OPPOSITION: PROPRIETORSHIP: DISTINCTIVENESS: DECEPTION AND CONFUSION: HONEST ADOPTION OF MARK: GOOD FAITH: AIPO)

Haddonstone Pty Ltd v. Haddonstone Ltd (ACCEPTANCE: OPPOSITION: PROPRIETORSHIP: MANUFACTURER OR DISTRIBUTOR: ROLE OF REGISTRAR: AIPO)

Evidence. See also under Extension of time to file evidence and *Evidence of use*

Australian Bacon Ltd v. Mulfric Foods Pty Ltd (APPLICATION FOR REMOVAL: OPPOSITION: NON-USE: Pat. Off.)

Australian Telecommunication Corporation v. Centec International Corp. Pty Ltd (OPPOSITION: ADDRESS FOR SERVICE: SERVICE OF EVIDENCE: Pat. Off.)

Bee Tek (Import & Export) Pte Ltd v. Kenner Parker Toys Inc. (APPLICATION FOR EXTENSION OF TIME TO FILE EVIDENCE IN REPLY: PUBLIC INTEREST: WHETHER INDULGENCES ALREADY GIVEN EXCESSIVE: Pat. Off.)

Black & Decker Corporation v. Akarana Abrasive Industries Ltd (APPLICATION FOR EXTENSION OF TIME TO FILE EVIDENCE-IN-SUPPORT: USUAL TIME REQUIRED FOR PREPARATION OF EVIDENCE: INCONVENIENCE OF APPLICANT: PUBLIC INTEREST: COSTS: Pat. Off.)

Bristol-Myers Co.'s Application (DISTINCTIVENESS: ACQUIRED DISTINCTIVENESS: ADAPTED TO DISTINGUISH: GEOGRAPHIC NAME: Pat. Off.)

Cafe Do Brasil SpA v. Scrava Pty Ltd (REMOVAL: NON-USE: PRIMA FACIE CASE: SPECIAL CIRCUMSTANCES: Pat. Off.)

D'Urban Inc. v. Canpio Pty Ltd (EFFECTIVE SERVICE: EVIDENCE SERVED OUT OF TIME: FAILURE TO SEEK EXTENSION OF TIME: SPECIAL CIRCUMSTANCES: Pat. Off.)

Decina Bathroomware Pty Ltd's Application (APPLICATION: DISTINCTIVENESS: EVIDENCE NECESSARY: INHERENTLY ADAPTED TO DISTINGUISH: Pat. Off.)

Decor Corporation Pty Ltd v. Deeko Australia Pty Ltd (WHETHER INTENTION TO USE FOR ALL GOODS SPECIFIED: ABSENCE OF CLEAR EVIDENCE TO THE CONTRARY: Pat. Off.)

Dimtsis v. Agricultural Dairy Industry Authority of Epirus, Dodoni SA (APPLICATION FOR EXTENSION OF TIME TO FILE EVIDENCE: OBJECTION TO: SPECIAL CIRCUMSTANCES CONSTITUTED BY ERRORS OR OMISSIONS BY AGENTS OF PARTIES: Pat. Off.)

Effem Foods Pty Ltd v. Design Concepts Pty Ltd (OPPOSITION: APPLICATION TO EXTEND TIME TO FILE EVIDENCE-IN-SUPPORT OF OPPOSITION: EXTENSION OPPOSED: INTENTION TO OPPOSE A SECOND APPLICATION FOR REGISTRATION INSUFFICIENT GROUND TO JUSTIFY FURTHER EXTENSIONS: Pat. Off.)

Figgins Holdings Pty Ltd v. Parfums Christian Dior (EXTENSION OF TIME FOR FILING EVIDENCE: Pat. Off.)

Flagstaff Investments Pty Ltd v. Guess? Inc. (USE: FOREIGN PUBLICATIONS ADVERTISING: DECEPTION OR CONFUSION: ABSENCE OF EVIDENCE: Pat. Off.)

Foodland Associated Ltd v. John Weeks Pty Ltd (EVIDENCE: SERVICE: EXTENSION OF TIME LIMITS: Pat. Off.)

Herron Pharmaceuticals Pty Ltd v. Sterling Winthrop Pty Ltd (ADMISSION OF FURTHER EVIDENCE: AIPO)

International Computers Ltd's Application (TRADE MARK: APPLICATION: DRS: DISTINCTIVENESS: Pat. Off.)

Johnson & Johnson Australia Pty Ltd v. Sterling Pharmaceuticals Pty Ltd (SURVEY EVIDENCE: Fed. Ct)

Jonathan Sceats Design Pty Ltd's Application (OBJECTION TO ALLOWANCE OF EXTENSION OF TIME FOR SERVICE OF EVIDENCE IN SUPPORT OF OPPOSITION: Pat. Off.)

Liederman's Application (EVIDENCE OF OVERSEAS DISTINCTIVENESS: Pat. Off.)

Matsushita Electric Industrial Co. Ltd's Application (EVIDENCE OF SALES FIGURES: Pat. Off.)

Murdock Overseas Corporation v. Saramar Corporation (APPLICATION OUT OF TIME FOR EXTENSION OF TIME FOR FILING EVIDENCE: OMISSION BY ATTORNEY: PUBLIC POLICY: Pat. Off.)

O'Brien and Associates v. Orton & Burns Engineering Pty Ltd (PART B REGISTRATION: OPPOSITION: Pat. Off.)

Orton & Burns Engineering Pty Ltd v. John L. O'Brien and Associates (APPLICATION FOR SPECIAL LEAVE TO ADDUCE FURTHER EVIDENCE: MEANING OF FURTHER EVIDENCE: UNAVAILABLE TO APPLICANT WHO HAS FILED NO EVIDENCE: Pat. Off.)

Pacific Dunlop Ltd v. Fruit of the Loom Inc. (APPLICATION FOR EXTENSION OF TIME TO FILE EVIDENCE IN ANSWER: TIME NEEDED TO GATHER EVIDENCE ON USE: Pat. Off.)

Paragini Footwear Pty Ltd v. Paragon Shoes Pty Ltd (APPLICATION FOR LEAVE TO LODGE FURTHER EVIDENCE: Pat. Off.)

Pelikan International Handelsgesellschaft mbH & Co. KG v. Lifinia Pty Ltd (SUBSTANTIALLY IDENTICAL: AIPO)

Polo Textile Industries Pty Ltd v. Domestic Textile Corporation Pty Ltd (SUFFICIENCY OF USE: GOODS OF THE SAME DESCRIPTION: Fed. Ct)

Prosimmon Golf (Aust.) Pty Ltd v. Dunlop Australia Ltd (PERSON AGGRIEVED: ADEQUACY: Pat. Off.)

Rollbits Pty Ltd v. Rowntree Mackintosh PLC (SERVICE OF DOCUMENTS: EXTENSION OF TIME: PUBLIC INTEREST: PRESENTATION OF EVIDENCE AND ARGUMENTS: Pat. Off.)

Rowntree PLC v. Rollbits Pty Ltd (EVIDENCE OF REPUTATION: BURDEN OF PROOF: S.C.(NSW))

Royale & Co. (Aust.) Pty Ltd v. Maxims Ltd (EXTENSION OF TIME LIMITS: Pat. Off.)

Sabra International Pty Ltd's Application (SUFFICIENCY: Pat. Off.)

Selskar Pty Ltd's Application (HONEST CONCURRENT USE: CONFLICTING EVIDENCE: AIPO)

Sew Hoy & Sons Ltd v. Skill Print Pty Ltd (PERSON AGGRIEVED: PRIMA FACIE CASE OF NON-USE: SUFFICIENCY OF EVIDENCE: Pat. Off.)

Small's Application (NO EVIDENCE TO SHOW ACQUIRED DISTINCTIVENESS: Pat. Off.)

Société des Produits Nestlé SA v. Penaten Pharmazeutische Fabrik Dr Med Rieze & Co. GmbH (EXTENSION OF TIME LIMIT TO LODGE EVIDENCE: Pat. Off.)

Sterling Pharmaceuticals Pty Ltd v. Johnson & Johnson Australia Pty Ltd (ADMISSIBILITY AND RELEVANCE OF EVIDENCE: HEARSAY EVIDENCE: SURVEY EVIDENCE OF PUBLIC AS TO KNOWLEDGE AND USE OF TRADE MARK: ADMISSIBILITY OF EVIDENCE OF MEANINGS OF WORDS TO AID STATUTORY CONSTRUCTION AND FOR OTHER PURPOSES: INADMISSIBILITY OF EVIDENCE AS TO ULTIMATE ISSUE: Fed. Ct)

Studio SrL v. Buying Systems (Aust.) Pty Ltd (FURTHER EVIDENCE: SPECIAL LEAVE: Pat. Off.)

Trepper v. Miss Selfridge Ltd (PERSON AGGRIEVED: ONUS: SPECIAL CIRCUMSTANCES: Pat. Off.)

Universal City Studios Inc. v. Frankenstein Pty Ltd (OPPOSITION: EVIDENCE IN SUPPORT: AIPO)

Virtual Reality and Reality v. W. Industries Ltd (OPPOSITION: AIPO)

Weller v. TGI Friday's Application (OPPOSITION: OPPONENT SEEKING SPECIAL LEAVE TO ADDUCE FURTHER EVIDENCE: AIPO)

Evidence of use and *Evidence of non-use*

Advanced Hair Studio of America Pty Ltd v. Registrar of Trade Marks (RELATIONSHIP BETWEEN THE MARK AND THE CHARACTER OR QUALITY OF THE SERVICES: INVENTED WORD: INHERENTLY DISTINCTIVE: S.C.(Vic.))

American Chemical Society's Application (EVIDENCE OF LONG USE: DISTINCTIVE OF ORIGIN OF USE TO RELEVANT SECTION OF COMMUNITY: Pat. Off.)

925

Ex parte order

Golf Lynx v. Golf Scene Pty Ltd (INFRINGEMENT: PASSING OFF: ANTON PILLER ORDER: S.C.(NSW))

Extension of time

Ampex Corp. v. Amper SA (OPPOSITION: EXTENSION OF TIME TO SERVE EVIDENCE: SETTLEMENT NEGOTIATIONS: PUBLIC INTEREST: AIPO)

Atomic Skifabrik Alois Rohrmoser v. Sasdor Pty Ltd (LODGING NOTICE OF OPPOSITION: Pat. Off.)

Atomic Skifabrik Alois Rohmoser v. Registrar of Trade Marks (PERIOD FOR OPPOSITION: Fed. Ct)

Australian Broadcasting Corporation's Application (FILING NOTICE OF OPPOSITION: INCORRECT REASONS: SECOND APPLICATION FILED: WHETHER AMENDMENT OR SUBSTITUTION NECESSARY: MATERIAL SUFFICIENT TO DISCHARGE ONUS: PUBLIC INTEREST: Pat. Off.)

Australian Olympic Committee Inc. v. Brennan (OPPOSITION: APPLICATION FOR EXTENSION OF TIME FOR SERVICE OF EVIDENCE: FACTORS TO BE CONSIDERED: AIPO)

AWA Ltd v. Future Software Pty Ltd (OPPOSITION: APPLICATION WITHIN TIME PRESCRIBED OPPOSED: PUBLIC INTEREST: Pat. Off.)

Bee Tek (Import & Export) Pte Ltd v. Kenner Parker Toys Inc. (FILING EVIDENCE IN REPLY: PUBLIC INTEREST: WHETHER INDULGENCES ALREADY GIVEN EXCESSIVE: Pat. Off.)

Bentley Lingerie Inc. v. Greta Lingerie (Aust.) Limited (OPPOSITION: LATE APPLICATION FOR EXTENSION OF TIME TO FILE EVIDENCE: SPECIAL CIRCUMSTANCES: AIPO)

Black & Decker Corporation v. Akarana Abrasive Industries Ltd (FILING EVIDENCE IN SUPPORT: USUAL TIME REQUIRED FOR PREPARATION OF EVIDENCE: INCONVENIENCE OF APPLICANT: PUBLIC INTEREST: Pat. Off.)

Branov v. Sleep Better Bedding Mfg Pty Ltd (EXTENSION OF TIME TO LODGE OPPOSITION: AIPO)

Bundy American Corp. v. Rent-A-Wreck (Vic.) Pty Ltd (INTER-PARTY NEGOTIATION: PUBLIC INTEREST: Pat. Off.)

Carlton & United Breweries Ltd v. Miller Brewing Co. (OPPOSITION: REASONS: Pat. Off.)

D'Urban Inc. v. Canpio Pty Ltd (EVIDENCE SERVED OUT OF TIME: FAILURE TO SEEK EXTENSION OF TIME: SPECIAL CIRCUMSTANCES: Pat. Off.)

Dimtsis v. Agricultural Dairy Industry Authority of Epirus, Dodoni SA (FILING EVIDENCE: OBJECTION TO: SPECIAL CIRCUMSTANCES CONSTITUTED BY ERRORS OR OMISSIONS BY AGENTS OF PARTIES: Pat. Off.)

Effem Foods Pty Ltd v. Design Concepts Pty Ltd (FILING EVIDENCE-IN-SUPPORT OF OPPOSITION: EXTENSION OPPOSED: INTENTION TO OPPOSE A SECOND APPLICATION FOR REGISTRATION INSUFFICIENT GROUND TO JUSTIFY FURTHER EXTENSIONS: Pat. Off.)

Esselte Letraset Ltd's Application (OPPOSITION: CIRCUMSTANCES BEYOND CONTROL: Pat. Off.)

Farchione & Scrimizzi's Application (NON-PAYMENT OF REGISTRATION FEE: UNDUE DELAY: AIPO)

Figgins Holdings Pty Ltd v. Parfums Christian Dior (FILING EVIDENCE: Pat. Off.)

Food Marketers Pty Ltd v. Maconochie Seafoods Ltd (LODGING NOTICE OF OPPOSITION: SPECIAL CIRCUMSTANCES: PUBLIC INTEREST: Pat. Off.)

Foodland Associated Ltd v. John Weeks Pty Ltd (SERVICE OF EVIDENCE: Pat. Off.)
Gatward's Application (LODGING NOTICE OF OPPOSITION: FAILURE DUE TO ERROR BY AGENT, NOT BY REASON OF CIRCUMSTANCES BEYOND THE CONTROL OF THE PERSON CONCERNED: Pat. Off.)
Gordon & Rena Merchant Pty Ltd v. Barrymores Pty Ltd (OPPOSITION: EXTENSION OF TIME: EVIDENCE IN ANSWER: SPECIAL CIRCUMSTANCES: ONUS OF PROOF: AIPO)
Halbach & Braun v. Polymaze Pty Ltd (EXTENSION OF TIME TO SERVE EVIDENCE IN ANSWER TO OPPOSITION: AIPO)
Jonathan Sceats Design Pty Ltd's Application (OBJECTION TO ALLOWANCE OF EXTENSION OF TIME FOR SERVICE OF EVIDENCE IN SUPPORT OF OPPOSITION: Pat. Off.)
K.T. Technology (S.) Pte Ltd v. Tomlin Holdings Pty Ltd (OPPOSITION: Pat. Off.)
Lind Engineering Pty Ltd v. Leeton Steel Works Pty Ltd (OPPOSITION: SUFFICIENCY OF REASON: Pat. Off.)
Lord Bloody Wog Rolo v. United Artists Corporation (OPPOSITION: Pat. Off.)
Lyons v. Registrar of Trade Marks (APPLICATION: Fed. Ct)
Mayfair International Pty Ltd's Application (APPLICATION: OPPOSITION WITHDRAWN: ADVERTISEMENT OF ACCEPTANCE BUT FAILURE TO REGISTER WITHIN PRESCRIBED TIME: DISCRETION: AIPO)
Meditex Ltd v. New Horizonz Pty Ltd (OPPOSITION: AIPO)
Metropolitan Dairies Pty Ltd v. Pura Natural Spring Waters Pty Ltd (TRADE MARKS: REGISTRATION: RENEWAL: LAPSED REGISTRATION: EXTENSION OF TIME: ERROR OR OMISSION: NATURAL JUSTICE: *Locus standii*: PUBLIC POLICY: Pat. Off.)
Murdock Overseas Corporation v. Saramar Corporation (APPLICATION OUT OF TIME FOR EXTENSION OF TIME FOR FILING EVIDENCE: OMISSION BY ATTORNEY: PUBLIC POLICY: Pat. Off.)
Pacific Dunlop Ltd v. Fruit of the Loom Inc. (OPPOSITION TO APPLICATION FOR REMOVAL: FILING EVIDENCE-IN-ANSWER: TIME NEEDED TO GATHER EVIDENCE ON USE: PUBLIC INTEREST: Pat. Off.)
Playground Supplies Pty Ltd's Application (OPPOSITION: PUBLIC INTEREST: Pat. Off.)
Ritz Hotel London Ltd's Application (OPPOSITION: NOTICE: Pat. Off.)
Rohrmoser v. Registrar of Trade Marks (OPPOSITION: Fed. Ct)
Rollbits Pty Ltd v. Rowntree Mackintosh PLC (SERVICE OF DOCUMENTS: PUBLIC INTEREST: PRESENTATION OF EVIDENCE AND ARGUMENTS: Pat. Off.)
Royale & Co. (Aust.) Pty Ltd v. Maxims Ltd (EXPUNGEMENT FOR NON-USE: EVIDENCE: Pat. Off.)
Société des Produits Nestlé SA v. Penaten Pharmazeutische Fabrik Dr Med Rieze & Co. GmbH (LODGING EVIDENCE: Pat. Off.)
Stafford-Miller Ltd v. Jean Patou Parfumeur (LODGING NOTICE OF OPPOSITION: Pat. Off.)
Tandy Corporation's Application (OPPOSITION: Pat. Off.)
Universal City Studios Inc. v. Frankenstein Pty Ltd (OPPOSITION: EVIDENCE IN SUPPORT: AIPO)
Virtual Reality and Reality v. W. Industries Ltd (OPPOSITION: EVIDENCE: AIPO)

Hearing fees

Foodland Associated Ltd v. John Weeks Pty Ltd (REFUND: STATUTORY PROVISIONS: Pat. Off.)
Tattilo Editrice SpA v. Playboy Enterprises Inc. (OPPOSITION: WITHDRAWAL: T.M.Reg.)

Injunction

Australian Design Council v. Peter Borello (INFRINGEMENT: CONTEMPT: FALSE REPRESENTATION: CONDUCT: CONTINUING USE OF TRADE MARK IN BREACH OF INJUNCTION: DELIBERATE BREACH: PUBLIC INTEREST FACTORS: HONESTY IN ADVERTISING: FINE: Fed. Ct)

Hogan v. Koala Dundee Pty Ltd (MERCHANDISING RIGHTS: ASSIGNMENT OF RIGHT TO USE IMAGE: LOSS NECESSARY TO FOUND INJUNCTION: FORM OF INJUNCTION: DAMAGES: WHETHER PROOF OF FRAUD NECESSARY: Fed. Ct)

Interlocutory injunction—adequacy of damages

Digby International (Australia) Pty Ltd v. Beyond Imagination Pty Ltd (INFRINGEMENT: EXTREME/POWERADE EXTREMISTS: SERIOUS QUESTION TO BE TRIED: BALANCE OF CONVENIENCE: Fed. Ct)

Interlocutory injunction—balance of convenience

Crusta Fruit Juices Pty Ltd v. Cadbury Schweppes Pty Ltd (INFRINGEMENT: CRESTA/CRUSTA: IMPERFECT RECOLLECTION: Fed. Ct)

Digby International (Australia) Pty Ltd v. Beyond Imagination Pty Ltd (INFRINGEMENT: EXTREME/POWERADE EXTREMISTS: SERIOUS QUESTION TO BE TRIED: Fed. Ct)

Miniskips Ltd v. Sheltan Pty Ltd (SERIOUS QUESTION TO BE TRIED: Fed. Ct)

Interlocutory injunction—serious question to be tried

Digby International (Australia) Pty Ltd v. Beyond Imagination Pty Ltd (INFRINGEMENT: EXTREME/POWERADE EXTREMISTS: BALANCE OF CONVENIENCE: Fed. Ct)

Miniskips Ltd v. Sheltan Pty Ltd (BALANCE OF CONVENIENCE: Fed. Ct)

Jurisdiction

Browne v. S. Smith & Son Pty Ltd (INFRINGEMENT: REMOVAL FOR NON-USE: JURISDICTION OF FEDERAL COURT: Fed. Ct)

Figgins Holdings Pty Ltd v. Registrar of Trade Marks (ASSIGNMENT OF APPLICATION: REGISTRATION OF PROPRIETORSHIP: Fed. Ct)

John Weeks Pty Ltd v. Foodland Associated Ltd (REGISTRATION: RECTIFICATION: NON-USE: Fed. Ct)

McDonald's Corporation v. Coffee Hut Stores Ltd (APPEAL: OBJECTION TO INCORRECT CORPORATE NAME ON APPLICATION: SURNAME: FAMILY OF MARKS: Fed. Ct)

Oehlschlager's Opposition (REMOVAL: USE ON INVOICES AND BUSINESS CORRESPONDENCE: FIELD OF USE: COPYRIGHT: Pat. Off.)

Leave

Weller v. TGI Friday's Application (OPPOSITION: OPPONENT SEEKING SPECIAL LEAVE TO ADDUCE FURTHER EVIDENCE: AIPO)

Locus standii

Herron Pharmaceuticals Pty Ltd v. Sterling Winthrop Pty Ltd (PERSON AGGRIEVED: *Locus standii* BASED ON PRIOR REGISTERED MARKS: AIPO)

Kraft Foods Inc. v. Gaines Pet Foods Corporation (REMOVAL FOR NON-USE: PERSON AGGRIEVED: ONUS OF PROOF: Fed. Ct)

Metropolitan Dairies Pty Ltd v. Pura Natural Spring Waters Pty Ltd (REGISTRATION: RENEWAL: LAPSED REGISTRATION: EXTENSION OF TIME: ERROR OR OMISSION: NATURAL JUSTICE: *Locus standii*: PUBLIC POLICY: Pat. Off.)

Natural justice

Metropolitan Dairies Pty Ltd v. Pura Natural Spring Waters Pty Ltd (REGISTRATION: RENEWAL: LAPSED REGISTRATION: EXTENSION OF TIME: ERROR OR OMISSION: *Locus standii*: PUBLIC POLICY: Pat. Off.)

Objection by examiner

Cling Adhesive Products Pty Ltd's Application (OBJECTION BY EXAMINER: WHETHER DESCRIPTIVE: WORDS JOINED BY HYPHEN: INHERENT DISTINCTIVENESS: EVIDENCE OF USE: AIPO)

Fastrack Racing Pty Ltd's Application (OBJECTIONS BY EXAMINERS: POWER OF REGISTRAR TO SET DOWN FOR HEARING: APPLICATION IN MULTIPLE CLASSES: AMENDMENT OF CLASS: DIVISIONAL FILINGS: DESCRIPTIVE MARK: AIPO)

Personal Prating Meters Pty Ltd's Application (APPLICATION: PART A: EXAMINATION: OBJECTION: LACK OF INHERENT ABILITY TO DISTINGUISH: AIPO)

Sunraysia Natural Beverage Co. Pty Ltd's Application (APPLICATION: OBJECTION BY EXAMINER: WHETHER CAPABLE OF BECOMING DISTINCTIVE: AIPO)

Tatra Nominees Pty Ltd's Application (APPLICATION: OBJECTION BY EXAMINER: WHETHER DESCRIPTIVE: EXISTING REGISTRATIONS: AIPO)

Toro Company's Applications (DESCRIPTIVE MARK: CONSISTENCY BY REGISTRAR: AIPO)

Onus of proof

Kraft General Foods Inc. v. Gaines Pet Foods Corp. (REMOVAL FROM REGISTER: NON-USE: EFFECT OF CONTRACTUAL TERMS: PERSON AGGRIEVED: DISCRETION: AIPO: Fed. Ct)

Person aggrieved

Kraft Foods Inc. v. Gaines Pet Foods Corporation (REMOVAL FOR NON-USE: *Locus standii*: ONUS OF PROOF: Fed. Ct)

Power of registrar

Fastrack Racing Pty Ltd's Application (OBJECTIONS BY EXAMINERS: POWER OF REGISTRAR TO SET DOWN FOR HEARING: APPLICATION IN MULTIPLE CLASSES: AMENDMENT OF CLASS: DIVISIONAL FILINGS: DESCRIPTIVE MARK: AIPO)

Role of registrar

Haddonstone Pty Ltd v. Haddonstone Ltd (ACCEPTANCE: OPPOSITION: PROPRIETORSHIP: MANUFACTURER OR DISTRIBUTOR: ESTOPPEL: DECEPTION OR CONFUSION: AIPO)

Stamp duties

Carnations Australia Pty Ltd v. Commissioner of Stamp Duties (WHETHER TRADE MARK PROPERTY OUTSIDE QUEENSLAND: S.C.(Qd))

Stay

Vulcan Australia Ltd v. M.L. D'Astoli & Co. Pty Ltd (INFRINGEMENT: CO-PENDING APPLICATION FOR SIMILAR MARK: Fed. Ct)

Summary judgment

Sceats v. Jonathan Sceats Design Pty Ltd (REMOVAL FOR NON-USE: DISCRETIONARY
REMEDY: EXERCISE OF DISCRETION: Fed. Ct)

Survey evidence

Domino's Pizza Inc. v. Eagle Boys Dial-a-Pizza Australia Pty Ltd (OPPOSITION:
DECEPTION AND CONFUSION: PROPRIETORSHIP: AIPO)
Johnson & Johnson Australia Pty Ltd v. Sterling Pharmaceuticals Pty Ltd (Fed. Ct)
Sterling Pharmaceuticals Pty Ltd v. Johnson & Johnson Australia Pty Ltd
(ADMISSIBILITY AND RELEVANCE OF EVIDENCE: SURVEY EVIDENCE OF PUBLIC
AS TO KNOWLEDGE AND USE OF TRADE MARK: Fed. Ct)
Toro Company's Applications (OBJECTION: DESCRIPTIVE MARK: CONSISTENCY BY
REGISTRAR: AIPO)

Prior Registrations

Anheuser-Busch Inc. v. Castlebrae Pty Ltd (APPLICATION: PRIOR REGISTRATION BY
RESPONDENT: CHARACTER MERCHANDISING: Fed. Ct)
Approved Prescription Services Ltd's Application (REGISTRABILITY: LETTERS AND
INITIALS: OFFICE PRACTICE: Pat. Off.)
Athol Thomas Kelly's Application (LIKELIHOOD OF DECEPTION OR CONFUSION:
HONEST CONCURRENT USE: IMPERFECT RECOLLECTION DOCTRINE: Pat.
Off.)
Bodegas Rioja Santiago SA v. Barossa Co-operative Winery Ltd (OPPOSITION:
COMMON DESCRIPTIVE ELEMENTS: Pat. Off.)
Camiceria Pancaldi and B. Srl v. Le Cravatte Di Pancaldi Srl (OPPOSITION: PRIOR
INCONSISTENT REGISTRATION: DECEPTION AND CONFUSION: AIPO)
Cougar Marine Ltd v. Roberts (OPPOSITION: DIVISIONAL APPLICATION:
PROPRIETORSHIP: ABANDONMENT BY PRIOR USERS: GOODS OF THE SAME
DESCRIPTION: HONEST CONCURRENT USER: AIPO)
Dow Chemical Co. v. C.H. Boehringer Sohn KG (OPPOSITION: SIMILAR WORD:
IMPERFECT RECOLLECTION: Pat. Off.)
Kirra Collectables Pty Ltd v. Pewter Products Pty Ltd (OPPOSITION: KIRRA:
WHETHER GOODS OF THE SAME DESCRIPTION: AIPO)
Legal & General Life of Australia Ltd v. Carlton-Jones & Associates Pty Ltd
(OPPOSITION: PRIOR REGISTRATION REMOVED: DISCLAIMER: EFFECT: Pat.
Off.)
W.D. & H.O. Wills (Australia) Ltd and Benson & Hedges Co. Pty Ltd's Application
(OBJECTION: SUBSTANTIAL IDENTITY: DECEPTIVE SIMILARITY: Pat. Off.)

Prior Use

Algie v. Dorminy (OPPOSITION: WHETHER DECEPTIVE OR CONFUSING: AIPO)
Boundy Insulations Pty Ltd's Application (OPPOSITION: PRIOR USE BY FOREIGN
OPPONENT: OVERSEAS USE: Pat. Off.)
Buying Systems (Australia) Pty Ltd v. Studio Srl (OPPOSITION: PROPRIETORSHIP:
PRIOR USE BY OPPONENT: CONNECTION IN THE COURSE OF TRADE: AIPO)
Logan v. Coulter (OPPOSITION: DECEPTIVE SIMILARITY: INTENTION TO USE:
AIPO)
Marston Fastener Corp.'s Application (OPPOSITION: RELEVANT PRIOR USE: Pat.
Off.)

Rael Marcus v. Sabra International Pty Ltd (OPPOSITION: APPEAL: OVERSEAS VENDOR: EFFECT OF PREVIOUS, NOW-LAPSED REGISTRATION OF MARK AND LICENCE TO USE IT: DISTINCTION BETWEEN NON-USE AND ABANDONMENT: Fed. Ct)

Technicolor Inc. v. R. & C. Products Pty Ltd (OPPOSITION: PROPRIETORSHIP: REGISTRAR'S DIRECTION: Pat. Off.)

Proprietorship

Agricultural Dairy Industry Authority of Epirus Dodoni SA v. Dimtsis (OPPOSITION: USE LIKELY TO DECEIVE OR CAUSE CONFUSION: REGISTRABILITY: Pat. Off.)

Alexander v. Tait-Jamison (OPPOSITION: WHETHER MARKS NEARLY OR SUBSTANTIALLY IDENTICAL: WHETHER GOODS OF THE SAME DESCRIPTION: USE OF BUSINESS NAME: WHETHER USE AS MARK: AIPO)

Allworth Constructions Pty Ltd v. Dixon Investments Pty Ltd (USE OF TRADE MARK: GOODS OR SERVICES: AIPO)

Alpha Industries Pty Ltd v. Vita-Craft Ltd (SCANDALOUS AND IMPROPER: Pat. Off.)

Big Country Developments Pty Ltd v. TGI Friday's Inc. (ACCEPTANCE IN PART A: OPPOSITION: USE BY OPPONENT AS A MARK: Pat. Off.)

Bodyline Cosmetics Ltd v. Brot Bodyline (OPPOSITION: FIRST USE: HONEST CONCURRENT USE: AIPO)

Buying Systems (Australia) Pty Ltd v. Studio Srl (OPPOSITION: PRIOR USE BY OPPONENT: CONNECTION IN THE COURSE OF TRADE: AIPO)

Carnival Cruise Lines Inc. v. Sitmar Cruises Ltd (SERVICE MARKS: OPPOSITION: DECEPTIVE SIMILARITY: Fed. Ct)

Cole v. Australian Char Pty Ltd (OPPOSITION: ABANDONMENT: INTENTION TO USE: LIKELIHOOD OF DECEPTION OR CONFUSION: BLAMEWORTHY CONDUCT: AIPO)

Comlink Information Systems Inc. v. Technology One Pty Ltd (OPPOSITION: FINANCE ONE: LOGO: AIPO)

Cougar Marine Ltd v. Roberts (OPPOSITION: DIVISIONAL APPLICATION: ABANDONMENT BY PRIOR USERS: PRIOR REGISTRATION: GOODS OF THE SAME DESCRIPTION: AIPO)

Crooks Michell Peacock Pty Ltd v. Kaiser (OPPOSITION: PROPRIETORSHIP: DISTINCTIVENESS: DECEPTION AND CONFUSION: ESTOPPEL: HONEST ADOPTION OF MARK: GOOD FAITH: AIPO)

Daimaru Pty Ltd v. Daimaru KK (OPPOSITION: INTENTION TO USE: USE LIKELY TO DECEIVE OR CAUSE CONFUSION: Pat. Off.)

Daimer Industries Pty Ltd v. Daimaru KK (OPPOSITION: FIRST USE BY OPPONENT ONLY BRIEFLY BEFORE APPLICATION BY APPLICANT: AIPO)

Dana Corp. v. Unidrive (APPLICATION: OPPOSITION: DISTINCTIVENESS: SUBSTANTIALLY IDENTICAL OR DECEPTIVELY SIMILAR: AIPO)

Domino's Pizza Inc. v. Eagle Boys Dial-a-Pizza Australia Pty Ltd (OPPOSITION: DECEPTION AND CONFUSION: SURVEY EVIDENCE: AIPO)

Dunlop Olympic Ltd v. Cricket Hosiery Inc. (APPLICATION: OPPOSITION: DISTINCTIVENESS: LIKELIHOOD OF DECEPTION OR CONFUSION: USE OF MARK OVERSEAS: Pat. Off.)

Figgins Holdings Pty Ltd v. Registrar of Trade Marks (ASSIGNMENT OF APPLICATION: REGISTRATION OF PROPRIETORSHIP: JURISDICTION TO ORDER: Fed. Ct)

First Tiffany Holdings Pty Ltd v. Tiffany and Company (OPPOSITION: AUTHORISED USE AND CONTROL: CONNECTION IN THE COURSE OF TRADE: Pat. Off.)

Flagstaff Investments Pty Ltd v. Guess? Inc. (APPLICATION: GUESS?: OPPOSITION: USE: FOREIGN PUBLICATIONS ADVERTISING: Pat. Off.)

Haddonstone Pty Ltd v. Haddonstone Ltd (APPLICATION: ACCEPTANCE: OPPOSITION: MANUFACTURER OR DISTRIBUTOR: ESTOPPEL: ROLE OF REGISTRAR: AIPO)

Hearst Corp. v. Pacific Dunlop Ltd (APPLICATION: OPPOSITION: LIKELIHOOD OF DECEPTION OR CONFUSION: Pat. Off.)

Jamieson v. American Dairy Queen Corporation (APPLICATION: OPPOSITION: Pat. Off.)

Johnson & Johnson v. S.C. Johnson & Son Inc. (WHETHER CONFUSING: HONEST CONCURRENT USE: T.M.Reg.)

Keith Harris & Co. Ltd's Application (OPPOSITION: FIRST USE: USE LIKELY TO DECEIVE OR CAUSE CONFUSION: JOINT USE OF TRADE MARKS: Pat. Off.)

Koh Electronics Trading v. Libra Electronics Pty Ltd (OPPOSITION: PROPRIETORSHIP: FIRST USE: LIKELIHOOD OF DECEPTION OR CONFUSION: BLAMEWORTHY CONDUCT: IDENTICAL MARKS: COPYING OF OVERSEAS MARK: COPYRIGHT PROPRIETORSHIP ON MARK: GOODS OF SAME DESCRIPTION: AIPO)

Legal & General Life of Australia Ltd v. Carlton-Jones & Associates Pty Ltd (OPPOSITION: PRIOR REGISTRATION REMOVED: TRAFFICKING: Pat. Off.)

Martin Cellars Pty Ltd v. Kies Pty Ltd (OPPOSITION: LIKELIHOOD OF DECEPTION OR CONFUSION: AIPO)

MCT Unilabels SA v. Peter Katholos (OPPOSITION: DECEPTIVELY SIMILAR: SUBSTANTIALLY IDENTICAL: AIPO)

Meditex Ltd v. New Horizonz Pty Ltd (OPPOSITION: EXTENSION OF TIME: COSTS: AIPO)

Mobil Oil Corp. v. Foodland Associated Ltd (APPLICATION: OPPOSITION: AMENDMENT OF MARK: DISCLAIMER: T.M.Reg.)

Natural Paper v. Spastic Centre of New South Wales (OPPOSITION: LACK OF INTENTION TO USE: NON-USE: DECEPTION OR CONFUSION: AIPO)

Nissan Motor Co. (Australia) Pty Ltd v. Vector Aeromotive Corporation (APPLICATION: OPPOSITION: USE OF TRADE MARK: GOODS OR SERVICES: AIPO)

O'Brien and Associates v. Orton & Burns Engineering Pty Ltd (ACCEPTANCE FOR PART B: OPPOSITION: EVIDENCE: DISTINCTIVENESS: Pat. Off.)

Reich v. Country Life Bakeries Pty Ltd (OPPOSITION: LIKELY TO DECEIVE OR CONFUSE: DIVISIONAL APPLICATION: REGISTRAR'S DISCRETION: AIPO)

Riviera Leisurewear Pty Ltd v. J. Hepworth & Son PLC (APPLICATION: OPPOSITION: REPUTATION: DECEPTION AND CONFUSION: Pat. Off.)

Saturno's Norwood Hotel Pty Ltd's Application (OPPOSITION: FIRST USE BY APPLICANTS: LIKELIHOOD OF DECEPTION OR CONFUSION: Pat. Off.)

Settef SpA v. Riv-Oland Marble Co. ((Vic.) Pty Ltd (INFRINGEMENT: WHETHER DISTINCTIVE, DECEPTIVE AND CONFUSING: RECTIFICATION: NON-USE: USE IN GOOD FAITH: ABANDONMENT: S.C.(Vic.))

Sigma, Kabushiki Kaisha, v. Olympic Amusements Pty Ltd (OPPOSITION: WHETHER SUFFICIENT ACTIVITY IN AUSTRALIA TO ESTABLISH PROPRIETORSHIP: AIPO)

Société des Produits Nestlé SA v. Strasburger Enterprises Inc. (OPPOSITION: QUIX QUIK: DECEPTION OR CONFUSION: AIPO)

Sportscraft Consolidated Pty Ltd v. General Sportcraft Co. Ltd (OPPOSITION: DECEPTION: CONFUSION: SUBSTANTIALLY IDENTICAL: DECEPTIVELY SIMILAR: AIPO)

Stingray Surf Co. Pty Ltd v. Lister and Brown (OPPOSITION: HONEST CONCURRENT USER: AIPO)

Studio Srl v. Buying Systems (Australia) Pty Ltd (APPLICATION: OPPOSITION: PRIOR FOREIGN PROPRIETORSHIP BY OPPONENT: WHETHER CONFUSION: Pat. Off.)

Stylesetter International Co. Pty Ltd v. Le Sportsac, Inc. (APPLICATION: OPPOSITION: PROPRIETORSHIP: USE PRIOR TO APPLICATION: Pat. Off.)

Sundream Pty Ltd v. Hartland Investments Pty Ltd (OPPOSITIONS TO REGISTRATION: LIKELIHOOD OF DECEPTION OR CONFUSION: ONUS OF PROOF: Pat. Off.)

Surf Shirt Designs Pty Ltd (OPPOSITION: USE LIKELY TO DECEIVE OR CAUSE CONFUSION: Pat. Off.)

Tavefar Pty Ltd v. Life Savers (Australasia) Ltd (OPPOSITION: LIKELIHOOD OF DECEPTION OR CONFUSION: Pat. Off.)

Thai Gypsum Products Co. Ltd v. Waring and Gillow Pty Ltd (PROPRIETOR OF MARK: LEVEL OF USE: USE IN CONNECTION WITH GOODS: USE ON BROCHURES: Fed. Ct)

Triple Three Leisure Ltd v. Turkovic (APPLICATION: OPPOSITION: INHERENT DISTINCTIVENESS: USE OUTSIDE AUSTRALIA: AIPO)

Unidrive v. Dana Corp. (OPPOSITION: DECEPTION OR CONFUSION: AIPO)

Untell Pty Ltd v. Manenti Holdings Pty Ltd (OPPOSITION: DISTINCTIVENESS: INHERENT ADAPTABILITY TO DISTINGUISH: Pat. Off.)

Vamuta Pty Ltd (t/a Sogo Jewellers) v. Sogo Co. Ltd (IDENTICAL MARKS: SOGO: USE AS ADVERTISEMENTS: AIPO)

Warner-Lambert Co. v. Harel (OPPOSITION: DECEPTION OR CONFUSION: BLAMEWORTHY CONDUCT: AIPO)

Public Interest

Australian Broadcasting Corporation's Application (EXTENSION OF TIME TO FILE NOTICE OF OPPOSITION: INCORRECT REASONS: SECOND APPLICATION FILED: WHETHER AMENDMENT OR SUBSTITUTION NECESSARY: MATERIAL SUFFICIENT TO DISCHARGE ONUS: Pat. Off.)

Australian Design Council v. Peter Borello (INFRINGEMENT: CONTEMPT: CONTINUING USE IN BREACH OF INJUNCTION: DELIBERATE BREACH: PUBLIC INTEREST FACTORS: Fed. Ct)

AWA Ltd v. Future Software Pty Ltd (EXTENSION TO TIME FOR OPPOSITION: APPLICATION WITHIN TIME PRESCRIBED OPPOSED: Pat. Off.)

Bee Tek (Import & Export) Pte Ltd v. Kenner Parker Toys Inc. (EXTENSION OF TIME TO FILE EVIDENCE-IN-REPLY: WHETHER INDULGENCES ALREADY GIVEN EXCESSIVE: Pat. Off.)

Black & Decker Corporation v. Akarana Abrasive Industries Ltd (EXTENSION OF TIME TO FILE EVIDENCE-IN-SUPPORT: Pat. Off.)

Bundy American Corp. v. Rent-A-Wreck ((Vic.) Pty Ltd (EXTENSION OF TIME LIMITS: INTER-PARTY NEGOTIATION: Pat. Off.)

Food Marketers Pty Ltd v. Maconochie Seafoods Ltd (EXTENSION OF TIME FOR LODGING NOTICE OF OPPOSITION: SPECIAL CIRCUMSTANCES: Pat. Off.)

Pacific Dunlop Ltd v. Fruit of the Loom Inc. (REMOVAL: APPLICATION FOR EXTENSION OF TIME TO FILE EVIDENCE-IN-ANSWER: TIME NEEDED TO GATHER EVIDENCE ON USE: Pat. Off.)

Playground Supplies Pty Ltd's Application (EXTENSION OF TIME LIMIT: Pat. Off.)

Rollbits Pty Ltd v. Rowntree Mackintosh PLC (SERVICE OF DOCUMENTS: EXTENSION OF TIME: PRESENTATION OF EVIDENCE AND ARGUMENTS: Pat. Off.)

Public Policy

Metropolitan Dairies Pty Ltd v. Pura Natural Spring Waters Pty Ltd (REGISTRATION: RENEWAL: LAPSED REGISTRATION: EXTENSION OF TIME: ERROR OR OMISSION: NATURAL JUSTICE: *Locus standii*: Pat. Off.)

933

Quality or Character

Courtaulds Textiles (Holdings) Ltd's Application (ADJECTIVAL COMPOUND INDICATING QUALITY OR CHARACTER: SIGNIFICANT OVERSEAS USE: CAPABLE OF BECOMING DISTINCTIVE: AIPO)

Kettle Chip Co. Pty Ltd v. Pepsico Australia Pty Ltd (KETTLE THINS/DOUBLE CRUNCH KETTLE COOKED POTATO CHIPS: DESCRIPTIVE WORDS: Fed. Ct)

Registrability

Agricultural Dairy Industry Authority of Epirus Dodoni SA v. Dimtsis (OPPOSITION: PROPRIETORSHIP: USE LIKELY TO DECEIVE OR CAUSE CONFUSION: Pat. Off.)

Approved Prescription Services Ltd's Application (LETTERS AND INITIALS: INVENTED WORK: ADAPTED TO DISTINGUISH: Pat. Off.)

Aussat Pty Ltd (Re) (APPLICATION: SUBSTANTIALLY IDENTICAL: DECEPTIVELY SIMILAR: AIPO)

Beatrice Companies Inc.'s Application (INHERENTLY DISTINCTIVE: CAPABLE OF BECOMING DISTINCTIVE: USE IN AUSTRALIA: Pat. Off.)

Business Marketing Australia Pty Ltd v. Australian Telecommunication Commission (GENERIC TERMS: DISTINCTIVENESS: DIRECT REFERENCE: AIPO)

Findlay v. Rimfire Films Ltd (APPLICATION: CROCODILE DUNDEE: OPPOSITION: USE LIKELY TO DECEIVE OR CAUSE CONFUSION: T.M.Reg.)

Fischer Pharmaceuticals Ltd's Application (INVENTED WORD: DESCRIPTIVENESS: AIPO)

Grolsch NV's Application (BOTTLE SHAPE: DISTINCTIVE: INHERENT ADAPTABILITY: Pat. Off.)

Hans Continental Smallgoods Pty Ltd's Application (DESCRIPTIVE: UNCOMMON COMBINATION OF WORDS: AIPO)

Hong Kong and Shanghai Banking Corp. Ltd's Applications (CHINESE CHARACTERS: REGISTRABILITY UNDER SECTION 24: Pat. Off.)

JGL Investments Proprietary's Application (ADAPTED TO DISTINGUISH: INHERENT ADAPTABILITY: Pat. Off.)

Maxam Food Products Pty Ltd's Application (INVENTED WORD: DESCRIPTIVE: CAPABLE OF BECOMING DISTINCTIVE: Pat. Off.)

McGloin (J.) Pty Ltd's Application (DESCRIPTIVE MARK: EVIDENCE OF USE: PART B: Pat. Off.)

Mobil Oil Corp. v. Registrar of Trade Marks (INVENTED WORD: S.C.(NSW))

Paragold Distributors Pty Ltd's Application (OBJECTION TO REGISTRATION: DIRECT REFERENCE TO CHARACTER OR QUALITY OF GOODS: NON-REGISTRABILITY IN PART A AND PART B: AIPO)

Queensland Rugby Football League (APPLICATION: DISTINCTIVENESS: GENERIC TERMS: AIPO)

Springs Industries Inc.'s Application (DISTINCTIVE: DESCRIPTIVE: ADAPTABILITY TO DISTINGUISH: Pat. Off.)

Tandy Corp.'s Application (ORDINARY MEANING: Pat. Off.)

Taylor's Application (DISTINCTIVE: Pat. Off.)

Teleflora (Australia) Inc.'s Applications (SUBSTANTIALLY IDENTICAL: DECEPTIVELY SIMILAR: GOODS AND SERVICES OF SAME DESCRIPTION: AIPO)

Tooheys Ltd's Application (SURNAME: DISTINCTIVE: CAPABLE OF BECOMING DISTINCTIVE: Pat. Off.)

Westco Jeans (Aust.) Pty Ltd's Application (ADAPTED TO DISTINGUISH: INHERENT ADAPTABILITY: DESCRIPTIVE: Pat. Off.)

Yamaha Corp.'s Application (OBJECTION: DESCRIPTIVE: NON-DISTINCTIVE: Pat. Off.)

Registration

Sterling Winthrop Pty Ltd v. Stephen Hunter Pty Ltd (OPPOSITION: PHARMACEUTICAL: WORD COMMON TO THE TRADE: SIMILARITY: USE: DECEPTION: CONFUSION: AIPO)

Removal from Register

Anstoetz's (Jab Josef's) Application (NON-USE: PERSON AGGRIEVED: USE BY DISTRIBUTOR: Pat. Off.)

Atomic Skifabrik Alois Rohrmoser v. Sasdor Pty Ltd (EXTENSION OF TIME TO LODGE NOTICE OF OPPOSITION: Pat. Off.)

Australian Bacon Ltd v. Mulfric Foods Pty Ltd (OPPOSITION: EVIDENCE: NON-USE: Pat. Off.)

Briggs v. Jaden Marketing Pty Ltd (NON-USE: UNAUTHORISED USE: DISCRETION: AIPO)

Browne v. S. Smith & Son Pty Ltd (INFRINGEMENT: REMOVAL FOR NON-USE: Fed. Ct)

Cafe Do Brasil SpA v. Scrava Pty Ltd (NON-USE: EVIDENCE: PRIMA FACIE CASE: SPECIAL CIRCUMSTANCES: Pat. Off.)

D'Urban Inc. v. Canpio Pty Ltd (NEED TO PROVE NON-USE: Pat. Off.)

ECONOVENT Trade Mark (NON-USE: ONUS OF PROOF: Pat. Off.)

Fawns & McAllan Pty Ltd v. Burns-Biotec Laboratories Inc. (OPPOSITION: NON-USE: PERSON AGGRIEVED: T.M.Reg.)

Gordon & Rena Merchant Pty Ltd v. Ocky Docket (Aust.) Pty Ltd (OPPOSITION: NON-USE: PERSON AGGRIEVED: ONUS: Pat. Off.)

Herron Pharmaceuticals Pty Ltd v. Sterling Winthrop Pty Ltd (PERSON AGGRIEVED: *Locus standii* BASED ON PRIOR REGISTERED MARKS: AIPO)

Kraft General Foods Inc. v. Gaines Pet Foods Corp. (NON-USE: ONUS OF PROOF: EFFECT OF CONTRACTUAL TERMS: PERSON AGGRIEVED: DISCRETION OF REGISTRAR: DEROGATION FROM GRANT: AIPO: Fed. Ct)

Kraft Foods Inc. v. Gaines Pet Foods Corporation (PRACTICE: *Locus standii*: PERSON AGGRIEVED: ONUS OF PROOF: Fed. Ct)

Lane v. Diners Club International Ltd (NON-USE: OPPOSITION: ONUS OF PROOF: NEED FOR APPLICANT TO ESTABLISH PRIMA FACIE CASE: Pat. Off.)

Murray Goulburn Co-operative Co. Ltd v. New South Wales Dairy Corporation (LIKELIHOOD OF DECEPTION: CONFUSION: GROUND FOR REMOVAL: ASSIGNMENT WITHOUT GOODWILL: Fed. Ct)

Murray Goulburn Co-operative Company Ltd v. New South Wales Dairy Corporation (NON-USE: EXERCISE OF DISCRETION TO EXPUNGE BALANCE OF A MARK WHERE THE MARK HAD BEEN USED ONLY IN RELATION TO TWO TYPES OF GOODS: SUFFICIENT REASON FOR LEAVING THE MARK ON THE REGISTER: Fed. Ct)

Murray Goulburn Co-operative Company Ltd v. New South Wales Dairy Corporation (NON-USE: GOODS OF THE SAME DESCRIPTION: NO USE IN GOOD FAITH: Fed. Ct)

Murray Goulburn Co-operative Company Ltd v. New South Wales Dairy Corporation (NON-USE: PREVIOUS EXPUNGEMENT OF PART OF GOODS ORDER: WHETHER COURT SHOULD EXERCISE ITS DISCRETION TO EXPUNGE BALANCE OF REGISTRATION: Fed. Ct)

Oehlschlager's Opposition (OPPOSITION: USE ON INVOICES AND BUSINESS CORRESPONDENCE: FIELD OF USE: Pat. Off.)

Pacific Dunlop Ltd v. Fruit of the Loom Inc. (OPPOSITION TO APPLICATION FOR REMOVAL: APPLICATION FOR EXTENSION OF TIME TO FILE EVIDENCE-IN-ANSWER: TIME NEEDED TO GATHER EVIDENCE ON USE: Pat. Off.)

Pierre Fabre SA v. Marion Laboratories Inc. (NON-USE: OPPOSITION: ONUS OF PROOF: T.M.Reg.)

Prosimmon Golf (Aust.) Pty Ltd v. Dunlop Australia Ltd (NON-USE: PERSON AGGRIEVED: Pat. Off.)

Ritz Hotel Ltd v. Parfums Yves Saint Laurent Ltd (ORDERS SERVED ON REGISTRAR: Fed. Ct)

Sasdor Pty Ltd v. Atomic Skifabrik Alois Rohrmoser (NON-USE: OPPOSITION: PERSON AGGRIEVED: Pat. Off.)

Sceats v. Jonathan Sceats Design Pty Ltd (NON-USE: DISCRETIONARY REMEDY: Fed. Ct)

Sew Hoy & Sons Ltd v. Skill Print Pty Ltd (OPPOSITION: PERSON AGGRIEVED: PRIMA FACIE CASE OF NON-USE: SUFFICIENCY OF EVIDENCE: Pat. Off.)

Small & Associates Pty Ltd v. Robert Half Incorporated (REGISTRATION: NON-USE: AIPO)

Smith Pty Ltd v. E.A. Browne (INTENTION TO USE: NON-USE: Pat. Off.)

Studio Australia Pty Ltd v. Softsel Computer Products Inc. (ALLEGED NON-USE: EVIDENCE OF STATEMENT FROM TRADE MEMBERS: FAILURE TO SHOW PRIMA FACIE CASE: Pat. Off.)

Studio Australia Pty Ltd v. Softsel Computer Products Inc. (NON-USE: *Locus standii*: ADEQUACY OF EVIDENCE: Pat. Off.)

Vulcan-Hart Corporation v. Vulcan Australia Ltd (CORRECTION OF REGISTER: MISNOMER IN ORIGINAL APPLICATION: AIPO)

Reputation. *See also* Goodwill

Commissioner of Taxation v. Just Jeans Pty Ltd (SALE OF UNREGISTERED TRADE MARK WITHOUT GOODWILL: EFFECT: Fed. Ct)

Heller Financial Services Ltd v. John Brice (TRANSFER: SALE OF BUSINESS: SUBSISTENCE: S.C.(Qd))

Merv Brown Pty Ltd v. David Jones (Aust.) Pty Ltd (REGISTRATION: VALIDITY: REPUTATION AND GOODWILL: ASSIGNMENT WITHOUT GOODWILL: SUFFICIENCY: Fed. Ct)

Merv Brown Pty Ltd v. David Jones (Aust.) Pty Ltd (INFRINGEMENT: VALIDITY OF ASSIGNMENT WITHOUT GOODWILL: Fed. Ct)

Murray Goulburn Co-operative Co. Ltd v. New South Wales Dairy Corporation (GROUND FOR REMOVAL FROM REGISTER: ASSIGNMENT WITHOUT GOODWILL: Fed. Ct)

Murray Goulburn Co-operative Company Ltd v. New South Wales Dairy Corporation (RECTIFICATION: ASSIGNMENT WITHOUT GOODWILL: Fed. Ct)

Ocean Pacific Sunwear Ltd v. Ocean Pacific Enterprises Pty Ltd (PASSING OFF: REPUTATION AND GOODWILL IN MARKS: FIELDS OF USE: Fed. Ct)

Scandalous and Improper

Alpha Industries Pty Ltd v. Vita-Craft Ltd (PROPRIETORSHIP: Pat. Off.)

Second-hand Goods

Fender Australia Pty Ltd v. Beck (INFRINGEMENT: AUSTRALIAN TRADE MARK RIGHTS IN A U.S. MARK ASSIGNED TO DISTRIBUTOR IN AUSTRALIA: WHETHER SALE IN AUSTRALIA OF SECOND-HAND GOODS BEARING OVERSEAS MANUFACTURER'S MARK INFRINGES AUSTRALIAN MARK: Fed. Ct)

Wingate Marketing Pty Ltd v. Levi Strauss & Co. (INFRINGEMENT: PHONETIC SIMILARITY: LEVI'S/REVISE: PASSING OFF: SECOND-HAND JEANS: ALTERATIONS: CONFUSION AS TO ORIGIN: Fed. Ct)

Series of Marks

Dempster's Application (WHAT CONSTITUTES SERIES: EFFECT OF HYPHEN: DIVISIONAL APPLICATION: Pat. Off.)

Johnson & Johnson's Application (WHAT CONSTITUTES: AIPO)

Lyson Australia Pty Ltd's Application (WHAT CONSTITUTES SERIES: Pat. Off.)

Services and Service Marks

Allworth Constructions Pty Ltd v. Dixon Investments Pty Ltd (USE OF TRADE MARK: GOODS OR SERVICES: AIPO)

Carnival Cruise Lines Inc. v. Sitmar Cruises Ltd (OPPOSITION: DECEPTIVE SIMILARITY: PROPRIETORSHIP: Fed. Ct)

Caterpillar Tractor Co. v. Caterpillar Loader Hire (Holdings) Pty Ltd (INFRINGEMENT: GOOD FAITH: S.C.(S.A.))

Computer People Pty Ltd (APPLICATION: AMENDMENT: DISCLAIMER: DESCRIPTION OF APPLICANT'S SERVICES: Pat. Off.)

Estate Agents Co-operative Ltd v. National Association of Realtors (USE IN RESPECT OF SERVICES: CLASSIFICATION OF SERVICES PROVIDED TO MEMBERS OF AN ASSOCIATION: Pat. Off.)

Foodland Associated Ltd v. John Weeks Pty Ltd (APPLICATION FOR GEOGRAPHICAL RESTRICTION: APPEAL FROM REGISTRAR FOLLOWING COMMENCEMENT OF NEW STATUTE: TRANSITIONAL PROVISIONS: Pat. Off.)

Informed Sources Pty Ltd's Application (OBJECTION: INFORMED SOURCES DESCRIPTIVE OF INFORMATION SERVICES: LACK OF INHERENT DISTINCTIVENESS: Pat. Off.)

Small's Application (DIRECT REFERENCE TO CHARACTER OF SERVICES: Pat. Off.)

Shape

Grolsch NV's Application (REGISTRABILITY: BOTTLE SHAPE: DISTINCTIVE: INHERENT ADAPTABILITY: DISTINCTIVE THROUGH USE: Pat. Off.)

Signature

Belle Jardiniere's Application (SIGNATURE OF LIVING PERSON NOT THAT OF APPLICANT: WHETHER CONSENT TO USE SIGNATURE: Pat. Off.)

Similar Goods or Services. *See also under* Deceptively Similar

Alexander v. Tait-Jamison (OPPOSITION: USE OF BUSINESS NAME: WHETHER USE AS MARK: AIPO)

Allied Colloids Ltd v. S.C. Johnson & Son Inc. (EARLIER MARK REGISTERED FOR OVERLAPPING GOODS: Pat. Off.)

Aussat Pty Ltd (Re) (SUBSTANTIALLY IDENTICAL: DECEPTIVELY SIMILAR: CLOSELY-RELATED GOODS AND SERVICES: AIPO)

Bull SA v. Micro Controls Ltd (OPPOSITION: PRIOR REGISTERED MARK: LIKELIHOOD OF DECEPTION OR CONFUSION: Pat. Off.)

Chan Li Chai Medical Factory (H.K.) Ltd's Application (CHINESE CHARACTERS: MARKS DECEPTIVELY SIMILAR: Pat. Off.)

Chanel Ltd v. Chronogem Ltd (EARLIER PART B MARK REGISTERED FOR SAME GOODS: Pat. Off.)

Chanel Ltd v. Produits Ella Bache Laboratoire Suzy (DECEPTIVE SIMILARITY: BLAMEWORTHY CONDUCT: AIPO)
Caltex Petroleum Corp. v. Veedol International Ltd (APPLICATION ACCEPTED: OPPOSITION: WHETHER MARKS DECEPTIVE OR CONFUSING: WHETHER SUBSTANTIALLY IDENTICAL WITH OTHER REGISTERED MARKS: AIPO)
Dana Corp. v. Unidrive (OPPOSITION: PROPRIETORSHIP: DISTINCTIVENESS: AIPO)
Jonsered Motor AB's Application (CITATION: DECEPTIVE SIMILARITY: GEOGRAPHICAL NAME: TRADE MARK USED IN PLURAL FORM: AIPO)
Prince Manufacturing Inc. v. Abac Corp. Australia Pty Ltd (TRADE PRACTICES: PASSING OFF: TENNIS RACQUETS: Fed. Ct)
Selson (Europe) Pty Ltd v. Selson (Australasia) Pty Ltd (OPPOSITION: CONFUSION: SIMILAR GOODS: Pat. Off.)
Simac SpA Macchine Alimentari's Application (OPPOSITION: DECEPTIVE SIMILARITY: SAME GOODS: USE: EVIDENCE: RELEVANT DATES: Pat. Off.)

Special Circumstances. *See* **Practice** (*Extension of time*)

Stamp Duties. *See* **Practice** (*Stamp duties*)

Substantially Identical

Canon KK v. Brook (OPPOSITION: DECEPTIVELY SIMILAR: GOODS OF THE SAME DESCRIPTION: HONEST CONCURRENT USE: AIPO)
Champagne Louis Roederer v. Resourse Management Services Pty Ltd (OPPOSITION: DECEPTIVELY SIMILAR: GOODS OF THE SAME DESCRIPTION: BLAMEWORTHY CONDUCT: DISENTITLEMENT TO PROTECTION: PRACTICE: AIPO)
Karu Pty Ltd v. Jose (REGISTRATION: OPPOSITION: APPEAL: GOODS IN DIFFERENT CLASSES: SUBSTANTIALLY IDENTICAL MARKS: Fed. Ct)
Little Tykes Co. v. Ciardullo (OPPOSITION: LITTLE TYKE/LITTLE TIKES: DECEPTIVELY SIMILAR: GOODS OF THE SAME DESCRIPTION: CHARACTER MERCHANDISING: AIPO)
Pelikan International Handelsgesellschaft mbH & Co. KG v. Lifinia Pty Ltd (ACCEPTANCE: OPPOSITION: DECEPTIVE OR CONFUSING: EVIDENCE: AIPO)
Sterling Winthrop Pty Ltd v. Stephen Hunter Pty Ltd (OPPOSITION: REGISTRATION: PHARMACEUTICAL: WORD COMMON TO THE TRADE: USE: DECEPTION: CONFUSION: AIPO)
Teleflora (Australia) Inc.'s Applications (REGISTRABILITY: SUBSTANTIALLY IDENTICAL: DECEPTIVELY SIMILAR: GOODS AND SERVICES OF SAME DESCRIPTION: AIPO)

Summary Judgment. *See* **Practice** (*Summary judgment*)

Surname or Nickname

Ada Productions Pty Ltd's Application (SURNAME: DISTINCTIVENESS: Pat. Off.)
Amco Wrangler Ltd v. Jacques Konckier (APPLICATION: PART B: OPPOSITION: LIKELIHOOD OF DECEPTION OR CONFUSION: SURNAMES: Pat. Off.)
Gordon & Rena Merchant Pty Ltd v. Ocky Docket (Aust.) Pty Ltd (NICKNAME: Pat. Off.)
Hillier Parker May & Rowden's Applications (DISTINCTIVENESS: WORD COMBINATIONS: TWO SURNAMES: Pat. Off.)
Kenner Parker Toys Inc.'s Application (OBJECTION: SURNAME: EXTENSIVE "HOUSE" MARK USER: Pat. Off.)

Lee Man Tat and Lee Man Lok Application (SURNAMES: DISTINCTIVENESS: Pat. Off.)

Liederman's Application (EXAMINER'S OBJECTIONS: SURNAME: CAPABLE OF BECOMING DISTINCTIVE: EVIDENCE OF OVERSEAS DISTINCTIVENESS: Pat. Off.)

McDonald's Corporation v. Coffee Hut Stores Ltd (FAMILY OF MARKS: Fed. Ct)

Polo Textile Industries Pty Ltd v. Domestic Textile Corporation Pty Ltd (DISTINCTIVENESS OF MARK: FOREIGN SURNAME: EXPUNGEMENT: Fed. Ct)

Red Tulip Imports Pty Ltd's Application (No. 2) (REGISTRATION: SURNAME: DISTINCTIVENESS: Pat. Off.)

Red Tulip Imports Pty Ltd's Application (REGISTRATION: SURNAME: ORIGINAL MEANING: Pat. Off.)

Tooheys Ltd's Application (REGISTRABILITY: SURNAME: DISTINCTIVE: CAPABLE OF BECOMING DISTINCTIVE: Pat. Off.)

Survey Evidence. *See* **Practice** (*Survey evidence*)

Trade Marks Considered

AMEX/AMEV: American Express Co. v. NV Amev (Pat. Off.)

BATH TIME: R. & C. Products Pty Ltd v. Bathox Bathsalts Pty Ltd (Pat. Off.)

CAPLETS: Johnson & Johnson Australia Pty Ltd v. Sterling Pharmaceuticals Pty Ltd (Fed. Ct)

CASSINI: Golden Era Shirt Co. Pty Ltd v. Cassini (S.C.(NSW))

CATERER'S CHOICE: Lorraine's Application (Pat. Off.)

CHANEL/CHANTAL: Chanel Ltd v. Chantal Chemical & Pharmaceutical Corp. (Pat. Off.)

COMMAND/COMMAND PERFORMANCE: Radford Chemical Company Pty Ltd's Application (Pat. Off.)

COMPUTA-PAY: Mayne Nickless Ltd's Application (Pat. Off.)

COWABUNGA: Mirage Studios v. Thompson (AIPO)

CRESTA/CRUSTA: Crusta Fruit Juices Pty Ltd v. Cadbury Schweppes Pty Ltd

CROCODILE DUNDEE: Findlay v. Rimfire Films Ltd (T.M.Reg.)

DAIMARU/DAIMER: Daimer Industries Pty Ltd v. Daimaru Kabushiki Kaisha (AIPO)

DAIMER/DAIMARU: Daimer Industries Pty Ltd v. Daimaru Kabushiki Kaisha (AIPO)

DIAL-AN-ANGEL/GUARDIAN ANGEL: Dial-An-Angel Pty Ltd v. Sagitaur Services Systems Pty Ltd (Fed. Ct)

DORADO: Fabriques de Tabac Réunis SA's Application (Pat. Off.)

DRS: International Computers Ltd's Application (Pat. Off.)

EXTREME/POWERADE EXTREMISTS: Digby International (Australia) Pty Ltd v. Beyond Imagination Pty Ltd

FAME: Gay and Lunetta's (Gianfrancos) Application (Pat. Off.)

GARDEN/GARDENIA: Gardenia Overseas Pte Ltd v. The Garden Co. Ltd (AIPO)

GUARDIAN ANGEL/DIAL-AN-ANGEL: Dial-An-Angel Pty Ltd v. Sagitaur Services Systems Pty Ltd (Fed. Ct)

GUESS?: Flagstaff Investments Pty Ltd v. Guess? Inc. (Pat. Off.)

HI-TEC: Inter-footwear Ltd's Applications (Pat. Off.)

INFORMED SOURCES: Informed Sources Pty Ltd's Application (Pat. Off.)

KANGAROO (device): Brandella Pty Ltd's Application (Pat. Off.)

KETTLE THINS/DOUBLE CRUNCH KETTLE COOKED POTATO CHIPS: Kettle Chip Co. Pty Ltd v. Pepsico Australia Pty Ltd

KNOCKOUT: Westco Jeans (Aust.) Pty Ltd's Application (Pat. Off.)
LASER DISC: Pioneer KK's Application (Pat. Off.)
LEVI'S/REVISE: Wingate Marketing Pty Ltd v. Levi Strauss & Co. (Fed. Ct)
LITTLE TYKE/LITTLE TIKES: Little Tykes Co. v. Ciardullo
OXFORD: Oxford University Press v. Registrar of Trade Marks (Fed. Ct)
PERMACRAFT: Holmes's Application (Pat. Off.)
PINE ACTION/PINE-O-CLEEN: R. & C. Products Pty Ltd v. Sterling Winthrop
    Pty Ltd (Fed. Ct)
PIVOT: Wilkinson Sword Ltd's Application (Pat. Off.)
POLO/POLO CLUB: Polo Textile Industries Pty Ltd v. Domestic Textile
    Corporation Pty Ltd (Fed. Ct)
PORTABLE CARRY-ALL: Nexoft Corporation's Application (AIPO)
PROFESSIONAL: Brian Davis & Co. Pty Ltd's Application (Pat. Off.)
QUIX:QUIK: Société des Produits Nestlé SA v. Strasburger Enterprises Inc
REALTOR: Estate Agents Co-operative Ltd's Application (Pat. Off.)
REVISE/LEVI'S: Wingate Marketing Pty Ltd v. Levi Strauss & Co. (Fed. Ct)
ROARING FORTIES: McManamey (David Fraser)'s Application (Pat. Off.)
ROLLING STONES: Musidor BV v. Tansing (Fed. Ct)
SIDELIFTER: Steel Bros (N.Z.) Ltd's Application (Pat. Off.)
SORBOLITE: Visco Sport Ltd's Application (Pat. Off.)
STC: STC PLC's Application (Pat. Off.)
SUPERNODE: Northern Telecom Ltd's Application (AIPO)
SUPERSWITCH: Mitel Corp.'s Application (Pat. Off.)
TELETEX: Siemans AG's Application (Pat. Off.)
TIMELESS CREATION: Hawke (Aust.) Ltd's Application (Pat. Off.)
TRADEMARK: Gencorp's Application (AIPO)
VOGUE: Spiritual Sky Group Co. Pty Ltd v. Bernard Leser Publications Pty Ltd (Pat.
    Off.)
WATERFORD: Waterford Glass Group Ltd's Application (Pat. Off.)
WATERWELL: Brian Davis & Co. Pty Ltd's Application (Pat. Off.)
WYANDRA GOLDEN CRUMPETS: Hardings Manufacturers Pty Ltd's
    Application (Pat. Off.)

Use

Carnival Cruise Lines Inc. v. Sitmar Cruises Ltd (SERVICE MARKS: OPPOSITION:
    APPEAL: FUN SHIP: WHETHER SUFFICIENT IDENTITY BETWEEN MARKS AND
    SERVICES: Fed. Ct)
Cole v. Australian Char Pty Ltd (APPLICATION: OPPOSITION: ABANDONMENT:
    INTENTION TO USE: LIKELIHOOD OF DECEPTION OF CONFUSION:
    BLAMEWORTHY CONDUCT: AIPO)
Pacific Dunlop Ltd v. Bonny Sports Corp. (OPPOSITION: REGISTRATION:
    COMPOSITE MARK: BONNY PLUS DEVICE: ESSENTIAL FEATURES:
    DECEPTION: CONFUSION: DISTINCTIVENESS: AIPO)
Sigma, Kabushiki Kaisha, v. Olympic Amusements Pty Ltd (WHETHER SUFFICIENT
    ACTIVITY IN AUSTRALIA TO ESTABLISH PROPRIETORSHIP: AIPO)
Sterling Winthrop Pty Ltd v. Stephen Hunter Pty Ltd (OPPOSITION: REGISTRATION:
    PHARMACEUTICAL: WORD COMMON TO THE TRADE: SIMILARITY:
    DECEPTION: CONFUSION: AIPO)
Thai Gypsum Products Co. Ltd v. Waring and Gillow Pty Ltd (PROPRIETOR OF
    MARK: LEVEL OF USE: USE IN AUSTRALIA: USE IN CONNECTION WITH GOODS:
    USE ON BROCHURES: Fed. Ct)
Vamuta Pty Ltd (t/a Sogo Jewellers) v. Sogo Co. Ltd (PROPRIETORSHIP: SOGO:
    IDENTICAL MARKS: USE AS ADVERTISEMENTS: AIPO)

Use in Course of Trade

Carnival Cruise Lines Inc. v. Sitmar Cruises Ltd (SERVICE MARKS: OPPOSITION: APPEAL: FUN SHIP: WHETHER SUFFICIENT IDENTITY BETWEEN MARKS AND SERVICES: Fed. Ct)

Use in Company Name

Winning Appliances Pty Ltd v. Dean Appliances Pty Ltd (WHETHER MISLEADING AND DECEPTIVE CONDUCT: ASSIGNMENT OF TRADING NAME: WHETHER GOODWILL ASSIGNED: Fed. Ct)

Use Overseas

Courtaulds Textiles (Holdings) Ltd's Application (ADJECTIVAL COMPOUND INDICATING QUALITY OR CHARACTER: SIGNIFICANT OVERSEAS USE: CAPABLE OF BECOMING DISTINCTIVE: AIPO)

Visual Similarity. *See also under* Confusion or Deception

Astra (AB) v. Schering Corporation (APPLICATION: OPPOSITION: DECEPTIVELY SIMILAR: CONFUSION: HABITS OF MEDICAL PRACTITIONERS IN WRITING PRESCRIPTIONS AND PHARMACISTS IN READING THEM: HEALTH CONSEQUENCES OF DECEPTION OR CONFUSION: Pat. Off.)

Word Common to the Trade

Sterling Winthrop Pty Ltd v. Stephen Hunter Pty Ltd (OPPOSITION: REGISTRATION: PHARMACEUTICAL: SIMILARITY: USE: DECEPTION: CONFUSION: AIPO)

BRUNEI

Patents

Compulsory Licensing

Blackburn v. Boon Engineering & Construction Sdn Bhd (TERM: WHETHER P.A.49 APPLICABLE: H.C.)

Patents Act 1949 (U.K.), Applicability of

Blackburn v. Boon Engineering & Construction Sdn Bhd (TERM: COMPULSORY LICENSING: H.C.)

Term

Blackburn v. Boon Engineering & Construction Sdn Bhd (COMPULSORY
LICENSING: WHETHER P.A.49 APPLICABLE: H.C.)

CANADA

Confidential Information, Breach of Confidence and Trade Secrets

Agreement

Lac Minerals Ltd v. International Corona Resources Ltd (ABSENCE OF
CONFIDENTIALITY AGREEMENT NOT FATAL: S.C.)

Breach of Confidence, Test for

Lac Minerals Ltd v. International Corona Resources Ltd (TEST FOR BREACH:
REVERSE ONUS BY RECIPIENT TO SHOW NO MISUSE: ABSENCE OF
CONFIDENTIALITY AGREEMENT NOT FATAL: S.C.)

Breach of Duty

Lac Minerals Ltd v. International Corona Resources Ltd (TRADE SECRETS: TRUST
AND TRUSTEES: FIDUCIARY RELATIONSHIP: CONSTRUCTIVE TRUST: S.C.)
Stenada Marketing Ltd v. Nazareno (FRANCHISES: PUBLIC DOMAIN:
INTERLOCUTORY INJUNCTION: S.C.(B.C.))

Business Relationship

Stenada Marketing Ltd v. Nazareno (RELATIONSHIP GIVING RISE TO PROTECTED
INFORMATION: INTERLOCUTORY INJUNCTION: EQUITY: S.C.(B.C.))

Constructive Trust

Lac Minerals Ltd v. International Corona Resources Ltd (FIDUCIARY RELATIONSHIP:
CONFIDENTIAL INFORMATION: BREACH OF DUTY: MINING EXPLORATION
RESULTS: ACQUISITION OF PROPERTY: S.C.)

Equity

Stenada Marketing Ltd v. Nazareno (INTERLOCUTORY INJUNCTION: PURCHASE OF
MACHINE: WHETHER UNIQUE SYSTEM DEVELOPED BY PLAINTIFF:
DISCLOSURE FOR PURPOSE OF SALE OF FRANCHISE: MATERIAL AVAILABLE TO
PUBLIC: SPRINGBOARD PRINCIPLE: S.C.(B.C.))

Evidence. *See* **Practice** (*Evidence*)

Expert Evidence. *See* **Practice** (*Expert evidence*)

Fiduciary Relationship

Lac Minerals Ltd v. International Corona Resources Ltd (TRUST AND TRUSTEES:
BREACH OF DUTY: CONSTRUCTIVE TRUST: MINING EXPLORATION RESULTS:
ACQUISITION OF PROPERTY: S.C.)

Interlocutory Injunction. *See* **Practice** (*Interlocutory injunction*)

Material Available to Public

Stenada Marketing Ltd v. Nazareno (DISCLOSURE FOR PURPOSE OF SALE OF FRANCHISE: SPRINGBOARD PRINCIPLE: S.C.(B.C.))

Misuse

Lac Minerals Ltd v. International Corona Resources Ltd (TEST FOR BREACH: REVERSE ONUS BY RECIPIENT TO SHOW NO MISUSE: INDUSTRY PRACTICE: S.C.)

Onus. *See* **Practice** (*Onus*)

Practice

Evidence

Computer Workshops Ltd v. Banner Capital Market Brokers Ltd (C.A. (Ont.))
Lac Minerals Ltd v. International Corona Resources Ltd (EXPERT EVIDENCE: INDUSTRY PRACTICE: S.C.)

Expert evidence

Lac Minerals Ltd v. International Corona Resources Ltd (INDUSTRY PRACTICE: S.C.)

Interlocutory injunction

Stenada Marketing Ltd v. Nazareno (NON-DISCLOSURE COVENANT: S.C.(B.C.))
Stenada Marketing Ltd v. Nazareno (EQUITY: SPRINGBOARD PRINCIPLE: S.C.(B.C.))

Onus

Lac Minerals Ltd v. International Corona Resources Ltd (MISUSE: TEST FOR BREACH: REVERSE ONUS BY RECIPIENT TO SHOW NO MISUSE: S.C.)

Public Domain

Stenada Marketing Ltd v. Nazareno (FRANCHISES: INTERLOCUTORY INJUNCTION: NON-DISCLOSURE COVENANT: S.C.(B.C.))

Springboard Principle

Stenada Marketing Ltd v. Nazareno (DISCLOSURE FOR PURPOSE OF SALE OF FRANCHISE: MATERIAL AVAILABLE TO PUBLIC: UNIQUE FEATURE CREATED BY PLAINTIFF NOT USED BY DEFENDANTS: S.C.(B.C.))

Trade and Contractual Relationships

Stenada Marketing Ltd v. Nazareno (RELATIONSHIP GIVING RISE TO PROTECTED INFORMATION: S.C.(B.C.))

Trust and Trustees

Lac Minerals Ltd v. International Corona Resources Ltd (FIDUCIARY RELATIONSHIP: BREACH OF DUTY: S.C.)

Copyright

Adaptation

Mackintosh Computers v. Apple Computer Inc. (COMPUTER PROGRAMS: REPRODUCTION: CONTRIVANCE: MACHINE PARTS: Fed. Ct: C.A.)

Assignment

FWS Joint Sports Claimants v. The Copyright Board (INTERPRETATION OF CONTRACT: ASSIGNMENT OF PARTIAL RIGHTS: Fed. C.A.)

Broadcasts

FWS Joint Sports Claimants v. The Copyright Board (COMPILATION OF TELEVISION PROGRAMS: RETRANSMISSION OF TELEVISION SIGNALS: Fed. C.A.)

Télé-Métropole Inc. v. Bishop (INFRINGEMENT BY BROADCAST PRE-RECORDING: EPHEMERAL RECORDINGS: STATUTORY INTERPRETATION: S.C.)

Co-ownership

Spiro-flex Industries Ltd v. Progressive Sealing Inc. (INDIRECT COPYING: REPRODUCTION OF THREE-DIMENSIONAL REPRESENTATION OF ORIGINAL DRAWINGS: SALES BROCHURE: S.C.(B.C.))

Computer Program

115778 Canada Inc. v. Apple Computer Inc. (PROGRAM STORED IN ELECTRONIC FORM ON CHIP: REPRODUCTION: MERGER OF IDEA AND EXPRESSION: TRANSLATION: S.C.)

Mackintosh Computers Ltd v. Apple Computer Inc. (PROGRAM STORED IN ELECTRONIC FORM ON CHIP: REPRODUCTION: MERGER OF IDEA AND EXPRESSION: TRANSLATION: S.C.)

Mackintosh Computers v. Apple Computer Inc. (INFRINGEMENT: REPRODUCTION: ADAPTATION: CONTRIVANCE: MACHINE PARTS: Fed. Ct: C.A.)

Designs

Bayliner Marine Corp. v. Doral Boats Ltd (INFRINGEMENT: PLANS FOR BOAT HULLS: WHETHER REGISTRABLE AS DESIGNS: Fed. C.A.)

Implied Consent

Télé-Métropole Inc. v. Bishop (INFRINGEMENT BY BROADCAST PRE-RECORDING: EPHEMERAL RECORDINGS: IMPLIED CONSENT NOT INCLUDED IN LICENCE TO PERFORM WORK: S.C.)

Indirect Copying

Spiro-flex Industries Ltd v. Progressive Sealing Inc. (REPRODUCTION OF THREE-DIMENSIONAL REPRESENTATION OF ORIGINAL DRAWINGS: S.C.(B.C.))

Infringement

1682330 Ontario Inc. v. Cineplex Odean Corp. (PLEADINGS: SCULPTURE: MORAL RIGHTS: PASSING OFF: FCTD)

Bayliner Marine Corp. v. Doral Boats Ltd (PLANS FOR BOAT HULLS: WHETHER
REGISTRABLE AS DESIGNS: STATUTORY EXCLUSION: NOVELTY: Fed. C.A.)

Mackintosh Computers v. Apple Computer Inc. (COMPUTER PROGRAMS:
REPRODUCTION: ADAPTATION: CONTRIVANCE: MACHINE PARTS: Fed. Ct:
C.A.)

Télé-Métropole Inc. v. Bishop (BROADCAST PRE-RECORDING: EPHEMERAL
RECORDINGS: STATUTORY INTERPRETATION: IMPLIED CONSENT NOT
INCLUDED IN LICENCE TO PERFORM WORK: EFFECT OF U.K. COPYRIGHT
LAW: S.C.)

Merger of Idea and Expression

115778 Canada Inc. v. Apple Computer Inc. (SUBJECT-MATTER: COMPUTER
PROGRAM: PROGRAM STORED IN ELECTRONIC FORM ON CHIP: S.C.)

Mackintosh Computers Ltd v. Apple Computer Inc. (SUBJECT-MATTER:
COMPUTER PROGRAM: PROGRAM STORED IN ELECTRONIC FORM ON CHIP:
S.C.)

Moral Rights

1682330 Ontario Inc. v. Cineplex Odean Corp. (PLEADINGS: INFRINGEMENT:
SCULPTURE: PASSING OFF: FCTD)

Ownership of Copyright

Planet Earth Productions Inc. v. Rowlands (PHOTOGRAPHS AND NEGATIVES:
SEIZURE: PHOTOGRAPHS ORDERED BY ANOTHER: S.C.(Ont.))

Spiro-flex Industries Ltd v. Progressive Sealing Inc. (INDIRECT COPYING:
REPRODUCTION OF THREE-DIMENSIONAL REPRESENTATION OF ORIGINAL
DRAWINGS: SALES BROCHURE: S.C.(B.C.))

Photographs and Negatives

Planet Earth Productions Inc. v. Rowlands (SEIZURE: OWNERSHIP OF COPYRIGHT:
PHOTOGRAPHS ORDERED BY ANOTHER: S.C.(Ont.))

Pleadings. *See* Practice *(Pleadings)*

Practice

Pleadings

1682330 Ontario Inc. v. Cineplex Odean Corp. (INFRINGEMENT: SCULPTURE:
MORAL RIGHTS: PASSING OFF: FCTD)

Recordings and Broadcasts. *See* Broadcasts

Registrability

Bayliner Marine Corp. v. Doral Boats Ltd (PLANS FOR BOAT HULLS: STATUTORY
EXCLUSION: NOVELTY: Fed. C.A.)

Reproduction

Mackintosh Computers v. Apple Computer Inc. (INFRINGEMENT: COMPUTER
PROGRAMS: ADAPTATION: CONTRIVANCE: MACHINE PARTS: Fed. Ct: C.A.)

Sculpture

1682330 Ontario Inc. v. Cineplex Odean Corp. (PLEADINGS: INFRINGEMENT: MORAL RIGHTS: PASSING OFF: FCTD)

Seizure

Planet Earth Productions Inc. v. Rowlands (PHOTOGRAPHS AND NEGATIVES: OWNERSHIP OF COPYRIGHT: PHOTOGRAPHS ORDERED BY ANOTHER: S.C.(Ont.))

Three Dimensional Representations

Spiro-flex Industries Ltd v. Progressive Sealing Inc. (REPRODUCTION OF THREE-DIMENSIONAL REPRESENTATION OF ORIGINAL DRAWINGS: S.C.(B.C.))

Translation

115778 Canada Inc. v. Apple Computer Inc. (COMPUTER PROGRAM: REPRODUCTION: MERGER OF IDEA AND EXPRESSION: S.C.)

Mackintosh Computers Ltd v. Apple Computer Inc. (COMPUTER PROGRAM: PROGRAM STORED IN ELECTRONIC FORM ON CHIP: REPRODUCTION: MERGER OF IDEA AND EXPRESSION: S.C.)

United Kingdom Copyright law, Effect of

Télé-Métropole Inc. v. Bishop (INFRINGEMENT BY BROADCAST PRE-RECORDING: EPHEMERAL RECORDINGS: STATUTORY INTERPRETATION: S.C.)

Passing Off

Appearance of Wares

Stiga AB and Noma Outdoor Products Inc. v. SLM Canada Inc. (TRI-SKI SNOW SLED: SECONDARY MEANING IN GET-UP A PREREQUISITE FOR ACTION: Fed. Ct)

Confusion

Searle Canada Inc. v. Novapharm Ltd (TRADE MARK: GET-UP: TABLETS: INTERLOCUTORY INJUNCTION: BALANCE OF CONVENIENCE: Canada: C.A.)

Walt Disney Productions v. Fantasyland Hotel Inc. (COMPONENTS OF CAUSE OF ACTION: REPUTATION: MISREPRESENTATION: DAMAGES: ISSUE ESTOPPEL: EVIDENCE: USE OF WORD ASSOCIATION: RELEVANCE TO CONFUSION: Q.B.)

Copyright Infringement

1682330 Ontario Inc. v. Cineplex Odean Corp. (PLEADINGS: SCULPTURE: MORAL RIGHTS: FCTD)

Get-up

Searle Canada Inc. v. Novapharm Ltd (TRADE MARK: TABLETS: CONFUSION: INTERLOCUTORY INJUNCTION: BALANCE OF CONVENIENCE: C.A.)

Misrepresentation

Walt Disney Productions v. Fantasyland Hotel Inc. (TRADE NAME: COMPONENTS OF CAUSE OF ACTION: REPUTATION: DAMAGES: ISSUE ESTOPPEL: EVIDENCE: USE OF WORD ASSOCIATION: RELEVANCE TO CONFUSION: Q.B.)

Moral Rights

1682330 Ontario Inc. v. Cineplex Odean Corp. (COPYRIGHT: PLEADINGS: INFRINGEMENT: SCULPTURE: FCTD)

Pleadings. *See* Practice *(Pleadings)*

Practice

Balance of convenience

Searle Canada Inc. v. Novapharm Ltd (TRADE MARK: GET-UP: TABLETS: CONFUSION: INTERLOCUTORY INJUNCTION: C.A.)

Damages

Walt Disney Productions v. Fantasyland Hotel Inc. (COMPONENTS OF CAUSE OF ACTION: REPUTATION: MISREPRESENTATION: ISSUE ESTOPPEL: EVIDENCE: Q.B.)

Evidence

Walt Disney Productions v. Fantasyland Hotel Inc. (COMPONENTS OF CAUSE OF ACTION: REPUTATION: MISREPRESENTATION: DAMAGES: ISSUE ESTOPPEL: USE OF WORD ASSOCIATION: RELEVANCE TO CONFUSION: Q.B.)

Interlocutory injunction

Searle Canada Inc. v. Novapharm Ltd (TRADE MARK: GET-UP: TABLETS: CONFUSION: BALANCE OF CONVENIENCE: C.A.)

Issue estoppel

Walt Disney Productions v. Fantasyland Hotel Inc. (COMPONENTS OF CAUSE OF ACTION: REPUTATION: MISREPRESENTATION: DAMAGES: EVIDENCE: USE OF WORD ASSOCIATION: RELEVANCE TO CONFUSION: Q.B.)

Pleadings

1682330 Ontario Inc. v. Cineplex Odean Corp. (COPYRIGHT INFRINGEMENT: SCULPTURE: MORAL RIGHTS: FCTD)

Reputation

Walt Disney Productions v. Fantasyland Hotel Inc. (TRADE NAME: COMPONENTS OF CAUSE OF ACTION: MISREPRESENTATION: DAMAGES: ISSUE ESTOPPEL: EVIDENCE: USE OF WORD ASSOCIATION: RELEVANCE TO CONFUSION: Q.B.)

Sculpture

1682330 Ontario Inc. v. Cineplex Odean Corp. (MORAL RIGHTS: FCTD)

Secondary Meaning

Stiga AB and Noma Outdoor Products Inc. v. SLM Canada Inc. (APPEARANCE OF WARES: SECONDARY MEANING IN GET-UP A PREREQUISITE FOR ACTION: Fed. Ct)

Tablets

Searle Canada Inc. v. Novapharm Ltd (TRADE MARK: GET-UP: CONFUSION: INTERLOCUTORY INJUNCTION: BALANCE OF CONVENIENCE: C.A.)

Trade Marks

Searle Canada Inc. v. Novapharm Ltd (GET-UP: TABLETS: CONFUSION: INTERLOCUTORY INJUNCTION: BALANCE OF CONVENIENCE: C.A.)

Walt Disney Productions v. Fantasyland Hotel Inc. (COMPONENTS OF CAUSE OF ACTION: REPUTATION: MISREPRESENTATION: DAMAGES: ISSUE ESTOPPEL: EVIDENCE: USE OF WORD ASSOCIATION: RELEVANCE TO CONFUSION: Q.B.)

Patents

Ambiguity

Hoffmann-La Roche Ltd v. Apotex Inc. (IMPEACHMENT: ANTICIPATION: OBVIOUSNESS: CLAIMS FAIL TO STATE EXPLICITLY WHAT IS THE INVENTION: CLAIMS BROADER THAN THE INVENTION MADE: Fed. C.A.)

Anticipation

Hoffmann-La Roche Ltd v. Apotex Inc. (IMPEACHMENT: OBVIOUSNESS: CLAIMS AMBIGUOUS: CLAIMS FAIL TO STATE EXPLICITLY WHAT IS THE INVENTION: CLAIMS BROADER THAN THE INVENTION MADE: REISSUE: Fed. C.A.)

Stiga AB and Noma Outdoor Products Inc. v. SLM Canada Inc. (INFRINGEMENT: OBVIOUSNESS: REGISTRATION OF ASSIGNMENT: Fed. Ct)

Application

Pioneer Hi-Bred Ltd v. Commissioner of Patents (SUFFICIENCY OF DISCLOSURE: S.C.)

Assignment

Stiga AB and Noma Outdoor Products Inc. v. SLM Canada Inc. (REGISTRATION OF ASSIGNMENT: Fed. Ct)

Claims and Claim Construction

Eli Lilly and Co. v. Novopharm Ltd (PROCESS: MANUFACTURE OF PHARMACEUTICAL: WHETHER INFRINGING PROCESS USED: DOCTRINE OF EQUIVALENTS: PURPOSIVE CONSTRUCTION: Fed. Ct)

Hoffmann-La Roche Ltd v. Apotex Inc. (IMPEACHMENT: ANTICIPATION: OBVIOUSNESS: CLAIMS FAIL TO STATE EXPLICITLY WHAT IS THE INVENTION: CLAIMS BROADER THAN THE INVENTION MADE: Fed. C.A.)

O'Hara Manufacturing Ltd v. Eli Lilly & Co. and Thomas Engineering Ltd (INFRINGEMENT: CLAIM CONSTRUCTION: PITH AND SUBSTANCE: Fed. C.A.)

Construction. See also under Claims and Claim Construction

Disclosure

Pioneer Hi-Bred Ltd v. Commissioner of Patents (APPLICATION: SUFFICIENCY OF DISCLOSURE: S.C.)

Evidence and Evidentiary Burden. *See* **Practice** (*Evidence and evidentiary burden*)

Impeachment

Hoffmann-La Roche Ltd v. Apotex Inc. (ANTICIPATION: OBVIOUSNESS: CLAIMS AMBIGUOUS: CLAIMS FAIL TO EXPLICITLY STATE WHAT IS THE INVENTION: CLAIMS BROADER THAN THE INVENTION MADE: Fed. C.A.)

Infringement

Eli Lilly and Co. v. Novopharm Ltd (PROCESS: MANUFACTURE OF PHARMACEUTICAL: WHETHER INFRINGING PROCESS USED: DOCTRINE OF EQUIVALENTS: PURPOSIVE CONSTRUCTION: Fed. Ct)

Le Bloc Fibre Quebec Inc. v. Les Entreprises Arsenault & Frs (JOINDER OF PARTIES: Fed. Ct)

O'Hara Manufacturing Ltd v. Eli Lilly & Co. and Thomas Engineering Ltd (CLAIM CONSTRUCTION: PITH AND SUBSTANCE: Fed. C.A.)

Stiga AB and Noma Outdoor Products Inc. v. SLM Canada Inc. (OBVIOUSNESS: ANTICIPATION: REGISTRATION OF ASSIGNMENT: Fed. Ct)

Joinder of Parties. *See* **Practice** (*Joinder of parties*)

Obviousness

Hoffmann-La Roche Ltd v. Apotex Inc. (IMPEACHMENT: ANTICIPATION: Fed. C.A.)

Stiga AB and Noma Outdoor Products Inc. v. SLM Canada Inc. (INFRINGEMENT: ANTICIPATION: Fed. Ct)

Pith and Substance

O'Hara Manufacturing Ltd v. Eli Lilly & Co. and Thomas Engineering Ltd (INFRINGEMENT: CLAIM CONSTRUCTION: Fed. C.A.)

Practice

Evidence and evidentiary burden

Tye-Sil Corporation Ltd v. Diversified Products Corporation (VALIDITY: PRESUMPTION: EVIDENTIARY BURDEN: Fed. Ct)

Joinder of parties

Le Bloc Fibre Quebec Inc. v. Les Entreprises Arsenault & Frs (INFRINGEMENT: Fed. Ct)

Presumption of validity

Tye-Sil Corporation Ltd v. Diversified Products Corporation (EVIDENTIARY BURDEN: Fed. Ct)

Process

Eli Lilly and Co. v. Novopharm Ltd (MANUFACTURE OF PHARMACEUTICAL: WHETHER INFRINGING PROCESS USED: DOCTRINE OF EQUIVALENTS: PURPOSIVE CONSTRUCTION: STATUTORY NOTICE UNDER PATENTED MEDICINES REGULATION: PROHIBITION ON ISSUE: Fed. Ct)

Presumption. *See* **Practice** (*Presumption of validity*)

Reissue

Hoffmann-La Roche Ltd v. Apotex Inc. (CLAIMS AMBIGUOUS: CLAIMS FAIL TO
  EXPLICITLY STATE WHAT IS THE INVENTION: CLAIMS BROADER THAN THE
  INVENTION MADE: Fed. C.A.)

Sufficiency of Disclosure. *See* **Disclosure**

Validity

Tye-Sil Corporation Ltd v. Diversified Products Corporation (PRESUMPTION:
  EVIDENTIARY BURDEN: Fed. Ct)

Practice

Appeals

Meredith & Finlayson v. Canada (Registrar of Trade Marks) (SUMMARY
  EXPUNGEMENT: SCOPE OF APPEAL FROM REGISTRAR'S DECISION: SUMMARY
  PROCEEDINGS: FCTD)

Damages

Eleanor A. Consulting Ltd v. Eleanor's Fashions Ltd (TRADE MARK: INFRINGEMENT:
  INTERLOCUTORY INJUNCTION: HONEST CONCURRENT USER: FCTD)

Evidence

Computer Workshops Ltd v. Banner Capital Market Brokers Ltd (BREACH OF
  CONFIDENCE: IMPLIED: C.A. (ONT.))
Lac Minerals Ltd v. International Corona Resources Ltd (CONFIDENTIAL
  INFORMATION: TEST FOR BREACH: EXPERT EVIDENCE: INDUSTRY PRACTICE:
  S.C.)
Searle Canada Inc. v. Novapharm Ltd (TRADE MARK: SUBSTITUTION: INDUCING
  SUBSTITUTION: FCTD)

Evidence of Use

Registrar of Trade Marks v. Hawg Iron Inc. (SUMMARY EXPUNGEMENT: HAWG
  FOR MOTOR CYCLES: T.M. Sr Hearing Officer)

Evidentiary Burden

Tye-Sil Corporation Ltd v. Diversified Products Corporation (PATENT: VALIDITY:
  PRESUMPTION: Fed. Ct)

Expert Evidence

Lac Minerals Ltd v. International Corona Resources Ltd (CONFIDENTIAL
  INFORMATION: TEST FOR BREACH: INDUSTRY PRACTICE: S.C.)

Interlocutory Injunction

Aristograf Graphics Inc. v. Northover (EX-EMPLOYEE: CUSTOMERS: FIDUCIARY
  RELATIONSHIP: H.C.(Ont.))

Eleanor A. Consulting Ltd v. Eleanor's Fashions Ltd (TRADE MARK: INFRINGEMENT: DAMAGES: HONEST CONCURRENT USER: FCTD)

Keybrand Foods Inc. v. Guinchard (EX-EMPLOYEE: PRODUCT RECIPE: PROOF: Ont. Ct (Gen.) Div.))

Novapharm Ltd v. Syntex Inc. (CONSIDERATIONS BEFORE GRANT: MERITS NOT TO BE DECIDED: INFRINGEMENT OF TRADE MARKS NOT *per se* IRREPARABLE HARM: Fed. C.A.)

Purolator Courier Ltd v. Mayne Nickless Transport Inc. (TRADE MARKS: COMPARATIVE ADVERTISING: FALSE AND MISLEADING STATEMENTS TENDING TO DISCREDIT A COMPETITOR: GOODWILL IN MARK: FCTD)

Searle Canada Inc. v. Novapharm Ltd (PASSING OFF: GET-UP: TABLETS: CONFUSION: BALANCE OF CONVENIENCE: C.A.)

Stenada Marketing Ltd v. Nazareno (FRANCHISES: CONFIDENTIALITY: PUBLIC DOMAIN: NON-DISCLOSURE COVENANT: S.C.(B.C.))

Joinder of Parties

Le Bloc Fibre Quebec Inc. v. Les Entreprises Arsenault & Frs (PATENTS: INFRINGEMENT: Fed. Ct)

Onus

Lac Minerals Ltd v. International Corona Resources Ltd (CONFIDENTIAL INFORMATION: MISUSE: TEST FOR BREACH: REVERSE ONUS BY RECIPIENT TO SHOW NO MISUSE: S.C.)

Pleadings

1682330 Ontario Inc. v. Cineplex Odean Corp. (COPYRIGHT: INFRINGEMENT: SCULPTURE: MORAL RIGHTS: FCTD)

Proof

Keybrand Foods Inc. v. Guinchard (EX-EMPLOYEE: PRODUCT RECIPE: INTERLOCUTORY INJUNCTION: Ont. Ct (Gen.) Div.))

Registrar's Decision, Appeal from. *See* **Appeals**

Seizure

Planet Earth Productions Inc. v. Rowlands (COPYRIGHT: PHOTOGRAPHS AND NEGATIVES: OWNERSHIP: PHOTOGRAPHS ORDERED BY ANOTHER: S.C.(Ont.))

Summary Proceedings

Meredith & Finlayson v. Canada (Registrar of Trade Marks) (TRADE MARKS: EXPUNGEMENT: SCOPE OF APPEAL FROM REGISTRAR'S DECISION: FCTD)

Trade Marks

Adoption of Foreign Mark. *See also under* **Foreign Mark**

Bousquet v. Barmish Inc. (DIFFERENT WARES: PREVIOUS USE IN CANADA REQUIRED: FIVE YEAR DELAY CREATES HIGHER BURDEN: F.C.)

Appeal. *See* **Practice** (*Appeal*)

Certification Mark

Life Underwriters Association of Canada v. Provincial Association of Quebec Life Underwriters (INFRINGEMENT: CLU: Fed. C.A.)

Comparative Advertising

Purolator Courier Ltd v. Mayne Nickless Transport Inc. (FALSE AND MISLEADING STATEMENTS TENDING TO DISCREDIT A COMPETITOR: GOODWILL IN MARK: FCTD)

Composite Mark

Osler, Hoskin & Harcourt v. Southwestern Bell Telecommunications, Inc. (SUMMARY EXPUNGEMENT: FREEDOM PHONE FOR TELEPHONE EQUIPMENT: USE: T.M. Hearing Officer)

Confusion and Confusing Trade Marks

Ports International Ltd v. Ipco Corp. (OPPOSITION: SURROUNDING CIRCUMSTANCES: OUTLET FOR PRODUCT: T.M. Opp. Bd)
Searle Canada Inc. v. Novapharm Ltd (PASSING OFF: GET-UP: TABLETS: CONFUSION: INTERLOCUTORY INJUNCTION: BALANCE OF CONVENIENCE: C.A.)

Damages

Eleanor A. Consulting Ltd v. Eleanor's Fashions Ltd (INFRINGEMENT: INTERLOCUTORY INJUNCTION: HONEST CONCURRENT USER: FCTD)

Descriptive Mark

Telesat Canada v. Ogden (OPPOSITION: TELEPORT 1 & DESIGN: USE AS REGISTERED: T.M. Opp. Bd)

Distinctiveness

Bousquet v. Barmish Inc. (ADOPTION OF FOREIGN MARK ON DIFFERENT WARES: PREVIOUS USE IN CANADA IS REQUIRED: FIVE-YEAR DELAY CREATES HIGHER BURDEN: Fed. Ct)

Entitlement

United States Shoe Corp. v. Premiere Vision Inc. (OPPOSITION: PERSON NOT ENTITLED: T.M. Opp. Bd)

Evidence. *See* **Practice** (*Evidence*)

Evidence of use. *See* **Practice** (*Evidence of use*)

Expungement. *See also under* **Practice** (*Summary expungement*)

Bousquet v. Barmish Inc. (DISTINCTIVENESS: MESSAGE TO THE PUBLIC: NAME OF DESIGNER: SIGNIFICANT REPUTATION REQUIRED: F.C.)

Foreign Mark

Bousquet v. Barmish Inc. (ADOPTION ON DIFFERENT WARES: PREVIOUS USE IN CANADA REQUIRED: FIVE-YEAR DELAY CREATES HIGHER BURDEN: Fed. Ct)

Goodwill

Purolator Courier Ltd v. Mayne Nickless Transport Inc. (COMPARATIVE ADVERTISING: FALSE AND MISLEADING STATEMENTS TENDING TO DISCREDIT A COMPETITOR: INTERLOCUTORY INJUNCTION: FCTD)

Honest Concurrent User

Eleanor A. Consulting Ltd v. Eleanors Fashions Ltd (INFRINGEMENT: INTERLOCUTORY INJUNCTION: DAMAGES: FCTD)

Inducing Substitution

Searle Canada Inc. v. Novapharm Ltd (EVIDENCE: FCTD)

Infringement

Eleanor A. Consulting Ltd v. Eleanor's Fashions Ltd (INTERLOCUTORY INJUNCTION: DAMAGES: HONEST CONCURRENT USER: FCTD)
Life Underwriters Association of Canada v. Provincial Association of Quebec Life Underwriters (CERTIFICATION MARK: CLU: Fed. C.A.)

Interlocutory Injunction. *See* Practice *(Interlocutory injunction)*

Message to the Public

Bousquet v. Barmish Inc. (DISTINCTIVENESS: EXPUNGEMENT: Fed. Ct)

Non-use. *See* Use

Official Marks—Olympic

Canadian Olympic Assoc. v. Konica Canada Inc. (PRE-EXISTING RIGHTS: NOT ACCEPTED BY PUBLIC NOTICE: USE WITH OTHER WARES NOT PERMITTED: Fed. Ct)

Opposition

Ports International Ltd v. Ipco Corp. (CONFUSING TRADE MARK: SURROUNDING CIRCUMSTANCES: OUTLET FOR PRODUCT: T.M. Opp. Bd)
Telesat Canada v. Ogden (DESCRIPTIVE MARK: TELEPORT 1 & DESIGN: USE AS REGISTERED: T.M. Opp. Bd)
United States Shoe Corp. v. Premiere Vision Inc. (PERSON NOT ENTITLED: PREVIOUS USE: NON-USE: T.M. Opp. Bd)

Outlet for Product

Ports International Ltd v. Ipco Corp. (OPPOSITION: CONFUSING TRADE MARK: SURROUNDING CIRCUMSTANCES: T.M. Opp. Bd)

Passing Off

Searle Canada Inc. v. Novapharm Ltd (GET-UP: TABLETS: CONFUSION: INTERLOCUTORY INJUNCTION: BALANCE OF CONVENIENCE: C.A.)

Practice

Appeals

Meredith & Finlayson v. Canada (Registrar of Trade Marks) (SUMMARY EXPUNGEMENT: SCOPE OF APPEAL FROM REGISTRAR'S DECISION: SUMMARY PROCEEDINGS: FCTD)
Oy v. Canada (Registrar of Trade Marks) (REGISTRATION: WHETHER DECISION TO REGISTER APPEALABLE: FCTD)

Evidence

Registrar of Trade Marks v. Hawg Iron Inc. (SUMMARY EXPUNGEMENT: EVIDENCE FILED DEMONSTRATING MARK IN USE: T.M. Sr Hearing Officer)
Searle Canada Inc. v. Novapharm Ltd (SUBSTITUTION: INDUCING SUBSTITUTION: FCTD)

Evidence of use

Registrar of Trade Marks v. Hawg Iron Inc. (T.M. Sr Hearing Officer)

Interlocutory injunction

Eleanor A. Consulting Ltd v. Eleanor's Fashions Ltd (INFRINGEMENT: DAMAGES: HONEST CONCURRENT USER: FCTD)
Novapharm Ltd v. Syntex Inc. (CONSIDERATIONS BEFORE GRANTING: MERITS NOT TO BE DECIDED: INFRINGEMENT OF TRADE MARKS IS NOT *per se* IRREPARABLE HARM: Fed. C.A.)
Purolator Courier Ltd v. Mayne Nickless Transport Inc. (COMPARATIVE ADVERTISING: GOODWILL: FCTD)
Searle Canada Inc. v. Novapharm Ltd (BALANCE OF CONVENIENCE: C.A.)

Summary expungement

Meredith & Finlayson v. Canada (Registrar of Trade Marks) (SCOPE OF APPEAL FROM REGISTRAR'S DECISION: FCTD)
Osler, Hoskin & Harcourt v. Southwestern Bell Telecommunications, Inc. (FREEDOM PHONE FOR TELEPHONE EQUIPMENT: USE OF COMPOSITE MARK: T.M. Hearing Officer)
Registrar of Trade Marks v. Hawg Iron Inc. (HAWG FOR MOTOR CYCLES: EVIDENCE FILED DEMONSTRATING MARK IN USE: T.M. Sr Hearing Officer)

Summary proceedings

Meredith & Finlayson v. Canada (Registrar of Trade Marks) (SUMMARY EXPUNGEMENT: SCOPE OF APPEAL FROM REGISTRAR'S DECISION: FCTD)

Pre-existing Rights

Canadian Olympic Assoc. v. Konica Canada Inc. (OFFICIAL MARKS: OLYMPIC: NOT ACCEPTED BY PUBLIC NOTICE: USE WITH OTHER WARES NOT PERMITTED: Fed. Ct)

Previous Use. *See* **Use**

Registrability and Registration

Oy v. Canada (Registrar of Trade Marks) (WHETHER DECISION TO REGISTER APPEALABLE: FCTD)

Reputation. *See also* **Goodwill**

Bousquet v. Barmish Inc. (ADOPTION OF FOREIGN MARK ON DIFFERENT WARES: DISTINCTIVENESS: SIGNIFICANT REPUTATION REQUIRED: F.C.)

Shape and/or Colour

Novapharm Ltd v. Syntex Inc. (INFRINGEMENT: SHAPE AND COLOUR OF TABLET OF MEDICINE: Fed. C.A.)

Substitution

Searle Canada Inc. v. Novapharm Ltd (INDUCING SUBSTITUTION: EVIDENCE: FCTD)

Summary Expungement. *See* **Practice** (*Summary expungement*)

Summary Proceedings. *See* **Practice** (*Summary proceedings*)

Use (including **Non-use** and **Previous Use**)

Bousquet v. Barmish Inc. (ADOPTION OF FOREIGN MARK ON DIFFERENT WARES: PREVIOUS USE IN CANADA IS REQUIRED: FIVE-YEAR DELAY CREATES HIGHER BURDEN: DISTINCTIVENESS: F.C.)

Canadian Occidental Petroleum Ltd v. Oxychem Canada Inc. (OPPOSITION: NON-USE: T.M. Opp. Bd)

Canadian Olympic Assoc. v. Konica Canada Inc. (OFFICIAL MARKS: OLYMPIC: PRE-EXISTING RIGHTS: NOT ACCEPTED BY PUBLIC NOTICE: USE WITH OTHER WARES: Fed. Ct)

Osler, Hoskin & Harcourt v. Southwestern Bell Telecommunications, Inc. (SUMMARY EXPUNGEMENT: FREEDOM PHONE FOR TELEPHONE EQUIPMENT: USE OF COMPOSITE MARK: T.M. Hearing Officer)

Telesat Canada v. Ogden (OPPOSITION: DESCRIPTIVE MARK: TELEPORT 1 & DESIGN: USE AS REGISTERED: T.M. Opp. Bd)

United States Shoe Corp. v. Premiere Vision Inc. (OPPOSITION: PERSON NOT ENTITLED: PREVIOUS USE: NON-USE: T.M. Opp. Bd)

HONG KONG

Confidential Information and Breach of Confidence

Appeal. *See* **Practice** (*Appeal*)

Breach of Fiduciary Duty. *See* **Fiduciary Duty**

Crown Servant

Attorney-General v. South China Morning Post Ltd (BALANCING COMPETING INTERESTS OF PUBLIC SECURITY AND FREEDOM OF SPEECH: FREEDOM OF SPEECH: PUBLIC SECURITY: C.A.)

***Ex Parte* Injunction.** *See* **Practice** (*Ex parte injunction*)

Ex-employee

Gillman Engineering Ltd v. Simon Ho Shek On (DUTY: S.C.)

Fiduciary Duty

Attorney-General v. South China Morning Post (*Spycatcher*: AVAILABLE OUTSIDE HONG KONG: SERIAL RIGHTS: BALANCING COMPETING INTERESTS OF PUBLIC SECURITY AND FREEDOM OF SPEECH: S.C.: C.A.)

Attorney-General v. South China Morning Post Ltd (FORMER CROWN SERVANT: C.A.)

Gillman Engineering Ltd v. Simon Ho Shek On (DUTY OF EX-EMPLOYEE: S.C.)

Freedom of Speech

Attorney-General v. South China Morning Post (BALANCING COMPETING INTERESTS OF PUBLIC SECURITY AND FREEDOM OF SPEECH: S.C.: C.A.)

Attorney-General v. South China Morning Post Ltd (BALANCING COMPETING INTERESTS OF PUBLIC SECURITY AND FREEDOM OF SPEECH: C.A.)

Information Available Outside Hong Kong

Attorney-General v. South China Morning Post Ltd (C.A.)

Interlocutory Injunction. *See* **Practice** (*Interlocutory injunction*)

Leave to Appeal. *See* **Practice** (*Leave to appeal*)

Practice

Appeal

Attorney-General v. South China Morning Post (LEAVE TO APPEAL TO PRIVY COUNCIL: S.C.: C.A.)

Arguable case

Attorney-General v. South China Morning Post Ltd (INTERLOCUTORY INJUNCTION: CONTINUING INTEREST WORTHY OF PROTECTION AND ARGUABLE CASE FOR PERMANENT INJUNCTION AFTER TRIAL DEMONSTRATED BY PLAINTIFF: C.A.)

Ex parte injunction

Attorney-General v. South China Morning Post (DISCHARGE: APPEAL: LEAVE TO APPEAL TO PRIVY COUNCIL: S.C.: C.A.)

Interlocutory injunction

Attorney-General v. South China Morning Post Ltd (CONTINUING INTEREST WORTHY OF PROTECTION AND ARGUABLE CASE FOR PERMANENT INJUNCTION AFTER TRIAL DEMONSTRATED BY PLAINTIFF: INJUNCTIVE RELIEF TO CONTINUE UNTIL TRIAL OF ACTION: C.A.)

Leave to appeal

Attorney-General v. South China Morning Post (*Ex parte* INJUNCTION: DISCHARGE: LEAVE TO APPEAL TO PRIVY COUNCIL: S.C.: C.A.)

Privy Council, leave to Appeal to. *See* **Practice** (*Leave to appeal*)

Public Security

Attorney-General v. South China Morning Post (BALANCING COMPETING INTERESTS OF PUBLIC SECURITY AND FREEDOM OF SPEECH: S.C.: C.A.)
Attorney-General v. South China Morning Post Ltd (BALANCING COMPETING INTERESTS OF PUBLIC SECURITY AND FREEDOM OF SPEECH: INTERLOCUTORY INJUNCTION: CONTINUING INTEREST WORTHY OF PROTECTION AND ARGUABLE CASE FOR PERMANENT INJUNCTION AFTER TRIAL DEMONSTRATED BY PLAINTIFF: INFORMATION AVAILABLE OUTSIDE HONG KONG: C.A.)

Unauthorised Disclosure. *See* **Breach**

Copyright and Designs

Abandonment of Copyright

Interlego AG v. Tyco Industries Inc. (INFRINGEMENT: LEGO TOYS: DESIGNS: NOVELTY: ORIGINALITY: PUBLIC ESTOPPEL: EXPIRY OF REGISTRATION: ADDITIONAL DAMAGES: C.A.)

Additional Damages. *See* Practice (*Damages*)

Alteration

Interlego AG v. Tyco International Inc. (INFRINGEMENT: LEGO BRICKS: ARTISTIC WORK: ORIGINALITY: ALTERATIONS TO ENGINEERING DRAWINGS: NON-EXPERT DEFENCE: REGISTERED DESIGN: WHETHER DESIGN CAPABLE OF REGISTRATION: NOVELTY: EYE APPEAL: WHETHER FEATURES OF BRICK DICTATED SOLELY BY FUNCTION: P.C.)

Anton Piller Order. *See* **Practice** (*Anton Piller order*)

Arguable Case. *See* **Practice** (*Arguable case*)

Artistic Merit

R. v. Chan Hing-Kin (COMPUTER PROGRAMS: CASINGS FOR PERSONAL COMPUTERS: INFRINGEMENT: FUNCTIONAL WORKS: North Kowloon Magistrates' Court)

Artistic Work

Interlego AG v. Tyco Industries Inc. (INFRINGEMENT: ORIGINALITY: MOULDS AS ENGRAVINGS: NON-EXPERT DEFENCE: S.C.)

Interlego AG v. Tyco International Inc. (INFRINGEMENT: LEGO BRICKS: ORIGINALITY: ALTERATIONS TO ENGINEERING DRAWINGS: NON-EXPERT DEFENCE: REGISTERED DESIGN: WHETHER CAPABLE OF REGISTRATION: NOVELTY: EYE APPEAL: WHETHER FEATURES DICTATED SOLELY BY FUNCTION: P.C.)

Burden of Proof. *See* **Practice** (*Burden of proof*)

Computer Programs

R. v. Chan Hing-Kin (CASINGS FOR PERSONAL COMPUTERS: INFRINGEMENT: North Kowloon Magistrates' Court)

Consumables

Canon KK v. Green Cartridge Company (Hong Kong) Ltd (INFRINGEMENT: REPLACEMENT PARTS: NON-DEROGATION FROM GRANT: EXTENT OF RIGHT TO REPAIR: S.C.)

Copyright Act 1956 (U.K.)

Mattel Inc. v. Tonka Corp. (MEANING OF "IMPORT" IN SECTION 5(2) OF COPYRIGHT ACT 1956 AS EXTENDED TO HONG KONG)

Damages. *See* **Practice** (*Damages*)

Designs. *See* **Registered Designs**

Drawings

Interlego AG v. Tyco International Inc. (INFRINGEMENT: ALTERATIONS TO ENGINEERING DRAWINGS: NON-EXPERT DEFENCE: P.C.)

Engravings

Interlego AG v. Tyco Industries Inc. (MOULDS AS ENGRAVINGS: NON-EXPERT DEFENCE: ADDITIONAL DAMAGES: S.C.)

Estoppel

Interlego AG v. Tyco Industries Inc. (INFRINGEMENT: PUBLIC ESTOPPEL: EXPIRY OF REGISTRATION: ABANDONMENT OF COPYRIGHT: C.A.)

Evidence. *See* **Practice** (*Evidence*)

***Ex Parte* Order.** *See* **Practice** (*Ex parte order*)

Expiry of Design Registration

Interlego AG v. Tyco Industries Inc. (ABANDONMENT OF COPYRIGHT: C.A.)

Eye Appeal

Interlego AG v. Tyco International Inc. (WHETHER CAPABLE OF REGISTRATION: NOVELTY: WHETHER FEATURES DICTATED SOLELY BY FUNCTION: Pat. Ct)

Functional Works and **Features Dictated Solely by Function**

Interlego AG v. Tyco International Inc. (LEGO BRICKS: REGISTERED DESIGN: WHETHER CAPABLE OF REGISTRATION: WHETHER FEATURES DICTATED SOLELY BY FUNCTION: P.C.)
R. v. Chan Hing-Kin (COMPUTER PROGRAMS: CASINGS FOR PERSONAL COMPUTERS: ARTISTIC MERIT: North Kowloon Magistrates' Court)

Implied Licence

R. v. Chan Hing-Kin (COMPUTER PROGRAMS: CASINGS FOR PERSONAL COMPUTERS: INFRINGEMENT: POSSESSION: LAY RECOGNITION TEST: North Kowloon Magistrates' Court)

Import

Mattel Inc. v. Tonka Corp. (MEANING OF: AGENT: PROCUREMENT OF BREACH: PROCUREMENT OF PRINTING OF PACKAGING: H.C.)
(MEANING OF "IMPORT" IN SECTION 5(2) OF COPYRIGHT ACT 1956: S.C.)

Infringement

Canon KK v. Green Cartridge Company (Hong Kong) Ltd (REPLACEMENT PARTS: CONSUMABLES: NON-DEROGATION FROM GRANT: EXTENT OF RIGHT TO REPAIR: S.C.)
CBS/Sony (Hong Kong) Ltd v. Television Broadcasts Ltd (TAPE RECORDINGS: REPRESENTATIVE ACTIONS: STRIKING OUT: H.C.: S.C.)
Interlego AG v. Tyco Industries Inc. (LEGO TOYS: DESIGNS: NOVELTY: ORIGINALITY: PUBLIC ESTOPPEL: EXPIRY OF REGISTRATION: ABANDONMENT OF COPYRIGHT: ADDITIONAL DAMAGES: C.A.)
Interlego AG v. Tyco International Inc. (LEGO BRICKS: ARTISTIC WORK: ORIGINALITY: P.C.)
Koo (Linda Chih Ling) v. Lam Tai Hing (QUESTIONNAIRES USED IN SCIENTIFIC SURVEY: S.C.)
Phonographic Performance (South East Asia) Ltd v. California Entertainments Ltd (OWNERSHIP: BURDEN OF PROOF: C.A.)

Lay Recognition Test. *See* **Practice** (*Non-expert or lay recognition test*)

Non-Derogation from Grant

Canon KK v. Green Cartridge Company (Hong Kong) Ltd (INFRINGEMENT: REPLACEMENT PARTS: CONSUMABLES: EXTENT OF RIGHT TO REPAIR: S.C.)

Non-Expert Test. *See* **Practice** (*Non-expert or lay recognition test*)

Novelty

Interlego AG v. Tyco International Inc. (WHETHER DESIGN CAPABLE OF REGISTRATION: EYE APPEAL: WHETHER FEATURES DICTATED SOLELY BY FUNCTION: P.C.)

Originality

Interlego AG v. Tyco Industries Inc. (INFRINGEMENT: ARTISTIC WORK: MOULDS AS ENGRAVINGS: NON-EXPERT DEFENCE: S.C.)

Interlego AG v. Tyco International Inc. (LEGO BRICKS: ARTISTIC WORK: P.C.)

Ownership

Phonographic Performance (South East Asia) Ltd v. California Entertainments Ltd (BURDEN OF PROOF: INFRINGEMENT: C.A.)

Possession

R. v. Chan Hing-Kin (COMPUTER PROGRAMS: CASINGS FOR PERSONAL COMPUTERS: INFRINGEMENT: North Kowloon Magistrates' Court)

Practice

Anton Piller order

Mattel Inc. v. Tonka Corp. (DISCHARGE OF ORDER FOR MISLEADING EVIDENCE: SERVICE OUT OF THE JURISDICTION: S.C.)

Arguable case

Mattel Inc. v. Tonka Corp. (IMPORT, MEANING OF: AGENT: PROCUREMENT OF BREACH: H.C.)

Burden of proof

Phonographic Performance (South East Asia) Ltd v. California Entertainments Ltd (OWNERSHIP: INFRINGEMENT: C.A.)

Damages

Interlego AG v. Tyco Industries Inc. (INFRINGEMENT: NON-EXPERT DEFENCE: ADDITIONAL DAMAGES: S.C.)

Evidence

Mattel Inc. v. Tonka Corp. (DISCHARGE OF ANTON PILLER ORDER FOR MISLEADING EVIDENCE: SERVICE OUT OF THE JURISDICTION: S.C.)

Ex parte order

Mattel Inc. v. Tonka Corp. (SERVICE ABROAD: WHETHER ORDER GRANTED ON INNOCENT MISTAKE OF FACT SHOULD BE DISCHARGED: H.C.) (DISCHARGE OF ORDER FOR MISLEADING EVIDENCE: S.C.)

Non-expert or lay recognition test

Interlego AG v. Tyco Industries Inc. (INFRINGEMENT: ARTISTIC WORK: ORIGINALITY: MOULDS AS ENGRAVINGS: S.C.)

Interlego AG v. Tyco International Inc. (INFRINGEMENT: LEGO BRICKS: ALTERATIONS TO ENGINEERING DRAWINGS: P.C.)

960

R. v. Chan Hing-Kin (COMPUTER PROGRAMS: CASINGS FOR PERSONAL COMPUTERS: FUNCTIONAL WORKS: ARTISTIC MERIT: IMPLIED LICENCE: North Kowloon Magistrates' Court)

Representative actions

CBS/Sony (Hong Kong) Ltd v. Television Broadcasts Ltd (INFRINGEMENT: TAPE RECORDINGS: STRIKING OUT: H.C.: S.C.)

Service out of the jurisdiction

Mattel Inc. v. Tonka Corp. (*Ex parte* ORDER: H.C.: S.C.)

Striking out

CBS/Sony (Hong Kong) Ltd v. Television Broadcasts Ltd (INFRINGEMENT: TAPE RECORDINGS: REPRESENTATIVE ACTIONS: H.C.: S.C.)

Procurement of Breach

Mattel Inc. v. Tonka Corp. (H.C.)

Recordings

CBS/Sony (Hong Kong) Ltd v. Television Broadcasts Ltd (INFRINGEMENT: REPRESENTATIVE ACTIONS: STRIKING OUT: H.C.: S.C.)

Registered Design

Interlego AG v. Tyco Industries Inc. (INFRINGEMENT: ARTISTIC WORK: ORIGINALITY: MOULDS AS ENGRAVINGS: REGISTRABILITY: S.C.)
Interlego AG v. Tyco Industries Inc. (INFRINGEMENT: LEGO TOYS: NOVELTY: ORIGINALITY: PUBLIC ESTOPPEL: EXPIRY OF REGISTRATION: ABANDONMENT OF COPYRIGHT: C.A.)

Replacement Parts

Canon KK v. Green Cartridge Company (Hong Kong) Ltd (INFRINGEMENT: CONSUMABLES: NON-DEROGATION FROM GRANT: EXTENT OF RIGHT TO REPAIR: S.C.)

Representative Actions. *See* Practice (*Representative actions*)

Right to Repair

Canon KK v. Green Cartridge Company (Hong Kong) Ltd (EXTENT: INFRINGEMENT: REPLACEMENT PARTS: CONSUMABLES: NON-DEROGATION FROM GRANT: S.C.)

Service out of the Jurisdiction. *See* Practice (*Service out of the jurisdiction*)

Striking Out. *See* Practice (*Striking out*)

Subject-Matter

BARBIE DOLL

Mattel Inc. v. Tonka Corp. (H.C.: S.C.)

Computer programs

R. v. Chan Hing-Kin (North Kowloon Magistrates' Court)

LEGO toys

Interlego AG v. Tyco Industries Inc. (S.C.)
Interlego AG v. Tyco Industries Inc. (C.A.)

Questionnaires used in scientific survey

Koo (Linda Chih Ling) v. Lam Tai Hing (S.C.)

Tape recordings

CBS/Sony (Hong Kong) Ltd v. Television Broadcasts Ltd (HC: S.C.)

Tape Recordings. *See* **Recordings**

United Kingdom Copyright Act 1956, Effect of in Hong Kong

Mattel Inc. v. Tonka Corp. (MEANING OF IMPORT IN SECTION 5(2): S.C.)

Passing Off

Common Descriptive Words

Land Power International Holdings Ltd v. Inter-Land Properties (H.K.) Ltd (TRADE
    MARK: COMMON DESCRIPTIVE WORDS USED AS MARK: LITTLE DIFFERENCES
    SUFFICE TO AVOID CONFUSION: C.A.)

Damages. *See* **Practice** (*Damages*)

Get-up

Interlego AG v. Tyco Industries Inc. (INTERLOCUTORY INJUNCTION:
    MISREPRESENTATION: H.C.: C.A.)

Interlocutory Injunction. *See* **Practice** (*Interlocutory injunction*)

International Reputation. *See* **Reputation**

Jurisdiction. *See* **Practice** (*Jurisdiction*)

Misrepresentation

Interlego AG v. Tyco Industries Inc. (GET-UP: INTERLOCUTORY INJUNCTION:
    MISREPRESENTATION: H.C.: C.A.)

Practice

Damages

Ten-Ichi Co. Ltd v. Jancar Ltd (WHETHER RECOVERABLE: H.C.)

Interlocutory injunction

Interlego AG v. Tyco Industries Inc. (GET-UP: MISREPRESENTATION: H.C.: C.A.)
Riley Leisure Products Pty Ltd v. Dokyo Co. Ltd (TRADE NAME: C.A.)

Jurisdiction

Ten-Ichi Co. Ltd v. Jancar Ltd (TRADE MARK: WHETHER ACTION LIES WHERE NO
    ACTIVE BUSINESS IN JURISDICTION: INTERNATIONAL REPUTATION:
    WHETHER DAMAGES RECOVERABLE: H.C.)

Reputation

Ten-Ichi Co. Ltd v. Jancar Ltd (TRADE MARK: WHETHER ACTION LIES WHERE NO
ACTIVE BUSINESS IN JURISDICTION: INTERNATIONAL REPUTATION: H.C.)

Trade Mark or Trade Name

Riley Leisure Products Pty Ltd v. Dokyo Co. Ltd (TRADE NAME: INTERLOCUTORY
INJUNCTION: C.A.)
Ten-Ichi Co. Ltd v. Jancar Ltd (TRADE MARK: WHETHER ACTION LIES WHERE NO
ACTIVE BUSINESS IN JURISDICTION: INTERNATIONAL REPUTATION: H.C.)

Patents

Catnic Components v. Hill & Smith Principles

Improver Corporation v. Raymond Industrial Ltd (RECONCILIATION OF
PRINCIPLES IN *Catnic*: OBVIOUSNESS: H.C.)

Certainty

Improver Corporation v. Raymond Industrial Ltd (DEPILATORY DEVICE:
CONSTRUCTION OF CLAIM: OBVIOUSNESS: C.A.)

Construction of Claim

Improver Corporation v. Raymond Industrial Ltd (DEPILATORY DEVICE:
OBVIOUSNESS: CERTAINTY: C.A.)

European Patent Convention

Improver Corporation v. Raymond Industrial Ltd (EUROPEAN PATENT: PROTOCOL
ON INTERPRETATION: INFRINGEMENT: VALIDITY: PURPOSIVE
CONSTRUCTION: EUROPEAN PATENT CONVENTION: INCONSISTENT PRIOR
EUROPEAN DECISIONS: H.C.)

Infringement

Canon KK v. Green Cartridge Company (Hong Kong) Ltd (STATUTORY
INTERPRETATION: EFFECT OF P.A.77 IN H.K.: EXTENT OF RIGHT TO REPAIR:
S.C.)
Improver Corporation v. Raymond Industrial Ltd (EUROPEAN PATENT: PROTOCOL
ON INTERPRETATION: VALIDITY: PURPOSIVE CONSTRUCTION:
RECONCILIATION OF PRINCIPLES IN *Catnic Components v. Hill & Smith*:
OBVIOUSNESS: H.C.)
Improver Corporation v. Raymond Industrial Ltd (DEPILATORY DEVICE:
CONSTRUCTION OF CLAIM: OBVIOUSNESS: CERTAINTY: C.A.)
Pfizer Inc. v. Jiwa International (H.K.) Co. (REGISTRATION OF U.K. PATENT UNDER
LOCAL ORDINANCE: EFFECT: POSITION OF LICENSEE: H.C.)

Licensee

Pfizer Inc. v. Jiwa International (H.K.) Co. (INFRINGEMENT: REGISTRATION OF
U.K. PATENT UNDER LOCAL ORDINANCE: EFFECT OF: COMMON LAW: H.C.)

Obviousness

Improver Corporation v. Raymond Industrial Ltd (EUROPEAN PATENT: PROTOCOL
ON INTERPRETATION: INFRINGEMENT: VALIDITY: PURPOSIVE
CONSTRUCTION: RECONCILIATION OF PRINCIPLES IN *Catnic Components v.
Hill & Smith*: H.C.)
Improver Corporation v. Raymond Industrial Ltd (DEPILATORY DEVICE:
CONSTRUCTION OF CLAIM: CERTAINTY: NO INFRINGEMENT: C.A.)

Protocol on Interpretation

Improver Corporation v. Raymond Industrial Ltd (EUROPEAN PATENT: EUROPEAN
PATENT CONVENTION: INCONSISTENT PRIOR EUROPEAN DECISIONS: H.C.)

Purposive Construction

Improver Corporation v. Raymond Industrial Ltd (INFRINGEMENT: VALIDITY:
RECONCILIATION OF PRINCIPLES IN *Catnic Components v. Hill & Smith*:
OBVIOUSNESS: EUROPEAN PATENT CONVENTION: INCONSISTENT PRIOR
EUROPEAN DECISIONS: H.C.)

Patent (U.K.)—Effect of Registration of Under Local Ordinance

Pfizer Inc. v. Jiwa International (H.K.) Co. (INFRINGEMENT: POSITION OF
LICENSEE: EFFECT OF PATENT IN HONG KONG UNDER COMMON LAW: H.C.)

Patent Act 1977 (U.K.)

Canon KK v. Green Cartridge Company (Hong Kong) Ltd (EFFECT IN H.K.: S.C.)

Validity

Improver Corporation v. Raymond Industrial Ltd (EUROPEAN PATENT: PROTOCOL
ON INTERPRETATION: INFRINGEMENT: PURPOSIVE CONSTRUCTION:
RECONCILIATION OF PRINCIPLES IN *Catnic Components v. Hill & Smith*:
OBVIOUSNESS: H.C.)

Practice and Miscellaneous Subjects

Anton Piller Order

Guess? Inc. v. Lee (NON-DISCLOSURE: C.A.)
Mattel Inc. v. Tonka Corp. (DISCHARGE OF ORDER FOR MISLEADING EVIDENCE:
SERVICE OUT OF THE JURISDICTION: S.C.)

Appeal

Attorney-General v. South China Morning Post (*Ex parte* INJUNCTION: DISCHARGE: LEAVE TO APPEAL TO PRIVY COUNCIL: S.C.: C.A.)

Arguable Case

Attorney-General v. South China Morning Post Ltd (CONTINUING INTEREST WORTHY OF PROTECTION AND ARGUABLE CASE FOR PERMANENT INJUNCTION AFTER TRIAL DEMONSTRATED BY PLAINTIFF: C.A.)
Mattel Inc. v. Tonka Corp. (H.C.)

Burden of Proof

Phonographic Performance (South East Asia) Ltd v. California Entertainments Ltd (C.A.)

Evidence

Mattel Inc. v. Tonka Corp. (*Ex parte* ORDER: GRANT ON INNOCENT MISTAKE OF FACT: H.C.) (DISCHARGE OF ANTON PILLER ORDER FOR MISLEADING EVIDENCE: S.C.)

Ex Parte Order or Injunction

Attorney-General v. South China Morning Post (DISCHARGE: APPEAL: LEAVE TO APPEAL TO PRIVY COUNCIL: S.C.: C.A.)
Mattel Inc. v. Tonka Corp. (SERVICE ABROAD: GRANT ON INNOCENT MISTAKE OF FACT: H.C.) (DISCHARGE OF ANTON PILLER ORDER FOR MISLEADING EVIDENCE: S.C.)

Interlocutory Injunction

Attorney-General v. South China Morning Post Ltd (BALANCING COMPETING INTERESTS OF PUBLIC SECURITY AND FREEDOM OF SPEECH: CONTINUING INTEREST WORTHY OF PROTECTION AND ARGUABLE CASE FOR PERMANENT INJUNCTION AFTER TRIAL DEMONSTRATED BY PLAINTIFF: C.A.)
Interlego AG v. Tyco Industries Inc. (MISREPRESENTATION: H.C.: C.A.)
Riley Leisure Products Pty Ltd v. Dokyo Co. Ltd (C.A.)

Jurisdiction. *See also under* Service out of the Jurisdiction

Ten-Ichi Co. Ltd v. Jancar Ltd (WHETHER ACTION LIES WHERE NO ACTIVE BUSINESS IN JURISDICTION: H.C.)

Leave to Appeal

Attorney-General v. South China Morning Post (*Ex parte* INJUNCTION: DISCHARGE: LEAVE TO APPEAL TO PRIVY COUNCIL: S.C.: C.A.)

Mareva Injunction

Ka Wah International Merchant Finance Ltd v. Asean Resources Ltd (PROCEDURE: FOREIGN ASSETS: H.C.)

Representative Actions

CBS/Sony (Hong Kong) Ltd v. Television Broadcasts Ltd (TAPE RECORDINGS: STRIKING OUT: H.C.: S.C.)

Service out of the Jurisdiction

Mattel Inc. v. Tonka Corp. (DISCHARGE OF ANTON PILLER ORDER FOR MISLEADING EVIDENCE: S.C.)

Striking Out

CBS/Sony (Hong Kong) Ltd v. Television Broadcasts Ltd (COPYRIGHT: INFRINGEMENT: REPRESENTATIVE ACTIONS: H.C.: S.C.)

Trade Marks

Anton Piller Order. *See* **Practice** (*Anton Piller order*)

Copyright Act 1956

Mattel Inc. v. Tonka Corp. (MEANING OF IMPORT IN SECTION 5(2) AS EXTENDED TO HONG KONG: S.C.)

Criminal Penalties

R. v. Ng Wen Chein (INFRINGEMENT: FORGERY: IMPRISONMENT: S.C.)

Damages. *See* **Practice** (*Damages*)

Ex Parte **Order.** *See* **Practice** (*Ex parte order*)

Forgery

R. v. Ng Wen Chein (INFRINGEMENT: CRIMINAL PENALTIES: IMPRISONMENT: S.C.)

Good Arguable Case. *See* **Practice** (*Good arguable case*)

Import

Mattel Inc. v. Tonka Corp. (MEANING OF UNDER SECTION 5(2) OF U.K. COPYRIGHT ACT 1956 AS EXTENDED TO HONG KONG: DISCHARGE OF ANTON PILLER ORDER FOR MISLEADING EVIDENCE: SERVICE OUT OF THE JURISDICTION: S.C.)

Imprisonment

R. v. Ng Wen Chein (INFRINGEMENT: FORGERY: CRIMINAL PENALTIES: S.C.)

Infringement

Mattel Inc. v. Tonka Corp. (GOOD ARGUABLE CASE: WHETHER DEFENDANT PROCURED PRINTING OF PACKAGING: *Ex parte* ORDER: SERVICE ABROAD: GRANT ON INNOCENT MISTAKE OF FACT: H.C.)

R. v. Ng Wen Chein (FORGERY: CRIMINAL PENALTIES: IMPRISONMENT: S.C.)

Injunction. *See* **Practice** (*Injunction*)

Interlocutory Injunction. *See* **Practice** (*Interlocutory injunction*)

International Reputation

Ten-Ichi Co. Ltd v. Jancar Ltd (PASSING OFF: WHETHER ACTION LIES WHERE NO ACTIVE BUSINESS IN JURISDICTION: H.C.)

Jurisdiction. *See* **Practice** (*Jurisdiction*)

Passing Off

Land Power International Holdings Ltd v. Inter-Land Properties (H.K.) Ltd (COMMON DESCRIPTIVE WORDS USED AS MARK: LITTLE DIFFERENCES SUFFICE TO AVOID CONFUSION: C.A.)

Riley Leisure Products Pty Ltd v. Dokyo Co. Ltd (TRADE NAME: INTERLOCUTORY INJUNCTION: C.A.)

Ten-Ichi Co. Ltd v. Jancar Ltd (WHETHER ACTION LIES WHERE NO ACTIVE BUSINESS IN JURISDICTION: INTERNATIONAL REPUTATION: H.C.)

Practice

Anton Piller order

Mattel Inc. v. Tonka Corp. (INFRINGEMENT: *Ex parte* ORDER: SERVICE ABROAD: GRANT ON INNOCENT MISTAKE: H.C.) (DISCHARGE OF ORDER FOR MISLEADING EVIDENCE: S.C.)

Damages

Ten-Ichi Co. Ltd v. Jancar Ltd (WHETHER ACTION LIES WHERE NO ACTIVE BUSINESS IN JURISDICTION: INTERNATIONAL REPUTATION: WHETHER RECOVERABLE: H.C.)

Ex parte order

Mattel Inc. v. Tonka Corp. (SERVICE ABROAD: GRANT ON INNOCENT MISTAKE OF FACT: DISCHARGE: H.C.) (DISCHARGE OF ANTON PILLER ORDER FOR MISLEADING EVIDENCE: S.C.)

Good arguable case

Mattel Inc. v. Tonka Corp. (INFRINGEMENT: WHETHER DEFENDANT PROCURED PRINTING OF PACKAGING: *Ex parte* ORDER: H.C.: S.C.)

Injunction

Ten-Ichi Co. Ltd v. Jancar Ltd (PASSING OFF: WHETHER ACTION LIES WHERE NO ACTIVE BUSINESS IN JURISDICTION: H.C.)

Interlocutory injunction

Riley Leisure Products Pty Ltd v. Dokyo Co. Ltd (PASSING OFF: TRADE NAME: C.A.)

Jurisdiction

Ten-Ichi Co. Ltd v. Jancar Ltd (WHETHER ACTION LIES WHERE NO ACTIVE BUSINESS IN JURISDICTION: H.C.)

967

Service Abroad

Mattel Inc. v. Tonka Corp. (*Ex parte* ORDER: GRANT ON INNOCENT MISTAKE OF FACT: H.C.) (DISCHARGE OF ANTON PILLER ORDER FOR MISLEADING EVIDENCE: SERVICE OUT OF THE JURISDICTION: S.C.)

Procurement

Mattel Inc. v. Tonka Corp. (INFRINGEMENT: PROCUREMENT OF PRINTING OF PACKAGING: H.C.)

Reputation

Ten-Ichi Co. Ltd v. Jancar Ltd (WHETHER ACTION LIES WHERE NO ACTIVE BUSINESS IN JURISDICTION: INTERNATIONAL REPUTATION: H.C.)

Service Abroad. *See* **Practice** (*Service Abroad*)

INDIA

Confidential Information and Breach of Confidence

Applicability of English Authorities

Brady v. Chemical Process Equipment Pvt. Ltd (COPYRIGHT: INFRINGEMENT: INTERIM INJUNCTION: H.C.)

Machine Drawings

Brady v. Chemical Process Equipment Pvt. Ltd (COPYRIGHT: INFRINGEMENT: INTERIM INJUNCTION: H.C.)

Copyright

Ad interim **Injunction.** *See* **Practice** (*Ad interim injunction*)

Agreement to Assign

Heptulla v. Orient Longman Ltd (JOINT AUTHORSHIP: GHOST–WRITTEN MEMOIRS: DEFINITION OF AUTHOR: HEIRS OF AUTHOR: H.C.)

Appeal. *See* **Practice** (*Appeal*)

Author and Authorship

Heptulla v. Orient Longman Ltd (JOINT AUTHORSHIP: GHOST–WRITTEN MEMOIRS: DEFINITION OF AUTHOR: HEIRS OF AUTHOR: H.C.)
Smt Mannu Bhandari v. Kala Vikas Pictures Pvt. Ltd (FILMING RIGHTS: ASSIGNMENT: H.C.)

Balance of Convenience. *See* **Practice** (*Balance of convenience*)

Brochure

Lamba Brothers Ltd v. Lamba Brothers (INFRINGEMENT: NO CLAIM TO COPYRIGHT: H.C.)

Cable TV Network, Exhibition of Video Films Over. *See* **Films**

Cartoon Characters. *See* **Films**

Cinematograph Films. *See* **Films**

Cognizance of Complaint. *See* **Practice** (*Cognizance of complaint*)

Complaint, Cognizance of

Consent Decree in United States

Copyright Notice

Lamba Brothers Ltd v. Lamba Brothers (INFRINGEMENT: BROCHURE NOT INDICATING CLAIM TO COPYRIGHT: H.C.)

Criminal Action

Flower Tobacco Co. v. Mottaahedah Bros (INFRINGEMENT: H.C.)
Jogendra Nath Sen v. State (INFRINGEMENT: H.C.)
Sumeet Machines Pvt. Ltd v. Sumeet Research & Holdings Ltd (INFRINGEMENT: SIMULTANEOUS LAUNCHING OF CIVIL AND CRIMINAL PROCEEDINGS: H.C.)

Design. *See* Indian **Design**

Destruction of Work

Amar Nath Sehgal v. Union of India (ARTISTIC WORK: MURAL: DETERIORATION: *Ex parte* INTERIM INJUNCTION TO PREVENT LOSS: H.C.)

Deterioration of Work

Amar Nath Sehgal v. Union of India (ARTISTIC WORK: MURAL: DETERIORATION: *Ex parte* INTERIM INJUNCTION TO PREVENT LOSS: H.C.)

English Authorities, Applicability of. *See* **Practice** (*English authorities, applicability of*)

Estoppel. *See* **Practice** (*Estoppel*)

Exclusive licence. *See* **Licence**

Ex-employee

Thomas (V.T.) v. Malayala Manorama Co. Ltd (CARTOONS: PREVENTION OF PUBLICATION AFTER TERMINATION OF EMPLOYMENT: *Ad interim ex parte* INJUNCTION VACATED: H.C.)

Exhibition of Video Films over Cable TV Network. *See* **Films**

Ex Parte **Injunction.** *See* **Practice** (*Ex parte injunction*)

Filming Rights

Smt Mannu Bhandari v. Kala Vikas Pictures Pvt. Ltd (ASSIGNMENT: AUTHOR'S RIGHTS: H.C.)

Films

Everest Pictures Circuit v. Karuppannan (INFRINGEMENT: H.C.)
Garware Plastics & Polyester Ltd v. Telelink (INFRINGEMENT: EXHIBITION OF VIDEO FILMS OVER CABLE TV NETWORK: INJUNCTION: H.C.)
Madhavan v. S.K. Nayar (ALLEGED COPYING OF NOVEL BY CINEMATOGRAPH FILM: INFRINGEMENT: APPEAL: H.C.)
Smt Mannu Bhandari v. Kala Vikas Pictures Pvt. Ltd (FILMING RIGHTS: ASSIGNMENT: AUTHOR'S RIGHTS: H.C.)
Thomas (V.T.) v. Malayala Manorama Co. Ltd (CARTOONS: EX-EMPLOYEE: PUBLICATION AFTER TERMINATION OF EMPLOYMENT: *Ad interim ex parte* INJUNCTION VACATED: H.C.) (PETITION FOR STAY OF *ex parte* INJUNCTION: H.C.)

Get-up

Camlin Pvt. Ltd v. National Pencil Industries (TRADE MARK: INFRINGEMENT: PASSING OFF: CAMLIN FLORA/TIGER FLORE: MARK AND CARTON DIFFERENT: GET-UP AND DESIGN OF PENCIL LIKELY TO CONFUSE SMALL CHILDREN: INTERIM INJUNCTION: H.C.)
Shri Prem Singh v. Ceeam Auto Industries (INFRINGEMENT: PIRACY: LACK OF EQUITY: H.C.)

Ghost-written Memoirs

Heptulla v. Orient Longman Ltd (JOINT AUTHORSHIP: DEFINITION OF AUTHOR: H.C.)

Heirs of Author. *See* **Author and Authorship**

Importation

Gramaphone Co. of India Ltd v. Birendra Bahadur Pande (MUSICAL RECORDS: S.C.)
Grammophone Company of India Ltd v. Pandey (INTERNATIONAL COPYRIGHT: S.C.)

Information

Glaxo Operations U.K. Ltd v. Rama Bhaktha Hanuman Candle & Camphor Works (JOINDER OF CAUSE OF ACTION: JURISDICTION: INTERIM INJUNCTION: H.C.)

Infringement

Brady v. Chemical Process Equipments Pte Ltd. (BREACH OF CONFIDENCE: MACHINE DRAWINGS: THREE-DIMENSIONAL REPRODUCTION: APPLICABILITY OF ENGLISH AUTHORITIES: H.C.(Delhi))
Brooke Bond (India) Ltd v. Balaji Tea (India) Pvt. Ltd (TRADE MARK: PASSING OFF: INJUNCTION: H.C.)

Brooke Bond India Ltd v. Raj Kamal Enterprises (REGISTERED DESIGN: PACKAGE LABEL: INTERIM INJUNCTION: H.C.)

Burroughs Wellcome (India) Ltd v. G.K. Sharma & King Scientific Research Centre (JURISDICTION OF COURT TO ENTERTAIN COMPOSITE SUIT: INTERIM INJUNCTION: H.C.)

Charan Dass & Veer Industries (India) v. Bombay Crockery House (DESIGN: INTERIM INJUNCTION: H.C.)

Chawrana Tobacco Co. v. Bhagwandas (INTERIM INJUNCTION: H.C.)

Everest Pictures Circuit v. Karuppannan (CINEMATOGRAPH FILM: H.C.)

Flower Tobacco Co. v. Mottaahedah Bros (CRIMINAL ACTION: H.C.)

Garware Plastics & Polyester Ltd v. Telelink (EXHIBITION OF VIDEO FILMS OVER CABLE TV NETWORK: INJUNCTION: H.C.)

Gold Seal Engineering Products Pvt. Ltd v. Hindustan Manufacturers (TRADE MARK: PASSING OFF: JURISDICTION: JOINDER OF CAUSES OF ACTION: H.C.)

Gramaphone Co. of India Ltd v. Electroband (India) Pvt. Ltd (RECORDS, CASSETTES: INTERIM ORDER: H.C.)

Gramaphone Co. of India Ltd v. The Oriental Gramophone Records Co. (RECORDS, CASSETTES: INTERIM INJUNCTION: H.C.)

Gurshant Engineering Co. Pvt. Ltd v. DLF Universals Ltd (PASSING OFF: APPEAL: H.C.)

Habeebur Rehman & Sons v. Ram Babu & Brothers (TRADE MARK: PASSING OFF: COPYRIGHT IN LABEL: DEFENDANT PRIOR REGISTRANT: INTERIM INJUNCTION: APPEAL: H.C.)

Heptulla v. Orient Longman Ltd (PUBLICATION OF EXTRACT: INTERIM INJUNCTION: H.C.)

Hindustan Pencils Pvt. Ltd v. India Stationery Products Co. (TRADE MARK: INTERIM INJUNCTION: REGISTRATION UNDER COPYRIGHT ACT: *Ex parte* INJUNCTION: DELAY, LACHES AND ACQUIESCENCE: H.C.)

Jogendra Nath Sen v. State (CRIMINAL COMPLAINT: H.C.)

Kissan Industries v. Punjab Food Corp. (TRADE MARK: PASSING OFF: INFRINGEMENT: H.C.)

Lamba Brothers Ltd v. Lamba Brothers (BROCHURE NOT INDICATING CLAIM TO COPYRIGHT: H.C.)

Madhavan v. S.K. Nayar (ALLEGED COPYING OF NOVEL BY CINEMATOGRAPH FILM: APPEAL: H.C.)

Mohanlal Gupta v. The Board of School Education, Haryana (H.C.)

Monsoon Ltd v. India Imports of Rhode Island Ltd (PRINTED FABRICS: SECONDARY INFRINGEMENT: PERIOD OF GRACE BEFORE FIXED WITH KNOWLEDGE: Ch.D.)

Nirex Industries (Pvt.) Ltd v. Manchand Footwears (TRADE MARK: JURISDICTION: INTERIM INJUNCTION: H.C.)

P.M. Diesels Ltd v. S.M. Diesels (TRADE MARK: COPYRIGHT IN MARK: FIELD MARSHAL/SONAMARSHAL: TRADING STYLE: INTERIM INJUNCTION: H.C.)

Parkash Roadlines Ltd v. Parkash Parcel Services (Pvt.) Ltd (TRADE MARK: PASSING OFF: INTERIM INJUNCTION: H.C.)

Penguin Books Ltd v. India Book Distributors (CONSENT DECREE IN UNITED STATES APPEAL: INTERLOCUTORY INJUNCTION: H.C.)

Pidilite Industries Pvt. Ltd v. Mittees Corporation (INTERIM INJUNCTION: THREATS: H.C.)

Richardson Vicks Inc. v. Vikas Pharmaceuticals (PASSING OFF: *Ad interim* INJUNCTION MADE ABSOLUTE: H.C.)

Shri Prem Singh v. Ceeam Auto Industries (GET-UP: PIRACY: LACK OF EQUITY: H.C.)

Sumeet Machines Pvt. Ltd v. Sumeet Research & Holdings Ltd (TRADE MARK: SIMULTANEOUS LAUNCHING OF CIVIL AND CRIMINAL PROCEEDINGS: H.C.)
Tata Oil Mills Co. Ltd v. Reward Soap Works (INTERIM INJUNCTION: H.C.)
Tobu Interprises Pvt. Ltd v. Tokyo Cycle Industries (PASSING OFF: H.C.)

Interim Injunction. *See* **Practice** (*Interim or interlocutory injunction*)

Interlocutory Injunction. *See* **Practice** (*Interim or interlocutory injunction*)

International Copyright

Grammophone Company of India Ltd v. Pandey (IMPORTATION: S.C.)

Joint Authorship. *See* **Author and Authorship**

Jurisdiction. *See* **Practice** (*Jurisdiction*)

Label

Brooke Bond India Ltd v. Raj Kamal Enterprises (REGISTERED DESIGN: INFRINGEMENT: INTERIM INJUNCTION: H.C.)
Habeebur Rehman & Sons v. Ram Babu & Brothers (INFRINGEMENT: DEFENDANT PRIOR REGISTRANT: INTERIM INJUNCTION: APPEAL: H.C.)
William Grant & Sons Ltd v. McDowell & Co. Ltd (DESIGN AND DEFINITION OF LABEL: GET-UP: H.C.)

Licence

K.I. George v. Cheriyan (EXCLUSIVE LICENCE: JURISDICTION: H.C.)

Machine Drawings

Brady v. Chemical Process Equipment Pvt. Ltd (INFRINGEMENT: BREACH OF CONFIDENCE: INTERIM INJUNCTION: H.C.)

Mural

Amar Nath Sehgal v. Union of India (ARTISTIC WORK: DESTRUCTION: DETERIORATION: *Ex parte* INTERIM INJUNCTION TO PREVENT LOSS: H.C.)

Music

Gramaphone Co. of India Ltd v. Birendra Bahadur Pande (RECORDS: IMPORT: S.C.)
Super Cassette Industries Ltd v. Bathla Cassettes India (Pvt.) Ltd (THREATS: INJUNCTION: APPEAL TO VACATE: H.C.)

PhD Thesis

Fateh Singh Mehta v. O.P. Singhal (INJUNCTION TO PREVENT UNIVERSITY FROM AWARDING PhD: H.C.)

Piracy

Shri Prem Singh v. Ceeam Auto Industries (INFRINGEMENT: GET-UP: LACK OF EQUITY: H.C.)

Period of Grace. *See* **Practice** (*Period of grace*)

Petition. *See* **Practice** (*Petition*)

Practice

Ad interim Injunction

Richardson Vicks Inc. v. Vikas Pharmaceuticals (*Ad interim* INJUNCTION MADE ABSOLUTE: H.C.)

Appeal

Gurshant Engineering Co. Pvt. Ltd v. DLF Universals Ltd (H.C.)

Habeebur Rehman & Sons v. Ram Babu & Brothers (TRADE MARK: INFRINGEMENT: PASSING OFF: COPYRIGHT IN LABEL: INFRINGEMENT: DEFENDANT PRIOR REGISTRANT: INTERIM INJUNCTION: H.C.)

Madhavan v. S.K. Nayar (ALLEGED COPYING OF NOVEL BY CINEMATOGRAPH FILM: H.C.)

Penguin Books Ltd v. India Book Distributors (INFRINGEMENT: CONSENT DECREE IN UNITED STATES: INTERLOCUTORY INJUNCTION: H.C.)

Super Cassette Industries Ltd v. Bathla Cassettes India (Pvt.) Ltd (SONGS OF PAKISTANI ARTIST'S: THREATS: APPEAL TO VACATE INJUNCTION: H.C.)

Balance of convenience

Heptulla v. Orient Longman Ltd (JOINT AUTHORSHIP: GHOST-WRITTEN MEMOIRS: DEFINITION OF AUTHOR: HEIRS OF AUTHOR: AGREEMENT TO ASSIGN COPYRIGHT: PUBLICATION OF EXTRACT: H.C.)

Cognizance of complaint

Brundaban Sahu v. Rajendra Subudhi Subudhi (UNREGISTERED MARK AND LABEL: H.C.)

Delay, laches and acquiescence

Hindustan Pencils Pvt. Ltd v. India Stationery Products Co. (TRADE MARK: INFRINGEMENT: INTERIM INJUNCTION: REGISTRATION UNDER COPYRIGHT ACT: *Ex parte* INJUNCTION: H.C.)

English authorities, applicability of

Brady v. Chemical Process Equipments Pte Ltd. (INFRINGEMENT: BREACH OF CONFIDENCE: THREE-DIMENSIONAL REPRODUCTION: H.C.(Delhi))

Equity

Shri Prem Singh v. Ceeam Auto Industries (INFRINGEMENT: GET-UP: PIRACY: LACK OF EQUITY: H.C.)

Estoppel

Heptulla v. Orient Longman Ltd (AGREEMENT TO ASSIGN COPYRIGHT: PUBLICATION OF EXTRACT: INTERIM INJUNCTION: BALANCE OF CONVENIENCE: H.C.)

Ex parte injunction

Amar Nath Sehgal v. Union of India (ARTISTIC WORK: MURAL: DESTRUCTION: DETERIORATION: H.C.)

Hindustan Pencils Pvt. Ltd v. India Stationery Products Co. (TRADE MARK: INFRINGEMENT: INTERIM INJUNCTION: REGISTRATION UNDER COPYRIGHT ACT: DELAY, LACHES AND ACQUIESCENCE: H.C.)

Thomas (V.T.) v. Malayala Manorama Co. Ltd (CARTOON CHARACTERS: PETITION FOR STAY OF *ex parte* INJUNCTION: H.C.) (*Ad interim ex parte* INJUNCTION VACATED: H.C.)

Interim or interlocutory injunction

Camlin Pvt. Ltd v. National Pencil Industries (H.C.)

Charan Dass & Veer Industries (India) v. Bombay Crockery House (H.C.)

Chawrana Tobacco Co. v. Bhagwandas (H.C.)

Glaxo Operations U.K. Ltd v. Rama Bhaktha Hanuman Candle & Camphor Works (TRADE MARK: INFORMATION: JOINDER OF CAUSE OF ACTION: JURISDICTION: H.C.)

Gramaphone Co. of India Ltd v. The Oriental Gramophone Records Co. (INFRINGEMENT: RECORDS, CASSETTES: H.C.)

Habeebur Rehman & Sons v. Ram Babu & Brothers (TRADE MARK: INFRINGEMENT: PASSING OFF: COPYRIGHT IN LABEL: INFRINGEMENT: DEFENDANT PRIOR REGISTRANT: APPEAL: H.C.)

Hindustan Pencils Pvt. Ltd v. India Stationery Products Co. (TRADE MARK: INFRINGEMENT: REGISTRATION UNDER COPYRIGHT ACT: *Ex parte* INJUNCTION: DELAY, LACHES AND ACQUIESCENCE: H.C.)

Nirex Industries (Pvt.) Ltd v. Manchand Footwears (H.C.)

Penguin Books Ltd v. India Book Distributors (H.C.)

Parkash Roadlines Ltd v. Parkash Parcel Services (Pvt.) Ltd (TRADE MARK: INFRINGEMENT: PASSING OFF: H.C.)

Pidilite Industries Pvt. Ltd v. Mittees Corporation (H.C.)

P.M. Diesels Ltd v. S.M. Diesels (TRADE MARK: COPYRIGHT IN MARK: INFRINGEMENT: FIELD MARSHAL/SONAMARSHAL: TRADING STYLE: H.C.)

Tata Oil Mills Co. Ltd v. Reward Soap Works (H.C.)

William Grant & Sons Ltd v. McDowell & Co. Ltd (H.C.)

Interim order

Gramaphone Co. of India Ltd v. Electroband (India) Pvt. Ltd (INFRINGEMENT: RECORDS, CASSETTES: H.C.)

Joinder of causes of action

Glaxo Operations U.K. Ltd v. Rama Bhaktha Hanuman Candle & Camphor Works (TRADE MARK: INFORMATION: JURISDICTION: INTERIM INJUNCTION: H.C.)

Gold Seal Engineering Products Pvt. Ltd v. Hindustan Manufacturers (TRADE MARK: INFRINGEMENT: PASSING OFF: JURISDICTION: H.C.)

Jurisdiction

Burroughs Wellcome (India) Ltd v. G.K. Sharma & King Scientific Research Centre (INFRINGEMENT: TRADE MARK: PASSING OFF: JURISDICTION OF COURT TO ENTERTAIN COMPOSITE SUIT: H.C.)

Glaxo Operations U.K. Ltd v. Rama Bhaktha Hanuman Candle & Camphor Works (TRADE MARK: INFORMATION: JOINDER OF CAUSE OF ACTION: INTERIM INJUNCTION: H.C.)

Gold Seal Engineering Products Pvt. Ltd v. Hindustan Manufacturers (TRADE MARK: INFRINGEMENT: PASSING OFF: JOINDER OF CAUSES OF ACTION: H.C.)

K.I. George v. Cheriyan (EXCLUSIVE LICENCE: H.C.)

Mohan Meaking Ltd v. Kashmiri Dreamland Distilleries (TRADE MARK: PASSING OFF: M.M.B./M.B.B.: H.C.)

Nirex Industries (Pvt.) Ltd v. Manchand Footwears (INFRINGEMENT: TRADE MARK: H.C.)

Overseas consent decree

Penguin Books Ltd v. India Book Distributors (INFRINGEMENT: CONSENT DECREE IN UNITED STATES: H.C.)

Period of grace

Monsoon Ltd v. India Imports of Rhode Island Ltd (PRINTED FABRICS: SECONDARY INFRINGEMENT: PERIOD OF GRACE BEFORE FIXED WITH KNOWLEDGE: Ch.D.)

Petition

Thomas (V.T.) v. Malayala Manorama Co. Ltd (PETITION FOR STAY OF *ex parte* INJUNCTION: H.C.)

Stay

Thomas (V.T.) v. Malayala Manorama Co. Ltd (PETITION FOR STAY OF *ex parte* INJUNCTION: H.C.) (*Ad interim ex parte* INJUNCTION VACATED: H.C.)

Printed Fabrics

Monsoon Ltd v. India Imports of Rhode Island Ltd (SECONDARY INFRINGEMENT: PERIOD OF GRACE BEFORE FIXED WITH KNOWLEDGE: Ch.D.)

Prior Registration as Trade Mark

HMT Ltd v. Girnar Ltd (ARTISTIC WORK: Cprt Brd)

Publication of Extract

Heptulla v. Orient Longman Ltd (AGREEMENT TO ASSIGN COPYRIGHT: H.C.)

Records, Cassettes

Gramaphone Co. of India Ltd v. Electroband (India) Pvt. Ltd (INFRINGEMENT: INTERIM ORDER: H.C.)

Gramaphone Co. of India Ltd v. The Oriental Gramophone Records Co. (INFRINGEMENT: INTERIM INJUNCTION: H.C.)

Registered Design

Brooke Bond India Ltd v. Raj Kamal Enterprises (PACKAGE LABEL: INFRINGEMENT: INTERIM INJUNCTION: H.C.)

Registration

D'Vaiz Chemical v. Kundu Coatar Co. (TRADE MARK: PRIOR RIGHTS: PRIOR USER: INTERLOCUTORY INJUNCTION: H.C.)

Hindustan Pencils Pvt. Ltd v. India Stationery Products Co. (TRADE MARK: INFRINGEMENT: INTERIM INJUNCTION: *Ex parte* INJUNCTION: DELAY, LACHES AND ACQUIESCENCE: H.C.)

Removal from Register

Associated Electronics & Electricals Industries Pvt. Ltd v. Sharp Tools (ARTISTIC WORKS: APPEAL: H.C.)

Reputation

William Grant & Sons Ltd v. McDowell & Co. Ltd (PASSING OFF: COPYRIGHT: INTERLOCUTORY INJUNCTION: SINGLE MALT SCOTCH WHISKY: DESIGN AND DEFINITION OF LABEL: GET-UP: TRANS-BORDER REPUTATION OF PRODUCT AVAILABLE IN INDIA: EROSION OF REPUTATION: GENERIC NATURE OF PRODUCT: H.C.)

Secondary Infringement. *See also under* **Infringement**

Monsoon Ltd v. India Imports of Rhode Island Ltd (PRINTED FABRICS: SECONDARY INFRINGEMENT: PERIOD OF GRACE BEFORE FIXED WITH KNOWLEDGE: Ch.D.)

Stay. *See* **Practice** (*Stay*)

Threats

Pidilite Industries Pvt. Ltd v. Mittees Corporation (INFRINGEMENT: INTERIM INJUNCTION: H.C.)
Super Cassette Industries Ltd v. Bathla Cassettes India (Pvt.) Ltd (THREATS: INJUNCTION: APPEAL TO VACATE: H.C.)

Three-dimensional Reproduction

Brady v. Chemical Process Equipments Pte Ltd (INFRINGEMENT: APPLICABILITY OF ENGLISH AUTHORITIES: H.C.(Delhi))

Trade Mark, Copyright in

P.M. Diesels Ltd v. S.M. Diesels (INFRINGEMENT: FIELD MARSHAL/ SONAMARSHAL: TRADING STYLE: INTERIM INJUNCTION: H.C.)

Trading Style

P.M. Diesels Ltd v. S.M. Diesels (TRADE MARK: COPYRIGHT IN MARK: INFRINGEMENT: FIELD MARSHAL/SONAMARSHAL: INTERIM INJUNCTION: H.C.)

Video films. *See* **Films**

Design

Appeal. *See* **Practice** (*Appeal*)

Cancellation

Domestic Appliances v. Globe Super Parts (INFRINGEMENT: CANCELLATION: H.C.)
Engineering & Pulp Producers Pvt. Ltd v. Raj Kumar Shah & Cons (H.C.)

Joginder Singh v. M/s Tobu Enterprises (P.) Ltd (TRICYCLES AND SEATS: CANCELLATION: PRIOR PUBLICATION: LACK OF NOVELTY: H.C.)

Khaitan (India) Ltd v. Metropolitan Appliances (SUBSEQUENT REGISTRATION OF IDENTICAL DESIGN: H.C.)

Plastella M/s v. Controller of Patents and Designs (CANCELLATION: PRIOR PUBLICATION: APPEAL: H.C.)

Expiry

Hindustan Lever Ltd v. V.V. Dhanushkodi Nadar & Sons (INFRINGEMENT: PASSING OFF: INTERIM INJUNCTION: TRANSFER OF SUIT: H.C.)

Infringement

Bansal Plastic Industries v. Neeraj Toys Industries (INTERIM INJUNCTION: H.C.)

Brooke Bond India Ltd v. Raj Kamal Enterprises (PACKAGE LABEL: INTERIM INJUNCTION: H.C.)

Charan Dass & Veer Industries (India) v. Bombay Crockery House (TRADE MARK: PASSING OFF: INTERIM INJUNCTION: H.C.)

Domestic Appliances v. Globe Super Parts (CANCELLATION: H.C.)

Hindustan Lever Ltd v. V.V. Dhanushkodi Nadar & Sons (PASSING OFF: INTERIM INJUNCTION: EXPIRED: TRANSFER OF SUIT: H.C.)

Niky Tasha India Pvt. Ltd v. Faridabad Gas Gadgets Pvt. Ltd (INTERLOCUTORY INJUNCTION: H.C.)

Smt Moneka Chawla v. National Trading Co. (INTERIM INJUNCTION: APPLICATION TO VACATE: H.C.)

Interim or Interlocutory Injunction. *See* **Practice** *(Interim or interlocutory injunction)*

Jurisdiction. *See* **Practice** *(Jurisdiction)*

Lack of Novelty

Joginder Singh v. M/s Tobu Enterprises (P.) Ltd (TRICYCLES AND SEATS: CANCELLATION: PRIOR PUBLICATION: H.C.)

Package Label

Brooke Bond India Ltd v. Raj Kamal Enterprises (INFRINGEMENT: INTERIM INJUNCTION: H.C.)

Practice

Appeal

Plastella M/s v. Controller of Patents and Designs (CANCELLATION: PRIOR PUBLICATION: H.C.)

Interim or interlocutory injunction

Bansal Plastic Industries v. Neeraj Toys Industries (INFRINGEMENT: H.C.)

Brooke Bond India Ltd v. Raj Kamal Enterprises (PACKAGE LABEL: INFRINGEMENT: H.C.)

Charan Dass & Veer Industries (India) v. Bombay Crockery House (TRADE MARK: INFRINGEMENT: PASSING OFF: H.C.)

Hindustan Lever Ltd v. V.V. Dhanushkodi Nadar & Sons (INFRINGEMENT: PASSING OFF: H.C.)

Niky Tasha India Pvt. Ltd v. Faridabad Gas Gadgets Pvt. Ltd (INFRINGEMENT: H.C.)

Smt Moneka Chawla v. National Trading Co. (INFRINGEMENT: APPLICATION TO VACATE: H.C.)

Jurisdiction

Samir Senray's Design Application (PRELIMINARY OBJECTION ABOUT LACK OF JURISDICTION TO HEAR THE MATTER: Pat. Off.)

Preliminary objection

Samir Senray's Design Application (LACK OF JURISDICTION TO HEAR THE MATTER: Pat. Off.)

Transfer of suit

Hindustan Lever Ltd v. V.V. Dhanushkodi Nadar & Sons (INFRINGEMENT: PASSING OFF: INTERIM INJUNCTION: EXPIRED: H.C.)

Preliminary Objection. *See* **Practice** (*Preliminary objection*)

Prior Publication

Joginder Singh v. M/s Tobu Enterprises (P.) Ltd (TRICYCLES AND SEATS: CANCELLATION: LACK OF NOVELTY: H.C.)

Plastella M/s v. Controller of Patents and Designs (CANCELLATION: APPEAL: H.C.)

Registration

D'Vaiz Chemical v. Kundu Coatar Co. (TRADE MARK: PRIOR RIGHTS: PRIOR USER: INTERLOCUTORY INJUNCTION: H.C.)

Hindustan Pencils Pvt. Ltd v. India Stationery Products Co. (TRADE MARK: INFRINGEMENT: INTERIM INJUNCTION: *Ex parte* INJUNCTION: DELAY, LACHES AND ACQUIESCENCE: H.C.)

Removal from Register

Associated Electronics & Electricals Industries Pvt. Ltd v. Sharp Tools (ARTISTIC WORKS: APPEAL: H.C.)

Subsequent Registration of Identical Design

Khaitan (India) Ltd v. Metropolitan Appliances (CANCELLATION: H.C.)

Transfer of Suit. *See* **Practice** (*Transfer of suit*)

Passing Off

Acquiescence. *See* **Practice** (*Acquiescence*)

***Ad Interim* Injunction.** *See* **Practice** (*Ad interim injunction*)

Appeal. *See* **Practice** (*Appeal*)

Common Field of Activity

Apple Computer Inc. v. Apple Leasing Industries Ltd (RESTRAINT OF USE OF UNREGISTERED MARKS IN PROVISION OF SERVICES: INTERNATIONAL REPUTATION: H.C.)

Common to the Trade

Thapsons Pvt. Ltd v. Ashoka Food Industries (TRADE MARK: INFRINGEMENT: SIMILAR MARKS: *Ad interim* INJUNCTION: H.C.)

Conflict Between Licencees

Wander Ltd v. Antox India Pvt. Ltd (TRADE MARK: INTERIM INJUNCTION: APPEAL AND FURTHER APPEAL: H.C.)

Confusion

Camlin Pvt. Ltd v. National Pencil Industries (TRADE MARK AND CARTON DIFFERENT: GET-UP AND DESIGN LIKELY TO CONFUSE SMALL CHILDREN: INTERIM INJUNCTION: H.C.)

Deception

National Garments v. National Apparels (TRADE MARK: GET-UP: COVER OF BOXES: INTERIM INJUNCTION: APPEAL: H.C.)

MRF Ltd v. Metro Tyres Ltd (TRADE MARK: INFRINGEMENT: NYLOGRIP/ RADIALGRIP: INTERIM INJUNCTION: H.C.)

Deceptively Similar Trade Marks

Carew Phipson Ltd v. Deejay Distilleries Pvt. Ltd (PRE-MIXED ALCOHOLIC DRINKS: RIVAL MARKS NOT DECEPTIVELY SIMILAR: INTERIM INJUNCTION: H.C.)

Declaration. *See* Practice *(Declaration)*

Drug Controllers Licence

Fleming (India) v. Ambalal Sarabhai Enterprises (TRADE MARK: USE OF BRAND NAMES UNDER DRUG CONTROLLER'S LICENCE: INJUNCTION: APPEAL: H.C.)

Ex Parte Injunction. *See* Practice *(Ex parte injunction)*

Export

Brooke Bond India Ltd v. Balaji Tea (India) Pvt. Ltd (TRADE MARK: INFRINGEMENT: RED LABEL: RED APPLE TEA: PACKETS FILLED IN INDIA AND EXPORTED: H.C.)

Family Business

Power Control Appliances Co. v. Sumit Machines Pvt. Ltd (RIVAL BUSINESS ESTABLISHED BY FAMILY MEMBER: INTERIM INJUNCTION: APPEAL: H.C.)

Family Name. *See* Trade Marks and Trade Names

First to Enter Market

Duncan Agro Industries Ltd v. Somabhai Tea Processors (Pvt.) Ltd (TRADE MARK: FIRST TO ENTER MARKET: INTERIM INJUNCTION: APPEAL: H.C.)

Foreign Plaintiff or Proprietors

Agarwal (M.K.) v. Union of India (NEWPAPERS WITH IDENTICAL NAMES: FOREIGN PROPRIETORS: H.C.)

Revlon Inc. v. Kemco Chemicals (FOREIGN PLAINTIFF: NO LOCAL IMMOVABLE ASSETS STRIKING OUT: SECURITY FOR COSTS: H.C.)

Get-up

Camlin Pvt. Ltd v. National Pencil Industries (COPYRIGHT: INFRINGEMENT: TRADE MARK AND CARTON DIFFERENT: GET-UP AND DESIGN OF PENCIL LIKELY TO CONFUSE SMALL CHILDREN: H.C.)

National Garments v. National Apparels (TRADE MARK: COVER OF BOXES: DECEPTION: H.C.)

William Grant & Sons Ltd v. McDowell & Co. Ltd (DESIGN AND DEFINITION OF LABEL: TRANS-BORDER REPUTATION OF PRODUCT AVAILABLE IN INDIA: EROSION OF REPUTATION: H.C.)

Goods of Different Description

Daimler Benz AG v. Hybo Hindustan (TRADE MARK: INFRINGEMENT: BENZ: INTERIM INJUNCTION: H.C.)

Goodwill

Apple Computer Inc. v. Apple Leasing Industries Ltd (INTERNATIONAL REPUTATION: COMMON FIELD OF ACTIVITY: NATURE OF GOODWILL: H.C.)

House Mark. *See* Trade Marks and Trade Names

Identical Goods

Hindustan Radiators Co. v. Hindustan Radiators Ltd (IDENTICAL TRADING STYLE: INTERIM INJUNCTION: H.C.)

Interim and Interlocutory Injunction. *See* Practice *(Interim and interlocutory injunction)*

International Reputation. *See* Reputation

Injunction

Blue Cross & Blue Shield Association v. Blue Cross Health Clinic (TRADE MARK: INFRINGEMENT: H.C.)

Brooke Bond (India) Ltd v. Balaji Tea (India) Pvt. Ltd (TRADE MARK: INFRINGEMENT: H.C.)

Fleming (India) v. Ambalal Sarabhai Enterprises (TRADE MARK: USE OF BRAND NAMES UNDER DRUG CONTROLLER'S LICENCE: APPEAL: H.C.)

Indian Institute of Human Resources Development v. National Institute of Human Resources Development (INSTITUTES CARRYING ON UNAUTHORISED BUSINESS OF TRAINING AND AWARDING DIPLOMAS: INJUNCTION AGAINST BOTH FOR FRAUDULENT ACTIVITIES: H.C.)

Kopran Chemicals Co. Ltd v. Kent Pharmaceuticals (India) Pvt. Ltd (TRADE MARK: INFRINGEMENT: RIFINEX/RIFISON: INFRINGEMENT: H.C.)

Parkash Metal Works v. Square Automation (Pvt.) Ltd (TRADE MARK: INFRINGEMENT: HOT FLO/PMW HOT FLO: H.C.)

Institutes Training and Awarding Diplomas

Indian Institute of Human Resources Development v. National Institute of Human Resources Development (INJUNCTION AGAINST BOTH FOR FRAUDULENT ACTIVITIES: H.C.)

Jurisdiction. *See* **Practice** (*Jurisdiction*)

Laches. *See* **Practice** (*Laches*)

Likelihood of Deception or Confusion

Apple Computer Inc. v. Apple Leasing Industries Ltd (RESTRAINT OF UNREGISTERED MARKS IN THE PROVISION OF SERVICES: INTERNATIONAL REPUTATION: COMMON FIELD OF ACTIVITY: H.C.)

Newspapers with Identical Names

Agarwal (M.K.) v. Union of India (FOREIGN PROPRIETORS: H.C.)

Permanent Injunction

Amrutanjan Ltd v. Amrachand Sobachand (TRADE MARK: INFRINGEMENT: NO SALE UNDER INFRINGING MARK: JURISDICTION: H.C.)

Practice

Acquiescence

Apple Computer Inc. v. Apple Leasing Industries Ltd (LACHES: H.C.)

Ad interim injunction

Ceat Tyres of India Ltd v. Jay Industrial Services (TRADE MARK: INFRINGEMENT: H.C.)
Hidesign v. Hi-Design Creations (TRADE MARK: HIDESIGN/HI-DESIGN CREATIONS: H.C.)
Lakshmi PVC Products Pvt. Ltd v. Lakshmi Polymers (TRADE MARK: H.C.)
Thapsons Pvt. Ltd v. Ashoka Food Industries (TRADE MARK: INFRINGEMENT: SIMILAR MARKS: COMMON TO THE TRADE: H.C.)

Appeal

Bajaj Electricals Ltd v. Metal & Applied Products (INTERIM INJUNCTION: H.C.)
Camlin Pvt. Ltd v. National Pencil Industries (TRADE MARK: INFRINGEMENT: INTERIM ORDER: H.C.)
Canon KK v. Canon Electronics Pvt. Ltd (TRADE MARK: INFRINGEMENT: *Ex parte ad interim* INJUNCTION: H.C.)
Deekonda Pedda Chinniah v. Mangalore Ganesh Beedi Works (TRADE MARK: INFRINGEMENT: INTERIM INJUNCTION: H.C.)
Duncan Agro Industries Ltd v. Somabhai Tea Processors (Pvt.) Ltd (TRADE MARK: FIRST TO ENTER MARKET: INTERIM INJUNCTION: H.C.)
Exxon Corporation, USA v. Exxon Packing Systems Pvt. Ltd, Hyderabad (THREATS: INTERIM APPLICATION: H.C.)
Fleming (India) v. Ambalal Sarabhai Enterprises (TRADE MARK: USE OF BRAND NAMES UNDER DRUG CONTROLLER'S LICENCE: INJUNCTION: H.C.)
Gurshant Engineering Co. Pvt. Ltd v. DLF Universals Ltd (TRADE MARK: INFRINGEMENT: COPYRIGHT: H.C.)
Habeebur Rehman & Sons v. Ram Babu & Brothers (TRADE MARK: INFRINGEMENT: COPYRIGHT IN LABEL: INFRINGEMENT: DEFENDANT PRIOR REGISTRANT: INTERIM INJUNCTION: H.C.)
Johnson & Johnson v. Christine Hoden India (P.) Ltd (INTERIM INJUNCTION: H.C.)
Kamal Trading Co. v. Gillette U.K. Ltd (INTERLOCUTORY INJUNCTION: H.C.)

Mohan Meakin Ltd v. The Pravara Sahakari Sakhar Karkhana Ltd (STATUTORY NOTICE PERIOD: JURISDICTION: H.C.)

Power Control Appliances Co. v. Sumit Machines Pvt. Ltd (FAMILY BUSINESS: RIVAL BUSINESS ESTABLISHED BY FAMILY MEMBER: INTERIM INJUNCTION: H.C.)

Wander Ltd v. Antox India Pvt. Ltd (TRADE MARK: CONFLICT BETWEEN LICENSEES: INTERIM INJUNCTION: APPEAL AND FURTHER APPEAL: H.C.)

Composite suit

Burroughs Wellcome (India) Ltd v. G.K. Sharma & King Scientific Research Centre (TRADE MARK: COPYRIGHT: INFRINGEMENT: PASSING OFF: LETTERS PATENT: JURISDICTION OF COURT TO ENTERTAIN COMPOSITE SUIT: H.C.)

Declaration

Kali Aerated Water Works v. Rashid (TRADE MARK: INJUNCTION: H.C.)

Ex parte injunction

Canon KK v. Canon Electronics Pvt. Ltd (TRADE MARK: INFRINGEMENT: *Ad interim* INJUNCTION: APPEAL: H.C.)

White Horse Distillers Ltd v. The Upper Doab Sugar Mills Ltd (TRADE MARK: INFRINGEMENT: APPEAL: H.C.)

Injunction, limitation

East India Pharmaceutical Works Ltd v. G.G Pharmaceuticals (TRADE MARK: INFRINGEMENT: STAY REFUSED: H.C.)

Interim and interlocutory injunction

Amrutanjan Ltd v. Ashwin Fine Chemicals & Pharmaceuticals (TRADE MARK: INFRINGEMENT: AMRUTANJAN/ASHWIN: H.C.)

Apple Computer Inc. v. Apple Leasing & Industries Ltd (TRADE MARK: H.C.)

Aravind Laboratories v. Padmini Products (TRADE MARK: H.C.)

Bajaj Electricals Ltd v. Metal & Applied Products (APPEAL: H.C.)

Britannia Industries Ltd v. Bharat Biscuits Co. Pvt. Ltd (INTERIM INJUNCTION REFUSED: H.C.)

Burroughs Wellcome (India) Ltd v. G.K. Sharma & King Scientific Research Centre (H.C.)

Carew Phipson Ltd v. Deejay Distilleries Pvt. Ltd (PRE-MIXED ALCOHOLIC DRINKS: RIVAL MARKS NOT DECEPTIVELY SIMILAR: H.C.)

Charan Dass & Veer Industries (India) v. Bombay Crockery House (H.C.)

Daimler Benz AG v. Hybo Hindustan (TRADE MARK: INFRINGEMENT: BENZ: GOODS OF DIFFERENT DESCRIPTION: H.C.)

Deekonda Pedda Chinniah v. Mangalore Ganesh Beedi Works (TRADE MARK: INFRINGEMENT: APPEAL: H.C.)

Duncan Agro Industries Ltd v. Somabhai Tea Processors (Pvt.) Ltd (TRADE MARK: FIRST TO ENTER MARKET: APPEAL: H.C.)

Exxon Corporation, USA v. Exxon Packing Systems Pvt. Ltd, Hyderabad (APPEAL: H.C.)

Habeebur Rehman & Sons v. Ram Babu & Brothers (TRADE MARK: INFRINGEMENT: COPYRIGHT IN LABEL: INFRINGEMENT: DEFENDANT PRIOR REGISTRANT: APPEAL: H.C.)

Hindustan Lever Ltd v. V.V. Dhanushkodi Nadar & Sons (H.C.)

Hindustan Radiators Co. v. Hindustan Radiators Ltd (IDENTICAL TRADING STYLE AND MARK FOR IDENTICAL GOODS: H.C.)

Jain & Bros KK v. Paras Enterprises (H.C.)

Johnson & Johnson v. Christine Hoden India (P.) Ltd (APPEAL: H.C.)

Kamal Trading Co. v. Gillette U.K. Ltd (APPEAL: H.C.)

Manoj Plastic Industries v. Bhola Plastic Industries (H.C.)

MRF Ltd v. Metro Tyres Ltd (TRADE MARK: INFRINGEMENT: NYLOGRIP/ RADIALGRIP: DECEPTIVE USE OF TYRE TREAD PATTERN: H.C.)

National Garments v. National Apparels (APPEAL: H.C.)

Parkash Roadlines Ltd v. Parkash Parcel Services (Pvt.) Ltd (TRADE MARK: INFRINGEMENT: H.C.)

Power Control Appliances Co. v. Sumit Machines Pvt. Ltd (FAMILY BUSINESS: RIVAL BUSINESS ESTABLISHED BY FAMILY MEMBER: APPEAL: H.C.)

R.J. Reynolds Tobacco Co. v. ITC Ltd (H.C.)

Ranbaxy Laboratories Ltd v. Dua Pharmaceuticals Pvt. Ltd (H.C.)

Rawal Industries (Pvt.) Ltd v. Duke Enterprises (H.C.)

Regency Industries Ltd v. Kedar Builders (H.C.)

Richardson Vicks Inc. v. Vikas Pharmaceuticals (*Ad interim* INJUNCTION MADE ABSOLUTE: H.C.)

Rightway v. Rightways Footwear (H.C.)

S.P.S. Jayam & Co. v. Gajalakshmi (TRADE MARK: INFRINGEMENT: JOINDER OF PARTIES: H.C.)

Tata Oil Mills Co. Ltd v. WIPRO Ltd (H.C.)

Tinna Enterprises Pvt. Ltd v. International Rubber Industries (H.C.)

Virendra Dresses v. Varindera Garments (H.C.)

Wander Ltd v. Antox India Pvt. Ltd (TRADE MARK: CONFLICT BETWEEN LICENSEES: APPEAL AND FURTHER APPEAL: H.C.)

William Grant & Sons Ltd v. McDowell & Co. Ltd (H.C.)

Interim order

Camlin Pvt. Ltd v. National Pencil Industries (TRADE MARK: INFRINGEMENT: APPEAL: H.C.)

Joinder of causes of action

Gold Seal Engineering Products Pvt. Ltd v. Hindustan Manufacturers (TRADE MARK: INFRINGEMENT: JURISDICTION: H.C.)

Joinder of parties

S.P.S. Jayam & Co. v. Gajalakshmi (TRADE MARK: INFRINGEMENT: INTERIM INJUNCTION: H.C.)

Jurisdiction

Amrutanjan Ltd v. Amrachand Sobachand (TRADE MARK: INFRINGEMENT: NO SALE UNDER INFRINGING MARK: PERMANENT INJUNCTION: H.C.)

Burroughs Wellcome (India) Ltd v. G.K. Sharma & King Scientific Research Centre (JURISDICTION OF COURT TO ENTERTAIN COMPOSITE SUIT: H.C.)

Gold Seal Engineering Products Pvt. Ltd v. Hindustan Manufacturers (TRADE MARK: INFRINGEMENT: JOINDER OF CAUSES OF ACTION: H.C.)

Mohan Meaking Ltd v. Kashmiri Dreamland Distilleries (TRADE MARK: M.M.B./ M.B.B.: H.C.)

Mohan Meakin Ltd v. The Pravara Sahakari Sakhar Karkhana Ltd (STATUTORY NOTICE PERIOD: APPEAL: H.C.)

Laches

Apple Computer Inc. v. Apple Leasing Industries Ltd (ACQUIESCENCE: H.C.)

Pleadings

Cormandel Fertilizers Ltd v. Cormandel Cements Ltd (TRADE MARK: INFRINGEMENT: AMENDMENT OF PLEADINGS: H.C.)

Public interest

Astra/IDL Ltd v. The Pharma Ltd (TRADE MARK: INFRINGEMENT: BETALONG/ BETALOC: PRESCRIPTIONS: WEIGHT TO BE ATTRIBUTED TO: H.C.)

Security for costs

Revlon Inc. v. Kemco Chemicals (FOREIGN PLAINTIFF: NO LOCAL IMMOVABLE ASSETS STRIKING OUT: H.C.)

Statutory notice period

Mohan Meakin Ltd v. The Pravara Sahakari Sakhar Karkhana Ltd (JURISDICTION: APPEAL: H.C.)

Stay

East India Pharmaceutical Works Ltd v. G.G. Pharmaceuticals (TRADE MARK: INFRINGEMENT: INJUNCTION: LIMITATION: STAY REFUSED: H.C.)

Striking out

Revlon Inc. v. Kemco Chemicals (FOREIGN PLAINTIFF: NO LOCAL IMMOVABLE ASSETS SECURITY FOR COSTS: H.C.)

Transfer of suit

Hindustan Lever Ltd v. V.V. Dhanushkodi Nadar & Sons (H.C.)

Pre-mixed Alcoholic Drinks

Carew Phipson Ltd v. Deejay Distilleries Pvt. Ltd (RIVAL MARKS NOT DECEPTIVELY SIMILAR: INTERIM INJUNCTION: H.C.)

Prescriptions, Weight to be Attributed to

Astra/IDL Ltd v. The Pharma Ltd (TRADE MARK: INFRINGEMENT: BETALONG/ BETALOC: PUBLIC INTEREST: H.C.)

Public Interest. *See* **Practice** (*Public interest*)

Reputation

Apple Computer Inc. v. Apple Leasing Industries Ltd (RESTRAINT OF UNREGISTERED TRADE MARKS IN RESPECT OF PROVISION OF SERVICES: INTERNATIONAL REPUTATION: COMMON FIELD OF ACTIVITY: NATURE OF GOODWILL: H.C.)

Calvin Klein Inc. v. International Apparel Syndicate (INTERNATIONAL FASHION GARMENTS: NO LOCAL BUSINESS: OVERSEAS REPUTATION: INJUNCTION: H.C.)

William Grant & Sons Ltd v. McDowell & Co. Ltd (SINGLE MALT SCOTCH WHISKY: DESIGN AND DEFINITION OF LABEL: GET-UP: TRANS-BORDER REPUTATION OF PRODUCT AVAILABLE IN INDIA: EROSION OF REPUTATION: H.C.)

Rival Business Established by Family Member

Power Control Appliances Co. v. Sumit Machines Pvt. Ltd (FAMILY BUSINESS: INTERIM INJUNCTION: APPEAL: H.C.)

Similar Services

MRF Ltd v. Metro Tyres Ltd (TRADE MARK: INFRINGEMENT: NYLOGRIP/ RADIALGRIP: DECEPTIVE USE OF TYRE TREAD PATTERN: INTERIM INJUNCTION: H.C.)

Similar Trade Marks

Thapsons Pvt. Ltd v. Ashoka Food Industries (TRADE MARK: INFRINGEMENT: COMMON TO THE TRADE: *Ad interim* INJUNCTION: H.C.)

Statutory Notice Period. *See* Practice (*Statutory notice period*)

Threats

Exxon Corporation, USA v. Exxon Packing Systems Pvt. Ltd, Hyderabad (INTERIM APPLICATION: APPEAL: H.C.)

Trade Marks and Trade Names

Amrutanjan Ltd v. Amrachand Sobachand (INFRINGEMENT: NO SALE UNDER INFRINGING MARK: PERMANENT INJUNCTION: JURISDICTION: H.C.)

Amrutanjan Ltd v. Ashwin Fine Chemicals & Pharmaceuticals (INFRINGEMENT: AMRUTANJAN/ASHWIN: INTERIM INJUNCTION: H.C.)

Apple Computer Inc. v. Apple Leasing & Industries Ltd (INTERIM INJUNCTION: H.C.)

Apple Computer Inc. v. Apple Leasing Industries Ltd (RESTRAINT OF UNREGISTERED MARKS IN RESPECT OF PROVISION OF SERVICES: INTERNATIONAL REPUTATION: H.C.)

Aravind Laboratories v. Padmini Products (INTERIM INJUNCTION: H.C.)

Astra/IDL Ltd v. The Pharma Ltd (INFRINGEMENT: BETALONG/BETALOC: PRESCRIPTIONS: WEIGHT TO BE ATTRIBUTED TO: PUBLIC INTEREST: H.C.)

Bajaj Electricals Ltd v. Metal & Applied Products (INFRINGEMENT: USE OF FAMILY NAME: INTERIM INJUNCTION: APPEAL: H.C.)

Bata India Ltd v. m/s Pyarelal & Co. (INFRINGEMENT: BATA:BATAFORM: H.C.)

BK Engineering Co. v. UBHI Enterprises (USE OF HOUSE MARK: H.C.)

Blue Cross & Blue Shield Association v. Blue Cross Health Clinic (INFRINGEMENT: INJUNCTION: H.C.)

Britannia Industries Ltd v. Bharat Biscuits Co. Pvt. Ltd (INFRINGEMENT: BRITANNIA SNAX/BHARAT SNACKS: INTERIM INJUNCTION: REFUSED: H.C.)

Brooke Bond (India) Ltd v. Balaji Tea (India) Pvt. Ltd (INFRINGEMENT: INJUNCTION: H.C.)

Brooke Bond India Ltd v. Balaji Tea (India) Pvt. Ltd (INFRINGEMENT: RED LABEL: RED APPLE TEA: PACKETS FILLED IN INDIA AND EXPORTED: H.C.)

Burroughs Wellcome (India) Ltd v. G.K. Sharma & King Scientific Research Centre (SEPTRIN/CETRAN: COPYRIGHT: INFRINGEMENT: JURISDICTION OF COURT TO ENTERTAIN COMPOSITE SUIT: INTERIM INJUNCTION: H.C.)

Camlin Pvt. Ltd v. National Pencil Industries (INFRINGEMENT: APPEAL: INTERIM ORDER: H.C.)

Canon KK v. Canon Electronics Pvt. Ltd (INFRINGEMENT: *Ex parte* AD INTERIM INJUNCTION: APPEAL: H.C.)

Ceat Tyres of India Ltd v. Jay Indutrial Services (INFRINGEMENT: *Ad interim* INJUNCTION: H.C.)

Chandra Bhan Dembla Trading v. Bharat Sewing Machine Co. (INFRINGEMENT: H.C.)

Charan Dass & Veer Industries (India) v. Bombay Crockery House (COPYRIGHT: DESIGN: INFRINGEMENT: PERFECT/SWASTIK PERFECT: INTERIM INJUNCTION: H.C.)
Cormandel Fertilizers Ltd v. Cormandel Cements Ltd (INFRINGEMENT: AMENDMENT OF PLEADINGS: H.C.)
Daimler Benz AG v. Hybo Hindustan (INFRINGEMENT: BENZ: GOODS OF DIFFERENT DESCRIPTION: INTERIM INJUNCTION: H.C.)
Deekonda Pedda Chinniah v. Mangalore Ganesh Beedi Works (INFRINGEMENT: INTERIM INJUNCTION: APPEAL: H.C.)
Duncan Agro Industries Ltd v. Somabhai Tea Processors (Pvt.) Ltd (FIRST TO ENTER MARKET: INTERIM INJUNCTION: APPEAL: H.C.)
East India Pharmaceutical Works Ltd v. G.G. Pharmaceuticals (INFRINGEMENT: INJUNCTION: LIMITATION: STAY REFUSED: H.C.)
Fleming (India) v. Ambalal Sarabhai Enterprises (USE OF BRAND NAMES UNDER DRUG CONTROLLER'S LICENCE: INJUNCTION: APPEAL: H.C.)
Globe Super Parts v. Blue Super Flame Industries (INFRINGEMENT: INJUNCTION: H.C.)
Gold Seal Engineering Products Pvt. Ltd v. Hindustan Manufacturers (INFRINGEMENT: JURISDICTION: JOINDER OF CAUSES OF ACTION: H.C.)
Habeebur Rehman & Sons v. Ram Babu & Brothers (INFRINGEMENT: COPYRIGHT IN LABEL: INFRINGEMENT: DEFENDANT PRIOR REGISTRANT: INTERIM INJUNCTION: APPEAL: H.C.)
Hidesign v. Hi-Design Creations (HIDESIGN/HI-DESIGN CREATIONS: Ad interim INJUNCTION: H.C.)
Himachal Pradesh Horticulture Produce Marketing v. Mohan Meakin Breweries Ltd (INFRINGEMENT: H.C.)
HMT Ltd v. Olympic Agencies (INFRINGEMENT: HMT-SONA, HMT-ASHA/ OLYMPIC SONA, OLYMPIC ASHA: FOR WATCHES: H.C.)
Jain & Bros KK v. Paras Enterprises (INFRINGEMENT: INTERIM INJUNCTION: H.C.)
Jawahar Engineering Co. v. Jovahar Engineers Pvt. Ltd (INFRINGEMENT: H.C.)
Johnson & Johnson v. Christine Hoden India (Pvt.) Ltd (INFRINGEMENT: STAYFREE: INJUNCTION: H.C.)
Kali Aerated Water Works v. Rashid (KALI MARK/SRI NEW KALI MARK AERATED WATER: DECLARATION: INJUNCTION: H.C.)
Kamal Trading Co. v. Gillette U.K. Ltd (INFRINGEMENT: 7 O'CLOCK: INTERLOCUTORY INJUNCTION: APPEAL: H.C.)
Kissan Industries v. Punjab Food Corp. (COPYRIGHT: INFRINGEMENT: H.C.)
Kopran Chemicals Co. Ltd v. Kent Pharmaceuticals (India) Pvt. Ltd (INFRINGEMENT: RIFINEX/RIFISON: INFRINGEMENT: INJUNCTION: H.C.)
Kwality Icecreams Ltd v. India (USE OF LICENCED MARK AFTER TERMINATION OF AGREEMENT: H.C.)
Lakshmi PVC Products Pvt. Ltd v. Lakshmi Polymers (Ad interim INJUNCTION: H.C.)
Manoj Plastic Industries v. Bhola Plastic Industries (SAME TRADE MARK FOR IDENTICAL GOODS: INTERIM INJUNCTION: H.C.)
Mohan Meakin Ltd v. The Pravara Sahakari Sakhar Karkhana Ltd (INFRINGEMENT: STATUTORY NOTICE PERIOD: JURISDICTION: APPEAL: H.C.)
Mohan Meaking Ltd v. Kashmiri Dreamland Distilleries (M.M.B./M.B.B.: JURISDICTION: H.C.)
MRF Ltd v. Metro Tyres Ltd (INFRINGEMENT: NYLOGRIP/RADIALGRIP: DECEPTIVE USE OF TYRE TREAD PATTERN: INTERIM INJUNCTION: H.C.)
National Garments v. National Apparels (GET-UP: COVER OF BOXES: DECEPTION: INTERIM INJUNCTION: APPEAL: H.C.)
Parkash Metal Works v. Square Automation (Pvt.) Ltd (INFRINGEMENT: HOT FLO/ PMW HOT FLO: INJUNCTION: H.C.)

Parkash Roadlines Ltd v. Parkash Parcel Services (Pvt.) Ltd (INFRINGEMENT: INTERIM INJUNCTION: H.C.)

Pavunny v. Mathew (INJUNCTION: H.C.)

R.J. Reynolds Tobacco Co. v. ITC Ltd (NOW: INFRINGEMENT: INTERIM INJUNCTION: H.C.)

Ranbaxy Laboratories Ltd v. Dua Pharmaceuticals Pvt. Ltd (CALMPOSE/ CALMPROSE: INFRINGEMENT: INTERIM INJUNCTION: H.C.)

Rawal Industries (Pvt.) Ltd v. Duke Enterprises (INFRINGEMENT: TRADING STYLE: INTERIM INJUNCTION: H.C.)

Regency Industries Ltd v. Kedar Builders (USE OF PLAINTIFF'S NAME FOR BUILDINGS: INTERIM INJUNCTION: H.C.)

Richardson Vicks Inc. v. Medico Laboratories (INFRINGEMENT: INJUNCTION: H.C.)

Rightway v. Rightways Footwear (PRIOR USE: INTERIM INJUNCTION: H.C.)

S.P.S. Jayam & Co. v. Gajalakshmi (INFRINGEMENT: JOINDER OF PARTIES: INTERIM INJUNCTION: H.C.)

Tata Oil Mills Co. Ltd v. WIPRO Ltd (INFRINGEMENT: INTERIM INJUNCTION: H.C.)

Thapsons Pvt. Ltd v. Ashoka Food Industries (INFRINGEMENT: SIMILAR MARKS: COMMON TO THE TRADE: *Ad interim* INJUNCTION: H.C.)

Tinna Enterprises Pvt. Ltd v. International Rubber Industries (INFRINGEMENT: TINNA/TANY: INTERIM INJUNCTION: H.C.)

Tobu Interprises Pvt. Ltd v. Tokyo Cycle Industries (COPYRIGHT: INFRINGEMENT: TOBU/TOHO: H.C.)

Wander Ltd v. Antox India Pvt. Ltd (CONFLICT BETWEEN LICENSEES: INTERIM INJUNCTION: APPEAL AND FURTHER APPEAL: H.C.)

White Horse Distillers Ltd v. The Upper Doab Sugar Mills Ltd (INFRINGEMENT: *Ex parte* INJUNCTION: APPEAL: WHITE HORSE/FLYING HORSE: H.C.)

Trading Style

Hindustan Radiators Co. v. Hindustan Radiators Ltd (IDENTICAL TRADING STYLE AND MARK FOR IDENTICAL GOODS: INTERIM INJUNCTION: H.C.)

Rawal Industries (Pvt.) Ltd v. Duke Enterprises (TRADE MARK: INFRINGEMENT: INTERIM INJUNCTION: H.C.)

Transfer of Suit. *See* **Practice** (*Transfer of suit*)

Unregistered Trade Marks. *See* **Trade Marks and Trade Names**

Use of Licenced Mark after Termination of Agreement

Kwality Icecreams Ltd v. India (H.C.)

Patents

Appeal. *See* **Practice** (*Appeal*)

Application

Gajjar's Application (PRIOR PUBLICATION: H.C.)

Philips Petroleum Co. v. Joint Controller of Patents & Designs (PROCESS AND PASSIVE AGENT: OBJECTIONS RAISED AFTER ACCEPTANCE AND ADVERTISEMENT OF COMPLETE SPECIFICATION: H.C.)

Ram Pratap v. The Bhabha Atomic Research Centre (DIFFUSION PUMP: Pat. Off.)
Ratheon Company v. Comptroller of Patents & Designs (IMAGE SYSTEM: H.C.)
Thomas Brandt v. Controller of Patents & Designs (PROCESS PATENT: REJECTION BY CONTROLLER: APPEAL: REMAND BACK TO CONTROLLER: H.C.)
Thomson Brandt's Application (PROCESS: STATUTORY INTERPRETATION: Pat. Off.)

Assignment

International Control Automation Finance v. Controller of Patents & Designs (REASSIGNMENT: RECORDAL OF PROPER ASSIGNEE: H.C.)

Evidence. *See* Practice *(Evidence)*

False Claim of Improvement

Unique Transmission Co. India Ltd v. ESBI Transmission Pvt. Ltd (FLEXIBLE COUPLINGS: REVOCATION: INVENTION NEITHER NEW, NOR NOVEL, BEING FREELY USED BY MANUFACTURERS: H.C.)

Infringement

Bishwanath Prasad Radhay Sham v. Hindustan Metal Industries (PERMANENT INJUNCTION: S.C.)
Burroughs Wellcome (India) Ltd v. G.K. Sharma & King Scientific Research Centre (TRADE MARK: COPYRIGHT: INFRINGEMENT: PASSING OFF: JURISDICTION OF COURT TO ENTERTAIN COMPOSITE SUIT: INTERIM INJUNCTION GRANTED: H.C.)
Fabcon Corporation Inc. USA v. Industrial Engineering Corpn Ghaziabad (TRANSFER OF SUIT: H.C.)
Godrej Soaps Ltd v. Hindustan Lever Ltd (INTERIM INJUNCTION: APPEAL: MANUFACTURE OF PRODUCT PRIOR TO GRANT OF PATENT: H.C.)

Interim Injunction. *See* Practice *(Interim injunction)*

Jurisdiction. *See* Practice *(Jurisdiction)*

Manufacture of Product Prior to Grant

Godrej Soaps Ltd v. Hindustan Lever Ltd (INFRINGEMENT: INTERIM INJUNCTION: APPEAL: H.C.)

Novelty

Polar Industries v. The Jay Engineering Works Ltd (REVOCATION: H.C.)
Unique Transmission Co. India Ltd v. ESBI Transmission Pvt. Ltd (FLEXIBLE COUPLINGS: REVOCATION: H.C.)

Objections

Philips Petroleum Co. v. Joint Controller of Patents & Designs (APPLICATION: PROCESS AND PASSIVE AGENT: OBJECTIONS RAISED AFTER ACCEPTANCE AND ADVERTISEMENT OF COMPLETE SPECIFICATION: H.C.)

Opposition

Ahmedabad Textile Industries Research Association v. The Bombay Textile Research Association (PROCESS PATENT: Pat. Off.)

Press Metal Corp. Ltd v. Noshir Sorabji (PRIOR PUBLICATION: H.C.)

Permanent Injunction. *See* **Practice** *(Permanent injunction)*

Practice

Appeal

Godrej Soaps Ltd v. Hindustan Lever Ltd (INFRINGEMENT: INTERIM INJUNCTION: MANUFACTURE OF PRODUCT PRIOR TO GRANT OF PATENT: H.C.)
Thomas Brandt v. Controller of Patents & Designs (APPLICATION: PROCESS PATENT: REJECTION CONTROLLER: REMAND BACK TO CONTROLLER: H.C.)

Evidence

Guest Keen Williams Ltd v. Controller of Patents & Designs (PROCEEDINGS BEFORE CONTROLLER: H.C.)

Interim injunction

Burroughs Wellcome (India) Ltd v. G.K. Sharma & King Scientific Research Centre (H.C.)
Godrej Soaps Ltd v. Hindustan Lever Ltd (INFRINGEMENT: APPEAL: MANUFACTURE OF PRODUCT PRIOR TO GRANT OF PATENT: H.C.)

Jurisdiction

Ajay Industrial Corp. v. Kanao (PATENT: REVOCATION: JURISDICTION: India: H.C.)
Burroughs Wellcome (India) Ltd v. G.K. Sharma & King Scientific Research Centre (JURISDICTION OF COURT TO ENTERTAIN COMPOSITE SUIT: H.C.)

Permanent injunction

Bishwanath Prasad Radhay Sham v. Hindustan Metal Industries (INFRINGEMENT: S.C.)

Proceedings before controller

Guest Keen Williams Ltd v. Controller of Patents & Designs (EVIDENCE: H.C.)

Transfer of suit

Fabcon Corporation Inc. USA v. Industrial Engineering Corpn Ghaziabad (INFRINGEMENT: H.C.)

Prior Publication

Gajjar's Application (APPLICATION: H.C.)
Press Metal Corp. Ltd v. Noshir Sorabji (OPPOSITION: H.C.)

Proceedings Before Controller. *See* **Practice** *(Proceedings before controller)*

Process Patent

Ahmedabad Textile Industries Research Association v. The Bombay Textile Research Association (OPPOSITION: Pat. Off.)
Philips Petroleum Co. v. Joint Controller of Patents & Designs (APPLICATION: PROCESS AND PASSIVE AGENT: OBJECTIONS RAISED AFTER ACCEPTANCE AND ADVERTISEMENT OF COMPLETE SPECIFICATION: H.C.)
Thomas Brandt v. Controller of Patents & Designs (REJECTION BY CONTROLLER: REMAND BACK TO CONTROLLER: H.C.)

Thomson Brandt's Application (Pat. Off.)

Reassignment

International Control Automation Finance v. Controller of Patents & Designs
(ASSIGNMENT: RECORDAL OF PROPER ASSIGNEE: H.C.)

Recordal of Proper Assignee

International Control Automation Finance v. Controller of Patents & Designs
(ASSIGNMENT: REASSIGNMENT: H.C.)

Rectification

Bayer AG v. Controller of Patents (H.C.)

Rejection

Thomson Brandt v. Controller of Patents & Designs (APPLICATION: APPEAL: Pat.
Off.)

Revocation

Ajay Industrial Corp. v. Kanao (JURISDICTION: H.C.)
Polar Industries v. The Jay Engineering Works Ltd (NOVELTY: H.C.)
Unique Transmission Co. India Ltd v. ESBI Transmission Pvt. Ltd (INVENTION
NEITHER NEW, NOR NOVEL, BEING FREELY USED BY MANUFACTURERS:
FALSE CLAIM OF IMPROVEMENT ON EXISTING INVENTION: H.C.)

Right to Lodge

Anup Engr Ltd v. Controller of Patents (H.C.)

Transfer of Suit. *See* **Practice** (*Transfer of suit*)

Practice

Acquiescence

Apple Computer Inc. v. Apple Leasing Industries Ltd (LACHES: H.C.)
Hindustan Pencils Pvt. Ltd v. India Stationery Products Co. (TRADE MARK:
INFRINGEMENT: INTERIM INJUNCTION: REGISTRATION: *Ex parte*
INJUNCTION: DELAY AND LACHES: H.C.)

Ad Interim Injunction including *Ad Interim Ex Parte* Injunction

Coromandel Fertilizers Ltd v. Coromandel Cements Ltd (*Ad interim* INJUNCTION
VACATED: H.C.)
Nucron Pharmaceuticals Pvt. Ltd v. International Pharmaceuticals (TRADE MARK:
INFRINGEMENT: SEPMAX/SELMAX: APPLIED TO MEDICINES FOR
DIFFERENT MEDICAL CONDITIONS: DECEPTIVE SIMILARITY: LIKELIHOOD OF
DISASTROUS CONSEQUENCES: LEAVE TO APPLY FOR *ad interim* INJUNCTION:
H.C.)
Richardson Vicks Inc. v. Vikas Pharmaceuticals (*Ad interim* INJUNCTION MADE
ABSOLUTE: H.C.)

Thomas (V.T.) v. Malayala Manorama Co. Ltd (PREVENTION OF PUBLICATION AFTER TERMINATION OF EMPLOYMENT: *Ad interim ex parte* INJUNCTION VACATED: H.C.)

Affidavit of Service

India Videogram Association Ltd v. Patel (WRIT: SERVICE BY INSERTION THROUGH DEFENDANT'S LETTER BOX: NO AFFIDAVIT OF DUE SERVICE: DEFENDANT OUTSIDE JURISDICTION: LEARNING OF WRIT ON HER RETURN PRIOR TO ITS EXPIRY: WHETHER SERVICE EFFECTED DURING CURRENCY OF WRIT: R.S.C. ORDER 10, R.1(3)(B)(I): Ch.D.)

Appeal

Anglo-French Drug Co. (Eastern) Ltd v. Hony-N-Bois (TRADE MARK: OPPOSITION: APPEAL TO HIGH COURT ALLOWED: H.C.)

Bajaj Electricals Ltd v. Metal & Applied Products (INTERIM INJUNCTION: H.C.)

Canon KK v. Canon Electronics Pvt. Ltd (TRADE MARK: INFRINGEMENT: PASSING OFF: *Ex parte ad interim* INJUNCTION: H.C.)

Exxon Corporation, USA v. Exxon Packing Systems Pvt. Ltd, Hyderabad (TRADE MARK: THREATS: PASSING OFF: INTERIM APPLICATION: H.C.)

Fairdeal Corp. (Pvt.) Ltd v. Vijay Pharmaceuticals (*Ex parte* INJUNCTION: H.C.)

Farbenfabriken Bayer AG v. Christopher John (TRADE MARK: OPPOSITION: H.C.)

Gurshant Engineering Co. Pvt. Ltd v. DLF Universals Ltd (TRADE MARK: INFRINGEMENT: PASSING OFF: COPYRIGHT: H.C.)

Hiralal Parudas v. Ganesh Trading Co. (TRADE MARK: RECTIFICATION: H.C.)

Johnson & Johnson v. Christine Hoden India (P.) Ltd (INTERIM INJUNCTION: H.C.)

Kamal Trading Co. v. Gillette U.K. Ltd (INTERLOCUTORY INJUNCTION: H.C.)

Khanshiram Surinder Kumar v. Thakurdas Deomal Rohira (TRADE MARK: RECTIFICATION: H.C.)

Madhavan v. S.K. Nayar (COPYRIGHT: INFRINGEMENT: H.C.)

Mohan Meakin Ltd v. The Pravara Sahakari Sakhar Karkhana Ltd (STATUTORY NOTICE PERIOD: JURISDICTION: H.C.)

National Garments v. National Apparels (INTERIM INJUNCTION: H.C.)

Penguin Books Ltd v. India Book Distributors (CONSENT DECREE IN USA: INTERLOCUTORY INJUNCTION: H.C.)

Plastella M/s v. Controller of Patents and Designs (DESIGN: CANCELLATION: H.C.)

Thakur Ayurvedic Pharmacy v. Pandit D.P. Sharma (TRADE MARKS: OPPOSITION: REVIEW PETITIONS: H.C.)

White Horse Distillers Ltd v. The Upper Doab Sugar Mills Ltd (TRADE MARK: INFRINGEMENT: *Ex parte* INJUNCTION: H.C.)

Complainant's Qualifications

Vishwa Mitter of Vijay Bharat Cigarette Stores v. O.P. Poddar (STATUTORY OFFENCE: S.C.)

Consent Decree in United States

Penguin Books Ltd v. India Book Distributors (APPEAL: INTERLOCUTORY INJUNCTION: H.C.)

Costs

Hind Azad Factory v. Azad Factory (DELAY IN FILING EVIDENCE: REVIEW: T.M.Reg.)

Declaration

Bijoli Grill Spencer's Products v. Spencers & Co. Ltd (TRADE MARK: INJUNCTION: H.C.)

Kali Aerated Water Works v. Rashid (TRADE MARK: PASSING OFF: INJUNCTION: H.C.)

Sidharth Wheels Pvt. Ltd v. Bedrock Ltd (TRADE MARK: THREATS: H.C.)

Defendant Outside Jurisdiction

India Videogram Association Ltd v. Patel (WRIT: SERVICE BY INSERTION THROUGH LETTER BOX: NO AFFIDAVIT OF DUE SERVICE: DEFENDANT LEARNT OF WRIT ON RETURN PRIOR TO ITS EXPIRY: WHETHER SERVICE EFFECTED: Ch.D.)

Delay

Hind Azad Factory v. Azad Factory (DELAY IN FILING EVIDENCE: T.M.Reg.)

Hindustan Pencils Pvt. Ltd v. India Stationery Products Co. (TRADE MARK: INFRINGEMENT: INTERIM INJUNCTION: REGISTRATION UNDER COPYRIGHT ACT: *Ex parte* INJUNCTION: DELAY, LACHES AND ACQUIESCENCE: H.C.)

Progro Pharmaceuticals (Pvt.) Ltd v. Deputy Registrar of Trade Marks (DELAY IN FILING COUNTER-STATEMENT: EXTENSION OF TIME LIMITS: H.C.)

English Authorities, Applicability of

Brady v. Chemical Process Equipments Pte Ltd (H.C.)

Estoppel

Heptulla v. Orient Longman Ltd (COPYRIGHT: GHOST-WRITTEN MEMOIRS: AGREEMENT TO ASSIGN COPYRIGHT: BALANCE OF CONVENIENCE: H.C.)

Evidence

Hind Azad Factory v. Azad Factory (DELAY IN FILING: COSTS: REVIEW: T.M.Reg.)

Guest Keen Williams Ltd v. Controller of Patents & Designs (PROCEEDINGS BEFORE CONTROLLER: H.C.)

Ex Parte Injunction

Canon KK v. Canon Electronics Pvt. Ltd (TRADE MARK: INFRINGEMENT: PASSING OFF: APPEAL: H.C.)

Fairdeal Corp. (Pvt.) Ltd v. Vijay Pharmaceuticals (TRADE MARK: INFRINGEMENT: APPEAL: H.C.)

Hindustan Pencils Pvt. Ltd v. India Stationery Products Co. (TRADE MARK: INFRINGEMENT: INTERIM INJUNCTION: REGISTRATION UNDER COPYRIGHT ACT: DELAY, LACHES AND ACQUIESCENCE: H.C.)

R.P. Locks Co. v. Sehgal Locks Co. (TRADE MARK: INFRINGEMENT: INTERIM *ex parte* INJUNCTION: H.C.)

Thomas (V.T.) v. Malayala Manorama Co. Ltd (COPYRIGHT: PETITION FOR STAY OF *ex parte* INJUNCTION: H.C.)

Thomas (V.T.) v. Malayala Manorama Co. Ltd (COPYRIGHT: EX-EMPLOYEE: PREVENTION OF PUBLICATION AFTER TERMINATION OF EMPLOYMENT: *Ad interim ex parte* INJUNCTION VACATED: H.C.)

White Horse Distillers Ltd v. The Upper Doab Sugar Mills Ltd (TRADE MARK: INFRINGEMENT: PASSING OFF: *Ex parte* INJUNCTION: APPEAL: H.C.)

Extension of Time Limits

Progro Pharmaceuticals (Pvt.) Ltd v. Deputy Registrar of Trade Marks (DELAY IN FILING COUNTER-STATEMENT: H.C.)

Injunction

Anglo French Drug Co. (Eastern) Ltd v. Belco Pharmaceuticals (TRADE MARK: INFRINGEMENT: H.C.)

Bijoli Grill Spencer's Products v. Spencers & Co. Ltd (TRADE MARK: DECLARATION: H.C.)

ESSCO Sanitations v. Mascot Industries (TRADE MARK: INFRINGEMENT: H.C.)

Garware Plastics & Polyester Ltd v. Telelink (COPYRIGHT: INFRINGEMENT: EXHIBITION OF VIDEO FILMS OVER CABLE TV NETWORK: H.C.)

East India Pharmaceutical Works Ltd v. G. & G. Pharmaceuticals Ltd (TRADE MARK: GEOGRAPHICAL EXTENT: H.C.)

East India Pharmaceutical Works Ltd v. G.G. Pharmaceuticals (TRADE MARK: INFRINGEMENT: PASSING OFF: STAY REFUSED: H.C.)

Globe Super Parts v. Blue Super Flame Industries (PASSING OFF: TRADE MARK: INFRINGEMENT: H.C.)

Johnson & Johnson v. Christine Hoden India (Pvt.) Ltd (TRADE MARK: INFRINGEMENT: PASSING OFF: H.C.)

Kali Aerated Water Works v. Rashid (TRADE MARK: PASSING OFF: DECLARATION: H.C.)

Pavunny v. Mathew (PASSING OFF: TRADE NAMES: H.C.)

Pioneer Hi-bred International Inc. USA v. Pioneer Seed Company Ltd (TRADE MARK: REGISTERED USER ARRANGEMENT: REFUSAL TO GIVE INSPECTION: SUIT FOR PERMANENT INJUNCTION AGAINST REGISTERED USER: H.C.)

Injunction Vacated

K.R. Jadayappa Mudaliar v. K.S. Venkatachalam (TRADE MARK: UNLICENSED USE: H.C.)

P.M. Diesels Pvt. Ltd v. Thukral Mechanical Works (TRADE MARK: RECTIFICATION: ENTITLEMENT TO USE MARK: H.C.)

Interim Application

Exxon Corporation, USA v. Exxon Packing Systems Pvt. Ltd, Hyderabad (TRADE MARK: THREATS: PASSING OFF: APPEAL: H.C.)

Interim *Ex Parte* Injunction

R.P. Locks Co. v. Sehgal Locks Co. (TRADE MARK: INFRINGEMENT: H.C.)

Interim Injunction

Appliances Emporium v. M/s Usha Industries (India) New Delhi (TRADE MARK: INFRINGEMENT: H.C.)

Bajaj Electricals Ltd v. Metal & Applied Products (TRADE MARK: INFRINGEMENT: PASSING OFF: USE OF FAMILY NAME: APPEAL: H.C.)

Bansal Plastic Industries v. Neeraj Toys Industries (REGISTERED DESIGN: INFRINGEMENT: H.C.)

Bombay Oil Industries Pvt. Ltd v. Ballarpur Industries Ltd (TRADE MARK: INFRINGEMENT: H.C.)

Britannia Industries Ltd v. Bharat Biscuits Co. Pvt. Ltd (TRADE MARK: INFRINGEMENT: PASSING OFF: INTERIM INJUNCTION REFUSED: H.C.)

Burroughs Wellcome (India) Ltd v. G.K. Sharma & King Scientific Research Centre (TRADE MARK: COPYRIGHT: INFRINGEMENT: PASSING OFF: JURISDICTION OF COURT TO ENTERTAIN COMPOSITE SUIT: INTERIM INJUNCTION GRANTED: H.C.)

Camlin Pvt. Ltd v. National Pencil Industries (TRADE MARK: COPYRIGHT: INFRINGEMENT: PASSING OFF: H.C.)

Charan Dass & Veer Industries (India) v. Bombay Crockery House (TRADE MARK: COPYRIGHT: DESIGN: INFRINGEMENT: PASSING OFF: H.C.)

Chawrana Tobacco Co. v. Bhagwandas (TRADE MARK: COPYRIGHT: INFRINGEMENT: H.C.)

Glaxo Operations U.K. Ltd v. Rama Bhaktha Hanuman Candle & Camphor Works (COPYRIGHT: TRADE MARK: INFORMATION: JOINDER OF CAUSE OF ACTION: JURISDICTION: H.C.)

Griffon Laboratories (P.) Ltd v. Indian National Drug Co. P. Ltd (TRADE MARK: INFRINGEMENT: H.C.)

Hindustan Lever Ltd v. V.V. Dhanushkodi Nadar & Sons (REGISTERED DESIGN: INFRINGEMENT: PASSING OFF: TRANSFER OF SUIT: H.C.)

Hindustan Pencils Pvt. Ltd v. India Stationery Products Co. (TRADE MARK: INFRINGEMENT: REGISTRATION UNDER COPYRIGHT ACT: *Ex parte* INJUNCTION: DELAY, LACHES AND ACQUIESCENCE: H.C.)

Jain & Bros KK v. Paras Enterprises (TRADE MARK: INFRINGEMENT: PASSING OFF: H.C.)

Johnson & Johnson v. Christine Hoden India (P.) Ltd (TRADE MARK: PASSING OFF: APPEAL: H.C.)

Manoj Plastic Industries v. Bhola Plastic Industries (PASSING OFF: TRADE MARK: H.C.)

National Garments v. National Apparels (PASSING OFF: TRADE MARK: GET-UP: COVER OF BOXES: DECEPTION: APPEAL: H.C.)

Nirex Industries (Pvt.) Ltd v. Manchand Footwears (TRADE MARK: COPYRIGHT: INFRINGEMENT: JURISDICTION: H.C.)

Philip Morris Belgium SA v. Golden Tobacco Co. Ltd (TRADE MARK: INFRINGEMENT: H.C.)

Pidilite Industries Pvt. Ltd v. Mittees Corporation (TRADE MARK: INFRINGEMENT: COPYRIGHT: THREATS: H.C.)

R.J. Reynolds Tobacco Co. v. ITC Ltd (TRADE MARK: INFRINGEMENT: PASSING OFF: H.C.)

Ranbaxy Laboratories Ltd v. Dua Pharmaceuticals Pvt. Ltd (TRADE MARK: INFRINGEMENT: PASSING OFF: H.C.)

Rawal Industries (Pvt.) Ltd v. Duke Enterprises (TRADE MARK: PASSING OFF: INFRINGEMENT: TRADING STYLE: H.C.)

Regency Industries Ltd v. Kedar Builders (PASSING OFF: USE OF PLAINTIFF'S NAME FOR BUILDINGS: H.C.)

Rightway v. Rightways Footwear (TRADE MARK: TRADE NAME: PASSING OFF: PRIOR USE: H.C.)

Tata Oil Mills Co. Ltd v. Reward Soap Works (TRADE MARK: COPYRIGHT: INFRINGEMENT: H.C.)

Tata Oil Mills Co. Ltd v. WIPRO Ltd (TRADE MARK: INFRINGEMENT: PASSING OFF: H.C.)

Tinna Enterprises Pvt. Ltd v. International Rubber Industries (TRADE MARK: INFRINGEMENT: PASSING OFF: H.C.)

Vacated Enterprises v. Hyderabad Lamps Ltd (TRADE MARK: CHOKES FOR FLUORESCENT TUBES: INFRINGEMENT: INTERIM INJUNCTION VACATED: H.C.)

Virendra Dresses v. Varindera Garments (PASSING OFF: H.C.)

Vrajlal Manilal & Co. v. N.S. Bidi Co. (TRADE MARK: INFRINGEMENT: H.C.)

Interlocutory Injunction

Kamal Trading Co. v. Gillette U.K. Ltd (PASSING OFF: TRADE MARK: INFRINGEMENT: APPEAL: H.C.)

Niky Tasha India Pvt. Ltd v. Faridabad Gas Gadgets Pvt. Ltd (DESIGNS: INFRINGEMENT: H.C.)

Penguin Books Ltd v. India Book Distributors (COPYRIGHT: INFRINGEMENT: CONSENT DECREE IN UNITED STATES: APPEAL: H.C.)

Sidharth Wheels Pvt. Ltd v. Bedrock Ltd (TRADE MARK: THREATS: DECLARATION: NATURE: H.C.)

Synthetic Moulders Ltd v. Semperit AG (TRADE MARK: INFRINGEMENT: H.C.)

Interlocutory Injunction—Balance of Convenience

Heptulla v. Orient Longman Ltd (H.C.)

Interlocutory Petition

Cipla Ltd v. Unicure Pharmaceuticals (TRADE MARK: RECTIFICATION: JURISDICTION: T.M.Reg.)

Joinder of Cause of Action

Glaxo Operations U.K. Ltd v. Rama Bhaktha Hanuman Candle & Camphor Works (COPYRIGHT: TRADE MARK: INFORMATION: JURISDICTION: INTERIM INJUNCTION: H.C.)

Gold Seal Engineering Products Pvt. Ltd v. Hindustan Manufacturers (TRADE MARK: INFRINGEMENT: COPYRIGHT: PASSING OFF: JURISDICTION: H.C.)

Jurisdiction

Ajay Industrial Corp. v. Kanao (PATENT: REVOCATION: H.C.)

Burroughs Wellcome (India) Ltd v. G.K. Sharma & King Scientific Research Centre (TRADE MARK: COPYRIGHT: INFRINGEMENT: PASSING OFF: JURISDICTION OF COURT TO ENTERTAIN COMPOSITE SUIT: H.C.)

Cipla Ltd v. Unicure Pharmaceuticals (TRADE MARK: RECTIFICATION: INTERLOCUTORY PETITION: T.M.Reg.)

Glaxo Operations U.K. Ltd v. Rama Bhaktha Hanuman Candle & Camphor Works (COPYRIGHT: TRADE MARK: INFORMATION: JOINDER OF CAUSE OF ACTION: INTERIM INJUNCTION: H.C.)

Mohan Meakin Ltd v. The Pravara Sahakari Sakhar Karkhana Ltd (STATUTORY NOTICE PERIOD: APPEAL: H.C.)

Nirex Industries (Pvt.) Ltd v. Manchand Footwears (TRADE MARK: COPYRIGHT: INFRINGEMENT: INTERIM INJUNCTION: H.C.)

Samir Senray's Design Application (DESIGN: PRELIMINARY OBJECTION ABOUT LACK OF JURISDICTION TO HEAR THE MATTER: Pat. Off.)

Seal Engineering Products Pvt. Ltd v. Hindustan Manufacturers (TRADE MARK: INFRINGEMENT: COPYRIGHT: PASSING OFF: JOINDER OF CAUSES OF ACTION: H.C.)

Laches

Apple Computer Inc. v. Apple Leasing Industries Ltd (LACHES AND ACQUIESCENCE: H.C.)

Hindustan Pencils Pvt. Ltd v. India Stationery Products Co. (TRADE MARK: INFRINGEMENT: INTERIM INJUNCTION: REGISTRATION UNDER COPYRIGHT ACT: *Ex parte* INJUNCTION: DELAY, LACHES AND ACQUIESCENCE: H.C.)

Leave to Apply

Nucron Pharmaceuticals Pvt. Ltd v. International Pharmaceuticals (TRADE MARK: INFRINGEMENT: SEPMAX/SELMAX: APPLIED TO MEDICINES FOR DIFFERENT MEDICAL CONDITIONS: DECEPTIVE SIMILARITY: LIKELIHOOD OF DISASTROUS CONSEQUENCES: LEAVE TO APPLY FOR *Ad interim* INJUNCTION: H.C.)

Mandamus

Antox India (Pvt.) Ltd v. State Drug Controller, Tamil Nadu (TRADE MARK: STATE MANUFACTURING LICENCE: H.C.)

Notice Period

Mohan Meakin Ltd v. The Pravara Sahakari Sakhar Karkhana Ltd (STATUTORY NOTICE PERIOD: JURISDICTION: APPEAL: H.C.)

Permanent Injunction

Bishwanath Prasad Radhay Sham v. Hindustan Metal Industries (PATENT: INFRINGEMENT: S.C.)

Petition

Thomas (V.T.) v. Malayala Manorama Co. Ltd (COPYRIGHT: STAY OF *ex parte* INJUNCTION: H.C.)

Proceedings before Controller of Patents & Designs

Guest Keen Williams Ltd v. Controller of Patents & Designs (EVIDENCE: H.C.)

Public Interest

Astra/IDL Ltd v. The Pharma Ltd (TRADE MARK: INFRINGEMENT: BETALONG/ BETALOC: PASSING OFF: PRESCRIPTIONS: WEIGHT TO BE ATTRIBUTED TO: H.C.)

Service

India Videogram Association Ltd v. Patel (WRIT: INSERTION THROUGH LETTER BOX: NO AFFIDAVIT OF DUE SERVICE: DEFENDANT OUTSIDE JURISDICTION: LEARNING OF WRIT ON RETURN PRIOR TO ITS EXPIRY: WHETHER SERVICE EFFECTED: Ch.D.)

Stay

Durai Swamy v. Subhaiyam (TRADE MARK: INFRINGEMENT: THREATS: RECTIFICATION: H.C.)

East India Pharmaceutical Works Ltd v. G.G. Pharmaceuticals (TRADE MARK: INFRINGEMENT: PASSING OFF: INJUNCTION: LIMITATION: STAY REFUSED: H.C.)

Thomas (V.T.) v. Malayala Manorama Co. Ltd (PETITION FOR STAY OF *ex parte* INJUNCTION: H.C.)

Transfer of Suit

Fabcon Corporation Inc. USA v. Industrial Engineering Corpn Ghaziabad (PATENT: INFRINGEMENT: H.C.)

Hindustan Lever Ltd v. V.V. Dhanushkodi Nadar & Sons (REGISTERED DESIGN: INFRINGEMENT: PASSING OFF: INTERIM INJUNCTION: H.C.)

Writ

India Videogram Association Ltd v. Patel (SERVICE BY INSERTION THROUGH LETTER BOX: NO AFFIDAVIT OF DUE SERVICE: DEFENDANT OUTSIDE JURISDICTION: LEARNING OF WRIT ON RETURN PRIOR TO ITS EXPIRY: WHETHER SERVICE EFFECTED: Ch.D.)

Trade Marks

Abandonment

Banik Rubber Industries v. Sree K.B. Rubber Industries (REGISTRATION: OPPOSITION: RECTIFICATION: H.C.)

Abandonment of Opposition

Pfizer Inc. v. Chemo-Pharma Laboratories Ltd (OPPOSITION: LATE FILED EVIDENCE: T.M.Reg.)

Acquiescence. *See* **Practice** (*Acquiescence*)

Ad Interim **Injunction.** *See* **Practice** (*Interim and interlocutory injunction*)

Agreement

Raj Steel Rolling Mills v. Vij Iron & Steel Co. (APPLICATION: OPPOSITION: REQUEST FOR REVIEW REFUSED: H.C.)

Appeal. *See* **Practice** (*Appeal*)

Application

American Home Products Corp. v. Mini Pharma (OPPOSITION: PARIN/SPARINE: T.M.Reg.)

Anglo French Drug Co. (The) v. Brihans Laboratories (OPPOSITION: BRIPLEX/ BEPLEX: H.C.)

Anglo-French Drug Co. (Eastern) Ltd v. Hony-N-Bois (OPPOSITION: HEPASYP/ HEPAX: DISMISSAL: APPEAL TO HIGH COURT: H.C.)

Borachem Industries Pvt. Ltd v. Fabril Gasosa (OPPOSITION: BONITA/BONILA: T.M.Reg.)

Burroughs Wellcome (India) Ltd v. American Home Products Corp. (OPPOSITION: ACTICEPH/ACTIFED: T.M.Reg.)

Ciba-Geigy Ltd v. Torrent Laboratories Pvt. Ltd (OPPOSITION: ULCIBAN/CIBA: H.C.)

Colgate Palmolive Co. v. Erasmo De Sequeria (OPPOSITION: FABRIL/FAB: T.M.Reg.)

Farbenfabriken Bayer AG v. Christopher John (OPPOSITION: APPEAL: H.C.)

Flower Tobacco Co. v. Wajidsous Pvt. Ltd (OPPOSITION: T.M.Reg.)

GTC Industries Ltd v. ITC Ltd (OPPOSITION: WINEX/WINNER: APPEAL: H.C.)

Galfa Laboratories Pvt. Ltd v. Rekvina Pharmaceuticals (OPPOSITION: PRIOR REGISTRATION: PETITION TO CANCEL OPPONENTS REGISTRATION: STAY: H.C.)

J. & W. Hardie Ltd v. Joseph E. Seargram & Sons Inc. (ANTIQUE/THE ANTIQUARY: HONEST CONCURRENT USER: H.C.)

J.N. Nicholas (Vimto) Ltd v. Rose & Thistle (WIMTO: CONFUSION WITH VIMTO AND VINTO: APPLICATION TO EXPUNGE VINTO FOR NON-USE: SPECIAL CIRCUMSTANCES: APPEAL: H.C.)

Johann A. Wulfing v. Chemical Industrial & Pharmaceutical Laboratories Ltd (OPPOSITION: CIPLAMINA/COMPLAMINA: H.C.)

Pharma Research & Analytical Labs v. Jal Pvt. Ltd (OLIN: T.M.Reg.)

Raj Steel Rolling Mills v. Vij Iron & Steel Co. (OPPOSITION: AGREEMENT: REQUEST FOR REVIEW REFUSED: H.C.)

Rolex Chemical Industries Application (OPPOSITION: ROLEX: T.M.Reg.)

Surjit Singh v. Alembic Glass Industries Ltd (OPPOSITION: IDENTICAL MARK: DIFFERENT GOODS: H.C.)

Thakur Ayurvedic Pharmacy v. Pandit D.P. Sharma (OPPOSITION DISMISSED: REVIEW PETITIONS ALSO DISMISSED: APPEAL: H.C.)

Uniroyal Inc. v. Maxpharma (OPPOSITION: VITAMAX/VITAVAX: T.M.Reg.)

Arbitration Award

Allied Industries (Jaipur West) v. Allied Industries (Jaipur South) (DECLARATION OF EQUAL RIGHTS: RECTIFICATION: APPLICATION: T.M.Reg.)

Assignment

Aravind Laboratories v. V.A. Samy Chemical Works (INFRINGEMENT: QUALIFICATION TO FILE SUIT: VALIDITY OF ASSIGNMENT AND RENEWAL OF TRADE MARK: INJUNCTION: H.C.)

Associated Mark

Rose & Thistle v. J.N. Nicholas (VIMTO) Ltd (VIMTO: NON-USE: USE OF ASSOCIATED MARK: RECTIFICATION TO ALLOW REGISTRATION OF WIMTO: H.C.)

Cancellation

Galfa Laboratories Pvt. Ltd v. Rekvina Pharmaceuticals (OPPOSITION: PRIOR REGISTRATION: PETITION TO CANCEL OPPONENT'S REGISTRATION: STAY: H.C.)

Cognizance of Complaint

Brundaban Sahu v. Rajendra Subudhi Subudhi (COPYRIGHT: UNREGISTERED MARK AND LABEL: H.C.)

Common Field of Activity

Apple Computer Inc. v. Apple Leasing Industries Ltd (PASSING OFF: UNREGISTERED MARKS: SERVICES: INTERNATIONAL REPUTATION: H.C.)

Common to the Trade

Thapsons Pvt. Ltd v. Ashoka Food Industries (INFRINGEMENT: PASSING OFF: SIMILAR MARKS: *Ad interim* INJUNCTION: H.C.)

Confusion

J.N. Nicholas (Vimto) Ltd v. Rose & Thistle (APPLICATION: WIMTO: CONFUSION WITH VIMTO AND VINTO: APPLICATION TO EXPUNGE VINTO FOR NON-USE: SPECIAL CIRCUMSTANCES: APPEAL: H.C.)

Copyright in Mark

P.M. Diesels Ltd v. S.M. Diesels (INFRINGEMENT: FIELD MARSHAL/SONAMARSHAL: TRADING STYLE: INTERIM INJUNCTION: H.C.)

Costs. *See* **Practice** (*Costs*)

Criminal Action or Application

Arumugam v. State of Tamil Nadu (FORGERY AND COUNTERFEITING: H.C.)
Flower Tobacco Co. v. Mottaahedah Bros (COPYRIGHT: INFRINGEMENT: H.C.)
Mohamad Khalil v. The State of Maharashtra (REVISION: H.C.)
SPS Selvaraj v. Muthuswamy Naicker (INFRINGEMENT: CIVIL AND CRIMINAL PROCEEDINGS: CONTEMPT: H.C.)
Sumeet Machines Pvt. Ltd v. Sumeet Research & Holdings Ltd (INFRINGEMENT: SIMULTANEOUS LAUNCHING OF CIVIL AND CRIMINAL PROCEEDINGS: H.C.)

Deception

National Garments v. National Apparels (PASSING OFF: GET-UP: COVER OF BOXES: INTERIM INJUNCTION: APPEAL: H.C.)

Deceptive Similarity

Nucron Pharmaceuticals Pvt. Ltd v. International Pharmaceuticals (INFRINGEMENT: SEPMAX/SELMAX: APPLIED TO MEDICINES FOR DIFFERENT MEDICAL CONDITIONS: LIKELIHOOD OF DISASTEROUS CONSEQUENCES: LEAVE TO APPLY FOR *ad interim* INJUNCTION: H.C.)
Rahim (M.A.) v. Aravind Laboratories (INFRINGEMENT: EYETEX/EYERIS: INTERIM INJUNCTION: RECTIFICATION: EXPUNGEMENT: APPEAL: DESIGN OF LABEL AMENDED TO AVOID CONFLICT: WITHDRAWAL OF INTERIM INJUNCTION: H.C.)

Declaration. *See* **Practice** (*Declaration*)

Delay. *See* **Practice** (*Delay*)

Design of Label, amended to Avoid Conflict

Rahim (M.A.) v. Aravind Laboratories (INFRINGEMENT: EYETEX/EYERIS: DECEPTIVE SIMILARITY: INTERIM INJUNCTION: RECTIFICATION: EXPUNGEMENT: APPEAL: WITHDRAWAL OF INTERIM INJUNCTION: H.C.)

Different Goods

Brij Mohan Dutta v. Jallo Subsidiary Industries Co. (India) Pvt. Ltd (INFRINGEMENT: LION BRAND/LION ELEPHANT: INTERIM INJUNCTION: APPEAL: H.C.)

Cartier International BV Co. Ltd v. Ramesh Kumar Sawhney (INFRINGEMENT: CARTIER: INTERNATIONAL REPUTATION: INTERIM INJUNCTION: H.C.)
Daimler Benz AG v. Hybo Hindustan (INFRINGEMENT: PASSING OFF: BENZ: INTERIM INJUNCTION: H.C.)
Sony Corporation v. Elite Optical Co. (OPPOSITION: T.M.Reg.)
Surjit Singh v. Alembic Glass Industries Ltd (APPLICATION: OPPOSITION: PROPRIETOR OF IDENTICAL MARK: H.C.)

Distinctiveness

Ciba-Geigy Ltd v. Sun Pharmaceuticals Industries (INFRINGEMENT: ANAFRANIL/ CLOROFANIL: INTERIM INJUNCTION: APPEAL: H.C.)
Hami Brothers v. Hami & Co. (RECTIFICATION: H.C.)
Reckitt & Colman of India Ltd v. Medicross Pharmaceuticals Pvt. Ltd (INFRINGEMENT: DISPRIN/MEDISPRIN: NOTICE OF MOTION: H.C.)

Drug Controller's Licence

Fleming (India) v. Ambalal Sarabhai Enterprises (PASSING OFF: USE UNDER DRUG CONTROLLER'S LICENCE: INJUNCTION: APPEAL: H.C.)

Entitlement to Enforce

Finlay Mills Ltd v. National Textile Corp. (UNAUTHORISED USE BY MANAGED COMPANY: H.C.)

Entitlement to Use. *See* Use

Ex Parte Injunction. *See* Practice (*Ex parte injunction*)

Export

Brooke Bond India Ltd v. Balaji Tea (India) Pvt. Ltd (INFRINGEMENT: PASSING OFF: RED LABEL: RED APPLE TEA: PACKETS FILLED IN INDIA AND EXPORTED: H.C.)
Philip Morris Inc. v. GTC Industries Ltd (INFRINGEMENT: BAN ON IMPORTS: EXPORT OF PRODUCTS USING PLAINTIFF'S NAME: INTERIM INJUNCTION: H.C.)

Expungement

Hardie Trading Ltd v. Addison Paints & Chemicals Ltd (NON-USE: APPEAL: SPECIAL CIRCUMSTANCES: IMPORT BAN: H.C.)
J.N. Nicholas (Vimto) Ltd v. Rose & Thistle (APPLICATION: WIMTO: CONFUSION WITH VIMTO AND VINTO: APPLICATION TO EXPUNGE VINTO FOR NON-USE: SPECIAL CIRCUMSTANCES: APPEAL: H.C.)
Rahim (M.A.) v. Aravind Laboratories (INFRINGEMENT: EYETEX/EYERIS: DECEPTIVE SIMILARITY: INTERIM INJUNCTION: RECTIFICATION: APPEAL: DESIGN OF LABEL AMENDED TO AVOID CONFLICT: WITHDRAWAL OF INTERIM INJUNCTION: H.C.)

Extension of Time Limits. *See* Practice (*Time limits*)

Family Name

Bajaj Electricals Ltd v. Metal & Applied Products (BAJAJ: INFRINGEMENT: INTERIM INJUNCTION: APPEAL: H.C.)

First to Enter Market

Duncan Agro Industries Ltd v. Somabhai Tea Processors (Pvt.) Ltd (PASSING OFF: INTERIM INJUNCTION: APPEAL: H.C.)

Foreign Plaintiff

Revlon Inc. v. Kemco Chemicals (PASSING OFF: NO LOCAL IMMOVABLE ASSETS: STRIKING OUT: SECURITY FOR COSTS: H.C.)

Forgery and Counterfeiting

Arumugam v. State of Tamil Nadu (CRIMINAL OFFENCE: H.C.)

Goods of Different Description. *See* **Different Goods**

Get-Up

Camlin Pvt. Ltd v. National Pencil Industries (COPYRIGHT: INFRINGEMENT: PASSING OFF: CAMLIN FLORA/TIGER FLORE: TRADE MARK AND CARTON DIFFERENT: GET-UP AND DESIGN OF PENCIL LIKELY TO CONFUSE SMALL CHILDREN: INTERIM INJUNCTION: H.C.)

National Garments v. National Apparels (PASSING OFF: COVER OF BOXES: DECEPTION: INTERIM INJUNCTION: APPEAL: H.C.)

P.M. Diesels Ltd v. S.M. Diesels (COPYRIGHT IN MARK: INFRINGEMENT: FIELD MARSHAL/SONAMARSHAL: INTERIM INJUNCTION: H.C.)

Rawal Industries (Pvt.) Ltd v. Duke Enterprises (PASSING OFF: INFRINGEMENT: TRADING STYLE: INTERIM INJUNCTION: H.C.)

Sushil Vasudev (t/a Kwality Ice Cream Co.) v. Kwality Frozen Foods Pvt. Ltd (KWALITY: REGISTRATION: PRIOR USER: INTERIM INJUNCTION: H.C.)

Goodwill

Apple Computer Inc. v. Apple Leasing Industries Ltd (PASSING OFF: UNREGISTERED MARKS: SERVICES: INTERNATIONAL REPUTATION: COMMON FIELD OF ACTIVITY: LIKELIHOOD OF DECEPTION OR CONFUSION: NATURE OF GOODWILL: H.C.)

Government Policy

Duke & Sons Ltd v. Union of India (USE OF FOREIGN BRAND NAMES: PROHIBITION: HYBRID NAME: PEPSI LAHER: H.C.)

Honest Concurrent Use

J. & W. Hardie Ltd v. Joseph E. Seargram & Sons Inc. (APPLICATION: ANTIQUE/ THE ANTIQUARY: H.C.)

Sandoz Ltd v. Pharmaceutical & Chemical Industries (OPPOSITION: *Res judicata:* T.M.Reg.)

Import Ban

Hardie Trading Ltd v. Addison Paints & Chemicals Ltd (EXPUNGEMENT: NON-USE: APPEAL: SPECIAL CIRCUMSTANCES: H.C.)

Philip Morris Inc. v. GTC Industries Ltd (INFRINGEMENT: EXPORT OF PRODUCTS USING PLAINTIFF'S NAME: INTERIM INJUNCTION: H.C.)

Toshiba Appliances Co. v. Toshiba KK (RECTIFICATION: NON-USE FOR FIVE
YEARS: NON-INTENTION TO USE: H.C.)

House Mark

BK Engineering Co. v. UBHI Enterprises (PASSING OFF: USE OF HOUSE MARK:
H.C.)

Infringement

Amrutanjan Ltd v. Amrachand Sobachand (PASSING OFF: NO SALE UNDER
INFRINGING MARK: PERMANENT INJUNCTION: JURISDICTION: H.C.)
Amrutanjan Ltd v. Ashwin Fine Chemicals & Pharmaceuticals (AMRUTANJAN/
ASHWIN: PASSING OFF: INTERIM INJUNCTION: H.C.)
Anglo French Drug Co. (Eastern) Ltd v. Belco Pharmaceuticals (INJUNCTION: H.C.)
Appliances Emporium v. M/s Usha Industries (India) New Delhi (INTERIM
INJUNCTION: H.C.)
Aravind Laboratories v. V.A. Samy Chemical Works (QUALIFICATION TO FILE SUIT:
VALIDITY OF ASSIGNMENT AND RENEWAL OF TRADE MARK: INJUNCTION:
H.C.)
Arumugam v. State of Tamil Nadu (CRIMINAL OFFENCE: FORGERY AND
COUNTERFEITING: H.C.)
Bajaj Electricals Ltd v. Metal & Applied Products (BAJAJ: PASSING OFF: USE OF
FAMILY NAME: INTERIM INJUNCTION: APPEAL: H.C.)
Bata India Ltd v. M/s Pyarelal & Co. (PASSING OFF: BATA/BATAFORM: H.C.)
Bijoli Grill Spencer's Products v. Spencers & Co. Ltd (INJUNCTION: DECLARATION:
H.C.)
Blue Cross & Blue Shield Association v. Blue Cross Health Clinic (PASSING OFF:
INJUNCTION: H.C.)
Bombay Oil Industries Pvt. Ltd v. Ballarpur Industries Ltd (SAFFOLA/SHAPOLA:
INTERIM INJUNCTION: H.C.)
Brij Mohan Dutta v. Jallo Subsidiary Industries Co. (India) Pvt. Ltd (LION BRAND/
LION ELEPHANT: INTERIM INJUNCTION: APPEAL: DISSIMILAR PRODUCTS:
H.C.)
Britannia Industries Ltd v. Bharat Biscuits Co. Pvt. Ltd (BRITANNIA SNAX/
BHARAT SNACKS: PASSING OFF: INTERIM INJUNCTION: REFUSED: H.C.)
Brooke Bond (India) Ltd v. Balaji Tea (India) Pvt. Ltd (PASSING OFF: INJUNCTION:
H.C.)
Brooke Bond India Ltd v. Balaji Tea (India) Pvt. Ltd (PASSING OFF: RED LABEL:
RED APPLE TEA: PACKETS FILLED IN INDIA AND EXPORTED: H.C.)
Brooke Bond India Ltd v. Raj Kamal Enterprises (MARK AND ARTISTIC LABEL: H.C.)
Burroughs Wellcome (India) Ltd v. G.K. Sharma & King Scientific Research Centre
(SEPTRIN/CETRAN: COPYRIGHT: PASSING OFF: JURISDICTION OF COURT
TO ENTERTAIN COMPOSITE SUIT: H.C.)
Camlin Pvt. Ltd v. National Pencil Industries (COPYRIGHT: PASSING OFF: CAMLIN
FLORA/TIGER FLORE: MARK AND CARTON DIFFERENT: GET-UP AND
DESIGN OF PENCIL LIKELY TO CONFUSE SMALL CHILDREN: INTERIM
INJUNCTION: H.C.)
Camlin Pvt. Ltd v. National Pencil Industries (PASSING OFF: APPEAL: INTERIM
ORDER: H.C.)
Canon KK v. Canon Electronics Pvt. Ltd (PASSING OFF: *Ex parte ad interim*
INJUNCTION: APPEAL: H.C.)
Cartier International BV Co. Ltd v. Ramesh Kumar Sawhney (CARTIER:
INTERNATIONAL REPUTATION: GOODS OF DIFFERENT DESCRIPTION:
INTERIM INJUNCTION: H.C.)
Ceat Tyres of India Ltd v. Jay Industrial Services (PASSING OFF: *Ad interim*
INJUNCTION: H.C.)

Chandra Bhan Dembla Trading v. Bharat Sewing Machine Co. (PASSING OFF: H.C.)

Charan Dass & Veer Industries (India) v. Bombay Crockery House (COPYRIGHT: DESIGN: PASSING OFF: PERFECT/SWASTIK PERFECT: INTERIM INJUNCTION: H.C.)

Chawrana Tobacco Co. v. Bhagwandas (COPYRIGHT: INTERIM INJUNCTION: H.C.)

Chemicals Co. Ltd v. Kent Pharmaceuticals (India) Pvt. Ltd (RIFINEX/RIFISON: PASSING OFF: INJUNCTION: H.C.)

Ciba-Geigy Ltd v. Sun Pharmaceuticals Industries (ANAFRANIL/CLOROFANIL: DISTINCTIVENESS: INTERIM INJUNCTION: APPEAL: H.C.)

Cipla Ltd v. Unicure Pharmaceuticals (PIROX: RECTIFICATION: INTERLOCUTORY PETITION: JURISDICTION: T.M.Reg.)

Cormandel Fertilizers Ltd v. Cormandel Cements Ltd (PASSING OFF: AMENDMENT OF PLEADINGS: H.C.)

Coromandel Fertilizers Ltd v. Coromandel Cements Ltd (*Ad interim* INJUNCTION VACATED: H.C.)

Crystal Knitters v. Bombay Vestors (CRYSTAL/COASTAL: INTERIM INJUNCTION: THREATS: H.C.)

Daimler Benz AG v. Hybo Hindustan (PASSING OFF: BENZ: GOODS OF DIFFERENT DESCRIPTION: INTERIM INJUNCTION: H.C.)

Deekonda Pedda Chinniah v. Mangalore Ganesh Beedi Works (PASSING OFF: INTERIM INJUNCTION: APPEAL: H.C.)

Durai Swamy v. Subhaiyam (THREATS: RECTIFICATION: STAY: H.C.)

ESSCO Sanitations v. Mascot Industries (INJUNCTION: H.C.)

Fairdeal Corp. (Pvt.) Ltd v. Vijay Pharmaceuticals (*Ex parte* INJUNCTION: APPEAL: H.C.)

Flower Tobacco Co. v. Mottaahedah Bros (CRIMINAL ACTION: COPYRIGHT: H.C.)

Globe Super Parts v. Blue Super Flame Industries (PASSING OFF: INJUNCTION: H.C.)

Gold Seal Engineering Products Pvt. Ltd v. Hindustan Manufacturers (PASSING OFF: JURISDICTION: JOINDER OF CAUSES OF ACTION: H.C.)

Griffon Laboratories (P.) Ltd v. Indian National Drug Co. P. Ltd (SORBILINE/SORBITON: INTERIM INJUNCTION: H.C.)

Gurshant Engineering Co. Pvt. Ltd v. DLF Universals Ltd (PASSING OFF: COPYRIGHT: APPEAL: H.C.)

Habeebur Rehman & Sons v. Ram Babu & Brothers (PASSING OFF: COPYRIGHT IN LABEL: DEFENDANT PRIOR REGISTRANT: INTERIM INJUNCTION: APPEAL: H.C.)

Himachal Pradesh Horticulture Produce Marketing v. Mohan Meakin Breweries Ltd (PASSING OFF: H.C.)

Hindustan Pencils Pvt. Ltd v. India Stationery Products Co. (INTERIM INJUNCTION: REGISTRATION UNDER COPYRIGHT ACT: *Ex parte* INJUNCTION: DELAY, LACHES AND ACQUIESCENCE: H.C.)

HMT Ltd v. Olympic Agencies (TRADE MARKS: PASSING OFF: HMT-SONA, HMT-ASHA/OLYMPIC SONA, OLYMPIC ASHA—FOR WATCHES: H.C.)

Jain & Bros KK v. Paras Enterprises (PASSING OFF: INTERIM INJUNCTION: H.C.)

Jawahar Engineering Co. v. Jovahar Engineers Pvt. Ltd (PASSING OFF: H.C.)

Johnson & Johnson v. Christine Hoden India (Pvt.) Ltd (PASSING OFF: STAYFREE: INJUNCTION: H.C.)

K.R. Jadayappa Mudaliar v. K.S. Venkatachalam (UNLICENSED USE: INJUNCTION VACATED: H.C.)

Kali Aerated Water Works v. Rashid (PASSING OFF: KALI MARK/SRI NEW KALI MARK AERATED WATER: DECLARATION: INJUNCTION: H.C.)

Kalyani Breweries Ltd v. Khoday Brewing & Distilling Industries Ltd (KALYANI BLACK LABEL: KHODAY BLACK LABEL: INJUNCTION: H.C.)

Kamal Trading Co. v. Gillette U.K. Ltd (PASSING OFF: 7 O'CLOCK: INTERLOCUTORY INJUNCTION: APPEAL: H.C.)

Kissan Industries v. Punjab Food Corp. (PASSING OFF: COPYRIGHT: H.C.)

Kopran Chemicals Co. Ltd v. Kent Pharmaceuticals (India) Pvt. Ltd (RIFINEX/ RIFISON: PASSING OFF: INJUNCTION: H.C.)

Manoj Plastic Industries v. Bhola Plastic Industries (PASSING OFF: SAME TRADE MARK FOR IDENTICAL GOODS: INTERIM INJUNCTION: H.C.)

Mohan Meakin Ltd v. The Pravara Sahakari Sakhar Karkhana Ltd (PASSING OFF: STATUTORY NOTICE PERIOD: JURISDICTION: APPEAL: H.C.)

MRF Ltd v. Metro Tyres Ltd (NYLOGRIP/RADIALGRIP: PASSING OFF: DECEPTIVE USE OF TYRE TREAD PATTERN: INTERIM INJUNCTION: H.C.)

Nirex Industries (Pvt.) Ltd v. Manchand Footwears (COPYRIGHT: JURISDICTION: INTERIM INJUNCTION: H.C.)

Nucron Pharmaceuticals Pvt. Ltd v. International Pharmaceuticals (SEPMAX/ SELMAX: APPLIED TO MEDICINES FOR DIFFERENT MEDICAL CONDITIONS: DECEPTIVE SIMILARITY: LIKELIHOOD OF DISASTROUS CONSEQUENCES: LEAVE TO APPLY FOR *ad interim* INJUNCTION: H.C.)

Optrex India Ltd v. Optrex Ltd (USE AS MARK AND PART OF COMPANY NAME: PREVENTION OF USE AFTER TERMINATION OF REGISTERED USER AGREEMENT: INTERIM INJUNCTION: H.C.)

P.M. Diesels Ltd v. S.M. Diesels (COPYRIGHT IN MARK: FIELD MARSHAL/ SONAMARSHAL: TRADING STYLE: INTERIM INJUNCTION: H.C.)

Parkash Metal Works v. Square Automation (Pvt.) Ltd (PASSING OFF: HOT FLO/ PMW HOT FLO: INJUNCTION: H.C.)

Parkash Roadlines Ltd v. Parkash Parcel Services (Pvt.) Ltd (PASSING OFF: INTERIM INJUNCTION: H.C.)

Pepsico Inc. v. Express Bottlers Services Pvt. Ltd (PEPSI/PEPSICOLA: NON-USE: RECTIFICATION PROCEEDINGS PENDING: INJUNCTION REFUSED: APPEAL: H.C.)

Philip Morris Belgium SA v. Golden Tobacco Co. Ltd (INTERIM INJUNCTION: H.C.)

Philip Morris Inc. v. GTC Industries Ltd (BAN ON IMPORTS: EXPORT OF PRODUCTS USING PLAINTIFF'S NAME: INTERIM INJUNCTION: H.C.)

Pidilite Industries Pvt. Ltd v. Mittees Corporation (FEVICOL/TREVICOL: COPYRIGHT: INTERIM INJUNCTION: THREATS: H.C.)

Poddar Tyres Ltd v. Bedrock Sales Corporation (PASSING OFF: USE IN CORPORATE NAME: INTERIM INJUNCTION: H.C.)

R.J. Reynolds Tobacco Co. v. ITC Ltd (NOW: PASSING OFF: INTERIM INJUNCTION: H.C.)

R.P. Locks Co. v. Sehgal Locks Co. (HARRISON/HARICON: INTERIM *ex parte* INJUNCTION: H.C.)

Rahim (M.A.) v. Aravind Laboratories (EYETEX/EYERIS: DECEPTIVE SIMILARITY: INTERIM INJUNCTION: RECTIFICATION: EXPUNGEMENT: APPEAL: DESIGN OF LABEL AMENDED TO AVOID CONFLICT: WITHDRAWAL OF INTERIM INJUNCTION: H.C.)

Ranbaxy Laboratories Ltd v. Dua Pharmaceuticals Pvt. Ltd (CALMPOSE/ CALMPROSE: PASSING OFF: INTERIM INJUNCTION: H.C.)

Rawal Industries (Pvt.) Ltd v. Duke Enterprises (PASSING OFF: TRADING STYLE: INTERIM INJUNCTION: H.C.)

Reckitt & Coleman of India Ltd v. Medicross Pharmaceuticals Pvt. Ltd (DISPRIN/ MEDISPRIN: DISTINCTIVENESS: NOTICE OF MOTION: H.C.)

Richardson Vicks Inc. v. Medico Laboratories (PASSING OFF: INJUNCTION: H.C.)

Richardson Vicks Inc. v. Vikas Pharmaceuticals (COPYRIGHT: PASSING OFF: *Ad interim* INJUNCTION MADE ABSOLUTE: H.C.)

S.M. Enterprises v. Hyderabad Lamps Ltd (SOLAR: CHOKES FOR FLUORESCENT TUBES: INTERIM INJUNCTION VACATED: H.C.)

Injunction. *See* **Practice** *(Injunction)*

Intention to Use. *See* **Use**

Interim *Ex Parte* Injunction. *See* **Practice** *(Interim and interlocutory injunction)*

Interim Injunction. *See* **Practice** *(Interim and interlocutory injunction)*

Interlocutory Injunction. *See* **Practice** *(Interim and interlocutory injunction)*

International Reputation

Jurisdiction. *See* **Practice** *(Jurisdiction)*

Laches. *See* **Practice** *(Laches)*

Lack of Equity. *See* **Practice** *(Equity)*

Licence

Licensees

Wander Ltd v. Antox India Pvt. Ltd (CONFLICT BETWEEN LICENSEES: PASSING OFF: INTERIM INJUNCTION: APPEAL AND FURTHER APPEAL: H.C.)

Likelihood of Deception or Confusion

Apple Computer Inc. v. Apple Leasing Industries Ltd (UNREGISTERED MARKS: SERVICES: INTERNATIONAL REPUTATION: COMMON FIELD OF ACTIVITY: NATURE OF GOODWILL: H.C.)

Likelihood of Disastrous Consequences

Nucron Pharmaceuticals Pvt. Ltd v. International Pharmaceuticals (INFRINGEMENT: SEPMAX/SELMAX: APPLIED TO MEDICINES FOR DIFFERENT MEDICAL CONDITIONS: DECEPTIVE SIMILARITY: LEAVE TO APPLY FOR *ad interim* INJUNCTION: H.C.)

Marks in Issue

501/507 Tata Oil Mills Co. Ltd v. Reward Soap Works (H.C.)

7 O'CLOCK Kamal Trading Co. v. Gillette U.K. Ltd (H.C.)

ACTICEPH/ACTIFED: Burroughs Wellcome (India) Ltd v. American Home Products Corp.

AMRUTANJAN/ASHWIN: Amrutanjan Ltd v. Ashwin Fine Chemicals & Pharmaceuticals

ANAFRANIL/CLOROFANIL: Ciba-Geigy Ltd v. Sun Pharmaceuticals Industries

ANTIQUE/THE ANTIQUARY: J. & W. Hardie Ltd v. Joseph E. Seargram & Sons Inc.

BAJAJ: Bajaj Electricals Ltd v. Metal & Applied Products

BATA/BATAFORM: Bata India Ltd v. M/s Pyarelal & Co.

BENZ: Daimler Benz AG v. Hybo Hindustan

BETALONG/BETALOC: Arumugam v. State of Tamil Nadu

BIDIS: Vrajlal Manilal & Co. v. N.S. Bidi Co.

BLACK KNIGHT/ROYAL KNIGHT: Mohan Meakin Ltd v. The Pravara Sahakari Sakhar Karkhana Ltd

BONITA/BONILA: Borachem Industries Pvt. Ltd v. Fabril Gasosa

BRIPLEX/BEPLEX: Anglo French Drug Co. (The) v. Brihans Laboratories

BRITANNIA/SNAX/BHARAT SNACKS: Britannia Industries Ltd v. Bharat Biscuits Co. Pvt. Ltd

CALMPOSE/CALMPROSE: Ranbaxy Laboratories Ltd v. Dua Pharmaceuticals Pvt. Ltd

CAMBRIDGE: Rothmans of Pall Mall Ltd v. New Tobacco Co. Ltd

CAMLIN FLORA/TIGER FLORE: Camlin Pvt. Ltd v. National Pencil Industries

CARTIER: Cartier International BV Co. Ltd v. Ramesh Kumar Sawhney

CIPLAMINA/COMPLAMINA: Johann A. Wulfing v. Chemical Industrial & Pharmaceutical Laboratories Ltd

CRYSTAL/COASTAL: Crystal Knitters v. Bombay Vestors

DISPRIN/MEDISPRIN: Reckitt & Colman of India Ltd v. Medicross Pharmaceuticals Pvt. Ltd

EYETEX/EYERIS: Rahim (M.A.) v. Aravind Laboratories

FABRIL/FAB: Colgate Palmolive Co. v. Erasmo De Sequeria

FEVICOL/TREVICOL: Pidilite Industries Pvt. Ltd v. Mittees Corporation

FIELD MARSHAL: P.M. Diesels Pvt. Ltd v. Thukral Mechanical Works

FIELD MARSHAL/SONAMARSHAL: P.M. Diesels Ltd v. S.M. Diesels

FORMIS/CHARMIS: BK Products Application
GARAMYCIN/GAMAMYCIN: Schering Corp. v. Perk Pharmaceutical Services
HARRISON/HARICON: R.P. Locks Co. v. Sehgal Locks Co.
HEPASYP/HEPAX: Anglo-French Drug Co. (Eastern) Ltd v. Hony-N-Bois
HIDESIGN/HI-DESIGN CREATIONS: Hidesign v. Hi-Design Creations
HMT-SONA, HMT-ASHA/OLYMPIC SONA, OLYMPIC ASHA: HMT Ltd v.
  Olympic Agencies
HOT FLO/PMW HOT FLO: Parkash Metal Works v. Square Automation (Pvt.)
  Ltd
JEEP/CHHAP: Jeep Corp. v. Lion Industries
KALI MARK/SRI NEW KALI MARK: Kali Aerated Water Works v. Rashid
KALYANI BLACK LABEL: KHODAY BLACK LABEL: Kalyani Breweries Ltd v.
  Khoday Brewing & Distilling Industries Ltd
KWALITY: Sushil Vasudev (t/a Kwality Ice Cream Co.) v. Kwality Frozen Foods
  Pvt. Ltd
LION BRAND/LION ELEPHANT: Brij Mohan Dutta v. Jallo Subsidiary
  Industries Co.
M.M.B./M.B.B.: Mohan Meaking Ltd v. Kashmiri Dreamland Distilleries
MEGAVITE/MEGAVIT: Geoffrey Manners & Co. Ltd v. Mega Pharma
  Laboratories
MJTONE/M2TONE M.J. Exports Pvt. Ltd v. Charak Pharmaceuticals
M.M.B./M.B.B.: National Garments v. National Apparels
NOW: R.J. Reynolds Tobacco Co. v. ITC Ltd
NYLOGRIP/RADIALGRIP: MRF Ltd v. Metro Tyres Ltd
OLIN: pharma Research & Analytical Labs v. Jal Pvt. Ltd
PARIN/SPARINE: American Home Products Corp. v. Mini Pharma
PEPSI LAHER: Duke & Sons Ltd v. Union of India
PEPSI/PEPSICOLA: Express Bottlers Services Pvt. Ltd v. Pepsico Inc.
PEPSI/PEPSICOLA: Pepsico Inc. v. Express Bottlers Services Pvt. Ltd
PERFECT/SWASTIK PERFECT: Charan Dass & Veer Industries (India) v.
  Bombay Crockery House
PIROX: Cipla Ltd v. Unicure Pharmaceuticals
QUADRIDERM/CORIDERM: Schering Corp. v. Kilitch Co. (Pharma) Pvt. Ltd
RAJA/MAHRAJA: S.M. Chopra & Sons v. Rajendra Prosad Srivastava
RED LABEL: RED APPLE: Tea: Brooke Bond India Ltd v. Balaji Tea (India) Pvt.
  Ltd
RIFINEX/RIFISON: Kopran Chemicals Co. Ltd v. Kent Pharmaceuticals (India)
  Pvt. Ltd
ROLEX: Rolex Chemical Industries Application
SAFFOLA/SHAPOLA: Bombay Oil Industries Pvt. Ltd v. Ballarpur Industries Ltd
SEPMAX/SELMAX: Nucron Pharmaceuticals Pvt. Ltd v. International
  Pharmaceuticals
SEPTRIN/CETRAN: Burroughs Wellcome (India) Ltd v. G.K. Sharma & King
  Scientific Research Centre
SOLAR: S.M. Enterprises v. Hyderabad Lamps Ltd
SONY: Sony KK v. Shamrock Maskar
SORBILINE/SORBITON: Griffon Laboratories (P.) Ltd v. Indian National Drug
  Co. P. Ltd
STAYFREE: Johnson & Johnson v. Christine Hoden India (Pvt.) Ltd
SUPER DUST TEA: Brooke Bond India Ltd v. Balaji Tea (India) Pvt. Ltd
TINNA/TANY: Tinna Enterprises Pvt. Ltd v. International Rubber Industries
TOBU/TOHO: Tobu Interprises Pvt. Ltd v. Tokyo Cycle Industries
ULCIBAN/CIBA: Ciba-Geigy Ltd v. Torrent Laboratories Pvt. Ltd
VIMCO/SIMCO: Simla Chemicals Pvt. Ltd v. MJSP Products (India)

VIMTO/VINTO: J.N. Nicholas (Vimto) Ltd v. Rose & Thistle
VIMTO/VINTO: Rose & Thistle v. J.N. Nicholas (Vimto) Ltd
VITAMAX/VITAVAX: Uniroyal Inc. v. Maxpharma
WHITE HORSE/FLYING HORSE: White Horse Distillers Ltd v. The Upper
    Doab Sugar Mills Ltd
WIMTO: J.N. Nicholas (Vimto) Ltd v. Rose & Thistle
WIMTO Rose & Thistle v. J.N. Nicholas (Vimto) Ltd
WINEX/WINNER: GTC Industries Ltd v. ITC Ltd

Non-Intention to Use

Pankaj Group v. The Good Year Tyre and Rubber Co. (RECTIFICATION: T.M.Reg.)
Toshiba Appliances Co. v. Toshiba KK (RECTIFICATION: NON-USE FOR FIVE
    YEARS: IMPORT BAN: H.C.)

Non-Use

DRISTAN Trade Mark (RECTIFICATION: REGISTERED USER: H.C.)
DRISTAN Trade Mark (RECTIFICATION: OVERSEAS PROPRIETOR: INDIAN
    SUBSIDIARY: BONA FIDE INTENTION TO USE AT DATE OF REGISTRATION:
    REGISTERED USER: S.C.)
Fatima Tile Works v. Sudarson Trading Co. Ltd (RECTIFICATION: USE BY
    SUBSIDIARY COMPANY: H.C.)
Hardie Trading Ltd v. Addison Paints & Chemicals Ltd (EXPUNGEMENT: APPEAL:
    SPECIAL CIRCUMSTANCES: IMPORT BAN: H.C.)
J.N. Nicholas (Vimto) Ltd v. Rose & Thistle (APPLICATION: WIMTO: CONFUSION
    WITH VIMTO AND VINTO: APPLICATION TO EXPUNGE VINTO FOR NON-
    USE: SPECIAL CIRCUMSTANCES: APPEAL: H.C.)
Pepsico Inc. v. Express Bottlers Services Pvt. Ltd (INFRINGEMENT: PEPSI/
    PEPSICOLA: RECTIFICATION PROCEEDINGS PENDING: INJUNCTION
    REFUSED: APPEAL: H.C.)
Rose & Thistle v. J.N. Nicholas (Vimto) Ltd (VIMTO: USE OF ASSOCIATED MARK:
    RECTIFICATION TO ALLOW REGISTRATION OF WIMTO: H.C.)
Rothmans of Pall Mall Ltd v. New Tobacco Co. Ltd (CAMBRIDGE FOR
    CIGARETTES: NON-AVAILABILITY OF MARK: H.C.)
Toshiba Appliances Co. v. Toshiba KK (RECTIFICATION: NON-USE FOR 5 YEARS:
    NON-INTENTION TO USE: IMPORT BAN: H.C.)
Vishnudas Kishindas Zarda Factory v. Vazir Sultan Tobacco Co. Ltd
    (RECTIFICATION: NON-USE: REGISTRABILITY: H.C.)

Opposition

American Home Products Corp. v. Mini Pharma (PARIN/SPARINE: T.M.Reg.)
Anglo French Drug Co. (The) v. Brihans Laboratories (BRIPLEX/BEPLEX: H.C.)
Anglo-French Drug Co. (Eastern) Ltd v. Hony-N-Bois (APPLICATION: HEPASYP/
    HEPAX: DISMISSAL BY REGISTRAR: APPEAL TO HIGH COURT ALLOWED:
    H.C.)
Banik Rubber Industries v. Sree K.B. Rubber Industries (REGISTRATION: ABAN-
    DONMENT: RECTIFICATION: H.C.)
Bharaj Manufacturing Co. v. Shiv Metal Works (REGISTRATION: T.M.Reg.)
BK Products' Application (FORMIS/CHARMIS: T.M.Reg.)
Borachem Industries Pvt. Ltd v. Fabril Gasosa (BONITA/BONILA: T.M.Reg.)
Burroughs Wellcome (India) Ltd v. American Home Products Corp. (ACTICEPH/
    ACTIFED: India: T.M.Reg.)
Ciba-Geigy Ltd v. Torrent Laboratories Pvt. Ltd (ULCIBAN/CIBA: H.C.)

Colgate Palmolive Co. v. Erasmo De Sequeria (FABRIL/FAB: T.M.Reg.)
Farbenfabriken Bayer AG v. Christopher John (APPLICATION: APPEAL: H.C.)
Flower Tobacco Co. v. Wajidsous Pvt. Ltd (APPLICATION: T.M.Reg.)
GTC Industries Ltd v. ITC Ltd (WINEX/WINNER: APPEAL: H.C.)
Galfa Laboratories Pvt. Ltd v. Rekvina Pharmaceuticals (PRIOR REGISTRATION: PETITION TO CANCEL OPPONENT'S REGISTRATION: STAY: H.C.)
Geoffrey Manners & Co. Ltd v. Mega Pharma Laboratories (MEGAVITE/ MEGAVIT: H.C.)
Hardie Trading Ltd v. Addison Paints & Chemicals Ltd (OVERSEAS PROPRIETOR: USE BY AGENT: REGISTERED USER: APPLICATION BY INDIAN COMPANY: APPLICATION FOR STAY: H.C.)
Hind Azad Factory v. Azad Factory (DELAY IN FILING EVIDENCE: COSTS: REVIEW: T.M.Reg.)
Johann A. Wulfing v. Chemical Industrial & Pharmaceutical Laboratories Ltd (APPLICATION: CIPLAMINA/COMPLAMINA: H.C.)
M.J. Exports Pvt. Ltd v. Charak Pharmaceuticals (REFUSAL OF REGISTRATION: MJTONE/M2TONE: APPEAL: H.C.)
Pfizer Inc. v. Chemo-Pharma Laboratories Ltd (LATE FILED EVIDENCE: ABANDONMENT OF OPPOSITION: T.M.REG.)
Progro Pharmaceuticals (Pvt.) Ltd v. Deputy Registrar of Trade Marks (DELAY IN FILING COUNTERSTATEMENT: EXTENSION OF TIME LIMITS: H.C.)
Raj Steel Rolling Mills v. Vij Iron & Steel Co. (AGREEMENT: REQUEST FOR REVIEW REFUSED: H.C.)
Rolex Chemical Industries' Application (APPLICATION: ROLEX: T.M.Reg.)
Sandoz Ltd v. Pharmaceutical & Chemical Industries (HONEST CONCURRENT USE: Res judicata: T.M.Reg.)
Simla Chemicals Pvt. Ltd v. MJSP Products (India) (VIMCO/SIMCO: T.M.Reg.)
Singh v. Alembic Glass Industries Ltd (APPLICATION: IDENTICAL MARK: DIFFERENT GOODS: H.C.)
Sony Corporation v. Elite Optical Co. (GOODS TOTALLY DIFFERENT: T.M.Reg.)
Sony KK v. Shamrock Maskar (SONY: H.C.)
Thakur Ayurvedic Pharmacy v. Pandit D.P. Sharma (TRADE MARKS: APPLICATION: OPPOSITION DISMISSED: REVIEW PETITIONS ALSO DISMISSED: APPEAL: H.C.)
Uniroyal Inc. v. Maxpharma (APPLICATION: VITAMAX/VITAVAX: T.M.Reg.)
Universal Pharmacy v. Classic Pharmaceuticals (REQUEST FOR FURTHER EXTENSION OF TIME TO FILE EVIDENCE: OPPOSITION DEEMED ABANDONED: PETITION FOR REVIEW: REGISTRAR'S POWER: T.M.Reg.)

Overseas Proprietor

Hardie Trading Ltd v. Addison Paints & Chemicals Ltd (USE BY AGENT: REGISTERED USER: APPLICATION BY INDIAN COMPANY: OPPOSITION: APPLICATION FOR STAY: H.C.)

Passing Off

Amrutanjan Ltd v. Amrachand Sobachand (INFRINGEMENT: NO SALE UNDER INFRINGING MARK: PERMANENT INJUNCTION: H.C.)
Amrutanjan Ltd v. Amrachand Sobachand (TRADE MARK: INFRINGEMENT: NO SALE UNDER INFRINGING MARK: PERMANENT INJUNCTION: JURISDICTION: H.C.)
Amrutanjan Ltd v. Ashwin Fine Chemicals & Pharmaceuticals (INFRINGEMENT: AMRUTANJAN/ASHWIN: INTERIM INJUNCTION: H.C.)
Apple Computer Inc. v. Apple Leasing & Industries Ltd (INTERIM INJUNCTION: H.C.)
Aravind Laboratories v. Padmini Products (INTERIM INJUNCTION: H.C.)

Thapsons Pvt. Ltd v. Ashoka Food Industries (INFRINGEMENT: SIMILAR MARKS: COMMON TO THE TRADE: *Ad interim* INJUNCTION: H.C.)

Tinna Enterprises Pvt. Ltd v. International Rubber Industries (INFRINGEMENT: TINNA/TANY: INTERIM INJUNCTION: H.C.)

Tobu Interprises Pvt. Ltd v. Tokyo Cycle Industries (COPYRIGHT: INFRINGEMENT: TOBU/TOHO: H.C.)

Wander Ltd v. Antox India Pvt. Ltd (CONFLICT BETWEEN LICENSEES: INTERIM INJUNCTION: APPEAL AND FURTHER APPEAL: H.C.)

White Horse Distillers Ltd v. The Upper Doab Sugar Mills Ltd (INFRINGEMENT: *Ex parte* INJUNCTION: APPEAL: WHITE HORSE/FLYING HORSE: H.C.)

Permanent Injunction. *See* **Practice** (*Permanent injunction*)

Petition for Review. *See* **Practice** (*Petition for review*)

Piracy

Shri Prem Singh v. Ceeam Auto Industries (COPYRIGHT: INFRINGEMENT: GET-UP: LACK OF EQUITY: H.C.)

Practice

Acquiescence

Apple Computer Inc. v. Apple Leasing Industries Ltd (LACHES AND ACQUIESCENCE: H.C.)

Hindustan Pencils Pvt. Ltd v. India Stationery Products Co. (INFRINGEMENT: INTERIM INJUNCTION: REGISTRATION UNDER COPYRIGHT ACT: *Ex parte* INJUNCTION: DELAY, LACHES AND ACQUIESCENCE: H.C.)

Ad interim injunction

Ceat Tyres of India Ltd v. Jay Industrial Services (INFRINGEMENT: PASSING OFF: H.C.)

Hidesign v. Hi-Design Creations (PASSING OFF: HIDESIGN/HI-DESIGN CREATIONS: H.C.)

Lakshmi PVC Products Pvt. Ltd v. Lakshmi Polymers (PASSING OFF: H.C.)

Nucron Pharmaceuticals Pvt. Ltd v. International Pharmaceuticals (INFRINGEMENT: SEPMAX/SELMAX: APPLIED TO MEDICINES FOR DIFFERENT MEDICAL CONDITIONS: DECEPTIVE SIMILARITY: LIKELIHOOD OF DISASTROUS CONSEQUENCES: LEAVE TO APPLY FOR *ad interim* INJUNCTION: H.C.)

Thapsons Pvt. Ltd v. Ashoka Food Industries (INFRINGEMENT: PASSING OFF: SIMILAR MARKS: COMMON TO THE TRADE: H.C.)

Appeal

Anglo-French Drug Co. (Eastern) Ltd v. Hony-N-Bois (APPLICATION: OPPOSITION: HEPASYP/HEPAX: DISMISSAL BY REGISTRAR: APPEAL TO HIGH COURT ALLOWED: H.C.)

Bajaj Electricals Ltd v. Metal & Applied Products (BAJAJ: INFRINGEMENT: PASSING OFF: USE OF FAMILY NAME: INTERIM INJUNCTION: H.C.)

Brij Mohan Dutta v. Jallo Subsidiary Industries Co. (India) Pvt. Ltd (INFRINGEMENT: LION BRAND/LION ELEPHANT: INTERIM INJUNCTION: DISSIMILAR PRODUCTS: H.C.)

Camlin Pvt. Ltd v. National Pencil Industries (INFRINGEMENT: PASSING OFF: INTERIM ORDER: H.C.)

Canon KK v. Canon Electronics Pvt. Ltd (INFRINGEMENT: PASSING OFF: *Ex parte ad interim* INJUNCTION: H.C.)

Ciba-Geigy Ltd v. Sun Pharmaceuticals Industries (INFRINGEMENT: ANAFRANIL/ CLOROFANIL: DISTINCTIVENESS: INTERIM INJUNCTION: H.C.)

Deekonda Pedda Chinniah v. Mangalore Ganesh Beedi Works (INFRINGEMENT: PASSING OFF: INTERIM INJUNCTION: H.C.)

Duncan Agro Industries Ltd v. Somabhai Tea Processors (Pvt.) Ltd (PASSING OFF: FIRST TO ENTER MARKET: INTERIM INJUNCTION: H.C.)

Exxon Corporation, USA v. Exxon Packing Systems Pvt. Ltd, Hyderabad (THREATS: PASSING OFF: INTERIM APPLICATION: H.C.)

Fairdeal Corp. (Pvt.) Ltd v. Vijay Pharmaceuticals (INFRINGEMENT: *Ex parte* INJUNCTION: H.C.)

Farbenfabriken Bayer AG v. Christopher John (APPLICATION: OPPOSITION: H.C.)

Fleming (India) v. Ambalal Sarabhai Enterprises (PASSING OFF: USE OF BRAND NAMES UNDER DRUG CONTROLLER'S LICENCE: INJUNCTION: H.C.)

GTC Industries Ltd v. ITC Ltd (APPLICATION: OPPOSITION: WINEX/WINNER: H.C.)

Gurshant Engineering Co. Pvt. Ltd v. DLF Universals Ltd (INFRINGEMENT: PASSING OFF: COPYRIGHT: H.C.)

Habeebur Rehman & Sons v. Ram Babu & Brothers (INFRINGEMENT: PASSING OFF: COPYRIGHT IN LABEL: INFRINGEMENT: DEFENDANT PRIOR REGISTRANT: INTERIM INJUNCTION)

Hardie Trading Ltd v. Addison Paints & Chemicals Ltd (EXPUNGEMENT: NON-USE: SPECIAL CIRCUMSTANCES: IMPORT BAN: H.C.)

Hiralal Parudas v. Ganesh Trading Co. (RECTIFICATION: H.C.)

J.N. Nicholas (Vimto) Ltd v. Rose & Thistle (APPLICATION: WIMTO: CONFUSION WITH VIMTO AND VINTO: APPLICATION TO EXPUNGE VINTO FOR NON-USE: SPECIAL CIRCUMSTANCES: H.C.)

Johnson & Johnson v. Christine Hoden India (P.) Ltd (PASSING OFF: INTERIM INJUNCTION: H.C.)

Kamal Trading Co. v. Gillette U.K. Ltd (PASSING OFF: INFRINGEMENT: 7 O'CLOCK: INTERLOCUTORY INJUNCTION: H.C.)

Khanshiram Surinder Kumar v. Thakurdas Deomal Rohira (RECTIFICATION: H.C.)

M.J. Exports Pvt. Ltd v. Charak Pharmaceuticals (REFUSAL OF REGISTRATION: OPPOSITION: MJTONE/M2TONE: H.C.)

Mohan Meakin Ltd v. The Pravara Sahakari Sakhar Karkhana Ltd (INFRINGEMENT: PASSING OFF: STATUTORY NOTICE PERIOD: JURISDICTION: H.C.)

National Garments v. National Apparels (PASSING OFF: GET-UP: COVER OF BOXES: DECEPTION: INTERIM INJUNCTION: H.C.)

Rahim (M.A.) v. Aravind Laboratories (INFRINGEMENT: EYETEX/EYERIS: DECEPTIVE SIMILARITY: INTERIM INJUNCTION: RECTIFICATION: EXPUNGE-MENT: DESIGN OF LABEL AMENDED TO AVOID CONFLICT: WITHDRAWAL OF INTERIM INJUNCTION: H.C.)

S.M. Chopra & Sons v. Rajendra Prosad Srivastava (RAJA/MAHRAJA: RECTIFICATION: H.C.)

Schering Corp. v. Kilitch Co. (Pharma) Pvt. Ltd (INFRINGEMENT: QUADRIDERM/CORIDERM: H.C.)

Schering Corp. v. Perk Pharmaceutical Services (INFRINGEMENT: GARAMYCIN/ GAMAMYCIN: PRACTICE INTERIM RELIEF: H.C.)

Thakur Ayurvedic Pharmacy v. Pandit D.P. Sharma (APPLICATION: OPPOSITION DISMISSED: REVIEW PETITIONS ALSO DISMISSED: H.C.)

Toshiba Appliances Co. v. Toshiba KK (RECTIFICATION: NON-USE FOR FIVE YEARS: NON-INTENTION TO USE: IMPORT BAN: EXPUNGEMENT CONFIRMED: H.C.)

Apple Computer Inc. v. Apple Leasing & Industries Ltd (PASSING OFF: H.C.)
Aravind Laboratories v. Padmini Products (PASSING OFF: H.C.)
Bombay Oil Industries Pvt. Ltd v. Ballarpur Industries Ltd (INFRINGEMENT: H.C.)
Brij Mohan Dutta v. Jallo Subsidiary Industries Co. (India) Pvt. Ltd (INFRINGEMENT:
 LION BRAND/LION ELEPHANT: APPEAL: DISSIMILAR PRODUCTS: H.C.)
Britannia Industries Ltd v. Bharat Biscuits Co. Pvt. Ltd (INFRINGEMENT: PASSING
 OFF: INTERIM INJUNCTION REFUSED: H.C.)
Brooke Bond India Ltd v. Balaji Tea (India) Pvt. Ltd (INFRINGEMENT: PASSING OFF:
 RED LABEL: RED APPLE TEA: PACKETS FILLED IN INDIA AND EXPORTED:
 H.C.)
Burroughs Wellcome (India) Ltd v. G.K. Sharma & King Scientific Research Centre
 (COMPOSITE SUIT: INTERIM INJUNCTION GRANTED: H.C.)
Camlin Pvt. Ltd v. National Pencil Industries (COPYRIGHT: INFRINGEMENT:
 PASSING OFF: H.C.)
Cartier International BV Co. Ltd v. Ramesh Kumar Sawhney (INFRINGEMENT:
 CARTIER: INTERNATIONAL REPUTATION: GOODS OF DIFFERENT
 DESCRIPTION: H.C.)
Charan Dass & Veer Industries (India) v. Bombay Crockery House (COPYRIGHT:
 DESIGN: INFRINGEMENT: PASSING OFF: H.C.)
Chawrana Tobacco Co. v. Bhagwandas (COPYRIGHT: INFRINGEMENT: H.C.)
Ciba-Geigy Ltd v. Sun Pharmaceuticals Industries (INFRINGEMENT: ANAFRANIL/
 CLOROFANIL: DISTINCTIVENESS: APPEAL: H.C.)
Coromandel Fertilizers Ltd v. Coromandel Cements Ltd (INFRINGEMENT: Ad interim
 INJUNCTION VACATED: H.C.)
Crystal Knitters v. Bombay Vestors (INFRINGEMENT: CRYSTAL/COASTAL:
 THREATS: H.C.)
D'Vaiz Chemical v. Kundu Coatar Co. (REGISTRATION: PRIOR RIGHTS: PRIOR
 USER: H.C.)
Daimler Benz AG v. Hybo Hindustan (INFRINGEMENT: PASSING OFF: BENZ:
 GOODS OF DIFFERENT DESCRIPTION: H.C.)
Deekonda Pedda Chinniah v. Mangalore Ganesh Beedi Works (INFRINGEMENT:
 PASSING OFF: APPEAL: H.C.)
Duncan Agro Industries Ltd v. Somabhai Tea Processors (Pvt.) Ltd (PASSING OFF:
 FIRST TO ENTER MARKET: APPEAL: H.C.)
Exxon Corporation, USA v. Exxon Packing Systems Pvt. Ltd, Hyderabad (THREATS:
 PASSING OFF: APPEAL: H.C.)
Glaxo Operations U.K. Ltd v. Rama Bhaktha Hanuman Candle & Camphor Works
 (INFORMATION: PRACTICE JOINDER OF CAUSE OF ACTION: JURISDICTION:
 H.C.)
Griffon Laboratories (P.) Ltd v. Indian National Drug Co. P. Ltd (INFRINGEMENT:
 H.C.)
Habeebur Rehman & Sons v. Ram Babu & Brothers (INFRINGEMENT: PASSING OFF:
 COPYRIGHT IN LABEL: INFRINGEMENT: DEFENDANT PRIOR REGISTRANT:
 APPEAL: H.C.)
Hindustan Pencils Pvt. Ltd v. India Stationery Products Co. (INFRINGEMENT:
 REGISTRATION UNDER COPYRIGHT ACT: Ex parte INJUNCTION: DELAY,
 LACHES AND ACQUIESCENCE: H.C.)
Jain & Bros KK v. Paras Enterprises (INFRINGEMENT: PASSING OFF: H.C.)
Johnson & Johnson v. Christine Hoden India (P.) Ltd (PASSING OFF: APPEAL: H.C.)
Kamal Trading Co. v. Gillette U.K. Ltd (PASSING OFF: INFRINGEMENT: APPEAL:
 H.C.)
Manoj Plastic Industries v. Bhola Plastic Industries (PASSING OFF: SAME MARK FOR
 IDENTICAL GOODS: H.C.)
MRF Ltd v. Metro Tyres Ltd (INFRINGEMENT: NYLOGRIP/RADIALGRIP:
 PASSING OFF: DECEPTIVE USE OF TYRE TREAD PATTERN: H.C.)

National Garments v. National Apparels (PASSING OFF: GET-UP: COVER OF BOXES: DECEPTION: APPEAL: H.C.)

Nirex Industries (Pvt.) Ltd v. Manchand Footwears (COPYRIGHT: INFRINGEMENT: JURISDICTION: H.C.)

Optrex India Ltd v. Optrex Ltd (INFRINGEMENT: USE AS MARK AND PART OF COMPANY NAME: PREVENTION OF USE AFTER TERMINATION OF REGISTERED USER AGREEMENT: H.C.)

P.M. Diesels Ltd v. S.M. Diesels (COPYRIGHT IN MARK: INFRINGEMENT: FIELD MARSHAL/SONAMARSHAL: TRADING STYLE: H.C.)

Parkash Roadlines Ltd v. Parkash Parcel Services (Pvt.) Ltd (INFRINGEMENT: PASSING OFF: H.C.)

Philip Morris Belgium SA v. Golden Tobacco Co. Ltd (INFRINGEMENT: H.C.)

Philip Morris Inc. v. GTC Industries Ltd (INFRINGEMENT: BAN ON IMPORTS: EXPORT OF PRODUCTS USING PLAINTIFFS NAME: H.C.)

Pidilite Industries Pvt. Ltd v. Mittees Corporation (INFRINGEMENT: COPYRIGHT: THREATS: H.C.)

Poddar Tyres Ltd v. Bedrock Sales Corporation (INFRINGEMENT: PASSING OFF: USE IN CORPORATE NAME: H.C.)

R.J. Reynolds Tobacco Co. v. ITC Ltd (INFRINGEMENT: PASSING OFF: H.C.)

Rahim (M.A.) v. Aravind Laboratories (INFRINGEMENT: EYETEX/EYERIS: DECEPTIVE SIMILARITY: RECTIFICATION: EXPUNGEMENT: APPEAL: DESIGN OF LABEL AMENDED TO AVOID CONFLICT: WITHDRAWAL OF TRADE MARK: H.C.)

Ranbaxy Laboratories Ltd v. Dua Pharmaceuticals Pvt. Ltd (INFRINGEMENT: PASSING OFF: H.C.)

Rawal Industries (Pvt.) Ltd v. Duke Enterprises (PASSING OFF: INFRINGEMENT: TRADING STYLE: H.C.)

Richardson Vicks Inc. v. Vikas Pharmaceuticals (COPYRIGHT: INFRINGEMENT: PASSING OFF: *Ad interim* INJUNCTION MADE ABSOLUTE: H.C.)

Rightway v. Rightways Footwear (TRADE NAME: PASSING OFF: PRIOR USE: H.C.)

S. M. Enterprises v. Hyderabad Lamps Ltd (SOLAR: CHOKES FOR FLUORESCENT TUBES: INFRINGEMENT: INTERIM INJUNCTION VACATED: H.C.)

SPS Jayam & Co. v. Gajalakshmi (TRADE MARK: INFRINGEMENT: PASSING OFF: JOINDER OF PARTIES: H.C.)

Sidharth Wheels Pvt. Ltd v. Bedrock Ltd (THREATS: DECLARATION: NATURE: H.C.)

Sushil Vasudev (t/a Kwality Ice Cream Co.) v. Kwality Frozen Foods Pvt. Ltd (KWALITY: TRADING STYLE: REGISTRATION: PRIOR USER: H.C.)

Synthetic Moulders Ltd v. Semperit AG (INFRINGEMENT: H.C.)

Tata Oil Mills Co. Ltd v. Reward Soap Works (COPYRIGHT: INFRINGEMENT: H.C.)

Tata Oil Mills Co. Ltd v. WIPRO Ltd (INFRINGEMENT: PASSING OFF: H.C.)

Tinna Enterprises Pvt. Ltd v. International Rubber Industries (INFRINGEMENT: PASSING OFF: H.C.)

Vrajlal Manilal & Co. v. N.S. Bidi Co. (BIDIS: INFRINGEMENT: H.C.)

Wander Ltd v. Antox India Pvt. Ltd (CONFLICT BETWEEN LICENSEES: PASSING OFF: APPEAL AND FURTHER APPEAL: H.C.)

Interim order

Camlin Pvt. Ltd v. National Pencil Industries (INFRINGEMENT: PASSING OFF: APPEAL: H.C.)

Interim relief

Schering Corp. v. Perk Pharmaceutical Services (INFRINGEMENT: GARAMYCIN/ GAMAMYCIN: APPEAL: H.C.)

Injunction

Anglo French Drug Co. (Eastern) Ltd v. Belco Pharmaceuticals (INFRINGEMENT: H.C.)

Bijoli Grill Spencer's Products v. Spencers & Co. Ltd (DECLARATION: H.C.)

Blue Cross & Blue Shield Association v. Blue Cross Health Clinic (INFRINGEMENT: PASSING OFF: H.C.)

Brooke Bond (India) Ltd v. Balaji Tea (India) Pvt. Ltd (INFRINGEMENT: PASSING OFF: H.C.)

East India Pharmaceutical Works Ltd v. G. & G. Pharmaceuticals Ltd (GEOGRAPHICAL EXTENT: H.C.)

ESSCO Sanitations v. Mascot Industries (INFRINGEMENT: H.C.)

Fleming (India) v. Ambalal Sarabhai Enterprises (PASSING OFF: USE OF BRAND NAMES UNDER DRUG CONTROLLERS LICENCE: APPEAL: H.C.)

Heptulla v. Orient Longman Ltd (H.C.)

Kali Aerated Water Works v. Rashid (PASSING OFF: KALI MARK/SRI NEW KALI MARK AERATED WATER: DECLARATION: H.C.)

Kalyani Breweries Ltd v. Khoday Brewing & Distilling Industries Ltd (INFRINGEMENT: KALYANI BLACK LABEL: KHODAY BLACK LABEL: H.C.)

Kopran Chemicals Co. Ltd v. Kent Pharmaceuticals (India) Pvt. Ltd (INFRINGEMENT: RIFINEX/RIFISON: INFRINGEMENT: PASSING OFF: H.C.)

Parkash Metal Works v. Square Automation (Pvt.) Ltd (INFRINGEMENT: PASSING OFF: HOT FLO/PMW HOT FLO: H.C.)

Richardson Vicks Inc. v. Medico Laboratories (INFRINGEMENT: PASSING OFF: H.C.)

Joinder of cause of action

Glaxo Operations U.K. Ltd v. Rama Bhaktha Hanuman Candle & Camphor Works (INFORMATION: JURISDICTION: INTERIM INJUNCTION: H.C.)

Gold Seal Engineering Products Pvt. Ltd v. Hindustan Manufacturers (INFRINGEMENT: PASSING OFF: JURISDICTION: H.C.)

Joinder of parties

S.P.S. Jayam & Co. v. Gajalakshmi (INFRINGEMENT: PASSING OFF: INTERIM INJUNCTION: H.C.)

Jurisdiction

Amrutanjan Ltd v. Amrachand Sobachand (TRADE MARK: INFRINGEMENT: PASSING OFF: NO SALE UNDER INFRINGING MARK: PERMANENT INJUNCTION: H.C.)

Burroughs Wellcome (India) Ltd v. G.K. Sharma & King Scientific Research Centre (JURISDICTION OF COURT TO ENTERTAIN COMPOSITE SUIT: H.C.)

Cipla Ltd v. Unicure Pharmaceuticals (RECTIFICATION: INTERLOCUTORY PETITION: T.M.Reg.)

Glaxo Operations U.K. Ltd v. Rama Bhaktha Hanuman Candle & Camphor Works (INFORMATION: PRACTICE JOINDER OF CAUSE OF ACTION: INTERIM INJUNCTION: H.C.)

Gold Seal Engineering Products Pvt. Ltd v. Hindustan Manufacturers (INFRINGEMENT: PASSING OFF: JOINDER OF CAUSES OF ACTION: H.C.)

Mohan Meaking Ltd v. Kashmiri Dreamland Distilleries (PASSING OFF: M.M.B./ M.B.B.: H.C.)

Mohan Meakin Ltd v. The Pravara Sahakari Sakhar Karkhana Ltd (STATUTORY NOTICE PERIOD: APPEAL: H.C.)

Nirex Industries (Pvt.) Ltd v. Manchand Footwears (COPYRIGHT: INFRINGEMENT: INTERIM INJUNCTION: H.C.)

Laches

Apple Computer Inc. v. Apple Leasing Industries Ltd (LACHES AND ACQUIESCENCE: H.C.)

Hindustan Pencils Pvt. Ltd v. India Stationery Products Co. (INFRINGEMENT: INTERIM INJUNCTION: REGISTRATION UNDER COPYRIGHT ACT: *Ex parte* INJUNCTION: DELAY, LACHES AND ACQUIESCENCE: H.C.)

Late-filed evidence

Pfizer Inc. v. Chemo–Pharma Laboratories Ltd (OPPOSITION: ABANDONMENT OF OPPOSITION: T.M.Reg.)

Late receipt of application for rectification

Pankaj Group v. The Good Year Tyre and Rubber Co. (NON-APPEARANCE DURING RECTIFICATION PROCEEDINGS: T.M.Reg.)

Leave to apply

Nucron Pharmaceuticals Pvt. Ltd v. International Pharmaceuticals (INFRINGEMENT: SEPMAX/SELMAX: APPLIED TO MEDICINES FOR DIFFERENT MEDICAL CONDITIONS: DECEPTIVE SIMILARITY: LIKELIHOOD OF DISASTROUS CONSEQUENCES: LEAVE TO APPLY FOR *ad interim* INJUNCTION: H.C.)

Mandamus

Antox India (Pvt.) Ltd v. State Drug Controller, Tamil Nadu (STATE MANUFACTURING LICENCE: H.C.)

Non-appearance during rectification proceedings

Pankaj Group v. The Good Year Tyre and Rubber Co. (LATE RECEIPT OF APPLICATION FOR RECTIFICATION: T.M.Reg.)

Notice of motion

Reckitt & Colman of India Ltd v. Medicross Pharmaceuticals Pvt. Ltd (INFRINGEMENT: DISPRIN/MEDISPRIN: DISTINCTIVENESS: H.C.)

Permanent injunction

Amrutanjan Ltd v. Amrachand Sobachand (INFRINGEMENT: PASSING OFF: NO SALE UNDER INFRINGING MARK: H.C.)

Petition for review

Thakur Ayurvedic Pharmacy v. Pandit D.P. Sharma (OPPOSITION DISMISSED: REVIEW PETITIONS ALSO DISMISSED: APPEAL: H.C.)

Universal Pharmacy v. Classic Pharmaceuticals (REQUEST FOR FURTHER EXTENSION OF TIME TO FILE EVIDENCE: OPPOSITION DEEMED ABANDONED: REGISTRAR'S POWER: T.M.Reg.)

Pleadings

Cormandel Fertilizers Ltd v. Cormandel Cements Ltd (INFRINGEMENT: PASSING OFF: H.C.)

Public interest

Arumugam v. State of Tamil Nadu (CRIMINAL OFFENCE: FORGERY AND COUNTERFEITING: H.C.)

Qualification to file suit

Aravind Laboratories v. V.A. Samy Chemical Works (INFRINGEMENT: VALIDITY OF ASSIGNMENT AND RENEWAL OF TRADE MARK: H.C.)

Registar's power

Universal Pharmacy v. Classic Pharmaceuticals (PETITION FOR REVIEW: T.M.Reg.)

Request for review

Raj Steel Rolling Mills v. Vij Iron & Steel Co. (OPPOSITION: AGREEMENT: REQUEST FOR REVIEW REFUSED: H.C.)

Res judicata

Sandoz Ltd v. Pharmaceutical & Chemical Industries (OPPOSITION: HONEST CONCURRENT USE: T.M.Reg.)

Security for costs

Revlon Inc. v. Kemco Chemicals (PASSING OFF: FOREIGN PLAINTIFF: NO LOCAL IMMOVABLE ASSETS: STRIKING OUT: H.C.)

Special circumstances

Hardie Trading Ltd v. Addison Paints & Chemicals Ltd (EXPUNGEMENT: NON-USE: APPEAL: IMPORT BAN: H.C.)

J.N. Nicholas (Vimto) Ltd v. Rose & Thistle (APPLICATION: WIMTO: CONFUSION WITH VIMTO AND VINTO: APPLICATION TO EXPUNGE VINTO FOR NON-USE: APPEAL: H.C.)

Statutory notice period

Mohan Meakin Ltd v. The Pravara Sahakari Sakhar Karkhana Ltd (JURISDICTION: APPEAL: H.C.)

Stay

Durai Swamy v. Subhaiyam (INFRINGEMENT: THREATS: RECTIFICATION: H.C.)

Galfa Laboratories Pvt. Ltd v. Rekvina Pharmaceuticals (APPLICATION: OPPOSITION: PRIOR REGISTRATION: PETITION TO CANCEL OPPONENT'S REGISTRATION: H.C.)

Hardie Trading Ltd v. Addison Paints & Chemicals Ltd (OVERSEAS PROPRIETOR: USE BY AGENT: REGISTERED USER: APPLICATION BY INDIAN COMPANY: OPPOSITION: APPLICATION FOR STAY: H.C.)

Striking out

Revlon Inc. v. Kemco Chemicals (PASSING OFF: FOREIGN PLAINTIFF: NO LOCAL IMMOVABLE ASSETS SECURITY FOR COSTS: H.C.)

Time limits

Progro Pharmaceuticals (Pvt.) Ltd v. Deputy Registrar of Trade Marks (DELAY IN FILING COUNTERSTATEMENT: EXTENSION OF TIME LIMITS: H.C.)

Universal Pharmacy v. Classic Pharmaceuticals (REQUEST FOR FURTHER EXTENSION OF TIME TO FILE EVIDENCE: PETITION FOR REVIEW: REGISTRAR'S POWER: T.M.Reg.)

Prior Use

Rightway v. Rightways Footwear (TRADE NAME: PASSING OFF: INTERIM INJUNCTION: H.C.)

Qualification to File Suit. *See* Practice (*Qualification to file suit*)

Quality Control

Cycle Corp. of India Ltd v. T.I. Raleigh Industries Ltd (RECTIFICATION: NON-OBSERVANCE OF QUALITY CONTROL: H.C.)

Prior Registrant

Habeebur Rehman & Sons v. Ram Babu & Brothers (INFRINGEMENT: PASSING OFF: COPYRIGHT IN LABEL: INFRINGEMENT: INTERIM INJUNCTION: APPEAL: H.C.)

Prior Registration

Galfa Laboratories Pvt. Ltd v. Rekvina Pharmaceuticals (APPLICATION: OPPOSITION: PETITION TO CANCEL OPPONENT'S REGISTRATION: STAY: H.C.)

Prior Rights

D'Vaiz Chemical v. Kundu Coatar Co. (REGISTRATION: PRIOR USER: INTERLOCUTORY INJUNCTION: H.C.)

Prior User

D'Vaiz Chemical v. Kundu Coatar Co. (REGISTRATION: PRIOR RIGHTS: INTERLOCUTORY INJUNCTION: H.C.)
Sushil Vasudev (t/a Kwality Ice Cream Co) v. Kwality Frozen Foods Pvt. Ltd (KWALITY: TRADING STYLE: REGISTRATION: INTERIM INJUNCTION: H.C.)

Prohibition of Use of Foreign Brand Names

Janak Mathuradas v. Union of India (LICENCE: PROHIBITION NOT A BAR TO GRANT: H.C.)

Rectification

Allied Industries (Jaipur West) v. Allied Industries (Jaipur South) (ARBITRATION AWARD DECLARING EQUAL RIGHTS: T.M.Reg.)
Banik Rubber Industries v. Sree K.B. Rubber Industries (REGISTRATION: OPPOSITION: ABANDONMENT: H.C.)
Cipla Ltd v. Unicure Pharmaceuticals (PIROX: INTERLOCUTORY PETITION: JURISDICTION: T.M.Reg.)
Cycle Corp. of India Ltd v. T.I. Raleigh Industries Ltd (NON-OBSERVANCE OF QUALITY CONTROL: H.C.)
DRISTAN Trade Mark (NON-USE: REGISTERED USER: H.C.)
DRISTAN Trade Mark (OVERSEAS PROPRIETOR: INDIAN SUBSIDIARY: NON-USE: BONA FIDE INTENTION TO USE AT DATE OF REGISTRATION: REGISTERED USER: S.C.)
Durai Swamy v. Subhaiyam (INFRINGEMENT: THREATS: STAY: H.C.)

Express Bottlers Services Pvt. Ltd v. Pepsico Inc. (PEPSI/PEPSICOLA: WHETHER SALES TO EMBASSIES AMOUNT TO BONA FIDE USE OF MARK: H.C.)
Fatima Tile Works v. Sudarson Trading Co. Ltd (NON-USE: USE BY SUBSIDIARY COMPANY: H.C.)
Hami Brothers v. Hami & Co. (DISTINCTIVENESS: H.C.)
Hiralal Parudas v. Ganesh Trading Co. (APPEAL: H.C.)
Khanshiram Surinder Kumar v. Thakurdas Deomal Rohira (H.C.)
P.M. Diesels Pvt. Ltd v. Thukral Mechanical Works (FIELD MARSHAL: ENTITLEMENT TO USE MARK: INJUNCTION VACATED: H.C.)
Pankaj Group v. The Good Year Tyre and Rubber Co. (NON-INTENTION TO USE: T.M.Reg.)
Pepsico Inc. v. Express Bottlers Services Pvt. Ltd (INFRINGEMENT: PEPSI/ PEPSICOLA: NON-USE: RECTIFICATION PROCEEDINGS PENDING: INJUNCTION REFUSED: APPEAL: H.C.)
Rahim (M.A.) v. Aravind Laboratories (INFRINGEMENT: EYETEX/EYERIS: DECEPTIVE SIMILARITY: INTERIM INJUNCTION: EXPUNGEMENT: APPEAL: DESIGN OF LABEL AMENDED TO AVOID CONFLICT: WITHDRAWAL OF INTERIM INJUNCTION: H.C.)
Rose & Thistle v. J.N. Nicholas (Vimto) Ltd (VIMTO: NON-USE: USE OF ASSOCIATED MARK: RECTIFICATION TO ALLOW REGISTRATION OF WIMTO: H.C.)
S.M. Chopra & Sons v. Rajendra Prosad Srivastava (RAJA: MAHRAJA: APPEAL: H.C.)
Toshiba Appliances Co. v. Toshiba KK (NON-USE FOR 5 YEARS: NON-INTENTION TO USE: IMPORT BAN: H.C.)
Toshiba Appliances Co. v. Toshiba KK (NON-USE FOR 5 YEARS: NON-INTENTION TO USE: IMPORT BAN: APPEAL: EXPUNGEMENT CONFIRMED: H.C.)
Vishnudas Kishindas Zarda Factory v. Vazir Sultan Tobacco Co. Ltd (NON-USE: REGISTRABILITY: H.C.)

Refusal of Registration

M.J. Exports Pvt. Ltd v. Charak Pharmaceuticals (OPPOSITION: MJTONE/ M2TONE: APPEAL: H.C.)

Registered User

DRISTAN Trade Mark (RECTIFICATION: NON-USE: H.C.)
DRISTAN Trade Mark (RECTIFICATION: OVERSEAS PROPRIETOR: INDIAN SUBSIDIARY: NON-USE: BONA FIDE INTENTION TO USE AT DATE OF REGISTRATION: S.C.)
Hardie Trading Ltd v. Addison Paints & Chemicals Ltd (OVERSEAS PROPRIETOR: USE BY AGENT: APPLICATION BY INDIAN COMPANY: OPPOSITION: APPLICATION FOR STAY: H.C.)
Optrex India Ltd v. Optrex Ltd (INFRINGEMENT: USE AS MARK AND PART OF COMPANY NAME: PREVENTION OF USE AFTER TERMINATION OF REGISTERED USER AGREEMENT: INTERIM INJUNCTION: H.C.)
Pioneer Hi-Bred International Inc. USA v. Pioneer Seed Company Ltd (REFUSAL TO GIVE INSPECTION: SUIT FOR PERMANENT INJUNCTION AGAINST REGISTERED USER: H.C.)

Registrability

Vishnudas Kishindas Zarda Factory v. Vazir Sultan Tobacco Co. Ltd (RECTIFICATION: NON-USE: H.C.)

Registration

Banik Rubber Industries v. Sree K.B. Rubber Industries (OPPOSITION: ABANDONMENT: RECTIFICATION: H.C.)

Bharaj Manufacturing Co. v. Shiv Metal Works

D'Vaiz Chemical v. Kundu Coatar Co. (PRIOR RIGHTS: PRIOR USER: INTERLOCUTORY INJUNCTION: H.C.)

General Motors Holden's Ltd v. Premier Automobiles Ltd

HMT Ltd v. Girnar Ltd (ARTISTIC WORK: EARLIER REGISTRATION OF HMT: COPYRIGHT BOARD)

Hindustan Pencils Pvt. Ltd v. India Stationery Products Co. (INFRINGEMENT: INTERIM INJUNCTION: *Ex parte* INJUNCTION: DELAY, LACHES AND ACQUIESCENCE: H.C.)

Jeep Corp. v. Lion Industries (JEEP/CHHAP: T.M.Reg.)

Sushil Vasudev (t/a Kwality Ice Cream Co) v. Kwality Frozen Foods Pvt. Ltd (KWALITY: TRADING STYLE: PRIOR USER: INTERIM INJUNCTION: H.C.)

Renewal

Aravind Laboratories v. V.A. Samy Chemical Works (QUALIFICATION TO FILE SUIT: VALIDITY OF ASSIGNMENT AND RENEWAL OF MARK: H.C.)

Review Petitions. *See* Practice (*Petition for review*)

Revision

Mohamad Khalil v. The State of Maharashtra (CRIMINAL APPLICATION: H.C.)

Services

Apple Computer Inc. v. Apple Leasing Industries Ltd (USE OF UNREGISTERED MARKS IN RESPECT OF SERVICES: INTERNATIONAL REPUTATION: COMMON FIELD OF ACTIVITY: H.C.)

Similar Marks

Thapsons Pvt. Ltd v. Ashoka Food Industries (INFRINGEMENT: PASSING OFF: COMMON TO THE TRADE: *Ad interim* INJUNCTION: H.C.)

Special Circumstances. *See* Practice (*Special circumstances*)

Statutory Notice Period. *See* Practice (*Statutory notice period*)

State Manufacturing Licence

Antox India (Pvt.) Ltd v. State Drug Controller, Tamil Nadu (MANDAMUS: H.C.)

Statutory Offence

Vishwa Mitter of Vijay Bharat Cigarette Stores v. O.P. Poddar (COMPLAINANT'S QUALIFICATIONS: S.C.)

Threats

Crystal Knitters v. Bombay Vestors (INFRINGEMENT: CRYSTAL/COASTAL: INTERIM INJUNCTION: H.C.)

Durai Swamy v. Subhaiyam (INFRINGEMENT: RECTIFICATION: STAY: H.C.)

Exxon Corporation, USA v. Exxon Packing Systems Pvt. Ltd, Hyderabad (PASSING OFF: INTERIM APPLICATION: APPEAL: H.C.)

Pidilite Industries Pvt. Ltd v. Mittees Corporation (INFRINGEMENT: FEVICOL/ TREVICOL: COPYRIGHT: INTERIM INJUNCTION: H.C.)

Sidharth Wheels Pvt. Ltd v. Bedrock Ltd (DECLARATION: INTERLOCUTORY INJUNCTION: NATURE: H.C.)

Trading Style. *See* Get-up

Unlicensed Use. *See* Use

Unregistered Marks

Apple Computer Inc. v. Apple Leasing Industries Ltd (PASSING OFF: USE IN RESPECT OF PROVISION OF SERVICES: INTERNATIONAL REPUTATION: NATURE OF GOODWILL: H.C.)

Brundaban Sahu v. Rajendra Subudhi Subudhi (COPYRIGHT: UNREGISTERED MARK AND LABEL: COGNIZANCE OF COMPLAINT: H.C.)

Use. *See also under* Non-use

Duke & Sons Ltd v. Union of India (USE OF FOREIGN BRAND NAMES: GOVERNMENT POLICY: PROHIBITION: HYBRID NAME: PEPSI LAHER: H.C.)

Express Bottlers Services Pvt. Ltd v. Pepsico Inc. (PEPSI/PEPSICOLA: RECTIFICATION: WHETHER SALES TO EMBASSIES AMOUNT TO BONA FIDE USE OF MARK: H.C.)

Fatima Tile Works v. Sudarson Trading Co. Ltd (USE BY SUBSIDIARY COMPANY: RECTIFICATION: NON-USE: H.C.)

Finlay Mills Ltd v. National Textile Corp. (UNAUTHORISED USE BY MANAGED COMPANY: ENTITLEMENT TO ENFORCE: H.C.)

Fleming (India) v. Ambalal Sarabhai Enterprises (USE UNDER DRUG CONTROLLER'S LICENCE: PASSING OFF: INJUNCTION: APPEAL: H.C.)

Hardie Trading Ltd v. Addison Paints & Chemicals Ltd (USE BY AGENT OVERSEAS PROPRIETOR: REGISTERED USER: APPLICATION BY INDIAN COMPANY: OPPOSITION: APPLICATION FOR STAY: H.C.)

K.R. Jadayappa Mudaliar v. K.S. Venkatachalam (UNLICENSED USE: INJUNCTION VACATED: H.C.)

Kwality Icecreams Ltd v. India (PASSING OFF: USE AFTER TERMINATION OF AGREEMENT: H.C.)

Optrex India Ltd v. Optrex Ltd (INFRINGEMENT: USE AS PART OF COMPANY NAME: PREVENTION OF USE AFTER TERMINATION OF REGISTERED USER AGREEMENT: INTERIM INJUNCTION: H.C.)

P.M. Diesels Pvt. Ltd v. Thukral Mechanical Works (FIELD MARSHAL: RECTIFICATION: ENTITLEMENT TO USE: INJUNCTION VACATED: H.C.)

Poddar Tyres Ltd v. Bedrock Sales Corporation (INFRINGEMENT: USE IN CORPORATE NAME: PASSING OFF: INTERIM INJUNCTION: H.C.)

Rose & Thistle v. J.N. Nicholas (Vimto) Ltd (VIMTO: NON-USE: USE OF ASSOCIATED MARK: RECTIFICATION TO ALLOW REGISTRATION OF WIMTO: H.C.)

Use of Family Name. *See* **Family Name**

Use of House Mark. *See* **House Mark**

ISRAELI

Copyright

Computer Software

Apple Computer Inc. v. New-Con Technologies Ltd (INFRINGEMENT: PRINTED CIRCUITS: D.C.)

Infringement

Apple Computer Inc. v. New-Con Technologies Ltd (COMPUTER SOFTWARE: PRINTED CIRCUITS: D.C.)

Printed Circuits. *See* **Computer Software**

Patent

Discovery

Hydroplan Engineering Ltd v. Naan Metal Works (INFRINGEMENT: VALIDITY: OBVIOUSNESS: NATURE AND SCOPE OF DISCOVERY: PATENT AGENTS: PRIVILEGE: Div. Ct)

Infringement

Hydroplan Engineering Ltd v. Naan Metal Works (DISCOVERY: VALIDITY: OBVIOUSNESS: NATURE AND SCOPE OF DISCOVERY: PATENT AGENTS: PRIVILEGE: Div. Ct)

Obviousness

Hydroplan Engineering Ltd v. Naan Metal Works (INFRINGEMENT: PRACTICE: DISCOVERY: VALIDITY: NATURE AND SCOPE OF DISCOVERY: PATENT AGENTS: PRIVILEGE: Div. Ct)

Patent Agents

Hydroplan Engineering Ltd v. Naan Metal Works (INFRINGEMENT: PRACTICE: DISCOVERY: VALIDITY: OBVIOUSNESS: NATURE AND SCOPE OF DISCOVERY: PRIVILEGE: Div. Ct)

Privilege

Hydroplan Engineering Ltd v. Naan Metal Works (INFRINGEMENT: PRACTICE: DISCOVERY: VALIDITY: OBVIOUSNESS: NATURE AND SCOPE OF DISCOVERY: PATENT AGENTS: Div. Ct)

Validity

Hydroplan Engineering Ltd v. Naan Metal Works (INFRINGEMENT: PRACTICE: DISCOVERY: OBVIOUSNESS: NATURE AND SCOPE OF DISCOVERY: PATENT AGENTS: PRIVILEGE: Div. Ct)

MALAYSIA

Copyright

Goodyear Tire & Rubber Co. v. Silverstone Tire & Rubber Co. Sdn Bhd (INFRINGEMENT: SCOPE OF PROTECTION: TRADE MARK: PASSING OFF: GET-UP OF TYRES: REPUTATION AND GOODWILL: H.C.)

Acquisition of Copyright

Foo Loke Ying v. Television Broadcasts Ltd (FOREIGN CINEMATOGRAPH FILMS: S.C.)

Affidavit. *See* **Practice** (*Affidavit*)

Anton Piller. *See* **Practice** (*Anton Piller*)

Appeal. *See* **Practice** (*Appeal*)

Censorship

Asia Television Ltd v. Vina Video Sdn Bhd (CINEMATOGRAPH FILM: VIDEO TAPES: H.C.: Fed. Ct)

Cinematograph Film. *See* **Film**

Collection

Penerbit Fajar Bakti Sdn Bhd v. Cahaya Surya Buku dan Alat Tulis (SHORT STORIES AND POEMS: SUBSISTENCE OF COPYRIGHT: H.C.)

Contempt. *See* **Practice** (*Contempt*)

Copyright Act 1969

Prosecution under

Public Prosecutor v. Oh Teck Soon (TIME FOR PROSECUTION: S.C.)

1025

Statutory construction

Foo Loke Ying v. Television Broadcasts Ltd (ACQUISITION OF COPYRIGHT IN FOREIGN CINEMATOGRAPH FILMS: S.C.)

Cross-examination on Affidavit. *See* **Practice** (*Cross-examination on affidavit*)

Damages. *See* **Practice** (*Damages*)

Entitlement

Asia Television Ltd v. Mega Video Recording Supply Centre (FOREIGN OWNERS: H.C.)

Film

Asia Television Ltd v. Vina Video Sdn Bhd (CINEMATOGRAPH FILM: VIDEO TAPES: CENSORSHIP: H.C.) (APPEAL: Fed. Ct)
Foo Loke Ying v. Television Broadcasts Ltd (ACQUISITION OF COPYRIGHT IN FOREIGN CINEMATOGRAPH FILMS: S.C.)

Foreign Owners

Asia Television Ltd v. Mega Video Recording Supply Centre (ENTITLEMENT: H.C.)

Infringement

Mokhtar Haji Jamaludin v. Pustaka Sistem Pelajaran (DAMAGES: H.C.)
Polygram Records Sdn Bhd v. Phua Tai Eng (INJUNCTION: CONTEMPT: H.C.)
Public Prosecutor v. Basheer Ahmad (PROCEDURE: Fed. Terr. Cr. App. Ct)
Television Broadcasts Ltd v. Mandarin Video Holdings Sdn Bhd (ANTON PILLER PRACTICE: PRIVILEGE AGAINST SELF-INCRIMINATION: H.C.)
Television Broadcasts Ltd v. Seremban Video Centre Sdn Bhd (APPEAL: ANTON PILLER ORDER: H.C.)

Injunction. *See* **Practice** (*Injunction*)

Practice

Affidavit

Chong Loy Sen v. Public Prosecutor (CROSS-EXAMINATION ON AFFIDAVIT: H.C.)

Anton Piller Practice

Television Broadcasts Ltd v. Mandarin Video Holdings Sdn Bhd (PRIVILEGE AGAINST SELF-INCRIMINATION: H.C.)
Television Broadcasts Ltd v. Seremban Video Centre Sdn Bhd (INFRINGEMENT: APPEAL: H.C.)

Appeal

Asia Television Ltd v. Vina Video Sdn Bhd (CINEMATOGRAPH FILM: VIDEO TAPES: CENSORSHIP: Fed. Ct)
Television Broadcasts Ltd v. Seremban Video Centre Sdn Bhd (ANTON PILLER ORDER: H.C.)

Contempt

Polygram Records Sdn Bhd v. Phua Tai Eng (INFRINGEMENT: INJUNCTION: H.C.)

Cross-examination

Chong Loy Sen v. Public Prosecutor (CROSS-EXAMINATION ON AFFIDAVIT: H.C.)

Damages

Mokhtar Haji Jamaludin v. Pustaka Sistem Pelajaran (INFRINGEMENT: H.C.)

Injunction

Polygram Records Sdn Bhd v. Phua Tai Eng (INFRINGEMENT: CONTEMPT: H.C.)

Privilege against self-incrimination

Television Broadcasts Ltd v. Mandarin Video Holdings Sdn Bhd (ANTON PILLER PRACTICE: H.C.)

Procedure

Public Prosecutor v. Basheer Ahmad (INFRINGEMENT: Fed. Terr. Cr. App. Ct)

Privilege against Self-incrimination. *See* **Practice** (*Privilege against self-incrimination*)

Procedure. *See* **Practice** (*Procedure*)

Prosecution under Copyright Act 1969. *See* **Copyright Act 1969** (*Prosecution under*)

Publication

Foo Loke Ying v. Television Broadcasts Ltd (SUBSISTANCE: ACQUISITION OF COPYRIGHT IN FOREIGN CINEMATOGRAPH FILMS: S.C.)

Statutory Construction. *See* **Copyright Act 1969** (*Statutory construction*)

Subsistance

Foo Loke Ying v. Television Broadcasts Ltd (PUBLICATION: ACQUISITION OF COPYRIGHT IN FOREIGN CINEMATOGRAPH FILMS: STATUTORY CONSTRUCTION: S.C.)
Penerbit Fajar Bakti Sdn Bhd v. Cahaya Surya Buku dan Alat Tulis (COLLECTION OF SHORT STORIES AND POEMS: H.C.)

Video Tapes. *See* **Film**

Passing Off

Adequacy of Damages. *See* **Practice** (*Interlocutory injunction*)

Balance of Convenience. *See* **Practice** (*Interlocutory injunction*)

Business Name

Dun & Bradstreet (Singapore) Pte Ltd v. Dun & Bradstreet (Malaysia) Sdn Bhd (IDENTICAL BUSINESS NAMES: DIFFERENT SCOPE OF ACTIVITY: H.C.)

Mun Loong Co. Sdn Bhd v. Chai Tuck Kin (BUSINESS NAME: MONOPOLY RIGHT: H.C.)

Revertex Ltd v. Slim Rivertex Shn Bhd (REGISTRAR OF COMPANIES REFUSAL NOT TO REGISTER SIMILAR NAME: H.C.)

Confusion

Excelsior Pte Ltd v. Excelsior Sport (C.) Pte Ltd (TRADE NAME: H.C.)

Regent Decorators Sdn Bhd v. Chee (FORMER EMPLOYEES: CONFUSION: MAREVA INJUNCTIONS: S.C.)

Essential Features

Fraser & Neame Ltd v. Yeo Hiap Seng Ltd (TRADE MARK: INFRINGEMENT: ESSENTIAL FEATURES: H.C.)

Fancy Name. *See* Trade Mark or Trade Name

Foreign Plaintiff

Westpac Banking Corp. v. Goodmaker Leasing Corp. Berhad (GOODWILL: FANCY NAME: H.C.)

Former Employees

Regent Decorators Sdn Bhd v. Chee (CONFUSION: MAREVA INJUNCTIONS: S.C.)

Get-up

A. Clouet & Co. Pte Ltd v. Maya Toba Sdn Bhd (TRADE MARK: INFRINGEMENT: PASSING OFF: SIMILARITY OF LABELS AND GET-UP: AYAM BRAND/BOTAN BRAND: LABEL COMMON TO THE TRADE: PRACTICE: LIMITATION PERIOD: H.C.)

Goodwill

Westpac Banking Corp. v. Goodmaker Leasing Corp. Berhad (FOREIGN PLAINTIFF: FANCY NAME: H.C.)

Injunction. *See* Practice (*Injunction*)

Labels

A. Clouet & Co. Pte Ltd v. Maya Toba Sdn Bhd (TRADE MARK: INFRINGEMENT: PASSING OFF: SIMILARITY OF LABELS AND GET-UP: AYAM BRAND/BOTAN BRAND: LABEL COMMON TO THE TRADE: PRACTICE: LIMITATION PERIOD: H.C.)

Mareva Injunction. *See* Practice (*Mareva injunction*)

Monopoly Right

Mun Loong Co. Sdn Bhd v. Chai Tuck Kin (BUSINESS NAME: H.C.)

Overseas Manufacture

Winthrop Products Inc. v. Sun Ocean (M.) Sdn Bhd (TRADE MARKS: PARALLEL IMPORTS: PRODUCT MANUFACTURED IN U.K.: H.C.)

Parallel Imports

Winthrop Products Inc. v. Sun Ocean (M.) Sdn Bhd (PRODUCT MANUFACTURED IN U.K.: H.C.)

Practice

Injunction

Heublein Inc. v. Paterson Simons & Co. (S.) Pte Ltd (TRADE MARK: BALANCE OF CONVENIENCE: C.A.)

Interlocutory injunction—adequacy of damages

Chong Fok Shang v. Lily Handicraft (SERIOUS QUESTION TO BE TRIED: BALANCE OF CONVENIENCE: H.C.)

Interlocutory injunction—balance of convenience

Americaya Singapore Pte Ltd v. Americaya Malaysia Shn Bhd (TRADE MARK: INFRINGEMENT: APPLICATION FOR STAY PENDING HEARING OF APPLICATION TO EXPUNGE: H.C.)
Chong Fok Shang v. Lily Handicraft (SERIOUS QUESTION TO BE TRIED: WHETHER DAMAGES ADEQUATE COMPENSATION: H.C.)
Heublein Inc. v. Paterson Simons & Co. (S.) Pte Ltd (TRADE MARK: INJUNCTION: C.A.)

Interlocutory injunction—serious question to be tried

Chong Fok Shang v. Lily Handicraft (BALANCE OF CONVENIENCE: WHETHER DAMAGES ADEQUATE COMPENSATION: H.C.)

Limitation period

A. Clouet & Co. Pte Ltd v. Maya Toba Sdn Bhd (TRADE MARK: INFRINGEMENT: PASSING OFF: SIMILARITY OF LABELS AND GET-UP: AYAM BRAND/BOTAN BRAND: LABEL COMMON TO THE TRADE: H.C.)

Mareva injunction

Regent Decorators Sdn Bhd v. Chee (FORMER EMPLOYEES: CONFUSION: S.C.)

Reputation and Goodwill

Dun & Bradstreet (Singapore) Pte Ltd v. Dun & Bradstreet (Malaysia) Sdn Bhd (TRADE MARK: IDENTICAL BUSINESS NAMES: DIFFERENT SCOPE OF ACTIVITY: H.C.)

Scope of Activity

Dun & Bradstreet (Singapore) Pte Ltd v. Dun & Bradstreet (Malaysia) Sdn Bhd (IDENTICAL BUSINESS NAMES: DIFFERENT SCOPE OF ACTIVITY: H.C.)
Seet Chuan Seng v. Tee Yih Jia Foods Manufacturing Pte Ltd (SIMILAR NAME AND MARK: DISTINCTIVENESS AND LIKELIHOOD OF DECEPTION: GOODS IN DIRECT COMPETITION: S.C.)

Serious Question to be Tried. *See* Practice *(Serious question to be tried)*

Similarity

Hille International Ltd v. Tiong Hin Engineering Pty Ltd (TRADE MARK: INFRINGEMENT: DECEPTIVE SIMILARITY: H.C.)

Seet Chuan Seng v. Tee Yih Jia Foods Manufacturing Pte Ltd (TRADE MARK: SIMILAR NAME AND MARK: GOODS IN DIRECT COMPETITION: S.C.)

Trade Mark or Trade Name

A. Clouet & Co. Pte Ltd v. Maya Toba Sdn Bhd (INFRINGEMENT: SIMILARITY OF LABELS AND GET-UP: AYAM BRAND/BOTAN BRAND: LABEL COMMON TO THE TRADE: PRACTICE: LIMITATION PERIOD: H.C.)

Americaya Singapore Pte Ltd v. Americaya Malaysia Shn Bhd (APPLICATION FOR STAY PENDING HEARING OF APPLICATION TO EXPUNGE: INTERLOCUTORY INJUNCTION: BALANCE OF CONVENIENCE: H.C.)

Dun & Bradstreet (Singapore) Pte Ltd v. Dun & Bradstreet (Malaysia) Sdn Bhd (IDENTICAL BUSINESS NAMES: DIFFERENT SCOPE OF ACTIVITY: REPUTATION AND GOODWILL: H.C.)

Excelsior Pte Ltd v. Excelsior Sport (C.) Pte Ltd (TRADE NAME: CONFUSION: H.C.)

Fraser & Neame Ltd v. Yeo Hiap Seng Ltd (INFRINGEMENT: ESSENTIAL FEATURES: H.C.)

Heublein Inc. v. Paterson Simons & Co. (S.) Pte Ltd (INJUNCTION: BALANCE OF CONVENIENCE: C.A.)

Hille International Ltd v. Tiong Hin Engineering Pty Ltd (INFRINGEMENT: DECEPTIVE SIMILARITY: H.C.)

Revertex Ltd v. Slim Rivertex Shn Bhd (REGISTRAR OF COMPANIES REFUSAL NOT TO REGISTER SIMILAR NAME: H.C.)

Seet Chuan Seng v. Tee Yih Jia Foods Manufacturing Pte Ltd (SIMILAR NAME AND MARK: GOODS IN DIRECT COMPETITION: S.C.)

Westpac Banking Corp. v. Goodmaker Leasing Corp. Berhad (FOREIGN PLAINTIFF: GOODWILL: FANCY NAME: H.C.)

Winthrop Products Inc. v. Sun Ocean (M.) Sdn Bhd (PARALLEL IMPORTS: PRODUCT MANUFACTURED IN U.K.: H.C.)

Patents

Agricultural Methods

Rhône-Poulenc AG Co. v. Dikloride Herbicides Sdn Bhd (AGRICULTURAL METHODS: INFRINGEMENT: VALIDITY: H.C.)

CIMETIDINE

Smith Kline & French Laboratories Ltd v. Salim (Malaysia) Sdn Bhd (DRUG MANUFACTURED IN BRITAIN AND OTHER COUNTRIES: PATENTS IN RESPECT OF DRUG REGISTERED BY PLAINTIFFS IN UNITED KINGDOM AND THEN IN MALAYSIA: DEFENDANTS IMPORTING AND RESELLING DRUG IN MALAYSIA WITHOUT NOTICE OF ANY RESTRICTION IN RESPECT OF IMPORT AND RESALE: WHETHER PLAINTIFFS RIGHTS INFRINGED: H.C.)

Importing

Smith Kline & French Laboratories Ltd v. Salim (Malaysia) Sdn Bhd (IMPORT AND RESALE WITHOUT NOTICE OF RESTRICTION: WHETHER RIGHTS INFRINGED: H.C.)

Infringement

Rhône-Poulenc AG Co. v. Dikloride Herbicides Sdn Bhd (VALIDITY: H.C.)

Smith Kline & French Laboratories Ltd v. Salim (Malaysia) Sdn Bhd (IMPORT AND RESALE WITHOUT NOTICE OF RESTRICTION: WHETHER RIGHTS INFRINGED: H.C.)

Manufacture Overseas

Smith Kline & French Laboratories Ltd v. Salim (Malaysia) Sdn Bhd (PATENTS IN U.K. AND IMPORT AND RESALE WITHOUT NOTICE OF RESTRICTION: WHETHER RIGHTS INFRINGED: H.C.)

Notice of Restriction

Smith Kline & French Laboratories Ltd v. Salim (Malaysia) Sdn Bhd (PATENTS IN U.K. AND IMPORT AND RESALE WITHOUT NOTICE OF RESTRICTION: WHETHER RIGHTS INFRINGED: H.C.)

Novelty

Rhône-Poulenc AG Co. v. Dikloride Herbicides Sdn Bhd (AGRICULTURAL METHODS: INFRINGEMENT: VALIDITY: H.C.)

Reselling

Smith Kline & French Laboratories Ltd v. Salim (Malaysia) Sdn Bhd (PATENTS IN U.K. AND IMPORT AND RESALE WITHOUT NOTICE OF RESTRICTION: WHETHER RIGHTS INFRINGED: H.C.)

Practice and Miscellaneous Subjects

Affidavit

Chong Loy Sen v. Public Prosecutor (CROSS-EXAMINATION ON AFFIDAVIT: H.C.)

Anton Piller Practice

Television Broadcasts Ltd v. Mandarin Video Holdings Sdn Bhd (PRIVILEGE AGAINST SELF-INCRIMINATION: H.C.)
Television Broadcasts Ltd v. Seremban Video Centre Sdn Bhd (APPEAL: H.C.)

Appeal

Asia Television Ltd v. Vina Video Sdn Bhd (Fed. Ct)
Television Broadcasts Ltd v. Seremban Video Centre Sdn Bhd (ANTON PILLER ORDER: H.C.)

Balance of Convenience

Americaya Singapore Pte Ltd v. Americaya Malaysia Shn Bhd (INFRINGEMENT: PASSING OFF: APPLICATION FOR STAY PENDING HEARING OF APPLICATION TO EXPUNGE: H.C.)

Chong Fok Shang v. Lily Handicraft (SERIOUS QUESTION TO BE TRIED: WHETHER DAMAGES ADEQUATE COMPENSATION: H.C.)
Heublein Inc. v. Paterson Simons & Co. (S.) Pte Ltd (C.A.)

Burden of Proof

Hock Choo Hoe Sdn Bhd v. Public Prosecutor (FALSE TRADE DESCRIPTION: CORPORATION: WHETHER STATUTORY DEFENCE AVAILABLE: H.C.)

Corporation

Hock Choo Hoe Sdn Bhd v. Public Prosecutor (FALSE TRADE DESCRIPTION: WHETHER STATUTORY DEFENCE AVAILABLE: BURDEN OF PROOF: H.C.)

Cross-examination

Chong Loy Sen v. Public Prosecutor (CROSS-EXAMINATION ON AFFIDAVIT: H.C.)

Delay

Malaysian Milk Sdn Bhd's Registered Design (STRIKING OUT: RECTIFICATION OF REGISTER: ESTOPPEL: Ch.D.)

Estoppel

Malaysian Milk Sdn Bhd's Registered Design (STRIKING OUT: RECTIFICATION OF REGISTER: DELAY: Ch.D.)

Ex Parte Application

Tohtonku Sdn Bhd v. Superace (M.) Sdn Bhd (PENANG: H.C.)

Limitation Period

A. Clouet & Co. Pte Ltd v. Maya Toba Sdn Bhd

Mareva Injunction

Regent Decorators Sdn Bhd v. Chee (FORMER EMPLOYEES: S.C.)

Privilege Against Self-incrimination

Television Broadcasts Ltd v. Mandarin Video Holdings Sdn Bhd (ANTON PILLER PRACTICE: H.C.)

Serious Question to be Tried

Chong Fok Shang v. Lily Handicraft (BALANCE OF CONVENIENCE: WHETHER DAMAGES ADEQUATE COMPENSATION: H.C.)

Stay

Americaya Singapore Pte Ltd v. Americaya Malaysia Shn Bhd (INFRINGEMENT: PASSING OFF: APPLICATION FOR STAY PENDING HEARING OF APPLICATION TO EXPUNGE: H.C.)

Striking Out

Malaysian Milk Sdn Bhd's Registered Design (RECTIFICATION OF DESIGN REGISTER: DELAY: ESTOPPEL: Ch.D.)

Whether Damages Adequate Compensation

Chong Fok Shang v. Lily Handicraft (PASSING OFF: SERIOUS QUESTION TO BE TRIED: BALANCE OF CONVENIENCE: H.C.)

Trade Marks

Agent

Sanita Manufacturing (Malaysia) Sdn Bhd v. Chanchai Aroonratanawongse (REGISTRATION BY AGENT: ALTERATION WITHOUT AUTHORITY: APPLICATION TO EXPUNGE ALTERATION: S.C.)

Alteration Without Authority

Sanita Manufacturing (Malaysia) Sdn Bhd v. Chanchai Aroonratanawongse (REGISTRATION BY AGENT: APPLICATION TO EXPUNGE ALTERATION: S.C.)

Application

Wall (T.) & Sons Ltd v. Rasa Sayang Ice Cream (INFRINGEMENT: OPPOSITION: STAY: BALANCE OF CONVENIENCE: H.C.)

Burden of Proof. *See* **Practice** (*Burden of proof*)

Class of Goods

Hai-O Enterprise Bhd v. Nguang Chan (WHETHER NON-REGISTRATION IN CORRECT CLASS RESULTED IN NON-USER OF MARK: H.C.)

Confusion

Excelsior Pte Ltd v. Excelsior Sport (C.) Pte Ltd (PASSING OFF: H.C.)

Criminal Offence

Socoil Corp Bhd v. N.G. Brothers Import and Export Co. (INFRINGEMENT: FALSE TRADE DESCRIPTION: Pat. Ct)

Ex Parte Application. *See* **Practice** (*Ex parte application*)

Expungement

Americaya Singapore Pte Ltd v. Americaya Malaysia Shn Bhd (INFRINGEMENT: PASSING OFF: APPLICATION FOR STAY PENDING HEARING OF APPLICATION TO EXPUNGE: H.C.)

Hai-O Enterprise Bhd v. Nguang Chan (IMPORTER REGISTERING IN OWN NAME: WHETHER MARK WRONGLY REGISTERED: WHETHER NON-REGISTRATION IN CORRECT CLASS RESULTED IN NON-USER OF MARK: H.C.)

Sanita Manufacturing (Malaysia) Sdn Bhd v. Chanchai Aroonratanawongse (REGISTRATION BY AGENT: ALTERATION WITHOUT AUTHORITY: APPLICATION TO EXPUNGE ALTERATION: S.C.)

False Trade Description

Socoil Corp Bhd v. N.G. Brothers Import and Export Co. (INFRINGEMENT: CRIMINAL OFFENCE: Pat. Ct)

1034

Marks in Issue

AYAM BRAND/BOTAN BRAND
A. Clouet & Co. Pte Ltd v. Maya Toba Sdn Bhd (H.C.)

Non-user

Hai-O Enterprise Bhd v. Nguang Chan (REGISTRATION IN WRONG CLASS: WHETHER NON-REGISTRATION IN CORRECT CLASS RESULTED IN NON-USER OF MARK: H.C.)

Opposition

Wall (T.) & Sons Ltd v. Rasa Sayang Ice Cream (INFRINGEMENT: APPLICATION: STAY: BALANCE OF CONVENIENCE: H.C.)

Overseas Manufacture

Hai-O Enterprise Bhd v. Nguang Chan (MANUFACTURER OWNER IN CHINA: MALAYSIAN IMPORTER OF CHINESE PRODUCT REGISTERING MARK IN OWN NAME: H.C.)
Winthrop Products Inc. v. Sun Ocean (M.) Sdn Bhd (PARALLEL IMPORTS: PRODUCT MANUFACTURED IN U.K. SOLD IN MALAYSIA: INFRINGEMENT: PASSING OFF: H.C.)

Parallel Imports. *See* **Imports and Importer**

Passing Off

A. Clouet & Co. Pte Ltd v. Maya Toba Sdn Bhd (INFRINGEMENT: PASSING OFF: SIMILARITY OF LABELS AND GET-UP: AYAM BRAND/BOTAN BRAND: LABEL COMMON TO THE TRADE: PRACTICE: LIMITATION PERIOD: H.C.)
Americaya Singapore Pte Ltd v. Americaya malaysia Shn Bhd (APPLICATION FOR STAY PENDING HEARING OF APPLICATION TO EXPUNGE: INTERLOCUTORY INJUNCTION: BALANCE OF CONVENIENCE: H.C.)
Dun & Bradstreet (Singapore) Pte Ltd v. Dun & Bradstreet (Malaysia) Sdn Bhd (IDENTICAL BUSINESS NAMES: DIFFERENT SCOPE OF ACTIVITY: REPUTATION AND GOODWILL: H.C.)
Excelsior Pte Ltd v. Excelsior Sport (C.) Pte Ltd (CONFUSION: H.C.)
Fraser & Neame Ltd v. Yeo Hiap Seng Ltd (INFRINGEMENT: ESSENTIAL FEATURES: H.C.)
Heublein Inc. v. Paterson Simons & Co. (S.) Pte Ltd (INJUNCTION: BALANCE OF CONVENIENCE: C.A.)
Hille International Ltd v. Tiong Hin Engineering Pty Ltd (INFRINGEMENT: DECEPTIVE SIMILARITY: H.C.)
Revertex Ltd v. Slim Rivertex Shn Bhd (REGISTRAR OF COMPANIES REFUSAL NOT TO REGISTER SIMILAR NAME: LIKELIHOOD OF DECEPTION: H.C.)
Seet Chuan Seng v. Tee Yih Jia Foods Manufacturing Pte Ltd (SIMILAR NAME AND MARK: DISTINCTIVENESS AND LIKELIHOOD OF DECEPTION: GOODS IN DIRECT COMPETITION: S.C.)
Winthrop Products Inc. v. Sun Ocean (M.) Sdn Bhd (PARALLEL IMPORTS: PRODUCT MANUFACTURED IN U.K. SOLD IN MALAYSIA: INFRINGEMENT: H.C.)

Practice

Balance of convenience

Americaya Singapore Pte Ltd v. Americaya Malaysia Shn Bhd (INTERLOCUTORY INJUNCTION: APPLICATION FOR STAY PENDING HEARING OF APPLICATION TO EXPUNGE: H.C.)

Wall (T.) & Sons Ltd v. Rasa Sayang Ice Cream (INFRINGEMENT: APPLICATION: OPPOSITION: STAY: H.C.)

Burden of proof

Hock Choo Hoe Sdn Bhd v. Public Prosecutor (FALSE TRADE DESCRIPTION: CORPORATION: WHETHER STATUTORY DEFENCE AVAILABLE: H.C.)

Ex parte application

Tohtonku Sdn Bhd v. Superace (M.) Sdn Bhd (INFRINGEMENT: Penang: H.C.)

Limitation period

A. Clouet & Co. Pte Ltd v. Maya Toba Sdn Bhd (INFRINGEMENT: PASSING OFF: SIMILARITY OF LABELS AND GET-UP: AYAM BRAND/BOTAN BRAND: LABEL COMMON TO THE TRADE: PRACTICE: LIMITATION PERIOD: H.C.)

Stay

Americaya Singapore Pte Ltd v. Americaya Malaysia Shn Bhd (PASSING OFF: APPLICATION FOR STAY PENDING HEARING OF APPLICATION TO EXPUNGE: H.C.)

Wall (T.) & Sons Ltd v. Rasa Sayang Ice Cream (INFRINGEMENT: APPLICATION: OPPOSITION: BALANCE OF CONVENIENCE: H.C.)

Proprietor

Tohtonku Sdn Bhd v. Superace (M.) Sdn Bhd (INFRINGEMENT: *Ex parte* APPLICATION FOR RELIEF: Penang: H.C.)

Registration

Americaya Singapore Pte Ltd v. Americaya Malaysia Shn Bhd (INFRINGEMENT: PASSING OFF: APPLICATION FOR STAY PENDING HEARING OF APPLICATION TO EXPUNGE: H.C.)

Seizure of Goods

Hai-O Enterprise Bhd v. Nguang Chan (MANUFACTURER OWNER IN CHINA: MALAYSIAN IMPORTER OF CHINESE PRODUCT REGISTERING MARK IN OWN NAME: TRADE DESCRIPTION ORDER: SEIZURE OF GOODS: H.C.)

Stay. *See* **Practice** (*Stay*)

Trade Description Order

Hai-O Enterprise Bhd v. Nguang Chan (MANUFACTURER OWNER IN CHINA: MALAYSIAN IMPORTER OF CHINESE PRODUCT REGISTERING MARK IN OWN NAME: SEIZURE OF GOODS: H.C.)

NEW ZEALAND

Confidential Information and Breach of Confidence

Account of Profits. *See* **Practice** (*Account of profits*)

Assignment

Millwell Holdings Ltd v. Johnson (EX-EMPLOYEE: DIRECTOR: H.C.)

Client List

Peninsular Real Estate Ltd v. Harris (EX-EMPLOYEES: NO RESTRAINT OF TRADE CLAUSE: H.C.)

Damages

Aquaculture Corp. v. New Zealand Green Mussell Co. Ltd (No. 2) (ASSESSMENT OF DAMAGES: EVALUATION OF LOST OPPORTUNITY: EXEMPLARY DAMAGES: ACCOUNT OF PROFITS REFUSED: H.C.)

Aquaculture Corporation v. New Zealand Green Mussel Co. Ltd (AVAILABILITY OF DAMAGES FOR BREACH OF DUTY OF CONFIDENCE: WHETHER EXEMPLARY DAMAGES MAY ALSO BE AWARDED: C.A.)

Fiscal Technology Co. Ltd v. Johnson (NON-DISCLOSURE AGREEMENT: BREACH OF CONTRACTUAL OBLIGATIONS: APPROPRIATENESS OF EXEMPLARY DAMAGES: H.C.)

Wilson v. Broadcasting Corporation of New Zealand (FORMAT OR CONCEPT FOR A TELEVISION PROGRAMME: FEASIBILITY STUDY: EXEMPLARY DAMAGES: H.C.)

Declaration. *See* **Practice** (*Declaration*)

Defence of Iniquity. *See* **Practice** (*Iniquity*)

Delivery-up. *See* **Practice** (*Delivery-up*)

Director

Millwell Holdings Ltd v. Johnson (EX-EMPLOYEE: ASSIGNMENT: H.C.)

Disclosure

Silvercrest Sales Ltd v. Gainsborough Printing Co. Ltd (SIMPLE SECRET: NO CONTRACT NECESSARY: CIRCUMSTANCES OF DISCLOSURE: NEGOTIATIONS: H.C.)

Document

Corporate Group Holdings Ltd v. Corporate Resources Group Ltd (RESTRAINT ON USE: H.C.)

Equitable Duty

Attorney-General v. Wellington Newspapers Ltd (GOVERNMENT SECRETS: STATUS OF INTELLIGENCE AGENTS: FIDUCIARY OBLIGATION OF CONFIDENCE: H.C.: C.A.)

Ex-employee and Ex-client

Effem Foods Pty Ltd v. Trade Consultants Ltd (INTERNATIONAL TRADE ADVISOR: DUTIES OWED TO EX-CLIENT: *Quia timet* INJUNCTION: H.C.)

Elley Ltd v. Wairoa-Harrison & McCarthy (EX-EMPLOYEE: DELIVERY-UP OF DOCUMENTS: H.C.)

Millwell Holdings Ltd v. Johnson (EX-EMPLOYEE: DIRECTOR: ASSIGNMENT: H.C.)

Peninsular Real Estate Ltd v. Harris (CLIENT LIST: NO RESTRAINT OF TRADE CLAUSE: H.C.)

Exemplary Damages. *See* Damages

Fiduciary Obligation

Attorney-General v. Wellington Newspapers Ltd (GOVERNMENT SECRETS: PUBLIC INTEREST IN RESTRAINING PUBLICATION: H.C.: C.A.)

Format or Concept

Wilson v. Broadcasting Corporation of New Zealand (FORMAT OR CONCEPT FOR TELEVISION PROGRAMME: FEASIBILITY STUDY: H.C.)

Freedom of the Press

Attorney-General v. Wellington Newspapers Ltd (GOVERNMENT SECRETS: STATUS OF INTELLIGENCE AGENTS: EQUITABLE DUTY OF CONFIDENCE: FIDUCIARY OBLIGATION OF CONFIDENCE: PUBLIC INTEREST IN RESTRAINING PUBLICATION: H.C.: C.A.)

Government Secrets

Attorney-General v. Wellington Newspapers Ltd (FREEDOM OF THE PRESS: STATUS OF INTELLIGENCE AGENTS: EQUITABLE DUTY OF CONFIDENCE: FIDUCIARY OBLIGATION OF CONFIDENCE: PUBLIC INTEREST IN RESTRAINING PUBLICATION: H.C.: C.A.)

Injunction

Aquaculture Corp. v. New Zealand Green Mussel Co. Ltd (No. 2) (H.C.)

European Pacific Banking Corporation v. Fourth Estate Publications Ltd (INIQUITY RULE: PUBLIC INTEREST: EFFECT OF DOCUMENTS ALREADY IN PUBLIC DOMAIN: H.C.)

Intelligence Agents, Status of

Attorney-General v. Wellington Newspapers Ltd (GOVERNMENT SECRETS: EQUITABLE DUTY OF CONFIDENCE: FIDUCIARY OBLIGATION OF CONFIDENCE: PUBLIC INTEREST IN RESTRAINING PUBLICATION: H.C.: C.A.)

Interlocutory Injunction. *See* Practice (*Interlocutory injunction*)

Lost Opportunity, Evaluation of. *See* Practice (*Lost opportunity*)

Non-disclosure Agreement

Fiscal Technology Co. Ltd v. Johnson (BREACH: DAMAGES: APPROPRIATENESS OF EXEMPLARY DAMAGES: H.C.)

Practice

Account of profits

Aquaculture Corp. v. New Zealand Green Mussel Co. Ltd (No. 2) (ASSESSMENT OF DAMAGES: EVALUATION OF LOST OPPORTUNITY: EXEMPLARY DAMAGES: ACCOUNT OF PROFITS REFUSED: H.C.)

Attorney-General v. Wellington Newspapers Ltd (GOVERNMENT SECRETS: INTELLIGENCE AGENTS: EQUITABLE DUTY: FIDUCIARY OBLIGATION: H.C.: C.A.)

Declaration

Attorney-General v. Wellington Newspapers Ltd (GOVERNMENT SECRETS: INTELLIGENCE AGENTS: EQUITABLE DUTY: FIDUCIARY OBLIGATION: ACCOUNT OF PROFITS: H.C.: C.A.)

Delivery-up

Elley Ltd v. Wairoa-Harrison & McCarthy (EX-EMPLOYEE: H.C.)

Iniquity

Attorney-General v. Wellington Newspapers Ltd (GOVERNMENT SECRETS: MATERIAL IN PUBLIC DOMAIN: EFFECT OF PUBLICATION OUTSIDE NEW ZEALAND: H.C.: C.A.)

European Pacific Banking Corporation v. Fourth Estate Publications Ltd (INJUNCTION: PUBLIC INTEREST: EFFECT OF DOCUMENTS ALREADY IN PUBLIC DOMAIN: H.C.)

Interlocutory injunction

Silvercrest Sales Ltd v. Gainsborough Printing Co. Ltd (SIMPLE SECRET: NO CONTRACT: CIRCUMSTANCES OF DISCLOSURE: NEGOTIATIONS: H.C.)

Lost opportunity, evaluation of

Aquaculture Corp. v. New Zealand Green Mussel Co. Ltd (No. 2) (ASSESSMENT OF DAMAGES: EXEMPLARY DAMAGES: H.C.)

Quia timet injunction

Effem Foods Pty Ltd v. Trade Consultants Ltd (INTERNATIONAL TRADE ADVISER: DUTIES OWED TO EX-CLIENT: H.C.)

Privacy

Bradley v. Wingnot Films Ltd (FILM: SCENE SHOT IN CEMETERY INCLUDING FAMILY TOMBSTONE IN BACKGROUND: EMOTIONAL DISTRESS: H.C.)

Private International Laws

Attorney-General v. Wellington Newspapers Ltd (GOVERNMENT SECRETS: FREEDOM OF THE PRESS: PUBLIC INTEREST IN RESTRAINING PUBLICATION: MATERIAL IN PUBLIC DOMAIN: EFFECT OF PUBLICATION OUTSIDE NEW ZEALAND: H.C.: C.A.)

Publication outside New Zealand, Effect of

Attorney-General v. Wellington Newspapers Ltd (PUBLIC INTEREST IN RESTRAINING PUBLICATION: PRIVATE INTERNATIONAL LAWS: MATERIAL IN PUBLIC DOMAIN: H.C.: C.A.)

Public Domain

Aquaculture Corp. v. New Zealand Green Mussel Co. Ltd (MUSSEL PREPARATION FOR TREATMENT OF ILLNESS: H.C.)

Attorney-General v. Wellington Newspapers Ltd (PUBLIC INTEREST IN RESTRAINING PUBLICATION: PRIVATE INTERNATIONAL LAWS: EFFECT OF PUBLICATION OUTSIDE NEW ZEALAND: H.C.: C.A.)

European Pacific Banking Corporation v. Fourth Estate Publications Ltd (INJUNCTION: INIQUITY RULE: PUBLIC INTEREST: H.C.)

Public Interest

Attorney-General v. Wellington Newspapers Ltd (PUBLIC INTEREST IN RESTRAINING PUBLICATION: H.C.: C.A.)

European Pacific Banking Corporation v. Fourth Estate Publications Ltd (INJUNCTION: INIQUITY RULE: EFFECT OF DOCUMENTS ALREADY IN PUBLIC DOMAIN: H.C.)

Quia Timet Injunction. *See* **Practice** (*Quia timet injunction*)

Restraint of Trade

Peninsular Real Estate Ltd v. Harris (EX-EMPLOYEES: CLIENT LIST: NO RESTRAINT OF TRADE CLAUSE: H.C.)

Simple Secret

Silvercrest Sales Ltd v. Gainsborough Printing Co. Ltd (NO CONTRACT: CIRCUMSTANCES OF DISCLOSURE: NEGOTIATIONS: INTERLOCUTORY INJUNCTION: H.C.)

Spycatcher

Attorney-General v. Wellington Newspapers Ltd (GOVERNMENT SECRETS: FREEDOM OF THE PRESS: STATUS OF INTELLIGENCE AGENTS: EQUITABLE DUTY OF CONFIDENCE: FIDUCIARY OBLIGATION OF CONFIDENCE: PUBLIC INTEREST IN RESTRAINING PUBLICATION: PRIVATE INTERNATIONAL LAWS: MATERIAL IN PUBLIC DOMAIN: EFFECT OF PUBLICATION OUTSIDE NEW ZEALAND: EXEMPLARY DAMAGES: DECLARATION: ACCOUNT OF PROFITS: DEFENCE OF INIQUITY: H.C.: C.A.)

Use of Information

Smith Kline & French Laboratories Ltd v. Attorney-General (CONFIDENTIAL INFORMATION SUPPLIED TO HEALTH DEPARTMENT BY PHARMACEUTICAL MANUFACTURER: USE TO GRANT CONSENT TO RIVAL GENERIC DRUG: USE INTERNAL TO DEPARTMENT: USE NOT UNAUTHORISED NOR DETRIMENTAL TO PLAINTIFFS: SUPPLY OF SAMPLE TO HEALTH DEPARTMENT IN SUPPORT OF APPLICATION FOR CONSENT TO DISTRIBUTE GENERIC DRUG PRIOR TO EXPIRY OF PATENT: H.C.)

Van Camp Chocolates Ltd v. Aulsebrooks Ltd (MISUSE: TORT: C.A.)

1040

Copyright

Acquiescence. *See* **Practice** (*Acquiescence*)

Adaptation

Fiscal Technology Co. Ltd v. Johnson (INFRINGEMENT: ADAPTATION INVOLVING
  SIGNIFICANT SKILL AND EXPERTISE: RELIEF: INJUNCTION: DELIVERY-UP:
  DAMAGES: APPROPRIATENESS OF EXEMPLARY DAMAGES: H.C.)

Anton Piller Order. *See* **Practice** (*Anton Piller order*)

Artistic Works

Bonz Group (Pty) Ltd v. Cooke (INFRINGEMENT: MODEL: HAND-KNITTED
  GARMENTS: PROTOTYPE: OBJECTIVE SIMILARITY: INDEPENDENT SKILL,
  EFFORT AND LABOUR: ORIGINALITY: H.C.)
Lilypak Industries Ltd v. Poly Containers (N.Z.) Ltd (DISPOSABLE PLASTIC CUPS: USE
  WITH PLASTIC HOLDERS: H.C.)
Mono Pumps (New Zealand) Ltd v. Amalgamated Pumps Ltd (INFRINGEMENT:
  INJUNCTION: WHETHER DRAWINGS ILLUSTRATING AN IDEA CAPABLE OF
  COPYRIGHT PROTECTION: H.C.)
Pop-A-Shot Inc. v. Filtration and Pumping (Commercial) Ltd (REPRODUCTION:
  H.C.)
Thornton Hall Manufacturing Ltd v. Shanton Apparel Ltd (ORIGINALITY: CAUSAL
  CONNECTION: INFRINGEMENT: C.A.)
Thornton Hall Manufacturing Ltd v. Shanton Apparel Ltd (INFRINGEMENT: DRESS:
  SAMPLE: WHETHER THREE-DIMENSIONAL REPRODUCTION OF AN ORIGINAL
  ARTISTIC WORK: SUBSISTENCE OF COPYRIGHT: H.C.: C.A.)
Thornton Hall Manufacturing Ltd v. Shanton Apparel Ltd (No. 2) (SUBSISTENCE:
  SKETCHES, PATTERNS AND SAMPLE DRESS: ORIGINALITY: OWNERSHIP:
  INFRINGEMENT: H.C.)

Assignment

Anvil Jewellery Ltd v. Riva Ridge Holdings Ltd (SUBSISTENCE: AGREEMENT FOR
  SALE OF ASSETS: CONSTRUCTION: INTERLOCUTORY INJUNCTION: ANTON
  PILLER ORDERS: H.C.)

Authorisation

Brintons Ltd v. Feltex Furnishings of New Zealand Ltd (No. 1) (INFRINGEMENT:
  INDEMNITY AND CONTRIBUTION: STRIKING OUT: H.C.)

Balance of Convenience. *See* **Practice** (*Interlocutory injunction*)

Causal Connection

Thornton Hall Manufacturing Ltd v. Shanton Apparel Ltd (ARTISTIC WORKS:
  ORIGINALITY: INFRINGEMENT: C.A.)

Commissioned Work

Plix Products Ltd v. Frank M. Winstone (Merchants) (INFRINGEMENT: KIWI FRUIT
  "POCKET PACKS": PUBLIC LICENCE: INEVITABLE DESIGN: H.C.: C.A.)

Compilation of Common Features

Artifakts Design Group Ltd v. N.P. Rigg Ltd (H.C.)

Compilation of Extracts

Longman Group Ltd v. Carrington Technical Institite Board of Governors (BOOKS BY TUTOR AT TECHNICAL INSTITUTE: INFRINGEMENT: DEFENCE OF FAIR DEALING: ADMISSIBLE EVIDENCE TO DETERMINE FAIR DEALING: REASONABLE PROPORTION: H.C.: C.A.)

Computer Subjects

Barson Computers (N.Z.) Ltd v. John Gilbert & Co. Ltd (INFRINGEMENT: COMPUTER PRODUCTS: IMPORTATION: IRRELEVANCE OF HYPOTHETICAL MAKER: H.C.)

International Business Machines Corporation v. Computer Imports Ltd (INFRINGEMENT: COMPUTER TECHNOLOGY: THREE-DIMENSIONAL REPRODUCTION OF CABINET AND INTERNAL LAYOUT OF PERSONAL COMPUTER AND BY COPYING OF COMPUTER PROGRAM: IMPORTATION AND SALE: SOURCE CODE: WHETHER OBJECT CODE: H.C.)

Consent Order. *See* **Practice** (*Consent order*)

Conversion Damages. *See* **Practice** (*Conversion damages*)

Crown Use

Longman Group Ltd v. Carrington Technical Institute Board of Governers (INFRINGEMENT: SUBSTANTIALITY OF REPRODUCTION: FAIR DEALING: RESEARCH OR PRIVATE STUDY: USE BY AGENT OF CROWN: H.C.)

Damages. *See* **Practice** (*Damages*)

Declaration. *See* **Practice** (*Declaration*)

Delay. *See* **Practice** (*Delay*)

Delivery-up. *See* **Practice** (*Delivery-up*)

Design. *See* **Design Cases**

Dramatic Copyright

Television New Zealand Ltd v. Newsmonitor Services Ltd (INFRINGEMENT: TELEVISION BROADCASTS: SCRIPT OF NEWS: LITERARY COPYRIGHT: COPYING FOR PRIVATE PURPOSES: FAIR DEALING: PRIVATE RESEARCH OR STUDY: IMPLIED LICENCE: REPRODUCTION FOR JUDICIAL PROCEEDINGS: C.A.)

Drawings in Patent Specification

Inglis v. Mayson (INFRINGEMENT: SUBSTANTIAL REPRODUCTION: H.C.)

Election Between Account of Profits or Damages. *See* Practice *(Account of profits)*

Evidence. *See* Practice *(Evidence)*

Fair Dealing

Longman Group Ltd v. Carrington Technical Institite Board of Governors (COMPILATION OF EXTRACTS FROM BOOKS BY TUTOR AT TECHNICAL INSTITUTE: INFRINGEMENT: ADMISSIBLE EVIDENCE TO DETERMINE FAIR DEALING: REASONABLE PROPORTION: H.C.: C.A.)

Longman Group Ltd v. Carrington Technical Institute Board of Governers (INFRINGEMENT: SUBSTANTIALITY OF REPRODUCTION: RESEARCH OR PRIVATE STUDY: USE BY AGENT OF CROWN: H.C.)

Television N.Z. v. Newsmonitor Services Ltd (INFRINGEMENT: TELEVISION PROGRAMMES: RECORDING BY NEWS MONITORING SERVICE: TRANSCRIPTS: IMPLIED LICENCE: H.C.)

Features Common to the Trade

Klissers Farmhouse Bakeries Ltd v. Harvest Bakeries Ltd (No. 2) (H.C.)

Forum. *See* Practice *(Forum)*

Idea and Expression

Mono Pumps (N.Z.) Ltd v. Karinya Industries Ltd (INFRINGEMENT: LICENSEE OF OVERSEAS PATENT: INTERLOCUTORY INJUNCTION: H.C.)

Implied Licence

Mono Pumps (New Zealand) Ltd v. Amalgamated Pumps Ltd (INFRINGEMENT: INJUNCTION: ORIGINAL ARTISTIC WORK: WHETHER DRAWINGS ILLUSTRATING AN IDEA CAPABLE OF PROTECTION: LICENSING AGREEMENT: IMPLIED TERMS: H.C.)

Television N.Z. v. Newsmonitor Services Ltd (INFRINGEMENT: TELEVISION PROGRAMMES: RECORDING BY NEWS MONITORING SERVICE: TRANSCRIPTS: FAIR DEALING: H.C., C.A.)

Importation

Barson Computers (N.Z.) Ltd v. John Gilbert & Co. Ltd (INFRINGEMENT: COMPUTER PRODUCTS: IRRELEVANCE OF HYPOTHETICAL MAKER: H.C.)

International Business Machines Corporation v. Computer Imports Ltd (INFRINGEMENT: COMPUTER TECHNOLOGY: THREE-DIMENSIONAL REPRODUCTION OF CABINET AND INTERNAL LAYOUT OF PERSONAL COMPUTER AND BY COPYING OF COMPUTER PROGRAM: H.C.)

1043

Samsung Electronics Co. Ltd v. ASDA Holdings Ltd (WORKS FROM NON-CONVENTION COUNTRY: PARALLEL IMPORTATION: EXCLUSIVE DISTRIBUTORSHIP: UNAUTHORISED IMPORTATION: H.C.)

Indemnity and Contribution

Brintons Ltd v. Feltex Furnishings of New Zealand Ltd (No. 1) (INFRINGEMENT: AUTHORISATION: STRIKING OUT: H.C.)

Indirect Copying

Crystal Glass Industries Ltd v. Alwinco Products Ltd (INFRINGEMENT: THREE-DIMENSIONAL REPRODUCTION: JOINT TORTFEASORS: CONVERSION DAMAGES: C.A.)

Engineering Dynamics Ltd v. Reid & Harrison (1980) Ltd (INFRINGEMENT: TEST: SUBSTANTIAL PART: VERBAL AND VISUAL INSTRUCTIONS: CONVERSION DAMAGES: H.C.)

Inevitable Design

Plix Products Ltd v. Frank M. Winstone (Merchants) (INFRINGEMENT: KIWI FRUIT "POCKET PACKS": PUBLIC LICENCE: COMMISSIONED WORK: H.C.: C.A.)

Infringement

Atkinson Footwear Ltd v. Hodgskin International Services (INTERLOCUTORY INJUNCTION SOUGHT TO RESTRAIN ACTS IN NEW ZEALAND AND AUSTRALIA: JURISDICTION *in personam, in rem:* H.C.)

Barson Computers (N.Z.) Ltd v. John Gilbert & Co. Ltd (COMPUTER PRODUCTS: IMPORTATION: IRRELEVANCE OF HYPOTHETICAL MAKER: H.C.)

Bleiman v. News Media (Auckland) Ltd (COMPETITION BASED ON RESULTS OF SPORTING EVENTS: COPYING: SUBSTANTIAL PART: TEST FOR ASSESSING BREACH: INTERIM INJUNCTION: C.A.)

Bonz Group (Pty) Ltd v. Cooke (ARTISTIC WORK: MODEL: HANDKNITTED GARMENTS: PROTOTYPE: OBJECTIVE SIMILARITY: INDEPENDENT SKILL, EFFORT AND LABOUR: ORIGINALITY: H.C.)

Brintons Ltd v. Feltex Furnishings of New Zealand Ltd (No. 1) (AUTHORISATION: INDEMNITY AND CONTRIBUTION: STRIKING OUT: H.C.)

Brintons Ltd v. Feltex Furnishings of New Zealand Ltd (No. 2) (INNOCENT INFRINGEMENT: KNOWLEDGE: MEASURE OF DAMAGES: LOSS OF PROFIT: CONVERSION DAMAGES: MEASURE OF CONTRIBUTION BY THIRD PARTY: H.C.)

Busby v. Thorne EMI Video Programmes Ltd (ANTON PILLER ORDER: PRIVILEGE AGAINST SELF-INCRIMINATION: SEARCH AND SEIZURE: JURISDICTION: CONDITIONS: C.A.)

Colonial Arms Motor Inn Ltd v. Twentieth Century-Fox Films Corp. (PRACTICE: ANTON PILLER: JURISDICTION: FORUM: C.A.)

Dominion Rent A. Car Ltd v. Budget Rent A. Car System (1970) Ltd (LICENCE: ACQUIESCENCE: LACHES: DELAY: INTERFERENCE WITH TRADE: UNFAIR TRADING: C.A.)

Engineering Dynamics Ltd v. Reid & Harrison (1980) Ltd (TEST: SUBSTANTIAL PART: INDIRECT COPYING: VERBAL AND VISUAL INSTRUCTIONS: CONVERSION DAMAGES: H.C.)

Fiscal Technology Co. Ltd v. Johnson (ADAPTATION INVOLVING SIGNIFICANT SKILL AND EXPERTISE: INJUNCTION: DELIVERY-UP: DAMAGES: APPROPRIATENESS OF EXEMPLARY DAMAGES: H.C.)

Green v. Broadcasting Corporation of New Zealand (PASSING OFF: U.K. TELEVISION PROGRAMME: *Opportunity Knocks*: LITERARY OR DRAMATIC WORK: FEATURES OF FOREIGN PROGRAMME COPIED: GOODWILL IN NEW ZEALAND: SCRIPTS: SUBSISTENCE: WRITING OR OTHER MATERIAL FORM: VIDEO TAPES: C.A.: P.C.)

Inglis v. Mayson (SUBSTANTIAL REPRODUCTION: DRAWINGS IN PATENT SPECIFICATION: H.C.)

International Business Machines Corporation v. Computer Imports Ltd (COMPUTER TECHNOLOGY: THREE-DIMENSIONAL REPRODUCTION OF CABINET AND INTERNAL LAYOUT OF PERSONAL COMPUTER AND BY COPYING OF COMPUTER PROGRAM: IMPORTATION AND SALE: H.C.)

Longman Group Ltd v. Carrington Technical Institite Board of Governors (COMPILATION OF EXTRACTS FROM BOOKS BY TUTOR AT TECHNICAL INSTITUTE: FAIR DEALING: ADMISSIBLE EVIDENCE TO DETERMINE: REASONABLE PROPORTION: H.C.: C.A.)

Mayceys Confectionery Ltd v. Beckmann (FLAGRANCY: CONVERSION DAMAGES: DAMAGES: ADDITIONAL DAMAGES: H.C.)

Mono Pumps (New Zealand) Ltd v. Amalgamated Pumps Ltd (INJUNCTION: ORIGINAL ARTISTIC WORK: WHETHER DRAWINGS ILLUSTRATING AN IDEA CAPABLE OF PROTECTION: H.C.)

Mono Pumps (N.Z.) Ltd v. Karinya Industries Ltd (LICENSEE OF OVERSEAS PATENT: IDEA AND EXPRESSION: INTERLOCUTORY INJUNCTION: H.C.)

PDL Packaging Ltd v. Labplas (N.Z.) Ltd (MOULD OF BOTTLE: H.C.)

Plix Products Ltd v. Frank M. Winstone (Merchants) (KIWI FRUIT "POCKET PACKS": PUBLIC LICENCE: INEVITABLE DESIGN: COMMISSIONED WORK: H.C.: C.A.)

Thornton Hall Manufacturing Ltd v. Shanton Apparel Ltd (ARTISTIC WORKS: ORIGINALITY: CAUSAL CONNECTION: DAMAGES: TIME FOR MAKING ELECTION BETWEEN ACCOUNT OF PROFITS OR DAMAGES: TRIAL LIMITED TO LIABILITY: INCIDENTAL FINDINGS OF "FLAGRANCY": WHETHER PRE-DETERMINATION OR BIAS FOR SUBSEQUENT DAMAGES TRIAL: C.A.)

Television N.Z. v. Newsmonitor Services Ltd (TELEVISION PROGRAMMES: RECORDING BY NEWS MONITORING SERVICE: TRANSCRIPTS: FAIR DEALING: IMPLIED LICENCE: H.C., C.A.)

Thorn EMI Video Programmes Ltd v. Kitching (ANTON PILLER PRACTICE: PRIVILEGE AGAINST SELF-INCRIMINATION: H.C.: C.A.)

Thornton Hall Manufacturing Ltd v. Shanton Apparel Ltd (ARTISTIC WORK: DRESS: SAMPLE: WHETHER THREE-DIMENSIONAL REPRODUCTION OF AN ORIGINAL ARTISTIC WORK: SUBSISTENCE: H.C.: C.A.)

Thornton Hall Manufacturing Ltd v. Shanton Apparel Ltd (No. 2) (SUBSISTENCE: SKETCHES, PATTERNS AND SAMPLE DRESS: ARTISTIC WORKS: ORIGINALITY: OWNERSHIP: H.C.)

Tony Blain Pty Ltd v. Splain (POP CONCERTS: ANTON PILLER ORDER AGAINST PERSONS UNKNOWN: H.C.)

Watson v. Dolmark Industries Ltd (COPYING OF PART OF BOOK: DEGREE OF ORIGINALITY: INTERIM INJUNCTION: H.C.)

Wellington Newspapers Ltd v. Dealers Guide Ltd (FLAGRANT COPYING: PUNITIVE OR EXEMPLARY DAMAGES: C.A.)

Wham-O Manufacturing Co. v. Lincoln Industries Ltd (PATENT DRAWINGS: ACQUIESCENCE: DAMAGES: H.C.: C.A.)

Wilson v. Broadcasting Corporation of New Zealand (FORMAT OR CONCEPT FOR A TELEVISION PROGRAMME: BREACH OF CONFIDENTIALITY: FEASIBILITY STUDY: EXEMPLARY DAMAGES: H.C.)

Injunction. *See* **Practice** (*Injunction*)

Innocent Infringement

Brintons Ltd v. Feltex Furnishings of New Zealand Ltd (No. 2) (KNOWLEDGE: MEASURE OF DAMAGES: LOSS OF PROFIT: CONVERSION DAMAGES: MEASURE OF CONTRIBUTION BY THIRD PARTY: H.C.)

Interim Injunction. *See* **Practice** (*Interlocutory or interim injunction*)

Interlocutory Injunction. *See* **Practice** (*Interlocutory or interim injunction*)

Joint Tortfeasors. *See* **Practice** (*Joint tortfeasors*)

Jurisdiction. *See* **Practice** (*Jurisdiction*)

Knowledge. *See* **Practice** (*Knowledge*)

Laches. *See* **Practice** (*Laches*)

Licence

Mono Pumps (New Zealand) Ltd v. Amalgamated Pumps Ltd (AGREEMENT: IMPLIED TERMS: H.C.)

Mono Pumps (N.Z.) Ltd v. Karinya Industries Ltd (INFRINGEMENT: LICENSEE OF OVERSEAS PATENT: IDEA AND EXPRESSION: INTERLOCUTORY INJUNCTION: H.C.)

Plix Products Ltd v. Frank M. Winstone (Merchants) (INFRINGEMENT: KIWI FRUIT "POCKET PACKS": PUBLIC LICENCE: INEVITABLE DESIGN: COMMISSIONED WORK: H.C.: C.A.)

Literary or Dramatic Work

International Business Machines Corporation v. Computer Imports Ltd (INFRINGEMENT: COMPUTER TECHNOLOGY: THREE-DIMENSIONAL REPRODUCTION OF CABINET AND INTERNAL LAYOUT OF PERSONAL COMPUTER AND BY COPYING OF COMPUTER PROGRAM: IMPORTATION AND SALE: TRANSFER OF LITERARY WORK: H.C.)

Television New Zealand Ltd v. Newsmonitor Services Ltd (INFRINGEMENT: TELEVISION BROADCASTS: SCRIPT OF NEWS: COPYING FOR PRIVATE PURPOSES: FAIR DEALING: PRIVATE RESEARCH OR STUDY: IMPLIED LICENCE: REPRODUCTION FOR JUDICIAL PROCEEDINGS: H.C., C.A.)

Loss of Profit. *See* **Practice** (*Loss of profit*)

Object Code. *See* **Computer Subjects**

Originality

Bonz Group (Pty) Ltd v. Cooke (INFRINGEMENT: ARTISTIC WORK: MODEL: HAND-KNITTED GARMENTS: PROTOTYPE: OBJECTIVE SIMILARITY: INDEPENDENT SKILL, EFFORT AND LABOUR: H.C.)

Thornton Hall Manufacturing Ltd v. Shanton Apparel Ltd (ARTISTIC WORKS: CAUSAL CONNECTION: C.A.)

Thornton Hall Manufacturing Ltd v. Shanton Apparel Ltd (No. 2) (SUBSISTENCE: SKETCHES, PATTERNS AND SAMPLE DRESS: ARTISTIC WORKS: H.C.)

Watson v. Dolmark Industries Ltd (INFRINGEMENT: COPYING OF PART OF BOOK: DEGREE OF ORIGINALITY: H.C.)

Ownership

Thornton Hall Manufacturing Ltd v. Shanton Apparel Ltd (No. 2) (SUBSISTENCE: SKETCHES, PATTERNS AND SAMPLE DRESS: ARTISTIC WORKS: ORIGINALITY: H.C.)

Parallel Importation

Samsung Electronics Co. Ltd v. ASDA Holdings Ltd (WORKS FROM NON-CONVENTION COUNTRY: EXCLUSIVE DISTRIBUTORSHIP: UNAUTHORISED IMPORTATION: H.C.)

Practice

Account of profits

Thornton Hall Manufacturing Ltd v. Shanton Apparel Ltd (INFRINGEMENT: TIME FOR MAKING ELECTION BETWEEN ACCOUNT OF PROFITS OR DAMAGES: TRIAL LIMITED TO LIABILITY: INCIDENTAL FINDINGS OF "FLAGRANCY": WHETHER PRE-DETERMINATION OR BIAS FOR SUBSEQUENT DAMAGES TRIAL: C.A.)

Acquiescence

Dominion Rent A Car Ltd v. Budget Rent A Car System (1970) Ltd (INFRINGEMENT: LICENCE: LACHES: DELAY: C.A.)

Wham-O Manufacturing Co. v. Lincoln Industries Ltd (INFRINGEMENT: PATENT DRAWINGS: DAMAGES: H.C.: C.A.)

Anton Piller order

Anvil Jewellery Ltd v. Riva Ridge Holdings Ltd (ASSIGNMENT: AGREEMENT FOR SALE OF ASSETS: CONSTRUCTION: INTERLOCUTORY INJUNCTION: DISCHARGE: H.C.)

Busby v. Thorne EMI Video Programmes Ltd (PRIVILEGE AGAINST SELF-INCRIMINATION: INFRINGEMENT: SEARCH AND SEIZURE: JURISDICTION: CONDITIONS: C.A.)

Colonial Arms Motor Inn Ltd v. Twentieth Century-Fox Films Corp. (INFRINGEMENT: JURISDICTION: FORUM: C.A.)

Thorn EMI Video Programmes Ltd v. Kitching (INFRINGEMENT: PRIVILEGE AGAINST SELF-INCRIMINATION: H.C.: C.A.)

Tony Blain Pty Ltd v. Splain (PASSING OFF: INFRINGEMENT: POP CONCERTS: ANTON PILLER ORDER AGAINST PERSONS UNKNOWN: H.C.)

Balance of convenience

Pop-A-Shot Inc. v. Filtration and Pumping (Commercial) Ltd (IMPECUNIOUS DEFENDANT: H.C.)

Consent order

Franklin Machinery Ltd v. Albany Farm Centre Ltd (INTERLOCUTORY INJUNCTION: APPLICATION FOR DECLARATION THAT REVISED PRODUCTS FELL OUTSIDE TERMS OF ORDER OR VARIATION OF ORDER: PRINCIPLES TO BE APPLIED: H.C.)

Conversion damages

Brintons Ltd v. Feltex Furnishings of New Zealand Ltd (No. 2) (INNOCENT INFRINGEMENT: KNOWLEDGE: MEASURE OF DAMAGES: LOSS OF PROFIT: MEASURE OF CONTRIBUTION BY THIRD PARTY: H.C.)

Crystal Glass Industries Ltd v. Alwinco Products Ltd (INFRINGEMENT: THREE-DIMENSIONAL REPRODUCTION: INDIRECT COPYING: JOINT TORTFEASORS: C.A.)

Engineering Dynamics Ltd v. Reid & Harrison (1980) Ltd (INFRINGEMENT: TEST: SUBSTANTIAL PART: INDIRECT COPYING: VERBAL AND VISUAL INSTRUCTIONS: H.C.)

Damages

Brintons Ltd v. Feltex Furnishings of New Zealand Ltd (No. 2) (INNOCENT INFRINGEMENT: KNOWLEDGE: MEASURE OF DAMAGES: LOSS OF PROFIT: CONVERSION DAMAGES: MEASURE OF CONTRIBUTION BY THIRD PARTY: H.C.)

Mayceys Confectionery Ltd v. Beckmann (INFRINGEMENT: FLAGRANCY: CONVERSION DAMAGES: ADDITIONAL DAMAGES: H.C.)

Thornton Hall Manufacturing Ltd v. Shanton Apparel Ltd (INFRINGEMENT: TIME FOR MAKING ELECTION BETWEEN ACCOUNT OF PROFITS OR DAMAGES: TRIAL LIMITED TO LIABILITY: INCIDENTAL FINDINGS OF FLAGRANCY: WHETHER PRE-DETERMINATION OR BIAS FOR SUBSEQUENT DAMAGES TRIAL: C.A.)

Wellington Newspapers Ltd v. Dealers Guide Ltd (INFRINGEMENT: FLAGRANT COPYING: PUNITIVE OR EXEMPLARY DAMAGES: C.A.)

Wham-O Manufacturing Co. v. Lincoln Industries Ltd (INFRINGEMENT: PATENT DRAWINGS: ACQUIESCENCE: H.C.: C.A.)

Wilson v. Broadcasting Corporation of New Zealand (INFRINGEMENT: FORMAT OR CONCEPT FOR A TELEVISION PROGRAMME: BREACH OF CONFIDENTIALITY: FEASIBILITY STUDY: EXEMPLARY DAMAGES: H.C.)

Declaration

Franklin Machinery Ltd v. Albany Farm Centre Ltd (APPLICATION FOR DECLARATION THAT REVISED PRODUCTS FELL OUTSIDE TERMS OF CONSENT ORDER OR VARIATION OF ORDER: H.C.)

Delay

Dominion Rent A Car Ltd v. Budget Rent A. Car System (1970) Ltd (INFRINGEMENT: LICENCE: ACQUIESCENCE: LACHES: C.A.)

Delivery up

Fiscal Technology Co. Ltd v. Johnson (INFRINGEMENT: ADAPTATION INVOLVING SIGNIFICANT SKILL AND EXPERTISE: RELIEF: INJUNCTION: H.C.)

Evidence

Longman Group Ltd v. Carrington Technical Institte Board of Governors (ADMISSIBLE EVIDENCE TO DETERMINE FAIR DEALING: H.C.: C.A.)

Forum

Colonial Arms Motor Inn Ltd v. Twentieth Century-Fox Films Corp. (INFRINGEMENT: ANTON PILLER: JURISDICTION: C.A.)

Injunction

Atkinson Footwear Ltd v. Hodgskin International Services (INFRINGEMENT: INTERLOCUTORY INJUNCTION SOUGHT TO RESTRAIN ACTS IN NEW ZEALAND AND AUSTRALIA: JURISDICTION *in personam, in rem*: H.C.)

Fiscal Technology Co. Ltd v. Johnson (INFRINGEMENT: ADAPTATION INVOLVING SIGNIFICANT SKILL AND EXPERTISE: DELIVERY UP: H.C.)

Mono Pumps (New Zealand) Ltd v. Amalgamated Pumps Ltd (INFRINGEMENT: ORIGINAL ARTISTIC WORK: WHETHER DRAWINGS ILLUSTRATING AN IDEA CAPABLE OF PROTECTION: H.C.)

Interlocutory or interim injunction

Anvil Jewellery Ltd v. Riva Ridge Holdings Ltd (SUBSISTENCE: ASSIGNMENT: AGREEMENT FOR SALE OF ASSETS: CONSTRUCTION: ANTON PILLER ORDERS: DISCHARGE: H.C.)

Bleiman v. News Media (Auckland) Ltd (INFRINGEMENT: COMPETITION BASED ON RESULTS OF SPORTING EVENTS: COPYING: SUBSTANTIAL PART: TEST FOR ASSESSING BREACH: C.A.)

Pop-A-Shot Inc. v. Filtration and Pumping (Commercial) Ltd (ARTISTIC WORKS: REPRODUCTION: BALANCE OF CONVENIENCE: IMPECUNIOUS DEFENDANT: H.C.)

Joint tortfeasors

Crystal Glass Industries Ltd v. Alwinco Products Ltd (INFRINGEMENT: THREE-DIMENSIONAL REPRODUCTION: INDIRECT COPYING: CONVERSION DAMAGES: C.A.)

Jurisdiction

Atkinson Footwear Ltd v. Hodgskin International Services (INFRINGEMENT: INTERLOCUTORY INJUNCTION SOUGHT TO RESTRAIN ACTS IN NEW ZEALAND AND AUSTRALIA: JURISDICTION *in personam, in rem*: H.C.)

Colonial Arms Motor Inn Ltd v. Twentieth Century-Fox Films Corp. (INFRINGEMENT: ANTON PILLER: FORUM: C.A.)

Knowledge

Brintons Ltd v. Feltex Furnishings of New Zealand Ltd (No. 2) (INNOCENT INFRINGEMENT: H.C.)

Laches

Dominion Rent A. Car Ltd v. Budget Rent A. Car System (1970) Ltd (INFRINGEMENT: LICENCE: ACQUIESCENCE: DELAY: C.A.)

Loss of profit

Brintons Ltd v. Feltex Furnishings of New Zealand Ltd (No. 2) (INNOCENT INFRINGEMENT: KNOWLEDGE: MEASURE OF DAMAGES: H.C.)

Privilege against self-incrimination

Busby v. Thorne EMI Video Programmes Ltd (ANTON PILLER ORDER: INFRINGEMENT: SEARCH AND SEIZURE: JURISDICTION: CONDITIONS: C.A.)

Thorn EMI Video Programmes Ltd v. Kitching (INFRINGEMENT: ANTON PILLER PRACTICE: H.C.: C.A.)

Search and seizure

Busby v. Thorne EMI Video Programmes Ltd (ANTON PILLER ORDER: PRIVILEGE AGAINST SELF-INCRIMINATION: INFRINGEMENT: JURISDICTION: CONDITIONS: C.A.)

Striking out

Brintons Ltd v. Feltex Furnishings of New Zealand Ltd (No. 1) (INFRINGEMENT: AUTHORISATION: INDEMNITY AND CONTRIBUTION: H.C.)

Privilege Against Self-incrimination. *See* **Practice** (*Privilege against self-incrimination*)

Prototype

Bonz Group (Pty) Ltd v. Cooke (INFRINGEMENT: ARTISTIC WORK: MODEL: HAND-KNITTED GARMENTS: OBJECTIVE SIMILARITY: INDEPENDENT SKILL, EFFORT AND LABOUR: ORIGINALITY: H.C.)

Research or Private Study

Longman Group Ltd v. Carrington Technical Institute Board of Governers (INFRINGEMENT: SUBSTANTIALITY OF REPRODUCTION: FAIR DEALING: USE BY AGENT OF CROWN: H.C.)
Television New Zealand Ltd v. Newsmonitor Services Ltd (INFRINGEMENT: TELEVISION BROADCASTS: SCRIPT OF NEWS: LITERARY COPYRIGHT: DRAMATIC COPYRIGHT: FAIR DEALING: IMPLIED LICENCE: REPRODUCTION FOR JUDICIAL PROCEEDINGS: C.A.)

Search and Seizure. *See* **Practice** (*Search and seizure*)

Source Code. *See* **Computer Subjects**

Striking Out. *See* **Practice** (*Striking out*)

Subsistence

Anvil Jewellery Ltd v. Riva Ridge Holdings Ltd (H.C.)
Green v. Broadcasting Corporation of New Zealand (INFRINGEMENT: U.K. TELEVISION PROGRAMME: *Opportunity Knocks*: LITERARY OR DRAMATIC WORK: FEATURES OF FOREIGN PROGRAMME: C.A.: P.C.)
Thornton Hall Manufacturing Ltd v. Shanton Apparel Ltd (INFRINGEMENT: ARTISTIC WORK: DRESS: SAMPLE: H.C.: C.A.)
Thornton Hall Manufacturing Ltd v. Shanton Apparel Ltd (No. 2) (SKETCHES, PATTERNS AND SAMPLE DRESS: ARTISTIC WORKS: ORIGINALITY: H.C.)

Substantial Part

Bleiman v. News Media (Auckland) Ltd (INFRINGEMENT: COMPETITION BASED ON RESULTS OF SPORTING EVENTS: COPYING: TEST FOR ASSESSING BREACH: INTERIM INJUNCTION: C.A.)
Engineering Dynamics Ltd v. Reid & Harrison (1980) Ltd (INFRINGEMENT: TEST: INDIRECT COPYING: VERBAL AND VISUAL INSTRUCTIONS: H.C.)

Three-dimensional Reproduction

Crystal Glass Industries Ltd v. Alwinco Products Ltd (INFRINGEMENT: INDIRECT COPYING: JOINT TORTFEASORS: CONVERSION DAMAGES: C.A.)

International Business Machines Corporation v. Computer Imports Ltd (INFRINGEMENT: REPRODUCTION OF CABINET AND INTERNAL LAYOUT OF PERSONAL COMPUTER: IMPORTATION AND SALE: H.C.)

Thornton Hall Manufacturing Ltd v. Shanton Apparel Ltd (INFRINGEMENT: ARTISTIC WORK: DRESS: SAMPLE: SUBSISTENCE OF COPYRIGHT: H.C.: C.A.)

Video Tapes

Green v. Broadcasting Corporation of New Zealand (INFRINGEMENT: U.K. TELEVISION PROGRAMME: *Opportunity Knocks*: SUBSISTENCE OF COPYRIGHT: WRITING OR OTHER MATERIAL FORM: C.A.: P.C.)

Writing or Other Material Form

Green v. Broadcasting Corporation of New Zealand (INFRINGEMENT: U.K. TELEVISION PROGRAMME: *Opportunity Knocks:* SUBSISTENCE OF COPYRIGHT: VIDEO TAPES: C.A.: P.C.)

Design

Commissioned Work

Plix Products Ltd v. Frank M. Winstone (Merchants) (COPYRIGHT: INFRINGEMENT: KIWI FRUIT "POCKET PACKS": PUBLIC LICENCE: INEVITABLE DESIGN: H.C.: C.A.)

Distinctiveness

Klissers Farmhouse Bakeries Ltd v. Harvest Bakeries Ltd (PASSING OFF: MISREPRESENTATION: GET-UP: BREAD BAGS: ELEMENTS COMMON TO TRADE: C.A.)

Elements Common to Trade

Klissers Farmhouse Bakeries Ltd v. Harvest Bakeries Ltd (PASSING OFF: MISREPRESENTATION: GET-UP: DISTINCTIVENESS: BREAD BAGS: DESIGN: ELEMENTS COMMON TO TRADE: PROTECTION WITHIN LIMITED GEOGRAPHICAL AREA: C.A.)

Industrial Designs, Protection of

Franklin Machinery Ltd v. Albany Farm Centre Ltd (COPYRIGHT: *Obiter* OBSERVATIONS ON EXTENT TO WHICH COPYRIGHT HAS BEEN AND SHOULD BE USED TO PROTECT INDUSTRIAL DESIGNS IN NEW ZEALAND: H.C.)

Inevitable Design

Plix Products Ltd v. Frank M. Winstone (Merchants) (COPYRIGHT: INFRINGEMENT: KIWI FRUIT "POCKET PACKS": PUBLIC LICENCE: COMMISSIONED WORK: H.C.: C.A.)

1051

Infringement

UPL Group Ltd v. Dux Engineers Ltd (TESTS: DEGREE OF NOVELTY ORIGINALITY RELEVANT TO SCOPE OF DESIGNS: WHETHER INFRINGEMENT: C.A.)

Novelty

UPL Group Ltd v. Dux Engineers Ltd (INFRINGEMENT: TESTS: DEGREE OF NOVELTY ORIGINALITY RELEVANT TO SCOPE OF DESIGNS: WHETHER INFRINGEMENT: C.A.)

Originality

Lewis & Co. Ltd v. Trade Winds Furniture Ltd (REGISTRABILITY: H.C.)

Registrability

Lewis & Co. Ltd v. Trade Winds Furniture Ltd (ORIGINALITY: H.C.)
Mono Pumps (New Zealand) Ltd v. Amalgamated Pumps Ltd (COPYRIGHT: INFRINGEMENT: INJUNCTION: ORIGINAL ARTISTIC WORK: WHETHER DRAWINGS ILLUSTRATING AN IDEA CAPABLE OF COPYRIGHT PROTECTION: LICENSING AGREEMENT: IMPLIED TERMS: H.C.)

Passing Off

Anton Piller Order. *See* **Practice** (*Anton Piller order*)

Balance of Convenience. *See* **Practice** (*Balance of convenience*)

Breach of Injunction. *See* **Practice** (*Breach of injunction*)

Champagne

Wineworths Group Ltd v. Comite Interprofessional du Vin de Champagne (WHETHER CHAMPAGNE GENERIC IN NEW ZEALAND FOR SPARKLING WINES WHEREVER PRODUCED: PROPRIETARY RIGHT IN NAME: C.A.)

Coloured Capsules

Bayer AG v. Pacific Pharmaceuticals Ltd (GET-UP: DISTINCTIVENESS: INTERLOCUTORY INJUNCTION: H.C.)

Common Field of Activity

Taylor Bros Ltd v. Taylors Group Ltd (COMPANY NAME: TRADE PRACTICES: MISLEADING OR DECEPTIVE CONDUCT: SIMILAR TRADES: DIFFERENT GEOGRAPHICAL AREAS OF OPERATION: DRYCLEANING LINEN HIRE: H.C.: C.A.)

Common Features, Compilation of

Artifakts Design Group Ltd v. N.P. Rigg Ltd (COPYRIGHT: COMPILATION OF COMMON FEATURES: GOODWILL IN GET-UP: H.C.)

Company Name. *See also under* **Trade Mark and Trade Name**

Esanda Ltd v. Esanda Finance Ltd (INTERIM INJUNCTION: OVERSEAS REPUTATION: H.C.)

Taylor Bros Ltd v. Taylors Group Ltd (TRADE PRACTICES: MISLEADING OR DECEPTIVE CONDUCT: SIMILAR TRADES: DIFFERENT GEOGRAPHICAL AREAS OF OPERATION: DRYCLEANING LINEN HIRE: WHETHER COMMON FIELD OF ACTIVITY: H.C.: C.A.)

Confusion

Taylor Bros Ltd v. Taylors Group Ltd (FAIR TRADING ACT PROCEEDINGS: CONSTRUCTION OF INJUNCTION: BREACH: INTERIM INJUNCTION PERMITTING RESPONDENTS TO TRADE UNDER THE NAME "TAYLORS" PROVIDED CERTAIN CONDITIONS MET: SUBSEQUENT PERMANENT INJUNCTION RESTRAINING TRADING "UNDER AND BY REFERENCE" TO "TAYLORS": RESPONDENTS TRADING AS "LAYTONS" IN MANNER AIMED AT CREATING IMPRESSION OF CONTINUITY AND WHILE CONTINUING TO USE "TAYLORS" ON GOODS HIRED TO CUSTOMERS: WHETHER USE OF "LAYTONS" IN THE CIRCUMSTANCES A BREACH OF THE PERMANENT INJUNCTION: NO CONTINUING CONFUSION: REMEDIES: C.A.)

Construction of Injunction. *See* Practice *(Construction of injunction)*

Damages. *See* Practice *(Damages)*

Descriptive Trade Mark. *See* Trade Marks

Distinctiveness

Bayer AG v. Pacific Pharmaceuticals Ltd (GET-UP: COLOURED CAPSULES: INTERLOCUTORY INJUNCTION: H.C.)
Blue Boats Ltd v. Gulf Tourist Services (1982) Ltd (SIMILARLY-COLOURED HARBOUR SHIPS: OTHER SHIPS SIMILARLY COLOURED: WHETHER DISTINCTIVE GET-UP: H.C.)
Klissers Farmhouse Bakeries Ltd v. Harvest Bakeries Ltd (MISREPRESENTATION: GET-UP: BREAD BAGS: DESIGN: ELEMENTS COMMON TO TRADE: PROTECTION WITHIN LIMITED GEOGRAPHICAL AREA: C.A.)

Duty to Account

Watson v. Dolmark Industries Ltd (WHETHER CAUSE OF ACTION ESTABLISHED: FIDUCIARY DUTY: LICENSOR'S MOULDS AND DIES BAILED TO LICENSEE: USE OF DIES FOR LICENSEE'S OWN PURPOSES: BREACH OF DUTY: UNFAIR SPRINGBOARD ADVANTAGE: LIABILITY OF SUBSTANTIAL PROPRIETOR OF LICENSEE: C.A.)

Elements or Features Common to Trade

Klissers Farmhouse Bakeries Ltd v. Harvest Bakeries Ltd (No. 2) (COPYRIGHT: H.C.)
Klissers Farmhouse Bakeries Ltd v. Harvest Bakeries Ltd (MISREPRESENTATION: GET-UP: DISTINCTIVENESS: BREAD BAGS: DESIGN: PROTECTION WITHIN LIMITED GEOGRAPHICAL AREA: C.A.)

Elements of Passing Off

Tot Toys Ltd v. Mitchell (TRADE MARKS: KIWI BEE/BUZZY BEE: ELEMENTS OF PASSING OFF: TRADE MARK: ASSIGNABILITY OF MARK: H.C.)

Evidence. *See* **Practice** (*Evidence*)

Features Common to Trade. *See* **Elements or Features Common to Trade**

Foreign Plaintiff. *See* **Practice** (*Foreign plaintiff*)

Geographical Area, Protection Within

Klissers Farmhouse Bakeries Ltd v. Harvest Bakeries Ltd (C.A.)
Prudential Building & Investment Society of Canterbury v. Prudential Assurance Co.
    of N.Z. Ltd (INSURANCE COMPANY WHICH OPERATED NATIONALLY AND A
    BUILDING SOCIETY WHICH OPERATED PROVINCIALLY BOTH USED THE NAME
    PRUDENTIAL: GEOGRAPHICAL EXPANSION OF BUSINESS AND EMPHASIS
    ALTERED ON PART OF NAME: C.A.)

Geographical or Descriptive name

Totara Vineyards Sye Ltd v. Villa Maria Estate Ltd (INTERIM INJUNCTION: H.C.)

Get-up

Artifakts Design Group Ltd v. N.P. Rigg Ltd (COPYRIGHT: COMPILATION OF
    COMMON FEATURES: GOODWILL IN GET-UP: H.C.)
Bars Products International Ltd v. Holt Lloyd Ltd (MISLEADING AND DECEPTIVE
    CONDUCT: WINDSCREEN CLEANERS: INTERLOCUTORY INJUNCTION:
    RECALL OF PRODUCT DISTRIBUTED: H.C.)
Bayer AG v. Pacific Pharmaceuticals Ltd (COLOURED CAPSULES: DISTINCTIVENESS:
    INTERLOCUTORY INJUNCTION: H.C.)
Blue Boats Ltd v. Gulf Tourist Services (1982) Ltd (SIMILARLY-COLOURED
    HARBOUR SHIPS: OTHER SHIPS SIMILARLY COLOURED: WHETHER
    DISTINCTIVE GET-UP: H.C.)
Plix Products Ltd v. Frank M. Winstone (Merchants) (COPYRIGHT: INFRINGEMENT:
    KIWI FRUIT "POCKET PACKS": PUBLIC LICENCE: INEVITABLE DESIGN:
    COMMISSIONED WORK: H.C.: C.A.)

Goodwill

Artifakts Design Group Ltd v. N.P. Rigg Ltd (COPYRIGHT: COMPILATION OF
    COMMON FEATURES: GOODWILL IN GET-UP: H.C.)
Auckland Harbour Cruise Co. Ltd v. Fullers Captain Cook Cruises Ltd (TOURIST
    YACHT CRUISES: SAIL COLOURS AND VESSELS' NAMES SIMILAR: TERRITORIAL
    NATURE OF GOODWILL: INTERIM INJUNCTION: H.C.)
Green v. Broadcasting Corporation of New Zealand (COPYRIGHT: INFRINGEMENT:
    U.K. TELEVISION PROGRAMME: *Opportunity Knocks*: GOODWILL IN NEW
    ZEALAND: H.C.: C.A.: P.C.)
Pop-A-Shot Inc. v. Filtration and Pumping (Commercial) Ltd (COPYRIGHT:
    ARTISTIC WORKS: REPRODUCTION: MISLEADING AND DECEPTIVE CONDUCT:
    GOODWILL AND REPUTATION: H.C.)

Interim Injunction or Interlocutory Injunction. *See* **Practice** (*Interim injunction or interlocutory injunction*)

Breach of injunction

Taylor Bros Ltd v. Taylors Group Ltd (CONSTRUCTION OF INJUNCTION: BREACH: REMEDIES: C.A.)

Construction of injunction

Taylor Bros Ltd v. Taylors Group Ltd (BREACH: REMEDIES: C.A.)

Damages

Noel Leeming Television Ltd v. Noel's Appliance Centre Ltd (PASSING OFF: MISREPRESENTATION: CONFUSION: REPUTATION: OWN NAME: SURVEY EVIDENCE: INJUNCTION: DAMAGES: H.C.)

Evidence

Levi Strauss & Co. v. Kimbyr Investments Ltd (EXPERT EVIDENCE: SURVEY EVIDENCE: ADMISSIBILITY: H.C.)
Noel Leeming Television Ltd v. Noel's Appliance Centre Ltd (SURVEY EVIDENCE: H.C.)

Foreign plaintiff

Crusader Oil N.L. v. Crusader Minerals N.Z. Ltd (REPUTATION: H.C.)
Dominion Rent A Car Ltd v. Budget Rent A Car System (1970) Ltd (INTERNATIONAL REPUTATION: SHARED REPUTATION: C.A.)

Interim injunction or interlocutory injunction

Auckland Harbour Cruise Co. Ltd v. Fullers Captain Cook Cruises Ltd (TOURIST YACHT CRUISES: SAIL COLOURS AND VESSELS' NAMES SIMILAR: TERRITORIAL NATURE OF GOODWILL: H.C.)
Bars Products International Ltd v. Holt Lloyd Ltd (WINDSCREEN CLEANERS: RECALL OF PRODUCT DISTRIBUTED: H.C.)
Bayer AG v. Pacific Pharmaceuticals Ltd (COLOURED CAPSULES: DISTINCTIVENESS: H.C.)
Compusales Holdings N.Z. Ltd v. Sperry Ltd & Burroughs Ltd (COMPUTER DEVELOPMENT COMPANIES: TRADE NAME: UNISYS: UNDERTAKING AS TO DAMAGES: H.C.)
Coronet Property Group Ltd v. Coronet Equities Ltd (SERIOUS QUESTION TO BE TRIED: BALANCE OF CONVENIENCE: PARTIES' ACTIVITIES NOT IN COMPETITION WITH EACH OTHER: H.C.)
Esanda Ltd v. Esanda Finance Ltd (COMPANY NAME: OVERSEAS REPUTATION: H.C.)
Griffin & Sons Ltd v. R. (1988) Ltd (SIMILAR PACKAGING FOR CONFECTIONERY: H.C.)
Klissers Farmhouse Bakeries Ltd v. Harvest Bakeries Ltd (H.C.: C.A.)
Taylor Bros Ltd v. Taylors Group Ltd (CONSTRUCTION OF INJUNCTION: BREACH: REMEDIES: C.A.)
Totara Vineyards Sye Ltd v. Villa Maria Estate Ltd (GEOGRAPHICAL OF DESCRIPTIVE NAME: H.C.)

Serious question to be tried

Coronet Property Group Ltd v. Coronet Equities Ltd (INTERIM INJUNCTION: BALANCE OF CONVENIENCE: PARTIES' ACTIVITIES NOT IN COMPETITION WITH EACH OTHER: H.C.)

Survey evidence

Noel Leeming Television Ltd v. Noel's Appliance Centre Ltd (H.C.)

Undertaking as to damages

Compusales Holdings N.Z. Ltd v. Sperry Ltd & Burroughs Ltd (H.C.)

Recall of Product

Bars Products International Ltd v. Holt Lloyd Ltd (WINDSCREEN CLEANERS: INTERLOCUTORY INJUNCTION: H.C.)

Reputation

Crusader Oil N.L. v. Crusader Minerals N.Z. Ltd (FOREIGN PLAINTIFF: REPUTATION: H.C.)

Dominion Rent A Car Ltd v. Budget Rent A Car System (1970) Ltd (FOREIGN PLAINTIFF: INTERNATIONAL REPUTATION: SHARED REPUTATION: C.A.)

Esanda Ltd v. Esanda Finance Ltd (PASSING OFF: COMPANY NAME: INTERIM INJUNCTION: OVERSEAS REPUTATION: H.C.)

Noel Leeming Television Ltd v. Noel's Appliance Centre Ltd (MISREPRESENTATION: CONFUSION: OWN NAME: SURVEY EVIDENCE: H.C.)

Pop-A-Shot Inc. v. Filtration and Pumping (Commercial) Ltd (GOODWILL AND REPUTATION: H.C.)

Sail Colours, Vessels' Names and Ships' Colours

Auckland Harbour Cruise Co. Ltd v. Fullers Captain Cook Cruises Ltd (TOURIST YACHT CRUISES: SAIL COLOURS AND VESSELS' NAMES SIMILAR: TERRITORIAL NATURE OF GOODWILL: H.C.)

Blue Boats Ltd v. Gulf Tourist Services (1982) Ltd (SIMILARLY-COLOURED HARBOUR SHIPS: OTHER SHIPS SIMILARLY COLOURED: WHETHER DISTINCTIVE GET-UP: H.C.)

Serious Question to be Tried. *See* Practice (*Serious question to be tried*)

Shared Reputation

Dominion Rent A Car Ltd v. Budget Rent A Car System (1970) Ltd (FOREIGN PLAINTIFF: INTERNATIONAL REPUTATION: SHARED REPUTATION: C.A.)

Status Quo

Franklin International Export Ltd v. Wattie Exports Ltd (INJUNCTION AGAINST: WHAT QUALIFIES AS STATUS QUO: WHETHER GET-UP SUFFICIENTLY RESEMBLES THAT OF PLAINTIFF: H.C.)

Survey Evidence. *See* Practice (*Survey evidence*)

Tabs on Jeans Pockets. *See* Labels

Television Programme

Green v. Broadcasting Corp. of N.Z. (TV PRODUCTION: INTERNATIONAL GOODWILL: H.C.)

Green v. Broadcasting Corporation of New Zealand (INFRINGEMENT: PASSING OFF: U.K. TV PROGRAMME: *Opportunity Knocks*: LITERARY OR DRAMATIC WORK: FEATURES OF FOREIGN PROGRAMME COPIED: GOODWILL IN NEW ZEALAND: C.A.: P.C.)

Territorial Nature of Goodwill. *See* **Goodwill**

Trade Mark or Trade Name

Compusales Holdings N.Z. Ltd v. Sperry Ltd & Burroughs Ltd (COMPUTER DEVELOPMENT COMPANIES: UNISYS: H.C.)

Levi Strauss & Co. v. Kimbyr Investments Ltd (TABS ON JEANS POCKETS: H.C.)

Levi Strauss & Co. v. Robertsons Ltd (GET-UP AND LABELLING OF JEANS: H.C.)

Shotover Gorge Jet Boats Ltd v. Marine Enterprises Ltd (MARK DESCRIPTIVE OF SERVICE: SECONDARY MEANING: H.C.)

Taylor Bros Ltd v. Taylors Group Ltd (INTERIM INJUNCTION PERMITTING RESPONDENTS TO TRADE UNDER THE NAME "TAYLORS" PROVIDED CERTAIN CONDITIONS MET: SUBSEQUENT PERMANENT INJUNCTION RESTRAINING TRADING "UNDER AND BY REFERENCE" TO "TAYLORS": RESPONDENTS TRADING AS "LAYTONS" IN MANNER AIMED AT CREATING IMPRESSION OF CONTINUITY AND WHILE CONTINUING TO USE "TAYLORS" ON GOODS HIRED TO CUSTOMERS: WHETHER USE OF "LAYTONS" IN THE CIRCUMSTANCES A BREACH OF THE PERMANENT INJUNCTION: NO CONTINUING CONFUSION: REMEDIES: C.A.)

Taylor Bros Ltd v. Taylors Group Ltd (COMPANY NAME: TRADE PRACTICES: MISLEADING OR DECEPTIVE CONDUCT: SIMILAR TRADES: DIFFERENT GEOGRAPHICAL AREAS OF OPERATION: DRYCLEANING LINEN HIRE: WHETHER COMMON FIELD OF ACTIVITY: H.C.: C.A.)

Tot Toys Ltd v. Mitchell (KIWI BEE/BUZZY BEE: ELEMENTS OF PASSING OFF: ASSIGNABILITY OF MARK: H.C.)

Wineworths Group Ltd v. Comite Interprofessional du Vin de Champagne (WHETHER CHAMPAGNE GENERIC IN NEW ZEALAND FOR SPARKLING WINES WHEREVER PRODUCED: PROPRIETARY RIGHT IN NAME: C.A.)

Undertaking as to Damages. *See* **Practice** *(Undertaking as to damages)*

Use of Own Name

Noel Leeming Television Ltd v. Noel's Appliance Centre Ltd (MISREPRESENTATION: CONFUSION: REPUTATION: SURVEY EVIDENCE: INJUNCTION: DAMAGES: H.C.)

Patents

Adequate Remuneration. *See* **Extension**

Appeal. *See* **Practice** *(Appeal)*

Application

Wellcome Foundation Ltd v. Commissioner of Patents (NEW USE OF KNOWN DRUG: TREATMENT: C.A.)

Douglas Pharmaceuticals Ltd v. Ciba-Geigy AG (CELOTEX CONDITIONS: APPLICATION IN NEW ZEALAND: PROTECTION AGAINST CLAIMS OF INFRINGEMENT BETWEEN EXPIRY OF PATENT AND ORDER EXTENDING IT: INADEQUATE REMUNERATION: EXTENSION: RELEVANCE OF FOREIGN REMUNERATION: C.A.)

Glaxo Group Ltd v. Commissioner of Patents: (COMPULSORY LICENCE: PRIMA FACIE CASE: JUDICIAL REVIEW: EVIDENCE FOR FINDINGS: C.A.)

Celotex Conditions

Douglas Pharmaceuticals Ltd v. Ciba-Geigy AG (APPLICATION IN NEW ZEALAND: PROTECTION AGAINST CLAIMS OF INFRINGEMENT BETWEEN EXPIRY OF PATENT AND ORDER EXTENDING IT: INADEQUATE REMUNERATION: EXTENSION: RELEVANCE OF FOREIGN REMUNERATION: C.A.)

Compulsory Licence

Glaxo Group Ltd v. Commissioner of Patents: (APPLICATION: PRIMA FACIE CASE: JUDICIAL REVIEW: EVIDENCE FOR FINDINGS: C.A.)

Confidentiality. *See* **Practice** (*Confidentiality*)

Discovery. *See* **Practice** (*Discovery*)

Discretion. *See* **Practice** (*Discretion*)

Drawings in Specification, Copyright in

Inglis v. Mayson (H.C.)
Wham-O Manufacturing Co. v. Lincoln Industries Ltd (HC: C.A.)

Evidence. *See* **Practice** (*Evidence*)

Exceptional Case. *See* **Extension**

Experimental Use

Monsanto Co. v. Stauffer Chemical Co. (N.Z.) (INFRINGEMENT: INTERLOCUTORY RELIEF: H.C.)

Expiry

Smith Kline & French Laboratories Ltd v. Attorney-General (INFRINGEMENT: IMPORTATION: SUBMISSION TO GOVERNMENT BODY FOR APPROVAL AFTER EXPIRY: WHETHER SUBMISSION "USE": C.A.)

Extension

Ciba-Geigy AG v. Douglas Pharmaceuticals Ltd (APPEAL FROM REFUSAL: ADEQUATE REMUNERATION: NOTIONAL ROYALTY: ONUS OF PROOF: WORLDWIDE PROFITS: WHETHER EXCEPTIONAL CASE: H.C.)
Douglas Pharmaceuticals Ltd v. Ciba-Geigy AG (PROTECTION AGAINST CLAIMS OF INFRINGEMENT BETWEEN EXPIRY OF PATENT AND ORDER EXTENDING IT: INADEQUATE REMUNERATION: RELEVANCE OF FOREIGN REMUNERATION: C.A.)
E.R. Squibb & Sons Inc. v. Pacific Pharmaceuticals Ltd (FACTORS RELEVANT: ADEQUATE REMUNERATION OF: RELATIONSHIP OF NATURE AND MERITS OF INVENTION TO THE PUBLIC GOOD: H.C.)
Hassle (A.B.) v. Pacific Pharmaceuticals Ltd (DISCOVERY: CONFIDENTIALITY: FINANCIAL INFORMATION: PROFESSIONAL PRIVILEGE: H.C.)
Merck & Co. Inc. v. Pacific Pharmaceuticals Ltd (INADEQUATE REMUNERATION: OPPOSITION: NOTICE: ONUS OF PROOF: H.C.)
Merrell Dow Pharmaceuticals Inc. (LOST TIME IN EXPLOITATION: NO FAULT OF PATENTEE: EFFECT OF DELAYS IN REGULATORY APPROVAL: H.C.)

Pacific Pharmaceuticals Ltd v. Merck & Co. Inc. (INADEQUATE REMUNERATION: DISCRETION: H.C.)

False Suggestion

Dow Chemical Co. v. Ishihara Sangyo Kaisha Ltd (REVOCATION: PARTICULARS OF OBJECTION: APPLICATION TO STRIKE OUT: INSUFFICIENCY: H.C.)

Foreign Remuneration. *See* **Extension**

Importation

Smith Kline & French Laboratories Ltd v. Attorney-General (N.Z.) (INFRINGEMENT: IMPORTATION OF SAMPLE OF INFRINGING DRUG SOLELY FOR PURPOSE OF APPLYING FOR HEALTH DEPARTMENT APPROVAL FOR DISTRIBUTION: C.A.)

Smith Kline and French Laboratories Ltd v. Douglas Pharmaceuticals Ltd (INFRINGEMENT: CIMETIDINE: IMPORT OF SAMPLE FOR PURPOSES OF APPLICATION FOR PRODUCT LICENCE: USE FOR COMMERCIAL ADVANTAGE: INFRINGEMENT ESTABLISHED: C.A.)

Infringement

Douglas Pharmaceuticals Ltd v. Ciba-Geigy AG (CELOTEX CONDITIONS: APPLICATION IN NEW ZEALAND: PROTECTION AGAINST CLAIMS OF INFRINGEMENT BETWEEN EXPIRY OF PATENT AND ORDER EXTENDING IT: INADEQUATE REMUNERATION: EXTENSION: RELEVANCE OF FOREIGN REMUNERATION: C.A.)

Glaxo Group Ltd v. Apotex NZ Ltd (PRACTICE: APPLICATION TO STRIKE OUT: ALLEGED ABUSE OF PROCESS: EVIDENCE IN SUPPORT: AFFIDAVITS: H.C.)

Inglis v. Mayson (ESSENTIAL INTEGERS: INVALIDITY: H.C.)

Interpress Associates Ltd v. Pacific Coilcoaters Ltd (PLEADINGS: APPLICATION FOR FURTHER AND BETTER PARTICULARS AS TO ESSENTIAL INTEGERS: H.C.)

Monsanto Co. v. Stauffer Chemical Co. (N.Z.) (EXPERIMENTAL USE: INTERLOCUTORY RELIEF: H.C.)

Smith Kline & French Laboratories Ltd v. Attorney-General (SUPPLY OF SAMPLE MEDICINE TO HEALTH DEPARTMENT IN SUPPORT OF APPLICATION FOR CONSENT TO DISTRIBUTE GENERIC DRUG PRIOR TO EXPIRY OF PATENT: NO INFRINGEMENT: H.C.)

Smith Kline & French Laboratories Ltd v. Attorney-General (N.Z.) (IMPORTATION OF SAMPLE OF INFRINGING DRUG SOLELY FOR THE PURPOSES OF APPLYING FOR HEALTH DEPARTMENT APPROVAL FOR DISTRIBUTION: C.A.)

Smith Kline & French Laboratories Ltd v. Attorney-General (EXPIRY: IMPORTATION: SUBMISSION TO GOVERNMENT BODY FOR APPROVAL AFTER EXPIRY: WHETHER SUBMISSION "USE": C.A.)

Smith Kline and French Laboratories Ltd v. Douglas Pharmaceuticals Ltd (CIMETIDINE: IMPORT OF SAMPLE FOR PURPOSES OF APPLICATION FOR PRODUCT LICENCE: USE FOR COMMERCIAL ADVANTAGE: INFRINGEMENT ESTABLISHED: C.A.)

Insufficiency

Dow Chemical Co. v. Ishihara Sangyo Kaisha Ltd (REVOCATION: PARTICULARS OF OBJECTION: APPLICATION TO STRIKE OUT: FALSE SUGGESTION: H.C.)

Interlocutory Relief. *See* **Practice** (*Interlocutory relief*)

Judicial Review. *See* **Practice** (*Judicial review*)

Lack of Inventive Step

Smale v. North Sales Ltd (REVOCATION: INFRINGEMENT: PRIOR PUBLICATION AND OBVIOUSNESS: WHETHER INVENTION WAS NEW: H.C.)

Licence of Right

Smith Kline & French Laboratories Ltd v. Attorney-General (CIMETIDINE: CONFIDENTIAL INFORMATION: PRODUCT LICENCE: H.C.)

Manner of New Manufacture

Wellcome Foundation Ltd v. Commissioner of Patents (APPLICATION: METHOD OF TREATMENT: C.A.)

Method of Treatment

Wellcome Foundation (Hitching)'s Application (NEW THERAPEUTIC USE FOR KNOWN DRUG: C.A.)
Wellcome Foundation Ltd v. Commissioner of Patents (APPLICATION: MANNER OF NEW MANUFACTURE: C.A.)

New Use of Known Drug

Wellcome Foundation (Hitching)'s Application (NEW THERAPEUTIC USE FOR KNOWN DRUG: C.A.)
Wellcome Foundation Ltd v. Commissioner of Patents (APPLICATION: NEW USE OF KNOWN DRUG: TREATMENT: C.A.)

Notice. *See* **Practice** (*Notice*)

Novelty

Smale v. North Sales Ltd (REVOCATION: INFRINGEMENT: PRIOR PUBLICATION AND OBVIOUSNESS: LACK OF INVENTIVE STEP: H.C.)

Obviousness

Smale v. North Sales Ltd (INFRINGEMENT: PRIOR PUBLICATION: WHETHER INVENTION WAS NEW: LACK OF INVENTIVE STEP: H.C.)

Onus of Proof. *See* **Practice** (*Onus of proof*)

Opposition

Merck & Co. Inc. v. Pacific Pharmaceuticals Ltd (EXTENSION: INADEQUATE REMUNERATION: NOTICE: ONUS OF PROOF: H.C.)

Pharmaceutical Patent

Glaxo Group Ltd v. Apotex N.Z. Ltd (DIFFERENT CRYSTALLINE FORMS: APPLICATION FOR PRE-TRIAL DISCOVERY TO OBTAIN DETAILS OF CRYSTALLINE FORM AND ROUTE OF SYNTHESIS: H.C.)

Practice

Abuse of process

Glaxo Group Ltd v. Apotex NZ Ltd (INFRINGEMENT: APPLICATION TO STRIKE OUT: ALLEGED ABUSE OF PROCESS: EVIDENCE IN SUPPORT: AFFIDAVITS: H.C.)

Affidavits

Glaxo Group Ltd v. Apotex NZ Ltd (INFRINGEMENT: APPLICATION TO STRIKE OUT: ALLEGED ABUSE OF PROCESS: EVIDENCE IN SUPPORT: H.C.)

Appeal

Ciba-Geigy AG v. Douglas Pharmaceuticals Ltd (EXTENSION OF TERM: APPEAL FROM REFUSAL: H.C.)

Confidentiality

Hassle (A.B.) v. Pacific Pharmaceuticals Ltd (DISCOVERY: EXTENSION: FINANCIAL INFORMATION: PROFESSIONAL PRIVILEDGE: H.C.)

Discovery

Hassle (A.B.) v. Pacific Pharmaceuticals Ltd (CONFIDENTIALITY: PATENT EXTENSION: FINANCIAL INFORMATION: PROFESSIONAL PRIVILEDGE: H.C.)
Interpress Associates Ltd v. Pacific Coilcoaters Ltd (INFRINGEMENT: APPLICATION FOR FURTHER AND BETTER PARTICULARS AS TO ESSENTIAL INTEGERS: H.C.)

Discretion

Pacific Pharmaceuticals Ltd v. Merck & Co. Inc. (EXTENSION: INADEQUATE REMUNERATION: H.C.)

Evidence

Glaxo Group Ltd v. Apotex NZ Ltd (INFRINGEMENT: APPLICATION TO STRIKE OUT: ALLEGED ABUSE OF PROCESS: EVIDENCE IN SUPPORT: AFFIDAVITS: H.C.)
Glaxo Group Ltd v. Commissioner of Patents: (APPLICATION: COMPULSORY LICENCE: PRIMA FACIE CASE: JUDICIAL REVIEW: EVIDENCE FOR FINDINGS: C.A.)

Interlocutory relief

Monsanto Co. v. Stauffer Chemical Co. (N.Z.) (INFRINGEMENT: EXPERIMENTAL USE: H.C.)

Judicial review

Glaxo Group Ltd v. Commissioner of Patents: (APPLICATION: COMPULSORY LICENCE: PRIMA FACIE CASE: EVIDENCE FOR FINDINGS: C.A.)

Notice

Merck & Co. Inc. v. Pacific Pharmaceuticals Ltd (EXTENSION: INADEQUATE REMUNERATION: OPPOSITION: ONUS OF PROOF: H.C.)

Onus of proof

Merck & Co. Inc. v. Pacific Pharmaceuticals Ltd (EXTENSION: INADEQUATE REMUNERATION: OPPOSITION: NOTICE: H.C.)

Pleadings

Interpress Associates Ltd v. Pacific Coilcoaters Ltd (APPLICATION FOR FURTHER AND BETTER PARTICULARS AS TO ESSENTIAL INTEGERS: H.C.)

Professional priviledge

Hassle (A.B.) v. Pacific Pharmaceuticals Ltd (DISCOVERY: CONFIDENTIALITY: PATENT EXTENSION: FINANCIAL INFORMATION: H.C.)

Striking out

Dow Chemical Co. v. Ishihara Sangyo Kaisha Ltd (REVOCATION: PARTICULARS OF OBJECTION: FALSE SUGGESTION: INSUFFICIENCY: H.C.)

Glaxo Group Ltd v. Apotex NZ Ltd (ALLEGED ABUSE OF PROCESS: EVIDENCE IN SUPPORT: AFFIDAVITS: H.C.)

Prior Publication

Smale v. North Sales Ltd (INFRINGEMENT: YACHT SALES: REVOCATION: OBVIOUSNESS: H.C.)

Professional Privilege. *See* Practice (*Professional privilege*)

Revocation

Dow Chemical Co. v. Ishihara Sangyo Kaisha Ltd (PARTICULARS OF OBJECTION: APPLICATION TO STRIKE OUT: FALSE SUGGESTION: INSUFFICIENCY: H.C.)

Smale v. North Sales Ltd (INFRINGEMENT: PRIOR PUBLICATION AND OBVIOUSNESS: WHETHER INVENTION WAS NEW: LACK OF INVENTIVE STEP: H.C.)

Striking Out. *See* Practice (*Striking out*)

Treatment. *See* Method of Treatment

Practice and Miscellaneous Subjects

Account of Profits

Aquaculture Corp. v. New Zealand Green Mussel Co. Ltd (No. 2) (ACCOUNT REFUSED: H.C.)

Attorney-General v. Wellington Newspapers Ltd (H.C.: C.A.)

Thornton Hall Manufacturing Ltd v. Shanton Apparel Ltd (TIME FOR MAKING ELECTION BETWEEN ACCOUNT OF PROFITS OR DAMAGES: C.A.)

Acquiescence

Dominion Rent A Car Ltd v. Budget Rent A Car System (1970) Ltd (C.A.)

Wham-O Manufacturing Co. v. Lincoln Industries Ltd (H.C.: C.A.)

Anton Piller Order

Anvil Jewellery Ltd v. Riva Ridge Holdings Ltd (DISCHARGE: H.C.)

Busby v. Thorne EMI Video Programmes Ltd (PRIVILEGE AGAINST SELF-INCRIMINATION: SEARCH AND SEIZURE: JURISDICTION: CONDITIONS: C.A.)

Colonial Arms Motor Inn Ltd v. Twentieth Century-Fox Films Corp. (JURISDICTION: FORUM: C.A.)

Thorn EMI Video Programmes Ltd v. Kitching (PRIVILEGE AGAINST SELF-INCRIMINATION: H.C.: C.A.)

Tony Blain Pty Ltd v. Splain (POP CONCERTS: ANTON PILLER ORDER AGAINST PERSONS UNKNOWN: H.C.)

Balance of Convenience

Coronet Property Group Ltd v. Coronet Equities Ltd (INTERIM INJUNCTION: SERIOUS QUESTION TO BE TRIED: H.C.)
Levi Strauss & Co. v. Dino Clothing Co. Ltd (INTERLOCUTORY INJUNCTION: H.C.)
Pop-A-Shot Inc. v. Filtration and Pumping (Commercial) Ltd (IMPECUNIOUS DEFENDANT: H.C.)

Breach of Injunction

Taylor Bros Ltd v. Taylors Group Ltd (CONSTRUCTION OF INJUNCTION: REMEDIES: C.A.)

Consent Order

Franklin Machinery Ltd v. Albany Farm Centre Ltd (INTERLOCUTORY INJUNCTION: APPLICATION FOR DECLARATION THAT REVISED PRODUCTS FELL OUTSIDE TERMS OF ORDER OR VARIATION OF CONSENT ORDER: PRINCIPLES TO BE APPLIED: H.C.)

Construction of Injunction

Taylor Bros Ltd v. Taylors Group Ltd (C.A.)

Declaration

Attorney-General v. Wellington Newspapers Ltd (H.C.: C.A.)
Franklin Machinery Ltd v. Albany Farm Centre Ltd (APPLICATION FOR DECLARATION THAT REVISED PRODUCTS FELL OUTSIDE TERMS OF CONSENT ORDER OR VARIATION OF ORDER: H.C.)

Delay

Dominion Rent A Car Ltd v. Budget Rent A Car System (1970) Ltd (C.A.)

Delivery-up

Elley Ltd v. Wairoa-Harrison & McCarthy (EX-EMPLOYEE: DELIVERY-UP OF DOCUMENTS: H.C.)

Discovery

Hassle (A.B.) v. Pacific Pharmaceuticals Ltd (CONFIDENTIALITY: PATENT EXTENSION: FINANCIAL INFORMATION: PROFESSIONAL PRIVILEGE: H.C.)
Interpress Associates Ltd v. Pacific Coilcoaters Ltd (PATENT: INFRINGEMENT: APPLICATION FOR FURTHER AND BETTER PARTICULARS AS TO ESSENTIAL INTEGERS: H.C.)

Evidence

Glaxo Group Ltd v. Commissioner of Patents: (JUDICIAL REVIEW: EVIDENCE FOR FINDINGS: C.A.)
LaBounty v. Hydraulic Machinery Company of New Zealand Ltd (H.C.)
Levi Strauss & Co. v. Kimbyr Investments Ltd (EXPERT EVIDENCE: SURVEY EVIDENCE: ADMISSIBILITY: H.C.)

Longman Group Ltd v. Carrington Technical Institite Board of Governors (DEFENCE OF FAIR DEALING: ADMISSIBLE EVIDENCE TO DETERMINE: H.C.: C.A.)
Noel Leeming Television Ltd v. Noel's Appliance Centre Ltd (SURVEY EVIDENCE: H.C.)

Foreign Plaintiff

Crusader Oil N.L. v. Crusader Minerals N.Z. Ltd (PASSING OFF: REPUTATION: H.C.)
Dominion Rent A Car Ltd v. Budget Rent A Car System (1970) Ltd (PASSING OFF: INTERNATIONAL REPUTATION: C.A.)

Forum

Colonial Arms Motor Inn Ltd v. Twentieth Century-Fox Films Corp. (ANTON PILLER: JURISDICTION: C.A.)

Judicial Review

Glaxo Group Ltd v. Commissioner of Patents: (EVIDENCE FOR FINDINGS: C.A.)

Iniquity

Attorney-General v. Wellington Newspapers Ltd (H.C.: C.A.)
European Pacific Banking Corporation v. Fourth Estate Publications Ltd (PUBLIC INTEREST: H.C.)

Interference with Contractual Relations

New Zealand Industrial Gases Ltd v. Oxyman (H.C.)

Interlocutory or Interim Injunction

Anvil Jewellery Ltd v. Riva Ridge Holdings Ltd (ANTON PILLER ORDERS: DISCHARGE: H.C.)
Auckland Harbour Cruise Co. Ltd v. Fullers Captain Cook Cruises Ltd (H.C.)
Bars Products International Ltd v. Holt Lloyd Ltd (RECALL OF PRODUCT DISTRIBUTED: H.C.)
Bayer AG v. Pacific Pharmaceuticals Ltd (H.C.)
Chemby Marketing Ltd v. Willoughby (WHETHER A SERIOUS QUESTION TO BE TRIED: EFFECT OF UNDERTAKING BY DEFENDANT: H.C.)
Compusales Holdings N.Z. Ltd v. Sperry Ltd & Burroughs Ltd (UNDERTAKING AS TO DAMAGES: H.C.)
Coronet Property Group Ltd v. Coronet Equities Ltd (SERIOUS QUESTION TO BE TRIED: BALANCE OF CONVENIENCE: H.C.)
Esanda Ltd v. Esanda Finance Ltd (H.C.)
Griffin & Sons Ltd v. R. (1988) Ltd (H.C.)
Klissers Farmhouse Bakeries Ltd v. Harvest Bakeries Ltd (H.C.: C.A.)
Levi Strauss & Co. v. Dino Clothing Co. Ltd (BALANCE OF CONVENIENCE: H.C.)
Pop-A-Shot Inc. v. Filtration and Pumping (Commercial) Ltd (BALANCE OF CONVENIENCE: IMPECUNIOUS DEFENDANT: H.C.)
Silvercrest Sales Ltd v. Gainsborough Printing Co. Ltd (H.C.)

Taylor Bros Ltd v. Taylors Group Ltd (CONSTRUCTION OF INJUNCTION: BREACH: C.A.)
Tony Blain Pty Ltd v. Splain (PROCEDURE: H.C.)
Totara Vineyards Sye Ltd v. Villa Maria Estate Ltd (H.C.)

Joint Tortfeasors

Crystal Glass Industries Ltd v. Alwinco Products Ltd (C.A.)

Jurisdiction

Apple Computer Inc. v. Apple Corps. SA (EXISTENCE OF CONTRACTUAL DISPUTE BETWEEN IDENTICAL PARTIES IN U.K. PROCEEDINGS: SOLE JURISDICTION CLAUSE IN U.K. AGREEMENT: H.C.)
Colonial Arms Motor Inn Ltd v. Twentieth Century-Fox Films Corp. (ANTON PILLER: FORUM: C.A.)

Knowledge

Brintons Ltd v. Feltex Furnishings of New Zealand Ltd (No. 2) (COPYRIGHT: INNOCENT INFRINGEMENT: H.C.)

Laches

Dominion Rent A Car Ltd v. Budget Rent A Car System (1970) Ltd (ACQUIESCENCE: DELAY: C.A.)

Loss of Profit

Brintons Ltd v. Feltex Furnishings of New Zealand Ltd (No. 2) (MEASURE OF DAMAGES: CONVERSION DAMAGES: H.C.)

Malicious Falsehood

Alan H. Reid Engineering Ltd v. Ramset Fasteners (N.Z.) Ltd (TRADE LIBEL: RULE AGAINST RESTRAINT OF PUBLICATION WHERE JUSTIFICATION CLAIMED: COMPARATIVE ADVERTISING: INTERLOCUTORY INJUNCTION: H.C.)
Bradley v. Wingnut Films Ltd (WHETHER FILM SUGGESTED PLAINTIFFS INVOLVEMENT: WHETHER FILM PRODUCED IN SUCH A WAY AS TO CAUSE HARM AND DISTRESS TO PLAINTIFF: H.C.)

Notice

Merck & Co. Inc. v. Pacific Pharmaceuticals Ltd (PATENTS: EXTENSION: OPPOSITION: ONUS OF PROOF: H.C.)

Onus of Proof

Merck & Co. Inc. v. Pacific Pharmaceuticals Ltd (PATENTS: EXTENSION: OPPOSITION: ONUS OF PROOF: H.C.)

Privilege against Self-incrimination

Busby v. Thorne EMI Video Programmes Ltd (ANTON PILLER ORDER: JURISDICTION: CONDITIONS: C.A.)
Thorn EMI Video Programmes Ltd v. Kitching (ANTON PILLER PRACTICE: H.C.: C.A.)

Procedure

Tony Blain Pty Ltd v. Splain (INTERIM INJUNCTION: H.C.)

Professional Privilege

Hassle (A.B.) v. Pacific Pharmaceuticals Ltd (DISCOVERY: CONFIDENTIALITY: PATENT EXTENSION: FINANCIAL INFORMATION: H.C.)

Quia Timet Injunction

Effem Foods Pty Ltd v. Trade Consultants Ltd (INTERNATIONAL TRADE ADVISER: DUTIES OWED TO EX-CLIENT: H.C.)

Search and Seizure

Busby v. Thorne EMI Video Programmes Ltd (ANTON PILLER ORDER: PRIVILEGE AGAINST SELF-INCRIMINATION: JURISDICTION: CONDITIONS: C.A.)

Serious Question to be Tried

Chemby Marketing Ltd v. Willoughby (INTERIM INJUNCTION: EFFECT OF UNDERTAKING BY DEFENDANT: H.C.)
Coronet Property Group Ltd v. Coronet Equities Ltd (INTERIM INJUNCTION: BALANCE OF CONVENIENCE: H.C.)

Striking Out

Brintons Ltd v. Feltex Furnishings of New Zealand Ltd (No. 1) (COPYRIGHT: INFRINGEMENT: AUTHORISATION: INDEMNITY AND CONTRIBUTION: H.C.)
Dow Chemical Co. v. Ishihara Sangyo Kaisha Ltd (PATENTS: REVOCATION: PARTICULARS OF OBJECTION: APPLICATION TO STRIKE OUT: FALSE SUGGESTION: INSUFFICIENCY: H.C.)

Survey Evidence

Levi Strauss & Co. v. Kimbyr Investments Ltd (H.C.)
Levi Strauss & Co. v. Kimbyr Investments Ltd (EXPERT EVIDENCE: ADMISSIBILITY: H.C.)
Noel Leeming Television Ltd v. Noel's Appliance Centre Ltd (H.C.)

Trade Libel

Alan H. Reid Engineering Ltd v. Ramset Fasteners (N.Z.) Ltd (MALICIOUS FALSEHOOD: RULE AGAINST RESTRAINT OF PUBLICATION WHERE JUSTIFICATION CLAIMED: COMPARATIVE ADVERTISING: INTERLOCUTORY INJUNCTION: H.C.)

Undertaking as to Damages

Compusales Holdings N.Z. Ltd v. Sperry Ltd & Burroughs Ltd (INTERIM INJUNCTION: H.C.)

Undertaking, Effect of

Chemby Marketing Ltd v. Willoughby (INTERIM INJUNCTION: WHETHER A SERIOUS QUESTION TO BE TRIED: H.C.)

Trade Marks and Trade Names

Application

Penfolds Wines (N.Z.) v. Leo Buring Pty Ltd (OPPOSITION: DECEPTIVE OR CONFUSING: Pat. Off.)

Assignment

Tot Toys Ltd v. Mitchell (ASSIGNABILITY OF MARK: H.C.)

Balance of Convenience. See Practice (*Interlocutory injunction*)

Comparative Advertising

Villa Maria Wines Ltd v. Montana Wines Ltd (INFRINGEMENT: SUGGESTION OF PARITY OF QUALITY: CONNECTION IN THE COURSE OF TRADE: H.C.: C.A.)

Confusing Similarity

Levi Strauss & Co. v. Kimbyr Investments Ltd (INFRINGEMENT: SCOPE OF PROTECTION OF REGISTERED MARK: PICTORIAL REPRESENTATION AND WRITTEN DESCRIPTION: STATUTORY INTERPRETATION: H.C.)

Confusion and Deception. See Likelihood of Deception or Confusion

Connection in the Course of Trade

Villa Maria Wines Ltd v. Montana Wines Ltd (INFRINGEMENT: COMPARATIVE ADVERTISING: SUGGESTION OF PARITY OF QUALITY: C.A.)

Damage

Levi Strauss & Co. v. Kimbyr Investments Ltd (INFRINGEMENT: SCOPE OF PROTECTION OF REGISTERED MARK: H.C.)

Deceptive or Confusing. See Likelihood of Deception or Confusion

Descriptive of Service

Shotover Gorge Jet Boats Ltd v. Marine Enterprises Ltd (PASSING OFF: MARK DESCRIPTIVE OF SERVICE: SECONDARY MEANING: H.C.)

Distinctiveness

Arthur Martin (Sales) Ltd v. Electra Mechanics (1975) Ltd (MARK INITIALLY BELONGING TO MANUFACTURER CAN BECOME DISTINCTIVE OF DEALER: H.C.)

Evidence. See Practice (*Evidence*)

Expert Evidence. See Practice (*Evidence*)

Expungement

Apple Computer Inc. v. Apple Corps. SA (EXISTENCE OF CONTRACTUAL DISPUTE BETWEEN IDENTICAL PARTIES IN U.K. PROCEEDINGS CONCERNING THE SAME MARKS: SOLE JURISDICTION CLAUSE IN U.K. AGREEMENT: H.C.)

Get-up and Labelling

Levi Strauss & Co. v. Robertsons Ltd (INFRINGEMENT: DIFFERENCE BETWEEN WRITTEN DESCRIPTION AND PICTORIAL REPRESENTATION IN CERTIFICATE OF REGISTRATION: REMOVAL: H.C.)

Import

South Pacific Tyres N.Z. Ltd v. David Craw Cars Ltd (SECOND-HAND TYRES IMPORTED INTO AND SOLD IN NEW ZEALAND BEARING IDENTICAL MARKS TO THE PLAINTIFFS' REGISTERED NEW ZEALAND MARKS: H.C.)

Infringement

Levi Strauss & Co. v. Dino Clothing Co. Ltd (TABS ON JEANS: ARCUATE STITCHING: INTERLOCUTORY INJUNCTION: BALANCE OF CONVENIENCE: H.C.)

Levi Strauss & Co. v. Kimbyr Investments Ltd (SCOPE OF PROTECTION OF REGISTERED MARK: PICTORIAL REPRESENTATION AND WRITTEN DESCRIPTION: STATUTORY INTERPRETATION: H.C.)

Levi Strauss & Co. v. Robertsons Ltd (GET-UP AND LABELLING OF JEANS: TRADE MARK: DIFFERENCE BETWEEN WRITTEN DESCRIPTION AND PICTORIAL REPRESENTATION IN CERTIFICATE OF REGISTRATION: H.C.)

New Zealand Industrial Gases Ltd v. Oxyman (INSERTING GAS INTO CONTAINERS BELONGING TO PLAINTIFF AND MARKED WITH ITS TRADE MARKS WAS NOT USE OF THE MARK: INTERFERING WITH CONTRACTUAL RELATION: H.C.)

South Pacific Tyres N.Z. Ltd v. David Craw Cars Ltd (SECOND-HAND TYRES IMPORTED INTO AND SOLD IN NEW ZEALAND BEARING IDENTICAL MARKS TO THE PLAINTIFFS' REGISTERED NEW ZEALAND MARKS: MARKS APPLIED TO TYRES IN JAPAN: LACK OF CONNECTION OR ARRANGEMENT WITH OWNER OR LEGITIMATE USER OF MARKS IN JAPAN: H.C.)

Tony Blain Pty Ltd v. Splain (INTERIM INJUNCTION: COMMERCIAL EXPLOITATION OF NAMES AND ACTIVITIES OF ARTISTS AND OTHERS: PROTECTION OF LICENSEES: PROCEDURE: H.C.)

Villa Maria Wines Ltd v. Montana Wines Ltd (COMPARATIVE ADVERTISING: SUGGESTION OF PARITY OF QUALITY: CONNECTION IN THE COURSE OF TRADE: H.C.: C.A.)

Wham-O Manufacturing Co. v. Lincoln Industries Ltd (H.C.: C.A.)

Interference with Contractual Relations

New Zealand Industrial Gases Ltd v. Oxyman (INFRINGEMENT: INSERTING GAS INTO CONTAINERS BELONGING TO PLAINTIFF AND MARKED WITH ITS TRADE MARKS WAS NOT USE OF THE MARK: H.C.)

Interim Injunction. See **Practice** (*Interim or interlocutory injunction*)

Interlocutory Injunction. See **Practice** (*Interim or interlocutory injunction*)

Jurisdiction

Jurisdiction. See **Practice** (*Jurisdiction*)

Likelihood of Deception or Confusion

Levi Strauss & Co. v. Kimbyr Investments Ltd (REGISTRATION: PICTORIAL REPRESENTATION: WRITTEN DESCRIPTION: SCOPE OF REGISTRATION: INFRINGEMENT: RECTIFICATION: H.C.)

Penfolds Wines (N.Z.) v. Leo Buring Pty Ltd (APPLICATION: OPPOSITION: Pat. Off.)

Non-use

Levi Strauss & Co. v. Kimbyr Investments Ltd (INFRINGEMENT: SCOPE OF PROTECTION OF REGISTERED MARK: PICTORIAL REPRESENTATION AND WRITTEN DESCRIPTION: STATUTORY INTERPRETATION: CONFUSING SIMILARITY: SURVEY EVIDENCE: DAMAGE: H.C.)

Opposition

Natural Selection Clothing Ltd v. Commissioner of Trade Marks (REGISTRATION: OVERSEAS OPPONENT: STRUCK-OFF COMPANY: *Locus standii*: H.C.)
Penfolds Wines (N.Z.) v. Leo Buring Pty Ltd (APPLICATION: DECEPTIVE OR CONFUSING: Pat. Off.)

Overseas Opponent

Natural Selection Clothing Ltd v. Commissioner of Trade Marks (REGISTRATION: OPPOSITION: STRUCK OFF COMPANY: *Locus standii*: H.C.)

Overseas Proprietor

South Pacific Tyres N.Z. Ltd v. David Craw Cars Ltd (INFRINGEMENT: SECOND-HAND TYRES IMPORTED INTO AND SOLD IN NEW ZEALAND BEARING IDENTICAL MARKS TO THE PLAINTIFFS' REGISTERED NEW ZEALAND MARKS: MARKS APPLIED TO TYRES IN JAPAN: PLAINTIFFS HAD NO CONNECTION OR ARRANGEMENT WITH OWNER OR LEGITIMATE USER OF TRADE MARKS IN JAPAN: H.C.)

Practice

Evidence

Levi Strauss & Co. v. Kimbyr Investments Ltd (INFRINGEMENT: SCOPE OF PROTECTION OF REGISTERED MARK: CONFUSING SIMILARITY: NON-USE: DAMAGE: H.C.)
Levi Strauss & Co. v. Kimbyr Investments Ltd (REGISTRATION: PICTORIAL REPRESENTATION: SCOPE OF REGISTRATION: EXPERT EVIDENCE: SURVEY EVIDENCE: ADMISSIBILITY: H.C.)

Interim or interlocutory injunction

Chemby Marketing Ltd v. Willoughby (SERIOUS QUESTION TO BE TRIED: EFFECT OF UNDERTAKING BY DEFENDANT: H.C.)
Levi Strauss & Co. v. Dino Clothing Co. Ltd (INFRINGEMENT: TABS ON JEANS: ARCUATE STITCHING: BALANCE OF CONVENIENCE: H.C.)
Tony Blain Pty Ltd v. Splain (INFRINGEMENT: INTERIM INJUNCTION: COMMERCIAL EXPLOITATION OF NAMES AND ACTIVITIES OF ARTISTS AND OTHERS: PROTECTION OF LICENSEES: PROCEDURE: H.C.)

Interlocutory injunction—balance of convenience

Levi Strauss & Co. v. Dino Clothing Co. Ltd (INTERLOCUTORY INJUNCTION: H.C.)

Interlocutory injunction—serious question to be tried

Chemby Marketing Ltd v. Willoughby (SERIOUS QUESTION TO BE TRIED: EFFECT OF UNDERTAKING BY DEFENDANT: H.C.)

Jurisdiction

Apple Computer Inc. v. Apple Corps. SA (PROCEEDINGS FOR EXPUNGEMENT OF NEW ZEALAND TRADE MARK: EXISTENCE OF CONTRACTUAL DISPUTE BETWEEN IDENTICAL PARTIES IN U.K. PROCEEDINGS CONCERNING THE SAME MARKS: "SOLE JURISDICTION" CLAUSE IN U.K. AGREEMENT: H.C.)

Locus standi

Natural Selection Clothing Ltd v. Commissioner of Trade Marks (REGISTRATION: OPPOSITION: OVERSEAS OPPONENT: STRUCK-OFF COMPANY: H.C.)

Survey evidence

Levi Strauss & Co. v. Kimbyr Investments Ltd (INFRINGEMENT: SCOPE OF PROTECTION OF REGISTERED MARK: PICTORIAL REPRESENTATION: WRITTEN DESCRIPTION: CONFUSING SIMILARITY: H.C.)
Levi Strauss & Co. v. Kimbyr Investments Ltd (PICTORIAL REPRESENTATION: WRITTEN DESCRIPTION: SCOPE OF REGISTRATION: LIKELIHOOD OF DECEPTION OR CONFUSION: SURVEY EVIDENCE: ADMISSIBILITY: H.C.)

Undertaking, effect of

Chemby Marketing Ltd v. Willoughby (INTERIM INJUNCTION: SERIOUS QUESTION TO BE TRIED: H.C.)

Procedure

Tony Blain Pty Ltd v. Splain (INFRINGEMENT: INTERIM INJUNCTION: H.C.)

Protection of Licensees

Tony Blain Pty Ltd v. Splain (INFRINGEMENT: INTERIM INJUNCTION: COMMERCIAL EXPLOITATION OF NAMES AND ACTIVITIES OF ARTISTS AND OTHERS: PROTECTION OF LICENSEES: H.C.)

Rectification

Levi Strauss & Co. v. Kimbyr Investments Ltd (PICTORIAL REPRESENTATION: WRITTEN DESCRIPTION: SCOPE OF REGISTRATION: INFRINGEMENT: LIKELIHOOD OF DECEPTION OR CONFUSION: EXPERT EVIDENCE: SURVEY EVIDENCE: ADMISSIBILITY: H.C.)

Registration

Levi Strauss & Co. v. Kimbyr Investments Ltd (PICTORIAL REPRESENTATION: WRITTEN DESCRIPTION: SCOPE OF REGISTRATION: H.C.)
Levi Strauss & Co. v. Robertsons Ltd (INFRINGEMENT: PICTORIAL REPRESENTATION: WRITTEN DESCRIPTION: REMOVAL: H.C.)

Removal

Levi Strauss & Co. v. Robertsons Ltd (INFRINGEMENT: PICTORIAL REPRESENTATION: WRITTEN DESCRIPTION: H.C.)

Repackaging

New Zealand Industrial Gases Ltd v. Oxyman (INFRINGEMENT: INSERTING GAS
INTO CONTAINERS BELONGING TO PLAINTIFF AND MARKED WITH ITS TRADE
MARKS WAS NOT USE OF THE MARK: INTERFERING WITH CONTRACTUAL
RELATION: H.C.)

Scope of protection of Registered Mark

Levi Strauss & Co. v. Kimbyr Investments Ltd (INFRINGEMENT: PICTORIAL
REPRESENTATION: WRITTEN DESCRIPTION: STATUTORY INTERPRETATION:
H.C.)

Second-hand Goods

South Pacific Tyres N.Z. Ltd v. David Craw Cars Ltd (INFRINGEMENT: SECOND-
HAND TYRES IMPORTED INTO AND SOLD IN NEW ZEALAND BEARING
IDENTICAL MARKS TO THE PLAINTIFFS' REGISTERED NEW ZEALAND MARKS:
MARKS APPLIED TO TYRES IN JAPAN: LACK OF CONNECTION OR
ARRANGEMENT WITH OWNER OR LEGITIMATE USER OF MARKS IN JAPAN:
H.C.)

Secondary Meaning

Shotover Gorge Jet Boats Ltd v. Marine Enterprises Ltd (MARK DESCRIPTIVE OF
SERVICE: H.C.)

Serious Question to be Tried. *See* **Practice** (*Interlocutory injunction*)

Survey Evidence. *See* **Practice** (*Survey evidence*)

Tabs on Jeans

Levi Strauss & Co. v. Dino Clothing Co. Ltd (ARCUATE STITCHING: H.C.)
Levi Strauss & Co. v. Kimbyr Investments Ltd (TABS ON JEANS POCKETS: H.C.)

Undertaking, Effect of. *See* **Practice** (*Undertaking, effect of*)

SAUDI ARABIA

Trade Marks

Confusion

Beecham Group PLC v. Banafi' (INFRINGEMENT: HAIR PREPARATIONS:
BRYLCREEM/STELLACREAM: WHETHER CONFUSION POSSIBLE BY
CONSUMER OF AVERAGE PRODUCT: Court of Grievances)

Extent of Protection

Beecham Group PLC v. Banafi' (INFRINGEMENT: HAIR PREPARATIONS:
BRYLCREEM/STELLACREAM: WHETHER CONFUSION POSSIBLE BY
CONSUMER OF AVERAGE PRODUCT: Court of Grievances)

Get-up

Beecham Group PLC v. Banafi' (INFRINGEMENT: HAIR PREPARATIONS: BRYLCREEM/STELLACREAM: EXTENT OF TRADE MARK PROTECTION: WHETHER CONFUSION POSSIBLE BY CONSUMER OF AVERAGE PRODUCT: Court of Grievances)

Import

Beecham Group PLC v. Banafi' (INFRINGEMENT: HAIR PREPARATIONS: BRYLCREEM/STELLACREAM: INJUNCTION: IMPORT AND SALE ENJOINED: Court of Grievances)

Infringement

Beecham Group PLC v. Banafi' (HAIR PREPARATIONS: BRYLCREEM/ STELLACREAM: Court of Grievances)

Practice

Injunction:

Beecham Group PLC v. Banafi (INFRINGEMENT: IMPORT AND SALE ENJOINED: Court of Grievances)

SINGAPORE

Confidential Information and Breach of Confidence

Adequacy of Damages. *See* **Practice** (*Adequacy of damages*)

Elements of Tort

Chiarapurk Jack v. Haw Paw Brothers International Ltd (INTERLOCUTORY INJUNCTION: PARTICULARS OF INFORMATION REQUIRED: C.A.)
X Pte Ltd v. CDE (EQUITABLE OBLIGATION OF CONFIDENCE: INTERLOCUTORY INJUNCTION: SERIOUS QUESTION TO BE TRIED: APPROPRIATENESS OF DAMAGES: H.C.)

Equitable Obligation of Confidence

X Pte Ltd v. CDE (ELEMENTS TO BE SATISFIED: INTERLOCUTORY INJUNCTION: SERIOUS QUESTION TO BE TRIED: APPROPRIATENESS OF DAMAGES: H.C.)

Form of Order. *See* **Practice** (*Adequacy of damages*)

Injunction. *See* **Practice** (*Injunction*)

Manufacturing Process

Chia v. Haw Par Brothers International Ltd (WHETHER PLAINTIFF SEEKING INJUNCTION IS REQUIRED TO SPECIFY THE CONFIDENTIAL ASPECTS OF THE PROCESS: C.A.)

Practice

Adequacy of damages

Chia v. Haw Par Brothers International Ltd (FORM OF ORDER: C.A.)

Form of order

Chia v. Haw Par Brothers International Ltd (ADEQUACY OF DAMAGES: C.A.)

Injunction

Chia v. Haw Par Brothers International Ltd (MANUFACTURING PROCESS: WHETHER PLAINTIFF SEEKING INJUNCTION IS REQUIRED TO SPECIFY THE CONFIDENTIAL ASPECTS OF THE PROCESS: C.A.)

Interlocutory injunction—appropriateness of damages

X Pte Ltd v. CDE (GROUNDS: BREACH: ELEMENTS TO BE SATISFIED: EQUITABLE OBLIGATION OF CONFIDENCE: SERIOUS QUESTION TO BE TRIED: H.C.)

Interlocutory injunction—particulars of information required

Chiarapurk Jack v. Haw Paw Brothers International Ltd (ESSENTIAL ELEMENTS OF CAUSE OF ACTION: C.A.)

Interlocutory injunction—serious question to be tried

X Pte Ltd v. CDE (ELEMENTS TO BE SATISFIED: EQUITABLE OBLIGATION OF CONFIDENCE: APPROPRIATENESS OF DAMAGES: H.C.)

Copyright

Assignment

Singapore Broadcasting Corporation v. The Performing Right Society Ltd (LICENSING SCHEME: MUSIC COMPOSERS ASSIGNING PERFORMING RIGHTS TO BODY: BODY DEMANDING ROYALTY PAYMENT FROM BROADCASTING CORPORATION FOR THE BROADCASTING OF ITS REPERTOIRE: Cprt Trib.)

Bona Fide Purchaser for Value Without Notice. *See* Practice *(Defences)*

Broadcasting

Singapore Broadcasting Corporation v. The Performing Right Society Ltd (LICENSING SCHEME: ROYALTY FOR BROADCASTING REPERTOIRE: Cprt Trib.)

Cinematographic Films. *See* Films

Compilation

Robert John Powers School Inc. v. Tessensohn (INFRINGEMENT: SCOPE OF PROTECTION: INVERSE PASSING OFF: H.C.) (APPEAL: C.A.)

Composers

Singapore Broadcasting Corporation v. Performing Right Society Ltd (LICENSING SCHEME: Cprt Trib.)

Computer Software

Federal Computer Services Sdn Bhd v. Ang Jee Hai Eric (SCOPE OF PROTECTION: INTERPRETATION OF STATUTE: H.C.)

Novell, Inc. v. Ong Seow Pheng (SCOPE OF PROTECTION: SOFTWARE AND MANUALS: FIRST PUBLICATION IN UNITED STATES: INJUNCTION: H.C.)

Copyright Act 1911

Construction

Butterworths & Co. (Publ.) Ltd v. Ng Sui Nam (INFRINGEMENT: H.C.)

Costs. *See* Practice (*Costs*)

Computer Sound Cards

Aztech Systems Pte Ltd v. Creative Technology Ltd (INFRINGEMENT: DESIGNING COMPATIBLE SOUND CARDS: FAIR DEALING FOR THE PURPOSE OF PRIVATE STUDY: DEROGATION FROM GRANT: IMPLIED LICENCE: H.C.)

Derogation from Grant

Aztech Systems Pte Ltd v. Creative Technology Ltd (INFRINGEMENT: COMPUTER SOUND CARDS: DESIGNING COMPATIBLE SOUND CARDS: FAIR DEALING FOR THE PURPOSE OF PRIVATE STUDY: IMPLIED LICENCE: H.C.)

Equitable Owner. *See* Ownership

Exhibition

Television Broadcasts Ltd v. Golden Line Video & Marketing Pte Ltd (CINEMATOGRAPHIC FILMS: RENTAL WITHOUT LICENCE: VIDEOTAPES NOT PIRATED COPIES: H.C.)

Fair Dealing

Aztech Systems Pte Ltd v. Creative Technology Ltd (INFRINGEMENT: COMPUTER SOUND CARDS: DESIGNING COMPATIBLE SOUND CARDS: FAIR DEALING FOR THE PURPOSE OF PRIVATE STUDY: DEROGATION FROM GRANT: IMPLIED LICENCE: H.C.)

Films

Television Broadcasts Ltd v. Golden Line Video & Marketing Pte Ltd (CINEMATOGRAPHIC FILMS: EXHIBITION: RENTAL WITHOUT LICENCE: VIDEOTAPES NOT PIRATED COPIES: H.C.)

First Publication

Novell, Inc. v. Ong Seow Pheng (FIRST PUBLICATION IN UNITED STATES: ADDITIONAL DAMAGES: TRADE MARK: INFRINGEMENT: INJUNCTION: H.C.)

Implied Licence

Aztech Systems Pte Ltd v. Creative Technology Ltd (INFRINGEMENT: COMPUTER SOUND CARDS: DESIGNING COMPATIBLE SOUND CARDS: FAIR DEALING FOR THE PURPOSE OF PRIVATE STUDY: DEROGATION FROM GRANT: H.C.)

Importation

Public Prosecutor v. Teo Ai Nee (PARALLEL IMPORTATION: INFRINGEMENT: SCOPE OF PROTECTION: SUBSISTENCE: ONUS OF PROOF: H.C.)

Infringement

Aztech Systems Pte Ltd v. Creative Technology Ltd (COMPUTER SOUND CARDS: DESIGNING COMPATIBLE SOUND CARDS: FAIR DEALING FOR THE PURPOSE OF PRIVATE STUDY: DEROGATION FROM GRANT: IMPLIED LICENCE: H.C.)

Butterworths & Co. (Publ.) Ltd v. Ng Sui Nam (CONSTRUCTION OF 1911 COPYRIGHT ACT: H.C.)

Essex Electric (Pte) Ltd v. IPC Computers (U.K.) Ltd (Ch.D.)

Expanded Metal Manufacturing Pte Ltd v. Expanded Metal Co. Ltd (*Ex parte* APPLICATION FOR INJUNCTION: ANTON PILLER ORDER: PRIVILEGE AGAINST SELF-INCRIMINATION: INFERENCE TO BE DRAWN: C.A.)

Public Prosecutor v. Teo Ai Nee (SECONDARY INFRINGEMENT: KNOWLEDGE: TEST: REQUISITE STATE OF MIND: H.C.)

Public Prosecutor v. Teo Ai Nee (COPYRIGHT: PARALLEL IMPORTATION: SCOPE OF PROTECTION: SUBSISTENCE: ONUS OF PROOF: H.C.)

Remus Innovation MbH v. Hong Boon Siong (PARALLEL IMPORTATION: PRACTICE: INTERLOCUTORY INJUNCTION: STANDARD OF PROOF: DISCRETION: CHANCE OF INJUSTICE: H.C.)

Robert John Powers School Inc. v. Tessensohn (SCOPE OF PROTECTION: COMPILATION: INVERSE PASSING OFF: MISLEADING ACCOUNT OF ACHIEVEMENT IN RÉSUMÉ: H.C.) (APPEAL: C.A.)

Interest. *See* **Practice** (*Interest*)

Licensing Scheme

Singapore Broadcasting Corporation v. Performing Right Society Ltd (REASONABLENESS: AMOUNT OF ROYALTIES TO BE PAID BY NATIONAL BROADCASTER: COSTS: INTEREST: Cprt Trib.)

Logo

Auvi Pte Ltd v. Seah Siew Tee and Chai Foh Min (EQUITABLE OWNER: H.C.)

Ownership

Auvi Pte Ltd v. Seah Siew Tee and Chai Foh Min (LOGO: EQUITABLE OWNER: H.C.)

Tai Muk Kwai v. Luen Hup Medical Company (RIVAL CLAIM OF OWNERSHIP: DEFENCE OF BONA FIDE PURCHASER FOR VALUE WITHOUT NOTICE: H.C.)

Parallel Importation

Remus Innovation MbH v. Hong Boon Siong (INFRINGEMENT: PRACTICE: INTERLOCUTORY INJUNCTION: STANDARD OF PROOF: DISCRETION: CHANCE OF INJUSTICE: H.C.)

Piracy

Television Broadcasts Ltd v. Golden Line Video & Marketing Pte Ltd (CINEMATOGRAPHIC FILMS: RENTAL WITHOUT LICENCE: VIDEOTAPES NOT PIRATED COPIES: H.C.)

1076

Practice

Anton Piller

Expanded Metal Manufacturing Pte Ltd v. Expanded Metal Co. Ltd (INFRINGEMENT: *Ex parte* APPLICATION FOR INJUNCTION: PRIVILEGE AGAINST SELF-INCRIMINATION: INFERENCE TO BE DRAWN: C.A.)

Appeal

Robert John Powers School Inc. v. Tessensohn (INFRINGEMENT: INVERSE PASSING OFF: C.A.)

Costs

Singapore Broadcasting Corporation v. Performing Right Society Ltd (LICENCE SCHEME: INTEREST: Cprt Trib.)

Damages

Novell, Inc. v. Ong Seow Pheng (ADDITIONAL DAMAGES: H.C.)

Defences

Tai Muk Kwai v. Luen Hup Medical Company (BONA FIDE PURCHASER FOR VALUE WITHOUT NOTICE: H.C.)

Discretion

Remus Innovation MbH v. Hong Boon Siong (INFRINGEMENT: PARALLEL IMPORTATION: INTERLOCUTORY INJUNCTION: STANDARD OF PROOF: CHANCE OF INJUSTICE: H.C.)

Ex parte injunction

Expanded Metal Manufacturing Pte Ltd v. Expanded Metal Co. Ltd (INFRINGEMENT: ANTON PILLER ORDER: PRIVILEGE AGAINST SELF-INCRIMINATION: INFERENCE TO BE DRAWN: C.A.)

Interest

Singapore Broadcasting Corporation v. The Performing Right Society Ltd (LICENCE SCHEME: ROYALTIES: COSTS: Cprt Trib.)

Interlocutory injunction—chance of injustice

Remus Innovation MbH v. Hong Boon Siong (INFRINGEMENT: PARALLEL IMPORTATION: STANDARD OF PROOF: DISCRETION: H.C.)

Interlocutory injunction—standard of proof

Remus Innovation MbH v. Hong Boon Siong (INFRINGEMENT: PARALLEL IMPORTATION: DISCRETION: CHANCE OF INJUSTICE: H.C.)

Knowledge

Public Prosecutor v. Teo Ai Nee (INFRINGEMENT: SECONDARY INFRINGEMENT: TEST: REQUISITE STATE OF MIND: H.C.)

Originality

Risis Pte Ltd v. Polar Gems Pte Ltd (WHETHER DESIGN NEW OR ORIGINAL: INFRINGEMENT: NOVELTY: PRINCIPLES IN JUDGING: H.C.)

Practice

Anton Piller

Hung Ka Ho v. A-1 Office System Pte Ltd (APPLICATION TO DISCHARGE: INTERROGATORIES: PRIVILEGE AGAINST SELF-INCRIMINATION: H.C.)

Interrogatories

Hung Ka Ho v. A-1 Office System Pte Ltd (PRIVILEGE AGAINST SELF-INCRIMINATION: H.C.)

Privilege against self-incrimination

Hung Ka Ho v. A-1 Office System Pte Ltd (ANTON PILLER: APPLICATION TO DISCHARGE: INTERROGATORIES: H.C.)

Search warrants

Lance Court Furnishings Pte Ltd v. Public Prosecutor (SCOPE OF PROTECTION: DESIGNS INDUSTRIALLY APPLIED: WHETHER PROPERLY OBTAINED: H.C.)

Scope of protection

Lance Court Furnishings Pte Ltd v. Public Prosecutor (DESIGNS INDUSTRIALLY APPLIED: SEARCH WARRANTS: WHETHER PROPERLY OBTAINED: H.C.)

Passing Off

Adequacy of Damages. *See* **Practice** (*Adequacy of damages*)

Bona Fide Purchaser for Value Without Notice. *See* **Practice** (*Defences*)

Costs. *See* **Practice** (*Costs*)

Deception and Confusion

Jordache Enterprises Inc. v. Millenium Pte Ltd (PRONUNCIATION OF TRADE NAME: DECEPTION AND CONFUSION: REPUTATION: PRACTICE: COSTS: H.C.)

Mechanical Handling Engineering (S.) Pte Ltd v. Material Handling Engineering Pte Ltd (SHARED REPUTATION DOCTRINE: WHETHER RELEVANT: INITIALS: MHE: EVIDENCE OF CONFUSION: H.C.)

Saga Foodstuffs Manufacturing (Pte) Ltd v. Best Food Pte Ltd (GET-UP: SIMILARITY: RELEVANCE OF INTENTION TO DECEIVE: EVIDENCE: MARKET SURVEY: HEARSAY: H.C.)

Tong Guan Food Products Pte Ltd v. Hoe Huat Hng Foodstuffs Pte Ltd (GET-UP: SIMILARITY: REPUTATION: C.A.)

Elements of Tort

Pernod Ricard SA v. Allswell Trading Pte Ltd (GET-UP: MERE COPYING OF UTILITARIAN FEATURES INSUFFICIENT: H.C.)

Get-up

Chia v. Haw Par Brothers International Ltd (SIMILARITY OF GET-UP: FORM OF
ORDER: ADEQUACY OF DAMAGES: C.A.)

Pernod Ricard SA v. Allswell Trading Pte Ltd (ELEMENTS OF TORT: MERE COPYING
OF UTILITARIAN FEATURES INSUFFICIENT: H.C.)

Saga Foodstuffs Manufacturing (Pte) Ltd v. Best Food Pte Ltd (SIMILARITY:
CONFUSION OF PUBLIC: RELEVANCE OF INTENTION TO DECEIVE: EVIDENCE:
MARKET SURVEY: HEARSAY: H.C.)

Tong Guan Food Products Pte Ltd v. Hoe Huat Hng Foodstuffs Pte Ltd (SIMILARITY:
DECEPTION OR CONFUSION: REPUTATION: C.A.)

Goodwill and Reputation

Essex Electric (Pte) Ltd v. IPC Computers (U.K.) Ltd (EXCLUSIVE DISTRIBUTION
AGREEMENT IN U.K.: WHETHER OWNERSHIP OF U.K. GOODWILL VESTED IN
PLAINTIFF OR EXCLUSIVE DISTRIBUTOR: Ch.D.)

Jordache Enterprises Inc. v. Millenium Pte Ltd (PRACTICE: COSTS: H.C.)

Mechanical Handling Engineering (S.) Pte Ltd v. Material Handling Engineering Pte
Ltd (TRADE MARK: NAMES OF CORPORATIONS: DESCRIPTIVE NAME: SAME
INDUSTRY: REPUTATION: DATE EXTABLISHED: SHARED REPUTATION
DOCTRINE: WHETHER RELEVANT: INITIALS: MHE: EVIDENCE OF
CONFUSION: DELAY: LACHES, ACQUIESENCE AND ESTOPPEL: H.C.)

Tong Guan Food Products Pte Ltd v. Hoe Huat Hng Foodstuffs Pte Ltd (GET-UP:
SIMILARITY: C.A.)

Intention to Deceive

Saga Foodstuffs Manufacturing (Pte) Ltd v. Best Food Pte Ltd (GET-UP: SIMILARITY:
CONFUSION OF PUBLIC: EVIDENCE: MARKET SURVEY: HEARSAY: H.C.)

Inverse Passing Off

Robert John Powers School Inc. v. Tessensohn (COPYRIGHT: INFRINGEMENT:
SCOPE OF PROTECTION: COMPILATION: MISLEADING ACCOUNT OF
ACHIEVEMENT IN RÉSUME: H.C.) (APPEAL: C.A.)

Practice

Acquiescence

Mechanical Handling Engineering (S.) Pte Ltd v. Material Handling Engineering Pte
Ltd (H.C.)

Adequacy of damages

Chia v. Haw Par Brothers International Ltd (SIMILARITY OF GET-UP: FORM OF
ORDER: C.A.)

Costs

Jordache Enterprises Inc. v. Millenium Pte Ltd (PRONUNCIATION OF TRADE NAME:
DECEPTION AND CONFUSION: REPUTATION: H.C.)

Defences

Tai Muk Kwai v. Luen Hup Medical Company (BONA FIDE PURCHASER FOR VALUE
WITHOUT NOTICE: H.C.)

Delay

Mechanical Handling Engineering (S.) Pte Ltd v. Material Handling Engineering Pte Ltd (H.C.)

Estoppel

Mechanical Handling Engineering (S.) Pte Ltd v. Material Handling Engineering Pte Ltd (H.C.)

Evidence

Saga Foodstuffs Manufacturing (Pte) Ltd v. Best Food Pte Ltd (GET-UP: SIMILARITY: CONFUSION OF PUBLIC: RELEVANCE OF INTENTION TO DECEIVE: MARKET SURVEY: HEARSAY: H.C.)

Form of order

Chia v. Haw Par Brothers International Ltd (SIMILARITY OF GET-UP: ADEQUACY OF DAMAGES: C.A.)

Interlocutory injunction—balance of convenience

Reed Exhibitions Pte. Ltd v. Khoo Yak Chuan Thomas (RESTRAINT OF TRADE: LICENSEES' COVENANT NOT TO ENTER TRADE SIMILAR TO LICENSOR FOR ONE YEAR FROM TERMINATION OF LICENCE: SERIOUS QUESTION TO BE TRIED: WHETHER DAMAGES AN ADEQUATE REMEDY: C.A.)

Interlocutory injunction—serious question to be tried

Reed Exhibitions Pte. Ltd v. Khoo Yak Chuan Thomas (RESTRAINT OF TRADE: LICENSEES' COVENANT NOT TO ENTER TRADE SIMILAR TO LICENSOR FOR ONE YEAR FROM TERMINATION OF LICENCE: WHETHER DAMAGES AN ADEQUATE REMEDY: BALANCE OF CONVENIENCE: C.A.)

Interlocutory injunction—whether damages an adequate remedy

Reed Exhibitions Pte. Ltd v. Khoo Yak Chuan Thomas (RESTRAINT OF TRADE: LICENSEES' COVENANT NOT TO ENTER TRADE SIMILAR TO LICENSOR FOR ONE YEAR FROM TERMINATION OF LICENCE: SERIOUS QUESTION TO BE TRIED: BALANCE OF CONVENIENCE: C.A.)

Laches

Mechanical Handling Engineering (S.) Pte Ltd v. Material Handling Engineering Pte Ltd (H.C.)

Market survey

Saga Foodstuffs Manufacturing (Pte) Ltd v. Best Food Pte Ltd (GET-UP: SIMILARITY: CONFUSION OF PUBLIC: RELEVANCE OF INTENTION TO DECEIVE: EVIDENCE: HEARSAY: H.C.)

Reputation. *See* **Goodwill**

Trade Mark or Trade Name

Jordache Enterprises Inc. v. Millenium Pte Ltd (INFRINGEMENT: JEANS: PRONUNCIATION: DECEPTION AND CONFUSION: REPUTATION: COSTS: H.C.)

Mechanical Handling Engineering (S.) Pte Ltd v. Material Handling Engineering Pte Ltd (NAMES OF CORPORATIONS: DESCRIPTIVE NAME: SAME INDUSTRY: REPUTATION: DATE EXTABLISHED: SHARED REPUTATION DOCTRINE: WHETHER RELEVANT: INITIALS: MHE: EVIDENCE OF CONFUSION: H.C.)

Tai Muk Kwai v. Luen Hup Medical Company (RIVAL CLAIM OF OWNERSHIP OF TRADE MARKS: GOODS MANUFACTURED BY PLAINTIFFS AND EXCLUSIVELY SOLD AND DISTRIBUTED BY DEFENDANT AS SOLE IMPORTER: WHETHER ASSIGNMENT OF MARKS CONFERS OWNERSHIP: DEFENCE OF BONA FIDE PURCHASER FOR VALUE WITHOUT NOTICE: H.C.)

Practice and Miscellaneous Subjects

Acquiescence

Mechanical Handling Engineering (S.) Pte Ltd v. Material Handling Engineering Pte Ltd (H.C.)

Adequacy of Damages

Chia v. Haw Par Brothers International Ltd (CONFIDENTIAL INFORMATION: PASSING OFF: SIMILARITY OF GET-UP: FORM OF ORDER: C.A.)

Anton Piller

Expanded Metal Manufacturing Pte Ltd v. Expanded Metal Co. Ltd (PRIVILEGE AGAINST SELF-INCRIMINATION: INFERENCE TO BE DRAWN: C.A.)

Costs

Jordache Enterprises Inc. v. Millenium Pte Ltd (H.C.)
Singapore Broadcasting Corporation v. Performing Right Society Ltd (INTEREST: Cprt Trib.)

Defences

Tai Muk Kwai v. Luen Hup Medical Company (BONA FIDE PURCHASER FOR VALUE WITHOUT NOTICE: H.C.)

Delay

Mechanical Handling Engineering (S.) Pte Ltd v. Material Handling Engineering Pte Ltd (H.C.)

Estoppel

Mechanical Handling Engineering (S.) Pte Ltd v. Material Handling Engineering Pte Ltd (H.C.)

Evidence

Ng Chye Mong Pte. v. Public Prosecutor (CRIMINAL OFFENCE: COUNTERFEITING: LACK OF EVIDENCE THAT GOODS NOT GENUINE: H.C.)

Saga Foodstuffs Manufacturing (Pte) Ltd v. Best Food Pte Ltd (MARKET SURVEY: HEARSAY: H.C.)

Ex Parte Injunction

Expanded Metal Manufacturing Pte Ltd v. Expanded Metal Co. Ltd (ANTON PILLER ORDER: PRIVILEGE AGAINST SELF-INCRIMINATION: INFERENCE TO BE DRAWN: C.A.)

Form of Order

Chia v. Haw Par Brothers International Ltd (ADEQUACY OF DAMAGES: C.A.)

Interest

Singapore Broadcasting Corporation v. Performing Right Society Ltd (COSTS: Cprt Trib.)

Interlocutory Injunction—Appropriateness of Damages

X Pte Ltd v. CDE (CONFIDENTIAL INFORMATION: SERIOUS QUESTION TO BE TRIED: H.C.)

Interlocutory Injunction—Balance of Convenience

Reed Exhibitions Pte. Ltd v. Khoo Yak Chuan Thomas (PASSING OFF: RESTRAINT OF TRADE: LICENSEES' COVENANT NOT TO ENTER TRADE SIMILAR TO LICENSOR FOR ONE YEAR FROM TERMINATION OF LICENCE: SERIOUS QUESTION TO BE TRIED: WHETHER DAMAGES AN ADEQUATE REMEDY: C.A.)

Interlocutory Injunction—Chance of Injustice

Remus Innovation MbH v. Hong Boon Siong (STANDARD OF PROOF: DISCRETION: H.C.)

Interlocutory Injunction—Discretion

Remus Innovation MbH v. Hong Boon Siong (STANDARD OF PROOF: CHANCE OF INJUSTICE: H.C.)

Interlocutory Injunction—Serious Question to be Tried

Reed Exhibitions Pte. Ltd v. Khoo Yak Chuan Thomas (PASSING OFF: RESTRAINT OF TRADE: LICENSEES' COVENANT NOT TO ENTER TRADE SIMILAR TO LICENSOR FOR ONE YEAR FROM TERMINATION OF LICENCE: WHETHER DAMAGES AN ADEQUATE REMEDY: BALANCE OF CONVENIENCE: C.A.)
X Pte Ltd v. CDE (APPROPRIATENESS OF DAMAGES: H.C.)

Interlocutory Injunction—Standard of Proof

Remus Innovation MbH v. Hong Boon Siong (DISCRETION: CHANCE OF INJUSTICE: H.C.)

Interlocutory Injunction—Whether Damages an Adequate Remedy

Reed Exhibitions Pte. Ltd v. Khoo Yak Chuan Thomas (PASSING OFF: RESTRAINT OF TRADE: LICENSEES' COVENANT NOT TO ENTER TRADE SIMILAR TO LICENSOR FOR ONE YEAR FROM TERMINATION OF LICENCE: SERIOUS QUESTION TO BE TRIED: BALANCE OF CONVENIENCE: C.A.)

Costs. *See* **Practice** (*Costs*)

Counterfeit Goods

Trade Facilities Pte Ltd v. Public Prosecutor (IMPORTATION: SALE ABROAD: GOODS
RETURNED BY FOREIGN BUYER: JURISDICTION: H.C.)

Counterfeit Labels

Ng Chye Mong Pte Ltd v. Public Prosecutor (EXPLANATION OF: WHETHER NEED
TO PROVE THAT CONTENTS OF BOTTLES ALSO NOT GENUINE: NATURE OF
CRIMINAL OFFENCE: CONSTRUCTION: H.C.)

Criminal Offence

Challenger Technologies Pte Ltd v. Public Prosecutor (FALSE APPLICATION OF
REGISTERED MARK: ACTUAL OR IMPLIED CONSENT OF PROPRIETOR: H.C.)
Heng Lee Handbags Co. Pte Ltd v. Public Prosecutor (SEARCH WARRANT:
JUSTIFICATION: APPLICATION TO QUASH: H.C.)
Ng Chye Mong Pte Ltd v. Public Prosecutor (COUNTERFEIT LABELS: NATURE OF
CRIMINAL OFFENCE: CONSTRUCTION: H.C.)
Oh Cheng Hai v. Ong Yong Yew (CRIMINAL PROCEDURE: PRIVATE
PROSECUTION: *Locus standii*: COSTS: POSSESSION OF INLAY CARDS FOR AUDIO
TAPES: WHETHER OFFENCE UNDER STATUTE: H.C.)

Deception and Confusion

Davidoff Extension SA v. Davidoff Commercio E Industria Ltda (USE OF ANOTHER
COMPANY'S MARK: DISCRETION: H.C.)
Jaguar Trade Mark (SIMILARITY BETWEEN MARKS: INTENTION TO DECEIVE:
LIKELIHOOD OF CONFUSION: H.C.)
Jordache Enterprises Inc. v. Millenium Pte Ltd (INFRINGEMENT: JEANS:
PRONUNCIATION OF TRADE NAME: H.C.)

Descriptiveness

Econlite Manufacturing Pte Ltd v. Technochem Holdings Pte Ltd (PASSING OFF:
TRADE NAME: ECONOLITE: LIKELIHOOD OF CONFUSION OR DECEPTION:
OVERLAP IN FIELD OF ACTIVITY: DAMAGES: H.C.)

Equitable Owner. *See* **Ownership**

Expungement

Beyer Electrical Enterprise Pte Ltd v. Swanfu Trading Pte Ltd (ALOHA SWANFU:
APPLICATION TO EXPUNGE: BONA FIDE USE: ONUS OF PROOF: H.C.: C.A.)
Davidoff Extension SA v. Davidoff Commercio E Industria Ltda (USE OF ANOTHER
COMPANY'S MARK: REPUTATION: DECEPTION OF PUBLIC: DISCRETION:
H.C.)
Jaguar Trade Mark (APPLICATION TO EXPUNGE: DISCRETION: SIMILARITY
BETWEEN MARKS: H.C.)

Macy & Co. Inc. v. Trade Accents (FALSE CLAIM TO PROPRIETORSHIP OF TRADE MARK: H.C.)

Tai Muk Kwai v. Luen Hup Medical Company (RIVAL CLAIM OF OWNERSHIP: WHETHER ASSIGNMENT CONFERS OWNERSHIP: BONA FIDE PURCHASER FOR VALUE WITHOUT NOTICE: H.C.)

Passing Off

Econlite Manufacturing Pte Ltd v. Technochem Holdings Pte Ltd (TRADE NAME: ECONOLITE: WHETHER DESCRIPTIVE: LIKELIHOOD OF CONFUSION OR DECEPTION: OVERLAP IN FIELD OF ACTIVITY: DAMAGES: H.C.)

Heublein Inc. v. Paterson Simons & Co. (Singapore) Pte Ltd (FRANCHISE: KENTUCKY FRIED CHICKEN: INJUNCTION: COUNTERCLAIM: BALANCE OF CONVENIENCE: C.A.)

Mechanical Handling Engineering (S.) Pte Ltd v. Material Handling Engineering Pte Ltd (NAMES OF CORPORATIONS: DESCRIPTIVE NAME: SAME INDUSTRY: REPUTATION: H.C.)

Phonetic Similarity

Jordache Enterprises Inc. v. Millenium Pte Ltd (INFRINGEMENT: JEANS: PRONUNCIATION OF TRADE NAME: H.C.)

Karrimor International Ltd v. Ho Choong Fun (EXPUNGEMENT: OWNERSHIP OF MARK: WORLDWIDE REPUTATION OF APPLICANT: SIMILARITY OF APPEARANCE BETWEEN PRODUCT: H.C.)

Practice

Anton Piller

Reebok International Ltd v. Royal Corp. (*Riddick* PRINCIPLE: WHETHER ARTICLES SEIZED UNDER ANTON PILLER ORDER CAN BE USED IN FOREIGN CIVIL PROCEEDINGS AGAINST THIRD PARTIES: H.C.)

Acquiescence

Mechanical Handling Engineering (S.) Pte Ltd v. Material Handling Engineering Pte Ltd (H.C.)

Balance of convenience

Heublein Inc. v. Paterson Simons & Co. (Singapore) Pte Ltd (COUNTERCLAIM: C.A.)

Contempt

Cartier International BV v. Lee Hock Lee (APPLICATION FOR COMMITTAL: H.C.)

Costs

Jordache Enterprises Inc. v. Millenium Pte Ltd (H.C.)

Oh Cheng Hai v. Ong Yong Yew (POSSESSION OF INLAY CARDS FOR AUDIO TAPES: WHETHER OFFENCE UNDER STATUTE: H.C.)

Counterclaim

Heublein Inc. v. Paterson Simons & Co. (Singapore) Pte Ltd (INJUNCTION: BALANCE OF CONVENIENCE: C.A.)

Damages

Econlite Manufacturing Pte Ltd v. Technochem Holdings Pte Ltd (OVERLAP IN FIELD OF ACTIVITY: H.C.)

Defences

Tai Muk Kwai v. Luen Hup Medical Company (BONA FIDE PURCHASER FOR VALUE
  WITHOUT NOTICE: H.C.)

Delay

Mechanical Handling Engineering (S.) Pte Ltd v. Material Handling Engineering Pte
  Ltd (H.C.)

Discovery

Guccio Gucci SpA v. Sukhdav Singh (POST-JUDGMENT-DISCOVERY: PAST ACTS OF
  INFRINGEMENT: PRIVILEGE AGAINST SELF-INCRIMINATION: H.C.)
Reebok International Ltd v. Royal Corp. (ANTON PILLER: *Riddick* PRINCIPLE:
  WHETHER ARTICLES SEIZED UNDER ANTON PILLER ORDER CAN BE USED IN
  FOREIGN CIVIL PROCEEDINGS AGAINST THIRD PARTIES: H.C.)

Discretion

Davidoff Extension SA v. Davidoff Commercio E Industria Ltda (H.C.)
Jaguar Trade Mark (APPLICATION TO EXPUNGE: H.C.)

Estoppel

Mechanical Handling Engineering (S.) Pte Ltd v. Material Handling Engineering Pte
  Ltd (H.C.)

Evidence

Cartier International BV v. Lee Hock Lee (PRESUMPTION: CONTEMPT:
  APPLICATION FOR COMMITTAL: SUFFICIENCY: HEARSAY: ADMISIBILITY:
  H.C.)
Louis Vuitton v. Lee Thin Tuan (PRODUCTION OF DOCUMENTS: H.C.) (APPEAL:
  PRIVILEGE AGAINST SELF-INCRIMINATION: C.A.)
Ng Chye Mong Pte. v. Public Prosecutor (CRIMINAL OFFENCE: COUNTERFEITING:
  LACK OF EVIDENCE THAT GOODS NOT GENUINE: H.C.)

Jurisdiction

Trade Facilities Pte Ltd v. Public Prosecutor (COUNTERFEIT GOODS: IMPORTATION:
  SALE ABROAD: GOODS RETURNED BY FOREIGN BUYER: H.C.)

Laches

Mechanical Handling Engineering (S.) Pte Ltd v. Material Handling Engineering Pte
  Ltd (H.C.)

Locus standi

Oh Cheng Hai v. Ong Yong Yew (CRIMINAL PROCEDURE: PRIVATE
  PROSECUTION: H.C.)

Onus of proof

Beyer Electrical Enterprise Pte Ltd v. Swanfu Trading Pte Ltd (ALOHA SWANFU:
  BONA FIDE USE: H.C.: C.A.)

Pleadings

Saga Foodstuffs Manufacturing (Pte) Ltd v. Best Food Pte Ltd (ASSIGNMENT OF APPLICATION BEFORE DATE OF WRIT: AMENDMENT: H.C.)

Privilege against self-incrimination

Guccio Gucci SpA v. Sukhdav Singh (POST-JUDGMENT DISCOVERY: PAST ACTS OF INFRINGEMENT: H.C.)

Louis Vuitton v. Lee Thin Tuan (APPEAL: PRODUCTION OF DOCUMENTS: C.A.)

Search warrant

Heng Lee Handbags Co. Pte Ltd v. Public Prosecutor (JUSTIFICATION: APPLICATION TO QUASH: H.C.)

Pronunciation of Mark or Name. *See* **Phonetic Similarity**

Rectification

Arnold Palmer Trade Mark (BONA FIDE INTENTION TO USE: TRAFFICKING: H.C.)

Auvi Pte Ltd v. Seah Siew Tee and Chai Foh Min (PERSONS AGGRIEVED: LOGO: EQUITABLE OWNER: H.C.)

Macy & Co. Inc. v. Trade Accents (AGGREIVED PERSON: INTERNATIONAL AND LOCAL GOODWILL AND REPUTATION: FALSE CLAIM TO PROPRIETORSHIP OF TRADE MARK: H.C.)

Registration

Arnold Palmer Trade Mark (RECTIFICATION: BONA FIDE INTENTION TO USE: TRAFFICKING: H.C.)

Reputation

Davidoff Extension SA v. Davidoff Commercio E Industria Ltda (USE OF ANOTHER COMPANY'S MARK: APPLICATION FOR EXPUNGEMENT: DECEPTION OF PUBLIC: DISCRETION: H.C.)

Jordache Enterprises Inc. v. Millenium Pte Ltd (INFRINGEMENT: JEANS: PRONUNCIATION OF TRADE NAME: DECEPTION AND CONFUSION: H.C.)

Karrimor International Ltd v. Ho Choong Fun (EXPUNGEMENT: OWNERSHIP: WORLDWIDE REPUTATION: PHONETIC SIMILARITY: H.C.)

Macy & Co. Inc. v. Trade Accents (RECTIFICATION: INTERNATIONAL AND LOCAL GOODWILL AND REPUTATION: H.C.)

Similarity of Appearance

Karrimor International Ltd v. Ho Choong Fun (EXPUNGEMENT: OWNERSHIP: WORLDWIDE REPUTATION: PHONETIC SIMILARITY: H.C.)

Trafficking

Arnold Palmer Trade Mark (REGISTRATION: RECTIFICATION: BONA FIDE INTENTION TO USE: H.C.)

Use

Arnold Palmer Trade Mark (BONA FIDE INTENTION TO USE: TRAFFICKING: H.C.)

Beyer Electrical Enterprise Pte Ltd v. Swanfu Trading Pte Ltd (ALOHA SWANFU: APPLICATION TO EXPUNGE: BONA FIDE USE: ONUS OF PROOF: H.C.: C.A.)

Worldwide Reputation. *See* **Reputation**

SOUTH AFRICA

Confidential Information and Breach of Confidence

Anton Piller Orders. *See* **Practice** (*Anton Piller orders*)

Customer Lists

Van Castricum v. Theunissen (UNLAWFUL COMPETITION: EX-EMPLOYEE: TPD)

Directors. *See also under* **Employees**

Sage Holdings Ltd v. Financial Mail (Pty) Ltd (EMPLOYEES: PUBLIC POLICY: WLD)
Sibex Construction (S.A.) (Pty) Ltd v. Injectaseal C.C. (UNLAWFUL COMPETITION:
    EX-EMPLOYEES: PRICE LIST : DUTY OF FIDELITY: TPD)

Discovery and Inspection. *See* **Practice** (*Discovery and inspection*)

Duty of Fidelity

Sibex Construction (S.A.) (Pty) Ltd v. Injectaseal C.C. (UNLAWFUL COMPETITION:
    EX-EMPLOYEES: PRICE LIST: DIRECTORS: TPD)

Enforcement. *See* **Practice** (*Enforcement*)

Employees. *See also under* **Directors**

Knox D'Arcy Ltd v. Jamieson (EX-EMPLOYEE: DISTINCTION BETWEEN TRADE
    SECRETS AND OTHER CONFIDENTIAL INFORMATION: WLD)
Sage Holdings Ltd v. Financial Mail (Pty) Ltd (DIRECTORS: PUBLIC POLICY: WLD)
Sibex Construction (S.A.) (Pty) Ltd v. Injectaseal C.C. (UNLAWFUL COMPETITION:
    EX-EMPLOYEES: PRICE LIST: DUTY OF FIDELITY: DIRECTORS: TPD)
Van Castricum v. Theunissen (UNLAWFUL COMPETITION: EX-EMPLOYEE:
    CUSTOMER LISTS: TPD)

Fiduciary Relationship

Meter Systems Holdings Ltd v. Venter (UNLAWFUL COMPETITION: RESTRAINT OF
    TRADE: ENFORCEMENT: EX-EMPLOYEE: WLD)

Interim Injunction. *See* **Practice** (*Interim injunction*)

Master and Servant

Multi Tube Systems (Pty) Ltd v. Ponting (INTERIM INJUNCTION: D&CLD)

Practice

Anton Piller orders

Waste-Tech (Pty) Ltd v. Wade Refuse (Pty) Ltd (DISCOVERY AND INSPECTION: NATURE AND SCOPE: WLD)

Discovery and inspection

Waste-Tech (Pty) Ltd v. Wade Refuse (Pty) Ltd (ANTON PILLER: NATURE AND SCOPE: WLD)

Enforcement

Meter Systems Holdings Ltd v. Venter (UNLAWFUL COMPETITION: FIDUCIARY RELATIONSHIPS: RESTRAINT OF TRADE: EX-EMPLOYEE: WLD)

Interim injunction

Multi Tube Systems (Pty) Ltd v. Ponting (MASTER AND SERVANT: D&CLD)

Price list

Sibex Construction (S.A.) (Pty) Ltd v. Injectaseal C.C. (UNLAWFUL COMPETITION: EX-EMPLOYEES: DUTY OF FIDELITY: DIRECTORS: TPD)

Public policy

Sage Holdings Ltd v. Financial Mail (Pty) Ltd (EMPLOYEES: DIRECTORS: WLD)

Restraint of Trade

Meter Systems Holdings Ltd v. Venter (UNLAWFUL COMPETITION: FIDUCIARY RELATIONSHIPS: ENFORCEMENT: EX-EMPLOYEE: WLD)

Unlawful Competition

Knox D'Arcy Ltd v. Jamieson (EX-EMPLOYEE: DISTINCTION BETWEEN TRADE SECRETS AND OTHER CONFIDENTIAL INFORMATION: WLD)

Sibex Construction (S.A.) (Pty) Ltd v. Injectaseal C.C. (EX-EMPLOYEES: PRICE LIST: DUTY OF FIDELITY: DIRECTORS: TPD)

Van Castricum v. Theunissen (EX-EMPLOYEE: CUSTOMER LISTS: TPD)

Unlawful Interference with Trade

Hacharis Heat Treatment (Pty) Ltd v. Iscor (TPD)

Copyright

Abridgement

Galago Publishers (Pty) Ltd v. Erasmus (INFRINGEMENT: TEST OF: OBJECTIVE SIMILARITY: ASSIGNED COPYRIGHT: STATUS OF AUTHOR: A.D.)

Account of Profits. *See* **Practice** (*Account of profits*)

Adaptations

Bosal Afrika Pty Ltd v. Grapnel Pty Ltd (INFRINGEMENT: DRAWINGS: PROTOTYPE: CPD)

Additional Damages. *See* **Practice** (*Damages*)

Artistic Work

Da Gama Textile Co. Ltd v. Vision Creations C.C. (INFRINGEMENT: SCOPE OF PROTECTION: THREE-DIMENSIONAL REPRODUCTION OF ARTISTIC WORK: D&CLD)

Waylite Diaries C.C. v. First National Bank Ltd (SUBSISTENCE: DRAWINGS: LITERARY WORK: WRITTEN TABLES AND COMPILATIONS: DIARY: WLD: A.D.)

Assignment

Galago Publishers (Pty) Ltd v. Erasmus (INFRINGEMENT: TEST OF: OBJECTIVE SIMILARITY: ASSIGNED COPYRIGHT: STATUS OF AUTHOR: A.D.)

Payen Components S.A. Ltd v. Bovic Gaskets C.C. (COMPUTERISED CATALOGUING SYSTEM: WORK PRODUCED BY PROGRAM: ASSIGNMENT TO OVERSEAS PARENT COMPANY: WLD)

Author and Authorship

Fax Directories (Pty) Ltd v. S.A. Fax Listings C.C. (SUBSISTENCE: LITERARY WORK: D&CLD)

Galago Publishers (Pty) Ltd v. Erasmus (ASSIGNED COPYRIGHT: STATUS OF AUTHOR: A.D.)

Nintendo Co. Ltd v. Golden China TV-Game Centre Ltd (PARALLEL IMPORTATION: VIDEO GAMES: S.C.)

Broadcast

South African Music Rights Organisation Ltd v. Svenmill Fabrics (Pty) Ltd (INFRINGEMENT: MUSIC: CPD)

Cinematographic Film. *See* **Film**

Compilation

Waylite Diaries C.C. v. First National Bank Ltd (SUBSISTENCE: ARTISTIC WORK: DRAWINGS: LITERARY WORK: WRITTEN TABLES AND COMPILATIONS: DIARY: WLD, A.D.)

Computer-related Subjects

Greenberg v. Pearson (INFRINGEMENT: DISCOVERY: PRODUCTION OF DOCUMENTS: COMPUTER PRINTOUTS: SOURCE CODES: INVOICES AND OTHER SECONDARY DOCUMENTS: WLD)

Payen Components S.A. Ltd v. Bovic Gaskets C.C. (COMPUTERISED CATALOGUING
SYSTEM: WORK PRODUCED BY PROGRAM: WLD)

Creation of Work from Photograph

Bress Designs (Pty) Ltd v. G.Y. Lounge Suite Manufacturers (Pty) Ltd (DIMENSIONAL
WORK: LOUNGE SUITE: WLD)

Criminal Offences

S. v. Nxumalo (SALE OF INFRINGING COPIES: *Mens rea*: FORM: KNOWLEDGE: TPD)

Damages. *See* **Practice** (*Damages*)

Design. *See* South African **Design**

Dimensional Work

Bress Designs (Pty) Ltd v. G.Y. Lounge Suite Manufacturers (Pty) Ltd (LOUNGE
SUITE: CREATION FROM PHOTOGRAPH: WLD)
Da Gama Textile Co. Ltd v. Vision Creations C.C. (INFRINGEMENT: SCOPE OF
PROTECTION: THREE-DIMENSIONAL REPRODUCTION OF ARTISTIC WORK:
D&CLD)
Tolima (Pty) Ltd v. Cugacius Motor Accessories (Pty) Ltd (THREE-DIMENSIONAL
FORM OF TWO-DIMENSIONAL DRAWING: INDIRECT COPYING: WLD)

Drawings

Appleton v. Harnischfeger Corporation (SUBSISTENCE: ENGINEERING DRAWINGS
MADE OVERSEAS: APPLICABLE LEGISLATION: A.D.)
Bosal Afrika Pty Ltd v. Grapnel Pty Ltd (INFRINGEMENT: PROTOTYPE:
ADAPTATIONS: CPD)
Waylite Diaries C.C. v. First National Bank Ltd (SUBSISTENCE: ARTISTIC WORK:
LITERARY WORK: WRITTEN TABLES AND COMPILATIONS: DIARY: WLD:
A.D.)

Evidence. *See* **Practice** (*Evidence*)

Exclusive Distributor

Frank & Hirsch (Pty) Ltd v. A. Roopanand Brothers (Pty) Ltd (INFRINGEMENT:
IMPORTATION: D&CLD)

Exclusive Licence

Fulton (J.K.) (Pty) Ltd v. Logic Engineering Enterprises (Pty) Ltd (NOT NECESSARY
FOR LICENCE TO COVER ALL ACTS MENTIONED IN RELEVANT ACT: WLD)
Paramount Pictures Corp. v. Video Parktown North (Pty) Ltd (FILM: RIGHTS: TPD)
Video Parktown North (Pty) Ltd v. Paramount Pictures Corp. (INFRINGEMENT:
CINEMATOGRAPHIC FILM: TPD)

Film

Paramount Pictures Corp. v. Video Parktown North (Pty) Ltd (EXCLUSIVE LICENSEE:
RIGHTS: TPD)
Video Parktown North (Pty) Ltd v. Paramount Pictures Corp. (INFRINGEMENT:
TPD)

Foreign Law. *See* **Practice** (*Foreign law*)

Get-up

Frank & Hirsch (Pty) Ltd v. A. Roopanand Brothers (Pty) Ltd (INFRINGEMENT: IMPORTATION: EXCLUSIVE DISTRIBUTOR: TRADE DRESS: LABELS: D&CLD)

Importation

Frank & Hirsch (Pty) Ltd v. A. Roopanand Brothers (Pty) Ltd (INFRINGEMENT: EXCLUSIVE DISTRIBUTOR: D&CLD)

Nintendo Co. Ltd v. Golden China TV-Game Centre Ltd (PARALLEL IMPORTATION: VIDEO GAMES: AUTHORSHIP: S.C.)

Twentieth Century Fox Film Corp. v. Anthony Black Films (Pty) Ltd (INFRINGEMENT: PARALLEL IMPORTS: WLD)

Indirect Copying

Tolima (Pty) Ltd v. Cugacius Motor Accessories (Pty) Ltd (COPYRIGHT: THREE-DIMENSIONAL FORM OF TWO-DIMENSIONAL DRAWING: WLD)

Infringement

Bosal Afrika Pty Ltd v. Grapnel Pty Ltd (DRAWINGS: PROTOTYPE: ADAPTATIONS: CPD)

Butt v. Schultz (UNFAIR COMPETITION: USE OF BOAT AS MOULD: ECD)

Columbia Pictures Industries Inc. v. Videorent Parkmore (COPYRIGHT: INFRINGEMENT: KNOWLEDGE: H.C.)

Da Gama Textile Co. Ltd v. Vision Creations C.C. (SCOPE OF PROTECTION: THREE-DIMENSIONAL REPRODUCTION OF ARTISTIC WORK: D&CLD)

Fax Directories (Pty) Ltd v. S.A. Fax Listings C.C. (SUBSISTENCE: LITERARY WORK: AUTHOR OWNERSHIP: COMPANY: TELEFAX DIRECTORY: D&CLD)

Frank & Hirsch (Pty) Ltd v. A. Roopanand Brothers (Pty) Ltd (IMPORTATION: EXCLUSIVE DISTRIBUTOR: GET-UP: TRADE DRESS: LABELS: D&CLD)

Greenberg v. Pearson (PRACTICE: DISCOVERY: PRODUCTION OF DOCUMENTS: COMPUTER PRINTOUTS: SOURCE CODES: INVOICES AND OTHER SECONDARY DOCUMENTS: WLD)

Galago Publishers (Pty) Ltd v. Erasmus (TEST OF: OBJECTIVE SIMILARITY: ASSIGNED COPYRIGHT: STATUS OF AUTHOR: ABRIDGEMENT: A.D.)

Harnischfeger Corporation v. Appleton (EVIDENCE: OWNERSHIP: FOREIGN LAW: WLD)

Insamcor (Pty) Ltd v. Maschinenfabriek Sidler Stadler AG (ORIGINALITY: PROOF: EVIDENCE: SUFFICIENCY: WLD)

Juta & Co. Ltd v. De Koker (SUBSTANTIAL PART: TPD)

Klep Valves (Pty) Ltd v. Saunders Valve Co. Ltd (SUBSISTENCE OF: TRADE MARK: INFRINGEMENT: A.D.)

Payen Components S.A. Ltd v. Bovic Gaskets CC (SUBSTANTIAL PART: REMEDIES: INJUNCTION: BREACH: INTERFACE BETWEEN UNLAWFUL COMPETITION AND COPYRIGHT, TRADE MARK, DESIGN AND PASSING OFF ACTIONS: A.D.)

Priority Records (Pty) Ltd v. Ban-Nab Radio and TV (DAMAGES: ADDITIONAL DAMAGES: D&CLD)

Saunders Valve Co. Ltd v. Klep Valves (REMEDIES: PRESUMPTION OF ORIGINALITY: TPD)

South African Music Rights Organisation Ltd v. Svenmill Fabrics (Pty) Ltd (MUSIC: BROADCAST: CPD)

Twentieth Century Fox Film Corp. v. Anthony Black Films (Pty) Ltd (PARALLEL IMPORTS: WLD)

Video Parktown North (Pty) Ltd v. Paramount Pictures Corp. (CINEMATOGRAPHIC FILM: EXCLUSIVE LICENSEE: REMEDIES: ACCOUNT OF PROFITS: TPD)

Knowledge. *See* **Practice** (*Knowledge*)

Labels

Frank & Hirsch (Pty) Ltd v. A. Roopanand Brothers (Pty) Ltd (INFRINGEMENT: IMPORTATION: EXCLUSIVE DISTRIBUTOR: GET-UP: TRADE DRESS: D&CLD)

Literary Work

Fax Directories (Pty) Ltd v. S.A. Fax Listings C.C. (SUBSISTENCE: AUTHOR OWNERSHIP: COMPANY: INFRINGEMENT: TELEFAX DIRECTORY: D&CLD)

Payen Components S.A. Ltd v. Bovic Gaskets C.C. (SUBSISTENCE: COMPUTERISED CATALOGUING SYSTEM: WORK PRODUCED BY PROGRAM: ASSIGNMENT OF COPYRIGHT TO OVERSEAS PARENT COMPANY: WLD)

Mens rea. *See* **Practice** (*Mens rea*)

Music

South African Music Rights Organisation Ltd v. Svenmill Fabrics (Pty) Ltd (INFRINGEMENT: BROADCAST: CPD)

Objective Similarity

Galago Publishers (Pty) Ltd v. Erasmus (INFRINGEMENT: TEST OF: ASSIGNED COPYRIGHT: STATUS OF AUTHOR: ABRIDGEMENT: A.D.)

Originality

Insamcor (Pty) Ltd v. Maschinenfabriek Sidler Stadler AG (INFRINGEMENT: PROOF: EVIDENCE: SUFFICIENCY: WLD)

Ownership

Fax Directories (Pty) Ltd v. S.A. Fax Listings C.C. (SUBSISTENCE: LITERARY WORK: COMPANY: INFRINGEMENT: TELEFAX DIRECTORY: D&CLD)

Harnischfeger Corporation v. Appleton (EVIDENCE: INFRINGEMENT: FOREIGN LAW: WLD)

South African Broadcasting Corporation v. Pollecutt (PERFORMERS' RIGHTS: RESTRICTION ON USE OF PERFORMANCE: SOUND RECORDING: STATUTORY INTERPRETATION: A.D.)

Parallel Imports. *See also* **Importation**

Nintendo Co. Ltd v. Golden China TV-Game Centre Ltd (VIDEO GAMES: AUTHORSHIP: S.C.)

Twentieth Century Fox Film Corp. v. Anthony Black Films (Pty) Ltd (INFRINGEMENT: WLD)

Performers' Rights

South African Broadcasting Corporation v. Pollecutt (RESTRICTION ON USE OF PERFORMANCE: SOUND RECORDING: OWNERSHIP: STATUTORY INTERPRETATION: A.D.)

Photograph

Bress Designs (Pty) Ltd v. G.Y. Lounge Suite Manufacturers (Pty) Ltd (DIMENSIONAL WORK: LOUNGE SUITE: CREATION FROM PHOTOGRAPH: WLD)

Practice

Account of profits

Video Parktown North (Pty) Ltd v. Paramount Pictures Corp. (TPD)

Damages

Priority Records (Pty) Ltd v. Ban-nab Radio and TV (INFRINGEMENT: ADDITIONAL DAMAGES: D&CLD)

Discovery

Greenberg v. Pearson (PRODUCTION OF DOCUMENTS: COMPUTER PRINTOUTS: SOURCE CODES: INVOICES AND OTHER SECONDARY DOCUMENTS: WLD)

Evidence

Harnischfeger Corporation v. Appleton (INFRINGEMENT: OWNERSHIP: FOREIGN LAW: WLD)
Insamcor (Pty) Ltd v. Maschinenfabriek Sidler Stadler AG (PROOF: SUFFICIENCY: WLD)

Foreign law

Harnischfeger Corporation v. Appleton (EVIDENCE: INFRINGEMENT: OWNERSHIP: WLD)

Injunction

Payen Components S.A. Ltd v. Bovic Gaskets CC (BREACH: INTERFACE BETWEEN UNLAWFUL COMPETITION AND COPYRIGHT, TRADE MARK, DESIGN AND PASSING OFF ACTIONS: A.D.)

Knowledge

Columbia Pictures Industries Inc. v. Videorent Parkmore (INFRINGEMENT: H.C.)
S. v. Nxumalo (OFFENCES: SALE OF INFRINGING COPIES: *Mens rea*: FORM: TPD)

Mens rea

S. v. Nxumalo (OFFENCES: SALE OF INFRINGING COPIES: FORM: KNOWLEDGE: TPD)

Presumption of originality

Saunders Valve Co. Ltd v. Klep Valves (INFRINGEMENT: REMEDIES: TPD)

Proof

Insamcor (Pty) Ltd v. Maschinenfabriek Sidler Stadler AG (INFRINGEMENT: ORIGINALITY: EVIDENCE: SUFFICIENCY: WLD)

Presumption of Originality. *See* **Practice** (*Presumption of Originality*)

Proof. *See* **Practice** (*Proof*)

Prototype

Bosal Afrika Pty Ltd v. Grapnel Pty Ltd (INFRINGEMENT: DRAWINGS: ADAPTATIONS: CPD)

Sale of Infringing Copies

S. v. Nxumalo (OFFENCES: *Mens rea*: FORM: KNOWLEDGE: TPD)

Scope of Protection

Da Gama Textile Co. Ltd v. Vision Creations C.C. (INFRINGEMENT: THREE-DIMENSIONAL REPRODUCTION OF ARTISTIC WORK: D&CLD)

Sound Recording

South African Broadcasting Corporation v. Pollecutt (PERFORMERS' RIGHTS: RESTRICTION ON USE OF PERFORMANCE: OWNERSHIP: STATUTORY INTERPRETATION: A.D.)

Subsistence

Appleton v. Harnischfeger Corporation (ENGINEERING DRAWINGS MADE OVERSEAS: APPLICABLE LEGISLATION GOVERNING RECOGNITION OF COPYRIGHT IN DRAWINGS: A.D.)

Fax Directories (Pty) Ltd v. S.A. Fax Listings C.C. (LITERARY WORK: AUTHOR OWNERSHIP: COMPANY: INFRINGEMENT: TELEFAX DIRECTORY: D&CLD)

Klep Valves (Pty) Ltd v. Saunders Valve Co. Ltd (INFRINGEMENT: A.D.)

Payen Components S.A. Ltd v. Bovic Gaskets C.C. (LITERARY WORK: COMPUTERISED CATALOGUING SYSTEM: WORK PRODUCED BY PROGRAM, ASSIGNMENT OF COPYRIGHT TO OVERSEAS PARENT COMPANY: WLD)

Waylite Diaries C.C. v. First National Bank Ltd (ARTISTIC WORK: DRAWINGS: LITERARY WORK: WRITTEN TABLES AND COMPILATIONS: DIARY: WLD: A.D.)

Substantial Part

Payen Components S.A. Ltd v. Bovic Gaskets CC (INFRINGEMENT: REMEDIES: INJUNCTION: BREACH: INTERFACE BETWEEN UNLAWFUL COMPETITION AND COPYRIGHT: TRADE MARK, DESIGN AND PASSING OFF ACTIONS: A.D.)

Three-Dimensional Reproduction

Da Gama Textile Co. Ltd v. Vision Creations C.C. (INFRINGEMENT: SCOPE OF PROTECTION: D&CLD)

Trade Dress

Frank & Hirsch (Pty) Ltd v. A. Roopanand Brothers (Pty) Ltd (LABELS: D&CLD)

Unfair Competition

Butt v. Schultz (INFRINGEMENT: USE OF BOAT AS MOULD: ECD)

Payen Components S.A. Ltd v. Bovic Gaskets C.C. (SUBSISTENCE: LITERARY WORK: COMPUTERISED CATALOGUING SYSTEM: WORK PRODUCED BY PROGRAM: ASSIGNMENT OF COPYRIGHT TO OVERSEAS PARENT COMPANY: EXCLUSIVE LICENSEE: WLD)

Schultz v. Butt (COPYRIGHT: REGISTRATION: BOAT HULLS: A.D.)

Use of Work as Mould

Butt v. Schultz (INFRINGEMENT: UNFAIR COMPETITION: ECD)

Schultz v. Butt (TRADE MARK: UNFAIR COMPETITION: REGISTRATION: BOAT HULLS: A.D.)

Written Tables and Compilations

Waylite Diaries C.C. v. First National Bank Ltd (SUBSISTENCE: ARTISTIC WORK: DRAWINGS: LITERARY WORK: DIARY: WLD: A.D.)

Designs

Expungement

Sportshoe (Pty) Ltd v. Pep Stores (S.A.) (Pty) Ltd (ADAPTED TO DISTINGUISH: INFRINGEMENT: A.D.)

Fraudulent Imitation

A.C. Components Pty Ltd v. Jadon Investments Pty Ltd (INFRINGEMENT: VALIDITY: NO OBVIOUS IMITATION: DESIGN REGISTRATION VALID: AIR CONDITIONING DIFFUSER: S.C.)

Functional Integer

Robinson v. Cooper Corp. of S.A. (Pty) Ltd (INFRINGEMENT: TPD)

Infringement

A.C. Components Pty Ltd v. Jadon Investments Pty Ltd (VALIDITY: NO OBVIOUS IMITATION: FRAUDULENT IMITATION FOUND: REGISTRATION VALID: AIR-CONDITIONING DIFFUSER: S.C.)

Robinson v. Cooper Corp. of S.A. (Pty) Ltd (FUNCTIONAL INTEGER: TPD)

Registrability

Homecraft Steel Industries (Pty) Ltd v. Hare & Sons (Pty) Ltd (COPYRIGHT: A.D.)

Validity

A.C. Components Pty Ltd v. Jadon Investments Pty Ltd (INFRINGEMENT: NO OBVIOUS IMITATION: FRAUDULENT IMITATION FOUND: REGISTRATION VALID: AIR-CONDITIONING DIFFUSER: S.C.)

Passing Off, including Trade Dress and Get-up

Anton Piller Order. *See* **Practice** (*Anton Piller order*)

Association in Minds of Public

Hollywood Curl (Pty) Ltd v. Twins Products (Pty) Ltd (No. 1) (UNREGISTERED MARK: REPUTATION: SIMILAR GET-UP: A.D.)

Character Merchandising

Federation Internationale de Football v. Bartlett (CONCEPT: REPUTATION: TRADE MARK: WORLD CUP USA '94: AMENDMENT: DISCLAIMER: MATTER COMMON TO THE TRADE: TPD)

Confusion. *See also* Likelihood of Confusion or Deception

Reckitt & Colman S.A. (Pty) Ltd v. S.C. Johnson & Son (S.A.) (Pty) Ltd (TRADE MARK: UNFAIR COMPETITION: DECEPTION AND CONFUSION AS TO ORIGIN OF GOODS: SIMILARITY OF MARKS: NEUTRA AIR/NEUTRA FRESH: APPLICATION FOR INTERIM INTERDICT: TPD)

Rovex Ltd v. Prima Toys (Pty) Ltd (TRADE MARK: DOLL: FIRST LOVE/BABY LOVE: PASSING OFF: CPD)

Sportshoe (Pty) Ltd v. Pep Stores (S.A.) (Pty) Ltd (TRADE MARK: EXPUNGEMENT: ADAPTED TO DISTINGUISH: INFRINGEMENT: PRODUCTS NOT COMPETING WITH ONE ANOTHER: DIFFERENCES IN PRICES, DESIGN, STRUCTURE AND OUTLETS OF PRODUCTS: A.D.)

Connection in Trade

Royal Beech-Nut (Pty) Ltd v. United Tobacco Co. Ltd t/a Willards Foods (TRADE MARK: SIMILAR MARKS: IMPLIED REPRESENTATION OF CONNECTION IN TRADE: A.D.)

Damages. *See* **Practice** (*Damages*)

Deception. *See also* Likelihood of Confusion or Deception

Boswell-Wilkie Circus (Pty) Ltd v. Brian Boswell Circus (Pty) Ltd (TRADE MARK: USE OF OWN NAME: NPD)

Rizla International BV v. L. Suzman Distributors (Pty) Ltd (NAME: GET-UP: PUBLIC DOMAIN: TEST: WHETHER USE CALCULATED TO DECEIVE: EXTENT OF LEGITIMATE IMITATION: DUTY TO DISTINGUISH GOODS FROM COMPETITOR: C.P.D.)

Sportshoe (Pty) Ltd v. Pep Stores (S.A.) (Pty) Ltd (TRADE MARK: EXPUNGEMENT: ADAPTED TO DISTINGUISH: INFRINGEMENT: PRODUCTS NOT COMPETING WITH ONE ANOTHER: DIFFERENCES IN PRICES, DESIGN, STRUCTURE AND OUTLETS OF PRODUCTS: A.D.)

Descriptive Words, Secondary Meaning

Van der Watt v. Humansdorp Marketing C.C. (USE OF OWN NAME: SECLD)

Evidence. *See* **Practice** (*Evidence*)

Form of Interdict. *See* **Practice** (*Form of interdict*)

Get-up

Frank & Hirsch (Pty) Ltd v. A. Roopanand Brothers (Pty) Ltd (TRADE DRESS: LABELS: D&CLD)

Hollywood Curl (Pty) Ltd v. Twins Products (Pty) Ltd (No. 1) (UNREGISTERED MARK: REPUTATION: SIMILAR GET-UP: ASSOCIATION IN MINDS OF PUBLIC: A.D.)

Reckitt & Colman S.A. (Pty) Ltd v. S.C. Johnson & Son S.A. (Pty) Ltd (TRADE MARK: LIKELIHOOD OF CONFUSION OR DECEPTION: EVIDENCE OF PSYCHOLOGISTS AND LINGUISTIC EXPERTS: ROLE: MARKET OR PUBLIC OPINION SURVEY: EVIDENCE: A.D.)

Rizla International BV v. L. Suzman Distributors (Pty) Ltd (NAME: GET-UP: PUBLIC DOMAIN: TEST: WHETHER USE CALCULATED TO DECEIVE: EXTENT OF LEGITIMATE IMITATION: DUTY TO DISTINGUISH GOODS FROM COMPETITOR: C.P.D.)

Union Wine Ltd v. E. Snell & Co. Ltd (COMPARISON: D&CLD: CPD)

Weber-Stephen Products Co. v. Alrite Engineering (Pty) Ltd (TRADE MARK: DISTINCTION BETWEEN ARTICLE AND ITS GET-UP: REPUTATION OF PRODUCT ATTACHING TO ITS SHAPE: TPD)

Goodwill

Moroka Swallows Football Club Ltd v. The Birds Football Club (TRADE MARK: NAME OF SOCCER TEAM: WLD)

Likelihood of Confusion or Deception

Reckitt & Colman S.A. (Pty) Ltd v. S.C. Johnson & Son (S.A.) (Pty) Ltd (TRADE MARK: UNFAIR COMPETITION: DECEPTION AND CONFUSION AS TO ORIGIN OF GOODS: SIMILARITY OF MARKS: NEUTRA AIR/NEUTRA FRESH: APPLICATION FOR INTERIM INTERDICT: TPD)

Reckitt & Colman S.A. (Pty) Ltd v. S.C. Johnson & Son S.A. (Pty) Ltd (TRADE MARK: PASSING OFF: GET-UP: EVIDENCE OF PSYCHOLOGISTS AND LINGUISTIC EXPERTS: ROLE: MARKET OR PUBLIC OPINION SURVEY: EVIDENCE: A.D.)

Mala Fides. *See* **Practice** (*Mala fides*)

Market Surveys. *See* **Practice** (*Public opinion or market surveys*)

Name

Rizla International BV v. L. Suzman Distributors (Pty) Ltd (NAME: GET-UP: PUBLIC DOMAIN: TEST: WHETHER USE CALCULATED TO DECEIVE: EXTENT OF LEGITIMATE IMITATION: DUTY TO DISTINGUISH GOODS FROM COMPETITOR: C.P.D.)

Onus of Proof. *See* **Practice** (*Onus of proof*)

Practice

Anton Piller application

Easyfind International (S.A.) (Pty) Ltd v. Instaplan Holdings (WLD)

Damages

Haggar & Co. v. S.A. Tailorscraft (Pty) Ltd (TRADE MARK: REPUTATION: EVIDENCE: QUANTUM: TPD)

Evidence

Haggar & Co. v. S.A. Tailorscraft (Pty) Ltd (REPUTATION: TPD)
Hoechst Pharmaceuticals (Pty) Ltd v. The Beauty Box (Pty) Ltd (MARKET SURVEYS: WEIGHT: A.D.)
Reckitt & Colman S.A. (Pty) Ltd v. S.C. Johnson & Son S.A. (Pty) Ltd (LIKELIHOOD OF CONFUSION OR DECEPTION: EVIDENCE OF PSYCHOLOGISTS AND LINGUISTIC EXPERTS: ROLE: MARKET OR PUBLIC OPINION SURVEY: A.D.)

Form of interdict

Weber-Stephen Products Co. v. Alrite Engineering (Pty) Ltd (EFFECT OF NOTICE ON DEFENDANTS PRODUCT: INTERDICT INFRINGED: S.C.)

Mala fides

Scott v. Watermaid (Pty) Ltd (CPD)

Onus of Proof

Pepsico Inc. v. United Tobacco Co. Ltd (REPUTATION: PRE-LAUNCH PUBLICITY: WLD)
(INTERLOCUTORY INJUNCTION: WLD)

Public opinion or market surveys

Hoechst Pharmaceuticals (Pty) Ltd v. The Beauty Box (Pty) Ltd (MARKET SURVEYS: WEIGHT: A.D.)
Reckitt & Colman S.A. (Pty) Ltd v. S.C. Johnson & Son S.A. (Pty) Ltd (MARKET OR PUBLIC OPINION SURVEY: A.D.)

Public Domain

Rizla International BV v. L. Suzman Distributors (Pty) Ltd (NAME: GET-UP: PUBLIC DOMAIN: TEST: WHETHER USE CALCULATED TO DECEIVE: EXTENT OF LEGITIMATE IMITATION: DUTY TO DISTINGUISH GOODS FROM COMPETITOR: C.P.D.)

Public Opinion Survey. *See* Practice *(Public opinion or market surveys)*

Reputation

Federation Internationale de Football v. Bartlett (CHARACTER MERCHANDISING: CONCEPT: TRADE MARK: WORLD CUP USA' 94: TPD)
Haggar & Co. v. S.A. Tailorscraft (Pty) Ltd (EVIDENCE: TPD)
Johnson & Son Inc. v. Klensan (Pty) Ltd t/a Markrite (TPD)
Pepsico Inc. v. United Tobacco Co. Ltd (ONUS OF PROOF: PRE-LAUNCH PUBLICITY: WLD)
(ONUS OF PROOF: INTERLOCUTORY INJUNCTION: WLD)

Weber-Stephen Products Co. v. Alrite Engineering (Pty) Ltd (DISTINCTION BETWEEN ARTICLE AND ITS GET-UP: REPUTATION OF PRODUCT ATTACHING TO ITS SHAPE: TPD)

Similar Names or Get-up. *See also under* Get-up

Cambridge Plan AG v. Moore (DIETARY PREPARATION: SIMILAR PRODUCT APPELLATION: DISCLAIMER IN REGISTRATION: D&CLD)
Hollywood Curl (Pty) Ltd v. Twins Products (Pty) Ltd (No. 1) (UNREGISTERED MARK: REPUTATION: SIMILAR GET-UP: ASSOCIATION IN MINDS OF PUBLIC: A.D.)

Test of Passing Off

Searles Industrials (Pty) Ltd v. International Power Marketing Ltd (SALIENT FEATURES: TPD)

Trade Dress

Frank & Hirsch (Pty) Ltd v. A. Roopanand Brothers (Pty) Ltd (GET-UP: LABELS: D&CLD)

Trade Marks and Trade Names

Boswell-Wilkie Circus (Pty) Ltd v. Brian Boswell Circus (Pty) Ltd (USE OF OWN NAME: DECEPTION: NPD)
Cambridge Plan AG v. Moore (INFRINGEMENT: DIETARY PREPARATION: SIMILAR PRODUCT APPELLATION: DISCLAIMER IN REGISTRATION: D&CLD)
Federation Internationale de Football v. Bartlett (CHARACTER MERCHANDISING: WORLD CUP USA '94; AMENDMENT: DISCLAIMER: MATTER COMMON TO THE TRADE: TPD)
Frank & Hirsch (Pty) Ltd v. A. Roopanand Brothers (INFRINGEMENT: D&CLD)
Haggar & Co. v. S.A. Tailorscraft (Pty) Ltd (REPUTATION: TPD)
Hoechst Pharmaceuticals (Pty) Ltd v. The Beauty Box (Pty) Ltd (A.D.)
Hollywood Curl (Pty) Ltd v. Twins Products (Pty) Ltd (No. 1) (UNREGISTERED MARK: REPUTATION: A.D.)
Johnson & Son Inc. v. Klensan (Pty) Ltd t/a Markrite (REPUTATION: TPD)
Moroka Swallows Football Club Ltd v. The Birds Football Club (NAME OF SOCCER TEAM: GOODWILL: WLD)
Philip Morris Inc. v. Marlboro Shirt Co. S.A. Ltd (EXPUNGEMENT: A.D.)
Reckitt & Colman S.A. (Pty) Ltd v. S.C. Johnson & Son S.A. (Pty) Ltd (GET-UP: LIKELIHOOD OF CONFUSION OR DECEPTION: A.D.)
Reckitt & Colman S.A. (Pty) Ltd v. S.C. Johnson & Son (S.A.) (Pty) Ltd (UNFAIR COMPETITION: DECEPTION AND CONFUSION AS TO ORIGIN OF GOODS: SIMILARITY OF MARKS: NEUTRA AIR/NEUTRA FRESH: APPLICATION FOR INTERIM INTERDICT: TPD)
Rovex Ltd v. Prima Toys (Pty) Ltd (DOLL: FIRST LOVE/BABY LOVE: CONFUSION: CPD)
Royal Beech-Nut (Pty) Ltd v. United Tobacco Co. Ltd t/a Willards Foods (SIMILAR MARKS: IMPLIED REPRESENTATION OF CONNECTION IN TRADE: A.D.)
Scott v. Watermaid (Pty) Ltd (MALA FIDES: CPD)
Searles Industrials (Pty) Ltd v. International Power Marketing Ltd (INFRINGEMENT: TEST: SALIENT FEATURES: TPD)
Sportshoe (Pty) Ltd v. Pep Stores (S.A.) (Pty) Ltd (EXPUNGEMENT: ADAPTED TO DISTINGUISH: INFRINGEMENT: CONFUSION OR DECEPTION: A.D.)

Weber-Stephen Products Co. v. Alrite Engineering (Pty) Ltd (DISTINCTION BETWEEN ARTICLE AND ITS GET-UP: TPD)

Unlawful Competition

Bress Designs (Pty) Ltd v. G.Y. Lounge Suite Manufacturers (Pty) Ltd (DIMENSIONAL WORK: LOUNGE SUITE: WLD)

Reckitt & Colman S.A. (Pty) Ltd v. S.C. Johnson & Son (S.A.) (Pty) Ltd (DECEPTION AND CONFUSION AS TO ORIGIN OF GOODS: SIMILARITY OF MARKS: NEUTRA AIR/NEUTRA FRESH: APPLICATION FOR INTERIM INTERDICT: TPD)

Unregistered Trade Mark. *See* Trade Marks and Trade Names

Use of Own Name

Boswell-Wilkie Circus (Pty) Ltd v. Brian Boswell Circus (Pty) Ltd (DECEPTION: NPD)

Van der Watt v. Humansdorp Marketing C.C. (OWN NAME OR MERE DESCRIPTIVE WORDS: SECONDARY MEANING: SECLD)

Patents

Amendment

Water Renovation (Pty) Ltd v. Gold Fields of S.A. Ltd (REVOCATION: DISCRETION: PRIOR ART: RESEARCH PAPER: A.D.)

Appeal. *See* Practice (*Appeal*)

Application

Colgate-Palmolive Co. v. Unilever Ltd (PERSON SKILLED IN THE ART: TPD)

Kurosaki Refractories Co. Ltd v. Flogates Ltd (OPPOSITION: WITHDRAWAL OF OPPOSITION: COSTS: PARTY AND PARTY: TAXATION: TPD)

Selero (Pty) Ltd v. Mostert (CONVERSION TO PATENT OF ADDITION: REGISTRARS POWER TO AUTHORISE: TPD)

Claims

De Beers Industrial Diamond Division (Pty) Ltd v. General Electric Company (VALIDITY: INCORPORATION BY REFERENCE: APPEAL: TPD: A.D.)

G.I. Marketing CC v. Fraser-Johnston (VALIDITY: LACK OF NOVELTY: CLAIMING: DISTINCTION BETWEEN WORDS DESCRIBING PURPOSE OF INVENTION AND WORDS IMPORTING LIMITATION OR QUALITY OF ESSENTIAL INTEGER OF INVENTION: STATUTORY INTERPRETATION: A.D.)

Clarity

Roman Roller CC v. Speedmark Holdings (Pty) Ltd (VALIDITY: OBVIOUSNESS: LACK OF CLARITY: STATUTORY INTERPRETATION: A.D.)

Construction

Raubenheimer v. Kreepy Krauly (Pty) Ltd (INFRINGEMENT: PITH AND MARROW: A.D.)

Selero (Pty) Ltd v. Chauvier (INFRINGEMENT: A.D.)

Costs. *See* **Practice** (*Costs*)

Delivery-up. *See* **Practice** (*Delivery-up*)

Essential Features

G.I. Marketing CC v. Fraser-Johnston (VALIDITY: LACK OF NOVELTY: CLAIMING: DISTINCTION BETWEEN WORDS DESCRIBING PURPOSE OF INVENTION AND WORDS IMPORTING LIMITATION OR QUALITY OF ESSENTIAL INTEGER OF INVENTION: STATUTORY INTERPRETATION: A.D.)
Multotech Manufacturing (Pty) Ltd v. Screenex Wire Weaving Manufacturers (Pty) Ltd (VALIDITY: A.D.)

Exclusive Licensee

Hoover S.A. (Pty) Ltd v. Fisher & Paykel Ltd (EXTENSION: INADEQUATE REMUNERATION: PROFITS MADE BY EXCLUSIVE LICENSEE: TPD)

Executor. *See* **Practice** (*Executor*)

Expiry

South African Druggists Ltd v. Bayer AG (EXTENSION: POST-EXPIRY APPLICATION: TPD)
Stauffer Chemicals v. Chesebrough-Ponds (Pty) Ltd (INFRINGEMENT: REMEDIES: DELIVERY-UP: TPD)

Extension

De Beers Industrial Diamond Division (Pty) Ltd v. General Electric Co. (INADEQUATE REMUNERATION: A.D.)
Hoover S.A. (Pty) Ltd v. Fisher & Paykel Ltd (INADEQUATE REMUNERATION: PROFITS MADE BY EXCLUSIVE LICENSEE: TPD)
South African Druggists Ltd v. Bayer AG (POST-EXPIRY APPLICATION: TPD)
South African Railways & Harbours v. Standard Car Truck Co. (INADEQUATE REMUNERATION: A.D.)

Inadequate Remuneration. *See* **Extension**

Incorporation by Reference

De Beers Industrial Diamond Division (Pty) Ltd v. General Electric Company (INSTRUCTIONS CONTAINED IN SPECIFICATION AS TO HOW INVENTION WORKS, OR HOW TO MAKE OR OPERATE IT: AVAILABILITY OF OTHER PATENT SPECIFICATION: TPD: A.D.)

Infringement

Chauvier v. Pelican Pools (Pty) Ltd (*Locus standii*: PATENTEE DECEASED: EXECUTOR: DOMINIUM IN PATENT VESTING IN EXECUTOR WHO SHOULD SUE IN HIS OWN RIGHT IN RESPECT OF ANY INFRINGEMENT: TPD)
Continental Linen Co. (Pty) Ltd v. Kenpet Agency (Pty) Ltd (THREATS: JUSTIFICATION: RELIEF: TPD)

Par Excellence Colour Printing (Pty) Ltd v. Ronnie Cox Graphic Supplies (Pty) Ltd (VALIDITY: ONUS: A.D.)

Raubenheimer v. Kreepy Krauly (Pty) Ltd (CONSTRUCTION OF SPECIFICATION: PITH AND MARROW: A.D.)

Selero (Pty) Ltd v. Chauvier (SECURITY FOR COSTS: TPD) (CONSTRUCTION: A.D.)

Stauffer Chemical Co. v. Safsan Marketing & Distributing Co. (Pty) Ltd (PITH AND MARROW: PRACTICE: COSTS: A.D.)

Stauffer Chemicals v. Chesebrough-Ponds (Pty) Ltd (REMEDIES: DELIVERY-UP: EXPIRY OF PATENT: TPD)

Inutility

Selas Corp. of America v. Electric Furnace Co. (VALIDITY: A.D.)

Locus Standii. See **Practice** (*Locus standii*)

Novelty

G.I. Marketing CC v. Fraser-Johnston (VALIDITY: LACK OF NOVELTY: CLAIMING: DISTINCTION BETWEEN WORDS DESCRIBING PURPOSE OF INVENTION AND WORDS IMPORTING LIMITATION OR QUALITY OF ESSENTIAL INTEGER OF INVENTION: STATUTORY INTERPRETATION: A.D.)

Obviousness

Roman Roller CC v. Speedmark Holdings (Pty) Ltd (VALIDITY: LACK OF CLARITY: STATUTORY INTERPRETATION: A.D.)

Onus. See **Practice** (*Onus*)

Opposition

Kurosaki Refractories Co. Ltd v. Flogates Ltd (APPLICATION: WITHDRAWAL OF OPPOSITION: COSTS: PARTY AND PARTY: TAXATION: TPD)

Patent of Addition

Selero (Pty) Ltd v. Mostert (APPLICATION: CONVERSION TO PATENT OF ADDITION: REGISTRAR'S POWER TO AUTHORISE: TPD)

Person Skilled in the Art

Colgate-Palmolive Co. v. Unilever Ltd (APPLICATION: TPD)

Pith and Marrow

Raubenheimer v. Kreepy Krauly (Pty) Ltd (INFRINGEMENT: CONSTRUCTION OF SPECIFICATION: A.D.)

Stauffer Chemical Co. v. Safsan Marketing & Distributing Co. (Pty) Ltd (INFRINGEMENT: PRACTICE: COSTS: A.D.)

Practice

Appeal

De Beers Industrial Diamond Division (Pty) Ltd v. General Electric Company (VALIDITY: CLAIMS: INCORPORATION BY REFERENCE: TPD: A.D.)

Pfizer Inc. v. South African Druggists Ltd (EXTENSION: APPLICATION: TPD)

Costs

Kurosaki Refractories Co. Ltd v. Flogates Ltd (WITHDRAWAL OF OPPOSITION: PARTY AND PARTY: TAXATION: TPD)
Stauffer Chemical Co. v. Safsan Marketing & Distributing Co. (Pty) Ltd (INFRINGEMENT: PITH AND MARROW: A.D.)

Delivery-up

Stauffer Chemicals v. Chesebrough-Ponds (Pty) Ltd (INFRINGEMENT: REMEDIES: EXPIRY OF PATENT: TPD)

Discretion

Water Renovation (Pty) Ltd v. Gold Fields of S.A. Ltd (REVOCATION: AMENDMENT: PRIOR ART: RESEARCH PAPER: A.D.)

Executor

Chauvier v. Pelican Pools (Pty) Ltd (*Locus standii*: PATENTEE DECEASED: DOMINIUM IN PATENT VESTING IN EXECUTOR WHO SHOULD SUE IN HIS OWN RIGHT IN RESPECT OF ANY INFRINGEMENT: TPD)

Locus standii

Chauvier v. Pelican Pools (Pty) Ltd (PATENTEE DECEASED: EXECUTOR: DOMINIUM IN PATENT VESTING IN EXECUTOR WHO SHOULD SUE IN HIS OWN RIGHT IN RESPECT OF ANY INFRINGEMENT: TPD)

Onus

Par Excellence Colour Printing (Pty) Ltd v. Ronnie Cox Graphic Supplies (Pty) Ltd (INFRINGEMENT: VALIDITY: A.D.)

Registrar's power

Selero (Pty) Ltd v. Mostert (APPLICATION: CONVERSION TO PATENT OF ADDITION: REGISTRAR'S POWER TO AUTHORISE: TPD)

Relief

Continental Linen Co. (Pty) Ltd v. Kenpet Agency (Pty) Ltd (INFRINGEMENT: THREATS: JUSTIFICATION: TPD)

Remedies

Stauffer Chemicals v. Chesebrough-Ponds (Pty) Ltd (DELIVERY-UP: TPD)

Security for costs

Selero (Pty) Ltd v. Chauvier (INFRINGEMENT: TPD)

Taxation

Kurosaki Refractories Co. Ltd v. Flogates Ltd (WITHDRAWAL OF OPPOSITION: COSTS: PARTY AND PARTY: TPD)

Prior Art

Water Renovation (Pty) Ltd v. Gold Fields of S.A. Ltd (REVOCATION: RESEARCH PAPER: A.D.)

Reasonable Certainty

De Beers Industrial Diamond Division (Pty) Ltd v. General Electric Company (SPECIFICATION: FUNCTION: SKILLED ADDRESSEE: TEACHING: INCORPORATION BY REFERENCE: AVAILABILITY OF OTHER SPECIFICATION: TPD: A.D.)

Rectification

Pressings and Plastics (Pty) Ltd v. Sohnius (FRAUDULENT APPLICATION: TPD)

Registrar's Power. *See* **Practice** (*Registrar's power*)

Relief. *See* **Practice** (*Relief*)

Remedies. *See* **Practice** (*Remedies*)

Revocation

Water Renovation (Pty) Ltd v. Gold Fields of S.A. Ltd (AMENDMENT: DISCRETION: PRIOR ART: RESEARCH PAPER: A.D.)

Security for Costs. *See* **Practice** (*Security for costs*)

Skilled Addressee

De Beers Industrial Diamond Division (Pty) Ltd v. General Electric Company (SPECIFICATION: FUNCTION: REASONABLE CERTAINTY: TEACHING OF: TPD: A.D.)

Specification

De Beers Industrial Diamond Division (Pty) Ltd v. General Electric Company (FUNCTION: REASONABLE CERTAINTY: SKILLED ADDRESSEE: TEACHING OF: INCORPORATION BY REFERENCE OF THE TEACHING OF ANOTHER PATENT: AVAILABILITY OF OTHER SPECIFICATION: TPD: A.D.)
Kreepy Krauly (Pty) Ltd v. Hofmann (ADDRESSEES: IMPLEMENTATION: A.D.)
Raubenheimer v. Kreepy Krauly (Pty) Ltd (INFRINGEMENT: CONSTRUCTION: PITH AND MARROW: A.D.)

Taxation. *See* **Practice** (*Taxation*)

Threats

Continental Linen Co. (Pty) Ltd v. Kenpet Agency (Pty) Ltd (JUSTIFICATION: RELIEF: TPD)

Validity

De Beers Industrial Diamond Division (Pty) Ltd v. General Electric Company (CLAIMS: INCORPORATION BY REFERENCE: APPEAL: TPD: A.D.)
G.I. Marketing CC v. Fraser-Johnston (LACK OF NOVELTY: CLAIMING: DISTINCTION BETWEEN WORDS DESCRIBING PURPOSE OF INVENTION AND WORDS IMPORTING LIMITATION OR QUALITY OF ESSENTIAL INTEGER OF INVENTION: STATUTORY INTERPRETATION: A.D.)

Multotech Manufacturing (Pty) Ltd v. Screenex Wire Weaving Manufacturers (Pty) Ltd (ESSENTIAL FEATURES: A.D.)

Par Excellence Colour Printing (Pty) Ltd v. Ronnie Cox Graphic Supplies (Pty) Ltd (INFRINGEMENT: ONUS: A.D.)

Roman Roller CC v. Speedmark Holdings (Pty) Ltd (OBVIOUSNESS: LACK OF CLARITY: STATUTORY INTERPRETATION: A.D.)

Selas Corp. of America v. Electric Furnace Co. (INUTILITY: A.D.)

Practice and Miscellaneous Subjects

Account of Profits

Montres Rolex S.A. v. Kleynhams (TRADE MARK: INFRINGEMENT: CPD)

Video Parktown North (Pty) Ltd v. Paramount Pictures Corp. (COPYRIGHT: INFRINGEMENT: TPD)

Anton Piller Orders

Easyfind International (S.A.) (Pty) Ltd v. Instaplan Holdings (TRADE MARK: INFRINGEMENT: PASSING OFF: WLD)

Waste-Tech (Pty) Ltd v. Wade Refuse (Pty) Ltd (CONFIDENTIAL INFORMATION: NATURE AND SCOPE: WLD)

Appeal

De Beers Industrial Diamond Division (Pty) Ltd v. General Electric Company (PATENT: VALIDITY: TPD: A.D.)

Pfizer Inc. v. South African Druggists Ltd (PATENT: EXTENSION: TPD)

Silver Seiko Co. Ltd v. Kaisha (TRADE MARK: APPLICATION: TPD)

Costs. See also under Security for Costs

Kurosaki Refractories Co. Ltd v. Flogates Ltd (PATENT: WITHDRAWAL OF OPPOSITION: PARTY AND PARTY: TAXATION: TPD)

Stauffer Chemical Co. v. Safsan Marketing & Distributing Co. (Pty) Ltd (PATENT: INFRINGEMENT: A.D.)

Delivery-up

Stauffer Chemicals v. Chesebrough-Ponds (Pty) Ltd (PATENT: INFRINGEMENT: TPD)

Discovery and Inspection

Waste-Tech (Pty) Ltd v. Wade Refuse (Pty) Ltd (CONFIDENTIAL INFORMATION: ANTON PILLER ORDERS: NATURE AND SCOPE: WLD)

Enforcement

Meter Systems Holdings Ltd v. Venter (CONFIDENTIAL INFORMATION: FIDUCIARY RELATIONSHIPS: RESTRAINT OF TRADE: EX-EMPLOYEE: WLD)

Evidence

Haggar & Co. v. S.A. Tailorscraft (Pty) Ltd (TRADE MARK: PASSING OFF: REPUTATION: TPD)

Harnischfeger Corporation v. Appleton (COPYRIGHT: INFRINGEMENT: WLD)
Hoechst Pharmaceuticals (Pty) Ltd v. The Beauty Box (Pty) Ltd (TRADE MARK: PASSING OFF: MARKET SURVEYS: WEIGHT: A.D.)
Insamcor (Pty) Ltd v. Maschinenfabriek Sidler Stadler AG (COPYRIGHT: INFRINGEMENT: ORIGINALITY: PROOF: SUFFICIENCY: WLD)
Reckitt & Colman S.A. (Pty) Ltd v. S.C. Johnson & Son S.A. (Pty) Ltd (TRADE MARK: PASSING OFF: LIKELIHOOD OF CONFUSION OR DECEPTION: EVIDENCE OF PSYCHOLOGISTS AND LINGUISTIC EXPERTS: ROLE: MARKET OR PUBLIC OPINION SURVEY: A.D.)

Executor

Chauvier v. Pelican Pools (Pty) Ltd (PATENT: *Locus standii*: PATENTEE DECEASED: DOMINIUM IN PATENT VESTING IN EXECUTOR WHO SHOULD SUE IN HIS OWN RIGHT IN RESPECT OF ANY INFRINGEMENT: TPD)

Foreign Law

Harnischfeger Corporation v. Appleton (COPYRIGHT: OWNERSHIP: WLD)

Form of Interdict

Weber-Stephen Products Co. v. Alrite Engineering (Pty) Ltd (PASSING OFF: EFFECT OF NOTICE ON DEFENDANTS PRODUCT: S.C.)

Hearing *In Camera*

Continental Wholesalers v. Fashion Fantasy (Pty) Ltd (TRADE MARK: INFRINGEMENT: INTERIM INJUNCTION: D&CLD)

Injunction—Breach

Payen Components S.A. Ltd v. Bovic Gaskets CC (INTERFACE BETWEEN UNLAWFUL COMPETITION AND COPYRIGHT, TRADE MARK, DESIGN AND PASSING OFF ACTIONS: A.D.)

Injurious Falsehood

Aetiology Today C.C. v. Van Aswegen (UNLAWFUL COMPETITION: PUBLIC POLICY: COMPETITION BETWEEN SCHOOLS: TEACHERS MOVING TO NEW SCHOOL: WLD)

Interim Injunction

Continental Wholesalers v. Fashion Fantasy (Pty) Ltd (TRADE MARK: INFRINGEMENT: HEARING *in camera*: D&CLD)
Multi Tube Systems (Pty) Ltd v. Ponting (CONFIDENTIAL INFORMATION: MASTER AND SERVANT: D&CLD)

Joinder

Wistyn Enterprises (Pty) Ltd v. Levi Strauss & Co. (TRADE MARK: EXPUNGEMENT: REGISTERED USER: TPD)

Jurisdiction

Spier Estate v. Die Bergkelder BPK (TRADE MARK: INFRINGEMENT: CANCELLATION PROCEEDINGS: S.C.)

Knowledge

Columbia Pictures Industries Inc. v. Videorent Parkmore (COPYRIGHT: INFRINGEMENT: H.C.)

S. v. Nxumalo (COPYRIGHT: OFFENCES: SALE OF INFRINGING COPIES: *Mens rea*: FORM: OFSPD)

Locus Standii

Chauvier v. Pelican Pools (Pty) Ltd (PATENT: INFRINGEMENT: PATENTEE DECEASED: EXECUTOR: DOMINIUM IN PATENT VESTING IN EXECUTOR WHO SHOULD SUE IN HIS OWN RIGHT IN RESPECT OF ANY INFRINGEMENT: TPD)

Danco Clothing (Pty) Ltd v. Nu-Care Marketing Sales and Promotions (Pty) Ltd (TRADE MARK: EXPUNGEMENT: AGGRIEVED PERSON: TPD: A.D.)

Mala Fides

Scott v. Watermaid (Pty) Ltd (TRADE MARK: PASSING OFF: CPD)

Market Surveys

Hoechst Pharmaceuticals (Pty) Ltd v. The Beauty Box (Pty) Ltd (TRADE MARK: PASSING OFF: EVIDENCE: WEIGHT: A.D.)

Reckitt & Colman S.A. (Pty) Ltd v. S.C. Johnson & Son S.A. (Pty) Ltd (TRADE MARK: PASSING OFF: GET-UP: LIKELIHOOD OF CONFUSION OR DECEPTION: EVIDENCE OF PSYCHOLOGISTS AND LINGUISTIC EXPERTS: ROLE: MARKET OR PUBLIC OPINION SURVEY: EVIDENCE: A.D.)

Mens Rea

S. v. Nxumalo (COPYRIGHT: OFFENCES: SALE OF INFRINGING COPIES: KNOWLEDGE: OFSPD)

Onus

Par Excellence Colour Printing (Pty) Ltd v. Ronnie Cox Graphic Supplies (Pty) Ltd (PATENT: INFRINGEMENT: VALIDITY: A.D.)

Tri-ang Pedigree (S.A.) (Pty) Ltd v. Prime Toys (Pty) Ltd (TRADE MARK: INFRINGEMENT: A.D.)

Presumption of Originality

Saunders Valve Co. Ltd v. Klep Valves (COPYRIGHT: INFRINGEMENT: REMEDIES: TPD)

Proof

Insamcor (Pty) Ltd v. Maschinenfabriek Sidler Stadler AG (COPYRIGHT: INFRINGEMENT: ORIGINALITY: EVIDENCE: SUFFICIENCY: WLD)

Public Policy

William Grant & Sons Ltd v. Cape Wine & Distillers Ltd (TRADE MARK: UNLAWFUL COMPETITION: CONDUCT: REPRESENTATION: CONFUSION OR DECEPTION: CPD)

Relief

Continental Linen Co. (Pty) Ltd v. Kenpet Agency (Pty) Ltd (PATENT: INFRINGEMENT: THREATS: JUSTIFICATION: TPD)

1110

Remedies

Stauffer Chemicals v. Chesebrough-Ponds (Pty) Ltd (PATENT: INFRINGEMENT: DELIVERY-UP: EXPIRY OF PATENT: TPD)

Restraint of Trade

Concept Factory v. Heyl (REASONABLENESS: DESIGN AND IDEAS IN PUBLIC DOMAIN: COPYING: TPD)

Security for Costs

Selero (Pty) Ltd v. Chauvier (PATENT: INFRINGEMENT: TPD)

Taxation

Kurosaki Refractories Co. Ltd v. Flogates Ltd (PATENT: WITHDRAWAL OF OPPOSITION: COSTS: PARTY AND PARTY: TPD)

Trade Libel

Caston Ltd v. Reeva Forman (Pty) Ltd (RIGHT TO SUE: DAMAGES: SPECIAL DAMAGES: QUANTITY: A.D.)

Unlawful Boycott

Times Media Ltd v. South African Broadcasting Corporation (TRADE MARK: UNLAWFUL COMPETITION: PUBLIC BROADCASTING CORPORATION REFUSING TO TELEVISE ADVERTISEMENT: GOODWILL: WLD)

Trade Marks

Abandonment

Image Enterprises C.C. v. Eastman Kodak Co. (MARKS REGISTERED IN SOUTH AFRICA: DECISION TO WITHDRAW: APPLICATION FOR SAME MARKS: S.C.)

Account of Profits. *See* **Practice** (*Account of profits*)

Adapted to Distinguish

Sportshoe (Pty) Ltd v. Pep Stores (S.A.) (Pty) Ltd (EXPUNGEMENT: INFRINGEMENT: A.D.)

Aggrieved Person

Danco Clothing (Pty) Ltd v. Nu-Care Marketing Sales and Promotions (Pty) Ltd (EXPUNGEMENT: *Locus standii*: TPD: A.D.)

Alteration of Goods

Television Radio Centre (Pty) Ltd v. Sony KK (INFRINGEMENT: REGISTERED USER: A.D.)

Amendment

Federation Internationale de Football v. Bartlett (WORLD CUP USA '94: DISCLAIMER: MATTER COMMON TO THE TRADE: TPD)

Anton Piller. *See* **Practice** (*Anton Piller*)

Appeal. *See* **Practice** (*Appeal*)

Application

Estée Lauder Cosmetics Ltd v. Registrar of Trade Marks (ESTÉE LAUDER
  BEAUTIFUL: REGISTRATION: DISCLAIMER OF PART OF MARK: NON-
  DISTINCTIVE CHARACTER: TPD)
Kentucky Tobacco Corp. (Pty) Ltd v. Registrar of Trade Marks (KENTUCKY:
  GEOGRAPHICAL SIGNIFICANCE: COMPOSITE MARK: TPD)
Mars Incorporated v. Candy World (Pty) Ltd (EXPUNGEMENT: PERSON AGGRIEVED:
  DEFENSIVE REGISTRATION: A.D.)
Silver Seiko Co. Ltd v. Kaisha (APPEAL: PRACTICE: TPD)

Association in the Mind of the Public

Hollywood Curl (Pty) Ltd v. Twins Products (Pty) Ltd (No. 1) (UNREGISTERED
  MARK: REPUTATION: SIMILAR GET-UP: A.D.)

Cancellation

Spier Estate v. Die Bergkelder BPK (INFRINGEMENT: JURISDICTION: S.C.)

Classes

Sodastream Ltd v. Bermon Brothers (Pty) Ltd (INFRINGEMENT: SIMILAR GOODS:
  DIFFERENT CLASSES: A.D.)

Common to the Trade

Federation Internationale de Football v. Bartlett (WORLD CUP USA '94: TPD)

Composite Mark

Kentucky Tobacco Corp. (Pty) Ltd v. Registrar of Trade Marks (APPLICATION:
  KENTUCKY: GEOGRAPHICAL SIGNIFICANCE: TPD)

Confusion

Decro Paint & Hardware (Pty) Ltd v. Plascon-Evans Paints (Tvl) Ltd
  (INFRINGEMENT: P.D.: A.D.)
Philip Morris Inc. v. Marlboro Shirt Co. S.A. Ltd (PASSING OFF: EXPUNGEMENT:
  USE: A.D.)
Reckitt & Colman S.A. (Pty) Ltd v. S.C. Johnson & Son (S.A.) (Pty) Ltd (DECEPTION
  AND CONFUSION AS TO ORIGIN OF GOODS: SIMILARITY OF MARKS:
  NEUTRA AIR/NEUTRA FRESH: APPLICATION FOR INTERIM
  INTERDICT: TPD)
Rovex Ltd v. Prima Toys (Pty) Ltd (DOLL: FIRST LOVE/BABY LOVE: PASSING
  OFF: CPD)
Sportshoe (Pty) Ltd v. Pep Stores (S.A.) (Pty) Ltd (EXPUNGEMENT: ADAPTED TO
  DISTINGUISH: INFRINGEMENT: PASSING OFF: CONFUSION OR DECEPTION:
  PRODUCTS NOT COMPETING WITH ONE ANOTHER: DIFFERENCES IN PRICES,
  DESIGN, STRUCTURE AND OUTLETS OF PRODUCTS: A.D.)
William Grant & Sons Ltd v. Cape Wine & Distillers Ltd (UNLAWFUL COMPETITION:
  CONDUCT: REPRESENTATION: CONFUSION OR DECEPTION: PUBLIC POLICY:
  CPD)

Container Mark

Cointreau et Cie S.A. v. Pagan International (INFRINGEMENT: BOTTLE: SHAPE: THREE-DIMENSIONAL MARK: UTILITARIAN OR FUNCTIONAL FEATURE: LACK OF DISTINGUISHING FEATURES: A.D.)

Damages. *See* **Practice** (*Damages*)

Deception

Boswell-Wilkie Circus (Pty) Ltd v. Brian Boswell Circus (Pty) Ltd (PASSING OFF: USE OF OWN NAME: NPD)

Reckitt & Colman S.A. (Pty) Ltd v. S.C. Johnson & Son (S.A.) (Pty) Ltd (DECEPTION AND CONFUSION AS TO ORIGIN OF GOODS: SIMILARITY OF MARKS: NEUTRA AIR/NEUTRA FRESH: APPLICATION FOR INTERIM INTERDICT: TPD)

Sportshoe (Pty) Ltd v. Pep Stores (S.A.) (Pty) Ltd (EXPUNGEMENT: ADAPTED TO DISTINGUISH: INFRINGEMENT: PASSING OFF: CONFUSION OR DECEPTION: PRODUCTS NOT COMPETING WITH ONE ANOTHER: DIFFERENCES IN PRICES, DESIGN, STRUCTURE AND OUTLETS OF PRODUCTS: A.D.)

William Grant & Sons Ltd v. Cape Wine & Distillers Ltd (UNLAWFUL COMPETITION: CONDUCT: REPRESENTATION: CONFUSION OR DECEPTION: PUBLIC POLICY: CPD)

Defensive Registration

Mars Incorporated v. Candy World (Pty) Ltd (EXPUNGEMENT: PERSON AGGRIEVED: APPLICATION: A.D.)

Disclaimer

Cambridge Plan AG v. Moore (INFRINGEMENT: PASSING OFF: DIETARY PREPARATION: SIMILAR PRODUCT APPELLATION: D&CLD)

Estée Lauder Cosmetics Ltd v. Registrar of Trade Marks (DISCLAIMER OF PART OF MARK: ESTÉE LAUDER BEAUTIFUL: NON-DISTINCTIVE CHARACTER: TPD)

Federation Internationale de Football v. Bartlett (WORLD CUP USA '94; AMENDMENT: MATTER COMMON TO THE TRADE: TPD)

Smithkline Beecham Consolidated S.A. (Pty) Ltd v. Unilever plc (EFFECT OF: WHETHER DISCLAIMED MATTER TO BE CONSIDERED IN COMPARISON WITH LATER APPLICATION FOR SIMILAR MARK: STRIPED TOOTHPASTE: A.D.)

Distinctiveness

Heublin Inc. v. Golden Fried Chicken (Pty) Ltd (EXPUNGEMENT: ITS FINGER LICKIN GOOD: TPD)

Evidence. *See* **Practice** (*Evidence*)

Exclusive Distributor

Frank & Hirsch (Pty) Ltd v. A. Roopanand Brothers (INFRINGEMENT: IMPORTATION: PASSING OFF: D&CLD)

Taylor & Horne (Pty) Ltd v. Dentall (Pty) Ltd (UNFAIR COMPETITION: LEGITIMATE SALE OF GOODS BY THIRD PARTY: A.D.)

Expungement

Danco Clothing (Pty) Ltd v. Nu-Care Marketing Sales and Promotions (Pty) Ltd (*Locus standii*: AGGRIEVED PERSON: TPD: A.D.)

Heublin Inc. v. Golden Fried Chicken (Pty) Ltd (ITS FINGER LICKIN GOOD: distinctiveness: TPD)

Mars Incorporated v. Candy World (Pty) Ltd (PERSON AGGRIEVED: APPLICATION: DEFENSIVE REGISTRATION: A.D.)

Philip Morris Inc. v. Marlboro Shirt Co. S.A. Ltd (PASSING OFF: USE: CONFUSION: A.D.)

Sportshoe (Pty) Ltd v. Pep Stores (S.A.) (Pty) Ltd (ADAPTED TO DISTINGUISH: INFRINGEMENT: PASSING OFF: CONFUSION OR DECEPTION: PRODUCTS NOT COMPETING WITH ONE ANOTHER: DIFFERENCES IN PRICES, DESIGN, STRUCTURE AND OUTLETS OF PRODUCTS: A.D.)

United Bank Ltd v. Standard Bank of South Africa Ltd (NO BONA FIDE USE FOR A PERIOD OF FIVE YEARS: TPD)

Wistyn Enterprises (Pty) Ltd v. Levi Strauss & Co. (REGISTERED USER: JOINDER: USE: TPD)

Geographical Significance

Kentucky Tobacco Corp. (Pty) Ltd v. Registrar of Trade Marks (APPLICATION: KENTUCKY: COMPOSITE MARK: TPD)

Get-up

Hollywood Curl (Pty) Ltd v. Twins Products (Pty) Ltd (No. 1) (PASSING OFF: UNREGISTERED MARK: REPUTATION: SIMILAR GET-UP: ASSOCIATION IN MINDS OF PUBLIC: A.D.)

Hearing *In Camera*. See **Practice** (*Hearing in camera*)

Imports and Importation

Frank & Hirsch (Pty) Ltd v. A. Roopanand Brothers (INFRINGEMENT: EXCLUSIVE DISTRIBUTOR: PASSING OFF: D&CLD)

Vinide Ltd v. National Home Products (Pty) Ltd (STATUTORY PROVISIONS: RESTRICTIVE PRACTICES: H.C.)

Infringement

Beecham Group PLC v. Southern Transvaal Pharmaceutical Pricing Bureau (Pty) Ltd (USE IN THE COURSE OF TRADE: GOODS FOR WHICH TRADE MARK REGISTERED: INTERPRETATION OF STATUTE: WLD)

Beecham Group PLC v. Southern Transvaal Pharmaceutical Pricing Bureau (Pty) Ltd (USE IN COURSE OF TRADE: REFERENCE TO TRADE IN GOODS IN CLASS FOR WHICH MARK REGISTERED: COMPUTER SOFTWARE SYSTEM PROVIDING INFORMATION ON GENERIC ALTERNATIVE MEDICINES AVAILABLE AFTER EXPIRY OF PATENT: A.D.)

Cambridge Plan AG v. Moore (PASSING OFF: DIETARY PREPARATION: SIMILAR PRODUCT APPELLATION: DISCLAIMER IN REGISTRATION: D&CLD)

Cointreau et Cie S.A. v. Pagan International (CONTAINER MARK: BOTTLE: SHAPE: THREE-DIMENSIONAL MARK: UTILITARIAN OR FUNCTIONAL FEATURE: LACK OF DISTINGUISHING FEATURES: A.D.)

Continental Wholesalers v. Fashion Fantasy (Pty) Ltd (INTERIM INJUNCTION: HEARING IN CAMERA: D&CLD)

Decro Paint & Hardware (Pty) Ltd v. Plascon-Evans Paints (Tvl) Ltd (CONFUSION: P.D.: A.D.)

Easyfind International (S.A.) (Pty) Ltd v. Instaplan Holdings (PASSING OFF: ANTON PILLER APPLICATION: WLD)

Esquire Electronics Ltd v. Executive Video (PRE-RECORDED VIDEO TAPES: A.D.)

Esquire Electronics Ltd v. A. Roopanand Brothers (Pty) Ltd (MAGNETICALLY RECORDED IMAGES: WHETHER REPRODUCTION ESTABLISHED: D&CLD: S.C.)

Frank & Hirsch (Pty) Ltd v. A. Roopanand Brothers (EXCLUSIVE DISTRIBUTOR: IMPORTATION: PASSING OFF: D&CLD)

Hampo Systems (Pty) Ltd v. Audiolens (Cape) (Pty) Ltd (APPLICATION TO PREVENT AUTHORISED DEALER FROM PARALLEL SELLING: CPD)

MCT Labels S.A. v. Gemelli C.C. (USE AS TRADE MARK: UNAUTHORISED USE: D&CLD)

Metal Box South Africa Ltd v. Midpak Blow-Moulders (Pty) Ltd (USE OF CONTAINER: RELEVANCE OF BELIEF OF PUBLIC AS TO ORIGIN OF GOODS: TPD)

Miele et Cie GmbH & Co. v. Evro Electrical (Pty) Ltd (USE IN THE COURSE OF TRADE: A.D.)

Montres Rolex S.A. v. Kleynhams (ACCOUNT OF PROFITS: CPD)

Plascon-Evans Paints Ltd v. Van Riebeeck Paints (Pty) Ltd (NOTIONAL USE: A.D.)

Searles Industrials (Pty) Ltd v. International Power Marketing Ltd (PASSING OFF: TEST: SALIENT FEATURES: TPD)

Sodastream Ltd v. Berman Brothers (Pty) Ltd (GAS CYLINDERS: TPD)

Sodastream Ltd v. Bermon Brothers (Pty) Ltd (SIMILAR GOODS: DIFFERENT CLASSES: A.D.)

Spier Estate v. Die Bergkelder BPK (CANCELLATION PROCEEDINGS: JURISDICTION: S.C.)

Sportshoe (Pty) Ltd v. Pep Stores (S.A.) (Pty) Ltd (EXPUNGEMENT: ADAPTED TO DISTINGUISH: PASSING OFF: CONFUSION OR DECEPTION: PRODUCTS NOT COMPETING WITH ONE ANOTHER: DIFFERENCES IN PRICES, DESIGN, STRUCTURE AND OUTLETS OF PRODUCTS: A.D.)

Television Radio Centre (Pty) Ltd v. Sony KK (REGISTERED USER: ALTERATION OF GOODS: A.D.)

Tri-ang Pedigree (S.A.) (Pty) Ltd v. Prime Toys (Pty) Ltd (ONUS: A.D.)

Upjohn Co. v. Merck (LIKELIHOOD OF CONFUSION: TPD)

Interim Injunction. *See* **Practice** (*Interim injunction*)

Joinder. *See* **Practice** (*Joinder*)

Lack of Distinguishing Features

Cointreau et Cie S.A. v. Pagan International (INFRINGEMENT: CONTAINER MARK: BOTTLE: SHAPE: THREE-DIMENSIONAL MARK: UTILITARIAN OR FUNCTIONAL FEATURE: A.D.)

Likelihood of Confusion

Upjohn Co. v. Merck (INFRINGEMENT: TPD)

Likely to Deceive or Confuse

Ritz Hotel Ltd v. Charles of The Ritz (RECTIFICATION: PERSON AGGRIEVED: QUALITY CONTROL: IMPORTED PACKAGING: A.D.)

Locus Standii. See **Practice** (*Locus standii*)

Mala Fides. See **Practice** (*Mala fides*)

Market Surveys. See **Practice** (*Market surveys*)

Non-Distinctive Character

Blockbuster Entertainment Corporation v. Registrar of Trade Marks (REGISTRATION: NON-DESCRIPTIVE AND PURELY DESCRIPTIVE MARK: BLOCKBUSTER/CHARTBUSTER: VIDEO RENTAL INDUSTRY: SERVICE MARK: TPD)

Estée Lauder Cosmetics Ltd v. Registrar of Trade Marks (REGISTRATION: DISCLAIMER: APPLICATION: ESTÉE LAUDER BEAUTIFUL: TPD)

Notional Use. See **Use**

Onus. See **Practice** (*Onus*)

Ordinary or Laudatory Words

Sea Harvest Corp. (Pty) Ltd v. Irvin & Johnson Ltd (UNLAWFUL COMPETITION: CPD)

Origin of Goods

Reckitt & Colman S.A. (Pty) Ltd v. S.C. Johnson & Son (S.A.) (Pty) Ltd (DECEPTION AND CONFUSION AS TO ORIGIN OF GOODS: SIMILARITY OF MARKS: NEUTRA AIR/NEUTRA FRESH: TPD)

Parallel Selling

Hampo Systems (Pty) Ltd v. Audiolens (Cape) (Pty) Ltd (INFRINGEMENT: APPLICATION TO PREVENT AUTHORISED DEALER FROM PARALLEL SELLING: CPD)

Passing Off

Boswell-Wilkie Circus (Pty) Ltd v. Brian Boswell Circus (Pty) Ltd (USE OF OWN NAME: DECEPTION: NPD)

Cambridge Plan AG v. Moore (INFRINGEMENT: DIETARY PREPARATION: SIMILAR PRODUCT APPELLATION: DISCLAIMER IN REGISTRATION: D&CLD)

Easyfind International (S.A.) (Pty) Ltd v. Instaplan Holdings (INFRINGEMENT: ANTON PILLER APPLICATION: WLD)

Frank & Hirsch (Pty) Ltd v. A. Roopanand Brothers (INFRINGEMENT: EXCLUSIVE DISTRIBUTOR: IMPORTATION: D&CLD)

Haggar & Co. v. S.A. Tailorscraft (Pty) Ltd (REPUTATION: EVIDENCE: DAMAGES: QUANTUM: TPD)

Hoechst Pharmaceuticals (Pty) Ltd v. The Beauty Box (Pty) Ltd (EVIDENCE: MARKET SURVEYS: WEIGHT: A.D.)

Hollywood Curl (Pty) Ltd v. Twins Products (Pty) Ltd (No. 1) (UNREGISTERED REPUTATION: SIMILAR GET-UP: ASSOCIATION IN MINDS OF PUBLIC: A.D.)

Johnson & Son Inc. v. Klensan (Pty) Ltd t/a Markrite (REPUTATION: TPD)

Moroka Swallows Football Club Ltd v. The Birds Football Club (NAME OF SOCCER TEAM: GOODWILL: WLD)

Philip Morris Inc. v. Marlboro Shirt Co. S.A. Ltd (EXPUNGEMENT: USE: CONFUSION: A.D.)

Reckitt & Coleman S.A. (Pty) Ltd v. S.C. Johnson & Son S.A. (Pty) Ltd (GET-UP: LIKELIHOOD OF CONFUSION OR DECEPTION: EVIDENCE OF PSYCHOLOGISTS AND LINGUISTIC EXPERTS: ROLE: MARKET OR PUBLIC OPINION SURVEY: EVIDENCE: A.D.)

Reckitt & Coleman S.A. (Pty) Ltd v. S.C. Johnson & Son (S.A.) (Pty) Ltd (UNFAIR COMPETITION: DECEPTION AND CONFUSION AS TO ORIGIN OF GOODS: SIMILARITY OF MARKS: NEUTRA AIR/NEUTRA FRESH: APPLICATION FOR INTERIM INTERDICT: TPD)

Rovex Ltd v. Prima Toys (Pty) Ltd (DOLL: FIRST LOVE/BABY LOVE: CONFUSION: CPD)

Royal Beech-Nut (Pty) Ltd v. United Tobacco Co. Ltd t/a Willards Foods (SIMILAR MARKS: IMPLIED REPRESENTATION OF CONNECTION IN TRADE: A.D.)

Scott v. Watermaid (Pty) Ltd (MALA FIDES: CPD)

Searles Industrials (Pty) Ltd v. International Power Marketing Ltd (INFRINGEMENT: TEST: SALIENT FEATURES: TPD)

Sportshoe (Pty) Ltd v. Pep Stores (S.A.) (Pty) Ltd (EXPUNGEMENT: ADAPTED TO DISTINGUISH: INFRINGEMENT: CONFUSION OR DECEPTION: PRODUCTS NOT COMPETING WITH ONE ANOTHER: DIFFERENCES IN PRICES, DESIGN, STRUCTURE AND OUTLETS OF PRODUCTS: A.D.)

Van der Watt v. Humansdorp Marketing C.C. (USE OF OWN NAME OR MERE DESCRIPTIVE WORDS: SECONDARY MEANING: SECLD)

Weber-Stephen Products Co. v. Alrite Engineering (Pty) Ltd (DISTINCTION BETWEEN ARTICLE AND ITS GET-UP: REPUTATION OF PRODUCT ATTACHING TO ITS SHAPE: TPD) (FORM OF INTERDICT: EFFECT OF NOTICE ON DEFENDANT'S PRODUCT: INTERDICT INFRINGED: S.C.)

Person Aggrieved

Mars Incorporated v. Candy World (Pty) Ltd (EXPUNGEMENT: APPLICATION: DEFENSIVE REGISTRATION: A.D.)

Ritz Hotel Ltd v. Charles of The Ritz and Registrar of Trade Marks (RECTIFICATION: QUALITY CONTROL: IMPORTED PACKAGING: LIKELY TO DECEIVE OR CONFUSE: A.D.)

Practice

Account of profits

Montres Rolex S.A. v. Kleynhams (CPD)

Anton Piller application

Easyfind International (S.A.) (Pty) Ltd v. Instaplan Holdings (INFRINGEMENT: PASSING OFF: WLD)

Appeal

Silver Seiko Co. Ltd v. Kaisha (APPLICATION: TPD)

Damages

Caston Ltd v. Reeva Forman (Pty) Ltd (TRADE LIBEL: RIGHT TO SUE: SPECIAL DAMAGES: QUANTITY: A.D.)

Haggar & Co. v. S.A. Tailorscraft (Pty) Ltd (PASSING OFF: REPUTATION: EVIDENCE: QUANTUM: TPD)

Evidence

Haggar & Co. v. S.A. Tailorscraft (Pty) Ltd (PASSING OFF: REPUTATION: TPD)

Hoechst Pharmaceuticals (Pty) Ltd v. The Beauty Box (Pty) Ltd (PASSING OFF: MARKET SURVEYS: WEIGHT: A.D.)

Reckitt & Coleman S.A. (Pty) Ltd v. S.C. Johnson & Son S.A. (Pty) Ltd (PASSING OFF: LIKELIHOOD OF CONFUSION OR DECEPTION: EVIDENCE OF PSYCHOLOGISTS AND LINGUISTIC EXPERTS: ROLE: MARKET OR PUBLIC OPINION SURVEY: A.D.)

Form of interdict

Weber-Stephen Products Co. v. Alrite Engineering (Pty) Ltd (PASSING OFF: EFFECT OF NOTICE ON DEFENDANTS PRODUCT: INTERDICT INFRINGED: S.C.)

Hearing in camera

Continental Wholesalers v. Fashion Fantasy (Pty) Ltd (INFRINGEMENT: INTERIM INJUNCTION: D&CLD)

Interim injunction

Continental Wholesalers v. Fashion Fantasy (Pty) Ltd (INFRINGEMENT: HEARING *in camera*: D&CLD)

Joinder

Wistyn Enterprises (Pty) Ltd v. Levi Strauss & Co. (EXPUNGEMENT: REGISTERED USER: TPD)

Jurisdiction

Spier Estate v. Die Bergkelder BPK (INFRINGEMENT: CANCELLATION PROCEEDINGS: S.C.)

Locus standii

Danco Clothing (Pty) Ltd v. Nu-Care Marketing Sales and Promotions (Pty) Ltd (EXPUNGEMENT: AGGRIEVED PERSON: TPD: A.D.)

Mala fides

Scott v. Watermaid (Pty) Ltd (PASSING OFF: CPD)

Market surveys

Hoechst Pharmaceuticals (Pty) Ltd v. The Beauty Box (Pty) Ltd (PASSING OFF: WEIGHT: A.D.)

Reckitt & Coleman S.A. (Pty) Ltd v. S.C. Johnson & Son S.A. (Pty) Ltd (LIKELIHOOD OF CONFUSION OR DECEPTION: EVIDENCE OF PSYCHOLOGISTS AND LINGUISTIC EXPERTS: ROLE: MARKET OR PUBLIC OPINION SURVEY: EVIDENCE: A.D.)

Onus

Tri-ang Pedigree (S.A.) (Pty) Ltd v. Prime Toys (Pty) Ltd (INFRINGEMENT: A.D.)

Public Policy

William Grant & Sons Ltd v. Cape Wine & Distillers Ltd (UNLAWFUL COMPETITION: CONDUCT: REPRESENTATION: CONFUSION OR DECEPTION: CPD)

Public policy. *See* **Practice** (*Public policy*)

Rectification

Ritz Hotel Ltd v. Charles of The Ritz (PERSON AGGRIEVED: QUALITY CONTROL: IMPORTED PACKAGING: LIKELY TO DECEIVE OR CONFUSE: A.D.)

Registration

Action Bolt (Pty) Ltd v. Tool Wholesale Holdings (Pty) Ltd (VALIDITY: SELLING OF GOODS DOES NOT CONSTITUTE A SERVICE: REGISTRATION FOR RETAIL AND WHOLESALE SERVICES CONTRARY TO STATUTE: TPD: A.D.)

Blockbuster Entertainment Corporation v. Registrar of Trade Marks (NON-DESCRIPTIVE AND PURELY DESCRIPTIVE MARK: BLOCKBUSTER/CHARTBUSTER: VIDEO RENTAL INDUSTRY: SERVICE MARK: TPD)

Cambridge Plan AG v. Moore (INFRINGEMENT: PASSING OFF: DIETARY PREPARATION: SIMILAR PRODUCT APPELLATION: DISCLAIMER: D&CLD)

Estée Lauder Cosmetics Ltd v. Registrar of Trade Marks (DISCLAIMER: ESTÉE LAUDER BEAUTIFUL: NON-DISTINCTIVE CHARACTER: TPD)

Smithkline Beecham Consolidated S.A. (Pty) Ltd v. Unilever plc (DISCLAIMER: EFFECT OF: WHETHER DISCLAIMED MATTER TO BE CONSIDERED IN COMPARISON WITH LATER APPLICATION FOR SIMILAR MARK: STRIPED TOOTHPASTE: A.D.)

Weber-Stephen Products Co. v. Registrar of Trade Marks (SHAPE AND CONFIGURATION: TPD)

Registered User

Television Radio Centre (Pty) Ltd v. Sony KK (INFRINGEMENT: ALTERATION OF GOODS: A.D.)

Wistyn Enterprises (Pty) Ltd v. Levi Strauss & Co. (EXPUNGEMENT: JOINDER: TPD)

Reproduction

Esquire Electronics Ltd v. Executive Video (INFRINGEMENT: PRE-RECORDED VIDEO TAPES: A.D.)

Esquire Electronics Ltd v. A. Roopanand Brothers (Pty) Ltd (INFRINGEMENT: MAGNETICALLY RECORDED IMAGES: D&CLD: S.C.)

Restrictive Practices

Vinide Ltd v. National Home Products (Pty) Ltd (STATUTORY PROVISIONS: IMPORTS: H.C.)

Secondary Meaning

Van der Watt v. Humansdorp Marketing C.C. (PASSING OFF: USE OF OWN NAME OR MERE DESCRIPTIVE WORDS: SECLD)

Services and Service Marks

Action Bolt (Pty) Ltd v. Tool Wholesale Holdings (Pty) Ltd (REGISTRATION: VALIDITY: SELLING OF GOODS DOES NOT CONSTITUTE A SERVICE: REGISTRATION FOR RETAIL AND WHOLESALE SERVICES CONTRARY TO STATUTE: TPD: A.D.)

Blockbuster Entertainment Corporation v. Registrar of Trade Marks (REGISTRATION: NON-DESCRIPTIVE AND PURELY DESCRIPTIVE MARK: BLOCKBUSTER/CHARTBUSTER: VIDEO RENTAL INDUSTRY: SERVICE MARK: TPD)

Shape. *See* **Three-dimensional Mark**

Special Damages. *See* **Damages**

Three-dimensional Mark

Cointreau et Cie S.A. v. Pagan International (INFRINGEMENT: CONTAINER MARK: BOTTLE: SHAPE: UTILITARIAN OR FUNCTIONAL FEATURE: LACK OF DISTINGUISHING FEATURES: A.D.)

Weber-Stephen Products Co. v. Registrar of Trade Marks (REGISTRATION: SHAPE AND CONFIGURATION: TPD)

Unauthorised Use

MCT Labels S.A. v. Gemelli C.C. (INFRINGEMENT: USE AS TRADE MARK: D&CLD)

Unlawful or Unfair Competition

Escherich Developments (Pty) Ltd v. Andrew Mentis Steel Sales (Pty) Ltd (WLD)

Knox D'Arcy Ltd v. Jamieson (CONFIDENTIAL INFORMATION: EX-EMPLOYEE: DISTINCTION BETWEEN TRADE SECRETS AND OTHER CONFIDENTIAL INFORMATION: WLD)

Long John International Ltd v. Stellenbosch Wine Trust (Pty) Ltd (MISREPRESENTATION: CHARACTER, COMPOSITION OF ORIGIN OF GOODS: REPUTATION: D&CLD)

Schultz v. Butt (COPYRIGHT: REGISTRATION: BOAT HULLS: A.D.)

Sea Harvest Corp. (Pty) Ltd v. Irvin & Johnson Ltd (ORDINARY OR LAUDATORY WORDS: CPD)

Silver Crystal Trading (Pty) Ltd v. Namibia Diamond Corp. (D&CLD)

South African Historical Mint (Pty) Ltd v. Sutcliffe (FORMER EMPLOYEE: TRADE SECRETS: CPD)

Taylor & Horne (Pty) Ltd v. Dentall (Pty) Ltd (EXCLUSIVE DISTRIBUTION AGREEMENT: LEGITIMATE SALE OF GOODS BY THIRD PARTY: A.D.)

Times Media Ltd v. South African Broadcasting Corporation (PUBLIC BROADCASTING CORPORATION REFUSING TO TELEVISE ADVERTISEMENT: GOODWILL: UNLAWFUL BOYCOTT: WLD)

Van Castricum v. Theunissen (CONFIDENTIAL INFORMATION: EX-EMPLOYEE: CUSTOMER LISTS: TPD)

William Grant & Sons Ltd v. Cape Wine & Distillers Ltd (CONDUCT: REPRESENTATION: CONFUSION OR DECEPTION: PUBLIC POLICY: CPD)

Unregistered Trade Mark. *See also under* South African **Passing Off**

Hollywood Curl (Pty) Ltd v. Twins Products (Pty) Ltd (No. 1) (PASSING OFF: REPUTATION: SIMILAR GET-UP: ASSOCIATION IN MINDS OF PUBLIC: A.D.)

Use

MCT Labels S.A. v. Gemelli C.C. (INFRINGEMENT: USE AS TRADE MARK: UNAUTHORISED USE: D&CLD)

Philip Morris Inc. v. Marlboro Shirt Co. S.A. Ltd (PASSING OFF: EXPUNGEMENT: CONFUSION: A.D.)

Plascon-Evans Paints Ltd v. Van Riebeeck Paints (Pty) Ltd (INFRINGEMENT: NOTIONAL USE: A.D.)

United Bank Ltd v. Standard Bank of South Africa Ltd (EXPUNGEMENT: NO BONA FIDE USE FOR A PERIOD OF FIVE YEARS: TPD)

Wistyn Enterprises (Pty) Ltd v. Levi Strauss & Co. (EXPUNGEMENT: REGISTERED USER: JOINDER: TPD)

Use as a Trade Mark

MCT Labels S.A. v. Gemelli C.C. (INFRINGEMENT: UNAUTHORISED USE: D&CLD)

Use in the Course of Trade

Beecham Group PLC v. Southern Transvaal Pharmaceutical Pricing Bureau (Pty) Ltd (INFRINGEMENT: GOODS FOR WHICH TRADE MARK REGISTERED: INTERPRETATION OF STATUTE: WLD) (REFERENCE TO TRADE IN GOODS IN CLASS FOR WHICH MARK REGISTERED: COMPUTER SOFTWARE SYSTEM PROVIDING INFORMATION ON GENERIC ALTERNATIVE MEDICINES AVAILABLE AFTER EXPIRY OF PATENT: A.D.)

Miele et Cie GmbH & Co. v. Evro Electrical (Pty) Ltd (INFRINGEMENT: A.D.)

Use of Container

Metal Box South Africa Ltd v. Midpak Blow-Moulders (Pty) Ltd (INFRINGEMENT: RELEVANCE OF BELIEF OF PUBLIC AS TO ORIGIN OF GOODS: TPD)

Use of Own Name

Boswell-Wilkie Circus (Pty) Ltd v. Brian Boswell Circus (Pty) Ltd (PASSING OFF: DECEPTION: NPD)

Van der Watt v. Humansdorp Marketing C.C. (PASSING OFF: USE OF OWN NAME OR MERE DESCRIPTIVE WORDS: SECONDARY MEANING: SECLD)

Utilitarian or Functional Feature

Cointreau et Cie S.A. v. Pagan International (INFRINGEMENT: CONTAINER MARK: BOTTLE: SHAPE: THREE-DIMENSIONAL MARK: LACK OF DISTINGUISHING FEATURES: A.D.)

Validity

Action Bolt (Pty) Ltd v. Tool Wholesale Holdings (Pty) Ltd (REGISTRATION: SELLING OF GOODS DOES NOT CONSTITUTE A SERVICE: REGISTRATION FOR RETAIL AND WHOLESALE SERVICES CONTRARY TO STATUTE: TPD: A.D.)

TRINIDAD AND TOBAGO

Patents

Know-how

IMH Investments Ltd v. Trinidad Home Developers Ltd (LICENCE AGREEMENT: CONSTRUCTION: C.A.)

Licence Agreement

IMH Investments Ltd v. Trinidad Home Developers Ltd (KNOW-HOW: CONSTRUCTION: UNPAID ROYALTIES: SUMMARY JUDGMENT: C.A.)

Misrepresentation:

IMH Investments Ltd v. Trinidad Home Developers Ltd (LICENCE AGREEMENT: RECISSION BY LICENSEE: ESTOPPEL: C.A.)

Royalties

IMH Investments Ltd v. Trinidad Home Developers Ltd (LICENCE AGREEMENT: UNPAID ROYALTIES: SUMMARY JUDGMENT: LICENCED PATENTS NEVER REGISTERED BUT ROYALTIES PAID FOR SEVEN YEARS: C.A.)

Practice

Appeal

IMH Investments Ltd v. Trinidad Home Developers Ltd (UNPAID ROYALTIES: SUMMARY JUDGMENT: STATUTORY AND CONTRACTUAL INTEREST: DISCRETION: C.A.)

Discretion

IMH Investments Ltd v. Trinidad Home Developers Ltd (KNOW-HOW: LICENCE AGREEMENT: STATUTORY AND CONTRACTUAL INTEREST: C.A.)

Estoppel

IMH Investments Ltd v. Trinidad Home Developers Ltd (LICENCE AGREEMENT: LICENCED PATENTS NEVER REGISTERED BUT ROYALTIES PAID UNDER AGREEMENT FOR SEVEN YEARS: RECISSION BY LICENSEE: JUDGMENT: C.A.)

Interest

IMH Investments Ltd v. Trinidad Home Developers Ltd (LICENCE AGREEMENT: CONSTRUCTION: UNPAID ROYALTIES: STATUTORY AND CONTRACTUAL INTEREST: DISCRETION: C.A.)

Judgment

IMH Investments Ltd v. Trinidad Home Developers Ltd (KNOW-HOW: LICENCE AGREEMENT: C.A.)

Summary Judgment

IMH Investments Ltd v. Trinidad Home Developers Ltd (KNOW-HOW: LICENCE AGREEMENT: C.A.)

UNITED STATES

Confidential Information and Trade Secrets

Computer Software

Computer Associates International, Inc. v. Altai, Inc. (FEDERAL PRE-EMPTION: C.A.)

Federal Pre-emption

Computer Associates International, Inc. v. Altai, Inc. (COMPUTER SOFTWARE: C.A.)

Copyright

Assignment

Stewart v. Sheldon Abend, DBA Authors Research Co. (ASSIGNMENT OF RENEWAL RIGHTS: DEATH OF AUTHOR BEFORE RENEWAL: S.C.)

Authorisation

Lewis Galoob Toys Inc. v. Nintendo of America Inc. (INFRINGEMENT: DERIVATIVE WORKS: WHETHER MODIFICATION OF VISUAL DISPLAYS BY A DEVICE NOT AFFECTING THE COMPUTER PROGRAM ITSELF IS AN INFRINGEMENT: D.C.)

Blank Form Doctrine

George L. Kregos v. The Associated Press (INFRINGEMENT: PROTECTABILITY OF COMPILATION OF FACTS: ORIGINALITY: MINIMAL CREATIVITY: IDEA/ EXPRESSION MERGER DOCTRINE: SPORT STATISTICS FORM: C.A.)

Classroom Guidelines

Basic Books Inc. v. Kinkos Graphics Corp. (INFRINGEMENT: CLASSROOM GUIDELINES: EXCESSIVE COPYING: FAIR USE: D.C.)

Commercial Purpose

American Geophysical Union v. Texaco Inc. (INFRINGEMENT: PHOTOCOPYING: SCIENTIFIC JOURNALS: CORPORATE RESEARCH: FAIR USE: D.C.: C.A.)
Basic Books Inc. v. Kinko's Graphics Corp. (INFRINGEMENT: CLASSROOM GUIDELINES: EXCESSIVE COPYING: DEFENSES: WILFUL INFRINGEMENT: FAIR USE: MARKET EFFECT: FACTUAL MATTER: D.C.)

Compilation

Feist Publications, Inc. v. Rural Telephone Service Co. Inc. (INFRINGEMENT: COPYING OF ORIGINAL ELEMENTS: LACK OF CREATIVITY: FACT/EXPRESSION DICHOTOMY: S.C.)

George L. Kregos v. The Associated Press (INFRINGEMENT: ORIGINALITY: MINIMAL CREATIVITY: IDEA/EXPRESSION MERGER DOCTRINE: BLANK FORM DOCTRINE: SPORT STATISTICS FORM: C.A.)

Computer-Related Subjects

Audiovisual displays

Lewis Galoob Toys Inc. v. Nintendo of America Inc. (WHETHER MODIFICATION OF VISUAL DISPLAYS BY A DEVICE NOT AFFECTING THE COMPUTER PROGRAM ITSELF IS AN INFRINGEMENT: D.C.)

Circuit layouts

Atari Games Corp. v. Nintendo of America Inc. (CIRCUIT IN SILICON CHIP: SUBSISTENCE: SCOPE OF PROTECTION: MERGER OF IDEA AND EXPRESSION: INFRINGEMENT IN REVERSE ENGINEERING: D.C.)

Brooktree Corporation v. Advanced Micro Devices Inc. (MASK WORKS: WHETHER CIRCUIT LAYOUT DICTATED BY FUNCTION: D.C.)

Computer programs

Apple Computer, Inc. v. Microsoft Corp. (LOOK AND FEEL: SUBSISTENCE OF COPYRIGHT IN VISUAL DISPLAYS: D.C.)

Atari Games Corp. v. Nintendo of America Inc. (CIRCUIT IN SILICON CHIP: SUBSISTENCE OF SCOPE OF PROTECTION: MERGER OF IDEA AND EXPRESSION: INFRINGEMENT IN REVERSE ENGINEERING: D.C.)

Computer Associates International, Inc. v. Altai, Inc. (NON-LITERAL ELEMENTS PROTECTABLE: SUBSTANTIAL SIMILARITY TEST: C.A.)

Lewis Galoob Toys Inc. v. Nintendo of America Inc. (AUDIOVISUAL DISPLAYS: INFRINGEMENT: AUTHORISATION: DERIVATIVE WORKS: FAIR USE: D.C.)

Lotus Development Corporation Paperback Software International (USER INTERFACE: COPYRIGHTABILITY OF NONLITERAL ELEMENTS: D.C.)

NEC Corporation v. Intel Corporation (MICROCODE IN MICROPROCESSOR CHIPS: SUBSISTENCE: MINIMAL VERBAL STRUCTURES: WHETHER MODIFICATION OF EARLIER COPY AVOIDS INFRINGEMENT: D.C.)

Wheelan Associates Inc. v. Jaslow Dental Laboratories Inc. (INFRINGEMENT: COPYING OF STRUCTURE: SUBSTANTIAL PART: C.A.)

Xerox Corpn v. Apple Computer Inc. (LOOK AND FEEL: USER INTERFACE: S.C.)

Look and feel

Apple Computer, Inc. v. Microsoft Corp. (SUBSISTENCE OF COPYRIGHT IN VISUAL DISPLAYS: D.C.)

Lotus Development Corporation Paperback Software International (NON-LITERAL ELEMENTS: IDEA/EXPRESSION: D.C.)

Xerox Corpn v. Apple Computer Inc. (USER INTERFACE: INFRINGEMENT: REMEDIES: WHETHER ORDER STRIKING OUT COPYRIGHT REGISTRATION AVAILABLE: S.C.)

Mask works

Brooktree Corporation v. Advanced Micro Devices Inc. (CIRCUIT LAYOUTS: WHETHER CIRCUIT LAYOUT DICTATED BY FUNCTION: D.C.)

Microcode in microprocessor chips

NEC Corporation v. Intel Corporation (SUBSISTENCE: MINIMAL VERBAL STRUCTURES: WORKS DICTATED BY FUNCTION: D.C.)

User interface

Lotus Development Corporation v. Paperback Software International (NONLITERAL
   ELEMENTS: IDEA/EXPRESSION: LOOK AND FEEL: D.C.)
Xerox Corpn v. Apple Computer Inc. (LOOK AND FEEL: INFRINGEMENT:
   REMEDIES: S.C.)

Concept and Feel

Dawson v. Hinshaw Music Inc. (INFRINGEMENT: PRIMA FACIE CASE: SUBSTANTIAL
   SIMILARITY: TWO-PRONG TEST: TOTAL CONCEPT AND FEEL: ORDINARY OR
   LAY OBSERVER VERSUS INTENDED AUDIENCE: EVIDENCE: SUBSTANTIAL
   SIMILARITY OF COPYRIGHTABLE WORKS: TESTIMONY FROM MEMBERS OF
   INTENDED AUDIENCE: EXPERT TESTIMONY ON INTENDED AUDIENCE: SHEET
   MUSIC VERSUS AUDIO RECORDINGS: C.A.)

Constructive Trust

Xerox Corpn v. Apple Computer Inc. (COMPUTER PROGRAMS: LQOK AND FEEL OF
   USER INTERFACE: REMEDIES FOR INFRINGEMENT: WHETHER ORDER
   STRIKING OUT COPYRIGHT REGISTRATION AVAILABLE: WHETHER REMEDY
   OF CONSTRUCTIVE TRUST AVAILABLE: S.C.)

Copying

Excessive copying

Basic Books Inc. v. Kinko's Graphics Corp. (INFRINGEMENT: CLASSROOM
   GUIDELINES: DEFENCES: MISUSE: ESTOPPEL: REMEDIES: WILFUL
   INFRINGEMENT: FAIR USE DOCTRINE: D.C.)

Original elements

Feist Publications, Inc. v. Rural Telephone Service Co. Inc. (INFRINGEMENT:
   COMPILATION: LACK OF CREATIVITY: FACT/EXPRESSION DICHOTOMY: S.C.)

Structure

Wheelan Associates Inc. v. Jaslow Dental Laboratories Inc. (INFRINGEMENT:
   COMPUTER PROGRAMS: SUBSTANTIAL PART: C.A.)

Corporate Research

American Geophysical Union v. Texaco Inc. (INFRINGEMENT: PHOTOCOPYING:
   SCIENTIFIC JOURNALS: COMMERCIAL PURPOSE: FAIR USE: D.C.: C.A.)

Death of Author

Stewart v. Sheldon Abend, DBA Authors Research Co. (ASSIGNMENT OF RENEWAL
   RIGHTS: DERIVATIVE WORKS: PRE-EXISTING WORKS: TERMINATION
   PROVISIONS: S.C.)

Defences

Basic Books Inc. v. Kinko's Graphics Corp. (INFRINGEMENT: CLASSROOM
   GUIDELINES: EXCESSIVE COPYING: MISUSE: ESTOPPEL: REMEDIES:
   INJUNCTION: STATUTORY DAMAGES: D.C.)
Lasercomb America Inc. v. Job Reynolds (INFRINGEMENT: MISUSE: EQUITABLE
   DEFENCE: LIMITED MONOPOLY: C.A.)

Lotus Development Corporation Paperback Software International (NON-LITERAL ELEMENTS: IDEA/EXPRESSION: LOOK AND FEEL: D.C.)

Infringement

American Geophysical Union v. Texaco Inc. (PHOTOCOPYING: SCIENTIFIC JOURNALS: CORPORATE RESEARCH: COMMERCIAL PURPOSE: FAIR USE: D.C., C.A.)

Atari Games Corp. v. Nintendo of America Inc. (CIRCUIT IN SILICON CHIP: SUBSISTENCE: SCOPE OF PROTECTION: MERGER OF IDEA AND EXPRESSION: REVERSE ENGINEERING: D.C.)

Basic Books Inc. v. Kinko's Graphics Corp. (CLASSROOM GUIDELINES: EXCESSIVE COPYING: WILFUL INFRINGEMENT: FAIR USE DOCTRINE: D.C.)

Brooktree Corporation v. Advanced Micro Devices Inc. (STANDARD OF SIMILARITY REQUIRED: SUBSTANTIALLY COPIED: REVERSE ENGINEERING: D.C.)

Data East USA Inc. v. Epyx Inc. (SUBSTANTIAL SIMILARITY: C.A.)

Dawson v. Hinshaw Music Inc. (PRIMA FACIE CASE: SUBSTANTIAL SIMILARITY: TWO-PRONG TEST: TOTAL CONCEPT AND FEEL: ORDINARY OR LAY OBSERVER VERSUS INTENDED AUDIENCE: EVIDENCE: SUBSTANTIAL SIMILARITY OF COPYRIGHTABLE WORKS: TESTIMONY FROM MEMBERS OF INTENDED AUDIENCE: EXPERT TESTIMONY ON INTENDED AUDIENCE: SHEET MUSIC VERSUS AUDIO RECORDINGS: C.A.)

Feist Publications, Inc. v. Rural Telephone Service Co. Inc. (COPYING OF ORIGINAL ELEMENTS: COMPILATION: LACK OF CREATIVITY: S.C.)

George L. Kregos v. The Associated Press (PROTECTABILITY OF COMPILATION OF FACTS: ORIGINALITY: MINIMAL CREATIVITY: IDEA/EXPRESSION MERGER DOCTRINE: BLANK FORM DOCTRINE: SPORT STATISTICS FORM: C.A.)

Lasercomb America Inc. v. Job Reynolds (MISUSE: EQUITABLE DEFENCE: LIMITED MONOPOLY: C.A.)

Lewis Galoob Toys Inc. v. Nintendo of America Inc. (AUTHORISATION: DERIVATIVE WORKS: WHETHER MODIFICATION OF VISUAL DISPLAYS BY A DEVICE NOT AFFECTING THE COMPUTER PROGRAM ITSELF IS AN INFRINGEMENT: FAIR USE: D.C.)

NEC Corporation v. Intel Corporation (WHETHER MODIFICATION OF EARLIER COPY AVOIDS INFRINGEMENT: D.C.)

Wheelan Associates Inc. v. Jaslow Dental Laboratories Inc. (COMPUTER PROGRAMS: COPYING OF STRUCTURE: SUBSTANTIAL PART: C.A.)

Xerox Corpn v. Apple Computer Inc. (REMEDIES: WHETHER ORDER STRIKING OUT COPYRIGHT REGISTRATION AVAILABLE: S.C.)

Injunction. See Practice (*Injunction*)

Lack of Creativity

Feist Publications, Inc. v. Rural Telephone Service Co. Inc. (INFRINGEMENT: COPYING OF ORIGINAL ELEMENTS: COMPILATION: FACT/EXPRESSION DICHOTOMY: S.C.)

Licence

Apple Computer, Inc. v. Microsoft Corp. (SCOPE: INTERPRETATION: COMPUTER PROGRAMS: LOOK AND FEEL: D.C.)

Lasercomb America Inc. v. Job Reynolds (RESTRICTIONS: NON-COMPETITION PROVISIONS: C.A.)

1128

Notice

NEC Corporation v. Intel Corporation (FORFEITURE: NON-USE OF COPYRIGHT NOTICE: D.C.)

Pre-existing Works

Stewart v. Sheldon Abend, DBA Authors Research Co. (ASSIGNMENT OF RENEWAL RIGHTS: DEATH OF AUTHOR BEFORE RENEWAL: DERIVATIVE WORKS: TERMINATION PROVISIONS: FAIR USE: SUBSTANTIAL PORTION: S.C.)

Remedies

Xerox Corpn v. Apple Computer Inc. (INFRINGEMENT: WHETHER ORDER STRIKING OUT COPYRIGHT REGISTRATION AVAILABLE: WHETHER REMEDY OF CONSTRUCTIVE TRUST AVAILABLE: S.C.)

Renewal Rights

Stewart v. Sheldon Abend, DBA Authors Research Co. (ASSIGNMENT OF RIGHTS: DEATH OF AUTHOR BEFORE RENEWAL: S.C.)

Reverse Engineering

Atari Games Corp. v. Nintendo of America Inc. (COMPUTER PROGRAMS: CIRCUIT IN SILICON CHIP: INFRINGEMENT: D.C.)

Brooktree Corporation v. Advanced Micro Devices Inc. (CIRCUIT LAYOUTS: MASK WORKS: INFRINGEMENT: STANDARD OF SIMILARITY REQUIRED: SUBSTANTIALLY COPIED: D.C.)

Scope of Protection

Atari Games Corp. v. Nintendo of America Inc. (COMPUTER PROGRAMS: CIRCUIT IN SILICON CHIP: MERGER OF IDEA AND EXPRESSION: D.C.)

Statutory Damages

Basic Books Inc. v. Kinko's Graphics Corp. (INFRINGEMENT: CLASSROOM GUIDELINES: D.C.)

Striking Out Copyright Registration

Xerox Corpn v. Apple Computer Inc. (REMEDIES FOR INFRINGEMENT: WHETHER ORDER STRIKING OUT COPYRIGHT REGISTRATION AVAILABLE: S.C.)

Subsistence

Apple Computer, Inc. v. Microsoft Corp. (SUBSISTENCE OF COPYRIGHT IN VISUAL DISPLAYS: D.C.)

Atari Games Corp. v. Nintendo of America Inc. (COMPUTER PROGRAMS: CIRCUIT IN SILICON CHIP: D.C.)

NEC Corporation v. Intel Corporation (COMPUTER PROGRAMS: MICROCODE IN MICROPROCESSOR CHIPS: MINIMAL VERBAL STRUCTURES: WORKS DICTATED BY FUNCTION: D.C.)

Substantial Part

Stewart v. Sheldon Abend, DBA Authors Research Co. (FAIR USE: S.C.)

Wheelan Associates Inc. v. Jaslow Dental Laboratories Inc. (INFRINGEMENT: COMPUTER PROGRAMS: COPYING OF STRUCTURE: C.A.)

Substantial Similarity

Computer Associates International, Inc. v. Altai, Inc. (COMPUTER SOFTWARE: NON-LITERAL ELEMENTS PROTECTABLE: C.A.)

Data East USA Inc. v. Epyx Inc. (INFRINGEMENT: RELATIONSHIP BETWEEN IDEAS AND EXPRESSION: SUFFICIENCY OF EVIDENCE OF CONTENTS OF AUDIO-VISUAL WORK: C.A.)

Dawson v. Hinshaw Music Inc. (INFRINGEMENT: TWO-PRONG TEST: TOTAL CONCEPT AND FEEL: ORDINARY OR LAY OBSERVER VERSUS INTENDED AUDIENCE: C.A.)

Wilful Infringement. *See Infringement*

Work Made for Hire

Community for Creative Non-Violence v. James Earl Reid (EMPLOYEE: INDEPENDENT CONTRACTOR: AGENT: C.A.)

Works Dictated by Function

NEC Corporation v. Intel Corporation (COMPUTER PROGRAMS: MICROCODE IN MICROPROCESSOR CHIPS: SUBSISTENCE: MINIMAL VERBAL STRUCTURES: D.C.)

Patents

Infringement

Rite-Hite Corp. v. Kelly Co. Inc. (DAMAGES: LOST PROFITS: INJUNCTION: FAILURE TO PRACTICE INVENTION: C.A., Fed. Ct)

Practice

Damages

Rite-Hite Corp. v. Kelly Co. Inc. (LOST PROFITS: INJUNCTION: FAILURE TO PRACTICE INVENTION: C.A., Fed. Ct)

Injunction

Rite-Hite Corp. v. Kelly Co. Inc. (LOST PROFITS: INJUNCTION: FAILURE TO PRACTICE INVENTION: C.A., Fed. Ct)

Trade Marks

Inherent Distinctiveness

Two Pesos Inc. v. Taco Cabana Inc. (INHERENT DISTINCTIVENESS: SECONDARY MEANING NOT REQUIRED: S.C.)

Secondary Meaning

Two Pesos Inc. v. Taco Cabana Inc. (INHERENT DISTINCTIVENESS: SECONDARY MEANING NOT REQUIRED: S.C.)

Trade Dress

Two Pesos Inc. v. Taco Cabana Inc. (INHERENT DISTINCTIVENESS: SECONDARY MEANING NOT REQUIRED: S.C.)

E. SPECIAL INTEREST SUBJECTS: WORLDWIDE CASES

COMPUTER-RELATED SUBJECTS

Adaptations

Accounting Systems 2000 (Developments) Pty Ltd v. CCH Australia Ltd (COPYRIGHT: INFRINGEMENT: REPRODUCTION OR ADAPTATION: REPRODUCTION OF SUBSTANTIAL PART: EFFECT OF EXPENDITURE OF TIME AND EFFORT IN DEVELOPING COMPUTER PROGRAM: Australia: Fed. Ct)

Apple Computer Inc. v. Computer Edge Pty Ltd (COPYRIGHT: INFRINGEMENT: ADAPTATIONS: Australia: Fed. Ct)

Apple Computer Inc. v. Computer Edge Pty Ltd (COPYRIGHT: INFRINGEMENT: MICRO COMPUTER PROGRAMS: WHETHER SOURCE CODE ADAPTATION OF SOURCE CODE: Australia: Fed. Ct)

Mackintosh Computers v. Apple Computer Inc. (COPYRIGHT: INFRINGEMENT: REPRODUCTION: CONTRIVANCE: MACHINE PARTS: Canada: Fed. Ct: C.A.)

Alteration of Data

R. v. Cropp (HACKING: UNAUTHORISED ACCESS: UNAUTHORISED MODIFICATION: ALTERATION OF DATA ON COMPUTER: INTERPRETATION OF STATUTE: U.K.: Crown Court, Snaresbrook)

Assignment of Rights

Acorn Computer Ltd v. MCS Microcomputer System Pty Ltd (COPYRIGHT: REQUIREMENT OF WRITING: EQUITABLE OWNERSHIP: JOINT OWNERSHIP: Fed. Ct)

Payen Components S.A. Ltd v. Bovic Gaskets C.C. (COPYRIGHT: SUBSISTENCE: LITERARY WORK: COMPUTERISED CATALOGUING SYSTEM: WORK PRODUCED BY PROGRAM: ASSIGNMENT OF COPYRIGHT TO OVERSEAS PARENT COMPANY: EXCLUSIVE LICENSEE: UNLAWFUL COMPETITION: South Africa: WLD)

Audiovisual Displays. *See* Visual Displays

Back-Up Copies, Right to Make

Artware (Sárl) v. Groupe D'Utilisation Francophone D'Informatique (SOFTWARE SALES: COPYRIGHT: ANTI-PROTECTION PROCESSES: France: S.C.)

Chip. *See* Silicon Chip

Circuits

Apple Computer Inc. v. New-Con Technologies Ltd (COPYRIGHT: INFRINGEMENT: SOFTWARE: PRINTED CIRCUITS: Israel: D.C.)

Atari Games Corp. v. Nintendo of America Inc. (CIRCUIT IN SILICON CHIP: SUBSISTENCE OF COPYRIGHT: SCOPE OF PROTECTION: MERGER OF IDEA AND EXPRESSION: INFRINGEMENT IN REVERSE ENGINEERING: United States: D.C.)

Autodesk Inc. v. Dyason (COPYRIGHT: WHETHER ELECTRICAL CIRCUIT IS A COMPUTER PROGRAM: WHETHER SET OF INSTRUCTIONS AND DATA PROCESSING DEVICE NEED BE SEPARATE: INFRINGEMENT: REPRODUCTION: AUTHORISATION: DEVICE ENABLING BREACH OF SHRINK-WRAP LICENCE: Australia: Fed. Ct)

Avel Pty Ltd v. Wells (CIRCUIT LAYOUTS: PARALLEL IMPORTATION OF ELIGIBLE
   LAYOUTS FOR VIDEO GAMES: COPYRIGHT: ELIGIBLE LAYOUTS CONTAINING
   SUBSTANTIAL PARTS OF COMPUTER PROGRAMS, THE COPYRIGHT IN WHICH
   WAS OWNED BY ONE OR OTHER OF THE APPELLANTS: WHETHER
   IMPORTATION OF SUCH ELIGIBLE LAYOUTS CONSTITUTED AN
   INFRINGEMENT OF APPELLANTS' COPYRIGHT IN COMPUTER PROGRAMS:
   Australia: Fed. Ct)
Brooktree Corporation v. Advanced Micro Devices Inc. (CIRCUIT LAYOUTS: MASK
   WORKS: COPYRIGHT: WHETHER CIRCUIT LAYOUT DICTATED BY FUNCTION:
   INFRINGEMENT: STANDARD OF SIMILARITY REQUIRED: SUBSTANTIALLY
   COPIED: REVERSE ENGINEERING: United States: D.C.)
Centronics Systems Pty Ltd v. Nintendo Co. Ltd (CIRCUIT LAYOUT: INTEGRATED
   CIRCUIT: COMMERCIAL EXPLOITATION: INTERPRETATION OF STATUTE:
   IMPORTATION: INFRINGEMENT: Australia: Fed. Ct)
Centronics Systems Pty Ltd v. Nintendo Co. Ltd (CIRCUIT LAYOUT: INTEGRATED
   CIRCUIT: OWNER OF E.L. RIGHTS IN AN ORIGINAL CIRCUIT LAYOUT:
   INFRINGEMENT: WHETHER MADE IN ACCORDANCE WITH ORIGINAL
   LAYOUT: PURPOSE OF EVALUATION OR ANALYSIS: SHRINKING/SCALING:
   KNOWLEDGE: Australia: Fed. Ct)
Dyason (Martin Peter) v. Autodesk Inc. (COPYRIGHT: WHETHER ELECTRICAL
   CIRCUIT CAN BE A COMPUTER PROGRAM: INFRINGEMENT: REPRODUCTION:
   AUTHORISATION: WHETHER SUPPLY OF DEVICE ENABLING COMPUTER
   PROGRAM TO BE USED ON MORE THAN ONE COMPUTER AT A TIME MAY BE
   AUTHORISATION OF INFRINGEMENT: Australia: Fed. Ct)

Compatible Equipment

Aztech Systems Pte Ltd v. Creative Technology Ltd (COPYRIGHT: INFRINGEMENT:
   DESIGNING COMPATIBLE SOUND CARDS: FAIR DEALING FOR THE PURPOSE OF
   PRIVATE STUDY: DEROGATION FROM GRANT: IMPLIED LICENCE: Singapore:
   H.C.)

Computer Hacking. *See* Hacking

Computer Printout. *See* Printout

Computer Program. *See* Program

Computerised Database. *See* Database

Computerised Teaching System

Avtex Airservices Pty Ltd v. Bartsch (COPYRIGHT: OWNERSHIP: COMPUTERISED
   TEACHING SYSTEM OF WORKBOOKS, SLIDES AND COMPUTER PROGRAMS:
   Australia: Fed. Ct)

Confidential Information

Series 5 Software Ltd v. Philip Clarke (SOURCE CODES: SOLICITATION OF
   CUSTOMERS: INTERLOCUTORY RELIEF: DELAY: INTERLOCUTORY
   INJUNCTIONS: PRINCIPLES: HISTORICAL SURVEY OF *American Cyanamid*
   CASES: Ch.D.)

Contracts

Nottingham Building Society v. Eurodynamics Systems plc (SOFTWARE: REPUDIATION: DELIVERY-UP OF SOFTWARE: DISPUTED DEBT: INTERLOCUTORY ORDER FOR DELIVERY-UP: APPLICATION FOR LEAVE TO ADDUCE FURTHER EVIDENCE: INTERNAL COMPANY DOCUMENTS: RELEVANCY: C.A.)

Salvage Association (The) v. CAP Financial Services Ltd (BREACH: LIMITATION CLAUSE: APPLICABILITY OF UNFAIR CONTRACT TERMS ACT: Q.B.D.)

St Albans City & District Council v. International Computers Ltd (SOFTWARE: NEGLIGENT MISSTATEMENT: DEFICIENCY IN SOFTWARE RESULTING IN REDUCED REVENUE: WHETHER LOSS RECOVERABLE: LIMITATION CLAUSE: REASONABLENESS: WHETHER SOFTWARE GOODS: WHETHER PARTIES DEALING ON STANDARD TERMS: Q.B.D.)

Contributory Infringement. *See* Infringement and Breach

Criminal Offence

Grant v. Procurator Fiscal (CONFIDENTIAL INFORMATION: COPIES OF COMPUTER PRINT-OUTS: WHETHER DISHONEST EXPLOITATION OF THE CONFIDENTIAL INFORMATION OF ANOTHER A CRIME: Scotland: H.C.)

Irvine v. Carson (COPYRIGHT: POSSESSION OF INFRINGING COPIES OF COMPUTER PROGRAMS FOR THE PURPOSE OF DISTRIBUTING: CONVICTION: APPROPRIATE PENALTY: ORDER FOR FORFEITURE OF COMPUTERS USED FOR MAKING INFRINGING COPIES: Australia: Fed. Ct)

Irvine v. Hanna-Rivero (COPYRIGHT: INFRINGING COPIES OF COMPUTER PROGRAMS MADE FOR SWAP TRADE: DEFENDANT PLEADED GUILTY: CONSIDERATION OF APPROPRIATE PENALTY: ORDER FOR FORFEITURE OF SOME HARDWARE EQUIPMENT USED IN MAKING INFRINGING COPIES: Fed. Ct)

Police v. B (GAINING ACCESS TO COMPUTER CENTRE WITHOUT AUTHORISATION: USE OF MECHANICAL MEANS THROUGH INNOCENT AGENT: OFFENCE: New Zealand: C.A.)

R. v. Whiteley (COMPUTER HACKING: CRIMINAL DAMAGE: INTANGIBLE DAMAGE TO TANGIBLE PROPERTY: CONVICTION UPHELD: C.A., Crim. Div.)

Data-Processing Device

Autodesk Inc. v. Dyason (COPYRIGHT: WHETHER ELECTRICAL CIRCUIT IS A COMPUTER PROGRAM: WHETHER SET OF INSTRUCTIONS AND DATA PROCESSING DEVICE NEED BE SEPARATE: INFRINGEMENT: REPRODUCTION: AUTHORISATION: DEVICE ENABLING BREACH OF SHRINK-WRAP LICENCE: Australia: Fed. Ct)

Database

CCOM Pty Ltd v. Jiejung Pty Ptd (COPYRIGHT: COMPILATION OF CHINESE CHARACTERS IN DATABASE: INFRINGEMENT: CAUSAL LINK BETWEEN MATERIAL AND ALLEGED COPY: PATENT: COMPUTER PROCESS FOR ASSEMBLING CHINESE LANGUAGE CHARACTERS: VALIDITY: INFRINGEMENT: WHETHER SALE OF PROGRAM FOR USE IN STANDARD COMPUTER INFRINGES PATENTED APPARATUS CLAIM: CONTRIBUTORY INFRINGEMENT: Australia: Fed. Ct)

Derby & Co. Ltd v. Weldon (No. 9) (PRACTICE: DISCOVERY: INSPECTION: WHETHER DOCUMENT: EXTENT TO WHICH INSPECTION TO BE ORDERED: Ch.D.)

Dun & Bradstreet Ltd v. Typesetting Facilities Ltd (COPYRIGHT INFRINGEMENT: BREACH OF CONFIDENCE: APPLICATION FOR INSPECTION: INFORMATION IN ELECTRONIC FORM, SO VISUAL INSPECTION OF DISKS USELESS: DISCLOSURE OF CONTENTS REQUIRED: PRACTICE: INSPECTION BEFORE SERVICE OF STATEMENT OF CLAIM: REQUIREMENTS: INSPECTION ORDERED: Ch.D.)

Paxus Services Ltd v. People Bank Pty Ltd (PRACTICE AND PROCEDURE: DISCOVERY BEFORE ACTION: CONFIDENTIAL INFORMATION IN COMPUTER DATABASES: WHETHER COMPUTER DATABASE A DOCUMENT: CONSIDERATIONS FOR EXERCISE OF DISCRETION: Australia: Fed. Ct)

Dedicated ROM. *See* ROM

Diskettes

Computermate Products (Aust.) Pty Ltd v. Ozi-Soft Pty Ltd (COPYRIGHT: LICENCE TO IMPORT COPYRIGHT MATERIAL: NATURE AND DEFINITION OF LICENCE WITHIN STATUTORY DEFINITION: LICENCE INTERCHANGEABLE WITH CONSENT AND PERMISSION: ONUS OF PROVING EXISTENCE OF LICENCE: Australia: Fed. Ct)

Ozi-Soft Pty Ltd v. Wong (COPYRIGHT: CONTRIBUTORY INFRINGEMENT: IMPORTATION OF DISKETTES PURCHASES FROM COPYRIGHT OWNERS: IMPLIED LICENCE: DOCTRINE OF NATIONAL TREATMENT: Australia: Fed. Ct)

Electrical Circuit. *See* Circuits

Employee (As Creator)

Missing Link Software v. Magee (COPYRIGHT: INFRINGEMENT: WORK MADE IN COURSE OF EMPLOYMENT: TO WHOM DOES WORK OF MOONLIGHTING EMPLOYEE BELONG: Ch.D.)

Enabling Breach. *See* Infringement and Breach

Equitable Ownership. *See* Ownership

Fair Dealing

Aztech Systems Pte Ltd v. Creative Technology Ltd (COPYRIGHT: INFRINGEMENT: SOUND CARDS: DESIGNING COMPATIBLE CARDS: PRIVATE STUDY: DEROGATION FROM GRANT: IMPLIED LICENCE: Singapore: H.C.)

File Transfer Program

Ibcos Computers Ltd v. Barclays Mercantile Highland Finance Ltd (COPYRIGHT: SOFTWARE: SOURCE CODE: SUBSISTENCE AND EXTENT OF PROTECTION: INFRINGEMENT: SUBSTANTIAL PART: BREACH OF CONFIDENCE: BRITISH LEYLAND DEFENCE: RESTRICTIVE COVENANT: CONSTRUCTION: Ch.D.)

Hacking

R. v. Cropp (UNAUTHORISED ACCESS: UNAUTHORISED MODIFICATION: ALTERATION OF DATA ON COMPUTER: INTERPRETATION OF STATUTE: U.K.: Crown Court, Snaresbrook)

R. v. Whiteley (CRIMINAL DAMAGE: INTANGIBLE DAMAGE TO TANGIBLE PROPERTY: CONVICTION UPHELD: C.A., Crim. Div.)

Idea and Expression

115778 Canada Inc. v. Apple Computer Inc. (COPYRIGHT: SUBJECT-MATTER: COMPUTER PROGRAM: PROGRAM STORED IN ELECTRONIC FORM ON CHIP: REPRODUCTION: MERGER OF IDEA AND EXPRESSION: TRANSLATION: Canada: S.C.)

Apple Computer Inc. v. Microsoft Corp. (COPYRIGHT: COMPUTER PROGRAMS: LOOK AND FEEL OF VISUAL DISPLAYS OF PROGRAM: SUBSISTENCE OF COPYRIGHT IN VISUAL DISPLAYS: MERGER OF IDEA AND EXPRESSION: INDISPENSABLE EXPRESSION: *Scenes a faire*: MERE FUNCTIONALITY: United States: D.C.)

Atari Games Corp. v. Nintendo of America Inc. (COPYRIGHT: COMPUTER PROGRAMS: CIRCUIT IN SILICON CHIP: SUBSISTENCE OF COPYRIGHT: SCOPE OF PROTECTION: MERGER OF IDEA AND EXPRESSION: INFRINGEMENT IN REVERSE ENGINEERING: United States: D.C.)

John Richardson Computers Ltd v. Flanders (COPYRIGHT: SUBSISTENCE: OWNERSHIP: INFRINGEMENT: SUBSTANTIAL PART: COMPUTER PROGRAM: COMPILATION: IDEA AND EXPRESSION: ESTOPPEL: Ch.D.)

Legal Protection of Computer Programs Regulations 1993 (PROTECTION OF COMPUTER PROGRAMS AS LITERARY WORKS: ENACTMENT OF E.C. COUNCIL DIRECTIVE 91/250: ORIGINALITY: NON-PROTECTION OF UNDERLYING IDEAS AND PRINCIPLES: ENUMERATION OF RIGHTHOLDER'S EXCLUSIVE RIGHTS: RESTRICTIONS ON USE OF INFORMATION: ACTIONABLE INFRINGEMENTS: Ireland: minister for Enterprise and Employment)

Lotus Development Corporation Paperback Software International (COPYRIGHT: USER INTERFACE: COPYRIGHTABILITY OF NON-LITERAL ELEMENTS: IDEA/EXPRESSION: LOOK AND FEEL: COPYRIGHT ACT 1976 (U.S.): United States: D.C.)

Lotus Development Corporation v. Paperback Software International (COPYRIGHT: USER INTERFACE: COPYRIGHTABILITY OF NON-LITERAL ELEMENTS: IDEA/EXPRESSION: LOOK AND FEEL: United States: D.C.)

Mackintosh Computers Ltd v. Apple Computer Inc. (COPYRIGHT: SUBJECT-MATTER: PROGRAM STORED IN ELECTRONIC FORM ON CHIP: REPRODUCTION: MERGER OF IDEA AND EXPRESSION: TRANSLATION: Canada: S.C.)

Thomas and Stohr's Application (PETTY PATENT: OPPOSITION TO EXTENSION OF TERM: COMPUTER INVENTION: OBVIOUSNESS: IDEA: ANTICIPATION: Pat. Off.)

Total Information Processing Systems Ltd v. Daman Ltd (COPYRIGHT: SOFTWARE INTERFACE: MERGER OF IDEA WITH EXPRESSION: WHETHER PRINCIPLE OF DEROGATION FROM GRANT CONFINED TO COMPANIES WITH DOMINANT POSITION: EVIDENCE FOR INTERLOCUTORY APPLICATION: Ch.D.)

Imports and Importation

Atari Inc. v. Fairstar Electronics Pty Ltd (TRADE MARK: INFRINGEMENT: VIDEO COMPUTER SYSTEMS: PARALLEL IMPORTATION: Australia: Fed. Ct)

Avel Pty Ltd v. Wells (CIRCUIT LAYOUTS: INTEGRATED CIRCUIT: DEFENCE TO PARALLEL IMPORTATION OF COPYRIGHT MATERIAL: COPYRIGHT: COMPUTER PROGRAMS: INFRINGEMENT: PARALLEL IMPORTATION AND SALE: STATUTORY DEFENCE: Australia: Fed. Ct)

Avel Pty Ltd v. Wells (CIRCUIT LAYOUTS: PARALLEL IMPORTATION OF ELIGIBLE LAYOUTS FOR VIDEO GAMES: COPYRIGHT: ELIGIBLE LAYOUTS CONTAINING SUBSTANTIAL PARTS OF COMPUTER PROGRAMS, THE COPYRIGHT IN WHICH WAS OWNED BY ONE OR OTHER OF THE APPELLANTS: WHETHER IMPORTATION OF SUCH ELIGIBLE LAYOUTS CONSTITUTED AN INFRINGEMENT OF APPELLANTS' COPYRIGHT IN COMPUTER PROGRAMS: Australia: Fed. Ct)

Barson Computers (N.Z.) Ltd v. John Gilbert & Co. Ltd (COPYRIGHT: INFRINGEMENT: IMPORTATION: IRRELEVANCE OF HYPOTHETICAL MAKER: New Zealand: H.C.)

Broderbund Software Inc. v. Computermate Products (Australia) Pty Ltd (COPYRIGHT: INFRINGEMENT: PARALLEL IMPORTATION AND SALE: IMPLIED LICENCE OF IMPORTER: WHETHER DISTRIBUTOR AN EXCLUSIVE LICENSEE: EVIDENCE: MARKET SURVEY: RESTRICTIVE PRACTICES: MARKET POWER: EXCLUSIONARY PROVISIONS: ANTI-COMPETITIVE AGREEMENTS: EXCLUSIVE DEALING: USE OF SURVEY EVIDENCE: Australia: Fed. Ct)

Centronics Systems Pty Ltd v. Nintendo Co. Ltd (CIRCUIT LAYOUT: INTEGRATED CIRCUIT: COMMERCIAL EXPLOITATION: INTERPRETATION OF STATUTE: IMPORTATION: INFRINGEMENT: Australia: Fed. Ct)

Computermate Products (Aust.) Pty Ltd v. Ozi-Soft Pty Ltd (COPYRIGHT: LICENCE TO IMPORT: DISKETTES: NATURE AND DEFINITION OF LICENCE WITHIN STATUTORY DEFINITION: LICENCE INTERCHANGEABLE WITH CONSENT AND PERMISSION: ONUS OF PROVING EXISTENCE OF LICENCE: Australia: Fed. Ct)

International Business Machines Corporation v. Computer Imports Ltd (COPYRIGHT: INFRINGEMENT: COMPUTER TECHNOLOGY: THREE-DIMENSIONAL REPRODUCTION OF CABINET AND INTERNAL LAYOUT OF PERSONAL COMPUTER AND BY COPYING OF COMPUTER PROGRAM: IMPORTATION AND SALE: SOURCE CODE: WHETHER OBJECT CODE (SILICON CHIP): TRANSFER OF LITERARY WORK: New Zealand: H.C.)

Ozi-Soft Pty Ltd v. Wong (COPYRIGHT: CONTRIBUTORY INFRINGEMENT: IMPORTATION OF DISKETTES PURCHASES FROM COPYRIGHT OWNERS: IMPLIED LICENCE: DOCTRINE OF NATIONAL TREATMENT: Australia: Fed. Ct)

Roland Corporation v. Lorenzo & Sons Pty Ltd (COPYRIGHT: DRAWING OF SINGLE LETTER: COMPUTER PRINTOUT: ORIGINAL CREATED ON FLOPPY DISK: TRADE MARKS: DESIGNS: DEFENCE: PHOTOGRAPH IN BOOK: IMPORTATION: TRADE MARK: COPYRIGHT IN LOGO DEVICES REGULATED UNDER STATUTE: Australia: Fed. Ct)

Star Micronics Pty Ltd v. Five Star Computers Pty Ltd (COPYRIGHT: WHETHER ROM IN COMPUTER PRINTER A COMPUTER PROGRAM: ORIGINALITY: SECONDARY INFRINGEMENT: SALE OF IMPORTED PRINTERS INCLUDING COMPUTER PROGRAM IN ROM: PASSING OFF: SUPPLY OF FOREIGN SUPPLIED PRINTERS AS ASSOCIATED WITH AUSTRALIAN SUPPLIER: SUPPLY OF 220v COMPUTER PRINTERS AS INTENDED BY MANUFACTURER FOR DISTRIBUTION IN AUSTRALIA: Australia: Fed. Ct)

Infringement and Breach

Accounting Systems 2000 (Developments) Pty Ltd v. CCH Australia Ltd (COPYRIGHT: REPRODUCTION OR ADAPTATION: REPRODUCTION OF SUBSTANTIAL PART: EFFECT OF EXPENDITURE OF TIME AND EFFORT IN DEVELOPING COMPUTER PROGRAM: Australia: Fed. Ct)

Apple Computer Inc. v. Computer Edge Pty Ltd (COPYRIGHT: MICRO: WHETHER SOURCE CODE ADAPTATION OF SOURCE CODE: Australia: Fed. Ct)

Apple Computer Inc. v. New-Con Technologies Ltd (COPYRIGHT: SOFTWARE: PRINTED CIRCUITS: Israel: D.C.)

Atari Games Corp. v. Nintendo of America Inc. (COPYRIGHT: CIRCUIT IN SILICON CHIP: SUBSISTENCE OF COPYRIGHT: SCOPE OF PROTECTION: MERGER OF IDEA AND EXPRESSION: INFRINGEMENT IN REVERSE ENGINEERING: United States: D.C.)

Atari Inc. v. Fairstar Electronics Pty Ltd (TRADE MARK: VIDEO COMPUTER SYSTEMS: PARALLEL IMPORTATION: Australia: Fed. Ct)

Atari Inc. v. Philips Electronics Ltd (COPYRIGHT: INSPECTION: PRACTICE: Ch.D.)

Australian Computer Evaluation Consultants Pty Ltd v. Datbury Pty Ltd (COPYRIGHT: INFRINGEMENT: COMPUTER PROGRAM: PASSING OFF: Australia: Fed. Ct)

Autodesk Australia Pty Ltd v. Cheung (COPYRIGHT: SALE OF UNAUTHORISED REPRODUCTIONS: DAMAGES: MEASURE OF COMPENSATORY DAMAGES: ADDITIONAL DAMAGES: CLAIM BY COPYRIGHT OWNER AND AUSTRALIAN DISTRIBUTOR: Australia: Fed. Ct)

Autodesk Inc. v. Dyason (COPYRIGHT: ORIGINALITY: SUBSTANTIAL PART: APPELLANTS' DEVICE TO PREVENT ITS COMPUTER PROGRAMS BEING RUN ON A COMPUTER WITHOUT DEVICE: Australia: H.C.)

Autodesk Inc. v. Dyason (COPYRIGHT: WHETHER ELECTRICAL CIRCUIT IS A COMPUTER PROGRAM: WHETHER SET OF INSTRUCTIONS AND DATA PROCESSING DEVICE NEED BE SEPARATE: REPRODUCTION: AUTHORISATION: DEVICE ENABLING BREACH OF SHRINK-WRAP LICENCE: Australia: Fed. Ct)

Autodesk Inc. v. Dyason (No. 2) (COPYRIGHT: COMPUTER PROGRAM: ORIGINALITY: SUBSTANTIAL PART: APPELLANT'S DEVICE TO PREVENT ITS COMPUTER PROGRAMS BEING RUN ON A COMPUTER WITHOUT DEVICE: Australia: H.C.)

Avel Pty Ltd v. Wells (CIRCUIT LAYOUTS: INTEGRATED CIRCUIT: DEFENCE TO PARALLEL IMPORTATION OF COPYRIGHT MATERIAL: COPYRIGHT: PARALLEL IMPORTATION AND SALE: STATUTORY DEFENCE: Australia: Fed. Ct)

Avel Pty Ltd v. Wells (CIRCUIT LAYOUTS: PARALLEL IMPORTATION OF ELIGIBLE LAYOUTS FOR VIDEO GAMES: COPYRIGHT: ELIGIBLE LAYOUTS CONTAINING SUBSTANTIAL PARTS OF COMPUTER PROGRAMS, THE COPYRIGHT IN WHICH WAS OWNED BY ONE OR OTHER OF THE APPELLANTS: WHETHER IMPORTATION OF SUCH ELIGIBLE LAYOUTS CONSTITUTED AN INFRINGEMENT OF APPELLANTS' COPYRIGHT IN AUSTRALIA: Australia: Fed. Ct)

Aztech Systems Pte Ltd v. Creative Technology Ltd (COPYRIGHT: SOUND CARDS: DESIGNING COMPATIBLE SOUND CARDS: FAIR DEALING FOR THE PURPOSE OF PRIVATE STUDY: DEROGATION FROM GRANT: IMPLIED LICENCE: Singapore: H.C.)

Barson Computers (N.Z.) Ltd v. John Gilbert & Co. Ltd (COPYRIGHT: COMPUTER PRODUCTS: IMPORTATION: IRRELEVANCE OF HYPOTHETICAL MAKER: New Zealand: H.C.)

Barson Computers Australasia Ltd v. Southern Technology Pty Ltd (COPYRIGHT: OPERATING SYSTEMS IN ROM: SUBSISTENCE: REVERSE ENGINEERING BY DISASSEMBLY: SUBSTANTIAL PART: CONTRIBUTORY USE OF GENUINE COPY FOR TESTING AND DEMONSTRATION: TRADE PRACTICES: MISLEADING OR DECEPTIVE CONDUCT: ADVERTISING OF FUTURE PRODUCT: Australia: Fed. Ct)

Beecham Group PLC v. Southern Transvaal Pharmaceutical Pricing Bureau (Pty) Ltd (TRADE MARK: USE IN COURSE OF TRADE: REFERENCE TO TRADE IN GOODS IN CLASS FOR WHICH MARK REGISTERED: COMPUTER SOFTWARE SYSTEM PROVIDING INFORMATION ON GENERIC ALTERNATIVE MEDICINES AVAILABLE AFTER EXPIRY OF PATENT: South Africa: A.D.)

1137

Broderbund Software Inc. v. Computermate Products (Australia) Pty Ltd (COPYRIGHT: PARALLEL IMPORTATION AND SALE: IMPLIED LICENCE OF IMPORTER: WHETHER DISTRIBUTOR AN EXCLUSIVE LICENSEE: EVIDENCE: MARKET SURVEY: RESTRICTIVE PRACTICES: MARKET POWER: EXCLUSIONARY PROVISIONS: ANTI-COMPETITIVE AGREEMENTS: EXCLUSIVE DEALING: USE OF SURVEY EVIDENCE: Australia: Fed. Ct)

Brooktree Corporation v. Advanced Micro Devices Inc. (CIRCUIT LAYOUTS: MASK WORKS: COPYRIGHT: WHETHER CIRCUIT LAYOUT DICTATED BY FUNCTION: STANDARD OF SIMILARITY REQUIRED: SUBSTANTIALLY COPIED: REVERSE ENGINEERING: United States: D.C.)

CCOM Pty Ltd v. Jiejung Pty Ptd (COPYRIGHT: COMPILATION OF CHINESE CHARACTERS IN DATABASE: CAUSAL LINK BETWEEN MATERIAL AND ALLEGED COPY: PATENT: COMPUTER PROCESS FOR ASSEMBLING CHINESE LANGUAGE CHARACTERS: VALIDITY: WHETHER SALE OF PROGRAM FOR USE IN STANDARD COMPUTER INFRINGES PATENTED APPARATUS CLAIM: CONTRIBUTORY INFRINGEMENT: Australia: Fed. Ct)

Centronics Systems Pty Ltd v. Nintendo Co. Ltd (CIRCUIT LAYOUT: INTEGRATED CIRCUIT: OWNER OF E.L. RIGHTS IN AN ORIGINAL CIRCUIT LAYOUT: WHETHER MADE IN ACCORDANCE WITH ORIGINAL LAYOUT: PURPOSE OF EVALUATION OR ANALYSIS: SHRINKING/SCALING: KNOWLEDGE: Australia: Fed. Ct)

Centronics Systems Pty Ltd v. Nintendo Co. Ltd (CIRCUIT LAYOUT: INTEGRATED CIRCUIT: COMMERCIAL EXPLOITATION: INTERPRETATION OF STATUTE: IMPORTATION: Fed. Ct) (APPEAL: KNOWLEDGE OR CONSTRUCTIVE KNOWLEDGE OF LICENCE OR OF PROPERTY RIGHT: Australia: H.C.)

Dun & Bradstreet Ltd v. Typesetting Facilities Ltd (COPYRIGHT: BREACH OF CONFIDENCE: COMPUTERISED DATABASE: APPLICATION FOR INSPECTION: INFORMATION IN ELECTRONIC FORM, SO VISUAL INSPECTION OF DISKS USELESS: DISCLOSURE OF CONTENTS REQUIRED: PRACTICE: INSPECTION BEFORE SERVICE OF STATEMENT OF CLAIM: REQUIREMENTS: INSPECTION ORDERED: Ch.D.)

Dyason v. Autodesk Inc. (COPYRIGHT: WHETHER ELECTRICAL CIRCUIT CAN BE A COMPUTER PROGRAM: REPRODUCTION: AUTHORISATION: WHETHER SUPPLY OF DEVICE ENABLING COMPUTER PROGRAM TO BE USED ON MORE THAN ONE COMPUTER AT A TIME MAY BE AUTHORISATION OF INFRINGEMENT: Australia: Fed. Ct)

Express Newspapers Ltd v. Liverpool Daily Post (COPYRIGHT: ORIGINALITY: WORK PERFORMED BY COMPUTER: LOTTERIES: Ch.D.)

Format Communications Manufacturing Ltd v. ITT (U.K.) Ltd (BREACH OF CONFIDENCE: COPYRIGHT: PRACTICE: DISCOVERY AND INSPECTION: SAFEGUARDS: C.A.)

Ibcos Computers Ltd v. Barclays Mercantile Highland Finance Ltd (COPYRIGHT: SOFTWARE: SOURCE CODE: SUBSISTENCE AND EXTENT OF PROTECTION: SUBSTANTIAL PART: BREACH OF CONFIDENCE: FILE TRANSFER PROGRAM: *British Leyland* DEFENCE: RESTRICTIVE COVENANT: CONSTRUCTION: Ch.D.)

International Business Machines Corporation v. Computer Imports Ltd (COPYRIGHT: COMPUTER TECHNOLOGY: THREE-DIMENSIONAL REPRODUCTION OF CABINET AND INTERNAL LAYOUT OF PERSONAL COMPUTER AND BY COPYING OF COMPUTER PROGRAM: IMPORTATION AND SALE: SOURCE CODE: WHETHER OBJECT CODE (SILICON CHIP): TRANSFER OF LITERARY WORK: New Zealand: H.C.)

Irvine v. Carson (COPYRIGHT: CRIMINAL OFFENCE: POSSESSION OF INFRINGING COPIES OF COMPUTER PROGRAMS FOR THE PURPOSE OF DISTRIBUTING: CONVICTION: APPROPRIATE PENALTY: ORDER FOR FORFEITURE OF COMPUTERS USED FOR MAKING INFRINGING COPIES: Australia: Fed. Ct)

Irvine v. Hanna-Rivero (COPYRIGHT: INFRINGING COPIES OF COMPUTER PROGRAMS MADE FOR SWAP TRADE: DEFENDANT PLEADED GUILTY: CONSIDERATION OF APPROPRIATE PENALTY: ORDER FOR FORFEITURE OF SOME HARDWARE EQUIPMENT USED IN MAKING INFRINGING COPIES: Australia: Fed. Ct)

John Richardson Computers Ltd v. Flanders (COPYRIGHT: SOFTWARE: MINOR INFRINGEMENTS: FORM OF ORDER AND INJUNCTION: DAMAGES: PLAINTIFF'S RIGHT TO INQUIRY WHERE INFRINGEMENT SLIGHT: DEFENDANT'S RIGHT TO INQUIRY AS TO DAMAGES ON PLAINTIFF'S CROSS-UNDERTAKING: COSTS: APPROPRIATE ORDER WHERE WHOLESALE INFRINGEMENT ALLEGED BUT ONLY MINOR ESTABLISHED: Ch.D.)

John Richardson Computers Ltd v. Flanders (COPYRIGHT: SOFTWARE: TITLE TO PORTIONS OF PROGRAM WRITTEN BY INDEPENDENT CONTRACTORS: WHETHER COPYING: WHETHER SUBSTANTIAL PART REPRODUCED: NO COPYING OF SOURCE CODE: APPROPRIATE TEST: ESTOPPEL: Ch.D.)

John Richardson Computers Ltd v. Flanders (COPYRIGHT: SUBSISTENCE: OWNERSHIP: SUBSTANTIAL PART: COMPUTER PROGRAM: COMPILATION: IDEA AND EXPRESSION: ESTOPPEL: Australia: Fed. Ct)

Lasercomb America Inc. v. Job Reynolds (COPYRIGHT: MISUSE: EQUITABLE DEFENCE: LIMITED MONOPOLY: SOFTWARE LICENSING RESTRICTIONS: NON-COMPETITION PROVISIONS: United States: C.A.)

Leisure Data v. Bell (COPYRIGHT: PRACTICE: MANDATORY INJUNCTION: C.A.)

Lewis Galoob Toys Inc. v. Nintendo of America Inc. (COPYRIGHT: AUDIOVISUAL DISPLAYS: AUTHORISATION: DERIVATIVE WORKS: WHETHER MODIFICATION OF VISUAL DISPLAYS BY A DEVICE NOT AFFECTING THE COMPUTER PROGRAM ITSELF IS AN INFRINGEMENT: FAIR USE: United States: D.C.)

Mackintosh Computers v. Apple Computer Inc. (COPYRIGHT: REPRODUCTION: ADAPTATION: CONTRIVANCE: MACHINE PARTS: Canada: Fed. Ct: C.A.)

Missing Link Software v. Magee (COPYRIGHT: WORK MADE IN COURSE OF EMPLOYMENT: TO WHOM DOES WORK OF MOONLIGHTING EMPLOYEE BELONG: Ch.D.)

M.S. Associates Ltd v. Power (COPYRIGHT: INTERLOCUTORY INJUNCTION: TRANSLATOR PROGRAMS: SIMILARITIES: ARGUABLE CASE: BALANCE OF CONVENIENCE: Ch.D.)

NEC Corporation v. Intel Corporation (COPYRIGHT: MICROCODE IN MICROPROCESSOR CHIPS: SUBSISTENCE: MINIMAL VERBAL STRUCTURES: WORKS DICTATED BY FUNCTION: FORFEITURE OF COPYRIGHT: NON-USE OF COPYRIGHT NOTICE: SCOPE OF LICENCE: WHETHER MODIFICATION OF EARLIER COPY AVOIDS: United States: D.C.)

Novell, Inc. v. Ong Seow Pheng (COPYRIGHT: SCOPE OF PROTECTION: COMPUTER SOFTWARE AND MANUALS: FIRST PUBLICATION IN USA: ADDITIONAL DAMAGES: TRADE MARK: INFRINGEMENT: INJUNCTION: Singapore: H.C.)

Ozi-Soft Pty Ltd v. Wong (COPYRIGHT: CONTRIBUTORY INFRINGEMENT: IMPORTATION OF DISKETTES PURCHASES FROM COPYRIGHT OWNERS: IMPLIED LICENCE: DOCTRINE OF NATIONAL TREATMENT: Australia: Fed. Ct)

R. v. Chan Hing-Kin (COPYRIGHT: CASINGS FOR PERSONAL COMPUTERS: POSSESSION: FUNCTIONAL WORKS: ARTISTIC MERIT: IMPLIED LICENCE: LAY RECOGNITION TEST: Hong Kong: North Kowloon Magistrates' Court)

Star Micronics Pty Ltd v. Five Star Computers Pty Ltd (COPYRIGHT: WHETHER ROM IN COMPUTER PRINTER A COMPUTER PROGRAM: ORIGINALITY: SECONDARY SALE OF IMPORTED PRINTERS INCLUDING COMPUTER PROGRAM IN ROM: PASSING OFF: SUPPLY OF FOREIGN SUPPLIED PRINTERS AS ASSOCIATED WITH AUSTRALIAN SUPPLIER: SUPPLY OF 220v COMPUTER PRINTERS AS INTENDED BY MANUFACTURER FOR DISTRIBUTION IN AUSTRALIA: Australia: Fed. Ct)

Star Micronics Pty Ltd v. Five Star Computers Pty Ltd (DAMAGES: BREACH OF COPYRIGHT, PASSING OFF AND MISLEADING OR DECEPTIVE CONDUCT: MEANING OF FRAUD IN CONTEXT OF PASSING OFF: WHETHER ESTABLISHED: LACK OF CLEAR EVIDENCE OF ACTUAL DAMAGE: DAMAGES FOR LOSS OF REPUTATION: DAMAGES FOR DIMINUTION IN VALUE OF COPYRIGHT: Australia: Fed. Ct)

Thrustcode Ltd v. WW Computing Ltd (COPYRIGHT: INTERLOCUTORY INJUNCTION: WHETHER COPYRIGHT CAN SUBSIST IN A COMPUTER PROGRAM: DIFFICULTY IN ESTABLISHING EVIDENCE OF COPYING: BALANCE OF CONVENIENCE: Ch.D.)

VDU Installations Ltd v. Integrated Computer Systems and Cybernetics Ltd (COPYRIGHT: ANTON PILLER ORDER: IMPROPER EXECUTION: NEGLIGENT IMPROPRIETY: CONTEMPT: Ch.D.)

Waterlow Directories Ltd v. Reed Information Services Ltd (COPYRIGHT: INTERLOCUTORY INJUNCTION: LEGAL DIRECTORIES: COPYING OF NAMES AND ADDRESSES FOR COMPUTER MAIL-SHOT TO COMPILE OWN DIRECTORY: WHETHER REPRODUCTION: WHETHER SUBSTANTIAL: EURO-DEFENCES: NON-DEROGATION FROM GRANT: QUANTIFIABILITY OF DAMAGE: ADEQUACY OF UNDERTAKINGS: BALANCE OF CONVENIENCE: Ch.D.)

Wheelan Associates Inc. v. Jaslow Dental Laboratories Inc. (COPYRIGHT: COPYING OF STRUCTURE: SUBSTANTIAL PART: United States: C.A.)

Willemijn Houdstermaatschappij BV v. Madge networks Ltd (PATENT: COMPUTERS: CONSTRUCTION: ESSENTIAL INTEGER: INESSENTIAL VARIANT: C.A.)

Xerox Corpn v. Apple Computer Inc. (LOOK AND FEEL OF USER INTERFACE: REMEDIES FOR WHETHER ORDER STRIKING OUT COPYRIGHT REGISTRATION AVAILABLE: WHETHER REMEDY OF CONSTRUCTIVE TRUST AVAILABLE: United States: S.C.)

Inspection

Atari Inc. v. Philips Electronics Ltd (COPYRIGHT: INFRINGEMENT: COMPUTER PROGRAM: PRACTICE: Ch.D.)

Derby & Co. Ltd v. Weldon (No. 9) (COMPUTER DATABASE: PRACTICE: DISCOVERY: WHETHER DOCUMENT: EXTENT TO WHICH INSPECTION TO BE ORDERED: Ch.D.)

Dun & Bradstreet Ltd v. Typesetting Facilities Ltd (COPYRIGHT INFRINGEMENT: BREACH OF CONFIDENCE: COMPUTERISED DATABASE: INFORMATION IN ELECTRONIC FORM, SO VISUAL INSPECTION OF DISKS USELESS: DISCLOSURE OF CONTENTS REQUIRED: PRACTICE: INSPECTION BEFORE SERVICE OF STATEMENT OF CLAIM: REQUIREMENTS: INSPECTION ORDERED: Ch.D.)

Format Communications Manufacturing Ltd v. ITT (U.K.) Ltd (BREACH OF CONFIDENCE: COPYRIGHT: INFRINGEMENT: PRACTICE: DISCOVERY AND INSPECTION: SAFEGUARDS: C.A.)

Integrated Circuit. *See* **Circuits**

Interfaces

Lotus Development Corporation v. Paperback Software International (COPYRIGHT: USER INTERFACE: COPYRIGHTABILITY OF NON-LITERAL ELEMENTS: IDEA/EXPRESSION: LOOK AND FEEL: COPYRIGHT ACT 1976 (U.S.): United States: D.C.)

Total Information Processing Systems Ltd v. Daman Ltd (COPYRIGHT: SOFTWARE: COPYRIGHT IN SOFTWARE INTERFACE: MERGER OF IDEA WITH EXPRESSION: WHETHER PRINCIPLE OF DEROGATION FROM GRANT CONFINED TO COMPANIES WITH DOMINANT POSITION: EVIDENCE FOR INTERLOCUTORY APPLICATION: Ch.D.)

Xerox Corpn v. Apple Computer Inc. (LOOK AND FEEL OF USER INTERFACE: REMEDIES FOR INFRINGEMENT: WHETHER ORDER STRIKING OUT COPYRIGHT REGISTRATION AVAILABLE: WHETHER REMEDY OF CONSTRUCTIVE TRUST AVAILABLE: United States: S.C.)

Joint Ownership. *See* Ownership

Look and Feel

Apple Computer Inc. v. Microsoft Corp. (COPYRIGHT: VISUAL DISPLAYS OF PROGRAM: SUBSISTENCE OF COPYRIGHT IN VISUAL DISPLAYS: MERGER OF IDEA AND EXPRESSION: INDISPENSABLE EXPRESSION: *Scenes a faire*: MERE FUNCTIONALITY: United States: D.C.)

Apple Computer, Inc. v. Microsoft Corp. (COPYRIGHT: SUBSISTENCE VISUAL DISPLAYS: LICENCE: SCOPE: INTERPRETATION: United States: D.C.)

Lotus Development Corporation v. Paperback Software International (COPYRIGHT: USER INTERFACE: COPYRIGHTABILITY OF NON-LITERAL ELEMENTS: IDEA/EXPRESSION: COPYRIGHT ACT 1976 (U.S.): United States: D.C.)

Xerox Corpn v. Apple Computer Inc. (USER INTERFACE: REMEDIES FOR INFRINGEMENT: WHETHER ORDER STRIKING OUT COPYRIGHT REGISTRATION AVAILABLE: WHETHER REMEDY OF CONSTRUCTIVE TRUST AVAILABLE: United States: S.C.)

Manuals

Novell, Inc. v. Ong Seow Pheng (COPYRIGHT: SCOPE OF PROTECTION: COMPUTER SOFTWARE AND MANUALS: FIRST PUBLICATION IN UNITED STATES: ADDITIONAL DAMAGES: TRADE MARK: INFRINGEMENT: INJUNCTION: Singapore: H.C.)

Micro Computer Programs

Apple Computer Inc. v. Computer Edge Pty Ltd (COPYRIGHT: INFRINGEMENT: WHETHER SOURCE CODE ADAPTATION OF SOURCE CODE: Australia: Fed. Ct)

Microcode

NEC Corporation v. Intel Corporation (COPYRIGHT: MICROCODE IN MICROPROCESSOR CHIPS: SUBSISTENCE: MINIMAL VERBAL STRUCTURES: WORKS DICTATED BY FUNCTION: FORFEITURE OF COPYRIGHT: NON-USE OF COPYRIGHT NOTICE: SCOPE OF LICENCE: INFRINGEMENT: WHETHER MODIFICATION OF EARLIER COPY AVOIDS INFRINGEMENT: United States: D.C.)

Object Code. *See also* **Source Code**

International Business Machines Corporation v. Computer Imports Ltd (COPYRIGHT: INFRINGEMENT: COMPUTER TECHNOLOGY: THREE-DIMENSIONAL REPRODUCTION OF CABINET AND INTERNAL LAYOUT OF PERSONAL COMPUTER AND BY COPYING OF COMPUTER PROGRAM: IMPORTATION AND SALE: WHETHER OBJECT CODE (SILICON CHIP): TRANSFER OF LITERARY WORK: New Zealand: H.C.)

Open Industry Standard

X/Open Group (RESTRICTIVE PRACTICES: COMPUTER OPERATING SYSTEM: "UNIX": AGREEMENT TO STANDARDISE: INTENTION TO APPROVE: NOTICE: E.C. Comm.)

Operating System

Barson Computers Australasia Ltd v. Southern Technology Pty Ltd (COPYRIGHT: OPERATING SYSTEMS IN ROM: SUBSISTENCE: INFRINGEMENT: REVERSE ENGINEERING BY DISASSEMBLY: SUBSTANTIAL PART: CONTRIBUTORY INFRINGEMENT: USE OF GENUINE COPY FOR TESTING AND DEMONSTRATION: TRADE PRACTICES: MISLEADING OR DECEPTIVE CONDUCT: ADVERTISING OF FUTURE PRODUCT: Australia: Fed. Ct)

X/Open Group (RESTRICTIVE PRACTICES: UNIX: AGREEMENT TO STANDARDISE: OPEN INDUSTRY STANDARD: INTENTION TO APPROVE: NOTICE: E.C. Comm.)

Originality

Autodesk Inc. v. Dyason (COPYRIGHT: INFRINGEMENT: COMPUTER PROGRAM: SUBSTANTIAL PART: APPELLANT'S DEVICE TO PREVENT ITS COMPUTER PROGRAMS BEING RUN ON A COMPUTER WITHOUT DEVICE: Australia: H.C.)

Autodesk Inc. v. Dyason (No. 2) (COPYRIGHT: INFRINGEMENT: COMPUTER PROGRAM: SUBSTANTIAL PART: APPELLANT'S DEVICE TO PREVENT ITS COMPUTER PROGRAMS BEING RUN ON A COMPUTER WITHOUT DEVICE: Australia: H.C.)

Express Newspapers Ltd v. Liverpool Daily Post (COPYRIGHT: INFRINGEMENT: WORK PERFORMED BY COMPUTER: LOTTERIES: Ch.D.)

Star Micronics Pty Ltd v. Five Star Computers Pty Ltd (COPYRIGHT: WHETHER ROM IN COMPUTER PRINTER A COMPUTER PROGRAM: SECONDARY INFRINGEMENT: SALE OF IMPORTED PRINTERS INCLUDING COMPUTER PROGRAM IN ROM: PASSING OFF: SUPPLY OF FOREIGN SUPPLIED PRINTERS AS ASSOCIATED WITH AUSTRALIAN SUPPLIER: SUPPLY OF 220V COMPUTER PRINTERS AS INTENDED BY MANUFACTURER FOR DISTRIBUTION IN AUSTRALIA: Australia: Fed. Ct)

Ownership

Acorn Computer Ltd v. MCS Microcomputer System Pty Ltd (COPYRIGHT: ASSIGNMENT: REQUIREMENT OF WRITING: EQUITABLE OWNERSHIP: JOINT OWNERSHIP: Australia: Fed. Ct)

Autodesk Australia Pty Ltd v. Cheung (COPYRIGHT: INFRINGEMENT: SALE OF UNAUTHORISED REPRODUCTIONS: DAMAGES: MEASURE OF COMPENSATORY DAMAGES: ADDITIONAL DAMAGES: CLAIM BY COPYRIGHT OWNER AND AUSTRALIAN DISTRIBUTOR: Australia: Fed. Ct)

Avel Pty Ltd v. Wells (CIRCUIT LAYOUTS: PARALLEL IMPORTATION OF ELIGIBLE LAYOUTS FOR VIDEO GAMES: COPYRIGHT: ELIGIBLE LAYOUTS CONTAINING SUBSTANTIAL PARTS OF COMPUTER PROGRAMS, THE COPYRIGHT IN WHICH WAS OWNED BY ONE OR OTHER OF THE APPELLANTS: WHETHER IMPORTATION OF SUCH ELIGIBLE LAYOUTS CONSTITUTED AN INFRINGEMENT OF APPELLANT'S COPYRIGHT IN AUSTRALIA: Australia: Fed. Ct)

Avtex Airservices Pty Ltd v. Bartsch (COPYRIGHT: COMPUTERISED TEACHING SYSTEM OF WORKBOOKS, SLIDES: Australia: Fed. Ct)

Centronics Systems Pty Ltd v. Nintendo Co. Ltd (CIRCUIT LAYOUT: INTEGRATED CIRCUIT: OWNER OF E.L. RIGHTS IN AN ORIGINAL CIRCUIT LAYOUT: INFRINGEMENT: WHETHER MADE IN ACCORDANCE WITH ORIGINAL LAYOUT: PURPOSE OF EVALUATION OR ANALYSIS: SHRINKING/SCALING: KNOWLEDGE: Australia: Fed. Ct)

Cope Allman (Marrickville) Ltd v. Farrow (COPYRIGHT: COMMISSIONED WORK: ENGRAVINGS: CONFIDENTIAL INFORMATION: Australia: S.C.(NSW))

John Richardson Computers Ltd v. Flanders (COPYRIGHT: SUBSISTENCE: INFRINGEMENT: SUBSTANTIAL PART: COMPUTER PROGRAM: COMPILATION: IDEA AND EXPRESSION: ESTOPPEL: Ch.D.)

Ozi-Soft Pty Ltd v. Wong (COPYRIGHT: CONTRIBUTORY INFRINGEMENT: IMPORTATION OF DISKETTES PURCHASES FROM COPYRIGHT OWNERS: IMPLIED LICENCE: DOCTRINE OF NATIONAL TREATMENT: Australia: Fed. Ct)

Passing Off

Australian Computer Evaluation Consultants Pty Ltd v. Datbury Pty Ltd (COPYRIGHT: INFRINGEMENT: COMPUTER PROGRAM: Australia: Fed. Ct)

Patents and Patentability

Beecham Group PLC v. Southern Transvaal Pharmaceutical Pricing Bureau (Pty) Ltd (TRADE MARK: INFRINGEMENT: USE IN COURSE OF TRADE: REFERENCE TO TRADE IN GOODS IN CLASS FOR WHICH MARK REGISTERED: COMPUTER SOFTWARE SYSTEM PROVIDING INFORMATION ON GENERIC ALTERNATIVE MEDICINES AVAILABLE AFTER EXPIRY OF PATENT: South Africa: A.D.)

CCOM Pty Ltd v. Jiejung Pty Ptd (COPYRIGHT: COMPILATION OF CHINESE CHARACTERS IN DATABASE: INFRINGEMENT: CAUSAL LINK BETWEEN MATERIAL AND ALLEGED COPY: PATENT: COMPUTER PROCESS FOR ASSEMBLING CHINESE LANGUAGE CHARACTERS: VALIDITY: INFRINGEMENT: WHETHER SALE OF PROGRAM FOR USE IN STANDARD COMPUTER INFRINGES PATENTED APPARATUS CLAIM: CONTRIBUTORY INFRINGEMENT: Australia: Fed. Ct)

Computer Generation of Chinese Characters (APPLICATION: COMPUTER PROGRAM: CHINESE CHARACTERS: WHETHER PATENTABLE: WHETHER APPLICATION OF TECHNICAL NATURE: APPLICATION REFUSED: Germany: S.C.)

Gale's Application (APPLICATION: COMPUTER RELATED INVENTIONS: DEDICATED ROM: WHETHER EXCLUDED FROM PATENTABILITY: Pat Off: Pat. Ct: C.A.)

Hitachi Ltd's Application (COMPUTER-RELATED INVENTION: WHETHER PATENTABLE: Pat. Off.)

Honeywell Bull Inc.'s Application (COMPUTER PROGRAM: MATHEMATICAL ALGORITHM: MANNER OF MANUFACTURE: Pat. Off.)

IBM (Barclay & Bigar)'s Application (SECOND GRANT: PRACTICE: C.–G.)

Thomas and Stohr's Application (PETTY PATENT: OPPOSITION TO EXTENSION OF TERM: COMPUTER INVENTION: OBVIOUSNESS: IDEA: ANTICIPATION: Pat. Off.)

Wang Laboratories Inc.'s Application (PATENTABILITY: COMPUTER-RELATED INVENTION: TECHNICAL CONTRIBUTION: Pat. Ct)

Willemijn Houdstermaatschappij BV v. Madge networks Ltd (INFRINGEMENT: COMPUTERS: CONSTRUCTION: ESSENTIAL INTEGER: INESSENTIAL VARIANT: C.A.)

Printed Circuits. *See* **Circuits**

Programs

115778 Canada Inc. v. Apple Computer Inc. (COPYRIGHT: SUBJECT-MATTER: PROGRAM STORED IN ELECTRONIC FORM ON CHIP: REPRODUCTION: MERGER OF IDEA AND EXPRESSION: TRANSLATION: Canada: S.C.)

Accounting Systems 2000 (Developments) Pty Ltd v. CCH Australia Ltd (COPYRIGHT: INFRINGEMENT: REPRODUCTION OR ADAPTATION: REPRODUCTION OF SUBSTANTIAL PART: EFFECT OF EXPENDITURE OF TIME AND EFFORT IN DEVELOPING COMPUTER PROGRAM: Australia: Fed. Ct)

Accounting Systems 2000 (Developments) Pty Ltd v. CCH Australia Ltd (COPYRIGHT: REPRODUCTION OF SUBSTANTIAL PART: Australia: Fed. Ct)

Apple Computer Inc. v. Computer Edge Pty Ltd (COPYRIGHT: INFRINGEMENT: MICRO WHETHER SOURCE CODE ADAPTATION OF SOURCE CODE: Australia: Fed. Ct)

Apple Computer Inc. v. Microsoft Corp. (COPYRIGHT: LOOK AND FEEL OF VISUAL DISPLAYS OF PROGRAM: SUBSISTENCE OF COPYRIGHT IN VISUAL DISPLAYS: MERGER OF IDEA AND EXPRESSION: INDISPENSABLE EXPRESSION: *Scenes a faire:* MERE FUNCTIONALITY: United States: D.C.)

Apple Computer Inc. v. Rowney (COPYRIGHT: PRACTICE: ANTON PILLER PROCEEDINGS: FORM OF ORDER: Australia: S.C.(NSW))

Apple Computer Inc. v. Segimex Sárl (COPYRIGHT: France)

Apple Computer Inc. v. Microsoft Corp. (COPYRIGHT: LOOK AND FEEL: SUBSISTENCE OF COPYRIGHT IN VISUAL DISPLAYS: LICENCE: SCOPE: INTERPRETATION: United States: D.C.)

Atari Games Corp. v. Nintendo of America Inc. (COPYRIGHT: CIRCUIT IN SILICON CHIP: SUBSISTENCE OF COPYRIGHT: SCOPE OF PROTECTION: MERGER OF IDEA AND EXPRESSION: INFRINGEMENT IN REVERSE ENGINEERING: United States: D.C.)

Atari Inc. v. Philips Electronics Ltd (COPYRIGHT: INFRINGEMENT: INSPECTION: PRACTICE: Ch.D.)

Autodesk Australia Pty Ltd v. Cheung (COPYRIGHT: INFRINGEMENT: SALE OF UNAUTHORISED REPRODUCTIONS: DAMAGES: MEASURE OF COMPENSATORY DAMAGES: ADDITIONAL DAMAGES: CLAIM BY COPYRIGHT OWNER AND AUSTRALIAN DISTRIBUTOR: Australia: Fed. Ct)

Autodesk Inc. v. Dyason (COPYRIGHT: INFRINGEMENT: ORIGINALITY: SUBSTANTIAL PART: APPELLANT'S DEVICE TO PREVENT ITS COMPUTER PROGRAMS BEING RUN ON A COMPUTER WITHOUT DEVICE: Australia: H.C.)

Autodesk Inc. v. Dyason (COPYRIGHT: WHETHER ELECTRICAL CIRCUIT IS A COMPUTER PROGRAM: WHETHER SET OF INSTRUCTIONS AND DATA-PROCESSING DEVICE NEED BE SEPARATE: INFRINGEMENT: REPRODUCTION: AUTHORISATION: DEVICE ENABLING BREACH OF SHRINK-WRAP LICENCE: Australia: Fed. Ct)

Autodesk Inc. v. Dyason (No. 2) (COPYRIGHT: INFRINGEMENT: ORIGINALITY: SUBSTANTIAL PART: APPELLANT'S DEVICE TO PREVENT ITS COMPUTER PROGRAMS BEING RUN ON A COMPUTER WITHOUT DEVICE: Australia: H.C.)

Avel Pty Ltd v. Wells (CIRCUIT LAYOUTS: INTEGRATED CIRCUIT: DEFENCE TO PARALLEL IMPORTATION OF COPYRIGHT MATERIAL: COPYRIGHT: INFRINGEMENT: PARALLEL IMPORTATION AND SALE: STATUTORY DEFENCE: Australia: Fed. Ct)

Avel Pty Ltd v. Wells (CIRCUIT LAYOUTS: PARALLEL IMPORTATION OF ELIGIBLE LAYOUTS FOR VIDEO GAMES: COPYRIGHT: ELIGIBLE LAYOUTS CONTAINING SUBSTANTIAL PARTS OF COMPUTER PROGRAMS, THE COPYRIGHT IN WHICH WAS OWNED BY ONE OR OTHER OF THE APPELLANTS: WHETHER IMPORTATION OF SUCH ELIGIBLE LAYOUTS CONSTITUTED AN INFRINGEMENT OF APPELLANTS COPYRIGHT IN AUSTRALIA: Australia: Fed. Ct)

Avtex Airservices Pty Ltd v. Bartsch (COPYRIGHT: OWNERSHIP: COMPUTERISED TEACHING SYSTEM OF WORKBOOKS, SLIDES: Australia: Fed. Ct)

Barson Computers Australasia Ltd v. Southern Technology Pty Ltd (COPYRIGHT: OPERATING SYSTEMS IN ROM: SUBSISTENCE: INFRINGEMENT: REVERSE ENGINEERING BY DISASSEMBLY: SUBSTANTIAL PART: CONTRIBUTORY INFRINGEMENT: USE OF GENUINE COPY FOR TESTING AND DEMONSTRATION: TRADE PRACTICES: MISLEADING OR DECEPTIVE CONDUCT: ADVERTISING OF FUTURE PRODUCT: Australia: Fed. Ct)

Broderbund Software Inc. v. Computermate Products (Australia) Pty Ltd (COPYRIGHT: INFRINGEMENT: PARALLEL IMPORTATION AND SALE: IMPLIED LICENCE OF IMPORTER: WHETHER DISTRIBUTOR AN EXCLUSIVE LICENSEE: EVIDENCE: MARKET SURVEY: RESTRICTIVE PRACTICES: MARKET POWER: EXCLUSIONARY PROVISIONS: ANTI-COMPETITIVE AGREEMENTS: EXCLUSIVE DEALING: USE OF SURVEY EVIDENCE: Australia: Fed. Ct)

CCOM Pty Ltd v. Jiejung Pty Ptd (COPYRIGHT: COMPILATION OF CHINESE CHARACTERS IN DATABASE: INFRINGEMENT: CAUSAL LINK BETWEEN MATERIAL AND ALLEGED COPY: PATENT: COMPUTER PROCESS FOR ASSEMBLING CHINESE LANGUAGE CHARACTERS: VALIDITY: INFRINGEMENT: WHETHER SALE OF PROGRAM FOR USE IN STANDARD COMPUTER INFRINGES PATENTED APPARATUS CLAIM: CONTRIBUTORY INFRINGEMENT: Australia: Fed. Ct)

Computer Generation of Chinese Characters (PATENT: APPLICATION: CHINESE CHARACTERS: WHETHER PATENTABLE: WHETHER APPLICATION OF TECHNICAL NATURE: APPLICATION REFUSED: Germany: S.C.)

Cope Allman (Marrickville) Ltd v. Farrow (COPYRIGHT: OWNERSHIP: COMMISSIONED WORK: ENGRAVINGS: CONFIDENTIAL INFORMATION: S.C.(NSW))

Dyason (Martin Peter) v. Autodesk Inc. (COPYRIGHT: WHETHER ELECTRICAL CIRCUIT CAN BE A COMPUTER PROGRAM: INFRINGEMENT: REPRODUCTION: AUTHORISATION: WHETHER SUPPLY OF DEVICE ENABLING COMPUTER PROGRAM TO BE USED ON MORE THAN ONE COMPUTER AT A TIME MAY BE AUTHORISATION OF INFRINGEMENT: Australia: Fed. Ct)

Federal Computer Services Sdn Bhd v. Ang Jee Hai Eric (COPYRIGHT: SCOPE OF PROTECTION: INTERPRETATION OF STATUTE: Singapore: H.C.)

Format Communications Manufacturing Ltd v. ITT (U.K.) Ltd (BREACH OF CONFIDENCE: COPYRIGHT: INFRINGEMENT: PRACTICE: DISCOVERY AND INSPECTION: SAFEGUARDS: C.A.)

Honeywell Bull Inc.'s Application (PATENT: APPLICATION: MATHEMATICAL ALGORITHM: MANNER OF MANUFACTURE: Pat. Off.)

Ibcos Computers Ltd v. Barclays Mercantile Highland Finance Ltd (COPYRIGHT: SOFTWARE: SOURCE CODE: SUBSISTENCE AND EXTENT OF PROTECTION: INFRINGEMENT: SUBSTANTIAL PART: BREACH OF CONFIDENCE: FILE TRANSFER PROGRAM: *British Leyland* DEFENCE: RESTRICTIVE COVENANT: CONSTRUCTION: Ch.D.)

International Business Machines Corporation v. Computer Imports Ltd (COPYRIGHT: INFRINGEMENT: COMPUTER TECHNOLOGY: THREE-DIMENSIONAL REPRODUCTION OF CABINET AND INTERNAL LAYOUT OF PERSONAL COMPUTER AND BY COPYING OF COMPUTER PROGRAM: IMPORTATION AND SALE: SOURCE CODE: WHETHER OBJECT CODE (SILICON CHIP): TRANSFER OF LITERARY WORK: New Zealand: H.C.)

Irvine v. Carson (COPYRIGHT: CRIMINAL OFFENCE: POSSESSION OF INFRINGING COPIES OF PROGRAMS FOR THE PURPOSE OF DISTRIBUTING: CONVICTION: APPROPRIATE PENALTY: ORDER FOR FORFEITURE OF COMPUTERS USED FOR MAKING INFRINGING COPIES: Australia: Fed. Ct)

Irvine v. Hanna-Rivero (COPYRIGHT: INFRINGING COPIES OF PROGRAMS MADE FOR SWAP TRADE: GUILTY PLEA: CONSIDERATION OF APPROPRIATE PENALTY: ORDER FOR FORFEITURE OF SOME HARDWARE EQUIPMENT USED IN MAKING INFRINGING COPIES: Australia: Fed. Ct)

John Richardson Computers Ltd v. Flanders (COPYRIGHT: INFRINGEMENT: SOFTWARE: TITLE TO PORTIONS OF PROGRAM WRITTEN BY INDEPENDENT CONTRACTORS: WHETHER COPYING: WHETHER SUBSTANTIAL PART REPRODUCED: NO COPYING OF SOURCE CODE: APPROPRIATE TEST: ESTOPPEL: Ch.D.)

John Richardson Computers Ltd v. Flanders (COPYRIGHT: SUBSISTENCE: OWNERSHIP: INFRINGEMENT: SUBSTANTIAL PART: COMPILATION: IDEA AND EXPRESSION: ESTOPPEL: Ch.D.)

Legal Protection of Computer Programs Regulations 1993 (PROTECTION OF COMPUTER PROGRAMS AS LITERARY WORKS: ENACTMENT OF E.C. COUNCIL DIRECTIVE 91/250: ORIGINALITY: NON-PROTECTION OF UNDERLYING IDEAS AND PRINCIPLES: ENUMERATION OF RIGHTHOLDER'S EXCLUSIVE RIGHTS: RESTRICTIONS ON USE OF INFORMATION: ACTIONABLE INFRINGEMENTS: Ireland: Minister for Enterprise and Employment)

Leisure Data v. Bell (COPYRIGHT: INFRINGEMENT: PRACTICE: MANDATORY INJUNCTION: C.A.)

Lewis Galoob Toys Inc. v. Nintendo of America Inc. (COPYRIGHT: AUDIOVISUAL DISPLAYS OF INFRINGEMENT: AUTHORISATION: DERIVATIVE WORKS: WHETHER MODIFICATION OF VISUAL DISPLAYS BY A DEVICE NOT AFFECTING THE COMPUTER PROGRAM ITSELF IS AN INFRINGEMENT: FAIR USE: United States: D.C.)

Lotus Development Corporation Paperback Software International (COPYRIGHT: USER INTERFACE: COPYRIGHTABILITY OF NON-LITERAL ELEMENTS: IDEA/EXPRESSION: LOOK AND FEEL: COPYRIGHT ACT 1976 (U.S.): United States: D.C.)

Lotus Development Corporation v. Paperback Software International (COPYRIGHT: USER INTERFACE: COPYRIGHTABILITY OF NON-LITERAL ELEMENTS: IDEA/EXPRESSION: LOOK AND FEEL: United States: D.C.)

Mackintosh Computers Ltd v. Apple Computer Inc. (COPYRIGHT: SUBJECT-MATTER: COMPUTER PROGRAM: PROGRAM STORED IN ELECTRONIC FORM ON CHIP: REPRODUCTION: MERGER OF IDEA AND EXPRESSION: TRANSLATION: Canada: S.C.)

Mackintosh Computers v. Apple Computer Inc. (COPYRIGHT: INFRINGEMENT: REPRODUCTION: ADAPTATION: CONTRIVANCE: MACHINE PARTS: Canada: Fed. Ct: C.A.)

Milltronics Ltd v. Hycontrol Ltd (COPYRIGHT: CANADIAN AUTHOR: QUALIFYING PERSON: C.A.)

M.S. Associates Ltd v. Power (COPYRIGHT: INFRINGEMENT: INTERLOCUTORY INJUNCTION: TRANSLATOR PROGRAMS: SIMILARITIES: ARGUABLE CASE: BALANCE OF CONVENIENCE: Ch.D.)

NEC Corporation v. Intel Corporation (COPYRIGHT: MICROCODE IN MICROPROCESSOR CHIPS: SUBSISTENCE: MINIMAL VERBAL STRUCTURES: WORKS DICTATED BY FUNCTION: FORFEITURE OF COPYRIGHT: NON-USE OF COPYRIGHT NOTICE: SCOPE OF LICENCE: INFRINGEMENT: WHETHER MODIFICATION OF EARLIER COPY AVOIDS INFRINGEMENT: United States: D.C.)

Novell, Inc. v. Ong Seow Pheng (COPYRIGHT: SCOPE OF PROTECTION: FIRST PUBLICATION IN UNITED STATES: ADDITIONAL DAMAGES: TRADE MARK: INFRINGEMENT: INJUNCTION: Singapore: H.C.)

Ozi-Soft Pty Ltd v. Wong (COPYRIGHT: CONTRIBUTORY INFRINGEMENT: IMPORTATION OF DISKETTES PURCHASES FROM COPYRIGHT OWNERS: IMPLIED LICENCE: DOCTRINE OF NATIONAL TREATMENT: Australia: Fed. Ct)

Payen Components S.A. Ltd v. Bovic Gaskets C.C. (COPYRIGHT: SUBSISTENCE: LITERARY WORK: COMPUTERISED CATALOGUING SYSTEM: WORK PRODUCED BY PROGRAM: ASSIGNMENT OF COPYRIGHT TO OVERSEAS PARENT COMPANY: EXCLUSIVE LICENSEE: UNLAWFUL COMPETITION: South Africa: WLD)

R. v. Chan Hing-Kin (COPYRIGHT: CASINGS FOR PERSONAL COMPUTERS: INFRINGEMENT: POSSESSION: FUNCTIONAL WORKS: ARTISTIC MERIT: IMPLIED LICENCE: LAY RECOGNITION TEST: Hong Kong: North Kowloon Magistrates' Court)

Sega Enterprises Ltd v. Richards (COPYRIGHT: COMPUTER PROGRAM: INTERLOCUTORY RELIEF: Ch.D.)

Star Micronics Pty Ltd v. Five Star Computers Pty Ltd (COPYRIGHT: WHETHER ROM IN COMPUTER PRINTER A PROGRAM: ORIGINALITY: SECONDARY INFRINGEMENT: SALE OF IMPORTED PRINTERS INCLUDING PROGRAM IN ROM: PASSING OFF: SUPPLY OF FOREIGN SUPPLIED PRINTERS AS ASSOCIATED WITH AUSTRALIAN SUPPLIER: SUPPLY OF 220v PRINTERS AS INTENDED BY MANUFACTURER FOR DISTRIBUTION IN AUSTRALIA: Australia: Fed. Ct)

Thrustcode Ltd v. WW Computing Ltd (COPYRIGHT: INFRINGEMENT: INTERLOCUTORY INJUNCTION: WHETHER COPYRIGHT CAN SUBSIST IN A PROGRAM: DIFFICULTY IN ESTABLISHING INFRINGEMENT: EVIDENCE OF COPYING: BALANCE OF CONVENIENCE: Ch.D.)

Unicomp Srl v. Italcomputers Srl (COPYRIGHT: CREATIVE WORK: Italy: Magistrates Ct: Pisa)

Wheelan Associates Inc. v. Jaslow Dental Laboratories Inc. (COPYRIGHT: INFRINGEMENT: COPYING OF STRUCTURE: SUBSTANTIAL PART: United States: C.A.)

Xerox Corpn v. Apple Computer Inc. (LOOK AND FEEL OF USER INTERFACE: REMEDIES FOR INFRINGEMENT: WHETHER ORDER STRIKING OUT COPYRIGHT REGISTRATION AVAILABLE: WHETHER REMEDY OF CONSTRUCTIVE TRUST AVAILABLE: United States: S.C.)

Reverse Engineering

Atari Games Corp. v. Nintendo of America Inc. (COPYRIGHT: CIRCUIT IN SILICON CHIP: SUBSISTENCE OF COPYRIGHT: SCOPE OF PROTECTION: MERGER OF IDEA AND EXPRESSION: INFRINGEMENT IN REVERSE ENGINEERING: United States: D.C.)

Barson Computers Australasia Ltd v. Southern Technology Pty Ltd (COPYRIGHT: OPERATING SYSTEMS IN ROM: SUBSISTENCE: INFRINGEMENT: REVERSE ENGINEERING BY DISASSEMBLY: SUBSTANTIAL PART: CONTRIBUTORY INFRINGEMENT: USE OF GENUINE COPY FOR TESTING AND DEMONSTRATION: TRADE PRACTICES: MISLEADING OR DECEPTIVE CONDUCT: ADVERTISING OF FUTURE PRODUCT: Australia: Fed. Ct)

Brooktree Corporation v. Advanced Micro Devices Inc. (CIRCUIT LAYOUTS: MASK WORKS: COPYRIGHT: WHETHER CIRCUIT LAYOUT DICTATED BY FUNCTION: INFRINGEMENT: STANDARD OF SIMILARITY REQUIRED: SUBSTANTIALLY COPIED: United States: D.C.)

ROM

Barson Computers Australasia Ltd v. Southern Technology Pty Ltd (COPYRIGHT: OPERATING SYSTEMS IN ROM: SUBSISTENCE: INFRINGEMENT: REVERSE ENGINEERING BY DISASSEMBLY: SUBSTANTIAL PART: CONTRIBUTORY INFRINGEMENT: USE OF GENUINE COPY FOR TESTING AND DEMONSTRATION: TRADE PRACTICES: MISLEADING OR DECEPTIVE CONDUCT: ADVERTISING OF FUTURE PRODUCT: Australia: Fed. Ct)

Gale's Application (PATENT APPLICATION: COMPUTER-RELATED INVENTIONS: DEDICATED ROM: WHETHER EXCLUDED FROM PATENTABILITY: APPLICATION REFUSED: Pat Off: Pat. Ct: C.A.)

Star Micronics Pty Ltd v. Five Star Computers Pty Ltd (COPYRIGHT: WHETHER ROM IN PRINTER A COMPUTER PROGRAM: ORIGINALITY: SECONDARY INFRINGEMENT: SALE OF IMPORTED PRINTERS INCLUDING PROGRAM IN ROM: PASSING OFF: SUPPLY OF FOREIGN SUPPLIED PRINTERS AS ASSOCIATED WITH AUSTRALIAN SUPPLIER: SUPPLY OF 220V PRINTERS AS INTENDED BY MANUFACTURER FOR DISTRIBUTION IN AUSTRALIA: Australia: Fed. Ct)

Set of Instructions

Autodesk Inc. v. Dyason (COPYRIGHT: WHETHER ELECTRICAL CIRCUIT IS A COMPUTER PROGRAM: WHETHER SET OF INSTRUCTIONS AND DATA-PROCESSING DEVICE NEED BE SEPARATE: INFRINGEMENT: REPRODUCTION: AUTHORISATION: DEVICE ENABLING BREACH OF SHRINK-WRAP LICENCE: Australia: Fed. Ct)

Shrink-wrap Licence

Autodesk Inc. v. Dyason (COPYRIGHT: WHETHER ELECTRICAL CIRCUIT IS A COMPUTER PROGRAM: WHETHER SET OF INSTRUCTIONS AND DATA-PROCESSING DEVICE NEED BE SEPARATE: INFRINGEMENT: REPRODUCTION: AUTHORISATION: DEVICE ENABLING BREACH OF SHRINK-WRAP LICENCE: Australia: Fed. Ct)

Beta Computers (Europe) Ltd v. Adobe Systrems (Europe) Ltd (SUPPLY OF SOFTWARE: NO CONCLUDED CONTRACT UNTIL ACCEPTANCE OF LICENCE CONDITIONS BY PURCHASER: NO NEED FOR IMPLIED TERM: LICENCE CONDITIONS IMPOSED BY COPYRIGHT OWNER: SCOTTISH DOCTRINE OF *Jus quaesitum tertio*: Scotland: O.H.)

Silicon Chip

115778 Canada Inc. v. Apple Computer Inc. (COPYRIGHT: SUBJECT-MATTER: COMPUTER PROGRAM: PROGRAM STORED IN ELECTRONIC FORM ON CHIP: REPRODUCTION: MERGER OF IDEA AND EXPRESSION: TRANSLATION: Canada: S.C.)

Atari Games Corp. v. Nintendo of America Inc. (COPYRIGHT: CIRCUIT IN SILICON CHIP: SUBSISTENCE: SCOPE OF PROTECTION: MERGER OF IDEA AND EXPRESSION: INFRINGEMENT IN REVERSE ENGINEERING: United States: D.C.)

International Business Machines Corporation v. Computer Imports Ltd (COPYRIGHT: INFRINGEMENT: COMPUTER TECHNOLOGY: THREE-DIMENSIONAL REPRODUCTION OF CABINET AND INTERNAL LAYOUT OF PERSONAL COMPUTER AND BY COPYING OF COMPUTER PROGRAM: IMPORTATION AND SALE: SOURCE CODE: WHETHER OBJECT CODE (SILICON CHIP): TRANSFER OF LITERARY WORK: New Zealand: H.C.)

Mackintosh Computers Ltd v. Apple Computer Inc. (COPYRIGHT: SUBJECT-MATTER: COMPUTER PROGRAM: PROGRAM STORED IN ELECTRONIC FORM ON CHIP: REPRODUCTION: MERGER OF IDEA AND EXPRESSION: TRANSLATION: Canada: S.C.)

NEC Corporation v. Intel Corporation (COPYRIGHT: MICROCODE IN MICROPROCESSOR CHIPS: SUBSISTENCE: MINIMAL VERBAL STRUCTURES: WORKS DICTATED BY FUNCTION: FORFEITURE OF COPYRIGHT: NON-USE OF COPYRIGHT NOTICE: SCOPE OF LICENCE: INFRINGEMENT: WHETHER MODIFICATION OF EARLIER COPY AVOIDS INFRINGEMENT: United States: D.C.)

Software Sales

Artware (Sárl) v. Groupe D'Utilisation Francophone D'Informatique (COPYRIGHT: RIGHT TO MAKE BACK-UP COPIES: SOFTWARE: ANTI-PROTECTION PROCESSES: France: S.C.)

Beta Computers (Europe) Ltd v. Adobe Systrems (Europe) Ltd (SHRINK-WRAPPED LICENCE: NO CONTRACT UNTIL ACCEPTANCE OF LICENCE CONDITIONS: LICENCE CONDITIONS IMPOSED BY COPYRIGHT OWNER: DOCTRINE OF *Jus quaesitum tertio*: Scotland: O.H.)

Nottingham Building Society v. Eurodynamics Systems plc (CONTRACT: REPUDIATION: DELIVERY-UP OF SOFTWARE: DISPUTED DEBT: INTERLOCUTORY ORDER FOR DELIVERY-UP: APPLICATION FOR LEAVE TO ADDUCE FURTHER EVIDENCE: INTERNAL COMPANY DOCUMENTS: RELEVANCY: C.A.)

St Albans City & District Council v. International Computers Ltd (CONTRACT: NEGLIGENT MISSTATEMENT: DEFICIENCY IN SOFTWARE RESULTING IN REDUCED REVENUE: WHETHER LOSS RECOVERABLE: LIMITATION CLAUSE: REASONABLENESS: WHETHER SOFTWARE GOODS: WHETHER PARTIES DEALING ON STANDARD TERMS: Q.B.D.)

Software

Apple Computer Inc. v. New-Con Technologies Ltd (COPYRIGHT: INFRINGEMENT: PRINTED CIRCUITS: Israel: D.C.)

Artware (Sárl) v. Groupe D'Utilisation Francophone D'Informatique (SOFTWARE SALES: COPYRIGHT: RIGHT TO MAKE BACK-UP COPIES: ANTI-PROTECTION PROCESSES: France: S.C.)

Beecham Group PLC v. Southern Transvaal Pharmaceutical Pricing Bureau (Pty) Ltd (TRADE MARK: INFRINGEMENT: USE IN COURSE OF TRADE: REFERENCE TO TRADE IN GOODS IN CLASS FOR WHICH MARK REGISTERED: SYSTEM PROVIDING INFORMATION ON GENERIC ALTERNATIVE MEDICINES AVAILABLE AFTER EXPIRY OF PATENT: South Africa: A.D.)

Computer Associates International, Inc. v. Altai, Inc. (COPYRIGHT: NON-LITERAL ELEMENTS PROTECTABLE: SUBSTANTIAL SIMILARITY TEST: TRADE SECRETS: FEDERAL PRE-EMPTION: United States: C.A.)

Federal Computer Services Sdn Bhd v. Ang Jee Hai Eric (COPYRIGHT: SCOPE OF PROTECTION: INTERPRETATION OF STATUTE: Singapore: H.C.)

Ibcos Computers Ltd v. Barclays Mercantile Highland Finance Ltd (COPYRIGHT: SOURCE CODE: SUBSISTENCE AND EXTENT OF PROTECTION: INFRINGEMENT: SUBSTANTIAL PART: BREACH OF CONFIDENCE: FILE TRANSFER PROGRAM: *British Leyland* DEFENCE: RESTRICTIVE COVENANT: CONSTRUCTION: Ch.D.)

Intergraph Corp. v. Solid Systems CAD Services Ltd (COPYRIGHT: PRACTICE: APPLICATION TO DISCHARGE ANTON PILLER ORDER: MATERIAL NON-DISCLOSURE: MISREPRESENTATION: DELAY: Ch.D.)

Jian Tools For Sales Inc. v. Roderick Manhattan Group Ltd (SOFTWARE FOR BUSINESS PLANS: BIZPLAN BUILDER: WHETHER DESCRIPTIVE: COMPANY WITH NO U.K. PLACE OF BUSINESS: REPUTATION: ADEQUACY OF DAMAGES ON ROYALTY BASIS: EFFECT OF FORCED CHANGE OF NAME: BALANCE OF CONVENIENCE: DEFENDANT'S AWARENESS OF PLAINTIFF'S OBJECTIONS: PRESERVATION OF STATUS QUO: Ch.D.)

John Richardson Computers Ltd v. Flanders (COPYRIGHT: INFRINGEMENT: TITLE TO PORTIONS OF PROGRAM WRITTEN BY INDEPENDENT CONTRACTORS: WHETHER COPYING: WHETHER SUBSTANTIAL PART REPRODUCED: NO COPYING OF SOURCE CODE: APPROPRIATE TEST: ESTOPPEL: Ch.D.)

John Richardson Computers Ltd v. Flanders (COPYRIGHT: MINOR INFRINGEMENTS: FORM OF ORDER AND INJUNCTION: DAMAGES: PLAINTIFF'S RIGHT TO INQUIRY WHERE INFRINGEMENT SLIGHT: DEFENDANT'S RIGHT TO INQUIRY AS TO DAMAGES ON PLAINTIFF'S CROSS-UNDERTAKING: COSTS: APPROPRIATE ORDER WHERE WHOLESALE INFRINGEMENT ALLEGED BUT ONLY MINOR ESTABLISHED: Ch.D.)

Lasercomb America Inc. v. Job Reynolds (COPYRIGHT: INFRINGEMENT: MISUSE: EQUITABLE DEFENCE: LIMITED MONOPOLY: LICENSING RESTRICTIONS: NON-COMPETITION PROVISIONS: United States: C.A.)

Nottingham Building Society v. Eurodynamics Systems plc (CONTRACT: REPUDIATION: DELIVERY-UP OF SOFTWARE: DISPUTED DEBT: INTERLOCUTORY ORDER FOR DELIVERY-UP: APPLICATION FOR LEAVE TO ADDUCE FURTHER EVIDENCE: INTERNAL COMPANY DOCUMENTS: RELEVANCY: C.A.)

Novell, Inc. v. Ong Seow Pheng (COPYRIGHT: SCOPE OF PROTECTION: SOFTWARE AND MANUALS: FIRST PUBLICATION IN UNITED STATES: ADDITIONAL DAMAGES: TRADE MARK: INFRINGEMENT: INJUNCTION: Singapore: H.C.)

Società Italiana Degli Autori ed Editori (SIAE) v. Domenico Pompa (COPYRIGHT: INTELLECTUAL PRODUCT: BASIS OF PROTECTION: Italy: S.C.)

St Albans City & District Council v. International Computers Ltd (CONTRACT: NEGLIGENT MISSTATEMENT: DEFICIENCY IN SOFTWARE RESULTING IN REDUCED REVENUE: WHETHER LOSS RECOVERABLE: LIMITATION CLAUSE: REASONABLENESS: WHETHER SOFTWARE GOODS: WHETHER PARTIES DEALING ON STANDARD TERMS: Q.B.D.)

Toby Construction Products Pty Ltd v. Computer Bar Sales Pty Ltd (SALE OF GOODS: WHETHER "GOODS": S.C.(NSW))

Total Information Processing Systems Ltd v. Daman Ltd (COPYRIGHT: COPYRIGHT IN SOFTWARE INTERFACE: MERGER OF IDEA WITH EXPRESSION: WHETHER PRINCIPLE OF DEROGATION FROM GRANT CONFINED TO COMPANIES WITH DOMINANT POSITION: EVIDENCE FOR INTERLOCUTORY APPLICATION: Ch.D.)

Sound Cards

Aztech Systems Pte Ltd v. Creative Technology Ltd (COPYRIGHT: INFRINGEMENT: SOUND CARDS: DESIGNING COMPATIBLE CARDS: FAIR DEALING FOR THE PURPOSE OF PRIVATE STUDY: DEROGATION FROM GRANT: IMPLIED LICENCE: Singapore: H.C.)

Source Code. *See also* Object Code

Series 5 Software Ltd v. Philip Clarke (CONFIDENTIAL INFORMATION: SOLICITATION OF CUSTOMERS: INTERLOCUTORY INJUNCTIONS: HISTORICAL SURVEY OF *American Cyanamid* CASES: Ch.D.)

Storage

115778 Canada Inc. v. Apple Computer Inc. (COPYRIGHT: SUBJECT-MATTER: COMPUTER PROGRAM: PROGRAM STORED IN ELECTRONIC FORM ON CHIP: REPRODUCTION: MERGER OF IDEA AND EXPRESSION: TRANSLATION: Canada: S.C.)

Mackintosh Computers Ltd v. Apple Computer Inc. (COPYRIGHT: SUBJECT-MATTER: COMPUTER PROGRAM: PROGRAM STORED IN ELECTRONIC FORM ON CHIP: REPRODUCTION: MERGER OF IDEA AND EXPRESSION: TRANSLATION: Canada: S.C.)

Translator Programs

M.S. Associates Ltd v. Power (COPYRIGHT: INFRINGEMENT: INTERLOCUTORY INJUNCTION: SIMILARITIES: ARGUABLE CASE: BALANCE OF CONVENIENCE: Ch.D.)

Unauthorised Modification

R. v. Cropp (COMPUTERS: HACKING: UNAUTHORISED ACCESS: ALTERATION OF DATA ON COMPUTER: INTERPRETATION OF STATUTE: U.K.: Crown Court, Snaresbrook)

UNIX. *See* Operating System

User Interface. *See* Interface

Visual Displays

Apple Computer Inc. v. Microsoft Corp. (COPYRIGHT: LOOK AND FEEL: SUBSISTENCE: MERGER OF IDEA AND EXPRESSION: INDISPENSABLE EXPRESSION: *Scenes a faire*: MERE FUNCTIONALITY: United States: D.C.)

Apple Computer, Inc. v. Microsoft Corp. (COPYRIGHT: LOOK AND FEEL: SUBSISTENCE: LICENCE: SCOPE: INTERPRETATION: United States: D.C.)

Lewis Galoob Toys Inc. v. Nintendo of America Inc. (COPYRIGHT: AUDIOVISUAL DISPLAYS: INFRINGEMENT: AUTHORISATION: DERIVATIVE WORKS: WHETHER MODIFICATION BY A DEVICE NOT AFFECTING THE COMPUTER PROGRAM ITSELF IS AN INGRINGEMENT: FAIR USE: United States: D.C.)

1151

VDU Installations Ltd v. Integrated Computer Systems and Cybernetics Ltd (COPYRIGHT: INFRINGEMENT: ANTON PILLER ORDER: IMPROPER EXECUTION: NEGLIGENT IMPROPRIETY: CONTEMPT: Ch.D.)

MASTER and SERVANT, including RESTRICTIVE COVENANTS, EMPLOYEES and RESTRAINT OF TRADE

Abuse of Process. *See* **Practice** (*Abuse of process*)

Anton Piller. *See* **Practice** (*Anton Piller*)

Breach of Confidence

A Company's Application (FORMER EMPLOYEE OF COMPANY PROVIDING FINANCIAL SERVICES: THREAT TO DISCLOSE CONFIDENTIAL INFORMATION TO REGULATORY BODY: NO THREAT OF DISCLOSURE TO PUBLIC: ENTITLEMENT TO INJUNCTION: Ch.D.)

Angus & Coote Pty Ltd v. Render (EX-EMPLOYEE: WHETHER INFORMATION HAS QUALITY OF CONFIDENCE: NO PROOF INFORMATION TAKEN IN WRITTEN FORM: EMPLOYEES FIDUCIARY DUTY AND DUTY OF GOOD FAITH: S.C.(NSW))

ANI Corp. Ltd v. Celtite Australia Pty Ltd (DUTIES OF EMPLOYEES AFTER EMPLOYMENT: WHETHER INFORMATION GAINED DURING EMPLOYMENT HAS QUALITY OF CONFIDENCE: PUBLICATION BY PATENTS: INTERLOCUTORY INJUNCTION: EX-EMPLOYEES: Australia: Fed. Ct)

Attorney-General v. Heinemann Publishers Australia Pty Ltd and Wright (*Spycatcher*: BOOK IN MANUSCRIPT FORM: BREACH OF FIDUCIARY DUTY: NATURE OF DEFENDANT'S EMPLOYMENT BY CROWN: NATURE OF DUTY OF CONFIDENTIALITY: WHETHER INFORMATION IN PUBLIC DOMAIN: PRIOR PUBLICATION OF INFORMATION BY THIRD PARTY: Australia: S.C.(NSW): C.A.(NSW))

Balston Ltd v. Headline Filters Ltd (BREACH OF DUTY OF GOOD FAITH: EX-EMPLOYEE: Ch.D.)

Berkeley Administration Inc. v. McClelland (EX-EMPLOYEES: FINANCIAL INFORMATION: WHETHER CONFIDENTIAL: WHETHER USED: Q.B.D.)

Faccenda Chicken Ltd v. Fowler (CONSPIRACY: SALES INFORMATION: MASTER AND SERVANT: DUTY OF FIDELITY: Ch.D.: C.A.)

Ixora Trading Incorporated v. Jones (BREACH OF DUTY OF FIDELITY: EX-EMPLOYEES: STATEMENT OF CLAIM FRIVOLOUS AND VEXATIOUS: Ch.D.)

J.A. Mont (U.K.) Ltd v. Mills (EX-EMPLOYEE'S SEVERANCE AGREEMENT: VALIDITY OF COVENANT: FORM OF INJUNCTION: APPROACH TO CONSTRUCTION OF RESTRICTIVE COVENANTS: GOOD FAITH: C.A.)

Johnson & Bloy (Holdings) Ltd v. Wolstenholme Rink PLC (EX-EMPLOYEE: NATURE OF INFORMATION: SCOPE OF INJUNCTION: C.A.)

Mainmet Holdings PLC v. Austin (EX-EMPLOYEE: NOT IN COMPETITION WITH EX-EMPLOYER: TRADE SECRETS: MALICIOUS FALSEHOOD: WHETHER INJUNCTION APPROPRIATE: Q.B.D.)

Multi Tube Systems (Pty) Ltd v. Ponting (MASTER AND SERVANT: INTERIM INJUNCTION: South Africa: D&CLD)

Confidential Information. *See also* Breach of Confidence

Conspiracy

Contempt. *See* Practice (*Contempt*)

Contracts of Employment

Lawrence David Ltd v. Ashton (RESTRAINT OF TRADE: CONFIDENTIAL
  INFORMATION: TRADE SECRETS: INTERLOCUTORY INJUNCTION: EX-
  EMPLOYEE: PERIOD OF RESTRAINT: C.A.)
Poly Lina Ltd v. Finch (FORMER EMPLOYEE: EMBARGO ON ENGAGEMENTS WITH
  COMPETITOR: WIDTH OF COVENANT: ADEQUACY OF UNDERTAKING NOT TO
  DISCLOSE: Q.B.D.)
PSM International Ltd v. Whitehouse (BREACH OF CONFIDENCE: RESTRAINT OF
  EX-EMPLOYEE FROM FULFILLING CONTRACT ALREADY MADE WITH THIRD
  PARTY: C.A.)

Contracts of Service. (*See also under* Recording Contracts)

Community for Creative Non-Violence v. James Earl Reid (COPYRIGHT: WORK
  MADE FOR HIRE: EMPLOYEE: INDEPENDENT CONTRACTOR: AGENT: United
  States: C.A.)
De Garis v. Neville Jeffress Pidler Pty Ltd (COPYRIGHT: ARTICLE IN NEWSPAPERS:
  PRESS-CLIPPING AND MEDIA MONITORING SERVICE: ARTICLE WRITTEN ON
  COMMISSIONER WRITTEN BY JOURNALIST EMPLOYED UNDER CONTRACT OF
  SERVICE: OWNERSHIP OF COPYRIGHT: FAIR DEALING DEFENCE: WHETHER
  IMPLIED LICENCE TO REPRODUCE: Australia: Fed. Ct)
Warren v. Mendy (RESTRAINT OF TRADE: INJUNCTION: INTERLOCUTORY:
  BOXER'S MANAGER SEEKING TO RESTRAIN DEFENDANT FROM ACTING FOR
  BOXER: RELATIONSHIP DEPENDENT ON MUTUAL TRUST AND CONFIDENCE:
  WHETHER EFFECT OF GRANTING RELIEF TO COMPEL BOXER TO PERFORM
  CONTRACT WITH MANAGER: WHETHER RELIEF APPROPRIATE: C.A.)
Watson v. Prager (PROFESSIONAL BOXER AND MANAGER: RESTRAINT OF TRADE:
  REASONABLENESS: IMPARTIALITY OF BRITISH BOXING BOARD OF CONTROL
  AS ARBITRATOR: Ch.D.)

Copyright Infringement

Private Research Ltd v. Brosnan (INTERLOCUTORY INJUNCTION: BREACH OF
  CONFIDENCE: EMPLOYER AND EMPLOYEE: MISUSE OF CONFIDENTIAL
  INFORMATION: WHETHER FAIR QUESTION TO BE TRIED: ADEQUACY OF
  DAMAGES: BALANCE OF CONVENIENCE: Ireland: H.C.)

Covenants. *See* Restrictive Covenants

Crown Employee

Attorney-General v. Brandon Book Publishers Ltd (CONFIDENTIAL INFORMATION:
  FIDUCIARY DUTY: IRELAND: BRITISH SECURITY SERVICE EX-EMPLOYEE:
  BOOK: *One Girl's War.* CONSTITUTIONAL RIGHTS: Ireland: H.C.)
Attorney-General v. Guardian Newspapers Ltd and The Observer Ltd (*Spycatcher.*
  NEWSPAPER ARTICLE OUTLINING ALLEGATIONS TO BE PUBLISHED IN BOOK:
  NEWSPAPERS NOT HAVING ACCESS TO AUTHOR'S MANUSCRIPT: PRIOR
  RESTRAINT OF PUBLICATION: PUBLIC INTEREST: ALLEGATIONS OF
  MISCONDUCT BY SECURITY SERVICE: AUTHOR'S DUTY OF CONFIDENTIALITY
  TO CROWN: MATERIAL IN PUBLIC DOMAIN: FORM OF INJUNCTION: Ch.D.:
  C.A.)

Attorney-General v. Heinemann Publishers Australia Pty Ltd and Wright (*Spycatcher*:
BOOK IN MANUSCRIPT FORM: BREACH OF FIDUCIARY DUTY: INJUNCTIONS:
NATURE OF DEFENDANT'S EMPLOYMENT BY CROWN: NATURE OF DUTY OF
CONFIDENTIALITY: WHETHER INFORMATION IN PUBLIC DOMAIN: PRIOR
PUBLICATION BY THIRD PARTY, WITH AGREEMENT OR ACQUIESCENCE OF
BRITISH GOVERNMENT: PUBLIC POLICY: PUBLIC INTEREST: EVIDENCE:
CREDIBILITY OF CROWN WITNESS: Australia: S.C.(NSW): C.A.(NSW))
Kerr v. Morris (RESTRAINT OF TRADE: NHS DOCTOR: VALIDITY OF COVENANT:
PUBLIC INTEREST: C.A.)
Strack v. E.C. Commission (SECRECY: CIVIL SERVICE: EURATOM EMPLOYEE
EXPOSED TO RADIOACTIVE CONTAMINATION: PROCEEDINGS FOR
RECOGNITION OF INDUSTRIAL DISEASE: ACCESS TO MEDICAL INFORMATION:
NOT ON PERSONAL FILE: MADE AVAILABLE TO CLAIMANT'S DOCTOR BUT NOT
TO CLAIMANT: ADEQUATE COMPLIANCE WITH RULE OF ACCESS:
COMMISSION'S GRUDGING AND UNINFORMATIVE REPLY TO REQUESTS FOR
ACCESS: MALADMINISTRATION: COMMISSION WINS CASE BUT ALL COSTS
AWARDED AGAINST IT: ECJ)

Customers and Customer Lists

Aristograf Graphics Inc. v. Northover (EX-EMPLOYEE: CUSTOMERS: FIDUCIARY
RELATIONSHIP: INTERLOCUTORY: INJUNCTION: Canada: H.C.(Ont.))
Faccenda Chicken Ltd v. Fowler (BREACH OF CONFIDENCE: CONSPIRACY: SALES
INFORMATION: MASTER AND SERVANT: DUTY OF FIDELITY: Ch.D.: C.A.)
Peninsular Real Estate Ltd v. Harris (CONFIDENTIAL INFORMATION: EX-
EMPLOYEES: CLIENT LIST: NO RESTRAINT OF TRADE CLAUSE: New Zealand:
H.C.)
Roger Bullivant Ltd v. Ellis (BREACH OF CONFIDENCE: EX-EMPLOYEE:
SPRINGBOARD DOCTRINE: CUSTOMER CARD INDEX: C.A.)
Universal Thermosensors Ltd v. Hibben (BREACH OF CONFIDENCE: STOLEN
CUSTOMER INFORMATION: EX-EMPLOYEES' COMPETING BUSINESS:
ASSESSMENT OF DAMAGES: INTERLOCUTORY ORDER BY CONSENT: SCOPE OF
INJUNCTIONS IN BREACH OF CONFIDENCE: SPRINGBOARD DOCTRINE:
DISCRETION: ANTON PILLER PRACTICE: Ch.D.)
Van Castricum v. Theunissen (TRADE MARK: UNLAWFUL COMPETITION:
CONFIDENTIAL INFORMATION: EX-EMPLOYEE: CUSTOMER LISTS: South
Africa: TPD)

Damages. *See also under* **Practice** (*Adequacy of damages*)

Lock International PLC v. Beswick (ANTON PILLER ORDER: PLAINTIFF TO PAY
DAMAGES: CONFIDENTIAL INFORMATION: EX-EMPLOYEE: INJUNCTION:
TRADE SECRETS: Ch.D.)
Pioneer Concrete Services Ltd v. Lorenzo Galli (CONFIDENTIAL INFORMATION:
IMPLIED OBLIGATION: RESTRAINT OF TRADE: INJUNCTION: DECLARATION:
S.C.(Vic.))
Schindler Lifts Australia Pty Ltd v. Debelak (TRADE LIBEL: INJURIOUS FALSEHOOD:
INDUCING BREACH OF CONTRACT: GENERAL SOLICITING OF BUSINESS:
EMPLOYEES DUTY: INJUNCTION: Australia: Fed. Ct)
Universal Thermosensors Ltd v. Hibben (BREACH OF CONFIDENCE: STOLEN
CUSTOMER INFORMATION: EX-EMPLOYEES' COMPETING BUSINESS:
ASSESSMENT OF DAMAGES: Ch.D.)
Zang Tumb Tuum Records Ltd v. Johnson (POP GROUP: RECORDING AGREEMENT
AND PUBLISHING AGREEMENT: UNREASONABLE RESTRAINT OF TRADE:
ENFORCEABILITY: WAIVER OF OBJECTION: SCOPE OF INQUIRY AS TO
DAMAGES: C.A.)

Directors

Millwell Holdings Ltd v. Johnson (CONFIDENTIAL INFORMATION: DEVICES ASSEMBLED FROM COMMONPLACE COMPONENTS AND ON PUBLIC VIEW: EX-EMPLOYEE: DIRECTOR: ASSIGNMENT: New Zealand: H.C.)

Sage Holdings Ltd v. Financial Mail (Pty) Ltd (CONFIDENTIAL INFORMATION: EMPLOYEES: DIRECTORS: PUBLIC POLICY: South Africa: WLD)

Sibex Construction (S.A.) (Pty) Ltd v. Injectaseal C.C. (CONFIDENTIAL INFORMATION: UNLAWFUL COMPETITION: EX-EMPLOYEES: PRICE LIST: DUTY OF FIDELITY: DIRECTORS: South Africa: TPD)

Discovery. *See* Practice (*Discovery*)

Employer's Liability

Supply Of Ready Mixed Concrete (No. 2) (CONTEMPT: BREACH OF INJUNCTION BY EMPLOYEE: LIABILITY OF EMPLOYER: H.L.)

Estoppel. *See* Practice (*Estoppel*)

Ex-employee

A Company's Application (CONFIDENTIAL INFORMATION: BREACH OF CONFIDENCE: PUBLIC INTEREST: FORMER EMPLOYEE OF COMPANY PROVIDING FINANCIAL SERVICES: THREAT TO DISCLOSE CONFIDENTIAL INFORMATION TO REGULATORY BODY AND REVENUE: NO THREAT OF DISCLOSURE TO PUBLIC: WHETHER COMPANY ENTITLED TO INJUNCTION: Ch.D.)

Angus & Coote Pty Ltd v. Render (CONFIDENTIAL INFORMATION: WHETHER INFORMATION HAS QUALITY OF CONFIDENCE: NO PROOF INFORMATION TAKEN IN WRITTEN FORM: EMPLOYEE'S FIDUCIARY DUTY AND DUTY OF GOOD FAITH: CONTRACT OF EMPLOYMENT: IMPLIED TERM OF GOOD FAITH: INJUNCTION: LENGTH OF RESTRAINT: DELIVERY-UP: CLEAN HANDS: Australia: S.C.(NSW))

ANI Corp. Ltd v. Celtite Australia Pty Ltd (CONFIDENTIAL INFORMATION: DUTIES OF EMPLOYEES AFTER EMPLOYMENT: WHETHER INFORMATION GAINED DURING EMPLOYMENT HAS QUALITY OF CONFIDENCE: PUBLICATION BY PATENTS: INTERLOCUTORY INJUNCTION: Australia: Fed. Ct)

Aristograf Graphics Inc. v. Northover (CUSTOMERS: FIDUCIARY RELATIONSHIP: INTERLOCUTORY: INJUNCTION: Canada: H.C.(Ont.))

Attorney-General v. Brandon Book Publishers Ltd (CONFIDENTIAL INFORMATION: FIDUCIARY DUTY: IRELAND: BRITISH SECURITY SERVICE EX-EMPLOYEE: BOOK: *One Girl's War.* CONSTITUTIONAL RIGHTS: Ireland: H.C.)

Attorney-General v. Guardian Newspapers Ltd (CONFIDENTIAL INFORMATION: BOOK: *Spycatcher.* FORMER CROWN EMPLOYEE: INTERLOCUTORY INJUNCTION: SUBSEQUENT PUBLICATION OUTSIDE JURISDICTION: Ch.D.)

Balston Ltd v. Headline Filters Ltd (BREACH OF CONFIDENCE: BREACH OF DUTY OF GOOD FAITH: Ch.D.)

Berkeley Administration Inc. v. McClelland (BREACH OF CONFIDENCE: FINANCIAL INFORMATION: WHETHER CONFIDENTIAL: WHETHER USED: Q.B.D.)

Computer Machinery Co. Ltd v. Drescher (CONFIDENTIAL INFORMATION: INTERLOCUTORY INJUNCTION: EVIDENCE: Ch.D.)

Elley Ltd v. Wairoa-Harrison & McCarthy (CONFIDENTIAL INFORMATION: DELIVERY-UP OF DOCUMENTS: New Zealand: H.C.)

Gillman Engineering Ltd v. Simon Ho Shek On (CONFIDENTIAL INFORMATION: DUTY OF EX-EMPLOYEE: Hong Kong: S.C.)

Fidelity. *See* Good Faith

Fiduciary Relationship or Duty

Aristograf Graphics Inc. v. Northover (EX-EMPLOYEE: CUSTOMERS: Canada: H.C.(Ont.))

Attorney-General v. Brandon Book Publishers Ltd (CONFIDENTIAL INFORMATION: BRITISH SECURITY SERVICE EX-EMPLOYEE: Ireland: H.C.)

Attorney-General v. Heinemann Publishers Australia Pty Ltd and Wright (BREACH OF CONFIDENCE: *Spycatcher.* BOOK IN MANUSCRIPT FORM: NATURE OF DEFENDANT'S EMPLOYMENT BY CROWN: Australia: S.C.(NSW): C.A.(NSW))

Faccenda Chicken Ltd v. Fowler (BREACH OF CONFIDENCE: CONSPIRACY: SALES INFORMATION: MASTER AND SERVANT: Ch.D.: C.A.)

Meter Systems Holdings Ltd v. Venter (CONFIDENTIAL INFORMATION: UNLAWFUL COMPETITION: RESTRAINT OF TRADE: ENFORCEMENT: EX-EMPLOYEE: South Africa: WLD)

Prout v. British Gas PLC (PATENT: INFRINGEMENT: VALIDITY: BREACH OF CONFIDENCE: WHETHER DISCLOSURE BY EMPLOYEE UNDER EMPLOYEES' SUGGESTION SCHEME BINDING ON DEFENDANT: SPRINGBOARD DOCTRINE: Pat. C.C.)

Franchise Agreement

Kall-Kwik Printing (U.K.) Ltd v. Frank Clarence Rush (RESTRICTIVE COVENANT: CONSTRUCTON: ENFORCEABILITY: REASONABLENESS: INTERLOCUTORY INJUNCTION: Ch.D.)

Good Faith, Duty of

Angus & Coote Pty Ltd v. Render (CONFIDENTIAL INFORMATION: EX-EMPLOYEE: WHETHER INFORMATION HAS QUALITY OF CONFIDENCE: IMPLIED TERM: CONTRACT OF EMPLOYMENT: Australia: S.C.(NSW))

Balston Ltd v. Headline Filters Ltd (BREACH OF CONFIDENCE: EX-EMPLOYEE: Ch.D.)

J.A. Mont (U.K.) Ltd v. Mills (EX-EMPLOYEE'S SEVERANCE AGREEMENT: VALIDITY OF COVENANT: BREACH OF CONFIDENCE: FORM OF INJUNCTION: CONSTRUCTION OF RESTRICTIVE COVENANTS: C.A.)

Inducing Breach of Contract

Schindler Lifts Australia Pty Ltd v. Debelak (TRADE LIBEL: INJURIOUS FALSEHOOD: GENERAL SOLICITING OF BUSINESS: EMPLOYEES DUTY: INJUNCTION: DAMAGES: Australia: Fed. Ct)

Inquiry as to Damages. See **Practice** (*Inquiry as to damages*)

Inspection. See **Practice** (*Inspection*)

Interim Injunction. See **Practice** (*Interim or interlocutory injunction*)

Interlocutory Injunction. See **Practice** (*Interim or interlocutory injunction*)

Ireland

Private Research Ltd v. Brosnan (COPYRIGHT: INFRINGEMENT: INTERLOCUTORY INJUNCTION: BREACH OF CONFIDENCE: EMPLOYER AND EMPLOYEE: MISUSE OF CONFIDENTIAL INFORMATION: WHETHER FAIR QUESTION TO BE TRIED: ADEQUACY OF DAMAGES: BALANCE OF CONVENIENCE: H.C.)

Mareva Injunctions. *See* **Practice** (*Mareva injunctions*)

Master and Servant

Faccenda Chicken Ltd v. Fowler (BREACH OF CONFIDENCE: CONSPIRACY: SALES INFORMATION: DUTY OF FIDELITY: Ch.D.: C.A.)
Multi Tube Systems (Pty) Ltd v. Ponting (CONFIDENTIAL INFORMATION: INTERIM INJUNCTION: South Africa: D&CLD)
Speed Seal Products Ltd v. Paddington (BREACH OF CONFIDENCE: STRIKING OUT: ACTIONABLE ABUSE OF PROCESS: PLEADINGS: Ch.D.)

Pleadings. *See* **Practice** (*Pleadings*)

Practice

Abuse of process

Speed Seal Products Ltd v. Paddington (BREACH OF CONFIDENCE: MASTER AND SERVANT: STRIKING OUT: PLEADINGS: Ch.D.)

Anton Piller

Lock International PLC v. Beswick (PLAINTIFF TO PAY DAMAGES: CONFIDENTIAL INFORMATION: EX-EMPLOYEE: INJUNCTION: TRADE SECRETS: Ch.D.)
Universal Thermosensors Ltd v. Hibben (STOLEN CUSTOMER INFORMATION: EX-EMPLOYEES' COMPETING BUSINESS: ASSESSMENT OF DAMAGES: INTERLOCUTORY ORDER BY CONSENT: SCOPE OF INJUNCTIONS IN BREACH OF CONFIDENCE: SPRINGBOARD DOCTRINE: DISCRETION: Ch.D.)

Contempt

Supply Of Ready Mixed Concrete (No. 2) (BREACH OF INJUNCTION BY EMPLOYEE: LIABILITY OF EMPLOYER: H.L.)

Discovery

Redic Industries Pty Ltd v. JAL Chemicals Pty Ltd (CONFIDENTIAL INFORMATION: INSPECTION OF FINANCIAL AND SALES RECORDS OF COMPANY OF FORMER EMPLOYEES: Australia: S.C.(Vic.))

Discretion

Carlton & United Breweries Ltd v. Tooth & Co. Ltd (CONTRACT: IMPLIED TERMS: GOODWILL OF BUSINESS: INDUCEMENT TO BREAK CONTRACT: RESTRAINT OF TRADE: AGENCY: Australia: S.C.(NSW))
Group Inc. v. Eaglestone (EMPLOYMENT CONTRACT: RESTRICTIVE COVENANT: HIGHLY-PAID SERVICES BROKER: WORKING RELATIONSHIP VERY PROFITABLE FOR EMPLOYER: GOODWILL: INTENTION TO FLOUT NOTICE PERIOD: INJUNCTION: ADEQUACY OF DAMAGES: BALANCE OF CONVENIENCE: Ch.D.)
Universal Thermosensors Ltd v. Hibben (BREACH OF CONFIDENCE: STOLEN CUSTOMER INFORMATION: EX-EMPLOYEES' COMPETING BUSINESS: ASSESSMENT OF DAMAGES: INTERLOCUTORY ORDER BY CONSENT: SCOPE OF INJUNCTIONS IN BREACH OF CONFIDENCE: SPRINGBOARD DOCTRINE: ANTON PILLER PRACTICE: Ch.D.)

Estoppel

Silvertone Records Ltd v. Mountfield (CONTRACT: POP GROUP: RECORDING AGREEMENT AND PUBLISHING AGREEMENT: RESTRAINT OF TRADE: WHETHER UNREASONABLE: WAIVER OF OBJECTION: WHETHER AGREEMENTS SEVERABLE: Q.B.D.)

Zomba Music Publishers Ltd v. Mountfield (CONTRACT: POP GROUP: RECORDING AGREEMENT AND PUBLISHING AGREEMENT: RESTRAINT OF TRADE: ENFORCEABILITY: WAIVER: SEVERABILITY OF AGREEMENTS: Q.B.D.)

Inquiry as to damages

Zang Tumb Tuum Records Ltd v. Johnson (SCOPE: CONTRACT: POP GROUP: RECORDING AGREEMENT AND PUBLISHING AGREEMENT: UNREASONABLE RESTRAINT OF TRADE: ENFORCEABILITY: WAIVE OF OBJECTION: C.A.)

Inspection

Redic Industries Pty Ltd v. JAL Chemicals Pty Ltd (CONFIDENTIAL INFORMATION: DISCOVERY: INSPECTION OF FINANCIAL AND SALES RECORDS OF COMPANY OF FORMER EMPLOYEES: Australia: S.C.(Vic.))

Interim or interlocutory injunction

ANI Corp. Ltd v. Celtite Australia Pty Ltd (CONFIDENTIAL INFORMATION: WHETHER INFORMATION GAINED DURING EMPLOYMENT HAS QUALITY OF CONFIDENCE: PUBLICATION BY PATENTS: Australia: Fed. Ct)

Attorney-General v. Guardian Newspapers Ltd (CONFIDENTIAL INFORMATION: BOOK: *Spycatcher*: FORMER CROWN EMPLOYEE: SUBSEQUENT PUBLICATION OUTSIDE JURISDICTION: Ch.D.)

Attorney-General v. Guardian Newspapers Ltd and The Observer Ltd (*Spycatcher*: NEWSPAPER ARTICLE OUTLINING ALLEGATIONS TO BE PUBLISHED IN BOOK: NEWSPAPERS NOT HAVING ACCESS TO AUTHOR'S MANUSCRIPT: PRIOR RESTRAINT OF PUBLICATION: PUBLIC INTEREST: ALLEGATIONS OF MISCONDUCT BY SECURITY SERVICE: AUTHOR'S DUTY OF CONFIDENTIALITY TO CROWN: MATERIAL IN PUBLIC DOMAIN: FORM OF INJUNCTION: Ch.D.: C.A.)

Austin Knight (U.K.) Ltd v. Hinds (EMPLOYMENT CONTRACTS: RESTRICTIVE COVENANT: NON-SOLICITATION CLAUSE: WHETHER PLAINTIFF'S BUSINESS PROTECTABLE: WHETHER RESTRICTION REASONABLE: MISUSE OF CONFIDENTIAL INFORMATION: Ch.D.)

Computer Machinery Co. Ltd v. Drescher (CONFIDENTIAL INFORMATION: FORMER EMPLOYEES: EVIDENCE: Ch.D.)

John Michael Design PLC v. Cooke (RESTRAINT OF TRADE: EMPLOYMENT: AGREEMENT: TIME LIMITATION: C.A.)

Keybrand Foods Inc. v. Guinchard (EX-EMPLOYEE: PRODUCT RECIPE: PROOF: Canada: Ont. Ct (Gen.) Div.))

Kall-Kwik Printing (U.K.) Ltd v. Frank Clarence Rush (FRANCHISE AGREEMENT: RESTRICTIVE COVENANT: CONSTRUCTION: ENFORCEABILITY: REASONABLENESS: Ch.D.)

Lansing Linde Ltd v. Kerr (CONFIDENTIAL INFORMATION: EX-EMPLOYEE: RESTRAINT OF TRADE: RESTRICTIVE COVENANT IN CONTRACT OF EMPLOYMENT: BREACH: WHETHER INFORMATION ACQUIRED BY EMPLOYEE PROTECTABLE AS TRADE SECRETS: C.A.)

Lawrence David Ltd v. Ashton (CONTRACT: RESTRAINT OF TRADE: CONFIDENTIAL INFORMATION: TRADE SECRETS: EX-EMPLOYEE: PERIOD OF RESTRAINT: C.A.)

Multi Tube Systems (Pty) Ltd v. Ponting (CONFIDENTIAL INFORMATION: MASTER AND SERVANT: South Africa: D&CLD)

Stenada Marketing Ltd v. Nazareno (FRANCHISES: CONFIDENTIALITY: PUBLIC DOMAIN: NON-DISCLOSURE COVENANT: Canada: S.C.(B.C.)

Universal Thermosensors Ltd v. Hibben (BREACH OF CONFIDENCE: STOLEN CUSTOMER INFORMATION: EX-EMPLOYEES' COMPETING BUSINESS: ASSESSMENT OF DAMAGES: INTERLOCUTORY ORDER BY CONSENT: SCOPE OF INJUNCTIONS IN BREACH OF CONFIDENCE: SPRINGBOARD DOCTRINE: DISCRETION: ANTON PILLER: Ch.D.)

Mareva injunctions

Regent Decorators Sdn Bhd v. Chee (PASSING OFF: FORMER EMPLOYEES: CONFUSION: Malaysia: S.C.)

Pleadings

Speed Seal Products Ltd v. Paddington (BREACH OF CONFIDENCE: MASTER AND SERVANT: STRIKING OUT: ACTIONABLE ABUSE OF PROCESS: Ch.D.)

Price List

Sibex Construction (S.A.) (Pty) Ltd v. Injectaseal C.C. (CONFIDENTIAL INFORMATION: UNLAWFUL COMPETITION: EX-EMPLOYEES: DUTY OF FIDELITY: DIRECTORS: South Africa: TPD)

Public Interest

A Company's Application (CONFIDENTIAL INFORMATION: BREACH OF CONFIDENCE: FORMER EMPLOYEE OF COMPANY PROVIDING FINANCIAL SERVICES: THREAT TO DISCLOSE CONFIDENTIAL INFORMATION TO REGULATORY BODY AND REVENUE: NO THREAT OF DISCLOSURE TO PUBLIC: WHETHER COMPANY ENTITLED TO INJUNCTION: Ch.D.)

Attorney-General v. Guardian Newspapers Ltd and The Observer Ltd (INTERLOCUTORY INJUNCTION: *Spycatcher*. ALLEGATIONS OF MISCONDUCT BY SECURITY SERVICE: AUTHOR'S DUTY OF CONFIDENTIALITY TO CROWN: MATERIAL IN PUBLIC DOMAIN: FORM OF INJUNCTION: Ch.D.: C.A.)

Attorney-General v. Heinemann Publishers Australia Pty Ltd and Wright (BREACH OF CONFIDENCE: *Spycatcher*. NATURE OF DEFENDANT'S EMPLOYMENT BY CROWN: NATURE OF DUTY OF CONFIDENTIALITY: PRIOR PUBLICATION OF INFORMATION BY THIRD PARTY: PUBLIC POLICY: Australia: S.C.(NSW): C.A.(NSW))

Kerr v. Morris (RESTRAINT OF TRADE: NHS DOCTOR: VALIDITY OF COVENANT: C.A.)

Recording Agreements

Panayiotou v. Sony Music Entertainment (U.K.) Ltd (RESTRAINT OF TRADE: CHALLENGE TO ENFORCEABILITY OF AGREEMENT: ENTITLEMENT: EARLIER COMPROMISE OF PROCEEDINGS: REASONABLENESS OF TERMS: CONDUCT OF DEFENDANT: Ch.D.)

Silvertone Records Ltd v. Mountfield (RECORDING AGREEMENT AND PUBLISHING AGREEMENT: RESTRAINT OF TRADE: WHETHER UNREASONABLE: ESTOPPEL: WAIVER OF OBJECTION: WHETHER AGREEMENTS SEVERABLE: Q.B.D.)

Zang Tumb Tuum Records Ltd v. Johnson (POP GROUP: RECORDING AGREEMENT AND PUBLISHING AGREEMENT: RESTRAINT OF TRADE: REASONABLENESS: ENFORCEABILITY: WAIVER OF OBJECTION: C.A.)

Zomba Music Publishers Ltd v. Mountfield (POP GROUP: RECORDING AGREEMENT AND PUBLISHING AGREEMENT: RESTRAINT OF TRADE: ENFORCEABILITY: ESTOPPEL: WAIVER: SEVERABILITY OF AGREEMENTS: Q.B.D.)

Restrictive Covenants

Austin Knight (U.K.) Ltd v. Hinds (EMPLOYMENT CONTRACTS: NON-SOLICITATION CLAUSE: WHETHER PLAINTIFF'S BUSINESS PROTECTABLE: WHETHER RESTRICTION REASONABLE: MISUSE OF CONFIDENTIAL INFORMATION: INTERLOCUTORY INJUNCTION: Ch.D.)

Deacons v. Bridge (RESTRAINT OF TRADE: SOLICITORS: PARTNERSHIP: WIDTH OF COVENANT: Hong Kong: Pat. Ct)

Evening Standard Co. Ltd v. Henderson (EMPLOYEE: C.A.)

Group Inc. v. Eaglestone (EMPLOYMENT CONTRACT: HIGHLY-PAID SERVICES BROKER: WORKING RELATIONSHIP VERY PROFITABLE FOR EMPLOYER: GOODWILL: INTENTION TO FLOUT NOTICE PERIOD: INJUNCTION: ADEQUACY OF DAMAGES: BALANCE OF CONVENIENCE: DISCRETION: Ch.D.)

J.A. Mont (U.K.) Ltd v. Mills (EX-EMPLOYEE'S SEVERANCE AGREEMENT: VALIDITY OF COVENANT: BREACH OF CONFIDENCE: FORM OF INJUNCTION: APPROACH TO CONSTRUCTION OF RESTRICTIVE COVENANTS: GOOD FAITH: C.A.)

Kall-Kwik Printing (U.K.) Ltd v. Frank Clarence Rush (FRANCHISE AGREEMENT: CONSTRUCTION: ENFORCEABILITY: REASONABLENESS: INTERLOCUTORY INJUNCTION: CH.D.)

Kerr v. Morris (RESTRAINT OF TRADE: NHS DOCTOR: VALIDITY OF COVENANT: PUBLIC INTEREST: C.A.)

Lansing Linde Ltd v. Kerr (CONFIDENTIAL INFORMATION: EX-EMPLOYEE: INTERLOCUTORY INJUNCTION: RESTRAINT OF TRADE: ACTION FOR BREACH: WHETHER INFORMATION ACQUIRED BY EMPLOYEE PROTECTABLE AS TRADE SECRETS: WHETHER INTERIM INJUNCTION TO BE GRANTED: C.A.)

Poly Lina Ltd v. Finch (FORMER EMPLOYEE: EMBARGO ON ENGAGEMENTS WITH COMPETITOR: WIDTH OF COVENANT: ADEQUECY OF UNDERTAKING NOT TO DISCLOSE: Q.B.D.)

Reed Exhibitions Pte. Ltd v. Khoo Yak Chuan Thomas (PASSING OFF: RESTRAINT OF TRADE: LICENSEES' COVENANT NOT TO ENTER TRADE SIMILAR TO LICENSOR FOR ONE YEAR FROM TERMINATION OF LICENCE: PRACTICE: INTERLOCUTORY INJUNCTION: SERIOUS QUESTION TO BE TRIED: WHETHER DAMAGES AN ADEQUATE REMEDY: BALANCE OF CONVENIENCE: Singapore: C.A.)

Talk of the Town Pty Ltd v. Hagstrom (COPYRIGHT: ENGRAVING: FUNCTIONAL OBJECTS: DRAWINGS AND DIES: RESTRAINT OF TRADE: Australia: Fed. Ct)

Taylor v. Rotowax Trading Ltd (RESTRAINT OF TRADE: SALE OF COMPANY: NON-COMPETITION CLAUSE IN BREACH OF COVENANT: ACQUISITION OF GOODWILL OF VENDOR COMPANY: New Zealand: C.A.: P.C.)

Restraint of Trade

Aetiology Today C.C. v. Van Aswegen (UNLAWFUL COMPETITION: PUBLIC POLICY: COMPETITION BETWEEN SCHOOLS: TEACHERS MOVING TO NEW SCHOOL: INJURIOUS FALSEHOOD: INTERDICT: South Africa: WLD)

Botha v. Carapax Shadeports (Pty) Ltd (CESSION OF BUSINESS: SALE OF GOODWILL: TRANSFER OF RESTRAINT OF TRADE OBLIGATIONS: South Africa: A.D.)

Carlton & United Breweries Ltd v. Tooth & Co. Ltd (CONTRACT: IMPLIED TERMS: GOODWILL OF BUSINESS: INDUCEMENT TO BREAK CONTRACT: AGENCY: DISCRETION: Australia: S.C.(NSW))

1162

Concept Factory v. Heyl (REASONABLENESS: DESIGN AND IDEAS IN PUBLIC DOMAIN: COPYING: UNLAWFUL COMPETITION: GENERAL PRINCIPLES: South Africa: TPD)

Deacons v. Bridge (SOLICITORS: PARTNERSHIP: WIDTH OF COVENANT: Hong Kong: Pat. Ct)

John Michael Design PLC v. Cooke (EMPLOYMENT: AGREEMENT: TIME LIMITATION: INTERLOCUTORY INJUNCTION: C.A.)

Kerr v. Morris (NHS DOCTOR: VALIDITY OF COVENANT: PUBLIC INTEREST: C.A.)

Lansing Linde Ltd v. Kerr (CONFIDENTIAL INFORMATION: EX-EMPLOYEE: INTERLOCUTORY INJUNCTION: RESTRICTIVE COVENANT IN CONTRACT OF EMPLOYMENT: ACTION FOR BREACH: WHETHER INFORMATION ACQUIRED BY EMPLOYEE PROTECTABLE AS TRADE SECRETS: C.A.)

Lawrence David Ltd v. Ashton (CONTRACT: CONFIDENTIAL INFORMATION: INTERLOCUTORY INJUNCTION: TRADE SECRETS: INTERLOCUTORY INJUNCTION: EX-EMPLOYEE: PERIOD OF RESTRAINT: C.A.)

Meter Systems Holdings Ltd v. Venter (CONFIDENTIAL INFORMATION: UNLAWFUL COMPETITION: FIDUCIARY RELATIONSHIPS: ENFORCEMENT: EX-EMPLOYEE: South Africa: WLD)

Panayiotou v. Sony Music Entrtainment (U.K.) Ltd (CONTRACT: RECORDING AGREEMENT: CHALLENGE TO ENFORCEABILITY OF AGREEMENT: ENTITLEMENT: EARLIER COMPROMISE OF PROCEEDINGS: REASONABLENESS OF TERMS: CONDUCT OF DEFENDANT: Ch.D.)

Peninsular Real Estate Ltd v. Harris (CONFIDENTIAL INFORMATION: EX-EMPLOYEES: CLIENT LIST: NO RESTRAINT OF TRADE CLAUSE: New Zealand: H.C.)

Perceptual Development Corporation v. Versi Pty Ltd (CONTRACT: INFORMATION IN PUBLIC DOMAIN: TECHNIQUE FOR DIAGNOSIS AND TREATMENT OF DYSLEXIA: Australia: Fed. Ct)

Pioneer Concrete Services Ltd v. Lorenzo Galli (CONFIDENTIAL INFORMATION: IMPLIED OBLIGATION: INJUNCTION: DECLARATION: DAMAGES: Australia: S.C.(Vic.))

Silvertone Records Ltd v. Mountfield (CONTRACT: POP GROUP: RECORDING AGREEMENT AND PUBLISHING AGREEMENT: REASONABLENESS: ESTOPPEL: WAIVER OF OBJECTION: WHETHER AGREEMENTS SEVERABLE: Q.B.D.)

Talk of the Town Pty Ltd v. Hagstrom (COPYRIGHT: ENGRAVING: FUNCTIONAL OBJECTS: DRAWINGS AND DIES: VALIDITY OF COVENANT: Australia: Fed. Ct)

Taylor v. Rotowax Trading Ltd (COVENANT: SALE OF COMPANY: NON-COMPETITION CLAUSE IN BREACH OF COVENANT: ACQUISITION OF GOODWILL OF VENDOR COMPANY: New Zealand: C.A.: P.C.)

Warren v. Mendy (BOXER'S MANAGER SEEKING TO RESTRAIN DEFENDANT FROM ACTING FOR BOXER: RELATIONSHIP DEPENDENT ON MUTUAL TRUST AND CONFIDENCE: WHETHER EFFECT OF GRANTING RELIEF TO COMPEL BOXER TO PERFORM CONTRACT WITH MANAGER: INTERLOCUTORY INJUNCTION: WHETHER RELIEF APPROPRIATE: C.A.)

Watson v. Prager (AGREEMENT BETWEEN PROFESSIONAL BOXER AND MANAGER: WHETHER UNREASONABLE: IMPARTIALITY OF BRITISH BOXING BOARD OF CONTROL AS ARBITRATOR: WHETHER ACTION INVOLVED ALLEGATION OF FRAUD: Ch.D.)

Zang Tumb Tuum Records Ltd v. Johnson (CONTRACT: POP GROUP: RECORDING AGREEMENT AND PUBLISHING AGREEMENT: ENFORCEABILITY: WAIVER OF OBJECTION: SCOPE OF INQUIRY AS TO DAMAGES: C.A.)

Zomba Music Publishers Ltd v. Mountfield (CONTRACT: POP GROUP: RECORDING AGREEMENT AND PUBLISHING AGREEMENT: ENFORCEABILITY: ESTOPPEL: WAIVER: SEVERABILITY OF AGREEMENTS: Q.B.D.)

Singapore

Reed Exhibitions Pte. Ltd v. Khoo Yak Chuan Thomas (PASSING OFF: RESTRAINT OF TRADE: LICENSEES' COVENANT NOT TO ENTER TRADE SIMILAR TO LICENSOR FOR ONE YEAR FROM TERMINATION OF LICENCE: PRACTICE: INTERLOCUTORY INJUNCTION: SERIOUS QUESTION TO BE TRIED: WHETHER DAMAGES AN ADEQUATE REMEDY: BALANCE OF CONVENIENCE: C.A.)

Springboard Doctrine

Prout v. British Gas PLC (PATENT: INFRINGEMENT: VALIDITY: BREACH OF CONFIDENCE: WHETHER DISCLOSURE BY EMPLOYEE UNDER EMPLOYEES' SUGGESTION SCHEME BINDING ON DEFENDANT: FIDUCIARY RELATIONSHIP: Pat C.C.)

Roger Bullivant Ltd v. Ellis (BREACH OF CONFIDENCE: EX-EMPLOYEE: CUSTOMER CARD INDEX: C.A.)

Universal Thermosensors Ltd v. Hibben (STOLEN CUSTOMER INFORMATION: EX-EMPLOYEES' COMPETING BUSINESS: ASSESSMENT OF DAMAGES: INTERLOCUTORY ORDER BY CONSENT: SCOPE OF INJUNCTIONS IN BREACH OF CONFIDENCE: DISCRETION: ANTON PILLER PRACTICE: Ch.D.)